THE OXFORD DICTIONARY OF WORLD RELIGIONS

THE OXFORD DICTIONARY OF WORLD RELIGIONS

EDITED BY

John Bowker

Oxford New York

OXFORD UNIVERSITY PRESS

1997

Oxford University Press, Great Clarendon Street, Oxford OX2 6DP
Oxford New York
Athens Auckland Bangkok Bogota Bombay
Buenos Aires Calcutta Cape Town Dar es Salaam
Delhi Florence Hong Kong Istanbul Karachi
Kuala Lumpur Madras Madrid Melbourne
Mexico City Nairobi Paris Singapore
Taipei Tokyo Toronto

and associated companies in
Berlin Ibadan

Oxford is a trade mark of Oxford University Press

First published by Oxford University Press 1997

British Library Cataloguing in Publication Data
Data available

Library of Congress Cataloging in Publication Data
Data available
ISBN 0–19–213965–7

1 3 5 7 9 10 8 6 4 2

Typeset by Interactive Sciences Ltd, Gloucester
Printed in Great Britain
on acid-free paper by
The Bath Press

For Margaret

'Kind is my Love today, tomorrow kind,
Still constant in a wondrous excellence'

PREFACE

WHEN Mr Brooke, in *Middlemarch*, stated that if he went into Parliament, he would emulate Wilberforce and work at philanthropy, 'Mr Casaubon bowed, and observed that it was a wide field.' Religion is even wider; and while this Dictionary would not be able to keep pace with Mr Brooke's 'impetuous reason', it has been written for those who wish to pause and to understand religion and religions better. Vague impressions of religion can do great harm, not least by giving offence to the adherents of religions by seeming to be casual about the things that matter to them. Even the choice of an illustration for the dust jacket of this book shows how difficult these things can be. The photograph of a Thai Buddhist meditating was chosen because it suggests a general religious atmosphere of prayer. Prayer and meditation, however, are not the same thing, and this image ignores the fact that many Buddhists regard their following of the Buddha's teaching as a non-theistic philosophy and not as a religion. It seems perhaps a trivial detail, but detail, in the case of religion, matters.

The details, however, are daunting. Each religion has a long history of its own, with its attendant people and texts and ideas. The Dictionary was planned, therefore, to help those who have an interest in religions, but who find the subject vast. At the time we began, the first-year course at Lancaster University on the Introduction to Religions had more than a hundred students on it. They, and others who come to religions for the first time, find themselves, not simply in Baudelaire's 'forest of symbols', but in a forest also of concepts, texts and practices, languages and histories, teachers and preachers, guides, gurus and gods. The purpose of the Dictionary is to provide initial bearings on new and unfamiliar ground, not just for students, but for the general reader as well. Some entries are brief, because such items as Congé d'élire or Dalmatic do not, in this context, need more than a short definition. But in most articles an attempt has been made to offer something more than a definition, so that the reader can gain some sense of what the item is and why it has been included, even though a full treatment is obviously impossible. I have attempted to give at least a few salient quotations, since these often convey more of the feeling of a belief or of a person than an abbreviated biography can do. Many of these I have translated for the purpose.

The Dictionary has been far too long in the making. It was delayed by the sheer volume of the work; even the headword lists took far longer than I had expected. It was delayed further by my return to Cambridge and by my illness. But all clouds have linings, and during this period, I have written almost exactly half the book. I have also supplied most of the brief suggestions for further reading. In a book covering so much ground in so many entries, it was clearly impossible to provide full bibliographies. The books listed are, therefore, *only suggestions*: they are limited to one or at the most two, offering a possible 'next step' for those who require further information. Some were suggested by contributors, but most come from myself, and thus represent a highly personal reading list, the illustration no doubt of a misspent life. There will surely be other and more recent books, which a library catalogue will disclose. As it is, I broke my own rule, and I have listed more than two books on a number of major topics where the pressure on space made it impossible to do more than point at a large horizon.

Pressure on space: given that there are multi-volume encyclopedias on each of the religions, and one-volume dictionaries on many, it was rash to attempt a one-volume work on the major world religions. But neither general readers nor students have a reference library beside them all the time. We therefore decided to give the maximum space to text, rather than to illustrations. Religions are expressed as much in pictures and signs as they are in words, and although entries on art and music have been included, it was out of the question to do justice to these areas in a single-volume work. There remains yet to be written a companion dictionary of religious art and music. In the mean time I have edited for Dorling Kindersley *World Religions*, which is based on illustration, and gives a glimpse of that other side of religion.

Pressure on space has also meant that a careful system of cross-reference has been used, so that information is not too often repeated. If major concepts (for example, karma) were to be explained each time they appear, we would be back with the many volumes. For the same reason, I have also compiled an Index of major themes. This has reduced the number of times an article ends with 'See also . . .' In the case of such things as cosmology or mysticism, the book would otherwise have been greatly lengthened, since each 'See also' list would have had to be repeated at the end of several entries. The making of the Index was an immense task in its own right. It was made possible, first through the generosity of Gresham College, London (who paid for both the hardware and software involved), and secondly through the skills of Dr Martin Richards, of the Computer Laboratory of Cambridge University. My gratitude to them is great indeed.

My thanks go also to many others: to the contributors, and especially for their patience in accepting the delay in publication; to Lamea Abbas Amara, Krishan Bhugtiar, David Bowker, Gene d'Aquili, Sean Hughes, and Professor C. F. D. Moule who offered advice or corrections on particular entries; to Lavinia Cohn-Sherbok for undertaking a whole area of the Dictionary when another, at a late stage, withdrew; to Dr Christopher Hancock, Dr Newman Brooks, and Dr Margaret Bowker who rescued the book, when, at the very end, promised articles failed to turn up; to Professor Roger Corless who gave me the will to go on when it seemed impossible; to Trinity College for lending me books; to the late Peter Nailor, and to Gresham College, for support and friendship; and to Dr Stephen Wroe and Mrs Sarah Brunning who, among many others, have cared for me through my illness and enabled me to take up this work again. In the early years, Dr J. F. Coakley, in addition to being a contributor, undertook the immense work which was necessary to get the whole project under way. His admirable efficiency and care laid the foundations on which the rest could be built. My thanks go also to the Press (not least, again, for their patience), to the skill of those in India who typed in a difficult manuscript, to proof-readers, and to the development editor, Pam Coote, and the copy-editor, Jane Robson. Above all, my thanks go to Alysoun Owen, and her production and design colleagues John Mackrell and Nick Clarke: this book was extremely complicated to design and set, with many substantial changes at very late stages: her dedication to getting things right has been extraordinary.

Finally, words cannot possibly express adequately my thanks to my wife Margaret. Quite apart from the entries she has written, she has sustained me at every point. It is certain that without her, the Dictionary would have been abandoned long ago. She is, in a real way, the joint-author of it.

John Bowker

Cambridge, 1996

EDITORS

JOHN BOWKER, Gresham Professor, Gresham College, London
and Adjunct Professor at the University of Pennsylvania and
North Carolina State University; formerly Professor of Religion,
University of Lancaster and Fellow of Trinity College,
University of Cambridge, UK
General editor and contributor

ADRIAN ABBOTTS, Head of Religious Studies,
Sir Jonathan North Community College,
Leicester, UK
Consultant editor and contributor for Tibetan religion

DR PETER B. CLARKE, Professor of the History and Sociology
of Religion and Director, Centre for New Religions,
King's College, University of London, UK
Consultant editor and contributor for new religious movements

LAVINIA COHN-SHERBOK, Honorary Research Fellow,
University of Kent, Canterbury, UK
Consultant editor and contributor for Judaism

PROFESSOR JOHN R. HINNELLS, Professor of Comparative Religion,
University of London and Head of the Department of the
Study of Religions, School of Oriental and African Studies, UK
Consultant editor and contributor for Zoroastrianism/Parsis

JOSEPH KITAGAWA, lately of the Divinity School, University of Chicago, USA
Consultant editor for Far Eastern religions

DR ELEANOR NESBITT, Lecturer in Education,
Warwick Religions and Education Research Unit, University of Warwick, UK
Consultant editor and contributor for Sikhism

DR HAROLD TURNER formerly Founder-Director of Interact Centre,
Selly Oak Colleges, Birmingham, UK
Consultant editor and contributor for new religious movements

DR MARTIN WILTSHIRE, Department of Religion and Philosophy,
Edith Cowan University, Western Australia
Consultant editor and contributor for Buddhism

CONTRIBUTORS

Dr Gina Alexander
Jungian analyst
British Association of Psychotherapists
UK
Jung

Claire Baillargeon
Santa Barbara
California
USA
Hinduism

Revd P. M. Ballaman
Anglican deacon
UK
Modern Christian thought

Dr Jerome H. Bauer
Department of Asian and Middle Eastern Studies
University of Pennsylvania
USA
Indian civilization; South Asian religion and philosophy; Hinduism

Revd Dr Jeremy Begbie
Vice Principal
Ridley Hall
Cambridge
UK
Calvin and Calvinism; modern systematic theology

David Bowker
Teacher of religious studies
UK
Religions; religious studies

Dr Margaret Bowker
Emeritus Reader
University of Lancaster
UK
Church history; Christianity

Andrew Braddock
Ridley Hall
Cambridge
UK
Church history

Dr Peter Newman Brooks
Fellow
Robinson College
Cambridge
UK
Reformation

Dr Raymond Brown
Sometime Principal
Spurgeon's College
London
UK
Christianity

Mr Robert F. Campany
Associate Professor
Department of Religious Studies
Indiana University
USA
Chinese religion

Professor D. R. Catchpole
St Luke's Foundation Professor of Theological Studies
University of Exeter
UK
New Testament

Professor Henry Chadwick
Emeritus Professor
University of Cambridge and
Former Master of Peterhouse
Cambridge
UK
Anglican-Roman Catholic International Commission

The Late Professor K. S. Chen
Former Chairman of the Department of Oriental Languages
University of California
Los Angeles
USA
Chinese Buddhism

Professor Julia Ching
University of Toronto
Canada
Chinese religion

Professor J. P. Clayton
Professor of Religious Studies
University of Lancaster
UK
Religious studies

Dr J. F. Coakley
Senior Lecturer in Near Eastern Languages
Harvard University
USA
Christianity

Professor R. J. Corless
Associate Professor of Religion
Duke University
USA
Buddhism (general) and Far Eastern Buddhism

The Revd Canon C. F. Coussmaker
Anglican chaplain in Moscow
Russia
Orthodox Christianity

Dr Kenneth Cragg
Former Anglican bishop in Jerusalem and
Warden of the Central College, Canterbury
UK
currently Visiting Professor
Union Theological Seminary
New York
USA
Islam

David Craig
Head of Religious Broadcasting
BBC World Service
UK
World religions

Dr Brian Davies, OP
Regent
Blackfriars, Oxford, and
University Research Lecturer
University of Oxford
UK
Christianity

Dr Wade Dazey
Associate Professor
Department of Philosophy and Religious Studies
University of Wisconsin-Whitewater
USA
General Hinduism and Advaita Vedanta

Professor J. C. Dobbins
Associate Professor of Religion and East Asian Studies
Oberlin College
Ohio
USA
Japanese Buddhism

Professor Richard H. Drummond
Florence Livergood Warren
Professor of Comparative Religions
University of Dubuque Seminary
USA
Christian mission

Professor Gary L. Ebersole
Associate Professor
History of Religions

CONTRIBUTORS

University of Chicago
USA
Japanese religion

Dr Gavin Flood
Lecturer in Religious Studies
Department of Theology and Religious Studies
University of Wales
Lampeter
UK
Hinduism

Ed Gilday
Formerly Research Student
Centre for Far Eastern Studies
University of Chicago
USA

Dr David Gosling
Cambridge Teape Fellow
Clare Hall
University of Cambridge
UK
South-East Asian Buddhism

Mary Griffith
Santa Barbara
California
USA
Hinduism

Mr John S. Guest
Trustee Emeritus
Robert College of Istanbul
Turkey
Yezidi religion

Revd Dr C. D. Hancock
Holy Trinity Church
Cambridge
UK
Anglicanism

Dr F. E. Hardy
Reader in Indian Religions
King's College
University of London
UK
Indian religions

Dr Ian Harris
Reader in Religious Studies
University College of St Martin
Lancaster
UK
Buddhism

Dr Paul Heelas
Reader in Religion and Modernity
Department of Religious Studies
University of Lancaster
UK
Study of religion

Professor Y. T. Hosoi
Associate Professor
Oregon State University
Corvallis
Oregon
USA
Japanese religion

Most Revd Trevor Huddleston
Former Archbishop of the Indian Ocean and President
Anti-Apartheid Movement
Africa

Zahid Hussein
Former research student
University of Lancaster
UK
Islam

Professor Paul Ingram
Professor of Religion
Pacific Lutheran University
Tacoma
Washington
USA
Japanese Buddhism

Dr Penelope Johnstone
Tutor in Arabic
Oriental Institute
University of Oxford
UK
Islam

Dr H. A. Kanitkar
Lector
Department of Anthropology and Sociology
School of Oriental and African Studies
University of London
UK
Hinduism

Mr V. P. Hemant Kanitkar
Former schoolmaster and author of books on Hinduism
UK
Hinduism

Professor T. Kasulis
Professor of Comparative Studies in the Humanities
Ohio State University
Columbus
USA
Japanese Buddhism

Dr Ruth Katz
Former Associate Professor of Religion
Florida State University
USA
Hinduism

Dr Damien Keown
Lecturer in Indian Religion
Department of Historical and Cultural Studies
Goldsmith's College
University of London
UK
Buddhism

Professor H. J. Kim
Professor Emeritus
Department of Religious Studies
University of Oregon
USA
Korean Buddhism

Professor H. Kiyota
Chairman
Buddhist Studies Program
Department of South Asian Studies
University of Wisconsin-Madison
USA
Buddhism

Dr Linda L. Lam-Easton
Associate Professor
Department of Religious Studies
California State University
Northridge
USA
Chinese religions; history of religions

Dr Gerald J. Larson
Professor of Religious Studies
University of California
Santa Barbara
USA
Hindu and Buddhist traditions; history of religions

Professor Andrew Louth
Professor of Cultural History
Goldsmith's College
University of London
UK
Christianity

Professor Theodore M. Ludwig
Professor of Theology
Valparaiso University
Indiana
USA
Japanese religion

Dr Nancy McCagney
Assistant Professor of Philosophy
Department of Philosophy
University of Delaware
USA
Indian Mahayana Buddhism

Mark MacWilliams
Assistant Professor
Religious Studies

Bucknell University
USA
Japanese religion

Professor M. M. J. Marasinghe
Professor of Buddhist Philosophy
University of Kelaniya
Sri Lanka
Buddhism

Dr F. Matchett
Honorary Research Fellow
in Indian Religions
Department of Religious Studies
University of Lancaster
UK
Hinduism

Professor Jeffrey J. Meyer
Professor and Chair of Religious
Studies Department
UNC Charlotte
North Carolina
USA
Chinese religion

Dr Alan John Milbank
University Lecturer and Fellow
of Peterhouse
University of Cambridge
UK
Christianity

Professor Alan L. Miller
Professor of Religion
Miami University
Oxford
Ohio
USA
Japanese folk religion

Revd Gareth Moore, OP
Prior
Couvent de l'Épiphanie
Rixensart
Belgium
Christian ethics

Dr P. E. Nosco
Formerly, Institute of Asian
Studies
St John's University
New York
USA
Shinto

The late Maurice Oldfield
Cumbria
UK
Jainism

Emily Groszos Ooms
Elementary school teacher
The Willows Community School
Los Angeles
USA
Japanese religion

Jeanne Openshaw
Research Fellow
Lucy Cavendish College
University of Cambridge
UK
Bauls

Professor Roger O'Toole
Professor of Sociology
University of Toronto
Canada
Sociology of religion

Dr Lloyd Pflueger
Assistant Professor of Philosophy
and Religion
Truman State University
Kirksville
USA
South Asian philosophy and religion

Dr Richard B. Pilgrim
Associate Professor
Department of Religion
Syracuse University
New York
USA
Japanese religion

Professor Don A. Pittman
Associate Professor of the History
of Religions
Tainan Theological College and
Seminary
Tainan
Taiwan
Chinese religion

Dr Y. Raef
Professor of Arabic and Islamic
Studies
American University in Cairo
Egypt
Islam; Islamic thought

Revd Chris Russell
UK
Charismatic movement

Dr P. J. Sherry
Reader
Religious Studies Department
University of Lancaster
UK
Christianity; philosophy of religion

Dr Peter Smith
Visiting Professor in History and
Social Sciences
International Students
Degree Program
Mahidol University
Thailand
Babi; Baha'i

Mr P. J. Stewart
Lecturer in Ecology
University of Oxford
UK
Contemporary Islam

Dr Laurence G. Thompson
Professor Emeritus of East Asian
Languages and Cultures
University of Southern California
Ventura
USA
Confucian classics; Chinese religion

Very Revd Simon Tugwell, OP
President of the Dominican
Historical Institute
Rome
Italy
Dominicans

Professor Taitetsu Unno
Jill Ker Conway Professor
of Religion
Smith College
Northampton, Massachusetts
USA
East Asian Buddhism

Professor Manabu Waida
Professor of the History of
Religions
University of Alberta
Edmonton
Canada
Japanese religion

Dr Michael Walsh
Librarian
Heythrop College
University of London
UK
Christianity

Professor L. H. Yearley
Walter Y. Evans-Wentz Professor
Stanford University
USA
Chinese religion

Professor D. C. Yu
Formerly, Department of Religion
Maryville College
Tennessee
USA
Chinese religion

NOTE TO READER

ENTRIES are arranged in letter-by-letter alphabetical order up to the first punctuation in the headword. For example, the entry on **Jerusalem** comes before **Jerusalem, Synod of**, which in turn precedes **Jerusalem Conference**. Some longer entries have been divided into sections each of which deals with an individual religion. These sections are either arranged in the logical order for the specific entry and discussion, or grouped as Semitic religions (Judaism, Christianity, Islam), Asiatic religions (Hinduism, Jainism, Buddhism, Sikhism, Chinese, Japanese); other religions (e.g. Zoroastrianism) usually appear at the end. The religions of the former group are referred to by the abbreviation W. (western), and the latter by E. (eastern), although all religions are now found in eastern and western parts of the world.

Cross-references are indicated by an asterisk or the use in brackets of 'see' followed by the entry headword, or part of the headword, to which the reader is being referred. Sometimes the flagged word in the text will differ from the exact form of the headword, but it is always clear where the reader is being directed. For example, *Ecumenical Movement is asterisked, but the actual form of the entry is Ecumenism. 'See also' followed by a headword in small capitals is also used at the end of an entry to cross-refer the reader to subjects of related interest. The reader is also cross-referred to the Topic Index at the back of the book. So, under the entry **Meditation** there are in-text cross-references *inter alia* to *contemplation and *Jesuits and at the end of the entry: See also MENPEKI; ZAZEN; Index, Meditation.

A cross-reference item is normally marked with an asterisk only at its first appearance in any entry and is included only where reference is likely to increase understanding of the entry being read. Frequently recurring terms (such as God and the names of the major religions, all of which have their own entries) are not cross-referenced. Signpost entries (i.e. entries which simply direct the reader to a main entry where the discussion of them appears) include short descriptions to enable readers to decide whether they wish to pursue the cross-reference. Thus: **Hsing** (human nature): see HSÜN TZU and **Vaudois** (adherents of Christian reform movement): see WALDENSES.

Use of italics The titles of books and texts are in italics except for some foundational texts, such as the Adi Granth, Bible (and its individual books) and Qur'an. These are in normal text (roman) type. Foreign and transliterated terms are usually in italics, unless they are asterisked as cross-references and thus have their own entry, in which case they are in roman type throughout the entry. The text includes a large number of transliterated terms which may be unfamiliar to the reader; for ease of reading we have tried to keep the use of italics to a minimum.

Foreign words Foreign scripts have been transliterated. However, there are often different systems of transliteration for each language, and preferred transliterations are often changing. Most obviously, Chinese transliteration has changed from the Wade–Giles system to Pinyin. Most older books will have followed the Wade–Giles system, and for that reason it is usually used in the Dictionary, since it is the form readers will most frequently meet. But an index has been provided at the back of the book that lists all Chinese headwords with their Pinyin alternatives. With other languages, we have tried to provide the form that a general reader is most likely to encounter today.

This leads to a necessary inconsistency in the case of diacriticals. In the case of some languages (e.g. Greek, Hebrew) diacriticals are now almost always left out in books for the general reader, whereas in the case of others (e.g. Sanskrit, Pali) they are increasingly being added. Plurals are given in English form.

Some words have alternative transliterations which conform to general patterns. For example, words starting with **c** may also commonly begin **ch** as for cela or chela; caitya or chaitya. Likewise, **sh** may also appear as ṣ or ś ; **ḥ** as **ch**. Other common variants are b / v; f / ph; g / gh; k / q; v / w. The form used sometimes varies across entries, and for major items the alternative spellings are given. This has, clearly, not been possible in every instance, and readers who fail to find an entry are advised, in the above instances, to look for the alternative spelling.

In the case of the Arabic definite article al- ('the'), the letter 'l' is assimilated to the letters known as *alhuruf ashshamsiya* (i.e. the Sun letters), t, th, d, dh, r, z, s, sh, ṣ, ḍ, ṭ, ẓ, l, n. Thus al-shams, the sun becomes ash-shams. Since these forms are less commonly followed in English books, the form al- has been retained in the dictionary, including the alphabetical order—thus al-Razi not ar-Razi, al-Shaf'i not ash-Shaf'i. Note also that such entries appear under 'A', not under the first capital letter: R, Sh, etc.

Further reading suggestions appear at the end of some entries (see Preface, p. vii). Titles are abbreviated, where lengthy, to the point where they can be easily found in a catalogue or bibliographical database. So, under **Satan**, J. W. Boyd, *Satan and Mara . . .* (1975) is listed; the full title is *Satan and Mara: Christian and Buddhist Symbols of Evil*.

Abbreviations In order to make the text as readable as possible abbreviations have been kept to a minimum (but see also Index under Acronyms and Abbreviations). The following have been used:

Languages

Arab.	Arabic	Ital.	Italian
Aram.	Aramaic	Jap.	Japanese
Chin.	Chinese	Lat.	Latin
Eng.	English	Pers.	Persian
Fr.	French	Skt.	Sanskrit
Germ.	German	Syr.	Syriac
Gk.	Greek	Tib.	Tibetan
Heb.	Hebrew	Yid.	Yiddish

Others

AH	After the Hijra, *Anno Hegirae* (see entry HIJRA)
b. [in names]	ben, ibn (son of)
B.	*Babli* (Babylonian Talmud)
BCE	before the common era
CE	in the common era
P. or *J.*	Palestinian or Jerusalem Talmud
R.	Rabbi
$\sqrt{\ }$	from the root of

RELIGION

The Meaning of Religion

A strange thing about religion is that we all know what it is until someone asks us to tell them. As *Augustine said of *time: 'What, then, is time? If no one asks me I know; but if I have to say what it is to one who asks, I know not.' That has not stopped people trying to define religion, but their definitions are clearly different:

Religion is the sigh of the oppressed creature, the heart of a heartless world, just as it is the spirit of a spiritless situation. It is the opiate of the people (Karl *Marx)

Religion is a daughter of Hope and Fear, explaining to Ignorance the nature of the Unknowable (Ambrose Bierce)

A religion is a unified system of beliefs and practices relative to *sacred things, that is to say, things set apart and forbidden—beliefs and practices which unite into one single moral community called a *Church, all those who adhere to them (Émile *Durkheim)

It seems best to fall back at once on this essential source, and simply to claim, as a minimum definition of religion, the belief in Spiritual Beings (Edward *Tylor)

*Psychoanalytic investigation of the unconscious mental life reveals that religious beliefs correspond closely with the phantasies of infantile life, mainly unconscious ones, concerning the sexual life of one's parents and the conflicts this gives rise to (Sigmund *Freud)

Religion is what the individual does with his own solitariness (A. N. *Whitehead)

A brief, handy definition of religion is considerably more difficult than a definition of evolution, so, for limited purposes only, let me define religion as a set of *symbolic forms and acts which relate man to the ultimate conditions of his existence (R. N. Bellah)

Viewed systemically, religion can be differentiated from other culturally constituted institutions by virtue only of its reference to superhuman beings. All institutions consist of *belief systems*, i.e., an enduring organisation of cognitions about one or more aspects of the universe; *action systems*, an enduring organisation of behaviour patterns designed to attain ends for the satisfaction of needs; and *value systems*, an enduring organisation of principles by which behaviour can be judged on some scale of merit. Religion differs from other institutions in that its three component systems have reference to superhuman beings (Melford Spiro)

Without further ado, then, a *religion* is: (1) a system of symbols which acts to (2) establish powerful, pervasive and long-lasting moods and motivations in men by (3) formulating conceptions of a general order of existence and (4) clothing these conceptions with such an aura of factuality that (5) the moods and motivations seem uniquely realistic (Clifford *Geertz)

Religion is the human attitude towards a sacred order that includes within it all being—human or otherwise—i.e., belief in a cosmos, the meaning of which both includes and transcends man (Peter Berger)

Pure religion and undefiled before God and the Father is this: to visit the fatherless and widows in their affliction, and to keep oneself unspotted from the world (Letter of *James).

These and the many other definitions of religion (J. H. Leuba began his book *A Psychological Study of Religion* . . . (1912), with nearly fifty of them, sorted into three different types) tell us much about religion, but because of their diversity, none of them on its own can tell us what religion is. Some emphasize the personal, others the social; some the beliefs, others the uses; some the structures, others the functions; some the private, others the public; some the mundane, others the transcendent; some the truth, others the illusion. We might, perhaps, attempt to put them all together, but that would produce a juggernaut (*jagganatha) even more unwieldy than the lumbering giant of Orissa.

Would the origins of the word itself take us any further? The Latin *religio* refers to the fear of *God or the gods, and (much later) to the ceremonies and rites addressed to the gods. But it does so through its reference also to the scrupulous and often over-anxious way in which *rituals are conducted. The Latin poet Lucretius addressed strong words against religion:

> Tantum religio potuit suadere malorum . . .
> Religio peperit scelerosa atque impia facta.
> (*De rerum natura*, 1.101, 183)

(How many evils has religion caused! . . . Religion has brought forth criminal and impious deeds.)

But Lucretius had in mind the sacrifice of Iphigenia at Aulis as a demonstration of the disastrous consequences of an over-scrupulous insistence on the exact detail of ritual. So the Latin word supports the modern sense of 'doing something religiously', i.e. with an obsessive attention to detail (when it was reported in 1995 that Honda UK was supplying air conditioning kits containing the highly pollutant R12 refrigerant, despite the Montreal Protocol which looked for its elimination, Honda UK issued a statement saying: 'The Montreal Protocol is being religiously adhered to by Honda UK. . . . The only R12 kits being sold are from existing stocks held', *Daily Telegraph*, 12 Aug. 1995, p. C3). But this sense of the word is far too restricted. When people do things religiously, they not only do them scrupulously: they do them devotedly, generously, *ecstatically, *prayerfully, *sacrificially, superstitiously, *puritanically, ritualistically, and in many other ways as well.

So does the underlying etymology of the word help us further? A problem is that the etymology of *religio* is not certain. Cicero took it from *relegere*, to gather things together, or to pass over the same ground repeatedly. But most have taken it from *religare*, to bind things together. And if that is so, it certainly draws attention to one of the most obvious and important features of religion: it binds people together in common practices and beliefs: it draws them together in a common enterprise of life—so much so that Durkheim regarded religion as being the social in symbolic form (hence his definition above): religion is the social fact (and the experience of it by individuals as being real and greater than themselves) being made objective outside the lives of individuals. As a result, the social has a legitimate and emotional demand on them:

> Society is a reality *sui generis*; it has its own peculiar characteristics, which are not found elsewhere and which are not met with again in the same form in all the rest of the universe. The representations which express it have a wholly different content from purely individual ones and we may rest assured in advance that the first add something to the second. . . . Religion ceases to be an inexplicable hallucination and takes a foothold in reality. In fact we can say that the believer is not deceived when he believes in the existence of a moral power upon which he depends and from which he receives all that is best in himself: this power exists, it is society. . . . It is society which classifies beings into superiors and inferiors, into commanding masters and obeying servants; it is society which confers upon the former the singular property which makes the command efficacious and which makes *power.* So everything tends to prove that the first powers of which the human mind had any idea were those which societies have established in organising themselves; it is in their image that the powers of the physical world have been conceived. (*The Elementary Forms of the Religious Life* (1912), tr. J. W. Swain (New York: Collier, 1961), 28, 257, 409)

Durkheim may have concentrated too much on the entirely speculative origin of religion. He hoped that by examining the acorn he would be able to understand the oak. He may also, as *Weber thought, have paid too little attention to the creation of religious meaning, innovation, and change. But his grasp of the importance of the social in understanding religion was a breakthrough. Religions are organized systems which hold people together.

Religions as Systems: Natural Selection and Survival

The question then becomes obvious: why are these systems necessary? The basic answer to that lies in the most fundamental condition of human life and survival, as we now understand it. Natural selection through the sifting process of evolution sets an impartial rule against the experiments of life. Those which are best adapted to the environmental conditions survive long enough to replicate more of their genes into another generation; those which are ill adapted may not survive at all. It is from this perspective that bodies have been regarded (admittedly in too casual and inaccurate a way) as gene-survival machines: a chicken is an egg's way of making another egg (Samuel Butler). So the skin is the first defensive boundary of the gene-replication process. But humans have then built a second defensive system outside the boundary of the body, in their shared cultural achievements; so that *culture is the second defensive skin in which the gene-replication process sits.

Religions are the earliest cultural systems of which we have evidence for the protection of gene-replication and the nurture of children. Obviously, our early ancestors knew nothing of how gene-replication works. But that is irrelevant to the evolutionary point. It is not understanding, but successful practice which is measured by survival. That is why religions have always been preoccupied with *sex and *food, creating food laws and systematic agriculture, and taking control of sexual behaviour, *marriage, and the status of *women. Sometimes the close relation between sexual and religious emotion has been promoted, on occasion exploited. This necessary connection between religion, sex, and food is the reason also why the family is the basic unit of religious organization, even in religions where *celibacy is seen as a higher vocation. On this basis, sociobiology (the study of the interaction of genes and culture which claims that culture can be best understood as a consequence of choices which have proved beneficial in protecting gene-replication) has claimed that religions have had value, not because their beliefs might happen to have been true (though sociobiologists generally assume that they are not), but because they have served the purposes of survival and selection

There is much about sociobiology that is clearly wrong (for a critical survey, see J. W. Bowker, *Is God a Virus? Genes, Culture and Religion* (London: SPCK, 1995), but it is at least correct in observing that religions are highly organized protective systems. And they have worked. For millennia religions have been the social context in which individuals have lived their lives successfully, success being measured in terms of survival and replication. Even now, more than three-quarters of the population of the world regard themselves as being attached to some religion, however much or little they do about it.

Gene-Protein Process and Preparation for Religion

But still the question has to be asked, why *religious* systems? After all, animals, birds, and fish live in many different kinds of social organization without saying their prayers (so far as we know, though some religions have thought otherwise). But that is simply to say that the emergence of the human brain carries with it immensely greater possibilities, not least in the development of consciousness and language. It is here that we can locate the emergence and development of religion. These possibilities are latent in the brain, in the sense that they are a consequence of the particular structures and substances which the gene-protein process builds in the brain—and builds, therefore, not in a random way, but with great stability and consistency from generation to generation. This means that although there are differences in human populations which are derived from the gene-protein process (for example, skin pigmentation, colour of eyes, average height), there is much more that is held in common. That is why *biogenetic structuralism can claim that humans are prepared from the gene-protein process for many of their characteristic behaviours: they are prepared, for example, for sexual development and behaviours, for sleeping and waking, for eating and drinking, for linguistic competence. The gene-protein process does not *determine* what individuals will do with their preparedness, but it does give stable opportunities to create in culture both the expression and the control of what that process has prepared in the human brain. Biogenetic structuralism makes the point that humans are also prepared, in this gene-protein sense, for those characteristic behaviours which have been called religious. This at once explains why there is much that is universal and common in religious behaviour, but why, nevertheless, there are many different religions and why there are radical differences among them: that happens because what people in societies and cultures do with their preparedness is not determined. But the basic universality, at the level of brain/body competence and opportunity, means that whereas the sign held up in the crowd used to read, 'Prepare to meet thy God', it should now be amended to read, 'Prepared to meet thy God'. It means also that religion, or what is sometimes called 'religiosity', is inevitable in the human case unless there are major alterations in the human DNA.

Somatic Exploration and Discovery

So the basic argument of sociobiology is correct, that religions are early and, for millennia, successful protective systems tied to the potentialities of the brain and body, and to the necessity for survival. The point then becomes obvious, that once successful protective systems are established, people are given the confidence and security to do many other things as well. They are set free to explore their own nature and society, as well as the world around them. These explorations of human possibility, and of the environments in which it is set, opened the way to the specifically religious. Where human possibility is concerned, the exploration is primarily of the human body. It is therefore known, from Greek *soma* = 'body', as 'somatic exploration'. What is this body capable of experiencing? What is it capable of being and of becoming? In some religions, the emphasis has been on exploration inwards: they have sought and found truth within the body, in terms of *enlightenment, peace, emptiness (see e.g. *śunyata), the *Buddha-nature, and are therefore known as 'inversive systems'. The exploration of what *Thoreau called 'the private sea', the streams and oceans of our inner nature, has led to such religions as *Jainism and *Buddhism. In other religions, the emphasis has been on exploring the meaning and value of what has been discovered outside the body, and of the relationships into which people enter. It was this which culminated in communion, or even union, with God. This exploration of the value in relationship has produced religions like *Judaism, *Christianity, and *Islam. These systems, in which value and meaning are found in relationship, are known as 'extraversive systems'. In both cases, it is a matter of emphasis: an inversive system is never unattentive to that which concerns extraversive systems, and vice versa. In both cases, also, the realities of evil and wickedness are recognized and mapped as well.

The consequences of somatic exploration are vast. They are indeed the subject matter of this book. The system, or more often subsystem, of a religion provides the context within which sanctions and rewards, approval and disapproval, inspiration and ideation are held in common. As a result, the context becomes one of security, a security within which people are set free from a great deal of anxiety and uncertainty. As they internalize the constraints of the system, they are able, if they wish, to move on into further exploration and discovery of their own (on the importance of 'constraint', see further p. xxii). What might give rise to these discoveries, or what, in other words, might exist waiting to be discovered, is described in faltering languages, and it is approached through imperfect practices. However, both words and practices are winnowed, corrected, and reinforced through time. No language, whether verbal or non-verbal, can encompass God or the Buddha, *heaven or enlightenment, but language opens up the way to these and other possibilities. The languages are corrected and reinforced precisely because that to which they point interacts so consistently with those who seek, that frequently, though not invariably, they find a truth or a reality far beyond their languages and independent of them. To find God or the Buddha is more like being found by them.

As the consequences of somatic exploration in the past are realized in the present, so the characteristic practices of religions become apparent, in *worship, *meditation, *prayer, *yoga, *zazen, and much else. All of these are appropriations of past and tested achievements and experience, realized and extended in the present. The consequent power and peace are, for many, so real and unequivocal that all else in human life fades in comparison. The Buddha-nature is intelligible to anyone as a proposition; but the Buddha-nature as the universe and one's own appearance within it is true in a transforming sense only to those who have realized it by the ways so carefully preserved and transmitted. God may be the subject of philosophical debate; but God as source and goal of life is known only to those who receive him as gift, demand, and invitation—so much so that Rudolph *Otto could offer the distinct experience of the *Holy, of *mysterium tremendum et fascinans* (the wholly other who both terrifies and yet attracts, who 'appears and overthrows, but who is also the mystery of the self-evident, nearer to me than my *I*', Martin *Buber) as a *Kantian a priori category of human judgement (see esp. *The Idea of the Holy*, chs. xiv and xvii):

> We conclude, then, that not only the rational but also the non-rational elements of the complex category of 'holiness' are *a priori* elements and each in the same degree. Religion is not in vassalage either to morality or to teleology, '*ethos*' or '*telos*', and does not draw its life from postulates; and its non-rational content has, no less than its rational, its own independent roots in the hidden depths of the spirit itself. (p. 140)

Paradoxically, therefore, somatic explorations require human initiatives, but all of them, whether inversive or extraversive, have ended up with the realization that human initiatives cannot achieve the furthest goals without profound help which is not of their own making: guides, *gurus, and *grace take us further than even the furthest exploration can imagine.

Even so, somatic exploration *has* made supreme discoveries about human possibility. It has led people into assurance, union, trance, and ecstasy, and it has enabled them to understand and reverence the cosmos as the bearer of meaning and value. So religions open people up to possibility in this life, and now beyond *death as well. Initially, the latter point did not obtain: the belief that there will be a worthwhile life after death is late in religious history. This means that the great religious traditions of both East and West did not *in origin* have any strong belief that the purpose of life and religion is to obtain rewards or avoid punishments after death. It follows that the enduring religious traditions of the world were not, as so many assume, established on the basis of an offer of 'pie-in-the-sky'. They were established on the basis of this-life experience and exploration, not on the promise of a reward after death (for the detail of this, see J. W. Bowker, *The Meanings of Death* (Cambridge: Cambridge University Press, 1991)).

Yet eventually the belief that there will be enduring consequence through and beyond death became firmly established. This was mainly a matter of inference from the nature and quality of what had been discovered in the process of somatic exploration. Since those discoveries were so many and so diverse, it is not surprising that the subsequent beliefs differ greatly in their descriptions of what may be the case through and after death. This is reinforced by the fact that the different somatic explorations, which have led to different religions, have produced radically different accounts of human nature, that is, different religious anthropologies. Here already we can begin to see that the different religions really are different: religious differences *do* make a difference. But all of them protect and transmit important discoveries about the possibilities of human life.

The consequences of somatic exploration are not simply a matter of practice: there is also somatic exegesis, the interpretation of what has been discovered which produces elaborate belief systems and world pictures, as also it produces texts to sustain them. Somatic exegesis points to worlds vivid with gods and spirits, full of power and presence. To enquire further (for example, into their *ontology or existence) leads into those human reflections, so important in the history of religions, of *philosophy and *theology.

The importance of all this begins to explain why religions are protective systems: they protect much that is indispensable for human life and flourishing of a kind, and in ways, which necessarily evoke a distinctive word ('religion'). Religions in fact have even more to protect and transmit than all that has so far been described, but that alone, ranging from sex to salvation, is far too important to be left to chance. It is information which has to be organized if it is going to be saved and shared. Religions are systems for the monitoring, coding, protecting, and transmitting of information which has proved to be of the highest possible value, from person to person and (even more important) from generation to generation.

The Organization of Religions

The ways in which religions do this are again extremely varied. So far as organization is concerned, religions may be large-scale and coherently organized and hierarchical: an example is *Roman Catholicism, which has a strong centre of authority and control, the *Vatican, and a clear hierarchy of *Pope, *cardinals, *bishops, *priests, male *religious orders, female religious orders, *laity, running in parallel with a spiritual hierarchy of *apostles, *saints, *martyrs, *confessors, *doctors. But equally, they may be large-scale and *loosely* organized, with virtually no overall structure at all: an example is *Hinduism; but among Hindus there are extremely strong subsystems, based, for example, on gurus or *temples or holy places. Or again, they may be small-scale and local, extending perhaps only to the borders of a village. Between the extremes, there are many variations on the theme of protecting information and transmitting information, of allowing or denying access to the religious system (a powerful means for controlling aberrant beliefs or practices, see e.g. *excommunication, *heresy), and of sharing or restricting knowledge with the wider outside world. For that last reason, religions vary between mystery religions and *missionary religions: the former set and maintain conditions before access is allowed; the latter feel impelled to share what has been entrusted to them. Organization also evokes many different kinds of religious specialist—*priests, *witches, *shamans, *gurus, *imams, *rabbis, *monks, *nuns, *bhiksus—an almost endless list.

The organization of religions is so important for some that the preservation and efficiency of the system become for them an end in itself. The risk involved in this is that they may become curators of a museum, or persecutors of those who do not conform. The system as an end is reinforced by the fact that religion is extremely big business. The numbers alone of those who secure all or part of their livelihood from religion make religion one of the largest global industries. When the Pope made his six-day visit to Britain, a company, Papal Visits Ltd., was set up to raise the costs estimated at £1 million per day. When it appointed Mark McCormack of the International Management Group, better known for managing the investments of sporting millionaires, he commented in an interview: 'They said that when the Pope had visited the Church in Ireland a couple of years ago, it cost the Church several million pounds and that everyone and his brother had made money except the Church.' On this occasion, it was estimated that the Church would make money and that McCormack would make, from his 20 per cent share of the profits, £1 million. With money inevitably goes power. It is an observation at least as old as Polybius (*c.*125 BCE) that 'since the masses of the people are inconstant, full of unruly desires, passionate and reckless of consequence, they must be filled with fears to keep them in order; the ancients did well therefore to invent the gods and the belief in punishment after death'. The financial exploitation of this is a familiar theme in religious history. Money is the root of much religion. A history of religion might well be written as a history of authority, control, and power, since the sanctions and rewards of religious systems are pervasive, and often subtle, in the extreme.

Life as Project: Ethics and the Nature of Time

It is easy, therefore, for religious organizations to become an end in themselves. But the creative health of religions lies in the recognition that the system is not an end, but a means to ends which transcend the organization—indeed, a means to *the* End (*eschatology), the final destiny of all that is. All human life is lived as project. That is so because humans are conscious that there is a future, but they know extremely little about it. Life as project (towards acknowledged but largely unknown futures) means that evaluation is built into the formation of human actions: is this wise or is it foolish? is it rash or is it prudential? is it harmful or is it beneficial? is it good or is it bad? This is clearly the foundation of *ethics and of evaluating behaviours and people as moral or immoral, and religions have done much to create stable ethical evaluations which obtain throughout a particular system and culture.

It is a reason also why acceptance and rejection, approval and disapproval, are so central to religious life: the terms on which these obtain are fundamental, for good and for ill, in the forming of human lives, groups, and societies. They include the ways in which self-approval and self-acceptance become possible. Religions, each in different ways, map the conditions and terms of approval and disapproval, and of acceptance and rejection. This may, of course, create major difficulties, social as well as psychological, for those who cannot accept or meet the terms. But on the other hand, it has had the huge advantage of making life as project less unpredictable.

Religions have done even more to make the future less unknown: they have produced, despite Augustine's perplexity, descriptions of the nature of time which allow the process of time to tell a significant story: the experience of moving from past to present to future is no longer 'one damn thing after another', but a vehicle of destiny in which people and societies are characterized in particular ways. The ways vary greatly, because the understandings of time vary greatly. Thus in the broadest division (for examples, see TIME), time in some religions is regarded as cyclical (but with lives being lived linearly, with as many as 84 million *rebirths or reappearances), while in others time is linear, moving from creation to end (but with lives lived cyclically, going round repeated years of commemorative *festivals). In many religions, both the past and the future can be visited: the past in order that it may continue to live in the present, and so that wrongdoing may be repaired and forgiven (*retrogressive rituals, which 'visit' past events and enable people to relive or deal with them, are common), the future so that it is not wholly unknown. Religions have produced a multitude of different ways in which the future can be foretold, and they have also portrayed what the ultimate future will be like—and by what ways that future state can be reached. They have even attempted to create proleptic societies which anticipate the final state.

In these ways, religions make life as project a little easier. They protect and transmit the means to attain the most important goals imaginable. Some of these goals are proximate: they are goals which can be attained within this life (a wiser, more fruitful, more charitable, more successful, way of living) or within the process of rebirth. But others are ultimate, and have to do with the final condition of this or any other human person, and of the cosmos itself. These ultimate goals may be at the extremes of joy or pain, of reward or punishment; which means that death, for most religions, is the threshold of judgement, or the place of judgement itself. The picture is complicated by the fact that for religions with a belief in rebirth or reappearance, such as Hinduism, Jainism, Buddhism, the possibility of punishment after death, in the equivalent of *hell, is only a proximate goal: it is not an ultimate destiny; and even in religions like Christianity or Islam, where the judgement after death is ultimate, it has always been a matter of debate whether punishment is eternal (*universalism). But even with the many qualifications which the immense diversity of religions always makes necessary, the general point remains that religious systems protect and transmit the means through which the proximate and ultimate goals of life, as they are designated within the systems themselves, can be attained. Furthermore, they give accounts of the state of the dead of such a kind that the living can either remain in some form of communication or communion with them, or can have assurance about them and can continue to care for them. Religions extend the family beyond the grave (or funeral pyre: see *ancestors).

Text, Tradition, and Story

How is all this information to be secured and conveyed? The family is of paramount importance, but so too is the social gathering, in forms which emerge eventually in *ekklesia* and its equivalent in other religions. The Greek word *ekklesia,* which means a summoning out of individuals into a group, refers often to political organizations; but it came to be the word used for the Christian Church—as in the English 'ecclesiastical' or *ecclesiology. But there is an ecclesial necessity in all religions, whether in village assembly, *synagogue, *mosque, *gurdwara, or *temple. Religion binds people together in a common enterprise; and it is in the forms and modes of religious assembly that much of the transmission of religious information takes place. Much is transmitted orally, and much, again, is entirely non-verbal: that is why so much of religion is expressed in gestures, symbols, *art, and silences; even that most fundamental of human necessities, *breathing, becomes a vehicle of religious exploration and discovery.

But the precious nature of religious information, whether verbal or non-verbal, means that writing became of paramount importance: in the beginning was the Word, or Sound, *Logos, or *Śabda. The Word extends its powers when it is written down, and Sound becomes more repeatedly accessible when it is translated into text. Text always runs in parallel to oral transmission, and by no means all religions became text-based. But text as authority and *revelation builds into religious life one of its most powerful constraints. The *Bible says . . . ; but so also does *Tanach (Jewish *Scripture), the *Qur'an, *Śruti, the *Angas, the *Guru Granth Sahib, the Book of *Mormon. The fact that they do not all say the same thing, and may indeed contradict each other, reinforces the radical divide between religions; but it also means, more simply, that revelation is always contingent—that is, no matter how strong the claims may be that a particular text or collection of texts comes from heaven or from God, it is always related to the particular historical circumstances in which it first appeared. And that means, in turn, that it is related to the transmission of a particular system.

The importance of texts extends beyond revelation. The work of *exegesis is continuous in all religions, which means, in other words, that the working out of the meaning of any particular tradition is a continuing task. Again, much of this is practical, a working out in life of what the tradition requires, enables, and expects. But much is committed to writing, so that the *scribe (especially before the invention of printing), although sometimes feared, is almost invariably honoured as a midwife of meaning. Text as the protector of information immediately creates the problems of exegesis and *hermeneutics (whose meaning is the true meaning of the text? and who decides which it is?), but it also creates opportunity: it becomes a transforming constraint on individual lives, and it releases the possibility of a brilliant kaleidoscope of different kinds of writing, in philosophy, poetry, story and drama, all of which owe much to the religious contexts in which they came into being.

In these ways religions have protected and transmitted the information which has been tested and winnowed through time, and they have thus created worlds of confidence: they have created worlds in which people can recognize who they are, why they are, where they are, and where they are going. They can know how they should live and behave. Religions establish codes of recognition, so that in potentially hostile environments, people can recognize whether those approaching them are friends or foes, whether their intentions are hostile or friendly. Religions create extended families—extending them, in some cases, far beyond even the kinship group and tribe, to make into one community 'all the nations of the earth' (see, for example, 'UMMA). Religions are usually tribal, but the tribe may be extremely large and metaphorical. The codes of recognition and of expected behaviour, even beyond the scope of ethics, bring order into society, often organizing hierarchies. Even more importantly, from a religious point of view, they give to all members, including the poorest and least privileged, the opportunity of religious success, however that is described. The codes of recognition and behaviour need to be secure and well established for that to be possible. In all these many ways, religions make life a little more predictable. They enable people to recognize the many different kinds of limitation which lie before the project of their lives, and how to accept or deal with them.

So important is the role of religions in creating meaning that the great pioneer of the modern study of religion, Max Weber, regarded it as their primary function. In his view, religions create theodicies. '*Theodicy' usually has a more restricted meaning, that of justifying claims made about the love and power of God in the face of suffering and evil. In Weber's usage, theodicies are explanations which will account for the inequalities and injustices of life: you live long, I die young; you are rich, I am poor; you are male, I am female; you are well, I am sick. Religions pour meaning and explanation into the gaps of inequality, and organize societies so as to be a living expression of a particular theodicy.

But although Weber extended the sense of the word, he did not really extend it enough. The meanings and values which religions create and sustain extend far beyond the range of even his understanding of theodicy, important though that is. Religions create entire worlds of order and entertainment, in which the place of each part can be recognized and identified. The biography of any individual is set within a far larger narrative, the components of which are constantly translated into that biography, thereby completely transforming its nature and outcomes. Much of this translation into life will be entirely unconscious, but much also will be a deliberate appropriation of the ways in which a religion makes the story, or components of the story, available—for example, in scripture-reading, preaching, *liturgy, or *pilgrimage. 'Religion as story' (to quote the title of the book edited by J. Wiggins, University Press of America, 1985) may be applied literally through story-telling, with the story-teller highly valued in all religions (see e.g., K. Narayan, *Storytellers, Saints and Scoundrels: Folk Narrative in Hindu Religious Teaching* (Delhi: Motilal Banarsidass, 1992)), but it may also lead to imaginations of time and space on such a large scale that they provide the conceptual context of life in a particular religion. Thus, for example, religions create cosmogonies and *cosmologies. Often these have been evaluated as quasi-scientific accounts, and have then been measured for worth against current cosmological theories in the natural sciences. In fact, a religion may have many cosmogonies, often contradictory of each other, each of which serves a different purpose. There are at least five creation stories in Jewish Scripture, and many more than that among Hindus. The point is that religions devise and elaborate cosmogonies and cosmologies, not in order to anticipate the brief episode of twentieth-century science, but in order to display the universe as an arena of opportunity, the opportunity to live in the ways and for the purposes which a religion suggests or demands. By providing maps of time and space, religions enable people to deal with (or to accept) the many limitations which stand across the project of their lives.

The cosmos as the bearer of meaning demands particular ways of acting and living. Religions, therefore, regard people as being both responsible and accountable: their lives move to some reckoning, whether it is spoken of as *Judgement or as *Karma (or in other ways), and whether the dialectic is described as *sin and *salvation, or as ignorance (*avidya) and enlightenment; and all religions have an imagination of hell. Religions may stress the inadequacy of human actions without help (grace and *redemption, or their equivalents, in other religions, of rescue and repair). But the belief that humans should do nothing and leave it all to God, guru, or grace, the extreme versions of which end up in *antinomianism, is rare.

Religious Creativity: Myth, Ritual, and Symbols

So religions (as Weber insisted) pour into the gaps not only meaning but also actions; and that is why religions are a constant force for change, despite the fact that they are also, as systems, necessarily conservative. But as in biology, so here: constraints are the condition of freedom, and once the constraints of a religion are internalized, people are set free to act and think in creative ways (on the meaning and importance of constraint in biology and religion, see J. W. Bowker, *A Year to Live*, Introduction (London: SPCK, 1991); *Is God a Virus . . . ?*, 96 ff.)

The supreme intellectual instruments of this religious creativity are *myth, *ritual, and *symbol. The word 'myth' has been debased in recent years so that it is now, in popular usage, another word for something false or invented. Yet myth is in fact one of the greatest of human achievements. Myths are narrations, usually stories, which point to truths of a kind that cannot be told in other ways—for example, in the categories of natural science. That is why myth was seized upon in the nineteenth century by those like Wagner who accepted that science has a true story to tell, but a limited one: it cannot, for example, tell us anything about the experienced truths of human love and suffering. Myth places individual biographies and local events into a much larger context and story, thereby giving them meaning and significance. Myth may provide explanations of ritual, but rituals may also be independent of myth. Rituals are actions repeated in regular and predictable ways which create order in the otherwise random process of time. They may therefore be entirely secular (as, for example, on New Year's Eve or at the opening of an Olympic Games), but they are extensive in religions. Some are *rites of passage (marking the movement of individuals or groups through significant moments of life and death), others mediate protection into dangerous worlds; some initiate, others terminate membership of a religious group; some seek to effect change, others to express meaning. Ritual is the enacted language through which human hopes and fears are articulated and dealt with, and life is constantly renewed. So much is expressed through ritual that it is impossible to summarize all that it means and does.

So too with symbols: language is important (to say the least) in expressing religious beliefs and ideas, but symbols are at least as much so. Symbols are compressed expressions of religious beliefs and ideas in visible form, some of which are enacted, but many of which are transcribed. Symbols rarely attempt to portray what they purport to be about, because they are economies of statement, feeling, and belief, usually achieved and established in religions and simply appropriated by particular individuals. Rather than reproducing something, they act as entrances to religious worlds and imaginations, much as the Looking Glass admitted Alice to wonder and delight—and to terror. Symbols are possessed of power and may encompass a universe in a space not much larger than a small room—or God in a *host the size of a coin.

From all this flows religious art and architecture, and much more besides. Religions are the resource and inspiration of virtually all the most enduring and timelessly moving of human creations—not just in art and architecture, but in agriculture, *music, *dance, *drama, poetry, and in the explorations of the cosmos which issued eventually as the natural sciences (it is only in very recent centuries that science has become decoupled from religion as a way of exploration). In practice and presentation, religions in human experience have been fun and they have been entertainment. Long before Hollywood began to dream in dollars, religions were mounting spectacles, heightened, often, by terror, and enhanced by high degrees of audience participation.

Boundaries and Border Incidents: Religions and Conflict

The protection and transmission of all of this requires organized systems, which religions necessarily are, and systems require boundaries. The boundaries may be literal, being established in relation to particular geographies, or they may be metaphorical. In either case, boundaries will be required; and where there are boundaries, there will be border incidents. Whenever boundaries come under threat, religions are likely to become either offensive or defensive. The threat may be one of literal invasion and displacement, or it may be metaphorical, as, for example, when it seems that *secular values and interests are displacing those of the inherited religion. In either case, at least some religious people will seek to hold, or even to extend, their ground. For this reason, religious wars are common, either between subsystems within the same religion, or between religions, or between religions and the non-religious world. The seriousness of the issues affords a powerful reinforcement of *fundamentalism, that is, the determination to identify and maintain certain fundamental and non-negotiable markers of true or legitimate religious identity. Maintaining that identity and defending boundaries against invasion or erosion leads repeatedly to religious wars, or wars in which religions are involved. All religions defend the legitimacy of war in some circumstances (see *Just War), even those religions which insist on non-violence or on **ahimsa*. The circumstances are restricted, and careful rules of limitation are usually specified. But war, particularly in defence, is recognized.

That is one reason why virtually all the long-running and apparently insoluble problems in the world, in Northern Ireland, Bosnia, Cyprus, the Middle East, Kashmir, *Khalistan, Sri Lanka, India and Pakistan, East Timor, the Philippines, have deep religious roots. If you wish to see where future conflicts will occur, draw on a map of the world the lines where religions, or subsystems of religions, meet. It is true that religions are capable of coexisting with each other, and often have done so for long periods of time: that has been the case, for example, until very recently, with Jewish communities in Muslim lands. But they do so only so long as the continuity of each of the religions in question does not seem to be threatened.

The reason why religions are so intransigent is because they protect and transmit all that information which is of such high and tested value, at least to those who see things that way. People would rather die than abandon such inherited treasure, especially when they have often tested it and proved it to be of worth in their own case. This is the paradox of religious urgency: religions are such bad news (when they are) only because they are such good news: they protect so much that is so important and so well tested through time that people would die rather than lose it. There is no doubt that one can point to many kinds of damage which religions have done, in terms, for example, of spiritual terrorization or of the subordination of women, in most aspects of their lives, to the decisions and determinations of men. But religions also remain now as they have been in the past, the major resource for the transformation of life and the transfiguration of art. There will always, therefore, be many who will resist a threat to their religion and the ruin of all that goes with it.

The Future of Religion

War and fundamentalism, however, are not the only responses to novelty. Religions are open to change, and have indeed changed much through the centuries. Change is invariably resisted by some, as being the kind of threat summarized in the previous paragraphs. Sometimes it is so strongly resisted that new *sects, new *cults, even *new religions split off and begin a history of their own. But because religions protect and transmit information of such high value and proven worth in the transformation of life, the appropriation of that information into life often demands transformation and change in the institution. The procedures of change are different in each religion, but the fact of change is a part of religious history, even though change has often, perhaps usually, been resisted. Religions are the custodians of collective memory: they carry the constraints from the past which control human life into distinct, but within the boundaries shareable, outcomes, so that a Buddhist, for example, is recognizable in any country or any generation, even though no Buddhist is identical with any other. But collective memory may demand change in order that the values and goals of a system can be appropriated and lived in new circumstances. The importance of collective memory is that it enables religions to maintain identity while at the same time being open to change.

What of the future of religion? Human religiosity will not diminish except by way of atrophy (by non-use, if that happens), because the preparation for it is so deeply embedded in the brain—and, many would say, because it then develops and flourishes in relation to what is truly discovered, however approximately and corrigibly this is described. Thus the extraordinary discoveries of somatic exploration and exegesis will not become unattainable, even if, for the sake of argument, the neurophysiology of the underlying brain events is better understood. But the forms of expression will certainly change. Partly that is a matter of language, and partly one of organization. All our languages about anything, even about something as relatively obvious as the universe, are approximate, provisional, corrigible, and frequently wrong, at least from the point of view of later generations; and yet, as in the case of the natural sciences, they can be extremely reliable. If that is true of the universe, it will certainly be true also of God, *Brahman, and the Buddha-nature: what we say will always be approximate and incomplete, but it will continue to achieve great reliability. It is the corrigibility and approximate nature of all languages which opens up the necessity of faith. But faith, as trust in the tradition and the teacher, then sets out on journeys which for many (not inevitably, and certainly not for all) reveal the truth of that for which it yearns. 'Eternity in time', to quote the phrase of Henry *Vaughan, is no longer a paradox but a persuasion. Meditation enters into meaning far beyond common senses, and rests in that supreme condition which leaves behind it even such treasures as beauty, excitement, and delight. Prayer is presence, before One who elicits praise, thanksgiving, and joy, as well as *penitence and sorrow. Because prayer is the greatest of the human languages of love, it connects others to God as well.

The truth of all this is so well known and practised that it will endure, even in the midst of great changes. So far as organization is concerned, we are on the edge of unimaginable transformations in the methods and speed of communication. The *ecclesia* of the internet does not require physical presence. And yet humanity does. The ecclesial necessity which helped to bring religions into being may yet serve purposes of humanity which could scarcely be envisaged until the last decade.

What, finally, of the definition of religion? Has it

come any closer into our sights? Clearly not. We have simply shown that *Wittgenstein was right when he observed of games that it is easier to recognize a game than to define it—or at least, than it is to define the word 'game' in such a way that all the characteristics of all games are embraced within it (see e.g. *Philosophical Investigations,* nos. 66 f., on 'family resemblances'). We can recognize a religion when we see one because we know what the many characteristics of religion are; but we would not expect to find any religion which exhibited all the characteristics without exception. That process of discerning the characteristics is the first level of *phenomenology, and it is the reason why Ninian Smart (*The World's Religions* . . . (Cambridge: Cambridge University Press, 1989), 12–21) has proposed that we can gain a more balanced and comprehensive view of 'the luxurious vegetation of the world's religions' by observing what is the case in seven different dimensions: the practical and ritual; the experiential and emotional; the narrative or mythical; the doctrinal and philosophical; the ethical and legal; the social and institutional; and the material (art, architecture, and sacred places). It will still remain the case that the second level of phenomenology remains to be done, the testing and examination of what has brought the brilliant and majestic creation of religion into being in the first place, and has sustained it to the present. Religion is a risk of intolerance, cruelty, bigotry, social oppression, and self-opinionated nastiness. Within that 'luxurious vegetation' are ruthless predators of power and ambition. But religion also remains, as that first definition of Marx recognized, the heart and soul of what might otherwise be (and in the twentieth century all too often has been) a heartless world.

John Bowker

A

A (1) Symbol of emptiness (*śūnyatā) and of the undifferentiated source of appearance in *Zen Buddhism. In Japanese esoteric Buddhism (*mikkyō), *aji*, the first sound in the Sanskrit alphabet, contains the epitome of all truth, and as such is a key element in meditation: *aji-kan* (meditation on the letter A) involves sitting in the lotus or half-lotus position (*padmāsana) concentrating on an image of the moon in the middle of which is drawn the Skt. letter A. The sound of it is repeated with each breath (in and out) until the letter in the moon is visualized even with eyes closed. If this is maintained, all dualities are overcome, all states of appearance are destroyed, and the buddha-nature is attained.

A (2) (Gk., alpha). First letter of the Greek alphabet, combined with the last, *Ω* (omega), to refer to God as the beginning and the end, the all-encompassing.

A (3) Letter of negation in several languages, as in, e.g., *atheism, *adharma.

Aaron (*c.*13th cent. BCE). Elder brother of *Moses. By acting as Moses' mouthpiece, he contributed to the freeing of the Israelites from slavery in Egypt (Exodus 1–10). Subsequently he made the *golden calf for the people to console them for Moses' absence on Mount *Sinai (Exodus 32). He was consecrated *priest of the *Sanctuary (Exodus 28–9, Leviticus 8–9) and was perceived in biblical literature as the archetypal *priest and the founder of the hereditary priesthood (see AARONIDES). In *rabbinic Judaism Aaron was perceived as one close to the people, a peace-maker. *Hillel commanded, 'Be a disciple of Aaron, loving and pursuing peace, loving your neighbours and drawing them to *Torah.' Biblical criticism sees a less unified picture, with the priestly, military, and other roles coming from different sources.

In the Qur'ān, he appears as Hārūn, a *prophet and helper to his brother Mūsā (Moses). Mūsā prays: 'Appoint for me a helper (*wazīr) from my family, my brother Hārūn' (20. 29–30). He is mentioned among the prophets (4. 164), and in sūra 20 which narrates the episode of the golden calf. Hārūn opposes this idolatry (verse 90), but is none the less rebuked by Mūsā on his return.

A. Cody, *A History of Old Testament Priesthood* (1969); H. Valentin, *Aaron . . .* (1978).

Aaron ben Elijah (?1328–69). *Karaite Jewish philosopher and exegete. His greatest work was the trilogy *Ez Hayyim* (Tree of Life), *Gan Eden* (Garden of *Eden), and *Keter Torah* (Crown of the Law). This covered the range of philosophy of religion, Karaite law, and a commentary on the *Pentateuch. The aim of Aaron's philosophy was to produce a Karaite counterpart to *Maimonides' *Guide to the Perplexed*. Extracts of his work in Eng. tr. can be found in L. Nemoy (ed.), *Karaite Anthology* (1952).

Aaron ben Jacob ha-Kohen of Lunel (13th/14th cent. CE). French Jewish *Talmudist. His most famous work, *Orhot Ḥayyim* (Ways of Life), was a compilation of Jewish law which was widely quoted by, for example, Joseph *Caro and Simeon *Duran. The anonymous **Kol Bo* (Compendium) is generally thought to be an abbreviated form of *Orhot Ḥayyim*.

Aaronides. Descendants of *Aaron and members of the Israelite *priesthood. According to Numbers 18. 1–7, there is a clear distinction between members of the house of *Levi whose function is to 'minister to you while you and your sons with you are before the tent of testimony' (v. 2) and the direct descendants of Aaron who 'shall attend to your priesthood for all that concerns the altar and that which is within the veil' (v. 7). Most scholars believe this is an oversimplification since other sources, such as Deuteronomy 10. 8–9, imply that the entire Levite tribe had priestly status. It is possible that the Aaronides were an Egyptian priestly family who followed Moses before the tribe of Levi—certainly many Egyptian names can be found in the records of the Aaronic priesthood (e.g. Exodus 6. 25, 1 Samuel 1. 3, Jeremiah 20. 1). For reading, see AARON.

Aaron of Baghdad (mid-9th cent. CE). A Babylonian Jewish scholar who lived in Italy and is regarded as a link between the Babylonian *academies and W. Jewish culture. Although none of his writings survive, stories were told of his magical powers and his possession of certain *mystical secrets. He is described by *Eleazar ben Judah of Worms in the 13th cent. as *av kol ha-sodot* ('the father of all secrets').

Ab-. For words beginning Ab-, check also alternative spelling, AV-, e.g. 'Abodah is under 'Avodah.

Abaddon (Heb.). Place of destruction, mentioned in the *Wisdom literature (e.g. Job 31. 12, Psalm 88. 12). In the *Talmud, it is a name given to *Gehenna.

'Abādites (Muslim sect): see 'IBĀDIYA.

Abangan (Javanese, 'brown coloured'). Javanese who are culturally (rather than observantly) Muslim. They are, e.g., adept practioners of *wayang kulit/purwa* (see THEATRE). They have come under increasing pressure from observant Muslims (*santri*) to conform, but remain resistant to the eradication of indigenous customs.

C. Geertz, *Religion of Java* (1960).

Abarbanel (Jewish statesman): see ABRABANEL.

Abba (1) (Aram., 'Father'). An address to God used by *Jesus. That Jesus addressed God in prayer in this familiar way is one of the best-attested features of his recorded words (e.g. Luke 11. 2), and was perhaps blasphemous in the ears of the religious authorities (John 10. 33–6). The Aramaic word itself is found in the New Testament in Mark 14. 36, Romans 8. 15, and Galatians 4. 6; it is a term both of a child's respectful relation to its father and of a confidential relation to an esteemed person. It is thus oversimple to regard it as a child's intimate word of affection. In Orthodox Christianity, 'Abba' is used to address the superior in a (male) religious community; Abbas is the title of a Coptic bishop.

J. Barr, 'Abba Isn't Daddy', *Journ. of Theol. Studies*, 39 (1988); J. Jeremias, *The Prayers of Jesus* (1967).

Abba (2) (late 3rd/early 4th cent. CE). Jewish Babylonian *amora. He is mentioned as a disciple of R. Huna and R. Judah. He later settled in *Israel, is described as 'our teacher in the land of Israel' (*B.Sanh.* 17b), and his teachings are to be found in the *Talmud and *Midrash. Because he often visited Babylonia, he was seen as a link between the two centres. In his view, 'God is strict, even to the weight of a hair, with his loved ones.'

Abba bar Kahana (late 3rd cent. CE). Jewish Palestinian *amora. He was regarded as one of the greatest exponents of *aggadah of his era, and many of his statements are thought to reflect the problems facing the Jews at the time—e.g. 'No serpent ever bites below unless it is incited from above . . . , nor does a government persecute a man unless it is incited from above' (*Eccles. R.* 10. 11) probably refers to the persecution of the Jewish community at the time.

Abbahu (3rd/4th cent. CE). Jewish Palestinian *amora. He held a prominent position in the Jewish community of Caesarea and was well-known for his generosity, wealth, and excellent relationship with the Roman authorities. He issued proclamations and introduced customs such as the order of *blessing the *shofar on *Rosh ha-Shanah. He was particularly opposed to sectarianism within the community, and was equally severe about Christians and *Samaritans. He insisted 'it was ordained that, "Blessed be the name of his glorious Kingdom for ever and ever", be recited in a loud voice—to offset any false charges by Sectarians' (*B.Pes.* 56a).

J. Neusner (ed.), *Christianity, Judaism and Other Greco-Roman Cults*, iv (1975), *ad loc.*

ʿAbbās (uncle of *Muḥammad and source of the *ʿAbbāsid dynasty): see AL-ʿABBĀS.

Abba Saul (mid-2nd cent. CE). Jewish Palestinian *tanna. He passed on traditions concerning the human embryo and the structure and furnishing of the *Temple. He may well have been a disciple of R. *Akiva. He called himself a gravedigger and he described many current burial practices. As a general principle, he held that 'moral life and action are more important than learning'.

ʿAbbās Effendi (one-time head of Bahāī faith): see SHOGHI EFFENDI.

ʿAbbāsids (Arab., *al-dawlah al-ʿabbāsiya*, from *Banū al-ʿAbbās*). Muslim dynasty in power 749–1258 CE (AH 132–656). Their name is derived from their ancestor *al-ʿAbbās, the uncle of *Muḥammad. After the death of *ʿAlī b. Abī Tālib, the fourth and last of the Rāshidūn or 'rightly guided' caliphs (*Khalīfa), the rule passed to the *Umayyads with their capital in *Damascus (660–750 CE (AH 41–132).) Social, economic, political, and religious factors combined led to an uprising with strong Persian and *Shīʿite elements, and the Umayyads were ousted, nearly all of them killed, and al-Saffāḥ ('the spiller', i.e., of Umayyad blood) took over power as the first of the ʿAbbāsid rulers. The next caliph, al-Manṣūr, founded the city of Baghdād, to be the capital of the Muslim empire and a centre of learning, culture, and fashion. One of the most famous of the ʿAbbāsid caliphs was Hārūn al-Rashīd (764–809 (AH 147–194); his splendid court is reflected in *The Thousand and One Nights*). His son al-Maʾmūn (813–33 (AH 198–218)) founded the *Bayt al-ḥikma* (house of wisdom) for the translation from Gk. of classical texts of philosophy, science, and medicine. Under the ʿAbbāsids, the *Muʿtazilite school of theology enjoyed a brief period of supremacy, but the more orthodox schools eventually regained their dominant place. Although the ʿAbbāsids were the nominal rulers throughout the Muslim empire, various dynasties gained effective control of parts of this vast region. The Buwayhids, from Persia, actually entered Baghdād and controlled affairs from 945 (AH 334) for just over a century. The *Fāṭimids in Egypt, a *Shīʿa dynasty, took power in 909 (AH 297) but were finally ousted by the Ayyūbids under *Ṣalāḥ al-Dīn (Saladin) in 1171 (AH 567). One survivor of the massacre of the Umayyads, ʿAbd al-Raḥmān, made his way to Spain (al-Andalus) and founded an independent dynasty with its capital at Cordoba.

In 1258 (AH 656) the Mongols captured and sacked Baghdād, rolled up the body of the last caliph in a carpet and rode their horses over it. Thus the ʿAbbāsid caliphate came to an end, although another branch reigned in Cairo 1261–1517 (AH 659–923), when they were supplanted by the *Ottomans.

H. Kennedy, *The Abbasid Caliphate* (1981); J. Lassner, *The Shaping of Abbasid Rule* (1980); M. J. L. Young *et al.* (ed.), *Religion, Learning and Science in the ʿAbbasid Period* (1991).

Abbaye (late 3rd/4th cent. CE). Jewish Babylonian *amora. As head of the *academy at *Pumbedita, he debated legal points with the most prominent scholars of his time. His discussions with his colleague *Rava are recorded at length in the *Talmud. He also was familiar with popular maxims and common folk remedies. In his teachings, Abbaye was the first to make explicit the distinction between the literal and the figurative meaning of a text. In both his teachings and his actions, he stressed the importance of promoting harmony in social relationships 'so that one may be beloved above and well-liked below' (*B.Ber.* 17a).

J. Neusner, *A History of the Jews in Babylonia*, iv (1966–70), *ad loc.*

Abbé (French). Title for a clergyman. It was originally restricted to the *abbot of a monastery, but in the 16th cent. many secular clerics were appointed nominal abbots, and the term came to be transferred to *secular priests in general.

Abbess. Feminine form of *abbot, dating back to 6th cent. An abbess is elected by a community of *nuns as its superior. The title was used originally in certain *Benedictine communities, and was later extended to *Poor Clares and other communities adhering to stability in a particular place. Abbesses exercised wide authority, sometimes using various pontifical insignia (even occasionally hearing the confessions of other nuns). These powers were restricted in the Code of Canon Law in 1917. The Rite for the Blessing of an Abbess (post-*Vatican II) prays that 'her manner of life may show clearly what she is, a mother'.

Abbey. Building or buildings used (or once used) by a religious order of *monks or *nuns. The name was originally used of *Benedictine orders (e.g. Benedictines, *Cistercians, *Carthusians, *Trappists). Under the Benedictine Rule, each abbey is a 'family' under the authority of its *abbot.

Abbot (Aram., Syr., *abba*, 'father'). The head of a Christian monastic community, especially in the *Benedictine or *Cistercian traditions. The term is used in translation for the head of communities in other religions: e.g. *roshi. The Tibetan *mkhan-po* (also, following the pronunciation, *khenpo*) is often translated 'abbot': he is the senior official who presides at the ordination of new monks.

ʿAbd (Arab., 'servant' (pl. *ʿibād*) or 'slave' (pl. *ʿabīd*). In the religious sense, a 'servant' or 'worshipper' of *Allāh. ʿAbd is often found in combination with one of the names of Allāh, as a name for a Muslim, e.g. ʿAbdallāh, ʿAbd al-Nāṣir, ʿAbd al-Karīm. In the secular sense, the *Qurʾān speaks of *slaves, of 'a slave possessed (by a master)' (*ʿabd mamlūk*, 16. 75). The Qurʾān accepts slavery as a fact, but encourages kind treatment of slaves, and to free them is an act of piety (2. 177). Women slaves could be taken as concubines, but could also become legal wives.

Abdal (Arab., 'substitutes'). A numerical set of seventy *Sūfī holy people, constant in number until the end of the world, when their number diminishes and the world ends. The central figure (known only to God) is the *qutb, or axis, of the world; around him are four pegs (*awstād*), so that together the abdal form a tent of protection for the world.

ʿAbd al-Bahā (one-time head of Bahāī faith): see ʿABDUʾL-BAHĀ.

ʿAbd al-Jabbār (*c*.935–*c*.1025 (AH 322–415)). A leading Muslim *Muʿtazilite theologian. Born in Iran, he was educated according to the schools of *al-Shāfiʿī and *al-Ashʿarī. He moved in a rationalist direction, and wrote many books, of which the best-known is *al-Mughnī fī abwāb al-tawhīd waʾl-ʿadl*: *tawḥīd and ʿadl are the first two of the five Muʿtazilite principles.

G. F. Hourani, *Islamic Rationalism* . . . (1971).

ʿAbd al-Karīm al-Jīlī (*c*.1365/6–*c*.1412 (AH 767–815)). A Muslim mystic who was a follower of *Ibn al-ʿArabī's system and wrote the *Sūfī treatise **Al-Insān al-Kāmil* (The Perfect Man), dealing with cosmic, metaphysical, and ontological problems. His ideas were widely influential. According to Jīlī, 'Being is one; all apparent differences are modes, aspects and manifestations of reality. The phenomenal is the outward expression of the real. The essence (*dhat*) of God is unknowable. Pure Being as such has neither name nor attribute; only when it gradually descends from its absoluteness and enters the realm of manifestation, do names and attributes appear. The phenomenal world, the world of attributes, is no illusion; it really exists as the self-revelation of Pure Being.'

In Jīlī's *ontology, *Allah, the Pure Being, reveals itself in the following line of descent. *ʾAma* is the unknowable Pure Essence (*Ilahīyya*); the Absolute in its absoluteness before its first manifestation. *Ahadīyya* is the first manifestation (*tajallī*) of Abstract Oneness exclusive of attributes, qualities, or relations and is followed by *Wahidīyya* (Unity in plurality), which comprises all attributes and qualities under the aspect of unity. The fourth stage of descent is *Rububīyya* (Lordship), which is the principle of order for the next series of individualizations, and maintains them in their proper place. The fifth level is *Rahmanīyya*: here the Lord through an act of mercy brings the universe into existence from himself, and manifests his Attributes (*sifat*): 'The Lord is the one substance of the universe. The universe is ice and the Lord is the water of which the ice is made.' The differentiation of universal phenomena is the result of mutual relationships of Divine attributes such as the Creator and the Destroyer, the Knower and the Known.

Jīlī also elaborated the doctrine of *Muḥammad as the *Logos, the Perfect Man *(al-Insān-al-Kāmil): Man is the microcosm in which all attributes are united, and in him alone does the Absolute become conscious of itself in all its diverse aspects. The Perfect Man is the place where all opposed terms of reality and appearance are harmonized. The Lord, having completely realized itself in the human nature of the Perfect Man, returns into itself through the medium of human nature. For Jīlī, this absolutely Perfect Man is the Prophet Muḥammad, and in every age the Perfect Men are an outward manifestation of the essence of Muḥammad. Muḥammad should be loved and adored as the most perfect manifestation of the Lord.

Nicholson, *Studies in Islamic Mysticism* (1978), 83.

ʿAbd Allāh ibn Maimūn al-Qaddāḥ (*c.*10th cent./AH 3rd cent.). A revered figure among *Shīʿa Muslims, who did much to establish and organize *Ismāʿīliya; but the details of his own life remain obscure. Even the meaning of al-Qaddaḥ is uncertain: it may be from *qadaḥ*, 'a bowl', one who makes occult preparations; or *qaddaḥ*, flint, the striker of sparks of divine guidance.

ʿAbd Allah ibn Yāsīn (Muslim revivalist): see ALMORAVIDS.

ʿAbd al-Muṭṭalib ibn Hāshim (of the tribe of Quraysh). Grandfather of *Muḥammad. He was born in *Madina but was taken to *Mecca by his mother while still a child, soon after his father Hāshim's death, and cared for by his uncle. He became a merchant, and probably had a certain influence in Mecca. He had the monopoly of supplying pilgrims with water, and was responsible for digging out the well of *Zamzam. When Muḥammad's father died, he became guardian of the child, but himself died when Muḥammad was aged 8, and the guardianship passed to his uncle *Abū Ṭālib the father of *ʿAlī.

ʿAbd al-Qādir al-Jīlī (more often Jīlānī, 1077–1166 (AH 470–561)). Preacher, *Ḥanbalite theologian, and supposed founder of the *Qādirīya *Sūfī order. He was born in Naif in Jīlān province, south of the Caspian Sea. He studied in Baghdād, remaining there until his death. He came to be recognized as the leading authority in religious sciences, but it was not until he was 50 years old (521/1127) that he first appeared in public as a preacher. His fame as an orator attracted students from all over the Muslim world. It is said that his sermons converted many Jews and Christians to Islam, and many Muslims to the spiritual life. Financial support from his many followers enabled him to establish a *ribāt* (Sūfī centre), where the poor and needy were cared for. He served as *muftī, teacher of Quranic exegesis, *ḥadīth, and *fiqh.

ʿAbd al-Qādir's Sūfī path consists in fighting the 'greater *jihād' against the lower self, rather than the 'lesser jihād' of the physical struggle against the enemies of Islam. His way is to eradicate the idolatry of the self, to recognize in all that happens, whether of good or evil, the will of God, and to live in submission to his will according to his Holy Law. ʿAbd al-Qādir's major works are *al-Fath al-Rabbanī* (Victory of the Lord) and *al-Futūḥ al-Ghayb* (Glimpses of the Unseen, tr. A. D. Ahmad, 1958): 'To take anything on the basis of desire without any order from God is swerving from duty and opposing the truth; and to take anything without being prompted by desire is harmony and agreement with truth; and to discard it is insincerity and hypocrisy' (sermon 39, *Futūḥ al-Ghayb*). ʿAbd al-Qādir's sober Sufism gained wide acceptance amongst the orthodox circles, and therein lies the reason for the great spread of the Qādirīya order throughout the Muslim world. He was given the title Ghawth-al-Aʿẓam (the greatest of all helpers) and his tomb in Baghdād still attracts many devotees. His service to Islam is summarized in the story of a sick man who called on him to help him sit up. When ʿAbd al-Qādir did so, the sick man grew to immense size, saying that he was Islam, who had wasted away, but was now restored to strength.

M. A. Aini, *Un grand saint de l'Islam* . . . (1938); ed. S. H. Nasr, *Islamic Spirituality*, II, (1991).

ʿAbd al-Rāziq, ʿAlī (1888–1966). Egyptian writer and scholar whose *Islām wa Usūl al-Hukm* (Islam and the Principles of Government) caused a sensation in 1825. Responding to the demise of the *Ottoman Caliphate the previous year, he claimed that Islam had never been essentially political, that the Caliphate was dispensable, and that Islam was a purely spiritual loyalty.

Fr. tr. in *Revue des Études Islamiques* (1933 and 1934).

ʿAbduh, Muḥammad (1849–1905 (AH 1266–1322)). Egyptian Muslim theologian, known as *al-ustad al-iman* (master and guide). He was the founder of the Egyptian Muslim modernist school. He was from a peasant family in lower Egypt, and studied at *al-Azhar University, and in Paris, where he met *al-Afghānī and became his closest disciple (founding with him the *Salafiyya). Under al-Afghānī's influence, ʿAbduh broke away from religious traditionalism and set about the task of presenting Islamic tenets (in a way that would be acceptable to the modern mind), of reforming Islamic institutions, and of allowing the pursuit of knowledge. ʿAbduh emphasized the important function of reason in Islam, that although faith and reason operate in different spheres, they must not conflict but must positively co-operate in human advancement. By restating Islam in such a way, ʿAbduh attempted to open the door, by way of *ijtihād, to new influences and the acquisition of modern knowledge. Furthermore, he worked for the removal of the apparent impediment, in the vast *ḥadīth literature, to the way of modernization.

ʿAbduh's major work, *Risālat-al-Tawhid* (1897), and the journal *al-Manār* (1897), were widely read and supported by many Muslims, but also provoked bitter hostility from orthodox circles. In 1899, ʿAbduh obtained the highest religious position in Egypt, that of state *muftī, which he held till his death. ʿAbduh used this powerful position to push through many reforms. In his endeavour to promote ijtihād and *ijmāʿ, he launched a strong attack on *taqlīd, (acceptance of authority from the past), and initiated new laws in changing times for the common good (maṣlaḥa) in Egypt (e.g. ʿAbduh's *fatwā on permitting the consumption of meat slaughtered by Jews and Christians, and legalizing loan interests). He condemned what he regarded as the malpractices of the *Sūfī Orders, such as excessive veneration and worship of saints, and withdrawal from worldly life. ʿAbduh also rejected the hairsplitting of the *ʿulamā in matters of *sharīʿa over trivial matters such as nail-cutting and ritual ablution.

He regarded his commentary (*tafsīr) on the *Qur'ān as his most important work, but it was unfinished at his death, and was completed (and revised) later, by Muḥammad Rashīd Riḍā.

C. C. Adams, *Islam and Modernism in Egypt* (1933); M. H. Kerr, *Islamic Reform . . .* (1966).

ʿAbdu'l-Bahā (1844–1921, lit. Servant of Bahā). Title of ʿAbbās Effendi, eldest son and appointed successor of *Bahā'u'llāh as head (1892–1921) of the *Bahā'ī faith. Successfully rebutting a challenge to his leadership from his half-brother, Mīrzā Muḥammad ʿAlī, he superintended the expansion of the Bahā'ī religion to North America and Europe, delineated its further expansion, and guided the Iranian Bahā'ī community through the turbulent years of the constitutional movement. In addressing contemporary social and economic issues, he gave expression to a distinctive Bahā'ī programme of social reform. He remained under restriction in the *Ottoman prison-city of Akka until the freeing of religious and political prisoners in 1908 by the Young Turks. Thereafter he made extended missionary journeys to visit his followers and sympathizers in Egypt, Europe, and North America (1910–13). Giving hundreds of public talks, he called for wide-ranging social reform, warned of the impending threat of world war, and advocated the establishment of an international court of arbitration. He died in Haifa on 28 November 1921, having appointed his eldest grandson, *Shoghi Effendi Rabbānī to be his successor. His writings, which cover a wide range of doctrinal, philosophical, and social topics, consist mainly of letters to his followers. Almost 27,000 of his letters have so far been collected. His followers also collected and published the transcripts of many of the talks he gave in Palestine, Europe, and North America.

Eng. trs., M. Gail; E. G. Browne; H. M. Balyuzi, *ʿAbdu'l-Bahā*, (1971).

Abel. A herdsman, in Jewish *scripture, the younger son of the first human beings, *Adam and *Eve. According to Genesis 4. 1–9 he was murdered by his elder brother, the farmer, *Cain. Cain was jealous that Abel's *sacrifice had been accepted while his was rejected. This has been interpreted as symbolizing the conflict between the agricultural and the nomadic way of life, but this is an inference from the text. Rabbinic exegesis took Cain's offence to be a denial of eternal life and thus of ultimate accountability.

Abelard, Peter (1079–1142). Christian philosopher and theologian. Born at Pallet, near Nantes, he was one of the most brilliant and controversial theologians of his day. His academic career was cut short after his love-affair with Héloïse in Paris, where he was a popular lecturer. He challenged current philosophical orthodoxy, preparing the way for *nominalism, and was condemned for his teaching on the *Trinity. His doctrine of the *atonement, emphasizing the love of Christ, manifest in his life and passion, which calls forth a human response of love, has had a continuing influence: 'The purpose and cause of the *incarnation was that God might illuminate the world by his wisdom and stir it to the love of himself.' His works include *Christian Theology, Ethics*, and his letters to Héloïse.

E. M. Buytaert (ed.), *Peter Abelard* (1974); D. E. Luscombe, *Peter Abelard* (1979).

Abercius, St (d. *c.*200 CE). Christian *bishop of Hieropolis in Phrygia Salutaris. He is known from an important inscription apparently set up by him over his future tomb. It mentions a trip to Rome, where 'I saw a people bearing the splendid seal' (=*baptism), and beyond the Euphrates, where 'everywhere I had associates'. He also mentions the currency of the *eucharist with bread and wine.

Abgar V, 4 BCE–50 CE, King of Edessa. According to a popular tradition as early as *Eusebius (and also in the *Doctrine of *Addai*) he wrote a letter to *Jesus asking him to visit and heal him. A letter from Jesus in return promised to send an apostle. Some versions add that Jesus sent back a portrait of himself. *Egeria recorded in the 4th cent. that Jesus' letter was preserved at Edessa, and copies were used as talismans.

Abhabba-ṭṭhāna (Pāli, 'condition of being incapable'). A characteristic of the *Arhat in Buddhism, who is regarded as incapable of certain kinds of moral transgression, e.g. transgressing against the pañca-śila. The doctrine of the Arhat's 'incapability' reinforces the idea of the inseparability of 'religious' from 'moral' perfection.

Ābhāsa-caitanya (Skt., 'reflection' + 'consciousness'). The way in which, in Hinduism, absolute consciousness (*cit) is reflected in human awareness.

The world-entangled self (*jīva) takes this reflection to be the reality and thus fails to break through to the true realization of *Brahman, and of the true self (*ātman) as Brahman.

Abhava (Skt.). In Hinduism, the non-reality or non-existence of manifest appearances, hence (by the realization that this is so) release (*mokṣa) from entanglement in them. In Buddhism, abhava reinforces *Nāgārjuna's argument for *śūnyatā.

Abhayākaragupta (11th/12th cent.). Buddhist monk and scholar, especially of *Tantric Buddhism. He was born a *brahman, but became Buddhist in response to a vision. He was initiated into tantra, but remained a monastic scholar. He wrote many works on monastic discipline, issues in *abhidhamma, and tantra. The tr. of his works into Tibetan began under his own supervision, thus extending his influence.

Abhaya-mudra (Skt., 'fearlessness' + *mudra). The gesture of being without fear (only acquired in full in the condition of *mokṣa). In Hinduism it is characteristic of *Viṣṇu; in Buddhism it is common in representations of the *Buddha.

Abhaya-vacana (Skt., 'fearlessness' + 'words'). The capacity in Hinduism to speak without mortal or bodily fear, when one has achieved spiritual insight.

Abheda-bodha-vākya (Skt., 'identity' + 'alertness' + 'utterance'). A formula in Hinduism to invoke the absolute truth.

Abhibhāvayatana (Skt.; Pāli *abhibhāyatana*). Eight fields of mastery or control of the perception of manifest appearances, an early practice in Buddhism. They are mastery of the perceptions of: (i) form in relation to one's own body and of limited forms outside it; (ii) the same and of forms without limit outside it; (iii) no form in relation to one's own body and of limited forms outside it; (iv) the same and of forms without limit outside it; (v)–(viii) different manifestations of beauty.

Abhibhāyatana (control of perceptions): see ABHIBHĀVAYATANA.

Abhicāra (Tantric form of Durga): see CHINNAMASTA.

Abhidhamma (Pali; Skt., *abhidharma*, 'special teaching'), *Buddhist reflection, often analytic, on the meaning of the Buddha's teaching. The *Abhidhamma Piṭaka thus forms one of the 'three baskets' (*Tripiṭaka) of Buddhist text collections. The abhidhamma of the different Buddhist schools varies in detail, but in general it is concerned with the more exact description and analysis of the dhamma/ *dharmas which constitute appearance (and in particular of the *skandhas), and also with the whole process of *paticca-samuppāda (conditioned arising of phenomena). One consequence of this is a careful survey of different types of human character as these relate to Buddhist teaching and *meditation. The purpose is practical, not simply speculative, since the analysis will promote a wiser pursuit of both proximate and ultimate goals.

H. V. Guenther, *Philosophy and Psychology in the Abhidharma* (1974); Nyanaponika Thera, *Abhidhamma Studies* (1965).

Abhidhamma Piṭaka (Pāli; Skt., Abhidharma Piṭaka). The third and final section of the Buddhist *canon (*tripiṭaka). Each school of early Buddhism had its own particular version of the Abhidhamma Pitaka, though the only complete versions now extant are those of the *Sarvāstivādins (in Chinese and Tibetan) and the *Theravādins (in Pāli). Although generally conceded to be later in composition than the *Vinaya and Sutta-Piṭakas, achieving their final form in *c.*1st cent. BCE, the books contained within the Abhidhamma Piṭaka are regarded as genuine buddha-vācana, and, for this reason, have been incorporated within the Canon. According to Theravādin tradition, the Buddha first taught the Abhidhamma books to the Tāvatiṃsa-*devas and *Māyādevī during the solitary months of the rain-retreat (see VASSA); he then repeated them to *Sāriputta, from whom they passed into Buddhist tradition.

In the early cents. CE, there grew up a voluminous tradition of commentaries and manuals on the Abhidhamma. One relatively late school, however, the *Sautrāntikas, acquired its name from its refusal to recognize the Abhidhamma as authoritative.

The contents are mainly concerned with philosophical and psychological issues. Of particular importance for the history of Buddhist thought is (Pāli) bk. 7, *Kathāvatthu* (Points of Controversy), dealing with 219 contested issues.

Eng. trs. Pali Text Society; S. Z. Aung, *Points of Controversy* (1915); H. V. Guether, *Philosophy and Psychology in the Abhidharma* (1957); N. Mahathera, *Guide through the Abhidhamma-Piṭaka* (1957); C. Willemen, *The Essence of Metaphysics* (1975).

Abhidharma-kośa Śāstra. A systematic *Sarvāstivāda Buddhist treatise composed by (or attributed to) *Vasubandhu in the period before he embraced *Mahāyāna Buddhism. The work comprises two parts: verse (*Abh.k. kārikā*) and prose commentary (*Abh.k. bhāṣya*). The verse expresses *Sarvāstivāda *Abhidharma teaching; the prose, *Sautrāntika interpretation of that teaching. As an encyclopaedia of Abhidharma, the work became absolutely central to the tradition of study within Buddhism in subsequent cents. A Skt. version was discovered in Tibet in 1934.

Fr. tr. E. Lamotte (1976); L. de la Vallée-Poussin (1923–6).

Abhijñā (supernatural powers): see ABHIÑÑĀ.

Abhimāna (Skt., 'self-esteem'). The self in Hinduism that has made a declaration of independence, i.e. of self-sufficiency, and is therefore far removed from the true realization of the unity of all appearance in relation to *Brahman.

Abhinavagupta (960–1050 CE). A Hindu theologian of *Kashmir *Śaivism who wrote extensively on poetics, aesthetics, and religious doctrine and practice. In his work *Tantrism finds its philosophical articulation. His comprehensive *Light on Tantra* (*Tantrāloka*, Ital. tr. R. Gnoli *Lucce delle sacre scritture*, 1960) is a synthesis of the traditions, teaching, and practice of Kashmir Śaivism in which the absolute (Maheśvara, Paramaśiva) is conceived as pure consciousness (*saṃvit*, *caitanya) which is the union of light (*prakāśa*) and awareness (*vimarśa*). The hierarchical cosmos is an appearance (*ābhāsa*) concealing the true nature of pure consciousness from which it emanates. For Abhinavagupta, cosmogony is a process of the gradual coagulation of the absolute into sound (*vācaka*) and objects (*vācya*) or *tattvas. The goal of religious practice (*sādhana, *pūjā and *yoga) is the recognition (*pratyabhijñā*) of the identity of the self (*aṇu) with the pure consciousness of Maheśvara. His ideas are summarized in his *Essence of Supreme Meaning* (*Paramārthasāra*, Fr. tr. L. Silburn, 1957). He also contributed to aesthetics (*rāsa), writing a commentary (*locana*) on the great aesthetician Ānandavardhana's *Dhvanyāloka* and Bharata's *Nātya Śāstra* (Eng. tr. R. Gnoli, *The Aesthetic Experience According to Abhinavagupta*, 1956). Abhinavagupta was probably the first Indian philosopher to link aesthetic and religious experience, maintaining that the aesthetic emotions (rāsa) originate in the aesthetic emotion of tranquility (*śāntarasa*) which is also an experience of the absolute. Applying the categories of aesthetic to religious experience was developed much later by the Gosvamins, *brahmans who are descendants of Nityāndanda.

K. C. Pandey, *Abhinavagupta* (1959, rev. 1963).

Abhiniveṣa (love of the world): see ASMITA.

Abhiññā (Pāli), **Abhijñā** (Skt., 'higher knowledge'). In Buddhism, any of six supernormal powers: (i) psycho-kinesis, (ii) clairaudience, (iii) telepathy, (iv) knowledge of the rebirth of others and of the karmic factors, (v) knowledge of one's own former rebirths, (vi) knowledge of the extinction of the *āsavas. The first five are reckoned 'mundane' (*lokiya*) because they are attainable by non-Buddhist as well as Buddhist ascetics by the practice of *samādhi; normally they supervene upon the attainment of the fourth *jhāna. The sixth is a spiritual or 'supramundane' (lokuttara) knowledge and is synonymous with the realization of *nirvāna. The last three are otherwise known as the 'threefold knowledge' (*tevijjā*). See also IDDHI.

Abhirati. The *paradise of the *Buddha *Akṣobhya, the 'Realm of Joy'. It is the Eastern paradise (see SUKHĀVATI), but in the sense that Buddhist heavens or hells have only the degree of reality that humans confer upon them. They seem real to those who are still in ignorance.

Abhisamayālankāra (The Treatise on the Exposition of the Perfection of Wisdom). An important commentary work of the Buddhist Mahāyāna tradition attributed to *Maitreya and probably composed in the 4th cent. CE. The text is a commentary on the 'Large Treatise on the Perfection of Wisdom' (*Mahāprajñāpāramitā-sūtra*), the teachings of which are summarized in 274 stanzas into a scheme of eight ascending stages (abhisamaya) to enlightenment. Due to its brevity and popularity the text has itself been the subject of numerous subcommentaries, most importantly in Skt. by Haribhadra (8th cent.) and in Tibetan by *Tsong-kha-pa (1357–1419 CE).

Abhiṣek(a) (Skt., *abhi* + *ṣich*, 'sprinkle water'). In Hinduism, a general word for anointing or sprinkling, especially in order to consecrate: 'Then the sprinkling of Rama's head, which began with the happy tears of the two Queen Mothers, was completed by the ministers using waters from holy streams' (*Raghuvaṃsha* 14. 7). It is thus used particularly of water used at the inauguration or coronation of a king (**Taittirīya Brāhmaṇa* 1. 7. 5). The besprinkler himself was listed in a list of victims for human sacrifice (*puruṣamedha*): *Taittirīya Brāhmaṇa* 3. 4. 8. 1. Abhiṣeka in later Hinduism is transferred to a religious context and is sometimes a synonym for *dīkṣa or sometimes follows from dīkṣa. There are various kinds of abhiṣeka: for example, in *Śaivism, after the *nirvāna dīkṣa* (see DĪKṢA), the adept can eventually take either the ācārya-abhiṣeka and become a *guru or the *sādhaka-abhiṣeka and become a follower of the way of enjoyment (*bubukṣu*) and power (*siddha).

In Buddhism, abhiṣeka is the means by which the guru transmits the power and authority to a pupil to engage in specific forms of meditation. It is important especially in Tibet (Tib., *dbang.bskur*, 'empowerment'), where it is an *initiation ritual in Tibetan Buddhism preceding *Tantric practice. When a *lama has decided that a particular practice suits a student yogin, the student undergoes five stages of preparation. The first stage, called Preparation, involves reflective contemplation on the purpose of the practice. When this is deemed satisfactory, a minor abhiṣeka is conducted called Authorization (permission to do the practice). The third stage of abhiṣeka proper, which establishes a relationship between the practitioner and the deity involved, is divided into four substages, the first of which, called 'Master' or 'Flask' consecration, is further divided into six minor consecrations. This is the most well known, where a golden flask with peacock feathers is used to dispense blessed water (or alcohol) to the *yogin to drink, clearly revealing the origin of the rite in the coronation of ancient Indian kings—although sometimes *tormas are used, being touched onto the yogin's head. Each action is repeated three times to empower the body, speech, and mind, since all three are used in tantric practice. The three further subdivisions of the third stage are called 'Secret', 'Wisdom', and 'Fourth', though the flask (*bum.pa*) itself may be used in each. All four are heavily ritualized and involve taking of vows. Empowerment to perform a tantric practice is not complete however until the completion of the last two stages; of these, the fourth, Textual Explanation, is just as important as the abhiṣeka, since it joins the yogin to the lineage from which the text of the practice came. It takes place in a ceremonial atmosphere, with a ritual recitation preceding the exegesis. The final stage, Oral Instruction, involves clarification by the lama of the formal details of *visualization, *mantra, *mudrā, etc. It is quite common for 'lower' consecrations to be given to hundreds of people at once, even if the associated practice (the minimum requirement of which is 100,000 mantras) is not immediately performed. This is done to sow the seed of a bond with the deity which may ripen in a future life, and in this case the first and last two stages would not be thought necessary. For 'higher' consecrations, such as those associated with *'wrathful' deities, adherence to the five stages is rigid.

Abhiṣeka-bhūmi (highest stage of perfection): see BHUMI.

Abhuta-dharma (miracle): see ABUDATSUMA.

Abi (Jap.; Skt. *avīci*). The lowest part of Buddhist *hell, a place of such pain that no one cries out, and anguished silence prevails. However, as with all Buddhist hells, it is not a place of everlasting torment, since there is nothing permanent in the Buddhist perspective.

Abidatsuma-kusha-ron. Jap. for *Abhidharma-kośa-bhāṣya*, the survey of *Theravāda teaching by *Vasubandhu.

Abidatsumazō. Jap. for *Abhidhammapiṭaka, one of the three (*sanzō*) or five (*gozō*) divisions of Buddhist texts or 'scriptures'.

Abimelech (date uncertain, 19th–16th cents. BCE). King of Gerar, whom both *Abraham and *Isaac tried to deceive by presenting their wives as their sisters (Genesis 20, 26. 1–11). He also appears in connection with both *patriarchs in disputes over wells (Genesis 21. 25, 26. 15–21). Because of the similarities between the stories, most scholars regard them as different versions of the same incidents. According to the *aggadah, Abmilech is described as a *'righteous gentile' (*Mid. Ps.* 34).

Abimelech (12th cent. BCE). In the Jewish scriptures, the son of *Gideon by his Shechemite concubine (Judges 8. 31). He slaughtered sixty-nine of the seventy sons of Gideon and became ruler of the city of Shechem (Judges 9. 1–5). Subsequently he destroyed the city, but was mortally wounded during the siege of Thebez (Judges 9. 39–54). Although Abimelech is not counted as one of the judges, his story may reflect the changing attitude of Israelites towards the institution of monarchy at that time.

Abjad. Muslim method of calculating from the numerical value of letters—alif = 1, ba' = 2, etc. The letters are moved on squares, or the numbers are substituted for letters, to gain secret meanings, predictions, and the like. In that respect it resembles Jewish *gematria.

Ablutions. Ritual cleansings to remove impurity and to mark transitions from profane to sacred states, etc. They are often, therefore, associated with *rites of passage. In Judaism, ablution is ritual washing intended to restore or maintain a state of ritual *purity is rooted in *Torah. In the Jewish tradition, ablution can involve total immersion, washing of hands and feet, or washing hands only. Total immersion must take place in 'living water', i.e. the sea, a river or a spring, or in a *mikveh. It was practised by the *priests in *Temple times, by *proselytes to Judaism as part of the conversion ceremony, and by *women seven days after their menstrual period. Washing of hands and feet was required of priests before taking part in Temple services and the ritual washing of hands is performed before and after meals and on many other occasions. A complete list of when it is required was compiled by Samson b. Zadok (13th cent. CE): see Joseph *Caro's *Shulḥan Arukh.* OH 4. 18.

In Christianity, in addition to the general sense in which *baptism might be regarded as 'an ablution', the word has a technical sense. The ablutions are the washing of the fingers and of the *communion vessels after the communion. The custom was established by the 11th cent., and was regulated by the *Missal of Pius V: ablutions are to be in two parts, the chalice by the wine, and then the chalice and fingers by wine and water. Subsequently the *paten was washed also by water. The necessity for this is related to reverence for the *real presence of Christ after the consecration of the bread and wine.

In Islam, ritual purity (*ṭahāra) is required before carrying out religious duties, especially *ṣalāt (worship). Ablution is of two kinds: *ghusl and wuḍū' (regulations being given in the *Qur'ān, 5. 7), with a third kind substituting for the others where necessary:

1. Ghusl, major ablution: complete washing of the body in pure water, after declaring the *niyya (intention) to do so. It is obligatory after sexual relations whereby a state of *janāba* (major ritual impurity) is incurred. It is recommended before the prayer of Friday and the two main feasts (*ʿid al-aḍḥā and *ʿīd al-fiṭr), and before touching the Qur'ān. For the dead, ghusl must be carried out before burial.

2. Wuḍū', minor ablution, is required to remove

*ḥadath, minor ritual impurity which is incurred in everyday life. After the niyya, the face is washed with pure water, mouth and nose being also rinsed; then the hands and the arms are washed up to the elbow; the head is rubbed with water; and the feet are washed up to the ankles. Wuḍū' should usually be carried out before each of the five times of daily prayer.

3. Where water is not available, clean sand may be used, rubbed upon the body; this method, tayammum, can be substituted for wuḍū' and, occasionally, for ghusl. Every *mosque is supplied with running water for wuḍū'.

For ablution among Hindus, see TARPAṆA, ŚODHANA. Since Sikhs concentrate on inner cleanliness ('True ablution consists in the constant adoration of God', Ādi Granth 358), ritual ablutions are much diminished.

M. Douglas, *Purity and Danger* . . . (1966); *Natural Symbols* (1970).

Aboab, Isaac (end of 14th cent. CE). A Jewish *rabbinic writer. He was a member of a prominent *Sephardic family which produced several outstanding scholars. Isaac was the author of *Menorat ha-Ma'or* (Candlestick of Light) composed 'for the ignorant and the learned, the foolish and the wise, the young and the old, for men and for women', which was widely popular. Using the image of the seven-branched candlestick, he used traditional *aggadic material to illustrate (i) guarding against evil feelings, (ii) guarding against evil speech, (iii) observing *mitzvot* (*mitzvah), (iv) studying *Torah, (v) repentance, (vi) cultivating *shālōm, and (vii) humility. Aboab used a wide variety of aggadic sources and he cites passages from many works now lost.

Abodah (Jewish ritual): see AVODAH.

Abomination of Desolation. Tr. of the Gk. *Bdelugma erēmōseōs* from 1 Maccabees 1. 54 and the Heb. *shiqquz shomen* from Daniel 12. 11. It refers to something *idolatrous which was set up on the *altar of the *Jerusalem *Temple in obedience to the command of Antiochus IV (Epiphanes)—possibly an image of Antiochus. It is then picked up in the New Testament (Matthew 24. 15, Mark 13. 14), where again the exact reference is uncertain.

Abō Rasetsu. A guardian of *hell in Japanese Buddhism. Rasetsu is taken from *rākṣasa, but he has the specific appearance of a hybrid, with the head and legs of an ox, but the hands and torso of a human.

Abortion. The artificial termination of an established pregnancy. In all religions, there is a general tendency to disapprove, but the fact and severity of disapproval varies with circumstances. Thus it may depend on the stage which the pregnancy has reached; on the welfare of the pregnant woman; on the status, value, or (in more recent times) rights of the unborn human life; the assumed gender of that life; the interests of others (e.g. the father); the requirements of whatever is authoritatively determinative of decisions in this area (e.g. scripture). Some religions are thus more definite, in so far as they have normative scriptures in which prescriptions can be found (or from which they can be derived). Thus according to Jewish law, abortion is permitted if the foetus threatens the life of the mother, but some authorities are considerably more liberal: Jacob *Emden stated that abortion is permissible as long as the foetus has not emerged from the womb, even if not in order to save the mother's life, but only to save her from the harassment and great pain which the foetus causes her. In general, the earlier the pregnancy, the more acceptable the abortion (according to the *Talmud, a foetus is not formed until the 41st day). In general, abortion is not permitted because the foetus is deformed, but it is allowed if there is evidence that giving birth will cause the mother mental anguish.

In Islam, while the prevention of pregnancy for valid reasons is allowed, the abortion of a formed foetus is forbidden (see al-halal wa'l-ḥaram) and is also a crime against a living human being. Thus blood recompense (*diya*) must be paid if the infant is aborted alive and then dies, less if it is aborted dead. But as with Judaism, the life and well-being of the mother take precedence. In Eastern religions, the offence of abortion rests on the grounds of reverence for life (*ahiṁsā). The bad *karma accruing from an abortion varies according to the stage of pregnancy reached, and may be minimal if it is necessary in order to save the mother's life. Even so, a mother may relate to the aborted life as having gone on through rebirth to another appearance. This is esp. prominent in Japan, where the *bodhisattva Jizo (*Kṣitigarbha) has special care of dead children. The 'children who are not born' are known as *mizugo*, and a special ritual has been developed to prevent harmful consequence from an abortion by bringing peace to all parties involved (including the unborn child: see D. Miura, *The Forgotten Child* . . . , 1983). The general disapproval of abortion can be seen in the fact that if a Buddhist monk assists in the bringing about of an abortion, he must be expelled from the *saṅgha. In Christianity, abortion falls within the condemnation of the killing of innocent persons, but it is not agreed when the status of 'person' obtains. Thus Thomas *Aquinas stated that the sin of homicide occurs, if one strikes a pregnant woman and an abortion results, only if the foetus is formed and ensoulment has occurred—after forty days for a male foetus, ninety for a female; Luther and Calvin held that both soul and body exist immediately at conception. In a very recent development (1869), Roman Catholics have regarded the embryo as having human status from the moment of conception, and have thus regarded any abortion as unlawful killing. However, abortions have been allowed (by the principle of double-effect) if the procedures designed to protect the mother have had the secondary effect of destroying the foetus (as in the removal of a cancerous but pregnant uterus, or in the removal of a fallopian tube in which an ectopic pregnancy has formed). However, other Christians are more in line with other religions in holding to an incremental view of human development, and in allowing that there are circumstances (e.g. after rape or incest) in which abortion is permissible. A more far-reaching view of incremental development which looks at the good of the continuing family and the child's place in it, has only just begun to establish itself.

Abot(h) (Jewish treatise): see AVOT.

Abrabanel (Abravanel). Isaac ben Judah (1437–1508), Jewish statesman, commentator, and philosopher. He succeeded his father as treasurer to the Portugese king Alfonso V, but was compelled to flee to Spain when he was suspected of participating in rebellion against his successor. Although in the service of Ferdinand and Isabella of Spain, he failed to prevent the expulsion of the Jews in 1492, and went into exile, eventually settling in Venice where he died. His exile he held to be a gain: 'When I lived in royal courts I had time to dally with books. It was only when I became a wanderer on the face of the earth, going destitute from kingdom to kingdom, that I became a student of the Book of God.' By the age of 20 he had written *Ateret Zekenim* (The Crown of Elders) examining divine providence. In *Rosh Amanah* (The Principles of Faith) he defended *Maimonides, although he also maintained that the isolation of some dogmas as seemingly more important than others is wrong, since the whole of *Torah is a seamless robe, 'and we must believe everything in the holy Torah'. He resisted, in a trilogy, scepticism about the coming of the *Messiah, anticipating his arrival in 1503. The Jews would return to the land of Israel, there would be *resurrection and judgement, and a new, more spiritual, humanity would emerge, for 'humanity is the purpose of creation'. His conjectures, based on careful exegesis, did much to inspire the messianic movements of the 16th and 17th cents. He wrote commentaries on many biblical books. His exegesis is characterized by his preoccupation with Christian biblical understanding and his interest in comparing the social institutions of biblical times with those of the 15th cent. He held that prophecy is not to be evaluated only as foretelling, since some apparent predictions had not come to pass. He also pointed out that there are faults of style and language in *Jeremiah and *Ezekiel, thereby calling in question (at least implicitly) strictly verbal inspiration.

B. Netanyahu, *Don Isaac Abravanel . . .* (1968).

Abrabanel, Judah (also known as Leo Hebraeus, *c.*1460–*c.*1523). Jewish Portuguese philosopher, poet, and physician. He served as personal physician to the Spanish viceroy in Naples and was the author of *Telunah ʿal ha-Zeman* (Complaint against Time) and four poems about his father *Isaac. His most famous work was a philosophical dialogue on the theme of love (*Dialoghi di amore*). Humans come to know love at three levels, 'of pleasure, of profit, of virtue'. From these they come to realize that love is the ultimate goal of the universe, which can, in its fullest sense, be found only in union with God. This work was widely published and translated in the latter part of the 16th cent.

Tr. F. Fredeberg-Seeley and J. H. Barnes (1937).

Abraham (originally named Abram). *Patriarch of the Israelite people. *Genesis records how Abraham left *Ur to move to *Canaan. He was promised that he would be the father of a great nation, and the divine call, first made at Haran (Genesis 12. 1–4), was repeated at Shechem (12. 6–7), in the land of Canaan (13. 14–17), when an elaborate *covenant was made (15. 1–21), when the covenant of *circumcision was introduced (17. 9–22), and when *Isaac's birth was foretold (18. 1–15) By this time, Sarah, Abraham's wife, was past the age of childbearing, but she none the less produced a son, Isaac (21. 1–5) and insisted that Abraham's concubine, Hagar, and her son *Ishmael be expelled from the camp (21. 9–21). Subsequently Abraham was commanded by God to sacrifice Isaac (the *Akeda) who was only saved by an *angel at the last moment. In consequence Abraham was again promised that his descendants would be as numerous as the stars of *heaven (22. 1–19).

In the biblical tradition, Abraham is thus perceived as the patriarch of the Jewish people. In the *aggadah, Abraham is seen as an ideal figure who kept the *oral law even before it had been revealed. As the first to recognize God, he is the father of all *proselytes and he is compared with *Job, as one who argued with God when he pleaded for the cities of *Sodom and Gomorrah (Genesis 18. 14–29). He is described as a *prophet and 'God omitted no blessing in the world with which he did not bless him' (*SER* 6). According to **Tanḥuma*, 'Abraham was a prototype: his experiences were a symbol of all that was to happen to Israel.'

Jewish philosophers used Abraham to illustrate their ideas. *Philo argued that reason should be subordinated to *faith, on the basis of the verse that 'Abraham believed the Lord; and he reckoned it to him as righteousness' (Genesis 15. 6). *Maimonides argued that Abraham was the first to accept that the world came into being from nothingness and to accept the existence of God on the basis of reason. Legends about Abraham can also be found in the *midrash covering his birth and childhood, and these stories were in wide circulation in the Middle Ages. The biblical story has proved the inspiration for pictorial, musical, and literary compositions for both Jewish and Christian artists.

In Christianity, Abraham is an exemplar of the

efficacy of faith without law (Romans 4, Galatians 3. 6–9) and of faith as such (Hebrews 11. 8 ff.). In James 2. 20–4, his faith (in his willingness to sacrifice *Isaac) is an illustration of *justification by works. He was believed to have been one of the just liberated by *Christ on his descent into *hell. See also ABRAHAM'S BOSOM.

In Islam, his name (in the Qur'ān) is Ibrāhīm. He is seen as a *prophet and the one who together with his son Ismā'īl (Ishmael) restored the original monotheistic worship at the *Ka'ba in *Mecca: 'We covenanted with Ibrāhīm and Ismā'īl that they should sanctify My House . . . ' (Qur'ān 2. 125). By the time of *Muḥammad however the cult of the Ka'ba had reverted to pagan rites. Ibrāhīm is considered as the original Muslim, who submitted to *Allāh as a *ḥanīf (monotheist) and muslim (3. 67). Islam is itself referred to as the 'religion of Ibrāhīm' (*millat Ibrāhīm*, 2. 130). The Qur'ān describes or alludes to various episodes of his early life, notably his refusal to worship idols (37. 33–98, 21. 51–70). The sacrifice asked of him, his obedience, and the rescue of his son (not named but generally held to be Ismā'īl), (37. 102–11) are significant as an example of perfect submission (*islām*) to Allāh, and he is commended as a 'model' (16. 120).

J. van Seters, *Abraham in History and Tradition* (1975).

Abraham, Apocalypse of. A literary work of the 2nd cent. CE. It tells the story of *Abraham's visit to the seven heavens. It only exists in a Slavonic version of a Greek translation, but is undoubtedly Jewish in origin and is possibly influenced by IV *Ezra. It includes speculation on the relationships of God with the world and attempts to calculate the date of the end of the world.

Tr. G. H. Box (1918).

Abraham, Testament of. A book of unknown date containing the apocryphal story of the death of *Abraham. There are many other testaments of biblical figures. The book uses *midrashim about Abraham and *aggadah about Moses. Jewish in origin, it survives in two Greek versions.

Trs. M. R. James (1892), G. H. Box (1927).

Abraham bar Hiyya (d. *c.*1136). Jewish Spanish philosopher and translator. He produced several works of philosophy, the best known of which are *Hegyon ha-Nefesh ha-Azuvah* (Meditation of the Sad Soul), the encyclopaedic *Yesodei ha-Tevunah u-Migdal ha-Emunah* (Foundation of Understanding and Tower of Faith), a book of astronomy *Hokhmat ha-Hizzayon* (Wisdom of the Revelation), and one on *astrology, *Megillat ha-Megalleh* (Scroll of the Revealer). Influenced by Neoplatonism, he did much to transmit Arabic science to the Christian world, and in general he saw possible virtue in the non-Jewish world: 'Israel was advantageously endowed with belief in God's unity and with acceptance of *Torah, but all have capacity to believe the same.'

Meditation of the Sad Soul, tr. G. Wigoder (1969).

Abraham ben David of Posquières (*c.*1125–98 CE, also known as Rabad). Jewish French *Talmudist. A man of great wealth, he founded a *yeshivah in Posquières which educated such distinguished scholars as Meir b. Isaac and Abraham's own son, *Isaac the Blind. *Naḥmanides commented on his piety and erudition. His criticism of *Maimonides' *Mishneh Torah* (especially for not giving sources or explanations, and for the very tendency to codify) established his reputation, and his most famous work, the *Ba'alei ha Nefesh* (Masters of the Soul) discussed the laws related to *women. He also wrote commentaries on the *Mishnah and *Talmud as well as *hassagot* (critical glosses) on the works of several contemporary scholars.

I. Twersky, *Rabad of Posquieres* (1962).

Abraham ben Moses ben Maimon (1186–1237 CE). Leader of Egyptian Jewry, philosopher, and son of *Maimonides. On his father's death he became *nagid of the Egyptian community and the position remained hereditary until the end of the 14th cent. He introduced various new ritual practices, influenced by the Muslim *Sūfīs, and therefore aroused strong opposition. He defended his father's works in various publications and produced an encyclopaedic work on Judaism entitled *Kifayat al-Abidin* (Comprehensive Guide for the Servants of God).

Abrahamites. A Christian Judaizing sect flourishing in Bohemia between 1747 and 1781. They rejected the doctrine of the *Trinity, kept Saturday as the *Sabbath, did not eat pork, and even occasionally practised *circumcision. Their leader, Jan Pita, was executed in 1748, and, because they had contact with the local Jewish community, several Jewish leaders were also tried. Toleration of non-Roman Catholics was allowed in 1781, but because the Abrahamites refused to describe themselves as either Jews or Christians, the men were deported and the sect collapsed.

Abraham's bosom (Heb., *be-heiko shel Avraham*). An expression indicating the location of righteous souls. It appears in *aggadic literature in the *Midrash and in the *Talmud. *Jesus used the phrase in the parable of Dives and Lazarus (Luke 16. 22–31). In Christian mythology, it came to stand for *limbo where unbaptized babies dwell. It led to the famous 'malapropism' of the Hostess in Shakespeare's *Henry V*: 'Nay, sure he's [Falstaff] not in hell; he's in Arthur's bosom, if ever a man went to Arthur's bosom.'

Abram (Jewish Patriarch): see ABRAHAM.

Abravanel (Jewish statesman): see ABRABANEL.

Abrogation (Muslim): see NASKH.

Absalom. Son of *David. After the rape of his sister Tamar by their half-brother Amnon, Absalom murdered Amnon and fled the court. Having raised rebellion against his father David, he was killed in the subsequent battle, causing his father to lament, 'Oh my son Absalom, my son, my son Absalom! Would I had died instead of you, O Absalom, my son, my son!' (2 Samuel 13–18). Counselled by the treacherous Achitophel, their names supplied the title of Dryden's 'Absalom and Achitophel': 'In pious times, ere priestcraft did begin, Before polygamy was made a sin. . . .'

Absolute Dependence, Feeling of: see SCHLEIERMACHER, F.

Absolute unitary being: see BIOGENETIC STRUCTURALISM.

Absolution. The statement and the enactment of the forgiveness of *sins, and of release from them. It is a sacrament in the *Roman Catholic and *Orthodox (Gk., *metanoia, exomologesis*) Churches, with absolution being pronounced by a *priest or *bishop. In *Russian Orthodoxy, the form of absolution is in the form of a prayer (precatory), 'May our Lord and God *Jesus Christ forgive you', followed by the statement (indicative), 'I, n., through the power given to me by him, forgive you and absolve you. . . .' In the Catholic tradition, the indicative form became standard from the time of the Council of *Trent onward, 'I absolve you in the name of the Father, and of the Son and of the Holy Spirit.' When the rite of penance was revised after *Vatican II, a precatory form was added.

Abstinence. The practice of not eating certain foods: see also ASCETICISM; CELIBACY. As a Christian technical term it is distinguished from fasting (eating little or nothing). Traditionally Roman Catholics abstain from meat on Fridays and certain other days in the year, but the discipline has been relaxed since 1966. In Orthodox churches abstinence from animal foods extends beyond *Lent to (in theory) *c.*150 days of the year.

Abu (1). A mountain in Rājasthān, sometimes called the 'Olympus of India'. It is especially noted for Jain temples of great beauty, an important place of *pilgrimage for Śvetāmbara Jains. The Hindu custodians of the mountain allowed a Jain temple to be built there only after Vimala had covered their land with gold coins; and both Hindu and Jain temples are to be found there still. It is particularly sacred to devotees of *Viṣṇu and *Śiva.

Abu (2) (Arab.). In Muslim names, 'father of'.

Abubacer (Muslim philosopher): see IBN TUFAYL.

Abu Bakr (d. 634 (AH 13)). The first adult male convert to Islam, a close friend of the Prophet *Muḥammad, and first Caliph (*Khalīfa) of the Islamic *'umma. His faithfulness to Muḥammad at *Mecca earned him the title of *al-Siddīq* ('the truthful one'). When others doubted (e.g. over the Night Journey (*Miʿrāj) of the Prophet, or concerning the need for the Treaty of Hudaibiyya) he remained unshaken in his belief in Muḥammad's prophethood. He was Muḥammad's companion in the *hijra from Mecca to al-*Madīna. At Madīna, when Muḥammad married the daughter of Abu Bakr, the tie between the two men was further strengthened.

At Madīna, Abu Bakr's sound advice and intelligence brought him to the forefront as Muḥammad's right-hand man. He distinguished himself through his expertise in genealogy, considered vital for the political administration of a tribal society. He aided the Prophet in successfully building alliances with the neighbouring tribes, and in the eventual isolation of Meccan opposition.

Upon Muḥammad's death in 632 (AH 11), the forceful *Umār persuaded the Madinans to accept Abu Bakr as the Prophet's successor. Abu Bakr guided the young Muslim community through the difficult and dangerous period following the death of Muḥammad, especially in the wars of the *Ridda. A major victory at Ajnadin against the Byzantines heralded the dawn of the Islamic conquests.

Abu Bakr accelerated Arab integration under Islam: captured tribal leaders were treated with respect, and consequently became active supporters of Islam (i.e. a united, God-fearing community). Thus Abu Bakr gave to Islam, the religion, the means of political expression, and therein lies his greatness. On his death he was buried beside Muḥammad.

Abudatsuma (Jap., for Skt., *abhuta-dharma*). An unusual or praeternatural event, a miracle performed by a deity in Hinduism, or by a *Buddha in Buddhism.

Abū Dāwūd al-Sijistānī (817–89). Muslim compiler of one of the six *ṣaḥīḥ, or canonical, collections of aḥādīth (see ḤADĪTH). He is said to have learnt 500,000 traditions, of which he took 4,800 for his collection *Sunan*. *Ibn Ḥanbal, who taught him, is said to have approved of his work, and it was also said that if one possesses the *Qur'ān and abū Dāwūd's *Sunan*, nothing further is needed. The main interest of the traditions is in judicial matters.

Abū Dharr al-Ghifāri (d. 652/3 CE (AH 31/2)). Close companion of the Prophet Muḥammad. The Prophet named him 'the shining truth' because of his unswerving belief in the oneness of *Allāh. He was famed for the piety and asceticism in which he lived his life. He transmitted 281 *ḥadīths, mainly pertaining to moral and metaphysical matters. He is regarded highly by the *Shīʿa branch of Islam, and has recently acquired a considerable cult among Islamic socialists, Muslim reform movements, and Iranian revolutionaries.

Traditions state that his character bore great similarity to that of ʿIsa/*Jesus. During the rule of the third *khalīfa *ʿUthmān, Abū Dharr's vociferous condemnation of the pleasure-loving people of

Damascus brought him to public notice: 'This gold and silver of yours shall one day be heated in the fire of hell and therewith shall be scarred in your foreheads, you ungodly spendthrifts! Wherefore, spend now the same in alms, leaving yourself enough but for your daily bread.' Apprehensive of public disorder, *Mu'āwiyya, governor of Syria, dispatched Abu Dharr to *Madīna, informing 'Uthmān that he was a sincere but misguided enthusiast. Abu Dharr argued his case before 'Uthmān, stating that the great and wealthy should be forced to give up their riches. 'Uthmān tried to reason with him: 'After men have completely fulfilled their obligations, what power remains with me to compel them to any further sacrifice?' Abu Dharr persisted in his 'communistic' interpretation of Islam, and was ultimately banished to the desert village of al-Rabadha. Thus ended a phase in the struggle between the idealists and the pragmatists in early Islam.

A. J. Cameron, *Abu Dharr al-Ghifari* (1973).

Abū Ḥanīfa (d. 767 (AH 150)). Muslim theologian and jurist, and founder of the *Ḥanafites (Kufan) law school (*sharī'a). He came from Central Asia, and became established as a leading religious authority in Kūfa. Although Abū Ḥanīfa never held an official post of *qādī, he played the important role of theoretical systematizer in technical legal thought, with much influence over his students in Kūfa, especially Abū Yūsuf. Abū Ḥanīfa's use of *qiyās (analogy), *istiḥsān (juristic preference), ra'y (personal judgement) to resolve new legal problems arising in the expanding Muslim world, characterized his law school, in contrast to the other *schools of law. Furthermore, he stressed the idea of an international Muslim community, unified by the *Qur'ān and *Sunna, avoiding extremes. In his personal life, he suffered punishment and imprisonment at the hands of the Umayyads and *'Abbāsids because of his independent viewpoint and his refusal to accept the official post of qādī in Kūfa. He died in prison in Baghdād. His school of law is extensively followed and applied in the Muslim world.

M. S. Nu'amani, *Imām Abū Ḥanīfah* . . . (1889; tr. M. H. Hussain, 1972).

Abū Huraira (d. 676–8 (AH 57 or 58). Companion of the Prophet *Muḥammad, and prolific transmitter of *Ḥadīth: nearly 3,500 ḥadīth have come down from him. He was a late convert to Islam (629 (AH 7)), and he lived in the Prophet's house. His powerful memory and intelligence were recognized by Muḥammad, who gave him permission to record Ḥadīth (written and oral). During the early conquests, he refused to accept administrative posts, and instead preferred to live as a private citizen in *Madīna, where he died at the age of 78.

Abulafia, Abraham ben Samuel (1240–*c*.1291). A wandering Spanish *kabbalist. He wrote a number of *mystical essays, and in 1280 went to Rome to persuade the pope to relieve the sufferings of the Jews. He was condemned to death, but was reprieved after the pope's death. He attracted a considerable following and announced that the *messianic era would begin (according to Jewish calculation) in 5050 (i.e. 1290). Arousing the opposition of Solomon ben Abraham *Adret, he responded with various polemical works.

Abulafia, Me'ir (1170?–1244, also known as Ramah). Spanish *Talmudic Scholar. He was prominent in the Toledo community and carried the title of *nasi. His *Sefer Peratei Peratin* (Book of Minute Details) was a detailed Talmudic commentary and he produced many hundreds of *responsa. He is best known for his controversy with *Maimonides on the doctrine of the *resurrection, but, despite this dispute, he had great respect for the philosopher, as is shown by the elegy he composed for him after his death.

Abu Madyan, Shu'aib b. al-Ḥusain (1126–98 (AH 520–94)). *Ṣūfī poet, teacher, and adept. Born in Spain of a poor family, he travelled to Morocco to learn weaving as a trade. He began to travel in search of teachers, among them *'Abd al-Qādir al-Jīlīnī. He settled in Biijayah (Bougie) in Algeria, where disciples gathered to him. He was recognized as the *qutb al-Ghawth (the axis on whom the mystical support of the world turns), and he remains the spiritual guardian of Algeria.

Abuna (Ethiopic and Arab., 'our father'). The *patriarch of the *Ethiopian church. An alternative title is Aba Salama (Father of Peace), the name given to St Frumentius (4th cent.), the *metropolitan of Aksum and primate of Ethiopia who had been consecrated by *Athanasius.

Abu Sufyān b. Harb b. Umayyā (d. 653 (AH 32)). A notable Quraysh aristocrat, a wealthy merchant and financier, with hardly any equals in *Mecca for intelligence and business acumen. Like most of the Meccan merchants, he was originally hostile to Muḥammad and Islam. He led the caravan which escaped from the Muslims at the battle of *Badr, and it was he who took over the command of the Meccans after that defeat. Under his leadership, the Meccans scored a military success at Uhud. The failure of the great confederacy to take *Madīna in 627 (AH 5) led him to lose heart, and resistance to Islam came to be directed by others. When the Meccans broke the peace of al-Hudaybiyya in 630 (AH 8), Abu Sufyān went to Madīna to negotiate. He played an important role in the peaceful occupation of Mecca by Muḥammad. Possibly Muḥammad's marriage to Abu Sufyān's daughter may have eased the reconciliation process. He became a Muslim at the fall of Mecca, and then supported Islam with vigour and enterprise—he fought bravely in the battle of Hunain and at the siege of al-Taif where he lost an eye. The Prophet made him governor of Najrān, and later, during the Islamic conquests, he saw active service against the Byzantines as a military general. He fought in the historic battle of Yarmuk (636 CE), and died in Palestine.

Abū Ṭālib (d. 619 CE). An uncle of the Prophet *Muḥammad. He was the chief of the Hāshim clan of the Quraysh tribe. Though Abū Ṭālib remained loyal and protected his kinsman Muḥammad from his enemies, he never converted to Islam. It was his son *Alī, raised by the Prophet, who brought fame to his name.

Abu ʿUbaida b. al-Djarrah (d. 639 (AH 18)). One of the earliest converts to Islam, he distinguished himself by his piety, intelligence, bravery, and devotion to the Prophet *Muḥammad. The Prophet nicknamed him 'al-Amin' (The Trustworthy), and promised him paradise. Abu ʿUbaida's remarkable courage in all the early battles, coupled with his leadership qualities, made him a powerful figure among the *Companions. Later he was sent as a preacher to Najran to train the newly converted tribes in Islam. During the time of Abu Bakr he served as a commander in Syria, and in ʿUmār's caliphate, he was made supreme commander over the Syrian army. He conquered *Damascus, Hims, Antioch, and Aleppo, and successfully administered those territories. He died of the plague which claimed the lives of many Muslim warriors.

Abū Yūsuf, Yaʿkūb (Muslim writer on law): see ḤANAFITES.

Academies. An established gathering of Jewish scholars. The *Talmudic terms are yeshivot ('sitting'), also *bet ha-midrash (Heb., 'House of Study'), *bet din gadol (Heb., 'the great house of law'), and *metivta rabba* (Aram., 'the great session'). As *Hillel put it in the 1st cent. CE, 'the more *Torah, the more life, the more yeshivah, the more wisdom' (*Avot* 2. 7). In the early days, the *halakhah was decided after discussion in the academies and in the second *Temple period (1st cent. BCE–1st cent. CE) the Great *Sanhedrin was described as a yeshivah from which Torah goes forth to all *Israel. After the destruction of the Temple in 70 CE, several academies were founded, the most famous being that of *Johanan b. Zakkai at *Jabneh. Discussions at Jabneh were presided over by the *nasi and were conducted in front of students and other members of the public. Later academies were established in Babylonia at *Sura and *Pumbedita which survived until approximately the middle of the 11th cent. CE. Their purpose was to produce expert scholars in the field of *oral law. A *rosh yeshivah* (head of the academy) was elected by the sages whose role was to give lectures to the students and to discuss halakhic matters. The Academy on High (*yeshivah shel ma'lah*) is a rabbinic belief in an assembly in heaven of scholars and others who acquired merit on earth, by studying and keeping Torah. To be 'summoned by the Academy on High' is a euphemism for death.

Acamana (Skt., 'cleansing of mouth'). Washing out the mouth, in Hinduism, in order to purify what enters and what leaves it. It is thus an aspect of *pūjā through which the Hindu transfers from the world to God.

Ācāra. Hindu term for custom and for law and behaviour according to custom—as in *Manusmṛti, where, e.g., rules of behaviour for different *castes are laid down. The opposite are *viruddha-ācār* (conduct contrary to custom) and *bhrashṭācār* (fallen out of customary use). See also ĀCĀRYA.

Ācāra-aṅga (one of the twelve Aṅgas): see AṄGA.

Ācariya-muṭṭhi (Pāli, 'teacher's fist'). A teacher's reluctance to impart the whole of his knowledge and skill to his pupils. Buddhism stresses that its founder is definitely not this kind of a teacher: 'I have preached the truth without making any distinction between exoteric and esoteric doctrine; for in respect of the truths, the *Tathāgata has no such thing as the closed fist of a teacher, who keeps some things back' (D. II. 100).

Ācārya (Skt., 'one who knows or teaches the *ācāra, the rules of right conduct'). 1. The title ācārya is primarily applied to a Hindu teacher who invests the student with the sacrificial thread (*vajñopavīta*) and instructs him in the *vedas and the religious law (*dharma). By extension it is applied to a spiritual preceptor, or to anyone learned in the Hindu tradition. This title is frequently affixed directly to the proper name, e.g. *Śaṅkarācārya.

2. In particular, a group of Tamil *Vaiṣṇava teachers regarding the *Āḻvārs as incarnations of *Viṣṇu's instruments/weapons. The first was *Nāthamuni (9th cent. CE).

3. In Buddhism Pāli, *ācāriya*), teacher of the *dhamma, in contrast to *upāydhyāya*, who taught discipline and the rules.

4. Among Jains, the ācārya holds a vital place in teaching and in the transmission of lineage (for an example, see BHIKṢU, ĀCĀRYA); 'As the most lavishly equipped ship can, without a captain, easily sink, so a monk can have excellent faith, but without a good ācārya, can drown in the ocean of rebirth.'

Accidie (Gk., *akēdia*, 'negligence', 'indifference'). In ascetical terminology, one of the principal temptations, or deadly sins. It occurs in the list of eight such in *Evagrius of Pontus (with analysis), and is frequently mentioned in the stories of the *Desert Fathers. *Cassian provides a classic W. discussion, owing much to Evagrius. Accidie is a listlessness tempting one to give up prayer and the spiritual life. In the later English tradition it is translated as sloth, which is an oversimplification.

S. Wenzel, *The Sin of Sloth: Acedia in Medieval Thought* . . . (1967).

Acedia (lack of commitment): see ACCIDIE.

Acinteyyāni (Pāli, *acinteyya*, 'that which cannot or should not be thought'). Certain notions or thought-topics considered by *Theravāda Buddhism to lie beyond the scope of imagination or speculation. Prolonged reflection on them is discouraged because it leads to no satisfactory answers, only to frustration and anguish. They are the notions of what it is like to be a Buddha; what a higher state of consciousness is like (see SAMĀDHI); what are the particular fruits of *karma; who created the world. See also AVYĀKATĀNI.

Acintya-śaktī (Skt., *acintya*, 'unthinkable, incomprehensible, the Absolute'). The literally incomprehensible force associated with a *mantra, which cannot be contained by reason or by bodily power.

Acit (Skt., opposite of *cit, 'consciousness'). That which is inert, the material universe. In *Rāmānuja's system, acit forms the body of God.

Acoemetae (Gk., *akoimētai*, 'sleepless ones'). *Orthodox ascetics in general, and in particular monks following the rule of *Basil. They were founded in the 5th cent., first on the Euphrates, later in *Constantinople. They observed strict poverty, a missionary apostolate, and (whence their name) continual and *antiphonal singing of psalms. They were defenders of *Chalcedon against the *Monophysites, but adopted *Nestorian views and were excommunicated in 534. The term may be applied more generally to Eastern Christian *ascetics.

Acolyte, In the W. Church, one of the minor *orders, first heard of in 251 in Rome. His function is to assist the priest and deacon at the *mass, but later, acolytes and *subdeacons take over most functions in the liturgy of the other minor orders. As early as the 9th cent. boys took over the duties of carrying and lighting candles at the mass, and ordination as acolyte usually became a step to the diaconate and priesthood. This changed in 1972, and now the order may be conferred on laymen. In E. Christianity, the order (of attendant) is incorporated in the ordination to the lowest order of a specific rite. A further development has been the RC acceptance of the practice of allowing girl and women servers in the sanctuary.

Acquisition, doctrine of (Muslim): see QADAR.

Action Française, a political group, with a journal (from 1908 a daily newspaper) of the same name, having strong *Roman Catholic connections. It was founded in 1898, after the *Dreyfus affair. It sought the restoration of French national unity and pride, under a restored monarchy. The nation, France, has a soul and character which had been damaged by the Republic when it allowed a place to Jews, foreigners, freemasons, and Protestants. Although its leaders, especially Charles Maurras, included atheists or freethinkers, the movement valued the conservative traditionalism of R. Catholicism and its powerful social control. Many RCs were attracted to it, but the extremity of its views, in the context of the rise of other Fascist movements in Europe, alarmed others. Attempts to have it condemned by Rome were delayed by the 1st World War, but the involvement of RCs was prohibited in 1926. The movement revived during the period of the Vichy government in France, 1940–4. Maurras was imprisoned in 1945, released in 1951, and died in 1952.

P. C. Capitan, *Charles Maurras et l'idéologie d'Action Française* (1972); M. Sutton, *Nationalism, Positivism and Catholicism* . . . (1982).

Acts of the Apostles, The. Fifth book of the New Testament. It recounts the history of the earliest church at Jerusalem and in Palestine (chs. 1–8, 12); the first preaching of the gospel to Gentiles (10–11); and the conversion of *Paul and his missionary work as far as Rome (9, 12–28). It is almost the only source for Christian history in the period 30–64 CE, though in using it the reader must reckon with the author's idealized picture of the earliest church as a unified body under the *Apostles and guided by the *Holy Spirit, and with his liberty in composing speeches. Acts is generally accepted as the work of the same author as the third gospel. The 'we'-sections of Acts (starting with 16. 10–17) suggest that he was one of Paul's companions, such as *Luke, but some scholars hold that the author's portrait of Paul is too distorted for this to be credible. Dates from as early as 64 CE (before Paul's death) up to the 2nd cent. have consequently been argued.

Acupuncture. One of the nine branches of Chinese traditional medicine. Chinese medicine derives its ethos from both Confucianism (regarding the body as a sacred legacy from the ancestors, which inhibited intrusive procedures and autopsies) and Taoism, where the search for immortality promoted a wide range of experiments. Since the body acts as a channel, especially for *ch'i, the points of insertion of the needles of acupuncture do not have to be proximate to the place of pain and disorder: they stimulate and promote the body's own ability to treat itself; thus the carefully mapped points of insertion (the numbers vary from 350 to 450) are related to the body's internal system of communication and control.

F. Mann, *Acupuncture* . . . (1973).

ʿĀd (pre-Islamic people): see HŪD.

Adalbert of Prague, St (*c*.956–97). Christian *bishop and martyr. His name was Voytech, but he adopted the name of Adalbert, the bishop of Magdeburg. Although young, he was made bishop of Prague in 982, but the political conflict and opposition made him withdraw to Rome in 990. Pope John XV sent him back to his diocese, where he founded the *abbey of Brevnor, but continuing opposition forced him once more to return to Rome. This time he was sent to the unconverted Pomeranians, by whom he and his fellow-missionaries were killed. His influence remained extensive. He was canonized in 999. Feast day, 23 April.

Adam (Heb., 'man'), In W. tradition, the first human being. According to the first creation account in Genesis, Adam was created in the image of God (1. 27) on the final day of creation. In Genesis 2, he is said to have been made from the dust of the earth (Heb., *adamah*, 'earth') and to have become a living *soul after God had breathed into him (2. 7) He was given power over the birds and animals, and the plants and vegetables were to serve him for food. All went well until Adam's wife, *Eve, tempted by the serpent, encouraged the man to eat of the fruit of the Tree of Knowledge of Good and Evil, which they had been expressly forbidden to touch. As a result, they became conscious of their nakedness and hid from God. God punished them by evicting them from the Garden of *Eden and condemning the man to toil for his living (Genesis 2. 5–3. 24). Despite the punishment, Judaism does not understand the *fall of Adam as having created a radical fault, as does Christianity, requiring the second Adam (i.e., *Christ) to deal with the fault and its effects. The 'fall' is a fall upwards, into new opportunities of action and knowledge. The *aggadists described Adam as more beautiful than the sun, for 'Adam was created for the service of the Holy One and the orb of the sun for the service of humanity', but after his disobedience he was thought to have lost his radiance (see L. Ginzberg, *The Legends of the Jews, ad loc.*). In medieval philosophy, Adam is frequently regarded as the prototype man, *Adam Kadmon, and much discussion is devoted to the meaning of 'being created in God's image'. The story of Adam and Eve has inspired both Jewish and Christian art.

In Islam, Adam is not only the first human being but the first *prophet, entrusted by *Allāh with a message for humankind. The *Qur'ān describes his creation very briefly: he is made of 'clay' (7. 12, 15. 26–8). The *angels protested when Allāh proposed to create a being who, they pointed out, would rebel against him (see 2. 30–8). Allāh, however, taught Adam the 'names of all things', whereupon the angels agreed to bow down before him, all except Iblīs (*Satan). Adam and Eve were told to dwell in the Garden, but forbidden to eat of a particular tree. Both were deceived by Satan who 'made them slip' from their former state. The connection with the 'serpent' comes in later tradition. There is no doctrine in Islam of a 'fall' from a previously perfect condition, and a consequent inherited *original sin. Adam repents, and is taught words—interpreted as words which will bring down Allāh's mercy upon him. Humanity thereafter needs only 'guidance' towards the right path. Adam is supposed to have wandered in the earth, to have performed the rites of *ḥajj (pilgrimage) at *Mecca, and to have built the first *kaʿba there. He later died, and was buried, at Mecca. Allāh is said to have made a *covenant with Adam and with his descendants (7. 172), and he is thus in a special sense the father of all humankind.

Adam, Books of. Apocryphal books. They include the *Book of the Life of *Adam and *Eve* (probably composed in Palestine between 100 BCE and 200 CE), the *Cave of Treasures* (a Syriac work), the Ethiopic *Book of Adam and Eve*, and various Armenian compositions dealing with the Adam and Eve legend. These are mainly Christian reworkings of the *aggadic stories, but there are also similarities with *apocalyptic writings such as the books of *Jubilees and *Enoch.

Adam Kadmon (Heb., primordial Man). A *kabbalistic notion, summarizing, in mystical terms, the divine symbolism of the human body. According to the kabbalah, the first man *Adam was made in the image of 'adam elyon' (the supreme man). The term Adam Kadmon first appeared in an early 13th cent. treatise, and the idea was developed by later writers. Isaac *Luria described Adam Kadmon as the most perfect manifestation of God that the human mind can contemplate, and his followers contrasted Adam Kadmon with *Satan, 'adam beliyya'al' (the evil man). Later still Adam Kadmon was identified with the *messiah, and *Shabbetai Zevi was regarded as an incarnation of Adam Kadmon by his disciples.

Adam's Bridge or **Rāma's Bridge.** The chain of small islands linking S. India to N. Śri Lankā, which could be crossed on foot until the 15th cent., when storms widened the gaps. According to **Rāmāyaṇa*, *Hanumān built the link to enable *Rāma to cross and rescue *Sītā. According to Muslim tradition, *Adam crossed here after his expulsion from the Garden of *Eden.

Adam's Peak. Śrī Pada. Sacred mountain in Śri Lankā, at the top of which (a place of *pilgrimage) a hollow shape is identified by adherents of the relevant religions as the *footprint of *Adam, the *Buddha, *Śiva, or the *apostle *Thomas.

Adar: see CALENDAR (JEWISH).

Adat. Traditional, often unwritten, law, the customary part of legal regulation in Muslim countries, which often comes from pre-Islamic times, and has therefore to be integrated (so far as it can be) with *sharīʿa.

B. ter Haar, *Adat Law in Indonesia* (tr. 1948); M. B. Hooker, *Adat Laws in Modern Malaya* (1972).

Addai. Traditional founder of the important church of Edessa in N. Mesopotamia. According to the Syriac *Doctrine of Addai* he was one of *Jesus' seventy disciples (Luke 10. 1) and was sent by St *Thomas to heal the local King *Abgar. It is probably an invention no earlier than the 3rd cent. to give the church an apostolic pedigree.

The Syriac 'liturgy of Addai and Mari', still the

chief *liturgy of the *Church of the East, has some very ancient features, e.g. the *eucharistic prayer addressed to the Son and probably the lack of the 'words of institution'; but it hardly goes back to the day of *Pentecost as church tradition declares.

Ādhān. The call to worship (*ṣalāt) given by the mu'adhīn (Muezzin) traditionally from the manāra (minaret), before each of the five daily times of ṣalāt. It is said that *Muḥammad chose this form of summons to prayer some two years after the *Hijra (622 CE). His first mu'adhīn was *Bilāl, an Abyssinian slave.

The Ādhān is given as a long-drawn-out chant, which ensures its carrying over a long distance; the words incorporate the *Shahāda (profession of faith):

(i) *Allāhu Akbar* (God is most great)
(ii) *Ashhadu anna lā ilāha illā Allāh* (I bear witness there is no god but God)
(iii) *Ashhadu anna Muḥammadan rasūl Allāh* (I bear witness Muḥammad is the messenger of God)
(iv) *Ḥaiya 'alā al-ṣalāt* (Come to prayer)
(v) *Ḥaiya 'alā al-falāḥ* (Come to wellbeing)
(vi) *Al-ṣalāt khayrun min al-nawm* (Prayer is better than sleep)
(vii) *Allāhu Akbar* (God is most great)
(viii) *Lā ilāha illā Allāh* (There is no god but God)

All except the last phrase are generally said twice; (vi), only for the dawn prayer. Nowadays, especially in city mosques, the Ādhān is usually relayed by a loudspeaker fixed at the top of the minaret, and in many cases the voice is recorded. The Ādhān is recited into a child's right ear soon after birth, thus symbolically marking its entrance into the Muslim community. In *Shī'ite communities an additional call is characteristically inserted between (v) and (vi), *ḥaiya 'ala ḥair al-'amal* (Come to the best work).

Ādhāra (Skt., 'container'). The Hindu understanding of the way in which *ātman is contained in the five *kośas or sheaths.

Adharma (Skt.). In Hinduism, the opposite of *dharma, synonym of *pāpa: evil, sin, what is not right or natural, or according to *śāstras. Adharma is complementary to dharma—one cannot exist without the other, and both are necessary in the evolution of the universe.

Adharma is personified in Hindu mythology as the son of *Brahmā and brother of *Dharma, born from Brahmā's back. According to one myth, Adharma's wife is *Nirṛti (Destruction), who bears him three sons—Evil, Terror, and Death. According to another, Hiṁsa (injury, opposite of *ahiṁsā) is Adharma's wife, who bears him a son, Anṛta (Falsehood) and a daughter Nirṛta (Destruction), who marry each other and bear various evils, which in personified form bear the other evils of the world. *Kalki* *Purāṇa* holds *Kālī to be a descendant of Adharma. 'A man of wicked conduct (*adharmas*) is looked upon as an animal by society'. Adharmacārin (opposite of *brahmacarya) is one practising wickedness.

Adhvaryu (performer): see SACRIFICE (HINDU).

Adhvenak (image): see FRAVASI.

Adhyāropa (Skt., 'false covering'). The way in which in Hinduism, illusory or false understandings impose themselves on what is truly the case, which ultimately must be *Brahmān. The classic example is that given by *Śaṅkara of a rope on a path which is believed to be a snake, an error which arises from *avidyā (ignorance). It follows that release from ignorance requires instructed attention to what is real, and to the ways leading to that knowledge.

Adhyāsa (Skt.). In philosophical Hinduism, superimposing reality on what is not real. It is false attribution, as when a rope is mistaken for a snake. It is thus the fundamental ignorance which prevents the true perception of *Brahmān as that which alone is real.

Adhyātma (Skt., 'that which pertains to the *ātman'). 1. In Hinduism the inner self or soul of the individual; but because of the relation of ātman to *Brahmān, it is also the supreme self, or (theistically conceived) the deity.

2. In Jainism, the inner self, which *Banārsīdās discovered could be cultivated to the realization of supreme truth. It is the name of a movement devoted to that end, which preceded Banārsīdās, although he so reorganized it that he is often regarded as its founder.

***Adhyātma Rāmāyaṇa*.** A version of **Rāmāyaṇa* composed by different authors, based on the original Skt. work of Vālmīkī. These authors include: (i) Rāghavadāsa, a disciple of Nijānanda; (ii) Shivarāma Pūrnānanda (1628–98)—related to Eknātha and Mukteshwer, he lived at Kalyāṇī in Mahārāshtra; there are 5,135 verses in this version, completed in 1685; (iii) Dattavarada Viṭṭhal (1748–98), a resident of Akolā in Mahārāshtra, he composed 3,040 verses for his version of *Adhyātma Rāmāyaṇa*; another author, (iv) Govind Harī, has also entitled his composition *Adhyātma Rāmāyaṇa*, but it ranks below those of Shivarāma and Dattavarada. Its tendency is to move the epic in an *Advaitin and spiritualized direction.

Ādhyātma-Yoga. A yogic discipline in Hinduism which elucidates the difference between *ātman and its *kośas (containers), thus leading to the state of *ādhyātma-prasāda*, which is equivalent to the liberated self (*jīvanmukti).

Ādi (Skt., 'original'). The first, primordial or archetypical, found in many compound words.

Adiaphora (Gk., 'things indifferent'). The view that certain items in a controversy are not sufficiently central to warrant continuing division or dispute. Adiaphorism is thus of importance in *ecumenical discussions or arguments, and particularly in the attempts to hold together many varied views in *Anglicanism (see especially B. J. Verkamp, *The Indifferent Mean: Adiaphorism in the English Reformation to 1554*, 1977). Adiaphorists also appear in the Continental *Reformation, both with reference to doctrine (brought to an end by the Formula of Concord, 1577, which ruled that nothing is adiaphoristic in times of persecution, but that otherwise certain ceremonies could be regarded as such) and to pleasures or entertainments in the world.

Ādibrahmacariyaka-sīla (Pāli, 'conduct regarding the fundamentals of the holy life'). Collectively, the three precepts of the Eightfold Path (see AṢṬAṄGIKA-MARGA) relating to ethical behaviour: right speech, right action, and right livelihood.

Ādi Brāhma Samāj. The 'original' *Brahmo Samāj (according to its adherents) when the movement split.

Ādi Buddha (Skt.; Tib., *dang.po'i.sangs.rgyas*). Primordial Buddha, the highest being in Tibetan Buddhist cosmology. Although teachings regarding the Ādi Buddha existed in India at least as early as the 7th cent. CE, they did not enter Tibet until the arrival of *Atiśa in 1042, after which the Ādi Buddha, known in India as Vajradhāra, became identified as Dorje Chang (Tib., *rDor.rje.ch'ang.*, 'Holder of the Thunderbolt') by all schools except the *Nyingma, who know him as Kuntu Zangpo (Tib. *kun.tu. bzang.po.*, 'Goodness in all Ways'; Skt.: *Samantabhadra).

The development of the Ādi Buddha is connected with the development of Buddhist docetism. The Kāraṇḍavyūha Sūtra (probably 7th cent. CE in verse form) portrays him as the personification of pure *śūnyatā, who transforms himself into *Avalokiteśvara in order to create the world, and who, as Avalokiteśvara, then projects himself onto the world stage as both the historical Buddha and as various Hindu deities, for the purpose of teaching different people according to their needs. The creation theme of the Kāraṇḍavyūha was not developed by later texts, however, and the Ādi Buddha is now connected more specifically with the *Tathāgatas than with the world. In Tibet he is the original 'enlightened mind' (Skt., *jñānakāya*), the fusion of wisdom and emptiness; the five *jinas of the *maṇḍala are conceived as his *skandhas, and all buddhas and their doctrines are seen as aspects of his nature.

In both India and Tibet the doctrine of the Ādi Buddha has been rooted in the *tantra rather than the *sūtra traditions, and his is a philosophical rather than a folk notion. The Tibetan traditions have avoided the attribution to him of theistic qualities by stressing his nature as śūnyatā, and by seeing his purpose as essentially that of a device within the confines of tantric practice. His *bīja *mantra is OM.AH.HUM., which represents the *body, speech, and mind of all buddhas.

Ādi Granth (Pañjābī, 'first volume', the second being *Dasam Granth, i.e. 'tenth book'). Sikh scriptures. The Ādi Granth is usually called the Gurū Granth Sāhib in recognition that it is the embodiment of the *Gurū. Sikhs also call it *Gurbāṇī (the Gurū's utterance). They believe that before his death Gurū *Gobind *Siṅgh declared the Ādi Granth his successor. The *Ardās concludes with the injunction 'Gurū mānio granth' ('acknowledge the Granth as Gurū'). Any room in which the Ādi Granth is appropriately installed is a *gurdwārā. The scriptures are treated with the same detailed devotion as would be shown to a human Gurū—e.g. a *chaurī is waved over it and the volume is ceremonially laid to rest at night. *Marriage is solemnized in its presence. It is consulted for daily advice (*hukam) and when *naming children. Sad and joyful occasions are marked by *akhaṇḍ pāṭh (continuous reading).

The Ādi Granth consists of 1,430 pages, each copy having standard page length and numbering. The script throughout is *Gurmukhī, although the language is varied. The basic language, akin to modern Hindī or Pañjābī, is the medium of North Indian poet-mystics mostly of 15th–16th cents. CE (i.e. Sādhukaṛī or Santbhāṣā), but its regional colour varies from poet to poet; and words from e.g. Sanskrit, Sindhī, *Arabic, and Marāṭhī occur.

The contributors are: (i) *bhagats and *sūfīs, i.e. Hindu and Muslim mystics predating the Sikh Gurūs. These are Jaidev, Sheikh Farīd, *Nāmdev, Trilochan, Parmānand, Sadhnā, Beṇī, *Rāmānanda, Dhannā, Pīpā, Saiṇ, *Kabīr, *Ravi Dās; (ii) Gurūs *Nānak, *Aṅgad, *Amar Dās, *Rām Dās, *Arjan Dev, *Tegh Bahādur (including one *śalok sometimes attributed to Gobind Siṅgh); and (iii) poets contemporary with the Gurūs i.e. Bhīkhaṇ, *Sūrdās, Sundar, *Mardānā, Satta and Balvand, and at least eleven bards in the Gurūs' entourage.

The contents are metrical and, excepting the opening *Japjī, are intended for singing. After the hymns comprising the *Rahirās and *Sohilā the subsequent compositions are divided into thirty-one *rāgs (in the order listed). Thereafter follow a series of śaloks and *Savayye, the Mundāvaṇī ('seal'), and Rāgamālā. Each rāg is subdivided as follows: (i) *chaupads and hymns of two, three, five, or six stanzas; (ii) *aṣṭapadīs; (iii)*chhants; (iv) vārs of Gurūs in serial order followed by bards; and (v) bhagat *bāṇī, i.e. hymns of pre-Nānak saints, usually beginning with Kabīr and Nāmdev. Each section commences with the *Mul Mantra.

There are three extant versions (*bīṛ*) of the Ādi Granth: (i) the *Kartārpur version, dictated to *Gurdās Bhallā by Arjan Dev, incorporating the Mohan pothīs of Amar Dās, hymns by himself, Rām Dās, and contemporary bards; (ii) the *Banno version; and (iii) the *Damdamā version which is currently used. According to tradition, Gobind

Siṅgh's request to see the Kartārpur manuscript was refused, so he dictated a copy from memory to *Manī Siṅgh, adding fifty-nine hymns and fifty-six śaloks by Tegh Bahādur. This manuscript was lost in battle although copies survived.

Despite the diversity of authorship and language, the message of the Ādi Granth is unanimous: salvation depends not upon *caste, ritual, or asceticism, but upon constant meditation on God's name (*nām) and immersement in his being:

Lord, mighty River, all-knowing, all-seeing,
And I like a little fish in your great waters,
How shall I sound your depths?
How shall I reach your shores?
Wherever I go, I see you only,
And snatched out of your waters I die of separation (Ādi Granth, p. 25)

The Sikhs' awareness of God draws upon the mystical, sometimes paradoxical, poetry of the Ādi Granth. Gurū Nānak's luminous insights, most economically stated in the *Mul Mantra, find further expression in the compositions of later Gurūs. Many names are used for God, some familiar to Hindus (e.g. *Hari, Śiv, Brahma, Rām, Mohan) and others to Muslims (e.g. Rabb, *Allāh, Khudā, Sāhib), but God is emphatically One (*ik oṅkār) and does not become incarnate as an *avatāra. Above all, God's name is Truth (*sat(i)nām). He is the *Sat(i)gurū by whose *grace the way of *salvation from *rebirths is revealed. He is the *creator of all and everything occurs in accordance with his will (hukam). He is beyond attributes (*nirguṇ) and possesses all attributes *śāgun* (see ŚĀGUNA BRAHMAN), both transcendent and immanent. Gurū *Tegh Bahādur asked, 'Why do you go to the forest to find God? He lives in all and yet remains distinct. He dwells in you as fragrance resides in a flower or the reflection in a mirror.' (Ādi Granth p. 684.)

God is sustainer and destroyer—even of death. He is *nirañjan (unentangled in *māyā). He is sovereign, eternal, omnipresent, and omniscient; beyond measure, utterance, or visual representation. He is the source of light, beauty, and mercy. He dispels fear and anxiety. By the Gurū's grace and by devoted repetition of God's name he can be realized.

Gurū Gobind Siṅgh's *Jāp sings God's glory. Elsewhere Gobind Siṅgh's epithets such as *sarvloh* (all-steel) and *bhagautī* (sword) mark a new emphasis. See also VĀHIGURŪ; DASAM GRANTH.

Trs. Gopal Singh (1962), Mannohan Singh (1969); S. S. Kohli, *A Critical Study of the Ādi Granth* (1969); C. Shackle, *A Guru Nanak Glossary* (1981).

Ādinātha (Skt. 'first lord'). Title given to first Jain *tīrthaṅkara of this present time span (*avasarpiṇī*), *Ṛṣabha. The Ādinātha temple on Mount *Abu in S. Rajasthan provides an outstandingly beautiful example of Jain architecture and is a major centre of Jain pilgrimage today. As a title of *Śiva, see SIDDHA.

Ādi-purāṇa. 1. An occasional title of *Brahma purāṇa*.

2. A Jain work in Skt. on the 'origin' and past history of the world. It was written by *Jinasena in S. India, and completed by his disciple Guṇabhadra who also continued the narrative in the *Uttara-*purāṇa*, which his own disciple Lokasena finished in *c.*892 CE. These two parts, also called together *Mahā-purāṇa*, contain the Jain world history, from its beginnings up to the time of the *Mahāvīra, the last *tīrthaṅkara (and historical founder of Jainism). Within the framework of the (mythical) adventures of the sixty-three *śalākā-puruṣas* (lit. 'staff-men', denoting here 'heroic men'), a vast store of Indian and specifically Jain story material has been arranged. During the subsequent centuries, many versions of *Mahā-purāṇa* were produced in different vernaculars: by Puṣpadanta *c.*965 in Apabhraṃśa (S. India), by Cāvuṇḍarāya *c.*978 in Kannada, and in Tamil the anonymous *Śrī-Purāṇa* as late as the 14th cent. All these belong to the *Digambara tradition; on the Śvetāmbara side is *Triṣaṣṭiśalākāpuruṣacaritra*, again in Skt., by the famous *Hemacandra (12th cent.) from Gujarat. An almost incalculable amount of literature arose, by dealing with individual 'heroes' of the set of sixty-three on a grand epic scale, in many Indian languages.

Jinasena's intention was to provide, in an increasingly 'Hindu-conscious' southern Indian environment, a Jain answer to the Hindu *purāṇas. Starting with the 'origin' of the world (which means, since time and the universe themselves are without beginning, with the beginning of the cosmic cycle in which we find ourselves), he introduced the figure *Ṛṣabha or *Ādinātha ('the First Emperor'). Through him, and various other secondary heroes and anti-heroes, the Jain religion, the heterodox belief-systems (like 'Hinduism'), the *caste-system, etc. were instituted. By virtue of carrying the eternal truth of Jain teaching into the current cosmic cycle, Ṛṣabha is the first of the twenty-four tīrthaṅkaras, promulgators of the true teaching. The series, as does *Mahā-purāṇa*, comes to an end with the twenty-fourth tīrthaṅkara, the (historical) Mahāvīra. By envisaging the *jīva of Ṛṣabha's grandson Marīci re-embodied, i.e. as Tripṛṣṭha (the first of the nine *Vāsudevas), and then as the Mahāvīra, an overarching continuity is provided for the whole pattern. From archaic *Kṛṣṇa material, a set of Vāsudeva (= Kṛṣṇa), Baladeva (= Kṛṣṇa's half-brother), and Prati-Vāsudeva (= Kṛṣṇa's main antagonist) is derived, which—once projected onto the story of *Rāma—could be multiplied further, so that in each category we find now nine representatives. Finally, a set of twelve *cakravartins, 'universal emperors', is woven into the pattern. Since three of these 'emperors' are also tīrthaṅkaras, we obtain the total of sixty-three for these heroes. To varying extent, the 'life-stories' of all of them, including prior chains of lives, are narrated. By this device the Jains could incorporate the whole of Kṛṣṇa and Rāma mythology, the famous epic stories of the **Mahābhārata* and the **Rāmāyaṇa*, the *Bṛhatkathā*, and innumerable further myths, legends, and stories into one coherent chronological (and ideological) framework.

Tr. of Hemacandra, H. M. Johnson (6 vols., 1962).

Aditi (Skt., 'boundlessness'). Unlimited space and consciousness, hence infinity, eternity. Manifested as a goddess (frequently mentioned in the **Ṛg Veda*), she is the inexhaustible source, the mother of the *Ādityas under whose constraint the universe is alone possible; and she is also the consumer of all things, i.e. death. She is the mother of all the gods (*deva-mātṛ*). In the Epics and *Purāṇas, she is herself one of the thirteen daughters of Dakṣa (ritual skill) and the wife of *Kaśyapa, by whom she became the mother of *Viṣṇu in his manifestation as *Vāmana. Aditi represents a caution already apparent in the *Vedas about attributing the origin of the universe to a personal agent, such as a god: see further COSMOLOGY.

Ādityas. In Hinduism, the ruling principles which constrain the universe into its outcomes. In personified form, they are the sons of *Aditi. They are associated closely with the sun as the source of life, and became eventually twelve in number to correspond to the twelve solar months. Initially, there were eight sons, of whom one, Mārtāṇḍa, was born as a lifeless egg (or misshapen foetus), but was given the shape and life of the sun by the other Ādityas, who thus share in the power of the sun. The eight are identified with the Vasus, the eight spheres of existence. When the number was extended to twelve (e.g. *Taittirīya Āraṇyaka* 1. 13 and subsequent texts) and they were identified with the twelve ruling principles, they were usually (but with occasional variants) listed as Aṁsā (the share of the gods), Aryaman (generous nobility), Bhaga (due inheritance), Dakṣa (ritual skill), *Mitra (constancy in friendship), Pūṣan (prosperity), Śakra (courage), Savitṛ (power of words), Tvaṣṭṛ (skill in craft and technique), *Varuṇa (fate), *Viṣṇu (cosmic law), Vivasvat (social law). In later times, the name Āditya came to be applied to any god (so fundamental are the twelve principles to the sustenance of the cosmos), though it was especially applied to *Sūrya, the sun. Āditya-sūnu, son of the Sun, was the name of Sugrīva, the monkey-king of the **Rāmāyaṇa*, and of others. In Buddhism, Āditya is a name given to the Buddha.

Ādityavarṇa. A Hindu spiritual practice and experience based on the intense light of the sun. Cf. NŪR in Islam.

Adloyada (Heb.). *Purim carnival. The expression derives from the Hebrew *'ad de-lo-yada'* (until one no longer knows). According to the *rabbis, participants should celebrate on Purim until they no longer know the difference between 'Blessed be Mordecai' and 'Cursed be Haman'. The celebration involves processions of carnival floats through major *Israeli towns.

Adonai (Heb., 'my Lord'). Jewish title of God. It is commonly used in the Jewish tradition to replace the *tetragrammaton (JHWH) when reading the text of the Hebrew scriptures, and its vowels, inserted into JHWH, thus produce the form Jehovah.

Adon 'Olam (Heb., 'Lord of the World'). A Jewish hymn praising God's greatness. Although attributed to Solomon ibn *Gabirol, its authorship is unknown. It has appeared in both the *Sephardic and *Ashkenazic liturgy since the 14th cent. CE, and is now normally placed at the end of the *Sabbath and *Festival *Musaf service. A version appears in George Borrow's *Lavengro*.

Adoptianism. A Christian *heresy in 8th-cent. Spain. According to its main proponent, Archbishop Elipandus of Toledo, the *Logos, as true Son of God, must be distinguished from *Christ, who is Son in a different sense, as a consequence of the Word 'adopting' humanity.

More generally, the term, usually spelt adoptionism, refers to the view that *Jesus was a man whom God adopted as his son. The earliest *christologies may be called adoptionist in that they speak of divine status for Christ only at his resurrection (e.g. Acts 2. 36). Some sects, e.g. the *Ebionites, seem to have located Jesus' adoption at his baptism (Luke 3. 22). But such views were progressively ousted as christology came to insist on the pre-existence of Christ and his identification with God. In modern times adoptionist views have been revived by liberal theologians as a way of safeguarding Jesus' humanity.

Adoptionism: see ADOPTIANISM.

Adret, Solomon ben Abraham (Shelomoh b. Avraham, *c.*1235–*c.*1310, commonly known as Rashba). Spanish Jewish scholar. He was considered the outstanding student of *Naḥmanides, and for forty years held the position of *Rabbi of Barcelona. He was the author of many *responsa which were gathered together for future guidance. These responsa are a major source of information for the history of the Jews of the late 13th cent., as his influence spread throughout Europe. He defended *Maimonides and attacked the *messianic pretender, Abraham *Abulafia. Although a traditionalist, he permitted his students to study physics and *metaphysics after the age of 25, and put no restriction on astronomy and medicine, though always under the control of past authority: 'What is founded on tradition or God's inspiration cannot be dislodged by any science in the world.' Besides his responsa, he wrote novellae to various tractates of the *Talmud which are still consulted today. He also refuted the attempt of Raimundo Martini in *Pugio Fidei* to argue from the Talmud against the Jews; and he argued against *ibn Ḥazm, contesting the divine origin of the *Qur'ān.

I. Epstein, *The Responsa of Rabbi Solomon ben Adretha Barcelona* . . . (1925); J. Perles, *R Salomo ben Abraham* . . . , *Sein Leben* . . . (1863).

Adrian IV (*c.*1100–59). The first and so far only Englishman to be *pope. He was born Nicholas Breakspear, and after education partly in France, he became a monk near Avignon. In 1137, he was elected *abbot. The community complained of his severity, and Pope Eugene III moved him to be cardinal-bishop of Albano. In 1150–3 he was *papal legate in Scandinavia, where his skill in reordering the church led him to be called 'The Apostle of the North'. He was elected pope in 1154. In the conflicts of the time, he sought an alliance with the German king, Frederick I Barbarossa, crowning him in front of his army as Holy Roman Emperor in 1155, in a ceremony designed to emphasize Frederick's subservient position. However, Frederick had his own ideas, informed by dreams of restoring the empire of Charlemagne and Otto I. Adrian looked south for an ally in William I of Sicily, whom he had at one time excommunicated: he recognized him as king in return for tribute, and felt able to confront Frederick once more. Frederick claimed rights over N. Italy and Corsica at the diet of Roncaglia (1158); Adrian refused to approve his nominee to the see of Ravenna and threatened to excommunicate him unless he withdrew the Roncaglia claims within forty days; but within that period, Adrian died. It has been claimed that he encouraged Henry II to incorporate Ireland into the English Kingdom, but the authenticity of the *bull *Laudabiliter* is doubtful.

W. Ullmann, 'The Pontificate of Adrian IV', *Cambr. Hist. Journ.* 11: 233–52.

Adṛṣṭa (Skt., 'unseen'). Unseen force; in Indian philosophy related to and sometimes synonymous with *karma. It designates an imperceptible constraint on any given event, accounting for such forces as gravity and magnetic attraction as well as the unseen causes of one's present life-situation, i.e. actions performed in previous lives. The *Sāṃkhya system believed adṛṣṭa to reside in *prakṛti. For the *Vaiśeṣikas it is a necessary condition for the arising of another body after death and is created by the contact between the internal organ (*antaḥ karaṇa*) comprising *buddhi, *ahaṃkāra, and *manas, and the soul (*ātman), though this is rejected by the *Nyāya. There is some contention among Nyāya-Vaiśeṣika philosophers as to whether adṛṣṭa is a quality of atoms (*aṇu) and therefore material, or not. In *Pūrva-mīmāṃsā, adṛṣṭa is found as a synonym for *apūrva, the force produced by a sacrifice which gives results at a later date.

Adultery. The way in which religions have played so vital a role in the protection of what would now be recognized as gene-replication and the nurture of children has contributed to a strong condemnation of adultery in all religions—though what counts as adultery is diversely defined: thus, according to Jewish law, sexual relationship between a married man and an unmarried woman, although sinful, is not considered adulterous; In Islam (see ZINĀ'), there is no distinction between men and women (Qur'ān 24. 3), but there has been considerable dispute about the permissibility of extra-marital sex between Muslim men and their unmarried slave women. At issue in the religious evaluation of marriage and adultery has been the stability of families within the continuing structure of society (hence the importance of known parentage and descent), along with the predictability and reliability of humans in relations of commitment to each other. The offence of adultery is the disruption of that fidelity, which traditionally carries with it well-defined roles for husbands and wives. These again affect the religious evaluation of adultery. Thus in the Hindu religion of the *Dharma Sūtras and Śastras, as of the Epics, it is assumed that the character of women not only defines their role, but is of such weakness that they cannot be regarded as responsible for an act of this kind: 'When comitting an act of adultery, only a man becomes unclean through offence.' Because of the social consequences of adultery, religions are at a far extreme from the opinion of Voltaire, that 'adultery is an evil only if it is a theft, but we do not steal that which is donated to us'. Because of the involvement of others by implication, consent does not erase the offence. According to Jewish scripture, adultery was punishable by death, although the adulterer seems to have been able to buy himself off by paying compensation to the husband. The relationship between God and his *chosen people was often described as that of a faithful husband pursuing a faithless wife (see particularly Hosea 1–3).

In Buddhism, adultery is included in the forms of illicit sexual intercourse, any of which is a cause of bad *karma. In *Sutta Nipāta* 106–8, adultery is singled out as the most seriously wrong in a series of examples of wrongdoing. A monk involved in this, as in other sexual misdemeanours, is expelled from the *saṅgha.

Adultery is likewise forbidden by Sikh teaching. 'Do not cast your eyes on the beauty of another's wife' (Ādi Granth p. 274). According to the *Gurus both men and women are responsible: see KHĀLSĀ; POLYGAMY; RAHIT.

Advaita (Skt., 'not-dual'). The state in which there is only, without differentiation, whatever there is, in which all appearances of distinction (e.g. between subject and object, perceiver and perceived) are known to be a consequence and product of inadequate understanding, or ignorance (*avidyā, *adhyāsa). This state can only be ascribed to God or to *Brahman as Absolute. This perception of non-duality underlies *Advaita Vedānta.

Advaita Vedānta. One of the three major philosophical/theological systems in Hindu *Vedānta, whose leading protagonist was *Śaṅkara. *Brahman is the Absolute and underlying ground of all appearance: for those with (trained) eyes to see, Brahman can be perceived as the real and the unchanging lying within or behind the manifold appearances which the senses encounter. There cannot, therefore, be any truth in the human propensity to differentiate objects, or parts of objects, as though they have the reality of their superficial appearance. There is only Brahman, which is necessarily undifferentiated. It follows that there cannot even be a difference, or duality, between the human subject, or self, and Brahman, for Brahman must be that very self (since Brahman is the reality underlying all appearance). The goal of human life and wisdom must, therefore, be the realization that the self (*ātman) *is* Brahman—hence the famous formula (*mahāvākya), *tat tvam asi*, thou art that. Meanwhile, before that realization (which is *mokṣa, release) occurs, the self is entangled in the world of appearances, and in that state is known as *jīva. Like two birds on a tree, the true self (ātman) sits serene and detached, the other (jīva) immerses itself in activity. It also superimposes (*adhyāsa) on the world false impressions of reality, as (in the most famous example) when it sees what is truly a rope on a path, but imposes on it the belief that it is a snake (see also ADHYĀROPA). But when the jīva sees the rope for what it truly is (Brahman), it becomes *jīvanmukti, liberated self. Śankara summarized his system in a single sentence, 'Brahman alone is real, the world is appearance, ātman is nothing but Brahman'. See also AJĀTIVĀDA; ŚRĪ HARṢA; Index, Advaita.

E. Deutsh and J. A. B. van Buitenen, *A Source Book of Vedānta* (1971).

Advaya (Skt., non-duality). The essential nature of things when truly understood, according to Buddhist thought. The term itself is not met with in the Pāli *Tripiṭaka, although the *Buddha does deny the duality (*dvayatā*) of existence (*atthitā*) and non-existence (*nātthitā*) (*Samyutta Nikāya* 2. 17). This effectively means that the Buddha's teachings avoid the two extremes of eternalism (*śāśvatavāda*) and nihilism (*ucchedavāda*), without at the same time admitting a sole reality such as the Upaniṣadic *Brahman. It is this recognition of non-duality (advaya) which gave the impetus to *Siddhartha to strive for Buddhahood (*Mahāvastu* 1. 237. 14), and because of the centrality of the notion to his teaching the Buddha is often referred to as a teacher of non-duality (advaya-vādin).

The term is more commonly encountered in the literature of the *Mahāyāna. In the *Prajñāpāramitā* (see PERFECTION OF WISDOM) corpus it is often found as a synonym of suchness (*tathatā) since, from the ultimate point of view, reality cannot be determined on the basis of dichotomies, such as subjectivity and objectivity, which operate according to worldly convention. The *Ratnagotravibhāga* of *Asaṅga goes further and holds reality (*tattva) to be ultimately non-dual (advaya) on the grounds that it is devoid of both action (*karman) and defilement (*kleśa).

Advent (Lat., *adventus*, 'coming', i.e. of Christ). The season of the church year preceding *Christmas. Originally a season of fasting, in the *Orthodox Church it begins in November. In the W. Church, fasting is no longer obligatory, and the season is shorter, beginning on the Sunday closest to 30 Nov. Concerned with the *Four Last Things, Advent prepares for the *parousia, as well as for Christmas.

Adventists. Members of Christian sects who believe that the Second Coming of *Jesus Christ is literal and imminent. Seventh Day Adventists, derived from William Miller (1781–1849) who predicted the end of the world in 1843–4, believe that the Advent is delayed because of the failure to keep the *Sabbath. Sabbath-keeping was confirmed in the visions of Ellen G. White (d. 1915), who was a prolific writer of Adventist literature. *Dietary laws from the Old Testament are also observed, and the further belief, that the Advent will occur when the *gospel has been proclaimed throughout the world, leads to vigorous proselytization.

E. S. Gaustad, *The Rise of Adventism* (1974).

Advocatus Dei: see DEVIL'S ADVOCATE.

Advocatus diaboli: see DEVIL'S ADVOCATE.

Advowson. The right, in the Christian Church, to present to a *bishop a nominee for appointment to a *parish or other benefice. This right may be in the hands of the bishop, in which case it is usually described as 'collating'. Often such right was a result of local land ownership and was in lay hands, or in those of religious communities. In neither case can they canonically 'appoint' to an ecclesiastical office: they can nominate or present to a bishop a person for appointment, and this can only be refused on defined grounds which relate to the suitability either of the candidate or of the patron. In the Middle Ages, if certain conditions were not met and the candidate was deemed 'unsuitable', the right might go to the bishop (as it did if the presentation was not made within a given period, usually six months). These rights were highly contested in the Middle Ages, not least because local interests might be overridden by other interests, papal or royal. The right was often coveted, not least by the *pope, who sought on occasions to intervene in order to promote to a benefice his own nominee. In the 14th cent. in England, the pope's right to take to himself some advowsons was restricted, and in the 16th cent., this was also done in France and Spain. When rights over land changed hands, the associated advowsons changed as well. Hence at the English Reformation, many advowsons were transferred from the monasteries to the Crown or to secular patrons. In the 20th cent. in England the right of advowson or patronage has been increasingly concentrated in the hands of ecclesiastical authorities (though lay patronage survives), and has been limited: the interests of the parish have been more effectively secured. In other parts of Europe varying conditions obtain, often to the advantage of the diocesan bishop.

Ādya-śrādha. A Hindu anticipatory funeral rite, performed during their lifetime by those who have no son to perform the appropriate rites for them after death, or by those who for some other reason believe that the rites will not be performed after death.

Aelia Capitolina. The post-135 CE Roman name for *Jerusalem. After the *Bar Kokhba revolt, the Emperor Hadrian tried to deprive the city of its Jewish character. A sanctuary dedicated to the god Jupiter Capitolinus was constructed on the *Temple mount, and Jews were prohibited from entering the city, which was then called Aelia Capitolina in all official edicts.

Aelred, St (1109–67). *Cistercian monk of Rievaulx; author, as novice-master, of *Speculum Caritatis* (The Mirror of Love), emphasizing God's love as restoring fallen humans into their true image: the initiative comes from the grace and vocation of God. 'You called me, Lord, you called, you shouted, you assailed me, . . . you broke up the hard places of my heart, you sweetened and softened and dispelled my bitterness.' He was *abbot of Revesby in 1143 and of Rievaulx in 1147. He wrote a major work on Christian friendship, based on Cicero's *De Amicitia*, but showing how friendship is transformed and spiritualized in relation to Christ (hence the title, *De Spirituali Amicitia*). He has, consequently, been adopted as the equivalent of a *patron saint by some gay (*homosexual) Christians. He made the outward journey of the itinerant hermit into an analogy of the inner journey of the Christian person of prayer, while emphasizing the quality and importance of friendship: 'Friend adhering to friend in the spirit of Christ is made with Christ into a single heart and soul, and so rises higher through degrees of love to friendship with Christ.' He was known as 'the *Bernard of the north'.

Trs. G. Webb and A. Walker (1962); M. E. Walker (1974).

Aeon: see TIME.

Aetiology (account of causes or origins): see MYTH.

Aetos (Gk.). In Greek Orthodoxy, the inset in the choir floor which marked the position of the emperor's throne. From this it became a decorated mat on which *bishops stand at their consecration in order to recite the *Creed and their profession of faith.

Affective prayer. A way of prayer which makes use of the emotions or feelings or the will, as opposed to prayer of the intellect. It is sometimes thought of as a stage higher than prayer which relies on thinking about things, but still a form of prayer in which human activity is paramount.

Affirmative way. The approach to God which affirms that something can be discerned of his being and nature through reason and from the created order. It is therefore in contrast to the *via negativa. A classic expression occurs in Christianity in the five arguments advanced by St *Thomas Aquinas (*Quinque Viae) from which he concluded that 'the existence of God can be demonstrated from those of his effects which are known to us' (*Summ. Theol.* 1, qu. 2, art. 2): it can be known *that* God is, but not, without revelation, *what* God is. The affirmative way is even stronger in some other religions, especially in Islam, where creation offers demonstrations of God subsumed under the same word (*ayā) as that which is used for the verses of the *Qur'ān; and in Hinduism, where the cosmic appearance may be the body of God (see e.g. *Rāmānuja), and where in any case the true reality underlies all appearance. The affirmative way then becomes highly important in spiritual life, since the created order offers the opportunity of advance into the discernment of God and may indeed be regarded as a ladder of ascent. A classic example in Christianity is St *John of the Cross: 'My beloved is the mountains and lonely wooded valleys, remote islands and resounding rivers, the sigh of love-evoking breezes, the still of night before the dawn, silent music, sounding solitude, the meal that refreshes and deepens love' (*Spiritual Canticle*, 14 f.). The affirmative way is thus the foundation of kataphatic theology in contrast to *apophatic, though the two are necessarily linked, since even the ultimate kataphatic claim of *Jesus, that 'he who has seen me has seen the Father' (John 14. 9) does not produce God as an object among objects.

Affliction, cults of. Cults and their associated ritual activities which deal with the occurrence of affliction, especially disease. The cause may be thought to be human or supernatural. The rituals often take the form of contest against the cause of the affliction and thus merge into possession and *exorcism. Although particularly common in Africa, such cults have occurred in all parts of the world (e.g. in connection with *śītalā in India). Because of the pronounced use of drums, these cults are sometimes known as 'the drums of affliction', the title of V. S. Turner's study of the Ndembu (1968).

F. D. Goodman, *How About Demons?* (1988); I. M. Lewis, *Ecstatic Religion* (1971).

Afghānī: see AL-AFGHĀNĪ, JAMĀL AL-DĪN.

Afikomen (Heb.). The middle of three pieces of *mazzah which is broken and set aside during the

*Passover *Seder and is left to be eaten at the end. In *Ashkenazi households, it has become the custom for the children to hide the afikomen from the leader and only return it after a ransom has been paid.

African-American religion. The religious beliefs of so large and diverse a population cannot be unified into a single, artificial scheme. The African dispersion has now mingled with many other sources, and black Americans look to more roots than those of their African origin (thus *black Muslims may absorb Islam *ab origine*, not simply via Africa, and black Catholics advert to St Martin de Porres, a 17th-cent. Peruvian of Afro-Hispanic descent); and in any case, the nature of the religion in any particular area depends on a creative interaction with existing beliefs and customs. To take only one example, in Haiti religious themes from Dahomey, the Yoruba, and Bakongo have created 'vodun' (*vodou, usually transliterated 'voodoo'), in which the RC saints (with whom vodun is connected) are always subordinate in terms of Catholic orthodoxy. Nevertheless, the African roots, the long experience of slavery and of continuing prejudice, and the ambivalent relation of Christianity to the struggle for emancipation and equality (both enforcing and justifying slavery, yet also inspiring and leading emancipation, both providing consolation with acquiescence yet also leading protest), have produced vivid and deeply moving forms of religious life. In relation to Christianity, they have been marked by a strong independence (for the first African-American Church, see AFRICAN METHODIST EPISCOPAL CHURCH), ranging from the 'storefront churches' to the African Orthodox Church (founded by Marcus *Garvey and an Episcopalian priest, G. A. McGuire), in which the *Madonna and *Christ are visualized as black. In relation to the mainstream denominations and churches, the *Baptist Church, with its emphasis on autonomy for local congregations and less formal requirements for ministry, has proved particularly attractive, and at one stage (*c.* 1960) the National Baptist Convention numbered more than 6 million members. In relation to Islam, see NATION OF ISLAM, BLACK MUSLIMS.

Despite the extreme vitality and diversity of African-American religion, H. A. Baer and M. Singer (*African-American Religion in the 20th Century*, 1992) have suggested that African-American religion falls into four broad types: (i) messianic-nationalist (cf. MESSIAH); (ii) *thaumaturgic; (iii) conversionist; (iv) mainstream. In addition, it is clear that all types are united by a profound involvement in the religious possibilities of music and dance. R. F. Thompson (*Flash of the Spirit*, 1983) has singled out as recurrently characteristic the dominance of a percussive style, propensity for multiple metre, overlapping call and response, inner pulse control, suspended accentuation patterning, and songs and dances with social allusion.

M. J. Adler (ed.), *The Negro in American History* (1969); O. Alho, *The Religion of the Slaves* (1976); A. B. Cleage, *Black Messiah* (1969); J. H. Cone, *My Soul Looks Back* (1986) and *God of the Oppressed* (1975); H. Courlander, *Negro Folk Music USA* (1963); W. E. B. Dubois, *Souls of Black Folk* (1903); J. H. Evans *Black Theology: . . . a Bibliography* (1987); L. H. Fishel (and) B. Quarles, *The Black American: A Documentary History* (1970); R. F. Johnston, *The Development of Negro Religion* (1954); B. Mays, *The Negro's God* (1968); P. Oliver, *Songsters and Saints* (1984); A. Raboteau, *Slave Religion . . .*, (1978); H. Thurman, *The Negro Spiritual Speaks of Life and Death* (1947) and *Deep River* (1955); J. Washington, *Black Religion* (1964); G. S. Wilmore and J. H. Cone, *Black Theology: A Documentary History, 1966–79* (1979); J. W. Work, *American Negro Songs and Spirituals* (1940).

African Apostles. Two distinct independent Christian movements in central Africa, both beginning in Zimbabwe in 1932, the Masowe Apostles and the Maranke Apostles. The former derive from John Masowe (?1910–73), baptised as an *Anglican, who had a mystic call experience, called himself *John the Baptist, and proclaimed an *apocalyptic message of imminent judgement and moral reform. His followers became called VaPostori (Shona, 'the Apostles'), but their anti-government and anti-church attitudes led to harassment which drove them to seek freedom by settling as the Apostolic Sabbath Church of God in the Korsten slum of Port Elizabeth, South Africa, in 1947. Here their manual skills led to the popular name of the Basketmakers' Church. Deported in 1962, they moved north *en route* to Ethiopia and Jerusalem, but most settled in Zambia near Lusaka, where they established a range of small industries; others established the church in some nine adjacent countries, and Masowe died in Tanzania. The church is notable for its migrant history, its emphasis on Bible study, the absence of drums, dancing, or instruments to support its singing, spiritual healing without holy water or a healing medium, and a women's 'convent of sisters' to serve as guardian of the tradition.

The Maranke Apostles were founded by Johane Maranke (1912–63), brought up in the American *Methodist mission, who had a *pentecostal experience and also visions of going to heaven, which were later recorded in 'The New Revelation of the Apostles' as an addition to the Bible.

The outpouring of the Spirit on Maranke, and his healings, exorcisms, and prophecies, led to a mass movement, also called VaPostori, and later the African Apostolic Church. As a well-organized body, with provision for training new leaders at its headquarters and for sending out young people on missionary travels for two years, it has become the largest such church in Zimbabwe, and has spread across central Africa as far as Zaire, with an estimated half-million members. Its main ceremonies are the baptism in 'Jordan' and the annual Pasika (*Passover), a holy *communion celebration held at official, central, enclosed Pasika sites with strict testing of members at the entrance gates for unconfessed sins. Schisms occurred after Masowe's death but have remained small.

B. Jules-Rosette, *African Apostles* . . . (1975).

African Greek Orthodox Church. A complex development from E. *Orthodoxy around an *Anglican Ugandan, Reuben Mukasa (1899–1982), nicknamed Spartas. After hearing of Marcus *Garvey's independent African Orthodox Church in America, he founded his own counterpart in Uganda in 1929. Upon finding the Garvey Church to be heterodox, Spartas separated and affiliated in 1933 with the Greek Orthodox Patriarchate in Alexandria. He added the word 'Greek' to the name of his church, which was accepted into membership by the Patriarchate in 1946, along with Orthodox churches with a similar history in Kenya. The whole African Greek Orthodox Church thus came directly under the first Greek Orthodox *Metropolitanate for E. Africa when this was established in 1959. After allegations of paternalism and of inadequate material aid, Spartas led a secession in 1966, to become the African Orthodox Autonomous Church South of the Sahara, with some 7,000 members. Most of this church returned with Spartas when the Greeks consecrated him auxiliary bishop of Uganda in 1972, with other African auxiliary bishops for Tanzania and Kenya. The total community within the Greek-related church in E. Africa is over a quarter of a million. It represents a prolonged search for a Christianity that is both African and in an authentic Christian tradition, as well as the first major contemporary expression of Greek Orthodox missionary concern.

African Instituted Churches. Indigenous churches in Africa, characterized by their independence from the history (and originally missionary) churches. Hence they were first known as African Independent Churches. The initials AIC became common, so that the new and current name (adopted by the churches in question to emphasize that they are founded and led by Africans, and are not to be defined by their relationship to the historic and missionary churches) allows the same initials to be used. AIC are also characterized by cultural renaissance, a de-emphasis on the high verbalization of mainstream churches, and an emphasis on the *Holy Spirit and on biblical warrant for African cultural norms (e.g. the importance of dreams, prophecy, and visions; whether this includes *polygamy is disputed). For examples, see AFRICAN APOSTLES; AFRICAN ISRAEL CHURCH NINEVEH; AIYETORO; ALADURA; BAYUDAYA; BRAID(E); BWITI; DÉÏMA; EAST AFRICAN REVIVAL; ETHIOPIANISM; FEDEN; GODIANISM; GOD'S KINGDOM SOCIETY; HARRIS MOVEMENT; JAMAA; KIMBANGU; KITAWALA; LUMPA CHURCH; MAI CHAZA'S CHURCH; MARIO LEGIO; MUSAMA DISCO CRISTO; NAZARITE CHURCH; PROVIDENCE INDUSTRIAL MISSION; ZION CHRISTIAN CHURCH; ZIONIST CHURCHES. Some of these movements may be seeking an expression of (or be in communion with) established forms of Christianity—e.g. African Greek Orthodox Church, in relation to Greek Orthodoxy; Order of Ethiopia in relation to *Anglicanism. Less common are breakaway movements from Islam; but see e.g. HAMALLISM and MOURIDES.

D. B. Barrett, *Schism and Renewal in Africa* . . . (1968); H. W. Turner, *Bibliography of New Religious Movements in Primal Societies, i. Black Africa* (1977).

African Israel Church Nineveh. An early independent church in Kenya, mainly among the Luhya and the Luo. It was founded by the highly charismatic David Zayako Kivuli (1896–1974) who was baptized in 1925 in the Pentecostal Assemblies of East Africa (a Canadian mission), had a mystic experience in 1932, became a teacher and evangelist, and led a small peaceful secession in 1942. By 1960 it was spreading to Uganda and Tanzania, and in 1975, when it joined the *World Council of Churches, it claimed 76,000 members. The headquarters north of Kisumu are a 'holy city', like the church, called Nineveh, after the biblical city that repented. Public confession of sin occurs on Thursday evenings before the long *pentecostal forms of worship on Fridays. Although orthodox in beliefs, there is only spiritual *baptism, without water, and no holy *communion. Healing by herbal, Western, or spiritual methods is accepted; monogamy is taught and *alcohol and tobacco banned. They are known in public for vigorous evangelistic processions with drums and flags.

African Methodist Episcopal Church. The first church in the USA to be made up entirely of African-Americans. It came into being in 1787 when those with black skin refused to be segregated in the seating in St George's church in 4th St, Philadelphia. There was some scuffling, and as Richard Allen (to be elected the first *bishop of the ensuing church) recalled, 'By this time prayer was over, and we all went out of the church in a body, and they were no more plagued with us there. . . . Here was the beginning and rise of the first African church in America.' The church was reorganized in 1816, expanding greatly after the Civil War. In 1841, it founded the first African-American publishing house.

African Orthodox Church: see AFRICAN-AMERICAN RELIGION.

African religion. No single religion corresponds to the term 'African religion', nor could it. The geography of Africa ranges from rain forests to uninhabitable deserts; its peoples are organized in many different social ways, from itinerants to villages to tribes to urbanized communities; and the vast continent has been invaded by other religions which frequently dominate particular areas, especially Christianity and Islam, but also to a lesser degree Hinduism. These in turn have often been appropriated and given a new and distinctive African style and content (see e.g. AFRICAN INSTITUTED CHURCHES).

Nevertheless, although there is no such 'thing' as 'African religion', attempts have been made to draw out some of the recurrent and characteristic emphases to be found in Africa.

1. There is strong reverence for a supreme God, the source and support of life; frequently this is combined with a belief in a hierarchy of lesser spirits or beings through whom one approaches God, rather than through direct prayer or worship; indeed, the closer one comes to God (or the closer God comes to the world), the more disturbing and unusual happenings there are likely to be.

2. The power of God (as an example of this disturbing effect) to inspire particular individuals or functionaries is emphasized; possession and divination, and also the readiness with which prophetic religions have grown up in Africa, are contemporary illustrations of this theme.

3. Religion is important in maintaining both social and cosmic order; God, the intermediary spirits, humans, and even animals form a network of mutual support, in which issues of personal salvation are not prominent; community and tribal identity are paramount.

4. The importance of *ancestors is noted. 'Ancestor worship' is too strong and too misleading a term; in fact it is commonly believed that each individual is made up of several different 'souls', including the continuing effects of the ancestors as guardians; the ancestors are not saved out of the world, but rather continue to be related to the ongoing family, and remain a part of it—until they are removed by the extending gap of succeeding generations; therefore, just as one must respect living members of the family for the sake of order and harmony, so one must do the same for those members of the family who are now ancestors. This reinforces a great respect for the old, since these are close to the ancestors, both chronologically and in experience.

5. *Rites of passage maintain stability and order; puberty and initiation rites are of obvious importance here, but all these rites have a vivid importance in African life.

6. *Magic and witchcraft are emphasized. These activities were much misunderstood by W. observers so long as they followed J. G. *Frazer in regarding them as poor technology born of ignorance; in fact, they combine an expressive role with a functional, often therefore saying more about the maintenance of order than about the explanation of particular events; while at the same time they persist in their efficacy, even in modernized and literate Africa. Mediums, diviners, magic-workers, and witches are of great importance, often expressing patterns and networks of relationship, and functioning as powerful methods of social control.

7. The oral tradition is powerful; not only is Africa rich and eloquent in *myth (see especially I. Okpewho, *Myth in Africa*, 1983)—a giftedness which is continued in modern literature, as pointed out by W. Soyinka *Myth, Literature and the African World*—but sound is regarded as bearing great effect.

8. There is emphasis on the sacred and often sacrosanct nature of the environment, almost any aspect of which may carry religious meaning.

D. Forde (ed.), *African Worlds*; M. Fortes and G. Dieterlin, *African Systems of Thought* (1965); E. B. Idowu, *African Traditional Religion* (1973); J. S. Mbiti, *An Introduction to African Religion* (1975); P. E. Ofori, *Black African Traditional Religions . . .: A Bibliographical Survey* (1975); B. Ray, *African Religions* (1976); J. V. Taylor, *The Primal Vision* (1963); D. Zahn, *The Religion, Spirituality and Thought of Traditional Africa* (1979); E. M. Zuesse, *Ritual Cosmos* (1979).

Afro-Brazilian cults. New (syncretist) religions based on survivals of African religions among the black slave population, originally in the north-east but now over most coastal areas and in southern cities. Some exhibit traditional Yoruba religion little changed from W. Africa. Candomblés are the forms developed in Bahia early in the 19th cent. (also called Xango, i.e. *Shango). These vary according to whether the African origins are Congolese-Angolan, Yoruba, or Islamic Negro (Hausa, etc.), and to the presence of Amerindian or Catholic elements. 'Macumba', more in Rio de Janeiro and São Paulo, emphasizes possession by ancestral spirits rather than deities, and tends to pass over into *magic and to forms known as Quimbanda. Batuque in Belem is more Brazilianized, with songs in Portuguese and members from all races, although lower class. These cults usually feature spirit possession, mediums, divination, animal *sacrifices, *dances, and cult centres with *altars and ritual paraphernalia. They are not *messianic or reformist, but concerned with daily problems and are often simply added on to folk Catholicism; now they are being eroded by the development of *Umbanda.

R. Bastide, *The African Religions of Brazil . . .* (1978).

Afscheiding (Dutch Reformed separation): see DUTCH REFORMED CHURCH.

Afterlife. The condition awaiting humans and the cosmos after death or at the end of time. Beliefs vary greatly between religions, though in origin the major continuing religious traditions, both East and West, had no belief that there would be a worthwhile existence after death. They could not deny that in some sense there is a trace of the dead, in memory and dreams, or in the resemblance of offspring to ancestors; but whatever state the dead may be in, it is a condition of extreme weakness, in which all connection with God and with the living is cut off, and certainly to be avoided or postponed as long as possible: it is, in Sophocles' words, *ton apotropon Haidan*, Hades to be shunned. The most militant reaction to this occurred in China, in the quest for immortality; and gradually both traditions came to realize that there may be about us that which does endure through the process of time and therefore perhaps through the event of death.

The Jewish tradition has come to believe that the life of human beings continues through death, and that there will be a consummation of the purposes of God in the *messianic age. But in the biblical period, there was no such belief until the very latest time. Then it seemed incoherent to have experienced the faithfulness (*ḥesed*) of God in creation and history, and to suppose that God was incapable of continuing it beyond death. The dead had been thought to maintain nothing but a shadowy existence beneath the earth in *Sheol, with all relations with God severed. For that reason, the *Sadducees, relying on the absence of such teaching in Torah, could deny *resurrection. In the later biblical books and in the *apocryphal literature, the doctrine of the resurrection of the dead emerges, and the 1st-cent. CE philosopher *Philo taught that the individual *soul was immortal. In the *Talmudic period, the *rabbis had many opinions, but in general it was believed that after the messianic redemption, the person would be reconstituted before judgement and the righteous would enjoy God's presence forever. The wicked, however, would be punished. In the Middle Ages, *Maimonides taught that the belief in the resurrection of the dead was a fundamental *principle of the Jewish faith, but some philosophers understood immortality in terms of the intellectual contemplation of God while others claimed it was the love of God which was all important. Today, *Orthodox Jews still maintain a belief in bodily resurrection, but most Reform Jews are only concerned with spiritual survival. The Jewish equivalent of *hell is derived from the mundane 'valley of Hinnom', *Gehinnom, Gk., Gehenna.

Christian beliefs were formed in the context of acute Jewish debates, in the period of the second *Temple, about the likelihood and nature of the afterlife, and are controlled by the astonished and grateful acceptance of the resurrection of *Jesus Christ. Jesus himself had affirmed belief in life after death, arguing against the Sadducees, but not going into detail. Early Christianity put together the two Jewish forms of speculation, thereby talking of the resurrection of the body, but also of the continuing life of the soul in the interval before the resurrection body is restored to it—a 'gap' which eventually allowed the doctrine of *purgatory. The New Testament is not detailed in its descriptions of the afterlife, apart from the visionary poetry of the Book of Revelations. *Heaven and *hell are filled out somewhat in later Christian imagination, but there remains a necessary agnosticism as regards detail in Christian accounts (see also LIMBO). It has become an issue (of *universalism) in Christianity whether hell is an eternal condition, or whether the objectivity of Christ's *atonement will eventually bring all to salvation.

The afterlife in Islam is known as *al-akhira*. The Muslim understanding of the afterlife is based on vivid and literal pictures in the *Qur'ān. After an interval in the grave (*barzakh), the dead will be raised by the summoning angels, *Munkar and Nakir, and, with souls and bodies reunited, will be taken to the day of judgement (*yaum al-dīn). Deeds will be weighed so exactly that nothing will be overlooked, even to the weight of the thread on a date-stone. The intercession of Muḥammad will help those who are on an exact balance. Those for whom the judgement is adverse will burn in fire (*jahannam*: see HELL, ISLAM) with new skins being prepared for them when the old are scorched. The fire may not be eternal (the issue is disputed). Those for whom the judgement is favourable will enter the Garden, with cool streams and beautiful maidens (*hūr); how far these are to be understood metaphorically is again an issue.

The early understandings in India of human nature and its destiny much resemble in attitude those of the Jewish Bible. The *Vedic imagination could conceive only of this life as a place of guaranteed worth, though they recognized that the gods worked hard (with the help of sacrifices) at maintaining their own (limited) immortality; and that death had been handed over to *Yama as a part of this process. According to *Taittirīya Brāhmaṇa* 3. 9. 15. 53–6, 'through special sacrifices, the gods became immortal. Death was apprehensive: "What shall be my portion?" They said, "None shall be immortal in the body. . . . Those who do not know or do not perform this sacrificial action will come to life again and again after death, and become food for Death." ' This revolutionary passage introduces a hint of an immortal soul and of recurrent rebirth (*samsāra). Neither samsāra nor *ātman as immortal soul are present in the *Vedas. The advance to ātman was made in the *Brāhmaṇas and *Āraṇyakas via *prāṇa, breath—the recognition that prāṇa is the support of life. Prāṇa is like the *logos in the W., since it not only supports life, but is the creator of sound (*vāc, see e.g. *Jaiminīya Upaniṣad Brāhmaṇa* 8. 2. 6), and becomes equated with Brahman as creator. Thus the life-principle in humans (and other manifestations) is eventually believed to be not other than the undying Brahman—so that ātman is Brahman. A transitional passage in the *Śankhayana Āraṇyaka* (3. 1–7) describes the soul's reception in heaven, coming in the end before Brahman who says, 'That which you are, that I am'—an anticipation of the *mahāvākyas of the Upaniṣads. In these early texts, Brahman oscillates between the masculine and neuter (i.e. between being understood personally and impersonally, e.g. *Aitareya Āraṇyaka* 2. 6. 1; 3. 2. 2–4), a division which was formalized and never reconciled in subsequent faith. On the one side (*advaita), the afterlife is a final realization that there is not other than Brahman, so that the 'afterlife' is as a drop merged with the entire ocean; on the other side (e.g. the theistic religion of the *Śaivites and the *Vaiṣṇavites, and indeed virtually the whole of Hinduism as lived), the afterlife is a personal relation with the object of devotion in this life; the 'heaven' thus attained is variously described. For both positions, rebirth has become an evil to be brought to an end. The many hells belong firmly within the process of rebirth, not to any eternal destiny—an understanding which is true of Eastern religions in general.

For Jains, the afterlife is mapped onto a cosmography in which the Middle World includes the part inhabited by humans. Below are a series of hells of increasing unpleasantness; above are a series of heavens of increasing brightness, including the abode of the gods. But those heavens are not the desirable state: this is the Isatpragbhara, the slightly curved (shaped somewhat like curved space in a parabola), where the *jīvas which have ceased to be encumbered by bodies abide.

Buddhists pressed further in resisting the Hindu move toward an eternal ātman. While there is continuity of consequence through samsāra, there is no eternal and undying subject of this process (*anātman). The process may move through heavens and hells, but these are no 'abiding city'. They are, nevertheless, vividly described, and are often the goals (or avoidances) in practice of the majority of Buddhists, for whom the ultimate goal of *nirvāna is too remote. It was this observation which led M. Spiro to describe Buddhism as a religion of proximate and ultimate salvation (*Buddhism and Society*). The afterlife may involve being reborn as an animal or attaining the condition of *arhat: between the two, many *Theravādin Buddhists aim for a better outcome in the next birth without aiming too far. In Mahāyāna, the realization of the ultimate goal was brought closer within reach, particularly through devotion to *bodhisattvas, whose role it is to save all sentient beings. This is dramatically illustrated in devotion to *Amida/Amithāba. The heavens described in devotional Buddhism (e.g. *Sukhāvatī) are as attractive as the Garden of Islam. While sharing Hindus' presuppositions about rebirth, Sikh teaching emphasizes the possibility of attaining *mukti during one's present life.

In the case of the religious traditions, both East and West, the development of beliefs in an afterlife was tentative and extremely reluctant to advance beyond the evidence of experience in this life. Once those beliefs had become established, attempts were often then made to use them as coercive instruments in the control of human behaviour. Even then, humans have remained robustly resistant to the misuse of the largely unknown, continuing to behave in ways that are scarcely consistent with a knowledge of hell and heaven. See Index, Afterlife.

J. W. Bowker, *The Meanings of Death* (1991).

Agadut Israel (Jewish movement): see ḤAFETS ḤAYYIM.

Aga Khan (Pers., Āghā Khān). Title conferred on the *Ismāʿīlī *imām (spiritual leader), Ḥasan ʿAlī Shāh (d. 1881) and to his successors as leaders of the Nizārī Ismāʿīlīs. They claim descent from *ʿAlī and *Fāṭima (the daughter of *Muḥammad).

W. Frischauer, *The Aga Khans* (1970).

Āgama (Skt.). In Hinduism, a general term for scripture, but more specifically, a body of medieval *Vaiṣṇava (specifically *Pāñcarātra), *Śaiva, and *Śakta literature in Sanskrit and Tamil, called respectively the Pāñcarātra Saṃhitās, the Śaiva Āgamas, and the Śakta Tantras. There is also a collection of Jain Āgamas. In a narrower sense, Āgama refers to the dualist and non-dualist Śaiva texts and is sometimes used interchangeably with *Tantra. The Āgamas traditionally contain four sections: (i)*Jñāna or *vidya pada, concerning higher knowledge and providing a theoretical substructure; (ii) *yoga pada, concerning concentration and the knowledge of *subtle bodies; (iii) *kriyā pada*, concerning *temple building, installing the deity, and ritual; and (iv) *carya pada* concerning behaviour, *festivals, and *caste. However, the distinction between these categories is often vague. Though regarded as non-*Vedic (*avaidika*) by the orthodox, the Āgamas use Vedic terminologies, and there is considerable *Sāṃkhyan influence. Common concerns are the three realities (*tattvatrayam*), of God, Souls, and World; liberation (*mokṣa, *mukti); initiation (*dīkṣa and *abhiṣeka); *mantra; *nyāsa; *tattvas; and a cosmology of pure, pure-impure, and impure creation.

In Buddhism, āgama is the *Mahāyāna name for the collections of writings known in Pāli as *nikāya. Thus Dirghāgama is equivalent to Digha Nikāya; Madhyamāgama to Majjhima Nikāya; Samyuktāgama to Samyutta Nikāya; Ekottarikāgama to Anguttara Nikāya. The Nikāyas add a fifth collection, Khuddaka Nikāya, the Short Collection. In Jap., āgama is *agon*, as in *agon-gyō*, the four Chinese collections of *sūtras. In Jainism, it is the term, along with *siddhānta* (established teachings); for the 'canonical' texts: see AṄGA.

J. A. B. van Buitenen (tr.), *Yamuna's Āgama Prāmānyam* (1971); J. Gonda, *Medieval Religious Literature in Sanskrit* (1971).

Āgāmi-karma: see KARMA.

Agape (Gk.). 1. 'Love' (avoiding the sexual associations of *erōs*), the word used in the New Testament for the love of God or Christ, or of Christians, of a new and different quality.

2. The 'love feast' celebrated by early Christians (1 Corinthians 11. 17–34). It may originally have derived from Jesus' ordinary meals with his disciples (rather than the *Last Supper). In the 2nd to 5th or 6th cents. it appears in various forms as a meal complementary to the *eucharist itself, e.g. in *Hippolytus as a celebration in private homes but with a minister present.

Agastya or **Agasti**. A great *Vedic sage said to have been born of Mitra and *Varuṇa in a large earthenware pot (*kumbha*), hence known as

Kumbhayonī. He is the legendary pioneer of the *Āryan occupation of peninsular India. According to *Rāmāyaṇa*, *Rāma, when in exile, was his guest, and he received *Viṣṇu's sword and a bow with inexhaustible quivers from Agastya. He is said to have drunk the oceans and digested the two demon brothers Ātāpi and Wātāpi. Identified with a later Agastya, he is believed by many *Tamil Hindus to be still alive, dwelling (invisibly) on Agastya Malai (his sacred hill). But in fact, the Tamil legends of Agastya, the author of the first Tamil grammar, are used to explore the origins of Tamil culture. In Shulman's comment, 'Agastya is a symbol of Tamil learning, not as independent from or opposed to Sanskrit, but rather in harmony and conjunction with it.'

D. D. Shulman, *Tamil Temple Myths* (1980).

Aggadah/Haggadah (Heb., 'narrative'). Rabbinic teaching which is not *halakhah and which includes stories, legends, history, ethical maxims, and witticisms. The *rabbis themselves maintained that aggadah was not authoritative and insisted that 'no halakhah may be derived from the aggadot' (*TJ Pe'ah* 2. 6, 17a); but its status in relation to insight and piety is high: 'Do you wish to know him by whose word the world came into being? Study aggadah' (*Sifre*). Aggadic literature developed in Palestine from the era of the second *Temple until the end of the *Talmudic period. It expresses the ideas and sentiments of the *tannaim and the *amoraim and draws on old myths and legends as well as popular teaching. For example, Rabbi *Hillel was supposed to know 'the conversations of trees and clouds, and of the beasts and animals', (*Sof.* 19. 9), while Rabbi *Meir was said to have known 300 fox fables. Discourses of the rabbis on biblical teaching were preserved, and sermons seem to have been delivered at *Festivals, after reading the *Torah scroll in the *synagogue, on occasions of family joy and sorrow, and at other public functions. These discourses were preserved in the aggadic literature and were used subsequently by later preachers. In addition, an aggadic history developed which involved additions and supplements to the biblical stories, many of which appear highly fanciful to modern readers—for example, the contrast between *Esau and *Jacob in Genesis 27: 22 is seen as a contrast between Esau and Jacob's descendants, namely the Romans and the Jews. Theological doctrines were also discussed as the sages attempted to answer such questions as to whether the heavens or the earth were the first to be created, how *proselytes should be treated or whether Israel's salvation was dependent on prior repentance. Much later mystical speculation has its roots in aggadic teaching.

Thus although the aggadah does not have the same authority as the halakhah, it must be seen as an invaluable treasury of Jewish thought and feelings over a period of nearly a thousand years. On one occasion, *Eleazer b. Azariah is reported to have said to R. *Akiva, 'What have you to do with the aggadah? Cease your talk and turn to the laws of Nega'im ('Plagues') and Oholot ('Tents')' (*B. Hag* 14a), but in general expertise in aggadah was highly regarded—as R. Johanan stated: 'Whenever you find the works of R. Eleazar b. R. Jose [the great aggadist], shape your ears like a funnel.'

L. Ginzberg, *The Legends of the Jews* (7 vols., 1909–38). A modern anthology, *Sefer ha-Aggadah* (1910) was compiled by H. N. Bialik and Y. H. Ravnitzky, Eng. tr. 1993.

Aggadat Bereshit. An *aggadic *midrash ('commentary') on the book of *Genesis. It probably should be dated in the 10th cent. CE. It consists of interpretations of verses from Genesis, followed by interpretations of relevant extracts from the *Prophets and the *Psalms.

Aggadic. Pertaining to *aggadah.

Aggiornamento (Ital., 'updating'). The renewal of the *Roman Catholic Church which Pope *John XXIII hoped would come from the Second *Vatican Council and would lead to the reunion of all Christians; especially the renewal of the religious life of Catholics, and the bringing up to date of the Church's teaching, discipline, and organization.

Aggregates, Five (composition of human beings): see SKANDHA.

Āghā Khān (spiritual leader): see AGA KHAN.

Aghlabids. Muslim dynasty in N. Africa and Sicily, 800–909 (AH 184–296), after when they were overthrown by the *Fāṭimids. Their power was theoretically delegated from the *'Abbāsids, though in effect they were independent. They conquered both Sicily and Malta, before losing both to the Normans.

Aghorī (Skt., 'non-terrific'). A *Tantric *Śaiva sect existing to the present day, renowned for *antinomian practices which include consuming ordure and corpse-flesh. They venerate a tradition of *gurus and worship *Śiva as Aghora, or the goddess as *Śītalā, Parnagīrī, or *Kālī. Like their predecessors, the *kāpālikas, they carry a skull which they use as a bowl, dwell in cremation grounds, and cover themselves in the ashes of corpses. Some take an intoxicating drink of *bhanga. Aghorī gurus were not cremated but buried in an upright meditation posture.

J. P. Parry in M. Bloch and J. P. Parry (ed.), *Death and the Regeneration of Life* (1982).

Agnes, St. Christian virgin and martyr. There is no certain information about her death or its date, but she has been venerated in Rome since the 4th cent. She is represented with a lamb (Lat., *agnus*). Feast day, 21 Jan.

Agni (Skt., 'fire'; cf. Lat., *ignis*). The god of fire in Hinduism, of great importance, especially in the *Vedic period. As *sacrifice is at the centre of Vedic religion, Agni is at the centre of sacrifice. As messenger of the gods, Agni is mediator between humankind and the heavenly realm. All offerings must pass through the sacred fire to reach their divine destinations. Agni is the witness of all sacred transactions, the benefactor and protector of people and their homes, and guardian (*loka-pāla*) of the south-east quadrant of the universe. His three principal forms include not only fire on earth, but also lightning in the atmosphere and the sun in the sky. In a sense Agni personifies all the gods, the power of the divine, immanent in all things. He is understood as the source of knowledge (the *Veda), both god of priests and priest of the gods, and potent enemy of darkness. Ever youthful, he bestows life and immortality.

In the Veda, Agni is depicted as seven-tongued, golden-toothed, having a thousand eyes and flaming hair. He is dressed in black and carries a flaming javelin in one of his four hands. His smoke-bannered chariot is drawn by red steeds; its wheels are the seven winds. *Iconographically Agni is shown riding on or accompanied by the ram (*aja*). Mythologically he takes various forms, including son of Dyaus and Pṛthivī, Kaśyapa and Aditi, and of Aṅgiras and *Brahma and Śāndilī as well. He is said to be king of the *Pitṛs, a *Marut, and one of the seven *ṛṣis during the reign of Manu Tāmasa. Another legend has it that Agni was brought down to earth by the wind god, Mātariśvan on the command of ṛṣi Bhrigu. Agni's progeny include Skanda (by his wife Svāhā) and Pāvaka, Pavamāna, and Śuci. Various heroes and later descendants are linked with him by the designation Āgneya or Agniveṣa. Agni is the first word of the Veda, and, as the world-consuming subterranean fire (Vadabāgni) or the flame of the funeral pyre, is the ultimate expression of life, human and divine.

D. M. Knipe, *In the Image of Fire* (1975); F. Staal, *Agni: The Vedic Ritual* . . . (1983).

Agnihotra. Hindu daily ritual of offering milk, oil, and gruel, in the morning and the evening, to *Agni, in the domestic (*gārhapatya*) and sacrificial (*āhavanīya*) fires.

Agnihotri (1859–1928). Hindu founder of the Dev Samaj. Originally called Shiv Narayan, he was born into a *brahman family and became a teacher in Lahore. He joined the *Brahmo Samāj, and was a fiery opponent of *Ārya Samāj. He broke away from Keshub Chandra Sen in 1887, but his Dev Samaj only took on distinctive ideas when he adapted Herbert Spencer to ideas of *Brahman/*ātman, thus viewing ātman as an 'inanimate' life-force, evolving to altruism. His *Dev Śāstra* (1917) emphasizes scrupulous morality and strict vegetarianism. Through his first wife, Lilavati, a strong commitment was made to women's education. Dev Samaj has a continuing but small support.

S. P. Kanal, *An Introduction to Dev Dharma* (1965).

Agnosticism (Gk., *a* + *gnōstos*, 'not know'). A position distinguished from *theism and *atheism equally, by its view that neither in principle nor in fact is it possible to know God's nature or even whether he exists. In its broadest sense, agnosticism is compatible with deep religious commitment, as in the case of *Nicholas of Cusa or of Henry Mansel (1820–71); in its narrower and more specific sense, however, it normally implies a certain detachment in matters religious. The term itself was coined by T. H. Huxley (1825–95), who defined its basic principles as repudiation of all metaphysical speculation and of most Christian doctrine as unproven or unprovable, and the application of scientific method to the study of all matters of fact and experience. Other leading 19th-cent. agnostics included W. K. Clifford (1845–79), Charles Darwin, John Stuart Mill (1807–73), Herbert Spencer (1820–1903), and Leslie Stephen (1832–1904). Agnosticism has had a renewed influence in the 20th cent. through the logical positivists and their heirs, although not all would be equally happy to be called 'agnostic'.

Agnus Dei (Lat., 'Lamb of God'). The hymn derived from John 1. 29 sung or said during or after the breaking of the bread at *communion in W. churches. It consists of the line 'Lamb of God, you take away the sins of the world, have mercy upon us' repeated three times, but (since the 11th cent.) with 'grant us peace' instead of 'have mercy upon us' the third time; and at *Requiems, 'grant them rest'.

Agon[-gyō]: see ĀGAMA (Buddhist).

Agra. City on the Yamuna river in India, capital city for some of the *Mughal rulers. It is particularly famous for the *Taj Mahal, and for the fort containing the Pearl Mosque (Moti Masjid) of Shah Jehan.

R. Nath, *Agra and its Monumental Glory* (1977).

Agrapha (Gk., 'unwritten [sayings]'). Words of Jesus recorded outside the four *gospels. Some appear elsewhere in the New Testament (e.g. Acts 20. 35), others in *apocryphal gospels and the writings of the *Church fathers.

Agudat Israel (Yisra'el). 'Union of Israel', abbreviated as Agudah, a world movement of *Orthodox Jews. It was founded in 1912, from a number of Orthodox communities as a counterweight to the programmes of the *Zionist Congresses. Its name is derived from the liturgy of the High Holy Days which speaks of all creatures forming 'one union' to do God's will. Although it is not a party with a programme, it has developed *da'at Torah*, the understanding of Torah on particular matters—i.e. the application by scholars of Torah to all aspects of life. See also ḤAFETS ḤAYYIM.

G. S. Schiff, *Tradition and Politics: The Religious Parties of Israel* (1977).

Agunah (Heb., 'tied woman'). A married woman who cannot remarry, either because her husband has not given her a divorce, or because there is no proof of his death. The term is also applied to a widow who cannot obtain release from a *levirate *marriage. There has been much *halakhic discussion on the problem of the agunah, but no satisfactory solution has been found. The term does not apply to men, because if a man's wife disappears without trace, Jewish law permits a man to contract an additional marriage. No such dispensation exists for woman, and any children born to such women are deemed *mamzerim; however, the Chief *Rabbinate in Israel has inclined to a liberal acceptance of circumstantial evidence, from which death can be presumed. For Reform Jews, the problem does not exist, because this detail of *halakhah is not accepted.

AH (Muslim dating): see HIJRA.

Ahad ha-'Am ('One of the People'). Asher Hirsh Ginsberg. (1856–1927), essayist and Jewish *Zionist leader. His article *Lo Zeh ha-Derekh* (The Wrong Way), published in 1889, argued that educational work should take place before an immediate indiscriminate settlement in the land of *Israel. He became spiritual leader of the secret order of Benei Moshe ('sons of Moses') and the editor of the monthly literary periodical, *Ha-Shilo'ah* (The Coming One) which contributed to the development of modern Hebrew literature. Although he had a role in the obtaining of the *Balfour Declaration, he favoured group action rather than negotiation: 'Israel's salvation will be achieved by *prophets, not by diplomats.' He was aware of the problem of Arab rights, observing on one occasion, 'I am very careful in the choice of my enemies.' His thought has been influential in Zionist thinking, both in Israel and in the *diaspora.

L. Simon, *Ahad ha'Am* . . . (1960).

Aḥai of Shabḥa (Jewish writer on law): see CODIFICATIONS OF LAW.

Ahalyā (also called Maitreyi). The wife of the *ṛṣi Gautamā. She committed adultery with *Indra, the King of the Heavenly region. When Gautamā discovered her infidelity, he cursed her and, in some versions, made her invisible; in others he turned her into stone as a punishment. According to **Rāmāyaṇa*, she was restored to her original form when Rāmā, in his exile in the Daṇḍaka forest, touched the stone with his foot.

Aham Brahman asmi (i.e. aham brahmāsmi). 'I am Brahman' (*Bṛhadāraṇaya Upaniṣad* 1. 4. 10). Hindu formula through which the identity of the self (*ātman) with *Brahman is proclaimed. It is one of the *mahāvākyas, great precepts.

Ahaṃkāra (Skt., 'I maker'). In Indian (especially *Sāṃkhya) philosophy, the principle of the ego. In general ahaṃkāra is the ego or ego principle responsible for one's individuality, one's self-awareness. In Sāṃkhya, ahaṃkāra is understood as the second evolution of unmanifest *prakṛti and the immediate product of the *buddhi (or *mahat) principle. *Sāṃkhya-Kārikā* 24 equates ahaṃkāra with *abhimāna, 'conceit' or 'self-assertion', and details the products of the ahaṃkāra principle. These products are of three kinds, according to the dominant *guṇa (constituent mode of prakṛti). Those predominant in *sattva are the more subjective principles of *manas, mind, the five sense capacities, and the five action capacities. Those products of ahaṃkāra predominant in *tamas (also called *bhutādi*) are the five subtle elements (*tanmātras*), the building blocks of the objective world. The form of ahaṃkāra predominant in *rājas, the *taijasa*, provides the energy for both these subjective and objective products. Along with buddhi and manas, ahaṃkāra makes up the threefold 'inner instrument', *antaḥkaraṇa*. Ahaṃkāra is thus the element of 'me' or 'mine' within our intellect and mind.

Āhāra ('food' or 'nutrition'). In the Pāli *Nikāyas, āhāra sums up the whole teaching of the *Buddha in relation to the living being, including the 'Doctrine of Dependent Origination', *paticca-samuppāda. The basic perception is that 'all beings live on food' (*sabbe sattā āhāraṭṭhitika, Digha Nikāya* iii. 211). This statement covers the whole nature of a living organism, which depends not only on material food but also psychic food, for its sustenance. This is because a living being is a psycho-physical entity (*nāmarūpa). Therefore, four kinds of foods are mentioned in relation to the living being. The physical part of a being is sustained by 'material food' (*kabaliṅkāro āharo*), and the mental part is fed by three kinds of psychic food—namely, 'the food of contact' (*phasso āhāro*), 'the food of mental volition' (*manosañcetanā āharo*), and 'the food of consciousness' (*viññāna āharo*). The psychic foods are necessary not only for the sustenance of a living being, but also for those who seek rebirth (*Samyutta Nikāya* 2. 11)

'The food of contact' is mentioned in the Nikāyas as the combination of eye (*cakkhu*), forms (*rūpa), and visual consciousness (*cakkhu viññāna*). When these three factors are present and brought in relation to each other, it is called contact (*phasso*: *Samyutta Nikāya* 2. 73). This contact is said to have six sources as to its origin: eye contact, ear contact, and so on. Feeling (*vedanā*) is the outcome of contact, and this is divided into three—namely, pleasure (*sukha*), displeasure (*dukkha), and indifference (*upekkha). Craving (taṇhā) is the outcome of feeling, and such craving is the force of 'becoming' (*bhava*) and reappearing (*punabbhava). Such contact initiates not only feelings but all sorts of mental activity. According to *Samyutta Nikāya*, 4. 68, when one is subject to contact one feels (vedeti), one thinks (*ceteti*), one forms mental images (*sañjānāti*).

'The food of mental volition' is the 'will to act'. 'Will' is the food of the mind through which action (*karma) is formed by means of the body (*kāyena*), the word (*vācāya), and the mind (*manasā): *Anguttara Nikāya* 3. 415. This action is divided into two, wholesome (*kusala) and unwholesome (akusala). The action precipitates reappearance in the various worlds, such as in hell (*niraya), in the animal world (*tiracchāna yoni*), and in the human world (*manussa loka*), and so on (*Anguttara Nikāya* 3. 415).

'The food of consciousness' is the main link between life and reappearance based on *karma, and this consciousness feeds both the mind and the corporeality (*viññāna paccayā nāmarūpaṃ*) in the new life. It is said that if consciousness does not descend into the mother's womb, a psycho-physical component will not be constituted. In the same manner, if the projected consciousness were to be extinguished, then there would not be a child birth. If the consciousness of a child were to be cut off there would not be further development of that psycho-physical entity called the young child (*Digha Nikāya* 3. 63). Thus the four kinds of foods are the main sustenance behind a being's life.

Aharonim (Heb., 'later ones'). Later (from Middle Ages onward) rabbinic authorities—contrasted with earlier authorities, the *Rishonim.

Āhavanīya (sacrifice): see AGNIHOTRA.

Ahikar, Book of. An *Aramaic folk-work, known during the period of the Assyrian Empire. Part of the text was discovered among the *Elephantiné documents, and several other versions have survived. It consists of the life of Ahikar (also mentioned in the *apocryphal book of *Tobit) and his sayings to Nadan his adopted son. Ahikar was the wise hero of a folk-story widely known in the Ancient Near East.

A. Yellin, *Sefer Ahikar he-Hakham* (1938).

Ahiṁsā (Skt., 'not-harming'). Avoiding injury to any sentient creature through act or thought, a principle of basic importance for Indian religions, but especially for Jains and Buddhists. In Hinduism, it is not much discussed in early texts, perhaps because it was recognized that it might be in conflict with *dharma (e.g. the duty of the warrior). According to *Manusmṛti* 11. 222, a *brahman should make daily offerings, observe ahiṁsā, tell the truth, eradicate anger, and be trustworthy; ahiṁsā appears in *Chandogya Upaniṣad* 3. 17. 4 (in a passage making sacrifice a controlling metaphor for human life) as part of the equivalent of *dakṣinā, in *Patañjali's *Yoga Sūtra* 2. 35, ahiṁsā is one of the five restraints (*yama). Both Buddhism and Jainism give much more emphasis to ahiṁsā, perhaps because ahiṁsā reinforced their rejection of sacrifice (since sacrifice necessarily involves violence against animals). It is the first of the five precepts of Buddhist life (*śīla), and *Aśoka regarded his adoption of ahiṁsā as 'the greatest progress' he had made (7th Pillar Edict). For Jains, it is the first of the *Five Great Vows. It is regarded as the single, controlling principle from which the details of ethical life and of vows embodying them are derived. Good conduct (*carita*) is ahiṁsā put into practice. It was a Jain, Śrīmad *Rājacandra, who greatly influenced *Gāndhī, through whose teaching, practice, and example non-violence became a powerful instrument of dissent and political action in the 20th cent. Gāndhī was aware of the conflict with dharma (especially in the advice of *Kṛṣṇa in the *Bhagavad-gītā), and made some attempt to historicize the application of dharma. It was observant Hindus, attentive to dharma, who nevertheless assassinated him. See Index, Ahiṁsa.

Ahl al-Hadith (People of the Tradition). A relatively small but vigorous Islamic reform movement. It first appeared in India at the end of the 19th cent., and its characteristics are similar to the *Wahhābī movement of Arabia. Their creed is 'whatever the Prophet *Muḥammad taught in the *Qur'ān and the authentic traditions, that alone is the basis of our religion'. They emphasize *tawḥīd (Unity) of Allāh, and deny occult powers and knowledge of hidden things to any of his creatures. This is a direct attack on the claimed supernatural powers of mystics and saints and the exaggerated veneration paid to them. The movement exerts every effort to eradicate customs that may be traced to innovation (*bidʿa) or non-Islamic influences. On matters of Islamic law, the ahl-al-Hadith far exceed Wahhābī puritanism. They cast aside the four orthodox schools of law, and instead contend that every believer is free to follow his own interpretation of the Qur'ān and the traditions, provided that he has sufficient learning to enable him to give a valid interpretation. Consequently, they do not accept the consensus (*ijmāʿ) of the preceding generations as binding on them. As a result, they have fallen foul of the orthodox *Hanafī school, who constitute the majority of Muslims in Pakistan and India.

Ahl al-Kitāb. 'People of the Book', i.e. possessing a *scripture; the name given by the Qur'ān to the Jewish (Banū Isrā'īl) and Christian (*Naṣārā) communities, possessors respectively of the *Tawrāt (Torah) and Zabūr (Psalms) and of the *Injīl (Gospel), and later extended by Muslim law to the Sabeans and the *Zoroastrians. To these people was given the status of *dhimma, 'protection'. In the Qur'ān, the term may refer to Jews only (e.g. 4. 153), or Christians only (e.g. 4. 171), though the distinction is not always clear, or may designate both groups. The Jewish community is said to have received the *Covenant (*mīthāq*) from Allāh (Qur'ān 3. 187) but to have rejected it (4. 155).

The People of the Book are summoned to believe in the new scripture (Qur'ān 4. 47, 3. 28, 5. 21), and there are among them those who believe and are friendly towards the Muslims (3. 113–15, 199, 29. 47).

However, they are blamed for some form of 'corruption' of their scripture (see TAḤRĪF), and for committing evil deeds (5. 68). They are accused of wishing to turn the Muslims from their allegiance (2. 109, 3. 69, 72). Although the Qur'ān allows them to keep their own religion, and affords them protection, they are expected to pay a special tribute, the *jizya (9. 29). Because of this special status, it is a vital issue in community relations whether the category can be extended to include others, e.g., Hindus.

Ahl al-Mantalka (Arab., 'people of the girdle'). *Copts and Syrian Jacobites, so called as a mark of humility (cf. HABIT, RELIGIOUS), but also as a sign of humiliation, from the Muslim insistence that Christians in Egypt should wear a girdle, in order to be identified.

Ahl al-Suffa. A group of poor Muslims, who were given permission by the Prophet *Muḥammad to live in a corner of the *Madīna mosque. They lived in extreme poverty and were constantly engaged in prayers and *Qur'ān recital. The ahl al-Suffa are often regarded as the Islamic equivalent of Christian monks, but they differed in that they married and supported families. Later generation of Muslims, especially the *Sūfīs, venerated the pious and ascetic character of the ahl al-Suffa as a model for themselves.

Ahl al-Sunna wa'l-jamā'a (non-Shi'ite Muslims): see SUNNA.

Ahl-i-Haqq ('People of the Truth'). A secret religious sect found in W. Persia and Kurdistan, dating back to the 11th cent. It incorporates *Zoroastrian, *Manichaean, Jewish, Christian, and *Sūfī ideas into a popular *messianic cult. The Ahl-i-haqq is not a single entity but a loosely knit federation of associated movements sharing the following: they await the advent of the Lord of Time 'who shall come to accomplish the desires of the Friends and embrace the Universe'; and the belief in the seven successive manifestations of divinity in a human form (worn as a garment), including *Jesus Christ, *'Alī, and Sultan Sohak. This cult, supported mainly by the lower classes, peasants, and nomads, is rich in folklore and miraculous elements. Post-revolutionary Iran witnessed sections of the Ahl-i-haqq claiming Imām *Khumayni to be a precursor for the final reincarnation, but this claim was later denied by the authorities, and the movement was heavily criticized for its un-Islamic ideology. Since it includes a belief in reincarnation, the opposition is not surprising.

Aḥmad al-Badawī, Sidi (*c.* 1199/1200–1276 (AH 596–675)). *Sūfī adept, immensely revered in Egypt. Boisterous in youth, he underwent some kind of inner conversion in *c.*627 and withdrew from human contact, including marriage, to seek God alone. He made pilgrimage to the tombs of many of the great Sūfīs, e.g. *al-Jīli and *al-Ḥallāj. Settling finally at Tanditā in Egypt, he developed even more ascetic ways. After his death, 'Abd al-'Āl became his *khalīfa, and organized his followers under strict rule.

Ahmed il-Bedawī, tr. E. Littmann (1950).

Aḥmad al-Tijānī (1737–1815). Founder of the African *Sūfī order, the Tijāniya. He was born in Algeria, and early in life joined several Sūfī orders before withdrawing for five years to a remote community. In 1781, he saw *Muḥammad in a vision, and received from him the command to establish his own order. He attracted little support until he received royal support in Morocco. After his death, the order spread rapidly in N. and W. Africa, becoming increasingly aggressive against French colonialists and non-Muslims. This use of the *jihād, combined with the personal cult of al-Tijānī, makes the order suspect to other Muslims.

J. Abun-Nasr, *The Tijaniyya* (1965).

Aḥmadīy(y)a. The movement founded by Mirzā Ghulām Aḥmad Qādiyānī (*c.*1835–1908), hence the later name Qādī. In *Barāhīn-i-Aḥmadiyya* (1880), Aḥmad claimed to be *al-Mahdī, and in due course also the *Messiah, the *avatāra of *Kṛṣṇa, and the reappearance of *Muḥammad. The Aḥmadīya believe, with other Muslims, that 'Isa/*Jesus did not die on the cross, but they do not believe that he was received into heaven. Rather, they hold that he visited India to preach, and died there, aged about 120. His tomb is at Srinagar. While sharing many Muslim beliefs, they are nevertheless regarded by Muslims as heretical and to be treated as such. They have, therefore, suffered considerable persecution. When Aḥmad died, Nūr al-Dīn succeeded as *Khalīfa. On his death, the movement split, with the Qādīs regarding him as a *prophet (in clear conflict with orthodoxy which describes Muḥammad as 'the seal of the prophets', i.e. the Last), but with the Lahore group regarding him as a reformer, and thus staying closer to mainstream Islam. The Lahore group (Aḥmadīya Anjuman-i-Ishā'at-i-Islam) has spread widely and established the Woking mosque as its UK centre.

S. Lavan, *The Ahmadiyah Movement* (1974).

Ahmad Khan, Sir Sayyid (1817–98). Often known simply as Sir Sayyid, founder of Islamic Indian modernism and an educational reformer. Sir Sayyid's greatness lies in restoring Muslim confidence and bringing them into the modern age through a practical programme of social and educational reform. He recognized the weakness of Indian Muslims and the futility of armed insurrection against strong British rule (e.g. the failure of the Indian Mutiny, 1857). The only course of action for him was to recognize British rule and raise the standard of the Muslims by working from within. Thus he pursued social and educational reforms in a spirit of reconciliation towards Western civilization, on which he modelled his ideas. His insistence on the importance of the English language in education, the inauguration of a literary and scientific society, and the establishment of a Muslim college at Aligarh (1875) modelled on the lines of Cambridge and Oxford, provoked violent reaction from *al-Afghānī, the *Shīa, and the orthodox *ʿulamā. However, Sir Sayyid's sincerity, and the strength of his belief that an intellectual awakening is necessary before political awareness develops, pacified the opposition. His two major works *Essays on the life of Mohammed* (1870) and a Quranic commentary (1880–95) were attempts to demythologize the *Qur'ān, and to offer psychological and naturalistic interpretations of Islam. He also, unusually, wrote a *Bible commentary, *Tabyīn alkalām*.

C. W. Troll, *Sayyid Ahmad Khan* . . . (1978).

Aḥmad Sirhindī (b. 1563 (AH 971)). A leading figure in the *Naqshbandi *Sūfī order, who did much to restore Sunni orthodoxy to *Mughal India. Having spent some years in the court of *Akbar, he came to think that religious observance must begin at the top: 'The ruler is the soul and the people are the body: if the ruler goes astray, the people will surely follow.' He became a Naqshbandi adherent of Khwāja Bāqī bi'llah in 1600 and succeeded him as *shaykh in 1603. His claim to strong spiritual authority led to a period in prison, but his followers recognized him as 'the Renewer'. In his teachings (mainly collected in his letters), he abandoned the pervasive Sūfī doctrine, derived from *ibn ʿArabī, of *waḥdat al-wujūd*, the oneness of being: this claims that everything which exists can only do so because it is created by God, and might therefore be regarded as an aspect of Divine Reality—'Wherever you turn, there is the face of God' (Qur'ān 2. 115). The obvious risk here is that of *pantheism, so close to the surrounding Hinduism which Sirhindī contested strongly. Instead, he emphasized *waḥdat al-shuhūd*, the unity of witnessing consciousness, a single awareness. He equally opposed Akbar's experiments in religious ecumenism, and elicited a promise from the emperor that he would 'defend the law of Islam'. More positively, he achieved far greater precision in the definition of mystical terminology, and he described his own experience and the way to it so clearly that it was as a map to a well-known town.

ed. S. H. Nasr, *Islamic Spirituality*, II, (1991).

Ahriman (Pahlavi): see ANGRA MAINYU.

Ahura Mazda. The Wise Lord (or possibly more correctly 'The Lord Wisdom'), God in *Zoroastrianism. There has been much debate whether *Zoroaster dramatically reformed the teaching concerning an existing deity or introduced a totally new god. Most scholars argue for the former (*medha* means 'wise' in the *Vedic tradition). Certainly the doctrinal emphasis was different from the tradition he inherited. Whereas in pre-Zoroastrian times the gods appear to have been thought of as remote beings who must be placated. Zoroaster was convinced he had seen Ahura personally and had been called by him. This injected into the foundations of Zoroastrianism a concept of a personal God. In the *Gāthās, Ahura is referred to as the creator of all things, of the heavens, of humanity, both materially and spiritually. In the developed Zoroastrian tradition, the emphasis is on Ahura Mazda's goodness and knowledge, but not on his *omnipotence, for he is restricted by the activities of the wholly independent evil *Angra Mainyu. The first creations of Ahura were the *Amesa Spentas, the heavenly forces. Beneath them in the heavenly hierarchy are the *yazatas*, or worshipful beings. Mostly these consist of the old pre-Zoroastrian deities, such as *Mithra. They are now the servants and creations of Ahura Mazda who is alone worthy of worship in his own right, although veneration is offered to the others by devout worshippers. In modern Zoroastrian exegesis, the Amesa Spentas are often compared to the archangels and *angels of Judaism and Christianity (not inappropriately, since scholars have often argued that the Iranian tradition influenced the Semitic faiths). Ahura Mazda is said to wear a 'star decked robe', his fairest forms are the sun on high and the light on earth. He is the Good Creator (*Bundahisn) who will ultimately triumph over evil (*Frasokereti). In that battle he has his helpers (*hamkars*) chief among whom are humans.

M. Boyce, *Zoroastrians* (1979); H. Gray, *The Foundations of the Iranian Religions* (1925); J. R. Hinnells, *Persian Mythology* (1973); R. C. Zaehner, *The Dawn and Twilight of Zoroastrianism* (1961).

Ai. 1. Love in *Mo Tzu's system, usually in the form chien ai, universal love: 'To give peace to the world is the reason why the wise exist . . . What is the cause of disorder? It is the absence of love for each other.' Confucians criticized universal love for being less discriminating than *jen (e.g. Wang Ying-ming: 'Mo Tzu's universal love has no gradations: father, son and members of one's own family are looked on as the same as a passer-by'). However, universal love is in a different category from jen, being more related to utilitarian considerations: altruism has benefits running in both directions.

2. In Japanese Buddhism, ai (lust as well as love) is fundamental desire which may go in either of two opposite directions. It may become self-interested and self-satisfying, in the pursuit of sexual fulfilment or temporal achievement, and it may thus become one of the twelve causes linking a person to existence and reappearance. On the other hand, it may be self-denying and disinterested in the pursuit of the good of another, and is thus supremely the love of a *buddha or *bodhisattva, a transfigured love.

AIC: see AFRICAN INSTITUTED CHURCHES.

Aidan, St (d. 651). Christian *apostle to Northumbria. He was a monk of Iona brought to *Lindisfarne as bishop by King Oswald to evangelize his territory. His gentle commitment and personal asceticism made his many missionary journeys successful. He educated a small group of boys to be church leaders, among them St Chad. Feast day, 31 Aug.

Ailred (Cistercian monk): see AELRED.

Ainu. A Japanese people and religion. They were early inhabitants of Japan, driven northward from *c.*7th cent. CE. They are now mainly assimilated into mainstream Japanese culture, though some of their beliefs and practices can be traced in later religion—e.g. their animistic belief that spirits or spiritual powers (*kamuy*) are causative in natural events

N. G. Munro, *Ainu Creed and Cult* (1962).

ʿĀ'isha bint Abī Bakr (d. 678 CE (AH 59)). Daughter of *Abu Bakr, born in *Mecca about 614 CE, and wife of *Muḥammad. She was married to him not long after the death of his first wife *Khadīja, and he admitted freely that she was his favourite wife of all those he subsequently married. She seems to have been very attractive and possessed of a lively mind. The *revelation often came to Muḥammad while he was in her company.

On one of Muḥammad's expeditions, in 627, ʿĀ'isha was left behind at one of the stopping places on the return journey, and only rejoined the main party next day, in the company of a young man. The resultant scandal was largely created by Muḥammad's enemies, and caused him great distress. The matter was only cleared up when a revelation assured him of his wife's innocence, and he strongly censured those who had accused her (Qur'ān 24. 11–20).

At Muḥammad's death in 632, ʿĀ'isha was only about 18 years old, and because of her status as one of the Prophet's wives, she would not have been permitted to marry again (Qur'ān 33. 55). She played no part in political life until towards the end of the reign of *ʿUthmān, the third Caliph, when she joined the growing opposition party. In 656, ʿUthmān was assassinated; ʿĀ'isha, together with Ṭalḥa and al-Zubayr, took control of Baṣra, and in Dec. 656 fought against *ʿAlī b. Abī Ṭālib, the successor of ʿUthmān. This event was known as the Battle of the Camel, because the camel-litter carrying ʿĀ'isha was in the thick of the fighting. Ṭalḥa and al-Zubayr were killed, but ʿĀ'isha survived, and from then on kept to her house in *Madīna, where she died in 678. She was said to be both pious and learned, and is quoted as the source for many (1,210) *ḥadīth, especially those concerning Muḥammad's personal life.

N. Abbott, *ʿĀ'isha the Beloved of Mohammed* (1942).

Aitareya Upaniṣad. A short work of three chapters: the first deals with creation of all things from the One (*ātman), bringing out the correspondences between macro- and microcosm; the second with the three births, conception, natural birth, and extension through one's son; and the third with the nature of ātman.

For trs., see UPANIṢAD.

Aiyetoro (Yoruba, 'happy city'). A utopian Christian community, the Holy Apostles, in Nigeria, founded by a group of persecuted members of the *aladura-type Cherubim and Seraphim society. In 1947 they migrated to a mudbank in the coastal lagoons 160 miles east of Lagos, built a model town on piles, and set up a radical form of economic communism under a priest-chief. With incredible labour they became one of the most prosperous peasant communities in Nigeria, with their own school, adult education, technical training, electricity generation, and industries making soap, shoes, furniture, and clothing, in addition to engaging in deep-sea fishing. Within twenty years they reached some 2,000 members and had achieved an economic and social transformation informed by a Christian ideal of a happy and peaceful life, including the belief that death had been conquered. The day opens with worship, and offenders against the strict ethic are sent away. Several branch communities developed, but by the 1970s internal dissension and litigation had appeared and the original impetus had faded.

Aizen-myō-ō (Jap.; Skt., Rāgarāja or Vajrarājapriya). In Japanese esoteric Buddhism, a protective deity who destroys all evils and passions. Aizen-myō-ō is depicted with one head, three eyes, and six arms that hold various weapons such as a bow and arrow; usually painted dark red, he is fierce in appearance. In Japan, he is popularly known as the god of love.

Aja Ekapād (Skt., 'the one-footed goat'). A *Vedic god. The exact nature of Aja Ekapād is obscure. He is mentioned only six times in *Ṛg Veda*, usually in connection with Ahi Budhnya, an atmospheric deity. Aja Ekapād is also mentioned in connection with the thundering flood, the ocean, *Sarasvatī, the atmosphere, and all the gods. **Atharva Veda* refers to him as making firm the two worlds; *Taittirīya* **Brāhmaṇa* notes that he is born in the east. Later traditions connect Aja Ekapād with *Agni or the sun. He has been interpreted as Agni in the form of lightning.

Ajaṇṭā. An impressive series of about twenty-eight (numbers vary because of interconnections) humanly constructed caves in W. India, cut into a cliff overlooking the Waghora River, Maharashtra. Started in the 2nd cent. BCE and continued until the 6th cent. CE Ajaṇṭā is a series of monastic residences (*vihāras) with four associated *caitya halls. Five caves belong to the *Theravāda phase of Buddhism, the rest represent the *Mahāyāna. At its peak Ajaṇṭā accommodated 200 monks. The wall-paintings, from all periods of construction, reached a peak of achievement during the Gupta era (320–650 CE).

This Gupta style celebrates a fusion of the sacred and the aristocratic, and, through the visits of Chinese pilgrims, exercised a powerful influence on the painting of the T'ang (618–906 CE).

G. Yazdani, *Ajanta* (1931–55).

Ajapa-mantra (Skt.). Hindu *Haṭha-Yoga belief that every breathing creature must repeat a *mantra with every *breath in and out: *seham*, He am I, *hamsa*, I am He. This may therefore be an involuntary affirmation.

Ajari. Jap. tr. of *ācārya, hence title of a Buddhist monk in general, or teacher in particular, especially among *Tendai or *Shingon Buddhists.

Ajātivāda (Skt., 'the doctrine of non-origination'). According to the teaching of the early *Advaita Vedānta philosopher *Gauḍapāda, as propounded in his *Kārikā* (Commentary) on the *Māṇḍukya *Upaniṣad*, the entire phenomenal world characterized by the objects of sense experience is unreal, a mere appearance like the visions experienced in a dream, and the Self is not separate from the objects of experience. There is only one changeless Reality (Consciousness, *vijñāna, or *Brahman, or *ātman), and all causality is mere appearance. 'That which is ever-existent appears to pass into birth through illusion (*māyā) and not from the standpoint of Reality (*tattva)' (3. 27). 'As are dreams and illusions or a castle in the air seen in the sky, so is the universe viewed by the wise in the *Vedānta. There is no dissolution, no birth, none in bondage, none aspiring for wisdom, no seeker of liberation, and none liberated. This is the absolute truth.' (2. 32).

Aji-kan (meditation on A): see A (1).

Ajita Kesakambala. One of the notorious six heretical teachers criticized by the Buddha for propounding false doctrines. The epithet 'kesakambala' derives from the hair garment worn by Ajita which the Buddhists described as foul-smelling and repellent. In spite of his austere garb Ajita was a materialist who denied the doctrine of the retribution of actions (*karma) and the purpose of the religious life. In Pāli sources he is recorded as teaching that *almsgiving and *sacrifice are useless, that there is no future life, and that at death the four elements which compose the body separate, resulting in the total annihilation of the individual. In the Tibetan and Chinese sources Ajita, perhaps confused with another heretical teacher *Makkhali Gosala, the leader of the *Ajīvaka sect, is portrayed as holding a deterministic theory involving a specific number of rebirths before annihilation—moral and religious action being powerless to alter this preordained sequence of events. In terms of Buddhist doctrine Ajita's teachings were heretical on two grounds: (i) the denial of the fruit of good and evil deeds (*akiriyavāda*); and (ii) the belief that the individual is annihilated at death (*ucchedavāda).

Ajīva (Skt. 'not jīva', i.e. 'not living'). In Jainism the insentient constitution of the physical universe which forms one of the two major divisions of all existing things, the other being *jīva (the sentient soul). The Jains delineate five categories of ajīva: (i) *pudgala, matter which is made up of atoms which are uncreated, indestructible, and real; (ii) *dharma-dravya*, the principle of motion; (iii) *adharma-dravya*, the principle of rest; (iv) *ākāśa*, space; (v) *kāla, time, which coexists with space. Jīva is seen in Jainism as already in contact with ajīva from beginningless time and together they constitute reality. The ajīva holds the jīva in bondage, and the goal of Jainism is to release the jīvas entangled in *karmic matter by restraining the body through penances and ascetic practices which make up the Jain path of purification.

Ājīvaka (Skt., 'one who practises a way' (?)). A heterodox sect founded by *Makkhali Gosala, a contemporary and opponent of the *Buddha. Makkhali was for six years the itinerant companion of *Mahāvīra, the Jain leader, before they parted company after a disagreement. There are similarities in the practices of both sects: initiation is by tearing out the hair, and the lifestyle is one of extreme austerity involving nakedness, penances, and ordeals. In matters of belief, however, they differ: whereas the Jains along with the Buddhists accept the doctrine of *karma, the Ājīvakas deny the existence of free will. In their deterministic system every soul must follow willy-nilly a long chain of existences preordained by fate (*niyati*); neither good nor evil deeds have the power to hasten or retard this process or affect the circumstances of life. According to Buddhist sources, Makkhali compared the course of a man's life to a ball of string which, when thrown down, rolls along unwinding in a preordained course until it reaches its end. At the time of the Buddha the Ājīvakas were an important sect and remained so for several hundred years. After this they declined, and by the medieval period had disappeared altogether, perhaps reabsorbed into Jainism or the South Indian devotional cults in which Makkhali enjoyed an ephemeral deification.

A. L. Basham, *History and Doctrines of the Ājīvakas* (1951).

Ajñāna (Skt.). In Hinduism, the opposite of *jñāna, but particularly ignorance of the identity of *ātman and *Brahman, and thus in consequence equivalent to *avidyā.

Ājur Veda (sacrificial prayer): see YAJUR VEDA.

Akāl (timeless): see AKĀL PURUKH; AKĀL TAKHT; AKĀLĪ.

Akalanka (8th cent. CE). A *Digambara Jain philosopher and logician. According to biographies written centuries after his death, he regarded Buddhists as his greatest intellectual opponents, and he organized his arguments to eradicate their viewpoint. The relativism of his outlook required a careful defence of Jain epistemology. His main achievement was to realize that the traditional division of inference (*svārthānumāna* and *parārthānumāna*) can be extended, so that something akin to the abductive inference of Peirce is anticipated.

Akālī (Pañjābī, 'deathless'). Designation by Gurū *Gobind Siṅgh of those devotees of Akāl (i.e. God), the Timeless one, who were prepared to die for the Sikh cause. Their fearlessness won the title *'Nihaṅg', although the two terms have since gained widely differing connotations. Akālīs assumed guardianship of the Sikh faith. They reappeared from relative obscurity into which they had fallen during the 19th cent. as the name was adopted by campaigners for *gurdwārā reform. *Jathās of Akālīs, co-ordinated in 1920 in the Shiromaṇī Akālī Dal, protested non-violently against the *mahants' corrupt control of gurdwārās such as *Tarn Tāran. The Akālī Dal (political party) first met in 1926 and, despite division, has continued to dominate the *Shiromaṇī Gurdwārā Parbandhak Committee and to campaign actively—e.g. for a Pañjābī-speaking state (achieved in 1966) and for greater Sikh autonomy.

Akāl Purukh. 'Being beyond time', Sikh designation of God. 'Akāl Purukh' is the theological affirmation of God's absolute transcendence: 'You are Akāl Purukh (the Timeless One), death does not hang over your head' (Ādi Granth 1038). *Vāhigurū is the designation more common in devotion, but Akāl Purukh is the foundation on which Sikh faith and confidence rest: 'Having cast down, God builds up, and having built, casts down; having filled the ocean, God dries it up, having dried it up, he empties it. The One who is beyond anxiety has power to do this' (Ādi Granth 934). Although 'he' is traditionally used of God, God is without form (*niraṅkār*) and beyond gender distinctions. Indeed, s/he is often addressed as both: 'You are my mother, you are my father, you are my family, in all places you are my protector, why then should I be afraid?' (Ādi Granth 103).

Akāl Takht (Pañjābī, 'immortal throne'). The foremost *takht among Sikh shrines, located in *Amritsar. The Akāl Takht was founded by Gurū *Hargobind for the organization of the *panth's secular and military affairs. Many of the *Gurus' and *śahīds*' (martyrs) weapons were housed in this *gurdwārā, and formative *gurmatās originated here. Each night, the *Ādi Granth is transferred here from the neighbouring *Harimandir. Four storeys were added by mahārājā Rañjīt Siṅgh. In June 1984, during fighting between the Indian army and supporters of Jarnail Siṅgh *Bhindrānwāle, the Akāl Takht was severely damaged, but it has since been rebuilt.

Ākāśa (Skt., 'open space, vacuity, ether'). 1. One of the five gross elements (*mahābhūtas) of Hindu philosophy (albeit the finest), the ether which pervades the universe and is the vehicle of life and sound. Ākāśa is the subtlest of the mahābhūtas, and in *Chandogya Upaniṣad* is equated with *Brahma. See also BHŪTA.

2. In *Matsya* *Purāṇa, Ākāśa is a god of house-building.

3. In Buddhism, space, either as limited by the boundaries of bodies, or unlimited space.

4. For Jains, see ASTIKAYA.

Akathistos (Gk., 'not sitting', because it is sung standing). A *Greek hymn in twenty-four stanzas in honour of the Virgin *Mary. It is sung in *Orthodox churches on the fifth Saturday in *Lent, but was perhaps composed originally for the feast of the *Annunciation. It belongs to the genre of hymns called *kontakia* (collect hymns which express the theme of the day's feast), and although anonymous it has been attributed by some scholars to the 6th-cent. master of this genre, *Romanos. If not by him, it is at least no later than the 9th cent. It is considered one of the finest of Orthodox hymns.

Tr. D. Attwater, *The Akathistos Hymn* (1934).

Akbar the Great (Jalāl ud-Dīn Muḥammad, 1542–1605). One of the ablest rulers of *Mughal India, who built a durable base for stable Muslim rule. Akbar ruled for forty-eight years and created a strong central government to administer the vast Mughal empire; he extended it from Afghanistan to the Godavari river in S. India. He promoted arts, learning, and music. Agra and Delhi became flourishing centres of culture, trade, and commerce. Akbar's main achievement was to secure effective support of the Hindu majority in the empire through a policy of toleration; he abolished *jizya (levied on Hindus), appointed talented Hindus (especially the Rajputs) as governors, as military commanders, and as advisors (e.g. Todar Mall masterminded the revenue reforms). In return, the Hindus, on the whole, provided him with co-operation and faithful service.

During the latter part of his reign, Akbar, while maintaining that he remained Muslim, promulgated Dīn-i-Ilāhī (Divine Faith, also called Tawḥīd-i Ilāhī) as a new religion for his empire. It was a syncretization of various creeds and an attempt to create a pure theism. Although he was illiterate himself, he founded an 'Ibādat-khāna (house of worship) where leaders of different religions could discuss their faiths. It appears that Akbar was genuinely interested in reconciling religions: 'I try to take good from all opinion with the sole object of ascertaining the truth!' However, Akbar's Dīn-i-Ilāhī met with very little success (it was strongly opposed by *Aḥmad Sirhindī), and it died with him.

The early accounts by Abū al-Fazl 'Allāmī have been translated (in part) by H. Beveridge (1907–39; repr. 1977), and by H. Blochmann and H. S. Jarrett (1873–94), revised by D. C. Phillot and J. N. Sarkar (1939–49); R. Sharma,

The Religious Policy of the Mughal Emperors (1972); V. A. Smith, *Akbar . . .* (2nd edn., 1966).

Akdamut Millin (Heb., 'Introduction'). Introductory words of an *Aramaic poem written by R. Meir b. Isaac Nehorai. It consists of ninety lines, praising God, the Creator and Lawgiver. In the *Ashkenazi liturgy, it is recited on *Shavu'ot before the reading of the *Torah portion (Exodus 19–20).

'Akeda/'Aqeda (Heb., 'Binding' (of *Isaac)). The story of *Abraham's intended *sacrifice of Isaac. According to Genesis 22, Abraham was commanded by God to sacrifice his beloved son, on Mount Moriah. At the last moment, an *angel told Abraham that it was merely a test, and a ram was offered in place of the child. In Jewish thought, this incident is regarded as the supreme example of obedience to God's will, while modern *biblical critics have explained it in terms of ancient practices of child sacrifice. Traditionally the *Temple was believed to have been built over the site where the 'akeda took place. The story is referred to in the *Rosh ha-Shanah liturgy, and one explanation for the blowing of the *shofar is that it is a reminder of the ram sacrificed in place of Isaac. In *rabbinic literature, the 'akeda is described as the last of the ten trials of Abraham, and the story was compared with many examples of real martyrdom. The incident is also much discussed in Jewish philosophy: *Naḥmanides, for example, used the 'akedah to examine the problem of God's foreknowledge and human free will. The story is also frequently used by moralists, and has been the inspiration for Christian and Jewish works of art.

À Kempis (Christian writer): see THOMAS À KEMPIS.

Akhaṇḍ Kīrtanī Jathā (Pañjābī, 'continuous hymn-singing group'). A non-political organization emphasizing strict allegiance to Sikh discipline. The Jathā draws inspiration from the devout and learned fighter for Indian independence, Bhāī Randhīr Singh (1878–1961). Members abstain from all non-vegetarian food, narcotics, and intoxicants, and prefer to eat from iron utensils. They argue that one of the *five Ks is the *keskī*, a turban to cover the uncut hair (*kesh*) which other Sikhs regard as one of the Ks. Females wear the *keskī* under their *chunnī* (scarf). Members hold *akhaṇḍ pāṭh and twelve hour sessions of *raiṇ sabhāī kīrtan* (overnight hymn-singing). From the Akhaṇḍ Kīrtanī Jathā have come many members of the more political and militant Babbar Khālsā, campaigning for an independent state, *Khālistān.

Akhaṇḍ pāṭh (Hindī, Pañjābī). 'Uninterrupted reading' of the *Ādi Granth. Akhaṇḍ *pāṭh is a relatively recent Sikh practice. Anyone wishing to mark a happy or sorrowful family occasion may arrange for akhaṇḍ pāṭh, providing food for all who read or attend during the forty-eight hours. Shifts of readers read, day and night, at an unhurried pace. Akhaṇḍ pāṭh also introduces *gurpurbs, concluding early on the anniversary morning. Akhaṇḍ pāṭh is preceded by six verses of *Anand *Sāhib, the *Ardās, a *hukam, and the preparation of *kaṛāh praśād. Many people gather for the concluding ceremony which is called *bhag.bhog*. In some large *gurdwārās, the akhaṇḍ pāṭhs are continuous, with one succeeding another.

Akhārā ('wrestling arena', i.e. a monastery): see NIRMALĀ.

Akhlāq (ethics): see ETHICS (Islam).

Akhun(d): Persian for *Mulla.

Aki Matsuri (harvest festival): see NIINAME-SAI.

Aki no Higan (festival): see FESTIVALS AND FASTS.

Aki no Shanichi (protective festival): see FESTIVALS AND FASTS.

Akiva/Aqiba (*c.*50–135 CE). Jewish scholar and *martyr. Akiva was one of the leading scholars of his age and is credited with systematizing the *midrash. He set up his own school at Bene Barak, and his pupils included R. *Meir and R. *Simeon bar Yoḥai. He recognized Simeon bar Kokhba as the *messiah in his revolt against the Romans in 132 CE, applying to him the verse 'a star shall come forth out of *Jacob, and a sceptre shall rise out of Israel' (Numbers 24. 17). Ultimately he died as a martyr, being flayed alive by the Romans. Akiva's prominence among the sages is indicated in R. *Johanan's famous statement, 'The author of an anonymous *mishnah is R. Meir, of an anonymous *tosefta, R. Nehemiah, of an anonymous *sifra, R. Judah . . ., and all are taught according to the views of Akiva.'

L. Finkelstein, *Akiva, Scholar, Saint and Martyr* (1962).

Akṣara (Skt., 'unchangeable'). That which cannot perish, the immutable, hence a name for *Brahman.

Akṣara-puruṣa (Skt., 'unchangeable' + *puruṣa). The uninvolved Self which keeps aloof and detached from the changes which occur in *prakṛti, and simply observes its processes.

Akṣobhya (Skt., 'imperturbable'). In Buddhism, one of the five Jinas or *Dhyāni-Buddhas who inhabits the pure land of the East (*Abhirati). Akṣobhya is mentioned briefly in the earliest *Mahāyāna sources but comes to prominence in later *Tantric Buddhism. His paradise in the East is described, in a manner similar to the *pure land of Amitābha/*Amida in the West, as a utopia without evil, ugliness, or suffering, wherein the virtuous are reborn.

In Tantric Buddhism he is the father of the

spiritual lineage which has Vajrapāni for *bodhisattva and Kanakamuni as the earthly Buddha. His consort is the earth goddess Locanā, and he is usually depicted in iconography in the gesture (*mudra) of touching the earth to call witness to his enlightenment. He is symbolically associated with the colour blue and with the aggregate (*skandha) of consciousness.

Aku-byōdō (Jap., 'bad-sameness'). A subtle error in Zen Buddhism whereby the sameness of all things when they are experienced in enlightenment (*byōdō), is confused with a belief that all things are the same—thereby overlooking their provisional distinctions.

Akum (non-Jewish star worshipper): see GENTILE.

Akuśala (Skt., opposite of *kusala. Unskilful action. Actions are called 'unskilful' because of their undesirable effects, since they contain the seed of unhappy destiny or rebirth. These actions are rooted in greed (*lobha), hatred (*dosa), or delusion (*moha), the three unfavourable roots (akuṣala-mūla). While kuśala requires deliberate, conscious effort, as it goes against the natural inclination of the senses for giving in to the stimuli which continuously flow in through the sense doors, akuśala results from giving in to this natural inclination by seeking to satisfy the sensory thirst. The resulting distraction weakens the capability of the individual for spiritual effort and thereby makes him inefficient for the purpose of *nirvāna.

Explained in terms of the individual's moral conduct, akuśala consists of ten actions: (i) destruction of life (*pānātipātā*), (ii) theft (*adinnādānā*), (iii) unchastity (*kāmesumicchācārā*), (iv) lying (*musāvādā*), (v) slander (*pisunāvācā*), (vi) rough speech (*pharusāvācā*), (vii) idle talk (*samphappalāpā*), (viii) covetousness (*abhijjā*), (ix) malice (*vyāpāda*), and (x) wrong views (*micchādiṭṭhi*): *Majjhima Nikāya* I. 489. The result which is generated by an akuśala action is *pāpa, but this distinction between the cause and its effect seems to have disappeared even in the later portions of the Pāli canon, with akuśala being equated with pāpa. See also KARMA/KAMMA.

Akusō (Jap., 'evil monk'). Common term from the Heian period in Japan for monks who had abandoned their monastic orders (and rules) and had become warriors. They constituted the *sōhei*, soldier-monks who were only overcome in the 16th cent.

Akuśu-kū (Jap., 'wrong understanding' + 'emptiness'). A wrong understanding, in Zen Buddhism, of the true nature of ku (Skt., *śūnyatā. In this error, ku is understood as equalling 'nothing', the negation of existence. But Ku/śūnyatā is the repository and source of all appearance, so that appearance is neither more nor less than it. Thus 'form is not other than emptiness, and emptiness is not other than form'. (**Heart Sūtra*).

al-'Abbās b. 'Abd al-Muṭṭalib (d. 652–3 (AH 32)). An uncle of the Prophet *Muḥammad. The *'Abbāsid dynasty took its name from him, being descended from his son. 'Abbās was a prosperous merchant entrusted with the right of supplying drinking water to the pilgrims at *Mecca. Though he refused to recognize Muḥammad as a prophet, 'Abbās protected him from his Meccan enemies. He fought against the Muslims at *Badr, was taken prisoner and then released. He accepted Islam, when Muḥammad marched on Mecca in 630 (AH 8) and is said to have acted bravely in the battle of Hunayn and turned the tide of the battle in the Muslims' favour. He settled in *Madīna and contributed to the finances of the expeditions against the Byzantines, though he was never given any administrative post.

Aladura (Yoruba, 'praying people'). The general name for a wide range of prophet-healing independent churches that have developed in W. Nigeria since about 1918, spread as far as the Cameroon and Sierra Leone, and established branches in Britain. The largest is the Christ Apostolic Church, which earlier had assistance from Faith Tabernacle, Philadelphia, and the Apostolic Church in England, and grew through the mass healing revival under Joseph Babalola (1904–60) from 1930. One of its founders (later Sir) Isaac Akinyele, became Olubadan ('king') of Ibadan. It is a well-organized church, a member of the Nigerian Christian Council, with its own schools and teacher training, and several hundred thousand members. Another section of Aladura consists of the many forms of Cherubim and Seraphim Societies deriving from a Yoruba prophet, Moses Tunolase (?1885–1933) and a young *Anglican woman, Victorianah Abiodun Akinsowon (b. 1907). They separated from the *Anglican Church in 1928, and all sections stress revelation and healing. The third main group, the Church of the Lord (Aladura), was founded in 1930 by an Anglican catechist, Josiah Oshitelu (1902–66), dismissed for his deviationist practices. Although never more than 15,000 members, it has spread widely in W. Africa and into Britain, and its second head, E. O. A. Adejobi, became a member of the Central Committee of the World Council of Churches in 1983. The whole movement includes many small secessions from the above sections and numerous smaller churches.

J. D. Y. Peel, *Aladura* (1968).

al-Afghānī, Jamāl al-Dīn (1838–97 (AH 1254–1314)). A Muslim modernist and reformer, and strong anti-colonialist. He was born in Iran, but his formative years were spent in Afghanistan. From 1871, he taught in Cairo, but subsequently travelled widely, following political opportunity. For a time he worked with Muḥammad *Abduh (founding the *Salafiyya), but he broke away, preferring political intrigue to the reform of Islam. He continued to travel, leaving a tremendous influence and impression upon the people he visited. He aimed to rally the Muslim world to realize its power as an international community, and by raising its political and intellectual standards, to combat Western colonialism. Freedom and liberation from foreign rule were to be followed by the establishment of a pan-Islamic state, the union of the Muslim people under one *khalīfa. The pan-Islamic state would carry out socio-economic and religious reforms to improve the life and condition of the Muslims. This programme would be in accordance with an open and progressive Islam.

Al-Afghānī argued that Islam was not incompatible with Western reason or science (he contested, in particular, E. Renan's lecture 'Islam and Science'), but as a Muslim rationalist, he repudiated blind faith and conjecture, and instead believed that true happiness sprang from wisdom and clear-sightedness. Life in this world has to be improved in order to gain a peaceful life in the hereafter. His *Al-Radd ʿalā al-Dahriyīn* (The Refutation of the Materialists, tr. N. R. Keddie, 1966) reasserted faith in the transcendental truth of Islam. The Arabic language was regarded by al-Afghānī as of primary importance in promoting the unity of the Muslim world. But in the end, politics rather than reform claimed him.

N. R. Keddie, *Sayyid Jamāl al-Dīn . . .: A Biography* (1972).

al-Aḥsā'ī (Muslim founder of the Shaykhīs): see SHAYKH AHMAD IBN ZAYN AL-DĪN.

al-Akhira (the hereafter): see AFTERLIFE.

al-ʿAqīqah (sacrifice at time of a birth): see SACRIFICE.

al-Aqṣā Mosque: see JERUSALEM.

al-Arbaʿayn (commemoration of departed): see FUNERALS RITES (Islam).

al-ʿArsh (the throne of God): see KURSĪ.

al-Ashʿarī, Abū 'l-Ḥasan ʿAlī ibn Ismāʿīl (873–935 (AH 260–324)). Foremost Muslim theologian, who is often regarded as the founder of *kalām. In early life, he was a *Muʿtazilite, but he became doubtful about the power of human reason to solve theological problems when he raised the issue of the condemnation of those whom God might have brought to death earlier (thus avoiding the deeds for which they were condemned). He moved more toward the *Ḥanbalites and contested the arguments of the Muʿtazilites, while using some of their methods. He insisted that the *Qur'ān is uncreated (against the view that anything which appears in or through material form must be created). In affirming attributes of God (e.g. the hand of God), al-Ashʿarī held that they are truly posited (they are not metaphors), but that it is impossible to say in exactly what way they pertain to God—thus producing the famous formula, *bilā kaif(a)*, 'without knowing how'. He also dealt with the problem of how humans can be accountable for their actions if God determines all things, by developing the doctrine of acquisition (*kasb*, see QADAR): God creates all possibilities, but humans acquire a particular act in the action itself. If that suggests that God creates evil, al-Ashʿarī replied, 'Nothing can be evil on the part of God: a thing becomes evil for us because we transgress the limit set for us, . . . but because the Creator is subject to no one and is bound by no command, nothing can be evil on his part.' Among many works, he wrote *al-Ibānah ʿan Uṣūl al-Diyānah* (Discourse on the Foundations of Religion, tr. W. C. Klein, 1940) and *Maqālāt al-Islāmiyyīn* (The Treatises of the Islamic Schools).

M. Allard, *le Problème des attributs divins . . .* (1965); R. J. McCarthy, *The Theology of al-Ashʿari* (texts and trs., 1953).

al-Asmā' al-Ḥusnā (names of Allāh in Islam): see NINETY-NINE BEAUTIFUL NAMES OF GOD.

Alawi (a Shīʿa Muslim movement): see NUṢAIRĪ.

ʿAlawiyya (Sūfī movement): see SHĀDHILIYYA.

Ālaya-vijñāna ('receptacle-consciousness'). In Yogācāra (Buddhist Idealism, also known as *Vijñānavāda) the continuum of subjective consciousness underlying cognition and personal experience through time (given that there is no 'self' supplying this continuity). The concept was introduced by *Asaṅga in the 4th cent. CE as an elaboration of the *Abhidharmic notion of a stream of consciousness (*bhavaṅga-sota*) which constitutes personal continuity over a series of lives. The ālaya may be conceived of in the terms of early Buddhism as an extension of the aggregate of consciousness (*vijñāna). Asaṅga specifies three levels or strata within this aggregate: (i) the operational consciousness of the six senses, (ii) the self-referential intellect or ego (*manas), and (iii) the substratum or receptacle-consciousness (ālaya-vijñāna) within which experience is stored, matured, and re-emitted in the *karmic cycle in the form of new perceptions. These are the eight functions of consciousness of which the ālaya is the most basic.

In the unenlightened consciousness the imperfect functioning of perception and cognition in stages (i) and (ii) above leads to the depositing of defilements or seeds (*bīja) in the ālaya which taint or 'perfume' it. In the course of time these seeds mature and are projected from the ālaya as new perceptual phenomena. In this way the ālaya serves as the support of sentient existence and the mechanism of karmic retribution. As progress is made towards enlightenment the defiled seeds are gradually replaced by undefiled ones until there occurs a reversal or revolution within the ālaya (*āśrayaparāvṛtti*) and the maturation and propagation of karmic seeds comes to a halt. Thus the traditional concepts of *saṃsāra and *nirvāna are reinterpreted idealistically as functional modes of the ālaya. See also ANĀTMAN; ARAYASHIKI.

al-Azhar (Arab., 'the most resplendent'). One of the principal *mosques in Cairo, also a centre of learning and later a university. It was founded in 969 CE by the *Fāṭimid rulers of Egypt. Since they were Isma'īlī, al-Azhar was (for two centuries) a centre for Isma'īlī teaching, until the Ayyubids under Ṣalāḥ al-Dīn (*Saladin) deposed the Fāṭimid dynasty in the late 12th cent. For a while al-Azhar was in decline, but was restored under the Mamluks (late 13th cent. onwards) and subsequently became a centre of religious teaching for the whole Sunnī (see *Sunna) Islamic world. In particular, it was a centre for training missionaries. At first only the religious sciences were taught, and until the 19th cent. this was on the mediaeval pattern of rote learning and personal instruction by *shaykhs who gave their own *ijāza* (certificate) to satisfactory students. The *primus inter pares*, the Shaykh al-Azhar, emerged as an office in the 17th cent. With government intervention, in 1872 a diploma and examinations were instituted; under the influence of Muḥammad *'Abduh, further regulations were introduced in 1896 regarding qualifications, courses, and examinations. Even then al-Azhar remained largely independent and was opposed to modern methods and studies, although some further subjects were added to the curriculum. In the 1950s, and especially in the reform of 1961, further expansion added facilities for a much wider range of studies (including sciences, languages, and business studies) and in the 1970s a section for women was opened. Al-Azhar remains to this day one of the leading and most influential universities in the Islamic world, and accepts numerous students from abroad, thus helping to spread its ideals and standards and influencing Islamic teaching outside Egypt.

Alb. A Christian eucharistic *vestment, derived from the Graeco-Roman *tunica talaris*. It is a long white (Lat., *albus*) garment usually with tight-fitting sleeves and held in at the waist by a cord ('girdle'). It may be ornamented near the hem with coloured strips called 'apparels'. Traditionally, it symbolizes purity, and the celebrant may say 'Make me white ...' when putting it on. In the RC Church, the development of the lace industry led to the addition of elaborate decoration, with lace from waist to ankles, and on the cuffs.

al-Baiḍāwī. 'Abdallah b. 'Umar al-Baiḍāwī, of Persian origin, author of one of the best known works of *tafsīr (*Qur'ān commentary), a comprehensive work based largely on *al-Zamakhsharī's *Kashshāf*. It is deliberately a compilation designed to be of help to the student and scholar, and as such gained considerable popularity; numerous later works of tafsīr were based on it. Al-Baiḍāwī belonged to the *Shāfi'ī school of law, and wrote on law, grammar, and scholastic theology. He became chief *qāḍi (judge) in Shirāz, and died in 1286 CE.

A. F. L. Beeston, *Baiḍāwī's Commentary on Sūrah 12 of the Qur'ān* (1983).

Alban, St. The first Christian *martyr in Britain. The date of his death is either *c.*209 or *c.*305. He was converted to Christianity by a fugitive priest he sheltered, in whose cloak he was arrested. He was subsequently put to death. His shrine is in St Albans Abbey. Feast day, 20 June.

al-Bannā (founder of Sūfī movement): see HASAN AL-BANNĀ'.

al-Baṣrī (Sūfī): see HASAN AL-BAṢRĪ.

Albertus Magnus, St (*c.*1205–80). Christian philosopher and theologian. He was born in Bavaria, studied at Padua and Bologna, and became a *Dominican in 1222/3. He held one of the Dominican chairs of theology at the University of Paris, where Thomas *Aquinas was one of his pupils, and later (1260–2) he became bishop of Ratisbon. Allowed to resign, he resumed teaching at Cologne. He preached a *crusade in Germany, 1263–4. As well as Magnus, he was called Doctor Universalis. He was canonized and proclaimed a Doctor of the Church in 1931. His major work consisted in the application of Aristotle (fused as by then he was with *Neoplatonism) to Christian theology. He wrote paraphrases of Aristotle, regarding God as the necessary being in whom essence and existence are identical, and demonstrating his existence from motion and the impossibility of an infinite chain of principles. However, he allowed that creation is best accounted for by a theory of *emanations leading to this world. While metaphysics deals with God as first being, and theology deals with God as revealed, both end in *apophatic mystery: philosophy and empirical enquiry are of value, but cannot contradict revelation. He wrote commentaries on the Sentences of *Peter Lombard and on Pseudo-*Dionysius, and a *Summa de Creaturis*. He left incomplete a *Summa Theologica*.

S. Tugwell, *Albert and Thomas* (1988).

Albigenses. A branch of the *Cathars of S. France. Christian *dualist heretics, Pope Innocent III failed to convert them; a savage *Crusade, led by Simon de Montfort, went on until 1218; and in 1233, the *Dominican *Inquisition undertook to eliminate them. Their main centre was Albi (hence the name); they may have had remote ancestry in the teaching of *Mani.

al-Bīrūnī, Abū Rayḥān (973–1049 (AH 362–442)). Muslim scholar of wide-ranging interests, not least in other religions. His parents were Persian-speaking, and he came from the area now known as Uzbekistan. When attached to the court of Maḥmūd of Ghaznah, he went to India where he learnt Skt. (translating *Patañjali's Yoga into Arab.) and studied Indian science and philosophy—he particularly admired their achievements in astronomy and mathematics. His study culminated in *Kitāb al-Hind* (The Book of India). On this basis, he developed work of his own on a wide scale, particularly, but by no means exclusively, in astronomy. His extraordinary achievements were not followed by other Muslims—perhaps because they seemed too threatening to orthodox belief. Yet al-Bīrūnī himself, while concerned to understand other faiths, did not waver in his adherence to Islam.

Tr. E. C. Sachau (1888; 1964).

al-Bistāmī, Abū Yazīd/Bāyazīd (d. 875 (AH 261)). A Persian *Sūfī, who was given to a life of asceticism and solitude. His only desire in life was to attain a direct experience of divine reality. He wrote no work, but his ecstatic utterances have been preserved in writing by such contemporaries as *Dhu'l-nūn and *al-Junaid. It appears that he possessed extraordinary powers of intellectual and imaginative speculation. 'As soon as I attained to oneness, I became a bird with a body of unity and wings of everlastingness, and I continued flying in the air of quality . . . I thought that I had arrived at the very throne of God and I said to it, "O throne, they tell us that God rests upon you", "O Bāyazīd," replied the throne, "We are told here that he rests in a humble heart." ' His particular method of attainment was one of subtraction, or stripping away, of the attributes of personality until not even personality is left—as when a snake finally sloughs its skin; 'If I could say—and absolutely mean it—"There is no God but *Allāh", there would be nothing to concern me after that.' Al-Bistāmī is much quoted by the Sūfīs, and had a far-reaching influence upon the development of Sufism in the direction of a pantheistic doctrine.

M. A. Rabb, *Persian Mysticism: Abū Yazīd al-Bistāmī* (1971).

Albo, Joseph (15th cent. CE). Spanish Jewish preacher and philosopher. Albo was the author of *Sefer ha-'Ikkarim* (Book of Principles), a reasoned presentation of the articles of the Jewish *faith, explained in the light of contemporary ideas: '*Torah does not require us to believe absurdities.' He was familiar with Islamic philosophy and Christian *scholasticism and was greatly influenced by the teaching of Hasdai *Crescas. Against the *thirteen Principles of *Maimonides and six of Crescas, he formulated three principles of Judaism—the existence of God (though 'God has no definition'), divine *revelation, and reward and punishment (though he added eight further derivative principles). Subordinate to the principles are six dogmas, namely the creation of the world *ex nihilo*, the status of *Moses as supreme *prophet, the validity of Mosaic law, the possibility of attaining human perfection, the *resurrection of the dead and the coming of the *messiah. The work achieved great popularity and went through many edns.

Text and Eng. tr., I. Husik (5 vols., 1929–30).

al-Bukhārī, Muḥammad b. Ismā'īl (810–70 (AH 194–256)). Compiler of one of the main collections of *ḥadīth, known as *Ṣaḥīḥ* ('sound', 'genuine'). He was born at Bukhārā, and began to study ḥadīth at the age of 10. He had a fine memory and became recognized as one of the chief authorities on ḥadīth. He travelled extensively in search of ḥadīth, which he subjected to careful scrutiny—much needed, since spurious ḥadīth were circulating. Al-Bukhārī is said to have interviewed a thousand *shaykhs, and to have examined more than 200,000 ḥadīth, rejecting many. The *Ṣaḥīḥ* contains over 7,000 narratives, though because some are repeated, the total is under 3,000. These are mainly arranged according to subject-matter, for ease of reference, in ninety-seven 'books' and further divided into 3,450 chapters. Together with the *Ṣaḥīḥ* of *Muslim (d. 875 (AH 261)), al-Bukhārī's collection is accepted as the main definitive compilation of reliable ḥadīth, and as such, comes second only to the *Qur'ān as a source of principles for legislation and religious practice.

Eng. tr. of the *Ṣaḥīḥ* by M. M. Khan (9 vols., 4th edn. 1979).

Alchemy (Arab., perhaps from Gk. via Syriac, *al-kīmiyā*). The endeavour (minimally) to find the key to the transformation of chemical substances, especially of base metals into precious ones; and beyond that, to find 'the elixir of immortality'. The word and practice of 'alchemy' thus underlie modern chemistry. In its earlier forms it pervades all religions, though moving increasingly to interior and spiritual transformations. Thus in Taoism, there were two different levels: practitioners of Wai-tan (external alchemy) sought a potion for immortality, based on a belief that a person's vital energy (*yüan-ch'i) was a particular balance of *yin-yang, which, if it is disturbed, produces illness and death; gold and cinnabar have the power to restore the balance. The practitioners of Nei-tan (internal alchemy) aimed to develop an immortal soul from *ching, *ch'i, and *shen, by meditative exercises, especially breathing and control of bodily functions.

European alchemy seems to have begun in Hellenistic Egypt around the 1st cent. CE, and possibly even earlier. It enjoyed flourishing periods in 2nd- and 3rd-cent. Greece, and in various parts of the Arab world in the 7th and 8th cents., thus taking its name from the Arab. *al-kīmiyā*, the Syriac *kīmīyā*, and the Gk. *chēmeia*. In the 10th cent., alchemy re-entered Europe via Islamic Spain, where it also received influence from the *Kabbalah. At its peak in Renaissance Europe, in addition to having produced a well-developed medical system under such as Paracelsus, alchemy came for some to rival the Church as the epitome of *Hermetic philosophy; its adherents counted themselves as the true Christians, and pointed to the necessity of transformative experience for spiritual realization. Their pretensions were mocked in Ben Jonson's *The Alchemist* (1610), which identifies all alchemists as charlatans and deluded mystics; but strong cases have been made for *The Tempest* (1611) as a reply to Jonson (Frances Yates, *Shakespeare's Last Plays*, 1975) and also for *King Lear* (1605) as an alchemical allegory *par excellence* (Charles Nicholl, *The Chemical Theatre*, 1980).

Alchemical theory in this period involved the belief that all metals in the ground are steadily evolving into gold, and that similarly all men are evolving into Christs. The alchemists saw themselves as only speeding up a natural process, a vision in which *Jung saw the inherent implication of God's imperfection and need for redemption by Man (a fact which he suggested the alchemists themselves did not fully recognize). Alchemical practice correspondingly involved a dynamic *cosmology whereby the process of creation was re-enacted in the alchemical process and, mystically, within the alchemist himself by meditative identification with that process (Jung describes this as the 'projection of the psychic contents' on to the working material). The return of matter to its pre-creation state (termed 'chaos', 'massa confusa', or 'prima materia') was achieved by the application of heat to a retort containing the material (which was not always lead: sometimes eggshells, or the alchemists' faeces, fingernails, hair, etc., were used), which released the spirit from matter and, by identification, from the alchemist himself. The goal of the process was to reconstitute the original matter in a transmuted state (hence, lead into gold) whereby it—and consequently the alchemist—would be a more suitable vessel to receive the *Holy Spirit again. Gerhard Dorn, *Philosophia Meditativa* (1602), explains the rationale:

> Knowest thou not that heaven and the elements were formerly one, and were separated from one another by divine artifice that they might bring forth thee and all things? . . . Again, in every generation such a separation is necessary, and needs to be effected of thyself, before thou settest sail towards the true philosophy. Thou wilt never make from others the one which thou seekest, except first there be made one thing of thyself.

A guarantee of the success of the process was believed to be the 'philosopher's stone', whose mere presence would ensure positive results but which also symbolized the completion of the process. It is not known whether an identification of the philosopher's stone with *Christ was overtly made before Petrus Bonus did so in his *Pretiosa Margarita Novella* (*c*.1330–9), but this was certainly a strong current in alchemy from then until its demise, being forcefully repeated by such as Jacob *Boehme (1575–1624) and Robert Fludd (1574–1637). It is thus evident that many alchemists sincerely believed in (or at least, hoped for) the presence of Christ during their work, and saw their goal as the transmutation of their own mundane personality into Christhood.

A strengthening of church roles in government in 17th-cent. Europe contributed to the suppression of many great alchemical and Hermetic intellects. In England, John Dee was condemned to a life of poverty; in Italy, Giordano Bruno was burned at the stake. To a large extent alchemy was driven underground, resulting in the birth of Rosicrucianism. However, it was essentially the growth of rationalism, the development of chemistry out of alchemy as a material, not spiritual, enquiry, and works such as Robert Boyle's *The Sceptical Chymist* (1661) which undermined the alchemical theory of the elements, which were seminal in the death of alchemy as a spiritual pursuit.

A. Coudert, *Alchemy . . .* (1988); M. Eliade, *The Forge and the Crucible* (1978); J. Needham, *Science and Civilization in China*, v/2 (1974); A. Pritchard, *Alchemy: A Bibliography of English Language Writings* (1980); P. Ray, *A History of Hindu Chemistry* (1904–9; rev. 1956).

Alcohol (Arab.). Intoxicants which in some religions are prohibited. In Islam, they are *harām* (see KHAMR), and in Buddhism, abstention from alcohol is one of the five basic principles of moral conduct (pañca-*śīla): 'I take on myself to abstain from alcohol and drugs [since they lead to carelessness in moral life].' Among Hindus, *surāpāna*, drinking intoxicants, is the second of the five great sins (*mahāpātaka), although there is much commentarial discussion on what counts as an intoxicant (*śūdras can drink liquor without incurring sin). It is the power of alcohol to obliterate judgement and self-control which makes it dubious in religious eyes. Thus among Sikhs, alcohol is consumed, but the *Gurūs taught, 'By drinking wine one loses sanity and becomes mad, loses the power of discrimination and incurs the displeasure of God' (Ādi Granth 554). Drinking alcohol is forbidden for initiated *khālsā Sikhs, as is the taking of drugs—though *Nihaṅg Siṅghs take an infusion of cannabis ritually to aid meditation. In Judaism and Christianity, wine is extolled as part of the bounty of God, but again, in moderation. The problem of keeping in moderation the advice to Timothy ('Take a little wine for your stomach's sake', 1 Timothy 5. 23) and the recognition of the social damage caused by alcohol abuse, has led to Temperance Movements, and the taking of the Pledge to abstain: for an example, see BOOTH, W.

Al-Dajjāl (Arab.). The perjurer or false accuser, a figure in Islamic *eschatology, the '*anti-Christ' whose wiles and deceptions 'cover' (a root meaning) and resist the truth. He is not mentioned in the *Qur'ān, but tradition in Islam seems indebted to Christian eschatology, in part, for its *mise-en-scène*. *Jesus, known as *al-Masīḥ in Islam, raptured to heaven in rescue from the cross, will one day return, preach Islam, and slay al-Dajjāl, before his ultimate burial in *Madīna alongside the tomb of *Muḥammad. In some versions the slayer is the *Mahdī. Traditionalists present al-Dajjāl in a variety of guises and descriptions as to his age, his schemes, his residence, and his retinue. He sleeps only with his eyes. By some he is identified with *al Shaytan al-Rajīm, 'the accursed Satan', whom pilgrims on the *ḥajj repudiate by hurling stones against his 'pillar' outside *Mecca.

Aleinu le-Shabbe'ah (Heb, 'It is our duty to praise'). *Prayer now recited at the end of the prayerbook services. According to tradition, it was composed by *Joshua, but probably dates back to the period of the second *Temple. It expresses Israel's unique status and looks forward to the coming of God's Kingdom on earth. In the *Ashkenazi *liturgy, it is customary to prostrate oneself during the recital of the Aleinu on *Rosh ha-Shanah and *Yom Kippur. It begins, 'It is our duty to praise the Lord of all things, to ascribe greatness to the Creator, that he has not made us like the nations of other lands, nor placed us like the other families of earth'.

Alexandria. City in Egypt, notable in Christian tradition (stemming, traditionally, from St *Mark) for its catechetical school in the 2nd and 3rd cents. and in the 4th and 5th cents. especially for the 'Alexandrian theology' represented by *Origen, *Athanasius, and *Cyril. This is in general characterized by the influence of *Neoplatonism (e.g. in Origen's ability to speak of the Trinity almost as three gods), and by its mystical and allegorical methods of interpreting the *Bible. In *christology it held that Christ's divine nature was basic if he was to have saved us, while his human nature tended to be restricted to the flesh which was its vehicle. See also ANTIOCH; MONOPHYSITES. The *patriarchs of Alexandria have jurisdiction over Catholic *Copts, Copts who do not accept *Chalcedon, and Orthodox Copts; the patriarchs of the latter two have existed in continuous line since 567 CE.

al-Fārābī, Abu Nasr Muḥammad Ibn Tarkhān (*c*.870–950 (AH 257–339)). A philosopher-mystic of Turkish origin who lived during the height of *'Abbāsid rule in Baghdād. His philosophy contained elements of Aristotelanism, Platonism, and *Sufism. Al-Fārābī wrote on many diverse subjects—e.g. mathematics, medicine, psychology, politics, metaphysics, and music. Among Muslim philosophers he is considered the Second Teacher (*al-mu'allim ath-thāni*) after Aristotle, from whom he derived three arguments for the existence of God, namely, the first mover, the first cause, and necessary being. Al-Fārābī's chief work, *Attainment of Happiness*, defends the basis of *revelation (i.e. *prophecy) against the strong attacks of such free-thinkers as Al-Rawandī who rejected revelation and prophets, resurrection and the afterlife, and who believed that reason is sufficient for seeking knowledge and truth. Al-Fārābī argued that prophets possessed remarkable faculties through which they could commune with the Active Intellect, so that, whereas philosophers expressed the truths derived from the Active Intellect through reason and logic, the prophets expressed the same knowledge in religious utterance and symbolism. Furthermore, he allocated to prophets an important function as law-givers for society, and felt that religion was needed by the ruler and teachers for the non-philosophical masses. However, he agreed with the philosophers that logic has religious as well as philosophical importance (because intellectual perfection is part of the religious goal) and that prophecy is secondary to the perfect philosopher, who receives divine illumination (*nūr) to see truth.

He reconciled the various modes of human reflection and enquiry by dividing the intellect (the extension of Being into the human) into three: the active intellect, the potential intellect and the acquired intellect. In this way he could affirm the equal validity of many human arts and skills. His *Kitāb al-Musiqa* (The Book of Music) laid the foundations for an Islamic theory of music, drawing attention to relations between mathematics and music; and his *Risalah fi ara' ahl alMadina al-fadilah* (Treatise on the . . . Virtuous City) was widely influential in the development of political science.

N. Rescher, *Al-Farabi: An Annotated Bibliography* (1962).

Alfasi, Isaac ben Jacob (known as Rif, 1013–1103). N. African codifier of Jewish law. His *Sefer ha-Halakhot* (Book of the Commandments) was the best known code before the *Mishneh Torah* (Second Law Code) of *Maimonides. It was much admired: as Maimonides wrote, 'The *Halakhot of the great *rabbi, our teacher Isaac of blessed memory . . ., contains all the decisions and laws we need in our day . . .'. The code extracted all the decisions from the *Talmud and summarized all the laws which remained relevant to the time. Joseph *Caro regarded Alfasi, Maimonides, and *Asher b. Jehiel as the three pillars of learning on which Judaism rested, and he used their work as a foundation for his own **Shulḥān Arukh* (Arranged Table).

al-Ghaz(z)ālī, Abū Hāmid Muḥammad (d. 1111 (AH 505)). The 'Proof of Islam' (*hujjat al-Islam*), often considered the greatest religious authority after the Prophet *Muḥammad. As a result of the esteem accorded to him by his contemporaries, al-Ghaz(z)ālī deeply influenced the direction of Islamic thought, in particular Islamic jurisprudence (*sharī'a), dialectical theology (*kalām), philosophy, and mysticism (*taṣawwuf).

He was born at Tūs and was educated there and at Nishapur. He rose to be a distinguished professor at the Baghdād Nizamiya, a formidable scholar in Islamic law and theology. However, in 1095, he underwent a crisis brought on by a search for inner conviction, and by an awareness that although he was lecturing *about* God, he did not know God. He therefore abandoned his high position for the life of a *Sūfī, seeking to know the reality of which, hitherto, he had only spoken. After ten years, he returned to Nishapur and wrote his *magnum opus*, *'Ihyā 'ulūm al-dīn* (The Revival of the Religious Sciences) and other key works, such as *Mishkāt al-anwār* (Niche of the Lamp), *al-Qistās al-mustaqīm* (The Just Balance), *Kīmiya' al-Sa'āda* (The Alchemy of Happiness), and *Tahāfut al-Falāsifah* (The Incoherence of the Philosophers) in which the inadequacy of reason outside its appropriate spheres points to the necessity for revelation and mystical knowledge. On three matters, faith concludes where reason cannot adjudicate: the eternity of the world; the specificity of God's knowledge; and the *resurrection of the body. Orthodoxy also led him to espouse *Occasionalism. In *Munqidh min al-Dalāl* (The Deliverance from Error), al-Ghaz(z)ālī recorded his own experience of inner conversion or change: 'That which is most distinctive of mysticism is something which cannot be apprehended by study, but only by immediate experience, by ecstasy and moral change. What a difference there is between knowing the definition of health and satiety (together with their causes and presuppositions) and being healthy and satisfied.' For al-Ghaz(z)ālī, speculative systems were no substitute for direct knowledge and divine illumination, and the highest seekers of knowledge are those who combine subjective and objective knowledge. Since mystical experiences are thus heightened levels of consciousness, they must, when the individual returns to ordinary consciousness, translate themselves into good works and actions. Thus al-Ghaz(z)ālī emphasized ethics in the attainment of truth and happiness. He also considered the ordinary person's simple devotion to be as important as the religious understanding of the élite: 'Trust the religion of the old women', he observed at the end of his life. He therefore supported Sūfī orders, with their populist support, as a form of social order that would preserve the Islamic spirit through difficult and turbulent times. It was his achievement that he successfully harmonized Sufism into the field of orthodoxy and gave it acceptance as an inner dimension of Islam. At the same time, his emphasis on the limits of reason in relation to faith led eventually to a withdrawal of Islam from the leadership it had given to the world in science and philosophy.

Trs. of various works: C. Field, W. H. T. Gairdner, S. A. Kamili, W. M. Watt; O. Leaman, *An Introduction to Medieval Islamic Philosophy* (1985); W. M. Watt, *Muslim Intellectual* . . . (1963).

al-Hakim (Druze holy figure): see DRUZES.

al-Halal wa'l-Harām. The permitted and the forbidden in Islam. This constitutes the fundamental division between what *Allāh permits and what he forbids. The creation principle *(asl)* is that everything which God has created is for human use (Qur'ān 2. 29; 31. 20; 45. 13), but that for specific reasons in each case, some things are prohibited, hence the *ḥadīth: 'What Allāh has made lawful in his Book is halal, and what he has forbidden is harām, and that concerning which he is silent is, by his mercy, allowed.' The 'map' of halal and haram is then the description of every aspect of Muslim life. The *exact* details may be disputed between the different schools of *sharīʿa, but to alter the categories in either direction is an offence as culpable as *shirk.

More particularly, the word halal is used as a short-hand for the permitted way of slaughtering animals—by severing blood-vessels, while naming the name of Allāh over the animal. This is usually done by cutting through the throat of the animal until the jugular veins are severed. The meat is then halal, permitted. Cf. SHEḤITAH.

Y. al-Qaradawi, *The Lawful and the Permitted in Islam* (n.d.).

al-Hallāj, Abu 'l-Mughīth al-Ḥusain b. Mansur (d. 922 (AH 309)). One of the most controversial figures in Islam: he was acclaimed as a saint by the masses and condemned as a heretic by the jurists. It is said that he was called Hallāj al-asrar (Carder of Consciences) because he could read the secret thoughts of others. He embraced the doctrine of *fanā' (extinction of personal consciousness) and other notions such as *hulul* (union and identity with God). Al-Hallāj aimed to bridge the abyss between humans and God: 'I am He whom I love and He whom I love is I. We are two spirits dwelling in one body. When you see me, you see Him.' However, to the jurists of his time, he appeared blasphemously to contradict the Islamic notion of *tanzīh (transcendence of God), and even to threaten the social order.

Al-Hallāj deliberately chose and taught the path of mystical union with God to shake the dry, 'lawbound' theologians of that era. He was a powerful public preacher, reducing many to tears with words which flowed from unmistakable experience: 'O you [who hear me], save me from God! He has ravished me from myself, and does not restore me to myself. Alas for anyone who finds himself abandoned after such a presence, alone after such a union.' He paid the supreme penalty for his choice. After many years of extensive teaching and travelling throughout Central Asia and India, he was arrested, imprisoned and finally brutally executed in Baghdād. His last words are treasured by the Sūfīs, who have made him their *martyr *par excellence*: 'Forgive the people, and do not forgive me. Do with me what you will . . . all who have known ecstasy long for this, alone with the Alone.' His only work to have survived is *Kitāb al-Tawāsīn* (902 CE). This contains the famous phrase *'ana' l-Haqq* (I am the Truth). It is important to read it in its proper context: 'If you do not recognize God, at least recognize his signs. I am that sign, I am the Creative Truth (*'ana' l-Haqq*) because through the Truth I am a truth eternally.' (*Kitāb al-Tawāsīn*, pp. 51–2). Cf. also AL-INSĀN AL-KĀMIL.

L. Massignon, *The Passion of al-Hallāj* . . . (1922; tr. 1981).

al-Ḥaqq (the True, i.e., God): see HAQQ.

al-Hasan b. 'Ali (d. 669–70 (AH 49)). Second *Shīʿa *Imam, son of *ʿAlī and *Fāṭima, and claimant to the Caliphate until he renounced the office in favour of *Muʿāwiyyah. As a child he was a particular favourite of his grandfather, the Prophet *Muḥammad. He is said to have physically resembled the

Prophet. According to traditional accounts, he was a mild, generous, peace-loving man, who evidently spent most of his youth making and unmaking marriages: about 100 are recorded, along with 300 concubines! Such deeds earned him the title of *al-mitlāq* (the Divorcer) and involved ʿAlī in serious enmities. After his father's assassination he was claimed Caliph, but upon realizing Muʿāwiyyah's strength and his own lack of military support (coupled with his distaste for bloodshed and war), he decided to stand down in favour of Muʿāwiyyah. Consequently, Muʿawiyyah rewarded him with a generous settlement and a subsidy of a million dirhams. The Shīʿa contend that Hasan was a *martyr by being poisoned to death by Muʿāwiyyah. However, this is unlikely since Muʿāwiyyah had already neutralized him and Muʿāwiyyah was not a man to commit an unnecessary crime when his design had already succeeded. It is more likely that he died of consumption.

al-Ḥasan b. al-Sabbah (d. 1124 (AH 518)). Founder of the *Nizārīs (popularly known as *Assassins). Very little is known of his early life. His followers captured the strong mountain fortress of Alamūt in 1091 (AH 483) and established it as a power centre of the Assassin movement. He did not introduce assassination as a religious duty, for it had already been practised by other sects; nor is it clear that he even advocated this. But from him derived a movement which gained considerable strength, and which terrorized parts of the Muslim world, until Alamūt was captured and destroyed by the *Mughals in the 13th cent.

ʿAl Het (Heb., 'for the sin'). First words of a Jewish prayer of confession recited on *Yom Kippur. ʿAl het consists of an alphabetical list of sins expressed in the first person plural. Each section concludes with the words, 'and for all these God of forgiveness, forgive us, pardon us, grant us *atonement'.

al-Ḥusain b. ʿAli (626–80 (AH 4–61)). Third *Shīʿa *Imām, known from his death as Sayyid al-Shuhadā', 'the Chief of Martyrs'. He was the son of *ʿAlī and *Fāṭima, and, acc. to numerous *ḥadīth, was much loved by *Muḥammad. During his youth, Ḥusain distinguished himself for his devotion and service to his father. He remained in the background during *Muʿāwiyya's reign, but refused to acknowledge Yazīd as heir-apparent. Upon Yazīd's accession (680), he escaped from *Madīna with his family and relatives to Mecca, and then headed for Kūfa to muster support for his cause. However, Ḥusain and his party were intercepted by Umayyad troops near Karbalā. They were surrounded, and cut off from access to water for ten days. On 10 Muḥarram, Ḥusain's weary supporters (92 males) gave battle against 4,000 soldiers. During the fierce engagement, Ḥusain's party was annihilated. The tragedy was worsened by the massacre of Ḥusain's male children and infants (only one young, sick son of Ḥusain, Zayn-al-Abidin survived), and by the rough treatment of the females of the Prophet's family. The magnitude of the violence committed on the Prophet's family shocked the Muslim world and raised questions about the nature of Umayyad rule, and the direction of Islam as a religion.

The Karbalā tragedy became the focus of the Shīʿa faith: Ḥusain, impelled by a desire to fulfil the demands of true Islam, had stood up against the evil Umayyads; his sacrifice was to redeem Islam, and to teach people the need of revolt against an unjust (*zalim*) government. Thus Ḥusain, along with ʿAlī, became the focus of a religio-political movement (i.e. Shīʿa) that sought the restoration of ʿAlī's descendants to the political leadership of the Islamic community. Sunni and Shīʿa sources agree that Ḥusain was a pious and fearless man, and that he spent his nights in religious devotions, possessed great humility and generosity. Furthermore, he was noted for his eloquence and nobility.

ʿAlī b. Abī Tālib (d. 661 (AH 40)). Cousin and son-in-law of the Prophet *Muḥammad, and the fourth Caliph (*Khalīfa) in Islam. ʿAlī was one of the ten to whom paradise was promised by Muḥammad. He distinguished himself in all the early battles as a courageous warrior and was consequently nicknamed Haidar (lion) and Murtada (he in whom God is well pleased). During the rule of the first three Caliphs, ʿAlī served as an adviser (e.g. over the adoption of the *hijra as the starting-point to the Islamic calendar). After ʿUthmān's murder, ʿAlī was proclaimed *khalīfa* (Caliph) by the Medinans. However, ʿAlī's reign was an unhappy and frustrating one, marked by the first civil war in Islamic history, the beginnings of the overt *Sunni/*Shīʿa split in Islam which persists to the present (Shīʿa being the party of ʿAlī). ʿAlī was opposed by the bulk of the Quraysh (Meccan ruling élite), the first group being led by *ʿĀ'isha (the Prophet's favourite wife) with Talha and Zubayr, who were easily defeated by ʿAlī. The second group, led by the astute *Muʿāwiyya (governer of Syria and kinsman of the murdered ʿUthmān) posed a serious threat, as Muʿāwiyya denied ʿAlī's legitimacy to the office of Caliph on the grounds of complicity in ʿUthmān's murder.

Inconclusive military conflict at Siffīn (657 (AH 37)) led to the famous incident where the Syrians hoisted copies of the Qur'ān on spears, and invited the combatants to resolve the problem by recourse to the Holy Book. ʿAlī was forced to accept arbitration by most of his army, and was thus politically outmanœuvred by Muʿāwiyya's stratagem. ʿAlī's support diminished, a section of his army rebelled (those averse to arbitration) and these were crushed at Nahrawan (658 (AH 38)). The remnants of this defeated group later became known as the *Kharijites. ʿAlī attempted a programme of internal reorganization of the Islamic state, but was continually beset by internal friction and the ever-present threat of war issuing from Syria. During ʿAlī's preparations for further battle, he was assassinated by a Kharijite in the mosque of Kūfa (661 (AH 40)).

Since the period of ʿAlī's caliphate is a controversial time in Islamic history, it is open to various interpretations. Both Sunni and Shīʿa sources agree that ʿAlī was a powerful orator, a leading authority on the Qur'ān and the *Sunna of the Prophet Muḥammad, and that his piety was beyond question. ʿAlī's sermons, lectures, and discourses have been preserved in *Nahj-ul-Balagha* (collected in the 11th cent.), which gives glimpses of his austere life: 'The world is carrion, whoever wants a part of it must be satisfied to live with dogs'; 'Blessed are those who renounce the world and only aspire for the world to come.' Both Shiʿa and *Sūfī sources exalt ʿAlī to a superhuman figure and trace their chain of transmission (*shijra*) back to him. Historically, it seems clear that ʿAlī played a large part in the creation of the Islamic state. However, while Muḥammad, *Abu Bakr, and *ʿUmar had displayed great pragmatism in the handling of worldly affairs, ʿAlī lacked political insight: on the assumption of authority, he reversed all of ʿUthmān's policies, appointed new governors, initiated a programme of tribal reorganization, and moved the capital to Kūfa which was the centre of political unrest and intrigue, meanwhile having no sound basis of support for implementing these ideals. The nomads, who constituted the bulk of ʿAlī's army, were not homogeneous; wild and unruly by habit, they took pride in their individuality. ʿAlī's opponents constituted the Quraysh élite, particularly the Umayyah clan who had proved their administrative skills in the rapidly expanding empire. The Syrian Arabs came, not from the desert, but from settled town dwellings, and were more stable and reliable than those on whom ʿAlī depended. Moreover Muʿawiyya possessed great skill in handling men and had proven himself an outstanding governor of Syria. The Arab-Islam polity could only function with the co-operation of the Quraysh. The Muʿawiyya/ʿAlī struggle had deeper implications for the Islamic community than merely the avenging of ʿUthmān's murder, or the dominion of Syria or Iraq; it opened up the two different directions of the Muslim community. ʿAlī's programme was utopian, looking for the pure Islamic state, whereas that of Muʿawiyya was more of a secular nature.

In Shiʿite understanding, ʿAlī is *walī Allah*, 'the friend of God', closest to him in sanctity. As such he is distinguished from Muḥammad, who is (merely!), *nabī, prophet. In a sermon on his return from his last *ḥajj, Muḥammad said: 'I leave among you two important things: the first and more important is the Qur'ān, the second is my family.' The family descent via ʿAlī designates the legitimate *Imām, which can never, for a Shiʿite, be a matter of election—the most fundamental division from the Sunnis.

G. Enkiri, *Les Deux Héros de l'Islam* (1969).

Ali Hujwīrī (Sūfī): see SŪFĪS.

al-Ikhwān al-Muslimūn. 'The Muslim Brotherhood', a religio-political movement founded in Egypt by *Ḥasan al-Bannā' (1904–49) in 1928. Its adherents urge a return to the fundamentals of Islam. The Ikhwan's main objectives were to free Egypt from British domination and then to establish an Islamic state in accordance with the *Qur'ān, dedicated to reforming Egyptian life; this would involve eliminating such Western influences as night-clubs, discos, casinos, and pornography. A parallel women's movement, 'The Muslim Sisters', seeks to restore the Islamic status of women. Between 1933 and 1953, the Ikhwan had a widely based popular following in Egypt. Their activities involved preaching in *mosques and public places, founding schools at various levels to combat illiteracy, organizing courses in religious education, building mosques, setting up hospitals and dispensaries in cities and villages, and even participating in industrial and commercial enterprises to increase the standard of living in Egypt. The Ikhwan's rising power posed a real threat to the military régime, and the movement was outlawed in 1954. Its leading cadre were executed after an attempt to assassinate President Nasser. Though under continual harassment by the authorities, the movement survived. After Egypt's humiliating defeat in the Six-Day War in 1967, the Ikhwan's slogan, 'Egypt's defeat is a sign of God's punishment for leaving the path of Islam', again brought it to the public's notice. President Sadat acknowledged the Ikhwan as a political party and tried to use them as a tool against the left, but the Ikhwan/Sadat alliance was broken when Sadat made the Camp David Accord with Israel, and they accused him of treachery against Islam and the Palestinian people. In 1981, Sadat was assassinated by a militant group within the Ikhwan, and again many of its leading members were executed or imprisoned. All previous attempts by the authorities to liquidate the Ikhwan have met with failure, for as soon as one group is eradicated, another springs up and takes its place. Moreover, persecution has increased their prestige and popularity amongst Egyptians, for they are honoured as martyrs in the defence of Islam and enjoy grassroot support.

I. M. Husaini, *The Moslem Brethren* (1956); R. P. Mitchell, *The Society of the Muslim Brothers* (1969).

al-Insān al-Kāmil (The Perfect Man). An expression perhaps first compounded by *Ibn ʿArabī in *Fuṣūṣ al-Ḥikam* (*Bezels of Wisdom*): 'Everything the world contains is subject to man. This is known to him who knows, that is to say, to the Perfect Man, and is not known by him who does not know, that is to say, to man the animal. He (The Perfect Man) is the mirror by which God is revealed to himself.' Ibn ʿArabī identified the Perfect Man with the Prophet *Muḥammad the archetype of the universe and humanity; the first symbol of the Lord was Nūr Muḥammad (Light of Muḥammad), and it is in him and through him that prophets and saints find their perfection. *'Abd al-Karīm al-Jīlī elaborated this notion further: 'The Perfect Man is the pole (*qutb) around which the spheres of existence turn, from the first to the last.' For al-Jīlī, he (the Perfect Man) is unique for all time but appears in different guises and names: there is no reincarnation but merely the irradiation of the reality of Muḥammad on each occasion upon the most perfect of men, who thus become Muḥammad's representatives on the plane of manifestation. In another development (cf. AL-HALLĀJ), the Creator (al-*Ḥaqq) and the Perfect Man (al-Ḥalq) are seen as complementary constituents of total or absolute Being: 'Man unites in himself both the form of God and the form of the universe . . . God is necessary to us in order that we may exist, but we are necessary to him in order that he may be manifested to himself' (Ibn 'Arabī). Such a way of union was of profound importance in *Sūfism.

'Aliyah (Heb., 'ascent'). 1. Emigrating from the *diaspora to the land of *Israel to become a permanent resident.

2. The calling up of a member of the congregation in a *synagogue to recite a *blessing or to read from the *Torah scroll (in full, ʿaliyah la-Torah).

3. Making *pilgrimage to *Jerusalem.

al-Jamāl wa'l-Jalāl (mercy and majesty): see NINETY-NINE BEAUTIFUL NAMES OF GOD.

al-Jīli (Jilāni) (Sūfī philosopher): see ʿABD AL-KARĪM AL-JĪLĪ; ʿABD AL-QĀDIR AL-JĪLĪ.

al-Junaid, Abū 'l-Qāsim (d. 910 (AH 298)). *Sūfī teacher, who influenced *al-Hallāj, and who laid the foundations of much of the development of Sufism. He studied at the *Shāfiʿite school of law in Baghdād, and first came in contact with Sufism through his uncle, Sarīʿ al-Saqatī. He was further instructed by *al-Muḥāsibī, and from both his instructors he received his strong insistence that religious law and orthodox behaviour and belief control Sūfī experience. He thus distanced himself from the extreme statements of such men as al-Hallāj, and has therefore been known as the advocate of 'sober Sufism'. Little of his own writing has survived, apart from fragments collected in a work given the general title of an Epistle, *Rasa'il*. He believed that because all things are derived from God as their creator, they will finally return to him and live in him. This 'return' is anticipated by the Sūfī in the state of *fanā'.

A. H. Abdel-Kader, *The Life, Personality and Writings . . .* (1976).

al-Khamriyya (The Wine Ode): See OMAR KHAYYAM.

al-Kharkī (Sūfī master): see MAʿRŪF AL-KARKHĪ.

al-Kursi (the footstool/throne of God): see KURSĪ; THRONE OF GOD.

Allāh. Arab. for God: if from earlier Semitic languages (e.g. Aram., *alāhā*), perhaps *the* God (Arab. *al* = 'the'). Before the birth of *Muḥammad, Allah was known as a supreme, but not the sole, God. Muḥammad became aware, early in his life, of conflict between religions and of contest, therefore, between 'gods'. From his experience in the cave on Mount *Ḥirā' (with possible influence from *ḥanīfs), Muḥammad saw that if God is God, it is God that God must be: there cannot be division of God into separate or competing beings. From this absolute realization of *tawḥīd (oneness of God), the whole of Islam is derived—as indeed is the whole of the created order. Hence the fundamental mark of *islām* (allegiance to God) is the *shahāda, *lā ilāha illā Allāh* . . . This involves Islam in necessary conflict with polytheism, idolatry, and what was taken to be the Christian understanding of the *Trinity.

In the *Qur'ān, Allah is described by many epithets, contributing eventually to the *ninety-nine beautiful names of God. Controlling all are the two descriptions (occurring in the *basmala) *rahmān* (merciful) and *rahīm* (compassionate). In later Islam, fierce arguments developed: about the status of the attributes of God (too much status would confer ontological, or truly existent, reality on them, thus converting them into something like independent parts of God); about anthropomorphic statements (e.g. the Qur'ān says that God sits on a *throne: to take this literally would limit God in space. This particular issue was resolved agnostically by saying that he does so, *bilā kaifa wa lā *tashbīh*, without knowing how and without comparison, sc. with our way of sitting; and also by *tanzīh); and about the power of God to determine all things. This last issue is focused on the term *qadar. The Qur'ān emphasizes the absolute power of God to determine all things, which suggests strong *predestination (as held e.g. by the Jabriya); in that case, how can humans be held accountable for their deeds and be judged accordingly (the question raised e.g. by the Muʿtazilites)? The eventual solution (at least for the Ashʿarites (acquisition) was formulated in the doctrine of *iktisāb*, see AL-ASHʿARI).

Theological and rational reflection on God is complemented, in Islam, by the direct and immediate relation of the believer with God, above all in *salāt: to everyone, God is closer than the vein in the neck (50. 16). This close and direct relation to God led into the cultivation of the experiential awareness of God, which culminated in *Sūfism. The sense among Sūfīs of the presence of God everywhere and not least in the self seemed at times to carry with it *pantheistic implications (see e.g. AL-HALLĀJ), and might have led to tension with the practical and obedient side of Islam associated with *sharīʿa. Yet in fact the two remained close to each other, not least because of the work of reconciliation undertaken by *al-Ghaz(z)ālī.

For the controlling and all-important Sūra of

Unity (112), which, if a Muslim says it with conviction, leads to the shedding of sins as a tree sheds its leaves in autumn, see TAWḤĪD.

Allāhābād (Hindu place of pilgrimage): see PRAYĀGA.

Allāhu Akbar. 'God is great' (literally, 'greater'), fundamental and repeated proclamation by Muslims of the absolute supremacy of God.

al-Lāt. Meccan goddess, apparently recognized in the verse of the *Qur'ān insinuated by Shaitān/ *Satan, but repudiated by *Muḥammad. See SATANIC VERSES.

al-Lawḥ (tablet): see UMM AL-KITĀB.

Allegory

Judaism A narrative expressing abstract ideas as concrete symbols; a description of a topic or subject under the guise of another which is suggestive of it, an extended comparative metaphor. There is little distinction in biblical Heb. between an allegory, a *parable, a simile, or a metaphor. Many of the *prophets used allegory, such as *Ezekiel's description of sheep and shepherds referring to the kings of *Israel (34. 2–16). The *Song of Songs has been interpreted allegorically, as a description of the relationship between God and his people. The Bible furnishes further examples in Isaiah 5. 1–7 and Daniel 7. Allegory is also to be found in *Talmudic and *kabbalistic literature. It was especially prominent in *Philo, who regarded allegory as 'the rules of a wise architect'. Yet he also insisted that the literal sense and practice must be maintained (see e.g. *De Abrahamo*, 89–93).

Christianity Allegorical exegesis is that which treats a text as if it were an allegory, and was thus important for Christians as a way of relating Jewish scripture (from their point of view, the Old Testament) to Christianity.

Allegorical exegesis is already apparent in the gospels (e.g. Mark 4. 14–20). It became part of the classic medieval theory of Old Testament exegesis, according to which a text has four senses: the literal, allegorical (applying it to Christ or the Church), tropological (applying it to the soul and its virtues), and *anagogical (applying it to heavenly realities). Modern scholarship generally repudiates the allegorical interpretation of the Bible, but it may occasionally be heard, especially in sermons. In modern usage it is often distinguished from *typology.

Alleluia, Lat. and Gk. form of the acclamation *hallelujah, used in many places in Christian worship. In Catholic but not Orthodox practice, it is omitted from the liturgy at certain penitential times of the year.

Allen, Richard (first bishop of the African Methodist Episcopal Church): see AFRICAN METHODIST EPISCOPAL CHURCH.

All Saints' Day. The feast which celebrates *all* the Christian *saints, whether known by name or not. The date in the W. is 1 Nov., and in the E. the first Sunday after *Pentecost. The W. 'All Souls' Day' is a commemoration of the faithful departed on the following day (or on 3 Nov. if 2 Nov. is a Sunday); the *mass on this day, as in *requiem masses, includes the *sequence **Dies irae*.

Almagest (Lat. form of Arab., *al-majisti*, which in turn is the Arab. form of Gk. *megalē syntaxis*). Ptolemy's work on astronomy, which became the basis of the extensive Muslim work in that field. It was through the Muslim/Arab. appropriation of Ptolemy that Ptolemy was reintroduced into medieval Europe. The term also became a general word for any of the great medieval works on other topics, e.g. *alchemy.

al-Mahdī (Arab., 'the guided one'). In *Sunni Islam, one who receives guidance from God (God is al-Hādī, the Guide, Qur'ān 22. 54; 25. 31). The term may apply to figures in the past (e.g. the first four caliphs; see KHALĪFA; cf. AR-RĀSHIDŪN), or to those who revive Islam, but more often it refers to a future, *eschatological figure, who will come to herald in the end of all things. This may be ʿĪsā/ *Jesus, who will restore the observance of Islam after a period of decline, when the *Kaʿba will have disappeared and copies of the *Qur'ān will have become blank paper. The belief in al-Mahdī as the future Restorer is not essential in Sunni Islam, but it is nevertheless widely held at a popular level.

In Shīʿa Islam, even stronger beliefs surrounding al-Mahdī as the hidden Imām, who will emerge at the end of time, developed among the Twelvers (*Ithna ʿAshariy(y)a). The twelfth Imām, ʿAli ibn Muḥammad Simmarī, was born in Samarra' in 869 (AH 255). On the death of his father in AH 260, he became Imām but was kept in seclusion (the first so-called occultation, *ghaiba, *ghaibat-i-sughra*), being seen (if at all) on rare occasions only by senior figures. He answered questions through a succession of deputies (*wakīl*). Shortly before the death of the fourth *wakīl* in 939 (AH 329), it was announced that there would be no further Imām, that the major occultation would occur (*ghaibat-i-kubra*), and that the Imām would remain hidden until God gave him permission to manifest himself. This is in accord with a *ḥadīth which says: 'If there were but one day remaining for the world, God would lengthen that day until he sends to it a man from my [*Muḥammad's] house and community. His name will be the same as mine. He will fill the earth with justice and equity where before it was filled with tyranny and injustice.' Meanwhile, the hidden Imām gives guidance, hears prayers, and intercedes. al-Mahdī is also known as Imām-i-ʿAṣr (the Imām of the Period), al-Muntazar (the Awaited), and Ṣāḥib al-Zamān (the Lord of the Age). See also MUḤAMMAD AḤMAD (the Mahdi of the Sudan).

A. A. Sachedina, *Islamic Messianism* (1980).

al-Majlisī, Muḥammad Bāqir ibn Muḥammad al-Tāqī (1628–99 (AH 1038–1111)). Leading *Shiʿite theologian (ʿalim, see *ʿulamā), whose opinions became a formative influence on the development of Twelver Shiʿite (*Ithna ʿAshariyya) practice and organization. He was strongly opposed to the rationalizing of religion through philosophy, to the *Sūfīs and to the Sunnis, whom he saw as intransigent competitors, and whom he succeeded in persuading the Shah to have banned from Isfahan. He wrote in Persian as well as Arabic, and thus secured a far wider audience for his fierce support for the Twelvers. His major work was *Biḥār al-anwār* (The Ocean of Lights), a many-volumed work assembling *ḥadīth. He encouraged, both the cult of the *Imāms, and the elaboration of rituals (e.g. the devotion to the martyrs, *shahīd) and pilgrimages. His opposition to the Sunnis may have induced the Afghan invasion of 1722, but this in turn opened the way to the reconquest by the Qajars: they established a dynasty in 1794 (AH 1209) which endorsed the programme of al-Majlisī, making Teheran the capital. They in turn were overthrown by Reza Khan, whose short-lived Pahlavi dynasty could not possibly capture the Shiʿite devotion of the old order, still less displace the authority of the Hidden Imām exercised through the *mullas as al-Majlisī had established it. Part of his *Ḥayat al-Qulūb* was translated by J. Merrick, *The Life and Religion of Mohammed* (1850).

K.-H. Pampus, *Die theologische Enzyklopädie . . .*, (1970).

Almanac. Especially in China, an annually published lunar calendar containing weather and harvest prognostications, lucky and unlucky days, festival dates and birthdays of the gods, moral maxims, and, most thumbed, a variety of fortune-telling systems. As an extended set of written instructions and diagrams for synchronizing human activity with the cosmic order of the universe, almanacs were popularly accorded the dignity of literature and the efficacy of protective charms. In the West, almanacs were originally connected with *astrology, suggesting a rational order in the cosmos. Almanacs mediated this to a large readership, combining the encyclopaedic with the sermonizing and moralizing. Their influence was as wide as their scope: 'The almanac-makers of early modern England boldly took as their subject the whole of Creation' (B. Copp, *Astrology and the Popular Press*, 1979).

al-Masīḥ (name for Jesus in Islam): see MESSIAH (ISLAM).

al-Māturīdī, Abū Mansūr Muḥammad (d. 944 (AH 333)). Contemporary of *al-Ashʿarī, and founder (like him) of an important school of orthodox, conservative theology, which admitted a place for human reason, but not a paramount one. He therefore attacked the *Muʿtazilites, using their own styles of argument to defeat them. The differences between Ashʿarites and Maturidites were reckoned as thirteen, of which the most substantial was the former's emphasis on the absolute power of the will of *Allāh, and the latter's emphasis that humans have freedom and responsibility. Thus the Ashʿarites must say, 'I am a believer if God wills' (*'insh'Allah*), but the Muʿtazilites can say, 'I know with truth [*ḥaqqan*] that I am a believer'. Even so, al-Ashʿarī could endorse a (slightly different) doctrine of acquisition (*kasb*: see QADAR). al-Māturīdī affirmed the attributes of God as found in the *Qur'ān, though he accepted that we cannot 'know how' (i.e. bilā kaif: see ALLĀH) God sits on his throne, etc.

Almemar. Platform in *synagogue where the reading stand is placed. In *Ashkenazi circles, it is usually described as the *bimah, and among the *Sephardim as the *tebah*.

Almohads (Arab., *al-muwwaḥḥidūn*, 'those who espouse Oneness'). Spanish name of a Muslim dynasty in N. Africa and Spain, 1130–1269 (AH 524–667). Their name summarizes their character as protestants against the lax style of prevailing Islam, especially under the *Almoravids. They derived their inspiration from *ibn Tumart, but it was his successor, ʿAbd al-Mu'min, who extended territorial control. In 1170 (AH 566) Muslim Spain fell to them, and they made Seville their capital (for a time). Under the Almohads, both philosophy and architecture flourished (e.g. *ibn Tufayl, *ibn Rushd, and *ibn ʿArabī). The 'Almohad arch' is sometimes interpreted as a physical manifestation of sūra 94 in the *Qur'ān, 'Did we not widen your chart for you and lift from you your burden, the burden that was breaking your back?' The Grand Mosque in Seville, the Giralda, is now a cathedral, but still illustrates the vision. After their defeat at Las Navas de Tolosa in 1212 (AH 609), their eclipse was only a matter of time.

Almoravids (Arab., *al-murābiṭūn*, 'those who espouse defence'). Spanish name of a Muslim dynasty in N. Africa and Spain, 1056–1147 (AH 448–541). Initially a rigorist revival movement in Sudan under ʿAbd Allāh ibn Yāsīn, the territorial expansion set out from a ribāṭ (fortress for the defence of Islam) in the Niger. Invited into Spain, the Almoravids defeated Alfonso VI at Sagrajas in 1086 (AH 479)—thereby initiating among Christians a determination to create a more united front against Islam. From their initial austerity and zeal, the Almoravids declined into a more lax and ostentatious lifestyle, until supplanted by the *Almohads—providing thereby a consummate illustration of *ibn Khaldūn's theory of recurrent patterns in historical and social change.

Almsgiving. A work of merit, and sometimes of obligation, in most religions. In part, it establishes reciprocity, as in the N. American Kwakiutl potlatch ceremony, where 'a whole people was caught up in an exchange system that conferred greatest prestige on the individual who gave away the greatest amount of the most valuable goods' (M. Harris, *The Rise of Anthropological Theory*, 1968, which summarizes, pp. 306 f. the interest of anthropologists in potlatch: see also M. Mauss, *The Gift*, 1909, 1959). In terms of reciprocity, the formality of exchange issued in systems of merit, whereby especially benefits could be transferred to the dead (see e.g. DĀNA; INDULGENCE). In Buddhism, this was elaborated into a social structure of mutual support between laity and *saṅgha. But equally, almsgiving is evoked by a religious sense of charity, where there is no calculation of consequence beyond the good of the recipient. This is prominent in Judaism and in important respects (though it is blurred by issues of reward) in Christianity. In Islam, *zakāt is an obligation, and one of the *Five Pillars.

al-Muḥāsibī ('he who examines his conscience'), Abū 'Abd Allāh Ḥārith (*c.*781–857 (AH 165–243)). *Shāfi'ite theologian who turned to ascetic renunciation and moral purification, and is regarded as the first *Sunni mystic (*Sūfī) to organize a theologically systematic approach to God. He placed much emphasis on the Day of Judgement, but balanced it with a vision of the glory of the heavenly reward. He was a prolific writer, with about 200 works ascribed to him. His *Kitāb al-ri'āya li-ḥuqūq Allah* (The Book of Observance of that which is Owed to God) is a book of spiritual advice, which includes the importance of self-examination (Arab., *muḥāsaba*), hence his name.

al-Nasā'ī, Abu 'Abd al-Raḥmān Aḥmad (d. 915 (AH 303)). Muslim collector of *Ḥadīth: his collection became one of the six Ṣaḥīḥ (Sound) collections. He lived first in Egypt, then in Damascus. His collection is concerned with details in the application of law, and was admired particularly by the *Shāfi'ites.

al-Naẓẓām, Ibrahīm b. Saiyār (d. *c.*840 (AH 225)). Leading *Mu'tazilite theologian and accomplished poet. In some ways, he is closer to the eventual position of al-Ash'arī than other Mu'tazilites, especially in his emphasis on *Qur'ān as the only source of theology and ethics, and in his willingness to recognize restrictions on human freedom within the limits set by God (cf. kasb in QADAR). But he was strongly rejected, even by other Mu'tazilites, for his dogmatic style.

al-Niffarī, Muḥammad (d. *c.*965 (AH 354)). *Sūfī who developed the notion of *waqfa*, a condition in which the mystic hears God directly—and perhaps is moved to write automatically at God's will. He claimed also that the vision of God is possible in this world.

Tr. A. J. Arberry, 1935.

Alobha (Pāli). Being without greed, one of the three root or conditioning attitudes which produce good *karma in Buddhism.

A-lo-pen (7th cent. CE). Chinese name of a Persian Christian monk who was a missionary in China. According to a stele discovered by Jesuits in 1625, the emperor Tai-tsung (627–50) gave permission to A-lopen and sixty-seven others to work as missionaries in Sian-fu. Nestorian missions established an extensive church which was ended by Ming persecutions.

Alphonsus Liguori (moral theologian): see LIGUORI.

al-Qadam al-Sharīf (the noble footprint, i.e. example, of Muḥammad): see FOOTPRINT OF MUḤAMMAD.

al-Qamar (the crescent moon): see CRESCENT MOON.

al-Quds (the Holy [Place]): see JERUSALEM (ISLAM).

al-Rāshidūn (first four 'rightly guided' caliphs in Islam): see KHALĪFA.

al-Rāzī, Abū Bakr Muḥammad ibn Zakariyyā (850–925 (AH 236–313)). Muslim philosopher, physician, and pre-eminent medical writer; in Europe he became known as Rhazes (Rasis in Chaucer). He learnt medicine in Baghdād where he spent most of his career. He wrote a large number of books, including *Kitāb al-Mansūrī* (tr. into Lat. as *Liber Almansoris*), *Kitāb al-Mulūkī* (*Liber Regius*) and a vast encyclopaedia, completed after his death by his pupils, *Hāwī* (*Continens*, first tr. in 1279 and later one of the first books to be printed, five times between 1488 and 1542). He recognized the complexity of causes in the case of illnesses, and was aware that the will of the patient played so prominent a part that charlatans could often effect cures (though the competence of physicians was in any case limited). He placed great emphasis on reason ('The Creator, praised be his name, bestowed upon us reason and gave it to us in order that we might thereby attain and achieve every benefit that it lies within our nature to attain and achieve, whether in this world or the next'), and in one of his books, on prophecy, claimed that reason is of a higher order than prophecy; the book has not survived. He ended his days blind, and refused treatment, saying that he had been in the world so long that he had seen enough of it.

A. J. Arberry, *The Spiritual Physick of Rhazes* (1950).

al-Rāzī, Fakhr al-Dīn (1149–1209 (AH 543–606)). Prominent Muslim theologian and philosopher, who contested *Mu'tazilites until compelled into exile, eventually settling in Herāt. There he founded a *madrasa and was accorded the title of *Shaykh al-Islām. He attracted many pupils, but because of his determination to show how theology and philosophy can be reconciled, he was accused by some of betraying Islam. His death may have been caused by poison.

al-Sādiq, Jaʿfar (sixth Shīʿa Imām): see ISMĀʿĪLIYYA.

al-Sanūsī, Sīdī Muḥammad (1791–1859 (AH 1206–76)). Founder of the Sanūsiya order (the Senusis). After a period in *Mecca, he returned to N. Africa, and at Jaghbūb, made freed slaves welcome. He was initiated into *Qadiriya mysticism, and attempted to harmonize orthodox practice with mystical attainment, with special emphasis on *dhikr.

al-Shāfiʿi, Abū ʿAbd Allāh Muḥammad (d. 820 (AH 204)). Founder of the *Shāfiʿite school of Muslim law (*sharīʿa). He was taught by *Mālik b. Anas (amongst many others), but differed from him in paying particular attention to the methods of applying Qur'ān and *sunna, and for that reason is regarded as the founder of uṣūl al-*fiqh (the principles of fiqh). Thus he attempted to establish rules governing the exercise of *qiyās (analogy); but having done so, he was prepared to use it to establish a middle way between conservative traditionalism and innovation.

al-Shaikh al-Akbar: see IBN (AL)-ʿARABĪ.

al-Shaybānī, Muḥammad b. al-Ḥasan: see HANAFITES.

al-Shaytan: see SATAN (ISLAM).

al-Shibli, Abū Bakr Dulaf b. Jahdar (*c*.861–945 (AH 247–334)). *Sūfī mystic of Baghdād. He was originally a high government official but turned to the mystic life at the age of 40. Although he belonged to *al-Junaid's sober school of Sufism, he distinguished himself as an extreme and eccentric Sūfī, whose excessive behaviours and practices (e.g. rubbing salt in his eyes to prevent sleep) led to his committal to a lunatic asylum, where he would offer discourses on the Sūfī way to distinguished visitors from all over the Muslim world. Shibli also gained fame for condemning *al-Hallāj, even at the scaffold, for the reason that he had divulged esoteric secrets to the uninitiated masses. He left no works, but his aphorisms and mystical utterances have been preserved in the classical Sūfī literature such as *Kashf al-Mahjūb* (Unveiling of the Hidden) by al-Hujwiri. Shibli is an important link in the transmission chain (silsilah) of many of the Sūfī orders. His tomb in Baghdād is still venerated.

al-Sirhindī: see SŪFĪS.

al-Tabarī, abū Jaʿfar Muḥammad ibn Jarīr (*c*.839–923 (AH 224–310)). Prominent Muslim scholar, best known for his history of the world, *Ta'rīkh al-Rusul wa'l-Mulūk* (Chronicle of Apostles and Kings). He also composed a vast commentary (*tafsīr) on the *Qur'ān, in which he gathered together earlier exegesis on an equally large scale. It became a standard work of reference for later exegetes, and is used to the present day. He also founded a school of *sharīʿa, known as Jariyya, but it was so close to the *Shāfiʿites that it did not persist.

Altar (Lat., *altare*, 'to raise up'). A structure, often raised, either natural or humanly made, usually with a flat surface, on which offerings are made to God or gods. Because of the association with sacrifice, it became an issue in Christianity whether the structure on which the *elements for the *eucharist/ *mass/*Lord's Supper (the diverse names express the same dispute) are set and prepared, should be called 'the table' or 'the altar', and whether the structure should be free-standing as a table, or should be a solid structure made of stone or metal. Until the *General Instruction of the Missal* of Pope *Paul VI no longer made the practice obligatory, *relics of *martyrs were incorporated into RC altars, thus reinforcing the association with sacrifice. In Hinduism, the *vedi* (altar) is the centre of the world, *axis mundi*, because the divine comes into the world at that point. Instructions for the construction and ordering of altars are contained in **Śatapatha Brāhmaṇa* and **Yajur Veda*. They were often constructed with an hour-glass shape, like that of a woman's torso, thus emphasizing the life-giving function of the altar. Altars were a feature of ancient Near Eastern worship, and thus long precede the altars of the *Jerusalem *Temple. Although prophets contested local altars, and Deuteronomy attempted to centralize all worship in *Jerusalem, it is clear that the *patriarchs and tribes frequented them. When the Jerusalem Temple was built, the *tabernacle contained an altar in the courtyard as well as one in the tent, and there is a full description of the sacrificial altar in the vision of a new temple in Ezekiel 43: 13–17, which possibly corresponded to one remembered in *Solomon's Temple. It was believed that temple and *sacrifice were only legitimate in the Jerusalem sanctuary, and after the destruction of this in 70 CE, the family table in the home took the place of the sacrificial altar: 'Now that there is no altar, a man's table atones for him' (*B. Ber.* 55a).

Christianity The designation of the *eucharistic table as an altar has been general in Catholic Christianity since the 2nd cent. It gave rise to controversy at the Reformation, however, owing to its association with the doctrine of the *sacrifice of the mass. Protestants in general do not use it, preferring to speak of 'the table', as of the Last Supper. The earliest 'altars' were presumably of wood, if they were tables in private houses; stone altars may be derived from the celebration of the eucharist on the tombs of *martyrs, from this custom also derives the rule in RC churches (until 1977) that all altars should contain relics. In the W., the practice of celebrating private masses led to churches having more than one altar, the original one being then known as the 'high altar'. In the E., the major components were laid down before the schism of East and West: altars are usually made of stone (sometimes of wood). The word *bēma* (Gk., 'altar') may refer to the whole sanctuary, *hiera/hagia trapeza* ('sacred/holy table') being reserved for the altar. In some Churches (e.g. E. Syrian, W. Syrian) there may be more than one altar, for prayer and for the *gospel, as well as for the eucharist.

Hinduism The Skt. *pīṭha* ('seat') is the stand on which rest representations of divinity; *vedi* is the elevated ground (or sometimes trench) where offerings are made. The orientation of the altar, representing the six directions, was as important as its construction, which should be if feasible of brick (hence the Jewish early synonym for idolatry, 'setting up a brick'; see J. Bowker, *Targums and Rabbinic Judaism*, 1969, on *Ps. Philo* 6. 2). The home hearth (*āyatana*) is of paramount importance for family ritual.

Altar of Earth. A structure built to the north of the old Inner City of Beijing (Peking) in 1530 CE, as a counterpart in symmetrical relationship to the *Altar of Heaven in the south. The original name of the complex was *fang tse* (literally, 'square watery place') altar, indicating that Sovereign Earth, worshipped there by late Ming and Ch'ing emperors on the summer solstice, was conceived as the chthonic spirit which ruled over the entire sublunary world, and thus the counterpart of Heaven. The most important element in the complex was the two-tiered and square altar, surrounded by a moat, on which the Emperor worshipped Sovereign Earth, together with the other important earthly spirits: the four seas, the four rivers, and various mountains deemed especially sacred in Chinese tradition. In building the altar, the *yin or earthly numbers of six and eight and their multiples were repeatedly used. Throughout most of Chinese history, there was no separate Altar of Earth. The spirits of both Heaven and Earth were worshipped together at the Altar of Heaven, and the construction of the northern altar came as a result of ritual controversies which took place in the late Ming dynasty during the Chia Ching reign period (1522–60 CE).

Altar of Heaven. An architectural complex located south of the old Inner City of Beijing (Peking), just to the east of the north–south axial way. Venerated Chinese writings such as the *Classic of History* and the *Book of Rites* mention the Shang and early Chou emperors worshipping at 'suburban altars', and each of the succeeding dynasties built an Altar of Heaven south of their capital city for this purpose. Although Beijing's Altar of Heaven, as the most recent example, contains the often photographed 'Temple of Heaven' together with many other buildings in its spacious grounds, the most important structure was the Altar of Heaven itself, a roofless, three-tiered circular platform constructed of concentric circles of paving stones. Numerical symbolism was prevalent, particularly the yang (see YIN-YANG) or heavenly numbers of nine, five, three, and the cosmic numbers 72, 108, 360. On this platform, the greatest imperial sacrifice was offered each year, in the pre-dawn darkness on the day of the winter solstice. Surrounded by his retinue of ministers, courtiers, and members of the royal family, the Emperor faced north and worshipped *Shang-Ti, the God of Heaven, and the other heavenly spirits: those of the sun, moon, stars, clouds, rain, wind and thunder. See also ALTAR OF EARTH.

Altered States of Consciousness. Neurophysiological states in which ordinary consciousness is suspended or replaced by other states. In this broad sense, sleep itself is an altered state of consciousness, but the phrase is used more often of induced states, ranging from those induced by drugs to those induced by meditation practices. Controversy has arisen over whether the states so induced are identical, or whether there is a difference in those which occur in religious contexts. However, the debate has made it clear that the phrase itself may be a category mistake, by giving the impression that there are discrete brain states which can be subsumed under this single heading.

Alternative Service Book 1980. *Church of England service-book. It is an 'alternative' to the *Book of Common Prayer to which it corresponds in content, and which it has extensively replaced in use. The 'ASB' services embody liturgical changes introduced for theological and historical reasons, and (most obviously in 'Holy Communion Rite A') they modernize the 16th-cent. language of the BCP. The book embodies twenty-five years of committee-work as well as revisions by the General Synod; its language has accordingly been criticized as prosaic and awkward.

al-Tirmidhī, Abu ʿĪsā Muḥammad (d. *c.*889 (AH 275)). Author of one of the six authoritative collections of *ḥadīth, which is known sometimes as *Ṣaḥīḥ*, but more often as *Jāmiʿ*. As well as traditions on law, much space is devoted to religion and theology. He was attentive to the reliability of the *isnād, as well as the content, and, as a result, his collection is shorter (and less repetitious) than those of *al-Bukhārī and *Muslim. Of his life, virtually nothing is known, except that he was either born blind, or became blind in later life.

al-Ṭūsī, Muḥammad ibn Ḥasan (995–1067 (AH 385–460)). Leading *Shiʿite scholar. Born in Ṭūs (hence the name), he played an important part in stabilizing the religion in practice after the occultation of the twelfth *Imām. He collected Shiʿite traditions in *al-Istibṣār* (The Examination) and in *Taḥdhīb al-Aḥkām* (The Correcting of Judgements), which form part of the 'Four Books' of authoritative traditions. Even more influential was his *Kitāb al-Nihāya* (The Book of Method), which lays out the basis of Shiʿite legal procedure, and which became the foundation of a legal school which endured for centuries after his death. After riots, during which his library was burnt, he moved to al-Najaf where he died.

al-Ṭūsī, Nasīr al-Dīn (1201–74 (AH 598–673)). Shiʿite scholar and theologian. Born in Ṭūs (hence the name), he worked under an *Ismāʿīlī ruler in Alamūt (the centre for the *Assassins), and wrote Ismāʿīlī works of accepted and great authority, but his own personal allegianace is uncertain. When the *Mughals, under Hūlāgū Khān, captured Alamūt in 1256, he worked under Hūlāgū as an astrologer—and saved many libraries from destruction. He compiled the astronomical tables known as *Zīj al-Khānī*, and introduced into astronomy 'the Ṭūsī couple'. Writing on virtually all subjects, his most enduring works were *al-Akhlāq al-Nāsiriyya* (1235, The Nasiriyyan Ethics) and *Tajrīd al-Iʿtiqādāt* (The Definition of the Articles of Faith).

al-Tustarī (Muslim theologian and mystic): see SAHL AL-TUSTARĪ.

Alumbrados (Span., also known from Lat., as *Illuminati). Movements for reform, based on personal holiness and enlightenment, in 16th/17th cent. Spain. At least three different groups have been identified, attracting both educated and uneducated adherents. Because of their supposed connection with *Lutheranism, they were fiercely persecuted by the *Inquisition; yet prominent figures (e.g. *Ignatius Loyola, *John of the Cross, *Teresa of Avila) were all accused of illuminism, illustrating how close were the goals of holiness for these diverse figures.

A. Hamilton, *Heresy and Mysticism in 16th Century Spain* (1992).

A-luo-ben (Persian Christian monk): see A-LO-PEN.

Āḻvārs (Tamil, 'saintly masters'). A group of (allegedly) twelve Hindu poets of the 6th to 9th cent. CE from South India. They wrote in the vernacular *Tamil on *Viṣṇu/*Kṛṣṇa religion, and their works were collected in the **Nāl-āyira-divya-prabandham*. Like their *Śaivite contemporaries (the *Nāyaṇmār), they promulgated a new, *bhakti-oriented form of religion in the South which soon gained enormous popularity. This upsurge of Hindu devotionalism has to be seen against the background of an earlier Jain and Buddhist dominance and the emergence of two new kingdoms (the Pāṇḍyas in Maturai, and the Pallavas in Kāñcī) which were consciously 'Hindu'. They absorbed a large number of religious professionals after the collapse of the Gupta empire in the 6th cent. CE who built a large number of Viṣṇu (and *Śiva) temples to accommodate the immigrant *brahmans. These temples with their images of Viṣṇu (see *arcâvatāra*, in AVATĀRA) provided the concrete setting for most of Āḻvār religion, which in content derives from classical texts like **Bhagavad-gītā*. The poems reveal a knowledge of most of the ('classical ten') avatāras, but due to the influence of earlier *Māyōṉ cults, the emphasis is predominantly on Kṛṣṇa (whose status in relation to Viṣṇu remains rather nebulous). At least from the time of *Nammāḻvār, who is the most outstanding in the group as theologian, mystic, and poet, the much older and originally secular poetic tradition of the Tamil *caṅkam* literature is used to give form to a religious poetry of high sophistication and intense eroticism. As far as Āḻvār theology is concerned, it can be regarded as preshadowing in various ways the later school tradition of *Śrī-Vaiṣṇavism which, however, adopted a very different form of devotion, shunning the erotic, ecstatic, and aesthetic features of the Āḻvārs in favour of sober *prapatti, meditation, and ritual. The Śrī-Vaiṣṇavas accepted the Āḻvārs in their lineage of past teachers, and evolved both a large store of legendary accounts of their lives and a theological interpretation of them. Here they are regarded as avatāras of various weapons which Viṣṇu wields, and of heavenly beings like *Lakṣmī, and this is set in the context of Viṣṇu's desire to be as close as possible to humanity. The same desire motivates the temple-images, and the choice of the vernacular Tamil for the poems dedicated to them. The legends are colourful, but lack the more violent aspects of *Śaivite *hagiography. They tell, for example, about Parakālaṉ, a robber-knight who used his plundered wealth to feed devotees of Viṣṇu and build temples; about Āṇṭāḷ who refused to get married to any mortal man and chose Viṣṇu of Śrī-Raṅgam as her husband; or about the untouchable Pāṇ, a musician who through divine intervention was allowed inside that same temple. Very little biographical information can be found here; and also what the Āḻvārs themselves tell us (in the stereotyped concluding stanzas of a poem) is very meagre. No external historical document about them is known. The traditional number is twelve, but because not all poems are 'signed' (in the concluding stanza), this cannot be verified from the *Divya-Prabandham* itself. Many of the traditional names by which they are referred to are honorific titles and differ from the names actually mentioned. The most important Āḻvārs are: *Nammāḻvār ('Our Saintly Master', real name: Caṭakōpaṉ); Tirumaṅkai-Āḻvār ('the Saintly Master from the region of Tirumaṅkai [near modern Sirkazhi]', real names: Parakālaṉ, Kalikaṉṟi); Periyâḻvār ('the Great Saintly Master', real name: Viṭṭucittaṉ); Āṇṭāḷ ('the Lady', real name: Kōtai); and Kulacēkaraṉ ('Peak of his Lineage', his real name). Thus there is one woman among them (Āṇṭāḷ, allegedly the adopted daughter of Periyâḻvār). No more than three belong definitely to the *brahman *varna (who, at the same time, are the most colloquial, popular poets), two could have been rulers (chieftains or petty kings), and one a *śūdra landlord (Nammālvār, the most complex and sophisticated poet of the group). All this suggests that we are not dealing here with a popularist, mass movement attacking brahman élitism, but on the contrary with a non-brahman élite which only through brahman contributions acquired a wider and more popular dimension. see also *Bhāgavata-Purāṇa*.

Tr. of Nammālvār, A. K. Ramanujan (1981); see also F. E. Hardy, *Virahabhakti*, pp. 239–479; J. S. M. Hooper, *Hymns of the Ālvārs* (1929).

Alwah (works of prophet-founder of Bahā'ī Faith): see BAHĀ'U'LLĀH.

al-Zamakhsharī, Abu'l-Qāsim Maḥmūd ibn ʿUmar (1075–1144 (AH 467–538)). Muslim grammarian and *Qur'ān commentator. He was born in the Khwārizm province of N. Persia, where, apart from a period of study in *Mecca, he spent most of his life. His commentary on the Qur'ān, *al-Kashshāf ʿan Ḥaqā'iq Ghawāmid al-Tanzīl* (The Unveiler of the Truths of the Sciences of Revelation), takes each verse, phrase by phrase, and gives an interpretation which goes back to the theological rationality of the *Muʿtazilites. Thus free will is defended and the idea of the created Qur'ān is espoused. At the same time, al-Zamakhsharī's linguistic interests allowed him to make many points about the rhetorical and literary beauty of the Qur'ān, and this endeared the commentary to subsequent generations. It became the subject of many commentaries on itself, which, in general, eliminated the rationalizing theology.

Ama, et fac quod vis (love and do what you will): see ETHICS (Christianity).

Amal (ritual power): see MAGI.

Amarakośa (Skt., 'deathless vocabulary'). Dictionary of classical Sanskrit, compiled by Amara-simha, a Buddhist of *c.*7th cent. CE. It is an important resource, not just of linguistic meanings, but of cultural information. Many supplements/commentaries were subsequently produced.

Amarāvatī (Skt., 'abode of the deathless'). 1. The 'deathless' are the gods, hence A. is the abode of the gods, i.e., heaven. It is more specifically the capital of *Indra's domain, also known as *Svarga, to the east of Mount Meru. Access is limited to those who have undergone *tapas, have been brave in battle, and have offered *ghṛta. 'To enter Amarāvatī' = 'to die'.

2. A Buddhist ceremonial and pilgrimage centre situated along the Kistna river, Andhra Pradesh. The site dates from the Śuṅga period (185–75 BCE). However, the central building, the Great *Stūpa, is the most important structure dating from the late Āndhra (25 BCE–320 CE). This is the largest of all stūpas. Although now partially ruined, the brick core was originally covered with carved marble slabs depicting scenes from the lives of the *Buddha. The animated style of these bas-reliefs was a great influence on later Indian, Sri Lankan, and SE Asian art. The architectural style differs from the northern stūpas notably in its lack of elaborate gateways (*toraṇa*), and its possession of four structural offsets at the base pointing in the cardinal directions. Legend, supported by a nearby inscription, has it that *Nāgārjuna may have been associated with Amarāvatī. In the *Puraṇas, the name is Umarāvatī.

Amarāvikkhepikas (Pāli, 'eel-wrigglers'). A name in the Buddhist *Nikāyas for a school of sceptical philosophers who were contemporaries of the *Buddha. They are supposed to have refrained from giving any categorical answers on questions relating to ethics and speculative knowledge. They adopted the stance that things are intrinsically unknowable, and that, as a consequence, the only remaining worthwhile goal is the pursuit of subjective states of tranquillity. The uncertainty relating to propositions and theories is itself inimical to peace of mind and the principle of tranquillity. They were called 'eel-wrigglers' because their evasiveness when questioned resembled the quick movements of the Amarā fish, notoriously difficult to catch. In spite of their sharp dismissal in the texts, there is some evidence to suggest that the Buddha may have come under their influence. His chief disciples, *Sāriputta and *Moggallāna, are alleged to have been followers of *Sañjaya Belaṭṭhiputta, a renowned sceptic, immediately prior to their conversion to Buddhism; and the Buddha himself adopted an at least superficially comparable style to the eel-wrigglers on certain speculative questions (see AVYĀKATA); and, when in debate, he resorted to the same fourfold formula (catuṣkoti) as they used in putting their case.

Amar Dās, Gurū (1479–1574 CE). Third Sikh *Guru. Gurū Amar Dās, the son of Tej Bhān, was born into a Bhallā *Khatrī family to Lachhmī in Bāsarke village, *Amritsar District, *Pañjāb. He married Mansā Devī who bore him two sons, Mohan and Mohrī and two daughters, Bhānī and Dānī. According to tradition Amar Dās was a devout *Vaiṣṇavite Hindu, who observed fasts and made an annual *pilgrimage to the *Gaṅgā, but had no guru. Impressed with the words of the *Japjī, which he heard his nephew's wife Amro (Gurū *Aṅgad's daughter) singing, he visited Aṅgad at Khaḍūr. Despite his advanced age he remained here serving the Gurū by day, even when commanded to spend each night in the newly built town of *Goindvāl. His devotion was frequently tested by his master. For twelve years he brought a vessel of water for the Gurū's ablutions. One stormy night he stumbled over a weaver's loom peg, but still persevered. In 1552 Amar Dās was installed as Gurū by Aṅgad who bade him continue living at Goindvāl. His succession was challenged by Aṅgad's son, Dātū, who even kicked him from his seat. Then Amar Dās respectfully observed, 'This must have hurt your foot.' However Amar Dās hid himself in his native village, Bāsarke, until rediscovered by Bhāī *Buḍhā, who had followed the Gurū's mare to his hiding place.

As Gurū, Amar Dās was responsible for establishing practices distinctively Sikh yet reminiscent of Hindu custom: (i) he instructed Sikhs to gather to worship the one God on the first days of the Hindu months, *Vaiśākhi (April–May), Māgha (Jan.–Feb.) and on *Dīvālī; (ii) he had a deep well dug at Goindvāl as a Sikh *tīrath; (iii) he provided distinctive rituals for birth and *death, replacing the Sanskrit *śaloks with *hymns of the Gurūs; (iv) also ascribed to Gurū Amar Dās is the *Mohan Pothī*, a two-volume collection of hymns (composed by himself, his two predecessors, and six bhagats, *Kabīr, *Nāmdev, Trilochan, Seiṇ, *Ravidās, and Jaidev), which served as a nucleus for Gurū *Arjan Dev's compilation of the Ādi Granth; (v) Gurū Amar Dās emphasized the importance of the *Gurū-kā-laṅgar in the motto '*pahale paṅgat picche saṅgat*', i.e. 'First sit in a laṅgar row, then sit in the congregation.' This denial of *caste distinction antagonized the *brahmans.

Reflecting Akbār's imperial administration Gurū Amar Dās divided the areas where his followers lived into twenty-two *mañjīs, and appointed preachers (including women) for missionary work. Regarding his sons as unfit for Gurūship, Amar Dās rigorously tested his sons-in-law, Rāmā and Jethā, to see which should succeed him, deciding upon the latter, Rām Dās, Gurū. Aged 95, Amar Dās died at Goindvāl. Although miracles are traditionally ascribed to him, for surer insight into his nature and teaching one must turn to his 869 hymns in the Ādi Granth. Of these the most celebrated is the *Anand Sāhib. Like his predecessors, Amar Dās taught that salvation could not result from ritual, caste observance, and penance, but only by mental concentration upon God's Name (see NĀM).

Amaterasu-ō-Mikami (Jap., 'heavenly-shining-deity'). The central deity (*kami) of the classical Shinto tradition. This female deity, usually associated with the sun, plays a central part in the most important myth cycles of Shinto, and subsequently in the ritual traditions of Shinto—especially as connected to the imperial household and the sense of a national religion. The mythologies tell us that she was born of the original parent deities, *Izanagi and Izanami, and became the ruling deity in the 'high heavenly plain' (*takama-no-hara*) where the myriad heavenly deities dwell. Subsequently, she sent her grandson, Ninigi, to subjugate and rule the land of Japan. Out of this process the earthly kami were subjugated to the heavenly kami, and the imperial line came into being.

As the ancestral deity of the imperial family, Amaterasu was enshrined in the central shrines of Shinto at *Ise. There, through the centuries, emperors and peasants alike have worshipped her, sought her help in times of trouble, and appealed to her life-giving power of renewal—especially on behalf of the whole nation.

Amba. Title of the Christian *Coptic *patriarch. Traditionally, the one chosen to be patriarch is dragged to his consecration in chains, to indicate his unwillingness to be promoted, not an attitude normally found among Christian clergy. Ideally, he is the first son of a first husband, unmarried, one who lives in the desert, and not a *bishop—in which case any lower orders (deacon, priest, and archpriest, *kummus*) can be bestowed on successive days. A new patriarch is chosen by an assembly of twelve bishops, but if there is not unanimity, an old *Nestorian method was to take three slips of paper, each bearing a name, plus a fourth bearing the name of 'Jesus Christ the Good Shepherd', and to place them beneath the *altar for three days. A child selects one: if it is that of Jesus Christ, the three are thought unworthy, and the procedure is repeated with three other names.

Ambā, Ambikā. One of the names of the Hindu Goddess. Literally it means 'mother', like the related *ammā/ammaṉ. A particular goddess-figure is denoted by it only in the context of regional cults centred around temples. For example, in Mahārāṣṭra we find Ambe-Jogāī, an important *kula-devatā of *brahmans. In Gujarāt, the temple of Ambajee (where the goddess is called Ambā-jī ± *mātā* or Ambā-Bhavānī) is one of the three regional *pīṭhas* (where *Satī's heart is supposed to be located). There is a tendency here to identify Ambājī with Mahā-Lakṣmī, who killed *Mahiṣa.

Ambapālī. A beautiful courtesan of Vesali and devotee of the *Buddha. She is said to have been born miraculously at the foot of a mango tree in the royal gardens at Vesali and was named accordingly (Pāli, *amba*, 'a mango'). Many princes sought her hand, and to end the rivalry it was decided she should become a courtesan. In later life she became a devout follower of the Buddha and built a monastery (*vihāra) in her own garden which she donated to the order. The Buddha stayed there shortly before his death, and having accepted an invitation to dine with her declined a second invitation from the local princes. Ambapālī had a son who became an elder in the order, and she herself eventually renounced the world, gained insight into impermanence through contemplating the ageing of her own body, and attained *arhatship.

Ambedkar, Bhīmrāo Rām (1891–1956). Indian lawyer and politician, also known as Babasaheb. Born the fourteenth child of untouchable (Mahar) parents in Indore State he succeeded, against all the odds, in graduating from Elphinstone College in 1912. His career developed on two fronts: he was called to the bar in 1923, and became Principal of the Government Law College, Bombay. Politically, he became active fighting for the rights of untouchables. In 1924 he founded an organization for the 'moral and material progress of untouchables' and employed the technique of *satyāgraha (passive resistance) in a successful attempt to allow untouchable access to Hindu temples and tanks. His deep-seated mistrust of *caste Hindus led to disagreements with *Gāndhī, and in 1935 he announced an intention to lead untouchables out of the Hindu fold altogether. He finally embraced Buddhism in 1956, an action which led to sudden, mass conversions, particularly in Mahārāshtra. In Britain his followers are chiefly Pañjābīs of the same (*chamār) caste as the *Ravidāsī. Ambedkar was a prolific writer and a major influence in the development of modern India. He founded the Independent Labour Party of India (1936) and was an uneasy participant, as Law Minister, in the Nehru Government (1946–51). Shortly before his death he initiated the Bharatiya Buddha Mahasabha as an organization to promote the spread of Buddhism in India. Deprived of his strong leadership many untouchable converts to Buddhism have since reverted to Hinduism.

B. R. Ambedkar, *The Buddha and his Dhamma* (1957); his writings are being collected and published by V. Moon; D. Keer, *Dr. Ambedkar, Life and Mission* (1954).

Ambrose, St (*c*.339–97). *Bishop of Milan. He was trained in rhetoric and law, and assumed the *see in *c*.374, after having been civil governor. He was famous as a preacher and champion of orthodoxy (e.g. against the *Arians). He protested against the execution of *Priscillianist heretics, and he excommunicated Theodosius after a massacre: 'An emperor is within the church, not over it.' His most important works are treatises on the literal and metaphorical importance of virginity/purity (*De Virginibus*, 377), on the sacraments (*De Sacramentis*, the earliest witness to the present Roman *canon of the mass), and on ethics with special reference to the clergy. He was a strong advocate of *monasticism, writing on asceticism, and also interpreting Eastern theology for the West. He is one of the four original *Doctors of the W. Church. Feast day, usually 7 Dec.

F. H. Dudden, *The Life and Times of St. Ambrose*, (1935); A. Paredi, *Saint Ambrose* . . . (Eng. tr. 1964).

AMDG (Lat., Ad Maiorem Dei Gloriam, 'to the greater glory of God'). The motto of the *Jesuits, but it appears more widely as well.

Amen (Heb., 'So be it'). An individual or congregational endorsement of a *prayer or *blessing. The response dates back at least to the days of the second *Temple when 'Amen' was said after the songs chanted by the Levites. In contrast to the Christian custom, the person who recites the blessing does not usually say 'Amen', but traditionally even God himself 'nods Amen' to the blessings offered to him by human beings (*B. Ber.* 7a). In Islam, the form is *āmīn*, spoken as a form of inclusion and assent to the words of prayer.

Ame no Koyane. One of four *kamis of the Kasuga shrine in *Nara. Ame no Koyane co-operated with *Amaterasu and *Hachiman to establish and then endorse the Japanese imperial system.

American Jewish Committee. Oldest Jewish defence organization, founded in 1906. It was formed in response to the extensive Russian *pogroms of the time, and it lobbied for a liberal US immigration policy. From this committee grew the American Jewish Relief Committee and other philanthropic organizations, and it has sponsored numerous publications including *The American Jewish Yearbook*. It has consistently combated *anti-Semitism, both in America and worldwide, and since the Second World War has also concerned itself with civil liberties for non-Jewish groups.

Amesa Spentas. The 'Bounteous' (or Holy) Immortals in Zoroastrianism. *Zoroaster mentions a number of heavenly forces, the creations of, and therefore subservient to, *Ahura Mazda, but powers through which Ahura and his worshippers are linked. In the later tradition they form a coherent system of seven beings, although there is some difference about which figures are included in the seven, notably whether Ahura is himself one of the seven or not (in which case the ancient figure of Sraosa becomes one instead). Each of the seven protects one of the seven creations which is represented in major rituals by its symbol. The Amesa Spentas are, therefore, part of theology and liturgy.

Apart from Ahura Mazda, and his unique Holy Spirit (Spenta Mainyu) each of these forces represents both an aspect of Ahura and a feature of the good Zoroastrian. Ahura is said to receive prayer and praise through each of them, and each can represent *paradise. They are, therefore, the means by which worshippers approach Ahura, and the means by which Ahura approaches the worshipper. So it is that whoever gives heed to Ahura and obeys (Sraosa) him, will attain wholeness and immortality through the deeds of the Good Mind (*Ys.* 45. 4). It is through the Good Mind that worshippers follow the paths of right, gain wholeness and immortality, and therefore attain the dominion.

In the *Pahlavi literature, these figures are described in mythological language, having golden thrones in the House of Song (heaven). But some at least of this is present in Zoroaster's teachings, for he uses masculine forms for some and feminine for others. The older scholarly tendency to contrast an abstract prophetic teaching and a medieval mythology is almost certainly wrong. In Indo-Iranian thought, myth and abstraction merge into each other. Scholars often compare them to archangels in Judaeo-Christian thought, a belief which Zoroastrianism probably influenced. The six other than

Ahura are: (i) Vohu Manah, the Good Mind who appeared to Zoroaster in his visions and led him into the divine presence, and who similarly conducts the soul to heaven after judgement, the personification of Ahura's wisdom; (ii) Asa, righteousness or truth, who represents the divine law and moral order; the righteous are called *asavan*, followers of Asa, but those who do not know Asa forfeit heaven, for they are outside the order of God; Asa is represented in ritual by the fire, the focal point of devotion; (iii) Armaiti, spoken of as feminine, represents devotion; she is the personification of faithful obedience, harmony, and worship, and is said to have appeared visibly to Zoroaster; (iv) Khsathra, the personification of Ahura's might, majesty, dominion, and power, might be termed 'the kingdom of God' on earth which establishes the divine will in helping the poor and weak by overcoming evil; (v) and (vi), Haurvatat and Ameretat, two feminine beings, always mentioned together in the texts, representing wholeness, totality, or fullness (often translated as integrity). Haurvatat is the personification of what salvation means to the individual. Ameretat, literally deathlessness, is the other aspect of salvation—immortality. Some of these figures clearly derive from the India-Iranian tradition,—e.g. Asa is clearly related to *Vedic *Ṛta. Others appear to have been the part of the original inspiration of Zoroaster, e.g. Vohu Manah. In the ritual, the pure priest, duly endowed with ritual power (*amal*), concentrates his gaze on the objects representing the Amesa Spentas as he recites their names with devotion, and so it is thought they become really present, strengthening the worshipper and the world.

M. Boyce, *Zoroastrians* (1979); J. Hinnells, *Persian Mythology* (1973).

ʿAm ha-Arez (Heb., 'people of the land'). In biblical Hebrew, the term refers to the general population, particularly that of Palestine, which harassed the returning Jewish *exiles (see Ezra 3. 3, Nehemiah 10. 29). In some contexts, e.g. 2 Kings 2. 18 ff., it seems to identify a representative body within the nation. In the era of the second *Temple, the ʿam ha-arez were contrasted with the observant *pharisees, and in rabbinic times the term was pejorative to indicate those who were not scholarly and well-versed in *Torah: 'A scholar though he be, a *mamzer takes precedence over a *high priest if he be an ʿam ha-arez' (Hor. 3. 8).

Amice. A Christian *eucharistic vestment. It is an ornamented linen neckcloth worn above the *alb so as to form a kind of collar.

Amida or **Amita.** In Far Eastern Buddhism the name of the principal *Buddha of the *Pure Land lineages, the Jap. pronunciation of the Chinese transliteration (O-mi-t'o) of the Skt. (Amita, 'Immeasurable One'). According to *Jōdo Shinshū, the largest Japanese Pure Land lineage, Amida is, in the *Trikāya system, the *Sambhoga-Kāya, *Śākyamuni Buddha (Jap. *Shaka Butsu*), and is the Nirmāṇakāya, while the Dharmakāya is ineffable. The titles Amitābha (Skt., 'He of Immeasurable Light') and *Amitāyus (Skt., 'He of Immeasurable Life') are, contrary to the Tibetan tradition, regarded by the Japanese as synonyms for Amida. The invocation (*nembutsu) to Amida is *namu Amida butsu*, 'veneration to the Buddha Amida', the 'Original Vow'. In Chinese, it is *namo o-mi-to-fo*, 'veneration to Amitābha'.

According to tradition (recounted in e.g. *Sukhāvatī-vyuha*), immeasurably long ago a king heard the preaching of a Buddha, and renouncing his throne, he became a monk with the name Dharmākara (Jap., Hōzō). Instructed by the Buddha Lokeśvararaja (Sejizaiō), he resolved with forty-eight vows to found a buddha-land. He surveyed many existing lands, noting the perfections of each, in order to create one land containing them all, which became *Sukhāvatī (Gokuraku), of which he has become ruler. For innumerable *kalpas he devoted himself to good deeds and the service of others, and ten kalpas ago he became the Buddha Amida. He is now attended by the *bodhisattvas *Avalokiteśvara and Mahāsthāmaprapta. He sits on a lotus, emitting rays of golden light, surrounded by an aura larger than a billion worlds. He has 84,000 marks, which are the materialization of corresponding virtues. Appeal to Amida at the moment of death, or concentration on Amida for ten moments, or (according to *Shinran) faith in the efficacy of the vow of commitment to Amida, cancels the *karmic consequence of evil deeds, and leads to rebirth ('again-becoming', *punabhava) in the Pure Land. The major text, the Lotus Sūtra, states repeatedly, 'There is only One Way, not two or three', and that Way is devotion to Amida. For the basic text, *Amida-kyō*, see SUKHĀVATĪVYŪHA. See also AMITĀYUS.

ʿAmidah (Heb., 'standing'). A Jewish prayer consisting of eighteen *benedictions which is a core part of the structure of each of the three daily services. It is also known as the *Shemoneh-Esreh ('eighteen') or, in *Talmudic sources, as *ha-tefillah* ('the prayer'). It is said standing (facing in the direction of Jerusalem), and is recited in different forms on weekdays, *Sabbaths, and *festivals. God is blessed as 'the shield of *Abraham', as the one 'who revives the dead', as the 'holy God', as the 'giver of knowledge', as the one who 'delights in repentance', who is 'gracious and abundantly forgiving', as the 'redeemer of *Israel', as the 'healer of the sick', as the one 'who blesses the years', 'who gathers the banished ones of his people Israel', as the one who 'loves righteousness and judgement', 'who breaks his enemies and humbles the arrogant', who is 'the support and trust of the righteous', who 'rebuilds *Jerusalem', 'who hearkens to prayer', 'who returns the divine presence to *Zion', 'whose name is good', and finally 'who blesses his people Israel with peace'. On the sabbath and festivals, only the first three and the last three blessings are recited, and, during the prayer, the worshipper 'must see himself as if God's presence was opposite him' (*B. Sanh.* 22a).

Āmīn (so be it): see AMEN.

Amish. A group of strict *Mennonites now settled mainly in the eastern USA, particularly in Ohio, Pennsylvania, and Indiana. The sect originated at the end of the 17th cent. with Jacob Ammann (*c*.1644–*c*.1725), a Swiss minister who insisted on strict discipline, including avoidance of those under the ban of excommunication, even within the family. Members of the sect began to emigrate to N. America soon after 1700. They now number about 130,000.

The 'Old Order' Amish separate themselves from the society around them by retaining the dress and customs of that early period: beards and broad-brimmed hats for men, bonnets and aprons for women, no motor transport, no electricity in homes. They refuse military service, have their own schools, and decline Social Security benefits. Sunday worship rotates among the houses of the congregation. There is no missionary activity, and marriage is always within the Amish community; the growth or maintenance of their numbers is due to the large size of families. Some other Amish groups, in various ways more liberal, have separated from the Old Order Amish.

J. A. Hostetler, *Amish Society* (1963).

Amitābha (Pure Land Buddha): see AMIDA.

Amitābha-Sūtra. One of the three basic *sūtras of the *Pure Land School (with **Amitāyurdhyāna-Sūtra* and **Sukhāvatīvyūha*). It survives in Chinese translations, and describes the fundamental practice of reciting Amitābha's name (*Amida). Constant repetition and concentration will mean that the believer will be undisturbed, because unsurprised, when Amitābha and his retinue appear at his deathbed.

Amitāyurdhyāna-Sūtra ('Sūtra on Contemplation on *Amitāyus'). One of the three basic *sūtras of the *Pure Land School (with **Amitābha-Sūtra* and **Sukhāvatīvyūha*). It describes the pure land and the moral life which prepares for it, associating the legend of the formation of the pure land with the sixteen visualizations which lead to rebirth in the Pure Land, starting with the natural order (sun, water, earth, trees), leading through celestial appearances, to the forms of the *buddhas and *bodhisattvas.

Amitāyus (Skt.; Tib., *tshe.dpag.med*, 'Limitless Life'). In Tibetan Buddhism an aspect of *Amida/Amitābha (Skt.; Tib., *'d.dpag.med*, 'Limitless Light') concerned with long life. In Buddhism in general, human life is especially precious, since only as a human, and not as an animal, demon, or god, can one best practise compassion and hear the teachings. If one desires a longer life for these reasons, then one would practise a meditation centred on Amitāyus, perhaps also increasing one's chances of rebirth in Amitābha's *Pure Land of *Sukhāvatī, where the life span is considerably longer than our one hundred years. Iconographically depicted as red, as is Amitābha, but with a crown and ornaments, Amitāyus is generally portrayed surrounded by his 108 *emanations, each of which have separate names which, recited together, form the *mantra of the practice devoted to him. In Japanese Buddhism, Amitāyus is simply an epithet, rather than an aspect of Amitābha.

Ammā (Skt., Marathi, etc.), **Ammaṉ** (Tamil, etc.). Literally 'mother' (compare AMBĀ, AMBIKĀ). It is frequently used with reference to Hindu goddesses, and appears in compound names of regional and local *grāmadevatās, etc., e.g. *Māriyamnam, *Yellammā.

Ammann, Jacob: see AMISH.

Amoghasiddhi (Skt., 'the unerring achiever of the goal'). One of the five transcendent *Buddhas in *Mahāyāna and *Zen Buddhism. His *mudra is that of fearlessness, and his emblem is *vajra, the absolute and indestructible, as a diamond.

Amoghavajra (Chin., *Pu-k'ung Chin-kang*; Jap., *Fukū (kongō)*). An influential teacher of esoteric Buddhism in 8th cent. China, 6th patriarch of Chen-yen (*Shingon). His early life is uncertain, before he went to Java at about the age of 10. He studied under Vajrabodhi, and the two together went to China in 720 and established esoteric Buddhism there. He spent about five years in India from 740, collecting Skt. texts, and on his return, he engaged in a major work of translation, numbering in the end more than 100 works. He received support from the emperor in building temples and in teaching and performing esoteric rituals. Among his pupils was *Hui-k'o, who transmitted the teaching to *Kūkai, and thus to Japan. He based his own teaching especially on *Vajraśekhara-Sūtra*, a wisdom text. He was given the title Kuang-chih San-tsang (Kōchi Sanzō) in 765.

Amoraim (Aramaic, 'spokesmen'). Jewish scholars who interpreted the *Mishnah in Palestine and Babylonia between 200 CE and 500 CE. The *Talmud records their discussions, and they are distinguished from the *tannaim whose debates are chronicled in the Mishnah. Their *halakhic decisions are considered to have the same validity as those of the tannaim, and they also continued and developed the *aggadic tradition. Communication was maintained between the Palestinian and Babylonian schools by messengers and visiting scholars and this accounts for the sayings of Babylonian amoraim appearing in the Palestinian Talmud and vice versa. Those scholars ordained by the *nasi and the *Sanhedrin in Palestine were given the title *'Rabbi' whereas the Babylonian scholars were known as 'Rav'. Besides teaching, the amoraim fulfilled community duties such as acting as judges and dispersing charitable funds. Over 2,000 amoraim can be identified over a period of 300 years, but there is inevitable confusion over some names.

Amos (8th cent. BCE). A *prophet of the northern kingdom. The biblical book of his prophecy is considered to be the earliest of the prophetic books. Amos is said to have been a herdsman from Tekoa who prophesied during the time of Uzziah, king of *Judah, and Jeroboam, king of *Israel. He inveighed against the nations of the earth (1. 2–2. 6); he prophesied Israel's punishment (2. 7–6. 14); he described incidents in his own life (7. 1–9. 6) and he prophesied future comfort for the nation (9. 7–15). He thundered against social injustice: 'For three transgressions of Israel and for four, I will not revoke punishment; because they sell the righteous for silver, and the needy for a pair of shoes' (2. 6). He foretold foreign invasion and insisted that God was not primarily interested in religious observance—instead, 'let justice roll down like water and righteousness like an overflowing stream' (5. 24). He appears (7. 14 f.) to dissociate himself from the cult prophets, having received a direct call from God, but the verse may in fact be a strong affirmative, to be translated, 'I not a prophet? I not a son of a prophet? [sc., I certainly am].'

ʿAmr b. ʿUbaid (co-founder of Islamic theological school): see MUʿTAZILITES.

ʿAmr ibn al-ʿĀṣ (d. 663 (AH 42)). Muslim statesman. A Qurayshite, ʿAmr was a late convert to Islam, but the Prophet *Muḥammad recognized his talents and immediately sent him as an envoy to Oman where he met with great success. *Abu Bakr dispatched him as a commander to Palestine. In the military conquests and administrative organization of Syria and Palestine ʿAmr played a prominent role. However, his real fame rests as the conqueror of Egypt during *ʿUmar's caliphate. He held Egypt by his political skills and even seems to have gained the support of the *Coptic Church. At the battle of Siffin, ʿAmr commanded *Muʿawiyyah's cavalry against *ʿAlī, and devised the plan of arbitration by *Qur'ān. Muʿawiyyah rewarded ʿAmr's faithful service by appointing him governor of Egypt, where he remained until his death.

Amrit (Pañjābī, 'undying'; Skt., 'ambrosia'). The nectar of immortality. For Sikhs, amrit has several related meanings. 'Taking amrit' (amrit *chhakaṇā*) means receiving initiation (*amritsanskar*) at the *khaṇḍe-dī-pāhul ceremony with sweetened baptismal water. According to tradition, Gurū *Gobind Siṅgh first prepared amrit to initiate the *khālsā in 1699 CE. During the preparation of amrit for the *naming ceremony, only the first five verses of the *Japjī *Sāhib are recited. In popular usage, amrit is often holy water believed to have healing properties, especially water which has been close to the *Ādi Granth during a *pāṭh (reading). Used metaphorically in the Ādi Granth, amrit suggests both immortality and sweetness particularly as a result of meditation upon God's name (*nām simaran), e.g. 'Ambrosial (amrit) is the True Name' (Ādi Granth 33). The 'amrit velā' is the hour before dawn especially precious for prayer. See AMRITDHĀRĪ; AMRITSAR.

Amritdhārī (*Pañjābī, 'one who has received amrit'). An initiated Sikh. Amritdhari Sikhs have accepted *amrit at the *khaṇḍe-dī-pāhul ceremony and so are committed to keeping the rules of the *khālsā, in particular the *Five Ks.

Amritsanskar (Sikh initiation): see KHAṆḌE-DĪ-PĀHUL.

Amritsar (*Pañjābī, 'pool of nectar'). Sikhs' spiritual capital. Amritsar, *Pañjāb, is 400 km. NNW of Delhi and 30 km. from Pakistan. It is especially holy to Sikhs on account of the *Harimandir (Golden Temple). Amritsar, first known as Gurū kā Chak, Rāmdāspur, and Chak Rām Dās, was founded 1577 CE by Gurū *Rām Dās, who built a brick temple there. The site, surrounding a sacred pool, had been granted, according to one tradition, by Emperor *Akbar to Rām Dās' wife, Bībī Bhānī. Gurū *Arjan Dev extended the temple. The city took its name from the pool. *Vālmīki reputedly composed the *Rāmāyaṇa* near the Amritsar pool, and in his *āśram received the banished *Sītā and taught her sons. See also BĀLMĪKĪ.

In the 18th cent. Amritsar was sacked several times, notably by the Afghan invader Ahmed Shāh Abdālī. Subsequently the city was divided between Sikh *misls until Mahārājā *Rañjīt Siṅgh captured and rebuilt Amritsar. In 1984, the Indian army stormed the Harimandir to dislodge Sikh militants.

Apart from the Harimandir and *Akāl Takht, other sites venerated by Sikhs include Bābā Atal, a nine-storeyed shrine to Gurū *Hargobind's son of that name, and holy pools, e.g. Kaulsar. In 1919, many Sikhs who, disregarding the Rowlatt Acts, had gathered on *Vaisākhī in Jalliānwālā Bāgh, were killed by British soldiers under the command of Brigadier General Dyer. This event, of great significance for the Independence movement in India, and for establishing 'minimum force' as a rule in crowd control, is known as the Amritsar massacre.

Amṛta (Skt., 'not-death'). The nectar of immortality, as in *Amrit; but in Hinduism (especially *Vedas), it is *soma.

Aṁśa (share of the gods): see ĀDITYAS.

Aṃśāvatāra (partial incarnation of Hindu deity): see AVATĀRA.

Amulets: see CHARMS.

Anabaptists ('re-baptizers'). Various *radical or left-wing *Reformation groups who reinstated the *baptism of believers on profession of personal faith. Two Zürich Reformers, Conrad Grebel and Felix Manz, formed the first congregation at Zollikon in 1525 (later called 'the Swiss Brethren'). Others were established in Moravia, led by Jacob Hutter (so Hutterites), in S. Germany, led by Balthasar Hubmaier and Hans Denck, and in NW Germany and the Low Countries, inspired by Melchior Hoffmann, a leader who combined unorthodox *christology and *millenarianism with deep piety. Forced by persecution to leave their homes, many Anabaptists came to regard baptism as initiation into Christian suffering, with Christ as the proto-martyr of their faith. Some Anabaptist exiles, influenced by the fanatical views of Jan Matthys and Jan Bockelson (John of Leyden), introduced polygamy in the city of Münster (1533–5) which was eventually besieged. The episode was not only a stigma on Anabaptism, but led inevitably to increased persecution with the loss of many thousands of lives. The Münster débâcle also issued in a fresh definition of Anabaptist thought by writers such as Dirk Philips, and especially Menno Simons, whose spirituality, pacifism, and social ideals continue to be treasured by the *Mennonites. In general, Anabaptists were marked by radical discipleship (*Nachfolge*), separation from the world (refusing military service and civil *oaths) and simplicity and holiness of life: 'Foremost, apply love, Through which we overcome, while on life's course; It is the bond of perfection. Love is God himself, It remains in eternity' (*Aussbund*, Anabaptist Hymnal, 1583, no. 124).

H. S. Bender, *Conrad Grebel* . . . (1950); C.-P. Clasen, *Anabaptism: A Social History* . . . (1972); R. Friedmann, *The Theology of Anabaptism* (1973); H. J. Hillerbrand, *A Bibliography of Anabaptism (1520–1630)* (1962); G. H. Williams, *The Radical Reformation* (1962).

Anāgāmin (Skt., Pāli, 'not-returner'). Theravādin Buddhist who is free of the five fetters (*saṃyojana) and is on the third stage of the path towards attainment (*ārya-mārga); when he dies, he will 'not return' (hence the name) to this world; but because he is not free of the bond of existence (*bhava-yoga*), he will continue in a higher realm.

Anāgārika (Pāli, 'without home'). Groups in India, before and during the time of the *Buddha, who had left home for a more ascetic life. They became formally organized, with their own ritual and teaching traditions. In Buddhism, the term was adapted to those who adopt a homeless life, but who do not enter the *saṅgha.

Anagogical Interpretation (Gk., *anago*, 'I lead up'). Interpretations of scripture (*hermeneutics) which point to the meaning of a text in relation to its eternal or heavenly meaning: it is the spiritual sense of scripture which anticipates what the Church is or will be in heaven. In a looser sense, the term is sometimes used of interpretations which point to a mystical or spiritual meaning. See ALLEGORY.

Anahana (Jap., from Skt., *ānāpāna). Awareness of *breathing in *Zen Buddhism, as a natural rhythm. It is not regulation of breathing, which would imply effort to exercise control, but resting in the rhythm until awareness is transcended.

Anāhata-śabda (Skt., 'not-struck sound'). Awareness of pure sound beneath audible sounds (as of *Brahman underlying appearances), attained through the appropriate *cakra (close to the heart). *Om may be described by this term.

Analects. Accepted English rendering of *Lun Yü*, the *Dialogues* or *Conversations* of *Confucius and his personal disciples. It is one of the *Confucian Classics, considered by scholars to be the most nearly contemporary, verbatim transcription of some of the Master's sayings. It is extremely terse, has little continuity, and seldom provides background or extended discussion. Nevertheless, close study rewards the student with a good idea of the basic philosophy of Confucius, and even considerable insight into his character and personality. The *Analects* is not only the cornerstone of the Confucian School, but has been one of the most influential books in all human history, studied and revered as much in other E. Asian civilizations as in China itself.

The *Analects* emphasize the importance of *ritual, with its implications for order and conservation of the past ('Tzu Kung proposed abolishing the lamb-sacrifice at the new moon; Confucius said, "Tzu, you love the lamb, but I love the rite" ', 3. 17), but otherwise are religiously cautious, concentrating on present duty rather than speculation ('Tzu Lu asked about worshipping ghosts and spirits; Confucius said, "We do not know how to serve other people, how can we know about serving the spirits?" ', 11. 11).

Trs., among many, D. C. Lau; J. Legge; A. Waley.

Analogy. A proportional similarity. Most theological discussion of analogy has been concerned with analogical predication, a mode of predication in which terms familiar in one context are used in an extended sense elsewhere. Thus it is claimed that terms like 'love', 'wisdom', and 'living', which are learnt in everyday contexts, are applied to God by analogy because of some relationship (e.g. likeness, exemplarity, participation, and causation) between God's perfections and these human attributes. Clearly, the use of analogical predication presupposes some knowledge of God's perfections, and of the relationship between them and human attributes.

According to Thomas *Aquinas, such a mode of predication is midway between univocity and equivocation (*Summa Theologiae*, 1a, xiii. 5). Later Thomists attempted to classify different types of analogy, especially Analogy of Attribution (e.g. the various senses of 'healthy') and Analogy of Proper Proportionality (e.g. our knowledge: created beings: God's knowledge: God's essence). They also spoke of the analogy of being (*analogia entis*) underlying Thomistic metaphysics, a phrase not used by Aquinas, although he did specify that 'being' is predicated analogically. Terms like 'family resemblance', 'open texture', and 'systematic equivocation', used in 20th-cent. analytic philosophy, may be regarded as akin to analogy. See also TANZĪH; NYĀYA (for *upamana*).

Anamchara (soul-friend): see CELTIC CHURCH.

Anamnesis (Gk., 'remembrance'). A prayer in the Christian *eucharist which follows the words of institution, commemorating the *passion, *resurrection, and *ascension of *Christ. In the *Apostolic Tradition* of *Hippolytus it begins, 'Remembering therefore his death and resurrection, we offer to You this bread and this cup'. The interpretation of this prayer, and the drafting of modern versions of it, are always controversial, since it is here that views of the eucharistic *sacrifice may find expression.

Ananaikyo. A New Sect Shinto organization (see SECT SHINTO) founded in 1949 by Nakano Yonosuke. It is deliberately eclectic: the name means 'the teaching' (*kyo*) of 'the three' (*ana*) and 'the five' (*nai*), referring to the religious traditions from which it draws inspiration. It is *eschatological, looking (literally) for the signs of the end, having established observatories for this purpose. It also practises *kami possession and ecstasy, through a technique known as *chinkon kishin*, 'stilling the self to become one with the kami'. The principal kami worshipped is Kuni Tokotachi no Mikoto.

Anan ben David (8th cent. BCE). Jewish Babylonian sage, regarded as the founder of *Karaism. According to Karaite legend, when the *exilarchate of Babylon was bestowed on Anan's younger brother, Anan consequently founded an alternative sect. His immediate followers, the Ananites, rejected the *Talmudic tradition and relied on the *Bible alone as the source of divine law. Anan's own book, *Sefer ha-Mitzvot* (Book of Precepts), became an important text in the later Karaite movement. He himself led an ascetic life, and he stressed that a strict interpretation of the law should always be preferred over a more lenient one.

L. Nemoy, *A Karaite Anthology* (1952).

Ānanda (Skt.). 1. A chief disciple and first cousin of the *Buddha. He was personally commissioned by him and served as his devoted aide and constant companion, assisting in travelling and helping with discourses. As the Buddha lay dying, he consoled the weeping Ānanda: 'Weep not . . . Long have you been close to me by your acts, your words, your thoughts of love and infinite tenderness that never changed. You have done well . . .' (*Mahāparinibbāna-Sutta*).

After the Buddha's death, Ānanda advanced from a learner (sekha) to an *arhat and took a prominent role in the first *Council, though he was criticized by other members for the role he had taken in encouraging the admission of *women into the *saṅgha, and for other faults as perceived by the Council. Though not an intellectual, Ānanda could explain the 60,000 words of the Buddha and was known as the Dhammabhaṇḍāgārika, 'treasurer of the Teachings'.

2. Initially a qualitative attribute of *Brahmā, it became, especially in *Vedānta, the consciousness that is free from all entanglements in *samādhi. It is usually found in association with *sat and *cit, hence in the fused form, Satchidānanda, Being, Consciousness, Bliss. A *saṁnyāsin in the Śankara tradition is given the word ānanda as part of his name—e.g. Vivekānanda.

Ananda Marga (Skt., 'path of bliss'). Movement founded in India in 1955 by Shree Shree Anandamurti, known to his followers as Baba and regarded by them as a *thaumaturge or miracle-worker. Imprisoned in India in 1971 on a charge of murder and later released when Indira Gandhi fell from power, Anandamurti's career, as well as that of his movement, evoked controversy.

The principal goal of this strictly hierarchical movement is stated as 'the liberation of self and service to humanity' or 'inner realization and social development', which when achieved on a sufficiently wide scale will permit the establishment of a world government of 'enlightened', 'realized', individuals. This world government will mercilessly fight 'sin', mainly by the use of meditational techniques of a *Tantra yogic kind, but also by all other means deemed necessary. The stress placed on this form of meditation derives from the belief that this spiritual technique not only liberates the individual but also develops within the person a universalistic outlook and an all-consuming passion and concern for social justice. Though it has been suggested that this 'revolutionist' movement has several million adherents, the actual membership is undoubtedly very much smaller.

Ānandamayī Mā (1896–1982). Hindu responsive teacher and spiritual attainer, who reached the goal without studying the scriptures, and without a *guru. She was married at 12, but gave priority to spiritual development. She passed through the attainments of *yoga within six years, and she became known as 'the mother filled with bliss', instead of her original name, Nirmala Sundari Devi. Her followers built an *āśram in Decca in 1929, and another at Dehradun in 1932. After that, she travelled extensively in India, never giving formal lectures, but responding to questions, and never regarding the one to whom she spoke as 'an-other', but as part of the whole, which is the true realization (i.e. *advaita).

Sri Ānandamayī Mā, *The Words of Sri Ānandamayī Mā* (1982).

Anandamurti (founder): see ANANDA MARGA.

Anand Karaj (Sikh marriage): see MARRIAGE (SIKH).

Anand Marg: see ANANDA MARGA.

Anaṇḍpur (Sāhib) (*Pañjābī, '(respected) city of bliss'), Sikh holy place, in NE *Pañjāb. Gurū *Tegh Bahādur founded Anaṇḍpur in 1664, and it was here that in 1675 his son *Gobind received his severed head. This was cremated where *Gurdwārā Śīś Gañj now stands. After several years in Paontā, Sāhib Gurū Gobind Siṅgh returned to Anaṇḍpur where on *Baisākhī 1699 he instituted the *khālsā. The *khaṇḍā used in preparing the *amrit and many other historic weapons are preserved in Gurdwārā Keśgaṛh Sāhib, a *takht. Gobind Siṅgh fortified Anaṇḍpur and was besieged there, 1701–4, until its devastation, when he evacuated the town. For *Holā Mahallā, thousands flock to Anaṇḍpur and witness the *Nihaṅgs' swordplay in what is now an impressive Sikh centre. In 1972, the *Akālī Dal met at Anaṇḍpur and drew up the Anaṇḍpur Sāhib Resolution, which summarized Sikh aspirations for the designation of an enlarged Pañjāb as a Sikh homeland.

Anand Sāhib (Pañjābī, 'bliss'). Composition by Guru *Amar Dās, included as part of the *Ādi Granth. It can be found on pp. 917–22. Words from it are used in the *Kaṛāh praśād ceremony. It is forty stanzas in length, in Rāmkali *rāg, declaring that bliss springs from attunement with God. The first five verses and the last precede *Ardās at the end of all Sikh ceremonies. See also NITNEM.

Ananites (movement): see ANAN BEN DAVID.

Ananta. *Śeṣa, 'the infinite one', the constantly coiling cosmic snake on which *Viṣṇu reclines.

Ānāpāna (Skt.). Control of *breathing in Hindu *yoga. Ānāpānasati (Pāli) is a corresponding Buddhist technique (in sixteen stages or ways), counting breaths in and out, which calms the mind and is a preparation for attainment of the *dhyānas. Cf. also Anahana in *Zen Buddhism.

Ānāpānasati: see ĀNĀPĀNA.

Anaphora (Gk., 'offering'). The central part of the Christian *eucharist, known in the West as the *canon), and in the East as the Eucharistic Prayer. The word is mainly used with reference to the liturgies of Eastern and *Oriental Orthodox churches, who use a sometimes large number of alternative anaphoras. It is believed that there was early established a common structure, which can be discerned in *Hippolytus' *Apostolic Tradition*, of an introductory dialogue, thanksgiving, Institution, *anamnesis, *epiclesis, and *doxology. The W. Syrian Annaphuras are variant liturgies which are claimed to go back to early days, even to the *apostles (e.g. the *Annaphura of St *James, the brother of our Lord*, which was known to St *Cyril of Jerusalem in the 4th cent.

'Anas b. Mālik (d. 709/11 (AH 91/3)). A prolific transmitter of *ḥadīth who served the Prophet *Muḥammad as his servant from an early age, and grew up in his house. 'Anas supported the anti-Umayyad figures, such as *'Alī and 'Abd Allah b. Zubayr, and consequently suffered punishment. He was later pardoned and died when about 100 years old.

Anat Anath. A Goddess worshipped widely in the ancient Near East, the consort of *Baʿal. She is not mentioned in the Bible except in place-names, Beth-Anath and Anathoth (in the *Ugaritic texts, she is distinguished from the Goddesses Ashtoreth and *Asherah). However, her cult seems to have been practised in the Jewish colony at *Elephantiné in the 5th cent. BCE.

U. Cassuto, *The Goddess Anath* (1971).

Anathema. A sentence of separation from a Christian congregation. The word is the equivalent of Heb. *ḥerem. Paul pronounces this sentence on, for example, those preaching a gospel different from his (Galatians 1. 8–9), though he also knows the word as a general curse (1 Corinthians 12. 3). From the 4th cent. heretics were regularly 'anathematized'. *Cyril's twelve anathemas against *Nestorius were issued in 431. From the 6th cent. a distinction was made between anathematization (complete separation from the congregation) and *excommunication, though this distinction has not always been clearly maintained.

Anātman (Skt., 'not-self'; Pāli *anatta*). Fundamental perception in Buddhism that since there is no subsistent reality to be found in or underlying appearances, there cannot be a subsistent self or soul in the human appearance—in contrast to Hinduism, where the understanding of *ātman and *jīva is equally fundamental to its understanding of the human predicament and how to escape it. If all is subject to *dukkha (transience and the grief that arises from trying to find the non-transient within it), then human appearance is no exception. The human is constituted by five aggregates (*skandha) which flow together and give rise to the impression of identity and persistence through time. Thus even if there is 'no soul', there is at least that which has the nature of having that nature. There were major disputes about the best candidates for constituting this impression (see especially PUDGALA; ĀLAYA-VIJÑĀNA), but agreement was in general reached that there is no soul which, so to speak, sits inside the human body, like the driver of a bus, and gets out at the end of the journey. There is only the aggregation of components, which is caused by the previous moment and causes the next. Thus while there is momentarily some one person who is rightly identified as the Dalai Lama, there is no one person who the Dalai Lama always is (cf. **Milindapañha*). In *Mahāyāna Buddhism, this term was extended to apply to all appearance which arises from *Śūnyatā and is therefore devoid of substance, empty of self.

S. Collins, *Selfless Persons*.

Anatta: see ANĀTMAN.

Anbhav Prakash. Experience of *enlightenment among Sikhs. It is the perception of reality which means that a person has become centred on God (*gurmukh).

Ancestors. The maintaining of ancestors in memory is a fundamental part of religious life and practice. Even during the millennia in which belief in personal life after death was extremely rare, this remembering—and often veneration—of ancestors was extensive. Yet the term 'ancestor-worship' is usually misleading (see AFRICAN RELIGION) it is not so much that ancestors were worshipped as that they continued in relation to the living family, both sustaining it (provided they were in fact appropriately remembered) and being sustained by it. If they were forgotten or neglected, they might well turn into restless or hungry or avenging figures. Rituals therefore developed to ensure proper respect to these continuing members of the family, as well as to provide means of consulting them. For this reason, there is a stress in many traditions on the importance of having a son who will become the guardian of the rituals. In developed religions, especially Christianity, conflict developed over the appropriateness of maintaining contact with the dead: thus 'prayer for' or 'with' or 'from' the dead seemed to some Christians to be incompatible with the sole saving efficacy of *Christ; in Islam, elaborate memorials seem to trap the deceased in a world which they have left. Yet almost everywhere, from gravestones to elaborate rituals, religions make it clear that death neither terminates existence nor severs the ties of family. Care for the ancestors (*pitṛ) devolves, among Hindus, on to the eldest son, and formal rites support the ancestors in their domain (see CARDINAL DIRECTIONS; ŚRĀDDHA).

To illustrate this with only one example: in China, according to ancient belief, people have two kinds of soul. The spiritual one, *hun, is composed of *yang* (see YIN-YANG), vital breath (*ch'i), and when death takes place it ascends to the ethereal realm of Heaven. The physical one, called *p'o, is composed of *yin, vital breath, and when death takes place it returns to the gross realm of Earth, accompanying the corpse to the grave. Later theories of *Taoism and Buddhism greatly complicated this belief, but did not displace it. Still today the spirit of the deceased is associated with two tablets, that for the hun on the altar of the family home, and that for the p'o at the tomb. As in life, so in death, the family seniors, especially the parents, command respect and obedience (*hsiao, the cardinal duty of filiality). When properly interred in a grave with good *feng-shui, given the specified ritual sacrifices, and in general remaining the object of the solicitous attentions of their descendants, the ancestors will use their spiritual power to confer blessings. If neglected, of course they will show their resentment by bringing misfortunes upon their unfilial offspring. The hope that ritual sacrifices will result in the souls of the dead becoming benevolent spirits (*shen) and the fear that neglected souls will become malevolent ghosts (*kuei) are basic principles of wide extension in Chinese religion. The practices of the ancestral cult thus consist of ritual sacrifices. These were prescribed in great detail in the ritual codes of the *Confucian Classics, especially the *Records of Rites* (**Li-Chi*). They comprise funerary rituals, mourning rituals, and continuing sacrifices to the *manes*. The classical rituals still remain more or less in force today, complemented by rituals of Taoism and Buddhism, and by popular religion.

The ancestral cult is also of the greatest social significance as the religious tie that binds the family and the patrilineage (*tsu*). All males, together with their wives and unmarried children, are united in the cult of their common ancestors. The ultimate symbol of their unity is their founding ancestor, who may be enshrined, together with the host of less memorable ancestors, in a lineage temple. The identity of the patrilineage, with its many constituent families, is reaffirmed through such practices as participation in funerals, where each member wears distinctive costume indicating precisely his or her relationship to the deceased according to the degrees of mourning prescribed for five generations. Headship of the patrilinear family devolves upon the eldest son, whose most important ritual function is maintenance of the ancestral sacrifices. This religious requirement is the chief reason why the Chinese have always felt the absolute necessity of having sons. It is also obviously a contributing factor to the dominance of males in Chinese society: '*Mencius said: "There are three things which are unfilial, and the greatest is to have no posterity" ', *Meng Tzu*, IVA. 26.

W. H. Newell (ed.), *Ancestors* (1976).

Anchorite, Anchoress (Gk., *anachōreō*, 'withdraw'). One who withdraws from the world in order to offer prayer and mortification, frequently understood in sacrificial terms. Anchorites are precursors of the development of *monasticism, and are related to the hermits who are attached to monastic orders (e.g. among *Camaldolese or *Carthusians). The term became more strictly applied to those who live in a cell (restricted dwelling-place). In the later M. Ages, such cells were sometimes attached to parish churches. *Julian of Norwich is (thought to be) a notable example.

Andrew, St. One of the twelve *apostles of *Jesus. He was the brother of *Peter, and is mentioned by name in several stories in the gospels (e.g. John 6. 8). According to the *Acts of Andrew*, a 3rd-cent. work now partly lost, he was crucified in Patras in Greece. The tradition that his cross was X-shaped goes back no further than the 10th cent. He is *patron saint of Russia and of Scotland. Feast day, 30 Nov.

Andrewes, Lancelot (1555–1626). *Anglican *bishop. Born in Barking, he was educated at Cambridge where he stayed on to teach. In 1601 he became Dean of Westminster, was consecrated bishop in 1605, becoming bishop of Winchester in 1619. He was famous as a preacher, and it is on his sermons and his *Preces Privatae* (Private Prayers) that his importance rests. Both betray his great *patristic learning, and the influence of the Greek Fathers. According to the 17th cent. historian, Thomas Fuller, 'The world wanted learning to know how learned this man was, so skilled in all (especially oriental) languages, that some conceived he might (if then living) have almost served as an interpreter-general at the Confusion of Tongues.' His style and method is reminiscent of the *Metaphysical poets, with their delight in paradox, especially the twin paradoxes of God's incarnation and human deification: 'Grant, O Lord, that Christ Himself may be formed in us, that we may be made conformable to His image, that when we are lukewarm in prayer and stand in need of any grace or heavenly consolation, we may remember His appearance in the presence of God, and His intercession for us.' T. S.*Eliot regarded his sermons as ranking 'with the finest English prose of their time, of any time' (*For Lancelot Andrewes*): 'He takes a word and derives a world from it.'

N. Lossky, *Lancelot Andrewes the Preacher* (1986; tr. 1993).

Anekāntavāda (Skt., *anekānta* = 'non-one-sidedness' or 'manysidedness'). In Jain philosophy, the doctrine of the manysidedness of reality. This doctrine is a combination of the kindred Jain doctrines of *nayavāda (viewpoints) and *syādvāda (maybe). The teaching shows itself in embryo in the debates held by *Mahāvīra, but it has been developed and sophisticated by Jain philosophers since, probably because of its practical relevance to a minority community living in a diverse society. If we approach any reality recognizing that what we know is only partial, like blind men attempting to describe an elephant from an encounter with but a part of it, then all views become acceptable and valid in some respect. The doctrine claims that seven assertions, apparently contradictory, but perfectly true, can be made about anything: (i) *syādasti*, maybe it truly is (for example, a cold room); (ii) *syānnāsti*, maybe it truly is not (if you enter it from a colder one); (iii) *syādastināsti*, maybe it truly is and is not (two different people's opposite statements could be true); (iv) *syādavaktarya*, maybe it is exhaustively indescribable (if two opposite statements are relatively true); (v) *syādastyavaktarya*, maybe it is and is indescribable; (vi) *syānnāst yavaktavya*, maybe it is not and is undescribable; (vii) *syādastināstyavaktavya*, maybe it is and is not and is indescribable. The last three appear to be later, and are not accepted by all Jains. Although a cumbersome systematization, this doctrine does represent a very practical outlook, and reflects a humility and tolerance which has served the Jains well and has helped them to coexist happily with the kaleidoscope of religious and philosophical viewpoints in India.

Aṅga (Skt., 'limb, part'). 1. The eight steps of *Rāja-Yoga in Hinduism.

2. A Jain term to denote the twelve 'limbs' of revered and basic texts. Among Jains, 'scripture' is a fluid, even a contested, concept (see DIGAMBARA). The Śvetāmbara have a *'canon', defined by 19th-cent, European scholars as the '45 text canon', but while this defines the core texts, more texts are revered, and groups among the Śvetāmbara do not identify identical texts. Nevertheless, the basic texts for both Digambara and Śvetāmbara are the Twelve Aṅgas, but Śvetāmbara believe (xii) below to be lost: (i) *Ācāra-aṅga* ('Behaviour', rules for ascetics); (ii) *Sūtrakṛta-aṅga* ('On Heretical Views', attitudes to rituals, and to other views); (iii) *Sthāna-aṅga* ('Possibilities', options especially, in relation to *jīva, and numerical descriptions; (iv) *Samavāya-aṅga* ('Combinations', similarities, as in (iii), also describing the aṅgas); (v) Digambara, *Vyākhyā-prajñapti-aṅga*; Śvetāmbara, *Bhagavatī-aṅga* ('Explanations Expounded', 60,000 questions, and answers, to, and from, the *tīrthaṅkaras); (vi) *Jñātradharma-katha-aṅga* ('Accounts of *Jñāna and *Dharma'); (vii) *Upāsakādhayna-aṅga* ('Ten Chapters on Lay Responsibilities', the vows and rules of conduct for lay people, especially for the eleven stages of a householder's life); (viii) *Antakṛddaśā-aṅga* ('Ten Chapters on End-Achievers', the extreme methods of ten ascetics who freed themselves from *karma); (ix) *Anuttaraupapādikadaśa-aṅga* ('Ten Chapters on Arisers in Heaven', on ten ascetics who are reborn in the five heavens, *anuttaravimāna*); (x) *Praśnavyākaraṇa-aṅga* ('Questions and Expositions', instructions on how to reply to questions); (xi) *Vipākasūtra-aṅga* ('Text on Ripening', an exploration of Karma); (xii) *Dṛṣṭi-pravāda-aṅga* ('Disputation about Views, parts only, divided into five parts, *Parikarma* (on the geography of earth and sky), *Sūtra* (on false views), *Prathamānuyoga* (on sixty-three illustrious figures), fourteen *Pūrvagata* (in fourteen sections), and five *Cūlikā* (on magical skills).

Associated with the twelve aṅgas, are for Śvetāmbara, twelve dependent texts (*upaṅgas*). Also revered are six Cedasūtras, four Mūlas ('Root') sūtras (the foundation of an ascetic life), ten Prakīrṇakas and two Cūikāsūtras. The Śvetāmbara 'canon' is said to have been fixed at the Assembly at

Valabhī (453 or 466 CE), but there is no list of what was actually agreed.

3. In Buddhism, the nine (or twelve) 'branches' within the *canon of literary types: *sutta* (*sūtra), *geyya* (recitation), *veyyākaraṇa* (prophecies), *gāthā* (verse), *udāna* (solemn pronouncement), *ittivuttaka* (discourses beginning, 'This has been said by the master'), *jātaka, *abhutadhamma* (stories of accomplishments), *vedalla* (analysis and explication). In N. (Skt.) Buddhism the three additional aṅgas are *nidāna* (linking introduction), *avadāna (biographies), and *upadeśa* (explanations).

N. Tatia, *That Which Is: Tattvārtha Sūtra*, app. 6 (1994).

Aṅgad, Gurū. (1504–52). Second Sikh Gurū. Lehṇā (Lahaṇā) as he was originally called, a Trehaṇ *Khatrī, lived at Khaḍūr, *Pañjāb. His devotion to *Durgā turned to loyal service of Gurū *Nānak at *Kartārpur. Impressed by his selfless obedience, Nānak renamed him Aṅgad (Pañjābī *aṅg*, 'part of one's body'), and proclaimed him his successor rather than the disappointed *Srī Chand.

In Khaḍūr, as Gurū from 1539, Aṅgad built on Nānak's foundations. He organized the *Gurū-kā-laṅgar on a larger scale. To him, too, is generally attributed the *Gurmukhī script and a collection of Nānak's *hymns, a nucleus for the later *Ādi Granth, which contains only sixty-two of Aṅgad's compositions. He encouraged wrestling and physical fitness, as only the healthy could perform *sevā (service).

All the *janam-sākhī sources emphasize Aṅgad's unquestioning humility when tested by his master. For example, Aṅgad uncomplainingly ruined his new clothes by carrying a muddy bundle at Nānak's command. His wife, Khīvī, bore him two daughters and two sons, Dātū and Dāsū, in preference to whom he elected *Amar Dās as successor.

Angel (Gk., *angelos*, 'messenger'). An intermediary between heaven and earth. In the early religious imagination of the Jews, the connection between heaven and earth was thought to be literal, as in the attempt to build a tower of Babel (Genesis 11. 1–9). For that reason, *Jacob had a vision of angels ascending and descending a ladder between *heaven and earth (Genesis 28. 12). It was only later (perhaps under Persian influence) that they developed their own means of propulsion with wings. There are various references to angels (Heb., *malakhim*, 'messengers') in the *Bible. One, for example, appears to Hagar (Genesis 16. 7); one intervenes in *Abraham's sacrifice of *Isaac (Genesis 22. 11); another wrestles with Jacob (Genesis 32), and the angel of the Lord appears to *Moses in the burning bush. In *Isaiah's vision (6. 2), the Lord was seated surrounded by the seraphim. Angels are mentioned frequently in the book of Psalms, and in the books of Ezekiel, Daniel, and Zechariah. The tradition continued in the *Apocrypha, in the *Talmud and *midrash, in the liturgy, in the mystical tradition and in Jewish philosophy. Many are named (e.g. *Gabriel, *Michael, *Metatron, *Raphael, *Raziel, *Uriel): they carry prayers to God, they teach *Torah to each embryo in the womb, and they accompany Jewish fathers as they walk home on the evening of *Sabbath. Most modern Jewish commentators, however, regard angels as products of an earlier world view. While belief in their existence is not denied altogether, they tend to be understood as symbolic or poetic figures, taking a cue from *Maimonides, 'Everyone entrusted with a mission is an angel; all the powers of the body are angels.'

Jewish angelology was taken over by early Christianity. According to the *gospels, angels announce *Jesus' birth, strengthen him in his trials, attend his *resurrection, and will accompany his *parousia. In the book of Revelation, angels play an especially important part as announcers and heavenly worshippers. There was probably an early speculation that *Christ himself was an angel, rejected in Hebrews 1. 4 ff. In *patristic times the most influential treatment of angels came from Ps.-*Dionysius who ranked the angels in three hierarchies of three choirs each: *Seraphim, *Cherubim, Thrones; Dominions, Virtues, Powers; Principalities, Archangels, Angels. Catholic teaching includes few pronouncements on angels, but enjoins a cult similar to that of the *saints. In Christianity, the notion of fallen angels is developed further. These refuse to return or acknowledge the sovereignty and love of God: they are not destroyed but have a limited scope of subversive activity.

In Islam, angels (Arab., *malā'ika*, pl., of *malak*) are 'messengers with wings' (Qur'ān 35. 1, the *sūra of angels). They were created before humans, and protested to Allāh at his plan to create human beings (2. 30–3), though they agreed to bow down to *Adam (2. 34), except for Iblīs (see DEVIL).

One of their functions is to record good and bad deeds; one sits at the right and one at the left (50. 17–18). They are sent down to warn human beings (16. 2), and they 'praise the glory of their Lord and seek forgiveness on behalf of those on earth' (42. 5). They will be sent down on the Day of Judgement (25. 25).

The angel of revelation is Jibrīl (*Gabriel), who 'brings down (the revelation) to your heart, by Allah's permission' (2. 97), and he is mentioned together with Mikā'īl (2. 98). The angel of death (32. 11) is not named, but tradition calls him 'Izrā'il, while the angel who will announce the Day of Judgement is Isrāfīl. Two angels, *Munkar and Nakīr, question people, on their first night in the grave, about Muḥammad: if they answer that he is *rasūl *Allāh, the messenger of God, they are left in peace until *Yaum al-Qiyama, the day of Resurrection. For others, there ensues the 'punishment in the tomb'.

M. J. Adler, *What About Angels?* W. Eickmann, *Angelologie und Dämonologie des Korans* (1908); G. MacGregor, *Angels* (1988); G. Davidson, *A Dictionary of Angels* (1967).

Angel of Death. God's messenger who brings *death to human beings. There is no constant figure of the angel of death in the *Bible, but in the *Talmud, *Satan and the evil *inclination are both identified with him. In folk literature, he is all-seeing ('the Angel of Death is all eyes'), a fugitive, a wanderer, and an old man holding a poisoned sword. Various heroes, such as R. Joshua b. Levi, have succeeded in defeating this terrifying figure, but for the ordinary person, he is a source of dread: R. Naḥman in the Talmud is reported to have said, 'Even if the Almighty were to order me back upon earth to live my life all over again, I would refuse because of horror of the Angel of Death' (*BMK* 28a). For Islam, see ANGEL.

Angelus. A Catholic thrice-daily devotion (early morning, noon, and evening), consisting of three *Ave Marias with *versicles and a *collect. A bell is rung (three times for each Ave and nine times for the collect) as a reminder of the *incarnation to those at work outside—hence the familiar painting by Millais. The devotion came into general use in the 17th cent.

Angelus Silesius (1624–77). Joannes Scheffler, Christian mystical writer and controversialist. A *Lutheran who, in 1653, became RC, he was ordained priest in 1661. Remembered for his mystical poems, the collection *Heilige Seelenlust* (1657) interprets the mystical life in the imagery of the *Song of Songs; and *Der Cherubinische Wandersmann* (1675) is deeply influenced by the tradition of German mysticism inspired by *Eckhart ('Be not—God is, | Do nothing—And His word is done'). Silesius uses extremely bold language of the mutually dependent love between God and the soul: 'Though Christ a thousand times in Bethlehem is born, | Unless he's born in you, you stay forlorn'.

Angkor. Capital in central Cambodia of the Khmers, a people of N. Indo-Chinese origin, established by Yaśovarman II (889–910 CE). A successor in the dynasty, Sūryavarman II (1112–52), raised Angkor Wāt (*wāt*, 'city temple') on the site as a fortress-temple dedicated to Devarāja and to himself as an *avatāra of *Viṣṇu. A tiered-pyramid structure, interconnected by a labyrinth of galleries and staircases, and surrounded by a moat 2½ miles in circumference, Angkor Wāt rises 200 ft from the jungle floor like a gigantic *maṇḍala. The interior walls are richly adorned with sculpture in relief depicting scenes from the **Rāmāyaṇa* and the legends of Viṣṇu and *Kṛṣṇa.

Close by is Angkor Thom which was established as a new capital by Jayavarman VII (1181–*c*.1210), with the Bayon as its ceremonial centre. Dedicated for *Mahāyāna Buddhist worship the workmanship of the Bayon is more crudely executed than at Angkor Wāt and the decoration was never completely finished. Nevertheless, the enigmatic masks of the *Bodhisattva Lokeśvara crowning the structure represent the apogee of Cambodian sculpture.

B. P. Groslier and J. Arthand, *Angkor: Art and Civilisation* (1966).

Anglican Chant. The music of the Psalms and canticles as sung in many Anglican churches, developed out of the *plainchant psalm-tones about the end of the 17th cent. See also liturgical use of PSALMS.

Anglicanism, from the Latin *Anglicana ecclesia* (lit., English Church), as found in clause 1 of *Magna Carta*, 1215, used to differentiate the 'English Church' from the Church elsewhere in Europe even if under the jurisdiction of the king of England: it was subsequently, in the Act of Supremacy in 1534, described as the *Church of England, which Henry VIII also described as *Anglicana Ecclesia* to distinguish it as the Church over which he alone had the power of authority and reform. 'Anglicanism' is now used to describe the diverse character, practice, and faith of 37 autonomous Churches of the international Anglican Communion and its *c*.70 million members world-wide. It is held together by the *Lambeth Conferences, Primates' meetings, and the Anglican Consultative Council. Structurally, therefore, it resembles the diffused but collegial responsibilities of the *Orthodox Church much more than it does the centralizing control of the *Vatican in *Roman Catholicism. In different parts of the Anglican Communion it may carry a different name, as e.g. ECUSA (the *Episcopal Church in the USA), the Church of Ireland, the Scottish Episcopal Church, Nippon Sei Ko Kai (the Holy Catholic Church of Japan). In addition to the Provinces of Canterbury and York, the main Churches and Provinces are in Aotearoa, New Zealand and Polynesia; Australia; Brazil; Burundi; Canada; Central Africa; Indian Ocean; Ireland; Japan; Jerusalem and the Middle East; Kenya; Korea; Melanesia; Mexico; Myanmar; Nigeria; Papua New Guinea; Philippines; Rwanda; Scotland; SE Asia; S. Africa; S. Cone of America; Sudan; Tanzania; Uganda; USA; Wales; W. Africa; W. Indies; Zaire.

Anglicanism is an episcopal (with *bishops) Church, in continuity with Catholicism, but also accepting much from the *Reformation. It is thus described as 'both Catholic and reformed', though both of those two extremes generally regard it as insufficiently either. It is in communion with *Old Catholics, but not with the Roman Catholic Church, the Orthodox Church or, in the main, with the Reformed or non-episcopal Churches, any more than they are in communion with each other. It did, however, become part of the Churches of South and North India (though not without controversy).

A number of attempts have been made to describe the particular ethos of Anglicanism, but they are too limited in application to be satisfactory on their own. Thus Anglicanism can be traced historically, from its pre-Reformation roots to the present day, but there has been much change in the course of time and in relation to the communities which it has sought to serve: the Church of England in the late 16th cent. has connections and similarities with the Church of England in the 20th, and with, e.g., the Church of the Province of S. Africa, but the differences are also obvious. Or again, there is an Anglican identity located in the *liturgy, with a shared source in the **Book of Common Prayer*, but each Province now has its own Prayer Book, revised for its own needs. Attempts have been made to identify an Anglican spiritual tradition, but these run the risk of omitting as many important figures as they include. The theology and philosophy of the Anglican Church are sometimes claimed to have a distinct style, but without an Anglican *magisterium, the style is bound to endorse freedom in enquiry and diversity as virtues. Some have laid stress on Britain's imperial past: it is true that Anglican *missionary initiatives followed trade and colonization, fleetingly alluded to in the Prayer Book (1662) provision 'for the baptising of Natives of our plantations', but the view that Anglicanism is defined by the British imperial past hardly does justice to Nippon Sei Ko Kai (see above), still less to the autonomy of the Churches in the Anglican Communion. Mission has played an important part in Anglicanism, not least in such societies as *SPCK (1698), *(U)SPG (1701), and *CMS (1799). Founded initially to educate and support clergy and laity in English colonies, especially at first in America, they soon became an independent outreach of the gospel, with missionaries often being well-informed critics of colonial policies. The independence of mission now sees England as a mission-field. All these themes are important, but insufficient on their own to characterize Anglicanism. To avoid distortion, therefore, it is necessary to describe Anglicanism as it presents itself (*phenomenology at the first level), shot through as it is with variation and differences—which some claim to be its strength.

Looked at in this way, there emerges, historically and in the present, an Anglicanism possessed of four discernible strands which may present themselves as 'parties' or movements: (1) The '*evangelical' which traces its roots to a putative process of *protestantizing and *puritanizing of the English Church in the mid-16th cent.; it persists as a simple (but not unscholarly), pious, biblical tradition committed to personal devotion and to proclaiming the saving work of Christ by word and deed, though often containing divergent views on Church, ministry, *sacraments and (more recently) on the *charismatic movement. (2) The 'catholic' which argues consistently for theological and ritual continuity through the English reformation and thence, through the *Oxford and later Anglo-Catholic Movements, for the essential participation of Anglicanism, as a member or 'branch' of the one universal Church, in the apostolicity of its bishops, the validity of its *orders, and the sacramentality of its worship and life. (3) The 'liberal' which continues the veneration of reason, conscience, and private judgement (found in e.g. the *Cambridge Platonists), subjecting theology and practice to rigorous examination, allowing that wisdom and insight arise in the world outside the boundaries of the Church (not least in other religions, but also in science, art, music, literature, etc.), and accepting the constraints of biblical criticism. (4) The 'radical' which espouses the option for the poor (see LIBERATION THEOLOGY) and adopts the revisionist *hermeneutics associated with justice and love according to which radical change is demanded in many areas (e.g. of orders in relation to the *ordination and *consecration of women as priests/bishops; of politics in relation to racism, ecology, and the distribution of resources; of sexual ethics in relation to blessing 'same-sex' unions and the ordination of practising *homosexuals; and of liturgy in relation to inclusive language) if the radical commitment of Jesus to those on the margins of society is to be realized in the present as well.

Despite (or perhaps because of) the strength of these varying positions, a process of accommodation and a commitment to 'comprehensiveness' has been as formative of Anglicanism as critical differentiation, not least because this is in keeping with the original spirit of the Church of England in the 16th cent. The *via media* 'Reformed Catholicism' of the 17th cent. 'Caroline Divines' is thus deemed more in keeping with the spirit of Anglicanism than the strong Protestantism of Bishop Jewel's earlier *Apology of the Church of England* (1562); and *via media* has often been used as a description of Anglicanism. This 'comprehensiveness' is the experience of shared and tolerating faith which characterizes such Anglicans as Richard *Hooker, William *Temple and Desmond *Tutu. But it means that the theology which underpins Anglicanism is elusive. Authority is dispersed and theological resources are many. There is no Anglican *Summa, nor any institutional forum for theological statements. But there is no lack of probing theological investigation. This finds expression in the Church of England's Doctrine Commission Reports (of which note especially *Believing in the Church*, 1981, which explores the Anglican style of corporate believing, i.e., of what it means to be a Church), statements from the Houses of Bishops, sermons and books by individuals. It is expressed also in a rich poetic, literary, and artistic heritage. The contributions to music and architecture, not least through patronage and commissioning, have been immense. All this is characterized by a virtue of generosity (at least in theory; the reality is often different) which withholds or even suspends judgement in the interests of unity within pluralism. Pluralism is extended also by different provinces drawing on local experience to reach differing conclusions—e.g., the Church in Wales initially reached a conclusion over the ordination of women different from that of the Church of England.

There is nevertheless a common focus in that Anglican theology is based on an appeal to scripture, tradition, and reason, expanded in the dictum of Lancelot *Andrewes: 'One *canon, . . . two *testaments, three *creeds, four general *councils, five centuries and the series of *fathers in that period . . . determine the boundary of our faith.' The influence of the Enlightenment changed the order and favoured the critical role of rational judgement alongside scripture and tradition. In recent years, an appeal to post-modernism has turned against the individualizing consequences of the Enlightenment; but this has as yet been a matter of defensive slogans, not of serious analysis. More disruptive of the 'threefold' method has been the popular appeal to 'experience' (privately and culturally defined) to which the other traditional sources are accountable.

When appealing to the Bible, Anglicans affirm its holiness as God's inspired word, its sufficiency for knowledge of salvation through Jesus Christ, its authority as the foundation of faith, and its power in the lives of individuals (hence the widespread importance of private Bible reading) and in the Church (hence the emphasis in public worship). The appeal to tradition seeks to establish the Anglican Church in the faith and wisdom of the early Church, and it identified 'Historic Formularies' (Creeds, *Thirty Nine Articles, Prayer Book Homilies) to ensure unity, apostolicity, sound teaching, and the discernment of error. The appeal to reason reflects doctrinally potent convictions about the nature of truth in relation to God, and of human ability to discern it, with consequences ranging from Hooker's common-sense and *Locke's rational defence to mere reasonableness or the privilege of private judgement: here again Anglican theological method has been shaped by doctrinal convictions. On this basis, the Lambeth Conference of 1930 spoke of 'the ideals for which the Church of England has always stood', and listed 'an open Bible', a pastoral priesthood, a common worship, a standard of conduct consistent with that worship and a fearless love of truth.' The core characteristic is a capacity, deliberately nurtured, to comprehend diversity. Such 'comprehensiveness' is always under severe political, philosophical, and theological pressure, and is open (since centralizing regulation is understandably mistrusted) to manipulation. Nevertheless, although difficult to define, comprehensiveness involves a necessary agreement on certain 'Fundamentals' (as the 1968 Lambeth report stressed) and a containing of both Protestant and Catholic elements in a national Church. It may thus still be 'the privilege of a particular vocation', as the 1948 Lambeth Conference held, for the Anglican Communion to contain in microcosm the diversity elsewhere divided into disparate denominations.

Anglicanism's pioneering role in *ecumenicism had an early start (e.g., individual explorations of reunion with the Orthodox), but takes its rise in modern times from the Chicago-Lambeth Quadrilateral (usually referred to simply as the Lambeth Quadrilateral) of 1888, prompted by W. R. Huntingdon's *The Church Idea* (1870). It identifies four elements 'on which approach may be, by God's blessing, made toward Home Reunion', namely, the holy scriptures as containing all things necessary for salvation, the Creeds as the sufficient statement of Christian faith, the sacraments of *baptism and *Holy Communion, and 'the Historic Episcopate, locally adapted in the methods of its administration to the varying needs of the nations called of God into the Unity of His Church.' There have been some practical results, as in the former Churches of N. and S. India: Methodists and Anglicans are close to recovering the unity from which they began; in 1993, conversations between British and Irish Anglican Churches and Nordic and Baltic Lutheran Churches produced the Porvoo *Common Statement* (the Porvoo Declaration, 1993), which called for a relationship of communion, with structures for collegial consultation and interchangeable ministries; this was approved by participating Churches in 1995. Otherwise, there have been continuing agreed statements and conversations, as with Lutherans, Reformed Churches, Orthodoxy and Roman Catholics (see ARCIC).

Underlying all of the foregoing has been a long and deep commitment to a practical spirituality, epitomized in George *Herbert's poem, 'Teach me, my God and King', with its lines, 'Who sweeps a room, as for Thy laws, Makes that and the action fine.' In its rich and varied history, it has extended into fields as diverse as *Christian Socialism (see also MAURICE, F. D.) on the one hand, and artistic endeavour on the other. It lies behind the spiritual tradition that includes William *Law's *A Serious Call to a Devout and Holy Life* (1728), John *Donne's *Holy Sonnets*, and R. S. Thomas's *Collected Poems* (1993), a consequence of an unremitting honesty in the presence of God so often evidently absent, in a technological age:

> . . . God,
> looking into a dry chalice,
> felt the cold touch of the machine
> on his hand, leading him
> to a steel altar. 'Where are you?'
> he called seeking himself among
> the dumb cogs and tireless camshafts.

It is a tradition in which a creationist poet like Thomas *Traherne, an apologist like C. S. *Lewis, or a writer like T. S. *Eliot can equally explore God's truth in Christ in relation to the glory and misery and mystery of life; it is a tradition which turned *Wilberforce to the abolition of slavery and Archbishop Trevor Huddleston to the abolition of apartheid. It is the theological and spiritual context in which an incarnational sacramentalism prevails.

P. D. Avis, *Anglicanism and the Christian Church* (1989); H. G. G. Herklots, *Frontiers of the Church: The Making of the Anglican Communion* (1961); H. R. McAdoo, *The Spirit of Anglicanism* (1965); J. R. H. Moorman, *The Anglican*

Spiritual Tradition (1983); S. C. Neill, *Anglicanism* (1954); W. L. Sachs, *The Transformation of Anglicanism* (1992); ed. S. W. Sykes and J. E. Booty, *The Study of Anglicanism* (1988); ed. W. J. Wolf *et al.*, *The Spirit of Anglicanism* (1986).

Anglican/Roman Catholic International Commission: see ARCIC.

Anglo-Catholics. *Anglicans who embrace *Catholic doctrines, especially of the *church and *sacraments, stressing continuity from the early Church. The name is conveniently used within an ecclesiology which speaks of a single catholic church with various branches ('Roman', 'Anglican', etc.). This theory, and the currency of the word 'Anglo-Catholic', are the product of the *Oxford Movement. Anglo-Catholics most often refer to themselves as 'Catholic Anglicans' or simply 'Catholics'. In the 1980s, a movement for 'Catholic Renewal' sought to reassert the place of this party in the Church of England, but in the public mind it has been associated mainly with opposition to the ordination of women and to union with *Free Churches. See also HIGH CHURCHMEN.

O. Chadwick (ed.), *The Mind of the Oxford Movement* (1960).

Angra Mainyu (Pahlavi Ahriman). The 'Destructive Spirit' or 'devil' in *Zoroastrianism. He is thought to have existed 'from the beginning', independent of *Ahura Mazda (i.e. he is coeval). In the Gāthās, *Zoroaster declared, on the basis of his vision, 'Then shall I speak of the two Primal Spirits of existence, of whom the Very Holy thus spoke to the Evil One: "Neither our thoughts nor teachings nor wills, neither our choices nor words nor acts, not our inner selves nor souls agree" ' (*Ys.* 45. 2). Angra Mainyu is the source of all that is evil, of pollution (e.g. the smoke afflicting the good flame of the fire), of that which destroys (e.g. decay and rust), of misery, suffering, and death. By instinct his will is to destroy. To aid him in his conflict with the Good Creation he (mis-)created the demon forces, the *daevas, such as Wrath, Greed, Procrastination. In the material world, his work is carried out by the creatures who embody his destructive aims, the *khrafstras*—e.g. the marauding lion, the venomous snake, the rat, and not least the fly. But since the material form is essentially the creation of Ahura Mazda, then there is a real sense in which Angra Mainyu does not exist in the world, save only in the bodies of people in the forms of the demons. If everyone would cast out the demons lodging within them, then evil would be ejected from the world and good would triumph. The bodies of men and women are therefore the battleground in which the opposing forces contend. *Hell is the 'Abode of the Lie', and the Lie is a synonym for evil; it is that which is not as it should be. That which evil creates cannot be said to be life, it is rather 'not life'. Azi Dahaka is the personification of the Lie, often depicted in mythology as a terrible dragon with three heads, six eyes, and three jaws, whose body is full of *khrafstras*. In modern Zoroastrian thought, Angra Mainyu is commonly demythologized and interpreted as an evil tendency within human nature, and the rich mythological tradition is taken, at best, as colourful imagery for an abstract idea.

L. H. Gray, *The Foundation of the Iranian Religions* (1925); J. R. Hinnells, *Persian Mythology* (1979); R. C. Zaehner, *The Dawn and Twilight of Zoroastrianism* (1961), and *The Teachings of the Magi* (1956).

Anguttara-Nikāya (Pāli, 'graduated collection'). The fourth part of the Sūtra-*piṭaka of the Buddhist Pāli canon.

Tr. F. L. Woodward, *The Book of the Gradual Sayings* (1932–6).

Angya (Jap., 'wander on foot'). Pilgrimage of *unsui (Zen monk who has completed the first phase of his training), preferably through dangerous territory, as a test of his detachment. He wears a *kasa*, a broad-brimmed hat which compels him to look down and not gaze around. When he reaches the monastery of his appointed destination, he may well be refused entry, to test still further his determination. If he persists, he is tested further within the monastery before final acceptance.

Anicca (Pāli, 'impermanent', 'not enduring'), **Anitya** (Skt.), One of the *Three Marks of Existence in Buddhism. The teaching of the impermanence or transitoriness of all things is central to the whole of Buddhist philosophy and practice. It involves the affirmation, as a truth statement, that all phenomena, both mental and physical, are without exception impermanent. Furthermore, despite this truth being everywhere evident and verifiable, we ourselves are in a state of ignorance (*avijjā) regarding it. The transition from this ignorance to the awareness (and personal acceptance) of the impermanence of all things constitutes, along with the acceptance of the other two marks of existence, the Buddhist path of salvation; and the transition is effected by the aid of the Buddha and his teaching.

There are various ways in which the truth of the universality of impermanence is spoken of. Figuratively, the action of time is compared to the wheel of a moving chariot (which only touches the ground at one point at a time), an ever-flowing mountain stream, a bubble, a mirage, the sound of a bell. Introspectively, we can verify the truth by observing that our thoughts and feelings never remain the same but are in perpetual flux (e.g. the extreme brevity of a single thought, which never persists but always runs on to another thought). Analytically, 'impermanence', is to be observed in the fact that all things exist in dependence on something else, arise out of and become something else: no thing exists in isolation, no thing possesses stability. It is precisely in this respect that *nirvāna is to be understood as the direct antithesis of anicca, that is, as comprising duration, stability, and permanence, and why it is regarded as worthy of our aspiration, unlike the things of this world. The teaching on anicca links up with the Buddhist doctrine of 'dependent origination' (*paticca-samuppāda) which states that 'all things have a beginning' and that 'all things with a beginning must have an end'; the doctrine of anicca draws attention to the fact of their demise. The paramount importance of anicca in Buddhist teaching is spotlighted in the Buddha's last words, 'decay is inherent in all things'.

In consequence of all this, Buddhism teaches the practice of *aniccānupassanā* ('contemplation of impermanence'; cf. VIPASSANĀ) as the way of realizing the truth of impermanence. Indeed, tradition holds that to practise *aniccānupassanā* for only the time it takes to snap one's fingers is an invaluable exercise, indicating by this how little attention people in general give to the notion of impermanence. The apprehension of impermanence is not a matter of academic interest but is important to the process of continuity because it liberates a person from *attachment* to objects (mental and physical) within the world. If things are impermanent they have no intrinsic value; therefore they are unworthy of our preoccupation. In particular, emphasis is placed upon the impermanence of body, feelings, and mind-states (painful, pleasurable, and neutral) as these are not only objects of experience always with us but the channels through which objects in the world at large are perceived. The actual process of contemplation involves 'watching' the rise or appearance of a given datum, verifying its 'dependent' or 'caused' origin; then, by the same token, 'watching' its subsidence or disappearance and verifying its transient characteristic. Here, a given object of experience is not only 'seen' to be impermanent but is also 'deduced' to be such on the basis of the fact that it is 'dependent' for its existence on something else which itself is impermanent; so, for example, 'feeling' is impermanent because it is 'dependent' on 'body' which is impermanent, and so on. It is a process by which one moves from the particular to the general and from the general back to the particular, until ultimately one arrives at the insight (*paññā*) that 'all is impermanent' (*sabbaṁ aniccaṁ*).

Acceding intellectually to the truth of impermanence is termed in Buddhism the acquisition of 'right view' (*sammā-diṭṭhi*; see AṬṬANGIKA-MĀRGA) and is synonymous with entry on to the path to enlightenment. The discernment of impermanence correspondingly represents the 'explosion' or 'dissolution' of all wrong views (cf. *diṭṭhis) because the construction of any metaphysical system necessarily rests upon the assumption of some notion of 'permanence' or of some element of 'permanence' within it; therefore the acceptance of anicca works counter to the tendency to superimpose constructions on reality.

The *Abhidhamma tradition sought to give an account and explanation of the mechanics of the empirical doctrine of anicca by suggesting physical theories of the precise life-span or momentariness of things. And therefore, according to the *Mahāyāna (see especially *Nāgārjuna), it fell into the trap of erecting a *metaphysical theory about something whose very purpose was to extirpate such theories. The *Mahāyāna, on the other hand, took the fact of the totality or universality of impermanence to imply the relativity of all things, an interpretation which contributed significantly to the design and formulation of its *śūnyatā doctrine.

Ani Ma'amin (Heb., 'I believe'). A short Jewish creed of unknown authorship. It is based on *Maimonides' principles of the Jewish faith (*articles of faith), and dates back at least to the 15th cent. In most *Ashkenazi *prayer books, it is printed at the end of the Morning Service. More particularly, it is the title of Elie Wiesel's cantata, for which see the HOLOCAUST.

Animals. The resemblances between many animals and humans, not least in their dependence on food and air, has given to animals a special status in all religions. Thus it has been widely believed that suprahuman realities, not least divine and diabolic, can take on the form of animals. They can also epitomize, in the form of *totems, the networks of relationship which constitute a human society. Bearing, as they do, the obvious signs of vitality, animals have been a major part of *sacrifice, becoming instrumental in expressing the many needs which humans have felt in their relation to God and to each other. Some religions (e.g. Islam) have retained animal sacrifice (*'Id al-Aḍḥā), but others have reacted strongly against the efficacy of such acts (e.g. Buddhism and Jainism; Christianity saw the purpose of all sacrifices more efficaciously fulfilled in the death of *Christ). However, even in religions where the sacrifice of animals has taken, or does take, place, animals may be given a high and revered status. Judaism and Islam emphasize that they come from the hand of the Creator, and while they are to some extent given to humans for their use and food (e.g. Qur'ān 16. 5–8), this is within limits, and must always be in the context of kindness. Judaism envisages a hierarchy in creation, with the higher levels expected to exercise responsibility (Genesis 2. 15; Genesis 1. 28 and Psalm 115. 16 were understood as humans being entrusted with responsibility as stewards). Domestic animals are included in the *Sabbath rest of the Decalogue (*Ten Commandments), and the prohibition on causing distress to animals is contained in the principle, tsa'ar ba 'alei ḥayyim. Comparably, in the *Qur'ān 'there is not an animal on earth, nor a bird that flies on its wings which is not a community like you, . . . and they shall all be gathered to their Lord in the end' (6. 38). Animals may be kept for food, transport, etc., but not in any way that involves cruelty: they may not be mutilated while still alive, which forbids much animal experimentation. Among Hindus, there is a controlling sense that that which alone is truly real (whether conceived of as *Brahman or as God) underlies and guarantees the subsistence of all appearance: 'This form is the source and indestructible seed of innumerable incarnations within the cosmos, and from it the appearances of all different living beings are created, heavenly beings, animals, humans, and all other kinds. . . . Thus you should regard deer, camels, monkeys, donkeys, rats, reptiles, birds and flies as though they are your own children' (*Śrimad-Bhagavatam*). This underlying attitude is epitomized in the sacred cow (*go). Not surprisingly, animals can be the focus of worship and in particular can be the forms of incarnation (*avatāra). Many of the gods and goddesses have particular animals associated with them, often expressed as their mounts—thus the lion and *Durgā, the elephant and *Gaṇeśa (and *Indra), the bull and *Śiva, the owl and *Lakṣmī, etc. The principle of *ahiṁsā, emphasized and reinforced among Jains and Buddhists, led to a strong preference for vegetarianism (for this issue in general, see FOOD). The fact that people in all religions treat animals badly does not alter what is in theory (and often with considerable threat) required of them. An attempt to mobilize the resources of religion for greater care of the environment and of animals within it was made in the Assisi meetings and declarations in 1986.

M. Batchelor and K. Brown (eds.), *Buddhism and Ecology* (1992); E. Breuilly and M. Palmer (eds.), *Christianity and Ecology* (1992); J. B. Callicott and R. T. Ames (eds.), *Nature in Asian Traditions of Thought* (1989); (for texts of the Assisi declarations and fuller discussions of religions and environmental issues), O. P. Diwivedi, *World Religions and the Environment* (1989); J. Holm and J. W. Bowker (eds.), *Attitudes to Nature* (1994); F. Khalid and J. O'Brien, *Islam and Ecology* (1992); R. Prime (ed.), *Hinduism and Ecology* (1992); T. Regan (ed.), *Animal Sacrifices* (1987); A. Rose (ed.), *Judaism and Ecology* (1992).

Anima naturaliter Christiana ('naturally Christian soul'): see TERTULLIAN.

Animism. The belief that perhaps all appearances, but certainly living appearances, are animated by spirits (are made vital by an *anima*, Lat., 'spirit'). *Tylor introduced the term as part of his explanation of the origin of religions, and for decades his view dominated the *anthropology of religion. Now, at most, animism would be, either a recognition of soul-beliefs in particular societies, or a casual synonym for pre-literate societies and their religions.

E. A. Nida and W. A. Smalley, *Introducing Animism* (1959).

Ānimitta (Skt., 'signless'). In *Mahāyāna Buddhism a synonym for both emptiness (*śūnyatā) and the desireless (*apraṇihita*). In the Pāli **Tripiṭaka* the signless comprises one of the three entrances to liberation (*vimokṣa-mukha*): *Majjhima Nikāya* I. 297. In his **Visuddhimagga* (21. 67) *Buddhaghoṣa holds that the signless entrance to liberation (*animitta-vimokṣa-mukha*) is achieved by the contemplation of *anicca, impermanence (*aniccānupassanā*). This attainment leads in turn to the signless element (*animittādhātu*) which is *nirvāna.

The three entrances to liberation are also mentioned in many Mahāyānasūtras, but another important usage of the term ānimitta is in connection with the notion of the elements of existence (*dharma). The **Ratnakuṭa Sūtra* considers all dharmas to be ānimitta since they are devoid of any own-nature (*niḥsvabhāva*). As such, dharmas can be neither measured (*aprameya*) nor differentiated and consequently are empty (*śūnya) of all determining signs (*nimitta*).

Aniruddha (manifest power of Viṣṇu): see VIṢṆU.

Anitya (Skt., 'not-permanent'). In Hinduism, the characteristic of *māyā, understood not in its derived sense of 'illusion', but as transitory nature of all appearance. In Buddhism (Pāli *anicca), the concept became even more fundamental.

Anjin, Anshin (Jap.). Peace in mind-consciousness (*kokoro), attained in *Zen Buddhism especially through the unsuccessful search for the mind: if the mind cannot be found, 'it' cannot give rise to disturbance. Also known as *dai-anjin*, great peace.

Annaphura (W. Syrian liturgies): see ANAPHORA.

Annapurna (Skt., 'one who gives nourishment'). Household Goddess for Hindus, who guarantees to her worshippers that food will not fail. She is a beneficent aspect of *Durgā and the *Śakti of *Śiva, and is a 'divine mother'; hence the name of the mountain range in the *Himālayas, 'the Goddess of the Harvests'.

Aññatitthiya Paribbājakas (Pāli), **Anyatirthika Parivrājakas** (Skt.). Wanderers of other views. In Buddhist scriptures, the name for groups of non-Buddhist *ascetics that were contemporaries of the *Buddha. Because they were seen as rivals and competitors to Buddhism, they are generally represented unfavourably, though there is some evidence to suggest that the Buddha himself may have regarded them more highly than his own followers. In the *Pāli canon they are depicted as rowdy, garrulous, disputatious, lacking decorum, and as speculators purveying the doctrines of *Eternalism or Annihilationism (*ucchedavāda). The Buddha and his disciples are reported to have held many dialogues with them in the parks where they assembled. On these occasions they are invariably represented as putting questions either to him or to the disciples, not the other way round, so that the opportunity always occurs for the Buddhist side of interpretation to be put. It is the partial, one-sided doctrines of the aññatitthiya paribbājakas which the Buddha was refuting when he taught the famous parable of the blind men and the elephant (that each describes a part by touch, and thus claims a wrong identification of the whole). They illustrate the many and varied philosophies and pedantries that existed in NE India at the time of the Buddha, and formed much of the backcloth for the shaping of his own teaching. Sometimes Buddhism made converts from them; if so, it was a *Vinaya rule that they should serve four months probation before entering the order (*saṅgha).

Anne, St. Mother of the Virgin *Mary, of whom nothing certain is known: she does not appear in the Bible, but only in legends beginning with the *Protogospel of *James*. Her cult, by then widely popular, was attacked by the Reformers. Feast day, in the W. (with St Joachim her husband), 26 July; in the E., 25 July.

Annihilationism (doctrine of no afterlife): see UCCHEDAVĀDA.

Annunciation. The announcement to the Virgin *Mary by the angel *Gabriel that she would conceive a son *Jesus (Luke 1. 26–38). The Christian festival, also called 'Lady Day', is celebrated on 25 Mar., exactly nine months before *Christmas, even though the date falls in *Lent.

Anointing

Judaism Pouring oil on a person symbolizes their elevation of status, especially in relation to God. In *Israel, it was performed at the inauguration of kings, the consecration of *priests, and the cleansing of lepers. The Hebrew term *mashiaḥ* ('anointed one') came to mean king or *high priest, and was then transliterated into English as *messiah. Associated with the anointing of kings was the bestowal of God's spirit ('and the Spirit of the Lord came mightily upon *David', 1 Samuel 16. 13). The anointing of priests, in contrast, sanctified them and removed them into the realm of the holy ('You shall . . . anoint the tabernacle . . . and it shall become holy . . . You shall bring *Aaron . . . and you shall anoint him . . . that he may serve me as priest', Exodus 40. 9–13). According to the *Talmud, there was only a limited supply of anointing oil, and therefore it was not used after the reign of King *Josiah.

Christianity In the New Testament anointing is found as a *charismatic means of healing: see UNCTION. From early times anointing has also been used in the rites of *baptism, *confirmation, and *ordination, as well as in the consecration of churches, altars, bells, etc. See also CHRISM.

Anonymous Christians (view that all in the exercise of humanity are related to Christ): see RAHNER, K.

Ansar (early supporters of Muḥammad in Madīna): see HELPERS.

Anselm (*c*.1033–1109). Monk and *archbishop of *Canterbury. Born in Aosta, the son of a Lombard landowner, he left Italy and became a monk of Bec, Normandy, in 1060. In 1063 he succeeded Lanfranc as prior, and in 1078 became abbot. In 1093 he succeeded Lanfranc as archbishop of Canterbury, inheriting a conflict with the king. He was in exile 1098–1100 and on his return was involved in the Investiture controversy (see GREGORY VII), spending a further period in exile 1103–7. A prolific theologian, he stands firmly in the W. tradition of *Augustine, and defended the doctrine of the double procession of the *Holy Spirit against the Greeks. His theological method is marked by a delight in the new-found powers of human reason which can operate without total subordination to scriptural and patristic 'authority'. His two most famous works were the *Proslogion* (1078–9) and **Cur Deus Homo* (1097–8): in the former, starting from the concept (or name) of God as 'that than which nothing greater can be conceived', he proceeded to demonstrate God's existence (ch. 2), his necessary existence (chs. 3–4; *ontological argument), and his attributes, especially his ineffability; in the latter, he demonstrated the rational necessity (or coherence) of the death of God-made-man, if the human offence against God through *sin is to be forgiven, rejecting much of the imagery of traditional patristic doctrine (e.g. of a combat with the *devil). Two famous phrases express his conjunction of faith and reason: *fides quaerens intellectum* ('faith seeking understanding', his first proposed title for the *Proslogion*) and *credo ut intelligam* ('I believe in order that I may understand', cf. *Augustine, *Comm. on John*, 40. 9). The *Proslogion* is addressed to God, and Anselm composed several other prayers and meditations which unite theological insight and personal devotion: 'God often works more by the unlearned seeking the things of God than by the learned seeking the things that are their own.'

R. W. Southern, *St Anselm and his Biographer* (1963).

An Shih-kao (2nd cent. CE). Buddhist monk, converted when crown prince in Parthia, who went to China and undertook and organized the first translations of Buddhist texts into Chinese. Since they were mainly concerned with *dhyāna, he became the founder of the *Dhyāna School of Buddhism. His use of *Taoist terms greatly helped the transition of Buddhism into China.

Antakṛt-daśa-aṅga: see AṄGA.

Āṇṭāḷ (S. Indian bhakti poetess): see ĀḺVĀR.

Antarā-bhava (Skt., 'intermediate state'). The period, according to Hindus, which intervenes between death and rebirth. The term was taken into Buddhism, although there is no soul (*ātman) being reborn. In Japanese, the intermediate state is *chūu* or *chūin*.

Anthem (from Gk., *antifōnon*, 'that which is sung by alternate voices'). A musical setting of words usually from the *Bible, sung by a choir in church.

The Prayer Book of 1559 requires *Anglican services to include 'an hymn, or such-like song, to the praise of Almighty God'; hence the Prayer Book of 1662 which states that after the 3rd collect of *Mattins or *Evensong, 'in Quires and Places where they sing here followeth the Anthem'. Anthems became a major part of musical repertory, and were attempted often at the level of parish church (as in Gray's 'Elegy . . . in a Country Churchyard', 'the pealing anthem swells the note of praise').

N. Temperley, *The Music of the English Parish Church* (1979).

Anthony: see ANTONY.

Anthony, Susan (advocate of women's suffrage): see FRIENDS, THE SOCIETY OF.

Anthropology of religion. In the co-ordinating of anthropology as a discipline in the later 19th cent., the study was concerned with what were thought to be 'primitive' religions, i.e. those which were believed to be closer to an original state, cruder and simpler than developed, historical religions. Few anthropologists today think that the religions of non-westernized small-scale societies are different in kind from religions of the *great traditions. Instead, they tend to be impressed by the fact that similar beliefs, *rituals, *myths, etc., can be found in both contexts. More fundamentally, anthropology itself has increasingly ceased to be an isolated discipline. The long-standing divide between anthropology and sociology, for example, has lost its force. Partly because of the realization that there are not two types of society ('civilized' and 'primitive', nor even 'rational' and 'irrational') to be studied in different ways, anthropologists and sociologists now work in both Western and non-Western contexts.

For these reasons, the anthropology of religion has effectively ceased to be a distinct 'subject'; rather, religion is seen as a major part of the ways in which individuals and societies organize and sustain their lives. Anthropologists continue to regard long-term field-work as important (with notable exceptions, e.g. C. *Lévi-Strauss), and they tend to focus on such issues as kinship organization, myth, ritual and *symbols, *magic and *witchcraft. During the first half-century, anthropologists of religion developed both structuralism and functionalism, and debated which has controlling priority: to study a skeleton (i.e., structure) establishes what functions are possible in the body which it sustains; but to study what a body does (i.e., its functions) allows one to determine what structure is necessary for those functions. But structure/function has ceased to dominate analysis, and in recent years there has been a return to the social and individual construction of meaning and significant space. While studies of particular societies and practices continue to make individual contributions of great worth, the overall view scarcely exists. Thus a recent 'Introductory Text', *Anthropological Studies of Religion* (Brian Morris, 1987), commended by another anthropologist as 'the best text on religion thus far' tells us extremely little about religion and much about other anthropologists assessing religion. Until the 19th-cent. ghost of reductionism is exorcised, the anthropology of religion is likely to remain introspective.

Anthropomorphism (Gk., 'of human form'). The attribution of human qualities to the divine, as also to other items in the environment, hence the conceiving of God or the gods, or of natural features, in human form. Anthropomorphism is extremely ancient, and is clearly a major strategy of the religious imagination. From Xenophanes (*c*.570–475 BCE, 'If oxen, lions and horses had hands with which to make images, they would fashion gods after their own shapes and give them bodies like their own') to Rupert Brooke (1887–1915, 'Immense, of fishy form and mind, Squamous, omnipotent, and kind; And under that Almighty Fin, The littlest fish may enter in'), it has been recognized that anthropormphism is a necessary consequence of the inadequacies of human language in relation to God, and that religion is a constant refinement of that anthropomorhic necessity. The status of such language and descriptions has been a matter of fierce debate in those religions which rely on revelations which describe God in terms of human qualities—e.g. sitting on a throne (in Islam, see TANZĪH). In general the limitations of *analogical language and of *symbols led in the direction of the *via negativa. That is true even of Hinduism, but in that case the prevailing sense of God underlying all appearance makes the occurrence of anthropomorphism deceptive: there is a real presence through the image, and thus through sound and language (see e.g. ŚABDA; MANTRA; MAṆḌALA).

Anthroposophical Society, The. Organization founded by the Austro-Hungarian Rudolf Steiner (1861–1925) in 1912, which has for its principal aim the development of new perspectives for the study of humanity. Matter, in Steiner's view, is a necessary evil, for without descending into matter, spirit cannot rise up and acquire an individuated form. Humans are the high point of this process of the evolution of spirit. Doctrines derived from Hinduism and Christianity have been grafted on to this basic teaching. For example, Christ is seen as the archetype of spiritual individuality, and at his Second Coming spirit, until then trapped in matter, will be liberated, thus allowing a gradual process of spiritual evolution involving countless reincarnations to unfold.

In addition to the General Anthroposophical Society with its headquarters in Switzerland, the Society's other institutions include the Waldorf Schools for Children and the Anthroposophical Church known as the Christian Community, and established by Steiner in 1922. The extensive rituals of this Church have an esoteric rather than an orthodox character, and it has both men and women priests. It provides the ceremonial and worship for the village communities organized by the Camphill Movement.

Another important Anthroposophical institution is the School of Spiritual Science situated near Basel in Switzerland. The school gives lectures, conducts group spiritual research, and teaches a three-tier system of meditation in which one passes through the first stage (designated imagination) to that of inspiration, and finally to the intuitive stage.

The membership is about 25,000 worldwide and of these some 8,000 are to be found in West Germany.

J. Hembeben (ed.), *Rudolf Steiner in Selbstzeugnissen und Bilddokumenten* (1963); G. Wachsmuth, *Life and Work* (1955).

Antichrist. An eschatological figure first mentioned in the epistles of John in the New Testament. He is described as a pseudo-*messiah who stands against Jesus at the end of days. Similar ideas can be found in Jewish *eschatology where the powers of evil are finally overcome in the ultimate great battle. The Christian Antichrist tradition draws on Jewish notions of an evil, arrogant, eschatological ruler, and the Antichrist frequently carries anti-Jewish traits. The concept may have grown out of the continued Jewish *messianic hopes, cast by Christians into a demonic mode.

In the *New Testament, the Antichrist is mentioned by name only in 1 John 2. 18 and 22, 4. 3, 2 John 7, but the images of Revelations (e.g. the beasts of ch. 13) and 2 Thessalonians 2. 3–10 (the 'man of sin' who will appear and claim to be God but then be destroyed by Christ) have given colour to the concept. All these passages probably derive from Jewish eschatology which knew at least of a wicked king to come (see e.g. Daniel 11. 36). In later Christian tradition Antichrist has been identified with *Satan; with the emperor Nero *redivivus*; with other particular enemies of the faith; and sometimes by Protestants with the pope.

In Islam, al-Dajjāl is an anti-religious figure who is often identified with Shaitān/Satan. In particular, he is the opponent and tempter of 'Īsā/*Jesus, who will fight a final battle with him when 'Īsā returns at the end of days. Recognizable from his gross build, he has a single eye set in his forehead like a floating grape, and above it is inscribed *Kāfir.

W. Bossuet, *The Antichrist Legend* (1896).

Anticlericalism. Hostility (expressed usually by laypeople) against the privileges enjoyed by the Christian clergy, and a criticism of their failure to maintain the undertakings of their calling, to look after those committed to their care and to preach and teach the Christian gospel: 'There are none harder nor hungrier than men of Holy Church' (Langland). The extent of anticlericalism in pre-*Reformation Europe varied: it was widespread in Germany (often associated with heresy); the *Lollards in England and the followers of *Hus in Bohemia voiced anticlerical sentiments, but so, at times, did *Erasmus and other reformers who were Catholic in their beliefs. In the 18th cent., it became associated with the emancipation of knowledge and inquiry from the attempted control of the Church, and with an increasing emphasis on the rights and autonomy of individuals, and led to widespread freeing of the State from Church control. In the French revolution, the RC establishment was removed (1792–3), and although a concordat in 1801 (only later implemented) restored the position of the Church, anticlericalism persisted and increased until in 1905 the recognition of the Church was withdrawn. In the American Constitution (and subsequent amendments), Church and State were rigorously separated, with anticlericalism playing a part: 'Ecclesiastical establishments tend to great ignorance and corruption, all of which facilitate the execution of mischievous projects' (James Madison, 'father of the Constitution', 1774: see J. Lasley, *Priestcraft and the Slaughterhouse Religion*). The consequent marginalization of the Church and the diminution in the public role of the clergy led to a reduction in anticlericalism. However, the attacks made by Pope *John Paul II on the *Enlightenment as the source of 'the culture of death' (which now, in his view, is dominant), combined with issues of celibacy and child abuse among the clergy, have led to a resurgence of anticlericalism, as clergy become identified with an authoritarian Church not open to criticism. 'Anticlericalism' has also been applied in other religions to opposition to institutional figures of authority, although there are no clergy of exactly the same kind.

E. Cameron, *The European Reformation* (1991).

Anti-cult movement. Collectively, those groups and organizations that began to emerge in the 1970s in the United States, Europe, Australia, and elsewhere, in response to what were considered to be the harmful effects of *new religions on recruits.

These bodies, which include the Spiritual Counterfeits Project (SCP) in the USA, FAIR (Family Action Information and Rescue) in Britain, and ADFI (Association pour la defénse de la famille et de l'individu) in France, disseminate literature on new religions, carry out research, and seek to counsel and advise those distressed by the fact that a friend or relative has become a member of a new religion.

Antidoron (Gk., 'instead of the gift'). In the Byzantine *liturgy the part of the *eucharistic loaf which is not consecrated, but is blessed and distributed to the congregation at the end of the service. Non-Orthodox thus receive it 'instead of' communion, and it is considered a symbol of *ecumenical fellowship. A similar custom ('pain bénit') survives in the Roman Catholic Church in France. Members of a congregation may take the antidoron home and consume a part of it each day as a part of their morning prayer.

Antinomianism (Gk., *anti*, 'against', + *nomos*, law) A tendency in all religions, for some among those who believe to regard themselves as so possessed of grace/salvation/enlightenment, etc., that existing laws are no longer applicable. It may also apply to an attitude which regards the keeping of rules and laws as an impediment on the way to freedom/release/salvation, etc., because it produces a legalistic understanding of actions and rewards. See Index, Antinomianism.

Antioch (modern Antakya in SE Turkey). City associated in Christian tradition with a tendency in theology opposed to that of *Alexandria. Its exponents include John *Chrysostom, *Theodore of Mopsuestia, *Nestorius, and *Theodoret. 'Antiochene' exegesis of scripture looked for historical rather than for hidden meanings, and was critical in holding some parts of the Bible more valuable than others. In *Trinitarian thinking, the Antiochenes insisted on the oneness of God, and thus saw the 'persons' as being in effect three modes of operation. In the *christological controversy of the 5th cent., the Antiochene position appears as an emphasis on the duality of natures united (too loosely, in their opponents' view) in Christ and the integrity of his humanity. The Council of Antioch (341) attempted to modify the *Nicene settlement. Antioch is now the *see of five *patriarchs, the *Greek Orthodox, Syrian Orthodox, *Melkite, *Maronite, and Syrian Catholic.

Antiphon (Gk., *antiphōnon*, 'responsive'). 1. In the W. Church, sentences, usually from the *Bible, recited before and after the *Psalms and *canticles in the divine *office, by alternative choirs or voices. They vary with the season or feast.

2. In the Orthodox liturgy, in addition to responsories, it may be any of the three anthems at the beginning of the *eucharist; or any 'alternate utterance' in which psalms or other words are sung alternately. The custom is said to go back to *Ignatius of Antioch, but by the time of *Basil, the antiphon had become more of a dialogue between a reader and congregation.

Antipope. A person in Christianity who claims (or exercises) the office of *pope illegitimately. The RC Church lists thirty-seven, from Hippolytus (d. *c*.235) to Felix V, who abdicated in 1449. The major and serious conflict over the papacy took place in the W. schism, 1378–1417. After the election of Urban VI in 1378, some cardinals, claiming that he was mentally unstable, elected Clement VII, who returned to Avignon as the centre of papal authority. Attempts to heal the schism included the election of a third pope, Alexander V, at Pisa. The attempt to locate continuing authority in these circumstances led directly into the conciliar controversy, raising the possibility that a general council, or the college of *cardinals (with or without such additional figures as certain university professors), had the ultimate authority—a position condemned by Pius II in the Bull *Exsecrabilis*, and also by the First *Vatican Council. The schism was ended by the elevation of Oddo at the Council of Constance (1414–18) to become Martin V.

Anti-semitism. Hostility against the Jewish people. The term was first used by Wilhelm Marr in Germany) in 1879, but prejudice against the Jews appeared in ancient times. The Roman emperor Claudius, for example, described the Jews as a people who spread 'a great plague throughout the world', and the destruction of the second *Temple in 70 CE was seen as evidence that God was punishing them. The Christian *gospels stress the responsibility of the Jews for the *crucifixion of *Jesus ('And all the people answered, "His blood be on us and on our children" ', Matthew 27. 25) and identify the Jews with the *devil ('you are of your father, the devil': John 8. 14). With the triumph of Christianity, Jews were increasingly persecuted, marginalized, and deprived of civil rights. In 1215, the 4th Lateran Council decreed special clothing for Jews, thereby increasing their isolation. They were accused of desecrating the Christian *host, of poisoning wells, and of killing Christian children. As the 16th cent. theologian *Erasmus put it, 'If it is incumbent upon a good Christian to detest the Jews, then we are all good Christians'. The *Reformation made little difference initially to these attitudes, especially in the case of *Luther, whose work *Against the Jews and Their Lies* (1543) proposed radical measures, e.g. burning synagogues, which were later implemented under Hitler. There was some amelioration in the *Enlightenment, when Lessing and others saw a core of truth in all religions. But 19th-cent. anti-Semitism was reinforced on racist grounds, especially by Gobineau and Chamberlain.

Although Jews fared somewhat better in Islamic lands, they did not achieve full civil rights in Christian Europe until the 19th cent. Anti-Semitic feelings did not disappear then, however, as is illustrated by the *Dreyfus case in France in 1894, the pronouncements of Richard Wagner in Germany, the circulation of such spurious works as *The Protocols of the Elders of Zion*, and the huge numbers of Jews who emigrated to the United States to escape the *pogroms of E. Europe. Cartoons of the period show the Jew as avaricious, lascivious, and power-mad. Anti-Semitism was a fundamental tenet of German National Socialism which culminated in the *Holocaust. The foundation of the state of Israel was believed by Zionists to be the only solution to anti-Semitism, but as a result of the Arab–Israeli conflict, Muslim anti-Semitism is today even more virulent than its Christian counterpart. The tenacious persistence of anti-Semitism is summarized in the melancholy prediction of V. Adler, 'The last anti-semite will die only with the last Jew.'

G. I. Langmuir, *History, Religion and Antisemitism* (1991); L. Poliakov, *The History of Antisemitism* (1974–85).

Antony, St (also called 'the Great' or 'of Egypt', *c*.250–356). Christian hermit whose life and actions lie at the foundation of *monasticism. He withdrew into the desert in *c*.285, in order to develop holiness of life away from the distractions of the world. In the desert, he is said to have wrestled with demons in the form of wild beasts. As word spread, he was joined by other solitaries, until eventually his advice and encouragement provided a *rule. They remained individual and solitary and did not come together in a common life. His withdrawal did not mean a lack of interest in church affairs, and he took the side of *Athanasius in the *Arian dispute. Athanasius wrote the *Vita Antonii*, from which details of his life are derived. He is regarded as 'the father' of Christian monasticism.

R. T. Meyer, *The Life of Antony* (1950).

Antony of Padua, St (?1195–1231). Christian *Franciscan, *patron saint of the poor. Well-educated, he joined the Franciscans in search of simplicity and perhaps *martyrdom. But he was summoned to become the first official professor or teacher of the Order. His zeal, especially against the Cathars, earned him the title of *malleus haereticorum*, 'hammer of heretics'. His power as a preacher led to widespread renewal of Christian commitment. He became regarded as a worker of miracles, and, as his cult developed, he became associated with the power to restore or locate lost property—perhaps because of an incident in which a novice was forced, by an apparition, to return a psalter which he had taken. He was canonized in 1232 and made a Doctor of the Church in 1946. Feast day, 13 June.

J. Toussaert, *Antonius von Padua* (1967).

Antyeṣṭi, Antyeshti ('cremation'). The sixteenth sacrament in Hinduism, dealing with funeral rites. There is no other *saṃskāra for the body after the last rites. *Aśwalāyana Gṛhya Sūtra* gives the following procedure for the final rites of cremation: the dead person, if male, should be bathed by males, and, if female, should be bathed by females. Paste of rubbed sandalwood should be applied to the corpse and it should be dressed in new clothes. The following items should be used for burning: saffron, musk, sandalwood, camphor, sufficient wood for fuel, and these things should be taken to the cremation ground which is usually near a river. If there is a permanent *kunda* (a rectangular structure in stone with a rectangular hollow in the centre) it should be used. In its absence a temporary one may be dug near a river bank. Wood fuel should be neatly arranged on the stones as if building a wall. Large spoons should be tied to long staves so that oblations of molten ghī may be offered to the fire from a distance. When the pyre is ready, the body should be laid on it and covered over with more wood. The head of the corpse should be pointing to the north. Male corpses should be shaved before bathing. A lamp burning ghī should be lit, and the man officiating at the funeral should light a little camphor with the flame of the lamp and with it should light the pyre. The pyre should be first lit at the north end and gradually at other points until the whole is completely ablaze. Five oblations should be offered to *Agni, *Soma, Loka, Earth, and the other world, with the words: 'Dear departed! After death, may the power of your sight be absorbed in the sun, your soul into the atmosphere; may you go to the luminous region or the earth, according to your religious merit, or go to the waters if it be your lot, or to the plants, assuming different bodies.'

Following the instructions of the **Rg Veda*, seventeen oblations are offered by four persons standing at each corner of the pyre. Afterwards, following the **Yajur Veda*, sixty-three oblations are offered to the following: the five airs of vitality with their strength; the earth; the firmament; the heavenly region; the ten directions; fire; air; the sun; the moon; the asterisms; purity; the two eyes; the two ears; hair; skin; blood; fat; flesh; sinews; bones; marrow; semen; rebirth; perseverance; good effort; various activities; uplift; the waters; the navel; the tongue; cleanliness; purifying; enlightenment; sadness; austerity; agencies of austerity; day; vengeance; repentance; medicine; time; death; the supreme spirit; physical forces; spiritual forces; heaven and earth.

In ancient times, ghī was readily available as a secondary fuel. The idea of putting so much ghī on the pyre is that the whole pile should continue to burn vigorously so that the corpse is reduced to ashes. In modern times, when cremation can be by gas or electricity, only a token ceremony is performed and *mantras are recited, but generally no oblations can be offered.

On the third day, the near relatives go back to the funeral ground and collect the few remaining bones and either bury them in the ground nearby or throw them in the river. The *Vedas do not mention any rites, yet in practice on the twelfth day, relations and friends are invited for the feast of the wake. The annual *śrāddha (ancestor veneration) is performed by the surviving relatives.

Aṇu (Skt., 'tiny, minute'). In *Vaiśeṣika, a point in space without dimension which evolves from the subtle elements (*tanmātras*). Aṇus are eternal, invisible, and intangible, and are in a constant state of disintegration and reintegration. The material universe is evolved through the coming together of aṇus: a combination of two aṇus (*dvyaṇuka*) creates a form with length and breadth but not thickness; combined with a third atom (*tryaṇuka*), this form becomes a particle. At the highest atom stage (*paramāṇu*) the aṇus become material. There are four basic *paramāṇus* which are the essential components of earth, water, fire, and air. These correspond to the *mahābhūtas of other Indian philosophical systems. In *Kashmir Śaivism, aṇu is the soul or basic particle of *Śiva. For the application among Terapanth Jains, see BHIKṢU, ĀCĀRYA.

Anubhava (Skt., 'experience'). In *Vedānta, 'experience' or 'intuition' as the basis of an individual's knowledge of *Brahman, the Absolute. For *Śaṅkara brahman-anubhava, the 'intuition of Brahman', is the ultimate experience—impersonal, transcendental, and abstract. This anubhava is different from all other experience in that it is non-dual, beyond the distinction of subject and object, yet characterizable in essence as *sat-cit-ānanda, of the nature of unchanging bliss-consciousness. The intuition of Brahman is *enlightenment and liberation; it is the experience of one's self as Brahman (*brahmātmabhāva*). According to Śankara this experience is available for those properly prepared only if triggered by the hearing of certain great scriptural utterance, *mahāvakyas, such as *tattvamasi*, 'Thou art That'. In *Advaita Vedānta, enlightenment is not a matter of speculation or emotion, but a direct and immediate anubhava.

Anubhāvi-guru (Skt.). The *guru who is witness of the highest truth, because he has direct experience of it.

Anubhūti (direct experience of Brahman): see REVELATION.

Anu Gītā. The miniature Gītā, a summary and recapitulation of the **Bhagavad-gītā*, given to *Arjuna by *Kṛṣṇa at the end of the Great War, because, as Arjuna says, 'the instruction already given has gone out of his degenerate mind'. It is selective (e.g. it does not recapitulate the devotional parts of the *Gītā*), and inclines to an emphasis on *jñāna-yoga.

Tr. K. T. Telang (1882; repr. 1965); A. Sharma, *The Hindu Gītā* . . . (1986).

Anugraha (uncompelled action, grace): see RĀMĀNUJA.

Anumāna (inference): see RĀMĀNUJA; NYĀYA.

Anupassanā (Pāli), **Anupaśyanā** (Skt., *anupaśyati*, 'look at'). Contemplation, observation; the mode of meditation in Buddhism through which insight (*vipassanā) takes place. Anupassanā works on the basis of looking at the object of thought not in terms of the quality or attribute which it seems to the natural, unenlightened mind to possess but in terms of its contrary or opposite, that is, its *true* characteristic. So, for example, the abandonment of the perception of permanence takes place by means of the contemplation of impermanence (*anicca), of the perception of self by means of the contemplation of no self (*anatman), and so on. **Visuddhimagga* (p. 694) lists eighteen such topics.

Anupodisesa-nibbāna (nirvāna with no conditions remaining): see NIRUPADHIŚEṢA-NIRVĀṆA.

Anurādhapura. Capital of Sri Lanka until 10th cent. CE. The Mahāvihāra monasteries were established here, along with many temples and *stūpas. Of particular importance are the two great dagobas, Ruwanweli and Thūparāma, which are early stages in the development of stūpas. A branch or cutting of the *Bo tree (under which the *Buddha became enlightened) was planted in the 3rd cent. BCE, which survives to the present as (reputedly) the oldest tree in the world.

Anuruddha. 1. A close companion of the *Buddha, who was present at his death. To him is attributed the recitation and thus preservation of *Anguttara-Nikāya.

2. Theravādin Buddhist scholar of uncertain date (but within centuries either side of 10th cent. CE), author of *Abhidhammattha-sangaha* which summarizes Theravādin teaching; cf. *Buddhaghosa's *Visuddhimagga*.

Anusaya (Skt., *anuśaya*). In Buddhism a latent tendency or disposition towards vice. The standard list includes seven such factors: sensuous lust (*kāmarāga*), hostility (*patigha*), speculative views (*diṭṭhi), sceptical doubt (*vicikicchā*), conceit (*māna*), craving for continued existence (*bhavarāga*), and ignorance (*avijjā).

These factors are the dormant predisposing conditions for corresponding forms of manifest conduct (*paryutthāna*) which are symptomatic of mental and emotional turbulence. Until the underlying anusaya is eradicated, the harmful dispositions will subsist (*anu-si*) as personality-traits. According to Buddhist psychology these dispositions are carried over to the next life and exist even in the newly born infant. On the path to enlightenment they are eradicated in a particular sequence, with the disappearance of the last two marking the attainment of *Arhatship. Cf. also ĀSAVA.

Anusim (Heb., 'forced ones'). People compelled unwillingly to convert from Judaism to another faith. Instances of forced conversion have occurred throughout Christian history and include the baptism of the Jewish community of Clermont-Ferrand in 576 CE, compulsory conversions in the Rhineland in the 10th cent. and the Conversos or *Marranos of Christian Spain. In many cases, these converts tried to retain their Jewish heritage and attempted in secret to teach their children their ancestral beliefs and practices. Forced conversion also took place in Islamic countries, where there were similar attempts to retain Jewish identity.

Anussati (Pāli, 'recollection'). Contemplative practices in Buddhism which break attachment to the three destructive roots (*akuśala). Initially six, they are now reckoned as ten: contemplation on (i) the *Buddha; (ii) *dharma; (iii) the *saṅgha; (iv) *sīla;

(v) *dāna (or detachment); (vi) *devas; and (vii) death; (viii) the body; (ix) breathing (see ĀNĀPĀNA); (x) peace.

Anussava (Pāli), **Anuśrava** (Skt., 'that which has been heard or reported'). Tradition: according to early Buddhism, that which is passed on by word of mouth from one person to another and from one generation to another. In the *Nikāyas it is chiefly used with reference to the *brahmans who appealed to tradition as sacrosanct, believing their own *Vedas to be divine revelation and the exclusive source of all knowledge and truth. However, Buddhism maintained that the claim for any doctrine or teaching to represent knowledge or truth cannot rest exclusively on the fact that it is part of or belongs to tradition. In order for a body of teaching to be regarded as valid knowledge three criteria need to be met: the teacher or transmitter of the doctrine must be observed as someone who is free of attachment (*rāga), hate (*dosa), and delusion (*moha); the meaning of the teaching should be tested by the pupil independently of the teacher; and the teaching has to be tested in practice.

Anuttaravimāna. The five heavens of the Jains. The detail of how ten great ascetics attained these heavens is found in *Anuttoropapādaka-daśa-anga* (see AṄGA).

Anuttarayogatantra (division of tantric texts): see TRIPIṬAKA.

Anuttoropapādaka-daśa-aṅga: see AṄGA.

Anuvrata. The 'lesser vows' which Jain lay-people take, as a kind of parallel to the great vows of the ascetics. They are applied to the practice of daily life. Thus (i) *ahiṁsā: whereas the ascetic avoids all violence, the lay-person tries to avoid wanton destruction of life-forms; (ii) *satya*, truthfulness: this is applied esp. to business and trade dealings; (iii) *asteya*: this is applied to modern temptations such as tax-avoidance; (iv) *brahmacarya: celibacy is by definition irrelevant to the married man, but he attempts control, perhaps abstaining from sex after a son is born who will continue and fulfill obligations; (v) *aparigraha*: instead of abandoning all possessions, he is required to be moderate and to give the surplus to religious needs. The *gunavratas* are three supplementary vows, restricting unnecessary travel (in the light of (i) above, and counteracting self-indulgence and extravagance). The *śikṣavratas* are three vows of instruction, relating to specific religious duties.

Aṇuvrata Movement, (Skt., *aṇu*, 'lesser', + *vrata*, 'vows'). Indian moral revival movement based on the *anuvrata vows of Jains. Founded in 1948 by Acharya Tul(a)si, head of the Jain Śvetāmbara Terāpantha sect, the movement aims to purge corruption and uplift the moral tone of the life of individuals and the nation. By restating the five ancient Jain values embodied in the vows, the movement, which has had considerable impact in India, seeks to bring about a non-violent revolution in human values and foster goodwill, tolerance and universal love. To further these goals, an international branch of the movement was established in Jaipur in 1984. See further BHIKṢU, ĀCĀRYA.

Anuvyañjana. In Buddhism, one of the secondary or minor physical attributes of a 'Great Man' (*mahāpurusa*), and especially of the *Buddha. There are said to be eighty such features of the bodily grace and beauty of such a person: these include perfectly formed and proportioned limbs, elegance of gait, a melodic voice, and auspicious signs on the palms of the hands and soles of the feet. Several versions of the full list occur in textual sources although the specific attributes and the order of the items vary: see LAKṢAṆA.

Apacāyana (respect to elders): see DASAKUSALAKAMMA.

Apadāna (part of Pāli canon): see KHUDDAKANIKĀYA.

Āpaddharma (Skt., *āpad*, 'misfortune', + *dharma*, 'law'). In Hinduism, a practice only permissible in time of calamity, distress, or misfortune; the *dharma of emergencies. For example, in time of civil disorder a king may violate the laws applying in peacetime, and in time of famine a *brahman may violate the food prohibitions of his *caste. In Hindu mythology, āpaddharma commonly involves the reversal of caste roles: brahmans behave according to the *svadharma of *outcastes, and are rebuked by outcastes, whose āpaddharma is to uphold the institution of caste.

Apara-vidya (Skt., 'not-direct knowledge'). Knowledge by hearsay or report in Hinduism, as opposed to para-vidya, direct knowledge by way of experience, hence also known as Brahma-vidya.

Aparigraha (Skt.). 1. The state in Hinduism of detachment from all possessions and desires, one of the five virtues required on the first step of *Rāja-Yoga, according to *Patañjali's account. The others are *satya* (truthfulness), *ahiṁsā (non-injury of others), *asteya* (not stealing), and *brahmacarya (continent and holy life). They constitute the Mahāvrata, the Great Vow which remains in force for all the other steps.

2. Jain vow of detachment: see FIVE GREAT VOWS.

Apartheid (policy of separate development): see DUTCH REFORMED CHURCH.

Apasmāra (Skt., 'epilepsy'). The demonic dwarf who in Hindu mythology personifies ignorance and forgetfulness. In Hindu *iconography, *Śiva as Natarāja is depicted dancing on Apasmāra, breaking the back of forgetfulness. According to the *Suśruta* **Saṁhitā*, Apasmāra is the personification of epilepsy.

Apāya (Skt.). The four lower modes of rebirth possible for humans. They are animals, *narakas (beings in torment), *pretas (hungry ghosts), and *asuras (roughly, demons, but only in the sense that they are complementary to *devas, and may thus be reckoned as among the good, or higher, modes of existence, *gati).

Aphrahat, Aphraates (early 4th cent.). 'The Persian sage', earliest of *Syriac church *fathers. He was a *bishop in Persia during the persecutions of Shapur II (310–79). His twenty-three *Demonstrations*, dated between 337 and 345, give a survey of the Christian faith. They are notable for their emphasis on celibacy and asceticism generally, primitive theology uninfluenced by Gk. expressions, and mildness of polemic against the Jews.

Apikoros (probably from Gk., 'Epicurean'). A person who abandons the *rabbinic *tradition. The term first occurs in the *Mishnah, and it is defined by *Maimonides as one who rejects divine *revelation and *prophecy, or who insists that God has no knowledge of human activity. Today it is used to describe anyone with heretical or heterodox views.

Apocalypse, Apocalyptic (Gk., 'revelation'). Jewish and Christian literature of revelations, making known the features of a heavenly or future time or world, or, in general, things hidden from present knowledge; hence 'apocalyptic books' or literature. Between the 2nd cent. BCE and the 2nd cent. CE, *prophecy was supposed to have ended. Apocalyptical literature therefore tends to be set in the earlier period of prophecy. Frequently *eschatological in orientation, such books as Daniel, Baruch, 4 Ezra, Enoch, and some among the *Dead Sea Scrolls, look forward to the last days when wickedness will finally be overthrown and God will be supreme. After the destruction of the second *Temple in 70 CE, there was increased emphasis on the meaning of the political upheavals. Such works as *Apocalypse of *Abraham*, *Life of *Adam and *Eve*, and *Apocalpyse of Baruch* exerted an influence on the *midrash of the day and on the development of mystical thought within Judaism.

In Christianity, the controlling example is the Book of Revelation, although apocalyptic words are attributed to *Jesus: thus Mark 13 is often referred to as 'The Markan Apocalypse'. Because apocalyptic is often concerned with catastrophic events, e.g. the end of the world, it lends itself to such titles as *Apocalypse Now*, a film exploring the Vietnam War on the basis of Joseph Conrad's *Heart of Darkness*.

B. McGinn, *Apocalyptic Spirituality* (1979); C. Rowland, *The Open Heaven . . .* (1982); D. S. Russell, *The Method and Message of Jewish Apocalyptic* (1964); *Apocalypse: The Morphology of a Genre*, special issue of *Semeia*, 14 (1979).

Apocalypse of Ezra: see ESDRAS, BOOKS OF, 3 and 4.

Apocatastasis (Gk., *apokath'istēmi*, 'to restore'). The restoration of the created order to a condition, either of its intended perfection, or to its source (e.g. God as creator). It is thus associated with the end of the present cosmos. However, it has also been adopted by those who hold that creation is eternal (see COSMOLOGY): in that case, apocatastasis refers to the phase in which the absolute condition of perfection is attained. Thus, *Origen linked the belief to a view that all will eventually be saved. In Jewish *kabbalah, the belief appears in the form of the return of the emanations (*sefirot) into God, so that all is in him. In Islam, it was developed to resolve the issue of whether creation is eternal or a single initiative: if God creates, then it must always have been an inherent and necessary part of his nature, since otherwise he would have made a quasi-human decision, and would thus have changed in his intention and act; but if creation is eternal, then God in himself is not Absolute. Apocatastasis resolves the issue by saying that, even in an infinite sequence of creations, there will always be a 'moment' (itself unmeasurable, because there is no time, which is relative) when the possibility of creation is inherent but not actual, and when God is Absolute. In Hinduism, something akin to apocatastasis occurs in the *mahāpralaya. In Buddhism, the equivalent is the point at which the condition of nirvāna is universally realized.

Apocrypha (Gk., 'hidden things'). Jewish books associated with the *Bible, but not included in the Jewish *canon. These are works regarded by the sages as *Sefarim hizonim* (extraneous books). They include (i) *Esdras; (ii) *Tobit; (iii) *Judith; (iv) additions to *Esther; (v) *Wisdom of Solomon; (vi) Ecclesiasticus; (vii) *Baruch; (viii) *Song of the Three Children; (ix) *Susanna; (x) *Bel and the Dragon; (xi) The Prayer of *Manasseh; (xii) 1 *Maccabees; (xiii) 2 Maccabees. In addition, there are many other books, known as *Pseudepigrapha (frequently *apocalyptic in character), which were written in the same period. During the *Talmudic period, there seems to have been little knowledge of these books in Jewish circles. They were preserved in the Christian Church, and it was only in the time of the Renaissance that Jewish scholars again came into contact with the original works. Meanwhile, the Apocrypha, but not the Pseudepigrapha, became incorporated into the canon of *scripture for the *Roman Catholic Church (except for 1 and 2 Esdras and The Prayer of Manasseh). The E. Church accepts Tobit, Judith, Ecclesiasticus, and Wisdom. Since the apocryphal books were included in the *Septuagint, they appeared inevitably in the *Vulgate. The Council of *Trent anathematized those who do not regard these books as canonical. *Luther, followed by reformed parts of the Church, included a translation of them in the Bible, but regarded them as not equal to scripture: they are 'profitable and good to read'.

L. H. Brockington, *A Critical Introduction* . . . (1961).

Apocryphal. Of the same form as a book of scripture but excluded from the *canon as doubtful or spurious. Among Jewish writings the word is best applied not to the *Apocrypha proper but to the wider class of *Pseudepigrapha, and thus to the 'Apocryphal Old Testament'. The 'Apocryphal New Testament' includes gospels, acts of apostles, epistles, and apocalypses. Among the gospels, The Gospel according to the *Hebrews and The Gospel of *Thomas may include trustworthy traditions, but most simply set out to satisfy popular curiosity with tales of *Jesus' childhood, post-resurrection life, etc. The Acts—of *Peter, Paul, *John, Andrew, and *Thomas—are likewise largely romance. The most famous of the epistles are the spurious letters of Paul known as 3 Corinthians and Laodiceans; and of apocalypses, that of Peter.

E. Hennecke and W. Schneemelcher, *New Testament Apocrypha* (Eng. tr. 1963); M. R. James, *The Apocryphal New Testament* (1924); H. F. D. Sparks (ed.), *The Apocryphal Old Testament* (1984).

Apollinarius or **Apollinaris** (*c.*310–*c.*390). Christian *heretic. Although as *bishop of Laodicea he was an orthodox opponent of *Arianism, his *christological teaching was condemned, finally in 381 at the Council of *Constantinople. He left the church *c.*375. Apollinarianism is the view which defends the divine nature in *Christ by refusing to allow that there could be moral development during his lifetime. There can be a human body and soul, but the *Logos replaces the human spirit and is thus not subject to change. Such a view, according to opponents, means that Christ was not fully human.

A. Grillmeier, *Christ in Christian Tradition*, i (1975, *ad loc.*).

Apollonian and Dionysiac religion. Contrasted forms of religion, the former being reflective and rational, the latter ecstatic and fervent. The distinction does not altogether rest in consistent distinctions in Greek religion, though they can be illustrated *from* Greek religion. The distinction in its modern form derives from the work of *Nietzsche, who, in *The Birth of Tragedy*, argued that the achievement of Greece did not rest on Apollonian calm alone but on its fusion with the passion of Dionysus—a blend which Greek tragedy exhibits. Apollonian art is a quest for rationality in an irrational world; Dionysiac art tears the veil from the surface and allows a glimpse into the nihilism and destructiveness below. Tragedy is the highest art, because it unites the two. It was rapidly realized that religions exhibit these two styles, and they became a frame of reference for the analysis of religious behaviour. Thus Ruth Benedict (*Patterns of Culture*, 1948) applied them to indigenous American cultures of N. America, contrasting the Apollonian emphasis on moderation, sobriety, and restraint which she found among the Pueblo Indians with the Dionysiac desire for exaltation in personal experience, recklessness, and states of emotional excess (sometimes assisted by drugs) which she found in most other tribes.

Apologetics (Lat., *apologia*, 'defence'). The defence, or commendation, of a religion. Among Jews, there is an extensive literature defending the Jewish people and religion against adverse criticism. It inevitably reflects the pattern of relationships between Jews and their neighbours through the centuries. In Hellenistic times, the emphasis was on the defence of the Jewish tradition against paganism, often claiming (e.g. *Josephus) that Judaism fulfilled the quest of pagan philosophy and religion. In the Middle Ages, Jewish scholars held disputations with Christian ecclesiastics, and such works as *Judah Halevi's *Sefer ha-Kuzari* (The Book of the Khazars) compared Christian, Islamic, and Jewish *revelation. With the growth of secularism in the modern era, Jewish apologetic has been used in the battle to gain religious toleration and civil rights, to combat *antisemitism in its many guises, and to defend the state of *Israel.

Among Christians, the name 'Apologists' is given to, the earliest group of Christian writers who (*c.*120–220) composed defences of Christianity addressed to educated outsiders. They include Athenagoras, *Justin Martyr, *Minucius Felix, *Tatian, and *Tertullian. They were concerned especially to refute charges that Christianity was a new religion and that it might be polytheistic or immoral or politically dangerous. Some also drew attention to good features in pagan life, and claimed that the work of the *Logos could effect such results. After the establishment of the Church under *Constantine, the work of apologetics continued, endeavouring to establish the validity of Christian claims. A notable example is *Augustine's **City of God*. *Calvin's *Institutes of the Christian Religion* is addressed to Francis I (the French King) to persuade him that he was in error in pursuing a policy of persecution.

K. Werner, *Geschichte der apologetischen und polemischen Literatur* . . . (1861–7).

Apologists: see APOLOGETICS.

Apophatic theology. Another name for 'theology by way of negation', according to which God is known by negating concepts that might be applied to him, stressing the inadequacy of human language and concepts to say anything of God. *Philo and *Plotinus influenced the Christian apophatic tradition, which is found in e.g. *Gregory of Nyssa and Pseudo-*Dionysius the Areopagite; it is characteristic of mystical theology and Eastern *Orthodoxy, and shows parallels with Indian *Advaita Vedānta: see e.g. NETI, NETI.

Apostasy, (Gk., 'stand away from'). The act or state of rejecting one religious faith for another. In the books of *Maccabees, those Jews who adopted

*Hellenistic practices were described as apostates. Once Christianity became the dominant religion of the Roman Empire, the fear of persecution or expulsion was a frequent cause of apostasy from Judaism, although there were some converts to Christianity, such as Judah ha-Levi of Cologne, who were motivated by genuine religious conviction. Apostasy was regarded with horror by the Jewish community, although a distinction was always made between apostates who converted for gain and the *anusim or *Marranos who were forced to convert and tried to maintain their Judaism secretly. Since the 18th cent., the motivation for abandoning Judaism has tended to be a desire for *assimilation into mainstream society—so, for example, the German poet Heinrich Heine was baptized in order to contribute to the culture of his day. According to the *halakhah, an apostate remains a Jew: he can contract a valid Jewish marriage, and the child of an apostate mother is considered a Jew. However, as the law stands at present, an apostate Jew is not entitled to immigrate to *Israel under the *law of Return.

In Christianity, the debate mainly took the form of the ability of one elected to salvation to fall from *grace (see e.g. ARMINIUS). In Islam, the issue is extremely prominent, involving the argument whether it requires the death penalty: see MURTADD.

Apostle (Gk., *apostolos*, 'one sent out'). 1. An important early Christian title, used in two senses: (i) an authoritative missionary; and (ii) one of *Jesus' chosen twelve disciples. Sense (i) is the earlier, and Paul's claim to apostleship in his letters (e.g. 1 Corinthians 9. 1) has secured him the title even though sense (ii) early superseded it (e.g. Matthew 10. 2). (Pioneer missionaries are sometimes also styled 'apostle'—e.g. St *Patrick, the 'apostle of Ireland'.) According to the doctrine of *apostolic succession, the authority of *bishops and correctness of doctrine is guaranteed by their descent through a succession from the apostles (and thence from Christ). The need for any such succession is denied by *Protestants. For (ii) see Index, Apostles.

2. The name given to the *Epistle in the *Orthodox liturgy.

3. An official of the *Catholic Apostolic Church.

G. Klein, *Die Zwölf Apostel* (1961); W. Schmithals, *The Office of the Apostle* . . . (1969).

Apostle of the North: see ADRIAN IV.

Apostles' Creed. A statement of faith used in W. Christian Churches. It runs:

I believe in God, the Father almighty, creator of heaven and earth. I believe in Jesus Christ, his only Son, our Lord. He was conceived by the power of the Holy Spirit and born of the Virgin Mary. He suffered under Pontius Pilate, was crucified, died, and was buried. He descended to the dead. On the third day he rose again. He ascended into heaven, and is seated at the right hand of the Father. He will come again to judge the living and the dead. I believe in the Holy Spirit, the holy catholic Church, the communion of saints, the forgiveness of sins, the resurrection of the body, and the life everlasting. Amen.

There is no basis to the tradition that it was composed by the *apostles; rather, it evolved from the baptismal *creed used at Rome in the 2nd cent. In modern use it figures in the rite of *baptism and in the daily *offices. It is less theologically developed than the *Nicene Creed, and in the 20th cent. has been treated as a basis for *ecumenical agreement.

Apostles of the Southern Slavs (Christian missionary brothers): see CYRIL AND METHODIUS.

Apostle to the apostles: see MARY MAGDALENE.

Apostolicae Curae. Bull issued by *Leo XIII in 1896, declaring that *Anglican *ordinations 'are absolutely null and utterly void', because of double defect of form and intention.

Apostolic Council. The meeting in Jerusalem described by *Paul in Galatians 2. 1–10 between himself, *James, *Peter, and *John. It approved Paul's missionary preaching to gentiles independent of the Jewish law. The account in Acts 15. 1–21 minimizes the opposition from the *Judaizers, and also attributes to the council a set of minimal stipulations (to abstain from anything polluted by idols, from fornication, from meat of strangled animals, and from blood: the so-called 'apostolic decree') made to gentile churches. The event is usually dated to 48, less often to 51 CE.

Apostolic Delegate. A papal appointment to represent the pope in those countries which do not have diplomatic relations with the *Holy see (cf. NUNCIO). Permanent apostolic delegations were established in the USA in 1893, and in Great Britain in 1938.

Apostolic Fathers. The Christian fathers of the period immediately after the New Testament. They are *Clement of Rome, *Ignatius, *Hermas, *Polycarp, and *Papias, and the authors of *The Epistle of *Barnabas*, *The Epistle to *Diognetus*, 2 **Clement*, and the **Didache*.

There are many trs.; L. W. Barnard, *Studies* . . . (1967); J. Lawson, *A Theological and Historical Introduction* . . . (1961).

Apostolic Succession. A belief in Christianity that the authority of the ordained ministry, in word and *sacrament, is protected by the continuous transmission of that authority through successive ordinations by those who were themselves validly ordained. It is claimed by *Orthodox Christianity, *Roman Catholicism, *Anglicanism, and others. **Apostolicae Curae* repudiated the Anglican claim, declaring its orders null and void, but its arguments are seen increasingly as tainted by the polemic needs of the time. On the other hand, the whole concept is attacked by other Christians, on the grounds that there is no basis in the *New

Testament for transmission through a validly ordained *bishop alone.

Apotheosis (Gk., *apo*, 'from', + *theoun*, 'to deify'). The elevation of a human being to the rank and status of a god. While many religious cultures exhibit the promotion of heroes and rulers in this way, the term is especially associated with the divinization of Roman emperors (at first after their deaths, but eventually during their lives); the refusal by Christians of the cult of the emperor led to persecution in the early centuries. See also EUHEMERISM.

Appar (Late 6th or 7th cent. CE). A *Tamil poet, one of the sixty-three *Nāyaṇmārs. A devotee of *Śiva, his 312 surviving hymns remain in use. He is a model of the self-effacing servant of the Lord. In early life, he became a Jain, but he reverted to *Śaivism after the intercession of his sister. Much of his poetry is self-castigation for his Jain apostasy, in contrast to his devotion to Śiva.

Apratiṣṭhita-nirvāna (Skt., 'not-fixed nirvāna'). The state, in *Mahāyāna Buddhism of one who has attained *nirvāna, but suspends final attainment in order to help those who are still on the path to liberation—i.e. a *bodhisattva. He is completely removed from *karma (the causality of previous works) and *saṃsāra (the cycle of reappearance), and also from natural law, so that he can manifest himself in any form he chooses.

Apsarā (Skt., 'move in water'). The dancers in *Indra's *svarga (heaven) in Hinduism. They emerged, on one account, from the *Churning of the Ocean, and since neither the *devas nor the *asuras wished to marry them, they became available for all, and were called Sumad-Ātmajas, daughters of joy. According to other accounts, they (and the *gandharvas) came from *Prajāpati's dismembered body, or from *Vāc (Word). They are sent by the gods to tempt *ṛṣis, and *Atharva-veda* 4. 37 offers a spell to resist them. They are also invoked to bring good fortune to weddings. Their estimated members vary, though according to **Mahābhārata* they number 42,000, and yet they can dance on the point of a sacrificial post. They are frequently depicted in Hindu relief art. In Buddhism, they are depicted as richly adorned attendants on *Sakka (i.e. Indra).

Apsarasa: see GANDHARVA.

Apse (Gk., *apsis*). The rounded end of a church, especially in Greek Orthodoxy: it is derived from the Constaninian basilicas which incorporated the pagan *apsis* where judges and legal advisers sat.

'Aqeda(h) (Abraham's intended sacrifice of Isaac): see 'AKEDA.

Aqib[v]a (Jewish scholar and martyr): see AKIVA.

'Aqīda (articles of faith): see CREED (ISLAM).

Aqṣā Mosque: see JERUSALEM.

Aquila (2nd cent. CE). Translator of the Hebrew *Bible into Greek. A convert to Judaism, Aquila intended his translation to replace the *Septuagint, which had been appropriated by Christians. His translation, finished *c.*130, was literal, to the point of frequently obscuring the sense of the text. It survives only in fragments. Rabbinic sources confuse Aquila and Onkelos, the author of the *Targum on the Pentateuch.

Aquila. Italian town, which was the scene of the anti-Jewish preaching of Bernadino de Siena in 1438, Giacomo dello Marca in 1466, and Bernadino da Feltre in 1488. The remaining Jewish families were expelled in 1510.

Aquinas, Thomas, St (*c.*1225–74). *Dominican philosopher and theologian, recognized as one of the greatest thinkers of the Catholic Church. He was *canonized in 1323 and declared a *Doctor of the Church in 1567. Feast day, 28 Jan. Aquinas's major works include commentaries on Aristotle and the Bible, general treatises (*Summae*) on Christian doctrine, and discussions of particular topics such as Truth and Evil. Central to his outlook is the notion of God as Creator *ex nihilo* (out of nothing). On Aquinas's account, God is the cause of there being anything apart from himself. In the light of this view, Aquinas further argued that God is not one of a class of spiritual beings; he is *sui generis*, not an individual, omniscient, omnipotent, changeless (meaning 'timeless'), perfect, incomprehensible, and the cause of all that comes to pass, including the choices of his creatures. Aquinas rejected determinism and believed in free will, but he also insisted that the free actions of creatures are directly caused by God as Creator of everything.

In the areas of ethics and psychology Aquinas resembles Aristotle. He rejected a sharp mind–body dualism, and he held that criteria of human goodness are discovered by a study of human nature which is essentially bodily and social. But according to Aquinas, human beings can be transformed by *grace to a level not anticipated by philosophy: 'Since men are ordered by divine providence to a higher good than human frailty can experience in the present life, the mind has to be called up to something higher than our reason can attain presently, so that it may learn to desire, and study to aim at something which altogether surpasses the state of our present life' (*Summa contra Gentiles* 1. 5). He also held that by faith one can have access to truths about God not themselves demonstrable philosophically. These truths include doctrines like the *Trinity and the *Incarnation, which Aquinas believed to be revealed by God. The business of theology, Aquinas held, is to meditate on such truths, to draw out their implications, and to indicate against objectors that they are not believed unreasonably. See also THOMISM; QUINQUE VIAE.

V. J. Bourke, *Aquinas' Search for Wisdom* (1965); M.-D. Chenu, *Toward Understanding Saint Thomas Aquinas* (1964); F. C. Copleston, *Aquinas* (1955); B. Davies, *The Thought of Thomas Aquinas* (1992); E. Gilson, *The Christian Philosophy of St Thomas Aquinas* (1956); R. McInery, *Saint Thomas Aquinas* (1977).

'Arabi (Sūfī mystic): see IBN (AL-)ʿARABĪ.

Arabic. The language of the *Qur'ān, and thus the most sacred language for all Muslims, since it is the language of the final and uncorrupted language of revelation. For that reason, the Qur'ān cannot be translated: it can only be interpreted or paraphrased in other languages. The beauty of Arabic is held to be incomparable: according to a proverb, Persian is the language of *paradise, but Arabic is the language of God. The Qur'ān is recited according to developed rules, and forms the basis for education. The recitation of the Qur'ān is learnt even by those who know no Arabic, and Arabic is the language of the obligatory prayers (*ṣalāt).

Ārādhana (Skt.). Adoration of God in Hinduism, and aspiration to attain union with him, especially by repetition of his name.

Ārādhya: see LIṄGĀYAT.

ʿArafā(t). Muslim place of *pilgrimage, a plain about 19 km. from *Mecca. According to tradition, after *Adam and *Eve were expelled from *paradise, they separated, but met again at this place, and recognized (Arab., *ʿarifa*, 'know') each other. Pilgrims on the *ḥajj assemble here toward the end of the obligatory duties for at least a short time. The massive assembly is said to resemble, in anticipation, the Day of Judgement.

Ar(a)ha(n)t (in Buddhism, one worthy of reverence, having reached the stage before nirvana): see ARHAT.

Arai Hakuseki (1657–1725). Confucian statesman and scholar during Japan's Tokugawa (1600–1868) period. From 1709 to 1715 he served as adviser to two Tokugawa shōguns, Ienobu and the infant Ietsugu. He exerted considerable influence on government policy and administration, and in his later years he devoted himself to scholarship, especially in the fields of ancient Japanese history, Shintō theology, and historical linguistics. He also wrote Japan's first autobiography. With wise appreciation of the ephemeral worth of contemporary evaluations, he wrote: 'I am deeply reluctant to entrust my writings to publication; I am really entrusting myself to the judgements of people 2 or 3 centuries after my death.'

Arakan. Jap. for *arhat.

Arama, Isaac b. Moses (*c.*1420–94). Jewish communal leader in Spain. He was the author of *Akedat Yizhak* (Binding of *Isaac; see ʿAKEDA), a philosophical and *allegorical commentary on the *Pentateuch. It consists of a series of 105 sermons each in two parts—an investigation of the chosen text and a scriptual commentary, philosophical in tone but full of homely wisdom (e.g. 'While the rope is in your hand, pull the cow'; 'A beginning is more than half of the whole'). It was reprinted many times and has influenced the style of Jewish preaching to this day. He also wrote a polemic dealing with the relationship between philosophy and religion ('Reason must surrender some rights to revelation'), one commentary on the Five Scrolls, and another on Proverbs. In his philosophy, he was critical of *Maimonides' rationalism and was influential on such thinkers as Isaac *Abrabanel.

Aramaic. A Semitic language written generally in *Hebrew script. Ancient (from 700 BCE) inscriptions have been found as far afield as Afghanistan, Turkmenistan, and the Caucasus. In the later period of the second *Temple, the *Pentateuch was translated into Aramaic (these translations are known as *targumim* (*targums)). Several of the *Dead Sea Scrolls are in Aramaic; and Aramaic words, such as 'Talitha cumi' (little girl, get up) (Luke 5. 41), are to be found in the New Testament. A W. dialect of Aramaic appears to have been the language *Jesus spoke, as it was also the language of the Jerusalem *Talmud and the *aggadic *midrashim. The Babylonian Talmud was largely written in the E. Aramaic dialect, which was spoken by Christians and Jews in what is now Iraq. Aramaic words entered the Hebrew and Arabic language, and Aramaic dialects are still spoken today in a few areas.

Āraṇyaka (Skt., 'that which pertains to the forest'). In Hinduism, the genre of texts within the *Vedic corpus developed as an adjunct to the *Brāhmaṇas. They are explanatory and speculative in nature, intending to give the secret aspects of rituals obtainable only by the advanced student instructed in the seclusion of the forest. The Āraṇyakas are transitional texts still greatly influenced by their predecessors, the Brāhmaṇas and overshadowed by the later *Upaniṣads. They are generally listed as being four in number: the *Aitareya*, *Kausītaki*, *Taittirīya*, and *Jaiminīya Āraṇyakas*.

Eng. tr. of parts, A. B. Keith (1908, 1909).

Ārati, Aratrika (Skt.). Evening *pūjā (worship) in Hinduism, with incense, flowers, and chant, and with lights swung in front of the image.

Araya-shiki (Jap., for Skt., *ālaya-vijñāna, 'storehouse-consciousness'). The eighth and foundational level of consciousness in the Buddhist Hossō (see DŌSHŌ) school. It stores impressions received from other forms of consciousness and retains them as a potential for further actions and thoughts. It is thus the potential energy which constitutes appearances.

Arba'ah minim (four plants used in Jewish rite of Sukkot): see FOUR SPECIES.

Arbada (mountain in India): see ABU.

Arba kosot (Heb., 'four cups'). Four cups of wine traditionally drunk at the *Passover *seder. The tradition is based on a *midrashic interpretation of Exodus 6. 6–7, where four different terms for deliverance are used: 'I will bring you out . . . I will deliver you . . . I will redeem you . . . I will take you.' According to the *Mishnah, even the poorest person is expected to observe this obligation (*Pesaḥim*. 10. 1).

Arba Kushiyot: see FOUR QUESTIONS.

Arcāvatāra: see AVATĀRA.

Archbishop. Title of certain Christian *bishops, approximately equivalent to *metropolitan. In the *Roman Catholic Church, however, it is also given to bishops of sees of special importance, bishops personally so honoured by the Holy See, and some non-residential ('titular') bishops of the Roman *curia or diplomatic corps.

Archdeacon. In *Anglican churches, a priest having administrative charge over part of a diocese. He exercises a general supervision of the parish clergy and deals with matters of church buildings and other property. He is styled 'Venerable'. Anciently, the archdeacon was a chief *deacon appointed by the bishop. Gradually the office increased in power and independence until it was restricted by a series of councils (finally, *Trent) and displaced in the *Roman Catholic Church by that of *Vicar-General. In the E. Church, an archdeacon may not necessarily be a priest.

Arches, Court of. The *consistory court of the province of *Canterbury, so-called because formerly it met in the E. London church of St Mary-le-Bow (Lat., *S. Maria de Arcubus*). Until 1534 an appeal from this court lay only to the pope, but in that year was transferred to the king in chancery.

Archetypes: see MYTH.

Archimandrite (Gk., *archi*, 'ruler of', + *mandra*, 'fold'). Title given in the early church (later also Archimandret, Slavonic) to a monastic superior, equivalent (but slightly higher) to *hegumenos* and to the Western *abbot, either of a single monastery or of a group of monasteries. In the *Orthodox Church it has become a title of honour; for the Copts, an archimandrite is second only to a *patriarch.

Archimedean point: see CULTURAL RELATIVITY AND RELIGION.

Architecture: see ART.

Archpriest. A title of certain clerics in the *Roman Catholic and *Orthodox Churches. From the 5th cent. on, the archpriest was the senior *presbyter of a city, who might take the *bishop's place at liturgical functions. In the W. his office became transformed into those of *dean and *rural dean, and the title now survives as honorary in certain European cathedrals. In the Orthodox Church the title may or may not entail any specific duties. It is the highest rank which a married priest can attain. The title appears to have been used first by *Jerome (stating that a church may have only one archpriest).

ARCIC (*Anglican/*Roman Catholic International Commission). Created by Pope Paul VI and Archbishop Michael Ramsey of Canterbury in consequence of the Second *Vatican Council's positive decree on *ecumenism (1965). Past dialogue among non-Roman Catholics had been mainly multilateral. The RC Church, now entering ecumenical conversations as never before with churches influenced by the Reformation, thought bilateral dialogue more likely to achieve clarity and less liable to become diffuse if and when the parties shared much of their understanding of the Christian tradition. From 1971 to 1981 ARCIC produced four agreed statements on *eucharist, ministry, and *ordination, and (in two stages) authority. Principles governing the conversations were (*a*) avoidance of polemical language inherited from late medieval and 16th-cent. formulas designed to exclude; (*b*) avoidance of statements on essential doctrines which could be interpreted in incompatible senses by the two parties. After initial 'range-finding' the goal was soon formulated as authentic consensus, not merely juxta-position of divergences with a shrug of the shoulders at their insolubility. In eucharist and ministry, ARCIC believed that consensus was achieved on the most basic questions and even ventured to claim 'substantial agreement' (in the sense that if so much was agreed, remaining problems would be soluble). Authority was more difficult, but remarkable convergence was certainly found.

The decision to avoid emotive and polemical terms of the past made the reception of the agreed statements difficult for those on either side of the divide whose understanding of the issues was determined by the language of the 16th cent. RCs could be upset by a eucharistic statement affirming the objectivity of Christ's presence in the consecrated elements, yet not holding the category of substance wholly necessary in articulating the nature of change, or by a statement on ordination which, while accepting 'indelible character' (approved not only by official RC definitions but in major Anglicans such as Hooker), avoided those words. Protestants were upset by a footnote positive towards *transubstantiation; but, in view of the equally full acceptance of 'signification', critics could not restate the 16th-cent. problem that if transubstantiation means the total abolition of the signs, the nature of the *sacrament is destroyed.

On eucharistic *sacrifice ARCIC affirmed that the sacrament is no repetition of Christ's once for all sacrifice, yet 'enters into the movement of the self-offering' (a phrase borrowed from J. A. Jungmann) and entreats the benefits of his passion on behalf of the whole Church. That was to say that in the power of the Spirit the offering is made to the Father by *Christ and his people as members in him.

On ministry and ordination, ARCIC affirmed that, while not all ministries need special authorization, some functions need ordination, a sacramental act which in turn requires the corporate recognition given by the episcopate in due succession: ordination is not the private commissioning by a local congregation or regional community but should receive recognition from the whole Church. The function of the eucharistic president in presenting the offering makes it natural to use priestly terms, and this *priesthood is related to but not identical with the Spirit's gift of priestliness to the whole Church.

Four years after the agreed statement on ministry, American Anglican women were ordained to the priesthood. ARCIC was aware of the debate on the issue, but, considered that the 'subject' of ordination did not affect the fundamental theology of ministerial priesthood, even if it clearly had repercussions for the practicability of shared sacramental life and therefore could render ARCIC's communion ecclesiology (present in Vatican II's *Lumen Gentium*) only a paper ideal.

In the two statements on authority ARCIC mainly focused on points disputed between Canterbury and Rome. The conciliar fellowship of all Churches through a universal episcopate could be readily agreed (ARCIC did not affirm guaranteed inerrancy of general *councils). The Anglican problems with Roman primacy were reduced to four, *viz.*, claims deductively to ground papal authority on *'Petrine texts' in the New Testament; to base primacy on 'divine right' (not merely, as Orthodox theologians would urge, on conciliar canon law or proved utility in the experience of church history); to be endowed with the charism of 'infallibility' in teaching independently of the universal *episcopate; and, thorniest of all, to a universal immediate ordinary jurisdiction inherent in the office of the Roman see. The Anglican question thus becomes: 'Is the centralized authority of the *Pope so integral to the very concept of a visible universal Church that it becomes one of the objects of divine faith?' To a conservative RC, the Anglican estimate of papal authority seemed minimizing: Vatican I and II used terms stronger than that of a primacy inductively discerned from history and seen, by the eye of faith, to be providentially active, indeed indispensable, for ecclesial unity, for the faithful transmission of the faith, and for the upholding of local *bishops against secular pressures. On authority the agenda was obviously set by the Anglicans, and at ARCIC the RCs did not press questions about, e.g., apparently unlimited pluralism in faith and practice or about the divisiveness of the 'royal *supremacy' in England (not an issue for other provinces of the Anglican Communion).

Although Anglican official endorsement of the agreed statements came reasonably rapidly after a period of astonishment, critical observations came from *Evangelical Protestants restating *Calvinist positions, and from Liberal Protestants for whom the doctrinal statements about the eucharist and especially about the Church and authority were too conservative—e.g., in holding the Church in history not to be in error in affirming the doctrine of God the holy *Trinity. For some, any statement satisfactory to one partner must for that reason be insufficient to satisfy the other—a reaction found among both RCs and Anglicans for whom *ecumenism was a polite name for treachery. The Roman Congregation for the Doctrine of the Faith under Cardinal Ratzinger accompanied the publication of the four reports (*Final Report*, 1982) with predominantly negative 'Observations'. The official Vatican verdict (December 1991) was in tone less negative than the 1982 Observations, being positive especially about the eucharistic statement, but left a cold impression, rejection of women priests (on which ARCIC had said nothing very significant) being prominent, together with the Anglican reserve towards the dogmas of 1854 and 1950 which had declared obligatory the beliefs that Christ's mother was so prepared by divine grace to bear the Redeemer and shape his humanity that she was free from the taint of original sin and that she was both redeemed by her Son and received by him in glory.

After 1982 ARCIC was continued with largely new members and was increased in size, from 18 to 24. The large agenda assigned to it began with the most intricate of all articles of faith, *Justification. An agreed statement, *Salvation and the Church*, appeared (1987), followed by *Church as Communion* (1991), and, after further changes in membership, by a statement on moral issues, *Life in Christ: Morals, Communion and the Church* (1994), recognizing differences on divorce and contraception but denying that the issues are church-dividing.

C. Hill and E. Yarnold, *Anglicans and Roman Catholics* . . . (1994).

Ardās (Pañjābī, 'petition' from Persian 'arż-dāsẖt). The Sikh Prayer. The Ardās marks the conclusion of Sikh congregational worship in the *gurdwārā and is to be repeated daily after the *Rahirās and *Kīrtan *Sohilā. Its contents are as follows: (i) invocation of God; (ii) injunction to remember each of the ten *Gurūs, to meditate on the *Ādi Granth, to recall the *pañj pyāre and *Sāhibzāde, the 'forty saved ones' (see MUKTSAR), other faithful Sikhs, martyrs who suffered torture, those who sacrificed their lives for the integrity of the gurdwārās, the *takhts, all gurdwārās; (iii) God is requested to keep his *khālsā faithful, to protect them, that they may be victorious, to bestow the gifts of discipleship, *keś*, Sikh discipline, discernment and faith, the greatest gift of God's *Nām, bathing in *Amritsar (since partition of India in 1947) access to shrines now in Pakistan, to fulfil specific requests (e.g. for sick persons or a marriage), and to pardon mistakes. The Ardās is punctuated with the injunction to proclaim *Vāhigurū. An exhortation to acknowledge the Ādi Granth as Gurū follows.

The Ardās is not in the Ādi Granth, and only the opening passage (concluding with veneration of Gurū *Tegh Bahādur) is attributable to Gurū *Gobind Siṅgh. The prayer evolved in the 18th cent., providing insight into contemporary ideals although lines have been added since. It is printed as part of *Nitnem.

In congregational worship the Ardās follows verses of the *Anand Sāhib, and is offered by any devout *amritdhārī Sikh standing facing the Ādi Granth in front of the people. For this prayer all stand hushed, heads bowed, hands together, reverently murmuring 'Vāhigurū' when bidden, and kneeling to touch the floor with their brows at the end. Recitation of Ardās is followed by a *hukam and distribution of *kaṛāh praśād. See NIRAṄKĀRĪ; RAVIDĀSĪ.

Ardhanārī (Skt., 'half-female'). The androgynous form of a Hindu deity, especially of *Śiva as Ardanārīśvara, 'Hermaphrodite Lord'. In painting or sculpture, the ardhanārī is represented with the left side of the body as female and the right side as male. On the one hand, this symbol of the union of male and female polarities within the Supreme Being is an image of erotic desire (*kāma) and divine creativity. On the other hand, ardhanārī symbolizes the perfect balance of male and female, of all dualities and limitations within the transcendent, impersonal *Brahman. In *Tantric belief the balance of male and female elements within the individual, achieved by various techniques (sexual and non-sexual), results in *enlightenment and bliss. Although the most common ardhanārī is that of Śiva, *Viṣṇu, *Kṛṣṇa, and other deities are also portrayed in this form.

Ardhanārīśvara: see ARDHANĀRĪ.

Arendt, Hannah (1906–75). Philosopher and political scientist. She was born in Germany, but emigrated to the USA in 1941. She worked as Research Director for the Conference on Jewish Relations (1944–6), as chief editor for Schocken Books (1946–8), and as executive director of Jewish Cultural Reconstruction. She then embarked on a university career, ending as Professor in the Graduate Faculty of the New School for Social Research in New York. She was deeply concerned with the way in which the atomization, alienation, and anomie of mass society left it open to totalitarian take-over. In her view, freedom and thought depend on the separation of political life (the public realm) from social and economic life (the private realm)—as in the Greek polis or in the system envisaged in the American revolution. The modern world has seen the advent of the opposite, with public and private realms coerced together into the social and economic sphere, depriving thought of its necessary privacy and converting politics into economic administration. This allows totalitarian *ideology to take over, and opens the way to 'the banality of *evil'. All this keeps pace with *anti-semitism, since the stateless Jew cannot rely on any vague notion of human rights: rights are subordinated to ends.

E. Young-Breuhl, *Hannah Arendt* . . . (1982).

Arghya (Skt.). Sacrificial offering during Hindu *pūjā (worship).

Arhat (*arhati*, 'be worthy of'; Pāli *arahat*). In Buddhism, one who is worthy of reverence because he has attained the penultimate state of perfection (Chin., *alohan, lohan*; Jap., *arakan*; Korean, *arahan, nahan*). The term was originally applied to all ascetics, but it came to be applied to those who are no longer bound to *punnabhava ('again-becoming') and have become completely detached from the Triple World of sense, form, and formlessness. Since, in *Theravāda, there can be only one *Buddha in each world cycle, the condition of arhat is the highest to which one can aspire in this cycle (since the Buddha has already appeared). The arhat is, according to *Dhammapada*, one, 'whose ex-pressions are utterly extinguished, who is free of basis [for reappearance], whose terrain is emptiness, signlessness and freedom: his track is as difficult to know as that of the birds in the sky' (93). The arhat is portrayed 'dignified, bald, and with a certain severity' (Conze). In China, they are transformed into the *lo-hans (Jap. *rakan*).

Arhats are on the fourth and highest stage leading to *nirvāna and are in the condition known as *sopadhiśeṣa-Nirvāṇa, nirvāna with a shadow of conditions remaining. They possess four faculties of discernment and exegesis not possessed by ordinary mortals, and five kinds of transcendent knowledge, so that they are characterized by supreme wisdom, and are known as *prajñāvimukta*. They can hear and understand all sounds in the universe, know the thoughts of others, and remember previous existences.

*Mahāyāna Buddhism, in contrast, regards the notion, especially the limited goal, of arhat as selfish. The development of the *bodhisattva, who might attain the goal but returns to help others, is held to be the logical application of the example of the Buddha and of his teaching.

Among Jains, the arhat is one who is worthy of absolute reverence. In effect, these are the *tīrthaṅkaras.

I. B. Horner, *The Early Buddhist Theory of Man Perfected* (1934).

Ari (acronym): see LURIA, ISAAC BEN SOLOMON.

Arianism. The Christian *heresy according to which the Son of God was a creature and not truly

God. In the Arian system the Son could be called 'God', but only as a courtesy title; he was created (not begotten) by the Father, and he achieved his divine status by his perfect obedience to him. As a creature, it must be said of Christ *ēn pote hote ouk ēn* (a famous slogan), 'there was once when he was not'. The chief proponent of the doctrine was the Alexandrian priest *Arius (*c.*250–*c.*336), who composed popular songs embodying it. The doctrine was condemned at a synod at Alexandria (*c.*320) and definitively at the Council of *Nicaea (325) by means of the *homoousion formula. The Arians returned to influence in the Roman Empire under Constantius (337–61), when various formulas, such as the 'homoean' position (that the Son was 'similar' to the Father) were subscribed to in synods. But the brilliant theology of the *Cappadocians led to the final victory of Nicene orthodoxy at the Council of Constantinople in 381. Arianism kept a foothold among the Germanic tribes in the W. empire until 496.

R. C. Gregg and D. E. Groh, *Early Arianism* (1981); R. C. Gregg, *Arianism* (1985).

Aridity. A state of emptiness or listlessness in which it is difficult to pray. Its cause may be physical illness or sinfulness. But much W. (as opposed to E.) Christian spirituality teaches that such aridity may mark the beginning of the *dark night of the soul (cf. JOHN OF THE CROSS).

Aristeas, Letter of. An anonymous Jewish composition written probably in the late 2nd cent. BCE. It is supposedly composed by Aristeas, a Greek at the court of Ptolemy II Philadelphus (285–246 BCE) and describes the translation of the Hebrew scriptures into Greek. It explains how it was accomplished by seventy-two scholars in seventy-two days. This story is based on a legend about the *Septuagint, and the attitude of the writer reflects the outlook of the *Hellenized educated Jews of Alexandria. It seems to be designed to enhance the status of a Gk. translation.

Aristotle (384–322 BCE). Greek philosopher whose influence on W. theology and philosophy has been prodigious—though it was not so much by a strict exegesis of his ideas as by an eclectic adaptation combined particularly with *Neoplatonism. But the influence and adaptation are not surprising. In his own thought, a theology or science of God is the primary form of knowledge, partly because God is the source (*arche*) of all things, and partly because God alone possesses knowledge in the highest degree. The human desire to know is thus the highest truth of our being, and is potentially a sharing in God's knowledge of himself. This aspiration may in the past have been handed down in *myth, but through *nous* (intellect or intelligence which is the essence of God's nature) humans attain to God. Although subsequent W. philosophy has paid much attention to Aristotle's logic, his philosophy is in fact deeply religious: it is not confined to postulating an unmoved Mover 'in order to complete his metaphysics' (A. N. Whitehead, *Science and the Modern World*, 1925). Whitehead went on to claim that 'it did not lead him very far towards the production of a God available for religious purposes'. Yet in fact the insistence on the rationality of God and of the human possibility of entering into union with God through *nous* laid foundations for a theological and rational spirituality which flourished especially in Islam—albeit by then in a form which was Platonic. So far as Christianity is concerned, there was little Aristotelian influence on early theology: the logical treatises were known, but were interpreted in Neoplatonist categories, the metaphysical treatises were treated as 'advanced' works, as were the scientific works. *Boethius translated the logical works into Latin in the 6th cent. and preserved them for the W. The real influence of Aristotle on W. Christian theology came in the 13th cent., mediated by Jews and Muslims, becoming a source of controversy (Aristotelianism was condemned in Paris in 1277), but providing nevertheless the philosophical basis for *scholasticism, especially in St Thomas *Aquinas.

J. M. Cooper, *Reason and Human Good in Aristotle* (1975); M. Grene, *A Portrait of Aristotle* (1963); J. Lear, *Aristotle* (1988).

Arius (*c.*250–*c.*336). Christian theologian who gave his name to the Arian heresy. Based in Alexandria, he was involved in controversy with the local *bishop, but only fragments, or quotations, of his own work survive. The view associated with him protects the absolute sovereignty and transcendence of God: it is impossible for *God* to be present in a human life. If Christ is divine, it can only be in the sense that he is 'divinized' by his association with God, but he remains subordinate to God, as a son to a father. The Son is thus a creature, however unique and perfect: 'there was a time when he was not'. Strongly opposed by *Athanasius, this view had wide support, but was eventually condemned at the Council of *Nicaea in 325. The Arian controversy was renewed in later centuries and has been a recurrent interpretation of the person of Jesus by those who fear that otherwise they will compromise the transcendence and unity of God.

A. Grillmeier, *Christ in Christian Tradition* (1965).

Ariyaratne, A. Y. (founder): see SARVODAYA.

Ariya-satta/sacca (foundation of the Buddha's teaching): see FOUR NOBLE TRUTHS.

Arjan Dev, Gurū (1563–1606). Fifth Sikh *Gurū, poet and first Sikh *martyr. Arjan Mal, the youngest son of Gurū *Rām Dās and Bībī Bhānī, was born in *Goindvāl, *Pañjāb. He married Gaṅgā who bore one son, *Hargobind. In preference to his elder brother, *Prithī Chand, Arjan was invested as Gurū in 1581 by *Bhāī *Buḍhā at the request of Gurū Rām

Dās. Prithī Chand's jealousy proved a continuing source of harassment to Arjan.

Gurū Arjan Dev completed the excavation of sacred pools at Rāmdāspur, later renamed *Amritsar, extended the town and superintended the construction of the *Harimandir. He raised the necessary funds from tithes brought annually by the *masands. In 1601 the *temple was completed.

In 1590 Arjan had another sacred pool dug. This was *Tarn Tāran which became a leprosarium and place of pilgrimage. He next built *Kartārpur and Srī Hargobindpur on the Beās River, both in Pañjāb.

In 1594 he returned to Amritsar and, finding that Prithī Chand was composing hymns to further his ambition, Arjan decided to make an authentic collection of hymns. These *Bhāī *Gurdās wrote down at his dictation. To the *Mohan Pothī*, *Amar Dās' compilation, Arjan Dev added his father's hymns, his own compositions, and hymns by Indian saints and bards. This volume, the *Ādi Granth, was completed in 1604 and installed at Amritsar but is now at Kartārpur in the possession of the *Sodhī family. Having heard that Arjan's anthology included hymns disparaging Islam the Emperor, *Akbar, asked to see it, but was so pleased with the random excerpts read to him by Gurdās and Buḍhā that he remitted local taxes at the Gurū's request. Akbar later visited the Gurū.

However, Akbar's successor, Jahāṅgīr, resented the increasing power of Arjan Dev, now known as the 'True Emperor'. His hostility was fuelled by the Gurū's enemies, both Muslim and Hindu, notably, according to a Sikh tradition, the finance minister, Chandū, whose hopes of marrying his daughter to Hargobind had been dashed by the Gurū. As Arjan Dev had allegedly given financial assistance to Jahāṅgīr's rebel son Khusro, he was charged with sedition as well as with creating communal dissension. He was subjected to prolonged torture. According to Sikh tradition he had to sit in a red hot cauldron and was bathed in boiling water. Before his death he appointed Hargobind to succeed him.

Gurū Arjan Dev's 2,216 hymns are the largest contribution to the Ādi Granth. In the spirit of his predecessors his verses proclaim the saving power of God's name (*nām), the blindness of sinful man, the greatness of God, and the need for constant devotion to God. Of his compositions, the greatest is the *Sukhmanī.

Arjuna. In the **Mahābhārata*, the third, or middle, *Pāṇḍava, a fabulous warrior best known for his skill as an archer, in many ways the hero *par excellence* of the epic. Son of *Kuntī by the god *Indra, Arjuna wields the bow Gāṇḍīva, carries the monkey *Hanumat on his battle standard, and rides a chariot drawn by white horses. Among other early feats, Arjuna wins *Draupadī as a common wife for the Pāṇḍavas in a bow-bending contest, strives with *Śiva to win weapons before the *Kurukṣetra war, and visits Indra's heaven. During the war itself, he is responsible for the deaths of the *Kaurava generals *Bhīṣma and *Karṇa, and many other victories.

Arjuna's close friendship with *Kṛṣṇa is central to the *Mahābhārata*'s structure. Among Arjuna's wives is Subhadrā, Kṛṣṇa's sister: the son of Arjuna and Subhadrā is Abhimanyu, who dies in the Kurukṣetra war. During the Kurukṣetra war, Kṛṣṇa serves as Arjuna's charioteer and adviser, often inciting him and the other Pāṇḍavas to tricky means to their end of victory. Perhaps the most famous incident in the *Mahābhārata* is Arjuna's failure of nerve before the war, in which he will have to kill his Kaurava relatives, resulting in Kṛṣṇa's expounding of the **Bhagavad-gītā* to encourage him to fight. In truth, the *Mahābhārata* tells us, Arjuna and Kṛṣṇa are incarnations of *Nara and Nārāyana; it is as though Arjuna's friendship with (devotion to) Kṛṣṇa brings him beyond the human state to semi-divinity.

Ark. 1. The vessel in which *Noah supposedly saved his family and a breeding pair of each animal and bird species from the destruction of the great flood (Genesis 6. 1–9. 18).

2. The 'ark of the *covenant' (*aron ha-berith*) was a container, made by God's command during the Wilderness wandering of Israel, to contain the tablets of the covenant. Captured by the Philistines, it was recovered and brought to *Jerusalem, where it was installed in the *Holy of Holies (1 Kings 8. 1–11). It was not restored to the second *Temple.

3. The niche in the *synagogue in which the *Torah Scrolls (*Scrolls of the Law) are kept. It is located on the wall which faces towards the Temple Mount in Jerusalem and is considered the holiest part of the building. It is usual to stand when the doors of the Ark are open—while certain prayers are recited as well as when the scrolls are removed for reading or are being replaced. A *ner tamid* ('eternal light') is kept burning in front of the Ark. In *Ashkenazi circles, the Ark is called the *aron* or *aron kodesh* ('holy Ark'), and among the *Sephardim, it is known as the *heikhal* ('sanctuary').

Arkān ud-Dīn (fundamentals of Muslim life): see FIVE PILLARS OF ISLAM.

Armageddon. In Christian *eschatology, the scene of the last battle between good and evil. The name appears only in Revelation 16. 16, where it is said to be 'Hebrew'; it is usually taken to be from Har Megiddo, mountain of Megidda.

Armaiti (one of the Holy Immortals): see AMESA SPENTAS.

Armenian Church. One of the *Oriental churches, sometimes incorrectly called 'Armenian Orthodox'. Armenia was the first country to adopt Christianity as a state religion, after the conversion of King Tiridates III by St Gregory 'the Illuminator' *c.*294 (hence the name 'Armenian Gregorian Church' which is sometimes used). Gregory established the chief see at Etchmiadzin near Mount Ararat, close to the present city of Yerevan. In 390 the country was partitioned between the Byzantine and Persian Empires, and in 430 the monarchy disappeared. Armenia has subsequently had many rulers, though it blossomed as an independent state in the 9th–11th cents. A major factor in the preservation of Armenian national consciousness has been membership of the Church, and non-ethnic Armenians cannot be admitted to membership, though this does not prevent children becoming members by baptism if one parent is Armenian.

The stance adopted by the Armenian Church in the *christological controversies of the 5th–6th cents. is obscure, but the church has been more or less *Monophysite (though regarding itself simply as non-Chalcedonian) since the Council of *Chalcedon was repudiated at a synod of *c*.506. The translation of the Acts of the Council into Armenian was said to be so inaccurate that the Church was right in considering them heretical! Pressure to revert to the Chalcedonian christology of the Byzantine Empire ceased with the Islamic conquest of the country from 639 on.

The Armenian Church was much influenced by contact with the *Crusaders, of which one result was a temporary (12th–13th cents.) union of much of the Church with Rome. Another was the adoption of the *mitre as the liturgical headgear of its *bishops. The present *Uniat church, the Armenian Catholic Church of *c*.100,000 members, goes back only to 1740.

Under the Ottoman Turks the Armenians suffered notorious persecutions, culminating in massacres as late as 1920 which left practically no Armenians in Turkish territory. Of the $3\frac{1}{2}$ million Armenians, most live now in the ex-Soviet Republic of Armenia, where conflict with Azerbaijan over the disputed territory of Nagorno-Karabakh is exacerbated by memories of persecution. There is a large *diaspora, including $\frac{1}{2}$-million in the USA. It is generally held that the Armenian Church during the period of the Soviet Union was relatively fortunate, and enjoyed more privileges than the Church of *Georgia, for example. But in the diaspora this encouraged a schism between pro-Soviet and anti-Soviet parties, which is now slowly beginning to heal.

The Armenian Church has two classes of *priests: the *vardapets* or doctors, who are unmarried, and the *parish priests who, unless monks (*monasticism) must be married before *ordination as *deacons. Bishops are usually chosen from among the *vardapets*. The Armenian *liturgy is celebrated in the ancient Armenian language, having been translated (with the Bible) in the early 5th cent. by St *Mesrob, who himself invented the Armenian alphabet. For the *eucharist the Armenians use unleavened bread, and do not mix water with the wine. They follow the Julian *calendar. Following the ancient Eastern practice, the birth of Christ is not celebrated as a separate feast at *Christmas, but at *Epiphany. The sign of the cross is made in the Latin fashion. There is a strong prohibition against *icons/iconography, and the churches are thus simple and plain in style, though pictures of Christ, and of the *saints and mysteries of the Church are often found hanging from the walls. The *altar is usually on a stage at the east end of the church, and a curtain is drawn for the duration of the communion of the clergy. An organ or harmonium is often used to accompany the choir, in contrast to the *Orthodox churches, where such instruments are forbidden.

Armenian Massacres: see ARMENIAN CHURCH.

Arminius, Jacobus (1560–1609). Dutch theologian who gave his name to the system of theology known as Arminianism. After studying with *Beza, he became (in 1588) minister in Amsterdam, at a time when Holland was a stronghold of *Calvinism. After disputes, he became professor at Leiden, where there were further arguments over *predestination, leading to severe divisions. Arminius held that God willed that all people should be saved, and that it is only because God foresaw the belief or unbelief of individuals that he can be said to have predestined some to salvation, others to damnation. After his death, his followers issued the Remonstrance of 1610, from which the major differences from strict Calvinism can be discerned: (i) Christ died for all; (ii) God's saving grace can be resisted; (iii) Christians can fall from grace; (iv) the Holy Spirit is necessary to help the achievement of what is good; (v) salvation is for those who believe in Christ and who persist in holiness, obedience, and faith. Arminius and Arminianism had a wide (though always contested) influence, including such figures as Grotius and John *Wesley.

C. Bangs, *Arminius* . . . (1985).

Armour of Faith (Zoroastrian): see NAUJOTE.

Armstrong, Herbert W. (b. 1892). Leader of the 'Worldwide Church of God'. Armstrong began as a preacher on radio in the USA in the 1930s, and became widely known through the radio programme 'The World Tomorrow', after 1955 continued by his son Garner Ted. The Armstrong organization also includes the free magazine *The Plain Truth* on current affairs, and Ambassador College in Pasadena, California. The Worldwide Church of God itself has an apparently small membership, and has traditionally met locally in rented halls rather than built its own churches.

Armstrong's doctrines owe much to British Israelism. Their major theme is the reference of biblical prophecy to Britain and America and to current events (e.g. war in the Middle East as a 'sign of the times' and precursor of *Armageddon). Worship is on the Sabbath (Saturday), and Jewish festivals are observed rather than Christmas and Easter; the *Ten Commandments figure prominently; several *tithes are required of church members. Medicine is deprecated in favour of spiritual healing. Since the 1970s the organization has suffered from scandals over the style of life of some of its leaders.

See further J. M. Hopkins, *The Armstrong Empire* (1974).

Arnauld, Antoine (known sometimes as 'the Great', 1612–94). Christian philosopher and controversialist. He studied and taught at the Sorbonne until he was expelled (1656) for his *Jansenist views. In 1643 he had published a book on frequent communion (of that title) stressing the need for thorough preparation and appropriate disposition, and in 1644 an anonymous apology for Jansen. Despite his enforced retirement, he continued to write, and in 1669 he was restored by Louis XIV. After this period of acceptance in France, he was eventually compelled to take refuge in the Netherlands. His major writings were *The Art of Thinking* (with Pierre Nicole, 1662), also known as the *Port Royal Logic*, and *Concerning True and False Ideas* (1683). He developed (while criticizing) Cartesian logic and views, pointing out, for example, the circularity in one of *Descartes arguments: the idea of God depends on the clarity and distinctness of our perception of him, while the truth of our clear and distinct perceptions depends on God's existence. In theology, he, more than anyone else, was responsible for diffusing Jansenist ideas.

Aron: see ARK (2).

ar-Rāshidūn (the (first) four caliphs): see KHALĪFA.

Art. Although religions are usually studied through their words and texts, religious people live at least as much (probably more) through their non-verbal modes of expression—through *ritual at least as much as through *myth, through rhythm as much as through song. Beyond ritual, religious art extends the human ability to communicate through complex sign-systems, locking on, especially, to the imagination of worlds and states which cannot be directly seen. Thus religious art recovers the past (often portraying past events which have present significance), and it mediates between the present and the future, whatever that future may bring: enlightenment, *nirvāna, death, *heaven, *hell. Religious art also generates power and consequence, sometimes of destruction and malevolence, and it captures the many moods of human experience (joy, sorrow, penitence, love, hope, resignation), relating them to the continuing codes of evaluation which each religion carries. Religious art is profoundly connected to the human ability to recognize and take delight in truth, beauty, and goodness. What *counts* as beautiful or good may differ from one religion to another (or from one age to another in any religion), but not the human ability to recognize those absolutes within the change and contingency of human circumstance. Thus religious art is extensively concerned with celebration, worship, thanksgiving, and praise. Above all, the demands of religious art have offered the supreme challenge and opportunity to the human ability to create—to be the creator of artefacts, to be an artist. Not surprisingly, religions have been the resource and inspiration of almost all the most enduring art and architecture throughout the whole of human history, at least until very recently; and religions (i.e. religious people or institutions) have been evocative of art through patronage on a massive scale.

Yet at the same time, each religion develops its own distinctive art, *dance, architecture, and *music. That is because such art cannot be detached from the entire network of 'information' which constitutes the characteristic nature, form, and content of each religion (obviously, the sub-systems of any religion may themselves be competitive in such a way that the very status of art may itself be contested). Thus Judaism produces synagogues, Christianity produces churches, Islam mosques, Hinduism temples, Buddhism *stūpas, etc. Partly this is a function of available materials and current technology. But also (and much more), these characteristic 'shapes' are controlled into their outcome by the ideology (represented through signs, *symbols, and *icons) of the religion in question (see H. W. Turner, *From Temple to Meeting House* . . . , 1979). These sign-systems provide the controlling metaphors for religious art; but then, conversely, religious art mediates those basic, controlling metaphors back into the lives of believers, transforming them into outcomes that could not otherwise occur.

Religious art does this at many different levels and in equally many different ways. At its most basic (and often most banal), religious art can be propaganda; not far beyond that, it can be exploitation (the attempt to elicit religious emotions at an immature level, what Rose Macaulay summarized as 'bleeding hearts in convent parlours'). It can be coercive (Doré's engravings of heaven are perfunctory, of hell terrifying), it can be repetitive and dull, it can simply be illustration. But moving again beyond that, religious art can both be, and be the instrument of, a reawakening of forgotten or abandoned truths about ourselves and our possibilities: it can open eyes to a new seeing of an otherwise prosaic world. At this level, the controlling metaphors become, not restriction, but opportunity, not least because they evoke contrasted meanings. Thus the crucifixion may be the young hero, the *Christus Miles*, or it may be the suffering servant, the bearer of our pain: Christ is *both* victim *and* victor, but rarely both at once. Finally, the manifestations of religious art can be epiphany: they can *be* what they purport to be about, the incursion of whatever it is that is true into the midst of time and space. Art is then holy rather than religious. See also Index, Art; Aesthetics.

Judaism Jewish art is a dialectic between strong prohibitions against making images or likenesses of living creatures (Exodus 20. 4, Deuteronomy 4. 16–8, 5. 8) and the celebration of craftsmanship in the building of the Temple and its appurtenances. Archaeology (especially revealed through the work of E. R. Goodenough, *Jewish Symbols in the Graeco-Roman Period*) have shown how far the prohibition was ignored, e.g. in synagogue decoration (note, especially Dura-Europus, hard though that is to evaluate, J. Gutman, *The D.-Europus Synagogue*). Not until the 19th cent. did Jewish artists break out into the style and techniques surrounding them. From M. Oppenheim (1799–1882) onward, Judaism has taken the *assimilationist risk, with moving consequences in the case of such artists as Chagall. But in general, Jewish art has focused on the synagogue and its contents, and on Torah manuscripts and Torah ornaments (e.g. the *keter* or crown, the *rimmonim*, the finials on the rollers holding the scroll). Jewish symbols reconnect with the lost temple, most recurrently through the *menorah. Among other books beautifully produced, the Passover Haggadah has been the most frequent.

Synagogue architecture has seen many different styles of hall or building appropriated through the ages. Apart from the necessity to separate women from men (in Orthodox synagogues), the main requirement is to give prominence (and protection) to the Torah Scroll, and to provide a pulpit for the reading of scripture.

Thus far, Jewish art illustrates the dictum, 'Paganism sees its God, Judaism hears him.' But the God of Israel also hears his people, and a further dimension of Jewish art has flowed from the command of the Psalmist, 'Serve the Lord with gladness, and come before his presence with a song' (Psalms 100. 1). According, therefore, to the Talmud, 'Song is obligatory in the ritual of the sanctuary' (*B. Arak*. 11a). A preference was given for chant and the human voice over instruments. Among the *Ḥasidim, music and dance were regarded as a most important way of quickening the divine spark within, so that even wordless melodies were encouraged to uplift the soul. Instrumental music and polyphony made slow progress until the advent of *Reform, where some imitation of Protestant hymns and chorales was made. This created a bridgehead from which Jewish musicians could stand on level ground with their Gentile counterparts, leading to their great contribution to modern European music—e.g. Milhaud or Bloch, who said: 'I aspire to write Jewish music. . . . It is the Jewish soul that interests me, the complex, glowing, agitated soul that I feel vibrating through the Bible.'

A. Eisenberg, *The Synagogue Through the Ages* (1974); J. Gutman, *Beauty and Holiness* . . . (1970); S. S. Kayser and G. Schoenberger, *Jewish Ceremonial Art* (1959); L. A. Mayer, *Bibliography of Jewish Art* (1967).

Christianity Beginning from simple emblems of identity and allegiance (e.g. the sign of a fish, since the Gk. for 'fish' is *ichthus*, the letters of which stand for Jesus Christ, God and Saviour) Christian art and architecture developed into the most diverse forms of expression. The representation of biblical scenes, and of the Last Judgement, were visual aids in the instruction of largely illiterate or uneducated populations. But the power inherent in such representations led directly to the development of *icons—and to the eventual controversy about the extent to which, if at all, they were/are idolatrous. Mosaics (those of Ravenna being especially fine early examples) and wall-paintings were reinforced in churches by stained glass. But church buildings themselves summarized Christian truths and affirmations in their layout: thus the secular basilica, or assembly hall, was adapted to draw attention to the celebration of the *eucharist, and to the role of the *bishop in presiding; or again, Gothic cathedrals extended the shape to make it cruciform, and to enhance the vast and mysterious unknowability of God who can only be approached in penitence and praise. In contrast, many modern churches have returned the emphasis to the gathering of the people of God, bringing the *altar or table into the midst of the people, and reducing the emphasis on what the poet Larkin called 'the holy end'. Christian art simply cannot be summarized: resting frequently on a strong doctrine of creation (as also on developing systems of patronage and commissioning), it is, at its best, a deliberate extension of the work of the Holy Spirit in bringing order and beauty out of chaos and ugliness. At its worst, it is the illustration of a text, sometimes allied to the spiritual terrorization which can on occasion characterize Christian missionary zeal. Yet even at the level of illustration, the work can (as in the case of illuminated manuscripts, to give only one example) be both inspired and inspiring; and in the case of *music, the Christian text has supplied to composers the challenge which has evoked some of the most enduring compositions.

P. Hammond, *Liturgy and Architecture* (1960); M. Miles, *Image as Insight* . . . (1985); E. Newton and W. Neil, *2000 Years of Christian Art* (1966); J. Walton, *Art and Worship* (1988).

Islam Muslim art is controlled by the *ḥadīth which tells how *Muḥammad returned one day to his tent and found his favourite wife, *ʿĀ'isha, sewing a saddle-cloth. When he saw that she was decorating it with human figures, Muḥammad threw her and the cloth out of the tent. When she asked why, he said, 'Give life to that which you have created'—i.e. it belongs to God alone to create life. The work of the artist or architect in Islam is limited, therefore, to the work of giving praise to *Allāh, or to expressing allegiance (*islam). Supremely this is seen in *mosque architecture, which may be extremely simple—nothing more than a hut—or classically elegant and cool. It needs little more, internally, than the niche indicating the direction of prayer towards *Mecca (*mihrab*; see MOSQUE) and the pulpit for the delivering of the sermon (*khuṭba), and externally the minaret from which the faithful are summoned to prayer. But it calls also for the reminder of the primacy of the *Qur'ān over life through the carving of texts from the Qur'ān. This, as also the writing of copies of the Qur'ān, led to the most distinctive of Islamic art forms, *calligraphy.

T. Burckhardt, *The Art of Islam* . . . (1976); C. J. du Ry, *Art of Islam* (1970); R. Ettinghausen and O. Grabar, *The Art and Architecture of Islam, 650–1250* (1987), O. Grabar, *The Formation of Islamic Art* (1973); M. Lings, *The Quranic Art of Calligraphy and Illumination* (1976); G. Michell (ed.), *Architecture of the Islamic World* (1978); A. Papadopoulo, *Islam and Muslim Art* (1979); Y. H. Safedi, *Islamic Calligraphy* (1978); A. Schimmels, *Calligraphy and Islamic Culture* (1984); D. Talbot Rice, *Islamic Art* (1975).

Hinduism Of all religions, Hinduism is most vivid in its *iconography, because of its belief that the underlying source of all appearance (*Brahman) is present in all appearance. Thus the work of the sculptor, etc., is to make manifest what is already there in the material, not simply to illustrate a story about the gods. The gods are of course 'illustrated', in the sense that the 'real presence' of theistic being in the cosmos (and therefore in the material which the artist is using) can reach the worshipper (in what Christians would recognize as a sacramental way) through these representations. They can thus produce the state of *rasananda* (see RASA), blissful union with the god, often regarded as the equivalent of *samādhi. But the same is possible in all the arts (e.g. *dance, *music, drama) because there is nothing in the cosmos which is not sustained in being by Brahman. The recognition of this is equally obvious in the attention paid to the sacred orientation of space. The order made apparent in astronomy, geometry, mathematics (hence the early Hindu commitment to these arts which the West would regard as sciences) led to a mapping of that cosmic order on to space in miniature (e.g. through the *maṇḍala) or in the planning of towns, but above all in the architecture of temples and shrines.

The temple is the major source and expression of Hindu art. Its shape, laid down in the *śāstras, was originally a square, designed to concentrate force. Above the shrine is a tower (the *śikara*, a symbolic mountain), channelling the deity into the shrine and the worshipper, and radiating power upward as well. From the temple derive carving (to entice the deities or spirits), dance, the creation of manuscripts, and the decoration of textiles. The temple then reaches out into everyday life through the corresponding decoration of house and body. Thus the creation of the classical music, the *rāga, is understood as the 'building of a temple': 'In the improvised pieces, you start like building a temple: you lay the foundations, then gradually you build up the building, then you do the decorative things, like the painting and carving. Finally you bring out the deity, into that temple.'

Indian art is thus the making manifest of the real and the true which is already the guarantor of all appearance: it is the alignment of appearance with truth: 'The Hindu temple is the sum total of architectural rites performed on the basis of its myth. The myth covers the ground and is the plan on which the structure is raised' (Kramisch).

T. Bhattacharya, *The Canons of Indian Art* (1963); S. Kramisch, *The Hindu Temple* (1976); B. Rowland, *The Art and Architecture of India* . . . (1970); H. Zimmer, *The Art of Indian Asia* (1960).

Jainism Jain art is devoted mainly to the decoration of temples (*sāmavasarāna*, regarded as assemby halls of the *jinas, not as places where God or gods are worshipped) and to reverence for the jinas. While Jain art shares much of the styles and techniques of Indian art in general, it is different in important respects. Above all (since a controlling metaphor of paramount importance for Jains is *ahiṁsā), the atmosphere of Jain art is one of great peacefulness. For the same reason, materials are avoided which might involve the taking of life, e.g. clay and ivory. The main figures represented are those of the jinas, but the *śāsanadevatās are also common. Also distinctive are *ayagapata*, small carvings, incorporating elaborate symbolism, which express devotion. They may be related to *yantras and *maṇḍalas.

P. Pal, *The Peaceful Liberators: Jain Art from India* (1994).

Sikhism See ICONOGRAPHY.

Buddhism Buddhist art, with the possible exception of *Zen art (see below), did not arise from such deep theoretical considerations as did the Hindu. It arose from grateful recognition of the work of the *Buddha in teaching the way to the cessation of *dukkha. The Buddha is therefore represented increasingly with the marks indicating his status or his achievement of *nirvāna. He is thus usually represented in serene posture, often on a *lotus leaf; but there examples of the emaciated Buddha, indicating the austerity of his long search for enlightenment. The elaboration of saviour-figures in Mahāyāna and Tibetan Buddhism led to an immense proliferation of sculpture and wall-painting, with extremely careful codes of iconographic symbols. The devotion of thanksgiving to the Buddha (and eventually to buddhas and *bodhisattvas) led to the building of *caityas and stūpas; and the formal organization of Buddhism into communities of monks (*bhikṣu) required the building of accommodation in monasteries (*vihāra). The development of these into large temple and monastic complexes is particularly impressive in Japan (see further P. Popham, *Wooden Temples of Japan*, 1990).

Ch'an/Zen art occupies a special place in Buddhism. Ch'an/Zen is a way of seeing through the superficial claims of appearance in reality, enticement, endurance, etc., to the true buddha-nature of all appearance. The approach to enlightenment may be via many different routes (e.g. based on *sūtras or opposed to sūtras), but in all cases the realization of truth is necessarily expressed in all manifestations of life—since there is only one buddha-nature, including oneself within it (*buddhatā, *busshō). Zen realization, therefore, is both attained and expressed through the arts. Architecture of monasteries is thus related to environment, especially by the development of *gardens leading into the natural landscape: 'The art [of gardens] was definitely used in China and Japan to express the highest truths of religion and philosophy' (L. Warner, *The Enduring Art of Japan*). Rock gardens, with carefully swept sand, challenge the perception of the ordinary; the tea-garden surrounded the tea-ceremony (see CHADŌ).

In addition to architecture, *calligraphy is central in Ch'an/Zen art. Calligraphy precedes Ch'an in China, but it was raised to new heights by Ch'an practitioners, especially in the Sung period. In Japan, it was known originally as *shojutsu*, but later as *shodō*. The importance for Zen lies in the complete connection between the artist and the art: nothing serves so well to overcome the opposition between worker and work: the medium is the messenger; the connection from heart-mind, through brush and ink, to paper realizes the unity of the one buddha-nature. Moreover, the Zen emphasis on training, discipline, and control as the necessary conditions of freedom and enlightenment are perfectly summarized in calligraphy—and in Zen painting—because there is no possibility of correction or starting again: each stroke remains as it is put down. Painting extends calligraphy, as is visibly obvious, though it may move in the direction of the illustration of Zen themes, rather than the expression of Zen.

T. Hoover, *Zen Culture* (1977); N. W. Ross, *The World of Zen* (1962); D. Seckel, *The Art of Buddhism* (1984).

Artha (Skt., 'goal', 'advantage', 'wealth'). 1. In Hinduism, a goal of life. There are four traditional arthas; *dharma (duty, law), artha (advantage, utility, goal-oriented activity), *kāma (erotic or aesthetic expression), and *mokṣa (release, liberation). The end of artha, the pursuit of wealth and advantage, is the end of life proper to a ruler (*kṣatriya) or householder (*gṛhastha). Artha is success in one's worldly pursuits. See also ARTHAŚĀSTRA.

2. In *Sāṁkhya and *Yoga philosophy, the object of the senses.

Arthaśāstra (Skt., *artha*, 'advantage' + *śāstra*, 'teaching'). A Sanskrit text concerned with *artha, worldly advantage, especially the advantage of the prince (*rājanya*) and universal monarch (*cakravartin).

One of the most influential works of political philosophy, it is attributed to Kāuṭilya (or Caṇakya) a minister of Candragupta Māurya. His historical existence is disputed, as is the attribution of the *Arthaśāstra* to a single author and a single century; but most scholars agree that the work was compiled between the 4th cent. BCE and the 2nd cent. CE. It is a manual of political and administrative theory for kings, a work treating not only *daṇḍanīti* or the science of power and punishment, and *rajadharma*, or what is right for kings, but also the metaphysical foundations of *dharma and artha.

Kāuṭilya presupposes the traditional S. Asian concept of *matsyanyāya*, or 'law of the fishes', according to which large fish prey upon smaller fish.The role of the king, established through a pact made with the people, is to mitigate this law by providing protection for all *bhūtas, all human and non-human beings. When he performs his duty well he receives a portion of the merit of those under his protection, and when he performs it badly, he receives a portion of their demerit. It is the duty of the king to extend his dominion if possible, to bring order to the *Āryan world and to the entire world. Kāuṭilya develops a theory of world conquest based upon a *maṇḍala or circle of states, an organic power system. Kāuṭilya maintains that warfare or *daṇḍanīti* is necessary to uphold the sanctity of the pact, the basis of social and cosmic peace. For Kāuṭilya, peace is not the absence of war, but the order maintained through war.

Ed. and tr., R. P. Kangle (1960–5).

Arthur's Bosom (location of righteous souls): see ABRAHAM'S BOSOM.

Ārtī. Hindu offering of light during *pūjā (worship). It evoked from Gurū *Nānak the hymn *Sohilā, which remythologizes the ceremony: 'The sky is the ārtī dish: in it the sun and the moon are lamps, the mass of stars are the jewels, the sandalwood trees are the incense, the breeze, the *chaurī and the words are the flowers.'

Articles of faith (*ikkarim*, Heb., 'roots'). Formulations of Jewish belief. These are not as important as are *creeds in Christianity, since every person born of a Jewish mother is automatically a Jew irrespective of religious conviction. The *Shema', recited twice daily, is the fundamental Jewish article of faith. *Philo spoke of eight basic principles, Hananel b. Hushi'el isolated four articles, and *Maimonides set down thirteen *principles. The latter are (i) God's existence; (ii) his unity; (iii) his lack of a physical body; (iv) his eternity; (v) his unique claim to divinity; (vi) the validity of *prophecy; (vii) *Moses' status as chief prophet; (viii) Moses' reception of the whole *Torah; (ix) the completeness of Torah; (x) God's omniscience; (xi) reward and punishment; (xii) the coming of the *Messiah; and (xiii) the *resurrection of the dead. These thirteen principles became the basis of later formulations, including *ani ma'amin of the Prayer Book, the 'ikkarim' of David Kokhavi, Hasdai *Crescas' *'Or Adonai* (Light of the Lord), and Joseph *Albo's *Sefer ha-Ikkarim* (Book of Roots). In the 12th cent., the *Karaite Judah Hadassi produced ten articles of faith, and in the 19th cent., Moses *Mendelssohn, the pioneer of modernism within Judaism, identified three essential principles.

Articles, Thirty-Nine: see THIRTY-NINE ARTICLES.

Aruṇācala (Skt., 'red mountain'). A holy mountain in Tamil Nadu, S. India, at whose foot lies the Arunācalasvara temple dedicated to *Śiva. It was here that *Ramaṇa Mahārṣi settled, and his *āśram remains a centre for developing his teaching.

Arūpadhatu: see LOKA.

Arūpaloka: see LOKA (Buddhist).

Āryadeva or **Deva** (*c*.3rd cent. BCE; Tib., 'Phags-pa-lha). The foremost disciple of *Nāgārjuna and a leading exponent of the Buddhist *Mādhyamaka school of philosophy. Probably a native of Śrī Lankā, Āryadeva carried forward the work of his master by consolidating and defending the Mādhyamaka system against its opponents. His most celebrated work is the *Four Hundred Verses* (*Catuḥśataka*) which is in sixteen chapters: the first eight chapters expound the Mādhyamaka philosophy while the remaining eight are a refutation of rival Buddhist and non-Buddhist schools. It became a basic work for *San-lun.

V. S. Bhattacharya, *The Catuḥśataka of Āryadeva* (1931).

Aryaman (generous nobility): see ĀDITYAS.

Ārya-mārga (Pāli, *ariya-magga*). Sacred path to the full and final attainment in Buddhism. It has four stages, divided according to whether the *arya-pudgala* (person on the path) is still on the way or has gained the fruit (*phala*): (i) is the stream-enterer (*srotāpanna); (ii) is the once-returner (*sakrdāgāmin); (iii) is the not-returner (*anāgāmin); (iv) is the attainer (*arhat).

Āryans. A group of Indo-European speaking people who spread through Iran and N. India in the early 2nd millenium BCE. This is the so-called Aryan invasion, which overran the Dravidians and informed the combined texts, practices, and beliefs of *Vedic religion. The Aryans also introduced the classic division of society (*varna) into *brahmans, *kšatriyas, and *vaiśyas, with the indigenous population serving as *śūdras.

Arya-pudgala: see ĀRYA-MĀRGA.

Ārya Samāj. A Hindu reform movement founded by a *brahman, *Dayānanda Sarasvatī, in 1875. Ārya Samāj became very strong in the Puñjāb; its Bombay branch was started in 1876. The followers of Dayānanda are against idol-worship and meaningless rituals in modern Hinduism, and aim to return to the *Vedas in their beliefs and ritual. Dayānanda's interpretation of the Vedas is to be found in his book *Vedabhāshya*. Followers of Ārya Samāj do not tolerate *caste divisions in Hindu society, and they introduced the novel idea of converting people of other faiths to Hinduism. The followers of Ārya Samāj do invaluable work to remove social and religious injustices. It is now a worldwide organization.

K. W. Jones, *Arya Dharm* (1976); J. T. F. Jordens, *Dayānanda Sarasvatī* (1978); L. L. Rai, *The Ārya Samāj* (1932).

Ārya-satya (foundation of Buddha's teaching): see FOUR NOBLE TRUTHS.

Asa (one of the Holy Immortals): see AMESA SPENTAS.

Asahara Shoko (Japanese cult leader): see AUM SHINRIKYO.

Āsā kī Vār, Āsā dī Vār. *Hymn by *Gurū *Nānak, including some *śaloks by Gurū *Aṅgad. This *vār (heroic poem) in Āsā *rāg, praising God and true religion, is repeated daily in Sikh morning *worship after *Japjī. It consists of eighty-three verses (twenty-four *pauṛīs, each preceded by two or more śaloks). See MARRIAGE.

Asamprajñāta (Skt., 'non-differentiated', 'non-discerned') or **nirbīja** (Skt., 'without seed'). A stage of *samādhi in *rāja *yoga following from *samprajñāta ('differentiated') or *sabīja* ('with seed') samādhi. The **Yoga Sūtra* (1. 51) says that this state of consciousness is achieved upon the cessation (*nirodha) of all contents of consciousness (*citta), and that in it karmic impressions (*saṃskāras) are terminated. With the destruction of all *karma the soul (*puruṣa) attains liberation or isolation (*kaivalya) from *prakṛti.

Asaṃskṛta (Skt., 'not-conditioned'; Pāli *asankhata*). The state in Buddhism of anything that is beyond conditioned existence—the opposite, therefore, of saṃskṛta, the state in which all things are transient, coming into being, changing, and passing away. In Theravādin teaching (and also *Vātsīputrīya), asaṃskṛta applies only to *nirvāna, but for other schools the term was applied to that which cannot be weighed, measured, etc. Thus it could be applied to the content of fundamental teaching (e.g. the Eightfold Path, *aṣtangika-marga); or to the limitless state of mind in contemplation.

Āsana (Skt. 'sitting', 'posture'). A posture assumed for the practice of *yoga; the third 'limb' of *Patañjali's 'eight-limbed' (*aṣṭāṅga) or *rāja yoga. Āsana keeps the body still, regulates physical processes, and so allows the yogin to concentrate his mind. Patañjali says that the āsana should be 'steady and comfortable' (*sthira-sukham*) which results in the relaxation of tension (**Yoga Sūtra* 2. 46–8). There also occurs the elimination of opposites such as heat and cold, pain and pleasure etc. That is, the body becomes immobile and the yogin loses awareness of it, which allows him to develop one-pointed (*ekāgrata) consciousness (*citta). Āsana is found throughout Indian religious literature, in the *Upaniṣads, *Purāṇas, and **Mahābhārata*. For example, the **Śvetāśvatara Upaniṣad* (2. 8) speaks of the need during yoga to hold the body steady with the chest, neck, and head erect. Patañjali gives no precise instructions concerning posture; this would be given by the *guru. In *Haṭha-yoga, āsana takes on central importance, and Haṭha-yoga and *Tantric texts describe and give lists of different āsanas. Perhaps the most famous is the 'lotus posture' (*padmāsana) in which the yogin sits with the right foot placed on the left thigh and the left foot on the right thigh, soles facing upwards, with the hands placed between the thighs palms facing up. The eyes are directed to the tip of the nose and tongue placed at the root of the front teeth. Frequently āsanas, which can involve great physical exertion, are modelled on animals and natural phenomena, for example, the 'lion posture' (*siṃhāsana*), the 'tortoise posture' (*kurmāsana*), and the 'corpse posture' (*śavāsana*).

Asaṅga (Skt., 'not-bound'). 1. In Hinduism, the state of the true self (*ātman) which knows itself to be what it is—not bound to, or identified with, the mind or body.

2. 4th cent. CE. Founder of the Buddhist Yogācāra/*Vijñānavāda school of idealism and elder brother of *Vasubandhu, from whose biography the details of Asaṅga's life are known. Originally a follower of the *Theravāda form of Buddhism, he became dissatisfied with its teachings and, according to legend, received instruction in the *Mahāyāna teachings from the *bodhisattva *Maitreya. Asaṅga in turn converted his brother to the Mahāyāna, and the two composed many treatises expounding the Yogācāra system. Numerous works are attributed to Asaṅga including the monumental *Yogācārabhumiśāstra*, *Mahāyānasutrālaṃkāra*, and *Mahāyānasaṃgraha*.

E. Lamotte, *La Somme du grand véhicule d'Asanga* (1938–9).

Asankhata: see ASAṂSKṚTA.

Asaññasatta (Pāli, 'unconscious being'). In Buddhism, a class of celestial beings who through the practice of meditation have reached a lofty state of existence in which mental activity is suspended for great lengths of time. When their state expires, the conscious processes of conception and ideation recommence and these beings instantaneously fall to a lower level. The traditional Buddhist celestial hierarchy extends through thirty-one levels and the asaññasatta beings occupy level twenty-two. Their mode of existence is often erroneously identified with *nirvāna and can then become a hindrance to further spiritual progress.

Asat (Skt., 'not-being'). Linguistically the opposite of *sat (being), but not in the sense of annihilation or nihilism. Asat is the unimaginable, that which is in the absence of objects. It is thus the Absolute without qualities in *Advaita Vedānta.

Asava (in Buddhism, the destructive poison of desire): see DAŚABALA.

Āsava or **Āśrava** (Pāli/Skt., 'outflow', as from a sore). In Buddhism, a group of basic defects or defilements which are the cause of repeated rebirth. There is an original list of three which is often supplemented by a fourth. (i) sense-desires (*kāmāsava*), (ii) the desire for continued existence (*bhavāsava*), (iii) wrong views (*diṭṭhāsava*), and (iv) ignorance of the truth (*avijjāsava*). The āsavas summarize the cognitive and affective impediments to the state of full perfection, and their destruction (*āsavakkhaya*) is equated with the attainment of various desirable stages: eliminating (iii) = *Sotāpanna; (iii) + (i) = *Anāgāmin (non-returner); all four = *arhat. Among Jains, āśrava is the incursion of consequence from *karma, which has to be recognized by appropriate attention before it can be eliminated.

ASB (Church of England service book): see ALTERNATIVE SERVICE BOOK.

Ascama (rabbinic approval of halakhic decision): see HASKAMAH.

Ascension. The withdrawal of *Christ into heaven witnessed by the *apostles forty days after his *resurrection (Acts 1. 9). Writers earlier than *Luke do not mention it, and probably it was Luke's way of limiting Jesus' appearances to the past. Ascension Day, a major Christian festival, is observed forty days (i.e. the fifth Thursday) after Easter. In early times it was often celebrated with a procession to mark Jesus' journey to the Mount of Olives, the traditional site of the Ascension.

'Ascension' may also refer to the ascent of the Prophet *Muḥammad to heaven: see MIʿRĀJ.

'Ascension' is then applied to many descriptions of other-world journeys, especially among *shamans.

Ascetical theology (Gk., *askēsis*, 'exercise', 'training'). The theological discipline concerned with the ways of reaching Christian perfection, and especially with the human activities involved: ways of overcoming temptation, cultivating the virtues, fasting, and prayer. It overlaps with, and is with difficulty precisely distinguished from, moral theology and *mystical theology.

Asceticism (Gk., *askesis*, 'exercise', as of an athlete). The practice of self-denial or self-control as a means of religious attainment through discipline. Asceticism occurs in all religions, since in all religions there are more important things in life than living, and to attain particular goals, or to serve others, the giving up of some things on one's own behalf may be the only way forward. Nevertheless, asceticism is somewhat suspect in Judaism (but see BAḤYA BEN JOSEPH) and in Islam, because it seems to imply a denial of the goodness of God's creation. Even so, *ṣawm (fasting during the month of

Ramadhan) is one of the *Five Pillars of Islam; see also ZUHD.

In Hinduism, the most basic structure of ordinary life, the four stages of life (*āśrama) are marked by discipline, culminating in complete renunciation; the practice of asceticism is marked *pravrajya (going forth from home). The efficacy of self-mortification (*tapas) is so great that even the gods engage in it. This is even more marked in Jainism, where the ideal is the one who dies his death before it actually occurs (see SALLEKHANĀ). The practice of control becomes literally manifest in the many techniques of *yoga.

All of these were practised by Gautama in the early stages of the quest for enlightenment which culminated in his becoming the *Buddha. His description of two methods which he tried gives an early illustration of what was attempted. The 'All my limbs became like the joints of withered creepers . . . my gaunt ribs became like the crazy rafters of a tumble-down shed, my scalp became shrivelled and shrunk and the skin of my belly clung to my backbone' (*Majjhima Nikāya* 1. 240 ff.). A famous sculpture in the Lahore Museum depicts the Buddha in this wretched state.

Renouncing these practices as counterproductive the Buddha took food once again and realized the importance of an harmonious relationship between mind and body in the pursuit of the religious life. He had now experienced both the extremes of a life of ease and comfort (as a prince) and the life of extreme austerity and asceticism. Neither was satisfactory and the Buddha finally chose the 'middle way' between the two as the only sure path to liberation which he then quickly gained. Thus his own personal experience became central to the formation of Buddhist attitudes towards extreme attitudes and practices of all kinds, and asceticism thereafter found no real foothold in the Theravādin tradition.

The Buddha came to be critical of contemporary ascetic movements, and in several discourses he describes and criticizes their many and varied practices. Many went naked while others wore garments of cloth, hemp, rags, or hair; some imitated the behaviour of animals and slept on the ground or on beds of thorns; many restricted the type of food they would eat, the frequency of consumption, and the type of person they would accept it from. Although the Buddha prohibited extreme practices of the above kind he allowed twelve optional practices (*dhutanga) of a moderately ascetic kind but resisted the attempt to make five of them compulsory for monks; thirteen are listed in **Visuddhimagga* 11. It follows that, by Indian standards, asceticism in Buddhism is moderate, being a middle way (Skt., *madhyamā-pratipad*) between indulgence and denial, both of which confuse the mind. Its concern is with the overcoming of addictive attachment (Skt., *rāga*) to cyclic existence (Skt., **saṃsāra*). The test of good Buddhist asceticism is whether or not it brings freedom from one's own addictions so that one is free to help others with calmness, clarity, and compassion.

Among Jains, the commitment to asceticism is the central dynamic of the whole system. Those far enough advanced in the emancipation of *jīva from *karma (see GUNASTHĀNA) undergo initiation (*dīkṣa) and take the *Five Great Vows (*mahāvrata*); but the laity are closely integrated, by being on the same path, and by the formality of *dāna, gifts in support of the ascetics. The two immediate aims of the Jain ascetic counterbalance each other, *saṃyama being restraint, and *tapas being the generation of 'heat' (i.e. spiritual power). The centrality of asceticism for Jains can be seen in the ways in which formal and *ritual actions were introduced, epitomized in the six obligatory actions (*avaśyakas*) of equanimity, praise of the fordmakers, reverence of teachers, repentance, abandonment of the body by making it become as lifeless as feasible, abandonment of the world (in formal ways).

Among Sikhs, asceticism is viewed with caution: the *Gurus advocated for all Sikhs full involvement in family life coupled with self-discipline. For the *amritdhārī this frequently means a vegetarian diet and avoidance of *alcohol, but *celibacy is preached only by the *Udāsīs. 'One reaches not truth by remaining motionless like trees and stones, nor by being sawn alive' (Ādi Granth 952). Austerities and penances are considered painful, irrelevant and not conducive to spiritual development. (see GRAHASTI; NIRMALĀ; SRĪ CHAND; TOBACCO.)

In Judaism, ascetic abstention has never had a prominent place, although fasting is practised on the *Day of Atonement (Yom Kippur) and on various other specified days. However, the *prophets stressed that fasting in itself is not pleasing to God—God requires justice and righteousness rather than empty prayers and religious practices. Despite the existence of such ascetic groups as the *Nazirites and the *Essenes, in general the *rabbis regarded privation as a sin against the wishes of God: 'In the hereafter, we will be called to account for every enjoyment or pleasure which we declined here without sufficient cause' (*J.Kidd.* 4. 12). Later authorities were divided. *Abraham b. Hiyya went so far as to recommend sexual abstinence as the ideal. *Maimonides, on the other hand, argued for a middle way between self-indulgence and deprivation, and this pattern is generally followed in modern Judaism.

The origins of Christian asceticism are to be found in the strongly *eschatological consciousness of early Christians who looked forward to an imminent end of the world in which good would triumph over evil in a holy war. They were to prepare themselves by watchfulness, prayer, fasting, and, for many, sexual continence (cf. 1 Samuel 21. 5), anticipating martyrdom as the test of their faithfulness and a sign of the imminence of the final struggle. With the triumph of Christianity in the 4th cent. this attitude of eschatological awareness was inherited by the *monastic movement, and Christian asceticism became archetypically monastic. A systematic understanding of the demands of such asceticism on human nature was developed, notably by *Evagrius, and later by *Cassian and Dorotheus, drawing on Greek philosophy, especially Plato and the Stoics. Struggle against the demons preserved the notion of holy warfare, a characteristic of the Eastern Church. In the West, devotion to the humanity of Christ during the Middle Ages focused attention on the *imitation of Christ, especially his sufferings. The Renaissance brought a reaction against Christian asceticism, intensified by the Reformation with its tendency to suggest the worthlessness of human effort. See Index, Asceticism.

M. G. Bhagat, *Ancient Indian Asceticism* (1976); H. Chakraborti, *Asceticism in Ancient India* . . . (1973); R. Laidlaw, *Riches and Renunciation* . . . (1995). O. Chadwick (ed.), *Western Asceticism* (1958).

Aseity (Lat., *a se*, 'in himself', that which God is): see NOMINALISM.

Asenath. Daughter of the Egyptian high priest of On and wife of *Joseph. Her two sons, Manasseh and *Ephraim, were the *patriarchs of their eponymous tribes. According to the *rabbis, Asenath was the daughter of Dinah, Joseph's sister, and thus really an Israelite, but there is no biblical foundation for this.

Ash or **ashes.** In Western religions, ashes generally represent human frailty and mortality. Thus in Christianity, ashes are smeared on the forehead during the *Ash Wednesday ritual, with the words (traditionally: they are now more likely to be gender-neutral), 'Remember, O man, that thou art dust, and unto dust shalt thou return.' The words of committal in the Anglican **Book of Common Prayer* are, 'We commit this body to the ground, earth to earth, ashes to ashes, dust to dust.' But in Indian religions, and especially among Hindus, ash represents the pure substance left when the impure accidents of life have been removed. Ash is therefore smeared on the body as a mark of commitment to the process of liberating the true self from all that encumbers it. *Saivites are distinguished by three horizontal ash marks across the forehead.

Ashamnu (Heb., 'we have sinned'). Opening words of the Jewish penitential *prayers. Originally, it was the formula used by the *High Priest in the *Temple on the *Day of Atonement (Yom Kippur), and today is part of the *liturgy for that Day, *seliḥot and the New Moon fast.

Ash'arī (Muslim theologian): see AL-ASH'ARI.

Asher. One of the twelve tribes of Israel. According to Genesis 30. 12 f., the tribe is descended from *Jacob's eighth son.

Asherah. A Canaanite goddess and a wooden cult figure. Asherah was the mother Goddess and apparently the consort to *El, the father and creator of the gods. Jezebel, wife of King Ahab, brought her cult into the court worship of *Israel and the prophet *Elijah is said to have vanquished the 400 prophets of Asherah who 'dined at Jezebel's table' (1 Kings 18. 19). The asherah also seems to have been a cult figure placed near the altar. Its use is specifically forbidden in Deuteronomy 16. 21.

W. L. Reed, *The Asherah in the Old Testament* (1949).

Asher b. Jehiel/Yeḥi'el (also known as 'Asheri' and 'Rosh' *c*.1250–1327). Jewish *Talmudic authority. After the imprisonment of his teacher, *Meir of Rothenburg, he became the leader of the German Jewish community, but later fled from Germany and became *rabbi of Toledo. He encouraged the Spanish leaders to support Solomon *Adret's ban on the study of philosophy for those under the age of 25, and his *responsa were hugely influential throughout Europe. While he summarized the decisions of the earlier codifiers and produced commentaries on the *mishnayot and *tosafot of almost all the tractates of the Babylonian *Talmud, his purpose was one of continuing application: 'We must not be controlled in our decisions by an admiration of great men.'

Asher Hirsh Ginsberg (Jewish Zionist leader): see AHAD HA-'AM.

Asheri: see ASHER B. JEHIEL.

Ashes: see ASH.

Ashkenazim. German Jewry and its descendants in other countries. Originally the Ashkenaz referred to a small group of Jews settled on the banks of the Rhine. Gradually the term included all Jews from northern France, through Germany to Poland and Russia, and now includes their descendants in Israel, Australia, and the USA. The Ashkenazim are specifically contrasted with the *Sephardim, the Jews whose cultural origin was in Spain. As early as the 11th cent. CE, in *Rashi's commentry on the *Talmud, the term *erez Ashkenaz* (the land of Ashkenaz) refers to Germany. In the 14th cent., *Asher b. Jehiel described himself as 'adhering . . . to our own custom and to the tradition of our blessed forefathers, the sages of Ashkenaz'. Gradually, separate Ashkenaic and Sephardic customs, differences of pronunciation, *liturgical rites, and distinctive scripts were established, even though there was a cross-fertilization between the cultural centres of Germany and Spain. The approach of the Ashkenazi *tosafists to the Talmud was adopted by *Naḥmanides in Spain, and the Ashkenazi *ḥasidim were interested in the works of the Sephardic *Maimonides. Ashkenazi Jews were distinguished in E. Europe by their use of the *Yiddish language, and, before the Second World War, the Ashkenazim probably comprised about 90 per cent of the total of world Jewry. Although their numbers were greatly reduced in the *Holocaust and the USA is now their main centre, there is both an Ashkenazi and a Sephardi *Chief Rabbi in Israel, and Ashkenazi and Sephardi customs and rituals remain distinctive from one another.

Ashkenazi, Zevi Hirsch b. Jacob (also known as the Ḥakham Zevi, 1660–1718). Jewish *halakhist. Despite his *Ashkenazi origin, he adopted *Sephardi customs and was appointed *Ḥakham of the community of Sarajevo. He subsequently served as *rabbi of Hamburg, Wandsbeck, and Rothenburg, and then as rabbi of the Amsterdam Ashkenazi community. After a violent quarrel with the Sephardi rabbi, he moved to Opatow in Poland and then back to Hamburg. His chief work was a collection of responsa, *Ḥakham Zevi* (Rabbi Zevi) which dealt with such matters as the relationship between the Ashkenazim and Sephardim, and also with more specific questions—as, e.g., whether a *golem can be counted to make up the requisite number for prayer.

Ashoka (Indian ruler): see AŚOKA.

Ashram: see ĀŚRAMA.

Ashrei (Heb., 'happy are they'). First word of a reading from the book of Psalms used in the Jewish *liturgy. The reading includes Psalms 84. 5, 144. 15, 145, and 115. 18. It is read twice in the morning and once in the afternoon service, following the *Talmudic dictum that anyone who recites the Ashrei three times a day can be sure of a place in the world to come.

Ashtoreth or **Astarte.** Pagan Goddess. Frequently designated in the Bible as the feminine version of *Baʿalim and generally used to mean pagan worship. King *Solomon is said to have gone after 'Ashtoreth, goddess of the Sidonians' (1 Kings 11. 5). Astarte is the Greek name for Ashtoreth; she was a warrior and fertility deity, and her worship is known from *Ugaritic texts and from Egyptian sources, as well as from the Bible. She and *Anath were the sisters and consorts of Baʿal and may have been seen as different aspects of the same goddess. She may well have been the 'queen of heaven' whose worship *Jeremiah roundly condemned (Jeremiah 44).

ʿAshūrāʾ (Arab., from Heb., *ʿāsōr*, 'tenth [of the month]'). The Jewish *Day of Atonement, observed as a day of fasting by the early Muslim community in *Madīna, perhaps with the hope of identifying more closely with the Jews. The *Qur'ān speaks of fasting being decreed 'as it was decreed for those before you' (2. 183), possibly a reference to ʿAshūrāʾ; verse 185, however, specifies *Ramaḍān which replaced it in the second year of the *Hijra (624 CE). It then became a voluntary fast day on 10 *Muḥarram, often observed by the pious. For *Shīʿa Muslims, this is the anniversary of the death of *al-Husain at the hands of the Caliph Yazīd, and it is observed often with displays of self-inflicted wounds indicating willingness for martyrdom, and by martyrdom plays (*taʿziya).

M. M. Ayoub, *Redemptive Suffering in Islam . . .* (1978).

Ash Wednesday. So-called because of the practice of marking with *ash the foreheads of clergy and people at the beginning of *Lent (of which this is the first day). With Good Friday, it is the only day on which fasting is prescribed for *Roman Catholics.

Asmi-māna (Pāli, 'pride of "I am" '). In Buddhism, self-pride, egoism, conceit; considered to be a major obstacle to moral and spiritual development at any stage along the path to *nirvāna. One of the ten fetters (*saññojana*) and an important factor in Buddhist teaching on no-self (*anatta), it is combated specifically by meditation on impermanence (*anicca): 'Awareness of impermanence is to be cultivated for the removal of self-pride. In him who is aware of impermanence, awareness of what is not the self is established; he who is aware of what is not the self achieves the removal of self-pride, he attains nirvāna in this very life', *Ud.* 37. As distinct from its more basic counterpart, the (false) view of individuality (*sakkāya-diṭṭhi), asmi-māna represents the subtlest manifestations of self-delusion and persists until nirvāna is realized.

Asmita (Skt., 'I am-ness'). The error in Hinduism of supposing that the immediately experienced self is the true self: it is one of four kinds of error or ignorance (*avidyā), to be overcome in *yoga. The others are *rāga (attachment), dveṣa (aversion, which indicates that one is still involved, albeit by a feeling of revulsion), and *abhiniveṣa* (love of material and physical life).

Asmodeus or **Ashmedai.** An evil spirit. He first appears in Tobit and subsequently in the *Testament of Solomon*. In the later *agaddah, he is a lively, mischievous character even though he is described as 'king of the demons' (*B. Pes.* 110a). In folklore he often appears as the butt of jokes and is frequently seen as a kindly spirit and the friend of human beings.

Aśoka (3rd cent. BCE). Indian ruler of the Mauryan dynasty who converted to Buddhism and did much to promote the faith, while at the same time allowing freedom of worship to all creeds. Aśoka was the third incumbent of the Mauryan throne. By the time of his accession in 272, the Mauryan Empire (the first in Indian history) included the bulk of the subcontinent, except for parts of the south and the territory of Kalinga on the Bay of Bengal. After a victorious but bloody campaign against Kalinga in the eighth year of his reign, Aśoka underwent a conversion to Buddhism and replaced the policy of conquest by force (*digvijaya*) with one of conquest by righteousness (*dharmavijaya*). He proclaimed his ethical principles throughout his empire by means of

*Edicts inscribed upon rocks, pillars, and walls of caves. From the Edicts it may be seen that the content of Aśoka's *Dharma is essentially that of a lay Buddhist: it consists of 'Few sins and many good deeds, of kindness, liberality, truthfulness and purity' (Pillar Edict 2). In the Bhabru edict he conveys good wishes and greetings to the *Saṅgha. But no reference is made to the technical aspects of Buddhist doctrine as expounded in the *Four Noble Truths. Aśoka implemented the Buddhist virtues of compassion and non-harming (*ahiṁsā) by prohibiting the slaughter of animals in the capital, pardoning criminals, constructing civil amenities (such as roads, rest-houses and water-storage tanks), and appointing officials to promote the Dharma and have regard for the interests of his subjects. There is also evidence in the Edicts that he intervened to expel dissident elements from the Buddhist Order, and according to Buddhist sources he played a leading role in the Council of Pāṭaliputra in 250 BCE (see COUNCILS, BUDDHIST).

After Aśoka's death in 232 Mauryan rule rapidly declined and in the 2nd cent. BCE the N. and NW were extensively invaded by Greeks and Central Asian nomadic tribes.

B. G. Gokhale, *Asoka Maurya* (1966); E. Hultzsch, *The Inscriptions of Asoka* (transcriptions and trs., 1925); N. A. Nikam and R. McKeon, *The Edicts of Aśoka* (1959); J. S. Strong, *The Legend of King Asoka: A . . . Translation of the Aśokāvadāna* (1984); R. Thapar, *Aśoka and the Decline of the Mauryas* (1961).

Asparśa (Skt. 'non-touching). In Hinduism, keeping apart from the worldly and carnal influences of the world; a basic virtue subsumed under the relaxed *asceticism of *tyāga*, a passive rather than active approach.

Āśrama, Āśram. 1. A centre (usually Hindu) for religious study and meditation.

2. The four stages of life for a Hindu following the *Vedic way: *brahmacarya (receiving instruction), *gṛhastha (householder), *vānaprastha (forest dweller), *saṁnyāsa (renouncer).

P. Olivelle, *The Asrama System* (1993).

Āśrava (defilement): see ĀSAVA.

Āśraya (Skt., 'basis'). In Buddhist Sanskrit sources, a term used mainly in a philosophical sense to refer to the receptacle-consciousness (*alaya-vijñāna) as the basis or support of the other six consciousnesses (*vijñāna) or sense-modalities. It is through the restructuring or transformation (*parāvṛtti*) of the āśraya that enlightenment is attained. Less commonly the term is used of the body itself as the substrate or support for conscious experience.

Assassins (Fr., from Arab., *ḥashīshī*, 'one who consumes hashish'). An *Ismāʿīlī (Nizārī) sect at the time of the *crusades, founded by *al-Ḥasan b. al-Sabbah, who resorted to assassination supposedly under the influence of the drug (though the name *ḥashīshī* is not often used outside Syrian texts). Taking advantage of the confused conditions, the sect gained considerable strength, but was driven out of its mountain strongholds in the 13th cent. CE. The ruler of the Syrian assassins was known as *shaikh al-jabal*, 'the Old Man of the Mountain'.

M. G. S. Hodgson, *The Order of Assassins* (1955); B. Lewis, *The Assassins* (1968).

Assemblies of God. Christian denomination. It was organized in 1914 in Hot Springs, Arkansas, USA, from previously independent *Pentecostal churches. It became the largest white Pentecostal body in the USA, with 1.4 million adherents in 10,000 autonomous congregations throughout the country. It also has organizations in over 100 other countries, of which the largest are in Canada, England, France, Italy, Nigeria, and Brazil. Doctrinally, apart from the importance assigned to tongues (see GLOSSOLALIA) as evidence of baptism in the *Holy Spirit, the Assemblies of God are in the *Baptist tradition.

Assimilation. The process of so integrating with another culture that distinctive Jewish identity is lost. From biblical times, there has been a fear of Jews being assimilated into the pagan cultures of the surrounding nations, and early Christianity is seen by some Jewish communities as a process of assimilation of the early Jewish Christians into a *gentile mode of life. Since the second half of the 18th cent., assimilation has been a serious threat to the continued existence of Judaism and the Jewish people. The increasing separation of Church from State created a more neutral domain, which led to the belief (cf. MENDELSSOHN, MOSES) that one might be 'a Jew at home and a gentile in the street', or (J. L. Gordon), 'Be a Jew in your tent and a man outside.' In post-Enlightenment Europe, assimilation was seen as the means of attaining individual emancipation and social advancement, and *apostasy became commonplace. The *Reform movement, with its rejection of the traditional doctrine of the *messiah and the return to *Zion, was an attempt to preserve the distinctively religious element in Judaism while rejecting any form of social separation. Since the Second World War, acculturation of the Jews to the dominant culture has accelerated with increased intermarriage, greater educational and social opportunity, and increased secularism. On the other hand, a smaller group has preserved and maintained its Jewish identity, with more serious programmes of Jewish education, prompted by the survival of *anti-semitism and the establishment of the state of *Israel. Thus the modern community is increasingly polarized between the almost completely assimilated and those who are affirming their Jewish character more strongly than ever.

Association For Research and Enlightenment. A movement founded in Virginia Beach, Virginia, USA, in 1931 by the so-called 'sleeping prophet', Edgar *Cayce, and continued under Hugh Lynn Cayce, son of the founder. It is characterized by religious tolerance, holistic health practices, metaphysical teachings, and effective marketing techniques. Enquirers are directed to the Cayces' 14,256 discourses topically indexed under 10,000 categories and housed in the ARE library and Conference Center. Its publishing house has sold over 12 million books and booklets under 100 different titles.

The Center sponsors conferences on *New Age religious themes and holistic health. The ARE, with its occult practices, shares with many other New Age groups a belief in reincarnation, parapsychology, astrology, Atlantis, and novel interpretations of Christianity, such as the belief that *Jesus travelled to India, Tibet, and Egypt for training.

Assumption of the Virgin Mary. The Christian belief that *Mary was taken body and soul into heaven at the end of her life. The doctrine first emerged in various New Testament *apocrypha of the 4th cent., and on the strength of a passage in pseudo-*Dionysius became accepted in orthodox circles by the 7th cent. Finally in 1950 Pope *Pius XII, in the decree *Munificentissimus Deus*, defined it as a divinely revealed dogma, making claims that have little historical support: 'This truth is based on Sacred Scripture, . . . it has received the approval of liturgical worship from the earliest times, it is perfectly in keeping with the rest of revealed truth.' What is clearly true is the recognition that it is 'deeply embedded in the minds of the faithful' (or at least many of them), and on this basis it was declared and defined as a dogma revealed by God that 'Mary ever Virgin, when the course of her earthly life was finished, was taken up body and soul into the glory of heaven.' In Orthodox Churches, the belief is generally held but with less precise definition. Feast day in the W., 15 Aug.

Assyrian Church. A name used since the 19th cent. for the *Church of the East. It became popular especially in *Anglican circles as a way of avoiding the name *Nestorian, which was disliked by the Syrians themselves and appeared to prejudge their orthodoxy. The new name unfortunately carried with it the unprovable suggestion that the Christians were descendants of the ancient Assyrians of Nineveh. With this suggestion in mind, and in order to assert a cultural identity, *Syrian Christians of various denominations have recently started to call themselves 'Assyrians'.

Aṣṭamangala (Skt.). In Hinduism, eight objects to make auspicious an important occasion, e.g. the coronation of a king. They are variously listed, but a typical list includes: a lion, bull, elephant, banner, trumpet, water-jar, fan, lamp. For a lesser occasion the list might include: a king, *brahman, cow, sun, water, fire, gold, ghee.

In Buddhism, the practice was adapted to express veneration of the *Buddha as universal sovereign. The eight symbols are often placed before images of the Buddha. They are: parasol (power and protection); two fish (kingship); conch shell (conqueror); lotus blossom (purity); water-jar (nectar of *amṛta); banner (victory of the spirit); knot (endless eternity); wheel of teaching (*dharma-cakra).

Aṣṭāṇga-yoga (Skt., 'eight-limbed yoga'). A name in Hinduism for *Rāja-yoga, which has eight steps (aṅga): for details, see RĀJA-YOGA.

Aṣṭangika-mārga (Skt.; Pāli, *aṭṭangika-magga*). The eightfold path which leads, in Buddhism, to release from *dukkha (transience and the suffering involved in it). It is the last of the *Four Noble Truths, and one of the thirty-seven 'limbs' of enlightenment (*bodhipākṣika-dharma). Each of the eight is described as *samyak* (Skt.), *samma* (Pāli), often translated 'right'; but the meaning intended is not 'correct' as opposed to 'incorrect', but rather 'complete' or 'perfected'. The path is not intended to be a series of sequential steps, since in fact the perfected ways of behaviour (iii–v) precede all else; the eight summarize the necessary constituents in the process toward enlightenment and *nirvāna. They are: (i) perfected view (*samyak-dristhi / sammā-ditthi*), which understands the Four Noble Truths and their dependence on no persistent substantiality (*anātman); (ii) perfected resolution (*s.-kalpa / s.-sankappa*) in the direction of non-attachment, *ahiṁsā, etc.; (iii) perfected speech (*s.-vāc / s.-vāchā*), free from malice, gossip, lies, etc.; (iv) perfected conduct or action (*s.-karmānta / s.-kammanta*) in accordance with *śīla; (v) perfected livelihood (*s.-ājīva*), avoiding work which might harm others; (vi) perfected effort (*s.-vyāyāma / s.-vāyāma*) in setting forward that which produces good *karma / kamma; (vii) perfected mindfulness (*s.-smriti / s.-sati*), as summarized in *satipaṭṭhāna; (viii) perfected concentration (*s.-samādhi / s.-samādhi*), especially in *jhāna.

*Mahāyāna Buddhism makes its usual criticism of the *Theravādin understanding, namely, that it concentrates too selfishly on the individual's progress, with an emphasis on conduct and practice. Since suffering and rebirth arise, for Mahāyāna, from ignorance, the eight components are interpreted as means to dispelling ignorance. They become: (i) insight into *dharmakāya* (*trikāya); (ii) cessation of mental superimpositions; (iii) silence in absorption of *dharma; (iv) withdrawal from all actions with karmic consequence; (v) living in a way that dharma neither arises nor ceases; (vi) abandoning all intentionality; (vii) giving up reflection on unprofitable questions; (viii) no reliance on ideas or concepts at all.

Aṣṭapadī (Pañjābī, 'eight stanzas'). A poem of eight or occasionally more verses. In the *Ādi Granth, within each *rāg the *Gurūs' aṣṭapadīs are grouped between the last *chaupad and the first *chhant.

Aṣṭasāhasrikā-Prajñāpāramitā-Sūtra. Early (*c*.100 BCE) *perfection of wisdom *sūtra, 'The Sūtra of Perfect Wisdom in 8,000 Lines'. It became the basis of many later elaborations (into 18,000, 25,000, 100,000, etc., lines). It elevates the *bodhisattvas as the practitioners of the six perfections (*pāramitā), and therefore points the way to the practice of *jhāna (meditation).

Eng. tr. E. Conze (1975).

Aṣṭāvakra. The teacher of *Patañjali. He is held to be the author of *Aśtāvakra-Saṃhitā*, a fundamental work of *Advaita Vedānta. Born deformed, he became a *muni and engaged in great asceticism (*tapas).

Eng. tr. H. P. Shastri, *Ashtavakra Gita* (1978).

Aṣṭa-vimokṣa (Skt.). Eight liberations, a meditation exercise in Buddhism which leads to detachment from dependence on forms of appearance: (i) concentration on the defects in all forms of appearance; (ii) concentration on defects in external forms (reinforcing (i)); (iii) abandoning the appearance of beauty; (iv) attaining the limitlessness of space; (v) attaining the limitlessness of consciousness; (vi) attainment of no-thingness; (vii) moving beyond either perception or non-perception; (viii) cessation of perception and feeling which anticipates *nirvāna (*nirodha-samāpatti).

Asterisk (Gk., 'a star'). A metal (usually gold or silver) instrument used in Greek Orthodoxy to cover the *paten so that the covering veils do not touch the consecrated bread during the *eucharist.

Asteya (Indian vow against stealing): see APARIGRAHA (I).

Asthangika-mārga (Buddhist eightfold path): see AṢṬANGIKA-MARGA.

Āstika (Skt.). Hindu name for the six philosophical systems (*darśana) which adhere correctly to the *Vedas, acknowledging their authority. The opposite are the *nāstika systems.

Astikaya ('it exists' + 'a body'). The five elements of Jain ontology. According to Jains, there are five elements which pervade the universe (*loka) and which keep it in being: (i) *jīva, 'life-permeation'; (ii) *dharma, 'movement'; (iii) *pudgala*, 'atomic individuals'; (iv) *ākāśa*, 'space'; all of these making up the fifth category of non-jīva, *ajīva. The oddity of this arrangement probably arises from the fact that originally the Jains made a simple twofold division (jīva/ajīva), so that the more sophisticated analysis emerged only gradually. On the later analysis, the whole loka in every point is or has been filled with jīvas. If embodied, they are divided into moving (*trasa*) or stationary (*sthavara*). The atoms provide the space/time dimensions for jīva, including breath and language; and later, the *Digambaras added 'time' as a sixth element. *Ākāśa* offers the dimension of action, like a pot in which rice is cooked. All five elements are substantially real, because otherwise the universe would be one undifferentiated whole, about which nothing could be said—a notion akin to that of redundancy in information theory.

Astrology. The belief that the stars and planets have effects on human life and affairs. It is entangled in astronomy, and while the two, in some religions, reinforce each other, they may also be in serious conflict.

In Hinduism, decision-making on all serious matters (e.g. the date and time of a wedding) and on many everyday matters is referred to astrology (*jyotiṣa). The earliest surviving text is *Gargasaṃhitā* (1st cent. CE). Of great authority was *Pañca-siddhānta* (6th cent.), only a part of which has survived. Jyotiṣa is one of the six *vedāṅgas, where it is of particular importance in deciding the most auspicious time for a ritual or sacrifice.

In general, Buddhism adopted the Hindu scheme of astronomy but rejected the latter's preoccupation with astrology. The position and movement of the celestial bodies was of interest to Buddhists for pragmatic purposes only, such as calculating the time of day, the length of the lunar month and its holy days, and the period of retreat during the rainy season. Such skills were especially important in the case of forest-dwelling monks who were cut off from society: such monks were to learn 'the positions of the constellations, either the whole or one section, and to know the cardinal points'.

Astrology and divination are stigmatized as practices unworthy of a monk, and the *Buddha is singled out for praise as one not devoting himself to such 'low arts' (*tiracchāna-vijjā*). That such practices were rife in the time of the Buddha may be seen from the extensive list in the *Brahmajāla-sutta*, an early Buddhist discourse which describes numerous techniques of divination including astrology, augury, soothsaying, incantations, and charms. Monks were discouraged from practising magic, interpreting dreams and omens, and casting horoscopes. Despite this, one of the Buddha's chief disciples, *Moggallāna, is reputed to have been skilled in divination and sorcery and to have used these powers for the propagation of the faith. Although he was rebuked on several occasions for this by the Buddha, the practice of divination by monks was never eradicated. In practically all Buddhist cultures monks officiate as advisers to the laity and employ techniques of divination. In the Buddhism of Tibet and Central Asia, indigenous *shamanistic practices were incorporated with only superficial modifications, and in China a complex system of astrology and divination based on the Book of Changes (*I Ching*) found an accommodation within Buddhism.

Sikhs return to a more basic condemnation of astrology. Although some Sikhs may consult horoscopes, astrology is condemned by the *Rahit-Maryādā in accordance with the *Gurūs' teaching. 'You calculate auspicious days for marriage, but do not reflect that the one formless Lord is above and beyond these days' (Ādi Granth p. 904). See CALENDAR; SAṄGRĀND.

In both Judaism and Christianity, astrology is officially condemned (e.g. *Catechism of the Catholic Church* (1994), 2116), because it detracts from the sovereignty of God, as though stars and planets can be lesser creators in God's world; but unofficially, at the level of folk-religion, the consulting of horoscopes is simply one example of how tenacious these beliefs are. The historian *Josephus commented that astrology was common among the Jews even though the practice of star-gazing among the Babylonians was scoffed at by the prophets. (Isaiah 47. 13). The sages were not in agreement about astrology. R. *Johanan ben Zakkai said: 'There is no star for Israel' (*B. Shab.* 156a), while *Rava declared, 'Life, children and sustenance—these things depend not on merit, but on the stars' (*BMK* 28a). Later, there were several famous Jewish astrologers, such as Masha'allah, (8th cent.) and Abu Daud (10th cent.). Saadiah *Gaon believed in astrology, as did *Abraham bar Hiyya and Abraham ibn Ezra. Hasdai *Crescas, Joseph *Albo, and *Maimonides all rejected it, Maimonides declaring, 'The science which is called the decree of the stars . . . is no science at all, but mere foolery'. Much *kabbalistic literature, however, takes the validity of astrology for granted.

In Islam, the contest between astronomy and astrology (*ʿilm al-nujūm*) became explicit in *al-Ghaz(z)ālī: he commended astronomy as a part of the study of the signs of God in God's creation (*aya), but strongly condemned astrology as spurious. Even so, the same term was still being applied to both, *ʿilm ahkam al-nujūm*, and the practice of astrology did not abate, at least at the popular level. Astrology for the purposes of divination (*ʿilm al-tanjīm*) has remained widespread, defending itself from the charge of faithlessly failing to trust in the will of God (*qadar) by saying that the disposition of the stars is a part of God's creative act. See Index, Astrology.

Aśubha (Skt., 'not-beautiful'). The contemplation in Buddhism of disgusting objects, sometimes equated with reflection on the unpleasing features of the body, especially of corpses in different stages of decay. It is thus a dramatic instance of *memento mori*. Aśubha is described among the forty meditation exercises in the **Visuddhimagga*.

Asura (Skt.), power-seeking and power-hungry being, not unlike a *Titan, often, but somewhat misleadingly translated as 'demon'; or, *anārya* (non-*Āryan) people of ancient India. The derivation of asura is uncertain. Some scholars derive it from Ashur, the Assyrian god, or from the breath (*asu*) of *Prajāpati, or from the root *as* (to be). According to a *Hindu myth, a-sura is the negation of *surā*, an Indo-Āryan liquor, and refers to non-Āryan abstainers. In Hindu mythology, *sura* came to mean a minor god, in contrast to a-sura ('not-god', hence 'demon'), but this is believed to be a false etymology.

In the older parts of the **Ṛg-Veda*, asura refers to the supreme spirit, like the *Zoroastrian *Ahura Mazda, or to *Vedic deities (*devas) such as *Varuṇa, *Agni, *Mitra, and *Indra. In younger Vedic texts and in Hindu mythology, asuras are demons or titans who strive against the devas (gods) (cf., the Iranian tradition, in which *ahura* came to mean 'god' and *daeva* came to mean 'demon').

According to *Śatapatha *Brāhmaṇa*, the devas and asuras both sprang from Prajāpati, but the former chose true speech while the latter chose the lie. *Āitareya Brāhmaṇa* relates that the devas hold power by day and the asuras hold equal power by night.

The non-Āryan Dānavas and Lāityas were called asura. These may have been peoples who were opponents of the Indo-Āryans and who were mythologically equated with the titans and demons.

Asuras are not necessarily evil, nor are devas necessarily good. They are consubstantial, distinguished only by their mutual opposition, which is not conceived as an absolute ethical *dualism.

W. D. O'Flaherty, *The Origins of Evil in Hindu Mythology* (1976).

Aśvaghoṣa (2nd cent. CE). A court poet of the Kusāna king Kaniṣka and author of literary works in Sanskrit on Buddhist themes. He is known to be the author of three such works: *The Acts of the Buddha* (*Buddhacarita*), *Nanda the Fair* (*Saundarananda*), and *The Story of Sariputra* (*Sāriputraprakaraṇa*). His most famous work is the first of these, a biography of the *Buddha in epic *mahākāvya* style. Originally in twenty-eight cantos only seventeen survive in Skt., the remainder being preserved in Tibetan and Chinese translation. The author's deep respect and reverence for the Buddha is unmistakable in all of these compositions. Tradition also ascribes to him *Mahayanaśraddhotpāda-śastra*.

Germ. tr. F. Weller, *Das Leben des Buddha von Aśvaghoṣa* (1926–8); Eng. tr. D. T. Suzuki, *Acvaghosha's 'Discourse on the Awakening of Faith in the Mahāyāna'* (1900); E. H. Johnston (1936 and 1972).

Aśvamedha. A Hindu, *Vedic, ritual of horse-sacrifice. It was performed by kings as a symbolic representation of their supreme power and authority, as well as, sometimes, for such boons as the birth of a son to ensure succession. For one year the chosen horse might wander as he pleased, unmolested and protected by an armed guard. Should he trespass into another kingdom, its ruler would have to give battle or submit. At the end of the year the horse was brought back to the capital with due ceremony, and sacrificed along with other animals. The fertility element of the ceremony is evident from the way in which, symbolically, the senior queen would lie beside the dead horse. Jaya Siṉha II of Jaipur was the last prince to perform this sacrifice, in the 18th cent.

Aśvin(s) (Skt., *aśva*, 'horse'). Two Hindu, *Vedic, deities, who appear at dawn, drawn in a golden carriage by horses or birds. They are associated with light and the sun, and are particularly auspicious and helpful. They are frequently mentioned in the *Vedas, always inseparable, though in later literature they are distinguished as Nāsatya and Dasra.

Atami (religious centre): see SEKAI KYŪSEIKYŌ.

Āṭānatiyā (part of Buddhist Pāli canon): see DIGHA-NIKĀYA.

Atas. Fire, in *Zoroastrianism one of the seven Good Creations of *Ahura Mazda, the one most commonly bound up with worship. There are many levels to the symbolism. In ancient Iran, trial by ordeal was part of the judicial process whereby the witness either had fiery molten metal poured on the chest or was made to pass between two banked walls of flame. If the testimony was true, then it was believed Ahura Mazda would protect him. Judgement is, therefore, one element in the symbolism. So too was protection, because of the fires which guarded the nomads from the threat of wild animals at night. Fire, be it in the form of the sun or the warmth of the living body, was further associated with life. In Indo-Iranian practice, sacrificial offerings were poured on the fire which blazed high and conveyed the worshipper's gifts to God. The fire, therefore, had a mediating role. An ancient 'hymn' (*Atash Nyayes*) addresses prayers to the fire and refers it as 'son of God'. The ritual fire is the focal point of Zoroastrian ceremonies, interpreted by some as radiating the power of God, and by others as the best symbol of 'He who is himself pure undefiled light'. All Zoroastrians believe that when they stand in purity and in devotion before the sacred fire, they stand in the presence of God. The common label 'fire-worshipper' is offensive to them, because they rightly believe it fails to do justice to the richness of the symbolism and the religion.

True to its nomadic roots, Zoroastrian worship was essentially carried out in the presence of the divine creations of the waters (e.g. by a river) and on mountain tops. Temples, and the associated cultic use of statues, were probably introduced during the Achaemenid era (6th–4th cent. BCE), perhaps an Imperial imitation of the splendours of rival empires, such as the Babylonians. They proliferated under the Parthians and became splendid foci of royal patronage under the Sasanians, but whether they ever replaced the tradition of domestic worship before the household fire among the general public may be doubted. When the *Parsis first settled in India, they maintained only one permanently burning ritual fire for many centuries. In Muslim Iran, many temples were desecrated and destroyed, and mosques were built on the ruins to highlight the Muslim triumph. The home, therefore, continued to be the main setting for much Zoroastrian devotional life. However, in the 19th cent., the new-found wealth of the Parsis, plus the introduction of pollution into the home by the employment of non-Zoroastrian servants, resulted in the building of many temples in India and in some centres of the *diaspora (e.g. Aden and Zanzibar).

There are three categories of fire, and two types of fire temple. The different grades of fire are distinguished by the manner of their consecration. The highest, the *Bahram* fire, involves the bringing together and consecrating of sixteen different types of fire (e.g. fire which has cooked dead matter and has thus been involved in the greatest pollution, goldsmith's fire, a shepherd's fire, and one caused by lightning). The rites are so complex they last a year. Temples housing such fires are sometimes referred to as 'Cathedral Fire Temples' because of their status. There are four such temples in Iran, and eight in India (four in Bombay and the oldest of all, which has burnt for over 1,000 years, at Udwada). They are treated as royalty, with a crowning dome, and the wood is laid on them in the shape of a throne.

The second grade of fire, the *Adaran* fire, is the one which burns in most temples, and its consecration is much less complicated, combining only four types of fire (that of priests, warriors, farmers, and artisans). Like the Atas Bahram it can be tended only by a ritually pure priest. The third grade of fire, the *dadgah*, may be tended by a lay person in the home, but is also used in the 'inner' or 'higher' ceremonies in the temple where it is tended by the priest. In both Iran and India, temples are commonly referred to as *Dar-i-Mihrs* (Gateway or Court of Mithra), or in India by the Gujarati as *Agiary*, or 'House of fire'.

M. Boyce, *A Persian Stronghold of Zoroastrianism* (1977).

Atatürk (Turkish Leader known as 'father of the Turks'): see OTTOMAN EMPIRE.

Athanasian Creed. A statement of faith formerly widely used in W. churches. It begins: 'Whosoever will be saved, before all things it is necessary that he hold the Catholic faith. Which faith except everyone do keep whole and undefiled, he shall perish everlastingly.' The opening words thus furnish the alternative title 'Quicunque Vult'. It was composed in the 4th or 5th cent. (certainly after the time of *Athanasius) in Latin. It expounds the doctrines of the *Trinity and the *Incarnation (the latter part including a list of Christ's works as in the *Apostles' Creed). It is printed in the Latin *Breviary and the **Book of Common Prayer* for recital in worship on certain occasions, but its archaism, great length, and 'damnatory clauses' (as in the second sentence above) have led to its general disuse.

J. N. D. Kelly, *The Athanasian Creed* (1964).

Athanasius, St (*c*.296–373). Bishop of *Alexandria and important church *father. He opposed any compromise with *Arianism at the council of *Nicaea (325), and so was repeatedly deposed and exiled from his *see while that party was in the ascendant. He was finally restored in 366. Athanasius's most important work (written before *c*.318) was *On the *Incarnation*, in which he expounds how God the Word, by his union with manhood, restored fallen humanity to the image of God (Gen 1.27), and by his death and *resurrection overcame death, the consequence of *sin. From 339 to 359 he wrote a series of works defending the true deity of God the Son and attacking the theology and ecclesiastical politics of the Arians. From about 361 he sought to reconcile the semi-Arian party in Alexandria to the *homoousion formula. Athanasius's (probably genuine) *Life of *Antony* stimulated the monastic movement in Egypt and made it known in the West.

Tr. of most of the works in the Library of Nicene and Post-Nicene Fathers, iv (1892); F. L. Cross, *The Study of Athanasius* (1945); C. Kannengiesser, *Athanase d'Alexandrie . . .* (1983); A. Pettersen, *Athanasius* (1995).

Atharvan. The priest who in Indian religion was the first to generate fire, to institute its worship, and to offer *soma (*Ṛg Veda* 1. 83. 5). For those reasons he was called 'the father of fire'. His descendants, the Atharvānas, have inherited his responsibilities in relation to domestic rituals. See also ATHARVA VEDA.

Atharva Veda (Skt.). The *Vedic collection of hymns used by the *Atharvan priests in the domestic rituals. Because of its lack of connection to the larger, more public Vedic sacrifices, the *Atharva Veda* early on was relegated to a secondary position and denied the title *Veda accorded the *trayī vidyā* (threefold knowledge), i.e. the **Ṛg*, **Sāma*, and **Yajur Veda*. The Atharvan school responded by claiming the office of the domestic priest (*purohita) and officiating priest (*brahman), by adding a final section of hymns (book 20) devoted specifically to one of the major sacrifices, the *soma sacrifice, and by expounding a tradition of the fourfold Veda. Originally the collection had the title *'Atharvāṅgirasaḥ'*, referring to the two families of priests, the Atharvans and Āṅgirasas, to whom the collection belonged. This double title also indicated the supposedly twofold nature of the collection. The Atharvans traditionally were regarded as performing appeasing and auspicious rites, the Āṅgirasas hostile and imprecatory rites. In actuality the Atharva Veda consists of sundry hymns not easily divided into these categories. Charms, curses, hymns intended for healing, recovering, or inflicting injury are mixed with hymns of praise and speculation. The speculative hymns in particular are important for the history of Indian philosophy. The speculation is more advanced than that of the *Ṛg Veda*, and points toward the philosophical tendencies of the later *Āraṇyakas and *Upaniṣads.

Tr. W. D. Whitney (1905); M. Bloomfield (1897).

Atheism. Disbelief in the existence of God; to be distinguished from *agnosticism, which professes uncertainty on the question. The biblical reference to the fool who says in his heart 'There is no God!' (Psalm 14. 1) suggests that it is no new phenomenon. Modern atheists make a variety of claims to defend their position: that there is little or no real evidence for the existence of God, that *theism is refuted by the existence of *evil in the world, that it is meaningless because unverifiable, that it is inauthentic because it attacks human autonomy, and that it is unscientific. Many follow *Feuerbach and *Marx in seeing the concept of God as a human construct, a 'projection' of whatever qualities are admired in a particular society.

Many Christian theologians regard atheism as culpable, citing Romans 1. 19–21 in support of their view. Others (e.g. J. Maritain, *The Range of Reason*, 1952) allow that many atheists are really 'pseudo-atheists', because they are only rejecting inadequate concepts of God, and that in their pursuit of goodness and truth they may be regarded as implicit theists.

In Indian religion and philosophy, atheism is addressed to different understandings of what God is and does (according to those who believe), and is often more subtle. Thus Jains and Buddhists allow that within the domains of appearance, that which might be labelled 'God' is no less (but no more) real than other transient appearances, and is of effect; but in practice, 'God' must be left behind for true progress to be made. Among Hindus, several systems interpreted the tradition without involving God, e.g. Carvaka; Saṁkhya was initially atheistic, though God was later able to be accommodated in the system; and Pūrva and Uttara Mīmāṃsā debated the worth of arguments pointing to God.

Athos, Mount. Peninsula in NE Greece (*c*.48 × 10 km. in area), named for the mountain at its end. Known as the 'Holy Mountain' (Hagion Oros), it is the principal centre of *Orthodox monasticism. It is an autonomous monastic district, in effect a theocratic republic from 1927. Its importance dates from the foundation of the monastery of the *Lavra in 962. In the 11th cent. the number of monasteries is said to have been 180. Under Turkish rule Mt. Athos was instrumental in keeping alive the intellectual tradition of Orthodoxy, and especially *Hesychasm. Presently there are twenty 'ruling monasteries' plus dependent houses of various sizes including hermits' dwellings. Most are *coenobitic, with the 'idiorrhythmic' houses, in which each monk arranges his own work and meals, gradually disappearing. Monastic life is austere and traditionalist. The total number of monks declined in 1980 to *c*.1,300 from the 7,432 recorded in 1903; but that trend has been reversed, particularly after the collapse of communism which led to a considerable influx of monks. This has created a complex problem for Orthodoxy and for the Greek government: the independence of Mt. Athos has made this seem a way of immigrating without the usual controls. In 1994, the *patriarch in Istanbul sent an exarchate (delegation of three bishops) to preside over the Holy Community (the representative leaders of the communities) in order to discuss the status of new arrivals, but this was angrily rejected as interference. Lying behind the immediate issue is the fear of Mt. Athos that they are to be silenced before a move is made to reunion with Rome.

Of the twenty monasteries, seventeen are Greek; there is one Russian, one Serbian, and one Bulgarian. A rule forbids women, or even female animals, to set foot on the peninsula.

S. Kados, *Mount Athos* (1980).

Atiśa (also Atīśa and Dīpaṅkaraśrījñāna; *c.*982–1054). Indian teacher who strongly influenced the development of Buddhism during its 'second diffusion' in Tibet. Having turned to the spiritual path while a young boy, following a vision of his tutelary divinity *Tārā, Atiśa is reputed to have studied in his youth with many members of the *Siddha tradition, such as *Nāropa, Maitrīpa, and Ḍombhipa, before spending twelve years studying Buddhism in Sumatra and eventually becoming abbot of the monastic university of Vikramaśīla. As one of the most revered teachers in India, Atiśa left to enter Tibet in 1042 at the invitation of King Byang.chub.' od, and stayed until his death.

On arrival in Tibet, Atiśa found that Buddhism was only beginning to reassert itself there following the earlier persecution by King Langdarma, and that the monks lacked guidance on interpretation of the 'old' *tantras such as Atiśa found at Samye, and the 'new' tantras being freshly introduced by the great traveller-translators such as Rinchen Zangpo. The extent of the ignorance regarding these teachings was such that, believing all dharmas to be essentially pure, monks were not conceiving of any actions as being marked by impurity, and consequently Atiśa's main task was to correct their superficial interpretations. Atiśa accomplished this essentially by emphasizing monastic discipline, the grounding of *Tantrism in the philosophy and ethics of the *sūtras, and the need for a pupil to devote himself to a single teacher. When his own disciple, Dromdon, asked Atiśa which was the more important, a text or a teacher, Atiśa replied that without a teacher 'the doctrine and the man will go separate ways'; this sentiment has pervaded Tibetan Buddhism ever since.

As well as emphasizing tantras related to *Ādi Buddha, such as *Sarvatathāgata tattvasamgraha tantra* (introduced by Rinchen Zangpo), Atiśa is credited with the introduction into Tibet of the worship of Tārā, and of the popular system of meditation and philosophy known as Lojong (*blo.sbyong*, 'mind training'), which involves such meditations as the consideration of all beings as having been one's mother in a previous existence. The arising desire to repay the kindness of one's mother is by this meditation extended to all beings, generating a sense of universal responsibility and transforming 'wishful' *bodhicitta into 'effective' bodhicitta. Of more than 200 works ascribed to Atiśa, his most famous is *Bodhipathapradīpa* (A Lamp for the Path to Enlightenment), elucidating the correct development of the *bodhisattva. In 1056 Dromdon, who was noted for his strict observance of the moral and monastic code, founded the *Kadam ('Advice') school, aimed at 'following the advice of Atiśa'.

Eng. tr. R. Sherburne, *A Lamp for the Path and Commentary by Atīśa* (1983); A. Chattopadhyaya, *Atiśa and Tibet* (1967).

Atiyoga (exceptional or perfect yoga): see DZOGCHEN.

Atlanteans. A philosophical society founded in 1957 from the teachings of a 'spirit guide' named Helio-Arcanophus. These teachings place emphasis upon the importance of the individual and the need to find a meaning to life which can help sweep aside frustration and allow one to develop spiritually. Acknowledging God as an ultimate thought or intelligence, the philosophy, without dogma, examines such subjects as reincarnation, *karma, healing, *meditation, the *deva, and elemental kingdoms, the significance of Atlantis, the future of the world, psychology, dreams, and astrology. Members are encouraged to explore the potential of their psychic natures and to help the planet positively by sending thoughts of love and healing to individuals and world situations.

Ātmabodha. A short treatise on 'knowledge of the Self', attributed to *Śaṅkara. In sixty-eight verses (*ślokas*) it covers the most important points of *Advaita-Vedānta.

Tr. T. Leggett, *The Chapter of the Self* (1978); V. P. N. Menon, *Atma Bodha* (1964).

Ātman (Skt.). For Hindus and Sikhs, the real or true Self, which underlies and is present in human appearance. In the Vedas, that sense had not developed. In the **Ṛg Veda* it means breath, or the whole body, as opposed to parts of it. It may even simply be a reflexive pronoun (cf. *nafs in Arabic). It was only in the period of the *Āraṇyakas and *Upaniṣads that attempts were made to define and describe the nature of this 'self' more precisely. *Brihādaranyaka Upaniṣad* 1. 3. 22 states that the vital force, ātman (now much more than breath) is present and operative in every form of life, not just in humans. Ātman is therefore necessarily identical with *Brahman. But clearly Brahman cannot be reduced to the material and contingent involvements of human life, which produce a sense of self-independence. The self of this independence is *jīva. Thus ātman becomes the uninvolved observer of the jīva in its entanglements in the world, which bind it to countless rebirths: hence the image of the two birds: 'Two birds, companions, always united, cling to the same tree. Of these two, the one eats the sweet fruit, while the other looks on without eating' (*Śvetasvatāra Upaniṣad* 4. 6). Ātman attains its final release (*mokṣa) when it realizes that it is, what it always has been, Brahman: *tat tvam asi*, thou art that.

In Buddhism, this idea of ātman was profoundly contradicted: see ANĀTMAN (= *anatta*). For Sikhs, the immortal ātman is the means of relation to God—indeed, the union (for those who attain it) is so close that it comes close at times to identity: 'God abides in the ātman, and the ātman abides in God' (*Ādi Granth 1153).

Atonement

Judaism (Heb., *kapparah*). Reconciliation with God. According to Jewish belief, human sin damages the relationship with God and only the process of atonement can restore it. According to biblical teaching, *sacrifice was the outward form of atonement (Leviticus 5), provided human beings also purified themselves spiritually (e.g. Isaiah 1. 11–17). After the destruction of the *Temple in 70 CE, (the only means of atonement were *prayer, repentance, fasting, *charity, and full restitution. See also DAY OF ATONEMENT. Atonement is also set in the context of more general considerations of forgiveness. Although the ancient Israelites believed that sacrificial ritual could lead to forgiveness (*meḥilah, seliḥah*), human contrition was essential, and the act of forgiveness was accomplished by God alone: 'When a man or woman commits any of the sins . . . , he shall confess his sin . . . , and he shall make full restitution for his wrong . . . in addition to the ram of atonement with which atonement is made for him (Numbers 5. 5–8). Repeatedly the *prophets emphasized that the act of sacrifice was insufficient and that repentance must be accompanied by a change of heart (e.g. Jeremiah 4. 4). None the less, the Israelites could be confident of God's forgiveness because of the *covenant relationship and because it is in God's nature, as a father and shepherd, to forgive his people (see Hosea 11. 1–9)—hence Heine's deathbed statement (wrongly taken as a jest), 'God will forgive me—it's his business.' Although one of *Maimonides thirteen *principles of the Jewish faith is that God rewards the righteous and punishes the wicked, the *Talmud insists that 'He who sins and regrets his act is at once forgiven' (*B.Ḥag.* 5a). However, the tradition also emphasizes that sins against fellow human beings can only be forgiven by the injured party. Before the Day of Atonement, therefore, it is customary to seek forgiveness from those one has wronged. The Talmud (*B.Taʿan.* 20b) expects a willingness to be forgiven: the injured person must be 'pliant as a reed, not hard as a cedar'.

Christianity In Christian theology, atonement is the reconciliation ('at-one-ment') of men and women to God through the death of Christ. The word was introduced by W. *Tyndale (in 1526) to translate *reconciliatio*. The need for such reconciliation is already apparent in the Old Testament: in the system of sacrifices which removed ritual and moral uncleanness; in the prophecies of a 'new covenant' (Jeremiah 31. 31); and in the *servant songs which speak of the servant being 'wounded for our transgressions' (Isaiah 53. 5). Jesus' recorded words about his death—to some degree authentic, e.g. Mark 10. 45, 1 Corinthians 11. 25—placed it in this theological context. Thus the earliest Christian preaching expounded Christ's death as 'for our sins' (1 Corinthians 15. 3). The idea is elaborated particularly by *Paul. For him Christ's death and resurrection were the means by which we were redeemed from the effects of the law and its transgression, namely sin, from God's condemnation, and from death. A new peace was made between God and humanity 'through the blood of his cross' (Colossians 1. 20). Hence the death of Christ was a 'propitiation' or 'expiation' (Romans 3. 25; the translation of *hilastērion* here and elsewhere is a delicate question). A different exposition of the atonement, in sacrificial language, is found in Hebrews.

Although there have been no official Church definitions of the doctrine of the atonement, there have been many accounts of how the life, death, resurrection, and ascension of Jesus effect for others the forgiveness and reconciliation with God which he clearly mediated to many during his lifetime and ministry: in other words, these accounts attempt to answer the questions of what the death of Jesus adds to his life, or of how the 'atonements' effected in his life are still achieved after his death. In general, these accounts claim that the death of Jesus universalizes what would otherwise have been a local and restricted transaction. There are five major accounts falling into two groups, objective and subjective theories. Objective theories claim that something factual has been done for us which has dealt with the reality of sin, and which we could not have done for ourselves. The penal (or juridical) theory claims that Christ has borne the penalty instead of us, so that God can now forgive freely: sin, being an infinite offence against God, required a correspondingly infinite satisfaction which only God could make (see ANSELM). Literally interpreted, this may lead to claims that Christ is a substitute for each individual who deserves the penalty, hence substitutionary theories of atonement. Equally objective are sacrificial theories, which claim that Christ is the sinless offering who makes a universal expiation of the stain of sin—or, with less biblical and religious warrant, that he propitiates the deserved wrath of God; in neither of these cases is Christ a substitute: the New Testament seems to think more in terms of Christ as the representative of human beings. Again objectively, the atonement has been understood as a victory (perhaps by way of being a ransom or a 'bait') against evil and sin personified in the Devil: this is often called the classic or dramatic theory, also the Christus Victor theory (the title, in English, of G. Aulén's influential article, subsequently book, *Den kristna forsonnigstanken*, 1930/1). Subjective theories, also known as moral or exemplary theories, claim that the extent of God's love revealed in Christ and especially in his acceptance of a brutal and unjust death, move us to repentance. This theory is especially associated with *Abelard. All these theories have an individualistic emphasis, as has the missionary appeal based on them. The advent of the *sociology of religion has led in the 20th cent. to an increasing stress on the corporate nature of atonement, on the death and resurrection of Christ, recapitulated in *baptism and the *eucharist, constituting people as his body. *Weber saw all religions as salvific, since 'every need for salvation is an expression of some distress': through *theodicy, atonement is effected as reconciliation, which, by application in the Christian case, must be demonstrated as a living fact. Thus atonement is much more than individual conversion and rescue: it is the transformation of the social context through the redeeming act of Christ. This social understanding of atonement has been expressed especially through *Liberation Theology.

All these interpretations can be grounded in the Bible. But the Bible propounds no 'theory'. Atonement in general is expressed in the Bible most obviously in 'the face of God': God turns his face from sinners; those who long for reconciliation 'seek his face'; in Christ, God turns his face to his people once more; and as a result, they will in the end know him as they are known, and see him face to face (see J. W. Bowker, *A Year to Live*, 1991). This is poetry rather than dogma, but it is perhaps the only way of expressing experience and hope. See Index, Atonement.

F. W. Dillistone, *The Christian Understanding of Atonement* (1968); M. Hengel, *The Atonement: A Study of the Origins . . . in the New Testament* (1981); V. Taylor, (1937, 1946, 1952); H. E. W. Turner, *The Patristic Doctrine of Redemption* (1952).

Attangika-magga (Buddhist eightfold path): see AṢṬANGIKA-MĀRGA.

ʿAṭṭār, Farīd al-Dīn (d. *c.*1229 (AH 627)). Persian mystic (*Sūfī) and poet. He is particularly remembered for *Mantiq al-Ṭāʾir* (The Language of the Birds, tr. S. C. Nott), which takes its point of departure from *Qurʾān 38. 19. 'The birds assembled and all were turning to God.' ʿAṭṭār composed an allegory of the spiritual journey, with all the birds following the Hudhud (Hoopoe) bird. In the end they come to an indivisible union with the King. But he wrote many other, often epic, poems, e.g. *Muṣībatnāmah* (Book of Affliction, Fr. tr. I. de Gastines, 1981), *Ilāhīnāmah* (Divine Book, tr. J. A. Boyle, 1976).

H. Ritter, *Des Meer der Seele* (1955).

Aṭṭha-loka-dhamma (Pāli, 'eight worldly concerns'). Buddhism teaches that there are eight matters which are common human preoccupations. They are 'gain and loss, fame and obscurity, praise and blame, happiness (*sukha*) and suffering (*dukkha)'. Looking at the world in these terms, however, is regarded as inherently unsatisfying, and perfect happiness (*paramasukha*) is not possible until they are abandoned.

Auden, Wystan Hugh (1907–73). A poet increasingly involved in the exploration and expression of Christian themes. After his time at Oxford (1925–8), he taught for five years and emigrated to the USA in 1938, becoming a naturalized citizen in 1946. After attachment to various colleges, he became Professor of Poetry at Oxford (1956–61) and ended his days there. His poetry often renews an early interest in geology by seeing landscape as a metaphorical geography of the spiritual condition, reinforced by a love of Norse myths and sagas (qualities evident in his verse-plays, written with C. Isherwood, *The Dog Beneath the Skin, The Ascent of F6, On the Frontier*). After the death of his mother (a committed Anglo-Catholic) in 1941, he became increasingly concerned with religion. This is particularly evident in a Christmas oratorio (written for Benjamin Britten), *For the Time Being* (1944) and a reflection on Good Friday, *Horae Canonicae* (1955). Acknowledgement of guilt becomes the ground of freedom: to live in the tangle of human history makes one, inevitably, an accomplice, but to acknowledge complicity is the beginning of *grace. Of God and theology he wrote (*A Certain World*, 1971): 'Theologians are in the difficult position of having to use language, which by its nature is anthropomorphic, to deny anthropomorphic conceptions of God. Dogmatic theological statements are neither logical propositions nor poetic utterances. They are "shaggy dog" stories; they have a point, but he who tries too hard to get it will miss it.'

J. Fuller, *A Reader's Guide to Auden* (1970); C. Osborne, *W. H. Auden . . .* (1980).

Augsburg Confession. A summary of the Christian faith drawn up during the *Reformation for the Diet of Augsburg, and presented to the emperor Charles V. It was written by *Luther, *Melanchthon, and two others. The original was submitted to twenty Catholic theologians who approved nine articles, approved six with qualification, and condemned thirteen. This 'Papalist Confutation' was then responded to by Melanchthon, and this response was attached to the Confession. A final authorized text was issued, to create the document which remains of foundational importance in Lutheranism. The first twenty-one articles deal with similarities and dissimilarities between Lutherans and Roman Catholics, the last seven with abuses in the existing church.

G. W. Forell, *The Augsburg Confession* (1968).

Augustine of Canterbury, St (d. 604 or 605). Missionary to England and first *archbishop of *Canterbury. He was sent by Pope *Gregory in 596 to re-establish the church in England. A few months after his landing in 597, Christianity was formally adopted by King Ethelbert of Kent. About 603 he attempted but failed to reach an agreement with the Celtic Church on matters of discipline and practice. At Canterbury, he helped to establish the monastery of Sts Peter and Paul, where the first ten archbishops were buried.

M. Deansely, *Augustine of Canterbury* (1964).

Augustine of Hippo, St (354–430). Christian *father and *doctor of the Church. He was a native of Tagaste in N. Africa. His mother *Monica was a Christian, but as a young man he gradually abandoned what Christian belief he had. For nine years he was associated with the *Manichaeans, but had left this religion also by the time he came to Rome as a teacher of rhetoric. Becoming a professor of rhetoric at Milan, he became a Neoplatonist and, under the influence of *Ambrose, was converted to Christianity in 386, after responding to a command, 'Tolle, lege', and opening the New Testament at Romans 13. 13 f. He returned to N. Africa, was ordained priest in 391 and became *bishop of Hippo (modern Bōne in Algeria) *c.*396. His own life and conversion were the subject of his deeply moving *Confessions* (many trs., but note F. J. Sheed, H. Chadwick).

Augustine's influence on Christian thought and theology, especially down to the 13th cent., has been immense. His own theology was formulated in controversy with three opponents in particular. First, against Manichaeism, he defended the essential goodness of all that God, as sole creator, has created. Thus evil could only be *privatio boni*, the absence of the good which ought to be. Moral evil is a consequence of freewill, whereas physical evil results from imperfection. Second, the *Donatist controversy caused him to formulate systematic doctrines of the church and *sacraments. He held that sinners could not be excluded from the institutional church but would be identified and dealt with only on the last day. Augustine's last battle was with the *Pelagians, clarifying his teaching on the *fall, *original sin, and *predestination. He held that man's original endowment from God was lost by the fall of *Adam, so that now all suffer from an inherited defect and liability from Adam's sin; and from this the whole human race is justly *massa damnata*, to be saved only by the grace of God. Since God knows what he intends to do, Augustine is inevitably predestinarian to some extent, and this influenced especially *Calvin and other Reformers. Apart from his polemical works, the *Confessions* and *The *City of God* are most important. The former (*c.*400) is basically autobiographical, and is also a kind of introspective thanksgiving for his conversion. It is a classic analysis of the emotional side of Christian experience in the face of sin. The latter, written 413–26 in the light of the sack of Rome in 410, deals with the contrast between Christianity and the world, with the two contrasting standards involved in the two loves, the love of God to the contempt of the world, and the love of the world to the contempt of God. Feast day, 28 Aug.

Tr. of most of Augustine's writings in the Library of Nicene and Post-Nicene Fathers (8 vols., 1887–92); Loeb; Library of Christian Classics, etc.; C. Andresen, *Bibliographia Augustiniana* (1962); G. Bonner, *St Augustine of Hippo* (1986); P. Brown, *Augustine of Hippo* (1967); J. Burnaby, *Amor Dei* (1938); H. Chadwick, *Augustine* (1986); E. teSelle, *Augustine the Theologian* (1970).

Augustinians. Augustinian or Austin Friars, a Christian religious order drawn together from disparate orders of hermits in 1256. It was based on the Rule of St *Augustine, with a constitution drawn from the *Dominicans. The Rule (*Regula Sancti Augustini*) appears to have been drawn up by one of Augustine's followers, perhaps during his lifetime. Augustine intended monasteries to be places where the mutual love of the monks would build up the Body of Christ. They would act as 'physicians' of the Church, following *Christus medicus*. The Rule emphasizes union with others in a common love of God, with the superior as a servant of others. The Rule seeks to make practicable its own prayer: 'May the Lord grant that you adhere to all these things in love, as lovers of spiritual beauty, bearing up the sweet perfume of Christ from your good way of life, not as those enslaved under law, but as freemen established under grace.' Among those adopting the Rule were *Canons Regular, Premonstratensians, and *Dominicans. The Rule was also adopted by Orders for women (e.g. the Augustinians of the Assumption of Mary, known as Assumptionists, Bridgettines, Salesian Sisters, and Ursulines). The Order of St Augustine became less eremetical (the Discalced Augustinians emerged in the 16th cent. emphasizing *contemplation, and became independent in 1931), and undertook practical work, e.g. founding schools and hospitals. Locally based reformed congregations emerged, to one of which (the German Reformed Congregation) Martin *Luther belonged. They are identified by the initials OSA.

G. Lawless, *Augustine of Hippo and Monastic Rule* (1987).

Aulén, G.: see ATONEMENT; CHRISTUS VICTOR.

AUṂ: see OṂ.

Aumbry. A recess in the wall of a church or sacristy in which sacred items (and sometimes the *reserved Sacrament) are kept.

Aum Shinrikyo, Supreme Truth Movement. A Japanese syncretistic movement, with a strong eschatological emphasis. Under its leader, Asahara Shoko, to whom dedication as to a guru was required, it became notorious in 1995 because of its claimed association with two attacks using poison gas on a random population. The second of these, on the Tokyo subway, killed or injured hundreds of people. The members of the movement believed that the end of the world cycle was due in 1997; in preparation for the end, new recruits were required to demonstrate their loyalty by arduous programmes of self-denial—including near-starvation.

Its main headquarters were near Mount Fuji (*Fuji-san), an association which has linked the movement (inappropriately) with the older Shinrikyo. Shinrikyo was founded by Sano Tsunihiko (1834–1906), who had belonged to Ontakekyo, one of the mountain worship cults. He claimed that his family had received and transmitted particular traditions, which could only be learnt from him. Shinrikyo, however, while being eclectic, is nevertheless conservative: it worships *Amaterasu and the **kojiki* deities, it emphasizes loyalty to emperor and family, and it requires participation in rituals as well as the practice of kado (flower meditation: see IKEBANA) and *chadō (tea ceremony). Shinrikyo has given rise to at least four break-away groups, but none of a radical, 'end of world' kind.

Auraṅgzéb (1618–1707) 6th Mughal emperor in India, son of Shāh Jahān and Mumtāj Mahal. He was well-versed in Arabic and Persian and had a working knowledge of Hindi, as well as Chagatāi and the Turkī languages. He served as Subhādār of Daulatābād, Gujarat, Balkh, Multān, and Burhāṇpur between 1636 and 1652.

When Shāh Jahān became ill in 1657, Auraṅgzéb attacked and captured Agrā, imprisoned his aged father and declared himself Emperor, assuming the title 'Alamgīr Gazī'. The coronation was celebrated lavishly in 1659 and from that time the Hijari year replaced the Persian Navaroz in India. Between 1662 and 1682 he lived at Delhi, consolidated his power, and marched against the Marāṭhās in 1682. He struggled unsuccessfully to conquer the Marāṭhās for twenty-five years and died, supposedly of a broken heart, at Ahamadnagar in 1707.

Among historians, he is a particularly controversial figure. One view praises him for maintaining the Islamic character of the Mughal Empire, while the other holds him responsible for the downfall of the Mughals because of his religious fanaticism. It is clear that he identified the interests of the Muslim *Sunnī orthodoxy with that of the Mughal Empire, and his efforts were directed towards the restoration of Islamic law in Mughal India. He outlawed drinking, gambling, and prostitution, and he banned music; he reimposed *jizya (poll tax) on non-Muslims (in contrast to *Akbar) and forbade *sati. He waged ceaseless war against heresy and idolatry. Such a religious policy alienated the powerful Hindu Rajputs, who were a vital pillar of support for the Mughals, and provoked active resistance—from the Jats and *Sikhs in the Puñjāb, and the Marhattas in the Deccan. Moreover, his puritanical commitment even divided the Muslims (*'ulamā from *Sūfīs), and Iranian Shi'as from Tarani Sunnis and Hindustani Muslims. Overcome by religious zeal, he failed to note the practical requirements of administering a multi-religious community, especially of a Muslim minority ruling over a Hindu majority.

Auraṅgzéb's simple lifestyle found no imitators among his officers. The Mughals had become used to a life of luxury, and factionalism had become rampant. Auraṅgzéb checked these forces in the first twenty years of his reign, but they became active in the period (over twenty-five years) of the Deccan Wars during his absence from the capital Delhi. He thus enlarged the Empire to its greatest extent, but it was so weakened internally that it fell apart soon after his death. Auraṅgzéb bequeathed an empty treasury and a divided India to his successor.

J. Sarkar, *History of Aurangzib* (1912–30).

Aureole (symbol or mark of holiness): see HALO.

Aurobindo, Śri (1872–1950). Born Aurobindo Ghose in Calcutta, he became a widely known Hindu teacher. His father was influenced by *Brahmo Samāj, and he gave his son a Western education, at St Paul's School and King's College, Cambridge. He returned to India in 1893 and became Professor of English at Baroda College. Committed to prison for a year for his work against British rule, he there had his first spiritual experiences. On his release, he turned to the practice of *yoga, but he came to regard the classical ways of yoga as too one-sided: they aim to raise the yogi towards a goal, whereas in his view, the true technique should be to integrate the goal into life. Hence his system became known as Pūrna-Yoga, or Integral Yoga.

Threatened with further arrest, he took refuge in 1910, in the French enclave of Pondicherry, and remained there until his death. He met there Mira Richard (Alfassa) who became his constant support and companion. She established the Aurobindo-ashram (*āśrama) and, after his death, a town, Auroville, to embody his teaching. She is known as 'the Mother'.

The chief works (among many) of Śri Aurobindo are *The Life Divine*, a commentary on the **Bhagavad-gītā*, and *The Synthesis of Yoga*. His teaching seeks the discovery and expression of the Absolute (cf. BRAHMAN) in a series of grades of reality, from matter to spirit. He thus strongly opposed *Advaita tendencies to regard appearances as illusory: 'Individual salvation can have no real sense if existence in the cosmos is itself an illusion.' Nevertheless, the power of *māyā to impede progress remains, if it is not properly understood. Māyā, according to Aurobindo (and in his view, 'the Vedic seers') is 'the power of infinite consciousness to comprehend, contain in itself and measure out . . . name and shape out of the vast illimitable truth of infinite existence'. The human goal is to prepare, through Integral Yoga, for the Supreme Being to bring us to our final goal.

R. A. McDermott, *Six Pillars: An Introduction to the Major Works* . . . (1974); A. B. Purani, *Life of Sri Aurobindo* (1964).

Aurva. In Hindu mythology, the son of *Cyavana and the grandson of *Bhṛgu. His birth was remarkable: because the sons of Kṛtavīrya, the Bhṛgu clan's traditional enemies, were killing even children in the womb, his mother transferred her embryo to her thigh, from which, after a hundred years, Aurva emerged with a flash of light which blinded his enemies. From his angry desire for vengeance he produced a flame which could devour the whole world, but he was persuaded by his ancestors to cast this flame into the ocean. There, the Aurva-fire, sometimes called *vāḍavāgni* (Skt., 'mare-fire') because it has a mare's head, awaits the time when it is unleashed to destroy the universe.

Auschwitz. The largest Nazi concentration camp. Established in 1940 on the outskirts of Oseiecim, Poland, it was both a labour and an extermination camp. Between one million and two and a half million Jews are estimated to have died there, and Auschwitz has thus become a symbol of the horrors of the *Holocaust—as also of the extreme issues of *theodicy, of 'Theology after Auschwitz' (see HOLOCAUST).

Authorized Version. An English translation of the *Bible published in 1611. It was ordered by King James I (hence the American name 'King James Version') and was the work of *c.*50 scholars. It is indebted, through various earlier versions, to the work of W. *Tyndale. The words 'Appointed to be read in Churches' appear on the title-page, but it has never otherwise been 'authorized'. Only in the 20th cent. has the Authorized Version lost ground to modern versions for use in churches, and it is still defended against them, e.g. for the familiar beauty of its language by traditionalists, and for the alleged superiority of its text by some *fundamentalists.

Autocephalous (Gk., *autos*, 'self' + *kephalē*, 'head'). Term describing an *Orthodox church whose hierarchy is independent of any other. Thus 'the Orthodox Church' comprises a variable number of autocephalous 'Orthodox churches', whose *patriarchs are ranked only in honour (1. Constantinople, 2. Alexandria, 3. Antioch, 4. Jerusalem, 5. Moscow, etc.). Some autocephalous churches are very small, e.g. Sinai (one monastery) and Czechoslovakia (autocephalous since 1951).

Auto-da-fé (Portuguese, 'act of faith'). The elaborate public ceremony of the *Inquisition, especially in Spain, at which, after a showy procession, mass, and sermon, the sentences were read. Heretics were dressed in a yellow gown and mitre. Those sentenced to death were handed over to the secular power.

Autonomy of the liminal (independence in ritual of the transitional stage): see RITES OF PASSAGE.

Auto Sacramental (Spanish religious plays): see THEATRE AND DRAMA.

Av, Ninth of (Heb., *Tishah be-Av*). A day of *mourning in the Jewish calendar for the destruction of the Jerusalem *Temple. According to the *Talmud, five disasters occurred on 9 Av: (i) the Israelites could not enter the *Promised Land; (ii) and (iii) the first and second Temples were destroyed; (iv) the last Jewish stronghold in the *Bar Kokhba war was destroyed; (v) Emperor Hadrian established a heathen temple in Jerusalem. Traditionally, all mourning rites are observed from sunset to sunset and the book of Lamentations is read in the *synagogue.

Avadāna literature. One of the twelve types of literary composition traditionally found in Buddhist Sanskrit literature. The Avadānas are essentially popular moral tales which seek to inspire the believer to exertion in the faith and the performance of good deeds. The stories avoid complex doctrinal matters and depict instead the ways in which good deeds motivated by love and devotion are rewarded, and bad deeds performed out of ill will and hatred are punished. The recipient of the good and evil actions is often the *Buddha himself in a previous life, a member of the Order, or an object of religious significance.

The Avadāna style of literature seems to have become popular among the schools of early Buddhism prior to the rise of the *Mahāyāna, which would date it approximately at the beginning of the Christian era. In the Avadānas we see the beginning of a devotional attitude towards the Buddha which was to become more pronounced in the Mahāyāna. The absence of *bodhisattva-figures and the down-to-earth flavour and setting of the tales also argues for a pre-Mahāyāna date. There is no reference to a doctrine of salvation through the intercession of the Buddha: instead the Avadānas stress the necessity of a long process of moral development in which the individual is personally responsible for his spiritual progress. The most important examples of this type of literature include the **Avadāna-Śataka*, the *Aśoka-Avadāna*, *Divya-Avadāna*, and the later *Avadāna-Kalpalatā*.

Avadāna-Śataka (Skt. 'the 100 Avadānas'). An ancient collection of tales or moral stories from the *Theravāda Buddhist tradition, dating to 1st or 2nd cents. BCE. Probably the oldest work in the tradition of *Avadāna literature, its authorship is uncertain but its popularity resulted in a Chinese translation being made at a very early date. The work is divided into ten chapters each containing ten stories on a particular theme. The central preoccupation is with the consequences of good and evil deeds and their maturation and effect upon the doer in later lives. The Buddha himself is the hero of many of the tales in the manner of the Pāli *Jātaka literature, and reverence and devotion to him is undisguised. Other protagonists are *Arhats, gods, and ghosts (*preta) who are reaping the consequences of their moral or immoral deeds.

Avadhūt-Gītā ('Song of an Illumined One'). A Hindu work of 193 verses composed by Mahātmā Dattatraya. Nothing is known of him, except that he lived within some centuries around the 4th cent. BCE. The *Avadhūt-Gītā* is a compressed summary of the way in which the *Upaniṣads were moving in the direction of *Advaita Vedānta.

Avalokiteśvara (Skt., 'the lord who looks in every direction', or 'of what is seen'). One of the most important *bodhisattvas in *Mahāyāna Buddhism. He embodies compassion (*karuṇā), and is thus called Mahākarunā (the other necessary constituent of a *buddha being wisdom, *prajña, which is embodied in Mañjuśri). Avalokiteśvara is the manifestation as bodhisattva of the power of the equally compassionate buddha, Amitābha (*Amida). He is the supremely compassionate helper, and is often depicted with a thousand arms and a thousand eyes for that purpose. He is also eleven-headed, because when he looked at suffering humanity, his head split open from pain. From a single tear shed by Avalokiteśvara, *Tārā was born who ferries the faithful across on their way to *nirvāna, or to the Western Paradise (see SUKHĀVATĪ). He responds instantly to all who 'with all their mind call on his name'.

In China, Avalokiteśvara is known as Kuan-yin, 'he who hears the sound of the world'. In addition to the characteristics and representations of Avalokiteśvara, Kuan-yin frequently has a child on one arm, and appears (under Taoist influence of complementary properties) increasingly with feminine characteristics. She becomes the all-compassionate mother-goddess, perhaps the most popular deity in China, represented in a flowing white robe, holding a *lotus. In Ch'an, her aid is spiritualized, dealing with all that impedes 'developing the compassion of Kuan-yin'. Her birth, enlightenment, and death are celebrated in annual festivals.

In Japan, 'he' (see below) is known as Kannon (Kanzeon, Kwannon), the Bodhisattva of Compassion, one of the most popular deities in Mahāyāna Buddhism. According to the **Lotus Sūtra*, Kannon perceives the sufferings of all sentient beings and devises ways to assist them, to answer their prayers, and to lead them to salvation. This compassion of the Bodhisattva is reflected in his fuller name Kanzeon, meaning 'He Who Regards the Cries of the World'. The *Pure Land scriptures present Kannon as one of two attendants of the Buddha Amida (Skt., Amitābha) another of Mahāyāna's eminent deities of compassion. The link between the two is often depicted iconographically by a small image of Amida appearing in Kannon's crown. In Japan, as in China, Kannon was frequently portrayed in feminine form, possibly stemming from the *Lotus Sūtra*'s statement that the Bodhisattva will take on the guise of a woman or any other figure in order to lead sentient beings to salvation, and perhaps suggesting feminine representation to be more expressive of compassion.

In Tibet, he is known as sPyan-ras-gzigs, or in the West as Chenrezi. He is the protector of the land of snows, who becomes present in different individuals to initiate or sustain buddha-teaching. Thus the king Songsten-Gampo who brought Buddhism into Tibet (see TIBETAN RELIGION) is regarded as an incarnation of Avalokiteśvara, as are the successive *Dalai Lamas. The Skt., formula associated with him, *om mani padme hum* becomes in Tibet *om mani peme hung*, and was the first *mantra introduced there. Iconographically, he still appears eleven-headed with a thousand arms, but more often with four arms sitting on a lotus.

M. T. de Mallmann, *Introduction à l'étude d'Avalokiteçvara* (1948).

Avanti: see SACRED CITIES, SEVEN.

Avasthā (Skt. 'condition', 'state'). In Hinduism a state of consciousness or condition in a world (*loka, *bhuvana*). A common classification of different states of consciousness (*avasthā*) is found in the *Upaniṣads, notably **Māndūkya*, namely the four levels of waking (*jagrat*), dreaming (*suṣupti*), deep sleep (*svapma*) and the 'fourth' (*turīya). Through *yoga the fourth state is attained which is a concentrated absorption (*samādhi) sometimes equated with liberation (*mokṣa). However, later Tantrism postulates a condition 'beyond the fourth' (*turīyatīta*). In *Māṇḍūkya Upaniṣad* the three states of consciousness correspond to three levels of the hierarchical cosmos and three levels of the sound *om (see PRAṆAVA). The fourth state corresponds to *Brahman, the absolute. Thus the psychology expressed by the avasthās corresponds to cosmology. Avasthā also refers to the four periods of human life, childhood, youth, adulthood, and old age.

Avatamsaka literature. An important and extensive literary compilation in *Mahāyāna Buddhism centring on the *Avatamsaka-sūtra*, also known as *Buddhāvatamsaka-sūtra* (Sutra of the Garland of Buddhas; Chin., *Hua-yen ching*; Jap., *Kegon-kyo*). Most of the Skt. original of the work, reputedly extending to 100,000 verses, has been lost, but several translations exist in Tibetan and Chinese. The Chinese translation of the Tang Dynasty is the most popular and is divided into thirty-nine chapters, in the course of which the *Buddha and great *bodhisattvas such as *Mañjuśrī and Samantabhadra preach to nine assemblies. The first assembly centres on the Buddha's enlightenment under the Bodhi tree and describes how myriads of supernatural beings came to praise him on this occasion. Several of the other chapters became revered as important sūtras in their own right, such as 'The Ten Stages of a Bodhisattva's Career' (*Daśabhūmika-sūtra*) and the 'Entry into the Absolute' (*Gaṇḍavyūha-sūtra*), these being the only parts, in consequence, which survive in Sanskrit.

Throughout the text the Buddha is portrayed as the focal point of all the spiritual energies of the universe which coalesce into a magnificent cosmic unity. The *Avatamsaka-sūtra* rapidly became popular in China with the Hua-Yen school, in Korea, and especially in Japan with the development of the

Kegon school. Doctrinally it embraces Yogācāra/ *Vijñāvāda idealism, *Mādhyamaka, and *Tantric elements, which it weaves together into a rich metaphysical tapestry. Underlying the apparent diversity in the world is a complex mesh of interdependence and interpenetration of phenomena illuminated and energized by the compassion of the cosmic Buddha (*Vairocana). No part of the whole exists in isolation and there is complementarity and mutual identification between all entities in a grand harmonious unity. Elements which appear to be separate are in fact subtly linked like jewels which reflect their brilliance upon one another. Even in a speck of dust the Buddha-nature manifests itself: 'There is not a single sentient being which is not endowed with the knowledge of the *Tathāgata. But because sentient beings are attached to false and deluded views, they cannot see this. . . . If all things in the cosmos were recorded on a sūtra-scroll as large as the universe, the truth about them is contained in a single speck of dust—and it is contained in each speck of dust, as much in one as in any other.' The teachings of the *Avatamsaka-sūtra* are open to interpretation at many levels and it has been the subject of extensive commentarial and exegetical literature. The most important developments in the study and interpretation of the Avatamsaka were completed by about 1,000 CE.

G. C. C. Chang, *The Buddhist Teaching of Totality* (1971); T. Cleary, *The Flower Ornament Scripture: A Translation. . .*(1984).

Avatāra (Skt., 'descent'). The earthly manifestations (or 'incarnations') of a Hindu deity. While it is popularly but wrongly believed that the concept is first expressed in the famous verse of the **Bhagavad-gītā*, 'I [Kṛṣṇa] come into being age after age . . .' (iv. 8), it was indeed the figure of *Kṛṣṇa, and his relationship with the deity *Viṣṇu, which triggered off the subsequent conceptual developments.

By about the 4th cent. CE this development culminated in 'avatāra', denoting an earthly manifestation of Viṣṇu due to his free choice (i.e. not due to the laws of *karma or a curse) and taking the form of a full human life (including conception, birth, and natural death), for the sake of a specific cosmic purpose. Although not all traditions and theological schools accepted such a non-transcendental status for Kṛṣṇa, the pattern proved extremely productive in other areas, because it allowed for the inclusion of other popular heroes and figures of worship under the general umbrella of Viṣṇu religion. Already at a relatively early stage, the *Vedic figure of Trivikrama was included, now under the name of *Vāmana, 'the Dwarf'. By widening the definition of the term, cult-figures like the *Varāha (Boar), *Kūrma (Tortoise), *Matsya (Fish), and Nṛsiṃha/*Narasiṃha (Man-Lion), could be included. Somewhat later also *Rāma, *Balarāma or Baladeva (Kṛṣṇa's half-brother), and *Paraśurāma (Rāma with the Axe) entered the group. Even the *Buddha was appropriated by certain traditions. All the figures listed so far are manifestations of Viṣṇu in the past; with the future—in fact the end of the present cosmic cycle—is connected the arrival of *Kalkin.

Many other figures were regionally, or at times envisaged as avatāra of Viṣṇu, e.g. Nayagrīva, *Dattātreya, the Haṃsa (Goose), etc. But by the close of the first millennium CE a set of ten had acquired the widest currency (Baladeva, the Buddha, and Paraśurāma being somewhat less rigidly included in such lists of ten). The arrangement shows an interesting 'evolutionary sequence'. We move from pure sea-animal (Matsya) to more amphibian creatures (Kūrma, Varāha); then from semi-human (Nṛsiṃha) and deformed human (Vāmana) to fully human beings (Kṛṣṇa, Balarāma, Rāma, Paraśurāma, the Buddha) of the past, and of the future (Kalkin).

The concept also began to appear in forms of Hinduism other than *Vaiṣṇavism. For example, many figures of local goddesses became regarded as avatāras of *Durgā; regional deities like *Khaṇḍobā get 'Sanskritized' by being interpreted as avatāras of *Śiva. Another extension of the concept that proved particularly useful was the idea of an *arcâvatāra*, viz., the descent and permanent residence of a deity (particularly Viṣṇu) in the sculpture of a temple image (*arcā*).

Finally, various religious movements have tended to regard their founder or their sages as avatāras of their own specific deity (or of some other divine paraphernalia, like Viṣṇu's weapons who became avatāras as the *Āḻvārs). For example, in the case of *Caitanya, in some strands of the movement founded by him he was regarded as the dual avatāra of *Rādha and *Kṛṣṇa, in one person. The concept of an *aṃśâvatāra*, 'partial incarnation', remained unproductive outside the circles of the scholastics; in some areas *aṃśa* is actually used as a synonym of avatāra.

In recent times, the concept of avatāra, especially in relation to animal figures, has been challenged by reforming and rationalizing movements (e.g. *Brahmo Samāj); at the same time, the belief put forward in **Bhāgavata-purāṇa*, that humans can become avatāras by a divine infilling, has allowed the title to be extended to religious leaders, such as *Gāndhī and Satya *Sai Baba, or to non-Hindus, such as *Jesus or *Muḥammad.

C. Dimmitt and J. A. B. van Buitenen, *Classical Hindu Mythology* . . . (1978); G. Parrinder, *Avatar and Incarnation* (1970).

Avelei ha-Rahamim (Heb., 'Merciful Father'). Memorial *prayer for Jewish martyrs which is found in a *Prayer Book* of 1290. The prayer emphasizes the merits of those who sacrificed their lives for **kiddush ha-shem* (sanctification of God's name), and calls for divine retribution. It is recited as part of the *Sabbath morning service after the *Torah reading.

Avelei Zion (Heb., 'Mourners of Zion'). Groups of Jews dedicated to mourning the destruction of the

*Temple in Jerusalem. Derived from Isaiah 61. 3, they are mentioned in the *Talmud and seem to have revived in the 9th cent. They lived in poverty, depending on the charity of pilgrims. Groups existed in Germany, Italy, and the Yemen, as well as in Israel. Many of the Jerusalem *Karaites seem to have followed the pattern of behaviour of the Avelei Zion, but with the conquest of Palestine by the Seljuk Turks in 1071, they disappeared from Jerusalem. Among them was R. Meir b. Isaac Nehorai, author of **Akdamut Millin*.

Ave Maria. Christian, mainly Catholic, salutation and invocation addressed to *Mary: Ave Maria, gratia plena, Dominus tecum. Benedicta tu in mulieribus, et benedictus fructus ventris tui, Jesus. Sancta Maria, mater Dei, ora pro nobis peccatoribus, nunc et in hora mortis nostrae. Hail Mary, full of grace, the Lord is with you. Blessed are you among women, and blessed is the fruit of your womb, Jesus. Holy Mary, mother of God, pray for us sinners now and at the hour of our death.

Averroes (Spanish Muslim theologian): see IBN RUSHD.

Averroism. The views associated with Averroes (*Ibn Rushd), which became influential in Jewish and Christian philosophy from 1230 onward. Since these attributed views included the absolute separation of God from his creation, the eternity of matter and its potentiality, and the notion of 'double truth', one (literal in relation to revelation) for the uneducated and the other allegorical, much of the Christian response became hostile: Averroism was condemned in 1270 and 1277, and was strongly criticized by *Aquinas. Nevertheless, Averroist philosophers continued to defend this outlook, the most prominent being Siger of Brabant (*c.*1235–1284). Since he also held that the active intellect is a common principle and not separately individuated, thereby ruling out personal immortality, his condemnation by papal legates is unsurprising. He was summoned to answer charges of *heresy, but he fled from France. The manner and date of his death are uncertain, although he is said to have been murdered. *Dante (*Paradise* 10. 133 f.) placed him, not among the heretics, but among the twelve wise of old.

Avesta. The holy book of *Zoroastrianism (the word probably means 'The Injunction [of Zoroaster]'). Only approximately one-quarter of the original is extant (judging from summaries of that original in later works). Much was lost during centuries of Islamic persecution in Iran, when books along with temples were destroyed. That which has survived is basically the liturgical material which continued in use in regular worship. The alphabet in which it is written was evolved specifically for this purpose. It is very precise, with forty-nine letters (including fourteen for vowels). That alphabet was invented in the Sasanian period, and reports that old copies of the Avesta were stored in the Achaemenid palace of Persepolis are probably fictional, for the material then existed only in oral form. The content of the 'canon' includes material from many ages. There are some pre-Zoroastrian 'hymns' (some of the *Yásts*, such as *Yt.* 10 to Mithra) and 'Litanies' (*Nyayes*), although some of these have a Zoroastrian veneer (e.g. by the use of an introductory formula). Some *Yasts* were composed in Achaemenid, possibly even in Parthian times (e.g. *Yt* 1 to Ohrmazd: see AHURA MAZDA). The anti-demonic law, the *Vendidad*, contains much ancient material, although its present structure was probably Parthian. The liturgy of the *Yasna* is especially ancient, probably much of the substance deriving from Indo-Iranian times. Embedded in the *Yasna* are the seventeen hymns of Zoroaster, the *Gāthās*. They are in two blocks (*Ys.* 28–34 and 43–53) either side of the *Yasna Haptanhait* liturgy, which, if not by Zoroaster, is certainly early. The *Gāthās* are embedded in the *Yasna* the 'act of [daily] worship', because that is the liturgical context within which the prophetic hymns have been preserved. The phrase Younger Avesta is used to denote the material of later composition, and it has generally been interpreted as the reassertion of pre-Zoroastrian 'paganism' undermining the abstract monotheism of the prophet. A Zoroastrian cast is given to it by including a fictional introduction asserting that the material was revealed to Zoroaster by *Ahura Mazda. Undoubtedly the *Gāthās* have a disinctive personal style, but recent scholarship has questioned many of the assumptions behind this polarizing of Gathic and Younger Avestan religion (e.g. by emphasizing that since Zoroaster was himself a practising priest, it is likely that he accepted the priestly traditions this literature reflects). The imagery of an ancient 'pagan' tradition and abstract prophetic reform perhaps owe more to a stage in biblical scholarship than to a dispassionate study of the Iranian materials. In Zoroastrian tradition, the whole Avesta is attributed to the prophet.

Although Avestan manuscripts have been deposited in European libraries (e.g. the Bodleian) for many years (the oldest manuscript is dated 1323 CE), they were first studied by Thomas Hyde in 1700. But it was only when the Frenchman, Anquetil du Perron, returned from extensive fieldwork in Gujarat that serious study began, despite the withering scepticism of the Oxford Orientalist, Sir William Jones, who dismissed Anquetil's Avesta as spurious. In the 19th cent., European scholars began to appreciate the significance of Anquetil's discoveries. The translation is particularly difficult, above all with the *Gāthās*. Although the language is close to the *Vedas, these are the only known texts in that language. Their fragmentary nature, combined with the allusive poetic imagery and metrical form, make them extremely difficult to translate. They are intensely personal in style, passionate outpourings of an individual spirit, following visions of God. For

Zoroastrians, they are the most powerful holy *manthras*.

In modern religious practice, Zoroastrians use a *Khorda Avesta*, a collection of essential prayers for daily use by lay people. Much older are the commentaries (*Zand*) on the Avesta, which, because they were often preserved alongside the Avesta, came to be referred to as *Zend Avesta*, as though the two were synonymous, which they are not. However, these ancient *Zand* provide an important insight into the early interpretation of the Avesta, and in some cases a lost work is known only through its *Zand*.

M. Boyce, *Sources for the Study of Zoroastrianism* (1984); I. Gershevitch, 'Old Iranian Literature' in B. Spuler (ed.), *Handbuch der Orientalistik* (1968).

Avicebron (Jewish poet): see GABIROL, SOLOMON.

Avicenna (Muslim philosopher): see IBN SĪNĀ.

Avidyā (Skt.) or **avijja** (Pāli), Literally 'non-knowledge' or ignorance. A term in Indian religions which, in its broadest connotation, means that which keeps a person bound on the wheel of transmigration (*saṃsāra) due to his/her action (*karma) and so is a condition of suffering (*duḥkha). This is ignorance of liberation (*mokṣa, *nirvāna), the meaning of which is formulated variously by different traditions.

1. Avidyā in Hinduism. Although all agree that ignorance is that which keeps a person bound, there are nevertheless within Hinduism various understandings of how and why ignorance arises and of how to eradicate it.

In the *Vedas avidyā means ignorance of ritual and moral obligations and so implies absence of knowledge rather than an ontological condition of bondage. In the *Upaniṣads it comes to mean spiritual delusion and the non-knowledge of *Brahman, thus the **Katha* (1. 2. 4 and 5) and the **Maitri* (7. 9) *Upaniṣads* compare those who live in ignorance while thinking themselves wise with blind men leading each other. To reach Brahman, ignorance which is an 'inner crookedness' (**Praśna Upaniṣad* 1. 16) must be eradicated. The same idea is found in the **Bhagavad-gītā* 5. 16, which says that knowledge eradicates ignorance (*ajñāna*). In *Sāṃkhya-*yoga ignorance, which is the cause of bondage and suffering, is regarded as the non-discrimination of the individual self (*puruṣa) from matter (*prakṛti) in which it appears to be entangled. For *Advaita Vedānta bondage is similarly due to beginningless ignorance which, in contrast to Sāṃkhya, is the creation of distinctions where none exist; in reality there being only Brahman. For *Śaṅkara ignorance is equated with superimposition (*adhyāsa), the power of projecting on to the non-dual reality that which is unreal, as when one takes a rope to be a snake or a shell to be silver (**Brahma-sūtra-bhaṣya* 1. 1). Thus ignorance is the perception of plurality where there is unity. A serious problem for the Advaita understanding is proposed by the *Nyāya-*Vaiśeṣika tradition, namely that if the plurality of selves is due to ignorance, to whom does this ignorance belong? If to Brahman then he is not all-knowing, if to individual selves then their individuality must be admitted. For *Rāmānuja's Viśiṣtādvaita, ignorance is the absence of knowing that the self (*jīva) is distinct from, yet also merged into, Brahman, while for the *Dvaita school of *Madhva, avidyā is ignorance of the self's eternal distinction from God.

2. In Buddhism, avijja/avidyā is ignorance of the true nature of reality, the non-emancipated state of mind; it is specifically expressed in Buddhist writings as lack of experiential knowledge of the *Four Noble Truths. Ignorance is identified as the root source of all sorrow and suffering, and for this reason is usually made the first in the links of causation (*paticca samuppāda) resulting in old age and death. False views (*diṭṭhi) and delusion (*moha) are especial features of avijja but the term has the widest usage, encompassing the whole range and nature of human activity. It is combated by the Noble Eightfold Path (*aṣṭangika-mārga), a life of purity (*brahmacarya), the idea of impermanence (*aniccasanna*), and insight meditation (*vipassanā). Avijja refers to moral and spiritual ignorance, not ignorance of a factual and scientific kind, and is only finally extinguished with the attainment of nirvāna.

Avinu Malkenu (Heb., 'Our Father, our King'). A Hebrew liturgy recited on the Ten Days of *Penitence, and in some communities on other fast days. Its origin is R. *Akiva's prayer, 'Avinu Malkenu, we have no king but you: Avinu Malkenu, for your sake have compassion on us' (*B.Taʿan* 25b). The number and order of the verses varies according to the different rites.

Av kol ha-sodot (the father of all secrets): see AARON OF BAGHDAD.

Avodah (Heb., 'Service'). Description of the complicated sacrificial ritual practised in the Jerusalem *Temple on the *Day of Atonement, and now recited as the central part of the *Musaf service on that day. It is based on Leviticus 16, and is described in the *Mishnah (*Yoma* 1–7). The reading is enriched by various *piyyutim composed in the Middle Ages.

Avodah Zarah (Heb., 'idolatrous worship'). Tractate of the *Mishnah, *tosefta, and *Talmud, assigned to the order of 'Nezikim' (torts). It includes both *halakhic and *aggadic material, and deals with the laws concerning *idolatry and relations with idol-worshippers.

Avot (Heb., 'Fathers'). A treatise of the *Mishnah placed at the end of the order of 'Nezikim' (torts). Often known as *Pirkei Avot* (the Chapters of the Fathers), it presents a series of sayings of the sages going back from the *tannaim in an unbroken chain to *Moses' revelation on Mount *Sinai. The text is included in some editions of the traditional *Prayer Book, and it is regularly studied in the *synagogue on the *Sabbath. It covers teaching on the fundamental aspects of life, and is the best known of all *Talmudic works. Its opening words summarize the rabbinic enterprise: 'Be attentive in establishing justice, raise up many disciples, and make a fence around *Torah.'

Avvakum (1620–82). Archpriest of the Russian Church, leader, and eventually *martyr, of the Raskolniki, or *'Old Believers'. He was the son of a village priest, and after his own ordination, became a friend of the Tsar Alexis. As *archpriest of Our Lady of Kazan in Moscow, he opposed the liturgical reforms of *Patriarch *Nikon, while establishing the ascetical and highly moral group of 'The Old Believers'. For his opposition, he was exiled to Siberia in 1653. He returned on the death of Nikon (1664), but was again exiled, imprisoned, and punished for refusing the continuing reforms. Finally he and his companions were condemned to death at the stake. He wrote a fine autobiography.

Avvakum, *The Life Written by Himself* (1979) and tr. P. Pascal, *La Vie . . .* (1938); P. Pascal, *Avvakum et les débuts du Raskol . . .* (1938).

Avyākata (Pāli; Skt., *avyākṛtavastūni*, 'that which cannot be expressed'). The four issues or questions on which the *Buddha was pressed, but concerning which he remained silent. The silence was not because the questions are unanswerable, but because any answer would lead to a false sense of apprehension within the limits of his hearers' understanding. The issues are: (i) whether the world is eternal, or not, or both, or neither; (ii) whether the world is finite in space, or not, or both, or neither; (iii) whether the *Tathāgata exists after death, or not, or both, or neither; (iv) whether the soul is identical with the body or is different from it. The Buddha refused to become what he called 'an eel-wriggler', seeking dogmatic certainty by way of sophisticated equivocation on matters which are not open to that kind of certainty (*Brahmajāla Sutta* 28); but it does not follow from that that he was agnostic. The true answers require insight which is itself a consequence of enlightenment or of considerable progress toward it.

T. R. V. Murti, *The Central Philosophy of Buddhism* (1955).

Avyākṛta(vastūni) (inexpressible issues): see AVYĀKATA.

Avyakta. The unmanifest in Hinduism, either the power of God, or of *prakṛti, before it becomes manifest in created appearance or *Brahman.

Awakening of Faith (Mahāyāna Buddhist text): see MAHĀYĀNAŚRADDHOTPĀDA-ŚASTRA.

Awliya' (pl., friends of God): see WALĪ.

Axial age. Period around the 6th cent. BCE, when religions were instrumental in effecting great changes in history and civilization. The term was used by Karl Jaspers to draw attention to the rise to prominence of great religious leaders and innovations which established the basis of the great civilizations until the disturbance of those patterns by the European enlightenment and expansion of trade and empire. He drew attention to *Zoroaster, the *Upaniṣads, the *Buddha, *Mahāvīra, *Confucius, the emergence of *Taoism.

Axis mundi. The central pivot of the earth or of the entire cosmos. For examples, see BODHIMAṆḌA; TEMPLE (JAIN); MERU. The idea is applied in the *Sūfī *qutb. See Index, Axis mundi.

Ayā (pl. *āyāt*; Arab., 'sign' or 'mark'). In the *Qur'ān, a mark of Allāh's existence and power (2. 248; 3. 41; 26. 197), and especially 'a *miracle'. The greatest sign and miracle of Allāh is the Qur'ān, and sections of the Qur'ān, shorter than *suras, are referred to as *āyāt* (e.g. 2. 99; 3. 58; 3. 164; 28. 87; 45. 5). From this usage, the word has come to mean the verses of the Qur'ān. See also ʿILM.

Ayam Ātman Brahman (Skt., 'This Self is Brahman': *Bṛhadāraṇyaka Upaniṣad* 4. 4. 5) one of the *Mahāvākyas in Hinduism, the realization that *ātman is *Brahman.

Aya Sofya (mosque, formerly basilica): see HAGIA SOFIA.

Ayatollah (Arab., 'sign of God'). Title of high-ranking Shiʿite Muslim authorities, especially in Iran. It is a recent (20th cent.) title for exceptional jurists (*mujtāhid*), whose authority rests on that of the infallible *Imām—though in 1979, the Ayatollah Khomeini (see KHUMAYNI) adopted the title of Imām for himself. Since he did not claim to be the Hidden Imām, this was a new development in hierarchical practice and theory. An Ayatollah's decisions (*fatwā) have authority only for those who examine and agree with them—in theory; in practice, Ayatollahs gain personal followings, among whom their decisions are accepted as binding. The extension of these personal followings to even wider communities is again a recent innovation.

Ayatollah Khomeini (figure head of Islamic Revolution in Iran): see KHUMAYNI, RUḤ ALLAH.

Ayn al-Quzat (Persian Sūfī of 12th cent.): see SHARĪʿATĪ, ʿALĪ.

Ayodhyā ('Invincible'). One of the Hindu seven *sacred cities (equally sacred to Jains and Buddhists) in Uttar Pradesh. Founded, according to tradition, by Manu (or Ikṣvaku), it is regarded as the capital city of *Rāma, and his birthplace in manifestation to this world. It has become a place of bitter conflict between Muslims and Hindus, since the Muslims built a mosque on the site of the temple dedicated to Rāma. Hindus have recently made repeated attempts to take back the whole site, destroying the mosque in 1992.

Āyur veda (Skt., 'Knowledge of Life'). The ancient and traditional Hindu school or system of healing, regarded as a supplement to the **Atharva Veda*. The major early works are the *Caraka-saṃhitā* and the *Suśruta-saṃhitā*, 1st–4th cents. CE. Hindu medicine is based on an analysis of a correspondence between the macro- and micro-cosmos. Like the macrocosmos, the human body is composed of the five elements, earth, air, fire, water, and ether. In different combinations, these produce the three characteristic expressions of vitality (*doṣa*), which are related to the three qualities (*guṇas). The maintenance of relationship and balance is the principle of cure and care in ayurvedic medicine, which continues to be widely practised. For a spiritual equivalent, cf., BHŪTAŚUDDHI.

J. Filliozat, *The Classical Doctrine of Indian Medicine* (1964); C. Leslie (ed.), *Asian Medical Systems* . . . (1976).

Azalī Bābīs. Followers of Mīrzā Yaḥyā Nūrī, called Ṣubḥ-i Azal (Morn of Eternity) (1830/1–1912), the appointed successor of the Bāb (see BĀBĪS). After the Bāb's execution (1850), Babism ceased to be a united movement. Ṣubḥ-i Azal was involved with the militant faction which unsuccessfully plotted the assassination of the Shah (1852). In the consequent purge he went into hiding, later joining his older half-brother *Bahā'u'llāh in Baghdād. Increasingly overshadowed by Bahā'u'llāh, he maintained the leadership of a small radical faction of *Bābīs. He was exiled to Ottoman Cyprus in 1868 and died in Famagusta on 29 Apr. 1912. Some of his younger disciples became freethinkers and were prominently involved in the political opposition to the Qajar regime which culminated in the Iranian constitutional movement of the early 1900s.

Azazel. Place to which the *scapegoat was consigned on the *Day of Atonement. According to Leviticus 16. 8, '*Aaron shall cast lots upon the two goats, one lot for the Lord and the other lot for Azazel.' The custom was that, after one goat was slaughtered, the other was sent into the wilderness, carrying away the peoples' sins. A description of the ritual is to be found in the *avodah. There is a dispute as to the exact meaning of Azazel; some rabbis identified it as a cliff or a place of rocks, while others saw it as a supernatural power, perhaps made up of two fallen *angels, Uza and Azael. 'Go to Azazel!' is the equivalent in modern Hebrew of 'Go to hell!'

Azhar (Cairo mosque): see AL-AZHAR.

Azharot (Heb., 'exhortations'). Jewish didactic poems used in liturgy. The earliest example begins, 'In the beginning you gave azharot to your people'—hence the name. Azharot, via *gematria, equals 613. Connection is then made with the classification made by R. Simlai: '613 commands were given to Moses, 365 negative according to the days of the solar year, 248 positive according to the limbs in the human body.' Azharot as compositions summarize and celebrate *halakot, and were recited initially at *Shavu'ot, itself the thanksgiving for the giving of *Torah.

Azi Dahaka (the Lie): see ANGRA MAINYU.

Azymites. A name given to the *Roman Catholic Church by the *Orthodox at the time of the *schism of 1054. It refers to the Latin use of unleavened bread (Gk., *ta azyma*) in the *eucharist, which was a special object of attack from the Eastern side, since it was held to invalidate the eucharist.

B

Baʿal (Phoen., Ugaritic, etc., 'Lord'). The weather god of the western Semites. It is possible that 'Baʿal' was not a proper name since 'the Baʿalim' (Judges 2. 11) seems to refer to a group of local gods, and the weather god is frequently referred to as 'the baal'. According to *Ugaritic myths, Baʿal defeated the sea-god, Yamm, and this is echoed by the biblical belief, 'In that day the Lord ... will punish Leviathan the fleeing serpent ... and he will slay the dragon that is in the sea' (Isaiah 27. 1). Baʿal worship seems to have been very seductive to the Israelites—as witnessed by the condemnation of Baʿal worship by the Israelite prophets (e.g. Isaiah 53. 3–10, Hosea 13. 2), and by the confrontation between *Elijah and the prophets of Baʿal (1 Kings 18). Several of the Israelite kings, such as Ahaz and Manasseh, actually encouraged Baʿal worship, and the change from a nomadic to an agricultural way of the life inevitably made the Baʿal cult attractive. Many of Baʿal's attributes were ascribed to the Israelite God, and certain aspects of Baʿal liturgy were taken over and adapted to the praise of the God of Israel.

M. D. Coogan (ed.), *Stories from Ancient Canaan* (1978).

Baʿal ha-Tanya (founder of Jewish movement): see SHNE'UR ZALMAN OF LYADY.

Baʿal ha-Turim (Jewish halakhic authority): see JACOB BEN ASHER.

Baʿal Shem (Heb., 'master of the divine name'). Title given in *ḥasidic and *'kabbalistic literature to those who possess secret knowledge of God's name. The term was also used for writers of *amulets. The baʿalei (pl.) shem were particularly known as healers and exorcists from the 17th cent. onwards, and many of their deeds were passed down in legend particularly in ḥasidic communities. See also ISRAEL BEN ELIEZER, who, as a founder of ḥasidism, assumed the title Baʿal Shem Tov.

Baʿal Shem Tov (founder of E. European Jewish Ḥasidism): see ISRAEL BEN ELIEZER.

Baʿal teshuvah (Heb., 'master of repentance'; also *chozer bi-teshuvah*). One who returns to the observance of religion, and also (more recently) a Jew who is newly observant. The Baʿal Teshuvah movement was a reaction in Israel to the miraculous outcome of the Six Day War, and elsewhere to what seemed to be the excesses of personal freedom in society.

Bāb: see BĀBĪS.

Bābā (Pañjābī term of endearment for old man). Sikh title given to Gurū *Nānak and other saintly men regardless of age—e.g. Bābā Aṭal Rāi, son of Gurū Har Gobind, who died at the age of 9. The same honorific is given to the *Ādi Granth and to some contemporary spiritual leaders.

Babasaheb (Indian lawyer and politician): see AMBEDKAR, B. R.

Babbar Khālsā (Sikh organization): see AKHAṆḌ KĪRTANĪ JATHĀ.

Babel, Tower of. The enterprise which, acc. to the Bible, was the cause of the multiplicity of languages in the world. According to Genesis 11. 1–9, human beings decided to build a tower which would touch the sky. God prevented the project by introducing the confusion of different languages, and people were then scattered throughout the world. In the *aggadah, the tower was built for idolatrous purpose and was in fact a rebellion against God.

Bābīs. Followers of Sayyid ʿAlī Muḥammad Shīrāzī (1819–50), a merchant from southern Iran who ultimately claimed to be the bearer of a new religion in succession to Islam. His initial claim, made in the spring of 1844 after a series of revelatory visions, was that he was the *Bāb* ('gate') to the *Hidden Imám of Twelver Shiʿism (see ITHNĀ ʿASHARĪYA). Later he claimed to be the Imām himself, returned as *al-Mahdī at the end of the age. Finally he claimed to be the *Nuqta* ('point') of a new revelation from God. Teaching a complex combination of esoteric and messianic ideas, the Bāb initially attracted many *Shaikhīs to his cause, but the movement soon gained a wider following, becoming well established in many parts of Iran. Orthodox religious leaders sought to stem its growth, and in response to persecution the Bābīs steadily became more militant. At the order of the government, the Bāb was imprisoned in remote fortresses in the north-western province of Azerbaijan. Then, during the political crisis of 1848, fighting broke out between a group of Bābīs and orthodox Muslims. Government intervention against the Bābīs gave them the status of self-proclaimed holy *martyrs, whilst their fanatical resistance led the government to regard them as insurrectionaries. Further armed struggles followed (1850–1), and on government orders, the Bāb was executed (8/9 July 1850), and the movement was suppressed. The movement then fragmented, a small group making an unsuccessful attempt to assassinate the Shah (Aug. 1852), whilst a variety of individuals advanced claims to theophanic authority. Ultimately most of the remaining Bābīs gave their allegiance either to Ṣubḥ-i Azal (*Azalī Bābīs), the Bāb's designated successor and an advocate of continued militancy, or to *Bahā'u'llāh (see also BAHĀ'Ī FAITH), who proclaimed a new religion and demanded obedience to government and an end to militancy. Given the short and troubled history of early Babism, much documentary material has been lost, but copies of the Bāb's major writings have survived, several—notably the Persian *Bayān*—having been published in French translation.

Abbas Amant, *Resurrection and Renewal: The Making of the Babi Movement in Iran, 1844–1850* (1982); H. M. Balyuzi, *The Bāb* (1973); Mīrzā Ḥuseyn of Hamadan, *The Tarīkh-i-Jadīd or New History of Mīrzā ʿalī Muḥammad the Bāb*, tr. and ed. E. G. Browne (1893); Denis MacEoin, *The Sources for Early Babi Doctrine and History: A Survey* (1992); M. Z. Nabīl, *The Dawnbreakers*, tr. and ed. Shoghi Effendi (1932); P. Smith, *The Babi and the Bahai Religions* (1987).

Babu (Skt., 'Lord'). Honorific title of respect in India, especially for a holy person.

Babylonian captivity. Period (586–538 BCE) during which many Israelites were held in exile in Babylon. The phrase was applied by Petrarch to the Church during the period when the papacy was at Avignon (1309–77): see ANTIPOPE.

Babylonian Talmud (Jewish authoritative development of Mishnah): see TALMUD.

Bach, J. S. (German composer): see MUSIC.

Bacharach, Jair (1638–1702). German *Talmudist. Under his leadership thirteen scholars met to study and prepare themselves for *redemption. Serving as the *rabbi of Koblenz and Worms, he collected the writings of *Shabbeti Tzevi and was the author of collections of *responsa, mainly of a conservative trend: thus, he forbade the crossing of a river on the *Sabbath to attend *synagogue, as also the request of a man in his will that his only child (a daughter) should recite *kaddish for him. His anxiety was that individuals might make their own interpretations of *halakot: 'As a rule, he who asks questions is ignorant.'

Bacon, Roger (*c.*1214–92). *Franciscan philosopher. Born in England, he studied at Paris and perhaps, earlier, at Oxford. He was one of the first to show interest in *Aristotle's scientific works, then becoming known in the West. Back in England *c.*1247, under the influence of Robert *Grosseteste, he devoted himself to languages, mathematics, and experimental science, and became a Franciscan. Later, in Paris, he wrote his encyclopaedic work, the *Opus Maius*, for Pope Clement IV, after whose death in 1268 he came under suspicion of novelty and dangerous doctrine.

Badā' (Arab., 'appearance'). The occurrence of new circumstances which bring about the alteration of an earlier determination on the part of God. The issue related to this term is extremely controversial in Islam, because it implies that God can 'change his mind'—i.e. it threatens the attribution of immutability, omnipotence, and *qadr (see ALLĀH). It is of particular importance for *Shiʿa Muslims, but only extreme sects drew the conclusion of mutability in God. For others, apparent change is still in the foreknowledge of God, who knows that only at such-and-such a time will a particular determination be possible. Thus, the *Qur'ān cannot speak of the battles of *Badr and Uhud before they have occurred, but what is to be said of them is always known to God. This developed into the view that contingent circumstances alter the option which God espouses and brings into being. Thus *Ismāʿīl was predestined to succeed as 7th Imām, but God brought about instead that his brother should succeed.

Badā' rests particularly on the Quranic claim that God will change his determination to punish sinners, provided that they repent. It is reinforced by mansukh (*naskh, abrogation of one part of the Qur'ān by another).

Bādarāyaṇa ('descendant of Badara'). The ancient Indian sage, living around the 1st cent. BCE (though some suggest much later, e.g. 3rd/4th cent. CE), who propounded the basic teachings of *Vedānta which are expressed in the *Brahmasūtra* and later developed by *Śaṅkara, *Rāmānuja, and their successors. Although Śaṅkara attributed the authorship of the *Brahmasūtra* to Bādarāyaṇa, and this attribution is accepted by many modern Vedāntins, several early commentators on the *Brahmasūtra* (such as Vācaspatimiśra and Ānandajñāna, as well as Rāmānuja, *Madhva, and others) have attributed the work to the legendary compiler of the **Mahābhārata* epic, Vedavyāsa. It is unlikely that Bādarāyaṇa and Vedavyāsa are two names for the same person, but the later tendency to identify these two may be seen as a way of reconciling divergent views and endowing the *Brahmasūtra* with additional authority. It is more likely that Bādarāyaṇa's teachings were systematized in the *Brahmasūtra* by a later anonymous author. These teachings, as given in the *Brahmasūtra* passages mentioning Bādarāyaṇa by name, can be summarized as follows: (i) the aim of human life is liberation (*mokṣa); (ii) liberation is effected by the direct knowledge of *Brahman; and (iii) direct knowledge of Brahman is independent of, and not subordinate to, ritual acts.

Badr. Small town SW of *Madīna, the site of the first victory of the Muslim community after the *Hijra. This success, against numerical odds, was claimed by the Muslims as a sign of *Allāh's favour, and is thus described in the *Qur'ān, mainly in *sūra 8: 'It was not you who slew them, but Allāh slew them' (v. 18): the division of booty, and its uses, are decreed (vv. 42–3); the day itself is referred to as a 'day of *furqān*' (here, *furqān is taken to mean deliverance from judgement).

M. Hamidullah, *The Battlefields of the Prophet Muhammad* (1953).

Baeck, Leo (1873–1956). German *rabbi and leader of *progressive Judaism. He was a rabbi in Berlin from 1912 (serving as an army chaplain during the First World War). From 1933 he defended the rights of Jews in Nazi Germany and, refusing all invitations to leave, he was deported in 1943 to Theresienstadt concentration camp. After the war he moved to London, and then to the USA, to continue teaching. His best known work was *Wesen des Judentums* (The Essence of Judaism, 1905) in which, reacting against *Harnack's *Essence of Christianity*, he argued that Judaism was essentially a dialectic between 'mystery' and 'command' within a system of ethical monotheism: 'Through faith, man experiences the meaning of the world; through action, he is to give to it a meaning.' He rejected Christianity as a 'romantic' religion longing for spiritual redemption, in contrast to Judaism, which he saw as a 'classical' religion striving for the improvement of this world.

A. Friedlander, *Leo Baeck* (1973).

Bahā'ī Faith. A religion founded by *Bahā'u'llāh in the 1860s. After his death in 1892, it was led successively by his eldest son, *'Abdu'l-Bahā (from 1892 to 1921), his great-grandson, *Shoghi Effendi (from 1922 to 1957), and then (in 1963, after a brief 'interregnum') by an elected body, the *Universal House of Justice.

Claiming to be the promised one of all religions, and preaching a message of global socio-religious reform, Bahā'u'llāh initially drew his followers from amongst the *Bābīs, most of whom became Bahā'īs. The religion soon expanded beyond the social and conceptual universe of Iranian Shiʿism, attracting converts from elsewhere in the Middle East, and from the 1890s onwards, in North America and Europe. Though small in numbers, the Western Bahā'ī communities played a crucial role in the further diffusion of the religion, and from the 1920s in the establishment of its 'Administrative Order'. Significant expansion in the non-Muslim Third World began in the 1950s and 1960s, Bahā'īs from these areas now constituting the majority of the world's five million Bahā'īs. There were also large-scale conversions in North America in the late 1960s/early 1970s particularly amongst southern US blacks. Regarded as heretics by Islamic authorities, Bahā'īs have been subject to persecution, especially where they have been seen as the exponents of a Western and anti-Islamic ideology.

Bahā'ī is monotheistic, but as God is regarded as in essence completely transcendent and unknowable, religious doctrine centres on the belief in a series of 'Manifestations of God' (*mazāḥir-i ilāhī*). These individuals reflect and manifest the attributes of God and progressively reveal the divine purpose for humankind. Their teachings vary in accord with the receptivity and maturity of the people of their era, but all represent one single 'religion of God'. The Manifestations include *Abraham, *Moses, *Zoroaster, Gautama *Buddha, *Jesus, *Muḥammad, the *Bāb, and for the present age, Bahā'u'llāh. Further divine messengers will periodically appear for the remainder of humanity's existence as a species. The divine teachings concern both the eternal spiritual quest of the individual and the onward progress of humanity. Each individual human soul is created to know and reflect the attributes of God in both this world and the afterlife. Spiritual progress is potentially unlimited, and 'heaven' and 'hell' are states of soul. The concept of reincarnation is rejected. Spiritual progress requires recognition of the Manifestations of God, obedience to their commands, and well-motivated good deeds. At a societal level, the present age is regarded as unique. The unity of all the peoples and religions of the earth is the destined hallmark of the age. Governments and peoples must work to secure world peace, a world auxiliary language, a world government, the abolition of all forms of racial, national, and religious prejudice, the ending of all forms of economic and chattel slavery, the abolition of extremes of wealth and poverty, and the equality of the sexes. The harmony of true religion and true science is asserted.

Religious life centres on various individual acts of devotion (daily obligatory prayer and moral self-accounting, an annual nineteen-day fast), and a communal 'Feast' held once every nineteen days at the beginning of each month in the Bahā'ī calendar, and comprising devotional, consultative, and social sections. There are no set meditational techniques, but a large number of prayers composed by Bahā'u'llāh and his successors are thought to possess a special potency. Missionary activity and work (especially in the spirit of service to others) are also regarded as devotional acts. Besides Feasts, Bahā'ī communities come together to commemorate various Holy Days, including the Bahā'ī New Year at the vernal equinox (usually 21 Mar.), and the Riḍvān festival (21 Apr.–2 May) marking the anniversary of Bahā'u'llāh's first declaration of his mission (1863). There are also home-based regular teaching meetings ('firesides'). There are Bahā'ī Houses of Worship in various parts of the world, but Bahā'ī devotions may be held anywhere. Smaller communities usually meet in each others' homes. Many Bahā'īs make a pilgrimage to the Bahā'ī shrines in Haifa and Akka.

In terms of the regulation of social life, the importance of stable family life is much emphasized. Marriage is monogamous, and conditional on the consent of both the bride and groom and their parents. Divorce is strongly discouraged, but is permitted after a set 'year of waiting'. The planning of family size is regarded as a matter of personal decision. All extramarital sexual relations are forbidden. Also forbidden are homosexual relationships, gambling, begging, the use of alcohol and narcotics, and involvement in partisan politics or sedition. Bahā'īs are bidden to be loyal to duly established governments, to value education and work, and to practise personal cleanliness. Backbiting is morally condemned, the importance of personal conscience is emphasized, and much stress is placed on the principle of consultation as a means of resolving problems. With no priesthood, administration rests with locally and nationally elected councils ('Spiritual Assemblies'), supreme authority resting with the *Universal House of Justice.

The contemporary Bahā'ī community is not static. As the religion has become more established, contacts with other religious and social groups, and with organizations such as the agencies of the United Nations have steadily increased. Internally, the growing predominance of Third World Bahā'īs has led to changes in leadership and to an increasing stress on grassroots social and economic development projects. Bahā'ī schools, literacy programmes, and radio stations are proliferating. See Index, Bahā'ī.

J. Ferraby, *All Things Made New* (1975); P. Smith, *The Babi and Baha'i Religions* (1987), and *A Short History of the Bahā'ī Faith* (1995).

Bahā'u'llāh (1817–92) (Arab., 'the Glory/Splendour of God'), Religious title adopted by Mīrzā Ḥusayn ʿali Nūrī, the prophet-founder of the *Bahā'ī Faith. Born into a wealthy landowning family in N. Iran, he chose to follow a life of religious involvement rather than that of a courtier. In 1844 he became a *Bābī. Imprisoned in the Black Pit of Tehran in 1852, he experienced a number of revelatory visions, and after his exile to Ottoman Iraq withdrew to the mountains of Kurdistan where he lived as a pious ascetic. Returning to Baghdād in 1856, he soon became the leading figure in a revival of Babism. Although he demanded that his followers should abandon militancy, the Iranian government was alarmed, and sought his removal from Iraq. Accordingly in 1863 he was summoned to Istanbul, and thence dispatched to Edirne (Adrianople) (1863–8) and then to the prison-city of Akka (Acre) in Ottoman Syria (1868–92). Immediately before his departure from Baghdād he apparently made the first declaration of his claim to be a new messenger from God, the promised one foretold by the Bāb. In Edirne this claim was made openly (1866), that he was 'he whom God shall manifest'; and the Bābī community soon became divided between the followers of Bahā'u'llāh (Bahā'īs) and those of his half-brother Ṣubḥ-i Azal (*Azalīs). By the 1870s, most Bābīs had become Bahā'īs, energetic missionary endeavour thereafter augmenting their numbers both in Iran and elsewhere in the Middle East. Turning over much of the task of organizing the movement to his eldest son and eventual successor, ʿAbbās Effendi (*ʿAbdu'l-Bahā), Bahā'u'llāh devoted his final years to his writings. These were now all regarded as revelations from God, and besides thousands of letters to his followers, included a number of lengthy books and 'Tablets' (*alwāḥ*). Whilst in Baghdād, his works had been primarily concerned with ethical, mystical, and doctrinal themes (as in the *Hidden Words*, *Seven Valleys*, and *Book of Certitude*), his later writings were more diverse. In his 'Tablets to the Kings' he proclaimed his mission and called for the establishment of world peace. In his *Most Holy Book* (*c.*1873), he formulated the basis for a distinctive Bahā'ī Holy Law, and in a number of final works he delineated his principles for social reconstruction in a new world order (*Tablets of Bahā'u'llāh*). He died in the vicinity of Akka on 29 May 1892. His remains were buried at the Bahjī, which is now a shrine for pilgrims, and the direction of prayer for believers (*qibla).

H. M. Balyuzi, *Bahā'u'llāh, the King of Glory* (1980); Shoghi Effendi, *Gleanings from the Writings* . . . (1976) and *God Passes By* (1974).

Bahir, Sefer ha (Book of Light). An early Jewish *kabbalistic work. It was ascribed to R. Nehunya, and it is an anthology of statements attributed to various *tannaim and *amoraim; probably it has been handed down in a mutilated form. It is the earliest work which deals with the *sefirot (divine attributes) which are given symbolic names. Much of scripture is interpreted as being concerned not with the created world, but with the divine realm which is seen as the area for the activity of the sefirot. The *Sefer ha-Bahir* seems to have appeared in S. France at the end of the 12th cent. CE and some portions seem to have been influenced by the writings of *Abraham b. Hiyya. It is, in certain aspects, similar to the speculations of the *gnostics, but it is not known whether there is an historical link. In later kabbalistic circles, it was regarded as an authoritative source, 'composed by the mystic sages of the *Talmud' (Jacob b. Jacob ha-Kohen), but those who were opposed to the kabbalah regarded it as heretical.

Edns. by G. Scholem (Germ.) and R. Margaliot (Heb.), which divide the work differently.

Baḥīrā. A Syrian monk who in Islamic tradition is said to have recognized the signs of prophethood on the young *Muḥammad, when the latter was on a trading journey to Syria. Some have seen in this legend an attempt to compensate for the apparent lack of any prophecy concerning Muḥammad in previous scriptures, considered important for the acceptance of a prophet.

Bahiraṅga-sādhana (Skt.). The development in Hinduism of an increasing detachment from the external world. The first three stages (*yama, *niyama, and *āsana) of *Patañjali's yoga are means to this end.

Bahubali (first person to achieve liberation in this world cycle): see PILGRIMAGE (JAIN); DIGAMBARA.

Bahya ben Asher (13th cent. CE). Jewish commentator and *kabbalist. Serving as *Dayyan in Saragossa, he produced a commentary on the *Pentateuch (*Beʾurʿal ha-Torah*, 1291) which interpreted the text literally, homiletically, rationally and kabbalistically. It was very popular. He is important in the history of Kabbalah in that he preserves and quotes the mystical teaching of *Naḥmanides' contemporaries. He adopted a four-level interpretation of scripture: (i) *peshat*, plain or literal; (ii) *midrash, homiletical; (iii) *sekhal*, reasoned and argued; (iv) *sōdh*, derived from mystical union with God. This approach is summarized under the mnemonic, pardes. In his view, all is to be understood as a consequence of the intention of God: 'Those who ascribe events to chance are like birds that see a net and think it has no special purpose.' All commentary is to light the way to God: 'The light of a candle serves a purpose when it is held in front, none when it is held behind one's back.'

Baḥya ben Joseph ibn Paquda (Pakuda) (late 11th cent. CE). Jewish philosopher, known only through his major work *Kitab al-Hidaya ila Fara'd al-Qulub* (tr. into Heb. as *Ḥovot ha-Levavot*, Duties of the Hearts). It discusses the ritual and ethical obligations of the *Torah, and attempts to lead the reader through various mystical stages towards union with God. The title is derived from a distinction between 'works of the limbs', i.e. visible behaviours, and 'duties of the heart', the development of interior wisdom. The work is unusual in Judaism in that it allows the benefits of *asceticism: 'Abstainers are physicians of faith and healers of souls.' The author was clearly influenced by Muslim spirituality, but was immensely popular and had an important influence on later Jewish devotional works.

M. Mansoor, *The Book of Direction to the Duties of the Heart* (1973); G. Vajda, *La Théologie ascétique de Baḥya Ibn Paquda* (1912).

Bāhya-pūjā (Skt.). The external forms of devotion in Hinduism, especially to *avatāras; but equally constituting the *karma-kāṇḍa (ritual requirements) of the *Vedas.

Baidawi (Islamic scholar): see AL-BAIḌĀWĪ.

Baigan, Ishida (founder of Japanese religious movement): see SHINGAKU.

Baimasi (Buddhist monastery): see PAI-MA-SSU.

Bairāgī. An order of Hindu *yogis, derived from Bhatrahāri, a ruler who was persuaded by *Gorakhnāth to give up his throne and become a disciple. The term is more often encountered in the Sikh reinterpretation, in which the bairags are those who devote themselves to God while remaining with their families.

Baisākhī, V(a)isākhī. Hindu spring festival. The first day of the Hindu solar month Vaiśākha (Apr.–May), it is New Year's Day by the solar calendar of S. India and a spring harvest festival in N. India, celebrated with *melās, dances, and folksongs. Celebrated on or near 13 Apr., Baisākhī is of special importance to Sikhs. *Gurū *Amar Dās enjoined Sikhs to assemble in the presence of the Gurū. After abolishing the *masand order *Gobind *Siṅgh bade Sikhs to contribute directly to the treasury of the Gurū on Baisākhī. In 1699 he instituted the *khālsā on Baisākhī. Sikhs everywhere commemorate this event with *akhaṇḍ pāṭh and *kīrtan. The previous year's *Niśān *Sāhib is replaced and the flagpole cleaned. Often new initiates receive *amrit, and *gurdwārā presidents and management committees are elected. The *Harimandir Sāhib, Amritsar, is illuminated. On several occasions tragedy has befallen Baisākhī celebrations in Amritsar. In 1721 *Manī Siṅgh prevented fighting between Sikh factions. In 1762 Ahmed Shāh Abdālī desecrated and destroyed the Harimandir. In 1919, many Sikhs who had gathered in Jalliānwālā Bāgh, Amritsar, were shot by General Dyer's soldiers. The spelling 'Vaisakhi' is now favoured by many Sikh leaders in Britain, as evidenced by 'logos' on recent festival T-shirts. See GURPURB; SAṄGRĀND.

Baker, Augustine (1575–1641). Influential Benedictine (see BENEDICT) writer, especially on spirituality and *asceticism, in particular through his *Holy Wisdom* (*Sancta Sophia*, 1657). He lived and worked in the tradition of the 14th-cent. English mystics, e.g. Walter Hilton, emphasizing detachment even from liturgy and formal devotion, if these become an end rather than a means. The mystical union with God is best achieved through *affective prayer.

Bala (Skt., Pāli). The five powers developed in Buddhism by the strengthening of the five roots (*indriya), which lead to enlightenment: (i) the bala of faith (*śraddhā) which eradicates false views; (ii) the bala of effort (*virya) which eradicates unwholesome views; (iii) the bala of concentration through the four foundations (*satipaṭṭhāna); (iv) the bala of absorption in the object of contemplation (*samādhi); (v) the bala of wisdom (*prajña) which penetrates the *Four Noble Truths.

Balaam. A biblical character. He was instructed by Balak, king of Moab, to curse Israel, but after a vision of an *angel he blessed the Israelites instead (Numbers 22. 1–24. 25) uttering the prophecy, 'How fair are your tents, O Jacob, your encampments, O Israel! . . . God brings him out of Egypt; he has, as it were, the horns of the wild ox, he shall eat up the nations his adversaries, and shall break their bones in pieces.' The oracles of Balaam, which are archaic in language and therefore probably of an early date, were highly influential on the eschatology of Ezekiel 38 and 39. In *aggadic literature, opinion is divided between those who saw Balaam as a great prophet and those who saw him as a man with 'an evil eye, a haughty spirit and a proud soul' (*Avot* 5. 19).

Bālak Siṅgh (1797–1862). Spiritual preceptor of *Rām Siṅgh, who founded the *Nāmdhārī Sikh movement. He exhorted his followers to live simply and practise no religious ritual apart from repetition of God's name (*Nām, hence the name of the movement). Devotees regard Bālak Siṅgh as a reincarnation of Gurū *Gobind Siṅgh. He chose Rām Siṅgh to succeed him, thereby recognizing the reality of an organized movement.

Balarāma. In Hindu mythology, *Kṛṣṇa's elder brother, son of *Vāsudeva and *Devakī. The latter's kinsman, *Kaṃsa, intended to kill her children at birth, so Balarāma was miraculously transplanted from Devakī's womb into that of her co-wife Rohiṇī. He grew up with Kṛṣṇa among the cowherds of Vṛndāvana, was associated with him in his youthful exploits, and eventually helped him to kill Kaṃsa. He is also called Saṃkarṣaṇa (Skt., 'extraction, ploughing'), a name which in the Kṛṣṇa story is related to the circumstances of his birth, but which is more likely to spring from the fact that he was once originally an independent divinity connected with agriculture, wine, and snake cults. These connections survive within the Kṛṣṇa mythology, in that Balarāma's characteristic weapon is the plough, he is frequently depicted as drinking heavily, and he is often said to be a manifestation of the cosmic serpent *Śeṣa. He is also said to be a manifestation of *Viṣṇu, and his name sometimes appears in the eighth place in the standard *avatāra list. In the *Pañcarātra system, Saṃkarṣaṇa is the second *vyūha, who proceeds from Vāsudeva-Kṛṣṇa—even though the tradition that he was older than Kṛṣṇa may point to a time when he was the more important deity of the two.

Bālā Sandhū. *Bhāī Bālā, Hindu companion of Gurū *Nānak. In Sikh tradition, Bālā was Gurū Nānak's constant companion on his travels. In popular iconography he is shown fanning his master while *Mardānā plays the *rabāb*. The Bālā *janamsākhīs are the only evidence for Bālā's existence, which is historically uncertain.

Baldachino. In Christian churches, originally in *Coptic-rite churches, a domed canopy supported on four columns and covering the main *altar. It is usually highly gilded and decorated.

Balfour Declaration. British declaration of sympathy with *Zionism. It was made in a letter of 2 Nov. 1917, from the British Foreign Secretary (i.e. Balfour) to Lord Rothschild: 'His Majesty's Government view with favour the establishment in Palestine of a national home for the Jewish people . . .'. It was qualified by a clause 'that nothing be done which may prejudice the civil and religious rights of existing non-Jewish communities in Palestine'. But at the time, the British supported the idea of a Jewish commonwealth in Palestine under British protection in order to detach Palestine from the Turkish Empire, and as a means of encouraging Russian Jews to pressurize the new Bolshevik government to stay in the First World War. According to Field-Marshal Smuts (in 1947), it had been passed to 'rally Jewry on a worldwide scale to the Allied cause'. The declaration was endorsed in 1920 by the allies at the San Remo Conference. It was, however, in apparent conflict with the McMahon correspondence, which made commitments to the Arabs. Sharif Hussein and ibn Saʿud were 'courted' in order to secure their help against the *Ottoman Turks. Thus are the seeds of conflict sown by politicians who (as almost always in post-Enlightenment countries) neither understand nor care about religions.

Bali. An offering, in Hinduism and Buddhism, of grain or rice to gods and spirits, in particular, part of the daily offering of the *gṛhastha (householder) which ensures that at death he will attain *Brahman.

Bali. In Hindu mythology, one of the leaders of the *daityas (demons) and grandson of Prahlāda. Having acquired sovereignty over the triloka (Skt., 'triple world' see LOKA), he was tricked out of it by *Viṣṇu in his *Vāmana form. He was bound and consigned to the nether regions, but according to some versions of the story, was promised by Viṣṇu that he should become the *Indra of the next *manvantara*. According to one legend he was offered the choice of entering heaven with one hundred fools, or hell with one wise person. He chose the latter, because a hundred fools will turn heaven into hell, but one wise person will turn hell into heaven.

Bālmīkī. Pañjābī community venerating *Vālmīki. This movement, of Hindu/Sikh origin, gives enhanced identity to devotees of chūhṛā (sweeper) status in the *caste hierarchy. Bālmīkis revere both the *Rāmāyaṇa* and the *Ādi Granth, celebrating both *Gurpurbs and Hindu *festivals, especially the birthday (in Oct.) of Vālmīki. In Britain there are temples in Coventry, Bedford, Southall, and Birmingham. Bālmīkī leaders in Britain prefer the spelling 'Vālmīkī'. See also Mazhabī, Raṅghṛetā, Ravidāsī.

M. Juergensmeyer, *Religion and Social Vision* (1982).

Balokole (Christian renewal movement): see EAST AFRICAN REVIVAL.

Balthasar, Hans Urs von (1905–88). *Roman Catholic theologian. After a basically philosophical education, with special reference to German studies, he became a *Jesuit in 1929. He studied theology at Lyons, 1933–7, and was ordained in 1939. During the war (and until 1948), he was chaplain at Basel University. In 1950, he left the Jesuits and became a secular priest in the Swiss diocese of Chur. In 1969, he was appointed to the International Theological Commission, and in 1988 was nominated to be a *cardinal but died before this could be put into effect. As a philosophical theologian, von Balthasar emphasized the necessary openness of human nature to exploration and creativity. In his *Herrlichkeit: Eine theologische Asthetik* (Eng. tr., *The Glory of the Lord: A Theological Aesthetics*, 1982, 1984, 1986), he insisted on the importance of the form which is more than the sum of its parts: to perceive the beauty of an object or of a harmony is to grasp the wholeness of it which is never exhausted. In the appreciation of beauty, the cause may remain the same, and yet it never *is* the same as it is appreciated: a person is constantly drawn on into a transcendence which is perfectly illustrated (and enacted) in the *Incarnation. Thus God reveals himself, not simply in truth and goodness, but as beauty. Here is the perfected form of love, which is so urgent in its self-giving that it draws the one who contemplates it into a corresponding act of unreserved giving. On this basis, von Balthasar completed his massive trilogy with his *Theodramatik* (1973, 1976, 1978) and *Theologik* (1985, 1985, 1987): because God has dramatically expressed his love and displayed his glory in his Son, so we can know that he has spoken a definitive word of truth. Along this route, humanity can transcend those points of departure which may have in them much that is fine but nothing which is absolute in its definition of the good, the beautiful, and the true: 'The opposition between what is profane and what is sacred is indeed fully justified in its place, else there could be no movement. Yet in this openness and this reciprocally flowing movement the opposition is transcended by the unity of him in whom and for whom all things have been created, and who has been charged by the Father to bring them home.' This process of discernment did not evade the realities of pain and evil, particularly after von Balthasar met, and received into the RC Church, Adrienne von Speyr, with whom he founded the Community of St John (Johannesgemeinschaft), and from whom, he maintained, he received much more than he gave. In particular, he received from her the insight she acquired from a mystical sharing, each *Holy Week, in Christ's Passion and Descent into Hell. She died in 1967; and in the end, von Balthasar failed to follow her in the path of reversed transcendence, and continued to see the existing Church as the intended form of Christian being derived from Christ. His awareness of the transcendental form of human religiousness remained perfunctory, and his immense knowledge of European intellectual history appears to have left him less aware of the demands of that wider ecumenism to which the logic of his position pointed.

M. Kehl and W. Loser (eds.), *A von Balthasar Reader* (1983); J. O'Donnell, *Hans Urs von Balthasar* (1922); J. Riches (ed.), *The Analogy of Beauty . . .* (1986).

Baluan Native Christian Church (Papua New Guinean Church): see PALIAU MALOAT.

Bāmiyān. Buddhist holy place with carved and decorated caves, in Afghanistan. The caves served as *caityas for the Buddhist monks who lived nearby. The decorations are mainly of paradises of the *Pure Land school and of their presiding *Buddhas. Outside are the remains of two large Buddha figures. The Buddhism of Bāmiyān disappeared with the spread of Islam.

Banāras (sacred city of India): see KAŚI.

Banārsīdās (1586–1643). Jain layperson and reformer, who maintained that spiritual development and experience are not a specialist preserve. He was a trader in Agra, who was a devout layman in his youth, but who became disenchanted with ritual and image-reverence, and joined instead the *Adhyātma ('inner soul') movement. He reorganized this to such an extent that he is sometimes regarded as its founder. He subordinated ritual and monastic authority, allowing them only a preliminary place on the path that leads to personal realization of truth: 'I achieved a vision with which I could see everything with the same untroubled eye: everything was equal, nothing high or low. As God is my witness, I had indeed attained a knowledge akin to supreme realization.' He made a record of progress in *Ardhkathanak*, his *Half a Story*, so-called because it is an autobiography of his first fifty-five years, half the ideal life-span. It is a remarkable and vivid record, ranking with the spiritual autobiographies of *Augustine and *al-Ghaz(z)ali.

M. Lath, *Ardhakathanaka: Half a Tale* (1981).

Bancroft, Richard (1544–1610). *Archbishop of *Canterbury. He was born at Farnworth, Lancs, educated at Christ's and Jesus Colleges, Cambridge, and served in many posts before, in 1597, he became bishop of London. He had increasing episcopal responsibility because of Whitgift's poor health. Bancroft succeeded him as archbishop in 1604. His aversion to *Puritanism is expressed in his writings. An uncompromising man of considerable academic ability, he was committed to the importance of clerical learning.

Tracts Ascribed to R. Bancroft, ed. A. Peel (1953).

Bandā Siṅgh Bahādur (1670–1716 CE). Sikh military leader. Bandā Siṅgh, originally Lachman Dās, became a *bairāgī (Hindu renunciant) in early youth, adopting the name Mādho Dās. He settled as a hermit at *Nander where he later became Gurū *Gobind Siṅgh's ardent follower, renamed Bandā (slave). The gurū authorized him to punish the persecutors of the Sikhs. Followed by increasing numbers of peasant supporters, he subjugated the Pañjab east of Lahore, devastating places associated with Muslim tyranny, e.g. Sirhind. After eight years of fighting against the Mughals he was besieged at Gurdās-Naṅgal and cruelly executed in Delhi. Historians differ in their assessment of Bandā. For many contemporaries, he was emperor, issuing coins from his headquarters at Mukhlisgaṛh. His followers were the Bandeīs. See MANĪ SIṄGH.

Bāṇī ('speech'). Common abbreviation among Sikhs for *gurbāṇī, the writings contained in the *Ādi Granth. See also BHAGAT BĀṆĪ.

Banka (Jap., 'evening portion'). The recitation in Zen monasteries of the evening *sūtra (also 'bansan'). Banka-zoji, which follows, is the careful cleaning of the monastery.

Bankei Eitaku (Yōtaku), also **KOKUSHI** (1622–93). Japanese *Zen teacher of the *Rinzai school. When young, he wandered through Japan, attending various Zen teachers, and then retired into seclusion to practise *zazen. Neglecting his health, he had an enlightenment experience at a moment of critical illness: 'I felt a congestion in the throat: I spat out a lump of black phlegm, and at that moment I realized what had escaped me: "All things are entirely resolved in the Unborn (*fushō)." ' He received further instruction from Dōsha Chōgen, who bestowed on him the seal of recognition (*inkashōmei), but Bankei seized it and tore it up—he had no need of written authority. When he began to teach, he found that no one could understand the words that arose from his experience, so he went again into seclusion, until he was discovered as a Zen master and many pupils gathered around him. In 1672, he was appointed abbot of Myōshin-ji (monastery) in *Kyōto, and at this point the extreme simplicity of his teaching led to a Rinzai revival, in which ritual preoccupations were transcended. Although he prohibited the recording of his teaching, some instructions and dialogues have survived. He continued to travel extensively to different monasteries, especially to those needing restoration. When he told his disciples that his death was approaching, and they asked for the customary farewell poem, he replied that they should listen to the sounds of everyday life, as his teaching is thus summarized: 'Awaken to the unborn in the midst of everyday life.'

Bankei's understanding (and realization) of the unborn Buddha-mind rests on Zen understanding of the undifferentiated permeation of the buddhanature (*bussho) in all appearance, empty of self (*śūnyatā): 'The unborn is the ground of all appearance, and the source of all appearance. . . . Thus the unborn is the foundation of all buddhas.' That means that all talk of 'not-dying' is 'a waste of time: there cannot be death for what is not born'. The goal is therefore the realization of the unborn in oneself: 'My message to everyone is that the Buddha mind is innate in them. From their parents, nothing else is innate. The Buddha mind is unborn because it is always there, innate, and it enlightens the mind.'

N. Waddell, *The Unborn: The Life and Teaching of Zen Master Bankei* (1984).

Banno, Bhāī (16th–17th cents. CE). Disciple of Sikh Gurū *Arjan Dev; early version of *Ādi Granth. According to tradition, Arjan Dev either entrusted his compilation to Banno for binding in Lahore or reluctantly lent it on condition he did not keep it for more than one night in his village, Māṅgaṭ. By travelling extremely slowly Banno contrived to copy the entire Ādi Granth before returning it. Unlike the *Kartārpur version, the Banno version, also known as the Māṅgaṭ version or bitter version (*khārī bīṛ*), contains a *hymn by *Mīrābāī, a hymn of Sūr Dās of which only the first line appears in the Kartārpur version and a hymn by Arjan Dev in Rāmakalī *Rāg of which the Kartārpur version has only a couplet. The reasons for these discrepancies are uncertain.

Banū Isrā'īl (children of Israel): see AHL AL-KITĀB.

Baoli (place of ritual bathing): see PILGRIMAGE.

Bapak (father): see SUBUD INTERNATIONAL BROTHERHOOD.

Baptism. The rite of admission into the Christian church, practised by all denominations. Its origin is probably to be sought in (i) the Jewish practice of baptizing proselytes; and (ii) the baptism administered by *John the Baptist 'for the forgiveness of sins' (Mark 1. 4). *Jesus underwent this latter baptism (Mark 1. 9) and may even have baptized his own followers for a time (John 3. 22), but did not make baptism part of his ministry. Christian tradition, however, looks back to Jesus' post-resurrection command to baptize in the name of the Father, Son, and Holy Spirit (Matthew 28. 19–20) as the institution of the rite.

The doctrine which attended baptism in the early church was variable. Baptism might be, for example, the washing away of sins (Acts 2. 38), a dying with Christ (Romans, 6. 4), a rebirth (John 3. 5), or the occasion of the gift of the Holy Spirit (1 Corinthians 12. 13). This plurality of themes, as well as the vagueness of passages speaking of the baptism of 'households' (e.g. Acts 16. 33), make it difficult to say whether infants were baptized (the question continues to be debated: see J. Jeremias, *Infant Baptism in the First Four Centuries*, Eng. tr. 1960, and K. Rengstorf, *Did the Early Church Baptize Infants?*, Eng. tr. 1961).

The theology of baptism gained precision in the 3rd and 4th cents., notably in the West in the writings of *Augustine. The Catholic view which emerged was of a rite which works *ex opere operato, which confers a 'character' on the recipient (who thus can never be rebaptized, even after *apostasy), and which is valid even if administered in *heresy or *schism. Infant baptism became the norm, alongside the developing theology of *original sin, thus displacing the earlier common practice of delaying baptism until one's deathbed. These views were subsumed into the medieval theology of the *sacraments.

The 16th-cent. Reformers modified that theology: *Luther, reconciling the necessity of baptism with his doctrine of justification by faith alone, regarded baptism as a promise of divine grace after which a person's sins are no longer imputed to him or her. *Zwingli, on the other hand, saw baptism only as a sign of admission to the Christian community. *Calvin taught that baptism can only be of effect for the elect, who have faith (without which the rite is vacuous). The radical *Anabaptists understood baptism exclusively as a response of faith on the part of the individual to the gospel, and thus rejected infant baptism.

Except among those denominations which now practise only the baptism of believers (chiefly *Baptists, Disciples, *Jehovah's Witnesses, some *Pentecostals, and Plymouth *Brethren), baptism forms the first part of Christian initiation, which is then completed in *confirmation (although in the *Orthodox church this is immediate).

In the most usual form of early Christian baptism, the candidate stood in water, and water was poured over the upper part of the body. This is technically called 'immersion', but the word is now more often used to refer to the method (used e.g. by Baptists and Orthodox) of dipping the whole body under water. The method in most W. churches is a threefold pouring of water over the head ('affusion'). Exceptionally baptism may be by 'aspersion', or sprinkling of water over the head.

G. R. Beasley-Murray, *Baptism in the New Testament* (1962); G. W. and M. Thurian, *Baptism and Eucharist* (1983); G. Wainwright, *Christian Initiation* (1969); World Council of Churches, *Baptism, Eucharist and Ministry* (1982).

Baptism, forced. see ANUSIM.

Baptist Churches. Christian denomination. Baptists form one of the largest *Protestant bodies with a worldwide membership of over 40 million, plus a greater number of adherents. Its beginnings can be traced among the *Anabaptists, and to the ministry of the English *Puritan John Smyth (*c.*1554–1612), and his fellow separatist exiles, who made believers' *baptism the basis of their gathered church fellowship in Amsterdam. Most of Smyth's members applied with him to join the *Mennonites and were eventually accepted by them, though not in Smyth's lifetime. His colleague, Thomas Helwys, accompanied by other members, returned to England in 1612, despite the dangers, and formed the first Baptist church on English soil at Spitalfields, London. *Arminian in theology, they ultimately became known as *General Baptists. Another Baptist group developed from a London *Calvinistic *Independent church from which some members, persuaded concerning believers' baptism, broke away sometime in the 1630s to form a church of believers baptized on profession of faith. This was the first of the *'Particular' Baptist churches, so named because of their emphasis on 'particular' redemption and their belief that Christ died only for the elect. The Particular Baptists continued to treasure their congregational autonomy, whilst General Baptists developed a slightly more connexional form of church polity, using their annual Assembly for more than deliberative purposes and appointing 'Messengers' who had responsibilities of oversight as well as of church planting. Baptist work in Wales can be traced to the formation of a church at Ilston, Gower, Swansea in 1649. Churches were also established in Ireland in the mid-17th cent., and in Scotland by the mid-18th cent. In England a Baptist 'General Union', formed in 1813, was gradually transformed into the Baptist Union of Great Britain and Ireland (1873).

Concerned, since the publication of Helwys's *Mystery of Iniquity* (1612), about religious liberty, some early 17th-cent. Baptists sought freedom in America. Roger Williams began Baptist work at Rhode Island in 1639 which, after early difficulties, spread rapidly throughout the USA, largely inspired by the mid-18th-cent. *Great Awakening in New England. The 18th cent. witnessed continuing expansion so that by 1900 there were 4 million Baptists in the USA, 12 million by 1950. The majority of their present congregations belong to either the 'American Baptist Churches in the USA' (originally the Northern Baptist Association) with 1.6 million members in 1983, the *Southern Baptist Convention with 13.9 million, and two (largely black) National Conventions with a combined membership of 10.3 million. Additional smaller bodies provide a total Baptist membership in the USA of 26.7 million.

The denomination's concern for world mission in the 19th cent. resulted in the establishment of Baptist work in India (William Carey 1761–1834), Burma (Adoniram Judson 1788–1850), Germany (J. G. Oncken 1800–84), and elsewhere in Europe. Baptists form an important body in the former Soviet Union, though precise numbers are difficult to estimate; their 5,000 churches affiliated to the All-Union Council of Evangelical Christians and Baptists have a membership of 545,000 (1983). Baptist work in Australia and New Zealand began in the 19th cent., and in the present century there has been considerable expansion in Africa, Asia, and South America. The Baptist World Alliance, formed in 1905, provides an international forum for the exchange of Baptist thought, paying special attention to matters concerning Christian education, missions, religious freedom, and human rights.

W. H. Brackney, *The Baptists* (1988); R. Torbert, *A History of the Baptists* (1963).

Baqā' (Sūfī state of attainment): see FANĀ'.

Baraita (Aram., for Heb., *hizonah*, 'outside'). Every Jewish tradition of the *tannaim which is found outside Judah ha-Nasi's *Mishnah. The beraitot (pl.) were used to supplement mishnaic teaching or to solve a new problem which had arisen. Later beraitot were derived from the *amoraim although they were generally cited in the name of a particular sage. There were many compilations of beraitot including the *Tosefta which was designed as a companion to the Mishnah.

Baraka. *'blessing' (Arab., cf. Heb., *bārakh*). In Islam, a quality or force emanating originally from *Allāh but capable of transmission to objects or to human beings. The word appears in the *Qur'ān in the plural, *barakāt*, 'blessings' (7. 94; 11. 50, 76), and the term *mubārak*, 'blessed', is used, for example, of the Book (6. 92, 155), the *Kaʿba (3. 90), an olive tree (24. 33). *Muḥammad, *prophets, and holy persons in general are especially credited with baraka, and in popular Islam baraka can be acquired by touching a shrine or the tomb of a *walī (holy person), and above all from the *Black Stone in the Kaʿba. A baraka from God initiates a *Sūfī order: see SILSILAH. Great Sūfī *shaykhs also become possessed of baraka which is transmitted to others and may remain associated with their tombs, thereby evoking *pilgrimage.

Baramon-sōjō (Indian Buddhist monk): see BODHISENA.

Barbarossa (German King): see ADRIAN IV.

Barclay, Robert (exponent of Quaker beliefs): see FRIENDS, THE SOCIETY OF.

Bardaisan or **Bardesanes of Edessa** (154–222). Christian speculative thinker, by the 4th cent. classed as a *heretic. His Syriac *Book of the Laws of Countries* is a more or less orthodox treatment of fate; and he opposed *Marcion. The attacks of *Ephrem on him, however, show that his own system included a cosmological myth and *gnostic-like ideas of salvation. Bardaisan's disciples persisted for several centuries.

Bardo (Skt., *antarabhāva*, 'intermediate state'). In *Tibetan Buddhism, the state after death and before rebirth. A distinction is made, however, in the *Nyingma, *Kagyü, and *Sakya traditions (which follow the **Tibetan Book of the Dead*) between six bardos, three of life and three of death. Those of life are the After Birth (*skyes.nas*) bardo, the Dream (*rmi.lam*) bardo, and the bardo of Deep Meditation (*bsam.gtan*); those of death are the Time of Death (*'chi.kha*) bardo, the Reality (*chos.nyid*) bardo, and the bardo of Seeking Rebirth (*srid.pa*, literally, 'existence'). The subject experiencing these bardos is not an unchanging soul (which concept does not exist in Buddhism) but the constantly changing continuum of consciousness which, according to spiritual advancement, becomes either sharpened or bewildered after disjunction from the body. The duration of the inter-life state is given (largely symbolically) as forty-nine days, although there are slightly varying doctrines among Tibetan schools as to the nature of the experience therein.

According to the *Geluk school (which does not include the *Tibetan Book of the Dead* in its tradition), the forty-nine days divide into seven seven-day periods; in each period the deceased, having already assumed the form of his future body, determines his future birth by attraction to his appropriate circumstance. A being destined for rebirth in a hot hell will be attracted to heat, for example. If a place of birth is not found after seven days, a 'small death' is experienced and another seven-day period is entered, but the maximum time spent in the inter-life state is forty-nine days. An important feature of the Geluk teaching regarding the bardo is the connection between the manner of death and the future rebirth. According to this doctrine, because the consciousness remains closely associated with the body for three or four days after death, a peaceful death in which mourners do not reveal their grief is particularly desirable, and to interfere with the body in this time is not considered good as this could precipitate the consciousness into a lower rebirth. Strong emphasis is placed by the Geluk on the determining power of the state of mind at death (i.e. virtuous, non-virtuous, or neutral), and also on the negative influences of desire, hatred, and ignorance during the bardo itself. See further J. Hopkins and Lati Rinpoche, *Death, Intermediate State and Rebirth in Tibetan Buddhism.*

Bardo Todrol (Tibetan afterdeath state): see TIBETAN BOOK OF THE DEAD.

Barelvi. Indian and Pakistani school of Muslim thought with over 200 million followers. The Dar-al-uloom was founded in 1904 by the Qadiri *Sūfī master, Imām Ahmad Reza (d. 1921) at Barelvi in N. India. Imām Ahmad Reza perceived the moral and intellectual decline of Indian Muslims at the beginning of the 20th cent. His solution was to strengthen the ordinary person's Islam by having the *Hanafi *sharīʿa propagated through well-respected channels such as Sūfī *shaykhs and *ʿulamā.

Barelvi is a stronghold of *Sunni orthodoxy against the *Wahhābī and *Ahmadīyya movements. The Barelvi *ʿulamā are conservative, but appreciate that a thousand years of Indian Islamic tradition cannot be given up by the masses overnight. Instead they argue that traditional institutions, such as the Sūfī orders with their Pir-murid structure, should be used to bring the masses closer to the *sunna of the Prophet.

The charismatic Barelvi divines, such as Syyed Madani-Muhaddith Azam, Mawlana Arshad Qadri, Mawlana Mustafa, Sheikh Madani and Mawlana Hashmi Madani, have a massive populist support. All are fiery orators and formidable scholastic theologians. Politically Barelvi is neutral to the Indian Congress Party and is pro-Pakistan. See also DEOBAND.

Baresnum (purification): see PURITY.

Bar-Ilan (Orthodox Jewish University): see BERLIN, N. Z. J.

Bar Kokhba, Simeon (d. 135 CE). Leader of Jewish revolt against Rome. His name ('Son of a Star') seems to have been understood as a fulfilment of the verse in Numbers 24. 17, 'A star shall come forth out of *Jacob, and a sceptre shall rise out of *Israel'. He was accepted as *messiah by R. *Akiva, the leading authority of his day, and the revolt seems to have lasted for three years, 132–5 CE, after the Emperor Hadrian had built a temple to Jupiter in Jerusalem. Bar Kokhba seems to have united the people, seized Jerusalem, established an administration, and even struck coins. However, he was eventually killed by the Roman army after a siege at Bethar which traditionally was taken on the 9 *Av: the Jewish population of Judea was either scattered or slaughtered.

Barlaam and Joasaph, Sts. Heroes of a medieval Christian romance. In it, an 'Indian' king Abenner tries to keep his son Joasaph from becoming a Christian as a seer had prophesied at his birth. The boy is brought up in a palace alone in strict ignorance of any of the ills of life and of Christianity. He is eventually allowed to go for a drive, sees men who are maimed, blind, and old, and becomes troubled. A Christian ascetic Barlaam, disguised, then preaches to him a series of parables and converts him. The story continues with a contest between Christianity and paganism and with Abenner's own conversion. The dependence of the tale on the legendary life of the *Buddha is obvious. Probably the basic story circulated in central Asia and *Abbāsid Iraq before being Christianized in the *c.*10th cent. The extant *Georgian version of the story seems earliest, then those in Greek and Latin. Barlaam and Joasaph (or Josaphat) became popular Christian saints; feast day, 27 Nov. For a Jewish version, see IBN HASDAI.

Eng. trs. G. R. Woodward and H. Mattingly; D. M. Lang.

Barmecides (Muslim government adviser): see WAZĪR.

Barmen Declaration. Document issued in May 1934 by the Confessing Synod of Barmen (in present-day Wuppertal, Germany) attended by *Lutheran, *Reformed, and *United delegates during the German *Kirchenkampf. It was drafted by K. *Barth, and consists of a preamble and six theses. Each thesis quotes, then expounds, a New Testament text, then rejects an opposing thesis; e.g. in § 3 'We reject the false doctrine as though the church were permitted to abandon the form of its message and order, to its own pleasure or to changes in prevailing ideological and political convictions.' 'Barmen' marked the beginning of organized opposition by the *Confessing Church to the Nazi government; however, its concern is ecclesiastical and theological, and is not yet sensitive to events leading in the direction of the *Holocaust.

Bar mitzvah (Heb., 'Son of the Commandment'). The ceremony and status of attaining religious adulthood in Judaism. According to Eleazar b. Simeon (2nd cent. CE), a father ceases to be responsible for the deeds of his son once the son reaches the age of 13. Traditionally the boy is called up to read the Torah *Scroll and the *haftarah in the *synagogue. This is followed by some sort of party, including a festive *kiddush. Girls are considered to have reached religious maturity at the age of 12, but except in *Progressive Judaism, this tends to be a fairly muted occasion. See BAT MITZVAH.

Ed. M. Paterson, *The Bar Mitzvah Book* (1975).

Barnabas, St. A Jew of Cyprus who became a member of the earliest Christian church at Jerusalem and was the companion of *Paul on his first missionary journey (Acts 4. 36, 9. 27, 13. 2, etc.). He parted from Paul to go to Cyprus (Acts 15), and among other traditions he is said to have been martyred there in 61 CE. According to *Tertullian and some modern scholars, he was the author of the letter to the Hebrews. Feast day, 11 June.

The *Letter of Barnabas* is an anonymous treatise seeking to attack Judaism by claiming the *Old Testament for Christians alone. The author explains the ritual laws as *allegories and finds various concealed prophecies of Christ. It may be dated *c.*70–100 CE.

Eng. tr. in *Early Christian Writings*.

Barth, Karl (1886–1968). Christian theologian, of dominating importance in 20th cent. Beginning his career at the end of the long 19th-cent. ascendancy of liberal and reductionist theology in Germany (e.g. *Feuerbach, *Schleiermacher, and *Strauss), epitomized for Barth in the figure of *Harnack, Barth entered his first and massive protest against this in his *Der Römerbrief* (1919). This introduced what came to be known as 'dialectical theology', or 'the theology of crisis' (Gk., *krisis*, 'judgement'). God cannot be found by humans as the conclusion of an argument, or as the experience at the end of a religious or mystical quest. God, rather, speaks his Word through the words of 'the strange new world of the Bible'. God takes the initiative in seeking that which is lost, finally coming to humanity in *Jesus Christ, the Word made flesh. There is an infinite, qualitative difference between the Creator and his creatures, and only God can re-establish such relationship as is possible, now that the intended relationship of the creation order has been disrupted by sin. Revelation is thus an 'event', and the Church is (or should be) utterly dependent on it.

From 1921 to 1935, Barth was Professor of Theology at Göttingen, Münster, and then Bonn. His resistance to the rise of the Nazis led to his expulsion to Switzerland, where he became Professor at Basle. Although he published many works, his major commitment was to the many-volumed *Church Dogmatics*. The first volume appeared in 1932; 13 volumes later, it was unfinished at his death. He increasingly stressed the human vocation to co-operate with the initiatives of God in creation, and saw a place for human wisdom and knowledge as a prolegomenon to the acknowledgement of the sovereignty of God. In a much-quoted remark, he observed, 'Whether the *angels play only Bach when praising God, I am not quite sure. I am sure, however, that *en famille* they play Mozart.'

G. W. Bromiley, *Introduction to the Theology of Karl Barth* (1979); C. Brown, *Karl Barth and the Christian Message* (1967); E. Busch, *Karl Barth: His Life* . . . (1976); G. Hunsinger, *How to Read Karl Barth* (1991). E. Jungel, *Karl Barth* (1982, 1986).

Bartholomew, St. One of the twelve *apostles (Mark 3. 18). The name means only 'Son of Tolmai' and he is sometimes identified with Nathanael (John 1. 45–51). He is traditionally said to have been flayed alive at Albanopolis in Armenia. Feast day in W., 24 Aug.; in E., 11 June.

Baruch. Scribe and companion of the *prophet *Jeremiah. He wrote the prophet's words at his dictation and read them before the community and the court (Jeremiah 36). He kept the deeds of a field which Jeremiah had bought and he accompanied him into exile in Egypt. In the *aggadah, he was perceived as a priest as well as a prophet and was the teacher of *Ezra. In *apocryphal literature, several books are attributed to him, and further fragments of such books have been found among the *Dead Sea Scrolls.

The Book of Baruch (*1 Baruch*) is one of the additions to the book of Jeremiah in the *Septuagint. It is a collection of short partly liturgical pieces set against the fall of Jerusalem in 587 BCE, supplied with an introduction professedly by Baruch (1. 1.–14). It is however usually dated to post-*Maccabean times, and some have suggested it was either written or adapted for use in the cycle of Sabbaths commemorating national disasters which began to be observed after 70 CE.

2 Baruch (Syriac *Apocalypse of Baruch*) describes the Babylonian capture of Jerusalem. Originally written in Greek or Hebrew, it survives in only one manuscript in Syriac. It is usually supposed to have been written in the period 70–135 CE to encourage Jews after the destruction of the second *Temple.

3 Baruch (Greek *Apocalypse of Baruch*) describes Baruch's vision of the seven heavens. It is apparently of Jewish origin but worked over by a Christian hand. It may date from the 2nd cent. CE.

The *Rest of the Words of Baruch* (*4 Baruch* or *Paralipomena Jeremiae*) is a legendary account of Jeremiah's return from exile and his death. It is also probably a Greek work of the 2nd cent. CE, originally Jewish but with Christian additions.

Barukh Shem (Heb., 'Blessed be his name'). The beginning of an ancient Jewish doxology probably based on Nehemiah 9. 5, 'Bless the Lord your God from everlasting to everlasting. Blessed be your glorious name which is exalted above . . .'. It is regularly used after the first verse of the *Shema', and in the *Orthodox tradition, it is pronounced in a whisper.

Barzakh (Arab., 'an obstacle', 'separation', 'hindrance', or 'barrier'. The word is found three times in the Qur'ān (23. 100, 25. 53, 55. 20), and is understood differently by commentators, with moral, physical, and metaphysical interpretations. In 23. 100 it is the barrier preventing unbelievers, after death, from returning to the earth to accomplish the good they have left undone. The physical sense is that of a barrier between hell and paradise; and of the grave, which lies between this life and the next. The Qur'ān also mentions two seas (one fresh, the other salt) between which there is a barzakh which prevents them being mixed. The *Sūfīs add a metaphysical interpretation of barzakh in their ontology, in the sense of space between the physical world (*'alam-al-jism*), the angelic world (*'alam-al-malakūt*), and the world of Power and Dominion (*'alam-al-jabarūt*). A mystic who spans the abyss between divine and human knowledge may also be called a barzakh.

Basava or Basavaṇṇa (*c.*1106–67/8). A Hindu religious reformer, associated with the founding of the *Liṅgāyata, also known as Vīraśaivism. He was a devotee of *Śiva from an early age, but he soon found *caste and ritual impeding progress: 'Love of Śiva cannot live with ritual.' He left his home and wandered until he came to Kappaḍisaṅgama, where three rivers meet. He became a devotee of the Lord of the Meeting Rivers, Kūḍalasaṅgamadēva, to whom reference is made in almost all his poems. After study of the *Vedas under a *guru, he began to worship with his own chosen *liṅga, *iṣṭaliṅga*, later to become characteristic of the Liṅgāyats. He returned to life in the world and became a minister in the court of Bijjala, becoming 'not only the king's treasurer, but the treasurer of the Lord's love'. His egalitarian community of followers grew rapidly, evoking the opposition of traditionalists. Basava espoused non-violence, but when he could not control his followers, he returned to Kappaḍisaṅgama, where he died. His most practical and characteristic teaching aimed to re-establish the body as the true temple, a theme which he often expressed in poems of the vacana style—*vacana* ('that which is said') being a religious lyric in Kannada free verse:

> The rich
> Will make temples for Śiva:
> What shall I,
> A poor man,
> Do? My legs are pillars,
> The body is the shrine,
> The head Is the cupola,
> Of gold.
> Listen, O Lord of the meeting rivers,
> Things standing shall fall,
> But the moving shall ever stay.

P. B. Desai, *Basaveśvara and His Times* (1968); S. C. Nandimath, *A Handbook of Vīraśaivism* (1942); A. K. Ramanujan, *Speaking of Śiva* (1973).

Base Communities: see LIBERATION THEOLOGY.

Bashō (Matsuo Bashō, Japanese poet): see HAIKU.

Basil, St, 'the Great' (*c.*330–79). One of the three *Cappadocian fathers, and the first of the three Holy Hierarchs of the E. Church. After a good education he became a monk, and, after a tour in Syria and Egypt, a hermit. He returned, *c.*364, to assist the bishop of Caesarea (in Cappadocia) in the fight against the *Arian emperor Valens, and in 370 succeeded to the see. Besides his eloquence and personal holiness, Basil was known for his talent for administration. His two monastic rules (see below) determined the structure of E. Christian monasticism ever since. He built hospitals and hostels alongside church buildings in Caesarea, and organized relief for the poor. His writings, in addition to letters, are a treatise *On the Holy Spirit*, three anti-Arian books *Against Eunomius*, and homilies. Feast day in W., 2 Jan.; in the E., 1 Jan.

The *Rule of Basil* has two forms, each set out as a series of questions and answers about the monastic life. Stopping well short of the extreme deprivations of the desert hermits, it prescribed liturgical prayer at fixed hours, manual work, poverty and chastity, community life, care for the poor, and the education of children. The present form of the rule is a revision by *Theodore of Studios (d. 826).

The Liturgy of Basil is used in the E. Church in place of that of *Chrysostom on a few fixed days (e.g. the Sundays in *Lent) each year. It may go back to Basil but has been continually modified at least since the 9th cent. and probably before.

Trs. B. Jackson, W. K. L. Clarke, R. J. Deferrari, M. Wagner, A. C. Way; P. J. Fedwick (ed.), *Basil of Caesarea* (1981).

Basilica of Notre Dame de Paix. A vast church built at Yamoussoukro in the Ivory Coast, at the instigation of President Felix Houphouet-Boigny. It is 17 metres taller than St Peter's in Rome, and its dome is about three times the size of St Paul's in London. It holds 7,000 people seated and 11,000 standing. Although much of it is imitative and perhaps not well designed to withstand the African climate, visitors are usually impressed by the quality and consequence of the stained glass in creating atmosphere.

Basilides (2nd cent. CE). An Alexandrian Christian theologian who inclined to *gnosticism. According to *Hippolytus he taught that under the supreme God were various good world-rulers, including the God of the Jews. *Jesus was endowed with a heavenly light to summon the elect, who will ascend to the highest heaven. His followers formed a separate sect, but his own views are uncertain, being reported by opponents.

Basketmakers Church: see AFRICAN APOSTLES.

Basle, Council of (1431–49). The council which inherited the problems of the council of *Constance, convened by Martin V and dissolved by his successor, Eugenius IV, later in the year. It refused to be dissolved and reaffirmed the decrees of Constance on the superiority of a general *council over the *pope. Under pressure, the pope recognized the council in 1433. In 1437 it settled the *Hussite question against the papal view, by conceding *communion in both kinds to the Bohemians; but in the same year the break with the *Orthodox occurred, when they and the papal party moved to Ferrara (see FLORENCE, COUNCIL OF). The continuing council of Basle deposed the pope and elected the *antipope, Felix V, in 1439. After his abdication, the council submitted to the pope in 1449.

Basmala (Arab.). The saying of *Bismi'llah*, 'in the Name of *Allāh', invoking a blessing upon every action and undertaking of a Muslim. The full form is *bismillāhi (ar-)raḥmāni (ar-)raḥīm*, 'in the Name of Allah the merciful the compassionate', and it precedes every *sūra of the *Qur'ān except the ninth (see FĀTIḤA). The basmala can be used in lawful 'magic'. In *Sūfī teaching the letters of the basmala have a mystic significance. It is said that the basmala was inscribed on *Adam's thigh, *Jibrīl's wing, *Solomon's seal, and the tongue of ʿIsā (*Jesus). It is much used in architectural and manuscript ornamentation. Cf. also ḤAMDALA, the saying of *al-ḥamdu li 'illāh*, 'praise belongs to Allāh', which precedes the writing of any formal document.

Baso Dōitsu (leader of Ch'an/Zen school): see MA-TSU TAO-I.

Bassevi, Joseph (prominent Jew allied to ruler in Prague): see COURT JEWS.

Bassui Zenji (Tokushō) (1327–87). Jap. Zen teacher of the *Rinzai school. When he was 7, his father died, and this prompted him into *dai-gidan, probing questions based on doubt which form one of the three foundation pillars of *zazen, especially after *Hakuin. This led to a number of enlightenment experiences, and to monastic ordination, though he did not enter a monastery, because of monastic ritual and comfort. He was then instructed by Kohō Zenji and received the mark of recognition (*inka-shōmei), but resisted those who sought to make him a master of instruction. He eventually consented to become abbot of a monastery, and died sitting in the lotus position (see PADMĀSANA), saying, 'Do not be deceived: Look closely: what is this?' His letters and some of his *dharma instruction have been preserved: see P. Kapleau, *The Three Pillars of Zen* (1980). The single thread to his teaching is that when we wake from the dream of ignorance, we find that we always were where we wished to be: 'If you are dreaming that you are lost and cannot find the way home, and you pray to God or to the

Buddha and you are still lost, wake up from your dream and you will find yourself in your original place.'

Bast (Arab., 'expand', cf. Qur'ān 2. 245). In *Sūfī Islam, a technical term describing a state of exalted joy: 'The fear of God contracts me, the hope for him expands me . . . When he expands me through hope, he restores me to myself' (*al-Junaid). It is a state contrasted with *qabd (cf. MASHHAD). According to ibn 'Ata'illah, 'God gives you bast so as not to leave you in qabd, and he gives qabd so as not to leave you in bast, and he leads you on from both, so that you may belong only to himself.'

Bāṭinīy(y)a (Arab., *batana*, 'conceal'). Name for several Muslim sects, characterized by their seeking the inner, or secret, or esoteric meaning of the *Qur'ān. Bāṭinī is any doctrine which is esoteric or secret, and the term may, therefore, be used as a term of abuse—since the Qur'ān is 'an open book'. See e.g. ISMĀ'ĪLĪ, SEVENERS. More precisely, the Bāṭinīy(y)a may refer to a movement derived from one who refused to reveal his identity, and who appeared in Kufa, in 891 (AH 278), fasting by day and worshipping by night, and inviting conversion to the Ismā'īlīs. He appointed twelve guides or authorities (*naqib*), set out on a journey to Damascus, and disappeared. His place was taken by Aḥmad the Qarmite, who instituted new teachings and practices (e.g. two daily prayers, not five, the permissibility of wine, no ablutions after sexual intercourse): see further QARMATIANS.

Bat Kol or **Qol** (Heb., 'daughter of a voice). A divine voice which reveals God's will. According to the *rabbis, it was frequently heard during the biblical period, such as before the death of *Moses, and to rebuke *Solomon in his emulation of Moses. After the cessation of *prophecy, it became the only direct means of communication between God and human beings and occurred at the death of martyrs and occasionally in dreams.

Bat mitzvah (Heb., 'daughter of the commandment'). The status for a girl of attaining religious adulthood (cf. BAR MITZVAH for a boy). No ceremonies are laid down in the law, but from the mid-19th cent., apparently at the initiative of Jacob Ettlinger, chief rabbi of Altona, a ceremony was devised, though not as part of the *synagogue service. Mordecai *Kaplan extended the ceremony to the synagogue service, where it is located in *Reform synagogues: a liturgy is contained in the Reform *New Union Prayer Book* (1975); the ceremonies are more elaborate in *Progressive Judaism.

Batuque: see AFRO-BRAZILIAN CULTS.

Baugs (places for worship): see PARSIS.

Bāul (Bengali, 'mad'). In India a kind of minstrel, mystic, and/or adept in esoteric practice, as well as a category of 'folk-song' composed and sung by such people. Those called 'Bāul' belong to the Bengali-speaking region of S. Asia: W. Bengal (India) and Bangladesh.

Since the end of the 19th cent., Bāuls have become increasingly important to urbanized, upper-class Bengalis in search of their roots. Previously ignored or despised as low-class entertainers of the common folk, they came to be seen as the bearers of a glorious indigenous heritage, be it Hindu, *Sūfī, (secular) Indian, or Bengali. The expectations of non-Bāul patrons of 'folk' music and indigenous spirituality have fostered a variety of cultural phenomena: notably a class of high-profile, semi-professional Bāul performers, who may be contrasted with (less visible) initiates into esoteric practice, also called 'Bāul'. An important practice is the singing of devotional songs to a one-stringed instrument (*ek-tara*).

'Bāuls' are to be found among both Hindus and Muslims, and some Bāul lineages recruit from both these communities. The overt influence of Sūfīs is most discernible among Bāuls of Muslim origin (also called 'Fakir'), while that of Bengali Vaiṣṇavism (especially of the *Sahajīyā cult) tends to predominate among those of Hindu origin. The ancestry of Bāuls is often traced back to Buddhist *Tantra by scholars, who also connect them with a variety of other traditions, mainly Vaiṣṇava and Sūfī, but also with *Yoga, Hindu *Tantra, the *Lokāyata ('Materialist' school), and the Sant movement of northern India.

One meaning of the word 'bāul' is 'mad', and Bāuls are associated with madness in part through their liminal status. Their challenge to and partial transcendence of conventional structures and boundaries has caused them to be both extolled and vilified. They not only tend to blur distinctions between Hindu and Muslim, but between the various *castes (they recruit from all) and, to some extent, between male and female. They may technically be householders or renouncers of householder life, or their status may be ambiguous. They share a common belief that God is located within a person in the heart, known as 'the caged bird', or as 'the Man of my heart' (*moner mānush*), who can only be found by following 'the contrary path' (*ulṭa *sādhana*), which leads away from the world. Thus conventional religiosity is usually rejected by Bāuls, who represent an eclectic and fluctuating tradition of reinterpretation, criticism, and outright rejection of orthodoxies and orthopraxies of various kinds, Muslim and Hindu. For example, rather than worship images of deities (a practice associated with Hindus) or the transcendent god of orthodox Islam, they tend to divinize human beings and the human body. Although the *guru may play a fundamental role, importance is generally placed on one's own experience, rather than on external sources of authority, such as *Veda or *Qur'ān, temple or mosque, priest or mullah: 'What need do we have of temples when our bodies are temples where the Spirit abides?' They often wear tattered clothes, indicating a rejection of worldly values.

Most of their practices are esoteric (often classified as Tāntric) and are centred on the human body, almost invariably in conjunction with a partner of the opposite sex. Particular emphasis is placed on the generative male and female fluids, and other substances emerging from the body. While they often accept the esoteric anatomy of *cakras and *nāḍīs, experienced through *Kuṇḍalinī yoga, they are more devotionally inclined than other Tantric traditions.

D. Bhattacharya, *Songs of the Bards of Bengal* (1969); Upendranāth Bhaṭṭācārya, *Bāṅlār bāul o bāul gān* (1981); S. B. Dasgupta, *Obscure Religious Cults* (1969).

Baur, Ferdinand Christian (1792–1860). German Protestant theologian, who was Professor of Theology at Tübingen from 1826 to his death, and founded the *'Tübingen school'. Influenced by F. D. E. *Schleiermacher and by G. W. F. *Hegel's understanding of history, he saw conflict and synthesis as the key to understanding early Christianity. So, e.g. in his controversial work on Paul (1845; Eng. tr. 1873–5), he held that only the letters reflecting his life-long opposition to the older disciples (viz., Galatians, 1–2 Corinthians, Romans) were authentic. He applied similar historical criticism to the development of Christian doctrines, especially the *atonement, *Trinity, and *incarnation.

W. Geiger, *Spekulation und Kritik* . . . (1964); H. Harris, *The Tübingen School* (1975); P. C. Hodgson, *The Formation of Historical Theology* . . . (1966).

Baxter, Richard (1615–91). *Puritan writer and theologian. Shropshire born and largely self-educated, Baxter was influenced by two *Nonconformist preachers, Joseph Symons and Walter Craddock. Ordained *deacon in 1638 by the bishop of Worcester, he served as curate at Kidderminster with outstanding success as teacher and pastor. For a short period in the Civil War he worked with the parliamentary soldiers, but he became increasingly estranged from Cromwell. At the Restoration he refused the bishopric of Hereford, taking his place with other ejected Nonconformists. In the persecution period he was 'forced 5 or 6 years . . . to practice Physick', spent some time in prison and, 'but a pen in God's hand', gave himself to extensive writing ('I was but a Pen, and what praise is due to a pen?'). His total literary output of 141 books and pamphlets includes such outstanding works as *The Saints' Everlasting Rest* (1650) and *Gildas Salvianus: The Reformed Pastor* (1656). His lengthy autobiography, *Reliquiae Baxterianae*, was edited by Matthew Sylvester and published posthumously in 1696. Some of his hymns are still in use (e.g. 'Ye holy *angels bright').

G. F. Nuttall, *Richard Baxter* (1962). F. J. Powicke, *A Life* (1924).

Bay 'at (pact among Sūfīs): see INITIATION.

Bayram. In Turkey denotes *ʿīd, feast: as in kurban bayramı or büyük bayram for *ʿīd al-aḍḥā (the feast of sacrifice, also known in Arab. as *ʿīd al-qurbān*); and in şeker bayramı or küçük bayram for *ʿīd al-fiṭr, feast of breaking of the fast at the end of *Ramaḍān.

Bayudaya (Luganda, 'the Jews'). An African community in E. Uganda, officially known as 'The Propagation of Judaism in Uganda—Moses Synagogue'. The founder, Semei Kakungulu (?1850s–1928), was an outstanding Ganda political and military leader who became a *Protestant in the 1880s, but when disappointed in not being made Kabaka ('king'), he turned to religion and joined the semi-Christian, anti-medicine Bamalaki movement which had Judaic features. After deep study he took the *Old Testament literally and left in 1919 to form his own Bayudaya movement which insisted on *circumcision, the biblical festivals, and ritual slaughter. Between 1923 and 1937 he met several foreign Jews who instructed him more fully; he then shed the remaining Christian elements such as the *New Testament, *baptism, *Sunday observance, and recognition of *Jesus Christ. The movement declined to about 300 in 1961 through intermarriage, reversions to Christianity, and the influence of Christian schools. Since then, some contacts with world Jewry have provided limited assistance, prompted the acceptance of medicines, and encouraged an increase to about 1,000 in the 1970s.

BCP: see BOOK OF COMMON PRAYER.

Bdud-joms Rin-po-che or **Dudjom Rinpoche** (1904–87). Head of the *Nyingma order of Tibetan Buddhism. When 3 years old, he was recognized as the reappearance of the 'treasure-finder', Bdud-joms gling-pa (1835–1903). He was educated at many of the major centres in Tibet, becoming a prolific author and poet. As a refugee in 1959, he settled first in Darjeeling and in Nepal, but then increasingly in the USA, and Europe, where he established Nyingma centres. He was thus a major figure in securing the Tibetan *diaspora.

Dudjom Rinpoche, *The Nyingma School of Tibetan Buddhism* (1990).

Beard: see HAIR.

Beas (river providing name of religious movement): see RĀDHĀSOĀMĪ SATSAṄG.

Beatification. In the *Roman Catholic Church, the penultimate stage in the process which leads to the *canonization of a *saint. After this stage, the *pope allows the local veneration of the person in question. If there is evidence of two miracles then the canonization can proceed. A person who has been beatified receives the title of 'Blessed'. In the Russian Church there is a similar process for authorizing the local cult of deceased Christians.

Beatific vision. The vision of God granted to the redeemed in *heaven. The term is used mainly in Catholic theology where it was the subject of much debate in the later Middle Ages. Benedict XII (1336) defined that the blessed in heaven 'see the Divine Essence by an intuitive vision and face to face, so that the Divine Essence is known immediately, showing itself plainly, clearly and openly, and not mediately through any creature'. According to Thomas *Aquinas, the beatific vision was granted briefly to *Moses and *Paul in this life. In Islam, the vision of God is the culminating experience of the rewarded in heaven, though the impossibility of seeing God directly is usually defended by affirming that a general manifestation of God is interpreted in the forms of habitual devotion.

Beatitudes. Promises of blessing, and specifically the sequence of eight or nine sentences beginning 'Blessed are the poor in spirit' in *Jesus' *Sermon on the Mount (Matthew 5. 3–11). The version in Luke's 'sermon on the plain' (6. 20–2) is shorter with more marked contrast of present and future.

Beautiful Names of God (in Islam): see NINETY-NINE BEAUTIFUL NAMES OF GOD.

Becket, Thomas à, St (*c*.1117–70). *Archbishop of *Canterbury and *martyr. He was born in London, educated at Merton Priory, Paris, and, possibly, Bologna. He entered the service of Archbishop Theobald, and subsequently became *archdeacon of Canterbury. A friend of Henry II, who appointed him chancellor in 1154 and, despite his protestations, archbishop of Canterbury in 1162. Thomas almost immediately came into conflict with the king over Henry's claim to judge 'criminous clerks', and, receiving little or no support from the other English *bishops, he had to flee abroad in 1164. An apparent reconciliation was achieved in 1170, but in a fit of temper Henry expressed the wish to be rid of the archbishop (according to tradition, 'Will no one revenge me of the injuries I have sustained from one turbulent priest?'), and four of his knights took him at his word: they murdered Thomas in Canterbury Cathedral on 29 Dec. Whether Thomas' interpretation of the necessary powers of the Church was innovative or simply ill-advised is a matter of continuing debate. His successors, notably Hubert Walter, managed to reach an accommodation with their kings on this matter, which clearly eluded Becket. He was canonized three years after his death (feast day, 29 Dec.), and his tomb rapidly became a centre of pilgrimage. When it was razed by Henry VIII in 1538, it was reported to have yielded many cartloads of jewels and precious metals, and by royal proclamation it was ordered that Becket 'shall not be . . . reported, nor called, a saint, but Bishop Becket'. His life has evoked powerful dramatic interpretations, especially by Anouilh and *Eliot (*Murder in the Cathedral*).

F. Barlow, *Thomas Becket* (1986).

Bede, St, 'the Venerable' (*c*.673–735). English scholar. He spent his life as a monk at Jarrow in Northumbria. His most important work is the *Ecclesiastical History of the English People*, a main source for early English history, and also for an understanding of spiritual life at the time, focused on death and judgement. He is said to have repeated on his deathbed an Old English poem:

> Before the journey that awaits us all,
> No man becomes so wise that he has not
> Need to think out, before his going hence
> What judgement will be given to his soul
> After his death, of evil or of good.

He also wrote commentaries on much of the Latin Bible. In the 11th cent., his bones were moved to Durham cathedral. In 1899 he was made a *Doctor of the Church. Feast day, 27 May.

P. H. Blair, *The World of Bede* (1970); A. H. Thompson, *Bede* (1935).

Bedikat ḥamez (search for leaven): see LEAVEN.

Bedwardites. Followers of Alexander Bedward (1859–1930), a prophet-healer at August Town, Kingston, Jamaica. He was successor to an American Negro, Woods, founder of the Jamaica *Baptist Free Church in 1891, who had appointed his convert Bedward as *bishop with the title 'Shepherd'. Shepherd Bedward emphasized prayer, fasting, baptism by the *Holy Spirit, prophecy, and healing through water from the Mona River. In 1920 he proclaimed he was now the Christ, Bedwardism would rule the earth, and the whites would be destroyed. In 1921 the Bedwardites marched on Kingston but were dispersed, and he was committed to a mental asylum where he died. A remnant worshipped into the 1970s beside the ruins of a fine stone church destroyed in a hurricane.

Beelzebub. A name equivalent to *Satan found in the gospels (Mark 3. 22–6 and par.). The Gk. text is *Beelzeboul*, which may correspond to Heb. *Baal-zebel*, 'lord of filth'. The English form -bub is due to the influence of Baal-zebub ('lord of flies') in 2 Kings 1. 2.

Beghards (lay Christian movements): see RHENO-FLEMISH SPIRITUALITY.

Beguines (lay Christian movements): see RHENO-FLEMISH SPIRITUALITY.

Behemoth. A monster described in the book of Job. In Job 40. 15–24, 'he eats grass like an ox . . . his bones are tubes of bronze, his limbs like bars of iron'. Initially he may have been an existing animal (the hippopotamus has been suggested) like the *leviathan, but in later literature, he became a mythical beast. At the end of time, he will be served at the banquet of the righteous (*Targ.Yer.*, Numbers 9. 6).

Behrends, L. (prominent Jewish administrator/banker): see COURT JEWS.

Beijing. Capital of China for most of the last seven centuries under Yüan, Ming, Ch'ing dynasties, and currently under the People's Republic. Built according to ancient cosmic principles, it was oriented to the four directions, bisected by a North-South axial way, and modelled on the capital city of the God (*Shang Ti) in the Heavens. The latter was conceived as located in a group of stars which included the Pole Star and was called the Purple Forbidden Enclosure. From his throne there, Shang Ti faced south and ruled the universe. Beijing's palace city was modelled on this Heavenly archetype and called the Purple Forbidden City. From there the emperor ruled the world as vice-gerent of Heaven. Religiously, the most important monuments of the capital were the *Altar of Heaven to the south of the city, the *Altar of Earth to the north, the Imperial Ancestral Temple and the Altar to Land and Grain, and the *T'ai Ho Tien* or Imperial Hall of Audience, where the emperor sat on his 'dragon throne' and symbolically ruled the entire world facing south. Less important (but part of the city's cosmic symmetry) were the altars of the Sun and Moon, to the east and west, and the Altar of Agriculture where the emperor performed a ritual ploughing ceremony every spring.

Being-itself: see TILLICH, PAUL.

Beit (house of, as in Beit-Hillel): see BET.

Bektāshīy(y)a. Turkish Derwish order, originating in about the 12th cent. CE, of a particularly eclectic kind. The traditional founder was Hajji Bektash Vali, but very little is known of him. He is said to have come from Khurasān, where his father was ruler, and to have been already dead by the end of the 13th cent.; but even that is doubtful. They are *Shi'ite in so far as they acknowledge the Twelve Imāms, but different from other Muslims in disregarding such obligations as *ṣalāt, and in allowing *women to take part in rituals without the veil. They borrowed, probably from Christianity, forms of initiation, and confession and absolution. In Turkey, the movement was dissolved in 1925. See also ḤURŪFĪ.

J. K. Birge, *The Bektashi Order of Dervishes* (1937; 1994).

Bel and the Dragon. Two stories which appear together in the *Apocrypha, and at the end of *Daniel in *Roman Catholic Bibles. They are directed against idolatry. Bel was an idol who was supposed to consume food, but the prophet *Daniel exposed the cult as a fraud. The dragon was killed by Daniel, who was thrown into a den of lions, but miraculously survived. The book appears to have been written in Babylon in the 4th or 5th cent. BCE, and the Gk. version in the *Septuagint appears to have been translated from the *Aramaic.

Belial (Heb., 'worthlessness'). A description of people acting in a worthless manner and, in post-biblical literature, the name of the Prince of Evil. He is the Spirit of darkness; he opposes God's will; he dominates wicked people and the world is his kingdom. According to the **Testaments of the Twelve Patriarchs*, he will be chained by God's *Holy Spirit and he will ultimately be defeated by God's armies. Many scholars believe that the idea of Belial as God's opponent owes something to Persian dualism.

Bellarmine, Robert, St (1542–1621). Italian *Jesuit *cardinal and controversialist. He was born in Montepulciano, Tuscany, and entered the Society of Jesus at Rome in 1560. He was ordained priest in 1570 in Louvain—where he was the first Jesuit to hold a chair—but shortly afterwards returned to the Roman College, now the Gregorian University, to teach controversial theology to priests destined for England and Germany. His lectures provided the basis for his famous work, *De Controversiis* or *Controversies*, published at Ingolstadt between 1586 and 1593. The first volume of this was about to be placed on the *Index when the *pope died: Bellarmine's theory, that the popes enjoyed only indirect authority in temporal affairs, proved unacceptable to Sixtus V, and this held up his *canonization until 1930, though his cause had been introduced in 1627. He was made a cardinal in 1599, and briefly (1602–5) served as *archbishop of Capua. After his return to curial duties in Rome he engaged in debate with James I of England over the *divine right of kings, and with William Barclay over papal authority. In 1616 he was obliged to censure Galileo, although he had considerable sympathy for his views. In later life Bellarmine produced a number of popular devotional works. He was declared a *Doctor of the Church in 1931.

J. Brodrick, *The Life and Work* (1928).

Benamozegh, Elijah ben Abraham (1822–1900). Italian *rabbi and philosopher. Serving as rabbi in Leghorn, he produced numerous books and articles which attempted to reconcile traditional Judaism, including *Kabbalah, with the secular philosophy of his day: 'For me, *Torah is a reflection of the universe.' His most popular book was *Israël et l'humanité*. He argued that Israel uniquely combines ethics and national identity, thus exhibiting to the world, by its adherence to the law, the way in which righteousness is removed from abstraction to practicality: 'Humanity cannot discern the essential principles on which society must rest unless it meets with Israel. But Israel cannot plumb the depths of its own national and religious tradition unless it meets with humanity.'

Benares: see KĀŚI.

Ben Asher, Aaron ben Moses (called Abu Sa'id; early 10th cent. CE). Jewish biblical scholar. A contemporary of Saadiah *Gaon, he was well known as a masorete (see MASORAH). Although a *Karaite, his vocalization of the scriptures carried enormous prestige. *Maimonides referred to a biblical manuscript as one which 'all relied on since it was corrected by Ben Asher'. His *Sefer Dikdukei ha-Te'amim* (Book of the Decreed Grammar) laid the basics of Hebrew grammar.

Ben Asher, Jacob (author of Jewish law text): see CODIFICATIONS OF LAW.

Bene Berith (Jewish charitable organization): see B'NAI B'RITH.

Benedicite (Lat., 'bless ye'). The song of praise beginning 'O all ye works of the Lord, bless ye the Lord'. It forms part of the *Song of the Three Children. It has been used as a Christian *canticle from very early times. In the **Book of Common Prayer* it is an alternative to the *Te Deum at *mattins.

Benedict, St (*c*.480–*c*.550). Christian monastic leader. Little is known of his life. He withdrew from the world to live in a cave at Subiaco in *c*.500, where a community grew up around him. He moved with a small number of monks *c*.525 to Monte Cassino, where he remained and composed his Rule—although he does not seem to have intended to found an order. Feast day in W., 11 July; in E., 14 Mar.

The *Rule of St Benedict* is a fundamental rule of W. Christian monasticism. The opening chapters seem to have been based on the anonymous *Rule of the Master* (see S. Tugwell, *Ways of Imperfection*, 1984) emanating from a smaller monastery in SE Italy; *Basil, *Pachomius, and *Augustine were also influential. It consists of seventy-three terse chapters, dealing with both spiritual matters and questions of organization, liturgy, and discipline. Stability and obedience are paramount: 'Obedience is a blessing to be shown by all, not just to the abbot, but to one another, since we know that it is by the way of obedience that we go to God.' The Rule envisages a monastery under the direction of an elected abbot, in which all possessions are held in common. The central occupation (detailed since 'idleness is the enemy of the soul') is the divine *office (*opus dei*); this, with private prayer, reading, and work fills the day. The regime is simple but not strongly ascetical. Life is lived very much under the eye of God, the Judge who nevertheless (or thereby) protects the weak from tyranny.

The Rule was used in many communities, underlying attempts at greater obedience (e.g. *Cluny, *Carthusian, *Cistercian). Endeavours to unify the Benedictines in a single order (e.g. Fourth *Lateran Council, 1215) could not initially overcome a preference to found local congregations as a means to the reformation of life. From the mid-19th cent., the number of Benedictine communities has multiplied. Benedictine nuns (founded by Benedict and his sister, St Scholastica) live by the same Rule. See Index, Benedictine.

Latin text of the Rule with Eng. tr. by J. McCann (rev. 1966); P. Balsetier (ed.), *Saint Benedict* (1981); E. C. Butler, *Benedictine Monasticism* (1961); T. Kardong, *The Benedictines* (1988) and *Commentaries on Benedict's Rule* (1987); A. de Vogüé, *The Rule . . . A Doctrinal and Spiritual Commentary* (Eng. tr. 1983); A. Wathen, *Silence . . .* (1973).

Benedict XV (1854–1922). *Pope from 3 Sept. 1914. He was born Giacomo Della Chiesa and became the protégé of Cardinal Rampolla, whom he served in the papal nunciature (*nuncio) in Spain, and in the Secretariat of State, before being appointed archbishop of Bologna. His pontificate was dominated by the First World War: the first of Benedict's twelve *encyclicals dealt with peace, he was deeply distressed by the failure of his 1917 peace initiative, and he was forced to close his missing persons bureau after charges had been made that it was a centre for espionage. He speeded the publication of the first code of *canon law, worked for an understanding between the *Holy See and the kingdom of Italy, and fostered better relations between the *Roman Catholic Church and the churches of the East, establishing as part of the Gregorian University a Pontifical Oriental Institute.

Benedictines: see BENEDICT, ST; Index, Benedictine.

Benediction (with the Blessed Sacrament). Catholic eucharistic devotion. As a separate evening service, benediction is first found in the 15th cent. In the modern service in its most solemn form, the consecrated host is exposed to view in a *monstrance placed on or above the *altar; hymns are sung; the sacrament is incensed twice; and the priest blesses the congregation with it. In recent years, benediction has become less common, and has frequently given way to evening masses. See also REAL PRESENCE; EXPOSITION.

Benedictions. Formulas of blessing. Among Jews, according to the *Talmud, the formulation of benedictions goes back to the time of *Ezra. Although this is legend, blessings can be found in the *Bible, as when *David said to Abigail, 'Blessed be the Lord the God of *Israel, who sent you this day to me!' (1 Samuel 25. 32). The various benedictions seem to have originated in different communities; the blessings said in the *'amidah, for example, can be traced back to a variety of different sources. Blessings follow a certain formula: 'Barukh attah Adonai' ('Blessed are you, O Lord') and, at the start of a prayer, 'Eloheinu, melekh ha-'Olam' ('Our God, King of the universe'). Various *laws grew up concerning benedictions—*Rav, for instance, taught that every blessing must include the name of God. Before performing a particular *mitzvah it is necessary to use the formula *'asher kiddishanu b'mitzvotav v'itzivanu'* ('who has sanctified us with his commandments and commanded us . . .'). According to R. *Meir, every Jew has a duty to pronounce one hundred benedictions every day (*B. Men.* 43b). Special benedictions are grouped in three categories: (i) *birkhot ha-nehenim*, blessings for enjoyment (e.g. before and after meals, over fragrant odours); (ii) *birkhot ha-mitzvot*, blessings on performance of commandments; (iii) *birkhot hoda'ah*, blessings of gratitude (e.g. on witnessing natural phenomena, such as thunderstorms, rainbows, earthquakes, or on ritual occasions). Everything in life, whether it gives rise to sorrow or to joy, has its ultimate source in God.

Benedictus. Title of two Christian liturgical hymns. 1. The song of Zechariah at the birth of *John the Baptist (Luke 1. 68–79), sung in the daily *office (e.g. at Anglican *morning prayer). 2. The 'Benedictus qui Venit', forming the end of the *Sanctus at the *eucharist ('Blessed is he who comes in the name of the Lord').

Bene Israel (Heb. 'Sons of Israel'). Early Jews (of the biblical period), but more particularly a Jewish community in India. Indian Jews claim their community dates back to the days of the *Maccabees and survived in complete isolation. They clung to the practice of *circumcision, some *dietary *laws, the *Sabbath, and recited the *Shemaʿ. Various conjectures have been made about their origin, such as that they were descendants of refugees from Muslim persecution or offshoots of the Jewish communities of Yemen. They only made contact with the Jews of Cochin in the mid-18th cent. and from this contact, the Bene Israel gradually became integrated into mainstream Jewish life. By 1969, 12,000 had emigrated to *Israel, although the religious establishment initially raised questions of personal status and legitimacy: in 1964, the Chief Rabbinate declared them 'full Jews in every respect'.

Ben'en; also **Enni Ben'en** (also known as Shoichi Kokushi; 1202–80). Japanese *Zen master of the *Rinzai Yogi school. When 8 years old, he began to study in the *Tendai and *Shingon schools, and in 1235 visited China. He was instructed by Wu-chun Shih-fan (Jap., Bushun Shiban), and received the mark of recognition (*inka-shōmei). He returned to Japan in 1242 and became abbot of the Tōfuku-ji (monastery) in Kyōto. Enni was thus a man of wide education, but while he was prepared to take part in Tendai and Shingon rituals, he believed that Zen was the true way to the goal. In *Jisshūyōdōki* (Essentials of the Way of the Ten Schools), he claimed that Zen was not simply 'a school among schools', but that it was the 'bowl which carries the Buddha mind' through history: 'Zen is the Buddha mind. The precepts (*śīla) are its outward means; the teachings are its explanatory means; the invocation (*nembutsu) is its effective means (*upāya-kauśalya). These three proceed from the Buddha mind, and this way is thus the foundation.'

Ben Gurion, David (1886–1973). First prime minister of *Israel. On 14 May 1948, he proclaimed the birth of the independent state of Israel, serving as minister of defence and prime minister. His intention was that 'there will not simply be peace between us and the Arabs, but friendship and cooperation'. Tactically he pursued this aim, though in practice force was frequently necessary. His own faith he summarized as, 'We have preserved the Book, and the Book has preserved us.'

Ben ha-matserim (between the disasters commemorated by Jews on 17 Tammuz and 9 Av): see THREE WEEKS.

Benjamin. Youngest son of the patriarch *Jacob, full brother to *Joseph and forefather of the tribe of Benjamin. According to the *Genesis narrative, Joseph used Benjamin's special relationship with his father to test his half-brothers' integrity (see Genesis 42–5). The territory of the tribe was in the south and eminent Benjamites include the judge Ehud (Judges 3) and the first king, Saul (1 Samuel 9). According to the *aggadah, Benjamin was the only brother not to participate in the selling of Joseph, with the result that he had the privilege of having the *Temple built on his territory (*Gen.R.* 99. 1).

Bensh (Yid., 'Bless'). Jewish expression used for making a *blessing. A bensh can refer to grace after meals, blessing a child, or other *benedictions.

Ben Sira, Wisdom of (also called *Ecclesiasticus*, the Church (book), and *Sirach*, the Gk. for Sira). Book of the *Apocrypha. It was probably composed in the 2nd cent. BCE. It is divided into eight sections and includes maxims, psalms, and eulogies on the great figures of the Hebrew scriptures. It directs humanity to the ways of wisdom, virtue, and moderation, and emphasizes the importance of well-ordered family life. It was much quoted in *Talmudic literature and is the source of several customs (such as pronouncing a *benediction when seeing a rainbow) which subsequently became part of the *halakhah. It includes the passage which begins, 'Let us now praise famous men, and our fathers that begat us.' No Hebrew text was known until 1896, when a part was found in the *Cairo Genizah; since then much of the original has been recovered.

Ben sorer u-moreh (Jewish Commandment): see REBELLIOUS SON.

Beraitot (paragraphs): see TOSEFTA; BARAITA.

Berakhot (Heb., 'benedictions'). The first tractate of the *Talmud. The tractate discusses prayers and *blessings, including the laws involved in the recital of the *Shemaʿ, the *ʿAmidah and the various *benedictions. The *gemāra of the Babylonian *Talmud enlarges on the *halakhah of the *Mishnah and adds considerable *aggadic commentary. The tractate is placed at the beginning of the order *Zera'im (seeds) and there is much scholarly discussion as to why this tractate should be so positioned when it has nothing to do with agriculture.

Berdyaev, Nicolas (1874–1948). Russian philosopher. Originally a sceptic with Marxist sympathies, he embraced *Orthodoxy after the revolution of 1905, and from 1922 lived as an *émigré* in Paris, warning against the false optimism of Marxist socialism, which takes no account of the realities of human nature: 'Socialism is no longer a Utopia or a dream: it is an objective threat, and a warning to Christians to show them unmistakeably that they have not fulfilled the law of Christ.' His religious philosophy was deeply influenced by *Dostoevsky and also *Boehme, whom he saw as a formative influence on German Idealism. Human freedom is seen as ambiguous, a tragic burden, and redemption exploits the polarity of man and woman—woman's weakness, receptivity, and innocence being the source of the apprehension of redemption. There is thus a *gnostic tinge to his philosophy, which attracted the suspicion of the Orthodox hierarchy.

O. F. Clarke, *Introduction to Berdyaev* (1950); M. Spinka, *Nicolas Berdyaev* (1950).

Bereshit (Heb., 'in the beginning'): see GENESIS.

Berit (Heb., 'covenant'): see COVENANT.

Berkowits, E. (Jewish writer): see HOLOCAUST (3).

Berlin, Naphtali Zevi Judah (known as ha-Neziv, 1817–93). Jewish *Talmudic scholar. From 1854, he was head of the *yeshivah at Volozhin which became the spiritual centre of Russian Jewry. He resisted the attempts of the maskilim (i.e. proponents of the *Haskalah) to introduce secular studies and concentrated on the teaching of the *Torah and the Babylonian *Talmud. At the same time he rejected any form of *Orthodox separatism, declaring 'such advice is as painful as a dagger in the body of a nation', since all Jews are commanded to form 'one union'. Ultimately he was exiled by the Russian authorities and the yeshivah was closed.

His son, Meir Berlin (Bar-Ilan), 1880–1949, was prominent in religious Zionism, and became a leader in the *Mizraḥi movement, first in Berlin, then (1915–26) in the USA. From 1926 he settled in Palestine, where he was involved in initiating the Talmud Encyclopedia. The Orthodox university, Bar-Ilan, was established in 1955 to honour his memory.

Bernadette, St (1844–79). Bernadette Soubirous was born into a humble family at *Lourdes, where, at the Massabielle Rock, she received eighteen apparitions of the Virgin *Mary between 11 Feb. and 16 July 1858. 'The lady' Bernadette saw caused a spring of water to appear, and commanded that a chapel be built; at last she identified herself as the *Immaculate Conception. Initially harassed, not least by publicity, she joined and remained with the sisters of Notre Dame at Nevers. She was beatified in 1925 and canonized in 1933. The importance of Lourdes as a place of pilgrimage, and its association with healing, has made her among the most popular modern *saints.

Bernard of Clairvaux, St (1090–1153). Christian monastic reformer and mystical writer. He joined the *Cistercian monastery at Citeaux in *c.*1111, and established at Clairvaux in 1115 a daughter house in which he insisted on rigorous observance and discipline. He combined an emphasis on the love and mercy of God with vehement controversy on this earth. He was officially charged with preaching the Second *Crusade, whose failure he felt deeply. Several Latin hymns are ascribed to him, among them being (in translation), 'Jesu, the very thought of thee | With sweetness fills my breast', and 'O Sacred Head now wounded'. He was canonized in 1174 and proclaimed *Doctor of the Church in 1830.

Bernard's understanding of spiritual life is *affective, dominated by the way in which the human freedom to consent is met by God's *grace so that the consequence of love flows forth. The God who is longed for and loved is the God who longs for and loves: Christ is the bridegroom and the Holy Spirit is his kiss. Therefore, 'the reason for loving God is God himself'. In contrast to *Anselm's *fides quaerens intellectum*, Bernard wrote of *anima quaerens Verbum* (the soul seeking the Word). Feast day, 20 Aug.

G. Evans, *The Mind of Saint Bernard* . . . (1983); B. Scott-James, *Saint Bernard of Clairvaux* (1957).

Bertinoro, Obadiah ben Abraham Yare (*c.*1450–*c.*1516). Italian Jewish commentator on the *Mishnah. In 1488–90, he travelled through Italy to Egypt, via Rhodes, and on to the land of Israel where he became leader of the *Jerusalem community. Of Jerusalem, he observed: 'The wind blows in all directions in Jerusalem—because all winds come first to Jerusalem before going elsewhere, so that they can prostrate themselves before the Lord.' His commentary on the Mishnah became the standard work, comparable to *Rashi's commentary on the *Talmud and drawing heavily on it. His acronym is Ra'av (Rabbenu Ovadyah mi-Bartenura).

Beruryah (2nd cent. CE). Jewish woman scholar of the *Talmud. The wife of R. *Meir, she was the only woman in Talmudic literature whose *halakhic opinions were respected. Stories were circulated about her great learning (e.g. *B.Pes.* 62b). In the midst of many misfortunes (her father was tortured to death by the Romans, her sister was forced into prostitution, her brother was killed by robbers), the culminating one was the death of her two sons one *Sabbath afternoon. Only when the Sabbath ended did she tell her husband, by asking whether a precious object, deposited with her for safe-keeping, should be returned to its owner. R. Meir replied, 'Of course!' She then told him the news, quoting Job 1. 21. In the so-called Beruryah Incident, R. Meir tested her integrity by sending to her a student to seduce her into adultery: after submitting, she committed suicide.

D. M. Goodblatt in W. S. Green (ed.), *Persons and Institutions in Early Rabbinic Judaism* (1977).

Besant, A.: see THEOSOPHICAL SOCIETY.

Beshara. *Sūfī-inspired movement, started in London *c.*1970. The name of the founder, a Turk, is unknown, and while members stress that there is no leader as such, Beshara teaching is grounded in the writings of the mystics *Ibn Arabi (1165–1240) and *Jalāl al-Dīn Rūmī (1207–73). Beshara presents itself as being of the 'real', esoteric Sūfī tradition, which is beyond religion, and through the practice of *dhikr ('remembrance'), meditation, and study, it seeks to bring people to a full and constant awareness of reality and of God.

Besht (founder of E. European Ḥasidism): see ISRAEL BEN ELIEZER (i.e. Baaʿl Shem Tov).

Bet Din (Heb., 'house of judgement'). Jewish court of *law. Traditionally the establishment of the bet din as an institution is ascribed to *Ezra. Battei din (pl.) were local courts while the *Jerusalem *Sanhedrin was the supreme court. After the destruction of the *Temple in 70 CE, the bet din in *Jabneh became the central authority while local battei din were established throughout the *Diaspora. The huge literature of *rabbinic *responsa grew out of the judgements of the bet din which generally were composed of three judges learned in Jewish law and which covered every area of dispute. Today the bet din is concerned with religious matters, such as the supervision of *kashrut and the granting of divorce. In *Israel, the bet din is the rabbinic court which has jurisdiction in such areas as personal status, while the bet mishpat (also 'house of judgement') deals with secular cases.

Bet (ha-)Midrash (Heb., 'house of study'). Houses of study in Judaism go back at least to the second century BCE, when Simeon Ben Sira asked people to 'dwell in my bet midrash' (*Ecclesiasticus* 51. 47). They were the community centre where Jewish culture and learning were preserved and disseminated. Attendance at a bet ha-midrash was a meritorious act, and he who goes from the *synagogue after prayer to study at the bet ha-midrash is considered worthy of entering synagogues and battei ha-midrash (pl.) in the world to come. It was often merged with the synagogue, but a distinction was maintained between the function of prayer and the function of study.

Bethel. Town approximately 10 miles north of Jerusalem. Archaeological evidence points to settlement dating back to 3,000 BCE. According to Genesis, *Abraham built an altar between Bethel and Ai (12. 6–8), and *Jacob had a vision of *angels ascending and descending on a ladder stretching between heaven and earth (28. 10–22). The name Bethel means literally 'house of God' and the place was said to have been so called by Jacob. For a short period, during the era of the *Judges, the *tabernacle rested at Bethel (Judges 20. 18) and Jeroboam established it as a major shrine (1 Kings 12. 1–14. 16) to the fury of the *prophets.

Bet Hillel. One school of Jewish interpretation of the oral *law. It is frequently contrasted with the other school, Bet Shammai. The schools existed in the 1st and 2nd cents. CE, and *tannaitic literature records many of the controversies. In general, Bet Hillel was considered to be the more lenient of the two: for example, Bet Hillel maintained that a woman could be remarried even if only one person testified to her husband's death, while Bet Shammai demanded more than one witness (*B.Yev.* 122a). Ultimately the Bet Hillel school gained ascendancy and it was said, 'A *bat kol went forth and declared, "The *halakhah is according to the words of Bet Hillel" ' (*TJBer.* 1. 7, 36). By the *amoraic period, it was said, 'The opinion of Bet Shammai, when it conflicts with that of Bet Hillel, is no *Mishnah' (*B.Ber.* 36b).

Bethlehem. Town located 5 miles south of Jerusalem. Traditionally *Jacob buried his favourite wife, Rachel, near Bethlehem (Genesis 35. 19); it was the scene of the story of *Ruth; and King *David was anointed by the prophet *Samuel there (1 Samuel 16. 1–13). According to Micah 5. 2, 'You, O Bethlehem Ephrathah, who are little to be among the clans of Judah, from you shall come forth for me one who is to be ruler in Israel.' On the basis of this, *Jesus' birth in the city is understood by Christians as the fulfilment of prophecy (Matthew 2. 1–12; Luke 2. 1–20).

Bet mishpat: see BET DIN.

Betrothal (in Judaism): see SHIDDUKHIN.

Bet Shammai: see BET HILLEL.

Betsugedatsukai. Jap. ('individually liberating precepts') for *prātimokṣa, the precepts for Buddhist monks.

Beza, Theodore (1519–1605). French-born successor to *Calvin in Geneva as the leader of Reformed Protestantism (see REFORMATION). Educated for a legal career, he renounced *Roman Catholicism after a severe illness in 1548. Academically, he devoted himself to biblical study, especially to study of the Greek text. During the wars of religion (1560–98) he provided a theological argument and basis for resistance to usurped political authority. His strong defence of biblical literalism, double predestination and firm church discipline laid deep foundations for Calvinism and initiated what has been called 'Reformed Scholasticism'. However, the precise connection of Beza with this has been much disputed.

P. F. Geisendorf, *Théodore de Bèze* (1949).

Bezalel. Head builder of the *tabernacle (Exodus 31. 1–11; 36–9). He is described as being 'filled with the *Spirit of God, with ability and intelligence, with knowledge and all craftsmanship' (Exodus 31. 3). According to the *aggadah, although he was divinely appointed, God told *Moses to seek the Israelites' approval, since no leader should be accepted without the people's agreement (*B.Ber.* 55a).

Bhadrakalpika-sūtra (Skt., 'Sūtra of the Fortunate Age'). *Sūtra of *Mahāyāna Buddhism of a type which became extremely popular: it focuses on the legends of the thousand *buddhas of the fortunate age, of which the Buddha *Śākyamuni is the fifth.

Bhaga (due inheritance, social order): see ĀDITYAS.

Bhagat (Pañjābī form of Skt., *bhāgavata). Among Sikhs, those whose compositions are included in the *Ādi Granth, but who are either non-Sikhs or Sikhs who are not *Gurūs. These include *Nāmdev, *Kabīr, *Ravidāsi, and *Sūrdās. The material written by them is known as bhagat *bāṇī. The inclusion of such material demonstrates the claim of Gurū *Nānak that revelation and truth are to be found in all religions. In consequence, the *scriptures of other religions should be held in respect by Sikhs.

Bhagavā, Bhagavant, (Pāli, Skt.). 'Lord', 'Master', 'Exalted One', 'Blessed One'; reverential title used of the *Buddha by his disciples and others. Used subsequently by followers to open, for example, *pansil and *triśaraṇa recitals: *Namo tassa Bhagavato Arahato Sammāsambuddhassa*: 'Homage to the Lord, the Worthy One, the Perfectly Enlightened One.'

Bhagavad-gītā (Skt., 'the song of the *Bhagavā'). A fundamental text for Hindus—for many, the most sublime. It forms part of book vi of the **Mahābhārata*, and in eighteen sections of 700 verses, it explores the situation which has brought the warrior Arjuna to a crisis of conscience: he is opposed in battle by members of his own family; should he attack and perhaps kill them? Offered the assistance of *Kṛṣṇa Devakīputra, he accepts and receives instruction on appropriate conduct and attitudes. The main part of the *Gītā* records this instruction. In part, this is pragmatic: it is Arjuna's *dharma as a warrior to fight (2. 33); if he does not do so, he will lose status (2. 34); a war justly fought 'opens the door to heaven' (2. 32). But these considerations are best viewed as *upāya-kauśalya (skill-in-means in teaching, which draws a pupil on, through provisional teaching which is going to be transcended), since Kṛṣṇa then offers teaching which goes far beyond. Only deeds done without attachment to consequences, and through devotion (*bhakti) to *Īśvara (God in personified form), and with trust in his grace (*prasāda) can lead to the realization of *Brahman. The supreme manifestation of that grace is in the incarnation (*avatāra) of God, i.e. in the *Gītā*, of Kṛṣṇa as the *avatāra of *Viṣṇu. In order to move to the complete realization of this, Kṛṣṇa points Arjuna to the three paths (*marga), of knowledge (*jñāna-marga), of action with detachment (*karma-marga), and of devotion to God (*bhakti-mārga). Since these are ways of being united to the ultimately true and real, they are also known as karma-yoga, jñāna-yoga, and bhakti-yoga, the latter amounting to *rāja-yoga; thus *yoga may serve in *Bhagavad-gītā* as an abbreviation for the three mārgas. However, yoga is an extremely rich term in the *Gītā*, meaning also the work and effort involved, the person who undertakes it, the course of action chosen, the way chosen and the goal envisaged.

The *Gītā* appears to have been addressed (the date is uncertain, but *c.*200 BCE is likely) to a situation in which major unease about the excessive and costly rituals of *Brahmanical religion had led to a reaction so severe that it had isolated both Buddhism and Jainism as separate religions; and it had led also to a reaction within the continuing tradition, in the *Āraṇyakas and the *Upaniṣads. At the same time, philosophical systems were being developed which seemed to make unnecessary the postulate of God (e.g. *Sāṁkhya). The *Gītā* appears to make a deliberate attempt to show the worth of the major ways of the continuing tradition (though obviously it corrects any non-theistic system if taken in isolation). This means that the *Gītā* can be 'read' (i.e. interpreted) as articulating (and ultimately endorsing) virtually all Hindu ways of progress toward the goal (*mokṣa). In particular, it can be read as an expression of *Advaita Vedānta, *Viṣiṣṭadvaita, and *Dvaita: it therefore reads as a deliberate attempt to reconcile and hold the line against further schism. But are the options all, in the end, equally valid? The question is much debated. Van Buitenen (see bibliography below) concluded:

> How, finally, is Kṛṣṇa's teaching of bhakti related to his teachings of action and knowledge? I do not believe that he wishes to present them as equally valid options, or he would have done so. He has given new meaning to, and with it new hope for, the ordered life of action according to class and life stage; on the surface he has advocated the stoicism of acting for its own sake. He has rather ignored the benefits of knowledge and sharply warned against the dangers of blanket renunciation for the sake of release. Now he supplants the stoicism with the enthusiasm of the believer acting in God's name and for his glorification, and replaces the salvation-seeking knowledge with that knowledge of God that only bhakti can bring. . . . Tradition sees the summation of his teaching in his *caramaśloka*, the 'last' verse: 'Abandon all the Laws and instead seek shelter with me alone: be unconcerned, I shall set you free from all that is evil' (18. 66).

But even if the Gītā seems in the end to be endorsing one way over the others, nevertheless it achieves a profound reconciliation; not surprisingly, therefore, it is the most revered and influential text among Hindus. R. B. Minor, *The Bhagavad Gītā* (1982) summarizes the many possible ways in which the words and text have been interpreted, by both classical and modern commentators.

Of many translations, that of J. B. van Buitenen was the product of a lifelong study of the Mahābhārata, and is printed with a transcription of the original text. For classic Indian interpretations, see A. Sharma, *The Hindu Gita* (1986); for more recent interpretations, see R. B. Minor, *Modern Indian Interpreters of the Bhagavadgita* (1986); J. C. Kapoor, *Bhagavad-Gītā: An International Bibliography . . . 1785–1979* (1983).

Bhagavān (Skt., 1st person nom. of *bhagavat*, 'having shares', from √*bhaj*, 'distribute, partake'). Hindu epithet for God as constantly concerned for human well-being, and as 'one who receives his share' (sc., of offerings and honour): 'He who understands the rise and dissolution, the coming and going, the wisdom and ignorance, of all beings should be called Bhagavan' (*Viṣṇu Purāṇa* 6. 5. 78). Although the term can be used as a title of respect for honoured individuals, especially teachers (it is used of the *Buddha, see BHAGAVĀ, or more recently in the form 'Bhagwan' in *Rajneeshism), it is most commonly used of God as Lord (*Īśvara), in particular of *Viṣṇu-Nārāyana or *Vāsudeva-Kṛṣṇa. A Bhāgavata is one who is devoted to Bhagvān, in a disposition of *bhakti. Major texts of this devotion are *Bhagavad-gītā* and **Bhāgavata-purāṇa*.

Initially, Bhāgavatas were not organized as a movement or sect. The earliest such organization seems to have been that of *Pāñcarātra. Subsequently many bhakti movements of Bhāgavatas came into being, e.g. the *Āḻvārs, the Sant tradition, the followers of *Nimbārka, of Vallabha, of *Madhva, of *Caitanya. By this time, Bhāgavatas are virtually synonomous with Vaiṣṇavites.

J. Gonda, *Die Religionen Indiens . . .*, ii (1963).

Bhāgavata. One devoted to *Bhagavān.

***Bhāgavata-purāṇa*.** A Hindu mythological work in Skt., one of the eighteen *mahapurāṇas. The title must be derived from *Bhagavān, which means here *Kṛṣṇa/*Viṣṇu, the central deity of the text. It is usually included in the list of the eighteen mahāpurāṇas (Major Purāṇas), but among these it is the most idiosyncratic and unusual work—which very likely suggests single authorship. There is ample evidence for its origin in the *Tamil-speaking area of S. India, and it must have been written in the later 9th or earlier 10th cent. CE. At least from the early 11th cent. it is also known in North India, and soon evolved as one of the single most important sacred scriptures of medieval Hinduism. Innumerable versions of it were produced in almost all vernaculars of India, and many religious movements (among them the schools of *Caitanya and Vallabhā) made it their scriptural authority. It is a complex work, fusing many different traditions, hence its wide popularity. Its basic structure and content derive from the **Viṣṇu Purāṇa* (with traces of influence also from the **Mārkaṇḍeya-purāṇa*). But unlike that source, and the earlier purāṇas generally, it uses highly sophisticated lyrical metres and descriptions (often presented as songs). Also, the form of devotion it advocates—an intense emotionalism that aims at *ecstasy—is quite different from earlier *bhakti texts (such as the **Bhagavad-gītā* or the *Viṣṇu Purāṇa*). These two features have been shown to derive from the vernacular tradition of the Tamil *Āḻvārs, whose poems are actually paraphrased or translated in numerous passages. Traces also of Jain influence are not absent, e.g. in the inclusion of certain Kṛṣṇaite myths. The (earlier) **Ādi-purāṇa* may well have served as a stimulus for the *Bhāgavata-purāṇa*. That the work understands itself nevertheless as 'orthodox' Hindu scripture is clear not only from its title but also from its archaizing language which imitates *Vedic grammar. Finally, to complete this grand synthesis of religion in S. India, the whole is presented within a metaphysical frame of reference which is derived from the *advaita tradition, but is modified here to represent a theistic Kṛṣṇa-Viṣṇu advaita. Book x (and far less xi), which deals with the earlier part of Kṛṣṇa's life and includes very lengthy accounts of his love-affairs with the *gopīs, has greatly overshadowed in popularity the remaining parts of the text. Furthermore, the whole purāṇa is said to have been composed by *Vyāsa in order to make good his deficiency in not having formerly sung Kṛṣṇa's praises; Kṛṣṇa appears even in book i; and the bulk of the work is said to have been recited by Vyāsa's son Śuka to Parikṣit, who owes his life to Kṛṣṇa. Kṛṣṇa is undoubtedly the Supreme Godhead throughout the whole work, and even the mischievous pranks of his childhood are invested with cosmic significance. The whole purāṇa is written in an archaic style which suggests that the circles which produced it wished to give it an appearance of Vedic authority. The movements led by Caitanya and Vallabha were largely based upon the *Bhāgavata-purāṇa*, and its influence is still felt today, not only in India, but—because of its use by the Kṛṣṇa Consciousness movement—throughout the world.

Trs. J. M. Sanyal; G. V. Tagare; see also F. Hardy, *Viraha-bhakti*, pp. 481–651.

Bhāgo, Mātā or Māī (Pañjābī, 'mother'; b. 17th cent. CE). Sikh heroine. Māī Bhāgo rallied the 'forty immortals' at *Muktsār, vowing that she would, if necessary, die for Gurū *Gobind Siṅgh. Wearing men's clothing, she fought bravely, killing several men of the local Mughal governor, Wazir Khān, and was blessed by the Gurū. Apparently she subsequently lost her reason and died at *Nander.

Bhagwan (founder of Indian-based movement): see RAJNEESH.

Bhāī (Pañjābī, 'brother'). Title for Sikh men which indicates particular esteem. Examples of men so honoured are Bhāī *Buḍhā, Bhāī *Gurdās, and Bhāī Ghanīyā. The title is one of popular acclaim, not of any formal process. The equivalent for women is *bībī.

Bhāī Kanayhā (model of selfless Sikh): see SEVĀ.

Bhairava (Skt.). 1. A ferocious form of *Śiva, akin to *Kālī, revered in *Tantrism especially by the Kāpālikas and in *Kashmir Śaivism. By meditating on this terrible form of the deity, the adept (*sādhaka) eventually sees through the ferocity and apprehends the transcendent beyond form. That is, liberation (*mokṣa) is achieved through embracing the terrible aspects of existence and realizing that these too are manifestations of the absolute consciousness (*caitanya) of Śiva. Bhairava is also equated with the absolute *Parameśvara, being regarded as the union (*yāmala) of light (*prakāśa*) and awareness (*vimarśa*) who projects, maintains, and destroys the cosmos. The *Netra Tantra* describes him for the purposes of meditation (*dhyāna) as black with five faces, ten arms, clad in an elephant skin, and seated in the lotus posture (*padmāsana) on a corpse. He is accompanied by his *śakti *Bhairavī who is likewise terrible.

2. The name/title of one who seeks to enter a Tantric sect.

Bhairavī (Skt.). A ferocious form of the Goddess (*Devī) in Hinduism especially in *Tantrism, the *śakti of *Bhairava. Like *Kālī, Bhairavī is described as having a terrible appearance, garlanded with severed heads. She is the active principle of the cosmos dancing on the passive principle of *Śiva, often represented as a corpse. In the *Tantras Bhairavī asks questions of Bhairava, though in one text (the *Tāra Tantra*) she gives answers to Bhairava. The 14th-cent. poet, Vidyāpati, describes her as dancing wildly on the corpse of Śiva, devouring and disgorging demons, her mouth foaming with blood. Like Kālī, Bhairavī represents the terrible aspects of existence which have to be embraced in order to achieve liberation (*mokṣa).

Bhaiṣajyaguru (more fully: Bhaiṣajyaguru vaiḍūryaprabha tathāgata, 'Radiant lapis-lazuli Master of Healing Buddha'; Tib. sman.bla; Chin., Yao Shih Fo; Jap., Yakushi Nyōrai; Korean, Yaksa). The *Buddha of healing, frequently called 'Medicine Buddha', popular in the *Mahāyāna Buddhism of Tibet, China, and Japan, whose dispensation also includes longevity, protection from disasters, and the transmutation of negative states of mind (all illnesses in Buddhism, by virtue of their *karmic origin, being considered to some extent psychosomatic). It is important to note that the predicament of humans in the Buddhist world has always been seen in terms of suffering, and the historical Buddha *Śākyamuni has always been seen in the role of physician; illness, old age, and death were three of the four sights which impelled Śākyamuni to seek *enlightenment, and the product of his enlightenment—the formulation of the teaching as the *Four Noble Truths—followed the traditional methodology of a doctor: diagnosis of the disease (suffering), location of the cause (poisoning by desire, hatred, and delusion), assessment of prognosis, and prescription. The particularly Mahāyāna development of the Buddha of healing is thus a close focus on one of the fundamental aspects of Buddhahood itself.

The earliest evidence of the Healing Buddha is the Chinese translation from the Skt. of *Bhaiṣajyagurusūtra* (early 4th cent. CE), and as this has close similarities with the **Lotus Sūtra* (*c.*2nd cent. CE) in which the *bodhisattva King of Healing (Bhaiṣajyarāja) is prominent, it is likely that Bhaiṣajyaguru was a development bestowing increased importance to Bhaiṣajyarāja. As a subject for meditation, Bhaiṣajyaguru is depicted holding a lapis-lazuli (understood as a healing stone) medicine bowl containing nectar (*amṛta) in his lap, cupped in the dhyāna *mudrā (meditation-gesture) of his left hand, to indicate the importance of meditation for healing. In his right hand he holds the yellow medicinal myrobalan fruit between his thumb and index finger, with three fingers downpointed to bestow blessings. (Some Japanese representations have him holding his bowl standing, with his right hand in the gesture of fearlessness.) Occasionally Bhaiṣajyaguru is depicted with six 'brothers', and although these may be shown in varying shades of red and yellow, Bhaiṣajyaguru himself is always depicted in the deep, healing blue of lapis-lazuli.

According to a Tibetan sūtra (also extant in Chinese), he took twelve vows which epitomize his work: to radiate light to all beings; to proclaim his healing power; to fulfil the desires of all beings; to lead all by the *mahāyāna (way); to reinforce all in observing *sīla; to heal; to lead all to enlightenment; to change women into men in their next appearance; to ward off false teaching and endorse the truth; to save all beings from a bad rebirth; to feed the hungry; to clothe the naked. He presides over the *Pure Land of the East (cf. *Sukhāvatī, the Western Paradise).

R. Birnbaum, *The Healing Buddha* (1979).

Bhājā (Buddhist monastic establishment): see VIHĀRA.

Bhajana (chant): see MANDIR(A).

Bhajana (song of praise): see WORSHIP.

Bhakti (Skt., either from √*bhaj*, 'to share, be loyal', or √bhañj, 'to separate'). Devotion in love and adoration, especially to one's chosen manifestation of the divine (*iṣṭadeva); but it may be guru-bhakti (surrender to a guru) or vaidhi-bhakti (willing acceptance of a guru's instructions). In its theistic form, it perhaps appears in the **Ṛg Veda* (5. 85. 7 f.; 7. 87. 7), in hymns imploring *Varuṇa to forgive the offences of his devotees. But it became a major way of Indian religious life (owing much to the religion of *Tamil-Nadu), in which the grace (*prasāda) of God modifies the strict causality of *karma. Bhakti-marga (the way of bhakti) has produced some of the world's most moving theistic poetry, as well as the formalization of the stages through which union with God can be attained, in Bhakti-yoga (see e.g. Vivekānanda, *Karma-Yoga and Bhakti-Yoga*, 1955). The **Bhagavad-gītā* is the foremost exposition and expression of bhakti addressed to *Kṛṣṇa. The theory and stages of bhakti are elaborated by Nārada in the *Bhaktisūtras* (with eleven stages) and in **Bhāgavata-purāṇa* (with nine stages: *śravaṇa* (listening), *kīrtana (singing), *smaraṇa* (recollecting), *arcana* (worshipping), *pādasevana* (serving), *vandana* (praising), *dasya* (service), *sakhya* (friendship), *ātmanivedana* (self-surrender)). The analogical base of erotic passion and union is frequently explored: see e.g. **Gītāgovinda*. Devotion to Śiva is most elaborately expressed in the *Tamil Śaivasiddhānta. See also VAIṢṆAVA; ŚAIVA; ŚRI-VAIṢṆAVISM; Index, Bhakti.

M. Dhavamony, *Love of God According to the Śaiva Siddhānta* (1971); F. E. Hardy, *Viraha Bhakti . . .* (1981); K. Werner (ed.), *Love Divine: Studies in Bhakti and Devotional Mysticism* (1993).

Bhaktivedanta Swami Prabhupada (founder of ISKCON): see PRABHUPADA.

Bhandarkar, Ramkrishna Gopal (1837–1925). Eminent Indian academician, who was Professor of Sanskrit at Deccan College, Puné, 1884–93, and Vice-Chancellor of Bombay University 1893–5. His writings are numerous, and he is especially noteworthy for his search for Skt. manuscripts in Western India and Rajasthan, and the editing of Bhavabhūti's *Mālatī Mādhuva*. He was an authority on the early history of the Deccan and the *Vaiṣṇavite and *Śaivīte branches of Hinduism. He was also a leader of a reformist religious movement in Maharashtra, the Prarthana Samaj.

R. G. Bhandarkar is commemorated by the Bhandarkar Oriental Research Institute in Puné, which was founded in 1917, and to which he presented his library. In 1918 the then Bombay Government donated its collection of over 20,000 Skt. and Prakrit manuscripts to the Institute, and passed to it the responsibility of the Bombay Sanskrit and Prakrit Series which began in 1868. In 1966 the Institute completed its outstanding critical edition of the **Mahābhārata*. Its journal, the *Annals of the Bhandarkar Oriental Research Institute*, was begun in 1919, coincident with the holding of the first All India Oriental Conference, which was organized by the Institute. The Institute is now recognized as a postgraduate research and teaching institution by Puné University.

Bhanga or **bhang.** A narcotic (*cannabis sativa*) used in India to assist divination and produce ecstatic states. According to **Atharva Veda* 9. 6. 15, it is one of the five kingdoms of plants ruled by *Soma.

Bharata. The tribe which took part in the war described in the *Mahābhārata, and the name of several notable *Āryans; hence also the name (Bharat) of modern India.

Bharata natya. S. Indian *dance, performed originally by *Deva-Dāsīs. Although it fell into disuse, it has been reconstructed by following the dance poses as they are sculpted in Indian temples.

Bharatya Janata Party. Indian political party committed to the preservation of Hindu identity. At Independence, India was made, constitutionally, a secular state. Minority religions have specific rights, as do minorities within the Hindu context (e.g. *untouchables, for whom positive discrimination has been enacted). The BJP emerged as itself a minority protest against the erosion of Hindu values and status. In 1984, it had only two members of Parliament, but subsequently, it became the largest opposition party. Committed to the Constitution, it has nevertheless run the risk of being taken over on the streets by far more extreme groups, e.g. Rashtriya Svayamsevak Sangh (RSS), founded as a self-defence militia in pre-Independence days; and Viśva Hindu Paraśad (VHP), which has tried to give 'Hinduism' a more systematic ideology. These and other groups were involved in the destruction of the *Ayodhyā mosque.

Bhārhut. In Madhya Pradesh, this is the earliest surviving Buddhist *stūpa. Based on a Mauryan relic mound, the stūpa was decorated in the Śuṅga period, about 100 BCE. The carvings found at Bhārhut are archaic and represent the earliest examples of Buddhist *iconography, *yakṣas and tree motifs being particularly prominent. The presence of 102 lamp-niches around the dome is a peculiar feature.

Bhāsa (early: *c.* 4th cent. CE?). Hindu dramatist. His works were lost until 1912, when thirteen plays attributed to him were published, including the admired *Svapna-vāsavadatta*.

Bhāṣya. Hindu commentary on sacred texts, especially *sūtras. Because sūtras are compressed and aphoristic, bhāṣyas are a vital key to understanding them. They represent a natural application of the campaign against *avidya (ignorance) as the great impediment standing in the way of enlightenment and release (*mokṣa). There is no single agreed 'meaning', so that bhāṣyas are likely to represent schools of interpretation.

Bhāṭṛā, N. Indian pedlar community claiming *brahman descent. They trace their origin to Mādho Mal of Śri Lankā, whose descendant, Chaṅgā Bhāṭṛā, reputedly became a disciple of Gurū *Nānak when the latter visited the island. Many Bhāṭṛās are Sikhs. In the first decades of 20th cent. Bhāṭṛā Sikhs pioneered migration to Britain and live chiefly in

British ports. There is no intermarriage between Bhāṭṛā Sikhs and Sikhs of other *castes, and in some cities they have formed separate *gurdwārās. Their marriages are characterized by subsidiary rituals unfamiliar to other Sikhs. Bhāṭṛā women are generally more restricted than other Sikh women in Britain, being discouraged from work outside the home and, if married, covering their faces in the gurdwārā.

Bhāṭṭa (Skt.). A follower of *Kumārila Bhaṭṭa; also in Hinduism, an honorific title given to learned *brahmans.

Bhattaraka (Skt., 'learned man'). Head of a group of naked monks in *Digambara Jainism. Buildings (*maṭha*) to accommodate these ascetics began to be built from about the 5th cent. BCE, and the bhattarakas became in effect the presidents of them, organizing the education, the library, the taking of vows, etc., and representing the community to the outside world. For this reason they wore garments (the saffron robe: see MONASTICISM, BUDDHIST) even inside the community—except at meals or when initiating another bhattaraka. Bhattarakas have persisted to the present day, though they have become more like advocates for Jainism in general, rather than for the communities in relation to the outside world.

Bhāva (Skt.). 1. In *Sāṃkhya, a set of psychological predispositions either eight or fifty in number. The more concise numbering renders them as virtue (*dharma), vice (adharma), knowledge (*jñāna), ignorance (ajñāna), non-attachment (*vīrāga*), attachment (*rāga), power (*aiśvarya*), and impotence (*anaiśvarya*).

These dispositions are an inherent part of human nature. They reside in the intellect (*buddhi) and are carried with one throughout the entire series of births in a gradual process of evolution which leads ultimately to the transcendence of the bhāvas. The bhāvas are not specific *karmic tendencies, but are even more basic than these. They create the environment in which karma is accumulated or overcome.

In *Sāṃkhyakārikā*, in which the eight bhāvas are described, reference is made to fifty bhāvas which are comprised of five types of ignorance (*vi paryaya*), twenty-eight types of incapacity (*aśakti*), nine types of complacency (*tuṣṭi*), and eight types of perfection (*siddha).

All of the bhāvas except knowledge (jñāna) dominate and bind to endless rebirths. Like the others, jñāna is not a specific quality but rather a general characteristic of mind. It is the realization—not simply intellectual—of the distinction between *puruṣa and *prakṛti and liberates one from the other bhāvas, and ultimately life itself.

2. The emotional dispositions in Hinduism of the bhakta (one engaged in *bhakti) to the chosen deity (*iṣṭadeva): (i) *śanta*, peace; (ii) *dāsya*, servant to master; (iii) *sākhya*, friend to friend; (iv) *vātsalya*, parent to child; (v) *madhura*, wife to husband, lover to beloved.

3. In Buddhism, 'being', every kind of manifestation in the three domains of appearance (triloka: see LOKA). It is also the tenth link in chain of conditioned-arising (*paticca-samuppāda).

4. For Jains, bhāva, with *dravya, enters deeply into the dynamic of lay and ascetic life. In the quest to disentangle *jīva from *karma, bhāva represents the spiritual elements whose priority must be secured over against the physical constituents of material appearance (dravya). For those who have already taken the greater vows, the whole of life and ritual (since they have renounced the world) assumes the distinction of bhāva from dravya; but for laypeople, dravya may be brought into their rituals in order to set the distinction in motion.

Bhavacakra (Skt., the 'wheel of existence'). Buddhist, and especially Tibetan, painting which portrays the relentless process of recurrent birth, death, and rebirth, *saṃsāra, as a wheel. Pictures on the wheel convey the conditions of saṃsāra together with the moral and mental factors which cause the individual to remain within saṃsāra. The wheel is shown clasped by the hands and feet and being devoured by a demon monster, *Māra, symbolizing the all-pervasive nature of death and impermanence. The wheel itself is divided into four concentric circles. At the centre is depicted a cockerel, snake, and pig, signifying respectively the cardinal vices of passion (*rāga), ill-will (*dosa), and delusion (*moha); these vices thus form the hub upon which the whole wheel turns. In the next ring, humans with bad *karma are shown on their way to *hell, descending from top right to bottom, while ascending from bottom left to top are shown humans with good karma on the way to *nirvāna. The next circle, the largest surface area on the wheel, is divided into six segments, depicting the realms of rebirth: as gods, *asuras, *pretas, hells, animals, and humans; here, at the top centre, the Buddha is portrayed preaching the *dharma. The outermost ring, in twelve sections, has pictures portraying each of the links which make up the chain of dependent origination (*paticca-samuppāda). Nirvāna is nowhere depicted, of course, since it is the antithesis of bhāva or saṃsāra; though a figure of the Buddha is sometimes featured outside the wheel, indicating his emancipation from the wheel of birth and death.

According to the *Divyāvadāna*, the Buddha himself instituted the drawing of the bhavacakra as a pedagogic device for the instruction of the non-literate in Buddhist truths. The earliest known example of the bhavacakra is a fresco (*c*.6th cent. CE) of *Ajaṇṭā. Bhavacakras are principally found painted inside the doorways of Tibetan temples and on Tibetan painted-scrolls (*thankas*): see TIBETAN WHEEL OF LIFE.

Bhāvanā (Pāli, Skt., 'to make become', 'to nurture', 'to develop', $\sqrt{bhu}$ = 'to be'). In early Buddhism, *meditation in the broadest sense: methods of mental training and discipline leading to mind-control and spiritual insight. They fall into two categories: mind-development (*citta-bhāvanā) leading to tranquillity (*samatha) and insight-development (*vipassanā-bhāvanā). Bhāvanā is also regarded as a form of meritorious action (*puṇya). According to **Vissudhimagga*, there are 40 exercises leading to śamatha, which must precede vipassanā-bhāvanā.

Bhavanga-sota (stream of consciousness): see Ālaya-vijñāna.

Bhavānī. A name of the Hindu Goddess. Theoretically it can be derived from Bhava, a synonym of *Śiva. This would then denote the goddess as Śiva's consort, similar to *Pārvatī, *Durgā, or Gaurī. However, in the context of regional cults connected with temples, Bhavānī may figure independently from Śiva. For example, in Mahārāṣṭra we find Tuljā-Bhavānī of Tuljāpur.

Bhāvaviveka (also 'Bhāvya' and 'Bhāviveka'; *c.*500–70 CE). Major Indian philosopher of the *Madhyamaka school of Buddhism, who criticized the Mādhyamika *Buddhapālita on the grounds that the latter's *prāsaṅgika mode of reasoning (revealing to one's opponent that the consequences of his view involve a logical absurdity) is insufficient for generating in one's opponent the correct understanding of one's thesis. According to Bhāvaviveka, because a consequence (prasaṅga) alone lacks the support of a logical reason (*liṅga*) and example (*dṛṣṭānta*) which are necessary for valid syllogistic inference, it cannot also accomplish the simultaneous denial of any alternative theses which the opponent may present. On this basis, Bhāvaviveka developed a syllogistic mode of reasoning (utilizing the logical theory of *Dignāga) which stressed 'independent inference' (*svatantrānumāna*); this led to the retrospective identification of his school by the Tibetans as *Svatantrika-Madhyamaka.

A major mark of Bhāvaviveka's thought is the division of reality into ultimate truth (*paramārthasatya*) and conventional truth (*saṃvṛtisatya*), by which self-existence (*svabhāva) is asserted as a conventional truth but not as an ultimate one. Thus the perception by an ordinary man of the horns of a bull as being self-existent should be accounted as a conventionally valid cognition, in contradistinction to the illusory cognition of the horns of a hare, even though the self-existence of the horns of the bull is refuted with the arrival of ultimate insight.

For both his logical methodology and his assertion of a conventional 'svabhāva', Bhāvaviveka attracted strong criticism from *Candrakirti, which polarized Madhyamaka into two principal schools of Svatantrika and Prāsaṅgika. Bhāvaviveka's principal works are the *Prajñāpradīpa* (Light of Wisdom), which is a commentary on *Nāgārjuna's *Mulamadhyamakākarikās*, and the *Madhyamakahṛdayakārikās* (Verses on the Essence of the Middle Way), with his own commentary the *Tarkajvāla* (Blaze of Reasoning), which assesses the *brahmanical systems.

Bhave, Vinoba: see VINOBA BHAVE.

Bhāvya: see BHĀVAVIVEKA.

Bhīkanji: see BHIKṢU, ĀCĀRYA.

Bhikkhu, bhikkhunī: see BHIKṢU/BHIKṢUṆĪ.

Bhikṣu/bhikṣuṇī (Skt.; Pāli, *bhikkhu*, *bhikkhunī*; Chin., *pi-ch'iu*; Jap., *biku*; Korean *pigu*). Male/female members of the Buddhist *saṅgha, usually translated as 'monks', 'nuns'. Originally, the saṅgha formed 'the advance guard' of Buddhism, since only those who renounced the world could attain *nirvāna. In time, a balance of exchange between lay-people and monks was established (see e.g. *dāna), through which both could advance by mutual support; and this relationship has formed the dynamic of *Theravādin societies. It is required (or at least desirable) that a layman should spend a period during the rainy season living as a bhikṣu.

The life of the saṅga is laid down in the rules of the *Vināya-piṭaka, underlying the basic principles of poverty, chastity, and peacefulness. The bhikṣu relies on begging for his food, and his clothing, made of three parts (*tricīvara*), is preferably ragged. Initially, all bhikṣus spent their lives wandering, but were then allowed to spend the rainy season in a monastery (*vihāra), which has now become the norm for the saṅgha.

The *Buddha initially resisted the formation of an order of bhikṣuṇīs, fearing for distraction and moral disorder. But this was introduced by Mahāprajāpati Gautami, the Buddha's stepmother. Although the transmission lineage of Theravādin bhikkhunīs has been broken, that of Mahāyānist bhikṣuṇīs has been preserved. There is no difference in principle between Theravada and Mahāyāna monastic observances, but the Mahāyāna list of precepts is longer. Mahāyāna bhikṣus observe 250 precepts while bhikṣuṇīs observe 348. Theravādin nuns adopt the habit and tonsure but observe only the ten precepts (Pāli, *dassasīla*) of the novice (Pāli, *sāmaṇari*) and are called *dasasīlavanti*, 'those of the ten precepts'.

Bhikṣu, Ācārya (also Bhīkanji, 1726–1803). Founder of the Jain reforming sect, the Terapanth. He was born in Rajasthan, where the sect's main strength has remained. His family was Śvetāmbara (for which see DIGAMBARA), but he felt that his parents belonged to a sect that was defective in ethical care. He came under the influence of the *ācārya, Raghunathji, and was initiated by him in 1751. However, he came to regard his teacher as too complacent (e.g. in his view that since the world is in the age of the fifth spoke of the wheel, the age of decadence, no one can be expected to meditate for more than an hour), and Bhikṣu broke away in 1759 to found the Terapanth on the basis of extreme discipline and rigour. He followed the life of a wandering beggar, and by the time he died, he had initiated forty-nine monks and fifty-six nuns.

The name 'Terapanth' is variously explained: *tera* means (in Rajasthani) both 'thirteen' and 'your'. Thus the 'Thirteen Path' may be the reliance on the thirteen basic elements of ascetic practice which Bhiksu was restoring (the *Five Great Vows, the Five Attentive Actions, *samiti*, and the Three Protections, *gupti*); or it may be the number of early followers (thirteen monks and thirteen laymen); or it may be the devotion to '*you*, Lord *Mahāvīra'. In any case, Bhikṣu demanded absolute discipline and effort. He elevated the role of the ācārya, to become the sole authority over adherents, and to appoint his own successor. In this way he hoped to prevent the fission of the movement into further sects. He emphasized the difference between actions within the world, which, however meritorious, have no connection with the transcendent realm of attainment (*lokottara) which is the proper objective of the religious person. Thus in his extreme emphasis on *ahiṁsā (non-violence), he held that some characteristic Jain actions, such as buying animals from butchers in order to set them free, affect society, but do not achieve the profound transformation which a religious apprehension and practice of ahiṁsa opens up. It is necessary to penetrate the ensouled nature of *all* appearance. The eighth ācārya, Tulsi, who succeeded in 1936, took this out into the world (especially of politics and economics), arguing that the accelerating power of humans to destroy must be counteracted by an accelerating power to reform spiritually. He therefore founded the *Anuvrata Movement, from *aṇu ('atom', with deliberate reference to 'atom bomb') and *vrata, 'vow': 'A small, or atomic, vow alone has the power to ward off and counter the threat of an atom bomb.'

Bhīma or **Bhīmasena.** in the **Mahābhārata*, the second oldest *Pāṇḍava, of the strong and wild warrior type, whose weapon, when not simply a tree trunk, is the mace. A tremendous eater, Bhīma's most common epithet is Vṛkodara (Wolf-Belly). Bhīma is the son and incarnation of the wind god, *Vāyu, and therefore the half-brother of *Hanumat. Violently anti-*Kaurava, and propelled by bloody oaths he has taken against *Duryodhana and Duḥśāsana (to break Duryodhana's thigh and drink Duḥśāsana's blood), it is Bhīma who is responsible for the death in the *Kurukṣetra war of one Kaurava brother after another, and finally of Duryodhana in hand-to-hand mace combat. But Bhīma also has a gentler side, displayed primarily in his relationship to *Draupadī, for whom he performs many favours. A talented *rākṣasa killer, Bhīma also has a rākṣasī wife, Hiḍimbā, and is by her the father of the good rākṣasa, Ghaṭotkaca.

Bhindrānawāle, *Sant Jarnail Siṅgh (1947–84). Controversial Sikh leader. Jarnail Siṅgh was the leader of a religious institution, Damdamā Sāhib Taxāl, which was reputedly founded by the 18th-cent. Sikh hero, Bābā Dīp Siṅgh. His rise to political prominence resulted from the desire of Congress Party politicians to split the *Akālīs. He opposed the Sant *Nirañkārīs, and inspired militant support for *Khālistān. He was killed in the *Akāl Takht by the Indian army during Operation Blue Star.

Bhīṣma. In the **Mahābhārata*, the 'Grandfather' of the *Pāṇḍavas and *Kauravas. Really the sky god *Dyaus (one of the eight Vasus: see ĀDITYAS) incarnate, Bhīṣma is born as the son of King Śaṃtanu and the river Ganges (*Gaṅga). His name, Bhīṣma ('Terrible') is actually an epithet which he earns, when grown, by vowing celibacy, and renouncing kingdom and progeny, as a favour to his father. His father rewards him with *svacchandamaraṇam*, the ability to die as he chooses. While waiting to die, he rests on a bed of arrows, and exhorts Yudhiṣṭhira with the legal and spiritual instruction which constitutes books xii and xiii of the *Mahābhārata*, the **Śānti-* and *Anuśāsanaparvans*.

Bhog (Pañjābī, 'enjoyment, climax'). Among Sikhs, the ceremonial conclusion of a complete reading of the *Ādi Granth. As the *pāṭh nears its close people gather for the bhog. *Śaloks of Gurū *Tegh Bahādur, the Mundāvanī and Rāgamālā, are read followed by *Anand Sāhib (verses 1–5 and last verse), *Ardās and a *hukam. *Karāh Praśād is distributed.

Bhoga (Skt.). In Hinduism, food offered to a form of God; also sensory pleasure.

Bhṛgu. In Hindu mythology, a divine seer, son of *Brahmā (or of *Varuṇa, or of *Indra, or of *Prajāpati), and eponymous ancestor of the Bhṛgu or Bhārgava clan. The term bhṛgu occurs twenty-six times in the **Ṛg Veda*, apparently with reference to a whole race of beings who are connected with fire in various ways (Bhṛgu may be connected with *bhrāj*, Skt., 'to shine'). In epic and *purāṇic mythology, members of the Bhṛgu clan have the power to restore the dead to life, and are frequently either victims or aggressors in violent confrontations, particularly with *kṣatriyas of the Haihaya clan, who are traditionally seen as both their patrons and their enemies. They are also often portrayed as showing hostility to the gods. Besides Bhṛgu and Śukra, other prominent Bhārgavas are *Cyavana, *Aurva, and *Paraśurāma. The importance of these figures in the **Mahābhārata* led V. S. Sukthankar to postulate the theory that this epic as we know it today consists of an earlier work about the Pāṇḍava–Kaurava war, thoroughly revised and expanded by historical members of the Bhārgava family of *brahmans who wished to glorify their mythical ancestors.

Bhubaneswar (formerly Bhuvaneśvara, 'Lord of the world', an epithet of Śiva). City in Orissa with many temples dedicated to Śiva, especially Lingavaj temple.

Bhūmi (Skt., 'ground', 'level', 'stage'). In *Mahāyāna Buddhism, a stage in a systematized scheme of progress to spiritual maturity and perfection in enlightenment (*nirvāna). Most schools of Buddhism recognize a scheme of states or stages which are passed through, beginning with conversion and the taking up of the religious life and ending in enlightenment. *Theravāda lists the four stages of the *arya-mārga, and the theory of the bhūmis may be thought of as an outgrowth of this or as an extension of the scheme of progress in the Eightfold Path (*aṣtangika-mārga) through morality, meditation, and wisdom. The most popular sequence involves a list of ten bhūmis although some texts refer only to seven. After the first six stages the devotee achieves the realization of personal selflessness (*anātman) and after the tenth stage the realization of the selflessness of all phenomena (*dharmaśūnyatā*). Thus personal liberation, the goal of Theravāda Buddhism, is supplemented by Mahāyāna metaphysics with its vision of the 'higher truth' of universal selflessness. The ten stages, which are linked to the practice of the ten Perfections, are as follows:

1. Joyful (*pramuditā*): A *bodhisattva embarks upon his religious career with the production of the thought of enlightenment (*bodhicitta).

2. Pure (*vimalā*): All immoral conduct and dispositions are eradicated.

3. Luminous (*prabhākarī*): Through meditation the bodhisattva strengthens and deepens his insight.

4. Brilliant (*arciṣmatī*): All good qualities are vigorously pursued.

5. Hard to Conquer (*sadurjayā*): The bodhisattva devotes himself to his own development and to the welfare of others.

6. Facing Forward (*abhimukhī*): Great wisdom is attained and insight into the true nature of all phenomena.

7. Going Far (*dūrangamā*): The power of 'skilful means' (*upāya-kauśalya) is attained.

8. Immovable (*acalā*): The possibility of falling back is gone forever.

9. The Good (*sādhumatī*): The bodhisattva preaches the doctrine and converts beings.

10. Cloud of the Dharma (*dharmamegha*): The bodhisattva reaches full perfection and is consecrated as a fully enlightened Buddha. He sits, surrounded by bodhisattvas, on a lotus in the Tuṣita heaven. This stage is also known as abhiṣeka-bhūmi.

H. Dayal, *The Bodhisattva Doctrine in Buddhist Sanskrit Literature* (1932).

Bhumi ('earth'): see LOKA.

Bhūta (Skt., √*bhu*, 'being'). 1. In S. Asian philosophy, an element, especially a *mahābhūta (gross element) but also a tanmātra (subtle element: see AHAṂKARA). Hindu systems of philosophy list five gross elements: ether (*ākāśa), air, fire, water, and earth.

2. Spirits; in the *Brāhmaṇas, human and non-human beings; in later texts, malignant spirits or goblins. Bhūtas are distinguished from *asuras (demons), *yakṣas (sprites), and *rākṣasas (ogres). **Manusmṛti* prescribes a morning and evening offering as propitiation to the bhūtas, who will otherwise plague one's household with misfortune, strife, and disease.

Bhūtas have become equated with *pretas or ghosts of people who died violently or who lacked descendants to perform the *śrāddha ceremony. They haunt houses and forests, casting no shadow and never touching the ground. Their contact may be avoided by lying on the ground, and they may be driven off by burning turmeric.

Bhūtaśuddhi (Skt., 'purification of the elements'). The ritual purification of the body in *Tantrism, so as to render the body sacred in order to worship a deity. The gross body is made up of five elements (earth, water, fire, air, ether), and through *visualization and *mantra repetition each element is systematically dissolved into its subtle source. Each element is associated with a particular area of the body (though correspondences vary in different texts): earth from the feet to the knees, water from the knees to the navel, fire from the navel to the heart, air from the heart to between the eyes, and ether (*ākāśa) from between the eyes upwards. So beginning with the feet and working upwards, the *sādhaka dissolves the gross body and merges into *Śakti in form of the *bīja mantra. The sādhaka then emerges with a pure body made of *sattva, having burnt away the impurity of the gross body. The next stage of the *pūjā is the formal assimilation of the divine mantra body of the deity to his own through *nyāsa. Thus the sādhaka's body becomes the deity's body and the deity enters his heart, the idea being that only a god can worship a god. The body corresponds to the cosmos, so bhūtaśuddhi recapitulates at a personal level the process of cosmic dissolution (*pralaya). Bhūtaśuddhi is a preliminary rite in all forms of Tantric pūjā.

Bhūtatathatā (Skt., 'suchness of existents'). In Buddhism, the true nature, as opposed to the appearance, of the manifest world. It is 'that which really is', in contrast to all that is transient, and thus in *Mahāyāna, it is the *buddha-nature.

Bhuvaneśvara ('Lord of the world', title of Śiva): see BHUBANESWAR.

Bībī. Honorific title for Sikh women, e.g. Bībī Nānakī, Gurū *Nānak's elder sister.

Bible. The collection of sacred writings of Jews, or that of Christians. The word derives from Gk. *biblia*, 'books', which came to be used as a singular noun as the books of the Bible were thought of as a unity. See also CANON and articles on individual books. The Hebrew Bible is divided into three sections, *Torah (law), Nevi'im (*prophets) and Ketuvim (*writings). From the initial letters, the acronym Ta Na Kh is formed, which thus becomes a common name for the Bible i.e. Tanach, Tanak, etc. Torah includes *Genesis, *Exodus, *Leviticus, *Numbers, and *Deuteronomy (collectively known as the *Pentateuch). Nevi'im includes *Joshua, *Judges, *1 and 2 Samuel, *1 and 2 Kings, *Isaiah, *Jeremiah, and the twelve prophets. The Ketuvim are *Psalms, * Proverbs, *Job, the five *scrolls (the *Song of Songs, *Ruth, *Lamentations, *Ecclesiastes, *Esther), *Daniel, *Ezra, *Nehemiah, and *1 and 2 Chronicles. This division into three parts goes back at least to the 2nd cent. BCE. Other books which are not regarded as canonical are to be found in the *Apocrypha and *pseudepigrapha. Much was translated into Greek (*Septuagint) and Aramaic (*Targum) before Christian times.

The earliest Hebrew term for the Bible was *ha-seferim* (the books), the Greek translation of which is *ta biblia*. The notion of a canon of scripture is distinctively Jewish, and the Jews saw themselves as separate from other people in their devotion to the Bible (cf. the aphorism of BEN GURION). The scriptures were perceived as a witness to the nation's history and the guarantee of God's promise to them in the future. It is not known why some books survived and entered the canon while others, such as the 'Chronicles of King David' (mentioned in 1 Chronicles 27. 24), disappeared, but the sacredness and authority of the existing books were beyond dispute among the Jewish people. The text was interpreted from the time of Ezra by *scribes who checked and rechecked that the text was correct. Later the *tannaim and the *amoraim formulated *midrash, (interpretations and explanations of the biblical text), and biblical exegesis has constituted a major theme in Jewish literature until the present day. Of the great commentators, *Rashi remains outstanding.

The focus of the *Sabbath morning service in the *synagogue is the appointed *reading from the Torah Scroll. This is followed by the *haftarah reading (again a fixed extract) from a prophet book which in some sense illumines the Torah reading. During the course of a year, the entire Pentateuch is read. Many of the liturgical *prayers are based on the psalms and other biblical verses, and it is probable that the poetic texts were originally preserved through the repertoire of the professional guild of *Temple singers. Biblical stories have also been a constant inspiration for both Jewish and Christian art.

The Christian Bible consists of two parts, the Old and the New Testaments. The Christian Old Testament corresponds to the Hebrew Bible. *Roman Catholic and *Orthodox Bibles also include other books and parts of books which belonged to the *Septuagint version of the Jewish scriptures. Until recently Roman Catholics usually cited the names of books in the *Vulgate form. Protestant Bibles restrict the Old Testament to the Hebrew canon, segregating these other writings as the Apocrypha, or omitting them as is the practice of the Bible Societies.

The New Testament was formed as the second part of the Christian Bible when at an early date churches began to regard certain of their own writings in Greek, especially if of apostolic origin, as of equal authority and inspiration to those inherited from Judaism. It attained its present form in the 4th cent., comprising four *Gospels, Acts, thirteen epistles of Paul, seven catholic epistles, and Revelation. By the 5th cent. there were translations of the New Testament into Syriac, Armenian, Coptic, Latin (see VULGATE), and Ethiopic. See also CANON.

The most important English versions of the Bible still in use are (with dates of New and Old Testaments):

1. The Rheims-Douai version (1582, 1610): a Roman Catholic translation based on the Vulgate.

2. The Authorized or King James Version (1611): the only familiar version to the mass of English-speaking people until the mid-20th cent.

3. The Revised Version (1881, 1885): an eventually unpopular revision of the foregoing, in the same style but following better manuscripts.

4. The Revised Standard Version (1946, 1952): an American revision deriving from the Authorized Version, eliminating archaisms but keeping close to the words of the original text.

5. The New English Bible (1961, 1970; revised 1989 as The Revised English Bible): a departure from the tradition of the Authorized Version supported by most non-Catholic British churches and aiming at a timeless literary style.

6. The Jerusalem Bible (1966; revised as The New Jerusalem Bible, 1985): the English version of an originally French Catholic translation, notably modern as in its translation of the *tetragrammaton as 'Yahweh' rather than 'the LORD'.

7. The Good News Bible (1966, 1976): a version in simple non-ecclesiastical language published by the Bible Societies.

8. The New American Bible. A translation (1952–70) undertaken by R. Catholics in response to the *encyclical, *Divino afflante Spiritu*, which encouraged attention to the original text and meaning. The NT was revised in 1978.

9. The New Revised Standard Version (1989, 1995). This translation is remarkable for its attention to gender-inclusive language.

10. The New American Standard Bible (1960–3, but with subsequent editions containing corrections, etc.).

11. The New International Version (1965–75, revised 1985), a widely used version aiming at natural English style and conformity to conservative evangelical understanding.

In Christianity, the Old Testament retained its authority although the details of law were superseded by *grace. Taken together, the Old and New Testaments form a single and continuous record of God's revelation. While different styles of interpretation were allowed (*hermeneutics), the fundamental inerrancy of the Bible seemed to be demonstrated by the Divine authorship. Critical historical study of the Bible has changed this outlook since the 19th cent., at least in the W. Church outside *fundamentalist circles. The use of tools such as *form criticism is now generally recognized as a prerequisite for interpreting the Bible. Despite the rigidity of earlier statements, this consensus may be said now to include the Roman Catholic Church. Papal teaching on biblical interpretation has concentrated on the need of interpreters to follow the teaching authority of the Church in matters of faith. See also HERMENEUTICS.

Thus Christian understandings of the provenance of the Bible are unlike that of Muslims of the *Qur'ān. While recognizing the initiative of God (especially through (the agency of) the Holy Spirit) in bringing these words into being, they have largely abandoned theories of 'divine dictation', as though the human author/poet/prophet, etc., simply 'took down' the words dictated. The process is seen as one in which the work is concursive, with God not by-passing, or overruling, the human competence and social circumstances of the writer. For this reason, Muslims, who acknowledge Jews and Christians as 'people of the Book' (*ahl al-kitāb), regard the Bible as defective and compromised when compared with the Qur'ān.

For a list of books, see Index, Biblical books.

The Cambridge History of the Bible, ed. P. R. Ackroyd (1963–70); A. S. Herbert, *Historical Catalogue of Printed Edns. of the English Bible, 1525–1961* (1968).

Bible Belt. The southern states of the United States of America, where the mainstream of Christianity is characteristically *fundamentalist, stressing the literalism and inerrancy of the Bible. See also BRANCH DAVIDIANS.

Biblical theology. A movement in Christian theology, especially in the 1930s–1950s, which sought to expound a common, 'biblical' (usually, 'Hebraic') viewpoint and language in the Old and New Testaments. In so far as some technical terms in the latter acquired shades of meaning from the Old Testament (through the *Septuagint), the insight was valid. But its proponents often exaggerated the difference between 'Hebrew' and 'Greek' thought; built too much on studies of single words; and did not appreciate the diversity among the different biblical writers and periods.

Bidʿa (Arab., 'innovation'). Belief or practice for which there is no precedent in the *sunna of Prophet *Muḥammad. Generally speaking, bidʿa as 'innovation' has a bad sense, since it implies unconsidered disruption of what God has revealed and intended in *Qur'ān. However, jurists such as Imām *al-Shāfiʿi recognized that allowances must be made for changes in environments and other conditions, and in the development of knowledge. He therefore taught that there were good and even necessary innovations as long as they did not contradict Qur'ān, *sunna, and *ijmāʿ. Thus a distinction came to be made between bidʿa which was good (*ḥasanna*) or praiseworthy (such as the study of Quranic philology, rhetoric, and *fiqh), and one which was bad (*sayyiʿa*) or blameworthy, such as discos and free mixing of the sexes in public. In some Muslim countries, such as Iran, even such aspects of Westernization as the use of *tobacco are denounced as bidʿa. However, even amongst the most conservative *ʿulamā, modern scientific knowledge and technology are viewed as good bidʿa.

Big Wild Goose Pagoda: see SIAN.

Bihbahānī, Vahid (Aqa Muḥammad Baqir ibn Muḥammad Akmal, 1706–92 (AH 1118–1207)). Shiʿite scholar and definer of the Uṣūlī system of jurisprudence. He was born in Isfahān and spent his early life in Bihbahān, but when he settled in *Karbalā' in 1746, his influence extended widely. In contrast to the traditionalist Akhbārīs (who required precedent for all decisions), he recognized the legitimacy of *ijtihād and of the work of the mujtāhidūn, who apply principles to current issues and arrive at novel and unprecedented decisions. Aggressive in the extreme, he declared the Akhbārīs to be *kāfirs (expelling them to a marginal existence in such places as S. Iraq), and he employed a religious police (*mirghadabs*, 'executors of wrath') to enforce his views— a kind of precursor of the Revolutionary Guards. He also greatly strengthened the authority of the *ʿulamā, allowing the *Mullas to follow his example and to declare themselves Mujtāhids and representatives of the Hidden *Imām on earth. This theory of ijtihād, which led to the authoritarian development of Shiʿite Islam, is set forth in *Risalat al-ijtihad wa'l-akhbar*.

Bīja (Skt., 'seed, potency'). In both Hinduism and Buddhism, the latent power underlying every manifest appearance. In particular, bīja is the power concentrated in a symbolic sound, which a *guru has learnt in experience, and which he passes on to a pupil in a bīja *mantra (seed syllable). As aspect of the absolute reality is thus concentrated in the mantra.

Biku. Jap. for *bhikṣu.

Bilā kaif(a): see ALLĀH; AL-ASHʿARĪ.

Bilāl b. Rabāḥ. (d. *c.*641 AH 20). One of the first Muslims, best known as the first *muezzin of *Muḥammad. Of African origin, he was a slave in *Mecca and possibly the first adult convert after *Abu Bakr. He suffered persecution for his faith, was freed by Abu Bakr, and became a personal servant to Muḥammad, whom he followed to *Madīna. When the *ādhān (call to prayer) was instituted, in the first year of the *hijra, he became the first to give it; after the conquest of Mecca in 630 (AH 8) it was Bilāl who gave the first adhān from the roof of the *Kaʿba. He accompanied Muḥammad on his military expeditions, and after his master's death spent most of the rest of his life on campaign in Syria.

Bimah (Heb., 'elevated place'). *Synagogue platform on which the *Torah reading stand is placed. Sermons may be preached from the bimah, the Torah is chanted there, and the *shofar is blown. Reading the Torah from a raised platform goes back to the days of *Nehemiah (Nehemiah 8. 4). In most synagogues, it is placed in the centre of the building but among *Progressive congregations, it is sited directly in front of the *Ark. Alternative names for the bimah are *almemar or *tevah*.

Bimbisāra, Seniya. King of Magadha at the time of the *Buddha. He had ruled for fifteen years when Gautāma, at the age of 30, passed through his capital on his quest for enlightenment. Thereafter the two had a long and cordial relationship, and after hearing the Buddha preach, Bimbisāra gained the stage of *srotāpanna (stream-enterer). He became a patron of the Buddhist *saṅgha and donated a park for the use of monks. The relationship developed along reciprocal lines, with the Buddha offering advice to the king on religious matters and accepting it in return on questions of monastic practice and jurisprudence. Bimbisara abdicated in favour of his son Ajātasattu, but was imprisoned and tortured by him. According to tradition, after his death, which preceded that of the Buddha by eight years, Bimbisāra was reborn in a heavenly world where he continued his practice of the Buddhist way.

Binding of Isaac: see ʿAKEDA.

Bindu (Skt., 'drop' or 'particle'). A complex term of varied though related meanings in Hinduism and especially in *Tantrism.

1. In a general sense it is the expression of the highest consciousness (*samvid*) as *Śakti which is subtle, eternal, and pervades the whole universe, yet is also the centre of creation.

2. More specifically in *Śāivism and *Śaktism, bindu is a technical term for the material cause of pure creation (see KASHMIR ŚAIVISM). It is contrasted with *māyā, the material cause of impure creation, though both must be regarded as two aspects of one reality which interpenetrate each other. Thus there is nothing in māyā which does not contain some trace of bindu and nothing in bindu without a trace of māyā. This allows for the possibility of transformation from one to the other. Bindu is equated with *Śiva *tattva, the top of pure creation, out of which emerges *nāda or śakti tattva. In other Tantric classifications, however, bindu is said to emerge from nāda. It then becomes threefold, *tribindu* or *kāmakalā*, which comprises bindu, nāda, and *bīja. From the tribindu evolves the *matṛkas* (mothers), which are subtle sounds, and from them the gross letters (*varṇa*). At a great dissolution (*mahāpralaya) all manifestation collapses back into bindu. Pure beings (such as Vijñānakalas) who have gone beyond māyā are said to have a pure body made of bindu.

3. Bindu is equated with the *anusvāra*, the nasalized vowel in Sanskrit (ṃ) represented in devanāgarī as a dot with the letter. It has great symbolic significance in *mantra as the absolute contracted to a point, the pure potential out of which the universe emanates and to which it returns. For example, *ahaṃ ('I') is a Śaiva mantra symbolizing the going out and withdrawal of the cosmos.

4. Cosmic evolution (the macrocosm) is located within the body (the microcosm) in Tantrism. Thus bindu is located between the eyebrows as a drop which is the object of meditation. It is sometimes identified with *Kuṇḍalinī, within which *laya yoga* is called bindu *sādhana.

5. In its grossest sense, bindu is a synonym for semen, cosmic potential reduced to an individual level. Like thought (*citta) and breath (*prāṇa), semen is ever restless. Through yoga and meditation, semen, thought, and breath are controlled and the lower bindu is transformed to the higher bindu between the eyebrows.

6. Bindu is depicted as the point in the centre of the *Śrī yantra.

Literature concerning bindu is found in the *Āgamas, *Tantras, and related texts. There are different interpretations of bindu. The monistic Trika, or Kashmir Saivism, maintains that bindu is identical with the absolute consciousness (*parāsaṃvid*), whereas the dualistic *Śaiva Siddhānta maintains that bindu is part of *pāśa* which is quite distinct from the Lord (*pati*) and from individual souls (**paśu*).

Biogenetic structuralism and religion. Biogenetic structuralism is an account of the way in which the gene-protein process in the formation of the human body, and especially of the brain, prepares human beings for characteristic behaviours and for a range of different competence. It thus prepares us for linguistic, sexual, musical, etc., competence, without dictating what we do with each competence. The claim is that we are prepared also for religious competence, and that religious beliefs and behaviours are consequently an inevitable part of human life. Biogenetic structuralism proposes two operators arising from different parts of the brain: the inferior parietal lobule on the dominant side, the anterior convexity of the frontal lobes (primarily on the dominant side), and their reciprocal neural interconnections account for causal sequencing of elements of reality abstracted from sense perceptions—especially in the operation of cross-modal transfer. This is the causal operator, which operates in the same way as a mathematical operator: it organizes a given 'strip of reality' into what is subjectively perceived as causal sequences taken back to the initial source of that strip. If the initiating source is not given by sense data, the causal operator generates a source automatically. When these are personalized, they produce the religious consequence of gods, powers, spirits, devils, demons, etc. When the strip of reality is the entire universe, the initial source produced by the causal operator is *Brahman, the unproduced Producer of all that is *Aristotle's unmoved Mover, and the like. While this accounts for those religious phenomena which allow interaction with personalized sources of power (e.g. *myth, *ritual, *sacrifice, *symbol), it does not eliminate the issue of *ontology, i.e. whether there is in reality (in addition to the strip of reality which has evoked the causal operator) that which is claimed to be the source, allowing that it is necessarily described in approximate and corrigible language (see J. Bowker, *Licensed Insanities*, 1987): that is, the second level of *phenomenology, to which the theory points. The second operator is distinct from that concerned with control. It produces those states commonly described as *mystical. In the human autonomic system are two subsystems, the sympathetic (concerned with short-term energy expending, e.g. 'fight or flee', hence called ergotropic) and parasympathetic (concerned with energy-conserving in body-function maintenance, hence called trophotropic). Rhythmicity in the environement, whether visual, auditory, tactile, or propriocentive, drives the sympathetic-ergotropic system to maximal capacity with intermittent spillover and simultaneous activation of the parasympathetic-trophotropic system, thus creating unusual subjective states. The non-dominant parieto-occipital region of the brain is progressively activated, and this constitutes the second operator, the holistic operator, creating an increasing sense of wholeness which dominates progressively over the sense of multiplicity in ordinarily sensed reality. The suspension, or suppression, of rhythmicity produces the same consequence via the parasympathetic-trophotropic system. Other effects (e.g. the use of *incense), by stimulating the pleasure system, reinforce the attainment of ecstatic unitary states. Of these, the sense of absolute unitary being (often summarized as AUB) is described in virtually all religions: the difference between one's self and any other is obliterated, there is no sense of the passing of time, and all that remains is a perfect, timeless, undifferentiated consciousness. The state may in fact (and in time) be extremely brief, but qualitatively it leads to self-transcendence of such a kind that the contingencies of life (including death) seem comparatively unimportant. This is reported even by those (e.g. Bertrand Russell) who remain atheist. Since these fundamental constituents of religion have a gene-protein base in the brain, religions (for all that they do much more than this) will persist in human life in some form. Whereas the sign held up by prophets of doom used to read, 'Prepare to meet thy God', biogenetic structuralism rewrites the sign to read, 'Prepared to meet thy God'.

E. G. d'Aquili *et al.*, *The Spectrum of Ritual* (1979); C. D. Laughlin and E. G. d'Aquili, *Biogenetic Structuralism* (1974); C. D. Laughlin *et al.*, *Brain, Symbol and Experience* . . . (1990).

Birkat ha-mazon: see GRACE.

Birkat ha-minim (Heb., '*benediction concerning heretics'). The twelfth benediction of the Jewish *Amidah. It invokes God's wrath on the 'kingdom of arrogance'. It originates from the time of the second *Temple and has been used against collaborators, *Sadducees, and Judaeo-Christian sects. Although Jews have been accused of specially inveighing against Christians in their liturgy, the prayer is only directed against Jewish heretics and *gentile persecutors of the community: 'For apostates who have rejected your *Torah, let there be no hope, and may the Nazarenes and heretics perish in an instant . . . Blessed are you, O Lord, the one who shatters his enemies and humbles the proud.'

Birkat ha-Torah (Heb., '*Blessing of the *Law'). The blessing required by Jewish law before reading or studying the *Torah. The formula for the *benediction is, 'Blessed are you, Lord, our God, King of the Universe . . . who has chosen us from all nations and has given us your Law'. This should be pronounced both publicly in the *synagogue and privately at home before individual study.

Birth and population control. In general, religions give to birth the highest possible value. In W. religions, it tends to be seen as a matter of responsibility, aligned with the will of God: it is indeed a matter of pro-creation. In E. religions, birth continues the sequences of reincarnation or of reappearance (*punabbhāva). Although, to varying degrees and in different ways, each religion allows contraception, the emphasis is on the marvel and opportunity of birth.

In Judaism, the first command in the Bible is, 'Be fruitful and multiply' (Genesis 1. 28). Thus any measure to prevent conception involves breaking a positive command. The only biblical reference is the sin of Onan (Genesis 38. 9 f.) who was punished for spilling his seed on the ground instead of fulfilling his duty to raise children in the name of his dead brother. Hence male contraception is forbidden. However, in some circumstances, some (not all) methods of contraception are allowed. The most general circumstances are those which involve threat to the woman or a potential foetus. *B.Ket.* 39a requires contraception for those under 12 (at that time able to be married), pregnant mothers, and nursing mothers. The methods of contraception tend to favour those used by women (i.e. not the condom), since women may not be under the obligation of the command. *Progressive Judaism extends the notion of welfare to include the existing family, allowing family planning.

Christianity has followed the same instinct to forbid contraception, though (generally) without the same attention to detail. Churches apart from the *Roman Catholic Church have come to emphasize the whole marriage act, including the sustenance of the family, as a matter of love-endowed responsibility. The RC Church was moving in the same direction until 1968, when Pope Paul VI issued the *encyclical, **Humanae Vitae*, which reaffirmed the condemnation of artificial measures to prevent conception (against the majority advice of the commission set up in 1963 to assess the issue) which had appeared in the encyclical *Casti Connubii* (1930): 'Any use of marriage, whatever, in the exercise of which the act is deprived through human industry of its natural power of procreating life, violates the law of God and of nature.' It follows that the sexual act at times (e.g. in the monthly cycle) of natural infertility is permitted, even though it is not open to the possibility of conception.

In Islam, 'the preservation of the human species is unquestionably the primary objective of marriage' (al-Qaradāwi), but contraception is allowed for valid reasons: danger to the mother or a potential foetus, the burden of a further child on the existing family, protecting a suckling infant. According to *ibn Ḥanbal, the consent of the woman is required. While *coitus interruptus* (condemned in Judaism as 'the sin of Onan and Er') is the method most commonly discussed in *ḥadīth, there is no ban on modern methods.

Biruni (Muslim scholar): see AL-BĪRŪNĪ.

Birushan(a) (Jap.) (transcendent Buddha): see VAIROCANA.

Bishop (Anglo-Saxon via Lat. from Gk., *episkopos*). In Christian Churches, recognizing a threefold ministry (*deacons, *priests, bishops), the bishop is the highest order. In New Testament times, the offices of *episkopos* (literally, 'overseer') and *presbyteros* ('elder') are not distinguished (e.g. Titus 1. 5, 7). 'Monepiscopacy', in which a church is governed by a single bishop presiding over the lower orders of *presbyters (priests) and deacons, first appears in the letters of *Ignatius. By the middle of the 2nd cent. this government spread throughout *Catholic Christianity and the succession of bishops in their sees (*apostolic succession) became a matter of theological importance. Episcopal organization ceased to be universal at the *Reformation, but was retained by certain *Lutheran churches. Among other Protestants, the *Moravians and, in America, *Methodists, also have bishops. In Protestant use, the title does not always imply a claim to identity with the ancient office.

In Catholic doctrine, bishops are distinguished from priests chiefly by their authority to confer holy *orders and to administer *confirmation. They are normally 'consecrated' at the hands of a *metropolitan and two other bishops. The bishop's duties are the general oversight of the diocese, including the supervision of the clergy. He may have assistants known as *suffragan, auxiliary, coadjutor, or assistant bishops. In E. Churches (excluding in the past the *Assyrian Church) bishops, unlike other priests, must be celibate (but if he is a widower, he may enter a monastic state and become eligible to be chosen). This requirement means in practice that bishops are recruited from the ranks of monks.

Among the insignia traditional to the bishop are the throne in his *cathedral, *mitre, pastoral staff, pectoral cross, and ring. The most usual style of bishops is 'Right Reverend', or for *archbishops 'Most Reverend'.

For individual bishops, see Index, Bishops.

Bismillah ('in the Name of Allāh'): see BASMALA; SŪRA.

Bistāmī (Persian Sūfī): see AL-BISTĀMĪ.

Bitter herbs (eoder at Jewish Passover): see MAROR.

Bittul ha-tamid (Heb., 'abolition of the daily offering'). Interruption of *synagogue *liturgy to draw attention to a wrong. The purpose of bittul ha-tamid was to arouse 'public scandal for the rights of the individual'. According to *Gershom b. Judah, 'a plaintiff may not stop the morning prayers and reading of the *Torah, unless he has first three times stopped the evening services', but exceptions were made for widows and orphans. It was a custom mainly practised by *Ashkenazi Jews in the Middle Ages.

Bittul ha-yesh (the presence of God alone in creation): see ḤABAD.

BJP (Indian Political Party): see BHARATYA JANATA PARTY.

Black American religion: see AFRICAN-AMERICAN RELIGION.

Blackfriars. A specifically English medieval nickname given to the *Dominicans because of the black cape they wear. Designation of different orders of monks by the colour of their habit was common in other languages, but in English the practice included *canons and *friars as well.

Black Jews. Members of cults that emerged in Harlem, New York City, shortly after the First World War. Prophet F. S. Cherry, one of the first leaders of the Black Jews, maintained that his followers were the true Israelites of the Bible, and that *Jesus was black. Another important early Black Jewish figure was Arnold Ford from Barbados. Though grouped into a number of different sects, all Black Jews claim that they are descendants of Ethiopian Hebrews (cf. FALASHAS) who were deprived of their religion, sacred language (Hebrew), and names, during the era of slavery. Some are strictly *kosher* (see DIETARY LAWS), celebrate all the principal Jewish festivals, and hold services, which are characterized by sobriety and restraint, on Friday nights and Saturdays; others are more eclectic, drawing on Christian *Pentecostal traditions, as well as *kabbalistic and rabbinic sources. There appears to be little historical or social connection with the mainstream Jewish community.

Black Mass. Usually a blasphemous caricature of the *mass, with an inversion of symbols and a worship of *Satan, not God. But the term is also used colloquially for the requiem mass for the dead when black vestments are used.

H. F. T. Rhodes, *The Satanic Mass* (1965).

Black Muslims. Members of the Nation of Islam, established in Detroit in the 1930s by Wallace D. Fard (sometimes Ford); the movement is unorthodox in relation to Islam. Proclaiming himself 'the Supreme Ruler of the Universe', and later to be identified with God, Allāh, Fard hailed black people as the founders of civilization, and predicted the destruction of Caucasians and Christianity and the establishment of a Black Nation after the final judgement of the white race.

*Elijah Muhammad took over the movement on Fard's disappearance in 1934, assuming the titles 'Minister of Islam' and 'Prophet'. *Malcolm X became Elijah Muhammad's chief aide in 1963 before breaking away to found the Muslim Mosque, Inc., and the Organization of Afro-American Unity. He was assassinated in Feb. 1965.

Less dedicated now than in its past to the goal of establishing a separate black nation, the Nation of Islam confines itself for the most part to the pursuit of social justice and equality for blacks. Use is made of both the *Qur'ān and the *Bible, and services are held both in Arabic and English.

Black Pagoda (Konārak temple): see SŪRYA.

Black shamanism (contest against malevolent spirits): see SHAMANS.

Black Stone (*al-ḥajar al-aswad*). A stone said to be of meteoric origin, variously thought to be of lava or basalt, and reddish-black in colour, some 12 inches in diameter, embedded in the eastern corner of the *Kaʿba in *Mecca. As the Kaʿba is the focus of Muslim devotion, being the 'house of *Allāh', so is the Black Stone the holiest object, and during the *ḥajj (pilgrimage) the pilgrims try to kiss or touch it as they walk seven times around the Kaʿba. See also BARAKA.

Blake, William (1757–1827). Poet, artist, and visionary. Trained as an engraver, he soon combined his talent for illustration with his poetic gifts and, with *Songs of Innocence* (1789), began a series of works, engraved and combining text and coloured illustration. His vision combined a positive acceptance of, and delight in, the world of the senses, both the immediately pleasing and that which is darker and more threatening: it was expressed through verbal and visual imagery that became increasingly complex and allegorical. The key to all this Blake found in various occult traditions—hermetic, *Neoplatonic, *gnostic, and especially the theosophy of *Swedenborg. He was opposed to what he saw as the lifeless, mechanical applications of the science of Newton, and equally to the rational, conceptual religion of the 18th cent. In this he prefigured Romanticism and shared its horror for the damage done by the Industrial Revolution to any genuinely human life: 'Let every Christian, as much as in him lies, engage himself openly and publicly, before all the World, in some mental pursuit for the Building up of Jerusalem.'

Blasphemy (Gk., 'speaking evil'). Impious or profane talk, especially against God; and in many W. legal systems, the offence of reviling God or *Jesus Christ or an established church. To be blasphemous, a publication must be intended to shock and endanger the moral fabric of society; one that is merely anti-religious (e.g. denying the existence of God) is not. In England in 1977 the editor of *Gay News* was convicted of blasphemous libel for publishing a poem which portrayed Jesus as a practising homosexual. This was the first successful prosecution for blasphemy since 1922, and showed the difficulty of objectively applying the common-law definition. The appearance of Salman Rushdie's *The *Satanic Verses*, raised the issue whether blasphemy should be extended to become a more general offence (in the UK), or whether it is an offence in the domain of inciting unrest.

In Judaism, 'blasphemy' is speaking scornfully of God (Heb., *gidduf, ḥeruf*) and is described euphemistically as *birkat ha-Shem* ('blessing the Name', i.e. God). According to Leviticus 24. 10–23, the penalty for cursing God is death, but in discussing this passage, the *rabbis defined blasphemy in such a way that it became an improbable crime—and thus the death penalty did not need to be invoked. Excommunication (*ḥerem) became the punishment in any case once legal autonomy had been lost. See further L. W. Leary, *Treason Against God: A History . . .* (1981).

The nearest equivalent in Islam is *sabb*, offering an

insult to God. Qur'ān 9. 74 condemns those who 'swear by God that they said nothing but in fact spoke a word of rejection (*kalimat al-kufr*) after they had become Muslim'. This relates blasphemy closely to apostasy (*ridda). The expression of contempt for God, the Prophet *Muḥammad, the angels, or the traditional religious explications of revelation constitutes the offence. Accidental blasphemy is not usually excusable (though *Mālikites allow it if it is expressed by a recent convert to Islam). The punishment varies between the different *Schools of Islamic Law—e.g. the *Ḥanafites remove the offender's legal rights, declare his marriage invalid, and declare any claims to inheritance or property void; the Mālikites demand immediate execution of the death penalty.

Blavatsky, H. P.: see THEOSOPHICAL SOCIETY.

Blessing. A two-way movement of (from humans to God) thanksgiving and praise, and of (from God to humans) power and goodness/good fortune. Blessings (in both senses) are prominent in Judaism, where it is said that there is a blessing for every occasion. The formula for invocation is *barakh* and for good luck *berakhah* (blessing), *shālōm (peace), or *tov* (good). A blessing was perceived as a source of power and the *rabbis taught that 'the blessing' or *cursing of an ordinary person should not be lightly estimated (*B.Meg.* 15a). See also BENEDICTIONS.

In Christianity, blessings occur especially in worship and in the *liturgy—e.g. at the end of the *eucharist and other services, where the congregation is blessed. Often the words of Numbers 6. 24–6 or Philippians 4. 7 are used. Objects are also ritually blessed: *vestments, oil for *unction, etc., and even purely secular objects (e.g. as the clergyman's part in a civic ceremony).

In Islam, *baraka was associated originally with fecundity and having many descendants. From this it came to mean success or prosperity in more general terms. The source is always God, even when it is mediated through people or places close to him in *islām*.

C. Westermann, *Blessing: In the Bible and the Life of the Church* (1978).

Blondel, Maurice (1861–1949). French *Roman Catholic philosopher. His *Letter on Apologetics* (1896; Eng. tr. 1964) and *History and Dogma* (1904; Eng. tr. 1964) concern issues raised by the *Modernist crisis, though their importance transcends this context. His deepest influence on RC philosophy and theology has come through his analysis of the way in which human willing and action may embody an implicit acknowledgement of God (see especially *L'Action*, 1893). Blondel thought that there is a desire for the supernatural immanent in the dynamism of the will, and that therefore our mental life is directed to possession of the *Beatific Vision.

R. Virgoulay and C. Troisfontaines, *Maurice Blondel: Bibliographie* (1975).

Blood. Commonly held in religions to be the sign and condition of life, and therefore a fundamental constituent of *sacrifices. Because of its importance in relation to God's gift of life, the Jewish *Bible contains an absolute prohibition against swallowing the blood of an animal (see Leviticus 3. 17; Deuteronomy 12. 15–16). The justification for this is the belief that the blood contained life (Leviticus 17. 11). The Israelites were also commanded to drain the blood when sacrificing animals because it was through the blood that expiation for *sin was effected. The prohibition was regarded as one of the seven *Noachide Laws, hence its appearance as a minimal requirement in early Christianity for converts (who would not be required to observe the whole of *Torah: see Acts 15), and as a mark of ethical monotheism in pre-Islamic *Mecca. The prohibition leads directly to laws of *kashrut* (see DIETARY LAWS) and *sheḥitah (the method for slaughtering animals). Eating meat was itself a concession on the part of God after the *Flood.

In Christianity, the shedding of the blood of *Christ came to be understood as the continuation and culmination of the *Temple sacrifices, achieving completely that which they had partially anticipated (see especially Hebrews). At the *eucharist, the words of institution are repeated ('This is my blood . . .'), so that Christians participate in the divine life, the eternal in the midst of time (John 6. 25–71). From this developed devotion to the Precious Blood (from the *Vulgate tr. of 1 Peter 1. 19), decreed as a feast day for the whole Church by Pius IX in 1859, though transferred to a votive mass after *Vatican II.

Bloodguilt. In Judaism the liability for punishment of those who have shed blood. Deliberate murder is punishable by death, and God is the final guarantor that homicide will be avenged. In Genesis 9. 5–6 God explains, 'For your lifeblood I will surely require a reckoning . . . Whoever sheds the blood of man, by man shall his blood be shed.' The blood-avenger is known as *goel ha-dam* (see e.g. Judges 8. 18–21, 2 Samuel 3. 27, 13. 28 ff.). If someone has killed accidentally, he must flee to a *city of refuge until the natural death of the *high priest acts as a substitute for his death (Numbers 35. 9–28). No bloodguilt, however, is incurred by killing in self-defence (Exodus 22. 1), nor as a result of execution (Leviticus 20. 9–16), nor in the course of war (1 Kings 2. 5–6).

Blood-libel. The accusation that *Jews murder non-Jews to obtain *blood for *Passover rituals. Rumour of the blood-libel allegation goes back at least to the 2nd cent. BCE. The first distinct case was in Norwich in 1144 when the Jews were said to have tortured a Christian child before Easter 'in hatred of our Lord'. This accusation was repeated in many places in the Middle Ages and was the cause of anti-Jewish riots and massacres. The Jews themselves consistently and vehemently denied it, but blood-libel cases by the 17th cent. had spread to E. Europe and were a regular motif in *anti-Semitic propaganda until the Second World War.

Blood of the martyrs, seed of the Church (Christian evaluation of martyrdom): see PERSECUTION; TERTULLIAN.

Blue Cliff Record (Chinese Ch'an verses): see HSÜEH-TOU CH'UNG-HSIEN.

B'nai B'rith (Heb., 'Sons of the *Covenant'). Oldest and largest Jewish *charitable organization. It was founded in 1843 in New York, and its aim is 'to unite persons of the Jewish faith in the work of promoting their highest interests and those of humanity' (the B'nai B'rith Constitution). The work is effected through local lodges, and today the organization has a total membership of approximately half a million people throughout the world.

E. E. Grusd, *B'nai B'rith: The Story of a Covenant* (1967).

Bo, as in Bo Tree: see BO TREE.

Boanerges. The surname given by *Jesus (Mark 3. 17) to *James and *John. According to Mark, it means 'sons of thunder', but its derivation and significance are both uncertain.

Bodai. Jap. version of Skt., *bodhi, via Chinese. It is thus the state of *kokoro, the completely enlightened mind and complete *Buddha realization. Bodaishin is the 'enlightenment mind', the determination to find complete enlightenment.

Bodaidaruma. Jap. for *bodhidharma.

Bodhgāya. On the Nairañjana River, Bihar, the legendary site of the *Bo Tree under which the *Buddha gained final enlightenment. A major place of pilgrimage, tradition ascribes the foundation of a temple on this spot to *Aśoka. Foundations certainly exist from the Kushan era (114–241 CE), when a temple was erected to house an image of the Buddha in his Earth-Witnessing posture. Although much of the original appearance is lost, the present Mahābodhi Temple contains elements from virtually every period of Buddhist art. It was substantially restored at the beginning of this century by Singhalese Buddhists, and now consists of one central tower surrounded by four smaller towers at the corners. See also DHARMAPĀLA.

As Gayā, it is sacred to Hindus as one of the seven *sacred cities. Its temple is dedicated to the lotus feet of *Viṣṇu.

Bodhi (Skt., Pāli, 'awakened'). In Hinduism, perfect knowledge, personified as Bodha, a son of Buddhi (intellect).

In Buddhism, it is the experience of enlightenment, which, unlike *nirvāna, can be given an approximate description: it is the attainment of perfect clarity of mind in which things are seen as they really are—as in the experience of Gautāma under the tree (hence called Bodhi or *Bo tree) through which he became the Buddha. Cf. BODAI.

In later Buddhism, the bodhis are the four stages of the *ārya-mārga (the path to perfection), and in Theravāda they were equated with realised understanding of the *Four Noble Truths. The consequent enlightenment is of three different kinds, that of a *srāvaka (one who seeks through the ordinary route of hearing and learning), that of *pratyekabuddha (one who seeks on his own), and that of samyaksaṃbuddha (one who seeks and finds after the *dhamma has disappeared from the world).

In *Mahāyāna, bodhi is wisdom based on insight into the undifferentiated sameness of all appearance, which leads to awareness of one's own *bussho (buddha-nature), as well as to the realization of *śūnyatā, the uncharacterizable 'emptiness' from which appearance arises. Mahāyāna also recognizes three different kinds of bodhi: for oneself (the b. of an *arhat), for others (a *bodhisattva), of a *Buddha.

Bodhicaryāvatāra (Entering upon the Practice of Awakening). A practical work by Śantideva on the Buddhist six perfections (*pāramitā), which include, as the fifth, *jhāna (meditation). Of Śantideva, nothing certain is known, apart from the fact that he was the supposed author of an analytic work, *Śikshāsamuccaya*. *Bodhicaryāvatāra* is a much revered and used work. It is basically *enstatic in emphasis, pointing to ways in which body and mind can be withdrawn from the world, and then how, in the exchange of self and other, the sense of independence in the self can also be overcome: 'Whoever wishes to give protection in the quickest possible way to himself and others should put into practice the supreme secret, the exchange of self and others.' Thus if a person sees someone lying by the road, robbed and beaten by thieves, he should minister to that person, not as the one giving help, but as the one receiving what is needed, while seeing 'another' as the one giving the help. In this way, all sense of being 'a self' is obliterated in a practical way.

Eng. trs.: from the Skt., M. L. Matics; from the Tibetan, S. Batchelor.

Bodhicitta (Skt., 'thought of enlightenment'). An important concept in *Mahāyāna Buddhism, having both a personal and a cosmic aspect. In the personal sense it denotes the spontaneous generation of the resolve to strive for enlightenment, especially with the altruistic objective of bringing benefit to other beings. The cosmic aspect of the doctrine locates the seed or first stirrings of this impulse in a transpersonal matrix or resource along absolutistic lines. Here it is reality itself, under its various denominations such as the 'Body of Truth' (*dharmakāya), the 'Womb of *Tathāgatas' (*tathāgatagarbha), or 'True

Suchness' (*bhūtatathatā), which engenders the possibility of enlightenment. The personal bodhicitta is the reflection of this potential in the human heart and is thought of as the buddha-nature latent in all beings.

In *Tantric Buddhist symbology bodhicitta is identified with the seed or semen which is produced through the union of male and female, representing the fusion of wisdom (*prajña) with compassion (*karuṇā) in the bliss of perfect enlightenment.

Bodhidharma (Chin., *P'u-t'i-ta-mo* or *Tamo*; Jap., *Bodaidaruma* or *Daruma*, *c.*5th cent. CE). The 28th successor (*hassu) in line from Śākyamuni Buddha, and the first Chinese patriarch of Ch'an/Zen Buddhism. According to the traditional accounts, he travelled from India to China, and after meeting with no success in his missionary endeavour in the south, he wandered slowly to the north (crossing the Yang-tse on a reed), and settled at the *Shao-lin monastery on Mount Shung-shan (Jap., Sūzan, Sūsan). He engaged in motionless *zazen for nine years (hence the name of this period, *menpeki-kunen, nine years facing the wall). Hui-k'o joined him as a pupil, and became the second patriarch. The forms of meditation taught by Bodhidharma were based on the *Mahāyāna sūtras, with especial emphasis on **Laṅkāvatāra-sūtra*. It produced *Dhyāna Buddhism, with dhyāna (meditation) understood in a broad sense: it was this which fused with Taoism to produce the distinctive form of Ch'an. According to tradition, Bodhidharma decided to return to India, but died (or was poisoned) before he could do so. Nevertheless, Sung Yun, on his way back from a journey to India to collect sūtras, met Bodhidharma wearing one sandal. When Sung Yun returned to China, he told Bodhidharma's followers, who opened his grave, only to find it empty, except for one sandal.

Tradition also attributes six treatises to Bodhidharma, of which one, *The Two Ways of Entrance*, is translated by D. T. Suzuki, *Essays in Zen Buddhism*, iii (1970). But this, and the whole tradition about Bodhidharma is extremely uncertain. H. Dumoulin (*Zen Buddhism*, i. 89), states that 'as far as I know, no Japanese historian of Zen has denied the historicity of Bodhidharma'; but that simply emphasizes how tenuous are any details about him. Nevertheless, to him is attributed the famous verse (actually composed much later) which summarizes Zen: 'A special transmission outside the scriptures | Not established on words and letters; | By pointing directly into the mind | It allows one to see into [the nature of one's own] nature and thus attain Buddhahood.'

Bodhidharma is usually portrayed with an appearance of fierce concentration, and Daruma-dolls are given in Japan to those who have attained a goal through perseverance.

H. N. McFarland, *Daruma: The Founder of Zen in Japanese Art and Popular Culture* (1987); Yanagida Seizan, *Daruma* (1981).

Bodhimaṇḍa. The site of the *Buddha's enlightenment under the *Bo Tree. Sometimes used to refer only to the spot on which the Buddha actually sat, and other times to the surrounding area of land with the tree at its centre. Mythologically this point becomes the point of enlightenment of all Buddhas, past, present, and future; the bodhimaṇḍa is conceived of as the centre or navel of the world, and the tree as the *axis mundi*. In iconography the Buddha is depicted as seated on the bodhimaṇḍa with his right hand touching the earth to call it to bear witness to his enlightenment.

Bodhipakkhiya-dhamma: see BODHIPĀKṢIKA-DHARMA.

Bodhipākṣika-dharma (Pāli, *bodhipakkhiya-dhamma*, 'things pertaining to enlightenment'). In Buddhism, the thirty-seven necessities for the attainment of enlightenment. They are divided into seven groups: (i) the four foundations of right attention (*satipaṭṭhāna); (ii) the four perfect efforts (*sammā-padhāna); (iii) the four components of concentrated power (*iddhi-pāda); (iv) the five roots (*indriya); (v) the five powers (*bala); (vi) the seven contributions to enlightenment (*bojjhanga); (vii) the Eightfold Path (*aṣṭangika-mārga).

Bodhiruci (translator of Buddhist scriptures): see PURE LAND SCHOOLS.

Bodhisattva (Skt.; Pāli, *bodhisatta*, 'Enlightenment-Being'; Chin., P'u-sa; Jap., Bosatsu; Korean, Posal; Tib., byang.chub sems.dpa, 'Hero of the Thought of Enlightenment'). In *Theravāda Buddhism a title exclusively identifying historical *Buddhas (i.e. *Śākyamuni) in their previous lives, before their Buddhahood was attained; and in *Mahāyāna Buddhism to describe any being who, out of compassion, has taken the *bodhisattva vow to become a Buddha for the sake of all sentient beings. The Theravādin concept involves the belief that there is only one Buddha (for this world cycle), and that the highest an ordinary man can aspire to is to be *arhat or *pratyekabuddha; the Mahāyāna concept involves the belief that the attainment of Buddha by way of being bodhisattva, is a possibility for everyone.

Within the Mahāyāna, different levels or *bhūmi (as opposed to different types) of bodhisattva are understood. Strictly, an ordinary person who has 'engendered *bodhicitta' (generated a desire for enlightenment in order to save all beings from suffering) and taken the bodhisattva vow is a bodhisattva, but there are also 'celestial bodhisattvas', such as *Mañjuśrī and *Avalokiteśvara, who are almost Buddhas in their attainments. Connecting these extremes is the series of bhūmis, or stages, of a bodhisattva's development. These are standardized as ten by **Daśabhūmika-sūtra* (Sūtra on the Ten Stages), which describes in detail the transformations in a bodhisattva's understanding as he progresses towards Buddhahood.

A bodhisattva's progress is determined by his practice of the six (sometimes given as ten) perfections (*pāramitās) which are: generosity and morality; patience and energy; meditation and wisdom. Taken in successive pairs, these perfections indicate the primary qualities which a bodhisattva seeks to unify: compassion, skilful means (*upāya-kauśalya), and wisdom. Of these, compassion is in a sense the most important since it provides the whole motivation for entering the bodhisattva path. It is also said that practising the first five perfections results in an 'accumulation of merit' (*punyasambhara*), and that development of the sixth perfection results in an 'accumulation of insight' (*prajñāsambhara*); the dual cultivation of these as 'accumulations of enlightenment' (*bodhisambhara*) creates within the bodhisattva the necessary inner disposition towards Buddhahood.

This contrast between the bodhisattva and the arhat or pratyekabuddha ideals is the principal distinction between the Mahāyāna and Theravāda schools, since the overwhelming message of the Mahāyāna is that the *nirvāna with which the arhats and pratyekabuddhas content themselves is not the highest goal. Also, the *prajñāpāramitā* (*perfection of wisdom) doctrine that *saṃsāra and nirvāna are in some sense coextensive implies that nirvāna cannot be a negation of saṃsāra and that the world therefore is not a thing to be abandoned. Thus, in *Astasāhasrikā-sūtra* the Buddha says of the bodhisattva: 'Without becoming absorbed in nirvāna, he applies his mind to the external world and determines to achieve perfect wisdom.' *Daśabhūmika-sūtra* says that the sixth stage, 'Facing', is so called because at this stage the bodhisattva 'turns away from the pratyekabuddha and *śrāvaka attainments and faces the wisdom of Buddhahood', and that the bodhisattva 'does not absorb himself in nirvāna because (he knows) there are yet more stages towards enlightenment'.

The rejection of such a blissful state indicates that the primary concern of the bodhisattva is not his own comfort. He turns his back on the lower goal of absorption in nirvāna (arhatship) in favour of the higher goal of Buddhahood, which will more greatly enable him to enter wilfully the uncomfortable situations of suffering beings in order to save them. Some bodhisattvas, such as *Avalokiteśvara, who in some Tibetan schools is considered to have already attained Buddhahood, even enter the hell-realms in order to alleviate pain there. The poet-philosopher *Śāntideva encapsulates the bodhisattva's attitude: 'So long as transmigrating beings suffer, may I become their medicine, their doctor and their nurse until everyone is healed . . . In order to attain the goals of all beings, I shall give up without reserve my body, and all my accumulated virtue of the past, present and future, to be used towards this end.' The Mahāyāna notion of the bodhisattva as a being who views his own comfort (and sometimes his vows) as concerns subordinate to the needs of others, thus increased the social dimension of Buddhism and emphasized the value of lay life alongside monkhood. In *Vimalakīrtinirdeśa-sūtra* (*c.*2nd–3rd cents. CE), for example, it is the lay bodhisattva Vimalakīrti who is the hero, and *Mañjuśrī is the only other bodhisattva deemed wise enough to converse with him. For examples, see Index, Buddhas, Bodhisattvas.

H. Dayal, *The Bodhisattva Doctrine . . .* (1932).

Bodhisattva-śīla (Skt.). Rules of discipline for the forming of a *bodhisattva, which are obligatory in *Mahāyāna Buddhism for both monks and laypeople. They are laid down in the **Brahmajala-sūtra* and the first ten have particular importance: no killing, stealing, lapse in proper (especially sexual) behaviour, lying, intoxicants, gossip, boasting, envy, malice, slander of the *Three Jewels. These rules are undertaken at a formal ordination ceremony, which includes the *moka* (burning in of a symbolic sign). They are not rigid, in the sense that they can be broken if the welfare of another is at stake.

Bodhisattva vow (Skt., *praṇidhāna*). The vow in *Mahāyāna Buddhism to follow the six *pāramitās (perfections) and attain Buddhahood, the taking of which is deemed as the first entering of the Mahāyāna path. On entering the monkhood in any Buddhist country a set of vows (*prātimokṣa) are taken and a new name received because, even in a Mahāyāna monastery, initial entry on the Buddhist path is via *Hīnayāna; taking the *bodhisattva vow and receiving a further name mark a subsequent entry into Mahāyāna. In Tibet, there are further, stricter, vows (and the taking of another name) when entering the *Vajrayāna (*tantric) division of Mahāyāna. The core of the bodhisattva vow is: 'I vow to attain enlightenment for the sake of all sentient beings'. It expresses the idea that *all* bodhisattvas *must* attain Buddhahood in order to be fully able to serve the world. It also amplifies the Mahāyāna in contradistinction to Hīnayāna, because enlightenment now overrides *nirvāna as a higher goal, and is desired not for one's own sake, but for others. For the 'four great vows' in Zen, see SHIGUSEIGAN.

Bodhisattva-yāna. The 'Vehicle of the *Bodhisattvas', an alternative designation for the *Mahāyāna or 'Great Vehicle', is the way, means or method by which bodhisattvas pursue their religious career. It distinguishes itself from the two methods employed by the *Hīnayāna or 'Small Vehicle', namely the way adopted by the Buddha's early disciples or the 'Vehicle of the Hearers' (*śrāvaka-yāna*); and the goal of personal enlightenment in seclusion (*pratyekabuddha-yāna*). Both of these earlier methods are thought to display a lack of concern for others and were superseded for the Mahāyāna by the 'Vehicle of the Bodhisattvas' within which the interests of others are given priority over one's own.

Bodhisena (704–60). Indian Buddhist monk, commonly referred to as Baramon-sōjō (Jap., 'the *brahman abbot'). He originally went to China where he met members of a Japanese embassy to the T'ang, and at their invitation returned with them to Japan in 736. He resided at Daian-ji monastery, a centre for foreign monks in Nara, and in 752 was appointed the chief celebrant at the grand dedication ceremony of the Great Buddha (*daibutsu) at Tōdai-ji. Tōdai-ji was the central monastery (Sōkokubun-ji), unifying all the provincial monasteries and nunneries built by imperial edict. The casting of the Great Buddha was a monumental undertaking that drained the government treasury, but it demonstrated the majestic power of the emperor and the unity of the nation. Bodhisena, Emperor *Shōmu (who conceived the idea), Rōben (the first chief abbot), and *Gyōgi, a charismatic monk, are known as the four founders of Tōdaiji.

Bodhi Tree (tree under which Buddha gained enlightenment): see BO TREE.

Bodhyanga (in Buddhism, the seven contributions to enlightenment): see BOJJHANGA.

Body as temple (teaching of Basava): see BASAVA.

Body/bodies in Hinduism: see ŚARĪRA.

Body, speech, and mind: A frequent division, especially in *Tibetan Buddhism, of the sentient being into his three functional aspects which *tantric practice or *sādhana practice aims to transmute into the body, speech, and mind of a *Buddha. Tantric practices are correspondingly divided into practices of body (*yoga, *mudra, prostrations), practices of speech (*mantra, liturgy) and practices of mind (*samādhi). Implicit in this division is the recognition that the *trikāya (three-body) macrocosm (*nirmāna-kāya, *sambhoga-kāya, *dharmakāya) is represented within the microcosm (body, speech, mind) of the individual. This threefold division is symbolized in ritual texts in the seed syllables (*bīja) OM. AH. HUM.

Boehme, Jakob (1575–1624). German *Lutheran theosophical writer. Son of a farmer, from 1599 to 1613 he lived as a cobbler in Görlitz in Silesia. He claimed to be a mystic, writing under direct divine inspiration. From the publication of his first work, *Aurora* (1612), he provoked official opposition. Most of his works were published posthumously, including the famous *Signatura Rerum* and *Magnum Mysterium*. Boehme is obscure and difficult, using much abstruse terminology. The origin of all (sometimes identified with the Father) is the *Ungrund*, beyond good and evil. This *Ungrund* or 'abyss' knows itself in the Son, who is light and wisdom, and expresses itself in the *Holy Ghost: 'I saw the Being of all Beings, the Ground and the Abyss; also, the birth of the Holy *Trinity, the origin and first state of the world and of all creatures'. Good and evil, 'love' and 'wrath', equally stem from the abyss, and their interaction leads to the formation of the world. Redemption through *Christ is the triumph of good. Boehme was enormously influential, especially on German idealism, and also in England.

Eng. tr. J. Ellistone and J. Sparrow (rev. 1762–84); A. Weeks, *Boehme*; J. J. Stoudt, *Sunrise to Eternity* (1957).

Boethius (*c.*480–*c.*524). Roman philosopher and statesman. His most famous work, *On the Consolation of Philosophy*, is not specifically Christian, but was popular among Christians for its description of the soul attaining knowledge of the vision of God through philosophy. Regarded now as the author of other theological works, and therefore himself a Christian, he was put to death by the *Arian emperor Theodoric, and has therefore been considered a *martyr. He was canonized as 'St Severinus'.

H. Chadwick, *Boethius: The Consolations* . . . (1981); M. Gibson (ed.), *Boethius* . . . (1981).

Boethusians. A Jewish sect of the 1st cent. BCE/CE. The Boethusians were probably founded by the *high priest Simeon b. Boethius. Like the *Sadducees, they did not accept the doctrine of the *resurrection of the dead, but politically, unlike the Sadducees, they seem to have supported the dynasty of King *Herod. They may be the Herodians referred to in the New Testament. In *Talmudic times, they were described as deceitful, exploitative priests, and in terms of *Sabbath practices, were not even regarded as Jews.

Boff, C. and L.: see LIBERATION THEOLOGY.

Bogomils. A *dualist Christian sect which flourished in Bulgaria from the 10th to as late as the 17th cent., and more widely in the Byzantine Empire in the 11th–12th cents. The name comes from their founder, a priest who took the name Bogomil (= Gk., *Theophilos*). A source of *c.*950 describes it as 'Manichaeism mixed with Paulicianism': the accusation of *Manichaeism is conventional among orthodox writers, and probably there was no historical connection between the two systems; but the derivation from the Paulicians, who had missionaries in Bulgaria, is certainly correct. As a *heresy Bogomilism is unusual in having appeared in a newly (since 864), and insecurely, Christianized territory, but probably can be seen to some extent as a popular protest against an imported church order.

Accordingly, Bogomils are said to have been hostile both to the civil authorities and to most of the apparatus of the Orthodox church: *sacraments, *icons, Sunday worship, church buildings, etc. In their doctrine they espoused the dualist and neo-*gnostic doctrines of the Paulicians (e.g. belief in the devil as the creator of humanity and the world, *docetic ideas of Christ, rejection of the Old Testament). They were also strongly ascetic, rejecting sex, marriage, and possessions, and not eating meat, believing that the soul must be freed from evil and thus the body. Bogomil influence can be discerned in the later *Catharism of W. Europe.

Bohemian Brethren (Christian movement): see MORAVIAN BRETHREN.

Bojjhanga (Pāli; Skt., *bodhyanga*). The seven contributions, in Buddhism, to enlightenment. They emphasize equanimity and the exercise of the human capacity to distinguish right from wrong. See also BODHIPĀKṢIKA-DHARMA.

Bōkatsu (Jap., 'stick' + 'shout'). Zen Buddhist training technique, using blows from a stick (*kyosaku) or a shout (*ho), not as a punishment, but—at the exactly right moment—to help the breakthrough to enlightenment.

Bokuseki (Jap., 'marks of ink'). Zen Buddhist *calligraphy. The purpose is not aesthetic, but to express Zen experience. The words executed are usually those of the Zen masters (*hōgo), but the text may be simply one letter or one word. Outstanding practitioners were *Muso Soseki, *Ikkyu Sōjun, *Hakuin Zenji, and more recently *Yamamoto Gempō.

Bokushū Chinsonshuku (Ch'an teacher): see MU-CHOU CH'EN-TSUN-SU.

Bollandists. A small group of Belgian *Jesuit scholars of hagiology. It was begun by John van Bolland (1596–1665) to publish the *Acta Sanctorum*, a massive critical collection of the lives of Christian *saints, arranged in the order of their feasts in the calendar. By 1773, when the Jesuits were suppressed in Belgium, it had run to 50 volumes (to 7 Oct.). Work resumed in 1837; 10 Nov. was reached in 1925, and in 1940 an introduction to Dec. was published. Since 1882 they have also edited the journal *Analecta Bollandiana*.

Bön (Tib., 'invocation'). The non-Buddhist religion of Tibet which was indigenous and unorganized before the first diffusion of Buddhism there (7th cent.), but which became organized at the time of the second diffusion (11th cent.). In spite of claims of uninterrupted continuity, however, any connection between ancient and modern Bön is extremely tenuous.

The nature of original Bön—beyond probable *animism and *shamanism and definite non-literacy—is hard to determine, since all early descriptions of it are Buddhist and intended to discredit, while modern Bön (using the Tibetan script itself only designed for the express purpose of translating Indian Buddhist texts) appears to have been so in awe of Buddhism that its entire *cosmology, doctrines of enlightenment, distinctions between *sūtra and *tantra, and so forth were lifted from it. Both use the same title, *sangs.rgyas* (eminently purified) to refer to their founder, Shenrab having the role of *Śākyamuni (*Gshen-rab mi-bo-che) and a remarkably similar life-story. Snellgrove's (1967) point is valid, however, that since 'by far the greater part would seem to have been absorbed through learning and then re-told . . . this is not just plagiarism'. Thus, contrary to the popular misconception that Buddhism was significantly influenced by Bön when it entered Tibet, it is clear that what is known of Bön today is almost completely influenced by *Mahāyāna Buddhism, which was itself transplanted from India into Tibet virtually unchanged.

In spite of their being doctrinally (where they owe most to the *Nyingma, including their highest teachings of *Dzogchen) and structurally (their monastic system is almost identical to the *Geluk) quasi-Buddhist, Bön-pos guard jealously their non-Buddhist self-image. Amongst Buddhists a distinction is made between white Bön (*bon.dkar*) and black Bön (*bon.nag*), owing to the practice by some of animal sacrifice. It is atypical practices such as this, and the greater frequency in Bön of shamanism (where it may have a legitimate claim of priority), which are the only clues to original Bön. The term itself—originally used by Buddhists to distinguish themselves as *chos.pas* (followers of the *Dharma) from their 'unenlightened' neighbours—was always happily accepted by Bön-pos. It may be related to *Bod* ('Tibet'—i.e. 'religion of Tibet') or, as Bön-pos themselves prefer, to the verb *bon* ('to invoke'—i.e. 'religion of the invokers'), which is not unlike the use of the term *Mantrayāna.

P. Kvaerne, *Tibet, Bon Religion: A Death Ritual* (1984); D. Snellgrove, *The Nine Ways of B'on* (1967); D. Snellgrove and H. E. Richardson, *A Cultural History of Tibet* (1968).

Bon (rituals, festival of the dead): see ULLAMBANA; FESTIVALS.

Bonaventura (1221–74). Govanni di Fidanza, Christian mystic and saint. Born near Viterbo in Italy, he believed that he had been rescued from illness by the intercession of St *Francis. He entered the order of the Friars Minor, and became minister-general in 1256. His *Itinerarium Mentis in Deum* describes the way that leads to God by the path of his illumination. Nothing exceptional is required except the willingness to pray and to pay the price of complete devotion. Humans are made with three possible orientations: to the world through the body; to oneself through consciousness; to truth, Christ, and God through the mind. For those who turn in that last direction, there are seven levels of ascent, by apprehending: (i) the world as God's work; (ii) the presence of God through the world; (iii) the self made in God's image; (iv) the self renewed by God as his mirror; (v) the light emanating from God; (vi) *Jesus Christ the Mediator; (vii) union in love and mystical rest. *Leo XIII called Bonaventura 'the prince of mystics'; E. *Gilson called him 'a St Francis of Assisi gone philosopher and lecturing at the university of Paris'.

Trs. P. Boehner and M. F. Laughlin; E. Gilson, *The Philosophy of St. Bonaventure* (1938); J. F. Quinn, *The*

Historical Constitution of Saint Bonaventure's Philosophy (1973).

Bonfire of vanities (burning of frivolous or lewd items): see SAVŌNAROLA, GIROLAMO.

Bonhoeffer, Dietrich (1906–45). German pastor and Christian (*Lutheran) theologian. Educated at Tübingen and Berlin, and coming under the influence of people as diverse as *Harnack and *Barth, he felt called initially to pastoral work. In London, he became acquainted with George Bell, bishop of Chichester, with whom he shared growing unease about the rise of the Nazis, and the attempt of the Nazis to control the Church. Bonhoeffer, therefore, took a leading part in drafting the *Barmen Declaration. He attempted to found a seminary for pastors of the *Confessing Church, but this was soon closed down. He continued to oppose Hitler, searching with Bell for some resolution of the conflict. He was arrested in Apr. 1943. His *Letters and Papers from Prison* are a moving testament. He was executed on 9 Apr. 1945, commemorated in the nearby church by a tablet which states, 'Dietrich Bonhoeffer, a witness of Jesus Christ among his brethren.'

His theological work was, obviously, unfinished. He accepted with Barth that religion as a human enterprise was an inevitable failure; but in contrast, indeed, he envisaged a 'religionless Christianity', commensurate with 'a world come of age'. For a Lutheran, there are strong Calvinist notes in what he wrote. Yet equally, he stressed Lutheran themes of the two kingdoms and of a consequential salvation by faith. In his *Ethics* he seems to be going even further in a *Kierkegaardian direction by stressing the unimportance of law once the primacy of the ethical act in relation to God is recognized. But manifestly it would be absurd to seek consistency in one whose work was absorbed into titanic issues of good and evil, where many compromised, and he did not. He endeavoured to live—and die—in the pattern of discipleship, which must accept the possibility of crucifixion: 'Jesus is there only for others, God in human form—not in the Greek "divine-human" form of "man in himself", but "the Man for others", and therefore the crucified.'

E. Bethge, *Dietrich Bonhoeffer* . . . (1970); A. Dumas, *Dietrich Bonhoeffer* . . . (1972); C. J. Green, 'Bonhoeffer Bibliography: English Language Sources', *Union Seminary Quart. Rev.* 31 (1976).

Boniface, St (680–754). Christian 'apostle to Germany'. He was a native of Devon who, after earlier missionary visits, received the support of the pope for his work in Germany in 722. The challenge involved in felling the Oak of Thor at Geismar led to a breakthrough in recognition, and not much later he laid the foundations of church organization in Germany. After becoming archbishop of Mainz, he returned to missionary work in Frisia where he was martyred. Feast day, 5 June.

T. Schieffer, *Winifrid Bonifatius und die christliche Grundlegung Europas* (1972).

Boniface VIII (*c.*1235–1303). *Pope from 24 Dec. 1294. He was born Benedict Gaetani, and after studying law, served in a variety of posts in the Roman *curia. As a *cardinal he was instrumental in 1294 in persuading Celestine V to resign the papacy, and was elected in Celestine's place. His pontificate was dominated by the struggle with Philip the Fair of France, compounded by Philip's support for Boniface's arch enemies, the Colonnas. The *bull *Clericis Laicos* of 1296 forbade taxation of the clergy without papal approval. Philip promptly forbade the export of monies from France, and the pope, who depended upon this income, backed down. But when the king prevented French *bishops from attending a *council in Rome on the reform of the French Church, Boniface responded with the bull *Unam Sanctam* which proclaimed that there is no salvation or remission of sins outside communion with the bishop of Rome (see EXTRA ECCLESIAM NULLA SALUS). Boniface was on the point of excommunicating Philip in Sept. 1303 when his palace at Anagni was attacked by the Colonnas and French-led mercenaries. The pope was briefly held captive, and died a month later as a consequence of his treatment.

T. S. R. Boase, *Boniface VIII* (1933); C. T. Wood, *Philip the Fair and Boniface VIII* (1967).

Bonpu-no-jōshiki (Jap., 'every person's awareness'). According to Zen Buddhism, ordinary, everyday consciousness, which is fraught with delusion (*mayoi)—as opposed to the enlightened mind. This state of sickness precludes the awareness of one's own buddha-nature (*bussho). At the same time, the strong stress on the undifferentiated sameness of all appearance, arising from *śūnyatā, means that there are not two 'consciousnesses': unenlightened and enlightened consciousness are identical in nature, but in the former state it is ignorant of its nature.

Book of Changes: see I-CHING.

Book of Common Prayer (often *BCP*). The major prayer book of the *Anglican Church, and official service book of the *Church of England. It contains daily offices, the rite for the celebration of the *Lord's Supper, offices for *rites of passage, the psalter, the ordinal, the calendar and lectionary, the *thirty-nine articles, and other supplementary material. It was formed from earlier offices, etc., with much influence from Thomas *Cranmer. The first book appeared in 1549, the second in 1552 (revised in a Protestant direction). It was suppressed by Queen Mary in 1553 and reinstated with modifications under Elizabeth I in 1559. Parliament abolished the Prayer Book in 1645, but it was reinstated with the restoration of the monarchy in 1662—from which date it is frequently named. An attempt to revise it in 1928/9 was rejected by Parliament, but parts of the revision came into use. An **Alternative Service Book* (1980) was produced (ASB) on the basis of a new act in 1975, which allowed General Synod to introduce such reforms without recourse to Parliament. But BCP remains in parallel and in use, and it continues as one of the exemplars of doctrine in the Church of England. Its centrality and continuing use is advocated by the Prayer Book Society.

Book of Heavenly Commandments (Chin., *T'ien-t'iao shu*). A key religious document in the *T'aip-'ing rebellion which began around 1850 in China. Citing both the Chinese classics and the Bible, heavily influenced both by traditional Chinese morality and by *Protestant missionary work, the text lays down rules to govern the lives of members of the T'ai-p'ing ('Great Peace') community, including 'ten commandments' which approximate to those of Exodus 20.

Book of Jashar. A lost Israelite book of poetry. It was probably the source of *Joshua's command to the sun and the moon (Joshua 10. 12–13) and *David's lament for *Saul and Jonathan (2 Samuel 1. 19–27). However, the *Talmud identifies the *Book of Jashar* with the 'books of *Abraham, *Isaac and *Jacob'—presumably Genesis, because the *patriarchs were 'upright' (Heb., *yshr*).

Book of life (Heb., *Sefer ha-Ḥayyim*). A book in *heaven in which Jews believe the names of the righteous are inscribed. In Psalm 69. 28, the poet declares that his enemies should be 'blotted out of the book of the living; let them not be enrolled with the righteous'. This belief may go back to the ancient ideas of the Sumerians who thought that their gods kept tablets recording the activities of mortals. According to the *Talmud, three books are open in heaven on *Rosh ha-Shanah—the book of life for the names of the righteous, the book of death for the totally wicked, and an intermediate book which is only closed on Yom Kippur (*Day of Atonement). Consequently in the *Amidah for the Ten Days of *Penitence, extra *blessings are inserted for 'inscription in the book of life'. *Judah ha-Nasi warned: 'Know what is above you: an eye that sees, an ear that hears, and a Book in which all your deeds are set down' (**Avot* 2. 1). According to *Ashkenazi belief, God's judgement is sealed during *Sukkot, when a slip of paper recording each person's fate falls from heaven—hence the Yiddish greeting, 'A gute kvitl', 'A good slip / seal!'

Book of the Covenant. The laws found in Exodus 20. 22–23. 33. They include cultic instructions (20. 22–6); legal prescriptions concerning slavery, capital offences, and theft (21. 2–22. 16); religious and moral instructions involving idolatry, caring for the poor, respect for rulers, social justice, and the religious calendar (22. 17–23. 19) and a final concluding passage (23. 20–33). It is generally thought to date from the pre-monarchical era.

Book of the Dead: see TIBETAN BOOK OF THE DEAD.

Book of the Yellow Emperor (Chin., *Huang-ti nei-ching*, 'The Inner Classic of the Yellow Emperor'). 'The first systematic description of the system of correspondences that has remained valid in Chinese medicine to this day' (M. Porkert, *The Theoretical Foundations of Chinese Medicine*, 1974). Compiled sometime during the Han era (206 BCE–220 CE), this work, consisting of two parts (the *Su-wen* or 'Candid Questions' and the *Ling-shu* or 'Spiritual Pivot'), expounds a comprehensive theory of medicine based on systems of 'correspondence', 'correlation', or 'resonance' among various parts and aspects of the human person, and between those and other parts and aspects of the larger world.

Eng. tr. chs. 1–34 of the first part, J. Veith, *Huang Ti Nei Ching Su Wên: The Yellow Emperor's Classic of Internal Medicine* (1949; 2nd edn. 1966).

Booth, William (1829–1912). Founder and first General of the *Salvation Army. Born in Nottingham, apprenticed to a pawnbroker, he had firsthand experience of poverty, often speaking of his 'blighted childhood'. He became a *Methodist New Connexion Minister, but in 1854 his itinerant preaching caused him to leave the denomination, later to establish evangelistic and social work in East London. His Whitechapel 'Christian Mission' changed its name in 1878 to the 'Salvation Army'. Booth's social concern is expounded in his best-selling book, *In Darkest England and the Way Out* (1890). After the death of his wife, Catherine, he travelled the world encouraging Salvationist activity in many countries, continuing his preaching even when he was almost blind. A strong advocate of rousing music (and of denying to the *devil all the best tunes), he also introduced 'the standard of the London cab-horse', pointing out that many had to live on less money than was expended on maintaining cab-horses: the standard of the London taxi produces a similar result.

St J. Ervine, *God's Soldier* (1935).

Borobudur. The largest of Buddhist monuments, situated in mid-Java. Probably built in the 9th cent. CE by the dynasty established in that region by Śailendra, a S. Indian king, little is known of its subsequent history. Constructed around a natural hillside, Borobudur forms a terraced pyramid, five levels high, surmounted by three circular platforms on which are positioned seventy-two miniature *stūpas, themselves clustered around a massive central stūpa. A hidden ninth basement level has recently been excavated. The whole structure is believed to represent the Buddhist cosmology as a *maṇḍala, successive levels corresponding to stages on the path. The meaning of the name Borobudur is unclear.

L. Gomez and H. W. Woodward, *Borobudur: History and Significance of a Buddhist Monument* (1981).

Bosatsu (abbr. of Jap., *bodaisatta*). Jap. equivalent of Skt., *bodhisattva; also a title of respect given by emperors to outstanding monks, the first instance being *Gyōgi.

Bossey. An *ecumenical institute near Geneva in Switzerland, run by the World Council of Churches, including a graduate school of ecumenical studies. It was founded in 1946, with a particular emphasis on lay and youth training, aiming at the mediation of Christian convictions 'into all realms of life'.

Bo Tree, Bodhi Tree (Skt., *bodhi*, 'enlightenment'). The tree (*ficus religiosa*) under which the *Buddha is believed to have gained enlightenment. Situated in Bodhgaya, Bihar, the present tree is not particularly large and is unlikely to be the original. In India the tree is generally regarded as a potent symbol of sacrality, and Buddhist mythology holds the Bodhi Tree to have come into being at the same time as the Buddha's final birth. Further it is held that each Buddha is associated with a particular Bodhi Tree. Since the earliest accounts of the Buddha's enlightenment fail to mention a tree it has been suggested that the cult of the enlightenment tree is the result of mythological accretion. This theory is supported by the later versions of the story which tend to contradict one another over the length of time spent under the tree by the Buddha. The cult is nevertheless early. An *Aśokan edict records a visit to the site by the emperor, and a jealous queen of Aśoka is said to have damaged the tree *c.*240 BCE. To symbolize the establishment of Buddhism in Śri Lankā, a cutting, sent by Aśoka, was planted at *Anurādhapura where it still flourishes.

It became customary to plant a Bodhi Tree (a cutting when possible), usually surrounded by a low railing, in the courtyard of a *vihāra to signify the presence of the *Dharma, and this practice continues to the present day. In early Buddhist art, particularly in the carved reliefs at *Sāñchī and Bhārhut, the image of the tree was used as a symbol of the Buddha, since at this period his depiction was not considered permissible.

Boxer Rebellion. A major anti-foreign uprising in north China in 1899–1900 by a Chinese secret society known to Westerners as the 'Boxers'. The I-ho ch'uan, or 'Righteous and Harmonious Fists', was a secret religious society associated with the *Eight-Trigram Society. It was noted for its practice of the old-style Chinese callisthenics, the movements of which suggested to Westerners the name 'Boxers'. Worshipping a number of deities popular in Chinese folk religion, the Boxers claimed through spiritual discipline and magical arts to achieve special supernatural powers, such as invulnerability to bullets and the ability to fly. In the early 1800s, the Boxers were fundamentally an anti-Ch'ing sect. However, unequal treaties forced on China by foreign governments, increasing numbers of Christian missionaries in the country, and the terrible economic hardships of the post-*Taiping era, led to a Boxer redefinition of the primary source of China's humiliation and despair: foreigners ('Hairy Men') and their arrogant, heterodox faith (Christianity). Progressive Chinese leaders urged political, social, and economic reform, as well as accommodation in some respects to Western ways, as the most promising path to the creation of a stronger modern China. Conservative reactionaries, however, urged the Chinese court to encourage the violent, anti-foreign programme of the Boxers. The Empress Dowager, Tz'u-hsi, in hopes of preserving Ch'ing rule while purging China of foreign powers, chose to act in support of the Boxers. With court patronage, they destroyed churches and foreign residences, murdered missionaries and Chinese Christians, and attacked foreign legations. In Aug. 1900, a large allied Western force defeated the Boxers, demanding punishment of Ch'ing government officials clearly involved in the uprising, significant financial reparations for the loss of life and property, and new political and military measures to ensure the future security of foreigners in China. The Boxer Rebellion thus ended with an even further debilitated Ch'ing dynasty and, consequently, new popular support for the radicals' call for a republican revolution and a new China.

Brahmā (to be distinguished from *Brahman or its alternative Brahma). In Hinduism, a post-*Vedic deity. Brahmā is the god of creation and first in the Hindu triad of Brahmā, *Viṣṇu and *Śiva. He is represented as red in colour, with four heads and four arms, the hands holding, respectively, a goblet, a bow, a sceptre, and the *Vedas. He is said to have once had five heads, and there are varied mythological accounts explaining the loss of one of them: *Śaivite devotees claim it was struck off by Śiva because of Brahmā's arrogance; others claim Brahmā's daughter, *Sarasvatī (ultimately his chief consort) destroyed it through a curse because of his incestuous desire for her. Other wives of Brahmā include: *Aditi, *Sāvitrī, and *Gāyatrī. Brahmā's vehicle is the *Haṁsa, a white swan or goose, and his dwelling is *Brahmaloka.

Just as Śaivites have claimed the pre-eminence of Śiva, so *Vaiṣṇavites have represented Viṣṇu as superior to Brahmā; he is often portrayed as sitting on a lotus springing from the navel of Viṣṇu. Today Brahmā is seldom worshipped, and his shrines are few; only two major temples in India are dedicated to him: one at Pushkar, near Ajmere, the other at Khedbrahmā. Nevertheless, Brahmā does figure in both Buddhism and Jainism.

Brahmā had several sons, including Dakṣa and the four Kumāra, Sanat-Kumāra, Sānanda, Sanaka, and Sanātana, who determined to remain celibate and pure for eternity. To Brahmā's sons is attached the epithet 'mind-born', since they are personifications of his thought as universal creator-spirit. In mythology, Brahmā, in the form of Āpava (water-mover) is said to have divided into two forms: the first male, *Puruṣa, and the first female, Virāj. Another version of the creation myth tells how these two sprang from each other. The union of Brahmā and Virāj gave birth to the Manu Svāyaṁbhuva (genetically self-reproducing Man).

Epithets of Brahmā include: Abja-bhū (lotus-born); Ādi-kavi (first poet); Ashṭa-Karṇa (eight-eared); Chatur-ānana (four-mouthed); Chatur-mukha (four-faced); Dhātṛi (creator); Druhina (avenger); Kiñja-ja (lotus-born); Lokeśa (world-ruler); Nābhi-ja (navel-born); Pitāmaha (great father); Sanat (the ancient one); Sarojin (lotus-like); Srashṭṛi (originator); Vedhas (wise); Vidhātṛi (creator); Vidhi (fate).

G. M. Bailey, *The Mythology of Brahmā* (1983).

Brahmacarin. In Hinduism, following a pathway of discipline to attain an end, e.g. in *Yoga or *Tantra. It became equated with *celibacy, brahmacārin, and is the first of the four *āśramas, or stages of life, of a Hindu. The term indicates an unmarried student who is still under the tutelage of his *guru. Formerly abstinence from sex, rather than the unmarried state, seems to have been enjoined for the brahmachārin; the *Dharmaśāstras, for instance, state that a married man who abstains from sex on certain days of the lunar month may be a brahmachārin, and *Buddha also achieved this status before his enlightenment, although he was at that time married. See also BRAHMACARYA.

Brahmacarya (Skt., 'behaviour or conduct (*caryā*) appropriate to Brahman'), 1. In Hinduism, the mode of life of an unmarried student of the *Vedas, characterized especially by sexual continence and service to the teacher (*guru). The Upaniṣadic ideal of brahmacarya was codified in the early literature on Hindu law as the first of the four stages in life (the four *āśramas). During a period of study (usually specified as twelve years) the religious student (*brahmacārin) lives in the home of his teacher, maintains his sacred fire, tends his cattle, collects offerings given by the nearby villagers, and learns by rote that portion of the Veda recited by the teacher. At the conclusion of this period of studentship, and before returning home to marry and take up the responsibilities of a householder, the religious student bestows a gift (often a cow) upon the teacher.

In later Hindu monastic traditions the statement of *Jābāla Upaniṣad* is accepted, that one may proceed directly from the first life-stage of brahmacarya to the final stage of complete renunciation (*saṁnyāsa) if one has a burning desire to renounce the world. In these monastic traditions, brahmacarya is considered a probationary period for young monks prior to taking the final vows of renunciation (saṁnyāsa).

There is also the practice of *naiṣṭhika brahmacarya* according to which the individual remains a life-long celibate student without any intention of eventually becoming a householder or of being initiated into the stage of complete renunciation (saṁnyāsa).

Frequently the term brahmacarya is encountered in modern Hindu literature as a synonym for celibacy and self-control.

2. In Buddhism, a life lived in accordance with Buddhist rules of conduct (*śīla), especially by *bhikṣus.

3. Among Jains, it is one of the *Five Great Vows.

Brahmachari, Dhirendra (1925–94). Hindu *guru and teacher of *yoga, who exercised much influence on Indira Gandhi—he was known by those who mistrusted him as India's Rasputin. He was born into a poor family in E. India, and was employed in a minor capacity in the Central Planning Commission. During this time, he began to study yoga, and in his thirties, he left Delhi for Mantalai, a place of great beauty, where he set up an *āśrama. He became renowned for his demonstration of yogic control, especially in his commitment to wearing only a dhoti in all temperatures: he wore it without distress during a visit to Russia, when the temperature fell to −18°. In 1968, Mrs Gandhi visited Mantalai and was deeply impressed. When her son, Sanjay, was killed in an air-crash, she seemed to relate to Brahmachari almost as a surrogate son. He taught her yoga and persuaded her that yoga classes should be introduced into Indian schools. He became immensely wealthy (his accusers claiming that he benefited from Congress Party funds), and developed extensive business interests. He lived in a wealthy style, but pointed out that this, to a true *sādhu, is a matter of complete irrelevance and indifference. He believed that he could, as a yogin, live, if he wished, for two centuries, and had prepared a cave for this purpose at Mantalai. He died, having never married.

Brahmajala-sūtra (Sūtra of the Net of Brahman). A *Mahāyāna Buddhist *sūtra, containing basic instruction on the rules of moral life (*śīla). It contains fifty-eight rules, of which the first ten are esp. important: see BODHISATTVA-ŚĪLA.

Eng. tr. B. Bodhi, *The Discourse on the All-Embracing Net of Views* (1978).

Brahmajijñāsā (Skt., literally, 'the desire to know *Brahman' or 'the enquiry into Brahman'). The subject-matter of the **Brahmasūtra* is pronounced in its famous first verse: *athāto brahmajijñāsā*, 'Then therefore the enquiry into Brahman.' In his commentary on this verse, *Śaṅkara explains that the knowledge of Brahman is the highest aim of humans, yet the desire for knowing Brahman depends on certain antecedent conditions already having been fulfilled (hence the use of the word 'then' in the verse). These prior conditions are: (i) the discrimination of what is eternal from what is non-eternal; (ii) renunciation of all desire to enjoy the fruit of one's actions both here in this life and hereafter; (iii) cultivation of tranquillity, self-restraint, and the other virtues of quietude, patience, concentration, and faith; and (iv) desire for final release from the cycle of rebirth. The enquiry into Brahman proceeds through hearing the revelation of Brahman contained in the scriptures (i.e. the *Vedas, especially the *Upaniṣads), reasoning concerning the meaning of these scriptural statements, and then profound meditation conferring direct intuition (*sākṣātkāra*) into Brahman. These three (hearing, reasoning, and profound meditation) are called in Skt. *śravaṇa*, *manana*, and *nididhyāsana*.

Brahma Kumari. A Hindu-oriented movement composed in the main of unmarried women and founded in Hyderabad in 1937 by the one-time Sind diamond merchant, Dadi LeKray. Women are clearly the spiritual and moral leaders in this *millennial movement, in which the traditional role of wives and husbands has been reversed. Moreover, the orthodox Hindu belief in the possibility of escape from *saṁsāra is rejected in favour of the idea of the golden age: after humanity has been destroyed by a nuclear catastrophe, purified souls only will live as deities in a state of complete happiness.

Through the practice of celibacy and *yoga, souls can attain unity with the founder, Shiv Baba as he came to be known, and a right of entry to the golden age. In the late 1960s the movement, with headquarters in Mount Abu, India, began to acquire a following in the West.

Brahmaloka (Skt., 'domain of Brahmā'). Hindu *heaven in the company of Brahmā and the gods.

Brahman or **Brahma** (Skt., literally, 'growth' or 'expansion'). The one supreme, all-pervading Spirit; the impersonal Absolute, beyond attributes, which is the origin and support of the visible universe. This neuter noun, Brahman (or Brahma) should be distinguished from the masculine form, *Brahmā, the personal Creator-god in the Hindu triad of *Brahmā, *Viṣṇu and *Śiva.

The etymology of Brahman is obscure, but is traditionally derived from the verb root *bṛh* or *bṛṁh*, 'to grow great', 'to increase'. In the earliest use of the word in the *Vedas, and especially in **Atharva Veda*, the meaning of Brahman is the mysterious force behind a magical formula. It then means the sacred utterance through which the *devas become great, and thus also ritual power and those in charge of it (i.e. *brahmans). In the *Śatapata Brāhmaṇa*, and then in the Upaniṣads, the word Brahman comes to mean the source of power, and thus the impersonal, supreme, eternal principle behind the origin of the universe and the gods. It is this later meaning that is developed in the systematic philosophy of *Vedānta which teaches that Brahman, the impersonal Absolute, is the essence, the Self (*ātman), of all beings. Ātman and Brahman are one, and the knowledge of Brahman (*brahmavidyā*; see APARA-VIDYA) is the supreme goal of human life as it confers liberation (*mokṣa) from the ongoing cycle of suffering and rebirth (see e.g. ŚAṄKARA).

The move to the impersonal, Absolute understanding of Brahman created issues for theistic Hindus, for whom the experience of personal relationship with the unproduced Producer of all that is, is paramount. One solution was to regard Brahmā, Viṣṇu, and Śiva as three manifested aspects of Brahman (*trimurti); another was to regard the gods as manifestations of appearance (*māyā) of such a kind that they can create and command worship; another was to modify an austere *advaita (non-dualist) account of Brahman, and regard Brahman as bearing within itself the characteristic of relationship: see VIŚIṢṬĀDVAITA, DVAITA; Index, Brahman.

Brahman (often Anglicized as brahmin; Skt., *brāhmaṇa*). A member of the highest of the four *varna, or categories, of *Vedic society, hence *Brahmanism.

The brahmans were traditionally the custodians, interpreters, and teachers of religious knowledge, and, as priests, acted as intermediaries between humans, the world, and God. They alone knew and could perform the rituals of correct worship, making them acceptable to God. Since the brahmans were the most highly literate section of society, they moved into other professions too, e.g. law and medicine. Because of their high ritual status, brahmans were expected to be meticulous in observing dietary rules, e.g. vegetarianism, abstinence from alcohol, etc. Being considered to be always in a state of ritual purity, Brahmans became ceremonial cooks, as all could eat the food prepared by them for feasts with no fear of accidental pollution. Brahmans enjoyed the patronage of the rulers they served, and some became rich landowners as a result. Because of traditions of literacy and education, brahmans, even in modern India, are prominent in the ranks of professionals and administrators.

B. S. Khare, *The Changing Brahmans* (1970); A. D. Moddie, *The Brahmanical Culture and Modernity* (1968).

Brāhmaṇa (Skt., 'that pertaining to *brahman*'). In Hinduism, the explanatory portion of the *Veda developed as a commentary on the *mantra portions of the text. The word brāhmaṇa has the general meaning of 'explanation of the sacred power (*brahman) contained in the mantras'. More specifically, the word came to be used for a genre of texts, mostly prose in style, attached to the four *saṁhitās of the Veda. They are valuable for their explication of ritual and their inclusion of various legends, myths, and philosophical speculations. Commonly they are dated between 1,000 BCE and 650 BCE. The most important are the following: the *Aitareya* and *Kausītaki* (*Śāṅkhāyana*) Brāhmaṇas of the **Ṛg Veda*; the *Jaiminīya* and *Pañcaviṃsa* (*Tāṇḍyamahā*) Brāhmaṇas of the **Sāma Veda*; the *Taittirīya* Brāhmaṇa of the Black and the *Śatapatha* Brāhmaṇa of the White **Yajur Veda*; the *Gopatha* Brāhmaṇa of the **Atharva Veda*. To the Brāhmaṇas were then added the *Āraṇyakas.

Trs. J. Eggeling (1882–1900); A. B. Keith; W. Caland (1955); S. Bhattacharji, *Literature in the Vedic Age*, ii. *Brāhmaṇas, Āranyakas* . . . (1986); J. Gonda, *Vedic Literature* (1975).

Brahmānanda. In Hinduism. 1. The absolute, undifferentiated bliss of *Brahman.

2. Disciple of Svāmi *Vivekānanda (born Rakhal Candra Ghosh) who succeeded him as head of the *Rāmakrishna Mission.

Brahmanical religion: see BRAHMANISM.

Brahmanirvana (Skt.). Final union with *Brahman in which all traces of dual relationship have been eradicated.

Brahmanism. Religion of early India which came to prominence in the *Vedic period, and is effectively to be identified with Vedic religion and its continuity. It emphasized sacrifice and ritual under the control of the *brahmans as those who have access to the rituals and control of them.

Brahman satyam, jagat mithya (Skt.). A sentence which summarizes for Hindus the entire teaching of *Advaita Vedānta: Brahman is the real reality (cf. SAT), the world is deceptive (because its apparent reality is superimposed on Brahman.

Brahmārandhra (Skt.). The place in the crown of the head through which, according to Hindus, the self escapes at death (though through the arms in the case of a wicked person), and through which, in *yoga, consciousness can ascend to higher levels (cf. KUṆḌALINĪ).

Brahma-samādhi (Skt.). An absorption state (*samādhi) of *brahman-consciousness attained through the repetition of a *mantra (*japa).

Brahmasūtra. An ancient Indian work which systematizes the teachings of the *Upaniṣads concerning *Brahman, Ultimate Reality, in 555 elliptic verses or *sūtras. It is attributed to *Bādarāyaṇa, a sage of the 1st cent. BCE, but may have been compiled in its final form several centuries later. The *Brahmasūtra*, together with the principal Upaniṣads and the **Bhagavad-gītā*, forms the *prasthānatrava*, the 'threefold source' of *Vedānta philosophy. Commentaries have been written to interpret the meaning of the terse and sometimes ambiguous sūtras, thus giving rise to several divergent philosophical traditions within Vedānta, all claiming to be based on the *Brahmasūtra*. The most famous of these traditions are those of *Śaṅkara, *Rāmānuja, and *Madhva. Other names for the *Brahmasūtra* are encountered in Indian literature: the *Vedāntasūtra* or *Uttaramīmāṁsāsūtra*, because it outlines the philosophy of Vedānta; the *Bādarāvaṇasūtra*, named after its supposed author; the *Vyāsasūtra*, so-named by another tradition which credits its authorship to the sage Vyāsa; and the *Śārīrakasūtra*, because it is an investigation of 'that which is embodied', i.e. the individual self according to Śaṅkara, or Brahman according to Rāmānuja. See also BRAHMAJIJÑĀSĀ.

Tr. G. Thibaut, *Vedānta-Sūtras* (Sacred Books of the East, 34, 38).

Brahma-vidya (knowledge by hearsay in Hinduism): see APARA-VIDYA.

Brahma-vihāra (Skt., Pāli, 'dwellings of Brahmā'). Meditational states and attitudes in Hinduism, taken up and reapplied in Buddhism as central meditation practice: the meditator brings into being four attitudes, and radiates them out: (i) kindness to all beings (*metta/*maitrī); (ii) compassion to all suffering (*karuṇā); (iii) joy over those who are rescued (*muditā); (iv) equanimity to friend and foe (*upekkha). In *Mahāyāna, these are included in the perfect virtues (*pāramitā), which dispose a *bodhisattva to bring about the salvation of others. Those who meditate on the brahma-vihāras will attain reappearance after death in the Brahmā-heaven, far short of *nirvāna, but an advance on reappearance as a human or worse. For an exposition, see *Buddhaghoṣa, *Visuddhimagga* 9.

Brahmin: see BRAHMAN.

Brahmo Samāj. 19th-cent. Hindu reform movement. It had its antecedent in the Brahmo Sabha (1828) of Rām Mohan Roy (1772–1833), who was impressed by Western achievements, but who believed that Indian spirituality was greater. He was sent to a Muslim university, where he became attracted by *Sūfism: this turned him against what he took to be idol-worship. His father insisted that he study for twelve years at *Kāśi (Benares), where he began to see the *Upaniṣads as the basis of a reformed Hinduism. He made connection with Christian missionaries, but when he published *The Precepts of Jesus: The Guide to Peace and Happiness*, Christians turned against him for Indianizing Christianity, and Hindus turned against him for advocating Christianity. His major reform was to persuade the British that *sati (widow-burning) was not part of original *dharma: both he and his opponents travelled to England in 1833 (where he died), but the practice was banned. The Brahmo tradition of reinterpreting early Hinduism in the light of new knowledge led to the organizing of Brahmo Samāj in 1843 by Debendranath *Tagore (father of the poet). The presence of Keshub Chandra *Sen in the movement led to Tagore continuing with the Adi Samāj, while Sen led the Brahmo Samāj to further division and a cult-like focus on himself—though he also engaged in much social reform. The movement continued into the 20th cent., but rapidly declined in influence and membership.

S. D. Collet, *The Life and Letters of Raja Rammohun Roy* (rev. D. K. Biswas and P. C. Ganguli, 1962); S. C. Crawford, *Ram Mohan Roy* . . . (1987); D. Kopf. *The Brahmo Samaj* . . . (1979); M. C. Parekh, *The Brahmo Samaj* (1992).

Braid(e) Movement. The first modern prophet and revival movement in Nigeria, and one of the first in Africa. It arose in Nov. 1915 at Opobo, within the semi-independent *Anglican community among the Ijaw people in the E. Niger delta, through the healing and prayer ministry of a lay leader in the Bakana parish, Garrick Braid (*c.*1880–1918). This led to mass *baptisms, *Sunday observance, rejection of magic rituals, and reduction in the extensive gin trade. Although at first welcomed by the African assistant-bishop, excesses and attacks on traditional shrines ended church support and alienated the colonial administration, which was already nervous of seditious activities in the early stages of the First World War. Braid was twice imprisoned on charges that later seemed unjustified. The independent 'Christ Army' churches that appeared continued after his death, and many churches in E. Nigeria now claim him as founder.

Brain-washing. Coercive methods of conversion or changes in behaviour. Based on (i) Pavlov's discovery that fear among his laboratory dogs (induced by floods) led to the erasing of certain learned behaviours and to relatively greater ease in implanting new ones; and (ii) the use of deprivation techniques in breaking down political and other prisoners, it was argued that religious threats of hell-fire (e.g.), followed by promises of salvation (accompanied by rhythmic and emotional music), produced conversion by comparable mechanisms. W. Sargant's *Battle for the Mind* popularized this argument. Subsequently, the term has been used in relation to new cults/religions, which have been accused of stripping would-be converts of their previous identities (especially by 'love-bombing', surrounding them with acceptance and love) and then 'programming' them into total allegiance to the movement. See also DEPROGRAMMING, which has been accused of being brain-washing in reverse.

Branch Davidians. Cult derived from Seventh Day *Adventists, whose centre, at Waco in Texas, was destroyed after an FBI siege intended to arrest its leader, David Koresh. The name of the cult goes back to the promises of Isaiah 11. 1, 'A branch will spring from the stock of Jesse [the father of David], a new shoot will grow from his roots: on him will rest the spirit of the Lord, the spirit of wisdom and insight . . .'. After an Adventist preacher, Victor Houteff, was expelled from his congregation in 1929, he set up a separate Adventist movement, from which many schisms in turn occurred. One of these was joined by Vernon Howell in 1981, who took the name of David Koresh when he became its leader: he identified himself with the Lamb of the book of Revelation (5 *et passim*). Based on strongly authoritarian guidance from biblical texts, the movement recruited mainly from existing Adventist congregations. Described by its opponents as being far out, even by the standards of the *Bible belt in the southern states (of America)—'at the buckle end of the belt'—the siege ended when an attempt to flush the cult members out resulted in a conflagration and many deaths.

Braslav Ḥasidim (Jewish leader): see NAḤMAN.

Brautmystik (bridal or nuptial mysticism): see RHENO-FLEMISH SPIRITUALITY.

Breastplate. Metal pendant hung in front of the covered *Torah scrolls among the Jewish *Ashkenazim. It is reminiscent of the breastplate traditionally worn by the *high priest (Exodus 28: 15 ff.), and, like it, sometimes contains twelve precious stones representing the twelve tribes of Israel.

Breath. As a necessary and manifest condition of life, breath and breathing have a literal and metaphorical importance in religions. Basic words which come to identify a real and continuing self originate as 'breath' (see e.g. *ruaḥ* in Hebrew, RŪḤ (NAFS), ĀTMAN); and 'breath' becomes the vehicle of divine communication and presence—hence Ruaḥ ha-Qodesh, i.e. the *Holy Spirit, and the invocation, 'Breathe on me, Breath of God, Fill me with life anew . . .'. In *Ṛg Veda* 10. 90. 13, the breath (*prāṇa) of the primordial Man, *Puruṣa, becomes the origin of vāyu, the wind, whose manifest form is *Vāyu. Prāṇa as the source and persistent sustainer of life thus became the link between ātman as (in the *Vedic period) a reflexive pronoun and ātman as the indestructible soul or self. The understanding and control of breath is therefore an important part of *yoga, especially within *Haṭha-yoga, and as prāṇayama, the fourth in the eight stages (mentioned by *Patañjali, 1. 34, 2. 29 and 49, but later much elaborated). The control of breath, recognized as highly dangerous, has led to claims of extraordinary feats of retention, with practitioners being buried alive or submerged in water. But the purpose is not wonder-working, but the suffusion of the whole body with the divine, especially through the repetition, synchronized with the breathing in and out, of the *Haṁsa *mantra, thereby sending the breath through the myriad channels of the body (*nāḍī). In *Tantrism, the even more specific object is to arouse the energies of *kuṇḍalinī. The importance of breathing in meditation was accepted by Buddhists, but also adapted. Ānāpānasati (*ānāpāna) is a relatively straightforward set of techniques; but in Tibet, breathing is a key means to *visualization. In all these cases, breathing exercises are preparatory, but in China they are an end in themselves. They appear early (at least 6th cent. BCE), and evidently underlie the Taoist practices which were aimed at the control of the energies (especially sexual energies) of the body, with the aim of achieving *ch'ang sheng* ('long life', the material immortality of the bodily elements): that would require, through practice, retention of breath for a period as long as a thousand normal breaths. Short of achieving that, the practice produces calmness through a deep breathing which imitates the hibernation of animals, or, more often, the breathing of an embryo in the womb: see further CH'I. In W. religions, breathing is used for the control of the mind and for bringing a person without reserve or distraction into the presence of God. In Christianity, see JESUS PRAYER; HESYCHASM; in Islam, see DHIKR, in which a common technique is that of saying *la ilaha* ('there is no God') while breathing in, and *illa Allah* ('except God') while breathing out. See also Index, Breathing.

B. K. S. Iyengar, *Light on Yoga* (1966); S. Kuvalayananda, *Pranayama* (1966); C. Luk, *Taoist Yoga, Alchemy and Immortality* (1970).

Breeches Bible (Calvinist Bible): see GENEVA.

Brethren, Plymouth. A Christian body which takes its name from the place where their first congregation was formed in 1831. The movement traces its beginning to the initiative of Edward Cronin, a Dublin medical student, who gathered a group of likeminded friends. Their ideals came to be shared by A. N. Groves and J. N. Darby (formerly an Anglican priest) whose teaching gifts were quickly recognized. Two other leaders, Francis Newman and B. W. Newton, came under Darby's forceful influence. Newton exercised an influential ministry in Plymouth, which was criticized by Darby and a breach occurred. Continuing differences also resulted in a serious division in Bristol, after which 'Open Brethren' maintained congregational autonomy, whilst Darby's followers, the 'Exclusive Brethren', pursued a more centralized form of church life, generally disassociating themselves from Christians of other persuasions. A major division in the Exclusive Brethren was caused by the radical separatist teaching of James Taylor (d. 1970). Most Open Brethren meetings are happy to unite with evangelical Christians in other traditions, and many Exclusive Brethren meetings, whilst maintaining a segregation policy, do not identify with the Taylorite excesses. The Open Brethren Assemblies practise believers' *baptism, but infant baptism within Christian 'households' is common among Exclusive Brethren groups. Preferring to be known as 'Christian Brethren', members of Open Brethren congregations have maintained a strong commitment to worship (with a 'breaking of bread' service each Sunday morning), regular Bible study, personal evangelism, and overseas missionary work.

Brethren of Purity (secret movement founded in Iraq): see IKHWĀN AL-ṢAFĀ'.

Brethren of the Common Life (Christian community): see GROOTE, G.

Breviary. The book containing the divine *office of the *Roman Catholic Church. As a combination of earlier books (the Hymnary, Lectionary, etc.) it began to appear in the 11th cent. It remained essentially unchanged in structure until 1971 (although there were important reforms in 1568 and 1911) when a completely new breviary was issued by Pope *Paul VI. The revision was aimed at removing the predominantly monastic stamp of the offices (e.g. by reducing their number and distributing the psalter over four weeks instead of one) and at enriching the repertory of texts to be read. The Breviary is usually published in several volumes, each covering part of the year. Various religious orders have their own breviaries which differ somewhat from the Roman one.

Bṛhadāraṇyaka Upaniṣad (Skt., 'of the Great Forest'). The longest and perhaps oldest of the principal Upaniṣads. Composed in prose style between *c.*8th and 6th cents. BCE, it consists of six chapters attached to the final book of the **Śatapatha Brāhmaṇa*. The traditional division of this Upaniṣad into forty-seven sections according to subject-matter indicates the wide range of philosophical speculation it embraces. It begins with a meditation on the esoteric correspondence between the parts of the sacrificial horse (*Aśvamedha) and the components of the natural world; it then considers the origin of the world, the course of the soul after death, and returns again and again to profound reflection on the one, all-pervading Absolute which is the Self of all beings. (see BRAHMAN). The central religious and philosophical themes adumbrated in this Upaniṣad have been variously interpreted in important commentaries by *Śaṅkara, *Rāmānuja, and other pivotal religious thinkers of Hinduism. For tr. see UPANIṢAD.

Bṛhaspati (Skt., *bṛh*, 'prayer', + *pati*, 'Lord'). 1. A *Vedic god who embodies, not a natural phenomenon, but reason and moral judgement. He also holds on behalf of the gods the benefits produced by sacrifices, as a kind of banker of the cosmic order.

2. A Hindu teacher of materialism: see CĀRVĀKA.

Bricolage (Fr., 'doing odd jobs'). A characteristic (according to C. *Lévi-Strauss) of the early human mind, in contrast to modern scientific thinking. But bricolage is entirely rational (i.e. not pre-rational) in its own way. He introduced the term in *The Savage Mind*. A *bricoleur* is one who improvises and uses any means or materials which happen to be lying around in order to tackle a task: 'The *bricoleur* is adept at executing a great number of diverse tasks; but unlike the engineer, he does not subordinate each of them to the availability of raw materials and tools, conceptualized and procured specifically for this project; his instrumental universe is closed, and the rule of his game is to make do with the means at hand.' In the making of *myth, bricolage is the use of whatever happens to be 'lying around', so that myth is both rational and also improvisatory.

Bridegroom of the Law. In Judaism, strictly the reader who is called up to read the last portion of the *Pentateuch (Deuteronomy 33. 27–34. 12) in the morning service on the Jewish festival of *Simḥat Torah ('the Rejoicing in the Law'). The reader who starts the first chapter of Genesis in the same service is the 'bridegroom of the beginning'. Different customs are practised in different communities, but it is common for the 'bridegrooms' to give a party for the congregation after the service.

Bridget of Sweden, St (d. 1373). Founder of the Brigittines. She was the daughter of the governor of Uppland who married at the age of 13 and bore eight children. After the death of her husband in 1344, she retired from the world to a life of prayer. She experienced visions (whose content she dictated to the abbot of a nearby monastery), one of which commanded her to found the Order of the Most Holy Saviour, later known as Brigittines. The Order followed the *Augustinian rule, and was organized in parallel communities of women and men. It flourished until the *Reformation, but was banished from Sweden in 1595. It was reintroduced to Sweden in 1923. Bridget was canonized in 1391.

J. Jörgensen, *St Bridget of Sweden* (1954).

Bridgid, St. Regarded by many as the second *patron saint of Ireland, but there is no unequivocal evidence that she existed. A *Life* was written in the 7th cent. by Cogitosus, and she is said to have founded the Abbey of Kildare in the 5th cent. Despite this hazy background, she has been prominent especially as the one who protects families and crops against evil, and she may therefore have taken over the functions of the Celtic goddess Brigit. Her festival is at the start of spring ploughing and sowing (1 Feb.), and is marked by young men (known as Biddies) visiting houses in disguises to ward off evil.

D. O. Cathasaigh, 'The Cult of Brigid', in J. J. Preston (ed.), *Mother Worship* (1982).

Brigittines: see BRIDGET OF SWEDEN.

British Israelites: see TEN LOST TRIBES.

Broad Churchmen. Christians who seek to avoid narrow theological definitions and interpret the creeds and other formulae in a 'broad', liberal sense. In distinction, in Anglicanism, from *high and *low church, they have affinities with the later *modernists.

Bronze vessels. Containers of food and drink for ritual use, produced from the Shang to the Chou dynasties in China. About two dozen different types have been identified by Chinese art historians, those of the Shang period being most highly prized both for their antiquity and their workmanship. Their association with the ancestral cult is certain, since they are primarily found in aristocratic burials; in addition, such relatively late texts as the **Li Chi* (Book of Rites) have numerous passing references to 'sacrificial vessels', although little direct attention is given to them. Thus the exact usages to which the various types were put is not known with any precision, although it seems safe to conclude that some were used for water and later wine from which libations were poured and from which ritual participants ceremonially drank; others were used to boil soups or stews containing both animal and vegetable ingredients. The contents of the vessels were clearly meant primarily for the deceased ancestral spirits or for other powerful spiritual beings to which sacrifices were addressed. Some vessels have inscriptions which not only help to date them but also indicate that they were often cast to celebrate some service to kings or princes as well as to commemorate the virtues of illustrious *ancestors. Possibly they were used, in Shang times, in sacrificial rites to royal ancestors, who were expected to intercede with *Shang Ti for the people. A most impressive, as well as controversial, aspect of these vessels is the (usually) low-relief decoration using stylized and elaborate animal motifs. Many art historians reject the notion that these have significant symbolic meaning, while many historians of religions seek to read them as an elaborately encoded sacred world-view (so e.g. P. Ackerman and C. Hentze, who claim connections with the religions of ancient Mesopotamia and Iran). The bronzes are perhaps most famous for the so-called *t'ao-t'ieh* ('ogre masks'), which show, in split representation, an animal with a single head and two bodies extending out more or less flatly toward the two adjoining sides of the vessel. Also characteristic is the composite nature of the animals represented, which makes them difficult to identify. Tigers will have ram's horns and feathered bodies, or buffaloes will show feline and ornithological features. The animals depicted seem to be both those traditionally sacrificed in religious rites and those, such as the tiger and dragon, not sacrificed but of religious significance. For the most part, scholars have seen in these motifs symbols of life renewal, fecundity, sacred sovereignty, and cosmic order; but equally, these zoomorphic forms may represent animal helpers or 'familiars' connected with *shamanistic activities which were of great importance in ancient China for communicating between *Heaven and Earth.

Brothers and Sisters of the Common Life (Christian community): see GROOTE, G.

Brunner, Heinrich Emil (1889–1966). Christian (Swiss Reformed) theologian, for most of his working life Professor of Theology at Zurich. He maintained a distinct position from Karl *Barth, but endeavoured to retain a dialectical theology, with the utter distinctiveness of God nevertheless already 'prepared for', by way of recognition, in his creation. Thus in *The Mediator* (1927, 1934) he claimed that the command to love God wholly and solely is unrealistic apart from Christ's own fulfilment of it which opens the way to our own. But precisely because of the complete incommensurability between Creator and creature, revelation can only be oblique or indirect, because it is mediated through the creature, and is not a direct revelation of the Creator (if it were, God would have been turned into an 'object' which we can encounter in revelation). He also held out for a place in Christian belief for natural theology, where the fact *that* the Creator is, can be discerned. Arising from theology is the necessary demand of ethical behaviour, both social and individual.

H. E. Brunner, *The Divine Imperative* (1932, 1937) and *Man in Revolt* (1937, 1939); C. W. Kegley (ed.), *The Theology of Emil Brunner* (1962).

Bsam. yas (first monastery in Tibet): see SAMYÉ; TUCCI, G.

Bstan-'dzin-rgya-mtsho (current Dalai Lama): see DALAI LAMA.

Buber, Martin (1878–1965). Jewish philosopher and *Zionist leader. As a Zionist, influenced by *Aḥad ha-ʿAm, Buber emphasized the importance of education. In 1916, he founded the periodical *Der Jude* (The Jew) which was an important organ in the Jewish Renaissance movement in Central Europe between the two World Wars. As a 'Hebrew humanist', he emphasized the rights of the Arabs, stating 'the Jewish people proclaims its desire to live in peace and brotherhood with the Arab people and to develop the common homeland'. His *Ich und Du* (I and Thou) was published in 1923 (Eng. edn. 1937) and contains his famous philosophy of dialogue. He distinguished between 'I–It' relationships, which are impersonal interactions designed to achieve a particular end, and 'I-thou' relationships which are mutual, direct, and open. This leads to the characterisation of God as the 'eternal thou'—the one who is only known through direct personal relationship. Buber settled in *Israel in 1938, where he was the first president of the Israel Academy of Sciences and Humanities. He frequently lectured in Europe and the United States and his work has been profoundly influential on both Jewish and Christian theologians. He was an early proponent of Jewish-Christian *dialogue, referring to *Jesus as 'my brother', and seeing a similar commitment to suffering and prophetic service: 'We Jews, we of the blood of *Amos and *Jeremiah, of Jesus and *Spinoza and all the earth-shatterers who, when they died, were unsuccessful, we know a different world from this one which subscribes only to success.'

M. Cohn and R. Buber, *Martin Buber: A Bibliography* (1980); M. S. Friedman, *Martin Buber, The Life . . .* (1976); P. S. Schilpp and M. Friedman (eds.), *The Philosophy of Martin Buber* (1967).

Bucer, Martin (1491–1551). Christian Reformer and theologian. A *Dominican friar, he was attracted in 1518 to *Luther's teaching. Released from his monastic vows in 1521, he led the *Reformation in Strasbourg and was noted for his tolerance and diplomacy in theological debates. His teaching and organization made a deep impression on *Calvin during his exile from Geneva (1538–41). Bucer sought to mediate in debates among the Reformers concerning the *eucharist, and also gave significant leadership in discussions between *Protestants and *Roman Catholics. As guest of Thomas *Cranmer, he came to England in 1549 and was appointed Regius Professor of Divinity at Cambridge. His liturgical influence is clearly evident in the Anglican Ordinal (1550) and the revision of the Prayer Book. His *De Regno Christi* offers a stimulating interpretation of ideal Christian society.

Eng. tr. W. Pauck, *Library of Christian Classics*, 19 (1967); H. Eells, *Martin Bucer* (1931); R. Stupperich, *Bibliographia Bucerana* (with H. Bornkamm, *Martin Bucers Bedeutung für die Europäische Reformationsgeschichte*, 1952).

Buchman, Frank (1878–1961). Founder of *Moral Re-Armament. A *Lutheran pastor in Pennsylvania, Buchman embarked for Europe in 1908 after a disagreement. There he began a campaign along evangelical lines. In Oxford in 1921 he founded the 'First-Century Christian Fellowship' or Oxford Group Movement, the chief activity of which was house parties including group confessions, prayers and listening for God's guidance, having as their aim the 'changing' of lives. Buchman's preaching began to emphasize the need to 'change' world leaders if a war was to be avoided. His preference, accordingly, for association with the influential and rich attracted criticism, and his reputation suffered much from his reported remark, 'I thank God for a man like Hitler who has built a front-line defence against the anti-Christ of communism.' The Oxford Group became Moral Re-Armament in 1938.

Buddha (Pāli, Skt.; Chin., *fo*; Jap., *butsu*; Korean, *pul*). 1. An enlightened person, literally, 'one who has awakened' to the truth. Traditional Buddhism teaches that there are two sorts, samyaksaṃbuddha (see SAMMASAMBUDDHA) and *pratyekabuddha; and that *Gotama is one in a series of the former kind. *Mahāyāna Buddhism extends the notion of a buddha into a universal principle: all beings possess a 'buddha-nature' and are therefore prospective buddhas.

2. Title applied to Gotama (Skt., Gautama), the historical founder of Buddhism (hence, the Buddha Gotama or Gotama Buddha) and to other samyakbuddhas (e.g. the Buddha *Maitreya or Maitreya Buddha) by virtue of their being buddhas par excellence (as in (1) above). When occurring by itself, the expression 'the Buddha' is generally used to mean Gotama, though he is referred to by adherents of the *Theravāda tradition as simply 'Buddha'. The *Pāli canon suggests that, in his lifetime, Gotama (after his enlightenment) was not referred to so much as Buddha as *Tathāgata, his own preferred form of self-reference.

Gotama Buddha, also known, especially in Mahāyāna, as Buddha *Sākyamuni (i.e. the Wise

One, or Sage, of the Śakya clan) was not the first Buddha. Theravādin texts know of six preceding Buddhas, Vipaṣyin (Vipassi), Śikin (Sikhi, Viśvabhu (Vessabhū), Krakuccanda (Kakusandha), Konagāmara, and Kaśyapa (Kassapa), Nor is he the last. The Buddha who comes in the future and renews the *dhamma is Maitreya (see BUDDHAS OF THE THREE TIMES).

In Mahāyāna (for the reasons in (1) above), there are recognized many more (indeed countless) transcendent Buddhas. Because of the three-body (*trikāya) doctrine, the buddha-nature can manifest itself in accessible form. For examples of these, who are teachers of *bodhisattvas, and who reign over a paradise (*Pure land, see AKṢOBHYA; AMIDA; AMOGHASIDDHI; VAIROCANA; RATNASAṂBHAVA. They can also appear in an earthly appearance, the 'body of transformation' (*nirmāna-kāya) of trikāya. In the development of *Vajrayāna, each of five transcendent buddhas is linked to an earthly buddha and a bodhisattva, in ways which satisfy the need for both transcendence and immanence at the same time—a problem also addressed in the development of the Christian *Trinity.

In Hinduism, the Buddha (i.e. Gotama) is the ninth in the standard list of *Viṣṇu's *avatāras. Earlier lists do not include his name, and the first suggestion of any kind of identification with Viṣṇu is a story in the **Viṣṇu Purāṇa*, of how the latter emitted an illusory form which went about converting the demons to Jain and Buddhist heresies, thus weakening them in their warfare against the gods. It is only later that positive reasons are given for Viṣṇu's manifestation as the Buddha, e.g. in order to abolish sacrifices, out of compassion for animals.

Returning to Gotama who became the Buddha of recent manifestation: there are uncertainties about his dates. According to the Long Chronology, he lived just over 200 years before *Aśoka, giving approximate dates of 566–486 BCE. According to the Short Chronology, he lived 100 years before Aśoka, i.e. *c.*448–368. He was born Siddhārtha Gotama or Gautama, in *Kapilavastu, in modern-day Nepal. After his enlightenment, he became known as the Buddha, the Enlightened One. Although many stories of his life are told, and immense bodies of teaching are attributed to him, it is not possible to reconstruct his biography or his own teaching with any historical certainty—nor, from a Buddhist point of view, is it in the least desirable. The Buddha is a physician who diagnoses illness and suggests treatment; but the worth or the value lies, not in the biography of the physician, but on whether the patient is cured.

Buddhist biographies are late (see e.g. **Buddhacarita*, **Lalitavistara*). They, and texts in the *Pāli canon, suggest that Gotama was brought up in a royal household (perhaps son of the rāja of Kapilavastu), and that he married (perhaps more than one wife). His wife Yaśodharā bore a son, Rāhula. Although his father tried to protect Gotama from disturbing experiences, he ordered a carriage and saw, on separate occasions, a sick man, an old man, and a dead man. Disturbed by the thought that these conditions awaited him, he wondered how to escape them. On a fourth trip, he saw an emaciated religious *ascetic. Gotama abandoned his wife and son, and embarked on extreme asceticism. He discovered that such practices attain their goal—but no more than their goal; and these goals do not lead to escape from suffering and death.

In disillusionment at the limited attainments of asceticism, Gotama reverted to 'the middle way' (a characteristic name for 'Buddhism') and sat beneath a tree (*Bo Tree), concentrating on 'seeing things as they really are'. He passed through the four stages or layers of progressive insight (*jhānas), and reached enlightenment.

His initial response was to remain where he was, aware of the true nature of *dukkha, and of how it arises, and of how it ceases, and of the path leading to its cessation (*Four Noble Truths). Since this included awareness that there is no self or soul (no Hindu *ātman or *jīva) seeking rescue from the process of change and death, but only the process itself, he realized that he would be greeted with hostility or derision if he attempted to share this truth with others. But eventually he was prevailed upon (by the god *Brahmā) to share the truth, on the grounds that humans are like lotuses in a pool: all are rooted in mud; most are swamped below the surface; but a few are struggling to the light and some have already blossomed. The Buddha agreed to teach according to the capacity of his audiences (*upāya-kauśalya).

The rest of his life (when he had in fact attained *nirvāna, but the residual appearances of *karma kept him in apparent form on this earth) was spent wandering, with an increasing band of disciples, in the area of the larger Ganges basin; the rainy months were usually spent in community, the beginning of the *vihāra, and of the custom for *Theravādin Buddhist men to spend part of at least one rainy season as a member of a Buddhist monastic community (*saṅgha). According to *Majihima Nikāya*, his last words before death were, 'Decay is inherent in all compounded things, so continue in watchfulness' (or '. . . work out your own salvation with diligence'). See Index, Buddha's life; Buddhas, Bodhisattvas.

R. H. Drummond, *Gautama the Buddha* (1974); F. E. Reynolds, *Guide to Buddhist Religion* (1981); E. J. Thomas, *The Life of the Buddha as Legend and History* (1927, 1975), and *The History of Buddhist Thought* (1933, 1951).

Buddhabhadra (359–429). Buddhist *Sarvāstivāda monk, who was born in Kashmir, and entered the *saṅgha at 17. He met Chih-yen, who advised him to go to China. There he translated basic works (e.g. **Mahāparinirvāna-sūtra* and *Vināya-piṭaka), but came into conflict with *Kumārajīva monks, and took refuge, away from the capital, in *Lu-shan.

There he became an interpreter of the teaching of *Hui-yuan.

Buddhacarita. 'The Acts of the Buddha', a biography of the Buddha in the style of Sanskrit epic poetry (*mahākāvya*) written by *Aśvaghoṣa about the 2nd cent. CE. Of the seventeen cantos which survive in the original, only the first thirteen are by Aśvaghoṣa, the remaining four being added in the 19th cent. and extending the narrative as far as the Buddha's return home to Lumbinī after his enlightenment. The complete version of the epic is preserved in Tibetan and Chinese translations which both extend to twenty-eight cantos.

The Buddhacarita is a literary and religious classic, the work of a talented and skilful poet who was also an adherent of the faith. The style is reverent yet restrained and relatively free of the fanciful hagiographic detail found in other sources. A translation of the earlier part is in E. Conze, *Buddhist Scriptures*.

Buddhadāsa (Skt; Thai, Putatāt). Thailand's most influential Buddhist scholar and reformist monk. Born in 1905, Buddhadāsa (i.e. 'servant of the Buddha') was ordained at the age of 20, but soon afterwards became disenchanted with conventional monastic life. He decided to embark on a career of *vipassanā (insight meditation), and established a centre for this purpose at Suan Mokkhabalārāma (The Grove of the Power of Liberation) near Chaiya in S. Thailand in 1932. He remained there, paying occasional visits to Bangkok and abroad. He gave a lecture at the Sixth Great Buddhist Council held in Rangoon, 1954–6.

Buddhadāsa is a painstaking scholar who has undertaken extensive research on the *Tripiṭaka, especially the Sutta-Piṭaka (discourses), with a view to presenting a rational and scientifically based exposition of *Buddha-dharma. His books, which fill a room at the National Library, have exerted considerable influence on generations of Thai students and young monks.

Following King Mongkut's disregard for the literal understanding of Buddhist cosmology, Buddhadāsa *demythologizes many traditional beliefs. Thus gods and demons become states of mind, rebirth a moment-to-moment experience, and the doctrine of *anatman (no-self) a statement of the need to move away from an existence characterized by 'ego' or 'self-ness' to *nirvāna (Pāli), here and now.

The notion of *śūnyatā (emptiness) becomes the means whereby apparent contradictions are transcended. Thus, to the busy professional who wants to know how both to work and practise vipassanā, Buddhadāsa's advice would be that there is a quality of work which can be attained when the mind is characterized by śūnyatā. This resembles the **Bhagavad-gītā*'s doctrine of *nishkāma karma*, though Buddhadāsa is reluctant to accept the similarity. His use of śūnyatā puts him partly within the Mahāyānist tradition, particularly the *Mādhyamaka school.

Buddha-dharma. Teaching of the *Buddha and thus an appropriate name for 'Buddhism'. In *Zen, buddha-dharma is *buppō*, and is no longer teaching which can be given orally or through books, but is the inner experience which gave rise to the Buddha's teaching and which can only be grasped by a corresponding enlightenment. In SE Asia, 'Buddhism' is also known as buddha-sāsana, the practice of Buddhist morality and meditation.

Buddha-family: see BUDDHAKULA.

Buddha-fields: see BUDDHA-KṢETRA.

Buddhaghosa (Pāli, Skt., 'Buddha-voice'). Theravādin Buddhist, who was born in a *brahman family at the end of the 4th cent., traditionally at *Bodhgāya. He was converted to Buddhism by reading Buddhist texts, and went for instruction to the Mahāvihāra monastery in Śri Lankā. He wrote commentaries on many works in the Pāli canon, but is best remembered for *Visuddhimagga, The Way of Purity,* a work of great importance in understanding post-canonical Buddhism. It lays out systematically the Theravādin teaching of the Mahāvihāra monastery: chs. 1–2 cover *śīla, 3–13 *samādhi, 14–23 *prajña.

Eng. tr. B. Nyanamoli, *The Path of Purification* (1976).

Buddha-kāya. The 'bodies' (i.e. forms of manifestation) of the buddha-nature, more usually known as *Trikāya.

Buddha-kṣetra (Skt., 'Buddha-field'). The sphere of influence and activity of a *Buddha. In Buddhist cosmology each world-system (*cakka-vāla*) is the domain of a particular buddha within which he arises and leads beings to liberation through his teachings. The concept came to prominence in the *Mahāyāna on the basis of early speculations about the range of a buddha's knowledge and the extent of his sensory powers. With the concept of a plurality of buddhas came the idea of an infinite number of 'buddha-fields' extending throughout the reaches of space in many dimensions. These fields vary in their degree of perfection and are divided into two basic categories, pure and impure. The world we inhabit now is an instance of an impure buddha-field since beings here are still subject to the basic vices of greed, hatred, and delusion. The most famous of the pure buddha-fields or *Pure Lands is the paradise of the Buddha Amitābha (*Amida) in the west, described in the *Sukhāvatívyūha Sūtras*, into which all may be reborn by calling upon the name of Amitābha. The existence of these pure buddha-fields became immensely important in the development of popular devotional Buddhism especially in China and Japan.

Buddhakula (Skt., 'buddha-family'). The five basic qualities found in the Mahāyāna buddhas, manifested (though the three-body system of appearance, *trikāya) in the 'body of delight' (*sambhoga-kāya), the body in a buddha-paradise, enjoying the truth which it embodies. The five qualities are different aspects of *prajña (wisdom). They are associated with five buddhas in particular, who are the heads of the buddha-families: *Vairocana, *Amoghasiddhi, *Akṣobhya, *Ratnasaṃbhava, and Amitābha (*Amida). They are represented, extremely frequently, in the form of a *maṇḍala, with Vairocana in the centre, Amoghasiddhi in the north, followed by the others in clockwise order.

Buddha-nature: see BUDDHATĀ; TATHĀGATA-GARBHA; and Index *ad loc*.

Buddhapālita. A teacher and commentator of the *Prāsaṅgika branch of the *Mādhyamaka school who lived most probably in the 5th cent. CE. He is the author of the *Mūla-mādhyamaka-vṛtti*, a commentary on the *Mādhyamaka-kārikā* of *Nāgārjuna, the 2nd-cent. CE. founder of the school. Buddhapālita's commentary, which survives in Tibetan, contains twenty-seven chapters and is divided into ten sections. Buddhapālita's interpretation of Mādhyamaka was criticized by the Svātantrika-Mādhyamaka author *Bhāvaviveka, who was in turn refuted by *Candrakirti, the most famous exponent of the Prāsaṅgika interpretation.

Buddha-sāsana. Buddha-discipline, a term embracing the practice and teaching of the Buddha, and thus is a name for 'Buddhism': see also BUDDHA-DHARMA.

Buddhas of the three times. The *buddhas of the three periods, past (Kaśyapa, but often in iconography *Dīpaṃkara), present (Śākyamuni, i.e. Gotama), and future (*Maitreya).

Buddha's tooth (Buddhist relic): see PILGRIMAGE (BUDDHISM).

Buddhatā (Skt., 'buddha-nature'). In Mahāyāna Buddhism, the real and undifferentiated nature of all appearance. Since this nature constitutes all beings, they all have equal opportunity to realize this fact and to attain enlightenment—no matter what their present form or level of appearance. This is in contrast to *Theravāda. Within Mahāyāna, it is disputed whether inanimate appearances also possess the buddha-nature in this way. In Zen Buddhism, the equivalent (Jap.) term is *bussho, or *hossho*, and the awakening to the truth of that nature and one's identity with it is *mujōdō-no-taigen. Since all arises from *śūnyatā, bussho is necessarily not other than that; which means, in turn, that the buddha-nature must be beyond description or conceptualization. See also HUA-YEN; TATHĀGATA-GARBHA; Index, Buddha-nature.

Buddhavacana: see BUDDHIST SCRIPTURES.

Buddhavaṃsa (stories of previous Buddhas): see KHUDDAKA-NIKĀYA.

Buddhāvatamsaka-sūtra (Mahāyāna sūtra): see AVATAMSAKA LITERATURE.

Buddhi (Skt., 'intellect'). In Skt. (Hindu) literature, the higher mental faculty, the instrument of knowledge, discernment, and decision. Buddhi is understood in slightly different ways in the different philosophical systems. On the whole, it contrasts with *manas, mind, whose province is ordinary consciousness and the connection of *ātman with the senses. Buddhi, however, is a higher faculty which acts in sense percepts organized by manas and furnishes intellectual discrimination, determination, reason, and will. As such buddhi is at the very core of our being, as sentient creatures, and the closest mental faculty to the ātman, our Self or spirit.

In *Saṁkhya-yoga philosophy, buddhi (or *mahat*, 'the great one') plays a key role. Buddhi is the first principle derived from unmanifest *prakṛti (and predominant in *sattva guna*, 'intelligence stuff'), virtually transparent reflector for pure consciousness (*puruṣa), with which buddhi mistakenly identifies. With this mistaken identification with the conscious principle, a fall into ignorance, buddhi produces the next principle, *ahaṁkāra, which in turn produces manas. The three together make up the 'internal instrument' or *antaḥkaraṇa*. For salvation, buddhi must attain the discriminative discernment between itself as unconscious matter, prakṛti, and the independent and transcendent principle of pure consciousness, puruṣa.

Buddhism. This began historically (although, of course, in its own account it has always been the truth, with a long pre-history) in the 6th and 5th cents. BCE, in India, with the enlightenment of Gotama, who became thereby *muni of the Śakya clan (i.e. Śākyamuni) and (in his own self-description) *Tathāgata. Initially reluctant to share the truth of and the way to that enlightenment, he was persuaded to do so by *Brahmā on behalf of the gods. His teaching (*dharma) then becomes the foundation, for which reason 'Buddhism' (a Western term) is better called *Buddha-dharma or Buddha-sāsana (its name in SE Asia). It has its followers, in two major divisions—Theravāda (an inaccurate name; see HĪNAYĀNA) and Mahāyāna, with many sub-divisions—mainly in Śri Lankā and SE Asia (Thera.), and in Tibet, Vietnam, China, Korea, and Japan (Mah.).

The Buddha regarded himself as a guide and a physician, diagnosing ailments and pointing out the path to recovery. As presented now in the texts, he taught in the context of the basic components of Hindu *cosmology and psychology (long cycles of time, and equally long periods through which a self or soul, *ātman, is reborn as it moves, controlled by *karma as cause, toward freedom or salvation, *mokṣa), but modified them drastically: he saw all appearance as characterized by *dukkha (transience, *anicca, accompanied by the suffering which arises if one seeks something permanent or eternal in its midst). It follows that there cannot be a soul, but only the sequence of one moment giving rise to the next, constituting appearances with characteristic possibilities (human, e.g., as opposed to animal, through the *skandhas, aggregations). The no-soul doctrine is referred to as *anātman. It follows equally that there cannot be an eternal God, independent of the cosmos, who creates it. There are many gods in Buddhism, which is, especially at the popular level, an extremely theistic religion; but God/gods are a part of the process, simply having that characteristic appearance, as opposed to that of, e.g. animals or humans.

The teaching of the Buddha is summarized in the *Four Noble Truths (the truth of dukkha and how to escape it), the Eightfold Path (*aṣṭangika-mārga) (the route to escape or enlightenment), and *paticca-samuppāda (the analysis of the twelve-step chain of cause which gives rise to entanglement in *saṃsāra, the continuing process of reappearance (*punabhāva). Although there is no ātman, the causal sequence, of one moment giving rise to the next, can continue through the moment and process of death. To understand this is to start to reverse the sequence of paticca-samuppāda; and to practise all that the Buddha indicated is to move toward enlightenment and to attainment of the cessation of all interaction with manifest appearance, i.e. *nirvāna.

Buddhist commitment can thus be summarized in the *Three Jewels or Refuges: I take refuge in the Buddha; I take refuge in the Dhamma (Pāli for Skt., dharma); I take refuge in the *Saṅgha. The saṅgha is the communal organization of the *bhikṣus (bhikkhus), or monks. Initially, it was they alone who could advance toward nirvāna, but later Buddhism developed a mutually supportive understanding of the lay–bhikṣu interaction, in which both could advance, and each could help the other. This was taken dramatically further in Mahāyāna, where the idea of the buddha-nature (*buddhatā) means that all are equally capable, at any moment, of realizing the truth of their identity with that nature.

The Buddha's teaching was gathered, over a long period, into canonical collections, especially the *Tripiṭaka and the *Sūtras, though the status, particularly of the latter, may be disputed (see BUDDHIST SCRIPTURES). From about the end of the 4th cent. BCE, different interpretations of the teaching were leading to different schools, and especially to the major difference between Theravāda ('teaching of the elders'), with its eighteen schools, and Mahāyāna ('great vehicle', hence their derogatory reference to Theravāda as Hīnayāna, 'minor vehicle), with its innumerable styles and divisions; for these, see BUDDHIST SCHOOLS. Inherently eclectic, Mahayāna schools may so assimilate other religious practices and beliefs that they become virtually a 'new religion'—see e.g. VAJRAYĀNA, in Tibet, Mongolia, and Japan. Some attempts were made in the early centuries to secure co-operative agreements at the Buddhist *Councils.

Out of the early tensions and disputes, two major groupings emerged: the majority who claimed to be maintaining the original teaching, the *Mahāsāṃghika, and those in the western regions of India (to which Buddhism was spreading), who were called *Sthaviravāda. The spread of Buddhism was greatly accelerated during the reign of *Aśoka (3rd cent. BCE), whose Magadhan Empire covered most of modern India except the south. He adopted the social ethic of Buddhism as the philosophy of his reign, and although his personal commitment to Buddhism is uncertain, he is regarded by Buddhists as the model of the just ruler. His policies are recorded in his famous carved edicts.

Under this endorsement, popular Buddhism flourished, especially in *pilgrimages, in the development of *stūpas and the rituals and beliefs associated with them, and in the proliferation of art and image-making. But philosophy (*abhidhamma) also began its quest for more exact analysis of Buddhist concepts: three major schools emerged in the 3rd cent. BCE): Puggalavāda (Skt., Pudgalavāda), Sarvastivāda (Pāli, Sabbatthivāda), and Vibhajjavāda (Skt., Vibhajyavāda). Later, and even more important, came the development of 'the Great Vehicle', Mahāyāna, between the 2nd cent. BCE and 1st CE. It was not a single school or movement, but a drawing out of elements of practice and belief which had been in Buddhism from the outset, but without formal elaboration. Nevertheless, as the implications of these elements *were* elaborated, a new style of Buddhism began to emerge. In particular, the emphasis was no longer on making one's own way as near to enlightenment as possible (*arhat), but on attaining what the Buddha promised and then turning back from selfish attainment in order to help others (*bodhisattva). This led to entirely new cosmologies, as the whole spectrum of buddhas and bodhisattvas was mapped into its place. But even more disjunctively, new philosophical realizations were achieved of what the true buddha-nature must be, and how there cannot be other than that nature which is empty of self and of all differentiation (*buddhatā; *bussho; *śūnyatā). A key figure here was *Nāgārjuna and the *Mādhyamaka school.

The reasons for the decline and virtual disappearance of Buddhism in India remain a matter of academic dispute, ranging from the deliberate Hindu assimilation of some Buddhist ideas along with the clarification of ritual practices which the Buddha had attacked, to the Muslim conquest and its general aggression against other religions. Long before the decline, Buddhism had began to expand, in three different geographical directions, which produced very different versions of Buddhism (for which see following articles and TIBETAN RELIGION):

north into Tibet; east into China, Korea, and Japan; and south-east into Śri Lankā, Burma, and Thailand. For the development of Buddhism through schools/sects, see BUDDHIST SCHOOLS.

P. Harvey, *An Introduction to Buddhism* (1990); F. E. Reynolds, *A Guide to Buddhist Religion* (1981); R. H. Robinson and W. L. Johnson, *The Buddhist Religion* (1977); A. K. Warder, *Indian Buddhism* (1970); P. Williams, *Mahāyāna Buddhism* (1989); Y. Yoo, *Books on Buddhism: An Annotated Subject Guide* (1976) and *Buddhism: A Subject Index to Periodical Articles . . .* (1973).

Buddhism in Britain. Buddhist interest in Britain started in the late 19th cent. with the works of the Pali Text Society founded by *Rhys Davids in 1881 and with scholarly works done by various European scholars. Charles H. A. Benett was the second British Buddhist monk, as Ananda Metteyya in Burma, and brought the first Buddhist mission to England in 1908. After the Second World War some young Britons went to the East and were ordained there. They followed the Buddhist way of life and returned with some eastern teachers. Growing interest has led to about a hundred Buddhist centres and societies in Britain.

Among them *Theravāda, the four *Tibetan Schools, and *Zen tradition are the most popular. Apart from these, other Japanese sects, such as *Nichiren, *Shingon, *Jōdo Shu and Shin are represented. All these Buddhist Groups follow their traditional methods with slight adaptations to the W. world. But there has been a new development to form a Buddhist way more suitable to the W. way of life. This is called the 'Friends of *Western Buddhist Order' (FWBO), which is mainly influenced by *Mahāyāna Buddhism.

Buddhism in China. Buddhism was introduced into China about the beginning of the Christian era by Buddhist monks who travelled the overland route across Central Asia. During the first two centuries it maintained a precarious existence in its new surroundings, but with the downfall of the Han dynasty in the 3rd cent., a period of disunity and social turmoil ensued which affected the fortunes of the religion. The message of Buddhism, that existence is suffering (*dukkha), that life is transitory (*anicca), that there is an iron law of rewards and retribution (*karma), and that all beings can achieve salvation, proved to be an attractive magnet drawing the Chinese to the religion. By the time China was unified again in 589, followers of the religion included members of Chinese society at all levels, rulers to the common people. Buddhism was now ready to enter its golden age under the T'ang dynasty (618–907). During its heyday, it provided spiritual protection to the ruling families, economic benefits to the rich and noble, social welfare for needy commoners, and a bewildering array of deities for every believer. This growth was all the more remarkable because, throughout the period, Buddhism was attacked as being anti-filial (advocating celibacy), a parasite on society (encouraging mendicancy), subversive (contending that Buddhist monks did not have to observe the secular laws of the land).

That the religion was able to counter these criticisms and flourish was due in large measure to its ability to adjust itself to the Chinese environment. To refute the charge of unfiliality, the Chinese Buddhists observed memorial services for the departed ancestors, just as the Chinese did. Indian deities (such as the future Buddha *Maitreya) took on a Chinese appearance as the fat jovial *Laughing Buddha with children climbing all over him, while the *bodhisattva *Avalokiteśvara became the female Kuan-yin, the giver of children, in which form she was worshipped by countless numbers of Chinese women anxious to have children.

The accommodation to the Chinese scene may also be seen in the two most popular Chinese schools of Buddhism which flourished during the T'ang dynasty, the *Pure Land and *Ch'an. The popularity of the Pure Land school was due primarily to its direct and simple message, that all beings, no matter how depraved, could achieve salvation in the Western Paradise (*Sukhāvati) by having faith in the saving grace of Amitābha (*Amida), presiding Buddha of the Western Paradise. Likewise the Ch'an, with its emphasis on meditation, its iconoclastic attitude toward all Buddhas and bodhisattvas, its disregard for the scriptures, and its bizarre methods of instruction, was a protest and reaction against the long periods of *sūtra study, the ascetic religious practices, and elaborate rituals of traditional Buddhism. For the Ch'an, sitting in meditation was the only prerequisite for a direct, instant, and spontaneous realization of the buddha-nature (*buddhatā) within us; though Ch'an schools eventually disagreed among themselves on this point.

The growth of Buddhism up to the 8th cent. was also stimulated by the steady traffic of monks between India and China. Chinese monks in India would travel extensively to visit the holy sites of their religion or learn Sanskrit from their Indian masters, and upon their return to China would embark on the gigantic task of translating into Chinese the sacred texts they brought back with them (e.g. *Kumārajīva and *Hsuan-tsang). The Indian masters would bring with them the knowledge of the latest developments in Indian Buddhism which they transmitted to their eager Chinese disciples. The concrete result of their efforts is the monumental Chinese Buddhist canon, the latest modern edition of which was printed in Japan during 1922–35, consisting of 55 volumes, each one approximately 1,000 pages in length.

Buddhist art also played a prominent role in the dissemination of the religion among the Chinese. Images of Buddhist deities were carved out of the rocks in such centres as *Yün-kang and *Lungmen which may still be seen today as mute testimony to the emotional fervour of the faithful devotees. Within the Buddhist temples, the visitor would be dazzled by the golden images of the Buddha on the altar, by the intricate carvings on the wooden or stone pillars supporting the soaring roof, by the countless ritual vessels made of precious metals, and by the magnificent paintings of the Western Paradise. It was no wonder that the ordinary Chinese upon entry into a temple would be awed by the spectacular artistic displays and the mysterious enchanting sounds accompanying the ritual worship of the deities. His interest was further enhanced when he learnt that those same deities would offer him solace and comfort in times of sorrow, compassion and mercy during unfortunate periods, and hope and expectation of relief in the future from the present burdens of mundane life, things that his native *Confucianism never promised him.

By the end of the 8th cent., however, the fortunes of Buddhism in China began to decline. Travel between India and China via the overland route was blocked at the western end by the Arabs, thus depriving the Chinese of the religious and intellectual stimulation from India. The persecution of 845 in China accelerated the process. Though the religious community in later centuries continued to ordain monks and carry on religious activities, it became clear that the religion was no longer a creative spiritual and intellectual force in Chinese society.

Reverting to the major schools of Chinese Buddhism: the earliest were Chinese versions of Indian schools, e.g. *San-lun ('Three Treatise') and *Fa-hsiang ('Dharma Characteristics'); Chen-yen, a form of Mantrayāna (stressing the effectiveness of the *mantra) died out in China under persecution, but was of importance in Korea and Japan.

The next stage is characterized by attempts at synthesis, stressing that the *Buddha Śākyamuni taught by skilful means (*upāya-kauśalya), and arranging the *Theravāda/Śrāvakayāna and *Mahāyāna sūtras on different levels, while designating one or more sūtras as the pinnacle. Thus *T'ien-t'ai designated the **Lotus Sūtra* and the *Parinirvāṇa Sūtra* at the height, while *Hua-yen designated the **Avatamsaka Sūtra* at the height. Others, e.g. the Lu or *Vinaya school, placed the reconciling emphasis on practice. All were concerned to reconcile Buddhism with Taoist religion and Confucian ethics.

Practical Buddhism, extending 'practice' to devotion and meditation, produced the two major schools, *Pure Land (Ch'ing-t'u) and *Ch'an/Zen. Both schools had a system of transmission through patriarchs, but Pure Land became so widespread that the system of patriarchs died out. Ch'an maintained the system, but sub-divided into many different (sometimes competing) lineages. The founder of Ch'an (apart from the Buddha and the lineage leading from him) is held to be *Bodhidharma. After four successors, the sixth patriarch was disputed between *Hui-neng (leading to the Southern school) and Shen-hsiu (Northern school)—though the differences actually precede this conflict, and cannot be mapped precisely onto it. In 796, the emperor decided in favour of the Southern school, and Hui-neng was promoted to become the second founder of Ch'an (especially through the biographical parts of the *Platform Sūtra*, **Liu-tsu-ta-shih* . . .).

Out of many further lineage divisions, two become dominant after the 11th cent.: Lin-chi (Jap., *Rinzai), emphasizing *kōans and sudden enlightenment; and *Ts'ao-tung (Jap., *Sōtō), emphasizing quiet meditation and gradual awakening. The two merged in China, but have remained separate in Japan.

K. K. S. Chen, *Buddhism in China* . . . (1964) and *The Chinese Transformation of Buddhism* (1973); Tsukamoto Zenryu, *A History of Early Chinese Buddhism* (1985); E. Zürcher, *The Buddhist Conquest of China* (1959, 1972).

Buddhism in Japan. The dominant religious tradition of Japan, Buddhism first entered Japan *c.*5th or 6th cent. CE, from the Chinese mainland (traditionally in 538 from Korea). Initially, a few powerful clans opposed the new religion, but by the end of 6th cent. the emperor himself embraced Buddhism, and it received the devotion and patronage of the highest levels of Japanese society. Shōtoku Taishi or Prince Shōtoku (574–622) was instrumental in consolidating Buddhism in Japan: he was an avid proponent of Chinese culture who studied and lectured on such important *Buddhist scriptures as the **Lotus Sūtra* and who reputedly founded some of the oldest Buddhist temples in Japan. The Japanese did not initially comprehend Buddhism's doctrinal subtleties, but perceived it, rather, as a religion of propitious spirits similar to the indigenous *Shinto deities.

Japan's schools of Buddhism are generally categorized according to the historical period in which they emerged: Nara period (710–84), Heian period (794–1185), and Kamakura period (1185–1333). During these periods the Japanese assimilated the content of Buddhism, while also adapting it to their own religious sensibilities. *Nara Buddhism consisted of six schools which were virtual transplants from China: Hossō, Kusha, Sanron, Jōjitsu, Kegon (Chin., *Hua-yen), and Ritsu. These were not separate sectarian organizations but mostly philosophies of Buddhism studied side by side in the major temples of the ancient capital of Nara. Though some of the philosophies were *Hīnayāna in origin, the overriding thrust of Buddhist thought in Japan was always *Mahāyāna. In the Nara period Buddhism was treated as a source of both religious and worldly power, and hence the ruling class sought to control it and to use it for protection of the state (*chingo kokka*) and for concrete benefits in this world (*genze riyaku*).

Heian Buddhism was comprised of two schools: *Tendai (Chin., *T'ien-t'ai) founded by *Saichō (767–822) and *Shingon founded by *Kūkai

(774–835). Saichō sought to liberate Tendai from strict government supervision and to give it an indisputable Mahāyāna flavour by basing its ordination vows exclusively on the *bodhisattva precepts (*bosatsukai*) instead of the Hīnayāna precepts used by the Nara schools. This was a clear departure from long-standing Buddhist tradition. He also instituted a twelve-year programme of rigorous training for all Tendai monks involving meditation, study of the *Lotus Sūtra*, and esoteric practices. In doctrine Tendai stressed the interrelatedness of all reality, suggested in its maxim, 'A single thought encompasses the three thousand worlds' (*ichinen sanzen*). To realize this was the aim of these practices. Kūkai built his religious movement around esoteric meditations, rituals, and incantations. Performing them required initiation into special *maṇḍala, *mudrā, and *mantra. The goal in Shingon was to 'achieve Buddhahood in this very body' (*sokushin jōbutsu*) through these practices. Both schools took an accommodating attitude toward Shinto, construing its deities as protectors of Buddhism or manifestations of buddhas and bodhisattvas. The complexity and sophistication of Tendai and Shingon made them accessible primarily to an aristocratic audience. The religious powers that they embodied also lent them to the government's endeavour to use Buddhism for the protection of the state. None the less, Tendai and Shingon represent an advance on the Nara schools in the emancipation of Buddhism from government control and in the adaptation of Buddhism to the Japanese context.

Japanese Buddhism reached its height in the Kamakura period with the *Pure Land schools of *Hōnen (1133–1212), *Shinran (1173–1262), and *Ippen (1239–89); the *Zen schools of *Eisai (1141–1215), known as Rinzai (Chin., Lin-chi), and *Dōgen (1200–53), known as Sōtō (Chin., *Ts'ao-tung); and the Nichiren school of *Nichiren (1222–82). Each of these was strongly sectarian in outlook, emphasizing one specific practice to the exclusion of others. Pure Land advocated the *nembutsu, or invoking the name of the Buddha *Amida; Zen stressed *zazen, or sitting in meditation; and Nichiren recommended the *daimoku, or chanting the title of the *Lotus Sūtra*. Compared to earlier Buddhist systems, these practices represent a radical simplification of religious observance. The Pure Land and the Nichiren schools proclaimed the need for simple and accessible paths to salvation, for they believed that Buddhism had passed into the age of *mappō, or the 'Latter-day Dharma', when human beings lack the capacity to achieve enlightenment by traditional means. Amalgamation with Shinto, pursuit of worldly benefits, rigorous observance of vows, celibacy, study and meditation, clerical rights all became less important, and simple practices aimed at personal salvation emerged as the central concern. These new forms of Buddhism appealed to ordinary believers who could not meet up to the requirements of the earlier schools. Hence, Kamakura Buddhism became the religion of the masses, and it eventually overshadowed the Nara and Heian schools. To this day the Kamakura schools claim the vast majority of Japan's population as adherents.

S. Bando, *A Bibliography on Japanese Buddhism* (1958); J. M. Kitagawa, *Religion in Japanese History* (1966); D. and A. Matsunaga, *Foundation of Japanese Buddhism* (1974–6).

Buddhism in Korea. Chinese Buddhism was officially introduced to Korea during the Three Kingdoms period (*c.*350–668) when the country was divided into Koguryŏ, Paekche, and Silla. The teachings were transmitted first to Koguryŏ, then to Paekche, both in the 4th cent. CE, and finally spread to Silla in the 6th cent. The new religion allied itself with the court, embraced indigenous *shamanism and folk religion, gradually penetrating to the populace. Buddhism in Silla contributed to the formation of the *Hwarang Do, a unique institution which trained young aristocrats in civil and military virtues, through devotion to Mirŭk (*Maitreya Bodhisattva) and observance of Buddhist precepts.

During the unified Silla period (668–935) Buddhism took root and flowered in Korean soil. Many monks went to China and even to India in pursuit of Buddhist truth. The five major schools were formed: Yŏlban (Nirvāna), Kyeyul (Vinaya), Pŏpsŏng (Dharma-nature), Hwaŏm (Hua-yen), and Pŏpsang (Consciousness-only). In addition, the nine lineages (Nine Mountains) of *Sŏn (Ch'an/Zen) were transmitted from China. However, Hwaŏm Buddhism played the crucial role: *Wŏnhyo (618–86) and *Ŭisang (625–702) contributed to making Silla Buddhism syncretic and nationalistic, traits which have since been the hallmarks of Korean Buddhism. Faith in Kwanŭm (Kuan-yin) was also widely held among the people.

The Koryŏ dynasty (935–1392) marks the zenith of Korean Buddhism. Many temples and monasteries were built through state funds. Court nobles entered monkhood, while a number of monks assumed influential social positions. The secular power of the Buddhist order increased with the accumulation of lands and serfs. Buddhism absorbed religious *Taoism and Buddhist *esotericism; the halls of the seven stars (of the Dipper) and the halls of mountain gods were built along with the Buddha halls. *Maṇḍalas of buddhas, bodhisattvas, and gods were painted. Two new sects were established in this period: the Ch'ŏnt'ae (*T'ien-t'ai) sect, by *Ŭich'ŏn (1055–1101), and the Chogye sect, by *Chinul (1158–1210), through a unification of the nine existing Sŏn lineages. The publication of the *Korean Tripiṭaka in the 13th cent. was a brilliant achievement of Koryŏ Buddhism. For all of this, Buddhism was plagued by increasing internal corruption and external discontent.

The rulers of the Yi dynasty (1392–1910), adopting *Neo-Confucianism as the state orthodoxy, advanced a series of anti-Buddhist policies which dealt a crippling blow to Buddhism. King T'aejong

(r. 1401–18) reduced the eleven existing sects to seven, and King Sejong (r. 1419–50) reduced those seven sects to just two: the doctrinal school (*kyojong*) and the meditational school (*sŏnjong*). The number of monasteries was drastically diminished. The purpose of all this was solely to curb the political, economic, and ecclesiastical power of established Buddhism; and yet it was Buddhist monk soldiers who spearheaded national defence against Japanese armies at the time of Toyotomi Hideyoshi's two invasions of Korea in 1592 and 1597.

During the period of Japanese rule (1910–45), Korean Buddhism, under the influence of its Japanese counterpart, made some reforms but also suffered serious set-backs. The two surviving Buddhist groups were forced in 1911 to merge with the Chogye sect. In 1919 countless Buddhists together with other religionists and patriots participated in the March First Movement against Japanese colonial rule.

Since Korea's independence in 1945, Buddhism has coped with the challenges of the modern world. Shedding its seclusion in deep mountains, it is nowadays active in the cities. The Chogye sect remains influential. Young people are involved in Buddhist studies, meditation, the monastic way of life, and social services. The activities of nuns are noteworthy. *Won Buddhism is the most popular lay Buddhist movement today.

R. E. Buswell, *The Korean Approach to Zen: The Collected Works of Chinul* (1983); H.-K. Kim (ed.), *Studies on Korea: A Scholar's Guide* (1980); L. R. Lancaster, *The Korean Buddhist Canon: A Descriptive Catalogue* (1979).

Buddhism in South-East Asia. SE Asian Buddhism is mostly *Theravāda and historically related to the *Sthaviras (i.e. elders) who emerged in the 3rd cent. BCE, in what is now Śri Lankā. During the following centuries monks carried the teaching of the *Tripiṭaka to Thailand, Burma, Laos, and Cambodia, where it flourished, though not without substantial accommodation to popular Hinduism and animism.

A major reason for the rapid spread of Buddhism in SE Asia was its acceptance by monarchs who modelled their role on that of the Indian emperor, *Aśoka Maurya. Cambodian, Thai, and Burmese kings were known as *cakravartin, the turners of the wheel of *saṃsāra, and the promoters of justice and good religion. Some were also regarded as *bodhisattvas, or buddhas-to-be, and as *Maitreya, an actual future Buddha. The fusion of such Hindu, Theravādin, and Mahāyānist beliefs enabled successive monarchs to ply an important integrative function linking the past and the future, spiritual and secular life. The continuing influence of the Thai kings and Cambodia's Norodom Sihanouk has its roots in such notions of monarchy.

The close association between *saṅgha and State in most parts of SE Asia has enabled Theravāda Buddhism to maintain a dominant position in relation to Hindu and animistic beliefs, though not without accommodation. In Burma, for example, the 11th-cent. king Anawrahta was able to suppress all *nats (guardian spirits) which did not conform to Buddhist principles. *Brahman priests play a major role in the consecration of Thai kings, and the Thai notions of *phii* and *winyān* (spirit, soul) are prominent in popular Buddhism. But Theravāda Buddhism was never pure, and practices such as the building of shrines to gods and the veneration of Buddha images date back to its inception in Śri Lankā. Psychologically they tend to compensate for the austere aspects of the Theravāda, as represented, for example, by the discipline undertaken by an *arhat.

Thai Buddhism owes much to King Mongkut (1804–68), who rejected much of the mythology associated with SE Asian ideas surrounding the monarchy, replacing them with rational and scientific explanations. A monk prior to ascending the throne, he reordained according to the strict Mon tradition and founded a new branch of the saṅgha known as the Dhammayutika Nikāya ('those who adhere to the Dhamma'). The older group subsequently became known as the Mahānikāya ('the great branch').

The Dhammayutika monks became popular among the educated élite, and a parallel group came into being in Cambodia. The former remained subject to a single patriarch, whereas the latter had one for each branch. Mongkut's insistence on the *Vinaya, the first of the Tripiṭaka (Skt.), as the cornerstone for reform, influenced Thai, Cambodian, and to a lesser extent Laotian monks by making them more careful to observe its detailed rules. Thus Thai monks and novices may not attend government schools or colleges because this would involve an inappropriate amount of contact with women. In Śri Lankā, however, this is much less of a problem.

Nuns are rare in SE Asia, though provision exists for women to ordain to the level of *anāgārika, which is intermediate between the five precepts for a lay Buddhist, and the ten undertaken by the novice. They wear white robes. In Thailand they are known as *mae chii*, and their role is gaining in importance.

In Laos and Cambodia the political events of the 1970s have severely curtailed the activities of Buddhist monks. In Burma, *pongyis* ('great glory') played a prominent role in the movement for independence from Britain, and supported U Nu in his 1960 election campaign. But more recently, since the advent of Ne Win, saṅgha and State have parted company.

Thailand's continuous tradition of monarchy and saṅgha unchecked by colonial powers produced some important manifestations of Buddhism. Mongkut's rejection of supernaturalism has encouraged educated members of the saṅgha to present Buddhism in modern scientific dress. *Buddhadāsa (Skt.;

Putatāt, Thai) has reformulated cardinal doctrines such as the notion of rebirth to make them acceptable to scientifically trained intellectuals. Less well-known, but greatly respected by young scholar monks at Mahachulalongkorn and Mahamakut Buddhist universities, are Phra Rajavaramuni and Paññānanda Bhikku.

Other leading monks share the progressive outlook of Buddhadāsa, but are famous primarily as meditation teachers (Achan Mun) or practitioners of development (Phra Maha Narong Cittasobhano). During the last decades of the 20th cent., the Government, the two Buddhist universities, and various individual temples have pioneered development programmes geared primarily to the needs of the rural poor. Dr Prawese Wasi, director of the Sirirath Hospital in Bangkok, organized training schemes for monks in primary health care, and plans were made to involve both monks and *mae chii* in support for people with AIDS and their families. Such activities raise in an acute form the issue of appropriate behaviour for a monk, and there has been much public debate. Other leading Buddhists include Phra Kittiwudho, the politically rightist director of Cittipawan College and a popular broadcaster, Phra Bodhirak, leader of the black-robed Santi Aśoke reformist group (which ordains women on equal terms with men), Phra Payom Kallayano, a student of Buddhadāsa who spices his sermons with street-level slang and is very popular with young Thais, and Sulak Sivaraksa, well-known leftist intellectual and social critic.

Laotian Buddhism has followed much the same history as Cambodia, and was the state religion under royal patronage until the Communist take-over in 1975. There was no division into 'orders', as in Thailand and Cambodia, and a single patriarch. Monks played a major role in public education.

Vietnamese Buddhism differs from that of other mainland SE Asian Buddhist countries in that it was both Theravādin and Mahāyānist from an early stage, and has been heavily influenced by Confucianism and Taoism. The comparatively high proportion of Theravādins in the south is the legacy of the Cambodian presence between the 15th and 19th cents. Vietnamese monks have been heavily involved in politics, and in 1963 Thich Quang Duc, a 73-year-old monk, performed self-immolation as a protest against the Diem regime. The United Vietnamese Buddhist Church, which came into being during the religious and political ferment of the 1960s, united Theravādins and Mahāyānists in a single ecclesiastical structure. Thich Nhat Hanh is representative of the moderate political wing of the Church.

*Cao Dai and *Hoa Hao are even more syncretistic than their parent Vietnamese Buddhism. The former, founded in 1926 by Ngo Van Chieu (1878–1932), tries to draw together Confucianism. Taoism, Buddhism, and Christianity into a single religion of the Way (Tao). Hoa Hao, founded by Huynh Phu So in 1939, is more distinctively Buddhist and reformed in its opposition to religious rituals.

Buddhism in Indonesia and Malaysia is very much a minority religion. Theravādins and Mahāyānists (mostly the former) in Indonesia belong to the All Indonesia Federation of Buddhist Organizations, which was founded in 1978 to promote unity among Buddhists. Buddhism in Singapore and Hong Kong has, not surprisingly, been strongly influenced by Taoism, Confucianism, and Chinese ancestor worship.

Thus SE Asia Buddhism is a highly complex system of interlocking historical, geographic, political, and cultural traditions. Although common features exist, such as the role of the monarchy and accommodation between Buddhism and pre-Buddhistic animism and Hinduism, there is an enormous diversity which characterizes not only the differences between countries in the region but also significant distinctions which exist between the Theravāda Buddhism of SE Asia and its historical parents in Śri Lankā and India.

Burma: N. Ray, *Theravāda Buddhism in Burma* (1956); M. E. Spiro, *Buddhism and Society* . . . (1970). Thailand: J. Bunnag, *Buddhist Monk, Buddhist Layman* . . . (1973); Phra Rajavaramuni, *Thai Buddhism* . . . (1985); S. J. Tambiah, *World Conqueror and World Renouncer* (1976); J. Kornfield, *Living Buddhist Masters* (1977); R. C. Lester, *Theravāda Buddhism in SE Asia* (1973).

Buddhism in Tibet: see TIBETAN RELIGION.

Buddhist Councils: see COUNCILS, BUDDHIST.

Buddhist lineages: see BUDDHIST SCHOOLS.

Buddhist schools (sometimes referred to as 'sects'). These are felt by Buddhists to be primarily a matter of lineage more than credal confession. A Buddhist is a *Bauddha* (Skt., 'Follower of *Buddha') and takes refuge in the *Three Jewels, thus becoming a part of the *saṅgha with a particular interpretation of the *dharma, and will often refer to a particular person as 'my teacher'. This teacher will have been certified by another teacher in a lineage which, if complete, can be traced back to the Buddha. Controversies then arise over the authenticity of a lineage and/or the correctness or completeness of its understanding of the dharma. Since divisions over the interpretation of dharma have often impressed scholars as philosophical, they have been called schools rather than sects, or the neutral term 'tradition' may be used. Within Tibetan Buddhism the theoretical divisions called *siddhānta* (Skt., 'finality', 'explanation') have been translated as 'system' although they come closest to being philosophical schools. No one term in Buddhism corresponds to any of these divisions, and for convenience the word 'lineage' will be used here.

There are two major lineage groups: *Theravāda and *Mahāyāna. *Vajrayāna is sometimes counted as a third grouping and sometimes as a subset of Mahāyāna. Theravāda is most simply viewed as a single major lineage. Mahāyāna is a family of lineages that may be grouped into two main cultural types: Tibeto-Mongol and Sino-Japanese. Tibeto-Mongol Buddhism sees itself as the inheritor of later Indian Mahāyānist scholar-monks and places much emphasis on philosophical precision. Sino-Japanese Buddhism (which includes Korean and Vietnamese forms) developed lineages independently of Indian Mahāyāna.

Any lineage may claim superiority over any other by various means. Theravādins often claim to have preserved the *ipsissima verba* of the Buddha to which, they say, Mahāyāna has made unwarranted additions. Tibetan Buddhists point to the complexity of their systems as evidence that they have the fullness of the teachings in comparison with which the so-called *Hīnayāna (Skt., 'lesser' or 'inferior vehicle'), which is superficially similar to Theravāda, is said to be deficient. Specifically, the teaching of the *Tantras, which form Vajrayāna, are said by Tibetans to have been taught by the Dharmakāya (see TRIKĀYA) to a select group of disciples and passed down in a special lineage. Vajrayāna is also known in the Far East, especially in Japan as *Shingon, but it differs significantly from the Tibetan forms. Japanese Buddhists often argue for the superiority of their forms of Buddhism with a botanical image: India is the root of Buddhism, China the stem, and Japan the flower. Thus, forms such as *Zen and *Jōdo Shinshū, outwardly very simple, are seen as the concentrated and evolved essence of the original teaching of *Śākyamuni.

Early Buddhism is said to have divided into eighteen lineages on the basis of scholarly disputes about the nature of all three of the Three Jewels. André Bareau, working in a slightly larger historical framework, has recovered the most probable outlines of thirty-four lineages (*Les Sectes Bouddhiques du Petit Véhicule*, 1955). None of the earliest lineages can be clearly identified in later Buddhism, but Theravāda may be seen as the oldest surviving lineage. It has become the dominant form of Buddhism in SE Asia. Śri Lankā has been Theravādin since it became Buddhist in 3rd cent. BCE and has had considerable influence on the mainland. Burma, Thailand, and Kampuchea first received Chinese Mahāyāna and some Vajrayāna. They became Theravādin in, respectively, the 11th, 13th, and 14th cents. CE. Laos received Theravāda from Kampuchea in the 14th cent. CE. Theravāda has been repeatedly split over questions of monastic discipline (see VINAYA) and ordination practice, and the relative importance of doctrine and meditation. The making and healing of these splits has often proceeded with the collaboration, or at the initiation, of the respective governments.

Tibetan Buddhism has four main lineages divided into two major groups: Nyingmapa (Tib., 'Ancient Ones'), a single lineage attributed to the Indian missionary *Padmasambhava (9th cent. CE), which arranges the dharma into nine vehicles (Skt., *Yāna); and Sarmapa (Tib., 'New Ones'), a group containing the three lineages of the Later Transmission: Kagyupa founded by Marpa (1012–*c*.1098), Sakyapa founded by Konchog Gyalpo (1034–1102), and the Gelugpa reform of Tsongkhapa (1357–1419). The Nyingma and Sarma groups differ over their understanding of *śunyatā and the interpretation of Tantra. The sub-divisions of the Kagyu are the most complicated. There are two main divisions, Shangpa and Dragpo. The famous teacher *Milarepa (1040–1123), whose life and songs have been translated into English, was a Dragpo. The Dragpo has four divisions, of which the Karma Kagyu is the best known. Another division, Phagtru, itself has eight divisions, of which the Drikung and Drukpa are best known. Drukpa has further sub-divided into three. Tsongkhapa's lineage, Gelugpa, attempts a synthesis of what it considers the best features of all Sarma groups. The *Dalai Lamas belong to the Gelugpa. The Tibetan lineages spread into Mongolia and mixed with the indigenous *shamanism but without producing distinctly new lineages.

Chinese Buddhist lineages may be divided into three main types: modifications of Indian lineages, native scholastic lineages, and native popular lineages. All these lineages interact with each other in complex ways and this classification, although designed to be helpful, is in no way absolute. The major lineages based on Indian forms are one Hīnayāna, Chü-shê or Ābhidharmika; and two Mahāyāna, San-lun or *Mādhyamaka, and Fa-hsiang or Yogācāra / Vijñānavāda. These, and many smaller lineages, provided the theoretical basis for the development of the two great comprehensive Chinese systems of *T'ien-t'ai, based on the **Lotus Sūtra* and founded by Hui-ssŭ (515–76); and Hua-yen, based on the **Avatamsaka Sūtra* and founded by Tu-shun (557–640). Lineages with a wider appeal among layfolk are *Zen (Chin., Ch'an), attributed to the Indian missionary *Bodhidharma (*c*.5th cent.) and *Pure Land (Chin., Ching-t'u), perhaps founded by Hui-yüan (334–416). During the Sung and Ming Dynasties Zen and Pure Land were synthesised to form the basis of modern Chinese Buddhism.

Korean Buddhist lineages were at first extensions of the Chinese, with the Hua-yen (Hwaŏm) being the most important and forming the doctrinal basis for all later Korean Buddhism. A distinctively Korean lineage, Popsong (Dharma Nature) was founded by *Wŏnhyo (617–86) who attempted a comprehensive system based on the Awakening of Faith (*Mahāyānaśraddhotpāda-śastra*) and the teaching of One Mind. Zen *Sŏn was introduced by Pŏmnang in *c*.630 and sparked a major controversy between itself and scholastic Buddhism (collectively known as Kyo) which still affects Korean Buddhism. Sŏn itself divided into nine lineages, called 'mountains', which disputed with each other. The highly respected Master *Chinul (1158–1210) attempted to resolve the controversies by teaching the identity of the enlightenment achieved through Sŏn practice and Kyo study, i.e. the identity of the 'tongueless' and the 'tongued' dharma transmissions. The government forcibly united the lineages at various times, and in 1935 all lineages were unified as the Chogye.

Japan received many of the Chinese lineages through Korea in the 6th cent. CE, with some importance again being given to Hua-yen (Kegon). *Kūkai (774–835) combined two streams of Chinese Chen-yen (Vajrayāna) to form *Shingon, an original synthesis which became considerably more popular than its parents, and with his ability to align Buddhism with native folk religion he became a cultural hero. Zen and Pure Land have remained distinct lineages in Japan, with three forms of Zen modified from Chinese forms (*Sōtō, *Rinzai, and *Ōbaku) and two main forms of Pure Land (*Jōdo and *Jōdoshin) developed indigenously by *Hōnen (1133–1212) and *Shinran (1173–1263) respectively. *Nichiren (1222–82) founded a vigorously exclusivist lineage of which a later subbranch, *Nichiren Shōshū, is socially (as *Sōka Gakkai) and politically (as the Kōmei Party) highly visible in present-day Japan. Many Japanese lineages trace their origin to the break-up of the commodious *Tendai, the Japanese form of T'ien-t'ai, in Kamakura times (*c.*12th cent. CE), and may be seen as selecting one element of Tendai as a central theme or practice. Thus, Zen sitting, Pure Land chanting of the Name of *Amida, and Nichiren's emphasis on the *Lotus Sūtra* are not inventions of their founders: their originality consists in the claim that a single practice could have supreme efficacy. As Korea has tried to reduce the number of lineages, so Japan has allowed them to proliferate. Nearly 170 lineages, divided amongst 14 major groupings, are currently listed by the Japanese Agency for Cultural Affairs.

Vietnam received lineages from the rest of SE Asia around 1st cent. CE and from China between the 6th and 17th centuries. The SE Asian lineages have formed a Hīnayāna base for Vietnamese Buddhist practice supporting a superstructure of Chinese Mahāyāna, chiefly Zen (Vietnamese *Thiền*). The *Tha'o-Đu'ò'ng* lineage, a form of the Chinese Sung Dynasty synthesis imported in the 11th cent., had great influence on the character of Vietnamese Buddhism as a harmony of Zen (emphasizing wisdom) and Pure Land (emphasizing compassion). An indigenous form of Lin-chi (Vietnamese, *Lâm-Tế*) was founded by Liễu-Quán (d. 1743) and became the dominant lineage. All lineages were merged into the Unified Buddhist Church of Vietnam (Vietnamese, *Việt-Nam Phật-Giáo Thống-Nhất Giáo-Hội*) in 1963.

Buddhist Scriptures. These are extensive and variously classified. The fundamental division is into the word of the *Buddha (Skt., *buddhavacana*) and the authorized commentaries. The written scriptural tradition is secondary to the oral transmission and there is no single body of texts that might be called a 'Buddhist Bible'. A Buddha is never at fault in any of the 'three activities' of body, speech, and mind. Therefore, he teaches as much by his body (his appearance, movements, and ethical conduct) as by his words, and both of these are the expression of his enlightened mind. A Buddha does not communicate information about reality so much as a therapeutic analysis of suffering (*Majjhima Nikāya* 63) and his own realization of enlightenment: he demonstrates the *quality* of the perfectly free mind. This allows certain Buddhists, such as the *Zen lineages, to sit lightly to, or even ignore, texts in favour of 'mind-to-mind transmission'; but even heavily textual traditions, such as *Theravāda and Tibetan Buddhism, emphasize the importance of the quality of the life of the teacher who expounds the texts. Typically, a Buddhist teaching session is a progressive unfolding of a portion of *buddhavacana* through the authorized commentaries of a particular lineage and culminating in the teacher's own experience and explanation. This feature is encapsulated in the inseparability of the *Three Jewels: the Buddha manifests *dharma and entrusts it to the *saṅgha which maintains and teaches it in his name. In Tibetan Buddhism the mind of the teacher is said to be non-dual with the mind of Buddha and so he is regarded as the unifying principle, or living sacrament, of the Three Jewels. For the basic canon, see TRIPIṬAKA.

E. Conze (rev. L. Lancaster), *Buddhist Scriptures: A Bibliography* (1982).

Buḍhā, Bhāī (16th cent. CE). Respected contemporary of the first six Sikh *Gurūs. According to tradition, as a boy Bhāī Buḍhā became a loyal disciple of Gurū Nānak who gave him the name Buḍhā (Pañjabi, 'old man'). His devotion was surpassed only by that of Lahaṇā whom he anointed with *tilak* as Gurū Nānak's successor, Gurū *Aṅgad. He similarly invested Gurū *Amar Dās, *Rām Dās, *Arjan Dev, and *Hargobind. He traced Amar Dās to his hiding place and was later appointed manager of the villages granted to the Gurū's daughter, Bībī Bhānī. During the Gurūship of Arjan Dev, Bhāī Buḍhā publicized the misconduct of the rival claimant, *Prithī Chand. In 1604 he became the first *granthī, upon the installation of Arjan Dev's compilation of the *Ādi Granth in the *Harimandir whose construction he had supervised. Following the Gurū's execution and during the imprisonment of Gurū Hargobind, whose adviser he was, Bhāī Buḍhā and Bhāī *Gurdās administered the Sikh community. From his initiative at this time derives the continuing daily practice of devotees circling the holy pool singing hymns before offering *Ardās at the entrance of the Harimandir—originally for the Gurū's release.

Budo (martial ways): see MARTIAL ARTS IN JAPAN.

Buffalo (icon, myth, and sacrifice): see MAHIṢA.

Bugaku (Jap., 'dance music' or 'dance entertainment'). Ceremonial *dance and *music used in

Shinto, Buddhist, and Imperial Court festivals and rituals of Japan since the early days of Japanese history. The music, when performed alone, is called *gagaku* ('refined/ceremonial music'). Both the music and the dances were imported from China at a very early date (4th or 5th cent. BCE).

Bugei (martial arts): see MARTIAL ARTS IN JAPAN.

Buji-zen. In Zen Buddhism an unwarranted self-confidence whereby an individual believes that since he is the universal buddha-nature (*buddhatā) as a matter of fact, there is no need to engage in discipline or meditation to realize it.

Bujutsu (martial skills): see MARTIAL ARTS IN JAPAN.

Bukan (Buddhist teacher): see HAN-SHAN.

Bukhārī (compiler of Muslim ḥadīth): see AL-BUKHĀRĪ.

Bukkyo or **Buppo:** Jap. for *buddha-dharma.

Bulgakov, Sergei or **Sergius** (1871–1944). Russian philosopher and Orthodox theologian. The son of a priest, he was first destined for the Church himself, but grew disillusioned and began to participate in socialist and Marxist movements. These in turn disillusioned him after the 1905 Revolution, and he became active as a layman in Church affairs. He was ordained in 1918, but was then expelled from Russia in 1923, ostensibly for unorthodoxy, but more probably for political reasons. He eventually settled in Paris in 1925, where he was Dean of the Russian Orthodox Theological Institute of St Sergius until he died. He sought to interpret all doctrine in the light of the divine Sophia, or Wisdom: God created the cosmos out of nothing, as an emanation of his own nature; mediating between the two is the Sophia. He regarded *Mary as the most perfectly created image of the uncreated Sophia, and saw the veneration of Mary as the key to reconciliation between the Churches. Of his many works, *The Orthodox Church* (1935) and *The Wisdom of God* (1937) summarize his main ideas.

L. Zander, *God and the World* . . . (1948).

Bull (Lat. *bulla*, 'seal'). A papal document or mandate, of greater importance than a 'brief', so-called because sealed officially—though since 1878 only the most solemn ones bear such a seal. For examples, see Index, Bulls, encyclicals, etc.

Bullinger, Heinrich (1504–57). Swiss Reformer. Biblical and patristic study, the reading of *Luther's and *Melanchthon's writings, and *Zwingli's preaching, led Bullinger to support the *Reformation movement. He succeeded Zwingli as Chief Minister in Zürich, devoting his energies to educational reform, participation in the eucharistic debate amongst Protestants, and voluminous literary activities including influential correspondence with the English Reformers. He befriended several leaders among the English exiles from Queen Mary's persecution, whilst in the Elizabethan period he gave his support to the English bishops in their conflict with Thomas Cartwright's *Presbyterian concepts. He also wrote a literary defence of Elizabeth against the papal *bull which excommunicated her in 1570.

Eng. trs. T. Harding; G. W. Bromiley.

Bultmann, Rudolf (1884–1976). Christian interpreter of the New Testament and its environment, associated especially with the programme of *demythologization. After study at Marburg, Tübingen, and Berlin, and teaching at Breslau and Giessen, he became Professor at Marburg. He pioneered the study of *form-criticism, developing scepticism about the possibility of recovering much, if any, historical detail about Jesus, beyond his summons to decision: 'In every moment slumbers the possibility of its being the eschatological moment: you must awaken it.' His commentary on John argued for dependence on *gnostic ideas, and in an essay on NT and mythology (circulated from 1941, but published in H. W. Bartsch, *Kerygm and Myth*, Eng. tr. 1953) he claimed that the pre-scientific world view of the Gospels and NT needed to be demythologized (decoded, so that its essential message could be extracted from the accidents of its environment); and he saw the resultant message in terms not unlike those of European (especially Heideggerian) existentialism. The implication that there is 'a message of the NT' which can be identified is itself doubtful; and since existentialism is as much a creation of its times as any other world-view, Bultmann's programme is better termed 'remythologization'. Since Bultmann, like many of his sceptical successors, held few serious conversations with historians, the lack of rigorous historiography underlying his work is obvious. For further reading, see DEMYTHOLOGIZATION.

Bundahisn. 'Creation' in *Zoroastrianism, and a text with this title which assumed its final form 9th/10th cents. CE in the Pahlavi language. However, it is clearly a (priestly) schematization of ancient (much pre-Zoroastrian) lore. It exists in two recensions deriving from different manuscript traditions: the shorter or Indian *Bundahisn* (tr. E. W. West in *Sacred Books of the East*, v); and the longer, Greater or Iranian *Bundahisn* (ed. and tr. B. T. Anklesaria, 1956). It is the latter which is the most important. It starts with the 'event' of creation (a Zoroastrian counterpart to Genesis); much of the central section is dedicated to priestly schematic classifications of types of creation (types of mountains, rivers, birds, animals, etc.) and concludes with an account of the end of history (*Frasokereti).

The Zoroastrian cosmology, as expounded in the *Bundahisn* and other Pahlavi works, encapsulates

Zoroastrian belief about God (*Ahura Mazda), the world, human nature, and destiny. In ancient Iranian thought the world was thought of as a round flat disc floating on a cosmic ocean within a spherical universe, encased like an egg in a shell. Originally Ahura Mazda and the evil *Angra Mainyu existed alone. Ahura, aware of evil, created the world first in 'spiritual' (*menog*), i.e. non-material, form, non-tangible and non-visible, as a means of overcoming his opponent. After 3,000 years, he created the world in visible tangible material form (*getig*). In Zoroastrian thought, therefore, the material is not opposed to the spiritual but is rather its continuation, indeed its fulfilment. The *getig* world was created perfect, as were the archetypal beast (an ox) and human (*Gayomart*). Angra Mainyu, reflecting his destructive nature and instincts, saw that which was good and attempted to defile and destroy it. He broke in through the outer shell of the world causing it to shake, introducing motion so that the sun no longer stood still at the ideal noonday position but rotated, resulting in night as well as day. He caused the stars to rotate, and the violence of his onslaught caused valleys to emerge and mountains to grow. Motion and change were introduced into the ideal stillness of the Good Creation. Further he afflicted pollution on the waters and the fire, and assaulted humanity with suffering, misery, disease, and death. The world was created as a snare in which evil was trapped so that it may ultimately be defeated (Frasokereti). So as the first creature and first man died, they emitted sperm, and from it other creatures and humans grew. From death came life and life more abundantly.

Zoroastrian ethics are founded on this understanding of cosmogony. By nature men and women are perfect, free of all suffering, and sinless. As evil is in essence destructive, it is humanity's duty to expand the Good Creation both through expanding the world (e.g. in farming), and by having children. It is a religious obligation to enjoy the Good Creation, and to refrain from despoiling or abusing it. In the Pahlavi literature, this fundamental Zoroastrian conviction is expressed in terms like *Aristotle's teaching on the 'golden mean'. Virtue is defined as the mid-point between opposing vices, sin is thought of as 'excess' and 'deficiency'. Thus marriage is a religious obligation, the mean between the vices of ascetic *celibacy and debauchery. Fasting and gluttony are both sins, virtue is the middle path between the extremes. By eradicating the principles of disharmony, violence and excess, humanity is fighting for the good in the conflict with evil. Ultimately this will result in the eradication of suffering and death at Frasokereti when the cosmic forces of good and evil pair off in the ultimate battle. The creation is, therefore, in Zoroastrianism the good creation of Ahura Mazda, and as such it is to be venerated and cared for, enjoyed and expanded.

B. T. Anklesaria, *Zand Akasih: Iranian or Greater Bundahisn* (1956); J. R. Hinnells, *Persian Mythology* (1979); R. C. Zaehner, *Teaching of the Magi* (1956) and *The Dawn and Twilight of Zoroastrianism* (1961).

Bungan. A revitalization movement among the Kenyah and Kayan peoples of Indonesian Borneo and Sarawak. In the early 1940s, Jok Apui (d. 1955), a poor villager from central Borneo, had a vision of the goddess Bungan Malan in which she encouraged him to abandon traditional taboos and auguries, and pray simply to her. The increased agricultural efficiency brought about by the removal of taboos, and the simplified ritual of Bungan, led to the rapid spread of the movement in Central Borneo in the 1950s. Bungan has been variously interpreted as an attempt to revitalize traditional religion, a reaction to the threat posed by the encroachment of Christianity into the area, and an egalitarian social movement against the ritual stratification of local society. Though declining by the 1970s, Bungan has still not died out entirely.

Bunyan, John (1628–88). *Puritan preacher and writer. Born into a poor home at Elstow, Bedfordshire, he served in the Parliamentary army for a period during the Civil War and later worked as a travelling brazier. His early experience as a Christian was influenced by Lewis Bayly's *Practice of Piety*, Arthur Dent's *Plain Man's Pathway*, and *Luther on *Galatians*, as well as the beliefs and lifestyle of the members of the Bedford Independent Church, which he joined in 1653. He became one of its preachers in 1657 ('I preached what I felt, what I smartingly did feel'), but was partially 'silenced' during the Restoration period, spending most of twelve years in prison. Calvinist in ethos, he was a prolific writer, his main works, *Grace Abounding to the Chief of Sinners* (a spiritual autobiography, 1666), *Pilgrim's Progress* (part i, 1678; part ii, 1684), and *The Holy War* (1682) have become spiritual classics, leaving many phrases embedded in the English language and memory—'To be a pilgrim'; 'Doubting Castle and Giant Despair'; 'So he passed over, and all the trumpets sounded for him on the other side.' His literary style was shaped by his extensive knowledge of the English Bible and *Foxe's *Book of Martyrs*.

R. L. Greaves, *John Bunyan*, (1969); *John Bunyan, A Reference Guide* (1982).

Buppō (Jap., 'Buddhist instruction'). Buddhist teaching, i.e. Buddhism. Hence buppō-sha, one who studies and practises Buddhism, a Buddhist.

Buraku, or **burakumin.** Category of people in Japan outside the social orders. They were involved in contaminating work (especially involving dead bodies), who thereby transmitted impurity. They were known as *eta* ('great filth') and later (during the Tokugawa period, 1600–1868) as *hinin* ('non-persons'). In 1871, the Meiji government classified them as belonging to the lowest orders of recognized society, but discrimination persists to the present (cf.

the Indian attempts to ameliorate the condition of *outcastes).

G. De Vos and Hiroshi Wagatsuma, *Japan's Invisible Race* . . . (1966).

Burāq. The winged beast which the Prophet *Muḥammad is said to have ridden during the miraculous Night Journey and the Ascension (*mi'rāj). The name burāq is connected with the Arab. root *baraqa* ('to lighten', 'to flash') and suggests that the beast received its name 'the lightning flash' on account of its fantastic speed and fleetness of movement.

Burdah (Arab.). 1. A mantle, but especially one of the Prophet *Muḥammad's mantles, given away as a gift. One of these was given to the poet Ka'b ibn Zuhayr, who had been driven out for denouncing Islam in a poem, but who composed a eulogy to the Prophet as a way of asking pardon: 'I stand on a spot, where, if an elephant stood, the sides of his neck would be shaking in terror—if there is no forgiveness from the Messenger of *Allāh.' Ka'b's mantle is said to have been destroyed in the sack of Baghdad by the Mughals in 1258 CE (AH 656). However, the *Ottomans claimed to possess a cloak of the Prophet, perhaps this one, and this *khirqa-i-sharif* formed part of their claim to be authentic caliphs (*khalīfa).

2. The name of a famous, often-recited, poem, al-Burdah, praising the Prophet, by al-Buṣīrī (1213–96 CE (AH 610–95)), a *Sūfī who was suffering from paralysis. He dreamt that the Prophet placed his mantle on him, and when he woke, he was cured. It is a widespread custom to recite this poem on the anniversary (*mawlid*) of the Prophet's birth. He is (v. 56), 'like a flower in gentleness, like the full moon in splendour, like the ocean in fulness, and like all of Time brought to a single point'. Eng. tr. in A. Jeffrey, *Reader on Islam* (1962).

Burials: see FUNERAL RITES.

Burning bush. The plant from which occurred God's revelation to *Moses in Exodus 3. 1–4. 17. The bush is described as 'burning, yet it was not consumed'. Several plants, such as the wild jujube, acacia, or the bramble, have been identified as the bush. A bush growing in St Catherine's monastery on the (traditional) site on Mount Sinai is identified by the monks as derived from the original burning bush. During the Middle Ages, the burning bush became a Christian symbol for *Mary, as e.g. in Chaucer, Prologue to the Prioress' Tale.

Burning of books. A recurrent political and religious activity, indicating the power of words and ideas to call in question the validity and authority of existing systems. Familiar examples are 'the burning of the books' under Ch'in Shih Huang Ti (Qin Shihuangdi) (213 BCE), Ch'eng Yi (*Ch'eng Hao), the burning of the library of *Alexandria, the burning of the works of *Maimonides, the burning of books under the Nazis, of which J. Goebbels proclaimed (1933): 'The past is lying in flames, but the future will rise from the flames within our hearts.' The loss of particular works is irreparable, but the truth, in contrast to empty rhetoric, was better expressed by *Akiva, when he and the *Torah were burned together, 'The paper burns, but the words fly away.'

Burnt offerings: see SACRIFICE.

Bushidō or **Warrior Code** (Jap., 'Way of the Warrior'). The code of honour, valour, and duty governing the behaviour of the *samurai (warrior class) in Japan. The origins of bushidō are as obscure as the origins of the class it governs. It appears to have arisen during the 11th and 12th cents., when the central government proved incapable of maintaining order in the provinces, and warrior bands arose to provide security and protection of property. These gradually organized themselves into large clan-like organizations and displaced the old aristocracy as the politically pre-eminent elements in Japanese society, a position they formally maintained until the end of the 19th cent. Bushidō, as a code of behavior, was not systematized until the 17th cent. when Yamaga Sokō (1622–85), a masterless samurai or rōnin, wrote a series of works that detailed the obligations and responsibilities of the samurai class.

The central virtue of bushidō is loyalty. The samurai was obliged to provide unswerving loyalty to his lord and to be prepared to die if necessary to accomplish his lord's objectives. The noblest way to die was in battle, but bushidō included more than training in martial arts. The samurai considered capture in battle to be a disgrace, and so he was trained to avoid capture by ritual disembowelment or *seppuku* (popularly called *hara-kiri). Combat itself was likewise ritualized, with an emphasis on close-in fighting that disdained the use of weapons like the musket, known in Japan from the mid-16th cent. but banned shortly thereafter. Other values in bushidō, like austerity, self-control, and contempt for possessions or personal gain, all served to reinforce the core virtue of loyalty.

During the Tokugawa (1600–1868) period, the martial qualities of the samurai were enervated to a degree as a result of the unusually long peace that prevailed, making the samurai somewhat superfluous. The code of bushidō, however, served to preserve the samurai's value to society as the paragon of antiquated yet socially useful virtues. The values of bushidō continue to be evident in modern Japanese society, even though the class that spawned those values has disappeared. See further MARTIAL ARTS.

Inazo Nitobe, *Bushidō: The Soul of Japan* (1980); W. L. King, *Zen and the Way of the Sword: Arming the Samurai Psyche* (1994); G. R. Storry, *The Way of the Samurai* (1978); S. R. Turnbull, *The Samurai: A Military History* (1977); H. P. Varley *et al.*, *The Samurai* (1970).

Busshi (Jap., 'son of the Buddha'). A disciple of the *Buddha (i.e. a 'Buddhist'). More generally, busshi embraces all living beings, since the Buddha regards them as his family and children. Thus busshi also includes all *bodhisattvas.

Bussho. Jap., for *buddhatā, the buddha-nature in *Zen Buddhism. There is only buddha-nature constituting all appearance, thus one's self cannot be differentiated from it. The aim of Zen is to cultivate awareness and realization of this truth. See Index, Buddha-nature.

Busshō-dento Kokushi. Posthumous name of *Dōgen.

Busso (Jap., 'patriarchs'). The *Buddha and the patriarchs (*soshigata), from whom *Zen Buddhism is derived. Busso may also refer to the Buddha Śākyamuni.

Bu-ston (1290–1364). Tibetan teacher, translator, and historian of Buddhism belonging to the Bkah-brgyud-pa ('ka-ju-pa') sect. Schooled from his childhood by his parents in the esoteric and exoteric teachings of Tibetan Buddhism (*Tibetan religion), he became a novice at 17, and was ordained a monk at 23. By the age of 30 he had studied under all the great teachers of his day and began to compose treatises in his own name and to translate and edit the canon. By the age of 32, he completed his *History of Buddhism in Tibet* (Eng. tr. E. Obermiller, 1931–2) to which he appended a theoretical classification of the canon based on a distinction between the direct teachings of the *Buddha or *Bkah-ḥgyur* ('Kan-jur'), and the treatises of commentary thereon or *Bstan-ḥgyur* ('Ten-jur'). This became the accepted form of classification for the Tibetan canon. In addition he and his disciples compiled detailed catalogues of existing treatises and translations updating information and making corrections where necessary. Bu-ston's works number over 200 items, and the impetus he gave to Buddhist scholarship in Tibet was considerable and especially timely in view of the imminent extinction of Buddhism in India.

D. S. Ruegg, *The Life of Bu-ston Rinpoche* (1966).

Butler, Joseph (1692–1752). Anglican *bishop and philosopher. Born in Wantage of Presbyterian parents, in 1714 he became an *Anglican. From 1718 to 1726 he was preacher at the Rolls Chapel, where his sermons won him fame. He then became a parish priest in Co. Durham, where he wrote his *Analogy of Religion* (1736). He was consecrated bishop of Bristol in 1738 and became bishop of Durham in 1750. His *Sermons at the Rolls Chapel* (1726) present a basically Aristotelian view of morality, virtue being based on a true understanding of human nature guided by conscience. His *Analogy of Religion* defended a theistic and doctrinally orthodox Christianity against the prevailing *deism, his fundamental argument being that there are no greater difficulties in revealed religion than there are in understanding nature. It had a profound influence on the development of Anglican theology, *Newman, amongst others, acknowledging his indebtedness. His own mistrust of the irrational and of appeal to the praeternatural in religion is contained in his remark, 'The pretending to extraordinary revelations and gifts of the Holy Ghost is a horrid thing, a very horrid thing.'

A. Duncan-Jones, *Butler's Moral Philosophy* (1952); T. Penelhum, *Butler* (1985).

Butler, Josephine Elizabeth (1828–1907). Christian social reformer. She was initially committed to the improvement of educational opportunities and facilities for women, but she became equally concerned with the desperate plight of women made destitute in various ways. She particularly contested the consequences of sexual hypocrisy and the sexual exploitation of women by men. She led specific campaigns, one of which led to the repeal of the Contagious Diseases Act, another to the raising of the age of consent to 16. She is recognized in the *Anglican calendar of Lesser Commemorations on 30 Dec., as 'Social Reformer, Wife, and Mother'.

Butsu, or **Butsuda.** Jap. for *Buddha.

Butsudan. Japanese shrine or altar in Buddhist temples (or, in smaller versions, in homes).

Butsuden (Jap., 'Buddha-hall'). The building in which the images of *buddhas and *bodhisattvas are placed.

Butsudō (Jap., 'buddha-way'). The teaching of the Buddha (cf. BUKKYO, BUPPO), but with emphasis on the practical aspects of the path to enlightenment. In *Zen, it may refer to the attainment of that enlightenment.

Butsumyō-e (Jap., 'a buddha's name'). The former annual ceremony in Japan of reciting the names of buddhas in the past, present, and future to expiate sins. It was introduced by *Kūkai, and was held in the imperial palace, but ceased in the 14th cent. Initially about 13,000 names were recited, but the number was later reduced to 3,000.

Butterfly dreaming: see CHUANG-TZU.

Butto Kokushi (Zen master): see JAKUHITSU GENKŌ.

Bwiti. A range of *syncretist movements among the Fang and other tribes in Gabon and neighbouring territories. It began in the late 19th cent. as a creative synthesis of elements from traditional and Christian sources. Since the 1940s, the latter have been increasingly used to create a new mythology and ritual in which human life is shown as broken and then restored by *Jesus as a saviour. This process is related to traditional Fang concerns to establish good relations with the ancestors, secure fertility, and deal with witchcraft. Worship is focused on the Saturday all-night rites in which ceremonial dancing to traditional forms (but with new songs) portrays the life and death of Christ, and fatigue is suppressed by consumption of the root bark *iboga*; this is non-narcotic, but when used in large doses, in the initiation of members, produces visions of meeting the *ancestors or heavenly beings and experiencing the death and resurrection of Christ. Worship leads to 'one-hearted' solidarity and is followed by a communal meal. The religion is highly decentralized, with diffused male leadership and considerable variety among its many sections. Its impressive reformers and theological thinkers show a capacity for progressive development of Bwiti to meet new needs and move in a more Christian direction.

Byakuren-sha. Jap., for *Pai-lien-tsung, the White Lotus School.

Byams pa (earthly buddha): see MAITREYA.

Byōdō (Jap., 'sameness'). The undifferentiated nature of all manifest appearance, in *Zen Buddhism, since it arises from *śūnyatā and is the same buddha-nature (*buddhatā). Byōdō-kan is the experience of all things in this way.

Byrd, William (1543–1623). Composer especially of liturgical music, who remained a Roman Catholic although writing often for the Church of England. He was born perhaps at Lincoln, where he was appointed organist in 1563. He later became fellow-organist with *Tallis at the Chapel Royal. He was known as 'the Nightingale's own brother'.

O. Neighbour, *The Consort and Keyboard Music* . . . (1978); J. Kerman, *The Masses and Motets* . . . (1981).

Byzantine. That which pertains to the Church and the *patriarchate of *Constantinople; though the term in practice is often used to refer to the whole Eastern *Orthodox Church.

C

Cabasilas (Greek Orthodox theologian): see CAVASILAS.

Cabbala(h) (teachings of the Jewish mystics): see KABBALAH.

Cab-horse, standard of: see BOOTH, W.

Cabrini, Frances-Xavier, St (1850–1917). Founder of the Missionary Sisters of the Sacred Heart, and first saint of the USA. She was born in Italy and had hoped to become a missionary in China, but she was rejected on grounds of health. In 1880, therefore, she founded her own missionary society, taking as her controlling text Philippians 4. 13, 'I can do all things in the One who strengthens me.' Sent to New York by Pope Leo XIII, she began work among Italian immigrants in 1889, producing a network of support in practical form. She was known as Mother Cabrini, and she became the *patron saint of immigrants and displaced persons. She was canonized in 1946. Feast day, 13 Nov.

Cain. Eldest son of *Adam and *Eve and brother of *Abel. His sacrificial offering was unacceptable to God, in contrast to his brother's; in revenge he killed Abel and was condemned to wander the earth as a social pariah (see Genesis 4. 1–16). In the *aggadah, the story is expanded, and the 'mark of cain' (v. 15) was said to be a pair of horns which made other creatures fear him (*Gen.R.* 22. 12) and caused him eventually to be shot as an 'animal with horns' by his blind grandson Lamech.

Cairo (Arab., al-Qāhira, 'the victorious', but also from al-Qāhir, Mars, the city of Mars). Capital city of the *Fāṭimids, established by al-Muʿizz in 969 (AH 358). The city was founded according to careful astrological calculations, somewhat disrupted when a raven alighted on the initiating signal bell just as the planet Mars was appearing on the horizon—or so legend has it. In fact it was originally called al-Manṣūriyya until al-Muʿizz entered it, and only then was it called 'the victorious city of al-Muʿizz'. Under the Mamluke dynasty (1250–1517 (AH 648–922)), many of the great *mosques were built, including *al-Azhar; the pre-eminence of al-Azhar led to the recognition of Cairo as one of the cultural and religious centres of the Muslim world.

Cairo Genizah (Heb., 'storing'). A storeroom attached to the Ezra *synagogue in Cairo which contained valuable Hebrew historical documents. It was rediscovered and explored by Solomon *Schechter in 1896. Its chief treasures included the Heb. original of the book of *Ben Sira, fragments of Aquila's Gk. translation of the *Bible, the **Covenant of Damascus*, collections of *piyyutim, and documents on the history of *Karaism and the early medieval Egyptian Jewish community. Many of the fragments are held in Cambridge University Library, but only recently has research on the Cairo Genizah fragments been co-ordinated.

S. Shaked, *A Tentative Bibliography of Genizah Documents* (1964).

Caitanya (Skt.). 1. In Hinduism, the spiritually awakened consciousness; hence among followers of *Ramakrishna it is the title of the initiated *bhakticaitanya.

2. A devotee of *Kṛṣṇa, and source of the Caitanya or Gauḍīya Sampradaya (movement), who lived *c.*1485–1533, and was a major influence on the development of devotion to Kṛṣṇa (Kṛṣṇa-bhakti). He was born as Viśvambhara Misra, in Bengal, and was originally a scholar, but a powerful experience of religious love led him to renounce *brahmanical learning. In 1510, he was initiated as an *ascetic and took the name Śrī Kṛṣṇa Caitanya. He rapidly became renowned for his ecstatic devotion, expressed in dance and song, and was believed to be an *avatāra of the joint figure of Kṛṣṇa and *Rādhā, so that he was later depicted in cult images as (like Rādhā) fair, and not (like Kṛṣṇa) dark. His ecstatic, even wild, forms of devotion were later thought (by his disciple, Rūpa Gosvāmī) to be a participation in the divine *līlā, or play, the source of creativity itself. The so-called 'Six Gosvāmīs' were disciples who gave some order and structure to the inspiration which Caitanya left, and which continue to the present, not least in the Hare Krishna (see INTERNATIONAL SOCIETY . . .) movement.

Eng. tr. of Kṛṣṇadāsa Kavirāja's *Life*, A. C. Bhaktidevanta (1974–5); S. K. De, *Early History of the Vaiṣṇava Faith . . . in Bengal* (1961); W. Eidlitz, *Kṛṣṇa-Caitanya: Sein Leben und seine Lehre* (1968); O. B. L. Kapoor, *The Philosophy and Religion of Sri Caitanya* (1976); M. T. Kennedy, *The Chaitanya Movement* (1925); A. K. Majumdar, *Caitanya . . .* (1969).

Caitya (Skt., 'a shrine', also **cetiya**). 1. In Indian religions, a shrine or monument, a place of worship, a burial mound.

2. In Buddhism, any object of veneration such as a burial mound, a sacred tree, a robe, etc., but more specifically a particular kind of Buddhist temple.

Mainly found carved out of rock cliffs in the area surrounding Bombay (i.e., the Western Ghats), these caitya halls are among the earliest places constructed for Buddhist worship. Constructed as an imitation of free-standing, barrel-vaulted buildings, the caitya hall consists of a narrow nave illuminated solely by the rock entrance, at the end of which is a small *stūpa. An ambulatory generally follows the walls of the nave, with an apse at the furthest end. Very often, as at *Ajaṇṭā, the caitya hall is associated with a rock-carved monastery (*vihāra). A peculiarity of Ajaṇṭā (6th cent. CE) is the incorporation of a Buddha image into the stūpa. Most caitya halls are richly carved.

Caityagiri (Buddhist centre in India): see SĀÑCHĪ.

Caityavandana (interior devotion in Jainism): see PŪJĀ.

Cajetan, Tommaso De Vio (1464–1534). *Dominican scholar and exponent of *Aquinas. He entered the Dominican order in 1484 against his parents' wishes, and became a prolific author, with more than 100 works attributed to him. The best-known, *De Ente et Essentia*, attacked *Averroism. He strongly defended the monarchical authority of the *pope at the (Ps.-)Council of Pisa, and was accordingly made cardinal in 1517. In 1518, he held three disputations with *Luther, but failed to convince him. He paid careful attention to language, and argued for the importance of *analogy in *metaphysics. The two main types of analogy are those of attribution and proportionality. Some forms of the latter involve metaphor (the laughing sea), but others involve the application of terms to both analogates without metaphor, but with proportionality, as in the form 2 is to 4 as 4 is to 8. Thus to say that 'God is love' means that the love which exists in creatures pre-exists in God, but proportionally. His commentary on the *Summa Theologica* of Aquinas led to a revival of Thomism.

J. F. Groner, *Kardinal Cajetan* (1951).

Cakra (Skt., 'wheel'). A centre of psychic energy in the body conceived as a *lotus, especially in *Tantrism. Six main cakras connected by the *suṣumnā* *nāḍī (in Buddhism called *avadhūtī*) came to be recognized in Hinduism, the *mūlādhāra* ('root support') at the base of the spine, the *svādhiṣṭhāna* ('own place') in the genital region, the *maṇipūra* ('jewel city') at the navel, the *anāhata* ('unstruck') at the heart, the *viśuddha* ('pure') at the throat, and the *ājña* ('command') between the eyebrows. Just above here are two minor cakras: the *manas and *soma*. Above the top of the head is the thousand-petalled lotus (*sahasrāra padma*; or *ūṣṇīṣa kamala* for Buddhists), the abode of bliss which is not classified as an ordinary cakra. Each cakra has a certain number of petals, and is associated with a particular colour, shape, *tattva, and *bīja *mantra. For example, the *maṇipūra* at the navel has ten petals, is red, and contains a triangle, *Rudra is the presiding deity, *rūpa tattva dissolves in it, and its bīja is *raṃ*. Thus the cosmos and all beings therein are contained in the totality of the cakras: 'all beings that exist in the seven worlds are to be found in the body', says the *Śiva Saṃhita* (2. 4). Tantric Buddhism (*Vajrayāna) only accepts four cakras, the *maṇipūra, anāhata, viśuddha*, and *uṣṇiṣa kamala*.

The texts are ambiguous as to whether the cakras are situated along the spinal column or at the nervous plexuses of the physical body. Indeed, there are discrepancies in the texts concerning the number and descriptions of the cakras, and it is unclear whether they are meant to be actually existent or whether they are heuristic devices of Tantric *yoga used in *visualization; see also MAṆḌALA.

For its meaning in non-Tantric Buddhism, see DHAMMA-CAKRA.

Cakra pūjā (Skt.). 'Circle-worship', *Tantric worship by an equal number of male and female disciples of the same line of *gurus (guru *paramparā), who form a closed circle. The pūjā involves the *pañca-makāra, namely the ritual use of cooked meat and fish, parched grain, alchohol, and sexual intercourse (*maithuna). The female adept becomes the embodiment of *Śakti who grants the fulfilment of all the male adept's desires. Only those who have undergone the necessary initiation may partake in this ritual, and there must be no drunkenness or behaviour regarded as improper.

Cakravartin (Skt., 'wheel-turner'). A 'universal ruler'. In Hinduism, it refers to a ruler, in the ordinary sense, in this world, but an ideal ruler, one who creates a union between heaven and earth. In Buddhism (and in Jainism), it is extended to ethical sovereignty (e.g. in the *Edicts of Aśoka); and it became an epithet for a *buddha whose teaching is universally true throughout the cosmos. He is known by thirty-two marks (*dvātriṃśadvara-lakṣana).

Calcutta. Kālīghāt, the place in India where the major temple to *Kālī was built in the 16th cent. CE. The existing chief temple dates from 1809. A scattering of villages became a trading centre for the British, being transformed into a vast city and, for a time, the capital of India.

Calderón, P. (Christian dramatist): see THEATRE AND DRAMA.

Calendar

Judaism The Jewish calendar is fixed according to the number of years since the creation of the world (traditionally 3761 BCE. For the complexity of the different calculations, see E. Frank, *Talmudic and Rabbinical Chronology* (1956)). Thus the year 5000 began on 1 Sept. 1239 CE. When using the secular calendar, Jews use the terms BCE (before common era) and CE (common era) rather than BC and AD. The year follows a 354 day year of twelve lunar months. To harmonize this with the solar year of 365¼ days, an extra month, Adar II, is added into seven of every nineteen years. The months received Babylonian names during the *Exile: Tishri (Sept./Oct.), Heshvan (Oct./Nov.), Kislev (Nov./Dec.), Tevet (Dec./Jan.), Shevat (Jan./Feb.), Adar (Feb./Mar.), Adar II (see above), Nisan (Mar./Apr.), Iyyar (Apr./May), Sivan (May/June), Tammuz (June/July), Av (July/Aug.), Elul (Aug./Sept.). The year begins with 1 Tishri, Rosh ha-Shanah. With reference to its own past, Judaism also alludes to the periods of the Temples: the first Temple, completed by *Solomon but destroyed by the Babylonians at the beginning of the Exile (586–538 BCE), and the second Temple, from the restoration, especially associated with *Ezra and *Nehemiah, to the fall of Jerusalem at the end of the first Jewish revolt against Rome (66–70 CE)—although the levelling of the Temple site (ploughed up and sowed with salt) did not take place until the end of the second revolt, 132–5. Until the 16th cent., Jews in Oriental countries reckoned dates from the Seleucid era, which began in the autumn of 312 BCE.

A day begins and ends at sunset ('There was evening and there was morning, one day': Genesis 1. 5). Because there is some doubt as to which day will be the first of the month (*rōsh ḥōdesh*) all *festivals except Yom Kippur (*Day of Atonement) are celebrated for two consecutive days in the *diaspora by the *Orthodox. *Rosh ha-Shanah (the new year) is kept on 1 Tishri. It is followed by the days of repentance and Yom Kippur on 10 Tishri. The season of *Sukkot (tabernacles) begins on 15 Tishri and concludes with Shemini Azeret (the Closing Festival) and *Simḥat Torah (the rejoicing in the *law) on 22/23 Tishri. *Ḥanukkah (Lights) begins on 25 Kislev and ends on 2 Tevet. 10 Tevet is a fast day and 15 Shevat is the new year for trees. *Purim (Lots, the Feast of Esther) is celebrated on 14 Adar. It is preceded by the Fast of Esther (13 Adar) and succeeded by Shushan Purim (15 Adar). Pesaḥ (*Passover) begins on 15 Nisan and ends on 21/22 Nisan. 27 Nisan is Yom ha-Sho'ah (Day of the *Holocaust) and 5 Iyyar is Israel Independence Day. Lag ba-Omer (the thirty-third day of the counting of the *omer) is celebrated on 18 Iyyar and *Shavu'ot (Pentecost) takes place on 6/7 Sivan. There are fast days on 17 Tammuz and 9 Av, and 15 Av is a minor holiday.

Christianity In the Julian calendar, devised in 46 BCE, the length of the solar year was taken to be 365¼ days. It was thus slightly too long, and the seasons apparently advanced, so that by 325 CE, when the computation of Easter (for the varying dates, see EASTER) was fixed, the vernal equinox fell on 21 instead of 25 Mar. The calendar was reformed by Pope Gregory XIII in 1582 when it was realized that the Christian calendar was ten days in advance of the solar year. Pope Gregory XIII ordered that ten days in that year should be left out of October, and that henceforth each year divisible by 4 should have 366 days (to prevent a reoccurrence of the accumulated error)—hence the present leap years. Centenary years whose first two numbers are divisible by 4 are leap years, others are not: so that 2000 will be a leap year. The reformed calendar is known as the Gregorian (or New) Style, the unreformed as the Julian (or Old) Style. The Gregorian Style was accepted in Europe (except for Russia, Sweden, and England). England made the change in 1752; Russia changed in 1918, but adheres to the Old Style for ecclesiastical purposes, as do the patriarchates of Jerusalem and Serbia, as well as some Oriental Orthodox churches. There is also a *schismatic body of 'Old Calendarists' in Greece. The difference between the two calendars is now thirteen days, so that some Orthodox observe Christmas, 25 Dec. (Old Style), on 7 Jan. The Christian calendar follows each year the preparation for the coming of *Christ, his life, death, and *resurrection, and the being of God (see FESTIVALS AND FASTS). Thus, it begins with *Advent, which has four Sundays, and then either one or two Sundays after Christmas bridge the gap to the *Epiphany (6 Jan.). Thereafter 'Sundays after Epiphany' are reckoned until what used to be known as *Septuagisma, *Sexagesima, and *Quinquagesima (Sundays before Lent); Ash Wednesday introduces the forty days of *Lent, with its six Sundays; and five Sundays after Easter lead up to *Ascension day with its following Sunday and *Pentecost (Whitsunday). The remaining Sundays until Advent are numbered 'after Trinity' or 'after Pentecost'. The Sundays of the Orthodox year fall into three segments: *triodion* (the ten weeks before Easter), *pentecostarion* (the paschal season), and *octoechos* (the rest of the year). See also FESTIVALS AND FASTS.

The system of dating years AD (Lat., *Anno Domini*, 'in the year of the Lord') goes back to Dionysius Exiguus ('the Small'; *c.*500–50). In the *Easter tables drawn up by him years were numbered starting from the birth of Jesus which he placed (at least three years too late) in the year 753 of the city of Rome. The 'Christian Era' thus began with the *Annunciation on 25 Mar., AD 1. (The Gregorian calendar restored 1 Jan. as New Year's Day). The system was accepted at the Synod of Whitby in 664; it spread to Europe generally by the 11th cent. and to the Greek world in the 15th cent. Years BC (Before Christ) are counted backwards from 1 AD, there being no year 0. The abbreviations CE (Common Era) and BCE to replace AD and BC began with Jewish historians in the 19th cent., in order to avoid a religious confession within the words abbreviated.

Islam The Muslim calendar is lunar, with twelve months of twenty-nine or thirty days. Because this is not adjusted to the solar calendar (contrast the Jewish system), the religious festivals and holidays advance around the seasons: thus the month of fasting, *Ramaḍān, moves around the entire solar year, occurring sometimes in summer and sometimes in winter (intercalation is forbidden in the *Qur'ān 9. 37). Originally, the month could only begin when or if the new moon had been sighted, but for practical reasons this was soon formalized to a calendrical calculation. The months are: Muḥarram; Ṣafr, Rabīʿ al-Awwal, Rabīʿ al-Thāni, Jumādā al-Ūlā, Jumādā al-Thāniyya, Rajab, Shaʿbān, Ramadhān, Shawwal, Dhū al-Qaʿdah, Dhū al-Ḥijjah. The years are numbered from the *Hijra, the move of the Prophet *Muḥammad from *Mecca to *Madīna in 622 CE. 1 Muḥarram of that year was 16 July 622, which begins the first year of the Muslim era. The years are referred to as AH, i.e. 'after the Hijra'. The Hijri years are necessarily out of synchronicity with Christian calendar years (because there is no adjustment to the solar year), and in practice the Western Gregorian calendar is often followed: it is called *masihi* (of the messiah). For correspondences, see G. S. P. Freeman-Grenville, *The Muslim and Christian Calendars* (1963).

Hinduism The Hindu religious calendar is lunar, with the months divided into a bright (*śulapakṣa*) and a dark (*kṛṣṇapakṣa*) half, with fifteen *tithis* (days) in each. The correlation of human activity with the whole cosmic process (made evident in the movement of heavenly bodies) is of paramount importance. Consequently, the *tithis* are themselves divided into thirty *muhurtas*, of about 45 minutes each. The calculation of the auspicious time for important events then becomes a matter of subtle and complex calculation for which specialists are required. Overarching all is the necessity for securing the new moon, for which sacrifices of great importance are required. The religious calendar is then a proliferation of special observances, for some of which see FESTIVALS AND FASTS. There are six seasons (*ṛtu*): (i) Vasanta (spring); (ii) Grīṣma (hot season); (iii) Varṣa (rainy season); (iv) Śarad (autumn); (v) Hemanta (winter); (vi) Śiśira (cold). To each of these is allocated two months (Caitra, Vaiśākha; Jyaiṣtha, Aṣāḍha; Śrāvana, Bhādarapada; Aśvinā, Āśvayuja; Mārgaśīrṣa, Pauṣa; Māgha, Phālguna. Every two or three years a thirteenth month was added to adjust the lunar year to the solar year.

Buddhism The spread of Buddhism did not take with it a calendar which it then imposed on other countries; rather, it adapted to local calendars, and worked its own *festivals into the local scene. Buddhist calendars thus vary from culture to culture. Equally, no one theory of cosmic time or of the duration of its divisions is accepted by all schools of Buddhism, and speculation on such matters was discouraged by the *Buddha as not directly relevant to the quest for liberation. Such speculation as did occur was based upon Hindu notions of endlessly recurring cycles of time, and it is from this procession of *saṃsāra that the Buddhist seeks release. Thus time in itself has no eschatological significance and there is no doctrine of an apocalypse.

In Buddhism the most common theory of cosmic time takes the Great Aeon (*mahākalpa*) as the largest standard unit of measurement. This extends over a complete cycle of cosmic decline and renewal, and is said to last as long as it would take to erode a great mountain by brushing against it with a piece of silken cloth once every hundred years. The Great Aeon is divided into four 'Immeasurable Aeons' (*asaṅkhyeyakalpa*) which are each in turn subdivided into twenty 'Intermediate Aeons' (*antarakalpa*).

The first Immeasurable Aeon is characterized by decline and destruction, the second by chaos or emptiness, the third by renovation and renewal, and the fourth by comparative stability involving regular smaller cycles or ages (*yuga) of growth and decay. We are now in the first Intermediate Aeon of the fourth Immeasurable Aeon; the remaining nineteen will each undergo a phase of increase and decrease through four ages (yuga). There will be increase through the Iron, Bronze, Silver, and Golden Ages followed by decrease in the reverse order. The twentieth and final Intermediate Aeon will be of increase only, after which a new Great Aeon will commence with an Immeasurable Aeon of destruction.

Sikhism The Sikhs' religious calendar is a modified form of the Bikramī calendar. The year is solar (23 minutes 44 seconds shorter than the Christian year) and the months are lunar. Lunar month dates, varying within fifteen days, are used for *gurpurbs. So in 1984 Gurū *Gobind Siṅgh's birthday fell on both 10 Jan. and 29 Dec. Solar months, based on the twelve zodiac signs, are also used, e.g. for *saṅgrānds, *Baisākhī, and Lohṛī. The anniversaries of the battle of Chamkaur, martyrdom of the younger *sāhibzāde, and battle of *Muktsar are solar dates. Because of the discrepancy between the Bikramī and Christian solar year these dates advance one day in sixty-seven years.

Chinese The Chinese have traditionally followed both a solar and a lunar calendar. These run concurrently and coincide every nineteen years. The solar calendar divides the year into twenty-four periods, named (mainly) according to the weather expected in that period in the N. China plain. The only festival fixed by the solar calendar is at the beginning of the fifth period, *Ch'ing Ming. The lunar calendar is used to record public and private events. Twenty-two times in every sixty-year cycle, an extra month is added, according to complex and strict rules. The New Year begins with the second new moon after the winter solstice, between 21 Jan. and 20 Feb. The months have no names and are known by numbers; but they are associated with the five elements of the cosmos, wood, fire, earth, metal, and water; and also with animals; hence each year is known as 'the year of'. Thus 1996 is the year of the rat; 1997 of the ox; 1998 the tiger; 1999 the hare; 2000 the dragon; 2001 the snake; 2002 the horse; 2003 the sheep; 2004 the monkey; 2005 the chicken; 2006 the dog; 2007 the pig; 2008 the rat; 2009 the ox; 2010 the tiger. The traditional starting-point for chronological reckoning is the year in which the minister of the emperor, Huang-ti, worked out the sixty-year cycle, i.e. 2637 BCE.

Zoroastrian See FESTIVALS AND FASTS.

Caliph (successor, representative): see KHALĪFA.

Calligraphy. The skill and art of writing is admired in all religions and advanced to a great height in some. In Judaism, the work of a *scribe was related to the proper transmission of judgements in courts of law, but it became isolated as a work of protecting the true transmission, not only of *Torah, but of the whole of what eventually became scripture. The scribe thus became a religious 'expert', associated in the New Testament with the *Pharisees. In Christianity, the same work of carefully transmitting sacred texts led to the illumination of manuscripts—mainly of scripture, but also works of prayer and contemplation, e.g. books of Hours. In Islam, the importance of calligraphy reflected the prominence of the absolute and uncorrupted nature of the Word of God expressed through the *Qur'ān. Not only in text, but also on buildings, the elaboration of the visible word became a major form of art (and worship), with many different styles developing. All this was reinforced by a ban on any representation of the human figure (see ART, MUSLIM). No less important was calligraphy in China, but here the motivation was entirely different. In China, the quest for strict representation in art has been virtually non-existent for the whole of its history: Chinese art is an expression of underlying philosophies in which word and painting are necessarily at one. Poetry in China is called 'the host', and painting 'the guest': they require each other. And since one of the major religious philosophies, Taoism, invites the artist to penetrate to the underlying truth of things, calligraphy (in that context) developed an immediate economy of touch and style, so as not to hinder, either the artist or the one who looks at his work. This was taken to a consummate level in *Zen calligraphy (see BOKUSEKI) where the very act of putting brush to paper is to participate in the single buddha-nature of all things: calligraphy eliminates the gap between subject and object if it is undertaken in the appropriate way and without hesitation: you become what you paint, because you were not other than that in the first place.

Chiang Yee, *Chinese Calligraphy* (1973). J. Fontein and M. L. Hickman, *Zen Painting and Calligraphy* (1970); M. Lings, *The Qur'ānic Art of Calligraphy* . . . (1976); Nakata Yujiro, *The Art of Japanese Calligraphy* (1973); Y. H. Safadi, *Islamic Calligraphy* (1978).

Call to prayer (Muslim): see ĀDHĀN.

Calvary, Mount (Lat., *calvaria*, 'skull', translating Heb., *Golgotha*). The place of *Jesus' crucifixion, outside the walls of *Jerusalem (John 19. 20) and near the tomb. The traditional site is within the church of the Holy Sepulchre. This is inside the modern city but was probably outside the walls standing in the 1st cent. A less likely site, 'Gordon's Calvary', advocated by General C. G. Gordon, is a cliff outside the N. wall of the city with weather-marks like a face; nearby is the 'Garden Tomb' which would then be Jesus's burial place.

Calvin, John (1509–64). Christian *reformer and theologian. He was born in Noyon, Picardy, and studied at Paris, Orleans, and Bourges, being taught in the methods of medieval *scholasticism and various forms of humanist learning. Under *Protestant influence in Paris, he experienced a decisive change in religious outlook: 'God by a sudden conversion subdued my heart to teachableness.' He devoted the rest of his life to teaching, writing, preaching, and pastoring. Under the threat of persecution, he was forced to leave Paris and spent about three unsettled years travelling between Europe's main cities. During this period he wrote his *Psychopannychia* (1534) and the 1st edn. (1536) of his finest work, the *Institutes of the Christian Religion*. Passing through *Geneva, a city which had already committed itself to reform, Calvin was persuaded to settle there by the reforming preacher, Guillaume Farel. Calvin was soon appointed a preacher and pastor, but the measures he and others proposed for church reform were such that Calvin and Farel were forced to flee. In exile in Strasbourg, Calvin ministered to a French refugee congregation and developed a close friendship with Martin *Bucer, whose influence is evident in the next edn. of the *Institutes*, translated into French in 1541, which had a decisive impact not only on theology in France but also on the development of the French language well into the 17th cent. In Feb. 1541 Calvin was invited to return to Geneva where he remained until he died. Images of Calvin as the 'dictator of Geneva' have been largely discredited by modern scholarship. Calvin never held any political office and was always answerable to the City Council (who frequently opposed him). Nevertheless, his ideas had an enormous impact on the political life of the city, and contributed to the vast improvement of Geneva's educational facilities and public welfare. The reform of the Genevan church was accomplished in large part through the *Ecclesiastical Ordinances* (1541), a work which demonstrates Calvin's grasp of the importance of structure and discipline for the church's survival in hostile conditions. A diligent correspondent and a fervent preacher with an intense pastoral concern, Calvin battled with constant ill-health, frequent opposition, and loneliness. He died at the age of 55, one of the most influential figures of the Western world.

Calvin's place in human history rests largely upon his theology, adumbrated in his biblical commentaries and successive edns. of the *Institutes* (the final edn. appearing in 1559). At the heart of the Christian life lies 'union with Christ', an utterly unmerited relationship effected through the Holy Spirit. God 'accommodated himself to our capacity' by becoming a human being in Jesus Christ. In the humanity of Christ, crucified and risen, our humanity has been turned back to God. By being bound to Christ in faith we are now enabled to be reconciled to God. Calvin maintained a lifelong commitment to the Bible's importance for reforming every aspect of Christian faith and life, and the primary purpose of the Bible was to focus attention on Jesus Christ: 'The Scriptures should be read with a view to finding Christ in them.' He came to lay great stress on the importance of the *Church as our 'Mother', and held a very high view of the *sacraments of *baptism and the *Lord's Supper. The doctrine of *predestination, with which Calvin has often been associated, was never the leading principle of his thought. It was a way of buttressing his belief that our salvation from first to last is a work of God's unearned grace. However, many of his followers developed systems of theology where this doctrine does assume a pivotal place. See CALVINISM.

F. L. Battles and S. Tagg (ed.), *The Piety of John Calvin* (1978); P. Helm, *Calvin and the Calvinists* (1982); R. T. Kendall, *Calvin and English Calvinism* (1980); T. H. L. Parker, *Calvin . . .* (1995); A. P. F. Sell, *The Great Debate* (1982); F. Wendel, *Calvin . . .* (1963).

Calvinism. The religious ideas of bodies and individuals who were profoundly influenced by the 16th-cent. church reformer John *Calvin, or by his writings. In Calvinism there is typically a strong stress on the sovereignty of God over every area of life, and on the supremacy of *scripture as the sole rule of faith and practice, an authority confirmed by the inward witness of the Holy Spirit. Without denying that there is a partial unveiling of God's power in both creation and providence, Calvinism maintains that it is impossible properly to discern God's unique revelation without the 'spectacles' which scripture provides. Inherently sinful men and women, lost in the labyrinth of iniquity, can only be delivered by the Bible's message which, like Ariadne's thread, leads them out to a totally undeserved salvation. These themes were all propounded by Calvin, but it is now generally recognized that 16th-cent. Calvinist theology developed lines of thinking quite distinct from the reformer. The doctrine of *predestination in particular was never a leading axiom of Calvin's thought: the heart of his theology was union with Christ through the Spirit, by which a person found peace with God and the beginning of a transformed life. But many of Calvin's early followers (e.g. Theodore *Beza) were quick to establish the divine 'decree' (to eternal life and death) as the principle from which all other ideas were derived, and on this basis elaborated logically rigorous theological systems. This new emphasis on predestination was due in part to a need to preserve the distinctive identity of the followers of Calvin over against the *Lutheran wing of the *Reformation, and to the resurgence of interest in *Aristotelian philosophy. Calvinist theology reached powerful expression in the *Helvetic Confession (1566) and at the Synod of Dort (1618–19). The latter expounded the so-called 'five points' of Calvinism: total depravity, unconditional election, limited *atonement, irresistible *grace, and the final perseverance of the *saints. By the middle of the 17th cent., Calvinism had spread from France and Holland to England and Scotland. Firmly espoused by many *Puritans, and transplanted to New England, Calvinism was exposed to much rationalistic attack in the 18th and 19th cents. Nevertheless, in many parts of the world it still shapes much church life, and as an historical force it has greatly affected European and N. American culture in the social, political, scientific, and artistic spheres. With its strongly world-affirming character, it has shown a remarkable ability to adapt to local situations and contexts and to address a variety of issues within these contexts (points observed and applied by *Weber in his thesis on the Protestant Ethic).

A. McGrath, *John Calvin . . .* (1990).

Calvinistic Methodists. Those members of the Church in Wales who responded to the revivalistic preaching of Griffith Jones (1684–1761), Howel Harris (1714–73), and Daniel Rowland (1713–90). Harris urged continuing loyalty to the *established Church, but, under the pressure of repeated opposition, formal secession took place in 1795. Their meeting-houses were registered as Dissenting Chapels and the first ministers were ordained in 1811. Theological colleges were opened at Bala (1837) and Trevecka (1842). Now known as the Presbyterian Church of Wales, the denomination has a membership of about 80,000.

Camaldolese (etym. uncertain, perhaps from *campus Romualdi*, 'field of Romuald'). A Christian monastic order derived from the reforms of Romuald (*c.*920–1027), who did penance for his father in Ravenna, and came into contact with monastic life of various kinds. He founded a number of communities, including the hermitage of Camaldoli in the mountains near Arezzo, below which developed the monastery which became the centre of the Camaldolese Order. *The Life of the Five Brothers*, by St Bruno-Boniface, was written before Romuald died and contains the short rule of Romuald: 'Sit in your cell as in paradise. . . . Watch your thoughts as a skilled fisherman watches for fish. . . . Remember always that you are in the presence of God. . . . Abandon everything and wait, dependent on the grace of God, like the fledgling who eats only what its mother brings it.' The Congregation of Camaldoli is part of the Benedictine (see BENEDICT) confederation, although it understands itself as rooted in the *Desert Fathers and Mothers, preceding both Benedict and Romuald. In the 16th cent., the Congregation divided between the strictly eremetical and the combined form, but both remain in relationship with each other.

T. Matus, *The Monastic Life of the Camaldolese Benedictines* (1985).

Cambridge Platonists. A group of Anglican philosophical theologians who flourished between 1633 and 1688. Prominent among them were Benjamin Whichcote (1609–83), John Smith (1618–52), Henry More (1614–87), and Ralph Cudworth (1617–88). They found in Platonism and the Greek Fathers a rational philosophical structure that enabled them to distance themselves from contemporary enthusiasm, whether *Puritan or *High Church, by submitting the claims of revelation to the bar of reason by which we participate directly in God's *Logos (word, reason): 'The spirit in man is the candle of the Lord, lighted by God, and lighting man to God' (Whichcote). Influenced by Descartes, they none the less rejected his sharp distinction between thinking and extended substance, seeing in nature an immanent world soul. It is there that God can truly be discovered, not in argument or discourse: 'To seek our Divinity merely in books and writings is to seek the living among the dead: we do but in vain seek God many times in these, where his Truth too often is not so much enshrined as entombed: no; seek for God within thine own soul' (Smith).

C. A. Patrides (ed.), *The Cambridge Platonists* (1969).

Camisard revolt: see HUGUENOTS.

Campbell, Alexander (1788–1866). Founder of the 'Campbellites' or 'Disciples of Christ', and the *Churches of Christ. After his Glasgow University education, he followed his father, a Presbyterian minister, to the USA. He was ordained in 1812 and later joined the *Baptists, but his published teaching caused a disruption in their churches. In 1827 his followers separated to establish congregations known as the Disciples of Christ or Campbellites. He taught at their Bethany College, established in 1841. A voluminous writer, Campbell rejected all credal formulas, being persuaded that Christianity's only demands are personal confession of Christ in baptism.

R. Humbert (ed.), *A Compend . . .* (1961).

Campbell, Joseph (writer on myth): see MYTH.

Campion, Edmund, St (*c*.1540–81). *Jesuit *priest and *martyr. He was born in London, and at 15 went to St John's College, Oxford, where he had a brilliant career, attracting the attention of Elizabeth I and the patronage of the Earl of Leicester. He was ordained *deacon in the *Church of England in 1569, but then left for Dublin. He returned to England two years later and went on to *Douai, then to Rome, where he entered the Society of Jesus. He was ordained in Prague in 1578 and shortly afterwards left for England with Robert Parsons. He landed at Dover in June 1580. He escaped arrest for a year, though his writings, especially *Decem Rationes*, won him considerable fame. He was arrested at Lyford Grange in Berkshire, and was hanged, drawn, and quartered at Tyburn on 1 Dec. 1581. He was *canonized as one of the *Forty Martyrs of England and Wales in 1970. Feast day, 20 Oct.

Cāmuṇḍā. A form of the goddess *Durgā appearing from her forehead in her fierce aspect as the destroyer of the demons Caṇḍa and Muṇḍa.

Canaan. Land which later became Palestine, promised, according to Jewish belief, by God to the Israelites. According to Genesis 10. 19, Canaan extended 'from Sidon, in the direction of Gerar, as far as Garza, and in the direction of *Sodom, Gomorrah, Admah and Zeboiim, as far as Lasha'. Its population seems to have consisted of different groups (see Genesis 10. 15–18) and at the time of the Israelite conquests seems to have been divided into city-states. Joshua 12 specifies thirty-one kings against whom the Israelites fought. The area was a constant battleground for influence among the great powers of Egypt, Babylon, the Hittites, etc. During the first centuries of the 2nd millennium BCE, W. Semitic tribes such as the Edomites, Moabites, Arameans, Phoenicians, Ammorites, and Israelites, penetrated the area and this may reflect the events recorded as the Israelite conquest in the books of Joshua and Judges. Early Canaanite religion is revealed particularly in the *Ugaritic texts.

J. Gray, *The Legacy of Canaan* (1965).

Caṇḍī (Skt., 'vicious, fierce, violent'). 1. One of the names of the Hindu Goddess (also Caṇḍikā). It does not denote a specific goddess and tends to be used with reference to the more violent manifestations of *Devī (e.g. when killing the demon *Mahiṣa). However, the Sanskrit court-poet Bāṇa (Kanauj, 8th cent.) added pregnancy to the name in his poem *Caṇḍī-śatakam*. Since in Skt. love-poetry caṇḍī denotes the woman in a state of anger, whom the lover has to pacify by falling at her feet, the poet modelled his own submission to the Goddess on this. Appropriately he altered the myth of her killing of Mahiṣa by having the demon killed (and finding his salvation) through the contact with her foot.

2. In Bengal, an originally autonomous folk Goddess (similar to *Manasā). From *c*.14th cent. onwards, this Goddess became increasingly drawn into the mythology of the *purāṇas and thereby got fused with the Skt. Caṇḍī (see (1) above). This process is documented in the literary genre of the *Caṇḍī-maṅgal*, which traditionally narrates two independent stories. One concerns the hunter Kālaketu, who through worshipping the Goddess becomes king and gets protected against all adversaries. The second is about a merchant Dhanapati, whose younger wife is helped by Caṇḍī to remain unharmed in a series of tribulations, and about his son Śrīmanta who rescues himself and his father

from execution by praying to the Goddess. In these stories Caṇḍī displays far greater benevolence than Manasā.

3. In N. India, an alternative title of the Devīmāhātmya in the **Mārkaṇḍeya Purāṇa*.

Candīdās, Baru. Author of *Srikrsnakitana*, an early *Vaiṣṇava text. Nothing is known of the author, not even his dates, which vary from the 14th to the 16th cents. (except that 'Candīdās' suggests a devotion to *Durgā/*Caṇḍī). Even the name of the work is a recent ascription, dating from the recovery of the work in 1910. Nevertheless, the text reveals an important unfolding of the erotic themes underlying the *Krishna-*Rādha myth, taking further the **Gītagovinda* of Jayadeva. He was an important influence on *Caitanya.

M. H. Klaiman, *Singing the Glory of Lord Krishna* . . . (1984).

Candlemas. A Christian festival kept forty days after *Christmas, i.e. on 2 Feb. in most churches. It is also known as the Purification of the Virgin Mary, the Presentation of Christ in the Temple, and in the East, *Hypapantē* ('meeting', *sc.* with *Simeon), all with reference to the story in Luke 2. 22–39. A procession with candles is the distinctive rite in the West, symbolizing Christ as the light of the world, and his entry into the Temple.

Candles

Judaism Traditionally oil was considered a more appropriate fuel for liturgical lights, because candles tended to be made from ritually unclean animals. However, by the Middle Ages, possibly influenced by their use in the *Roman Catholic Church, candles were employed for *Sabbath lights, for the *Havdalah (dividing) ceremony, for searching for leaven at *Passover, for *Ḥanukkah (Lights), for the *ner tamid* (*eternal light) hanging before the *synagogue *ark, and for *Yahrzeit (commemoration of the dead). In some communities it was customary to carry a candle in front of the *Scroll of the law to symbolize the law as the light of life. Candles are also lit on the anniversary of the death of scholars, and in some places for the *Hoshana Rabba vigil during the festival of *Sukkot. See MENORAH.

Christianity In liturgical churches it is usual to have two or more candles ('altar lights') on the *altar, and they may also be carried in procession. Votive candles are also lit before statues or *icons in churches (Catholic and Orthodox respectively) as personal offerings. This sentiment is summarized in the prayer commonly found before votive candles in France: 'Seigneur, cette flamme qui monte devant toi, c'est tout le désir de mon cœur' (Lord, this flame which rises before you is all the longing of my heart). Because of a suspected devotion to saints (or to the image/idol), Protestant churches frequently banned the use of candles. In the Church of England, the Lincoln Judgement (1890) allowed two candles on the holy table, and the Lambeth Opinion (1899) prohibited the carrying of candles in procession, but neither have been widely followed.

Candrakírti (Tib., *Zla-ba-grags-pa*; Chin., *Yüeh-cheng*; Jap., *Gesshō*). A distinguished Buddhist teacher of the *Mādhyamaka school who flourished in the 7th cent. CE. Candrakīrti championed the *Prāsaṅgika form of the Mādhyamaka doctrine in his commentaries on the work of *Nāgārjuna, the founder of the school, and *Āryadeva, his disciple. According to this, the method of the Mādhyamaka is to reduce to absurdity the position of the opponent through a dialectical process which reveals the internal contradictions of his argument. The alternative interpretation of Mādhyamaka, that of the Svātantrika-Mādhyamaka sub-school led by *Bhāvaviveka, was that the Mādhyamaka should seek to establish a positive thesis of its own, and that a purely negative dialectic was inadequate. As well as disagreeing over strategy, the two schools held different philosophical positions concerning the ontological status of phenomena: see J. Hopkins, *Meditation on Emptiness* (1984).

The contribution of Candrakīrti to an understanding of the terse aphorisms of Nāgārjuna, most notably through his 'Clear Words' (*Prasannapadā*) commentary cannot be overestimated. Also of great importance is his own composition, *An Introduction to the Mādhyamaka System* (*Mādhyamaka-Āvatāra*). Candrakīrti's writings were studied extensively in Tibet where the Prāsaṅgika interpretation of Mādhyamaka was championed by the dGe-lugs-pa (*Geluk) sect founded by *Tsong Khapa. Candrakīrti is revered to this day as one of the greatest masters of the lineage from Nāgārjuna.

Canisius, Peter, St (1521–97). *Jesuit theologian and controversialist. Born in Nijmegen, he studied theology in Cologne where he was instrumental in establishing the first Jesuit house in Germany, having joined the Society in 1543. After a brief period at the Council of *Trent, in Rome, and Messina, he returned to Germany and in 1556 became the first superior of the German province. His interest in education led him to publish, in 1555, the first of three *catechisms, the second (and perhaps most influential) of which appeared in 1556. In the latter part of his life he worked on a Roman Catholic response to the Centuriators of Magdeburg, but disagreement with his Jesuit colleagues over this work led to his removal to Fribourg in Switzerland where he took charge of the setting up of a college, and where he died. In 1925 he was both canonized and, on the strength of his catechetical writings, declared a *Doctor of the Church. Feast day, 21 Dec.

J. Brodrick, *St. Peter Canisius* . . . (1935).

Canon. 1. Title of a member of the *chapter of a cathedral or *collegiate church. In the Anglican Church, 'residentiary canons' form the permanent staff of a cathedral, who are responsible for its worship and upkeep; otherwise the title of canon may be honorary or may entail duties such as preaching occasionally in the cathedral. 'Minor canons' are clerics appointed to sing the cathedral services.

2. (Gk., *Kanon*, 'rule'). The determination of books which have authority in a religion, either because they are believed to be inspired or revealed, or because they have been so designated. In both Judaism (see BIBLE) and Christianity, the decision about which books were to be included or excluded was a long process—not leading to unanimity in Christianity, where Roman Catholics, relying on the Latin translation of the Greek translation of the Hebrew, included additional books not recognized by Jews or other Christians (*Apocrypha). In Judaism the question of the canon was of practical importance: following the principle *metame et hayadayim* ('renders the hands unclean'), anyone who touches a biblical book contracts ritual uncleanness. According to the legend in 2 Esdras and *Pirqe Aboth the canon of the Hebrew Bible was closed by the *Great Synagogue starting with Ezra after the return from *exile. In fact the *Pentateuch may have been fixed this soon; the prophetic books followed by the 4th cent. BCE; uncertainty about some of the *Writings persisted among the rabbis until the 2nd cent. CE, although the synod of *Jabneh (*c.*100 CE) is usually said to have fixed the whole Hebrew Bible in its present form.

The Christian Church took over as the 'Old Testament' a larger corpus than the Hebrew Bible, based on the usage of Jews in Alexandria. As a whole, the Church from the time of *Marcion's attacks has defended the scriptural status of the Jewish canon. For attitudes to the books outside the Hebrew Bible, see APOCRYPHA.

The kernel of the New Testament canon, the four gospels and thirteen letters of Paul, had come to be accepted *c.*130 and were united with the Old Testament between 170 and 220 (cf. the collocation of Paul's letters with the 'other scriptures' in 2 Peter. 3. 16.) The controversy with Marcion probably hastened this process of determination. Doubts about some of the *Catholic epistles and *Revelation continued until later (and have never been settled in some oriental churches). On the other hand, **Barnabas* and **Hermas* were occasionally and locally admitted to the canon. The earliest witness to the present canon of the New Testament is the *Festal Letter* of *Athanasius for 367 CE; and the canon of both Testaments was probably finally fixed in Rome in 382.

The term 'canon' is then frequently applied to collections of sacred or holy texts in other religions, although they are not usually regarded as revealed by God in the same (diverse) ways as they are in Western religions—e.g. Hindu scriptures are eternal, Buddhist texts record the teaching of the *Buddha and are not divinely inspired or revealed. For Hinduism, see ŚRUTI; SMṚTI; VEDA; VEDĀNTA; and further refs. *ad loc.* For Buddhism (Pāli canon, etc.), see BUDDHIST SCRIPTURES; TRIPIṬAKA. The term 'canon' has been applied to revered and authoritative Jain texts (e.g. 'the 45 text canon'), but the term is particularly awkward in this case: see DIGAMBARA; AṄGA. For Sikhs, see ĀDI GRANTH. For the Taoist canon, see TAO-TSANG. In Japan, the **Nihongi* and **Kojiki* were given a status which made them effectively 'canonical'. See also Index, Canonical Collections.

H. Coward, *Sacred Word and Sacred Text: Scripture in World Religions* (1988).

3. The central prayer of consecration in the Roman *mass, and in all *eucharistic liturgies in different forms. It assumed its present form under *Gregory the Great (590–604). Unlike the practice in Eastern churches (see ANAPHORA), the RC Church maintained a single invariable prayer until recent times. From *c.*800 to 1967, most of it was recited silently by the celebrant. In 1967, permission was given for audible recitation and for the use of the vernacular. In 1968, three other forms of 'eucharistic prayer' were provided as alternatives to the canon; in the USA, there are nine permitted forms, including three for children's liturgies and two for the reconciliation of penitents. Applied to other liturgies, 'canon' is practically synonymous with the more usual term 'eucharistic prayer'.

4. A type of hymn sung at the E. (Byzantine) Orthodox morning *office. It consists of nine (or, in practice, eight) 'odes', each made up of from three to fourteen *irmoi* and *troparia* (stanzas). Their introduction is attributed to St Andrew of Crete (*c.*660–740). The odes originally came in between the nine *canticles, but in time they were detached from the canticles to which they correspond.

Canonization. The action by which the Christian church declares a deceased person to be a *saint. (The word can also refer broadly to a church's official approval of a doctrine, writing, etc.) In the Roman Catholic Church since *c.*13th cent. it has been reserved to the pope. According to present canon law the process begins with *beatification. The 'cause' of a deceased 'servant of God' must be argued before the Congregation of the Causes of Saints, having come to it from a *bishop attesting the person's local fame of sanctity or martyrdom. Investigation is then made of the servant's 'heroic practice of virtue' and of alleged miracles done by God through his or her intercession. In all this a Promotor Fidei (or 'Devil's Advocate') is appointed to present objections. A favourable verdict allows the pope to confer the title 'Blessed' and to permit the public veneration of the beatified person in a particular place or among a religious order. Thereafter, if further miracles are attested, the cause may be taken up again, and if it is favourably concluded, the servant of God is declared a saint and commended to be venerated in the whole Church. A special *mass and an *office are authorized. A process of 'equivalent canonization' operates for persons whose causes cannot now be rigorously argued but who have long-established cults. Canonization is regarded as irrevocable. In the Orthodox Church canonizations are usually made by synods of bishops of an *autocephalous church, but sometimes a cult comes to be accepted without formal authority.

Canon law. The body of rules or laws developing gradually, imposed by church authority in matters of its own organization and discipline (extending also to matters of belief). Its beginnings were in the practice of *councils which issued canons or pronouncements on immediate matters of discipline: thus, twenty canons were promulgated at *Nicaea (325), which gained authority throughout the Church; other councils were less authoritative. A second source of canon law was the pronouncements of influential bishops in 'canonical letters', and in the case of the popes, *decretals.

In the Catholic West, the standard text of canon law became the *Decretum* of *Gratian (*c.*1140), which organized nearly 4,000 patristic texts, consular decrees, and papal pronouncements into a legal system. This formed the first part of the larger *Corpus Iuris Canonici* (1st printed edn. 1499), which was in turn replaced by the *Code of Canon Law* (*Codex Iuris Canonici*), a comparatively small volume with 2,414 canons (1917). A revision commissioned after *Vatican II and published in 1983 further reduces the number to 1,752.

In E. churches there are various more or less authoritative collections of canons, e.g. the *Pedalion* ('rudder'; 1800) of *Nicodemus of the Holy Mountain. In the Church of England the canons presently in force (in addition to the laws of England) were published in 1969 and almost entirely repealed the only earlier collection of post-Reformation law, the 141 canons of 1604.

J. Coriden *et al.* (eds.), *The Code of Canon Law: A Text and Commentary* (1985).

Canons Regular. Roman Catholic *priests following a quasi-monastic form of common life, which first received formal approval at the Lateran Synod of 1059 and then spread quickly from Rome to most parts of W. Europe. By the middle of the 12th cent. the so-called *Rule of St *Augustine* had been generally adopted. There are today some nine congregations of Canons Regular in the RC Church, also known as Augustinian (hence Austin) Canons.

Canopy (for Jewish marriage ceremony): see HUPPAH.

Canossa (place): see GREGORY VII.

Canterbury. In Kent, SE England, chief see of the *Church of England. Its history goes back to 597 with the arrival of *Augustine in England. He had been ordered to organize the church into two provinces with *archbishops at London and York, but Canterbury displaced London from the first. The struggle for precedence with York was ended in Canterbury's favour in the middle of the 14th cent. The archbishop is styled *Primate of All England. He is, however, also head of the *Anglican Communion (of which the Church of England is a numerically small part), and some expect to see a non-English archbishop in the future.

Canticle. A song or prayer from the Bible (other than a *Psalm) used in Christian worship. Examples are the Song of *Moses and *Benedicite from the Old Testament; and the *Magnificat, *Benedictus, and *Nunc Dimittis from the New Testament. The Canticle of the Sun is a hymn of praise to God revealed in nature, composed by St *Francis, probably in 1225.

Cantillation. The musical reading of the Jewish Bible, *Talmud, or other liturgical passages. There is no scholarly agreement over the cantillation of Jewish liturgy. The biblical texts are read in accordance with the Masoretic (see MASORAH) tradition, and talmudic cantillation is also, to some extent, standardized only by custom.

Cantonists. Jewish children conscripted into the Russian army between 1827 and 1856. The children were snatched from their homes to fulfil the government quota. Taken far away from their villages, they were forcibly converted to Christianity. If they survived, at the age of 18 they were drafted into the regular army units, where they were compelled to serve for twenty-five years.

Cantor (Heb., *ḥazzan*). One trained to lead the Jewish *synagogue prayer service. Originally, the duties included the instruction of children (e.g. *Sotah* 7. 7 f.), but the later elaboration of synagogue services, with the addition of chants and *piyyutim (combined with a declining general knowledge of Hebrew) led to the development of cantors with musical skills. In Europe, cantor music was richly developed, leading at the end of the 19th cent. to 'the golden age of the *ḥazzanut*', with well-known individuals almost corresponding to operatic 'stars'.

Cao Dai (Vietnamese, 'supreme palace' or 'altar', and now the name for the supreme God). Syncretist religious and nationalist movement arising in the Mekong delta of Vietnam from spirit seances giving a new 'third revelation' through a civil servant, Ngo Van Chieu, in 1919. The first and second revelations had produced *Confucianism, *Taoism, Spirit worship, *Buddhism, and *Christianity, but Cao Dai would now unite and complete them. All their deities or founders are revered, together with an open-ended lower pantheon that includes Joan of Arc and Sun Yat Sen. God continues to speak through a divinatory device. Worship four times daily is required, and there is a Confucian and Buddhist form of ethic. In 1923, a businessman, Le Van Trung, began to develop Cao Dai as a strong organization on the *Roman Catholic model under a pope, although this later split into several sects, each with holy cities, like the main one at Tay Ninh City where there is an eclectic temple. Reaching a peak of some two million members, Cao Dai has been a political and even a military force, and has been in conflict with the various governments. Its fortunes since the end of the Vietnam War are not yet clearly known.

V. L. Oliver, *Caodai Spiritism* . . . (1976); J. Werner, *Peasant Politics and Religious Sectarianism: Peasant and Priest in the Cao Dai* (1981).

Capital punishment. This was the penalty for serious offences in the ancient world, summarized in the biblical injunction, 'Life for life' (Exodus 21. 23; cf. Genesis 9. 6). The Bible mentions stoning (e.g. Leviticus 20. 2), burning (e.g. Leviticus 20. 14), and hanging (Ezra 6. 11). According to the *Talmud, there was an obligation to give even criminals a humane death (*B.Sanh.* 45a), and execution should not involve mutilation (*B.Sanh.* 52a). The four modes of death specified are stoning, burning (only for an adulterous priest's daughter or for certain kinds of incest), slaying with a sword, and strangulation. It is not known whether Talmudic discussions reflected theory or actual practice. The Romans had removed the right of imposing capital punishment from the *Sanhedrin early in the 1st cent. CE, but previously there were executions (see *Sanh.* 6. 4). Certainly some *rabbis were against capital punishment—R. Tarfon and R. *Akiva said, 'If we had been in the Sanhedrin, no death sentence would ever have been passed' (*Mak.* 1. 10).

Christianity inherited the biblical injunctions, and lived in a world where executions were practised: hence the acceptance in Romans 13. 1–7 that such executions may be instruments of God's wrath. However, Christianity derived itself far more from the demand of *Jesus to forgive enemies and not to pursue vengeance. Christians have therefore been divided over the permissibility of capital punishment, although for most of their history Christians have supported and enacted it. Muslim attitudes are controlled by the verse in the *Qur'ān, 'Do not take the life which Allāh has made sacred except for justice' (6. 151). In practice, capital punishment is required for *murtadd (apostasy which has been followed by an attack on Islam), *zinā' (adultery), and unjust murder (see QIṢĀṢ).

Capital sins: see DEADLY SINS.

Cappadocian Fathers. Three 4th-cent. Christian theologians, *Basil of Caesarea, his brother *Gregory of Nyssa, and *Gregory of Nazianzus. They were all born in Cappadocia (now in modern Turkey). They were engaged in opposing *Arianism after the Council of *Nicaea, and were influential in its defeat at the Council of *Constantinople in 381. More than this, the Council also canonized their doctrine of the *Trinity which defended the deity of the Holy Spirit alongside the Father and Son as three persons in one substance.

Capsali, Moses ben Elijah (1420–96). Turkish *rabbi. He served as rabbi of Constantinople during the Muslim conquest of the city in 1453 and was much respected by Sultan Mehmet II. He was falsely accused of misinforming the community on family law, but was completely exonerated, and he ended a long-standing dispute by forbidding the teaching of *Talmud to the *Karaites.

Capuchins. Reformed branch of the Christian *Franciscan order. In 1525, Matteo da Bascio (1495–1552) sought to return to the greater simplicity of the early Franciscans. He wore the pointed cowl or hood (*capuce*, hence the name) of St Francis, and he and his companions devoted themselves to care of plague victims. Despite opposition and near-suppression when their third superior/general became a *Protestant, their zeal and preaching made them powerful in the *Counter-Reformation.

Cardinal. A member of the 'Sacred College' of priests selected by the pope to assist him in governing the *Roman Catholic Church. They comprise: (i) the 'cardinal bishops' of the seven titular sees around Rome; (ii) 'cardinal priests', formerly parish priests of Rome, but now bishops and archbishops of sees around the world; and (iii) 'cardinal deacons', formerly the district *deacons of Rome but now bishops holding posts in the Roman *curia. In 1994 there were 167 cardinals in all. On the death of a pope they meet in secret session to elect his successor; since 1971 those over the age of 80 may not vote.

Cardinals have the title of 'Eminence', and insignia including a red biretta and red skull cap. The cardinal's red broad-brimmed hat was abolished in 1969.

Cardinal directions. The division of space in Hindu cosmology, of great importance in sacrifice, orientation of towns and buildings, etc. With the *triloka* (see LOKA), they make up 'all this', i.e. the totality of space. According to *Śatapatha Brāhmaṇa* II. 1. 6. 20–4, the four directions, North, East, South, and West, gave birth to the three lokas. N. is the realm of human beings, often opposed to the E., which is the domain of the gods: the gods come from the E. to meet humans when they sacrifice. The S. is the domain of the *ancestors, and thus also of beings associated with death, e.g. *Maruts. The W. is the domain of animals, and especially of snakes, because they can slough their dead skins. Since it is the direction from which come food and sustenance, it is also the domain of wives and children, i.e., of fruitfulness.

B. K. Smith, *Classifying the Universe* . . . (1994).

Cardinal virtues (Lat., *cardo*, 'hinge'). Four particular virtues in Christianity, on which all others are said to depend: prudence, justice, fortitude, temperance. They are said to be derived by *Ambrose from the four virtues of the Greeks (e.g. of Plato). They were extended by the *Scholastics to seven, by adding to the four 'natural virtues' the three 'theological virtues' of faith, hope, and charity.

J. Pieper, *The Four Cardinal Virtues* (1966).

Cargo cults. The popular name for *millennial movements in Melanesia. During the last 100 years, hundreds of these have come into being from Fiji to Irian Jaya, and also in other tribal cultures. Local myths of a golden age encourage *prophets to announce the imminent return of *culture heroes or ancestors bringing spiritual or material 'cargo' of the kind discovered through Western contacts. This will inaugurate a new era of human fulfilment and equality with whites, who have proved disappointing through not sharing fully their great powers and resources. Airstrips, wharves, and storehouses may be built to receive the 'cargo'; old customs and farming are usually replaced by new rituals and moral reforms to prepare for the event. The social effects and anti-white aspects often lead to conflict with governments and churches. 'Cargoism' ranges from overt cults to implicit attitudes as to how development will come. Some movements are more religious in form, as with *Manseren cults, the *Vailala Madness, and *Jon Frum. Others also attempt realistic development, as with *Paliau and *Yali, and the Peli and Pitenamu Societies. Many movements are short-lived, and in the 1970s the cargo form seemed to be overshadowed by indigenous revival movements of a *pentecostal nature within Christian communities. Cargo cults have been the subject of much analysis and discussion in both anthropology and sociology.

G. Cochrane, *Big Men and Cargo Cults* (1970); I. C. Jarvie, *The Revolution in Anthropology* (1964); P. Lawrence, *Road Belong Cargo* (1964); E. Ogan, *Business and Cargo* (1972); F. Steinbauer, *Melanesian Cargo Cults* (1979); P. Worsley, *The Trumpet Shall Sound* (1957).

Cariyā-pitaka (part of Buddhist Pāli canon): see KHUDDAKA NIKĀYA.

Carlstadt or **Karlstadt** (*c.*1480–1541). Radical German *Reformer, Andrew Bodenstein, who took his name from his birthplace in Bavaria. He became teacher at Wittenberg, was several times Dean, and came to support *Luther's teaching. Luther's initial conservatism and Carlstadt's radical views were soon in conflict, especially during Luther's refuge in the Wartburg, when Carlstadt married, abandoned *vestments, celebrated *Communion in both kinds, disparaged infant *baptism, destroyed pictures and statues, and removed music from the *liturgy. He was compelled to leave Wittenberg (1528–9) for Switzerland where he finally taught in Basle.

Carmelites. Christian (Roman Catholic) religious order, deriving from hermits on Mount Carmel in Palestine, *c.*1200. Migrating to Europe as the failure of the Crusades began to lead to a break-up of the Latin Kingdom (*c.*1240), they were organized along lines of solitude, abstinence, and prayer. They were joined by nuns in 1452 as the Carmelite Second Order. Increasing laxity prompted the radical reforms of *Teresa of Avila, earning the name Discalced (i.e. not wearing sandals). *John of the Cross extended the reform to male houses of the order. Central in Carmelite consciousness has been *Elijah, associated as he was with Mount Carmel. Equally important has been *Mary, to whom the first chapel was dedicated; Carmelites are known as 'Brothers/Sisters of the Blessed Virgin Mary of Mt. Carmel'. Not having a founding figure (as e.g. *Dominic, *Francis, or *Benedict), they take Elijah and Mary as their founders. See Index, Carmelites.

B. Edwards (ed.), *The Rule of Carmel* (1973); J. Smet, *The Carmelites* (1975–85).

Carnatic music: see MUSIC.

Caro, Joseph ben Ephraim (1488–1575). *Rabbinic authority and author of the **Shulḥān Arukh*. Having lived much of his life in Turkey, in 1534 he settled in Safed where he was regarded as the leading scholar. His *Beit Yosef* (House of Joseph, 1555), on which he worked for twenty years, was a commentary on the *Arbaʿah Turim* (Four Rows) of *Jacob b. Asher; he investigated every law, discussed its development, and gave a final decisive ruling. His aim was to lay down the definitive *halakhah so that there would be 'one Law and one *Torah'. *Shulḥān Arukh* (Prepared Table, 1597) was a digest of the *Beit Yosef* designed for 'young students'. It is very brief and consists of thirty sections, one designed to be read daily. It has been enormously influential, and it was his stated hope that 'as a result of this work, the world will be filled with the knowledge of the Lord'. Caro also produced many *responsa and a commentary on *Maimonides' *Mishneh Torah* (Second Law), the *Kesef Mishneh* (Silver Repetition) (1574). He was involved in *kabbalistic study and kept a spiritual diary. He stressed the importance of intention ('Better a little prayer with good intention than much without it') and self-control ('Never be subverted into anger, not even on matters pertaining to heaven').

R. J. Z. Werblowsky, *Joseph Karo, Lawyer and Mystic* (1962).

Caroline Divines (17th-cent. bishops in England): see ANGLICANISM.

Cartesian doubt: see DESCARTES, R.

Cartesian dualism: see DUALISM; DESCARTES, R.

Carthusians. Roman Catholic monastic order, so-called from their mother-house, La Grande Chartreuse (Lat., *Cartusia*, 'Charterhouse') near Grenoble, founded in 1084 by St Bruno of Cologne (1032–1101). Carthusian monasticism emphasizes *eremitic over *coenobitic elements. Monks gather only for daily *mass, a portion of the daily office, a communal meal on Sundays and feast-days, and a weekly period of fellowship. They spend all other time alone in their cells, where they engage in study, manual labour, and above all contemplative prayer. The diet is strict and meatless, and the rule of silence is observed. This austere form of life has changed little since being first codified *c.*1127 in the *Customs* of Guigo I, fifth prior of La Grande Chartreuse. Thus the Order is traditionally characterized as 'never reformed because never deformed'. In 1985 there were twenty-three Carthusian monasteries worldwide including six for nuns.

The Carthusians: Origins, Spirit, Family Life (1959).

Cārvāka. A school of Indian materialism, also known as Lokāyata dārśana (i.e. restricting truth to this world (*loka)). The traditional founder is said to have been Bṛhaspati, of uncertain date (*c.*6th cent. BCE?) to whom is attributed *Bārhaspati Sūtra*, a work which has long since disappeared, although it is quoted in later works. The person Carvaka, after whom the school is named, is said to have been the chief pupil of Bṛhaspati; but it may be that the name is not of a person but of the school, derived from √*carv*, 'eat'—i.e., concerned with the pleasures of this life alone; or who 'eats up' all ethical considerations; or derived from *caruvak*, 'smooth-tongued', one who is superficially plausible. Hindus regard the system as a *nāstika darsana; and *nāstika-shiromāni*, 'extreme heretic', is a synonym for a materialist. Carvakins see no permanence, but constant change, in all appearance, so that the self is nothing more than the sum of its parts. Thus where **Bṛhadāraṇyaka Upaniṣad* 2. 4. 12 affirms the eternity of *ātman by the simile of salt dissolved in water without disappearing, Carvakins simply pointed to the dissolution and to the impossibility of reassembling the original. Since there cannot be a future personal immortality, the only wise course is to grasp life now—but with the moral control that a good action is more likely to produce happiness than the reverse. *Sarvadarśanasaṁgraha* (1) summarized Cārvāka beliefs: 'There is no *svarga, no *mokṣa, no ātman in another world. The *Agnihotra, the *Vedas and smearing oneself with *ashes were a natural development to give life-support to those without skill and knowledge. . . . While life continues, let a person live happily, feeding on *ghi even if he runs into debt. When the body becomes ashes, how can it return here?'

H. P. Shastri, *Lokayata* (1925).

Caryatantra (division of tantric texts): see TRIPIṬAKA.

Cassian, John (*c.*360–435). Christian monk. He came from the East to Marseilles, where *c.*415 he founded two monasteries and where he wrote his two main books. The *Institutes* sets out the ordinary rules for the monastic life. It was the basis of many W. rules, being drawn on e.g. by *Benedict. The *Conferences* record his conversations with monastic leaders of the East. Cassian was also an exponent of 'semi-*Pelagianism', and wrote a refutation of *Nestorius (*On the Incarnation Against Nestorius*).

O. Chadwick, *John Cassian* . . . (1950).

Cassiodorus (*c.*485–*c.*580). Roman author and Christian monk. He retired from public affairs in 540 to a monastery of his own foundation at Vivarium. He made it a kind of academy of secular and religious learning, which, by its example, did much to protect and continue classical learning and culture through the so-called 'Dark Ages'. His writings include biblical commentaries, a history of the Church, a manual of theology and the liberal arts, and various secular works.

Cassock. Ankle-length garment worn by Christian clergy (and, in church, by vergers, choristers, etc.). It is black for priests, purple for bishops, and white for the pope. It is worn under the eucharistic vestments (unless a white 'cassock alb' is worn) and also as an ordinary outdoor garment. In the Church of England the cassock was the distinctive outdoor dress of the clergy until the mid-19th cent., Roman Catholic clergy being forbidden by law to wear it so that they would not be mistaken for Anglicans. The Orthodox *rason*, the normal dress of clergy and monks, corresponds with the W. cassock: the inner *rason* is often called the *anterion*; the outer (*exorason*, *paliya*, or *ryasa*) has wider sleeves and is usually black.

Caste (Portuguese, *casta*, 'breed kind'). Term which indicates the unique hierarchical structure of S. Asian society, which, although originating from Hindu belief, has permeated all religions and communities of the subcontinent, having as its bases and sanctions religious as well as secular tenets. In modern India, the more common word for caste is the indigenous term *jāti (Skt., *jāta*, 'race').

The castes (and sub-castes), numbering many thousands, fit into the divinely originated *varna framework, though their origin is later and usually based on secular criteria relating to occupation and area of origin. A slight alteration in work-style or method could result in the formation of a new sub-caste, and thus these proliferated. The caste system relied on five criteria for its maintenance: pollution, commensality, endogamy, hereditary occupation, economic interdependence. The caste formed an exclusive kind of trade-guild, guarding not only techniques and skills, but also ties of patronage. Ritual, and, formerly, secular, status in society was ascribed, since, once born into a caste, the individual stayed in it for life, unless *outcasted for a grave offence. An individual could not change this ritual status on his own, but a caste or sub-caste *in toto* might change its position in the hierarchy by adopting practices of a higher caste, e.g. banning widow-remarrying or alcohol, practising vegetarianism, etc., or effecting successful marriage negotiations with a higher caste. In modern India some castes may seek reclassification at a lower level as Scheduled castes, since these have certain educational and economic privileges now allocated which are denied the higher categories.

Criteria of caste maintenance such as pollution, hereditary occupation, and commensality are necessarily gradually disappearing in public places in urban, industrialized India, but in the countryside (where *c.*80 per cent of the populace still lives), and in home life, such beliefs and the discriminatory practices related to them still prevail. Endogamy is still generally observed, and as the older generation still takes the responsibility for arranging marriages it is likely to survive for many years yet. The functions of caste are changing and broadening in modern India, becoming significant in the political arena, agricultural and commercial development, employment and promotion.

Caste has long been the target of reforming groups, both within Hinduism and from the outside. Thus *Gāndhī attempted to alter attitudes to untouchables; and *Ambedkar proposed conversion to Buddhism as a way of practical protest. Earlier, Gurū *Nānak and successive Sikh Gurūs declared caste irrelevant to salvation. 'The pride of caste and glory of status are futile, for each of us shelters under the same God' (Ādi Granth, p. 83). The *Gurū-kā-laṅgar and initiation into the *Khālsā negate the requirements of caste segregation. However, intercaste marriage has always been rare among Sikhs, and at least at that level, caste is far from being eradicated among Sikhs: see BĀLMĪKĪ; BHĀṬṚĀ; JAṬ; KABĪR; KHATRĪ; MAZHABĪ; MISL; RĀMDĀSĪ; RĀMGAṚHĪĀ; RAVI DĀS; RAVIDĀSĪ. See also Index, Caste.

A. M. Hocart, *Caste: A Comparative Study* (1950); J. H. Hutton, *Caste in India* (1946); S. S. Kalsi, *The Evolution of a Sikh Community in Britain* (1991); P. Kolenda, *Caste in Contemporary India* . . . (1978); D. G. McGilvray (ed.), *Caste Ideology and Interaction* (1982); P. H. Prabhu, *Hindu Social Organisation* . . . (1940, 1963); M. N. Srinavas, *Caste in Modern India* (1962).

Casuistry. The art of applying principles of moral theology to particular instances (Lat., *casus*, 'case'). After *Trent, the study of cases of conscience was imposed upon all studying for the Roman Catholic priesthood. The term came to be identified with hair-splitting and evasion, and to have a pejorative sense. It drew the scorn of *Pascal, both upon the discipline as such, and upon the *Jesuits who were its leading proponents. But the practice of casuistry in the sense defined above is indispensable if the abstract norms of morality are to be applied to the practical decisions of Christian living.

B. Häring, *The Law of Christ*, i (1961).

Catacombs (Gk., *kata kumbas*, 'by the hollows', an area south of Rome). In these long underground burial chambers (outside the city walls as burial was not permitted within) the bodies of the departed were placed in coffin-like recesses, in rows usually about four deep. Christian catacombs seem to be copied from Jewish ones. Six Jewish catacombs have been found in Rome. Although the inscriptions are mainly in Greek and Latin, Jewish symbols such as the *menorah (seven-branched candlestick), *shofar (ram's horn), and *sefer Torah* (book of the Law) are depicted. Jewish catcombs have also been found in Venosa (S. Italy), and in Sardinia. Catacombs are found outside many cities, but the most famous and extensive—several hundred miles of them—are at Rome. Services commemorating *martyrs buried there were held, and they became centres of *pilgrimage as the cult of martyrs developed.

Catechism (Gk., *katēcheō*, 'instruct'). An elementary manual of Christian doctrine. In the Middle Ages books were produced containing explanations of the *Lord's Prayer and *creed, lists of mortal sins, etc. It was the *Reformation, however, with its insistence on religious instruction, which brought forth the catechisms known today. The most famous is *Luther's *Small Catechism* (1529), still the standard book of the Lutheran Church; the Heidelberg catechism (1563) has a corresponding place for Calvinists. The Anglican **Book of Common Prayer* included a catechism; and *Presbyterian churches generally follow the 'Humble Advice' of the Westminster Assembly of 1647. In competition with the Protestants, the *Roman Catholic Church too began to produce new catechisms: the 'Penny Catechism' (*A Catechism of Christian Doctrine*) was issued in 1898. Catechisms normally contain expositions of the creed, Lord's Prayer, and the Ten Commandments; RC ones add instructions on the *Hail Mary, *sacraments, virtues and vices, and extend into virtually every area of doctrine and behaviour. After *Vatican II, it was thought desirable that catechisms should be embedded in local contexts of language and culture. A number of specific catechisms (e.g. French and German) were produced, with the Dutch catechism being widely read and used. An *ecumenical endeavour succeeded in producing *The Common Catechism* (1973). In 1985, an Extraordinary Synod initiated the writing of a new *Catechism of the Catholic Church* (1992), which was eventually (1994) translated into English: the original Eng. translation was rejected, because it used inclusive language (i.e., language which respects the fact that women are an equal part of the human race). The revised and approved translation not only restored masculine nouns and pronouns, but added many at places where they did not appear in the original. The *Catechism* itself was regarded as being equally conservative of pre-Vatican II Catholicism, although some concessions to the Council necessarily had to be made.

Catechumen. One who is undergoing training and instruction (Gk., *katachesis*) prior to Christian *baptism. In the early *eucharist, catechumens were solemnly dismissed after the 'Mass of the Catechumens', i.e. before the offertory. There was an elaborate preparation during *Lent, after which candidates were baptized on *Easter morning. In 1962 the catechumenate was restored in the Roman Catholic Church. It is of importance especially in missionary churches where there are numbers of adult baptisms, and involves instruction as well as the 'Time of Purification and Enlightenment'. See also NEO-CATECHUMENATE.

Categorical imperative. In Kantian ethics, the universal moral law, by which all rational beings are by duty constrained to act. The term was introduced in the *Foundations of the Metaphysics of Morals* (1785), where *Kant offered at least two different formulations: 'Act only according to that maxim by which you can at the same time will that it should become a universal law' and 'Act so that you treat humanity, whether in your own person or in that of another, always as an end and never merely as a means.' In either case, however, the moral law entails obligations towards one's self as well as towards others. Suicide, for instance, is said by Kant to be contrary to the moral law both because it is not a course of action which could become a universal law (without leading to the possible self-destruction of all human beings) and because it is a course of action inconsistent with the idea of humanity as an end in itself ('Therefore, I cannot dispose of man in my own person so as to mutilate, corrupt, or kill him'). The categorical imperative—of which this is but one example—is binding upon all rational beings at all times in all circumstances. It is not, however, an empirical generalization nor is it in any way grounded in our experience of the way people behave or in our knowledge of their psychological make-up. Arising rather from a universal sense of 'ought', the categorical imperative is rationally self-legislated (autonomy) by a free will, which is then bound by the constraints of the moral law. It is, therefore, both freely legislated by rational human beings and also objectively binding upon them. Indeed, the categorical imperative is the supreme limiting condition upon one's freedom as a rational being.

Category mistakes: see MYTH.

Cathars (Lat., *Cathari*, from Gk., *katharoi*, 'pure ones'). Christian dualist *heresy in W. Europe, which, in the 13th–14th cents., was a serious threat to the Catholic Church especially in S. France (see ALBIGENSES) and N. Italy. The origins of the movement are obscure, and although its doctrines were influenced by the *Bogomils of Bulgaria, it remains a possibility that its dualism was an independent development or inheritance.

The inner circle of the Cathars were the 'perfects', who followed a life of rigorous asceticism and praying the *Lord's Prayer. Admission to this circle was by the rite of *consolamentum* after an arduous probation, but other adherents received it on their deathbed. Those thus 'consoled' saw themselves as the only true Christians and denied the title to Catholics. The anthropological study by E. Le Roy Ladurie, *Montaillou* (1975; Eng. 1978) has shown in some detail how the Cathars lived and worked in a small village in S. France; other recent studies have also raised questions of how far social and political factors (e.g. the independence of local nobles) fostered the growth of the movement.

The decline of Catharism in the 14th cent. may be partly attributed to: (i) discord between moderate and more radical dualist factions; (ii) repression by the *Inquisition; and (iii) the newly attractive Catholic piety and devotion associated with the *Franciscans.

Cathedral (Gk., *kathedra*, 'seat'). The Christian church building in which a *bishop has his official seat. It is thus the principal church in a diocese.

Catherine of Alexandria, St (*c.*4th cent.?). Christian *martyr. Despite her wide popularity in the Middle Ages, extremely little (some would say nothing) is known of her. She is said to have been martyred during the persecution under Maxentius, by being tied to a wheel (hence the Catherine wheel), tortured, and beheaded. The monastery on Mt. Sinai named after her was said to have been established because her body was transported there by angels, being discovered in the 9th cent.; however, the monastery was not founded until the 6th cent., and early pilgrims knew nothing of the association. Her feast day (25 Nov.) was suppressed in 1969.

Catherine of Genoa, St (1447–1510). Christian mystic. Born of a noble family, Caterinetta Fieschi married young. Ten years later she experienced a sudden conversion and gave herself to the selfless care of the sick in a hospital in Genoa, at the same time experiencing strange, almost pathological, religious experiences, and supposedly receiving the *stigmata. Her spiritual doctrine is contained in the *Dialogues on the Soul and the Body* and *Treatise on Purgatory*: *purgatory is the final cleansing of the soul from self-love, to be accepted, therefore, with joy. She is remarkable for her accounts of dereliction and torment, which is, however, seen as purifying, and through all her teaching there breathes a sense of inextinguishable hope, based on the sense of union with God: 'My being is God, not by simple participation, but by a true transformation of my being: God is my Being, my Me, my Strength, my Beatitude, my Good, my Delight.' She was the subject of a widely influential study by von *Hügel, *The Mystical Element in Religion* . . .

Eng. tr. C. Balfour and H. D. Irvine; S. Hughes, *Catherine of Genoa* . . . (1979).

Catherine of Siena, St (1347–80). Christian saint who saw a vision of Christ when she was 7, after which she took a vow of virginity. She became a member of the Third Order of *Dominicans when she was 16 (or perhaps 18), and committed herself to work among the poor and the sick. Her holiness became widely known and she attracted many followers. In 1376 she went to Avignon to persuade Pope Gregory XI to return to Rome, and in the Great Schism which followed his death, she urged support for Urban VI. She looked for a Church renewed in holiness ('The only desire of God is our sanctification'), united under the pope. Many of her letters survive, as does the *Dialogo* (tr. F. Noffke, 1980), a spiritual work in which she relates contemplation and action, starting in the 'cell of self-knowledge' in order to know the work and love of God in relation to oneself, but moving into the world on that basis because God is known beyond doubt as love. She placed great emphasis on the nobility of humans made in the image of God: 'I have created the soul in my image and likeness, in that I have given it memory, intelligence and volition; and intelligence is the noblest part of the soul.' Her spirituality is thus always trinitarian: 'When these three powers of the soul, memory, intelligence and volition, are gathered and drawn together in my name, then all other works, both outward and inward, . . . are drawn toward me and united in me through the sense of love, and thus a person mounts to the heights, following the crucified love.' This is the proper end of our creation: 'Open the eye of your intelligence and look on me.' She was canonized in 1461 and made a Doctor of the Church in 1970; feast day 29 Apr. (30 Apr. until 1969). Raymond of Capua's *Life* was translated by C. Kearns, 1980.

A. Levasti, *My Servant Catherine* (1954).

Catherine wheel: see CATHERINE OF ALEXANDRIA.

Catholic (Gk., *katholikos*, 'universal'). A term used variously with reference to Christian belief and institutions.

1. Most generally, of the *Church in the whole world, as distinct from local congregations. Thus, according to the (unrealized and unrealizable) *Vincentian Canon, Catholic doctrine is what is believed 'everywhere, always, and by all'.

2. Especially in historical writers, of the great body of Christians in communion with the major sees and not divided by *heresy or *schism.

3. Of churches, institutions, and doctrines which claim as their basis a continuous tradition of faith and practice from the *apostles—the claim is contrasted with *Protestant appeals to the *Bible alone. Hence Catholic also refers to Christians who accept traditional doctrines and practices (e.g. devotion to *Mary, *sacraments). The emergence of an emphasis on institutions and tradition generally in writers of the 2nd cent. is often called 'early Catholicism'. See also ANGLO-CATHOLICS.

4. As a synonym for *Roman Catholic; it then applies to all churches, including the *Uniat churches, in communion with the bishop of Rome. See also OLD CATHOLICS.

Catholic Action. The organization of non-clerical members of the *Roman Catholic Church for apostolic action. It was defined by Pius XI in 1922 as 'the participation of laymen in the hierarchical apostolate', and it required the mandate of local *bishops. It took a variety of forms, *Azione Cattolica* in Italy, 'Jocisme' in Belgium and France, and a number of groups with more specific aims, e.g. the Association of Catholic Trade Unionists. *Pius XII retained the tight juridical structure imposed by his predecessor, but more recent emphasis upon the role of the laity in the Church has led to a loosening of legalistic structures, and 'the lay apostolate' has become the preferred term.

T. Hesburgh, *The Theology of Catholic Action* (1946).

Catholic Apostolic Church. A Christian denomination founded in 1832 by followers of Edward Irving, and so also called Irvingites. Irving was a Church of Scotland pastor (expelled in 1833) and exponent of *millennarianism and of the gift of tongues (*glossolalia). The new church sought to re-establish a biblical church order with 'apostles', 'prophets', and 'evangelists', as well as, later, a local ministry of 'angels' (bishops), priests, and deacons. In 1835 the full 'college of Apostles', numbering twelve, met in London. Shortly afterwards they began missionary work in Europe (most successful in N. Germany and Holland) and America. *Catholic doctrines and practices were increasingly adopted. The service book of 1842 was a mixture of the Roman, Greek, and Anglican rites. Priests wore vestments and used incense. Subsequently were added anointing of the sick, a ceremony called 'sealing' (based on Revelations, 7. 3 ff.), reservation of the sacrament, and holy water.

In Britain, Catholic Apostolic influence diminished considerably after the death in 1901 of the last apostle, who had been expected to survive until the Second Coming. The substantial church built in Gordon Square, London (1853) became the Anglican chaplaincy to Univ. of London. See also NEW APOSTOLIC CHURCH.

C. G. Flegg, *Gathered Under Apostles . . .* (1992).

Catholic Israel (Jewish ecumenical concept): see KENESET YISRAEL.

Catholikos (Gk., *katholikos*). A title of the *patriarchs of the *Church of the East, the *Armenian Orthodox Church, and the *Georgian Church.

Caussade, J. P. de (1675–1751). French *Jesuit and ascetic writer. His extensive correspondence with the Visitandines at Nancy is a leading source of our knowledge of his doctrine. In the early 18th cent. de Caussade did much to rescue *mysticism from the suspicion of *quietism, directly by seeking justification in Bossuet, a noted opponent of quietism, and more fundamentally by his own teaching. His principal work is *Abandonment to the Divine Providence*. His teaching can be crystallized in his phrase 'the sacrament of the present moment', through which our will is to be united to God's at every moment through abandonment to, and trust in, God.

Cavasilas, Nikolaos, St (*c*.1320–95). Greek theologian and mystical writer in the Orthodox Church. He adopted the name of his uncle (Archbishop Nilus Cavasilas) in place of his own, Chamaetos. He followed a political career, linked with the pretender, John VI Cantacuzene, and in 1353, he was one of three elected candidates for the office of patriarch. After John VI abdicated, little is known of his subsequent life. He wrote *An Exposition of the Divine Liturgy* (tr. J. M. Hussey and P. McNulty, 1960) and *Life in Christ* (tr. C. J. de Catanzaro, 1974), both of which exerted an influence long after his death. In the former he makes the worship on earth an anticipation of the worship in heaven; the connection is real, since the participation in the *sacraments is not merely symbolic. In the latter, the incarnate life of Christ is continued into the lives of the faithful through the sacraments, leading into union with God. He was canonized in 1983; feast day, 20 June.

W. Völker, *Die Sacramentsmystik des Nikolaus Kabasilas* (1977).

Cave of Machpelah (burial place, Jewish): see MACHPELAH, CAVE OF.

Caves of a thousand Buddhas: see TAN-HUANG.

Cayce, Edgar (1877–1945). The 'Sleeping Prophet', an American psychic healer and clairvoyant. For the last thirty or so years of his life, Cayce gave some 14,000 'readings' throughout the USA. Able to fall into a 'sleep state', Cayce claimed the ability to function 'in the realm of psychic or mental forces'. Many of his readings had to do with diagnosing and prescribing treatment for specific complaints, both physical and psychological. However, Cayce was more than a simple technician. He saw his gifts as spiritual in origin, and used them to aid those 'who seek to know better their relationship to their Maker'.

E. and H. Cayce, *The Outer Limits of Edgar Cayce's Powers* (1977).

Cecilia, St (2nd–3rd cent.). A perhaps legendary virgin martyr of the Roman church. Her *Acts* date from the 5th cent., and she is unknown to earlier writers. Her traditional tomb is in the *catacomb of Callistus. Since the 16th cent. she has been best known as patron saint of music and musicians; hence the Ode of Alexander Pope, the Song of Dryden, and the Anthem of W. H. *Auden, all 'for St Cecilia's Day': 'Blessed Cecilia, appear in visions . . . Composing mortals with immortal fire' (Auden). She is usually depicted with an organ. Feast day, 22 Nov.

Celā or **ceṭa.** A student, especially in relation to a *guru, of whom complete trust and acceptance is required.

CELAM (Episcopal Conferences): see LIBERATION THEOLOGY.

Celestial Buddhas. Those Buddhas, or those manifestations of the one buddha-nature, who appear in the *trikāya forms of manifestation, in the *sambhoga-kāya. They are accompanied by *bodhisattvas. They are prolific in number, and are often generated from existing belief-systems in the countries to which Buddhism spread. Although celestial Buddhas are associated with *Mahāyāna, their roots are certainly earlier. Major celestial Buddhas are Amitābha/*Amida, *Akṣobhya, *Vairocana, *Ratnasaṃbhava, *Amoghasiddhi, and various Buddhas associated with *Vajrayāna. In *Tantric Buddhism, there are also terrifying or *wrathful Buddhas, e.g. *Heruka, Hevajra, and Śaṃvara.

D. L. Snellgrove (ed.), *The Image of the Buddha* (1978).

Celestial Kings (Skt. *devarāja*; Chin., *t'ien-wang*; Jap., *shi-tenno*). The four world protectors in Buddhism. They dwell on Mount *Meru and guard the four quarters of the world. Vaiṣravana protects the north, holding (iconographically) a scroll of *dharma (teaching) and the pagoda in which *Nāgārjuna found the Buddhist scriptures; his body is green. Dhritarāśtra protects the east, with a white body, playing a peace-bringing lute. Virūdhaka protects the south, with a blue body, holding out a sword against *avidyā (ignorance). Virūpākṣa guards the west, with a red body, holding a serpent (*nāga) before whom he holds the treasure (*cintāmani) that the enlightened, and not the nāgas, should properly have. Images of the Celestial Kings are widespread in China and Japan, and few monasteries are without them.

Celestial Master (founder of Taoist school of Wu-tou-mi): see CHANG TAO-LING; WU-TOU-MI TAO.

Celestial Master School (Taoist): see WU-TOU-MI TAO.

Celibacy. A state of life without marriage, undertaken for religious or spiritual reasons. Celibacy was not practised among the Jews. According to the **Shulḥān Arukh*, 'Every man is obliged to marry in order to fulfil the duty of procreation.' This rests on the command in Genesis 1. 28. In *Temple times the *High Priest had to be married (Leviticus 21. 13) and unmarried people were barred from holding various public offices (*B.Sanh.* 36b). However, *Josephus records that some of the *Essenes were celibate.

In Christianity, celibacy rests on the demand for the renunciation of family ties 'for the sake of the kingdom' (Mark 10. 29, Luke 18. 29). In the early church, it was an individual vocation (Matthew 19. 12, 'Whoever is able to receive this, let him receive it'), and marriage was not incompatible with ecclesiastical office and *ordination. In the Eastern Orthodox church, the norm became one of unmarried bishops; other clergy could be married. In the West, celibacy was increasingly imposed, until from the time of Pope Gregory VII (d. 1095) it was assumed to be the rule. The Protestant *Reformation abolished mandatory celibacy; the *Counter-Reformation reaffirmed it, but as an ecclesiastical institution, and therefore open to change. It is safe to predict from the state and scale of the argument that the Roman Catholic Church will continue to change on this matter (e.g. convert clergy who are married are nevertheless ordained).

In other religions, celibacy may also be a permanent vocation (e.g. for Buddhist monks, *bhikṣus, unless their ordination is temporary), or it may be a temporary stage (e.g. the fourth *āśrama for Hindus). It may be tolerated, as it is among Sikhs, though regarded as less than ideal: the *Gurūs advocated and exemplified married fidelity as the best state, but Bhāī *Gurdas and *Manī Singh died celibate; and two Sikh groups, *Udāsīs and *Nirmalās, regarded celibacy as the ideal. At the other extreme, religions, like Judaism (above), which emphasize the goodness of creation as coming from God tend to attack celibacy as something approaching a blasphemous act—e.g. Islam.

E. Schillebeeckx, *Celibacy* (1968).

Celsus (2nd cent.). Philosopher and opponent of Christianity. His *True Discourse* (*c*.178) is largely quoted in *Origen's reply *Against Celsus* (mid-3rd cent.). Celsus's attitude to religion was interested but detached, seeing sense in the *Logos doctrine and Christian morals, but ridiculing the miracles and grotesque episodes in biblical history. He also objected to the Christian refusal to participate wholly in the State, and he regarded the Church as too exclusive and intolerant.

Contra Celsum, tr. H. Chadwick (1953).

Celtic Church. The Christian Church in parts of Britain before the arrival of St *Augustine from Rome in 596–7. Its early history is uncertain, but it was sufficiently organized to send delegates to the Synod of Arles (314). By the 4th cent. it was spreading from the poorer people to the upper classes and the army. The Saxon invasions of the 5th cent. destroyed much of Christianity, and the communities which survived in Ireland, Isle of Man, Scotland, Cornwall, Wales, and elsewhere were cut off from the continent. The Celtic Christians resisted the Roman Christianity of Augustine, and although agreement was reached, e.g. over the date of Easter at the Synod of Whitby (664), the conformity to Roman practice was not accepted everywhere. Celtic Christianity is marked by a kind of heroic devotion, with a simplicity of prayer and art which extends its missionary outreach (another prominent feature) into contemporary lives. It was strongly *ascetical, and emphasized the importance of *anamchairdeas*, soul-friendship, and of the *anamchara*, soul-friend, for counsel in the spiritual life. Many prayers (e.g. *Loricae*, breastplate prayers, as of the one attributed to St *Patrick) have survived and are in increasingly common use today. While they are aware of the Last Judgement, they are marked by tenderness and delight in creation.

J. B. Bulloch, *The Life of the Celtic Church* (1963); N. K. Chadwick, *The Age of the Saints in the Early Celtic Church* (rev., 1963); J. T. MacNeill, *The Celtic Churches: A History . . .* (1974); C. Plummer, *Irish Litanies* (1925); F. Henry, *Irish Art . . .* (1965, 1967); J. Ryan, *Irish Monasticism* (1931).

Cenobitic (monasticism in community): see COENOBITE.

Cerinthus. Early Christian *heretic. *Irenaeus records the story that the apostle *John fled from a public bath at Ephesus crying out 'Let us escape, lest the bath should fall while Cerinthus the enemy of the truth is in it.' He seems to have been a *gnostic of *docetic tendencies, and may perhaps even have been the opponent denounced in 1 John (e.g. 4. 1–3).

Certain because it is impossible: see TERTULLIAN.

Ceṭa (student): see CELĀ.

Cetas (Skt.). In *Yoga, the power of consciousness. It is a general term, perhaps parallel to the *antaḥkarana* of *Sāṃkhya.

Cetasika (quality of mental experience): see CITTA.

Cetiya (earth-mound): see CAITYA.

Ch. May be spelt C; check at appropriate place (e.g. chela / cela; chaitya / caitya).

Chaddor (veil): see ḤIJĀB.

Chadō or **cha-no-yu** (Jap., 'tea-way'). Zen Buddhist way to overcome ordinary consciousness, in which entities are differentiated, in themselves, or in subject–object distinctions. The translation 'tea-ceremony' is thus misleading if it implies a ritual involving tea, although its actions and context are highly formalized. Like other forms of Zen practice in the aesthetic domain (e.g. flower-way—not flower-arranging, *kado*, *ikebana), it is a means of mind-realization of the single buddha-nature (*buddhatā) of all appearance. The preparation and drinking of tea (religiously) began in China, apparently for medicinal purposes (reviewed by Lu Yü in *Ch'a Ching*). Sen no Rikyū (1521–91) organized tea-drinking practices into a single system, and also instructed Hideyoshi, who became the great master of cha-no-yu. *Eisai is said to have introduced the practice into Japan and into Zen. The practice may originally have derived from the use of tea as a stimulant to keep meditators awake. According to legend, tea as a plant derived from the eyelids of *Bodhidharma, who tore them off and threw them to the ground (whence tea began to grow) to keep himself awake during his nine-year meditation. The taking of tea usually takes place in a specially built tea-room, Sukiya: the original ideographs mean 'abode of fancy', but probably in the sense of 'abode of vacancy' (*śūnyatā). The tea-room is built in a style of poverty (often, now, at great expense), including, as entrance, a small hole which can only be entered, as a mark of humility, on one's knees: the whole is meant to be reminiscent of the isolation of a mountain retreat; a focal text is hung up with a careful placing of flowers in an alcove (*tokonoma*) beneath it. The implements and pace are carefully ordered: by the 16th cent. a hundred rules had been elaborated. Not surprisingly, the way of tea can only be learnt from an adept.

R. Castile, *The Way of Tea* (1971); Fujikawa Asako, *Cha-no-yu and Hideyoshi* (1957); Okakura Kazuko, *The Book of Tea* (1906, 1956); A. L. Sadler, *Cha-no-yu* (1930, 1963).

Chai (Chin., 'fasting'). Formal fast in Taoism, especially before sacrifice. It developed into an occasion during which pupils confess their faults to their teacher or master. This may last for days. Generally, these rituals begin with the participants stepping into a designated space, dishevelled or smeared (e.g. with charcoal in *t'u-t'an chai*) to indicate penitence. They repeat the twelve vows of repentance, then confess their sins to the accompaniment of rhythmic dreams. This, combined with thrice-daily repetition and little food, produces physical and ecstatic states. Among the different Tao schools, chai ceremonies are especially important in *Ling-pao p'ai, *T'ai-ping tao, and *Wu-tou-mi tao; in these, the connection between sickness and sin is explicit, so that the repentance rituals are tied to healing expectations.

Chaitanya: see CAITANYA.

Chakugo (summary of kōan): see JAKUGO.

Chalcedon. City in Asia Minor near Constantinople and venue of the fourth ecumenical *council in 451. It revoked the decisions of the 'Robber Synod' of *Ephesus in 449 and condemned *Eutyches. By drawing up a statement of faith, the so-called Chalcedonian definition, it attempted to end the controversy between *Alexandrian and *Antiochene *christologies. It canonized the title *Theotokos for *Mary and two letters of *Cyril of Alexandria; but the burden of the definition comes from the *Tome* of Pope Leo which tended to emphasize the particularity of the divine and human natures in Christ. According to the definition, Christ is to be acknowledged 'in two natures ... concurring into one person and one subsistence (*hypostasis)'. The strong *Monophysite party in the E. never accepted the definition, and until Islamic times repeated attempts were made by 'neo-Chalcedonians' to remove its offence without actually rescinding it. The *Oriental Orthodox churches still remain 'non-Chalcedonian'.

Eng. tr. of the definition in J. Stevenson (ed.), *Creeds, Councils and Controversies* (1966), 334–8.

Chalice (Lat., *calix*, 'cup'). The vessel containing the wine at the *eucharist. Present Roman Catholic law requires a chalice to be made of strong (i.e. not breakable and not able to absorb liquid) materials, preferably those which are valued in the country of use.

'Cham (Tibetan ritual drama): see MUSIC.

Chamār. An untouchable *caste of leatherworkers common in N. and Central India, whose task is to tan and work the hides of dead animals, a job full of the pollution that comes from death. The abhorrence of the higher castes for this type of work transfers to those who do it, hence the untouchable status of Chamārs.

Champa (heavenly Buddha): see MAITREYA.

Ch'an. Chin. for Jap., *Zen.

Chānaṇī (Pañjābī, 'canopy'). Decorative awning. In some *gurdwārās a large square of cloth is suspended over the *Ādi Granth in lieu of a wooden canopy (*pālkī*).

Chancellor. An administrative officer in a Christian diocese. In the Anglican Church he is president of the *consistory court and accordingly must be a senior lawyer; he need not be a priest. In the Roman Catholic Church the diocesan chancellor is a priest who is sometimes the confidential secretary of the *bishop and does much of the work otherwise executed by *vicars-general.

Chandogya Upaniṣad. One of the earlier *Upaniṣads, attached to the Sāmaveda. In eight chapters, it reviews the origin of the cosmos, the relation between the universal and the individual soul, together with its destiny. It includes the dialogue between Uddālaka Āruni and his son Śvetaketu, in which the teaching on the way in which *Brahman, the Absolute, permeates the universe, culminates in the focal (*mahāvakya) sentence, *tat tvam asi*, That thou art.

Eng. tr. (among many) in R. E. Hume (1931), S. Radhakrishnan (1953).

Ch'ang (Chin., 'enduring'). The permanent and eternal in Taoism, as opposed to the transient and mutable, and as such, one of the symbols of Taoism. Enlightenment (*ming) is attained through the realization of ch'ang.

Ch'ang-an. Chinese capital of the Former Han (202 BCE to 9 CE) and Sui-t'ang (590–906 CE) dynasties. Like all Chinese capitals, the city was conceived of as lying at the centre of the world, modelled and oriented according to the motions and positions of the sun, moon, and stars. With its near-perfect gridwork pattern and placement of essential architectural components, Ch'ang-an is a classical example of the cosmic-religious ideal for the imperial capital. The present city on the site is *Sian (Xian).

Chang Chüeh (d. 184 CE). Founder of the Taoist school of *T'ai-p'ing tao (the way of supreme peace). In a period of conflict and famine, he urged reconciliation and the equality of all people. As a practical manifestation of the latter, he organized *chai ceremonies (with ritual healings and recitations, based on communal acknowledgement of fault). He attracted a huge following, and led the Yellow Turban rebellion, so-called from the yellow cloth (*huang-chin*) worn by his followers. The rebellion was suppressed and Chang Chüeh was killed.

P. Michaud, 'The Yellow Turbans', *Mon. Serica*, 17 (1958).

Chang Hsien (Chin., 'Chang the Immortal'). The immortal (*hsien) figure who protects children and bestows male offspring. He is often accompanied by Sung-tzu niang-niang, the lady who bestows children.

Chang Hsiu. Founder of a Taoist movement much like the *wu-tou-mi tao of *Chang Lu—who murdered him in 190 CE. The emphasis was on healing accompanied by sacrifices to the Three Rulers (*san-kuan): Earth, Water, and Heaven. The movement was based on **Tao-te ching*, and was strictly organized.

Chang Kuo-lao (one of eight Immortals): see PA-HSIEN.

Chang Ling (founder of Taoist school of wu-tou-mi): see CHANG TAO-LING.

Chang Lu. One of the secondary founder members, in the 2nd/3rd cent. CE, of the Taoist movement, *wu-tou-mi tao. With the help of *Chang Hsiu (whom he then removed), he established a strictly governed religious state in N. Szechwan. Because of the assumed connection between ill-health and sin (see CHAI), he required strict moral observance. Offenders were required to make practical reparation, e.g. by repairing public buildings, either in person or by payment of the cost. He called himself *t'ien-shih (Celestial Master or heavenly Lord), a title which was then assumed by his successors. He took further the organization of the 'Celestial Master's Way', introducing the *tao-shih (often translated as 'the Taoist priest'), with a local temple and a hierarchy leading up to the T'ien-shih. The 'five pecks of rice' was also extended into a more extensive system of fees, enabling the pervasive presence of the tao-shih in Chinese society—and the survival of religious Taoism in this form down to the present, at least in Taiwan.

Chang Po-tuan (practitioner and teacher): see NEI-TAN.

Chang san-feng. Taoist immortal and source of *Ch'üan-chen tao; he is also said to be the founder of a school of Chinese boxing. As with other immortals, he appears on earth in visible form—for those who have the religiously trained eyes to see—the last appearance having been during the 14th cent.

Ch'ang-sha Ching-ts'en (d. 868). Chinese Ch'an Buddhist master, successor (*hassu) of Nan-ch'üan P'u-yüan, from whom he received the seal of recognition (*inka-shomei). He had no set school or monastery, but wandered in China, allowing his teaching to arise from whatever he encountered.

Ch'ang-sheng Pu-ssu (Chin., 'long-lasting', 'immortal'). The goal of Taoism in many of its practices. Initially, Taoism was concerned with literal and physical immortality (see ALCHEMY), which involved the quest for substances and exercises which might produce this (e.g. *tao-yin* (see GYMNASTICS), *fang-chung shu). The attainer of immortality (*hsien) ascends to heaven (*fei-sheng) visibly, or else seems to die and is buried, but when the coffin is opened, it is found to be empty.

The more reflective Taoism of *Lao-tzu or of *Chuang-tzu regarded spiritual immortality as more important—and indeed as alone attainable. It involves union with Tao, by whatever of many means the various Taoist schools proposed (for the way in which alchemy was interiorized, see NEI-TAN). But since exterior language may be used as a code for interior quest (and vice versa), it is not always clear which path a particular school is actually pursuing. The immortality may, in any case, be provisional only—postponing death for a period.

Many symbols of immortality appear in Chinese art under Taoist influence. Particularly frequent are peaches (cultivated by *Hsi Wang mu), the herb or mushroom of immortality (*ling-chih*), a crane (often holding the *ling-chih*), pine trees, a gnarled stick of wood.

Chang Tao-ling or **Chang Ling** (2nd cent. CE). Founder of the Taoist school of *wu-tou-mi tao, which emphasized the connection between sin and suffering, and which introduced repentance and healing ceremonies (see CHAI), for which were required payment of five pecks of rice—hence the name for the school. The movement was further organized and developed by *Chang Hsiu and *Chang Lu. When he died, he ascended visibly to heaven (*fei-sheng), thereby demonstrating his immortality (*ch'ang-sheng pu-ssu). Chang Tao-ling's own teaching is now impossible to recover, as indeed are secure details of his life. It would appear from legends that by claiming and demonstrating authority over all powers, good and evil, he was acting as a classical *shaman; but what was certainly an innovation was his organization of his followers into twenty-four areas where they continued to be sustained and encouraged. After his death, he has continued to be revered as the Celestial Master (religiously as Chang T'ien Shih) down to the present day.

Chang T'ien Shih (Celestial Master): see CHANG TAO-LING.

Ch'an-na. Chin. for *dhyāna.

Channing, William Ellery (1780–1842). American Christian pastor, originally a *Congregationalist: in the schism between conservatives and liberals, Channing espoused the liberals, rejecting the *Trinity and the radical consequence of *original sin (i.e. affecting the root before any actual sin has been committed). He is thus regarded as a leading *Unitarian thinker, but he said that he belonged only to 'the community of free minds'. He was educated at Harvard College from 1794, and was elected Regent in 1801. He ministered at a *Baptist church in Boston from 1803. Drawn into defence of liberals, he published his 1819 ordination sermon (for Jared Sparks) as *Unitarian Christianity*: 'We do, then, with all earnestness, though without reproaching our brethren, protest against the irrational and unscriptural doctrine of the Trinity. . . . With Jesus, we worship the Father, as the only living and true God.' From this, the influence of John *Locke is evident, emphasizing as he did the importance of reason. He regarded Christ as morally perfect, and from this he was prepared to infer pre-existence. He supported social reform, though not at first the abolition of slavery. Rebuked for this, he published *Slavery* (1835), which became a key text for the opponents of slavery.

A. Delbanco, *William Ellery Channing* (1981); R. L. Patterson, *The Philosophy of W. E. Channing* (1952).

Cha-no-yu (way of tea): see CHADŌ.

Chantry. Provision (Christian) made for the saying (or singing) of *mass for the souls of the dead, especially for the one making the endowment, but also for family and friends. The term thus applies to the endowment and the office, and also on occasion (if the bequest was large enough) to the chapel in which the masses were said. The chantry in this sense could be within a church, or a separate building, in which case legal provision was made to regulate the relation of the chapel to the parish church. Chantries became numerous in England in the 14th and 15th cents., but endowment was falling off on the eve of the *Reformation. Chantry priests also took on additional responsibilities, such as acting as schoolmasters or curates. In 1545, the possessions of chantries were vested in Henry VIII during his life, and in 1547 an Act suppressed more than 2,000 chantries and guild chapels. The chantry monies which had an educational provision in the endowment were used to provide for schools, many of which are recognizable through the use of a prefix, 'King Edward VI Grammar School'.

Ch'an-tsung (Jap., *zenshu*, literally 'the Ch'an school'). By this term, the different routes or paths in Zen Buddhism are recognized. For details, see BUDDHIST SCHOOLS.

Chao-chou Ts'ung-shen or **Jōshū Jūshin** (778–897). Leading Ch'an/*Zen master in China, successor (*hassu) of Nan-chüan P'u-yüan (Jap., Nansen Fugan). He had a profound experience of enlightenment when he was 18, which simply indicated to him that there was a way worth pursuing further (i.e. enlightenment is not an end, but a step on a path). After forty years training with Nan-chüan, he wandered in China seeking other Ch'an masters. At the age of 80, he settled in Chao-chou, gathering pupils around him. He instructed gently and quietly, but in very sharp and short ways. Among his *kōans, his famous *Mu kōan is often given still to Zen pupils as their first kōan: 'A monk once asked master Chao-chou, "Does a dog have a buddha-nature [*buddhatā] or not?" Chao-chou said, "Wu" [Jap., Mu].'

Chao-chou was especially important in showing how Ch'an and *Tao relate together, opening the way to creative coexistence. When he asked Nan-chüan about the Tao, Nan-chüan replied, 'Ordinary mind is Tao.' Chao-chou asked how he should move toward it. 'If you try to move toward it, you go away from it.' 'But if we do not try, how do we know that it is Tao?' Nan-chüan replied: 'Tao does not belong to "knowing" or "not-knowing": knowing is illusion, not-knowing is blank emptiness. If you really attain to Tao of no-doubt, it is like the vast abyss, limitless, boundless. How, then, can there be right and wrong in the Tao?' At these words, Chao-chou was suddenly enlightened, and his enlightenment is known as *funi daidō*, 'the nonduality of the great Tao'—which is a near synonym for the buddha-nature empty of self and differentiation.

Chao-chou was also an intuitively profound Buddhist. In his early days of training, he was absent on one occasion when Nan-ch'üan held up a cat: 'Monks', he said: 'If you can speak one word of Zen, I will spare the cat; if not, I will kill it.' No one could speak, and Nan-ch'üan killed the cat. When Chao-chou returned, Nan-ch'üan told him of the incident, and Chao-chou at once put his sandal on his head and walked away. Nan-ch'üan said, 'If only you had been here, my cat had not died!' See also KISSAKO.

Chaos. The primordial condition from which (or onto which) order is imposed, according to many religions, so that the cosmos can appear. This is often a matter of creation, but it can equally be a matter of evolution. Chaos may remain behind, or below, the appearance of order, so that it, or its agents, constantly threatens to reappear. See further COSMOLOGY.

P. G. Kuntz (ed.), *The Concept of Order* (1968); C. H. Long, *Alpha: The Myths of Creation* (1963).

Chapter. The members of a Christian religious community or of any similar body. The word originally denoted a portion of the monastic rule read daily in religious houses; by extension it came to refer to the assembly of those present to listen, and then to assemblies of monks of a whole province or order. Outside monasticism it most usually refers to the body of clergy responsible for a *cathedral or *collegiate church. From the 9th cent. cathedrals often had separate 'chapter houses'.

Charan pāhul (Pañjābī, 'foot-initiation'). Hindu initiation ritual continued by Sikh *Gurūs. This entails the devotee drinking *charanamrit* (the water in which the feet of a *brahman or a *murtī have been washed). With a toe, Gurū *Nānak and his successors would touch water in a vessel, some of which was then drunk by the person wishing to become a Sikh. This demonstrated humility. Gurū *Gobind Siṅgh replaced charan pāhul with *khaṇḍe-dī-pāhul, initiation with the *khaṇḍā on *Baisākhī day 1699. See also AMRIT.

Chardin (French Jesuit theologian): see TEILHARD DE CHARDIN.

Chariot (of God, in Ezekiel's vision): see MERKABAH MYSTICISM.

Charismatic (movement). Christian belief that the *Holy Spirit imparts particular gifts and inspiration, which have visible and internally recognizable consequences. The Charismatic movement developed in the 1960s, beginning in an *episcopal church in North America, and soon spread to other denominations. Its roots lie in many different soils, in *Pentecostalism which had begun over fifty years previously, in a new understanding of the person and work of the Holy Spirit in the light of teaching from the holiness movement (see *Holiness Churches) of the 19th cent. (of e.g. John *Wesley) and in the influence of various individual figures. This move of the Holy Spirit in the historic denominations was characterized by experience of *'baptism in the Holy Spirit' or 'second baptism' and by a new informality in *liturgical worship, anticipation of the Second Coming of Christ, and renewed emphasis on the present reality of the gifts of the Spirit, especially *healing, *prophecy, and speaking in tongues (*glossolalia). The latter featured highly in the spread of the movement, but never became adopted as the distinguishing sign, or evidence of baptism in the Spirit, as it continues to be for Pentecostalism. Instead, 'charismatic renewal' emphasizes that the heart and the emotions should be just as much engaged in religion as the head and the intellect. There is great expectation on the dynamic and empowering presence of the Spirit, not only in personal holiness, but in the corporate gathering, leading to a new emphasis on encounter with God in and through the immanent presence of the Holy Spirit. The Charismatic movement has developed a distinct style of corporate worship particularly evident in its songs, in lay participation, and in styles of prayer. Many of these features have not remained confined to those who would identify themselves as Charismatics. At the end of the 1980s membership was estimated by D. B. Barrett at over 300 million people in 230 countries. The same survey estimated that the movement is growing annually at a rate of 19 million members. Many have stayed within the historic denominations, but a large minority, frustrated with the seeming lack of urgency felt by the denominations and the constraints placed upon them by formal liturgy etc., have begun their own denominations, generally called Independent or House churches. K. McDonnell characterized the movement as a prophetic movement whose major challenge is directed at the barrenness of traditional churches, which is due to a lack of expectancy of God's presence.

Charismatic renewal was endorsed by Pope Paul VI in 1973, and in a charismatic mass in St Peter's at Rome, in 1975, he urged charismatics everywhere to share the joy of the Holy Spirit with everyone.

P. Hocken, *Streams of Renewal: The Origins and Development of the Charismatic Movement* (1986); K. McDonnell (ed.), *Presence, Power, Praise: Documents on the Charismatic Renewal* (1980); J.-J. Suurmond, *Word and Spirit at Play: Towards a Charismatic Theology* (1994).

Charismatic authority. Type of leadership, not confined to religions, exercised by gifted individuals. It was defined by *Weber as 'a certain quality of an individual personality, by virtue of which he is considered as extraordinary and treated as endowed with supernatural, superhuman, or at least exceptional powers or qualities'. There may be a conflict between charismatic authority and hereditary (or elected) authority. A classic instance occurred at the death of *Muḥammad, when one party (that of *ʿAli) sought to establish a hereditary succession, while the majority sought to identify the most clearly qualified successor: the eventual result was the *Sunna/*Shiʿa divide in Islam.

Charity (Lat., *caritas*; Gk., *charis*). An openness and generosity to others, especially in the support of those in need. In all religions, charity is highly valued, usually with an emphasis on disinterestedness, but sometimes in a structure of mutual benefits (see also ALMSGIVING). In Judaism, the nearest Heb. word to express this concept is *ẓedekah*, linked to *ẓedek*, justice. In contrast to the wider *gemilut ḥasadim* ('acts of loving-kindness'), *ẓedekah* involves the obligation to give to the poor. The Bible emphasizes the duty of charity: 'You shall open wide your hand to your brother, to the needy and to the poor in the land' (Deuteronomy 15. 11) is only one example out of many. God himself 'executes justice for the fatherless and the widow, and loves the sojourner, giving him food and clothing' (Deuteronomy 10. 18), and the *prophets maintained that an acceptable day of the Lord was one in which the hungry were fed and the homeless housed (Isaiah 58. 7). In *talmudic times, *ẓedakah* was taken to indicate that the poor have a right to charity. It was said, 'the poor man does more for the householder [in accepting charity] than the householder does for the poor man' (*Lev.R.* 34. 8). The manner of giving was also important and, according to *Maimonides, the highest form of *ẓedakah* was to give in such a way that neither the donor nor the recipient knew each other's identity. The tradition of charitable giving continued in the Middle Ages until modern times through local, national, and international Jewish agencies. According to *B.Sukk.* 49b, 'There are three ways in which *gemilut ḥasadim* exceeds *ẓedekah*: *ẓ.* can be performed only with money, *g.ḥ.* with one's whole body as well; *ẓ.* is only for the poor, *g.ḥ.* for both poor and rich; *ẓ.* is for the living, *g.ḥ.* is for the living and the dead.' Charity is controlled by the thought, 'Never humiliate a beggar: God is beside him.'

In Christianity, charity came in English to be associated with the deeply characteristic virtue of *agape, through the Authorized Version translation of 1 Corinthians 13: 'Though I speak with the tongues of men and of angels, and have not charity, I am become as sounding brass, or a tinkling cymbal . . .. And now abideth faith, hope, charity, these three; but the greatest of these is charity.'

In Islam, charity is formalized through *zakāt, but generosity (*sadaqāt*) to those in need is meritorious, as are other gifts to support religious purposes (see WAQF). See e.g. Qur'ān 17. 24/25 ff.

In Hinduism, the nearest equivalents to charity lie in the obligations of *dharma: acts of charity will lead to good *karma. In Buddhism, the alleviation of *dukkha (suffering) is equally indispensable for progress toward the ultimate goal. It lies in the expression of *metta/maitri (generous kindness), *karuṇā (compassion), and *muditā (active approval and support of good deeds, such as caring for the sick). In *dāna, a mutual structure of support is established between laypeople and the *saṅgha (community of monks).

Charms and amulets. These are universal, in all religions, even those where they might be expected to compromise trust in God alone. In Judaism, an amulet might seem to come close to breaking the command against graven images. Yet so many charms were excavated from the rabbinic period that it almost seemed to some that they were observing an alternative Judaism. In fact amulets, seeking to encapsulate the need for help, are a simple necessity in popular and folk religion; and a distinction was made between those which are, and those which are not, *mi-darke ha-Emori*, 'of the ways of the Amorites' (involve recognition of gods or powers other than God). Amulets (Heb., *kemea*) continued as a part of Judaism, worn round the neck or attached to a wall. They have to be written or made by a holy person, expert in *kabbalah. Various decorations, such as the star of David (*magen), triangles, a hand or kabbalistic letters, were used. They may be to protect against devils, thieves, or enemies, to obtain love, wisdom, or an easy childbirth. Intellectuals like *Maimonides denounced them as empty superstitions, but that did not affect their use, and such authorities as Solomon ben Abraham *Adret and *Naḥmanides accepted them.

Similarly, in Islam amulets might be expected to be suspect, as derogating from the absolute authority of *Allāh to determine all things as he wills. But in fact, amulets (Arab., *ḥijab*, *ḥamā'il*; in W. Africa *gri gri*) are permitted in *ḥadīth, and are used everywhere in the Muslim world. Usually, they contain passages of the *Qur'ān, but they may also contain (especially in Africa) names of protective spirits or angels; cf. also HAND OF FĀṬIMA.

In other religions, amulets are equally common and less surprising. Thus in Hinduism, the way in which all appearance is permeated by the spiritual and the divine makes the amulet (Skt., *rakṣa*; from *rakṣ*, 'guard, protect') entirely natural. Even the infant *Kṛṣṇa needed one (which was given to him by Yaśodā) to protect him from the evils which are inherent in the Hindu cosmos.

Amulets are an equally indispensable part of Chinese folk religion. They are generally rectangular paper sheets containing written commands and symbols to warn away evil influences. Frequently pasted over doorways, they may also be worn, or else burnt, with the ashes being used to make a medicinal paste or drink. Charms are used for many purposes associated with the exorcism of evil spirits, such as healing illness, or disturbed mental states, or social relationships; protecting persons and property; for wealth, long life, and a prestigious career; and to influence the fate of children, new ventures, gambling, etc. While standard charms can be readily bought, special ones are written out by a Taoist or Buddhist priest or, in some areas, a temple *shaman, who, in trance, draws blood with which to inscribe them. Often styled as imperial edicts, charms issue from the highest gods of the popular pantheon or invoke the jurisdiction of deities with specialized functions. Some *Confucian Classics and other religious books can act as charms, a belief based in part on the positive power traditionally ascribed to the written word itself. As instruments of exorcism, protection, and command over seasonal pestilences, the use of charms is recorded in China's oldest written records.

Charoset (Jewish food): see ḤAROSET.

Charvaka (school of Indian materialism): see CĀRVĀKA.

Chasidim (members of Jewish devotional movement): see ḤASIDIM.

Chasuble. The outermost vestment, usually richly decorated, worn by the celebrant at the Christian *eucharist. It is derived from the outer cloak worn in the Graeco-Roman world (the *paenula*, cf. Gk., *phelonion*, the corresponding Orthodox vestment). It is worn in Roman Catholic, and some Anglican and Lutheran churches.

Chaturvarga-chintāmanī: see HÉMĀDRĪ.

Chaupad (Pañjābī, 'Four stanzas'). A poem of four stanzas. In the *Ādi Granth, the Gurūs' chaupads, plus some *hymns of two, three, five, and six stanzas, are grouped first in each *rāg, followed by the *aṣṭapadīs.

Chaupaī (Pañjābī, 'verse of four lines'). Sikh hymn; specifically, the Bentī Chaupaī or hymn of supplication, a composition of Gurū *Gobind Siṅgh which is included in the *Dasam Granth. As part of *Rahirās it is repeated by devout Sikhs each evening. The Lord of the universe is begged for his protection.

Chaur(ī). Indian symbol of authority, now typically Sikh. A chaurī is a ceremonial whisk made of the tail hair of a white horse or yak embedded in a wooden or silver handle. Hindu gods and kings are depicted fanned by the chaurī, and medieval Indian guilds carried these insignia. A chaurī is kept beside the *Ādi Granth. It is waved above it as a sign of respect.

Cheese Sunday. Amongst Greek Orthodox Christians, the last Sunday before *Lent on which cheese and eggs may be eaten. It is also known as Forgiveness Sunday, when, after Vespers, members of the congregation turn and bow to each other, saying, 'Forgive me, a sinner', and replying, 'God forgives us', thereby effecting reconciliation before the start of Lent. The equivalent Sunday in the West is *Quinquagesima.

Ch'eng (sincerity): see CHUNG YUNG.

Ch'eng-chu (Chinese philosopher): see CHU HSI.

Ch'eng Hao, also **Ming-tao** (1032–85). Brother of Ch'eng Yi (or I, also I-ch'uan, 1033–1107), with whom he formed the neo-Confucianism of the Sung dynasty. They came from the family of a government official and were educated at the national university at Kaifeng. Both of them opposed the far-reaching reform programme of Wang An-shih (Wang Anshi) (1021–86): Ch'eng Hao was dismissed in 1080 and went into retirement in Lo-yang; Cheng Yi was not in an official post until 1086, when he served as imperial tutor. His severity led to his transfer to a minor post. In 1093, the reform programme was reinstated and he was banished in 1097 to Szechwan: his teaching was prohibited, and it was ordered that his books should be burnt. Although the two brothers shared much in common in their outlook, especially the emphasis on *li as the foundation of their goal, a moral and virtuous life, they nevertheless made distinct contributions to the development of neo-Confucian thought. Ch'eng Hao took a strongly holistic view, emphasizing the unity of the cosmos: the goal of the person of *jen must be to achieve harmony with that wholeness, by overcoming the habit of making distinctions and by returning the life-force (*ch'i) to that moral and emotional neutrality which was its state at birth. As a consequence of this, a transcendentally powerful quality (*shen) is developed. In Ch'eng Hao's view, human nature does not change from one age to another, so that reform must be, not to innovate, but to recover 'the laws established by the wise kings of old, which were based on human feelings and were in harmony with the order of things'.

Ch'eng Yi, in contrast, believed that true insight can be achieved only by the minute analysis of all things, in order to discover their fundamental constitution and thus the part that each plays in the whole: 'Each blade of grass and the branch of every tree possesses li, and should be examined for it.' It does not follow that *everything* must be examined before anything can be understood: the patterns and principles can be inferred from samples.

A. C. Graham, *Two Chinese Philosophers . . .* (1958).

Ch'eng-huang. Chinese gods who protect a city, and who guide the souls (*hun, *p'o) of the dead out of torment.

Ch'eng I: see CH'ENG HAO.

Cheng-i tao (Chin., Tao of unity). The collective term for Taoist schools who use *fu-lu (talismans) or amulets (*charms). Having their roots in *wu-tou-mi tao and *ling-pao p'ai, they were drawn together (somewhat) in the 14th cent. CE. Magical skills are passed on by direct inheritance, and the practitioners have a powerful position in popular religion—extensively in Hong Kong and Taiwan; probably still in China, but information is scarce. The other major form of religious Taoism is *Ch'üan-chen tao.

Cheng-kuan (teacher in Hua-yen Buddhism): see HUA-YEN.

Ch'eng-shih (teacher): see SAUTRĀNTIKAS.

Cheng-yi (Taoist movement): see WU-TOU-MI TAO.

Ch'eng Yi: see CH'ENG HAO.

Chen jen (Chin., 'perfected' or 'true man'). A term used by both Buddhists and Taoists in China to denote a person who has achieved the highest religious ideal. The term was used by Buddhists as a translation of the Skt. *arhat, 'perfected one', a follower of the *Buddha who had extinguished desire and uprooted ignorance. In Taoism it has moral qualities (see TE), and it also denotes one class among the 'immortals' (*hsien) who had achieved the arduous goal of sloughing off mortality and who henceforth took their place in a vast bureaucratic hierarchy of celestial officials. The characteristics of the chen jen of old are described in **Chuang-tzu*, ch. 6. See also PA HSIEN.

Chenrezi (bodhisattva): see AVALOKITEŚVARA.

Ch'en T'uan (10th cent. CE). Taoist scholar of both outer and inner *alchemy, who lived on Mount Hua-shan as a hermit. On the face of the rock he carved the diagram of the supreme emptying, the ultimateless (*wu-ch'i-tu*). He is also reputed to have originated the other diagram of great importance to neo-Confucians, the diagram of the immortal heaven (*hsien-t'ien-tu*).

Chen-yen (Chinese Esoteric Buddhism): see BUDDHISM IN CHINA; SHINGON.

Cherub (from Heb., *keruv*). A winged heavenly creature. In the Bible cherubim appear as guards at the gate of the garden of *Eden (Genesis 3. 24), as gold figures to form the throne of God on the *Ark of the *Covenant (Exodus 25. 18–20), as decoration in *Solomon's *Temple (e.g. 1 Kings 6. 29), as a figure in a *parable told by *Ezekiel (Ezekiel 28. 13 f.), and as a mount for God (e.g. 2 Samuel 22. 11). There were no cherubim in the second Temple and, by this era, according to *Josephus, no one knew what they were like.

Cherubic hymn or **Cherubikon.** The hymn, probably of the 6th cent., sung at the *Great Entrance in the Orthodox liturgy. It begins, 'Let us, who mystically represent the cherubim, and sing the holy hymn to the life-giving Trinity, now lay aside all earthly cares.'

Chhant (Pañjābī, 'poem, song'). In the *Ādi Granth, the chhants are *hymns between a *chaupad and an *aṣṭapadī in length, i.e. usually four stanzas of six lines. Within each *rāg the chhants follow the aṣṭapadīs and precede the *vārs.

Ch'i (Chin., 'air, breath, strength'). The vital energy (in Chinese religion, medicine and philosophy) which pervades and enables all things. Beginning from the elementary observation that the secret of a long life is to keep on breathing, it underlies the central Chinese, especially Taoist, concern with breathing exercises in relation to prolonging life and attaining immortality. 'Nourishing the life spirit' (*yang ch'i*) by a variety of exercises, including diet, *breath control, and sexual control, became pervasive. It is thus closely associated with *yüan-ch'i and *nei-ch'i*. It is gathered in the human body in the 'ocean of breath' (*ch'i-hai*) just below the navel, where it must be carefully fostered, especially through breathing practices, above all *hsing-ch'i*, which allows the breath/energy to permeate the whole body, by imagining the breath as a visible line or lines moving through the body; or *t'ai-hsi* which reverts one's breathing to that of an embryo or foetus in the womb, and which, by transferring ordinary breathing (outer ch'i or *wai-ch'i*) to dependent but directed breathing, is powerful in leading to cures and immortality (see ALCHEMY). The harnessing of ch'i through breathing practices is thus indispensable to Taoist life, and to its understanding of what constitutes all manifest appearance: the cosmos is an expression of Tao, in which ch'i is brought into the balance of *yin-yang. Their separation brought heaven and earth into being, their reunion in different degrees or patterns of association brings 'the ten thousand things' (*wan-wu*)—i.e. the totality of all entities and creatures—into being: 'In the beginning there was only the One, before heaven and earth were separated. When this One was divided, yin and yang came into being. That which received *yang-ch'i* rose light and clear, and became heaven; that which received *yin-ch'i* sank dark and heavy, and became earth; that which received both in right balance became human' (M. Miyuki, *Die Erfahrung der goldenen Blüte* (1984), 185). Medically, ch'i was developed into the exercises of *ch'i-kung*, also known as outer exercises (*wai-kung*). See also FU-CH'I; LIEN-CH'I; T'IAO-CH'I; YEN CH'I.

J. Needham, *Science and Civilization in China*, ii (1956).

Chiang-I (Taoist ritual dress): see HABIT, RELIGIOUS.

Chiang Kai-shek (1887–1975). Military and political leader of the Chinese Kuomintang party and the Nationalist government on mainland China and Taiwan. As a young anti-Ch'ing radical, Chiang participated in the 1911 Republican Revolution and became a trusted follower and colleague of Sun Yat-sen, father of the Chinese Revolution. Despite his early association with members of the Communist party and education abroad in the Soviet Union, after 1926 Chiang Kai-shek turned decisively against the communists and became, in fact, one of the most prominent spokesmen of anti-communism in Asia. With the military success of his great Northern Expedition (1926–8), Chiang gained recognition throughout the world as the official leader of the Chinese republic. In order to foster national unity, Chiang Kai-shek promoted in 1934 the New Life Movement, which emphasized cardinal virtues both of the Confucian tradition and of the Christian faith, to which he had converted. During the period 1937–45, Chiang's primary concern was Japanese aggression in China and the Allied cause in the Second World War. With the defeat of Japan in 1945, his primary problems became national reconstruction and the rising influence and military might of Mao Tse-tung. The success of Mao's Red Army forced Chiang in 1949 to flee for refuge to the island of Taiwan. Although never able to realize his dream of regaining control of the mainland, and thus unifying China, Chiang Kai-shek was able to establish on Taiwan a stable and relatively prosperous Republic of China based on a constitutional democracy. He was, therefore, a major figure in 20th-cent. history and a symbol of the Chinese will to become a respected, powerful, and self-determining modern nation.

Chiao (teaching): see CHINESE RELIGION.

Chiao (Chin., 'sacrifice'). Originally a wine offering (or 'toast') at the coming of age of a son, or at a wedding. Later it became a more general ritual offering among Taoists for a wide range of purposes (e.g. to ward off illness, to protect from fire, to bring peace or to procure blessings). The offerings are made to the Three Supreme (or Pure) Ones, *San Ch'ing, rather than to local or popular deities. The Chiao offering is related to *nei-tan, the inner alchemy, since it realizes the energies of the macrocosm, in the microcosm of the celebrant's body. Chiao continues at least in Taiwan.

M. Saso, *Taoism and the Rite of Cosmic Renewal* (1972).

Chicago-Lambeth Quadrilateral (basis for ecumenicism): see ANGLICANISM.

Chief Khālsā Dīwān. Religio-political Sikh association, Amritsar. Established in 1902 as an offshoot of the *Siṅgh Sabhā movement, the Chief Khālsā Dīwān strove for the betterment of all Sikhs, especially through improved education.

Chief Rabbi. Central religious authority among Jews for a region. In the Middle Ages, it was not uncommon for a king to appoint a chief rabbi to act as intermediary between himself and the community. Hasdai *Crescas, for example, served as Chief Rabbi of Aragon, and *Meir b. Baruch of Rothenburg was appointed for the Holy Roman Empire. The office has existed in England since the mid-18th cent., and Israel has both a *Ashkenazi and a *Sephardi chief rabbi. In the USA, Jacob Joseph was chief rabbi of Orthodox communities in New York (1888–1902), but there was no continuation of the office.

Ch'ieh-lan, abbreviation of *ch'ieh-lan shen*, spirits of the *ch'ieh-lan* (monastic premises; Sanskrit: *saṅghārāma*). As tutelary deities of Chinese Buddhist monasteries, these spirits received prayers at appointed times of the day, and sometimes had shrines or halls dedicated to them within the monastery grounds. Best known among them was Kuan Kung, the red-faced god of war.

Chien ai (universal love): see JEN.

Chien-chen (Chinese Buddhist master): see GANJIN.

Ch'ien tzu wen (Chin., 'Thousand-Character Text'). An important Chinese primer for children written by Chou Hsing-te in the 6th cent. CE.

Chigū (Jap., 'rare encounter'). An encounter with a *buddha or with the *Buddha's teaching. Chigu ketsuen is the action of a Buddhist when opportunity presents itself which brings other people to accept the teaching of the Buddha for themselves.

Chih (Cardinal virtue in Confucianism): see WU-CH'ANG.

Ch'i-hai (ocean of breath): see CH'I.

Chih-i or **Chih-che** (538–97). The third patriarch, but in effect founder, of the *T'ien-t'ai Buddhist school in China (his Jap. name is Chigi Chisha). He showed special gifts as a child (e.g. on hearing a *sūtra once he could repeat it; or he could see events in the past). He entered a monastery to become a pupil of Hui-ssu (second patriarch). In 576 he withdrew to Mount T'ien-t'ai (hence the name of the school), where his fame attracted to him the title 'man of wisdom', *chih-che*. He completed the first organized system of Buddhist teaching in China, and developed the practice of *chih-kuan* (Jap. *shikan*), as extensively practised still as his works on meditation are widely read: e.g. *Liu-miao famen* (The Six Marvellous Gates of Dharma), *T'ung-meng chih-kuan* (Chih-Kuan for Beginners). It was thought that it was he who proposed the systematization of Buddhism in China as '*five periods and eight schools', but this may in fact have been a later classification. Nevertheless, he clearly achieved a remarkable synthesis of Buddhist teaching.

L. N. Hurvitz, *Chih-i . . .* (1962).

Chih-kuan (Skt., śamatha-*vipaśyanā; Jap., *shikan*). Meditation methods in the *T'ien-t'ai Buddhist school. 'Chih' is the calming of the restless and distracted mind; 'Kuan' is the insight which then arises. Established by *Chih-i, there are two parts: the first is preparation, especially the overcoming of hindrances (*nīvaraṇa) through the control of the body and its functions, and of the six sense organs. Kuan is the turning inward of the mind to become aware of its total absence of form, which leads to the realization of *śūnyatā.

Chih-tun or **Chih Tao-lin** (314–66). Founder of the Prajña (wisdom) School of Chinese Buddhism. His particular importance was his adaptation of Chinese concepts in a Buddhist direction, thereby enabling the rapid assimilation of Buddhism into China. Thus *li is a basic concept of order in the cosmos and in society. Chih-tun took it to be the fundamental givenness or 'being-such-as-it-isness' (*tathatā) of Mahāyāna Buddhism. He paid particular attention to **Chuang-tzu*, seeing it as a kind of *praeparatio Buddhica*.

Chijang. Korean for *Kṣitigarbha.

Chijō tengoku (heaven on earth): see SEKAI KYŪSEIKYŌ.

Chikamatsu Monzaemon (1653–1724). Playwright for the Kabuki theatre and puppet theatre (Jap., *ningyō jōruri* or *bunraku*), generally regarded as Japan's greatest dramatist. Though involved in the composition of about thirty Kabuki plays, Chikamatsu's reputation rests primarily on the nearly 100 plays he composed for the puppet theatre. Chikamatsu wrote plays with both historical and contemporary settings but is remembered largely for his works in the latter category which provide a view of the life of the various social classes, especially that of merchants and artisans, of Tokugawa society. The plays are deeply imbued with the teachings of both Confucianism and Buddhism. A major theme of almost all of them concerns the conflict between social obligation (*giri*) and human feelings (*ninjō*) within the context of the Confucian ethical structure of Tokugawa society. Most of Chikamatsu's characters are also followers of *Pure Land Buddhism. The plays dealing with love suicides, for instance, end with the characters committing suicide with the hope of being reborn together in *Amida's Pure Land. In addition to a wide range of general Buddhist notions such as *karma, the plays also depict a variety of notions, practices, and figures connected with *Shinto and Japanese folk religion.

Eng. tr. D. Keene (1961); *Bunraku: The Art of the Japanese Puppet Theatre* (1965).

Ch'i-kung (breathing exercises): see CH'I.

Children of God or **The Family.** A *cult founded in California in 1968 by David Berg (1919–94), who assumed the name David, and became known to his followers as Mo. The movement established a number of communes in the USA before moving to London in 1971. The movement grew rapidly: by the mid-1970s it had set up 185 communes in sixty different countries; by 1995 the estimated membership was made up of *c.*12,000 communes. The Family (the name 'Children of God' was given to it by a journalist) claims to be a truly Christian movement which now has guidance (in addition to the Bible) in the Mo letters (written by the founder) which are regarded as the equivalent of the letters of *Paul in the early Church. According to The Family, humanity is now living in the last days and the signs of the Second Coming of *Jesus are evident: the destruction of the materialistic culture of capitalism will follow that of communism (predicted by Mo), to be replaced with a 'godly socialism', with an emphasis (borrowed from *Acts) on sharing. This extends to the sharing of sexual partners, which includes the use of sex to attract new members (known as 'flirty fishing'). Reports of this led to strong opposition to The Family, which was accused also of encouraging and practising the abuse of children. However, no successful prosecutions were sustained (although children were taken into care in several countries, including Australia and France); and in 1995, a UK High Court judgement refused the claim of a grandmother to remove her grandson from one of its communes, on the grounds that the movement had eradicated the sexual excesses of the past, had begun to eradicate inappropriate forms of discipline, and had become more open and less of a closed society.

Chiliasm (Gk., *chilioi*, 'a thousand'). Another name for *millennialism, the theory that Christ will reign for a thousand years before the final consummation of all things.

Chimere. A silk or satin gown without sleeves worn over the rochet by *Anglican *bishops, both in church (though not with eucharistic *vestments) and on full-dress occasions.

Ch'in (musical instrument): see MUSIC.

China and Tibet (as 'patron and priest'): see 'PHAGS-PA.

Chinese religion. Religion in China is not a single system of belief and practice. It is a complex interaction of different religious and philosophical traditions, of which four main strands (themselves by no means uniform) are particularly important: popular or folk religion (vivid with festivals, spirit-worlds, procedures in crises, and care of the dead), *Confucianism, *Taoism, and Buddhism (see BUDDHISM IN CHINA). In addition, Islam and Christianity have substantial followings in different parts of China, but they are distinguished from the others by appearing to the Chinese to require separation from the other religions/philosophies. In contrast, the Chinese in general have no problem in being entirely eclectic, being, for example, a Confucian in public life, a Taoist in the quest for immortality, a Buddhist in relation to ancestors, and dependent on folk wisdom in crisis or illness, or when buying a house. Thus religion is defined more by cultural geography than it is by bounded systems of beliefs and practices (though schools or traditions of teaching were formally organized).

There is no exact equivalent in Chinese for the word 'religion' (i.e. the characteristics which have evoked that word; cf. Introduction). *Men* means 'door', i.e. door leading to enlightenment, immortality, etc.; *tao* means 'way', and both are used. But more usual now is *chiao*, 'teaching', 'guiding doctrine' (as in *fo-chiao*, the religion of the Buddha; *ju-chiao*, the way of Confucius; *tao-chiao*, religious Taoism), usually in combination with *tsung*, 'ancestral, traditional', 'devotion, faith': *tsung-chiao*, the nearest equivalent to 'religion'.

Traditionally, religious history in China has been divided into four stages named after the seasons of spring, summer, autumn, and winter. The foundations in the Spring period are largely legendary, but can be discerned archaeologically in the *oracle bone divinations of the rulers of the Shang dynasty *c.*1300 BCE. From *c.*1100 to 206, the Six Ways developed which constitute some of the main themes of Chinese religious history. The historian Ssu-ma Tan (d. 110 BCE) summarized them as complementary, but the rivalries and distinctions could in fact be severe (and he himself was leading to the conclusion that Taoism is the best):

> The Commentary on *The Book of Changes* [see *I ching*] says: 'There is one moving force, but from it come a hundred thoughts and plans. They have the same objective but different ways to it.' They all seek good government, but teach and follow different ways. . . . The *yin-yang school emphasises omens and the things to be avoided, thus binding people in fear; but its organisation of the four seasons is essential. The followers of *Confucius deal with broad issues but lack attention to detail, but its rules of behaviour between lord and subject and father and son, and its distinctions between husband and wife and the older and

the younger cannot be changed. The followers of *Mo-tzu are too stern in parsimony, but their emphasis on basic life-essentials and on being frugal must be observed. The Legalists [Fa-chia: they advocated deterrent law and punishment, especially in Han Fei Tzu, and in his work of that name, often compared to Machiavelli's *The Prince*; in Fa-chia, the Tao is simply the working out of power politics: the past is not revered as a repository of wisdom, as it was for Confucius and Mo Tzu: what matters is how the ruler exercises 'the two handles' of reward and punishment] are strict and unmerciful, but they maintain the distinctions between superior and inferior which cannot be changed. The Logicians are precise in reasoning but often miss the truth, but the way they distinguish between names and what is real must be kept in mind. The Taoists teach people to live with spiritual focus and to act in harmony with the unseen: their teaching covers all that is necessary.

The Summer flowering (206 BCE–900 CE) saw the introduction of Buddhism into China. Buddhism in general attempted not to supplant the religious and cultural world which it encountered, but rather to show the correspondences between Chinese and Buddhist concepts, even though it was claiming a better way to the realization of the goal. Equally, Buddhism learnt much from China, and took on forms very different from those of India and *Theravāda. Taoism was extended to take increasing control of the rituals of popular religion, leaving Confucianism with a comparable control over the ethics and organization of political and social life.

The Autumn period runs until the end of the imperial system of government in 1912. It is regarded as a period of reformation, with many attempts to recover the authentic nature of Chinese religion. It is a period characterized, therefore, by increasing individualism, not least in the setting up of movements and secret societies, many of which were deliberately syncretistic.

The Winter period of decline and subjection to persecution after the accession of the Communists to power is not regarded as the final chapter of a story, but rather as the prelude to rebirth. The tenacity of religion at the local level has been obvious and ineradicable.

W. T. de Bary (ed.), *Sources of Chinese Tradition* (1960); J. Ching, *Chinese Religions* (1993); L. G. Thompson, *Studies of Chinese Religion: A Comprehensive and Classified Bibliography* (1976), *Chinese Religion in Western Languages* . . . (1984), and *Chinese Religion* (1979); J. F. Pas (ed.), *The Turning of the Tide: Religion in China Today* (1989); C. K. Yang, *Religion in Chinese Society* (1967); D. C. Yu, *Guide to Chinese Religion* (1985).

Chinese Rites Controversy. A dispute in the Roman Catholic Church about the propriety of adopting Chinese customs and terms into Christian liturgy and vocabulary. *Jesuit missionaries (see especially RICCI, MATTEO) had attempted to build a bridge into Chinese culture for the purposes of evangelism. An investigation in 1693 led to the Apostolic Constitution of Clement XI, *Ex illa die*, in 1715, which forbade these practices. Disputes continued over implementation until Benedict XIV reaffirmed the earlier decision in 1742. Cf. also MALABAR RITES.

Chinese Tripiṭaka (Chin., *San-ts'ang*, 'Triple Treasury', or *Ta Ts'ang-ching*, 'Great Treasury of Scriptures'). The collection of *Buddhist scriptures in Chinese. Although known as Tripiṭaka (Skt., 'Triple Basket') it is not divided into three major collections as is the Pāli *Tripiṭaka. It contains versions of most of the texts found in the Tripiṭaka with the addition of *Mahāyāna *sūtras , commentaries, histories, biographies, encyclopaedias, and even some non-Buddhist writings. The number of texts is not fixed and there are often multiple versions, especially of translations of sūtras. Native Chinese lineages such as the *T'ien-t'ai treat the Tripiṭaka more as a library than a *canon and select certain texts to be studied in a certain order, choosing one or more as containing the most exalted teaching. Various editions have appeared since the 1st printed edn. in 10th cent. CE. The most commonly used is the *Taishō Shinshū Daizōkyō* (Tokyo, 1924–9 and reprs.) containing 2,184 texts in 55 vols. In 1982 the State Council of the Peoples' Republic of China established the Chinese Tripitaka Editorial Bureau, charged with producing a new version, which is projected to contain 4,100 texts in 220 vols.

Ching (Chin., 'semen'). One of the three life forces in Taoism, the others being *ch'i (breath) and *shen (conscious mind). Ching is both semen and the menstrual flow, not so much in their literal manifestation, as in the power inherent in them. Loss of ching is debilitating, and many Taoist practices encourage control (especially for men), as well as increase of it: see FANG-CHUNG SHU.

Ch'ing-ming (Chin., 'clear and bright'). The fifth of the twenty-four periods of the Chinese solar *calendar. It is also the name of the festival which is additionally called 'the sweeping of the tombs': families sweep and tidy the graves of ancestors, offering food to them—and afterwards consuming food with them near the site.

W. Eberhard, *Chinese Festivals* (1952).

Ch'ing-t'an (Chin., 'pure conversation'). The cultivation in China among the educated or literati or erudite and philosophical conversation. Sometimes referred to as a 'neo-Taoist school', they were in fact a tradition, embracing more than neo-Taoists (e.g. Buddhists), even though they were generally inspired and influenced by the transcendental tendencies of neo-Taoism. Thus they could regard K'ung-tzu (*Confucius) as a greater Taoist than, for example, *Chuang-tzu, because he knew the state of *wu of which Chuang-tzu could only write. They flourished between the 3rd and 6th cents. CE, and among many groups, the Seven Sages of the Bamboo Grove were especially famous.

Ching-te Ch'uan-teng-lu (The Passing on of the Lamp; Jap., *Keito-ku Dentō-roku*). An early work (1004) of Ch'an/*Zen Buddhism, describing the history, via biographies, of the transmission of enlightenment, up to *Fa-yen Wen-i, founder of the *Hōgen school. With sayings and biographies of more than a thousand teachers/masters, it contains the earliest forms of many *kōans.

Chang Chung-yuan, *Original Teachings* ... (1969) contains selections in translation.

Ching-t'u (Chin., Jap. *jōdo*). *Pure Land, or the untainted transcendent realm created by the *Buddha Amitābha (*Amida) to which his devotees aspire to be born in their next lifetime. Ching-t'u Tsung is thus the Pure Land School.

Chinju (Jap., *chin*, 'to pacify' + *ju*, 'a lord': to protect). A Japanese tutelary shrine, temple, or deity. Originally the chinju was the lord or master of a settlement area; the term came to refer to the apotheosized leader's spirit (chinju no *kami), whose guardianship ensured peace and prosperity for a village or district. Though in principle the chinju no kami is distinct from both the *ujigami and *ubusuna no kami*, in practice the meanings often merge, with usage depending on local custom. As a verb, chinju is the act of establishing and maintaining a secure defensive perimeter, and by extension the area thus secured. Early on, then, it designated an area where safe commerce was guaranteed by both politico-military authority and religious sanction. The religious element of this 'sanctuary' notion led to its standard meaning of 'tutelary'.

Chin-lien (Golden Lotus): see CH'ÜAN-CHEN TAO.

Chinnamasta ('the headless'). A Tantric Hindu form of *Durgā. She is the fifth *mahāvidya who represents the end of life, especially when a sacrificial victim is beheaded. The Buddhist Tantric equivalent is Vajrayoginī, who is also depicted iconographically without a head. She is of particular importance in *abhicāra* (magic ritual) directed to the injury of enemies, or to other maleficent ends.

Chin-tan (Chin., 'golden cinnabar'). The elixir of immortality in Taoist *alchemy, the transferred equivalent of the 'medicine of immortality' (*pharmakon athanasias*) in Christianity, i.e. the *eucharist.

Chinul (1158–1210). Reformer of Sŏn (Ch'an/*Zen) and revitalizer of *Buddhism in Korea during the Koryŏ period (935–1392). Chinul, known also as National Teacher, Puril Pojo ('Universal Illuminator of Buddha-sun'), integrated the nine lineages ('Nine Mountains') of Sŏn Buddhism into the Chogye order and synthesized Sŏn and Hwaŏm (Hua-yen) placing primacy upon the former. His teaching of 'sudden enlightenment and gradual practice' (*tono-chŏmsu*) became central to Sŏn in Korea.

See further (with trs.) R. E. Buswell, *The Korean Approach to Zen* (1983); H. S. Keel, *Chinul* (1985).

Chinzei. A school of Jōdo (*Pure Land) founded by Benchō. He was a pupil of *Hōnen, who then returned to his home in Kyushu and built Zendōji as a centre for training in *nembutsu. Of its many subsequent sub-divisions, Shirahata-ryū is the strongest continuing group, often regarded as the main-line continuity of Jōdo. Its centre is Chion-in, but Zōjōji in Tokyo is of particular importance. It survived the raids of the Second World War, but the garden is reconstructed; the golf-driving range is built over the burial ground of the Tokugawa Shoguns.

Chi-Rho. The Greek letters X and P, being the first two letters of the word *Christos*, 'Christ'. It was an ancient abbreviation of the name. Since the 4th cent. it has been a common monogram. It first appeared, in the form ☧, on the *Labarum standard of *Constantine. The form ⳩, assimilated to a cross, is also an early variant.

Chironomy (hand gestures in cantillation): see MUSIC.

Chisha: see CHIH-I.

Chishti, Mu'īn al-Dīn Muḥammad (1142–1236 (AH 537–633)). Indian Sūfī, who mediated an important order (*tarīqa) into India. He was much influenced by *Abd al-Qādir—who, as a traditionalist, once said, 'My foot is on the head of every holy man.' Chishti emphasized fear of *hell-fire as an important constraint in religious life, but he also encouraged *music and chant since 'song is the support and the sustenance of the soul'. The Sūfī movement derived from him, the Chishti(y)ya, continues to make music central: it developed the *qawwālī* (singers) whose songs of love and devotion to *Allāh are a feature of holidays and festivals. He died at Ajmer, and his tomb is a celebrated place of pilgrimage.

The name 'Chishti' is derived from Chisht in Persia, pointing to the earlier history of the tarīqa. It traces its line back to *Ḥasan al-Basra, but a key figure was Khawjah abu Ishāq (d. 940), who was born in Chisht.

Chishtiy(y)a: see CHISHTI.

Chi-tsang (549–623). Buddhist teacher of the *San-lun school, who wrote many commentaries on *Sūtras and *Mahāyāna texts. He entered the San-lun monastery at the age of 7 (or perhaps 10) and studied, under Fa-lang, *Mādhyamaka texts. He contributed particularly to the 'two truths' of Mādhyamaka analysis, the relative truth which must be grasped only as a necessary step to absolute or transcendent truth. Thus relative truth affirms existence; but properly understood, the nature of existence (*śūnyatā) demands the affirmation of non-existence. The relative truth of the excluded middle (either existence or non-existence) leads to the realization that both are required. Thus, the same relative truth might seem to require either the affirmation or the denial of both existence and non-existence; but spiritual insight enables one to see that neither affirmation nor denial is required. In this way, Chi-tsang built up the *Middle Way, where nothing is affirmed and nothing denied. '"It is existent, it is non-existent": that is two-fold affirmation. "It is not existent, it is not not-existent": that is two-fold negation. But to fall into affirmation and negation is to fall backward to *Confucius and *Mo Tzu . . . Two-fold affirmation begets a tiger in a dream, two-fold negation conjures up a flower in the air. Since originally there is nothing to affirm, there cannot subsequently be anything to negate' (*San-lun hsüan-i*). Of immense importance in the development of San-lun (Chin. for Mādhyamaka), Chi-tsang's pupil, Ekwan, took the San-lun school to Japan, where it is known as *Sanron.

Chöd or **gcod** (Tib., *gcod*, 'cutting'). A *meditation prominent in *Tibetan Buddhism, which is traced to the great female *yoginī Machig Labdron (*ma.gcig lab.sgron) and her teacher Father Dampa Sangye (pha.dam.pa.sangs.rgyas; equated in one legend with *Bodhidharma). The meditation is normally performed in a charnel ground or known haunted place, where the *yogin, with the aid of *mantra, hand-drum and human thigh-bone trumpet, *visualizes the cutting up of his own body and the offering of it to demons as sacrificial food. Three purposes are served by the correct practice of chöd: the development of fearlessness, the development of compassion to all beings, even demons, and the development of the yogin's insight into his own intrinsic non-existence (*śūnyatā). The practitioners of chöd once constituted a monastic tradition in their own right, but their teachings are now principally absorbed within the *Kagyü and *Nyingma traditions. However, there are still chöd yogins who separate themselves from monasteries, living wild, and behaving in unconventional ways. On a folk level, they are attributed with strange powers, and are likely to be called upon in matters such as *exorcism.

Chödrug: see NARO CHOS DRUG.

Ch'oe Che-u (founder of Tonghak): see KOREAN RELIGION.

Chogye (Buddhist sect): see BUDDHISM IN KOREA.

Chōhōji (Japanese temple): see ROKKAKUDŌ.

Choir. Singers assisting in worship. Known in Christianity from the 4th cent., they customarily sang the music which was too difficult for the congregation. Lay singers began to augment choirs in *c.*15th cent., and by the 18th cent. the singers were often skilled professionals. The *liturgical movement has, however, emphasized the role of the choir in leading the singing of the congregation. The *rubric in the **Book of Common Prayer*, 'In quires and places where they sing, here followeth the Anthem', is a reminder of the extensive contribution of the *Church of England to the development of choirs and choral music, not least in chanting of *psalms.

Choka (Jap., 'morning part'). The Zen Buddhist morning *sūtra recitation, part of the daily routine in a Zen monastery (*tera).

Cholent ('stew'). Traditionally a Jewish housewife would prepare cholent in advance and put it in the oven before the *Sabbath began. It cooked slowly overnight and thus provided something hot to eat on Sabbath morning without breaking the Sabbath law against kindling a light or cooking.

Ch'ŏndo-gyo or **Ch'ŏndo-kyo** (Sect of the Way of Heaven): see KOREAN RELIGION.

Chorepiscopus. In E. churches, a minister intermediate in rank between *priest and *bishop. In modern times it is practically an honorary title. In the early church, however, the chorepiscopus was the bishop of a country (Gk., *chōra*) district, subject to a diocesan bishop, and unable to ordain (except perhaps to the lowest orders).

Chōrō (Jap., 'elder'). A title of respect for a senior monk, and in *Zen for the head of a temple.

Chorten (*mchod.rten*, 'receptacle of offerings'). The Tibetan development of the Indian Buddhist *stūpa. The chorten is similar in function to the stūpa as a receptacle for the remains of a holy person and as a shrine containing texts, images, etc., but differs in its architectural development. The central feature, the dome (*bum.pa*, 'flask') containing the relics, is wider at the top than the bottom, and rests upon a five-tier base symbolizing the five elements of this world (*jig.rten*, 'container of destruction') in which Buddhahood is attained. This base itself is given a platform called a 'throne' (*khri*). Above the flask the spire consists of thirteen rings diminishing in size upwards, presenting thirteen stages on the path to Buddhahood, and is surmounted by a solar disc resting on a crescent moon symbolizing wisdom and compassion, while upon the solar disc a small orb called a 'drop' (*thig.le*; Skt., *bindu*) represents the fusion of wisdom and compassion in enlightenment

Along with the two types of stūpa common in India—the basic form and the form with a raised walkway (which in Tibet is usually too narrow to be anything more than symbolic)—a chorten comprising an archway may be found at the entrance to a city, and the uniquely Tibetan Multiple Door (*sgo.mang*) chorten is especially prolific. The initiative in this chorten of not sealing the inside allows objects to be continually added (such as the dust of erased *maṇḍalas and ritual objects which by their sanctified nature cannot be thrown away), and the simultaneous creation of interior decorated chapels brought the chorten closer in concept to the temple. The practice on encountering chorten, as with the Indian stūpa, is to pass by or circumambulate clockwise, and sometimes prostrations will be performed.

Chōsan (Jap., 'morning devotion'). The *zazen (meditation) with which each day begins in a Zen monastery (*tera).

Chos drug (Kagyu teaching): see NĀRO CHOS DRUG.

Chosen people. A designation for the Jewish people, though also used of groups or people in other religions who have a strong sense of election, e.g. Christians. According to Deuteronomy, 'You are a people holy to the Lord your God; the Lord your God has chosen you to be a people for his own possession' (7. 6). The essence of the *covenant relationship was that God chose *Israel, and, as a consequence, the Jewish people are obliged to 'keep his statutes and observe his *laws' (Psalms 105. 45). Thus chosenness involves responsibility as well as privilege. Through bearing witness to God by keeping his commandments, the Israelites will be 'a light to the nations' (Isaiah 49. 6). If responsibilities are neglected, punishment is sure to follow, but it is unthinkable that God will reject his people altogether: 'Yet for all that . . . I will not spurn them . . . for I am the Lord their God' (Leviticus 26. 44). The *rabbis taught that the *Torah was offered to other nations first, but only the Jews would accept it (*B.Av.Zar.* 2b–3a), and in the liturgy God is blessed for having 'chosen us from all peoples and given us your Torah'. Despite the Christian claim that the Jews had forfeited the right to be the true Israel, through centuries of persecution the idea of election persisted. *Judah Halevi in the *Kuzar* (The Khazar) argued that the Jewish people had inherited a unique religious faculty, and some *kabbalists argued that Jewish *souls came from God while *gentile souls are fashioned from baser material. The doctrine of chosenness has been caricatured by *anti-Semites, who argued that it was the basis of the world conspiracy for Jewish domination. In the 19th and 20th cents., many Jews have become uneasy with the concept, and the *Reconstructionists in particular have eliminated all references to it in their liturgy.

B. W. Helfgott, *The Doctrine of Election in Tannaitic Literature* (1954); S. T. Katz, *Jewish Ideas and Concepts* (1977); K. Kohler, *Jewish Theology* (1968).

Chöten: see CHORTEN.

Chou. Chin. for *mantra.

Chou Tun-(y)i, also **Chou Lien-ch'i** (1017–73). *neo-Confucian scholar, who reordered Confucian cosmogony. Creating a sequential process from *t'ai-chi, he accounted for the proliferation of appearance from one unproduced producer. He offered an explanation for the *yin-yang diagram (*t'ai-chi-t'u) which summarizes the balance between activity and passivity: 'When the reality of t'ai-chi and the essence of yin and yang and the five agents come into mysterious union, integration ensues: the *ch'ien* [heavenly principle] constitutes the male, the *k'un* [earthly] the female: the interaction of the two engenders and transforms the myriad things, which in turn reproduce, resulting in unending transformation.' A practical consequence of his thought was an emphasis on the interdependence of all phenomena: when he was asked why he did not cut the grass outside his door, he replied that the feelings of the grass were not other than his own.

Chrism (Gk., *chrisma*, from *chriō*, 'anoint'). A mixture of olive oil and balsam used in Catholic and (with other ingredients, including wine, nuts, and gum) Orthodox churches. It is used in anointings at *baptism, *confirmation, and *ordination, and at other consecrations (but not in the anointing of the sick: see UNCTION). It is solemnly consecrated on *Maundy Thursday by bishops in the W. and by *patriarchs in the E. (where the ceremony is so long and solemn that it is less frequent—about once every ten years). The strength-giving richness of the oil and the fragrance of the balsam made the chrism a suggestive subject for allegorical interpretation—e.g. by *Dionysius the Areopagite. The anointing is known also as Chrismation, especially after baptism (to be 'a seal of the heavenly gifts').

Christ (*christos*, 'anointed one'). The Gk. translation of Heb., *māshiach*: Messiah. Applied to *Jesus it was originally a title (John 7. 41, Acts 3. 20), but the forms 'Christ Jesus', 'Jesus Christ', and 'Christ' very soon became used indifferently by Christians as proper names (e.g. 1 Corinthians 1. 1–9). In careful modern writing 'Christ' as the object of faith is often distinguished from 'Jesus' about whom historical statements can be made, but more usually 'Christ' takes the place of 'Jesus' in any more or less religious context.

Christadelphians. Christian denomination founded by John Thomas (1805–71), a physician in Richmond, Virginia, who broke away from the Christian Church of Alexander *Campbell in 1844. The name Christadelphians ('Christ's brethren') reflects Thomas's claim to return to the beliefs and practice of the earliest disciples. The doctrines of the *Trinity and of the pre-existence of Christ are both rejected. The core of Christadelphian doctrine is *millennialism, and specifically the belief in the return of Christ in power and glory to set up a kingdom beginning in Jerusalem and spreading throughout the world. Christadelphians are divided into two camps on the question of whether all, or only the faithful, will be resurrected at the last day. Local congregations are known as 'ecclesias', each of which elects its own officers. Christadelphians take no part in politics, voting, or military service.

Christian Fellowship Church or **Etoism.** The main independent church in Melanesia, founded on New Georgia in the Solomon Islands in 1959 by Silas Eto (b. 1905). As a *catechist-teacher in the *Methodist mission, he developed deviationist practices from the 1930s, and, in disillusionment with staid mission forms, began his own true church. He remained an admirer of J. F. Goldie, founder of the mission, and claimed authority from both God and Goldie as revealed to him in a dream. Ecstatic worship was combined with healing, successful economic activities, and development of a model village, Paradise, as a 'holy city'. Despite incipient *messianism concerning Eto himself, relations with Methodists, now in the United Church, were being re-established in the 1970s.

Christianity. The origins of Christianity lie, historically, in the life and ministry of *Jesus, extended through his death, *resurrection, and *ascension. In its own estimate, its origins lie further back in the former *covenants (hence, from a Christian point of view, the Old Testament) made with Israel.

Christianity exists in a vast diversity of different styles and forms of organization, but all are agreed that the figure of Jesus is the disclosure of God and the means of human reconciliation with him. The life and ministry of Jesus seemed (to at least some of those who witnessed or experienced them at the time) to be a restoration in word and action of the power (Gk., *dunamis*) not of himself but of God, leading to the conclusion that 'he who has seen me has seen the Father'; 'I and the Father are one' (John 14. 9, 10. 30). The once fashionable argument is no longer tenable that Jesus was a simple Jewish teacher who was gradually promoted (see EUHEMERUS) into being the Son of God, as a result of *Paul transforming the teaching of Jesus into a *hellenized new religion. From the earliest writings in the New Testament, Jesus was closely associated with God, with extremely high titles and status in relation to God. The extraordinary way in which Jesus acted as one who was mediating the consequence of God through his own person produced 'the phenomenon of the New Testament': the ways in which these documents speak of Jesus, and which relate him uniquely to God, have clear connections with both Jewish and Hellenistic categories, and yet they are always distinctive and idiosyncratic.

In the early years, 'Christianity' was one interpretation, among many at that time, of what God's covenant with Israel and his purpose in creation should be; but in this interpretation, it was believed that Jesus was the promised *messiah (Heb., *ha-Mashiach* = messiah = Gk., *ho Christos*, hence the name 'Christianity', which was first used, according to Acts 2. 26, in *c.*40 CE). Since for other Jews, many of the marks of a messiah did not accompany Jesus, and since claims (impossible to them) were being made about Jesus in relation to God, the two religions separated, although for centuries a small number of Christians continued to believe that Jewish *Torah should still be observed. On the majority Christian side, the keeping of Torah was no longer regarded as a necessary condition of being in a covenant relation with God. The separation from Judaism was made by universalizing the consequences of Christ to all people. That process was accelerated by the fall of Jerusalem in 70 CE, after which an increasing hostility to Judaism led to a long (and still unended, though moderated) history of *anti-Semitism.

Characteristic Christian doctrines emerged from the demand of the New Testament evidence (and from the experience which brought it into being). Jesus mediated the consequence and effect of God, so that on the one hand it was evidently God who was acting and speaking in and through him, and yet on the other it was clear that Jesus addressed God (e.g. in prayer) as apart from himself, as Father (see ABBA): this produced a quest in the early centuries to find ways of speaking of these two natures in one person (*Christology; the willingness and obedience of *Mary in accepting the conception and birth of Jesus produced a widespread, though not universal, devotion to Mary, and a close association of her with the work of *redemption). At the same time, God was clearly present to the life of Jesus (e.g. at his birth and his baptism, and in the directing of his mission), in the ways traditionally spoken of as the *Holy Spirit. This led to a further quest to find ways of speaking of the interior nature of God, as being in itself, not an abstract unity, but social and relational (i.e. as *Trinity).

It was also recognized that what Jesus had done during his life for some particular people, in reconciling them to God when they had become estranged from him and from each other, was, as a consequence of his death, resurrection, and ascension, extended to others, and indeed made universal, at least as an opportunity for those who respond in faith. This led to doctrines of *atonement.

This extension of the consequence of Christ was made immediately realistic, and thus realizable, through the enacted signs of *baptism (taking believers into the death of Christ and raising them to a new life already here on earth) and of the *last supper (*eucharist). From the earliest days (*Pentecost), the followers of Christ felt that they had been empowered by the Holy Spirit conferring on them special gifts. Initially, they looked for an early return of Christ (Second Coming or *parousia), and although that expectation faded, it has remained as an important *eschatological component of Christian belief. The sense of being, in the meantime, the continuing Body of Christ led to the mystical interpretation of the *Church, which lies apart from the many divisions of Christians into separated Churches.

Diverse writings evoked by the event of Jesus (his life and ministry, and their consequences in the lives of believers) were gathered eventually into the New Testament. During the New Testament period, the *kelal of Jesus (the context-independent command of love) was made context-dependent by many applications to particular circumstances: that is, the general command to love God and one's neighbour was applied to the circumstances in which people found themselves, as they asked what the meaning of that love should be in practice. Consequently, the relation between the context-independent command and the context-dependent applications has left a tension between liberty and law in Christian *ethics.

During the New Testament period also, the nature of Christian community (the Church) changed dramatically: the original metaphor of the Church as the Body of Christ, with all parts being of equal importance under the headship of Christ (e.g. Colossians 1. 17 f.; 1 Corinthians 12. 12 ff.), was changed into a metaphor derived from the Roman army, with a hierarchical organization and vertical levels of authority of *bishops, *priests, and *deacons: the clericalization of the Church and the subordination of the *laity has remained characteristic of most parts of Christianity down to the present. However, the two models (of the priesthood of all believers, 1 Peter 2. 4 ff., and the controlling authority of ordained ministers) have remained in tension throughout Christian history, although the authoritarian model has been dominant (e.g. in *Roman or Vatican Catholicism, with the *pope assuming the title from the Roman Empire of Pontifex Maximus).

Initially Christianity was a small religious movement, though confident in itself because of the resurrection and the experience of empowerment from the Holy Spirit. In the early centuries, it was held in suspicion by some because it was 'a new and noxious superstition' (Tacitus), by others because of its exclusive monotheism which contrasted with the prevailing Graeco-Roman syncreticisms. This exclusive emphasis occasionally brought it into conflict with imperial authorities. Where martyrdom occurred, Christianity in fact gained great strength (see TERTULLIAN), and the witness and cult of *martyrs gained an importance which has continued to the present: on the basis of the numbers involved, the 20th cent. has been called 'the century of martyrs'. After the support of *Constantine and the recognition of Christianity as the religion of the Empire under Theodosius I (emperor, 379–95), Christianity became the major religion of the Roman world.

Sometimes in conflict with existing religions and philosophies (e.g. *gnosticism), it nevertheless, during this period, drew on many such sources (including gnosticism and Greek philosophy) to elaborate its faith. Equally, it reworked various 'pagan' images in the artistic sphere (e.g. Orpheus is represented as the Good Shepherd, and Hercules as a type of Christ); this 'baptism' of symbols has remained characteristic of Christian *art. Faith and practice were constantly disputed and contested, leading to a series of *Councils in which attempts were made to achieve unity and conformity, i.e. *Catholicity. However, it was never the case that there was in origin a universally agreed *Apostolic faith (cf. VINCENTIAN CANON). Creeds developed from baptismal formulae (which served as 'passwords') to summaries of approved and legitimized faith. But major divisions emerged, some of which (e.g. Monophysites) persist as continuing Churches to the present. Especially serious was the schism between E. and W. Christianity. Despite attempts at repair, the *Orthodox (i.e. E.) Church (itself comprising several different traditions, disciplines, and practices) remains resistant to the claims of the bishop of Rome (the pope) to teaching and jurisdictional authority. The claim to the primacy of the pope was made more absolute at the First *Vatican Council, with the definition of the pope's *infallibility in matters of faith and morals. The attempt of Vatican II to contextualize this in the collegiality of bishops was not sufficient to contribute to the healing of the schism. W. Christianity was disrupted by the *Reformation, with the Reformed Churches dividing further, and repeatedly, on issues of doctrine and practice. Attempts to recover unity (*ecumenism) have led to increased co-operation, but to few restorations of organic unity. In many countries, these divisions were amplified by close relations (sometimes virtual identity) between Church and State; increasing separation of the two, especially after the Enlightenment (see ANTICLERICALISM), has led to different attempts on the part of the Churches to remain involved in political life.

The early involvement of Christianity with the Roman Empire evoked a reaction on the part of some who saw in it a compromise between the gospel, with its injunction to forsake the things of this world, and the quest for temporal power which underlay Roman imperialism. The development of a religious life which was deliberately separated from the world began with the *desert fathers and spread across the known world. It eventually found expression in the *monastic orders, notably that of St *Benedict, and it gained its evangelical outreach in the *religious orders of the 13th cent. onward. The monasteries between the 7th and 11th cents. did much to preserve the books and learning, both of the Roman world and of the early Church, from the raids of the barbarians and Vikings who only gradually adopted the faith. To books and learning were brought the arts of illumination (see CALLIGRAPHY; LINDISFARNE), as well, in time, as the skills of criticism and study (e.g. *Scholasticism). By the 10th cent., the building of cathedrals and abbeys offered scope to architects, sculptors, painters, and other craftsmen. Their work continued through the ensuing centuries in characteristic styles (e.g. Romanesque, *Gothic, Perpendicular, Baroque) and is also to be found in the smaller *parish churches. The combination of these developments led also, especially after the 12th cent. renaissance, to schools and universities coming into being.

Throughout its history, the Christian quest to share the good news (*gospel) of Christ has produced an emphasis on *mission, especially in the 19th cent., 'the century of mission', culminating in the Edinburgh Conference, 1910. As a result, Christianity is found in all parts of the world, and makes up more than a quarter of the world's population. At present, there is a pronounced shift of numerical allegiance from North to South, with Christianity growing especially in Africa and S. America—so much so that some believe that the future of Christian strength and imagination lies in these areas.

Liturgically, Christians follow the life, death, resurrection, and ascension of Jesus throughout each year, marking particular days as *festivals, and celebrating also those who have been exemplary in faith and practice (*saints). Among RCs, there are formal procedures for designating saints; in other Churches, the process is less elaborate. The quest for holiness, and the more elementary desire to be 'in touch' with holy things or people, made *pilgrimage to shrines and to *relics popular. The practices of *prayer (in its many forms) and worship are fundamental in Christian life.

The continuing examination of Christian origins and their implications has led to a high value being placed on *theology, which in turn has ensured that conflict and debate continue (often of an angry and vicious kind, hence the phrase reflecting this characteristic, *odium theologicum*), since varying positions on major issues can all equally find support in scripture (see HERMENEUTICS) and tradition (the status of tradition in relation to scripture being one such issue). Where these divisions have been translated into Church life and politics, they have frequently led to animosities, wars and persecutions among Christians which have made a mockery of the early description of Christians, 'Behold, how they love one another.'

Yet Christianity is often redeemed from that unhappy aspect of its history. In practice, it is (or should be) the answer to the question of the rich young ruler, 'Good master, what must I do to inherit eternal life?' (Mark 10. 17). The answer which Jesus gave pointed him beyond the keeping of the basic commandments (*Ten Commandments) to a total generosity of self and substance. In the *parable/allegory of the sheep and the goats, and of the last *judgement (Matthew 25. 31–46), the single criterion of judgement is stated: 'Inasmuch as you have done it to the least of one of these, you have done it to me.' That criterion means that Christian life should be the manifestation of a pervasive quality of love (*agape). From this has arisen the recent view that *orthopraxy is at least as important as orthodoxy (perhaps more so): see LIBERATION THEOLOGY. It is this stress on the transformation of human life into love which has led through the centuries to the founding of schools and hospitals, and to the care of the poor, and to the recognition of such people as *Francis of Assisi as exemplary: 'The Brothers shall possess nothing. . . . This is the highest degree of that sublime poverty, which has made you, my dearly beloved brethren, heirs and kings of the kingdom of heaven, which has made you poor in goods but exalted in virtues' (*Rule of St Francis*, 1223).

A. J. Arberry (ed.), *Religion in the Middle East* (1969); W. O. Chadwick (ed.), *The Pelican History of the Church* (various authors, 1960–71); F. L. Cross, *The Oxford Dictionary of the Christian Church* (1996); W. H. C. Frend, *The Early Church* (1966); A. Grillmeier, *Christ in Christian Tradition* (1975); J. N. D. Kelly, *Early Christian Doctrines* (1978); H. Kung, *On Being a Christian* (1977); K. S. Latourette, *A History of the Expansion of Christianity* (1938–45); E. Molland, *Christendom* (1959); J. Pelikan, *The Christian Tradition* (1971–83).

Christian Science. The Church of Christ (Scientist) was founded by Mary Baker Eddy (1821–1910). She had been a semi-invalid who, in 1862, began to learn from Phineas Quimby the possibility of cures without medicine. In 1866 (the year in which Quimby died), she claimed a cure from a severe injury (after a fall on ice) without the intervention of medicine. She devoted herself to the recovery of the healing emphasis in early Christianity, and in 1875 she completed the 1st edn. of *Science and Health with Key to the Scriptures*. In 1879, the Church of Christ (Scientist) was incorporated with the purpose of 'commemorating the word and works of our Master': in her own view, 'the Bible has been my only authority'. She became chief pastor of the Mother Church, and wrote *The Manual of the Mother Church* to govern its affairs. The Bible and Mrs Eddy's works are the source of guidance and teaching, hence the importance of establishing reading rooms where these works can make their own appeal to the reader—along with the *Christian Science Monitor*. Services of healing are correspondingly central to religious practice. Christian Science shares with E. religions a belief that ignorance is at the root of human unease—and thus of dis-ease: 'All reality is in God and his creation, harmonious and eternal. That which he creates is good, and he makes all that is made. Therefore the only reality of sin, sickness or death is the awful fact that unrealities seem real to human, erring belief, until God strips off their disguise.' Health, happiness, and holiness are restored, not by going to doctors or psychiatrists, but by adopting and applying to the whole of life those practices and attitudes which are in accord with the already existent divine harmony: 'Both sin and sickness are error, and Truth is their remedy.'

D. John, *The Christian Science Way of Life* (1962); R. Peel, *Mary Baker Eddy* (3 vols., 1966–77).

Christian Socialists and **Christian Socialism.** A group led by F. D. *Maurice, and including Charles Kingsley, which rejected *laissez-faire* economics and competition as conforming to the will of God, and envisaged instead a kind of 'organic' society, in which co-operative societies and education would reduce poverty and class hostility. The group published pamphlets and set up co-operatives (which failed), and it only lasted from 1848 to 1854. In 1877, Stewart Headlam founded its successor, the Guild of St Matthew, and several other societies were established, many of which were short-lived. In 1960, surviving groups amalgamated as the Christian Socialist Movement. Roman Catholics have been inhibited from participation by papal condemnations of socialism, beginning with *Rerum Novarum* (1891; more recent *encyclicals, e.g. *Sollicitudo Rei Socialis*, 1987, have acknowledged the prime importance of unexploited labour), and by suspicions of an inappropriate marriage with Marx (see LIBERATION THEOLOGY). Fundamentally, Christian Socialism has resisted the reduction of 'people to things' in a capitalist pursuit of profit.

T. Christensen, *The Origin and History of Christian Socialism* (1962); E. R. Norman, *The Victorian Christian Socialists* (1987).

Christians of St John (name given to the Mandeans): see MANDEANS.

Christmas. The Christian feast of Jesus' birth, celebrated on 25 Dec. Its observance is first attested in Rome in 336. Probably the date was chosen to oppose the feast of the 'birthday of the unconquered sun' on the winter solstice. In the E. the date 6 Jan. for the nativity generally gave way to 25 Dec. by the 5th cent., although at Jerusalem the older custom was kept until 549 and the *Armenian Church still observes it (see also EPIPHANY). Christmas absorbed the festive atmosphere of the Roman Saturnalia and the other pagan festivals it replaced, and has continued to accumulate 'traditions', particularly in the 19th cent.

S. Samuelson, *Christmas: An Annotated Bibliography* (1982); F. X. Weiser, *Handbook of Christian Feasts* (1958) and *The Christmas Book* (1952).

Christology (Gk., *christos*, *Christ, + *logos*, 'reflection'). The attempt in Christianity to account for the relation of *Jesus to God, especially in his own nature and person. Since Jesus expressed in word and action a claim to the restoration of the power and effect (in Gk., the *dunamis* or dynamic) of God in human life, and since it was clearly observed that this *dunamis* made a real difference in the lives of those who stood in need of healing or forgiveness, the question inevitably arose of how Jesus was related to God in such a way that the effect of God was mediated so unequivocally through him (Mark 6. 1–6). From the outset, New Testament writers related Jesus so closely to God that he could be seen as the initiative of God in seeking and saving that which was lost, even to the extent of being the manifestation of God so far as that can be seen or conveyed in human form: 'He that has seen me has seen the Father' (John 14. 9). According to the *gospels, Jesus spoke of God as apart from himself and yet as the source and the agent in himself of what he said and did. This led inevitably to questions of how the being of God is related to the humanity of Jesus in such a way that both are truly contained and present in one person.

The answers given to those questions are necessarily speculative. They range across a spectrum (in the history of the Church) from a view that he was a remarkable teacher and healer who was promoted by the faith of the early Christians into God, to the view that the pre-existent Son is God as God always is, and that the eternal and unchanging nature of God was truly present to the humanity of Jesus, both as co-agent of his activity and subject of his experience, without the humanity being obliterated or the divine nature compromised. The former are known as *Euhemeristic or Adoptionist Christologies (see e.g. ARIUS). The latter culminated in the *Chalcedonian definition, which sees the person of Jesus as (in the words of *Aquinas) *instrumentum coniunctum divinitatis*, the conjoined instrument of the Godhead. Between the two are other attempts, which either diminish the divine nature or reduce the humanity to make way for the divine initiative within it. J. Bowker, *The Religious Imagination . . .* (1978) indicates how an understanding of information-process by way of constraint allows a Chalcedonian-type Christology in contemporary terms. See Index, Christology.

D. G. A. Calvert, *From Christ to God . . .* (1983); A. Grillmeier, *Christ in the Christian Tradition* (1975–95); W. Kasper, *Jesus the Christ* (1976) and *The God of Jesus Christ* (1983); J. Macquarrie, *Jesus Christ in Modern Thought* (1990); J. Meyendorff, *Christ in Eastern Christian Thought*; J. Pelikan, *Jesus Through the Centuries* (1987); K. Runia, *The Present-Day Christological Debate* (1984); E. Schillebeeckx, *Jesus: An Experiment in Christology* (1979); J. Sobrino, *Christology at the Crossroads* (1978).

Christus Victor. Christ as victor: Christian belief that *Jesus as Christ overcame all powers of evil and the devil. It underlay major theories of *atonement in the early Church. In a succinct study (*Christus Victor*, 1931), G. Aulén called it the classic theory, in contrast to subjective theories and those which involve Jesus in offering satisfaction to an angry God. His book was based on lectures given in Germany in 1930, offering much encouragement to the resistance to totalitarian regimes.

Chronicles, Book of (Heb., *divre ha-yamim*). Historical book (now generally divided into two books) in the Hebrew *Bible. It consists of lists of families, tribes, inhabitants of *Jerusalem, Levites, and Gibeonites (1–9). These are followed by an account of the reigns of *David and *Solomon (1 Chronicles 10–2 Chronicles 9) and the history of the kings of *Judah from Rehoboam to Zedekiah (2 Chronicles 10–36). They seem to have been based on various written sources, such as 'The Acts of the Kings of Israel'

(2 Chronicles 33. 18) and 'The Words of Samuel the Seer' (1 Chronicles 29. 29). There is much scholarly discussion as to the purpose of the book. It has been suggested that it is a *priestly document, designed to prove that Judah is the only legitimate kingdom and all worship must be centred in Jerusalem. Traditionally *Ezra was believed to be the author, but it is now generally accepted that it was composed in the 4th cent. BCE. The Gk. title is *Paraleipomena* ('things left over', *sc.* from Samuel and Kings), but the work is more of a *midrash on those books, having affinities with Ezra and Nehemiah.

Chronology: see CALENDAR.

Chrysostom, John, St (*c*.347–407). Bishop of Constantinople and *Doctor of the Church. He served as priest at Antioch from 386, where his great powers of oratory (the name Chrysostom means 'golden-mouthed', more often expressed as 'golden-tongued', whence 'silver-tongued Smith', of the 16th-cent. preacher Henry Smith) were directed against moral and paganizing lapses in the nominally Christian city. His homilies on New Testament books eschew allegorizing, but are prepared to see the spiritual meaning of a text, together with its practical implications. As patriarch of Constantinople from 398, his reforming zeal made him enemies. He was deposed at the 'Synod of the Oak' (403), recalled after a few days, then finally deposed and exiled in 404. Feast day in the W., 13 Sept.; in the E., 13 Nov.

The Liturgy of St Chrysostom has been, since the 13th cent., the *eucharistic liturgy in general use in the Orthodox Church, except on the few days for which that of *Basil is prescribed. It has little if any connection, in its present form, with Chrysostom, but owed its influence to its being the liturgy of Constantinople. It is used in several different languages, and is contained (with the Liturgies of St Basil and of the Presanctified) in the *Hieratikon* (in Slavonic, *Sluz(h)ebnik*).

Eng. tr. in P. Thompson, *The Orthodox Liturgy* (1939); C. Baur, *Der heilige Johannes Chrysostomus* . . . (1929–30; tr. 1959–60).

Chthonian religion (Gk., *chthon*, 'earth'). Religions and religious practices which are concerned with the gods and goddesses or life forces of the earth—in contrast to Olympian religion, which has to do with the gods and goddesses on high.

Chu. Korean for *mantra.

Ch'üan-chen tao (Chin., 'way of realizing truth'). A major form of religious Taoism also known as Pure Yang (*chung-yang*) and Golden Lotus (*chin-lien*). The school was founded by Wang Ch'un-yang (1112–70 CE), after he met a hermit, in 1159, who claimed to be an incarnation of two of the immortals (*pa-hsien) from whom he received secret teachings. The objective for every disciple is to realize Tao in experience, by understanding his own nature and mind in relation to Tao. To this end he drew on classic sources (e.g. *Prajñāpāramitā Sūtra*, outer *alchemy and inner *nei-tan), but also on sources outside the Taoist tradition, especially *Zen Buddhism, and to some extent *Confucianism. His system is thus eclectic. Of several movements derived from Ch'üan-chen tao, the most important (or at least enduring) has been Lung-men, the Dragon Gate school, with its monastery at *Pai-yün kuan.

Chuang-tzu, also **Chuang chou** (*tzu* means 'master', *c*.370–286 BCE). Considered by Taoists to be (with *Lao-tzu) one of the founders of philosophical Taoism. Little is known of his life: he is believed to have held a minor administrative post; but he was a fierce critic of *Confucianism, and was unwilling to serve under a ruler who would limit his thought and action. Offered a high sum to become a government official, he likened the offer to the fattening of an ox which is led to the temple for sacrifice; it is too late then to reflect that it would have been better to remain as a humble pig, unnoticed by anyone.

He is traditionally the author of the work bearing his name, *Chuang-tzu* (or *Nan-hua chen-ching*). Of its thirty-three chapters, 1–7 (the 'inner books') are perhaps his own, the fifteen 'outer' and eleven 'mixed' chapters are thought to be by his pupils. As with Lao-tzu, the *Tao and its *te are open to realization by all people. It requires well-directed and unattached action (*wu-wei) and meditative concentration on the constantly changing nature of the world, which, when realized and discarded, leaves only the Tao. It is thus non-political, and in a way supplements Confucianism rather than subverts it, because it offers to officials and those involved in the world a contemplative way of release. The Tao is present in all things equally, so that humanity is not a special pinnacle of creation—the mushroom which lives for only a day is intrinsically of equal worth with P'eng Tsu who lived for hundreds of years. Progress is made by rest, not by purpose and striving:

> The Tao operates, and things follow . . . He who wracks his spirit and intelligence trying to find unity in things which are already in harmony if only he could understand it, may be called 'three in the morning'. Why? Because a keeper of monkeys promised them a ration of 3 nuts in the morning and 4 in the evening. The monkeys were furious. So the keeper said, 'Of course, I understand. Why don't you have four in the morning and three in the evening, at which concession, the monkeys were delighted, although neither name nor reality was really affected.'

Wisdom consists in recognizing distinction and perceiving the relation:

> Chuang Chou dreamed that he was a butterfly, fluttering about, not knowing that it was Chuang Chou. He woke with a start, and was Chuang Chou again. But he did not know whether he was Chuang Chou who had dreamed that he was a butterfly, or a butterfly dreaming that he was Chuang Chou. Between Chuang Chou and the butterfly

there must be some distinction: this is what is called, 'the transformation of things'.

Many Eng. trs., e.g. H. A. Giles (1961); A. C. Graham (1981); J. Legge, in *The Texts of Taoism* (1962); B. Watson, *The Complete Works* . . . (1968).

Chu Hsi (1130–1200). Chinese philosopher, who developed the analysis of neo-Confucian concepts, accepting influence from both Buddhism and Taoism, in a form which persisted to the 20th cent. In particular, he explored the relationship between the formal aspect of an entity (*li) and its material expression (*ch'i). He argued that there must be a mutually necessary manifestation of reality lying behind each, *t'ai-chi. Human wisdom lies in discerning that reality and living in harmony with it. Since he attended closely to the work of his predecessor, Ch'eng Yi (see CH'ENG HAO), his school is often known as that—i.e Ch'eng-chu, though also as 'the school of principle', Li-hsüeh. In practical terms, he did much to establish the Four Classics as the basis of education. He wrote commentaries on the *Confucian Classics, insisting on a realism in the pursuit of *jen (true humanity) which he contrasted with Buddhism. He is therefore often held to be the beginning of positivistic or scientific method in Chinese thought, notwithstanding the obvious limitations in his own knowledge: 'To understand jen, look at seeds of grain or stones of peaches or apricots: if you sow them, they will grow, because they are not dead things. That is why they are called jen ['stone' and 'humanity']. This shows that jen involves the spirit of vitality. . . . To be impartial is to make jen possible, and jen brings into being both altruism and love.'

K. Shimada, *Die neo-konfuzianische Philosophie: Die Schulrichtungen Chu Hsis und Wang Yang-mings* (1979); Wang-tsit Chan (ed.), *Chu Hsi* . . . (1986).

Chu-hung (1535–1615). A Chinese monk who combined *Zen and *Pure Land Buddhism to produce a practical path for lay Buddhists. His initial ambition was to purify the *saṅgha through strict observance of *Vinaya rules. Although this seemed to be in wide contrast to *nembutsu (recitation of the name of Amitābha (*Amida) as a means to direct salvation), he came to realize that all paths must necessarily be paths to the same goal, if the goal is true. He therefore developed a way in which nembutsu, meditation on a *kōan, and a disciplined life, all reinforce each other, without any necessity for entering the saṅgha. His synthesizing vision, which remains characteristic of Chinese Buddhism to the present, extended (selectively) to Taoism, but not to the recently arrived Christian missionaries. His arguments against them are summarized in his *T'ien-shuo ssu-p'ien* (Four Chapters on the Teachings of *T'ien).

Yü Chün-fang, *The Renewal of Buddhism* . . . (1980).

Chūin or **chūu** (intermediate state): see ANTARĀBHAVA.

Chū Kokushi (Ch'an/Zen master): see NAN-YANG HUI-CHUNG.

Ch'un Ch'iu. The *Springs and Autumns*, one of the *Confucian Classics. The title was commonly used for official annals of feudal states during the Chou dynasty (?1111–256 BCE). However, after that age it is always used in reference to the annals of Lu, native state of *Confucius, which he is said to have edited for the period 722–484 BCE. He is supposed, in the course of this editing, to have passed judgement upon every act and every actor in this historical record, these judgements being implied by the most precise use of language. Whether or not such esoteric meanings are actually contained in the *Springs and Autumns*, the tradition that this was the Master's intention established the basic canon of Chinese historiography, namely, that the purpose of writing 'history' is to 'praise and blame'.

Tr. J. Legge, *The Ch'un Ts'ew with the Tso Chuen* (1872).

Chung-Kuo-Shih (Ch'an/Zen master): see NAN-YANG HUI-CHUNG.

Chung-li Chuan (one of eight Immortals): see PA-HSIEN.

Chung-yang (form of Taoism): see CH'ÜAN-CHEN TAO.

Chung Yüan. Chinese festival (predominantly Buddhist), held to assist the hungry ghosts. It is held on the fifteenth day of the seventh month, and from this day until the end of the month offerings are made, or gifts contributed, which will assist those who have died with none otherwise to remember them, those without graves, and those without descendants. Paper equivalents of money and desirable objects are burnt or are scattered in rivers (for those who have drowned). In Buddhist temples, a large paper boat of the *dharma is made and then ceremonially burnt in the evening in order to help any wandering ghosts to cross the sea of clinging (*taṇhā) and torment and to attain the goal of *nirvāna.

Chung Yung ('Central Norm', often referred to as 'The Doctrine of the Mean'). A work attributed to Tzu Ssu, *Confucius' grandson (5th cent. BCE), but more probably a compilation of two or more works, being extracted from **Li Chi*. It advocates the discernment of a basic norm of human action which, if then put into effect, will bring life into harmony with the process of the universe. This requires a life controlled by *ch'eng*, sincerity, genuineness, and integrity. In this way, the natural order embraces both cosmos and ethical life; and those who live accordingly experience a mystical union between heaven and earth. In this way, *Chung Yung* is a Confucian response to the *Tao as 'the Way'; and the text served as an important bridge between *neo-Confucianism (which valued this text highly) and Taoism and Buddhism. It contains specific prescriptions for regulating life and society, setting the detail in a natural understanding of order: 'That which is bestowed by Heaven is called human nature. To fulfil this nature is called The Way. To cultivate The Way is to be instructed in the truth. ... Only the one who incorporates *ch'eng* can bring his own nature to perfect completion.... He becomes capable of reinforcing the powers of Heaven and Earth to nourish and transform, and thus he forms a trinity with Heaven and Earth.'

Tr. J. Legge, in *The Chinese Classics* (1893–5); E. R. Hughes, *The Great Learning and the Mean in Action* (1942).

Chün tzu (ideal person): see ETHICS (CONFUCIAN).

Chuppah (canopy used at Jewish weddings): see ḤUPPAH.

Church (from Gk., *kuriakon*, 'belonging to the Lord'). The institution of *Christianity. The word may refer to the whole number of organized Christians everywhere, to a particular denomination, to a local congregation, or to a building where Christians assemble. Reflection on the nature of the church, 'ecclesiology', is also a traditional part of Christian teaching.

The word for church (Gk., *ekklēsia*) occurs only twice in sayings of Jesus (Matthew 16. 18, 18. 17, both much disputed). Outside the gospels the word refers usually to a local body (e.g. 1 Corinthians 16. 1), though occasionally to a wider group (Colossians 1. 18). The ways in which believers are addressed (e.g. by Paul) as Christ's body, or bride, or heirs of God's promises to Abraham, or the Israel of God, form the basis for the Christian doctrine of the Church. This excludes the view that it is a voluntary association of individuals.

In *Orthodox understanding, the Church must be constituted by the *apostolic succession, and be *episcopal in character. It must accept the first seven *Councils, and its doctrine is held within that parameter. Beyond that, the Church does not have to be centrally governed. Thus the Church in practice is made up of *autocephalous churches and autonomous churches. While there is consequently no central figure of supreme authority like the bishop of Rome as *pope, the *patriarch of Constantinople is recognized as the ecumenical or universal patriarch. The Church is the mediation of the life of God to the created order: it is human actuality permeated by the divinizing power that flows out of the *incarnation and the gift of the *Holy Spirit at *Pentecost. The human image of God is restored to its proper nature through its transformation by the divine energies at work in the Church.

For Catholics, the Church is characterized as 'one, holy, catholic and apostolic'. Thus conceived, it is a visible body; its membership, its orders of ministers, and its unity are all constituted by participation in visible *sacraments. In addition to the Church on earth, often called the Church Militant, there exists the Church of the faithful departed, often called (in its two parts) the Church Expectant (being purified in *purgatory) and the Church Triumphant (in heaven). Such a doctrine of one visible church runs into the fact of *heresy and *schism, and since the schism of E. and W., each church has maintained that it itself is the intended realization of the visible church, the other being in schism. An alternative 'branch theory' of the church is characteristic of *Anglo-Catholics. According to this, all churches which maintain *Catholic doctrine and the apostolic succession of bishops may be a branch of the one church of Christ, even though out of communion with one another.

The Reformation gave rise to two major doctrines of the Church: (i) that it is a visible body, and, in God's intention, one (though divided if corruption and error have demanded a reformation); and (ii) that the true church is an invisible body, since it is by the personal commitment of faith that a person is saved and made a member of it. In the view of some the visible unity of the church should be secured by the state or ruler accepting an 'established' religion—hence the national churches on *Lutheran or *Calvinist lines. Others have held that unity of organization between Christian congregations in different places is unnecessary, since each local congregation is already the Church. The quest for Church unity is usually known as the *ecumenical movement.

For individual Churches see Index, Churches.

Church Army. Anglican evangelizing organization of lay workers founded in 1882 by Wilson Carlile on the model of the *Salvation Army. Its social work includes the running of old people's homes, hostels, youth centres, etc. Full-time workers wear a grey uniform and are styled Captains and Sisters.

Church Commissioners. Body which manages the endowments of the *Church of England. It was formed in 1948 from the merger of an earlier body, the Ecclesiastical Commissioners, with *Queen Anne's Bounty. In 1985 its investment portfolio had a value of over £1,600m., making it a larger investor than most pension funds; however, at that point (and just before the collapse in property prices), the Commissioners borrowed in order to invest in large property projects, eventually losing about £800m. The ensuing inquiry suggested ways in which the management of the fund could be made more professional and accountable. *Working As One Body* (the *Archbishops' Commission) also known, from its chairman, as the Turnbull report, proposed a National Council under the two Archbishops which would take over most of the functions of the Commissioners (reduced in number from 95 to 15) apart from being 'trustees of the historic assets of the Church'.

Churches of Christ. Christian denomination, also known as 'Disciples' and 'Campbellites' after its founder A. *Campbell. Organized in the USA, the earliest 'Disciples' came to adopt *baptism by immersion and the weekly observance of the Lord's Supper for baptized believers; each local church practised a *Congregational form of church government. Autonomous churches came to be established in Great Britain in the early 19th cent. and Acts 2. 42 was adopted as a worship pattern, with its model of teaching, fellowship (expressed in the offering), 'breaking of bread', and prayers, the latter being offered by any who desired to participate—a practice which reflects the influence on 'Disciples' of the mid-18th-cent. Scotch Baptists and Glasites. Instrumental music was not used in their worship until this century. The movement relied on a part-time ministry undertaken by men employed in secular occupations, though from 1920 a theological education was offered to ministerial candidates. The Churches of Christ participated in ecumenical discussion in the present century, and in 1981 the majority of the Churches of Christ in Great Britain became part of the *United Reformed Church.

Church Fathers. Christian writers of the first eight centuries CE, regarded as 'orthodox', developing though that concept was. By about the 4th cent. CE, appeal was being made to earlier Church Fathers as reinforcing authority. The study of these writers is known as Patristics or Patrology.

Church Missionary Society (Anglican missionary society): see CMS.

Church of England. The Christian Church which is 'by law established' in England. The Church of England is a consequence of the Reformation, as this was mediated under the 16th-cent. Tudor sovereigns. As the expression of *Anglicanism, it is the continuity of Christianity from the earliest times (see e.g. CELTIC CHURCH), as that changes through time. The Protestant advance in England under Henry VIII and Edward VI was reversed under the Catholic Mary. The character of the Church was then settled in the reign of Elizabeth I (1558–1603) when obedience to the Roman see was finally repudiated, the monarch became 'Supreme Governor', the **Book of Common Prayer* became the service book, the Articles of Religion were reduced to thirty-nine, and Archbishop M. *Parker led the attempt to achieve a national uniformity in religion.

The 'establishment' of the Church implies, most importantly, that the monarch must be a communicant member; she or he is crowned by the archbishop of *Canterbury; twenty-six bishops sit in the House of Lords; the sovereign (on the advice of the prime minister) nominates bishops; the highest church court is the Judicial Committee of the Privy Council; and Parliament must ratify measures of church government (but excluding, since 1974, forms of service).

Since 1970 the governing body of the Church of England has been the General Synod, which enacts measures to go before Parliament and other legislation, and debates matters of public interest. It consists of separate houses of bishops, clergy, and laity. Clergy and lay members are elected from local diocesan and deanery synods and ultimately from parochial church councils. The house of clergy has been the most conservative, being responsible, e.g. for defeating measures to unite the church with the Methodist Church (1972) and to move toward a union with all the *Free Churches (1981).

Church of the East. The *Syrian Church, more popularly known as *Nestorian, or *Assyrian, which descends from the ancient church in the Persian Empire. Its foundation is traditionally associated with Mari, a disciple of *Addai, or with St *Thomas himself, but probably it owes more to anonymous merchants, refugees, and captives deported from the Roman Empire. The Church suffered outbursts of persecution, mostly at the instance of *Zoroastrian clergy in the 4th–5th cents.; and even thereafter, in order to avoid suspicion of collaboration with the Romans, the Church gradually distanced itself from churches in the W. In isolation it adopted a strongly dyophysite (*Antiochene) christology which by the 7th cent. hardened into Nestorianism.

The church undertook very extensive missionary work, and even had outposts in China from 635 until 'foreign' religions were expelled in 845 (see HSI-AN FU). Under the Caliphs (*khalīfa), the Church enjoyed periods of fairly good treatment; the patriarchal see was moved from Seleucia (Ktesiphon) to Baghdād *c.*775; the *Catholikos became a considerable political figure and was chief bishop over a vast area of Asia. Christian fortunes changed drastically in the 14th cent. after the conversion of the Mughals to Islam and the marauding of Timur (Tamerlane). A remnant fled to the mountains of Kurdistan (NW Persia and E. Turkey), and the patriarchal succession was maintained on a hereditary basis. Further losses came with the formation of the Uniat Chaldean Church and in the 19th cent. of a *Protestant body. The survival of the ancient hierarchy is partly due to *Anglican support in the period 1886–1914. At present, the Nestorians form a very small community in Iraq (the patriarchate was restored to Baghdād in 1976 with the election of Mar Denḥa IV), together with other small populations in the Middle E., N. and S. America, and S. India (this being a dissident body from the Syro-Malabar Church).

Church-sect typology. The attempt to classify religious groups according to their typical relationships with society. First developed by *Troeltsch, the distinction has been influential in the *sociology of religion. Together with other established churches of the nation-states of his time, Troeltsch saw the Evangelical Church in Germany as exemplifying those religious groups which accept and affirm the established social order: the Church 'utilizes the State and the ruling classes, and weaves these elements into her own life; she then becomes an integral part of the existing social order'. Sects, on the other hand, are protest groups (on this view; for a fuller typology, see SECTS). During the European Middle Ages, sects opposed the Church, its teachings, and its priests. More recently sects (e.g. the *Mormons) have opposed secular society as well. Rather than working to advance overall social cohesion and order, sects follow the injunction 'come out from among them and be ye separate'.

B. Wilson, *Religion in Sociological Perspective* (1982); J. Yinger, *The Scientific Study of Religion* (1970).

Churning of the ocean (*samudramathana*). A Hindu myth, which tells how a great flood covered the earth, as a result of which many precious objects were lost, especially *amṛta. In order to recover them, *Viṣṇu, in his incarnation (*avatāra) as a tortoise (*Kūrma) dived to the ocean floor so that Mount *Mandara could be set up on his back. The gods and demons then coiled the serpent Vāsuki round the mountain, and, by pulling on each end, churned up the ocean until the missing objects were recovered. However, a poison, Halāhala, was also churned up, which *Śiva drank, in order to protect humanity, with the consequence that his throat is dyed blue. A version of the myth was already known in *Vedic times (*Ṛg Veda* 10. 136), where it is *Rudra who is the saviour. Later developments took the churning to be the origin of all created things; or to be the religious process of passing through many processes and states in order to attain the immortal goal of *mokṣa.

Cintāmani (Skt.). 1. In Hinduism, a magical jewel which has the power to grant every wish, hence an epithet for God.

2. In Buddhism, the same jewel, but now an attribute of *buddhas and *bodhisattvas, hence a symbol for the mind which has attained its (proper) desire.

Circumambulation. The movement around a holy object, or of a holy object. The completion of a circle of protection, or of community, creates an integrity which is otherwise hard to find in this world. The application of this in religions is diverse: examples include *Ḥajj (the Muslim circumambulation of the *Kaʿba); the *Prayer Wheel (in Tibet); the *stūpa and the *Bo tree in Buddhism (see RELICS (BUDDHIST)); the respect shown to the *Ādi Granth on entering a *gurdwārā; *Lāvān; the Hindu 'following the sun' round the sacred fire and, in the temple (and, in *pradakṣina*, to go around any sacred object, person, or place, including the whole of India; the seven circuits (*hakkafot) around a cemetery before a burial by *Sephardi and *Hasidic Jews.

Circumcision

Judaism (Heb., *berit milah* '*covenant of circumcision'). According to the Hebrew Bible, *Abraham circumcised himself and all the male members of his household in obedience to God's command (Genesis 17. 11–12). According to the *rabbis, obeying the commandment of circumcision is so important that heaven and earth will not exist without the *blood of the covenant (*B.Shab.* 137b). Any child born of a Jewish mother is Jewish whether circumcised or not. None the less it is the duty of a Jewish father to have his son circumcised on the eighth day (*Shulḥān Arukh* YD 260. 1). The operation is done by a *mohel who must be an observant Jew (*Sh.Ar.* YD 264. 1), and traditionally it is part of a religious ceremony at which the baby's name is announced. Male *proselytes are expected to undergo circumcision as well as ritual immersion.

Islam *Khitān* is male circumcision. It is obligatory, though the details, and the age at which it is done, vary. *Khafḍ* is female circumcision, which is not obligatory, but which is nevertheless regarded by many as according to *sunna—i.e. customary in the strong and religious sense. It therefore has higher status than being merely a local custom which Islam has adopted from the territories it has overrun, although in fact it is common only in Egypt, Sudan, Saudi Arabia, Yemen, and Iraq. In so far as it is increasing in frequency in, e.g., Jordan, Ethiopia, Somalia, sub-Saharan Africa, the UK, it is because of arguments that it belongs to sunna. Three main types are practised: the first is the removing of the clitoral hood, which is thus akin to male circumcision and does not arouse the same degree of opposition as do the other two (opposition expressed by Muslims as well as non-Muslims). The second involves the excision of the clitoral glans, or of the clitoris, perhaps also of the labia minora. The third extends this excision to the labia maiora, with the stitching together of the vulva apart from a small opening; this is reopened when the woman is married. Opposition is based on the claim that this is non-Islamic, that it is psychologically and physically painful, and that it perpetuates the male control of women in ways that the Quranic precept of 'different but equal' forbids.

F. Bryk, *Circumcision in Man and Woman* (1930, 1974); E. Wallerstein, *Circumcision . . .* (1980).

Cistercians. *Roman Catholic monastic order, also called 'White Monks'. The mother-house, Cîteaux (Lat., *Cistercium*) in Burgundy, was founded in 1098. The early Cistercians' professed desire was to follow strictly the Benedictine Rule (*Benedict), of which their interpretation arose from 'a conviction that it is possible to lead a monastic life without any compromise with the world' (J. Leclerc). In contrast to the comparative luxury of the monasticism of *Cluny, then at its height, they were austere in diet, clothing, architecture, and liturgy. They abjured tithes and other feudal revenues, supporting themselves instead by their own manual labour and that of lay-brothers (*conversi*), and developing previously uncultivated land on the fringes of settled Europe. Expansion of the order during its first two centuries was phenomenal: 525 monasteries were established throughout Europe by 1200, 694 by 1300. In addition to the evident contemporary appeal of Cistercian ideals, factors in this expansion included the fame of St *Bernard of Clairvaux, a highly systematic and efficient form of organization, and the profitable role of Cistercian agriculture in the expansion of the European economy. After *c.*1300, conditions for growth were lacking and membership declined severely.

In the 17th cent. a party of 'Strict Observance' emerged, advocating, among other rigours, total abstinence from meat. Its most important figure was A. de Rancé (d. 1700), abbot of La Trappe, whence is derived the name *Trappists, applied from the 19th cent. onward to Cistercians of the Strict Observance. Since 1890 the latter have constituted an order in their own right, distinct from the others, who are known as Cistercians of the Common Observance. Among notable Cistercians are *Bernard of Clairvaux, William of St-Thierry, *Aelred of Rievaulx, Guerric of Igny (the so-called 'four evangelists' of Cîteaux), and more recently Thomas *Merton. See Index, Cistercians.

J. Lekai, *The Cistercians . . .* (1977).

Cit (Skt., 'See'). In Hindu thought, pure consciousness as the essential and irreducible quality of the eternal self or *Brahman. It is pure consciousness distinct from mental states or ideas. Though not identical with particular states of mind or thoughts, cit illuminates and gives life to these. It is the background or foundation to all states of consciousness and as such is eternal and unchanging. In *Vedānta, cit is often grouped together with being (*sat) and bliss (*ānanda) as a description of Brahman.

Citta (Skt., 'that which has been seen', i.e. belonging to consciousness, cf. CIT). In Hinduism, the reflective and thus conscious mind; in Buddhism, an equivalent to *manas (reflective mind) and *vijñāna (continuing consciousness). It belongs to all beings above the level of plant life. The nature of citta received particular analysis and emphasis in *Vijñanavāda (also known as Yogacāra)—so much so that the school is also known as Cittamātra, Mind only. In *Abhidhamma, the analysis differentiates 121 types of citta, each of which may be combined with any one of fifty-two *cetasikas* (the accompanying qualities of experience), thus producing the extremely large variety of mental events.

Cittamātra (mind only): see VIJÑĀNAVĀDA; VIJÑAPTI-MĀTRA.

Citt'ekaggata or **cittassa ekaggata** (Pāli, 'one-pointedness of mind'). The mark of having reached full concentration (*samādhi) during Buddhist meditation. The mind acquires perfect singularity of intention and purpose, and is capable of focusing and retaining attention upon the chosen subject of meditation (*kammaṭṭhāna) without distraction.

***City of God, The*:** see DE CIVITATE DEI.

City of Refuge. A place to which, in Judaism, those who have accidentally killed may flee. According to Numbers 35. 13, there were six cities of refuge in biblical times, where one who had killed could escape the vengeance of the people and earn his living. Roads to the cities had to be kept in good repair and clearly signposted (*Mak.* 10. 6, *Yad.* 8. 5). After the trial, if he was found guilty of accidental killing, he could return to the city and was not free to leave until the death of the officiating *high priest had avenged the life. Such a person could also seek refuge at the altar (e.g. 1 Kings 1. 5).

Cīvara (part of Buddhist dress): see HABIT, RELIGIOUS; MONASTICISM (BUDDHIST).

Civil religion. The term used by R. N. Bellah to describe the complex of symbolic meanings shared by many Americans and uniting them in a moral community. In the fashion of *Durkheim, Bellah pointed to the sacralization of the American Way of Life. But American civil religion is seen as more than merely a form of national self-worship: it entails 'the subordination of the nation to ethical principles that transcend it and in terms of which it should be judged'. Linking theism, patriotism, competitive individualism, and faith in progress, different sectors of American life have emphasized different components of the overarching religion. One sacred-cum-social theme, however, is widely held. This is the notion of America as a redeemer nation, a chosen people with a messianic world-saving mission. Bellah has written (1975) that American civil religion 'is an empty and broken shell'. President Reagan reactivated the complex, deliberately sacralizing America's mission. Beyond the specific use of Bellah, 'civil religion' has come to refer more loosely to the evident necessity of all communities to find symbols and rituals which will take the place of the religious rituals and symbols which no longer command adherence: see further SECULARIZATION.

R. N. Bellah, *Beyond Belief* (1970), *The Broken Covenant* (1975); R. N. Bellah and P. E. Hammond, *Varieties of Civil Religion* (1980).

Classics, Confucian: see CONFUCIAN CLASSICS.

Clement of Alexandria, St (*c.*150–*c.*215). Christian *father (patristic theologian). He was head of the catechetical school of *Alexandria from 190. His chief works are the *Protrepticus*, or 'Exhortation to the Greeks', the *Paedagogus* on Christian life and manners, and the *Stromateis*, or 'Miscellanies'. Like the *gnostics, Clement held that knowledge or illumination was the chief element in Christian perfection, although for him true 'gnosis' presupposed the faith of the Church. Equally, he believed that Greek philosophy was a preparation for the gospel: 'Philosophy was necessary to the Greeks for righteousness until the coming of the Lord; and even now it is useful for the development of true religion as a kind of preparatory discipline for those who arrive at faith by way of demonstration.' He shared the emphasis of the *desert fathers on the unknowability of God (see APOPHATIC THEOLOGY): 'We fling ourselves upon the majesty of Christ: if we then advance through holiness towards the abyss [*bathos*], we shall have a kind of knowledge of God who contains everything, knowing, not what he is, but what he is not.' His name occurs in the early martyrologies, but it was excised by Pope Clement VIII on the grounds of his doubtful orthodoxy.

S. R. C. Lilla, *Clement of Alexandria* . . . (1971).

Clement of Rome, St. Traditional third *bishop of Rome, perhaps to be connected with the fellow worker of *Paul (Philippians 4. 3). A letter from the Roman church to that of Corinth is ascribed to him and is known as *1 Clement*. The letter, a somewhat pompous appeal for peace in the church of Corinth, shows the beginning of Roman claims to authority over other churches. It may be dated *c*.70 or *c*.96 CE. It also mentions (ch. 5) the martyrdoms of *Peter and Paul. The work known as *2 Clement* (but certainly by a different author) is a homily on the Christian life and repentance.

A mass of other early Christian literature circulated under Clement's name. The most important are the *Clementine Homilies* and *Recognitions* (3rd–4th cents.). Both are versions of a romance in which Clement meets *Peter, witnesses his contests with *Simon Magus, and (in the *Recognitions*) is reunited with his lost family by Peter. The romance is a framework for theological discourses of Peter. Among other features, their primitive Christology (Jesus as true *prophet and *messiah) and interest in the Jerusalem church have persuaded some scholars that they have a very early, perhaps *Ebionite, source. The *Tübingen school went so far as to see the conflict with Simon Magus as a reflection of the opposition between Peter and Paul in the 1st cent.

Tr. in R. M. Grant and H. H. Graham, *The Apostolic Fathers*, ii (1965); J. B. Lightfoot, *Apostolic Fathers* (1890).

Clergy (Gk. *kleros*, an object used in casting lots, as by Jewish priests, Deuteronomy 18. 1 ff.). Designated religious leaders, especially in Christianity by means of ordination. The New Testament displays a varied pattern of religious ministry and leadership. By the end of the 1st cent., the *bishop (*episcopos*, from Gk., 'overseer'), had responsibility for worship and the care of the poor in a local area, in close association with elders. Their work of service was supported by *deacons. By the beginning of the 2nd cent., the New Testament model of the Church, as a body in which all parts are equally necessary under the headship of Christ, was being replaced by the metaphor of a hierarchical body on the model of the Roman army, with a clear command structure. Ordained leadership was consolidated in three ranks, bishops, priests (virtually displacing elders), and deacons. The clericalization of the Church subordinated the laity in decision-making, a situation partly, but unevenly, reversed in the *Reformation. A further distinction arose, with the development of monasticism, between secular clergy (who work in the *saeculum*, or world), and regular clergy (who live under a *regula*, or rule, usually in communities). The term 'clergy' is sometimes used of functionaries in other religions (e.g. mullahs in Islam), but none have anything like the same order or succession or duties.

Cloud of Unknowing, The. English mystical treatise of the 14th cent. The author, whose anonymity has remained inviolate, stands in the line of *Dionysian influence as mediated by the Victorines, especially Thomas Gallus whose Latin version of Dionysius' *Mystical Theology* he rendered into English. The author teaches that God cannot be known by human reason and that in *contemplation the soul is conscious of a 'cloud of unknowing' between itself and God which can only be penetrated by 'a sharp dart of love'. The author recommends the repetition of short phrases or single words to foster this loving attention to God, and is sharply critical of any reliance on sensible feelings in *prayer, perhaps having *Rolle in mind. The teaching on the entry into the cloud of unknowing has marked parallels with *John of the Cross's teaching about the onset of the *dark night of the soul.

Cluny. Benedictine (*Benedict) *abbey in Burgundy (France), founded in 909/10. It became a centre of renewal in the Church and in monastic practice, under a series of highly able abbots, especially St Odo. The emphasis was on simplicity and order (including the refusal of high office in the Church), which extended to church building. Cluniac houses were established in many parts of Europe, although the control from Cluny was not strong. During the 12th cent., the influence of Cluny began to decline, although the abbey itself survived until 1790.

J. Evans, *Monastic Life at Cluny* . . . (1931).

CMS or **Church Missionary Society.** Anglican society founded in 1799 'to proclaim the Gospel in all lands and to gather the people of all races into the fellowship of Christ's church'. It pioneered Christian missionary work in NW Canada, New Zealand, the Middle E., Africa, Persia, parts of India and Pakistan, Śri Lankā, S. China, and Japan. In 1985 it had a budget of more than £3m., and was sponsoring missionaries in twenty-eight countries, all at the invitation of indigenous churches and in many cases working as teachers, engineers, etc. Its theology has always been *evangelical.

Coal. A description among Coptic, Ethiopic, and E. Syrian Christians of the sacramental body of *Christ. The description is derived from Isaiah 6.

6 f., where a live coal is taken from the altar and laid on the lips of the prophet. By *typology, the consecrated *host becomes the true and living coal.

Cobb, J. (exponent of process theology): see PROCESS THEOLOGY.

Codex Iuris Canonici (Lat., Code of *Canon Law). The collection of all laws obtaining in the Roman Catholic churches of the Latin Rite—the Eastern or Oriental Rite churches have their own Codex. The first code was drawn up between 1903 and 1917, and was revised between 1965 and 1982, being promulgated in 1983. It contains 1,752 canons, in seven books, dealing with General Norms, the People of God, the Teaching Office of the Church, the Office of Sanctifying in the Church, the Temporal Goods of the Church, Sanctions, and Processes.

Codifications of Law. In Judaism, successive attempts to bring order to the proliferating interpretations and applications of the original *Torah. The commands of Torah are often context-independent ('Be holy') and need to be applied: what does it mean to keep the *Sabbath day holy, in practice? Thus it came to be said that the laws on the Sabbath are a mountain hanging from a hair. As applications proliferated, so attempts to organize and eventually codify these applications were made. Among the earliest were *Mishnah and *Tosefta, leading to the Palestinian and Babylonian *Talmuds, though these are not in the form of codes. Pioneers of the latter were the *She'iltot* of the Babylonian Aḥai of Shabḥa, and *Halakhot Pesukot* of Yehudai Gaon. Prominent in the transition to codes was *Saʿadiah Gaon. But the most ambitious was *Mishneh Torah* of *Maimonides. This remains a point of reference, but other codes have appeared, often condensing and reorganizing—e.g. Jacob ben Asher's *Arba'ah Turim* (Four Rows; *Tur* for short), which was the basis for **Shulḥān Arukh* of Joseph *Caro. An alternative form, in more recent times, has been the compilation of encyclopaedias, of which one, embracing rabbinic law, is in the process of publication in Jerusalem. For Jewish Codes and Codes in other religions, see Index, Codes.

L. Ginsberg, 'Law, Codification of', *Jewish Encyclopedia*.

Coenobite (Gk., *koinos*, 'common', + *bios*, 'life'; hence coenobitic). A religious who lives in a community, as opposed to a hermit. Organized monastic communities began in Egypt with *Pachomius in the 4th cent. The word is also used of *anchorites (e.g. *Carthusians) who reside in separate dwellings under a rule of silence, but who live otherwise as a community.

Cohen, Hermann (1842–1918). German Jewish philosopher. As a philosopher, he brought a new interpretation to the thought of Immanuel *Kant. In response to the historian, Treitschke, who in 1879 attacked the Jews for lack of patriotism, he maintained that German Jews were completely loyal to German society while practising their religion. He argued that as the *chosen people of God, Jews have a particular duty to bring about the unity of humanity and establish God's Kingdom on earth. This duty is linked specifically to Torah and the keeping of its commands: 'If Judaism had brought nothing to the world but the *Sabbath, it would have proved itself to be the producer of peace and promoter of joy for all people. The Sabbath is the first step on the road which leads to the abolition of *slavery.' This defence of Judaism led to a change in his philosophical position in which he saw reality as rooted in God's existence. His major work, *Die Religion der Vernunft aus den Quellen des Judentums* was published a year after his death.

J. Melker, *Hermann Cohen's Philosophy of Judaism* (1968).

Colenso, John William (1814–83). *Anglican *bishop of Natal. He is remembered principally for the controversy caused by his papers on *The Pentateuch and the Book of Joshua Critically Examined* (1862–79). His studies (prompted by the questions of his Zulu inquirers, to whom, like the prophet, he could not tell a lie) looked especially at the implications of numbers taken literally, and challenged the historical accuracy of the books and their authorship by *Moses. He thus became at the time practically the only English exponent of the historical criticism of the *Bible. He was censured by the English bishops and deposed by his *metropolitan. He contested the deposition, and a schism ensued in Natal which was eventually healed in 1911.

J. Guy, *The Heretic . . .* (1983).

Coleridge, Samuel Taylor (1772–1834). Poet and thinker. Born at Ottery St Mary in Devon, he studied (somewhat chaotically) at Cambridge where he met William Wordsworth. With him he published *Lyrical Ballads* in 1798. Already he had, with Robert Southey, attempted to set up a communal society, Pantisocracy, putting into practice the ideals of the French Revolution. In 1798, he went to Germany to study *Kant, and came under the influence of Schiller and Goethe. On his return he lectured and wrote. In religion he represents the Romantic reaction against both rationalism and dogmatic religious systems, seeing the heart of religion in human religious need. *Boehme and *Spinoza were important influences, and he found support for his stress on inwardness in *Platonism. His belief that Church and State form an organic unity and that Christianity is to be identified in ethical action, led him to believe that the reunion of Christendom is possible—for which reasons he is sometimes called the 'father of the *Broad Church'.

S. T. Coleridge, *Lay Sermons* (1816), *On the Constitution of Church and State* (1830), *Aids to Reflection* (1825), and *Confessions of An Enquiring Spirit* (1840); J. R. Barth, *Coleridge and Christian Doctrine* (1987); J. D. Boulger,

Coleridge as Religious Thinker (1961); D. Jasper, *Coleridge as Poet and Religious Thinker* (1985).

Collating (appointing to a benefice): see ADVOWSON.

Collect. A short variable prayer used in W. Christian worship. In the *eucharist it precedes the readings. The term seems to have denoted originally the 'collecting' of the petitions of members of the congregation into a single prayer. Collects are constructed from an invocation, a petition, and a pleading of Christ's name or ascription of glory to God. The collects in the **Book of Common Prayer* are partly adapted from Latin service books and partly composed by T. *Cranmer. In the *BCP*, at morning and evening prayers two invariable collects follow the collect of the day.

Collective representations. A theoretical term closely associated with *Durkheim, referring to forms of knowledge which exist over and above any particular member of society. Religious and moral systems, categories of space, time, and the person, even much scientific knowledge, have *sui generis* characteristics. As traditions, they transcend individuals: people come and go, traditions live on. Although Durkheim tended to reify and mystify the realm of the collective, he helped pave the way for those theorists who have treated the religious as an autonomous domain. He wrote, for example, of 'the way in which religious ideas . . . combine and separate and are transformed into one another, giving rise to contradictory complexes' (*Rules of Sociological Method*, tr. 1938). Religions have their *own* (albeit also socially informed) dynamics. Durkheim moved towards what today is known as the intrareligious approach. See also LÉVI-STRAUSS, C.

Collegiate church. A church which is governed by a *chapter of *canons, but is not, like a *cathedral, a bishop's see. Instances in England are Westminster Abbey and St George's Chapel, Windsor.

Colossians, Letter to the. An epistle of *Paul and book of the New Testament. Like *Philippians, it was written from prison. The church at Colossae in SW Asia Minor had apparently been founded by Paul's co-worker Epaphrus. The main purpose of the letter is to deal with a certain 'philosophy' which was making converts (2. 1 ff.). Allusions (e.g. to speculation about *angels) suggest a connection with later *gnosticism, but this is not certain. The passage 1. 15–20 is one of the important texts for *christology in the New Testament.

Colours, liturgical: see LITURGICAL COLOURS.

Columba, St (*c*.521–97). Christian abbot and missionary, trained in Irish monasteries, who, in *c*.563 established himself and twelve companions on the island of Iona. He remained there as a base for evangelizing the Scottish mainland and establishing monasteries on other nearby islands. Though not a bishop, he exercised ecclesiastical authority in the area, and consecrated the new king of the Scots in 574. He is also known for three Latin poems and for his skill as a scribe. Feast day, 9 June.

Columbus Convention: see REFORM JUDAISM.

Commandments: see MITZVAH; SIX HUNDRED AND THIRTEEN COMMANDMENTS; TEN COMMANDMENTS.

Common Life, Brothers and Sisters of (Christian devotional movement): see GROOTE, GEERT.

***Common Prayer, Book of*:** see *Book of Common Prayer*.

Communicatio idiomatum (Lat., 'interchange of properties'). A doctrine of *christology put forward by several *patristic writers. It emphasizes the separateness of the human and divine natures in Christ, but holds that what may only strictly be said of the one may also be said of the other, because of their union in the one person. It is most clearly stated in the *Tome* of Pope Leo (449) (see CHALCEDON).

Communion. The partaking of the consecrated elements at the Christian *eucharist. Along with *Lord's Supper it is also (as in the **Book of Common Prayer*) another name for the whole service of the eucharist. Communion is received from the minister differently in different churches: kneeling at the communion table, standing, or from a tray and cup or cups passed among the congregation. Communion 'in both kinds', i.e. by partaking of both bread and wine, was universal until the Middle Ages, but in the W. the wine came to be drunk only by the celebrant, the people partaking only of the bread. This practice continued in the Roman Catholic Church until the second half of the 20th cent. All the churches of the Reformation administer communion in both kinds. In the Orthodox Church it is usual to give communion from a spoon containing the bread sprinkled with a few drops of wine. It is a characteristic difference between E. and W. practice that E. churches (except the *Armenian) use 'leavened' bread (made with yeast) and W. churches 'unleavened' (see AZYMITE). But in Protestant churches and at informal eucharists leavened bread is usual. In churches of Puritan ancestry grape juice is used instead of wine.

In E. churches children are admitted to communion as soon as they are baptized. In the RC Church since 1910 the rule has been that children are admitted as soon as they can distinguish between the eucharistic bread and ordinary bread; the day of a child's first communion is sometimes an occasion of family celebration. In other churches *confirmation or believer's baptism is necessary to be admitted to communion.

In the later Middle Ages, communion once a year by laypeople was the norm. In post-medieval times nearly all religious revivals, both Catholic and Protestant, have aimed at increasing frequency of communion. At present, weekly communion is most usual among observant Anglicans and Catholics. Daily communion is practised in religious communities and among a very few of the laity. In Protestant churches a typical practice is to append a communion service to the ordinary service of worship once a month. The Orthodox Church retains infrequent communion, about four times a year or less.

Communion of Saints. A belief professed in the Christian *Apostles' creed. It points to the whole company of the faithful, living and dead, in union with Christ and with each other. The Latin *communio sanctorum* could also mean 'communion of holy things', i.e. a sharing especially in the *sacraments.

Companions (Arab. *Aṣḥāb* or *Ṣaḥāba*). The men closest to *Muḥammad during his time in *Mecca and *Madīna; foremost among these, the first four caliphs (*khalīfa): *Abu Bakr, *ʿUmar, *ʿUthmān, and *ʿAlī b. Abī Tālib. A line of transmission of *ḥadīth must be traced back to a Companion, or a wife of Muḥammad, or member of his household. The behaviour and words of the Companions are themselves normative, signs of the *sunna, as are their reports of the Prophet's words and actions.

The stricter definition of Companions restricts them to those who actually knew Muḥammad well, and spent much time with him; but the term was later extended to include others of his generation who had met him. Companions are sometimes classified into groups, such as *Emigrants (*Muhājirūn*, i.e. those who accompanied Muḥammad on the *Hijra from Mecca to Madīna), and Helpers (*Anṣār*, those in Madīna who became his followers). See also SAHĀBA.

Compassion (characteristic Buddhist virtue): see KARUṆĀ.

Compline. The traditional last of the day *hours in the W. Church, said before retiring at night. The corresponding office in the Orthodox Church is the *apodeipnon* (Gk., 'after supper'). The W. office begins with an evening hymn such as 'Before the ending of the day' and includes the *Nunc Dimittis. It was subsumed into the Anglican *evening prayer, but is often said separately, e.g. privately or in religious retreats. In the 1971 Catholic Breviary it is called 'night prayer'. The Apodeipnon begins with a prayer ('O Heavenly King, the Comforter . . ., take up your abode in us and cleanse us from every stain, and save our souls, You who are Good'), followed by the hymn (Trisagion), 'O holy God', the Lord's Prayer, psalms, the creed, and final hymns and prayers, which vary according to the season. The Grand Compline is a more elaborate service in Lent.

Compostela: see PILGRIMAGE.

Concelebration. The celebration of the *eucharist by a number of priests saying the eucharistic prayer, or the words of *consecration, together over the same bread and wine. After dying out in the W. (except at ordinations), the practice was revived in the RC Church by *Vatican II. It is also sometimes used as a device to allow priests and congregations from churches out of communion with one another to have a eucharist together.

Concept of positive freedom (space for human effort in a deterministic system): see SPINOZA.

Conciliar controversy (dispute about the relative authority of a council or a pope): see ANTIPOPE.

Concordat. An agreement between a religious group and the government of a country on matters of mutual concern. In Roman Catholic understanding, the purpose of a concordat is to protect the spiritual and material welfare of the Church. Thus the *Vatican entered into concordats with both Nazi Germany and Fascist Italy. An important model is the Pactum Callixtinum, or Concordat of Worms (1122) whereby the contest between the Popes and the Holy Roman Emperors over the right to appoint bishops was resolved in favour of the Popes. The Concordat of 1801 between Pope Pius VII and Napoleon Bonaparte (then First Consul) led to the formal restoration of the RC Church in France after the Revolution under a measure of state control and support.

Concrete logic or **science** (of Lévi-Strauss): see MYTH.

Concursive revelation (a co-operative (i.e. between God and humans) understanding of revelation): see REVELATION.

Confessing Church or **Bekennende Kirche.** The *Protestant church in Germany organized in opposition to the official Nazi church organizations and policies. (see KIRCHENKAMPF). It was at first known as the 'Confessional' Church (*Bekenntnis-Kirche*) because it claimed to take its stand on the historic Christian *confessions (and not on mere politics): this attitude is reflected in its theological manifesto, the *Barmen Declaration of 1934. But as it began to see itself as a church of *confessors under persecution, the name 'Confessing' Church came to be preferred.

Confession

Christianity 1. An affirmation or profession of faith: (i) the testimony of a *martyr or *confessor (e.g. 1 Timothy 6. 13); (ii) a doctrinal statement in the Orthodox Church, of which the following are of particular importance: the Orthodox Confession of Peter *Mog(h)ila (1643); the Answers of Jeremiah, *patriarch of *Constantinople, to *Lutherans (1576); the Confession of Metrophanes Critopulus to Protestants (1625). In the Russian Orthodox Church, the *Catechisms, especially the Longer C. of Philaret (1839), are comparably central; (iii) Protestant professions of faith, especially of 16th/17th cents. Among Lutherans, the *Augsburg Confession (1530), the Apology of the AC (1531), the Smalcald Articles (1537), the Treatise on the Power and Primacy of the *Pope (1537), the Small and Large Catechisms of Luther (1529), were included in *The Book of Concord* (1580). Calvinists and other reformed Protestants regarded the production of Confessions as a continuing work of faith, and wrote many. Of especial importance are: the Gallican Confession (1559), the Helvetic Confessions (1536, 1566), the *Westminster Confession (1647), the Helvetic Consensus (1675). The *Thirty-Nine Articles (1563) combine Catholic, Lutheran, and Calvinist elements. Confessions continue to be important in response to particular occasions (e.g. *Barmen Declaration, 1934), or in quest for agreed teaching via *Catechisms (e.g. the Catholic Catechism, 1992). From this doctrinal sense of confession, the term has also come to mean a religious body or denomination.

2. An acknowledgement of *sin. In Christianity, this may be made either in worship by a congregation ('general confession'), or privately to a priest ('auricular confession': Lat., *ad auriculam*, 'to the ear'), who mediates God's willingness to forgive, and pronounces God's *absolution. Auricular confession has been the normal Catholic and Orthodox practice, although since 1970 there has also been a general confession in the Roman *mass (see J. Dallen, *The Reconciling Community: The Rite of Penance*, 1986). The Fourth *Lateran Council (1215) laid down that confession should be made at least once a year, and observant Catholics may go to confession monthly or weekly. Confession is formally part of the *sacrament of *penance. The relation between penitent and confessor issues in the 'seal of confession', the priest's obligation to treat as absolutely secret anything revealed to him in the confessional.

The recognition and acknowledgement of fault occurs in all religions, and the term 'confession' is applied widely, although what is happening in the context of each religion may be very different.

Judaism Confession of sin in Judaism (Heb., *viddu'i*) is an essential prequisite of expiation. Individuals, such as David after the seduction of Bathsheba (2 Samuel 11–12), as well as groups (e.g. Ezra 9) made confession and sought God's forgiveness.The *Mishnah records the prayer of the *high priest on the *Day of Atonement when he prayed for the forgiveness of the nation (*Yoma* 3. 8). Prayers of confession are part of the *synagogue liturgy, particularly at *Rosh ha-Shanah and Yom Kippur, and well-known prayers include Ashamnu (We have incurred guilt) *'Al het (For the sin), and *Avinu malkenu (Our father, Our king). Individuals should also make confession. The *Talmud teaches that in particular the dying should be encouraged to confess their sins, and all individual confession is made directly to God with no intermediary.

Buddhism The acknowledgement of wrongful actions was recognized by the Buddha to be of value in psychological and spiritual development. Unlike other traditions, however, in Buddhism confession is not made to a divine power and there is no concept of absolution or the forgiveness of sins. The act of confession (*pāpa-desanā*) is the owning-up to one's failings or shortcomings in order to cultivate greater self-awareness and be freed from the burden of persecutory guilt. Feelings of shame (*hiri*) and remorse (*ottappa*), on the other hand, which may be described as reparatory guilt, are regarded as healthy rather than pathological reactions to evildoing and as powerful inhibitors of further wrongful deeds. The occasion for confession in monastic Buddhism is a formal public event which takes place at the *Uposatha ceremony. Here the rules of monastic discipline are read out to the assembled monks, each of whom is obliged to declare infringements of them either by himself or another. Thus as well as ensuring individual purity the collective purity of the Order is also preserved. There is no counterpart to this formal ceremony for lay Buddhists.

Jainism Confession (*alocana* and *pratikramaṇa*) occurs twice daily for monks; laypeople make confession to their *guru. Confession is a specific attack on *karma as Jains understand it. In Paryūsana, confession is central, even (by letter) to those absent.

R. Pettazzoni, *La confessione dei peccati* (3 vols., 1929–36; *La Confession des péchés* is a tr. (by R. Monnot) and enlargement of vol. i).

Confessor. 1. In the early church, a person who suffered for 'confessing' (i.e. maintaining) the faith but not to the point of *martyrdom. After the time of persecutions, the term was extended to apply to those whose lives were manifestly holy (as Edward the Confessor, declared to be so in 1161).

2. A Christian priest who hears (private) *confessions and administers the sacrament of *penance.

Confirmation. The Christian rite in which the *Holy Spirit is conveyed in a renewed or fuller way to those who have already undergone *baptism, derived from John 14. 15–21, and Acts 2. 37 f., which suggests a division between the two. In the Middle Ages it came to be counted as one of the seven *sacraments. It appears generally as a distinct rite in the 4th cent., involving the laying on of hands or *anointing with oil; originally these acts were associated with baptism itself. In the E., the immediate relation of baptism and confirmation has been retained, so that a baby receives baptism, confirmation, and Holy Communion in a single service; the bishop takes no part, except for having consecrated the *chrism used for the anointing. In the W., the bishop retained his function as minister of the rite (as he had been originally also of baptism). Confirmation, therefore, had to be left until the candidate could be presented to the bishop in person.

Modern Roman Catholic practice is to confer confirmation shortly after the seventh birthday. It is normally administered during *mass. The candidates renew their baptismal vows; the bishop extends his hands over them and prays they may receive the Holy Spirit; and he traces the sign of the cross on the forehead of each with *chrism. *Vatican II restored an old Byzantine form of words, 'N., be sealed with the gift of the Holy Spirit.' Anglican churches have a similar rite (with, in the **Book of Common Prayer*, the words, 'Defend, O Lord, this thy child with thy heavenly grace, that s/he may continue thine for ever, and daily increase in thy Holy Spirit more and more until s/he come unto thy everlasting kingdom'), with a laying on of the hands, but without chrism or the sign of the cross, and confirmation is preceded by a course of Christian instruction by the local priest. In the Anglican Church no one is admitted to communion until confirmed. Lutherans and some other Protestant churches also practice confirmation in a similar way.

G. Austin, *The Rite of Confirmation* . . . (1985); K. B. Cully (ed.), *Confirmation* . . . (1962).

Confucian Classics. A canonical collection of works whose prestige in traditional China was comparable to that of Greek and Roman classics in the W., and whose authority was as unassailable as that of biblical scripture. These texts were by far the most important moral and intellectual influence in Chinese society, memorized by every student, tested in the imperial examinations that led to civil office, extensively quoted as a matter of course in government documents as well as private literary writings.

Three of them predate *Confucius: the *Shih* (Song Lyrics), the **Shu* (Historical Documents of Archaic Times), and the **I* or *Yi* (Change). The **Ch'un Ch'iu* (Springs and Autumns) is supposed to be from the brush of the Master himself. Texts on ritually correct behaviour are collectively called **Li Chi* (Ritual Scriptures). A canon of ritual music (*Yüeh Ching*) is said to have been lost before the 3rd cent. BCE, but its contents can be surmised from other, surviving texts. All these works were supposed to have been edited by Confucius, or have him as their figure of authority; hence the term, Confucian Classics. Great confusion was introduced into the Confucian literature by the notorious 'burning of the books' under the first Emperor of Ch'in in 213 BCE. During the succeeding Han dynasty (206 BCE–220 CE), most of the energy of the Literati or Confucian scholars (*Ju) went into restoring the Classics (as they now became) and interpreting them. An imperial college was established to teach them; imperially convened conferences debated controversial points in them; and they were engraved on stone in 175 CE and again during 240–8 CE. They were eventually made widely available as block-printed books during 923–53 CE.

The corpus of Confucian Classics varied over the course of time. Confucius himself is said to have taught his students the *Shih*, *Shu*, *Li*, and *Yüeh*, and perhaps, to the most capable, the *Yi* and *Ch'un Ch'iu*. The appellation 'scripture' (*ching*) was unknown to him, first appearing in the book of the philosopher Chuang (**Chuang Tzu*) in the 3rd cent. BCE. The Five Scriptures taught in the state college of the Han dynasty (from 136 BCE–220 CE) were *Shih*, *Shu*, *Yi*, *Ch'un Ch'iu*, and *Li* (at first the **Yi Li*, or Ceremonials and Rituals, and later the **Li Chi*, or Records of Rituals). To these there were then added the *Lun Yü* or **Analects*, and the **Hsiao Ching*, or *Scripture of Filiality*, to make up Seven Scriptures. In the T'ang period (618–907) the Canon comprised Nine Scriptures, including *Shih*, *Shu*, *Yi*, the Three Ritual Collections (*Yi Li*, *Li Chi*, and *Chou Li* or *Chou Kuan*, an idealized description of governmental institutions in early Chou times, ?1111–256 BCE), and the Three Exegeses, meaning the *Ch'un Ch'iu* with its ancient exegeses (*chuan*) named for their putative authors: *Kung-yang Chuan*, *Ku-liang Chuan*, *Tso Chuan*. The final version of the Confucian Classics was the *Thirteen Scriptures with Notes and Commentaries*, which appeared at the very end of the 12th cent. In addition to all of the above enumerated texts, it included the book of the philosopher Meng (*Meng Tzu*, or **Mencius*) and the earliest dictionary, called *Er Ya*.

The neo-Confucian philosophers of the Sung dynasty (960–1279) identified a corpus within this corpus which they called the *Four Books, or Books of the Four Philosophers (*Ssu Shu*): the *Analects*, *Mencius*, *Ta Hsüeh* (**Great Learning*), and *Chung Yung* (*Doctrine of the Mean), the latter two being small texts extracted from *Li Chi*. The Four Books, equipped with the commentaries of the great Sung literatus Chu Hsi (1130–1200), were thereafter the very heart of the Confucian Classics.

Confucianism (Chin. equivalent, *ju-chia*, *ju-chiao*, *kung chiao*: School of Scholars or of *Confucius). The school and teaching of Confucius, which formed the mainstream in Chinese philosophy during most of the past 2,000 years. While Confucius' teachings are best found in the *Analects*, Confucianism regards as its special texts the Confucian Classics, for which see above. These are books of widely divergent genres, including a divination manual, a collection of speeches and documents, and a collection of ceremonial songs and love lyrics. The *Spring-Autumn Annals* include a dry account of events which is said to be compactly didactic. The *Book of Rites*, however, contains certain chapters that have more philosophical content, and two of these have been singled out for special attention: the *Great Learning* and the *Doctrine of the Mean*. Together with the *Analects*, a record of the conversations between Confucius and his disciples, and the *Book of Mencius*, a lengthier record of the conversations between *Mencius and his disciples, they make up the so-called Four Books, a smaller corpus of texts offering more coherent philosophical teachings, especially regarding the cultivation of moral character, with 'the Mean' discoursing more on what may be called the heart of Confucian spirituality: the practice of moderating our emotions in an effort to reach psychic harmony. These Four Books assumed special importance quite late, becoming the core of the examination syllabus, together with certain commentaries, in 1313. Long before that, the Five Classics had become the basis of civil service examinations (125 BCE), thus establishing the supremacy of the Confucian school. Even then, Confucian philosophy became dominant in Han China (206 BCE–220CE) only after much uncertainty, and by losing some of its doctrinal purity and integrity. At that time, its chief interpreters preferred the teachings of *Hsun-tzu (d. 238 BCE) who opposed Mencius' doctrine of the original goodness of human nature, and gave primary importance to rituals. His disciples included important Legalists, that is, scholars and politicians who taught an amoral doctrine aimed at helping the political ruler to gain and to keep power, regarding penal law as the mainstay of such. In becoming the established orthodoxy, Confucianism became also eclectic, accepting many elements from Legalism. The Confucian Classics became the basis for traditions of textual philology and exegesis, developing traditions of commentaries and sub-commentaries that sometimes obscured the original teachings of the Master. Nevertheless, and in spite of certain attempts, the man Confucius never became divinized. He was given many posthumous honours, including the recognition of having been an 'uncrowned king' who ruled history through his teachings and alleged writings. A cult was inaugurated, with its centre at his native place, Ch'u-fu, and with his descendants as sacrificial officials in possession of a mansion situated near the huge temple dedicated to him. Elsewhere too, in China as well as Korea and Japan, temples were dedicated to his memory, and, quite appropriately, schools were usually situated next to these temples, as education and cult became integral parts each of the other. In Chinese terms, Confucianism is a religion (*chiao*, literally, 'doctrine') as well as a philosophy (*chia*, literally, 'a school of transmission'). But it is different from those W. religions which emphasize revealed doctrines and belief in God. While Confucius appears to have believed in a supreme deity, he preferred to teach a doctrine of humanism open to the transcendent, and, in so doing, charted a course away from the earlier preoccupations with the supernatural, as witnessed by *oracle bones (see CHINESE RELIGION). But his teachings helped to keep alive the older cult of veneration for ancestors, and the worship of Heaven, a formal cult practised by China's rulers who regarded themselves, in Confucian terms, to be the keepers of Heaven's Mandate of government. And as Confucius and his immediate disciples addressed themselves primarily to the rulers, searching for someone who would use their advice, China's later generations of Confucian scholars, just as eager for government office, found themselves usually as teachers and cultural mediators, continuing to mould and transform an ancient heritage (for developments, see NEO-CONFUCIANISM). Although Confucianism was not always in power—there were times, even centuries, when Taoism, and especially Buddhism, were preferred by the ruling élite—it has left an indelible imprint on Chinese civilization which remains even today under Marxist government in mainland China, surviving the terrible onslaughts it suffered during the Cultural Revolution (1966–76) and the Anti-Confucius campaign. In recent years, Confucian work ethic and family loyalty have been given as partial reasons for the rapid economic development of the E. Asian Pacific rim (Japan, Korea, Taiwan, Hongkong, Singapore). See also Index, Confucians.

W. T. de Bary (ed.), *Sources of Chinese Tradition* (1960); H. G. Creel, *Confucius and the Chinese Way* (1960); H. Fingarette, *Confucianism: The Secular as Sacred* (1972); W.-c. Liu, *A Short History of Confucian Philosophy* (1955).

Confucius. The Lat. rendering of K'ung Fu-tzu (Master K'ung), whose name was K'ung Ch'iu and also styled Chung-ni. The Chinese sage was born in the small ancient state of Lu, near modern Ch'u-fu (Shantung), probably in 552 BCE. Little can be established about his life, forebears, and family, although legends (including very early ones) are abundant. The best source is probably the *Analects* (*Lun-yu*), or Confucius' recorded conversations with his disciples (compiled in 3rd cent. BCE), and this may be supplemented by the *Annals of Tso* (3rd cent. BCE), the *Book of Mencius* (2nd cent. BCE) and the *Historical Annals* of Ssu-ma Ch'ien (1st cent. BCE). K'ung is sometimes said to be a direct descendant of the Shang (1766?–1123 BCE) royal house, whose heirs were given the fief of the state of Sung by the Chou dynasty (1111–249 BCE). But his own family had moved to Lu three to five generations prior to his birth. The *Analects* report that he was of humble status. While nothing certain is known of his childhood, he said of himself that by age 15, he had fixed his mind on studying; and his humble circumstances were the occasion for his learning many menial things. K'ung probably served in a junior post at the Lu court around the age of 27. He later became a *ssu-k'ou* (police commissioner?) at about the age of 50, but only for about a year. It was the highest public position he ever occupied. In over ten years of travel (497–484 BCE), K'ung visited many other feudal states of his time, seeking a ruler who would use his services, but never finding one. He also occupied himself with music and poetry, especially the *ya* and the *sung*, which now make up two sections of the *Book of Poetry*, one of the five classics considered Confucian. The *Analects* record as well conversations with Duke Ai of Lu, and with others, on questions of government, ritual, and his disciples. K'ung is also described as informal and cheerful at home, affable yet firm. In his old age, he devoted more and more time to his disciples. But the last years of his life were saddened by the successive losses of his son, his favourite disciple Yen Hui, and the loyal but flamboyant disciple, Tzu-lu. According to the *Annals of Tso*, he himself died aged 73, in the sixteenth year of the reign of Duke Ai (479 BCE). While we have no details about his last hours, we know that at an earlier time when he was sick and his disciple Tzu-lu asked for prayers, the Master replied, 'My prayers have been for a long time.' His political ambitions remaining unfulfilled, K'ung was remembered especially as a teacher, and by many as *the* great moral teacher of E. Asia. While he is said to have had 3,000 disciples, a maximum of seventy is more likely. Traditionally, he has also been credited with the editing of the Five Classics (see CONFUCIAN CLASSICS). The *Spring-Autumn Annals*, which record the history of the state of Lu (722–481 BCE), allegedly came from his hand. But scholars today dispute this. All one can say is that he loved the ancients, above all the Duke of Chou, to whom the Chou dynasty owed its rituals and other institutions, read widely in the books left behind by the ancients, and passed on his knowledge to his disciples: in an age when only aristocrats had access to formal education, he was the first to make it available to a wider circle, without regard to social origin. Above all, he was interested in the difficult art of becoming a perfectly humane (*jen) person, and regarded those who made efforts in that direction as the real gentlemen, rather than those born of high rank. A new class would come into being: scholars (*ju), men who studied with the aim of serving in and improving their society. These came also to be called *shih* (a word which had earlier referred to warriors or knights), and formed a class of educated gentry, the top of the social ladder. The Confucian school is known in Chinese as the Ju school. His central doctrine was that of jen, translated variously as goodness, benevolence, humanity, and human-heartedness. Formerly a particular virtue (the kindness which distinguished the gentleman in his behaviour toward inferiors), jen became a universal virtue, that which *makes* the perfect human being, the sage. K'ung defined it as loving others, as personal integrity and as altruism. His teachings give primary emphasis to the ethical meaning of human relationships, grounding the moral in human nature and its openness to the transcendent. Although he was largely silent on God and the after-life, his silence did not bespeak disbelief. His philosophy was clearly grounded in religion—the inherited religion of the Lord-on-high or Heaven, the supreme and personal deity. He made it clear that it was Heaven which gave him his message and protected him: 'Heaven is the author of the virtue that is in me' (*Analects* 7. 23).

H. G. Creel, *Confucius and the Chinese Way* (1960); W.-c. Liu, *Confucius . . .* (1956); R. Wilhelm, *Confucius and Confucianism* (1931).

Congé d'élire (Fr.). 'Permission to elect' a *bishop, granted in the *Church of England by the Crown to the dean and *chapter of the cathedral of the diocese. However, the congé d'élire is accompanied by a 'letter missive' containing the name of the royal nominee who must be elected (until 1967, under the penalties of *Praemunire).

Congregational churches. Those churches which assert the autonomy of the local congregation. Their historical roots are in Elizabethan Separatism, with its insistence that the 'gathered church' in any given locality consists of those who commit themselves to *Christ and to one another. Its members believe in a *covenant of loyalty and mutual edification, emphasizing the importance of discerning God's will whilst 'gathered' together in Church Meeting. Its earliest apologist, Robert Browne (*A Treatise of Reformation without tarrying for any*, 1582) was followed by others, notably Henry Barrow, John Greenwood, and John Penry. Early 17th-cent. persecution robbed these churches of some outstanding leaders, many leaving England for the Netherlands and later for America. The Congregational Church was prominent in the USA, especially in New England, until it was included in the *United Church of Christ. As the 17th cent. progressed, Christians committed to this Congregational type of churchmanship became known as Independents, and several took a prominent lead on the Parliamentary side in the Civil War. Their views were given vigorous expression by five gifted 'Dissenting Brethren' at the Westminster Assembly (1643) and in the Savoy Declaration of 1658. Like other *Nonconformists, they suffered persecution in the Restoration period, but emerged with vigour and confidence having produced influential writers and theologians such as John Owen and Thomas Goodwin. Denied the privilege of graduating at universities, many of their ministers were educated at the 18th-cent. Dissenting Academies, such as that at Northampton under P. Doddridge's leadership. County 'Associations' provided a meeting-place for church leaders and opportunities for mutual help, and in 1831–2 they gave wider geographical expression to their unity in the formation of the Congregational Union. Concern for world mission was evident in the establishment of the London Missionary Society, whilst their worldwide partnership was indicated by the International Congregational Council, formed in 1949. Renamed the Congregational Church in England and Wales (1966), it joined with the Presbyterian Church of England in 1972 to form the *United Reformed Church. Those churches which maintained that this union threatened their congregational principles joined either the newly formed Congregational Federation or the Fellowship of Evangelical Congregational Churches.

G. G. Atkins and F. L. Fagley, *History of American Congregationalism* (1942); R. T. Jones, *Congregationalism in England, 1662–1962* (1962); W. Walker, *Creeds and Platforms of Congregationalism* (1893).

Congregation for the Doctrine of the Faith: see INQUISITION.

Congregations, Roman. The departments of the Roman *curia responsible for the central administration of the Roman Catholic Church. Each consists primarily of *cardinals under a 'Cardinal-Prefect'. They are presently ten in number, viz. the Sacred Congregations for the Doctrine of Faith (the former *Holy Office), for Bishops, for the Eastern Churches, for the Sacraments, for Divine Worship, for the Clergy, for Religious and Secular Institutes, for the Evangelization of the Nations (the 'Propaganda Fide'), for the Causes of *Saints, and for Catholic Education.

Congruism (between grace and will): see SUAREZ, F. DE.

Conscience: see ETHICS (CHRISTIANITY).

Consecration (*Lat.*, *cum*, 'with', + *sacrum*, 'sacred': i.e. making connection with the sacred). In Christianity: (i) the act in the *eucharist through which the elements become Christ's body and blood; (ii) the *ordination of bishops; and (iii) the dedication of altars, churches, and eucharistic vessels. In liturgical churches, the consecration of a church is a solemn rite performed by the bishop and held to set apart the building permanently for sacred use.

In a more general sense, consecration is the act or ritual which invests objects, places, or people with religious significance, often by way of power and holiness. Thus in Hinduism, particular rituals bring into actuality the divine presence in or through a representation (especially at the moment of *prāṇapratiṣtha, breathing breath into the representation; among Buddhists, the separation between laypeople and *saṅgha is marked by consecrating the area of the compound and installing, ritually, a boundary stone (*sīmā*). In addition to social consecration, individuals may consecrate themselves, often with vows.

Conservative Evangelicals. *Evangelical Christians whose view of the *Bible is 'conservative', i.e. who either reject critical study of the Bible or else hold that such study confirms its authority and historical accuracy. See also FUNDAMENTALISM.

Conservative Judaism. A progressive movement within mainstream Judaism. Conservative (originally 'Historical') Jews acknowledge that certain changes in the Jewish way of life are inevitable since the Enlightenment, but that the traditional forms of Judaism are valid; thus changes in religious practice should only be made with great reluctance. The movement arose in both Europe and the USA in the late 19th cent. After the *Reform *rabbinate had announced its radical programme in Pittsburgh in 1885, the Conservative rabbis founded the *Jewish Theological Seminary, the aim of which was to preserve 'the knowledge and practice of historical Judaism as ordained in the law of *Moses, expounded by the *prophets and sages in Israel in Biblical and Talmudic writings' (Articles of Incorporation). Despite its distance from the Reform movement, the Seminary was not accepted by the *Orthodox, and its rabbinic *ordination was not recognized. Early eminent conservative Jews include Isaac Leeser, Cyrus Adler, Louis Ginsberg and Solomon *Schechter. In 1913, *synagogues sympathetic to the conservative movement formed the *United Synagogue of America, although it was not initially clear whether the United Synagogue's role was to define conservative practice. The Jewish Theological Seminary has become an institution of great academic eminence over the years. None the less, the Conservative movement's rulings on divorce, the ordination of women, the celebration of the second day of festivals, and *conversion have not been accepted by the Orthodox. Today as many as one-third of all affiliated Jews in the USA belong to conservative synagogues. An offshoot of the Conservative movement is *Reconstructionism, founded by the Conservative rabbi Mordecai M. *Kaplan, which perceives Judaism as 'a "religious civilization" rather than as a system of religious belief'. See Index, Conservative Judaism.

M. Davis. *The Emergence of Conservative Judaism* (1963); E. N. Dorff, *Conservative Judaism* . . . (1977); N. Gillman, *Conservative Judaism* (1993); I. Klein, *A Guide to Jewish Practice* (1979).

Consistory

Judaism Official organization of the French Jewish Community. Its constitution was drafted at the Assembly of Jewish Notables called by the Emperor Napoleon in 1806, whose purpose was to integrate Jews as 'useful citizens'. France was divided into thirteen regional Consistories whose purposes was to register all Jews, to encourage obedience to French law, and to organize Jewish religious life. The religious precepts were confirmed as eternally binding, but the political statutes were suspended on the grounds that the Jews were no longer a nation—a dramatic instance of the separation of '*Church' (i.e. *synagogue) and State. Mixed marriages were recognized, but *rabbis were not obliged to officiate at them. The formerly independent chief rabbinate gave way to a Central Consistory of *grands-rabbins* and laymen, with local consistories to regulate congregational matters. Thus the consistory was the Jewish representative organization to the French government until the official separation of Church and State in 1905. The consistory continued in a voluntary capacity until the middle of the 20th cent. but its influence was greatly diminished.

Christianity Any of certain ecclesiastical courts (the consistory being the room in which Roman emperors administered justice). In the Roman Catholic Church, the consistory is the assembly of *cardinals convoked by the pope and conducted in his presence. It may be public (e.g. to appoint new cardinals) or private to consider Church business. In the Church of England the consistory court is the bishop's diocesan court. It is presided over by the *chancellor, who is, once appointed, independent of the bishop. These courts lost most of their importance with the removal of matrimonial and testamentary cases to the secular courts in 1857. In many Presbyterian churches the consistory court is the committee of the local minister and elders.

Constance, Council of (1414–17). Convened at the insistence of the Emperor Sigismund to end the *Great Schism, to reform the *Church, and combat heresy. There were three rival *popes: the council asserted its superiority to the papal office, the three rivals all resigned or were deposed, and in 1417 Martin V was elected pope. Among measures to promote reform, the council enacted that there should be regular General Councils. In these ways the council was important in the history of conciliarism (see ANTIPOPE). *Wycliffe (already dead) and *Hus were condemned as heretics, and Hus was burnt at the stake, although he had come to Constance under safe-conduct from the emperor.

Constantine I or **the Great** (*c.*288–337). First Roman emperor to accept Christianity. When his father died in 306, he was declared emperor in the West, but had to fight against Maxentius to secure his position. On the eve of the battle of the Milvian Bridge, in 312, he saw in a dream, according to Eusebius, a cross bearing the inscription, 'In hoc signo vinces': 'In this sign you will conquer'. Following his victory, he gave favoured status to the Church, but whether this was formalized (in, e.g., the Edict of Milan, 313) is disputed. He established a new imperial capital, or new Rome, on the site of Byzantium, henceforward called *Constantinople. He may have postponed *baptism until his deathbed, perhaps for fear that he would sin after baptism.

H. Dörries, *Constantine the Great*, (1972); R. MacMullen, *Constantine* (1969).

Constantinople (modern Istanbul). The chief see of the E. Roman Empire from the 5th cent. Since the 6th cent. the bishop has been styled the *Ecumenical Patriarch of the East. It fell to Turkish domination in 1453, and many of its ancient churches have become mosques. By the Treaty of Lausanne (1923) the Turkish Republic is bound to protect the Greek Christians in Constantinople; but the patriarch must be a Turkish citizen.

Constantinople was the venue for three *ecumenical councils. Constantinople I (381) marked the end of the *Arian controversy. The 186 bishops ratified the work of *Nicaea and condemned *Apollinarius. Although no W. representatives were present it ranks as the second ecumenical council. See also NICENE CREED.

Constantinople II (553) secured the condemnation of *Theodore of Mopsuestia, and certain writings of *Theodoret and Ibas of Edessa. These 'three chapters' had been earlier condemned by Justinian to conciliate the *Monophysites, but the action had angered the *Chalcedonian West. At the council the pope was induced to assent to the anathemas. The council also condemned *Origenism.

Constantinople III (680) was convoked to settle the *Monothelite controversy. In debates conducted chiefly by the papal envoys, it affirmed the doctrine of two wills in Christ, admitting only a moral unity resulting from the complete harmony between them in Christ.

Constitution of Madina: see MADĪNA.

Consubstantial. Of one and the same substance, hence also being. In Christian use the word refers especially to the relationship among the persons of the *Trinity. The Lat. *consubstantialis* is the Western counterpart of Gk. **homoousios*, the test-word of anti-*Arian orthodoxy.

Consubstantiation. The doctrine according to which the substances *both* of the body and blood of Christ *and* of the bread and wine coexist in the *eucharistic elements after their consecration. It was formulated (though he may not have used the term) by *Luther in opposition to the medieval teaching of *transubstantiation. He illustrated it by the analogy of an iron put into the fire: both fire and iron are united in the red-hot iron, but both are still present.

Contarini, Gasparo (1483–1542). Christian *cardinal, who led those proposing reform of the Church to Pope Paul III. By 1511, he had already come to the conclusion that humans are justified by faith, not works, and this conclusion enabled him to view *Protestant claims with sympathy. In 1536, he presided over a commission, composed mainly of reform-minded cardinals (known as *spirituali*), which issued the report *Consilium de emendanda ecclesia* commending measures against ecclesiastical abuse. *Luther derided the report, and the College of Cardinals invoked *canon law to defeat it. He was papal legate to the Regensburg Colloquy (1541), where Protestants and Roman Catholics sought terms on which to reunify the Church. Both sides rejected his proposal of double *justification. He died a year later as papal governor of Bologna.

E. G. Gleason, *Gasparo Contarini* (1994); J. B. Ross, 'The Emergence of Gasparo Contarini: A Bibliographical Essay', *Church History*, 41 (1972).

Contemplation. In modern Western use, mental *prayer that is non-discursive and thus distinct from *meditation. At this stage, prayer usually begins to be less the fruit of human effort and more the result of direct divine *grace, a distinction suggested by the traditional contrast between 'acquired' and 'infused' contemplation. The more traditional, *patristic, usage sees contemplation (Gk., *theōria*) as the highest, and natural, activity of the mind (*nous*) when freed from the disturbing influence of the passions and desires: it is a state of direct communion with God in which the mind transcends discursive activity and knows by presence or union—'a peering into heaven with the ghostly eye'.

Contraception: see BIRTH AND POPULATION CONTROL.

Conversion. Conversion is a process common to all religions in its preliminary sense of 'conversion of manners'—i.e. the turning of one's life more deliberately toward the goals of the religion in question. But conversion also has a stronger sense, namely, the transfer of a person (or group of people) from one religion to another, or from no religion to belief. Conversion in that stronger sense is an extremely complex phenomenon, having a different status and priority in different religions; it may even change its status in a particular religion during the course of history. Thus Judaism (or parts of Judaism, since the term 'Judaism' is misleading for this period) during the period of the second *Temple was actively missionary, seeking converts to the worship of the one true God; but later, Judaism became highly resistant to seeking converts, not least because Judaism is a particular vocation to one people, and gentiles are *already* members of the *Noachide covenant, and have no need to undertake the laws of *Torah in addition. If there is a conversion priority in Judaism, it lies in the sense which some Jews have (e.g. *Lubavitch Ḥasidim) that *all* Jews should convert to Judaism (to the observance of Torah in orthodox form). Another example would be Hinduism: in general, a Hindu is defined by birth (as is a Jew): since there may be many millions of rebirths before any continuing soul/self attains *mokṣa (release), there is no urgency to convert, only to live according to the *dharma (appropriate way) of one's existing circumstance. That may happen to be Jain or Buddhist; and although Hindus regard these as erroneous systems (*nāstika dārśana), one may advance beyond them in the next rebirth: there is no imperative to convert in this life. Nevertheless, and partly in response to Christian missionary approaches, Hindu missionary movements began to develop in the 19th cent. (see e.g. ĀRYA SAMĀJ; BRAHMO SAMĀJ).

In other religions the imperative to convert others is non-negotiable. In Christianity it is tied to the view that there is no other way to salvation: 'No one comes to the Father but by me' (John 14. 6). Such conversion involves *baptism (which incorporates the new member of the body of Christ into the death and resurrection of Christ), and during periods of Christian history, it has been held that without such a transition, the outcome after death will be one of condemnation. A minor exception might be infants who have not extended *original sin by actual sin, and who might therefore end up in *limbo. Yet this extreme view (pervasive though it has been in Christianity) has always been moderated by another theme, that the initiative in human salvation has been taken objectively by God (cancelling the consequence of sin), and that those who have a natural sense of God and live by it will not be condemned. This view is particularly associated with K. *Rahner and the concept of Anonymous Christians. In a comparable way, Muslims are under obligation to make known the will and the way of *Allāh, revealed in the *Qur'ān; yet 'There is no compulsion in religion' (Qur'ān 2. 256/7), and Muslims recognize that the People of the Book (*Ahl al-Kitāb) should be treated with respect, and that they are not obliged to convert to Islam.

The psychology and neurophysiology of conversion are understood, as yet, only in very preliminary ways. At one extreme, the techniques associated with the term *brain-washing were explored in connection with religious conversion by W. Sargant, *Battle For the Mind* (1957); and although his work was impressionistic and failed to grapple with the issue of the extent to which 'brain-washing' can in fact occur in the human case, he nevertheless drew attention to many of the techniques used in evangelistic campaigns to secure commitment. At the other extreme, conversion may be undramatic and a consequence of a long process of reflection: an intelligent example is Martin Gardner, *The Whys of a Philosophical Scrivener* (1983). Between the two is the phenomenon of 'snapping', in which a convert to one religion or religious movement is precipitated into several others in rapid succession. See also (with examples in other religions) Index, Conversion.

W. Conn (ed.), *Conversion* . . . (1978); F. Conway and J. Siegelman, *Snapping* (1978); E. Griffin, *Turning: Reflections on the Experience of Conversion* (1980); C. B. Johnson and H. N. Maloney, *Christian Conversions: Biblical and Psychological Perspectives* (1982).

Convocations. The two provincial assemblies (Canterbury and York) of the clergy of the *Church of England. Each has an 'upper house' (of bishops) and 'lower house'. The Synodical Government measure of 1969 transferred the major functions of the convocations, including the power to enact *canons, to the General Synod.

Coomaraswamy, Ananda (1877–1947). A philosopher of aesthetics, who worked from the basis of the history of art to develop a form of the 'perennial philosophy' (*philosophia perennis*). Treating art as an 'effective expression of metaphysical theses', he emphasized the inspirational rather than the purely aesthetic. For him, traditional art (especially from India and from his homeland, Śri Lankā) is a form of knowledge. More exactly it is a form of knowledge with the power to effect transformation of being. Coomaraswamy drew on Plato and other metaphysicians and mystics, and argued that art can bring life to philosophical or religious theses. Such is the path to 'the abandoned lands of the Spirit'.

R. Lipsey (ed.), *Coomaraswamy: Selected Papers* (2 vols., 1977); and *Coomaraswamy: His Life and Work* (1977).

Cope. Christian *vestment. It is an outer cloak in the form of a semicircular piece of decorated cloth, worn over the shoulders and fastened in front with a clasp. It is worn, usually, for special or important occasions, processions, etc.

COPEC (conference): see TEMPLE, WILLIAM.

Copper Scroll. A document found at *Qumran. The writing, beaten out on a copper scroll, dates from approximately 25–75 CE. It consists of an inventory of treasure, conjectured to be the treasure seized from the *Temple before the Jewish revolt of 67 CE. Its text was published in Eng. in 1960 (J. Allegro, *The Treasure of the Copper Scroll*) and adds to our knowledge of the topography of the area.

Coptic Church (Arab., *qibṭ*, from Gk., *Aigyptios*, 'Egyptian'). The national Christian church of Egypt. Christian origins in Egypt are very obscure. The legend that St *Mark founded the church in *Alexandria is not attested before *Eusebius, and then it is mentioned only as hearsay. The few remains of Christianity in the 2nd cent. are mostly linked to *gnosticism. Even the 'orthodox' *Clement of Alexandria was of a gnostic temperament, and Egypt was also the home of *Basilides and *Valentinus. The *Nag Hammadi library shows that gnosticism persisted underground for another three centuries.

From about the time of *Origen, however, the Orthodox Church began to play an important part in history. The institutions of Egyptian *monasticism, first of all, deriving from Anthony and *Pachomius, were exported to churches in both E. and W. The theology associated with Alexandria also determined the course of the *christological controversy in the 5th and 6th cents. The Egyptian church, especially in Coptic-language rural areas, was overwhelmingly *monophysite, and seems to have welcomed the Islamic conquest of 642 as an end to Byzantine persecution.

Its position under Islam has, however, always been difficult. There were occasional persecutions under the *khalīfas, besides the legal disabilities imposed on non-Muslims as *dhimmis. Many restrictions (e.g. on church building and publication) still exist.

The Coptic Church was a founder member of the World Council of Churches in 1948. Its vitality appears in its Sunday schools and in a recent repopulation of some of the ancient desert monasteries. The number of Copts in the 1976 census was given as 2.3 million, but Coptic leaders claim it is 5 million or more, and that the figures were falsified to serve the picture of Egypt as an Islamic state.

Coptic liturgies and ceremonial preserve some very archaic features. The traditional liturgical language is Coptic, although it gave way to Arabic as a spoken language as early as the 9th cent.

O. H. E. Burmester, *The Egyptian or Coptic Church* (1967); E. R. Hardy, *Christian Egypt* (1952); W. Kammerer, *A Coptic Bibliography* (1950).

Corban (Heb., 'oblation'). An obligatory or free-will offering at the temple altar (Leviticus 1. 2, etc.). It is specifically to free-will or votive gifts that Jesus seems to refer in Mark 7. 11: he objects to letting 'corban' take precedence over maintaining one's parents.

Cordovero, Moses (1552–70). *Kabbalistic scholar. Cordovero was a disciple of Joseph *Caro and the teacher of Isaac *Luria. He attempted to construct a speculative kabbalistic system based on traditional medieval philosophy and the teachings of the *Zohar*. He taught that God was the First Cause and that no positive attribute can be used to describe him. From the *Ein Sof, the hidden Godhead, emanate successive stages, so that 'God is all reality, but not all reality is God.' Thus the gulf between God and the world can only be bridged by the 'Sefirot' (emanations) which come from God. The emanations mean that 'all is one, and nothing is separated from him'. So the religious goal must be to find one's way back to the Source: 'The perfection of creatures lies in their union with him, the First Cause.' His two great systematic works were *Pardes Rimmonim* ('Orchard of Pomegranates') and *Ellimah Rabbati*; and he also wrote a long commentary on the *Zohar*, *Or Yaqar* (Precious Light). His *Tomer Devorah* (Palm Tree of Deborah, trs. L. Jacobs, 1960) is a popular work showing how Kabbalah is, in practice, a way leading to God.

L. Fine, *Safed Spirituality* . . . (1984).

Corinthians, Letters to the. Two epistles of *Paul and books of the New Testament. The two letters to Paul's church at Corinth come from the years *c.*52–5. 1 Corinthians was written to deal with various problems in the church such as party feeling, sexual abuses, and speculation about 'wisdom'. There are important passages dealing with Paul's earliest preaching (15. 11), the resurrection (15. 12–57), the *eucharist (11. 23–6), and love (*agape; ch. 13). 2 Corinthians is largely taken up with Paul's claims to being an *apostle, which a rival mission had called into question. The passages 6. 14–7. 1 and 10–13 seem out of place and may be fragments of otherwise lost letters.

Corpus Christi (Lat., 'body of Christ'). The Christian feast commemorating the origin of the *eucharist. It is celebrated in the W. church on the Thursday after *Trinity Sunday. Its origin lies in the increasing devotion to the Blessed *Sacrament especially after the Fourth *Lateran Council in 1215, and after a vision experienced by a nun, the Blessed Juliana (d. 1258). A *bull of Pope Urban IV (*Transiturus*, 1264) commanded its observance. Since the 14th cent. Corpus Christi has been celebrated by carrying the *host in procession.

Corpus Hermeticum: see HERMETICISM.

Correlation (the relating of questions and religious symbols): see TILLICH, P.

Cosmic embryo (source of creation): see HIRAṆYAGARBHA.

Cosmogony: see COSMOLOGY.

Cosmological arguments. A family of arguments for the existence of God, which start from the existence of the world or some very general feature of it, e.g. causality, change, or contingency, and argue thence to the existence of a First Cause or Necessary Being, which is identified with God. Examples of this kind of argument include the first three of St Thomas *Aquinas' 'Five Ways' *Quinque viae (*Summa Theologiae* 1a. ii. 3) and *Leibniz's *On the Ultimate Origin of Things* (1697). Such arguments were attacked by *Hume and *Kant in the 18th cent. and by subsequent thinkers; but they are still defended by many *neo-Thomists and some analytic philosophers. Critics of the arguments claim that it is improper to demand a cause or 'sufficient reason' for the whole universe (as opposed to particular things and events), that uncaused happenings and certain kinds of infinite regress are possible, and that the arguments are inconsistent in excluding the question of what caused God. Their modern proponents see the arguments as an expression of the human mind's search for total intelligibility in the world, and contend that we should not set *a priori* limits to the search for ultimate explanations.

Cosmology (Gk., *kosmos* + *logos*). Reflection on, and account of the world/universe as a meaningful whole, as embodying or expressing an order or underlying structure that makes sense: cosmogony is concerned with the coming into being of the cosmos, and cosmography with the description of its extent. A cosmology either manifests the character of the world as an independent organism or expresses the intentions of a transcendent being or beings. In some conceptions the present order remains stable until ended by a transcendent power, but in other conceptions it is liable, or even certain, to be replaced by other orders in an unending cycle. In the latter conception, the notions of cosmogony and cosmology may resemble each other closely. In most pre-modern religions, the cosmological order is thought to affect all the different levels and types of existence so that human action and society should, or must, reflect the more general order. The particular ideas in a cosmology are often both so basic to a culture's thought and so different from each other that the ideas of one scheme—e.g. a neo-Confucian one—may not be adequately expressible in the ideas of another scheme—e.g. a traditional Christian one. In so far as cosmologies are concerned with the origin of the cosmos or with the description of its nature and distribution, they are linked to (or include) cosmogony and cosmography.

It is rare for religions to give a single cosmology or cosmogony purporting to be a description of the origin of the universe, in the way in which a scientific cosmology might aim to give a critically realistic account of the origin and nature of the universe. Religious cosmologies give accounts of origin and nature, but principally in order to display the cosmos as an arena of opportunity; and for that reason, a religion may offer, or make use of, many cosmogonies without making much attempt to reconcile the contradictions between them. It is this aesthetic and spiritual relaxation which allows religions to address cosmological issues from the point of view of accountability and responsibility (as at the present time over issues of ecology), not as competitors with a scientific account: thus the Vancouver Assembly of the World Council of Churches (see ECUMENISM) decided 'to engage member churches in a conciliar process of mutual commitment (covenant) to justice, peace and the integrity of creation (subsequently known as JPIC)'; while this (especially the word 'covenant') depends on a particular understanding of creation, and thus of cosmogony, it has moved far beyond concerns about identifying the 'correct' account of the cosmos and its origins. See Index, Cosmology.

D. Maclagan, *Creation Myths* . . . (1977); C. H. Long, *Alpha: The Myths of Creation* (1963); C. Blacker & M. Loewe, *Ancient Cosmologies* (1975).

Judaism *Tanach (Jewish scripture) contains at least six different types of creation narrative, each of which 'gives voice to the viewpoints and values prevalent in diverse settings, priestly, agrarian, sapiential, prophetic, cultic, apocalyptic' (D. A. Knight, in R. W. Lowin and F. B. Reynolds (eds.), *Cosmogony and Ethical Order*, 1985), but all of which are integrated to the overriding cult of *Yahweh. Even within scripture, there is an exegesis going on, which changes the emphasis of cosmology. Thus it was early observed that the Bible begins with a grammatical anomaly: the word *bereshith*, 'in the beginning', is actually in the form, 'in the beginning of'; but the text does not state, 'in the beginning of what'. Attention to Proverbs 8. 22 disclosed that Wisdom is called *reshith*, 'the beginning', so that Genesis 1. 1 could be translated 'by means of Wisdom God created', thereby locating a Wisdom cosmogony in Genesis, in a way which was to be fruitful in the interpretation of Jesus in early Christianity. Nevertheless, the controlling accounts are those in Genesis: God created everything that exists in six days and rested on the seventh (1–2. 4). A second, more anthropocentric account (Genesis 2. 4–24), although differing in detail, also emphasizes that God is the origin of everything. These stories have been compared with Mesopotamian accounts, such as the Babylonian *Emuna Elish* and the *Gilgamesh* epic, but they differ in that the Hebrew God is portrayed as the single omnipotent creator. There are no primeval battles between deities (though traces of those cosmogonies are in Psalms and Job). The world is created solely in obedience to the divine will. The *rabbis of the *talmudic period were anxious to refute any *gnostic suggestions that the world was created by angelic intermediaries. Although influenced by the cosmogonies of their time (R. *Abbahu, for example, believed that there was a succession of experimental worlds), the rabbis insisted that the world was created out of nothing, solely by the word of God—'With ten words was the world created' (*Avot* 5. 1). In common with their Christian counterparts, Jewish philosophers tried to harmonize the biblical account with philosophical theories. *Philo, for example, based his ideas on Plato's *Timaeus*; *Saʿadiah Gaon was influenced by Aristotle; and Solomon ibn *Gabirol tried to reconcile the biblical view with *Neoplatonism. Speculations about the nature of the visible cosmos (*maʿaseh bereshit*) and the transcendent world (*maʿaseh merkabah*) are found in Jewish *mysticism; and the *kabbalists taught that the gulf between God and the material world is bridged by the 'sefirot' (emanations) which have their origin in God (see e.g. *Cordovero). The Jewish prayer book liturgy maintains that God is 'He who renews the work of creation every day', and 20th-cent. theologians have emphasized the continuing nature of creation: 'Creation happens to us, burns itself in us, recasts us in burning . . . We take part in creation, meet the Creator, reach out to him, helpers and companions' (M. *Buber, *I and Thou*, 1958).

A. Attmann, *Studies in Religious Philosophy and Mysticism* (1969).

Christianity Christians inherited the Jewish cosmology, but virtually from the outset (as early as *Paul's letters) they associated Christ with the activity of the Father in creation. He is 'the one Lord through whom all things exist and by whom we are' (1 Corinthians 8. 6). He is the Wisdom of God (ibid. 1. 24), the 'image of the invisible God and the first-born of all creatures', in whom all things were created and now subsist (Colossians 1. 15 f.). Furthermore, creation now has its end and purpose in him. Not surprisingly, therefore, Christian interest in cosmology and creation has seen them as a matter, not of technique, but of relationship—i.e. the relation of dependence which the created order has on its creator, not just for its origin, but for its sustenance. The General Thanksgiving in the **Book of Common Prayer* encourages Christians to give thanks 'for our creation, preservation and all the blessings of this life'; but creation and preservation are the same thing. The creativity of God is continuous: if God as creator withdrew his creative presence from an entity, it would cease to be. Thus God is the cause, not simply of things coming to be, but also of their being. For that reason, it became obvious, at least as early as the time of *Aquinas, that the Greek argument, to the effect that the created world need not necessarily have had a beginning, was correct, but that this did not militate against a theistic understanding of creation: it would still be in a relation (albeit an unending relation) of createdness to its creator—a point lucidly argued by Leibniz in *On the Ultimate Origination of Things* (1697); see also IBN RUSHD. However, it was also accepted that if revelation discloses a finite beginning, then on those grounds it should be accepted. It has become an issue subsequently whether revelation makes disclosures of that quasi-scientific kind at all. The claim that God creates the world *ex nihilo* (out of nothing) has sometimes confused the point: *ex nihilo* does not mean that 'nothing' is the sort of no-thing that God creates out of (which happens to be nothing rather than something), but rather that everything owes its existence to God, and that the creator and the created are *ontologically distinct. The prevailing cosmography for millennia was one of a 'three-decker' universe (heaven above, earth in the middle, and hell below), but its 'correction' by modern cosmologies has not affected the more fundamental point of the earlier (or of any) religious cosmology which mapped the universe as an arena of opportunity. For that reason, a three-decker universe may well persist indefinitely in liturgy. Nevertheless, alternative cosmologies have been developed to reflect changing scientific understandings of the cosmos: see e.g. PROCESS THEOLOGY. However, the necessity for these is not altogether apparent: from at least the time of Aquinas, a distinction has been made between God as first cause (as above) who produces and sustains a creation in which both natural and free causes (secondary causes) operate, and those effective and efficient causes which are real and not nominal.

K. Tanner, *God and Creation in Christian Theology* . . . (1988); T. F. Torrance, *Divine and Contingent Order* (1981).

Islam The Qur'ān strongly affirms God as creator and disposer of all that is. By a simple word, *kun* ('Be'), he commands and it is (2. 117, 6. 73). God is al-Khāliq (the Creator, from *khalaqa*, 'he created'), and has the power and authority to bring about all things as he disposes (*qadar, *Allāh). Everything that he has created is a sign (*ayā), not only *of* God for those who have eyes to see, but also *that* God has power to continue his creative act in relation to humans by bringing them from the grave for judgement (e.g. 50. 6–11). Because all things are derived from God, this becomes the fundamental argument that all people must constitute a single *'umma (community) in *islām* (allegiance which constitutes true safety) to God. So strong and immediate a doctrine of creation gave rise to many disputes (e.g. about the place of human freedom and responsibility, or about the direct involvement of God in his creation). Attempts to make God the first of a series of delegated emanations and causes (e.g. in *ibn Rushd or *ibn Sīnā) were resisted—so much so that it came to be held that God was the creator of each specific occasion or event, hence the name 'occasionalism'. The creation of a first man and first woman, and of the earth and seven heavens in two days, and of the cosmos in six, is described in such a way that, given the nature of the Qur'ān, any apparent conflict with other accounts (e.g. in the natural sciences) would have to be resolved in favour of the Qur'ān.

M. Fakhry, *Islamic Occasionalism and its Critique by Averroes and Aquinas* (1958).

Hinduism Vedic religion displays a clear sense of an ordered universe in which *ṛta prevails. There are many different accounts of how the universe came into being, some implying agency, others emanation from a pre-existing state in which there is neither beginning nor end. Important examples are: Brahmāṇḍa (the cosmic egg from which all creatures come forth: *Ṛg Veda* 10. 121. 1; *Kaṭha Upaniṣad* 3. 10); *Hiraṇyagarbha (the golden embryo, the everlasting plan), or *akṣara puruṣa*, the indestructible person, who becomes the vibrating energy from which all life is generated); Viśvakarma as creator (the first to come forth from Brahmāṇḍa, the architect of the gods, *Ṛg Veda* 10. 82); and *Brahmā ('the source of the universe, presiding over all creation, preserving like *Viṣṇu, destroying like *Śiva', *Mārkaṇḍeya Purāṇa* 46. 14). Equally well-known was the understanding of the universe coming forth from the primordial sacrifice, described in *Ṛg Veda* 10. 90: see PURUṢA. Yet the universe may also have had no point of origin, but may rather be an emanation (*anādi-sṛṣti*) from a ground or source of being, later to be identified as *Brahman. Thus *Śaṅkara understood the emanation as a progress from the subtle to the gross constituents of the world. But earlier than that, there had developed a sense of an unending process like a wave, with elements rising up into organized appearance, but then lapsing into a corresponding trough during 'the sleep of Brahmā', a period of dissolution (*pralaya). It was thus possible that the cosmos arose from infinite space and consciousness, a belief expressed through *Aditi. In truth, Indian religion accepted that the origin of the cosmos could not be known, but that the conditions of ordered life could be extremely well known. Cosmology lays out the terms for achieving that understanding—cosmology, again, as the arena of opportunity—while remaining agnostic about detail, as in the so-called 'Hymn of Creation' (*Nāsadīya Sūkta*, *Ṛg Veda* 10. 129): 'Neither being (*sat) nor non-being was as yet. There was no air, no sky that lies beyond it. What was concealed? And where? And in whose protection? . . . Who really knows? Who can declare it? Whence was it born, and whence came this creation? The gods were born later than this world's creation, so who knows from where it came into existence? None can know from where creation has arisen, and whether he has or has not produced it. He who surveys it in the highest heaven, he alone knows—or perhaps does not know.' In philosophy, the self-generating nature of the universe was worked out particularly in *Sāṃkhya. In theistic terms, the universe is produced through *māyā, the power to bring all things into appearance.

There was a greater confidence in cosmography. Vertically, the world was understood to be made up of seven continents (*dvipas*), ranged in circles with intervening oceans around the central point of Mount *Meru. Vertically, if one takes a cross-section of the Brahmāṇḍa, one finds a series of layers. At the top are the *lokas of the gods and high attainers; next are the planets, sky, and earth; then the underworlds, and finally the twenty-eight *narakas or hells. See also CARDINAL DIRECTIONS.

S. M. Ali, *Geography of the Purāṇas* (1966); C. Blacker and M. Loewe (eds.), *Ancient Cosmologies* (1975); W. Kirfel, *Die Kosmographie der Inder* (1920).

Jainism and **Buddhism** The Indian scepticism about the work of the gods or God in creating this cosmos was taken to a further extreme in both Jainism and Buddhism. Such gods as there are (and there are many, especially in Buddhism) are subject to rebirth and are certainly incapable of creating anything. The Jains inherited the *triloka* (see LOKA), and envisaged it as something like an hour-glass, squeezed in at the middle. Above (*Urdhvaloka*) are a series of heavens of increasing brightness, at the top of which is 'the slightly curved place' (*Iśatpragbhara*) where dwell the liberated and disembodied souls. In the middle is the *Madhyaloka*, which includes the continent inhabited by humans. Below is the *Adholoka*, a series of increasingly terrible hells—from which release is eventually certain, though the intervening time may be unimaginably long.

In Buddhism, there is an equal rejection of any kind of creator—though there are stories of how it came about that Brahmā (a kindly and well-disposed god in Buddhism, but just as much in quest of enlightenment as anyone else) deceived himself into thinking that he must have been the creator (*Digha Nikāya* 1. 18). Buddhism inherited the same basic cosmography, but adapted it greatly. It envisages a series of levels, all of which are open to the process of reappearance: at the summit are the four realms of purely mental rebirth, (*arūpa-avacara*); below them are the realms of pure form (*rūpa-avacara*), where the gods dwell in sixteen heavens, five of which are known as 'pure abodes' (*suddhāvāsa*), the remaining eleven of which arise out of the *jhānas (meditational states). Lower still are the sense-desire heavens, including those of the Tāvatiṃsa gods (the thirty-three Vedic gods, the chief of whom, *Indra, known as Sakka, has become a protector of Buddhism) and of the Tusita gods (where *bodhisattvas spend their penultimate birth, and in which *Maitreya now dwells). In the sense-desire realms are the levels on which live *asuras, humans and animals. Below these are *pretaloka and the hells of torment (niraya/naraka). All worlds are made up of transient and impermanent moments, and are therefore the product, neither of a creator, nor even of some eternal process, as in the interaction between Puruṣa and *Prakṛti in Sāṃkhya. The world is simply a process, passing through cycles (*kappa*) of immense length. In *Mahāyāna, beyond the three domains of *kāma, *rūpa, and arūpa, there are added a further dimension of the *Buddha-kṣetras (Buddha-fields).

C. Caillat and R. Kumar, *The Jain Cosmology* (1981); W. R. Kloetzli, *Buddhist Cosmology* (1983).

Costa, Uriel da: see DA COSTA, U.

Councils: Formal assemblies for religious purposes: see Index, Councils.

Buddhism According to tradition three important councils were held in the early centuries after the passing away of the *Buddha. There is considerable uncertainty surrounding the date, location, deliberations, and conclusions of these councils, and while the traditional account may be accepted as reliable in some respects it should not be regarded as historically accurate in all.

The First Council is reported to have been held at Rājagriha in the year of the Buddha's death (486 BCE) with the objective of establishing the canon or at least two or its three divisions or 'baskets' (*tripiṭaka). These include the collection of the Buddha's discourses or sermons (*sūtra/sutta) and the material relating to the organization and history of the Order (*vināya). This part of the account is certainly inaccurate since the canon did not receive its final form until many years after this time.

The Second Council took place 100 or 110 years after the first and was held at *Vaiśālī. It arose out of a dispute concerning monastic practices, and in particular the handling of money by monks. One faction, the Vajjians, claimed that this, together with nine other practices, was legitimate; the more orthodox, on the other hand, regarded them as illegal and prohibited by the Vināya. The council ruled against the Vajjians but it is unclear how far their practices were reformed as a result.

The Third Council at *Pāṭaliputra in 250 BCE is the most important of the three and resulted in the 'Great Schism' between the 'Elders' (*Sthaviras) and the 'Great Assembly' (*Mahāsāṃghikas), which was to have a profound effect upon the later tradition. The Elders concerned themselves with doctrinal purity and the preservation of the Buddha's teachings without innovation or alteration; they centred upon monasticism and the quest for personal liberation. The Mahāsāṃghikas, on the other hand, were open to doctrinal innovation and were socially extrovert, welcoming the laity into their activities. It is from the Mahāsāṃghikas that the movement of the 'Great Vehicle' (*Mahāyāna) arose, with its emphasis on other-centred concern epitomized in the figure of the self-sacrificing *Bodhisattva, and incorporating popular devotional religious practices. At the centre of the schism were five theses put forward by a monk named Mahādeva, to the effect that the Buddha was greatly superior in wisdom and compassion to the *Arhat. The Mahāsāṃghikas accepted these five points and emphasized the Buddha's compassion and supernatural qualities, while the Sthaviras rejected them and held to the notion of the Buddha's nature as essentially human.

According to tradition, the Third Council was convened by the Emperor *Aśoka who ordered that certain schismatics be excluded. However, scholars now incline to the view that the Mahāsāṃghika schism occurred prior to 250 BCE, at a previous council, also held at Pāṭaliputra a century earlier, and that Aśoka's involvement in 250 BCE was with a fourth council concerned with an internal dispute among the Sthaviras alone. Councils which occurred later in history are of minor importance in relation to those mentioned above.

A. Bareau, *Les Premiers Conciles bouddhique* (1955).

Christianity A council is a formal assembly of *bishops and representatives of churches, for determining doctrine or discipline. Local councils, as of provinces or *patriarchates, are more usually called *synods. The meeting described in Acts 15 is traditionally the first council. General, or *ecumenical, councils are those made up of bishops and other representatives from the whole world; but the term refers specifically to those seven whose decisions have been taken to represent a true consensus and to be authoritative. These are, with dates: 1. *Nicaea I (325) 2. *Constantinople I (381) 3. *Ephesus (431) 4. *Chalcedon (451) 5. Constantinople II (553) 6. Constantinople III (680–1) 7. Nicaea II (787): see ICONOCLASM. In *Orthodox teaching the decisions of these seven councils are regarded as fundamental data for *theology. According to *Roman Catholic reckoning there have been fourteen further councils with the same ecumenical authority, of which the last three are *Trent (1545–63), *Vatican I (1869–70), and II (1962–5). The 'conciliar theory' (see ANTIPOPE), which held that supreme authority lay with a general council rather than the *pope, had advocates in the 14th–15th cents., and was expressed at the council of *Constance (1415). However, the popes successfully resisted it, and in 1460 Pius II forbade any appeals from the pope to a future general council. In present *canon law an ecumenical council must be convened by the pope and its decrees promulgated by the *Holy See; they are then *infallible. *Protestant doctrine subjects the decisions of all councils to the general criteria of what is apostolic and scriptural. The first four councils are most generally known and accepted as authoritative.

G. Alberigo *et al.* (eds.), *Conciliorum Oecumenicorum Decreta* (1972); F. Dvornik, *The Ecumenical Councils* (1961); H. Leclerq *et al.*, *Histoire des conciles d'après les documents originaux* (11 vols., 1907–52, tr. and expanding German of K.-J. von Hefele and J. Hergenröther); E. I. Watkin, *The Church in Council* (1960).

Counsels of perfection. Certain injunctions of *Jesus taken in Christian tradition (in contrast to 'commandments') as a standard of perfection for only a few disciples (cf. Matthew 19. 21). They are specifically: poverty, the renunciation of property; chastity, abstinence from sexual relations; and obedience, the submission of the will in all things to a superior. These three form the basis for the monastic life.

Counterculture. The mainly middle-class, Western youth culture of the 1960s which opposed the *rituals, forms, structures, ideologies, calculating rationality, and leadership of the wider society. Participants of the counterculture turned to unconventional lifestyles and solutions to personal and social problems, creating an expressive, ritually anti-ritual, romantic cult—which, however, in many cases, led to existential anxiety and even anomie. It was from among these casualties of the counterculture that a number of new religions of total commitment, such as the Unification Church (see MOON, SUN MYUNG) and Hare Krishna (see INTERNATIONAL SOCIETY . . .), gained many of their first converts in the West.

Counter-Reformation. Movement of revival and reform in the *Roman Catholic Church during the 16th and early 17th cents. The term was used in the 19th cent. to describe that Church's response to the *Reformation and the rise of *Protestantism, but this is too limiting a concept. The early leaders of the Counter-Reformation (such as Cisneros in Spain, *Pole or Giberti in Italy), the revival of *religious orders such as the *Augustinians and the *Carmelites, or the foundation of new orders such as the *Jesuits, owed little or nothing to the reaction to Protestantism. However, the summoning of the *Council of *Trent was a consequence of the spread of *Lutheranism, and much of the debate at Trent, especially that on the *sacraments, took place in the light of positions adopted by the *Reformers. The Church emerged from Trent with a more efficient system of central government, a renewed *liturgy, a clearer statement of some of its beliefs, and a new vigour. This self-confidence spilled over into exuberant church architecture, decoration, music, and ritual, a new style of devotional literature (exemplified by Francis *de Sales, *Introduction to the Devout Life*), and a fervent *missionary zeal both inside and outside Europe. Poland and Germany were won back to allegiance to Rome, and the Congregation for the Propagation of the Faith (*Propaganda Fide), was founded in 1622 to co-ordinate the missionary enterprise. Even though the Counter-Reformation may not have owed its origin to *Luther's revolt, it had the effect of hardening the *schism between the two branches of W. Christianity, and it was responsible, at least in part, for the century of religious wars which ended in 1648.

Court Jews. Prominent Jews used by European rulers to administer estates and develop credit systems. The institution of the Court Jew emerged gradually in the 16th and 17th cents. Well-known examples include Joseph Bassevi of Prague, Samuel Oppenheimer of Vienna, and Leffmann Behrends of Hanover. Influential and *assimilated, they played a prominent part in the development of the banking system of Europe.

S. Stern, *Court Jew* (1950).

Covenant

Judaism In the Bible, covenants were established between individuals (such as Laban and *Jacob, Genesis 31. 44), between states (such as *Judah and Syria, 1 Kings 15. 19), between kings and subjects (*David and the Israelites, 2 Samuel 5. 3), between marriage partners (see Mal. 2. 14) and between God and *Israel. Covenants were frequently accompanied by signs: the *Sabbath at the creation, the rainbow after the *flood, and *circumcision, were all signs of covenants God made with his people. Circumcision itself is frequently known as *berit* (covenant). Some scholars believe that the ancient Israelites held an annual celebration of the Sinai Covenant (Exodus 19–24) and that the book of Deuteronomy was drawn up as a covenant document, analogous to the text of Hittite treaties which have been discovered. In any event, the idea of a covenantal relationship between the Israelites and their God was fundamental to the Jewish religion ('I . . . will be your God and you shall be my people': Leviticus 26. 12). Through the covenant, the Jews believe they were *chosen to fulfil a unique destiny in the unfolding of God's salvation. According to the *Zohar*, '*Torah, God and circumcision are all called "Covenant", so all three remain inseparably linked together.'

E. W. Nicholson, *God and His People* (1986).

Christianity In the New Testament the Gk. *diathēkē* is certainly to be translated 'covenant' in such passages as Luke 22. 20: Jesus refers to the 'new covenant' (recalling Jeremiah 31. 31) sealed, like the old one at Sinai, with blood—in this case, at his death. The idea is elaborated in *typological fashion, by the author to the *Hebrews (chs. 8, 9, 12) who stresses the perfect forgiveness of sins under the new covenant.

'Covenant theology', or 'federal theology' (Lat. *foedus*, 'covenant'), was a particular development of the New Testament doctrine in *Calvinism in the 16th–17th cents. According to the *Westminster

Confession, ch. 7, God first entered into a covenant 'of works' with Adam, bestowing eternal life in exchange for obedience; when this was broken at the *fall, God made another, the covenant 'of grace', offering salvation freely through Christ. Among other problems, the suggestion that God could ever have dealt with humankind other than by grace brought the conception into eventual disfavour.

Islam The *Qur'ān speaks of a covenant made in pre-existence with all of humanity, when Allāh summoned all *Adam's descendants, and commanded them to submit to him as Lord (7. 171). He also made a covenant with Adam himself (20. 115). A covenant was made with the *prophets (3. 81), and with the Children of Israel (5. 13, 2. 83, 3. 187); but since they rejected it, they were cursed (5. 14). Similarly a covenant was made with the *Christians (5. 15). Both these groups, according to the Qur'ān, 'forgot' part of the message entrusted to them. Consequently their hearts were hardened, and they could no longer be relied upon to transmit the true message of Allāh, henceforth obtainable from the Qur'ān. The actual terms of the covenant are not specified in detail, but imply the belief in, and worship and service of, the One God.

Covenant, Book of: see BOOK OF THE COVENANT.

Covenanters. Scottish *Presbyterians who expressed their convictions through the signing of covenants. In particular they signed the National Covenant of 1638 and the Solemn League and Covenant of 1643, defending the Reformed faith and in effect rejecting the imposition of *episcopacy. With the restoration of the Stuarts, the Covenants were pronounced illegal, and the execution and persecution of Covenanters ensued. Even when William III restored Presbyterianism to Scotland in 1690, some Covenanters refused to rejoin the national church (since William was not a covenanted king), and their successors persist in small numbers to the present day.

J. D. Douglas, *Light in the North* (1964).

Covenant Service. A *Methodist service of dedication, usually at the New Year. Its practice was inspired initially by the *Puritan custom of drawing up personal and corporate covenants with God. In compiling the service, John *Wesley was clearly indebted to Richard Alleine's *Vindiciae Pietatis* and Joseph Alleine's *An Alarm to Unconverted Sinners*, both of which appeared in his famous collection of devotional works, the 'Christian Library'. The first Methodist Covenant Service was held on 11 Aug. 1755, but the printed order, *Directions for Renewing our Covenant with God*, was not issued until 1779. This opportunity for renewal of the covenant always takes place within the context of the *communion service which forms a fitting climax to an important annual occasion. The commitment includes the words: 'I am no longer my own, but yours. Put me to what you will, rank me with whom you will; put me to doing, put me to suffering; . . . let me be full, let me be empty; let me have all things, let me have nothing.. . .So be it. And the covenant now made on earth, let it be ratified in heaven.'

Coverdale, Miles (1488–1568). Translator of the Bible. Ordained priest in Norwich (1514), he became a member of the pro-*Lutheran group which reputedly met at the White Horse Inn in Cambridge, and was forced into exile because of his zeal for reform. The English Bible of 1539, known as the 'Great Bible', was his work, based mainly on earlier translations rather than on the Heb. and Gk. The Psalms in the **Book of Common Prayer* derive from this version. A gifted preacher, in 1551 he became bishop of Exeter, was a Marian exile, but returned to England on the accession of Elizabeth, assisting at the consecration of Archbishop Matthew *Parker.

Cow, sacred: see GO.

Cranach, Lucas, 'the Elder' (1472–1553). German artist whose altar-pieces, drawings, woodcuts, and portraits of leading Reformers gained him wide recognition. Once attracted to the *Reformation cause, he became *Luther's protector, close friend, and godfather of his first son, Hans. He was Saxony's official court-painter for over forty years.

Cranmer, Thomas (1489–1556). *Archbishop of *Canterbury, *Protestant reformer, scholar, and liturgist. Cranmer played so crucial a part in the Henrician *Reformation in England and in shaping the English *catechism, *prayer books and Articles (see THIRTY-NINE ARTICLES), that the proper appraisal of his life has often been obscured by the religious interests of his biographers. Born in Aslockton in Nottinghamshire, he went to Cambridge in 1503, achieving his BA (1511) and MA and becoming acquainted with the work of *Erasmus and the insights of the new learning (made possible by knowledge of Hebrew and Greek in the understanding of the Bible). He was not particularly distinguished in his early Cambridge studies, and in *c.*1515 he married, thereby curtailing (as it seemed) a career in university or Church, but his wife died in childbirth. A fellowship at Jesus College and ordination allowed him to study for his doctorate in Divinity (1526) and to evaluate the work of Biblical scholars, including *Fisher, *Luther, and both Catholic and other Reformers. In 1527, Wolsey began to employ him on embassies (notably to Spain), and Henry VIII became aware of his usefulness as a diplomat and theologian. While escaping from the plague in Cambridge, he went to Waltham as a tutor and met Stephen Gardiner. Probably as a result of this, he came to the notice of Henry VIII as a theologian who thought that the question of the royal divorce should be decided by theologians on the basis of scripture, and not by *canon lawyers. Asked by Henry to put his views on the divorce into book-form, he was subsequently used by the king to argue for the divorce at Bologna, Rome, and eventually Ratisbon and Nuremberg. There he encountered German Lutherans, and also met and married Margaret, the niece of Andreas Osiander (a Reformation theologian) in 1532. This unusual and uncanonical step was thrown into high relief when he was summoned from these Lutheran circles to become archbishop of Canterbury in 1533. Of his reluctance to accept he later said, 'there was never man came more unwillingly to a bishopric than I did to that'. He was called upon to annul the marriage of Catherine of Aragon to Henry VIII, and thereafter those of Anne Boleyn and Anne of Cleves.

His belief in the scriptural warrant for the authority of the prince and not the *pope as head of the Church guaranteed a measure of protection from Henry VIII and Edward VI, to whom he acted as spiritual guide and tutor. This in turn enabled Cranmer to advance some reformed views, especially on the desirability of vernacular scriptures, the abolition of superfluous *saints' days, and the translation of the *liturgy and catechism into English. He achieved all these in time, but not without reverses. He had to contest the theologically conservative Six Articles, and with them the prohibition of clerical marriage (his own included), and he had to see the fall of his friend and fellow-reformer, Thomas Cromwell. But the proclamation for the Great Bible (see COVERDALE, MILES), and the introduction of an English *litany and the 1549 Prayer Book, together with its successor of 1552 with the Forty-Two Articles, testify to his ability to serve the Protestant cause within the constraints of the existing political and social circumstances. The limits of his loyalty to the Crown were tested by the accession of Queen Mary in 1553, who required his allegiance to the crown to be transferred to the papacy. He wavered and recanted at first, but finally came to the view that loyalty to the monarch had to be subordinate to loyalty to the word of God. He was accordingly burnt as a heretic on 21 Mar. 1556.

His views on *transubstantiation changed, and he veered toward the end of his life to understanding Christ's presence in the *eucharist as real but not literal. But he was always open to the ideas of others and sought for a consensus among evangelical Reformers. He longed for a greater understanding among the laity of scripture and of the scriptural basis of their faith. He wanted the assets from the dissolution of the *chantries to be used for educational purposes, and he urged Christians to take the Bible 'into thine hands, read the whole story; and that thou understandest, keep it well in memory; that thou understandest not, read it again and again'. He urged the bewildered or the doubting to go to their 'curate and preacher: show thyself to be desirous to know and to learn'. He aimed to teach at the pace of his pupils (cf. UPĀYA-KAUŚALYA), which may explain his apparent vacillations. English people could not make such momentous changes easily, from pope to king, from *missal to prayer book, from Latin *Vulgate to Great Bible, all in the space of two decades—or if they did, they might easily change back. Cranmer wrestled for truth and was reluctant to impose it on others until they too had wrestled. Such integrity should not be confused with time-serving or obsequiousness.

Miscellaneous Writings and Letters . . . , ed. J. E. Cox (1846); *Writings and Disputations* . . . (1844); P. Brooks, *Thomas Cranmer's Doctrine of the Eucharist* (1965); D. MacCullock, *Thomas Cranmer* (1996).

Craving (Buddhist): see TAṆHĀ.

Creation: see COSMOLOGY.

Creationism. 1. The view that the universe and all things in it were created directly by God and are not the result of a long evolutionary process; this applies with particular force to forms of life. It is based on the account of creation in the book of *Genesis, understood literally as a descriptive account, and thus has links with *fundamentalism. Claiming to be, as a theory, of the same status as any other proposed (scientific) account, it emerged in the 1960s in the USA (though with roots in the 19th cent.) in direct contest with the theory of evolution associated with Charles Darwin (who argued in *The Origin of Species*, 1859, that organisms produce more reproductive units than give rise to mature individuals, yet the numbers of individuals in species remain fairly constant, with the result that there must be a high rate of mortality; in the ensuing competition for survival, individuals in a species are not all identical, but exhibit variations in all characteristics, so that some variants will succeed better than others, and parents of the next generation will be selected from those whose variations have helped them most to adapt to the conditions of their environment; since offspring resemble parents, the assumption can be made that subsequent generations will maintain and improve on achieved adaptations, thus taking part in a process of gradual change which has produced the current variety of life-forms). Creationism raises objections to neo-Darwinian theory (e.g. gaps in the fossil record, or the absence of interim forms in the production of complex organs or organisms) and looks for confirmation in nature of the biblical account. The immediate ancestry of creationism can be found in the inter-war attempts of fundamentalists to get state laws passed which would ban the teaching of evolution in public schools. These attempts received a set-back in the Scopes trial in Tennessee (1925): John Scopes was convicted for teaching Darwin's theory, in contravention of a law passed in March of that year. However, the overwhelming strength of Clarence Darrow's defence (including a devastating cross-examination of the prosecutor, William Jennings Bryan) effectively ended the fundamentalist campaign (the conviction of Scopes was overturned by the state supreme court, which nevertheless upheld the original statute; the US Supreme Court declared a similar statute unconstitutional in 1968). Creationism emerged more specifically in the 1960s when creationists demanded equal time for the teaching of creationism (hence the importance of insisting on the equal validity of both as theories), since the teaching of evolution alone violated freedom of religion because it was advocating a rival religion, secular humanism. After some initial success, not least in amending curricula and text-books, equal-treatment bills (which became law in Arkansas and Louisiana in 1981) were declared unconstitutional by federal courts in 1982. The appeal of Louisiana was rejected by the Supreme Court in 1987 (7–2) because the law was a violation of Church–State separation. The Creation Research Society supports the publication of creation science papers, but these have not been recognized as serious science outside the movement.

P. Kitcher, *Abusing Science: The Case Against Creationism* (1983); T. McGowen, *The Great Monkey Trial* (1990); H. M. Morris, *Scientific Creationism* (1974); R. L. Numbers, *The Creationists* (1992); M. L. Settle, *The Scopes Trial* (1972).

2. The view that God creates a soul for each human being, in contrast to pre-existence (that souls pre-exist bodies and enter into them) and traducianism (that souls generate souls as and when bodies generate bodies).

Credence. A small table or shelf in the sanctuary of a church near the *altar, to hold the bread, wine, and water to be used at the *eucharist.

Credo quia absurdum est (Lat., 'I believe because it is absurd'). A saying frequently used to mock the 'credulity' or dogmatic irrationality of religious believers. The saying is sometimes attributed to *Tertullian, though his nearest statement has a different nuance: 'Et mortuus est Dei Filius; prorsus credibile, quia ineptum est' (in paraphrase, so paradoxical is it to say that the Son of God has died that it would have to be a matter of belief). Such a saying does not preclude the recognition of rational support or reasons making evident what has evoked the statement: cf. ANSELM. It appears also in the form, 'credo quia impossibile est'.

Credo ut intelligam (commitment to the coherence between rationality and belief): see ANSELM.

Creed. A concise statement of what is believed (Lat., *credo*, 'I believe'). For examples, see Index, Creeds.

Judaism See ARTICLES OF FAITH.

Christianity Creeds originated as confessions of faith by candidates for *baptism. Initially they served as something like passwords, as in the Latin *symbolum*, an early name for a creed. They soon stood on their own as summaries of belief. By the 4th cent. these had become more uniform and always had one section each for the Father, Son, and Holy Spirit. The Council of *Nicaea (325) put in a credal form the profession of faith as a standard of orthodoxy, and the use of creeds for this purpose rapidly spread. The most important creeds, the *Nicene Creed, *Apostles' Creed, and *Athanasian Creed, are also used liturgically.

J. N. D. Kelly, *Early Christian Creeds* (1972); J. H. Leith (ed.), *Creeds of the Church: A Reader* . . . (1982).

Islam The basic 'creed' is the *shahāda, but this affirmation of allegiance (*islām*) is not a credal profession, with articles of faith. The nearest equivalent to that is the *ʿaqīda*, several of which appeared in the early history of Islam. The earliest (*Fiqh Akbar I*), with 10 articles, is attributed to *Abu Ḥanīfa, and is clearly addressed to controverted issues of the time—e.g. does a Muslim who sins become an infidel? Was *ʿUthmān in the right, or *ʿAlī? Article 7 affirms that differences of opinion in the community are a token of divine mercy. Later *ʿaqāʾid* (pl.) become more dogmatic and theological.

W. M. Watt, *Islamic Creeds: A Selection* (1994); A. J. Wensinck, *The Muslim Creed* (1932).

Cremation. Method of disposing of dead bodies by burning. It is the natural method of disposal in those religions (e.g. Hinduism: see ANTYEṢṬI) which regard the body as a dispensable vehicle for an immortal soul (*soma sēma*, 'the body a tomb'), or, as in the case of Buddhism, where the process of reappearance alone continues. But in religions such as Judaism, Christianity, and Islam, where there is belief in resurrection of the body, burial has been preferred as, intuitively, suggesting an easier reconstitution of the parts.

In Judaism, the disposal of bodies by burning is prohibited by Jewish law and is traditionally regarded with abhorrence. It was associated in the Bible with human sacrifice (Deuteronomy. 12. 31, Isaiah 30. 33), and was allowed only for criminals (Leviticus 20. 14, 21. 9). Burial is required by Genesis 3. 19. *Orthodox Judaism is reluctant to allow even the ashes of one cremated to be interred in a Jewish cemetery, but *Reform are likely to allow this, as also the presence of a *rabbi at a cremation. Until recently (late 19th cent. onward), cremation was regarded in Christianity with repugnance and legal opposition. For Roman Catholics, the ban on cremation was lifted in 1963, and in the revised Code of Canon Law, cremation is allowed provided it is not done for reasons contrary to Christian faith. See also FUNERAL RITES.

J. W. Bowker, 'Death, Burial and Cremation', in *The Sense of God* (1973).

Crescas, Hasdai (*c.* 1340–*c.*1412). Jewish Spanish philosopher and statesman. Crescas became a member of the royal household of Aragon and took a position of active leadership in the Jewish community. He wrote *Or Adonai* (The Light of the Lord) to refute the philosophical teachings of *Maimonides and Jewish Aristotelianism. This was initially intended to be the first part of a larger work *Ner Elohim* (Lamp of God), and the second part, the *Ner*

Mitzvah (Lamp of Commandment), was intended to supersede Maimonides' *Mishneh Torah* (A Second Law). Although Crescas' ideas were rejected by Isaac *Abrabanel and Shem Tov ben Joseph, he was later influential on *Spinoza.

Crescas held strongly to the view that salvation is not by metaphysics: 'Salvation is attained, not by adherence to metaphysical propositions, but by the love of God expressed in action.' The foundation is belief in the existence, unity, and incorporeality of God, who does not override the conditions of his creation: 'God himself cannot alter the laws of *a priori* truth.' From this follow six necessary conditions of Israel's existence: (i) God's knowledge of all things, including the non-existent; (ii) his providence in response to his people's love; (iii) his omnipotence; (iv) prophecy as a gift of God's love; (v) human freedom; (vi) the purpose of *Torah—spiritual bliss—and of humanity—to love God. There are then 'true opinions', disbelief in which would create heresy, but would not alienate entirely from Judaism. They include creation *ex nihilo*, resurrection and immortality, reward and punishment, the coming of the *messiah and the efficacy of prayer. Finally there are 'probabilities' (e.g. the existence of *demons, *astrology), concerning which it is possible to be in error, but those who do not believe are not to be censured.

H. A. Wolfson, *Crescas' Critique of Aristotle* (1929).

Crescent moon (Arab., *al-qamar*). Religious emblem of Islam, derived from the Quranic (e.g. 36. 39) recognition of the waxing and waning of the moon as a sign of God's unchanging purpose and control. Whenever *Muḥammad saw the new moon, he would say, 'O crescent of good and of guidance, my faith is in him who created you.' The emblem is relatively late, not originating with the Arabs, but introduced by the *Ottomans. The crescent on the cupola of a mosque indicates the direction of *Mecca; if it is combined with three gold balls, these represent the three worlds of material, subtle, and angelic being.

Crosby, Fanny. Mrs F. J. Van Alstyne (1823–1915), American hymn-writer. She was blind from the age of six weeks. Her more than 2,000 hymns include '*Jesus, keep me near the cross', 'To God be the glory, great things he hath done', and 'Safe in the arms of Jesus'. Critically regarded, they are mostly 'very weak, and poor, their simplicity and earnestness being their redeeming features' (J. Julian). None the less they became immensely popular, largely through the inclusion of many in *Sankey's *Sacred Songs and Solos* (1873), and remain so in churches which sing gospel hymns.

Cross. Chief of Christian symbols, deriving from the *crucifixion of Christ. It is used in various forms (plain, *crucifix, *icon) in the furnishing of churches and *altars, and as an object of private devotion. The claimed wood of the 'true cross' (see INVENTION OF THE CROSS) was divided and redivided, and now most of the *relics are very small. In liturgical use, the sign of the cross is prescribed at *baptism and *confirmation, and is also used at *blessings. Outside worship, *Catholic and *Orthodox Christians make the sign of the cross by touching the forehead, breast, each shoulder, and breast. The W. custom is left shoulder, then right; the E., opposite. It can serve as a basic and inarticulate expression of religious sentiment on all sorts of occasions.

R. Schneider Berrenberg, *Kreuz, Kruzifix: Eine Bibliographie* (1973).

Crown of thorns. An instrument of Christ's passion (John 19. 2). He is frequently depicted wearing this in *passion art and music: 'O sacred head, sore wounded . . .'.

Crowther, Samuel Ajayi (*c.* 1806–91). Anglican *bishop and pioneering African Church leader. He was born a Yoruba at Oshogun, was captured as slave in 1821, but was liberated by the British navy and sent to Sierra Leone. He was baptized in 1825 and became a leading worker for the *CMS. Under the 'three-self' policy of Henry *Venn, he became the first African bishop of W. Africa beyond colonial limits, in 1864. Bitterly opposed by European missionaries, he was ready to resign in 1889. The conflict led to the formation of the secessionist United Native African Church in Lagos in 1891, when Crowther died.

J. Page, *The Black Bishop* (1908).

Crozier. The ceremonial staff carried by Christian bishops (and sometimes by abbots and abbesses). In the W. it resembles a shepherd's crook; in the E. it is surmounted by a cross between two serpents. In etymology the word is akin to Old High German *krucka*, 'crutch'.

Crucifix. A representation of the *cross of Christ, usually with the figure of Christ. In the Roman Catholic and Anglican Churches it is widely used in private devotion, and forms the central focus of the *altar in churches. In the Orthodox Church its place is taken by cross-shaped *icons, i.e. with flat likenesses. Among Protestants only the Lutheran Church uses the crucifix, and *Evangelicals sometimes have a horror of it as idolatrous or as suggesting a dead rather than a risen Christ; at best, therefore, for them the cross should be empty (i.e. not bearing a figure).

Crucifixion. The punishment of death suffered by *Jesus (and, traditionally, a few other Christian *martyrs). As a Roman punishment, used above all for dangerous outlaws, it raises the question of Jesus' possible involvement with anti-Roman dissidents. As a particularly cruel and humiliating death, it forms the basis for the 'scandal' of Christian preaching of salvation (as 'the word of the cross': 1 Corinthians 1. 18). It is striking that *Christ on the cross is not represented in art until the 5th cent., and even then in a victorious rather than suffering manner. Realistic crucifixion scenes emerged in the West with devotion to the passion, which developed in the 12th–13th cents.

Crusades (Lat., *cruciata*, 'cross-marked', i.e. *cruce signati*, those wearing the insignia of scarlet crosses). Military expeditions in the name of Christianity, directed chiefly against Muslim territories to recapture the Holy Land, but sometimes also against other non-Christians, and occasionally against Christian *heretics. Of the crusades to reconquer the Holy Land, the traditional count lists eight. The first was instigated by Urban II in 1095 and led to the conquest of *Jerusalem in 1099, and the establishment of the crusader states. In 1182 the fall of Jerusalem to the Muslim leader *Salāḥ ud-Dīn (Saladin) occasioned the third crusade which, like its predecessor, was unsuccessful in attaining its end. The fourth crusade journeyed no further than Constantinople, which was sacked (1204). The remaining expeditions had varying success, but with the fall of Acre in 1299, the crusader states finally disappeared. Theoretically, the crusades were not concerned to convert or coerce non-Christians into belief, but only to ensure the proper preservation of sacred sites and access to them. However, since the Christians of the Holy Land and pilgrims to the shrines were in no danger from Muslims, the crusaders' motives were difficult for Muslims to understand. The regions occupied by the four crusader states were neither large, nor heavily Islamic, but their existence posed a strategic threat to the land and sea routes of the Islamic Middle East, and had to be reconquered. The reconquest, however, does not seem to have given rise to renewed interest in *jihād as such, nor to an alliance among the Muslims similar to that among the W. Europeans.

Juridically, a crusader was one who had 'taken the cross', i.e. vowed to go on a crusade. Failure to fulfil the vow might entail *excommunication, but in return for it the Church granted *indulgences (crusade bulls by the mid-13th cent. promised full remission of temporal punishment incurred by *sin) and security of a crusader's property in his absence on the crusade. These privileges came to be offered by the *papacy to those engaging in almost any campaign which could be presented as a defence of the Church including, in the 13th and 14th cents., the defence of the Church's property in Italy.

A. S. Atiya, *The Crusade: Historiography and Bibliography* (1962; 1976); J. Riley-Smith, *What were the Crusades?* (1977).

Cry of dereliction (of Jesus on the cross): see SON OF MAN, THE.

Crypto-Jews. Jews who secretly practised their religion while officially converting to either Christianity or Islam. Crypto-Jews have existed since the 7th cent. when they were forced to accept Christianity under the Visigoths in Spain. Well-known examples are the *Almohads of Spain and N. Africa of the 12th cent, the neofiti of S. Italy (late 13th–16th cent.), the Conversos or *Marranos of Spain (15th and 16th cents.) and the Jadid al-Islam of Meshed, Persia (19th cent.). See ANUSIM.

Crystal night (Nazi terror against Jews): see KRISTALLNACHT.

Cudworth, R.: see CAMBRIDGE PLATONISTS.

Cuius regio, eius religio ('whose region, his religion'). A summary of the Peace of Augsburg (1555) whereby rulers decided whether the religion of their own area should be Roman Catholic or Lutheran.

Cūlavaṃsa (The Short Chronicle). The history of Śri Lankā from 302 CE to the 19th cent. It is a continuation of the *Mahāvaṃsa*, written by at least three authors. The titles do not occur in the works themselves, but were introduced by W. Geiger (ed. with German tr., 1935; Eng. tr. C. M. Rickmers, 1953).

Cult. A term which refers to many non-traditional religious movements. Academics sometimes contrast cults with sects (see CHURCH-SECT TYPOLOGY) on the grounds that the former (e.g. *Cargo cults) are more alienated from traditional religions than the latter (e.g. *Jehovah's Witnesses); or that cults are more innovatory. Academics also write of other characteristics: cults attach importance to searching for mystical experience, are weakly structured, are small, are led by a *charismatic leader, and participants feel that they are the final arbiters of what is or is not the truth. Recently, however, the term has been employed in a different way, as a part of the polemic against *new religious movements in the West. One anti-cult organization, for example, provides a list of 'marks of cults', including the fact that such movements 'systematically employ sophisticated techniques designed to effect ego-destruction, thought reform, and dependence'; on this, see further BRAIN-WASHING.

B. R. Wilson, *Religious Sects* (1970); J. M. Yinger, *The Scientific Study of Religion* (1970).

Cults of affliction: see AFFLICTION, CULTS OF.

Cultural relativity and religion. Compared with the social organization of any of the higher primates, human communities are clearly different to a marked degree in the ways in which they organize, protect, and transmit their beliefs, values, social orderings, technologies, expectations, or whatever it is that might belong to a definition of *culture. But 'culture' not only marks humans off from primates: it marks human communities off from each other. Given that the basic biology and its needs are virtually identical in all humans, what is the status of the differences in culture which can so readily be observed? At one extreme are anthropologists who regard cultural diversity as nothing much more than a change of clothes: the clothes worn are no doubt well-chosen (i.e. well-adapted for the ecological niche which a particular group inhabits), but they cover the same basic human body. Taken to its limit, this view might emerge as a kind of genetic determinism—that the genes 'build' bodies as survival machines to ensure the replication of the information which they carry, and that different cultures are simply different strategies to secure that end. At the other extreme are anthropologists (and philosophers) who regard cultural diversity as profound: there is no such thing as 'human nature' or 'the person'; there are only mental and linguistic constructions which create entirely different ways of understanding and interacting with the world. In the succinct statement of E. Sapir (which underlies the Sapir-Whorf hypothesis about the way in which different languages create different worlds): 'Human beings do not live in the objective world alone, nor alone in the world of social activity as ordinarily understood, but are very much at the mercy of the particular language which has become the medium of expression for their society. . . . No two languages are ever sufficiently similar to be considered as representing the same social reality. The worlds in which different societies live are different worlds, not merely the same world with different labels attached.' Taken to its furthest limit, this view might emerge as cultural determinism, regarding the absolute control of language as not merely influencing how people perceive the world, but dictating that perception.

It is the second of these views which leads to cultural relativity, since if each culture creates and then imposes its own view of what reality is, then there is no neutral ground (no 'Archimedean point'—as in Archimedes' observation, 'Give me a place on which to stand and I will move the earth') on which to stand in order to give a neutral account or evaluation of any society or culture. The belief that one could attempt (let alone arrive at) a value-free account of religions is absurd: the observer is immersed in her own culture which imposes its standards on her judgements. It may even be impossible, on this view, to understand any other culture or religion at all. Thus although cultural relativism emerged (in part) as a protest against allowing one religion or culture to be assumed as the true standard by which to measure all others, it may end by having no standards by which to measure anything.

Beyond the issue of the incommensurability of different cultures, cultural relativism has raised equal questions for morality and *ethics. For if judgements are relative to the context in which they are produced, there cannot be any universal agreement on the good or the beautiful—though oddly, there *is* more agreement on the true. In fact, it is clear that although it is the case that humans have radically different views on what counts as good and what counts as beautiful, they share (as a human universal) the ability to make such judgements. Moreover, humans are clearly highly adaptable, in the sense that they can move between different cultures with relative ease. Thus the intermediate position seems correct, that cultures elaborate different worlds in which differences make such a difference that they cannot be understood except on their own terms of reference; but on the other hand, limits are set upon viable worlds by the conditions set in nature—both in the external environment, and also in the human body. Religions can then be understood as consequences of extremely long-running transmissions of somatic exploration and exegesis (i.e. long-running explorations and interpretations of the competence of the human body and its possible experiences). The study of religion may remain value-free, in the sense that it does not offer value-judgements on the worth or otherwise of particular exegeses; but on the other hand, it may lend itself to the increasingly common human enterprise of seeking to establish the eudaimonic (see ETHICS) in human life.

M. Carrithers, *Why Humans Have Culture* . . . (1994); E. Hatch, *Culture and Morality* (1983).

Culture. A many-layered concept with at least three dimensions: the cultivation of human natural capacities, the intellectual and imaginative products of such cultivation, and the whole way of life of a group or a society. All three dimensions are present in contemporary usage, but each also has a varied development of its own. 'Culture' was used in Roman times principally in the sense of tending the land (as in the Eng. 'agriculture'), a meaning extended by Cicero who described philosophy as the training or cultivation of the mind (*cultura animi*). This view was rediscovered and popularized in the 18th-cent. European *Enlightenment by such people as Wilhelm von Humboldt (1767–1835) and F. *Schleiermacher. 'Culture' also came to be conceived as the product of cultivation: learning, art, and music. Johann Gottfried von Herder (1744–1803) was possibly the first to speak of different 'culture*s*' in a way that anticipated more recent usage within ethnography or anthropology. This third and most extended sense of the term received its classical formulation by E. B. *Tylor in his study of *Primitive Culture* (1871): 'that complex whole which includes knowledge, belief, art, morals, law, custom, and any other capabilities and habits acquired by man as a member of society'. This or even broader conceptions have persisted within cultural anthropology to the present, whereas more narrowly focused definitions have been preferred within social anthropology. However, C. *Geertz made an attempt to reformulate the concept of culture as a socially constructed and historically transmitted network of *symbol systems (*The Interpretation of Cultures*, 1974).

Cupitt, D. (reductionist theologian): see SECULARIZATION.

Curate. A Christian clergyman who has the charge ('cure') of a parish, and thus (in England) the incumbent of a benefice, a *vicar, *rector, or (in the case of a new parish) 'perpetual curate'. Non-technically, however, the word is more often used to denote an unbeneficed clergyman appointed to assist the incumbent, i.e. properly an 'assistant curate'.

Cur Deus Homo? The title of Anselm's famous treatise on the *Atonement (1097–8), meaning: Why did God become man? A recurrent concern of Christian theology, *Athanasius' *On the Incarnation* is a notable predecessor. Anselm's importance lies in his attempt to bypass metaphor and found the doctrine on rational considerations.

Curé d'Ars (French priest): see VIANNEY, J.-B. M.

Curia, Roman. The collective organization which conducts the day-to-day affairs of the Roman Catholic Church. Since its reorganization by Pope Paul VI in 1967, it has been divided into the Secretariat of State, Sacred *Congregations, Tribunals (courts), Secretariats (mainly for *ecumenical affairs), Commissions, and Offices.

Cursing. The reverse side of *blessing, and therefore believed to bring actual power to bear. For that reason, casual cursing is as much disapproved of as is the taking of oaths which bring the name of God into disrepute, or, even more, which imply a claim to control the power of God. Thus *Jesus was reported as correcting the biblical command to fulfil one's oaths by commanding an abstinence from oaths altogether (Matthew 5. 33–7). Similarly, in Islam, *Muḥammad told traders to avoid swearing oaths in general, but particularly if there was any deceit with which the name of *Allāh would be associated. In Judaism, because cursing invokes power, the *rabbis only permitted cursing when it was prompted by a religious motive, and the *Talmud teaches: 'Be rather of the cursed than of the cursing' (*B.Sanh.* 49a). One curse has nevertheless remained prevalent (derived from Psalms 109. 13) which is applied especially to persecutors of Israel, from *Haman to Hitler: *yimmaḥ shemo (vezikro)*: 'may his name (and his memory) be blotted out'. In Christianity, the formal cursing of enemies continued into the Middle Ages (e.g. see L. K. Little, *Benedictine Maledictions: Liturgical Cursing in Romanesque France*, 1994), but waned in the gradual appropriation of the instruction of Jesus to his followers that they should love their enemies.

Cusanus (Christian philosopher): see NICHOLAS OF CUSA.

Custom (Jewish): see MINHAG.

Cuthbert, St (d. 687). Bishop of *Lindisfarne from 685. After the synod of Whitby, he was instrumental in winning acceptance of Roman usages at Lindisfarne. He was an active preacher, teacher, and overseer of the diocese, and by reputation a prophet and healer. His *relics were eventually (999) moved to Durham, and were translated to the new cathedral there in 1104, at which time his body was found to be uncorrupt. The cult of Cuthbert was especially popular from this time in N. England. Feast day, 20 Mar.

Cuti-citta (Skt., 'death consciousness'). In the scholastic Buddhism of the Theravāda tradition, one of the fourteen functions of the life-continuum (*bhavaṅga* (see ĀLAYA-VIJÑĀNA)). According to the medieval commentators it is the final moment of consciousness in an individual's life and is followed immediately by the first moment of consciousness at conception (*patisandhi-citta*) in the new appearance. Thus the beginning, continuation, and end of a life are designated as the moments of rebirth-linking (*patisandhi*), life-continuum (bhavaṅga), and death (*cuti*) respectively. The other eleven functions of the *bhavaṅga* are related to the process of perception, which occurs in a series of almost instantaneous stages, and the psycho-moral response of the individual to what is perceived.

Cyavana. In Hindu mythology, son of *Bhṛgu. Disturbed in his ascetic practices by Sukanyā, the daughter of King Śaryāti, he asked for her in marriage. Sukanyā proved to be a faithful wife to her elderly husband, and repelled the advances of the *Aśvins, who happened one day to see her naked while bathing. Her fidelity resulted in the twin gods' restoring her husband's youth, while he in turn secured for them a portion of the *soma sacrifice.

Cyprian, St (d. 258). *Bishop of Carthage and *martyr. He was elected bishop only two years after his conversion to Christianity *c.*246. During the persecution of Decius (249–51) he ruled his church from exile. After his return he pursued the policy of reconciling the 'lapsed' (i.e. those who had *apostatized during the persecution), not easily, but after appropriate penance and delay. The subsequent schism of *Novatian gave rise to the question whether *schismatics returning to the Church needed rebaptism. In these policies, Cyprian was governed by his sense of the overriding importance of the *Church: 'No one can have God as Father who does not have Church as Mother.' In a letter occurs one of the first expressions of the belief, *extra ecclesiam nulla salus: 'Outside the Church there is no salvation.' Ironically, therefore, Cyprian's insistence on rebaptism, supported by two synods, brought him into conflict with the policy of Rome. But this controversy was cut short by the persecution of Valerian, in which he was martyred. Cyprian's writings in Latin include a number of short theological works, among them *On the Unity of the Catholic Church* (251), and letters. Feast days variously 16 and 26 Sept., 2 Oct.

Eng. trs. R. E. Wallis; T. A. Lacey; M. Bévenot; P. Hinchcliff, *Cyprian of Carthage* . . . (1974).

Cyril, St (d. 444). Patriarch of *Alexandria from 412, and church *father. His career after *c.*430 was dominated by the controversy over church authority (he drove out schismatic followers of *Novatian), *christology, and specifically by his opposition to *Nestorius. The *Neoplatonist philosopher, Hypatia, was murdered by the mob, *possibly* at Cyril's instigation. The episode evoked a novel by Charles Kingsley. The rivalry between Alexandria and Constantinople for precedence, the difference between Alexandrian and *Antiochene theological thought, and Cyril's love of conflict, resulted in his support for the title *Theotokos for *Mary which Nestorius had rejected. He presided at the Council of *Ephesus (431) at which Nestorius was deposed. The resulting breach with the more moderate Antiochenes was healed in 433. It was a source of complaint by the *Monophysites that Cyril's own christological ways of speaking, (e.g. of the 'hypostatic union' in Christ of the *logos with the flesh) were not used at *Chalcedon. Cyril's writings include a large collection of letters (three to Nestorius), commentaries, an apology against *Julian the Apostate, and some sermons. In the E. he is 'the Seal of the Fathers', in the W. a doctor of the Church (since 1882).

R. W. Wilken, *Judaism and the Early Christian Mind* . . . (1971).

Cyril and Methodius (d. 869, 885). Christian missionary brothers, known as 'the *apostles of the (southern) Slavs'. Their activity was mainly in Moravia, subsequently among Croats, Serbs, and Bulgars, and was constantly subject to rivalry and opposition. Cyril worked out the alphabet now known as Glagolitic, and may (if it was not done by his successors) have worked out the better-known Cyrillic alphabet. The work of translation, especially of the Bible, was thus made possible.

F. Dvornik, *Byzantine Missions* . . . (1970).

D

Daʿat Torah (Torah understanding): see AGUDAT ISRAEL.

Da Costa, Uriel (1585–1640). Rationalizing Jewish freethinker, a heroic (for those who think likewise) type of those who resist religious obscurantism on grounds of conscience. He was born in Portugal of a *Marranos family. After beginning a career as a church lawyer, he abandoned Christianity when he read the Hebrew Bible. In about 1615, he took refuge in Amsterdam and professed Judaism openly. However, he came in conflict with the local *Sephardi congregation, which demanded communal conformity. Da Costa insisted instead on *sola scriptura* ('by scripture alone'), and rejected later *halakhic accretions, as well as ritual. He cast doubt on the immortality of the *soul; his first publication (1624) was duly burnt, and he was excommunicated (*ḥerem). In 1633, he formally submitted, though remaining privately sceptical. In his autobiography, *Exemplar Humanae Vitae* (published after his death, 1687), he recorded how he began to question the divine origin of the law of Moses: 'I concluded that it was nothing but a human invention.' Such views led to a second excommunication (1633). His decision to recant required public humiliation and punishment, the thought of which led him to suicide.

Dādā Gurūs. Affectionate name (roughly, 'Grandad') of four Jain teachers (*suri*) in the Śvetāmbara (see DIGAMBARA) Kharatara *Gaccha (sect). The Gaccha traces its origins back to a monk, Vardhamana (d. 1031), who broke free from temple-dwelling monks in order to re-establish purity of teaching. Among his disciples was Jineśvara, whose skill in debate led to the name Kharatara, 'keen-witted'. His most celebrated successor was Jinadatta (1075–1154), who undertook hazardous missionary journeys into Muslim territory to win converts. Jinadatta, with three later *suris* make up the four Dādā Gurūs: Maṇidhāri Jinacandra (1139–65), the 'jewel-wearer', from the jewel in his forehead with which he performed miracles; Jinakuśala (1279–1331), who won many converts; and Jinacandra (1537–1612), who won concessions for Jains and protection for Jain holy places from Muslim rulers, perhaps from *Akbar. Places associated with the Dādā Gurūs are still the object of veneration.

Dādū Dayāl (c.1543–1603). A saint of N. India in the *Sant tradition who composed poetry in Hindi. Born into a Muslim family, he was a cotton carder by profession. Married with a family, he travelled in Gujarat, finally settling in Rajastān where he died peacefully. Dādū was revered as a holy man during his lifetime, and is said to have met the emperor, *Akbar, who was deeply impressed by Dādū's spiritual presence. Dādū gathered a group of disciples about him who collected his poems together in a volume called *Dāduvāṇi*. These poems, some of which are intensely personal, speak of devotion (*bhakti) to a God beyond qualities (*nirguṇa) and the anguish of separation from God. Devotion to God and constant remembrance of him leads to liberation from *saṃsāra: 'To what shall we compare him? There is no second, God is God. In remembrance of him is peace. He alone knows his own secret, no other knows it. Delight in him through constant remembrance, so shall you find happiness.' (2. 84. 85) This remembrance means bringing to mind the name (*nām) of God, the name or sound which is thought to manifest the cosmos (see NĀDA, ŚABDA). This name is reached through *meditation and by the grace of the sat *guru. Indeed, many of Dādū's poems are in honour of his guru who gave him initiation (*dīkṣa). For Dādū, God, his name (or sound), and the guru are identical and can be located in the body through devotion and meditation (*bichār*). *Sūfī, *Vaiṣṇava, and *Sāṃkhya influences can be found in Dādū's poetry. His biography was written by Jan Gopal, *Dādū Janam Līla*, (c.1620).

W. M. Callewaert, *The Hindi Biography of Dādū Dayāl* (1988).

Daena (conscience): see FRASOKERETI.

Daeva (Old Pers., *daiva*; Middle Pers., *dēv*: 'shining one'). One of a group of gods in Ancient Persia (cf. DEVA) who were denounced by *Zoroaster as demonic and as gods of war and strife.

Daf Yomi (Heb., 'daily page'). Prescribed daily passage of *Talmud study. Devised by R. Meir Shapira in 1928, a double page of Talmud is prescribed for study each day. The entire Babylonian Talmud can be completed in seven years, and at the end of this period, there is a worldwide celebration (*siyyum*, 'conclusion'). The first cycle was completed in 1931, the seventh in 1988. Other cycles have since been instituted, e.g. of *Mishneh Torah.

Dāgaba (Pāli *dhātu*, 'element, essence' + *garbha*, 'chamber, cave'). A Buddhist mound where *relics are kept, hence occasionally a relic-container. A dāgaba usually has the same form as a *stūpa but not all stūpas are dāgabas, because not all stūpas contain relics.

Dahara-vidya (Skt., 'small space' + 'knowledge'). The realization in Hinduism of *ātman within the body, specifically in the 'domain of *Brahman', the interior of the heart.

Dai-anjin (great peace): see ANJIN.

Daiba (datta). Jap. for *Devadatta (the Buddha's cousin).

Daibosatsu (Jap., 'great bodhisattva'). The title of *Hachiman understood as the incarnation of a great *bodhisattva. Daibosatsu is, therefore, any bodhisattva (Jap., *bosatsu) who has reached the stage (*futai*) of not falling back into a lower state, and who is thus assured of becoming a *buddha. It is used as a title of respect for an outstanding monk.

Daibutsu (Jap., 'great Buddha'). Statues of *Buddhas or *Bodhisattvas exceeding a height of 4.8 metres and found throughout Asia. The most famous of these in Japan are the seated, bronze images of Birushana (Jap., Skt., *Vairocana) at the Tōdaiji in Nara (15 metres) and of *Amida (Jap.; Skt., Amitābha) in Kamakura (11.5 metres).

Dai-funshi (Jap., 'great resolve'). One of the three pillars of *zazen, the determination to counterbalance, through development of the *bodhi-mind, *dai-gidan*, 'great doubt'. *Dai-gidan* is not mild scepticism, but rather the necessary concomitant of enlightenment certainty: the more one knows by experience the truth of Zen, the more insistent the continuing presence of pain, strife, and suffering in the world must be as a question. The question is not to be evaded, but wrestled with from the perspective of dai-funshi. The third pillar is *dai-shinkon*, 'great faith', which supplies dai-funshi with its dynamic. Without faith, especially that the Buddha did indeed achieve enlightenment, the Zen path could not open up. At this fundamental point, Zen Buddhism is more like a religion and less like a philosophy (despite claims to the contrary in the West).

Dai-gedatsu (Jap., 'great liberation'). In Zen Buddhism, the attainment of enlightenment, and thus of the realized buddha-nature. Hence, it is a synonym for *nirvāna.

Dai-gidan: see DAI-FUNSHI.

Daigon (Jap., 'great incarnation'). The appearing in, or as, the human form of a deity.

Daigo-tettei (profound enlightenment): see DAISHI.

Daigu Ryokan (Zen poet and monk): see RYŌKAN DAIGU.

Daiji (Jap., 'great compassion'). The great compassion which is the goal and practice of *bodhisattvas. It is often used as the title of particular bodhisattvas, e.g. daiji daihi no satta, 'of great compassion and mercy', is Jizō; daiji daihi no honji is Kannon.

Daiji (Jap., 'important matter'). The one thing necessary in Japanese Buddhism for the attainment of enlightenment, namely, the desire and intention to seek it. Daiji is also used as a shorthand for daiji innen, the most important reason why the *Buddha appeared in the world, namely, to teach the *dharma to save all sentient beings.

Daijō. Jap. term for *Mahāyāna.

Daijō-kai (Jap.). 'Rules of the great vehicle', i.e. rules for monks and laypeople in *Mahāyāna Buddhism, as e.g. in *jujukai.

Daijô-sai. The first First Fruits Ceremony (*Niiname-sai) following the accession of a new emperor in Japan. The connection between accession and the harvest festivals first appears in written sources during the 8th cent., though surely in earlier times as well the sovereign's role included divinatory and sacrificial functions associated with agriculture. Preparations for the festival begin during the preceding spring, with the selection of rice fields to be consecrated for the supply of grain to be used as sacred offerings during the daijô-sai. The entire sequence of official preparations and performances, promulgated during the 10th cent., is contained in *Engi-shiki Procedures of the Engi Era [Books VI-X]*, tr. F. Bock (1970), 27–56.

Daikoku. A Japanese deity (said to have been introduced to Japan by *Saichō, 767–822), identified in the popular mind as one of the seven gods of luck (Shichi-fuku-shin). The name is a Sino-Jap. tr. of the Skt. *Mahākāla, an Indian deity whose character in Japan is manifested variously as a deity of war, of wealth and agriculture, and of the underworld. Indian and Chinese influence is apparent in these characterizations and in their representations in painting and sculpture. A further aspect of Daikoku is revealed in his identification with the deity Jizaiten (Skt., Makeśvara). In Japanese syncretism, he is erroneously assimilated by a play on words to the native deity Ôkuni-nushi. Which aspect is emphasized depends on local tradition.

In esoteric Buddhism, Daikoku appears in the northern quadrant of the outer (Diamond) sector of the Womb *Maṇḍala. As one of the seven gods of luck, Daikoku is portrayed with a round cap and hunter's garb. Over his left shoulder (or in his left hand) he carries a large sack, and in his right hand is a rice mallet or a spatula. He is seen standing or sitting on a hefty bagful of rice.

Daikyō. The 'Great Doctrine' promulgated by the new imperial Japanese government in the late 19th cent., as part of its effort to create a state religion. With the Meiji Restoration of 1868, the ancient ideal of 'the unity of religion and government' (*saisei itchi*) was resurrected by state sponsorship of Shinto and its formal separation from Buddhism, which, due to its close association with the old Tokugawa feudalistic regime, fell into political disfavour. In 1870, an imperial rescript announced the government's support of the Great Doctrine as a set of principles that summarized the essence of the way of the *kami (*kannagara*). The Great Doctrine stated three central moral-religious tenets: (i) reverence for the national gods, (ii) the importance of the Law of Heaven and the Way of Humanity, and (iii) loyalty to the throne and authorities.

It soon became evident, however, that the government's policy of patronage of a state Shinto and persecution of popular Buddhist and syncretistic Shinto sects was politically unsuccessful. In 1872, the Dept. of Religion and Education was established as the new institutional arm for the propagation of the Great Doctrine. This replaced the Dept. of Shinto, attempting to enlist the support of the major Buddhist sects and other religious groups in its propaganda efforts, appointing their leaders as 'national priests' with official status. However, even in this new arrangement, the overemphasis on Shinto liturgy and ideology at the expense of the other religions caused tensions. Internal disputes, as well as the artificial nature of the state-controlled national religion of Daikyō and lack of popular appeal, led to the abolishment of the Dept. of Religion and Education in 1875.

Daimoku. (Jap., 'sacred title'). The practice of chanting the *mantra *namu myōhō renge kyō*, 'I take refuge in the Lotus of the Wonderful Law Sūtra' (*Lotus Sūtra) followed by *Nichiren Buddhists. The Japanese monk Nichiren (1222–82) believed all Buddhist teaching and practice is concentrated in this mantra, which he also calligraphically inscribed on a tablet called the *gohonzon*, 'object of worship'.

Dainichi (Jap.; Skt., *Mahāvairocana*). The cosmic *Buddha of *Shingon or esoteric Buddhism. All phenomena point to the reality of Dainichi, and at the same time they are all manifestations of that reality. More concretely, it is said that the six elements—earth, water, fire, wind, space, and consciousness—create all Buddhas, all sentient beings, and the material world, Dainichi revealing the six elements in perfect harmony. The basic practice of esoteric Buddhism is to integrate the microcosmic activities of the body, speech, and mind with the *samādhi of the macrocosmic Dainichi through contemplation of *maṇḍala (cosmogram), symbolic hand gestures (*mudra), and mystical utterances (*mantra). In this way, one realizes the 'self entering the Buddha and the Buddha entering the self'. The contents of Dainichi are manifested in two ways: the aspect of wisdom, indestructible and unchanging like the diamond, as Kongōkai (Vajradhātu) maṇḍala, and the aspect of the all-embracing principle, underlying and nurturing all phenomena like the womb, as Taizōkai (Garbhadhātu) maṇḍala.

Dainichi Nōnin or **Jimbō Zenji** (12th/13th cent.). Zen Buddhist Japanese master of the *Rinzai school. Initially introduced to *Tendai teaching, he reached enlightenment without formal instruction from a master, and founded the Sambō-ji (monastery). To guard against accusations that he was a private and unauthorized teacher, he submitted his teaching to Yü-wang Cho-an (Jap., Ikuō Setsuan) of the Rinzai school, who confirmed his enlightenment and authenticity. Extremely little is known of his life—perhaps only that he sent two disciples to China in 1189 to request recognition (which was granted) from Cho-an Te-kuang (1121–1203). He is also credited (e.g. by *Nichiren) with the founding of the Daruma-school. The term is somewhat confusing, since *Daruma is associated primarily with *Bodhidharma, and in Japan with various different Zen schools. *Eisai distinguished Daruma from Zen: 'Some foolishly identify Daruma-shu with Zen. . . . But adherents of Daruma say there are no precepts, no practices, no passions: we are already enlightened, and do not need even such practices as *nembutsu. . . . Eisai commented: "They are those who are described in the *sūtras as having a false view of *śūnyatā; they must be avoided absolutely." ' From this it may be inferred that Daruma teaching pushed the doctrine of all appearance being empty of attributes, and all therefore equally bearing the buddha-nature, to a logical extreme. Although Daruma-shu was repudiated by Jap. Zen, Nōnin was himself acknowledged as a profound master.

Dainihon Kannonkai. Early form of *Sekai Kyūseikyō.

Daiō Kokushi (Zen master): see NAMPO JŌMYŌ.

Daiosho (Jap., 'great priest'). Honorific title of Zen masters, used particularly in the daily recitation in Zen monasteries of the lineage of tradition running back to the *Buddha Śākyamuni.

Daishi (Jap., 'great master'). Buddhist title of respect for a *buddha or high official. It is used especially of *Kūkai.

Daishi (Jap., 'great death'). In Zen Buddhism, the death of (or to) the differentiated self, which leads to profound enlightenment (*daigo-tettei*). This is called 'the death on the mat' (*zagu*), the consequence of undertaking the Zen way which the *zagu* epitomizes.

Dai-shinkon (great faith): see DAI-FUNSHI.

Daitoku-ji. The Monastery of Great Virtue, one of the largest Zen Buddhist monasteries in Kyōto. It was built in 1319 and formed part of the Gosan (literally, 'five mountains'), a confederation of five monasteries, based on the model established by the Sung emperor, Ning-tsung. The Gosan was also organized elsewhere, e.g. in Kamakura. However, Daitoku-ji was detached from the Kyōto Gosan in order to become a monastery where prayer and ritual would be offered for the health of the emperor; and in time it became the centre for a complex of smaller monasteries, in which Zen arts, especially *chadō, flourished.

Daityas. Sons of the *Vedic Goddess, *Diti, and demons, or giants, in post-Vedic Hinduism. They opposed the *devas (gods)—though less mythologically, they are also indigenous tribes who opposed the Āryan invasion. In the legend of the *Churning of the Ocean, they are a further complication, because they steal *amṛta, only to lose it again when they fall to the charms of *Viṣṇu disguised as Mohinī, the enchantress.

Daiun Sōgaku Harada (1870–1961). Japanese Zen master. He entered a *Sōtō monastery at the age of 7, but also trained in a *Rinzai monastery, Shōgen-ji. He received the seal of recognition (*inka-shōmei) from Dokutan Rōshi, and became abbot of Hosshin-ji. His teaching was continued by his *dharma successor, Hakuun Ryōko Yasutani, whose 'Introductory Lectures' appear in P. Kapleau, *The Three Pillars of Zen* (1980).

Daiva (Skt.; cf. Lat., *deus*). Sacred or divine power at work, hence divinity itself; usually the influence of powers outside the observable workings of nature. *Daivī-māyā* is thus the way in which *Brahman brings manifestation into its apparent forms. In Zoroastrianism, daivas were taken to be malevolent and were condemned as *demons.

Dajjāl (Muslim form): see ANTICHRIST.

Ḍākinī (Skt., 'female witch'; Tib., *mkha'.'gro.ma*, 'Female one who moves through the sky'). A class of Goddesses in Tibetan Buddhism attendant upon *yogins. They have a male equivalent, *ḍākas*, which are however not frequently mentioned. Historically, ḍākiṇīs were known in India as flesh-eating attendants of *Kālī, and as the sexual partners of yogins; in Tibetan and *Vajrayāna Buddhism, although their form may vary from extreme ugliness to extreme beauty, their principal concern is to inspire the yogin and to transmit secret teachings in dreams. They may sometimes take human form. In the *Nyingma tradition, ḍākiṇīs are responsible for guarding and revealing hidden texts (*terma). Iconographically, ḍākiṇīs are usually consorts of other deities, but it is *only* iconographically that they correspond to the Hindu *śaktis: the ḍākiṇīs are associated with wisdom, not with power, for which reason they are referred to as *prajñas (wisdoms).

Dakṣa (ritual skill): see ADITI; ĀDITYAS.

Dakṣinā (Skt., *da*, 'give', or perhaps *dakṣ*, 'causing the incomplete to be completed'). The Indian gift offered to the priestly officiants by the initiator of a sacrifice. Originally, the gift was a cow (hence the word may mean that). Just as the *brahmans depend on dakṣinās for their livelihood, so the well-being of the cosmos depends on their sacrifices. Thus in time dakṣinas became detached from specific sacrifices and became the equivalent of *dāna (gift, from which mutual benefit is derived). Dakṣinā was also personified as a Goddess who is (mother nature) the giver of life and is propitious. Dakṣinā is associated with the right hand, the propitious or clean side, and thus with masculinity.

Dakṣinācāra (Skt., 'night hand' + 'custom'). *Tantric Hinduism of the pure kind, hence 'right-handed Tantra', as opposed to *vāmācāra, or 'left-handed Tantra'—the left hand being the one with which impure acts are undertaken.

Dakṣināgni. The southern of the three fires in which Hindu offerings are made, in this case to the *pitṛs (the ancestors who dwell in the south). It also supplies the fire for cremations, so it is called (*Ṛg Veda* 10. 16. 9) 'the flesh-devouring fire'. It is regarded as dangerous and threatening, because of its association with death. The *dakṣināyāna* is the southern path which leads to the domain of the dead, as opposed to *devayāna*, which leads to the *devas.

Dalada Maligawa (shrine of tooth relic): see TOOTH RELIC TEMPLE.

Dalai Lama. The office of temporal and spiritual leadership of the Tibetan peoples, of which the present holder, Tenzin Gyatso (Bstan-'dzin-rgya-mtsho) is the fourteenth. The history of the office begins with Gendun Drub (Dge-'dun-grub-pa, 1391–1475), the third successor of *Tsong Khapa as head of the *Geluk school, noted for his skill in avoiding the political intrigue with which the *Kagyü, *Sakya, and the regional kings were enmeshed following the decline of Sakya rule with Mongol interest in the 13th cent. Predicting his own rebirth, Gendun Drub was the first member of the Geluk to adopt the *tulku system of reincarnating *lamas. His successor was Gendun Gyatso, whose own successor Sonam Gyatso (1543–88) accepted an invitation to renew the Tibetan–Mongolian priest–patron relationship. In a respectful exchange by Lake Kokonor in 1578, Altan Khan gave Sonam Gyatso the Mongolian title 'Ta le' (Ocean [of Wisdom]) Lama, which, retrospectively applied to his two predecessors, made Gendun Drub the first 'Ta le' Lama ('Dalai' being a W. transcription).

Sonam Gyatso's establishment of relations with the Mongols may not have been a deliberately political move, but when his successor was discovered as the great-grandson of Altan Khan, the Geluk suddenly found themselves as a major political force. Without their having much say in the matter, the child Yontan Gyatso (1589–1616) was accompanied to Lhasa by a Mongol army, whose mere presence set off a series of internal wars. The

'Great Fifth' Dalai Lama, Ngawang Lobsang Gyatso (1617–1682), brought unity to Tibet by using the Mongol power to quell the internal dissent (and to keep the Chinese Manchu dynasty at bay), and afterwards distanced himself sufficiently from the Khans to leave the Geluk as the autonomously dominant secular force in Tibet. The head of the Kagyü, the tenth Karmapa Choying Dorje (1604–74) acknowledged the authority of the Dalai Lama, which has gone unchallenged by all Tibetans to this day.

It was during the Great Fifth's reign that the building of the Potala palace was initiated in *Lhasa. When Ngawang Lobsang Gyatso died, his regent Sangye Gyatso suppressed the news, announcing that the Dalai Lama had gone into retreat, for thirteen years (a period of retreat not unusual in Tibet) until the Potala was completed. The sixth Dalai Lama, Tsanyang Gyatso, reared in secret, had thus not been discovered in the normal way but was the personal choice of the regent, and although the present Dalai Lama has vouched for his authenticity he appeared singularly unsuited for the office, disdaining politics for wine, women, and the writing of romantic poetry—much of which was very fine:

> Over the eastern hill rises
> The smiling face of the moon.
> In my mind forms
> The smiling face of my beloved.

—and also humorous:

> People gossip about me.
> I am sorry for what I have done.
> I have taken three thin steps
> And landed myself in the tavern of my mistress.

As if recognizing himself as a political disaster, Tsanyang Gyatso surrendered to the latest wave of Mongolian militarism and died while being taken out of Tibet. A wealth of mythologies (he was a *Tantric master, who did not really die) has arisen from attempts to explain his behaviour.

The reign of the politically disinclined seventh Dalai Lama Kelsang Gyatso (1708–57) coincided with a period of Chinese occupation, and much of it was spent in exile. The eighth Dalai Lama Jampal Gyatso (1758–1804) was similarly more interested in religion than affairs of state, thus allowing his regents—with Chinese encouragement—to develop a taste for power. The ninth, tenth, eleventh, and twelfth Dalai Lamas all died before their majorities, probably poisoned by their Chinese-backed regents. It was not until the eminently skilful 'Great Thirteenth' Dalai Lama Thubten Gyatso (1876–1933) expelled his own regent that a Dalai Lama was able to have a great effect on his country for the first time since the Great Fifth, steering Tibet through the 'Great Game' of European expansion, which included the Younghusband British invasion (1904), a Chinese invasion (1910), and two consequent exiles before reasserting the Dalai rule in 1912.

The reign of the present Dalai Lama (b. 1935) is the most poignantly known. Faced with a Chinese invasion of his homeland in 1950 he was invested with the powers of office three years in advance of his majority. One month later, in December 1950, with a tidal wave of atrocities heading towards Lhasa through the Eastern province of Kham, he took the advice of his Oracle and sought exile in India, taking with him the seals of State. In May 1951 using seals forged in Beijing, the collaborator Ngapo Ngawang Jigme signed away Tibet's independence in a '17-point Agreement' in exchange for high office. Refusing to accept this but seeking compromise, Tenzin Gyatso returned to Lhasa in August 1951. In 1956, in response to forced collectivization and repeated atrocities, Kham again erupted. 150,000 Chinese troops were committed along with extensive bombing of all inhabited areas. By 1958 Lhasa was swollen with refugees, and the impetus of the Chinese soldiery bearing down on Lhasa forced the military regime in the capital to be seen to be doing more to subdue the Tibetans. In March 1959, the Dalai Lama was invited to a theatrical show in an army camp without his bodyguards. Word got round, and thousands of Lhasa citizens surrounded his summer palace, the Norbulingka, to prevent his attending. On March 17th he fled in disguise towards India, and three days later the Norbulingka was shelled. In the following three days of fighting, by Chinese statistics 84,000 people were killed, and a year later the International Commission of Jurists pronounced China guilty of genocide. To date over 1,200,000 Tibetans, from a previous population of six million, are estimated to have died as a result of the occupation.

Today, Chinese settlement in Tibet has made Tibetans a minority there, and refugees who continue to escape into India and Nepal speak of such attempts to further reduce the Tibetan population by forced sterilization, abortion, and inter-marriage. Environmentally, Tibet is used for both nuclear testing and disposal of nuclear waste, and has been deforested by 50 per cent since 1950, threatening many endemic species. Street protests in Lhasa (1987–9) resulted in Martial Law (1989–90), and were repeated again in 1993. Monks and nuns constitute a high proportion of Tibetan prisoners in Chinese jails.

The current Dalai Lama, Tenzin Gyatso, has based himself in Dharamsala, India, from where he has become well-known internationally, and been styled a 'god-king' by the Western press. This potentially misleading term stems from the Tibetan consideration of eminent beings as emanations of *Buddhas or *bodhisattvas, and the Dalai Lama in particular as an emanation of *Avalokiteśvara, the bodhisattva of compassion. Among Tibetans, he is more commonly called 'Gyalwa Rinpoche' (Precious Eminence), or simply 'Kundun' (Presence). An active statesman, Tenzin Gyatso continues to negotiate improved conditions for his people and terms for his own return, and has overseen the transformation of the previous theocratic government into a democratically elected autonomous body (albeit in exile). In 1989 he received the Nobel Peace Prize for his adherence to the Buddhist principle of non-violence in the Tibetan struggle, although in the 1990s a wing of the Tibetan Youth Congress advocating armed resistance has become more vocal.

R. Hicks and N. Chogyam, *Great Ocean: An Authorized Biography* (1984); G. Schulemann, *Die Geschichte der Dalai-lamas* (1959); Tenzin Gyatso, *Freedom in Exile: The Autobiography . . .* (1990).

Dalmatic. A Christian eucharistic *vestment. It is a decorated tunic reaching to the knees, worn over the *alb by the *deacon (while the priest is wearing the *chasuble and the *subdeacon the tunicle).

Damadamā Sāhīb Taxāl (Sikh movement): see BHINDRĀNAWĀLE, J. S.

Damaru. The drum of the Hindu god, *Śiva. It accompanies him as Naṭarāja, the Lord of the *Dance. It is shaped like an hour-glass, with each half representing the *liṅga and the *yoni. From the symmetry between the two, the cosmos is created.

Damascus or **Dimashq.** Capital of Syria, claimed to be the oldest continuously inhabited city in the world. It is mentioned in the Ebla tablet (*c.*3000 BCE), and according to Muslim legend, it was the first city to be built after the flood—by the prophet *Hūd. It stands on the R. Barada which gives the whole area great fertility. Saul was converted to Christianity on the way to Damascus (hence 'a Damascus road experience' for any life-changing event); and 'the street called Straight' (i.e. Via Recta, Acts 9. 11) still runs for about a mile E.–W., with Roman gates at each end. Many different Christian communities live in Damascus, and there are ancient *synagogues (especially the Jawbar). But Damascus is predominantly a Muslim city, following its capture by Khālid ibn Walīd in 635 (AH 14). When the *Umayyads came to power in 661 (AH 41), Damascus became their capital; but the capital shifted to Baghdad with the arrival of the *Abbāsids in 750 (AH 132). The greatest monument is the Umayyad mosque, now restored after fire in 1893.

Damascus Document. Manuscript of a Jewish sect which left *Judah to settle in 'Damascus'. Initially discovered by Solomon *Schechter, further fragments were found among the *Dead Sea Scrolls. It was probably composed in approximately 60 BCE, and reflects opposition to the *Hasmonean *high priesthood. Central figures include the '*teacher of righteousness', the 'preacher of falsehood', and the 'people of mockery'. The sect, which may have been identical with the *Qumran community, seems to have lived by strict laws, although these differ in some respects from those in the *Manual of Discipline*.

Damayantī. The heroine of *Nalopākhyānam*, the 'Story of Nala' in *Mahābhārata*, which was told to console Yudhiṣṭhira after his gambling losses. It is a story of constancy in devotion, in which Nala loses everything except Damayantī, but recovers his kingdom in the end.

Damdamā or **Damdama Sāhib** (Pañjābī, 'resting place'). Village in S. Pañjāb where Guru *Gobind Siṅgh dictated the *Ādi Granth. Damdamā Sāhib in Bhatiṇḍā District was originally Talvaṇḍī Sābo and was renamed in honour of Gobind Siṅgh's stay after the battle of *Muktsar 1705 CE. It gave its name to the Damdamā version of the Ādi Granth. Several other locations associated with Sikh Gurūs are similarly named.

Damian, Peter (monk and cardinal): see PETER DAMIAN.

Dan. One of the twelve tribes of *Israel. Dan was the fifth son of *Jacob by the maidservant Bilhah, and the territory of the tribe was in the extreme north of the *Promised Land.

Dāna (Pāli, 'gift'). In Indian religions, a gift, especially for a religious purpose. In Buddhism, it is an act of generosity to any creature, but more usually a particular gift to a *bhikṣu or to the *saṅgha, bringing *merit to the giver (or transferring that merit to others). In origin, it may have deliberately replaced the Hindu *dakṣinā offered to *brahmans officiating at sacrifices—no longer possible once the *Buddha had repudiated the efficacy of sacrifices. Any occasion which previously had needed either a sacrifice or other ritual offering could now get religious sanction through the dāna offering. A standard list of ten gifts is often given (see, e.g., the section on giving in *Anguttara Nikāya*, 4. 239), namely, food, drink, clothing, vehicle, garlands, perfumes, ointments, beds (or bedding), dwellings, lighting; but the gift to the saṅgha became established as the midday meal. In return, monks give their ritual skills, training, counselling, preaching, etc., to the community. Dāna is one of the Six Perfections (*Pāramitā), one of the Ten Contemplations (*anussati), and one of the most important works of merit (*puṇya).

Dance. Like all pervasive religious behaviours, the dominant importance of dance in religious and especially *ritual behaviours can be traced back to its genetic role (see Introduction and BIOGENETIC STRUCTURALISM). Ethologists describe 'choreographed' behaviours among animals, birds, insects, etc., for the purposes of sexual display, establishing hierarchies, marking territories, and threatening rivals. So primordial and universal is dance that such diverse figures as Wagner ('The most original of the arts was that of dancing: its peculiar essence is rhythm, and this has developed into music') and G. van der Leeuw regarded dance as the origin of religion—though the latter distinguished between the animal and the human, since the former is instinctual and the latter culturally controlled and modified. In his view the dance helped humans to relate to nature through magic, ecstasy, and aesthetics. While it is clear that human dance in connection with religion transcends any ethological base, it remains the case that dance, by its rhythm and exclusion of other external stimuli, induces brain behaviours (often leading to trance or ecstasy) which underlie claims to *shamanistic or divine possession. At the least, they become evidence of connection with the divine (e.g. dervishes/ *derwīsh, *ḥasidic dancers), or of a manifestation of the divine (e.g. in Hindu temple dance). Even when such dance develops a tradition of its own, the religious roots are easy to discern (e.g. *Nō Theatre in Japan; Beijing opera in China, with its links with early descriptions of shaman dancing). Among Hindus, dance reiterates the cosmic process, epitomized in Śiva, who, as Naṭarāja, the Lord of the Dance, is the patron of dancers, creating, sustaining, destroying, and bringing to birth. Much Hindu dance draws on the *Nāṭya Śastra* (*c.*1st cent. BCE or CE), which lays out the rules for the dramatic manifestation of the divine. *Kathak* (teller of tales) is an example in N. India, which syncretizes elements from Islam. *Kathākali* (story-tale) occurs at Kerala in S. India, drawing on the epics: its dancers train for at least seven years for the performance, which takes place throughout the night (see K. B. Iyer, *Kathkali* (1955); F. P. Richmond *et al.* (eds.), *Indian Theatre*; P. Zarrilli, *Demystifying Kathakali*). The vernacular *nāc* (for nāṭya) gave rise to the Eng. 'nautch dancers'. *Kṛṣṇa's dance among the gōpīs is reflected in dance in honour of Kṛṣṇa (e.g. *Caitanya), visible in the streets today in the Hare Krishna (*International Society . . .) movement. See also GHOST DANCE; DENGAKU.

J. L. Hanna, *To Dance is Human* (1979); B. T. Jones (ed.), *Dance as Cultural Heritage* (1983, 1985); G. van der Leeuw, *Sacred and Profane Beauty* (1963); F. P. Richmond *et al.* (eds.), *Indian Theatre: Traditions of Performance*; R. Singh and R. Massey, *Indian Dances . . .* (1967); W. Sorrell, *The Dance Through the Ages* (1967); K. Vatsyayan, *Classical Indian Dance . . .* (1968).

Dance of Death or **Danse Macabre** or **Totentanz.** A defiant reaction, principally in medieval Europe, to the unpredictable but inevitable occurrence of death. It was evoked especially by the spread of bubonic plague in the 14th cent., when sufferers danced in graveyards. In art and literature, death becomes one of the dancers, drawing all (but particularly those in high position, e.g. kings and bishops) into the inevitable dance—thus emphasizing the equality of all in the face of mortality. Of many illustrations, Holbein's woodcuts, 'Totentanz', are particularly well-known. This deliberate confronting of death has a remote parallel in the Buddhist contemplation of death and of the frailities in the body which lead to it: see e.g. DEVA-DŪTA; DHĀTU-VAVATTHĀNA; FOUR LAST THINGS.

F. Eichenberg, *The Dance of Death* (1983); L. P. Kurtz, *The Dance of Death and the Macabre Spirit in European Literature* (1934).

Daṇḍa (Skt.). Staff or rod, symbolizing power. In the hand of *Kālī, it symbolizes the irreversible power of time. Daṇḍa is also the personified form of punishment, especially as penitential, thus ameliorating the punishments of a future birth. *Yama's staff is a form of Yama himself, creating fear of the next life and better behaviour in this. A daṇḍa is bestowed during the sacred thread ceremony (*upanayana), and it is carried by a student (*brahmacarya) as a symbol of his renunciation of worldly, distracting pleasures.

Daṇḍadhara. The title of the Hindu god *Yama as judge of the dead.

Daṇḍin. 1. *Saṁnyāsin who carries a staff, and thus one who is on the fourth stage of life (*āśrama).

2. Early (*c.*7th cent. CE) writer of Sanskrit prose whose style is held out as a perfect model. His best known work is *Daśakumāracarita*, tr. A. W. Ryder, as *The Ten Princes*; according to A. L. Basham, 'Few works of Indian literature tell us so much about low life' (*The Wonder that was India*, p. 442).

Dan-Gyo (Zen work): see LIU-TSU-TA-SHIH FA-PAO-T'AN-CHING.

Daniel, Book of. A book numbered among the *Writings of the Hebrew Bible and among the prophets in the Christian Old Testament. The first part of the book (chs. 1–8) describes the experiences of a man Daniel and his three companions under Nebuchadnezzar and Belshazzar, kings of Babylon, and Darius the Mede. These include the companions' escape from the fiery furnace (3), the handwriting on the wall ('Mene, Mene, Tekel, Upharsin') at Belshazzar's feast (5), and Daniel in the lions' den (6). The second part (7–12) is a series of visions of the future of the Jewish people. The traditional belief that the author was Daniel, a Jewish exile in Babylon in the 6th cent. BCE, has generally been given up. Most scholars hold that the book was written between 168 and 165 BCE to encourage the Jewish victims of persecution by the Seleucid emperor Antiochus Epiphanes. The section 2. 4–7. 28 is written in Aramaic, not Hebrew. The book became the model for Jewish and Christian *apocalypses. The figure of a *son of man in the vision of 7. 13 became important in the Christian tradition of *Jesus' sayings. In RC Bibles, Daniel is supplemented by three Greek writings, the *Song of the Three Children, *Susanna, and *Bel and the Dragon.

Daniélou, Alain, or **Shiva Sharan** (1907–94). Musician and scholar of Indian religions. Finding early refuge in music from his mother's extreme religious devotion, Daniélou became an accomplished dancer. In 1932 he visited India, where he met *Tagore, and under his influence, he entered

Benares University in 1935, being made a research professor, a post which he held until 1953. He became director of research into Skt. literature in Madras until 1956, and then member of the French Institute of Indology at Pondicherry. Returning to Europe, he became adviser to the International Music Council of UNESCO. While in Benares, he converted to Hinduism, taking the name Shiva Sharan. He translated texts (notably *Kāma Sūtra*; see KĀMAŚASTRA) and wrote many books, notably *Hindu Polytheism* (1964), *La Musique de l'Inde du Nord* (1985), *Le Mystère du culte du Linga* (1993), and *La Sculpture érotique hindou* (1973). For Daniélou, polytheism surpasses monotheism because 'divinity can only be reached through its manifestations'. He put into practice his own theory, that the polytheist

> travels from the outward forms of ritual and morality towards the more abstract aspects of knowledge and nonaction. These are outwardly represented by the different groups of static symbols, that is, deities, and active symbols, that is, rites. The seeker chooses at each stage the deities and rites which are within his reach as he progresses on the path that leads toward liberation.

Dante Alighieri (1265–1321). Italian poet. Little is known of his early life, but as a child he met 'Beatrice' with whom he fell in love. She died in 1290, the wife of another, provoking a crisis for Dante resolved by his writing *Vita Nuova*. In that, he promised her a poem 'such as had been written for no lady before'. That poem was his *Divine Comedy*, written sometime between 1305 and 1314. It is set in a period over Easter 1300 during which Dante travels from a dark forest (in which he has lost his way) through *hell ('Lasciate ogni speranza voi ch'entrate': All hope abandon, you who enter here) and *purgatory to *paradise. The account is vivid and detailed and is marked by his intellectual sympathy with *Thomism (Aristotle is called 'The Master of them that know') and his political sympathy with the Ghibellines, who supported the emperor against the *pope. The poet Virgil leads Dante through hell and purgatory, and on the boundary of the earthly paradise cedes his role to Beatrice, who guides Dante through the planetary spheres of paradise, finally ceding her role in turn to the contemplative *Bernard of Clairvaux who presents him to the Blessed Virgin, whose *intercession gains for Dante a glimpse of the *Beatific Vision and recognition of 'L'amor che muove il sole e l'altre stelle', the love that moves the sun and the other stars.

Trs., several, e.g. D. Sayers, J. D. Sinclair, C. S. Singleton (with comm.); S. Botterill, *Dante and the Mystical Tradition* (1994); P. Boyde, *Dante Philomythes and Philosopher* (1981); S. Ellis, *Hell* (1994); K. Foster, *The Two Dantes* (1977); E. G. Gardner, *Dante and the Mystics* (1913); C. Slade, *Approaches to Teaching Dante's Divine Comedy* (1982); P. Toynbee, *Dante Dictionary* (rev. C. S. Singleton, 1968).

Daoism: see TAOISM.

Darajah (rank or degree): see MARRIAGE (ISLAM).

Dār al-ḥarb (Arab., 'abode of war'). Territory outside Muslim jurisdiction; the opposite of *dār al-Islām. In theory, *jihād is commanded, since inhabitants of such territory are at war with the Muslim *'umma. Qur'ān 9. 5 commands the Muslims to fight and slay the polytheists. In Islamic law, a non-Muslim living in dār al-ḥarb was a *ḥarbī*, one of the *ahl al-ḥarb* ('people of war'), those who, though invited to accept Islam, had refused. In recent years the concept has been much modified, and the creation of Arab, usually Muslim, nation-states has tended to mean that national consciousness takes priority over the specifically Islamic nature of the state, although Islamic solidarity is still important. There has been, therefore, an increased emphasis on a *third* category, the 'domain of covenant' or 'of agreement', *dār al-ṣulḥ, which recognizes those states/countries with which treaties have been signed, and in which Muslims are free to practise their faith.

M. Khadduri, *War and Peace in the Law of Islam* (1955).

Dār al-Islām (Arab., 'abode of Islam'). Territories within the Muslim *'umma's supremacy and in which Islamic law prevails. Jews, Christians, and some others are given status as *dhimmis (protected persons). Dār al-Islām is contrasted with *dār al-ḥarb (abode of war), non-Muslim territory; the whole concept is somewhat modified today. (Not to be confused with DARUL ISLAM.)

Dār al-ṣulḥ (Arab., 'abode of the Truce'). Non-Islamic territories no longer hostile but having a treaty agreement with the adjoining Muslim state, to which they pay tribute. The Christians of Najrān in Arabia were given by *Muḥammad a treaty of protection, which was taken as a norm for later agreements of this kind (see NAṢĀRĀ). Among early Muslim lawyers there was some dispute as to the precise status of such territories, though they were distinguished from *dār al-ḥarb, hostile nations, and *dār al-Islām, part of the Muslim *'umma.

Dārā Shikoh (1615–59). Muslim heir-apparent of Shāh Jahān, who sought common ground between Hinduism and Islam. He came under the influence of *Qādariy(y)a teachers, who confirmed him in the importance of experiencing that of which he spoke; and he engaged in conversations with a Hindu *ascetic, Bābā Lāl. He regarded the two religions as 'the confluence of two oceans' (Qur'ān 18. 65): his views issued in *Majma' al-Bahrayn* ('Mingling of the Two Oceans', 1655). He also believed that the *Upaniṣads were 'the book that is hidden' (56. 78). As a result he began to translate Upaniṣads into Persian, in a work issuing in *Sirr-i Akbar* ('The Great Secret', 1657)—a work which, when translated into French by Anquetil Duperron (1801–2), had a great influence on European (e.g. Schopenhauer) attitudes to the East: despite its dubious equations of concepts, it gave the impression of *ex oriente lux*, 'out of the East, light'. Dārā Shikoh represents the high point of Muslim attempts, at the level of political rule, to find an accord with Hindus. He was defeated in battle by his younger brother and executed on charges including apostasy.

Darazī. A founder of the *Druzes, when he recognized the *Khalīfa al-Ḥākim as the incarnation of the universal reason (or *Logos) which had first been bestowed on *Adam, and had then been transmitted through the prophets to *ʿAlī, and thence to the Fātimid caliphs (*khalīfa). His own teaching was *Bātinite, and he is said to have allowed wine and marriages prohibited by the orthodox, and to have taught rebirth. He was probably assassinated, but for reasons which are uncertain.

Darbār Singh (Divine Court). A name of the Golden Temple of *Amritsar, *Harimandir Sāhib.

Dardura-siddhi (Skt., 'frog' + 'praeternatural power'). The power to raise one's body through yogic practices, i.e. levitation.

Dark Night of the Soul. A term of Western mystical theology. The idea of divine darkness goes back to *Philo and is found in both E. and W. Christianity. According to the classical exposition of *John of the Cross, the dark night is the stage in which the soul is purified in preparation for union with God. A distinction is drawn between active nights (in which the soul purifies itself) and passive nights (in which God purifies the soul); a further distinction divides the night into the preliminary Night of the Senses and the more fundamental Night of the Spirit. The 'Dark Night of the Soul' is more technical, and a great deal more profound, than the colloquial usage, which debases the phrase into a general malaise. The Dark Night is the action of God purifying the soul of attachments as it experiences the impotence of human efforts and the necessity for the gift and grace of God. It is in utter darkness that the light of God can be discerned:

O living flame of love, That tenderly wounds My soul in its deepest centre . . . : O smooth burning! O luxuriant wounding! O soft hand, O delicate touch.—That tastes of eternal life And pays every debt, Killing, you change death to life. Oh lamps of fire, In whose brilliance The deep caverns of feeling, Once dark and blind, Now with rare beauty, Give heat and light to their Belovéd!

Darqawiy(y)a (Sūfī order): see SHĀDHILIYYA.

Darśana (Skt., 'viewing'). 1. In post-Vedic times, the term refers to the 'schools' or 'viewpoints' of Indian philosophy, both orthodox and heterodox. The orthodox (*āstika) Hindu darśanas include six different systems which share certain presuppositions, in particular the authority of the *Veda as an infallible source of knowledge. These six darśanas are traditionally listed in pairs in the following order: *Nyāya, founded by Gautama, and *Vaiśeṣika by *Kaṇāda; *Sāṃkhya, founded by *Kapila and *Yoga by *Patañjali; *Pūrva-mīmāṁsā founded by *Jaimini and *Vedānta by *Bādarāyaṇa. The oldest is said to be Sāṃkhya after which Yoga, Pūrva-mīmāṁsā, Vedānta, Vaiśeṣika, and Nyāya may follow—the order is difficult to determine with exactness. These orthodox darśanas rise between the 6th and 3rd cents. BCE. Their basic teachings are set down in succinct aphorisms, *sūtras, which are then explicated and elaborated on by commentators over the centuries.

In dynamic interaction with the orthodox systems are the three main heterodox (*nāstika) darśanas, *Cārvāka, *Jaina, and Buddhist, which modify and adapt traditional views and challenge the authority of the Veda as well as the *brahman priesthood. The lively debate among the various darśanas, whether orthodox or heterodox, have served to refine, systematize, and elaborate Indian thinking rather than to interrupt its progress. All systems (with the exception of materialist Cārvāka) aim at the common practical goal, variously understood, of liberation from the cycle of birth and death, an ultimate state of spiritual freedom.

2. Paying respect or homage to ('viewing' with respect) a holy image, person or place, and receiving merit or blessing in return. Among Sikhs, the 'viewing' is of the *Ādi Granth, and hearing its contents.

3. In Buddhism (Pāli, *dassana*), insight based on reason to defeat false views (*dṛṣti*; Pāli, *diṭṭhi*) and mental defects (*kleśa; Pāli, *kilesa*). Darśana-marga (the way of darśana) leads from unreasoning trust to comprehension, especially of the *Four Noble Truths, and makes the seeker a 'stream-enterer' (*śrotāpanna; Pāli, *sotāpanna*).

D. Eck, *Darsana* (1981).

Darshan (Heb., 'expounder'). A professional expounder of Hebrew scripture. Initially Darshanim could expound both *halakhically and *aggadically on scripture—Eleazar b. Simeon, for example, was commended as a 'reader of scripture, a *Mishnah teacher . . . and a darshan', but the emphasis was on the aggada (*Lev.R.* 30. 1). Later, the term came to be used for a preacher, and in some large *Ashkenazi communities, a darshan was appointed as well as a *rabbi and a *dayyan.

Darul Islam (from Arab., *dār al-Islām). A revolutionary movement in Indonesia whose aim was to establish an Islamic state. Its leader was Sekarmadji Maridjan Kartosuwirjo (1905–62), who declared the Islamic State of Indonesia in 1949. Its main area of success was in W. Java, but several other rebellions (with the same aim, but not much co-ordinated) achieved limited success in central Java. The movements were finally defeated in 1965.

C. van Dijk, *Rebellion Under the Banner of Islam* (1981).

Daruma. Jap. for *Bodhidharma, hence the occurrence in several terms: Daruma-ki, his date of death (5th day of 10th month); Daruma-shu, his school of teaching, hence a name for Zen; Daruma-sōjō, the authentic transmission of his teaching via dharma-successors (*hassu) and patriarchs in succession (*soshigata).

Daruma school (Zen school): see DAINICHI NŌNIN.

Darwin, C. (theory of): see CREATIONISM.

Darwīsh (member of Muslim religious fraternity): see DERWĪSH.

Daśabala (Skt.; Pāli, *dasabala*). The ten powers of a *Buddha which confer knowledge on him of: (i) what is possible and impossible; (ii) the consequence of actions (*vipāka); (iii) the abilities of other beings; (iv) the direction of their lives; (v) the constituents of manifest appearances; (vi) the paths leading to the different domains of existence; (vii) those leading to purity and impurity; (viii) the states of meditation (*samādhi) and absorptions (*dhyāna); (ix) deaths and reappearances; (x) the eradication of all defilements (the three destructive poisons, Skt., *āśrava* Pāli, *āsava*: of desire, *kāma, of becoming in manifest form, *bhāva, and of ignorance, *avidyā/avijja).

Daśabhūmika-sūtra: see AVATAMSAKA LITERATURE.

Daśahrā or **Dussehra.** Ten-day Hindu *festival, celebrated at the beginning of Āśvina (see CALENDAR) in recognition of conquests of evil, especially of *Durgā over Mahiṣa and of *Rāma over *Rāvaṇa. In the case of the latter, the *Rāmlīlā* of *Tulsīdās is performed.

Dasakusalakamma (Pāli, 'ten meritorious actions'). A common Buddhist list of activities which bring good kamma (*karma) into effect and acquire (and transfer) merit: (i) *dāna; (ii) *śīla; (iii) *bhāvanā; (iv) *apacāyana* (showing respect to elders); (v) *veyyāvacca* (attending to their needs); (vi) *pattidāna* (transferring merit); (vii) *pattānumodana* (delighting in the merit of others); (viii) *dhammasavaṇa* (attending to the *dharma/dhamma of the *Buddha); (ix) *dhammadesanā* (preaching the dhamma); (x) *diṭṭhijjukamma* (adhering to right beliefs).

Daśalakśanaparvan (Jain observance): see FESTIVALS AND FASTS.

Dasam Granth or **Dasven Pādśāh Kā Granth** (Pañjābī, 'tenth book, book of the tenth Gurū'). Compilation of compositions traditionally ascribed to Gurū *Gobind Siṅgh and venerated by Sikhs. Despite its one-time canonical status, much of the Dasam Granth is seldom read, although it is especially important to the *Nihaṅgs. According to tradition *Manī Siṅgh collected these writings after the death of Gobind Siṅgh whose works had been lost in the Sirsā river. According to some scholars, court poets contributed certain portions, e.g. Pakhyān Charitra. The whole Dasam Granth is in verse enriched by numerous stylistic devices. The language is predominantly Braj (a N. Indian vernacular), but Persian, Avdhī, Pañjābī, and Khaṛī Bolī are also represented. The *Gurmukhī script is used throughout. Four manuscript compilations exist, plus other manuscripts and printed versions which cannot be authenticated. These compilations are Bhāī Manī Siṅgh Vālī Bīr, Gurdwāra Motī Bāgh Vālī Bīr, Paṭnā Sāhibjī dī Misl, and Saṅgrur Vālī Bīr. The books, devotional and narrative, are as follows: (i) *Jāp(u), morning prayer; (ii) *Akāl Ustat*, hymn of praise to the Timeless One; (iii) *Bachitra Nātak* (*Granth*) i.e. 'wonderful drama', autobiographical account, including Gobind Siṅgh's genealogy and previous incarnation as an ascetic in the Himalayas; (iv) *Chaṇḍī Charitra Ukti Bilās*, exploits performed by Chaṇḍī in wars with demons, narrated in Braj; (v) *Chaṇḍī Charitra*, Braj verse on the same theme in a different metre; (vi) *Vār Srī Bhagautī Jī Kī (or Chaṇḍī dī Vār), Pañjābī ballad in praise of goddess Bhagautī; (vii) *Giān Parbodh Granth*, praise of God illustrated from Hindu mythology; (viii) *Chaubīs Avtār*, quatrains and couplets describing twenty-four incarnations of *Viṣṇu; (ix) *Mehdī Mīr Badh*, supplement to *Chaubīs Avtār*; (x) *Brahmā Avtār*, seven incarnations of *Brahmā; (xi) *Rudrā Avtār*, two incarnations of *Rudra; (xii) *Rām Kālī Patśāhī* (or *Śabad Hazāre*), ten hymns in seven *rāgs; (xiii) *Srī Mukhibāk Savaīyyē*, thirty-two hymns giving exposition of religions of India; (xiv) *Jo Kichh Lekh Likhiyo Bidhna Savayyā* (or *Khālsa Mahimā*), poem praising Khālsā; (xv) *Śāstrā Nām Mālā Purān*, inventory of weapons and their uses; (xvi) *Pakhyān Charitra*, 404 stories of women's wiles; (xvii) *Zafarnāmā, Persian letter to Auraṅgzeb; (xviii) *Hikāyāt*, eleven tales in Persian, resembling *Pakhyān Charitra*.

D. Ashta, *The Poetry of Dasam Granth* (1959).

Daśanāmī (Skt., 'having ten names'). A Hindu order of wandering monks founded by the great philosopher *Śaṅkara and upholding his philosophy of *Advaita Vedānta. It is a loose federation of *Śaivite *saṁnyāsins ('renouncers'), consisting of ten monastic lineages, the members of each lineage bearing a distinctive title or 'name' (*nāman*), which is suffixed to their individual monastic names at the time of initiation. The ten lineages are further arranged into four groups, each attached to one of the four principal monastic seats (*pīṭhas*) established by Śaṅkara, and each with its own clan (*gotra*), teaching tradition (*saṁpradāya), *Veda, and Great Saying (*mahāvākya). The monastic teachers (*ācāryas) in charge of these principal monasteries have the title Śaṅkarācārya', and enjoy a kind of spiritual primacy among the Daśanāmī monks by virtue of their position, great learning, and austere lives.

The names given to members of the ten lineages, arranged according to the monastery with which they are associated, are as follows: Giri, Parvata and Sāgara with Jyotirmaṭha monastery at Badarīnātha in the N.; Vana and Āraṇya with Govardhanamaṭha monastery at Purī in the E.; Purī, Bhāratī, and

Sarasvatī with Śṛṅgerimaṭha at Śṛṅgeri in the S.; and Tīrtha and Āśrama with Śaradāmaṭha at Dvārakā in the W. Only men of *brahman birth may belong to the three lineages of Tīrtha, Āśrama, and Sarasvatī. They are sometimes called *daṇḍin saṁnyāsins because they retain the monastic staff (*daṇḍa) at the time of initiation. The Bhāratī lineage, though predominantly brahman, has a non-brahman section. The remaining lineages are open to all twice-born Hindus who, filled with a burning sense of renunciation, are prepared to sever all ties to caste and family. The claim that Śaṅkara founded a further lineage based on *Kāñcīpura (near Madras in the S.) is disputed by the others.

The Daśanāmī Order serves the functions of teaching and preserving the tradition of Advaita Vedānta, and provides an alternative way of life for those seeking to attain the ideal of realization of non-dual Reality (*Brahman) and complete freedom (*mokṣa).

W. Cenkner, *A Tradition of Teachers: Śaṅkara and the Jagadgurus Today* (1983).

Dassana (Buddhist insight based on reason): see DARŚANA.

Dassera (period of Hindu festivals): see FESTIVALS AND FASTS.

Dastur (Zoroastrian high priest): see MAGI.

Daswandh. The Sikh donation of a tenth of one's income for the purposes of the *Panth. It was introduced as an obligation by Gurū *Amar Dās, but it has become voluntary, especially as a donation to support the local *gurdwārā, and as an offering in front of the *Ādi Granth.

Datsuma. Jap. for *dharma.

Dattātreya. A Hindu sage or god-figure. In the *Mārkaṇḍeya Purāṇa*, Dattātreya appears as an *antinomian sage. In other *purāṇas he is listed among the *avatāras of *Viṣṇu. Particularly in Mahārāṣṭra he has been an object of worship; in Mahur on the Sahyadri mountain stands his most important temple. The non-Vedic tradition of the Mānbhāvs (Mahānubhāvas) venerate a Dattātreya as the second member of their lineage of five ancient teachers and in fact as an incarnation of *Kṛṣṇa. Among Mahārāṣṭrian *brahmans there is a more institutionalized form of Dattātreya worship, with its scriptural basis in the *advaita-oriented *Guru-caritra* by Gangādhar (16th cent.). In popular religion he is seen as the single avatāra of the three gods, *Brahmā, Viṣṇu, and *Śiva. This relates him to the *trimūrti, without making him identical with that triad. *Iconography depicts him with three heads, although often in between Brahmā and Śiva.

Daughters of Zion. Biblical phrase: 'Daughter of Zion' generally refers to *Jerusalem or the Jewish people, as, for example, in, 'Rejoice greatly, O daughter of Zion ... lo, your king comes to you' (Zech 9. 9).

David

Judaism Second king of *Israel. David was the youngest son of Jesse, grew up in *Bethlehem and was said to be descended from *Ruth. According to 1 Samuel 16–30, he came to the notice of King *Saul, and, after killing the Philistine giant Goliath, was married to Michal, the king's daughter. After Saul's death, he became king of *Judah (2 Samuel 2) and subsequently (ch. 5) of Israel, thus uniting the two kingdoms under his kingship. He defeated the Philistines, the Moabites, the Arameans, the Ammonites, and the Edomites, and he made his capital in *Jerusalem. With the support of the religious establishment, the belief was fostered that God had chosen David and his descendants to rule over the Israelites forever (2 Samuel 7. 16), and he is traditionally believed to have written many of the *Psalms. There was, however, opposition to the centralization of David's government which found its focus in the revolt of *Absalom (2 Samuel 13–19) and in the uprising of Sheba the Benjamite (2 Samuel 20). His final days were marred by court and family intrigue, and he was eventually succeeded by his son by Bathsheba, *Solomon. In the *aggadah David is generally exalted as the great poet and scholar king. The unique status of the Davidic line of kingship is particularly emphasized; it was said that even God 'looks forward to David's being king until the end of the generations' (*Gen.R.* 88. 7). This longing for the return of the line of David is a prominent theme in Jewish liturgy: in, for example, one of the *blessings said after the *haftarah, 'Gladden us, O Lord our God ... with the kingdom of the House of David, your anointed. ... Suffer not a stranger to sit upon his throne ... Blessed are you, O Lord, the Shield of David.' In *Kabbalistic teaching, he symbolizes the tenth *sefirot (emanation), the quality of kingdom. It was believed that as a counterpart to the historical David, God had another David to govern the inhabitants of the upper world. The biblical stories of David have continued to provide inspiration for artists, writers, and musicians.

Islam Dāwūd or Daʿūd, is one of the line of *prophets, and listed as such in the *Qur'ān (6. 84). He is linked with *Solomon as one who gives judgement (21. 78), sings praises of *Allāh (21. 79, 38. 18–19), and makes coats of mail (34. 11). Allāh 'strengthened his kingdom and gave him wisdom and sound judgement' (38. 20). A somewhat longer passage alludes to one of his judgements, to his asking forgiveness for an (unspecified) offence, and his being made a 'deputy' (*khalīfa*) (38. 21–6). He is given the *zabūr*, a book—representing the Psalms—which is mentioned elsewhere in the Qur'ān as one of the former scriptures. Qur'ān commentaries, based on *ḥadīth, centre on his ability to sing, and on his piety, especially in prayer and fasting.

David ben Samuel/ha-Levi, or **Taz** (1586–1667). Jewish *halakhic authority. Based in Poland, he served several communities and participated in the meetings of the Council of the Four Lands. At the end of his life, persuaded by his sons, he seems to have given his support to *Shabbetai Zevi. His most important work, *Turei Zahav* (The Rows of Gold), a commentary on the four parts of Joseph *Caro's **Shulḥān Arukh*, has greatly influenced later halakhic decisions.

David ben Solomon Ibn Abi Zimra or **Radbaz** (1479–1573). Jewish *Talmudist and *kabbalist. Between 1517 and 1553, he was head of the Egyptian Jewish community and made several significant reforms. He subsequently moved to Safed. His most important works were collections of *responsa. He regarded *aggadah as equally holy as *halakhah, although he accepted it could have an esoteric as well as a literal meaning. He also used kabbalistic lore in his decisions, but only when it did not conflict with the teachings of the *Talmud.

Davven or **Davnen** (Yid., uncertain origin). 'To pray': widely used among *Ashkenazi Jews.

Daʿwa (Arab., from *daʿā*, 'call', 'summon'). Invitation, call; prayer (see DUʿĀ', from the same root). It is the 'summons' to the way of Allāh, to the true religion (Qur'ān 14. 46). The term daʿwa has also been used in the political sense of propaganda, at various periods of Islamic history, e.g. the cause of the *ʿAbbāsids, the *Ismāʿīliy(y)a, the *Fāṭimids. It is also used today to denote the effort to spread the teachings of Islam, and in this sense is roughly equivalent to the concept of 'mission' in Christianity.

K. Ahmad and D. Kerr (eds.), *Christian Mission and Islamic Daʿwah . . .* (1982).

Daxma. Often referred to as a 'Tower of Silence', the place where *Zoroastrians expose their dead to vultures. Because death and decay are seen as weapons of evil, a corpse is traditionally seen as the place where *Angra Mainyu and his forces are powerfully present. All dead matter is polluting, but especially the corpse of a righteous person, for that represents a great (albeit temporary) victory of evil. It cannot therefore be buried in the earth, cremated, or disposed of at sea, for each of these is the good creation of Ahura Mazda. In ancient times, the dead were exposed in a remote place for carrion-eating creatures to devour. It has been plausibly argued that it was the prevalence of an alien religion, Islam, in Iran which led to the construction of special structures for the rite of exposure in order to avoid abuse. Daxmas are circular structures open to the sky, generally about 30 feet high. The normal design is for three concentric circles of spaces, *pavis*, to be laid out. Men are normally exposed in the outer circle, women in the middle, and children at the centre. Channels drain away the bodily fluids into a central pit. After the flesh has been devoured, and the bones bleached and made powdery by the sun, they too are cast into the pit and nowadays acid is periodically poured into the pit, so leaving no remains. Some W. accounts of the rites have been oversensational and devoid of sensitivity. From the Zoroastrian perspective, this means of disposal is quick (the vultures normally take about twenty minutes), it does not waste land and it is natural for humanity to feed the creatures in death as they eat them in life. Such practices are, obviously, not possible in all countries because there are no vultures. *Diaspora Zoroastrians (e.g. in Britain, America, and Canada) generally accept W. methods of cremation; and in the 'old countries' of Iran and India, they bury the dead, often using stone-lined graves to prevent the pollution affecting the earth. Zoroastrian funerals have two main concerns: to care for the soul and to restrict the pollution. It is important that a priest is called quickly after death. Traditionally the priest is accompanied by the Zoroastrian holy animal, a dog, who both protects people from threatening forces and is especially sensitive to an alien presence, and who therefore ritually 'sees' the corpse (Sagdid rite). Once the body has been ritually washed (the Sachkar ceremony) and dressed in a clean *sudre* and *kusti* (*Naujote), the priest commences the prayers which continue until the time of the funeral, which should normally be the same day, though it must not be during the hours of darkness. The corpse is laid on the floor (traditionally stone: non-porous, so that it will not soak up the pollution), and a circle is marked round it with a nail. That marks out the area of intense pollution where only the corpse-bearers (*nasarsalas*) should go. Until the 19th cent. most rites were conducted in the home, but in India nowadays it is usual for the corpse to be taken immediately to the funeral grounds, where provision is made for the rites to be performed and the purity laws observed. When all is ready for the funeral, the *nasarsalas* carry the corpse on a bier made of (non-porous) iron, followed by priest and dog and mourners walking in pairs (*paiwand*), linked by a cord so that there may be mutual protection against the potent forces of evil associated with death. Before the daxma the corpse is laid on a marble (again non-porous) slab where the bereaved pay their last respects before the *nasarsalas* proceed alone with the corpse into the daxma. While the mourners return to the nearby prayer-hall, the corpse is stripped. As the *nasarsalas* leave the daxma, they clap and the prayers begin, which last for about twenty minutes. On returning home the mourners change out of their traditional white (symbol of purity) clothes and into their daily attire. There are prayers for the soul over the succeeding three days, as it is thought to be meditating on its life, prior to facing its judgement at the Chinvat Bridge (*Frasokereti). On the morning of the fourth day, the *uthumna* ceremony is held, at which it is traditional to announce a charitable bequest in memory of the deceased, for beneficence rather than gravestones is thought to be the proper memorial. Prayers are offered for the dead in annual memory of them, and are traditionally invoked at all joyous occasions. There is also an annual *muktad* ceremony where the souls of all the deceased are remembered.

K. Mistree, *Zoroastrianism: An Ethnic Perspective* (1982); J. J. Modi, *Religious Ceremonies and Customs of the Parsees* (1936).

Day, Dorothy (1897–1980). US Christian activist on behalf of the poor and underprivileged. She was a journalist writing originally for socialist and communist publications, but after she became a *Roman Catholic in 1927, she became increasingly concerned with Christian action on behalf of the poor. In 1933, she founded (with Peter Maurin) the journal and movement, the Catholic Worker. She organized hospitality houses to care for the homeless and hungry, identifying herself with them: 'The only way to live in any true security is to live so close to the bottom that when you fall you do not have far to drop.' Despite the inevitable criticism from the Catholic hierarchy of her commitment, not least of her attacks on the Church whenever it lent itself to the support of political injustice or tyranny (*Liberation Theology), she remained loyal to the Church, regarding its truth as more fundamental than the opinions of those clergy who happen to have authority in it. Always wary of the praise of others, she once said, 'Don't call me a saint! I don't want to be dismissed so easily!' Among many books, see *House of Hospitality* (1939), *Loaves and Fishes* (1963), and her autobiography, *The Long Loneliness* (1981).

W. D. Miller, *Dorothy Day* (1982) and *All Is Grace* . . . (1987); J. E. O'Connor, *The Moral Vision of Dorothy Day* (1991).

Dayāl Bābā (founder of Sikh reform movement): see NIRAṄKĀRĪ.

Dayānand(a) Sarasvatī (1824–83). Mul Shankara, founder of the neo-orthodox Hindu movement, *Ārya Samāj. Born in Gujarat, he was educated in strict Brahmanical, not Western, style, and having studied the *Vedas under a *guru, he became a *saṁnyāsin in 1848, in the Sarasvatī Dandi Order of *yogis, taking the name Dayānand. After a long period as a wandering yogi, he settled in 1860 in Mathura, studying with the *Vedic scholar, Virajananda. Under his influence, Dayānand rejected the accretions of post-Vedic Hinduism and started a public campaign for a return to Vedic values. He regarded the Vedas as the source of all human wisdom, including the natural sciences; and he saw them as insisting on social reform (e.g. the emancipation of women and the removal of the abuses of *caste). To recover the foundational importance of the Vedas in life and society, he founded Ārya Samāj in 1875. He contested the claims of other religions (e.g. in *Satyārth Prakaś*, 1874), and believed that Hinduism properly understood has a mission to the world. His polemical style, in life and argument, made him many enemies, and he died, reportedly, of poison.

K. S. Arya and P. D. Shastri, *Swami Dayanand* . . . (1987); J. T. F. Jordens, *Dayananda Sarasvati* (1978).

Day of Atonement (Heb., Yom Kippur). The most important day in the Jewish liturgical year. According to Leviticus 16. 30, 'on this day shall atonement be made for you, to cleanse you; from all your sins you shall be clean before the Lord'. In the second *Temple period, the ritual of *Avodah was the central feature of the day. The people were commanded to 'afflict' themselves (Leviticus 23. 27), and the sages interpreted that as abstaining from food and drink, from washing, from anointing the body, from wearing leather shoes, and from sexual intercourse (*Yoma* 8. 1). After the destruction of the temple, it was believed that the day itself rather than the temple ritual atoned for *Israel's sin. None the less, forgiveness must be sought from those who have been wronged, and *confession must be made. In many communities, the day before Yom Kippur is regarded almost as a feast day: much food is eaten, gifts are sent to the poor, and neighbours visit each other to ask forgiveness. The Day of Atonement liturgy begins in the evening of 9 Tishri (see CALENDAR) with the *Kol Nidrei (all the vows) service in the *synagogue. Services continue through the next day until sunset, when it is customary to blow the *shofar to indicate the end of the fast. According to the *aggadah, the Day of Atonement is the day when Moses was given the second tablets of the law, and it was said that even if all other *festivals were abolished, the Day of Atonement on which the Israelites resemble the angels would remain (*PRE* 46). Today, even very *assimilated Jews remember and to some extent observe the day.

L. Jacobs, *Guide to Yom Kippur* (1957).

Day of Judgement: see DAY OF THE LORD.

Day of Judgement (Islam): see YAUM AL-DĪN.

Day of the Lord. In Jewish understanding, day of God's judgement on the world. According to the Hebrew prophets, at some definite date in the future, God will reward the righteous and punish the wicked. The Day of the Lord is mentioned by *Isaiah, *Joel, *Amos, *Obadiah, *Ezekiel, *Zechariah, and *Zephaniah. Characteristic of the passages is a sense of warning that God will suddenly intervene and the current world order will be changed for ever. In later thought, detail is added—e.g. all the dead will be resurrected so that they can be judged; *Elijah will return (*Malachi* 4) to initiate the *yom ha-din* ('day of judgement').

Days of Awe. In Judaism, the twelve days which begin with *Rosh ha-Shanah and end with Yom Kippur (*Day of Atonement). According to Jewish tradition, all humanity stand before God's throne of judgement at the new year, and the *book of life is finally closed on the Day of Atonement.

Dayyan (Aram., 'judge'). Members of Jewish religious courts. The title of dayyan is given to all members of a *bet din except the chairman who is known as *av bet din* or *rosh bet din* (father/head of the house of judgement).

Dayyeinu (Heb., 'it would have satisfied us'). Title of the chorus of a Jewish *Passover song. The song lists all the good things God did for the Israelites in the *Exodus story, and each one is greeted with the response 'Dayyeinu'. It first appears in the *siddur* (*sedarot) of *Sa'adiah Gaon (9th cent. CE)

Dbang bskur (Tibetan, empowerment): see ABHIṢEKA.

Deacon (Gk., *diakonos*, 'servant'). Christian minister next below *priest. Its general sense is 'one who mediates', as e.g. Hermes was the deacon of the gods. The diaconate is traditionally traced to the story in Acts 6. 1–6 of seven men appointed 'to serve tables', although the title deacon is not used there. In the early church, as first shown by the letters of 1 Timothy and Titus, deacons were a separate class of ministers with administrative duties. Their office of collecting and distributing alms could give them considerable importance, and the *archdeacon, the chief deacon of a place, became the bishop's principal administrative officer. Their influence diminished in the Middle Ages, and in W. churches, until recently, the diaconate became merely a stage to the priesthood, a period of training 'on the job'. Vocation to the 'permanent diaconate' has now re-emerged; in the Roman Catholic Church since *Vatican II, some men not aspiring to the priesthood (e.g. because married) have been ordained as deacons; among Anglicans, women are ordained deacon. In E. churches there have always been lifelong deacons, including men in secular occupations. In some churches they are, unlike priests, clean-shaven. In the liturgy the deacon assists the celebrant and reads the gospel. His characteristic vestment is the *dalmatic, and the stole worn over one shoulder.

In Protestant churches the name deacon is variously applied: in the *Lutheran church to assistant parochial ministers, even though in full Lutheran orders; in *Presbyterian churches to lay people who administer alms; and in *Baptist and *Congregational churches to laypeople who conduct the business of the congregation and distribute the elements at *communion.

J. N. Collins, *Diakonia* . . . (1990).

Deaconess. A woman Christian having an office akin to that of *deacon. The office can claim to be found in the New Testament (Romans 16. 1; 1 Timothy 3. 11), but emerges clearly only in the 3rd and 4th cents. The deaconess had duties like those of a deacon, especially among the women of the congregation, and in particular assisted at baptisms of women. When adult baptism became rare, the office of deaconess declined in importance, and disappeared in both E. and W. in the Middle Ages. It was revived in the 19th cent. among Lutherans, Anglicans, and Methodists. In the *Church of England the office resembled that of lay reader rather than deacon, and was pronounced formally not 'one of the holy orders' (Canons of 1969). However, the ordination of women to the priesthood in some provinces has led to a re-evaluation of the relation of the permanent diaconate to the diaconate as a preparation for priesthood (transitional diaconate), and thus of the status of deaconess in relation to the ordained ministry as such.

Dead Ḥasidim (follower of Naḥman of Bratslav): see NAḤMAN OF BRATSLAV.

Deadly sins or **capital sins.** In Christianity the most destructive of sins, usually listed as seven: pride, envy, anger, sloth, avarice, gluttony, and lust. Sloth embraces two sins listed separately in early accounts, *acedia* (Lat., *accidie) and *tristitia*, melancholy, weariness or dissatisfaction. These 'sins' are not necessarily active products of the will, but conditions which give rise to separation from God. Cf. the three 'deadly' faults of Buddhism; the *five deadly sins; *gogyaku-zai; *five evil passions.

M. Bloomfield, *The Seven Deadly Sins* (1967).

Dead Sea Scrolls. Collection of manuscripts found in caves near the Dead Sea. The scrolls, discovered between 1947 and 1956, date mainly between *c.*150 BCE and 68 CE. They seem to have belonged to a succession of communities based at *Qumran, the last of which was destroyed by the Romans in the first Jewish revolt. Because of the difficulty of deciphering them, and because of the notorious 'restrictive practices' on the part of those possessing the scrolls, the material has been published very slowly. Most of the scrolls are now held in the Shrine of the Book in *Jerusalem, but photographs have been released for the benefit of foreign scholars. Included in the manuscripts were more than a hundred copies of books of the Hebrew *Bible (every book except Esther is represented) as well as fragments of the *Septuagint, also *apocryphal books such as *Tobit and Ecclesiasticus (*Ben Sira, Wisdom of) and *pseudepigrapha such as the *Book of *Jubilees* and **Enoch*. Previously unknown books were also found, such as the *Sayings of *Moses*, the *Vision of Amram*, and the *Psalms of *Joshua*. In addition, there were manuscripts which seemed to relate to a community or communities based in Qumran: the *Manual of *Discipline*, the **Damascus Document*, the **Thanksgiving Psalms*, and the **War Scroll*.

The identification of those who produced the sectarian documents has been much disputed. Scholarly consensus favours a group closely related to the *Essenes. However, it is at least equally likely that Qumran, because of its remoteness, was a haven of refuge for conservative groups in more than one period, who disapproved of (or were persecuted by) those who were running the *Temple in Jerusalem. The sectarian documents might then be a reinforcing accretion of conservative views. Attempts to connect early Christianity with the/a sect have proved unconvincing, though it may be that sectarians became Christian, importing some of their beliefs; and in any case, there is at least the connection that both illustrate the contested ways in which, during this period, attempts were made to achieve the true practice of God's covenant.

Texts and trs. in progress (*The Rules*, 1993; *Damascus Document, War Scroll*, 1995); *Graphic Concordance to the Dead Sea Scrolls*, ed. J. H. Charlesworth *et al.* (1991); G. Vermes, *The Dead Sea Scrolls in English* (1962).

Dead Sea sect: see DEAD SEA SCROLLS; QUMRAN COMMUNITY.

Dean. The title of various Christian officials, of which the most important are: (i) the head of the *chapter of a *cathedral, who ranks next to the *bishop and in the Anglican Church is considerably independent of him; and (ii) the head of the chapter of a *collegiate church which is a 'peculiar' (independent of any episcopal authority), e.g. Westminster Abbey.

Death. The human and religious imagination of the nature and meaning of death has been prolific: virtually everything that can be imagined about death has been imagined. Yet almost universally the major religious traditions did not in origin have any belief that there will be some worthwhile continuing life after death. This is in strong contrast to the popular impression that religions came into being to offer 'pie in the sky'—i.e. some compensation for the miseries and inequalities of this life. This erroneous view was elevated to a formal theory by such anti-religious theorists as *Marx and *Freud.

In fact, the early human imagination of death was entirely realistic: since the breath returns to the air and the body to the dust, there is nothing that *can* survive. Thus in both E. and W., the emphasis originally was on the positive worth of *this* life, not on some imagined heaven or hell. In *Tanach (Jewish scripture), belief in a life with God after death scarcely appears during the biblical period; in the *Vedic period in India, even the gods are not immortal but have to work hard to keep death at bay. Yet equally it was clear that those who have died do not disappear entirely: they continue in their descendants (especially when they are formally and deliberately remembered), and they continue to appear, albeit in residual and extremely shadowy form, in dreams. The maintenance of memory of the departed thus underlies the earliest (and in many parts of the world, continuing) rituals in connection with the dead (see ANCESTORS).

Death was extensively understood as unnatural, intruding, or breaking into life for a variety of reasons—many of them seemingly trivial, like the stealing of an apple; or because the gods realized the earth would get too full if death were not introduced. The significance of death was then explored above all through the practice of *sacrifice. The meanings of sacrifice are extremely diverse, but they include a recognition that life is only made possible through death: sacrifice epitomizes the view that life is given up, not simply *to* other life, but *for* other life, to enable its possibility. It is what Charles Williams called 'a way of exchange'. Thus although death may be seen as a penalty, or as a condition from which escape is desirable, it is also seen to be opportunity; hence death becomes connected with *atonement.

The development of beliefs that there may be life beyond death came about historically in different ways and with different anthropologies (accounts of human nature) in different religious traditions. In the Judaeo-Christian tradition, the belief developed in the 3rd or 2nd cent. BCE that the 'friendship with God' (as *Abraham's relationship with God was described) might perhaps be continued by God through death. The imagination of how God might bring that about then varied: for those who adhered to the tradition which was eventually to end up as scripture, the anthropology of the book of *Genesis required a reconstitution of the body and breath of the person in question, the *resurrection of the dead. But for those who had received a Greek or Hellenistic education (e.g. *Philo), it seemed more plausible to speak of an immortal soul. Both views were contested by *Sadducees in the period of the Second *Temple, because there was no warrant for them in what was becoming scripture. Among early Christians the belief in life after death received non-negotiable reinforcement from the appearance of *Jesus among them after they had known that he had most certainly died on the Cross. Because he appeared with sufficient continuing identity to be recognizable, and yet not with a body simply reconstituted as his earthly body, Christianity developed an imagination of both a soul and a resurrection body. Islam extended those ideas in the direction of an even more formal anthropology.

In the E., the sense that death can be contested and, in favourable circumstances (especially with the help of sacrifices), be postponed, led to the belief in Hinduism that a self or soul is reborn many millions of times as it moves toward *mokṣa (release). In early Buddhism, it was accepted that there is continuing reappearance, but no self or soul being reborn. There is only the production of one aggregated moment of appearance caused, or brought into being, by the immediately preceding moment. *Vijñānavāda (Yogacāra) already recognized that there must nevertheless be a sufficient nature of appearance, even though devoid of characteristics (*śūnyatā), opening the way to the buddha-nature of all appearance. In China, the caution of *Confucius was widely prevalent: 'Confucius said, "If we are not yet able to serve humans, how can we serve spiritual beings?" Tzu-lu then said, "Then let me ask you about death." Confucius said, "If we do not yet know about life, how can we know about death?" ' But in the Immortality Cult, and even more in the development of *Taoism, the quest for immortality was undertaken in the schools of *alchemy, sometimes literally, more often in spiritual terms.

Death, therefore, is recognized by religions as a constraint over life; but they also recognized, long before it became a fundamental observation in the natural sciences, that constraints are the necessary conditions for the attainment of greater degrees of freedom. Among Muslims and Sikhs, for example, death is to be accepted as the will of God, and elaborate displays of mourning are discouraged.

On the basis of these understandings of death, different religions have expressed different preferences in the treatment of dead bodies: see CREMATION; FUNERAL RITES. They have also been in agreement to a large extent that excessive grief or mourning is inappropriate. See Index: Death, beliefs; Death, funerals.

J. W. Bowker, *The Meanings of Death* (1991).

Death, anniversary of (Jewish commemoration): see YAHRZEIT; FUNERAL RITES.

Death, kiss of. According to traditional Jewish belief, the death reserved for the righteous. The most difficult death from asthma or croup was compared to pulling a thorn out of wool. The easiest death, the 'kiss of death' was like a hair being removed from milk (*B.Ber.* 8a).

Death of God. *Nietzsche proclaimed that the death of God was 'a recent event' in 1887. Belief in God had become *unglaubwürdig* (incredible). In that view he was anticipated by many major figures in the 19th cent., not least by the Young Hegelians: *Feuerbach, *Strauss, and *Marx. The first two attempted to 'deconstruct' theological language and to show that it is really language about ourselves; the last claimed that religion and theology are distorted and socially inhibiting reflections of unjust social and economic relations. In both cases, belief in a transcendent God, independent of this or any other universe, seemed to have become incredible. In the 20th cent., 'Death of God' theology (the view that theology is at best anthropology) was accelerated into prominence by the further considerations that, in a Newtonian universe, the God of traditional theism cannot intervene or make any difference in a universe of this kind; and that even if he could, he evidently has not, to judge from the enormity of such evil episodes as the *Holocaust. 'Death of God' theology then became associated with religionless Christianity.

Deborah. Hebrew judge. Deborah led the Israelites against Jabin, king of *Canaan (Judges 4 and 5). She encouraged her general, Barak, to attack the enemy while the river was in full flood. The Canaanites were incapacitated by their iron chariots and the Israelites won a famous victory. Deborah's song of triumph is thought to be one of the earliest Hebrew poems in existence. According to the *aggadah, she and Hannah, the mother of *Samuel, were the only two women who composed hymns to God unequalled by men (*Zohar, Lev.* 196).

Decalogue: see TEN COMMANDMENTS.

De Chardin, T. (French Jesuit theologian): see TEILHARD DE CHARDIN.

De Civitate Dei ('The City of God'), Christian work by St *Augustine, which has had a major influence on political and social theory: it explores the relations between heaven and earth, and between divine *providence and human history. It was written in response to the fall of Rome to Alaric in 410, and to claims that this disaster had occurred because of the rejection of the pagan gods and rituals in favour of Christ. Augustine worte it intermittently over a period of 14 years, completing it in 426. Books I–X are an apologetic work against the pagans, showing that calamities have come about in the past without neglect of the gods, and that no security can be gained, in this world or the next, by worshipping them. Books XI–XXII deal with the two cities, the city of God and the city of this world, 'the earthly city marked out by the love of self, even to the contempt of God, and the heavenly city marked out by the love of God, even to the contempt of self'. Humans cannot live in isolation, but the kinds of city they build depend on the objects of their love: 'A people is an assemblage of reasonable beings bound together by a common agreement as to the objects of their love'. Augustine pointed to a manifest distinction between the social life which follows the will of God and that which follows the values of Rome, in which the love of worldly things and of honour prevails. The division goes back to the *Fall and to the murder by *Cain, the city dweller, of his brother Abel, the pilgrim, a violence in earthly affairs which is reiterated constantly in history (Rome was founded by the Romulus who murdered his brother Remus). Augustine did not regard the communities of Christians as without fault (hence a certain ambivalence in the work about whether the equation City of God = Kingdom of Heaven = Church really works, an ambivalence ignored by later theorists who sought to justify the temporal power of the Church on this basis): particularly after the *Donatist controversy, he knew that wheat and tares grow together until the final harvest. Equally, he recognized the many benefits of the Roman empire ('Without justice, what are kingdoms but bands of robbers?'). Nevertheless, the citizens of the city of God know that on earth they are exiles waiting for their return to their true home (Philippians 3. 20), and that 'here we have no abiding city' (Hebrews 13. 14). The two cities are thus entangled in time and history. The pilgrims on earth play their part in civil life and follow the customs of their day, but they are users rather than lovers of this world. At the Last Judgement it will be made clear who the true citizens of the city of God are. The work ends: 'There we shall rest and we shall see; we shall see and we shall love; we shall love and we shall praise. Behold what will be in the end without end! For what is our end but to arrive in that Kingdom which has no end?'.

Tr. H. Bettenson (1972).

Decretal. A papal letter; strictly, one in response to a question. Decretals are an important source of Roman Catholic *canon law. The first decretal dates from 385, and the earliest influential collection was that of Dionysius Exiguus (*c.*520). About 850 appeared the collection known as the 'false decretals', containing (along with much genuine matter) many forged letters of early popes, partly to provide early evidence for papal supremacy, and partly to defend the rights of diocesan bishops. They were not proved to be forgeries until 1558. After *Gratian had systematized canon law in his *Decretum* (*c.*1140), collections of later decretals were published by popes in 1234, 1298, and 1317.

Deer Park (site of the Buddha's first sermon): see SĀRNĀTH.

De fide (Lat., 'of the faith'). In Roman Catholic parlance, a term used of a proposition that has been explicitly and formally declared and defined by the Church to be true.

De Foucauld, Charles Eugène (1858–1916). Hermit. A wealthy aristocrat, he served as a cavalry officer in Africa and became an explorer. Brought back to Roman Catholicism by Abbé Huvelin, he sought a life of poverty and solitude, finally as a hermit in the Sahara amongst the Muslim Tuaregs. He won their respect by his sympathy with their language and way of life, but was assassinated by one in 1916. His missionary ideal of prayerful presence, by way of commitment to a local circumstance, inspired the Little Brothers and the Little Sisters who follow a rule he composed, though in his lifetime no one joined him. See also PETITS FRÈRES.

R. Bazin, *Charles de Foucauld . . .*, (Eng. tr. 1923); E. Hamilton, *The Desert My Dwelling Place . . .*, (1968); ed. J. F. Six, *Spiritual Autobiography . . .*, (1964).

Deg teg (Pers., 'kettle', 'sword'). A summary of the Sikh obligation for the *Panth to provide food and protection for the hungry and the unprotected—hence the cry in the *Ardās (prayer), 'Deg, tegh, fateh' (victory to generosity and arms).

Deguchi Nao (1836–1918). Female *shaman and founder of the new Japanese religion, Ōmoto-kyō. Through an experience of spirit (Ushitora no Konjin) possession at the age of 55, she articulated a radical eschatological and millenarian world view critical of established religious doctrines and the contemporary society and government. Through spirit writing, originally scratching these communications with a nail, she began to attract a large following. She met Ueda Kisaburo in 1898, and in 1900 recognized him as the promised saviour. He married Sumi, Nao's daughter, and became known as Deguchi Onisaburo. Deguchi Nao is venerated as *Kaiso* (spiritual founder) and Onisaburo as *Kyōso* (doctrinal founder). In 1921 and 1935 he was imprisoned as a threat to the government, and Ōmoto's buildings were destroyed. After the Second World War, the movement was reorganized under the name Aizenen (community of love and virtue), now Ōmoto Aizenen. It has influenced many other new religious movements in Japan.

Déïma or **Dahima.** The largest (after the *Harris churches) of the new religions in the Ivory Coast, with some 50,000 members among the Godié, Dida, Bakwé, and Bété peoples. Guigba Dahonon (1892–1951), a childless Godié, widowed in 1922, had various mystical experiences before developing a new teaching and movement, the Église Déïmatiste (a neologism), in 1942. To her disciples she became Marie Lalou (ashes), or more formally Bagué Honoyo, and claimed to replace the Prophet Harris as well as the *Bible, which was regarded as dangerously magical. The religion is strongly anti-fetish and uses water and ashes in place of traditional methods for healing and protection. Worship in simple churches focuses on a stripped palm tree in the form of a cross, the Ku-Su (death tree). There is a strong hierarchical organization on a *Roman Catholic model but under a succession of female 'popes'. After her death, her teaching was collected and developed into a large corpus of 'gospels', prayers, *catechism, and doctrines, and much of this now forms an official *canon which has been tr. into French.

Deipara (mother of God): see THEOTOKOS.

Deism. The name of a heterogeneous 'movement' (it was not organized, and so-called Deist writers do not follow a single programme) of the late 17th and 18th cents., concerned to defend the rationality of religion and belief in God in the face of scepticism, or the perceived implications of Newton's laws. There is much emphasis on natural religion, and often on the irrationality of Christian claims, especially about *miracles. Deism, in general, accepted the universality and success of Newton's work, from which it seemed evident that the universe was governed by mechanistic laws. These seemed to leave little room for God to intervene, e.g. to answer prayer or work miracles. Thus Deism proposed a God who initiated creation and donated its laws, but then allowed it to pursue its own course. Yet also Deists argued that religion was natural to humanity, manifesting itself in worship and morality. Important works of Deist writers are: J. *Locke, *Reasonableness of Christianity* (1695); J. Toland, *Christianity not Mysterious* (1696); M. Tindal, *Christianity as Old as the Creation* (1730), the so-called 'Deist Bible'.

P. Gay, *Deism: An Anthology* (1968).

Delusion. A fault as fundamental in E. religions (e.g. *moha in Buddhism) as sin is in W. religions, especially in the Christian understanding of original sin. Delusion is to see and interpret manifest appearance, including one's own nature and being, in the wrong way, mainly by superimposing wrong perceptions or ideas upon it. It is thus ignorance (in Hinduism *avidyā, in Buddhism *avijja, in Jap. Zen *mayoi*), but not in a naïve sense of 'not knowing something', but in a more active sense of operating one's whole life on the basis of wrong perception. E. religions then offer routes and methods to the transformation of perception until it results in 'right-seeing' or enlightenment—with many stages of great worth and illumination on the way. See Index, Delusions.

Demiurge (Gk., *dēmiourgos*, 'craftsman'). The divine being in *Plato's account (in *Timaeus*) of the formation of the visible world. The Greek *fathers used the word to refer to God as creator, following Hebrews 11. 10. In *gnostic thought, however, it was used disparagingly of the inferior deity who created the material universe, distinguished from the supreme God; and mainstream Christianity abandoned the word when it rejected gnosticism.

Demon (Gk., *daimōn*, 'a spirit'). Originally an unseen reality influencing a person's life, speech, or actions (e.g. the *daimōn* of Socrates), it became associated with malevolence or evil. Sometimes identical with the *devil, demons (in the plural) become more often servants or agents of the devil. Demonic figures appear in all religions. Examples are: in Judaism (see EVIL SPIRITS), *dibbuks, *golems; in Christianity, fallen *angels; in Islam, *shaitāns; in Hinduism, *asuras, *rākṣasas; in Buddhism, *asuras, *yakkhas, *Māra; in China, *kuei. These personified descriptions of the forces of evil are clearly evoked by the universal human experience of encountering evil, not as an abstraction, but as more like the consequence of personal agency.

J. W. Boyd, *Satan and Mara* . . ., (1975); E. Langton, *Essentials of Demonology: A Study of Jewish and Christian Doctrines* (1949); J. B. Russell, *The Devil* . . . (1977) and *The Prince of Darkness* (1988).

Demythologization. A programme associated particularly with Rudolf *Bultmann which endeavoured to penetrate and re-express the meanings of biblical myths. The programme seemed controversial because it appeared to call in question the reliability of what purport to be historical narratives. In fact the programme was building on the 19th-cent. achievement (especially of *Strauss and Wagner) in disentangling the worth of myth from the issue of historicity. Bultmann pressed further in attempting to translate the truths and insights which had been expressed in myths tied to a particular (and outlived) world-view into a thought-form of perennial human concerns, and thus of contemporary accessibility. His choice of existentialism seemed to meet the first point, but carried with it the inevitable dilemma that existentialism itself was not 'timeless' but had a short 'shelf-life'; and far more seriously, that cultural relativity suggests that such disparate world-views may be incommensurable and thus not open to translation, the one to the other. He therefore attempted also to define myth in a way which relates it to claims about the ontological reality of God: 'Mythology is the use of imagery to express the otherworldly in terms of this world and the divine in terms of human life, the other side in terms of this side. For instance, divine transcendence is expressed as spatial distance' (*Kerygma and Myth*, 1953). Bultmann might well be writing of *analogy; for how else can one speak of God? In practical terms, 'myth is a mode of expression which makes it easy to understand the cultus as an action in which material means are used to convey immaterial power'. Demythologization is then the attempt to express the content of myth in the non-imaginative form of the analysis of existence. In his view, the account of existentialists, especially M. Heidegger, is 'no more than a secularised, philosophical version of the New Testament view of human life'. That it can be made to seem so is perhaps a Procrustean exercise. See also HERMENEUTICS.

A. Malet, *Mythos et Logos* . . . (1962; Eng. tr. *The Thought of Rudolf Bultmann*, 1969); H. P. Owen, *Revelation and Existence* . . . (1957).

Dengaku (Jap., 'field entertainments'). Ritual music and dance forms within the agricultural folk religion of medieval Japan (*c.*11th–17th cents.). Song, dance, and music have been central to both Shinto and Japanese folk religion. Dengaku forms took place primarily in the rice fields at transplanting time to entertain the *kami (Shinto 'gods'), to ensure a bountiful crop, and to relieve the drudgery of the work. Some of these forms became 'professional' entertainment forms in their own right, and helped influence the development of such prominent and classical performing arts as the *Nō drama in the 14th cent.

Dengyō Daishi (founder of Tendai): see SAICHŌ.

Denkō-Roku (Sōtō stories): see KEIZAN OSHŌ DENKŌ-ROKO.

Denne (also **Den'e**, **Den-i**). In *Zen Buddhism, the handing on of the robe as a symbol of the transmission of *buddha-dharma in the lineage of patriarchs (*soshigata) to a successor (*hassu).

De Nobili, Roberto (1577–1656). Christian *Jesuit missionary. Despite family opposition, he became a Jesuit in 1596/7 and was sent to India in 1605. In contrast to the established missions which sought a disjunctive conversion from all things Indian, de Nobili learnt the languages and adopted the style of a *saṁnyāsin. He insisted on the incompatibility of idolatry, but otherwise encouraged converts (the first was a *brahman, Śivadharma) to retain their caste and other Hindu characteristics. Other Christians objected on grounds of a betrayal of Christianity, and he was inhibited from activity. His appeal to Rome was eventually upheld, in *Romanae Sedis Antistes*. He resumed his missionary activity, bringing many, particularly from lower castes, into the Church. He spent his last years in poverty and near blindness. His pioneering attempt (like that of *Ricci in China) to distinguish the gospel from the external aspects of the Church was an important step on the path to the indigenization of Christianity.

V. Cronin, *A Pearl to India* (1959).

Denomination. A religious group within a major religion, having the same faith and organization. The use of the word in this sense goes back to the 18th cent. 'Non-denominational' schools, ceremonies, organizations, etc., are those which are broadly Christian, or sometimes only broadly theistic. In particular, the term 'denominations' is frequently used of non-Roman Catholic parts of the *Church, and now increasingly of Roman Catholicism as well (thereby calling in question its claim to be *the* Church as intended and founded by Christ). See also SECTS.

R. E. Richey, *Denominationalism* (1977).

Densetsu (Jap., 'explanations of tradition'). Narratives of Japanese tradition describing acts of prominent figures, especially holy men who have attained religious powers, and are not entirely legendary (i.e. they had historical existence). Most of them are Buddhist. The stories tell how through their powers they assist ordinary people or punish wrong-doers. Often they are aetiological, accounting for the origins of popular beliefs, holy places, and customs. Particularly well-known are *Kobo densetsu*, the tales of *Kūkai. Comparable as genres of religious stories are *engi* (which tell especially of miracles and portentous events associated with holy places) and *reigenki* (stories of Buddhas and *bodhisattvas, in particular, of their efficacous powers of intercession). See also SETSUWA; SHINWA.

Deoband. A seat of Muslim learning, situated in Saharanpur, India. It was founded by Mawlana Qasem Nanawtawi in 1867. During the 20th cent. it gained extensive influence throughout the Muslim world and ranks with *al-Azhar in importance. The Deoband tradition is *Hanafite, and is based on the 18th-cent. reform movement of *Shah Waliullah, and is a synthesis of *Qur'ān, *tafsīr, *ḥadīth, *fiqh, ʿilm al-*kalām, and philosophy. Its aim is to resuscitate classical Islam, and to rid the Muslims of theological corruption and ritual malpractices. It refuses *ijtihād, and a strict enforcement of the *Shariʿa is maintained. Socially, Deoband is progressive, in that it strives to eliminate caste differences and ignorance amongst Indian Muslims, but it blocks any innovation, e.g. it is resolutely opposed to compulsory education for Muslim girls. Politically, it has been an important ally of the Indian Congress Party and was both anti-British and anti-Pakistan, envisaging an independent India in which its own teachings would take effect. Deobandis have spread throughout the world: e.g. there is an Islamic Academy of Deobandis in Manchester, which publishes a monthly magazine in Urdu, *El-hillal*, and which spearheads the Deoband movement in Europe amongst Muslim migrants.

Z.-H. Faruqi, *The Deoband School and the Demand for Pakistan* (1963); B. D. Metcalf, *Islamic Revival in British India: Deoband, 1860–1900* (1982).

Deontological ethics (from Gk., *dei*, 'it is necessary'). *Ethics which are grounded in objective principles and demands, rather than in an evaluation of consequences. Deontology is associated in religions with the belief that what is right and wrong, good and evil, can be known and should be acted upon; hence it is associated with the revealed will of God, or with *dharma, or with natural law.

Dependent origination (nexus of cause in Buddhist analysis which brings appearances into being): see PATICCA-SAMUPPĀDA.

Deprogramming. A technique devised in the early 1970s by the American Ted Patrick as an antidote to the alleged *brain-washing or 'programming' methods used in recruitment by some *new religions. Deprogrammers maintain that since recruits have been deprived of their freedom to think (a natural right), it is necessary to revive this capacity to think by the use of shock tactics such as destroying photographs of a movement's leader in the presence of the recruits, and by challenging the latter with questions to which they have not been programmed to respond. In this way, it is said, the mind is reopened, begins to function again, and the recruits begin to question all that they have been supposedly programmed to believe. Deprogrammers, on the assumption that recruits have been deprived of the capacity to make rational choices, have used such methods as 'kidnapping' in order to 'rescue' members from a movement prior to deprogramming them. This is regarded by some as a violation of civil liberties.

Derash (Heb., 'interpret'). A Jewish method of interpreting scripture. Derash is contrasted with *peshāt as the homilectical rather than the literal exposition of the text. It is one of the four traditional methods of interpretation: see BAHYA BEN ASHER.

Derekh erez (Heb., 'way of the world'). In Judaism, acceptable behaviour. According to R. Ishmael b. Nahman, derekh erez preceded the giving of the *Torah by twenty-six generations (*Lev.R.* 9. 3). It involves courtesy, family harmony, concern for others, modesty, and etiquette. It can be summarized by *Maimonides' dictum, 'he shall never in his lifetime trouble his fellow'. Two minor tractates of the *Talmud, *D. E. Rabbah*, and *D. E. Zuta*, provide rules of conduct and guides to behaviour (included in Eng. tr., A. Cohen, 1965).

Derwīsh or **dervīsh** (Pers., 'beggar'). A member of a Muslim religious fraternity (although the word may mean simply a religious mendicant, in Arab. *faqīr). The fraternities perhaps began in the custom of groups gathering around a particular *Sūfī teacher. Each group has its own chain of succession (*silsilah, which every member must know) through which the esoteric teaching and practice have been transmitted. For that reason, the particular ritual of a group is as important as *ṣalāt (prayer). The practices and teachings of the many groups are too varied to be summarized, but central to all is *dhikr, the calling to mind of *Allāh and of the unseen world, and of the worshipper's dependence on it. The elimination of outward stimuli is achieved by many different techniques, of which the best-known is the whirling *dance—hence the 'whirling dervishes', more correctly known as *Mawlawīy(y)a, transliterated as Mevlevis.

I. Friedlander, *The Whirling Dervishes* (1975).

De Sales, Francis, St (1567–1622). Christian *bishop and spiritual director and, with St Jane Frances de Chantal (1572–1641), the founder of the Salesian style of spirituality. Educated at Paris and Padua his life after ordination was active and much involved in the world and his diocese; whereas Jane de Chantal was more inclined to contemplation and the creation of holy space in her life. Together they founded the community of the Visitation of the Holy Name. The purpose of Salesian spirituality is expressed at the opening of his *Introduction to the Devout Life* (1609):

> Almost all those who have hitherto written about devotion have been concerned with instructing persons wholly withdrawn from the world or have at least taught a kind of devotion that leads to such withdrawal. My purpose is to instruct those who live in town, within families, or at court, and who by their state of life are obliged to live an ordinary life as to outward appearances.

Despite this intention to establish an unenclosed community of women devoted to prayer and the poor, the archbishop of Lyons required it to become enclosed in 1618. Salesian spirituality seeks to recapitulate the death and resurrection of Christ in life, so that the living Christ shines forth in every detail of life:

> What becomes of the light of the stars when the sun appears on our horizon? It does not go to extinction, but is caught up and *raptured into the sun's sovereign light. . . . And what becomes of the human will when it is wholly given over to the will of God? It does not go to extinction, but is so lost and dispersed into the will of God that it no longer stands out, and has nothing other than the will of God. (*Treatise on the Love of God*, 1616).

A number of Salesian Orders were subsequently founded, e.g. the Salesians of St John Bosco, the Oblates of St Francis de Sales.

W. Wright, *Bond of Perfection* . . . (1985).

Descartes, René (1596–1650). Philosopher. Educated at the *Jesuit college of La Flèche, in 1613 he went to Paris. Having devoted himself to philosophy, he settled in Holland. In 1649, at Queen Christina's invitation, he went to Sweden, where he died. His philosophy—expounded principally in his *Meditations* (1641), *Principles* (1644), and *Discourse on Method* (1637)—is based on a method of radical doubt. But even doubt leaves an awareness of self—his famous *cogito ergo sum* ('I think, therefore I am')—which becomes the pivot of his philosophy. From this point Descartes established, by pursuing 'clear and distinct ideas', a radical distinction (Cartesian dualism) between mind and matter—'thinking' and 'extended' reality—the existence of God (principally by a form of the *ontological argument), and thence the reliability of the world perceived through the senses. Cartesian doubt formed a point of departure for E. Husserl (for whom the doubt was not sufficiently radical), and thus is of importance for the development of *phenomenology.

J. Cottingham, *A Descartes Dictionary* (1993); G. Sebba, *Bibliographia Cartesiana* (1964).

Descent (of Christ) into Hell. A subject of Christian affirmation in, e.g., the *Apostles' Creed. The belief that Christ descended into *hell between his death and resurrection is based, though quite uncertainly, on such passages as Matthew 27. 52 f. and 1 Peter 3. 18–20. Some have understood the descent as an expression of Christ's victory over the evil powers (the 'harrowing of hell', a favourite theme of medieval art and drama); others, as the occasion of Christ's preaching to the pre-Christian righteous waiting in *Sheol. It has frequently been interpreted in the myth and ritual context of the *dying and rising god (associated with fertility cults, e.g. Isis and Osiris), and with the descent of heroes to the underworld to contest death, or to seek some precious object.

Desecration of host: see HOST, DESECRATION OF.

Desert Fathers. The earliest Christian monks of Egypt, *c.*3rd–5th cents. Their names and way of life were made famous in the Greek and Latin world through *Athanasius' *Life of *Antony*, the writings of *Jerome, the *Life of *Pachomius*, the anecdotal *Lausiac History* (*c.*419) of *Palladius, a similar *History of the Monks of Egypt*, and the *c.*6th-cent. collections known as the *Apothegmata Patrum* (Sayings of the Fathers). The emphasis in all these works is one of *asceticism, tempered by quiet devotion. The theme of the desert as the place of extreme spiritual struggle, perhaps of aridity combined with dependence on God, underlies the Desert Fathers; it is epitomized in the forty days which *Jesus is said to have spent in the wilderness at the outset of his ministry.

Eng. tr. from medieval Latin versions by H. Waddell, *The Desert Fathers* (1936); B. Ward, *The Sayings of the Desert Fathers* and *The Wisdom of the Desert Fathers* (1975) are trs. from the *Apothegmata*; D. J. Chitty, *The Desert a City*, (1966); G. Gould, *The Desert Fathers on the Monastic Community* (1993). U. W. Mauser, *Christ in the Wilderness* . . . (1963).

Determinism. The view that events and behaviours are determined before they occur, by the laws of the universe or by God. In religions, determinism takes different forms: in Christianity, see *Augustine and *Calvin; in Islam, *qadar and *kasb, *Allāh; in Hinduism *et al.*, *karma. The religious problem is how to reconcile the omnipotence of God or the inevitable effect of karma with the freedom and responsibility of the human agent. See also PREDESTINATION.

Detraditionalization (the erosion of tradition in religion and society): see ENTTRADITIONALISIERUNG.

Detroit Conference (1975): see LIBERATION THEOLOGY.

Deus absconditus (Lat., 'hidden God'). The apparent absence of God from those who seek him, or from circumstances where the godly are in extreme trouble. Such circumstances are, in the Jewish case, the *Maccabean revolt or the *Holocaust. The opaqueness of the purposes of God, summarized in this phrase, goes back to Isaiah 45. 15, 'Truly, you are a God that hides himself . . .'. Sometimes, this phrase is used as an equivalent for the *via negativa, but the two serve different functions in theistic reflection.

Deus ex machina (Lat., 'God out of the machine'). The device in classical theatre of bringing God on to the stage and into the action to resolve a problem in the plot; hence the introduction of an artificial solution to a problem.

Deus otiosus (Lat., 'inactive God'). God understood as removed or detached from activity in relation to humans or the created order. The supreme God may remain in authority over other gods or heavenly beings, but activity in relation to creation is delegated to them. A familiar example is that of the supreme Canaanite God, *El, being 'promoted' into transcendence and displaced by *Yahweh in relation, first to Israel, and then to the whole cosmos.

J. Bowker, *The Religious Imagination and the Sense of God* (1978).

Deus sive Natura (God or Nature): see SPINOZA.

Deuterocanonical books. Biblical books belonging to a second or secondary *canon, and specifically the books of the *Apocrypha, accepted by the RC Church as belonging to the canon of the (Hebrew) Old Testament.

Deutero-Isaiah (Isaiah 40–55): see ISAIAH.

Deuteronomic history. The name given by scholars to the theory of history in the biblical books Deuteronomy–2 Kings and based on the hypothesis that these books were edited as a whole according to a consistent principle. The editor or editors ('Deuteronomists') believed that obedience to the commands of God led to success, and disobedience to disaster. Deuteronomy gives the commands and warnings, and the later books record Israel's history in the light of this theory. For succinct examples, see the farewell speeches of Moses (Deuteronomy 31) and Samuel (1 Samuel 12), and the remarks on the fall of Jerusalem (2 Kings 23. 26–7, 24. 2–4). The work will have had its last edition by *c.*550 BCE. See also SAMUEL, BOOKS OF; KINGS, BOOKS OF.

Deuteronomy. The fifth book of the *Pentateuch in the Hebrew Bible and Christian Old Testament. The English title ('second law') derives from the Septuagint Gk. version of 17. 18. The usual Hebrew title *Devarim* ('words') is the second word of the text. The book takes the form of long farewell addresses by Moses. These include the *Ten Commandments (5. 6–21), *Shemaʿ (6. 4–9), and a 'Deuteronomic Code' (12–26) dealing with religious duties, civil institutions, and various other laws. The end of the book includes the appointment of Joshua to succeed Moses, and the Levites' custody of the book of the law (31), the 'song of Moses' (32), the 'blessing of Moses' (33), and his death (34). The homiletic style and diction of Deuteronomy mark off both it and its sources from the rest of the Pentateuch. The usual scholarly view is that the book is probably the product of a long evolution largely completed in the 7th cent. BCE in some connection with the religious reforms of King Josiah (2 Kings 23).

Deva (Skt., perhaps connected with *dyaus*, 'bright sky'). 'Shining One'. In Hinduism, a deva is a celestial power (cf. *Chandogya Upaniṣad* 6.3), and particularly a manifestation (*not* a personification) of a natural power, generally beneficent, especially if propitiated through offerings (see SACRIFICE, HINDU). In that way, it became a term for all the Vedic gods, generally reckoned as thirty-three (*Ṛg Veda* 1. 139. 11, 1. 45. 2). The introduction of goddesses, *devīs, appears to have been secondary. The devas were believed originally to have emerged from the union of heaven and earth, but in the later and prevalent cosmogony, they come from *Prajāpati. They are not immortal in the strong sense, but they become immortal in a provisional sense, keeping death at bay, through the sacrifices offered to them (for which in return they confer a wide range of benefits) and through drinking *soma. When humans also consumed soma, they became death-postponing, and they came to know the devas. Thus 'deva' is used to describe enlightened people who have had direct experience of the devas; and it is also used as a description of *Brahman in the form of a personal god. See also DEVATĀ.

In Buddhism, devas are manifest forms of re-appearance (*punabhāva) in 'heaven', i.e. in one of the good domains of manifestation (*gati). As with all appearances, the devas are not eternal, and will eventually reappear in another form on the way to enlightenment. Buddhism thus incorporated the theistic system of Hinduism (the thirty-three gods live on Mt. *Meru, and the peaceful gods live in the *Tuṣita heaven), but adapted the provisional immortality to its own understanding of the transience (*dukkha) of all appearance.

Deva (Buddhist Madhyāmaka philosopher): see ĀRYADEVA.

Deva-dāsī. 'Slaves of the *deva', women in Hindu temples devoted to the God or gods, especially *Śiva, the lord of the *dance, hence temple-dancers. But their dedication was also understood as a marriage to the God, the sexual realization of which was enacted by *brahmans and by other devotees, until eventually they were liable to become temple prostitutes. The 'dedication' was not necessarily voluntary: some girls were prepared from infancy. In recent years, the trend has been reversed, and the cultural and religious importance of the dance has been restored, encapsulating the spiritual journey leading to God.

Devadatta ('god-given'). In Hinduism, (i) the name of *Arjuna's conch shell; (ii) the white horse that Pārāśraya (*Kalki as universal ruler) will ride; (iii) a *prāṇa (cosmic energy) stream initiated by yawning to distribute power/*breath to an exhausted body.

In Buddhism, the cousin of the *Buddha (known in Japanese as Daiba (datta)), who joined the *saṅgha after hearing a discourse of the Buddha, but who plotted to murder him. The plot failed, but he still created a schism in the embryonic community by insisting on a more *ascetic way of life. On his death-bed (on one account), he reverted to the Buddha, but he will still spend many millennia in torment.

Deva-dūta. The Buddhist 'messengers from the *deva', sickness, old age, and death. As with the *Buddha's early experience, these are signals of the fate which awaits us all, and are thus the first pointers to *dukkha.

Devagṛha (house of God): see MANDIR(A)

Devakī. In Hindu mythology, daughter of Devaka, and wife of *Vasudeva. She and her husband were imprisoned by her kinsman Kamsa, and forced to hand over their new-born children to be killed, because Kamsa had been told that her eighth son *Kṛṣṇa, would destroy him. As Kṛṣṇa's mother, Devakī is sometimes identified with *Aditi, who was the mother of *Viṣṇu in his *Vāmana form, while Vasudeva is identified with Aditī's husband, *Kaśyapa.

Devālaya (house of God): see MANDIR(A).

Devaloka. 'Domain of the devas', a rough equivalent to *heaven, in Indian religions.

Deva-mātṛ (mother of the gods): see ADITI.

Devapūjā (worship of deities): see PŪJĀ.

Devarāja (Skt., 'god' + 'ruler'). A cult developed at *Angkor, in which the king was recognized as divine, or perhaps as ruler of the gods. The Sdok Kak Thom Stele records how this new status of kingship was initiated by a *brahman with a view to sealing the unity and loyalty of the Khmer people. From that beginning, the term has declined to mean simply 'godlike' (i.e. despotic) 'power'.

H. Kulke, *The Devarāja Cult* (1978).

Devarāja (four world protectors): see CELESTIAL KINGS.

Devatā(s) (Skt.). In Hinduism, a group of lesser gods and spirits. The many classes of devatās include tree spirits, water spirits, village gods, demons of disease, etc. All have very specific attributes and powers, usually related to the life of the common villager: e.g. the Goddess Sinivali is called upon during childbirth; Sitala, to remove smallpox; Annapurna, to ensure a bountiful harvest. In the *Upaniṣads, devatā refers to potency within the cosmos.

Devayāna. 'The path of the deva', the way, in Hinduism, followed by the truly faithful after death, leading to the realization of *Brahman (*Chandogya Upaniṣad* 4. 15. 5. f.). It is narrow and dangerous, and much like the bridge which leads to the domain of *Yama. Less mythologically, it is the path of wisdom and spiritual knowledge.

Devekut (Heb., 'cleaving'). Communion with God, derived from Heb., *davak*, being devoted to God. The *Talmud asks the question, how can man cleave to God as he is commanded (Deuteronomy 4. 24)? The response is given, by helping scholars (*B.Ket.* 111b) or by emulating God's attributes (*B.Sotah* 14a). The concept is much used in *kabbalistic literature, where devekut is perceived as the highest step on the spiritual ladder by which the mystic embraces the lower *sefirot (emanations) in his search for communion with the divine. It is generally accepted that devekut in this world will be fleeting and incomplete, since it is only after death that true devekut can be achieved. It is a concept and an attainment of great importance in *Ḥasidism.

Devī. Hindu Goddess. The term can be applied to any of the many forms of the Goddess. Initially, they may simply have been the feminine counterpart of the *devas, but already by the *Vedic period they appear as manifestations of the power inherent in natural phenomena, as e.g. *Uṣas (dawn), Rātrī (night), *Gaṅgā (Ganges), and other sacred rivers. In the post-Vedic period, many of these features were assimilated in Mahādevī (Great Goddess), who is the source of energy in the cosmos (*śākti), the dynamic counterpart of *Śiva. For Śāktas, Mahādevī is more than a counterpart: she is the ultimate source, for whom the other gods are servants and agents. In mythology (especially *Devī-Bhāgavata-Purāṇa), Devī frequently does what the male gods are unable to do: see MAHIṢA. Devībhakti, devotion to, and worship of, Devī, takes two major forms, of either right-handed or left-handed *tantra. The major festival of right-handed worship is *Durgā-pūjā, a particularly important festival in Bengal. Devī is invoked:

By you this cosmos is born into life, by you this world has been created, by you it is protected, by you it will be consumed at the end. . . . You are the śakti, the energy of all things, sentient or insensible. Who can worthily praise you, you who give form to all things, to all of us, to *Viṣṇu, to Śiva, to myself?

For eight days various rituals and processions take place, and on the ninth day Devī is returned to the waters of a river. In left-handed tantra, Śiva and Śākti are produced by *Brahman, but being neuter, Brahman is incapable of reproduction and creation. Even Śiva without Śākti is lifeless (a play on words: Śākti is symbolized by the letter *i*, so that Śiva without *i* becomes *śava* a corpse). Śākti is identified with *prakṛti (matter), so that the material, especially the body, becomes the place of meeting with the energizing Śākti. The major forms of Devi are *Durgā, *Pārvatī, and *Kālī. See Index, Devi.

C. M. Brown, *God as Mother: A Feminine Theology in India* (1974); T. B. Coburn, *Devī-Māhātmya* . . . (1984); L. E. Gatwood, *Devi and the Spouse-Goddess* (1985); see also bibliography at DURGĀ.

Devī-Bhāgavata-Purāṇa. Hindu mythological work in Skt., belonging to the genre of the *purāṇas. The title will popularly be understood as meaning 'the purāṇa in which *Bhagavān [the Deity] is the Goddess', but historically it must be interpreted as 'the purāṇa that imitates the **Bhāgavata Purāṇa* but is dedicated to the Goddess'. Related to this ambiguity is its fragile status as one of the eighteen *mahā-purāṇas (Major Purāṇas) which rests merely on its claim to be the 'real' or 'true' *Bhāgavat Purāṇa*. Historically it must be regarded as a late reworking of the classical *Bhāgavata Purāṇa* in terms of a religious system, in which, instead of *Kṛṣṇa/*Viṣṇu the Goddess (*Devī) appears central. Benares may well have been its place of origin, with possible influences of Bengal traditions. Its date of composition will not be much earlier than the 15th cent. CE. The Goddess is envisaged as Bhuvaneśvarī, 'Empress of the World', and as residing in the supreme heaven of Maṇidvīpa. Yet to spell out her mythical deeds, no new material appears here. Naturally, the stories of the *Devī-māhātmya* (on this see MĀRKAṆḌEYA PURĀṆA) are rewritten at great length, but the author's main intention is to demonstrate how the Goddess, as activating and controlling force, is implied in traditional myths. Above all, it is in the delusion, egoism, and violence of the male gods and sages that her presence and activities can be recognized. Book ix, which contains a very lengthy account of secondary goddesses, appears to be adapted from the slightly earlier *Brahma Vaivarta Purāṇa* (Prakṛti or book ii). In its long ritualistic passages the work rebuffs '*tantric' features and is eager to emphasize its orthodox, Vedic position. Indeed its cult of *bhakti—a total surrender to the all-powerful Goddess—bears no connection with the *Tantras.

Eng. tr. Swami Vijnananda (1921–3).

Devil. In Jewish scripture, the figure of *Satan is that of an adversary (1 Kings 11. 14), allowed by God to engage in his probing work (Job 1–2, Zecheriah 3. 1 f., 1 Chronicles 21.1; cf. 2 Samuel 24. 1). In later Judaism, although Jewish folklore includes stories about Ashmedai, the king of *demons and Lilith his queen, the figure of the devil is not significant. *Maimonides ignores the whole subject of demons, and the *rabbis stressed that even evil spirits came from God. In rabbinic literature, Satan is identified with the *yeẓer ha-raʿ (the evil inclination) and was thus responsible for all the sins of the Bible (*PdRE* 13. 1). But, there are few references to him in the liturgy.

In both Christianity and Islam, the devil and Satan are at times identified, and yet also appear as separate figures. Belief in the devil arises as a consequence of the universal human experience that evil is frequently experienced as though it is a consequence of personal agency: 'Brethren, be sober, be vigilant: your adversary the devil goeth about like a roaring lion, seeking whom he may devour . . .' (1 Peter 5. 8).

The devil is named in the *Qur'ān Iblīs, perhaps from Gk., *diabolos*, though Muslims derive the name from Arab., *balasa*, 'he despaired' (*sc.* of the mercy of God). But he is also al-Shaitān, Satan, and 'the enemy of God'. When the angels were ordered to bow down before the newly created *Adam, Iblīs refused to do so, because, being created of fire, he thought himself superior to something made of earth. He continues to tempt humans, especially through the whisper (*waswasa*, 'he whispered') and the false suggestion (*hātif*). At the end, he will be cast into Jahannam (see HELL, ISLAM).

Although Iblīs and (al-)Shaitān are identified, Shaitan also has a distinct existence, perhaps as the leader of the *jinn, perhaps as a name for them (since there seem also to have been more than one). In a personified version of temptation (cf. YEẒER), it is believed that everyone has a personal *angel and shaitān, the one urging to good, the other to evil.

See also DEMON for near-equivalent figures in other religions.

J. B. Russell, *The Devil* . . . (1977).

Devil's advocate or **advocatus diaboli.** Person appointed by the Roman Catholic Congregation of Rites to contest the claims of those put forward for beatification or canonization (i.e. being recognized officially as saints). His more correct name is *promotor fidei* (promoter of the faith); the supporter of the proposal is known as *advocatus Dei* (advocate of God).

Devotio Moderna (Christian community): see GROOTE, G.

Dev Samaj (Hindu movement): see AGNIHOTRI.

Devshirme (young Christian conscripts to Islam): see JANISSARIES.

Dew, prayer for (Heb., *tefillat tal*). Supplication for moisture forming part of the Jewish *'Amidah during the dry season. The Bible frequently cites the bestowal of dew as a mark of God's providence. According to tradition, the 'heavenly stores of dew' are opened at the beginning of *Passover, so that a symbolism was developed relating the restoration of life to the land with the restoration of Israel. Among Sephardi, these supplications are known as *tikkun tal*.

Dge-'dun-grub-pa: see DALAI LAMA.

Dge lugs (school of Tibetan Buddhism): see GELUK.

Ḍhamaru (drum, Hindu): see GHAṆṬA.

Dhamma or **Dharma** (Pālī, Skt.). Check alternative spellings at appropriate place.

Dhammabhaṇḍāgārika (chief disciple of Buddha): see ĀNANDA (1).

Dhamma-cakka or **dharma-cakra** (Pālī, Skt.). 'The Wheel of the Doctrine'. The motif of the many-spoked wheel is the distinctive symbol of Buddhism. It originally signified the Buddha's act of proclaiming his doctrine (*dharma) to the world (see FIRST SERMON). The momentous significance of this event was portrayed in canonical sources by comparing the Buddha to a monarch who lays stake to universal sovereignty by driving the wheels of his chariot throughout the earth; in the course of time the dhamma-cakka has come to signify Buddhist teaching and doctrine generally. Buddhism seems to have derived the wheel symbol from ancient *Vedic ritual where it signified the sun's disc, symbolizing cosmic order, and the king's chariot wheel, symbolizing royal sovereignty; thereby it integrated the ideas of heavenly and earthly power into one single notion. In adopting the wheel as a symbol for themselves, Buddhists were thus seeking to show that the Buddha's act of teaching had a universal, cosmic significance.

In earliest *iconography (*c.*2nd cent. BCE), the dhamma-cakka features as an aniconic symbol for the Buddha. As such it is represented *either* on or above a vacant throne, flanked on either side by two or more gazelles, signifying the *Deer Park (*Sārnāth) where the Buddha first preached, *or* on top of a column (Skt., *cakrastambha*), the column signifying the *axis mundi (another cosmic symbol). In later, iconic, representation it is traced on the Buddha's body and the soles of his feet, or held in his hands. The dhamma-cakka is depicted over the entrance to Buddhist temples or their gateways throughout Asia. When eight spokes are depicted, this signifies the Eightfold Path (*aṣṭangika-mārga) or the cardinal points of the compass. In *Vajrayāna iconography, the wheel is placed on a lotus pedestal and encircled by a halo, and symbolizes the essential word of the Buddhas; in E. Asia, Buddhist priests use gilt bronze wheels as ritual implements.

Dhamma-cakkappavattana-sutta. 'The Setting in Motion of the Wheel of Dhamma', the title of what is regarded as the *Buddha's *First Sermon, preached in the Deer Park at Isipatana (*Sārnāth), near Benares. It contains his essential teaching on the avoidance of the extremes of indulgence and *asceticism, and the *Four Noble Truths and the Eightfold Path (*aṣṭangika-mārga). It is one of the four great events of the Buddha's life, the others being his birth, his enlightenment, and his passing into *parinibbāna* (final *nirvāna at death). The sermon is recorded in **Saṃyutta-Nikāya* 5. 420.

Dhammapada (Teaching of the Verses). A collection of 423 key Buddhist texts (verses), of wide influence and importance throughout the Buddhist world. Spiritual teachers in India were expected to conclude a discourse with a key verse (*gatha*), and the *Buddha frequently followed that custom. The *Dhammapada* is a collection of such verses. It is thus not a systematic work, and although some principles of organization can be discerned, there is no continuous argument.

Four major versions have survived in (mainly) Indian languages: Pālī (26 chapters, 423 verses); Gāndhāri (most of the 26 chs.); Udānavarga (expanded in a *Sarvāstivādin direction to nearly 1,000 verses, partially preserved in Skt., complete in Chinese and Tibetan); the version of the *Mahāsāṃghika. A traditional commentary, attributed to *Buddhaghosa, collects stories of the occasions on which the sayings were first delivered (tr. E. W. Burlingame, Harvard Or. Series, 1921).

The opening two verses summarize the dominant importance of *karma/kamma in Buddhist life.

> All states are the result of what we have thought, mind is their commander, they are made by our thoughts. If one speaks or acts with an evil thought, then suffering follows as surely as the wheel follows the foot of the ox which pulls the cart . . . If one speaks or acts with a good thought, then happiness follows like a shadow that cannot be detached.

Particularly valued is verse 183: 'The giving up of

all that is evil, the cultivating of all that is good, the cleansing of one's mind, this is the teaching of all the Buddhas.' The concentrated form of the *Dhammapada* is summarized in its own verse (100): 'Better than a thousand sentences composed of meaningless words is one sensible word, on hearing which one becomes peaceful.'

Trs.: among many, I. Babbitt (1936); S. Radhakrishnan (1950); G. Sparham (Tib., 1983); N. Thera (1954); F. L. Woodward (1921); J. R. Carter and M. Palihawadana (1987).

Dhanvantari. The physician of the gods in Hinduism, who emerged from the *Churning of the Ocean bearing the cup of *amṛta. As the teacher of medicine, the **Āyur Veda* is attributed to him.

Dharam yudh ('war of righteousness'). Sikh recognition that in some circumstances war is necessary. Gurū *Nānak insisted that tyranny and injustice must be resisted, and Gurū *Amar Dās told members of the *Kṣatriyas that it was their *dharma to establish a protective fence of justice. However, it was not until the time of Gurū *Gobind Singh (10th Gurū) that the rules of war were drawn up. He laid down five conditions of a justifiable war: (i) it must be action of the last resort, after all other means of settling an issue have been exhausted; (ii) the motives must be pure (e.g. free from revenge or enmity); (iii) it must not be for the purpose of gaining territory, and any gained in conflict must be returned after victory; (iv) the soldiers must be committed Sikhs who therefore conduct themselves according to Sikh standards—especially in the treatment of the non-combatants and defeated; (v) minimum force must be employed. See, in comparison, JUST WAR.

Dhāraṇā (Skt., 'support'). 1. One-pointed concentration (*ekāgrata) in *yoga; the fifth 'limb' of *Patañjali's 'eight-limbed' (aṣṭāṅga) or *rāja-yoga resulting from *prāṇāyāma. Patañjali defines dhāraṇā as 'the binding of consciousness to a (single) point' (*Yoga Sūtra* 3. 1). *Vyāsa's commentary on the **Yoga Sūtra* says that this concentration can be on the wheel (*cakra) of the navel, on the lotus of the heart, on light inside the head, on the tip of the tongue, or on any external object. Dhāraṇā leads into *dhyāna; it is the steadiness of mind requisite for meditation and higher spiritual experience, and to die in dhāraṇā is to help oneself and one's relations to enter *paradise.

2. A term denoting a level of sonic cosmogony in *Tantrism. For example, in *Kashmir Śaivism the Devanāgarī phonemes *ya, ra, la,* and *va,* which represent certain levels of the cosmic hierarchy, are dhāraṇās, the idea being that sound (*nāda, *śabda) is the support of manifestation.

Dhāraṇī. In Hinduism, the earth Goddess; and (as also in Mahāyāna and Tantric Buddhist sources), a magical formula often composed of random syllables, the recitation of which is thought to produce supernatural effects or bestow magic powers. They are comparable to, but longer than, *mantras, and eventually (in *Vajrayāna) became discourses: for their classification in relation to developed texts, see TRIPIṬAKA.

Dharma or **Dhamma** (Skt., Pālī): check alternative spellings at appropriate place in compound words.

Dharma (Skt., *dhar,* 'hold', 'uphold'). 1. In Hinduism, dharma is a fundamental concept, referring to the order and custom which make life and a universe possible, and thus to the behaviours appropriate to the maintenance of that order. Hindus therefore refer to what Westerners call 'Hinduism' as *sanātana dharma,* everlasting dharma. Initially, dharma applied more to ritual and religious rules (especially sacrifices) than to ethics (e.g. *Ṛg Veda* 3. 17. 1), but by the time of the *Brāhmaṇas, the term includes also the rules which govern (and enable) society. These were gathered in the *Dharmasūtras and *Dharmaśāstras, of which the most important are the law-codes of Manu (Eng. tr., *Sacred Books of the East,* 25) and Yajñavalkya; others are translated in *SBE* 33. In the *Upaniṣads, dharma is related more to the ways appropriate for the attainment of *Brahman, than to ethics. See P. V. Kane, *History of Dharmaśāstra* (1930–62).

2. In Buddhism (Pālī, *dhamma*), the Hindu sense of cosmic law and order is retained, especially as it works out in *karma and reappearance according to the law of karma. But it was rapidly applied also to the teaching of the *Buddha (*pariyatti*) who is himself a manifestation of the truth that is dharma. Dharma is then understood as the practice (*paṭipatti*) of that truth, and as its realisation in stages (*paṭivedha*) up to *nirvāna, of which in this way dharma becomes a synonym. Thus to take refuge in the Dhamma (the second of the *Three Jewels, *triśaraṇa) is already to take refuge in the first, the Buddha. Dharma then becomes a term for the norms or rules of behaviour (*śīla, *vinaya), and also for the manifestations of appearance, the constituents of existent entities. The dharmas, enumerated and analysed in Buddhism in great detail, exhibit the constitution of all appearances and the ways in which they function.

T. Stcherbatsky, *The Central Conception of Buddhism and the Meaning of the Word 'Dharma'* (1923; 1970).

3. Among the Jains, dharma may simply be the teaching of the *Jinas, so that *adharma* is its opposite—error and immorality. However, both of these are also regarded as basic constituents of the universe: dharma is the all-pervasive medium of motion or activity, and adharma, also pervasive, offers the circumstance of rest, 'like the shade of a tree, inviting the traveller to pause'. Both are understood as real substances, in the Jain sense that without the ontological truth of the Five Elements (*astikaya),

there could be no distinctions in the universe, which is palpably false.

See Index, Dharma.

Dharmacakra (Skt.). The wheel of *dharma, the teachings of the *Buddha. In his *First Sermon, the Buddha set this wheel in motion, which no power can stop; hence the title of the *sutta* of this sermon, 'Dhamma-cakka-parattana'. See (Pali) DHAMMA-CAKKA.

Dharma character school (school of Chinese Buddhism): see FA-HSIANG.

Dharma Contest (mutual encouragement between master and pupil in Zen Buddhism): see HOSSEN.

Dharmadhātu (Skt., element of phenomena'; Tib., *chos.kyi.dbyings*, 'expanse of phenomena'). A term in Buddhist philosophy which began as a *Hīnayāna concept, indicating the true nature of phenomena as ultimately specific entities subject to dependent origination (Skt., *pratītyasamutpāda*; Pālī *paticcasammupāda), but which grew in importance in the *Mahāyāna to describe the true nature of all phenomena collectively as indivisible and empty (*śūnyatā) of own-being (*svabhāvaśūnya*). Many texts talk of the dharmadhātu as of a 'substratum', upon which the apparent solidity and individuality of phenomena is seen as the fault of the imputing mind. Thus the *Mahaprajñāparamitāśastra* (Great Treatise on *Perfect Wisdom, attributed, doubtfully, to *Nāgārjuna) says: 'So it is with phenomena: multiple and diverse, they are separated by (mental) grasping.' This same text reveals how the term 'dharmadhātu' conveys the Prajñāpāramitā identification of form and emptiness, *nirvāna and *saṃsāra: 'The dharmadhātu is nirvāna; it is indivisible and unspeakable (*niṣprapañca*). The dharmadhātu is the root of all (*maulabhāga*). Just as a yellow stone has gold as its essence . . . so all phenomena of the world have nirvāna as their essence . . . the original unborn suchness untainted by words is called dharmadhātu.'

Although the concept dharmadhātu involves the doctrine that the ultimate status of things is empty even of emptiness (*śūnyatāśūnyatā*), its usage, like that of the *svabhāvikakāya* (body of own-being), possibly indicates ontologizing tendencies within the Mahāyāna. Although in Mahāyāna texts dharmadhātu is synonymous with terms such as *bhūtakoti* ('reality-limit') and *tathatā ('thusness'), in modern Western usage it generally, and perhaps inadequately, simply indicates 'the absolute'.

Dharmaguru (Orthodox Hindu): see NĀSIK.

Dharmakara (name of king who vowed to found a Buddha-land): see AMIDA.

Dharmakāya. (One of three aspects of the buddha-nature): see TRIKĀYA.

Dharmakīrti. A Yogācāra / Vijñānavāda Buddhist logician of the 7th cent. CE, and author of seven treatises originally intended as commentaries on the work of *Dignāga but eventually superseding the latter as the basic materials for the traditional study of Buddhist logic and epistemology. The chief of these works, the *Pramāṇa-vārttika*, contains four chapters dealing with inference, the validity of knowledge, sense-perception, and syllogisms. Few of Dharmakīrti's writings survive in the original Skt., but all are preserved in Tibetan translation. For an account of Dharmakīrti's life and works and a discussion of the technical aspects of his theories, see E. T. Stcherbatsky, *Buddhist Logic* (repr. 1962); this also contains a translation of the *Nyāya-bindu*, one of Dharmakīrti's works on logic.

Dharmapāla (Skt., 'guardian of the *dharma'). 1. *Vajrayāna Buddhist deities, called on by Vajrayāna to protect the dharma wherever it is under threat. Some are known individually (e.g. the wrathful form of *Avalokiteśvara, or *Mahākāla), but others are general (e.g. Lokapalas, guardians of domains). The individual can also invoke the help of the Dharmapālas in *sādhana (realization processes in meditation).

2. *Yogācāra Buddhist philosopher (*c.*7th cent. CE), who was abbot of the Mahābodhi monastery at *Bodhgayā. Almost all his commentary writing has been lost, apart from Chinese trs.

Dharmapala, Anagarika (1864–1933). Sinhalese Buddhist reformer who laid foundations for the revival of Buddhism. He was born Don David Hewavitarne and received an English-based education. But under the influence of the *Theosophists, Olcott and Blavatsky, he renounced his European name in 1881 and took the name 'Guardian of Truth'. He adopted the role of *anāgārika, a homeless ascetic committed to reform. In 1891, he founded the Maha Bodhi Society for the renaissance of Buddhism and for the rescue of Buddhist sites in India. He was exiled in 1915 for political activities, and ended his days an ordained member of the *saṅgha. His legacy is a vigilant Buddhism in Śri Lankā, combining this-worldly asceticism with a deep suspicion of other religions.

Dharmasagara (Jain controversialist): see GACCHA.

Dharmaśāstra (Skt., *dharma*, 'law' + *śāstra*, 'teaching'). Any of a class of Sanskrit texts concerned with rules of conduct and law. Dharmaśāstras tend to be longer and more systematically organized than *dharmasūtras, and treat some topics neglected in the dharmasūtras, such as *vratas (religious vows); *utsarga* and *pratiṣṭhā* (dedication of public utilities, shrines, and temples); *kāla* (auspicious times); and *tīrtha (pilgrimages to sacred places). Dharmaśāstras concern both *śrauta*, the dharma of *śruti (chiefly Vedic rites), and *smārta, the dharma of *smṛti (chiefly *varṇāśramadharma). Some dharmaśāstras also concern *sādhārana dharma* (universal law), such as non-injury, truth-telling, etc. Dharmaśāstra tends to be oriented more towards universal and practical law than dharmasūtras, which tend to be associated with particular Vedic schools and geographic locations.

The dharmaśāstras strictly so-called are composed entirely in verse, although the term sometimes includes the prose dharmasūtras. The dharmaśāstra tradition emphasizes *brahman interests, in contrast to the *arthaśāstra tradition, which concerns the worldly dharma of the prince.

Of the more than 2,000 surviving dharmaśāstras, the most influential is certainly the *Manusmṛti* or Laws of Manu (see DHARMA). The *Yājñavalkyasmṛti* has had an indirect influence upon modern Indian law *via* the commentary of Vijñāneśvara.

P. V. Kane, *History of Dharmaśāstra* (1930–62).

Dharma-successor (one in succession of Buddhist teachers): see HASSU.

Dharmasūtra (Skt., *dharma*, 'law' + *sūtra*, 'aphorism'). Any of a class of Sanskrit prose texts concerned with law and rules of conduct (*dharma). Dharmasūtras differ from *dharmaśāstras in that the former consist of prose or mingled prose and verse, while the latter consist exclusively of verse. Dharmasūtras tend to be briefer than dharmaśāstras, consisting of terse *sūtras or aphorisms which are seldom arranged in any systematic fashion. The older dharmasūtras, unlike the dharmaśāstras, do not claim to be of divine origin. Dharmasūtras contain more linguistic archaisms than dharmaśāstras, and are more likely to be partisan towards a particular Vedic school. Many scholars follow Max *Müller in dating the dharmasūtras before the dharmaśāstras, and consider the latter to be metrical recastings of the former. Although there is much evidence to suggest the priority of the dharmasūtras, this is disputed by some scholars.

Major dharmasūtras include the *Gāutama-dharmasūtra*, *Bāudhāyana-dharmasūtra*, *Āpastamba-dharmasūtra*, *Vasiṣṭha-dharmasūtra*, *Viṣṇusmṛti*, and *Vāikhānasa-smārtasūtra*. Despite the distinctions, these works are sometimes referred to by the more encompassing term dharmaśāstra. Dharmasūtra is considered a branch of *kalpa sūtra, an ancillary or *aṅga of the *Vedas, and like dharmaśāstra is considered *smṛti or 'remembered' in contrast to the revealed Vedas.

Dharmsālā (Sikh community): see SIKHISM.

Dhātu (Skt., Pāli, 'region, element'). A word occurring frequently as a component in longer Buddhist terms, e.g. as one of the three worlds or domains, *kāmadhātu*, *rūpadhātu*, *arūpadhātu*—see LOKA. In its own right, it refers to elements of many different kinds, e.g. the physical elements (earth, water, wind, fire), the eighteen elements of sentience and consciousness (eye, ear, nose, tongue, mental awareness, etc.), the six states of appearance (solid, liquid, temperature, moving, spatial, conscious or not), the remains of a body after *cremation—see DĀGABA.

Dhātu-vavatthāna (Pāli). Buddhist analysis of the elements of the body, and thus one of the forty meditation exercises advocated by the *Visuddhimagga* (for which see BUDDHAGHOSA). By reviewing the body and its processes, the awareness of transience (*dukkha) is enhanced, and the separate nature of the functions destroys the sense of being a substantial, single being.

Dhikr (Arab., 'remembrance'). Basically a Quranic word, commanding 'remembrance of God', an act of devotion during and after the *ṣalāt (prayer). However, the *Sūfīs consider dhikr a spiritual food, and it is one of their main practices. It is said that 'the heart of a man is like a tree which breathes and lives through Divine Love, while the nourishment for the roots is given by dhikr of Allāh'. The special importance of using Quranic words and verses to remember Allāh is derived from numerous Quranic injunctions, e.g. 'So remember me and I will remember you' (2. 152); 'O you who believe! Remember Allāh with much remembrance' (33. 41); and, 'Remind yourself of your Lord when you are forgetting' (18. 24). Each Sūfī order has a dhikr of its own, constructed by its founder; the litanies and incantations are derived from the Qur'ān and taught by the *murshid* (Sūfī guide) to the initiate. It is the *murshid* who selects the dhikr fit for the spiritual stage of the seeker. It is also believed that a dhikr done without the guide's permission is practically useless. There are two types of dhikr: *dhikr-i-jalī* (loud recitation) and *dhikr-i-khafī* (performed with either a low voice or silently): The value and power of the dhikr is dependent upon right concentration and intention which brings into play body, speech, and mind. Only when the adept becomes identified with the dhikr (i.e. unity of the object and the subject), is the heart illuminated by the divine light. It should be noted that the dhikr does not bring union with God: it is a device to purify the heart so that it may become a fit receptacle of the divine attributes. See also DERWĪSH.

Dhimma. Official protected status granted by the Muslim ruling power to the non-Muslims, known as Ahl al-Dhimma, an individual being termed a Dhimmī. These were in origin generally of the *Ahl al-Kitāb, People of the Book (scripture), i.e. Jews and Christians, a status extended to *Zoroastrians (Majūs) and others as time went on until it has come to refer to non-Muslims living in a Muslim state. Unlike pagans (*mushrikūn*), Dhimmīs are allowed to retain their religion and generally to practise it unhindered, though subject to certain legal restrictions, mostly in social and economic life, which vary in harshness and in the extent to which they are applied.

The official levy is the *jizya or 'poll tax', mentioned in the Qur'ān (9. 29): 'Fight against those who have been given the Scriptures (but) believe not in Allāh and the Last Day ... and follow not the Religion of Truth, until they pay the tribute (jizya)'. Dhimmīs in the past could, and often did, attain and keep high positions in administration and finance, and many were employed as physicians at court. However, the numerous restrictions have tended to reinforce the generally second-class nature of non-Muslim citizenship. Whereas a Muslim man can marry a Dhimmī woman of the ahl al-kitāb, a Muslim woman cannot marry a non-Muslim. In criminal law, the blood-money for a Dhimmī is much less than that for a Muslim. No Dhimmī is permitted to try to convert a Muslim; and while conversion to Islam is usually encouraged, and certainly approved, the reverse is considered *apostasy often in practice and carried the death penalty.

The principle of Dhimmī status kept the non-Muslim population to a great extent separated from the Muslims, and, in the case of Christians, these were often encouraged to keep within their national/religious boundaries, seen as individual 'nations' rather than forming one Christian community. This practice was continued and elaborated by the Ottoman 'millet' system.

A. R. I. Doi, *Non-Muslims Under Shari'ah*, (1983); A. S. Tritton, *The Caliphs and their Non-Muslim Subjects* (1930).

Dhīr Mal (17th cent. CE). A claimant to being the Sikh Gurū. Dhīr Mal, son of Gurū *Hargobind's son, Gurdittā, was Gurū *Har Rāi's elder brother. He turned against his grandfather and, among many others (e.g. Rām Rāi), challenged the succession of his uncle Tegh Bahādur in 1664. His followers were called Dhīrmalīās.

Dhītika (Buddhist sage): see NĀGASENA.

Dhoti. Loin-cloth, common in India, and compulsory in some temples, as a mark of *ascetic poverty before God.

Dhṛtarāṣṭra. In the **Mahābhārata*, the blind 'king', father of the *Kauravas (Dhārtarāṣṭras), who, despite the meaning of his name ('he whose kingdom is firm'), is too weak to stop his evil sons from playing their dice game against the *Pāṇḍavas and fighting the *Kurukṣetra war.

Dhṛtarāṣṭra's blindness has been interpreted as a metaphor for the blindness of fate. An adjective commonly applied to him is *prajñācakṣus* ('he whose eye is wisdom'). When Dhṛtarāṣṭra declines to accept sight offered to him by Vyāsa just before the Kurukṣetra war, divine sight is given instead to his charioteer, Saṃjaya, who is thus equipped to narrate the events of the war, including the **Bhagavad-gītā* episode, to Dhṛtarāṣṭra and the epic audience. It is through Saṃjaya, too, that Dhṛtarāṣṭra gains some knowledge of *Kṛṣṇa's divinity—knowledge which is lacking to his sons.

The *Mahābhārata* states that Dhṛtarāṣṭra was the incarnation of a *gandharva, and indeed knows a gandharva—and also a serpent—by this name. Dhṛtarāṣṭra's wife is Gāndhārī.

Dhruva (Skt., 'fixed, constant'). In Hindu mythology, the son of Uttānapāda and grandson of *Manu. In early childhood he was forbidden by his stepmother to sit with her own son upon their father's lap. The angry child vowed to obtain for himself a position in the world which would be higher than all others. He left his father's city for the banks of the *Yamunā, where he practised such fierce *asceticism that he won the favour of *Viṣṇu, who made him the Polestar, occupying the highest point in heaven. This constancy has made him the symbol of fidelity in Hindu marriage ceremonies.

Dhū'l-Ḥijja. The Islamic month of pilgrimage (*ḥajj). It is the last month of the Muslim calendar, and together with *Dhū l'Qa'da* (preceding) and *al-Muḥarram* (following; the first month of the year) constituted the three months of truce in pre-Islamic times. During this time no fighting was allowed, and the tribes could come to *Mecca for pilgrimage and for trade.

Dhū'l-Nūn (Arab., 'owner of the fish'). A name for the Prophet Yūnus (*Jonah), after whom sūra 10 is named. In the *Qur'ān, the story of Yūnus is related at 37. 139–48, and he is alluded to with other prophets in 4. 163 and 6. 86.

Dhu'l-Nūn al-Misrī (d. 859 (AH 245)). An Egyptian mystic who travelled widely in search of truth and certainty. He became a leading authority on *ma'rifa* (knowledge of inner truth) and was considered to be the *qutb (spiritual head) of the *Sūfīs of his time. He was reckoned to be the first to systematize the states of mystical attainment (sing., *ḥāl) and the stages of the Path (*maqāmāt*), and to establish the study of *ma'rifa* (often, but loosely, translated as 'gnosis'). Dhu'l Nun classified knowledge into three categories; (i) the knowledge of religious commands and observances, which is for both the elect and the common people; (ii) the knowledge gained by proof and demonstration, which is for the elect; and (iii) *ma'rifa*, which is beyond the power of human learning and reason (which is why so many reject it). 'This knowledge is acceptable to neither the elect nor the common folk, and I remained an outcast and alone. This belongs to the attributes of Unity, those who contemplate the face of God within their hearts, so that God reveals himself to them in a way in which he is not revealed to any others in the world.' He equated it with the love of God: 'God's lovers see without knowledge, without sight, without information received, without description, without veiling and without veil.

They are not themselves, but insofar as they exist at all, they exist in God. It is the most precious gift and the greatest of graces.' However, love of God was founded on love to humanity and righteousness, so that he also maintained a positive attitude towards the world, seeing the manifestation of God in the created order, even to the extent that birds flocked above his coffin to give it shade.

Dhūtanga (Skt., Pāli, 'shaking off'). Twelve optional practices allowed by the *Buddha (see further ASCETICISM): (i) wearing patched robes; (ii) wearing a robe made of three pieces (*tricīvara*); (iii) eating only begged-for food; (iv) eating once a day; (v) refraining from excess at any meal; (vi) taking only a single portion of food; (vii) living in seclusion; (viii) living where bodies are cremated; (ix) living under a tree; (x) living in the open; (xi) living in whatever place one chances to arrive at; (xii) sitting and not lying down.

Dhyāna (Skt., 'meditation', 'absorption'). In Indian religions, a term denoting both the practice of *meditation and a higher state of consciousness (generally involving *enstasy), though the term takes on more precise meanings in different traditions; thus the Buddhist use of the term is distinct from the Hindu—see JHĀNA.

In the *Upaniṣads, the use of the term varies from specific to more general understandings. In **Chandogya Upaniṣad* (7. 6. 1–2), dhyāna denotes one-pointed (*ekāgrata) concentration on a single object, a mental condition superior to the unconcentrated, fluctuating mind (*citta). In **Śvetāśvatara Upaniṣad* (1. 3), dhyāna yoga, which consists of repeating the *praṇava* (see OṂ) which is likened to a fire-stick, results in a vision of God: 'Having made Oṃ (the *praṇava*) the upper friction stick (*araṇi*) and one's own body the lower, due to practising the friction of dhyāna one sees God (*deva) who is hidden' (*Śvetāśvatara Upaniṣad* 1. 14). **Maitri Upaniṣad* (6. 18) uses the term in a more specific sense as part of a 'six-limbed' (*ṣaḍaṅga*) *yoga (comprising *prāṇāyāma, *pratyāhāra, dhyāna, *dhāraṇā, *tarka, and *samādhi) to achieve oneness with *Brahman.

In *Patañjali's **Yoga Sūtra*, dhyāna has a parallel meaning as the seventh 'limb' of 'eight-limbed' (*aṣṭāṅga) or *rāja-yoga, indicating a condition in which mental fluctuation (*cittavṛtti*) is overcome (*Yoga Sūtra* 2. 11) by fixing the mind on a single object. Here it follows dhāraṇā and leads to samādhi. According to Vijñānabhikṣu, a 16th-cent. commentator, the difference between dhyāna and samādhi is that in dhyāna it is still possible for mental fluctuation (*cittavṛtti*) to arise, whereas in samādhi it is not.

In *Tantrism dhyāna comes to mean *visualization of one's own deity (*iṣṭadevatā), *maṇḍala, centres (*cakra) of the subtle body (*liṅga/*sūkṣma śarīra), or *guru, accompanied by *mantra repetition (*japa) and symbolic hand gestures (*mudra). Dhyāna as visualization is thus the visual equivalent of auditory mantra and corporeal mudra and is an essential part of *sādhana. The *Tantras and *Āgamas contain detailed iconographic descriptions of deities for the purposes of visualization. As visualization there are two stages to dhyāna which occur during the 'mental' or 'inner' worship (*manasa* or *antara yāga*) of Tantric *pūjā. Firstly there is the projecting of the deity onto an inner screen, secondly the sādhaka's identification of himself with the deity, for to worship a god, one must become that god. That is, the sādhaka creates a mental reality which he then becomes part of. For example, the *Pañcarātra text, the *Jayākhya Saṃhitā* (10. 71–82), describes the visualization of the adept's own body being burnt to ashes which are then carried away in a flood, followed by meditation on himself as Lord *Nārāyana. Thus through dhyāna the adept transcends his individuality and identifies with the divine.

Dhyāni-Buddhas (Meditation Buddhas). Term coined by B. H. Hodgson, early 19th-cent. British diplomat in Nepal, to describe the jinas ('eminent ones') who appear in a *tantric context in the *Maṇḍala of the Five Jinas. Although the term 'Dhyāni-Buddhas' does not seem to occur in any Buddhist literature (other than *Dharmakośasamgraha* written by Vajrācārya Amṛtānanda in 1826 at the request of Hodgson), it has nevertheless been widely adopted by W. commentators, resulting in many speculations, as to the nature of these figures on the basis of their imputed name—e.g. 'beings who exist in the sphere of meditation', 'beings who sustain the world in their meditation', 'beings who project human buddhas into the world in their meditation', and so forth. More correctly, the five jinas are subjects for meditation upon; and, as their role in the Maṇḍala of the Five Jinas reveals, they are essentially symbolic representations of particular aspects of the psyche and the world. As named, they are Amitābha (*Amida), *Amoghasiddhi, *Akṣobhya, *Ratnasaṃbhava, and *Vairocana.

Diaconate. Pertaining to, or belonging to, the order of *deacon.

Dialogue. 'Is not the road to Athens made for conversation?' asked Walter Pater in his *Plato and Platonism*. One would be doubtful of the affirmative about the road to *Mecca, or *Jerusalem, or Vārāṇasī (see KĀŚI). Pilgrims *en route* to those cities are likely to be too faith-proud, rite-prone, and community conscious for any debate about themselves. Religions historically have been traditional discriminators within humanity, sacralizing identity by force of doctrine and culture, and establishing (indeed, being) systems for the protection and transmission of highly valued, non-negotiable information.

But in recent decades 'dialogue' has come to be a word in frequent currency among theologians—not the Socratic-style dialogue which assumed and sought the single thread of reason and logic, but a much more perplexing engagement with the authority and interrelation of truth-systems claiming disparate, if not rival, sanction in and by the transcendent.

There have, of course, been fascinating interactions between faiths through the centuries. There is nothing new in their liability to each other. What is new now is the general awareness that they have one physical world of technology, as also of tragic political and economic tensions, in which they are responsible, together with a new degree of conscious pluralism in which secularity tends to equate—and ignore—all religious options. It is hard for faiths to concede their optionality. At least they have in common the final question of their relevance—and the relevance of their not having it in common.

Through these factors the movement has grown for an opening out of Christian theology from 'domestic' criteria of its tasks, whether patristic, reformed, liberal, to take in an active cognizance of other faiths. Other faiths have registered the same impulse. For some Christian theologians there is an arguable extension of the ecumenical instinct from 'Christian', however diversely read, to 'religious'. Is not the *ecumene* (the whole world, see ECUMENISM) the *corpus Christianum*? If Catholic/Orthodox/Protestant learn to abate bigotry, repudiate caricature, and 'do' things together, may not Hindu/Buddhist/Jew/Muslim/Christian and the rest do likewise? Why not an *ecumene* of religions?

Plainly, the problems, intellectual and psychic, are vastly enlarged. For some, dialogue is a conspiracy of hidden syncretism to be strenuously resisted, for others a useful tool facilitating a still missionary interpretation, for others again an implied surrender of finality to be either welcomed or deplored. For others again it is a vocation of obedience, Abrahamic perhaps, which does not yet know where it is being led.

The Vatican Secretariat for Non-Christian Religions, the Unit on Witness and Dialogue of the World Council of Churches, and the Committee for Relations with People of Other Faiths of the British Council of Churches, have published studies in the theology of dialogue and guidelines for relations with other faiths and with the ethnic groups which hold them. Observers from other faiths, firmly excluded from the 1961 Assembly of the World Council of Churches, were officially invited and welcomed at its 1983 Assembly in Vancouver.

Practical problems are easier to resolve than intellectual. Faiths, after all, are people: they are in and of persons. The art of personal relationships requires genuine respect, sincerity, courtesy, and a receptive will. Faiths, inwardly known *on* the *other* side, are only outwardly studied *from* ours. The dialogue must allow for this basic fact, bring the necessary imagination and suspend the instinct to misread and decry. Tolerance has to be transmuted into love.

But given the authentic will to understand, what can we, should we, do with our courts of appeal, our canons of authority, our set of minds? Some insist that theology, like geology, or botany, is strictly a discipline within its data, in this case, e.g., 'revelation'. If the theologian ventures outside these he becomes a philosopher of religion. Talking with Buddhists, can he even be a theologian at all? Others, however, believe that theology properly includes within its faith-theme a doubt of itself, the sort of doubt which must be generated by a genuine concession of plurality of creeds and cults, which he/she has not, as it were, neutralized by seeing them as already anonymously, potentially, or indirectly, the same as the Christian.

Dialogue in some quarters may be too glib a word. There are masses in all faiths for whom it is virtually non-existent. But for those, however few, who have sensed its implications aright it can only be the growing edge of their theology and the shape of their obedience. As Richard Niebuhr wrote: 'There is no such thing as disinterestedness in theology'—a comment to warn complacency, forbid seclusion, and kindle endeavour.

M. Barnes, *Religions in Conversation* . . . (1989); J. W. Bowker, *Is God a Virus? Genes, Culture and Religion* (1995); F. Clark (ed.), *Interfaith Directory* (1987); K. Cragg, *The Christian and Other Religions* (1977), *The Christ and the Faiths* (1986); K. Cracknell, *Towards a New Relationship* (1986); S. I. David (ed.), *Christianity and the Encounter with Other Religions* (1988); *Guidelines on Dialogue* . . . (World Council of Churches; 1979); ed. D. G. Dawe and J. B. Carman, *Christian Faith in a Religiously Plural World* (1978); S. J. Samartha, *Faith in the Midst of Faiths* (1977); R. B. Sheard, *Inter-religious Dialogue in the Catholic Church since Vatican II* . . . (1987).

Diamond Cutter: see DIAMOND SŪTRA.

Diamond Maṇḍala: see TAIZO-KAI MANDARA; SHINGON.

Diamond Sūtra. A short Buddhist text from the corpus of the *'Perfection of Wisdom' (*prajñāpāramitā*) literature which compresses the essential teachings into a few short stanzas. Composed around 300 CE, it was translated into Tibetan and Chinese and has remained immensely popular as a summary of the doctrine of 'emptiness' (*śūnyatā) or 'voidness' which lies at the heart of the Perfection of Wisdom writings. The full title of the text is 'The Diamond-Cutter Perfection of Wisdom Sutra' (*Vajracchedika-prajñāpāramitā-sūtra*), and, as its name suggests, it is thought to have the power to cut through ignorance like a diamond for those who study and reflect upon its profound meaning.

Eng. tr., E. Conze, *Buddhist Scriptures* (1968).

Diaspora (Gk., 'dispersion'; Heb., *galut*, 'exile', is the nearest equivalent). Jewish communities outside the land of *Israel. During the period of the second *Temple, there were populous Jewish settlements in Babylonia and throughout the Roman Empire. After the destruction of the Temple and the second Jewish revolt (see BAR KOKHBA), Jewish religious life was maintained through the *academies, *yeshivot, and *synagogues of the diaspora communities. Until the middle of the 19th cent., the largest Jewish settlements were in Europe, particularly in the Austro-Hungarian empire, in Russia, and in W. Europe, but there were also communities in N. Africa (including the *Falashas of Ethiopia) and in Asia (including small groups in India and China). In the 19th cent., there was mass emigration to the USA, and by 1914, approximately one-third of Jewry lived there. As a result of the *Holocaust and the foundation of the state of Israel, the number of Jews living in Europe was enormously reduced. Today, Russia's Jewish population numbers approximately two million, and both France and the United Kingdom have nearly half a million. There are small communities in other European countries; the vast majority of Jews in Arab-speaking countries have emigrated to Israel, and the largest diaspora settlements are now in the USA, Australia, and S. Africa. Inevitably the Jews of the diaspora have taken on the manners and customs of their host nations, even though *anti-Semitism, persecution, minority status, and a strong sense of religious and cultural difference has kept Jewish identity alive: 'Israel's entire Galuth history is one vast altar, upon which it sacrificed all that men desire and love, for the sake of acknowledging God and his Law' (S. R. *Hirsch). Today, increased *assimilation, higher rates of intermarriage, low birth rates, and increased secularism are threatening that identity, except among the ultra-*orthodox. The *Zionist dream and support for the state of Israel, however, has proved a unifying focus for the diaspora communities.

Diaspora is also widely used for members of other faiths living outside their spiritual homeland, e.g. Hindus, Sikhs, Zoroastrians.

N. G. Barrier and V. A. Dusenbery (eds.), *The Sikh Diaspora* (1989); P. Bhachu, *Twice Migrants: E. African Sikh Settlers in Britain* (1985); J. Brown and R. Foot (eds.), *Migration: The Asian Experience* (1995); J. Y. Fenton, *Transplanting Religious Traditions: Asian Indians in America* (1988).

Diatessaron (Gk., 'through four'). The gospel story compiled into one narrative from the four gospels by *Tatian *c.*150–60 CE. It was the standard text in Syriac-speaking churches until the 5th cent. when it was suppressed in favour of the separate gospels. The *Diatessaron* had an ascetic colouring, e.g. in changing 'wine' to 'vinegar' in Matthew 27. 34. It may have also had some relation to the *Gospel of *Thomas*. The original work (whether in Gk. or probably Syriac) is lost, and has to be reconstructed from, among other sources, a commentary by *Ephrem and other derivative 'gospel harmonies' in Lat., Arab., Persian, and Dutch.

Dibbuk or **dybbuk.** An evil spirit in Jewish folklore. The term appeared in literature in Germany and Poland in the 17th cent. The spirit was supposed to enter a person as a result of a secret sin. It causes mental illness and speaks through its host's mouth. Complicated procedures for exorcism can be found in *kabbalistic texts, and the power to exorcise was given to learned *ḥasidim. The dibbuk is connected with belief in *ibbur*, a limited transmigration of souls: the *ibbur* is the birth in a good person of a righteous soul, thus reinforcing that person's goodness. It was a natural extension to suppose that an evil spirit could take up residence in another. The dibbuk is common in *ḥasidic stories, and is the subject of an often performed play, *The Dibbuk*, by S. An-Ski (1916).

Didache (Gk., 'teaching'). Christian instruction in prayer, ethics, church order, etc. It is distinguished from *kerygma, 'preaching'.

The *Didache of the Twelve Apostles* is a short early Christian manual of morals (chs. 1–6), church practice (7–15), and *eschatology (16). The latter chapters include instructions on *baptism (by immersion if possible), two primitive *eucharistic prayers, and instructions for receiving travelling *prophets and *apostles. Local *bishops and *deacons are treated as if they are only just replacing an itinerant leadership. Such early characteristics as these have led many scholars to assign it a date in the 1st cent. CE.

Dies Irae (Lat., 'day of wrath'). Opening words of the *sequence in the Catholic *mass for the dead. Composed in the 13th cent., it first appeared in a printed missal in 1485. Until 1969 it was obligatory also on All Souls' Day (2 Nov.). For English translation, see e.g. *English Hymnal*, no. 351. Although the emphasis is on the threatening character of the Day of *Judgement, it includes recognition of (and pleas for) the mercy of God: 'Qui Mariam absolvisti | Et latronem exaudisti | Mihi quoque spem dedisti' (You who absolved Mary, and heard the plea of the thief, to me also you give hope).

Dietary laws: In Judaism the term *kasher*, or *kosher*, refers to food that is ritually fit for consumption—hence *kashrut*, fitness. According to Genesis, God gave all fruits and vegetables for human food (1. 29). Dietary laws, therefore, are primarily concerned with animals, birds, and fish, and their products. Animals that have a cloven hoof and chew the cud, such as the ox, sheep, and goat are kosher (Deuteronomy 14. 6), but creatures that fulfil only one of those criteria, such as the pig or camel, are forbidden (14. 7–8). All birds of prey are forbidden. Nowadays, only birds which are customarily regarded as 'clean' can be eaten (*B.Hul.* 63b) because the Bible itself does not list the clean birds. Eggs may only be eaten from *kosher* birds, and they must be rejected if there is a spot of *blood in them. Only fish which have both fins and scales are permitted, and so all shellfish are excluded. All insects (with the exception of certain kinds of locusts) are forbidden. Creatures must be slaughtered (*sheḥitah) in the ritually correct manner, and this must be carried out by a trained and licenced slaughterer (*shohet*). After slaughter, the animal or bird must be hung so that as much blood as possible drains out. Leviticus specifically forbids the eating of blood (7. 26–7), so meat must be salted and washed before it is cooked. Because of the prohibition, 'you shall not seethe the kid in its mother's milk' (Exodus 23. 19), milk products and meat products may not be cooked or prepared in the same dishes. During the *Passover season, no *leaven of any kind may be eaten. The dietary laws are extraordinarily complicated in their details. They can be found in the *Talmud tractate *Hullin* and in 'Yoreh Deʿah' (the teacher of knowledge), one of the four sections of the **Shulḥān Arukh*. There is little to explain the dietary laws in Jewish literature. According to the *Pentateuch, the regulations are connected with holiness: 'you shall be people consecrated to me: therefore you shall not eat any flesh that is torn by beasts . . .' (Exodus 22. 31). *Maimonides argued that forbidden foods are unhygienic, and this was the reason for the regulations. Even with modern methods of food production, however, the *orthodox will not touch forbidden foods. *Reform Jews generally ignore the dietary laws.

For other Religions, see FOOD AND RELIGION.

S. H. Dresner and S. Siegel, *The Jewish Dietary Laws* (1966); I. Grunfeld, *The Jewish Dietary Laws* (1972); I. Klein, *A Guide to Jewish Religious Practice* (1979).

Digambara (Skt., 'clothed in air'). 1. A Hindu *sādhu who goes about naked, having left sexual identity and desire far behind; a title, therefore, of *Śiva in his naked *asceticism.

2. One of two major divisions among Jains, the other being Śvetāmbara. The major divisions between the two are not mainly doctrinal, and it was often Digambara Jains who took the lead on behalf of both in controverting Hindu and Buddhist opponents (e.g. Akalanka, 8th cent. CE). They can live harmoniously in close proximity, though serious disputes arise over the ownership of, and access to, holy places (e.g. Bahubali, in S. Maharashtra; over 130 places are currently in dispute).

The origins of the split are obscure (some traditions taking it back to a time preceding *Mahāvīra, historians connecting it with the austerities in the teachings of Gosāla), since both parties give their own version. According to Ś., the secession of the D. occurred as the last of eight 'concealments' of true doctrine, 609 years after the death of Mahāvīra. Śivabhūti, in arrogant confidence, took a unilateral decision to abandon his clothes (on the issue of nudity, see below) in imitation of the *tīrthaṅkaras ('ford-makers'). According to D., the schism began during a time of *durbhiksha*, famine or political disturbance. Under Bhadrabāhu, the Ś., migrated south and began the heretical practice of wearing clothes. The division appears to have been formalized at the Assembly of Valabhi (453 or 466 CE), which only Ś. attended, making an attempt to agree on what would count as scripture—a concept rejected by the D. in any case. Evidence of developing bitterness between the two can be seen in such disputes as that between the Ś. Vadideva and the D. Kumudacāndra, in 1125.

There are five major issues between them: (i) Ś. monks and nuns wear clothes, D. monks do not; (ii) Ś. use a bowl for begging and for eating, D. do not; (iii) according to Ś., the *kevalin (fully omniscient being) requires food, according to D., not so; (iv) according to Ś., women can attain deliverance, according to D., they must first be reborn as men; (v) Ś. accept ancient writings as *āgama/siddhanta (scripture), D. believe that scripture has been lost in the age of decline. On (i), it is likely that Mahāvīra and his followers went about naked to demonstrate renunciation of the world and conquest of passion, etc., and it is not until the 5th cent. CE that images of the tīrthaṅkaras are clothed (D. images remain naked, with the tīrthaṅkaras having downcast eyes, dead to the world, while Ś. tīrthaṅkara-images have a loincloth and are alert to the world with a single eye). For the D., this early example of nudity must not be given up, because it demonstrates abandonment and enhances the reverence for all living creatures, who will not be destroyed if they take up residence in clothing that is washed. Yet in early times (e.g. Ācāraṅga among the *aṅgas) nudity was optional, and the Ś. emphasize that nakedness may lead to the lighting of fires in cold weather, leading to even more destruction of life. Issues (ii) and (iii) are linked: for D., the restriction of food to what can be taken in cupped hands is a mark of the ascetic moving to the status of kevalin, who is beyond the need for food; for Ś., those who partake of food are precisely those who can attain the status of kevalin, who remains a *human*, not superhuman, model; in addition, Ś. allow ascetics to have fourteen possessions, including a loincloth, D. allow only two, a feather and a brush to sweep away any insect for fear that they should inadvertently kill it.

On (iv), the Ś. draw attention to the fact that Mahāvīra's *tīrtha contained twice as many women ascetics as men, and they claim that Malli, 19th tīrthaṅkara, was a woman. The only women who are forbidden to become nuns are those who are pregnant; otherwise, gender is irrelevant to religious life and liberation. For the D., it is self-evident that women cannot go around naked, if only for their own safety; yet nudity is necessary for the religiously devoted; therefore, women cannot attain enlightenment and liberation, though they can progress toward a better rebirth.

On (v), both groups believe that, from the tīrthaṅkaras' preaching, the most fundamental texts, the Purvas, are now lost. But D. believe that what remains of the tīrthaṅkaras' preaching is a kind of resonating echo, transmitted orally by successions of disciples, whereas the Ś. have a '45-text canon' (though actually they give equal respect to texts outside that boundary). However, the D. have sacred texts of their own (e.g. *Satkhandāgama*, 'Āgama of Six Parts' and *Kasayapahuda*, 'Treatise on the Passions'), and both D. and Ś. revere some texts in common, e.g. *Tattvārtha Sūtra, by a disciple of the D. Kundakunda (who, despite the above, observed, '*Sūtras state that anyone whose faith is without āgama is without constraint. How can anyone without constraint be an ascetic?').

There remain some differences concerning Māhavīra: Ś. hold that he was born with a miraculous change of wombs, D. do not; Ś. that he was a pleasure-loving prince who experienced sudden conversion, D. that he was always full of insight, but that he respected his parents' wishes, until they died, not to renounce the world; Ś. that he was married, D. that he was not.

P. Dundas, *The Jains* (1992).

Diggers. A radical expression of the mid-17th-cent. Leveller movement, whose adherents described themselves as 'True Levellers'. Inspired by the leadership of Gerard Winstanley and William Everard, the Diggers formed communal settlements, dug and sowed common land in several English counties (1649–50), vigorously maintaining that the earth was a common treasury. Winstanley held *millenarian views, and his pamphlets (advocating social and economic equality, universal suffrage, and education for all) served as the movement's main propaganda during its short life.

Dīgha Nikāya (Skt., *Dīrghāgama*). The '*Long Collection*', the first of the five nikāyas of the Sūtra/Sutta Piṭaka of the Pāli canon (see BUDDHIST SCRIPTURES). The Pāli version has thirty-four suttas, the Chinese (Mahāyāna) thirty; twenty-seven are common to both. It is divided into three sections, or 'books' (*vagga*): (i) ethical rules, and refutation of false views; (ii) the Great (Mahā-) section, in which some discourses (e.g. that on the final passing away, **Mahāparinibbāna-sutta*) have become important works in their own right; (iii) the Pāthika section, i.e. the section beginning with the *Pāthika*, of which two discourses, *Sīgalovāda* (code for lay Buddhists) and *Āṭānatiyā* (providing protection) often appear separately.

Eng. tr. T. W. and C. A. F. Rhys Davids, *Dialogues of the Buddha* (1899–1921; repr. 1956–66).

Dignāga or **Diṅṅāga.** Buddhist logician who flourished towards the end of the 5th cent. CE. Reputed to be a native of S. India, he travelled north to study under the great master *Vasubandhu and became one of his four senior students, and the greatest in the field of logic (*pramāṇa). His greatest work is the *Pramāṇa-samuccaya* which combines many of his earlier insights into a complete system of epistemology. It deals with the problems of sense-perception and its role in knowledge, the reliability of knowledge, and the relationship between sensations, images, concepts, and the external world. After Dignāga the lineage continued through his pupil Īśvarasena to the great *Dharmakīrti in the 7th cent. The theories of Dignāga and other Buddhist philosophers on these matters are discussed in T. Stcherbatsky, *Buddhist Logic* (repr. 1962).

R. Hayes, *Dignāga on the Interpretation of Signs* (1988); Hattori Masaaki (tr.), *Dignāga, On Perception . . .* (1968).

Dīkṣa (Skt.). Initiation; in Indian religions, the means of access into a religious tradition, religious or social condition. Dīkṣa is given by the preceptor or *guru and often involves the giving of a new name to the initiate which symbolizes the end of one condition and birth or entrance into a new.

In Hinduism, in the *Vedas, dīkṣa was a necessary prerequisite for the *soma sacrifice undergone by the sacrificer (*yajamāna*) and his wife, involving asceticism (*tapas) and fasting. Indeed, dīkṣa is personified as Soma's wife. (*Ṛg Veda* 25. 26). Initiation plays an important part in the *varṇāśrama-dharma system where the upper three classes (*varṇa), the *Brāhmaṇas, *Kṣatriyas, and *Vaiśyas, are called the '*twice-born' (*dvija*). This is due to their being initiated into the study of the Vedas (*upanayana) when they enter the first stage of the Hindu life-way (*āśrama), the student phase (*bramacarya). During this rite, open only to males, the boy is given a new name, his first Vedic *mantra, a staff, and the sacred thread. A further initiation occurs for one who reaches the fourth phase of renunciation (*saṁnyāsa), during which a new name is given, and the adept renounces all worldly ties and burns his sacred thread. In the *Upaniṣads, initiation into an ascetic life involves undergoing hunger, thirst, and abstention from all pleasure (**Chandogya Upaniṣad* 3. 17. 2). Dīkṣa is regarded as having divine origin coming from the supreme person (*puruṣa) (**Muṇḍaka Upaniṣad* 2. 1. 6) and resting on truth (**Bṛhadāraṇyaka Upaniṣad* 3. 9. 23). The importance of dīkṣa carries on into classical and medieval Hinduism where sub-traditions within the central traditions of *Vaiṣṇavism, *Śaivism, and *Tantrism all required dīkṣa.

There are different kinds and various stages of dīkṣa particularly in *Tantrism where the utmost secrecy is maintained. In *Śaivism the 'collective' (*samaya*) and 'particular' (*viśeṣa*) initiations give access to the cult of *Śiva. After this the initiate is called a *samayin* and has permission to perform certain rites and use certain texts and mantras. These are followed by the nirvāṇa dīkṣa which give access to liberation (*mokṣa). The disciple now becomes a *putraka*, a 'son' of Śiva or the guru, and is now capable of attaining liberation. All these initiations take place within a *maṇḍala. Following the nirvāṇa dīkṣa the *putraka* can undergo one of two consecrations (*abhiṣeka) to become either a guru himself (ācāryābhiṣeka) or to become a *sādhaka (sādhakābhiṣeka). In contrast to the Vedic tradition, Tantrism often allows the initiation of women and *śūdras.

In Jainism, dīkṣa is the ceremony whereby a person passes from lay status to being an ascetic. The ceremony varies slightly between *Digambara and Śvetāmbara. For both communities, there are probationary periods, which vary in length. Among the former, the person takes leave of his parents and asks his teacher permission to enter the order. He then removes his clothes and plucks out his hair, then takes the *five great vows (*mahāvrata*) and receives a new name, together with the whisk and waterpot. He is then decorated with painted symbols, in much the same way as an image when it is being consecrated. Among the Śvetāmbara, most of these elements are present, though distributed in a different way. The Śvetāmbaras alone hold that child initiation is permissible.

Dilthey, W.: see HERMENEUTICS.

Dimensions of religion: see Introduction.

Dīn (Arab.). Life-way or religion, most particularly Islam. The word as used in the *Qur'ān is probably derived from a Christian source which had already borrowed from the Iranian *dēn*, religion. Other Arabic meanings are: judgement or retribution (as in *yaum al-dīn, day of judgement); custom or usage (A. Jeffery, *Foreign Vocabulary of the Qur'ān* (1938), 131–3). The idea of debt or obligation came to signify judgement on the one hand, and on the other, the duties to be fulfilled—those of 'religion', i.e. both faith and practice (Qur'ān 39. 14).

In what is generally thought to be the final verse of the Qur'ān in chronological order, *Allāh is represented as saying: 'This day have I perfected for you your religion (*dīnukum*) and chosen for you Islam as (your) religion' (5. 4). Thus 'The religion before Allah is Islam' (3. 19), yet there is 'no compulsion in religion' (2. 256). Islam is called *dīn al-ḥaqq*, the religion of truth (61. 9, 28. 28). The whole system is sometimes referred to as dīn wa-dawla, 'religion and state (combined)', there being no distinction within Islam between 'religion and politics'.

Dina de malkutha dina (Aram., 'the law of the country is the law'). The Jewish *halakhic principle that the law of the land is binding. The rule, originally laid down by the *amora Samuel in the 3rd cent. CE, states that *diaspora Jews are bound to obey their country's code of law—even, on some occasions, if it conflicts with Jewish law. In particular Jews must pay government taxes and accept the king's authority. The rabbis argued that the principle dina de malkutha dina derives ultimately from the Bible: 'Its rich yield goes to the kings whom you have set over us because of our sins; they have power also over our bodies and over our cattle at their pleasure' (Nehemiah 9. 37).

Dīn-i Ilāhī (religion of unity based on the oneness of God): see AKBAR.

Din Torah (Heb., 'ruling of the law'). A Jewish legal judgement. According to Jewish law, a dispute may be tried before *dayyanim (judges) in a *bet din (Jewish court). Since the 18th cent., this right is seldom exercised except in matters of personal status. A European folk-song relates how Levi Yizḥak had a din Torah with God, in which he brings God to trial for allowing the Jewish people to suffer so much.

Dionysiac (religion): see APOLLONIAN AND DIONYSIAC RELIGION.

Dionysius the pseudo-Areopagite (*c.*500). The name given to the author of a corpus of theological writings; until the end of the 19th cent., their authorship was generally ascribed to the Dionysius whom Paul had converted (Acts 17. 34).

Four of his works (*The Celestial Hierarchy, The Ecclesiastical Hierarchy, The Divine Names*, and *The Mystical Theology*) and ten letters are extant. The central characteristic of these works is the synthesis of Christian and *Neoplatonic thought. According to the treatises on hierarchies, the descent and return of the divine goodness is mediated through the nine celestial choirs of *angels and the terrestial hierarchy: the *sacraments, and the three orders of *bishops, *priests, and *deacons. The treatise on the divine names deals with the being and attributes, and the essential unknowability of God, the way to union with whom is described in *The Mystical Theology.* The leading theme is that of the intimate union (*henōsis*) of God and the soul, and the progressive deification of the human (*theiōsis*), by a process of unknowing in an ascent to God through the three ways of the spiritual life: *purgative, *illuminative, and *unitive.

Dionysius exerted a profound influence on Christianity. In the E., his works were commented upon by St *Maximus the Confessor and by Andrew of Crete. In the W., they were approved by *Gregory the Great, Martin I, and the *Lateran Council of 649 CE. Translated into Latin by John Scotus *Erigena, they became one of the foundations of medieval theology. *Hugh of St-Victor, *Albertus Magnus, and Thomas *Aquinas drew upon them; and the medieval mystics, especially Meister *Eckhart, Johannes *Tauler, '*The *Cloud of Unknowing*', and Richard *Rolle are heavily indebted to them. See also NEOPLATONISM.

Eng. trs. J. Parker, C. E. Rolt, J. D. Jones, T. L. Campbell; A. Louth, *Denys the Areopagite* (1989); P. Rorem, *Pseudo-Dionysus: A Commentary.*

Dīpaṃkara (Skt., Pāli, Dīpankara). 'Kindler of lights', best-known and first of the twenty-four *Buddhas who preceded Buddha Śākyamuni. With him and *Maitreya, Dīpaṃkara is one of the Buddhas of the three ages, past, present, and future. See also FORMER BUDDHAS.

Dīpāvalī (Hindu festival): see DĪVĀLĪ.

Dipavaṃsa. 'Island Chronicle': account of the Buddhist history of Śri Lankā from its beginnings to the 4th cent. CE. The record is taken up in the *Cūlavaṃsa*, and is paralleled by the **Mahāvaṃsa*.

Trs. H. Oldenberg (1879).

Diptychs (Gk., *diptychon*, 'two-leaved folder'). The lists of names, contained originally on two-winged tablets of ivory or bone or metal, of living and dead Christians for whom special prayer is made in the *liturgy of both E. and W. churches. In early times they were recited publicly, so that the inclusion (or exclusion) of a name could be taken as an indication of those who are in communion or who have been excommunicated. In art, the term also applies to an altar-piece with two folding side-wings.

Dīrghāgama (Indian division of Sūtra Piṭaka): see TRIPIṬAKA.

Dīrghatamas (Skt., 'long darkness'). A Ṛg Vedic *ṛṣi. Dīrghatamas or Dirghatapas ('long austerity') is traditionally known as the author of *Ṛg Veda* I. 140 and I. 164, one of the most philosophical and obscure hymns. He is the son of Utathya, an Aṅgiras ṛṣi who drank up the waters of the world to get his stolen wife back from the god Varuṇa. His mother was Utathya's second wife Mamatā, who, pregnant with Dīrghatamas, was impregnated against her will a second time by the high priest of the gods, Bṛhaspati. Dīrghatamas, who even in the womb had already mastered the *Vedas and Vedāṅgas, finally succeeded in kicking out the offspring of Bṛhaspati, Bharadvāja, prematurely from the crowded womb, for which act Bṛhaspati cursed Dīrghatamas to be born blind. By long worship and penance directed to the god *Agni, his sight was eventually restored. As a result of marital strife, which nearly took his life, Dīrghatamas decreed that wives be totally subject to their husband's will and be allowed only one husband, even if widowed. Among his many sons are Dhanvantari, Dirghaśravas, and Kakṣīvat, another famous ṛṣi.

Discalced (not wearing sandals): see CARMELITES.

Disciplina arcani (Lat., 'discipline of the secret'). The practice of concealing certain rites and doctrines from outsiders. The Christian Church certainly exercised such a discipline in the 4th and 5th cents., but it is not well attested before that period. It used to be adduced by Catholic writers to explain the scarcity of early Christian evidences on such subjects as the *Trinity, *mass, and number of *sacraments.

Discipline, Manual of. One of the *Dead Sea Scrolls. It contains a description of the customs of the Dead Sea sect including the annual renewal of the *covenant. This is followed by an explanation of the spiritual status of the sect; humanity is divided into the 'sons of truth' and the 'sons of iniquity'. Eventually the pious will enjoy 'endless gladness in everlasting life' while the wicked will suffer annihilation in 'the shadowy place of everlasting fire'. After rehearsing the penal code, the organization of the community is explained and the document concludes with three hymns of praise. The *Manual* is thought to date from approximately 150 BCE and there have been some scholarly attempts to identify a connection between the sect who produced the scroll and the *havurot ('fellowships') of the early *Pharisees described in the *Talmud. On the other hand, there are clear similarities between the rules of the *Manual* and those of the *Essenes as described by *Josephus.

W. H. Brownlee, *The Dead Sea Manual of Discipline* (1951).

Dispensation. A licence granted by ecclesiastical authority to do some act otherwise canonically illegal or to remit the penalty for breaking such a rule. In Roman Catholic practice dispensations have since the Middle Ages usually been reserved to the pope. *Canon law, however, delegates some dispensing powers to diocesan bishops and even (e.g. in respect of the laws of *abstinence) to parish priests, and in 1966 these delegated powers were widened further. The chief subjects of dispensations are *marriage (e.g. the removal of canonical impediments) and divorce, the *ordination of clergy, and the translation of bishops.

Dispensationalism. *Millennial scheme of biblical interpretation: 'Even if one looks on it as a mess of myth and fiction, dispensationalism is a remarkable and in many ways original approach to the understanding of the Bible' (J. Barr). It divides history into seven 'dispensations', in which God deals differently, and progressively, with humanity: Innocency (until the *fall), Conscience (from the fall to Noah), Human government (Noah to Abraham), Promise (Abraham to Moses), Law (Moses to Christ), Grace (the 'church age'), and Kingdom (the millennium). The church age, the present time, forms a parenthesis of indefinite length within a continuum in which God's dealings are with Israel. Thus, unusually, Old Testament prophecies are not referred to the Church but to the future and last dispensation. Dispensationalism is earliest associated with the Plymouth Brother (*Brethren, Plymouth), J. N. Darby (1800–82), but it attained wide popularity—remarkable for so complex a system—through the *Scofield Reference Bible (1909).

G. Breshears, *Dispensationalism Bibliography, 1965–90* (1991).

Disruption, The. A split in the Church of Scotland in 1843 over the right of presbyteries to veto proposed appointments. 474 out of 1,203 ministers seceded and formed the *Free Church of Scotland.

Distensio (unfolding of the universe): see GILSON.

Distinctionists (alternative name of the followers of Vātsīputrīya): see VĀTSĪPUTRĪYA.

Diti. In Hindu mythology, daughter of Dakṣa and wife of *Kaśyapa. As her name suggests, Diti is the counterpart of *Aditi, who is her sister and rival wife. Whereas Aditi gives birth to gods, Diti's children, the *Daityas, are demons, and there is a state of permanent hostility between the two sets of offspring. Diti is also the mother of the *Maruts in some versions of the story of their birth.

Diṭṭhi (Pāli, 'seeing'; Skt., *dṛṣṭi*). Wrong seeing in Buddhism. A speculative view, especially the seven false views: (i) belief in a sub-stantial self; (ii) rejection of *karma; (iii) espousing eternalism or (iv) nihilism in relation to the destiny of a self; (v) endorsing false *śīlas; (vi) confusing good with bad karma; (vii) doubting the *dharma of the *Buddha. The *Brahma-jāla Sutta*, the first sutta in *Dīgha Nikāya, sets out sixty-two false views based on the premiss that there is a subsisting and persisting self.

Dīvālī or **Dīwālī** or **Dīpāvalī.** The most important Hindu *festival which, unlike other festivals (such as the New Year, Makar Sankrānta, or *Holī), lasts for four or five days (the variation depending on the lunar calculation). It falls in Oct.–Nov. each year. Dīvālī is a short form of Dīpāvalī—a line of lamps. Dīvālī is celebrated by all Hindus, but it is the most important festival for merchants, bankers, and businessmen, because the main religious event is the worship of *Lakṣmī, the Goddess of wealth in Hindu mythology.

DAY 1: *Dhana-Trayodashī*: The thirteenth day of the dark fortnight of the month of Aśvina. On this day a single lamp of a single flame is lit and placed in front of the house in the evening so that the flame is pointing south. This is an offering to *Yama, the god of death (otherwise, throughout the year, a single flame lamp must never point towards the south).

DAY 2: *Narak Chaturdashī*. This celebrates the victory of *Kṛṣṇa over the demon Narakāsura, who, because he had at one time acquired spiritual merit, was allowed one request before he was killed. His request was to institute Dīvālī. Kṛṣṇa then released the 16,000 young women whom Narakāsura had kidnapped, and they immediately considered Kṛṣṇa their Lord and Master, hence the legend that Kṛṣṇa had 16,000 wives. On this day, all Hindus rise earlier than usual. Their heads and bodies are rubbed with perfumed oil before they take a bath. After the bath they put on new or clean clothes and enjoy a large breakfast with friends and relations. Firecrackers are let off in the morning and in the evening, and the midday meal is a feast with special sweet dishes. The house is illuminated with oil lamps in the evening.

DAY 3: *Lakshmi-Pūjan*. On this day Lakṣmī is worshipped in every house, symbolized by a gold ornament or a silver rupee. All doors and windows are kept open so that Lakṣmī may enter the household. Attractive patterns called *rangoli* are drawn on the floor near the entrance to the house. There is usually a drawing of a lotus flower among other patterns, for the lotus is considered the favourite seat of Lakṣmī. It is a day of feasting. The house and its surrounds are illuminated with oil lamps so that Lakṣmī may see her way clearly. On this day, Indian merchants and bankers finalize their account books and, after ending the financial year, offer worship to Lakṣmī. The rest of the Dīvālī celebrations are in the following month, Kārtik.

DAY 4: *Bali-Pratipaddaa*. King Bali is remembered for his generosity. On this day a married woman receives a special gift, usually a gold ornament, from her husband. Being one of the most auspicious days for Hindus, new undertakings are started on this day and the financial year begins.

DAY 5: *Bhrātra-Dvitīyā* (*Bhāubeej*). Sister's Day. All men are forbidden to eat any food cooked by their wives and are told to visit their sister's house. When the brother arrives, he is welcomed with some sugar. Then there is a ceremonial bath, before which the sister will apply perfumed oil to his head, arms, and back. After the bath, she puts *kumkum* (a dot of red powder) on his forehead and moves a lamp in a circular motion before him to ward off evil. He then gives her a present. After the midday feast he is free to return home. The custom is based on the legend that Yama dined on this day at the house of his sister Yamunā. He was pleased with the welcome he received, so he said: 'Let every man dine at his sister's house on this day each year.'

The festival of Dīvālī is a joyous occasion during which there should be light in every heart as there is light everywhere else.

Sikhs share the Dīvālī celebrations. Like *Baisākhī and Māghī, Dīvālī was a festival ordained by Gurū *Amar Dās for Sikh congregations. According to tradition *Bhāī Buḍhā completed his reading of the *Ādi Granth on Dīvālī and Gurū *Hargobind was released from Gwālior gaol. See MANĪ SIṄGH.

P. V. Kane, *History of Dharmaśāstra* (v/1; 1958).

Dīvān (Urdū, Pañjābī, 'court, congregation'). Sikh assembly for worship, which takes its name from the royal audience of the Mughal emperors. The *sangat gather for worship in the *gurdwārā. See also KĪRTAN.

Divination. The art or skill of divining (*sc.*, by use of 'divinity' or deity) that which is unknown—e.g.

the future, the identity of culprits, lost items, the best partner for marriage, etc. Divination may be entirely divorced from the gods, and usually is undertaken by recognized and designated specialists who use mechanical means or manipulative techniques. J. Collins (*Primitive Religion*, 1978) attempted a classification of ten methods: (i) by dreams; (ii) by presentiments; (iii) by body actions; (iv) by ordeals; (v) by possession; (vi) by necromancy; (vii) by animals or parts of dead animals; (viii) by mechanical means, using objects; (ix) by patterns in nature; and (x) by observing other patterns, e.g. that death always comes in threes. See also ASTROLOGY; MAGIC; Index, Divination.

M. Loewe and C. Blacker, *Divination and Oracles* (1981); L. Thorndike, *A History of Magic* . . . (1923–58).

Divine Comedy, The (*La Divina Commedia*). A long poetic work by *Dante, describing the three domains of the life to come, Inferno, *Purgatory, *Paradise. Begun *c.*1307, it was completed shortly before his death in 1321. The poet is guided by Virgil through the circles of *hell to the rim of purgatory, and in company with Beatrice is granted a glimpse of the *beatific vision: 'High phantasy lost power and here broke off, Yet, as a wheel moves smoothly free from jars, My will and my desire were turned by love, The love that moves the sun and other stars.'

Trs., e.g. J. Ciardi (1977), A. Mandelbaum (1982–6), D. L. Sayers, C. S. Singleton (1970–5); J. D. Sinclair; S. Botterill, *Dante and the Mystical Tradition: Bernard of Clairvaux in the Commedia* (1994); P. Boyde, *Dante Philomythes and Philosopher* (1981); S. Ellis, *Hell* (1994); K. Foster, *The Two Dantes* (1977); E. G. Gardner, *Dante's Ten Heavens* (1899, 1973) and *Dante and the Mystics* (1913); C. Grayson, *The World of Dante* (1980); C. Slade, *Approaches to the Teaching of Dante* (1982); P. Toynbee, *Dante Dictionary* (rev. C. S. Singleton, 1968); E. H. Wilkins, *A Concordance* . . . (1965).

Divine Light Mission. Religious movement founded by Sri Hans Ji Maharaj in 1960. When he died in 1966, his son (8 years old) is reported to have said to the mourners, 'You who have been deceived by *māỵa (illusion): Maharaj Ji is here in your midst: Recognize him, worship him and obey him.' He was acclaimed Gurū Maharaj Ji (often Maharaji) and Satguru. The movement was largely run by his mother, Mata Ji, until a schism, with Maharaji renaming his part of the movement Elan Vital. Central to the movement's teachings is a belief that *Buddha, *Kṛṣṇa, *Christ, *Muḥammad, and a number of lesser masters have taught what is termed the Knowledge, which consists essentially of techniques of *meditation. This Knowledge is transmitted from one master to another, each one being the only perfect or true teacher, *satguru*, during his lifetime. Followers or 'premies' believe that Guru Maharaj Ji is the present satguru.

Admitted to the movement through a secret initiation ceremony conducted by an '*apostle' or '*mahātma' authorized by the Guru, premies are introduced first to satsang, and to discourses on such matters as spiritual realization, and then to the Knowledge, both of which, it is claimed, bring mental peace and tranquillity, and in time God-realization. Some premies live in *āśramas, others with their families or a small group of devotees, and all are obliged to renounce *alcohol, drugs, and the eating of meat. The movement is strictly controlled from the top, with little room left for debate or discussion regarding decisions made by the leader.

Divine messengers (the reminders of human destiny in Buddhism: sickness, old age, and death): see DEVA-DŪTA.

Divine right of kings. A high view of monarchy resting on biblical texts which associate kings closely with God through their anointing. Because of this sacramental association, the early view held that the character of the king was irrelevant: the virtue lay in the office, not in the person. Thus even under a bad ruler, only passive obedience, not active rebellion, is appropriate. However, under the Stuarts in 17th-cent. England, and under Louis XIV and his successors in France, greater emphasis was laid on the authority of the monarch in person: the king was outside the scope of human law, since he received authority directly from God; yet he was also responsible for the welfare of the people. Nevertheless, even if there was dispute about how effectively he was doing this, disobedience was not other than disobedience against God. In the homily, *Against Wilful Rebellion* (1569), it is maintained that a bad monarch is God's punishment against a sinful nation. The execution of Charles I did not break the hold of this belief (indeed, it contributed to the view that Charles I was a *martyr, to be remembered as such in the **Book of Common Prayer*); it persisted as a motive for many of the non-Jurors. They refused to accept the accession of William and Mary, on the ground that this involved breaking their previous oath to James II and his successors. The divine right of kings meant that at most they could engage in passive obedience to the usurper. Nine *bishops (including the *archbishop of Canterbury, W. Sancroft) and about 400 priests were deprived of their posts. Sancroft perpetuated the succession of non-juring bishops by securing the *congé d'élire from James II in exile. Gradually the non-Jurors were absorbed into the Anglican Church, the last bishop, Robert Gordon, dying in 1779.

Divorce: see MARRIAGE.

Divya-Prabandham (Tamil hymns and poems): see NAL-ĀYIRA-DIVYA-PRABANDHAM.

Divya-siddhis. Praeternatural powers in Hinduism arising through meditation, which may nevertheless be highly dangerous—either physically to the meditator, or by way of distraction, as of a child by toys.

Divyāvadāna. One of the earliest Buddhist literary compositions in the *Avadāna style, being a collection of moral stories relating how good and evil deeds receive their appropriate retribution in the course of time. The text is divided into thirty-eight sections, varying in literary quality, which were arranged in their present form some time between 200 and 350 CE. The work is in Skt. and most probably belongs to the *Sarvāstivāda school of Buddhism. It includes many of the stories found in the **Avadāna-śataka*. No Eng. tr. of the text is presently available.

Djinn (fiery spirits in Islam): see JINN.

Dmigs pa (component in Tibetan Buddhist meditation): see VISUALIZATION.

Dō (Jap., *michi* or 'way'; Chin., *tao*). Used in Japan to identify some particular practice or discipline as religious; as a spiritual path. The term was borrowed out of similar usage in China (*tao*) and came to be associated not only with all the religions of Japan (e.g. *Shinto as shin-dō or kami-no-michi, the 'way of the *kami'; Buddhism as *butsudō, or the 'way of *buddha'), but also the fine and the martial arts (e.g. *gadō*/*kadō*, or the 'way of flowers' (*ikebana); *chadō, of tea; and *kendō, of the sword). In general, an external skill is attained which helps the realization of an internal spiritual refinement. The room or hall where these are practised is known as dōjō.

Docetism (Gk., *dokeō*, 'I seem'). The doctrine that the humanity and sufferings of Christ were apparent rather than real. A tendency to this view may be inherent in all 'high' *christology, and has been discerned, e.g. in the gospel of John. More specifically the name Docetai was used from the 2nd cent. CE to refer to those *gnostics who claimed that the crucifixion was an illusion, since Jesus' body was not susceptible to suffering. The view that Jesus miraculously escaped death on the cross (such as, on the usual or orthodox understanding of the Arabic, in the Qur'ān, 4. 157) may also be termed docetic.

A. Grillmeier, *Christ in Christian Tradition* (1975).

Doctors of the Church. Title given by the Roman Catholic Church to certain *saints who were also outstanding theologians. The first to be named were *Gregory the Great, *Ambrose, *Augustine, and *Jerome, by Pope Boniface VIII in 1298. In later times the list has been gradually increased to over thirty.

The title *doctor* is also unofficially used with distinguishing adjectives for the various *scholastic teachers, e.g. *Doctor Angelicus* (Thomas *Aquinas), *Doctor universalis* (*Albertus Magnus), etc.

Doctrine of the Mean. Eng. rendering of **Chung Yung*, one of the group of *Four Books in the *Confucian Classics. Like the **Great Learning* (*Ta Hsüeh*) it was extracted from the *Records of Rites* (**Li Chi*) by the *neo-Confucians of the Sung dynasty (960–1279) because of its relevance to their pursuit of sainthood through self-cultivation. The text deals with the existential situation of humans as moral beings in a moral universe, and the burden on the noble individual (*chün tzu*) to act and live accordingly. This expressed exactly the religious philosophy of the neo-Confucians.

Trs.: E. R. Hughes (1943), Hung-ming Ku in Lin, Yutang (ed.), *The Wisdom of China and India*, (1942), J. Legge (1892); see also Wei-ming Tu, *Centrality and Commonality* (1976).

Doenmeh (Turk., 'apostates'). Followers of the Jewish false *messiah, *Shabbetai Zevi, who converted to Islam. Shabbetai Zevi himself converted to Islam in 1666, and a small group of his disciples felt it was their duty to follow his example. Without renouncing their Judaism, they were outwardly keen Muslims. After the death of Shabbetai, their activities were centred in Salonika, where Shabbetai's brother-in-law, Jacob Querido, was pronounced to be a reincarnation of Shabbetai. By the 1720s, there were three Doenmeh sects, the Izmirim, the Jakoblar, and the Karakashlar, probably numbering about 600 families. They concealed their activities both from the mainstream Jewish community who described them as 'minim' (sectarians), and from Turkish society. They seem to have believed that Shabbetai, as the messiah, had opened up a 'spiritual *Torah' in place of the Mosaic *covenant. They were generally believed to be sexually promiscuous and orgiastic ceremonies were claimed to have taken place on the Spring *Festival, Hag ha-Keves (Festival of the Lamb); but such accusations are common against *new religious movements. Although compelled to move from Salonika in 1924, and despite widespread *assimilation, the sect is still in existence.

Dōgen Kigen, Zenji (1200–53). Founder of the *Sōtō Zen school in Japan and a major figure in Japanese intellectual history. Dōgen came from an aristocratic family which suffered a decline due to the shifting political situation, and he entered the Mount Hiei *Tendai Shū monastery at the age of 13. Here he was assailed by 'the Great Doubt': if, as the *sūtras maintain, all beings are endowed with the buddha-nature, why is such strenuous effort and training necessary to attain enlightenment? He left and studied Zen under *Eisai (1141–1215), but went to Sung China in 1223 for further study. There he became a disciple of Jü-ching (Rujing) (1163–1268) of T'ien-t'ung-ssu, attaining enlightenment by realizing the truth of 'Mind and body dropped off; dropped off mind and body'. He received from Jü-ching the seal of recognition (*inka-shōmei). In 1227 he returned to Japan and embarked on a mission to spread Zen, but, frustrated in his plans because of oppositions from various quarters, he retreated to present-day Fukui Prefecture where he founded *Eihei-ji. He devoted his life to the training of his disciples and the writing of his major work, *The Treasury of the Eye of True Dharma* (*Shōbōgenzō*) in ninety-five chapters (of which **Genjō-Kōan* is an especially revered part). His sayings are collected in *Eihei Kōroku*, and his rules of discipline for the community are in *Eihei Shingi*. His introduction to *zazen is in *Fukan Zazengi*. He was given the posthumous name and title of Busshō-dento Kokushi in 1854, and of Jōyō Daishi in 1879.

Dogen is recognized as a towering figure in the development of Zen. His name is linked especially to the practice of zazen—indeed, his way is known as exactly that, *shikan taza*, zazen alone. Remembering the example of *Bodhidharma, he taught his disciples to seek enlightenment in this way:

If you wish to attain enlightenment, begin at once on zazen. You need a quiet room, with food and drink in moderation . . . Bring to rest the ten thousand things. Don't think of good or evil, don't judge right or wrong, maintain the flow of the mind, will and consciousness, bring to a stop all desire, all concepts, all judgements. To sit properly, put down a thick cushion and on top of that a second (round one). Sit either in the full or half cross-legged position. . . . Robe and belt should be loose but in order. The right hand is on the left foot, the back of the left hand rests on the palm of the right. The two thumbs are in juxtaposition. The body is upright, not leaning to left or right, forward or backward. . . . The tongue is against the palate, lips and teeth are closed, the eyes are always open. Now that the body is in order, regulate the breathing. If a desire arises, note it and send it on its way. If you practice in this way for a long time, all attachments will be forgotten, and concentration will come naturally. That is the art of zazen; and zazen is the *Dharma Gate of great peace and joy.

The Chinese figures at the end expressing rest and joy were vital for Dogen: they are the *natural* condition of humanity, not something alien that has to be struggled for. Dogen explained the 'flow of mind' by quoting the master Yüeh-shan Hung-tao: 'A monk asked him, "What does one think about while sitting?" He replied, "One thinks about not-thinking (*fu-shiryo*)." "How does one think of not-thinking?" "Without thinking (*hi-shiryo*)." '

Dogen did not deny the importance of religious ritual or devotion to *Buddhas and *bodhisattvas—indeed, he said the opposite: without a proper sense of gratitude and reverence, it is impossible to develop the buddha-mind. Equally, his way is not one of escape from the world: zazen is the root of an all-embracing ethic of compassion: 'There is an easy way to become a Buddha: abstain from all evils, do not cling to birth and death, work in unwearying compassion for all sentient beings, respect those over you, sympathise with those under you, neither detest nor desire, neither worry nor weep; that is what is called "Buddha". Do not search beyond it.' The truth is that in religion, ritual, and ethics, provided these are rooted in zazen, one is always in the midst of realizing the one buddha-nature (*bussho; *śūnyatā; *tathāgata-garbha). This is most profoundly worked out in Dogen, who made a simple but all-important shift from the formula he inherited, and thereby solved 'the Great Doubt'. Whereas it had been said that all things *have* the buddha-nature, he stated that all things *are* the buddha-nature. There is nothing to do but realize what you already are—and always have been. There is not an 'x' to which is added a buddha-nature; there is only what there is, devoid of characteristics, despite superficial appearances to the contrary. But the buddha-nature is not of such a kind that one can say it is 'no-kind'; and Dogen devoted patient and sophisticated analysis to the distinctions. In a radical application of *anicca/anitya, Dogen pointed out that impermanence is the buddha-nature:

The very impermanence of grass and trees, of woods and forests, is the buddha-nature. The very impermanence of humans and things, of body and mind, is the buddha-nature. All things are impermanent because they are the buddha-nature. Because it is the buddha-nature, supreme and complete enlightenment is impermanent. *Nirvāna itself, because it is impermanent, is the buddha-nature.

For the same reason, Dogen denied the reality of the experience of time, since there never can be a before or after in that which is without exception the same buddha-nature: being is time and time is being (*uji*). In all things and in all experiences, the buddha-nature can be realized, especially by not trying to realize it.

Hee-Jin Kim, *Dogen Kigen* . . . (1975); Y. Yokei, *Zen Master Dogen* (1976); Eng. tr. Masunaga Reiho, *A Primer of Soto Zen* . . . (1972); T. Cleary, *Record of Things Heard* (1960); F. D. Cook, *How to Raise an Ox* . . . (1978). N. Waddell and M. Abe, 'Fukanzazengi', *Eastern Buddhist* (Oct. 1973).

Dogma (Gk., 'opinion'). Originally a good or acceptable opinion of philosophers, it became also a decree of a public or political authority; in that latter sense it is found in both Septuagint and New Testament. In Christian history (attaining among *Roman Catholics a formal definition at the First *Vatican Council) it is a truth revealed by God and presented to the Church for belief, either through a *council or a *pope or the *episcopacy. It thus has a status and authority beyond that of doctrine, which is the teaching (often systematic) of truth and hence its content.

A. Dulles, *The Survival of Dogma* (1971); W. Kasper, *Dogma unter dem Wort Gottes* (1965).

Dōjō (room for dō): see DŌ; ZENDŌ.

Dokusan (Jap.). The meeting of a Zen pupil with his instructor, in private (as opposed to the group training sessions). The content of dokusan is necessarily secret, for it is the relation of heart-mind to heart-mind in a creative unity which is idiosyncratic to a particular partnership. Nevertheless, some of the exchanges (*mondō) ended up as *kōans, which give some idea of the content. Only one who has received the seal of recognition (*inka-shōmei) can be the senior partner. The dokusan is no longer prevalent, except in the *Rinzai school.

Dōkyō (Japanese Zen monk): see ICHIEN.

Dōkyō Etan (teacher of Hakui): see HAKUIN.

Doleantie (Dutch Reformed separation): see DUTCH REFORMED CHURCH.

Dome of the Rock (Arab., Qubbat al-Ṣakhra). A Muslim building which covers the rock from which *Muḥammad is believed to have ascended to heaven. The Night Journey (*isra') and the Ascent (*mi'rāj) are not described in detail in the *Qur'ān (see 17.1 and 53. 12–18), but they are much elaborated in *ḥadīth. From the Rock on which the earth is founded (*eben shetiyyah), Muḥammad was taken by *Jibrīl through the seven heavens to the furthest limit. The Rock split at that moment, because it longed to follow Muḥammad to heaven. His footprint can still be seen. The building is also known (piously, but unhistorically) as the Mosque of 'Umar. It is magnificently decorated (the gold leaf on the Dome was restored in 1994), with calligraphic exposition of texts from the Qur'ān, including some about 'Īsā (Jesus). Its octagonal shape became the pattern for sanctuaries and tombs throughout the Muslim world, and even (following the brief period when the Christian crusaders controlled Jerusalem and the *Templars turned the building into a church) some churches: one survives in the chapel of Castle Tomar in Portugal, and another in Segovia in Spain.

Dominic, St (1170–1221). Founder of the *Dominicans. Born in Old Castile, he became a *canon regular in Osma. With his bishop, Diego d'Azevedo, he initiated a new style of evangelization in Languedoc, characterized by humility and rigorous poverty. From this evolved the Order of Preachers, which he established in 1215. He yearned to spend himself utterly in the spiritual service of others, an ideal he expected his friars to share. Contemporaries found him generous and friendly, and noted his extreme fervour in prayer. Though he encouraged his friars to trust in divine inspiration, he also insisted on serious theological study. He was canonized in 1234: feast day, 7 Aug.

S. Tugwell, *Saint Dominic* (1995); 'Notes . . .', in *Archivum Fratrum Praedicatorem*, 65 (1995) 5–168.

Dominicans. The 'Order of Friars Preachers', founded by St *Dominic in 1215 and confirmed in 1216. From the first foundation in Toulouse it spread rapidly; today its members work in most regions of the world. The goal of the order is to proclaim the word of God by preaching and teaching. It espoused *mendicant poverty, simplified conventual life and study as its main observances. A major emphasis in its work has been on theological study; some of the church's greatest teachers and intellectuals, such as *Albertus Magnus and Thomas *Aquinas, have been Dominicans. Dominicans were used by *popes in various ways (e.g. as *crusade preachers and *inquisitors). In the 16th cent., the Dominicans gave a lead in defending the rights of the American Indians and contributed to the development of international law. The legal constitution of the Order, which balances central authority and decentralization, has been much admired. In spite of periodic tensions between the claims of regular observance and those of the apostolate, between spiritual aspirations and practical charity, the order never split. There are also monasteries of enclosed nuns under the jurisdiction of the order, and a large number of congregations of active sisters attached to the order, though juridically independent. There are also Dominican lay fraternities and secular institutes. See Index, Dominicans.

B. Ashley, *The Dominicans* (1990); W. Hinnebusch, *Dominican Spirituality*, (1965); *The History of the Dominican Order* (1965, 1973); S. Tugwell (ed.), *Early Dominicans* (1982); M.-H. Vicaire, *Saint Dominic and His Times* (tr. 1964).

Dominus vobiscum (Lat., 'the Lord be with you'). A formal Christian greeting, used especially in the *liturgy.

Donation of Constantine. A spurious document designed to strengthen the authority of the church and of Rome, purporting to report how Constantine conferred on Pope Sylvester I (314–35) the primacy over other sees and secular rule in the W. Empire, and also the authority to judge the clergy. The document came to be treated as authoritative even by opponents of the papacy, and was used by popes from 1054 on. It was proved to be spurious in the 15th cent.

Donatism. A *schism in Christian N. Africa in the 4th cent. The Donatists refused to accept the *consecration of Caecilian as *bishop of Carthage in 311 because his consecrator had been a *traditor* (one who had given up copies of the Bible for confiscation) in the recent persecution of Diocletian. The local bishops consecrated a rival to Caecilian, and he was soon succeeded by Donatus, from whom the schism is named. The Donatists claimed that a holy church required worthy ministers for the validity of the *sacraments; accordingly they also demanded the rebaptism of Catholics joining their church. Their opponents, especially *Augustine, held that the unworthiness of ministers did not invalidate the sacraments, since their minister was Christ. The Donatist church repeatedly lost its case before official inquiries (313, 314, 316, 411) and was occasionally persecuted, but persisted until the Islamic conquest of the 7th–8th cents. To some extent its strength derived from regional feeling against Rome and economic insecurity in the countryside.

W. H. C. Frend, *The Donatist Church* (1952).

Dönmeh (followers of Jewish false messiah): see DOENMEH.

Donne, John (1571/2–1631). Christian *Metaphysical poet and priest. Brought up a Roman Catholic, he became an Anglican in the 1590s, after studying at

Oxford and possibly Cambridge. After secular employment as a private secretary and as a literary controversialist, he was ordained in 1615, becoming Dean of St Paul's in 1621. He wrote both love poetry and religious verse, and gained fame as a preacher. All his writing is characterized by bold use of imagery and delight in paradox: the ingenious love poet becomes an explorer of the paradoxes of God's mercy and grace.

Door gods. Three Chinese tutelary deities, derived, traditionally, from three officials of the emperor T'ang Tai Tsung (d. 649), of whom the best known was Wei Cheng. When the emperor was afflicted by bad dreams, the three officials stood outside his door to ward off visiting spirits. They were later replaced by painted representations, and can be found in this form on the doorposts of Taoist temples, and sometimes of homes.

H. J. Wechsler, *Mirror to the Son of Heaven* (1974).

Dorje (Tib., *rdo-rje*). 'Lord of stones'. It was originally the thunderbolt (*vajra*) weapon of the Hindu god *Indra, and thus the source of the name for *Vajrayāna Buddhism. The dorje became identified with the immoveable and indestructible, as a diamond, and from there it shifted to the clear, translucent essence of all reality, which is emptiness of all qualities, *śūnyatā. In Tib. Buddhism, the dorje is the masculine symbol of the skilful (*upāya) path to enlightenment, while the ritual bell (*drilbu*) is the feminine symbol of the path of wisdom (*prajña).

Dort, Synod of: see DUTCH REFORMED CHURCH.

Dosa or **dveṣa** (Pāli, Skt.). Ill-will, hate; with attachment (*rāga) and delusion (*moha) forming the three dispositions of mind which, according to Buddhism, produce bad *karma. It can be directed upon oneself as well as others, and manifests itself as anger and injurious action. Whereas rāga arises from attraction, dosa arises from aversion to things. It is counteracted by the meditation on loving-kindness (*metta).

Dōshō (629–700). Japanese Buddhist monk who founded the Hossō school. While under instruction in Yogācāra (*Vijñānavāda) under *Hsüan-tsang (Jap., Genjo), he was directed toward the *Southern school of Zen. On his return to Japan, he established the first Zen meditation hall at *Nara, but the Hossō school did not secure a wide following in Japan. Hossō is 'the dharma-characteristics' school: it maintained that all appearances are reducible to the consciousnesses, which in turn are necessarily of the same nature. It was one of the six schools of the Nara period (710–94).

Dositheus (1641–1707). Orthodox patriarch of Jerusalem from 1669. His best-known achievement was the Synod of *Jerusalem convened in 1672 to resist Protestant influence in the Greek Church. The decrees of the Synod are also known as the 'Confession of Dositheus', and form an important Orthodox dogmatic text. His patriarchate was also marked by various reforms, and more especially by his vigorous defence of the Greeks against the Latins, as in the dispute with the Franciscans over their rights to the Holy Places.

Dōsojin (Sino-Jap., *dō*, 'way', + *so*, 'ancestor', + *jin*, 'deity'). A Japanese folk deity, especially associated with crossroads, mountain passes, and village entrances, attested from medieval times to the present, and having a complex syncretistic history. Probably in origin Dōsojin represents a very ancient belief in a sacred power which controlled and promoted fecundity in humans. As such it is connected in obscure ways with phallic and other sexual symbols and ritual practices which sought the cosmic powers' co-operation in the dangerous course of conception, childbirth, and child-rearing. It has no mythology which can be said to have originated with it, although later scholars and perhaps popular tradition have linked it with a number of classical *Shinto deities mentioned in **Kojiki* or **Nihonshoki*. Among these are Sarutahiko, the deity of the crossroads who sought to block the descent of *Ninigi to earth and later became his guide. This deity is described as having a very long, phallus-like nose. Again, Dōsojin is associated with the deified stone with which the primordial father *Izanagi sought to block the path from the land of death when pursued by his enraged spouse Izanami. The stone was thus associated with Izanagi's fecundating power, by which he sought to counter the powers of death let loose upon the earth. The name Dōsojin seems to come partly from this Shinto tradition (road or path deities) and partly from Chinese folk belief in ancestral influence upon the health and prosperity of subsequent generations. Stones carved with human couples and labelled 'Dōsojin' can still be found in Japan and are thought to be guardians of marital harmony and fecundity. Further complicating the picture is the amalgamation of Dōsojin and the Buddhist Jizō (*Kṣitigarbha), the *bodhisattva who leads the spirits of dead children to the land of the dead and ameliorates their sufferings there, widely venerated in simple roadside shrines containing a stone Buddha-image, or just a stone.

Dostoevsky, Fyodor Mikhailovich (1821–81). Russian novelist. Born in Moscow, he read widely in European literature as a youth, but in 1838, under parental pressure, he began training as a military engineer. He abandoned this in 1843 with the success of his first novel, *Poor Folk*. In 1849, he was arrested for suspected revolutionary activity and condemned to death (or at least was taken to the scaffold and to the last moments before execution before the true sentence of four years in prison and four years as a private in the Siberian army was read out). He was released from the army in 1858. The immediate fruit of this experience was his remarkable *House of the Dead* (1861). Other novels followed which display a profound understanding of the depths of the human soul. *Notes from the Underground* (1864) sets rational egoism (which proffers reasons for treating others as instruments) against irrational selfishness which treats others as enemies. On his own account, the censors prevented him including the third option which might have rescued his anti-hero, the force of Christian love: 'Those swines of censors! Where I mocked and sometimes blasphemed for form's sake—that is allowed; where I deduced from this the need for faith and Christ, that is suppressed.' But Dostoevsky did not restore the suppressed passages when later he might have done so. *Crime and Punishment* (1866), *The Idiot* (1868), and *The Devils* (also translated as *The Possessed*, 1871) led up to his great achievement, *The Brothers Karamazov* (completed in 1880; the notebooks for all four of these novels have been published by E. Wasiolek, 1967–71). Amongst much else, *The Brothers Karamazov* sets the dissolute father Karamazov against the admirable Father Zossima, for whom true goodness, which he represents, issues in happiness and joy: 'People are made for happiness . . . All the righteous, all the saints, all the martyrs, were happy people.' With the Slavophils, Dostoevsky venerated the *Orthodox Church, and was deeply impressed by *Staretz Amvrosy whom he visited at Optina. But his sense of goodness was neither facile nor naïve. He saw human freedom as something so awesome that most people are ready to relinguish it. This is epitomized in the Legend of the Grand Inquisitor, which follows Ivan's probing question to Alyosha, whether, if he foresaw the extreme suffering of even only one child, he would create a cosmos. Alyosha concedes that he would not, but suggests that Ivan has left out Christ. Ivan tells his story of the Grand Inquisitor to show how the Catholic Church has subjected Christ to its own ends: the miracle, mystery, and authority rejected by Christ in the wilderness are made instruments by the Church in order to take away from people the burden of free will and choice. Christ refused to rob people of their freedom, leaving them open to achieve that victory of beauty which some lives then achieve: 'The awful thing is that beauty is mysterious as well as terrible. God and the devil are fighting there, and the battlefield is the human heart.' In his speech accepting the Nobel Prize for Literature, *Solzhenitsyn quoted Dostoevsky, 'Beauty will save the world.' But the Church, in contrast, has continued, as Dostoevsky feared to the last that it would, on its path of authority and control.

P. Conradi, *Fyodor Dostoevsky* (1988); J. Frank, *Dostoevsky* (biography in continuing vol., 1977–86); A. B. Gibson, *The Religion of Dostoevsky* (1973); M. V. Jones and G. Terry (eds.), *New Essays on Dostoevsky* (1983); S. Linner, *Starets Zosima in 'The Brothers Karamazov* . . . (1975); E. Wasiolek, *Dostoevsky: The Major Fiction* (1964).

Douai. Town in N. France. In the 16th cent., when it formed part of the Spanish Netherlands, Douai was a gathering place for English *recusants. William Allen established a college there in 1568 to train clergy for the English *mission, and a translation of the Bible, still known as the Douai version (though much of the work was done at Rheims where the college was from 1578 to 1593, hence Douai-Rheims), was begun there.

Double predestination (of both condemnation and salvation): see PREDESTINATION.

Double truth (levels of truth appropriate for the capacity of different people): see IBN RUSHD.

Douglas, Mary (anthropologist): see SACRED AND PROFANE.

Doukhobors (Russ.). 'Spirit-fighters', a Russian sect of unknown origin, which seems to have appeared among peasants in the district of Kharkov, moving later to the Caucasus. They called themselves 'the People of God', and were called by their opponents 'doukhobors', i.e. spirit wrestlers. Its members believe in one God manifested in the human soul in memory (Father), reason (Son), and will (*Holy Spirit), have an adoptionist (*adoptionism) understanding of *Christ, believe in *transmigration of the human soul, and adopt an allegorical understanding of the *scriptures and Christian *dogmas. They also reject the notion of property, and registration of birth, death, and marriage, at times have embraced pacifism, and have been accused of moral laxity. Attracting the hostility both of the government and of the Orthodox clergy, they several times experienced exile. They found sympathy from *Tolstoy, who, with the *Quakers, arranged for most of them (*c*.8,000) to emigrate to Cyprus and Canada at the end of the 19th cent., where most survive—few only in Russia.

G. Woodcock and I. Avakumovic, *The Doukobhors* (1968).

Do ut des (reciprocal understanding of sacrifice): see SACRIFICE.

Dov Baar of Lubavitch (son of founder of Ḥabad): see ḤABAD.

Dov Baer of Mezhirech (d. 1772). An early *ḥasidic leader. A *Talmudic and *kabbalistic scholar, Dov Baer was generally recognized as the successor of the Baal Shem Tov (*Israel ben Eliezer). He lived an *ascetic life and, by his saintliness, set a pattern for future *Zaddikim (Ḥasidic leaders). He sent messengers to spread his teaching, and, under his leadership, Ḥasidism spread through Lithuania, the Ukraine, Poznania, and Poland. His doctrines have been preserved through collections of his sayings and through the works of his disciples. His activities were strongly condemned by the *Orthodox in Vilna, who pronounced a ban of excommunication (*ḥerem) on the movement, and this is said to have hastened Dov Baer's death.

He is also known as 'the Great Maggid' because of his powerful preaching and aphorisms: 'What sin have I committed that I should be so popular?'; 'A person does not own his soul, so if he bestirs himself to worship God, it is God bestirring his own possession'; 'Expect to be ferociously opposed: thieves hold up those who have jewels, not those driving a muck-cart.' His teachings were collected after his death in *Maggid Devarav le-Ya'aqov* (1781). Central is his affirmation that 'God fills all worlds: no space is unoccupied by him.' One must 'see through' the surface appearance of things to perceive the divine energy which infuses all things. As with other Ḥasidim, he emphasized the importance of cultivating joy and happiness in the presence of God.

M. Buber, *Tales of Hasidim* (1964).

Dove. A bird of the pigeon family. Much symbolism is focused on the dove which ancient natural history (wrongly) regarded as a gentle and humble bird, noted for its fidelity. As the bird that returned to the *ark with an olive-branch, it is a symbol of peace (cf. Genesis 8. 11); as the bird that descended on Christ at his baptism, it is a symbol of the Holy Spirit (cf. Mark 1. 10). The dove is also a symbol of the Church, the faithful human soul, or divine inspiration. The 'eucharistic dove' was a popular vessel in medieval Europe for the *reservation of the Blessed Sacrament.

Dowie, John Alexander (1847–1907). Founder of the 'Christian Catholic Apostolic Church in Zion'. An Australian *Congregational minister, he moved to the USA in 1888 after a personal healing experience. There he established divine healing homes, and then in 1896 his own healing and *adventist church in Chicago. Infant *baptism was disallowed as unscriptural, and a vegetarian ethic banned *alcohol, tobacco, doctors, and medicines. In 1901, he moved with some 5,000 followers and established Zion City, north of Chicago, where he ruled as First Apostle, and *Elijah the Restorer. Through his journal *Leaves of Healing*, and through missionaries, his influence reached many countries overseas, especially S. Africa. He was deposed shortly before his death, after which the Church suffered divisions. A continuing community of several thousand includes some Navajo Indians, but the Church no longer rules Zion City as a theocracy.

Doxology. A short hymn ascribing glory (Gk., *doxa*) to God, as in the hymn verse beginning 'Praise God from whom all blessings flow'. In the *eucharist the doxology is the ending of the eucharistic prayer. See also GLORIA, for the lesser doxology.

Dōzoku-shin (Sino-Jap., *dozoku*, 'family', + *shin*, 'deity'). A class of native Japanese deities, belief in whom combines social, geographical, and consanguinary relationships. Dōzoku is the extended family in traditional Japan, always consisting of a *honge*, or main family, and a number of branch families reckoned through the male line of descent. In addition, often a number of fictive branch families are included because of historical association of long standing. But dōzoku is also the smallest cultic unit, in that worship of the dōzoku-shin is only open to family membership. The character of the dōzoku-shin varies, but there are two primary types: the most basic is a survival of the ancient *uji-gami* (see *kami), the clan deity who was believed to be the prime ancestor and founder of the clan; but in many cases the ancestral character of the deity has been obscured by adoption of *hito-gami*, or borrowed deities, who, because of greater prestige or power, have replaced the older figure. Traditionally all members of the dōzoku live in the same village, so that family rituals can be carried out in a spirit of mutual co-operation. Thus dōzoku-shin may be said to combine *ancestor reverence with a sense of the sacredness of locality.

Dragon Gate Caves: see LONGMEN CAVES.

Dragon Gate school (Taoist movement): see CH'ÜAN-CHEN TAO.

Dragon kings (Taoist mythological figures): see LUNG-WANG.

Dragons (Chinese). These are imagined by the Chinese as supernatural expressions of natural forces, sky or water animals with 'horns of a deer, head of a camel, abdomen of a cockle, scales of a carp, claws of an eagle, feet of a tiger, and ears of an ox', in serpentine or curved form such as a rainbow. One of the twelve branches of the *calendar, the dragon has the ability to change shape, and is associated with the thunder and rain, east, wood and wind, Spring, the ruling dragon, the male yang (*yin-yang) principle of the *Tao; it appears also in the *feng-shui (geomancy), where it is united with the yin tiger or, coming from the sky or beneath the sea, it is married to humans. The 'dragon kings' who have jurisdiction over rain and funerals, are known as *Lung-wang. See also LUNG.

The Dragon Boat Festival (Tuan Yang Chien) takes place on the fifth day of the fifth lunar month, and commemorates the death by drowning of Chu Yüan (? 3rd/late 4th cent. BCE). He is said to have committed suicide as a protest against corruption in government, and against the incessant conflict of the warring states.

W. Eberhard, *Chinese Festivals* (1952).

Drama (religious): see THEATRE AND DRAMA.

Draṣṭṛ. The one who looks on, the true self in Hinduism, which observes the phenomenal involvement in the world, without getting entangled in it.

Draupadī. Also called Kṛṣṇā, the heroine of the *Mahābhārata*, princess of Pāñcāla. Born from a sacrificial altar, she is said to be an incarnation of the Goddess *Śrī (Prosperity). Arjuna wins her in marriage by a feat of archery, but it is soon agreed that all five brothers will share her equally in an unusual polyandrous marriage symbolizing the unified Pāṇḍava kingship and the Pāṇḍava–Pāñcāla alliance. During the great *Mahābhārata* dice game, Draupadī is wagered by a desperate Yudhiṣṭhira, and insulted by the *Kauravas. The *Kurukṣetra war is as much the Pāṇḍavas' effort to avenge the Kauravas' affront to Draupadī as to regain their lost kingdom. Outside the *Mahābhārata*, Draupadī is known as a S. Indian village Goddess.

Dravya (Skt., 'substance'). In Indian religions and philosophies, a term for the basic constituents of reality. The concept gave rise to philosophical debate and was a central factor in doctrinal divergence. For example the dualist *Śaiva Siddhānta maintained that the pollution (*mala*) covering the soul (*paśu*) was an eternal substance (dravya), whereas the monistic *Kashmir Śaivism denied this. In the *Nyāya-Vaiśeṣika tradition, substance is one of the six categories (*padārtha*), itself subdivided into nine types which are themselves categorized according to whether they are material or immaterial substances. The material substances comprise the elements earth, air, fire, and water along with the 'inner instrument' (*antaḥ karaṇa*, namely *ahaṃkāra, *manas, and *buddhi), while the immaterial substances comprise time (*kāla), space, ether (*ākāśa), and individual souls (*ātman). The former are transient, the latter eternal. The Nyāya-Vaiśeṣika also categorize substance according to size, thus material substances are either atomic (*aṇutva*) and particular or conglomerations of atoms, whereas immaterial substances are ubiquitous. God (*Īśvara) is a special kind of soul and is therefore a substance (indeed, there was debate as to whether Īśvara constituted a tenth type of substance). The *Advaita Vedānta philosopher *Śaṅkara criticized the Nyāya-Vaiśeṣika contention that substance and quality are distinct categories (*Brahmasūtra-bhāṣya* 2. 2. 17), maintaining that in reality there is only a single substance, namely *Brahman. Thus Advaita Vedānta argues for a unique substance, while Nyāya-Vaiśeṣika calls for a plurality of substances. Jainism maintained that everything is either substance or modification (*paryāya*), there being five substances: matter (*pudgala*), soul (*jīva), space or 'ether' (ākāśa), activity (*dharma), and inactivity (adharma). Time (kāla) was added later. For Jains, dravya represents the materiality of the cosmos from which the *jīva seeks to be emancipated. It is basically opposed to *bhāva, but for laypeople dravya must be related to bhāva, especially in ritual, as the base from which the ascent to *mokṣa necessarily begins. Dravya is thus related to bhāva in ritual. Early Buddhism denied the idea of substance, all objects being a linguistic construction.

Dreaming or **dream-time.** The sense of identity, in Australian aboriginal culture, with the primordial guarantee of life and land by commanding figures (deities), together with the actions which sustain that identity and relatedness. Many different terms (e.g. *alcheringa*, *bugari*, *djugurba*) express this sense of reverent relatedness to the land and the conditions of its peace and prosperity. The 'dream-time' is the state in which those of the present-day live, in the company of the ancestors, in this ideal (but realizable) state. The connection is often made real through a *totem figure. The term 'dream-time' was (apparently) first used by B. Spencer and F. J. Gillen, *The Northern Tribes of Central Australia* (1904).

Dreams. The interior consequences of continuing brain activity during periods of sleep; day-dreaming arises from the cessation (or suppression) of ordinary modes of consciousness or attentiveness, allowing other modes and contents of thought to take place. Both forms of dream have been important in religions, the former because it allows the possibility of insight, information and warning that would not otherwise be accessible, the latter because it exists on the edge of trance states and altered states of consciousness. Organized and systemic religions tend towards official disapproval of claims resting on dreams, since they lie outside official control. But at a popular level, dreams offer an avenue to the unknown: The connection of dreams with *divination is already apparent in the study by Artemidorus, *Oneirocritica* (2nd cent. CE; see C. Blum, *Studies in the Dream Book of Artemidorus*, 1936). Despite the disrepute into which S. *Freud brought dream studies (see especially *The Interpretation of Dreams*, 1900) through his narrow-minded understanding of human nature, the self-awareness of dreams has been increasingly encouraged in more recent psychotherapy, both religious and secular, as an access to latent and residual states of dis-ease.

J. S. Lincoln, *The Dream in Primitive Cultures* (1935); B. Tedlock (ed.), *Dreams in Cross-Cultural Perspective* (1984).

Dream yoga (one of the six teachings of Nāropa): see MILAM.

Dreidel (spinning top): see ḤANUKKAH.

Drepung monastery: see LHASA.

Dress: see HABIT, RELIGIOUS; and Index, Dress.

Dreyfus case. Alfred Dreyfus (1859–1935) was a Jewish officer in the French army accused of betraying French military secrets to the Germans in 1894 and condemned to life imprisonment. He remained on Devil's Island in solitary confinement until 1898, when it was discovered that much of the evidence against him had been forged. At a retrial, the military court refused to admit the error, and found

Dreyfus guilty, but with extenuating circumstances. He was sentenced to a further ten years imprisonment. Two weeks later he was pardoned and reinstated in the army. The affair prompted anti-Semitic riots on the one hand, and enormous liberal agitation on the other, including an open letter from the novelist Émile Zola. Dreyfus was completely exonerated, but the whole affair made a strong impact on the Jewish community and led Theodor *Herzl in particular to *Zionism. Among Roman Catholics, the affair (apart from evoking the latent anti-Semitism in pre-*Vatican II Catholicism) is usually held to have retarded the adaptation, which the Church eventually had to make, to being an independent institution within a secular society in France.

P. Birnbaum (ed.), *La France de l'affaire Dreyfus* (1994).

Dṛg-Dṛśya-Viveka. A Skt. Hindu work of forty-six ślokas, which initiate into the deepest understanding of *Vedānta. Attributed to (among others) *Śankara, the most probable author was Bhārati Tīrtha (14th cent. CE).

Drilbu (ritual bell): see DORJE.

Droṇa. In the **Mahābhārata*, a *brahman, the weapons-teacher of both the *Pāṇḍavas and the *Kauravas. He was *ayonija* ('born from no womb') (*Mahābhārata* 1. 61. 63, etc.); rather, he was born in a trough (*droṇa*), from the seed of the seer Bharadvāja, spilt at the sight of the *apsara Ghṛtācī. Said to be a partial incarnation of *Bṛhaspati, priest of the gods, Droṇa's own priestly (brahmanical) role appears to be connected with the *Mahābhārata*'s conception of war as sacrifice. Droṇa's battle standard bears the brahmanical insignia of an altar and black antelope skin.

The figure of Droṇa typifies, in his long-standing enmity against the Pāñcālas, the brahman/*kṣatriya rivalry in the *Mahābharata*, as well as reflecting its interest in questions of *dharma. Like *Bhīṣma, he is a respected elder, who nevertheless fights on the 'evil' side in battle. In addition, Droṇa has the peculiarity of being a fighting brahman, a contradiction brought out even more clearly in the ambiguous nature of his son, Aśvatthāman.

Dṛshti-pravāda-aṅga: see AṄGA.

Drugpa Künleg or **'Brug-pa Kun-legs** (1455–1570). Tibetan, best-known as one of the 'holy fools' of Tibet. He was trained in the Drugpa school of the *Kagyüpa, but he adopted the ascetic life of a wanderer, which was nevertheless demonstrated in consumption of beer and women—in a quasi-*Tantric style of non-attachment even in action. He is believed to be the reappearance in bodily form of Saraha and Śavaripa, two *mahāsiddhas.

Druzes (Arab., Durūz). Members of a religious group numbering about half a million, mainly in S. Lebanon, SW Syria, and Hawran district of Israel/N. Palestine. A closely knit community, mainly landowners and cultivators, the Druzes practise a secret religion which conceals doctrines and practices from the uninitiated, a fact which has prevented until modern times a clear understanding of its origins, doctrines, and practices.

The Druze religion was derived from *Ismāʿīlīya, and was established in the 11th cent. in Cairo, Egypt, around the cult of the Fāṭimid *Khalīfa al-Ḥākim (disappeared in 1021 (AH 411)). Al-Ḥākim was first recognized as incarnate reason by al-Darazī, from whom the name Druze derives. The two most sacred books of the Druzes are *Al-Naqd al-Khafi* (Copy of the Secret) by *Ḥamza b. ʿAlī, often regarded as founder of the faith; and *Al-Juz'al-Awwal* (Essence of the First) by al-Muqtāna Bahā'uddin (d. 1031 CE), its main propagator. They called themselves *Muwaḥḥidūn* ('Unitarians') and found strong support amongst the Shiʿā Ismāʿīlīya of Wadi-al-Taym at the foot of Mount Hebron. Persecution in Egypt and Syria by the orthodox forced them to adopt *taqīya (dissimulation) and also to make their creed hereditary; no one could be permitted into the fold or be permitted exit from it. Ḥamza b. ʿAlī abrogated the *sunna of Prophet Muḥammad and introduced many precepts and dogmas alien to Islam. The main dogmas of the Druze faith are: confession in the unity of God; belief in successive manifestations of the deity (or of the Universal Intelligence, al-ʿAql al-Kulli) in human form; acceptance of al-Ḥākim as the last and greatest of these divine incarnations; recognition of five ministers who manifest aspects of the Divine Essence, Ḥamza b. ʿAlī being the supreme saint (*wali-al-zaman*); belief in *metempsychosis and in predestination; and observance of the seven precepts of Ḥamza who, on behalf of al-Ḥākim, absolved his followers from the obligations of Islam. Ḥamza's seven precepts are: veracity in speech; protection and mutual aid to the Druze community; renunciation of all forms of former worship and false belief; repudiation of Iblīs (the devil) and all forces of evil; confession of the divine unity in humanity, concentrated in 'Our Lord', Ḥākim, who is not dead but hidden; acquiesence in all al-Ḥākim's acts no matter what they be; and absolute submission and resignation to his divine will.

The Druze community is divided into *ʿuqqāl* ('intelligent'), the initiates; and *juhhāl* ('ignorant'), the uninitiated lay majority. The *ʿuqqāl* alone participate in the religious meetings, which are held at night from Thursday to Friday. Before admission to the *ʿuqqāl* circle, the aspirant is subjected to rigorous trial and probation. The most meritorious of the *ʿuqqāl* become *Ajāwīd* ('Perfect') and they lead an almost ascetic life. The Ajāwīd is the religious chief and focus of devotion for the Druzes. The Druze community possesses the character of a religious fraternal order that acts in unison during times of crisis, and it is this quality that has enabled them to survive to the present day.

P. K. Hitti, *The Origins of the Druze People and Religion* (1928); S. N. Makarem, *The Druze Faith* (1974).

Dry shit stick (person, acc. to Zen, attached to this world): see KAN-SHIKETSU.

Du‘ā’ (Arab., *da‘ā*, ‘call’ or ‘summon’, whence *da‘wa). In Islam, supplication or personal invocation, ‘calling upon’ *Allāh; private request or prayer, as contrasted with *ṣalāt, the ritual worship. Although more personal, and generally for some special occasion or intention, du‘ā’ does not really correspond to spontaneous or mental prayer in the Christian tradition. There are set formulae and texts which are considered appropriate or efficacious, and rules to be followed by the individual or group making the du‘ā’. In the *Qur’ān, Allāh is described as the One who hears the du‘ā’ of the supplicant—as in the case of *Ibrāhīm, who says: ‘My Lord is the hearer of prayer (du‘ā’)’, and again: ‘O our Lord! accept my prayer (du‘ā’ī)’ (14. 39–40). Du‘ā’ which asks for deliverance from an oppressor may contain a curse on the wrongdoer. See also ISTIKHĀRĀ. Examples of prayer from many different sources are to be found in C. Padwick, *Muslim Devotions: A Study of Prayer Manuals in Common Use* (1961).

Dualism (Lat., *dualis*). The conjunction of two (usually opposing) entities or principles. The term was used by T. Hyde in 1700 (*The Ancient Persian Religions*) to describe the conflict between good and *evil (Ormazd and Ahriman) in *Zoroastrianism; but it is used of many religious and philosophical dualities, e.g. mind and matter (as in Cartesian dualism), material and spiritual (as in *Manichaeism), *yin and *yang. In most religions, a modified dualism appears, which expresses the basic human experience of oppositions (right/left, male/female, up/down, good/evil, etc.), and of contest between them, but which sees the ultimate source and/or resolution as unitary. Thus, to take one example, the belief that the universe is derived from two ultimate sources is not intrinsically or biblically Jewish. Nevertheless, conflict stories of creation (*cosmology) are included in the Bible; and Greek dualistic thinking influenced such philosophers as *Philo. But Judaism is a monotheistic system, and the *rabbis insisted that both the *yeẓer ha-ra‘ and the yeẓer ha-tov (the evil and good inclinations) are ultimately the creation of God. In some Jewish writings, such as those of the sect of the *Dead Sea Scrolls, a mitigated dualism appears in that contrasts are made between flesh and spirit, darkness and light, impurity and purity. Similarly, the *kabbalists often described the *sefirot (God’s emanations) in dualistic terms. Nevertheless, it was always emphasized that there is one unity which is the source of everything.

U. Bianchi, *Il dualismo religioso* (1983).

Dudjom Rinpoche (head of Tibetan Buddhist order): see BDUD-JOMS RIN-PO-CHE.

Dukhobors (Russian sect): see DOUKOBHORS.

Dukkha or **duḥkha** (Pāli, Skt.). The second of the *Three Marks of Existence in Buddhism and the subject of the *Four Noble Truths. There is no satisfactory equivalent to the word in English, and it has been variously translated as ‘suffering’, ‘unsatisfactoriness’, ‘frustration’, ‘unhappiness’, ‘anguish’, ‘ill’, ‘dis-*ease*’ (opposite: *sukha*, ‘ease, well-being’): it is essentially transience and all that arises from the experience of transience. For the Buddhist, the primary characteristic of all sentient existence is the fact of dukkha. This is signified in the first of the Four Noble Truths—‘there is dukkha’; this means that the truth about suffering is the fact of its universality. The Buddha is said to have made no other claim for himself than that he was a teacher of the fact of ‘suffering’, its origin, cure, and remedy (the Four Noble Truths).

Traditional Buddhism defines ‘dukkha’ in a number of different ways. 1. In the Four Noble Truths, dukkha is represented as ‘birth, old age, sickness and death; grief, sorrow, physical and mental pain, and despair; involvement with what one dislikes and separation from what one likes; not getting what one wants; in summary, the five groups of grasping (*pañc’upādānakkhandhā*, cf. SKHANDHA) are a source of suffering’. 2. Threefold dukkha is ordinary mental and physical pain (*dukkha-dukkhatā*), that is, pure or intrinsic suffering; suffering as the result of change (*viparināma-dukkhatā*), owing to the impermanent and ephemeral nature of things; and suffering due to the formations (*saṅkhāra-dukkhatā*; *sankhara), that is, the sense of *saṃsāra or our own temporality and finiteness. 3. It is maintained that all sentient beings—whether gods, humans, *pretas, animals, or inhabitants of hell—are subject to dukkha. Gods suffer the least in the hierarchy of different beings, and the inhabitants of hell the most. Humans, lying midway, experience a mixture of suffering and happiness; this makes them the best-fitted to achieve escape from saṃsāra, because the mixture gives them both the opportunity and the impetus to discriminate the nature of reality.

Although Buddhism asserts the universal nature of ‘suffering’ as a cardinal doctrine, this does not mean to say that it denies or fails to appreciate the existence of happiness (*sukha*) where it is found. What it does maintain is that people’s conception of happiness, their attachment to and yearning after it, will sooner or later only bring sorrow because the objects of happiness are impermanent (*anicca). Consequently, because it is short-lived, happiness itself is only a further testimony to the truth of dukkha.

It is by comparison with *nirvāna that everything is apprehended as suffering. Therefore, the ‘truth’ of suffering is something which has to be discerned or discovered, like the truth of anicca. Hence it figures as a subject of contemplation (*dukkhānupassanā*, cf. VIPASSANĀ) in Buddhist meditational practice. The discernment of 'suffering' involves precisely the recognition that even the things which appear to provide happiness are ephemeral and that attachment to them therefore only yields suffering. But so ingrained is our desire for mundane happiness, it is said, that it is harder to comprehend (*paṭivijjhati*) the truth of the universality of suffering than to split a single hair into one hundred strands.

Buddhism rejects the theories that dukkha is either 'self-caused' (the Upaniṣadic view) or 'caused by another' (e.g. God or Chance) but holds instead that it is 'caused' or has an 'origin'. The character of this causation is set out in its doctrine of *paticca-samuppāda. The notion of 'vicarious suffering' is central within *Mahāyāna Buddhism. The *bodhisattva volunteers to remain within the round of rebirths and postpone his entry to *nirvāna in order to identify with and help alleviate the suffering of other sentient beings. The most cherished example of 'vicarious suffering' in the Buddhist tradition is the *Jātakamālā tale of how the Buddha, in a former existence, was a tigress who gave her own body as meat for her cubs to feed upon, to save them from starvation. The tradition of 'voluntary sacrifice' as a feature of Mahāyāna Buddhism was instanced in recent times by Vietnamese monks and nuns publicly burning themselves to death as an act of witness to the suffering inflicted on the people by the war.

Duleep Singh (son of Rañjit Siṅgh): see RAÑJĪT SINGH.

Dumézil, Georges (1898–1986). French scholar of Indo-European thought and structure. Much influenced by *Durkheim and Mauss, he made wide-ranging comparative studies, seeking to demonstrate the underlying importance of tripartite structures and functions (for an example see PĀṆḌAVAS), and also of paired relations between heavenly beings and earthly counterparts. Thus fertility gods are related in ritual and social ways to farmers and herdspeople, warrior gods to warriors, sovereignty gods (powerful in magic, etc.) to priests and through them to rulers. The history of *mythology displays, in his view, a rejection of a supreme skygod in favour of a tripartite division of power which reflects the social organization of the peoples concerned. This common distribution, into three supreme gods beneath whom pantheons are organized, was broken up in various (again recurrent) ways. Thus the ambiguities of the heavenly powers are commonly articulated (e.g. the warrior god is both powerful in protection but fierce in anger against wrongdoing). Ritual and sacrifice emerge to control these ambiguities. Although accused of imposing patterns and 'shaving the corners', his views were influential for a time in the study of religion.

G. Dumézil, *The Destiny of a King* (1973); *The Destiny of the Warrior* (1970).

Dunhuang (town in NW China): see TAN-HUANG.

Duns Scotus, Johannes (*c*.1265–1308). Medieval Christian philosopher. Born in Scotland, he became a *Franciscan when very young and studied at Oxford and Paris. He lectured in Cambridge, Oxford, and Paris, and in 1307 was moved to Cologne where he died. His principal work was his commentary on the *Sentences* of *Peter Lombard, which survives in three versions. An extremely subtle thinker, he was critical of the *Thomist system, using the distinction between what God could logically have done and what he actually did (the doctrine of the 'two powers') to undermine the primacy of reason, replacing it with a primacy of will or love. In his metaphysics he developed the idea that the principle of individuation is not matter, but a kind of individual uniqueness (*haecceitas*), that by virtue of which any being is *this* being: 'By grasping just what things are of themselves, a person separates the essences from the many additional incidental features associated with them in the sense-image, and sees what is true . . . as a more universal truth.' He was also the first great theologian to defend the doctrine of the *Immaculate Conception of the Blessed Virgin.

A. B. Wolter, *Duns Scotus* (1962).

Duperron, A. (French translator): see DĀRĀ SHIKOH.

Duran, Simeon Ben Zemah, known as **Rashbaz** (1361–1444). *Rabbinic authority and philosopher. He emigrated from Majorca to Algeria in 1391 where he became *Chief Rabbi in 1408. He was regarded as a great legal authority and was well-known for his careful judgements. As he described it, 'In reaching my decisions, I do not grope like the blind along the wall, for I give a decision only after studying the case carefully. I have never given a decision which I later retracted'. He respected, but did not always agree with, the philosophy of *Maimonides. He attacked the doctrine of the *Karaites and engaged in disputations with Christians. His major philosophical work was *Magen Avot* (Shield of the Fathers), written as an introduction to **Avot*. He maintained that many so-called *dogmas were open to argument (and substantiation), but that Judaism must insist on three foundational beliefs which were not to be disputed: the existence of God; the divine origin of *Torah; and reward and punishment after death.

I. Epstein, *The Responsa of Rabbi Simeon b. Serriah Duran* (1930).

Durgā. The one who is difficult to approach, among Hindus the fearsomely protective aspect of *Śiva's consort (see Mahādevī in *Devī), a slayer of demons who threaten the *dharma of creation. Notable among these was the buffalo-demon *Mahiṣa, who could not be slain by man or beast. Durgā being both a woman and divine, slew the creature easily (hence her name, Mahiṣāsuramardiṇī), using weapons given her by the gods. She also killed Śumbha and Niśumbha, demon-twins; and, with her help, the demons Tuṇḍa and Vituṇḍa met their end.

Durgā, the ten-armed, is shown carrying a variety of weapons, and accompanied by her vehicle, a lion or tiger, symbolic of her ferocity and aggression. She is supported by eight demonesses (*yoginī), whose task it is to finish the destruction. Durgā is considered as another aspect of *Kālī, and, like her, is a popular deity in Bengal, where Durga-pūja (see P. V. Kane, *History of Dharmaśastra*, v, 1975), celebrated Oct.–Nov., is a major festival. Unlike Kālī, Durgā is shown as beautiful, though warlike. See also ŚAKTI; DAŚAHRĀ.

M. C. P. Srivastava, *Mother Goddess in Indian Art, Archaeology and Literature* (1979); J. N. Tiwari, *Studies in Goddess Cults in N. India* (1971).

Durkheim, Emile (1858–1917). Only rivalled by Max *Weber as the father of social science. He founded the Année Sociologique, a group which made major contributions to the study of religion, 'représentations collectives', modes of thought, and forms of classification. Jewish by birth, Durkheim adopted a positivistic attitude towards religion. His classic *The Elementary Forms of the Religious Life* (1912; tr. 1915) utilized Australian aboriginal material to attempt to show that religious life originates as a response to experiences of society: 'It is unquestionable that a society has all that is necessary to arouse the sensation of the divine in minds.' This theory of replication is bound up with the claims that religious phenomena symbolize social structures, the symbolic process functioning to restate, and so reaffirm, the values which sustain the social order. Durkheim's sociological determinism—both with regard to religion, and, more generally, with regard to the ways in which society ultimately forms people's minds and controls their behaviour—is not dissimilar to *Marx's emphasis. It has also been highly influential, as witnessed by the works of M. Douglas and P. Berger, and by the fact that it is now generally taken for granted that comprehensive understanding of religions involves a social perspective. See also SACRED AND PROFANE (including his definition of religion).

R. Bierstedt, *Emile Durkheim* (1966); W. S. F. Pickering, *Durkheim on Religion* (1975); *Durkheim's Sociology of Religion* (1984).

Durvāsas. In Hindu mythology, the son of Atri and Anasūyā. He is also regarded as a manifestation of *Śiva. There are various versions of the myth which explains his connection with Śiva. According to one, *Brahmā, *Viṣṇu and Śiva all tried in vain to tempt Anasūyā's virtue. Her chastity won from them the boon that each of them should be born as her son; she thus gave birth to *Soma (representing Brahmā), *Dattātreya (Viṣṇu), and *Durvāsas (Śiva). In epic and *purāṇic mythology seers are notoriously irascible, but Durvāsas is regarded as the most irascible of all, and there are many stories in which someone who slights him is doomed to suffer as a result of his curse.

Duryodhana. In the *Mahābhārata*, the eldest of the *Kauravas. From one perspective, Duryodhana is absolutely evil: towards the Pāṇḍavas he shows unremitting hostility, and he is violently stubborn in his refusal to accept *Kṛṣṇa as god. On the other hand, the epic expresses some admiration for Duryodhana, and the celestials applaud him when he states, at the time of his death, 'Who indeed has met a better fate than I?' Duryodhana's weapon is the mace; his arch-enemy the Pāṇḍava Bhīma. His magical ability to hide himself under the surface of a pool of water after most of his army has been destroyed suggests serpent affiliations, and has been identified by some as an Indo-European theme.

Dusserah. Alternative spelling of Dassera, nine-day Hindu celebrations: see FESTIVALS AND FASTS.

Dutch Reformed Church or **Hervomde Kerk.** Major Christian (Protestant) Church, originally in the Netherlands, but spreading to other parts of the world through missionary work. It was organized during the revolt of the Low Countries against Spain in the 16th cent. The Spanish were gradually driven out of the north, but the south remained Catholic, hence the persisting divisions. Many different threads of Reformed theology and church order were entangled together until the Synod of Dort (1618–19) led to the character of the Church as Calvinist in theology and Presbyterian in government. The synod produced the Canons of Dort, which became one of the doctrinal foundations of the Dutch Reformed Church. The synod was involved in political contest, and was directed against the *Arminians or Remonstrants (so-called because in 1610 the followers of Arminius issued a remonstrance against unconditioned *predestination). The Remonstrants refused to attend a synod packed with their opponents and were duly condemned on the basis of their writings. The Canons were written to express the strong Calvinist position, of the total depravity of humanity after the *fall; of unconditional election (no action can persuade God's choice); of limited *atonement (Christ died only for the elect); of irresistible *grace (it cannot be rejected by the elect); and of the perseverance of the saints (one cannot repudiate election). The Remonstrants were ejected, and in the 17th cent., during a period of Dutch power, the Dutch Reformed Church was of central importance. A decline during the 18th cent. culminated in the French 'liberation' after the French Revolution, which resulted in the privileged status of the Church being drastically reduced. During the 19th cent., the prolonged struggle between conservative and modernizing tendencies led to several splits (e.g. the *Afscheiding* ('Separation') in 1834, the *Doleantie* in 1886, forming with the earlier separatists the Gereformeerde Kerk), but the Dutch Reformed Church remained the largest. Meanwhile it had spread with colonization to the E. and W. Indies, and through settlement to the USA. Its most prominent settlement was in S. Africa, from 1652. When the Cape Colony came under British control, the Dutch, the Boers, trekked north and formed their own states, Orange Free State and Transvaal—carrying with them strong biblical associations with the move into a Promised Land. Equally biblical in its claimed foundations was the view (originally formulated in the Netherlands to justify the apparent anomaly of divisions in that territory) of apartheid. Apartheid as a religious doctrine rests in a debate in one of the 19th-cent. separatist churches, the Nederduitse Gereformeerde Kerk: in 1829, its synod declared that people of different colours (i.e. races) should receive communion together, but in 1857 its synod ruled that because of the weakness of some, segregation should be allowed. In 1974, the NGK produced a report, *Human Relations and the South African Scene in the Light of Scripture*, which offered justification of apartheid, but in 1982, the World Alliance of Reformed Churches declared apartheid to be heretical. An amended position appeared in *Church and Society* (1986), but it did not eradicate apartheid. At this stage, two groups (Nederduitsche Hervomde Kerk and Afrikaanse Protestante Kerk) seceded and refused to attend the consultation in 1990 which led to the Rustenburg declaration. This made a confession of guilt for the damage done by apartheid and proposed forms of restitution: 'Some of us are not in full accord with everything said in this conference, but on this we are all agreed, namely, the unequivocal rejection of apartheid as sin.' Thus all the churches have increasingly opposed apartheid, and much of the opposition within S. Africa has come from Christians.

Dūtī pūjā (Skt.). In *Tantrism, worship of a beautiful woman involving the use of the *pañcamakāra. The woman is ritually purified and elevated to the status of the Goddess (*Devi) by means of meditation and *nyāsa. Then each part of her is worshipped in turn, especially her face, breasts, and generative organ (*yoni). She is offered *alchohol, cooked meat, and fish, and the ritual culminates in the adept having sexual intercourse (*maithuna) with her. This union is symbolic of the union of *Śiva and *Śakti, and the bliss of sexual intercourse is said to be akin to the bliss of the absolute state.

Dvaita (Skt., 'dual'). The Hindu philosophy and religious attitude which maintains that the subject–object, *I–Thou, relationship between a worshipper and God persists, even in the final union; and that such union cannot be regarded as absorption (in contrast to *Advaita). Naïve duality must of course be transcended. This position is particularly associated with *Madhva, and is then known as Dvaitavedānta.

Dvārakā: see SACRED CITIES, SEVEN.

Dvātriṃśadvara-lakṣana (Skt.). The thirty-two marks of a *cakravartin, especially of one who is a *buddha of universal teaching. The marks feature in representations of the Buddha, and (with some of the common variants) are: (i) the cone-shaped (round in China, flame-shaped in Thailand) rise on the crown of the head; (ii) the lock of white hair between the eyebrows, from which streams enlightening wisdom; (iii) eyelashes like a bull's; (iv) blue (or black) clear eyes; (v) a voice like Brahmā's; (vi) broad tongue; (vii) saliva improving the taste of food; (viii) gums like a lion's; (ix) white teeth; (x) even teeth; (xi) forty teeth; (xii) strong shoulders; (xiii) erect body; (xiv) upper body (or jaw) strong as a lion's; (xv) well-formed shoulders; (xvi) well-shaped hands, shoulders and head; (xvii) soft skin; (xviii) a body giving off rays of illumination; (xix) a golden-hued body; (xx) thick and curled body hair; (xxi) strong body; (xxii) no narrowing of the penis (or genitals hidden in a sheath); (xxiii) arms (or hands) reaching to the knees; (xxiv) lower body (or limbs) like an antelope's; (xxv) arched feet; (xxvi) smooth (or webbed) hands and feet; (xxvii) curved (or soft) toes and fingers; (xxviii) broad heels; (xxix) long fingers; (xxx) hairy body; (xxxi) level feet; (xxxii) mark of a thousand-spoke wheel on the soles of the feet. For a typical list, see *Dīgha Nikāya* 3. 142. A common feature of Buddha-images is also the elongated ears, produced from the days of his royal upbringing (with gold earrings), and thus symbolizing his renunciation of that life.

Dveṣa (aversion): see ASMITA.

Dvija (Skt.). The twice-born in Hinduism, the members of the three upper castes (*varna).

Dyāl Dās (Sikh reformer): see SIKHISM.

Dyāvā-pṛthivi (Mother Goddess of Hindus): see PṚTHIVI.

Dybbuk (evil spirit in Jewish folklore): see DIBBUK.

Dying and rising Gods. Deities found in the Mediterranean world which suggested a general 'myth and ritual' pattern, which in turn was then applied to many other figures, including *Jesus. The pattern was supposed to be one in which the king represented God in a New Year ritual, in which he was symbolically slain, thereafter rising from the dead: this was supposed to have secured fertility. Figures such as Adonis, Isis and Osiris, Marduk, Tammuz/Dumuzi were claimed for this pattern. This particular instance of a myth and ritual pattern was largely the product of J. G. *Frazer's fertile, but anti-Christian and anti-religious imagination: more attention to evidence has not confirmed the existence of such a pattern.

Dynasties, Chinese. Legendary dynasties are the Three Sovereigns, the Five Emperors. In Ancient China the dynasties are Hsia/Xia (uncertain dates); Shang (Yin) (*c.*1766–1123 BCE); Chou/Zhou (*c.*

1122–256 BCE). The dynasties in Imperial China are as follows: Ch'in/Qin (221–207 BCE); Former Han (206/2 BCE–9 CE); Hsin (9–23); Latter Han (25–220); The Three Kingdoms (Wei, Shu, Wu: 220–80); Chin/Jin (divided, *c.*280–420); The Six Dynasties, with China divided (450–589); Sui (589–618); T'ang/Tang (618–907); The Five Dynasties (907–60); Sung (960–1279); Yuan (1260–1367); Ming (1368–1644); and Ch'ing (1644–1911). The Republic lasted 1912–49 and the People's Republic began in 1949.

Dynasties, Muslim. The dynasties frequently mentioned here are listed in chronological order, beginning with al-Rashidun/ar-Rashidun, the Four Orthodox Caliphs, 632–61 (AH 11–40): *Abu Bakr, 632–4 (AH 11–13), *ʿUmar, 634–44 (AH 13–23), *ʿUthmān, 644–56 (AH 23–35), ʿAlī, 656–61 (AH 35–40). Umayyad (*Damascus), 667–750 (AH 41–132); ʿAbbasid (Baghdād), 750–1258 (AH 132–656); Umayyad of Cordova, 756–1031 (AH 138–422); Fāṭimids (Mahdiya and Cairo), 909–1171 (AH 297–567); Mamluk(e)s: Bahri, 1250–1390 (AH 648–792) and Burji, 1382–1517 (AH 784–922); Seljuq (Persia and Iraq), 1037–1157 (AH 429–552). The Ottoman Empire lasted 1299–1923 (AH 699–1341). Shahs of Persia include: Safavid, 1502–1736 (AH 907–1148), Qajar, 1779–1909 (AH 1193–1327), and Pahlavi, 1925–79 (AH 1344–99). In India dynasties include the Ghaznavid, 976–1186 (AH 366–582), and Mughal (Mogul), 1526–1858 (AH 932–1276). For further detail, see Index, Dynasties.

C. E. Bosworth, *The Islamic Dynasties . . .* (1967).

Dyophysites (Gk., 'two natures'). Those Christians who maintain the *Chalcedon definition of two natures in the one person of Christ, in contrast to *monophysites. In 1984, the long division between the two parties was affirmed by the *pope (John Paul II) and by the Syrian Orthodox *patriarch (Mar Ignatius Zakka II) to have arisen only because of cultural and linguistic differences in terminology.

Dyoya-dṛṣṭi (Skt.). The third eye, or divine-seeing eye, which is located for Hindus between the eyebrows. It is a an organ of direct seeing, but of that which is not open to the five sensory organs. See, in contrast, EVIL EYE.

Dysteleology. A lack of purposiveness or design in the universe. If teleology is regarded as evidence for God's existence, then it would seem that dysteleology is *prima facie* evidence against it. This claim was propounded by *Hume in his critique of the *Teleological Argument for God's existence in his *Dialogues on Natural Religion* (1779). Others have taken an even stronger line, arguing that dysteleology and evil are a grave problem for theism in general, not just for natural theology (cf. J. L. Mackie *The Miracle of Theism*, 1982). Theists argue that dysteleology is only an *apparent* lack of purposiveness, or that it is caused by human sin or evil spirits, or that it is permitted by God as a test. See also EVIL, PROBLEM OF.

Dzogchen (Tib., rDzogschen). 'Great perfection', in the *Nyingma school of Tibetan Buddhism (*Tibetan religion), the highest of the nine *yānas (ways) which lead to perfect completion; and as the highest of the ways, it is also used sometimes as a synonym for Nyingmapa teaching itself. It is known also as *ati-yoga* (Atiyoga, exceptional *yoga), beyond which nothing is required (or indeed possible) in order to reach the goal. Dzogchen is transmitted partly in practice and partly in *tantra texts, in a secret tradition which is taken back to the *Buddha Śākyamuni. According to tradition, it was brought to Tibet by *Padmasambhava; it was reorganized, in a more systematic form, by Jigme Lingpa (1730–98), in a form that continues to the present day. The tantra texts and instructions are divided into three groups: *sems-sDe*, those concerned with the realization of mentality as such (*sems-nyid*); *klong-sDe*, those concerned with the realization of the emptiness of spatial appearances (cf. ŚŪNYATĀ); and *man-ngaggi-sDe*, those which integrate the others and develop meditational techniques for cutting through resistance. The attributes of the three *kāyas* (bodies: see TRIKĀYA) of buddha-realization are achieved as the condition of perfect attainment. Central, therefore, to Dzogchen is the realization that nothing, either mental or physical, has reality underlying its appearance, and that the mind, which cannot be measured or weighed, and is neither square nor round, is the threshold of truth (once it is disentangled from ignorance and delusion) because it is realized as being purely what it is. Dzogchen leads to the direct awareness of 'mind' as it is: the buddha-nature without qualification or attribute.

Tr. of some texts, J. Low, *Simply Being* (1994).

E

E (Jap., 'gather, understand'). An assembly or gathering in Japan, especially for religious purposes, or under a particular teacher. E is the understanding that develops in those circumstances.

E. The name of a putative source used in the composition of the Pentateuch. It is distinguished from J principally because E uses the word *Elohim (of God) where J uses the *tetragrammaton (i.e. Yhwh, transliterated as Jahveh or Jehovah)—hence E and J. See further PENTATEUCH.

East African Revival or **Balokole** (Luganda, 'saved ones'). A widespread Christian renewal movement with several independent origins. In the 1930s it spread among Ugandan *Anglicans and then into Kenya and Tanzania, working alongside the churches and avoiding schism, although meeting at first with a mixed reception from church leaders. It is essentially a lay movement, African in style and control, that has transcended tribal, racial, and church divisions, and has produced its own theology, organization, and hymns; one revival chorus, 'Tukutendereza' ('We praise thee, Jesus'), is now widely known. There has been a non-pentecostal emphasis on spiritual rebirth, repentance, *confession, testimonies, and deliverance through the death of *Jesus. Organization takes the form of team meetings, travelling evangelistic teams, and vast conventions of perhaps 30,000 people. In 1964 there arose a revival within the Revival, known as 'The Awakening', through unease over increasing organization and larger finances.

Easter. The Christian feast of the *resurrection of *Christ. According to *Bede, the name is connected with an Anglo-Saxon spring goddess 'Eostre'. The derivation is uncertain, but some Easter customs, e.g. the giving of eggs as gifts, are certainly pre-Christian. The importance of Easter in the liturgical year is evident in the preparation of *Lent and Passiontide, the ceremonies of *Holy Week, and the following Paschaltide.

The primitive Christian feast known in the 2nd–3rd cents. as the Pasch (Aramaic, *pasḥa*, '*Passover') formed the Christian counterpart to the Jewish festival. It celebrated Christ's death and resurrection together. By the late 2nd cent. it had, however, been removed from the Jewish date and attached to the following *Sunday, except among the *Quartodecimans. The Saturday night was celebrated by the illumination of churches and even whole cities; the *catechumens, after watching all night, were baptized early on Sunday and received Holy Communion.

Since the Council of *Nicaea (325) Easter has been fixed for the Sunday following the full moon after the vernal equinox. In practice the calculation is made with a table (such as the 'Table to Find Easter Day' in the **Book of Common Prayer*) which synchronizes the lunar and solar months. However, there is still a divergence between E. and W. Churches, mainly because almost all Orthodox Churches, even those who otherwise use the Gregorian *calendar, use the Julian date for the equinox. Thus the date of 'Orthodox Easter' sometimes coincides with the W. date, but it is usually one, four, or five weeks later.

The 'paschal vigil' is the principal celebration of Easter in liturgical churches, on the night of Saturday–Sunday. It derives from the early Pasch, but since the 4th cent., with the separate observance of *Good Friday, it has centred on the resurrection alone. About the same time the *paschal candle was introduced. The present Catholic rite includes the blessing and lighting of the candle outside the church; a procession with the candle through the darkened church during which the congregation light candles from it; the Exultet; nine readings from the Bible followed by a sermon; the blessing of the font, a service of baptism, and the renewal of baptismal vows; and the rest of the eucharist.

F. X. Weiser, *The Easter Book* (1954); *Handbook of Christian Feasts and Customs* (1958).

Eastern Catholic Churches: see UNIAT(E) CHURCHES.

Eastern Orthodox (Church). Those Christians who belong to the Churches which accepted the *Chalcedon definition of two natures in the one person of *Christ, and did not depart in the *great schism between E. and W. They are consequently *dyophysite as opposed to *monophysite. The term thus covers much more than the Greek Orthodox Church (for which it is nevertheless sometimes used as a synonym), and slightly less than all E. Christians. See further ORTHODOX CHURCH.

Eastern Paradise (Buddhist world of attainment): see BHAIṢAJYAGURU.

Eastern Rite Catholics. Christians who are in union with Rome, but who have followed rites other than the Latin rite. They are known also as Oriental Rite Catholics.

East Syrian Churches. Collective name for *Nestorian and Chaldaean Churches.

Easy Path: see PURE LAND SCHOOLS.

EATWOT (Ecumenical Association of Third-World Theologians): see LIBERATION THEOLOGY.

Eben Shetiyyah. The rock on which, according to Jews and Muslims, the world is founded. It is to be seen in Qubbat al-Sakhrah, the *Dome of the Rock (known piously, but inaccurately as 'The Mosque of 'Umar'), in *Jerusalem. From the dust of the rock on Mount Moriah Adam was created, and on to it Adam and Eve stepped when they were expelled from the Garden. On this Rock, Israel was founded, because here Abraham bound Isaac for sacrifice, thereby securing the covenant promises to Israel. From this Rock, *Muḥammad ascended to heaven on his Night Journey (*miʿraj): the rock split at that moment because it wanted to follow Muḥammad to heaven; the split can still be seen in the rock.

Ebionites (Heb. *ebyōnīm*, 'poor men'). A sect of Jewish Christians of the early centuries CE. Its nature and history cannot be reconstructed from surviving references. It appears to have existed east of the River Jordan. The sect emphasized the ordinary humanity of *Jesus as the human son of *Mary and Joseph, who was then given the *Holy Spirit at his *baptism; it also adhered to the Jewish *Torah. It is an open question whether they can have been direct descendants of the earliest Jerusalem church. The members were both poor and ascetic, and they remained outside the mainstream of church history. The so-called *Gospel of the Ebionites* (*apocryphal) survives only in quotations. See also ENCRATITES.

A. F. J. Klijn and G. J. Reinink, *Patristic Evidence for Jewish-Christian Sects* (1973).

Ebisu (Jap., of uncertain meaning, possibly 'foreigner'). A Japanese folk deity of good fortune especially associated with occupational success. In some parts of rural Japan, the mountain god or the field god is called Ebisu, while among those who live by fishing, many sea creatures as well as parts of the fishing nets are given this name. In the cities, the Ebisu festival is mostly the concern of merchants, although even here the god is often pictured as carrying a fish. Probably the deity originated in a cult of fishing luck. In some places, even today, at the beginning of the fishing season stones are brought up from the bottom of the sea and set up as Ebisu to be enshrined for the year; again, when casting the net fishermen are wont to shout 'Ebisu!' to invoke the power of the god. The curious fact that floating corpses are often called Ebisu seems connected to the idea of a visitor (foreigner), since all fish are visitors from the vastness of the sea to the shores near which they are caught.

Ecclesiastes (Heb., *Qoheleth*). A book in the Hebrew scriptures. Written by ha-Qoheleth (often tr. as 'the preacher', but more accurately 'the convoker'), 'Son of David, king in Jerusalem', the book is traditionally ascribed to *Solomon and is one of a group, collectively described as the five *scrolls. The writer argues that everything is ordained by God and that ultimately the life of humanity is transient: 'vanity of vanities! All is vanity!' (1. 2); and that 'there is nothing better for a man that he should eat and drink, and find enjoyment in his toil' (2. 24). It was contested whether the book should be included in the *canon of the *Bible (because it seemed to lack a sufficiently religious dimension), yet in fact, in a context where there was not yet a belief in life with God after death, it is a profoundly religious book: it affirms the worth of living life wholeheartedly on the only terms there are, with gratitude that there is life at all: 'A living dog is better than a dead lion!' The impression of scepticism is enhanced in the English by the translation of *ḥebel* as 'vanity': it is a word for 'mist' or 'steam in a bathroom', hence transience. There is much scholarly disagreement as to the origin of Ecclesiastes, but it is generally accepted that it was probably produced in the 3rd cent. BCE.

Ecclesiasticus (book of the Apocrypha / Bible): see BEN SIRA, WISDOM OF.

Ecclesiology (Gk., *ekkesia*, 'assembly'). Originally the study of Christian church architecture, but now reflection on the nature of the *Church. Such reflections are derived from the New Testament image of Christians as the Body of Christ, which was originally a metaphor of organic co-operation under the headship of Christ; but already by the 2nd cent., the metaphor was transposed and became one of an army (i.e. the Roman army), with a hierarchical emphasis. Thus ecclesiology points at one extreme to the hierarchical and authoritarian system of Vatican Catholicism (modified in theory, but not yet in practice, by conciliarity: see ANTIPOPE), and at the other to the *koinōnia* (communion) of the New Testament which is translated into house churches, local gatherings networked into monitoring organizations. Between the two extremes, a clearer understanding of systems and of the conditions of information protection, coding, and transmission suggests the possibility of a radically revised ecclesiology which the hierarchical church will undoubtedly resist.

E. Schillebeeckx, *Church: The Human Story of God* (1989, 1990).

Eck, John (1486–1543). German Roman Catholic theologian and opponent of *Luther. Eck was appointed Professor of Theology at Ingolstadt in 1510, a post he held throughout his life. After the *indulgence controversy, he opposed Luther's teaching, engaged in public debate with him and *Carlstadt at Leipzig in 1519, and exerted his influence to procure their condemnation in the papal *bull

Exsurge Domine of 1520. He wrote against Luther, *Melanchthon and *Zwingli, and defended the papacy. An excellent orator with a fine memory, he actively participated in Colloquies at Hagenau (1540), Worms (1541), and Rattisbon (1541).

T. Wiedermann, *Dr Johann Eck* (1865).

Eckankar (union with God). An occult *new religious movement 'revived' by Paul Twitchell (1908–71) in San Francisco in 1965. Its teaching is *pantheistic: God ('Sugmad') is everything and everywhere, the everlasting 'Eck' or cosmic current. To reach Sugmad one must use what is termed 'soul travel', and this can only be acquired by submitting to the living Eck Master who will burn away the person's debt of *karma. On the death of Paul Twitchell, Darwin Gross received from him the Rod of Power and became the living Eck Master. The movement has many centres in the USA and Europe, and reports a worldwide membership of 50,000 chelas or students.

Eckhart, Meister (*c.* 1260–1327). German Christian mystic. Born at Hochheim in Thuringia, he became a *Dominican at Erfurt as a youth, completing his studies at Paris in 1302. In 1311, after a period as provincial of the Order in Saxony, he returned to Paris to teach. He soon returned to Germany where he became famous as a preacher. Accused of *heresy in 1326, he died during the proceedings. In 1329 John XXII condemned sentences attributed to him as heretical or dangerous. Eckhart's work consists of Latin treatises and German transcripts of his vernacular sermons, from which latter the supposed 'heretical' utterances are largely drawn. His dogmatic work is traditional, even old-fashionedly *patristic, but in the 14th cent., his insistence on the reality of God's gift to humanity of himself in his son, a gift which deifies the human, sounded *pantheistic; conversely, his development of *seelenfünklein*, the spark of the soul, achieving union with God, sounded as though the two are merged:

> The soul may be led so near to God by the body of our Lord that all the angels, not excepting the Cherubim and Seraphim, shall not see any difference. . . . There never was another such union, for the soul is nearer to God than it is to the body which makes us human. It is more intimate with him than a drop of water put into a vat of wine, for that would still be water and wine; but here one is changed into the other so that no creature could ever again detect a difference between them.

Despite his condemnation, his influence, largely mediated by *Tauler and *Henry Suso, was considerable: 'To get into the core of God at his greatest, one must first get into the core of himself at his least; for no one can know God who has not first known himself.'

Meister Eckhart: The Essential Writings tr. and ed. E. Colledge and B. McGinn (1981); J. M. Clark, *Meister Eckhart* (1957), *The Great German Mystics* (1949); M. O'C. Walshe, *Meister Eckhart: Sermons and Treatises* (1979, 1981).

Ecology: see ANIMALS.

Ecstasy (Gk., *ek-stasis*, 'standing out of'). The experience, common in all religions, of being carried beyond ordinary, everyday experience into moments of extreme and intense transcendence. The word is used of such a wide range of such experiences that no common core can be identified. Thus it is used of the out-of-the-body experiences of *shamans, the third (and next to highest stage) of the analysis of mystical union of *Teresa of Avila, trance states, *fanā' among *Sūfīs, the *rapture of spirit possession. The neurophysiology of these (usually) brief states is not yet understood (but see BIOGENETIC STRUCTURALISM), though it is well-known that the inhibition or exclusion of external stimuli (even by the insistent repetition of one stimulus, e.g. by drumming) can lead to dramatic brain consequences, some of which approximate to some of the conditions defined as ecstatic. This inhibition may be achieved by drugs; but those who have experienced states which can claim to be ecstatic report that the differences between induced states and achieved states are, internally, extremely clear. I. M. Lewis, *Ecstatic Religion* (1971) claimed that such religion avoids the relegation of God to remoteness by demonstrating that humans can rise to the divine:

> Shamanistic religions assume . . . that, at least on certain occasions, man can rise to the level of the gods. And since man is thus, from the beginning held to participate in the authority of the gods, there is scarcely any more impressive power that he can acquire. What the shamanistic séance thus protests is the dual omnipotence of God and man. It celebrates a confident and egalitarian view of man's relations with the divine, and perpetuates that original accord between God and man which those who have lost the ecstatic mystery can only nostalgically recall in myths of creation, or desperately seek in doctrines of personal salvation.

The converse is *enstasy.

A. Hultkrantz and E. Arbman (eds.) *Ecstasy, or Religious Trance* (1963–70).

Ecumenical Councils: see COUNCILS (CHRISTIAN).

Ecumenical patriarch. Title of the patriarch of *Constantinople. In spite of its literal meaning, 'universal patriarch', he has only a primacy of honour over the other *Orthodox patriarchs. It was first assumed, in defiance of Pope *Gregory, by John IV (582–95).

Ecumenism or **ecumenicism** (Gk., *oikumene*, 'the inhabited world'). The Christian quest for recovered unity among the many different Churches of Christendom. The Ecumenical *Councils are claimed to represent the mind of the whole Church and thus to have distinct authority. The beginning of the modern ecumenical movement is usually traced to the Edinburgh Conference of 1910, when many (but no Roman Catholic) missionary societies met, at the end of a century of immense but competitive expansion, to explore the nature of mission and the ways to overcome debilitating divisions. The World

Council of Churches, a direct descendant, was formed in 1948: at the Canberra Assembly in 1991, 842 delegates from 317 Churches attended. Initially, the RC Church, believing itself to be already the one united church, held aloof, but after the Second *Vatican Council, authentic marks of grace were discerned in other churches, and a cautious but greater involvement in ecumenism began to take place, especially at the level of ecumenical theology. This preoccupation with internal Christian affairs already began to seem to some parochial, who called for a 'wider ecumenism', one which would explore the relations between religions. Spiritual ecumenism seeks to gather and share the spirituality of separated parts of the Church, or of religions. See Index, Ecumenicism.

G. Cashmore and J. Puls, *Clearing the Way: En Route to an Ecumenical Spirituality* (1990); R. F. Frazer, (ed.), *The Ecumenical Movement: A Bibliography* . . . (1983); E. Hillman, *The Wider Ecumenism* (1968); N. Lossky *et al.* (eds.), *Dictionary of the Ecumenical Movement* (1991).

Eddy, Mary Baker (1821–1910). Founder of the *Christian Science Movement. She was brought up in a New England *Calvinist environment, but reacted against its strong *predestinarianism. After reading of the *healings of Jesus, she was healed from an accident. She had already come to think of her recurrent illnesses as rooted in the mind, and at this point, with the help of a healer, Phineas Quimby, she studied scripture and embarked on a healing ministry. In 1875, she published *Science and Health* . . ., and in 1879, she founded the Church of Christ, Scientist, in Boston. The movement eventually (1891) became the First Church of Christ, Scientist. She started the publication of *The Christian Science Monitor* in 1908. The key to her movement and belief is contained in her statement, 'Both sin and sickness are error, and Truth is their remedy.'

R. Peel, *Mary Baker Eddy* . . . (1966–77).

Edels, Samuel Eliezer ben Judah Halevi (known as **Maharsha**, 1555–1631). Talmudic commentator. He lived successively in Posen, Lublin, and Ostrog, and was the founder of a large *yeshivah. The author of *Hiddushei Halakhot* (Tracts on the Commandments), he was held in high esteem, and on his tombstone was written, 'A holy man . . . His great work was a light to the eyes of the Sages of Israel'. The *Hiddushei* is one of the classics of Jewish literature and is printed in most editions of the Talmud. A further work, *Hiddushei Aggadot*, gives rationalizing exegesis of *aggadot, often explaining otherwise improbable claims as *parables.

Eden (perhaps Heb., 'be fruitful', or Sumerian 'flat plain'). The dwelling place created by God for *Adam and *Eve. According to Genesis 3. 1–22, the first human beings were cast out from Eden once they had eaten the fruit of the tree of knowledge of good and evil lest they also ate from the tree of life and lived for ever. The *rabbis described the ultimate destiny of the righteous as *gan Eden* (garden of *Eden), the opposite of *Gehinnom (as in *Avot* 5. 20). Thus Eden became, in the Jewish imagination, the epitome of perfection: see e.g. Ezekiel 28. 13, 31. 8–10, 36. 35.

Edict of Nantes (decree of toleration): see HUGUENOTS.

Edicts of Aśoka. A collection of inscriptions by the Buddhist emperor of India *Aśoka (*c.*274–232 BCE). A total of thirty-two have been found to date inscribed upon rocks, pillars, and caves in various parts of India. The edicts proclaim Aśoka's policy of rule by *dharma (righteousness) and his belief in the virtues of kindness, toleration, and upright conduct as the means to the happiness and well-being of his subjects both here and in the afterlife: 'This world and the next are hard to gain without great devotion to dharma, great self-awareness, great obedience, great care, great effort: through my instruction, reverence and love for dharma increase each day and will increase' (*1st Pillar Edict*). The Edicts may be more explicit: 'Here no animal is to be killed for sacrifice [cf. AHIṀSĀ], nor festivals [associations?] held . . . Of old many hundred thousand animals were killed in the kitchen of the Beloved of God, but now only three-two peacocks and a deer . . ., and even these may not be killed in future' (*1st Rock Edict*). His vision extended far: 'I am not satisfied with fulfilling the obligations of the state, for I reckon my work to be for the welfare of the whole world. . . . I do all I can, to clear my debt to all beings' (*6th Rock Edict*).

The language of the edicts is Prakrit, the connecting link between the classical language of Skt. and the modern Indo-European languages of India, and two different forms of script are used. Altogether there are sixteen Rock Edicts, three Minor Rock Edicts, seven Pillar Edicts, three Minor Pillar Edicts, two Pillar Inscriptions, and one Cave Inscription.

Tr. in Nikam and McKeon, *The Edicts of Asoka* (1966).

Edinburgh Conference (1910): see MISSION; ECUMENISM.

Edwards, Jonathan (1703–58). American *Calvinistic theologian and philosopher. Following his conversion at Yale, he was ordained into the *Congregational ministry and became pastor at Northampton, Mass., in 1724. His outstanding preaching there led to the 'Great Awakening' in 1734–5, which spread more widely in 1740–1. His *Faithful Narrative of the Surprising Works of God* (1737), which carefully describes the revival at Northampton, was widely influential. He became a close friend of G. *Whitefield who often met Edwards during his frequent visits to America. In 1758 he was elected President of the College of New Jersey (later Princeton), but only served a month before his death. A convinced Calvinist, he devoted much time in his later years to writing, taking every opportunity to oppose *Arminianism and *Socinianism. Several of his major theological works were published posthumously. His classic *Freedom of the Will* was influenced by John *Locke's analysis of the constitution of human nature, but that did not modify his insistence on salvation by sovereign *grace alone: grateful faith, by changing the emotional disposition of human character, can be instrumental in directing history toward its final destiny in the *kingdom of God. But the Calvinist emphasis remains: 'All children are by nature children of wrath, and are in danger of eternal damnation in *hell.' He followed *Aquinas in believing that 'the sight of hell-torments will exalt the happiness of the saints for ever'; and that includes observing the torment of those who have been loved ones on earth: 'Such will be their sense of justice that it will increase rather than diminish their bliss.'

R. W. Jenson, *America's Theologian* . . . (1988); M. X. Lerser, *Jonathan Edwards* (1981); P. Miller, *Jonathan Edwards* and *The Works* . . . (1957–).

Eel-wrigglers (philosophers): see AMARĀVIKKHEPIKAS.

Eger, Akiba ben Moses, known also as **Akiva Gins** (1761–1837). German *rabbi. Despite the opposition of the *reform movement, he became unofficial *chief rabbi of Posen where he established a large *yeshivah. Although he was strictly *orthodox, he made concessions in offering a more modern curriculum in Jewish schools, and he established a number of welfare institutions. Various editions of his *responsa were published both in his lifetime and after his death.

L. Wreschner, *R. Akiba Eger* (1906).

Egeria or ***Etheria, Pilgrimage of.*** An account of the journey of an abbess or nun (probably Spanish) to Egypt, Palestine, Edessa, Asia Minor, and Constantinople at the end of the 4th cent. Places and scenes are identified with the sites of biblical events. Liturgical matters, especially the services at Jerusalem and in the neighbourhood, are described, including accounts of the daily and Sunday night offices, *Epiphany (still at that time the only festival of Christ's birth), *Holy Week, *Easter, and *Pentecost. The text was discovered only in 1884.

Trs. M. L. McClure and C. L. Feltoe (1919), and J. Wilkinson (2nd edn. 1981).

'Ehad mi yode'a (Heb., 'Who knows one?'). A concluding *Passover song in the *Ashkenazi rite. The aim of the concluding songs 'is to keep children awake' (*B.Pes.* 108b). It is a progressive number song and probably originated in Germany in the 15th cent.:

Who knows 13? I know 13! 13 are the attributes of God; 12 are the tribes of Israel; 11 are the stars [that *Jacob saw in a dream]; 10 are the commandments; 9 are the months of pregnancy; 8 are the days before circumcision; 7 are the days of the week; 6 are the Orders of the *Mishnah; 5 are the books of *Torah; 4 are the Mothers of Israel; 3 are the Fathers of Israel; 2 are the Tables of law; 1 is our God in heaven and on earth.

Ehō (contingent and secondary consequences): see SHŌBŌ (2).

Eight auspicious symbols (in Hinduism): see AṢṬAMANGALA.

Eighteen benedictions (part of Jewish prayer): see ʿAMIDAH.

Eighteen Schools of Early Buddhism. According to Buddhist tradition, in the early centuries after the *Buddha's death the original unity of his followers quickly gave way to disagreement and schism, resulting in the formation of eighteen different schools. Eleven of these schools identified themselves with the conservative tradition of the 'Elders' (*Sthaviras), while the remaining seven constituted the innovative movement of the 'Great Assembly' (*Mahāsāṃghikas). These two branches are reported to have gone their separate ways following the convening of a council at Pāṭaliputra to decide the validity of five theses put forward by the monk Mahādeva (see COUNCILS). The schools of the Mahāsaṃghikas were united in their conception of the supramundane nature of the Buddha and elaborated various views in connection with his supernatural powers and the *docetic character of his mission. The schools of the Sthavira tradition were more concerned with the classification and analysis of points of doctrine, and debated amongst themselves on matters such as causation, the duration of phenomena, and the nature of personal identity and continuity. Chief among these schools were the *Theravāda, *Sarvāstivāda, *Sautrāntika, and Vātsīputrīya. Of the eleven schools of the Elder tradition only the Theravāda has survived, while the seven schools of the Great Assembly coalesced in the emergence of the *Mahāyāna.

Eightfold path (Buddhist way): see AṢṬANGIKA-MĀRGA.

Eight immortals (Taoist figures): see PA HSIEN.

Eight liberations (Buddhist meditation exercise): see AṢṬA-VIMOKṢA.

Eight masteries (Buddhist control of perception): see ABHIBHĀVAYATANA.

Eight Trigram Society. A general designation for various religious sects which staged a rebellion in N. China in 1813. The sects, which were closely related to the *millennarian White Lotus tradition, were galvanized into revolt by their belief that the millennium had arrived. See further BOXER REBELLION; and S. Naquin, *Millenarian Rebellion in China* (1976).

Eight Ways (Buddhist control of perception): see ABHIBHĀVAYATANA.

Eight ways of commendation (of the Jain way): see PRABHAVANA.

Eihei-ji. The Zen monastery of Eternal Peace, founded by *Dōgen Zenji in N. Japan, in 1243. With *Sōji-ji, it is one of the two main monasteries of the *Sōtō school. For its uneasy history with its companion monastery, see SŌJI-JI. It is now a major meditation centre, with about 15,000 linked centres worldwide.

Einhorn, David (1809–79). *Reform Jewish theologian. Because he could not find rabbinical employment in Europe on account of his radical views, he emigrated to the United States in 1855 and became *rabbi of Congregation Adath Israel, New York, in 1866. He strongly believed in introducing vernacular prayers and rejected the divine origin of the *Talmud. In his view, 'the doctrinal and moral law of Scripture' is 'the imperishable spirit of Judaism'; other laws are marks of the *covenant, which can change with the times if necessary: 'Like man himself, the child of God, the divine law has a perishable body but an imperishable spirit. The body is intended to be the servant of the spirit, and must disappear as soon as it is bereft of the latter.' It is not possible to reverse the unfolding history of the spirit: 'As little as the ripe fruit can be forced back into the bud or the butterfly into the chrysalis, so little can the religious idea, in its long process from generation to maturity, be bound to one and the same form.' But the cultivation of the spirit in worship and prayer is essential. His prayerbook, *Olat Tamid* (1856) was the model for the later reform *Union Prayer Book*, and his was the dominant voice at the Philadelphia Rabbinical Conference of 1869 which adopted a radical reform stance.

K. Kohler (ed.), *David Einhorn Memorial Volume* (1911).

Ein-Sof (Heb., 'the Infinite'). *Kabbalistic designation of God in his transcendence. The term first appeared in the 13th century in the circle of *Isaac the Blind. It was used to distinguish between God-in-himself and his *sefirot (emanations) by which humanity can know him. Initially, the term described the unlimited (i.e. infinite) range of God's thought. It was then applied to the Being of God as 'that which is not conceivable by thought'. In a loose sense, it might be said to be anticipated in the *Deus absconditus ('hidden God') theme of Isaiah: 'Truly, you are a God who hides yourself.' Yet in fact the kabbalistic understanding went much further, regarding Ein-Sof as so utterly hidden from human comprehension that it is not even mentioned in the Bible. For comparable reticence in other religions, see VIA NEGATIVA.

Eisai or **Yōsai** (1141–1215). A *Tendai monk who established the *Rinzai Zen Buddhist school in Japan. He began his career at Mount Hiei, studying Tendai esotericism, but went to China in 1168 for less than a year, studying *Ch'an and bringing back *T'ien-t'ai texts. He made a second trip to China in 1187 with intentions of going to India, but, unable to do so, he remained in China and studied the Ch'an of Lin-chi under Hsü-an Huai-ch'ang, and received the seal of recognition (*inka-shōmei). He returned to Japan in 1191 and built the first Rinzai Zen temple, Shōfukuji. In spite of the strong opposition from Mount Hiei against the establishment of Zen, he was successful in founding Kenninji (monastery) in Kyōto and Jufukuji in Kamakura. His polemical work, *Kōzen gokoku ron* (Dissemination of Zen for the Defence of the Nation), argues for the need of an independent Zen school, although he himself taught a synthesis of Tendai, esotericism, and Zen. He summarized 'true *dharma' as *en-mitsu-zen-kai*, 'perfect teaching-secret rituals-meditation-precepts'; though he also added, to *zen-kai, hannya* ('wisdom') and *mujokushin* ('flawless mind'). He is also famous for introducing the cultivation of tea (see CHADŌ) to Japan and writing the first book on the merits of tea drinking, *Kissa yōjōki*. He instructed *Dōgen, and for that reason, although his own lineage died out, he is often regarded as the founding figure of Zen in Japan. He was given the posthumous title of Senkō Kokushi.

M. Collcutt, *Five Mountains: The Rinzai Zen Monastic Institution in Medieval Japan* (1981).

Eisegesis (reading meanings into a text): see EXEGESIS.

Eisendrath, M. N. (1902–73). US *Reform *rabbi. While he was president of the *Union of American Hebrew Congregations, he presided over the change in direction of the Reform movement to a new *rapprochement* with tradition. He was also greatly involved in civil rights, social action, and interfaith activities. He was born in Chicago and educated at Hebrew Union College. From 1929 to 1943, he was rabbi in Toronto. In 1943, he took charge of the Union of American Hebrew Congregations, moving it in a Reform direction, especially when he established the Social Action Center in Washington.

Eka (Skt.). One; the unity (*Ṛg Veda* 10. 129) which precedes the manifestations of creation.

Eka (Second patriarch of Ch'an/Zen in China): see HUI-K'O.

Ekādaśi (Skt.). The eleventh day after a full or new moon, when Hindus fast and meditate, especially through the chanting of the name of God.

Ekāgrata (Skt.), 'one-pointedness'). Concentration on a single point in Hindu and Buddhist *yoga, especially *rāja yoga, which controls the fluctuations of the mind (*cittavṛtti*) generated by sense activity (*indriya) and karmic residues (*saṃskāras). Through concentration, all distractions are eliminated and the mind eventually achieves such one-pointedness that *samādhi is reached. Any object can be a locus for developing one-pointedness, whether physical (such as the space between the eyebrows, the tip of the nose, the Buddhist *kasiṇas, etc.) or mental (such as a thought (e.g. 'I am *Śiva'), a *mantra, God (*Īśvara), one's personal deity (*iṣṭadevatā), or inner light).

Eknāth or **Ekanātha** (*c.* 1535–99). *Marāṭhī Hindu scholar and poet. He was born at Paiṭhaṇ in Mahārāshtra. He is said to have been a disciple of Janārdana Swāmī of Devagirī, studied *Jnāneśverī* with him, and wrote many books on the legends from the *Purāṇas.

His most important service to the Marāṭhī language is undoubtedly the editing of *Jnāneśverī*. He obtained the manuscripts written 300 years previously and restored the famous commentary to its original form. He also restored Jñaneśvar's tomb at Āḷandī. He rendered *Bhāgavata* into Marāṭhī, and, when he was nearly 50 years old, he started his Marāṭhī translation of the **Rāmāyaṇa*. He was not able to complete this book, *Bhāvārtha Rāmāyaṇa*. He died at Paiṭhaṇ on the banks of the Godāvarī River, where a temple is dedicated to him.

W. S. Deming, *Eknāth* . . . (1933).

Eko (Jap.). The Buddhist transference of *merit to another, especially through a religious practice or gift (e.g. chanting a *sūtra). It may also be the transference of merit to a *buddha as a gift in order to attain the same state.

Ekoddiṣṭa. Post-Vedic funeral rites in Hinduism, performed after cremation of the body, to unite the deceased person with the ancestors (*pitṛ). After the Vedic view that the deceased joins the ancestors immediately, the belief prevailed that the deceased moves into a liminal stage, first of *ātivāhika śarīra*, 'fire form of body', which is one of great pain. A *pūraka* offering of a ball of rice is made to the *ātivāhika śarīra* which can then become a *preta. To enable the preta to progress, the ekoddiṣṭa rites are observed at six-monthly intervals, culminating in *sapiṇḍī karaṇa*, which transfers the preta into the *pitṛloka* ('domain of the ancestors').

J. W. Bowker, *The Meanings of Death* (1991).

Ekottarāgama (Indian division in Sūtra Piṭaka): see TRIPIṬAKA.

Ekwan (Korean monk): see SANRON.

El (Heb., 'God'). The name of the supreme God of the Canaanite pantheon (known e.g. from the *Ugaritic texts), which became the name of the God of Israel. In the early years of the settlement in Canaan of the kinship group, the descendants of Jacob, El was worshipped in his relation to places and powers of many kinds—e.g. El Elyon ('most high'), El 'Olam ('enduring'), El Shaddai ('Almighty'), El Berit ('of the covenant'); and also in the reinforcing form (plural), Elohim. The relation of Yhwh (transliteration uncertain, but conventionally Yahweh: see TETRAGRAMMATON) to El/Elohim was initially one of subordination: El delegated responsibilities and nations to lesser gods. But gradually Yhwh, Israel's God, displaced El as *the* God, assuming both function and status: Yhwh no longer 'sits in the council of El' but becomes 'who El is'. The distinction between El and Yhwh is discernible in the structure of the *Pentateuch, even though the 'Four Document hypothesis' (with *E and J two sources) has been increasingly questioned.

M. H. Pope, *El in the Ugaritic Texts* (1955).

Elan Vital (name of religious movement): see DIVINE LIGHT MISSION.

Elder

Judaism A group of respected citizens who form a consulting body. According to Deuteronomy, the elders of a city are involved in the laws of *blood *redemption (19. 12), expiation of an unsolved murder (21. 3), of a rebellious son (21. 19), of defaming a virgin (22. 15), and of *levirate marriage (29. 9). The elders of the people seem to have been regularly consulted by the king (see 1 Kings 20. 7) and participation in the counsel of the elders was regarded as a great honour (see Proverbs 29. 7–17). In the *Talmudic period, the term was used of scholars, particularly members of a *bet din ('The elder is none other than a sage'), and the word means 'one who has acquired wisdom' (*B.Kid.* 32*b*).

Christianity In the New Testament period, elders (Gk., *presbyteroi*) were church officials with a collective authority and oversight (they are called *episkopoi*, cf. *bishops, in Acts 20. 28, Titus 1. 5–7) over local congregations. In *Reformed churches, there are both teaching and ruling elders.

Elders of Zion, Protocols of the Learned. An *anti-Semitic forgery. The book purports to be the report of a conference of world Jewry in which the leaders plot world domination. Even the anti-Semitic Tsar, Nicholas II, perceived it to be a forgery. None the less, it was immensely influential between the two world wars and was used as a justification for Nazi policy. It was subsequently reissued in Arab and other Muslim countries.

Eleazar. The name of various prominent Jewish *tannaim and *amoraim. Eleazar ben Arakh (late 1st cent. CE) was the most outstanding pupil of R. *Johanan b. Zakkai who described him as 'a spring flowing with ever-increasing force'. He said, 'Be eager to study the *Torah, and know what you should answer to an unbeliever' (*Avot*. 2. 14). Eleazar ben Azariah (1st–2nd cent. CE) was a *priestly descendant of *Ezra and became *nasi to replace Rabban *Gamaliel II. Eleazar ben Damma (early 2nd cent. CE) was the nephew of R. *Ishmael. Eleazar ben Judah of Bartota (early 2nd cent CE) was a student of R. Joshua. He was famous for his generosity and is remembered for saying, 'Render unto Him what is His, for you and what you have are His' (*Avot* 3. 7). Eleazar ben Matya (early 2nd cent. CE) was a pupil of Tarfon. He is said to have understood seventy languages (*TJ, Shek* 5. 1, 48a). Eleazar ben Parta (early 2nd cent. CE) was arrested by the

Romans for publicly teaching Torah, but was miraculously delivered. Eleazar ben Shammua (*c.*150 CE) was a student of *Akiva and the teacher of *Judah ha-Nasi. Eleazar ben Simeon (late 2nd cent. CE) was thought to be the author of much of the *Zohar.* Eleazar ben Yose I (late 2nd cent. CE) is said to have exorcized the Roman emperor's daughter. Eleazar ben Zadok (late 1st cent. CE) practised *asceticism to try to prevent the destruction of the *temple in *Jerusalem. His grandson (also Eleazar ben Zadok) was the author of the maxim, 'No restriction may be imposed on the public unless the majority of the people can endure it'. In 1969 a lintel stone was found inscribed, 'This is the *bet midrash of Rabbi Eleazar ha-Kappar.' Eleazar Hisma (early 2nd cent. CE) transmitted *halakhot in the name of Joshua b. Hananiah, and Eleazar of Modin (late 1st cent. CE), said to be the uncle of Simeon *bar Kokhba, was much respected by R. *Gamaliel.

Eleazar ben Judah of Worms, known as **Eleazar Roke'aḥ,** (*c.*1165–*c.*1230). Medieval German Jewish scholar. Eleazar was a major scholar of the *Ḥasidei Ashkenaz movement. Based in Worms, he wrote many *piyyutim (liturgical poems) as well as works of theology, ethics, exegesis, and *halakhah. His family endured much suffering: during the Third *Crusade, his wife and daughters were killed and his son was mortally wounded. Nevertheless, he insisted that 'nothing is more beautiful than forgiveness'. In *Sefer ha-Ḥokhma* (The Book of Wisdom) he lamented the death of his teacher, Judah ha-Ḥasid, and of his children which deprived the world, both of the source of teaching about the mysteries of God (*sodh), and of its transmission in the future. In *Roke'aḥ* (the opening chapters of which were often reprinted as separate works), he explored the mystical meaning of halakot and prayers. In *Sodei Razayya* (The Secret of Secrets), he attempted to summarize the teachings of Ḥasidei Ashkenazim. Through his glory (*kabhodh*) God, who is utterly beyond human comprehension, 'is closer to all than the body is to the soul'. He makes his presence known through forms, or metaphors, which evoke appropriate response: 'If God, who is past all knowing, had not appeared to the prophets as a king on a throne, they would not have known how to pray to him at all.' The only true 'knowledge' is the relation of 'I and Thou' (as *Buber was later to develop it): 'The thoughts of one who is truly Jewish are as a pile of kindled coal, which love for God has fired and set alight.'

Election: see CHOSEN PEOPLE.

Elements. 1. In Christianity, the materials of bread and wine used in the *eucharist.

2. In Hinduism, the components and forces which constitute the universe: see *BHŪTA.

3. In Buddhism, constituents of appearance, *dharma (2).

Elephanta (Gharapuri). An island off the coast of Bombay, containing a famous representation of the *trīmurti *Śiva in a cave temple. The date is uncertain, but *c.*5th–7th cent. CE.

Elephantiné. City situated on an island in the Nile river. Elephantiné was the site of the discovery of a collection of papyri written in *Aramaic dating back to the 5th cent. BCE. They include legal documents, fragments of the *Book of Ahikar* and letters. The Elephantiné Jews desired to rebuild their own *Temple and seem to have been unconscious of the prohibition against a temple anywhere except *Jerusalem. Two goddesses seem to have been worshipped there as well as the Hebrew God, and *Passover (concerning the details of which they asked for information, suggesting that the fusion of Passover and Unleavened Bread was a recent event—perhaps initiated in *Josiah's reform, but not established until after the exile) was the only festival celebrated.

B. Porten, *Archives from Elephantiné* (1968).

Elevation. The lifting up of the *elements of the *eucharist by the celebrant. The purpose is both to symbolize their offering to God and to focus the devotion of the congregation. In the *Orthodox liturgy the priest says, 'Holy things for the holy', and then breaks the bread. In the Roman *mass, the bread and wine are each elevated in turn as they are consecrated.

Eliade, Mircea (1907–86). Advocate of what is called 'history of religions', which in his case is better seen as an attempt to discern elemental, timeless, patterns of religious life: 'The history of religions shows that we are not just biological cousins of the aboriginals, but friends and collaborators in a common human enterprise.' Religion is taken to be the manifestation of 'Being'. Symbolic forms, redolent of the sacred, are influenced by historical circumstances but are not themselves the product of history. The task is to use the comparative method to arrive at what is constant; to arrive at what goes beyond the contingencies of time.

Working with a model of the human as *homo religiosus*, of the human as motivated by an irreducible religious intentionality, Eliade drew most of his material from archaic cultures. Supposedly providing the most powerful evidence of the 'morphology of the sacred', these cultures are held to signal the contemporary need for greater *ontological rootage. Traditional humanity finds the meaning and value of its existence in basic *archetypes. The message is that Western men and women cannot afford to be as 'profane' as they are. The virtual destruction of the sense of the *sacred, the attenuation of *ritual and the relegation of *myth to the unconscious amounts to a new *Fall. 'A man of the pre-modern societies can attain to the highest spirituality, for, by understanding the *symbol, he succeeds in living the universal.'

Eliade has been criticized for his lack of historical sense, his lack of judgement in evaluating evidence, and his normative, if not theological, tendencies. Eliade's reply was to model himself on literary or art critics (e.g. Burckhardt), and to appeal to the value of a creative *hermeneutics, where the extension of meaning and insight does not depend on accuracy in every detail, nor on personal competence in every discipline and language. Of his own works, *The Sacred and the Profane* (1959) is accessible. See also SHAMANISM.

D. Allen and D. Doeing, *Mircea Eliade: An Annotated Bibliography* (1980); G. Dudley, *Religion on Trial* (1977).

Eliezer ben Hyrcanus (end of 1st cent. CE). Jewish *tanna. Eliezer was described by *Johanan b. Zakkai as outweighing all the sages of *Israel (*Avot* 2. 8). Both literally and metaphorically, he regarded the transmission of the Jewish inheritance as imperative: 'Those who bring no children into the world can be regarded as murderers.' He was the teacher of *Akiva, and his *yeshivah in Lydda was famous. Intensely conservative , he opposed the tendency of the council of *Jabneh to interpret *halakhot in the light of historical change. After his discussion with the *Sanhedrin on ritual purity, his view was rejected and he was excommunicated (*ḥerem). Only after his death was he reinstated as one of the foremost halakhists of his time: 'With the death of Eliezer, the *scroll of the Law was hidden away' (*B.Sof.* 49b). *Pirkei de-Rabbi Eliezer* (Sayings of Rabbi Eliezer) are ascribed to him.

J. Neusner, *Eliezer ben Hyrcanus* (1973).

Elijah (9th cent. BCE). Israelite *prophet. According to 1 Kings 17, Elijah warned King Ahab of a coming drought. He confronted the prophets of *Ba'al on Mount Carmel (ch. 18) and slaughtered them. Fleeing from the wrath of Queen Jezebel, God revealed himself to the prophet in a still small voice (ch. 19). He condemned the king for his theft of Naboth's vineyard and prophesied disaster for the house of Ahab (ch. 21). After choosing *Elisha as his successor, he was taken up to *Heaven in a fiery chariot (2 Kings 2. 1–18). According to the book of Malachi, he will return to earth 'before the great and terrible *day of the Lord' (4. 5). In *aggadic literature, Elijah was recognized as the forerunner of the *messiah. Consequently, the *gospels record speculation that John the Baptist, who wore the same clothes as Elijah (Mark 1. 6; 2 Kings 1. 8) was a reincarnation of the prophet. Subsequently Elijah was believed to be a partner of the messiah who will overthrow the foundations of the heathen (*Gen.R* 71. 9) and bring about the *resurrection of the dead. He also became a hero of Jewish folklore. He was seen as the champion of the poor and needy and it was told how he strangled a local *rabbi for stealing from collected charity. He most frequently was said to appear on the eve of *Passover to help the poor prepare for the *seder. It is customary to place a cup for Elijah in the middle of the table, and the door is opened during the seder for the prophet to come in and herald the days of the messiah. At *circumcision ceremonies, an unoccupied chair is placed for Elijah. According to the *midrash, when Elijah complained that the Israelites had forsaken the *covenant (1 Kings 19. 10, 14), God replied, 'Because of excessive zeal for me, you have brought charges against Israel . . .; therefore you shall have to be present at every circumcision ceremony' (*PdRE* 29: *Zohar*, Gen. 93a).

Later, it was believed that Elijah had left teachings of his own, and these are claimed to be contained in *Midrash Eliyahu Rabba* ('Great Midrash of Elijah'), and *M. R. Zuta* ('Small Midrash of Elijah').

Elijah ben Solomon Zalman (1720–97). The Vilna Gaon, known as Ha-Gra, a Lithuanian Jewish spiritual leader. Under the leadership of the Vilna *Gaon, the city of Vilna became the centre of opposition to the *Ḥasidic movement. He maintained, 'it is the duty of every believing Jew to repudiate and pursue them with all manner of afflictions and subdue them, because they have sin in their hearts and are like a sore on the body of Israel'. He was famous for his great learning and produced more than seventy works and commentaries on the *Bible, the *Talmud, the *midrashim, the **Zohar*, **Shulḥān Arukh*, on Hebrew grammar, and on scientific subjects. He believed totally in the eternity of the *Torah and declared, 'Everything that was, is and will be is included in the Torah. And not only principles, but even the details of each species, the minutest details of every human being, as well as of every creature, plant and mineral—all are included in the Torah.' He was a brilliant *halakhist, and was also devoted to the study of *Kabbalah. Philosophy he regarded as 'accursed', and he opposed all changes in customs and liturgy. Ḥasidism was rejected because he believed its emphasis on the love of God undermined the value of the Torah.

L. Ginzberg, *The Gaon, Rabbi Elijah* (1920).

Elijah Muhammad (1897–1975). Leader of the Nation of Islam, the American Black Muslim movement, called more fully 'The Lost-Found Nation of Islam', or, from 1976, 'The World Community of Islam in the West'. He was born in Georgia with the name Elijah Poole. Moving to Detroit, he became a follower of Wallace D. Hard (Wali Farad, known as Prophet Fard) who had founded the Temple of Islam to affirm 'the deceptive character of the white man and the glorious history of the black race'. He advocated self-help, especially through education, and he produced two manuals which guided the movement, *The Secret Ritual of the Nation of Islam* and *Teaching for the Lost Found Nation of Islam* . . . He became the chief aide of Fard, who gave him his new name, and when Fard disappeared in 1934, Elijah Muhammad took control. However, when the Detroit Temple was taken over by moderates, Elijah Muhammad moved to Chicago to found Temple No. 2 and the Nation of Islam. Fard was equated with *Allāh, at least as his emissary, so that prayers could be offered to him, and Elijah Muhammad took the titles of 'Prophet' and 'Messenger of Allah'. The work of self-help was rapidly extended, with special emphasis on the interior conversion of criminals and addicts. The Nation of Islam became politically prominent through the activities of *Malcolm X. Under Elijah Muhammad's successor, Wallace D. Muhammad, who took the title of *Imām, the movement became less aggressive, even allowing whites to become members. The aim was to allow other Muslims to recognize members of the movement as genuinely and legitimately Muslim. Its main publication, *Muhammad Speaks*, became later *Balalian News*. In 1985, it was announced that the American Muslim Mission was dissolved, since Islam is a single community (*'umma), not a coalition of sects. The original goals of the Nation of Islam were continued in what was originally a splinter group, but which rapidly grew in size, led by Louis Farrakhan (b. 1933). A fiery and inspiring orator, his attacks on Malcolm X (after his secession) were thought at the time to have helped to create the atmosphere leading to his assassination. Farrakhan has often been dismissed as a racist and anti-Semitic orator, but he speaks from great intelligence and culture. His political ambitions on behalf of the movement came to an end with the failure of Jesse Jackson (in the presidential nominations) in 1984, but the march of a million men in 1995 re-established Farrakhan and the nation of Islam as a political force. This was a rally in Washington, recalling that of Martin Luther *King in which the subordinate position of most blocks in the USA (graphically illustrated in statistics) was make the basis for a march of protest and pride.

J. Eure and R. Jerome, *Back Where we Belong* (1990); E. C. Lincoln, *The Black Muslims in America* (1963, rev. 1973); C. E. Marsh, *From Black Muslims to Muslims* (1984).

Elimelech of Lyzhansk (1717–87). Jewish *Ḥasidic leader. Elimelech was the pupil of *Dov Baer, and after some wanderings, settled in Lyzhansk in Galacia. He formulated the doctrine of the *Zaddik and taught that he should lead his community in all spheres of life, not merely the religious. He believed that the Zaddik had a direct connection with the higher world, and that 'every utterance of the Zaddik creates an *angel and influences higher spheres'. His main work was a commentary on *Torah, *No'am Elimelekh* (1787), but it is in effect an exposition of Ḥasidic ideology, and has remained an important guide for subsequent generations. While he endorsed characteristic activities (e.g. song and *dance, 'By means of songs and hymns, I open the way to the deeper world of mystical love'), he also offered simple and practical advice: 'How will our prayers raise us to higher and higher levels, bringing us ever nearer to you? Only if first you will give us the vision to see the good qualities in everyone and overlook his defects.'

M. Buber, *Tales of Hasidim* (1968).

Eliot, Thomas Stearns (1888–1965). Poet and critic. Born in St Louis, Missouri, he studied at Harvard, Paris, and Oxford. He settled in England and was naturalized in 1927. His religious background was Unitarian, which gave way to a despairing agnosticism which finds expression in his early poems and, especially, *The Waste Land* (1922). Many religious traditions appealed to him, including Hindu philosophy, *Neo-Thomism, and the classical Anglicanism of *Andrewes and the *Metaphysical poets (though an *anti-Semitic note is also evident), and in 1927 he was baptized and declared himself 'an *Anglo-Catholic in religion'. His later poems (especially *Four Quartets*, 1935–42) and his plays explore human doubt and scepticism within an intellectual framework, with deep traditional roots in the mystics, *Dante, and the Greek tragedians: what is believed is more readily lived than expressed in words. His concern for what he saw as the crisis of Western civilization found expression in essays, particularly, *Notes towards a Definition of Culture* (1948).

D. Gallup, *T. S. Eliot: A Bibliography* (1969); K. Smidt, *Poetry and Belief in the Work of T. S. Eliot* (1961).

Elisha (9th cent. BCE). Israelite *prophet. *Elijah chose Elisha to be his successor. He fulfilled Elijah's prophecy of destruction for the house of Ahab by sending a disciple to anoint Jehu king (2 Kings 9). He co-operated with Jehoram (ch. 3), he declared Hazael would be king of Syria (ch. 8), and there are several folk tales about him. In the *aggadah, it was taught that Elijah's promise to bestow a double portion on Elisha (ch. 2. 14) was fulfilled by Elisha's performing sixteen miracles to Elijah's eight.

Elisha ben Abuyah (early 2nd cent.). Jewish *tanna who subsequently renounced Judaism. Although he was the teacher of R. *Meir who quoted his sayings (e.g. *Avot* 4. 20), the reason for his *apostasy was not known. He is referred to in the Talmud (even by R. Meir when quoting him) as *aḥer*, 'another', in order to avoid mentioning his name. His life was the inspiration for several novels and poems of the *Haskalah period. A more recent treatment is M. Steinberg's novel, *As a Driven Leaf* (1939).

Elixir. (Arab., *al-iksīr*). Substances believed, especially in China, to confer immortality or simply longevity and magical powers, and as such the object of much herbal lore, myth, and *alchemy. In China, the elixir is based on preparations to unite *yin and yang and synchronize the microcosm and macrocosm. Ingestion was thought to afford eternal bodily regeneration or the internal germination of an 'immortal embryo' to be released at death.

In India, the nearest equivalents are *soma and *amṛta. When the quest for elixirs was transmitted via Islam to the West, the accompanying anthropologies could not be reconciled with belief-systems which placed emphasis (particularly in Christianity) on life after death as a consequence of the act and grace of God. It therefore became a minor part of alchemy.

A. Coudert, *Alchemy* . . . (1980).

Eliyyahu ben Shelomoh Zalman (Vilna Gaon): see ELIJAH BEN SOLOMON ZALMAN.

Elkesaites. A Jewish Christian group which arose *c.*100 CE in the country east of the Jordan, having affinities with the *Ebionites (e.g. in their *asceticism and in their use of only the gospel of *Matthew) and deriving their name from Elkesai who received a revelation from an angel 96 miles tall. Mani (see MANICHAEISM) belonged to an Elkesaite community in S. Babylon from the ages of 4 to 25. It is clear that a number of Manichean beliefs (e.g. in repeated incarnations of Christ, heavenly and earthly counterparts, and eating as sacramental) derive from the Elkesaites.

Ellorā or **Elūrā**. A complex of cave and rock temples in Maharashtra, India. Sacred to Hindus, Jains, and Buddhists, its thirty-four temples, monasteries, and sanctuaries come from all three religions. They were constructed from the 5th to the 9th cents.

P. Brown, *Indian Architecture* . . . (n.d.); J. Burgess, *Report on the Elura Cave Temples* (1882).

El male raḥamim (Heb., 'God full of compassion'). A Jewish prayer for the dead. It is normally recited at *funerals, for *Yahrzeit, and on visiting family graves: '. . . May the Compassionate One shelter her/him for ever under his protective wings, and may her/his soul be bound up in the bond of eternal life. The Lord is her/his inheritance: may s/he rest in peace; and let us say, Amen.' A special 'El male raḥamim' prayer is now often added to memorial services, to remember the victims of the *holocaust, 'our six million brethren, men, women and children, the holy and the pure, who were murdered, gassed, burned to death, and buried alive for the sanctification of God's name (*kiddush ha-Shem)'.

Elmo, St. The customary name for St Peter González (*c.*1190–1246), the patron saint of seamen. His 'fire' (i.e. electrical discharge on masts of ships) was taken as a sign of his protection. Feast day, 14 Apr.

Elohim (Heb., God(s)). A name for the God of the Jews. Its plural form may once have been literal—'mighty ones'—but it became subsumed in the accumulating Jewish sense that if God is indeed *God*, then there can only be what God is: One, and not a plurality of gods. See further EL.

Elūrā (sacred Indian cave temples): see ELLORĀ.

Ema (Jap.). Pictorial votive offerings. *Koema* (small ema) is a small flat wooden plaque, which may be rectangular, square, or pentagonal in shape, with a picture painted on its front surface. *Ōema* (large ema), which appeared after the 15th cent. is a work of art in many cases, painted by famous painters at the request of their rich patrons. Both *koema* and *ōema* are offered to the *kami of a shrine or to the deity of a temple for making wishes and for the fulfilment of the wishes.

The word *ema* (picture + horse) suggests its origin as a substitute for a live horse. Horses were offered to the kami on the occasion of excessive rainfall and severe drought in the Nara and Heian periods. From of old, they have also been regarded in Shinto tradition as a sacred animal on which the kami ride.

The gallery of ema exhibits all sorts of human problems and desires such as physical ailments, marriage, divorce, childcare, social success, improving skills in profession, and many others. Originally the picture of ema was nothing but a horse, but over the centuries a variety of pictures has come into use, each of which expresses directly or indirectly the content of a wish, for instance, a pair of eyes for the cure of eye disease.

Emaki (Jap.). A picture scroll. A long scroll, viewed from right to left, contains a series of pictures, often with the text that illustrates a story. The earliest extant emaki (a Japanese copy of a Chinese product) is *Kako genzai inga kyo emaki* (illustrated sūtra of past and present cause and effect) of the 8th cent. CE. With the subsequent development of painting in the Japanese style (*Yamato-e*) in the 9th cent., emaki became a favourite art medium combining painting with narrative in the 10th–16th cents.

Its motifs range from the secular to the religious. The classic romances of the Heian period (e.g. *The Tale of Genji* and *The Pillow Book*) ranked first among the former, and the war story became popular with the rise of the military class in the middle of the 12th cent. *Jigoku zōshi* (the Scroll of Hells), made in the 12th cent., is a religious emaki, in which the gruesome scenes of *hells based on Genshin's *Ōjōyōshū* (The Essentials for Salvation) are vividly illustrated. Temples and shrines supplied legends and miracle stories, and as a result of the spread of Buddhism in the Kamakura period, the lives of exemplary people were added to its themes (The Biography of the Revered Saigyō, The Biography of the Revered *Ippen, and the Biography of the Revered *Hōnen).

Emanation(s). Expressions of power or wisdom from a higher being, making connection between an uninvolved or uncontaminated source, and imperfect (because contingent) appearance. Emanations appear in different forms in many religions where the problem of relating the uncontingent and unconditioned to the contingent and conditioned was recognized. Emanations are characteristically *gnostic, and appear strongly in the *Neoplatonic system of *Plotinus. They appear with idiosyncratic genius in the poetry of *Blake. Under Neoplatonic influence, they are paramount in the *sefirot of *kabbalistic Judaism, protecting the unknowable 'nature' of God (see EIN-SOF). In contrast, although *Aquinas wrote of creation as 'the emanation of the whole of existence' (*Summa Theol.* I. 45. 1), he meant simply that God is the cause of all existence. In Tibetan Buddhism (*Tibetan religion), an emanation expresses either the profound influence of, or complete projection from, a higher being. The *Dalai Lama is said to be an 'emanation' of the *bodhisattva *Avalokiteśvara: this may be interpreted on various levels, either *docetically, whereby the form of the Dalai Lama is a complete projection from Avalokiteśvara, or symbolically, whereby, because of their close bond, the Dalai Lama is considered to embody the qualities of Avalokiteśvara (i.e. compassion). Thus the idea of emanation need not deny self-determination on the human level. The theory, though extensive in Tibetan Buddhism, is far from being of Tibetan origin; docetic interpretations of the historical Buddha, *Śākyamuni, were a key element in the *Mahāsāṃghika sects, from which the *Mahāyāna arose.

Emancipation, Jewish. Liberation from legal restrictions and political and social disabilities. Jewish emancipation depended on the political and social conditions of a particular country. In the USA, for example, the First Amendment of the constitution in 1791 in effect disestablished all religions, thus leading to Jewish emancipation. The cancellation of the final limitation against Jews was passed in Great Britain in 1871, and full emancipation was granted in France in 1791. It was achieved substantially later in E. Europe. Despite political emancipation, manifestations of *anti-Semitism have continued to occur. Campaigns for emancipation (as opposed to simply waiting for it to happen) were often fuelled by a perception of the dangers of *assimilation. Thus *Ahad ha'Am at the first Zionist Congress: 'There is only one object for which we have at present the strength, . . . and that is the *moral* object—the emancipation of ourselves from the inner slavery and spiritual degradation which assimilation has produced in us.'

Ember days (OE, *ymbren*). Four groups of three days (Wednesday, Friday, and Saturday) in the W. church year, fast days 'around' or 'about' four seasons, Advent (mid-Dec.), *Lent (*Ash Wednesday), *Pentecost, and Holy Cross Day (14 Sept.), kept as days of fasting and abstinence. They are now associated, as days of preparation, with *ordination.

Emden, Jacob, pen-name **Yavez** (1697–1776). Jewish *halakhist and *kabbalist. Emden was an indefatigable campaigner against the followers of *Shabbetai Zevi, and his most famous controversy was against Jonathan *Eybeschuetz, the *rabbi of Altona, Hamburg, and Wandsbek, whom he accused of secret Shabbateanism. From this, Emden went on to criticize and question the antiquity of some passages of the **Zohar*. However, although he was friendly with Moses *Mendelssohn, he did not accept the scientific study of religion, or the rabbinic domination of it—'Blessed be he who did not make me a rabbi!' He was an early exponent of the recovery of Jesus as a Jewish figure: 'The Nazarene brought a two-fold mercy to the world: he supported the *Torah of *Moses with all his strength, and he sought to raise the gentiles to greater perfection with ethical principles.' Indeed, he speculated what the relations between Jews and Christians might be if the latter lived according to those principles: 'Christians have many admirable characteristics and righteous principles: happy are they and happy are we when they treat us according to their faith.'

M. J. Cohen, *Jacob Emden, a Man of Controversy* (1937).

Emei (mountain in China): see PILGRIMAGE.

Emerald Buddha. The Buddha image, now in the Grand Palace in Bangkok, which epitomizes the Buddha's protection of the king and people of Thailand. The image, made of green malachite, was discovered in 1436, when a monument was split open by lightning. It was taken to Chiang-mai, to Laos, and then to Bangkok (in 1779). It was made *c.*1st cent. BCE, though legends date it much earlier.

C. Notton, *The Chronicle of the Emerald Buddha* (1932).

Emerson, Ralph Waldo (1803–82). Author and essayist, a leading figure among the New England Transcendentalists (the Transcendental Club met at his house from 1836 to give expression to revolutionary and visionary ideals). He was born in Boston in a *Unitarian family, and after study at Harvard, he became pastor of the Unitarian Second Church of Boston. However, his questioning of the tenets of faith, and a dispute over the administration of the Lord's Supper, led to his resignation. The break confirmed him in his conviction that the quest for truth can never be compromised. He gave up preaching in 1838, and regarded himself as 'God's child, a disciple of Christ', without ecclesiastical affiliation. The complexities of theology seemed to him hardly worth the investment of a life, given what they have led to: 'The history of persecution is a history of endeavours to cheat nature, to make water run up hill, to twist a rope of sand. . . . A mob is a society of bodies voluntarily bereaving themselves of reason.' Yet humans constantly transcend the irrationality of their creeds: 'Men are better than their theology: their daily life gives it the lie.' True 'religion', i.e. a transcendental humanity, is the realization of absolute value:

> The Universe has three children, born at one time, which reappear under different names, . . . whether they are called cause, operation and effect; or more poetically, Jove, Pluto, Neptune; or, theologically, the Father, the Spirit and the Son; but which we will call the Knower, the Doer and the

Sayer. These stand for the love of truth, the love of good, and the love of beauty. These three are equal.

To remain committed to these is necessarily to call in question all that is offered on the basis of authority: 'Whoso would be a man must be a nonconformist. . . . Imitation is suicide.'

G. W. Allen, *Waldo Emerson* (1981); W. S. Emerson, *Freedom and Fate* (1971).

Emic/etic (by analogy from phonemic/phonetic). The contrast in the study (mainly in anthropology) of peoples and their religion either according to the principles, methods, and interests of the observer (etic) or by an attempt to understand the viewpoint of the people themselves (emic). The emic/etic contrast raises acutely the issue of whose meaning is the meaning of the meaning (cf. HERMENEUTICS) since it is now recognized that the aim of a value-free account of religious beliefs and practices is unattainable. Emic and etic have been conveniently defined by M. Harris (*The Rise of Anthropological Theory*, 1969):

Emic statements refer to logico-empirical systems whose phenomenal distinctions or 'things' are built up out of contrasts and discriminations significant, meaningful, real, accurate, or in some other fashion regarded as appropriate by the actors themselves. . . . Etic statements depend upon phenomenal distinctions judged appropriate by the community of scientific observers. Etic statements cannot be falsified if they do not conform to the actor's notion of what is significant, real or meaningful.

N. Barley, *The Innocent Anthropologist* (1983) makes it abundantly clear why both are limited and why both are necessary.

Emigrants (Arab., *Muhājirūn*). Those who accompanied *Muḥammad on his emigration (*hijra) from *Mecca to *Madīna in 622 CE or followed shortly afterwards. The term became a title of respect, describing those who had left their homes and property; and it came to be applied also to those Meccans who in the next few years moved to Madina to join the Muslims. The *Qur'ān commends them for their piety and sincerity (2. 125, 3. 101, and especially 9. 20). Between the Emigrants and the *Helpers (Anṣār, the Muslims of Madīna) there was some friction, since the Emigrants had little means of support. The Qur'ān accordingly urges that they should be given money and assistance (59. 8–9), referring to 'the poor (among the) Emigrants, those who were expelled from their homes and their property'.

Emin Foundation. A *new religious movement started in London in 1973 by Raymond Armin (b. Shertenlieb), known to the members as Leo. The founder, whose supposed healing abilities rest on the use of electric force within peoples' bodies, is said to have discovered the laws that govern everything. Moreover, much of the Foundation's work involves studying Egyptology and E. religions. The declared aim of this Foundation is self-improvement, and members are encouraged to abandon what is described as the madness of the 20th cent. and turn instead towards what is real, definite, and of value which can be found in the ways and wisdom of the Great Mother of all, this planet. In this way the individual will acquire a true appreciation of both her/his nature and purpose in life.

All learning and discovery is carried on in groups, and without the use of books, members being encouraged to work things out for themselves. To underline the importance of group identity, members wear special tunics which are designed to symbolize unity and the principles of love, honour, and respect among members. This very strong emphasis on group identity can and apparently does pose problems for those who withdraw or wish to withdraw.

Empō Dentō-roku. A work of the Japanese Zen monk, Shiban Mangen (*c.*1627–1710), which contains the biographies of more than a 1,000 Zen monks.

Emptiness (the condition of all appearance being essentially devoid of characteristics): see ŚŪNYATĀ.

Enchin (founder of Jimon-shū): see TENDAI(-SHŪ).

Encratites. Groups of early Christians whose ascetic practices (and related teaching) were condemned by mainstream writers such as *Irenaeus. The term was apparently not used precisely but with reference to many *gnostics and *Ebionites who commonly rejected *alcohol, meat, and especially marriage. In these terms, much of the earliest Syriac Christianity may be said to have been 'encratite'.

Encyclical (Gk., *en*, 'in', + *kyklos*, 'circle'). A pastoral letter intended for circulation among all the churches of an area. By Roman Catholics they are restricted to letters sent out by the pope. They are cited by the first words of the Latin text, e.g. Pope John XXIII's encyclical **Pacem in terris* (1963). For examples, see Index, Bulls; encyclicals, etc. Among Anglicans, the term is used of the letters issued from the *Lambeth Conferences.

Engaku-ji. Zen Buddhist monastery of Complete Enlightenment (*engaku* is the enlightenment attained by a *buddha), founded in 1282 by the Chinese Ch'an master, Wu-hsüeh Tsu-yüan (Jap. Bukkō Kokushi or Mogaku Sogen). It was part of the Kamakura complex (*gosan), of the *Rinzai school, and it remains active to the present day.

Engi (Japanese stories): see DENSETSU.

Engishiki (Procedures of the Engi Era). A Japanese corpus of regulations for governmental administration and ceremonies in fifty books. The compilation of these procedures was initiated in 905 CE, under the leadership of Fujiwara no Tokihira at the command of Emperor Daigo (897–930). After Tokihira's death in 909, it was continued by his younger brother Tadahira through the Engi era (901–22) until it was completed and presented to the throne in 927.

The compilation of the *Engishiki* was perhaps the last effort made by the central government to restore and reinforce the ideal of the 7th-cent. state as a 'liturgical community'. Encyclopaedic in nature, this magnificent corpus is immensely valuable for the study of the liturgical community in ancient Japan.

The *Engishiki* can be divided into two parts in accordance with the two major divisions of the government: the *Jingi-kan* concerned with *kami (deities) affairs or Shinto religion for the well-being and prosperity of the national community, and the *Dajō-kan* dealing with all the 'secular' business of the government. All matters handled by the *Jingi-kan* are found in the first ten books of the *Engishiki*.

Books i and ii deal with the seasonal festivals for deities celebrated annually under the auspices of the *Jingi-kan* at all the official shrines. There are three categories of the festival: great, middle, and small. The place of the 'great' festival is occupied by only one festival, the enthronement festival (*daijōsai*) which occurs once in the reign of each emperor. This is mentioned at the beginning of book i, but concrete procedures for it are given in book vii. There are five national festivals of the 'middle' category, such as the praying for a good harvest (*toshigoi*), the tasting of the newly harvested rice grains (*niiname), and the festival at the Kamo shrines in Kyōto. There are thirteen festivals in the 'small' category.

Book iii contains procedures for the occasional festivals, as distinguished from the seasonal festivals (books i–ii). Book iv gives procedures to be followed at the Grand Shrine of *Ise where the sun goddess *Amaterasu, the primordial ancestress of the imperial family, is enshrined. Book v covers procedures for the Bureau of the Consecrated Princess of the Grand Shrine of Ise (*saigūryō*); whenever an emperor accedes to the throne, an unmarried royal princess is chosen by divination and sent to Ise as his personal representative to the Goddess Amaterasu. Book vi gives procedures for the Office of the Consecrated Princess of the Kamo Shrines (*saiinshi*), a cultic institution similar in nature to that mentioned in book v. Book vii deals with the procedures to be followed when the enthronement festival is celebrated. These procedures are also given in detail in many books of the *Engishiki* subsequent to book xi, for the festival involves all the ministries, bureaus, and offices of the government. Book viii records twenty-seven ritual prayers (*norito). Books ix and x present a register of the deities and the official shrines of varying rank and status throughout the nation. There are 3,132 deities to 2,861 shrines. See further, D. L. Philippi, *Norito: a New Translation*.

Engo Kokugon (Japanese name of Rinzai master): see YÜAN-WU K'O-CH'IN.

Enlightenment (attainment of insight, illumination, wisdom, truth, etc.): see Index, Enlightenment.

Enlightenment (Germ. *Aufklärung*). A period in European thought and art, *c.*1720–80. It is sometimes also called 'the Age of Reason'—misleadingly, since it implies that other 'ages' are, at least comparatively, irrational. It is thus sometimes a term of conflict, implying an emancipation from 'the dead hand of dogma'. See also DEISM; HASKALAH (Jewish Enlightenment).

G. R. Cragg, *Reason and Authority in the 18th Century*, (1964); P. Gay, *The Enlightenment* . . ., (1973).

Enni Ben'en (Zen master): see BEN'EN.

Ennichi (Jap., *en*, 'connection', + *nichi*, 'day'). An auspicious day; a holy day at Japanese shrines and temples. Believers who visit a shrine or temple associated with the particular deity or *bodhisattva being celebrated establish a special affinity with them and accumulate extraordinary merit as a result of their piety. Typical monthly feast days (with their associates) are 5 (Suiten), 10 (Konpira), and 25 (Kitano Tenjin); and 8 and 12 (Yakushi; Skt., *Bhaisajyaguru), 18 (Kannon); Skt., *Avalokiteśvara), 21 (Kobô-daishi), 24 (Jizô; Skt., *Ksitigarbha), and 28 (*Fudô; Skt., Acalanâtha) at Buddhist temples. Since similar feast days had already been instituted in China much earlier, most of those in Japan can be said to have derived from them.

Ennin (794–864). Third chief abbot (*zasu) of the Japanese *Tendai school, also known by his posthumous title, Jikaku Daishi. He became a disciple of *Saichō (767–822), the founder of Tendai, at the age of 15, and in 838 he went to China for further study of *T'ien-t'ai and Esoteric Buddhism (*Mikkyō). Visiting many holy sites and studying with various teachers, he experienced the Hui-ch'ang persecution of Buddhism which reached its height in 845, and he returned to Japan two years later. A record of his sojourn in China has been translated by E. O. Reischauer, *Ennin's Diary* (1955). His foremost contribution to history is the establishment of Tendai esotericism (Taimitsu) in contrast to the Shingon esotericism (Tomitsu) of *Kūkai (774–835), Saichō's great rival. No less important is his introduction of the *Pure Land practice of *Wu-t'ai-shan which initiated the Tendai Pure Land tradition. The bestowal of posthumous titles begins with Ennin, who preceded both Saichō (Dengyō Daishi) and Kūkai (Kōbō Daishi) in receiving the honour.

E. O. Reischauer, *Ennin's Travels in T'ang China* (1955); *Ennin's Diary* (1955).

En-no-gyōja (founder of mountain Buddhism): see SHUGENDŌ.

E'nō. Jap. for *Hui-neng.

Enoch. Descendant of *Adam (7th generation), in the Hebrew *Bible. According to Genesis 5. 24, he was one who 'walked with God and he was not; for God took him'. From this, he became central in *apocalyptic speculation. Many legends became attached to him and several pseudepigraphical books bear his name.

1 Enoch, or *Ethiopic Enoch* (so-called from its preservation in Ethiopic MSS of the Bible), contains a series of revelations to Enoch on the origin of evil, the angels and their destinies, and *Gehenna and Paradise. The book is composite, and chs. 37–71, the 'Similitudes' or 'Parables', have attracted special attention because of their use of the term '*Son of Man'. But this section alone of the book has not been found among MSS at *Qumran, and may be a Christian work. Other sections of the book are not later than the 1st cent. BCE.

2 Enoch, *Slavonic Enoch*, or *The Book of the Secrets of Enoch*, recounts a tour by Enoch of the seven heavens. It is a Christian work based on *1 Enoch*, variously dated from the 2nd to the 10th cents. CE.

3 Enoch is a Hebrew *Merkabah text to be dated perhaps to the 5th–6th cents. CE. It describes the vision of Rabbi *Ishmael b. Elisha, and is notable for its description of the angel *Metatron (elsewhere equated with Enoch).

In the Jewish *aggadic tradition, Enoch was frequently perceived as the guardian of secrets who eventually became king of the heavenly angels. However, when Christians seized on the figure of Enoch in order to demonstrate that *Torah is not necessary for salvation (because he was 'taken' by God before Torah was revealed), there was a rabbinic reaction, and Enoch was interpreted as very wicked, so that God 'took him' before he did more damage.

In Islam, the figure in the *Qur'ān (19. 57 f., 21. 85) of Idrīs is usually identified by Muslims with Enoch.

Tr. of the three books in J. H. Charlesworth (ed.), *The Old Testament Pseudepigrapha* (1983); M. A. Knibb and E. Ullendorff, *The Ethiopic Book of Enoch* (1978).

Enryaku-ji (centre of Tendai): see SAICHŌ; TENDAI SHŪ.

Ensō or **ichi-ensō** (Jap., 'circle'). The symbol especially in Zen Buddhism, of the absolute and uncontained reality, enlightenment. It occurs frequently in Zen painting, executed in a single, flowing stroke of the brush.

En Sof (the God beyond description in Judaism): see EIN-SOF.

Enstasy (Gk., *en-stasis*, 'standing into'). The experiences, or abolition of experience, arising as a consequence of those meditational, etc., techniques which withdraw the practitioner from the world, and even from awareness of the self. The word was coined in contrast to *ecstasy. Examples are *dhyāna, *jhāna.

Entelechy (Gk., *en* + *telos*, 'end', + *echein*, 'to have'). Aristotelian term pointing to the capacity of an entity to have complete reality and also the power to achieve through development completeness or perfection. The term was adopted by *Leibniz to describe his monads.

Enthusiasm. A religious attitude of extreme commitment, frequently leading to acts and utterances which (in the eyes of those outsiders who regard themselves as more sober) seem extraordinary. In general, therefore, it has become a term of disapproval, especially when used by those who regard authority and obedience as a necessary condition of true faith and practice—an example is the *Roman Catholic, Ronald Knox, in *Enthusiasm* (1950). *Holy fools often exhibit those characteristics which evoke the word.

Entia non sunt multiplicanda . . . ('entities ought not to be multiplied . . .'): see WILLIAM OF OCKHAM.

Entrance, Little and Great. In Orthodox Christianity, the processions which (i) lead up to the reading of the *gospel, and (ii) bring up the *elements to be consecrated.

Enttraditionalisierung (Germ., 'detraditionalization'). The phenomenon of the erosion of tradition in society in general and in religion in particular. Tradition has been a strong source of constraint and order, since religions are systems which protect information (both verbal and non-verbal) which has been tested through millennia and has proved effective (i.e. effective in relation to goals, some of which are set by evolution and natural selection at one extreme, others of which are set by ultimate attainments, such as the *beatific vision or *nirvāna at the other). The endorsement of individual choice and responsibility in democratic societies (which have had dominant economic power, and have thus increasingly made choice realizable), followed far more recently by the revolution in communications, has threatened and eroded the security of traditional boundaries which hitherto have protected (and often coerced) the transmission of information from one generation to another. Characteristically, religions have become a matter of choice in such societies where before a person 'belonged', even if he or she had little or no committed belief; and even within a religious tradition, the interpretation of that tradition becomes opened up to individuals rather than controlling authorities. The extent to which this creates tension depends on the structure of the religious tradition in question: thus the tension is greater for Vatican Catholics and Sunni Muslims than it is for Anglican Christians or Hindus (though subsystems in those cases may be extremely disturbed if they are themselves governed by strong boundary considerations).

Environment: see ANIMALS.

Ephesians, Letter to the. One of the epistles of *Paul and a book of the New Testament. Its opening theme is the common destiny of Jews and Gentiles alike in Christ (1–3). Then come admonitions (4–6) including a summary of the duties of members of a household (5. 21–33), and a final homily on the 'armour of God' (6. 10–20). Opinion is divided as to whether the letter could be the genuine work of Paul. Doubts arise, e.g., from the developed conception of 'the church' (1. 22 etc.). Unlike other letters of Paul, it has a lofty and generalized style throughout. Whether genuine or not it may have been originally written as a circular letter.

Ephesus. City in Asia Minor (near the W. coast of modern Turkey and now a ruin), and venue of the third *ecumenical council in 431. Under the leadership of *Cyril of Alexandria, it deposed and excommunicated *Nestorius and condemned his doctrines. The action was taken before the arrival of the Syrian bishops and papal legates, who protested and excommunicated Cyril. A reunion was however effected in 433.

A second synod was held in Ephesus in 449 to deal with *Eutyches. Presided over by the bishop of *Alexandria, it exonerated him; deposed instead the bishop of *Antioch; and refused to receive the *Tome* sent by Pope *Leo I. Its decisions were reversed by the Council of *Chalcedon in 451. The second synod is often known as the Latrocinium (Robber Synod).

Ephod (Heb.). A Jewish sacred garment. It was evidently part of the vestments of the *high priest. It was worn over the blue robe and under the sacred *breastplate and the *Urim and Thummim. *Divination was prohibited by Jewish law, but the ephod and Urim and Thummim were used as a means of seeking God's will. There are elaborate descriptions of the ephod in the *Talmud (e.g. *B.Yoma* 71b). Consultation of the ephod, however, had certainly died out by the time of the second *Temple.

Ephraem of Syria (Syriac church father): see EPHREM, ST.

Ephraim. Younger son of *Joseph. According to Exodus 48, the *patriarch *Jacob adopted Ephraim and *Manasseh, his brother, as his sons, ensuring their status as forefathers of *tribes. Ephraim's territory was in the hill country of central Palestine, and the name Ephraim was frequently used for the whole of the northern kingdom, *Israel. Eminent members of the tribe include *Joshua and king Jeroboam, who rebelled against the house of *David. According to the *midrash, the tribe of Ephraim left slavery in Egypt early, and many were killed by the *Philistines. In order to avoid their bones, God led the Israelites a circuitous route to the *Promised Land. It was these bones which came to life in *Ezekiel's vision of the valley of the dry bones (ch. 37) (*B.Sanh* 92b).

Ephrem, St (*c*.306–73). 'The Syrian', the most important of church *fathers in the *Syrian churches. He was born in Nisibis (Nusaybin in E. Turkey) where after his baptism he joined the ascetic and celibate circle in the church known as 'covenanters'. He attended the famous theological school in Nisibis, and was ordained *deacon (never *priest). After the Roman cession of Nisibis to Persia in 363 he moved to Edessa. His biblical commentaries (e.g. on the **Diatessaron*) and anti-heretical works (against *Bardaisan, Mani (see MANICHAEISM), *Arius) come from his last ten years. Ephrem is however best known in Syriac tradition for his large number of *hymns, which figure largely in liturgical books and which influenced later Syriac and even Greek hymnography. They are characterized by an elaborate use of *typology and symbolism which resists logical consistency and progression—a style in keeping with Ephrem's deep suspicion of philosophy and rationalism. Ephrem's reputation in the W. is shown by late legends in which he meets St *Basil and goes to Egypt. He was made a *Doctor of the Church in 1920.

Trs. C. W. Mitchell, H. Burgess, J. B. Morris, J. Gwynn; S. Brock, *The Luminous Eye* . . . (1985).

Epiclesis (Gk., 'invocation, prayer'). A prayer in the Christian *eucharist which asks the Father to send the *Holy Spirit upon the bread and wine to make them the body and blood of Christ. A prayer of this sort is found in the *Apostolic Tradition* of *Hippolytus (*c*.215). An explicit and solemn epiclesis is typical of Orthodox liturgies, and is regarded by commentators as the moment (rather than the earlier words 'This is my body' etc.) when the elements are consecrated. The Roman *canon of the mass contains no such reference to the Holy Spirit; an invocation of the Holy Spirit in the Anglican prayer book of 1549 was removed in 1552 and not restored in 1662. Modern W. liturgies, however, do include an epiclesis in the form of prayers for the operation of the Holy Spirit before and after the words of institution (but without speaking of either of these as a moment of consecration).

Epikoros (in Judaism, one with heterodox or heretical views): see APIKOROS.

Epiphanius, St (*c*.315–403). Church *father and bishop of Salamis in Cyprus. He was a strong supporter of *Nicaea, and opponent of *heresy. His most important writing was the *Refutation of all Heresies* (in Gk. the *Panarion*, 'medicine chest'), in which he attacked all heresies (or all that he knew) up to his own time. It is uncritical and disorganized but it preserves much valuable historical material. At the end of his life he was engaged in the opposition to *Origenism.

Epiphany (Gk., *epiphaneia*, 'manifestation'). An appearance of a divine or superhuman being. In Christian use it refers specifically to a feast celebrated on 6 Jan. It originated in the E., where it celebrated the baptism of Jesus and, at least in a secondary way, his birth. Since the 5th cent. when 25 Dec. took over as the date of *Christmas, it has remained the feast of Christ's baptism. Epiphany spread to the W. Church in the 4th cent., but here it became associated with the 'manifestation of Christ to the Gentiles' in the person of the *Magi of Matthew 2. 1–12.

F. X. Weiser, *Handbook of Christian Feasts and Customs* (1958).

Episcopacy. The system of church government by *bishops (*episcopoi*). *Anglican churches are, specifically, known as 'Episcopal' or 'Episcopalian', as in ECUSA, the Episcopal Church of the United States.

Episcopal Church in the USA or **Protestant Episcopal Church.** The *Anglican Church in the United States. Its organization dates from the consecration of Samuel Seabury as first bishop in 1784. A constitution and canons were drawn up, and the prayer book revised in 1789. There are ninety-six dioceses in the USA (1981), plus missionary dioceses mostly in US possessions and central America. Bishops are elected in diocesan conventions. The General Convention meets every three years. There are no archbishops, but there is a Presiding Bishop elected by the General Convention. The church adopted a new Book of Common Prayer in 1979. Most bishops ordain *women to the priesthood.

Episcopi vagantes (Lat., 'wandering bishops'). *Bishops who have been consecrated in an irregular manner or who, having been regularly consecrated, have ceased to be in communion with any major Church. The W. but not the E. theology of *orders has been generally ready to admit such consecrations as valid. A number of small churches derive their succession of bishops from such men, e.g. the 'Orthodox Church of the British Isles'.

P. F. Anson, *Bishops at Large* (1964).

Epistemology (reflection on how knowledge arises): see ONTOLOGY.

Epistle. The usual word for a letter, especially of the New Testament, and in liturgical use. In the *eucharist where there are two lections, they are traditionally called 'Epistle' and 'Gospel', even though the former may occasionally come from the Old Testament, Acts, or Revelation.

Epoche (bracketing out): see PHENOMENOLOGY.

Equiprobabilism (ethical choice where more than one possibility obtains): see LIGUORI, ALPHONSUS.

Erasmus, Desiderius (*c*.1466–1536). Christian humanist. Taught by the Brethren of the Common Life (see GROOTE, G.) at Deventer, Erasmus became an Augustinian monk in 1486 and was ordained priest in 1492. Widely travelled, friend of popes, kings, and nobility in several countries, he served for a period in the newly created Lady Margaret Professorship of Greek and Theology at Cambridge. Most of his later years were spent in Basle at the home of Froben the printer. A gifted writer, satirist, biblical translator, and editor of patristic works, Erasmus was Europe's most outstanding scholar in the early 16th cent. His merciless satire exposed ecclesiastical abuses, but he was not remotely tempted to join the *Reformers, fearing radicalism and the cost of change. He could identify the Church's faults, but was unable or unwilling to rectify them. Reproached for not fully observing the *Lent fast, he said of himself, 'I have a Catholic soul, but a Lutheran stomach.' His influential writings include *Adagia* (1500), a popular edn. of Gk. and Lat. proverbs (e.g. 'In the kingdom of the blind, the one-eyed man is king') frequently republished, *The Christian Soldier's Dagger or Handbook* (1504), and *The Praise of Folly* (1509). His reluctant controversy with *Luther issued in his *Freedom of the Will* (1524), a response to Luther's *Bondage of the Will*. Equally rejected by later *Roman Catholics, his satirical works were declared forbidden literature by some mid-16th-cent. *popes.

C. Augustijn, *Erasmus . . .*, (1991); R. H. Bainton, *Erasmus of Christendom* (1969); L.-E. Halkin, *Erasmus* (Fr. 1987; tr. 1993).

Erastianism. The view that the state has the right and responsibility to intervene in and control the affairs of the Christian Church as it appears in a particular State. The view was proposed by Thomas Erastus (Germ. Liebler, Lieber, or Lübler), 1524–83, against the *Calvinists: he argued that offending Christians should be punished by secular authority, and not by Church sanctions (e.g. withholding the sacraments). The most celebrated proponent has been Richard *Hooker. A modified Erastianism has characterized the Church of England.

Eremetical (Gk., *erēmos*, 'wilderness'). That which pertains to the life of those who go into solitary or isolated places to seek religious goals—hence hermits. The necessity to detach oneself from the world in order to seek higher goals is common in most religions—though in some (e.g. Judaism and some parts of Islam) it is regarded with suspicion as seeming to call in question the worth of God's creation: see ASCETICISM. For examples, see Index, Asceticism.

Erez Israel (Heb., 'Land of Israel'). The Jewish *Promised Land. Erez Israel was the Hebrew name given to the land governed by the British mandate, 1919–48.

Erhard Seminar Training: see EST.

Eriugena/Erigena, John Scotus (*c*.810–*c*.877). *Neoplatonic philosopher. He was an Irishman who became head of the palace school at Laon, but little else is known about his life. His importance lies mainly in his knowledge of Gk. and his work as translator and interpreter of *Dionysius the Areopagite, *Maximus the Confessor, and Gregory of

Nyssa. His influence was muted by his condemnation in the 13th cent., and the inherent difficulty of his thought. His own treatise, *Periphyseon* (On the Division of Nature), represents the first important influence of Neoplatonism on the W. since Boethius, depicting creation as a movement of emanation and return beginning and ending in God. Man is a microcosm of the universe, midway between animals and angels, redeemed by the incarnate *Logos: 'Man is the microcosm in the strictest sense of the word: he is the summary of all existence; there is no creature that is not recapitulated in man.'

M. Cappuyns, *Jean Scot Érigène* (1933; 1969); J. J. O'Meara, *Eriugena* (1969).

Erlebnis (lived experience): see HERMENEUTICS.

Eruv or **erubh** (Heb., 'mixing'). A symbolic act, by which *Sabbath restrictions can be circumvented. Such acts include carrying burdens on the Sabbath by amalgamating holdings; walking further than the permitted Sabbath distance by amalgamating boundaries, and cooking for the Sabbath on a Friday festival by amalgamating meals. The major eruvin are (i) *eruv hatserot*, the amalgamating of courtyards, creating a larger household, especially by handing over a loaf or other food and pronouncing a blessing; (ii) *eruv reshuyyot*, the enlarging of areas, even of entire towns, by encircling the area on poles at least 40 inches high—telephone poles can be utilized; (iii) *eruv tavshilin*, taking a piece of bread and an item of cooked food (e.g. a boiled egg) prepared before a festival and merging it with food prepared on the festival for an ensuing Sabbath (otherwise forbidden); the two items are reserved and eaten on the Sabbath; (iv) *eruv teḥumin*, enlarging the boundaries from a town to allow a longer Sabbath journey, by putting sufficient food for two meals at a place before the Sabbath, that place then counting as one's abode—a further 2,000 cubit's journey are allowed from that place. The tractate *Eruvin* follows naturally from *Shabbat* in the Order *Moʿed* in *Mishnah *et seq*.

Ervad (Zoroastrian priest): see MAGI.

Esau. Elder son of the patriarch *Isaac, and twin brother of *Jacob. According to Genesis, Esau gave his brother his birthright (25. 29–34) and then later Jacob also stole his blessing (ch. 27). Before the brothers were born, it was prophesied that 'two nations are in your womb, and two peoples, born of you, shall be divided; the one shall be stronger than the other, the elder shall serve the younger' (25. 23). Jacob was revered as the father of the Israelites, while Esau was the ancestor of the Edomites. The relationship between the two brothers was the subject of much *aggadot, particularly since Esau/Edom was taken to represent Rome and all hostile governments.

Eschatology (Gk., *eschatos*, 'last'). That which is concerned with the last things, the final destiny both of individuals and of humanity in general, and of the cosmos. The word was first used in the 19th cent., in discussing the Bible, but it refers to a concern in those religions which have a sequential (from a beginning to an end) understanding of time, and by application to religions which envisage an end to this particular cosmic cycle.

Judaism In the context of their vocation to be the *Chosen People of God, the Jews believe that the relationship between themselves and God will last for ever, and will be the means by which God's universal reign over all humanity will be established. The biblical *prophets looked forward to a great and terrifying *Day of the Lord (e.g. Amos 5. 18) when God's wrath against *Israel and the nations would be revealed. Only a faithful *remnant of the people would survive (e.g. Isaiah 11. 11), and an ideal ruler would arise descended from *David who would re-establish God's rule and usher in an era of peace and prosperity (e.g. Isaiah 11. 6–9). The same theories were prominent in the post-*exilic prophets and in the intertestamental literature. At various times in Jewish history, the end of time has been believed to be imminent—it is a prominent motif, for example, in the *Dead Sea Scrolls. By the *Talmudic period, there was a distinction made between 'the days of the *Messiah' and 'the world to come'—the former being a transition stage for the latter. Among *Maimonides' *articles of faith, belief in divine reward and punishment, in the coming of the messiah, and in the future *resurrection of the dead are all specified. In *Kabbalistic literature there are many complicated speculations, but, beyond the fundamental principles, there is no general agreement on the details of eschatological doctrines.

Christianity The message of *Jesus had an eschatological character, although whether it was primarily *apocalyptic (as in sayings like Matthew 25. 31 about the glorious coming of the *Son of Man) or more concerned to suggest that hopes were already fulfilled (as in sayings like Luke 11. 20; 'realized eschatology') is disputed. Apocalyptic ideas inherited by at least some circles in the early church were attached to the doctrine of the *parousia, but the belief that this was imminent faded by the second half of the 1st cent. Attempts thereafter were made to interpret the biblical themes allegorically, or more usually to translate them into individual terms (the *'Four Last Things': death, *judgement, *heaven, and *hell). Eschatology has been a chief subject of *demythologization, in which the urgent expectation of the end is re-expressed in terms of individual decisions or as a symbol of something outside history.

Islam The account of the last days is based on the *Qur'ān, elaborated in *ḥadīth, and varies slightly between *Sunni and *Shiʿa. In general, the last days will be initiated by Gog and Magog, often understood as fire and flood, who will devastate the world. The reign of *al-Mahdī will follow, restoring true *islām* to the earth. The *antichrist, *al-Dajjāl, will then usurp power until destroyed by ʿIsa (Jesus), though according to some by the Mahdi. The final judgement will then take place (*yaum al-Dīn).

S. G. F. Brandon, *Man and His Destiny in the Great Religions* (1962); J. A. T. Robinson, *In the End, God*, (1950); J. I. Smith and Y. Y. Haddad, *The Islamic Understanding of Death and Resurrection* (1981).

Esdras, Books of. Various Jewish biblical books. 'Esdras' is the Gk. and Lat. form of Ezra. Confusion results from the differences between the books of this title in the *Septuagint, *Vulgate (and hence some Catholic Bibles) and *Apocrypha in English Bibles. These correspond as follows:

Septuagint	*Vulgate*	*English Bibles*
Esdras A	3 Esdras	1 Esdras
Esdras B	1 Esdras	*Ezra
	2 Esdras	*Nehemiah
—	4 Esdras	2 Esdras

Using the titles of the English Apocrypha, *1 Esdras* is a retelling of the biblical history derived from 2 Chronicles, Ezra and Nehemiah with an interpolated story (3. 1–5. 6) of how Zerubbabel wins the assistance of Darius for the rebuilding of the temple. *2 Esdras*, and specifically chs. 3–14, is also known as the *'Ezra Apocalypse'*. It describes seven visions: the first three concern the destruction of Jerusalem and the problem of evil; the sixth (ch. 13) is of the victorious *Messiah, described as 'son of man'. It is usually dated toward the end of the 1st cent. CE.

Eshet hayil (Heb., 'A woman of valour'). Title, from opening words, of a Jewish song, derived from Proverbs, praising virtuous women. Proverbs 31. 10–31 describes a good woman in an alphabetic acrostic of twenty-two verses. It concludes, 'charm is deceitful and beauty is vain, but a woman who fears the Lord is to be praised'. Often (since *Tikkunei Shabbat* (1641) first commended the custom) the song is recited by the husband in a Jewish home before the *Sabbath evening *kiddush. It also forms part of the prayers for womens' funerals and is used on tombstones. In *Kabbalistic Judaism, *Eshet Ḥayil* is taken as applying to the *Shekhinah of God as his bride.

Eshin Sōzu (Japanese monk): see GENSHIN.

Esoteric Buddhism: see MIKKYŌ; SHINGON; and Index *ad loc.*

Essenes. Jewish sect, of a communal kind, active during the later part of the period of the second *Temple. The name was taken by *Philo (*Hypothetica* 11. 1–18, *Every Good Man is Free* 12. 75–13. 91) to mean 'holy ones', but others have suggested 'silent ones', 'healers', or 'pious ones'. In addition to Philo, the sect is known about from *Josephus (*War* 2. 119–61, *Antiquities* 18. 18–22, *Life* 2. 9–11), Pliny (*Natural History* 5. 73), and *Eusebius. Its beliefs and practices bear some resemblance to those described in the sectarian documents found at Qumran (see DEAD SEA SCROLLS), but it is too simple to identify the two: a more probable relationship is that they are variations on a theme, not least because of transient membership between the two.

In the early 1st cent. BCE, the sect numbered about 4,000. Only adult males were admitted after a three-year probationary period, when they swore an oath of obedience and secrecy about the teachings. Celibacy was enjoined, though Josephus knew of a group of Essenes who were married. Meals were eaten in common, and attention was paid to cleanliness and ritual purity, with the *Sabbath being observed with great strictness. They paid careful attention to ethics, and although they were critical of the Jerusalem Temple, they sent votive offerings to it. In defence of a true obedience to God and his *Torah, Essenes were among those who fought against Rome in the first Jewish revolt. Its failure in 70 CE removed them from the scene.

E. Schurer, rev. G. Vermes *et al.*, *The History of the Jewish People* (1979).

est. An acronym for Erhard Seminar Training. Established by Werner Erhard in 1971, seminars provide 'a sixty-hour educational experience which creates an opportunity for people to realize their potential to transform the quality of their lives'. As of Dec. 1984, when the original seminar closed, up to half-a-million in a number of countries had 'graduated'. est is especially popular in monied and middle-class America. It has been estimated that one out of twenty-six San Franciscan adults have taken the training. Best regarded as belonging to the human potential movement, more specifically as a self development religion, est has been at the forefront of fusing W. forms of psychological growth and E. (especially *Zen) forms of spirituality. est has also been influential in fusing self and social transformation. Attention is not limited to benefiting the isolated individual. The Centres Network, as Erhard's organization is now called, aims to eradicate hunger (The World Hunger Project), transform what it is to work, and in general make a difference to social life.

W. Bartley, *Werner Erhard* (1978); L. Rhinehart, *The Book of est* (1976).

Established Church. Any Church recognized by state law as the official religion of a country. An example is the *Church of England. Sometimes less formal arrangements give to a Church particular status, as with the Greek Orthodox Church in Greece. See also ETHIOPIAN ORTHODOX CHURCH.

Esther. Heroine of the Jewish Book of Esther. Esther (Heb., Ester), a beautiful Jewess, became the queen of the Persian king Xerxes I (486–65 BCE), called in this book Ahasuerus. When Haman, the prime minister, encouraged the king to issue an edict of extermination against the Jews, Esther, urged by her cousin Mordecai, begged for the life of her people. The king acceded to her pleas, and Haman himself was hanged on the gallows prepared for Mordecai. This story is read in the *synagogue on the feast of *Purim (also called the Feast of Esther), and children are encouraged to drown the sound of Haman with noisemakers whenever his name is read in the story. According to the *aggadah, Esther was descended from King Saul and was one of the four most beautiful women in the world (*B.Meg.* 13a, *B.Meg.* 15a). The day before Purim is known as the Fast of Esther. This is particularly celebrated by Russian Jews. Particular *seliḥot are recited, and the fast day portion of the *Torah is read in the synagogue (Exodus 32. 11–14, 34. 1–10).

The Book of Esther is the only book in the *Bible which does not mention the name of God. The name 'Esther' is therefore read as the Hebrew verb, 'I will hide': God is constantly active even when he does not directly reveal his action. Thus, although Esther was the wife of Ahasuerus, she was not involved in sexual relations with him, because God sent a spirit looking exactly like her to replace her on those occasions. The apparent absence of a religious context was made good in the Gk. translation with six additional passages: in the *Vulgate, and subsequent RC Bibles, 10. 4–16. 24.

Eta (category of excluded people): see BURAKU.

Eternalism. A belief refuted by Buddhism. In *Theravāda, it is the false belief that the self is independent of the body-mind continuum and therefore survives death unchanged (Pāli, *sassata-diṭṭhi*). In *Mahāyāna, it is the false belief in the inherent existence (Skt., *svabhāva, 'own-being' or 'essence') of anything whatsoever (Skt., *śāśvata-dṛṣṭi*). It is the opposite of *nihilism. See further SASSATAVĀDA.

Eternal light (Heb., *ner tamid*). The light kept burning before the *ark in the Jewish *synagogue. The *ner tamid* is a symbolic reminder of the golden seven-branched candlestick (*menorah) which burned continually in the *temple. Originally, it was placed in a niche in the western wall, but now is suspended in front of the Ark. It has been understood as symbolizing God's presence in the place of prayer. Alternatively, it is seen as representing a spiritual light emanating from *Jerusalem. In ancient times, it was created by burning a wick in olive oil; more recently *candles were used, and nowadays the *ner tamid* is generally fuelled by electricity.

Eternity. Not a long time, since 'eternity' does not enter into the dimension of time. *Brahman and God have been thought of as 'being' of that eternal state, where there is no passing of *time, although the passing of time is simultaneously present to Brahman/God. Thus Boethius defined eternity as *interminabilis vitae tota simul et perfecta possessio* ('the total, simultaneous and absolute possession of unlimited life'). Although this is the definitional truth of Brahman/God, it is also the possible perfection of the human *ātman/soul, because already it participates in eternity—ātman because it is not other than Brahman, the soul because the expression of the human mind is outside spatial and temporal definition, however much at present (i.e. in time) it is correlated with both; thus, putting it crudely, a thought cannot be weighed, measured, or located in space, however much it is correlated with particular brains. Philosophical reflections are usually far from the descriptive languages of religious texts, and the God of the Bible is portrayed as actively involved in time:

> Yet in truth, if God is not timeless and unchanging, then it is not *God* that God would turn out to be. If what we discern (albeit dimly and with very inadequate language if we try to talk about it), in and through the moments and occasions of absolute value, is not the timeless and unchanging source of that value, the unproduced Producer of all that is, then the term God is not worth using, because we would be affirming as absolute that which is not.... There is thus nothing in the least illogical in recognising that the timeless and unchanging can have complete awareness of the timeful and changing, and can have present to it even the fall of a sparrow, without losing that timeless and unchanging nature. It is to *that* nature that the fall of the sparrow is present—and Auschwitz and Golgotha—not to one who is subject to the changes and chances of this fleeting world (Bowker, *A Year to Live*, 1991).

A. N. Balslev, *A Study of Time in Indian Philosophy* (1983); T. F. Torrance, *Space, Time and Incarnation* (1969).

Etheria (early pilgrim to Jerusalem): see PILGRIMAGE, CHRISTIANITY.

Ethical monotheism. The worship of, and adherence to, one God which is based on practice, rather than arrived at as the conclusion of a philosophical argument. An example is the gradual insistence on *Yahweh to the exclusion of other gods in the biblical period of Judaism.

Ethics. The human concern for what is right and wrong, good and evil. Ethics arise from the human awareness of the future, combined with a lack of detailed knowledge about it. Lives and actions have to be projected into acknowledged but unknown futures, which at once makes evaluation inevitable: is a possible action right or wrong, wise or foolish, prudential or risky, good or evil? The attribution of value then extends to much else, and produces the characteristic recognition by humans of truth, beauty, and goodness, not as contingent or arbitrary, but as independent of the moment which gives rise to them—i.e. as absolutes. What *counts* as good or evil varies from age to age, culture to culture, though even then there is a considerable convergence which overrides what is known as *cultural relativity—which claims, in *Pascal's sentence, that what is true on one side of the Pyrenees is not true on the other. The anthropologist Fürer-Haimendorf exemplified cultural relativity in ethics thus: 'A European peasant, beheading a woman from a neighbouring village whom he happened to meet on her way home from the fields, would be locked up as a criminal lunatic; whereas in a Naga village, a youth returning with a human head captured under similar circumstances earns the insignia of a successful headhunter' (*Morals and Merit*, (1967), 1). What counts as right and wrong will always, to an extent, be culturally relative, but not the human ability to make such judgements, which is universal (those who cannot operate such judgements are recognized as ec-centric by such terms as 'psychopath') because it arises from the way the brain is built by the genes, in a body which can only live successfully in limits set by a planet of this kind. The gene-based brain and body is a human universal, however much particular lives are affected by their own histories and cultural contexts.

Religions are aware of these universals as a matter of experience. They know that thoughts and actions based on the absolutes of truth, beauty, and goodness are to be endorsed and encouraged, and perhaps are to be rewarded after death, even if not in this life (though in origin, there was no belief in a worthwhile life with God after *death in either the E. or the W. traditions: hence the far more prominent note in religions that good actions are to be undertaken and evil ones eschewed simply for what they are). But religions are equally aware of (and have different explanations for) the truth that humans frequently do what they know to be wrong. In Paul's memorable summary, 'The good that I would, I do not do; and the evil that I would not, that I do' (Romans 7. 19). Religious ethics are concerned, far more than secular ethics are, with the causes and consequences of evil.

On the basis of the experience of the human universal to make moral judgements and recognitions, religions have believed, in general, that there is a naturally good way to live and behave. In the E., this tends to be summarized under *dharma, in the W. under *natural law. Roughly speaking, if there is a consistent way for things to behave appropriately in the natural order (e.g. for stones to fall when dropped, or for the movement of planets to be predictable—hence the interest in the connections between those regularities and humans in *astrology), it would be extremely odd if there were not a naturally good way for humans to live with each other. In the W., this led Aristotle to propose what has subsequently been elaborated as eudaimonism—human flourishing. What has been a matter of contest, within religions as well as between them, is whether what counts as 'flourishing' has been fixed for all time (e.g. in the word of God in revelation, whether Vedic, Biblical or Quranic), or whether there is a constant exegesis of the eudaimonic—no doubt on the basis of previous experience and revelation (where applicable), but nevertheless prepared to move and change. Aristotle, after all, could not imagine a world without slaves and the subordination of wives to husbands—it was both natural and eudaimonic for those concerned; we do not agree, because the detail of the eudaimonic is not fixed for all time in all respects.

On the same basis of the human universal to make judgements of what is right and wrong, good and evil, religions have developed many different styles of moral living and accountability. They may see humans born with a radical deficit (*original sin) or with an accumulation of gain and loss from previous lives (*karma) or as balanced between good and evil and having always to choose, but with God having indicated where the right choice lies (through *Torah for Jews, *Qur'ān for Muslims, and *Ādi Granth for Sikhs). Thus the moral and ethical conflicts between religions are not essentially about issues so much as they are about differences in anthropologies (accounts of what human nature is and what its destiny may be). Religions, therefore, may differ in what they identify as a good action or a good person (though there is strong convergence, nevertheless). They certainly differ greatly in the status they give to laws and rules in the forming of moral life (at an extreme, this produces the recurrent theme of *antinomianism). But they agree very profoundly in their belief that human beings are capable of distinguishing between good and evil, or right and wrong, and of acting on those judgements. Those judgements may be strongly constrained by many things—by previous experience, by family upbringing, by genetic inheritance—and we may be limited in what we can actually do for ourselves. We may, in other words, need help, whether from God by way of command or *grace, or from *bodhisattva by way of compassionate assistance, or from spiritual guides and *gurus. But all religions believe that we have some competence to take charge of the lives we project into whatever futures there may be, and to allow moral considerations to act upon our decisions. This is what it means to be human. If there is a basic human right (concerning which, in such terms, religions say little), it is the right to be human in this way—to be sufficiently free to exercise responsibility and accountability in this way.

In a brief article, only an indication of characteristic emphases can be given for some of the major religions; but see also J. Holm and J. Bowker (eds.), *Making Moral Decisions* (1994); and Index, Ethics.

J. B. Carman and M. Juergensmeyer (eds.), *A Bibliographic Guide to the Comparative Study of Ethics* (1990); W. O. Cole, *Moral Issues in Six Religions* (1991); R. M. Green, *Religion and Moral Reason* (1988).

Judaism Jewish ethics are derived from *Torah as the God-given revelation of the way in which the broken human condition (described graphically in the opening chapters of *Genesis) can be repaired. Torah cannot be translated as 'law', but it is guidance which contains law, which in turn sets the conditions of the restored *covenant with God. Humans are not radically evil (the story of *Adam and Eve is not understood as Christians understand it): they are confronted by the two *inclinations. Torah is a language through which Jews (by their obedience to the laws) say 'Yes' to God and to his guidance, not for their own sake, but for that of the whole world, until 'the knowledge of God shall cover the earth as the waters cover the sea'. In this context, law merges with morality—and it was a dispute among the *rabbis whether an act to be moral had to go *beyond* what the law required (*lifnim mi-shurat ha-din*, 'beyond the boundary of the law'). It is perhaps simplest to say that law is the necessary, but not the sufficient, condition of the good life. In the vital *imitatio Dei* (*imitation of God), the details are all derived from Torah itself. However, written Torah does not cover every conceivable situation, so oral Torah (*oral law, which was believed also to have been given to *Moses on Mount Sinai) extended the source of moral authority into the rabbinic age. Even so, there is a continuing quest for legitimate decisions, especially when new issues arise—e.g. in bioethics. That is because Judaism, while based on law, is not legalistic. There are in fact only three moral absolutes, summarized in *kiddush ha-Shem; otherwise, much rabbinic discussion is devoted to ranking obligations in order of priority: saving life having precedent over keeping the *Sabbath is an example. In so far as there are differences between the major forms of Judaism, they mainly arise over the status given to the different styles of exegesis in the past, not over Torah and *halakhah as the source of the good life.

J. B. Agus, *The Vision and the Way* (1966); S. D. Breslauer, *Contemporary Jewish Ethics: A Bibliographical Survey* (1985, 1986), *Modern Jewish Morality: A Bibliographical Survey* (1986); S. Spero, *Morality, Halakah and the Jewish Tradition* (1983).

Christianity Christian ethics derive from the occasion when *Jesus was asked, as teachers, especially rabbis, often were at that time, to give his *kelal* of Torah (choice of verse which summarizes Torah). His choice, the love of God and the love of one's neighbour, was neither unique nor controversial. However, it was combined with strongly enacted claims to be manifesting the power (*dunamis*) of God to change people's lives in the direction of that command through healing and forgiveness—a claim which certainly threatened the *Temple as the locus of decision-making at that time, since it implied a direct relationship between God and humans, mediated through his own person. When this led to his crucifixion (see REBELLIOUS ELDER) and resurrection, the foundations for a radically different understanding of the covenant (the new testament) were laid. But the context-independent command of love had to be made context-specific: it had to be related to the circumstances in which the early and subsequent Christians found themselves. This is exactly what one finds *Paul and others doing in the writings which became eventually the New Testament. For example, in 1 Corinthians, Paul states how they should deal with a case of incest, with dietary scruples, with marriage and virginity, with support of ministry, with the behaviour of women in services, until he bursts out, almost in exasperation, 'I will show you a more excellent way'; and he reverts to the controlling, but context-independent, command of love. Christian ethics have oscillated through history between these extremes: on the one side, Situation Ethics, associated with Joseph Fletcher, emphasized the importance of each situation determining what is the most loving thing to do (echoing *Augustine's, *Ama, et fac quod vis*, 'Love, and do what you will'); on the other, when the *pope defines a matter of morals (as also of faith), it is infallibly decided; short of that, encyclicals (e.g. **Humanae Vitae*) offer advice which has such authority that some treat them as virtually infallible. Between the two, most Christians refer to the Bible (though with great division about whether or not the Bible, or at least the New Testament, should be treated as containing commands, applicable as non-negotiable law) and live their lives somewhere between the two extremes by the exercise of conscience. In the main forms of Christianity, conscience is the absolutely inviolable and sacrosanct centre of the person as human, as responsible for her or his decisions. In *Newman's insistent words, 'Conscience is the first of all the *Vicars of Christ.' Conscience should indeed be informed (see INVINCIBLE IGNORANCE; EXTRA ECCLESIAM), but it cannot be coerced. As *Bonhoeffer put it, 'Conscience is directed not towards a particular kind of doing, but towards a particular kind of being'—the self with God alone, in the communion of saints.

J. Macquarrie and J. Childress (eds.), *A New Dictionary of Christian Ethics* (1986).

Islam Since God has given to humans his guidance for their behaviour in the Qur'ān, Muslim ethics (*akhlāq*) are necessarily grounded in the Qur'ān. But as with all revelations, not every conceivable circumstance is covered in the Qur'ān. A second major source of guidance, therefore, lies in *ḥadīth: Muḥammad and his Companions were the first living commentaries on Qur'ān, and although ḥadīth is not in the same category of authority as the Qur'ān, nevertheless the example of *insān al-kāmil* (the perfect man) is of constant importance. The controlling concept of Muslim ethics is *tawḥīd, the absolute unity of God. From this derives the goal of creating a single *'umma (community of equals through the world), since all things and all people are derived from God who is One. Life as God desires it was eventually formulated more systematically in the schools of *sharīʿa (law), which detail the things which are lawful and prohibited (*al-halal w'al haram) for a Muslim. However, by no means all things are specified, and the principle applies that whatever God has not forbidden is allowed (as a mark of his generosity), though always within the boundaries of 'what God wills' as revealed in more general terms in the Qur'ān. Thus although Islam is regarded often by outsiders as an inflexible religion, there is much openness: the individual will have to account for his or her deeds on the final day to God, not to a Book. And even in relation to the Qur'ān, the meaning of the Arabic is not determined (there is always room for continuing exegesis); the traditional methods of application of Qur'ān and ḥadīth still apply: for these see IJMĀʿ, QIYĀS, IJTIHĀD.

Y. al-Qaradawi, *The Lawful and the Prohibited in Islam* (n. d.); A. R. I. Doi, *Shariah* . . . (1984); R. G. Hovannisian (ed.), *Ethics in Islam*, (1985).

Hinduism Hinduism is a coalition of widely differing styles in religious life and belief, but shared in common is the belief that humans are bearers of souls (*ātman) which are reborn many millions of times (*saṃsāra)—so long, in fact, as they are entangled in bodies which desire transient appearances more than the truth. In each life, *karma accumulates—for good and for ill—which is worked out in subsequent lives, until one orders one's life in the direction of release, which necessarily involves good actions. 'Hinduism' is a map of the many ways in which one may so live that the ātman attains its goal and obtains *mokṣa (release). In other words, Hinduism is a map of *dharma (appropriateness), and its own name for itself is *sanātana dharma*, everlasting dharma: in the Hindu way, it is dharma that has primacy as ethics, because it corresponds to *ṛta, the cosmic order in which natural law is grounded. Central to this in relation to ethical behaviour is *varṇāśramadharma, one's duty in relation to class/caste (*varna) and the four stages of life (*āśrama), which still obtains for many (though as always, not for all) Hindus. Within these concepts are contained the ritual obligations which sustain Hindu life. Although, therefore, much of dharma can be described in such works as the *Dharmaśāstras or the **Manusmṛti*, to each person there obtains *svadharma*, his or her own dharma. This may lead one to actions which may seem repugnant, as when *Arjuna shrank from battle, because it would involve killing his kinsfolk—yet *Kṛṣṇa insists that he must follow his dharma as a warrior, since in any case he cannot kill what is essential about any person, namely ātman. It is this which allows the Hindu to explore, in order to transcend by indifference, that which is normally (normatively) unethical in *Tantra. Only when the soul has overcome all attachment, whether of desire or of repugnance, can mokṣa be obtained.

C. Crawford, *The Evolution of Hindu Ethical Ideals* (1982); S. Jhingrom, *Aspects of Hindu Morality* (1989); P. H. Prabhu, *Hindu Social Organization* (1963).

Buddhism While the Buddha rejected the Hindu belief in an undying ātman passing from life to life, he nevertheless affirmed continuity of consequence flowing from one life to another, working out the consequences of karma and *taṇhā (thirst or clinging). His 'middle way' to enlightenment included the necessity for right conduct. This is summarized for laypeople in the Five Precepts (Pañca-*śīla), which are not so much commands as promises which a person makes to himself/herself each morning; and the Ten Precepts for the members of monastic communities. The Buddha's own lives are exemplary in defining what is good—the plural 'lives' being a reminder that the Buddha-to-be appeared in previous lives, stories concerning which are found in the *Jātaka collections. Of the Five Precepts, the first, *ahiṁsā (non-injury) has further implications, because no exception was made for the killing of animals for sacrifice. *Dāna (giving) developed as a substitute, leading to the characteristically dynamic relationship between laypeople and the *saṅgha (monastic community), and to generosity at the heart of ethical life. Mahāyāna Buddhism developed in too many different directions to allow summary, but central to all is the *bodhisattva ideal, which reinforces generous compassion at the heart of the good life. In what at first sight seems a startling contrast, there is the apparent use of deceit or of immoral methods by Buddhas and bodhisattvas to teach lessons. But this is *upāya-kauśalya (the use of skilful means) which operates at a preliminary level in order to bring home a higher truth. Thus the Buddha once encouraged *Mañjuśrī to kill him (against ahiṁsā) in order to emphasize that, since there is no self (*anātman), the Buddha cannot be 'killed'; indeed, to kill a person is to suppose that he has a soul, because he is then condemned to ignorance. This approach is taken to an extreme in *Vajrayāna, which resembles the attitude of Tantra (see Hindu ethics, above). The aim remains that of all Buddhist ethics, the development of mahā-*karuṇā, great and unlimited compassion.

G. Dharmasiri, *The Fundamentals of Buddhist Ethics* (1986); H. Saddhatissa, *Buddhist Ethics* (1970).

Confucianism The teaching of Confucius and of the Confucian school is addressed to the good of society, not simply to individual behaviour, or the attainment of individual goals. It is often summarized in the phrases, 'The Three Bonds' (between parent and child, husband and wife, ruler and subject), and 'The Five Relationships' (including those between brothers and between friends). Confucius believed that, with the help of heaven (*t'ien) or a positive moral force (*te), people can produce the all-important characteristics of *jen and *li. The moral issue can then be put as a question: 'How would the wise person (*sheng-jen) or ideal person (*chün tzu*) respond with te, and in accord with jen and li, in this situation?' Although Confucian ethics may seem to stress the desirability of hierarchical or vertical relationships, in fact the key factor stressed by Confucius is *shu* (reciprocity), even if the principle of authority has also been upheld in these relationships. Since Confucian thought was not insulated against influence from outside, it is the development of reciprocity which received stimulus from *Mencius. He stressed that 'no person is devoid of a heart sensitive to the suffering of others . . . : the heart of compassion is the seed of benevolence, of shame, of duty, . . . of right and wrong, of wisdom'. Confucianism was open to attack and criticism which also affected the development of the dominant school: see e.g. MO TZU, HSÜN TZU, and (at the root of Taoism) LAO TZU and CHUANG TZU.

Sikh 'Truthful living' is the aim of Sikh life which necessarily embraces ethics (Ādi Granth 62). It requires a positive action and effort (*kirat karna*) in a constant work of service (*seva) to others: 'Only by the self-forgetting service of others can God be reached' (AG 26). This is expressed particularly in *vand chakna*, sharing with others. Because all humans are subverted by *haumai, this effort is not easy to initiate or sustain, but Sikhs receive help from the grace of God, the teachings of the scriptures, and the example of the *Gurus.

S. S. Kohli, *Sikh Ethics*, (1975); Avtar Singh, *The Ethics of the Sikhs*, (1970).

Ethics of the Fathers: see AVOT.

Ethiopianism. A term used to identify one type of African independent church, which first emerged in the 1880s in Ghana, Nigeria (here called the 'African churches'), and in S. Africa, where the term was first used by Mokone's Ethiopian Church in 1892. It is based on references to Ethiopia in the Bible, especially in Psalm 68. 31, and on the ancient Christian kingdom of Ethiopia; together these provide a charter for dignity and independence. Ethiopian forms of the church also supported early nationalist movements and were sometimes involved in active revolt. 'Ethiopian' has become more of a religious classificatory term, in distinction from *Zionist in S. Africa or prophet-healing elsewhere. Ethiopian churches usually resemble the mission or older churches from which they secede in beliefs and practice, except for cultural features such as polygamy, leadership structure, or enthusiastic worship.

Ethiopian Jews: see FALASHAS.

Ethiopian Orthodox Church. The *monophysite national church of Ethiopia. The Church entertains legends of its origin in the preaching of Matthew or the eunuch of Acts 8. 26–39, but the planting of Christianity in the country actually dates from the 4th-cent. work of Frumentius at the royal court. Frumentius was consecrated the first *Abuna (patriarch) by Athanasius of Alexandria (*c.*340), thus establishing the dependence of the Church on the Church of Egypt. It became isolated from the rest of Christendom by the Islamic conquests of the 7th and 8th cents. There were periods of vitality under the Abuna Takla Haymanot (13th cent.) and the emperor Zara Jacob (1434–68) before a period of renewed Muslim pressure on the country in the 16th cent. Attempts at reunion with the Roman Catholic Church began at this time as a price of military help given by the Portuguese, but have never been successful and today there is only a small *Uniat body. The Church achieved independence from the Coptic Church with the advent of the first native Abuna in 1959. Until the revolution of 1974 the Church was part of the feudal, social, and economic system in Ethiopia. There were 200,000 priests, most of whom lived by farming church lands, and 827 monasteries. At the revolution the Church lost its established status and its lands were nationalized. Patriarch Tewoflos was arrested and was presumed dead. The socialist government has claimed not to be hostile to religion; churches are given an annual budget, and some congregations are active. Government interference and local persecutions are, however, constantly reported.

The Ethiopian Orthodox Church is in communion with the other *Oriental Orthodox Churches. It is unique, however, in its observance of Jewish practices, e.g. the keeping of the *Sabbath, *circumcision, and the distinction of clean and unclean meats. The Church also claims a connection with biblical Israel through the Queen of Sheba. How these Jewish themes and legends in Ethiopian Christianity are to be explained is very obscure. See also FALASHAS.

F. Heyer, *Die Kirche Äthiopiens . . .*, (1971); E. Ullendorf, *Ethiopia and the Bible* (1968).

Eto: see CHRISTIAN FELLOWSHIP CHURCH.

Etrog. Citron fruit used on the Jewish *festival of *Sukkot. The etrog is one of the *four species used as part of the liturgy. It was a frequent decorative motif in Jewish art in the second *Temple period; and it was believed to be the fruit of the tree of knowledge eaten by *Adam and Eve.

Eucharist (Gk., *eucharistia*, 'thanksgiving'). The principal service of Christian worship, at least in non-*Protestant churches. It is also variously called (Holy) *Communion, the *Lord's Supper, and the *Mass. The earliest account of the eucharist is *Paul's reference to the 'Lord's supper' in 1 Corinthians 11. 23–5, which attributes its institution to the words and actions of *Jesus at the *Last Supper and identifies the bread and the 'cup' with his body and blood. On the basis of other early texts (e.g. Luke 24. 30–5, **Didache* 9), some scholars suggest that a different kind of eucharist may have recalled other meals of Jesus with his followers. In any case it was the Pauline form of the eucharist which prevailed. It is usual, following G. Dix's influential book *The Shape of the Liturgy* (1945 and later edns.), to analyse the eucharist broadly into a 'four-action shape': '(1) The offertory; bread and wine are "taken" and placed on the table together. (2) The prayer; the president gives thanks to God over bread and wine together. (3) The fraction; the bread is broken. (4) The communion; the bread and wine are distributed together.'

Within this general outline, *liturgies of the eucharist are classified into *rites according to their ancestry in one or another of the major ancient Christian centres. The Byzantine and Oriental rites tend to be more elaborate than the Roman.

Two aspects of the theology of the eucharist in particular have been traditionally controversial in the West. First, in what sense do the elements of bread and wine become Christ's body and blood? Some of the *fathers wrote as if they believed in the persistence of the elements as bread and wine after consecration, and others as though they held them to be no longer there. The fourth *Lateran Council (1215) affirmed the *transubstantiation of the elements, and later in the century the doctrine was worked out, notably by St Thomas *Aquinas. The consequent idea of Christ's '*real presence' in the eucharistic elements led to an increase in devotion to the blessed *sacrament, shown e.g. by the institution of the feast of *Corpus Christi (1264). At the *Reformation, major controversies on the subject took place. M. *Luther argued for *consubstantiation (after the consecration, bread and wine coexist with the body and blood); *Zwingli maintained that the Lord's Supper was a memorial rite, with no change in the elements. *Calvin also denied that any change in substance took place, but held that the faithful receive the virtue (hence Virtualism), i.e. effect, of the body and blood of Christ which is really but spiritually present. Among Protestants these doctrines all have modern exponents.

The other controversy since the 14th cent. has been the doctrine of the eucharistic sacrifice: see SACRIFICE. Both these controversies have been eased by the *liturgical movement, which has shifted attention to the corporate nature of worship in the eucharist: it is now widely agreed that the eucharist commemorates the one and only sacrifice of Christ in such a way as to make its effects real. See Index, Eucharist.

L. Bouyer, *Eucharist* (1968); J. Emminghaus, *The Eucharist* (1978); R. C. D. Jasper and G. J. Cuming, *Prayers of the Eucharist: Early and Reformed* (3rd edn., 1987); J. Reumann, *The Supper of the Lord* (1985); B. Thompson, *Liturgies of the Western Church*.

Euchologion (Gk.). The book containing the text and rubrics for the Orthodox liturgy of the *eucharist, fixed parts of the daily *office, and the other sacraments and minor rituals.

Eudaimonism (human flourishing): see ETHICS.

Euhemerism. From Euhemerus (*c.*320 BCE), who argued that the gods developed out of elaborated legends concerned originally with historical people. Applied to Jesus, the question becomes, not **cur Deus homo?*, but *cur homo Deus?* Why (or how) was the man Jesus promoted to become the Son of God? The historical evidence supporting this interpretation of Jesus is negligible, not least since the letters of Paul, among the earliest writings of the New Testament, associate Jesus closely with God, with extremely high titles and claims. See also MYTH.

Eusebius (*c.*260–*c.*340). Bishop of Caesarea in Palestine and church historian. He called himself Eusebius Pamphilii after his teacher Pamphilius, a disciple of *Origen. He was sympathetic to *Arianism, and at the Council of *Nicaea the creed he proposed as a compromise between the parties was rejected. He accepted the *homoousion formula formally though never in earnest. Eusebius's most important work was the *Ecclesiastical History*, containing an immense range of material, including many extracts from earlier writers, about the Church from the beginning to his own time. It seems that books i–vii were published in 303, and the final edn. including books viii–x in 323. Among his other historical works are a *Chronicle*, containing tables synchronizing events in ancient history; a *Life of Constantine*, to whom he was theological advisor; and an account of the *Martyrs of Palestine* in the persecution of 303–10. His most important theological writings are the two apologetic works, *Preparation for the Gospel* (refuting Greek polytheism) and *Demonstration of the Gospel* (proving Christianity from the Old Testament).

R. M. Grant, *Eusebius as Church Historian* (1980); K. Lake et al., *Eusebius' Ecclesiastical History* (1927–8).

Eutyches (*c.*378–454). Christian *heretic, who opposed *Nestorianism so strongly that he was accused in 448 of the opposite error of confounding the two natures in Christ, and of denying that Christ's manhood was consubstantial with ours. He was deposed, then reinstated at *Ephesus in 449, and finally condemned at *Chalcedon in 451. 'Eutychianism' is thus repudiated by all Christian denominations, even though his confession of 'one nature' of Christ after the incarnation makes him akin to the *Monophysites.

Evagrius of Pontus (346–99). Christian spiritual writer. He was a noted preacher in *Constantinople, but left the temptations of the capital for Jerusalem and (in 382) the Nitrian desert of Egypt, to devote himself to prayer among the monks. He became a disciple of St *Macarius. His mystical works, largely in the form of aphorisms, were the main channel through which the ideas of *Origen passed to later writers like *Cassian, pseudo-*Dionysius, and *Maximus the Confessor. Few are preserved in Gk., owing to his condemnation from 553 onwards as Origenist. His *Centuries*, for example, is preserved in Syriac, where, however, it was heavily edited to alter the more Origenistic statements.

Tr. A. J. Mason, *Fifty Spiritual Homilies* (1921); D. J. Chitty, *The Desert a City* (1977).

Evam mayā śrutam ekasmin samaye or **evam me sutam ekam samayam** (Skt., Pāli). 'Thus have I heard. At one time . . .', the form of words occurring at the beginning of Buddhist *sūtras to show that a discourse of the Buddha is being related. It is followed by the name of the place where the discourse was given and often by the number of people who were present and a list of the prominent disciples who were there; then the discourse is related. The phrase gives an indication of how the Buddha's teaching came to be preserved: it is said by tradition that his disciples met after his death to recite what they could remember of his teaching. Each individual began his recital with these words which were retained in future transmissions of the teaching. Cf. Muslim methods of transmitting and safeguarding *ḥadīth.

Evangelical Alliance. An interdenominational body formed in 1846 as a response to *Tractarianism and as an expression of unity 'on the basis of great evangelical principles'. After initial problems over divergent views among Americans concerning slavery, the Alliance became established both in Europe and the USA. Its 19th-cent. enterprises included a vigorous campaign for human rights on behalf of small *Protestant groups who were suffering persecution in some parts of Europe. The Alliance's 20th-cent. work in England was given more vigorous expression after the Second World War by promoting evangelistic crusades, conferences for ministers, accommodation for overseas students, and active co-operation among interdenominational missionary societies. Prominent amongst its more recent achievements was the formation of TEAR Fund which raises *c.*£5–6 million a year for relief work throughout the world. A founder member of the World Evangelical Fellowship (1951), it continues each year to sponsor a week of prayer in early Jan.

Evangelical and Reformed Church. Formed in 1934 by a merger of two American churches of German background: the Reformed Church in the United States (called 'German Reformed Church' until 1869) which had originated in 18th-cent. migrations of German *Calvinists to the Middle Atlantic states, and the Evangelical Synod of North America, which was formed of congregations of 19th-cent. immigrants principally in the Midwest. Following the practice of the latter, the new denomination accepted *Reformed and *Lutheran standards of belief equally. In 1957 it merged with the *Congregational Christian churches to become the *United Church of Christ.

Evangelicals. *Protestant Christians who stress belief in personal conversion and salvation by faith in the atoning death of Christ, and in the Bible as the sole authority in matters of faith: stress is also laid on evangelism. Evangelicals typically uphold the importance of preaching in contrast to liturgical worship; reject such *catholic doctrines as the eucharistic *sacrifice; incline to *millenarian ideas; and entertain strong suspicions of the Roman Catholic Church in general. They may be said to be the most direct heirs of 'Protestant orthodoxy', and particularly *Calvinism. See also CONSERVATIVE EVANGELICALS.

In the Anglican Church, Evangelicals form a party rather than the whole membership. This party originated in the 'Evangelical revival' of the 18th cent., which renewed Christian commitment at a time when church life was at a low ebb. It survived within the Church of England after the separation of *Methodists and the Countess of *Huntingdon's Connexion, and in the 19th cent. showed its vitality especially in social reform and missionary work (see CMS). Anglican Evangelicals, however, continue to feel a kinship with members of other Protestant churches (see also LOW CHURCHMEN), and some began to raise questions of association after the decision was made to ordain women. The decline in the Catholic emphasis has led to a strong revival in the influence of Evangelicals.

D. W. Bebbington, *Evangelicalism in Modern Britain: A History from the 1730s to the 1980s* (1989); M. A. Noll, *et al.* (eds.), *Evangelicalism* (1994).

Evangelist. 1. In the New Testament (e.g. Ephesians 4. 11), an itinerant missionary.

2. Any of the authors of the four canonical *gospels: Sts *Matthew, *Mark, *Luke, and *John. This usage dates from the 3rd cent. The four evangelists are traditionally symbolized by a man, a lion, an ox, and an eagle, respectively, on the basis of Ezekiel 10. 14 and Revelation 4. 6–10. The four signs are known as (Gk.) tetramorphs.

Evans-Pritchard, Sir Edward (1902–73). British anthropologist who concentrated on religion and related cultural phenomena. Involved with fieldwork in the S. Sudan during the period 1926–39, Evans-Pritchard's main intention was to show the rationality and coherence of the cultural domain, in order to refute the Lévy-Bruhl thesis of primitive mentality. Received into the Roman Catholic Church in 1944, his later work tended to be more directed at those (following E. *Durkheim) who hold that religion cannot be studied in its own right but instead should be reduced to social and political matters. *Theories of Primitive Religion* (1965) is a sustained attack on scientific theories of religion, and *Nuer Religion* (1956) is one of the first detailed studies of a pre-literate religion in which the religious domain is treated non-reductionistically. By means of the semantic investigation of ideas, metaphors, and meaning-laden activities such as *sacrifice, the religious is conveyed as a largely *sui generis* system. Indeed, his intra-religious approach at times becomes theological in tone. In short, his in many ways innovatory emphasis on the study of meanings enabled him to make a stand against scientific reductionism. 'Social anthropology', he insisted, 'studies societies as moral or *symbolic systems and not as natural systems.' This approach (known as *hermeneutic explanation) is in strong contrast to *nomothetic explanation (Gk., *nomos*, 'a law') which seeks to find covering laws or generalizations—e.g.

Evans-Pritchard's near-contemporary, A. Radcliffe-Brown (1881–1955): 'Social Anthropology . . . is a theoretical or nomothetic study of which the aim is to provide acceptable generalisation.' Through what he called 'comparative sociology', Radcliffe-Brown sought to establish structural principles governing human relationships.

M. T. Douglas, *Edward Evans-Pritchard* (1980).

Evans-Wentz, Walter Yeeling (1878–1965). Pioneer in revealing and interpreting *Tibetan Buddhist philosophy to the West. Born in Trenton, New Jersey, of *Quaker-Spiritualist parents and himself a life-long sympathizer with *Theosophy, Evans-Wentz was born into and kept a strong dissatisfaction with established Western religious explanation. Having obtained an MA from Stanford, to which he left money in his will for the founding of a chair in Oriental philosophy, religion, and ethics, Evans-Wentz' doctorate at Jesus College, Oxford, under Sir John Rhys, resulted in the publication of his first book, *The Fairy Faith in Celtic Countries* (1911). In 1914 he began twenty-seven years of global travelling, financed by a prowess in real estate inherited from his father, during which he scarcely spent more than a few weeks in one place. In 1919 in Gangtok, Evans-Wentz met the Lama Kazi Dawa Samdup (former teacher of Alexandra David-Neel who wrote *Magic and Mystery in Tibet*, 1965) and together they began translating the **Tibetan Book of the Dead*, 1927, a totally unknown manuscript which Evans-Wentz had picked up in a Darjeeling bazaar. Other books haphazardly followed: *Tibet's Great Yogi*, **Milarepa*, (1928); *Tibetan Yoga and Secret Doctrines*, (1935); *Tibetan Book of the Great Liberation*, (1954) (pt. 2 of which he considered his most important work), and *Cuchama and Sacred Mountains*, (1981) (posthumously).

Eve (Heb., Ḥavvah). According to Jewish scripture, the first woman. In the book of Genesis, Eve was created from the rib of the first man, *Adam (2. 21–3). She was tempted by the serpent to disobey God and eat from the fruit of the tree of knowledge of good and evil. In consequence, she was condemned to labour in childbirth, to be subject to her husband, and, together with Adam, to be expelled from the Garden of *Eden. According to the *aggadah, Eve was Adam's second wife after *Lilith had left him, and the serpent approached Eve rather than Adam because it knew women are more easily tempted (*ARN* 1. 4). Eve is buried beside Adam on Mount *Machpelah.

In Islam the wife of Adam is mentioned in the *Qur'ān, but not by name. Together they were guilty of disobedience and were therefore expelled from Paradise (7. 19–25, 20. 120–3). Further details, including the name Eve (Arab., Hawwā'), are given in legends, probably from Rabbinic and Syriac sources. Ḥawwā' was created from Adam's rib, shared his punishment, and accompanied him on his wanderings through the earth. Both are said to have made the *ḥajj (pilgrimage) to *Mecca, instituting the rituals. Ḥawwā' died two years after Adam and was buried beside him at *Mecca.

Evening Prayer or **Evensong.** The evening office of the *Anglican Church. In the **Book of Common Prayer* it consists of: prayers, *versicles and responses, the *Lord's Prayer, Psalms, lessons, canticles (*Magnificat and *Nunc Dimittis), the *Apostles' Creed, *Kyrie, Lord's Prayer, versicles and responses, three *collects, *anthem, and further prayers. It is a conflation of the medieval *vespers and *compline. 'Evening prayer' is also a title for Roman Catholic vespers. See also MORNING PRAYER.

Even Shetiyyah (rock on which, according to Jews and Muslims, world is founded): see EBEN SHETIYYAH.

Evil. The furthest reach of wrongdoing and wrong being. Although *Kant maintained that the only evil thing is an evil will, there is much in human experience which evokes the word which is not a product of the will. Indeed, Hannah *Arendt, observing the Eichmann trial, spoke of the banality of evil, lying as it does so far outside the compass of will, and being 'excused' by the appeal that, in a totalitarian regime, to obey orders and not to think is the only behaviour possible (*Eichmann in Jerusalem: A Study in the Banality of Evil*, 1965). In a somewhat similar style, *Nietzsche argued that good and evil are not objective realities in the world, but are, rather, creations of the individual will as it seeks to avoid responsibility by identifying external reasons for action—e.g. in the will of God. A pure act of will, exercising its genuine freedom, takes one 'beyond good and evil' (*Jenseits von Gut und Böse*, 1886). Religions with a linear understanding of *time tend to see the defeat of evil in a consummation at the end of time; those with a cyclical view tend to see evil as an inevitable incursion at the end of a cycle (e.g. *Kali-Yuga, *mappō), beyond which the Phoenix will always arise from the ashes. In both cases, religions tend to see the occurrence of evil as the consequence of personal agency in the cosmic order (personified as *Satan, the Devil or Iblīs, *Māra, etc.), which if made absolute leads to *dualism, an eternal principle of evil; and in either case, religions offer resources both to recognize and combat evil, though they are the first to recognize that evil in its most lethal character wears the robes, cassocks, and garments of religious people. Yet there remains an overall optimism that the good, in human experience, outlasts and transcends the evil, as Graham Greene put it powerfully as the conclusion of his novel, *Monsignor Quixote* (1982):

> The Mayor didn't speak again before they reached Orense; an idea quite strange to him had lodged in his brain. Why is it that the hate of a man—even of a man like Franco—dies with his death, and yet love, the love which he had begun to feel for Father Quixote, seemed now to live and grow in spite of the final separation and the final silence—

for how long, he wondered with a kind of fear, was it possible for that love of his to continue? And to what end?

See also THEODICY; EVIL, PROBLEM OF.

J. Hick, *Evil and the God of Love* (1966); W. D. O'Flaherty, *Origins of Evil in Hindu Mythology* (1976); P. Ricoeur, *The Symbolism of Evil* (1967); R. Taylor, *Good and Evil* (1970).

Evil, problem of. If God is both almighty and perfectly good, why is there *evil in the world? This challenge, made by Epicurus (341–270 BCE), has been repeated over the centuries, either as a response to the *Teleological Argument for God's existence or, more radically, to attack *theism. The book of *Job is one of the earliest treatments of the question. Attempts to show that evil in the world can be reconciled with God's power and goodness are known as theodicies (*theodicy).

Modern treatments of the problem distinguish between moral and natural (or physical) evil. The most common theodicy in response to the former is the Free Will Defence: moral evil is regarded as the result of human freedom, a price worth paying either because freedom is an intrinsic good or because its good effects outweigh its bad ones. Strategies with regard to natural evil are more diverse: it, too, is sometimes treated as a result of the *fall; but more commonly it is seen as a necessary feature of a world which is to serve as an arena for character-building or 'soul-making'. Many thinkers consider that the only wholly satisfactory solution to the problem would be an *eschatological one.

For bibl., see THEODICY.

Evil eye. The capacity of the eye to see what happens, and to read, has made it a powerful metaphor of the ability of God to observe and judge all things, and (in association with light) of wisdom. The inner eye, or third eye (see DYOYA-DṚṢṬI), is, in E. religions, a spiritual capacity to discern truth which is physical and can be developed by appropriate exercises. But the eye equally has the power to convey mischief or damage, and is then known as the evil eye. According to Jewish sages, Sarah cast the evil eye (Heb., *ayin ra'ah* or *ayin ha-ra*) on Hagar (*Gen.R.* 45. 5), as did Joseph's brothers on *Joseph (*Gen.R.* 84. 10). Folk heroes had equal power—R. *Simeon b. Yoḥai, for example, reduced a wicked man to a heap of bones by gazing at him (*B.Shab.* 34a). Persons who have the evil eye were believed to be intensely jealous, so folk wisdom encouraged the avoidance of any expression of admiration which might provoke envy; and amulets and *charms were used to ward off the danger. In Islam, the evil eye (Arab., *ʿayn*) can take effect even without the intention of the person possessing it, causing harm or death to human beings or animals, damage to crops or goods, etc. Its reality and power are attested from the *ḥadīth: *al-ʿayn ḥaqq*, 'the Eye is true'. Another ḥadīth reports, 'Were anything able to counteract the decree (of Allāh) it would be the Eye', perhaps intended to modify the first statement.

The basic cause is said to be envy, expressed in words or look; hence one of the most effective measures recommended by *Muḥammad was to recite the *sūras 113 and 114 which 'seek refuge' from all evil including the 'evil of the envious when he envies' (113. 5). Other ḥadīth give prophylactic or curative measures. To repel magic or spells, religious and traditional remedies are often combined. The representation of the five fingers (*khamsa*, 'five') or the eye itself may be painted on a wall of a house or used as an amulet. The colour blue is effective, or a mixture of herbs and alum may be burnt as incense, and spells recited.

This whole concept is disapproved of by orthodox Islam since it seems to deny or bypass the absolute divine power and decree, but it is virtually impossible to eradicate, and survives today in folklore, on the fringes of religion and medicine.

T. Canaan, *Aberglaube und Volksmedizin im Lande des Bibel*; C. Maloney, *The Evil Eye*, (1978); O. G. S. Crawford, *The Eye Goddess* (1957); R. Pettazzoni, *The All-Knowing God* (tr. 1956); E. Westermarck, *Pagan Survivals in Muhammadan Civilisation*.

Evil spirits. The sense of evil being a consequence of active agents is common in all religions. They may be synonymous with *demons (q.v. for examples), but evil spirits take on many other forms. In Zoroastrianism, as *daevas, they form a fundamental part of the dynamic of the whole system. Evil spirits are frequently the spirits of the dead who have not received appropriate care from the living, and who are therefore restless until they receive support: for examples, see KUEI, PRETA. Evil spirits may take possession of other lives, not least those of humans. They are then contested through *exorcism or other rituals. They may also be contested by exclusion from the existing human community, a strategy which resulted in the execution of *witches and others believed to have been possessed. The contest may also take place between spirits themselves, as between good and evil *angels. Theistic religions usually resist *dualism, so that in the end (or End) evil spirits are subjected to the authority and power of God, hence the strong statements in the New Testament that all powers are subject to Christ (e.g. I Corinthians 15. 20–8; Ephesians 1. 18–23), statements which rest on the authority exercised by Jesus over demons during his ministry (e.g. Matthew 8. 16, 28–33; 9. 32–4; 15. 22–8). The New Testament attitude to evil spirits rests in turn on the accumulation of belief among the Jews. In the Bible, evil spirits live in the desert (Isaiah 34. 14), they spread sickness (Psalms 91. 6) and insanity (1 Samuel 16. 15), and they deceive people (1 Kings 22. 22). None the less, it is stressed that God is Lord of all and therefore even the evil spirit tormenting King *Saul (1 Samuel 16. 14) must be from God. Occasionally foreign gods, such as the *Canaanite Mavet or Reshev, were described as demons (as for example, *Hab.* 3. 5). In the inter-testamental period, demons seem to have become more prominent under their prince, *Belial. The *Talmud emphasizes that current beliefs held about demons in Babylon were not known in the land of *Israel. However, the Babylonian Jews were surrounded by spirits—'if the eye could see them no one could endure them. They surround one on all sides' (*B.Ber.* 6a), and details about demonic activity are to be found throughout the Babylonian Talmud and the *midrashim. Later commentators accepted these beliefs, and the philosopher *Maimonides was unusual in his scepticism. Similarly, the *kabbalists thought that the world was full of demons and they attempted to develop a systematical demonology, much of which drew on the popular folklore of the time. They compiled lists of *angels and demons with their various functions, and suggested amulets and remedies. Such magical beliefs only finally began to disappear after the Enlightenment, though at the level of folk-religion they persist. See Index, Evil agents.

R. Cavendish, *The Powers of Evil in Western Religion. . .* (1975); F. Gettings, *A Dictionary of Demons* (1988); D. P. Walker, *Unclean Spirits* (1981).

Exaltation of the Cross. The feast, also known as Holy Cross Day, kept in honour of the cross of Christ on 14 Sept. In the W. Church it commemorates the exposition of the true cross at Jerusalem by the emperor Heraclius in 629. The day is, however, that of an older feast in Jerusalem, for which see INVENTION OF THE CROSS.

Exarch. In some E. churches a *metropolitan whose office is of high status, though not as high as that of *patriarch.

Ex cathedra (Lat., 'from the seat/throne'). Authoritative statements in Roman Catholicism. *Vatican I stated that

> when he [the *pope] speaks ex cathedra, that is, when in discharge of the office of pastor and teacher of all Christians, he defines, by virtue of his supreme apostolic authority, a doctrine regarding faith or morals to be held by the universal church, he possesses, by the divine assistance promised to him in the person of blessed *Peter, the *infallibility with which the divine Redeemer willed his Church to be endowed in defining the doctrine concerning faith or morals.

Such definitions are 'irreformable', because they do not rely on the consent of the Church. The phrase colloquially has therefore come to refer to statements made with the kind of authority that brooks no argument.

Exclusive Brethren (Christian sect): see PLYMOUTH BRETHREN.

Excommunication. A censure imposed by the *Christian Church which deprives a person of the right to administer or receive the *sacraments or to hold office in the church. It is prescribed in Roman Catholic *canon law for such different offences as apostasy, heresy, and schism (canon 1364); and procuring an abortion (canon 1398). In early times, excommunication was a normal part of *penance, but developed as a separate discipline for impenitent sinners from the 6th–7th cents. Formerly, an excommunicated person who is *toleratus* (allowed to attend services and associate with the faithful) was distinguished from the exceptional offender declared by the *Holy See to be *vitandus*, 'to be shunned'.

The term is then applied to the process of expelling members from the, or a, community in other religions—e.g. the expulsion of a member of the Buddhist *saṅgha (monastic community) if he has committed one of the four offences which are known as *pārājika* (involving defeat): sexual misconduct, theft, murder, boasting of supernatural powers. See also (in Judaism) ḤEREM.

Exegesis (Gk., 'bring out'). 1. The task of 'bringing out' the meaning of a text. Exegesis raises immediately the central question of *hermeneutics, whose meaning is the meaning of the meaning? The belief that there is an original 'meaning' of the text (e.g. that which the author intended) will always be frustrated, partly because access to different minds, cultures, and historical periods is limited, partly because authors achieve more than they realize or intend, and partly because the meanings discovered in subsequent generations are not themselves meaningless. Even in religions with a strong sense of divine authorship of a sacred text (e.g. the relation of *Allāh to the *Qur'ān in Islam), it is recognized that the Arabic words are open to exegesis, so that previously unsuspected meanings become apparent. The task of exegesis is to seek out legitimate meaning in the light of continuing and developing understanding. As L. *Ginzberg put it, 'The dead letter needs to be made living by interpretation.' However, if the text does not exercise some control over proposed meanings, interpretation easily becomes eisegesis (reading meaning into a text).

2. A seminar-based organization devoted to 'the business of transformation'. Running from 1976 until 1984, Robert D'Aubigny's Exegesis Standard Seminar has attracted *c.*5,000 people. This *est-like manifestation of the human potential movement, the first of its kind to be developed in Britain, has also attracted considerable controversy. Critics claim that the one hundred hour seminars are excessively authoritarian, utilizing mind control techniques to establish unreflective commitment. Supporters claim that the seminars deprogramme members, confrontation being required to get members to see the extent to which they are conditioned or 'stuck'. The essentially *monistic teaching of the seminar is most in evidence among those graduates (some 300) who have opted to work together in various business contexts. Programmes Ltd., which became Europe's largest telephone marketing organization, is an exercise in 'the transformation of business'. Psycho-spiritual growth combines with mysticism in action

in the modern world—shades of *Gurdjieffian, 'the work', and an attempt to fulfil socially as well as individualistically envisaged human potential.

Exempla of the Rabbis. A medieval manuscript containing more than 300 Jewish stories. First published in 1924, ed. M. Gasler, the stories are largely similar to those found in *Talmudic and *midrashic literature. Other similar collections have survived, and their intention seems to have been to provide ethical models. Later, the pupils of Isaac *Luria and the Baal Shem Tov (*Israel ben Eliezer) compiled tales about their masters as edifying examples of admirable conduct.

Exilarch. Lay head of the Babylon Jewish community. The first clear evidence of the existence of the exilarch dates back to the 2nd cent. CE. Once the principle of *dina de malkutha dina (the law of the land is the law) was established in the 3rd cent., the Jewish government was secure in its administration of its own affairs. It was led by the exilarch (Aramaic *resh galuta*) and the office was hereditary; its holder was traditionally a member of the house of *David. He was recognized by the royal court as chief representative of the Jews; he was responsible for the collection of taxes from the community; he appointed judges and exercised criminal jurisdiction. There were both close ties and frequent conflicts between the exilarchs and the religious heads of the community, the geonim (*gaon). By the 13th cent., however, most of the powers of the exilarch had been transferred to the *academies.

Exile, Babylonian. Exile of the Jews in Babylon in the 6th cent. BCE. The northern kingdom of *Israel had been conquered by Assyria in the 8th cent. BCE, and many members of the ten northern tribes had been deported to other parts of the Assyrian Empire. Foreign elements were brought to Samaria and intermarried with the remaining population. By the early 6th cent., the kingdom of *Judah was part of the Babylonian Empire and, as a result of rebellion in 597 and again in 586 BCE, all but the poorest inhabitants in the land were transported to Babylon (see 2 Kings 24–5). Although the *Temple had been destroyed, the religious life of the nation continued, as is evidenced by the life and work of *Ezekiel, Deutero-*Isaiah, *Haggai, and *Zechariah. After the Persian conquest of Babylon, the Jewish exiles were allowed to return to *Jerusalem to rebuild the temple (see Ezra 1–4). However, many Jews remained in Babylon and communities grew up in every major city around the Mediterranean sea. From this experience and history derives the phrase, 'a Babylonian exile', to describe other periods of exile from a home circumstance. See also DIASPORA and GALUT.

P. R. Ackroyd, *Exile and Restoration* (1968); C. F. Whitley, *The Exilic Age* (1957).

Existence precedes essence: see NEO-THOMISM.

Existentialism. A disparate trend concentrated mainly in the second quarter of the 20th cent. but with roots in 19th-cent. European thought, especially in the writings of S. *Kierkegaard, F. *Dostoevsky, and F. *Nietzsche. Existentialism is more a pervasive 'mood' than a united movement or 'school' of thought. Its leading representatives were Rainer Maria Rilke (1875–1926), M. *Buber, F. Kafka (1883–1924), K. Jaspers (1883–1969), R.*Bultmann, P. *Tillich, G. Marcel (1889–1973), M. Heidegger, J.-P. Sartre (1905–80), and M. Merleau-Ponty (1908–61). There is no core of doctrines shared by these fiercely independent thinkers in virtue of which one calls them 'existentialists'; however, certain common themes run through their thought. Among them one would include at least the following: (i) deep suspicion of the claims of permanent systems or traditional ideologies, whether religious, metaphysical, or political; (ii) contempt for most academic philosophy as superficial and irrelevant to basic human needs and central human concerns; (iii) concern for the human condition as determined by the ever-present threat of death and ultimate meaninglessness; (iv) conception of human nature as unfixed and unfinished; (v) life as a series of ambiguous possibilities; and, (vi) disengagement from public issues and focus on the solitary individual and the decisions s/he is required to make in 'the moment'.

D. E. Cooper, *Existentialism: A Reconstruction* (1990).

Exodus. The Jewish liberation from *slavery in Egypt. The story of the Exodus is contained in a series of narratives in the book of Exodus. With the accession of an Egyptian Pharaoh, who 'did not know *Joseph' (Exodus 1. 8), the Israelites were reduced to slavery. As a result of divine intervention, and led by *Moses, the Israelites escaped and made a long, hazardous journey to the *Promised Land. Scholars do not agree on the date of these events or even whether there was a single sequence of events. Thus the narrative may be a consequence of a deliberate 'pooling' of memories (oral traditions) of members of the previously scattered kinship group (the *bene Jacob*) when they agreed to common action, perhaps at the time of David's expansion of territory. In that case, the Exodus tradition and the Wilderness traditions were originally separate and unconnected. So far as the Exodus is concerned, those scholars who identify the Israelites with the '*Habiru' of the Tell el-Amarna letters prefer a 15th-cent. dating, while others, relying on calculations from the Hebrew *Bible, believe that the Exodus took place in the first half of the 13th cent. BCE. It is also difficult to identify the Israelites' exact route. Although Numbers 33 gives a complete list of their stations when they were wandering in the desert, many of the places are not known. In addition, the biblical traditions differ, and Mount *Sinai has been identified as Jebel al-Halal, Jebel Sinn-Bishr, or another mountain deep in the south of the Sinai desert. During the course of the journey, the sea of reeds (Red Sea) miraculously parted (Exodus 14); the *Torah was given to the Jews and a new *covenant made on Mount Sinai (19–24); the *tabernacle was built (35–40), and Moses himself died (*Deuteronomy 34).

G. W. Shanks, *The Quest for the Historical Israel* (1981); H. Shanks (ed.), *Ancient Israel* (1988).

Exodus, Book of. The second book of the Hebrew Bible and Christian Old Testament. The English title follows that of the Septuagint Greek version, the usual short Hebrew title *Shemoth* ('names') being the second word of the text. The book describes the oppression of the Israelites, who had settled in Egypt in the time of Joseph, at the hands of a new king (ch. 1); the birth and preservation of Moses and his commission from God to deliver his fellow slaves (2–4); the refusal of Pharaoh to release the Israelites, even in the face of 'plagues' (the waters turned to blood, frogs, swarms of flies, etc.) until the loss of his firstborn made him relent, and the institution of the *Passover (5. 1–12. 36); the miraculous escape of the Israelites through the Red Sea (12. 37–18); their encampment at Mount Sinai and Moses' ascent to the summit where he received from God the *Ten Commandments and the Book of the Covenant and mediated a covenant between God and Israel (19–24); the episode of the *golden calf (32–4); the instructions for worship in the tabernacle (25–31) and its construction (35–40). Exodus thus describes the founding of all the main Israelite institutions except the monarchy. Like the rest of the *Pentateuch the book is traditionally ascribed to Moses but is held by modern critics to be a composite work of the 9th to 5th cents. BCE. Miriam's song in 15. 21 may be among the oldest passages in the Bible.

Ex opere operato (Lat., 'from the act done'). The objective mode of operation of the *sacraments as understood in Catholic theology. The claim that a sacrament is effective *ex opere operato* means that so long as the conditions of its institution are properly observed and fulfilled, the defective qualities of the minister and recipient are no impediment, and *grace is conferred. It is summarised in the title of Article XXVI (of the *Thirty-Nine Articles), 'Of the Unworthiness of the Ministers, which hinders not the effect of the Sacrament'.

Exorcism (Gk., *exorkosis*, 'out-oath'). The removing of that which has taken possession of a person or object or building. This is usually taken to be an *evil spirit or *demon. 'Possession' is a widespread phenomenon, and rituals of exorcism occur in virtually all religions. In Christianity, there was, until 1972, a minor order of exorcists. Exorcism now continues in mainstream Christianity under the oversight of a *bishop, and only with permission. In recent times, the issue has been raised whether the symptoms of possession are extreme states of brain disturbance, with chemical and neurophysiological explanations. While 'possession' must always have such a correlation, and while exorcism is sometimes used in manifestly inappropriate ways, it remains the case that phenomenologically 'possession' is an appropriate description of many cases, and that exorcism may be a legitimate part of the contest against grievous disturbance.

F. D. Goodman, *How About Demons? Possession and Exorcism in the Modern World* (1988); T. K. Oesterreich, *Possession, Demoniacal and Other* (1930).

Ex oriente lux (Lat., 'out of the East, light'). The belief that greater wisdom and deeper spirituality can be found in E. religions than in the materialistic West. The belief became strong in the 19th cent., when it formed part of the Romantic reaction against what were taken to be the scientistic pretensions of post-Newtonian science. Given impetus by such people as *Schopenhauer and Sir Edwin Arnold (his *Light of Asia* appeared in 1879: see B. Wright, *Interpreter of Buddhism to the West: Sir Edwin Arnold*, 1957), it led to an extensive and serious academic endeavour to study the religions of the East, and to publish texts and translations (e.g. *Müller, *Rhys Davids). The belief was shared by non-Westerners, and became a base for advocating the worth of E. thought and philosophy. Thus Rabindranath *Tagore made (unsuccessful) trips to both Japan and China in the hope that a spiritual alliance might be formed which would recover the world from 'the unholy feast' of the Western nations. See also DĀRĀ SHIKOH.

J. W. Bowker, *Hallowed Ground* (1993), ch. 6; S. N. Hay, *Asian Ideas of East and West: Tagore and his Critics* (1970).

Expiation. The removal of an offence by means of some act or offering by, or on behalf of, the offender. According to one understanding of *atonement in Christian theology, *Christ made expiation vicariously for the sins of human beings. The word is adopted in some modern versions of the New Testament to translate Gk. *hilasmos* and its cognates (e.g. in Romans 3. 25) where the traditional (e.g. **Book of Common Prayer*) translation 'propitiation' would suggest the authors thought of God as angry and in need of placating, rather than of himself as the one who initiated the process of atonement.

Exposition of the Blessed Sacrament. The displaying of the eucharistic *host for the purpose of devotion, e.g. by opening the doors of the *tabernacle where it is reserved, or in a *monstrance. See also BENEDICTION; CORPUS CHRISTI.

Exsurge Domine. A *bull issued in June 1520 by Pope *Leo X, threatening the excommunication of *Luther, 'the roaring boar' who had 'invaded the vineyard'. Its forty-one propositions deal with matters such as *indulgences, *penance, *purgatory, sacramental *grace, and papal authority. The *Reformer appealed for a general *council to discuss these issues but, having no success, burnt the bull publicly in Wittenberg, Dec. 1520. See also ECK, J.

Extra ecclesiam nulla salus (Est) (Lat., 'outside the church there is no salvation'). The view, expressed first by *Origen and *Cyprian, that formal membership of the Church is necessary for salvation. The *bull *Unam Sanctam* (1302) of Pope *Boniface VIII declared that 'there is one holy, catholic and apostolic Church, outside of which there is neither salvation nor remission of sins', and that 'it is altogether necessary to salvation for every human creature to be subject to the Roman pontiff'. The bull mentions specifically 'the Greeks' (i.e. the Greek Orthodox): *a fortiori*, those in other religions must be in equally great peril. This view has been repeated consistently: it was affirmed by Pius IX (1854) in *Singulari Quadam* ('It must, of course, be held as a matter of faith that outside the apostolic Roman Church no one can be saved') and by *Councils (e.g. Fourth Lateran, Florence); and the First *Vatican Council was only prevented from stating this position as a *dogma by the outbreak of the Franco-Prussian War.

The apparent severity to non-Christians and non-Catholics is modified by *invincible ignorance. Thus *Singulari Quadam* adds:

> It must likewise be held as certain that those who are affected by ignorance of the true religion, if it is invincible ignorance, are not subject to any guilt in this matter before the eyes of the Lord? (Who can) presume . . . to set the boundaries of such ignorance, taking into consideration the natural differences of peoples, lands, native talents, and so many other factors?

This caution issued in the teaching of Vatican II (especially *Lumen Gentium*) that those who live by conscience outside the Church may be saved. See also Anonymous Christians in RAHNER, K.

Extreme unction (rite of anointing): see UNCTION.

Eybeschuetz, Jonathan Ben Nathan/Nata also **Eybeschitz** (1690/5–1764). Jewish *talmudic and *kabbalistic scholar. When *rabbi of 'the three communities' (Altona, Hamburg, and Wandsbeck), he came into controversy with Jacob *Emden over his supposed leanings towards Shabbateanism (see SHABBETAI ZEVI). Eventually he was vindicated by the Council of the Four Lands in 1753. He was an outstanding preacher, and published several homiletic works, as well as thirty treatises on *halakhah. Scholars do not agree whether there is any substance in the Shabbatean charges. His book on the Kabbalah, *Shem 'Olam* (Everlasting Name) can be interpreted in different ways, and doubt has been cast on its authorship. Eybeschuetz published a refutation of the charges in *Luḥot Edut* (1755). In his work as a rabbi, he took the view that religion is not confined to 'the religious', i.e. that teaching and preaching must reach out to affect the conduct of public life: 'It is regrettable that our preaching is dealing constantly with our duties to God. Let the preacher protest, with a carrying voice, against the malpractices of prominent men, and the people will come to love him and to delight in his sermons.' At the same time, he was clear that the peacock parades of public office are of passing moment compared with eternity: 'The magnificent show of military parades may be of interest to government officials, but what, apart from wasting our time, can they possibly mean to us?'

Eye: see EVIL EYE.

Ezekiel. Hebrew prophet of the 6th cent. BCE and name of a prophetical book of the Hebrew Bible and Christian Old Testament. Ezekiel is the last of the three 'major prophets', after *Isaiah and *Jeremiah. He was a priest (Ezekiel 1–3) who received his vocation as a prophet in Babylon, to where he had probably been deported in 597 BCE. His prophecies seem to date from 593 to 571, some before and some after the fall of Jerusalem. They are marked by awe at the majesty and holiness of God (e.g. ch. 8); by a stress on the responsibility of each person for his own sin (18. 4 in tension with Exodus 20. 5b); and by a priestly preoccupation with details of the temple of the future (chs. 40–8). Ezekiel 37, among prophecies of redemption in chs. 33–9, describes the restoration of dry bones to life—an important image of the faithfulness of God to his covenant-people. To counteract extravagant speculation, the early *rabbis reduced its importance. R. Judah took it to be an allegorical vision, while R. *Eliezer insisted that 'the dead whom Ezekiel revived stood up, recited a song, and immediately died' (*B.Sanh.* 92 b). A further long-reaching effect was produced by Ezekiel's vision of the chariot (chs. 1 and 10): this created a literary type, and stands at the root of Jewish *merkabah mysticism, a type of mysticism practised by *Johanan b. Zakkai, and by Saul/*Paul—it appears to have been the context of the *Damascus road experience. As well as fears about mystical speculation, the book caused embarrassment because of the contradiction between chs. 40–8 and the laws of the *Pentateuch, as well as the fierce diatribes against Jerusalem in ch. 16. The Talmud (*B.Ḥag* 13a) records that the book was almost suppressed.

Ezra. A *priest and *scribe after whom a book in the Hebrew *Bible is named. Ezra himself was described as both a priest and scribe, and he had a major role in the rebuilding of the *Jerusalem *Temple after the Babylonian *exile. He is credited with persuading the people to keep the Torah, observe the *Sabbath, pay temple dues and refrain from *marriage with non-Jews. His dates are uncertain, because it is not clear whether the 'seventh year of King Artaxerxes' (7. 7) refers to Artaxerxes I or II. In the *aggadic tradition, Ezra was regarded as second in piety only to *Moses: 'If Moses had not anticipated him, Ezra would have received the

*Torah' (*Tosef., Sanh.* 4.7). The *rabbis also identified him with the prophet *Malachi (*B.Meg.* 15a).

Ezra and Nehemiah, Books of. Two books belonging to the *Writings of the Hebrew Bible and to the historical books of the Christian Old Testament. In some Roman Catholic Bibles the titles are 1 and 2 *Esdras respectively. The books continue the history of *Chronicles down to the end of the 5th cent. BCE, and are evidently the work of the same compiler ('the Chronicler'). The history relates the return of the Jewish exiles from Babylon and their efforts to rebuild the Temple in Jerusalem (Ezra 1–6); *Ezra's mission to Jerusalem and his reforms especially in the matter of mixed marriages (7–10); Nehemiah's plans for the restoration of Jerusalem (Nehemiah 1–7); the reading and acceptance of the Torah (8–10); arrangements for the occupation of the city (11–12); and further reforms of Nehemiah (13). The books draw on diverse sources. Ezra 4. 8–6. 18, 7. 12–26 are written in Aramaic, not Hebrew, and may have been taken from a collection of official Aramaic documents. The narratives are fragmentary and may, as some scholars hold, reverse the correct sequence, in which Nehemiah's work preceded Ezra's.

Ezrat Nashim (Heb., 'Court of Women'). A courtyard in the *Jerusalem *temple. *Women were not permitted to pass beyond the Ezrat Nashim, and later, the term was applied to the section of the *synagogue reserved for women.

F

Fa. Chin. for *dharma.

Face/body marks in Hinduism: see TILAKA.

Fa-chia (political philosophy): see CHINESE RELIGION.

Fackenheim, E. (Jewish writer): see HOLOCAUST; SHO'AH.

Fa-hsiang. A school of Chinese Buddhism, also known as Dharma-character, which continued the teaching of *Vijñavāda (Yogācāra), based on the writings of *Asaṅga and *Vasubandhu. It was founded by *Hsüan-tsang (600–64), whose work and translation, *Ch'eng wei-shih lun* (*Vijñaptimātratā-siddhi*) expounds the school's teaching. Everything is a *projection of mind, and possesses no reality in itself. Consciousness is analysed into eight types, in order to account for the different forms of appearance. These appear in 100 *dharmas, in five divisions, mind, mental functions, form, appearances not associated with mind, and non-created elements: 'Apart from what is transformed in consciousness, the self and the dharmas are certainly not existent, because apart from what apprehends and what is apprehended, there is nothing.' The understanding of how they give rise to the illusions of reality leads to the awareness of *tathatā, the entirely empty nature of reality; and that is the completed state (*tathāgata) of *nirvāna. The school began to decline in the 9th cent., but continued as a philosophical influence for many centuries.

Fa-hsien (*c*.338–*c*.422). Chinese Buddhist monk, who left China in 399 on pilgrimage to India, via the Himālayas. He collected Buddhist texts, and on his return to China in 414 he translated **Mahāparinirvāna-sūtra* and the *Mahāsāṃghika version of the *Vināya-piṭaka. But he is chiefly remembered for his account of his travels, *Fu-kuo chi*, for which see Li Yung-hsi, *A Record of the Buddhist Countries* (1957), H. A. Giles, *The Travels of Fa-hsien* . . . (1956).

Faith. The disposition of believers toward commitment and toward acceptance of religious claims. It has a distinct importance in Christianity because of *Paul's insistence on *justification by faith alone (Romans 4. 5, 9. 30; Galatians 3. 2), and his inclusion of faith in the three paramount virtues (along with hope and love, 1 Corinthians 13. 13). In this sense, faith can only be received from God as a gift of *grace, and becomes the means through which belief is formed (*fides qua creditur*, 'faith by which it is believed'). Faith in this sense (in contrast to works which persuade or coerce God into offering rewards) was much emphasized by the Reformers. This is faith as *fiducia*, trust. But faith also becomes 'the Faith', the gradual accumulation through time of that which is believed by Christians, faith as *assensus*, assent (*fides quae creditur*, 'faith which is believed'); and although the *Vincentian Canon has never actually obtained at any time, the *Creeds, as well as the canons of the early ecumenical *Councils, set parameters for the Christian faith in this sense. Faith in a far wider sense is necessary for human life and knowledge outside religion, since it is the basic acceptance that the universe is reliable, albeit unpredictable in many respects; indeed, F. R. Tennant regarded faith as the volitional element in all knowledge.

For faith in Buddhism, see ŚRADDHĀ; in Islam, see ĪMĀN.

H. Berkhof, *Christian Faith* (1986); J. Hick, *Faith and Knowledge* (1974); R. Swinburne, *Faith and Reason* (1981).

Fa-ju: see SOUTHERN AND NORTHERN SCHOOLS.

Fa-jung (Jap., Hōyū), 594–657, Ch'an Buddhist master, who founded the Gozu ('Oxhead') school, which is Ch'an/Zen related, but is not reckoned as belonging to the Five Houses/Seven Schools (*goke-shichishū) of the mainstream tradition. That is because, although Fa-jung is said to have been taught by *Tao-hsin, he was not granted the seal of recognition (*inka-shōmei). It is said that when Tao-hsin heard of the reputation of this holy man and went to seek him out, he found that the emanations from his mind in meditation were so powerful that birds flew to him bearing flowers in recognition. The Oxhead school appears to have been eclectic, drawing on what it regarded as wisdom in other traditions.

Fa-lang (507–81). *San-lun Buddhist teacher. He devoted himself to combining in practice *Vinaya rules and *dhyāna meditation. In 558 he established a school at (present-day) Nanking, and his teaching was continued by a pupil, *Chi-tsang.

Falashas. Jews of Ethiopian origin. The Falashas themselves claim to be descended from Menelik, the son of King *Solomon and the Queen of Sheba (1 Kings 10. 1–13). Most experts believe they belong to the Agau family of tribes to whom Judaism spread from S. Arabia. They call themselves 'Beta Esrael' (House of *Israel) and live in their own separate villages, the best known of which are near the town of Gondar. They keep the ritual *food law of the *Pentateuch; they *circumcise their sons on the eighth day; they observe the *Sabbath and *Day of Atonement, and they offer *sacrifice and eat unleavened bread (*mazzah) during the *Passover season. They know the twenty-four books of the Hebrew scriptures and many *apocryphal books, but they do not know the *Talmud. Their literature is written in Ge'ez, the language of the Ethiopian Church and their *Bible is translated from the *Septuagint rather than from the Hebrew. The mainstream Jewish community has known of the Falashas since the 15th cent. R. David b. Zimra believed they were descended from the tribe of *Dan. In response to the activities of 19th-cent. Christian missionaries, there was an attempt to protect the Falashas, and, after the establishment of the state of Israel in 1948, there was increased interest in them. Finally, as a result of famine and civil war, a large proportion of the community emigrated to Israel. Their precise personal status as Jews is still in some dispute among the Israeli religious establishment. In 1985, many Ethiopians demonstrated in Jerusalem against the *Chief Rabbi, who had demanded symbolic conversion for those among them who wished to marry—because of doubts about their divorce procedures and personal status. The insistence on symbolic recircumcision was withdrawn, but not ritual immersion.

W. Leslau (ed.), *Falasha Anthology* (1951).

Falk, Jacob (1680–1756). Jewish *halakhic authority. He began adult life as a businessman, but an explosion which killed close members of his family made him turn to study instead, emphasizing attention to God and to community, rather than attention to self: 'The Hebrew word for "I" contains the same letters as the word for "nothing" (*ayn*).' As *rabbi of Lemberg, his *yeshivah became the largest in Poland. He was a determined opponent of *Shabbateanism, siding with Jacob *Emden against Jonathan *Eybeschuetz. He is best known as the author of *Penei Yehoshuʿa* (The Face of Joshua) published in separate parts (1739, 1752, 1756, and 1780), which is a series of novellae on the *Talmud, and a defence of *Rashi, still respected and consulted.

Fall. The act of disobedience of *Adam and Eve which according to the Bible story in Genesis 2–3 was responsible for the human condition of pain, toil, and (already in ancient exegesis) mortality. The term is current especially in Christian theology, which beginning with *Paul (Romans 5. 12–21, 1 Corinthians 15. 22) used the Genesis story to explain the coming of *sin into the world. Paul made it a type of the redeeming work of Christ (*typology), but it formed a basis also in later theology for the doctrine of *original sin. A broadly accepted modern interpretation of the story of the Fall sees it as a *myth which teaches that sin arose from free human choice and that all human life has been thereby radically altered for the worse so that its actual state is different from that which God intended. The Jewish interpretation of the Genesis story does not see in it anything like the same radical, vitiating, fault: there is a sense in which 'the fall' is a fall upwards, into the opportunity of choice, action, and responsibility: see further references under *felix culpa.

Falsafa (Arab., *falṣafa*, from Gk. *philosophia*), the pursuit of philosophy in Islam. The Muslim delight in philosophy (at least in the early centuries) rests on a confidence that God is the creator of all things, and that *knowledge (*ʿilm) leads to a deeper understanding of him and of his works. Thus falsafa is a commitment to wisdom (*ḥikma*) in which all the sciences are necessarily involved. According to *al-Fārābī (*Iḥṣā' al-ʿulūm*, the Catalogue of Sciences), all the various sciences can be listed and described, but falsafa stands at the head, because it controls the rest. The commitment to philosophy led to the rescue and translation of many works of Greek philosophy, thereby preserving them from total loss, as also it led to thinkers and works of enduring stature (for examples, see Index, Philosophers; Philosophy; and Theologians and Philosophers; all under sub-heading Muslim). However, the pursuit of rational inquiry and reflection, beginning systematically with the *Muʿtazilites, led to a suspicion, culminating in *al-Ghaz(z)ali, that it might lead to the judgement of God by human reason, and to the subordination of revelation to reason. It was also increasingly felt (and here again al-Ghaz(z)ali was crucial) that the wisest knowledge of God lies in devotion to him, hence the extensive spread of *Sufism.

H. Corbin, *Histoire de la philosophie islamique* (1964); M. Fakhry, *A History of Islamic Philosophy* (rev. edn., 1983); O. Leaman, *An Introduction to Medieval Islamic Philosophy* (1985); J. P. Menasce, *Arabische Philosophie* (1948).

Fan (return to the source in Taoism): see FU.

Fanā'. 'Annihilation, dissolution', the *Sūfī state of attainment or perfection, achieved by the annihilation of all human attributes until God is all. It is 'to die before one dies'. In *Kashf al-Maḥjūb* (Revelation of Concealed Matters), al-Hujwīrī states: 'The Sūfī is he that has nothing in his possession, nor is himself possessed by anything. This is the essence of fanā'.' But if God is now 'all in all', he can, according to later Sūfīs, be discerned in the person in the state of fanā'. Thus abū Yazīd: 'When your creation, O God, sees me, it will say, "We have seen you": and you, O God, will be that, and I shall not be there at all.' It is the threshold of *baqā'*, perpetual being in relation to God, i.e. eternal life.

Fan Festival (Buddhist festival): see NARA BUDDHISM.

Fang-chang: see FANG-SHIH.

Fang-chung shu (Chin., 'arts of the inner chamber'). Taoist practices aiming at immortality (inner or outer, see ALCHEMY and NEI-TAN) through union with the powers of the opposite, i.e. through union of *yin and yang. This might be through union of *ch'i, breath, but the *ho-ch'i* practices (at new moon and full moon) were linked to sexual union—to which fang-chung shu refers as a general term. In sexual union, the male strengthens his yang by absorbing the female energy (yin) through union with as many partners as possible, combining female orgasm with no emission of semen (*ching); the woman conversely strengthens her own energy. These practices were particularly associated with *wu-tou-mi tao and *t'ai-ping tao, but the details have been largely lost, mainly due to their elimination from Taoist texts and practice under the pressure of *Confucian ethics.

Fang-shih (Fangshi) (Chin., 'master of techniques'). *Shamanistic controllers of *magic in China in the centuries BCE (though their techniques continued in popular religion long after). They were guides to the islands of the immortals (Fang-chang, P'eng-lai, and Ying-chou), and custodians of the techniques which secure both life and immortality. They were important predecessors of religious Taoism.

K. J. DeWoskin, *Doctors, Diviners and Magicians of Ancient China* (1983); N. V. Xuyet, *Divination, magie et politique dans la Chine ancienne* (1976).

Fang Yen-kou. Chinese Buddhist ceremony for the 'release of the burning mouths'. The 'burning mouths' are a type of hungry ghost (*preta). The monks break open the gates of hell (*naraka), with incantation and the ringing of bells. They pour out sweetened and consecrated water for the burning mouths, who can then take the three refuges (*Three Jewels) and the *bodhisattva vow. They can then be reborn as humans, or in the Western Paradise (*Sukhāvatī).

Fanon, F.: see LIBERATION THEOLOGY.

Faqih. One who possesses religious knowledge in Islam. The name refers more usually now to one well-versed in religious law (*fiqh, *sharīʿa). See also FUQAHA.

Faqīr (Arab., 'poor man', pl., *fuqarā*). One who has physical or spiritual needs. It may refer to a beggar in a miserable state, but within a religious context it implies dependence on God (Qur'ān 25. 15). For the *Sūfīs, the term faqīr is applicable to all those on the journey to God. It therefore indicates a need and dependence upon God for everything. See also DERWĪSH.

Fārābī (Muslim philosopher): see AL-FĀRĀBĪ.

Fara'zis (from Arab., *fard). Adherents of a movement in India, founded in 1818, to bring the observance of Islam to all sectors of society. It resisted the increasing tendency to allow a practical *syncretism between Hindus and Muslims, but it did not seek to overthrow established customs, and it did not regard *Sūfīs as threatening to the proper practice of Islam. The movement continues to the present day, but without the same revolutionary impetus.

M. A. Khan, *The History of the Fara'di Movement in Bengal, 1818–1906* (1965).

Fard (Arab., *farada*, 'prescribe'). That which is absolutely obligatory in Islam, as, particularly, the *Five Pillars. This is held to be the same as *wājib* (duty), except by *Ḥanafites who confine *wājib* to obligations imposed by law. A distinction is also made between farḍ al-ʿayn (obligation incumbent on all) and farḍ al-kifāya (obligation on all which is discharged if it is performed by some on behalf of all).

Fard (Arab., 'alone'). One who, in Islam, is filled with the realization of truth and illumination on his own—i.e. without belonging to a community or *Sūfī order. It is even possible that such a person might not belong to a religion derived from revelation at all, receiving the gift directly from God.

Farquhar, John Nicol (1861–1929). Christian student of Hinduism who argued for a 'fulfilment theory' of the relation of Hinduism to Christianity. He was introduced to the study of Indian religions at Oxford, by Max *Müller and Monier Monier-Williams. He went to India in 1891 to teach for the London Missionary Society. In 1902, he became Student Secretary of the Indian YMCA, and from 1912 its Literature Secretary. In 1913 he published his most influential work, *The Crown of Hinduism*. He left India in 1923 due to ill health, and became the second Professor of Comparative Religion at Manchester University.

E. J. Sharpe, *J. N. Farquhar* (1963).

Farrakhan, L. (leader of the Nation of Islam): see ELIJAH MUHAMMAD.

Fa-shun (patriarch of Chinese Buddhist school): see TU-SHUN.

Fasts, fasting: see FESTIVALS AND FASTS; ASCETICISM; SAWM.

Fateh (Urdu, Pañjābī, 'victory'). 1. Son of Gurū *Gobind Siṅgh. See SĀHIBZĀDE.

2. See VĀHIGURŪ.

3. Exchange of Sikh greeting. To the cry, 'Jo bole so nihāl' (anyone will be blessed who says), comes the response, '*Sat śrī akāl'.

Father. The ancient Christian title of a *bishop, from which two different modern senses derive.

1. Since the 19th cent. in English-speaking countries, the title has been used by and of all *Roman Catholic priests, and it is also customary in *Orthodox and *Anglo-Catholic usage.

2. The 'Fathers of the Church' are those Christian writers (not necessarily bishops) characterized by antiquity, orthodoxy of doctrine, holiness of life, and

the approval of the church. Their authority has in the past been held by some to be infallible in those matters where their teaching is unanimous: individuals were not protected from error. Thus some from the *patristic period are included among the Fathers, even though (as e.g. with *Tertullian and *Origen) some of their views are regarded as abnormal.

See also PATRISTICS; APOSTOLIC FATHERS; Index, Fathers.

Father of secrets (Babylonian Jewish scholar): see AARON OF BAGHDĀD.

Fathers (text in the Mishnah): see AVOT.

Fātiḥa, al-Sūra al-Fātiḥa, or **Fātiḥat al-Kitāb.** The 'opening *sūra' of the *Qur'ān, also sometimes called *Umm al-Kitāb ('mother of the book'), since it is said to contain the essentials of the entire Qur'ān. This is the most often recited of all passages: it features in the *ṣalāt five times daily, is spoken at auspicious occasions and to seal contracts, and may be used for *exorcisms and healing.

Bismillāh al-raḥmān al-raḥīm:
al-ḥamdu lillāh rabb al-ʿālamīn
al-raḥmān al-raḥīm
mālik yawm al-dīn;
iyāka naʿbudu wa-iyāka nastaʿīn.
ihdinā al-ṣirāṭ al-mustaqīm
ṣirāṭ alladhīna anʿamta ʿalayhim
ghayr al-maghḍūb ʿalayhim wa-lā al-ḍāllīn.

In the name of the Beneficent, the Merciful:
Praise be to Allah, the Lord of the worlds
the Beneficent, the Merciful,
Sovereign of the Day of Judgement
You (alone) we worship; You (alone) we ask for help.
Guide us in the straight path,
the path of those whom You have favoured,
not the (path) of those upon whom is wrath,
nor of those who go astray.

Fatima. Shrine of the Virgin *Mary in central Portugal. It was the scene of six appearances of Mary to three shepherd children from 13 May to 13 Oct. 1917. At the last of these, the Virgin revealed that she was Our Lady of the *Rosary. Only the children heard this, but others in the crowd on 13 Oct. described the sun seeming to fall and dance over their heads. After investigation, the bishop of Leiria authorized the cult of Our Lady of Fatima in 1930. A basilica was completed in 1953. Lucia Santos, one of the children, later (1936–42) made further disclosures about the revelations she received, e.g. that the Virgin had asked for a devotion to the Immaculate Heart of Mary, for the recitation of the rosary, and for penance. In 1952, *Pius XII put into effect the request to pray for the conversion of Russia, and in 1982 *John Paul II visited the shrine to give thanks for his surviving the attempt on his life. The reported 'secret' made known in the apparitions has not been disclosed publicly, despite many accounts of what it is.

Fāṭima. Daughter of *Muḥammad and *Khadīja who married Muḥammad's nephew *ʿAlī b. Abī Ṭālib. She bore him two sons, *al-Ḥusayn and *al-Ḥasan, and two daughters. Al-Ḥusayn, the younger son, was killed at the battle of *Karbalā' (680), and this defeat, the 'martyrdom' of al-Ḥusayn and his companions, marked the real beginning of the *Shīʿa party and sect. The Ahl al-Bayt, or 'family of the House' (of Muḥammad) are greatly venerated; the phrase is said to refer chiefly to five persons, Muḥammad, Fāṭima, ʿAlī, al-Ḥasan and al-Ḥusayn (Qur'ān 33. 33). Descent through Fāṭima is significant, and, for instance, gave the name to a Shīʿa dynasty in Egypt, the Fāṭimids (10th to 12th cent. CE). Fāṭima died some six months after her father Muḥammad in 632. Numerous legends have grown up around the person of Fāṭima, especially among the Shīʿa; Muḥammad is said to have named her as one of the four best women of Paradise, the others being Maryam (*Mary), *Khadīja, and the wife of Pharaoh.

Fāṭimids. *Ismāʿīlī dynasty, 909–1171 (AH 297–567), extending from Palestine to Tunisia, which founded *Cairo (al-Qāhirah) as its capital in 969 (AH 358). They also founded *al-Azhar University. The Fāṭimid *Khalīfas were Ismāʿīlī *Imāms, the means of God's presence in the world—though the claim of one of them, al-Hākim (d. 1021 (AH 411)) to *be* God was a claim too far. His equally excessive behaviour in destroying the Church of the Holy Sepulchre in *Jerusalem was a partial cause of the *Crusades. The dynasty was succeeded by the Ayyubids, founded by *Salāḥ ud-Dīn.

Fa-tsang or **Hsien-shou** (643–712). Third patriarch and major organizer of the *Hua-yen school of Chinese Buddhism. When he was 16, he made an offering of devotion before a relic of the Buddha by burning off one of his fingers. On hearing Chih-yen (the second Hua-yen patriarch) teach, he became his disciple 'as milk mixes with water'. He became a monk only after Chih-yen died, and began his work of translating and of systematically ordering the teaching of Hua-yen: he arranged Buddhist teachings into 'five levels and ten qualities', with Hua-yen at the height, and he integrated different teaching by affirming the interdependence and interpenetration of all phenomena.

Fatwā (Arab.). In Islamic law, a legal opinion, given on request to an individual or to a magistrate or other public official, concerning a point of law wherein doubt arises, or where there is not an absolutely clear ruling in existence. One qualified to give such an opinion is a *muftī, who would pronounce according to a particular *madhhab* ('school of law'). A fatwā may be contested, but only on the basis of existing precedent and law; it cannot, therefore, be regarded as an 'infallible pronouncement', but it commands assent where it can be seen to be well-grounded. See also SHAIKH AL-ISLĀM.

Faust. Initially a reprobate man who made a pact with the *devil and met a commensurate end. However, he became (through the *Enlightenment and into the 19th cent.) a heroic figure who sets his face against the supposed limitations of humanity. For Spengler, the adjective 'Faustian' described those defiant humans who set themselves to surpass the limits of their state. Major dramatic treatments are those of Christopher Marlowe (1604) and Goethe (1808, 1832).

F. Baron, *Doctor Faustus: From History to Legend* (1978); P. M. Palmer and R. P. More, *The Sources of the Faust Tradition* (1936).

Fa-yen Wen-i (Fayan Wenyi, Jap., Hōgen Bun'eki; 885–958). Chinese Ch'an/Zen Buddhist teacher, successor (*hassu) of *Lo-han Kuei-ch'en, whose work was continued by *T'ien-t'ai Te-shao (Jap., Tendai Tokushō). He was in the lineage of *Hsüan-sha Shih-pei, and because of his power as a teacher, the school subsequently became known as Fa-yen (Jap., Hōgen). He became a monk at the age of 7, studying Confucian texts and Buddhist *sūtras, but was attracted by the more experiential than intellectual emphasis of Ch'an. Taking refuge from a storm while travelling on *angya (the test of pilgrimage), he met Lo-han, and in the formative interaction (*mondō), he attained enlightenment through the words, 'The thickest is ignorance.' But his intellectual prowess lingered within him. Lo-han pointed to a stone: 'Is this stone in your consciousness or not?' He replied: 'In consciousness.' 'Why do you drag such a stone with you on your pilgrimage?' Few of his works survive. His sayings are gathered in a late work, *Ch'ing-liang Wen-i-ch'an-shih yü-lu*. They are characterized by paradox, and by the technique of answering a question with the same words—thus:

> Fa-yen asked Shao-hsiu, 'What does this saying mean, "A slight differentiation separates as between heaven and earth"?' Shao-hsiu replied, 'A slight differentiation separates as between heaven and earth.' The master asked, 'How can that be?' So Shao-hsiu asked, 'What, then, is your understanding?' The master replied, 'A slight differentiation separates as between heaven and earth.'

That exchange also illustrates Fa-yen's advocacy of the *Kegon principle of the interpenetration of all attributes, contemplated in the circle containing six attributes, totality and differentiation, sameness and difference, becoming and passing away. Through this contemplation, the experience of oneness is developed.

Fazl Allāh (founder of Shiʿa movement): see ḤURŪFĪ.

Feast of Fools (New Year Christian medieval festival): see HOLY FOOLS.

Feasts: see FESTIVALS AND FASTS.

Feden Church (Akan, 'children of Eden'). Formerly Eden Revival Church. A Ghanaian independent church founded by Yaw Charles Yeboa-Korie (b. 1938), a *Presbyterian secondary school teacher whose ill-health vanished after prayer, fasting, visionary experiences, and Bible study. In 1962 he founded an ancillary healing society, the Garden of Eden, at Nsawam, but his leadership qualities and travels abroad led to expansion and to the founding of Eden Revival Church, which became a member of the Ghanaian Council of Churches in 1970, and through a dream revelation became the Feden Church in 1975. There is an extensive school system, a church magazine, and many innovative rituals supported by bands and choirs, as well as *baptism by immersion and an annual *Lord's Supper; a branch exists in Britain. Yeboa-Korie is a powerful preacher with a biblical and moral message, as well as a *charismatic healer using physical contact extended by handkerchiefs, perfumed water, olive oil, etc., blessed by him for use at home; W. medical treatment is also accepted. He resisted political overtures by President Nkrumah, preferring to remain a modern prophet-healer, mediating between the older and the independent churches.

Feeling (of absolute dependence, as foundation of religion): see SCHLEIERMACHER, F.

Feinstein, Mosheh (1895–1986). *Orthodox Jewish *rabbi. Born in Russia, and rabbi of Luban, near Minsk, until he emigrated to the USA in 1937. As head of New York's Metivta Tiferet Jerusalem *yeshivah, Feinstein was a leading *halakhic authority (*posek). It was said that a newly ordained rabbi needed two things, his ordination certificate and Rabbi Mosheh's telephone number. Many of his *responsa covered questions raised by modern science and technology, and also by the *Holocaust and by air disasters, which magnified the problems of *agunah (a woman whose husband's fate is unknown). His responsa are published in *Iggerot Mosheh* (7 vols).

S. Finkelman, *Reb Moshe . . .* (1986).

Fei-sheng (Chin.). Ascending to heaven in daylight, one of the marks in Taoism of attaining immortality (see CH'ANG-SHENG PU-SSU).

Felix culpa (Lat., 'happy fault'). The Christian sense that sin has at least this to be said for it, that it evoked so great a redeemer. The phrase occurs in the *Missal, in the 'Exultet' on *Holy Saturday: 'O felix culpa, quae talem ac tantum meruit habere Redemptorem' (O happy fault, which deserved to have so great a Redeemer of such a kind). For a more general sense of this theme in Judaism, see INCLINATION; TESHUVA (repentance).

Fellowship of Isis. A *neo-pagan movement dedicated to the worship of female deities such as Isis, Venus, or Maia. This fellowship of *witches, occultists, and spiritualists has numerous centres and temples in the W., Africa, and elsewhere, and through *meditation and rituals strives to send both 'healing' and 'peace' energy to those parts of the world that are in turmoil.

Feminine symbols and religion. Although masculine images reflect the male control of religion for at least the last 2,000 years, the earlier pervasive and dominant importance of feminine imagery has not been entirely lost, persisting as it does in most religions (though less so in the later arrivals such as Islam). Early archaeological evidence is always open to speculation in the absence of text controls, but the abundance of images of the fruitful woman certainly suggests dominant cults of the Goddess rather than the God—enough so to suggest to M. Stone a period *When God was a Woman* (1976). Already the vulva is represented, not only realistically and as a flower, but also as the triangle which plays so important a part in the Hindu *yantra. Particularly dramatic are images of the Goddess, both modelled and depicted on walls, at the Neolithic site at Çatal Hüyük, in Turkey, on which J. Mellaart (*Çatal Hüyük* . . ., 1967) commented:

> As the only source of life she [woman] became associated with the processes of agriculture, with the taming and nourishing of domesticated animals, with the ideas of increase, abundance and fertility. Hence a religion which aimed at exactly that same conservation of life in all its forms, its propagation and the mysteries of its rites connected with life and death, birth and resurrection, were evidently part of her sphere rather than that of man. It seems extremely likely that the cult of the goddess was administered mainly by women, even if the presence of male priests was by no means excluded.

E. W. Gadon (*The Once and Future Goddess*, 1989) summarizes the findings at other early sites which confirm the same picture, and traces the persistence of the worship of the feminine even among the Hebrews. But equally, *Tanach (Jewish scripture) displays the passion and vigour with which the cult of *Yahweh, under the control increasingly of men, drove out the feminine in the cult, adapting myths to make woman the cause of fault, pain, and sorrow. The cult of the feminine persisted in Christianity in devotion to the Virgin *Mary (especially in syncretistic assimilation in such countries as Mexico), but even that image was reduced in male interpretations to one of submissive obedience (see e.g. Marina Warner, *Alone of All Her Sex* . . ., 1976).

In India, the same early reverence for the female as the source of life is evident from the archaeological remains, and here it would seem that the Goddess remained undiminished, with the cult of the Goddess still being of paramount importance, especially for *Śaktas (see e.g. DEVĪ, ŚAKTI, KĀLI, DURGĀ, RĀDHA, SARASVATĪ, LAKṢMĪ, GAṄGĀ, PĀRVATĪ, amongst many). Yet still the Goddess has often been brought into a relationship with the God, which means that most of her activities are expressed as extensions of his power, except, usually, when the power is negative (see S. G. Gombrich, 'Divine Mother or Cosmic Destroyer' in A. Joseph (ed.), *Through the Devil's Gateway*, 1990).

Even in ritual, where the feminine imagination achieved such brilliance in decoration, drama, and movement, the patriarchal takeover turned much of it into a kind of peacock parade of male ostentation: consider the way in which hierarchy and patriarchal control are expressed in the detail and flamboyance of ritual clothing in Roman Catholic ceremonial—only rivalled in the show put on by men in military clothing. Of particular pain (often literal) in women's experience has been the male takeover of ritual as a means of political and social control (see e.g. K. E. Paige and J. M. Paige, *The Politics of Reproductive Ritual*, 1981). The mutilation of female genitalia ('female circumcision') is the least happy example: not even required by the *Qur'ān, it has become nevertheless in a number of Muslim societies an embedded custom (against which many Muslim men protest, but without, yet, identifiable success; for the experience involved, see N. El Saadawi, *The Hidden Face of Eve: Women in Arab Society*, 1980). The reassertion of the feminine imagination of the sacred is gaining ground, but usually against much male resistance in the historical religions (hence the importance of Wicca and *witchcraft). The loss in the intervening centuries has been a kind of intellectual genocide—the eradication of the vision of half the human race. See also Index, Names of Goddesses; Women.

E. W. Gadon, *The Once and Future Goddess* (1989); J. S. Hawley and D. M. Wulff, *The Divine Consort: Rādhā and the Goddesses of India* (1982); D. Kinsley, *Hindu Goddesses* (1986); G. Lerner, *The Creation of Patriarchy* (1986); M. Oda, *Goddesses* (1981); C. Olson (ed.), *The Book of the Goddess, Past and Present* (1983); J. J. Preston (ed.), *Mother Worship* (1982); B. G. Walker, *The Woman's Dictionary of Symbols and Sacred Objects* (1988).

Feminist theology. Theological reflection which acknowledges from the outset that the greater part of theology so far in human history has been male-dominated, has been an expression of patriarchy, and has been saturated with masculine imagery, relegating feminine imagery to the edges. While the iconography of the feminine has remained more prominent in Eastern religions, theology is not the primary mode of discourse or reflection on the implications of patriarchy: see further WOMEN. In relation to the Judaeo-Christian tradition, G. Lerner calls this male domination 'the androcentric fallacy' (*The Creation Patriarchy*, 1986), which distorts the whole structure and life of the Church—though the same would be true, *mutatis mutandis*, of other theistic religions. *Apophatic theology emphasizes that all language about God must be incomplete, to say the least. Yet some language has to be used, however provisionally, not least in worship. The androcentric fallacy draws attention to the extreme distortions which result in life and imagination when only, or predominantly, masculine language and images are used. This cannot be corrected by using non-sexist language, or by adding 'sisters' to 'brothers' and 'mothers' to 'fathers'.

From this point of departure, there are many different styles of feminist theology. At one extreme, it is an expression of protest, which may reclaim the persistent thread of feminine religious awareness in Wicca or *witchcraft (which men have persecuted as a threat to their own domination). At the opposite extreme, feminist theology may be conservative, insisting that the difference between men and women (including the responsibility of men which takes precedence over women in status) is required by the documents of revelation and is set in natural distinctions: it tends to express itself in the formula, 'different but equal' (in the sight of God), and appeals, in the Christian case, to the Trinitarian language of Father, Son, and Holy Spirit in which the Father is the source though not the superior. Those holding the first position would not regard the latter as *feminist* theology at all. Between the two, feminist theology may be acknowledging the patriarchal constraints of revelation and history, but may then be seeking a co-operative transcendence of that point of departure under the overriding constraint of *agape as the realization of God's intention—when all divisive inequalities will be overcome and there will be 'neither Jew nor Greek, slave nor free, male and female' (Galatians 3. 28). This search for mutuality emphasizes the cultural relativity of the biblical period, in which the *incarnation did not obliterate circumstances, but set humans to the task of changing the world in the direction of love: the maintenance of patriarchy in Church or in society is then seen as precisely that demonic condition which has resulted from the *Fall, and from which Jesus has died to set humans free.

C. Bynum Walker, *Jesus as Mother: Studies in the Spirituality of the High Middle Ages* (1982); C. P. Christ, *Laughter of Aphrodite* (1987); E. S. Fiorenza, *In Memory of Her* (1983); N. R. Goldenberg, *Changing of the Gods: Feminism and the End of Traditional Religion* (1979); G. Lerner, *The Creation of Patriarchy* (1986); A. Loades (ed.), *Feminist Theology: A Reader* (1990); R. Radford Reuther (ed.), *Religion and Sexism . . .* (1974) and *New Woman, New Earth* (1975).

Fénelon, François de Solignac de la Motte (1651–1715). Spiritual writer. Born in Périgord of an aristocratic family, he studied at the seminary of Saint-Sulpice. As tutor to Louis XIV's grandson, he wrote his famous educational novel, *Télémaque* (1693), in which he condemned absolutism. In 1695 he became archbishop of Cambrai. Through his friendship with Mme Guyon and his defence of her doctrine of pure love, he became involved in the *Quietist controversy and was attacked by Bossuet, as a result of which he was banished from the court in 1697. His letters of spiritual direction have long been greatly valued, emphasizing disinterested love and passive contemplation, in which all aspects of life are valued, and the belief that anyone can live in a permanent union with God in contemplation is dismissed as 'a poisoned source of idleness and internal lethargy'. In contrast, 'We pray as much as we desire, and we desire as much as we love.'

M. de la Bedoyere, *The Archbishop and the Lady . . .* (1956); V. Leuliette, *Fénelon* (1970; tr. of P. Janet); M. Raymond, *Fénelon* (1967); F. Varillon, *Fénelon et le pur amour* (1957).

Feng-kan (Ch'an teacher): see HAN-SHAN.

Feng-shui (Chin., 'wind-water'). Chinese art or skill of *geomancy. Taking account of the five elements and the two forces of *yin and yang, the practitioners use a circular wooden plate on which the outline neo-Confucian cosmography is inscribed. They then determine the best site for buildings, graves, temples, etc.

S. D. R. Feuchtwang, *An Anthropological Analysis of Chinese Geomancy* (1974).

Fenollosa, Ernest Francisco (1853–1908). An American educator, poet, and pioneering scholar of E. Asian fine arts and culture. In 1878, he was appointed to the University of Tokyo, where until 1886 he lectured on Spencer, Hegel, and Emerson, exerting a lasting influence on a new generation of Japanese leaders. He is best known for the leading role he played in reviving Japanese interest in their own traditional arts, which eventually sparked a national cultural revival. This resurgence of pride and aesthetic appreciation of the traditional arts was inspired not only by Fenollosa's influential public lectures, but also by his own 'archaeological' discoveries, the most famous occurring in 1884, when he and his friend, Kakuzo Okakura, uncovered the long hidden statute of the *Bodhisattva Kannon in the Yumedono at Hōryūji. In 1886, Fenollosa helped to found the Tokyo School of Fine Arts, and was soon afterward appointed as an imperial commissioner to investigate art education in the USA and Europe. In 1890, he returned to the USA.

His published works include *East and West* (1893), a collection of poetry, *The Masters of Ukiyoe* (1896), and his *magnum opus*, *Epochs of Chinese and Japanese Art* (published posthumously in 1912).

Fen-yang Shan-chao (early collector of kōans): see KŌAN.

Feria. In Christian liturgical usage, a weekday on which no feast or *festival (despite Lat., *feria*, 'feast') falls. Since 1969, in Catholic churches, lessons are provided for every day of the year; the rest of the mass usually follows that of the previous Sunday. The word 'weekday' is now more common than feria.

Festivals and fasts. Festivals are celebrations, usually having an ordered and ritualized (see RITUAL) character. Festivals arise from the fact that 'no man is an island', or more exactly, from the fact that no one can live in isolation on an island in the midst of life: we are selves in a field of selves, requiring each other for the very process of life. Festivals give communal expression to the meaning of that process, in a shared affirmation of value and commitment. So universal is the religious fact of celebration that *Durkheim was able to make it a quintessential feature of religion itself: individuals experience the social as a fact over and above their own individuality, and therefore recognize this factual reality outside themselves in symbolic forms and ritual actions. It follows that festivals may not be specifically 'religious' (*civil religion): they may be secular in origin and intention (May Day parades in Moscow under the communist regime, or Martin Luther *King day in the USA under the separation of Church from State), but they will still exemplify the way in which the social exists as a real matter of experience in independence from the particular individuals who happen to make it up: the powerful effect of crowd emotion (e.g. at sports events or at a 'pop' concert) is a familiar example. Festivals arise from these recognitions of the social fact.

In that context, festivals manifest the demands of social existence in many different ways. At the simplest level, they affirm the worth of individuals in a social context (e.g. birthday parties, anniversaries). They mark *rites of passage; they express the dependence of human life on food and water, which are themselves uncertain in the context of the passing of seasons or the unpredictability of hunting; they mark occasions in the history of the community; they celebrate the epiphanies of power or grace which have offered the transformation of life in the direction of hope, especially when these have come from God or from the source of life itself—e.g. *ti'en, Heaven, or the *Tao. Such festivals are marked by trust and thanksgiving; and the dramatic nature of the celebration ties drama and the theatre to ritual in ways which have not yet been separated in India or China (see R. L. Grimes, *Beginning Ritual Studies*, 1982; R. Schechner, *Between Theater and Anthropology*, 1985).

But festival cannot be divorced from fast (see e.g. E. N. Rogers, *Fasting: The Phenomenon of Self-Denial* (1976). Fasts express the public recognition of unworthiness—to receive benefits, for example, or to participate in the community itself; or again, fasting may express a human desire to move beyond a present circumstance into some better outcome: little of worth is achieved without cost. Fasting may be isolated and specific (as when King *David fasted in the hope of saving his son's life, 2 Samuel 12. 16–20), or they may be prolonged over a regular period each year: *sawm, observed by Muslims during the daylight hours of the month of *Ramaḍān, is one of the *Five Pillars of Islam (i.e. one of the five indispensable conditions of being in the condition of *islām* in relation to God). Fasting may equally be a form of protest against perceived injustice or tyranny, as it may also be a form of preparation for some endeavour. The preparation of *Jesus for his ministry sent him for 'forty days and forty nights' into the wilderness—a preparation which was imitated by Christians during the seasons of (originally) *Advent and of *Lent.

But that last example shows how much festivals can change through time. Advent is now a preparation, not for *baptism, but for *Christmas; and Lent has become a period during which the advice of Herrick has increasingly been followed, to 'starve thy sin, And not thy bin, And that's to keep thy Lent' (i.e. the element of fasting has been almost eliminated). Many Jewish fasts and festivals show a comparable history of change and adaptation: thus *Passover and Unleavened Bread were originally two separate festivals at the same time of year, one for a population which tended flocks, the other for those who were settled and raised crops; the eventual settlement of the whole kinship group made a merger of the two festivals necessary; the attempt under *Josiah to make *Jerusalem the one centre of worship made them into pilgrimage festivals; and the growing sense of *Israel's vocation under God converted the one festival into a commemoration of the saving action of God in the escape from Egypt. The traces of this process of transformation can still be seen in the biblical documents. Thus although festivals and fasts often have reference to the past (so playing a vital part in the conservation and stability of social meaning), their significance is by no means fixed for all time. Even more sharply, the adoption of festivals and fasts by a new religion from its 'parent' (e.g. in the emergence of Jains, Buddhists, and Sikhs) shows both the tenacious hold of celebration and penitence in these public forms, and also the powerfully creative imagination which transforms human ritual.

At the same time, the conservative importance of festivals is precisely what seems negative about them to reformers. There is, in this respect, a constant tension in religions, exemplified in the Jewish *prophets and their protest against relying on the proper observance of festivals and fasts as the definition of appropriate behaviour before God: 'What are your endless sacrifices to me? says the Lord. I am sick of burnt offerings of rams and the fat of calves . . . Take your wrong-doing out of my sight: cease to do evil, learn to do good . . .' (Isaiah 1. 11, 16 f.). Yet even religious reformers find that the human need for festival and fast has to be satisfied, as can be seen in the proliferation of such occasions in the three religions mentioned above.

Judaism Among Jews, the festivals and fasts (following a lunar *calendar) are a mixture of agricultural and New Year observances, combined with those which commemorate the history of God's dealings with his people. The days of festival are known as (in the singular) *yom tov*, 'a good day'. Those commanded in the *Pentateuch include the three pilgrim festivals (*Passover, *Shavu'ot, and *Sukkot), the *New Year (*Rosh ha-Shanah), the *Day of Atonement (Yom Kippur), and the first day of the lunar month (Rosh Ḥodesh). Later festivals are the feast of *Esther (*Purim), the feast of Lights (*Ḥanukkah), and various memorial days. Festivals are celebrated with rejoicing, special meals (with the exception of the Day of Atonement), and often with abstention from work. There is special liturgy in the *synagogue, and the day is often marked by symbolic acts, such as lighting *candles (Ḥanukkah) or eating *mazzah (Passover). Again with the exception of Yom Kippur, it is customary among the *orthodox to celebrate the biblical festivals for two days in the *diaspora. The Bible records fasts being held to avert disaster (e.g. 2 Samuel 12. 22–3) and as a preparation for a divine encounter (e.g. Exodus 34. 28). Fixed fast days were first mentioned by the *prophet *Zechariah (ch. 8. 19); 10 Tevet commemorates the beginning of the siege of Jerusalem; 17 *Tammuz, the breaking of the walls; 9 *Av, the destruction of the *Temple, and 3 Tishri, the assassination of *Gedaliah. Many scholars believe even 10 Tishri was only fixed as the Day of Atonement at the end of the first temple period. The other two fasts of the Jewish calendar are 13 Adar, Fast of *Esther, and 14 Nisan, Fast of the Firstborn (commemorating the ten plagues in Egypt). Fasts are traditionally accompanied by prayer and confession, and involve abstention from food and drink, washing for pleasure, sexual intercourse, anointing, and wearing leather shoes. The purpose of fasting is 'to loose the bonds of wickedness' (Isaiah 58. 6), and it is pointless unless accompanied by sincere repentance. The *rabbis instituted modified fasting on other days, and it is customary to fast on the *yahrzeit of a parent's death, and before the ceremony on one's wedding day. But fasting is contained within the boundary of common sense: if its consequences are destructive, it holds no value: 'If the hunger of a fast makes you irritable, eat and be pleasant.'

See Y. Vainstein *Cycle of the Jewish Year*, 1961; S. J. Zevin, *The Festivals in Halakhah*, 1981.

Christianity Christian festivals follow an annual cycle, beginning with the advent of Christ and his birth, and tracing his life on earth: they culminate in his *ascension and status in the Holy and Undivided *Trinity. But at the same time, they commemorate and celebrate faithful followers of Christ, the *saints, *martyrs and *Doctors of the Church. Fasting is designed to strengthen the spiritual life by overcoming more immediate attractions of 'the world, the flesh and the *devil' (**Book of Common Prayer*). Jesus combined fasting with prayer (e.g. Matthew 6. 16–18) and the two were often subsequently combined (*asceticism). The observance of regular fasting began with weekly fast days, Wednesday and Friday. To these were added the fast of Lent; in the E., three further forty-day fasts throughout the year; and in the W., *vigil fasts and *ember days. In early times, fasting meant entire abstinence from food for the whole or part of the day. In E. and Oriental Churches fasting is still strictly observed, at least in Lent, by abstinence from all animal food products. In Catholic practice, fasting means one chief meal at midday and a small 'collation' in the morning and evening (see also ABSTINENCE); the only two fast days now are *Ash Wednesday and *Good Friday.

In addition to fasts in the calendar, the custom of a 'eucharistic fast' is also of ancient (*c.*3rd-cent.) origin. This called for the entire abstinence from food and drink before receiving *communion, because 'for the honour of so great a sacrament, the body and blood of the Lord should enter into the mouth of a Christian before other foods' (*Augustine). It is observed from the time of rising in Eastern and Oriental Churches. In the Roman Catholic Church, along with encouragement of frequent communion, the period of fasting was reduced to one hour.

Christian feasts are of three main kinds: (i) *Sunday, (ii) movable feasts, and (iii) immovable feasts. The movable feasts (*Easter, and *Pentecost seven weeks later) vary in date because of their origin in the Jewish lunar *calendar. The dates of certain other feasts, and the fast of Lent, also depend on that of Easter. The immovable feasts may have originated in the commemoration of *martyrs, extending to that of other *saints. By the 4th cent., the feasts of Christmas and *Epiphany were fixed, and various feasts of the Virgin *Mary and other feasts relating to *Christ were later added. The most extensive calendars are those of the RC and Orthodox Churches, but the 1969 RC calendar reduced the number of saints' days and restored the precedence of Sunday over them. The most important feasts, including all Sundays, are 'feasts of obligation' on which all Catholics are obliged to hear *mass. See also CALENDAR.

Islam Among Muslims (who follow a lunar calendar), the major festivals and fasts are linked to the command of the *Qur'ān or to the life of *Muḥammad. They are Ra's al-ʿĀm (New Year, 1 Muḥarram); ʿĀshūrā' (10 Muḥarram, for *Sunnis a day of blessing, but for Shiʿites the anniversary of the martyrdom of *al-Husain); Mawlid al-Nabī (12 Rabīʿ al-Awwal, Muḥammad's birthday); Laylat al-*Miʿrāj (27 Rajab, the Night Journey); Laylat al-Barāʿah (15 Shaʿbān, the night on which sins are forgiven and the destiny of the next year is fixed); Ramaḍān, a month of fasting during daylight hours which includes on the 10th the commemoration of the *Exodus, and on the 27th, *Laylat al-Qadr, the night of the descent of the Qur'ān; *ʿĪd al-Fiṭr (1 Shawwal, feast of fast-breaking); *ʿĪd al-Aḍḥā (10 Dhu -'l-Ḥijjah, feast of sacrifice, commemorating Ibrahīm's (Abraham's) willingness to sacrifice his son; 8–10 are the days of pilgrimage to *Mecca); ʿĪd al-Ghadīr (18 Dhu-'l-Ḥijjah, Shiʿites only, the designation by Muḥammad of *ʿAlī as his successor).

Hinduism It is said that Hindus have a festival (*vrata, celebration) for every day of the year. That is a serious underestimate. P. V. Kane, *History of Dharmasastra*, v/1, pp. 253–452, lists more than a thousand; and in addition, each temple will have its own local vrata (of which the pulling of the chariots (*ratha*) of *Jagannātha is simply one example). Major festivals which are likely to be observed by most Hindus are Kṛṣṇajayānti (*Janamaśtami, during Śrāvaṇa, Kṛṣṇa's birthday, celebrated at midnight after a day of fasting); Rakhi Bandhan (full moon of the same month, when friendships are renewed by tying a thread round the wrist, and when girls tie coloured threads round the wrists of their brothers to make them their protectors, following the example of *Indra, who was saved from the demon *Bali by the thread which his wife had tied on him); Ganeṣa Caturthī (during Bhadra, when the instruments of work are placed before *Ganeṣa to evoke his blessing); Dassera (the first half of the month Aśvina, a series of festivals, including Navarātri, the first nine days leading to Daśahrā— i.e. *Durgā *Pūjā; on the tenth day the victory of *Rāma and his monkey allies over Rāvaṇa is celebrated); *Dīvālī or Dipavālī (second half of Aśvina, the festival of lights); Nāgapañcami (mainly in S. India, the reverence of the cobra as guardian); Śivarātri (during Magha, devotion to Śiva and anointing of the *liṅga; a fast is kept, and worship is offered every three hours); *Holī (during Phalguṇa, a carnival of reversals and riot): see V. P. Kanitkar, *Hindu Festivals and Sacraments* (1984).

Buddhism Among Buddhists, festivals depend on the country and style of Buddhism: since Buddhism absorbed rather than obliterated the customs of the countries into which it spread, the accumulation of festivals makes it impossible to list them. However, certain major days are held by *Theravādin or *Mahāyāna Buddhists. Among Theravādins, the full moon dominates. New Year is observed with ceremonies of cleansing (sometimes partaking of the riotous character of the Hindu Holi): sand *stūpas are built to be washed away as a reminder of the transience of life. Full moon in the month Vesakha is the major celebration (Vesakha Pūjā) of the Buddha's birth, enlightenment, and parinibbana (*nirupadhiśeṣa-nirvāṇa). On the next full moon (in Śri Lankā) is Poson, celebrating the arrival of Buddhism in Śri Lankā; on the next full moon is Āsālha Pūjā, celebrating the Buddha's renunciation and First Sermon, and marking the beginning of the three month rain-period (*Vassa) during which laymen may join the *saṅgha, and during which the *bhikṣus stay in their monasteries. Mahāyāna adds many local festivals, but most Mahāyāna developments recognize the anniversaries of the birth, enlightenment, and parinirvana of the Buddha as separate occasions. The founding of the saṅgha and the power of Buddha relics are also celebrated. Fasting is regarded with a certain suspicion because of the Buddha's warning against the extremes of indulgence and *asceticism; but fasting is enjoined for bhikṣus from midday to the following morning, and may be followed by laypeople to gain merit, especially at new and full moon.

Jainism Jains have a large calendar (when local celebrations are included) which is complicated by the fact that few festivals are celebrated on the same day by *Digambaras and Śvetāmbaras. An exception is Mahāvīra Jayanti, the birthday of *Mahāvīra, which is celebrated on the 13th of the bright half of Caitra. Otherwise, the same feast or fast is observed at different times (e.g. Jñanapañcami honours scripture among the Śvetāmbaras, Śrutapañcami among the Digambaras) or the same goal is reached by different occasions: thus Paryushan (*Paryūsana) among Śvetāmbaras is an eight-day period of penitence, *confession, and effort to accomplish what should have been done during the year; the near equivalent for Digambaras is Daśalakśanaparvan, which starts exactly as Paryushan ends, and lasts for ten days during which ten virtuous qualities are recited and held out for emulation. The ritual year ends with Divālī, but the lights are reinterpreted as a commemoration of the lights lit to acknowledge the death of Mahāvīra.

Sikhism Sikh festivals are tied particularly to the Gurūs and to the founding of the *khālsā. Thus *Gurpurbs commemorate the births, accessions, or deaths of the Gurūs; and even those which have been received from Hinduism have been adapted: thus the lights on Divālī celebrate the release of Guru Hargobind on this day in 1619, and Hola-Mohalla (Holi) was given a specifically Sikh character by Guru Gobind Siṅgh in 1680. Of particular importance is *Baisakhi, commemorating the founding of the khālsā in 1699.

Zoroastrianism For Zoroastrians there are six seasonal festivals (*gahambars*) which together with New Year (No Ruz) constitute an annual cycle of religious obligation for all Zoroastrians. Along with the *sudre/kusti* prayers (*Naujote), they are in fact the only compulsory practices of the religion. Originally, they seem to have been celebrations of spring, summer, winter, harvest, the return of cattle from their summer pasture, and the annual visit of the souls of the departed. However, the Zoroastrian calendar has slipped back against the annual cycle (there was no equivalent of leap years), and so the original significance of the *gahambars* has been partly lost. What they do retain, however, is much of the traditional spirit of joyful worship of *Ahura Mazda (misery is a sin in Zoroastrianism), focusing on hospitality, the sharing of food and drink in which everyone has the religious obligation to undertake charitable giving to others, even if that be simply their labours. These festivals remain part of the living tradition in Iran but are not widely observed by *Parsis, partly because of the prohibition on large communal dining as an economy measure in newly Independent India. As Iranians and Parsis have come together in the diaspora, the ancient tradition has provided an effective means of bringing scattered Zoroastrian families together again. The spirits of the deceased are traditionally invited to be present so that they too can share in the community's joy. The festivities are preceded by religious ceremonies, in Iran in the temple, but in the diaspora in a community ritual, the *jashan*. In addition to denoting a specific ceremony *jashan* also refers to regular religious festivals in the calendar. The days of the month are named after certain Zoroastrian figures, as are the months of the year. Where the name of the day and month coincide, that is a *jashan* day marked by various rites. The last five days of the year are dedicated to each of the traditional five divisions of the *Gāthās (*Avesta) and are therefore known as 'Gatha days'. Other religious days of the year observed are Pateti (Parsi name for No Roz), when the Patet or prayer of repentance is recited seeking forgiveness for the past and affirming commitment to righteousness for the future. Khordadsal celebrates the birthday of *Zoroaster and Zarthoshtno Diso his death. The festival observed with particular care, not least in the diaspora, is the Farvardagan days (days of the 'Guardian Spirits' see FRAVASI), also known by Parsis as *muktad* (from Skt., 'the soul of the departed'). The dead are thought to be powerfully present, as their names are recited in community prayers, so those ceremonies are occasions when the purity laws have to be observed with particular care. The time of greatest merrymaking among diaspora Zoroastrians is probably Jamshedi No Roz which is generally celebrated on 21 Mar. There are three Zoroastrian calendars observed: Shenshais, followed by the majority of Parsis; Qadimi, which seeks to follow what is thought of as the ancient Iranian calendar; and the Fasli, a 19th-cent. attempt to adapt the Zoroastrian to the Gregorian calendar. These differences caused disputes in the past, but not in the 20th cent. The chart gives the majority Shenshais and the Fasli calendar, mainly observed by Iranian Zoroastrians, although they do not have all the ceremonies. The dates given are for 1995, but change slightly each year.

Festival	Shenshais	Fasli
(Iranian) Jamshedi Nau Roz		21 March
Khordad Sal	28 August	22 March
Farvardagan Jashan		8 April
Farvardegan/Muktad	13–22 August	
Zarthoshtno Diso	30 May	26 December
(Parsi) Nau Roz	23 August	

Notes: The Qadmi dates fall one month earlier than the Shenshais, both fall one day back each leap year. The Fasli dates remain constant, following the Gregorian calendar.

Sources: M. Boyce, *A Persian Stronghold of Zoroastrianism*, (1977); H. D. K. Mirza, *Outlines of Parsi History* (1974).

Japanese Since *Japanese religion is 'a brocade of religious traditions', the festivals (*matsuri) of all the religions involved will be a part of the Japanese scene. But there are also annual festivals which are more specifically Japanese, and which, in general (at least until recently) are observed by a large proportion of the population. Of the annual observances (*nenjū gyōgi*), the following are important: Shōgatsu (New Year, for about one week from 1 Jan., prepared for by cleaning homes and putting up a straw rope, *shimenawa*, symbolizing the binding of the home to divine power, and celebrated by special food and visits to shrines and superiors); Koshōgatsu (lesser New Year, following the lunar calendar, 15 Jan.); Setsubun (the turning of the seasons, held on the last day of winter, with the driving out of evil spirits from the home ('Oni wa soto') by the throwing of soybeans, and the inviting of good fortune ('Fuku wa uchi')); Hina matsuri (3 Mar., the doll festival, associating the girls of the family with illustrious figures, though originally it may have been the case that sins were transferred to the dolls which were then thrown into a river); Haru no shanichi (the day for the veneration of the protective deity, or *kami; the full veneration, Aki no shanichi, is held at the autumn equinox); Haru no higan (festival of the spring equinox; but because *higan* means, for Buddhists, 'the further shore', people visit their homes and ancestral graves; Aki no higan is held at the autumn equinox); Hana matsuri (8 Apr., the festival of flowers, observed by ascending a hill and gathering wild flowers, which, when they are brought home, lead the mountain deities (yama no kami) to follow); Tango no sekku (5 May, festival for celebrating the growth and achievements of boys); Suijin matsuri (15 June and 1 Dec., festivals of the kami of water, to seek their protection against the vindictive *goryō*); Tanabata (star festival, when craftsmen seek improvement in their skills by writing poems and floating them away on bamboo leaves on streams); Bon (sometimes O-bon, 13–16 July, feast for the dead, when the spirits of ancestors are welcomed back into the home and visits are made to attend to graves); Tsukimi (viewing the moon, 15 Aug. according to the lunar calendar, with offerings of the first-fruits of rice).

See Index, Festivals.

Festival of Light. Interdenominational movement founded in 1971 to promote action based on informed Christian opinion concerning declining moral values, particularly in the field of family ethics. Renamed, CARE (Christian Action Research and Education) in 1983, the organization aimed to raise moral standards and influence legislation in the direction of biblical ethics. Its educational work was pursued by means of literature, workshops, and rallies, by which it sought to draw attention to such matters as the influence of media violence and pornography, abortion, divorce, and euthanasia. The church-related work was that of the charitable body 'Care Trust'; the political pressure was exerted by 'Care Campaigns'.

Fetish (Port., *feitiço*, 'made thing'). An object held in awe or reverence. The term has had a wide range of uses and meanings. In origin, it derives from the observations made by early traders and travellers in W. Africa of objects (often worn) held in high regard.

From this it was concluded that a fetish was an idol. Already by the 18th cent., Charles de Brosses (in a comparison of ancient Egyptian and modern African religion) was suggesting that fetishism, as the worship of both inanimate and animate objects, was the first form of religion. It was then recognized that these objects were not so much worshipped as used to exercise power, and the word began to be used of objects containing force. Yet in fact it was clear that such objects are more often apotropaic, averting evil; thus a fetish became something like a good-luck charm. Beyond that, the word 'fetish' was taken up in psychoanalysis to refer to a sexual tendency to obtain erotic satisfaction from objects rather than people, even if only of objects associated with people. Colloquially, a fetish is an object of obsessive preoccupation, 'making a fetish of something'.

Feuerbach, Ludwig (1804–72). German philosopher and religious thinker whose theory of *projection greatly influenced, among others, Karl *Marx. Having himself studied with both *Hegel and *Schleiermacher at Berlin, Feuerbach was well-equipped later to lead an attack against the prevailing philosophy and theology. The attack came first in *The Essence of Christianity* (1841) and then again in *Principles of the Philosophy of the Future* (1843). Feuerbach sought by means of Hegel's own dialectic to undermine the master's system. Hegel, he suggested, had offered but a mirror-image of the world: to see the world as it is, one must simply reverse the picture given by Hegel. Among other things, this leads us to see that God is humanity's self-alienated essence projected onto a cosmic screen: in worshipping God, people are simply worshipping themselves. Among the world's religions, Christianity is most nearly true, in that in worshipping Christ it worships man as God; within Christianity, Protestantism comes nearest to the truth in that it is only really interested in God for us, the God-Man (*Christus pro nobis*), and not God in himself. For practical purposes, Protestantism is already atheistic, although it remains theoretically theistic; Feuerbach recommends that theory and practice be reconciled, that theology be reduced without remainder to anthropology. Anything less leads necessarily to contradictions.

E. Kamenka, *The Philosophy of Ludwig Feuerbach* (1970); M. Wartofsky, *Feuerbach* (1977).

Fideism. The view that true knowledge of God can be attained only by faith on the basis of revelation. Reason is therefore subordinated to faith where otherwise problematic issues or questions arise. Fideism might logically be refuted by reason, but a fideist could never accept that he had been refuted. More particularly, fideism is the view that faith precedes reason in the knowledge of God, so that reason and metaphysics are deficient in this respect. This view was condemned during the 19th cent., esp. as represented by L. E. Bautain (1796–1867): the Roman Congregation required his assent to five theses, opposed to fideism, in 1844.

Fides quaerens intellectum ('faith seeking understanding'): see ANSELM.

Fifth Monarchy Men. Members of a short-lived elitist *millennarian movement in England in the mid-17th cent. Its members, mainly artisans, journeymen, and apprentices, anticipated the establishment of the 'fifth monarchy' of Daniel 2. 44, in which Christ would reign for a thousand years. Opposed to the established church, they also rejected Oliver Cromwell when he became Protector. Following Venner's rebellion (1661) the movement died out.

Filaret of Moscow (1782–1867). *Russian Orthodox renewer of the Church, and Metropolitan of Moscow. He became a monk in 1808 and was ordained priest in 1809. He became archbishop of Moscow in 1821 and metropolitan in 1826. Through the Holy Synod from 1819, he worked for the independence of Church from State, but in 1842 he was excluded from the synod because of his support for translations of scripture into modern Russian, to be made (in the case of the Old Testament) from the Hebrew (and Aramaic), not from the Septuagint. He also supported the translation of the Church *Fathers, which he believed would return the Church to its roots, and he devoted much time to the reform of clergy education, producing *The Longer Catechism* (1823, rev., 1839; tr. R. W. Blackmore).

Filial piety (Confucian influenced virtue in E. Asian ethics): see HSIAO.

Filioque (Lat., 'and the Son'), the formula in the W. form of the *Nicene Creed which expressed the 'double procession' (i.e. from both Father and Son) of the *Holy Spirit. It was first added to the creed in Spain in the 6th or 7th cent., and by the 11th cent. became familiar to all Latin Christians as part of its rendition at the mass. Since the time of *Photius, a strong opponent, the *filioque* has been a central point of controversy between E. and W. Churches. The Orthodox point to the original creed omitting it, and to the need for a single 'fount of divinity' (*pēgē theotētos*, viz. the Father) within the Godhead. W. theologians emphasize instead the commonality of functions between the Father and Son; but there are indications that the E. position is increasingly recognized (e.g. its omission from the creed at the consecration of R. Runcie as archbishop of Canterbury).

W. A. Visse't Hooft, *Spirit of God, Spirit of Christ: Ecumenical Reflections on the Filioque Controversy* (1981).

Final solution. Nazi plan for the extermination of the Jews. The expression 'final solution' was first used in 1941. After the Wannsee Conference of 1942, Adolph Eichmann was authorized to implement the total destruction of European Jewry in the occupied lands. See HOLOCAUST.

Finkelstein, Louis (b. 1895). US *Conservative *rabbi. As president (1940–51) of the *Jewish Theological Seminary and the Rabbinical Assembly, his was the most prominent voice in the Conservative movement of his time. He was also a prolific writer, exploring the fundamental documents of Judaism, and also seeking to relate Jewish thought to the problems of his time. He believed that the intentions of the *Temple had been translated into the *synagogue: 'If Jewish life survived the destruction of the Temple, that was because the synagogue had been prepared to take over the whole burden and carry it onward for generations to come.' Believing that 'there is no sharp distinction in religious status between the rabbi and the layman', he saw Judaism as a model of spiritualized democracy. He envisaged 'an emerging, ordered, pluralistic universe of thought', in which there would be 'cooperation without imposing uniformity'. In that pluralism, there would be no compromise of principles: 'A Jew may not enter a building dedicated to idol-worship, not even to protect himself from inclement weather.' Under his leadership, Conservative Judaism became the largest organized body of American Jews.

H. Parzen, *Architects of Conservative Judaism* (1964).

Fiqh (Arab., 'intelligence, knowledge'). Jurisprudence, the science of the religious law in Islam. Fiqh originally indicated 'knowledge, understanding' (i.e. of the law ordained by God, the *sharīʿa) as opposed to *kalām, knowledge of theology. Fiqh covers all regulations of religious, political, civil, and social life; family, private, public, and criminal law. One who pursues the study of fiqh is a *faqih.

During the earliest period of Islam, legal matters as they arose were generally dealt with either by Arab customary law or by the legal systems in operation in the conquered territories. From the end of the 1st cent. AH/early 8th cent. CE, fiqh was studied and elaborated in the 'schools' of Madīna, Kūfā, and Syria. These differed in details and application of principles, but agreed on the importance of four sources of law (*uṣūl al-fiqh): the *Qur'ān, *Sunna (as exemplified in the *ḥadīth), *ijmāʿ (consensus), and *qiyās (analogy).

Four main schools of law (*madhāhib*, sing. *madhhab*) have survived, based on the teachings of *Shāfiʿī (d. 820 (AH 205)), *Mālik b. Anas (d. 795 (AH 179)), Aḥmad b. *Hanbal (d. 855 (AH 241)), and *Abū Ḥanīfa (d. 767 (AH 150)). Mālik's *Muwaṭṭa'* (The Path) is one of the earliest of all books of fiqh, and remained influential. Later law studies had to follow the basic principles already formulated, and it was increasingly argued that the right to *ijtihād (independent reasoning) had ceased with the death of the early generation of scholars. There was still room for some interpretation, and a legal expert might be called upon to give his considered opinion (*fatwā) on a difficult problem.

In addition to the Sunni schools, *Kharijites and *Shiʿites have their own schools. The major differences for the Shiʿites relate to the caliphate (*khalīfa) and to the constitutional consequences of their variant views, and also, to a lesser degree, to issues of marriage (see e.g. MUTʿA).

J. N. D. Anderson, *Islamic Law in the Modern World*; N. J. Coulson, *A History of Islamic Law* (1964).

Firdaws ('paradise'): see HEAVEN (ISLAM); PARADISE (ISLAM).

Firdawsi, Abu-l-Qasim Mansur (940–1020 (AH 328–411)). Iranian poet who preserved many Zoroastrian traditions. He placed little emphasis on religion beyond a vague monotheism compatible with Islam, but he was highly esteemed nevertheless for his *Shahnameh* (tr., A. G. and E. Warner; R. Levy), which celebrates Persian history. He was called Firdawsi by the Sultan Maḥmūd of Ghaznah, who said that his compositions turned the court into the rooms of paradise (*firdaws*, see PARADISE (ISLAM)).

Fire (in Hinduism): see AGNI.

Fire 'worship' (Zoroastrian): see ATAS.

First Amendment. The first amendment to the US Constitution, which states that 'Congress shall make no law respecting an establishment of religion, or prohibiting the free exercise thereof.' The 'free exercise' provision has been interpreted very broadly by the courts, only excluding e.g. polygamy and *snake-handling. The prohibition of 'establishment' has been held not to conflict with such institutions as tax exemption for church property, chaplains in the armed forces, and *Thanksgiving Day, but the Supreme Court ruled that it does exclude prayer and religious instruction in public schools and various kinds of government aid to church schools. In 1985, the Supreme Court ruled 6–3 that an Alabama law authorizing voluntary prayer or meditation in public schools violated the First Amendment: 'Just as the right to speak and the right to refrain from speaking are complementary components of a broader concept of individual freedom of mind, so also the individual's freedom to choose his own creed is the counterpart of his right to refrain from accepting the creed established by the majority.'

Firstborn. Jewish law gives first-born males a special status. According to Deuteronomy 21. 15–17, an eldest son is entitled to a double portion of the inheritance. Traditionally the first-born belonged to God: 'On the day that I slew all the first-born in the land of Egypt, I consecrated for my own all the first-born in *Israel, both of man and beast' (Numbers 3. 13). Consequently, first-born sons must be redeemed through the ceremony of *pidyon ha-ben* (redemption of the son). In exchange for five silver shekels (Numbers 18. 16), paid to a *kohen* (*priest) on the thirty-first day after birth, the child is ceremoniously returned to his father. First-born animals should also be given to a *kohen*. First-born males should also observe the Fast of the first-born on 14 *Nisan, the day before *Passover. This is to express gratitude to God for sparing the Israelites in the tenth plague, but this custom has largely disappeared. The detailed laws are in the tractate *Bekhorot* in the Mishnah *et al*.

First diffusion (period in history of Tibetan Buddhism): see TIBETAN RELIGION.

First fruits (Heb., *bikkurim*). The portion of harvest which, according to Jewish law, must be given to the *Temple. According to Deuteronomy 26. 1–11, every Israelite must 'take some of the first of all the fruit of the ground' and give it to the *priest on duty in the temple. A sheaf of the new barley harvest was traditionally offered on the second day of *Passover and the festival of *Shavu'ot, also called Hag ha-Bikkurim (the first-fruits festival) was the time for making the first-fruit offering. In Israel today first-fruit celebrations are still held on Shavu'ot and donations are made to the Jewish National Fund.

First Sermon. Of the *Buddha, preached at Benares. It expounded the *Four Noble Truths and the Eightfold Path (*aṣṭangika-mārga). It is known as 'the first turning of the *dharmacakra (wheel of dharma)': see DHAMMA CAKKAPPAVATTANA SUTTA.

Fiscus Judaicus. A tax on Jews levied in the Roman Empire. The fiscus Judaicus was a poll tax levied from 71 CE until the early 3rd cent. It was officially paid to Jupiter Capitolinus and took the place of the tax Jews had paid for the upkeep of the Jerusalem *Temple before its destruction in 70 CE.

Fish. As a Christian symbol, its use goes back to 2nd-cent. writers, e.g. *Tertullian who speaks of Christians as little fish following Christ the Fish, in connection with the water of baptism. The symbol itself may be derived from the acrostic spelling of *ichthus (Gk., 'fish') from the Gk. first letters of 'Jesus Christ, God and Saviour'. But it is possible that it could have a non-Christian origin. Certainly the religious use of fish was widespread in ancient religion, e.g. as an offering to the Syrian Goddess Atargatis. In this case the Christian acrostic is secondary, and probably a *gnostic invention. In the 4th and 5th cents. the fish became a symbol for the *eucharist, and appears in *catacomb paintings along with bread and wine.

Fisher, John, St (1469–1535). *Bishop of Rochester and *martyr. Born in Beverley, he went to Cambridge University where he became vice-chancellor and then, in 1504, chancellor. The same year he was appointed to the bishopric of Rochester. Though himself a severe critic of standards in the Church, he was a vigorous opponent of *Lutheranism, and greatly influenced the study of theology, especially in Cambridge. In 1529, to the considerable irritation of Henry VIII, he ably defended Catherine of Aragon. He was eventually imprisoned for refusing to take the oath attached to the Act of Succession on the grounds that it contained an admission of royal supremacy over the Church in England. Again to Henry's fury he was made a *cardinal in 1535. He was executed on 17 June that year, and canonized 400 years later. Feast day, 22 June.

R. Rex, *The Theology of John Fisher* (1991).

Fiṭra (Arab.). An important term in Islamic doctrine about humans and their moral constitution as creatures of God's creation. The pivotal passage is Qur'ān 30. 30 which uses the word in apposition to the command: 'Set your face to the religion as a *ḥanīf', followed at once by the words 'the nature of God on which he natured man'. Most exegesis takes fiṭra to mean human nature as designed and intended for 'religion'—understood as Islam. But some take fiṭra to mean Islam itself. Either way, fiṭra means that there is a congenial fitness of humanity to the right faith, and of the right faith to humanity. Hence the tradition that it is parents who make children something other than Muslim. Humans are by nature perfectible by law, amenable to divine will, not essentially liable to perversity or involved in *original sin. 'The nature of God' in Qur'ān 30. 30 means, not the divine 'image', but rather 'the nature God ordained'. Even so, the Qur'ān has very sombre comments on how misled and heinous humanity can be.

Five animals (Taoist exercises): see WU-CH'IN-HSI.

Five auspicious moments (Jain): see TRIŚALĀ.

Five Classics (of Shinto): see HONJISUIJAKU.

Five deadly sins. Five offences in Buddhism which deliver the offender (via *karma) into *naraka (hell): patricide, matricide, killing an *arhat, injuring a *buddha, creating schism in the *saṅgha. See also (in Japan) GOGYAKU-ZAI.

Five degrees (of enlightenment): see GO-I.

Five elements (in Chinese and Taoist understanding of the cosmos): see WU-HSING.

Five elements (Jain): see ASTIKAYA.

Five evil passions. In Sikh teaching, passions which typify the *manmukh (wayward individual) whose *man is prey to *haumai (egoism). They result in suffering and rebirth. They are *kām* (lust), *krodh* (anger), *lobh* (covetousness), *moh* (attachment to worldly things), and *haṅkār* (pride).

Five faces (of Śiva): see PAÑCĀNANA.

Five fetters: see SAṂYOJANA.

Five great vows (*mahāvrata*). Vows undertaken by Jain ascetics, accepted as fundamental to *Mahāvīra's teaching by both *Digambaras and Śvetambāras. Although not formally enunciated in the earliest literature, they have subsequently become the mark of those on the Jain *mokṣa-*mārga (path to liberation). They are (i) *ahiṁsā, the avoidance of killing any life-form (or, in extreme interpretations, ensouled beings: see *BHIKṢU), and of any act of violence (even in the mind). This involves e.g. care in walking and in eating and drinking. It underlies *caturmas*, the four-month retreat during the monsoon when life-forms proliferate; (ii) *satya*, speaking and thinking the truth, and avoiding lies; (iii) *asteya*, not taking what is not given, not just the avoidance of theft, but not occupying a location for too long, and not using alms without the teacher's permission; (iv) *brahmacharya, renunciation of all sexual activity, including any kind of contact with women; (v) *aparigraha*, detachment from all objects of the senses, and from possessions. A later sixth vow forbids eating after dark. For the lay (and less demanding) equivalents, see ANUVRATA.

Five heavens (Jain): see ANUTTARAVIMĀNA.

Five hindrances (Buddhist): see NĪVARAṆAS.

Five holy beings (Jain chant): see NAMASKĀRA-MANTRA.

Five Homages (basic Jain mantra): see FIVE SUPREME BEINGS.

Five houses. Five schools of Ch'an Buddhism (Tsung-men shih-kuei lun) during the later T'ang period and under the 'five dynasties'—though the roots of each are usually older: (i) *Ts'ao-tung (Jap., *Sōtō); (ii) *Lin-chi (Jap., *Rinzai); (iii) Yün-men (Jap., *Ummon); (iv) *Kuei-yang (Jap., Igyō; (v) Fa-yen (Jap., *Hogen).

The term was first used by *Fa-yen Wen-i (885–958), who described (i)–(iv).

H. Dumoulin, *Zen Buddhism: A History* . . ., I, (1988).

Five impediments (Buddhist): see JÑĀNA.

Five Ks, Pañj Kakke. Sikh symbols. *Khālsā Sikhs, male and female, are identifiable by five emblems which they wear. These are called the five Ks because their Pañjābī names all commence with 'kakkā' (k). According to tradition, after baptizing the *pañj pyāre on *Baisākhī day 1699, Gurū *Gobind Siṅgh commanded the observance of certain rules including the wearing of the five Ks. These would distinguish Sikhs from Muslims and Hindus, strengthening their sense of military discipline.

1. Keś, uncut hair. No hair may be removed from the body since this interferes with God's will. In contrast to the matted locks of Hindu ascetics, the Sikh's hair must be kept clean.

2. Kaṅghā, a small comb, usually of wood or ivory. This keeps the hair neat and so symbolizes controlled spirituality. Often a miniature kirpān (see below) is embedded in the kaṅghā.

3. Kirpān, steel sword. This is usually 20–5 cm. long, but kirpāns range from a miniature token worn around the neck or on the kaṅghā to 90 cm. long. The kirpān signifies courage in defence of right.

4. Kaṛā, steel bangle, worn on the right wrist. The symbolism of the circle arguably outweighs any historical use in warfare. The Kaṛā is a reminder of the wearer's unity with God and other Sikhs and of bondage to the Gurū, restraining the wearer from evil action.

5. Kachh, long shorts. These replaced the 'dhotī', customarily worn by men, enabling swift action in war. The kachh is worn as underwear by *amritdhārī Sikhs of both sexes and symbolizes continence.

See KHAṆḌE-DI-PĀHUL; SAHAJDHĀRĪ; TURBAN.

Five Mountains (Buddhist temples in Japan): see GOZAN.

Five Ms (actions ordinarily forbidden which induce power in Tantrism): see PAÑCA-MĀKĀRA.

Five Peaks (pilgrimage centres): see PILGRIMAGE.

Five pecks of rice (school of religious Taoism): see WU-TOU-MI TAO.

Five periods, seven stages (Taoist analysis of progress to the goal): see WU-SHIH CH'I-HOU.

Five Periods and Eight Schools. T'ien-t'ai classification, initiated by *Chih-i, of the *Buddha's teaching to reconcile the immense divergences that had grown up since his death. Controlled by the acceptance that the Buddha adapted his teaching to the levels of his audiences (*upāya-kauśalya), the five periods are chronological in his life, producing (i) **Buddhāvatamsaka-sūtra* in the first three weeks; (ii) the *Āgamas in the next twelve years; (iii) the Vaipulya-sūtras, the first level of *Mahāyāna, stressing superiority of *bodhisattva over *arhat, in the next eight years; (iv) *Prajñāpāramitā-sūtra* (*Perfection of Wisdom), unfolding *śūnyatā, in the next twenty-two years; (v) the **Lotus Sūtra* and **Mahāparinirvāṇa-sūtra* in his last eight years. But since the Buddha's teaching is indivisible, it was always present in each of the five periods, so that the stress on one aspect more than another led to eight different schools. T'ien-t'ai and the *Lotus Sūtra* re-establish the primordial unity.

Five Pillars of Islam (more literally, Pillars of the Faith, Arab., *arkān ud-Din*). These are the fundamental constituents of Muslim life. They are (i) ash-*Shahāda, the witness; (ii) *ṣalāt, formal prayer; (iii) *zakāt, tithe for the poor; (iv) *ḥajj, pilgrimage to *Mecca; (v) *sawm, fasting during *Ramaḍān. Although they are all derived from the *Qur'ān, it is uncertain when exactly they were formally organized. According to a *ḥadīth from Talḥāh ibn 'Ubayy, Muḥammad listed them to a man who enquired what the obligations of a Muslim are.

Five powers (Buddhist): see BALA.

Five precepts (Buddhist): see ŚĪLA.

Five Ranks (school of Ch'an/Zen Buddhism): see TS'AO-TUNG; GO-I.

Five roots (Buddhist): see INDRIYA; BALA; BODHIPĀKṢIKA-DHARMA.

Five Scrolls (books of Hebrew scriptures): see SCROLLS.

Five species. Varieties of cereals or grains which are indigenous to the land of Israel, and are therefore subject to biblical and rabbinic laws governing such produce. The basic requirement is that a portion of dough (*ḥallah) must be set aside for the priests (Numbers 15. 18–21).

Five Supreme Beings (*pañca paramesthin*, those at the highest stage), the five exemplary modes of being for Jains. Highest are the *tirthaṅkaras (also known as *arhat and *jina), who teach the way to liberation and found communities based on their teaching; next are the *siddhas, the liberated souls (*jīva); then the guides on earth (*acarya) who lead monks and nuns; then the teachers of monks and nuns (*upadhyāya*); then monks themselves. They are approached in reverence and homage through *pañca namaskāra* (the five homages), a *mantra which offers homage to each of the five groups. The mantra is believed to have great power and is fundamental in Jain ritual.

Five virtues (Hindu virtues): see APARIGRAHA.

Five virtues (in Confucianism): see WU-CH'ANG.

Five vows (Jain): see FIVE GREAT VOWS.

Five ways (arguments pointing to the existence of God): see QUINQUE VIAE.

Five ways of Ch'an/Zen. Early classification of five styles of meditation, made by Kuei-feng Tsung-mi (780–841), also known as Tsung-mi. He was the last patriarch of the *Hua-yen school of Chinese Buddhism, whose work *Yuan-jen lun* (The Original *Jen of Humanity) became a basic work in training Buddhist monks, precisely because of its analysis of the various schools and styles. The five styles are: (i) Bonpu, *zazen for restricted aims, e.g. improving health or mental relaxation; (ii) Gedō, meditation sharing Zen aims, but practised outside (e.g. by Hindus or Christians); (iii) Shōjō, aimed at emancipation from reappearance (*punabhava), and from a *Mahāyāna point of view, selfish; (iv) Daijō, 'great vehicle' (i.e. Mahāyāna) attainment of enlightenment (*kensho, *satori) etc.; (v) Saijōjō, highest form of Zen, in which the realization of the buddha-nature in all appearance (*bussho) occurs. The equation of (iv) with *Rinzai and (v) with Sōtō is artificial, since (iv) and (v) occur in both.

Fletcher, J. (exponent of Situation Ethics): see ETHICS (CHRISTIANITY).

Flight of the alone to the Alone: see NEOPLATONISM.

Flirty fishing (conversion technique of The Family): see CHILDREN OF GOD.

Flood. Deluge described in Genesis 6. 1–9. 18. According to the Hebrew scriptures, God decided to destroy humanity by sending a great flood. Only *Noah, his immediate family, and a pair of each animal species were saved in a huge *ark. When the rains finally subsided, Noah disembarked and offered God *sacrifice. God promised that never again would he attempt to destroy the earth, and he set a rainbow in the sky as a token of the *covenant. Flood legends can be found in other cultures such as those of the Australian Aborigines and the Pacific islanders. Similar to the biblical account are the Akkadian Epic of Atrahasis and the Babylonian Epic of Gilgamesh. The Israelite version, however, is unique in that it emphasizes the ethical demands of God. The flood is understood as a divine punishment, and Noah survives only because of his moral worthiness. For the flood of Manu in India, see PRALAYA.

Florence, Council of (1438–45). Council which effected a brief reunion of the Catholic and Orthodox Churches. An earlier reunion at the Council of Lyons (1274), which had been sought by the Greek Church in need of W. help against the Turks, lasted only until 1289. The same need, now more desperate with Constantinople itself threatened, brought a large delegation to Italy, headed by the Emperor John VIII and Patriarch Joseph of Constantinople. The party also included Bessarion of Nicaea, a proponent of union with Rome (later a cardinal in the RC Church) and Mark of Ephesus, a staunch opponent (later an Orthodox saint). Long sessions at Ferrara, then at Florence, discussed the problems of the *filioque, unleavened bread (see AZYMITES) in the *eucharist, *purgatory, the *epiclesis, and the primacy of Rome. The Orthodox, except Mark, accepted Roman statements on all these; their own use of unleavened bread and disuse of the filioque were not challenged. But returning home the Orthodox delegates found the union unpalatable to the faithful. In Constantinople it was said, 'Rather the Sultan's turban than the Pope's tiara'. Nor did the emperor receive much of the promised W. military aid. The union was doomed by the fall of the city in 1453 and was formally repudiated in 1472. The Council of Florence also established short-lived unions with other Eastern churches. See also LAETENTUR COELI.

J. Gill, *The Council of Florence* (1959) and *Personalities* . . . (1964).

Florenz, Karl A. (1865–1939). German scholar in the early 20th cent. who translated the ancient *Shinto texts into German and wrote extensively on Shinto and *Japanese religion and literature. He was professor at Hamburg, 1914–35. Among his major works are *Die historischen Quellen der Shinto-Religionen aus dem altjapanischen und chinesischen übersetzt und erklärt* (Leipzig, 1919), and 'Die Japaner', in *Lehrbuch der Religionsgeschichte*, founded by Chantepie de la Saussaye (Tübingen, 1925), i. 262–422.

Flower contemplation ('arrangement', Japanese religious practice): see IKEBANA.

Fo. Chin. for *buddha.

Folk religion. 1. Religion which occurs in small, local communities which does not adhere to the norms of large systems. Folk-urban typology was developed by Robert Redfield as a basis for the comparison of societies, and for the study of urbanization. Folk society is 'small, isolated, nonliterate and homogeneous, with a strong sense of group solidarity . . . Behaviour is traditional, spontaneous, uncritical and personal. . . . Kinship, its relationships and institutions, are the type categories of experience, and the familial group is the unit of action. The sacred prevails over the secular.' Folk religion is thus much studied by anthropologists.

2. In a wider sense, folk religion is the appropriation of religious beliefs and practices at a popular level. This may occur as much in urban as in rural environments, and may also be the way in which individuals or groups belonging to mainstream religions practise their religion: it may be at considerable variance from what is officially supposed to be the case, and is thus also referred to as non-official religion. In this sense, folk religion absorbs much that might be frowned upon by official religion. It is extremely eclectic, and picks up elements from popular culture, superstition, sentiment, the paranormal, the occult, astrology, etc., and it is characteristically unorganized. Nevertheless, it can form systems of belief and practice, as in the cult of Elvis Presley, whose home at Gracelands has become a shrine: see further NEW RELIGIOUS MOVEMENTS. Folk religion expresses the deep *religiosity which exists naturally in most people, and is therefore closely allied to implicit religion.

Food and religion. Religions, as systems of control and protection which were tested for efficacy (originally) in straightforward terms of selection, have as profound a concern in relation to food as they do in relation to sex. Consequently, the ways in which food is related to religious ideas and practices are extremely complex and varied—as in the following examples.

1. The rejection of particular foods: this can draw on ideas concerning the character of the rejected food, as for example in Hinduism where meat from the cow is shunned because (amongst other things) it has involved the murder of a sacred animal; or in *Manichaeism where meat is identified with the Flesh and thus with the realm of darkness generally. Such *taboos frequently operate on a social level also, defining the boundaries around the particular religious group: this is quintessentially the case with Judaism, though true also for certain Christian sectarian groups.

2. The association of abstinence with spiritual practices: *asceticism frequently extends to diet; as such it involves a mixture of the rejection of physical pleasure or luxury, a setting of the self apart from normal social life, and, frequently, a rejection of the bodily and non-spiritual by the denial or reduction of bodily needs. It is frequently paralleled by sexual asceticism.

3. The structuring of food according to religious categories: these can be categories of people, as in the Hindu caste rules or monastic observance; or they can be categories of time, as in yearly patterns of FESTIVALS AND FASTS such as *Lent or *Ramaḍān.

4. The use of food in religious ceremonies: food is one of the commonest forms of religious offering. As such it is enmeshed in a complex of particular symbolic patterns, although these frequently draw on ideas of sacrifice or of substitute sacrifice. Food is also central in ritual meals where participants eat together, as in the Mithraic cult or in aspects of the Christian eucharist, or where, as for example the *Passover, the meal enshrines a religious ceremony. The ingestion of food is a frequent feature of *rites of passage, many of which have, either directly or indirectly, religious significance. There are also folk foods consumed in association with religious festivals and sometimes retaining an element of religious symbolism—for example, *Shrove Tuesday or *Easter foods in Christianity.

5. A vital means through which *women have secured their own identity, and also degrees of control, in a male-dominated world: see e.g. C. Bynum, *Holy Feast and Holy Fast* (1987).

Hinduism Hindu food rites are embedded within a larger hierarchy of purity. In relation to food, this has three principal, though interrelated, aspects: as applied to the structured relations between the castes which are separated and ranked by means of such purity rules; as applied to states of the person (with, in general, impurity deriving from the organic aspects of life of which eating is one); and as applied to types of food or diet. Impurity is relational rather than absolute. Since the castes are ranked in a hierachy of purity, organic contact with lower castes (e.g. eating food prepared by or in the company of someone of lower caste) is polluting. Uncooked food (i.e. untransformed: raw, unmixed, dry, unpeeled), since it has not yet taken on the qualities of the preparer, is broadly acceptable from the hands of all, regardless of caste. *Pakka* food, i.e. cooked in clarified butter, one of the products of the cow and therefore relatively resistant to pollution, can be accepted from a relatively wide range of people. It is thus the food of feasts; in distinction to *kakka* (baked or cooked in water) which is only acceptable from someone of similar or higher caste. (This distinction is of less significance in S. India where pollution concerns are in general much stronger.) For the individual, purity is in a constantly precarious state. A high caste *brahman, for example, must before eating be in a ritually pure state (bathed, with bare torso, and free from casual contact with bearers of pollution), must eat only with the right hand (the left being reserved for sexual contact and excretion), and at the end of the meal will be in a less pure state than at the start. Among lower castes, the rules are similar in form though less strict. The hierarchy of castes is paralleled by a hierarchy of diets. The pattern of caste diets is one of great complexity and is much modified by regional differences; however, all Hindus would regard a vegetarian diet as superior, although only brahmans adopt it by rule. Vegetarianism in India both relates to concepts of purity and to the wider development of the ideal of *ahiṁsā. Among meats, beef is the lowest regarded, and is consumed only by *Untouchables and non-Hindus like Muslims, who often act as butchers. Meat-eating castes do not dispute this hierarchy, and on sacred occasions may adopt a vegetarian diet.

Sikhism The diet of most Sikhs is *Pañjābī, i.e. spiced vegetables, pulses, and the staple wheat chapātīs, plus dairy produce. Beef is avoided because of Hindu influence. Gurū *Gobind Siṅgh forbade *amritdhārī Sikhs to eat *halal* (see AL-HALAL) meat, and many abstain from all flesh and eggs. However, according to widely accepted tradition, Gurūs *Hargobind and Gobind Siṅgh hunted and ate meat. Gurū *Nānak preached against *brahman dietary taboos, pointing out that a person's whole life is fleshly and that upright conduct far outweighs avoiding meat (see Ādi Granth 1289). The *Gurū-kā-laṅgar is vegetarian. See also ALCOHOL; NĀMDHĀRĪ.

Buddhism The *Buddha's advice concerning dietary habits is addressed primarily to those who have embraced the monastic life rather than to lay society. An important principle underlying Buddhist monasticism is that monks should be dependent upon the laity for alms and should go out daily into the local community to beg for food. It is a familiar sight in the Buddhist countries of S. Asia to see a line of saffron-clad monks walking soberly in single file from house to house and pausing with downcast eyes while offerings of food are placed in their bowls by the laity. After completing their round the monks return to the monastery where they must consume their food before midday. Thereafter they may take only liquids before the next day. The Buddha commended the practice of eating once a day for its benefits in terms of overall mental and physical well-being.

As regards the type of food which may be consumed, the general principle is that monks should accept with gratitude whatever they are given and not be selective in preferring or rejecting particular dishes. In *Theravāda Buddhism there is no prohibition on eating meat, providing that the monk has not seen, heard, or suspected that the animal was slaughtered specifically on his behalf, thus avoiding complicity in the breaking of the First Precept against taking life. The Buddha himself is said to have died after consuming pork, although the precise nature of this dish has been disputed. Ten specific kinds of flesh, however, were thought to be inappropriate for human consumption, for instance the flesh of elephants, tigers, and serpents.

Under the influence of Mahāyāna Buddhism, which stressed the virtue of compassionate concern for all sentient beings, vegetarianism came to be regarded as the most appropriate diet. The development of certain philosophical doctrines, such as that all beings are united by their participation in the same fundamental nature (the *buddha-nature), also contributed to this tendency with the result that vegetarianism became the norm, especially in the countries of the Far East which were profoundly influenced by these views. Thus Buddhism contains no set taboos concerning diet except that which derives from the First Precept: the non-taking of life (*ahiṁsā). Although many Buddhist populations eat meat habitually, all would recognize a non-meat diet as a higher one, and many Buddhists would offer an intention that the consumed animal should have a good rebirth. In any case (and in distinction from Hindus), bad karma attaches to the killer, not the eater, of meat. Monastic orders vary as to whether they eat meat: certain maintain a strict vegetarian diet, while others accept whatever is offered to them provided an animal has not been expressly killed for their use. Beyond that, the Buddha had clear views on the importance of both psychic and material food (see ĀHĀRA), and urged moderation.

Judaism In Judaism the fundamental division is between food that is *kasher* (see DIETARY LAWS), fit, and that which is *terefah*, unfit. The categories are defined in *Torah, though they receive greater elaboration and definition in *Talmudic writings. The distinction between clean and unclean animals appears originally in Genesis in the context of sacrifice, though in Deuteronomy and Leviticus it becomes the foundation of the dietary law. Clean animals are quadrupeds that have divided hooves and chew the cud (e.g. ox, sheep, goat). Examples of unclean animals are hare, camel, pig—the latter becoming a particular focus of taboo. Clean fish are those with fins and scales: this excludes shellfish, eels, and whales. Unclean birds are defined by the Talmud, effectively excluding birds of prey and most water-fowl. Insects are forbidden, as are all creeping things such as lizards and snails. Carrion is always unclean. There are also certain rules concerning vegetable foods (Leviticus 19, 23; Deuteronomy 22).

Certain parts of the animal are also to be avoided: the sinews of the hip, and the fat covering the stomach and kidneys (originally sacrificed). The consumption of blood, which bears a powerful charge in Judaism representing the seat of life, is also to be avoided, and meat is treated prior to cooking to remove as much of it as possible.

Rules also focus on the preparation of foods, and in particular the rule forbidding the seething of a kid in its mother's milk is interpreted as the prohibition on the mixing of meat and milk, later extended within the rabbinical tradition to include rules governing the use of separate utensils for meat and milk preparation and their separation in the context of meals, three / six hours having to elapse between. Food that has been offered to pagan idols is also forbidden, as in later development is food prepared by idolaters.

Lastly, there are the rules concerning slaughter (*sheḥitah). For meat to be *kasher* it must be slaughtered according to the prescribed ritual rules of sheḥitah. Performed by a ritual slaughterman (*shoḥet*) it involves complex regulations, part of which at least aim at the removal of blood from the carcass. Particular foods are characteristic of particular festivals (e.g. *mazzah for Passover), and no cooking is allowed on the *Sabbath. As *diaspora Jews have settled round the world, they have adopted the tastes and recipes of their host nations; but all will still be under the constraint of Torah.

Islam Quranic food rules express a simplified form of Judaic rules. Muḥammad's commentary was made partly against the background of the taboos adopted by the different pagan tribes, and partly in correspondence to, though also in contradistinction to, those of rival monotheistic Christian and Jewish groups. According to the Qur'ān, Jewish laws were imposed as a punishment on the Israelites, and have been largely superseded by Islam. The Qur'ān defines which foods are lawful, *halal*, and which unlawful, *haram*. The unlawful include blood, pig meat, carrion, and the meat of sacrifices. The Qur'ān may seem equivocal over wine, praising it yet also forbidding it, but 5. 90–1/93–4 calls it 'an abomination of *Satan', and asks, 'Will you not then desist?' These regulations, in line with Islamic ethics generally, were subject to extensive commentary and elaboration in the post-Quranic period. The rules around Islamic slaughter (see AL-HALAL), which broadly follow the Jewish form, were given greater elaboration and extension, as were the categories of unclean foods, extended to include the impure parts of animals (faecal or sexual areas) or food prepared in an unclean way (e.g. by menstruating women, or by infidels). Explicitly forbidden foods were extended to include dog or human flesh. Observance varies in strictness between individuals (certain of the pious also avoid foods personally disliked, though not forbidden, by the Prophet: leek, garlic, onion) and between communities; the most widely followed are the Quranic strictures, with particular emphasis placed on the avoidance of pig meat.

Christianity The central rite of Christianity is a food rite (*eucharist), although one whose meal-like aspects are varyingly stressed. Protestant and Modernist interpretations tend to place greater emphasis on commensality and the shared meal, in distinction from more sacramental traditions in which the manifestation and incorporation of the divine in and through the bread and wine is of central significance. Dominant Christianity contains no explicit food taboos, though monastic observance—in general the avoidance of meat, particularly red meat—and the patterning of fast and feast days, extended to the laity in Friday fasting, draws on a more pervasive structure of meanings, which may owe something to a *Manichaean tendency. There is also a tradition of abstinence among certain Protestant sectarian groups, particularly those of 19th-cent. American origin. (e.g. Seventh Day *Adventists, *Mormons), from tea, coffee, tobacco, alcohol, and in some cases meat: all are interpreted as stimulants.

K. C. Chang (ed.), *Food in Chinese Culture* . . . (1977); M. Douglas, *Purity and Danger* . . . (1966); J. Goody, *Cooking, Cuisine and Class* . . . (1982); O. Prakash, *Food and Drinks in Ancient India* . . . (1961); R. Tannahill, *Food in History* (1973).

Fools: see HOLY FOOLS.

Footprint of Ibrāhīm (Abraham). An impression of a footprint claimed to be that of *Abraham, which is preserved near the *Kaʿba in *Mecca.

Footprint of Muḥammad. An impression in rock, said to be the point from which he took off on his ascent to heaven: see DOME OF THE ROCK. The metaphorical idea of 'following in the footprints of the Prophet' (*al-qadam al-sharīf*, 'the noble footprint') is strong in Islam, underlying as it does the importance of Muḥammad as the first living commentator on *Qur'ān. Cf. also MOSQUE.

Footprint of the Buddha: see PILGRIMAGE (BUDDHIST).

Forgiveness: see ATONEMENT.

Form criticism. A method of analysing a text in terms of its pre-history in oral tradition. It was first applied (1901) by H.*Gunkel to the narratives of Genesis, and has been most significantly used since then in studying the *Gospels, as well as the *Psalms and *Pentateuch. The term (Germ., *Formgeschichte*) comes from the preoccupation of the pioneer critics with the forms of oral material—e.g. in the case of the Gospels, 'miracle story', 'pronouncement story', 'legend'. Each form had a *Sitz im Leben*, a setting or purpose in the life of the community which preserved the material. The work of R. *Bultmann on the *Synoptic Gospels (1921 ff.) gave the method a reputation for scepticism, by its tendency to conclude that the early church created sayings of Jesus to serve its own purposes. It is now widely accepted that, if that view is too extreme, nevertheless there was some measure of influence on the traditions about Jesus by the churches which handed them on.

Former Buddhas. Members of a lineage of Perfectly Awakened Ones (*sammāsanbuddhas) who are alleged by tradition to have preceded *Gotama, the historical *Buddha. Earliest Buddhist texts record the names of six: Vipassi (the earliest), Sikhi, Vessabhu, Kakusandha, Konāgamana, and finally Gotama's immediate predecessor, Kassapa. Although these are purely mythological figures, *stūpas have been erected in their honour. It has been argued that the figure of seven buddhas in total has an intended astrological significance (six planets + the sun, i.e. Gotama) and represents early Buddhism's response to a growing popularity in astral cults.

In later texts the number of former buddhas becomes gradually multiplied: the **Buddhavaṃsa* lists twenty-four, the **Lalitavistara Sūtra* fifty-three, the *Larger *Sukhāvatīvyūha Sūtra* eighty-one, and the **Mahāvastu* five hundred. Eventually, in accordance with the expansive cosmology and mythology of the Mahāyāna, their number becomes incalculable. See also DĪPAṂKARA; MAITREYA.

Formgeschichte (form criticism): see FORM CRITICISM.

Forty hours devotion. A Christian (mainly Roman Catholic) adoration of the blessed sacrament in a *monstrance (i.e. exposed to view). The adoration may be only semi-continuous, and the 1973 instruction (on Holy Communion and Worship of the Eucharist outside the Mass) does not specify forty hours, but only an extended period, which should 'take place once a year, even though this period is not strictly continuous'. The practice seems to have originated in Italy, championed by (among others) Philip Neri; a *bull of approval, *Divina Disponente Clementia*, was issued in 1560.

Forty Martyrs of England and Wales. Forty Roman Catholics from England and Wales put to death between 1535 and 1680. The group is representative of a larger number of martyrs whose causes (see CANONIZATION) were in progress. The forty were drawn from the most familiar of the 199 beatified in 1886, 1895, and 1929. They were canonized by Pope Paul VI in 1970: feast day, 25 Oct. Like Protestant victims of the *Inquisition, the mode of their celebration became something of an *ecumenical embarrassment, but the more recent return, particularly in the RC hierarchy, to traditional positions, has restored their ecclesiastical importance. They should not be confused with the Forty Martyrs of Sebaste, who were members of the Thundering Legion, and who were frozen to death in *c.*320 CE.

Foucauld, C. de (founder of Little Brothers): see DE FOUCAULD, C.

Four Books **or** ***Ssu Shu.*** A group of texts within the *Confucian Classics, singled out for special attention by the literati (*ju) of the Confucian renaissance in the Sung period (960–1279). It included *Lun Yü* (**Analects*), *Meng Tzu* (**Mencius*), *Ta Hsüeh* (**Great Learning*), and *Chung Yung* (**Doctrine of the Mean*). These works, equipped with the commentaries of Chu Hsi (1130–1200), provided the classical authority for the neo-Confucian programme of self-cultivation for the attainment of sainthood.

Eng. tr. J. Legge.

Four Captives. A Spanish medieval story of four *rabbis captured by Muslim pirates. The rabbis, having been taken prisoner, were then redeemed by various Jewish communities. The story is preserved in Abraham *ibn Daud's *Sefer ha-Kabbalah* (The Book of Tradition, Eng. edn., 1967), and there is scholarly disagreement over its authenticity.

Four certainties (Hindu): see VAIŚARADYA.

Four Foundations (Buddhist): see SATIPAṬṬHĀNA.

Four goals of life (among Hindus): see PURUṢĀRTHA.

Four Horsemen of the Apocalypse. Biblical figures signalling the beginning of the *messianic age. They occur in Revelation 6 (cf. Zechariah 6. 1–7). Each colour stands for a form of destruction (black for famine, red for blood, pale for pestilence and death) except for the fourth, white, which has a crown and is sent to conquer.

Four Kings/Guardians (four world protectors in Buddhism): see CELESTIAL KINGS.

Four last things. The Christian awareness of the ultimate realities awaiting humanity and the cosmos. They are the second coming of Christ, the day of judgement, heaven, and hell, epitomized in death: *momento mori*, remembrance of one's death, has been, in Christian history, a summary of the awareness of one's destiny; thus death is often the first of the four last things, with the second coming and the day of judgement identified as the second. Hence:

> What Christian man is he, that hath wit and discretion, but he hath heard and, having any faith, believeth these four last things, of which the first, that is to say, death, we need no faith to believe, we know it by daily proof and experience? . . . The busy minding of thy four last things, and the deep consideration thereof, is the thing that shall keep thee from sin (Thomas *More).

The season of *Advent used to be associated with the four last things, but this has increasingly become a preparation for the commemoration of the first coming of Christ at *Christmas.

The mindfulness of death is a central part of Buddhist meditation. *Buddhaghosa's **Visuddhimagga* 8. 1–41 summarizes the method of realizing the imminence and inevitability of death, making it real and personal to *me*. The purpose is not so much avoidance of sin as detachment from all entanglement in, and reliance on, this world and body.

Four mountains. In China, sacred in association with *bodhisattvas: (i) Chiu-hua-shan / Ti-ts'ang (Skt., *Kṣitigarbha); (ii) P'u-t'o-shan / Kuan-yin (Skt., *Avalokiteśvara); (iii) O-mei-shan / P'u-hsien (Skt., *Samantabhadra); (iv) Wu-t'ai-shan / Wen-shu (Skt., *Mañjuśrī).

Four noble truths (Skt., *catvāri-ārya-satyāni*. Pāli, *cattari-ariya-saccāni*). The foundation of the *Buddha's insight and teaching: (i) the first truth is the recognition of the all-pervasive and universal nature of *dukkha; dukkha is often translated as 'suffering', but it is more accurately the fact and recognition of transience, with the suffering that is necessarily involved in transience; everything is in the condition of dukkha, but Buddhism does not deny that some things are genuinely pleasing (*sukha*); (ii) the second truth is the recognition of what gives rise to suffering, summarized in the thirst (*taṇhā, Skt., *tṛṣṇa) for satisfaction in things that necessarily pass away, or for permanence (e.g. a self or soul) in the midst of the transient; (iii) the third truth is that dukkha can nevertheless be brought to cessation, by the eradication of taṇhā, and that this cessation is *nirvāna; (iv) the fourth truth is the summary, in the Eightfold Path (*aṣṭangika-mārga), of the means to that eradication. This was set forth, in the *First Sermon of the Buddha after his Enlightenment.

Buddhaghoṣa, *The Path of Purity* (Eng. tr. P. M. Tin, 1971).

Four perfect efforts (Buddhist): see SAMMĀ-PADHĀNA; BODHIPĀKṢIKA-DHARMA.

Four questions (Heb., *arba kushiyot*). Questions asked at the *Passover *seder. Traditionally they are asked by the youngest competent person present, who asks why the night is different from other nights with its different customs (on this night, why only unleavened bread? Why only bitter herbs? Why do we dip them twice? Why not sitting but reclining?) In response the leader of the seder explains the Passover tradition.

Four species (Heb., *arba'ah minim*). The four plants which form part of the *Sukkot rite. The four species fulfil the biblical injunction, 'You shall take on the first day the fruit of goodly trees, branches of palm trees and boughs of leafy trees and willows of the brook' (Leviticus 23. 40). Traditionally the fruits are *etrog and the leafy trees are myrtle. During the ceremony, the branches are bound together and held in one hand while the etrog is held in the other. Different symbolic interpretations have been given of the four species; they may represent virtues, parts of the body, or features of the land of *Israel. The Bible itself gives no explanation.

Four stages of life (Hindu): see ĀŚRAMA.

Fourteen stages of Jain progress (Jain): see GUNASTHĀNA.

Fox, George (1624–91). Founder of the Society of *Friends (also known as *Quakers). As a young man he temporarily abandoned his family and friends whilst, in considerable anguish, he sought a genuine spiritual experience. By 1646 he was testifying to the reality of the *inner light of the living Christ, believing that he had discovered Christ 'experimentally, without the help of any man, book, or writing'. His teaching began to attract many followers who, under his forty years' leadership, became a stabilized community. In 1669 he married Margaret Fell (1614–1702), a widow, who in the northern counties had for some time encouraged the 'First Publishers of Truth', including many women. Despite poor health he travelled widely throughout England, Ireland, the West Indies, N. America (where *Penn found him 'civil beyond all forms of breeding'), and Holland. A charismatic figure with courage and integrity, he used his organizing skills to provide the Quakers with an effective structure, especially in a period of persecution. He spent six years in prisons, often under appalling conditions, which gave him an informed view on the need for prison reform and provided an example which inspired the social work of his successors among the Friends. His famous *Journal* was published three years after his death (ed. J. L. Nickalls, 1952; R. M. Jones, 1976).

W. C. Braithwaite, *The Beginnings of Quakerism* (1912; rev. 1955); *The Second Period of Quakerism* (1919; rev. 1961).

Foxe, John (1516–87). Author of 'Foxe's book of *martyrs'. Foxe wrote the book, *Acts and Monuments of matters happening in the Church*, while in exile in Europe during the reign of Queen Mary. Its chief purpose was to draw attention to the sufferings and endurance of the Protestant martyrs of Mary's reign.

Fraction. The breaking of the bread which, in all liturgies of the *eucharist, precedes *communion. It recalls Jesus' action at the *Last Supper (Matthew 26. 26) and reflects 1 Corinthians 10. 16b f. Its precise moment in the service varies, but is most usually just after the *Lord's Prayer. In the E., the bread is broken into four parts while the *koinonikon* (communion hymn) is sung. In the W. a *host is broken even if there are individual wafers of bread for the communion of the people. In the Roman mass, the *Agnus Dei is sung at the same time.

Francis, St, of Assisi (1181/2–1226). Christian ascetic and founder of the Franciscan order. Son of a wealthy textile merchant, Francesco Bernardone had dreams of chivalric heroism and a bent toward frivolity until, in his early twenties, he underwent a conversion. He began to devote himself to care of lepers, whom he had formerly found repellent, and soon renounced his patrimony in the public square, returning even his clothes to his father. Embracing poverty, which he spoke of as his bride, he acquired his food by begging, and applied himself to repairing ruined churches. In 1208 or 1209, after hearing at mass *Jesus' commission to the disciples (Matthew 10. 7–19), he set out to preach. Companions soon followed, forming with him a band that became the Franciscan Order. He drew up a simple Rule based on Gospel commands and sayings (the *Regula Primitiva*). In 1212, Clare followed him in establishing a group of women, the Second Order of St Francis, commonly known as *Poor Clares. In 1217, provinces were established, and in 1219 he went to Egypt, at the time of a *crusade, appearing before the Sultan to argue the case for Christ. In 1221, he established 'a third order', i.e. Tertiaries, for those living in the world, but aspiring to his ideals. As the Order grew, Francis opposed forces within which pressed for more thoroughgoing organization and discipline, a less extreme poverty, and greater accommodation to academic learning. He reasserted his ideals in his Rule of 1221 (*Regula Prima*), but was obliged to compromise in the definitive Rule (*Regula Bullata*) of 1223. Thereafter, increasingly ill, he withdrew somewhat from the affairs of the Order and spent periods in contemplative solitude, receiving the *stigmata in 1224. He dictated his *Testament* shortly before he died. He was canonized in 1228.

Whether or not Francis was 'after Jesus, the only perfect Christian' (E. Renan), his genius and appeal derive from a joyously radical conformity to Jesus' teaching and example. The appeal remains vast, sustained by a large body of hagiographical works, among which the Italian *Little Flowers of St Francis* (*c*.1375), a partial translation of a Latin work of *c*.1325 by Ugolino of Monte Giorgio, is especially popular, although unreliable for historical detail.

R. Armstrong and I. Brady, *Francis and Clare: The Complete Works* (1982); M. A. Habig, *St Francis . . .: Writings and Early Biographies* (1973); R. Manselli, *St Francis of Assisi* (1988); J. R. H. Moorman, *St Francis of Assisi* (1976).

Franciscans. Christian religious orders derived from St *Francis and St Clare of Assisi. Basic to them is the initial determination of Francis that they should be brothers and sisters 'living according to the form of the Holy Gospel'. The Franciscan Rule was first presented (*Earlier Rule*) to Innocent III in 1209, but it was a later version (*Final Rule*) which was confirmed in 1223. His Rule 'is neither an external code nor a propaedeutic to perfection, but an enunciation of the pure and full imitation of Christ in certain aspects of His life' (D. Knowles, *The Religious Orders in England*, 1948). Commitment to the poor and crucified Christ is made manifest in the relationships of the brothers and sisters, from which a mission to the world, in the guise of pilgrim and stranger, issues: this mission expresses a reverence for the created order which comes to humans as a gift. The Order of Friars Minor (OFM) divided later into the Friars Minor Capuchin (OFM Cap.) and Friars Minor Conventual (OFM Conv.). *Poor Clares are women in the Second Order of St Francis, and Tertiaries are those in the Third Order who remain laity in the world. A Franciscan Order was restored to the Church of England in 1931.

See Index, Franciscans.

L. I. de Aspurz, *Franciscan History* (1983); H. Holzapfel, *The History of the Franciscan Order* (1948); W. Short, *The Franciscans* (1989).

Francis Xavier, St (1506–52). Spanish *Roman Catholic (*Jesuit) priest and missionary to Asia, canonized, 1622: feast day 3 Dec. Xavier was born in Spanish Navarre as the third son of a Basque family of the lesser nobility. He was apparently attracted to the early *Protestant movement during his eleven years at the University of Paris, but he was eventually won over by his Basque fellow countryman, *Ignatius Loyola, to become one of the original band of the Society of Jesus (he was one of those who took vows with him at Montmartre in 1534). The goal of these men was at first to serve God and their neighbour through the historic vows of chastity and poverty and to make a pilgrimage to *Jerusalem. The five chapters, however, which condensed the rules of their society included the explicit one of a special vow of obedience to the pope. Xavier committed himself to obey the pope's command to serve in the already vast and growing overseas colonies of Portugal and sailed for India on 7 Apr. 1541, arriving in Goa a year later.

Xavier was still largely medieval in his religious and cultural orientation and often identified the glory of God and the glory of Portugal. His career, however, shows certain developments in both understanding and practice that were portents of more sophisticated later RC missiology. Xavier's first concern was with the spread of the faith, and he pushed on to areas where the Portuguese neither did nor could rule. In his plans to evangelize Japan and China, he clearly did not think of depending upon Portuguese political power or military force. He hoped to win the entire populace of Japan either by first converting the rulers or by gaining their favour and permission to preach freely to persons of every class.

Xavier went from the Portuguese Indian port of Goa to serve as a missionary priest among the Bharathas (Paravas) of the Coromandel coast of South India, a people who had been baptized *en masse* in 1534 in response to their appeal to the Portuguese for military protection against Muslim raiders.

Xavier's commission from both the king of Portugal and the pope extended to the whole of Asia, and he spent some months of 1546 and 1547 in what is now Indonesia. His primary goal, however, was Japan, and with a Japanese convert and a small band of co-workers landed on Kagoshima on 15 Aug. 1549. Xavier remained in Japan only two years and three months, leaving about 2,000 Christians to the ministrations of fellow Jesuits, after which he returned to

Goa and then came back to die on an island near the coast of China on 3 Dec. 1552. His body was taken to Goa, where it is still venerated.

Among Xavier's greatest contributions to the mission to Japan was his deep and growing respect for the Japanese as persons and as bearers of a high culture. His experience of Japan helped him to qualify the prevailing theological view that all who did not worship the true God, as known in Christian faith and the sacraments of the church, must go to hell. Earnest Japanese inquirers were greatly troubled because they could not reconcile the infinite goodness and mercy of God as taught by the Jesuits with the apparent fate of their ancestors according to this theological view. Xavier reported in a letter to Europe that the Lord himself helped the missionaries to deliver the Japanese from this terrible misgiving. They were able to explain that the moral law and knowledge of God were imprinted on human hearts from the beginning and that the Creator of all peoples had taught them apart from human mediation.

G. Schurhammer, *Francis Xavier* (1973–82).

Francke, A. H. (Pietist devoted to the poor): see PIETISM.

Frank, Jacob (1726–91). Founder of a Jewish sect. Born in Poland, Frank declared himself to be *messiah and the successor of *Shabbetai Zevi. He was *excommunicated in 1756 after he had attracted many disciples and had been accused of encouraging sexual immorality. Jacob appealed to the bishop of Kamenetz-Podolsk who offered protection in exchange for the Frankists renouncing the *Talmud. The Frankists also declared their belief in the Trinity of the three 'equal faces'. There was one public disputation between the new sect and the *rabbis in 1757 at Kamenetz-Podolsk, and another at Lvov in 1759, after which Frank was formally baptized, together with 500 of his followers. Although some leaders of the Jewish community were thankful for the formal separation of the Frankists, the Baal Shem Tov (*Israel ben Eliezer) commented that 'while the limb is joined to the body there is hope of a cure, but once the limb is amputated, there can be no possible remedy'. Frank was arrested in 1760, because the Church authorities discovered that the Frankists regarded Jacob rather than Jesus as their 'Lord of Holiness'. He was only released in 1772, when he settled in Offenbach which became a centre of baptism. Initially Frankists only married within the sect, but by the mid-19th cent., the number of mixed marriages increased and many of their descendants became prominent members of the Polish nobility.

N. M. Gelber, *The Messianic Idea in Judaism* (1920).

Frankel, Zacharias (1801–75). Bohemian *rabbi. Frankel was the first rabbi to preach in German; he acted as *Chief Rabbi of Dresden and founded what he called 'the positivist-historical school' which influenced the *Conservative movement. He interpreted texts in the light of historical knowledge, and refused to make a commitment on the origins of *oral Torah (*torah shebe'al peh*) on Sinai. In 1854 he became the director of the Juedisch-Theologisches Seminary at Breslau and was challenged by Abraham *Geiger and others on the *Reform side, and by Samson Raphael *Hirsch on the *Orthodox. The author of several books on *Talmudic literature, his work on the Jewish *oath led to its abolition in several German states. His seminary set a standard of rabbinic training which was imitated by all similar academies.

J. L. Blau, *Modern Varieties of Judaism* (1966).

Frankists: see FRANK, JACOB.

Frasokereti (Pahlavi, *Frasogird*). Literally, the 'making fresh' (or 'restored') in *Zoroastrian *eschatology. In Zoroastrian *cosmology (*Bundahisn*) the world and humanity are created perfect but are assaulted by evil. Zoroastrianism is, however, an optimistic religion and teaches that evil will ultimately be eradicated. Frasokereti is the process by which the good is triumphant. There are two aspects to Zoroastrian eschatology: individual and cosmic. At death, every individual faces judgement by the balances whereby good thoughts, words, and deeds are weighed against the evil committed in life. If the good outweigh the evil, then the soul is led by its *daena* (conscience) in the form of a beautiful maiden to the Bridge of Judgement (Chinvat Bridge) which it crosses safely and proceeds to a heavenly existence. If, however, the evil predominate, then the *daena* in the form of an ugly old hag leads the soul to the Bridge which changes its face to an ever-narrower side from which the soul falls into the deep, dark, smoky abyss of *hell, of stench, foul food, and punishment. However, this stay in hell (or heaven) is not eternal, for eternal punishment could not be corrective, as punishment should be. Zoroastrians, therefore, believe in a resurrection and a second judgement which forms part of the cosmic Frasokereti. This in turn is related to the teaching of the four ages.

Traditional Zoroastrian cosmology teaches that there are four periods each of three thousand years which together constitute the 'world year' of history. The first two periods are those in which the *menog* (material) and *getig* (spiritual) worlds existed in ideal form (Bundahisn). At the end of 6,000 years, *Angra Mainyu assaulted the world, and it then existed in mixed form (i.e. mixture of good and evil), or *gumezisn*. After 3,000 years in this state, the prophet *Zoroaster was born, and by bringing the revelation of the Good Religion from *Ahura Mazda, he ushered in the final period of 3,000 years, when the forces of evil are gradually removed. This final period is itself broken down into three periods, each of a thousand years, in which a saviour (*sōšyant*) is born. Each is conceived by a virgin by bathing in a lake wherein the sperm of the prophet is preserved. They are therefore of the line of the prophet, but the product of a virgin birth. Each of the first two overcomes a portion of evil, but at the end of the 3,000 years comes the ultimate conflict as evil in its death throes hurls its final onslaught against good. Cosmic and human worlds become chaotic, the sun, moon, and stars do not give their light, and the very foundations of ordered society are threatened as people fail to respect their elders, teachers, or family duties. Then the final Sōšyant appears, as the cosmic forces of good pair off in single combat with evil and destroy them. The saviour raises the dead and introduces the final judgement scene. Thus raised from the dead, from heaven or hell according to their individual judgement, all people now face the final judgement. Again they are dispatched to heaven or hell according to their lives. There is a logic to the two judgements in Zoroastrianism. Ahura Mazda created both the spiritual and material worlds and aspects of humanity. People must therefore be judged both in the spirit and in body. The first judgement (and consequent spell in heaven or hell) was evidently one of the spirit, for the body could be seen to remain on earth. The *resurrection facilitates the second judgement, and the second spell in heaven or hell represents the punishment in the body. But the punishment is corrective and again, therefore, cannot be eternal. Once corrected (the nature and extent of the punishments is determined by the nature and extent of the sin) then everyone passes through a stream of molten metal which finally either purges or tests that people are free of all sin. The world is restored to its primordial state as the metal in the hills is melted, they are lowered, and the valleys filled up. With evil expunged from the Good Creation all can finally dwell with God as the heaven and earth come together in what is the best of all possible worlds. Evil is defeated, and Ahura Mazda is now not only all-good, but also for the first time all-powerful.

J. R. Hinnells, *Persian Mythology* (1985); R. C. Zaehner, *Dawn and Twilight of Zoroastriaism* (1961).

Fravasi. The 'heavenly self' or 'external soul' in *Zoroastrianism. There are many Zoroastrian theological analyses of human nature. The most common is to divide a human being into five parts: the *tan* (body, i.e. the material or *getig* dimension); the vital spirit (*jan*); soul (*urvan*); 'image' (*adhvenak*); and fravasi. The *tan* is that which remains on earth after death, and the *urvan* is that which proceeds to the judgement to be confronted by its *daena* (conscience). The fravasi is thought of as the aspect of human nature which pre-exists birth. The doctrine of free will is so thoroughly pursued in Zoroastrianism that in the myth of creation the fravasis of humankind are collectively consulted to see whether they are willing to take part in the cosmic battle against evil and so assume human form. It is generally implied that even while the *urvan* may be punished in hell, the fravasi remains in its heavenly home, as the chief of the divine creations (humanity) cannot be fully separated from *Ahura Mazda. In some *Pahlavi literature there is a concept of human destiny. Each person has his/her *khwarr*, the destiny which Ahura has set before them, but all have the freedom to reject that destiny. The essence of a person is sometimes said to be his/her reason (*khrat*). Although there are these various parts of human nature, nevertheless the person is by nature a unity. *Angra Mainyu seeks to destroy that unity, that balance of the parts, and thus to destroy them, through greed, arrogance, despair, and the Lie.

H. W. Bailey, *Zoroastrian Problems in the Ninth Century Books* (1971); R. C. Zaehner, *The Dawn and Twilight of Zoroastrianism* (1961).

Frazer, Sir James George (1854–1941). A British cultural anthropologist whose views were, for a period, influential in the study of religion. His major work, *The Golden Bough* (13 vols., 1890–1937), relied on the comparative method (in his case, of a simple 'scissors and paste' variety) to explore subjects as diverse as *magic, sacred *kingship, *totemism, beliefs concerning the soul and immortality, and scapegoating—with the ultimate goal of developing what he called 'mental anthropology'. However, his psychological speculations are unduly intellectualistic, and are vitiated by crude evolutionary assumptions. As E. Leach pointed out, he wrote little of originality, except perhaps as concerns the ethnographic 'facts'; facts which he often devised so as to suit his picture of the 'savage'. Frazer did much to popularize his subject, and is still held in high esteem in some quarters, but he is best regarded as an Enlightenment dilettante who used his intelligence to denigrate what he refused to study and who ignored developments in the understanding of religion; he resembled Gibbon in his dismissive prejudices and eloquent English style.

R. Ackerman, *J. G. Frazer: His Life and Work* (1987); T. Besterman, *A Bibliography . . .* (1934).

Free churches. Churches free from state control; specifically, the Protestant churches of England and Wales other than the established church. The Free Church Federal Council, through which they cooperate, was founded in 1896. Separatist Protestant denominations have often adopted the adjective 'free' in their names. The Free Church of Scotland separated from the Church of Scotland at the *Disruption (1843). A minority, the 'Wee Frees', did not take part in the subsequent union which formed the United Free Church of Scotland (1900) and has survived as an independent body with 21,000 members (1980), mostly in the N. and NW of Scotland.

Freud, Sigmund (1856–1938). A major founding figure of psychoanalysis, with strong views on the mainly negative role of religion in human life and society. He was born of Jewish parents in Moravia, and after studying medicine in Vienna, he worked at the Brücke Institute for a year (1881–2) before joining the staff of the Vienna General Hospital. He worked with Joseph Breuer in the treatment of hysteria, by recall under hypnosis of traumas. In 1885 he studied under Jean Charcot in Paris. He began private practice in 1886. He now changed from neurology to psychopathology, although the change did not involve abandoning his *nomothetic ambition to become the first to uncover laws as invariant as those of Newton, but in his case governing, not cosmic, but psychological behaviour. Freud saw himself as having achieved, with Copernicus and Darwin, the last of the three revolutions which have humbled humanity: Copernicus displaced it from the centre of the universe, Darwin from distinction from other forms of life, and himself from control of mental life, since mental life is the product of unconscious forces which are not chosen and cannot be brought under rational control. Freud regarded the Unconscious as the ground of human life: 'Nothing can be brought to an end in the Unconscious; nothing is past or forgotten.' The effect of the Unconscious can be seen in the works of artists, but art is a neurotic retreat into fantasy: Freud believed that he had brought the Unconscious from neurosis to science. Psychopathology could then be seen as the consequence of traumatic events or of antisocial longings suppressed in the subconscious. Most of these are sexual in nature, going back to infancy, especially to the son's envy of the father and desire for the mother, issuing in the Oedipus Complex. An interior dynamic, described by Freud in *Das Ich und das Es* (1923), is set up between *das Es*, the basic, quantitatively fixed, instinctual drives, 'that cauldron of seething excitements'; then the gradually formed *Über-Ich*, which restrains *das Es*, acting as brake and a conscience ('It is the successor and representative of the parents and educators who superintended the actions of the individual in the first years of life'); and *das Ich*, the self which emerges as it mediates between the first two and the world, and which is a product of highly individual circumstances and events. These terms were translated into English (to reduce the metaphysical associations and to make Freud sound more scientific) as the Id, the Superego, and the Ego. This dynamic inevitably (i.e. with the force of a Newtonian law) produces constant compromise and repression. A way into the understanding of these repressions lies in 'the interpretation of dreams' (*Die Traumdeutung*, 1900): 'The majority of the dreams of adults deal with sexual material and express erotic wishes. . . . The dream is a disguised fulfilment of a suppressed or repressed wish.' Repression arises because each individual cannot pursue exactly what he (or she) desires, or lusts after, with libido: civilization is therefore a compromise which enables interactive life to proceed, but at a high individual price of inevitable neurosis. Such neurosis may reveal itself in small ways (e.g. wit, Freudian slips), or in more bizarre behaviours. The appropriate therapy for neurosis lies in a prolonged 'conversation' between patient and analyst, which aims to bring the buried causes to the light of awareness.

Religion, for Freud, emerges as a collective expression of neurosis, and as an attempt on the part of individuals to escape from the realities of a hostile and indifferent universe. Since individuals recapitulate the history of the human race ('The psychic development of the individual is a short repetition of the course of the development of the race'), the phylogenetic and ontogenetic explanations are variations on the same theme, as can be seen in one of his major analyses of religion, *Totem und Tabu: Über einige Übereinstimmungen im Seelenleben der Wilden und der Neurotiker* (1913; Totem and Taboo: Resemblances Between the Psychic Drives of Savages and Neurotics, 1917): religious solidarity and restraints begin in a primeval rebellion of the sons against the father. In *Der Mann Moses* . . . (1939; Moses and Monotheism, 1939), he drew on abandoned speculations of biblical historians to produce a theory of Moses as an Egyptian who tried to mediate to the Jews in Egypt the monotheism of Amenophis IV. The Jews resisted the demands of this ethical monotheism, preferring their own magic, and they killed Moses. But in later years, Mosaic religion, which had long been suppressed, reasserted itself. The long period of latency led to conflicts analogous to neurosis. In *Die Zukunft einer Illusion* (1927; The Future of an Illusion, 1928), he made his most explicit attack on the error of humanity in relying on the collective neurosis of religion. Religion rests on an attitude of *als-ob*, 'as-if', in which people seek comfort in a universe which is indifferent to them. They seek it, therefore, in the only place it can be found, in the illusory world of make-believe, in a heaven and God which they project. In a long correspondence with Oskar Pfister (*S. Freud/O. Pfister: Briefe 1909–1939*, 1963), Freud constantly reviewed his estimate of religion, expressing occasional doubt about detail but not about the fundamentally illusory and neurotic nature of religion. This itself was deeply embedded in his own lifelong fear of death. His account of religion is generally contradicted by evidence (e.g. his claim that ritual is obsessive neurosis 'writ large' is better understood as a product of redundancy), but his outlook and terminology have remained pervasive.

B. Bettelheim, *Freud and Man's Soul* (1983); A. Grinstein, *Sigmund Freud's Writings: A Comprehensive Bibliography* (1977); W. W. Meissner, *Psychoanalysis and Religious Experience* (1984); M. Schur, *Freud: Living and Dying* (1972).

Friar (Lat., *frater*, 'brother'). As applied to Christian religious, a usage which passed into the Romance languages and English. A friar was one who belonged to a mendicant order, as distinguished from those who belonged to monastic orders and were not itinerant. Since the *mendicant orders abandoned other terms like 'monk' and '*canon', it came to have particular application to them, but became exclusive and quasi-technical only with the obsolescence of other usages. The best-known orders of friars are the *Dominicans, *Franciscans, *Carmelites, and *Augustinians.

Friday prayer (of Muslims): see JUMʿA.

Friedlaender, David (1750–1834). A forerunner of *Reform Judaism. Through his marriage, he became part of a distinguished Prussian family of *Court Jews and he was one of Moses *Mendelssohn's circle. He believed the Jews were 'destined from time immemorial to guard and teach by example the pure doctrine of the unity and sanctity of God, previously unknown to other people'. He argued that prayers for friends and country should be substituted for the *messianic hope, and that secular law should be studied rather than *Talmud. He also was tireless in his efforts for Jewish political and civil rights in Prussia.

M. A. Meyer, *The Origins of the Modern Jew* (1967).

Friends, The (Religious) Society of, often called **Quakers.** A religious group of Christian derivation, emerging in the 17th cent. under the leadership of George *Fox. His followers first called themselves 'children of the light', following Fox's emphasis on the inner light which takes precedence over external guidance. They came to be called 'Friends' from the statement of Jesus (John 15. 14), 'You are my friends if you do what I command you.' They were first called Quakers in 1650, when Fox commanded a magistrate to tremble at the name of the Lord—though the name occurs earlier, of those who experienced tremors in a religious ecstasy. Because Fox believed that the churches were in apostasy from God's intention, and that even reformation could not recover the true apostolic faith and practice, he held that the Friends would relate directly to the risen Lord, without the intermediary function of priests, ministers, or sacraments, receiving the gifts of the Spirit and the inner light. Any meeting where two or three are gathered together (Matthew 18. 20) will experience the promise of Christ to be with them, enabling them to live in his style of love. For that reason, women are equal with men, since both alike are under the headship of Christ. Liturgy, sacraments, and clergy were abandoned as being an interposition between the believer and the Holy Spirit—though more recently some gatherings have reintroduced a pastor who leads the service. The Friends oppose warfare (partly on grounds of the command of Christ, partly because warfare demonstrates a diseased humanity), and refuse to take *oaths (since walking in the light means telling the truth). More positively, they have been notable in their practice of acting towards others in ways that will (or might) evoke the response of goodness. They were committed to the abolition of slavery (John Woolman, 1720–72), women's suffrage (Lucretia Mott, 1793–1880; Susan Anthony, 1820–1906), prison reform (Elizabeth Fry, 1780–1845), and the care of the mentally ill.

The resistance of the Friends to 16th-cent. laws of religion led to considerable persecution. Many fled to the American colonies, where William Penn (1644–1718) founded Pennsylvania. Asking Fox if he could continue to wear his family sword as a mark of honour, he was told, 'Wear it as long as you can.' Fox saw him some weeks later and asked him where his sword now was. Penn replied, 'I wore it as long as I could.' That spirit of personal truth was given classic expression in Robert Barclay's *Theologiae Verae Christianae Apologia* (1676: *Apology for the True Christian Divinity*, 1678). Despite Fox's *Rule for the Management of Meetings* (1688), which gave cohesion to the movement, there have been four subsequent divisions, especially that of the Hicksites, following Elias Hicks (1748–1830), but in recent years attempts at greater integration have been made. There are about a quarter of a million Friends, about half of whom are in the USA.

H. Barbour and J. W. Frost, *The Quakers*, (1988); L. S. Kenworthy (ed.), *Friends Face the World* (1987); D. V. Steere (ed.), *Quaker Spirituality: Selected Writings* (1984).

Friends of the Western Buddhist Order: see WESTERN BUDDHIST ORDER.

Fringes (to Jewish garments): see ZITZIT.

Frum (figure in cargo cult): see JON FRUM.

Fry, Elizabeth (prison reformer): see FRIENDS, THE SOCIETY OF.

Fu, also **fan** (Chin., 'return'). The movement of the *Tao in *Tao-te ching* (16), whereby all things return to their source. In meditation, this 'returning to the root' is the means to enlightenment: 'Returning to the source is stillness, which is the way of nature.' In *I Ching* (The Book of Changes), fu is the transformation of one into another, so that the completion of the *yin means the full return of the *yang. Hence the hexogram fu is one unbroken yang line below five broken yin lines.

Fu-ch'i (Chin., 'sustaining by breath'). Breathing (*ch'i) technique in Taoism, directing breath to all parts of the body. It precedes *t'ai-hsi*, embryonic breathing.

Fudō (Jap., 'immoveable'). One of the deities, in Japanese Buddhism and folk-religion, who protects Buddhism and its true adherents, or simply, those who appeal to him. These protective deities are known as *myōō*, and they usually take frightening forms. Fudō is the best-known of these: he is an emissary of *Dainichi, and appears with a sword in his right hand and a rope in the other. Fire is offered to him in Fudō-goma.

Fugen (a bodhisattva): see SAMANTABHADRA.

Fugyō-ni-gyō (Jap., 'doing by not doing'). Zen action which arises from deep enlightenment, and which is not intended or premeditated, but simply arises as the absolutely appropriate action in relation to the contingent circumstance. It is prepared for through *jōriki. It is comparable to its antecedent in Taoism, *wu-wei.

Fuhōzō (Jap.). The transmission of the *buddha-dharma in Zen Buddhism through the lineage of patriarchs (*soshigata), and also a person in that lineage (see HASSU).

Fujifuse (Jap., 'neither give nor accept'). A 'branch' (*ha*) of the *Nichiren school of Japanese Buddhism established by Nichiō (1565–1630) in 1595. This branch of Nichiren Buddhism teaches that both lay persons and monks and nuns should neither give nor receive alms from persons belonging to other schools and sectarian movements of Buddhism. Although originally suppressed by secular authorities, adherents of this sect continued practising their faith in secret, calling themselves *nai-shinja*, 'secret believers'. In 1874, the government finally granted the Fujifuse Branch legal recognition. Its headquarters temple is the Myōkakuji in Okayama Prefecture.

Fujikan. A meditation practice in Japanese Buddhism, in which Skt. letters, especially *A, are written on various parts of the body; their power is then absorbed into the body.

Fujisan. Mount Fuji (usually known in the W. as Fujiyama from a confusion arising from the Chinese character which can be pronounced 'yama' or 'san'), a cone-shaped dormant volcano, the highest mountain in Japan (3,776 metres), about 75 miles SW of Tokyo, greatly revered for its beauty and sacred character. Although adherents of all Japanese religions revere Mount Fuji, it was made particularly sacred by the Yamabushi, the mountain *ascetics. There are many shrines on the ascent, including a Shintō shrine at the summit. The ascent via the pilgrim routes takes two days; there is now, however, a bus service to a point halfway up the mountain.

Fujiyama: see FUJISAN.

Fukasetsu (Jap., 'the unsayable'). The Zen insistence that the experience of enlightenment (*kensho, *satori) cannot be described or communicated. Anyone who realizes his *bussho (buddha-nature) is like a dumb man after a beautiful dream. It follows also that words are always approximate and corrigible: they are the sign that points to the moon, but not the moon itself. Hence arises the famous formula of 'transmission outside the scriptures', i.e. through the direct interaction of *mondō or *hossen, attributed first to *Bodhidharma, but perhaps from *Nan-chuan Pu-yuan: *kyoge betsuden* (transmission outside the formal teaching), *furyu monji* (transmission outside the scriptures), and *jikishi ninshin* (direct pointing to the human being or heart) lead to the realization of one's buddha-nature (*kenshō jōbutsu*). In *Chuang-tzu*, the saying of Lao-tzu is recorded:

> If the *Tao [i.e. for Japanese, *dō*] could be handed over, a servant would hand it over to his master. If it could be given, a person would give it to his parents. If it could be communicated, everyone would tell of it to his brothers. . . . But for him who has not experienced the Tao in his innermost being, the way to heaven is not open.

Fukasetsu has its parallel in Zen, *fukashigi*, 'the unthinkable', that which can be experienced (enlightenment) but cannot be conceptualized.

Fukashigi: see FUKASETSU.

Fuke (flute-playing school of Zen): see KAKUSHIN; KOMUSŌ; P'U-HUA.

Fukko Shintō (from Chin., *fu-ku*, 'restore the ancient way'; Jap., 'Restoration Shintō'). A *Shinto movement that arose in the 18th cent. and sought to reconstruct ancient Japanese native religious practices as they were imagined to exist prior to the introduction of foreign creeds like Buddhism and Confucianism. Calling these practices the 'Ancient Way (*kodō*)', Fukko Shintō attempted to refashion them into a contemporary religion. The major figures of this movement include Kada Azumamaro (1669–1736), *Kamo no Mabuchi (1697–1769), *Motoori Norinaga (1730–1801), and Hirata Atsutane (1776–1843), all of whom were also known as 'National Learning' (*kokugaku) scholars.

Fuko (Buddhist teacher): see AMOGHAVAJRA.

Fukyo (Jap.). Communal recitation of *sūtras in Zen monasteries.

Fu-lu (pai). Apotropaic talismans in religious Taoism (especially *cheng-i tao, *t'ai-ping tao, and *wu-tou-mi tao). The fu-lu were also signs of contracts, first with the gods, but later in general. Fu-lu pai is the collective term for Taoist schools in which fu-lu are used.

Fumie. Japanese flat image of a Christian symbol, usually the crucifixion, designed to be stepped on. Suspected Christians were required to step on the representation to prove that they were not believers—a test at one time extended to whole populations, but discontinued in 1858. Surviving examples are often much worn.

Functionalism (accounts of religion which focus on the functions which religion serves): see SOCIOLOGY OF RELIGION.

Fundamentalism. In general, a description of those who return to what they believe to be the fundamental truths and practices of a religion. It can thus be applied to this attitude in all religions (e.g. the resurgence of conservative Islam is sometimes called 'Islamic fundamentalism'). But this use is often resented by such people, because of its more usual identification with those, in Christianity, who defend the *Bible against charges that it contains any kind of error. More specifically, it denotes the view of *Protestant Christians opposed to the historical and theological implications of critical study of the Bible.

The modern fundamentalist position developed in the USA in the late 19th cent. as a reaction to Liberal Protestantism. A 'Bible Conference' at Niagra (1895) issued a statement of belief affirming what were later called the five points of fundamentalism: the literal inerrancy of the *Bible, the divinity of Jesus *Christ, the *virgin birth, a substitutionary theory of the *atonement, and the physical *resurrection and bodily return of Christ. A series of twelve tracts entitled *The Fundamentals* (1910–14) were widely distributed in the English-speaking world, and in the 1920s nearly all the US Protestant churches were divided into 'Fundamentalist' and 'Modernist' camps. It was in this context that the Scopes trial attracted such public attention, and a number of new *Evangelical church bodies were formed.

To avoid overtones of closed-mindedness, Christians in the Fundamentalist tradition often prefer to be called *Conservative Evangelicals.

If the word (Arab. equivalents are *salafiyya and *uṣūliyya) is used of Muslims, when it refers to those who assert the literal truth of the *Qur'ān and the validity of its legal and ritual commandments for modern people (e.g. the prohibition of intoxicants, interests on loans, rate of inheritance, and divorce). While they do not oppose change, they insist that change must be governed by Quranic values and modes of understanding (i.e. in accordance with the *sharīʿa as a fixed corpus of clear directives. Moreover, it is an attitude of mind, a tendency amongst the educated classes who feel an affinity for the high culture of traditional Islam, and amongst groups, especially the *ʿulamā, who feel threatened by Westernization of society.

In an attempt to bring some ordered insight into a confused field, the American Academy of Arts and Sciences set up 'The Fundamentalism Project', which began to issue its reports in 1991. The key appeared to be that those who belong to what might be described as movements of reaction against modernity 'no longer perceive themselves as reeling under the corrosive effects of secular life: on the contrary, they perceive themselves as fighting back, and doing so rather successfully'. They fight back (resisting 'some challenge or threat to their core identity'); they fight for (for 'their conceptions of what ought to go on in matters of life and health'); they fight with (selectively with, not the whole of 'a pure past', but 'those features which will best reinforce their identity, keep their movement together, build defences around its boundaries, and keep others at some distance'); they fight against (not so much the outsider as the insider 'who would be moderate, would negotiate with modernity, would adapt the movement'); they fight under (mainly under God, but in a minority of non-theistic cases, under some transcendent reference). Fundamentalism is thus inevitably generated by the very process of time and change.

See Index, Fundamentalism.

M. E. Marty and R. S. Appleby (eds.), *Fundamentalisms Observed* (1991).

Funeral rites. From extremely early times (and possibly even among the Neanderthals), archaeology reveals that humans have treated the bodies of the dead with care and respect. However, despite much speculation, it is not possible to state what beliefs about the status of the dead accompanied these early practices. By the time texts mediate beliefs about the dead, it is clear that almost universally there was no belief that there would be a worthwhile life after death. The funeral rites of the major world religions now express and reflect the consequence of subsequent human experience and reflection in which a continuity of life beyond death is clearly more probable, and is certainly a matter of faith expressed through the rituals and liturgies.

On the importance of being buried/cremated in particular places see KAŚI; KARBALĀ'; MASHHAD. See also DEATH; CREMATION; RITES OF PASSAGE; Index, Death, Funerals.

J. W. Bowker, *The Meanings of Death* (1991); R. Chapman et al., *The Archaeology of Death* (1981).

Judaism In biblical times, the dead were buried preferably near their family graves—hence the expression, 'slept with his fathers' (e.g. 1 Kings 11. 43) became synonymous with 'dying'. The horror of being left unburied is conveyed in the story of Jezebel: 'When they went to bury her, they found no more of her than the skull and the feet and the palms of her hands' (2 Kings 9. 35). Jewish custom demands speedy burial after death, although funerals may not take place on the *Sabbath or *Day of Atonement. Traditionally, men are buried wrapped in their *tallit, and coffins were not used until the Middle Ages. Different communities observe different burial practices, but normally the coffin is escorted to the grave and *Kaddish is recited. Burial in the land of Israel is a desideratum, but failing that, earth from Israel should be placed on the head or under the body. Among *Reform Jews, embalming and cremation are permitted.

H. Rabinowicz, *A Guide to Life: Jewish Laws and Customs of Mourning* (1982).

Christian Christian respect for the body, and expectation of its resurrection, derive from the resurrection of *Christ. *Cremation was opposed and eventually became exceptional. Burial is often accompanied by a funeral *mass in those parts of the *Church where the mass is central; otherwise, funeral and committal services are generally simple and realistic about the immediate outcome for the body:

Forasmuch as it hath pleased Almighty God of his great mercy to take unto himself the soul of our dear brother/sister here departed, we therefore commit his/her body to the ground; earth to earth, ashes to ashes, dust to dust; in sure and certain hope of the Resurrection to eternal life, through our Lord Jesus Christ; who shall change our vile body, that it may be like unto his glorious body, according to the mighty working, whereby he is able to subdue all things to himself (*Book of Common Prayer*).

Opposition to cremation began to erode at the end of the 19th cent., and is now common; the prohibition against it among *Roman Catholics was lifted in 1963, and is now allowed provided it is not done for reasons contrary to the Christian faith.

J. W. Bowker, in *The Sense of God* (1973); D. Davies, *Cremation Today and Tomorrow* (1990).

Islam *Jināza/janāza* refers to the stretcher and to the corpse on it, and thus to the funeral itself. The *Qur'ān gives no detail, but much description occurs in *ḥadīth, and *fiqh is extremely detailed in its prescription. Generally speaking, burials should be carried out as speedily as possible. As soon as a Muslim is dead, he is laid on the stretcher with the head facing the *qibla. The *ghusl then takes place, and the body is covered in a shroud or shrouds (the number is disputed). *Ṣalāt is then said over the dead person, and if possible there should be recitation of the Qur'ān, or at least of *sūra 6. Mourning is restricted, because it disturbs the dead—though in practice lamentation (*niyaha*) occurs. It is an act of virtue to accompany the body to burial, on foot, since the *angels of death go on foot. The *shahīd (martyr) is differently treated: his body is not washed, and he is buried in the clothes he was wearing at the time of death, so that he continues to bear the marks of martyrdom. Prayers are said in the *mosque, including a prayer for the happiness of the departed soul. Forty days later, a family commemoration is held (*al-Arbaʿayn*, 'the Forty').

Hinduism see ANTYEṢṬĪ.

Buddhism Disposal of the body is preferably by cremation. An important feature is the interaction between officiants (e.g. *bhikṣus) and family, with gifts and transfer of *puṇya. Thus in Śri Lankā, the bhikṣus of the family temple are seated near the house of the deceased, under a canopy of white sheets or cloth. The body is brought out from the house and those present are invited to join in the thrice-repeated formula of faith, 'Namo tasso bhagavata arahato samma sambuddhassa' (Homage, be to him who is *arhat, the Enlightened One, the Buddha). The Five Precepts are then repeated (see *śīla f.), followed by a sermon on the nature of death and transience, and on the dead person. Cloth and cool drinks are offered to the monks, followed by the recitation of verses summarizing the impermanence of all things. Water is poured into a bowl placed before the monks and the dead body: as it fills and pours over the edge, the monks recite: 'As the rains fill the rivers and overflow into the ocean, so likewise may what is given here reach the departed.' That leads into a specific transfer of merit to the departed person, with the prayer, 'May the wealth of merit acquired by this effort be accepted by all the gods, and may it result in their welfare in every way.' The coffin is then closed and removed for either burial or cremation (for a monk, it is always cremation), and the mourners return for a funeral meal. On the evening of the sixth day afterwards, a monk is invited to the house again, to deliver a further address; and on the seventh day, a formal giving of alms to the monks (*sanghika-dāna*) takes place, which is again reciprocated by a transfer of merit to the dead. The same is repeated on the completion of three, and of six months, and sometimes at the anniversary.

Sikhism When a Sikh dies prayers (especially *sukhmāni sāhib) are said for the deceased. The body, washed and dressed and wearing the *five Ks, is cremated. During cremation *Kīrtan *Sohilā (the bedtime prayer) is recited. At home or in the *gurdwārā verses about death are read from the *Ādi Granth and the service concludes with *Ardās, a *hukam, and *kaṛāh praśād. The entire Ādi Granth is read—preferably at home—over a period of up to ten days (sahaj *pāṭh). On the final day the Rāmkalī Sad of Sundar is read. In India the ashes are usually immersed in a nearby river, especially nowadays in the Satluj at Kīratpur. Sikhs are to accept death as God's will and as a stage in the progress to him. Elaborate displays of mourning or of grief are therefore discouraged.

Chinese Most dead exist in perpetuity in the rituals of the living family. Usually the dead gain immortality of memory in the family unit, periodic offerings, and possible assistance of the 'soul' (in *Buddhist judgement); the family gains kinship cohesion by filial respect and blessings by the rites. Traditionally, the dead are buried with *ming chi* (spirit articles), a sustenance of some kind such as the urns and human sacrifices of the archaeological sites, or the burning of modern paper items of money and necessities. Thereafter, they are periodically offered incense and food in the family or hall shrines. Practices vary, including the purchase of a coffin well in advance of death as a sign of respect; laying of the dying on the ground; calling back of the soul at death; reporting the death to various divine figures; dressing the corpse and putting precious objects in the apertures; receiving guests in the house; and a funeral procession leading to interment in the grave. Mourning by wailing, leaping, and breast-beating, in varying degrees of severity, is performed by many, particularly by the eldest son who deteriorates in appearance and lives in a mourning hut serving the dead with the filial respect of the living. The grave is carefully chosen according to the *yin and yang 'geomantic' influences of *feng shui, and the body is often buried in a coffin, later disinterred, the bones put in a pot in the open air, and finally buried in the pot. Annual cleaning of the graves is done in the spring at *ch'ing ming. Buddhist and *Taoist rituals, which assist the judgement and rebirth of the soul, are often performed as well. This soul is often joined by conceptions of two others. The *p'o* (yin soul) transforms at death to the *kuei* and returns to the earth while the *hun* (yang soul) transforms at death into the *shen* and is located in the spirit tablet where it becomes the focus of family rituals. These rites and relationships vary considerably by location and historical period.

Fuqaha (Arab., pl. of *faqih), jurists possessing deep knowledge of *fiqh, such as the *ayatollahs and *ʿulamā of the Muslim world. In Egypt, the term encompasses a broader meaning, from a schoolmaster to a professional Qur'ān reciter.

Furqān. Generally translated as 'criterion' or 'distinction', sometimes 'deliverance'; an Arabic word of disputed origin. Jeffery (*Foreign Vocabulary of the Qur'ān*, (225–9) considers it is probably derived from the Aramaic *purqān*, 'deliverance' or 'salvation'. It is the name of *sūra 25 of the *Qur'ān, where it is a synonym for the Qur'ān itself: 'He who sent down the furqān to his servant' (25. 1); cf. 'He sent down . . . the Book, the Tawrāt and the Injīl . . . and the Criterion (furqān)' (3. 3). *Ramaḍān is described as the 'month in which was sent down the Qur'ān, as a guide . . . for guidance and criterion (furqān)' (2. 185). The meaning here is of some kind of scripture, though elsewhere it would seem to signify 'deliverance', as in the case of *Moses (Qur'ān 2. 53, 21. 48). The battle of *Badr, the first significant victory for the Muslims, is described as a 'day of furqān' (8. 41).

Furyū monji (transmission outside the scriptures): see FUKASETSU.

Fusatsu. Jap., for *uposatha.

Fushimi Inari (Jap., *Fushimi*, a place-name, + *inari*, ' the rice deity'). The most famous of the shrines to the Japanese rice god, *Inari, located in the SE suburbs of *Kyōto. Local tradition places its founding in 711 CE, as a result of the mysterious appearance of the deity, in the form of a bird, from a ball of rice. With the moving of the capital to nearby Kyōto in 794, the Fushimi shrine quickly grew in importance with the patronage of the aristocracy, until it was recognized as one of the three Great Shrines of the nation. In 908 three mythically important deities were enshrined also at Fushimi, namely, Ugatama, Sarutahiko, and Ame-no-uzume. Today, while the main shrine buildings occupy level ground at the base of Mount Fushimi, many paths wind around and over the low peak with hundreds of small shrines on either side. So many *torii (sacred Shintō gates) have been donated by worshippers that most of these paths are veritable tunnels of gates, and many of the small shrines have miniature gates placed within them, perhaps adding an aspect of feminine sexuality to the phallic fox-tails of the figures which attend Inari. Fushimi Inari shrine is also famous for the fact that one of its priests, Azumamaro Kada, in a petition to the Shogun government in 1728, helped launch the *kokugaku ('national learning') movement which not only revived interest in Shintō as a counterpoise to the dominance of Buddhism, but also contributed to the return of nominal direct rule by the emperor in the Meiji Restoration of 1869.

Fushizen-fushiaku (Jap.). Not thinking good, not thinking evil. The transcendence in Zen Buddhism of discrimination and differentiation in evaluation. The phenomenological value may inhere in appearance: it is the attitude which is transcendent.

Fushō (Jap., 'unborn'). Zen Buddhist term for the true nature of reality, in which there is no beginning or end, birth or becoming, passing away or death. There is only what there 'is', which is manifestation, arising from, and bearing the nature of, *śūnyatā. It is usually translated as 'Unborn': see e.g. BANKEI EITAKU.

Fusion of horizons (the relating of past text to present circumstance, thereby creating new meaning in lived experience): see HERMENEUTICS.

Futai (Jap., 'not falling back'; Skt., *avinivartanīya*). The stage in Buddhism of not falling back to a lower state, i.e. the securing of a stage in the spiritual path, especially at the higher levels: see e.g. DAIBOSATSU.

G

Gabirol, Solomon ben Judah ibn (*c.*1020–*c.*1057). Jewish Spanish poet and philosopher. Solomon ibn Gabirol was the author of many Hebrew poems. Using imagery from the Arab poetic tradition, he described himself as 'a violin to all singers and musicians'. Much of his secular poetry was composed for wealthy patrons and concerns nature, ethics, and wisdom. Many of his religious poems have been preserved in the *Sephardi and *Ashkenazi *prayer books and in *Karaite *liturgy; he was regarded as the outstanding poet of his time. According to Judah al-Harizi, 'All the poets before him were as nothing and after him none rose to equal him.' His poem, *Keter Malkhut* (The *Kingly Crown*, tr. B. Lewis, 1961) has been through many editions and describes the attributes of God and the 'predestined Will'. In addition, two philosophical treatises survive: *Mekor Hayyim* (The Source of Life) is a discussion of the principles of matter and form; and *Tikkun Middot ha-Nefesh* (The Improvement of the Moral Qualities) is concerned with ethics. He held that God lies beyond human knowledge and comprehension, but is nevertheless the goal of human life and aspiration, since without that aim, life is without meaning or order: 'My King, I wait upon you, my heart rests on you alone, like one who has dreamt a dark dream and relies on the interpreter. This is all I ask, that you hear my plea: this is what I seek, neither more nor less.' Many legends surround ibn Gabirol's life, one of which, published in 1587, being that he was murdered by an Arab.

Solomon ibn Gabirol, *Selected Religious Poems*, tr. I. Zangwill (1923); J. Schlanger, *La Philosophie de Solomon ibn Gabirol* (1968).

Gabriel (Heb., 'God is my warrior'). An archangel. He and Michael are the only angels named in the Jewish Bible (Daniel 8. 16; 9. 21; 10. 13; 12. 1; Raphael is mentioned in the *apocrypha, Tobit). In rabbinic and later Judaism, he is on the left hand of God, and guards the left side of humans while they sleep. He saved *Abraham from the fire into which Nimrod cast him, and was one of the three angels who visited him and rescued Lot from Sodom. He is the Prince of Fire, and will fight a mighty battle with Leviathan at the end of days. In Christianity, Gabriel announces the births of *John the Baptist and of *Jesus (Luke 1. 19, 26), suggesting the *eschatological importance of these events.

In Islam, Gabriel is Jibrīl or Jibrā'īl. He is one of the *angels (*malā'ika*), named three times in the *Qur'ān (2. 97, 98; 66. 4), once as the being who 'brought [the Qur'ān] down to your heart' (2. 97). Jibrīl has thus been identified as the one who transmitted the message. As the Qur'ān speaks more often of the spirit (*rūḥ*) acting as intermediary, Jibrīl has come to be identified with the spirit, and also with the vision of 'a noble messenger . . . before the Lord of the Throne' (8. 2, 19–23). It is believed that Allāh may send 'a messenger to reveal, by Allāh's permission, what he wills' (42. 51). In *tafsīr and hence in Muslim thought, it is Jibrīl who brought the revelation, and, as related in *ḥadīth, used to hold conversations with *Muḥammad. He is said to have taught him *wuḍū' and *ṣalāt, and to have been his guide on the *isra' or *mi'rāj (night journey to heaven). Jibrīl is said to have been Allāh's messenger to each *prophet, from *Adam onwards.

Gaccha (Skt., *gacchati*, 'goes'). Name of breakaway Śvetāmbara Jain sects. Originally, *ascetic communities were known as *kula* ('family') or *guna* ('throng'). The two major gacchas are Kharatara Gaccha (see DĀDĀ GURŪS) and Tapa Gaccha, derived from Jagaccandra Suri (1228), but owing its strength to Dharmasagara, a fierce controversialist—not least against the Kharatara. The latter are now a small remnant, but the Tapa Gaccha has about 4,000 monks and nuns.

Gadaffi, Colonel (Libyan leader): see QADHAFFI, MU'AMMAR.

Gadamer, H.-G. (philosopher): see HERMENEUTICS.

Gagaku (ceremonial music in Japan): see BUGAKU; MUSIC.

Gaki. Japanese term for restless or hungry spirits, Skt., *preta. In Zen monasteries, an offering of food is made to them before a meal. Gaki-dō is the domain of the hungry spirits, the second lowest of the ten realms of existence (*jikkai).

Galatians, Letter to the. An epistle of *Paul and book of the New Testament. It was prompted by news that Paul's converts were turning to a 'different gospel' (1. 6) which required adherence to the Jewish *Torah. Such a threat elicits Paul's strongest statement of the opposition between faith and the law (3. 1–5. 12), and plea that the Galatians having been set free would not return to that bondage. To justify his own preaching and independence from the church of Jerusalem Paul includes (1–2) an account of his career from his conversion onwards. The tone of the whole letter is passionate and self-defensive. Its placement in Paul's life is difficult and depends on which 'Galatians' are addressed. A date *c*.56 is suggested by its points of contact with *Romans.

Gallicanism. The assertion of more or less complete freedom in the *Roman Catholic Church from the authority of the *papacy. This was affirmed particularly for the Church in France (the old Gaul, hence the name). The theory was advocated in 1606 by Edmond Richer, appealing to (amongst others) *Gerson. His principle was maximum exclusion of the pope in order to strengthen the state church, but there were various types of Gallicanism beside his. The opposite is *Ultramontanism. The definition of papal infallibity at the first *Vatican Council made any further expression of Gallicanism impossible.

A. Gough, *Paris and Rome: The Gallican Church and the Ultramontane Campaign, 1848–1853* (1986); V. Martin, *Les Origines du gallicanisme* (1939).

Galloping Girls (name for IBVM): see INSTITUTE OF THE BLESSED VIRGIN MARY.

Galut (Heb., 'exile'). The state of being uprooted from the Jewish homeland. The word has connotations of alienation, degradation, and persecution. It reflects the despair of the Israelites in being exiled from *Erez Israel and their all-too-frequent experience in the *diaspora. By extension, Jewish mystics saw the evil inherent in the present world order as the result of the 'galut of the Divine Presence'. In contrast, trust in the providence and the promises of God is expressed in the hope, which underlies *Zionism, of *kibbutz galuyyot*, the ingathering of the exiles. However, the extent to which the wretchedness of the Jewish condition enters into the soul is epitomized in the saying of S. Levin (a Russian Zionist leader), 'It is easier to take the Jew out of Galut than to take Galut out of the Jew.'

Y. Baer, *Galut* (tr. 1947).

Gamaliel. Name of six Jewish sages, descendants of *Hillel, who filled the role of *nasi. Rabban Gamaliel ha-Zaken (the elder) (early 1st cent. CE) was responsible for many *takkanot, one of the most famous of which being his decision to allow a woman to remarry on the evidence of a single witness to her husband's death. According to Acts 22. 3, he was the teacher of the apostle *Paul. Rabban Gamaliel II (late 1st cent.) succeeded *Johanan b. Zakkai as nasi and was one of the greatest scholars of his generation. He concentrated on strengthening the centre at *Jabneh after the destruction of the *Jerusalem *Temple, and was responsible for determining the final version of the *Amidah. Gamaliel III (early 3rd cent.), the son of *Judah ha-Nasi, pronounced invalid the method of ritual slaughter of the *Samaritans. Rabban Gamaliel IV was nasi in the late 3rd cent., while Rabban Gamaliel V presided in the late 4th cent. Rabban Gamaliel VI (d. 426) was the final nasi. He was deprived of his position in 415 because he had built a *synagogue without permission and had defended the Jews against the Christians.

A. Guttmann, *Rabbinic Judaism in the Making* (1970); S. Kantner, *Rabban Gamaliel II* (1980).

Gampopa or **sGam-po-pa** (also known as Nyame Dagpo Lharje; 1079–1153). Tibetan monk and teacher, who drew on the *Kagyüpa and *Kadampa schools in establishing Dagpo Kagyu, and in the *lamrim work, *The Jewel Ornament of Liberation* (Eng. tr. H. V. Guenther, 1986). He held that the buddha-nature (*tathāgatha, *buddhatā, *bussho), or at least the capacity to become a *buddha is present in every sentient being, but that the human appearance forms the best base for this advance. To undertake the quest for attainment, a counsellor or spiritual friend is indispensable (*guru, *lama). His teachings (the scope of which are summarized) must be trusted, and they must be absorbed, not for one's own advancement alone, but with a view to helping others (*bodhisattva). He received his teaching in the Kadampa school, but especially from *Milarepa, from whom he received the *mahāmudrā teaching.

Gaṇadharas (Skt., 'leaders of the assembly'). In Jainism, the chief disciples of a *tīrthaṅkara who continued the teaching and organized the community after his death. Jain tradition names *Mahāvīra's eleven chief disciples, who were all drawn from the *brahman caste in the neighbourhood of Patna. Both *Digambara and Śvetāmbara tradition endows them with great *yogic powers.

Ganapati (Hindu God): see GAṆEŚA.

Gāṇapatya (Hindu sect): see GAṆEŚA.

Gaṇas (Hindu God): see GAṆEŚA.

Gaṇḍa-vyūha (Skt.). The cone-shaped elevation on the crown of the *Buddha Śākyamuni, one of the thirty-two marks of a buddha (*dvātriṃśadvaralakṣana). *Gaṇḍavyūha-sūtra* is part of the Buddhāvatamsaka-sūtra (*Avatamsaka literature), containing *bodhisattva vows of importance in the *Hua-yen school.

Gandhabba (heavenly beings): see GANDHARVA.

Gandhāra. A region in the NW of India (S. Afghanistan/N. Pakistan) which was a major centre of Buddhist art and culture. During the 2nd cent. CE the Buddha began to be represented, in idealized and Mahāyāna forms, which were based on his biography (and previous appearances, e.g. in *Jātaka episodes). Thus, while the Buddha is represented in the serene and compassionate style, he is also represented as the supreme ascetic, in emaciated form. Many of the thirty-two marks (*dvātriṃśadvara-lakṣana) also appear in symbolic form. By the

7th cent., according to Hsüan-tang on his pilgrimage, Buddhism in Gandhāra was extinct.

J. Marshall, *The Buddhist Art of Gandhara* (1960).

Gandharva (Skt., imbiber of song). 1. In Hinduism, sometimes a single god, who is the guardian of *soma. More often they are in the plural, described by the *Atharva Veda* as half-human, half-bird, and hairy. In later texts (e.g. *Mahābhārata*), they have become the musicians of the gods (with the *apsarasas*, the dancers) who also threaten to seduce *ascetics when they rival the gods.

2. In Buddhism, (Pāli, *gandhabba*) they continue as heavenly musicians, but they also have a role in sustaining the karmically governed accumulation of consequence from a previous life, through death, into a new appearance. They thus covered, mythologically, the 'gap' between death and new birth, somewhat like the (less mythological) 'subtle body', *liṅga-śarīra. They are in the lowest class of *devas, and attain this rebirth through only a minimal observance of duty.

Gāndhī, Mohandās Karamchand (1869–1948). Called Mahātmā, 'great soul', spiritual and practical leader of India (especially in pursuit of independence from British rule), of whom Rabindranath *Tagore said, 'The Mahātmā has won the heart of India with his love . . ., he has given us a vision of the *śakti of truth, and for that our gratitude to him is unbounded.' When asked for his message to the world, he said, 'My life is my message.' Born into the *Vaiśya caste, in a *Vaiṣṇavite family, with Jain friends (both of which influenced his later attitudes), he left a wife and infant son in 1888 to study law in London. He returned in 1891 to India, carrying with him Christian influences, but when he failed to establish his legal career in India, he went to S. Africa in 1893 (to assist a Muslim in a court case), where his experience of, and resistance to, racial abuse and oppressive government began. He founded the Natal Indian Congress, and began to develop his way of non-resistance, based on *ahiṁsā, *satyāgraha (lit., 'truth-insistence', a term which he coined and defined as 'soul-force'), *tapasya*, renunciation (cf. TAPAS), and *swaraj*, 'self-rule'. He was much influenced by (within his general Hindu perspective) the **Bhagavad-gītā*, and by such writings as the *Sermon on the Mount, *Tolstoy's *The Kingdom of God is Within You*, Ruskin's *Unto this Last*, Thoreau's *Civil Disobedience*. In 1914/15, he returned to India and adopted a simplified lifestyle, searching for a *dharma which would include and affirm the value of all, even of those who appeared as enemies (the British, separatist Muslims) or of those outside traditional dharma (*outcastes):

> My uniform experience has convinced me that there is no other God than Truth. And if every page of these chapters does not proclaim to the reader that the only means for the realisation of Truth is ahiṁsā, I shall deem all my labour in writing these chapters to have been in vain. . . . To see the universal and all-pervading Spirit of Truth face to face, one must be able to love the meanest of creation as oneself. And a man who aspires after that cannot afford to keep out of any field of life. . . . Those who say that religion has nothing to do with politics do not know what religion means (*Autobiography*).

But his inclusive style led to suspicion among orthodox Hindus, and he was shot on 30 Jan. 1948, uttering the name of *Rāma as he died. His assassins were motivated partly by fears for the integrity of *sanātana dharma, but more by Gandhi's generous attitude to Muslims, and especially his large monetary settlement on Pakistan.

Following his death, *Vinobā Bhāve continued his work, especially in transforming village life, and some of his settlements (e.g. Sabarmati Ashram and Sevagram) continue. But the enacting of his policies and ideology has not matched the revered status in which he is held. Hand-loom cloth and village industries have proved hard to integrate; and border disputes with China and Pakistan are of a different order from the eviction of increasingly reluctant imperialists. Yet Gāndhī remains an example and a rallying-point for those (e.g. Martin Luther *King, Nelson Mandela—see M. Benson, *Nelson Mandela*, 1994) who take up resistance against the self-serving obduracy of politicians. His life became the subject of a widely seen film, *Gandhi*, directed by Richard Attenborough.

J. Brown, *Gandhi's Rise . . .* (1972) and *Gandhi and Civil Disobedience* (1977); M. Chatterjee, *Gandhi's Religious Thought* (1983); D. Dalton, *Mahatma Gandhi* (1993); N. Pyarelal, *Mahatma* (1956, 1965).

Gan Eden (Garden of Eden; destiny of the righteous): see EDEN.

Gaṇeśa (Skt., 'Lord of the hosts'). Gaṇapati, Vināyaka (leader), Ekadanta (one-tusked), Lambodara (pot-bellied), Siddhadāta (the one who gives success), Vighnarāja (lord of obstacles), the elephant-headed god of wisdom and good fortune. Since early medieval times Gaṇeśa has been one of the most popular Hindu gods. He is invoked before all undertakings—from religious ceremonies (excluding funerals) to written compositions, and before the worship of other deities. Although Gaṇeśa has few temples solely to himself, his red-painted image is found everywhere, in homes, in shops, under trees, for he is known as the remover of obstacles, the very embodiment of success, good-living, peace, and wisdom. Gaṇeśa is represented as a pot-bellied king with the head of a one-tusked elephant. In his four hands he holds such objects as a shell (or water lily), a rope, an elephant goad, a mace, a discus, or a sweet rice-ball. His vehicle (*vāhana*) is the rat.

Gaṇesa's legends are numerous but do not appear until after the epics. His parents are *Śiva and *Pārvatī (although sometimes either deity alone is said to be his creator). His head was lost by envy of gods or demons, by a glance of Śani, or by the blow of Śiva himself. The first head that came to hand as a replacement was that of the elephant. Gaṇeśa's exploits show humour and cleverness. He is credited with writing the **Mahābhārata* by dictation from Vyāsa. As the Lord of Śiva's spirit hosts, the *Gaṇas*, Gaṇeśa may either curse or bless. Though his origins may be that of a tutelary village deity, today all sects claim him as their own. A few sectarians worship him exclusively (but all Hindus wish to enjoy his blessing), especially the Gāṇapatyas who produced the *Gaṇeśa-gītā* (a version of the **Bhagavad-gītā* in which Gaṇeśa replaces Kṛṣṇa) and the *Gaṇeśa-Purāṇa*.

P. B. Courtright, *Gaṇeśa* . . . (1985); A. Getty, *Gaṇeśa* . . . (1936).

Gaṇeśa Caturthi (Hindu festival): see FESTIVALS AND FASTS.

Gaṅgā. The river Ganges, sacred among Hindus. Its waters are employed in *pūjā (worship), and if possible, a sip from them is administered to the dying. Those who bathe in the Ganges will attain *Svarga (the paradise of *Indra), as will those who leave some part of themselves on the left bank (hair, bone, etc.). The river is said to flow from the toe of *Viṣṇu and to be spread into the world through the hair of *Śiva.

D. L. Eck, 'Gaṅga . . .', in J. S. Hawley and D. M. Wulff (eds.), *The Divine Consort* . . ., (1982) and *Banaras: City of Light* (1982); R. Singh, *Gaṅgā* . . . (1974).

Gaṅgeśa (Indian logician): see NYĀYA.

Ganjin (688–763). Japanese name of Chinese Buddhist master of *Vinaya school, Chien-chen, who went to Japan by invitation and founded the *Ritsu School. He joined the *saṅgha as a child, and taught a Buddhism based on Vinaya rules of discipline. The Chinese emperor prohibited his move to Japan in 742, but in 754 he succeeded in making the move, although in the mean time he had lost his sight. He lived in Tōdaiji, later in Toshodaiji, and gave formal instruction to many, including the emperor Shōmu and members of his family.

Gantō (Jap., 'the goose tower'). A tower built in Japan in honour of a *bodhisattva who had become manifest in the form of a goose, and who had sacrificed himself in order to instruct *Hīnayāna *bhikṣus. Thence it became a name in general for Buddhist towers.

Gaon (Heb., 'pride', Nahum 2. 3; pl. *ge'onim*). Honorific title of the heads of the Jewish *academies of *Sura and *Pumbedita. Between the 6th and 11th cents. CE, the geonim were recognized as the highest Jewish religious authorities. Scholars disagree when the title was first used. Traditionally there was competition between the two centres, and the geonim were appointed from within the academies by the *exilarch, although there seems to have been an element of heredity. The gaon presided over the supreme court (*bet din) of the *diaspora and was responsible for interpreting and establishing *Talmudic law worldwide. They had to support a large establishment and were maintained by taxes levied from the local communities and from voluntary contributions. By the 9th cent. their influence had declined, and other centres outside Babylonia delivered *responsa. In the 10th cent., the title of Gaon was also used by the head of the academy in *Israel, and in the 12th and 13th cents., it was also used in Damascus, Baghdād, and Egypt. The exact chronology of the geonim can no longer be established, and the list of Sherira ben Hanina Gaon contains contradictions and variants. Pre-eminent among the geonim were *Yehudai, *Sa'adiah, *Sherira, *Samuel b. Hophni, and *Hai ben Sherira.

L. Ginzberg, *Geonica*, 2 vols. (1909; repr. 1968).

Gapat (acronym for gemara, perush, and tosafot): see TOSAFOT.

Garbhagṛha (Skt., 'womb-container'). In Indian religions, a conceptualization of the inner source of life and truth, the origin of the universe; more particularly, the inner sanctuary of Hindu temples.

Garden, gardens. The creation of order, beauty, and utility, out of what would otherwise be wildness and perhaps wilderness, has supplied both a metaphor and a practice to religions. According to Francis Bacon ('Of Gardens') gardening is 'the purest of human pleasures, the greatest refreshment to the spirit of man'. This is particularly obvious in the landscape and the stone gardens of Zen Buddhism. These were influenced initially by Chinese gardens which often expressed the one nature of the Tao lying beneath all appearance, as well as the oppositions of *yin and yang (e.g. water and stones); but whereas the Chinese tended to regard the garden as a place to throw off the formalities of indoor life and of society, Zen saw the garden as an extension of the same life which seeks to discern and realize the buddha-nature inherent in all things. Thus early Zen gardens (e.g. in *Kyōto) create places for the extension of contemplation. This led into *kare sansui*, the dry landscape, creating gardens of sand and stone, where meditation, both in the making and in the observing, is paramount. Famous examples are at Daisen-in (*c.*1513) in Kyōto and Ryōan-ji (*c.*1490). In the West, gardens are inevitably a 'nostalgia for *paradise', for that harmonious condition summarized as the Garden of *Eden (Gan Eden). In Islam, nostalgia was replaced by anticipation and foretaste, with Muslim gardens representing proleptically what the *Qur'ān says of the gardens of heaven—hence the strong emphasis on water; they tend also to be symmetrically ordered. A memorable example can be found at Granada in the Generalife above Alhambra. See also PARADISE.

F. R. Cowell, *The Garden as Fine Art* (1978); M. L. Gothein, *A History of Garden Art* (1928; 1966); D. Graham, *Chinese Gardens* (1937); H. Inn, *Chinese Houses and Gardens* (1940); E. B. Macdougall and R. Ettinghausen (eds.), *The Islamic Garden* (1976); K. Nakane, *Kyōto Gardens* (1965); J. Prest, *The Garden of Eden* (1981); K. Shigemori, *Japanese Gardens* (1971); Teiji Ho, *The Japanese Garden* . . . (1972).

Garden of Eden: see EDEN.

Gārhapatya (Hindu domestic fire): see AGNIHOTRA.

Gartel (Yid., 'girdle'). Girdle worn by Jewish *ḥasidim. The gartel is worn at prayer by ḥasidic groups in fulfilment of the injunction to divide the upper and the lower body when praying. It also symbolizes the idea of girding the loins in the service of God.

Garuḍa. A fantastic creature of Hindu mythology, usually depicted either as a crowned bird or as a bird with a man's head. He is the son of *Kaśyapa and Vinatā, and the symbolic vehicle of *Viṣṇu. Featuring in many stories of Viṣṇu's (or *Kṛṣṇa's) wonderful deeds, he appears when summoned by his master's thought and fights with him against demons, especially those in serpent form.

In Buddhism, the predatory aspects of Garuḍa are emphasized. He is also the vehicle of *Amoghasiddhi, so that in context garuḍa may be a synonym of *buddha.

Garvey, Marcus Mosiah (1887–1940). Leading advocate of black advancement, and a central figure in *Rastafarianism. He was born in Jamaica where he trained as a printer. He founded the Universal Negro Improvement and Conservation Society and African Communities League, but his arguments and ambitions made little impact. He moved to the USA, via London, and founded businesses to advance Negro/black interests. He was opposed by the National Association for the Advancement of Coloured People, but pursued his own line, culminating (1920) in the 'Declaration of the Human Rights of the Negro People of the World'. After a two-year gaol sentence for fraud, he was deported to Canada in 1924. Taking literally the prophecy in Psalm 68. 31 ('Ethiopia shall soon stretch out her hands to God'), he affirmed Ethiopia and Africa as the source of civilization, and it is held by some that he also prophesied the enthronement of Haile Selassie as the returning *messiah.

R. Hill and B. Barr (eds.), *Marcus Garvey* . . . (1987).

Gasshō (Jap.). Placing the palms of the hands together in greeting, understood in Zen Buddhism as the reconciliation of the conflicting forces in the universe, in order to bring about (and invoke) peace and harmony.

Gatha (key verse in Buddhist text): see DHAMMAPADA.

Gāthās. The seventeen hymns of *Zoroaster, and thus texts of fundamental authority for *Zoroastrians, especially in the liturgy (*yasna). They were not written as instructions, but are, rather, hymns and prayers addressed to God. They are divided into groups called gāthās. In Hinduism, gāthās are poems which do not appear in the *Vedas.

S. Insler, *The Gathas of Zarathustra* (1975).

Gati (Skt., Pāli, 'mode of existence'). The various levels of existence in Buddhism, in which reappearance can take place through the process of *karma and *saṃsāra. There are six levels (three good, three bad), those of (i) gods (*devas); (ii) humans; (iii) spirits (*asuras); (iv) animals; (v) restless ghosts (*pretas); (vi) hell beings (*naraka). These levels of existence are distributed in the three domains (*triloka*, see LOKA).

Gauḍapāda. According to tradition, the author of the *kārikā* or commentary *Gauḍapādīyakārikā* (also known as *Āgama Śāstra*, or *Māṇḍūkyakārikā*) on the *Māṇḍūkya* **Upaniṣad*, and the teacher of Govindapāda, *Śaṅkara's teacher. This commentary is the earliest extant work to set forth the basic teachings of *Advaita Vedānta in systematic form. Nothing is known about his life, but, based on the tradition that he was Śaṅkara's *paramagura* ('teacher's teacher'), he may be assigned roughly to the 6th or 7th cent. CE.

V. Bhattacharya, *The Āgamaśāstra* . . . (1943); T. M. P. Mahadevan, *Gauḍapāda* . . . (1969).

Gauḍīya (devotee of Kṛṣṇa): see CAITANYA (2).

Gautama (traditional founder of Nyāya): see DARŚANA; NYĀYA.

Gautama, Indrabhuti. Early and prominent disciple of *Mahāvīra, still much revered among Jains.

Gautama Siddhārta (Skt.; Pali **Gotama Siddhatta**). The family name, plus the first name, of the *Buddha Śākyamuni.

Gayā (Hindu sacred city): see BODHGAYĀ.

Gāyatrī. A Hindu metre of 24 syllables, variously divided, but often 3×8. Many hymns in the **Ṛg Veda* are in this metre, one verse being of outstanding importance, and often called simply 'gāyatrī'; though it is also known as *sāvitṛ*, being addressed to the sun, Savitar (*Sūrya) as the supreme source of potency, life, and manifestation: 'Oṁ, tat savitur vareṇyaṁ bhargo devasya dhīmahi dhiyo yo naḥ pracodayāt, oṁ'; 'We meditate on the brilliant light of the One worthy of worship, source of all worlds: may he illuminate our minds' (*Ṛg Veda* 3. 62. 10). *Twice-born Hindus (i.e. of the three higher *castes) repeat this verse as a daily *mantra. Gāyatrī is then personified as the Goddess who presides over the three castes: she is the wife of *Brahmā and mother of the four *Vedas.

Gedaliah, fast of. Jewish fast commemorating the death of Gedaliah. Gedaliah was appointed governor of *Judah by the Babylonians after the fall of *Jerusalem in 586 BCE. He was assassinated by Ishmael b. Nethaniah, apparently in an attempt to overthrow Babylonian rule (2 Kings 25. 25–6; Jeremiah 41). A fast to commemorate this event is held on 3 Tishri.

Gedatsu (Jap., 'release'). In Zen Buddhism, release or liberation into enlightenment; hence also the equivalent of *zazen, the meditative way that leads to enlightenment. *Gedatsu no mon* is thus the gate that leads to enlightenment, and *gedatsu dōsō-e* is a name for the *kesa* as 'the garment of liberation', which is worn by officiants at ceremonies. Beyond gedatsu lies *dai-gedatsu, 'great' enlightenment.

Gedo (-zen) (Jap.). 'Outside' way of sharing Zen aims. see FIVE WAYS OF CH'AN/ZEN.

Geertz, Clifford (b. 1926). Influential American cultural anthropologist who advocates 'examining culture as an assemblage of texts'. This humanistic and *Weberian approach, of treating culture as the vehicle which enables participants to give form and meaning to their experiences, is most elaborately worked out in his view of religion as 'a system of symbols which acts to establish powerful, pervasive, and long-lasting moods and motivations in men by formulating conceptions of a general order of existence and clothing these conceptions with such an aura of factuality that the moods and motivations seem uniquely realistic' (*The Interpretation of Cultures*, 1973). The role of religion in organizing experience, in particular in providing responses to those experiences which lack 'interpretability', is explored in a number of works, including *The Religion of Java* (1960) and *Islam Observed* (1968). In general, his emphasis on meaning and experience has helped direct the *anthropology of religion away from traditional socio-structural concerns.

Gefühl (feeling): see SCHLEIERMACHER, F.

Gehenna, Gehinnom (Heb., Valley of Hinnom). A valley south of *Jerusalem, used as a waste tip. In the days of the Hebrew monarch, a cult which involved the burning of children was practised at Gehinnom. The cult was roundly condemned by the biblical *prophets (see Jeremiah 7. 31), and metaphorically the name came to mean a place 'where the fire smoulders unceasingly and the worm never ends its activity', i.e. a place where the wicked are abandoned with none to remember them, and where they are tormented after death. Gehenna is the Gk. form of the name.

Geiger, Abraham (1810–74). Leader of *Reform Judaism. In 1837 Geiger convened the first meeting of Reform *rabbis and as rabbi of the Berlin Reform congregation, he was director of the Hochschule für die Wissenschaft des Judenturms from 1872 until his death. He perceived Judaism to be solely a religion and was thus anxious to encourage *assimilation into the national life, as well as freedom of thought and enquiry: 'Priesthood was merely tolerated in Judaism, and the whole history of Judaism contains a continual war against it.' Because 'Judaism has not allowed the doctrine of *original sin to be grafted on to it', no mediator is needed between an individual and God. Humans must use God-given reason to advance their own understanding: 'Canonisation of ignorance has never been the rule in Israel.' Geiger was prepared to draw radical conclusions from these opinions, e.g. 'It is not birth but conviction . . . that makes the Jew', 'Let there be henceforth no distinction between obligations for *women and men, unless flowing from nature—no assumption of the spiritual minority of women.' Judaism has the same universal mission as had the *patriarchs of old. However, embedded as Geiger was in the German Romantic protest against Newtonian materialism, his vision tended towards a vague, transcendalist aspiration: 'Longing after the Highest and Noblest, attachment to the Whole, soaring up to the infinite . . ., this is religion.' He became more traditional in later life because he wished to avoid a split among the Jewish people—thus, although he regarded *circumcision as a 'barbaric act of bloodletting', he was opposed to its abolition. He summarized his view of Judaism in a popular series of lectures *Das Judenthum und seine Geschichte* (3 vols., 1865–7: Judaism and its History).

M. Weiner, *Abraham Geiger and Liberal Judaism* (1962).

Gelugpa: see GELUK.

Geluk (dge.lugs.pa, 'Virtuous Way'). One of the four principal schools of Tibetan Buddhism and that to which the *Dalai Lama belongs. Established in 1409 with the founding of the Riwo Ganden ('Joyous Mountain') monastery by *Tsong Khapa, the Geluk was the last of the great schools to be formed, and is now the largest. Tsong Khapa had in his middle years adopted the *Kadam school as his own, and in creating the Geluk (which he initially called the 'New Kadam') he was concerned with promoting the principles of *Atiśa on which the Kadam had been based. These principles, especially those of celibacy and of ensuring the purity of *tantric practice by relating it to the *sūtra tradition, were not at that time widely practised in Tibet where Tsong Khapa had himself been instructed in tantra before sūtra, and where celibacy was often actively discouraged. That Tsong Khapa was at pains to differentiate his school from the others is revealed by his prescription of *Yellow Hats for his monks, while the other schools wore Red.

Although in modern times all Tibetan schools have moved closer together, the Geluk is still noted for its adherence to *prāsangika-mādhyamaka, and for its educational system in which a monk progresses through a series of classes—each of which may last a minimum of two years—towards (for the most able) a Geshe ('Professor'; lit. 'Virtuous Friend') degree after some twenty-four years. These classes may typically teach the following subjects in progressive order: basic ritual, prayer, grammar, and discipline; logic, debate, and epistemology; *Perfectiion of Wisdom Prajñāpāramitā (using the *Abhisamayālankāra* attributed to Maitreyanātha); *Mādhyamaka (using the *Madhyamakalankāra* of *Śāntarakṣita and the works of *Candrakīrti and

Tsong Khapa); intensive logic and epistemology (using the *Pramānavārttika* of *Dharmakīrti); *Vinaya; phenomenology (using the *Abhidharmakośa* of *Vasubandhu); the Karam and Lharam stages of the Geshe degree which intensively review the foregoing. Most stages are accompanied by the textbook peculiar to the particular college of each monastic university. All major texts are learnt by heart, progression through the successive classes is determined through examination by debate, and only two monks may be passed out of the Lharam Geshe class each year. It should be noticed that advanced study of tantra is only begun after the Geshe degree is obtained.

The head of the Geluk school is not (as is commonly supposed) the *Dalai Lama, but the Khri Rinpoche (or throne-holder), an office passed on by educational attainment, not by incarnation. A recent head, Ling Rinpoche, died in Dec. 1983.

The Geluk tradition has had considerable success in taking root outside Tibet. At its centre in N. India, Dharmasala, an extensive publishing programme has been undertaken to preserve and disseminate Tibetan texts. Lama Thubten Yeshe (1935–84) taught many W. students, especially at his centre at Kopan near Kathmandu. Two of them, Harvey Horrocks and Peter Kedge, established the Manjushri Institute in the NW of England, the first European centre to offer training to the geshe level. Others are now established in France, Germany, Italy, Spain, and Switzerland, and in several places in the USA.

See Index, Geluk.

R. A. F. Thurman (ed.), *The Life and Teachings of Tsong Khapa* (1982); B. A. Wallace, *The Life and Teaching of Geshe Rabten* (1980).

Gemāra (Aram., 'completion'). The discussions of the Jewish *amoraim on the *Mishnah. Both the Babylonian and the Palestinian *Talmud contain gemāra, which is traditionally printed around the relevant Mishnah passage.

Gematria (Heb., *gimatriyya*, from Gk., *geometria*). Use or study of hidden meanings through numbers, especially the numerical equivalence of letters. The technique is widespread and ancient, being found among Greeks, Assyrians, and Babylonians. Sargon II built the wall of Khorsabad 16,283 cubits long because that was the numerical equivalent of his name.

Gematria first appeared in Jewish literature in the 2nd cent. CE. An example of the use of gematria in interpretation is R. Judah's inference from the verse 'because they are laid waste so that no one passes through . . .; both the birds of the air and the beasts have fled' (Jeremiah 9. 10) that no traveller passed through *Judah for fifty-two years. This is because the numerical value of the Heb. word *behemah* ('beast') is fifty-two. Gematria was much employed by the *kabbalists and was used to prove the *messiahship of *Shabbetai Zevi. Inevitably as time went on the system became more complicated; so, for example, Moses *Cordovero listed nine different systems of gematria. Despite criticism, its use was widespread in both *Sephardi and *Ashkenazi circles where its use is often less serious. Thus the Hebrew words for wine (*yayin*) and mystery (*sodh) both = 70, hence the saying, 'When wine goes in, the secret will come out'. *Charity is often distributed in multiples of eighteen because 18 = *ḥai*, 'life'.

In Islam, the equivalent techniques are known as *'ilm ul-ḥurūf*, based on *abjad (the numerical values of the letters). Thus Adam and Eve are specially related to God because their names = the Divine Name (of *Allāh).

F. Dornseiff, *Das Alphabet in Mystik und Magie* (1925).

Gemeinschaft (social ties of family and friendship): see IDEAL TYPE.

Gemilut ḥasidim (Heb., 'the bestowal of loving kindness'). The essential Jewish virtue of concern for one's fellow human beings. According to Simeon the Just in the *Talmud, the Jewish religion rests on the three pillars of *Torah, *Temple service, and gemilut ḥasidim (*Avot* 1. 2). Gemilut ḥasidim is more than *charity in that it can be given to the rich as well as to the poor, and can involve personal service as well as the mere gift of money. It is one of the major characteristics of Jewish ethics, and 'whosoever denies the duty of gemilut ḥasidim denies the fundamental of Judaism' (*Eccles.R.* 7. 1).

Gempon Sōgen Shintō (school of shinto): see YOSHIDA SHINTŌ.

General Baptists. The name given to those *Arminian Baptists who believed in 'general' redemption for all humanity. During the 18th cent. several of their English churches moved towards *Unitarianism so that in 1770 Dan Taylor, unhappy about these doctrinal changes, formed a New Connexion. This group united with the *Particular Baptists in 1891. See also BAPTIST CHURCHES.

General providence: see PROVIDENCE.

Genesis. The first book of the *Pentateuch and opening book of the Hebrew Bible and Christian Old Testament. The Eng. title follows that of the Septuagint Gk. version, the Hebrew title *Bereshith* being the first word of the text. The book contains the story of the Creation of the universe and the earliest human history (1–11) including the *Flood (6–8); and the stories of the *Patriarchs *Abraham (12–25. 18), *Isaac (25. 19–26), *Jacob (27–35), and *Joseph (37–50). According to a precise chronology (5. 3 ff., 11. 10 ff., 21. 5, 25. 26, 47, 28, etc.) the events of the book cover 2,307 years. A 'table of nations' in ch. 10 characterizes ancient peoples according to their descent from Noah after the Flood. God's *covenant with Abraham (22. 15–18) is fundamental to the idea of Israel as *chosen people. Traditionally Genesis, together with the other four books of the

*Pentateuch, is thought to have been of *Mosaic authorship, but the diversity of styles, the existence of duplicate accounts of the same stories, the use of different Hebrew names for God, and the presence of various anachronisms, led to the suggestion that it is a composite work derived from different, older documents. More recently, an even more diverse background has been suggested, of oral traditions associated with tribes, sanctuaries, etc. Whatever the origins, a coherence and clear theological theme emerges. Humanity is the climax of God's creation. From the nations of the world, Noah is singled out for salvation and a covenant relationship is established. This becomes the major theme of the book with the covenant with Noah's descendant Abraham, who is to become the father of a great people, the inheritors of the *Promised Land. The time sequence is highly schematized (ten generations from Adam to Noah and from Noah to Abraham) and the reader is left in no doubt that it is the unfolding of God's plan in history that is being described.

G. von Rad, *Genesis* (tr. 1961); R. N. Whybray, *The Making of the Pentateuch* . . . (1987).

Genesis Rabbah. Jewish *midrash on the book of *Genesis. Originating in Palestine, *Genesis Rabbah* is the earliest work of *aggadic midrash still extant. In its present form, it dates back before 425 CE, and provides a systematic commentary on Genesis.

Eng. tr. H. Freedman (1939).

Geneva. City in Switzerland, associated with J. *Calvin. The Geneva Academy and the Geneva Catechisms expounded Calvinist views; the Geneva Bible (usually known as the Breeches Bible for its translation of Genesis 3. 7) was issued with Calvinist commentary, and was widely read. A Geneva gown is a black, full-sleeved gown, still worn by some *Protestant ministers, to make a deliberate contrast with *vestments and their association with the *sacrifice of the *mass. Because of the austere character of Geneva, it is said that there is a cemetery in Switzerland half the size of Geneva and twice as much fun.

Genizah (Heb., 'storing'). A place or receptacle for storing the Jewish books or ritual objects which can no longer be used. According to Jewish law, any book or object containing the name of God cannot be destroyed. Therefore they were stored, often in a small room attached to a *synagogue, and thus many manuscripts of great antiquity have been preserved. See CAIRO GENIZAH.

Genjō (the wise and enlightened): see KENSHO.

Genjō (Jap. for Hsüan-tsang): see HSÜAN-TSANG.

Genjō-kōan. Text by Zen Buddhist master, *Dōgen Zenji, which became a part of **Shōbō-genzō*. It analyses the relation between *zazen and enlightenment, and is one of the most revered texts of the *Sōtō school.

Tr. (and comment.), H. T. Maezumi, *The Way of Everyday Life* (1978).

Genkan (Jap., 'hidden gate'). The entrance to the guest rooms in a Zen Buddhist monastery, hence, metaphorically, the entrance to the path leading to enlightenment, according to the different methods of training.

Genku (founder of Jodo): see HŌNEN.

Gennep, C.-A. K. van: see RITES OF PASSAGE.

Gensha Shibi (Ch'an/Zen master): see HSÜAN-SHA SHIH-PEI.

Genshin or **Eshin Sōzu** (942–1017). Japanese Buddhist monk of the *Tendai sect. Genshin was one of the most brilliant Tendai monks of his age, and left many important works of Tendai Buddhist doctrines, including the *Ichjō Yōketsu*, (Essentials of the One Vehicle), which argued that all beings are capable of attaining buddhahood. However, he is most famous as the author of the seminal Pure Land text, the **Ōjōyōshū* (Essentials of Birth in Pure Land). Although the Pure Land faith had been popularized by Genshin's earlier contemporary *Kūya (903–72), it was *Ōjōyōshū* which placed the Pure Land teachings on firm doctrinal footing. Genshin himself was also a serious follower of Pure Land Buddhism, and was instrumental in the formation of a society to seek rebirth in *Amida Buddha's Pure Land (*Sukhāvatī). For him, 'the social joys' of the Pure Land are the greatest of the ten pleasures of that Land: 'First is the pleasure of being welcomed by many saints.' Conversely, Genshin's descriptions of the many *hells are vivid and detailed.

A. A. Andrews, *The Teachings Essential for Rebirth* . . . (1973).

Gentile. A non-Jewish person. The term *goy*, although frequently used, is inappropriate, since the Heb. term means 'nation', and is used in the Bible of Israel. More accurate might be *nokhri*, a foreigner (or stranger), or *ger*, alien (see PROSELYTE). From early times, a distinction was made between *ger toshav* (lit., 'resident alien'), one who keeps the *Noachide laws, and *akum*, an acronym for those who worship stars and planets. In *Talmudic times, the Jewish attitude towards gentiles varied in response to the gentile attitude towards Jews. At one extreme, a gentile's friendship should be reciprocated (*BBK* 38b) and, at the other, the best of gentiles should be killed (*TJ*, *Kid.* 4. 11). It is believed that all gentiles should obey the seven Noachide laws, but they are not obliged to keep the *Six Hundred and Thirteen commandments; and a distinction is made between idolators and Christians and Muslims who, in the words of R. Menaḥem Meir, are 'peoples disciplined by religion'. Maimonides argued that Christians must be excluded on the ground that Trinitarian belief violated the first Noachide law, but most have disagreed. However inclusive the attitude has been ('righteous gentiles have a share in the world to come', *T.San.* 13. 2), the integrity of Israel must be preserved. Thus, dating back to the time of *Ezra, intermarriage between Jew and gentile was completely forbidden.

Genuflection (Lat., 'knee' + 'I bend'). Act of reverence performed by kneeling briefly on one knee. In Christianity it is performed before the sacrament (including when it is *Reserved) and at the point in the *Creed when it is said 'He became man'—though this is rapidly dropping out of use.

Geomancy. *Divination based on patterns or shapes drawn (or appearing) on 'the land' (Gk.), particularly on sand. The term is also applied to *feng-shui (winds and waters), the ancient Chinese proto-science of siting human habitations (for the living or the dead) in locations that will take maximum advantage of the currents of vital breath (*ch'i) that circulate throughout the landscape. This vital breath, like the positive and negative modes of electricity, embodies the *yin and yang forces that are basic to the functioning of the cosmos. It is the business of the geomancer to identify those topographical spots where yin and yang come together to produce a 'force field' with beneficial effects upon people. Such spots are in the first place recognizable to the expert eye by the conformation of their hills and water-courses. But an auspicious spot must also have the right concatenation of other celestial and terrestrial influences; these are determined by consultation with the elaborate geomancer's compass. The essential thing is that the site concentrate the vital breath without allowing it to disperse, so that it will focus directly upon tomb, home, temple, or palace. Even entire cities have often been located on the basis of feng-shui principles. Feng-shui is one of the several divinatory arts considered in traditional times to be suitable to the dignity of the literati élite because much of its lore was contained in texts not intelligible to the uneducated. Its influence has been, and continues to be, pervasive among Chinese communities everywhere.

R. Jaulin, *La Geomancie* (1966).

Geonim (pl.) (title for heads of Jewish academies): see GAON.

George, St. *Patron saint of England (and of soldiers, knights, etc.) and *martyr. Very little is known of his life or death, but he probably died at or near Lydda in Palestine *c.*303. His cult and legends did not become popular until the 6th cent. In the E. he is known as the great martyr, *megalomartyros*. The slaying of the dragon (a standard symbol of strength) is first credited to him only in the 12th cent., but became widely known in the W. through the **Golden Legend*. The saint became of great importance in England from the time of the *Crusades, when he was seen as a model of Christian chivalry. Richard I placed his army under his protection, and under Edward III he displaced St Edward the Confessor as patron of England.

Georgian Orthodox Church. The *autocephalous church of Georgia, the republic situated in the Caucasus between Russia and Armenia. The royal house of this small country was evangelized by a young girl St Nino *c.*330. The neighbouring Church of *Armenia became *monophysite, but the Church of Georgia has been *Chalcedonian since *c.*600. The Church became autocephalous in the 8th cent., but from 1811 to 1917 it lost its autocephalous status to the Russian Church. It suffered persecution on account of its resistance to the Bolshevik annexation of Georgia in 1921; church life declined under Soviet rule, with only forty churches reported to be functioning in 1975, but independence has seen a marked revival under the present Patriarch-Catholicos Ilya II. Religious life is again flourishing, with the reopening of a number of monasteries and convents, despite almost total suppression under Soviet rule.

Ger (a non-Jew living among Jews): see GENTILE.

Gereformeerde Kerk (Christian Protestant Church): see DUTCH REFORMED CHURCH.

Gerhardt, Paul (*c.*1607–76). German Christian hymn-writer. Apart from *Luther's own, his hymns are often held to be the finest of the Lutheran tradition. Those well-known in Eng. trs. include 'The duteous day now closeth', 'Jesus, thy boundless love to me', 'All my heart this night rejoices', and pre-eminently 'O sacred head, sore wounded' (from a Lat. poem attributed to St *Bernard). His hymns mark a transition from the objective orthodoxy of earlier Lutheran hymns to the personal piety of more modern compositions.

Gerizim. Mountain in *Israel. Mount Gerizim and Mount Ebal rise above the modern town of Nablus. According to Joshua 8. 30, Joshua's first act after the conquest was to build an *altar 'for a *blessing and a *curse' on the two mountains. Gerizim was the site of the *Samaritan *temple which was built about the time of *Nehemiah. It has remained the most sacred spot for the Samaritans and this has been a serious point of disagreement between the Samaritans and the Jews. After the Gerizim temple was destroyed in 129 BCE, the mountain became the site of various pagan shrines, a Christian church, and a Muslim cemetery. None the less, the Samaritans continue to hold their various festivals there, and the entire congregation stays on the mountain from 10 Nisan to the end of the *Mazzot feast.

Gerontius (poem by Newman): see NEWMAN, J. H.

Gershom ben Judah or **Me'or ha-Golah** ('light of the exile', *c.*960–*c.*1030). German Jewish *Talmudic scholar. Rabbenu Gershom was held in enormous reverence by later generations and *Rashi declared 'all *Ashkenazi Jewry are disciples of his disciples'. His name is connected with many *halakhic rulings, such as his ban against bigamy. Several Talmudic commentaries are ascribed to him; he transcribed the *Mishnah and was the first German scholar to compose *seliḥot and *piyyutim. His grave in Mainz is still visited by the pious.

Gerson, Jean le Charlier de (1363–1429). French churchman and spiritual writer. Born near Rethel in the Ardennes, he entered the college of Navarre at Paris in 1377 and in 1395 succeeded his friend, d'Ailly, as Chancellor of Notre-Dame and the University. All his life he was concerned for a true reform of the Church by a renewal of the spirit of prayer and sacrifice. He played a conciliatory role in the *Great Schism and was a supporter of conciliarism (see ANTIPOPE), attending the Council of *Constance. Although critical of, e.g., *Ruysbroek, his own spiritual writings belong to the tradition of *Catholic *mysticism, of which he was a synthesizer: of the three kinds of theology, symbolic, natural, and mystical, the latter is the most secure, depending on affective experience, and not on cognition. The end of contemplation is a union of love with God which is the work of the Holy Spirit.

Ger toshav (resident stranger): see GENTILE; NOACHIDE LAWS.

Gertrude of Helfta (Rhineland mystic): see RHENO-FLEMISH SPIRITUALITY.

Ge-sar (Tib., 'lotus temple'). A legendary hero in *Tibetan religion, who led the fight, in many dramatic episodes, against evil. He was adopted into Buddhism as the embodiment of *Avalokiteśvara, or of *Padmasambhava. As the bringer of future salvation, he became associated with the kingdom of *Shambhala.

Gesellschaft (social bonds of a formal kind): see IDEAL TYPE.

Geshe (Professor in Tibetan school): see GELUK.

Get (bill of divorce): see MARRIAGE AND DIVORCE (JUDAISM).

Gethsemane. The garden to which Jesus went with his disciples after the *Last Supper, in which he endured his 'agony' (Matthew 26. 37) and betrayal and arrest (26. 47–56). It lies in the valley between Jerusalem and the Mount of Olives, with the traditional site being supervised by *Franciscans.

Getig (materiality): see FRAVASI; FRASOKERETI.

Ge'ul(l)ah (Heb., 'redemption'). Title of several Jewish prayers. The section in the morning and evening liturgy between the *Shemaʿ and the *ʿAmidah is known as Ge'ullah. The term is also used for the *benediction recited at the end of the *Hallel during the *Passover *seder and for the seventh blessing of the ʿAmidah. The prayers invoke God, as 'mighty Redeemer' to regard Israel's affliction and deliver his people.

Gezerah (Heb., 'edict'). Command of several different kinds in Judaism. In general, they are commands of an unusual kind, either within Israel (e.g. a biblical command for which no reason is given, as in Numbers 19, or rabbinic commands to strengthen the integrity of Israel, as in *B.Shab.* 11a–17b, the eighteen gezerot (pl.) which reinforce distinctions between Jews and non-Jews), or from outside Israel (e.g. edicts of foreign rulers banning Jewish observances; hence the word becomes a synonym for pogroms, massacres, and persecutions). A gezerah, once (legitimately) enacted, cannot be rescinded.

Ghaiba (Arab., 'absence'). The state of one who has been withdrawn by God from visible appearance on earth, although he is still living invisibly on earth. The clearest example is the Hidden Imām (*al-Mahdī). It is also a *Sūfī stage on the way to *fanā', absent from self and present (*ḥaḍra*) only to God.

Ghaṇṭa. A bell, one of many objects used in Hindu ritual in association with *Śiva. The sound of his bell, or of his drum (*ḍamaru), encapsulates creation and is his 'form in sound' (*mantra (-svarūpa)). In the hands of Śiva's spouse, Ghaṇṭī (who is *Durgā), the bell is one of her twelve weapons to drive away threats and terrify enemies.

Ghāṭ. (Hindi; Skt., *ghaṭṭa*). A place of access, often by means of steps, to a river or lake, etc., for purposes of washing and for ritual cleansing (e.g. in *Gaṅgā). Some of these are reserved for dealing with the dead, especially for the dispersal of ashes.

Ghayba (hidden state): see GHAIBA.

Ghaz(z)ālī (Muslim philosopher and theologian): see AL-GHAZ(Z)ĀLĪ.

Ghetto. A compulsory urban residential area for Jews. The term 'ghetto' was probably first used for the Jewish quarter of Venice which was enclosed in 1516. Throughout Christian Europe, in the early modern age, city governments restricted Jews to living in a particular area of the city. After such regulations disappeared, the term continued to be used for predominantly Jewish areas which had been settled voluntarily. By extension, areas of cities occupied by non-Jewish ethnic minorities also came to be called ghettos. The idea of the Jewish ghetto was revived by the Nazis—Hitler said, 'Out with them from all the professions and into the ghetto with them; fence them in somewhere where they can perish as they deserve.' Those ghettos were used as holding places before the Jews were transported to the extermination camps.

The phrase 'ghetto mentality' refers to the (alleged) internalization of the attitudes of the outsider—humiliation, rejection, and contempt, and the acceptance of isolation. In fact, more often Mendele is correct: 'Israel is the Diogenes of the nations: he lives in a barrel, and his dwelling-place is narrow and restricted; yet under the dust and ashes of the ghetto, the flame of *Torah burns, giving light and heat for the whole people.' That vigour erupted in the uprising of the Warsaw ghetto against the Nazis on 19 Apr. 1943, which was put down by the destruction of the whole area.

Ghi or **ghee** (clarified butter, important in Hindu ritual): see GHṚTA.

Ghose, Aurobindo (Hindu philosopher and teacher): see AUROBINDO.

Ghost dance. The most famous *millennial movement among the N. American Indians, amongst the destitute tribes of the Great Basin and the Plains in 1889–90. The founder was Wovoka (*c.*1856–1932), a Paiute, also called Jack Wilson. After a mystic experience of visiting *heaven, he proclaimed the peaceful coming of a paradisal age in which the depleted buffalo and the ancestors (i.e. 'ghosts', hence the name) would return and the whites would depart. Its coming would be hastened by moral reform and the newly revealed round dance which, after several days of dancing, led to meeting the ancestors in a visionary trance. The movement among the Sioux was regarded by many whites as more militant; this culminated in the massacre of some 300 at Wounded Knee in Dec. 1890. With hopes thus crushed, the movement passed its peak by 1892; it lingers on among some tribes and provided the inspiration for the confrontation between Indians and government forces at 'Wounded Knee II' in S. Dakota in 1973.

W. La Barre, *The Ghost Dance* . . . (1970); R. Dewing, *Wounded Knee* (1984); A. B. Kehoe, *The Ghost Dance* . . . (1989); J. Mooney, *The Ghost-Dance Religion* . . . (1896).

Ghṛta (Skt.). Clarified butter, in modern Hindi *ghi*, often transliterated 'ghee'. It is produced by boiling butter and repeatedly skimming it until water, curds, and impurities have been removed, and a pure oil remains. It is used medicinally, especially when it has been kept for a great length of time, but its main use is in *pūjā, worship, and in fuelling the ghṛta lamps. It is a summary of the illumination which comes from *Indra, the light of divine knowledge become form. It is thus equivalent to *amṛta in *Ṛg Veda* 4. 58. 1.

Ghusl (Arab., 'to wash'). The major ritual of *ablution in Islam. It is commanded for major ritual impurity (*ḥadath), and consists in washing the whole body.

M. A. Quasem, *Salvation of the Soul and Islamic Devotions* (1983).

Ghwath-al-Aẓam (supposed founder of Sūfī order): see ABD AL-QĀDIR AL-JĪLĪ.

Giānī (Pañjābī, 'learned'). Scholar of Sikh scriptures. Sikhs use this title for any person regarded as proficient in expounding the teachings of the *Ādi Granth in the *gurdwārā. More specifically 'Giānī' denotes someone who has passed the *Pañjāb University's Honours examination in Pañjābī language and literature.

Gideon. One of the biblical *judges. His activities are recorded in the Book of Judges (6. 11–8. 32). He delivered the Israelites from the Midianites by leading a surprise attack with 300 picked men in the middle of the night. Subsequently Gideon decisively defeated the enemy and refused the offer of kingship, declaring 'The Lord will rule over you.' According to the *aggadah, Gideon, Jephthah, and *Samson were regarded as the three least worthy of the judges (*BRH* 25a).

Gifts: see ALMSGIVING.

Gijō. Jap. for **I Ching*.

Giku (Chinese Ch'an/Zen master): see I-K'UNG.

Gilbert of Sempringham (*c.*1083–1189). Founder of the Gilbertine Order of monks and nuns. While parish priest of his native Sempringham in Lincolnshire, he encouraged seven women of his congregation to form a community on the *Cistercian model. Other foundations followed. When the Cistercians refused to accept communities of nuns under their aegis, Gilbert arranged for the direction of his nuns by priests following the *Augustinian Rule, who together with the nuns, and the lay-brothers and lay-sisters, formed a double community, sharing their liturgical life. It was the only purely English medieval order.

Gilgit. 'A small unexplored country on the southern declivity of the Hindu Kush between Chitral on the West and Baltistan (Little Tibet) on the East' (H. Eliot). Since miscellaneous ruined *stūpas have been discovered in the area, particularly by Sir R. A. Stein in 1931, it has been thought likely that Gilgit was the seat of a Buddhist dynasty sometime between 5th and 6th cents. CE. Stein found in one of the stūpas important texts, including the earliest known list of Buddhist magical formulae (*dhāraṇīs) and miscellaneous *Vinaya writings subsequently ascribed to the Mūlasarvāstivādin school.

Gilgul (Heb., *gilgul neshamot*, 'transmigration of souls'). The Jewish doctrine of the transmigration of *souls. Although belief in the transmigration of souls was rejected by the major medieval Jewish philosophers, it was held by *Anan b. David, the founder of *Karaism, and it is expressed in many *kabbalistic texts. It was also believed by some that souls can be reborn in animals: Isaac *Luria identified a notorious, deceased fornicator in a large, black dog. His pupil, R. Ḥayyim *Vital wrote a systematic analysis of the soul which popularized gilgul. *Levirate marriage was seen as proof of gilgul; the doctrine solved the problem of innocent suffering and the Book of Job was interpreted in its light. The purpose of transmigration was the purification of the soul, and there were many different interpretations of the details of the doctrine. Some early kabbalists believed that transmigration occurred no more than three times, while others thought it occurred an endless number of times through all forms of existence.

N. E. David, *Karma and Reincarnation in Israelitism* (1908).

Gill, Eric (1882–1940). Artist and type-designer. Son of an assistant minister in the Countess of *Huntingdon's Connexion, he became a *Roman Catholic in 1913. From 1907 to 1924 he was associated with the Ditchling community and with its press, which occasioned his interest in printing. His main concern, however, was with sculpture. In the year of his conversion he was commissioned to produce the *stations of the cross in Westminster Cathedral, and later sculpted the statue of Ariel on the façade of Broadcasting House, London. In the last decade of his life he wrote a number of influential books defending the goodness of natural things, and the primacy of the spiritual, 'deepening our respect and admiration and love for the natural world . . . its sweetness and its terrors, even its comicality and, so to say, its Rabelaisian buffoonery and pig-style coarseness. All these things are good and holy.' His expression of this in his personal life created strain for those close to him.

Gilson, Étienne (1884–1978). French Roman Catholic philosopher and historian. He began his career with a study of Descartes, but research into *scholastic influence upon Descartes led him to medieval thought. After a period at the Sorbonne, he became in 1929 director of the Institute of Medieval Studies at Toronto. His special interest was the philosophy of Thomas *Aquinas, particularly the influence of *Aristotle on his thought. Though he was later to be criticized for underestimating the strength of *Platonism in the Middle Ages, his interpretation of the scholastics had a great impact upon modern RC philosophers. His view of the history of philosophy was dominated by a *teleological understanding of time:

> Christianity had put the end of man beyond the limits of this earthly life; it had affirmed at the same time that a creative God allows nothing to fall outside the designs of his providence; it therefore had to admit also that everything, both in the life of individuals and in the life of societies . . ., is ordered to this supraterrestrial end.

He therefore held, with *Augustine, that 'the universe is a kind of unfolding, a *distensio*, which imitates in its flowing forth the eternal present and total simultaneity of the life of God'. Such a view of order and providence cannot be concerned with a more dispassionate estimate of the actual history of the Church and its restrictive attitude to the quest for truth.

M. McGrath, *Étienne Gilson: A Bibliography* (1982); L. K. Shock, *Étienne Gilson* (1984).

Ginsberg, Asher Hirsh (Jewish Zionist leader): see AHAD HA-'AM.

Ginzberg, Louis (1873–1953). *Talmudic scholar. Born in Lithuania, he emigrated to the USA in 1899. After settling there, Ginzberg taught at the *Jewish Theological Seminary and was an important figure in the *Conservative movement. His major work was the 7-vol. *Legends of the Jews* (1909–38) in which he collected and combined hundreds of legends into a continuous narrative; and he was also the rabbinics editor for the *Jewish Encyclopaedia*. He took the view strongly that the law is not kept because one can find reasons for doing so (e.g. dietary laws for the waist-line, family laws for chastity): 'The law is not a means to an end, but the end in itself; the law is active religiousness, and in active religion lies what is specifically Jewish.' Judaism is thus a profoundly democratic religion, as he argued in *Students, Scholars, and Saints* (1928): 'The salvation of the Jews was never wrought by the rich.'

E. Ginzberg, *Keeper of the Law: Louis Ginzberg* (1966).

Giotto di Bondone (1266/7–1337). Italian fresco painter, often regarded as 'the founder of modern art'. Traditionally believed to be a pupil of Cimabue, *Dante observed, 'Now the cry is Giotto, And Cimabue's name is eclipsed.' According to Vasari, 'Giotto was born to throw light on the art of painting.' He did so especially by attention to perspective, and by making recognizable human figures and landscapes the bearers of Christian meaning; hence Boccaccio: 'People's eyes are deceived and they mistake the picture for the real thing.' His most famous (undisputed) work is in the Arena Chapel in Padua. The better-known frescos on the life of St Francis in Assisi may not be by him.

A. Martindale and E. Baccheschi, *The Complete Paintings . . .* (1969).

Giralda (Muslim dynasty in N. Africa and Spain): see ALMOHADS.

Girdle: see HABIT, RELIGIOUS.

Girsah (plain meaning): see PILPUL.

Gītā (Hindu text): see BHAGAVAD-GĪTĀ.

Gita. A *Maronite Christian veil, used to cover the paten, chalice, or oblation in the liturgy.

Gītāgovinda (Song of the Cowherd). A court poem by Jayadeva (12th cent. CE). Erotic in nature, it appears on the surface to be a straightforward account of the loves of *Kṛṣṇa for the gopīs, in contrast to his secret love for *Rādhā; it interweaves the themes of separation and consummation. But the poem is also read (and dramatically acted), especially by *Vaiṣṇavas, as a poem on the longing of the human for the divine, in which Rādhā is the *śakti of Kṛṣṇa. Nothing certain is known of Jayadeva's life.

L. Siegel, *Sacred and Profane Dimensions of Divine Love in Indian Traditions* . . . (1978); B. Stoler-Miller, *Love Song of the Dark Lord* (1977).

Gitanjali (poem by Indian poet Tagore): see TAGORE, R.

Glastonbury. In Somerset, one of the oldest English monasteries. Its history goes back to the 7th cent., but it became a famous Benedictine centre from *c.*940 under its abbot St Dunstan. About 1135 William of Malmesbury wrote its history, and in a 13th-cent. revision of this are the legends which associate it with *Joseph of Arimathea, King Arthur, and St *Patrick. These legends supported the abbey's claims to seniority, and also made England the earliest W. country to receive the gospel. The monastery was suppressed in 1539 and is now a ruin.

Glebe. Land which belongs to the endowment of a parish and which provides an income from farming by the priest himself or a tenant. In 1878 the income from glebe-lands in England was estimated at £400,000, but it has since declined to an insignificant share of church revenues.

Gloria. The first word in the Latin, and hence the common name, of a Christian hymn. It begins with the words of Luke 2. 14 'Glory be to God on high' (Lat. *Gloria in excelsis Deo*). It formed part of morning prayers in the 4th cent., and is still recited in the Greek morning *office. In W. liturgical churches it is sung or said in the eucharist on Sundays except in *Advent and *Lent. It is also known as the 'Greater *Doxology' or 'Angelic Hymn'. The 'Lesser Doxology', or *Gloria Patri*, is sung or said at the end of Psalms and *canticles. It runs, 'Glory be to the Father and to the Son and to the Holy Ghost/Spirit; as it was in the beginning is now and ever shall be, world without end. Amen.' It is also often sung in Protestant services.

Glossolalia (Gk., *glossa*, 'tongue', + *lalia*, 'speaking'). 'Speaking in tongues', the phenomenon, common in many religions, of a person speaking in words or word-like sounds which form a language unknown to the speaker. The utterances are often from people in an *ecstatic or trance state. Glossolalia is particularly familiar from the early Christian Church (Acts 2, 1 Corinthians 12–14); it has recurred consistently at moments of renewal, and it is strong in the contemporary Church where it is regarded, not as an enthusiastic aberration, but as a mark of the gift of the Spirit. Related phenomena are *xenoglossolalia*, speaking in a foreign language unknown to the speaker but known to the hearer; and *heteroglossolalia*, speaking in a language known to the speaker which the hearer hears in his/her own language.

F. D. Goodman, *Speaking in Tongues: A Cross-Cultural Study* . . . (1972); H. N. Maloney and A. A. Lovekin, *Glossolalia: Behavioral Science Perspectives* . . . (1986). W. J. Samarin, *Tongues of Men and Angels* (1972); C. Williams, *Tongues of the Spirit* (1981).

Gnosticism. A complex of religious movements, having at least some of its roots in Jewish and pagan thought but appearing in developed form as a Christian *heresy in the 2nd cent. Among the systems of that time, those of *Valentinus, *Basilides, and (somewhat apart from the rest) *Marcion are the best known. These systems ranged from the genuinely philosophical to the extensively mythological and magical. The *Bible was used and expounded, and *Jesus usually held a significant place, but much was different from mainstream Christianity.

Among these points of difference are (i) the distinction between the remote supreme Divine Being and the inferior *Demiurge or creator god responsible for the imperfect and perverted material world; (ii) the importance of *gnōsis* ('knowledge') as a means of redemption for at least some people (sometimes called the *pneumatikoi*, 'spiritual ones'); and (iii) a *christology of Jesus as the emissary of the supreme God in *docetic human form.

Opponents of gnosticism (e.g. *Irenaeus, *Tertullian, *Hippolytus) pointed to the plain sense of the scriptures and the unbroken tradition of the Church as proof against the legitimacy of esoteric revelations; to the absurdity of gnostic cosmology and especially its distinction between the creator and the supreme God; to the reality of Jesus' sufferings; and (apparently without good reason) to the immoral character of the gnostics themselves.

The study of gnosticism was transformed by the discovery of a library of Coptic gnostic texts at *Nag Hammadi in 1945–6. These have permitted for the first time a direct view of the movement. Recent study using these texts has supported two conclusions: first, gnosticism should probably be seen as an originally non-Christian phenomenon—mainly within Judaism but just possibly influenced by E. religions. In nascent form, it interacted with Christianity already in the 1st cent. (see e.g. 1 Timothy 6. 20), though *Bultmann's view that Christianity took over its christology from a gnostic 'redeemer myth' is still likely to be the reverse of correct. Second, the gnostics were ousted by the church in the 2nd–3rd cents., as much because of their élitism and opposition to an authoritarian discipline as because of their doctrines (some of which, like a liberal attitude to *women, seem attractive and defensible).

Reaction to gnosticism conduced to narrower definition within the *Catholic Church of ecclesiastical structures, the *canon of scripture, and tradition. The *Manichaeans, *Mandeans, and *Cathars may be in various ways descendants of the gnostics. The autobiography of C. G. *Jung shows the influence of gnosticism on his thought.

See Index, Gnostics.

G. Filoramo, *Gnosticism* (1990); H. Jonas, *The Gnostic Religion* (tr. 1963); B. Layton, *The Gnostic Scriptures* (1987); E. Pagels, *The Gnostic Gospels* (1980); K. Rudolph, *Gnosis* (1983).

Gō. Jap. for *karma.

Go (Skt., 'cow'). *Bos indicus*, in Hinduism, revered as the source of food and symbol of life. In the *Vedas, the cow is regarded as a gift from the gods, but there is no personification of the cow as a goddess. Aditi and Vāc are likened to cows because of their bounty (8. 89 and 90). The cow became associated with the sacrificial rituals through its designation as the appropriate gift (*dakṣinā) to the *brahmans, and thus its sacred and inviolable nature became established: to kill a cow is equal to killing a brahman. The point at which it became a sacrificial victim is uncertain, though it was clearly central in funeral rites; but in any case, substitutes (goats, birds, etc., and eventually rice) became prevalent. The five products (*pañcagavya*) of the cow (milk, curds, *ghṛta, urine, dung) are all used in *pūjā, worship, and also in apotropaic rites—e.g. *gokarīṣam*, in which dried cow-dung is placed on the heads of children possessed by evil spirits. For *Gāndhī, 'cow protection is the gift of Hinduism to the world', because it epitomizes the interrelation of all living things, and human dependence on the non-human for life.

The cultic worship of the cow takes place especially on the day of Gopastami, the 'cow holiday', when the cow is washed and decorated in the temple, and given offerings in the hope that her gifts of life will continue.

V. M. Dandekar, *The Cattle Economy of India* (1980).

Gobind Siṅgh, Gurū (1666–1708 CE). Tenth Sikh *Gurū. Gobind Rāi was born on 26 Dec. 1666, in Paṭnā, to Mātā *Gūjarī, while her husband, *Tegh Bahādur, was travelling further east. Later, the family returned to *Anaṇḍpur Sāhib, where, in Nov. 1675, Gobind Rāi received the severed head of his martyred father. As his father's chosen successor, he was installed as Gurū. He married Sundarī, Jīto, and Sāhib Devān (Mātā Sāhib Kaur). Of his sons, the *Sāhibzāde, Sundarī bore Ajīt, and Jīto bore Jujhār, Zorāwar, and *Fateh.

As a child Gobind Rāi had displayed a predilection for martial games. He was trained in swordsmanship and enjoyed hunting. He was educated in Hindī, Pañjābī, Skt., and Persian, and he composed prolifically, chiefly in Braj (a N. Indian vernacular). His poetry comprises the *Dasam Granth. Major themes are devotion to God, stories from Hindu mythology, and exhortation to military valour. To him flocked over fifty poets, including *Nand Lāl Goyā. These bards translated Hindu epics into Braj and Pañjābī.

Gobind Rāi moved from Anandpur further into the mountains, to Pāonṭā, which he fortified. Neighbouring hill rājās, nervous at his increasing power, unsuccessfully attacked his men at Bhaṅgāṇī. The Gurū returned to Anaṇḍpur and, with local hill chiefs, fought a Mughal force at Nadaun. He built the fortresses Anandgaṛh, Keśgaṛh, Lohgaṛh, and Fatehgaṛh. Realizing the corruption of the *masands, the Gurū excommunicated them and abolished the institution. With inspired foresight, on *Baisākhī 1699 (according to tradition) he inaugurated the *khālsā, and initiated with *amrit the *pañj pyāre to be the nucleus of a pure, casteless community, characterized by the *five Ks and a code of conduct (*rahat). He in turn received initiation (*Khaṇḍe-dī-pāhul) from them, assuming the name Siṅgh. Thousands more accepted this initiation.

Feeling increasingly threatened, the hill rājās approached emperor *Auraṅgzeb for military aid against Gobind Siṅgh's khālsā. After several engagements and the protracted siege of Anaṇḍpur, the Gurū accepted the Mughals' false promise of safe conduct, and evacuated Anaṇḍpur. The enemy pursued him to Chamkaur where his two elder sons died fighting. He escaped, at the insistence of his Sikhs, only to learn of the deaths of his mother and younger sons, the latter by order of Wazīr Khān, governor of Sirhind. From Dīnā he sent the *Zafarnāmā to Auraṅgzeb. At Khidrānā (*Muktsar) his followers were victorious against Wazīr Khān's men. The Gurū withdrew to Talvaṇḍī Sābo (*Damdama Sāhib) where he dictated the *Ādi Granth to *Manī Siṅgh.

On Auraṅgzeb's death in 1707 CE Gobind Siṅgh supported the succession of Bahādur Shāh who, however, would not take punitive action against Wazīr Khān. The Gurū proceeded to *Nandeṛ, where he commissioned *Bandā Siṅgh to inflict punishment upon Wazīr Khān and other persecutors of the Sikhs. Gobind Siṅgh was fatally wounded by two Pathān assassins. He bade his Sikhs regard the Ādi Granth as Gurū and died 7 Oct. 1708.

Gobind Siṅgh emphasized martial virtues in defending religious freedom against persecution. He believed he had been divinely ordained 'to spread the faith—go and extend true religion throughout the world and divert the people from evil paths'. (*Bachitra Nāṭak*). Adoration of God's holiness and majesty is expressed in new epithets (e.g. *akāl* (timeless), *sarvloh* (all-iron), 'Sword', and 'Punisher of Evil', as well as 'Gracious' and 'Benign'). Pious Sikhs daily recite his *jāp, *savayye, and *chaupaī in *Nitnem.

Our sources for Gobind Siṅgh's life are his *hukamnāmās (edicts) and autobiographical *Bachitra Nāṭak*, Mughal records of Auraṅgzeb's and Bahādur Shāh's reigns, and the later Sikh chronicles, Gur Bilās and Sūraj Parkāś. While affirming the insights of his predecessors, Gobind Siṅgh infused the Sikhs with a new discipline and transferred authority to the *panth (community) and *Granth (scriptures), so ending the line of human Gurūs.

See HOLĀ MAHALLĀ; NĀMDHĀRĪ; RAṄGHṚETĀ.

M. S. Deora, *Guru Gobind Singh: A Literary Survey* (1989); S. S. Kohli, *The Life and Ideals of Guru Gobind Singh* . . . (1986); J. S. Ramdev, *Guru Gobind Singh: A Descriptive Bibliography* (1967).

Gobutsu (Jap., 'five buddhas'). The five buddhas, distributed in the two *maṇḍalas, of Japanese esoteric Buddhism. They are *Dainichi in the centre, with, in the Diamond Realm mandala: Ashuku (east), Hōshō (south), *Amida (west), Fukūjōju (north); and in the Matrix Realm mandala: Hōdō (E.), Kaifukeō (S.), Muryōju (W.), Tenkuraion (N.).

God. The absolute and real who is, than which nothing greater can be conceived, the unproduced Producer of all that is, without whom nothing that is could be or could remain in being; or, alternatively, the *projection into supposed reality of human fears, neuroses, and abject needs (*Freud), or of human ideals which can never be realized (*Feuerbach), or of the requirements to perpetuate the conditions of alienation in the interests of some party (*Marx); in this second case, language about 'God' is a surrogate language about humanity or human persons ('Theology is anthropology'). The possibility of so wide a contrast between theistic realism and psychological unrealism arises because God (supposing God is) is not an object among objects in a universe, able to be discovered and/or explored, as are atoms, quasars, and the dark side of the moon. Nor is God the conclusion of an argument, although argument points to the probability of God, at least in the sense that the universe makes more sense if it exists as a consequence of one who produces and sustains it, than otherwise. For examples of such arguments, see QUINQUE VIAE. Since God cannot be produced as an object among objects, and since God is, whether this or any other universe happens to exist, it follows that God cannot be described in language, since God is far apart from humanly apprehended categories in time and space (i.e. is transcendent). In all theistic religions, this has led inevitably to *apophatic theology, to the recognition that we can only say with confidence what God is not, (e.g. *via negativa, *neti neti, *ein-sof). However, if God is indeed the creator of the universe we inhabit, then it would be reasonable to expect that there is some relation between his nature and that which it has produced, hence the importance of the *analogy and of analogy of being, *analogia entis*. Even so, if we cannot speak positively about God without always qualifying the words ('God is a Father, but not exactly as we understand and experience fathers'), then perhaps 'God' is qualified, so to speak, out of existence: in relation to suffering and *evil, this qualifying of the claim that God is Love (but not exactly as we understand love, because we would prosecute a parent who treated his children as God apparently treats his) led A. N. Flew to proclaim the death of God by a thousand cuts. Psychological unrealism (as above) then concludes that a God so qualified cannot have real, transcendent existence: 'God' is a projection, a way of speaking about, or justifying, other things and giving to them a supreme or ultimate status.

Theistic religions have always been aware of the inadequacy of human language about God, and of the ways in which people are prone to project onto God their own ideas and programmes. When people worship as God that which is less than God, this issues in *idolatry, which may take literal form. All theistic religions have condemned idolatry because it falls far short of what God would be if God were indeed and truly to be God. That condemnation of idolatry is made even by Hindus who are frequently accused by others, especially by Muslims, of worshipping idols. The distinction is instructive, since it means that even in the human affection of *worship, it is known that no words or images can contain or describe God, and yet the experienced consequence of God creates its own and continuing demand for, or invitation into, relationship. Religious and theological traditions then offer the inadequacies of language, sign, *symbol, *icon, etc. (or images in the case of Hindus), as a means of initiating an apprehension of God which is qualitatively *sui generis*—one which is capable of lifting life from the mundane (whose delights, satisfactions, and contentments are as real as its degradations, horrors, and betrayals) to a point of balance and rescue where the entire universe is seen as a start and not as a conclusion.

In the terms, therefore, of a critically realistic theology, religions accept that anything which is said about God is approximate, provisional, corrigible, and mainly wrong; but the question still remains, Is it wrong about some One? Even those religions which are most secure in their confidence that God has overcome the epistemic gap of transcendence, by revealing his word and his will, accept that all *revelation is conveyed contingently through words which are not identical with that concerning which they purport to be about—in terms which are approximate. In the end, all religions are bound to issue the invitation, 'Taste and see'. The experience and procedures of relatedness to what has been described in those approximate ways as *El, Zeus, *Allāh, *Viṣṇu, *Amida, *Brahman, etc., have built up through the millennia an impressive reliability of reference and relationship—and a reliability which has encouraged constant correction as successive generations have learnt, with increasing security, something more of the nature of the One with whom they have to deal. At the same time, that which is God has seemed, unequivocally, to be, so to speak, 'dealing with them': it is in this way that the major transformations in the human understanding of God have been made. In ways (which humans have tested and winnowed through time, and in virtually all cultures) of *prayer, *worship, *sacrifice, *contemplation, *meditation, *art, *music, artefact, the reliability of the communities of faith has been tested—and has been tested also against the extreme ease with which the transcendence of God can be exploited, so that religions are fruitful soil for the seeds of exploitation, profit, and deceit.

But no matter how easily religions are converted into a commercial confidence trick, the fact remains that such exploitation is parasitic on truth. Theistic religious traditions offer approximate characterizations of God which are themselves being winnowed through time. In each tradition, there emerge characterizations of God which impress themselves on the style in which its adherents live. In Judaism, the major emphasis is on holiness, in Christianity on the commitments of love which reflect a relatedness in the Godhead itself; in Islam on mercy and demand; among Hindus on the real presence of God in every circumstance. In no case is the human response to God a private or decontextualized affair. Other traditions have drawn attention to the misuse of God in human affairs which makes of God a substitute for the effort that is required of oneself if any advance is going to be made towards truth: thus Jains and Buddhists allow that theistic language has reference, but such theistic realities as there are, are themselves appearances on the way to their own release or enlightenment.

The logic of God, therefore, remains, that if God does indeed turn out to be God, it is God that God will turn out to be. While theistic religions sometimes deny this logic in the style of their relations to each other, the ways and the words of their attentiveness to God leave such a mark on the possibilities of life now, that the nature of the future remains open: it is necessarily the case that All remains yet to be known.

For names, see Index, Names of God, Names of Goddess.

W. P. Alston, *Perceiving God: The Epistemology of Religious Experience* (1991); J. W. Bowker, *The Sense of God . . .* (1973) and *Licensed Insanities: Religions and Belief in God in the Contemporary World* (1987); B. Davies, *Thinking About God* (1985); J. Holm and J. Bowker (eds.), *Picturing God (Themes in Religious Studies)* (1994); C. M. LaCugna, *God for Us: The Trinity and Christian Life* (1991); J. Pereira, *Hindu Theology: A Reader* (1976); R. Swinburne, *The Coherence of Theism*, (1977) and *The Existence of God* (1979).

God, name of in Judaism. According to Jewish theology God is One; there is no other (Deuteronomy 6. 4). All other gods are unequivocally rejected (Exodus 20. 3–5). God is unique; no likeness can be made of him (Exodus 20. 4). He is all-powerful (Job 42. 2), all-knowing (Job 28. 23), omnipresent (Psalms 139. 7–12), eternal (Isaiah 40. 6–8), and unchangeable (Isaiah 41. 4). As Isaiah put it, 'Who is God, but the Lord? And who is a rock, except our God?' Although, historically, this understanding was not achieved without struggle (see EL), it becomes biblically the paramount realization. First and foremost, God is the creator of everything that is. Nature reveals the glory of God (Psalms 19. 2), but God is not identical with his creation. Although the account in Genesis does not necessarily imply creation out of nothing, this has been the Jewish understanding. Besides creating the richness and diversity of nature which culminates in the creation of human beings (see ADAM and EVE), God also created the moral *law which is built into the fabric of the universe. Jews believe that God revealed himself in the unfolding of history and that he is king of all the nations (Jeremiah 10. 7). However, the Jews themselves are *chosen in a particular sense (Amos 3. 2) and, by making a *covenant with his people (e.g. Exodus 24. 7 ff.), *Israel remains God's witness (Isaiah 44. 8), and will be the agency of *salvation for all humanity. The covenant demands obedience to God's will, his *Torah, the *Six Hundred and Thirteen commandments and their explanations and interpretations as embodied in the *Mishnah, the *Talmud and the *responsa. In the Bible, God is portrayed as a Father, king, shepherd, judge, healer, guide, husband, predominantly masculine and patriarchal attributes; but God is also portrayed displaying female and maternal characteristics (e.g. and especially in Isaiah 24–7, 34–5, 40–66). Later Jewish philosophers, such as *Maimonides, argued that God has no attributes and that the biblical descriptions only reflect human reactions to his activities. In any case, the appropriate human response to God is love: 'You shall love the Lord your God with all your heart and with all your soul and with all your might' (Deuteronomy 6. 5), and prayer is the natural expression of this love. God is holy, and in so far as human beings are created in the image of God (Genesis 1. 26), they must seek to *imitate his holiness.

Inevitably, the biblical concept of God came to be discussed in ways affected by the philosophical cultures of later times. So *Philo, the learned Jew of 1st cent. Alexandria, was influenced by Plato; Maimonides in the 10th cent. by Aristotle; and the modern philosopher Franz *Rosenzweig by existentialism. Through the categories of the secular philosophers, such subjects as the attributes of God, the relationship of God to the world, the nature of God, and his existence were discussed. In its confrontations with paganism, Christianity, and Islam, Judaism was compelled to define the nature of monotheism and differentiate it from polytheism, dualism, trinitarianism, pantheism, and deism.

Because of God's exalted nature, his name is sacred. The *tetragrammaton is never pronounced, and *Adonai (the Lord) or Ha-Shem (the name) is substituted. In the Aramaic *targums, the name of God is often translated *memra* (word). Similarly, euphemisms are used by the *rabbis, such as *Rahmana* (the Merciful), *Ha-Makom* (the Place) or *Ha-Kadosh Barukh Hu* (the Holy One, blessed be He). The *Kabbalists called God *Ein-Sof (the infinite): there is nothing to be said about him, and he can only be known by his *Sefirot or emanations which are single facets of his revelation. Various Hebrew terms are used of God in the Jewish scriptures. Some of the terms such as *El (God) were also used by the Canaanites. God is described as El Elyon (God most high), El ʿOlam (the everlasting God), El Shaddai (God Almighty), El Berit (God of the Covenant), Elohim (God), and Adonai (the Lord). God's proper name, YHWH, is understood in the book of Exodus to derive from the Hebrew verb 'to be' (*hyh*) and is explained as Eheyeh (Exodus 3. 14: I-Am-Who-I-Am). It has been suggested that the tetragrammaton is in fact an abbreviation of Yahweh-Asher-Eheyeh (He brings into existence whatever exists).

According to Jewish law, only the *high priest could pronounce the tetragrammaton once a year on the *Day of Atonement. The name of God cannot be erased or discarded from any document (see GENIZAH), and it is forbidden to use any of the biblical names of God in a secular context. Among very *orthodox Jews, it is even customary to avoid writing God in the vernacular, and G-d is preferred.

A. Marmorstein, *The Old Rabbinic Doctrines of God: The Names and Attributes of God* (1968).

God, names of among Sikhs. The Name (*Nām) of God has particular importance for Sikhs. The Sikhs' awareness of God draws upon the mystical, sometimes paradoxical poetry of the Ādi Granth.

Lord, Thou mighty River, all-knowing, all-seeing,
and I like a little fish in Thy great waters,
How shall I sound Thy depths?
How shall I reach Thy shores?
Wherever I go, I see Thee only
And snatched out of Thy Waters I die of separation. (p. 25)

Gurū *Nānak's luminous insights, most economically stated in the *Mul Mantra, find further expression in the compositions of later Gurūs. Many names are used for God, some familiar to Hindus (e.g. *Hari, *Śiv, *Brahmā, *Rām, Mohan) and others to Muslims (e.g. Rabb, *Allāh, Khudā, *Sāhib), but God is emphatically One (*ik onkar) and does not incarnate as an *avatāra. Above all God's name is Truth (*sat(i)nām). He is the *Sat(i)gurū by whose *grace the way of *salvation from *rebirths is revealed. He is the creator of all, and everything occurs in accordance with his will (*hukam). He is beyond attributes (*nirguṇ) and possesses all attributes (*śāguṇ), both transcendent and *immanent. Gurū *Tegh Bahādur asked, 'Why do you go to the forest to find God? He lives in all and yet remains distinct. He dwells in you as fragrance resides in a flower or the reflection in a mirror' (Ādi Granth, p. 684).

God is sustainer and destroyer—even of death. He is *nirañjan (unentangled in *māyā). He is sovereign, eternal, omnipresent, and omniscient; beyond measure, utterance, or visual representation. He is the source of light, beauty, and mercy. He dispels fear and anxiety. By the Gurū's grace and by devoted repetition of God's name (*nām simaran) he can be realized.

Gurū *Gobind Siṅgh's *jāp sings God's glory. Elsewhere Gobind Siṅgh's epithets such as 'saryloh' (all-steel) and 'bhagautī' (sword) mark a new emphasis. See AKĀL PURUKH; VĀHIGURŪ.

God, names of in Islam: see NINETY-NINE BEAUTIFUL NAMES OF GOD.

Goddess. The source of life and being, once prevalent in religious imagination, but much suppressed during the millennia of male control of religions. The same observations about the provisionality of language and symbol apply here as in the case of God: they are compounded in the case of feminine imagery of the divine by the insistence on their inadequacies in the major monotheistic religions: see FEMININE SYMBOLS.

P. Berger, *The Goddess Obscured* . . . (1985); C. Downing, *The Goddess: Mythological Images of the Feminine* (1984); E. W. Gadon, *The Once and Future Goddess* (1989); P. Monaghan, *The Book of Goddesses and Heroines* (rev. 1990); C. Olsen (ed.), *The Book of the Goddess* (1983); M. Stone, *When God was a Woman* (1976); B. G. Walker, *The Woman's Book of Symbols and Sacred Objects* (1988).

Godianism. A Nigerian remodelling of African religions as a new modern faith, formed by amalgamation in 1963 between the Cult of Aruosa ('holy place' or 'altar') or Edo National Church and the National Church of Nigeria. The former was founded in 1945 by the Oba of Benin, Akenzua II, as a somewhat Christianized form of the ancient Bini faith. The latter began in 1948–50 among educated Ibos under K. O. K. Onyioha, as a sophisticated African religion with alleged origins in ancient Egypt and supporting the movement for political independence; despite borrowing many external Christian forms, the movement repudiates Christianity as a foreign religion. It represents pride in Africa, rather than a dynamic religious development.

Godō (Jap., 'back hall'). Part of the meditation hall in a Zen monastery, and thus also the senior monk who has charge of the godō.

Godparents. The sponsors of a child to be *baptized. They undertake responsibility for the child's Christian upbringing, and at the baptism of a baby they make the promises in its name, of renouncing the devil, of faith, and of obedience. In Roman Catholic canon law there may be at most two godparents, one of each sex; in the Church of England this is the minimum required.

God's Kingdom Society. A Nigerian sabbatarian movement resembling *Jehovah's Witnesses. It was founded in 1934 in the area south of Benin City by Gideon Urhobo, a former *Roman Catholic and ex-Jehovah's Witness, and by the 1960s had achieved over 2,000 members. It has a *unitarian view of *Jesus, and adapts Christian *hymns accordingly, replacing *Christmas with the Feast of Tabernacles (*Sukkah). The worship is plain and the ethic somewhat legalistic, with toleration of polygamy and subjection of women to husbands and elders. A holy city, Salem, near Warri, serves as headquarters for extensive printing of church and publicity materials, and for commercial activities such as transport and plantations.

Goel ha-dam (in Judaism liability for punishment of those who have shed blood): see BLOODGUILT.

Gog and Magog. *Apocalyptic character and territory in the vision of *Ezekiel. According to Ezekiel 36–8, God would wage war against 'Gog of the land of Magog' at the end of time. In the *aggadah, Gog and Magog are two parallel enemies against whom the Lord battles, and they are connected with the birthpangs of the *messiah (*Sif.Num.* 76). In the New Testament (Revelation 20) the war of Gog and Magog takes place one thousand years after the first resurrection. They are represented in giant statues at the Guildhall in London, as porters of the royal palace and descendants of giants.

Gogyaku-zai (Jap., 'five rebellious sins'). The five deadly sins in Japanese Buddhism: killing your father, killing your mother, killing an *arakan* (*arhat), causing the Buddha's appearance body to bleed, causing schism in the Buddhist order. Any of these leads to reappearance in hell (*jigoku), for torment of many *kalpas.

Gohei (Jap.), a wand-like implement used in Shinto observances. The gohei is formed by attaching strips of paper or cloth, usually white, to a sacred staff which may be waved by priests and their attendants over worshippers' heads to signal purification, or may be used to indicate the presence of a deity (*kami).

Gohonzon (tablet bearing Buddhist mantra): see DAIMOKU.

Go-i (Jap.). A classification in Zen Buddhism, first established by *Tung-shan Liang-chieh, of five degrees of enlightenment (*kenshō, *satori). They are laid out in pairs, each of which summarizes how the phenomenal is more truly to be understood: (i) *sho-chu-hen*, '*hen* in the midst of *shō*', the phenomena are immediate, but are understood as manifesting the underlying, true reality; (ii) *hen-chu-sho*, '*shō* in the midst of *hen*', non-differentiation is then achieved; (iii) *sho-chu-rai*, 'it coming out of *shō*', body and mind drop away as the realization of *śūnyatā obtains; (iv) *ken-chu-shi*, 'entering between the two', the realization of how śūnyatā itself vanishes (into phenomena); (v) *ken-chu-to* 'arrival in the midst of both', form and emptiness interpenetrate, in a realization of dynamic non-interaction.

Goi (non-Jewish person): see GENTILE.

Go-i-kōan (form of kōan in Rinzai): see KŌAN.

Goindvāl (Sāhib). Sikh place of *pilgrimage (*tīrath) 50 km. SE of *Amritsar. Its name is derived from Goindā who encountered obstacles in building the town until Gurū *Aṅgad commanded Amar Dās to assist him and subsequently to reside there. Here Emperor *Akbar later visited him. Traditionally his house was the now revered Chubārā Sāhib: here Rām Dās later lived, was installed as Gurū, and died, and here Gurū *Arjan Dev was born. In one room is preserved the palanquin in which Arjan Dev carried manuscripts when compiling the *Ādi Granth.

At Goindvāl in 1559 Gurū *Amar Dās instructed his Sikhs to dig a deep well (*bāolī*) with eighty-four steps for pilgrims to descend to the water, a number corresponding to the traditional 84,000,000 births and deaths in the cycle of transmigration. Near the well stands Bāolī Sāhib *Gurdwārā. Every autumn a local *melā commemorates the death of Gurū Amar Dās.

Gökalp, Ziya (1875–1924). A Turkish liberal reformer who prepared his country's orientation towards the establishment of a modern secular state. His programme of reform was a mixture of Turkish nationalism, socialism, secularism, and education. He supported Kemal Atatürk's policy of Westernization, and was one of his leading advisers. Turkish authorities have on occasion revived the cult of Ziya Gökalp to check the rising tide of conservative Islam in universities.

Goke-shichishū (Jap., 'five-houses, seven-schools'). A classification of the seven Ch'an Buddhist schools, during the T'ang period, which derived from five lineages: (i) *Rinzai from *Lin-chi I-hsuan (Jap., Rinzai Gigen); (ii) Igyo from Kuei-shan Ling-yu (Jap., Isan Reiyū) and from *Yang-shan Hui-chi (Jap., Kyōzan Ejaku); (iii) *Sōtō from *Tung-shan Liang-chieh (Jap., Tōzan Ryōkai) and from *Ts'ao-shan Pen-chi (Jap., Sōzan Honjaku); (iv) *Ummon from *Yün-Men Wen-yen (Jap., Ummon Bun'en); (v) *Hogen from *Fa-yen Wen-i (Jap., Hogen Bun'eki). Rinzai then split, to make up seven: (vi) *Yōgi from Yang-ch'i Fang-hui (Jap., Yōgi Hōe); (vii) Ōryō from *Huang-lung Hui-nan (Jap., Ōryō E'nan).

Gokhalé, Gopāḷ Krishna (1863–1915). An Indian political leader, born near Chipḷooṇ in the W. Indian region of Konkaṇ. He taught at Fergusson College, Poona, between 1884 and 1902, and considered Mr Justice M. G. *Rānadé as his mentor. His influence on religious matters (via politics) was great, because he was a staunch advocate of constitutional methods and reforms for Indian Home Rule, and was of importance for *Gāndhī. He visited England to represent Indian opinion and submit constitutional demands to the British Parliament many times between 1897 and 1915. He founded the Servants of India Society and encouraged educated Indians to become servants of India. Gāndhī considered Professor G. K. Gokhalé as his political *guru.

Gokuraku. Jap. for *Sukhāvatī.

Golden Book (mythology of Buddhist-influenced millennial movement): see TELAKHON.

Golden Calf. The golden statue made by *Aaron in Exodus 32. Anxious at the absence of *Moses on Mount *Sinai, Aaron was entreated by the Israelites to give them a god. When Moses saw the people worshipping the golden calf, he smashed the tablets of the *law, melted down the image, and scattered the gold powder over water which he compelled the Israelites to drink. Plague subsequently fell on the camp. According to the *aggadah, 'There is not a misfortune that *Israel has suffered which is not partly a retribution for the sin of the calf' (*B.Sanh.* 102a). According to *Pes.K.* 159a, 'The *High Priest would not enter the *Holy of Holies wearing any item of gold, lest it recall the Golden Calf.'

Golden Legend (Lat., *Legenda Aurea*). A manual consisting of lives of the *saints and of episodes in the lives of *Jesus and *Mary, making connection with Christian festivals, in the order of the Church *calendar. It was written by the *Dominican Jacob of Voragine between 1255 and 1266. It is of spiritual, not of historical, value. As a popular book of piety it was very successful, appearing in French in the 14th cent., and in edns. in many languages from the early printing-presses. It also furnished subjects for medieval artists.

Golden Lotus (form of religious Taoism): see CH'ÜAN-CHEN TAO.

Golden Rule. Epitome of ethical action, occurring, at least proverbially, in most religions, but associated particularly with Judaism and Christianity. In Judaism, it occurs most often in negative form: 'Whatever is hateful to you, do not do to another' (*Hillel in *B.Shab.* 31a, when asked by a *gentile to teach him the whole of *Torah while standing on one foot; cf. Tobit 4. 14); though Hillel said more positively, 'Love all creatures' (*Avot* 1. 12). In the New Testament, it appears, unpacking Leviticus 19. 18, 'Love your fellow as yourself', in the form: 'As you would that people should do to you, do likewise to them' (Matthew 7. 12; Luke 6. 31).

Golden Temple (Sikh holy place): see AMRITSAR; HARIMANDIR.

Golem (Heb., 'shapeless matter'). An embryo (Psalms 139. 16) or stupid person (*Avot* 5. 9), and eventually a creature brought into being artificially through the use of God's name. The Hebrew word is used for a wide range of incomplete states, and also for a robot-like creation. In medieval Jewish legends, the golem are created by use of the *tetragrammaton or by the power of the word *emet* ('truth'). At the outset, they are created as useful servants, but (as with comparable legends in other cultures), they either proved to be too stupid to do the work (e.g. on being asked to act as a *gentile and light the *Sabbath fire, a golem is likely to ignite the whole town), or they used their great strength malignantly and got completely out of control.

Golgotha (the place of Jesus' crucifixion): see CALVARY.

Goliath. *Philistine giant who was killed by young *David. According to 1 Samuel 17, David volunteered to fight against the Philistine champion, Goliath, felled him with a stone from his sling, and cut off his head with his own sword. As a result of this incident, David became known to King *Saul, although the text also indicates that David became known to Saul through playing soothing music when the king was disturbed by an evil spirit.

Goloka (Skt., 'Loka of cows'). Kṛṣṇa's paradise on Mount *Meru. It was added to the original seven *lokas, and it became for the *Vaiśnavites a term for eternal bliss.

Goma (Jap. for Skt., *homa). A burnt offering. Fire rituals (*gegoma*) are of particular importance in esoteric Buddhism, both for averting disasters and for increasing *merit. They should be accompanied by interiorized ritual (*naigoma*), which is in effect meditation. Fire represents the burning out of evil desires, etc.

Gomel blessing (Heb., *ha-Gomel*, 'he who bestows favours'). Jewish blessing offered in thanksgiving to God by one who has lived through a dangerous experience: 'Blessed are you, O Lord our God, King of the universe, who bestows favours on the undeserving and has bestowed favours on me.'

Gomi(-no)-zen: see CH'AN; ICHIMI-ZEN.

Gongen (Jap., temporary manifestation). An incarnation, e.g. of a *Shinto deity, or of a *buddha or *bodhisattva.

Gonsen-kōan (form of kōan in Rinzai): see KŌAN.

Good Friday. The Friday before *Easter commemorating Jesus' crucifixion. In liturgical churches it is a day of *penance. In the Roman Catholic Church, Good Friday and the following day (*Holy Saturday) are the only days in the year on which *mass is not celebrated. Instead the rite includes communion with *hosts consecrated on *Maundy Thursday. Also part of this rite is the *veneration of the cross. Besides the liturgy on this day, the most usual devotion is the *Three Hours' Service. In some Protestant churches, Good Friday is kept as a feast rather than a fast (as a thanksgiving for human redemption), and it is often a special day for the celebration of the Lord's Supper.

Good Samaritan. The *Samaritan in Jesus' *parable (Luke 10. 30–7) who, in contrast to two Jewish worthies who 'passed by on the other side', took it upon himself to care for a traveller who had been beaten and robbed on the road. His action demonstrates the answer to the question, 'Who is my neighbour?' (Luke 10. 29).

Good Shepherd. A title of *Christ derived from his discourse in John 10. 7–18 and the '*parable of the good shepherd' in Luke 15. 3–7. Elsewhere in the New Testament, the theme is taken up in Hebrews 13. 20 and 1 Peter 2. 25, 5. 4. In early Christian art, Christ was frequently represented as the Good Shepherd with a lamb on his shoulders.

Gopastami (cow festival): see GO.

Gopī (Skt., 'keeper of cows'). The women cowherds at *Vṛndāvana, who are involved with *Kṛṣṇa in the love-affairs of his youth. They come to symbolize, both the soul's devotion (*bhakti) to God, and also the legitimacy of flouting convention in the service of God:

> How wonderful was the yearning of the gopīs for Kṛṣṇa! They were seized with divine madness at the very sight of the black *tamāla* tree. Separation from Kṛṣṇa created such a fire of anguish in *Rādhā's heart that it dried up even the tears in her eyes: her tears would disappear in steam (Sri *Ramakrishna).

Gorakhnāth, Gorakṣa, or **Gorakṣanātha.** A Hindu yogin of *c.*10/11 cent. CE, of the Nātha *tantra cult, which claimed magical and occult powers through the practice of *yoga. He is said by some to have originated *Haṭha-yoga, and to have founded the order of Kānphaṭa yogīs (so-called from 'ear' + 'split': they wear heavy earrings after initiation; they are also called Gorakhnāthis). Gorakhnāth had the power to grow trees from seeds in a matter of hours, to revive the dead, to prolong his own life, etc. Tibetan Buddhists claim that he was originally a Buddhist. Two works in Skt. are attributed to him (*Siddhasiddhāntapaddhati* and *Gorakśa sátaka*), together with various hymns, but all are doubtful.

G. W. Briggs, *Gorakhnāth* . . . (1938); S. Dasgupta, *Obscure Religious Cults* (3rd edn., 1969).

Gordon, Judah (1831–92). Heb. writer. Through his poetry and journalism, Gordon inveighed against the rigidity of the *rabbinic leaders of his time. He was a prominent supporter of the *haskalah and, after moving to St Petersburg, he became the director of the Society for the Promotion of Culture among the Jews, and subsequently editor of the Hebrew daily newspaper *Ha-Meliz*. He believed that knowledge and technology must be spiritualized: 'With the redemption of the soil must go the redemption of the soul.' In his later years, disillusioned by the Russian *pogroms, he advocated emigration to W. Europe, but he came to realize that *anti-Semitism was endemic: 'The whole world is Israel's grave, and the books of Israel are but the epitaph inscribed on the tomb.' He urged the revival of the Hebrew language, and, although not a committed *Zionist, he proposed the founding of a society for those going to Palestine.

A. B. Rhine, *Leon Gordon: An Appreciation* (1910).

Gore, Charles (1853–1932). Anglican theologian and bishop of Oxford. As first principal of Pusey House, Oxford, he exercised great influence on students with his concern to bring *Catholic teaching to bear on personal holiness and social problems. He also mediated the importance of biblical criticism. Later, as canon of Westminster and as bishop (of Worcester, and then of Birmingham), his writings, especially on Christian apologetic (*Belief in God*, 1921; *Belief in Christ*, 1922; *The Holy Spirit and the Church*, 1924), were widely read. He also remained a strong, and increasingly conservative, exponent of *high-church principles. Of particular and far-reaching importance was his contribution to the establishment of the Community of the Resurrection, founded in 1892. This male Anglican community (whose members are often known as Mirfield Fathers, from the move made to Mirfield in 1898) aims to relate community life to the modern world, and did so to remarkable effect in S. Africa in sustaining resistance to apartheid.

J. Carpenter, *Gore* . . . (1960); G. L. Prestige, *The Life of Charles Gore* (1935).

Gorinsotoba (Jap., 'sotoba [*stūpa] with five sections'). Tombs (which became common after the Kamakura period in Japan) with five stone sections, of different shapes, placed on top of each other. The bottom stone is square, representing earth, inscribed with the Skt. letter *A; the next is round, representing water, inscribed VA; the next is triangular, fire, RA; crescent, wind, HA; jewel (*mani*) shaped, space, KHA.

Gosāla, Makkhali (founder): see AJIVIKAS.

Gosan or **Gozan.** 'Five mountains' (Chin., *wu-shan*), the federation of Ch'an/Zen monasteries, in groups of five, especially of Hang-chou, Ming-chou, and then in Japan of Kamakura and Kyōto. Because monasteries were often built on mountains, the word *shan* (Jap., *san* or *zan*) came to mean 'monastery'.

Gosan-bungaku (Jap., 'five-mountain literature'). Collective term for writings from the *gosan (federation) of Kyōto, during the Muromachi period (1338–1573).

Gose (Jap., 'the hereafter'). The afterlife in general; in particular, birth after death in the domain of *Amida.

Goseki (Jap.), 'Trace of enlightenment' in Zen Buddhism, of one who has had some experience of enlightenment, but still carries, 'the stench of enlightenment', i.e. has not yet learned to live as though he might or might not have had such experience, since he should be totally detached from it.

Goshichinichi mishiho. The annual Japanese *Shingon prayer ritual, called 'the latter seven days', since *Shinto ceremonies occupied the first week of the New Year, and this ceremony was held from the 8th to the 14th. Its purpose was prayer for the emperor, the state, peace and prosperity, etc., during the year to come. It was inaugurated by *Kūkai in 834, suspended during the *Meiji restoration, revived in 1883, and still continues.

Goso Hōen (Jap., for Wu-tsu Fa-yen): see KŌAN.

Gospel (Gk., *euangelion*; OE, *godspel*, 'good news'). 1. The content of Christian preaching. It is *Paul's usual word for his own message (e.g. Romans 1. 16, 1 Thessalonians 1. 5). In *Jesus' sayings it appears occasionally, e.g. Mark 8. 35.

2. A book containing sayings and stories of Jesus. This meaning apparently derives from Mark 1. 1, 'the beginning of the gospel'. Since there was only one Good News, the four separate gospels in the New Testament were distinguished as 'according to' *Matthew, *Mark, *Luke, and *John. How far the gospels resemble secular biographies is debatable, but the absence of biographical details and presence of theological interpretation are obvious. All four gospels were probably written for church use with preaching and teaching in mind. Other (*apocryphal) gospels more or less followed the model of the New Testament ones, but contribute little or nothing of historical value. See also SYNOPTIC GOSPELS; THOMAS; DIATESSARON; APOCRYPHA.

3. The reading from the gospels in the Christian *eucharist. It comes traditionally after all the other lections, and is read or intoned by the *deacon while the congregation are standing. In the Roman Catholic mass until 1964, a *Last Gospel, usually John 1. 1–14, was also read at the very end.

Gospel of Truth. A work on Christian life and salvation found among the Coptic texts of *Nag Hammadi. The title comes from the opening words, though the work is not properly a *gospel. It deals with the mission of *Jesus as 'the Word' or 'the Name' of the Father, with his teaching and his death. It is probably the work of this title by *Valentinus which *Irenaeus mentioned, in which case it must represent his early less unorthodox thought (before *c.*150 CE).

Tr. K. Goobel (1960).

Gosvamins (Hindu group concerned with aesthetics and religious experience): see ABHINAVAGUPTA.

Gosvāmīs (disciples of Caitanya): see CAITANYA.

Gotama or **Gautama** (Pāli, Skt.). 1. The clan (Skt., *gotra*) to which the historical *Buddha belonged. It is hence the name by which his non-Buddhist contemporaries refer to him, and a name used when distinguishing him from other Buddhas. His own tribe, the Śākyas, were imputed to be descendants of the Vedic *ṛṣi of that name.

2. The founder of the *Nyāya school of Hindu philosophy (*darśana), and author of a law book (*dharmaśāstra).

3. A Vedic *ṛṣi, to whom the composition of one of the finest hymns in the **Ṛg Veda* (1. 92) is attributed.

Gothic. An architectural style in N. Europe from early 12th cent. to 16th, and, as Gothic revival, in 19th cent. Thence it is applied to literature and religion to denote the opaquely mysterious—to some, grotesque. The term 'Gothic' was itself one of derogation when it was introduced during the Italian renaissance to describe the buildings and art of the Middle Ages as derived from the barbarian Goths. In fact, the Gothic styles arose from Romanesque and produced many spectacular achievements, not least in the innovations of rib vaulting and exterior flying buttresses which freed the walls to be vehicles of light, mediated, often, through stained glass. The cathedral at Chartres is a brilliant illustration of this achievement. Sculpture and carving followed the lead in exhibiting, not just the surface of the Christian story, but the feelings involved—thereby also evoking a passionate response.

L. Grodecki, *Gothic Architecture* (tr. 1977); S. Halliday and L. Lushington, *Stained Glass* (1982); E. Mâle, *The Gothic Image* (tr. 1958) and *Notre-Dame de Chartres* (1948); A Martindale, *Gothic Art from the 12th to the 15th Century* (1967) and *Gothic Art* (1985); C. Wilson, *The Gothic Cathedral* (1989).

Gotra. (Skt., 'cow-shed', 'assemblage', 'clan'). In India, the exogamous group of all persons (especially *brahmans) related by descent through the male line from a common male ancestor. According to an ancient text on Hindu law, the *Baudhāyanaśrautasūtra*, there are only eight gotras, namely the progeny of the seven great sages Viśvāmitra, Jamadagni, Bharadvāja, Gautama, Atri, Vasiṣṭha, and Kaśyapa, plus Agastya. In fact there are more gotras, though these eight may have been the primary ones. It is possible that in the earlier *Vedic period, descent was traced through teacher and pupil as well as through father and son. *Āpastamba Dharmasūtra* states that if a person does not know his own gotra he should take that of his teacher. In later times the word gotra came to mean, by extension, any family name or surname.

In *Mahāyāna Buddhism the term is employed to denote categories of religious practitioners on the basis of psychological, spiritual, and intellectual capacity. The *Sandhinirmocanasūtra* recognizes three gotras which seem to coincide with the three vehicles (*triyāna*) accepted by the Yogācāra (*Vijñanavāda). These are, in increasing order of attainment, the gotra of the auditors (*śrāvakayāna*), the gotra of the solitary *Buddhas (*pratyekabuddhayāna), and the gotra of the Thus-gone (*tathāgatayāna). Some texts add a further two classes; an indeterminate class (*aniyatagotra*) of spiritual beings, and for those outside the Buddhist communion—the so-called *agotra*. Some Buddhist commentators have suggested that this last class may be incapable of achieving enlightenment. *Daśabhūmikasūtra* speaks of a hidden intrinsic substance (*mahāmaṇiratna*) which may be mined and purified, in a clear parable of the Buddhist path. This precious substance is said to be found in a jewel mine (*ratnagotra*). Some recent scholars have concluded therefore that a subsidiary meaning of gotra may be mine or matrix. Such a view is reinforced by the statement in *Asaṅga's *Mahāyānasamgraha* that gotra is the seed of the dharma body (*dharmakāya*, see TRIKĀYA) in every living being. The term does not occur in any technical sense in the Pāli *Tripiṭaka but simply refers to all persons descended, or supposed to have descended, from a common ancestor. Thus the Buddha is held to be descended from the brahman clan or gotra of Gautama.

Gott-trunckener mensch ('God-intoxicated man'): see SPINOZA.

Govinda (Skt., 'cow-finder'). In Hindu mythology, another name for *Kṛṣṇa or *Viṣṇu. Although this name is often regarded as originating from the circumstances of Kṛṣṇa's early life as a cowherd, it is also possible that it may have been an epithet which was transferred to Viṣṇu from *Indra, whose great deed of killing *Vṛtra was believed to have freed the rain-clouds or cows of heaven. It is also sometimes connected with Viṣṇu's appearance as *Varāha, the boar which finds the earth (frequently personified as a cow) beneath the cosmic ocean.

Govinda, Lama Anāgārika (1898–1985). Interpreter of Tibetan Buddhism to the W. and founder of Ārya Maitreya Mandala. He was born E. L. Hoffmann of Bolivian and German parents. He studied art and archaeology and became an artist. He went to Śri Lankā in 1928, in pursuit of an interest in burial mounds, and was attracted by the Buddhism which he encountered. He became an *anāgārika. From a conference in Darjeeling, he felt a strong compulsion to go to Tibet, where he met his *guru, Tomo Geshe Rinpoche. He made many journeys in Tibet, and described both these and his reasons for transferring to Tibetan Buddhism, and for moving 'from the placid life of Ceylon's tropical paradise into the pandemonium of an Himalayan blizzard and the strange surroundings of a Tibetan monastery' in *The Way of the White Clouds* (1966). He gave a more technical introduction to Tibetan Buddhism in *Foundations of Tibetan Mysticism* (1960), and to the analysis of human nature in *The Psychological Attitude of Early Buddhism*, (1937, 1961).

Govindapāda. The teacher of *Śaṅkara, also known as Govindabhagavatpāda. Nothing is known about him apart from later traditional accounts, according to which he was born in Kashmir, and while wandering about India met his teacher, *Gauḍapāda, on the banks of the Narmadā River. He settled there in a cave-hermitage, where Śaṅkara happened to meet him later on and became his disciple. No works attributed to Govindapāda survive.

Goy (non-Jewish person): see GENTILE.

Goyim (non-Jewish people): see GENTILE.

Gozan (Jap., 'five mountains'). The five major *Zen temples designated by the Japanese government, in order of precedence (though this order changed from time to time). Initially (14th cent.) they were in *Kamakura: Kenchōji, Engakuji, Jufukuji, Jōchiji, Jōmyōji. Later in the same century, five further temples were designated in *Kyōto: Tenryuji, Shōkokuji, Kenninji, Tōkufuji, Manjuji.

Gozan Zen (form of Zen Buddhism in Japan): see RINZAI-SHŪ.

Gozu (school of Ch'an Buddhism): see FA-JUNG.

Grace. 1. In Christian theology, the expression of God's love in his free unmerited favour or assistance. According to the New Testament (mostly *Paul), it is conferred through faith (Romans 4. 16); is displayed in particular divine acts, especially in the death of Christ (Romans 3. 21–5; Hebrews 2. 9); and is an endowment of ministers (1 Corinthians 15. 10) and others (1 Corinthians 16. 23). The manner of its conferral has, however, been a subject of discussion since the 4th cent. and is now a characteristic matter of difference between *Roman Catholics and *Protestants.

In Catholic theology, grace is characterized as a supernatural power, lost by human beings at the *Fall, which elevates and sanctifies human nature so that it is capable of enjoying communion with God. Against a *Pelagian view, the distinction is made between prevenient grace, anticipating any move on a person's part toward God, and subsequent grace ('actual grace' for particular needs) in which God co-operates with a person after his conversion. Protestant theology rejects this view of grace along with the related conceptions of *merit and of the *sacraments. Instead it is seen primarily as God's action in his unmerited forgiveness and *justification of sinners.

'Grace' then becomes a category for describing free and uncoerced actions in other religions, especially of Kṛṣṇa in the **Bhagavad-gītā*: see e.g. PRASĀDA; RĀMĀNUJA (for *anugraha*); PRAPATTI. As a concept, grace is of great importance for Sikhs, in Gurū *Nānak's hymns and in all subsequent Sikh theology. Analogous to the benedictory glance of a human guru, this sense of God's loving favour is conveyed by the words *praśad, kirpā, nadar, bakhśīś*, *bhāṇā, daiā, mihar*, and *taras*. This concept of grace is not a denial of *karma, but God's initiative can override the result of bad actions. However, the individual must strive to improve. In *Japjī it is said that, whereas the nature of our birth springs from karma, the gate of *salvation results from grace (Ādi Granth 2). Through this grace one meets the Gurū and perceives the path to union with God through meditation on his *Nām. 'Only if one receives His grace does one obtain the Lord. Without his grace he cannot be obtained' (Ādi Granth 28).

R. Haight, *The Experience and Language of Grace* (1979); S. Kulandran, *Grace in Christianity and Hinduism* (1964).

2. Short prayers of invocation and thanksgiving, before and after meals. They are natural and characteristic in Judaism. The *rabbis taught that it was wrong to 'enjoy of this world without a prior *benediction'. The *blessing over bread ('who bringest forth bread from the earth') is based on Psalm 104. 14 and exempts the diner from further blessings. Grace after meals consists of four blessings—praising God for providing food, for the good land, a request for mercy on the Jewish people and thanks for God's goodness, coupled with various petitions. The *Birkat ha-Mazon* (blessing after meals) is a central liturgical practice in the observant Jewish home. It is modified on various occasions, and slightly different versions are used in different communities. It should only, however, be said after meals at which bread has been eaten—on other occasions other forms of grace are recited.

Gradual (Lat., *gradus*, 'step'). The *antiphons, usually from the Psalms, sung after the first lesson from the Bible in the *mass. The name derives from the practice of singing it on the altar steps or while the deacon was ascending the steps of the pulpit or dais from which the *Gospel is sung. Since 1969, a responsorial Psalm has become usual. In Anglican churches a hymn ('gradual hymn') is usually sung at this point.

Gradual enlightenment/sudden enlightenment. Schools within Ch'an Buddhism in China, derived from two pupils of *Hung Jen, Shen Hsiu, and *Hui-Neng. They correspond to the Northern and *Southern Schools.

***Gradual Sayings*.** Common Eng. name for **Anguttara-Nikāya*.

Graham, Billy (William Franklin; b. 1918). American Christian evangelist. He was ordained a *Southern Baptist minister and became a local pastor (1943–5), then a college president (1947–52). The first of his big evangelistic 'crusades', in which he preached to a series of mass meetings, was in Los Angeles in 1948. Many others have followed, notably one attended by hundreds of thousands in London in 1954, which made him a world figure. Since then he has preached in most parts of the world, even the USSR (1982 and 1984). A Billy Graham meeting includes *hymn- and solo-singing, and a sermon by Graham leading to an invitation to come forward and acknowledge *Christ as one's saviour. Those who do so are counselled and put in touch with a local church. Meetings are usually televised to a regional audience. Graham also has a weekly newspaper column, 'My Answer', and radio programme, 'Hour of Decision', and the Billy Graham Evangelistic Association publishes the monthly *Decision* (circulation 2 million). Graham took his message to a worldwide audience via satellite TV in his 1989–90 'Mission World' campaign and the 1996 'Operation Matthew' and 'Billy Graham World Television Series', which had estimated viewing figures of 2.5 billion people across 160 nations. He is notably able to preach a gospel that is traditionally *evangelical yet steers clear of crude politics and Americanism; though his friendships with US presidents have looked to some like a lapse.

Grahast(h)ī (Pañjābī, 'householder' = *gṛhasth āśram). The Sikh *Gurūs taught that God-realization is not to be sought by leading a reclusive life, but through fulfilling the responsibilities of family life. The Sikh must be involved in worldly activities yet detached like the lotus in water. In *Amar Dās' words, 'The true householder is he who restrains his passions, who seeks to . . . impose upon himself a rigorous discipline, who makes charity the outward expression. Such a householder is as *Gaṅgā water' (Ādi Granth 952). In the first verse of *Rām Dās' *Lāvān the grahastī state is affirmed (Ādi Granth 773). See CELIBACY; NIRMALĀ; UDĀSĪ.

Grail, The Holy, or **Sangreale** (perhaps Old Fr., from Lat., *gradale*, 'dish'). The legendary subject of several romances in the late Middle Ages. Some versions of the legend (principally the *Perceval* of Chretien de Troyes, ?1180–90) concern a knightly quest for the sacred object. In the *Parzival* of Wolfram von Eschenbach (*c*.1200) it is combined with the stories of King Arthur and the Round Table. Others (principally the *Estoire dou Graal* or *Joseph* of Robert de Boron, *c*.1200) tell its early history, in which it is the chalice or dish used at the *Last Supper which passed into the possession of *Joseph of Arimathea. The origin of the whole cycle of legends is obscure; it is not even clear whether the Christian elements are primary. In the 13th cent. it reinforced the ecclesiastical propaganda of *Glastonbury Abbey and later on was coupled with the legend of *Prester John. Legends of the grail remained within secular literature, however, and were never recognized by any church authority.

Grail Foundation. A movement started in the 1920s by the German-born Oskar Ernst Bernhardt (1875–1941), later known as Abd-ru-shin (also as Son of Light). After undergoing a 'conversion' experience in 1919, Abd-ru-Shin, who claimed to be in a previous life (in the time of Moses) a prince of an

Arabian tribe, began his mission, which was in essence to develop people's knowledge of creation as the means to resolving the problems of humanity. To this end *The Grail Message*, part of a series of public lectures, was published in 1923, to be followed by *In the Light of Truth*, consisting of 3 vols. of Abd-ru-Shin's lectures delivered between 1923 and 1937.

Though the movement's teaching covers a variety of social and economic as well as religious issues in great detail, its main concern is with explaining what is described as the immovable, automatic working of the Laws of Creation, knowledge of which, it is maintained, leads upwards to the Light. With headquarters at Vomperberg, Austria, the Grail Movement has circles in W. Europe, N. America, Africa, and throughout the world.

Grāmadevatā (Skt., 'local deity'). An image set up on the boundary of an Indian village to ward off evil. The chosen spirit may itself be a frightening figure, but one which has been propitiated by the villagers so that it turns its wrath against unwelcome intruders. They also serve as guardians against disease. They are usually female (cf. the frightening aspects of *Kālī and *Durgā), but some are male (e.g. Iyenar among the *Tamils, whose shrines often contain clay figures of horses on which he rides around the village during the night, warding off evil), and for a time included British tax collectors. The shrines are generally extremely simple and varied.

H. Whitehead, *The Village Gods of South India* (1921).

Grandmother Zen (gentle form of Zen): see RŌBA ZEN.

Granth (Pañjābī, 'book', from Skt., 'to knot together' since early books consisted of palm leaves strung together and tied). Sikh scripture. Granth refers primarily to the *Ādi Granth but see also DASAM GRANTH.

Granthī. Sikh who looks after the *Ādi Granth. A granthī should be skilled in reading the Ādi Granth and often acts as custodian of the *gurdwārā. His duties may include cleaning the gurdwārā and admitting visitors as well as daily reading of the scriptures and recitation of prayers. The granthī should be an *amritdhārī Sikh. The first granthī was *Bhāī Buḍhā. In Mughal times granthīs risked persecution. Consequently *Udāsī granthīs were appointed in many important Sikh shrines since they were usually clean-shaven and could save their lives by denying that they were Sikh.

Gratian (d. not later than 1159). Author of the *Decretum Gratiani* and thus the major source of Roman Catholic *canon law. He appears to have been a native of central Italy and a monk. His *Decretum* (c.1140) is a collection of early materials on all fields of church discipline, presented in a legal framework designed to harmonize the inconsistencies of the sources. It became the basic text on which subsequent teaching and development were based. Even without formal approval, it was used as an authority. Dante (*Paradiso* 10. 103–5) places Gratian in paradise. See also DECRETALS.

Great Assembly. The supreme authority of the Jewish people in the time of the second *Temple. The Great Assembly may be foreshadowed by the people of the Temple court who, under *Ezra, accepted the authority of the *Torah (Nehemiah 8–9). Traditionally it had 120 members, known as 'the men of the Great Assembly'. It was responsible for drawing up much of the text of the accepted *liturgy.

Great Awakening. A series of conversionary revivals of Christian religion in N. America, 1720–50. They were particularly associated with George *Whitefield, and proved divisive.

E. S. Gausted, *The Great Awakening in New England* (1957).

Great Bible: see COVERDALE, MILES.

Great doubt (of Dōgen): see DŌGEN KIGEN.

Great Entrance. In the *Orthodox liturgy of the *eucharist, the procession at which the bread and wine to be consecrated are carried in from the *prothesis table to the *altar. It is a solemn procession, going all around the church, and for many the high point of the whole service.

Great Learning. The *Ta Hsüeh*, one of the group of *Four Books* in the *Confucian Classics. A small work extracted from the collection called *Records of Rituals* (*Li Chi*). It was singled out for special attention by *neo-Confucian philosophers of the Sung dynasty (960–1279), who found it a perfect expression of their own programme of self-cultivation to attain saintliness and save the world: 'The Way of the Great Learning is to exemplify illustrious virtue, to love the people and to abide in the highest good.'

Trs. J. Legge (1892); E. R. Hughes (1943).

Great Perfection. Name given to the Tibetan tradition 'Great Perfection', i.e. *dzogchen.

Great Radiant Sūtra (Tantric Buddhist sūtra): see MAHĀVAIROCANA-SŪTRA.

Great sayings (of the Upaniṣads): see MAHĀVĀKYA.

Great schism. Either (1) the excommunication by Rome in 1054 of the *patriarch of *Constantinople, and the patriarch's excommunication of the *pope; or (2) the *schism in the W. Church, 1378–1417 when there were two, and for a time three, contenders for the title of pope.

1. The earlier event was occasioned by a legation to Constantinople, headed by Cardinal Humbert, in

an attempt to win Patriarch Cerularius' support against the Normans in Italy. While the papacy was trying to extend its influence over the traditionally Greek regions of S. Italy, the patriarch was unsympathetic, and he also claimed that the W. practice of using unleavened bread for the *eucharist was contrary to the *canons. The mutual *excommunications which followed were only the seal upon a rift which had been widening between the two churches over several centuries.

2. The papal schism in 1378 arose from the disputed election of Urban VI, though the election would probably not have been contested had Urban's behaviour been less high-handed. Disaffected *cardinals held a further conclave, and chose Clement VII, a cousin of the French king, who took up residence at Avignon. Urban and his successors became known as the Roman obedience, Clement and his as the Avignon obedience, the princes of Europe supporting one or the other according to their political interest. The two sides met at Pisa in 1409 to depose the popes of both obediences and elect a new pontiff, but as neither pope accepted deposition this created a third, Pisan, obedience. At the Council of Constance in 1415 the Pisan pope was deposed, and the Roman pope, Gregory XII, resigned, though his successor, Martin V, was not elected until after Gregory's death in 1417. The Avignon pope took refuge in Spain, where his successor was finally bribed to repudiate his claims in 1429.

Great synagogue. Perhaps better translated '*great assembly', a Jewish administrative council during the Persian period (538–331 BCE). Little is known of its activity. According to tradition, it was founded by *Ezra, it had 120 members (though others say 85), and it was responsible for preserving and applying *Torah.

Great tradition, little tradition. Categories introduced by the sociologist, Robert Redfield (*Peasant Society and Culture*, 1956) to distinguish between the major, continuing components of a religious tradition and the appropriation of them at local or village level. The distinction has often been applied, though usually without great methodological uniformity—e.g. by M. Singer (in *Traditional India . . .*, 1959) and by M. E. Spiro (in *Buddhism and Society: A Great Tradition and its Burmese Vicissitudes*, 1971, where he distinguishes between nibbanic Buddhism as a religion of ultimate salvation and kammatic Buddhism as a religion of proximate salvation, which, in practice, is the highest that most people can aim for).

Great vehicle (the development of Buddhism): see MAHĀYĀNA.

Great vow (commitment to first limb of Hindu yoga): see YAMA (2).

Great vows (basic Jain commitments): see FIVE GREAT VOWS.

Great Western schism: see ANTIPOPE; GREAT SCHISM.

Greek Orthodox Church. 1. The *autocephalous Christian church found mainly in Greece, a part of the *Orthodox Church whose belief and practice it shares. After the schism of 1054, the Orthodox Church in Greece remained under the *patriarch of Constantinople, but it became independent in 1833. It is governed by a Holy Synod of sixty-seven metropolitan bishops, presided over by the archbishop of all Greece whose *see is Athens. The Church is particularly strong in N. and S. America, and numbers *c.*15 million.

2. Incorrectly, but widely used prior to 1914, for all Orthodox churches, e.g. in Baedeker's *Guide to Russia*, 1914.

Green Book (revolutionary text of Libyan leader): see QADHAFFI, MUʿAMMAR.

Gregorian calendar, new calendar, or **new style.** The Julian *calendar as adjusted by Pope Gregory XIII in 1582 to make it cohere better with the solar year. It was not accepted in most *Orthodox Churches until 1924.

Gregorian Chant: see GREGORY I.

Gregory I, 'the Great', St (*c.*540–604). *Pope from 590 and founder of the medieval papacy. He was a man of wealth but sold his property for the relief of the poor and became a monk in 574. Later he was one of the seven *deacons of Rome, and a papal delegate at Constantinople. As pope at a time of great unrest, Gregory had to deal with the invasion of Italy by the Lombards, and with threats to the position of the Church from the claims of the Byzantine Empire. Politically, he followed a course independent of Constantinople, and by his aid to Italian cities established the temporal power of the papacy. He maintained the supremacy of the see of Rome, refusing to accept or recognize the title of *ecumenical patriarch, which the patriarch of Constantinople claimed. He also promoted *monasticism and granted particular privileges (*privilegia*) to monks in relation to *bishops, a move which later brought religious orders under the direct control of the papacy. He made important changes in the *liturgy (though the 'Gregorian' *Sacramentary is a later compilation) and promoted liturgical *music (hence the name 'Gregorian chant' for *plainsong). His many writings were mostly practical, including *Pastoral Care*, a *Commentary on Job* (expounding the literal, mystical and especially moral senses of the text), *Homilies on the Gospels*, and a collection of 854 letters. His own knowledge was more than theoretical: 'My sad mind, labouring under the weight of its engagements, remembers how it was with me of old in the monastery, . . . how it rose above all that was transitory, and, though still in the body, went out in contemplation beyond the boundaries of the flesh.' Gregory thus did much to establish the papacy as the supreme authority in the Church. He was canonized by popular acclamation when he died, and is one of the *Doctors of the Church Feast day, 12 Mar.

J. Richards, *Consul of God* (1980).

Gregory VII, St (*c.*1020–85). Originally Hildebrand, Christian pope who provoked the Investiture Controversy. Born in Tuscany, he was educated in Rome and became chaplain to Gregory VI (whom he accompanied into exile). He was summoned back to Rome by Leo IX and was sent on missions to France and Germany. Elected pope, he did not notify, still less seek the approval of, King Henry IV (of Germany, and Holy Roman Emperor). He set himself to the task of reform, making the power and mystique of the papacy central to his task. His *Dictatus Papae* (1075) not only emphasized the holiness of the pope in succession from *Peter, but also asserted the right of the pope to depose princes. His reform of the clergy reinforced decrees requiring *celibacy. He prohibited lay investiture (i.e. the right of laity to make appointments to certain church offices), which in effect envisaged the abolition of the royal control over bishops. Considerable unrest ensued, especially in France, England, and Germany. Henry IV continued to nominate bishops, convening a synod of German bishops at Worms and Piacenza in 1076 which deposed the pope. Gregory responded by excommunicating Henry and releasing his subjects from allegiance. Seeing the threat, Henry capitulated and sought absolution in penitent's attire at Canossa, near Reggio, in 1077. But this was the beginning, not the end, of conflict. When Henry seized Rome in 1084, Gregory was rescued by the Norman, Robert Guiscard, but the behaviour of the soldiers provoked even greater antagonism against Gregory. He fled to Monte Cassino, thence to Salerno where he died. His last words were, 'I have loved justice and hated iniquity, therefore I die in exile.' Whether a historian will agree with that verdict depends on the view taken of the centralization of papal power. He was canonized in 1606: feast day 25 May.

A. J. Macdonald, *Hildebrand* (1932); W. Ullmann, *The Growth of Papal Power in the Middle Ages* (2nd edn., 1962).

Gregory of Nazianzus, St (329–89). One of the *Cappadocian fathers, known in the Orthodox Church as 'the Theologian'. He was of aristocratic family, and as a student was a friend of *Basil. He shrank from the active life of a bishop, but in 379 he was summoned to Constantinople, where his preaching helped to restore the *Nicene faith at the council of 381. At this council he was recognized as bishop of Constantinople, but resigned the see almost at once. Gregory's writings include his forty-five *Orations*, of which nos. 27–31, the *Theological Orations*, are most important; the **Philocalia* of Origen; a collection of letters, some against *Apollinarius; and a number of religious and secular poems.

A.-S. Ellverson, *The Dual Nature of Man* (1981); T. Špidlík, *Grégoire de Nazianze* (1971); D. F. Winslow, *The Dynamics of Salvation: A Study in Gregory of Nazianzus* (1979).

Gregory of Nyssa, St (*c.*330–*c.*395). One of the *Cappadocian fathers, and younger brother of *Basil. As bishop of Nyssa, an unimportant town in his brother's metropolitan see, he was exiled by the *Arian party 376–8. At the Council of *Constantinople he was an eloquent supporter of the Nicene position. Gregory was the most profound and skilful writer of the Cappadocians. Apart from important polemical works his major writings are the systematic *Catechetical Orations*, a *Life of Moses* in which mystical exegesis is used, and ascetical works such as *On Virginity* in which he develops the thought that in virginity the soul becomes a spouse of Christ. The visible universe is a symbol of the unseen reality of God, to whom the soul ascends, especially in the discernment of spiritual beauty, 'to become oneself as beautiful as the Beauty which one has touched and entered'.

H. U. von Balthasar, *Présence et pensée* . . . (1942); W. Völker, *Gregor von Nyssa als Mystiker* (1953).

Gregory Palamas, St (*c.*1296–1359). Greek theologian and chief exponent of *hesychasm. Nobly born and well-educated, he became a monk, and *c.*1318 went to Mount Athos where he became familiar with hesychasm. With the advance of the Turks he fled to Thessalonica where he was ordained priest in 1326, and consecrated archbishop of Thessalonica in 1347. His fame stems from his controversy with Barlaam of Calabria, which began in 1337, over the nature of Christian contemplation. Against Barlaam's extreme statement of God's unknowability, he insisted, in his *Triads in Defence of the Holy Hesychasts* (*c.* 1338), that God really communicates knowledge of himself to humans, and that the experience of the uncreated light of the Godhead in contemplation, claimed by the hesychast monks, is veridical. Although initially Palamas was condemned, he was vindicated by councils at Constantinople in 1347 and 1351 and canonized in 1363. Feast days in E., 14 Nov. and the 2nd Sunday in Lent.

J. Meyendorff, *A Study of Gregory Palamas* (1964) and *Gregory Palamas and Orthodox Spirituality* (1974).

Gregory Thaumaturgus, St (miracle-worker): see THAUMATURGY.

Gregory the Illuminator, St (*c.*240–*c.*325). Apostle of Armenia. He converted the king Trdat (*c.*238–314) to Christianity, which was forthwith imposed as the official religion of the country. He was later consecrated the first bishop, and the episcopate remained for some generations in his family. The *Armenian Orthodox Church is sometimes styled 'Gregorian'.

Grey Earth monastery (school of Tibetan Buddhism): see THAUMATURGY.

Gṛhastha (Skt., 'standing in the home'). In Hinduism, the householder life-stage (*āśrama) described in *Manusmṛti*. Ideally, a *brahman enters into the gṛhastha stage at age 25, after completion of his Vedic studies and investiture with the sacred thread (*upanayana). During the gṛhastha āśrama, a man establishes a household, raises a family, and pursues worldly goals such as acquisition of wealth. At age 50 the householder is to retire to the forest.

According to *Manusmṛti*, the gṛhastha āśrama is the most important of the four āśramas, because people in the other three stages (student, forest hermit, wandering ascetic) are supported and maintained by the householder. *Manusmṛti* describes the duties of the brahman householder which involve accumulation of property through a pure and honest profession which does not involve injury to others and which is undertaken only for bare subsistence, by the standard of brahmans. The gṛhastha āśrama is appropriate only for the twice-born castes (dvijāti *varnas). Cf. *Grahast(h)i.

Gṛhyakarmani (home-based offerings or sacrifices): see SACRIFICES (HINDUISM).

Gṛhyasūtras (rules governing home rituals): see SŪTRA.

Griffiths, Bede, (1907–93). Christian monk and leading figure in the development of reinforcing spiritual practice from Christian and Eastern religious roots. On leaving Oxford University, he went with two companions in quest of simplicity in the Cotswolds, but this precipitated a personal crisis which led him into the Roman Catholic Church (a journey described in *The Golden String*). He became a Benedictine monk in 1933. After a period as prior of Farnborough (1947–52), he received permission to go to India to live a monastic life in the style of Jules Monchanin and Henri le Saux, who had been struggling to establish an Indian Christianity in the pattern of St *Francis and in the tradition of the Indian *saṁnyāsin. Griffiths said that he went to India to find the other half of his soul. In 1968, he became prior of the then failing Saccidananda Ashram (*Āśrama), putting into practice his vision of (as he entitled one of his books) *The Marriage of East and West*. In this he saw the only possible healing of the violently dualistic and exclusivist ideologies of the religious and political West. Towards the end of his life, he became intrigued by those W. scientists (especially Capra and Bohm) who seemed to point to an intuitive wisdom in the E. sense of the priority of perception over the perceived. He died revered in India though still suspect to some in the Vatican for an implicit syncretism—which in fact he always denied as a destruction of both traditions. For him, religions are routes to realization, the realization of the utter dependence of all life on God: 'Poverty—the poverty of spirit of the Sermon on the Mount—is a total detachment from the material world. It is to recognise that everything comes from God—our bodies, our breath, our very existence.'

Grodzinski, Ḥayyim Ozer (1863–1940). *Talmudic scholar. As *dayyan of Vilna, Grodzinski was one of the founders of the *Orthodox Keneset Israel Organisation. He also organized the Va'ad ha-*Yeshivot (council of the Yeshivot) for the support of Polish and Lithuanian yeshivot. He was an opponent of *Zionism and Jewish secular education, believing, 'Let him who is firm in spirit stay steadfast in his place . . . until God has mercy on his people and hastens his redemption.' The author of 3 vols. of *responsa, he believed 'the large and small yeshivot were the strongholds of Judaism'.

Groote, Geert, Gerard or **Gerard the Great** (1340–84), founder of the Brothers and Sisters of the Common Life. Born of a wealthy family in Deventer, he studied theology and law at Paris. After a somewhat worldly life, he spent three years in a *Carthusian monastery, and became attracted by the teachings of *Ruysbroek. He became a powerful preacher, attacking abuses in the Church. In 1380, he and his friend, Florentius Radewijns, established a group for the development of personal piety. From this group, the Brethren developed; and in 1383, he wrote a Rule for a similar community of women. In effect, this was the creation of the Devotio Moderna, the 'up-to-date devotion' which brought the practice of the presence of God into the midst of everyday life. He continued his friendship with Ruysbroek, translating works by him into Dutch and Latin. After his death from the plague, Radewijns extended the communities to include many followers, among whom *Thomas à Kempis is the best known, making the *Imitation of Christ a matter of practical, everyday possibility. His vision influenced both *Erasmus and *Luther.

T. Van Zijl, *Geert Groote* (1963).

Grossteste, Robert (*c*.1175–1253). Scholar, reformer, and bishop of Lincoln. One of the most successful teachers in the early 13th cent., in 1224–35 he lectured at the *Franciscan house of studies in Oxford. In 1235 he was appointed to Lincoln, and undertook a thorough visitation and reform of his diocese—which included Oxford. He was an outspoken critic of Rome's appointment of foreign prelates to English benefices. He translated a number of Greek works, including two by Aristotle, although in his own considerable philosophical writings he leant more heavily upon *Augustine and *Neoplatonism. He was also keenly interested in science, in which pursuit he was inspired, and encouraged, by Roger *Bacon. He took light to be the basic principle in the universe, able to be transformed into other elements, thereby allowing motion and intelligibility.

Gshen rab mi-bo-che. In *Tibetan Bon religion, the Enlightened One of the present era and source of the ordering of Bon religion. According to tradition, he was born 18,000 years ago, in 'Ol mo lung rings (in sTag zig, perhaps Persia, hence *dualistic elements below). He brought into more systematic order the rituals, customs, celebrations, and teachings of Bon religion. He has assumed a position in tradition not unlike that of Buddha *Śākyamuni, though with much more legendary accretion. He is known as *rNam mkhyen rgyal be gShen rab mchog*, 'the Omniscient Victor'. Moved by the compassion witnessed also in *bodhisattvas, he entered this world as manifestation (*rgyal tshab*) of the heavenly being, *gShen*. He engaged in stupendous battles with demons and with gods—who feared his power. He conquered them all, and acquired from them as spoil the sacred syllables of their strength. Three biographies of him remain religiously important.

gterma (class of Tibetan Buddhist texts): see TERMA.

gter. ston (discoverer of Tibetan Buddhist texts): see TERMA.

gtum mo ('Heat Yoga'): see NĀRO CHOS DRUG.

Gufu-shogyō-zen (Jap., 'fool's way of Zen'). The limited forms of Zen meditation. They are distinguished from *zazen because they focus on conventional concepts, e.g. *śūnyatā, *anātman, *anicca, etc. They have a preliminary use, for an extreme novice, but only in order to clear the way for zazen.

Guide For the Perplexed (work by Jewish philosopher): see MAIMONIDES, M.

Gūjarī, Mātā (d. 1704 CE). Wife of Gurū *Tegh Bahādur and mother of Gurū *Gobind Siṅgh. Mātā Gūjarī accompanied her husband to Paṭnā where she gave birth to her son and looked after him during Tegh Bahādur's travels further east. In the fighting which followed the siege of *Anaṇḍpur, she and the surviving *sāhibzāde reached Sirhind where she died after they had been betrayed to the authorities and walled up alive.

Gūji (Jap.). The chief priest of a *Shinto shrine. Originally the gūji was the chief fiscal officer of a shrine, but the term was later applied to the overall chief priest. Written with different characters, gūji also means a Buddhist temple or chapel attached to a Shinto shrine.

Guṇa (Skt., 'strand' or 'cord'). In Hindu *Sāṁkyha, the three components, qualities, or attributes (i.e. *sattva, *tamas, and *rājas) of material nature (*prakṛti). Everything mental and physical consists of these three guṇas in varying degrees; only pure consciousness (*puruṣa) is without attributes (*nirguṇa). Disturbance of the equilibrium of the guṇas is the cause of creation, and all of creation can be classified according to the predominance of one of the three guṇas.

A predominance of illumination (sattva), produced by the proximity of puruṣa to prakṛti, disturbs the equilibrium of the guṇas, thus initiating the creation process; from the unmanifest state (mūlaprakṛti), prakṛti evolves into the world. In the individual, the guṇas interact to create the mental faculties, the first being intellect (*buddhi) which contains the original predominance of sattva. The ego and eventually the sense capacities then evolve through the continual interaction with the guṇa of energy (rajas) and the guṇa of inertia (tamas).

A predominance of tamas produces the material world. The subtle elements first evolve and from these, according to the interplay of the three guṇas, the gross elements are produced. Reabsorption of the material world takes place when puruṣa is isolated from prakṛti and the three guṇas attain their original equilibrium. In the individual, this process occurs at liberation (*kaivalya). The *yogin retraces the evolutionary process; he strives to embody the original predominance of sattva and from this condition attain to the attributeless state of puruṣa.

In Jainism, guṇa is one of the qualities which apparent objects exhibit: any substance (*dravya) has certain guṇas which appear in different modes (*parāya*).

J. Larson, *Classical Sāṁkhya* . . . (1979).

Gunasthāna, Fourteen stages of Jain progress toward emancipation of the *jīva (cf. the Eightfold Path of Buddhism, *aṣṭangika-mārga): (i) *mithyātva*, having wrong belief; (ii) *sāśadana*, tending to right belief, but prone to backsliding; (iii) *miśra*, having a mixture of right and wrong belief; (iv) *avirata saṃyaktva*, having right belief but not acting upon it with a commitment through vows; (v) *deśa-vrata*, taking some vows; (vi) *pramatta-vrata*, taking all vows but impeded, e.g. by illness, from keeping them; (vii) *apramatta-vrata*, unimpeded vow-keeping; (viii) *apūrva-karaṇa*, new thought activity begins; (ix) *nirvṛtti-karaṇa*, is extended; (x) *sūkṣama-sāmparyāya*, only a residue of delusion remains; (xi) *upaśānta-moha*, delusion has subsided; (xii) *kṣīna-moha*, delusion is destroyed; (xiii) *sayoga-kevalī*, the jīva is omniscient in its last body; (xiv) *ayoga-kevalī*, the jīva passes through a brief stage of non-interactive omniscience, before its complete emancipation from *karma.

Gunavrata (supplementary Jain vows): see ANUVRATA.

Gunkel, Hermann (1862–1932). *Biblical scholar. Gunkel pioneered *form criticism of biblical study. He explored popular mythology in an attempt to uncover the original myth of creation. He classified the *psalms according to their liturgical use and life setting, by the methods known as *formegeschichtliche* ('form-historical') and *gattungsgeschichtliche* ('type-critical'). Often repeated phrases gave a clue to the 'setting in cultic life'. He distinguished five main types: (i) *Hymnus*, Hymn, including Songs of Zion and Enthronement Songs; (ii) *Klaglieder des Volkes*, Communal Laments; (iii) Königspsalmen, Royal Psalms; (iv) *Klaglied des Einzelnen*, Individual Lament; (v) *Danklieder des Einzelnen*, Individual Songs of Thanksgiving. Other proposed types (e.g. *Wallfahrtslieder*, Songs of Pilgrimage) are small in number. Although his categories have been much amended, his cultic interpretation of the Psalms, as a general approach, has endured. He also wrote an important study of *Esther.

Gupta dynasty. Established in N. India in 3rd cent. CE, and later covering a much larger area. It flourished *c*.350–510 CE. Under this dynasty, great heights of Hindu, Jain, and Buddhist religion and culture were achieved.

P. L. Gupta, *The Imperial Guptas* (1975, 1979); S. K. Maity, *The Imperial Guptas and Their Times* (1975).

Gurbāṇī (Pañjābī, 'utterance of the Gurū'). Usually, the words of the Sikh *Gurūs and *bhagats recorded in the *Ādi Granth, itself revered as Gurū; hence also a summary term for prayer.

Gurdās Bhallā, Bhāī, (c.1551–1637). Sikh writer contemporary with four *Gurūs. Bhāī Gurdās was the son of Gurū *Amar Dās' younger brother, and died unmarried. Although of varied literary quality, his compositions are highly regarded as the 'key to the *Ādi Granth'. They are not included in this, but, with the Dasam Granth and the poetry of *Nand Lāl 'Goyā', are approved for recitation in *gurdwārās. Bhāī Gurdās composed 556 briefer works (*kabitt*) and thirty-nine *vārs. Their subject is Sikh belief, history, and biography, the first vār in particular recounting in eulogistic style traditionally accepted episodes from Gurū *Nānak's life, as told in the *janam-sākhīs. His writings are of unique historical value as contemporary sources for the period of Gurūs Amar Dās, *Rām Dās, *Arjan Dev, and *Hargobind. Following formal initiation by Gurū Rām Dās, Bhāī Gurdās worked in Āgrā as a missionary until Arjan Dev's succession. When the latter compiled the Ādi Granth he served as his chosen amanuensis (1603–4). With Bhāī Buḍhā he took the scriptures to *Akbar, who wished to examine the contents. Bhāī Gurdās played a leading role during Gurū Hargobind's imprisonment, and supported his military style of leadership.

Gurdjieff, Georgy Ivanovich (*c*.1877–1949). Writer and one-time director of the Institute for the Harmonious Development of Man, in Paris. Born in Russia, Gurdjieff had already attracted a number of disciples from among his students by the time he left Moscow (just before the First World War) for Central Asia, the Middle East, and France.

In his lectures at the Institute for the Harmonious Development of Man, published posthumously as *All and Everything, or Beelzebub's Tales to His Grandson* (1973), Gurdjieff traced the development of the universe from its beginnings to modern times. Preoccupied with discovering the sense and significance of life on earth and in particular of human life, he maintained that these consisted essentially in people transforming themselves through a process of self-study and experience which would lead to inner growth in the form of qualitative changes in inner consciousness. Eventually they would become liberated, immortal souls, the goal, in Gurdjieff's view, of all religions.

Gurdjieff, who sought to synthesize Christianity and his own philosophical notions, has had a considerable influence on the thinking of such *new religious movements as the *metaphysical and *new age movements, and *Rajneeshism.

J. G. Bennett, *Gurdjieff* . . . (1973); P. D. Ouspensky, *In Search of the Miraculous* (1965).

Gurdwārā (Pañjābī, gurduārā, 'gateway of the *Gurū'). A building for Sikh congregational worship in which the *Ādi Granth is appropriately installed. A gurdwārā is characterized by its function of housing the Gurū, rather than by its architecture. An upstairs room in an ordinary house in which the Ādi Granth has been ceremonially installed can be a gurdwārā. Worshippers show appropriate respect, removing shoes and covering their heads before entry, and prostrating themselves before the Ādi Granth, as in a major shrine. In India each Sikh village boasts a gurdwārā—often a simple room. Most famous is the impressive *Harimandir, *Amritsar. Many gurdwārās have historical associations with the Sikh Gurūs e.g. *Rakāb Gañj, *Śīś Gañj, and the *takhts.

From the *janam-sākhīs and Bhāī *Gurdās we learn that *dharmsālas* ('resting-places') were established wherever Gurū *Nānak travelled. These buildings, sometimes donated by devotees, were specifically intended for devotional singing and prayer. Gurū *Hargobind visited many of these and restored them. However, many of the historical gurdwārā buildings date from the period of Mahārājā *Rañjīt Siṅgh and replace earlier constructions. Architecturally these famous shrines are a Mughal blend of Muslim and Hindu style. The parapets are surmounted by numerous *chatrīs* (open-sided kiosks). Apart from a central dome there may be smaller cupolas, fluted to resemble an inverted lotus. Domes may be topped with a *kalas* (short cylindrical ornament). These gurdwārās are generally two storeys high. Traditionally a gurdwārā has entrances on all four sides, symbolizing access to people of every sort. To reach the prayer hall one may pass a *dehrī* (threshold) with a high gate. Orientation is unimportant.

In Indian gurdwārās, white is the dominant colour, whatever the building materials used. Some gurdwārās are decorated with coloured stones inlaid in the marble slabs, with designs in gypsum covered with gold, with *Gurmukhi verses or with murals. A *niśān *sāhib indicates that a building is a gurdwārā.

In the 19th cent. gurdwārās were monopolized by *mahants backed by the British authorities. Following the *Siṅgh Sabhā and *Akālī pressure for reform of gurdwārā management, the Sikh community regained control of its shrines, each being run by a locally elected and registered managing committee. The most important historical gurdwārās in Pañjāb are managed by the *Shiromaṇī Gurdwārā Parbandhak Committee.

The gurdwārā is primarily the place where the *sangat gather daily for *kīrtan to worship in the presence of the Gurū as embodied in the Ādi Granth, and it has a vital social function. *Gurpurbs and family rites are often celebrated in the gurdwārā. This is especially true of marriages in Britain where, too, larger saṅgats gather on Sundays and *saṅgrānds. The gurdwārā depends on funds received from donations and offerings. These may be used to run schools or to give medical treatment in India. In British gurdwārās, elementary Pañjābī classes are run to familiarize Sikh children with Gurmukhī. In less deliberate ways too, the gurdwārās of diaspora Sikhs are centres of cultural reinforcement. Gurdwārās traditionally provide sustenance and accommodation for wayfarers as well as *Gurū-kā-laṅgar, so a kitchen, communal dining area, and restrooms and lavatories are important. There may be rooms for a resident *granthī. No *tobacco or *alcohol may be carried inside, and only vegetarian food can be cooked and eaten.

Inside the gurdwārā prayer hall, furniture is minimal. The scriptures are enthroned on cushions on a *mañjī beneath a canopy. In large Pañjāb gurdwārās this is usually in the centre of the rectangular hall. In village gurdwārās and British gurdwārās it is halfway along and a few feet away from a wall. To one side is an area for *rāgīs (musicians). The floor is carpeted for the congregation to sit, men on one side, women on the other, facing the Ādi Granth. Chairs are used in some American gurdwārās.

In Britain there are over 180 gurdwārās. Their increase in the 1960s and 1970s followed the immigration and establishment of Sikh families in industrial cities. Some are converted houses, schools, churches etc., and a number are purpose-built with no distinctive architectural features.

Gurmat. 'The teachings of the *Gurūs', the collective teaching and disciplinary instructions of the Sikh Gurūs, and thus the Sikh name for what in English is called 'Sikhism'.

Gurmatā (Pañjābī, 'Gurū resolution'). Decision affecting Sikh community, taken before the *Gurū—now in the presence of *Ādi Granth. Gurmatās taken in the *gurdwārā by a consensus of the *sangat are binding. Particularly authoritative are resolutions taken in the *Akāl Takht and issued as *hukamnāmās.

Gurmukh (Pañjābī, 'person oriented towards the *Gurū'). A pious Sikh responsive to the Gurū's word. In contrast to the *manmukh, the gurmukh embodies the living teaching of the *Ādi Granth. Continually remembering the Name of God (*Nām), the gurmukh loses all self-centredness (*haumai), leads a life of service, and attains the peace of ultimate union with God. See also RĀDHĀSOĀMĪ SATSAṄG.

Gurmukhī (Pañjābī, 'from the mouth of the *Gurū'). Sacred script of the Sikhs. The Gurmukhī alphabet consists of thirty-five letters and is simpler than, but closely related to, the Devanāgrī script used for Sanskrit and Hindī. Like Devanāgrī it is written from left to right and is totally phonetic. The origins of the Gurmukhī script are disputed but it is usually attributed to Gurū *Aṅgad, although it arguably originated much earlier than the Sikh Gurūs. Its development is closely associated with Sikhism, since a distinctive religious script confirmed the Sikhs' sense of an identity separate from both Hindus and Muslims.The script emphasized the accessibility of religious teaching to all regardless of *caste, unlike Skt. which was the preserve of the *brahmans. Gurmukhī is respected as the script of the *Ādi *Granth. It is the official alphabet for modern *Pañjābī, taught in the schools of Indian *Pañjāb. Competence in Gurmukhī is required of candidates for the Śiromaṇī Gurdwārā Parbandhak Committee. In Britain Gurmukhī classes are held in many *gurdwārās.

C. Shackle, *A Gurū Nānak Glossary* (1981) and *An Introduction to the Sacred Language of the Sikhs* (1983).

Gurpurb (Pañjābī, 'rising of a Gurū'). Sikh festival associated with an event in the *Gurūs' lives. The dates of Gurpurbs vary within twenty-eight days as they are lunar. In Britain, most gurdwārās celebrate Gurpurbs on the Sunday nearest the actual day. The most important Gurpurbs are Gurū *Nānak's birthday, celebrated on the full moon of Kārttika (Oct.–Nov.), Gurū *Gobind Siṅgh's birthday, celebrated in Pauṣa (Dec.–Jan.), and the *martyrdoms (*śahīd din*) of Gurū *Arjan Dev and Gurū *Tegh Bahādur, observed respectively in Jyaiṣṭha (May–June) and Mārgaśīrsa (Nov.–Dec.). The martyrdoms of the *Sāhibzāde are commemorated in Pauṣa. Many Gurpurbs are observed only or chiefly at the site of the original event—e.g. the birthday of Gurū *Har Krishan at Delhi (July) and the anniversary of the installation of the Gurū Granth Sāhib (*Ādi Granth) at *Amritsar (Sept.).

Celebration of a Gurpurb commences two days earlier with an *akhaṇḍ pāṭh which finishes on the morning of the Gurpurb. This is followed by *kīrtan and preaching on the life of the Gurū concerned. In India, the Ādi Granth is carried, strewn with flowers, through the streets in a procession headed by five armed representatives of the *pañj pyāre, and food is shared with the whole vilage. There are bands, lectures, and competitions.

See also BAISĀKHĪ; CALENDAR; DIVĀLĪ; HOLĀ MAHALLĀ; MELĀ; MUKTSAR.

Guru (Skt., 'heavy'). A teacher, initially of worldly skills or knowledge, hence a parent or a schoolteacher; but more often a teacher of religious knowledge or conveyor of spiritual insight and liberation (*mokṣa) in Indian religions, especially among Hindus and Sikhs. The term is often synonymous with *ācārya, though the latter is also used for the teacher of a skill. Guru should also be distinguished from *paṇḍita, a scholar or learned man.

The idea of a person as a channel for divine knowledge is found in the *Vedas with the *ṛṣis, the divinely inspired poets. The *Upaniṣads also have the idea of a teacher who conveys spiritual knowledge. For example, in *Chandogya Upaniṣad* (4. 9. 2–3), Satyakāma wishes his teacher (ácārya) to convey to him knowledge of *Brahman; indeed the very term 'upaniṣad' implies sitting at the feet of a teacher. The term guru appears in the *Dharma literature (e.g. **Manusmṛti* (2. 142 and 149), where the term is defined as a *brāhmaṇa who performs Vedic rites, which include Vedic initiation (*upanayana) and conception rites (*garbhādhāra*), and who teaches the Veda. In *Vaiṣṇavism, *Śaivism, and *Tantrism the guru is the means whereby the tradition is conveyed through the generations and teachings are authenticated through the guru lineage (*paramparā). With the development of *bhakti, devotion to the guru as a means of liberation became a central practice, especially in the *Sant tradition.

Buddhism has perhaps laid less stress on the guru than Hinduism, though the idea of the teacher as the conveyor of spiritual insight is still important. Indeed the *Buddha himself could be regarded as such a conveyor of insight, as is suggested by certain *arhats becoming enlightened after hearing a discourse by the Buddha (*Majjhima Nikāya* 1. 494). In *Mahāyāna Buddhism, the terms *mitra and *pratibhanika* convey the idea of a giver of spiritual insight, and the term guru is used in the *Vajrayāna, for example in the Kargyupa lineage of Tibetan Buddhism beginning with *Tilopa. The idea of the guru is now found in modern W. religious movements some of which have developed directly out of Indian traditions such as *Transcendental Meditation, the *Hare Krishna (*International Society . . .), and *Rajneesh movements.

Conceptions of the guru vary from that of one who is identical with God and conveys liberation (mokṣa), the *sat guru, to that of the guru as a guide, showing beings the way but not actually bestowing liberation. This variability of conceptions is constrained by the metaphysics of different traditions which determine the closeness of the guru to the source of manifestation. For example, in monistic *Kashmir Śaivism the guru is identical with God (*parameśvara), whereas in dualistic *Śaiva Siddhānta he is distinct from God (*Śiva).

The sat guru is liberated (*jivanmukti) and takes responsibility for his disciples, ensuring their eventual liberation, in one of several lifetimes, through purifying their accumulated *karma. He is the bestower of *grace (*anugraha*, *prasāda) which can be very immediate in *śaktipāta* (descent of power) or more gradual in meditation (*dhyāna). During initiation (*dīkṣa) given by the guru, the disciple (*śiṣya*) receives a *mantra which is energized by the guru, without whom it would not be efficacious. Tantrism and the Sant tradition stress the importance of submission to the guru. Even though various practices might be prescribed (such as meditation upon the guru's form or mantra repetition (*japa)), ultimately it is the guru's grace that bestows salvation. A touch or glance (*dṛṣṭi*) from him burns up the disciple's *karma, so looking at the guru (*darśana) is regarded as a highly beneficial spiritual practice. In such traditions the sat guru is the central focus of practice: thus the *Śiva Sūtra* of Kashmir Śaivism (2. 6) says 'the guru is the means'; and the **Kulārṇava Tantra* (1. 107) says 'One word from the guru gives liberation'. The guru who is regarded as a guide does not take on responsibility for his disciples; indeed in such traditions guru devotion is often discouraged, the guru being a helper rather than a means of liberation. Ramanamaharshi is an example of such a guru.

An important point to be stressed is that the guru occurs within a lineage (paramparā), the first guru (ādiguru) of which received spiritual knowledge directly from a divine source. Through the lineage the guru's authority as a channel for divine grace is vindicated and his action constrained. Disputes over succession can lead to the splitting off of sub-sects from the central lineage.

See Index, guru.

Among Sikhs, the term refers primarily to Gurū Nānak and his nine successors, *Aṅgad, *Amar Dās, *Rām Dās, *Arjan Dev, *Hargobind, *Har Rāi, *Har Krishan, *Tegh Bahādur, and *Gobind *Siṅgh. All manifested the one divine light, just as one lamp is lit from another. This belief in the essential oneness of the Gurūs is central to Sikhism. On the death of Gobind Siṅgh, Gurūship was vested in the *Ādi Granth (Gurū Granth *Sāhib) and the *Khālsā community. Sikhs venerate the Ādi Granth as Gurū. Only through the Gurū's gracious teaching may devotees achieve union with God (*Vāhigurū). In Nānak's hymns 'the Guru's voice' apparently refers to God's inner spiritual guidance. In poetic imagery the Gurū is the ferry across the ocean of existence. See NĀMDHĀRĪ; NIRAṄKĀRĪ; RĀDHĀSOĀMĪ; Index, Guru (Sikh).

Gurū Granth Sāhib (Sikh Scripture): see ĀDI GRANTH.

Gurū-kā-laṅgar. Sikh free kitchen, refectory. In every *gurdwārā vegetarian food is cooked and served free to people of any *caste, race, and creed with no order of precedence, although men and women usually sit separately. In major gurdwārās thousands are fed daily.

The *laṅgar not only emphasizes the equality and mutual responsibility of all, but demonstrates practically the ideal of *sevā (service). By contributing money, provisions, and labour in cleaning utensils, fetching water and fuel, cooking, and distribution, individuals discharge their corporate responsibility. By feeding the needy, one serves the *Gurū and worships God.

Originating in the earliest days of Sikhism the Gurū-kā-laṅgar developed from the example and teachings of Gurū *Nānak whose disciples gave hospitality in their *dharmsālās. Verses in the *Ādi Granth and numerous stories of successive Gurūs and their followers serving in the laṅgar are evidence of its continued centrality. Gurū *Amar Dās ordered all, including Emperor *Akbār, who came to see him, to eat first in the Gurū-kā-laṅgar, thus proving their humility. According to tradition one of Gurū *Gobind Siṅgh's last commands was to keep his laṅgar open. The *Pañjābī words 'paṅgat' (row) and 'deg' (cooking pot) refer to Gurū-kā-laṅgar in well-known verses.

See also KAṚĀH PRAŚĀD.

Gurumantra. The *mantra passed on to a pupil by a *guru, during initiation, which the pupil makes his own (by constant repetition), but also keeps secret.

Guruparampara (lineage of spiritual teachers): see PARAMPARĀ.

Gush Emunim. Organization of the faithful, a Jewish religious and nationalist group of the 20th cent. It was led by Tzevi Yehudah Kook (1891–1982), the only son of Abraham Isaac *Kook. He succeeded his father as head of the Merkaz ha-Rav *yeshivah, and shared his outlook. Gush Emunim put this into practice, and took the initiative in establishing Jewish settlements in the Administered Areas of Palestine/Israel after the Six Day War in 1967.

Gute kvitl (Yiddish greetin): see BOOK OF LIFE.

Gutiérrez, G. (theologian): see LIBERATION THEOLOGY.

Guṭkā (Pañjābī, 'manual'). Book of devotions. Sikhs use this term to refer to the breviaries including the *Nitnem and the *Sukhmanī. Unless Sikhs can set aside a room as a *gurdwārā in which the *Ādi Granth can be appropriately installed, they are likely to possess only the guṭkā for private prayer. The book is usually kept, wrapped in a cloth, on a high shelf.

Gymnastics, Taoist. This refers to the Chinese Tao-yin, meaning literally 'to guide' or 'conduct': stretching and bending exercises to facilitate permeation of 'vital breath' (*ch'i) throughout the body; a technique in cultivating immortal transcendency or at least longevity. Reference to such techniques is already made in the **Chuang Tzu* (3rd cent. BCE). The version best known today is the formalized, adagio-dance-like *t'ai-chi-ch'üan* practised daily by millions of people in E. Asia, and nowadays elsewhere as well.

Gymnosophists. 'Naked philosophers', referred to by Greek historians from the time of Alexander's invasion of India (327–326 BCE) to the 5th cent. CE. Pliny's description of them sitting naked in one posture and inflicting hardships on themselves, and being highly regarded by the people, suggests that they were possibly *Digambara Jain monks.

Gyōgi or **Gyōki** (668–749). Hossō (*Dōshō) monk who popularized Buddhism through his selfless activities. He was a descendant of a Korean king, and studied Buddhism at the Yakushi-ji. But instead of remaining monastery-based, he travelled about, building roads, temples, and bridges—and performing magical signs. Knowing of his high regard among the people, the emperor Shōmu asked him to undertake the building of the *daibutsu at Todai-ji. He argued that *kami are part of the same order as *buddhas and *bodhisattvas, thus doing much to make Buddhism acceptable in Japan. He administered the bodhisattva vows (*bosatsu-kai) to the imperial family, and received the title *daibosatsu. He was also believed popularly to be the incarnation of *Mañjuśrī.

H. H. Coates and R. Ishizuka, *Honen the Buddhist Saint . . .* (1949).

Gyō-jū-za-ga (Jap, 'walking, sitting, lying'). The Zen Buddhist emphasis that Zen attentiveness can and must be maintained, in all circumstances—as the *Buddha Śākyamuni maintained his concentration through a tremendous thunderstorm, during which the driver of a cart was struck by lightning and dropped down dead beside him. Hence when *Ikkyū Sōjun was asked to teach mindfulness in Zen, he took his brush and drew the word, 'Attentiveness'. 'Is that all?' he was asked: 'Can you add anything.' He took his brush and drew, 'Attentiveness, attentiveness'. 'But surely there is something more profound?' He drew a third time: 'Attentiveness, attentiveness, attentiveness.' 'Well, at least tell me what "attentiveness" means!' 'Attentiveness means attentiveness.'

Gyulü ('Illusory Body' in Tibetan Buddhism): see NĀRO CHOS DRUG.

H

Ha-Ari (Jewish kabbalist): see LURIA, ISAAC BEN SOLOMON.

Ḥabad (Heb., acronym of Ḥokmah, Bīnah, Da'at: wisdom, discrimination, knowledge). A religious and intellectual movement within Jewish *ḥasidism. Founded by *Shne'ur Zalman and based on Isaac *Luria's *Kabbalah and the doctrines of the Baal Shem Tov (*Israel ben Eliezer), the terms Ḥokmah, Binah, Da'at (ḤBD) are understood as *sefirot (emanations) in the divine mind. The Ḥabad *Zaddik is essentially a spiritual leader, and the Ḥabad were the first ḥasidic group to found *yeshivot. Shne'ur Zalman was succeeded by his son, *Dov Baer, who settled in Lubavich, with the consequence that Ḥabad and Lubavich are now interchangeable terms (though in fact there was a diffuse spread of Ḥabad movements). Today their main centres of activity are in Israel and the USA.

Central to Ḥabad is the belief that humans created in the image of God mirror the three sefirot within the divine mind. The lesser sefirot are the equivalent of emotional dispositions toward creation (as the Bible so often ascribes emotions to God). Religious life must reflect that order: emotions arise out of the intellectual process and are controlled by it; religious emotion is valid, but only if it arises from intellectual contemplation of God. To get it the other way round (to give priority to the production of religious feelings) is to lapse into mere emotionalism and uncontrolled enthusiasm. Dov Baer wrote a tract for followers of the movement (*Kuntres ha-Hitpa'alut*, Tract on Ecstasy) to help them distinguish genuine and spurious ecstasy.

But the fact remains that a profoundly joyous experience must be expected when 'like meets like', hence the celebratory nature of Ḥabad assemblies. This emerges from *bittul ha-yesh*, 'annihilation of that which is'. This is the loss of the individual, grasping ego in the adoration of God, but it is, also, the belief that a part of the *Ein-Sof lies within human nature: through annihilation of all else that surrounds it, the one is left with the One, and there is no distinction between them. Religious practices (e.g. the repetitive and quiet reciting of the *Shema') cut out the world and the internal clamour, and lead to this effect.

Bittul ha-yesh means also, in Ḥabad, that there is nothing in creation except the presence of God through his sefirot. Derived from Isaiah 6. 5 ('The whole earth is full of his glory'), it was held that the apparently substantial universe is in fact nothing but mist (cf., *ḥebel* in *Ecclesiastes) apart from God. On his deathbed, Shne'ur Zalman said, 'I see no room, no furniture, only the divine energy as truly real.' He maintained an extreme metaphysic of relationship: 'What is God? That which is apprehended. What is the world? That in which one apprehends. What is the soul? That with which one apprehends.'

R. Elior, *The Paradoxical Ascent to God: The Kabbalistic Theosophy of Habad Hasidism* (1992); R. A. Foxbrunner, *HABAD: The Hasidism of R. Shneur of Zalman . . .* (1992); L. Jacobs, *Seeker of Unity* (1966); L. Naftali, *Communicating 'the' Infinite: The Emergence of the Habad School* (1990).

Habakkuk, Book of (Vulgate *Habacuc*). One of the *Minor Prophets of the Hebrew Bible and Christian Old Testament. Chs. 1–2 are a dialogue between God and the prophet: God tells of the advent of the Chaldeans as punishment for sin, and then promises that they too will fall. Then there is a series of woes against various crimes. Ch. 3 is a prayer, with liturgical directions like those in the *Psalms, recalling God's past deliverance of his people. A date in the second half of the 7th cent. BCE seems most probable. A commentary on Habakkuk is among the most important of the *Dead Sea Scrolls. The words, 'the just shall live by his faith' (2. 4) have played an important part in Christian thought, starting from the quotation by *Paul in Galatians 3. 11.

Ḥaber (member of Jewish group): see ḤAVER.

Habiru ('*prw* of the Egyptian Tel el-Amarna letters, *hab/hapiru* in correspondence of Amenophis III and IV). A group or groups of people mentioned in Middle Eastern documents from the 18th to 12th cents. BCE. The Habiru seem to have been a class of dependents, either a group of soldiers attached to local rulers or as part of a list of enslaved people; sometimes they appear as marauders: the Tel-el-Amarna letters of the 15th–14th cents. portray them as a marauding band who plundered local settlements. There has been much scholarly speculation as to the connection between the Habiru and the Hebrews (Heb., *'ibri*), but it is highly unlikely that the Israelites' conquest of the *Promised Land can be identified with that of the Habiru in the Tel-el-Amarna letters; on the other hand, some distant echo of an uprising of a marginal people (i.e. kinship group) is not incompatible, especially with the opening chapters of *Joshua.

Habit, religious. Distinctive dress worn by members of religious orders. In W. Christianity, these are usually white (*Cistercians), brown (*Franciscans), or black (*Dominicans). In addition to the main garment, it usually includes a girdle (often with three knots for the vows of poverty, chastity, and obedience), scapular (a long piece of cloth worn on the shoulders and hanging down back and front, symbolizing the yoke of Christ), and a hood (for men) or veil (for women). Many orders have in recent years reduced or even abandoned the habit, to enable a greater freedom of commitment to the world; others have retained the habit as a sign of that commitment and its unequivocal nature.

In E. Orthodoxy, the different habits reflect different stages in the monastic life. A beginner wears the *proschema*, with an inner and outer *cassock-type garment (*rason*), with a leather belt, a round cap, and sandals. The next stage may substitute a cloak (*mandyas*) for the outer *rason*, which in any case will be fuller; a wooden cross is worn. The final stage introduces something like a scapular (*analavos*) which is decorated with representations of the instruments of the *Passion. There may also be a hood or cowl (*koukoulos*).

In E. religions, the equivalent of the religious habit appears with varying degrees of formality. In the Buddhist *saṅgha, a three-part dress was adopted: the lower body is clothed in the *antaravasaka* (a kind of sarong); the *uttarasaṅgha* or *cīvara* in Thailand (a length of woven cloth) surrounds the upper body; and the *saṅghati* or *kaṣāya* (a patchwork cloth to symbolize poverty) is worn over the left shoulder. *Kaṣāya* ('earth-coloured') refers to the 'impure' (aged or faded) colour of the cloth, in contrast to pure (bleached) white: it is the yellow dye used to create this effect which leads to the characteristic 'saffron robe'. For the Japanese habit, see SANNE.

Taoist ritual functionaries wear a cloak (*chiang-i*) which has on it symbols of the cosmos with which the ritual is making connection. These include symbols of the sun, moon, and stars, of the celestial heaven, the three Isles of the Immortals, and the gates of the earth.

In Judaism, the specialized garments of the *Temple functionaries ceased with the destruction of the Temple. A rabbi has no specialized ritual role, and therefore wears the same 'religious habit' in the *synagogue as any other man in the assembly: *tallit (prayer shawl with *zitzit, tassels), *tefillin (phylacteries), and kippah or *yarmulke (skull-cap).

Among Sikhs, formal dress requirements apply only to *amritdhārī Sikhs (see FIVE KS), but some customs have also established themselves. Thus Sikh dress is characteristically *Pañjābī, the women generally wearing a *salvār* (Indian trousers) and *kamīz* (long top) with a *chunnī* (finely woven scarf usually c.180 × 80 cm.) which covers the head in the *gurdwārā. Veiling of the face is forbidden in Sikh literature. W. clothes, especially trousers, are increasingly worn by younger women. Many men have adopted W. clothes too. For *keśadhārī men, the *turban is essential. *Sahajdhārī men cover their head with a handkerchief in the gurdwārā. Gurū *Gobind Siṅgh ordained the five Ks including the *kaṛā* (bangle) and *kachh* (drawers) for all amritdhārī Sikhs. See AKĀLĪ; BHĀṬṚĀ; KHAṆḌE-DĪ-PĀHUL; MARRIAGE; NĀMDHĀRĪ; NIHAṄG; UDĀSĪ.

For Muslim veiling, see HIJĀB. See also Index, Dress.

Hachimaki (white cloth of samurai): see KAMIKAZE.

Hachiman (Jap., 'eight banners'). A popular Shinto deity, often associated with good fortune in war. Hachiman seems to have come into being as the continuing *kami spirit of semi-legendary rulers of ancient Japan who were especially associated with conquering Korea and thus with military victory. The worship of Hachiman spread quickly in early Japan, and by the 8th cent. CE a distinctive Shinto cult devoted to Hachiman had developed. Primarily a deity of the military (*bushi*) classes, Hachiman became the patron kami of the Minamoto clan which defeated the Taira clan to bring the Heian Period to a close in the 12th cent. Subsequently, however, he has become a deity popular with all classes across the whole of Japan—especially in times of military conflict. See also KAMAKURA.

In Japanese Buddhism, Hachiman was integrated as H. *Daibosatsu, the Great *Bodhisattva, the first Shinto deity to be so treated. He is regarded as the incarnation of *Amida.

Hadad. A god of the Amorites and *Canaanites. The cult of Hadad was centred in Damascus and Baalbek and persisted up to Roman times. In Canaan, Hadad was identified with *Baʿal; the bull was sacred to him, and he was portrayed with thunderbolts and ears of corn as symbols of fertility.

Hadassah. The women's *Zionist organization of America. According to its constitution, Hadassah is dedicated to 'the ideals of Judaism, Zionism, American democracy, healing, teaching and medical research'. It was founded in the USA early in the 20th cent. It raises funds, runs educational programmes, and provides a focus of Jewish identification for American women, with the funds being used for medical care, training, and research in *Israel. Hadassah has also become involved in the Jewish National Fund, and in supporting young peoples' educational projects.

Ḥadath (Arab.). Ritual impurity for a Muslim, major or minor, which can only be eliminated by appropriate ablutions, *ghusl or *wuḍū'*.

M. A. Quasem, *Salvation of the Soul and Islamic Devotions* (1983).

Ḥadd (Arab., *hadda*, 'determine'; often in pl., *ḥudūd*). A boundary or limit set by God, in *Qur'ān of laws laid down, e.g. on fasting (2. 187), divorce (2. 229 f.). It came to mean unalterable punishments, especially stoning or beating for sexual intercourse outside the permitted relationships (*zinā'); beating for false accusations of adultery, or for drinking intoxicants; cutting off of the hand for theft.

Among *Sūfīs, ḥadd (but more often the part. *maḥdūd*) refers to the finiteness of humans in contrast to God.

Hadewijch of Antwerp (Christian mystical writer): see RHENO-FLEMISH SPIRITUALITY.

Ḥad Gadya (Aram., 'only one kid'). Folk-song chanted at the end of the Passover *Seder. It is a sequence poem (as 'This is the house that Jack built' or 'This is the nail'), tracing how God slew the angel of death that . . . ate the kid that father bought for only two *zuzim*, 'only one kid, only one kid' (or 'an only kid'). Sung no doubt for the amusement of the young, it has now an allegorical meaning in each detail, since the kid is Israel, bought on Sinai by the two tables of Law (or through Moses and Aaron).

Ḥadīth (Arab., 'narrative'). Muslim tradition—accounts of the 'words, deeds or silent approval' of *Muḥammad during the period of his preaching, but especially after the beginning of the *Qur'ān revelations. Although the plural is *ahādith*, Hadith is used in English as a collective for 'traditions', as well as the word for a single tradition. Ḥadīth report the *sunna (customary practice) of Muḥammad and his *Companions, and is given extra authority by the Quranic injunction to take Muḥammad as a 'fine example' (33. 21). The Qur'ān speaks of the 'Book and Wisdom' which Muḥammad would teach to the believers (2. 151, 3. 164), and this wisdom, *ḥikma*, was explained as referring to the ḥadīth. It became in time the second source of legislation, after the Qur'ān.

A ḥadīth—a single item of tradition—consists of two parts: *matn* ('text') and *isnād* or *sanad* ('chain of authorities'). The latter takes the form of: I heard from A who was told by B who heard from C that the Prophet said . . . An elaborate science of ḥadīth criticism grew up, mainly to ensure the authenticity of any given ḥadīth, and each one was classified as *ṣaḥīḥ* ('sound'), *ḥasan* ('good'), or *ḍaʿif* ('weak'), while more detailed classifications dealt with the authorities cited.

The law book of *Mālik b. Anas (d. 795) contains a large number of ḥadīth. The work of Aḥmad b. *Hanbal (d. 855) and other early works of ḥadīth were arranged according to the authorities cited, but later works were classified by subject-matter, since one main function of ḥadīth was to provide precedents and norms for legislation. The best known and most quoted is the Ṣaḥīḥ (Sound Collection) of *al-Bukhārī (d. 870), which contains thousands of ḥadīth, sifted from a much larger number which al-Bukhārī rejected. A second important collection is the Ṣaḥīḥ of *Muslim b. al-Hajjāj (d. 875), and those two are known as the 'two Ṣaḥīḥ'. Next in importance are those of *al-Tirmidhī (d. 892), *al-Nasā'ī (d. 915), Ibn Māja (d. 886), and *Abū Dāwūd (d. 888). Together these form the 'six books' of reference, which contain the ḥadīth generally accepted by Muslims as genuine and thus appropriate for guidance even today. Some ḥadīth do not necessarily date back to the time of Muḥammad but reflect the thinking of the community, while there were some ḥadīth constructed for political ends.

The *Shīʿa have their own collections of ḥadīth, which they accuse the *Sunnis of having deliberately ignored or concealed, which extol the virtues of *ʿAlī b. Abī Ṭālib and the Twelve *Imāms. The earliest authoritative collection is *Al-kāfī fī ʿIlm al-Dīn*, of Abu Jaʿfar.

See Index, Hadith.

Trs. of ḥadīth by K. Muhsin Khan, J. Robson (1963–5), E. Ibrahim and D. Johnson-Davies, and M. Zafrulla Khan; M. A. Anees and A. N. Athar, *Guide to Sira and Hadith Literature in W. Languages* (1986); M. M. Azami, *Studies in Hadith Methodology and Literature* (1977); A. Guillaume, *The Traditions of Islam* (1924); M. Hamidullah, *The Earliest Extant Work on Hadith . . .* (1961); J. H. A. Juynboll, *The Authenticity of the Tradition Literature* (1969); A. H. Siddiqi, *Sahīḥ Muslim* (1977); A. von Denffer, *Hadith: A Select and Annotated Guide to Materials in the English Language* (1979).

Hadj (pilgrimage): see ḤAJJ.

Ḥadra (present only to God): see GHAIBA.

Haeceitas (idea of individual uniqueness): see DUNS SCOTUS, J.

Haedong Kosŭng Jŏn (Lives of Eminent Korean Monks). One of the most important sources dealing with the history of *Buddhism in Korea. The work was compiled by scholar-monk Kakhun in 1215, in the hope that it would 'make the country and Buddhism prosper'. Only the first two chapters are extant today; these include eighteen major and seven minor biographies of eminent monks spanning a 500-year period from the time of Buddhism's initial introduction to Korea through the early centuries of its history.

Tr. P. H. Lee, *Lives of Eminent Korean Monks* (1969).

Ḥafets Ḥayyim or **Israel Meir ha-Kohen Kagan** (1838–1933). Jewish writer and source of inspiration for *Orthodox Jews. Born in Lithuania, he settled at Radun in Poland, where a group gathered around him which was known as the Ḥafets Ḥayyim *yeshivah of Radun. The name (by which he was subsequently known) was taken from his first book, which he published anonymously, in 1873, under that title. It is a work on gossip, tale-bearing, and slander. To guard the tongue is the all-important prerequisite of religious life: 'For each second of silence in which evil talk is renounced, there will be a blaze of eternal light in the hereafter.' He published other works (e.g. a guide for Jewish soldiers), of which the best known is a commentary on part of **Shulḥān Arukh*, providing a guide to the *halakhah of everyday life, where actions speak louder than theory: 'The Torah does not anywhere tell us to invite a visitor to pray, but it does tell us to invite him to receive food, drink and a bed.' He particularly encouraged the study of the tractate in the *Talmud, *Kodashim*, which deals with *Temple matters, since he held that the *messiah might return at any time and initiate the rebuilding of the Temple. He helped in the founding of an extreme Orthodox movement, *Agadut Israel, but he was clear that such movements are a means, never an end: 'On the Day of Judgement, God will not ask to what sect you belonged, but what kind of life you lived.'

L. S. Eckman, *Revered By All* (1974).

Ḥāfiẓ (one who learns the Qur'ān by heart): see QUR'ĀN.

Ḥafṣa. Wife of *Muḥammad. A daughter of *ʿUmar, she was born about 605 CE, and emigrated with her father from *Mecca to *Madīna. As the widow of a childless marriage, she was given as a wife to Muḥammad in 625 CE (AH 3). Although divorced after a domestic quarrel, she was later taken back. She is said to have owned the first written version of the Qur'ān. This was compiled at the orders of *Abu Bakr, was passed to ʿUmar, and, on his death, to Ḥafṣa, and later used as a foundation for the definitive version made during the caliphate (*khalīfa) of *ʿUthmān.

Haftarah (Heb., 'conclusion'). A *synagogue reading from the biblical *prophets. The second reading in the synagogue on *Sabbaths, *Festivals, and on the afternoons of fast days is taken from the prophetic books. It is chosen either because of its connection with the appointed *Torah reading or because of its relevance for the particular Festival. It is chanted in accordance with particular *cantillation, and one *blessing is said before and four are recited after it. The 'reading of the Law and the Prophets' is clearly as old as New Testament times (Luke 4. 17; Acts 13. 15), but the origin is not known. Traditionally, the haftarah is taken back to the persecutions of Antiochus Epiphanes in the Maccabean revolt (see MACCABEES, BOOKS OF) when the reading of Torah was forbidden; a passage from the Prophets having some connection was therefore substituted. But there is no direct evidence for this.

Hagar. The servant of *Sarah who was given as concubine of *Abraham and became the mother of *Ishmael (Genesis 16. 1–16). Conflict with Sarah led to her expulsion and miraculous rescue (21. 8–21). In Galatians 4, Paul used the story to argue that being enslaved under the old *covenant has been displaced by freedom under the new (*Isaac).

In Islam, Hagar is the wife of Ibrāhīm (*Abraham), who was sent out by him, with their son Ismāʿīl (Ishmael), into the desert. The story is not narrated in the *Qur'ān, but later legend, based on Jewish sources, describes their wandering and their eventual rescue. Hagar's running between two small hills, in search of water, is said to be the origin of the rite of *saʿy, 'running' between Ṣafā and Marwa, which is part of the ritual of *ʿumra.

Hagbahah, gelilah (Heb., 'lifting and rolling'). The ceremonial elevating and rolling up of the *Torah *scroll in the *synagogue. When the scroll is raised during the service, the congregation declares in Hebrew, 'This is the *law which *Moses set before the children of *Israel' (Deuteronomy 4. 44). Different groups follow different practices, but after the scroll has been raised, another person rolls it up and binds it. The *Talmud teaches that he who rolls the Torah scroll (*gelilah*) is even more honoured than those who are called up to read from it (*B.Meg.* 32a).

Haggadah (Heb., 'telling'; equivalent to *aggadah, and often used in that general sense). The order of service prescribed for the Jewish *Passover *seder. In the *Mishnah, it consists of the *kiddush which is said at all *festivals. The *mazzah is introduced as 'the bread of affliction', and the poor are invited to join the meal. Then the *four questions are asked by the youngest competent person present. In response, the story of the *exodus from Egypt is begun, and includes tales of the *rabbis, the *baraita of the four sons, and several *aggadic interpretations of the seder ritual. Commentaries of the *tannaim are recited on the stories of the ten plagues, the crossing of the Red Sea, and the significance of the Passover lamb, the unleavened bread, and the bitter herbs. The first part of the *Hallel is then recited, and, after the meal is eaten, *grace after the meal is said. The second half of the haggadah consists of a prayer for vengeance on the oppressing nations—'Pour out thy wrath'. This is followed by the latter part of the Hallel, a hymn of praise and the *benediction over the song. The Haggadah text is also divided according to the ritual acts of the seder. These involve the blessing over the wine, the washing of hands, the eating of the green herb, dividing the middle mazzah, narrating the exodus story, washing the hands before the meal, blessing the mazzah, eating the bitter herbs, eating the bitter herbs with mazzah, eating the meal, eating the *afikomen, grace after the meal, reciting the Hallel, and closing the proceedings.

Extra songs, poetry, and elaborations have been added to the original Haggadah over the years and, since the time of *Rashi, commentaries on the text have been produced. Many different manuscripts of the Haggadah have been preserved, the oldest version being in the 10th cent. *Prayer Book of *Saʿadiah Gaon. Since the 15th cent., more than 2,700 edns. of the Haggadah have been produced and it has been translated into every language used by

Jews. The *progressive movements have produced their own versions, amending the text in accordance with their own theology, and there is also a *Karaite version. Illustrated manuscript edns. tend to fall into one of three types: the Spanish which is decorated with full-page biblical miniatures, the *Ashkenazi which is decorated in the margins surrounding the liturgical text, and the Italian which is probably the earliest of the three. Of the printed edns., the best known are from Prague (1526), Mantua (1560), Venice (1599), Amsterdam (1695), Trieste (1864), Prague (1889), and Poona for the *Bene Israel congregation (1874).

J. Elias, *The Haggadah* (1980).

Haggai. Post-*exilic Jewish *prophet. Haggai is mentioned in Ezra 5. 1 as having a role in the rebuilding of the *Temple. The prophecies contained in Haggai can be dated to 520 BCE (the second year of King Darius) and are concerned primarily with the reconstruction of the Temple. Inspired by Haggai's words and led by *Zerubbabel, the governor of *Judah, and *Joshua, the *high priest, the people began to rebuild. In later oracles, the prophet promised that the second Temple would be more splendid that the first and that Zerubbabel would be the Lord's signet ring.

Hag ha-keves (Doenmeh festival): see DOENMEH.

Hagia Sofia, Aya Sofya, or **Sancta Sophia** ('Divine Wisdom'). The mosque, originally basilica or church of the Divine Wisdom, in Istanbul. It was commissioned in the 6th cent. by the emperor Justinian after the second church on the site (founded in 452 by Theodosius II) had been razed to the ground in the Nika revolts of Jan. 532. The chief architect was Anthemius of Tralles, the most distinguished mathematician and physicist of the age, assisted by Isidorus of Miletus. The original design combined architectural innovation and engineering skill to create a church in a manner and on a scale hitherto unknown in the Byzantine world. Dedicated on 26 Dec. 537, it was the most imaginative building ever built: a dome 100 feet wide hovered over a seemingly empty space. As the result of an earthquake in *c*.550, the dome collapsed, and Isidorus, a nephew of one of the original architects, restructured the building to give it greater stability. He increased the height of the external buttresses and of the dome itself. In 1317 huge buttresses were added on the north and south sides to strengthen the church. Sacked in 1204 by Catholic soldiers during the fourth *crusade, the church was desecrated, its relics were stolen, and a prostitute held court on the throne of the patriarch. In 1452 the Byzantine Church became Catholic in an attempt to gain W. support for an ailing Constantinople in the face of the might of the Turk. On 25 May 1453 Mehmet the Conqueror rode to the church, stopped the looting, cleared the building of relics, covered over its 'idolatrous images' (mainly mosaics), and converted it into a mosque—initially by the addition of a wooden minaret, and by the introduction of a miḥrāb and minbar (see MOSQUE). In the late 16th cent. as part of a restoration process, minarets were added by the architect Sīhān (see SULAIMĀN THE MAGNIFICENT). The last extensive restoration was commissioned by Sultan Abdul Mecit in 1847 by the Swiss brothers Fossati, and the Aya Sofia continued to function as a mosque until 1932 when it was opened as a museum.

Hagiographa (third section of Jewish scriptures): see WRITINGS.

Hagiography. The writing of the lives of Christian *saints (hence a derogatory sense, 'full of praise for, without sufficient criticism of, the subject'). Hagiographical writings can be divided into five types: (i) official records of the trials of *martyrs; (ii) accounts based on first-hand knowledge about a saint; (iii) accounts elaborating an earlier source of this kind; (iv) historical romances; and (v) romances in which the saint himself (or herself) is imaginary. At the zenith of the genre as pious literature in the late Middle Ages, the last two types were predominant. The work of H. Delehaye (e.g. *The Legends of the Saints*, tr. 1962) epitomizes the critical study of this literature by the *Bollandists since the 17th cent.

Ha-Gra (Jewish spiritual leader): see ELIJAH BEN SOLOMON ZALMAN.

Hahalis Welfare Society. A religious and economic development movement with some *cargo ideas on Buka Island, Papua New Guinea. In 1952, two former students in *Roman Catholic schools, John Teosin (b. 1938) and his brother-in-law, Francis Hagai, formed a family co-operative which in 1957 developed into a co-operative society involving half the Buka population in plantations, stores, transport, etc. In 1961, they set up their own 'church', with *Bible reading, *hymns, and rites and prayers focused on the ancestors. They also began 'Baby Gardens', extending the co-operative idea to increase of population through selected young people, ending the elders' monopoly of young women, and possibly hoping for a *messiah to be born. These were defended as 'matrimonial clubs' or 'trial marriage', but were criticized by both missions and administration. In 1962, refusal to pay head tax led to mass arrests. After 1965, relations improved, with more development activity through missions and government. Many members saw it as a cargo movement in line with earlier Buka movements, while the younger educated leaders were more concerned with hard work and rational organization.

Hai ben Sherira (939–1038). Jewish *gaon of *Pumbedita, hence also known as Hai Gaon. Hai succeeded his father as gaon and was regarded as a supreme *halakhic authority. According to Abraham *ibn Daud, 'he, more than all the geonim, propagated the *Torah in Israel. . . . No one among his predecessors can be compared to him.' Besides *responsa, he also wrote mystical *piyyutim, including five *seliḥot for 9 *Av, marked by a somewhat gloomy assessment of our present condition: 'Life is a severe illness, cured only by death.' His best known halakhic work was the Arabic *Kitab al-Shira wa-al-Baye* (Treatise on Commercial Transactions). Although he allowed the teaching of Arabic writing and arithmetic, he disapproved of the study of philosophy, and he had considerable influence on the leaders of Spanish Jewry such as *Samuel ha-Nagid.

Haibutsu kishaku. Jap. slogan, 'abolish Buddhism, destroy Buddhist images', adopted during (and as a consequence of) the *Meiji determination to establish Shinto as the state religion, in separation from Buddhism. This reversed many centuries during which there had been not only tolerance but considerable assimilation. The period of aggression lasted from 1868 to 1874.

Haiden (Jap.), The frontmost building in a Shinto shrine complex, used as an oratory or hall of worship.

Hai Gaon: see HAI BEN SHERIRA.

Haiku (Jap.). A verse form consisting of three lines: five, seven, and five syllables in length. Traditionally, each poem also contains an image or reference associated with one of the seasons in the year. The haiku has its historical origin as the opening triplet in a chain of linked verses called haikai. As such, it was traditionally called a *hokku*, the term haiku being of late 19th cent. provenance. Originally conceived as a form of amusement verse, the haikai utilized colloquialisms and words derived from Chinese, terms expressly forbidden in the more formal, high form of verse called *waka*. Only in the early 16th cent. did haikai come to be viewed as a legitimate poetic genre in its own right.

Because of its terseness and associations with wit, the haikai were considered the product of free association and verbal cleverness. In the 16th and 17th cents., contests were held to see which poet could generate the most verses in a single day. Mainly through the impact of Matsuo Bashō (1644–94) and his successors, however, the literary form assumed religious, specifically *Zen Buddhist, dimensions. In Zen Buddhism, enlightenment consists in the direct experience of phenomena, uncoloured by conceptual presuppositions. Bashō, a Zen Buddhist layman, understood the haiku to be the spontaneous verbal expression of that experience in the poet.

H. Henderson, *An Introduction to Haiku* (1958); Makoto Ueda, *Matsuo Basho* (1970); E. Miner, *Japanese Linked Poetry* (1979).

Hail Mary (tr. of Lat., *Ave Maria*). A prayer to the Virgin *Mary as follows: (*a*) Hail Mary, full of grace, the Lord is with you; blessed are you among women, and blessed is the fruit of your womb, Jesus. (*b*) Holy Mary, Mother of God, pray for us sinners now and in the hour of our death. Part (*a*) is based on the greetings of *Gabriel (Luke 1. 28) and Mary's cousin Elizabeth (Luke 1. 42). Its devotional use goes back to the 11th cent. The prayer with (*b*) added did not come into general use until the 16th cent. In this form it was included in the Roman *Breviary in 1568, but dropped in 1955. It remains a popular devotion. See also ANGELUS.

Hair. The treatment of hair is important in many religions. Hair is a visible and continuous sign of growth (or, in its cessation, of the approach of death), and as an indication of vigour, it lends itself to various statements of relationship to God or to other goals. The *Nazirite vow in Judaism, which includes letting the hair grow, gave to Samson his strength, which was only lost when Delilah cut his hair (Judges 16. 17; cf. Nazirite vow, Numbers 6. 1–18). Christianity adopted a sign of dedication in the opposite direction, by introducing the tonsure, the shaving of the top of the head of priests and monks. Tonsure has taken different forms, from the shaving of the whole head to only a part, often leaving a fringe to draw out the symbolism of the crown of thorns. The requirement of tonsure, which had in any case been abbreviated after the Council of *Trent to the cutting of five pieces of hair (often in the shape of a cross), was suppressed for the clergy in 1972 by the *motu proprio, *Ministeria Quaedam*, and by *Ad Pascendum*. Among nuns, the cutting short of the hair, either at entry to the novitiate or after the taking of vows, symbolized the cutting off of desire for the things of the world, but may also have had a practical reason, in that it enabled cleanliness under the veil.

In E. religions, comparable contrasts can be found. Thus among Hindus, *keśāntah*, the first shaving of the beard, is one of the *saṃskāras; but a Hindu *ascetic will leave his hair long and matted (*juṭā*): *Śiva, in particular, displays his contrasted modes of activity through the style of his hair. Among Sikhs, a *Khālsā Sikh is prohibited from cutting hair from any part of his body, and *keś* is one of the *Five Ks. Among *Rastafarians, a similar message of identity is sent through hairstyle, but this may be by 'dreadlocks' or by careful cutting (for the long locks of Jews see PEOT). A further extension can be seen in care taken to cover the head—for example, in the custom for some Jewish women of wearing a wig (*shaytl/sheitel*) in public (see HEAD, COVERING OF), which perhaps goes back to the implication of such covering in Numbers 5. 18, and was later understood as shame for the sin of Eve. It appears also in *Paul's instruction to women to keep their heads covered in church, in a passage of complex argument in 1 Corinthians 11. 2–16: 'Does it seem fitting that a woman should pray to God without a veil? Does not nature itself teach you that if a man has long hair, it is a disgrace to him, but when a woman has long hair, it is her glory? After all, her hair was given to her to be a covering.' Different again was the reason underlying the *Huguenot custom, as observed by André Gide:

> It fell to my lot to see the last representatives of that generation of men who addressed God as 'Thou', attending divine service with their great felt hats on their heads, raising them each time the pastor pronounced the name of God, and only taking them off during the Lord's Prayer. . . . They kept their heads covered in memory of the open-air services, held under a burning sky, in the secret recesses of the mountains, at a time when their ritual carried with it the danger of a capital penalty.

A particular place in the treatment of hair is reserved for beards. Beards mark the transition to manhood. In biblical Judaism, they mark also acknowledged status in society. To abuse a beard is a mark of contempt (2 Samuel 10. 4), and the neglect of the beard is a sign of mourning (2 Samuel 19. 24, Job 1. 20, etc.). Following both biblical precept (Leviticus 19. 27) and the custom of pagan philosophers, Christian clergy and monks have worn beards from the earliest times, a custom that still holds in the East. In the West, by the 9th cent., monks shaved regularly, a practice that spread to the clergy, and this difference became contentious between E. and W. Various W. medieval decrees require clergy to be clean-shaven. With the Renaissance, beards came again into fashion, and *Capuchin *friars, in particular, have continued to wear beards. Wearing of moustaches alone has no traditional authority. In Islam, the practice of Muḥammad in wearing a beard is necessarily followed, not least since he advocated it as a mark of distinction from the polytheists (*shirk): 'Be different from the *mushrikūn*: let the beard grow and trim the moustache.' From this arose the custom (now rare) of a man collecting the hairs from his beard if they fell out in order that they might be buried with him as a mark of Islam. But in recent centuries, the growing of a beard has increasingly been regarded as an opinion, not a compulsion.

To bring order into this diversity, E. Leach ('Magical Hair'), *Journ. of the R. Anth. Inst.* 1958) argued that the treatment of hair denotes social responses related to ideal social categories. Thus long hair is related to unrestrained sexuality, short or tightly bound hair is related to restricted sexuality, closely shaved hair is related to celibacy. C. R. Hallpike ('Social Hair', *Man*, 1969) argued that hair rituals cannot be mapped on to sexual opportunity alone. In his view, the treatment indicates relation to the acceptance or rejection of social control.

R. Bartlett, 'Symbolic Meanings of Hair in the Middle Ages', *Transactions of the Royal Hist. Soc.* (1994); W. Cooper, *Hair: Sex, Society, Symbolism* (1971).

Ḥajj (Arab.). Pilgrimage to *Mecca, specifically to the *Kaʿba, during the month *Dhū'l-Ḥijja. This is one of the *Five Pillars of Islam, a duty ordered in the *Qur'ān: 'Pilgrimage to the House (of Allāh) is a duty men owe to Allāh, for those who find a way thereto' (3. 91/97). This is incumbent upon every adult free Muslim, of sound mind, with sufficient funds to cover his journey and the expenses of his family during his absence. *Women should be suitably escorted.

The general term ḥajj includes the *ʿumra (lesser pilgrimage) to the Kaʿba, which can be performed at any time of the year but does not itself fulfil the obligations of ḥajj. The prescribed ceremonies are detailed in the *ḥadīth, and refer back largely to the rites of the 'Farewell Pilgrimage' of *Muḥammad in 632 CE, the year of his death. Many ceremonies are of pagan origin, but have been adapted to Islam—in particular by ascription to the practice and precepts of Ibrāhīm (*Abraham): 'We made a covenant with Ibrāhīm and Ismāʿīl that they should sanctify my House for those who go around it and who use it as a retreat, who there bend and prostrate themselves (in prayer)' (Qur'ān 2. 125).

The area around Mecca is designated *ḥarām (holy); the male pilgrim on reaching the boundary exchanges his usual clothes for two pieces of white cloth, covering the upper and lower parts of the body, and wears sandals; women, also in white, cover their whole body except face and hands. The pilgrim has now entered the state of *iḥrām, and until the end of the ḥajj ceremonies he must not put on other clothes, wear shoes, cut nails or hair, engage in sexual relations, take part in arguments, fighting, nor hunting of game. The *talbīyah is repeated frequently.

In Mecca itself the pilgrim goes first to the *Masjid al-Ḥarām for the rites of *ṭawāf, 'circumambulation' of the Kaʿba, and of *saʿy, 'running', and will if possible kiss the *Black Stone. Those rites, which form the ʿumra, are performed during the first few days of Dhū'l-Ḥijja. The ḥajj proper begins on the seventh day, with a *khuṭba (sermon) at the *mosque. On the eighth day, all pilgrims move eastwards from Mecca, spending that night at Minā or, further on, at *ʿArafāt. On the ninth day, the central and essential part of ḥajj takes place, the *wuqūf* ('standing') at ʿArafāt, before a small hill named Jabal al-Raḥma. Wuqūf begins at noon and continues till sunset. Then pilgrims hurry back to the small town of Muzdalifa within the Meccan boundaries, to stay overnight. On the tenth day, which is *ʿId al-Aḍḥā, they move to Minā, first to throw seven small stones (see RAJM) at a rock called Jamrat al-ʿAqaba, then to perform the ritual *sacrifice. From Minā the pilgrims return to Mecca to perform another ṭawāf; then the head can be shaved, or the hair cut, and the state of iḥrām is over. The next three days are spent visiting in and around Mecca, with the obligation to throw seven stones each day at each of three Jamras in Minā. Many pilgrims also go to *Madīna to visit the tomb of Muḥammad.

The ḥajj has a strong emotional appeal and great symbolic value in demonstrating the international solidarity of all Muslims. It is said to bring great blessings, and a common greeting to a returned pilgrim is 'may your pilgrimage be blessed and your sins forgiven'. In former times some pilgrims might spend several years on their way to Mecca, stopping at places to work, teach, or study.

D. Long, *The Hajj Today* (1979); M. Wolfe, *The Hadj*.

Hājjī Bektāsh Valī (founder of Turkish Derwish order): see BEKTĀSHĪYYA.

Ḥakham (Heb., 'wise'). *Rabbinic title. Originally the title ḥakham was used for scholars, especially in early days, who had not received rabbinic *semikhah. Later it was used as an alternative for rabbi and was used for those third in status after the *nasi and the *av bet din*. Among *Sephardi Jews the title is still used for the local rabbi. Ḥakham Bashi (Turk., 'chief') was the leader of Jewish communities recognized as such in the *Ottoman Empire. The title fell into oblivion at the end of the First World War.

Ḥakham Zevi (Jewish halakhist): see ASHKENAZI, ZEVI.

Hakhel (Heb., 'assemble'). The Jewish seventh year assembly. In Deuteronomy, *Moses commanded the Israelites, 'At the end of every seven years . . . when all *Israel comes to appear before the Lord your God . . . *assemble* the people . . . that they may hear and learn to fear the Lord your God' (31. 10–12). The *Mishnah connects this ceremony with the kings who had publicly to read selected passages from the *Torah. The practice has not been followed since the destruction of the *Temple, but since the establishment of the state of *Israel there has been an attempt to revive the ceremony. Thus in the hakhel in 1987 (5748), the President of Israel read from Torah at the Western Wall (*Wailing Wall), along with the *Ashkenazi and *Sephardi chief *rabbis.

Hākim (last and greatest of divine manifestations): see DRUZES.

Hakkafot (Heb., 'circuits'). Jewish ceremonial circular processions. According to Joshua 6. 14–15, the city of Jericho was circuited once a day for six days and seven times on the seventh, when the Israelites conquered the *Promised Land. According to the *Mishnah, the *lulav was carried around the *Temple on the seven days of *Sukkot (*Suk.* 3. 12). This practice is continued in the *synagogue when the *Torah *scrolls are carried round on *Simḥat Torah. Hakkafot are also performed in some communities by brides encircling their husbands during the *wedding ceremony, and round the coffin before the burial (see CIRCUMAMBULATION).

Hakuin (c.1685–1768). Ordination name of Nagasawa Ekaku, a major Japanese *Zen master, painter, and poet. Hakuin is especially noted for his vigorous revitalization of *Rinzai-shū spiritual training and for his bold style of inkwash painting. When a boy, he went with his mother to a Buddhist temple, and heard the torments of hell (*naraka) being recited in a *sūtra. He decided to set himself beyond that possibility by becoming a monk, and by becoming one whom 'fire could not scorch, nor water drown'. Opposed by his parents, he nevertheless entered a monastery at the age of 15. There he read of *Yen-t'ou Ch'uan-huo (Jap., Gantō Zenkatsu), whose murder by robbers, despite his advanced elimination of bad *karma, caused Hakuin to doubt the truth of Buddhism. But he persisted, and when he attained *satori, he realized that Gantō was alive and flourishing—as much as he had ever been. Engaged in the *mu kōan, he heard a bell and experienced the most profound enlightenment, but to his detriment, because he felt that he must be unique: 'My pride rose up like a mighty mountain, my arrogance swelled like a tidal wave' (*Orate-gama* 3). His teacher, Dōkyō Etan, refused to recognize the experience, and set him to more severe Zen training. In his own teaching, he emphasized the three pillars of Zen (see DAI-FUNSHI) and kōan practice: he is the source of the most frequently (in the W.) quoted kōan, 'What is the sound of one hand clapping?', which is known as *sekishu*. He was abbot of several monasteries, including Ryūtaki-ji, (active to the present day), and he emphasized disciplined meditation at all times (not just at chosen times) in order to achieve *kensho.

Tr. of parts of his writings, etc.: R. D. M. Shaw, *The Embossed Tea Kettle* (1963); P. B. Yampolski, *The Zen Master Hakuin: Selected Writings* (1971).

Hakushi (Jap., 'white paper'). The state of consciousness in Zen Buddhism attained through *zazen, which immediately precedes enlightenment. It is entirely empty and disconnected from all thought and experience.

Hakuun Ryōko Yasutani (1885–1973). Japanese Zen Buddhist master, who received the seal of recognition (*inka-shōmei) from Daiun Sōgaku Harada in 1943. He spent much time visiting the USA, and his instructions in Zen underlie P. Kapleau (ed.), *The Three Pillars of Zen* (1980).

Ḥāl (Arab., 'state', 'inner condition'; pl. *aḥwāl*). Among *Sūfīs, those thoughts and conditions which come upon the heart without intention or desire, such as sorrow, fear, pleasure, ecstasy, anger, or even lust. In their religious forms, they are such states, in relation to God, as confidence, peace, love, attentiveness, nearness, certitude. If these conditions are stable and not transient, they are called *maqām* (station); if they are fleeting and transient they are called ḥāl. Ḥāl is considered a divine gift, a direct illumination of the heart by God and sure cognizance of the 'Truth'. Its outer manifestation is ecstasy, rapture, and *dance. Cf. *kashf. See also DH'UL NŪN AL-MISRĪ.

Halāhala (poison drunk by Śiva): see CHURNING OF THE OCEAN.

Halakhah (Heb., from *halak*, 'he went'). A particular *law or the whole Jewish legal system. The halakhah is traditionally believed to go back in its entirety to *Moses. According to *Maimonides, 'In the two *Talmuds and the *Tosefta, the *Sifra and the *Sifrei, in all these are explained the permitted and the forbidden . . . as handed down from person to person from the mouth of Moses our teacher at *Sinai.' The halakhah is composed of the written law (the *six hundred and thirteen commandments of the *Pentateuch), the statements handed down by tradition (such as the words of the *prophets and the hagiographa (*Writings), the *oral law (which includes interpretations of the written law), the sayings of the *scribes, and established religious custom. Written law is *Torah she-bi-khetav*, oral law is *Torah she-be'al peh* ('. . . by mouth'). In the days of the second *Temple, a major point at issue between the *Pharisees and the *Sadducees was the validity of the oral law—the Sadducees adhering only to the written law. Even among the Pharisees, the schools of *Hillel and *Shammai differed in their interpretation of the biblical law and in their oral rulings. Various attempts were made to draw up collections of rulings. At the end of the 2nd cent. CE, however, R. *Judah ha-Nasi summarized the legal debates in a form that came to be regarded as authoritative, and this record of the final decisions of the *tannaim now constitutes *Mishnah. Once this text was established, further debate centred on its meaning and interpretation; these discussions of the Palestinian and Babylonian *amoraim are recorded in the two Talmuds. In the Middle Ages and subsequently, halakhah was codified. The final decisions of the Talmud and further *responsa were collected in such volumes as *Maimonides' *Mishneh Torah* (Second Law) and Joseph *Caro's **Shulḥān Arukh* (The Laid Table). The *Shulḥān Arukh* in particular became so authoritative that there was a marked reluctance to depart from its rulings.

The acceptance of the yoke of halakhah is seen by many as the distinctive essence of Judaism. According to the *Orthodox, halakhah is God-given and must be obeyed. The *Progressive movements, while reverencing the halakhah, do not accept its binding obligation in every aspect of life. In so doing, Progressive Jews are perceived by their Orthodox co-religionists as rejecting the point and purpose of the tradition. Hence *Reform *rabbis are not accepted as rabbis, and Reform *proselytes are not believed to be Jews. Thus it is in their unconditional adherence to halakhah, that Orthodox Jews define themselves and their commitment. For the extensions in oral Torah, see also GEZERAH; TAKKANOT; Index, Halakhah.

S. W. Baron, *A Social and Religious History of the Jewish People*, vi (1958); B. Cohen, *Law and Tradition in Judaism* (1959); M. Elon (ed.), *The Principles of Jewish Law* (1975); I. H. Herzog, *The Main Institutions of Jewish Law* (1965).

Halal (released from prohibition): see AL-HALAL WA'L-HARĀM.

Halevi, Judah (Jewish philosopher and poet): see JUDAH HALEVI.

Ḥaliza or **ḥalitsa** (Heb.). 'Taking off the shoe', part of the ritual arising from *levirate marriage if the brother of a dead man (without male descendant) wishes to repudiate his obligation to marry the widow. The description in Deuteronomy (25. 5–10) makes it clear that this was originally to shame the levir (brother-in-law) into fulfilling his obligation, but under the *rabbis opinion divided whether ḥaliza (i.e., repudiation) was to be expected, or whether the obligation was still coercive. The division continues to the present, with *Orthodox and Conservative Jews keeping the obligation (and thus ḥaliza if it is repudiated), and Reform (and others) generally abandoning levirate marriage and thus *ipso facto* ḥaliza unless a widow feels that she is not free to remarry without having been set free from a surviving brother-in-law in this way.

W. Rosenau, *Jewish Ceremonial Institutions and Customs* (1929).

Ḥallah. Type of dough or bread, or a portion, set aside for the *priest in ancient Judaism. According to Numbers 15. 18–21, a piece of dough was set aside for the priest as part of the grain *sacrifice. Today the practice of setting aside ḥallah is still maintained among the *Orthodox. It is usual to put aside a piece of dough the size of an olive and burn it. The laws governing ḥallah are found in the tractate of that name in *Mishnah and the subsequent writings dependent on Mishnah.

Hallāj (Sūfī): see AL-HALLĀJ.

Hallel. Psalms 113–18. The full Hallel is chanted in *synagogue on the first day of *Passover, on *Sukkot and on *Ḥanukkah. It is also recited in two parts during the Passover *seder. According to R. Eleazer, *Moses was the first to recite it, and according to the *Talmud, it was part of the liturgy of the synagogue from an early stage. The Hallel ha-Gadol (the great Hallel) is Psalm 136, and this is said on *Sabbaths and *Festivals.

Hallelujah. Hebrew (biblical) expression of praise. Hallelujah occurs twenty-three times in Psalms and means 'praise the Lord' (*halelu-Yah*).

Hallelujah religion. A group of new movements among Amerindian peoples in the interior of Guyana and across into neighbouring states. The 19th-cent. origins are obscure, pointing to Christian mission contacts and including a Makushi, Bichy Wung, who is believed to have visited England where, in a dream, God gave him the new Hallelujah religion (so-named from the shouting of 'Hallelujah' in worship). After his death, it spread to the

Akawaio whose own prophet Abel (d. 1911?), after visiting heaven and receiving prayer-songs, reformed the religion which had drifted back into traditional *shamanist forms. Since then, Amokokopai has developed as a central sacred village, and Abel's son Moses added dancing to the ritual. In the 1950s, English *Anglican missionaries re-established contact with Akawaio Hallelujah, which has moved in a more Christian direction, with preaching to interpret the Abel tradition and a cassava harvest rite resembling the *eucharist. The two religions co-operate and accept each other's *baptisms; with Anglican assistance, Hallelujah became affiliated in 1977 to the Guyana Council of Churches and secured more recognition from the government.

Halloween or **All Hallows Eve.** A Christian festival on 31st Oct., the evening before All Saints, 1 Nov. It absorbed and adopted the *Celtic new year festival, the eve and day of Samhain; as such, it was a time of reversals associated with liminality (see RITES OF PASSAGES), and much of this character has persisted in the now secularized customs associated with Halloween, especially in the USA.

R. and A. Linton, *Halloween Through Twenty Centuries* (1950).

Halo. Circular symbol of holiness or enlightenment, surrounding the head of the person thus distinguished. In Buddhist iconography, halos surround *arhats, *buddhas, and *bodhisattvas, often infilled with designs borrowed from *maṇḍalas. Halos were used in religious art in the (pre-Christian) ancient world for gods and, eventually, Roman emperors. They are found in Christian art from the 3rd cent. for Christ alone; then from the 5th cent. for Mary, saints, and angels also. In the Middle Ages Christ's nimbus was distinguished, usually with a cross. Living people were sometimes depicted with a square nimbus. In modern Roman Catholic practice the nimbus is permitted only for those whose cult has been officially approved. In the case of Christ and the Virgin Mary (and the Persons of the Trinity), the halo is extended to a gilt background, indicating glory, called the aureole. In early Byzantine art, it is of an oval shape and is known as *mandorla* (Ital., 'almond-shaped').

Ha-Maggid (Jewish ḥasidic leader): see DOV BAER.

Hamallism. A W. African Islamic brotherhood. It began from the attempt in Mali of a mystic within the *Sūfī and *Tijāniyya tradition, al-Akhdar (1909), to restore original Tijāni practices. In 1925 his saintly disciple, a half-Fulani, Hamahu'ullah ben Muhammad ben Seydina Omar (1886–1943), now known as Hamallah, formed a separate Tijāni brotherhood, whose aggressive reforming and missionary activities led to violent clashes with the Tijāniyya order and the French colonial regime. Later deviations from orthodoxy included noisy worship, the reorientation of prayer towards their holy city, Nioro, instead of *Mecca, abandonment of *ḥajj to the latter, and also of the *Qur'ān by some members, together with greater freedom for slaves, the lower classes, and women. Notable disciples include the learned Fulani, Tierno Bokar (1875–1940), and the Soninke, Yakouba Sylla, who developed his own villages, first in Mali and then from 1930 in the Ivory Coast, with an ascetic ethic, a prosperous communal economy and further religious deviations. As a modernizing African Islam, Hamallism appealed to young élites as an ally against Arab and French influence, and was identified with the struggle for political independence, but has since gone into decline.

Haman. Evil opponent of Jews in *Esther. When his name occurs during the reading of Esther, at *Purim, it is shouted down, because the name of evil-doers must be 'blotted out' (see CURSING). In tradition, the tree on which Haman was hanged (the one he had prepared for Mordecai) was a thorn tree, because all other trees refused the task; yet redemption took place among his family, since his grandchildren converted to Judaism, and some *rabbis claimed descent from them.

Ḥamdala (formula of blessing): see BASMALA.

Ḥamesh Megillot (five *books of Hebrew scripture): see SCROLLS, FIVE.

Ḥamez or **ḥamets** (raising agent forbidden to Jews in Passover): see LEAVEN.

Haṁsa. Wild goose (the bar-headed goose), which migrates to India from Central Asia. Its purity of colour and gracefulness in flight led to its becoming a symbol, in the *Upaniṣads, of the unity at the heart of all manifestation, e.g. one spirit in the midst of the world in **Śvetāśvatara Upaniṣad* 6. 15, and hence (in **Maitri Upaniṣad* 6. 8) *ātman. It is also the vehicle (*vāhana) of *Brahmā.

Haṁsa. Indian *mantra, often repeated, *so'ham*, 'He am I' (while *breathing in), *haṁsaḥ*, 'I am He' (while breathing out). It expresses the unity of the devotee with God. When the first part alone is repeated rapidly, it sounds like *haṁso*, the nominative of *haṁsa*, hence the name.

Ḥamza b. 'Alī b. Aḥmad. A founder of the *Druze movement, the details of whose life are uncertain. He lived in the 5th cent. AH (11th cent. CE). He is regarded by the Druzes as the last incarnation (*qā'im al-zamān*) of *'aql* (universal intelligence), and produced one of the two fundamental works of the movement, *Al-naqd al-Khafi* (copy of the Secret). For his seven precepts, see DRUZES.

Hanafi Muslims. A black American Muslim group, founded by Hamaas Abdul Khaalis in 1958, when he left the Nation of Islam (see ELIJAH MUHAMMAD; BLACK MUSLIMS). The movement aims to adhere to the *Ḥanafite school, regarding the parent movement as too much compromised by the American way of life.

Ḥanafites. The followers of a religious school named after the jurist *Abū Ḥanīfa, which grew out of the old Kufan and Basran law schools. Two of Abū Ḥanīfa's pupils, Abū Yūsuf Ya'kub (d. 795 (AH 182)) and Muḥammad b. al-Ḥasan al-Shaybānī (d. 805 (AH 189)) were more responsible for the authoritative development of the law school than Abū Ḥanīfa himself. The Ḥanafites are distinguished from the other law schools by recognizing that *Qur'ān and *ḥadīth are not sufficient for all issues, so that *qiyās and *ra'y* (personal opinion) are legitimate. This was reinforced by their recognizing local customs and whatever is intrinsically fair and just. It achieves this through preference for *istiḥsān in the process of legal decision-making. Abū Ḥanīfa recognized that particular aspects of Islamic law could not be put into practice in certain situations, because of local customs and traditions. He recommended the spirit of the law, rather than the word of law, in difficult cases. By recognizing the needs of changing and local circumstances, the Ḥanafite school, not surprisingly, prospered in non-Arab lands.

During the *'Abbāsid times, the Ḥanafite law code was the official code, and it spread to the E., where it flourished particularly in Central Asia and India. With the downfall of the 'Abbāsids, the Ḥanafite school also declined, but was revived by the rise of the Ottomans in Turkey and the Mughals in India. Nowadays this school prevails in Iraq, Syria, Turkey, USSR (Turkistan, Bukhara, and Samarkand), China, Afghanistan, India, and Pakistan.

Hana Matsuri (flower festival): see FESTIVALS AND FASTS (JAPANESE).

Ḥanbalites. One of the four main law schools of *sharī'a which developed from the teachings of the theologian Aḥmad *ibn Ḥanbal (d. 855 (AH 241)). Ḥanbal established no system of his own, but his pronouncements over legal problems were systematized by such followers as Abu Bakr al-Khallal (d. 924 (AH 311)). This school was an orthodox reaction against the excesses of esoteric *Sufism (though certainly not against all Sūfīs) and speculative theology. The Ḥanbalites rejected the *Mu'tazila (rationalist) view that the *Qur'ān was created in time and that God can best be described in negative terms (i.e. by saying only what he is not). The Ḥanbalite school is characterized by its literal and dogmatic nature. It recognizes no other source than the Qur'ān and the *Sunna in Islamic law; in its adherence to tradition (i.e. *ḥadīth), it sometimes has to admit weak ḥadīth as the basis of decision-making, since the other ways are rejected: thus the Ḥanbalites shun *qiyās (analogy) and *ra'y* (personal opinion), and make no concessions to prevailing local customs and habit. A weak ḥadīth is better than a strong qīyās. Their rigour in ritual and social matters, and especially their anti-*Shi'a sectarian attitude, gives them a more intolerant bias than the other orthodox law schools. The *Wahhābī reform movement of Saudi Arabia follows the Ḥanbalī law. The Ḥanbalites have been relatively small as a law school, restricted mainly to the Arabian peninsula and the Persian Gulf states; but their influence has been much more extensive because of their relation to conservative Islam. At the present time, because of their proselytizing efforts in Africa and the East, and because of secularizing threats to Islam, the Ḥanbalites are becoming increasingly influential.

Hand of Fāṭima (Arab., *yad Fāṭima*, also known as *al-kaff*, 'the palm'). Decorated hand or palm, common in Islam as a *charm. It is a symbol of power over disorder, and as such appears in other religions (under other names). It has no connection with *Fāṭima, the daughter of *Muḥammad.

Hands, laying on of. An action suggesting ideas of blessing, consecration, and the transmission of spiritual power. It is accordingly used in most Christian rites of *confirmation, *ordination, and *healing, biblical authority being found in e.g. Acts 8. 17, 1 Timothy 4. 14, Mark 6. 5 respectively. It also accompanies private blessings, on the model of Jacob's in Genesis 48. 14 ff. For the background in the Jewish laying on of hands, see SEMIKHAH.

Hands, washing of: see ABLUTIONS.

Handsome Lake or **Longhouse Religion,** a movement embracing some 5,000 Iroquois on Indian reservations in New York state, Ontario, and Quebec. It is probably the oldest continuing tribal prophet movement in the world. It was founded by Ganioda'yo (Seneca, 'Handsome lake') (1735–1815), an alcoholic Seneca chief with *Quaker contacts, whose heavenly relevations under trance in 1799 secured his own reform and initiated a new religion that transformed the demoralized Seneca. Belief in the Creator-God, *Jesus, *heaven, *hell and judgement was combined with reduction of Seneca divinities to ruling *angels and modification of traditional rituals, and of the longhouse into a 'church'. A modernizing and *puritan ethic attacked witchcraft and *alcohol, forbade further land sales, and encouraged farming and the nuclear-type family. Ganioda'yo's teaching became fixed in a Code which is recited once in two years by authorized 'preachers', and helps maintain 'Indianness'.

Ha-nerot hallalu (prayer): see ḤANUKKAH.

Han Hsiang-tzu (one of the Eight Immortals in Taoism): see PA-HSIEN.

Ḥanīf (Arab., pl. *ḥunafā'*; probably from Syriac *ḥanpē*, 'pagans'). In the *Qur'ān, a believer in the One God; a seeker after truth; it is sometimes equivalent to *muslim* in the broadest sense of a worshipper of *Allāh. The ḥanīf is also contrasted with the *mushrik*, (see SHIRK) 'idolator' (Qur'ān 2. 135), particularly when referring to Ibrāhīm (*Abraham), a model of the true believer (3. 67, cf. 2. 135, 16. 120). *Muḥammad and his community are commanded to follow his example (3. 95, 4. 125). In origin, the ḥunafā' appear to have been monotheists continuing a tradition which they derived from Ibrāhīm—perhaps as a consequence of Arabia being a place of refuge from persecutions of the aberrant among both Jews and Christians.

Hannya (Jap.). Direct and immediate insight in Zen Buddhism, based on (Skt.) *prajña. It is a necessary partner with *zazen, the one controlling the other in avoiding the aberrations of knowledge by intellect alone, or of experience as self-authenticating in claims to enlightenment.

Han-shan (Jap., Kanzan). A Chinese layperson, who practised Ch'an Buddhism in his own style, in approximately the 7th cent. CE. He wrote poems on any surface available, some of which were later collected in *Han-shan-shih* (Poems from Cold Mountain). He undertook no formal training or discipline, but did consult Feng-kan (Jap., Bukan) in the monastery, Ku'o-ching, in *dokusan. A cook's assistant, Shih-te, supplied Han-shan with food, and together the two realized the buddha-nature (*buddhatā) more profoundly than most of the monks. The two have become symbols (extremely common in Zen art) of the lay approach to enlightenment; they are sometimes represented with Feng-kan and a tiger, all lying down in sleep together.

Han Shu (History of the Han): see HISTORIES IN CHINA.

Ḥanukkah (Heb., 'Dedication'). Jewish Festival of Lights. Ḥanukkah begins on 25 Kislev and lasts for eight days. According to 1 *Maccabees* 4. 36–59, Judas *Maccabee purified the *Temple after the *Hellenistic desecration and rededicated it on 25 Kislev. Celebrations lasted for eight days. The story of one day's supply of the holy oil miraculously lasting eight days is legendary and dates back to the days of the *tannaim. In the days of the second Temple, it was customary to draw water and kindle torches and lamps in the temple courts. According to the *halakhah, the Ḥanukkah lights should be placed outside the entrance of the house or set on a windowsill overlooking the street. On lighting the lamp, two *benedictions are recited, one for the lights and one for the miracle. On the first night, one light is lit, on the second two, and so on until the eighth day, when all eight are lit. After the lamp is lit, a short prayer beginning, 'Ha-nerot hallalu' (These lamps) is recited. A short summary of the Ḥanukkah story is included in the *Amida and during the course of *grace after meals. On every day of the festival, the *Hallel is said in *synagogue and it is forbidden to fast or eulogize the dead. Ḥanukkah has been a highly popular festival since the Middle Ages. According to *Maimonides, 'Even he who draws his sustenance from charity should borrow or sell his cloak to purchase oil and lamps and kindle the Ḥanukkah lights.' In Christian countries, where Christmas is a major festival, Ḥanukkah has become a Jewish equivalent, with presents for children. It is also important in the State of Israel where it symbolizes the survival of Jewish people, the victory of the Jew over the many. Card-playing is traditionally associated with the festival, as is spinning the *dreidel* (spinning-top). The Ḥanukkah lamp or *menorah is a prominent ritual object in every Jewish household, and has become a vehicle for the display of artistic craftsmanship.

S. M. Lehrman, *A Guide to Hanukkah and Purim* (1958).

Hanumān, Hanumat, or **Sundara** (the beautiful). A major character in the **Rāmāyaṇa*, the monkey-king, or chief, Mahāvīra ('great hero'). He led a band of monkeys, or ape-like creatures, who gave vital assistance to *Rāma in the rescue of *Sītā from *Rāvaṇa's kingdom of Laṅkā. He is a symbol of strength and loyalty, and is patron of wrestlers; often at Indian fairs wrestlers will perform *pūjā at a small shrine of Hanumān before their contents. He was said to be learned in sciences, religion, and linguistics, and had the ability to fly and change shape at will; he also possessed an extremely long tail. When young he leapt into the sky in an attempt to capture the sun itself.

As Rāma's messenger he entered Rāvaṇa's kingdom to seek Sītā by leaping the intervening ocean. Finding Sītā, he gave her Rāma's ring as a token, but was captured and taken before Rāvaṇa, whom he annoyed by raising himself coil after coil on his tail, so that, however high Rāvaṇa raised his throne, Hanumān was still higher. To punish him Rāvaṇa ordered an oil-soaked cloth to be tied to his tail and ignited; unharmed, Hanumān rushed through city and countryside, setting fire to crops and buildings. During the ensuing great battle with Rāvaṇa, *Lakṣmaṇa, Rāma's brother, was mortally wounded; Hanumān was sent to fetch healing herbs from Mount Kailāsa. Uncertain which herbs were needed, Hanumān uprooted the whole mountain and brought it back with him, returning it that same night, thus saving Lakṣmaṇa's life. After the conquest of Rāvaṇa, Hanumān returned with Rāma to Ayodhyā, where he was rewarded by Rāma with long life and eternal youth.

For the *bhakta* (devotee to God, *bhakti), Hanumān is the symbol of *dāsya*, the servant in relation to the master.

K. C. and S. Aryan, *Hanumān in Art and Mythology* (n.d.).

Hanuman-nāṭaka or ***Mahānāṭaka.*** An epic play, in fourteen long acts, portraying the adventures of Hanumān.

Han Yü (786–824). Taoist writer, of exemplary prose style, who was a fierce defender of Confucianism, not simply against Buddhism, but also against the widespread and tolerant eclecticism which accepted Buddhism and Taoism as complementary to Confucianism. Although not effective in public life because of his uncompromising attitude, he was 'rediscovered' in the 10th-cent. Confucian revival, and became a hero of that movement. He looked back to an ideal age, when 'people faced many dangers, but wise men always came forward who taught them how to protect and sustain their lives, acting as their rulers and teachers: they drove off harmful insects and reptiles, birds and animals, and brought humanity to settle in the safe centre of the world'. His most violent polemic was directed against Buddhism, as in his 'Memorial Against the Bone of the Buddha', a protest against the placing of a supposed *relic of the Buddha in the imperial palace: 'If the Buddha does indeed have supernatural power to send down *curses and calamities, may he send them down on this, your servant, who appeals to High Heaven (*t'ien) to witness that he does not regret or withdraw a single word.' Han Yü ended his days in exile in S. China.

Ḥaqq (Arab.). The true, the real, that which is exactly opposite to *bāṭil*, the unreal, the transitory. Al-Haqq is thus supremely the title of God in the Qur'ān. He alone is absolute, all else is derived from him, and is dependent on him for each moment of its existence.

Hara (Skt., 'seizer'). A name of *Śiva. He is sometimes represented iconographically as Hari-Hara, appearing as a single god representing the two principal deities *Viṣṇu and Śiva; one side of the head wears a tiara, the other a plaited chignon. He is associated with sleep and the removal of pain.

Harai or **harae** (Jap., *harau*, 'to sweep or cleanse'). *Shinto rite of *exorcism or purification. It refers principally to ritual purification brought on by the waving of a sacred wand in order to prepare for worship. In other contexts, it may also refer to ritual cleansing (*misogi) or other acts of atonement.

Hara-kiri (Jap.). The means through which Japanese (Shinto and Zen) demonstrate mastery of death through *seppuku*, by cutting into the hara—the inner part of the body beneath the abdomen, which is believed to be the vital centre of life and control.

K. G. von Durckheim-Montmartin, *Hara, the Vital Centre* (1962).

Ḥaram (Arab., not to be confused with *ḥarām). A sacred enclave, or territory, whose sanctity makes it immune from certain practices (e.g. hunting, tree-felling, trading), being set apart and hallowed for purposes of pilgrimage. The ḥaram at *Mecca is the supreme example, the sacred enclosure, associated with *Adam and *Eve, and understood to have been built by *Abraham, housing the *Kaʿba, the focal point of the direction of Islamic *ṣalāt. In the Muslim *ḥajj to Mecca, pilgrims enter the state of ritual purity (*iḥrām*) as befits its ḥaram status, before greeting the city and the shrine. Pagan in Muḥammad's day, the prestige of the ḥaram enforced three months of truce from feuding, so that pilgrimage could be made. The vested interests of its guardians, the Quraish, were the greatest obstacle to Muḥammad's mission, an opposition he only overcame by establishing an alternative power base in *Madīna from which to conquer Mecca. The *Ḥaram al-Sharīf, or Dome of the Rock, in Jerusalem, is the third holiest sanctuary in Islam.

In a wider sense, it is the term used for *women's apartments inaccessible to strangers—i.e. the harem (*ḥarīm*).

Harām (things prohbited in Islam): see AL-HALAL WA'L-HARĀM.

Harappā. Archaeological site and modern name of a city of the *Indus Valley civilization, on the left bank of the Rāvī River in the Pañjāb, in what is now Pakistan. Harappā was the first of two major Indus Valley cities to be discovered by archaeologists; hence the Indus Valley civilization is designated the 'Harappā culture'. The site of Harappā was first excavated, 1924–1931, and again after the Second World War.

Harappā, like the other cities of the Indus Valley civilization, was laid out in a grid pattern, with a central acropolis, granaries, and a large bathing pool which may have had ritual purposes. Very little is known about the social structure and religion of the city, as the language is preserved only in a few commercial seals, which have not been deciphered.

The Harappā culture may have been Dravidian-speaking, though this is mere conjecture. Some scholars tend to assign textual anomalies to a non-Āryan, specifically Dravidian source located in the mysterious Indus Valley. For example, a Harappān statue of a man seated in a lotus posture has been dubbed 'the proto-Śiva', prototype of the Hindu deity *Śiva and precursor to the essentially non-Āryan *Yoga tradition. Such an identification is compelling, but until the Harappan language is deciphered, will remain a conjecture.

B. M. Pande and K. S. Ramachandran, *Bibliography of the Harappan Culture* (1971).

Hard, W. D. (founder of Temple of Islam): see ELIJAH MUHAMMAD; BLACK MUSLIMS.

Hardwār (Haridvāra, 'Viṣṇu's Gate'). One of the seven *sacred cities of Hindus. It is at the place where the *Gaṅgā leaves the mountains and begins its traverse across the plains. It is one of four places where drops of *amṛta, the nectar of immortality, fell to earth during a heavenly conflict, an event which is commemorated every twelve years in a *kuṁbhamelā.

Haredim (Heb., 'those who tremble'). Jews who observe the tenets of their religion with care. The word is derived from Isaiah 66. 5, 'Hear the word of the Lord, you who tremble at his word.' They do not constitute a distinct sect: the term, rather, covers those who seek to maintain traditional and *Orthodox Judaism in the midst, not only of a *secularizing world, but of those Jews who might be inclined to accommodate faith to modernity. They are described by Heilman and Friedman (in *Fundamentalisms Observed*: see FUNDAMENTALISM) as 'contra-acculturative activists'.

Hare Krishna (Hindu devotional movement): see INTERNATIONAL SOCIETY FOR KRISHNA CONSCIOUSNESS.

Harem (ḥarīm): see ḤARAM.

Hargobind, Gurū (1595–1644). Sixth Sikh *Gurū. Hargobind was born in *Amritsar to Gurū *Arjan Dev's wife, Mātā Gaṅgā, and survived *Prithī Chand's attempts on his life. In 1606 Bhāī *Buḍhā installed him as successor to his martyred father. He rejected the *selī*, a cord worn by earlier Gurūs, saying, 'My *selī* shall be the sword belt.' His two swords symbolized spiritual and temporal power ('pīrī' and 'mīrī'). The young Gurū's advisers were Bhāī Buḍhā and Bhāī *Gurdās.

Hargobind's martial, princely style marked a new emphasis in Sikhism. He trained soldiers and built Lohgaṛh (castle of steel), a fortress in Amritsar, and the *Akāl *Takht where heroic feats were sung. He requested contributions of arms and horses rather than money. Hargobind was imprisoned for over a year in Gwālīor, since a fine imposed on Arjan remained unpaid and the Gurū's power was increasing. He agreed to accept freedom only if the captive rājās were also liberated, and thus won the title 'Bandī Chhoṛ' (Holy Liberator). Hargobind's three wives, Dāmodarī, Nānakī, and Mahādevī bore him six children, a daughter, Vīro, and five sons, Gurdittā, Sūraj Mal, Anī Rāi, Aṭal Rāi, and *Tegh Bahādur.

Until Shāh Jahān's accession in 1627, Hargobind travelled in N. India, appointing *masands to teach the Gurūs' precepts, and raising *gurdwārās. He built his future retreat, Kīratpur (Abode of praise) in the Śivālik Hills to which he moved in 1634. Between 1628 and 1634 the Gurū was victorious in four engagements with Mughal forces. The first skirmish developed from a clash between the Gurū's and the emperor's hunting parties near Amritsar, the second over Śrī Hargobindpur, the third at Lahirā over the retrieval of horses from the emperor, and the fourth at *Kartārpur.

During Hargobind's final decade three sons died, including Gurdittā, whom he had probably regarded as his successor. Gurdittā's elder son, *Dhīr Mal, was hostile, so Hargobind appointed *Har Rāi, Dhīr Mal's brother, as his successor. The Gurū died in Kīratpur 1644. Contemporary sources contain minor inconsistencies regarding his life, and Hargobind wrote no hymns, but a clear picture, reinforced by *iconography, emerges of his impact on Sikhism.

Hari. Divine manifestation, in Hinduism, especially in the forms of *Viṣṇu and *Kṛṣṇa, but of innumerable different figures also—including *ṛṣis and lawgivers. Because Hari is the means through which *Brahman becomes manifest (*Viṣṇu Purāṇa* I. 22), he becomes equated with the personal form of God in general (*Īśvara).

Haribhadra (d. trad. 529 CE, perhaps later). Śvetāmbara Jain philosopher and teacher. Much about his life is uncertain, and indeed the accounts of other teachers of the same name may have been assimilated to him. He is said to have been a *brahman of great learning who was converted by a Jain nun, Yākinī, reciting a verse of mythical history which he could not understand. Appreciating that his spiritual education was not complete, he took the title of Yākinīputra ('spiritual son of Yākinī') in recognition of what she had done for him. A second title (perhaps indicating a second person) is Virahāṅka ('having the mark of separation'), referring to his separation from two nephews who had undertaken surreptitious instruction from Buddhists. On being discovered, one had been killed and the other had died of grief. Haribhadra engaged in angry dispute with a group of Buddhists, refuting them utterly and forcing them to the penalty of jumping into a vat of boiling oil. His teacher compelled him to penance for behaviour incompatible with Jainism. More than 14,000 works are attributed to him, and although many of these may be by others of the same name, the 'name' remains as a mark of the highest philosophical achievement and is still revered.

Haribhadra, also known as **Siṃhabhadra** (late 8th cent. CE). Indian Buddhist philosopher, a pupil of *Śāntarakṣita. A very important commentator on all aspects of *Mahāyāna *śāstra, his work presupposes knowledge of the *Pramāṇa school and of the **Abhidharma-kośa*. His school flourished during the reigns of the Pāla emperors Dharmapāla and Devapāla (*c.*765–850). Generally following *Dharmakīrti, Haribhadra is critical of the *Vijñānavādin writings of *Asaṅga and Vasubandhu, and in particular of the three-nature (*trisvabhāva*) doctrine, and the concept of dharma-element (*dharmadhātu). His principal works are the *Small Commentary* (*Sphuṭārtha*) and the *Great Commentary* (*Āloka*) on the Abhisamayālaṁkāra of Maitreya, and commentaries on all the major works of the Prajñāpāramitā (*Perfection of Wisdom) corpus, all of which are still indispensable materials for study in Tibetan monastic institutions. Haribhadra's main pupil seems to have been Buddhaśrījñāna.

Haridās, Svāmī (16th cent.). Hindu devotee of *Rādhā and *Kṛṣṇa, and founder (or inspiration) of a cult bearing his name. He wrote a small amount of Hindī verse (e.g. *Kelimāl*, 'Garland of Divine Play', in which he imagines himself as the attendant of Rādhā), but was remembered also for his skill as a musician. The Haridāsas have made vital contributions to Indian music, and include Purandaradāsa (1480–1564), who laid the foundations for Karnatak/Carnatic music of the modern period. The cult divided into two sects in the 17th cent., the one being ascetic, the other remaining based on the household. The two continue in *Vṛndāvana to the present day.

Hari-hara. A combination of Viṣṇu (Hari) and Śiva (Hara), to make clear (at least to *Advaita) the non-duality of all appearance, including theistic appearance. Hari-hara *mūrti is the combined image of the two, with Śiva, on the right, representing time, and Viṣṇu in the female form of *Mohinī, on the left, representing space.

Harijans ('Children of God'): see UNTOUCHABLES.

Ḥarim (forbidden area): see ḤARAM.

Harimandir (Sāhib) (Pañjābī, 'temple of God'). Name of several Sikh shrines, including the *gurdwārā marking Gurū *Gobind Siṅgh's birthplace at Paṭnā, and, most notably, the Sikhs' principal shrine, the Golden Temple or Sāhib Darbār at *Amritsar. Excavation of the sacred pool, commenced in 1577 by Gurū *Rām Dās, was completed 1589 by Gurū *Arjan Dev, and in 1601 the temple was completed. Following destruction and desecration, the gurdwārā was rebuilt and given its present appearance by Mahārājā *Rañjīt Siṅgh. Gilded copper sheets, inscribed with verses of the *Ādi Granth, encase the walls of the shrine, standing in the centre of a pool approximately 160 m. square. The shrine is reached by a marble causeway about 60 m. long, extending from the surrounding marble walkway in line with the *Akāl Takht. Certain historic sites are venerated within the complex—e.g. the Dukhbhañjanī tree and the place where the *martyr Dīp Siṅgh's head fell.

Hari Oṃ. Hindu *mantra to call forth the presence of God.

Harivaṃśa (Skt., 'the dynastic history of Hari [= Viṣṇu]'). A Hindu mythological text in Skt. It is a work of considerable text-historical complexities, with early layers reaching as far back as the 1st or 2nd cent. CE. The bulk of the work is constituted by material derived from two main traditions: (i) the *Purāṇa-pañcalakṣaṇa* (the archetype of the literary genre of the *purāṇas reconstructed by W. Kirfel; it could thus equally well be classified as a *purāṇa); and (ii) stories about the life of *Kṛṣṇa among the herdsmen of Vraja. This adaptation of an original 'herdsmen epic' is in fact one of the earliest extant versions of Kṛṣṇa's early life, and it includes (still very briefly, but in quite an earthly manner) his love-affairs with the *gopīs. Kṛṣṇa is here primarily a tribal deity or hero. Crucial to the subsequent textual history was the fact that it was adapted to serve as an appendix to the **Mahābhārata*. Being carried by that tradition, it took in a vast amount of later interpolations, including passages that developed the *avatāra concept. This extension of the text seems to have continued till after the 11th cent. and was partly influenced also by the conventions of Skt. court poetry.

The Jains also produced, in various languages, Harivaṃśa (Purāṇa)s which deal with their version of the Kṛṣṇa story.

Harivarman. Buddhist scholar of the 3rd cent. CE, originally a member of one of the subschools of the *Great Assembly (Mahāsaṃghikas) and perhaps also the founder of the Nominalist school (*Prajñaptivāda). Reputedly a native of Kashmir, he studied under the *Sautrāntika master Kumāralāta, before becoming dissatisfied with the conflicting views of the schools and desiring to reconcile their positions in a manner consonant with the original teachings of the *Buddha. To this end he composed a great *Abhidharma (scholastic) treatise entitled 'The Establishment of Truth' (*Satya-siddhi-śāstra*), which now survives in Chinese alone. An Eng. tr. based on the Skt. original as restored from Chinese has been made by N. Aiyaswami Sastri (Gaekwad's Oriental Series No. 159/165).

In this work, which is divided in accordance with the *Four Noble Truths, the author discusses a multitude of technical problems in Buddhist doctrine and rejects those opinions which are not sanctioned by scripture. He follows the interpretation of no single school and states that he wishes to establish his own conclusions independently. His views, however, are often close to those of the Bāhuśrūtīya and Dārṣṭāntika-Sautrāntika, while at the same time he argues strongly for the recognition of the role played by the mind in the construction of reality through the medium of concepts and intellectual constructions (*prajñapti).

Har Krishan, Gurū (1656–64 CE). Eighth Sikh *Gurū. As his brother, *Rām Rāi, had incurred the disfavour of their father, Gurū *Har Rāi, Har Krishan succeeded as Gurū in 1661 at the age of 5. The emperor Auraṅgzeb summoned him to Delhi, where he stayed in the house of Mirzā Rājā Jai Siṅgh of Jaipur. Here he died of smallpox. The site is now marked by Banglā *Sāhib *gurdwārā (near Connaught Place, New Delhi).

Various stories are told of the boy Gurū's powers (e.g. that when put to the test he recognized a queen disguised as a slave, and that he healed cholera sufferers with water from a well still believed to possess curative properties). In particular he indicated the provenance of his successor, Gurū *Tegh Bahādur, by saying, '*Bābā Bakāle', i.e. he would not be Rām Rāi or *Dhīr Mal, but would come from

Bakālā. In the *Ardās he receives special mention: 'Remember Śrī Har Krishan at whose sight sorrows vanish.'

Harmandir (Sikh shrines): see HARIMANDIR.

Harnack, Adolf Von (1851–1930). Christian theologian and historian. He gained his doctorate from Leipzig in 1873, and after a short period (1886–9) as professor at Marburg, he moved to Berlin where he remained until his retirement in 1921. The move to Berlin was challenged by the Lutheran Church because of the doubts expressed by Harnack in his *Lehrbuch der Dogmengeschichte* (History of Dogma, 1894–9) about the authorship of various New Testament books, *miracles, the *resurrection, and *Christ's institution of *baptism. The Prussian cabinet and emperor upheld his appointment, but he was refused recognition by the Church. Influenced by Ritschl, he regarded *hellenization as an intrusion into early Christianity, which had distorted the original, simpler gospel. What was that gospel? In the winter of 1899–1900 he delivered some public lectures in which he attempted an answer. These were published as *Das Wesen des Christentums* (The Essence of Christianity). These themselves have been summarized (though making a caricature of what Harnack wrote) as reducing the gospel to 'the Fatherhood of God and the brotherhood of man'; at the least should be added the dimension on which Harnack insisted: 'Eternal life lived in the midst of time, under the eye and by the help of God.' Harnack was a particular target of his pupil K. *Barth, for allowing liberal thought to control his understanding of early Christianity and of dogma.

G. W. Glick, *The Reality of Christianity* . . . (1967); K. H. Neufeld, *Adolf von Harnack* . . . (1977) and *Adolf von Harnacks Konflikt mit der Kirche* (1979).

Ḥaroset. Paste eaten at the Jewish *seder meal. Ḥaroset is made from fruit, spices, wine, and *mazzah meal. It symbolizes the mortar made by the Israelites while they were slaves in Egypt, and is eaten with bitter herbs (*maror) and mazzah during the *Passover seder service.

Har Rāi, Gurū (1630–61). Seventh Sikh *Gurū. Gurū Har Rāi was the second son of Gurū *Hargobind's son, Gurdittā (d. 1638) and brother of *Dhīr Mal. He was chosen as successor by his grandfather and became Gurū on his death in 1644, but was soon compelled to leave his birthplace, Kīratpur, for a remote mountain village. During his Gurūship, the ancestors of some leading *Pañjābī families became Sikh. Har Rāi returned to Kīratpur 1658 and aided Dārā Shikoh, Emperor Shāh Jahān's eldest son, thereby antagonizing his victorious younger son, Auraṅgzeb, who later summoned Har Rāi to Delhi. Instead he sent his son, *Rām Rāi, whose conduct caused Gurū Har Rāi to proclaim as successor his younger son, *Har Krishan. Gurū Har Rāi's words, that a temple or mosque can be repaired but not a broken heart, are indicative of his peaceable disposition.

Harris movement. A mass movement toward Christianity in the Ivory Coast and W. Ghana between 1913 and 1915, due to the itinerant ministry of a Grebo from Liberia, William Wadé Harris (*c.*1860–1929). Some 120,000 people of many tribes discarded traditional religious practices and magic, accepted his *baptism and elementary Christianity, built small churches, and waited for the whites he promised would come and teach the Bible. Only in 1924 did British *Methodist missionary W. J. Platt discover the movement in the Ivory Coast; systematic work gained the Methodist Church 32,000 members by 1926 in addition to some 36,000 already gained in W. Ghana. Other Harris converts became *Roman Catholics or developed a large range of Harris independent churches, especially the largest under John Ahui (b. 1894) with perhaps 150,000 members by 1980, and the Church of the Twelve Apostles under Grace Thannie (*c.*1880–1958) in W. Ghana. One of the best-known figures in the Ivory Coast is Albert Atcho (b. 1903), an Ebrié prophet-healer operating within the Harris context from his own village of Bregbo. The main Harris Church attracts some élites and is improving its organization. The brief work of its founder is the largest single influence in the development of Christianity and of a modern society in the Ivory Coast.

Harrowing of Hell. Medieval Christian term for the belief that on *Holy Saturday, *Jesus descended into *hell and defeated the powers of the devil. In consequence, he was able to set free the souls of those who had been faithful to God (and conscience) before the *incarnation and its associated *atonement. It thus epitomizes the *Christus Victor theme.

Hartshorne, Charles (b. 1897). American philosopher. His influence within religious thought has been mainly on those who call themselves '*process theologians'. This influence stems from his conception of God as 'dipolar': God encompasses such contraries as absoluteness *and* relativity, necessity *and* contingency, eternity *and* temporality. God is 'perfect being', not unchanging, but capable of being excelled by nothing other than himself: change, not permanence, is the fundamental nature of reality. This conception leads in Hartshorne's view to a panentheistic (see PANTHEISM) view of God–world relations: that is, one in which God is both world-inclusive *and* world-transcending (see e.g. *The Divine Relativity*, 1948). The second area of Hartshorne's influence has been in *natural theology. He has long championed a modal version of the *ontological argument for God's existence which is based on the form of argument in part 3 (but not part 2) of *Anselm's *Proslogion* (see e.g. *Anselm's Discovery*, 1965).

R. E. James, *The Concrete God* . . . (1967); D. W. Viney, *Charles Hartshorne and the Existence of God* (1985).

Hārūn (name of Aaron in the Qur'ān): see AARON.

Hārūn al-Rashīd (ʿAbbāsid caliph): see ʿABBĀSIDS.

Haru no Higan (festival): see FESTIVALS AND FASTS.

Haru no Shanichi (festival): see FESTIVALS AND FASTS.

Harvest Festival (Jewish): see SUKKOT.

Harvest Festival or **Thanksgiving** (Christian festival): see LAMMAS DAY.

Hasan (Jap.). The 'interruption' of Zen Buddhist training which comes about with the experience of enlightenment (*kensho, *satori). But it is *only* an interruption, a step along the way; and one who rests in the experience rapidly falls back (cf. the experience of *Hakuin).

Hasan (son of ʿAli): see AL-HASAN.

Ḥasan al-Bannā' (1906–49). The founder and leader of *al-Ikhwān al-Muslimūn in Egypt. He had a conservative religious upbringing and was drawn towards *Sufism as an initiate of the Hasafiy(y)a order. Ḥasan al-Bannā' studied at *al-Azhar and qualified as a teacher. In 1928, he founded the al-Ikhwān at Ismaʿiliyya. He attracted wide support for the Ikhwān among all classes. He believed that the sickness of Egyptian Islamic society could be cured 'only by a return to the regenerative springs of the *Qur'ān and the *Ḥadīth'. In 1936 he took up the cause of the Palestinians. After the Second World War, his activities were limited by the Egyptian government and he was arrested for short periods. Increasing tension between him and the government culminated in his assassination in 1949.

Ḥasan al-Baṣrī (642–728 (AH 21–110)). One of the earliest and most influential of the *Sūfīs. He was a freed slave, who was born in *Madīna but settled in Basra in 658, where he attracted many students. Most of the Sūfī lineages (*silsilah, *tarīqa) claim to pass through Ḥasan, and he appears also as a link in many *isnāds of *ḥadīth. His sayings are frequently quoted, making clear that he regarded the world as an arena in which we are tested in our devotion to God: 'God created fasting as a training ground that his servants might learn to run to him.' In a famous saying, he called the world a bridge on which we must set our feet, but on which it is foolish to build. In a letter addressed to ʿUmar II, he gave basic advice on *asceticism:

> Beware of this world with all its deceit: it is like a snake, smooth to the touch, but deadly in its poison. . . . This world has neither weight nor worth with God: it is so slight that it weighs with him less than a pebble or a flake of earth. . . . As the Word [i.e. *Jesus/ʿĪsā] used to say, 'My daily bread is hunger, my emblem is fear, my garment is wool, my steed is my foot, my lantern is the moon, my fire is the sun, my food is whatever the earth brings forth for the animals and cattle: by nightfall I have acquired nothing, but there is no one who is richer than I.'

He also insisted that true devotion cannot be for the sake of avoiding hell or gaining heaven, but only for the sake of God. He was an outspoken critic of the worldliness of the *Umayyad rulers, though he refused to support any rebellion against them, considering that an unjust ruler had nevertheless authority given by God. In his sermons he warned against all worldly ambition and counselled believers to keep death and the next life constantly in mind: 'Whoever knows God regards him as a friend, but whoever knows the world regards him as an enemy.' Sūfīs consider him the third master after *Muḥammad and ʿAlī, and as the founder of 'the science of hearts', *ʿilm al-qulūb*. He is perhaps the most frequently quoted of the early preachers, and his sermons are highly valued for their content and style.

Ha-Shelah ha-Kadosh (rabbi and kabbalist): see HOROWITZ, ISAIAH BEN ABRAHAM.

Ha-Shem (Heb., 'the name'). Way in Judaism of referring to the name of God without pronouncing it: it becomes a surrogate especially for the *tetragrammaton.

Hashemite or **Hāshimite.** A descendant of the clan (Banū Hāshim) to which *Muḥammad belonged. The term is sometimes restricted to those who are *shurafa* (*sharīf) descendants of the Prophet, since this accords added esteem, as in the case of the recently-founded dynasty of kings in Jordan.

Hashkivenu (Heb., 'cause us to lie down'). Beginning of second *benediction after the *Shemaʿ at Jewish evening *prayer. The prayer asks for God's protection during the night, and is mentioned in the *Talmud. According to the *Midrash on Psalm 6. 1, the Hashkivenu prayer is part of the evening prayer service because *zitzit (which are said to protect the wearer) are not worn at night. There are many musical settings of Hashkivenu of great beauty: 'Cause us, O Lord our God, to lie down in peace, and waken us, our King, once more to life. Spread over us the shelter of your peace, set us right with your good counsel, and deliver us for your Name's sake.'

Ḥasidei Ashkenaz. 12th- and 13th-cent. movement within German Jewry. The Ḥasidei Ashkenaz, which was made up of many like-minded groups, originated in Regensberg and spread to Speyer, Worms, and Mainz, and then to the rest of Germany. It produced ethical works, such as *Sefer Ḥasidim* (Book of the Pious), and esoteric mystical works, such as *Sefer Ḥayyim* (Book of Life). Prominent leaders include Samuel b. Kalonymus he-Ḥasid (late

12th cent.). The movement was influenced by *merkabah mysticism and by the works of Abraham ibn Ezra and *Sa'adiah Gaon. It rejected all anthropomorphic descriptions of God and maintained that divine powers were immanent in all creation, and could thus inspire prophets without affecting the eternal, unchanging reality of God. Adherents were expected to display extraordinary emotional fervour and complete purity of soul. The ultimate sign of love for God was believed to be *kiddush ha-shem (sanctification of the name), *martyrdom for the faith; and members of the Ḥasidei Ashkenaz showed enormous courage in the face of persecution. They were influenced by Christian *Pietism, and, in their turn, influenced mainstream medieval Jewry, including the Jews of Spain, Poland, and Lithuania.

J. Trachtenberg, *Jewish Magin and Superstition* (1939).

Ḥasidei ummot ha-ʿolam (Heb., 'the pious ones of the nations of the world'). *Gentiles perceived as righteous by the *rabbis (*Tos.Sanh.* 13. 2). *Maimonides defined the hasidei ummot ha-ʿolam as 'all who observe the Seven Commandments' (i.e. the *Noachide Laws). It is generally agreed that righteous gentiles have a place in the world to come, and R. Isaac Arama went so far as to state, 'Every true pious gentile is equal to a son of *Israel'. Since the Second World War, the term has been used to refer to those gentiles who helped Jews escape from Nazi persecution. Yad Vashem, the authority entrusted with the remembrance of national martyrs and heroes, includes a department to investigate and recognize those rescue activities, and it invites ḥasidei ummot ha-ʿolam to plant a tree in the Avenue of the Righteous in the Yad Vashem memorial in Jerusalem. Those recognized receive a medal inscribed with the text from *Sanh.* 4. 5: 'Whoever saves one life is regarded as having saved the whole world.' The name Yad Vashem is derived from two Heb. words in Isaiah 56. 5, 'I will give to them a monument [*yad*, 'hand'] and a manorial [*shem*, 'name'] better than sons and daughters . . .'

Ḥasidim (Heb., 'righteous'). Those described in Bible, especially Psalms, as close to God; the term was then used by the *rabbis to describe those leading particularly holy lives. The *ḥasidim ha-rishonim* ('first ḥasidim') were described in *Talmudic literature as fulfilling the *mitzvot with extreme scrupulousness and as being ever ready to offer sacrifice and undergo purification. Similar to the *ḥasidim ha-rishonim* were the *ḥasidim ve-anshei maʿaseh* ('the pietists and men of action') who were notable for their good deeds and miracles. Attempts have been made (e.g. by G. Vermes) to interpret *Jesus as a ḥasid, but the originality of Jesus is obvious in one who has connections with many aspects of Judaism (including this), and yet is not exactly like any of them. Later, in the *amoraic period, the ḥasid came to be associated with *asceticism. Not only was suffering and persecution to be accepted gladly, but also many of the pious afflicted themselves (although this was not universally approved). Simeon b. Lakish stated that a true ḥasid would always have his prayers for rain answered, but it was stressed that intelligence as well as piety was necessary to be pleasing to God. According to R. Joshua, a foolish ḥasid is to be found among those who bring destruction to the earth. See Index, Ḥasidim.

A. Buechler, *Types of Jewish-Palestinian Piety* (1922).

Ḥasidim, Sefer (Heb., 'Book of the Pious'). Medieval German Jewish book of ethics. The *Sefer Ḥasidim*, which is attributed to R. *Judah ha-Ḥasid (early 13th cent.), comprises the ethical lore of the *Ḥasidei Ashkenaz movement. Because it is concerned with everyday moral problems, the book is an important source for the social history of medieval German Jewry.

Hasidism (Heb., *ḥasidut*). Jewish religious movement which emerged in the late 18th cent. Hasidism first arose in S. Poland and Lithuania, with such charismatic leaders as *Israel b. Eliezer (Baʿal Shem Tov, the Besht), *Dov Baer of Mezhirech and Jacob Joseph of Polonnoye. These leaders drew groups of disciples around them, characterized by popular traditions of ecstasy, mass enthusiasm, and intense devotion to the leader, the *Zaddik. Hasidic groups travelled as far as *Erez Israel, and hasidic centres were to be found throughout E. Europe. By the 1830s, the majority of Jews in the Ukraine, Galicia, and central Poland belonged to the movement and there were sizeable groups in Hungary and Belorussia-Lithuania. With the great waves of immigration of the 1880s, Hasidism spread to the USA.

Initially there was considerable opposition to the movement from such figures as *Elijah b. Solomon Zalman, the Vilna Gaon. Early Hasidism was thought by opponents to be tainted with *Shabbateanism and Frankism (see FRANK, JACOB). Its mystical enthusiasm was also thought to detract from the sober study of *Torah. However, by the mid-19th cent., despite the different practices and rituals of the movement, the *Orthodox acknowledged Hasidism as a legitimate branch of Judaism. In the 20th cent., the Hasidic centres of E. Europe were destroyed by the Nazi *holocaust, and today the majority of Hasidim live either in the USA or Israel. The most numerous Hasidic groups are the *Lubavicher (under the Schneersohn dynasty) the Satmar, the Klausenburg-Sandz, the Telem, and the Skver.

Hasidic social life is centred on the court of the *zaddik who is seen as the source of all spiritual illumination (e.g. *devekut). Stories of past and present zaddikim are circulated as part of the mythology of the group. As in the root source, *Ḥabad, worship is characterized by joy, and is expressed in song and dance as well as prayer. A major goal is the individual *bittul ha-yesh* (the annihilation of selfhood) in which the worshipper is absorbed into the divine light. For the Hasid, all creation is really a manifestation of the divine vitality. It follows therefore that sorrow and despair have no true reality, so that 'burning enthusiasm' is a characteristic of Hasidic worship. The movement is profoundly influenced by the *kabbalistic teaching of Isaac *Luria, and it has spawned an extensive speculative, expository, kabbalistic, *halakhic, liturgical, and narrative literature of its own. The best-known modern expositor of Hasidism is Martin *Buber whose *Tales of Rabbi Nachman* (Eng. 1962), *Tales of the Hasidim* (1947–8), and *Legend of the Baal Shem* (Eng. 1969) interpreted the movement in the light of existentialism.

J. Don, *The Teachings of Hasidism* (1983); S. H. Dresner, *The Zaddik* (1960); L. Jacobs, *Hasidic Prayer* (1973); H. M. Rabinowicz, *Guide to Hasidism* (1960) and *World of Hasidism* (1970).

Haskalah (Heb., 'enlightenment'). The Enlightenment movement of the late 18th and 19th cents. in Judaism. Those who espoused the Haskalah were known as Maskilim. Related to the secular Enlightenment, Moses *Mendelssohn is generally considered to be the 'father of the Haskalah'. Although he was opposed to the education of Jewish and *gentile children together, he considered the translation of the Bible into German to be 'a first step towards culture'. The political conditions of the time contributed to the growth of the Haskalah. The absolute monarchs of Europe deprived local Jewish communities of their powers, and *court Jews and their families participated in non-Jewish circles. Jewish traders settled in non-Jewish areas, and educated Jews wished increasingly to gain expertise in secular culture and to work for Jewish emancipation.

Prominent Haskalah thinkers included Naphtale Herz Wessely, the educationalist, who believed that Jewish children 'were not all created to become *Talmudists', and David Friedlaender who rejoiced in the decline of the *yeshivot. Throughout Europe, rich Jews rejected *Yiddish and taught their children the language of their host nation. Haskalah scholars were also concerned with the revival and maintenance of biblical Hebrew. The first school founded on Haskalah principles was the Berlin Freischule which was opened in 1778; its curriculum included German, French, Mathematics, Science, History, Geography, Hebrew, and Bible. Similar schools were founded throughout Europe, and even the *Orthodox modified their schools' curricula. In some areas, Jews were ordered by the government to send their children to the state schools, and, increasingly, Jews were admitted to secondary schools and university.

In their desire for acceptance and emancipation, the Maskilim were particularly patriotic towards their host countries, and the *messianic hope was weakened. Mendelssohn himself continued to wait for the messiah, but did not believe the hope had 'any influence on our civic behaviour'. He emphasized his own German nationality, frequently referring to 'we Germans' and criticizing the expression 'Germans and Jews' (rather than 'Christians and Jews'). Members of the Assembly of Jewish Notables, set up by Napoleon in 1806, described themselves as 'Frenchmen of the Mosaic religion'. Coupled with this was a renewed interest in Jewish history and the nature of Judaism. The *diaspora was no longer seen as a punishment for *Israel's wickedness, but the result of historical and geographical factors. Judaism was understood as a spiritual and moral creed, and from this thinking grew the *Reform movement with its updated *Prayer Book and its rejection of the absolute claims of *halakhah.

The Haskalah spread throughout Europe as far as Russia by the 19th cent. As Jewish emancipation became a political reality, Jews increasingly became more involved in secular culture. Inevitably *assimilation and *apostasy became an option, as the traditional Jewish authorities could no longer exert their discipline over members. The community thus became more diverse with its divisions of Orthodox, *Progressive, and non-religious.

Haskamah (Heb., 'agreement'). Either *rabbinic approval of *halakhic decision, or rabbinic recommendation of a particular book (cf. in Christianity, the *imprimatur). The first haskamah appeared in the *Agur* by Jacob Landau (1490), and by 1554 the Rabbinical Synod of Ferrara declared that no book should be printed without the agreement of three rabbis. The haskamah had two functions, that of censorship (such as against *Shabbatean doctrines) and that of recommendation (similar to a publisher's endorsement today). The haskamah is still in use. Among *Sephardi in the West, it is spelt Ascama.

Hasmoneans. Name given to the *Maccabees in the *Talmud. The Hasmoneans were a priestly family who led the rebellion against the Selucid kings in the 2nd cent. BCE and established an autonomous Jewish kingdom. Mattathias started the revolt against the policies of King Antiochus Epiphanes, and, after his death, he was succeeded by his sons *Judah, Jonathan, and Simeon. Simeon became *high priest and hereditary ruler and was followed by his son John Hyrcanus and subsequently Aristobulus and Alexander Yannai (Jannaeus). The Hasmonean state was brought to an end in 67 BCE, when the land was annexed by the Romans. It was the last period of an independent Jewish state in the Holy Land until the founding of modern Israel.

Haso (sect founder): see NICHIREN SHŌSHŪ.

Hasso (Jap., 'eight aspects'). The eight major events of the Buddha's life. These are in fact differently listed, but a typical list is: (i) *gōtosotsu*, his coming down from the *Tuṣita heaven; (ii) *takutai*, his conception; (iii) *shusshō*, his birth; (iv) *shukke*, his renunciation of the world; (v) *gōma*, his defeat of evil powers; (vi) *jōdō*, his enlightenment; (vii) *tenpōrin*, his teaching of *dharma; (viii) *nyunehan*, his attaining of *nirvāna. Hasso no kegi is the Buddha's way of converting people by his manifestation of eight aspects.

Hassu (Jap., 'dharma-successor'). A Zen Buddhist pupil who has reached at least the same level of attained enlightenment as his master, and who is therefore given the seal of recognition (*inka-shōmei). He can then become a dharma-successor. The transmission involved is a personal interaction, not a handing over of items of information or of techniques. In early Ch'an, the transmission was symbolized by the handing over of the robe and bowl (*den'e).

Hasta. Hindu use of hand positions, especially to ward off evil. Closely associated with *mudra, the former strictly denotes arm and hand positions, the latter palm and finger positions.

Ḥatam Sofer (Jewish orthodox community leader): see SOFER, R. MOSES OF PRESSBURG.

Haṭha-yoga. Originally a part of *Rāja-yoga as taught by *Patañjali, but now frequently detached as a yoga to seek mental and physical health. Its purpose is to locate and activate the *cakras (centres of energy) and thus to raise the *kuṇḍalinī (dormant spiritual power) to life. It works especially through bodily postures (*āsana) and control of breath (*prāṇāyāma), uniting the *ha* (breath of the sun) with *tha* (breath of the moon). The reputed founder is *Gorakhnāth.

S. Dasgupta, *Obscure Religious Cults* (3rd edn., 1969).

Haṭha-Yoga-Pradīpikā (A lamp for Hatha-yoga). A work on *Haṭha-yoga which shows how Haṭha-yoga prepares the foundations for *Rāja-yoga.

Svātmārāma Yogindra, *Haṭhayogapradīpikā* (1933; 1974).

Ḥātim al-Aṣamm (Sūfī): see SŪFĪS.

Hatto (dharma-hall): see KYŌTO.

Haumai (Pañjābī, 'ego'). In the Sikh *Gurūs' teachings, something in human nature akin to self-centred pride, although there is no satisfactory English equivalent. Haumai is prominent in the *Ādi Granth, in the teaching of Gurū *Nānak, and of later Gurūs. It is the dominant force in the *manmukh (unregenerate person), obscuring the path towards union with God. Haumai pulls one away from ultimate truth and deeper into *māyā and the cycle of rebirth. From haumai spring sinful actions. However, through meditation upon the name of God (*nām simaran) one can loosen the grip of haumai and discern the divine order (*hukam): 'The pious (*gurmukh) shed their haumai, are inspired with the Name (Nām) and attain joy' (Ādi Granth, p. 29).

Haurvatat and Ameretat (two of the Holy Immortals): see AMESA SPENTAS.

Havdalah (Heb., 'separation'). *Blessings in Judaism recited at the end of *Sabbaths and *Festivals. Three blessings are said over wine, a candle, and spices, and then a final blessing for the separation of the holy and the profane. Different customs are practised in different communities, but the havdalah blessing is one of the most ancient and, according to the *Talmud, dates back to the 'men of the *Great Synagogue'.

Ḥaver or **ḥaber** (Heb., 'member, companion'). Member of a group which observed the Jewish laws of *tithing and heave-offering. The laws of membership date back at least to the 1st cent. BCE, and differ according to the schools of *Bet Hillel and Bet Shammai. The regulations for admittance into a group of Ḥaverim are similar to *Josephus' description of admittance into the *Essenes and the rules found in the *Manual of Discipline*. However, many Ḥaverim seem to have lived in the general community: 'At first they said that a haver who becomes a tax-collector is to be expelled. Later they said that as long as he is a tax collector, he is not trusted . . .' (*Tosef. Dem.* 3. 4). Later, in the geonic (see GAON) period, the term was used to describe important scholars, who were God-fearing but not sufficiently learned to be ordained as *rabbis.

Haviryajña (group of sacrifices): see SACRIFICES (HINDU).

Ḥavurah or **ḥaburah.** Mutual benefit society in Judaism. A ḥavurah is an association devoted to visiting the sick and burying the dead, or it may be simply a society for informal worship and fellowship. Modern ḥavurot tend to be formed by those who have found *synagogues impersonal or too large. In the period during the 1960s and 1970s when there was a massive increase in *new religious movements, especially in the USA, ḥavurot were often the equivalent of communes. They fulfilled a basic need of strong mutual support and affirmation.

Ḥawḍ (Arab., 'basin'). The place at which *Muḥammad will meet his *'umma (community) on the day of *resurrection. There is no reference to it in the *Qur'ān, but only in *ḥadīth, where it is said that the poor people who have not known the pleasures of life will join him near the basin which will be linked to the river of *paradise *al-Kawthar.* Its waters are as white as milk and as sweet as honey, and those who drink of it will taste and experience pleasure beyond the range of earthly experience.

Hawwā (wife of Adam): see EVE (Islam).

Hayagrīva. 1. A non-classical *avatāra of the Hindu god *Viṣṇu. When the *Vedas had been stolen by demons, Viṣṇu took on a form consisting of half-man, half-horse, dived into the ocean, and recovered the sacred scriptures. Iconography depicts him with a horse's head. He is worshipped in traditions influenced by the *Pañcarātra (e.g. among the *Śrī-Vaiṣṇavas). Envisaged as primordial teacher, he has absorbed features of the *Buddha.

2. A demon of Hindu mythology who stole the Vedas and was killed by Viṣṇu. The Jains also know this figure, and have him as one of their prati-Vāsudevas (see ĀDI-PURĀṆA).

Hayon, Nehemiah Hiyya ben Moses (*c.*1655–*c.*1730). *Kabbalist Jewish scholar. Hayon spent much of his life in *Erez Israel and was a prominent kabbalist. He was accused of *Shabbateanism and was the source of controversy both in Israel and in Amsterdam, where he was *excommunicated. He was the author of *Oz le-Elohim* (Strength to God) and a commentary on the pamphlet *Raza de-Meheimanuta* (The Mystery of the True Faith) which was attributed to Shabbetai Zevi. Ultimately he was rejected by most European communities and died in N. Africa.

Ḥayyim Vital (Jewish kabbalist): see VITAL, ḤAYYIM.

Ḥazal (our Wise of blessed memory): see SAGES.

Ḥazzan (leader of Jewish prayer service): see CANTOR.

Head, covering of. In Judaism, the custom of men covering their heads as a sign of humility before God, and of married women covering their heads as a sign of modesty before men, practised throughout the *Orthodox Jewish community. According to the *Talmud, it was optional for men to cover their heads, but by the 17th cent. bareheadedness was seen as a sign of frivolity and identification with *gentile customs. Today, Orthodox men wear at least a skull cap (Heb., *kippah*; Yid., *yarmulke) at all times; *Conservative Jews cover their heads for prayer; and it remains a matter of choice for *Reform Jews. The increasingly common practice of gentiles wearing a head-covering in Jewish company (especially on e.g. official visits) somewhat confuses the matter, since head-covering seems to have begun as a deliberate contrast to gentile practices (see YARMULKE), but it is presumably a matter of courtesy.

In *biblical times, women kept their hair hidden (see Numbers 5. 18). According to *Ket.* 7. 6, a man could divorce his wife without repaying her dowry if she walked down the street without a head covering. Since the early 19th cent., some married women followed the custom by wearing a wig (Yid., *shaytl*), although this was opposed in some circles. Today, only strictly Orthodox women keep their heads covered at all time. The Jewish custom is reflected in Paul's instruction (1 Corinthians 11. 10) that women should keep their heads covered in worship, an instruction which is only gradually dying out. See also HAIR.

Healing. In the religious perspective, disease and dis-ease are never far removed from each other. Since an aim of religions is to offer the means through which health in body, mind, and spirit may be attained (unless countervailing causes supervene, such as *karma, the will of God, invasion by *demons, etc.), the techniques and procedures of healing are extensive in all religions. In general, they are strong in diagnosis, natural remedies, and the mobilization of faith, especially in relation to a healing figure (e.g. *shamans): thus healing for Sikhs, for example, may lie straightforwardly in medicine, but it may lie also in *meditation on God (*nām simaran), in certain healing individuals, in the water from *Amritsar, *Tarn Tāran, and *amrit.

At the same time, the aetiology of disease is often located in the spiritual world. In part, of course, this is a consequence of ignorance. What might now be regarded as the specific causes of illnesses were not known at the time when religious systems were forming their accounts of the human condition. Thus *Augustine observed succinctly that 'all diseases of Christians are to be ascribed to demons'; and the contest with demons is familiar in the descriptions of the healing of particular disorders in the ministry of *Jesus, which was to him (and others) a demonstration that the *dunamis* (power or dynamic) of God is active in the world. He was living and operating in a context in which the view was widespread that 'where you see sickness, there you see sin': R. Ammi (3rd cent. CE) said, 'There is no death without sin, there is no sickness without sin' (*B.Shab.* 55a); Raba (4th cent.) said, 'If a man sees that painful suffering visits him, let him examine his conduct' (*B.Ber.* 5a). Jesus contested that view (e.g. Luke 13. 1–5, John 9. 1–7), but he did not contest the sense in which all suffering is 'of a piece': Jesus wept.

The contest against disease was continued in Islam, through which Greek medical knowledge was preserved and extended. *al-Ṭibb* ('medicine') became a major part of the Muslim commitment to *ʿilm (knowledge)—e.g. *al-Rāzī (Rhazes). Hospitals, or wards for the sick (*maristān*), were established next to holy places (e.g. the tomb of a *walī) in the hope that an effect would pass from the one to the other. But equally, a causative effect was believed to pass from conduct to health or ill-health.

In a comparable way, Hindus saw a connection between health and conduct—although in the Hindu case the causes of ill-health might lie in bad actions which occurred in previous births; for that reason, a moral stigma attached to people with leprosy or other visibly deforming diseases. Indian medical science is known as *Ayur veda ('the knowledge of longevity'), and is based on a theory of five elements (*bhūta) and three humours (*dośa*), wind, bile, and phlegm. Health consisted in maintaining all in balance and equilibrium, correcting imbalance by an array of herbal and other remedies. Thus health matters are not isolated from the general condition of life. *Carakasamhita* (ed. T. Y. Sarma, 1963) is a classic text on medicine (compiled in the 1st cent. BCE; *Suśruta Samhita* is a slightly later text on surgery): it combines health and medical matters with general instructions for the achieving of a good and satisfactory life. That is why René Dubos could conclude:

An intriguing characteristic of ancient medicine is that it incorporated most aspects of knowledge. Ancient physicians were concerned with the physiological effects of music, astronomical events, and religious beliefs, just as they were interested in anatomical structure, surgical techniques or the activities of drugs. Through the catholicism of their attitude, ancient medicine became the mother of the sciences, the inspiration of humanism and the integrating force of culture (*Man, Medicine and Environment*, 1970).

The same catholicity of attitude is evident in China, where the quest for immortality in religious Taoism (Tao-chiao/Daojiao) is not restricted to an endeavour to emancipate a self from society or a soul from a body. Taoists seek to relate the microcosm—which is present in the body in the three life-principles of breath (*ch'i/qi), vitality especially in semen (*ching/jing), and spirit (*shen)—to the macrocosm, so that the whole of life, internal and external, becomes an unresistant (*wu-wei) expression of that which alone truly is, namely, the Tao. It would thus be impossible to isolate some part of disease or disorder from its context. As early as the 6th cent. BCE, a text which surely rests on even earlier traditions, *Huang-ti Nei-ching* (The Inner Classic of the Yellow Emperor), was offering advice on health and healing which is entirely holistic: before healing comes proper nutrition, but before nutrition comes the calming and securing of the spirit. Since every aspect of nature is united in Tao, it follows that no suffering or distress can be isolated; nor can the alleviation of suffering be broken up into disparate parts. Thus the quest for immortality (even if only conceived of as longevity) takes many forms, some individual and some social: it may be addressed to inner hygiene and to control of the breath and of sexuality, but it may also be addressed to moral behaviour which is in harmony with the way of Tao.

Healing, therefore, in all religions takes place in a much larger context of life and its purposes, and remains closely related to modern insights into the psychosomatic unity of the human entity.

For the Buddhist 'Master of Healing', see BHAIṢAJYAGURU. See also Index, Healing.

R. Birnbaum, *The Healing Buddha* (1979); J. D. Bleich, *Judaism and Healing* (1981); T. Clifford, *Tibetan Buddhist Medicine and Psychiatry* (1984); M. W. Dols, *Medieval Islamic Medicine* (1984); J. Filliozat, *The Classical Doctrine of Indian Medicine* (Eng. 1964); D. Landy, *Culture, Disease and Healing* (1977); C. Leslie (ed.), *Asian Medical Systems* (1976); M. C. Sullivan, 'Bibliography of Religion and Medicine', in M. E. Marty and K. L. Vaux, *Health, Medicine and the Faith Traditions* (1982); G. P. Murdock, *Theories of Illness: A World Survey* (1980); M. Porkert, *The Theoretical Foundations of Chinese Medicine* (1974); R. E. Spector, *Cultural Diversity in Health and Illness* (1991); M. Ullmann, *Islamic Medicine* (1978); P. U. Unschuld, *Medicine in China* (1995–6).

Healthy, Happy, Holy Organization (3HO). A movement founded by Yogi Bhajan (Harbhajan Singh) in California in 1969. A Sikh-derived movement, 3HO aims at cleansing the subconscious mind and the whole person of all impurities principally through the practice of *kuṇḍalinī and *Tantric yoga, *meditation, and mantric chants, thereby preparing the individual for the reception of that 'pure consciousness' of which Yogi Bhajan is the vehicle. All is done in preparation for entry into the Aquarian Age which will be of a totally different era than the present Piscean Age. Both male and female members wear *turbans.

Heart, Sacred (object of Christian devotion): see SACRED HEART.

***Heart Sūtra* (*Mahāprajñapāramitā-hridaya-sūtra*).** A short Buddhist text, which, like the **Diamond Sūtra*, may be regarded as a distillation of the essential teachings on emptiness (*śūnyatā: it begins, 'Form is nothing but śūnyatā, but śūnyatā is nothing but form'), put forward in the vast corpus of the *Perfection of Wisdom (Prajñāpāramitā) literature. The *Heart Sūtra* was composed towards the end of this corpus and may be dated at around 350 CE.

Trs., many, e.g. E. Conze, *Buddhist Scriptures* (1958); E. J. Thomas (1952). See also A. Wayman in L. R. Lancaster (ed.), *Prajñaparamita and Related Systems* (1977).

Heaven

Judaism The biblical understanding of heaven is restricted to a cosmology which envisaged a realm or domain above the earth, where (initially) the gods and (subsequently) God and his agents dwell. Since there was no belief until the very end of the biblical period that there would be any life with God after death, 'heaven' is not a place of reward. As such beliefs developed, a distinction was drawn between *ʿolam ha-ba* (the world to come) and *ʿolam ha-zeh* (this world); and the former, associated with the *messiah and envisaging a world in which peace and plenty are restored, has some of the attributes which in Christianity and Islam were transferred to heaven. The Garden of *Eden is a controlling model, since this is *paradise lost—but able to be regained. In *kabbalah, a more elaborate series of heavens was envisaged through the effect of God's emanations. See also AFTERLIFE.

Christianity Heaven is held to be the domain of God and the *angels, and ultimately of all the redeemed, where they receive their eternal reward. In pre-scientific times this was conceived of as a place in or beyond the sky (as is presupposed by the story of Jesus' *ascension), although Christ is said in Ephesians 4. 10 to reign 'far above all heavens'; hence the recognition that heaven is not a place in the universe: 'Heaven ghostly is nigh down as up, and up as down; behind as before, before as behind, on one side as other' (*Cloud of Unknowing*). In Christian hope, the faithful disciple will eventually reign with Christ, either at the end of time (at Christ's second coming on earth and the *resurrection of the dead to meet him, 1 Thessalonians 4. 15–17), or as being 'with Christ' (Philippians 1. 23), i.e. in heaven already at one's death. Traditional Catholic doctrine holds that the souls of those who have died in a state of grace, which have been first purged of their stains in *purgatory, pass to heaven, where they enjoy perfect bliss; but, except for the Virgin *Mary, these souls still await reunion with their bodies at the general resurrection.

Islam The Arabic terms are *Janna*, 'garden', and *Firdaws*, 'paradise'. The Qur'ān mentions *jannāt al-na'īm* 'gardens of delight' (10. 9); *jannāt 'Adn*, 'gardens of Eden' (19. 62, 61. 12); 'gardens beneath which rivers flow' (3. 137, 61. 12). The delights of heaven and the punishments of *hell (*jahannam*, or *al-nār* = the fire) are vividly described in early *sūras of the Qur'ān. Topographical details include the gates of paradise (39. 73), its size (3. 133), and gardens (88. 10). Inhabitants include the *ḥūrīs, creatures of brilliant eyes and beautiful form (55. 72, 66. 23). Details are elaborated by the *ḥadīth (see e.g. ḤAWḌ). There are special gates of entry for those who have practised various forms of piety, such as fasting. Those who die in battle for Islam are assured immediate entry.

Some mode of 'vision' of *Allāh seems to be allowed for in the Qur'ān, which speaks of 'faces looking towards their Lord' (75. 23–4), but this only at intervals. The Qur'ān states that 'no soul knows what bliss is kept hidden, as a reward for their [the believers'] deeds' (32. 19), and the ḥadīth claim that Allāh has prepared rewards which 'no eye has seen, no ear heard'.

Some theologians preferred allegorical interpretation for all the descriptions given in Qur'ān and ḥadīth. The *Mu'tazilites in particular denied any form of 'seeing' Allāh; the Ash'arites (*al-Ash'ari) allowed for some form of divine vision, interpreted *bi-lā kayf*, without asking 'how'. *Sūfīs taught that although the joys of paradise would be real, the greatest of all would be the vision of Allāh. Some, such as *al-Ghaz(z)ālī, taught that there are three kinds of reward: the sensual, the imaginative, and the spiritual, to be granted to human beings according to their individual capacity. *Rābi'a even felt that the concept of reward could distract the believer from worshipping Allāh for his own sake. Modern exegesis is inclined towards a philological interpretation, based on the allegorical and metaphorical nature of the Arabic language: the joys of paradise, as described, are real, but belong to a different plane of existence which cannot be experienced in this life.

Other Religions for approximate equivalents see LOKA; SVARGA; TUṢITA; VAIKUṆṬHA (BAIKUNTH); PURE LAND; SUKHĀVATĪ; SACH KHAṆḌ; T'IEN; and Index, Heavens, Paradises.

ed. C. Blacker and M. Loewe (eds.), *Ancient Cosmologies* (1975); S. G. F. Brandon, *Man and His Destiny in the Great Religions* (1962); J. Hick, *Death and Eternal Life* (1976).

Heaven and earth, sacrifices to. The most important rituals of the Imperial Cult in China from most ancient times down to the 20th cent. In the earliest historically known period (late Shang dynasty, *c.*1300–?1111 BCE), the high god was called *Ti, or *Shang-Ti. He dwelt in Heaven where he presided, so to speak, over the council of ancestors of the incumbent king. The high god of the succeeding Chou dynasty (?1111–256 BCE) was called *T'ien, which means Heaven. Shang-Ti and T'ien gradually became assimilated as the supreme ruler, by whose mandate (*t'ien ming) every ruling dynasty was legitimated. In Chinese philosophy Heaven was the embodiment of *yang*, one of the two basic forces (*yin-yang) in the universe. By the same token Earth, mother of all and source of their nourishment, as well as ultimate devourer of their physical forms, was the embodiment of yin. From earliest times Earth, as localized, was also tutelary deity of political and administrative regions, population centres, and even individual households.

In worshipping Heaven and Earth, therefore, the emperor was on the one hand acknowledging the subordination and dependence of all humans in relation to the supreme powers of the universe, and on the other hand demonstrating his own supremacy as ruler of all, who alone had the right to act as their intermediary with those powers. Hence, these rituals were the sole prerogative of the emperor, their performance by anyone else being a declaration of rebellion. In view of all this, the sacrifices to Heaven and Earth were made as elaborate and impressive as possible. Some idea of their scope and magnificence can be got from viewing the sites at which they were performed, during the recent centuries, in Peking. There are also personal accounts by foreign observers that give a vivid picture.

Heavenly Master School (school of religious Taoism): see WU-TOU-MI TAO.

Hebraeus, Leo (alternative name of Jewish philosopher and poet): see ABRABANEL JUDAH.

Hebrews. Biblical term for those who became the Jews. The origin of the word and its connection with *Habiru are disputed, but the term subsequently became synonymous with 'Jew'.

Hebrews, Letter to the. Book of the New Testament. Along with moral encouragement, the main argument of the letter is that the institutions of Judaism are imperfect and point forward to *Christ. Thus the once-for-all *sacrifice of his death is superior to the sacrificial system of the Temple (e.g. 4. 14–10. 18). Such passages are the source of much familiar Christian *typology. The letter was probably addressed to a Christian congregation (in Rome?) in danger of relapsing into Jewish ways. In this case a time of persecution such as *c*.65 might be suggested. Hebrews was traditionally included among *Paul's letters, but it does not bear his name and nothing else points to him as the author.

Hebrew Union College—Jewish Institute of Religion. Oldest seminary in the USA dedicated to Jewish studies and the training of *Reform *rabbis. The Hebrew Union College was founded in Cincinnati, Ohio, by Isaac Meyer *Wise in 1875. The Jewish Institute of Religion was founded in New York by Stephen S. Wise in 1922, and the two schools were merged in 1950. The Los Angeles branch was formed in 1954 and a Jerusalem branch in 1963.

Ḥeder (Heb., 'room'). Traditional Jewish elementary school. The term ḥeder first occurred in the 13th cent. CE. The schools were privately owned and taught small children *Prayerbook, the *Pentateuch, and *Talmud. The teacher was known as the *melammed*, and the children were prepared for *yeshivah. These schools were much scorned by the Maskilim of the *Haskalah, leading to an attempt at modification (ḥeder metukkan, 'reformed ḥeder'), but the attempt failed. Conversely, attempts to transfer the ḥeder to the USA, as a supplement to the public schools equally failed to take root.

Hefker. Ownerless property. According to Jewish law, ownerless property (whether it has never been owned, such as a wild bird, or whether its original owner has irretrievably lost it) is exempt from the law of *tithes and heave-offering. There are many differences of opinion among the *rabbis as to the details of the law of Hefker, and, in any case, the law of the land supersedes Jewish law in this matter.

Hegel, Georg Wilhelm Friedrich (1770–1831). German philosopher, the most influential and arguably most significant in the 19th cent. He was born at Stuttgart, where he spent his youth and imbibed a strict *Lutheran *pietism from which he never fully escaped. Hegel attended university at Tübingen, where he studied theology and philosophy and where he formed a close friendship with two fellow students—the poet F. Hölderlin and the philosopher F. W. J. Schelling (who, following Hegel's death, succeeded him at Berlin as professor of philosophy). Hegel completed his formal education at Jena, where he also taught until the university was 'reorganized' by Napoleon (whom Hegel called 'the *Zeitgeist* on horseback') and where he wrote *The Phenomenology of Spirit* (1807). In this, his first major book, the dialectic of human experience is unfolded in a more lively and less wooden way than in his later lectures and writings as professor at Berlin. Spirit as pure potentiality (*An-sich-sein*), through its self-alienation and self-objectification in nature (*Dasein*) and then through its progressive self-reconciliation in the history of human self-consciousness, comes finally to full awareness of itself as pure or absolute Spirit (*Für-sich-sein*). Human self-consciousness is exhibited principally in the interlocking histories of science, art, religion, and philosophy. Philosophy is the highest activity of which the human spirit is capable, but it adds nothing substantial to what is already available in religion: philosophy re-expresses conceptually what religion has already expressed *mythologically. Hegel defined 'religion' with disarming simplicity as 'the consciousness of God'. Viewed *phenomenologically, 'consciousness of God' refers in Hegel's writings to a person's coming to be aware of essential unity with the divine Spirit. The development of this consciousness can be traced in the history of religions, culminating in Christianity, which is termed the 'revelatory' or 'absolute' religion. In it alone God is known 'as He is'. Viewed speculatively, however, 'consciousness of God' refers at the same time to God's own self-consciousness. The history of religions is likewise the means of God's coming to 'be-for-himself' in and through people's ever-developing consciousness of him. The history of religions, therefore, is, for God and humanity alike, the occasion of self-recognition ('Spirit knows Spirit . . .') and self-reconciliation ('. . . as identical with itself').

F. C. Beiser (ed.), *The Cambridge Companion to Hegel* (1993); W. Jaeschke, *Reason in Religion* (1990); C. Taylor, *Hegel* (1975).

Hegira (migration of Muḥammad): see HIJRA.

Hegumenos or **Igumen** (Gk., 'leader'). A title in E. Christianity for the leader of a *monastic community (equivalent of the W. *abbot or prior). He is usually elected by the community, and is not necessarily the spiritual father, or *staretz, of the community. In *Coptic Christianity, it may also be the *archpriest who has charge of a church or a *cathedral.

Heian Period (Japan, 794–1185): see BUDDHISM IN JAPAN; SAICHŌ.

Heifer, Red (animal used in Jewish ritual of purification): see RED HEIFER.

Heikan (Jap., 'closing the gate'). The Zen Buddhist ability to cultivate in *zazen an awareness of one's surroundings without involvement in them.

Heikhal (Sephardi name for the Ark): see ARK (3).

Heiler, Friedrich (1892–1967). Christian theologian and *phenomenologist of religion. He was originally a Roman Catholic, but became a Lutheran under the influence of Nathan *Söderblom. From 1922 until his retirement in 1960, he was professor of the comparative history of religions at Marburg. Pulled back in a more Catholic direction by the writings of von *Hügel, he founded an evangelical order of Franciscan tertiaries. His major work was

Das Gebet (1918; Prayer: A Study in the History and Psychology of Religion, 1932). In this he put into practice his understanding of phenomenology as a way to discovering common truths at the heart of different religions, beneath the surface. He saw the study of religion in this way as a path that could lead to reconciliation between religions. At the outset of *Erscheinungsformen und Wesen der Religion* (1961), he summarized his understanding of the phenomenological method: it could not be 'value-free', since every science has its presuppositions; thus the historian of religion must be inductive, but the phenomenologist must be deductive, building on the foundations of history, philology, etc., working always with empathy.

Heilsgeschichte (Germ., 'salvation-history'). The attempt (made initially by Christians) to discern a unifying thread in human, and especially in biblical, history, that thread being the initiatives and actions of God in saving his people and the world. Although it was introduced originally in a Hegelian context, it was revived, particularly by O. Cullmann (e.g. *Christ and Time*, 1964; *Salvation in History*, 1967), in order to resist the reduction of the Bible to the status of a document in the history of religions. A later development has looked at a kind of ecumenical heilsgeschichte, in which the different religions are seen as convergent routes toward a value-bearing world community.

E. C. Rust, *Salvation History* . . . (1962) and *Toward a Theological Understanding of History* (1967).

Hekdesh (Heb., 'consecrated'). Among Jews, consecrated property. In the period of the *Temple, Jews were expected to consecrate property for the upkeep of the Temple, and, unlike secular gifts, consecration could be effected simply by word of mouth. Consecration was voluntary ('If you are unwilling to *vow, it shall be no sin in you', Deuteronomy 23. 23), and whoever consecrated all his property 'acted contrary to the requirements of the law and committed a foolish rather than a pious act' (*Yad Arakhin* 8. 13). After the destruction of the Temple, the term hekdesh was used for the dedication of property to a *synagogue or a *charity. The laws concerning hekdesh, its purpose, administration, and legality, are highly complicated. Because of its connection with charity, a hekdesh came to mean a shelter for the sick and poor, the conditions of which often inspired horror in visitors—so that in Yiddish, *hekdesh* came to mean a slum or slovenly place.

Hekhalot and merkabah. Early Jewish magic and mysticism connected with the palaces of heaven (hekhalot) and the chariot (merkabah) of *Elijah by which he was carried up to heaven. Contemplation of the chariot chapters of Ezekiel are at least as early as *Johanan ben Zakkai, and, following the discovery among the *Cairo Genizah Fragments of an early text describing Johanan's experience, it seems clear that Saul (who became *Paul) practised this mysticism, and that this was the foundation of his many reported experiences, including the vision on the Damascus road. (For text, see J. Bowker, 'Merkabah Visions and the Visions of Paul', *Journ. of Semitic Studies*, 16, 1971). The other surviving treatises date from the 3rd to 7th cents., of which five were of particular importance in subsequent Jewish mysticism: *Hekhalot Zutartei* (The Smaller Book of Palaces), describing the ascension of *Akiva to heaven; *Hekhalot Rabbati* (The Greater Book . . .), describing the ascension of R. Ishmael; *Ma'aseh Merkabah* (The Work of the Chariot), an anthology of hymns sung by mystics during their ascent; *Sefer Hekhalot*, known also as the Third Book of Enoch,' in which R. Ishmael describes his ascension and meeting with *Metatron, *Sar ha-Panim*, the Prince of Countenances; and *Shi'ur Komah* (The Measurement of the Height), in which the vision of God is described in anthropomorphic terms derived particularly from Song of Songs. These early texts and practices profoundly influenced *kabbalah and such movements as *Ḥasidei Ashkenaz.

Hekigan-roku (Chinese Ch'an/Zen verses): see HSÜEH-TOU CH'UNG-HSIEN.

Hell

Christianity The word 'hell' in English Bibles translates both Heb. *sheol and Gk. *gehenna. The latter, which came to denote the divinely ordained place of punishment for the wicked after death, was decisive for Christian understanding. Traditional theology holds that unrepentant sinners go to hell after this life, while the redeemed go either to *purgatory or directly to *heaven. The character of hell is popularly, and often literalistically, inferred from such New Testament texts as Matthew 13. 42, 25. 30, 41, 46, and especially the description of the 'second death' in Revelation 21. 8 in terms of being cast into 'a lake which burns with fire and brimstone'. According to *scholastic theology, souls experience in hell both the loss of contact with God (*poena damni*) and *poena sensus*, usually taken to be an agent tormenting them. A conservative modern position would be that hell is the necessary consequence of human free will and cannot therefore contradict God's love or justice. But many theologians, if not critical of the whole notion of everlasting punishment (see UNIVERSALISM), are reticent about the doctrine of hell. See also JUDGEMENT; DESCENT OF CHRIST INTO HELL.

A. Bernstein, *The Formation of Hell* (1993).

Islam Jahannam (cf. Heb., *gēhinnōm*, Gk., *gehenna) is mentioned frequently in the *Qur'ān. It has seven gates (39. 71; 15. 43), and different levels, the lowest being the tree Zaqqūm and a cauldron of boiling pitch and fire. Punishments are in accord with the gravity of sins—a theme much elaborated by later commentators. The Qur'ān does not make it clear whether punishments of Muslim sinners are for ever, and *Muḥammad's statement, 'The condemned will be cast into fire, to dwell there so long as the heavens and the earth shall last, unless God wills otherwise', does not make it clear whether God ever would 'will otherwise' (the clause simply protects his omnipotent freedom); nor does it make clear whether new heavens and new earths will be created when the present ones are ended, in a way corresponding to God's renewal of the skins of the damned, so that the fire can burn them again. In contrast, a *kāfir is generally held to be punished eternally.

Other Religions For Buddhist and Hindu hells see NARAKA (Pālī, *niraya*); Index, Hell.

Hellenism. Greek life and culture in the period from the conquests of Alexander the Great (4th cent. BCE) to the death of *Constantine. For both Judaism and (in different ways) Christianity, Hellenism offered both threat and challenge. On the one side, it offered opportunity to enhance the Jewish understanding of God's nature and action toward his creation (as in the philosopher *Philo or the historian *Josephus), and it served as a vehicle for the missionary communication of Judaism which was recognized in the Roman Empire as being extensive and successful. On the other hand, the adoption of Hellenistic ways (ranging from town-planning and language to 'gymnastic' sports involving nudity—Gk., *gumnos* means 'naked') threatened the requirements of *Torah—and even the survival of Judaism itself at the time of the *Maccabean revolt. For Christianity, Hellenism offered a vehicle of missionary extension and of theological (and *christological) reflection. In the 2nd cent., Numenius of Apamea could ask, 'What is Plato but Moses in Greek form?' Yet at the same time there were those who thought that the involvement of the gospel in classical thought was an erosion of it. The question, 'What has Athens to do with Jerusalem?', came to expect the answer, 'Nothing'.

F. C. Grant (ed.), *Hellenistic Religions* . . . (1953); A. A. Long, *Hellenistic Philosophy: Stoics, Epicureans and Sceptics* (1974); F. W. Wallbank, *The Hellenistic World* (1981).

Helpers. The usual Eng. tr. of the Arab. *anṣār*, denoting those in *Madīna who had espoused Islam before and after the *Hijra of Muḥammad, and who helped or supported him and, indeed, made possible the Hijrah itself by the pact into which they had entered to secure Muḥammad's person and cause, should he migrate to them from Mecca. They were thus distinguished from the Muhājirūn (*Emigrants) who emigrated from Mecca to Madīna with Muḥammad. The Arabic root *nṣr* has to do with victory as well as aid, or, aid tending to success. The term is also used in the Qur'ān in the case of 'Īsā/Jesus to denote his disciples/apostles. (3. 52 and 61. 14) where, fortuitously or otherwise, it echoes the term *naṣāra* used of Christians in general by Islam, and associated with Nazareth. The muhājirūn/anṣār distinction among the first Muslims, skilfully managed by Muḥammad, persisted into the tensions of Muslim politics after his death.

Helvetic Confessions. *Confessions of Christian faith drawn up by the Swiss Protestant Churches. The First Helvetic (Swiss) Confession (1536) was drawn up by *Bullinger (and others), with the help of *Bucer, in the hope of reconciling the Swiss and the Lutherans. Based on scripture, it emphasizes church ministry and the role of the state in promoting true religion. The Second (1566) is a revision of Bullinger's personal Confession. Its strong emphasis on scripture is reinforced by its extension in preaching: 'The preaching of the Word of God is the Word of God.' It sought continuity in the Church, and has had a wide and continuing influence.

Hemacandra (1089–1172). Śvetāmbara Jain monk of great learning, who came to be known as 'the all-wise one of the degenerate age'. He was born as Caṅgadeva in a village near what is now Ahmedabad. His parents entrusted him to a Jain monk for education, and he was initiated into the ascetic life, being given the name Somacandra. In 1108, he was made *suri*, teacher of a group of monks with authority to expound scripture and appoint a successor. From this moment, he became known as Hemacandra. He was involved in complex relations with the rulers of Gujarat, who, although worshippers of *Śiva, nevertheless assimilated much of Jainism, leading to a brief period when there was a Jain kingdom, the only one to be established in India. His main surviving works recapitulate Jain history and principles, especially as exemplified in the past.

Triṣaṣṭiśalākāpuruṣacarita (The Deeds of the Sixty-Three Eminent Men, tr. H. M. Johnson, 1931–62) has a last section on *Mahāvīra which includes a kind of Jain utopia, in which the king will usually avoid prostitutes, and the queen will be chaste:

> When he eradicates all sin, the wild deer of the forest will chew the cud unharmed, like cows in a stall; . . . Even carnivorous animals will hear his command and will forget even the name of meat, as belonging to a nightmare. . . . Under his glorious rule, there will be no more pigeon-racing or cock-fighting throughout the earth. . . . He will establish his own era on the earth.

His *Yogaśastra* (Treatise on Yoga) takes *yoga in a very broad sense and becomes a compendium on appropriate Jain behaviour.

G. Buhler, *Life of Hemacandra* (1936).

Hémādrī. A learned scholar and a minister of the Yādava kings of Deogirī near Auraṇgābād, 1260–71. He possessed great powers of organization and a wide outlook directed towards the many-sided improvement of the people. He employed many scholars to prepare a compendium of religious observances, entitled *Chāturvarga-chintāmaṇī*. He introduced a code of private and official etiquette and forms of address in private and public correspondence. He introduced a cursive script called Moḍī for fast Marāṭhī writing, and a grain (Bājarī) as a cheap food-crop with plentiful yield.

Hémādrī invented the special art of constructing houses and temples with hewn stones, piled one upon another without the use of cement or mortar. He also wrote the history of the Yādava rulers, entitled *Yādava-Prashastī*. He was put to death by Rāmachandra Yādava about 1272 CE.

Hemkunt (Skt., *hemakuta*, 'golden peak'). Sikh shrine in N. India. According to the Bachitra Nāṭak in the *Dasam Granth of Gurū *Gobind Siṅgh it was here, at a height of 4,636 m. in the Gaṛhwāl Hills, that he had meditated during a previous incarnation. God had then commissioned him to spread his religion. Since the rediscovery of the site *c.*1930 it has become a place of summer *pilgrimage.

Hen-chū-shō (classification of five degrees of enlightenment: Zen Buddhism): see GO-I.

Henotheism (Gk., 'one God'). The worship of, and devotion to, one God, while allowing that other gods exist. The term was introduced by Max Müller, when he observed that the hymns in the *Vedas frequently describe the God to whom they are addressed as the One, the Supreme, etc., but that the God thus described is not the same from hymn to hymn. Kathenotheism is the worship of one god after another, but in the end Müller preferred the name 'henotheism'.

Henotikon (Gk., 'decree of unity'). The *christological formula sponsored by the Byzantine emperor Zeno in 482 to conciliate the *Monophysite party in the E. Empire. By the formula 'Christ was one and now two' it sought to avoid speaking of the number of 'natures' in Christ, and it went so far as to anathematize anyone who 'at *Chalcedon or anywhere else' sought to change the faith of *Nicaea. Such concessions were rejected by the see of Rome, and brought about a schism which lasted until 519. Moreover, the decree failed to satisfy all the Monophysites, who insisted on an explicit repudiation of Chalcedon.

Henry Suso (Seuse, *c.*1295–1366). German mystic. Of noble birth, he entered a Dominican convent at Constance at the age of 13. He studied under *Eckhart at Cologne between 1322 and 1325, and became his disciple. His defence of Eckhart led to censure. He won fame as a preacher and spiritual director, and from *c.*1347 lived at Ulm. His teaching, found especially in his life, and his *Little Books of Truth* and *Eternal Wisdom*, are expressed in vivid imagery. They manifest his debt to Eckhart and his opposition to the supposed immorality of the Brethren of the Free Spirit. He called himself 'The servant of the Eternal Wisdom', and experienced mystical states of which he said, 'If this is not heaven, I cannot know what heaven is.'

Herbert, Edward (1583–1648). First Lord Herbert of Cherbury, religious philosopher and early advocate of the idea that there is a universal religion natural to human beings. He was born in Shropshire and educated at Oxford. He went to Paris as ambassador in 1619, where he published, in 1624, *De Veritate* . . . While this displays a sophisticated epistemology, which refutes a crude empiricism, it also lays the foundations for his views on a common or natural religion, which he developed further in *De Religione Laici* (1645) and *De Religione Gentilium* (1663). He held that there are five beliefs which are innate and which are common to all people: (i) that there is a Supreme Being; (ii) that he is worthy of our worship; (iii) that virtue is the true mode of that worship or relationship; (iv) that sin is to be recognized and repented of; and (v) that justice demands that we receive a due reward or punishment after death for what we have done during this life. Since these beliefs are innate and universal, there is no need for revelation, and for this reason Herbert has been called 'the father of the *Deists'.

Herbert, George (1593–1633). *Anglican priest and *Metaphysical poet. From his days at Cambridge University, he impressed by his brilliance, and seemed destined for a court career. But, under the influence of Nicholas Ferrar, he turned to theology. In 1630 he was ordained priest and became rector of Bemerton. His *Priest to the Temple* presents an ideal of Anglican pastoral ministry; his collection of poems, *The Temple*, depicts the inner engagement between his soul and God in simple yet powerful verse, much influenced by the imagery of Scripture and the **Book of Common Prayer*, and owing a great deal to St *Augustine. Some are in use as hymns (e.g. 'Teach me, my God and King', 'Let all the world in every corner sing').

The Works of George Herbert, ed. F. E. Hutchinson (1941).

Here I stand (Luther's commitment): see WORMS, DIET OF.

Ḥerem (Heb., 'ban'). Excommunication from the Jewish community. Derived from the isolation of holy items in biblical times, the first reference to excommunication is in Ezra 10. 8. In the period of the *Talmud, four types of excommunication had developed: (i) *nezifah*, a rebuke, an expulsion for seven days (in Babylon for one) for such offences as keeping dangerous dogs and masturbation; (ii) *shamta*, now of uncertain meaning; (iii) *niddui*, 'separation', thirty days in *Erez Israel, seven in the *diaspora, but renewable without reform of ways; (iv) ḥerem, isolation: such a person was forbidden to hear or teach *Torah, and had to observe the laws of mourning. If a person died in this state, the coffin had placed on it a stone, to show that the person was worthy of stoning. The ceremony in the *synagogue was of awe-inspiring character, with black candles, the *ark open, and the *shofar blown. The excommunications of *Spinoza and of Acosta are particularly well-known. But frequently, the ḥerem was used as an instrument in communal arguments, as when Elijah Gaon excommunicated the *Ḥasidim. It is now little used in that way except by the extreme *Orthodox in Israel.

Heresy (Gk., *hairesis*, 'choice'). The adoption of false views and practices. Basically, the Gk. word may mean simply the adoption of a particular opinion or school of thought (e.g. Acts 5. 17), but in religious terms it is usually a choice of belief which is held to be aberrant (i.e. heretical) by the main continuing body of believers. Thus heresy is opinion or belief outside the boundary of accepted doctrine and practice. A heresiarch is the originator of a heresy or heretical movement. In Christianity, where the term is essentially located, *Roman Catholic theologians distinguish 'formal heresy' (the grave sin of wilful persistence in error) and 'material heresy' (the holding of heretical doctrines through no fault of one's own). Heresy is distinguished from *apostasy and *schism: as pertaining to 'choice', J. *Taylor regarded heresy as an error of the will rather than of the understanding. A doctrinal definition of heresy such as the above is, however, difficult to apply in unprejudiced discussion of actual historical controversies like those over *Arianism and *Nestorianism, since the claim of both sides to derive their doctrines from the Bible and the apostles cannot be judged *a priori*. In such contexts the 'heretics' are simply those whose doctrine was condemned by a consensus of the Church at a particular time (especially at an *ecumenical council). It remains possible to question the propriety of a council (e.g. *Chalcedon) or to ask whether the *gnostic heresy, for example, was repudiated for partly spurious reasons; while at the same recognizing the validity of the continuing consensus, and the necessity to confront issues of truth and responsibility. Within the continuity of Christianity, an appeal will usually be made to the guidance of the Holy Spirit as a guard against *cultural relativity and error.

In other religions, the term is not formally appropriate, but similar considerations, derived from the necessity for systems to have boundaries, can be found. Thus in Judaism, neither Bible nor *Talmud present creeds or dogmas to which Jews must conform. However, Deuteronomy 17. 8–13 isolates the *zaqen mamre*, the obstinate teacher (*rebellious elder), who persists in his opinion against the majority interpretation of the law. Such a person must be investigated and, if he persists, taken to the highest authority of the time. If he *still* persists, he must be executed, because otherwise two Israels will be created (two interpretations of *Torah). The gospel evidence portrays *Jesus being investigated in exactly that way. But at this early stage, there are no particular beliefs which have been isolated as necessary. Not until the time (12th cent.) of *Maimonides was an attempt made to define constitutive beliefs. Nevertheless, already in the *Mishnah serious aberrancy is recognized. Heresy now is belief in ideas condemned by the *Orthodox religious authorities. In Judaism, a heretic is still considered to be a *Jew, and is described by a number of terms such as *min, *apikoros, and *kofer* (cf. *kāfir). The attitude towards heretics is not consistent; on the one hand stories are told of scholars conversing amicably with heretics, and on the other that a Jew need not endanger his own life to save that of a heretic (*B.Av.Zar. 26a–b*). Traditionally heresy was punished by *ḥerem, and this was justified as avoiding divisiveness within the community. Prominent heretical opinions from the point of view of mainstream Judaism include *Samaritanism, Christianity, *Karaism, *Shabbateanism, sometimes *Hasidism, and the *Progressive movements.

The nearest equivalent in Islam is *ilḥād*, 'deviation'. Heretics are called *malāḥidah*. Right practice (*sunna) is as important as right belief, but in any case the heretic is, quintessentially, one who denies the reality of God. Thus the major offences in Islam are *shirk (associating anything or anyone with God as though equal to God) and *bidʿa (innovation, introducing any practice or claim which is not to be found in God's merciful revelation, the *Qur'ān). Almost as heinous is contempt of the prophets, especially Muḥammad. There are degrees of deviation: *Sunnis and *Shiʿites regard each other as deviant, but theoretically as still part of the same *'umma (community). One who denies God altogether is a kāfir and cannot be forgiven. One who forsakes Islam is an apostate (*murtadd), and if he turns against Islam in public attack, he should be executed. The condemnation of such views may be made in a *fatwā, and although a fatwā is informed advice which is accepted only when reflection agrees with it, in practice (particularly among Shiʿa) it has immediate authority.

In E. religions, it might seem, superficially, that there is little room for a concept equivalent to heresy. Resting on anthropologies which envisage many millions of rebirths or reappearances, guardians of truth might be expected to be more relaxed about conformity: if truth is denied or despised in this life, an appropriate rebirth will, through the workings of *karma, make amends. This impression is, in important respects, correct. 'Hinduism' and 'Buddhism' contain diversities of an even more spectacular kind than Christianity. Hinduism as *sanātana dharma (the unchanging map of how to live appropriately) is able to include conceptually even those breakaway religious movements, such as the Jains and Buddhists, which are usually described as separate religions. They are interpretations (*darśana) of the revelation in the *Vedas, but unorthodox ones—*nāstika as opposed to *āstika. They are by no means to be encouraged, but ironically, a nāstika can be left to the future, whereas an āstika who abandons *caste-regulated behaviour should be expelled. In a sense which is now eroded, the orthodox is defined geographically: it is the area in which *dharma can be observed. Thus **Manusmṛti*:

> The land between the two sacred rivers Sarasvati and Drsadvati, this land created by divine powers, is the Brahmavarta. The customs prevailing in this land, passed on from one generation to another, constitute right behaviour (*sadācāra*). From a *brahman born and bred in this land all people should learn how to live. . . . Beyond is the land of the mlecchas: a *twice-born should remain in this land; a *śūdra may, to gain his livelihood, live anywhere.

Buddhism was not even confined to territory, since it was, at least in terms of teaching, opposed to caste, sacrifice, and dharma determined by Vedas and brahmans. However, it was not on trivial issues that the early schools divided (see COUNCILS (BUDDHIST)); and the subsequent elaboration into *sūtra-based Buddhism (i.e. *Mahāyāna) led to an immense proliferation of schools and traditions. But although there has been considerable hostility between Mahāyāna and *Hīnayāna (witness the latter name itself), the different forms of Buddhism have in general flourished in different geographical areas. The definition of the heretic has therefore been extremely local, leading to expulsion from communities, especially of monks (see EXCOMMUNICATION). The nearest equivalent to heresy is 'false views': see DIṬṬHI; Index, Heresy, Heretics.

D. Christie-Murray, *A History of Heresy* (1989); G. Forkman, *The Limits of the Religious Community* (1972).

Hermas. Second-cent. Roman Christian and author of a work called *The Shepherd*. This purports to have been written in consequence of a series of visions. It is divided into five 'Visions', twelve 'Mandates', and ten 'Similitudes'. In the fifth Vision the Angel of Penance appears in the guise of a shepherd, whence the name of the treatise. The aim of the book is to show the necessity of *penance and the possibility of the forgiveness of sins at least once after *baptism. It also displays a primitive doctrine of the *Trinity. In the E. Church it was widely regarded as scripture, and is found in the Codex Sinaiticus after the New Testament. In the W. Church it was less valued, and the *Muratorian canon attributes it to a brother of Pope Pius (d. 154).

Hermeneutical circle: see HERMENEUTICS.

Hermeneutics (Gk., *hermeneutikos*, 'interpretation', from Hermes, the Greek messenger of the gods). The discipline arising from reflection on the problems involved in the transmission of meaning from text or symbol to reader or hearer. Since there is no privileged or 'correct' meaning of an utterance, hermeneutics has sometimes been summarized in the question, 'whose meaning is the meaning of the meaning?' For example, what does *Hamlet* mean? Whatever a grammatical and linguistic analysis of the words reveals? What Shakespeare intended? What a producer makes of it? What actors do with it in their own interpretation? What a critic understands by it? What an audience appropriates of it? On what grounds can any claimed understanding or interpretation be declared to be wrong? At what point can it be said that one 'understands' *Hamlet*? If translation from one language to another is required, how much meaning (of whose meaning?) is lost in the process—or gained? Translation may be so illuminating and suggestive that the remark is sometimes made, 'The original is unfaithful to the translation.'

The modern discussion of hermeneutics derives from the early Romantic movement (which sought to relate human creativity to the all-embracing ambitions of post-Newtonian explanation, either by bringing that creativity under Newtonian laws (*l'homme machine*) or, more often, by claiming that such creativity lies under its *sui generis* laws through which alone, and *not* by Newtonian, mechanistic reduction, can it be understood). In this latter endeavour, *Kant's emphasis on understanding was essential: *Verstand* (understanding) is the underlying human capacity for thought and experience, and *Verstehen* (acts of understanding), which are present in all thought and experience, are the expression of the distinctively human rationality. For *Schleiermacher (the key figure in the development of hermeneutics), hermeneutics could no longer be a matter of uncovering a single given meaning in a text by chipping away at the obstacles which at present obscure it. Rather, hermeneutics 'is an unending task of understanding'. Every utterance, verbal or non-verbal, belongs to a linguistic system (*Sprache*), but it belongs also to the lived experience (*Erlebnis*) of the one who utters: 'An act of speaking cannot be understood as a moment in a person's development unless it is also understood in relation to the language . . ., but an act of speaking cannot be understood as a modification of the language unless it is also understood as a moment in the development of the person.' There is thus a hermeneutical circle which it is the task of hermeneutics, conceived of as the art of understanding, to close.

Wilhelm Dilthey (1833–1911) took what he understood of Schleiermacher much further: 'Understanding and interpretation constitute the method used in the human sciences . . . At each instance, understanding discloses a world.' His *On the Construction of the Historical World in the Human Sciences* (1910) abandoned the view that understanding rests in human language-competence, and claimed instead that it rests in the whole life-process: it is a *Lebenskategorie* (a category of life). By this he meant that the process of life is a constant 'scan' of circumstances so that they can be understood and so that appropriate reactions can be initiated. What has to be 'understood', therefore, by the scientist of human behaviour is always a life-expression (*Lebensausserung*), which points back to a lived experience (*Erlebnis*) as its source. The expressed meaning

(*Ausdruck*) can be apprehended only by relating the two, but that in itself is a 'lived experience' on the part of the one who apprehends, part indeed of a continuing 'lived experience' which constitutes a 'pre-understanding'. The closing of the hermeneutical circle now becomes the connecting of two culturally and historically embedded lives, not to achieve '*the* meaning', but to create a new horizon of meaning from the connection, the fusion of horizons. There is no single 'meaning of the meaning' to be found, but a near-limitless opportunity of understanding—limits being set only by the lived experience and the consequent forms of utterance of those involved. For Emilio Betti (1890–1968), this offered the best hope for a tolerant society, since there is no one meaning, closed to all revision, ever to be attained.

Against what may seem to be a steady drift toward subjectivism ('meaning is for me'), ontological hermeneutics (associated especially with the later Heidegger and Hans-Georg Gadamer, *Wahrheit und Methode* . . ., 1972, 'Truth and Method', 1975) has sought to integrate the truth which lies behind language and which alone makes intelligible utterance possible. While it seems obvious to say that 'what are true are sentences', Gadamer insists (as do critical realists in the natural sciences) that there is what there is 'over and above our wanting and doing'. While all or most of what we say may indeed be approximate, provisional, corrigible, and mainly 'wrong', it is nevertheless wrong about something—theology would add, 'about Someone'. Thus where many assume that 'we find the truth', Gadamer argues that 'the truth finds us'. Language is the surface where truth becomes visible.

While hermeneutics is thus an issue in many disciplines, it is central to the interpretation of religious utterance, and of religious and sacred texts. In the Christian tradition, there have in fact been many different styles of exegesis of the Bible, some of which have seemed fanciful to later generations. Thus *allegory (e.g. as used by *Clement and *Origen) offered a meaning for the whole of the Bible controlled by the central fact of Christ. In the medieval period, scripture was expected to yield a fourfold meaning: the literal (letter) sense; the allegorical or *typological sense (the meaning in the context of the drama of salvation); the moral sense (the practical meaning in terms of conduct); the *anagogical sense (the meaning in relation to the purposes of God in eternity). For the Reformers, much of this had produced eisegesis (reading meaning into the text) rather than *exegesis. In the argument of Mathias Illyricus (*Clavis Scripturae Sacrae*, 1567), proper linguistic and historical attention to the text would yield its meaning, and the Bible as a whole should be used to interpret itself. One of the earliest (1737) uses of the word 'hermeneutics' in English reflects these extremes, warning against 'taking such liberties with sacred writ as are by no means allowable upon any known rules of just and sober hermeneuticks'. The fusion of horizons between text and reader reconciles these extremes by allowing the continuing creativity of the Holy Spirit to bring God's truth and the truth of God to the surface of a particular moment. For *Bultmann especially (who was deeply immersed in the history of hermeneutics), the biblical writings are not offering propositional statements about the nature and activity of God, but rather calling people to appropriate attitudes and responses in the orientation of life. Thus 'God will judge the world' is not so much a prediction about a future event as a summons to live responsibly and accountably now. More widely, hermeneutics is an invitation to the creation of community in which the *Logos is still articulate, closing the circle of Trinitarian love by the inclusion of otherwise disordered humanity and cosmos.

See Index, Hermeneutics.

R. J. Bernstein, *Beyond Objectivism and Relativism* . . . (1983); J. W. Bowker, *Licensed Insanities* . . . (1987); M. Ermarth, *Wilhelm Dilthey* . . . (1978); R. J. Howard, *Three Faces of Hermeneutics* . . . (1982); K. Mueller-Vollmer (ed.), *The Hermeneutics Reader* (1985); R. E. Palmer, *Hermeneutics* (1969).

Hermeneutics, rabbinic. The systems of biblical interpretation employed in rabbinic Judaism. The rabbis believed that the *Pentateuch was a divinely appointed, unified text, and that by following certain rules of interpretation, deeper meanings can be discovered. The three best-known sets of rules are the seven rules of *Hillel, the thirteen rules of R. *Ishmael, and the thirty-two rules of R. Eliezer b. Yose ha-Gelili. In addition, Nahum of Gurrizo developed a system based on the assumption that the marking on every letter has a specific meaning, and this idea was subsequently developed by R. *Akiva. Later, *kabbalists interpreted scripture on the basis of *gematria or the numerical values of words.

Hermeticism. System of *gnostic thought known from the *Corpus Hermeticum*, a collection of philosophical and magical texts dating from the 2nd and 3rd cents. CE. The Egyptian God, Thoth, is identified with the Greek Hermes who is called 'Thrice Greatest', i.e. Trismegistus. At one time they were thought to have been written by a contemporary of *Moses, whose wisdom anticipated the philosophical and religious wisdom of Plato and Jesus. Some of the texts (especially nos. 1, *Poimandres*, and 13, *The Secret Instruction on the Mountain*) are concerned to draw initiates through *ascetic self-discipline into a vision of God as Light, 'the first God':

> I can tell you nothing but this: I see that there has come to be in me a form which is not fashioned out of matter, and I have passed out of myself and entered into an immortal form. . . . I am no longer an object coloured and tangible, a thing of spatial dimensions. . . . To such eyes as yours, my son, I am not now visible.

The human and the divine are thus one: 'We must not be frightened of affirming that a man on earth is a mortal God, and that a God in heaven is an immortal man.' Hermeticism and the *Corpus* became immensely influential in the Renaissance when most of the texts were translated in Italy. The magical texts were taken up by John Dee, Robert Fludd, and Paracelsus, who developed 'man as microcosm' philosophies, and did much to open the way to the so-called scientific revolution: a magical world-view put humans at the centre of creative activity, no longer passive recipients of revelation and ecclesiastical control. The *Corpus* was correctly dated by Isaac Casaubon in 1614, and the texts rapidly waned in influence.

F. Bonardel, *L'Hermétisme* (1985); B. P. Copenhauer, *Hermetica* (1992); A.-J. Festugière, *La Révélation d'Hermès Trismégiste* (1950–4); G. Foden, *The Egyptian Hermes* (1986); F. A. Yates, *Giordano Bruno and the Hermetic Tradition* (1964) and *The Occult Philosophy in the Elizabethan Age* (1979).

Herod. Several rulers of Jud(a)ea bore this name.

1. Herod I (73–4 BCE, the Great) was appointed by his father to be governor of Galilee and, after his father's death, was appointed initially tetrarch by the Romans and, by 37 BCE, king. His official title was 'king, an ally and friend of the Roman people'. Married to the *Hasmonean princess, Mariamne, he none the less systematically set out to destroy all members of that dynasty including his wife and her two sons. During his reign he embarked on an extensive building campaign including the *Temple in Jerusalem. Despite this he was regarded by his Jewish subjects as a foreign agent and a destroyer of their institutions.

2. Herod II, grandson of Herod I and Mariamne, ruled as king of Chalcis, 41–8 CE. During this period, he had the right to appoint *high priests.

3. Herod Antipas, son of Herod I and Malthace, ruled as tetrarch of Galilee, 4 BCE–39 CE, until he was exiled by the Romans.

4. Herod Philip I, son of Herod I and Cleopatra of Jerusalem, ruled as tetrarch of Transjordan, 4 BCE–34 CE.

'That fox Herod' (Luke 13. 32) is thus Herod Antipas.

Herodians (Jewish party): see BOETHUSIANS.

Heruka (Skt.; Tib., *khrag.'thung*, 'Blood Drinker'). A class of *wrathful deity in Tibetan Buddhism who presides over *Tantric ritual. According to the texts, the Heruka serves not to 'protect' the ritual, but is rather a meditational 'tool' by which the *yogin, through identification with the Heruka, attacks his own egotistical grasping—the principal factor perpetuating the *paticca-samuppāda, limiting compassion and obstructing the attainment of enlightenment. The Heruka is most commonly represented as the wrathful mode of the Mandala of the five jinas: e.g. the 'Śrī-Heruka' Cakrasamvara and Vajravārāhī in ritual intercourse (*maithuna; *yab-yum) is a manifestation of *Vairocana.

Hervomde Kerk (Christian (Protestant) Church): see DUTCH REFORMED CHURCH.

Herzl, Theodor (1860–1904). Founder of the Jewish World *Zionist Organization. Born in Budapest, Herzl was brought up as a *progressive Jew, had a secular education, and trained as a lawyer in Vienna. As a newspaper correspondent, he attended the *Dreyfus trial in 1895 and became convinced that the only solution to the problem of *anti-Semitism was establishing a Jewish national homeland: 'There exists only one solution . . . We are talking about a simple old matter—the *Exodus from Egypt.' In 1896 he published *Der Judenstaat* (The Jewish State) which went through eighty editions in eighteen languages. Although he himself was prepared to consider a homeland in Argentina, he began to realize from Jewish reaction to his book that only *Erez Israel had sufficient attraction as a Jewish state. He travelled widely through Europe and the Middle East, and in 1897, the first Zionist Conference was held in Basle. Herzl was in the chair and was elected president of the new World Zionist Organization. Despite founding a Jewish bank to provide share capital for Zionist schemes, Herzl did not gain the support of the great Jewish banking families or of the liberal Jews. After negotiations with the German Kaiser and the Turkish Sultan came to nothing, Herzl held the fourth Congress in London and tried to gain the support of the British Government for Jewish settlement in the British terrotories of Cyprus and the Sinai Peninsula. Again no support was forthcoming, but instead Uganda in E. Africa was suggested. The Uganda scheme was rejected by the Zionist General Council in 1904. Herzl died of pneumonia later that year. He also wrote a novel, *Altneu Land* (Old New Land) about the yearning of the Jewish people for Zion, the motto of which was, 'If you will, it is no fairytale'. After the foundation of the State of Israel, his remains were reburied in Jerusalem, and the anniversary of his death, 20 Tammuz, is kept as a national memorial day.

A. Bein, *Theodor Herzl* (Eng. 1940).

Herzog, Isaac Halevi (1888–1959). First *Ashkenazi *Chief Rabbi of Israel (though not of Palestine). A brilliant scholar, he served as rabbi in Ireland, until he was elected in 1936 to succeed Abraham *Kook as Ashkenazi chief rabbi in Palestine. After the Second World War, he travelled widely to try to find and rescue Jewish children who had been hidden with *gentile families. Besides several volumes of *responsa, he published *Main Institutions of Jewish Law* (1936, 1939). His son, Chaim Herzog, was 6th President of Israel.

Heschel, Abraham Joshua (1907–72). US Jewish scholar. He was born in Poland, descended from *Ḥasidic rabbis. A close associate of Martin *Buber, he became a refugee from Nazi Germany, first in London, then in the USA. There he taught at the *Hebrew Union College and the *Jewish Theological Seminary. He wrote important studies on *kabbalah and was a highly influential philosopher of religion. In *Man is not Alone* (1951) and *God in Search of Man* (1956), Heschel tried to define the existential question to which Judaism provides the answer. It lies in the true use of freedom. God longs for his creatures but will not coerce them. Judaism exhibits the response of love and devotion when the commands of God are accepted in that style: 'God is of no importance unless he is of supreme importance.' Jewish history is the manifestation of degrees of success and failure in doing this, just as the Bible is the record of God's command and Israel's response. Revelation is not a matter of supposing that each mark in Torah came directly from God, but rather that Israel is a consequence of belief that God has made his will known. Thus 'man's good deeds are single acts in the long drama of redemption'. The laws of *halakhah are as essential as the musical notes without which a great symphony could not be played. Each individual has an indispensable part to play in realizing the *messianic kingdom: 'An architect of hidden worlds, every pious Jew is, partly, the Messiah.' His strong emphasis on ethical behaviour as the demonstration of religion took him into the Civil Rights movement, and into *dialogue with other religions, especially in the discussions which led to the revised attitude of *Vatican II to Judaism. What, in his view, is particularly distinctive about Judaism is that it has consecrated, not buildings, but time: 'Judaism is a religion of time, aiming at the sanctification of time. The sabbaths are our great cathedrals.' The Ḥasidic experience was never left behind, enabling him to keep faith, even when, as he put it, he kept his eyes on *Auschwitz.

J. C. Merkle, *The Genesis of Faith* . . . (1985); F. A. Rothschild (ed.), *Between God and Man* . . . (1965).

Hess, Moses (1812–75). German socialist and *Zionist. As an ethical socialist, Hess believed, in the early part of his life, that Jews should *assimilate into the majority culture. By 1862, he had published *Rome and Jerusalem* (Eng., 1918) which recommended the 'founding of Jewish societies of agriculture, industry and trade in accordance with Mosaic, i.e., socialist principles'. According to *Herzl, writing in 1901, 'I was enraptured and uplifted by him. . . . Since *Spinoza, Jewry has brought no greater spirit than this forgotten Moses Hess.'

I. Berlin, *Life and Opinions of Moses Hess* (1958).

Hesychasm (from Gk., *hesychia*, 'quietness'). Tradition of contemplative prayer associated above all with the monks of Mount *Athos. Many antecedents can be found in the early *Fathers, but its full expression is found in the 14th cent. in Gregory of Sinai, Nicephorus of Mount Athos, and especially *Gregory Palamas. Its central feature is constant recitation of the *Jesus Prayer, combined with optional physical techniques of a crouched posture and synchronization of such recitation with *breathing, so that the mind is united with the heart, and the whole person is drawn into 'prayer of the heart'. This leads to a vision by the bodily eyes of the Uncreated Light of the Godhead, the light that surrounded Jesus at the Transfiguration, none other than the uncreated energies of the Godhead. The distinction between the unknowable essence of God and his energies, identical with himself, by which he is genuinely known, is a central part of the intellectual defence of hesychasm made by Gregory Palamas. The **Philocalia* of *Nicodemus of the Holy Mountain and Macarius of Corinth (1782) is an anthology of hesychasm, now an accepted part of the tradition of E. Orthodoxy.

Heteroglossolalia (a form of speaking in tongues): see GLOSSOLALIA.

Hetu. In Buddhism, a 'root-condition', good or bad, which brings about a thought or action. It is not so much the cause as the conditioner of a thought or action when it arises, given a cause. The six root-conditions are *lobha, *dosa, and *moha and their opposites.

Hevra Kaddisha (Aram., 'holy brotherhood'). Jewish mutual benefit societies. By the late 17th cent. the term came to be used only for burial societies. Membership was regarded as an honour. According to Jewish law, no material gain may be made in disposing of the dead. Consequently it is forbidden to make money by burying the dead, and the duty thus devolves on the whole community. The Hevra was celebrated annually on a specific day (often 15 Kislev) with a fast followed by a banquet.

Hexapla (Gk., 'sixfold'). An edn. of the Old Testament produced by *Origen in *c.*245 CE. In it the Hebrew text, the Heb. text in Greek. letters, and four Gk. versions were arranged in six parallel columns. Its immense size meant that few complete copies were made: *Jerome used the original in Origen's library at Caesarea. The 'Hexaplaric' *Septuagint in the fifth column, was circulated on its own without Origen's critical symbols, and was carefully translated into Syriac (the 'Syro-Hexapla') in 616–17.

Hexateuch (Gk., *hex*, 'six', + *teuchos*, 'book'). A name given by J. *Wellhausen to the first six books of the Hebrew Bible, supposing that *Joshua was compiled from the same sources as the *Pentateuch.

Hicks(ites) (leader/followers of Quaker sect): see FRIENDS, THE SOCIETY OF.

Hidden Imām. A Shīʿa Muslim belief that the last Imām in succession from *ʿAlī did not die, but disappeared, and is now in a hidden state from which he helps believers and will return as *al-Mahdī at the end of time to return peace and justice to the earth. Different Imāms are identified as the Hidden Imām by different Shī'a groups. See AL-MAHDĪ; DRUZES; ITHNA 'ASHARIYYA; GHAIBA.

Hiden (Jap., 'field of compassion'). Buddhist actions of supporting the poor or needy. Since these produce *merit, they are compared to a field which brings forth a great harvest.

Hiei, Mt. (site of first Tendai temple): see MOUNT HIEI.

Hierarchy. A body of religious rulers organized in successive ranks. In Christianity, one may speak of the hierarchy of *bishops, *priests, and *deacons; but in Catholic use the word most usually refers to bishops and to other dignitaries whose authority derives from the pope. For the 'heavenly hierarchy', see ANGEL.

Hierophany (Gk., *hieros*, 'sacred', + *phainein*, 'to show'). The manifestation of the divine or the sacred, especially in a sacred place, object, or occasion. In the work of *Eliade, hierophanies serve to separate the *sacred from the profane: by virtue of its connection with locality, the sacred is no longer absolute, because the otherwise abstract absolute has limited itself in order to become manifest. Thus hierophany is in a paradoxical sense an act of divine or sacred veiling because of the inherent necessity for self-limitation. Because, therefore, only some aspect of the divine or sacred can be manifested, such manifestations may be named after the aspect revealed, e.g. theophany (of divinity), kratophany (of power).

High Churchmen. The group in the Church of England which gives a high place to the authority and antiquity of the *church, to the *episcopate, and to *sacraments. The title is first attested at the end of the 17th cent. Many High Churchmen went into *schism as Non-jurors (see DIVINE RIGHT OF KINGS) under William III. High Churchmanship was revitalized in 19th-cent. *Anglo-Catholicism deriving from the *Oxford Movement.

High Holy Days. The Jewish *festivals of *Rosh ha-Shanah and Yom Kippur (*Day of Atonement). The ten days between the two festivals are often known as 'the High Holy Day period'.

High Mass (Lat., *missa solemnis*). In W. churches the more ceremonial form of the *mass, in which the emphasis may be more on adoration than reception of communion. The *liturgical movement has conduced to a different style of worship, and since *Vatican II the term 'High Mass' has disappeared from official Roman Catholic documents.

High place. Place of worship. In biblical times, shrines were built on hills throughout *Erez Israel; though 'high place' may mean 'raised altar'. After the *Temple had been built in *Jerusalem, it was considered *idolatrous to worship at such shrines, and during the reigns of Hezekiah and *Josiah they were removed.

High priest. The chief priest (Heb., *kohen gadol*) of the *Jerusalem *Temple. According to Leviticus 21, the high priest was a descendant of *Aaron who had been anointed with holy oil as the first 'chief priest' (Exodus 28. 1). By the *Hellenistic period, the high priest was responsible for the religious life of the country, and was the recognized representative of the Jewish community. Thus even when the *Hasmoneans ruled as kings, they realized that they would also have to hold the high priesthood if they were to exercise real authority (a usurpation which caused the first schisms, leading to the community at *Qumran). By the end of the second Temple period, when the land was under Roman rule, the high priest was often considered merely an arm of the secular administration and was under constant criticism from the *Pharisees and *Zealots. Once the Temple was destroyed in 70 CE the office lapsed.

Hijāb (Arab.). Any partition which separates two things (e.g. that which separates God from creation), but usually the veil worn by Muslim *women. The *Qur'ān commands modesty in dress ('They should not display their adornment, except that which is apparent of it,' 24. 31), but it is not explicit about how much must be concealed. In a general way, whatever is not to be seen is the woman's *'awra*, but the extent of covering is disputed, and varies much from country to country. The almost total covering of the *chaddor* is not required by Qur'ān, The Qur'ān requires a comparable modesty in dress for men. See also PURDAH.

Y. al-Qaradāwi, *The Lawful and the Prohibited in Islam* (n.d.).

Hijiri. 1. (Jap., 'holy person, wise person'). Buddhist title for a monk of lower rank. In general, it is an epithet for any wise or virtuous person, but especially for devotees of a particular *buddha, etc., as in Amida-hijiri; or for one who dwells in a particular place, as in *Kūya-hijiri.

2. (Jap., 'he who knows the sun'). Lay *ascetics in Japanese religion, often in opposition to, and conflict with, officials in religion. Although in background they have some connections with *shamans, they emerge as lay-practitioners of many skills, particularly those which ward off evil spirits.

Hijra (Arab.). The 'emigration' of *Muḥammad from *Mecca to *Madīna in July 622 CE. Those who accompanied him on this move, or who joined him shortly after, were known as *emigrants (*muhājirūn*). The significance of the hijra was largely the severing of Muḥammad's previous ties with his own city and the tribe of Quraysh, and the setting up of the new community (*'umma), with religious affiliations. The hijra marks a stage in Muḥammad's own development, from a persecuted preacher to the leader of a socio-religious community with political and military power.

The Muslim calendar dates its years (H = *hijrīya*; AH = After the Hijra, or *Anno Hegirae* in W. usage) from the beginning of the lunar year in which the hijra took place.

Hilda, St (614–80). Abbess and founder of a Christian community at Whitby, to which both women and men belonged. She became a nun in 647, and in 649 she became abbess of a convent at Hartlepool. After she founded the community at Whitby, she remained there for the rest of her life. At the Synod of Whitby (664) she supported the Celtic party unsuccessfully (see WILFRID). She was much admired by *Bede: 'Her prudence was so great that even kings and princes . . . asked and received her advice. She required, of those whom she directed, constant attention to holy scripture, and the practice of justice, so that many among them might be fit for service in the church.' She was equally revered by those who knew her: 'All who knew her called her Mother, such were her amazing godliness and grace.' An Anglican community of nuns (Community of the Holy Paraclete) continues at Whitby at the present day. Feast day, 17 Nov.

Hildebrand (Christian pope): see GREGORY VII.

Hildegard (of Bingen), St (1098–1179). Medieval mystic and visionary. Brought up by a recluse, Jutta, in *c.*1116 she entered the Benedictine community that had gathered round her. In 1136 she succeeded Jutta as abbess. About 1150 she moved her community to Rupertsberg, near Bingen, on the Rhine. Encouraged by her confessor, she recorded some of her visions, and in 1147 Pope Eugenius III, under *Bernard of Clairvaux's influence, gave guarded approval to them. Gathered together in her *Scivias* ('Know Thy Ways'), her visions condemn contemporary vice and prophesy forthcoming disaster. But more importantly, they record an intelligent and direct seeing: 'These visions which I saw, I beheld neither in sleep, nor in dream, nor in madness, nor with the eyes of the body, . . . but wakeful, alert, with the eyes of the spirit and with inward ears.' She spoke of the disclosure as light 'more brilliant than the sun, . . . and I name it "the cloud of the living light". . . . Sometimes I behold within this light another light which I name "the living light itself". And when I look on it, every sadness and pain vanishes from my memory, so that I am again as a simple maid and not an old woman.' Hildegard was immensely accomplished: as an artist, she illustrated her own books; as a healer, she wrote a *vade mecum* of medicine, *The Book of Simple Medicine*; as a musician, she composed a Symphonia with many song settings, and a morality play with eighty-two melodies. She was also a splendid correspondent, who saw women and men as equal in their work for God in the 'creative greenness' of his Spirit. Feast day in Germany, 17 Sept.

B. Newman, *Sister of Wisdom* . . . (1987).

Hillel (late 1st cent. BCE–early 1st cent. CE). Leading Jewish *ḥakham* (*sage) of the second Temple period. He was born in Babylonia of a family claiming Davidic descent, but moved to Jerusalem where he studied under Shemaiah and Avtalyon. He had to support himself and his family, and was often in dire straits. One Friday, he did not have the fee for the lesson, but so avid was he for instruction that he climbed on the roof to listen through a skylight. He was seen in the morning blocking the light: because he was nearly frozen to death, he could not move. Shemaiah and Avtalyon brought him in and ordered a fire to be lit although it was the *Sabbath, saying that he was worthy of the Sabbath being broken for his sake. He rapidly emerged as a prominent interpreter of *Torah, developing his seven rules of *hermeneutics. He became *nasi (president) of the *Sanhedrin, and, with *Shammai, formed the last of the pairs (*zugot) of scholars. In general, Hillel adopted the less rigorous interpretations of Torah, though *B.Shab.* 77a refers to six issues where Hillel was more rigorous. In a famous contrast, a would-be *proselyte came to both, asking each to teach him Torah while he stood on one leg. Shammai drove him away for asking for the impossible. Hillel said, 'What is hateful to you, do not do to others. That is the whole of Torah; the rest is commentary on it. Now go and learn.' This negative form of the *Golden Rule is thus an instance of *kelal. His teaching could frequently be elliptical, challenging the hearer ('If I am not for myself, who will be for me? But if I am for myself alone, what am I? And if not now, when?'), but equally, his interpretations and style left behind him a school, *Bet Hillel. When he died, it was said of him, 'It was fitting that the *Shekhinah should rest on him, but his generation was unworthy of him.'

N. N. Glatzer, *Hillel the Elder* . . . (1959).

Ḥillul ha-Shem (Heb., 'profanation of the name'). Description of any action that profanes the name of God. Ḥillul ha-Shem must be avoided because it breaks the third of the *Ten Commandments and because it sets a bad example. The phrase is used to denote any action which might bring disgrace to Judaism or to the Jewish community—the converse, in fact, of *Kiddush ha-Shem.

Hilton, Walter (d. 1396). English mystic. After a period as a hermit, he became an Augustinian canon at Thurgarton Priory, Notts. His principal work, widely read in medieval England, is his *Ladder of Perfection*, which traces the soul's ascent to God in terms of the reformation of the image of God in the soul in two stages: reformation in faith, and in feeling, the former being the correction of false notions, the latter appropriation of the truth at the deepest level: 'For wit thou well, a bodily turning to God without the heart following is but a figure and a likeness of virtues and no soothfastness.' His inspiration is principally Augustinian and he stands apart from the growing *affective tradition represented esp. by *Rolle.

J. E. Milosh, *The Scale of Perfection and the English Mystical Tradition* (1966).

Himālaya ('abode of snow'). A vast mountain range on the northern border of India, regarded as sacred by Tibetans and Hindus alike. According to the **Mahābhārata*, the gods sacrifice on the summits, and Mount *Meru, the axis of the world and the source of its vitality, lies at its centre. No one should attempt to stand carelessly on the summits, because they are the transition from one domain to another. Sherpa Tenzing (who made, with Sir John Hunt, the first ascent of Everest) said: 'A lot of us found faith up there. We were trespassing on sacred ground. I only hoped the mountain would forgive the steps I chopped in her. The higher we went, the more we could hear her *mantra fighting with the wind.'

Himorogi (Jap., 'sacred hedge or enclosure'). In ancient times a particularly sacred place, such as a hill, grove, or the area surrounding some other unusual natural phenomenon. The sacral nature of the site can be manifested in various ways, both spontaneously and through divinatory rites.

When the natural site was discrete, as with a particular tree or rock formation, a circle of evergreen trees was planted around it to form a sanctuary for the purpose of preserving the area's sacrosanct status. Later, these sacred sites were marked by permanent enclosed shrines, and artificially established spaces within domestic compounds appeared as well. The meaning of the term has gradually been extended to include objects in which sacred power is concentrated, either naturally or through sacrificial acts. This manufactured locus for sacred manifestation has been conventionalized so that today its constructed form is generally fixed.

Contemporary groundbreaking ceremonies, known as *ji-(chin-)sai* or *koto-shizume no matsuri*, reflect in both form and intention the archaic ritual significance of himorogi. A derived usage refers to sacrificial offerings made at the sanctuary; a different Chinese ideogram is used for this meaning.

Hina matsuri (doll festival): see FESTIVALS AND FASTS.

Hīnayāna (Skt., 'small vehicle'). A name used by *Mahāyāna Buddhists for forms of early Buddhism, which they characterize as defective or preparatory in contrast to themselves, the 'Great Vehicle'—in particular because they regard adherents of Hīnayāna as being preoccupied, selfishly, with the advancement of their own aggregation of appearance towards the goal of *arhat, as opposed to that of *bodhisattva. Mahāyāna accepts that Hīnayāna rests on authentic teaching of the *Buddha Śākyamuni, but only on an extremely limited and introductory part of it, the fuller teaching being transmitted through the innumerable teachers and *sūtras which constitute Mahāyāna. A less aggressive name for the earlier forms of Buddhism is Theravāda, 'teaching of the elders', but this strictly is inaccurate, since Theravāda is the name of one particular school belonging to the *Sthavira group, itself one of the two parties into which early Buddhism split at the 3rd Council (see COUNCILS (BUDDHIST)) of Pātaliputra. However, Theravāda is the only surviving school of early Buddhism, so that the name (understood as a code for the diverse forms of early Buddhism) is at least less offensive than Hīnayāna. An alternative name is 'Pāli school', because early Buddhism rested on the Pāli canon. More accurate, but unlikely to displace Theravāda, is Śrāvakayāna, the vehicle of the disciple (i.e. who seeks to become *arhat, not buddha, or who 'hears', *śrāvaka, in the mode of personal disciple).

Hinduism. The major continuing and connected religions of India, which have now spread throughout the world. About 80 per cent of India's approx. one billion people regard themselves as Hindu, and there are about 30 million Hindus elsewhere in the world. The word 'Hinduism' derives from the Persian *hindu* (Skt., *sindhu*, 'river'), belonging to the Indus Valley, hence 'Indian'. The term is misleading if it gives the impression of a unified system of belief and practice: it was replaced for a time in academic circles by 'Indian religion', but even that has now become 'Indian religions' in the plural (though that too is ambiguous, since Jains, Sikhs, and Christians are also religions of India, as for many centuries was Buddhism). The term 'Hinduism' is used here and throughout this work as a convenient shorthand, and as at least a reminder that there are certain constituent characteristics of the connected 'Indian religions' which enable a Hindu to be picked out from a Muslim, say, or a Sikh, even though no particular Hindu movement or village, person or philosophy, will necessarily exhibit them all. A name for the tradition which is in common use among Hindus is *sanātana *dharma, everlasting dharma; another with more specific focus on the *brahmanical system is *varṇaśramadharma* (see VARNA; ĀŚRAMA).

Historically, Hinduism is seen as unfolding through successive stages, but this again is misleading, since many beliefs and practices from earlier stages persist through to the present, often little affected by subsequent developments. The roots (see H. D. Sankalia, *Prehistory and Protohistory in India and Pakistan*, 1961) are set down in the traditions of the original stone-age inhabitants of India; the *Indus Valley civilization; the more developed Dravidian culture, related to the Indus Valley, and persisting especially among the *Tamils; and the *Āryan invasion leading to *Vedic religion (the religions based on the *Vedas).

The Vedas (eternal truth) are believed to be eternal (sanātana). They are made known through *ṛṣis, who received them by a kind of intuition (*dṛṣti*). They were written down only because in the cyclic understanding of time (*yuga), the world comes to a period, as at the present, of degeneration and collapse (*Kali-yuga), during which the oral transmission of the Veda becomes erratic. The revealed scriptures are known as *śruti (revelation, that which has been perceived through hearing; for details see VEDA). *Āgama (scripture) denotes all writings which at least some Hindus regard as revealed, which may therefore extend beyond the core corpus: there are thus 108 Pāñcarātra or *Vaiṣṇava Āgamas, 28 *Śaiva Āgamas, and 77 *Śakta Āgamas; some sects regard the *Purāṇas as revealed (e.g. *Viṣṇu* and *Bhāgavata Purāṇas* among the Vaiṣṇavas). Revered by most Hindus is **Bhagavad-gītā*, and the majority regard it as revealed. Gathering śruti material are many *sūtras, but since they do not contain new material they are not usually cited as authorities in debate.

The second major source of authority is found in the texts of *smṛti ('that which has been remembered', tradition) which are much more closely concerned with the details of everyday life; among these texts, **Manusmṛti* is held in particularly high esteem. Much of śruti and smṛti has been gathered into *itihāsa-purāṇa (ancient histories), of which the two great epics **Mahābhārata* and **Rāmāyaṇa* probably have far greater direct influence on the population than the scriptures as such.

The Vedas gave rise to the elaborate ritual instructions and explanations of the texts known as *Brāhmaṇas, and this ritual-based religion is often referred to as brahmanical religion. It gave rise also to reflections on the meanings and implications of the rituals, in the *Āraṇyakas and the *Upaniṣads. Based on the consummations of the Veda in *Vedānta, the major forms of philosophical religion were elaborated (see ŚAṄKARA, RĀMĀNUJA, and MADHVA). But philosophical systems had already been established, some of them atheistic or materialist. There are traditionally six ways of orthodox (*āstika) insight (*darśana, for list); there is a continuing debate about those which should be considered *nāstika (unorthodox: not just, from a Hindu point of view, the obvious aberrations of the Jains and Buddhists, but perhaps also e.g. *Sāṁkhya).

But for the majority of Hindus, religious life is a matter, not so much of philosophy, as of ordering one's life according to the principles and practices which will lead to a better rebirth or even to *mokṣa (release). This 'ordering of life' is to live it according to dharma, or, less usually, to live it according to particular vows or devotions (see SĀDHU; TANTRISM). Dharma has many meanings, but in this case it means roughly 'appropriateness': 'Hinduism' as sanātana dharma is the map of how to live appropriately. It is this 'mapping' of the ways to live appropriately which is expressed in the divisions of labour (*varna), and even more specifically in the *caste-system (*jāti). In general, Hindus can aim legitimately for four goals (*puruṣārtha): within the bracket of controlling dharma and of mokṣa, the aims of *kāma and *artha are wholeheartedly endorsed. Thus Hinduism penetrates all aspects of life, from the humblest home to the polity of the state. A usual expectation is that a *twice-born Hindu will pass through four stages (*āśrama), embracing the responsibilities and delights of life and then letting go in the approach of death.

For death is not the end. Although the Vedas do not reveal any lively expectation of a worthwhile life after death, the concentration on *prāṇa (breath) in the period of the Brāhmaṇas and Āraṇyakas gave rise to the belief that there is an underlying self or soul (*ātman) which persists through the process of living and dying, and which subsists through all the changing appearances of a body. By the time of the Upaniṣads, this had become a belief that Brahman, the unproduced Producer of all that is, pervades the fleeting appearances of this or any other universe as ātman, as the underlying guarantor of appearance, but not in any way identical with it. While ātman is entangled in desire for the world, it continues to be reborn (*saṃsāra), at many different levels of appearance, in heavens and hells, as animals or as humans: the outcome, for better or for worse, is governed by a natural moral law of *karma, as inexorable as that of gravity. To be born as a human is a rare opportunity to advance toward mokṣa, release from the round of rebirth.

The nature of that attainment is variously described. At the philosophical end, *advaita envisages a reunion of undifferentiated reality, so that one can legitimately speak of fusion: *Brahman is unable to be described (*nirguṇa) and yet is characterized (*saguṇa) through the mode of presence to the created order; Brahman as ātman pervades all appearance, so that mokṣa consists in the realization that one's true self was never other than what Brahman is ('Thou art That': see MAHĀVĀKYA). At the theistic end of devotion to God (*bhakti), there is a realization of undisturbed relationship which one begins to anticipate in this life. In either case, the experience of the ultimate is that of sat-citānanda (*saccidānada).

Theism dominates Indian religion. Each person (or often region or village) is likely to have a particular focus of devotion (*iṣṭadevatā), but these will usually complement, not supplant the major deities. The sense of God as Lord (*bhagavān) is usually expressed as *Īśvara; but God may become manifest in many different forms, hence the (initially bewildering) proliferation of gods and goddesses from the Vedic period onward (see A. Daniélou, *Hindu Polytheism*, 1963). Attempts were made to systematize these, especially through the idea of *trimūrti (threefold manifestation of God), of which the most enduring has been that of *Brahmā as creator, *Viṣṇu as preserver, and *Śiva as destroyer (with a cyclic view of time, the cosmic appearance goes through endless recurrences of that process). Yet even here, it is still God who manifests himself in these ways: 'The only God, Janardana, takes the designation of Brahmā, Viṣṇu and Śiva as he creates, preserves or destroys. Viṣṇu as creator creates himself, as preserver preserves himself, as destroyer destroys himself' (*Viṣṇu Purāṇa* 1. 2. 66). It is the particular power of God to bring things into appearance (*māyā, often translated as 'illusion', which it may occasionally mean, but more often does not). A particular form of manifestation is that of 'incarnation', *avatāra. In *Bhagavad-gītā* 4. 7 f., Viṣṇu says, 'Whenever dharma is forgotten, whenever lawlessness prevails, I manifest myself: in every age I return to deliver the righteous, to destroy the wicked and to establish dharma.' Of the 'descents' of Viṣṇu (listed under avatāra) that of *Kṛṣṇa is the most popular. It is equally possible for incarnation to take place from 'down up', rather than 'up down', by a realization of the divine infilling of a true humanity (examples offered are *Gāndhī or *Jesus).

Amidst the myriad theistic devotions, three are of extensive importance: those to Śiva (*Śaivism, regarded by some as the oldest continuing Indian religion), to Viṣṇu (*Vaiṣṇava, numerically the largest, though divided into many subdivisions), and to *Śakti (see also ŚĀKTISM), in whom, as Goddess and divine mother, are gathered all the functions that Viṣṇu has for the Vaiṣṇavites and that Śiva has for the Śaivites. But the breakdown of these into particular traditions is prolific in its diversity. The traditions of devotion and teaching are transmitted through *gurus and protected in organized systems (*saṁpradāya).

Because theistic appearance is latent in all occasions and objects, devotion is possible in any circumstance. But much *pūjā (worship) begins with evoking the specific presence of the deity in this temple or this shrine or this object, etc. It is thus possible for the specific, focal presence to disappear at the end of the occasion of worship, so that the image, for example, is no longer holy in the same way. The evocation of the real presence of God is particularly important also in the focus of *mantra/ *maṇḍala and *yantra (sounds and diagrams); and in places or rivers closely associated with manifestations of God (see SACRED CITIES/SACRED RIVERS, SEVEN).

The three major paths (*mārga) of progress toward mokṣa are karmamārga (the way of works, following dharma), jñānamārga (the way of knowledge or of philosophical truth), and bhaktimārga (the way of devotion to God). *Bhagavad-gītā* makes an attempt to reconcile all three. All three are united also by being called *yoga. But yoga (particularly as associated with *Patañjali) has become a discipline of progress in its own right, with many forms of practice (though again yoga is likely to be complementary rather than competitive). In yoga, a person enters into a pattern of exercise and activity (much of it superficially extremely inactive), which rests on a sophisticated anthropology, but which the practitioner is trying to realize rather than understand.

In recent centuries., Hindu religion has been practised under foreign rule (Muslims, followed by the British). At Independence (1947), India was designated a secular state with recognition of all religions: the eclectic genius of Indian religion (which does not mean that there cannot be sharp conflicts and divisions) makes this a natural outcome. However, the remarkable ability of Indians to put this into practice (e.g. with the possibility of a Muslim president; contrast the status of Islam in Pakistan) has already come under strain with a growing sense that Hindus should affirm their identity over against the separatist tendencies of Sikhs and (in some areas) Muslims—hence the emergence of specifically Hindu political movements and parties (see BHARATYA JANATA PARTY). The contrast between these two attitudes (of inclusive toleration and Hindu self-affirmation) were already apparent in the many 19th-cent. attempts to revive and restate Hinduism: see ROY, RĀM MOHAN; BRAHMO SAMĀJ; SEN, KESHUB CHANDRA; DAYĀNANDA SARASVATĪ; ĀRYA SAMĀJ.

For many, the purpose of Hinduism is summarized in the prayer of *Bṛhadāraṇyaka Upaniṣad* 1. 3. 27, 'Lead me from the unreal to the real; lead me from darkness to light; lead me from death to immortality.'

W. T. de Bary (ed.), *Sources of Indian Tradition* (1958); S. Chennakesevan, *A Critical Study of Hinduism* (1980); D. J. Dell *et al.*, *Guide to Hindu Religion* (1981); G. Flood, *An Introduction to Hinduism* (1996); J. Gonda (ed.), *A History of Indian Literature* (1975–86) and *Religionen Indiens* (1960–3); B. Holland, *Popular Hinduism and Hindu Mythology: An Annotated Bibliography* (1979); T. J. Hopkins, *The Hindu Religious Tradition* (1971); J. M. Kanitkar, *Indian Anthropology* (1960); K. W. Morgan (ed.), *The Religion of the Hindus* (1958); B. Walker, *The Hindu World* (1968).

Hindu Sacred Cities: see SACRED CITIES, SEVEN.

Hindu Sacred Rivers: see SACRED RIVERS, SEVEN.

Hinin (non-persons): see BURAKU.

Hinnom, Valley of (*gey-hinnom*): see GEHENNA.

Hippolytus, St (*c.*170–*c.*236). Church *father. He was an important *priest in the Roman Church and an enemy of *Sabellianism. However, he criticized the lax policy of Pope Callistus (217–22) in readmitting penitents to *communion, and seems to have been elected by a party of right-wing dissidents as rival bishop of Rome. Probably he was reconciled to the pope's party before his death. The facts of his life, as well as his writings (the last from any W. father in Gk.) were later forgotten in Rome. He was imagined to have been a soldier converted by St Lawrence, and a *martyr.

Hippolytus's principal work is his *Refutation of all *Heresies* (largely discovered only in the 19th cent.), whose object was to show that all heresies derived from pagan philosophy. Historically more important is his treatise *The Apostolic Tradition* (known as the 'Egyptian Church Order' before 1916 when its authorship was proved): this was composed *c.*215, and contains detailed descriptions of the rites of *ordination, *baptism, and the *eucharist as practised at the time in Rome. Other partly preserved works of his include a chronicle of world history, various biblical commentaries, and homilies. Feast day, 13 Aug. (W.), 30 Jan. (E.).

Eng. trs. in Ante-Nicene Christian Library.

Ḥirā'. The mountain near Mecca to which, according to *ḥadīth, Muḥammad withdrew to meditate, and where, towards his fortieth year, he began to receive heavenly words which he was commissioned to announce to the Meccans. There were numerous caves in which a recluse could pray and muse. The mountain is not named in the Qur'ān, but 53. 1–11 is taken to refer to his experience there.

Hiraṇyagarbha or **Hiraṇyāṇḍa** (Skt., 'golden womb', 'golden embryo'). In early Hinduism, the source of all creation and life. In **Ṛg Veda* 10. 121. 1 ff., Hiraṇyagarbha becomes the unified source of the created order and is identified with *Prajāpati (though that final verse may be a later addition), after Prajāpati had emerged as the supreme creator, but before Prajāpati was merged with *Brahmā. Eventually all three were superseded by the less mythological cosmogony of *śakti and *brahman. See also KA; COSMOLOGY.

Hiraṇyakaśipu. In Hindu mythology, the son of *Kaśyapa and *Diti, and twin brother of *Hiraṇyākṣa. There are several versions of the events which lead up to his being killed by *Viṣṇu in his *Narasiṃha form. In some, Hiraṇyakaśipu obtains a boon from *Brahmā which makes him virtually indestructible, since the conditions under which he can be killed are so unlikely as to appear impossible. However, his tyrannical usurpation of world sovereignty, and in some versions his ill-treatment of his son Prahlāda, lead to his downfall when Narasiṃha attacks him and tears him apart. In some of the *Purāṇas Hiraṇyakaśipu is said to be reborn as *Rāvaṇa, who meets his death at the hands of *Rāma, and then as *Śiśupāla, who is killed by *Kṛṣṇa and thus attains *mokṣa. In the **Bhāgavata-Purāṇa*, Hiraṇyakaśipu and Hiraṇyākṣa are said to have once been Viṣṇu's attendants, who were cursed for their disrespectful behaviour and condemned to be born three times as demons before they could regain their position in heaven.

Hiraṇyākṣa. In Hindu mythology, son of *Kaśyapa and *Diti, and twin brother of *Hiraṇyakaśipu. In some versions of the *Varāha myth, he is said to carry off the earth and keep her captive beneath the waters, so that *Viṣṇu in boar form has to kill him in order to rescue her. In the **Bhāgavata-Purāṇa* it is Hiraṇyākṣa's death at Viṣṇu's hands which prompts Hiraṇyakaśipu to seek for vengeance, and this leads eventually to Viṣṇu's appearance as *Narasiṃha.

Hirata Atsutane (exponent of Japanese Studies movement): see KOKUGAKU.

Hiravijaya (1527–95). Śvetāmbara Jain teacher. He belonged to the Tapa *Gaccha, becoming head (*suri*) in 1566. In 1587, *Akbar summoned him to court to give an account of Jain teaching. Hiravijaya singled out compassion to all forms of life, and as a result, Akbar ordered that caged birds should be freed and that animals should not be slaughtered on the Jain festival of *Paryūṣana.

Vidyavijaya, *A Monk and a Monarch* (1942).

Hirsch, Samson Raphael (1808–88). Prominent exponent of Jewish *orthodoxy in 19th-cent. Germany. Hirsch served as a *rabbi at Oldenburg, Emden, Moraura, and Frankfurt-am-Main. His most important works, *Neunzehn Briefe ueber Judentum* (Nineteen Letters on Judaism) (1836; Eng. 1899) and *Choreb, oder Versuche ueber Jissroels Pflichten in der Zerstreuung* (Hobab-Essays on Israel's Duties in the *Diaspora) (1837; Eng. 1962), were designed for young adults as a defence of traditional Judaism. Although strictly Orthodox, Hirsch believed that the study of *Torah should be combined with *derekh erez (worldly occupation). To this end he founded Jewish schools which also taught secular subjects. He strongly opposed the emergent *Reform movement, defending, both Hebrew as the proper language for prayer, and also the traditional *synagogue organization. Initially he tried to prevent separation from the Reform movement, but from 1844, he recognized that 'Our *covenant of unity will no longer endure, and brother shall depart from brother in tears'. He believed that it was the people, rather than their religion, who were in need of reform, and he was convinced by the need of the community to elevate itself to match the ideals of Judaism, rather than adjust its practice to accord with comfortable secularism.

Z. H. Rosenbloom, *Tradition in an Age of Reform . . .* (1976); J. Rosenheim, *Samson Raphael Hirsch's Cultural Ideal and Our Times* (1951).

Hisbollah (party of God): see ḤIZBALLAH.

Historical Jesus: see QUEST FOR THE HISTORICAL JESUS.

Histories in China. The Chinese reverence for antiquity, ancestors, and precedent produced, as early as the Han dynasty (206 BCE–221 CE), not only Grand Historians as court officials, but also systematically organized histories which acquired a canonical status. *Shih chi* (Records of the Historian) set the pattern: it was begun by Ssu-ma T'an (d. 110 BCE) and completed by his son, Ssu-ma Ch'ien (145–90 BCE). The material is divided into five sections, Annals, Chronological tables, Discourses, Hereditary houses, and Memoirs. The Discourses cover rites, music, pipes, calendar, astronomy, Feng and

Shan sacrifices, Yellow river, economics. Ssu-ma Ch'ien, who was disgraced for supporting a defeated general, saw his work as compensating for his practical failure. In a letter to a friend he wrote: 'A man has only one death: it may be as weighty as Mt. T'ai or as light as the feather of a goose . . . I would be shamed to think that after my death my writings would not be available to posterity.' The historical work was continued by Pan Piao (3–54 CE) and his son Pan Ku (32–92), in *Han shu* (History of the Han). In this, they extended the Discourses to include punishments and laws, state sacrifices, geography, drainage of land, and literature. Subsequent Grand Histories followed these basic patterns.

B. Watson, *Ssu-ma Ch'ien . . .* (1958).

Hitbodedut (conversation with God): see NAḤMAN OF BRATSLAV.

Hitopadeśa (Indian collection of stories): see PAÑCATANTRA.

Ḥizb (Islamic prayers): see WIRD.

Hizballah or **Hisbollah** (Arab., *ḥizb Allah*, 'party of God'). Quranic term for Muslims as opposed to idolators, in the early struggle for Islam (5. 62, 58. 23). The term has been repeatedly adopted by movements within Islam (e.g. by Indonesian rebels in 1945), as, recently, by a radical group in the Lebanon, which retained links with Iran.

Ho. The ear-splitting shout of a Ch'an master, designed not only to startle into sudden enlightenment (*tongo*) but also to mark the line of transmission from teacher to pupil. The Japanese pronunciation of the Chinese character is *katsu*, and in Zen it is used in ways comparable to the *kyosaku, the 'wake-up stick'. It is also a manifestation of transmission without concepts, words, or symbols. It was introduced by *Ma-tsu, but established in teaching by *Huang-po Hsi-yün.

Ho (Chin., 'crane'). Taoist symbol of immortality and wisdom.

Ho. Jap., for *dharma.

Hoa Hao. A simplified neo-Buddhist religion in the Mekong Delta of Vietnam with *c.*1½ million followers. It arose in Hoa Hao village in 1939 when an infirm *Roman Catholic peasant, Huyan Phu So (1919–47), had a convulsive religious healing experience. He began vigorous teaching of the new faith in which he claimed to be the reincarnation of earlier religious leaders and uttered prophecies that were later fulfilled. His simplified religious practice for peasants, without need of monks or holy places, confined offerings to water, flowers, and incense, forbade *alcohol and opium, enjoined four prayers a day and required honour for parents, love for country and for one's fellow human beings, and respect for Buddhism. His mass following saw him as the 'Living *Buddha', but he was twice exiled and once placed in a mental hospital by the French. As a militant and nationalist religion, it set up its own virtually autonomous government in the Delta and joined the independence struggle, but opposed the Viet Minh which captured and executed the founder in 1947.

H.-T. Ho Tai, *Millenarianism and Peasant Politics in Vietnam* (1983).

Ho-ch'i (sexual union in Taoism): see FANG-CHUNG SHU.

Hodge, Charles (1797–1878). *Calvinistic theologian. Ordained into the *Presbyterian ministry (1821), he was educated at Princeton at which seminary he taught biblical studies, then theology, for most of his life. He wrote several New Testament commentaries as well as a 3-vol. *Systematic Theology*, and edited the *Biblical Repertory and Princeton Review* for over forty years. Firmly committed to the *Westminster Confession, he held to the verbal inspiration and infallibility of *scripture at a time when traditional *Calvinism was on the decline in America, though Hodge always remained tolerant to those who could not fully subscribe to his doctrinal position.

Hogen (Chin., Fa-yen-tsung; Jap., Hōgen-shū). Ch'an/Zen school, one of the *goke-shichishū, the revered early schools. It was founded by *Hsüan-sha Shih-pei (Jap., Gensha Shibi), dharma-successor (*hassu) of *Hsüeh-feng I-ts'un (Jap., Seppō Gison), so that it was originally called Hsüan-sha. But *Fa-yen Wen-i, in the next generation, far exceeded Hsüan-sha, so that the school became known as Fa-yen (Jap., Hōgen).

Hōgen Bun'eki (Chinese Ch'an Buddhist teacher): see FA-YEN WEN-I.

Hōge-sō: Zen Buddhist monks in Japan who renounced, not only worldly possessions, but also monastery-support (cf. *friars in Christianity). They wandered the countryside, chanting and begging for food. Because of their complete abandonment of the world, the term came to be used also for any wholly enlightened monk.

Hōgo (Jap., 'dharma word'). The sayings of Zen patriarchs and ancient masters in the Ch'an/Zen tradition. They are frequently the subject of *shodō* (way of the pen, *calligraphy).

Hoguk Sŭngdan. Monks' Militia for National Defence, organized by the national Chogye (see BUDDHISM IN KOREA) order in modern Korea. The participation of Korean monks in the military defence of their country has its roots in the character and history of Buddhism in Korea which, from the time of its inception, has, in the face of the constant threat of foreign invasion, been inextricably involved with the state and its fate.

Ho Hsien-ku (one of the eight immortals in Taoism): see PA-HSIEN.

Hōjin (Jap., for Skt., *sambhogakāya*). Body of delight, part of the *trikāya.

Hōjō (Jap., 'ten feet square'). The cell of a monk in a Zen Buddhist monastery; also the abbot, or the senior monk.

Hōjō-e (Jap., 'life-releasing ceremony'). A Japanese ceremony during which captive birds or fish are released into their natural environment. It was first held in the 8th cent. CE, and after falling into abeyance, it was revived in 1679.

Hoke-kyo. Jap., for **Lotus Sūtra*.

Hokkai (constituents of appearance). Jap., for *dharmadhātu.

Hokkeshū (Jap.): see TENDAI(-SHŪ).

Hokke-zanmai (ancestor rituals): see ZANMAI.

Hokkyō (Jap., 'dharma bridge'). A term for what, in the West, is called 'Buddhism'; cf. *Hinduism and sanātana dharma.

Hō koji goroku (lay Ch'an/Zen Buddhist): see P'ANG YÜN.

Hōkyōin-darani (Jap., 'the treasure-casket seal *dhāraṇī'). One of three spells chanted daily in *Shingon and Tendai temples. It is of great efficacy, since if its forty clauses are recited seven times, an ancestor in torment in hell (*jigoku*) will be released into the domain of *Amida. It is also efficacious in relation to illness.

Holā Mahallā (Pañjābī prob. masc. of Holī + place of attack). Sikh *festival, the day after *Holī. It was established by Gurū *Gobind Siṅgh as a day for military training through mock battles, a custom maintained by the *Nihaṅgs who gather in thousands at *Anaṇḍpur.

Holdheim, Samuel (1806–60). German *Reform Jewish leader. Holdheim served as a *rabbi in Frankfurt-on-the-Oder, in Mecklenburg-Schwerin, and ultimately in Berlin. He represented the extreme trend in Reform Judaism; he held *Sabbath services on a Sunday and defended the right of *uncircumcised children to be accepted as full *Jews. He argued that, just as *Talmud exhibited the application and transformation of Judaism by reference to the context of the time (appealing to *dina demalkhutha dina), so he was doing the same: 'The Talmud voices the convictions of its times, and from that standpoint it is right. I voice the convictions of my time, and from that standpoint, I am right.' Abraham *Geiger thought that he had gone too far, but nevertheless gave the eulogy at his funeral.

W. G. Plant, *The Rise of Reform Judaism* (1963).

Holī or **Holākā.** One of the important Hindu annual *festivals. Celebrated all over India at the beginning of spring, its precise form and motivation display enormous variety. On its basic level, it is a rural, agricultural festival of fertility. Typical features exhibit liminality (see RITES OF PASSAGE), as in the Occidental carnival: reversal of roles and ranks, merrymaking, and orgiastic licentiousness, spurting of coloured water, dressing up in weird manner, obscene jokes, etc. A straw figure of the witch Holikā (a child-eating *rākṣasī) is burnt in bonfires. On a different level, these rites were drawn into the myths and cults of the *purāṇic gods. Thus we find associations with the god of love, *Kāma, and with *Kṛṣṇa, whom popular mythology depicts as having himself celebrated the festival with the girls of the cowherds in Vraja.

Holiness (OE, *halignes*, 'without blemish'). The state of being set apart for God, or for religious purposes. For R. *Otto, the *Holy is *Ganz Andere*, the Totally Other, and all that relates to it must be separated from the profane and sinful. Holiness (Heb., *kedushah*) is a fundamental requirement of Jewish religion. The source of holiness is God, 'the Holy One, Blessed be He', who extends that condition (of separation from all that defiles) into the world, both in holy places (especially the Holy of Holies at the heart of the sanctuary in the *Temple) and in people. Israel is called to replicate this condition: 'You shall be holy, for I, the Lord your God, am holy' (Leviticus 19. 2). What does it mean to be holy? According to *Maimonides, 'When the Bible says, "Be holy", it means precisely the same as if it had said, "Keep my commandments".' To keep the commandments is to live in the condition which God intended for his creation, and in so far as it does this, Israel represents in miniature what will ultimately be the entire human case, when the knowledge of God will cover the earth as the waters cover the sea. Thus although it is often said (and written) that holiness means separation from unclean things, it more profoundly means closeness to God which involves separation from that which is incompatible with him. *Torah is thus the *syag* ('fence', a founding principle of rabbinic Judaism, *Pirqe* **Avot* 1. 1, 'Be reflective in judgement, raise up many pupils, and build a *syag* around Torah') which prevents diffusion into randomness and uncertainty.

Christianity inherited the hope of holiness from Judaism, but no longer saw Torah as either a necessary or a sufficient condition—*Paul indeed went further in regarding Torah as marking out in detail the impossibility of condition-based holiness. But holiness remains the goal, derived from Jesus: 'Conceived of the Holy Spirit, he will be holy' (Luke 1. 35). The Holy Spirit remains the source of the making holy (i.e. sanctification) of Christians, who become (or are meant to become) temples of the Holy Spirit (1 Corinthians 6. 11 and 20; 1 Peter 2. 9).

The word 'holiness' is then widely used for comparable vocations and goals in other religions, although it then loses its more specific constituents. In particular, it merges with considerations of *purity and *ablution: see also SACRED AND PROFANE.

J. Gammie, *Holiness in Israel* (1989).

Holiness Churches. Those churches which emphasize J. *Wesley's doctrine of perfection. Such groups usually teach that 'entire sanctification', involving the removal of inbred sin, follows conversion and is experienced instantaneously by faith. Following this crisis, the believer is empowered to live without deliberate sin, though not without 'weaknesses'. The doctrine played an important part in the development of early *Methodist spirituality. It spread quickly throughout the USA in the 19th cent., leading to the formation of several holiness denominations such as the Church of the *Nazarene and the Pilgrim Holiness Church. With his Methodist background, William *Booth naturally gave this teaching a significant place within the spiritual life of the *Salvation Army, whose Sunday morning services are still described as 'Holiness Meetings'.

Holiness Code. The collection of laws in Leviticus 17–26. The Holiness Code is so named because of the emphasis in the text that the Jewish people must be holy even as God is holy. However, some doubt whether these chapters constitute a separate Code, since they have a varied character and the word 'holiness' occurs only in 19–22 (and is in Leviticus outside this section). The structure of the Code parallels that of the laws of *Deuteronomy (12–28) and the Book of the Covenant (Exodus 20. 21–23. 33). It begins with laws related to *sacrifice (ch. 17), followed by laws concerning sexual conduct (18), a collection of ritual and ethical laws including the *Ten Commandments (19), more sexual laws (20), the laws of *priests and sacrifices (21–2), a list of holy days (23), a priestly section (24), laws concerning the *Sabbatical year (25), and admonitions, *blessings, and warnings (26). Those scholars who accept the Holiness Code date it from before the destruction of the first *Temple or early in the *Exile. It was probably composed by a single scribe, but arranged by the *priestly school.

Holocaust (Gk.). The burnt offering of Leviticus 1. 3, from which the word is applied to any offering which is consumed by fire.

Holocaust, Sho'ah (Heb., 'calamity'), or **Ḥurban** ('destruction'). The systematic destruction of European Jewry, 1933–45. In fact, the systematic extermination of other groups (e.g. homosexuals and gypsies) was also undertaken, but the term most often refers to the endeavour to make Europe 'Judenrein', free of Jews. *Anti-Semitism was a central platform of the Nazi party which gained power in Germany in 1933. 'It is our duty', wrote the Nazi leader Hitler, 'to arouse, whip up and to incite in our people the instinctive repugnance of the Jews.' From 1933 until war was declared in 1939, Jews were systematically eliminated from public office, intellectual and cultural life, and citizenship. During this period many Jews emigrated and their property was confiscated by the government. After the invasion of Poland in 1939, emigration was no longer practical. Instead the Jews were herded into *ghettos, deported east, and, from 1941 onwards, subjected to the 'Final Solution', systematic destruction in concentration camps (see AUSCHWITZ). The extermination of European Jewry was given priority (despite shortage of manpower and rolling stock): 'as a matter of principle, no consideration should be given to economic interests'. It is impossible to know the exact number of Jewish victims of the Holocaust, but losses are estimated at six million. Since 1951, 27 Nisan is kept as a Holocaust Remembrance Day (Heb., Yom ha-Sho'ah) in *Israel and the *diaspora. This day is publicly observed, and places of entertainment are closed. 10 Tevet is kept as the day of *kaddish on which *yahrzeit (memorial anniversary) of those whose date of death is unknown is commemorated.

Although there were many instances of *gentiles trying to save their Jewish neighbours from destruction, in general the official Christian churches, including the *Vatican, did little. The Holocaust finally destroyed the *Shtetl culture of E. Europe, and, since the Second World War, the primary focus of Jewish activity has been in *Israel and the USA. In the Holocaust, all theologians, including Jewish, are confronted with the problem of evil in its most acute form. A range of different responses has been made:

1. The third Ḥurban lies in the same providence of God which allowed the first two (the destructions of the two *Temples). I. Maybaum argued that Hitler could even be regarded as God's *messiah in the way that Deutero-*Isaiah interpreted Cyrus as 'God's messiah' (i.e. instrument of God's purpose) during the *Exile. Auschwitz becomes the analogue to Golgotha (*Calvary), and once more the Servant suffers to bring redemption. For some, this is evidenced in the establishment of the State of Israel.

2. Suffering, even on so immense a scale, is a punishment for sin (a traditional Jewish understanding of suffering): in the words repeated in the liturgy, 'Because of our sins we were exiled from our land' (*mi-p'nei ḥata'einu* . . .). On this account, the abandonment of God by so many Jews in the *galut (exile from the Holy Land) brought about a just punishment.

3. Rejecting so grotesque a view of God's character, E. Berkowits argued that God nevertheless had to allow the camps: 'God is mighty, for he shackles his omnipotence and becomes powerless so that history may happen' (*Faith After the Holocaust*). At the other extreme, he rejected also the obvious (to

many) conclusion that 'the death of God' has been demonstrated in the Holocaust. Indeed, he repudiated the Christian fascination with the Holocaust which was turning it into an intellectual game, even introducing university courses on 'The Holocaust': 'After Auschwitz, leave us alone.' It must be for the history of Judaism to come to terms with a Jewish event, however much Christianity prepared for it (and to some extent implemented it) by its *anti-Semitism, and however much, therefore, it has its own agenda of reflection and action as a result. For Berkowits, the Jews have accepted the vocation of exile, in order to bear the pain of freedom on behalf of a world which abuses it, thereby becoming themselves a moral vocation to the world to turn and repent:

> Yet all this does not exonerate God for all the suffering of the innocent in history. . . . Even if no answers could be found, we would still be left with the only alternative with which *Job too was left, of contending with God while trusting in him, . . . inquiring with our minds yet knowing in our hearts; and even as we search for the answer, praising him as the rabbis of old did: Who is mighty like you, our God, mighty in silence?

God is, but is beyond our understanding, as in the *Ein- Sof and *Deus absconditus traditions.

4. The presence of God in the Holocaust was affirmed also by E. Fackenheim (e.g. *God's Presence in History*, 1970) distinguishing between the two formative moments of Israel's origin, the Re(e)d Sea and Sinai, the saving presence and the commanding presence. God's saving presence was wholly absent from the camps, but his commanding presence was there. The commands are:

> Jews are forbidden to hand to Hitler posthumous victories. They are commanded to survive as Jews, lest the Jewish people perish. They are commanded to remember the victims of Auschwitz, lest their memory perish. They are forbidden to despair of man and his world, . . . lest they cooperate in delivering the world over to the forces of Auschwitz. Finally, they are forbidden to despair of the God of Israel, lest Judaism perish.

This amounts to a 614th commandment (the total in Torah being 613): Thou shalt survive.

5. R. J. Rubenstein has been accused of making that posthumous surrender to Hitler because of his belief that 'God' as characterized in the tradition is clearly dead. Yet Rubenstein (e.g. *After Auschwitz*, 1966) has made a thoroughly religious and Jewish response by suggesting that Judaism is called to a far more radical understanding of its inheritance: it cannot rely on the obviously bankrupt dependence on a God who intervenes when called upon in prayer to do so: in that sense (for Rubenstein, also a cultural sense) God is dead. But the necessity for community is all the more imperative (cf. *civil religion), and for that purpose, Jewish rituals, festivals, observances, etc., are vital:

> Judaism is the way in which we share the decisive times and crises of life through the traditions of our inherited community. The need for sharing is not diminished in the time of the death of God. We no longer believe in the God who has the power to annul the tragic necessities of existence; the need to religiously share that existence remains.

6. Elie Wiesel has offered an equally radical assessment of the Jewish tradition and belief in God. His sequence of three novels, moving from *Night*, to *Dawn* to Day (*Le Jour*, given the Eng. title, *The Accident*), marks the transition from the God-infused world which Wiesel had known as a child (born in 1928 in a Hungarian shtetl), through the camps (of which Wiesel was a survivor) where the search for God continues, to the world in which that God is dead: it is the transition from a world in which messianic redemption is 'around the next corner', to a world in which humans are clearly 'on their own'. Although Wiesel has been interpreted as maintaining the redemptive role of suffering, he has questioned the validity of that interpretation himself. In human terms of biography, there are heroic actions; on the scale of human history, this cannot be converted to an 'answer': 'Israel, an answer to the Holocaust? It is too convenient, too scandalous a solution.' Wiesel sees humanity after the Holocaust thrown into an abyss of non-meaning. Survival now means the forging of a new *covenant, no longer between Israel and God, because God has proved to be too unreliable a partner, but between Israel and its memories of suffering and death—of what *can* happen. The additional (not 'new', which would imply a different relation to the old) covenant will affirm the sanctification of life, witness, and solidarity. His Cantata, **Ani Ma'amin*, has been taken to show a more positive estimate of God, because it ends by blessing the fools who 'mock the man who mocks the Jew, singing over and over again, I believe, I believe in the coming of the messiah, and though he tarries, I will be waiting on any day that he comes'. But this is in the context of the inescapable polarity: 'The word of God continues to be heard. So does the silence of his dead children'; and overall, the presence of God to the questioning *patriarchs is one of a silent and enigmatic tear. There is a comparable note at the end of A. Schwarz-Bart's novel, *The Last of the Just*. The Holocaust calls in question the legend that the presence of thirty-six just men will be sufficient to preserve a generation. If the covenant has been broken, it is not by God's people. The novel ends, where all reflections on the Holocaust end, with this reminiscence of the characteristic Jewish response to life in *blessing:

> And praised. *Auschwitz*. Be. *Maidenek*. The Lord. *Treblinka*. And praised. *Buchenwald*. Be. *Mauthausen*. The Lord. *Belzec*. And praised. *Sobibor*. Be. *Chelmno*. The Lord. *Ponary*. And praised. *Theresienstadt*. Be. *Warsaw*. The Lord. *Vilna*. And praised. *Skarzysko*. Be. *Bergen-Belsen*. The Lord. *Janow*. And praised. *Dora*. Be. *Neuengamme*. The Lord. *Pustkow*. And praised . . .

While there has been a wide variety of Christian responses, few have taken the measure of the opening words of A. L. and A. R. Eckhardt (*Long*

Night's Journey into Day: A Revised Retrospective on the Holocaust, 1988): 'No event has made more clear the consequences of ideas than the German Nazi "Final Solution to the Jewish Problem". There could have been no "Jewish problem" to resolve had not almost two millennia of Christian teaching and preaching created it.' The absence of God from systematic *theology is nowhere more apparent than here. See also Index, Holocaust.

U. Adam, *Judenpolitik im Dritten Reich* (1972); H. J. Cargas, *The Holocaust: An Annotated Bibliography* (1985); R. Chartock and J. Spencer (eds.), *The Holocaust Years . . .* (1978); A. A. Cohen (ed.), *Arguments and Doctrines: A Reader . . .* (1970); A. J. and H. Edelheit, *Bibliography of Holocaust Literature* (1986); M. Gilbert, *The Macmillan Atlas of the Holocaust* (1982) and *The Holocaust: A History . . .* (1986); Y. Gutman (ed.), *Encyclopedia of the Holocaust* (1989); R. Hilberg, *The Destruction of the European Jews* (1961, rev. 1985); S. T. Katz, *Post-Holocaust Dialogues . . .* (1983) and *The Holocaust in Historical Context*, i. *The Holocaust and Mass Death before the Modern Age* (1994).

Holy. Term brought to prominence in the history of religions by N. *Söderblom and R. *Otto. For Söderblom, the distinction between the Holy and the Profane (cf. *Sacred and Profane) is the fundamental category of all religion. Otto saw the apprehension of the Holy through the operation of the religious *a priori* as the root of all religion: just as there must be *a priori* conditions which make possible such forms of human judgement as the scientific, the moral, and the aesthetic (and these different categories of judgement cannot be converted into each other, but give rise to different communities of human discourse), so, in Otto's view, there must be a priori conditions which give rise to the category of religious judgement, the human sense, different from the moral or the aesthetic sense, of a *mysterium tremendum fascinans et augustum*, an awe-inspiring depth of mysterious otherness, which attracts and yet terrifies. This is the *numinous. See also HOLINESS.

Holy fools. Figures who subvert prevailing orthodoxy and orthopraxis in order to point to the truth which lies beyond immediate conformity. The holy fool endeavours to express the insistence of all religions that detachment from the standards of the world is the *sine qua non* of advance into truth. Such figures are often, as one would expect, highly individual, but at the same time their witness is so important that whole communities may exemplify this style (e.g. the *Bāuls), or they may be valued as a tradition within a tradition, as in *Zen or among the Non-Possessors of Russian Orthodoxy (see POSSESSORS). Holy fools are also an important part of the reversals which are characteristic of the liminal stage of *rites of passage. Thus the Lord of Misrule (also known as the Abbot of Misrule) was elected in medieval Christianity to preside over Christmas festivities, often at the Feast of Fools. This was held at the New Year, and was so insistent in its reversals that it was repeatedly attacked by the official Church (e.g. at the Council of *Basle in 1435); the custom disappeared at about the time of the Reformation, but the traditional insights linger on in the figure of the clown. (For examples, see Index, Holy fools).

J. Saward, *Perfect Fools* (1980); E. Welford, *The Fool: His Social and Literary History* (1935); W. Willeford, *The Fool and His Sceptre* (1969).

Holy Ghost (third person of the Holy Trinity): see HOLY SPIRIT.

Holy Innocents. The children of Bethlehem who, according to Matthew 2. 16–18, were slaughtered by the order of King *Herod the Great in a vain attempt to kill the infant Jesus. They are commemorated as martyrs on 28 Dec.

Holy Office. The Roman *congregation established in connection with the *Inquisition by Pope Paul III in 1542 as the final court of appeal in trials of *heresy. In 1965 *Paul VI reformed it and changed its name to 'The Congregation for the Doctrine of the Faith'. It now has the task of promoting as well as monitoring the Church's teaching on faith and morals; but it continues to summon before it those whose teaching or practice appear to be aberrant.

Holy of Holies. Inner sanctum of the *Jerusalem *Temple. The Holy of Holies was windowless and had a raised floor. It was entered only once a year, by the *high priest on Yom Kippur (*Day of Atonment). During the period of the first Temple, it contained the *Ark of the Covenant and the two *Cherubim (1 Kings 19. 23–8), but these disappeared when that Temple was destroyed by the Babylonians (586 BCE). When the Temple was rebuilt, the Holy of Holies remained empty—to the surprise of Pompey, who entered the Holy of Holies when he captured Jerusalem and did not find the rich treasures which he had anticipated.

Holy Saturday. The Saturday in the Christian year between the *crucifixion and the *resurrection (i.e. *Good Friday and *Easter Day). Two contrasting themes characterize the day, that of waiting without knowledge of how grief is to be overcome, and that of the *harrowing of hell. It culminates in the Easter Vigil.

Holy see. A legal entity comprising the *pope and his *curia, recognized in international law as a sovereign body. It constitutes the central government of the *Roman Catholic Church and, since the *Lateran Treaty of 1929, has occupied the *Vatican City State.

Holy Spirit

Judaism In *Tanach (Jewish scripture), *ruaḥ ha-Qodesh/Kodesh* is the breath of God, and thus the effective and inspiring consequence of God at work in his creation. The Spirit 'broods over' the chaos out of which it brings forth order (Genesis 1. 2). The Holy Spirit is also known as *ruaḥ Elohim* and *ruaḥ Adonai*, indicating that no separate 'person' in relation to God is intended, but rather that this is the way in which God enables humans to do or say particular things—e.g. Bezalel to design the sanctuary (Exodus 35. 30 ff.), Saul to prophesy (1 Samuel 10. 10), Samson to kill a lion (Judges 14. 6). The Holy Spirit is thus God's presence to the world, as often in the Psalms (e.g. 41. 13; 51. 13; 143. 10). Increasingly, the Holy Spirit became linked with the final judgement of God, as in Joel 2, when he will pour out his spirit on the whole world, and 'your sons and your daughters shall prophesy, and your old men shall dream dreams, and your young men shall see visions'. The cessation of prophecy after the *Exile was a consequence of a determination that no such disaster as the Exile should occur again; but that meant a far tighter control on what counted as *covenantal behaviour (hence the development of *Halakhah and of priestly decision-making in the *Temple, while it survived). The claim to authority of those who bear the marks of inspiration and say, 'Thus says the Lord', was potentially subversive. In contrast, new interpretations of the Covenant (especially the sect(s) of the *Dead Sea Scrolls and Christianity) claimed authenticity by pointing to the return of the Holy Spirit—in the case of early Christianity through gifts of the Spirit and through such visible manifestations as direct inspiration in speaking with tongues—hence the claim to the fulfilment of the prophecy of Joel. However, mainstream Judaism and eventually rabbinic Judaism sharpened the claim that the Holy Spirit had been withdrawn at the time of the Exile as part of the punishment (*B.Yoma* 9b). It was recognized that the Holy Spirit had been the source of inspiration, so that whether a book had been so inspired was the criterion for inclusion in the *canon. Continuing communication with the Holy Spirit remained possible, but only after long religious discipline.

Christianity Formally, the Holy Spirit (or 'Holy Ghost', especially in liturgical use) is the third person of the Holy *Trinity. The Spirit is distinct from but coequal with the Father and the Son, and is in the fullest sense God. This understanding was canonized in the 4th cent.

The earliest Christian teaching on the Holy Spirit is found in *Paul's letters, where it seems to be almost identified with the risen Christ (e.g. 2 Corinthians 3. 17). Paul conceived of Christian life as life 'in the Spirit' (or 'in Christ') and he described the Spirit's gifts (Galatians 5. 22 f.). A similar exchange of functions between Jesus and the Spirit is found in the gospel of John (e.g. 16. 13; see PARACLETE). In the writings of *Luke the gift of the Holy Spirit appears as something more obviously demonstrable, e.g. in ecstatic speaking (Acts 19. 6; cf. 2. 4, the *Pentecost story), and in practical guidance received by the apostles (e.g. 15. 28; 16. 6).

In the *fathers before the 4th cent., the Holy Spirit is variously identified with the Son, or with the *Logos, or with God's *wisdom. No particular activity of God is consistently said to be that of the Spirit, although *Origen held that the characteristic sphere of the Spirit's operation was the Church, as contrasted with the whole creation which was that of the Logos. But from 360 CE onwards the doctrine of the Spirit became a matter of controversy when the Pneumatomach(o)i ('spirit-fighters') denied the full divinity of the Spirit. The *Cappadocian fathers argued against them, e.g. *Basil in his *On the Holy Spirit*, and were victorious at the Council of *Constantinople (381). In the West this doctrine was elaborated by *Augustine in his *On the Trinity*, especially in his understanding of the Spirit as the bond of unity in the Trinity. For the later divergence between Western and Orthodox language about the Holy Spirit, see FILIOQUE.

Modern theologians have lamented a poverty of interest in the Holy Spirit, at least in Western churches. Some have sought to understand the Spirit, as e.g., 'that power of communion which enables every other reality, and the God who is within and beyond all realities, to be present to us' (J. V. Taylor, *The Go Between God*, 1972). The *charismatic movement has, however, claimed to rediscover the 'baptism in the Holy Spirit' and its outward display in *healing, *exorcism, and speaking in tongues (*glossolalia). In any case, the Spirit is God in urgency and effect, wholly present to the creation and to individuals within it.

H. Berkhof, *The Doctrine of the Holy Spirit* (1964); A. Bittlinger (ed.), *The Church is Charismatic* . . . (1981); Y. Congar, *I Believe in the Holy Spirit* (3 vols., 1983); J. D. G. Dunn, *Jesus and the Spirit* (1975); W. Mills, *The Holy Spirit: A Bibliography* (1988); E. Schweizer, *The Holy Spirit* (1981).

Holy Synod. The supreme institution for the government of the *Russian Orthodox Church from 1721 to 1917. It was not like other synods, since it was in effect a committee composed of bishops, set up by Peter the Great to replace the patriarchate which he had abolished. The lay procurator, who attended as the Tsar's representative, was an important figure, though not a member. After the revolution, it was abolished and the patriarchate was restored. The governing body of the Church in Greece, a synod composed of bishops, is also called the 'Holy Synod'.

Holy war. Categorization of warfare in several religions (e.g. *jihād, *crusades), the war envisaged in the book of *Deuteronomy. It is distinct from the *just war, though they may overlap.

Holy water. In Christian usage, water which is blessed for use in certain rites, especially that which is blessed at the *Easter Vigil for baptism of *catechumens. The use of water (other than for baptism) goes back to the 4th cent. in the E. and the 5th cent. in the W. The custom of sprinkling the people with holy water at *mass (the *asperges*) dates from the 9th cent. At this time also 'stoups', basins for holy water with which the faithful could sprinkle themselves on entering a church, came into general use. Besides these practices, holy water is used at *blessings, dedications, *exorcisms, and burials.

Holy Week. The week preceding *Easter, observed in liturgical churches as a period of remembrance of, and attachment to the *passion of Christ. The most important days are *Palm Sunday, *Maundy Thursday, and *Good Friday. The rites for each day began to develop probably in Jerusalem in the 4th cent. A contemporary description is given by the *Pilgrimage of Etheria* (see PILGRIMAGE).

Holy Year. A year during which the pope grants, subject to particular conditions, a plenary *indulgence, the so-called Jubilee, to all those who visit Rome. A *bull specifies the particular purposes of the year and the conditions and benefits associated with it. A ceremony associated with the holy year is the opening of the Holy Door (*Porta Sancta*) in St Peter's basilica for the passage of those wishing to gain the indulgence, and its walling up a year later. The first holy year was in 1300; since 1475 they have usually been at twenty-five-year intervals, most recently in 1975, for renewal and reconciliation. But intervening years can be designated, e.g. 1983 in commemoration of redemption, and with reference to sacramental reconciliation, the theme of a *synod in that year.

H. Thurston, *The Holy Year of Jubilee* (1900).

Homa. The making of an oblation, in Hinduism, to the gods by throwing *ghṛta and other offerings on the sacrificial fire. This is particularly important in the effecting of the major *saṁskāras, e.g. *marriage. On that occasion, the bridegroom puts the offerings on the fire while the bride touches his right shoulder with her right hand while he does so. He says, 'May the fire of Homa bring safety to this bride, and may it bring children and a long life.' They *circumambulate the fire while the bridegroom recites a pledge from Paraskara's *Gṛhya Sūtra*, 'Let us love and revere each other, and protect each other with a generous heart; let us see, hear and live a hundred autumns.' The brother of the bride places her right foot on a stone slab before the fire while the bridegroom prays for her strength and stability. They then drop three oblations on the fire while the bridegroom pronounces the bride's transfer from one family to the other.

Homon (Jap., 'dharma gate'). The teachings of the *Buddha. In the Four Great Vows (*shiguseigan) of Zen, (part of the *bodhisattva vow), the third is: 'The dharma gates are manifold: I vow to enter them all.'

Homoousion (Gk., 'of one substance'). The word in the *Nicene Creed to express the relation in the one Godhead of the Father and Son. It was accepted as an anti-*Arian formula at the Council of *Nicaea at the urging of the emperor, although many bishops preferred the looser term *homoiousion*, 'of like substance'. Thus its sense may have been broadly 'of the same nature', rather than 'of the identical substance' as later theology took it. Homoousion was used again at *Chalcedon to express the relation of Christ to people; and it was extended to the *Holy Spirit during the 4th cent.

Homo religiosus (humans as religious beings): see ELIADE, MIRCEA.

Homosexuality. The attitude of religions to homosexuality is obscured by the extremely wide reference of the term (in some religions, for example, particular acts may be condemned, but not the disposition itself, and not all acts), by the ambiguities in the status of eunuchs, and by the uncertainty whether the term covers both males and females. In general, homosexuality is regarded as abnormal (standing outside the norms of nature and practice); there is then much difference concerning the 'normativeness of the norm'—i.e. how much it has to be covered by law. In Judaism, the main purpose of sexual relations, which should be within marriage, is procreation (Genesis 1. 28; 9. 1), but pleasure and delight are certainly important (see, e.g., *B.Yebamot* 118b). On the other hand, certain kinds of sexual activity are forbidden, including incest and adultery. The prohibitions against 'men lying with men as with a woman' occur in Leviticus (18. 22; 20. 13) and thus are a part of the *Holiness Code, and form a part of the general requirements for the securing of holiness. According to the *rabbis, the prohibition is a part of the *Noachide Laws, and thus applies to all people (i.e. to gentiles as much as to Jews). The penalties are *karet* (being cut off from the people of Israel, Leviticus 18. 29) and death (Leviticus 20. 13). *Talmud and the major *Codifications of Law reinforce this judgement. Very little is said about relations between women (known as *mesoleloth*): they are included in the prohibition against the practices of the Egyptians (Leviticus 18. 3), but are not included among *zenut*, improper sexual relations. Christianity inherited the prohibitions and amplified them with the condemnations of homosexual acts in Romans 1. 26–7 (including women), 1 Corinthians 6. 9, and 1 Timothy 1. 10. While some Christian exegesis has drawn attention to a distinction between (i) context-dependent applications and the more fundamental context-independent command to love, and (ii) the condition of homosexuality which lies in nature and particular acts which would have to be assessed for morality just as heterosexual acts have to be, the Roman Catholic Church has moved strongly to maintain the condemnation, describing the homosexual orientation as 'an objective disorder' (*On the Pastoral Care of Homosexual Persons*, 1986); the *Catechism of the Catholic Church* recognized that homosexuality is basically not a matter of choice, but insisted that homosexual persons are called to a life of chastity. In Islam, homosexuals (*qaum Lut*, the people of Lot, or Lutis) are condemned in the story of Lot's people in the Qur'ān (e.g. 15. 73 f.; 26. 165 f.), and in the last address of *Muḥammad. Some argue that since penetration has to be involved, homosexual acts between women should be less severely punished. In any case, *shariʿa is, as usual, concerned with public behaviour, so there is no strong condemnation of homosexuality if it is not displayed in public.

In India, the evaluation is more complex, because of the many strands of religious life. In general, it is clear that for *twice-born Hindus, 'homosexual acts' (*maithunaṁ puṁsi*) are condemned (e.g. **Manusmṛti* 11. 174 f., both men and women). But attitudes vary. While on the one hand oral sex is (in some texts) the equivalent of killing a *brahman, and homosexual acts may involve the loss of *caste, on the other hand the penalty may be a relatively small fine, and the act can be expiated by ritual washing. The **Kāma Sūtra* specifically states that physical sex between two people of the same sex (as also of the opposite) 'is to be engaged in and enjoyed for its own sake as one of the arts'. The evaluation depends on the context and on what is appropriate (i.e. *dharma) for it. Among Buddhists, the issue is subsumed under the general dynamic of Buddhist societies, in which the choice is between monastic celibacy and lay life. While consideration is given to homosexual acts within communities, there seems to have been little isolation of homosexuality as such. The issue is always the decision to act on the basis of accumulated *karma in the way that is appropriate for that moment. There is thus no blanket condemnation of homosexuality, still less of sexuality for enjoyment or for mutual fulfilment.

All these considerations were formed at a time when the 'natural nature' of homosexuality (and particularly of the genetic contribution to this widespread human condition) were not known. Religions which affirm the goodness of sexuality in its own right are adjusting more easily to new knowledge than those which hold that sexual acts must be open to life, and that the other functions of sex are always subordinate.

A. Swidler (ed.), *Homosexuality and World Religions* (1993).

Hōnen (1133–1212). Founder of the *Jōdo (Pure Land) sect of Japanese *Pure Land Buddhism. At the age of 13, he became a monk of the *Tendai sect. At the age of 43, he converted to the Pure Land teachings upon reading Shan-tao's *Kuan-wu-liang-shou-fo ching shu*. Subsequently he preached that everyone without exception can be reborn in *Amida Buddha's Pure Land by simply reciting the *nembutsu, and insisted that the Pure Land teachings be considered an independent sect. The older established sects' opposition to Hōnen's teachings led to his exile from the capital of *Kyōto in 1207. Although he was soon pardoned and returned to Kyōto in 1211, he died the following year. Among his major works are the *Senchaku Hongan Nembutsu Shu*, an outline of his Pure Land teachings, and the *Ichimai Kishomon*, a one-page summary of his teachings written or dictated on his deathbed:

> The method of final salvation that I have proposed is not a sort of meditation, . . . nor is it a repetition of the Buddha's name. . . . It is nothing but the simple repetition of *namu Amida Butsu*, with no doubt of his mercy: by this means one will be reborn in the Land of Pure Bliss. The simple repetition with absolute faith embraces such things as the three-fold preparation of the mind and the four practical rules. . . . Those who believe this, even though they have clear understanding of all that the Buddha Śākyamuni taught throughout his entire life, should live with the simplicity of ordinary people who cannot read a single letter, or like nuns and monks who are ignorant but whose faith is simple. Without pedantic attention to detail, they should practise the repetition of the name Amida with devotion—and that alone.

H. H. Coates and Ishizuka Ryugaku, *Honen the Buddhist Saint* . . . (1949).

Hongan (Jap., 'original vow'). The initial vow of a *bodhisattva, or more specifically, the eighteenth vow of *Amida:

> If it should be the case that, after I have attained buddhahood, those sentient beings in all ten directions with calm minds, pure faith and a desire to be born in my domain are not born there (even after ten recitations of the *nembutsu) may I not attain complete and perfected enlightenment; with the exception of those who have committed any of the five deadly sins (*gogyaku-zai) or who have destroyed *dharma.

Honganji (Jap., 'Temple of the Original Vow'). The headquarters temple of the Otani Branch (*ha*) of *Jōdo Shinshū or 'True Pure Land School' of Buddhism in *Kyōto. The temple was originally established by Kakushin-ni, the daughter of the founder of Jōdo Shinshū, *Shinran Shōnin, in 1272. Until the beginning of the 17th cent., there was only one Honganji. But Kyōmyo, the elder brother of the twelfth abbot of the Honganji, Junnyo, established a second temple bearing the same name under the patronage of the first Tokugawa Shōgun, Ieyasu, in 1602. Since this date, the original Honganji has been called Nishi ('West') Honganji and the newer temple Higashi ('East') Honganji. Both temples continue to remain institutionally separate in spite of little, if any, differences in teaching and practice.

Honi ha-Meʿaggel (1st cent. BCE). A Jewish miracle worker. According to the *Talmud, Honi ha-Meʿaggel ('the circle drawer') prayed for *rain in a time of drought and his prayer was fulfilled. Simeon b. Shetaḥ commented on this incident: 'As a son importunes his father, so God accedes to his request' (*Taʿan* 3. 8). Different stories are told about his death, including the legend that he slept for seventy years (*B.Taʿan* 23a) before finally dying. Some have seen him as exemplifying the kind of activity in which *Jesus engaged, but virtually no indication of his teaching has survived, nor is there any reason why that context should have compelled Jesus to move from Galilee to Jerusalem.

Honjisuijaku (Jap., 'original substance manifests traces'). Principle whereby Buddhism is reconciled with Shinto. In its original form, it stated that the *kami and gods or goddesses of Japan are *avatars of *Vairocana, the traces on earth of the original substance of divinity. Although the principle is associated with *Kūkai, its first known appearance is a century later. It became especially associated with *Shingon: not only was the 'original substance' of the gods linked to the thirteen Buddhas of Shingon, but the rituals and ceremonies of Shingon were adopted as well (according to *Kitabake Chikafusa, 'traditions from the age of the gods correspond most closely with Shingon'). *Ryōbu Shintō, 'dual Shinto', united the *maṇḍalas of Shingon and of the Shrines at *Ise. From the Middle Ages until the Meiji Restoration (1868), honjisuijaku was extensive: Buddhists controlled most of the shrines, and within the shrines, the images and practices of Buddhism coexisted with those of Shinto. On occasion, Shinto asserted itself as the senior partner—e.g. after the *kamikaze had driven off the Mongol invasions of 1274 and 1281; or again, in the composition of the Five Classics at about the same time, which are mainly about the history of the Ise shrine, but which also give an account of Shinto philosophy and ethics (leading to Ise Shinto). The Five Classics were used by adherents of 'Primordial Shinto' (Yuiitsu Shinto) in the 15th cent. to reverse the relationship. Thus Yoshida Kanetomo (1435–1511; see YOSHIDA FAMILY) interpreted honjisuijaku as meaning that the Japanese gods were the original substance and the Buddha and *bodhisattvas the manifest traces: 'Buddhism is the flower and fruit of all teaching, Confucianism the branches and leaves, but Shinto the trunk and roots: all foreign teachings are offshoots from Shinto.'

A. Matsunaga, *The Buddhist Philosophy of Assimilation* . . . (1969).

Honrai-no-memmoku (Jap., 'original face'). An expression through which Zen Buddhists penetrate through the superficial appearances to the unchanging, uniform buddha-nature (*buddhatā) present in all things. Thus, 'What is your face before your parents were born?'

Honshi (Jap., 'root-master'). Any master or teacher in Zen Buddhism who is the root or source of *hō* (*dharma). It may be the one who confers the seal of recognition (*inka-shōmei), or the founder of a Buddhist school, or *Buddha Śākyamuni.

Hooker, Richard (*c*.1554–1600). *Anglican theologian. As the apologist of the Elizabethan religious settlement in England, he was a decisively important interpreter of Anglicanism. His *Treatise on the Laws of Ecclesiastical Polity*, also a classic of English prose, was only partly published in his lifetime (books i–v of eight books). Starting from a broadly conceived philosophical theology appealing to natural law, he attacked the *Puritans for regarding the *Bible as a mechanical code of rules, since not everything that is right (e.g. *episcopacy) finds precise definition in the *scriptures. Moreover, the Church is not a static institution, and the method of Church government will change according to circumstances. Hence the Church of England, though reformed, possesses continuity with the early Church. He followed *Aquinas in distinguishing between eternal, natural, and positive law, and assigned to reason, as the discoverer of natural law and the interpreter of eternal law, a positive role. On this basis, he could look for the consensus of all reasonable people, and argued that the forms of government, ecclesiastic or civil, rest on public approval—whether that of the past (inherited in the present) or of the present. Church and State are aspects of the same government (since all authority is derived from God), so that consequently the State (or royal) power extends over religious as well as civil matters. He sought unity in Church and State with such zeal that Izaak Walton wrote of his 'Large preface or epistle to the Dissenting Brethren' that there was in it 'such bowels of love, and such a commixture of that love with reason, as was never exceeded but in holy writ'.

J. S. Marshall, *Hooker and the Anglican Tradition* . . . (1963); P. Munz, *The Place of Hooker in the History of Thought* (1949).

Hopkins, Gerard Manley (1844–89). Poet and *Jesuit priest. Educated at Balliol College, Oxford, where he came under the influence of *Tractarianism, he became a Roman Catholic in 1866 and a Jesuit in 1868. He taught, latterly, as Professor of Greek in Dublin. His poetry was a search after style which would match his vision of God's creation. From the 13th-cent. philosophy of *Duns Scotus, he developed the view that all things bear the inward stress of their particularity (what Scotus called *haecceitas*) and of their own God-given meaning, which he called 'inscape': 'As air, melody, is what strikes me most of all in music, and design in painting, so design, pattern, or what I am in the habit of calling "inscape" is what I above all aim at in poetry.' *Haecceitas* means, according to Scotus: 'By grasping just what things are of themselves, a person separates the essences from the many additional incidental features associated with them in the sense-image, and sees what is true . . . as a more universal seeing.' In 1874, Hopkins was sent to St Beuno's in N. Wales as part of his training, and during his three years there, his poetry took off from theory into celebration. His self-denying abstinence from poetry was broken by his poem, 'The Wreck of the Deutschland', occasioned by a disaster in which five nuns drowned: 'Thou mastering me | God giver of breath and bread; | World's strand, sway of the sea . . .'. He summoned the beauty in all things to give glory to their creator: 'The world is charged with the grandeur of God. | It will flame out, like shining from shook foil; . . .'. After he left Wales, he wrote little poetry until the final so-called 'black' sonnets/poems: 'To seem the stranger lies my lot, my life | Among strangers. . . . | This to hoard unheard, | Heard unheeded, leaves me a lonely began.' A mark of that isolation lies in the fact that his poetry was unpublished during his lifetime, appearing in 1918. But his devotion to God remained secure: 'He is so great that all things give him glory if you mean they should. So then, my brethren, live.'

J. F. Cotter, *Inscape* . . . (1972); T. Dunne, *Hopkins: A Comprehensive Bibliography* (1976).

Horaʿat sha'ah (Heb., 'ruling for the hour'). Legal ruling by Jewish authorities in an emergency, but not intended to have permanent validity. The precedent was set by *Elijah, when he offered a sacrifice on Mount Carmel at a time when sacrifice was supposed to be offered only in the *Temple—but by doing so he discredited the prophets of *Baʿal (1 Kings 18. 31–9). Many such rulings had to be made during the Second World War, even outside Nazi-occupied Europe—e.g. evacuees might be sent to places where *kosher* (see DIETARY LAWS) food was not available.

Horin. Jap. for *dharmacakra.

Horner, I. B. (1896–1981). Pioneer of Pāli Buddhist studies in the West. After graduating from Newnham College, Cambridge, in Moral Sciences in 1917, she worked in the College library until her first trip to Śri Lankā and India in 1921, which lasted for two years. At the end of this she returned to Newnham as Fellow and Librarian and published her first book on Buddhism, *Women under Primitive Buddhism*, in 1930. Subsequently, she edited and translated many Buddhist texts, in particular, the *Vinaya Piṭaka, the **Majjhima Nikāya*, and *Milinda's Questions*. She also wrote much on the teachings of early Buddhism. She became Honorary Secretary of the Pāli Text Society in 1942, and its President from 1949.

Horologion. In E. Christianity, a book of liturgical prayers and offices, somewhat like a *breviary. As well as the offices, it contains blessings, hymns, and the calendar.

Horowitz, Isaiah ben Abraham ha-Levi, also called **ha-Shelah ha-Kadosh** (The Holy Shelah, 1565–1630). *Rabbi and *kabbalist. Horowitz served as a rabbi in Dubno, Ostraha, Frankfurt-am-Main, and Prague before settling in 1621 in *Erez Israel. His main work is the *Shenei Luḥot ha-Berit* (Two Tablets of the Covenant, 1649: the title is abbreviated as Shelah, hence his name above) which combines *halakhah, sermon, and *kabbalah in teaching how to lead the good life. He advised, 'Let the man who wishes for eternal life repent all his life . . . let him perform . . . precepts . . . with animation of heart and with joy'. His book had great influence on the *Ḥasidic movement. In 1625, he was imprisoned by the *pasha, and following his ransom, he settled eventually in Tiberias. As a mark of respect, he was buried close to *Maimonides.

Horrid thing (claims to special gifts from the Holy Spirit): see BUTLER, JOSEPH.

Horse-sacrifice (Hindu ritual): see AŚVAMEDHA.

Hōryū-ji (temple-complex): see NARA BUDDHISM.

Hosanna (Gk., from Heb., *hoshana*, 'save, we beseech you'). An acclamation used in Christian worship from an early time (**Didache* 10. 6). It derives from the story of *Jesus' 'triumphal entry' into Jerusalem (Mark 11. 1–10, etc.) when the crowds called to him 'Hosanna! Blessed be he who comes in the name of the Lord! . . . Hosanna in the highest!' These words appear in many *eucharistic liturgies following the *Sanctus.

Hosea. First of the twelve books known as the minor *prophets in the Hebrew Bible and Christian Old Testament. Hosea was almost certainly produced in the Northern Kingdom of *Israel and, after the destruction of Israel in 721, subject to redaction in *Judah. It consists of a third-person account of a marriage with an unfaithful woman and the birth of three children, all of whom have symbolic names (chs. 1–2). This is followed by an autobiographical account of the same events (3). The relationship is understood as symbolic of God's relationship with his *chosen people. The prophet then inveighs against the moral corruption of the N. Kingdom (4–7), against the *idolatry and unfaithfulness of the people (8–13), and gives them instructions on how to turn back to God (14). It is generally accepted that chs. 1–3 have a different author from chs. 4–14. According to the *Aggadah, Hosea was a contemporary of *Isaiah, *Amos, and *Micah, but was the greatest of them because he taught his people to pray (*PR* 44. 23).

Hoshana Rabba (Heb., 'the great hoshana'). The seventh and last day of the festival of *Sukkot. In the *Temple ceremony, seven circuits of the *altar were made with the *lulav, and the festival is so named because of the numerous hoshana prayers which were recited. Hoshana Rabba was understood as a day of judgement and this is still expressed in various prayers. There is a widespread custom of staying up during the night of the festival to read the whole of the *Pentateuch. Special willow branches (known as 'hoshanot') are cut for the festival and beaten on the ground, and Hoshana Rabba is described in the *Talmud as the 'Day of the Willow'.

Ho shang (Chin. transliteration, possibly from Turk., *Udin*, language of Khotan, or the Kashgarian dialect, *Hwa Shie*, of the Skt., *upadhyāya*, 'self-taught teacher', or *upasaka* 'the tutor of Rahula': Ho,

'Harmony or Peace', + Shang, 'in charge of or ascend'). Any religious figure; or a reverent form used for an *abbot, *fang-chang*, or *bhikṣu in charge of a *saṅgha (community). Applications of the phrase range in China from specifics (such as an important, or retiring, or meat-eating, or married, or Ch'an religious figure) to its general use as a universal term for a religious figure.

Ho-shang Kung. A somewhat legendary Taoist figure, supposed to have written the commentary on the **Tao-te ching* which bears his name; but this is much later than the supposed date at which he lived.

Hoshanot (willow branches): see HOSHANA RABBA.

Hospitallers (Knights of Malta): see TEMPLARS.

Hossen (Jap., 'dharma contest'). Fundamental method in Zen Buddhism whereby a master and pupil move each other toward truth. The literal tr., 'contest', is inappropriate, since hossen is mutual encouragement, arising out of *zazen experience. It is thus like *mondō, except that hossen is usually a longer exchange. But like mondō, it contributes to the accumulated record of *kōans in Zen.

Hosshin. Jap., for *dharmakaya* in the three-body (*trikaya) understanding of the Buddha's manifestation.

Hosshin-kōan (creation of awareness of identity with Buddha-nature): see KŌAN.

Hossho (buddha-nature): see BUDDHATĀ.

Hossō school (Zen Buddhist school): see DŌSHŌ.

Hossu (Jap.). A small brush in Zen Buddhism, based on the brush used by Jains to sweep the path before them, in order to avoid killing an insect inadvertently. It was used (often in *kōans) by the master, and became a symbol of transmission. It was therefore passed on to a dharma-successor (*hassu).

Host (Lat., *hostia*, 'sacrifice, victim'). The bread of the *eucharist, especially the thin round wafer used by Roman Catholics and Anglo-Catholics (among whom the mass is most explicitly seen in relation to the death of Christ understood as *sacrifice).

Host, desecration of. Alleged profanation by Jews of the consecrated bread of the Christian eucharist. The accusation of the desecration of the host was first recognized by the Roman Catholic Church in 1215. In 1243 at Belitz, Germany, Jews were for the first time accused of desecration, and a number were burned at the stake. The accusation was made on many occasions throughout the Middle Ages and was revived in Romania as late as 1836.

Hotei (Chin., *Pu-tai*, 'cloth-bag'). A popular figure in the Ch'an or Zen Buddhist *iconography of China and Japan, as well as a popular deity in Chinese and Japanese folk religion. In Buddhist terms, Hotei represents both the *bodhisattva ideal and the iconoclastic spirit of *Mahāyāna (and Far Eastern) Buddhism. He is the Zen (and perhaps *Taoist) eccentric, wandering sage who bestows his spiritual goods on all he comes in contact with. He is well-represented in Zen literature and art, but perhaps most graphically as the fat, 'bliss-bestowing' figure of the tenth ox-herding picture in the Zen tradition. The Buddhist origins of this figure are unclear, but 10th-cent. China seems likely, and two theories have been put forward: (i) Hotei is an incarnation of the 'future' *buddha, *Maitreya; and (ii) he represents the semi-historical, 10th-cent. figure Chishi who was popularly called Master Cloth-Sack.

In Far Eastern folk religion he becomes associated with indigenous deities of happiness and good luck and, not unlike Santa Claus, represents both material and spiritual plentitude simply there for the asking—all symbolized by obesity and a large (cloth) sack on his back.

Hōtoku (Jap., 'repaying virtue'). A popular syncretic religious movement of the Tokugawa period (1600–1868) in Japan. Hōtoku was founded by Ninomiya Sontoku (1787–1856), whose mission was to uplift morally the life of farmers, while, at the same time, encouraging economic productivity. Sontoku's creed emphasized the *Confucian doctrine of filial piety, the virtue of manual labour (which was the human counterpart of the creative activities of the gods, *kami), and the practice of husbanding agricultural surpluses to protect against times of famine. Sontoku also advocated the formation of credit co-operatives in the local villages to provide interest-free loans to farmers in need. These Hōtoku societies, with their ethical principles of gratitude to parents, the emperor, and the gods, and the value of industry and frugality, exerted an important spiritual influence among the Japanese in the pre-modern period. He has remained an inspirational figure for those concerned with long-term consequences of short-term decisions in agriculture: 'The teaching of Hōtoku is entirely practical: the three most important constraints are to work, to be thrifty, and to pass on something to others. . . . Work and thrift are practised only for the purpose of passing on something to others.'

Hotṛ (group of Hindu priests): see ṚTVIJ; SACRIFICES (HINDUISM).

Ho-tse Shen-hui (Jap., Kataku Jin'e; *c.*680–*c.*760). Chinese Ch'an master, pupil of *Hui-neng, and founder of the Kataku school. In contrast to his predecessors, Ho-tse maintained that enlightenment was not attained by a gradual process through long stages of training, but rather through disengagement from mind and mentality (*mushin*) which leads directly into awareness of one's true nature (*kensho) and thus to sudden enlightenment. Despite this important breakthrough, the school did not last long.

Hō Un (lay Ch'an/Zen Buddhist): see P'ANG YÜN.

Houris (beautiful maidens of Paradise in Islam): see ḤŪR.

Hours, canonical. The individual services of the divine *office. In both E. and W. Christianity, these have traditionally been reckoned as seven, following Psalm 119. 164 ('Seven times a day I praise you'): *mattins and *lauds (counted together as one hour), *prime, terce, sext, none, *vespers, and *compline. The exact times cannot be given as a standard generalization, because the times of both meals and office varied between summer and winter, and between fasting days and others. For the principles and for illustrations from the early period in the W. Church, see D. Knowles, *The Monastic Order in England* . . . (1949), 448 ff. The *Constitution on the Sacred Liturgy* of *Vatican II envisaged that the praying of the Hours would return to the whole Church, and that the Hours 'may once again be genuinely related to the time of the day at which they are prayed'. An attempt to move in this direction was made in the revised *Breviary of 1971.

House Churches (local and communal gatherings of Christains): see ECCLESIOLOGY.

Hou-t'u (generative force of the earth in China): see T'U-TI.

Hōyū (Ch'an Buddhist master): see FA-JUNG.

Hōza (seated fellowship): see RISSHŌ KŌSEI KAI.

Hōzo (Jap. name for the monk, Dharmākara): see AMIDA.

Hṛdaya Sūtra (Buddhist text): see HEART SŪTRA.

Hsi-an Fu. In NW China, site of the discovery in 1625 of a stele usually called the '*Nestorian monument'. It is inscribed in Chinese with a text including a history of the Nestorian Church (see CHURCH OF THE EAST) in China up until the time of its erection in 781. According to this, a missionary A-luo pen (Abraham?) arrived at the T'ang court from the West in 635. Three years later a monastery with twenty-one monks was established. Probably the Nestorian presence in China was always that of a foreign religion (most of the proper names on the monument are Syriac) dependent on the imperial favour. It was suppressed along with Buddhism in 845.

F. V. Holm, *The Nestorian Monument* (1909); P. Y. Saecki, *The Nestorian Monument* . . . (1916).

Hsiang (incense): see INCENSE.

Hsiang-yen Chih-hsien (Jap., Kyōgen Chikan; d. *c.*900). Chinese Ch'an master; pupil and dharma-successor (*hassu) of *Kuei-shan Ling-yu. He is best known for the story of his breakthrough to enlightenment. After much text-based study and no progress, he went to Kuei-shan who asked him about his original face (*honrai-no-memmoku). He pored over his books, but, finding no answer, he asked Kuei-shan for it. 'I know it, but will not tell you', was his reply. Hsiang-yen gave up and withdrew to a hermitage. Sweeping his yard, he struck a pebble against a tree (or he heard the noise of a falling tile) and received immediate enlightenment, and gave thanks that Kuei-shan had refused an answer, since that would have become part of his intellectual *impedimenta*. He burned incense and bowed toward Kuei-shan's dwelling, and composed lines which begin: 'With one stroke all previous knowledge is obliterated | No careful cultivation is needed for this.' *Yang-shan criticized this for dependency, so Hsiang-yen composed: 'My poverty of last year was not real | This year it is poverty indeed | Last year left room for the point of a gimlet | This year even the gimlet is gone.' Yang-shan commented: 'You may have grasped the Zen of the perfected one, but you have not seen, even in a dream, the Zen of the patriarchs (*soshigata).' He replied: 'I have my secret | I look at you with twinkling eye | If you do not understand this | Do not call yourself a monk.' These three verses are the different Ch'an levels of inner realization. According to Hsiang-yen, the human predicament is summarized in the story of a man hanging by his teeth from the highest branch of a tall tree, who is asked why *Bodhidharma came from the West.

Hsiao (Chin., 'old age' + 'son'). Filial piety, a virtue considered most important in E. Asian social ethics, influenced by the school of Confucius, and by the ancient cult of *ancestral veneration. *The Classic of Filial Piety* (*Hsiao Ching*) has been associated with Tseng-tzu, a direct disciple of the sage himself. While filial piety appears to underscore the child's obligations of love and obedience to his or her parents, it actually implies as well the parent's obligations to love and educate the child, and refers therefore to the primacy of this familial bond in personal and social life. See also ETHICS (CONFUCIANISM).

Hsiao Ching (Scripture of Filiality). A small text included in the *Confucian Classics. It purports to be a lecture given by the Master (*Confucius) to his eminent disciple, Master Tseng (Tseng-tzu), who was noted for his filiality. The text is likely to be no earlier than the late Chou or early Han (roughly 5th–3rd cents. BCE).

Trs. J. Legge, *The Hsiao King* (1899); M. Makra, *The Hsiao Ching* (1961).

Hsien. Immortal beings depicted in Chinese art, literature, religion, and folklore since the 3rd cent. BCE. As bird-like people or wise old men lost in misty mountains, they could fly great distances or change their appearance at will. Though the sage *Chuang-tzu argued for acceptance of death as natural, the Chinese imagination often sided more with the first emperor, Ch'in Shih Huang-ti (ruled 247–210 BCE), who launched a grand but ill-fated expedition in search of *P'eng lai, an island abode of the immortals. The 4th-cent. scholar, *Ko Hung, reaffirmed belief in hsien and described various techniques to become immortal, including breathing exercises, dietary restrictions, sexual practices, and alchemical transmutations. Among the most popular immortals is *Hsi Wang Mu, Queen Mother of the West, whose famous peaches of immortality ripen once every 3,000 years. Her orchards were once raided by another renowned hsien, Sun Wu-k'ung, the monkey king. A Taoist group of 'Eight Immortals' (*Pa-hsien) contains the famous Lu Tung-pin with his gourd of immortal *elixir. Though hsien were somewhat eclipsed in medieval imagery by the 'perfected' (*chen-jen*) of Taoism and the *bodhisattvas and *arhats of Buddhism, they continued as evocative images in the arts.

M. Kaltenmark, *Le Lie-sien tchouan* (1953).

Hsien-t'ien (Chin., 'before heaven'). Taoist concept of 'before time', i.e. the absolute condition before the creation of heaven.

Hsin (trust): see WU-CH'ANG.

Hsing (human nature): see HSÜN TZU.

Hsing-ch'i (Chinese breathing practice): see CH'I.

Hsin-hsing (founder of school of Chinese Buddhism): see SAN-CHIEH-CHIAO.

Hsin-hsin-ming (Buddhist poem): see SENG-TS'AN.

Hsi Wang Mu. One of the most popular of the Chinese *hsien (immortals). She is the Queen Mother of the West, whose peaches of immortality ripen once every 3,000 years. She has many cosmic powers, and became the focus of a cult seeking her aid in salvation at the opening of the Common Era.

M. Loewe, *Ways to Paradise* ... (1979).

Hsi-yün (Ch'an teacher): see HUANG-PO HSI-YÜN.

Hsüan-Hsüeh (Chin., 'secret teaching'). An early stage of neo-*Taoism, in the 3rd and 4th cents. CE. Important figures were Wang Pi (226–49), Hsiang Hsiu (221–300), Ho Yen (d. 249), and Kuo Hsiang (d. 312), all of whom wrote commentaries on **Tao-te ching*. They developed *Ch'ing-t'an, reflective conversation, by which name the 'movement' is also known. Against their predecessors, they held that *Tao, as non-being, is not an agent bringing things into being; things arise spontaneously within the totality of all existent being, which they took to be the meaning of *ti'en, heaven:

The music of nature is not an entity existing outside of things. The different apertures, the pipes and flutes and the like, in combination with all living beings, together constitute nature. Since nonexistence is non-being, it cannot produce being. Then by whom are things produced? They spontaneously produce themselves, that is all (Kuo Hsiang).

Wang-pi in particular emphasized the equivalence of Tao to *wu (emptiness); wu is not 'nothingness', but pure form, and because it is pure form, it can impart perfection to all things. For that reason, the wise person does not withdraw from life, but learns to act appropriately with the norm of Tao, not initiating action, but going with the grain of Tao. That is the meaning of *wu-wei; and in that concept, Hsüan-hsüeh was able to assimilate *Confucian ethics, and to regard K'ung-tzu (*Confucius) as wiser than *Chuang-tzu or *Lao-tzu.

Hsüan-sha Shih-pei (Jap., Gensha Shibi; 835–908). A Ch'an/Zen master, the dharma-successor (*hassu) of *Hsüeh-feng I-ts'un, who began life as an illiterate fisherman. He received initial training in a monastery under *Vinaya rules, and lived an austerely ascetic life until he began pilgrimages to meet Ch'an masters. On one of these, he stubbed his toe against a stone in the road and experienced sudden enlightenment (*Ho-tse). As teacher of *Fa-yen Wen-i (Jap., Hogen Bun'eki), he became a distant founder of the Hogen school—it was known for some time as the Hsüan-sha school. When Wu-men Hui-k'ai wrote his famous *Wu-men-kuan*, (Gateless Barrier), he attributed his title to Hsüan-sha's summary: 'Have you not heard what Hsüan-sha said? "No-gate is the gate of emancipation; no-mind is the mind of the man of *Tao" .' See further KŌAN.

Hsüan-t'ien Shang-ti (Lord of the Dark Heaven). A Chinese deity. One of a family of five deities in antiquity, each in charge of a cardinal direction of the cosmos: Lord Green (East), Lord Red (South), Lord White (West), Lord Dark (North), Lord Yellow (Centre). Lord Dark has the power of driving away evil spirits. In the Han period (206 BCE–220CE), he was portrayed as tortoise and snake. In subsequent times, he became anthropomorphized and was given different names: Hsüan-t'ien Shang-ti, Hsüan-wu Sheng-chun (Dark Warrior of Sacred Lord), and, finally, Pei-chi Yu-sheng Chen-chün (Holy Lord-Protector of the North Pole Star). In 1118, he granted the imperial request and revealed himself to the *Taoist emperor Hui-tsung who painted a portrait of him. The religious Taoists, desirous of physical immortality, prayed to the stellar divinities for assistance for the making of the *elixirs. According to them, the North Pole Star (Plough or Dipper) is the central residence for the stellar deities headed by Hsüan-t'ien Shang-ti.

Hsüan-tsang, San-tsang, or **T'ang-seng** (*c*.600–64). A Chinese Buddhist monk and pilgrim, who was a major influence on the development of Buddhism in China through his translation of Skt. texts. He became a monk at the age of 13 and studied

*Mahāyāna under several teachers. The discrepancies led him to travel to India in order to return to the sources of the teaching. His famous pilgrimage is described in *Ta-t'ang hsi-yu chi* (Record of the Western Journey, tr. S. Beal, 1906), which became the basis for the 16th cent. novel *Hsi-yu chi* (tr. A. C. Yu, 1980; cf. also A. Waley, *Monkey*). At *Nālandā (then at its height), he immersed himself in Yogācāra, (*Vijñanavāda), and on his return to China, he became its protagonist, founding the *Fa-hsiang school. During the last twenty years of his life, he devoted himself to translating, in fluent style, at least seventy-five works. His pupil, K'uei-chi (636–82) wrote commentaries on many of the translations, using them to systematize the Fa-hsiang teachings.

S. Beal, *Life of Hsuan-Tsang* (1911); R. Grousset, *Sur les traces du Bouddha* (1929; tr. M. Leon, 1932; J. A. Underwood, 1971).

Hsüeh-feng I-ts'un (Jap., Seppō Gison. 822–908). Ch'an/Zen Buddhist master, dharma-successor (*hassu) of *Te-shan Hsüan-chien, from whom derived (via his pupils) the *Yün-men (Ummon) school and the *Fa-yen/*Hsüan-sha (*Hogen) school. His desire to become a monk at the age of 9 was frustrated by his parents, but three years later, during a visit to a monastery, he saw the *Vinaya teacher and declared, 'Here is my master'. He stayed, and after his full training, he began to wander as a *tenzo* (kitchen supervisor in a Ch'an monastery). He experienced profound enlightenment in *mondō with his dharma brother, *Yen t'ou Chuan-huo. Against his initial wishes, many monks gathered around him on Mount Hsüeh-feng (hence his name), and through them, Ch'an spread extensively. In his view, 'The whole immense earth, taken between the fingers, is the same size as a grain of rice.'

Hsüeh-tou Ch'ung-hsien (Jap., Setchō Jūken; 982–1052). Chinese Ch'an/Zen master of the *Yün-men (*Ummon) school, a great poet, who laid the foundations of the hundred verses of the *Pi-yen-lu* (Jap., *Hekigan-roku*; The Blue Cliff Record). Hsüeh-tou had begun the work of transforming the teaching of the masters (especially Yün-men) into poetic form. Yüan-wu K'o-ch'in took up and extended the work, making it into the most important collection (along with **Wu-men-kuan*) of Zen *kōans. To the two basic texts (the cases of enlightenment experience, and the verses) Yüan-wu added notes and a commentary. Thus for each of the hundred examples, there are seven parts: introduction, case, notes, commentary, verse, notes, commentary. In H. Dumoulin's view, 'To read the *Blue Cliff Record* in its given sequence and be guided by the spirit and imagination of the lively commentary W. Gundert [Ger., 3 vols.] has provided is to find a sure, albeit not easy, entrance into one of the foremost examples of religious world literature' (*Zen Buddhism*, p. 249).

Tr., T. and J. C. Cleary (1977); K. Sekida, *Two Zen Classics* (1977).

Hsü Kao-seng chuan (Chinese Buddhist biographical text): see TAO-HSÜAN.

Hsün Ch'ing: see HSÜN TZU.

Hsün Tzu (Xunzi). An important work of early Chinese philosophy attributed to Hsün Tzu or Hsün Ch'ing (b. *c.*300 BCE). His interpretation of *Confucian teaching, which became canonical (to be studied by court officials) during the former Han dynasty (206 BCE–9 CE), remained largely dominant until the rise of the *Neo-Confucian movement in the 11th cent. His interpretation of ritual also took on special authority by being absorbed into the **Li Chi*.

The book teaches that people are by nature 'evil'—not in any metaphysical way, but in the practical sense that without proper education people cannot rise to full participation in culture and society. At the root of this doctrine is a distinction between human 'nature' (*hsing*, 'that which cannot be learned or acquired by effort') and 'conscious activity' (*wei*, 'that which can be acquired by learning and brought to completion by effort', B. Watson tr., p. 158). *Hsün Tzu* stresses the importance of *wei*: people are not fully human until they have become imbued with a sense of moral and ritual propriety, and they are not born with that sense but must be taught it. This teaching was directed against that of *Mencius, that people are capable of learning to be moral because their nature is already 'good': it already contains the fonts of the sort of behaviour society wants to inculcate.

Hsün Tzu was influenced by the legalist school of his day, which stressed the necessity of law and coercion for maintaining social order. Since for Hsün Tzu education and the products of human culture are so essential, he naturally emphasized two realms of activity which defined the culture of the nobility in his time: rites and music. His famous interpretation of the mourning rites refrains from speaking explicitly about the actual fate of the deceased; instead it focuses on how the rites function to preserve the community, and both to express and to temper the emotions (*ch'ing*) of the living. The rites in general exemplify in highest form the power of human culture to transform, educate, and perfect—but not to eradicate—human nature. They exemplify, too, the resonant correspondence (often affirmed in Chinese tradition) between cultural and cosmic forms. 'Through rites Heaven and earth join in harmony, the sun and moon shine, the four seasons proceed in order, the stars and constellations march, the rivers flow, and all things flourish; men's likes and dislikes are regulated and their joys and hates made appropriate. . . . Are they not wonderful indeed?' (B. Watson tr., p. 94).

Tr. of parts, B. Watson, *Hsün Tzu: Basic Writings* (1963); H. H. Dubs, *The Works* . . . (1928).

Hsü-t'ang Chih-yü (Jap., Kidō Chigu; 1189–1269). Chinese Ch'an/Zen master of the *Rinzai tradition.

He was the teacher of Shōmyō who took his *dharma teaching to Japan. His discourses are collected in *Hsü-t'ang ko-shang yü-lu* (Jap., *Kidō oshō goroku*), and contain *kōans still used in Rinzai training. Self-portraits survive in Myōshin-ji and *Daitoku-ji in Kyōto.

Hua-Hu Ching (Chin., On the Conversion of Outsiders). Taoist work, *c.*300 CE, describing the missionary work of *Lao-tzu 'to the west', i.e. in India. Its main polemic claim is that Lao-tzu instructed the *Buddha, and that consequently Buddhism is a deviant variation on Taoism. Buddhists countered by claiming a much earlier date for the birth of Gautama.

Huai-nan Tzu. Chinese work of the 2nd cent. BCE, written and compiled by scholars of the court of Liu-an, prince of Huai-nan. It summarizes the main philosophies and schools, but proclaiming the superiority of Taoism. It originally contained twenty-one inner chapters on Taoism, and thirty-three outer chapters on other schools, but the outer chapters have not survived. It holds that each philosophy was appropriate to its time, but by penetrating more closely into the mysteries of the cosmos, this work will act as a better guide to rulers: 'I have tried to describe and illuminate the Tao and its inner power, and to clarify the tangle of human affairs. I have looked up to study heaven, and down to examine the earth, and around me to understand the principles of humanity.'

Huan-ching (Chin., 'allowing semen to return'). The control of semen, especially the prevention of ejaculation, as a redistribution of power in the body, a prelude to meditation in Taoism.

Huang-chin (yellow cloth worn by Tao group): see CHANG CHÜEH.

Huang-ch'üan (Chin., 'yellow springs'). The underworld to which, in Taoism, *yin-weighted souls descend after death. See further P'O.

Huang-lao Chün (Chin., 'ancient yellow Lord'). Taoist deity, and principal god of *T'ai-ping tao. Originally compounded from Huang-ti (one of the legendary emperors—the Yellow Emperor—and four founders of religious Taoism, *tao-chiao* and *Lao-tzu, he is the ruler of the world who appears in numerous incarnations of Taoist teachers to maintain the understanding of Tao.

A. K. Seidel, *La Divinisation de Lao-tseu dans le taoïsmedes Han* (1969).

Huang-lung Hui-nan (Jap., Ōryō E'nan, 1002–69). Ch'an/Zen master of the *Rinzai school. He was the dharma-successor (*hassu) of Shih-huang Ch'u-yüan, and founder of the Ōryō school of Zen within the Rinzai tradition. It was the first school of Zen to be carried from China to Japan—by *Eisai Zenji. He gathered around him 'a thick forest of pupils' and taught by way of the three barriers (Jap., *sankan*), in the style of *kōans:

Q. Each person, through causal contingency, has a native place: where is yours?
A. Early in the morning I ate white rice, now I feel hungry.
Q. In what ways are my hands like the Buddha's hands?
A. Playing the lute in moonlight.
Q. In what ways are my feet like those of a donkey?
A. When the heron stands in the snow, its colour is not the same.

Ōryō is one of the Seven Schools (*goke-shichishū) of Ch'an/Zen, but it died out in both China and Japan after a few generations.

Huang-po Hsi-yün, (Hsi-yün of the Huang-po mountain, Jap., Ōbaku Kiun; d. 850 CE). Ch'an/Zen master, dharma-successor (*hassu) of *Pai-chang Huai-hai and teacher of *Lin-chi I-hsüan, through whom he becomes one of the forefathers of the *Rinzai school. He sought instruction from *Ma-tsu, who died before he could reach him; instead, he was taught by Pai-chang. It was Huang-po who formalized the *Ho as a teaching/transmission method. His teachings were gathered by P'ei Hsiu (Jap., Haikyū) under the (shortened) title *Chu'an-hsin-fa-yao* (tr. J. Blofeld, *The Zen Teaching of Huang Po*, 1958), a classic text of the Ch'an tradition, which expounds the teaching of universal mind: 'In order to climb into the chariot of the Buddha, you must eradicate all dualist concepts and all attachment and revulsion.' Attainment may be by gradual or sudden enlightenment, since either way the end result is necessarily the same, because 'this state allows no degrees'; but the former is less satisfactory because it involves 'many *kalpas of unnecessary labour and suffering'.

Huang-ti (the Yellow Emperor): see HUANG-LAO CHÜN.

Huang-ti nei-ching (medical text): see BOOK OF THE YELLOW EMPEROR.

Huang-t'ing Ching (Chin., 'treatise on the yellow castle'). A Taoist work, *c.*3rd cent. CE, describing the deities of the body (*shen), and also the practices which lead to immortality (e.g. *ch'i and *fang-shih). The recitation of the title invokes the deities and wards off evil from the body.

Hua T'o (developer of Taoist exercises): see WU-CH'IN-HSI.

Hua-yen (Jap., *Kegon, lit., 'Flower Adornment' school). A major school of Chinese Buddhism, which derived its name from the title of the Chinese tr. of its main text, *Buddhāvatamsaka-sūtra* (see AVATATAMṢAKA). Its main organizer was *Fa-tsang (3rd Patriarch) (643–712), although its roots are earlier (e.g. *Tu-shun). Important teachers were Cheng-kuan (737–820), regarded as the incarnation of *Mañjuśrī, and Tsung-mi (780–841). Hua-yen was taken to Japan in 740 by Shen-hsiang, where it is known as *Kegon.

Hua-yen regarded itself as the culmination of the *Buddha Śākyamuni's teaching after his enlightenment. His listeners were initially struck 'deaf and dumb' with incomprehension. He therefore devised *Hīnayāna as an elementary introduction; elementary *Mahāyāna in the *Fa-hsiang and *San-lun schools, which still do not recognize the buddha-nature in all things; advanced Mahāyāna of the *T'ien-t'ai, where the emptiness of all things is recognized but their existence is maintained; the Ch'an/Zen stage of sudden, not gradual, enlightenment; the full teaching of Hua-yen. This teaching maintains the interdependence and equality of all appearance, the 'teaching of totality'. Appearances may be in different states, but they are necessarily interdependent in constituting the universe of phenomena, and in equally manifesting the Buddha-illumination of enlightenment. Thus when Fa-tsang was summoned by the formidable empress Wu to expound the sūtra, he took a golden lion in the room as illustration: the lion is the phenomenal world, *shih*, but it is constituted by gold, *li*, the underlying principle which has no form of its own. By analysis into *shih* and *li*, every manifestation is identical to every other, and is an expression of the buddha-nature (*buddhatā). This key perception of the interpenetration of all existences is expressed in Fa-Tsang's image of *Indra's net, which spreads across the universe, with a perfect jewel in each of its links: each jewel reflects every other jewel in the whole net. The image was given practical demonstration when he placed mirrors at eight points of the compass, above and below a Buddha image, which was lit by a candle in such a way that the mirrors reflected the image and each other backwards and forwards without termination. So it can be said that the true nature of the entire universe is contained in every least particle: 'Every living being and every minute thing is significant, because even the tiniest atom contains the whole mystery.'

T. Cleary (tr.), *Entry into the Inconceivable* (1983); F. D. Cook, *Hua-yen Buddhism* . . . (1977); the latter translated Fa-tsang's 'Treatise on the Five Doctrines', Ph.D. Wisconsin, (1970).

Hubbard, Lafayette Ron (1911–86). American science-fiction writer and founder of *Scientology. He became widely known with the publication in 1950 of his book *Dianetics: The Modern Science of Mental Health*, which is the basic textbook of Scientology. The Church of Scientology was founded in 1954. It has been involved in disputes about whether it is a religion or a psychotherapy, and over its methods of recruitment: in Australia, the High Court ruled in 1983 that it is a religion; in the UK, restrictions were placed (between 1968 and 1980) on those wishing to enter the country to work for, or to study, Scientology. Meanwhile, Hubbard withdrew increasingly from administration in order to write.

Hūd. A prophet, according to Qur'ān (in sūras 7, 11, 26, 46, 49), among the ʿĀd, demonstrating that God has sent messengers to more peoples than Jews and Christians.

Hudnan Pesobay (leader of the faithful): see MAGI.

Ḥudūd (limit set by God in Islam): see ḤADD.

Hügel, Baron Friedrich von (1852–1925). Roman Catholic philosopher, theologian, and spiritual writer. Of Austrian and Scottish parentage, he settled in England in 1876. Interested in the historico-critical study of the Bible, he befriended A. *Loisy and G. *Tyrrell, and played an important role in the *Modernist movement. His major works include *The Mystical Element of Religion as Studied in St *Catherine of Genoa and her Friends* (1908), *Eternal Life* (1912), *Essays and Addresses in the Philosophy of Religion* (2 vols., 1921, 1926), and *The Reality of God* (1931). Recent interest in him has concentrated on his connection with RC Modernism. His major works, however, all appeared after the Modernist crisis and deal with a wide diversity of topics: the importance of *ontology and history for religious belief, the relationship between Christianity and culture, immortality, and the role of *mysticism and sanctity in religion. 'Remember: no joy without suffering—no patience without trial—no humility without humiliation—no life without death.' Perhaps his abiding importance lies in the way in which he sought to link together theology, spirituality, and philosophy, particularly by delineating the experiential dimension of religion and its transformative power as manifested above all in the *saints: 'In the Scottish rivers, the salmon will leap and leap, and only after much leaping will they succeed in jumping up and into the higher reaches. Jump, Child, jump: *I* jump with you—look, we both manage it.'

M. de la Bedoyère, *The Life* . . . (1951).

Hugh, St (*c*.1140–1200). Bishop of Lincoln. Born in Burgundy, he was brought up to become a *canon regular, but was attracted to a more austere life and became a *Carthusian at the Grande Chartreuse in 1160. Henry II of England, impressed by his talents, persuaded him to become prior of the first English Carthusian house at Witham, Somerset, in 1175. In 1186, at the king's insistence, Hugh became bishop of Lincoln. As bishop he was very able and much loved. His shrine at Lincoln was among the most popular in medieval England.

Hugh of St-Victor (*c*.1096–1142). Medieval theologian, of whom little is known. About 1115 he entered St-Victor, a house of *Augustinian canons in Paris. Together with other later members of the Abbey, notably Richard of St-Victor and Thomas Gallus, he represents the distinctive and influential 'Victorine' school of theology, which is marked by the influence of *Dionysius the Areopagite (on whose *Celestial Hierarchy* Hugh wrote a commentary), and sees the whole created order as a set of symbols manifesting the glory of God and drawing people to contemplation. He had vivid experiences of God: 'It is joy unspeakable . . . I grasp something inwardly as with the embracement of love.'

Huguenots. (poss. from the name Hugues, or Swiss Eidgnosse, 'confederate'). French Calvinists. As *Calvinism spread rapidly in France during the 1540s, so persecution increased, especially under Henry II (1547–59). On his death, a more confused political situation ensued, leading to civil war. Militant Catholics (above all the family of the Guises) refused compromise: the massacre of St Bartholomew's Day (1572) was made the more repugnant by the fact that Protestant leaders had been invited to Paris to celebrate the marriage of a Huguenot leader, Henry of Navarre, to a Catholic, Margaret, sister of Charles IX. The reconciliation which that event might have introduced was nevertheless brought near by the accession of Henry, who turned Catholic to gain the throne (hence the saying of himself or perhaps of his minister Sully, 'Paris vaut bien une messe', 'Paris is well worth a mass'). He ended the civil war, and by the Edict of Nantes, in 1598, he extended toleration to the Huguenots, granting them civil rights and the power to hold certain fortified towns of their own. Nevertheless, it was not until 1787 that marriages before Huguenot ministers were recognized, and only in 1802, following the French Revolution, that the legal position of the Church was established. In the century before that, the Huguenots were subjected once more to fierce persecution and to enforced conversion. Many fled, particularly when, in 1685, the Edict of Nantes was revoked. The ensuing Camisard revolt persisted for twenty years, but again was suppressed with great violence. The differing groups were largely united in 1938 in the Reformed Church of France.

M. H. Baird, (1880, 1886, 1895); A. J. Grant, *The Huguenots* (1934); R. M. Kingdom, *Geneva and the Coming of the Wars of Religion in France* (1956).

Hui (brotherhoods): see SECRET SOCIETIES.

Hui-ch'ang persecution. Suppression of Buddhism in Korea by Emperor Wu-tsung of the T'ang dynasty during 842–5 in the Hui-ch'ang era (841–6). Countless monasteries were destroyed in 845, at which time the lands and serfs belonging to the monasteries were confiscated, and monks and nuns were laicized. The largest of its kind in the history of China, this anti-Buddhist campaign dealt the religion a crippling blow.

Hui-k'o (Jap., Eka; 487–593). Second patriarch (after *Bodhidharma) of Ch'an/Zen in China. His attempt to receive instruction from Bodhidharma is a famous story, summarized in *kōan form in **Wu-men-kuan* (41):

> Bodhidharma sat in *zazen facing the wall (*menpeki). The 2nd patriarch, who had been standing in the snow, cut off his arm and said, 'Your disciple's mind is not yet at peace: I beg you, my teacher, to give it peace.' Bodhidharma said, 'Bring the mind to me, and I will set it at rest.' The 2nd patriarch said, 'I have searched for the mind, and it is nowhere to be found.' Bodhidharma said, 'I have set it completely at rest for you.'

He then received six years of training, culminating in the seal of recognition (*inka-shōmei). He was driven to S. China by other Buddhist monks, and may perhaps have been assassinated by them. In addition to menpeki (wall-gazing), much emphasis was placed on the **Laṅkāvatāra-sūtra*. Hui-K'o equated it with *dharma, when he handed it to his successor at the end of his life with the words, 'The dharma that I received I now pass on to you: explain it to all people far and wide.'

Hui-kuo (Buddhist master): see KŪKAI.

Hui-neng or **Wei-lang** (Jap., E'nō; 638–713). Sixth patriarch of Ch'an/Zen in China, and dharma-successor (*hassu) of *Hung-jen. With his name is associated both a new orientation of Ch'an/Zen, and the only Chinese work to be accorded the status of a *sūtra, the *Platform Sūtra* (see LIU-TSU-TA-SHIH FA-PAO-T'AN-CH'ING). But much is legendary, and the autobiographical part of the *Platform Sūtra* (2–11) summarizes the traditions as they had accumulated in the 8th cent. According to these, he worked as a gatherer of firewood until he heard a man reciting (from the **Diamond Sūtra*), 'Let your mind flow freely without dwelling on anything', when he experienced enlightenment. The man sent him to Hung-jen, who set him to work in the kitchen. Hung-jen knew that he must find a successor, and asked the monks to write a poem summarizing Ch'an. Only Shen-hsiu responded, writing on a wall: 'The body is the *bodhi tree | The mind is a clear mirror: | At all times we must polish it | That no dust may collect on it.' Hung-jen warned Shen-hsiu that his verses showed that he had reached the gate but not entered it. Hui-neng heard the lines being recited, and being taken to the wall, he exclaimed: 'Fundamentally there is no bodhi tree | There is no stand with a clear mirror; | from the beginning not one thing exists; | To what, then, can a speck of dust cling?' Hung-jen summoned him by night and gave him the robe to mark the succession (*den'e), but sent him to S. China to avoid the jealousy of Shen-hsiu. Nevertheless, a schism developed between the Northern and the *Southern schools, with the N. emphasizing gradual progress, especially through attention to scriptures (*zengyō), and the S. emphasizing sudden enlightenment (*tongyō). Hui-neng is therefore represented in art tearing up the Sūtras. He told his disciples that his death was drawing near, and all, except Shen-hui, began to weep. He commended Shen-hui:

> You are young, but you have attained equanimity. You others have not understood: you weep because you do not know where I am going. If you knew where I was going, you would not weep. The nature itself is without birth or

death, without coming or going . . . Be the same as you would if I were here, and sit together in meditation . . . Even though I were still to be in the world, if you abandoned the teachings that I have entrusted to you, there would be no point in my presence.

P. B. Yampolsky, *The Platform Sutra of the Sixth Patriarch* (1967).

Hui Shih (4th cent. BCE). Chinese philosopher and friend of *Chuang-tzu, who taught by paradox and the unification of opposites. According to *Chuang Tzu* 33, 'Hui Shih was a man of so many ideas that his writings would fill five carts, but his teachings were contradictory, and his sayings missed the mark.' Everything is relative to something else, and thus is not absolutely great or small, etc.; but that suggests a standard of the infinitely great outside which nothing can lie, and of the infinitely small within which nothing can be contained.

Hui-tsung (1082–1135). Sung dynasty emperor in China, who strongly promoted Taoism. He encouraged the formation of the Taoist canon (*Tao-tsang) and built many monasteries. He bestowed on *Yü-huang the title *Shang-ti, god.

Hui-yuan (334–416). Buddhist monk of the early period of Chinese Buddhism. He was born into the Chia family in Yen-men (North Shansi). Although he studied the *Confucian Classics and *Taoist works in his youth, he became a disciple of *Tao-an (312–85), the most highly respected Buddhist monk of his time, at the age of 21. Sometime after he parted from Tao-an in 378, Hui-yuan took up residence on Mount Lu in S. China. Once he settled there, he never again left the mountain. In 402, he established the White Lotus School (*Pai-lien-tsung), a group of 123 monks and laymen bound together by vows to be reborn in *Amida Buddha's *Pure Land (*Sukhāvatī). This is considered the beginning of Chinese Pure Land Buddhism. Hui-yuan wrote the treatise, *Monks Do Not Pay Obeisance to Kings* (to argue for the independence of the Buddhist community from political authorities) and *San-pao-lun* (a treatise on *karma). At his invitation, Sanghadeva came from Kashmir to translate *Sarvāstivādin works into Chinese, and he corresponded with *Kumārajīva on many questions, especially related to *trikāya.

E. Zürcher, *The Buddhist Conquest of China* (1959).

Hukam (Pāñjābī, 'order' from Arab.). Sikh concept of divine order. For Gurū *Nānak and subsequent Sikh thinkers, hukam is a fundamental concept, recurring in the *Ādi Granth and prominent in the *Japjī *Sāhib, according to which nothing is exempt from God's hukam. Although it is beyond human understanding we know that it is the agent of creation, determining the physical universe and human existence—i.e. one's status, joys, and sorrows. By partial understanding of God's hukam one escapes egoism (*haumai) and achieves ultimate union with God. The hukam, God's constant self-revelation, corresponds to his word (*śabad); see also KARMA.

For Sikhs today hukam or *vāk* is the daily practice prescribed in the *Rahit Maryādā of consulting the scriptures. The Ādi Granth is opened at random and the portion appearing at the top of the left-hand page is read, if necessary from its opening on the previous page. If a *vār has been selected, the whole *paurī, including *śaloks, should be read as far as the sentence ending with 'Nānak'. In devout families, a *vāk* is read before breakfast. This is regarded as the directive for the day. Similarly in the *gurdwārā, after recitation of the Japjī and proper installation of the Ādi Granth, a *vāk* is read and may be prominently written up. Congregational worship commences with a *vāk* and always concludes with *Ardās followed by a *vāk*.

Hukamnāmā (Pañjābī, 'decree'). Historically the orders of the Sikh *Gurūs and *Bandā Siṅgh. Of the hundreds sent by the Gurūs and their families to congregations and individuals about one hundred are extant, including thirty-three dictated by Gurū *Gobind Siṅgh to scribes. Some from *Hargobind, *Har Rāi, and *Tegh Bahādur survive. These hukamnāmās are usually requests for financial, material, or military assistance, invitations to meet the Gurū at a festival, or warnings against the *masands. The hukamnāmās provide insights into the prevailing economic conditions. Such encyclicals may still be issued from *takhts enunciating a *gurmatā.

Ḥukkat ha-goi (Heb., 'custom of the *gentiles'). Idolatrous or heathen customs forbidden to Jews. Following the Leviticus 20. 23 commandment, 'You shall not walk in the customs of the nation', Jews were forbidden to follow any practices which are either idolatrous or foolish or leading to lewdness and unchastity. Thus the wearing of various kinds of clothing is regarded as ḥukkat ha-goi and many *Reform innovations, such as organ music and mixed choirs, were condemned by the *Orthodox on this basis.

Huligammā (Kannaḍa, *huli*, 'tiger', + Dravidian, *amman). One of the innumerable *grāmadevatās of S. India. One major temple of the Goddess is found in Raichur, Karṇāṭaka; it is associated with a special group of devotees—impotent or malformed men.

Humanae vitae. An encyclical written by Pope Paul VI in 1968 addressing the question of birth control, following the report of the commission set up by Paul's predecessor, John XXIII, to study the question of artificial contraception, principally the recently developed contraceptive pill. Paul recalls the serious duty of married couples to co-operate with God in the transmission of human life (§ 1). He takes note of increases in world population, of new thinking on the role of sex in marriage, and of scientific advances which have made possible artificial birth control (§ 2). He then (§ 3) mentions two reasons commonly put forward to legitimate artificial contraception. First, the sexual relations of married couples are important not only for procreation but also to express and strengthen their mutual love; the inability to engage in sexual relations because of the threat of unwanted pregnancy calls for a heroic sacrifice. Second, a couple's marriage can be understood in terms of a 'principle of totality', demanding only that they be open to new life, not each time they make love, but over the course of their fertile married life as a whole, by a planned spacing of children.

Paul begins his answer by asserting the right of the Church to pronounce on matters of natural law (§ 4); it is appeal to natural law that will form the basis of Paul's argument in the rest of the encyclical. He criticizes the findings of the commission set up by John XXIII, in which the great majority judged artificial contraception legitimate in certain circumstances (§§ 5, 6), and then sets out his own position by reference to the nature of conjugal love and of responsible parenthood.

Conjugal love is by nature (i) fully human, both of the senses and of the spirit; (ii) an unselfish sharing of life without undue reservation; (iii) faithful and exclusive until death; (iv) fulfilled in the begetting and raising of children (§ 9). From the last of these it follows that marriage requires awareness of the demands of responsible parenthood. These include (i) knowledge and respect of biological laws which are part of the human person; (ii) the dominion of reason and will over the passions; (iii) the possibility of deferring children, even indefinitely, for serious physical, economic or social reasons; (iv) recognition of God's moral order (§ 10).

On this basis Paul repeats the traditional view that 'each and every marriage act must remain open to the transmission of life' (§ 11). This is so because of the inseparable connection willed by God between the unitive and procreative aspects of the conjugal act, which not only closely unites husband and wife but also enables them to generate new life 'according to laws inscribed in the very being of man and of woman' (§ 12). People may not determine, by overriding the laws of their bodies, the beginning of human life; in this respect, as in all others, they are the ministers of God (§ 13). Hence, abortion and sterilization are inadmissible, as is any act before, during, or after intercourse designed to render it infertile (§ 14). Births may be spaced responsibly, but only in conformity with biological laws, by using the natural fertility cycle. A couple acting in this way acts according to nature, while a couple using artificial contraception acts against nature (§ 16).

The encyclical ends with an appeal to Catholics to follow and support its teaching on artificial contraception. However, its publication, while welcomed by some, was greeted with dismay and open dissent by many Roman Catholics, and its teaching on contraception has remained a matter of controversy, to the neglect of Paul's outline of the values of marriage and responsible parenthood.

Hume, David (1711–76). Philosopher, religious sceptic, historian, and leading figure of the Scottish Enlightenment. He is regarded today as one of the most important philosophers of the 18th cent., but he never held an academic post (he failed to get chairs in philosophy at the universities of Edinburgh and Glasgow), and in his own lifetime was most famous for his *History of England*. He worked as a librarian to the Faculty of Advocates in Edinburgh, but also spent some years at the British Embassy in Paris, where he encountered the French *philosophes*, and in London as an Under Secretary of State.

His most important philosophical works were: *A Treatise of Human Nature* (1739–40), *An Enquiry concerning Human Understanding* (1748), and *An Enquiry concerning the Principles of Morals* (1751). In them Hume took the empiricism of *Locke and Berkeley a stage further, reaching sceptical conclusions about the foundations of our knowledge of the external world, about inductive reasoning and rational *ethics (he pointed to the logical gap between 'is' and 'ought'), and about the existence of the self and a necessary causal nexus in nature. He attacked *metaphysics, and in general maintained that many of our fundamental assumptions cannot be justified intellectually, but rest ultimately on habit and custom.

A similar scepticism is seen in his works on religion. His *Natural History of Religion* (1757) foreshadows later anthropological accounts of religion in its investigation of the psychological and environmental factors influencing religious belief. Hume argues for the temporal priority of polytheism, which depends on fear of unknown causes and evolves towards rational *theism. But the latter is challenged in Hume's other works.

His essay 'Of Miracles' was originally written while Hume was in his early twenties, but not published until 1748 as section 10 of the first *Enquiry*. In it he argues that an appeal to *miracles cannot serve as the foundation of a religion, for it is always much more probable that our evidence for the universal and regular laws of nature will preponderate over the evidence for putative miracles, which Hume defines as violations of such laws. Thereby Hume sought to attack one strand of the conventional 18th-cent. apologetic, namely the appeal to prophecy and miracles as vouching for claimed revelations.

The other central support for such apologetics was attacked in Hume's most substantial work on religion, his *Dialogues concerning Natural Religion* (written in 1751–7, revised later, and published posthumously in 1779), much of which consists of a critique of Enlightenment *natural theology, especially the *teleological argument for the existence of God. Hume presents this argument, through its exponent Cleanthes, as an argument from *analogy; and then through another interlocutor, the sceptical Philo, attacks the drawing of the analogy, pointing to apparent *dysteleology in the universe, and suggests other explanations for the seeming order of the world. Moreover, Hume presents the problem of *evil as evidence against the claim that the world is designed. In the final *Dialogue* Philo allows that there is, after all, some force in the argument, for there *is* evidence of design in nature and it is likely that the cause or causes of order in the universe bear some remote analogy to human intelligence; but he concludes that the evidence is insufficient to support belief in a personal and benevolent deity, and therefore it cannot serve as the basis of a religion.

Thus already in the 18th cent. there is a radical questioning of the Enlightenment project of rational theism, through scepticism about natural theology and the appeal to miracles. Unlike many of the French *philosophes* of his own time, however, and also his own later followers, Hume did not claim to be an atheist, for he regarded *atheism too as going beyond the available evidence.

R. Wollheim (ed.), *Hume on Religion* (1963); J. C. A. Gaskin, *Hume's Philosophy of Religion* (2nd edn., 1988).

Ḥummash (Heb., 'five', = Gk., 'Pentateuch'). First five books of the Hebrew *Bible. For use in *synagogue, the Ḥummash is printed separately, sometimes with commentaries.

Hun. Constituent element in Chinese anthropology, one of two non-corporeal elements to make up the living human being (the other being *p'o). The two must interact harmoniously for life to continue; when they separate, death ensues.

For their destiny after death, see SHEN.

Hung-chih Cheng-chüeh (Jap., Wanshi Shōgaku; 1091–1157). Chinese Ch'an/Zen master of the *Sōtō school who clarified the distinction from *Rinzai Zen, in argument with his contemporary, Ta-hui Tsung-kao. He was the dharma-successor (*hassu) of Tan-hsia Tsu-ch'un. Where Ta-hui advocated the way of *kōan, Hung-chih valued more highly the way of silent illumination (*mo-chao ch'an*; Jap., *mokushō zen*), and responded to Ta-hui in a brilliant work of only 288 characters, *Mo-chao ming/Mokushomei*, (The Seal of Silent Illumination): silence is the mind's participation in the true nature of reality (i.e. appearance) and becomes thereby the shining illumination of what is the case. Ta-hui regarded this as idleness ('cold ashes and a withered tree'), in comparison with wrestling with kōans: 'A false Zen (*jazen*) has grown up in the forest of Zen: by confusing sickness with the remedy, they have denied the experience of enlightenment; what they have not experienced themselves they deny to others. . . . They call "peace" two meals of rice per day and sitting around without thoughts in meditation' (*Ta-hui yü-lu*). Hung-chih rejected Ta-hui's method as kōan-gazing Zen, *k'an-hua ch'an/kanna zen*, and the terms *mokushō zen* and *kanna zen* now designate the sides in this division; but the division is not absolute, and remains one of emphasis and of different understanding of the status of kōan and of *satori (enlightenment).

Hung Hsiu-ch'uan (ruler of Taiping's Heavenly Kingdom of Great Peace'): see TAIPING REBELLION.

Hung-jen (Jap., Gunin or Kōnin; 601–74). Fifth patriarch of Cha'n/Zen in China, dharma-successor (*hassu) of *Tao-hsin. Details of his life are legendary (e.g. he was accepted as a disciple through a *kōan conversation at the age of 6). He lived on Mount P'ing-jung, the East Mountain, hence his following were known as 'The Pure Gate of the East Mountain'. He did not exclude sudden enlightenment (*tongyō) but advocated progressive control of mind, especially by concentration on the figure one (Chinese character being a single horizontal line) as it merges in the horizon of perception. The One became a central concept in Ch'an/Zen, particularly in the realization by the mind of its buddhanature (*buddhatā). *Tsui-shang-ch'en lun* (Jap., *Saijōjō-ron*) is attributed to Hung-jen, but doubtfully. His successor was *Hui-neng.

Hungry ghosts (deceased who have not received appropriate or due support): see PRETA; LI-KUEI.

Huntingdon, Selina, Countess of (1707–91). Founder of the 'Countess of Huntingdon's Connexion', an association of Christian evangelicals. She lived at Donnington Park, Leicestershire, using that home and her London residences, as well as her wide influence, to promote the *Evangelical revival amongst contemporary aristocracy. Desiring to reach the upper classes, she opened chapels where the *Calvinistic preaching of her chaplains was combined with a liturgical form of worship. In 1768 she established a theological college at Trevecka, S. Wales. The Countess of Huntingdon's Connexion, formed in 1790, united her churches. In 1980, twenty-nine of these survived, with membership of 860.

Huppah (Heb., 'canopy'). Jewish marriage canopy. In the Jewish marriage service, the huppah represents the marriage chamber. In some communities, a *tallit is held as a canopy over the bride and groom. In the *Talmud, huppah is the term used for the legal domain of the man to which the woman becomes subject on her marriage.

Ḥūr, pl. **ḥawrā'** (Arab., 'white ones'). The beautiful maidens of *paradise, who are described in the *Qur'ān e.g. 2. 25, 3. 15, 4. 57, 55. 56 ff. They are often transliterated as 'houris'. Given the strong emphasis in Islam on the Goodness of all aspects of creation, it is not surprising to find the good of sexuality translated into paradise. But not all commentators (e.g. *al-Baiḍāwī) take the passages literally, and the *Sūfīs spiritualize the huris.

Ḥurban (destruction): see HOLOCAUST.

Ḥurūfī. A *Shiʿa movement founded by Fazl Allāh in the 14th cent. (8th cent. AH), later adopted by some *Bektāshīya. Their belief (summarized in *Maḥram-nāme*, AH 828) is that the universe moves in eternal cycles, from *Adam to the Day of *Judgement, with God becoming manifest through creation, especially in the human face which reflects the image of God. This manifestation is concentrated in the successive forms of prophet, saint, and (finally, in Fazl Allāh) the incarnation of God. They pay particular attention to hidden meanings in the relation between letters and numbers. Persecuted by the orthodox, one of their greatest poets, Nasimī, replied to one who was flaying him to death, and who asked why, if he was God, he grew pale as his blood drained away: 'I am the sun of love on the horizon of eternity: the sun always grows pale as it sets.'

Hus, Jan, or **John Huss** (1373–1415). Bohemian Christian Reformer. Educated at Prague University from 1390, he later taught in the Arts Faculty at the University, becoming its Rector in 1409. An ordained *priest and popular preacher, he came to accept some of *Wycliff's teachings as they were disseminated in early 15th-cent. Bohemia. The propagation of these views about reform coincided with the *Great Schism, and it was agreed to hold a Council at *Constance in 1414 to settle the controversy. The Emperor Sigismund promised Hus safe conduct and even guaranteed protection on his return journey if the charges against him were not lifted by the Council. Once in Constance, Huss was arrested and privately convicted of perpetrating Wycliffite ideas: extracts from his own *De Ecclesia* (1413) were used to accuse him of heresy. At a later public hearing he was not allowed to defend his own teaching but, charged with propagating views he did not hold, was condemned and burnt at the stake on 6 July 1415. He has remained a vital figure of Czech identity and resistance to foreign domination, especially in the 20th cent.

M. Spinka, *John Hus* (1941); *John Hus' Concept of the Church* (1966).

Husain (son of ʿAli and Imām): see AL-HUSAIN.

Huss, John: see HUS, JAN

Husserl, Edmund (philosopher): see PHENOMENOLOGY.

Hutterites (radical Reformation group): see ANABAPTISTS.

Huyan Phu So (founder): see HOA HAO.

Hwarang Do (Korean, 'The Way of Flower Youth'). An indigenous institution of young aristocrats residing in the kingdom of Silla in Korea. The Hwarang corps, founded during the reign of King Chinhŭng (540–76), was composed of aspiring leaders, schooled in civil and military virtues through their devotion to Mirŭk (*Maitreya, the future Buddha), their observance of Wŏn'gwang's 'Five Precepts for Laity', and the adoption of various *shamanic, *Taoist, and *Confucian values. Champions for the cause of the protection of the country, these men made significant political and military contributions during the critical period of Silla's nation-building.

Hyakujō Shingi (rules governing Ch'an/Zen monasteries): see PAI-CHANG-CH'ING-KUEI.

Hymn of Creation: see NĀSADĀSĪYA; COSMOLOGY (HINDU).

Hymns

Christianity The use of poetry, or metrical prose, in worship may be detected in the New Testament (e.g. Ephesians 5. 14, 19). A 3rd-cent. writer (perhaps *Hippolytus) refers to 'Psalms and odes such as from the beginning were written by believers, hymns to the Christ, the Word of God, calling him God' (*Eusebius, *History* 5. 28. 5). A few hymns survive from the pre-Nicene period, e.g. the *Phōs hilarion* ('Hail, gladdening light') still used in the Orthodox evening *office. In the 4th cent. hymns were often composed for controversial use, e.g. by *Arius and *Ephrem.

From the 5th cent. troparia (sing. *troparion*, a single-stanza hymn) are found in Greek service-books. Of these the best known are the *Cherubic Hymn and the *Monogenes* ('Only-begotten Son') sung in the eucharistic liturgy. Troparia were later joined together into the form of the kontakion, with 18–30 stanzas (e.g. the *Akathistos), and from the 7th cent. into *canons. Orthodox hymns used today are found in the various service-books; the best known Eng. trs. are by J. M. *Neale.

Latin hymns appear later than Greek. The most famous of early ones, the *Te Deum, is written in rhythmical prose. The simple and devotional hymns of *Ambrose fixed the style of Latin hymnody, and it was through his influence that hymns became a recognized part of worship in the West. Hymns were admitted into the Roman office in the 13th cent.: those of lauds, vespers, and mattins varied with the feast or season. Many ancient office hymns are now well known in translation, e.g. the *Pange lingua* ('Of the glorious body telling') and *Vexilla regis* ('The royal banners forward go'). The earliest hymns in the *mass were the *sequences.

The *Reformation affected greatly the development of hymns. Many were written by *Luther (imitating the pattern of medieval secular music), by P. *Gerhardt, and others. Since *Calvinism resisted anything but the words of *scripture in its services, the *Psalms were converted into metrical versions, of which the classical collection was the Geneva Psalter of 1563. In the *Church of England similar metrical Psalms were sung, the *New Version* of N. Tate and N. Brady (1696) surviving in use until the early 19th cent.

Modern hymn-writing and singing developed in

the 18th cent. The most important figures were the *Congregationalist Isaac *Watts, and John and Charles *Wesley, followed by P. Doddridge and W. Cowper. The practice of hymn-singing was encouraged and developed by the *Methodists, and soon spread among the Evangelical party of the Church of England.

The 19th cent. saw the establishment of hymn-singing in all parts of the Anglican church, partly under the influence of the *Oxford Movement and the translating of ancient and medieval hymns. Translations by Catherine Winkworth (1829–78) introduced a knowledge of German hymns. *Hymns Ancient and Modern* (1861) was an eclectic collection that set the pattern for most modern hymnals. In highly Protestant denominations, the progress of this eclectic trend has been slower; some hymn-books contain mostly 'gospel hymns' of the type popularized by D. L. *Moody and Ira *Sankey and collected in *Sacred Songs and Solos* (1873).

In all parts of the Roman Catholic Church there has been a surge in the use of vernacular hymns and guitar-accompanied religious songs in worship, especially since *Vatican II. The 1971 *Breviary also includes a rich and eclectic collection of hymns, some in Latin but most in English. In virtually all parts of the Church there has developed a wide use of chorus-type hymns in a modern idiom.

See also Index, Hymns.

Sikhism Sikh worship consists mainly of *kīrtan, singing the hymns comprising the *Ādi Granth. Gurū *Nānak is popularly represented singing his compositions to *Mardānā's accompaniment. See AṢṬAPADĪ; CHAUPAD; CHHANT; RĀG; RĀGĪ; ŚABAD; ŚALOK; SAVAYYE; VĀR.

Hypatia (Neo-Platonic philosopher): see CYRIL, ST.

Hypostasis (Gk.; pl. -ses). A technical term used in Christian formulations of the doctrine of the *Trinity and of *christology. In secular Gk. its most general meaning is 'substance', but it could also mean 'objective reality' as opposed to illusion (as in Aristotle), and 'basis' or 'confidence' (as in Hebrews 3. 14). In Christian writers until the 4th cent. it was also used interchangeably with *ousia*, 'being' or 'substantial reality'. The term also came to mean 'individual reality' hence 'person'. It was in this sense that it was enshrined, under the influence of the *Cappadocian fathers, in the orthodox doctrine of the Trinity as 'three hypostases in one ousia'. The word 'hypostatic' was also used by *Cyril of Alexandria to describe the union of the *Logos and flesh in Christ (hence hypostatic union), and this doctrine (although not Cyril's exact expression) was included in the definition of *Chalcedon. The *Nestorian Church however, understood the word (in Syriac translation) to mean 'nature', and continued to speak of two hypostases in Christ.

From this technical use, the term is applied to the substantiation of a metaphysical reality—e.g. the (possible) hypostasization of *Wisdom in Jewish Wisdom literature.

G. C. Stead, *Divine Substance* (1977).

I

I. A Chinese term often translated as 'righteousness'. It connotes that which is just, proper, in accord with moral and customary principles. Broader than the Eng. 'righteousness', it covers the right acts and intentions of an agent, the agent who does and intends what is right, and the duties of an agent. In meaning it is very close to a homophone which connotes ritual propriety, and it relates etymologically to the ritual sacrifice to the ancestors—those to whom one's principal duties were owed in the early tradition.

As a moral and philosophical concept, i is rooted in early *Confucian thought. For *Confucius himself, i seems to have been related to a more comprehensive value, *jen ('humanheartedness'). *Mencius placed greater stress on i, making it one of the four virtues each of which has a 'font' (*tuan*) in the heart or mind. Thus it is the presence in each person of 'the heart of shame' that, if properly cultivated, leads to the development of i. Mencius also frequently uses the compound *jen i* as a set phrase for 'morality'. *Hsün Tzu linked to the justification of hierarchical social distinctions, which he saw as necessary to a harmonious and secure social and cosmic order.

In early *Taoist thought, however, particularly in the **Chuang Tzu*, i is the condition in which all things, merely by following their nature, do the 'right' thing. 'When the Way is in all respects well ordered, we have i': 'perfect i takes no account of things' (*Chuang Tzu*). Positive rules which coerce people to behave in certain ways are not, in the Taoist way of thinking, part of i.

For early 'legalist' thinkers such as Han Fei Tzu, by contrast, i was seen as already a relic from the more harmonious past, bearing little relevance to the tumultuous realities of China in the 6th and 5th cents. BCE. Jen and i no longer suffice to order society, despite the fact that they were taught and practised by the sage kings and teachers of old; only coercion by force is effective: 'The people will bow naturally to authority, but few of them can be moved by i' (Han Fei Tzu).

These early schools of thought set the parameters for most subsequent moral and philosophical thought on i. Thus T'ang-period thinkers such as Han Yü (768–824) and Li Ao (fl. 798), in their revival of Confucian thought after a period of heavy Buddhist influence, stressed i along with jen as the essential values. And the so-called *neo-Confucian thinkers, beginning in the 11th cent., to a large extent appropriated the Mencian notion of i, specifying that it should be the sole guide of one's action no matter what one's fate.

ʿIbādāt (Arab., pl. of *ʿibāda*, 'service' or 'worship'). The rules governing worship in Islam. The singular is common in Qur'ān, e.g. 10. 29; 19. 65.

ʿIbādiy(y)a, ʿIbadites, or **ʿAbādites.** The only continuing branch of the *Kharijites, who are found particularly in Oman, and in N. and E. Africa. Their (probable) founder, ʿAbd Allāh b. ʿIbād (1st cent. AH) took a far more moderate line, not regarding non-Kharijites as *mushrikūn* (*shirk), and therefore rejecting political assassination as a weapon. Marriage with non-ʿIbādites was also allowed. It influenced other Muslim movements, of which the most enduring has been the *Wahhābīs.

The ʿIbādites are distinguished from *Sunnis by: (i) electing in secret their leaders (called *imāms), equally in contrast to *Shiʿites; several imāms may coexist, but if one were to be recognized, it would be equivalent to the Caliph (*khalīfa); (ii) believing that the *Qur'ān is created; (iii) praying with hands by the side (like Shiʿites, and also, among Sunnis, like *Mālikites).

Ibbur (Devil in Islam): see DIBBUK.

Iblīs (transmigration of souls): see DEVIL.

Ibn ʿAbd al-Wahhāb, Muḥammad (founder of conservative Muslim movement): see WAHHĀBĪYA.

Ibn (al-)ʿArabī, Muḥyi al-Dīn (1165–1240 (AH 560–638)). A great *Sūfī mystic and original thinker, called *al-shaikh al-akbar* (the Great Teacher, *Shaykh) by his followers. He profoundly influenced the development of Islamic mysticism and philosophy. He was born at Murcia in Spain and studied the Islamic sciences at Seville, where he gained fame as a leading scholar. In 1201–2 (AH 598), Ibn al-ʿArabī left Spain, never to return, and travelled from Tunis to Asia Minor, settling finally in Damascus where he died. He was generally well received, though in Egypt the *ʿulamā denounced him as a *heretic, and there was a movement to assassinate him.

Ibn al-ʿArabī synthesized Hellenic, Persian, and Indian systems of thought into his own particular system, emphasizing monistically *wahdat-al-wujūd* (Unity of Existence) and *al-Insān al-Kāmil (The Perfect Man). For him, Being is essentially one, and all phenomenal existence is a manifestation of the divine substance. For that reason he was suspected of pantheism, especially since he believed that he had the illumination of the divine light within himself, and that through this light he could see the mysteries of the Unseen. He wrote in *Tarjumān al-Ashwāq* (tr. R. A. Nicholson, repr. 1978):

> Within my heart, all forms may find a place, the cloisters of the monk, the idol's place, a pasture for gazelles, the *Kaʿba of God (to which all Muslims turn their face), the tables of the Jewish Law, the Word of God revealed to his Prophet true. Love is the faith I hold, and whereso'er His camels turn, the one true faith is there.

More than 800 works have been attributed to him, and it is claimed by some that about 400 have survived. His major works are *al-Futūḥāt al-Makkīya* (The Meccan Revelations, a complete system of mystical knowledge in 560 chapters), *Fuṣūṣ al-Hikām* (The Bezels of Wisdom, tr. R. W. J. Austin 1981, A. A. al-Tarjumana 1980), *Kitāb al-Ajwiba* (The Book of Answers), and *Tarjumān al-Ashwāq* (The Interpretation of Divine Love).

A. E. Affifi, *The Mystical Philosophy of Muhyid din-Ibnul Arabi* (1939); A. J. Arberry, *Sufism: An Account of the Mystics of Islam* (1950); W. Chittick, *The Sufi Path of Knowledge* (1989); H. Corbin, *Creative Imagination in the Sufism of Ibn ʿArabi* (1969); S. H. Nasr, *Three Muslim Sages* . . . (1964).

Ibn Adham, Ibrāhīm (Sūfī): see SŪFĪS.

Ibn al-Fāriḍ (Sūfī poet): see SŪFĪS; OMAR KHAYYAM.

Ibn Daud, Abraham ben David ha-Levi (Rabad; *c*.1110–80). Jewish philosopher, historian, and physician. Ibn Daud worked for most of his life in Toledo where he eventually died as a martyr. His most important books were *Sefer ha-Kabbalah* (The Book of *Kabbalah, G. D. Cohen, 1967), which defends Judaism throughout history against the *Karaite heresy, and *Al-ʿAqida al Rafiʿa*, tr. into Heb. as *Ha-Emunah ha-Ramah* (The Sublime Faith), which defends the doctrines of Judaism using Aristotelian modes of thinking. Both books have remained influential down to modern times. In his view, both Christianity and Islam support the truth of Judaism, while remaining themselves without assured foundation: 'The divine origin of *Torah is acknowledged by both *Jesus and *Muḥammad. It is not, therefore, incumbent on us to prove it. But the divine authority which they claim for its abrogation or change must be proved. But no proof has been given. Consequently, their claim must be rejected.'

G. D. Cohen, *Sefer ha-Qabbalah* (Eng., 1967); J. Guttmann, *Die Religionphilosophie des Abraham ibn Daud* (1879).

Ibn Ezra, Abraham (*c*.1089–1164). Jewish philosopher, poet, and biblical commentator. In his young manhood Ibn Ezra lived in Spain, but later he lived the life of a wandering scholar. Many epigrams and wise sayings are attributed to him in folk legend, and Jedaiah ha-Penini Bedersi speaks of 'the joy of the scholars of this country [France], its pious men and *rabbis when Ibn Ezra passed through their communities'. He was highly prolific and wrote both secular and religious poetry, commentaries on all the books of the Bible (those to the early prophets, Chronicles, Proverbs, Jeremiah, Ezekiel, Ezra, and Nehemiah are no longer in existence), books on Hebrew grammar, and two short works on philosophy. His life as well as his work was an inspiration to later generations. According to Joseph Delmedigo,

> This is the man, who all the days of his life, wandered around the world from the extremity of the western sea to Lucca and Egypt, Ethiopia and Elam. He had no money, not even a few coins, for he despised these all his days. He had only the garments he wore and the bag which contained his astrolabe, a stout heart and the spirit of God within him.

He may have been the model for R. Browning's 'Rabbi ben Ezra'.

M. Friedlaender, *Essays on the Writing of Abraham ibn Ezra* (1877).

Ibn Gabirol (Jewish Spanish poet): see GABIROL, SOLOMON.

Ibn Ḥanbal, Aḥmad (780–855 (AH 164–241)). The founder of a school of *sharīʿa of a highly conservative nature. He resisted the endorsement of *Muʿtazilite views and was therefore imprisoned (see MIḤNA). He was restored to favour under the caliph (*khalīfa) al-Mutawakkil. His most famous work was the *Musnad*, a vast collection of traditions edited from his lectures by his son. He did not formally establish a school of *fiqh, but laid the foundations built on by others. Rigorous against *bidʿa (innovation), his conservative theology made even fewer concessions than *al-ʿAsharī (see also HANBALITES); yet on many matters of law, he held two opinions, giving to his school a degree of flexibility, albeit within bounds.

Ibn Hasdai, Abraham ben Samuel ha-Levi (early 13th cent.). Spanish Jewish translator and poet. A staunch supporter of *Maimonides, ibn Hasdai wrote a letter in his support to the Jews of Castile, Aragon, Navarre, and Leon. He translated the work of the Muslim philosopher, *al-Ghaz(z)ālī, a work attributed to Aristotle, two texts of Maimonides, and the Arabic text **Barlaam and Joasaph*. Published as *Ben ha-Melekh ve-ha-Nazir* (The Son of the King and a Nazarite, 1518), in Ibn Hasdai's version went through many edns.

Ibn Ḥazm, Abu Muḥammad ʿAlī b. Aḥmad b. Said (994–1064 (AH 384–456)). Spanish Muslim philosopher, theologian, poet, and jurist, the chief codifier of the *Ẓāhirīya (literalist) school of law and theology. An intellectual giant, his tongue was said to be as sharp as a sword. Ibn Ḥazm is said to have written 400 works.

Born at Cordova, he lived during a period of crisis in Andalusian Islam, i.e. the collapse and disintegration of the *Umayyad political power. The turbulent nature of the times forced him to retire from political life and devote himself entirely to study and teaching. His radical non-conformity and dissatisfaction with the prevailing *Mālikite jurists, who always supported those in power, earned him popularity amongst the masses and the hatred of the ruling classes. Ibn Ḥazm's major work *Kitāb al-faṣl* (Book of the Harvest) dealt with the subject of God, his nature and attributes, freewill and predestination, faith, life after death, and the *Imamate. In addressing the gap between Islamic ideals and the evil practices of his times, Ibn Ḥazm's solution was a programme solely dependent on divine revelation, excluding everything subjective. For him, revelation is the ruler, and reason the worker; the basic need for divine guidance arises from the fact of human weakness, with its readiness to follow every temptation that appeals to the appetites, together with vanity and a mistaken sense of self-interest; this essential aspect of the human condition is illustrated in the allegory of Adam and Eve and their fall from grace. Furthermore, Ibn Ḥazm was convinced that the deviations of the theologians and jurists stemmed mainly from passions and personal preferences given legitimacy by the means of false reasoning. Moreover, he argued that without divine guidance the right way cannot be found: the *Qur'ān, therefore, and the genuine *ḥadīth must be taken as they are, literally (*ẓāhir*). For Ibn Ḥazm the only union possible with God is the union of understanding (*fahm*) and obeying his commands. The emotional consequences of life lived in *islām* (allegiance to God) were explored by him in *The Ring* [or *Necklace*] *of the Dove* (Eng. tr. A. J. Arberry).

I. Goldziher, *The Ẓāhiris* . . . (1971).

Ibn Isḥāq (author of life of Muḥammad): see MUḤAMMAD IBN ʿABD ALLAH.

Ibn Khaldūn, ʿAbd al-Raḥmān ibn Muḥammad (1332–1402 (AH 733–808)). Muslim historian and philosopher who discerned recurrent patterns in the movements of social groups in Muslim (and other) history, and who has therefore been called 'the father of sociology'. He was caught up in the turbulent vicissitudes of his time. He was born in Tunis, became a court official in Fez, and was imprisoned because of court intrigue. He moved to Granada, back to N. Africa, and eventually to Cairo. He became *Qāḍi of the *Mālikite school, and was frequently in conflict with the ruler. He was almost captured in Damascus by the army of Timur (Tamerlane). He returned to Cairo to teach at *al-Azhar, and died there, being buried (according to his contemporaries) in the *Sūfī cemetery; his grave has never been identified.

His greatest work is the *Muqaddima*, or *Prolegomenon*, to his *Kitāb al-ʿIbar* . . . (The Book of Examples and the Collection of Origins of the History of the Arabs and the Berbers). Going back to the biblical story of Cain (the hunter dwelling in space) murdering Abel (the sedentary dweller in time, who waits for the fruition of his labour, planting seeds), ibn Khaldūn discerned a constant conflict between desert and town. The nomads cannot fall into the decadence associated with towns, because the rigours of their life impose simplicity and austerity. Nevertheless, nomads periodically move towards the easier, or more predictable life on the edge of the deserts, herding sheep and goats, and beyond that, herding cattle, which demands fixed pastures. This creates an interior pressure toward the conquest of towns, bringing in a new regime. The new rulers bring with them vigour and innovation, but after three generations the first vigour is dissipated (the first generation is possessed of the vision of conquest, the second remembers the conquest and in large part participated in it, but the third knows of these things only by hearsay). The fourth generation believes that it possesses power 'as of right', as a consequence of birth: they receive all and give nothing, and thus open themselves to a new wave of conquest.

Correlated with this theory of human social forms (*ʿumrān*) emerging from the climatic and geographical conditions which support them, is a further observation about the nature of authority. As a body must be controlled by the head, which has an individual temper and character, so a society designates and accepts appropriate styles of authority, from local chieftain to king: the more powerful the king, the more isolated he becomes from his subjects, until they can perceive him only as a tyrant. As this occurs in the fourth generation of the cycle, so it creates the pressure which opens that particular rule to conquest and downfall.

Eng. tr., F. Rosenthal; Fr. tr., W. M. de Slane; A. Al-Azmeh, *Ibn Khaldūn in Modern Scholarship* (1981); M. Mahdi, *Ibn Khaldūn's Philosophy of History* (1957).

Ibn Rushd (1126–98 (AH 520–95)). Spanish Muslim theologian, philosopher, *Qur'ān scholar, natural scientist, and physician, known in the West as Averroes. He was born in Cordoba of an eminent Muslim family, and was educated in religious, legal, and medical sciences. Appointed a *qāḍi (judge) in Seville in 1169, in that capacity he also went to other towns in Islamic Spain. From 1182 he was chief physician to the ruler in Marrakesh.

He is known particularly for his commentary on Aristotle, and for other works dealing with many aspects of philosophy and theology. One concerns 'the convergence which exists between the religious law (*sharīʿa) and philosophy (*ḥikma*)'. Another work considers the problem of predestination. One of his most famous writings, *Tahāfut al-tahāfut* (The Incoherence of the Incoherence), criticizes *al-Gha(z)zālī's work, *The Incoherence of the Philosophers*, and upholds the value of philosophy as a wisdom applied to God's creation.

Among Ibn Rushd's doctrines, *Neoplatonist in origin, were the eternity and potentiality of matter (the world is eternal but caused, the *natura naturata* of God who is eternal and uncaused, *natura naturans*), and the unity of the human intellect, i.e. the doctrine that only one intellect exists in which every individual participates, to the exclusion of an isolated personal immortality. When his theories became known in N. Europe *c.*1230, the contradiction with Christian doctrine was not at first clear, and there emerged a party of 'Averroists' at the University of Paris led by Siger of Brabant (*c.*1240–*c.*1284). A treatise of Thomas *Aquinas was directed against them in 1270, and they were later accused of saying that 'things are true according to philosophy but not according to the Catholic faith, as though there were two contradictory truths', i.e. the theory of 'double truth'. Ibn Rushd's own understanding of 'double truth' was one of reconciliation. It rested on *ta'wīl, understood as producing, not two contradictory interpretations or truths, but rather the same single truth under two different styles of presentation. Religious truth is open and available to all, but in the form of *ta'wīl, it produces philosophy. It follows that there cannot be any conflict between faith and reason. See especially his *Fasl al-Maqal*, tr. G. Hourani, *Averroes, On the Harmony of Religion and Philosophy* (1961).

Trs. S. van den Bergh, G. F. Hourani, L. Gauthier, *Ibn Rochd* . . . (1948); O. Leeman, *Averroes and his Philosophy* (1988).

Ibn Sīnā, Abū 'Alī Ḥusayn (980–1037 (AH 370–429)). Muslim philosopher, scholar, theologian, physician, natural scientist, and statesman, known in the West as Avicenna. He was born in Bukhārā, of Persian origin, and from an early age studied the Qur'ān and religious sciences, then philosophy and medicine. His medical reputation was launched when, at the age of about 16, he successfully treated the Samanid ruler of Khurāsān, and was given access to his vast library. By the age of 18 he is said to have studied all that was then known in the way of natural science and philosophy and to have mastered Aristotle's metaphysics. He had a lively and somewhat disturbed career, since uncertain political conditions led him to several courts, including Hamadān and Isfahān, in search of patronage and protection. Even while exercising political functions, he continued to practise medicine and to write on science, medicine, and philosophy. He died at Hamadan, while accompanying the prince on a military expedition.

Of his large number of written works, most are in Arabic, with a few in Persian. Among his best known are works on philosophy and metaphysics, such as *Kitāb al-Shifā'* (Book of Healing, i.e. for the soul), and *Ḥayy ibn Yaqẓān*, a symbolic narrative. His belief in God as creator was combined with theories derived from *Plotinus (as conveyed in the 'theology of Aristotle'), particularly the idea of *emanation through various spheres of being. God as first cause and prime mover produces a single intelligence, which is able in turn to give rise to others; the chain of spiritual emanation extends to the tenth pure intelligence, which governs the terrestrial world of physical creation. He followed the Greek theory of the four elements (earth, air, fire, and water), each of which contains two of the natural qualities hot, cold, moist, and dry. The balance of elements is constantly being disturbed, and as each seeks to return to its original position, there arise change and movement. This Ibn Sīnā linked with the soul's search for the divine. Although he was sometimes accused by other Muslims of being an unbeliever and of contradicting Islamic teaching, Ibn Sīnā considered himself a Muslim attempting to show that philosophy was compatible with religious teachings.

His works were tr. into Latin under the name Avicenna, and had considerable influence in the later Middle Ages, e.g. on Thomas *Aquinas. Study of Avicenna's philosophy was banned for a while during the 13th cent. but again permitted by a decree of Pope Gregory IX in 1231. Ibn Sīnā's medical encyclopaedia the *Qānūn*, latinized as *Canon Medicinae*, gave rise to many commentaries, influenced the development of European medicine, and was not superseded until the arrival of modern W. medical theories and discoveries.

S. M. Afnan, *Avicenna* . . . (1958); A. J. Arberry, *Avicenna on Theology* (1951); W. E. Gohlman, *The Life of Ibn Sīnā* (tr. of Jūzjānī, 1974); S. H. Nasr, *Three Muslim Sages* . . . (1964).

Ibn Taimiy(y)a (Taymīyah), Taqī al-Din (1263–1328 (AH 661–728)). A Muslim theologian of conservative and literalistic views, who belonged to the *Ḥanbalite school, but so exceeded even them that he was considered by some heretical. Frequently imprisoned, he refused to compromise, and was an emphatic opponent of *bidʿa. He spurned taking refuge in *bilā kaif* (see ALLĀH), and once said, on descending from the pulpit of the *mosque in Damascus, 'God comes down from heaven to earth [to hear prayers] as I am coming down now.' He attacked sects, *Sūfīs, theologians (especially *al-Ghaz(z)ālī), reputations in the past and philosophy ('Does not philosophy lead to unbelief, and does it not produce the schisms that rend the heart of Islam?'). He also attacked Jews and Christians for failing to recognize that Islam has displaced those religions. His views were important in the emergence of the *Wahhābīs.

Ibn Tufayl, Abu Bakr (d. 1185 (AH 581)). Muslim philosopher and physician, known in the West as Abubacer. Born near Granada in Spain, he became *wazīr and physician to the *Almohads, introducing *ibn Rushd to the court. He developed his philosophical views in *Ḥayy ibn Yaqẓan*, (Alive, the Son of the Awake): Ḥayy represents humanity and Yaqẓan God. Ḥayy grows up on a desert island, and using his powers of observation, reason and reflection, he arrives at the truth and experience in relation to God which is usually associated with revelation. Detaching his lower soul from the world, he arrives at the mystical sense of God. However, the book accepts that for ordinary people, revelation and the structure of *sharīʿa *is* necessary to arrive at the same goal. The work was tr. into Lat. by E. Pococke in the 17th cent. (*Philosophicus Auotodidactus*) and was influential in the development of the idea of 'the noble savage' (Dryden) and of Rousseau's argument for a primitive simplicity which is corrupted by civilization. It may also have influenced Daniel Defoe's *Robinson Crusoe*.

Eng. tr. L. E. Goodman (1970, 1983).

Ibn Tumart (1077–1130 (AH 470–524)). A Muslim reformer in Morocco who was known as *al-Mahdī of the *Almohads. He grew up under the Almoravids who followed the *Mālikite understanding of *fiqh, in which reason is subordinate—a position contested by *al-Ghaz(z)ālī, whose works were burnt by the rulers. As ibn Tumart travelled in Spain, he came under the influence of the writings of *ibn Ḥazm; when he travelled east, he was comparably influenced by al-Ghaz(z)ālī. Returning home, he set about reform, especially of morals, 'by the hand [i.e. force] if possible; if not, by the tongue; and if not that, in the heart'. Opposition to this interference caused him to flee (to a Berber tribe) and then return—a recurrent pattern in his life. He was prepared to preach *jihād even against other Muslims, if their lax behaviour constituted, in effect, an attack on Islam. Gathering increasing personal authority to himself, he identified himself as al-Mahdi, calling his followers al-Muwaḥḥidūn (the Unitarians), hence the name Almohads.

Ibrāhīm: see ABRAHAM (ISLAM).

Ibrāhīm b. Adham (d. 777 (AH 160)). Born at Balkh in Central Asia into a royal family, he renounced his princely life after hearing a divine voice whilst out hunting, telling him, 'It is not for this that you were created.' From then on he became an ascetic and lived by the work of his hands. He became recognized as a great mystic. His views on meditation (*muraqaba*) and gnosis (*maʿrifa*) influenced the later *Sūfīs: 'Those who aspire to spiritual things are willing to stake both body and soul in the search for them, and they spend their years consumed by their love of God. The bird of their ambition has attained to fellowship with him; it has soared beyond temporal and spiritual things alike.' It is said that one of the three occasions of real happiness for him was when he looked at a fur cloak he was wearing and could not distinguish fur from lice, so numerous were the latter: 'Poverty is treasure which God keeps with him in heaven, and gives it only to those whom he loves.'

Iccā-mṛtyu (Skt., 'desired-death'). The Hindu ability to yield up life at a designated moment, not by suicide, but by concentration.

Ich'adon, also known as **Pak Yŏmch'ŏk, Yŏmch'ŏk,** or **Kŏch'adon** (503–27). A martyr during King Pŏphŭng's reign (514–40) in the kingdom of Silla, in Korea. When the king's desire to establish and propagate Buddhism was thwarted due to ministerial opposition, Ich'adon, the Grand Secretary to the king, offered to be executed in the hope that, by witnessing miraculous phenomena resulting from his death, the ministers might be persuaded to look favourably upon the disfavoured religion. Ich'adon's martyrdom did, in fact, immediately bring about Silla's official recognition of Buddhism, dated 527.

Ichien, also known as **Dōkyō,** or **Muju** (1226–1312). Japanese Zen monk of the *Rinzai school. He was primarily a student of *Ben'en, but he studied under several masters, and eventually produced an anthology of Buddhist stories, still used in training, *Shaseki-shu* (Collection of Sand and Stone).

Ichi-ensō (symbol in Zen Buddhism): see ENSŌ.

Ichigū o terasu undō (movement): see TENDAI SHŪ.

Ichiji-fusetsu (Jap., 'not a word said'). Zen term summarizing the fact that no teacher (including the *Buddha) has used a single word to describe ultimate truth or reality, since it is indescribable. For the elaboration of this, see FUKASETSU.

Ichiji-kan (Jap., 'one word barrier'). The culminating point (*wato) of a Zen *kōan when it consists in a single word.

Ichijitsu Shintō (one-truth Shintō): see TENDAI SHŪ.

Ichiji-Zen (Jap., 'one word Zen'). The use of a single word from a Zen teacher as a *kōan; cf. ICHIJI-KAN.

Ichimi-shabyo (Jap., 'one taste from bowl'). The authentic transmission of the buddha-dharma in Zen, from a master to his dharma-successor (*hassu).

Ichimi-Zen (Jap., 'one taste Zen'). The authentic Zen of the Buddha and the patriarchs (*soshigata), which consists in the experience of no distinction ('one taste') between form and emptiness. Its opposite (within Zen) is zen which relies on different types or goals of meditation (*five ways of Ch'an/Zen), known as *gomi (-no)-zen*.

Ichinen (Jap., 'one thought'). The instant moment of one thought in Zen, hence the exclusive 'thought' (i.e. without content) of true concentration. From this, it was applied to one recitation of the *nembutsu, and to unwavering and complete faith in *Amida.

Ichinen-fushō (Jap., 'a thought not arising'). The state of mind in Zen in which no distracting or wayward thought arises. It is attained through *zazen, and it is the 'mind' of a buddha.

Ichinen-mannen (Jap., 'one moment of *nen*, ten thousand years'). A summary of the Zen view that, in enlightenment, numerical sequences of endurance are irrelevant: if one is in a state of absolute enlightenment or bliss, it cannot be calculated whether it lasts a second or ten thousand (or more) years.

I-Ching (Jap., Gijō; 635–713). Chinese Buddhist monk and traveller. He entered the religious life when young, and travelled to India in 671. His journey took him through more than thirty countries, and he returned in 695 with relics and images, and also with texts which he set about translating, completing fifty-six works before he died. He also wrote a record of his travels, *Nankai-kiki-den*. He was given the title of *sanzō* (*san-tsang*), one well-versed in Buddhist teaching.

I Ching or ***Yi Ching*** (Scripture of Change(s)). One of the three pre-*Confucian Classics. Several ancient sages are supposed to have contributed to its complex structure, included the mythological culture-hero Fu Hsi, the founding ancestors of the Chou dynasty (?1111–256 BCE), and *Confucius. It seems originally to have been a diviners' manual, built on the symbolisms of eight trigrams (each composed of broken and unbroken lines, standing respectively for *yin and yang). These trigrams were later expanded to give sixty-four hexagrams. Each diagram was interpreted as a whole, and the component lines were also interpreted. Confucius is supposed to have added commentary, called the Ten Wings, which gave philosophical depth to the work. Although the devoted labour of many of China's most intelligent scholars throughout the centuries has failed to clarify the work in all its details, it has nevertheless been of the greatest influence upon Chinese thought.

Trs., J. Blofeld (1965), J. Legge (1899), R. Wilhelm (1950); see also H. Wilhelm, *Change: Eight Lectures on the I Ching* (1960).

Ichthus (Gk., 'fish'). An early emblem of Christianity, since the Gk. letters form the acronym of 'Jesus Christ, God [*theos*] and Saviour [*sōtēr*]'.

I-ch'uan (neo-Confucianist of the Sung dynasty): see CH'ENG HAO.

Icon (Gk., *eikon*, 'image' or 'picture'). Sacred pictures of the *Orthodox tradition. They are usually flat pictures, and painted in egg tempera on wood; but metal, ivory, and other materials may be used, and bas-relief and even high-relief icons are known, especially in Russia. They are used to decorate churches, where they are found on walls, ceilings, and stands (the *iconostasis separating the sanctuary from the nave being particularly prominent), and portable icons are used in private devotions. They depict *Christ, and the saints and mysteries of the Church: the scenes usually relate to liturgical celebration, rather than to historical events, though monasteries have icons of the legends of their foundation. The symbolism of the icon is held to effect the presence of the saint or mystery depicted, and in that presence prayer and devotion are made. The icon has been defined as 're-presenting that which it represents'. Candles are burnt before icons; they are venerated by kissing and prostration. Frequently they are held to have miraculous powers, and some to be of miraculous origin: to have been 'made without hands' (*acheiropoiētos*), or to have been miraculously transported from afar. The painting (or 'writing') of the icon is itself a religious act, prepared for by prayer and fasting, and was usually reserved for monks: such was Andrei Rublev (*c*.1370–*c*.1430), the greatest of all icon-painters. Suspicion of icons as idols led to *iconoclasm.

The word 'icon' also appears as a technical term in semiotics, with a transferred use: see SYMBOLS.

H. Brenske, *Icons* . . . (1990); P. Evdokimov, *L'Art de l'icône* (1970); G. Matthew, *Byzantine Aesthetics* (1963); L. Ouspensky, *Theology of the Icon* (1978) and *The Meaning of Icons* (1969); L. Ouspensky and V. Lossky, *The Meaning of Icons* (1982); D. and T. T. Rice, *Icons and their History* (1974).

Iconoclasm (Gk., 'image-breaking'). A movement which agitated the Church in the E. Roman Empire, *c*.725–843. The veneration of *icons had attracted an undercurrent of opposition for centuries (as early as *Epiphanius), but in the wake of a renewed Arab threat to Asia Minor it was widely blamed, especially in the army, for the weakness of the Christian empire. The opposition to icons was taken up by the emperors Leo III (717–41) and Constantine V (741–75). The latter convened a synod at Hieria in 753 at which the image-worshippers ('iconodules') were identified with *christological heretics, and all images of the saints were ordered to be destroyed as idols. A fierce persecution, especially of monks, ensued. Under the empress Irene (from 780), however, the position was reversed: at the seventh *ecumenical council at Nicaea in 787 the veneration of icons was officially reintroduced and the degree of veneration to be paid to them was defined.

After a politically unsettled period the new emperor Leo V (813–20) reasoned that iconoclasm ought to be reinstated. The policy was quickly made official and continued under his successors until 842. *Theodore of Studios, the foremost defender of images among the monks, was exiled, but persecution was in general less severe in this second phase of the controversy. An iconophile patriarch, Methodios, was elected in 843, and a great feast (since kept as the Feast of Orthodoxy) was celebrated on the first Sunday of Lent to mark the victory of the icons.

The *Armenian Church is unusual in having maintained a rejection of icons throughout its history, though paintings of Christ, the saints, and the mysteries of the Church do decorate their church buildings.

Iconoclasm then becomes a general word for opposition to, and destruction of, visible representations of the divine, and, more colloquially, for the destruction of that which is traditionally revered.

A. Bryer and J. Merrin (eds.), *Iconoclasm* . . . (1977); A. Graber, *L'Iconoclasme byzantin* (1984).

Iconography (Gk., *eikon*, 'image', + *graphe*, 'writing'). The study of the representation of otherwise unseen realities through coded means: such realities may include anything from God or gods to ideas; and the means may include statues, pictures, buildings, charms, or indeed anything which can hold the 'charge' of such representation. Iconography is typically concerned with identifying the codes which control such utterances into their characteristic outcomes. Since religions have differing attitudes to the representation of the holy or the divine, each religion has a different iconographical style and content. See further ART; and also Index, Iconography.

Judaism Jewish iconography is dominated by the prohibition on idols. While recurrent symbols occur in *Torah and *synagogue decoration, they are mainly to be found in manuscripts—and even there, iconography in Hebrew manuscripts is primarily restricted to Christian Europe—there is little from Muslim countries. *Haggadah manuscripts are illustrated with biblical and *aggadic scenes as well as pictures of ceremonial detail. Illustrations can also be found in *maḥzor and *siddur* manuscripts. The artwork is similar to medieval Christian iconography and varies according to community of origin.

Christianity The earliest Christian art was influenced by late Hellenistic realism, while in theme it was largely symbolic: *Christ represented by a fish (see ICHTHUS), or a young shepherd, etc. From the 4th cent., Christian art was influenced by Neoplatonic aesthetics which saw art as disclosing a higher, spiritual realm, and the highly conscious symbolism characteristic of *icons developed. Already one can detect a difference of emphasis between East and West, the E. stressing the liturgical function of the icon, while the W. saw images as pictorial illustrations of biblical events and religious doctrines. Even in the 4th cent., with Eusebius of Caesarea and others, there was resistance to the use of images. This came to a head in the 8th and 9th cents. with the *Iconoclastic Controversy, when, for a time, icons were banned by imperial authority and most were destroyed. The victory over *iconoclasm set the seal in the E. on the religious value of icons. In the W., partly under the influence of a growing devotion to Christ's sacred humanity, a more realistic, less symbolic style of painting developed from the 12th cent., about the same time as the symbolic use of form and colour reached its apogee in the stained glass of, e.g., Chartres Cathedral. The development of art in the W. has broken any *tradition* of Christian iconography: W. religious artists combine an arbitrary dependence on current artistic techniques with personally adopted symbolic schemes. As with other religions, Christianity also developed elaborate codes associated with events (e.g. *baptism, *crucifixion, *resurrection, etc.) and people, esp. *saints.

Islam See CALLIGRAPHY.

Hinduism Of all religions, Hinduism is the richest and most complex in its iconographical materials. Its strong sense of *Brahman, not simply underlying and guaranteeing all appearance, but actually pervading, and able to become focally manifest, in all appearance, means that any object can be charged with the divine. To make an image, therefore, is to bring the divine into that image—equally, the image may become 'dead' when the particular concentration of the divine is withdrawn from it at the end of the act of *pūjā (worship). Iconography is therefore a matter of interaction and of the means to its achievement. The most important *locus* of the interaction is the *mūrti (lit., 'embodiment', hence 'image'). Images are made in a bewildering number of different materials and styles, with a seemingly unending number of figures and postures. Yet in fact the designs and the ways in which the mūrtis are to be made are carefully detailed, both in texts and in the traditions of the craftsmen who make them—see especially Viśvakarman's *Viśvakarma Vāstuśāstra*, ed. V. K. Sastri and N. B. Gadre (1958) and S. Kramisch, *Indian Sculpture* (1933); and the postures carry meaning with extremely little redundancy, since the underlying sense of presence *is* the message to be conveyed.

Buddhism Early Buddhist icons are by no means as prolific as those of Hindus: the Buddha had pointed away from relying on outside help (e.g. gods), and he himself had attained *nirvāna, and is therefore not available to help directly. Nevertheless, the centrality of the Buddha in leaving guidance evoked icons of recognition (e.g. images of the Buddha in the attainment of enlightenment, often with the thirty-two marks of a Buddha *dvātriṃśadvaralakṣana) or of grateful remembrance (somewhat like having the photo of a loved one who has died: the *person* may no longer be in a position to help directly, but the image renews action through memory). *Stūpas are iconographic representations of Buddhist truth in this way. However, in Mahāyāna Buddhism (with the possible exception of Ch'an/Zen), the strong sense of the buddha-nature being present in all things (indeed, being all that there is of all things) led to developments comparable to those in Hinduism, but with utterly different purpose: in an interaction with images, the possibility of realizing the buddha-nature, not just in the image, but in (or as) oneself is enhanced. The connection is made in contemplation and in the chanting of *mantras. But in Mahāyāna, one is surrounded by a vast host of buddhas and *bodhisattvas, who are, so to speak, 'here' in order to assist those who reverence them. Each of these has an elaborate set of images and symbols, which reach a supreme height in Tibet.

Tibetan Religion Up to the 14th cent. CE., Tibetan iconography was primarily influenced by the developed Buddhist art forms of India (Bengal, Bihar, Kaśmir), Central Asia (Khotan), Nepal, and China, by which point—although regional developments continued—a synthesis of these influences was essentially sealed within a marked individuality, since preserved by strictly prescribed methodologies contained in the Tibetan canon. The reason for such concern over the precision of their iconographic expression is that all art, for the Tibetans, is not simply religiously aesthetic but also religiously functional, in the twin contexts of external ritual and of inner meditative practice.

In Tibetan painting (*ri.mo*), which is invariably of deities, holy people, and *maṇḍalas, and executed on scrolls, walls, stone, wood, and manuscripts, the outer purpose of the painting may be to lend the influence of the deity to the area of its presence; but privately it serves as a basis for a *yogin's *visualization. The execution of a painting is itself an act of meditation, which usually begins with the initiation of the artist by the *lama into the power of the deity. When the product is for the *Tantric meditation of one or a few people, the artist will work with the lama in secret using secret texts, and the yogin receiving the finished product is bound not to reveal it to any other person.

The most common form of Tibetan painting is the scroll (*thang.ka*) of cotton or silk, with cloth borders sewn around and covering flaps for protection. *Thangkas* are rectangular and generally a little over 1 m. in length, although for public display at festivals when hung from monastery walls they may be 20 m. *Thangkas* normally present a central deity surrounded by associated deities, or a holy person surrounded by other members of his lineage, creating a very rich effect. Figures represented are instantly identifiable by their particular colours, gestures, and symbols, which are altered only when an alternative aspect of that figure is intended. Although a gifted artist may be able to develop new styles, in the main, individuality of expression is simply not the purpose of Tibetan iconography, and is evidenced only in the subtleties of facial expression, or the more liberal frescos showing scenes from the lives of holy people. A result of this emphasis on symbolic precision is the boldness of primary colours, with no intention (or need) to depict mood through shades.

Tibetan statues, although their purpose is more for use on shrines than as bases for meditation, conform to the same strict modes of representation. Stonework, despite the ubiquity of material, is rare, though rock carvings are found, especially at places of danger (mountain paths, bridges, etc.); copper, bronze, and brass are much preferred, and are made by the 'lost wax' method, while statues of special value may be cast from eight metals (*aṣṭadhātu*) after the Indian practice. The practice of repeatedly gilding a *stūpa or statue for merit, found in Buddhist SE Asia, does not seem to have been common in Tibet: faces of statues are occasionally gilded; the hair of protective deities (*mGon.po*) is sometimes tinged red, as may be the lips of peaceful deities, whose hair may also be painted blue. Statues of *Mañjuśrī, *Avalokiteśvara, and *Tārā will be among those found in any shrine, where an image of Śākyamuni will always occupy the central position.

Sikhism Although Sikh *gurdwārās are much plainer than most Hindu *mandirs, pictures of Gurūs *Nānak and *Gobind Siṅgh feature prominently. Gurū Nānak is typically depicted as radiant, white-bearded, and turbaned, gazing in benediction. He may be attended by *Bālā Sandhū and *Mardānā. Gurū Gobind Siṅgh is usually mounted, holding a hawk and armed. Gurū Hargobind carries a bow and arrows. Sometimes all ten Gurūs are portrayed in a single picture, illustrating their essential unity. Individual Gurūs and scenes from Sikh history (e.g. the martyrdom of *Arjan Dev) are often shown. Less prominently displayed are pictures of other śahīds' *martyrdoms. A picture of *Harimandir Sāhib, *Amritsar, is popular and to be seen in many Sikh houses, as are paper calendar pictures of the Gurūs. Colours are bright and style unsophisticated. Earlier Indian gurdwārā decoration (i.e. *jaṛatkārī* or marble inlaid with coloured stones; 'gach' or gypsum designs covered with gold leaf; 'tukṛī' or coloured glass mirrors and stones inlaid in 'gach'; and frescos) are giving way to contemporary décor, marble with mirrorwork decoration.

T. P. van Baaren, *Iconography of Religions* (1970–); J. Banerjea, *The Development of Hindu Iconography* (2nd edn., 1956); L. Chandra, *Buddhist Iconography* (3rd edn., 1987); J. E. Cirlot, *A Dictionary of Symbols* (1972); A. N. Didron, *Christian Iconography . . . in the Middle Ages* (1851–86); M. H. Farbridge, *Studies in Biblical and Semitic Symbolism* (1923); G. Ferguson, *Signs and Symbols in Christian Art* (1954); A. Foucher, *L'Art greco-bouddhique du Gandhāra* (1905–23); A. Grabar, *Christian Iconography . . .* (1980); J. Hall, *Dictionary of Subjects and Symbols in Art* (1974); G. Hermeren, *Representation and Meaning in the Visual Arts* (1969); H. G. Kippenberg, *Visible Religion: Annual for Religious Iconography* (1982–); E. Kirschbaum and W. Braunfels (eds.), *Lexicon der christlichen Ikonographie* (1968–76); S. Kramisch, *The Hindu Temple* (1946); J. Leveen, *Hebrew Bible in Art* (1944); G. Liebert, *Iconographic Dictionary of Indian Religions* (1976); W. H. McLeod, *Popular Sikh Art* (1991); A. C. Moore, *The Iconography of Religions* (1977); T. A. G. Rao, *Elements of Hindu Iconography* (1914–16; 1968); C. Sivaramamurti, *The Art of India* (1977); D. L. Snellgrove (ed.), *The Image of the Buddha* (1978).

Iconostasis or **Eikonostasion** (Gk., 'a picture stand'). The screen in Eastern-rite churches separating sanctuary from nave. Since the 14th or 15th cents. the screen has been a wall of wood (a Russian innovation) or stone covered with *icons, which follow a prescribed arrangement. Through it are three doors, the central or Royal Door admitting to the altar, and those on the right and left respectively to the *diakonicon* (deacon's area) and *prothesis. The iconostasis conceals part of the liturgy from the view of the congregation.

Icons: see ICON.

ʿĪd (Arab., from Aram./Syriac, 'festival, holiday'). In Islam, feast or *festival. There are two main feasts, *ʿĪd al-Aḍḥā, the feast of *sacrifice, based on a part of the ceremonies of the *ḥajj; and *ʿĪd al-Fiṭr, the feast of the breaking of the fast (of *Ramaḍān). In each case the actual celebrations may extend over two or three days. The *ṣalāt for these two feasts takes a special form, and contains a *khuṭba, sermon.

Iḍā (Skt.). 1. Sacrificial food or libation in Hinduism. After the Flood, of which Manu was the only survivor, he collected from the waters butter, milk, whey, and curds, together called iḍā, which were then personified as his daughter (*Śatapata Brāhmaṇa* 1. 8. 1. 1 ff.) She asked Manu to allow her to assist at the sacrifices, since when she has been the mediator of benefits accruing through sacrifices.

2. One of the channels of subtle energy (*nāḍī) in the Hindu understanding of the body, which distributes the life-sustaining force (*prāṇa) throughout the body.

ʿĪd al-Aḍḥā, ʿĪd al-Qurbān or **al-ʿĪd al-Kabīr** (feast of the *sacrifice or the great feast). Muslim sacrifice of an animal—camel, sheep, or goat—forms part of the ceremony of *ḥajj, pilgrimage, and is carried out at Minā, near *Mecca, on the tenth day of *Dhū'l-Ḥijja. Muslims all over the world sacrifice an animal on this day, a ceremony which is intended to commemorate the sacrifice of Ibrāhīm (*Abraham). Generally part of the meat is eaten by the persons making the sacrifice, and part is given to the poor.

ʿĪd al-Fiṭr or **al-ʿĪd al-ṣaghīr** (the small feast). Feast of the breaking of the fast (of *Ramaḍān), second in importance to *ʿĪd al-Aḍḥā. It is celebrated on the first two or three days of Shawwāl, the month following Ramaḍān.

Iḍā-pātra (Skt.). The vessel used in Hinduism for the *iḍā offering. It is placed at the head of a corpse when the body and the sacrificial implements of the dead person are cremated.

'Idda (waiting period in relation to divorce): see MARRIAGE (ISLAM).

Iddhi, ṛddhi (Pāli, Skt.: *ardh*, 'grow', 'increase', 'prosper', 'succeed'). Paranormal, psychic, or magic power in Buddhism, where it is one of the six kinds of higher knowledge (*abhiññā). Canonical writings contain a standard list of eight forms of iddhi: the power to (i) replicate and project bodily-images of oneself, (ii) make oneself invisible, (iii) pass through solid objects, (iv) sink into solid ground, (v) walk on water, (vi) fly, (vii) touch the sun and moon with one's hand, (viii) ascend to the world of the god *Brahmā in the highest heavens. They are described in e.g. **Vissudhimagga* 12. These powers were said to become available to the meditator upon achieving the fourth *jhāna. They were possessed by the *Buddha and many of his monks and nuns. However, the Buddha regarded them equivocally because some non-Buddhist ascetics possessed them too; they were a sign of meditational attainment only, and not a spiritual qualification; and they could be put to bad as well as good use (see PĀṬIHĀRIYA). He, therefore, attempted to lessen their importance by making it an offence for monks or nuns to display them before the layfolk, and by providing an alternative interpretation of iddhi to mean the application of equanimity (*upekkhā) and mindfulness (*sati) in the face of all situations. Nevertheless, in *Vajrayāna they are prominent as a demonstration of perfect control over the body.

Iddhi-pāda (Pāli, 'ways of power'; Skt., *ṛddhipāda*). In Buddhism, the four components of concentrated power which result in supernatural powers (*iddhi), and bring about *samādhi (absorption in the object of contemplation): (i) intention (*canda*); (ii) will (*virya); (iii) mind (*cit); (iv) audacity in inquiry (*mīmāṃsā*). See also BODHIPĀKṢIKA-DHARMA.

Idealism (Buddhist school of): see VIJÑĀNAVĀDA.

Ideal type. A key concept and strategy in the study of religions, introduced by M. *Weber. Because of the complex and fluid nature of social (and thus of religious) phenomena, Weber realized that observations of actual instances have to be described through the isolation of characteristic features: examples are 'economic man', 'marginal man', *'sect', *'church', 'Gemeinschaft' (a group in which social bonds are based on close personal ties of kinship and friendship), 'Gesellschaft' (secondary relationships prevail, i.e. of a formal, contractual, specialized, impersonal, or expedient kind). Weber insisted that ideal types are never found in pure, uncontaminated form; in other words, ideal types differ from the way in which a particular cat is a type of cat (there are many cats, but each one exemplifies the type of cats, or is typically a cat). Ideal types are never found in reality: they are a methodological way of drawing attention to salient and differentiating characteristics. Thus Weber drew up a typology of action, according to which one type of action is more highly valued in the unfolding stages of social history: traditional, affectual (emotional), value-rational, and purpose-rational. The first two belong to pre-rational (i.e. pre-modern) societies, but Weber was careful to point out that all four appear in any society in any age, including the pre-rational in his own society.

Ideology. The organization of ideas and related practices into a more-or-less coherent belief-system, carrying with it commitment. Although the term was first used by Destutt de Tracy in 1796 to apply to the study of the way in which ideas are related to their base in sensations, it has come to refer to belief-systems which aim to achieve goals, justifying particular actions or policies on the way and vigorously excluding others. 'Ideology' is most naturally understood of a political system, e.g. Fascism, totalitarianism, Maoism. Although the definition lends itself most naturally to such religious organizations as *Vatican Catholicism, it is nevertheless an issue whether religions can rightly be thought of as ideologies. To Marx and Engels it was obvious that they can, and that in fact they supply the prime example of their understanding of ideology. For them, ideology is a system of ideas, which purports to be objective, but which reflects the unequal class structure and which (embodying 'false consciousness') is used to perpetuate the interests of the dominant class. Religions have been, historically, such ideologies. However, subsequent analysis (in the Marxian tradition) has drawn attention to the repeated ways in which religions have been the ideology of the oppressed and have been the motivation for revolution and change. In common to both positions is the belief that ideology serves interests. Not surprisingly, therefore, the term more recently has been reserved pejoratively for monopolistic and prescriptive belief-systems of such a kind that rational argument or dissent is precluded—of which, by a neat inversion, Marxism is taken to be a key example; and these have been *contrasted* with other belief and value systems which are open to pluralism, discussion, and dissent—including therefore religions where this obtains. The complexity, therefore, of using 'ideology' in the discussion of religious systems is that the term is contested; and that in any case most world religions exhibit both ideology and its opposite. Thus *Vatican II moved Roman Catholicism away from ideology in its pejorative senses; but the Vatican under Pope *John Paul II has made consistent efforts to take it back; some Roman Catholics support those efforts, but a great many do not. Thus it is impossible to generalize about a religion using a blanket term like 'ideology'. However, it may prove possible to analyse religions helpfully in terms of exactly this contest, for the realization of ideology and of resistance to it.

Far more loosely, ideology is used simply as a substitute for 'world-view', and in that general sense religions as ideologies are sometimes discussed in relation to *secularization—with secularization taken to be a contesting world-view. Popular though that usage is, it lacks rigour in dealing with the actual processes of change in belief-systems.

D. Apter (ed.), *Ideology and Discontent* (1964); M. Seliger, *Ideology and Politics* (1976).

Idiorrhythmic. Following the pattern of one's own life: monastic communities, especially on Mount *Athos, where the monks pursue separate lives, meeting for *offices and perhaps for communal meals on great feast days. Idiorrhythmic *skete is a community of cells or apartments (*kalyba*) gathered round a church (*kyriakon*). In each apartment there may be 'two or three gathered together', who elect a superior to the whole community.

Idolatry (Gk., *eidolon*, 'image', + *latreia*, 'worship'). The attributing of absolute value to that which is not absolute, and acting towards that object, person, or concept as though it is worthy of worship or complete commitment. In a religious context, this most usually means treating as God that which is not God; and in particular acting towards a representation of God as though it *is* God. Thus idolatry is associated with the worship of idols, as though these are the actuality of God. In that sense, idolatry is extremely rare, since most religious worshippers are well-aware that the signpost is not to be confused with that which is signified. The hymn which laments that 'the heathen in his blindness | Bows down to wood and stone' misses the point which is constantly exemplified in Hinduism: images of God bring the power and the presence of God into relation with the worshipper, but at the end of the act of worship, they do not have the same presence at all; indeed, in Indian villages, clay images will be discarded casually after their use in ritual. Nevertheless, strongly monotheistic religions have suspected that practice does not always live up to theory, and that idols are being regarded as God in reality. Thus biblical Judaism is unequivocally opposed to idol worship as is evidenced by the *Ten Commandments (Exodus 20). None the less, the ancient Israelites engaged in such idolatrous practices as the cults of *Baʿal and *Asherah which evoked the hostility of the *prophets (e.g. 1 Kings 18). Despite the purges of King Hezekiah and *Josiah, idol-worship persisted, including apparently child sacrifice to Moloch (2 Kings 16. 3), sacred prostitution (Ezekiel 16. 17), and astral worship (Amos 5. 26). *Rabbinic law deals with prohibitions concerning contact with an idolator (*Avodah Zarah*, passim). There can be no economic transactions before a pagan holiday, to preserve the Jew from any possible contact with a forbidden festival; no house or land in *Erez Israel may be sold or leased to an idolator; and no Jew may share food or wine with a worshipper of idols.

Islam is comparably opposed to idols (Arab., *wathan*, pl., *wuthun*; *sanam*, *asnam*), which must necessarily detract from the absolute supremacy and oneness of God. In pre-Islamic Arabia, the proliferation of images of the divine was immense. *Muḥammad's profound sense, derived from his experience in the Cave on Mount *Ḥirāʾ, that if there *is* God, there can only be what God is, made him particularly passionate against idolatry. The potential for conflict in India is alleviated only by the Muslim consideration that the final judgement on idolaters will lead to their just reward after death.

M. Halbertal and A. Margalit, *Idolatry* (1992).

Idrīs (Muslim Enoch): see ENOCH.

Iglesia ni Cristo (Tagalog, 'Church of Christ'). The largest *Protestant church in the Philippines, founded in 1914 by Felix Manalo (1886–1963), the 'angel from the East' of Revelations 7. 12, sent to restore the true church among the chosen Filipino people. Based on a literal reading of the Bible, *unitarian in christology, and highly polemical in relation to other churches, it uses Filipino language and music, and has beautiful churches all over the Philippines combining Buddhist and *Gothic motifs. A strong central organization, under Manalo's son, Erano, controls some half-million members, enjoys great wealth, and used its block vote to support ex-President Marcos. It has expanded into other parts of the world since 1968 through Filipino migrant workers, and some secessions at home have moved towards *trinitarian orthodoxy.

Iglesia popular ('church arising from the people'): see LIBERATION THEOLOGY.

Ignatian spirituality: see IGNATIUS (OF) LOYOLA.

Ignatius, St (d. *c.*107). Bishop of *Antioch. Nothing is known of his life beyond his journey under guard across Asia Minor to Rome to be martyred. He was received along the way by representatives of five local churches (Ephesus, Magnesia, Tralles, Philadelphia, Smyrna), and sent a letter back to each. These five letters, with one to the church at Rome and one to *Polycarp, were early collected and venerated (and other spurious letters added to them). The letters witness to the emergence of the office of *bishop, to which Ignatius was passionately committed as the best safeguard of the unity of the *Church: 'The Church is a choir and the bishop presides at her concerts which, like the concerts in heaven, cease not day or night. . . . Priests and people are joined to the bishop like the strings of a lyre to its frame, and so, in perfect union of thought and charity, a concert of praise goes up.' In this stress on the bishop as the centre of unity, he perhaps saw the danger as posed by one or more parties who practised Judaism and held *docetic views of *Christ. The letter to the Romans also shows Ignatius's ardent desire for *martyrdom. Feast day, 17 Oct. or 17 Dec. (W.); 20 Dec. (E.).

Trs., many (usually in collections of, e.g. *apostolic fathers).

Ignatius (of) Loyola (1491)/1495–1556). Founder of the Society of Jesus (*Jesuits). Born of a noble family, he became a soldier and was wounded during the siege of Pampeluna (1521). During a prolonged convalescence he read Ludolf of Saxony's *Life of Christ* and various lives of the saints which led him to abandon his military career. Upon recovery he went to Montserrat, made his confession, hung up his sword before a statue of the Blessed Virgin Mary, and exchanged clothes with a beggar. There followed a year (1522–3) of prayer and mortification at Manresa, the fruit of which profound experience is manifest in his *Spiritual Exercises*, probably written there. He then went on pilgrimage to the Holy Land, via Rome, and on his return studied for eleven years, first in Spain, then in Paris. In 1534, he and six companions (including *Francis Xavier) took religious vows. In 1540 the Society of Jesus was formally established, with Ignatius its first general. Unable to go to the Holy Land as originally intended, they offered their services to the pope and became a missionary order, preaching in India and the Far East, and the spearhead of the Counter-Reformation in Europe. The Ignatian way in prayer, based on the *Exercises*, moves religion from the head to the heart, in absolute devotion to God: 'Take, Lord, and keep, all my freedom, my memory, my understanding, and all my will, whatever I have and possess. You gave them to me, and I restore them to you . . . Give me your love and your grace: that is enough for me.' The *Exercises* are based on a dialogue between the person undertaking them and God, prompted by exchange with a director, the text of scripture, and the 'signs of the times'. They are divided into four weeks, which are based on the specific *grace sought and needed: the first corresponds to the *purgative way, the second to the *illuminative, the third and fourth to the *unitive. Any method is valid which contests or removes disordered affections or attachments. The claim of the *Exercises* is that the specific will of God for this person can be found, and that God will 'deal directly with the creature, and the creature directly with his/her Creator and Lord'. See also JESUITS.

C. de Dalmasas, tr. J. Aixala, *Ignatius of Loyola* . . . (1985); J. Munitiz, *The Spiritual Diary* . . . (1987); L. Puhl, *The Spiritual Exercises* . . . (1951); J. Tylenda (tr.), *A Pilgrim's Journey: The Autobiography* . . . (1985).

Ignorance: see AVIDYĀ; INVINCIBLE IGNORANCE.

Igyō-shu (school of early Ch'an/Zen): see KUEI-YANG-TSUNG.

Ihai. Japanese Buddhist mortuary tablets with which the spirits of deceased ancestors are associated. They are kept in the household shrine and are honoured with daily offerings. It is customary to ask a priest to chant a *sūtra on an anniversary or on the day of a funeral. *Reiyūkai has made the reverence of ancestors through ihai central to its practice.

Iḥrām (Arab., 'making forbidden or sacred'). In Islam, the state of ritual purity necessary for carrying out the rites of *ḥajj and *ʿumra (greater and lesser pilgrimage). This is achieved by statement of intent, rituals, and wearing a special garment of two pieces of unsewn cloth. Certain regulations have to be observed while in the state of iḥrām (for which see HAJJ).

IHS. Abbreviation of the name *Jesus by means of the first three letters in Greek (*H* being the uncial form of the letter *eta*). Later, however, attempts were made to understand the three letters as initials of words in Latin. Most popular was the interpretation *In Hoc Signo [vinces]*, 'in this sign [thou shalt conquer]', the inscription on the cross seen in a vision by the emperor *Constantine; or Iesus Hominum Salvator (Jesus, saviour of men).

I-Hsuan (Chinese master): see LIN-CHI I-HSÜAN.

Iʿjāz (Arab.). Inimitability or uniqueness of the *Qur'ān; literally 'incapacity', i.e. of others to imitate its style and content. The doctrine, based on the challenge in the Qur'ān itself (e.g. 2. 23 f., 10. 38, 11. 13, 52. 33 f.), was elaborated from the 3rd cent. AH, to uphold both the authority of the Qur'ān itself as the word of *Allāh, and the divine nature of *Muḥammad's mission and message. In addition, the Qur'ān was and is considered as the supreme example of literary style. The Qur'ān itself states that the whole of humanity and *jinn could not produce the like of it (17. 88), a challenge which was not taken up at the time; the Qur'ān's uniqueness has remained an article of faith among Muslims. See also MIRACLES (ISLAM).

Ijmāʿ. Principle of development in Islamic law. The root verb means 'to cause to gather', or 'converge', and yields the noun for a *mosque as a gatherer (*jāmiʿa*) of the faithful. It is by consensus of the community that the *sharīʿa in *Sunni Islam can be enlarged to respond to new situations. Only when the community of the faithful agrees, or converges, on a principle or practice is it legitimated. Ijmāʿ is always subject to being consistent with the prior sources *uṣūl al-dīn): the *Qur'ān, *ḥadīth, and *qiyās, or applied analogy. What is repugnant to the Qur'ān and the *Sunna cannot be argued from consensus. Sunni Muslims accept a tradition of Muḥammad that his community would never agree on error. They see the faithful as the repository of fidelity and the guarantors of a true Islam. The *Shīʿa do not accept ijmāʿ, relying instead on the light of the *Imāms and the authority of the *ayatollahs. Ijmāʿ in Sunni Islam must be initiated by *ijtihād or acknowledged expertise based on study and status. There is sharp debate as to whether the *bāb* (or door) of ijtihād is still open, and to whom, or whether—as rigorists prefer to claim—it is closed because earlier ijtihād has completed its task, and a final sharīʿa obtains, needing no further adaptation. This debate is part of what may be called a laicization of Islam.

Ijtihād (Arab., 'exertion'). An independent judgement concerning a legal or theological question, based on the interpretation and application of the roots of Islamic law (*Qur'ān, *Sunna), as opposed to *taqlīd. In practice it means reinterpretation, rather than following the legal norm. It is a logical deduction arrived at through individual enterprise by an expert with the right training to resolve a legal problem faced by the community. The *mujtāhid* (the one who makes and mediates such judgements) is particularly important in Shiʿa Islam, in contrast to the *ʿulamā.

Ikebana (Jap., 'living flowers'). The practice of flower-contemplation, often (but misleadingly) called the art of flower-arranging in Japan; also known as *kadō*, the 'Way of flowers'. By the 15th cent., informal traditions of floral arranging became formalized into distinct, stylistic 'schools'—each with their own oral and written teachings, and each with their own line of master teachers. These exist today as the Ohara, Ikenobo, and Sogetsu schools. Seen in terms of religion, the art of flower-arranging has been influenced by all the religions of Japan and has become, in its own right, an important part of a Japanese religio-aesthetic tradition, in which artistic disciplines and creativity carry important religious meaning as 'ways' (Chin., *tao*; Jap., *dō, michi*) of spiritual fulfilment.

S. G. Herrigel, *Zen in the Art of Flower Arrangement* (1958); D. Richie and M. Weatherby, *The Master's Book of Ikebana* (1966).

Ikeda Daisaku (b. 1928), Japanese third president of *Sōka Gakkai. With a strong missionary sense, he set out to raise the membership to three million, and to establish Sōka Gakkai International. In 1983, he received the UN Peace Award. His original intention had been to demonstrate in practice how religion can inform politics and remove corruption. To that end, he founded, in 1964, Kōmeitō (the Clean Government Party). Experience of political reality led him to abandon the attempt and to return to a separation of the two.

Ikhwān al-Muslimūn (Muslim Brotherhood): see AL-IKHWĀN AL-MUSLIMŪN.

Ikhwān al-Ṣafāʾ (Arab., 'Brotherhood of Purity'). A secret movement founded *c.*951 (AH 340) in Iraq. It had strong *Ismāʿīlī connections and views, which were summarized in the fifty-one (or fifty-two) letters, *Rasāʾil ikhwān al-Ṣafāʾ*, which deal, in encyclopaedic fashion, with sciences, theology, metaphysics, cosmology, etc., showing their relation to each other.

Ikkarim (basic principles of Jewish belief): see ARTICLES OF FAITH.

Ikkyu Sōjun (1394–1481). Zen master of the *Rinzai school in Japan. He experienced sudden enlightenment in 1418 when he heard (while meditating on a boat) the caw of a crow, of which he wrote: 'Violent anger and desire surge within me, For twenty years which is this moment. A crow caws, an *arahat from this transient world; What is the meaning of the beautiful face singing in the sun?' His teacher, Kaso Sōdon, bestowed the seal of recognition (*inka) on him, but he rejected it—perhaps even throwing it on the fire. He called himself 'the son of the wandering cloud', and although in later life he was appointed by the emperor abbot of *Daitoku-ji, he constantly and strongly rejected the decadent forms of Zen which he found around him. He expressed this critique in a highly unconventional lifestyle, and in his 'Mad Cloud' poetry, collected in *Kyōun-shu* (Germ. tr., Suichi and Thom, 1979). The many tales of his mocking style have made him one of the most popular figures in Japan—the holy madman, who frequented inns and brothels, and who danced down the street waving a skull. He was also noted for his dramatic *calligraphy.

S. Arntzen, *Ikkyu and the Crazy Cloud Anthology* (1986); J. C. Covell, *Unravelling Zen's Red Thread*; J. H. Sanford, *Zen Man Ikkyu* (1981).

Ikon (painted representation): see ICON.

Ik Onkar or **Ik Oaṅkār** (Pañjābi, 'one'; Skt., 'sacred syllable *oṃ'). Gurū *Nānak's statement that God is One. Ik Onkār is the Sikhs' most frequent statement about God, emphasizing the unity of the Primal Being as distinct from the three principles (*trimurti, *Brahmā, *Viṣṇu, *Śiva) of Hindu tradition. In its customary symbolic form the numeral stresses the divine singularity. It marks the beginning of the *Mul Mantra, and thus of *Japjī and the *Ādi Granth, and prefaces the *hymns of each *rāg—and within these the compositions, of each *Gurū and *Bhagat.

Iktisāb (acquisition of acts): see QADAR.

I-kuan Tao (Way of Pervading Unity). A Chinese Buddhist-*Taoist society, an offshoot of the *White Lotus Sect, founded by Wang Chüeh-i in the early 20th cent. It grew rapidly between the two World Wars under the leadership of Chang T'ien-jan (d. 1947), with most members recruited from the merchant class in the Japanese-occupied territories in N. China. Its main doctrine is *eschatological-*messianic: *Bodhisattva *Maitreya, at the command of Mother of No-birth (Wu-sheng Lao-mu), the creator-deity, will appear to the world imminently, at the end of the third and last *kalpa to save its members and all other human beings. It also believed that the existing world religions are but the different vehicles of the same Truth. Due to non-cooperation with the Communist government in the 1950s, many of its leaders suffered persecution and death. Like other similar sectarian groups in modern China which are regarded as being subversive by the state, I-kuan Tao was a secret society whose existence was deemed illegitimate.

I-k'ung (Jap., Giku; 9th cent.). Chinese Ch'an/Zen master of the *Rinzai school, who was invited by the empress, Tachibana Kachiko, to bring Ch'an to Japan. Danran-ji in *Kyōto was built for him, but he found no apt pupils, and he therefore returned to China. No further attempts were made at this translation until the 12th/13th cents.

Ilā. One of three Hindu goddesses (*Ṛg Veda* 1. 13. 9) who bring delight. Several conflicting stories are told about her, unified by the theme of changing sex between male and female. She was born from the horse-sacrifice (*aśvamedha) of Manu.

Ilḥād (deviation): see HERESY.

Illo tempore (that-ideal-time): see MYTH.

Illuminati. Either 16th-cent. Spanish mystical sects; or a German secret society founded in 1776. The Spanish illuminati or *alumbrados appear to have been founded by Antonio de Pastrana at the end of the 15th cent. They believed in a form of pure contemplation and absorption into God, practised severe mortifications, and claimed visions and the power of prophecy. They were harshly treated by the *Inquisition, and a number of *mystics, including *Ignatius Loyola and Teresa of Avila, were at some time suspected of being members. The German illuminati, founded by Johann Adam Weishaupt (1748–1830), pursued progressive illumination through initiation into the successive stages of their society, involving the study of philosophy and the arts. They believed themselves to be those who had received the illuminating grace of Christ, but (or 'therefore') they rejected other religions and organizations. They sought to establish a fraternal and classless society, on the basis of strict discipline (Weishaupt had been trained as a *Jesuit). They were also known as Perfectibilists. Though outlawed in 1784/5, the society re-emerged at the end of the 19th cent., only to disappear again under the Nazis.

Illuminationist (*ishraqi*) school: see SUHRAWARDĪ, SHIHĀB.

Illuminative Way. The second of the *Three Ways of the spiritual life. After being purified from sin in the *purgative way the soul is illuminated and enabled to attain a true understanding of created things ('natural contemplation') and thus prepared for the *unitive way.

Illuminism: see ALUMBRADOS; ILLUMINATI.

Illusion (in Advaita Vedānta philosophy): see MĀYĀ (2) and MITHYĀ.

'Ilm (Arab.). Knowledge, especially of *fiqh and *kalām. 'Ilm, of all kinds, has particularly high status in Islam, because a strong doctrine of creation (all things coming from God and potentially being revelatory of him, as *ayat) is combined with an absence of anything resembling *original sin (which might make humans incapable of appreciating God's self-revelation in the created order). The capacity for

ʿilm is thus a gift from God, which, when exercised, will lead to deeper knowledge of himself. Later speculations in philosophy led to a suspicion that 'knowledge for its own sake' was leading away from Islam, and this suspicion led to an increasing subordination of reason to revelation. See e.g. AL-GHAZ(Z)ĀLĪ; IBN TAIMIYYA.

F. Rosenthal, *Knowledge Triumphant: The Concept of Knowledge in Medieval Islam* (1970).

Ilm-i Kshnoom. Path of Knowledge, a Parsi occult movement: see PARSIS.

Ilyas, Mawlānā: see TABLĪGHĪ JAMĀʿAT.

Il-yŏn or **Iryŏn** (1206–89). Korean Buddhist scholar-monk. He compiled the *Samguk yusa* (Legends and History of the Three Kingdoms), a treasury of the history of Korean Buddhism, in or about the year 1285. At the time when Confucianism was beginning to gather strength in Koryŏ (935–1392), he endeavoured to revitalize Buddhism through this literary effort.

Images: see ICONOGRAPHY.

Imago Dei (Lat.). The image of God, in which, says Genesis 1. 26–7, humanity was created, but which is now marred as a consequence of the *Fall, according to Christians. In Catholic thought, what was lost at the Fall was not the 'image' but only the 'likeness' of God (also Genesis 1. 26), i.e. certain supernatural gifts such as immortality which are restored at baptism. The Reformers, however, held that this exegesis did not grasp the full seriousness of sin, and so insisted that the image, human nature itself, was deeply corrupted at the Fall.

In the *Qur'ān, man is created as the *khalīfa (caliph, or representative) of God on earth.

D. Cairns, *The Image of God in Man* (rev. edn., 1973).

Imām, (Arab., in the *Qur'ān 'sign', 'pattern', 'leader'). The leader of the Muslim congregational *ṣalāt, who can be any man of good standing in the community, but is often a theologically educated man who is engaged by the *mosque. There is no ordination, nor is the imām like the Christian *priest: he is only imām while acting as such.

2. Among Shiʿites, the Imām has an incomparably higher status. Initially, it is almost synonymous with 'rightful caliph' (*khalīfa), i.e. *ʿAlī and his descendants. The stress on succession led to the elaboration of the Imām as one who has received secret knowledge (*jafr), and who still receives (or may receive) direct divine guidance. There is dispute among Shiʿites whether the line ended with the seventh (*Seveners) or twelfth (Twelvers or *'Ithna 'Ashariyya) successor, complicated further by those who believe there is a Hidden Imām (see AL-MAHDĪ) whom the initiate can recognize, who may still give guidance, and who will become manifest at the End (see also ISMĀʿĪLIYA). As philosophical ideas spread which argued for the unity of Being, with the consequence that human (or perhaps all) manifestation is an incarnation of Being, so Imāms were regarded by some Shiʿite groups as incarnations of aspects of divine being. See also (al-)Zaidiy(y)a for their special understanding of Imām. See Index, Imams.

3. Among *Sūfīs (not always in distinction from (2)), the imām is the guide to true knowledge, and is thus equivalent to *pīr* (in Persian) or *murshid*.

4. The two larger beads in the *subḥa* (*rosary).

Īmān (Arab., 'be secure' 'trust'). The Muslim word for faith and trust in *Allāh, and in the Prophet *Muḥammad, and hence in the content of his message. In the *Qur'ān, therefore, īmān is sometimes the same as *islām* (allegiance to God). Does it follow, then, that īmān is all-important in relation to salvation, and that one who makes profession of īmān will be saved, no matter what his works? This was a deeply divisive issue in early Islam (cf. faith and works in Christianity), with the *Khārijites declaring that īmān accompanied by evil works designates such a person as no longer Muslim (and therefore to be treated as such) and the Murji'ites postponing the decision until Allāh reveals all secrets (and therefore treating as Muslims all who perform *ṣalāt facing the *qibla).

T. Izutsu, *The Concept of Belief in Islamic Thought* (1965); A. J. Wensinck, *The Muslim Creed* (1932).

Imitation of Christ. Basic Christian practice, the attempt of a disciple to follow the example of the Lord. It is also the title of a widely influential book on the spiritual life attributed to *Thomas à Kempis (15th cent.). Manuscripts of the book in the process of development have survived: the translation of C. Bigg (1898) is based on the autograph MS of 1441, from which it is clear that the author had not yet made his final revision. The work has also been known (from the Magdalen MS) as *De Musica Ecclesiastica* (On Ecclesiastical Music). The work emphasizes the absolute supremacy and perfection of God, and the importance of forsaking everything in order to attain union with God:

> Where can we find that which is truly good and which enduringly satisfies? Not in the multitude of things which distract, but in the One who gathers and unifies. For the One does not proceed from the many, but the many from the One . . . Compared with him, the creature is nothing, and only becomes anything in union with him. Whatever is not God is nothing, and should be reckoned as nothing.

Imitation of God. Jewish way of expressing the human obligation to imitate God in his actions. According to the Creation account in Genesis, humans are made in the image of God and, accordingly, they are commanded to 'walk in all his ways' (Deuteronomy 10. 12). The idea of the imitation of God is found in *rabbinic sources such as Hama bar Hanina, who explained the Deuteronomic verse thus:

How can a person walk after God? . . . What is meant is that one ought to walk after the attributes of God. Just as the Lord clothes the naked, so you shall clothe the naked [Genesis 3. 21]. Just as he visits the sick, so you shall visit the sick [Genesis 18. 1]. Just as he comforts mourners, so you shall comfort mourners [Leviticus 16. 1]. Just as he buries the dead, so you shall bury the dead [Deuteronomy 34. 6] . . . (*B.Sota* 14a).

The Codifiers made a similar point; *Maimonides lists among the Commandments, 'to emulate God in his beneficent and righteous ways to the best of one's ability'.

Immaculate Conception. The *dogma that the Blessed Virgin *Mary was, from the first moment of her being conceived, free from all stain of *original sin. Support for the doctrine in early Christian tradition is taken from *fathers such as *Justin and *Irenaeus who regarded Mary as the 'new Eve' corresponding to Christ as the 'new Adam'. It and the feast of the conception of the Virgin Mary were a matter of controversy in the West from the 12th cent. until its approval by Pope Sixtus IV in 1476. It became a general Roman Catholic belief in the 16th cent. and was formally defined by the *bull *Ineffabilis Deus* of Pius IX in 1854. The Feast of the Immaculate Conception is kept on 8 Dec.

E. D. O'Connor (ed.), *The Dogma of the Immaculate Conception* (1958).

Immanence (Lat., *immanere*, 'to inhabit'). The presence of actions, or of God, in the world, usually in such a way that the source of the action or presence remains distinct. Thus for the *scholastics, an immanent action is one in which the action remains within the subject and does not modify the object (such as seeing); for *Spinoza, a distinction between *causa immanens* and *causa transiens* allowed the causality of God to be immanent in nature. But more usually the word is used of the relation of God to the created order. The total transcendence of the unproduced producer of all that is would allow no relation to a created order; consequently, all theistic religions allow some degree, or mode, of immanence. At an extreme, the created order is understood to be the mode of God's self-manifestation, and thus to be the body of God. See also PANTHEISM; PROCESS THEOLOGY.

J. R. Illingworth, *Divine Immanence* (1898).

Immanuel or **Emmanuel** (Heb., 'God is with us'). The name of a son prophesied to be born of a young woman (or virgin) in Isaiah 7. 14. Christian tradition, starting with Matthew 1. 23, has interpreted the passage as a prophecy of the *virgin birth of Christ. The word 'Immanuel' does not figure in rabbinic literature. Jewish exegesis of Isaiah 7. 14 is directed against the Christian: e.g. David *Kimḥi pointed to the obvious difficulty of a birth centuries after Isaiah's time being, as the text states, a sign to King Ahaz.

Immortality: see AFTERLIFE.

Immortality, Chinese: see HSIEN; CH'ANG-SHENG PU-SSU.

Impassibility of God. The belief that because God is immutable, unchanging, and unchangeable (expressed in Art. 1 of the *Anglican *Thirty-Nine Articles by saying that he is 'without body, parts or passions'), he cannot suffer or be affected by what happens in, e.g., his creation. This view, which has dominated Christian theology for most of its history, was strongly influenced by philosophical considerations which insisted that for God to be absolute and perfect, he cannot be changed by effects from, so to speak, outside himself, e.g. by prayer or the cries of those who suffer. However, this is far removed from the biblical picture of God as one who feels and responds, and who can hardly be unaffected by the crucifixion of Jesus, if Jesus is indeed the Son of the Father. *Process theology reversed this emphasis by insisting that becoming is a necessary condition of being. Others have retained the traditional emphasis on the unchanging/unchangeable nature of God, but have insisted that change, suffering, petition, intercession, etc., are consequential to God and evoke response, but to and from one whose nature it is to make such response without his own nature changing: see ETERNITY.

Church of England Doctrine Commission, *We Believe in God* (1987), ch. 9; W. Maas, *Unveränderlichkeit Gottes* (1974); G. F. O'Hanlon, *The Immutability of God in the Theology of Hans Urs von Balthasar* (1990); RC Theological Commission, *Irish Theological Quarterly*, 49: 285–300.

Impermanence (in Buddhism): see ANICCA.

Imprimatur (Lat., 'let it be printed'). The permission granted in *Roman Catholicism by the appropriate authority for the approved publication of certain religious works: scripture and *liturgical works require permission from the *Holy See; textbooks on morality, theology, church history, canon law, and the like require permission from a bishop or competent ecclesiastical authority. *Canon law no longer requires any book on a religious subject to seek the imprimatur, but it encourages such books to be submitted for approval (cf. *haskamah in Judaism). The imprimatur requires the prior *nihil obstat ('nothing obstructs') of the officially appointed censor before it can be issued.

Imputation. The reckoning of qualities of one person as belonging to another. Traditional *Protestant theology emphasizes the imputation of *Adam's guilt at the *Fall to the whole human race, and in particular God's imputation of *Christ's righteousness to believers who have no righteousness of their own. Such a view works against the *Catholic concept of *merit actually conferred on a person ('imparted' rather than 'imputed') by God's sanctifying *grace. The term 'imputation' has, however, the disadvantage of suggesting that *justification is a kind of artificial legal fiction.

Inari (Jap., probably from a place-name). The most popular agricultural deity of Japan, especially associated with rice. Known to history only from the Nara period, Inari almost certainly originated among the early rice cultivators of the prehistoric Yayoi period. In the Heian period, Inari was increasingly associated with the official mythology of *Shinto, specifically with Ugatama, the female *kami (god) of food and clothing, Sarutahiko, the monkey kami (because of his sexual associations?), and Ame-no-uzume, the goddess whose kami-possession and ecstatic dance (in which she exposed her genitals) brought back the life-giving light of the sun. Inari shrines especially feature the fox whose life-size statues usually flank the worship centre and whose phallus-like tails again reinforce the motif of sexuality and fecundity. Probably the fox was originally thought to be the messenger of the god, but popularly it has become the form of the god himself. Like so many Japanese folk deities, Inari has drawn to himself many positive associations such as good fortune, abundant harvests, fecundity, and wealth. See also FUSHIMI INARI.

Incantation: see MAGIC.

Incarnation (Lat., *in carne*, 'in flesh/body'). The belief that God is wholly present to, or in, a human life and body. The term may be used to 'translate' the Hindu understanding of *avatāra, but is more commonly used of the belief that in *Jesus Christ, the divine and human natures were united in one person, and that God was, consequently, *in carne*, incarnated. See further CHRISTOLOGY. It may also (but more rarely) be used to speak of the *Mahāyāna Buddhist belief that the Buddha Śākyamuni manifests the eternal buddha-nature: see TRIKĀYA.

For examples in different religions, see Index, Incarnation.

Incense (Lat., *incendere*, 'to burn'). Substances which produce a sweet scent when burned, and are thus used in worship. Among many such substances are aloe, sandalwood, myrrh, frankincense, balsam, cedar, and juniper. In China, incense (*hsiang*) was used to enhance appreciation and thus (especially in Taoism) to assist in the realization of the *Tao—though incense was also used to ward off evil spirits or disease. In India, incense is used as an act of homage to the divine manifestation, especially in a *temple. In early Judaism, incense may have been associated with the smoke of sacrifice: the Heb. *ketoret* is derived from √*ktr*, 'cause to smoke', which may be the smoke from a sacrifice (1 Samuel 2. 15). In biblical times, the burning of incense accompanied all *sacrifices in the *Temple with the exception of the sin-offering of the poor and the meat-offering of the leper. The *high priest used to carry burning incense into the *Holy of Holies on the *Day of Atonement (Leviticus 16. 12–13) and there was a special incense *altar in the Temple Court. The ingredients of incense are presented in Exodus 30. 34–8 and elaborated in the *Talmud, although the use of incense declined from Talmudic times onwards. In Christianity, incense first appears in Christian worship *c.*500. Censing was at first an E. practice, as a preliminary to the opening prayers of the liturgy. In E. liturgies the offering of incense remains a part of the structure of the liturgy, whereas in the W. it is more like an accompaniment to other actions. In the present Roman rite, incense may (but need not) be used at the entrance procession, the *gospel, the offertory, and *elevation of the eucharistic elements. In the E. the altar, the elements on the *prothesis, the *icons, and the people are censed before the beginning of the liturgy, and further censings occur in its course. Incense is also used variously in the daily *offices (following Psalm 141. 2). See also THURIBLE.

Incense is an important part of Hindu offerings, both in the home and in the temple. It forms a part of the daily ritual in invoking the presence of God in preparation for worship. In Buddhism, this ritual was transferred to the representations of the *Buddha (or *bodhisattvas) as a part of *dāna.

E. G. C. F. Atchley, *A History of the Use of Incense in Divine Worship* (1909).

Inclination, good and evil. Instincts for good and evil in human nature, made formal in Jewish anthropology. According to Genesis 6. 5, 'The Lord saw . . . that every imagination of the thoughts of his heart was only evil continually'. The *rabbis taught that human beings were subject to two contradictory impulses, *yeẓer ha-ra*ʿ (evil inclination) and *yeẓer ha-tov* (good inclination). The evil inclination corresponds to natural passions and appetites and so should not be totally repressed or there would be no more *marriage, house-building, or children. None the less it must be controlled by regular study and observance of *Torah (*B.Kid.* 30b). The *yeẓer ha-tov* appears first at the age of 13, when the boy takes on the yoke of the Commandments (*Eccles.R.* 4. 13) and is the chief agent of the curbing of the *yeẓer ha-ra*ʿ.

Independence Day (Israel): see YOM HAATZMA'UT.

Independents. Another name for the English *Congregationalists. In the 1640s, it described those members of the Long Parliament and army officers who favoured religious toleration, as well as those who were committed to the idea of the autonomy of the local congregation as a gathered fellowship of believers.

Index (type of sign in Pierce's analysis): see SYMBOLS.

Index Librorum Prohibitorum (Lat., 'list of prohibited books'). The 'Index', the official list of books which Roman Catholics were, in general, forbidden to read or possess. The first Index was issued by the Congregation of the *Inquisition in 1557. Under *Leo XIII the control of literature likely to be contrary to faith and morals was delegated increasingly to diocesan bishops (*Officiorum ac Muneram*, 1897), and the importance of the Index accordingly declined. Its last edn. was in 1948, and in 1966 it was finally abolished. See also IMPRIMATUR.

R. Burke, *What is in the Index?* (1952).

Indian Ecumenical Conference. A movement for spiritual renewal among N. American Indians. The meetings began on the Crow Reservation, Montana, in 1970, with those attending coming from Alaska to Florida, and from many religions (*Catholic, *Protestant, *Bahā'ī, traditional and the new religions of Handsome Lake, and the Native American Church). Procedures were set up to follow traditional styles of meeting, including pow-wow dancing, tobacco offerings on the sacred fire, and the pipe ceremony and prayers at sunrise. The agenda has included concerns such as alcoholism, oppression by whites, ecology and Indian land, Indian identity and unity, and spiritual renewal under the Great Spirit. Attitudes have ranged from emphasis on 'Red Power' and anti-white, anti-Christian feelings, to more positive and forward-looking relationships with Christianity and W. culture.

Indian Shaker Church. A new *syncretist religion among Indians of NW USA and British Columbia. (There is no relation to white *Shakers or *Quakers.) John Slocum (?1840–97?) was a Squaxin logger near Olympia, baptized as a Roman Catholic. In 1881, he claimed to have visited heaven during a coma and to have been given a new way. In 1882, his wife Mary's shaking paroxysm was regarded as God's Spirit and cured John of an illness. Together they founded the Shaker Church, with moral reforms and spiritual healing through shaking and dancing rites in place of *shamanism. Their plain churches contain many crosses, and worship features prayers and dances, but no *sacraments. The *Bible is replaced by direct revelation (except for some secession groups co-operating with white Christians). After earlier persecution, they became incorporated in several states, and in the 1970s numbered about 2,000 members in over twenty congregations.

Indicative (form of absolution): see ABSOLUTION.

Indra. Supreme God of the Indo-Āryans, to whom (except for *Agni) more hymns are addressed in the *Ṛg Veda* than to any other. He is the dispenser of rain and source of fruitfulness, who is himself sustained by vast quantities of *soma. His strength is represented by his thunderbolt (*vajra*), and his forms are innumerable, because he can assume any shape. The rise of sects and of philosophical Hinduism led to a relegation of Indra to the less important, second level of gods, though he remained the chief of those. The Indraloka is the domain to which all heroic *kṣatriyas go after death. He is found also in Jain and Buddhist mythology (as Sakka).

Indra's net (image of the interconnectedness of all things): see HUA-YEN.

Indriya (Skt.). 1. In Indian philosophical systems, especially Sāṃkhya-yoga, the indriyas constitute the sense organs. There are ten indriyas divided into two categories: the organs of perception (buddhindriyas), and the organs of action (karmendriyas). The buddhindriyas are the capacity for seeing, hearing, smelling, tasting, and touching. They are thus the mediators between the manifested world and the intellect (*buddhi).

The karmendriyas are the capacities of speech, grasping, locomotion, excretion, and procreation. They are the instruments through which a person acts in the world. Neither the karmendriyas nor buddhindriyas are identical with physical parts of the body: the hands can become the instrument for locomotion and the feet for grasping. It is held that a *yogin, having 'withdrawn' his senses through meditation, can perceive the world without the mediation of physical organs, although he may still utilize the various buddhindriyas. In more mythological terms, the indriyas are the means provided by *Indra which allow humans to perceive the manifest world: the five sense organs, the five means of action, excretion, procreation, and thought. They thus contribute to *manas impressions of an external world.

2. In Buddhism, the controlling or directing powers in human life, often listed as the twenty-two physical and psychological capacities in humans, including the five roots which lead to the five powers (*bala), and culminating in the capacity of perfect knowledge—i.e. an *arhat. See also BODHIPĀKṢIKA-DHARMA.

Indulgence. In Roman Catholic practice, a remission by the Church of the temporal penalty due to sin, even when forgiven, in virtue of the merits of Christ and the saints. The granting of indulgences is now generally confined to the pope. The practice presupposes a retributive basis for God's justice, that sin must have a punishment even when the sinner is penitent and is absolved (see PENANCE); and the existence of a 'treasury of *merits' whose benefits can be administered by the Church.

The granting of indulgences became common in the 12th cent. 'Plenary indulgences' (i.e. remitting the whole of the punishment for a person's sins) are first known from their offer by Pope Urban II in 1095 to those who took part in the *Crusades. The unrestricted sale, in the later Middle Ages, of indulgences by professional pardoners, was an abuse against which the Reformation protested. Plenary indulgences are now less common (requiring a total conversion from all venial sin), and partial indulgences are no longer reckoned in years and days of remission from *purgatory.

Indus Valley civilization. Early civilization, known especially through the excavations of *Harappā and Mohenjodaro (both now in Pakistan), the religious characteristics of which continued into *Vedic religion after the *Āryan invasion. The civilization lasted *c.*2300–1750 BCE. Although much is extremely uncertain, excavations have revealed a considerable uniformity of culture, e.g. in the organization of town areas. The reconstruction of the religious beliefs is based mainly on the figures and images, and on scenes depicted on seals; the script has not been deciphered in a way that has met with universal assent. The worship of the Mother Goddess was prominent, in association with the tree of fertility; whether the male gods were all subordinate is disputed. The supreme God appears to have been the prototype of *Śiva as Paśupati, the lord of the animals, though many other suggestions have been made (e.g. that he is *Agni, or even a Jain or a pre-Buddhist *siddha). Tree and animal worship seem to have been prevalent. Various ways of disposing of the dead have been found, suggesting no uniform beliefs about the status of the dead, though the burial of pairs (male and female) of skeletons at Lothal has suggested to some an anticipation of *sati.

B. and R. Allchin, *The Birth of Indian Civilisation* (1968) and *The Rise of Civilization in India and Pakistan* (1982); W. A. Fairservis, *The Roots of Ancient India* (1971) and *Allahdino I: Seals and Inscribed Material* (1976); G. L. Possehl, *Ancient Cities of the Indus* (1979) and *Harappan Civilization . . .* (1982).

Infallibility. Inability to err, predicated by Roman Catholics of the *Church or of some teaching office within it, e.g. the *papacy or an ecumenical *council, when expounding the Christian revelation. The term is a negative one, signifying preservation from error rather than inspiration, and it is predicated properly of people or institutions rather than of the statements they make. The First *Vatican Council in 1870 proclaimed that the pope is infallible when speaking **ex cathedra*, that is when defining a doctrine on faith or morals to be held by the universal Church. The Second Vatican Council extended this claim to the body of bishops as a whole united with the pope (e.g. in an ecumenical council), and also proclaimed that Church as a whole is preserved from error by the *Holy Spirit when there is universal agreement within it on its fundamental beliefs. Hans *Küng has questioned the doctrine of infallibility, and suggested that instead the Church should be described as 'indefectible'. A comparable 'lust for certainty', can be seen in the *Meiji restoration and the elevation of the emperor.

In Islam, infallibility (Arab., *ʿiṣmah*) is predicated by all Muslims of the Prophet *Muḥammad when mediating God's revelation (i.e. the *Qur'ān), though otherwise he is an ordinary human, subject to error, etc.; by Sunni Muslims of the consensus of the community (*ijmaʿ), and by Shiʿa Muslims of the *Imāms.

Infancy Gospels. The *apocryphal gospels retailing stories about the birth and childhood of *Jesus. The best known are the *Protogospel of James* (2nd cent.), *Infancy Gospel of Thomas* (a little later?), and *Gospel of Pseudo-Matthew* (8th or 9th cent.). They are important for the study of iconography, legends, and Christmas carols, but devoid of historical value.

Tr. M. R. James.

Infant baptism: see BAPTISM.

Infralapsarians (relation of election to Fall): see PREDESTINATION.

Inga. The cause-and-effect nature of *karma (cf. *innen) in Zen Buddhism. A proper perception of the undifferentiated nature of reality will make it clear that cause and effect are not separated.

Ingathering of the exiles (Heb., *kibbutz galuyyot*). The return of Jewish exiles to the *Promised Land. The belief that the exiles of *Israel will be gathered back occurs frequently in the writings of the biblical *prophets (e.g. Isaiah 11. 12; Jeremiah 23. 3; Ezekiel 37. 21). In *Talmudic times, the *rabbis taught that the ingathering would be part of the *messianic era: 'The day of the Ingathering of the Exiles is as great as the day on which heaven and earth were created' (*B.Pes.* 8 8a). The tenth *blessing of the daily *Amida concludes: 'Blessed are you, O Lord, who gathers the dispersed of your people Israel.' Since the establishment of the modern State of Israel, the ingathering is often now understood as the immigration of Jews from over a hundred countries to the land of their forefathers, and is thus divested of the messianic character. See also GALUT.

Ingen (introducer of Ōbaku-shū to Japan): see ŌBAKU-SHŪ.

Initiation. The (usually *ritual) transfer of a person into a new state, and thus common in religions—either to bring a person into a new religious community, or to make transfers of status within such communities. Examples are *circumcision in Judaism, *baptism and *confirmation in Christianity, *bayʿat* ('pact') when a *Sūfī novice joins an order, *upanayana among twice-born Hindus, *abhiṣeka in Buddhism, *dbang.bskur* in Tibet (see ABHIṢEKA), *dīkṣa in all Indian religions, but of especial importance among Jains, *khaṇḍe-dī-pāhul among Sikhs. While it is clear that rites of initiation lie within the domain of *rites of passage (and have dominant symbolic reference to sexuality and new birth), there has been much debate about the focus of such rites: are they for the benefit (e.g. by way of social cohesion) of the group which performs them, or are they for the benefit of the individuals concerned? As acts of social drama, often of spectacular theatre, the answer may be 'both-and': at the very least, access to new knowledge, action and power is conferred, but conferred in such ways that the authority of the past (i.e. the inherited tradition) is reinforced. See Index, Initiation.

J. S. La Fontaine, *Initiation: Ritual Drama and Secret Knowledge across the World* (1985).

Injīl (Arab., from Gk., *euangelion*, 'gospel', via Ethiopic). In the *Qur'ān, the revelation given to 'Īsā/*Jesus, or a book given to him, or the scripture in the possession of the Christians. On the Quranic pattern, each *Prophet—from the time of *Adam down to *Muḥammad—received the message for the people of his time. Thus in the case of 'Īsā, *Allāh will teach him 'the Book and Wisdom, Tawrāt and Injīl' (3. 48).

As with the Quranic figure of 'Īsā, it is best to consider the Injīl independently of the Christian understanding. Essentially it is seen as a book revealed to 'Īsā (Qur'ān 57. 27), identical with the earlier revelations, since it 'confirms' what came before, and in turn is later 'confirmed' by the Qur'ān. The fact that the actual gospels do not correspond with the Qur'ān is explained by the theory of 'corruption' (see TAḤRĪF). Thus Muslims generally consider that the presently existing biblical texts are at the least unreliable, and very few are concerned to read the Christian scriptures.

Inka (-shōmei). The legitimating seal of recognition, in Zen Buddhism, that authentic enlightenment has been attained, and that a pupil has completed his training. Only on receiving inka can a person teach others, proclaim himself the dharma-successor (*hassu) of his master, and be addressed as *roshi. It is not the end of training, which extends over many lives, but it is a step towards the maintaining of the way of Zen.

Innen (Jap., 'cause and condition' *karma). The way, in Zen Buddhism, in which eventualities are brought into their being or appearance by constraints or causes, some of which are indirect or passive, while others are direct and active. Innen is also the account of events in the past which explain a person's present state. Innen-kegō applies the transitory nexus of cause and effect to the recognition that all appearances are temporary manifestations.

Inner Deity Hygiene school: see TAOISM.

Inner elixir (in Taoism): see NEI-TAN.

Inner light. In *Quaker vocabulary, the inward revelation of *Christ's will and presence. After years of intense searching, *Fox and his followers came to rely spiritually on 'the inner light of the living Christ' rather than external ceremonies, religious traditions, or even the *Bible itself. In second-generation Quakerism the term occasionally becomes synonymous with 'conscience'.

Innocent III (1161–1216). *Pope from 8 Jan. 1198. Born Lotario dei Conti, the youngest son of the Count of Segni, he became *cardinal during the pontificate of his uncle Clement III. As pope he refused for a decade to recognize the claims of Frederick Hohenstaufen to the imperial title, only doing so after falling out with his hitherto favoured candidate Otto IV. Otto was a nephew of the English King John, and Innocent was already at odds with John over his refusal to accept Stephen Langton, the pope's appointee, as archbishop of Canterbury. In 1208 Innocent put England under an *interdict, and four years later *excommunicated John, absolved his subjects from their allegiance, and handed the kingdom to the king of France. John capitulated. He made England a fief of the papacy, after which Innocent supported John, even against Langton over the Magna Carta. Innocent's pontificate is often held to be the zenith of papal power, and certainly the pope's training as a lawyer made him much in demand as arbitrator or judge. Innocent gave approval to the *Franciscan rule and summoned the fourth *Lateran council, but he also launched the campaign against the *Albigensians, and the disastrous fourth *crusade.

H. Tillmann, *Pope Innocent III* (1954; tr. 1980).

Inquisition. A Roman Catholic tribunal for the suppression of *heresy and punishment of heretics. Strictly speaking, one should speak of 'inquisitions', since there was no single institution. The earliest sanction was *excommunication, but the threat of the *Cathar heresy in W. Europe, led to the Church seeking help from the secular power. The Inquisition thus came into being under Pope Gregory IX in 1232, with papal inquisitors selected chiefly from among *Dominicans and *Franciscans because of their (theoretical) detachment from the world. They sought voluntary change, but if this was not forthcoming, secret trials were held, the accused having no counsel, and with no established rules of evidence: the justice of the proceeding depended therefore on the integrity of the inquisitor. An accused who resisted might be imprisoned under severe conditions or tortured to break his resistance. Sentence was pronounced at a public *sermo generalis* or *auto-da-fé. In the gravest cases the guilty person could be surrendered to the secular arm, which meant death at the stake. In 1542 the Congregation of the Holy Office was established, being reorganized in 1587 into the Congregation of the Roman and Universal Inquisition to supervise faith and morals in the entire church. After a further reorganization in 1908, in 1965 it became the Congregation for the Doctrine of the Faith and its role in censuring wrong belief has again become prominent.

The 'Spanish Inquisition' was a separate national institution, set up in 1478 (endorsed by Sixtus IV in 1483) against the *Marranos and *Moriscos but later directed against Protestants. The number of persons burnt under the first Grand Inquisitor, *Torquemada, was *c.*2,000. It was finally abolished in Portugal in 1821 and in Spain in 1834. See Index, Inquisition.

B. Hamilton, *The Medieval Inquisition* (1982); H. A. Kamen, *The Spanish Inquisition* . . . (1985); J. A. O'Brien, *The Inquisition* (1973); E. van der Vekene, *Bibliographie der Inquisition* . . . (1963).

Inquisition (Islam): see MIḤNA.

INRI. The initial letters of the Latin words *Iesus Nazarenus Rex Judaeorum* ('Jesus of Nazareth the King of the Jews'). These words, according to John 19. 19 f.), were written over the cross of Jesus in Hebrew, Latin and Greek.

Insān al-Kāmil (the Perfect Man): see AL-INSAN AL-KĀMIL.

Insang. Korean for *mudra.

Insh'Allah ('if God wills it'): see QADAR.

Institute of the Blessed Virgin Mary. Christian religious order for women, founded by Mary Ward (1585–1645) in 1611. She believed that the vocation of women cannot be confined to enclosed orders, and she therefore adopted the constitutions of the *Jesuits (Society of Jesus) as the basis for her Institute. It was known also as the Institute of the English Ladies, les Dames anglaises, or more dismissively as the Galloping Girls. They were strongly opposed by the papacy and were eventually suppressed. They did not receive papal approval until 1877.

H. Peters, *Mary Ward* (1991; tr. H. Butterworth, 1994).

Institutes, The. Short title of *Calvin's *Institutes of the Christian Religion*, a basic text of Christian Reformed theology.

Integral Yoga (Aurobindo's Yoga): see AUROBINDO, ŚRI.

Intention. A term in Catholic usage with several meanings, the most important of which are as follows.

1. The purpose of doing 'what the church does' in the *sacraments. Along with the right 'form' and 'matter', the right intention is held to be necessary for the validity of the sacrament. Otherwise, sacraments might be thought to be conferred by accident, e.g. when portrayed in religious drama.

2. The special object for which a prayer of intercession is made, or a *mass said.

In all religions, stress is laid on the importance of intention in the performance of religious duties or the pursuit of religious goals. For an example in Islam, see NIYYA.

Intentionality (Intentionalität): see PHENOMENOLOGY.

Intercession. *Prayer or petition on behalf of others. In Christian liturgies, intercessions are part of the *eucharist (in both the eucharistic prayer itself, and, emphatically in modern liturgies, in the *synaxis) and daily *office. They are often said *ex tempore*, with individual petitions ended by a response such as 'Lord in your mercy—Hear our prayer'.

L. Vischer, *Intercession* (1980).

Intercession (Islam): see SHAFĀʿA; WALĪ.

Interdict. A punishment in the Roman Catholic Church akin to *excommunication. Formerly, *canon law distinguished 'personal' and 'local' interdicts; the effect of the latter was the cessation of the administration of the *sacraments (except, e.g., for the dying) and of all solemn services in a place. In the Middle Ages it was a powerful weapon, occasionally used against whole countries, e.g. by Pope Innocent III in his struggles with Philip Augustus of France (1200) and John of England (1208).

Interim ethic/Interims Ethik: see SCHWEITZER, ALBERT.

International Society for Krishna Consciousness (ISKCON). A Hindu devotional movement, commonly known as Hare Krishna, founded in the USA in 1965 by Bhaktivedanta Swami *Prabhupada (1896–1977), a devotee of *Kṛṣṇa. It is in the tradition of *Caitanya. The movement's principal aim is to lead people, living in this demonic age, the age of *Kali-yuga, to attain salvation in the form of permanent Krishna-consciousness by the Way of *Bhakti-yoga, the highest of the three Ways of Knowledge, Works, and Devotion. Every concern, whether it be hunger or disease, is subordinated to the ultimate goal of Krishna-consciousness. It is believed that by adherence to a strict set of moral norms (one of which limits sexual intercourse to married people only and makes procreation its sole legitimate purpose); by dedicated missionary work by the continual recitation of the Kṛṣṇa mantra, (the Mahā-mantra); and by the practice of other prescribed devotions, the devotee can acquire, even here and now, a foretaste of eternal union with Kṛṣṇa. The Mahāmantra is: Hare Krishna, Hare Krishna; Krishna, Krishna, Hare, Hare; Hare Rama, Hare Rama; Rama, Rama, Hare, Hare. The devotees are vivid and obvious on the streets, in white or saffron robes (for men), and in coloured saris (for women), dancing and singing to traditional instruments. The movement, with an extensive worldwide membership, has offered rituals, not only to new converts, but to expatriate Hindus. The movement has been governed since the death of its founder by a Central Governing Board Committee which appoints a swāmi or representative to act as supreme authority in each of the various temples around the world, though there have been various schisms.

A. Burr, *I Am Not My Body: A Study of the International Hare Krishna Sect* (1984); F. J. Daner, *The American Children of Krishna* (1976); L. D. Shinn, *The Dark Lord* (1985); J. Stillson Judah, *Hare Krishna and the Counterculture* (1974).

Inter-Varsity Fellowship (IVF). Since 1974 the Universities and Colleges Christian Fellowship. It was established in 1927 to encourage links between student members of *evangelical Christian Unions in British universities and colleges. National conferences are held for students encouraging evangelistic outreach and Bible study. From the beginning there has been a strong missionary interest. The International Federation of Evangelical Students unites similar groups throughout the world.

Intinction. A method of administering *communion, by dipping the eucharistic bread into the wine. Its first use (3rd cent.) seems to have been to make communion easier for a sick person. Later it became a regular method of communion in both E. and W., and survives as the prescribed method in the Orthodox liturgy. In the W. it disappeared by *c.*1200, but has been revived in modern times, especially as a method of giving communion to the sick, or in the face of fear induced by the AIDS epidemic.

Introit (Lat. *introire*, 'go in'). The opening act in the *mass. It consists of a psalm or part of a psalm with *antiphon and *gloria Patri, sung as the celebrant enters the church. It was introduced to accompany the entrance procession and is not among the earliest parts of the eucharistic liturgy.

Invention of the Cross. The legendary discovery (Lat., *inventio*) of the cross of Jesus at *Calvary by St Helena, the mother of *Constantine. The legend developed from the 5th cent. on; earlier writers like *Cyril of Jerusalem imply at most that the cross was found in the time of Constantine. Much of the wood was distributed to different churches, with the main part being preserved in the Church of the Holy Sepulchre in Jerusalem. The Orthodox Church commemorates this event, along with the dedication of Constantine's basilica on the site of the Holy Sepulchre, on 14 Sept. The feast is now called the *Exaltation of the Cross in both E. and W. (a separate W. feast on 3 May having been suppressed in 1960).

Investiture controversy (dispute about the right of laity to make certain Church appointments): see GREGORY VII.

Invincible ignorance. Ignorance according to Roman Catholic understanding, which cannot be eradicated, even by the utmost effort, being a consequence of circumstances which were not chosen. In Christian thought, it means that acts or statements in this condition are involuntary and cannot be an offence against God. See also EXTRA ECCLESIAM NULLA SALUS (EST).

K. E. Kirk, *Ignorance, Faith and Conformity* (1925).

Invisible religion. Religious beliefs and practices which are held in parallel with (or in association with) those of the official religion to which the person concerned belongs: it is thus closely associated with non-official religion. They include such items as superstition and the paranormal, and also (since these are likely to be disapproved of by the official religion) beliefs and practices derived from other religions (see R. W. Bibby, 'Searching for the Invisible Thread . . .', *Journ. for the Sci. Study of Rel.* 1983). More broadly, the 'Invisible Religion thesis' is the argument of T. Luckmann (in the book of that title in its Eng. tr., 1967) that *Durkheim and *Weber were correct in identifying religion as the key to understanding society and the place of individuals in society. In his definition, religion is that which enables individuals to transcend their biological nature, thus making religion virtually synonymous with *culture:

> The organism—in isolation nothing but a separate pole of 'meaningless' subjective processes—becomes a self by embarking with others upon the construction of an 'objective' and moral universe of meaning. Thereby the organism transcends its biological nature. It is in keeping with an elementary sense of religion to call the transcendence of biological nature by the human organism a religious phenomenon. . . . This phenomenon rests upon the functional relation of self and society. We may, therefore, regard the social processes that lead to the formation of self as fundamentally religious. (pp. 48 f).

This is necessarily 'invisible' because it underlies, and is wider than, any particular visible religion.

Inyon. Korean for *karma.

In-zo. Jap. for *mudra.

Ippen or **Yugyō Shōnin,** 'wandering holy man' (1239–89). Founder of the Ji (Time) sect of Japanese *Pure Land Buddhism; he called his followers, *Jishū, Followers of the Timely Teaching; the 'time' is the six-hour invocation of the *nembutsu each day. Ippen is a representative example of the *hijiri, itinerant Buddhist practitioners, who travelled throughout Japan during the medieval period spreading the Pure Land teachings. As a youth, Ippen studied Pure Land Buddhism, but soon after the death of his father, he embarked on a life of wandering ministry which continued until his death. During his travels, he had an enlightenment experience at Mount Kumano. As a result of his experience, he took the name of Ippen ('one universality'). At the time of his death, Ippen burnt all of his writings, saying that they all revert to the phrase Namu Amida Butsu. Only a few of his writings, such as the letters and poems collected together in the *Ippen Shonin Goroku*, remain, which contains his final instruction: 'To all my followers: hold to my precepts to the end of the world. Make every effort and do not become neglectful. Every action, of body, speech or mind, has as its single end a total devotion to *Amida'.

D. Hirota, *No Abode . . .* (1986).

Iqbal, Sir Muhammad (1876–1938). Indian Muslim poet and philosopher. Iqbal's reinterpretation of Islam in the light of the *Sūfī heritage and W.

philosophy (especially Bergson's creative evolution) gave a fresh stimulus to Indian Islam. His powerful poetry in Urdu and Persian inspired a new generation of Indian Muslims to shape and improve their condition of life, and was one of the chief forces behind the creation of Pakistan. The salient features of Iqbal's thought are the notion of reality as pure duration, with God and man interrelating dynamically in the universe; and the marriage of intellect and love in transforming humans to a higher being. Iqbal's constant theme is, 'Arise, and create a new world'. For him, life is movement: to remain static and inactive is akin to death: 'A useless struggle is better than inaction'. He thus broke the stranglehold of fatalism: 'Destiny as assigned by God is identical with pure, non-serial time, and has, like it, a wide range of alternatives and possibilities'—i.e. humans are free to select the various possibilities open to them (cf. *kasb*, for which see QADAR). According to Iqbal (following *Jalāl al-Dīn Rūmī), love is the principle and driving force behind all creative evolution, while reason serves as a co-operating and organizing factor in this process. Moreover, Iqbal saw humans as creators, sharing that attribute of God, but only when they are purposeful and moral in their creativity. In this way, they fulfil their role as God's representatives (*khalīfa) on earth. Of his ten major works, *Bang-i-Dara* (1924), *Bal-i-Jibril* (1935), and *Zarb-i-Kalim* (1936) were well received by educated Indian Muslims. *The Reconstruction of Religious Thought in Islam* (1928) was a more systematic elaboration of Iqbal's Islamic vision, arguing for a return to *ijtihād and the establishment of *ijmāʿ through a legislative institution in the reformation of Islamic law. In the later part of his life, Iqbal emerged as an important political figure in the struggle of Indian Muslims for a Muslim homeland.

A. M. Schimmel, *Gabriel's Wing* . . . (1963).

Irenaeus, St (*c.*140–*c.*200). Church *father. He heard *Polycarp as a boy, so is generally supposed to have come from Asia Minor. He studied at Rome, then became presbyter and later (*c.*178) bishop of Lyons. The tradition that he was a martyr is late and unreliable. The most important work of Irenaeus is his *Detection and Overthrow of the Falsely Named 'Knowledge'* (usually known as *Against *Heresies*). This is a detailed attack on *gnosticism, especially the system of *Valentinus. Its interest lies in its descriptions (seemingly mostly fair) of gnostic doctrines; its use of earlier sources, many now lost; and its own exposition of Christian doctrine. The work relies partly on ridicule of the gnostics' fantastic mythological systems, but more importantly on the value of Christian tradition, as shown in the succession of *bishops from the *apostles, *canon of scripture, and the common 'hypothesis of faith'. Irenaeus may thus be called the first great *catholic theologian. With him is associated the notion of 'recapitulation': based on Romans 13. 9 and Ephesians 1. 10, the idea in Irenaeus is that Christ is the consummation and completion of God's purpose and design, summoning up all that God intended in creation and dealing in his own person with the defects which had entered in: 'The victory over the enemy would not have been effectively won if the conqueror had not been born as man from a woman . . ., but the Lord could not have made an end in his own person of that original enmity between man and the serpent . . . if he had come from another Father.'

J. Lawson, *The Biblical Theology of Saint Irenaeus* (1948); G. Wingren, *Man and the Incarnation* . . . (1959).

Irving(ites) (Christian movement): see CATHOLIC APOSTOLIC CHURCH.

Iryŏn (Korean Buddhist scholar-monk): see IL-YŎN.

ʿĪsā (Islamic name): see JESUS.

Īśa (Lord God): see ĪŚVARA.

Isaac. Son of the Hebrew *patriarch *Abraham by his wife Sarah. His name is derived from the fact that his mother laughed (*ẓahaka*) when told that she would bear a child (Genesis 18. 12). According to Genesis, Isaac was born after his mother had passed childbearing age and was the heir of the *covenant. He was the father of *Esau and *Jacob, lived as a semi-nomad in *Canaan and became wealthy with many flocks and herds (see Genesis 21–7). In the *aggadah, the sun shone with extraordinary splendour on the day of Isaac's birth, 'the like of which will only be seen again in the *messianic age' (*Tanḥ. B. Gen.*107). He is said to be one of only three men upon whom the evil *inclination had no influence (*BBB* 17a). See also ʿAKEDA.

In Islam, Isaac (Isḥāq) is listed in the *Qur'ān among the *prophets (e.g. 4. 163), and named as the son, a 'prophet, one of the righteous' (37. 112) promised to Ibrāhīm (Abraham) (cf. 6. 84, 21. 72). He is mentioned together with Ismāʿīl (*Ishmael) as Ibrāhīm's son granted in his old age (14. 39). Later Muslim tradition held that the son demanded in sacrifice was Ismāʿīl, though the Quranic account (37. 100–9) does not specify his name.

Isaac the Blind or **Sagi Nahor** (*c.*1160–1235). *Kabbalist. Isaac the Blind was the son of *Abraham ben David of Posquières. Described as 'the father of the Kabbalah', he was the author of several works including a commentary to the *Sefer *Yezirah* (ed. G. Scholem, 1963). He taught that, by contemplation, human beings could be in communication with divine emanations (the *sefirot). Very little is known of Isaac's personal life although stories of his mystical powers were circulated among his disciples.

Isaiah. Hebrew prophet of the 8th cent. BCE, and name of a prophetic book of the Hebrew Bible and Christian Old Testament. Isaiah, son of Amoz, exercised influence at the court of the kings of Judah and took a prominent part in foreign politics. His career as prophet covered the period from King Uzziah's death (*c.*740; Isaiah 6. 1) to the Assyrian invasion of Judah in 701. An early tradition relates his death as a martyr in the reign of Manasseh (*c.*690–*c.*640). He is called Shaʿya in Islamic tradition.

His teaching resembles that of *Amos and *Hosea in proclaiming the supremacy and moral demands of *Yahweh the God of Israel. He also stressed God's holiness (ch. 6). From these beliefs followed his political counsels, e.g. in urging Judah to keep out of foreign alliances. His expectations for the future were based on the survival of a 'remnant' (but perhaps *only* a remnant) of Judah and the promises made to the Davidic dynasty.

The book of Isaiah falls into three parts: chs. 1–35, 36–9, and 40–66. Chs. 1–35 are concerned especially with the Syrian pressure on Judah in the years 740–700 BCE. The *'Immanuel prophecy' of 9. 2–7 comes from this period. The oracles in 13. 1–14. 23, 24–7, and 34–5 appear to be from later than Isaiah's time. Chs. 36–9 is a section taken over from 2 Kings 18. 13–20. 19, plus the 'Song of Hezekiah' (Isaiah 38. 10–20). Chs. 40–66 take up the theme of the redemption of Israel and its mission in the world. Since the 19th cent. these chapters have been known as 'Deutero-Isaiah', on the recognition that they were written by a later author to encourage the Jewish exiles in Babylon shortly before their release in 537 BCE. Chs. 56–66 seem to presuppose that the *Temple had been rebuilt, and are therefore often distinguished as 'Trito-Isaiah'. See also SERVANT SONGS.

The *Ascension of Isaiah* is an *apocryphal work, originally Jewish, but now with Christian interpolations. It describes Isaiah's martyrdom, his ascent to heaven, and his visions there. The entire work survives only in Ethiopic; the date of the original is uncertain.

Īśā Upaniṣad. The shortest (eighteen verses) of the principal *Upaniṣads, so-called from its opening word, Lord, though also known from its full form as *Īśāvāsyam*. It contrasts the ignorant perception of manifestation as real with the true perception of undifferentiated reality. It is often regarded as containing the whole essence of the Upaniṣads.

Trs., many, e.g. Hume (1931), Nikhilananda (1949), Radhakrishnan (1953).

Ise. City in Japan containing the Ise shrines. The Inner Shrine is dedicated to *Amaterasu, and the Outer to Toyouke Okami, in addition to which there are various other shrines. Originally, only the imperial family could worship there, and it became the centre for imperial rites, e.g. *Niiname-sai, *Daijôsai. Under State Shinto, Ise became the shrine of the whole nation. Attempts were made here to absorb Buddhism (see HONJISUIJAKU) in Watarai Shintō, often known as Ise, or Outer Shrine, Shintō. The belief that pilgrimage to Ise can bring benefits to the nation can still be seen in visits of politicians to Ise. The pilgrimage is known as Ise Mairi.

Isḥāq (Muslim name for Abraham's son): see ISAAC.

Isḥāq Ṣafī al-Dīn (Sūfī shaykh): see ṢAFAVIDS.

Ishida Baigan (1685–1744). Founder of the Japanese movement, Shingaku ('education of the heart'). He was attracted to Shinto when young, but he studied other religions as well, especially neo-Confucianism and Buddhism. Applying himself to meditation, he had several experiences of a total identity of mind and body. He set up his own class, teaching that the true and attainable goal is the overcoming of self-centredness by the deliberate appropriation of the *Confucian virtues. The purification of the heart (*kokoro*) reiterated *Mencius (Meng Tzu), but he incorporated whatever of Buddhism or Ṭaoism or Shinto reinforced his message. In particular, he insisted that the middle-class elements are as essential to the well-being of a society as any others. Two of his works have survived, *Toimondo* (Town and Country Dialogues) and *Seikaron* (On Household Management).

Ishin-denshin (Jap., 'transmitting mind through mind'). Zen recognition of the transmission of buddha-dharma from master to pupil and to dharma-successors (*hassu), especially in the lineages of succession (*soshigata, *inka-shōmei). The term comes from the *Platform Sūtra* (**Liu-tsu-ta-shih* . . .), where *Hui-neng contrasts knowledge transmitted through books with the infectious transmission of immediate insight into the true nature of reality—hence his 'tearing up of the sūtras'.

Ishmael. Eldest son of the Jewish *patriarch, *Abraham, by his maidservant, Hagar. After the birth of *Isaac, Ishmael and his mother were driven from the camp, because Isaac, rather than Ishmael, was the heir of the *covenant (Genesis 16. 21). According to the *Aggadah, Ishmael dishonoured women, worshipped *idols, and tried to kill his younger brother (*Gen.R.* 53. 11; *Tosef.Sot.* 6. 6). He was said to be the ancestor of the Ishmaelites and, by extension, all the Arab peoples.

In Islam Ishmael (Ismāʿīl) is mentioned in the *Qur'ān as one of the *prophets (3. 84, 4. 163), and more specifically as a son of Ibrāhīm (*Abraham) (14. 39). The two are said to have rebuilt the *Kaʿba in *Mecca and instituted the rites of *ḥajj (pilgrimage). (2. 127–9).

Later Muslim tradition considers that the son demanded in sacrifice (not named in the Quranic account, 37. 100–9) was Ismāʿīl. It also relates the story of *Hagar and Ismāʿīl being sent away by Ibrāhīm. After wandering for some time, they stopped in a valley where Hagar ran to and fro between the two small hills of Ṣafā and Marwa—an action commemorated in the *saʿy ('running') part of the ritual of *ʿumra. The young Ismaʿil discovered a spring of water, *Zamzam. Isma'il is considered the ancestor of the northern Arabs, and thus of the later Arab tribes.

Ishmael ben Elisha (early 2nd cent. CE). Jewish sage. The son of a *priest, Rabbi Ishmael was one of the chief spokesmen of the sages of *Jabneh. He disputed with *Akiva on both *halakhic and *aggadic matters, and he expanded *Hillel's seven *hermeneutical rules to thirteen. In his view, 'we are required to *live* under the statutes [Leviticus 18. 5], not die under them' (*B.Sanh.* 74a). Many mystical sayings are also ascribed to him. According to legend, he was one of the *martyrs who was killed in the persecutions following the *Bar Kokhba rebellion, but this is doubtful.

Ishraqi or **Ishrāqiy(y)a** (illuminationist school): see SUHRAWARDĪ, SHIHĀB.

Ishvara (God): see ĪŚVARA.

Isidore, St (*c.*560–636). Archbishop of Seville. He is known mainly for his encyclopaedic writings, which were freely used by innumerable medieval authors. The most important of them is the *Etymologiae*, containing information on many secular subjects as well as on the books and offices of the Church and other theological matters. He has been wrongly identified as the compiler of the collection of partly spurious canonical documents known as the 'False *Decretals'. He was made a *Doctor of the Church in 1722.

E. Bréhaut, *An Encyclopaedist of the Dark Ages . . .* (1912).

Isis and Osiris: see DYING AND RISING GODS.

ISKCON: see INTERNATIONAL SOCIETY FOR KRISHNA CONSCIOUSNESS.

Islam (Islām). The religion of allegiance to God and to his *prophet *Muḥammad, the religion (*dīn) which God always intended for his creation, but which is derived in its present form from the prophetic ministry of Muḥammad (*c.*570–632 CE), and from the *revelation mediated through him, the *Qur'ān. The verbal noun *islām* appears eight times in the Qur'ān: derived from the same Semitic root as Heb. *shālom* (peace), it means 'entering into a condition of peace and security with God through allegiance or surrender to him'. *Islām* is closely related to *īmān (faithful trust), though 49. 14 implies a possible contrast between them: 'The Arabs say, "We believe [āmannā]". Say: "You do not believe, but you only say, We have given our allegiance [*aslamnā*]", but imān has not entered into your hearts.'

Islam began historically in the quest of Muḥammad to find the absolute truth of God in the midst of the many conflicting claims which he encountered in his environment about the nature of God. If Jews, Christians, Meccan idol-worshippers, etc., claimed to be worshipping God, it is *God* that they must be worshipping, so how could the conflicts arise? Influenced by earlier *ḥanifs (*ḥunafa'un*, monotheists who claimed to be adhering to the religion of *Abraham), Muḥammad went off for periods of increasing isolation during which he struggled in prayer to find *al-Haqq*, the true One; and in a cave on Mount *Ḥirā', there came to him the overwhelming sense of that reality pressing upon him, and the first of the utterances that later became the Qur'ān were spoken through him (96. 1). From this absolute sense of God, *Allāh, derived the insistence which is characteristic of Islam, that if God is indeed God, then there can only be what God is, the One who is the source of all creation and the disposer of all events and lives within it. The life of Muḥammad and the message of the Qur'ān then become a working out and application of that fundamental vision: all people (divided as they are from each other at present) should become a single *'umma (community), and every action and every aspect of life should become an act of witness that 'there is no God but God' and that 'Muḥammad is his messenger'.

Those latter affirmations, making up the basic witness (al-*Shahāda), form the first of the *Five Pillars of Islam, which together give form and structure to all Muslim lives. Muslim life and belief are derived directly from the Qur'ān, but since the Qur'ān does not deal with every issue or question which a Muslim might wish to ask, authoritative guidance is derived also from the traditions (*ḥadīth) concerning the words, deeds and silences of Muḥammad and his *companions: they were, in effect, a living commentary on Qur'ān. Even so, there remains much scope for application and interpretation. Methods of such interpretation emerged (see IJMĀ'; IJTIHĀD; QIYĀS), as also did major schools of interpretation, which drew up law-codes to govern Muslim life: see SHARĪ'A.

When Muḥammad died, no exact provision had been made for any successor to lead the new community, although Muḥammad had, during his final illness, asked *Abu Bakr to lead the prayers (*ṣalāt) instead of himself. There were two major forms of leadership in the communities of Arabia at that time: one looked for a person of high qualities if there was a crisis, and gave him allegiance for as long as the crisis lasted; on that basis, when Muḥammad died, there was no succession problem, because the tribes simply withdrew their allegiance and went back to their old ways; however, those who had grasped the message of giving allegiance (islām) to *God* immediately pursued them and brought them back into the fold (so that the first event of Muslim history is the War of Apostasy, al-*Ridda); those who thought in that way adopted the first form of leadership and chose Abu Bakr as their leader, known as caliph or *khalīfa. But there was also that second and more normal form of leadership, which was concerned with the running of everyday life in a community and which was hereditary: the obvious candidate for those who thought that this should be the model was Muḥammad's son-in-law (and nearest surviving blood-relative), *ʿAlī. Although there were four immediate successors (al-Rāshidūn; see KHALĪFA) before a final split, the strains were too great, and the party (*shīʿa*) of ʿAlī broke away from those who claimed to be following the custom (*sunna) of the Prophet, thereby creating the divide between Sunni and *Shīʿa Muslims which persists to this day.

The spread of Islam was extremely rapid. Within a hundred years of the death of Muḥammad, it had reached the Atlantic in one direction and the borders of China in the other. It now amounts to about a billion adherents, and is found in most countries of the world. Because of the relative simplicity of its requirements, its diffusion has been like that of water spreading over the ground, taking on the colour of the earth it flows over. Islam is thus found in many different styles, although always expressing the same basic characteristics. At one stage (from the 9th to the 13th cents. CE), the Muslim delight in creation led it into a passionate commitment to *knowledge (*ʿilm), which in turn led Muslims into spectacular achievements in philosophy (*falsafa) and the natural sciences, not only rescuing the Greek foundations which were in danger of being lost for ever, but making great advances of their own. These were mediated into Christian Europe, with consequences which are visible all around.

There were two major reactions to the achievements of Muslim philosophy and science. The first was a growing suspicion that perhaps the achievements of the human mind were taking priority over the revelation from God, and that philosophy was subjecting God to that final judgement which it is his prerogative alone to exercise. 'The Incoherence of Philosophy' was exposed by *al-Ghaz(z)ālī (1058–1111 (AH 450–505)), and since that time the prevailing tendency has been one of giving priority to revelation (and the sciences associated with it of exegesis) and obedience. The brief explorations of Islamic modernism, associated with such figures as *ʿAbduh and *Iqbal, have had little lasting consequence (see e.g. K. Cragg, *Counsels in Contemporary Islam*, 1965).

The second major reaction was a reinforcement of that style of Muslim life and devotion which is known as *Sufism. Sufism is a way of such attachment to God in love and worship that it can be regarded as the interior life which is founded on sharīʿa as the exterior. If Sufism seemed occasionally to the guardians of more traditional faith and practice (e.g. the *ʿulamā) to be outside the boundary of the acceptable (e.g. *al-Hallāj), far more often the two have been partners; and have persisted to the present day, attracting many, perhaps most, Muslims to some degree of membership.

Islam is necessarily a *missionary religion, since entrusted to it is the revelation of God's word and will for the world in a form which has not been corrupted (God has revealed the same content of Qur'ān through many other prophets, including *Moses and *Jesus, but all peoples before Muḥammad and the Arabs had corrupted what had been entrusted to them). The world is divided into three domains (see DĀR AL-HARB), with the clear expectation that in due course all will be unified in the single 'umma of God's intent. In the mean time, that quest for community is much complicated by the imposition, during the colonial period of European expansion, of nation-states. The caliphate, which had created the great *dynasties of the past (e.g. the *Umayyads, the *ʿAbbasids, culminating in the *Ottomans) lingered on in Turkey, but was abolished in 1924 during the attempt to establish Turkey as a secular state. The resulting ambiguities in countries where Muslims are in a majority (e.g. over the extent to which sharīʿa law should be introduced or extended), and the many problems for the recovery of authentically Muslim life in a world of rapid change, have not yet been resolved.

S. Azzam, *Islam and Contemporary Society* (1982); J. W. Bowker, *Voices of Islam* (1995); *The Cambridge History of Islam*, ed. P. M. Holt *et al.* (1970); D. Ede *et al.*, *Guide to Islam* (1983); J. L. Esposito, *Islam: The Straight Path* (new edn., 1991) and *Islam in Asia* (1987); C. L. Geddes, *Guide to Reference Books for Islamic Studies* (1985); M. G. S. Hodgson, *The Venture of Islam* (1974); A. Hussain, *Islamic Movements in Egypt, Pakistan and Iran: An Annotated Bibliography* (1983); I. M. Lapidus, *A History of Islamic Societies* (1988); *The Legacy of Islam*, ed. T. W. Arnold and A. Guillaume (1931), ed. C. E. Bosworth and J. Schacht (1974); F. Rahman, *Islam* (1966); A. Rippin, *Muslims* (1990); A. Schimmel, *Islam in the Indian Subcontinent* (1980).

Islamic law: see SHARĪʿA; FIQH.

Islands of the immortals (blissful home of the immortals): see FANG-SHIH.

Ismāʿīl (eldest son of Abraham): see ISHMAEL.

Ismāʿīliy(y)a or **Ismāʿīlīs.** An aggregation of Muslim groups, notable for esoteric teaching. Although the Ismāʿīlīs are associated with *Shīʿa Islam, they are more to be identified with their own teachings (which absorbed much from the remnants of *gnosticism in Persia) than with Shiʿite doctrines. Nevertheless, they emerged historically from disputes following the death of the sixth Shīʿa *Imām, Jaʿfar al-Sādiq. The succession should have passed to his eldest son, Ismāʿīl, but he died before his father. Nevertheless, some maintained that the authority had been transmitted to him as the first-born (and beyond him to his son). Others held that the succession should pass to Jaʿfar's eldest surviving son (his third), Mūsā al-Kāzim. The Twelvers (*ithnā ʿashariyya, majority Shīʿa) chose Mūsā and his successors, while those following Ismāʿīl came to be known as Ismāʿīlīs—and also as Seveners (*sabʿiyya*), partly for having chosen the Seventh Imām in direct succession, but also because of their belief that prophets always come in cycles of seven. Out of the Ismāʿīlīya there later arose many subsects e.g. *Qarmatians, Nizārīs (including *Assassins),

Mustaʿlīs, *Druzes, and Muqannʿah. These subdivisions were caused primarily over the various succession disputes (of the Imāms) which have characterized Shiʿism for most of its history. During the early 10th cent. CE, the Ismāʿīlīs established the powerful and prosperous Fāṭimid dynasty in N. Africa which extended its control, in the 11th cent., to Egypt, Palestine, Syria, Hijāz, Yemen, and Sind. The Fāṭimids were patrons of the arts and sciences and commerce, and they founded the first Islamic universities of *al-Azhar and Dār-al-Hikmah in Cairo. The Ismāʿīlī intellectuals, such as Qāḍī al-Nuʿmān (d. 974 CE) and al-Shahrastānī (d. 1153 CE) elaborated a complex view of knowledge: 'There is no *ẓāhir* [manifest outer] without its corresponding *bāṭin* [hidden or inner], just as there is no bāṭin without its *ẓāhir*.' It was in the interpretation of *bāṭin* (i.e. esotericism; see BĀṬINĪY(Y)A) that they produced a unique system of philosophy and science based on Islam and *Neoplatonic philosophy (effectively summarized in the encyclopaedia of *Ikhwān-al-Safā'). The feature which distinguishes them from other Muslim sects is their belief in seven (not five) *pillars of faith: belief, purification, prayer, almsgiving, fasting, pilgrimage, and struggle in Allāh's way. Their view, as regards the first (belief), is that faith (*imān) can only be achieved through allegiance to the Imām of the time; the Imām guides the believers to knowledge, and it is through knowledge that the Muslim becomes a true believer. Hence devotion to the Imām, is for the Ismāʿīlīs the most important of the seven pillars. The principle of ta'wīl (allegorical interpretation) of *Qur'ān by the Ismāʿīlī Imāms aroused strong opposition from the orthodox, especially *al-Ghaz(z)ālī.

The orthodox reaction, together with internal quarrels over the issues of succession, led to the decline and collapse of the Ismāʿīlī sect-power by the end of the 11th cent. At present the major Ismāʿīlī sect is the Nizārīs, numbering *c.*20 million, in India, Pakistan, E. Africa, Iran, Syria, and Lebanon. In India, they are known also as Khojas, from the Hindu *caste originally converted by a Persian Ismaʿīlī, Ṣadr al-Dīn. A highly organized and flourishing community, they are noted for the promotion of social, educational, and health enterprises within the Muslim world, which they finance through personal contributions and co-operative societies. Their Imām is the *Aga Khān.

F. Daftary, *The Ismaʿilis* ... (1990); S. H. Nasr (ed.), *Ismaʿili Contributions to Islamic Culture* (1977); I. K. Poonawalla, *Biobibliography of Ismāʿīli Literature* (1977); N. Tajdin, *A Bibliography of Ismailism* (1986).

Isnād. The chain of transmitters of a Muslim *ḥadīth.

Isra' (*al-Isra'*, Arab., 'the journey'). The miraculous journey of the Prophet *Muḥammad from *Mecca to Jerusalem. Qur'ān 17. 1 is taken as a reference to this journey ('Glory to him who caused his servant to journey by night from the sacred place of worship to the further place of worship, which we have encircled with blessings'), but no details are given. These are to be found in *ḥadīth, which tells of the way in which the angel Jibrāʿīl (*Gabriel) woke him from sleep and took him to *Burāq, an animal 'smaller than a mule but larger than an ass'. Together they travelled through the sky to Jerusalem, from where, after prayer and worship, he made the Ascent (al-*Miʿrāj). After that he was taken back to Mecca. al-Isra' and al-Miʿrāj together make up the Night Journey. See also AL-*MASJID AL-AQṢĀ'.

Israel. 1. Name given to the *patriarch *Jacob after he wrestled ('for you have striven', *sarita*, hence the name) with an angel near the ford of Jabbok (Genesis 32. 28–9).

2. Name used for the descendants of Jacob, and so for all the Jewish people, in full: *bene Israel*, sons of Israel.

3. The Northern Kingdom of the Jews. With the division of the kingdom during the reign of Rehoboam (*c.*930 BCE), the Southern Kingdom, which remained faithful to the House of *David, was known as *Judah, while the Northern Kingdom was called Israel. It included the territory of all the tribes except Judah and *Benjamin. It was eventually captured by the Assyrians in 721 BCE, and its people were scattered.

4. The Jewish homeland established in 1948. Israel was recognized by a United Nations resolution as an independent Jewish state. Under the *Law of Return, it provides a homeland for any Jew from any country in the world: but after the assassination in 1995 of the Prime Minister, Yitzhak Rabin, the first steps were taken to exclude those known to hold extremist views. See also EREZ ISRAEL; ZIONISM.

Israel ben Eliezer, **Baal Shem Tov,** or **Besht** (1700–60). Founder of E. European *Ḥasidism. Many legends are circulated about the life of Israel Ben Eliezer. On his thirty-sixth birthday, he is said to have revealed himself as a new charismatic leader. He worked as a teacher and a healer, travelling round the Jewish communities of E. Europe, attracting many followers by his charm and magnetism. His teachings were partly derived from the *Kabbalah, but his main emphasis was on individual salvation through which the world would be redeemed: 'For before one prays for general *redemption, one must pray for the personal salvation of one's own soul.' He taught that faith is the adhesion (*devekut) of the soul to God, 'and in all daily affairs, human beings must cling to God'. He stressed the importance of joy in prayer and worship, and believed that many fasts 'contribute to melancholy and sadness'. The study of *Torah was also emphasized; Israel taught that it should not only be understood 'for its own sake', but also by contemplating the significance of each individual letter which will 'make a man wise and radiate much light and true eternal life'. He maintained that 'every Jew is a limb of the *Shekhinah', but some individuals have superior spiritual qualities (the *Zaddik). Not only should the Zaddik teach his people to worship God, he should help the sinner to repent and, through special acts, restore the souls of sinners who have died. Israel ben Eliezer left no written teachings, but his disciples preserved many of his sermons and sayings (e.g. 'If you wish to live long, don't become famous'; 'There is no room for God in one who is full of himself'; 'If you want to help a friend out of the mud, don't be afraid of getting a little dirty'; 'When I die, I shall go out of one door and then in, through another.'). During his lifetime, his fame spread and, in some circles, aroused opposition. There is no evidence, however, that he was ever *excommunicated.

Shivhei ha-Besht (1814; Eng. edn., D. Ben Amos and J. R. Mintz, *In Praise of the Baal Shem Tov*, 1970); H. Rabinowicz, *The World of Hasidism* (1970).

Israeli, Isaac ben Solomon (*c*.855–955). Jewish philosopher. Israeli was court physician in Kairouan, the capital of the Maghreb. He was the author of *Kitāb al-Hudūd* (The Book of Definitions) which attempts to define such concepts as the soul, wisdom, the intellect, and nature. It was influenced by *Neoplatonism, and was popular, in a Latin version, with the Christian medieval schoolmen. He also conducted a lengthy correspondence with *Saʿadiah Gaon. He left advice for doctors which remains serviceable to the present day: 'Comfort the patient by the hope of healing, even when you are not certain, for thus you may assist the natural powers.'

Israelite Mission of the New Universal Covenant. A new movement in Peru, founded by Ezequiel Ataucuzi Gamonal. As a result of what he claims were divine revelations, Ezequiel considers himself called to lead God's chosen people to a new obedience to the *Mosaic law. By the early 1960s, a group of followers were meeting in Lima, and after legal recognition in 1969, the movement spread rapidly throughout Peru. Today it claims 80,000 members, though 25,000 may be more accurate. Its theology is largely from the Old Testament, but also contains Christian and Inca elements. Its distinctive features include worship on Saturday, blood sacrifices, celebration of the *Passover, belief that the Second Coming (*Parousia) and the New Jerusalem will be in Peru, and acceptance of Ezequiel as *Son of Man—superior to *Moses and *Paul, but not to *Jesus.

Isserles, Moses ben Israel or **Rema** (*c*.1530–72). Jewish legal authority. Isserles was one of the great *halakhic authorities of the time. He founded a *yeshivah and gained a worldwide reputation for his *responsa, being known as 'the *Maimonides of Polish Jewry' (on his tombstone is inscribed: 'From Moses [i.e. Maimonides] to Moses [Isserles] there has arisen no one like Moses'). He conducted a widespread correspondence with such scholars as Joseph *Caro, Solomon *Luria, and Samuel Judah, and his books include a supplement to the **Shulḥān Arukh*, a collection of responsa, and a collection of halakhic glosses. Although he aroused opposition for his emphasis on custom (*minhag) and his leniency (particularly when financial loss was involved), his rulings have become accepted as binding on *Ashkenazi Jews.

A. Siev, *Ha-Rema* (1957).

Isshi-injo (Jap., 'one vehicle'). The Zen insistence that a student can be taught (up to the level of the conferring of *inka-shōmei) by one master (*roshi) only. This is emphasized (especially in *Sōtō-shū) to stop students going from one teacher to another: since truth is transmitted from heart-mind to heart-mind (*ishin-denshin), it is highly personal, and cannot be left at one point and picked up at another, as though it were book-knowledge. Only when a pupil is recognized as equalling his teacher, can he then seek to deepen his realization of Zen through interaction (*mondō, *hossen) with other masters. The pilgrimage (*angya) is a preliminary for the finding of a roshi.

Isshin (Jap., 'one mind'). The universal mind which, in Buddhism, pervades all appearance—i.e. the Buddha-mind. 'One-mindedness' may also apply to unwavering devotion to *Amida, or in meditation.

Issur ve-hetter (Heb., 'forbidden and permitted'). All Jewish legal rulings about forbidden food (see DIETARY LAWS). Since the late 12th cent., a whole genre of literature grew up on the laws and customs of forbidden food. Examples include *Issur ve-Hetter* (1534) by Isaac b. Meir of Dueren and *Issur ve-Hetter he-Arokh* (1555) by Jonah Ashkenazi.

Iṣṭadevatā (Skt., 'beloved' + 'god'). The chosen deity, in Hinduism, of a temple, family, or cult; or the deity, either chosen by a worshipper, or given to a devotee by a *guru (along with a personal *mantra) who knows what aspect of divinity will help that person to attain progress, perhaps *mokṣa (release). This devotion underlies *bhakti-yoga, and it may be addressed to a holy person or to an *avatāra. The form of the chosen deity is known as *lakṣya*.

Iṣṭamantra (Skt.). Personal or chosen *mantra in Hinduism, employed in repetition (*japa), which brings into active being the god or power which it names. It may be allocated by a *guru, or it may be one of the many traditional mantras, e.g. *om namo Nārāyanāya*.

Istiḥsān (Arab.). A method of legal reasoning used in conjunction with *qiyās (analogy), especially by the *Ḥanafite law school. The principle of istiḥsān was incorporated for solving difficult legal cases arising out of complex conditions in a growing society, when strict adherence to the letter of the law would fail to meet the needs of the people. Istiḥsān can best be understood as juristic preference for a principle of law to promote the aims of the law. Hence, if any law deduced by qiyās is inequitable, inconvenient, or harsh, then the Ḥanafī jurist is at liberty to discard it and adopt one that is convenient and just. It is not an arbitrary opinion but a method to use the principle of law to fit the circumstances of a given case. It is closely related to *istiṣlāh.

Istikhārā (Arab.). The prayer (*du'ā') in Islam of one who is uncertain or undecided for divine guidance.

Istiṣlāh (Arab.). In Islamic law, the concept (not accepted by all schools of *sharī'a) of discerning the intended good of *Qur'ān and *ḥadīth injunctions in relation to the demands of human welfare (*maṣlaḥa*). For the *Mālikite law school it is an important method of legal reasoning used for resolving difficult cases. The Mālikites interpret istiṣlāh as consideration for what is aimed at for humanity in the divine law, and they apply it strictly to the following five areas: maintenance of religion, of life, of reason, of descendants, and of property. An example of istiṣlāh is the imposition of taxes above the normal rate on the rich in order to meet defence costs for the protection of the Muslim community. Despite their similarity, the relation between istiṣlāh and *istiḥsān was disputed between the different schools. The Mālikite jurists consider istiṣlāh to be a legal concept in terms of purely public interest (i.e. rule of necessity and need), while the Ḥanifites support the concept of istiḥsān primarily for promoting the principles of law.

Īśvara (Skt., *īś*, 'to have power'). The concept of a personal God as creator of the cosmos. In the *Vedas, īśvara is the power of a ruler, hence divine power (*Atharva Veda*, 7. 102. 1) and thus (19. 6. 4) a title of *Puruṣa as lord of immortality. In *Advaita Vedānta, Īśvara is *Brahman as Brahman is related to the manifest world of appearance, and is thus worthy of worship. All gods (including those of other religions, e.g. Islam) then became aspects of Īśvara according to the needs of the cosmos. In particular, Īśvara becomes manifest in the *trimūrti, or trinity, of *Brahmā, *Viṣṇu, and *Śiva. As, in effect, the personal god (i.e. the way in which God becomes personal to an individual), Īśvara evokes the attitude of *bhakti (devotion).

Īśvarakoti (Skt.). A perfected soul in Hinduism, which is reborn on earth to help others to realize truth; cf. AVATĀRA, or in Buddhism BODHISATTVA.

Iśvarakṛṣṇa (c.350–450). Author of the *Sāṃkhyakārikā*, a summary compilation of the *Sāṃkhya philosophy. A Chinese commentary by Paramārtha claims he was a *Brahman of the Kauśika family, and a reference in *Jayamaṅgalā*, a Skt. commentary, says that he was a wandering ascetic (*parivrājaka). He was probably a contemporary of Vindhyavāsin, Vārṣagaṇya, and *Vasubandhu.

Ithnā 'Asharīy(y)a (Arab., *ithna'ashar*, 'twelve'). The Twelvers, majority *Shi'a Islam, the official Shi'a religion of modern Iran. This Shi'a sect follows the cult of Twelve *Imāms, in distinction from the smaller Sab'īyya sect (*Seveners, see also ISMĀ'ĪLIYYA). The Ṣafāvids made the Ithnā 'Asharīy(y)a the state religion of Iran in 1500 (AH 906). The series of Twelve Imāms is: *'Alī, *al-Hasan, *al-Ḥusain, 'Alī Zayn, al-'Abidīn, Muḥammad al-Bāqir, Ja'far al-Ṣādiq, Mūsā al-Kāẓim 'Alī al-Riḍā, Muḥammad al-Taqī, 'Alī al-Naqī, al-Ḥasan al-'Askarī, and Muhammad *al-Mahdī. The Imāms are the chosen of God, who direct the destiny of humanity, and preserve and guide the world. Through them lies salvation, and without them is perdition. Those who die without knowing their Imām, die as unbelievers. The intercession of the Imāms to resolve human affairs, both for this life and for the afterlife, is indispensable. Special prayers are reserved for each of the Imāms during weekdays, and it is believed that pilgrimage to their tombs brings special rewards, especially at *Karbalā' and *Mashhad. Moreover, there is a strong eschatological element maintained by the Twelvers: the twelfth Imām, Muhammad *al-Mahdī, disappeared when a young child, and it is believed that he will come back again near the end of time, as *al-Mahdī, to herald the Day of Judgement and fill the trouble-torn earth with justice and peace. This is the Hidden Imām (*ghaiba).

I–Thou (in contrast to I–It). A distinction in ways of knowing, emphasized by M. *Buber: in the personal relationship, one subject, I, encounters or meets another subject, Thou; in connection with things, the subject observes or experiences an object, It: 'As experience, the world belongs to the primary word, *I–It*. The primary word *I–Thou* establishes the world of relation.' The relation with God may be I–It as a matter of discussion, but God can only be known in the I–Thou relationship.

M. Buber, *I and Thou* (1937).

Itihāsa (Skt., 'so indeed it was'). Early Hindu literature, comprising legends, myths, poems, etc., associated with epics and *purāṇas (especially the eighteen Mahāpurāṇas), which is then later called (e.g. *Chandogya Upaniṣad* 3. 4. 1 f.) the fifth *Veda. More generally the great epics (*Mahābhārata*, *Rāmāyaṇa*) are termed itihāsa. Collectively, Itihāsapurāṇa becomes the Veda which those who do not have access to the four Vedas are able to study (and enjoy).

M. Winternitz, 'The Popular Epics and the Purāṇas', in *A History of Indian Literature*, i (1963).

'Itikāf. 'Retreat' to a *mosque for a certain period of time, to engage in worship, fasting, and reading the *Qur'ān. This can be in fulfilment of a vow. It is particularly practised during the last ten nights of

*Ramaḍān, following the reported custom of *Muḥammad. The Qur'ān recommends ʿitikāf during the days of Ramaḍān (2. 187).

Itivuttaka (part of the Buddhist Pāli canon): see KHUDDAKA-NIKĀYA.

Itō Jinsai (1627–1705). A Japanese *Confucian scholar from the movement called Ancient Learning (*kokugaku). He opened his school in *Kyōto where he taught that the true message of the Confucian sages could only be apprehended by reading their ancient writings directly, without reliance upon the later Neo-Confucian commentaries of *Chu Hsi (1130–1200) and others. His school, known as the Kogidō or 'Hall of Ancient Meanings', was continued by his son, Itō Tōgai (1670–1736), with students drawn from all over Japan. See also Ogyū Sorai.

J. J. Spae, *Itō Jinsai* . . . (1948); Yoshikawa, *Kojiro, Jinsai, Sorai and Norinaga* (1983).

Ittai (Jap., 'one body'). The Zen experience of participating in (and indeed being) undifferentiated reality. It is thus the attainment of the goal of Zen training in which one's own body is not other than all that is, so far as 'is' is the appropriate word.

Iwasaka (Jap.). Proto-*Shinto sanctuary. The word appears only twice, once in the *Nihongi*, once in the *Kogoshūi*, both of which refer to the same myth narrating the descent of *Ninigi, the mythic ancestor of the imperial family. The texts infer that iwasaka stands for something to be set up, together with *himoroki* (meaning uncertain), for worship service, which implicitly suggests that it was not intended to be a permanent sanctuary. It may be taken as a synonym for *iwakura* (lit., 'rock seat') from which, some suggest, a priest-chieftain in ancient times delivered a divine message. Iwasaka, as it is written, is a compound of two Chinese characters 'rock' and 'boundary', which seems to indicate a type of stone formation, with or without the main sacred rock (*iwakura*) in the middle.

Iyenar (Tamil tutelary deity): see GRĀMADEVATĀ.

Izanagi and Izanami. The paired 'male who invites' and 'female who invites' in Japanese mythology. They are of the seventh generation of gods who are required to undertake creation—including, in the *Nihongi*, *Amaterasu. They stand on the floating bridge of heaven and stir up the matter of creation with a spear thrust into the depth of the ocean. Izanami is destroyed in the making of fire and goes to the land of Yomi (death). Izanagi searches for her, and when he finds her, he disobeys her command not to look at her. He lights a torch and sees her decaying body. Yomi tries to catch him so that he cannot return to the living and warn them about death, but he escapes. Izanami threatens in her anger to kill a thousand beings every day, but Izanagi responds by promising to bring one and a half thousand to birth. So begins the process of life and death.

Izmirim (Doenmeh sect): see DOENMEH.

ʿIzrāʾīl or **ʿAzrāʾīl** (Arab.). In Islam, the *angel of death. He is one of the four archangels, the one who 'appointed over you, will cause you to die' (Qur'ān 32. 12). He is entrusted by *Allāh with the task of taking the soul of each human being whose life-span has ended; and at the Day of Judgement he will be responsible for causing the death of all people then on the earth. *Ḥadīth and legend describe him as being of vast size and great strength.

J

J. The name given to a supposed source used in the composition of the *Pentateuch: it is an abbreviation of the Jahwistic (Yahwistic) source.

Jabneh (Yavneh, also known as Jamnia). Town to the east of *Jerusalem. It came to prominence after the Fall of Jerusalem in 70 CE, when R. *Johanan ben Zakkai was allowed by the Romans to establish a centre of learning—and, from the Jewish point of view, the *Sanhedrin. From here the continuity of Judaism in Israel was secured.

Jabriy(y)a (Muslim sect emphasising God's control): see QADAR.

Jacob (Heb., Yaʿakov). Third Hebrew *patriarch. Jacob was the younger twin son (with *Esau) of *Isaac and Rebekah. Before his birth it was predicted that both twins would be fathers of great nations, but the elder would serve the younger (Genesis 25. 22–3). Later, Genesis records how Jacob stole his brother Esau's birthright (25. 29–34) and blessing (27). Fleeing from his brother's anger, he had a vision at *Bethel (28. 10–15) and served his uncle Laban fourteen years for his daughter *Rachel (29). From his two wives and two concubines, Jacob had twelve sons who were to be the ancestors of the twelve *tribes. On his return to *Canaan, Jacob fought with a stranger at the ford of Jabbok and was given the new name of *Israel (32. 25–33). After being reconciled to Esau, Jacob settled finally in Canaan until he went down to Egypt to be with his son *Joseph (37–47). In the *aggadah, the story of Jacob is understood as symbolic of the later history of the Jews—so Esau struggling with Jacob in their mother's womb is interpreted as the conflict between Rome and Israel (e.g. *Gen.R.* 63. 8). There is a consistent tendency among the *rabbis to explain Jacob's conduct in the best possible light—so Jacob's desire for his brother's birthright was a desire for the privilege of offering the *sacrifices of the *first-born (*Gen.R.* 63. 13).

Jacob ben Asher or **Baʿal ha-Turim** (*c.*1270–1340). Jewish *halakhic authority. Jacob was the son of *Asher b. Jeḥiel. Working in poverty in Toledo, he compiled his halakhic masterpiece the *Arbaʿah Turim* (Four Rows, 1475) because he perceived 'reasoning had become faulty, controversy had increased, opinions had multiplied'. The *Turim* is divided into four parts: (i) *Oraḥ Ḥayyim* (The Path of Life), the laws concerning religious life through the whole day, including conduct in *synagogue and on fast and festival days; (ii) *Yoreh De'ah* (The Teaching of Knowledge), on *issur ve-hetter, including food, family, mourning, usury, oaths; (iii) *Even ha-Ezer* (The Stone of Help), on women, marriage, and divorce; (iv) *Ḥoshen Mishpat* (The Breastplate of Judgement), civil law. The work went through many edns., evoking commentaries and epitomes. In particular, it formed the basis of Joseph *Caro's *Beit Yosef* (House of Joseph), because in his view it contained 'most of the views of the *posekim'. Jacob also wrote a comprehensive commentary on the *Pentateuch, prefacing each section with explanations based on *gematria which have remained popular to the present day. His work was held in a bracket of attention to God—he prefaced the *Turim* with the observation, 'Better a little with devotion than much without it'—and was well aware that the more he wrote of his work, the more there remained to do: 'The road that leads to learning turns out to have no end.'

Jacob Joseph of Polonnoye (*c.*1710–84), *Ḥasidic teacher and author, known as Toledot (from his book *Toledot Yaʿakov Yosef*, 'The Generations of Jacob Joseph', 1780). Already a rabbi, he met and became a disciple of Baʿal Shem Tov (*Israel ben Eliezer) when he was about 35. He became a *zaddik (understanding the zaddik as 'the soul of the world, with the rest of his generation as the body; he is the channel through whom the influence of God flows into the lives of ordinary people'), and as such was a passionate defender and advocate of Ḥasidic teachings. Although he failed to oust *Dov Baer as the successor of Baʿal Shem Tov, he remains revered by Ḥasidim as one who transmitted his teachings faithfully and as the first (relatively) systematic exponent of Ḥasidism. His other major works (alluding to *Joseph in the title) were *Ben Porat Yosef* ('Joseph is a Fruitful Vine', 1781), *Tzafenat Pane'ah* (the name given to Joseph by Pharaoh in Genesis 41. 45, 1782), and *Ketonat Passim* ('Coat of Many Colours', pub. 1866). He emphasized the importance of humour and happiness in the service of God: 'Fasting and penance make one appropriately sad, but devotion can only be through joy.' Study is important, but equally so is mixing with people and enjoying their company: a zaddik cannot hope to raise people to God unless he is truly one of them ('He must have in him a particle of uncleanness'). The purpose of a human life is to become the temple of God.

S. H. Dresner, *The Zaddik: The Doctrine of the Zaddik according to the Writings of Rabbi Yaakov . . .* (1966).

Jacobson, Israel (1768–1828). Pioneer of *Reform Judaism. Jacobson worked for the emancipation of the Jews of the German states and was an enthusiastic supporter of Napoleon's Assembly of Jewish Notables. Jacobson himself summoned a similar assembly in Westphalia in 1808 and was instrumental in the founding of the first Reform *synagogues both in Westphalia and Berlin. These 'synagogues' borrowed, from *Lutheran churches, hymns and choirs, and ceremonies resembling *confirmation. He claimed to be working within the legitimate development of *halakhah, and to be restoring aesthetic vitality to otherwise dead assemblies.

Jacopone da Todi (*c.*1230–1306). *Franciscan poet. A lawyer of a somewhat worldly life, he was converted after the death of his wife. He became a Franciscan laybrother in 1278, joining the 'Spirituals' who sought to live according to the original rigour of the rule. As such he was imprisoned for a time by Pope Boniface VIII. He is famed for his deeply emotional devotional poems (*Laude*), in Latin and the Umbrian dialect, which became very popular (amongst them, probably, the *Stabat Mater*). Love draws us on through three heavens, in each of which the inadequacy of the preceding is made clear: 'I thought I knew you, tasted you, saw you under the image. Believing I held you in your completeness I was filled with delight and unmeasured love. But now I see I was mistaken: you are not as I thought and firmly held.'

E. Underhill, *Jacopone da Todi, Poet and Mystic* (1919).

Jaḍa-samādhi (Skt., 'insentient' + 'samādhi'). A defective condition in Hinduism, parasitic on two important goals: jaḍa is the highest state of yogin concentration, virtually equivalent to *vidyā, in which all false dualities are transcended; and *samādhi is the highest state of contemplation in which identity is achieved with the object of contemplation. But the two together refer to something more like 'dreamless sleep', a state of suspended consciousness.

Jade Emperor (Deity in Chinese folk religion): see YÜ-HUANG.

Jadid al-Islam (group of secretly practising Jews): see CRYPTO-JEWS.

Ja'far al-Sādiq (6th Shī'a Imām): see ISMĀ-'ĪLIY(Y)A.

Ja'farī Shi'ites. Those Shi'ite Muslims (Ithnā 'Ashariy(y)a, Twelvers) who follow the codes of religious law associated with Ja'far al-Sādiq.

Jafr. The belief of *Shī'a Muslims that there is a secret tradition of esoteric knowledge passed on through the succession of Imāms.

Jagaccandra Suri (Jain sect): see GACCHA.

Jagadguru (Skt., 'world-teacher'). Title assumed by sect leaders, as e.g. among the *Liṅgāyats.

Jagannātha (Skt., 'Lord of the Universe': often Anglicized as 'juggernaut'). Local name of the Hindu god *Viṣṇu/*Kṛṣṇa worshipped in the temple of Purī, Orissa. The temple is famous all over India and attracts large numbers of pilgrims, particularly to its *festivals. King Anantavarmā Coḍagaṅgā (*c.*1100 CE) began the construction of the actual building; there is good reason to believe that the god and his cult had tribal origins. Inside are found three images, made of wood in an abstract, geometrical style, typical of tribal art. Low-*caste priests participate in the daily ceremonies. But whatever the origins, Jagannātha was eventually interpreted as Kṛṣṇa/Viṣṇu, and the other two images as his half-brother *Balarāma and his 'sister' Subhadrā (in whom earlier cults of *Durgā/*Kālī were subsumed). The temple became notorious under colonial rule because of its festivals, during which period the wooden images are carried out in procession on huge wooden carts (up to 50 feet tall), requiring 4,000 or more men to pull them. Given the vast numbers of pilgrims present and the constraints of space, accidents did happen and people were caught under the wheels. The authorities of the time perceived this as intentional religious suicide. Yet it is doubtful that it was so in most cases. 'Juggernaut' came to denote blind, religious frenzy. But with memories of the huge festival carts lingering on, a more recent application of the word is to large, heavy lorries.

Jagjīt Siṅgh. A *Nāmdhārī Sikh who became leader in 1959. Jagjīt *Siṅgh, great-nephew of *Rām Siṅgh, succeeded his father, Partāp Siṅgh, as vice-regent until the long-awaited return of Rām Siṅgh. His title of *Sat gurū indicates his status. Although based at Bhainī *Sāhib, *Pañjāb, his commitment to the order led to much travel, promoting improved dairy farming, vegetarianism, and world peace.

Jahāṅgīr (1569–1626). *Mughal emperor from 1605, whose full title was Nūr-ud-din Mohāmmad Jahāṇgīr Gāzī. He had four sons and many wives and concubines, but he loved Nūr-Jahān best and ruled with her advice and active support. Towards the end of his reign he was under the influence of opium, which rendered him emperor in name only, and the real power was with Nūr-Jahān which she wielded with the ministers of her choice.

It was Jahāṇgīr who granted trading permission to Sir Thomas Roe, representing the East India Company and Elizabeth I at the Mughal court. Jahāṇgīr followed *Akbar's religious policy of tolerance so his reign was beneficial to his subjects. He was fond of natural beauty, hunting, and architecture. The intrigues of his son Khurram (later Emperor Shah Jehān, see TAJ MAHAL) and his wife Nūr-Jahān made Jahāṇgīr's last years full of misery and uncertainty. There was, however, no jarring event in his reign to upset the smooth working of the empire.

Jahannam: see HELL (ISLAM).

Jāhilīy(y)a (Arab., *jāhil*, 'untaught'). The state of ignorance understood to have characterized Arabian society prior to Islam. The *jāhil* is the ignorant person with (because of lack of the truth) an accompanying wildness or uncouthness. Islamic historiography saw the immediate time of *Muḥammad and the first four Caliphs as a golden age, never since renewed, and its antecedent years as totally dark and depraved. Pre-Islamic poetry does not wholly bear out this jāhilīya, with its evidence of *murū'a*, ('manly virtue'), its lament about feuding and the cheapness of life, and its register of human frailty. It is also necessary to keep in mind the presence of *ḥanīfs (implicit monotheists perhaps, who influenced Muḥammad and whom he celebrates), and the extent to which Muḥammad was himself a beneficiary of tribal and kinship systems of support. Broadly, however, Arabian society was beset by many ills—tribal conflict, bedouin poverty, Quraishi capitalism, and chronic disunity sanctioned by plural worship. Islam overcame some of these by harnessing *murū'a* to religious fervour and solidarity. In Islam today there are those who see in W. secularism a new jāhilīya and who anathematize some expressions of Islam itself by this term.

Jahnu. A Hindu prince who drank the Ganges (*Gaṅgā) when it flooded his sacrificial ground. The *ṛṣis and gods propitiated him, and he allowed the water to flow out of his ear, hence to be known in personified form as Jāhnavī, daughter of Jahnu. Hence also it is the name of the cave at the source of the Ganges.

Jaimal Siṅgh (founder of Hindu religious movement): see RĀDHĀSOĀMĪ SATSAṄG.

Jaimini. Name of several Hindu authors, the distinction between whom is not always clear. The *Mīmāṃsā-sūtras are attributed to a Jaimini (though they are from different dates), as is a Gṛhya Sūtra. Another Jaimini translated the **Aśvamedha parvan* of the **Mahābhārata* into Kanarese, and it is regarded as the finest example of poetry in that language.

Jainism. An ancient Indian *śrāmaṇic religious and philosophical tradition still vigorous today. The religion derives its name from the *jinas (spiritual victors), a title given to twenty-four great teachers or 'ford-makers' (*tīrthaṅkaras) whom Jains claim have appeared in the present half-cycle (*avasarpiṇī*) of time. In fact, Jain teaching is uncreated and eternal, being reactivated by the 'ford-makers' (as the *Three Jewels) in unending cycles. In the present cycle, historical evidence clearly reaches back to the last two of these teachers, *Mahāvīra (24th), who was a contemporary of the *Buddha, and *Pārśva (23rd), but it is evident that these teachers were reviving, restoring, and re-forming a thread of ancient śramaṇic teaching whose origins lie in Indian prehistory and may have links with the *Indus Valley Civilization (see ṚṢABHA). The aim of Jain spiritual endeavour is to liberate the soul (*jīva) by freeing it from accumulated *karma. Every soul is potentially divine and can aspire to *mokṣa by following a course of purification and discipline demonstrated by the tīrthaṅkaras. At the heart of Jainism lies a radical asceticism based on *five vows which monks and nuns follow wholeheartedly and which the laity attempt to the best of their ability. Of these five vows (*ahiṁsā (non-injury); *satya* (speaking the truth); *asteya* (not taking anything not given); *brahmacharya (chastity); *aparigraha (detachment from place, persons, and things)), the first is pre-eminent, involving a radical break from Hindu sacrifices, and also care not to injure living things. The major schism of Jainism between the *Digambara ('the atmosphere clad', i.e. naked) and Śvetāmbara ('white clad'), began to emerge as early as 300 BCE ostensibly over whether monks should go naked or wear a simple cloth; but the two schools came to embody differing views towards the scriptures (see AṄGA), women, and monastic practice.

In early years, the Jain movement diffused from its place of origin in the Ganges basin. Of particular importance was the settlement in *Mathurā, which was identified as the site of Pārśva's preaching. In the south, Jains seem to have formed a close relation with rulers, especially in Karnataka, and even to have allowed the possibility of war, but only if carried out for reasons of defence; though still it was more common to speak of the true warfare as that of the ascetic (cf. the inner *jihād of Islam). The diffusion of Jainism also accelerated the tendency to form separate groups (see GACCHA). Yet although differences have grown up over matters of ascetic discipline and (especially after the introduction of Islam into India) over the necessity or otherwise of images (see DIGAMBARA), there has been less dispute over the fundamental doctrines or philosophy. Jain philosophy forms a *nāstika school within the Indian philosophical tradition (i.e. from the perspective of the Hindus), since it rejects the authority of the *Vedas, *caste, and the idea of a God who creates. It is characterized by a realistic classification of being and a theory of knowledge which has connections with *Sāṃkhya and Buddhist thought. Jain philosophers have made many distinctive contributions to Indian philosophy particularly in the kindred doctrines of *nayavāda and *syādvāda which together form the doctrine of the manysidedness of reality (*anekāntavāda). This enables a tolerance which may account in part for the remarkable survival of Jainism in India. The wealth of the Jain laity and the scholarship of Jain monks through the ages has resulted in the Jains making notable contributions to Indian art, sculpture, and literature. Jain temples, particularly those at Mount Abu and

Ranakpur in Rajasthan, are among the most beautiful and breathtaking in the whole of Indian architecture. Jain libraries, many of them still not fully explored, house unique examples of local language, literature, and often fine miniatures and leaf-paintings. The keystone of Jain ethics, *ahiṁsā, gained international recognition in the 20th cent. through the life and work of Mohandas K. *Gāndhī, who, although a Hindu, was deeply influenced in his thinking by a young Jain layman, *Raychandbhai Mehta. Whilst accounting for less than 0.5 per cent of India's vast population, Jain influence on the religious, social, political, and economic life of the country has been and is quite out of proportion to their numbers. Jain education, wealth, concern for all life, and simple lifestyle have served as a powerful and morally uplifting factor in many Indian communities. Jains today are most heavily concentrated (about 3 to 4 million) in Maharasthra, Rajasthan, Gujarat, Madhya Pradesh, and Mysore, particularly in the business centres, which they tend to dominate. The initiation of the *Aṇuvrata Movement by the Śvetāmbara Terāpanth leader Acharya Tulasi in 1948, reflects the continuing influence and vitality of the Jain tradition in modern India. Until the last cent., Jainism was strictly an Indian phenomenon, but many Gujarati Jains, who had settled in E. Africa, migrated to Europe in the late 1960s and early 1970s as a result of pan-Africanization policies; so that today there are estimated to be 25,000 Jains in Europe, largely in the UK. Some estimates suggest a similar number may be found in N. America. The establishment of what became the Jain Samaj Europe in Leicester (UK) in 1973 witnessed to a thriving Jain community outside India despite its being deprived of contact with its ascetic leaders. This, and the fact that the central thrust of Jain teaching, ahiṁsā, has such direct relevance to the nuclear age, makes it all the more remarkable that relatively little W. scholarship has been devoted to this important, ancient religious tradition. See Index, Jains.

B. C. Bhattacharya, *The Jaina Iconography* (1974); N. N. Bhattacharya, *Jain Philosophy: A Historical Outline* (1976); P. Dundas, *The Jains* (1992); A. Ghosh, *Jaina Art and Architecture* (1974–5); M. U. K. Jain, *Jain Sects and Schools* (1975); P. S. Jaini, *The Jaina Path of Purification* (1979); J. Laidlaw, *Riches and Renunciation: Religion and Economy among the Jains* (1995); B. C. Nahar and K. C. Ghosh, *Encyclopedia of Jainism* (1986); Satyaprakash, *Jainism: A Select Bibliography* (1984).

Jakoblar (Doenmeh, Islamic sect): see DOENMEH.

Jakugo or **chakugo** (Jap., 'words of arrival'). A summary statement in Zen of the true understanding of a *kōan.

Jakuhitsu Genkō (1290–1367). Japanese Zen master of the *Rinzai school. He became a monk at the age of 15 and was taught by Yakuō Tokken in *Kamakura. When he asked Yakuō for his *matsugo* (his final, dying word, and also the word which will lead to enlightenment), Yakuō slapped him and he immediately experienced enlightenment. He went to China, 1320–6, where he was acknowledged as a master of Ch'an, although he himself felt that he received vital instruction, especially from Chung-feng Ming-pen. In particular, he developed the devotion to *Amida which appears in his poems—though the *Pure Land is to be sought and found within one's own mind, not as some 'place': 'Even though the *nembutsu and Zen are different in name, they are the same in essence.' On his return to Japan, he became an itinerant, seeking realization of truth in mountains and solitude. When Eigen-ji was built in 1361, he became the first abbot. After five years, during which many visitors were attracted, he resigned in favour of his disciple, Miten Eishaku. But in that period he contributed decisively to the *rinka* or *ringe* style of Zen monasticism, 'under the forest' or 'thicket', in which the ideal of simplicity and non-attachment was maintained.

Jakumetsu (Jap., 'stillness' + 'extinction'). Japanese pronunciation of the two Chinese characters which represent the Skt. for *nirvāna. It is thus an indefinable state of absolute attainment in which a buddha lives. It can be realized 'here' and 'now', so far as these are relevant words: it is not a state or condition which lies beyond or after this life.

Jalāl al-Dīn Rūmī or **Mawlānā/Mawlawī** ('our master', 1207–73 (AH 604–72)). A great mystic poet of Islam and founder of the *Mawlawīy(y)a (Mevlevi) *Sūfī order. He was born at Balkh, but his family migrated to Kōnya in Rūm, Anatolia, hence his surname. He rose to be professor of Religious Science at Kōnya. Rūmī's meeting with the Sūfī, Shams al-Dīn Tabrīzī, led him to abandon his teaching career and devote himself entirely to the mystic path. From then on, Rūmī, over a period of time, received divine illumination; and the love of God became the whole basis of his life: 'Love is the remedy for our pride and self-conceit, the physician of all our infirmities. Only he whose garment is rent by love becomes entirely unselfish.' Rūmī argues that rites and formulae are nothing, and that inner feeling is everything: ' "What can words do for me?" says God to Moses; "It is a glowing heart that I want; inflame the hearts with love and pay no heed to thought or expression." ' Contrary to general Muslim practice, Rūmī gave *music and *dance an important place in religious expression. He instituted the circular dance which represents the harmonious movement of heavenly bodies and an expression of cosmic love—i.e. all creation dancing in joy around the centre (God). In ideas also he extended the boundaries of orthodox Islam. Thus he suggested *metempsychosis:

> I die as a stone and become a plant; I die as a plant and I am raised up to be an animal; I die as an animal, and I am reborn as a man. . . . When I die as a man, I shall come to life as an angel . . . I will transcend even the angel to become what no man has seen, no thing, the Nothing.

He saw humans as virtually the extension (through a union of love) of God:

'We are the flute, the music you; | The mountain we, which echoes you; | The chessmen set in line by you, | To win or lose as moved by you; | We are the flags embroidered by the lion; | The unseen wind which ripples us is you.'

He even saw the ugly as manifesting the glory of God: 'The ugly says: "O King, Creator of the ugly, your power is as evident in the ugly which is despised, as in the beautiful which is admired." '

The best known of Rūmī's works are *Diwan-i-shams-Tabrizi* (The Poems of Shams-i-Tabriz) and *Mathnawī* (The Poem in Rhyming Couplets, tr. R. A. Nicholson, 1925–40), a great mystical poem considered by *Jāmī to be the essence of the Qur'ān rendered in Persian. He also wrote a prose treatise entitled *Fīhi mā fīhi* (What is within is within). His influence over the Sūfī orders of Turkey, Persia, Central Asia, and India reinvigorated Islam from within and helped it recover from the Mongol invasions (1258).

W. Chittick, *The Sufi Path of Love* (1983); R. A. Nicholson, *Rumi, Poet and Mystic* (1898); A. Schimmel, *The Triumphal Sun* . . . (1978); E. H. Whinfield, *Teachings of Rumi* . . . (1975).

Jalwah (return to the world to help others): see MULLĀ ṢADR.

Jamaa (Swahili, 'family'). A large *charismatic movement among African *Roman Catholics in Zaire. It was founded in the early 1950s among urban workers attached to the copper mines in the Katanga area, by a Belgian Franciscan missionary, Placide Tempels. It expressed the ideas in his influential book *Bantu Philosophy* (1945), which interpreted RC teaching in terms of African culture. Its informal intertribal local groups remained attached to the parish churches; members were almost all adult and married, except for *priests who participated. The teachings concerned deep personal and loving relationships, especially between husband and wife, a search for human dignity, and emphasis upon the life-force and fecundity. After a sympathetic beginning, relations with the RC hierarchy deteriorated, Tempels was withdrawn to Belgium in 1962, members were virtually *excommunicated from about 1970, and the government was exhorted to act, which it did with a formal banning in 1974. In spite of this Jamaa has spread widely into Kasai and beyond, and produced deviant secessions known as Katete.

W. de Craemer, *The Jamaa and the Church* . . . (1977).

Jamāʿat-i Islāmī (The Islamic Society). A highly disciplined and well-organized Muslim political party, founded in 1941 by Abul al-Aʿlā *Mawdūdī. It aims at establishing an observant Islamic state in Pakistan. The Jamāʿat's political platform offers an alternative to the secularists and the modernists, and in this lies its appeal (especially since 1977). The Jamāʿat advocates that Pakistan should be a theocratic state, ruled by a single man whose tenure of office and power are limited only by his faithfulness to Islam. The ruler should be assisted by a *shura* (advisory council), with no political parties and no provision for an opposition. General Zia al-Haqq, the military leader after the overthrow of Z. Bhutto (1977), used the Jamāʿat as a political prop for his 'back to Islam' campaign. The Jamāʿat has influence among the military, the middle-classes, and the college and university students. It publishes a monthly magazine, *Tarjuman al-Quran*, in Lahore that has a high circulation. On the international level, the Jamāʿat was on good terms with Imām *Khumayni and the oil-rich Arab states; the Saudis have supported the movement since the early 1970s.

Jamāl al-Dīn al-Afghānī (Muslim modernist reformer): see AL-AFGHĀNĪ.

James. The name of two or three early Christian figures. St James, the son of Zebedee, was brother of *John, and one of *Jesus' inner circle of disciples. He was martyred in 44 CE (Acts 12. 2). He was claimed in the Middle Ages to have been the apostle of Spain, and was supposed to have been buried at Santiago de Compostela (see PILGRIMAGE). St James, 'the Lord's brother' (Mark 6. 3), became the leader of the earliest Christian church at Jerusalem after the departure of *Peter. He took a moderate position at the *Apostolic Council in *c*.48. According to Hegesippus, who calls him 'James the Just', he was put to death by the *Sanhedrin in 62. Nothing is known of St James the Less (or 'the younger'; Mark 15. 40) unless he is to be identified with James the son of Alphaeus (Mark 3. 18) or Jesus' brother.

The Letter of James is the first of the *Catholic Epistles in the New Testament. It is almost entirely moral in content, without circumstantial notes or even (apart from 1. 1 and 2. 1) any specifically Christian features. A date as early as 40 CE and authorship by James the brother of Jesus are not impossible, although doubted by such early writers as *Origen. James was disliked by M. *Luther ('a right strawy epistle') and has been little valued by *Protestants generally on account of its words on the insufficiency of faith alone (2. 14–26).

James, William (1842–1910). American scholar whose contribution to the study of religion derives from his refusal to treat physiology, psychology, and philosophy as separate disciplines. What remains a major contribution to the psychology of religion, James's *The Varieties of Religious Experience* (1902), also benefited from the fact that he was equipped with 'religious musicality'. Always tending to be individualistic, *The Varieties* dwells on personal religious life rather than on institutional or social expressions. He introduced the phrase, 'stream of consciousness', and described the nature of the stream. This emphasis allowed him to further his aim of opening the reader to the whole range of experience. His empirically controlled and tested pragmatism ('By their fruits ye shall know them, not by their roots') makes it difficult to establish, in ontological terms, what James meant by 'religious'. But, like others after him (e.g. *Jung and Alan *Watts), he treated the conversion experience in psychological terms, as a breaking through to modes of consciousness which complete or bring to realization the 'spiritual Me' (see *The Principles of Psychology*, 1890). In general, the determination of both meaning and truth depends, for James, on the future—on the implications that propositions have for future (possible) experience. *The Will To Believe* (1897) is a commitment to struggle against evil and moral deficiencies, not an exercise in empty metaphysical speculation.

G. W. Allen, *William James, A Biography* (1967); G. E. Myers, *William James . . .* (1986); R. B. Perry, *The Thought and Character of William James* (1935).

Jāmi. A Hindu goddess of maternity and feminine attributes.

Jāmī, Mawlānā Nūr al-Dīn 'Abd al-Rahmān (1414–92 (AH 817–98)). Muslim *Sūfī poet of the *Naqshbandiy(y)a order, known as *khātam al-shu'arā'*, 'the seal of the poets'. He immersed himself in the teaching of *Ibn 'Arabī, but united this with the vision of *Jalāl al-Dīn Rūmī. His best-known poetic work (*Haft Awrang*, The Seven Thrones) explores, through classical examples, how human love is transformed into the symbol and vehicle of divine love: 'Ordinary human love is capable of raising us to the experience of real love.' His prose works expound Ibn 'Arabi, and his *Nafaḥāt al-Uns* (Breaths of Familiarity) became a standard history of Sufism.

'Jam.pa'i.dbyargs (bodhisattva): see MAÑJUŚRĪ.

Jan (spirit): see FRAVASI.

Janaka. Hindu king of Videha who was instructed by *Yajñavalkya, and who maintained that a pious *kṣatriya can perform sacrifices as much as the *brahmans. When ploughing a field to perform a sacrifice in order to obtain offspring, his daughter Sītā ('furrow') came fully formed from the earth, hence his epithet, Śīradhvaja, 'he of the plough-banner'. He remains an example of how to live serenely in the world after obtaining liberation.

Janamaśtami, also known as **Krishnajayānti.** Hindu *festival celebrating the birth of *Kṛṣṇa. It is held on the eighth day of the dark fortnight of the month of Śravana (Aug.). It is observed by many Hindus, and not just by *Vaiṣṇava devotees of Kṛṣṇa. The festival includes a nightlong vigil, concentrating on midnight, the time of Kṛṣṇa's birth. Stories of Kṛṣṇa are told, and sweetmeats are placed in his cradle as a gift: 'He who offers me with devotion as little as a leaf or a flower or a fruit, or even a drop of water, I will accept it from the longing soul, because it was offered with a pure heart in love' (*Bhagavad-gītā* 9. 26).

Janam-sākhī (Pañjābī, 'birth-testimony, biography'). Collection of hagiographic stories about Gurū *Nānak. Printed janam-sākhīs are later developments of underlying oral and manuscript traditions, not contemporary with Gurū Nānak. These manuscripts fall into the following groups: the popular *Bālā j.; the Purātan ('ancient') j., including the Vilāitvālī j. (India Office Library MS Panj. B6); the Ādi ('first') Sākhīs; the Miharbān j., attributed to Miharbān *Soḍhī; the Giān-Ratanāvalī of *Manī *Siṅgh; the Mahimā Prakāś ('light of glory') tradition and the B40 manuscript (India Office Library MS Panj. B40).

The janam-sākhīs are written in *Gurmukhī in Pañjābī prose ranging from an early, unrefined style to more sophisticated language and reflecting regional dialects. Between j. traditions there are discrepancies of events and sequence, some traceable to rivals' claims to Gurūship (e.g. Miharbān j.). *Miracles abound (e.g. to shade Nānak a tree's shadow remains stationary). Remembered episodes from the Gurū's life combine with elements from earlier traditions. There is an ascetic ethos, with stories providing a narrative context for Nānak's *hymns (variants of some in the *Ādi Granth).

The janam-sākhīs have contributed to Sikh corporate identity and popular devotion. They afford an invaluable insight into 17th- and early 18th-cent. Sikhism, rather than history of Gurū Nānak.

W. H. McLeod, *Early Sikh Tradition* (1980).

Janārdana: (Skt., 'giver of rewards'). One of the twenty-four *avatāras (incarnations) of *Viṣṇu. He takes the form of the planets, and distributes the consequences of actions to living beings.

Jaṅgamas (Liṅgāyat officiants): see LIṄGĀYAT.

Janissaries (Turk., *yeni cheri*, 'new troops'). Corps of highly trained Muslim soldiers who were raised from the *devshirme*, Balkan boys who, by levy, were compelled to become Muslims. They existed from the 14th cent. (8th cent. AH) to the 19th (13th). They usually numbered about 15,000, and religiously were associated with the *Bektāshīy(y)a. They were disbanded after a mutiny in 1826 (AH 1242).

Janna (garden): see HEAVEN (ISLAM).

Jansenism. A Christian religious movement of 17th- and 18th-cent. France which drew its inspiration from the *Augustinus* (1640) of Cornelius Jansen (1585–1638). This study of St *Augustine's doctrine of *grace adopted his most rigid views, and was accused of reiterating the teaching of *Calvin and of Baius. Jansen's views were propagated by Saint-Cyran, from 1635 the spiritual director of Mère Angélique *Arnauld, abbess of Port-Royal near Paris, and he also had a considerable influence on Angélique's youngest brother Antoine, encouraging him to write his attack on the practice of frequent *communion (1642). While emphasis on *predestination, the fewness of the number of the elect, and the perfect state necessary to receive the *sacraments, remained central, Jansenist teaching developed in a number of directions. Partly at least through the regular condemnation of its teachings by Rome, it became associated with *Gallicanism, and it attacked the *casuistry of the *Jesuits. The Jansenists were fortunate in having a number of able controversialists and spiritual writers among them, most notably *Pascal and Quesnel, and they gained considerable support among the French clergy despite the major rejection of their doctrine in Clement XI's *bull *Unigenitus* (1713). This condemned 101 propositions taken literally from Quesnel's *Nouveau Testament avec des réflexions morales* (1695), a book which had received the approval of Cardinal Noailles, the archbishop of Paris. The Cardinal died in 1729 without ever having formally accepted the condemnation of 1713. Jansenism spread outside France—particularly to Italy—and although it eventually died out as a discernible party within the Church, it long survived as a form of rigorist piety, characterized by the belief that a perfect love of God was a prerequisite for the proper reception of the sacraments.

N. Abercrombie, *The Origins of Jansenism* (1936); L. Cognet, *Le Jansénisme* (1961); A. Sedgwick, *Jansenism in 17th Cent. France . . .* (1977).

Jāp (Pañjābī, 'repetition'). *Hymn by Gurū *Gobind Singh. The Jāp is the introductory invocation to the *Dasam Granth and is included in *Nitnem for daily repetition. In a series of brief, rhyming, alliterative couplets, God's glory is proclaimed, often in negative statements, e.g. Jāp 80 (*Selections from the Sacred Writings of the Sikhs*, 1960, 267):

Nām thām nā jāt jākar, rup rang nā rekh
ād purakh udār mūrat, ajon, ād, asekh.

He has no name, no dwelling-place, no caste;
He has no shape, or colour or outer limits.
He is the Primal Being, Gracious and Benign,
Unborn, ever Perfect, and Eternal.

See also KHAṆḌE-DI-PĀHUL.

Japa (Skt., 'whispering', 'repetition'). The main constituent of *mantra yoga involving the repetition of a *bīja mantra, mantra, or series of mantras given by a *guru at initiation (*dīkṣa). Japa is accompanied by, or alternates with, *dhyāna, the concentration on, or visualization of, a form such as the guru or a deity. *Kulārṇava Tantra* (15. 15) says that 'when tired of japa one should perform dhyāna, when tired of dhyāna one should practice japa'. Japa leads to the apprehension of subtle inner sound which is known as 'repetitionless repetition' (*ajapa japa*). Often a *mālā (rosary) of ṛudrākṣa berries, or of various seeds, shells, or stones, is used to count the repetitions. The practice of japa leads to enlightenment, and to superhuman powers (*iddhis).

Japamāla (rosary): see MĀLĀ.

Japanese religion. A brocade of religious traditions developed over 2,000 years and consisting of indigenous folk religion, organized *Shinto, various schools of Buddhism, *Confucian teachings, *Taoist practices, and even Christian influences. There are original strands and added strands in Japanese religious history, none discarded, always changing and growing. The various strands intertwine and permeate each other, and Japanese people typically participate at different levels in several of these religious traditions. There are certain basic characteristics which are found throughout the different traditions, such as a sense of intimate relationship with the sacred reality in nature, an emphasis on local cults and festivals, veneration of ancestors with strong attachment to familial groups, and a clear sense of the unity of religion and the nation.

The indigenous folk religion, later called Shinto or kami no michi, revolved in prehistoric times around a feeling of awe for sacred powers called *kami which brought life and fertility to the land and to the human community. The social unit was the clan (*uji*), each of which had a tutelary kami (*ujigami*). When the imperial clan became dominant, a sacred national community was forged with the emperor as the divine head, supported by the myths collected in the *Kojiki* and the *Nihonshoki*. The central myths tell of the sun kami *Amaterasu Omikami sending her grandson *Ninigi to establish divine rule on earth, from which the imperial line descended. Based on that mythology the religious rituals (*matsuri) and the administration of government (*matsuri-goto*) were linked together and conducted in accord with the will of the kami. Eventually, with the advent of Confucian ideals from China, the emperor came to be considered as 'Manifest Kami' (*akitsu kami*) with the whole nation as a soteriological community (*kokutai) in a total unity of religion and government (*saisei itchi*).

New dimensions came to Japanese religion starting in the 6th cent. CE, with the advent of Sino-Korean culture with its system of writing, political models, and above all Buddhism, Confucianism, and Taoism, bringing about a major and lasting transformation of Japanese religion. The Japanese accepted all aspects of Chinese culture without discrimination: Confucian concepts such as filial piety and veneration of ancestors, Taoist divination and fortune-telling, and especially Buddhist rituals and teachings. Prince Regent Shōtoku (573–621), for example, advocated the continued veneration of the kami but at the same time, in his Seventeen Article Constitution of 593 CE, established both Confucianism and Buddhism as basic pillars of Japan. At first Buddhism was more the domain of the court and the élite, but by the Heian period it developed into the religion of all Japanese people, especially in the *Tendai and *Shingon forms. These two Buddhist schools synthesized many Buddhist traditions and also stressed esoteric practices, integrating these so thoroughly into the Japanese system that they also provided a theoretical basis for the Shinto-Buddhist amalgamation known as *Ryōbu Shintō and Sannō Ichijitsu, in which kami were understood to be manifestations of the Buddhas. As they accepted Buddhism, the Japanese transformed it in a practical, aesthetic direction. *Kūkai (773–835), for example, stressed aesthetic experience as the highest means of realizing union with the Mahavairocana Buddha (see VAIROCANA).

The most typically Japanese forms of Buddhism developed at the beginning of the feudal era in the Kamakura period, when classical Japanese court society was disrupted and people longed for security of faith and certainty of salvation in a time of confusion and degeneracy. New popular schools of Buddhism developed to meet their needs in this time of spiritual awakening: *Pure Land, *Nichiren, and *Zen Buddhism. These new schools (Pure Land and Zen had antecedents in China, but Nichiren was a unique Japanese movement) overcame the soteriological dualism which had separated clergy and laity in the older schools, universalized the religious path by focusing on the exemplary experience of the founder, and above all held out for the masses the experience of salvation not so much by spiritual discipline as by faith. Japanese Zen, newly introduced from China, did stress the spiritual discipline of meditation; however, *Dōgen (1200–53), founder of Sōtō Zen in Japan, shared with the other new sects a special view of the importance of faith, although he insisted that salvation lay not in flight to a saving Buddha power but in realizing the buddha-nature by sitting in meditation. Zen did not become the religion of the masses, but it did penetrate into the warrior class and became the driving force in a significant artistic culture that looked upon the practice of art as *geidō* ('the way of art'), a path of self-realization and enlightenment.

Western influences entered into Japanese religion with the introduction of Christianity by *Francis Xavier (1506–52) and other *Jesuit missionaries in the middle of the 16th cent. Within one century Christianity rose rapidly to be accepted by many feudal lords and their people and just as rapidly was destroyed, with some tenacious Christians forced underground to continue their faith as 'hidden Christians' (*kakure kirishitan*). In reaction to the foreign threat associated with Christianity, the Tokugawa rulers closed Japan to all foreign influences and gave to Buddhist temples the task of monitoring the religious practices of the people. As Buddhism became formalized and stagnant, a movement to restore Shintō arose, drawing on antecedents such as *Yoshida Shintō. Some used *neo-Confucian ideas, as in *Suiga Shintō and *Shingaku, but the scholars of the *Kokugaku ('national learning') movement such as *Motoori Norinaga (1730–1801) used a painstaking study of ancient philology in an attempt to return to the pure roots of Japanese culture and separate Shinto from Buddhism, thus creating *Fukko ('return to antiquity') Shintō. When pressure from the W. forced Japan to open up again in the 19th cent., the restoration government of Emperor *Meiji moved toward making State Shinto (*Kokka Shintō) the ritual and ideological support of the nation with the emperor as its symbolic head, to be served absolutely by all Japanese. New Shinto movements which had arisen in the turbulent days at the end of the Tokugawa era and beginning of the Meiji era were categorized as Sect Shinto (*Kyōha Shintō). While Buddhists, Christians, and Sect Shintoists had freedom of religion, allegiance to State Shinto was required of all. W. learning did penetrate deeply along with pressure to modernize, and Japanese thinkers like *Nishida Kitarō developed systems of philosophy combining W. methods with Japanese Buddhist ideas.

With Japan's defeat in the Second World War came the disestablishment of Shinto and the formation of the Association of Shinto Shrines independent of the government. The Sect Shinto groups have continued to attract large numbers of adherents, and many New Religions (*shinkō shūkyō*) have developed and are flourishing, drawing on ideas and practices from the various Japanese traditions. Some of these, like *Sōka Gakkai (from the Nichiren tradition), have attracted huge masses of followers, and promise to be significant factors in Japan for years to come. Buddhism continues to play a role in the lives of many people, and Christianity has had an impact on the values and thinking of the Japanese beyond its small numbers in Japan. Among many, however, there persists the sense that much of the spiritual heritage of Japan has been lost amid the *secularization of modern life.

See also BUDDHISM IN JAPAN; Index, Nichiren; Pure Land; Shinto.

M. Anesaki, *History of Japanese Religion* (1963); H. B. Earhart, *Religion in Japanese Experience* ... (1974); R. Ellwood and R. Pilgrim, *Japanese Religion* ... (1992); I. Hori (ed.), *Japanese Religion* (1972); J. M. Kitagawa, *Religion in Japanese History* (1966); K. Morioka, *Religion in Changing Japanese Society* (1975).

Japjī (Pañjābī, 'recitation'). Major Sikh religious poem composed by Gurū *Nānak. The Japjī introduces and epitomizes the *Ādi Granth. It is recited (not sung) each morning by devout Sikhs and during preparation of *amrit for *initiation (*khaṇḍe-dī-pāhul). Japjī commences with the *Mul Mantra, followed by a *śalok proclaiming *God's eternal truth. Thirty-eight *pauṛīs (stanzas) and a concluding śalok ensue, proclaiming God's greatness, the divine will (*hukam), and the need for all to obey him and to remember his name (*nām).

Jara. A Hindu *rākṣasī, able to change her form at will as she seeks flesh to eat. She is propitiated by being called Gṛhadevī (goddess of the household) and by being painted on walls surrounded by children.

Jaratkāru. A Hindu ascetic and *ṛṣi. According to the **Mahābhārata*, his austerity was so great that he travelled round the world living only on air and never eating. On this journey he came to a deep pit over which some men were suspended, head down, by a rope through which a rat was gnawing. He was told that these were his ancestors for whose predicament he was responsible, because he had had no son to perform the *ekoddiṣṭa rites (which sustain the ancestors). Jaratkāru agreed to marry if a bride with his own name could be found, for whom no bride-price was required. The daughter of the king of Nāga fulfilled the conditions, and they had a son, Āstīka.

Jaṭ. *Caste group dominant in Sikh *Panth. Although low in the Hindu caste hierarchy, the Jaṭs are economically powerful as landowners in *Pañjāb, with a martial and agricultural tradition. Among Sikhs in Pañjab, Jaṭs are numerically preponderant and significant numbers have emigrated, e.g. to Great Britain, Canada, and California. The *Gurūs were *Khatrī, but Jaṭ converts increased especially in Gurū *Gobind Siṅgh's time. Dharam Dās, one of the original *Pañj Pyāre, was a Jaṭ. Their influence grew under Mahārājā *Rañjīt Siṅgh. The hardy, independent character attributed to Sikhs is arguably Jaṭ in origin. See also RĀMGAṚHĪĀ.

Jaṭā. The state of *hair when a Hindu leaves it matted and uncared for, either as a sign of mourning, or as a mark of *asceticism. It is characteristic of *Śiva as the great yogin, whose jaṭā is also identified with Vāyu, the god of wind.

Jātaka ('birth-story'). A story of the previous incarnations of the *Buddha. Many of these stories exist, and it is thought that some may originally have been Indian, pre-Buddhist, fables and fairy tales. Some are found virtually unchanged in Aesop's collection. In the *Theravādin *Tripiṭaka, a collection of 547 Jātakas forms part of the *Khuddaka Nikāya*. They are arranged according to length, with the shortest first. Written in verse with prose settings, only the verse part, with the exception of *Kunālajātaka* (no. 536), is regarded as canonical. Some of these verses must be of great antiquity since they are found, not only in other parts of the Pāli canon, but also in many Skt. texts, both Buddhist and non-Buddhist. All of the Jātakas exemplify some positive quality exhibited by the Buddha in his multitude of former lives as a *bodhisattva. The longest and most important, *Vessantarajātaka* (no. 547), tells the story of the Buddha's life as Prince Vessantara who was so generous that he gave away everything, including a wife and two children. All the stories have been immensely popular and have been the source of much Buddhist *iconography. The Pāli Jātaka collection, which was itself originally one of the nine sections which made up the canon, does not exhaust all known Jātaka stories, and this suggests that different schools may have possessed dissimilar collections.

Trs., ed. E. B. Cowell (1895–1907).

Jātakamāla. A collection of thirty-four stories dealing with assorted former lives of the *Buddha (*jātaka). These moral tales, in a mixture of prose and poetry, treat various incidents of selflessness on the part of the Buddha during his period as a *bodhisattva. Written about the end of 2nd cent. CE, the work is ascribed to Śūra or Āryaśūra whom Tāranātha claimed to be the same person as Mātṛceta.

Jathā (Pañjābī, 'armed band'). Squad of Sikhs. In the 18th cent., the Sikh army, the Taruṇa Dal, divided into five jathās to counter Muslim aggression in *Pañjāb. In the 20th cent. Sikh jathās marched, demanding reform of *gurdwārā management and in protest at the partition of Pañjāb. See also MISL; TALVAṆḌĪ RĀI BHOI DĪ.

Jāti. The Hindu term for *caste. Its origin has been connected to the *varna classification, but whereas that was originally concerned with classification by occupation, jāti determines social status according to birth and lineage. Nevertheless, the two overlap, although the castes have now proliferated and no longer correspond to the original divisions (e.g. in some areas of Bengal, *śudra groups, those not considered 'twice-born', outrank the local *dvijāti*). Orthodox Hindus explain the proliferation of jātis as the result of miscegenation of varnas, which also accounts for the non-caste and *outcaste groups. A separate category exists for foreigners, e.g. Yavana, referring especially to Greeks. The protest of some modern Hindus against jāti has diminished its importance in urban areas, though everywhere it remains important in marriage. In the same way, although Gurū *Nānak set himself against caste, it has persisted among Sikhs, particularly in relation to marriage.

Jayadeva (Indian poet): see GĪTĀGOVINDA.

Jazen (false zen): see HUNG-CHIH.

Jehovah. Eng. vocalization of the four consonants that make up the *tetragrammaton. It is erroneous, since it took the vowels of *adonai* ('my lord') which were inserted into printed or written texts to prevent any attempt to pronounce the name of God.

Jehovah's Witnesses. A sect derived from Charles Taze Russell (1852–1916), emphasizing biblical literalism and the imminent coming of the kingdom of God. Jesus is not God but the son of God, the first of his creations. The fulfilment of the promise of God's kingdom will be inaugurated by the battle of *Armageddon, an event which was predicted for 1914—hence the saying of Rutherford, Russell's successor, that 'millions now living will never die'. 1914 is now interpreted as the establishment of the kingdom. Jehovah's Witnesses engage in persistent door-to-door proselytizing, endeavouring to sell *The Watchtower*, in which the movement's interpretation of world events is contained.

J. A. Beckford, *The Trumpet of Prophecy* . . . (1975).

Jen (Chin., 'benevolence'). A central virtue in the *Confucian tradition, also commonly tr. as 'humanity', 'human-heartedness', 'love', 'altruism', etc. The Chinese character is formed by combining the elements 'human' and 'two', suggesting a reference to the quality of human relationships. In early Confucian texts, jen is employed in two senses: (i) as the particular human virtue of benevolence or goodness which is embodied to some extent in all people (but perhaps especially in the nobility); (ii), and more importantly, as the moral life ideally embodied. In this latter sense, jen refers to a quality of living in relationship to others in the world which is extremely rare and precious. Indeed, Confucius averred that he had never known a person to whom the term truly applied.

Confucius, therefore, seems to have been the first to free jen from the exclusive possession of the nobility, rendering it a moral quality that can be pursued as a goal by human beings regardless of their social position (although Confucius certainly saw a hierarchically ordered society as the necessary context for learning and practising jen). As a general term, jen, for Confucius, embraces both *i ('righteousness') and *li ('propriety'). More specifically, he regarded jen as marked, above all, by an inner serenity, equanimity, and indifference to creaturely matters of fortune and misfortune over which one has no direct control. Like li, jen has an 'inner' and an 'outer' side. It comprehends all the outer-directed virtues and 'dispositions of soul' (*hsin*) which enable humans to have harmonious relations with others; it is also the capacity that infuses the li with their appropriate spirit, and that brings alive their potential spiritual power. At the same time, jen endows the individual with the 'inner dispositions' of equanimity, equilibrium, and self-sufficiency, which make those outer manifestations possible. Needless to say, jen does not 'happen by accident', but needs careful evocation and cultivation. Yao Xinzhong concluded his analysis of the Confucian understanding of jen:

> Jen, the central theme of Confucianism, is universal rather than partial, ethical rather than spontaneous, and essential rather than superficial . . . To be jen, one has to refine one's innate feelings in the context of family, cultivate one's potential in the context of society, and refine and extend natural love in the context of all human relationships. (*Asian Philosophy*, 5, 1995)

In the thought and teaching of *Mencius, jen is made into one of the four cardinal virtues, each of which has a 'source' (*tuan*) in the *hsin*. According to him, 'the heart of compassion is the fount of jen'. Mencius also used the compound expression 'jen i' as a set phrase meaning something like 'morality'. A passage from *Hsün Tzu exemplifies the closely interrelated nature of all three: 'If you want to become like the former kings and seek out jen and i, then li is the very road by which you must travel.'

Other schools of thought quickly criticized the Confucian understanding of jen. *Mo Tzu saw the Confucian jen as socially divisive because of what he took to be its partiality, and taught 'universal love' (*chien ai*, literally, 'a love that does not make distinctions') in its stead. Only within the context of universal love do partial loves (including the Confucian jen) become possible and remain within their proper limits.

Taoists such as *Lao-Tzu and *Chuang-Tzu challenged the Confucian understanding of jen on the grounds that it was part of *wei*, the sort of contrived action they sought to avoid. They linked jen to the fall from primordial simplicity. Thus a striking passage in Lao Tzu reverses the key concepts of Confucian morality: 'When the great Tao declined, the doctrine of jen and i arose; when knowledge and wisdom appeared, there emerged great hypocrisy'. Similarly in Chuang-Tzu:

> In a time of Perfect Virtue . . . men live the same as birds and beasts, group themselves side by side with the ten thousand things. . . . In uncarved simplicity the people attain their true nature. Then along comes the sage, huffing and puffing after benevolence [jen], and the world for the first time has doubts; mooning and mouthing over his music, snipping and stitching away at his rites [li], and the world for the first time is divided.

Nevertheless, chen-jen (real or perfect person) is admired as the one who bears all things with equanimity. Later analysis offers techniques to produce chen-jen.

In later neo-Taoist texts (*hsüan-hsüeh), jen refers to the universal extension of love, by which one forms mystically one body with Heaven and Earth.

N. J. Girardot, *Myth and Meaning in Early Taoism* (1983); B. I. Schwartz, *The World of Thought in Ancient China* (1985); X. Yao, *Confucianism and Christianity: A Comparative Study of Jen and Agape*, (1996).

Jeremiah. Second of the major Hebrew *prophets, after whom is named the prophetic book. Jeremiah was born in Anathoth *c.*650 (1. 1) of a priestly family (32. 2) and he never married (16. 1–4). He was deeply concerned with the historical events of his time which included the reforms of *Josiah, the Babylonian conquest, the destruction of the *Jerusalem *Temple, and the *exile of the people. Jeremiah was permitted to stay in the city, but after the murder of Gedaliah, many of the supporters of Gedaliah fled to Egypt and took the prophet with them (40–3). According to Christian tradition, he was stoned to death as a *martyr. The book contains *Baruch's scroll which includes Jeremiah's call, a condemnation of the nation, and warnings of coming disasters (1–6). This is followed by the first editorial addition to Baruch's scroll, including Jeremiah's temple sermon and condemnations of the people (7–10). The second editorial addition contains more preaching, the story of Jeremiah's persecution, various parables, and Jeremiah's confessions (11–20). Chs. 21–4 are oracles concerning the house of *David, and ch. 25 contains oracles against foreign nations. Chs. 26–44 describe various incidents in the life of the prophet which are interrupted by the Book of Consolations (30 and 31). Ch. 45 deals with Jeremiah's scribe, Baruch. Chs. 46–51 contain further oracles against foreign nations and ch. 52 describes the fall of Jerusalem. Traditionally the Book of Lamentations is also ascribed to Jeremiah.

Jeremy, Epistle of. Jewish *apocryphal book. The date is uncertain (4th–2nd cent. BCE). It purports to be a letter of the *prophet *Jeremiah to the Jewish *exiles in Babylon, inveighing against *idolatry. In the *Vulgate, it is added to *Baruch (ch. 6), and it was used by the *Marranos to justify their position.

Jericho (modern Tell esSultan). Ancient city which (according to the account in Joshua 6) succumbed to the conquest of Joshua and the Israelites with a dramatic fall of the walls at the sound of the trumpets, and with a complete destruction. Excavations revealed a very ancient settlement and then city, with some of the earliest known city fortifications. Although the archaeologist Garstang claimed to have found evidence, during his excavations of 1930–6, of destruction *c.*1400 BCE, and related this to the ʿapiru (*habiru) disruptions as evidence supporting the biblical account, this claim was disputed at the time and has subsequently seemed unsupportable. The walls which he attributed to a 14th-cent. destruction are structures which fell before the end of the 3rd millennium; and the site was at most occupied at the time; it was not a thriving city. A later Jericho (modern Tulul Abu al-ʿAlayiq) was the winter capital of *Herod, and was built slightly south of the site of the older city.

Jerome, St (*c.*342–420). Church *father. A native of Italy, he set out for Palestine in *c.*374 and spent four or five years as a hermit. Later (382–5) as secretary to Pope Damasus he successfully preached *asceticism in Rome. He eventually settled in Bethlehem in 386, where he devoted the rest of his life to study. Jerome's greatest scholarly achievement was the translation of most of the Bible into Latin (see VULGATE). He also advocated the Church's acceptance of the Heb. *canon of the Old Testament, excluding the *Apocrypha. His works include many learned biblical commentaries, Lat. trs. of *Eusebius and *Origen, a bibliography of ecclesiastical writers (called *On Illustrious Men*), and a number of historically important letters. He took part in such controversies of the time as that over *Origenism. Since the 13th cent. he has often been depicted in art with a red hat (in the belief that Damasus made him a *cardinal). He is also often represented with a lion at his feet. This goes back to the legend that Jerome helped a lion by removing a thorn from its foot. The lion subsequently assisted Jerome, e.g. by recovering a stolen ass. Feast day, 30 Sept.

J. N. D. Kelly, *Jerome* (1975).

Jerusalem

Judaism The capital of the State of *Israel. Jerusalem was captured by King *David from the Jebusites (see 2 Samuel 5) and became his capital. It was the site of *Solomon's *Temple and the royal palace, and remained the seat of the Davidic kings during the period of the monarchy. The city was captured and largely destroyed by the Babylonians in 587 BCE, but throughout the period of *exile, the people seem to have retained their faith: 'If I forget thee O Jerusalem, let my right hand forget its cunning' (Psalm 137. 5). The city was rebuilt in the Persian period. Now began the brilliant imagination of Jerusalem, containing virtually all beauty, the site of all important events from Creation to End. The Temple was reconstructed and remained the centre of social and religious life under the *high priest and was greatly enlarged by *Herod the Great. The Jewish revolt against the Romans in 66 CE, however, led to a prolonged siege of the city and its eventual destruction. Of the Temple only the western wall (*wailing wall) remained. After the *Bar Kokhba revolt in 135 CE, the city was renamed *Aelia Capitolina and no Jews were allowed to live there. When it became a Muslim city, a few Jewish families were allowed to settle; it continued to be a place of *pilgrimage for Jews of the *diaspora and there was a small *Karaite community. By the beginning of the 16th cent. it attracted *Kabbalists as well as scholars and *rabbis. In the diaspora, the hope of a return to Jerusalem was kept alive in the liturgy, particularly in the *Passover *seder ('Next year in Jerusalem'). When the State of Israel was created in 1948, Jerusalem was partitioned. In 1967 Israeli forces captured the Arab quarter and the united city was declared the capital of the State of Israel. See also ZION.

Christianity The Christian history of the city begins with Jesus' short ministry there; his crucifixion, resurrection, and (according to Luke and John) later appearances there to his disciples; and the events of *Pentecost. Jerusalem was the venue of the important meeting of *Paul with *Peter, *James, and *John in 48 or 51 CE (Acts 15. 4–29). The Jewish church there flourished at least until the war against Rome of 66–70 CE, and perhaps continued until the banishment of Jews from the city under Hadrian. The see of Jerusalem did not return to importance until the 4th cent. with the building of churches by *Constantine and the new fashion of pilgrimage to the Holy Places. The see never achieved the status of the other patriarchates, however, and the patriarch (a Greek, though the majority of the faithful are Arabs) has been permanently settled there only since 1845. The Christian centre of Jerusalem is the Church of the Resurrection, commonly known as the Church of the Holy Sepulchre. There are many other holy places within and outside the city, sometimes with rival claims to a particular identification by Orthodox and Roman Catholics: the former have usually the better claim, since the Latin sites were generally established no earlier than the *Crusades. The eventual failure of the Crusades had the incidental effect of transferring Jerusalem into the metaphorical imagination. Already Jerusalem had become more important as the heavenly Jerusalem, and had evoked superb Latin hymns, many of which were tr. by J. M. Neale in the 19th cent. with such skill that they became new works of art—e.g. 'Ye choirs of new Jerusalem'; 'For thee, O dear, dear country'; 'Light's abode celestial Salem'; 'Jerusalem the Golden'. For William Blake, Jerusalem was a powerful metaphor of protest and change.

Islam Jerusalem is not mentioned by name in the *Qur'ān, but 17. 5–7 is clearly referring to the two destructions of Jerusalem. On that basis, 17. 1 ties the Night Journey (*isra') and the Ascent (al-*Miʿrāj) to Jerusalem as the place of their occurrence: the footprint of *Muḥammad can still be seen, as can the Rock from which the Ascent was made—split, as it endeavoured to follow the Prophet to heaven. Jerusalem is thus tied to the demonstration of Muḥammad as the *Seal of the Prophets. Originally the *qibla (direction of prayer) was toward Jerusalem, only later being changed to *Mecca. Jerusalem thus becomes in Islam third in holiness to Mecca and *Madīna. Known originally as Iliya (i.e. Aelia) Madīna Bayt al-Maqdis, it became known from the 4th cent. AH as al-Quds, the Holy. Two major buildings were erected on the Temple Mount, al-Masjid al-Aqsa, 'the furthest mosque' referred to (in anticipation) in sūra 17; and Qubbat as-Sakhrah, the *Dome of the Rock (piously, but unhistorically, also called 'the Mosque of *ʿUmar'). The latter covers the *eben shetiyyah, the rock on which the world is founded and from which Muḥammad ascended to heaven. Jerusalem will be the scene of the events which initiate the end of the world and the final judgement. Yet for all this reverence for Jerusalem, there has also been in Islam an undercurrent of suspicion that the elevation of Jerusalem was introducing *bidʿa ('innovation'), a particularly disastrous sin, since it erodes the sufficiency of revelation. When *Salāḥ ud-Dīn recaptured Jerusalem from the crusaders, and Muslim buildings were restored, it had little significance beyond the Temple Mount. Its importance was as a centre of education and learning, and of *Sūfī devotion. The establishment of the State of Israel introduces new political considerations, but for some Muslims the major point remains the care of, and access to, the holy places.

J. Gutman (ed.), *The Temple of Solomon* (1976); F. E. Peters, *Jerusalem* (1985); Z. Vilnay, *Legends of Jerusalem* (1973).

Jerusalem, Synod of. A *council of the Orthodox church, convened by *Dositheus, patriarch of Jerusalem, in 1672 to reject Cyril *Lucar's sympathy with some aspects of *Calvinism. It emphasized church and sacraments, and with the Synod of Jassy (1642) it resembled the reaction to the Reformation of Tridentine Catholicism.

Jerusalem Conference (1928): see MISSION.

Jesse. Father of King *David (1 Samuel 16). His importance in Christian tradition derives from the messianic prophecy of Isaiah 11. 1 ('A shoot shall grow from the stock of Jesse'). This led eventually in the late Middle Ages to an iconographical composition showing a tree springing from Jesse and ending in Jesus, with intermediate descendants on scrolls of foliage on each side. It is at its most spectacular as a design for a stained-glass window, as may be seen in Chartres or Wells.

Jesuits. Properly called the Society of Jesus, a *religious order of clerks regular founded by *Ignatius Loyola. It received papal approval in 1540, and now has *c.*25,000 members, divided into a number of grades: the solemnly professed who take a fourth vow of obedience to the *papacy; the spiritual coadjutors (priests) and temporal coadjutors (lay brothers); and the scholastics—those in training for the priesthood, a training which may last up to a dozen years. The spirituality of the Society is based upon the *Spiritual Exercises* of Ignatius, a thirty-day series of retreat meditations which most Jesuits undertake twice during their training, and which is now increasingly shared with those outside the order (e.g. at St Beuno's, N. Wales). From its earliest years the Society has had a strong commitment to teaching at both secondary and tertiary levels, and to missionary work. The power of the Jesuits in the 17th and 18th cents. gave rise to considerable hostility in political circles of Europe, and also in some religious ones, particularly among the *Jansenists. In 1773 the Society was formally suppressed by Clement XIV, but restored again in 1814 by Pius VII shortly after his release from captivity. From then on the Society showed itself especially devoted to the Holy See, and lost some of its earlier flair and independence. In recent years, however, its members have made a significant contribution to the renewal of theological scholarship in the *Roman Catholic Church, and they are to the forefront of ecclesiastical developments in Latin America. For individual Jesuits, see Index, Jesuits.

W. V. Bangert, *A History of the Society of Jesus* (1972); J. de Guibert, *The Jesuits: Their Spiritual Doctrine and Practice* . . . (1964); J. O'Malley, *The First Jesuits* (1993).

Jesus (d. 30 or 33 CE). Jewish religious teacher, and in traditional Christian belief the unique *incarnation of God. (For the name 'Jesus Christ' see CHRIST.)

Sources for knowledge of Jesus' life and sayings are almost entirely of Christian provenance: of the two references to him by *Josephus (*Antiquities* 18. 3. 3, 20. 9. 1) the first is at least partly a Christian interpolation; the *Talmud offers at most two reports of value (*B. Sanhedrin* 43a, *B. Aboda Zara* 16b–17a), other references to Jesus in *rabbinic literature being based on much later anti-Christian invention. Roman legal sources are likewise non-existent, in spite of Christian writers' claims from the 2nd cent. on that there were records of Jesus' trial. Of Christian texts, little of historical value is found in *apocryphal gospels or other 2nd-cent. or later writings, and the four New Testament gospels remain practically alone as useful sources for the historian (see *Matthew, *Mark, *Luke, and *John for their individual characteristics). Even these, however, are the end products of an oral tradition which was passed on not for scholarly purposes but for use in preaching, teaching, liturgy, and the like. Christian *prophets also spoke words 'in the name of the Lord' (e.g. 1 Thessalonians 4. 15) which may have come to be treated on occasion as words of Jesus. Thus in various ways inauthentic and tendentious material certainly entered the gospels (although the scale of such an invasion is probably smaller than the early *form critics supposed), and for historical purposes, a critical reading of them is therefore essential. Such a reading is presumed in what follows.

Jesus was born before the death of King Herod (4 BCE), of pious parents Joseph and *Mary, of Nazareth in Galilee. According to Matthew and Luke, Mary conceived Jesus by the operation of the *Holy Spirit while remaining a virgin: see VIRGIN BIRTH. Jesus is once called a 'carpenter' (Mark 6. 3, unless the alternative reading referring to his believed father is preferred), but nothing is known of his life (apart from the fact that he had brothers and sisters) until he began to preach publicly. Probably his first work was alongside *John the Baptist in the Jordan valley (John 3. 22 ff.), Jesus himself having been baptized by John (Mark 1. 9). The gospels, however, place most of his career in Galilee and N. Palestine generally. Probably this career lasted only two or three years, before he was arrested and executed, having made a deliberate journey to Jerusalem for *Passover.

In reconstructing Jesus' message from his recorded words, many critics start by applying the 'criterion of dissimilarity', which identifies the most certainly authentic sayings as those which are foreign both to the Judaism of his day and to the early church's ways of speaking. This and other critical tools allow (in the view of most scholars) the main themes of Jesus' message to be seen. It is thus certain that Jesus preached about the *kingdom of God, and specifically of its imminent approach. Jesus, however, speaks of it sometimes as future (Matthew 6. 10), sometimes as already present (Matthew 12. 28, Luke 11. 20), and at other times as something which cannot be described except indirectly through *parables (Mark 4. 30). Of these various strains, probably the dominant one is that which considers the kingdom to be already present in Jesus' ministry and actions. Clearly, Jesus taught and acted (especially in healing) in a way which manifested the 'power' (*dunamis*) and 'authority' (*exousia*), not of himself but of God, whom he characterized as both king and father, addressing him as *Abba. This provoked the fundamental question of Mark 6. 2 which is the beginning of *Christology. Thus the *miracles, healings, and *exorcisms which he worked (and which also belong to the earliest traditions about him) had their significance in indicating the coming of the kingdom (Luke 11. 20) and as being the manifestation of the *dunamis* or power (or consequence) of God; likewise his association with those held by others to be the undesirables of society (Matthew 11. 19) was a symbol of the forgiveness and celebration associated with the new age. On the other hand, traditional esoteric sayings about an apocalyptic future (as in Mark 13) are less likely to be genuine.

How Jesus thought of himself in relation to this coming kingdom is uncertain. Clearly he mediated through himself an effect of God which transfigured his own life and transformed the lives of others. He seems to have been extremely reluctant to acknowledge the title *messiah, even though it appears this was given to him in certain circles (perhaps meaning 'anointed one' in a vague or general sense). From the well-attested fact that Jesus addressed God as Abba (Aramaic, 'father'), it could be inferred that he was Son of God; but Jesus did not use this expression as an exclusive title for himself. His most significant reference to himself seems to have been as 'the *son of man', which appears to embrace the two major senses in scripture and to be affirming that Jesus acts and speaks with God-related and God-derived authority, not as some special figure (an *angel or *prophet or messiah), but as one subject to death who nevertheless believes that in his obedient fulfilling of the vocation of Israel, he will be vindicated by God despite death (for details, see SON OF MAN).

Jesus selected an intimate band of twelve disciples (Mark 3. 14), but there are many sayings about the challenge of following him (e.g. Mark 8. 34) which seem to be addressed to his adherents generally. It is striking that there is no clear evidence that Jesus formed any kind of institution for his followers.

Jesus' position within the Judaism of his day was, broadly speaking, partly that of a teacher to whom legal and religious questions were referred, and partly that of a Galilean healer. In the former capacity he is recorded as challenging much of the *halakhah of the *Pharisees and criticizing current religious practices (Mark 7. 1–23), but still remaining within the Jewish religion of the *Torah (e.g. in attending synagogue, Matthew 4. 23, 9. 35; Luke 4. 16 ff.; John 6. 59). Often where he appears to criticize the biblical commandments themselves (e.g. Matthew 5. 21–48) his own dictates are more rather than less exacting, or even on a different plane altogether. His summary of Torah (*kelal) was in effect a context-independent command (see ETHICS, CHRISTIAN). However, Jesus spoke only in his own name from his own relation to God (he is often described as praying), and made no appeal to other authorities (though he had a deep understanding, not only of Torah, but of those works which were, or were becoming, Scripture); this characteristic, at least, separated him from other teachers (Mark 1. 22). In this respect, he stood in the tradition of the prophets, and as a prophet (Mark 6. 4) he could set aside the commandments of the Torah (as in Matthew 8. 22, Mark 2. 23–8) when they stood in the way of a greater proclamation.

The gospels record that Jesus was executed by *crucifixion by the Roman authorities in Judaea. This has suggested to some scholars that the offence of Jesus was political rather than (as the gospel writers insist) religious; and some incidents in the gospel story have then been interpreted as showing an anti-Roman, nationalist stance on the part of Jesus. However, this does not seem central to the issue of Jesus in Jerusalem. While there is much in the narratives of his trial which, if taken as a trial, is difficult to reconcile with historical probability, there is much which makes consistent sense of a twofold process. Jesus clearly made his way deliberately to Jerusalem (the Gk. uses strong words of necessity concerning his determination to leave the relative security of Galilee and to go to Jerusalem), because it was only in Jerusalem that the issue could be resolved, whether his teaching was 'from God or men'. It is equally clear that the initial offence of Jesus had to do with his threat to the authority of the Temple in deciding the true interpretation of Torah (the same issue which was raised by Stephen, Acts 7. 11 f.). This (as an offence) goes back to Deuteronomy 17. 8–13, which states that an obstinate teacher (see REBELLIOUS ELDER), who insists on his own opinion against the majority, must be brought before 'the judge who shall be in those days' (i.e. the highest authority), and if he rejects the decision on his teaching, he must be executed—because two interpretations of Torah must necessarily destroy Israel. The so-called 'trial' of Jesus was initially an investigation to see whether he came into the category of an obstinate teacher who insisted on his own opinion: for that reason, the offence of Jesus was not anything he said to the high priest ('the judge who shall be in those days'), but the fact that he said nothing: silence indicated his refusal to subordinate his God-derived authority to that of the high priest—who (not surprisingly) said, 'What need have we of further witnesses?' Whether it was necessary or simply convenient to hand Jesus over to the Romans for the punishment which Deuteronomy requires is uncertain; the charge then would have involved Jesus' threat to the Roman administration by his threat to the religious establishment which co-operated with the Romans.

There is good reason, therefore, to believe that Jesus anticipated his own death (the necessity of the journey to Jerusalem carries that implication, since Jesus knew that his teaching and actions came, not from himself, but from God, and that they were not subject to human authority). If the connection with Daniel 7 is correct, then he saw his death as the fulfilment of Israel's true destiny; and he saw it also as a *lutron* (ransom, in terms of a current dispute between Pharisees and Sadducees) for the sins of 'many' (Mark 10. 45). Such an interpretation is inherent above all in the *eucharistic words at the *Last Supper.

Jesus was executed and laid in a tomb on Friday; according to the gospels on Sunday morning his tomb was found to be empty. Beyond this point the three gospels Matthew, Luke, and John offer various and differing accounts of appearances of Jesus to his followers. These appearances are also mentioned by Paul (1 Corinthians 15. 5–8) as among the earliest traditions he knew, and (more than the empty tomb) lie at the basis of the Christian belief that Jesus had risen from the dead (see RESURRECTION OF CHRIST). For the later Christian doctrine involving this belief, see CHRISTOLOGY.

Even among Christians who accept the critical study of the gospels and its difficulties, the '*quest for the historical Jesus' is variously estimated. At one extreme is the view (associated with R. *Bultmann) that faith in Christ cannot depend on the results of historical inquiry into Jesus' life and character beyond what is contained in the New Testament *kerygma. On the other is the view (associated with J. Jeremias) that Jesus' message is recoverable with confidence and is itself at the basis of Christian faith. See Index, Jesus.

In Islam Jesus is generally called ʿĪsā ibn Maryam (Jesus, son of Mary) in the *Qur'ān. He is one of the *Prophets, a line which began with *Adam and ended with *Muḥammad. He is mentioned, together with Zakariyā, *John, and Elias, as one of the 'Righteous' (6. 85). Like Adam, he was created from dust (3. 59). The Qur'ān concentrates on the beginning and the end of ʿĪsā's earthly life; his actual teachings are not reported. He is conceived through the power of Allah, the message being conveyed to the virgin Maryam by 'Our Spirit' (19. 17–22), later identified with the angel Jibrīl *Gabriel (cf. 3. 45–7). He speaks in the cradle, to vindicate his mother's reputation (19. 30).

His miracles are said to include making birds out of clay, healing the sick, blind, and lepers, and raising the dead, (3. 49, 5. 113). The strange story of his making a 'table prepared' appear from heaven is thought by some to be an echo of the miracle of the loaves and fishes, or of the Last Supper (5. 115–18; sūra 5 is named 'the Table'). This is to be a 'solemn festival and a sign' (5. 117).

The crucifixion is apparently denied in the Qur'ān: 'They killed him not, nor crucified him, but so it was made to appear to them' (4. 157); but the Arabic can be taken to mean that the resurrection contradicted what they thought had happened. The Qur'ān is primarily concerned with upholding the power of Allāh, whose Prophets must always be victorious. The phrase 'made to appear to them' (*shubbiha lahum*) has caused much difficulty to the Muslim commentators, some saying that 'Īsā's place was taken by another (Judas, Simon of Cyrene, or an unnamed disciple), some that the whole event was unreal. On the usual understanding there is no concept of resurrection: the statement 'Allah raised him to Himself' (4. 158) and 'Īsā's declaration: 'Peace be upon me, the day I was born, the day I die, the day I am taken up alive' (19. 33) are seen as referring to the Ascension—cf. the statement: 'Allāh said: O 'Īsā; I shall take you and raise you to Myself' (3. 55). The word 'take you' (*mutawaffika*) could signify 'summon (in death)', but to Islam the death of 'Īsā will take place shortly before the end of the world. On the Day of Judgement he will be a witness against *ahl al-Kitāb (the People of the Book. 4. 159).

'Īsā has several titles: 'Word' from Allāh, and a 'Spirit' from him, though neither term corresponds to the Christian concept; 'Servant', 'Prophet', 'Messiah', 'Messenger', and 'only a messenger' (4. 171, 5. 78). He is 'strengthened by the Spirit of holiness' (*rūḥ al-qudus*; 5. 113, 2. 253). His humanity is emphasized, and the Christians are severely rebuked for ascribing divine status to him. In one passage 'Īsā is questioned by Allāh: 'Did you say to people, "Worship me and my mother as gods"?'; and his reply is: 'Glory to you! I could never say what I had no right to . . . I never said anything except what you commanded me, which is, Worship Allāh, my Lord and your Lord' (5. 119–20). The Christians are accused: 'They say: the Merciful One has taken a son!' This idea is violently rejected: 'The skies are ready to burst, the earth to split asunder . . . that they should invoke a son for the Merciful One' (19. 88–92). The Qur'ān, however, objects to ideas which are not orthodox Christian teaching. There is within Arabic a distinction between *ibn*, 'son', which can be used metaphorically or to denote a spiritual relationship, and *walad*, 'son' or 'offspring', in a more literal sense. It is this latter term which the Qur'ān employs in the verses just quoted, and the point is appreciated by some Muslim commentators.

'Īsā, as a Prophet in the Quranic scheme, comes with a message, the *Injīl, a book taught or revealed to him. Allāh says: 'We sent 'Īsā son of Maryam in the footsteps [of earlier Prophets] confirming the Tawrāt. We sent him the Injīl, containing guidance and light, and confirmation of the Tawrāt that came before' (5. 49). At his conception, Maryam is told: 'Allāh will teach him the Book and Wisdom, Tawrāt and Injīl (3. 48). Muslim tradition has elaborated on the Quranic data: 'Īsā will return before the Day of Judgement, kill the Dajjāl (*Antichrist), break the crosses, kill all swine, destroy churches and synagogues, and die after forty years, having inaugurated an era of peace on earth. *Sūfī teaching has taken 'Īsā as an example and inspiration, a model of piety, goodness, asceticism, and loving devotion to the Almighty (see e.g. the letter of *Ḥasan al-Basri to 'Umar).

For all that the Qur'ān, *ḥadīth, and later legend hold him in special reverence, he is less than Muḥammad the 'Seal of the Prophets'; and the 'Īsā of the Qur'ān has little resemblance to Jesus of the gospels. A link with Islam is made in Qur'ān 61. 6, where 'Īsā declares: 'I am the Messenger of Allāh to you, confirming the Tawrāt which came before, and giving glad tidings of a Messenger to come after me, whose name is Aḥmad.' Muslims hold that this messenger is Muḥammad.

J. B. Green *et al.* (eds.), *Dictionary of Jesus and the Gospels* (1992); A. E. Harvey, *Jesus and the Constraints of History* (1982); H. C. Kee, *Jesus in History* (1977) and *What Can We Know About Jesus* (1990); W. S. Kissinger, *The Lives of Jesus: A History and a Bibliography* (1985); G. Parrinder, *Jesus in the Qur'an* (1965); W. B. Tatum, *In Quest of Jesus* (1982); D. Wismer, *The Islamic Jesus: An Annotated Bibliography* (1977).

Jesus People. A variety of groups which flourished in the 1960s, differing somewhat in social organization, doctrine, and ritual, but all committed to a literal, *fundamentalist interpretation of scripture. For these groups, sometimes referred to as 'Jesus Freaks' or 'Street Christians', worship centred on the person of *Jesus and emphasized the continuing, direct activity of the *Holy Spirit, through his gifts (*charismata*, as in *charismatic movement), on the individual and community. While shunning many aspects of the *counterculture, such as drug-taking, they retained, none the less, many of the external trappings of that culture in the form of long hair, rock music, and communal lifestyle.

R. S. Ellwood, *One Way: The Jesus Movement and its Meaning* (1973).

Jesus Prayer or **Prayer of the Heart.** The prayer 'Lord *Jesus Christ, Son of God, have mercy on me' (or 'on me, a sinner'). The continual repetition of this prayer is specially important in *hesychasm, where it is often (though later) associated with a careful physical attitude—head bowed, eyes fixed on the place of the heart, control of breathing. The prayer may be abbreviated to the repetition of the name of Jesus. It is known from the 5th cent. and was commended by Diadochus and *John Climacus. A classic description of the place of the Jesus Prayer in Orthodox spirituality is the anonymous Russian account, *The Way of a Pilgrim* (Eng., 1941). 'The name of Jesus present in the human heart confers upon it the power of deification' (S. *Bulgakov).

L. Gillet, *The Prayer of Jesus* (1967); I. Hausherr, *The Name of Jesus* (1978).

Jetavana (Skt., Jeta or Jetri + *vana*, 'wood'). A grove on the outskirts of Śrāvastī, the capital city of Kośala, often frequented by the *Buddha. In many of the important dialogues, the Buddha is described as residing in the Jetavana grove. According to the Pāli *Tripiṭaka it was donated to the *saṅgha by a wealthy merchant, Anāthapiṇḍika, who paid its owner, Prince Jeta, enough gold pieces entirely to cover the ground. This incident is a frequent motif in the sculptural decoration of early Buddhist architecture. Jetavana was an important monastic site until the 11th cent. CE.

The Jetavana *dāgaba in Śri Lankā, 370 feet in diameter, is the largest dāgaba in existence. A splinter sect of the *Theravāda, the Jetavanīyas (formed 4th cent. CE, reabsorbed 12th cent.) take their name from this dāgaba.

Jew. A person descended from a Jewish mother or who has formally converted to Judaism. According to the *halakhah, Jewish decent is from the maternal line: 'Your son by an Israelite woman is called your son, but your son by a heathen woman is not called your son' (*B.Kid.* 68b), and such descent automatically brings with it the obligation to observe the commandments. Even an *apostate is counted as a full Jew. Gentiles who wish to identify with Judaism have to undergo full ritual conversion, including *circumcision for men, and *mikveh. The *Reform movement recognizes the children of Jewish fathers as Jews, and its conversion requirements are less stringent. Reform converts are not accepted as Jews by the *Orthodox, but can immigrate to *Israel under the *Law of Return.

Jewel net of Indra (image of the interconnectedness of all things): see HUA-YEN.

Jewel Ornament of Liberation (Tibetan Buddhist text): see GAMPOPA.

Jewish Theological Seminary (JTS). The educational centre of *Conservative Judaism. The Jewish Theological Seminary was founded in New York in 1887 for 'the preservation in America of the knowledge and practice of historical Judaism'. Under the leadership of Solomon *Schechter, the faculty and library were expanded and a teachers' institution was started. Today the Seminary trains *rabbis, cantors, teachers, and *synagogue administrators: it has a branch in California and sponsors many other educational activities for the Conservative movement. L. *Finkelstein defined the purpose of the JTS and of Conservative Judaism as a middle way: 'There are those who would think that we have but two alternatives, to reject or to accept the law, but in either case to treat it as a dead letter. Both of these are repugnant to the whole tradition of Judaism, and it is to combat them that the Seminary was brought into being.'

Jews' College. *Orthodox rabbinical seminary in London. Jews' College was founded in 1855 to train *rabbis and teachers for the English-speaking world.

Jhāna, dhyāna (Pāli, Skt., 'meditation', 'absorption'; Chin., *ch'an; Jap., *zen). In traditional Buddhism, the scheme of meditational practice which leads to *samādhi; the different stages within that scheme; any kind of mental concentration or effort.

The system of *meditation known as Buddhist Jhāna is composed of eight successive steps, called jhānas: the four lower jhānas or 'meditations on form' (*rūpajjhānā*) and the four higher jhānas or 'meditations on the formless' (*arūpajjhānā*). Jhanic meditation is not an end in itself (practitioners are warned of the danger of mistaking attainment of one of the stages for *nirvāna) but a means for achieving tranquillity (*samatha) which assists the development of insight (*vipassanā). The procedure involves progressive withdrawal from the activities of the senses together with their distractions, with a view to establishing 'one-pointedness of mind' or 'singularity of consciousness' (*ekaggatā-citta*, *ekāgrata); it is thus *enstatic.

Meditation proceeds with the selection of a suitable object (*kasiṇa) upon which to fix one's gaze. This object (parikamma-*nimitta, visual image) is then contemplated until one is capable of forming in the mind's eye a replica image as vivid as the sensation of the original object; this counterpart mental image (uggaha-nimitta) is in turn contemplated until it becomes transformed into a purified, idealized image or aura (paṭibhāga-nimitta) that is so fluid it can be either contracted into a single point or expanded to fill the entire universe, at one's bidding. On reaching this stage, the meditator is said to have achieved 'access' or 'entrance' (*upacāra-samādhi*) to the first jhāna. The attainment of this stage is also marked by the complete and final disappearance of the five factors relating to sensuality and unwholesome states of mind (see NĪVARAṆAS) which inhibit concentration, and their replacement by five factors of concentration: *vicāra* (the ability to advert one's attention to the subject of reflection): *vitakka* (the abilty to sustain one's attention upon the subject of reflection); *pīti* (ecstatic joy); *sukha* (tranquil joy), and *ekaggatā* (one-pointedness). The meditator continues to contemplate the idealized image until he finds that *vicara* and *vitakka* become a disturbance to him, and he eliminates them; by so doing he enters the second jhāna. He then enters the third jhāna by eliminating *pīti*; he has now reached what is regarded as the highest form of physical pleasure possible, composed of tranquil joy, equanimity (*upekkhā), a condition which is mindful (*sato*) and fully aware (*sampajāna*). The fourth jhāna is attained when all forms of pain and pleasure, sorrow and joy are transcended and upekkhā and mindfulness (*sati) alone remain. This jhāna is regarded as a crucial attainment because the meditator has now purified his mind of all sensuous dross and achieved a state of perfect concentration (*samādhi) and because he may now go on to develop the *brahmavihāra meditations, or the *abhiññās, or make the transition to the higher jhānas of the formless realm. This transition marks a shift from the physical to the supra-physical plane: the meditator expands his meditational image so that it fills the entire universe and then disposes of the image altogether; in so doing he is transcending the idea of discrete objects as a principle of thought. By now concentrating upon the infinite void or space left by the discarded image he is said to achieve the fifth jhāna. By shifting his concentration from the infinite space perceived to the act of infinite perception which does the perceiving, he enters the sixth jhāna. The seventh jhāna is marked by the removal of the act of perception itself, so that nothing at all remains. In the eighth and final jhāna the 'idea' of 'nothing' is removed and the meditator ceases conscious ideation altogether. There can be no further development beyond this stage in the sphere of conceptual thought. There does exist an additional attainment for one who embarks upon jhānic meditation, the cessation of all thought and feeling (*nirodha-samāpatti), but it is only possible for those who have already realized nirvāna.

Canonical sources themselves acknowledge that the jhānas are not exclusively Buddhist in origin, but are part of the general experience of *yoga: it is related that non-Buddhist sects utilized them, and that the Buddha attained the seventh and eighth jhānas under the teachers Alāra Kālāma and Uddaka Rāmaputta, prior to his *enlightenment.

H. Gunaratana, 'A Critical Analysis of the Jhānas . . .' (Ph.D., Am. Univ. Washington, 1980); Takeuchi Yoshinori, *Probleme der Versenkung in Ur-Buddhismus* (1972).

Jiba (plot of land where man was created, according to Shinto sect): see TENRIKYO.

Jibrīl (angel in Islam): see GABRIEL.

Jigoku. Jap. for *naraka, hell.

Jigme Lingpa ('Jigs-med gling-pa, Tibetan teacher): see KLONG-CHEN RAB-'BYAMS-PA.

Jihād (Arab., *jahada*, 'he made an effort'). More fully, *jihād fī sabīl *Allāh*, 'striving in the cause of God'. Jihād is usually translated as '*holy war', but this is misleading. Jihād is divided into two categories, the greater and the lesser: the greater jihād is the warfare in oneself against any evil or temptation. The lesser jihād is the defence of Islam, or of a Muslim country or community, against aggression. It may be a jihād of the pen or of the tongue. If it involves conflict, it is strictly regulated, and can only be defensive. Thus *Muḥammad said:

> In avenging injuries inflicted on us, do not harm non-belligerents in their homes, spare the weakness of *women, do not injure infants at the breast, nor those who are sick. Do not destroy the houses of those who offer no resistance, and do not destroy their means of subsistence, neither their fruit trees, nor their palms.

Jihād cannot be undertaken to convert others because there 'cannot be compulsion in religion' (Qur'ān 2. 256). If these regulations seem on occasion to be ignored, that failure is an offence to be answered for on the Day of Judgement (*yaum al-dīn). One who takes part in jihād is known as *mujtāhid*.

A. R. I. Doi, *Non-Muslims under Shariʿah* (1979).

Jijñāsā (Skt., 'desire to know'). In Hindu philosophy, an investigation or enquiry regarding a qualified object of knowledge. See BRAHMAJIJÑĀSĀ.

Jikaku Daishi (posthumous title): see ENNIN.

Jikishi ninshin (direct transmission of teaching in Zen): see FUKASETSU.

Jikkai. 1. Jap., 'the ten realms', i.e. the states of possible being: (i) *jigoku* of torment or hell; (ii) *gaki-dō, of hungry spirits; (iii) *chikusho*, of animals; (iv) *ashura*, that of *asuras; (v) *ningen*, of humans; (vi) *tenjō*, of heavenly beings; (vii) *shōmon*, of *śrāvakas; (viii) *engaku*, of *pratyekabuddhas; (ix) *bosatsu, of *bodhisattvas; (x) *butsu, of *buddhas. According to *Tendai, each of the ten realms contains in itself the other nine (*jikkaigogu*).

2. Jap., 'ten precepts', the ten precepts undertaken by a Buddhist monk: see ŚĪLA.

Jīlānī, al- (Muslim theologian): see ʿABD AL-QADIR AL-JĪLĪ.

Jīlī: see ʿABD AL-KARĪM AL-JĪLĪ; ʿABD AL-QADIR AL-JĪLĪ/JĪLĀNĪ.

Jimmu. The first emperor of Japan, a direct descendant from *Amaterasu, and the ancestor of subsequent emperors down to the present. According to tradition he was born in the west, but conquered the east, of Japan, ascending the throne of a united country in 660 BCE. But whether this is other than legend, or whether, indeed, Jimmu was a historical figure, is uncertain.

Jina (Skt., 'spiritual victor'). In the Indian religious tradition, a title given to great teachers and ascetics, and in Jainism a synonym for the twenty-four *tīrthaṅkaras. Jainism takes its name from jina: a Jain is a follower of the jina.

Jinacandra (Jain teacher): see DĀDĀ GURŪS.

Jinadatta Suri (Jain teacher): see DĀDĀ GURŪS.

Jinakuśala (Jain teacher): see DĀDĀ GURŪS.

Jinasena (9th cent. CE). *Digambara Jain writer. His major work was the *Mahāpurāṇa* (The Great *Purāṇa), an attempt at a universal history—Jinasena finished only the first part; it was completed by his pupils. The work gives an account of *Mahāvīra, but it serves also as a guide to kings. It also lays out the appropriate behaviours for laypeople, and as such it remains in use to the present day.

A. N. Upadhye, *Jinasena and his Works* (1968).

Jināza: see FUNERAL RITES (Islam).

Jineśvara (follower of Jain monk Vardhamana): see DĀDĀ GURŪS.

Jingikan (Jap., 'Department of *Shinto'). One of the two principal administrative branches of the centralized government, the so-called *ritsu-ryō state, of the pre-Nara (710–94) and Heian (794–1185) periods. The legal and political institutions, which were largely borrowed from Chinese T'ang dynasty models, comprised the Dept. of State (Dajōkan). The Jingikan, by contrast, was a Japanese bureaucratic innovation with legal precedence over the Dept. of State due to its antiquity and the importance of its religious activities. The Dept. of Shinto had jurisdiction over all matters pertaining to the worship of the gods (*kami). It supervised the rites of enthronement (Daijōsai), the rites of national purification (Oharae), the festivals of the first fruits and harvest, as well as the upkeep of shrines and the discipline of shrine priests. Suffering neglect during the long period of military rule after the Heian period, the Dept. of Shinto was briefly revived with the *Meiji Restoration of 1868, only to be abolished in 1871.

Jinja (Shinto shrine): see KAMI.

Jinja Shinto (category of Shinto organization): see SECT SHINTO.

Jinn (Arab., *junna*, 'be mad, furious, possessed'). Fiery spirits in Islam (Qur'ān 55. 15), particularly associated with the desert. While disruptive of human life, they may nevertheless be saved. A person who dies in a state of great sin may be changed into a *jinnī* in the period of the *barzakh. It was one of the jinn, Iblīs (see DEVIL), who refused to obey God in bowing down before Adam (Qur'ān 15. 31). However, the jinn may also be of service to humans in performing heavy labours. Thus, Solomon had an army of them as his helpers (21. 82, 27. 17).

Jinsei wa gejutsu de aru (living life as art): see MIKI TOKUHARU.

Jippō (Jap., 'ten directions'). The ten directions which encompass all possible places, the four cardinal points, the four intermediate points, up and down. Hence jippō-butsu, the *buddhas of the ten directions, i.e. all buddhas throughout the universe.

Jiriki and **tariki.** Japanese expressions referring to opposing methods of attaining salvation, jiriki, or salvation through one's own efforts, and tariki, salvation depending upon another power. In his teachings the *Buddha urged his followers not to look outside themselves for assistance in reaching the goal of the religious life; rather, they must find within themselves the will and strength needed for the task. Thus wise disciples must themselves walk the path (with the Buddha only showing the way), shaping their own destiny with their own *karma. In Japan, the *Zen school followed this tradition of jiriki. In *Mahāyāna Buddhism, however, the followers believed that it was inconceivable for the Buddha, being the compassionate and loving figure that he was, to restrict the results of his meritorious karma only to himself. Rather, they contended that that karma, accumulated by the Buddha over countless aeons, could be transferred to others to assist them in their quest for salvation. This idea of the transfer of *merits figured prominently in the teachings of the *Pure Land school, the most popular Mahāyāna school in China and Japan. This school emphasized that a devotee by himself was not able to win rebirth in the Western Paradise (*Sukhāvati) presided over by the Buddha Amitābha (*Amida), but if he were to have unqualified faith in the saving *grace of Amitābha and would abandon himself entirely to the power of that Buddha, then he would be able to gain rebirth in the Western Paradise, no matter how sinful or depraved he might be. Hence the expression tariki, depending on the other power of Amitābha. The common illustration of these concepts is the monkey and the cat. Infant monkeys cling to their mothers to be carried, but cats carry their young, lifting them by the back of the neck.

Jirinkan (Jap.). Meditation on Skt. letters. For an example, see A.

Jishū (Jap., 'the Time School'). A form of *Pure Land Buddhism founded by *Ippen in 1276. The main practice of Jishū is the constant repetition of the *nembutsu, as if, at each moment, one is on the point of death. Since Jishū originally had no temple, its adherents travelled about (like Ippen) encouraging the recitation of the nembutsu. For this reason, they are also known as Yugyō-ha, the school of wanderers.

Jisso (reality): see SEICHŌ NO IE.

Jīva (Skt., 'living'). In Hinduism, the living self which is engaged in the world and which identifies itself with mind and body as empirically real. The true self is *ātman, which is the One pervading all appearance. It is an issue in Hinduism whether jīva and ātman are, in the end, identical or whether some distinction remains between them: see JIVĀTMAN.

In Jainism, jīva is one of two categories into which all existing things must fall, the living as opposed to *ajīva. The concept of jīva is central to an understanding of Jainism, because of the way in which it credits all human beings, animals, insects, vegetation, and even earth, stones, fire, water, and air with living souls (jīvas). The universe is seen as being vibrant with innumerable jīvas, each of which is real, independent, and eternal, and characterized by consciousness (*caitanya), bliss (*sukha*), and energy (*virya). In its pure state each jīva is omniscient and possessed of infinite bliss, but through contact with ajīva and the ingress of *karma, which in Jainism is seen as material particles, these qualities are obscured and the jīva is bound to *saṃsāra, like gold in ore. The Jain path of purification offers a means of purifying the jīva through the pursuit of the *ratnatraya* (the *Three Jewels) of right faith, knowledge, and conduct; and with the help of strict ascetic discipline, the Jains believe that association with karma can be halted, just as 'a large pond when its influx of water has been blocked dries up gradually . . ., so the karmic matter of a monk . . . is annihilated by austerities— provided that there is no further influx' (*Uttarādhyayana Sūtra*). This teaching accounts for the enormous respect for life in all its forms which characterizes Jainism and is expressed in the keystone of Jain faith, *ahiṁsā.

Jivanmukta: see JĪVANMUKTI.

Jīvanmukti (Skt., 'liberated in this life'). In Indian religions, the condition of having attained enlightenment (*kaivalya, *mokṣa, *mukti, *nirvāna, etc.). A jivanmukta (one who has attained the condition) is in a state of being in the world but not of it, having reached beyond the human qualities of fear, desire, attachment, etc. Though his physical body is still subject to disease, he is enlightened, no longer living in nor dominated by time, but rather in an eternal present without personal consciousness but with complete lucidity of consciousness and the possessor of all the powers (*siddhis). He has reached the supreme goal and simply allows his life to run out like the fuel of a candle or the rotation of a potter's wheel after the potter has ceased to work.

A. G. K. Warrier, *The Concept of Mukti in Advaita Vedānta* (1961).

Jīvanmukti-viveka. 14th-cent. Hindu work by *Vidyaranya, which describes, in five chapters, the path to liberation, based on the *Vedas.

Jivātman (Skt., the 'living-self'). The personal or individual soul as distinct from the *paramātman, the 'Supreme-self'. According to *Advaita Vedānta, the distinction between the individual soul associated with the physical body and the one supreme self pervading all beings is only an apparent one due to spiritual ignorance and having no ontological basis. However, other schools of Indian philosophy, such as the *Viśiṣṭādvaita-vedānta and the various devotional (*bhakti) movements, affirm the reality of this distinction.

Jizō (bodhisattva who helps children): see KṢITIGARBHA; KAMAKURA; ABORTION.

Jizya (Arab., *jazā*, 'reward, requite'). The poll tax levied on non-Muslims in Muslim countries, based on e.g. Qur'ān 9. 29. It is, roughly, the equivalent of *zakāt, which Muslims have to pay. In return for jizya, the Muslim state has an obligation to protect those who pay it, since they are exempted from military service. Only male, competent adults are liable (which means, e.g., that slaves, the blind, and the crippled are not). Monks and nuns, having made a vow of poverty, are also exempt.

Jñāna (Skt., 'knowing').

Hinduism In the early period, jñāna was practical *knowledge or skill (e.g. of a warrior or farmer). It was also the practical ability to ward off personified evils or unseen powers (e.g. *asuras, *devas). But jñāna was rapidly extended to include all spiritual knowledge, and knowledge of the way to approach *Brahman or God (hence its appearance in the **Bhagavad-gītā*, as a way of progress, as jñāna-yoga). It then became detached as a reflection on the nature of knowledge as such: see JÑĀNAKĀṆḌA. More technically, jñāna is the cognitive episode or event in which knowledge can occur. Because the fundamental condition which prevents progress toward enlightenment or *mokṣa is *avidyā (ignorance), jñāna has a strong soteriological significance.

Buddhism (Pāli, *ñāṇa*). Early Buddhism possessed a thoroughgoing and radical critique of knowledge in response to the many and varied philosophies existing in India at the time of the *Buddha. It was mainly directed at two sorts of theories: those which were prepared to accept truth-claims solely on the basis of an appeal to faith, feelings, opinions, superficial reasoning, or to the notion of tradition (*anussava) and external authority (they were criticized for being either conjectural or uncritical); and those which were prepared only to accept sense-perception and extra-sensory perception (experientialists) or reason (rationalists) as valid sources of knowledge (they were adjudged right in basing themselves on direct experience, but were criticized for failing to take account of certain simple facts of human psychology. According to Buddhists, perception and reason cannot be totally relied upon since they are conditioned and distorted by our subjective attitudes—likes (*ruci*), dislikes (*aruci*), desire (*chanda*), fear (*bhaya*), ill will (*dosa), and delusion (*moha). Consequently, true knowledge (*aññā*) can only come about as a result of eliminating unwholesome mental and psychological factors; only then can perception and reason show us 'what exists as "existing" and what does not exist as "not existing" ' (*Atharva Veda* 36). Buddhism prescribes a programme for eliminating these factors: training in morality (*śīla), concentration (*samādhi), and understanding (*prajñaz). Therefore, the acquisition of knowledge becomes a practical not a theoretical issue, a principle which governs all Buddhist thinking and approach to existence, from its earliest phase, through *Nāgārjuna, to *Zen. Progress along the path to *nirvāna and the acquisition of knowledge are inseparable activities, so that each step of spiritual growth is accompanied by the appropriate form of cognitive awareness: 'In freedom the *knowledge* came to be: I am freed; and I *comprehended* that destroyed is birth, brought to a close is the Brahmafaring, done is what was to be done, there is no more of being such and such' (*Majjhima Nikāya* 1. 23). In terms of Buddhist doctrine, the true object of knowledge is to be found in the *Four Noble Truths and the law of causation (*paticca-samuppāda). These are not to be understood as dogmatic affirmations requiring credal assent, but as ways of summarizing the Buddhist experience of the world. Buddhism maintains that the source of this knowledge is both social and individual combined: it is to be found in the teaching (*dharma) of the Buddha which is proclaimed by his followers, and is also what each individual finds to be the case when he reflects systematically (*yoniso manasikara*) upon the nature of reality.

On this basis (especially in the analysis of the *Nikāyas), knowledge can be divided into three levels according to the explanation given in the Nikāyas: (i) sense-based knowledge of empirical phenomena, (ii) knowledge based on extra-sensory perception, and (iii) absolute knowledge. There are many kinds of knowledge explained in the Nikāyas and in the *Abhidhamma, though all kinds of knowledge can be subsumed under these three categories.

The Nikāyas explain that sense-perception is one source of knowledge, whereas materialists maintain that sense-perception is the only source of knowledge, a view which is criticized in the Nikāyas (*Digha Nikāya* 2. 328, 330). There are six faculties (eye, ear, nose, tongue, body, and mind) of sense-perception (*Samyutta Nikāya* 4. 104, 112). Based on these perceptions knowledge arises. This is normal or conventional knowledge (*sammuti ñāṇa, Digha Nikāya* 3. 277). *Kathavatthu* 310 defines conventional knowledge as a knowledge which accepts only object-related truth and nothing else. When a person sees an object he has the knowledge of that object as truth. Though Buddhism accepts this as a form of knowledge, it accepts other forms of knowledge also beyond normal sense-based knowledge.

Knowledge based on extra-sensory perception is one form of paranormal knowledge. This is called 'going beyond the human' (*atikkanta manusaka, Digha Nikāya* 1. 82). Five kinds of higher knowledge (*pañcabhiññā*) fall into this category (*Anguttara Nikāya* 2. 17–19). These are: (i) psychic power (*iddhividha*), (ii) divine ear (*dibbasota*), (iii) telepathic knowledge (*cetopariyaya nāṇa*) (iv) knowledge of previous existence (*pubbenivasanussati*), and (v) clairvoyance (*dibbacakkhu*). One can attain this state if one's mind is purified of five impediments (pañcanīvaraṇa, see NĪVARAṆAS—covetousness, ill will, sloth and torpor, restlessness and worry, and doubt, *Majjhima Nikāya* 1. 181, 270, 276) and on attaining the fourth *Jhāna.

Sometimes, a sixth kind of knowledge (*asavakkhya nāṇa*) is included in the reckoning of *pañcabhiññā*. This makes the series a sixfold higher knowledge (*calabhiññā, Digha Nikāya* 1. 83, *Vin*. 3. 88). This sixth *abhiññā* is the last of that series which is the knowledge of the destruction of defiling impulses (*asavakkhaya nāṇa*). With this knowledge one is able to verify the Four Noble Truths as well as the origin and cessation of the defiling impulses (*Digha Nikāya* 1. 84). Along with this, one's mind will be emancipated (*vimutti) (*Majjhima Nikāya* 1. 348) and this can be regarded as absolute knowledge.

Jñānadeva: see JÑĀNEŚVAR.

Jñānakāṇḍa (Skt., 'knowledge section'). Those portions, whether individual sentences or longer passages, of Vedic revelation (*śruti) dealing with knowledge (*jñāna), in which significant and authoritative statements are made concerning the nature of *Brahman. The knowledge section of the *Vedas is contrasted with the 'action section' (*karmakāṇḍa), which are those portions containing injunctions concerning the proper performance of Vedic ritual (*karma). The great philosopher of *Advaita Vedānta, *Śaṅkarācārya, stressed this distinction between the knowledge and action portions of the Vedas in order to reconcile apparent contradictions in Vedic teachings and to demonstrate that, although both portions are valid, the action portion leads only to worldly prosperity and heavenly rewards, goals of lower value than liberation (*mokṣa). This highest goal, according to Śaṅkara, can be realized only through knowledge of Brahman, the teaching of which is reserved to the knowledge portion of the Vedas, jñānakāṇḍa.

Jñāna-mudra. The Hindu *mudra (hand symbol) encapsulating knowledge: the index finger and thumb are joined, with the fingers outstretched; the finger (*jīva) is united with the thumb (*ātman), in the truth which points (outstretched fingers) beyond itself to what is real.

Jñanapañcami (Jain festival): see FESTIVALS AND FASTS.

Jñāneśvar or **Jñānadeva** (1275–96). *Marāṭhī Hindu writer and *yogi. His father, Viṭhobā, decided to renounce the material world, and, after giving false information about his family obligations, he became a *saṁnyāsin. When the truth was discovered by his *guru, he was forced to give up his new status and revert to the 'householder state' (see ĀŚRAMA) and live with his wife. The orthodox *brahmans did not approve of this reversal of status, and the couple and their children, when they were born, were all made *outcastes.

Jñāneśvar was one of four children. Although brahmans by birth, the boys were denied formal education since the whole family were social outcastes. The eldest brother, Nivṛattināth, became a yogi of the *Nāth sect (according to one tradition) and instructed Jñāneśvar, thus enabling him to be a yogi and attain knowledge. This tradition is mentioned in Jñāneśvar's composition on the *Bhagavadgītā*, where he lists the previous gurus as Ādināth, Mīnanāth, Gorakshanāth, Gaininā th, and Nivṛattīnath before himself. The children lived at Āḷandī after Jñāneśvar performed some minor miracles at Paiṭhaṇ to convince the orthodox brahmans of his yogic powers.

In the year 1290, at the age of 15, Jñāneśvar composed his Marāthī commentary entitled *Bhāvārtha-dīpikā* (The Lamp of Plain Meaning) on the **Bhagavad-gītā*. It was actually written down, as it was composed, by Nivṛattināth. It is the most revered work in Marāthī literature. Jñāneśvar is himself revered as a divine figure. Other important works attributed to him are *Amṛatānubhava*, *Yogavāsistha*, and *Advaitanirupana*. He gave up his life, following the yogic tradition, after burying himself alive in 1296. See also EKNĀTH.

S. Kripananda, *Jnaneshwar's Gita* (1989).

Jñātradharmakatha-aṅga (Jain text): see AṄGA.

Jō (Jap., 'meditation'). Buddhist concentration and meditation; also (a different Jap. word), a vehicle, i.e. a means of carrying people to salvation or *nirvāna; *jōjō* is the highest teaching.

Joachim of Fiore (*c*.1132–1202). Christian mystic and prophetic visionary. As a young man he became a *Cistercian, but later left and eventually founded his own monastery at Fiore in Calabria. He saw history divided into three ages: the age of the Father, in the Old Testament; the age of the Son, the period of the Church; and the shortly-to-be-inaugurated age of the Spirit, in which new religious orders would convert the world and usher in the 'Spiritual Church'. His views were influential among the new orders of the 13th cent., especially the Spiritual *Franciscans. He had two (perhaps three) experiences of mystical illumination which unfolded to him his *trinitarian understanding of history, and he was regarded by many (including *Dante) as a *prophet. He wrote a harmony of the Old and New Testaments, a commentary on the Apocalypse, and *The Psalter with Ten Strings*.

B. McGinn, *The Calabrian Abbot* (1985); M. E. Reeves, *Joachim of Fiore and the Prophetic Future* (1976).

Joan, Pope. Legendary female pope. The gist of the story is that about the year 1100 a woman in male disguise succeeded to the papacy. After reigning more than two years she gave birth to a child during a procession to the Lateran and died immediately afterwards. The tale is first attested in the 13th cent. and was widely believed in the Middle Ages.

Job, Book of. One of the books of *Writings (*Ketuvim*) in the Hebrew scriptures. It describes how the righteous Job was deprived by God of all his possessions including his children and was struck down with a vile disease (1–2). His three friends try to comfort him (3–26), but Job will not accept that he has sinned against the Lord (rightly, since he has been defined as innocent for the purpose of the book). Job laments his disastrous fate (29–31) and a fourth friend attempts consolation (32–7). Ultimately God speaks to Job (38–48) and all his fortune is restored. There has been much scholarly discussion as to the meaning, date, authorship, and message of the work, and it was much studied by the *rabbis. In the *aggadah, Job's sufferings are sometimes regarded as a punishment: 'Three took part in the consultation, *Balaam, Job and Jethro. Baalam, who advised slaying the male children, was slain, and Job, who was silent, was sentenced to suffering' (*B.Sot.* 11a). On other occasions they are seen as a test, and Job is compared with *Abraham. There is no hint of a solution in 'life after death': the passage (Job 19. 25 ff.) familiar from Handel's *Messiah*, beginning, 'I know that my redeemer liveth . . .', is obscure, but clearly envisages a court-scene in which God himself will vindicate Job as innocent: 'I know that my advocate is active on my behalf, and as the last speaker he will stand up in court: I will see my witness take his place in court, and my defending counsel I will see to be God himself.'

In Islam Job is known as Ayyūb. Qur'ān 21. 83–4 and 38. 41–4 refer briefly to his calamities, his patience, and his restoration to prosperity. Elsewhere his repute and qualities find mention in lists of biblical figures; 38. 44 suggests a play on words with his Quranic name, in that he was *awwāb*, one who turns again to God.

Jōbutsu (Jap., 'becoming a buddha'). The realization in Zen of one's own buddha-nature (*bussho). It is not possible to become a Buddha, only to realize what was always the case.

Jōdo (Jap.; Chin., *ching-t'u*). *Pure Land, Jap. equivalent of *Ching-T'u. See further PURE LAND SCHOOLS.

Jōdo Shinshū or **Shin-shu** (Jap., 'True *Pure Land School'). A school of Japanese Buddhism founded by *Shinran, and organized by Rennyo (1414–99). It is a lay movement, with no monks or monasteries, and it is based on simple but absolute devotion to *Amida, in which the *nembutsu (recitation of the name) is an act of gratitude, rather than one of supplicating trust. Reliance on Amida is all that is required for liberation, hence Jōdo-shin-shu is an extreme form of 'reliance on others' (tariki—see JIRIKI). It split into two factions, Ōtani and Honganji, in the 17th cent. Both have their main temples in *Kyōto, and both remain powerful in Japan today.

D. T. Suzuki, *Shin Buddhism* (1970); K. Yamamoto (ed.), *The Shinshu Seiten* (1978).

Jōdo-shu: see PURE LAND SCHOOLS.

Joel, Book of. One of the books of *minor prophets of the Hebrew scriptures and Christian Old Testament. The book of Joel consists of a description of a plague of locusts (1 and 2). The prophet urges the people to ask for God's mercy and promises an end to the plague. This is followed by a prophecy about 'the great and terrible *day of the Lord' when God's (*Holy) Spirit will be poured out on all flesh and only the faithful *remnant will escape destruction (3 and 4), a prophecy fulfilled, in Christian belief, at *Pentecost. The date of the book is uncertain and the two parts may have different authors.

Johanan ben Zakkai (1st cent. CE). Leading Jewish sage (*ḥakham) after the destruction of the second *Temple. According to legend, the life of Johanan ben Zakkai can be divided into three clear periods: 'For forty years he was in business, forty years he studied and for forty years he taught' (*B.Sanh.* 41a). As a teacher, Johanan is remembered for his precise examination of biblical texts and as the first sage known to have been engaged in *merkabah mysticism. During the siege of *Jerusalem, he managed to leave the city and was given permission by the Romans to join the sages of the *bet din at *Jabneh. Although he was not officially named *nasi, he raised the status of the Jabneh group. Numerous scholars settled there, and Johanan issued ordinances 'in remembrance the Temple' (*BRH* 4. 3). As a result of his efforts, it was possible for his successor, Rabban *Gamaliel, to be formally acknowledged as nasi. When Johanan died, it was said that 'the lustre of wisdom ceased' (*B.Sot.* 9–15). Thus despite the catastrophic loss of the Temple, the institutions of the Jewish faith continued to exist.

J. Neusner, *A Life of Rabban Yohanan ben Zakkai* (1962).

John, St. One of the twelve *Apostles and traditionally author of the fourth gospel, three epistles, and the book of *Revelation. John was the son of Zebedee (Matthew 4. 21), one of *Jesus' inner circle of disciples (Matthew 17. 1), and one of the 'pillar' apostles (Galatians 2. 9) of the early church. According to tradition he settled at Ephesus, whence he was temporarily exiled to Patmos under Domitian, and died a natural death as an old man. Feast day in the E., 26 Sept. (also 8 May); in the W., 27 Dec.

The Gospel according to John, the 'Fourth Gospel', differs considerably from the *Synoptic gospels. It contains: a prologue describing Jesus as God's *logos; a 'book of signs' including the testimony of *John the Baptist and Jesus' career in Judaea first and then Galilee (1. 19–12. 50); a 'book of glory' including Jesus' farewell to his disciples (13–17), death, and resurrection (18–20); and an epilogue (21). As well as giving a different account of the course of Jesus' ministry from that of Mark, John presents Jesus' words in long discourses dealing with his own identity and tending to obscure his human personality. The latter discrepancy was traditionally explained by John's having written a 'spiritual gospel' to supplement the other three. Many scholars, however, now suppose that John wrote independently of the others, and preserved traditions of high quality (e.g. Jesus' early association with John the Baptist), overlaid with the theology of his own circle. The gospel identifies the source of its tradition as the 'beloved disciple' (21. 24): there are good but not decisive reasons for identifying him with John son of Zebedee. The *christology of the gospel was, if not influenced by *gnosticism, at least congenial to it in the 2nd cent. For devotional reading, John has remained the most popular gospel: see e.g. 14. 13.

The three letters of John, among the 'Catholic epistles' of the New Testament, are usually ascribed to the same author or group as the gospel. They were not, however, universally considered authentic by ancient writers. The theological vocabulary (e.g. 'light', 'eternal life') is very close to that of the gospel, and 1 John appears to be attacking the *docetic interpretation of the gospel (4. 1–3). 1 John 5. 7 f., called the 'Johannine Comma' or 'Three Witnesses', displays an explicit doctrine of the *Trinity but is not part of the original text. 2 and 3 John are short; 3 John is notable as evidence that settled local churches early came to distrust wandering 'brethren' seeking hospitality.

The Acts of John belongs to the New Testament *Apocrypha. It is a 3rd-cent. work notable for the 'Hymn of Jesus' (set to music by Gustav Holst) and for colourful stories of John's later life in Ephesus.

John Climacus, St (*c.*579–*c.*649). Abbot of Sinai and Christian spiritual writer. The surname (Gk., *klimax*, 'ladder') comes from the work of his old age, the *Ladder of Divine Ascent*. The ladder has thirty 'steps' (chapters), treating the break with the world (1–3); virtues and vices of the active life (4–26); and the elements of the contemplative life (27–30), namely, stillness (*hesychia*), *prayer, dispassionateness (*apatheia*), and love. The work has been very influential in E. Christian spirituality, e.g. among the *Hesychasts, and is prescribed for reading in Lent in *Orthodox monasteries. It is also an early source for the *Jesus prayer.

Trs. L. Moore (1958); C. Luibheid and N. Russell (1982).

John of Damascus, St (*c.*675–*c.*749). E. Christian theologian, known as Chrusorroas, 'gold-flowing'. After holding a high official position in the Muslim government in Damascus for ten or twenty years, he moved to the monastery of St Sabas near Jerusalem, and became a priest. He came to prominence there after 726 on account of his *Three Apologies against those who Attack the Divine Images* (Eng., 1980; see ICONOCLASM). His other most important work, the *Fount of Wisdom* (Eng., 1958), has three parts, dealing with philosophy, *heresies, and the orthodox faith. Ch. 101 of the second part describes Islam, drawing on the author's first-hand knowledge and including it among the Christian heresies. The third part is a comprehensive presentation of the teaching of the Gk. fathers on the main Christian doctrines, which was an important source for subsequent writers, including *Aquinas. Among his other works are a number of poems which form part of the Gk. liturgy (though not all those ascribed to him are genuine). *The Life of *Barlaam and Joasaph* also used to be commonly ascribed to him. The writings of John of Damascus have been widely known in both E. and W. Christianity since the Middle Ages. He was declared a *Doctor of the Church in 1890, with a feast day on 27 Mar.; 4 Dec. in the E.

J. Nasrallah, *Saint Jean de Damas* . . . (1950); D. J. Sahas, *John of Damascus on Islam* . . . (1972).

John of God, St (1495–1550). *Holy fool and founder of the 'Brothers Hospitallers'. Born in Portugal and piously brought up, he became a soldier and abandoned religious practice. When he was about 40, he was converted and sought to atone for his former life. Unsuccessful in his bid for *martyrdom in Morocco, he returned to Spain and lived a life of sanctity marked by excesses of penitence and devotion. Under St John of Avila's influence, he diverted his energies to the care of the sick and poor. His order gradually took shape after his death.

John of the Cross (1542–91). Poet, mystic, and joint founder of the Discalced *Carmelites. He entered the Carmelite Order in 1563 and studied at Salamanca (1564–8). Faced with what he regarded as laxity in the order, he considered becoming a *Carthusian. *Teresa of Avila persuaded him to stay and undertake her own kind of reform. He spent the rest of his life furthering the reform and suffering imprisonment and banishment from those opposed to his and Teresa's vision. Out of his suffering his great works of mystical theology were born. All take the form of commentaries on his own poems, amongst the greatest in Spanish:

> O living flame of love
> That tenderly wounds
> My soul in its deepest centre:
> Since you are not disdainful,
> Come now, if you will,
> Break the veil of this sweet encounter.
> O smooth burning! O luxuriant wounding!
> O soft hand! O delicate touch—
> That tastes of eternal life
> And pays every debt:
> Killing, you change death to life.

The *Ascent of Mount Carmel* and the *Dark Night of the Soul* expound the *dark night, the *Spiritual Canticle* expounds the whole spiritual life through commentary on his long poem inspired by the Song of Songs, and the *Living Flame of Love* is concerned with the *unitive way. He died on 14 Dec., saying, 'Tonight I shall sing *mattins in heaven.'

E. Allison Pears, *Complete Works of St John of the Cross* (1953); C. de Jesus, *The Life* . . . (Eng. tr. K. Pond, 1958); E. W. Dicken, *The Crucible of Love* (1963); K. Kavanaugh and O. Rodriguez, *The Collected Works* . . . (1979); E. A. Peers, *Handbook* . . . (1954).

John Paul I (1912–78). *Pope from 26 Aug. to 28 Sept. 1978. He was born as Albino Luciano, in a family known for its socialist commitments. He was ordained in 1935, and taught at a seminary at Belluno, being also *vicar-general to the local *bishop. He was made bishop of Vittorio Veneto in 1958, and patriarch of Venice in 1969. He was made *cardinal in 1973. He was elected pope on the third ballot and was acclaimed as 'God's candidate', and as one who would develop *Vatican II while conserving the tradition—what he called 'the great discipline of the Church in the life of priests and of the faithful'. A man of obvious and self-communicating humility, he simplified the papal coronation drastically. He died of a heart attack while reading papers in bed. Subsequent theories (building in part on the absence of an autopsy) claimed that he was poisoned because of his determination to clarify the suspect dealings of the Vatican Bank (thereby implicating members of the *curia), but these have remained speculation; see e.g. D. Yallop, *In God's Name* (1984). He wrote *Catechesis in Easy Stages* (1949) and *Illustrissimi* (1978), letters addressed to figures in the past. The hope that the papacy would continue to develop the vision of Vatican II and would be committed, not just in rhetoric but in reality, to a gospel of commitment to the poor, faded under his successor: see JOHN PAUL II.

P. Hebblethwaite, *The Year of Three Popes* (1978).

John Paul II (b. 1920). Pope since 1978. Karol Wojtyla worked in a chemical factory during the Second World War and planned to become an actor. He was a professor at Lublin University and archbishop of Cracow before becoming the first non-Italian pope since 1523. An energetic man of engaging personality, he has become a well-known figure throughout the world because of his wide travels. He survived an attempt to assassinate him in Rome 1981. He has shown himself to be a conservative on moral and doctrinal issues, but to have concern for social questions and for the defence of human rights.

John the Baptist. A Jewish prophetic figure at the time of Jesus mentioned by *Josephus and frequently in the gospels. He preached on the banks of the Jordan demanding repentance and baptism in view of God's impending wrath (Matthew 3. 11). He denounced King Herod Antipas and was beheaded by him (Mark 6. 16–29). Jesus was among those baptized and it is possible that he belonged originally to John's circle (cf. John 3. 22–4). How far John saw himself as *Elijah the forerunner of the messiah, as Christian tradition early made him, is open to question. Probably at first there was some controversy between the Church and John's disciples who did not acknowledge this subordinate status. The *Mandeans, who revere John, may possibly have some remote connection with such disciples. In W. art he often bears a book or dish with a lamb on it (from John 1. 29). Feast days, 24 June (nativity; six months before Christmas according to Luke 1. 37) and 29 Aug. (death, or 'decollation').

In Islam, Yaḥyā is mentioned as a *prophet (6. 85, 19. 14 f.), and the prayer of his father, Zakariyya, for a child in his old age (21. 89) is held up as an example of prayer being answered.

C. H. Kraeling, *John the Baptist* (1951).

Bergamo, and was a *Vatican diplomat in Bulgaria, Turkey, and France before becoming patriarch of Venice in 1953. Because of his advanced age, he was expected to be only a stop-gap pope, but in fact he proved to be the most revolutionary pope of modern times. He announced the calling of the Second *Vatican Council in 1959, and presided over its first session in 1962–3. He established the Secretariat for Promoting Christian Unity in 1960. His encyclicals included **Mater et Magistra* and **Pacem in Terris* (addressed to all people of good will). A jovial, kindly, and witty man of wide culture, he was widely mourned at his death, both because of the hopes he inspired in his own church, and because of his openness to other Christians and indeed to all people. His *Journey of a Soul* illuminates the underlying quest of his whole life:

> This serenity of mine, this readiness to depart and appear before the Lord whenever he wills, seems to me to be such a sign of trust and love as to deserve from Jesus, whose *Vicar on earth I am called, the final gesture of his mercy. So let us continue, moving slowly towards him, as if he stood waiting with outstretched arms.

Z. Aradi *et al.*, *Pope John XXIII . . .* (1959); P. Hebblethwaite, *John XXIII . . .* (1985).

Jojitsu (Buddhist sect): see NARA BUDDHISM.

Jokhang ('House of the Lord'). Tibet's holiest temple, sometimes called the Tsuglakhang ('the Academy') and generally referred to by W. commentators as the 'Cathedral of Lhasa'. It was built by the thirty-third king of Tibet, Songsten Gampo (*c*.609–50), to house the statue of the Buddha Akṣobhya brought to him as dowry by his Nepalese wife, Princess Bhrikūti Trisun Devi, and was initially called the Trulnang ('place of transformation'). At the same time he took as tribute from the militarily weaker China a second wife, Princess Wen Cheng Kongjo, who brought as dowry the Jowo ('Lord', 'Master', or 'Elder Brother') *Rinpoche, an image of *Śākyamuni which had been a gift to her father, the T'ang Emperor T'ai Tsung, from a Bengali King. The Jowo was reputed to have been the product of the holy artist *Viśvakarman, and another temple, Ramoché (since 1474 the Upper Tantric College), was built to house it. When a renegade Chinese army threatened to invade Lhasa, Wen Cheng transferred the Jowo to the Trulnang; thereafter the statues were exchanged and the Trulnang acquired its present name. The statue of Akṣobhya was broken in two during the present Chinese occupation, and the upper half was transported to Beijing. In 1988 the lower portion was discovered in a Lhasa rubbish tip, and in 1989 the two halves were reunited and reconsecrated in Ramoché, which reopened following its Cultural Revolution closure in 1985. There is doubt as to whether either original statue survived the attack on Buddhism by the anti-Buddhist King Langdarma (*c*.803–42), but the present Jowo image appears to have survived the 1959 desecration of the Jokhang when 10,000 citizens of Lhasa, taking refuge from the three-day uprising, were slaughtered within its walls on the morning of 22 March. The Jokhang's contents were more systematically destroyed in 1966, and throughout the cultural revolution it was used as the Red Guard headquarters. At this time all religious activity, including *circumambulation of the Jokhang, was banned along with the use of Tibetan clothes, food bowls, writing, and all things non-Chinese. The prohibition on circumambulation and prostration in front of the Jokhang was relaxed in 1971, but it was not until 1984 that it began to function as a temple and a monastery again. In 1990 it had over a hundred monks, but in common with other 'newly functioning' monasteries in Tibet these include a number of police, and its ruling committee consists of non-ordained political appointees.

Jonah, Book of. One of the twelve books of the *Minor Prophets of the Hebrew scriptures and Christian Old Testament. Although Jonah is classified as a *prophetic book, it is mainly concerned with the narrative story of Jonah. Jonah was sent by God to Nineveh to proclaim judgement, but instead Jonah fled to Tarshish. When a storm blew up, it was recognized that Jonah was its cause and he was thrown overboard and swallowed by a great fish. After the fish regurgitated him, Jonah did obey God and went to Nineveh. He predicted the city's overthrow, but because the people repented, God was merciful. Jonah sulked because his prophecy had not come true, but was reproved by God because God cared for 'that great city'. The book is thus, along with *Ruth, a landmark on the way to the recognition of God's concern for all people, including *gentiles. Scholars disagree in their dating of it, but it must have been written before the 4th cent. BCE because it is referred to in the *Book of *Tobit*.

In Jewish liturgy, the book is read in the afternoon service for Yom Kippur. Jonah's stay in the fish's belly was taken in Christian tradition as a *type of Jesus' death and resurrection (Matthew 12. 40). In Islamic tradition the prophet is known as Yunus.

Jonang-pa. A school of Tibetan Buddhism prominent from the 13th cent. but closed down by the Great Fifth *Dalai Lama, allegedly for heresy, in the 17th-cent. reformation. The founding of the Jonang is attributed to the 12th-cent. Yumo Mikyo Dorje, and the school took its name from the Jomonang monastery founded by Thukje Tsondru, whose student Sherab Gyaltsen (1292–1361) was the first to systematize its teachings. The Jonang enjoyed good relations with other schools for some time—their historian Tāranātha was widely respected, and the *Geluk founder *Tsong Khapa studied *Kālacakra, for which the school was famous, at Jomonang. Yet their offending beliefs go back to Yumo Mikyo Dorje, who evolved the *zhen dong heresy during meditation on the Kālacakra and presented it supported by *sūtras 'indicating an essence' (*snying.po*; i.e. the *Tathāgatagarbha Sūtra*), but considered by other schools as 'requiring interpretation' (*neyārtha*) and not to be taken at face value (*nītārtha*). Because of this, and the fact that similar views were held for example in the *Nyingma which escaped the reformation largely unscathed, many scholars have suspected political rather than doctrinal reasons for their closure. Before the Great Fifth Dalai Lama established an ordered theocracy in 1642, Tibet was ridden with factional in-fighting, with sects and regional kings all jockeying for power. The kings of Tsang made great efforts to keep down the Geluk, and the Jonang along with the Karma *Kagyü had thrown in their lot with the kings of Tsang. That the Karma Kagyü came out of the Geluk victory with only heavy property confiscation is thought to be due to the skilful negotiations of their leader, the Karmapa, and to the Great Fifth's preference for a stronger Karma Kagyü than Drukpa Kagyü, who were equally troublesome to both sides but politically out of reach in Bhutan. It is ironic that, given the charge of heresy as a reason for their repression, the offending zhen dong doctrine was reactivated to underpin the 19th-cent. *Rimé movement, and has since become prevalent in all schools except the Geluk.

Jones, Eli Stanley (1884–1973). Christian missionary. Born in Maryland, USA, he was ordained Methodist minister and sent to work at the Lal Bagh English-speaking church in Lucknow. He adopted a travelling ministry, based on Sitapur, where he wrote the widely selling *Christ of the Indian Road* (1925). He went back to the USA where he was elected bishop, but he resigned before the consecration could take place in order to return to India. He was strongly committed to social justice—he became a friend of *Gāndhī—and to Indian Independence, for which he was, for a period, barred from the country. His equal commitment to Christianity ceasing to be an imported 'European' religion, and becoming Indian, issued especially in the Sal Tat ashram (*āśrama). This was originally an annual event, but it and other ashrams became permanent. In 1964, he was awarded the Gandhi Peace Prize.

R. W. Taylor, *The Contribution of E. Stanley Jones* (1973).

Jones, Sir William (1746–94). British jurist and orientalist, who began his broad linguistic studies at Oxford, where, in addition to European languages, he learnt Arabic, Persian, Chinese, and Hebrew. In 1774 he was called to the Bar, and nine years later was appointed judge at the Calcutta Supreme Court. He was Founder President of the Bengal Asiatic Society, which he headed until his death.

His work at the Calcutta Supreme Court convinced him of the need to consult Hindu legal source books in the original Skt., and this language he proceeded to learn, subsequently translating into English not only legal treatises such as the *Manusaṃhita* but also literary works such as **Śakuntalā*, *Hitopodeśa*, and **Gitágovinda*. He also produced a grammar of Persian, and wrote on the Islamic laws of succession and inheritance. Sir William Jones was one of the earliest European scholars to learn Skt., and his work was of major importance in enabling non-Indian academics to become aware of and appreciate the richness of the ancient Hindu contributions to Indo-European literature and philology.

Jones Church (Christian sect): see PEOPLES' TEMPLE.

Jon Frum (John Broom?). A *cargo cult in Vanuatu (formerly New Hebrides) which arose on Tanna Island in the late 1930s and has spread more widely and appeared intermittently ever since. A mysterious figure, Jon Frum (variously understood as an ancestor, the local mountain god, Karaperamun, or the 'King of America', after contact with affluent American troops in Second World War), was believed to be coming with a cataclysm that would sweep away the whites, unite Tanna and other islands, and introduce a world of plenty without need for farming or keeping pigs. The local *Presbyterian churches and European schools and money were rejected, and some traditional customs, such as dancing and kava drinking, were restored. In conflicts with the government, various individuals claiming to be Jon Frum, or his sons, have been gaoled, but the movement continues in an elusive fashion.

Jordanites or **White Robed Army.** A religious group located along the coast of Guyana. It traces its beginnings to Joseph MacLaren, an *Anglican Grenadian, who from 1895 preached 'pure *Protestantism' from the Bible in Guyana. This led to the establishment of the West Evangelist Millennial Pilgrim Church, but the main founder was E. N. Jordan (d. 1928), who was 'called' to join in 1917 through visions. Successive *bishops established friendly relations with the independent government, and by the 1970s claimed some 4,500 members. Being mainly Afro-Guyanese, they stress their African heritage and regard God as black. Their beliefs combine Hindu (reincarnation), Jewish, Christian, African and occult elements. Worship is on Saturdays and on a Jewish pattern; there are festivals of *Tabernacles, New Moon, and *Passover (but no *Christmas), and *circumcision is practised. Adult *baptism by immersion is important, and the end of the present age is expected. A strict ethic includes many food tabus, vegetarianism, no *alcohol, tobacco, or cola, and the banning of dances, the cinema, and radio music.

Jōrei (technique of faith-healing): see SEKAI KYŪSEIKYŌ.

Jōriki (Jap., 'power of mind'). The power that arises from *zazen, which enables instantaneous reactions to be perfectly composed and correct. Since it also gives access to *iddhis, it is regarded with circumspection by most Zen teachers.

Joruri-ji (temple-complex): see NARA BUDDHISM.

Joseph. The favourite son of the *patriarch *Jacob, borne by his wife Rachel. Genesis 37–47 describes how Joseph, having aroused the hatred of his brothers, was sold as a slave in Egypt. After a series of adventures, he rose to be second only to Pharaoh. His brothers were reconciled to him, and the whole family settled in Egypt. Ultimately both his two sons, *Ephraim and Manasseh, became founders of two Israelite tribes, reflecting Joseph's status among his brothers. The story of Joseph inspired much *aggadic discussion among the *rabbis and has been the inspiration for extensive artistic and literary treatment.

Joseph, St. The husband of the Virgin *Mary. In Matthew 1–2 and Luke 1–2 Mary is said to have been 'betrothed' to him when Jesus was born. According to Matthew 13. 55 he was a carpenter. His absence from stories of Jesus' public career would be explained (as it was in later legends) if he was an old man and had already died. The veneration of St Joseph was a development later in the W. than the E. Church. In art he usually appears with the child Jesus and a lily or staff. From 1479, his feast day in the W. was on 19 Mar. Between 1914 and 1955 his feast day was on the third Wednesday after Easter. In 1955 it was transferred (as St Joseph the Worker) to 1 May, to align it with the secular holiday. It ceased to be obligatory in 1969. In the E. it is the first Sunday after Christmas.

Joseph of Arimathea, St. The 'councillor' (Luke 23. 50) who buried the body of *Jesus after the crucifixion. (Arimathea was perhaps Ramlah.) John 19. 38 adds that he was a secret disciple of Jesus. According to a 12th-cent. source, he came to England with the Holy *Grail, building a church (the first in England) at *Glastonbury. The Holy Thorn is said to have sprung from his staff. Feast day in E., 31 July; in W., 17 Mar.

Joseph of Volokalamsk, St: see POSSESSORS.

Josephus (1st cent. CE). Jewish historian. From an aristocratic family, Josephus was appointed, during the Revolt against Rome, commander of Galilee as the envoy of the *Sanhedrin, but surrendered to the Romans in 67 CE. He accompanied Titus at the siege of *Jerusalem and, hated by the Jews as a traitor, he retired to Rome. He recorded the events of the Jewish rebellion in *The Jewish War* in which he declared he was writing without bias. His other great work was the *Jewish Antiquities* in which he tried to explain Jewish history and customs to the gentiles. He also attempted to explain his own conduct in *The Life*, and he composed a defence against *anti-Semitism in *Against Apion*. Josephus' histories are the only extensive surviving source, and, without them, little would be known of the history of the second *Temple.

Eng. trs. in Loeb library (1926–65); T. Rajak, *Josephus . . .* (1983); H. St. J. Thackeray, *Josephus, the Man and the Historian* (1967).

Joshua. Son of Nun, Hebrew/Israelite leader at the time of the conquest of *Canaan. The Hebrew scriptures describe how Joshua accompanied *Moses on his ascent of Mount *Sinai (Exodus 24. 13) and was one of the twelve spies sent to explore the *Promised Land. After Moses' death, he took over the leadership of the people and conquered and apportioned the land of Canaan. According to Numbers 27. 18–20, 'he was filled with the spirit of wisdom because Moses had laid his hands on him'. In the *aggadic tradition, 'the face of Moses was as the face of the sun, and the face of Joshua as the face of the moon' (*BBB* 75a). The fact that his name is that of (the Gk.) *Jesus made Joshua a type of *Christ in early Christian exegesis (e.g. Hebrews 4. 8 f.). In Islam, *al-Tabarī records traditions about Yushaʿ/Joshua.

Joshua, Book of. The book in the Hebrew scriptures and Christian Old Testament which describes the conquest and settlement of the land of *Canaan. The *Talmud teaches that 'Joshua wrote his own book' (*BBB* 15a) but this is not generally accepted by modern scholars, who generally either group it with the *Pentateuch to make the *Hexateuch, or regard it as the second book of the *Deuteronomic history. The work consists of three parts: the story of the conquest of the land (1–12), the division of the land among the *tribes and the establishment of the cities of the Levites and the *Cities of Refuge (13–21), and the final chapters (22–4) which include the *covenant at Shechem and an account of Joshua's death.

Jōshū Jūshin (Ch'an Zen Master): see CHAO-CHOU T'SUNG-SHEN.

Josiah (640–609 BCE). King of *Judah. The reign of King Josiah was marked by religious renewal. According to 2 Kings 23. 25, 'Before him there was no king like him . . . nor did any like him arise after him.' Josiah exploited the increased weakness of the Assyrian Empire: the kingdom of Judah expanded and worship was centralized in *Jerusalem. According to 2 Kings 22–3, the 'Book of the *Torah' was discovered and, in consequence, all traces of *idolatry and paganism were removed from the cult, the *high places were abolished, and the people undertook to keep the Law of God. Some scholars have identified the 'Book of the Torah' with *Deuteronomy. According to the *Aggadah, Josiah was an example of a truly repentant person (*OR* 24) and he was killed by being pierced by 300 arrows (*B.Taʿan.* 22b).

Josippon. 10th-cent. CE Hebrew history of the second *Temple period. Written in Italy, the book starts by listing the nations and ends with the siege of Masada. It was much quoted in medieval Bible and *Talmud commentaries.

Joss. An idol; the word is a pidgin corruption of the Portugese *deos*, taken back into European languages as a supposed Chinese word. Although it appears in various combinations (e.g. joss-house, a temple), it is most familiar now in 'joss-stick', a stick of incense used in temple ceremonies—or simply for its sweet smell.

Jōyō Daishi. Posthumous name of *Dōgen.

Jōzabu. Jap. for *Theravāda.

JPIC (Justice, Peace, and the Integrity of Creation): see COSMOLOGY.

JTS: see JEWISH THEOLOGICAL SEMINARY.

Ju (Jap., 'praise'). Eulogies of Zen masters often found attached to *kōan collections, e.g. *Pi-yen-lu*, *Wu-men-kuan*. The emotions of gratitude and reverence make these some of the finest examples of Buddhist poetry.

Ju. Jap. for *mantra.

Jubilee (Heb., *yovel*). Biblical law requiring the release of slaves and the restoration of family property every fifty years: 'Hallow the fiftieth year. . . . It shall be a jubilee to you, and you shall return every man to his possession and his family' (Leviticus 25. 10). The purpose of the law was to enable each Jew to begin life again on an equal basis and in possession of the original allocation of land at the time of the conquest of the *Promised Land. The agricultural laws of the sabbatical year (i.e. the seventh year of seven) applied in the Jubilee year, such as leaving the land to lie fallow. Since the law depended on the twelve tribes residing in the land of Israel, the law fell into disuse after the return from the Babylonian *Exile.

Jubilees, Book of. *Pseudepigraphic Jewish book. *The Book of Jubilees* dates from the second *Temple period and is supposedly the revelation of an *angel to *Moses. It consists of a recitation of the events of Genesis 1–Exodus 12, as dated according to *jubilee years. It warns against contact with *gentiles, and interprets the laws of the *Sabbath, offerings, and abstinence from blood and fornication, particularly strictly. The book ends with the expectation of both a *messiah from *Judah and one from Levi. It survived in Ethiopic, but fragments of the Hebrew text were found at *Qumran, and it greatly influenced later *midrashic literature. The *Falashas have based their *calendar upon its calculations.

Ju-chia. Chinese name for what is known in W. languages as *Confucianism. Meaning 'school' or 'tradition' of scholars, it referred originally to those who were trained and knowledgeable in matters of *li (rituals and appropriate behaviour); it came increasingly to refer also to those who were so-trained and worked in government. 'Confucianism' is also known as *ju-chiao* (*chiao* meaning those who belong to the same organization or social structure, e.g., a family, and who share common goals or interests; it is thus often translated as 'religion'). Since *chiao* involves educating or instructing a child, it became associated with those who belong to the same tradition. The later name Kung-chiao (tradition of *Confucius) is less common.

Ju-chiao (way of the followers of Confucius): see CHINESE RELIGION; CONFUCIANISM.

Judah. Fourth son of the Jewish *patriarch *Jacob and his wife Leah. Judah was the ancestor of the most prominent southern *tribe, and the name was used for the Southern Israelite kingdom which remained loyal to the *Davidic kingship.

Judah ben Samuel he-Ḥasid (*c.*1150–1217). Main teacher of the Jewish *Ḥasidei Ashkenaz movement. In *c.*1195, he moved to Regensburg, where he established an academy. Many legends were circulated about his life, but little for definite is known. His major works were *Sefer ha-Kavod* (Book of Divine Glory) of which only fragments survive, and *Sefer Ḥasidim*, to which he was only a contributor. He also wrote commentaries on prayer, a few magical treatises, and some works of ethics.

Judah Halevi (*c.*1075–1141). Jewish philosopher and poet. Judah spent much of his life travelling round the various Jewish communities of Spain. He was a close friend of Abraham *ibn Ezra who quoted his works of grammar and philosophy. Towards the end of his life, he travelled to *Erez Israel, but probably died on the way there in Egypt. According to legend, he was trampled to death in one of the gateways of Jerusalem, reciting his poem,

> O Zion, will you not ask me
> About the well-being of your captives,
> Those who seek after your peace
> And those who are the remnant of your flock?
> . . . I am like a jackal when I howl for your affliction,
> But when I dream of the return of your *exiles
> I am a lute for your songs.

About 800 of his poems have survived, including love poems, laments, lyric poetry, and songs of *Zion. His philosophy is contained in his *Kitab al-Hujja wa-al-Dalil fi Nasr al-Din al-Dhalil* (The Book of Argument and Proof in Defence of the Despised Faith, generally known as *Sefer ha-Kuzari* (The Book of the Kuzari, 1506; Eng. tr., H. Hirschfeld, 1945) which has gone through many edns. It is based on the legend of the king of the Khazars who invited an Aristotelian philosopher, a Muslim, a Christian, and a Jew to put forward their points of view. The *Kuzari* has been consistently popular and was particularly influential on *kabbalists in the Middle Ages, and, more recently, on the *Ḥasidim. For both Abraham Isaac *Kook and Franz *Rosenzweig it was seen as a most faithful picture of the unique attributes of Judaism.

I. I. Efros, *Judah Halevi as Poet and Thinker* (1941); R. Kayser, *The Life and Times of Judah Halevi* (Eng. 1949).

Judah ha-Nasi (late 2nd cent. CE). Jewish leader and legal expert. Judah ha-Nasi, a direct descendant of *Hillel, devoted his life as *nasi to building up the unity of the Jewish people in *Erez Israel and spreading the knowledge of *Torah. Many legends are told of his wisdom and holiness and of his friendly relations with the Roman emperor. He was said to have all righteous qualities (*Avot* 6: 8). His name is particularly associated with the redaction of the *Mishnah. The principles by which he made his selection of current *halakhah are not clear, though there is a tradition of 'thirteen different interpretations' from which he chose (*B.Ned.* 41a). None the less, the collection was fixed; no new material was added, and subsequent halakhah emerged only as commentary on Judah's Mishnah (see TALMUD). He was held in enormous reverence by his contemporaries, and it was said that 'not since the days of *Moses were learning and high office combined in one person until Rabbi' (*B.Git.* 59a). He was a strong advocate of receiving Torah with joy (cf. SIMḤAT TORAH): 'Fulfil the commands of God with joy, as Israel received Torah at Sinai with joy.' Life is lived under the eye of God: 'Remember three things and you will avoid transgressions: above you is an eye that sees, an ear that hears, and a faithful record of all your deeds.' His vocation as a teacher is clear in his remark, 'I have learned much from my teachers, more from my colleagues, and most from my pupils.'

Judah Loew ben Bezalel of Prague (**Der Hohe Rabbi Loew,** known as **Maharal mi-Prag,** *c.*1529–1609). Jewish leader and legal expert. Judah Loew served as *Chief Rabbi in Posen and Prague. He was the outstanding leader of his day, renowned for his piety, who produced highly influential works on ethics, philosophy, and homiletics. Without belonging to any particular school in his prolific output, he tried to solve the problems of the relationship of God with *Israel, the role of *Torah, and the reasons for *galut (exile). He was an early advocate of the view that 'the state' is an unnatural compromise, which will wither away when the true conditions of human freedom are realized. He recognized the pluralistic implications of this: 'It is wrong to suppress the views of an opponent: it is wiser to reflect on their meaning. Thus it would be wrong to silence someone who speaks out against religion.' He regarded Israel's vocation to be the proleptic representation of the harmony which will, eventually, be the world's final condition: 'Israel may be seen as contributing form to the otherwise chaotic and undisciplined character of the world. If Israel (God forbid!) should perish, the world would fall apart.' There has been a revival of interest in his work in the 20th cent., but the well-known legend that he was creator of the Prague *golem is unfounded.

A. Mauskopf, *Religious Philosophy of the Maharal of Prague* (1949); B. L. Sherwin, *Mystical Theology and Social Dissent: Life and Works* . . . (1982); F. Thieberger, *The Great Rabbi Loew of Prague* (1954).

Judah the Maccabee (2nd cent. BCE). Jewish warrior. Judah Maccabee was the third son of Mattathias, the *Hasmonean, who led the revolt against the rule of Antiochus Epiphanes in *Erez Israel. After defeating the Syrian forces in the battle of Beth-Zur, he took possession of *Jerusalem, purified the *Temple, and instituted the festival which is now celebrated as *Ḥanukkah. The story of his campaigns is told in the *Books of *Maccabees*. Judah defeated the Syrians again at Adasa in 161 BCE, but was subsequently killed at the battle of Elasa. His story has inspired many later writers, artists, and composers.

Judaism. The name 'Judaism' emerged at around the opening of the Christian era (*2 Maccabees* 2. 21, 8. 1, 14. 38; Galatians 1. 13). Like other aggregating names of major religions, it is misleading if it implies that there is uniformity of belief and practice among all Jews. Yet it is appropriate if it draws attention to a shared genealogy (identified through having a Jewish mother, and going back to 'our fathers *Abraham, *Isaac and *Jacob'; see PATRIARCHS) and to a sense of being a people chosen to receive God's guidance in *Torah—though the emphasis on being a *chosen people has itself been questioned during the 20th cent. Today a distinction is frequently drawn between 'secular' or 'cultural' Judaism (denoting those who accept the history and values of Judaism, but who do not observe the details of Torah: Torah is usually accepted according to *Hillel's summary, 'That which is hateful to you, do not do to your neighbour; all the rest is commentary', *B.Shab.* 31a) and 'religious' Judaism, which implies acceptance of Torah. Even then, there are major differences in the ways in which Torah is brought to bear on life, among the major divisions of *Orthodox, *Reform, *Conservative, *Progressive, *Reconstructionist, and Liberal Judaism. Attempts to define 'normative Judaism' have not met with extensive success; but at the least it can be said that Judaism is inseparable from the idea of the peoplehood of *Israel; and that adherence to another religion such as Christianity or Islam is incompatible with Judaism of any form (i.e. even with an ethnic or cultural sense of Judaism); those known as 'Jewish Christians' are those who accept that *Jesus was indeed the *Christ (i.e. *messiah) and are thus not accepted as Jews by Jews in general.

The origin of the Jewish people and of Judaism cannot be traced historically with any certainty. The major sources of information are contained in those books which came to be believed as having come from the initiative and inspiration of God, and which became *scripture, i.e. Torah, Nebi'im (*Prophets), and Kethubim (*Writings), hence the abbreviated name. *Tanach; this threefold division goes back to at least the 2nd cent. BCE: for details, see BIBLE. From these books, it seems clear that a kinship group, the bene Jacob (descendants of Jacob) gradually ceased to be nomadic and settled in areas of Canaan. Different parts of the kinship group followed different histories (a dramatic part of which was an enslavement in Egypt and an escape now commemorated in *Passover; another was a covenant with a god Yhwh at Sinai). As the tribes began to settle, so they began more formally to unite in the defence, and later conquest, of territory, making a covenant, not only with each other, but also under the demand and protection of Yhwh (how this name was originally pronounced is unknown; conventionally it is transliterated as *Yahweh, but Orthodox Jews would not attempt to pronounce it at all: see HA-SHEM). Yhwh had originally been a god in the council of the Canaanite supreme god, *El; but scripture reveals how Yhwh took over the powers and attributes of El, becoming 'that which God is': this extraordinary transformation is, more than anything else, the origin of Judaism.

The biblical version of the origins of Judaism gives a more coherent picture, of the creative act of God disturbed by increasing separations and conflicts (the opening chapters of Genesis), counterbalanced by a succession of *covenants which God made with a particular people (or their ancestors), culminating (but not ending) with the covenant with Moses: here the demand is made that Israel should be holy as God is holy, and that the people should obey the command, *Shemaʿ—'Hear, O Israel . . .'. When the people obey the commands of the covenant, all (especially according to Deuteronomy) will be well with them; if not, not. Thus Israel is a proleptic community, established by God in the midst of time, to represent that harmony which was intended by God in creation, and which will in the end be the whole human case, 'when the knowledge of God shall cover the earth as the waters cover the sea' (Habakkuk 2. 14). Under David, *Jerusalem was captured, and there the Lord's anointed (*haMāshiach* = the Messiah) mediated between God and people; there too the *Temple was built where worship and *sacrifices surrounded the *Holy of Holies, the inner sanctuary where only the *high priest entered on the *Day of Atonement (Yom Kippur). Yet ritual action and kingly control were never self-sufficient: they were monitored by prophets who spoke directly from God, *koh amar Adonai*, 'Thus says the Lord . . . '. In this way the triple cord of Israel's religion (prophet, priest, and king) was woven together.

Despite traumatic episodes, such as the *exile in Babylon after their defeat in battle, this faith continued and deepened—so much so that at the time when Jesus was alive, Judaism was a successful missionary religion, winning many converts to its ethical and obedient monotheism. During this period there were many conflicting interpretations of what it must mean in practice and in detail for Jews to fulfil the commands of the covenant. (e.g. *Sadducees, *Pharisees, *Dead Sea Scrolls). Nevertheless, there was a common sense that the final control and outcome of history is in the hand of God, and that God would send a messiah to restore the independent kingdom of the Jews, or of heaven; and this led to increasing restlessness under Roman occupation, culminating in two revolts against Rome, in 66–70/2 and 132–5 CE, which left the Jews a people no longer in possession of their holy land and places.

The reconstruction and continuity of Judaism was achieved by the *rabbis, beginning at *Jabneh. They sought and achieved a practice of Judaism which no longer possessed a Temple—the sabbath table, for example, becomes an altar; acts of charity replace sacrifices. In local communities, the *synagogue was reinforced as the centre of liturgy and education. The family and the synagogue became the centres of Jewish life. The period of Rabbinic Judaism saw a gathering together of the many interpretations of the original written Torah, which thus came to form a 'second' Torah, *Torah she beʿal peh* (oral Torah): this produced *halakhah, that by which Jews can walk in knowledge that this is the received application of Torah to life. This voluminous interpretation was gathered first in *Mishnah, then in *Talmuds; and eventually it was organized in Codes (*codifications of Law), notably the Code of *Maimonides and Joseph *Caro's *Shulḥān Arukh*. At the same time, Judaism was graphically expressed and sustained through its stories, *Aggadah, and its biblical exegesis, *midrash. But the fact remained that Jews were now dispersed throughout the world (*diaspora): the two major communities (between whom many differences, especially of custom, persist) were the *Sephardim (from Spain after the expulsion in 1492, and in the Mediterranean) and the *Ashkenazim (originally in Europe, but after the many *pogroms, culminating in the *Holocaust, now scattered again, but numerous in the USA). Both communities and traditions are present in Israel.

Although to the outsider Judaism may give the impression of being a religion preoccupied with law, it is not in any way legalistic. Through the centuries and down to the present, work is unceasing on the meaning of Torah and Talmud. But Jews keep the law (if they do) with care, not because they want to earn their way into God's favour, but simply because he has asked them to do so: Torah is a language of love, a way of saying 'Yes' to God (during almost the entire biblical period, there was not even a belief that life would continue with God after death—i.e. there was no reward for the faithful after death: see AFTERLIFE). Consequently the history of Judaism has thrown up two major explorations of this love of God which depend on Torah, but are not preoccupied with the keeping of the law as the *only* Jewish obligation: the first is *Kabbalah, the second is *Ḥasidism. At the same time, Jewish philosophers made important connections between the inherited faith and the quest for wisdom and truth (see Index, Philosophers: Jewish).

Throughout this whole period of *galut (exile) from the Jewish homeland, the memory of *Zion and the prayer for restoration and return (especially in the *liturgy) has been constant. The pogroms of 1881–2 forced many Jews to return to Palestine where the dreams of return began to take a practical form, and from where the *Zionist movement rapidly spread into Europe. Zionism received a major boost during the First World War, particularly through the *Balfour Declaration; and it became inevitable during and after the 'war against the Jews' waged by the Nazis and their followers from 1933 onward. Not all Jews agree with the Zionist interpretation of the restoration of Israel—some for reasons of strategy, others because only the return of the messiah can inaugurate the return (see M. Selzer (ed.), *Zionism Reconsidered*); but the Jewish commitment to Israel remains strong even among those who stay in the diaspora.

Since Judaism is not a *missionary religion (allowing converts, but not actively seeking them), the threats to its survival are structural, rather than theoretical. *Anti-Semitism remains a real and vicious illustration of the depravity of the human herd; but marrying out of Judaism threatens a serious dissipation of its numbers; and assimilation jeopardizes the identity of Jews in a pluralist and pluralizing world. But the tenacity of Jewish faith, which has endured millennia of hatred and murder, remains undiminished. As a Jewish woman put it (J. W. Bowker, *Worlds of Faith: Religious Belief and Practice in Britain Today*, 1983):

> Judaism is my inheritance. If I'm going to hand down an inheritance, the Jews have got to keep going—otherwise, what a terrible waste of suffering for all those thousands of years, if we're going to allow ourselves to disappear—through lack of effort, through lack of faith, through lack of love. I mean, what would God say? What would Abraham say? What a let-down.

S. W. Baron, *A Social and Religious History of the Jews* (1952–6); H. H. Ben-Sasson (ed.), *A History of the Jewish People* (1976); S. H. Bergman, *An Introduction to Modern Jewish Thought* (1963); A. A. Cohen and P. R. Mendes-Flohr, *Contemporary Jewish Religious Thought* (1987); A. J. and H. Edelheit, *The Jewish World in Modern Times: A Selected Annotated Bibliography* (1988); L. Finkelstein, *The Jews . . .* (1971); M. Gilbert (ed.), *The Illustrated Atlas of Jewish Civilization* (1991); J. Kaplan (ed.), *International Bibliography of Jewish History and Thought* (1984); J. D. Levenson, *Sinai and Zion* (1985); P. R. Mendes-Flohr and J. Reinharz, *The Jew in the Modern World* (1980); R. Seltzer, *Jewish People, Jewish Thought . . .* (1980); S. Sharot, *Judaism: A Sociology* (1976); A. Unterman, *Jews: Their Religious Beliefs and Practices* (1981).

Judaizers. Non-Jews and especially Christian groups who take up Jewish religious practices. Examples include the *Quartodecimans, the *Ethiopian Church, various descendants of English Puritanism including the Seventh-Day *Adventists, and a number of sects in Russia from the 15th cent. on. The term is also used of a group of Christian Jews in the earliest church of Jerusalem who insisted that gentiles embracing the gospel should also become Jewish *proselytes. They were defeated at the *apostolic council.

Judas Iscariot. The disciple who betrayed Jesus to the Jewish authorities (Mark 14. 10 f., 43 ff.; John 18. 2 ff., etc.). His motive is obscure; a popular theory, starting from the possible derivation of his name from *sicarius*, 'terrorist', is that Jesus had disappointed his hope of direct action against the Roman government. According to Matthew 27. 3–5 and Acts 1. 16–20 he committed suicide. He has been regarded with universal abhorrence in the Christian church, but more recently attempts have been made, especially by poets, to enter into so deep a fault: see, e.g., R. Duncan, *Judas* (1960); F. Kendon, *A Life and Death of Judas Iscariot* (1926).

Juddin (non-Zoroastrian): see PURITY.

Jude, St. One of the twelve *apostles ('Judas not Iscariot', according to John 14. 22). He is a popular saint in the Roman Catholic Church and is invoked in circumstances of special difficulty. Feast day in the E., 19 June; in the W., with St *Simon, 28 Oct.

The Letter of Jude is one of the *Catholic epistles of the New Testament. It denounces false and immoral teachers 'having not the Spirit'. Verse 14 quotes the book of **Enoch*. It is usually dated with 2 *Peter which it resembles.

Judenrein (free of Jews): see HOLOCAUST.

Judgement (of the Dead). Although religions differ in the extent to which they allow that humans are free in their choices and actions, they insist that humans are responsible and accountable for their thoughts and actions; and that in different ways their thoughts and actions now will affect their future outcome. In religions which believe in rebirth and *karma (Indian religions), a kind of judgement is always operating in and through this life, since (although karma itself is a neutral 'law' of moral consequence, and is not a system of reward and punishment) the consequences of present thought and behaviour affect what the next outcome after rebirth or reappearance will be. Even so, the next form of rebirth may be in a *heaven or *hell, and in that sense there is not only judgement through life but also of the dead. *Yama is thus associated with that judgement.

In W. religions, the status and descriptions of the judgement of the dead have become increasingly precise. Initially (in biblical Judaism), the idea scarcely exists, since there was no belief in a personal and substantial life after death. The moment of death (i.e. its circumstance and time, whether early or after a full 'three score years and ten' Psalm 90. 10) was long believed to be an act of judgement in itself; but apart from that, judgement was exercised on the people as a whole. As a result, the emphasis in later Judaism has been on the final eschatological judgement exercised by God on the world, especially in the return of the *messiah. At that stage, the righteous in Israel can expect their reward—a theme already present in the book of Daniel: see SON OF MAN. Early Christianity absorbed the Jewish perspective, but made the theme of judgement far more prominent as a consequence of the belief that the messiah (i.e. Christ) had arrived in the person of *Jesus. Jesus becomes the agent of God's judgement, especially in his second coming, *Parousia (e.g. Acts 10. 42, 17. 31; 2 Corinthians 5. 10). The issue of this judgement turns partly on belief and recognition of Jesus as Christ and as the Son of the Father (e.g. John 5. 22 ff.), but also on actions which exemplify the nature of *agape (active and disinterested love). This is particularly apparent in the *parable of the sheep and the goats in Matthew 25. 31–46.

Traditionally, a distinction is made between the final ('general') judgement of God on all people at the end of history (the Day of Judgement), and the 'particular judgement' on each individual soul immediately at its separation from the body. The general judgement is understood to take place at the resurrection of the dead at Christ's second coming. Some *millennarian schemes involve a whole series of judgements (see e.g. DISPENSATIONALISM). Some doctrine of particular judgement is entertained by most Christians, but it is most specific in Catholic teaching which holds that the soul is admitted at once either to the *Beatific Vision, to *purgatory, or to *hell.

In Islam, the precision of judgement in relation to the works which people have done is even more exact: 'We will set up the just balances, . . . so that no one will be wronged in anything: even if it is as slight as the weight of a mustard seed, we will produce it, for we know how to reckon' (Qur'ān 21. 49). The events of the Day of Resurrection and the Day of Judgement are described in literal detail, in both Qur'ān and *ḥadīth: see YAUM AL-QIYĀMA and YAUM AL-DĪN. The judgement of the dead has been a powerful instrument in the exercise of religious control over human life, and in pursuit of *conversion; see BRAIN-WASHING. Even so, the fact remains that humans pursued their customary ways of violence and ruthless self-interest at least as much in the ages when belief in the judgement of the dead was widespread as they do now in more secularized societies. The beliefs in karma and *original sin derive much of their credibility from this unhappy fact.

S. G. F. Brandon, *Man and His Destiny . . .* (1962), *Le Jugement des morts: Assour, Babylone, Israel, Iran, Islam, Inde, Chine, Japon* (Sources orientales, 1961), and *The Judgement of the Dead* (1967).

Judges, Book of. The second book of the Former Prophets in the Hebrew Bible and of the historical books in the Christian Old Testament. It is named for the series of heroes ('judges') who ruled Israel between the death of Joshua and the beginning of the monarchy and whose exploits are described in turn in the book. They include Othniel (3. 7–11), Ehud (3. 12–30), Shamgar (3. 31), *Deborah (4–5), *Gideon (6–8), Abimelech (9), Tola and Jair (10. 1–5), Jephthah (11–12), Ibzan, Elon, and Abdon (12. 8–15), and *Samson (13–16). The author has placed these probably independent stories in a historical framework in which the sequence of sin, punishment, penitence, deliverance is repeated. Judges professes (1. 1) to be a sequel to *Joshua, but in fact covers the same period (and probably more accurately) in describing the settlement in Palestine as gradual. The book is usually reckoned by critics to be the third book in the *Deuteronomic history.

Judith, Book of. *Apocryphal Jewish book dating from the second *Temple period. The story is set during the reign of the Assyrian King Nebuchadnezzar. Judith, a beautiful Jewish widow, lulled to sleep the Assyrian general Holofernes who was besieging the town of Bethulia. She then cut off his head and, without their general, the Assyrians were routed and departed. The book was probably written to encourage the people during the *Hasmonean campaigns, but other commentators (e.g. *Luther) regard it as a straightforward *allegory. Although originally written in Heb., it only survives in Gk. versions.

Juggernaut (name of Hindu god): see JAGANNĀTHA.

Jūgyū (-no)-zu. The Ten Oxherding Pictures, which portray the stages of Zen progress. There are several different cycles, all of great popularity.

P. Kapleau, *The Three Pillars of Zen* (1980); D. T. Suzuki, *Manual of Zen Buddhism* (1950).

Jujukai or **jujukinkai** (Jap.). The ten main precepts of Mahāyāna Buddhism. There are two sets, exoteric and esoteric. Exoteric: they forbid (i) taking life; (ii) stealing; (iii) unchasteness; (iv) lying; (v) trade in alcohol; (vi) gossip; (vii) praising self and deprecating others; (viii) reluctance in giving help to others; (ix) aggression; (x) slandering the *Three Jewels. Esoteric: one vows (i) not to abandon *dharma; (ii) not to abandon seeking enlightenment, (iii) not to covet; (iv) not to lack compassion; (v) not to slander any Buddhist teachings; (vi) not to be attached to anything; (vii) not to entertain false views; (viii) to encourage all to seek enlightenment; (ix) to instruct adherents of *Hīnayāna; (x) to practise responsive charity to *bodhisattvas.

Jujutsu: see MARTIAL ARTS.

Jukai. Receiving and granting the precepts (*kai), the formal initiation into the Zen Buddhist way.

Ju-lai. Chin. for *tathāgata.

Julian (332–63). Roman emperor from 361, known in Christian tradition as 'the Apostate'. His religious policy was to oppose Christianity and promote paganism (e.g. through education and the return of the old state cult). He also wrote *Against the Christians* (now lost), and attempted to create internal dissent by allowing all exiled bishops to return to their sees. He was killed on a military campaign against the Persians in 363; the story that he died with the words 'Vicisti, Galilaee' (Thou hast conquered, Galilean!') is a late invention.

Julian of Norwich (*c.*1342–after 1413). English mystic. Little is known of her life, except that she probably lived as an anchoress close to St Julian's church in Norwich. On 8 or 13 May 1373, while she was suffering from a severe heart attack, she had a series of fifteen visions relating to the Passion of Christ, followed the next day by a final vision. This she recorded in the shorter text of her *Showings*. More than fifteen years later she had a further revelation, after which she recorded a longer version in which she develops more deeply their significance, displaying considerable learning. 'Love was his meaning': a love both courteous and homely, reaching to the lowest point of our need, love creative and redeeming, the love of the Trinity itself, so that the 'ground of our beseeching' is the Son, dwelling in us, loving the Father. From her come the familiar words of consequent trust, 'All shall be well, and all shall be well, and all manner of thing shall be well'. She also laid great stress on the motherly nature and love of God: 'God is really our Mother as he is Father' (cf. FEMINIST THEOLOGY), and as a result she developed a sane optimism about the universe and the relative unimportance of *sin, compared with the good and grace which it allows.

E. Colledge and J. Walsh (eds.), *Julian of Norwich: The Showings* (1978); P. Molinari; *Julian of Norwich: The Teaching* . . . (1978); F. D. Sayer (ed.), *Julian and her Norwich* . . . (1973).

Jumʿa (Arab., *jamaʿa*, 'collect, unite'). The Muslim assembly for the midday prayer (*ṣalāt) on *yaum al-jumaʿ*, (day of assembly), Friday: 'When you are called to the "Friday" ṣalāt, make haste to the praise of *Allāh, and leave your business' (*Qur'ān 62. 9). It is obligatory on free, adult males (*women may attend, but will be strictly separated from men; it is held to be a mercy from God that they are excused this obligation). The ṣalāt is led by an *Imām, and it is preceded by a sermon (*khuṭba).

Junaid (Junayd): see AL-JUNAID (JUNAYD).

Jung, Carl Gustav (1875–1961). Psychiatrist and analytical psychologist, whose views have been thought by some to be more sympathetic to religion than those of *Freud. The son of a Swiss pastor, he studied medicine at the university of Basle before taking up his appointment to the Burghölzli psychiatric hospital in Zurich in 1900. Under Forel and Bleuler the Burghölzli had become world-famous, and until the end of his life Jung was grateful for the rigorous mode of observation he learned there. As a result of his years as an assistant psychiatrist, Jung concluded that there is meaning in the words and actions of psychotic patients. Building on the work first conceived by Galton, he expanded and developed the word-association test. Jung also studied under Pierre Janet in Paris in 1902–3. After an exchange of letters, Jung first met Sigmund Freud in 1907; they collaborated closely until 1913. By 1912, however, Jung could no longer conceal his differences from Freud and declared publicly that he disagreed with Freud's theories about the nature of the unconscious, on the aetiology of neurosis, and on infantile sexuality. In his old age Jung wrote that he could not accept Freud's insistence on his sexual theory 'as a dogma, an unshakeable bulwark' (*Memories, Dreams and Reflections*, 1963). After his break with Freud, Jung suffered a psychotic breakdown during which he believed that he confronted his own unconscious. The first fruit of this exploration was his formulation of a general theory of psychological types through which he hoped to distinguish the components of consciousness. In the construction of his typology Jung was applying his theory of opposites; he first distinguished between the two basic attitudes of introversion (when the individual is excited or energized by the internal world) and extraversion (when the individual is excited by the external world). He identified four properties or functions of consciousness (thinking, feeling, sensation, and intuition); these four functions divide into a rational pair (thinking and feeling) and an irrational pair (sensation and intuition). A person will have a primary mode (or superior mode) of functioning which will come from one of the two pairs of rational or irrational functioning. Using the two attitudes and the superior and auxiliary functions, it is possible to produce a list of sixteen basic types. Jung's typology has been the subject of debate and application, for example in the Myers Brigg's type indicator (MBTI) which has been widely used in church and other circles in order to enable a dispassionate awareness of one's preferences to be developed.

Many of the ideas of later analysts can be found to have been anticipated by Jung; for example, the concept of projective identification may be seen in Jung's term *participation mystique* which he borrowed from Lévy-Bruhl and which he used from 1912 onwards to refer to relations between *people* in which the subject (or part of him) attains an influence over the other, or vice versa. From his student days Jung was interested in philosophy, in mythology, and in the occult. Drawing on the tradition of the Platonic Idea, Jung developed his theory of archetypes in three stages, first using the term itself in 1919. Jung distinguished the archetype *per se* from the archetypal image realizable by human beings. Archetypes are recognizable in outer behaviours, especially those that cluster around the basic and universal experiences of life such as birth, marriage, motherhood, death, and separation; archetypal patterns wait to be realized within the personality, are capable of infinite variation, and are dependent upon individual expression. Jung declared that archetypal contents declared themselves first and foremost in metaphors. In his later middle age Jung became interested in *alchemy and collected many medieval and Renaissance alchemical texts, forming perhaps the most extensive collection since that of Sir Isaac Newton. Jung believed that alchemy, considered symbolically rather than scientifically, could be regarded as one of the precursors of the study of the unconscious and in particular of the analytical interest in the transformation of personality. Jung was also deeply interested in the *Gnostics (one of the *Nag Hammadi papyri was presented to the C. G. Jung Institute in Zurich in 1953 and named the Jung Codex.)

Jung felt humans to be naturally religious, the religious function being as powerful as the instinct for sex or aggression. He was not a supporter of established religions but he was interested in religious philosophies. Jung was deeply respectful of evil; his friendship with Father Victor White OP did not survive their disagreements about the doctrine of evil as *privatio boni*, which Jung felt to be profoundly inadequate. Jung could be said to have spent his whole life trying to relate human nature and beings to God. Jung distinguished between God and God-image:

> It is not for psychology, as a science, to demand a hypostatization of the God-image. But the facts being what they are, it does have to reckon with the existence of a God-image . . . the God-image corresponds to a definite complex of psychological facts, and is thus a quantity which we can operate with; but what God is in himself remains outside the competence of all psychology. (*Collected Works*, viii, para. 528)

On this basis, and especially from his theory of archetypes (which arise from the inherited tendency to respond to situations in ways that resemble the responses of human ancestors), and from his view that a collective personality is carried in the racial or collective subconscious, he claimed to have located the source which gives rise, not only to artefacts, but to dreams, myths, and religions:

> I am myself so profoundly convinced of this homogeneity of the human psyche that I have actually embraced it in the concept of the collective unconscious, as a universal and homogeneous substratum whose homogeneity extends even into a world-wide identity or similarity of myths and fairy-tales; so that a negro of the Southern States of America dreams in the motifs of Greek mythology, and a Swiss grocer's apprentice repeats in his psychosis the vision of an Egyptian gnostic.

Jung was not so much concerned with the ontological truth of religious assertions as with the role of religious symbols in enabling a healthy life. He ended his Yale lectures (*Psychology and Religion*, given in 1937, published 1938) by saying: 'Nobody can know what the ultimate things are. We must, therefore, take them as we experience them. And if such experience helps to make your life healthier, more beautiful, more complete and more satisfactory to yourself and to those you love, you may safely say: "This was the grace of God".' Thus Jung was happy, not *to* assert, but *in* asserting the truth of God's existence—but only (obviously) in his own symbolic sense. In the year before he died he made the same point in an interview:

> If you should find in yourself . . . an ineradicable tendency to believe in God or immortality, do not allow yourself to be disturbed by the blather of so-called 'free-thinkers'; but if you find in yourself an equally resistant tendency to deny all religious ideas, do not hesitate to deny them and see how that suits you.

P. Homans, *Jung in Context* (1979); A. Moreno, *Jung, Gods and Modern Man* (1970); L. Ress *et al.* (eds.), *General Bibliography* . . . (1979); A. Samuels *et al.*, *A Critical Dictionary of Jungian Analysis* (1986).

Justification. In Christian theology, God's act in redeeming men and women from a state of sin, and discounting its deserved effect. How this act is conceived is a matter of fundamental difference between traditional *Catholic and *Protestant theology.

According to the doctrine of *Augustine as elaborated by the *Scholastics, justification is the act which *makes* sinners righteous. It takes place by the infusion of sanctifying *grace, transmitted in the *sacraments. Men and women thus acquire righteousness which makes them worthy of *salvation.

M. *Luther, however, protested against any view which suggested that salvation could be a reward for a person's own worthiness, and insisted on the principle of 'justification by faith alone (*sola fide*)'. According to his conception, God *pronounces* righteous one who, although unworthy in himself, has faith in the atoning death of *Christ. The idea is that of a lawcourt in which a defendant is *declared* innocent or even in which the charge is simply cancelled; and this is indeed the semantic field of the Heb. root *ṣdk* behind the New Testament Gk., *dikaioō*, usually translated 'justify', as in Romans 3. 28 (cf. 8. 33–4). The Protestant doctrine has been elaborated in modern times by A. Ritschl, K. *Barth, and P. *Tillich among others.

Catholic and Protestant theologies have now approached each other *ecumenically. Protestant views, however insistent on God's unconditional acceptance of sinners, do not necessarily tend to a disregard of good works (*antinomianism) and of holiness. Catholic views, although based on God's justice and the rewards and punishment which must accompany it, do not deny that merit itself may be a gift of God.

J. Buchanan, *The Doctrine of Justification* (1961); A. E. McGrath, *Iustitia Dei: A History of the Christian Doctrine* . . . (1986); G. Reid (ed.), *The Great Acquittal* (1980).

Justin Martyr, St (*c*.100–*c*.165). Early Christian apologist (see APOLOGETICS). A native of Samaria, he became a Christian after a long search for truth in pagan philosophies, acquaintance with which helped his argument for Christianity. He taught first at Ephesus, and then as head of a Christian school in

Rome where *Tatian was one of his pupils. According to an authentic record of proceedings, he and some of his disciples were denounced as Christians and, on refusing to sacrifice, they were beheaded. Justin's *First Apology* (*c*.155) argues that traces of the truth are to be found in pagan thinkers, since all share in the 'generative word' (*logos spermatikos*), but Christianity alone is rationally credible, because the *logos became incarnate to redeem as well as to instruct. *His Dialogue with Trypho* (R. Tarphon) *the Jew* is considered one of the more fair-minded of ancient Christian rebuttals of Judaism.

Tr. in the Ante-Nicene Christian Library (1867); L. W. Barnard, *Justin Martyr* (1967); H. Chadwick, *Early Christian Thought* . . . (1966).

Just war. The belief that war is in some circumstances just, and that it must be conducted in ways limited by what is right. The two aspects of the Just War theory are called *ius ad bellum* and *ius in bello*. The Christian understanding of the Just War goes back to considerations of *iustum bellum* in the Roman Empire, and to the practice of warfare as commanded by God in the Old Testament, hence an inevitable relation to ideas of a holy war. Thus Judaism is not a pacifist religion: the Hebrew scriptures describe the wars fought by the Israelites against their neighbours from the time of the settlement in *Canaan (see S. Niditch, *War in the Hebrew Bible*, 1994); in the *diaspora, Jews have fought in armies of their host countries, and since 1948, thousands have volunteered and been conscripted to serve in the Israeli army for the defence of the Jewish state. The ideas of a holy war were modified by the New Testament commands of love and forgiveness (which to some Christians have meant that no war can be just, and that pacifism is an obligation) and the recognition that the state has legitimate functions and demands on its citizens. Although *Augustine made some attempt to draw together the threads of a Just War theory, the first systematic account appears in *Gratian's *Decretum*. The classic form of the theory, which had been consolidated by the time of the *Reformation, stated that *ius ad bellum* requires that there is (i) a just cause (of which three were recognized, to regain something wrongfully taken, to punish evil, and in defence against planned or actual aggression); (ii) a right authority initiating the war; (iii) a right intention on the part of those engaged; (iv) a proportional use of force, relevant to the issue and not doing more harm than good; and that the war should be undertaken (v) as a last resort, (vi) with the purpose of peace, and (vii) with a reasonable hope of success. *Ius in bello* limits warfare by the requirements of proportionality of means and discrimination of objects—often translated into noncombatant immunity. Whether these conditions can ever be fulfilled in modern warfare has been a matter of debate, as also has been the relation of terrorist actions to this theory.

In other religions, war can be regarded as 'just' (or at least as justifiable), but the criteria vary. In Islam and among Sikhs, the criteria are formal: see JIHĀD; DHARAM YUDH. In Indian-based religions, there is an overriding consideration of *ahiṁsā (non-violence). Nevertheless, in the long cycles of rebirth, there will always be those whose obligation (*dharma) it is to undertake warfare in certain circumstances (especially those of defence), even while those closer to the goal may be strict in their practice and advocacy of non-violence (see esp. ARTHAŚĀSTRA). This is the classic argument of *Kṛṣṇa to Arjuna in the **Bhagavad-gītā* (it must clearly be the dharma of a *kṣatriya to act as a warrior); but it is also found in Buddhism and among Jains (e.g. *Jinasena's *Mahāpurāṇa* contains instructions on how Jain kings should conduct warfare in defence of the Jain community and teaching). There is no religion in which the propriety of war in some circumstances is not admitted.

J. Ferguson, *War and Peace in the World's Religions* (1977); J. T. Johnson, *Just War Tradition and the Restraint of War* (1981) and *Can Modern War be Just?* (1984); T. Ling, *Buddhism, Imperialism and War: Burma and Thailand in Modern History* (1979); A. Noth, *Heiliger Krieg und heiliger Kampf in Islam und Christentum*; S. J. Tambiah, *Buddhism Betrayed? Religion, Politics and Violence in Sri Lanka*; M. Walzer, *Just and Unjust wars* (1977).

Jyeṣṭhā (Skt., 'elder sister'). Hindu goddess of misfortune. In classical works she is presented as the 'elder sister' of *Lakṣmī and as her opposite. In S. India, she may get fused with Yaśodā's daughter (see MĀYĀDEVĪ). She is known also as Śītalā, the Goddess of smallpox.

Jyotir-liṅga(m). The limitless *liṅga(m) of light, the form assumed by *Śiva which compelled *Brahma and *Viṣṇu to acknowledge his supremacy. For the twelve Jyotir-liṅga(m)s, see LIṄGA(M).

Jyotiṣa. Astronomy in Hinduism, one of the six *Vedāṅgas (supplements to the *Vedas). It is of particular importance in determining the most propitious time and day for sacrifices and for such enterprises as war or marriage.

K

K (Sikh requirement): see FIVE KS.

Ka (Skt.). Interrogative pronoun, 'who?', used as a summary of the inadequacy of language to describe God. *Ṛg Veda* 10. 121 concludes each stanza by asking, 'to whom shall we address our hymn?' The source and sovereign of all being was later identified with *Hiraṇyagarbha, and with *Prajāpati.

Kaʿba(h) (Arab., 'cube'). The building, deeply revered by Muslims, in the centre of the great *mosque at *Mecca, in the eastern corner of which, about 5 feet from the ground, is embedded the *Black Stone. The Kaʿba, about 35 feet by 40 feet and 50 feet high, is called 'the house of *Allāh', and is the focus of the daily *ṣalāt (ritual worship) of Muslims throughout the world, and of the annual *ḥajj (pilgrimage). In Islamic tradition, it is said to have been first built by *Adam, and rebuilt by Ibrāhīm and his son as a place for pilgrimage (Qurʾān 2. 125; 22. 126). By the time of *Muḥammad it had become a centre for pagan pilgrimage ceremonies (see ḤAJJ); after the conquest of Mecca in 630 CE, he cleansed the Kaʿba and threw out all the idols, of which there were said to be over 300. The Kaʿba is covered with a huge cloth (*kiswa) and is only entered once a year at the time of ḥajj. It is said to have been built directly under an equivalent Kaʿba in *heaven, and it is the exact point to which Muslims turn in their prayer (see QIBLA; ṢALĀT).

Kabbalah or **Qabbalah.** Teachings of Jewish mystics. The term encompasses all the esoteric teachings of Judaism which evolved from the time of the second *Temple. More particularly, it refers to those forms which evolved in the Middle Ages. Kabbalah draws on the awareness of the transcendence of God, and yet of his immanence. God can most closely be perceived through *contemplation and illumination. God both conceals and reveals himself. Through speculation and revelation, the hidden life of God and his relationship with his creation can be more nearly understood. Because mystical knowledge can so easily be misinterpreted its spread should be limited to those of a certain age and level of learning.

Traditionally it was taught that the kabbalah did not develop: it had been revealed in its perfection to *Adam, and new revelation was only given when original teaching was forgotten. Alternatively, it was thought that kabbalah was the secret part of the *oral law given to *Moses on Mount *Sinai. Once the *halakhah was fixed, there was a tendency by the kabbalists to transform the law from a code of conduct for the Jewish people to a universal secret law, and the mystical quest was to unravel the whole mystery of the relationship of God with the world.

Although the influence of kabbalah was limited in the area of halakhah, the kabbalists created fresh *aggadic material and completely reinterpreted much early *midrashic aggadot. The classic anthology of kabbalistic aggadah is Reuben Hoeshke's *Yalkut Re'uveni* (1660). Kabbalistic teaching and motifs entered the various *prayer books and thus spread to every *diaspora community. Nathan Hannover's *Shaʿarei Ziyyon* (1662) lists prayers which include such doctrines as the transmigration of *souls, the achievement of *tikkun, and the activities of powers of the upper world. Popular customs were also affected by kabbalah, and kabbalistic ideas were absorbed as folk beliefs. These customs and beliefs were described by Jacob Zemah in *Shulḥan Arukh ha-Ari* (1661). Popular ethics were also influenced by kabbalism, as is evidenced by such works as Elijah de Vidas' *Reshit Hokhmah* (1579). From the 15th cent., attempts were made to harmonize kabbalistic ideas with Christian doctrines, and, although this tendency was derided by the Jewish kabbalists, it did serve to spread kabbalah beyond the Jewish community. K. von Rosenroth's version of kabbalah texts (*Kabbala Denudata*, 1677–84) led the way to a popular appropriation of kabbalah outside Judaism, at least in *Theosophy.

From the late 18th cent., scholarly work on kabbalah has frequently been polemical. It was felt that the kabbalists had too much influence on Jewish life. Jacob *Emden's *Mitpahat Sefarim* (1768) attempted to prove that many passages from the **Zohar* were later interpolations and grew out of the author's struggle with *Shabbateanism. Similarly, 19th-cent. works were directed against the kabbalistic teachings of *ḥasidism. Since the beginning of the 20th cent., however, with the rise of *Zionism, there has been a growing interest in kabbalah, and in 1925 an international centre for kabbalistic research was founded in the Hebrew University of *Jerusalem. See also Index, Kabbalah.

A. Bension, *The Zohar in Moslem and Christian Spain* (1974); P. S. Berg, *Kabbalah for the Layman* (1982–8); J. Dan and R. Keiner (eds.), *The Early Kabbalah* (1986); P. Epstein, *Kabbalah* (1978); M. Idel, *Kabbalah . . .* (1988); G. Scholem, *On the Kabbalah and its Symbolism* (1965) and *Kabbalah* (1974); S. A. Spector, *Jewish Mysticism: An Annotated Bibliography on the Kabbalah in English* (1984).

Kabhod (Kavod) (Holiness): see KEDUSHAH.

Kabīr (d. 1518). An Indian saint-poet. His birth and origins are uncertain. He may have been the son of a high-*caste *brahman girl who was brought up by a low-caste Muslim weaver (though this story may have been told to show his derivation from diversity). He is said to have been a disciple of the Vaiṣṇava sage, *Rāmānanda. Certainly the differences between Hinduism and Islam meant nothing to him: *Allāh and *Rāma are but different names for the same Godhead. He thus promulgated a religion of love in which all castes and classes would be seen to be wrong ('If you consider yourself to be superior to other castes,' he said to a brahman, 'why were you not born by some different route, instead of from a mother like everyone else?'), and creeds would be unified. It was a religion of *bhakti (personal devotion to a personal God), in which the influence of *Sufism is apparent. Much of his life is legendary: most famous is the story that, after his death, his Hindu and Muslim disciples argued over the form of his funeral rites. They pulled aside the cloth covering his body and found nothing but flowers. Half were cremated and half were buried.

Kabīr was a sant, claiming to derive spiritual awareness from direct experience of the *śabad spoken by the Satgurū in the depth of the *soul. This alone transcends *death. To this goal, rigorous yogic exercises, caste, brahmanical learning, ritual, naked austerity, are all alike irrelevant: if it is possible to gain *mokṣa by going without clothes, then the deer of the forest should be the first to attain God. Devotees must remember God's name (*nām simaran). Kabīr used *Nām and *Rām interchangeably for God.

Kabīr sought to express and experience the love of God through *bhajans* and mystical songs. His verses are preserved in the *Ādi Granth, *Bījak* (of the Kabīr-panthīs), *Kabīr-Granthāvalī*, and in oral tradition. He chiefly composed couplets (*dohās*, also called *sākhīs and *śaloks), of which the Ādi Granth contains 243, and short lyrics (*pada* or *śabad*). His language was a vigorous vernacular, sometimes highly paradoxical. Many current proverbs are couplets attributed to Kabīr. His verses abound in images from ordinary life. Like the *satī, one must sacrifice life itself for the spiritual ascent. The soul's anguished separation from its Lord is like the young bride's awaiting her husband.

> *Hari (God) is like sugar spilled in the sand
> that an elephant cannot pick up.
> Says Kabīr: The *Gurū gave me the hint:
> Become an ant and eat it!

Sources for Kabīr's life include the Kabīr-panthī literature and Bhakta-mālā of Nābhājī.

N. Dass, *Songs of Kabir from the Adi Granth* (1991); F. E. Keay, *Kabir and his Followers* (1932); R. Tagore, *One Hundred Poems of Kabir* (1961); C. Vaudeville, *Kabir* (1974) and *Kabīr-vān* (1983); G. H. Westcott, *Kabir and the Kabir Panth* (1953).

Kachh (shorts): see FIVE KS.

Kada (Hagura) no Azumaro (Jap., 1669–1739). A *Kokugaku scholar and poet. His achievements owed as much to his own talent as to his family background and its tradition—the family having served the Fushimi Inari Shrine in Kyōto for many generations. At the age of 29 he taught poetry (*waka*, see HAIKU) at the court bureau of Prince Myōhōin, the son of the emperor Reigen. Two years later, he left Kyōto for Edo (modern Tokyo), where he devoted himself to Japanese studies and lectured on *Shinto studies, the Japanese classics, and poetry to his followers, many of whom were Shinto priests. As his fame as scholar in Kokugaku rose, the Shōgun Yoshimune called on him to work for his official library and himself heard his lectures. His writings were mainly the exegesis of the Japanese classics and of the works related to ancient rituals and laws. As for the method of his study, he followed the Keichū's path (see KOKUGAKU). In 1723, passing his post to his adopted son, Arimaro, he returned to Kyōto to spend the rest of his life in study and writing. Among his many disciples, *Kamo no Mabuchi distinguished himself. Though the *Petition to Establish a School* may have been written by one of his disciples, there is no reason to doubt that he desired to establish an accredited institution for the exclusive study of Kokugaku.

Kadam (*bka'.gdams*, 'advice'). A school of Tibetan Buddhism which gave rise to the *Geluk school under *Tsong Khapa in the 15th cent. CE. The Kadam school was founded by Dromdon ('brom-.ston), a pupil of *Atiśa, with the establishment of the Radreng monastery in 1056, in answer to a need felt by Atiśa and Dromdon for monastic reform and discipline, while Buddhism was reasserting itself in Tibet following the 9th-cent. persecution by King Langdarma. At this time the *saṅgha was not well ordered, and the interpretation of both 'new' *tantras flowing in from India, and of 'old' tantras already in Tibet, was not always well disciplined. The value of tantric practice was not denied by the Kadampas—indeed, Atiśa said some higher practices should not be undertaken by strict celibates—but its students were given greater guidance as to the symbolic nature of the tantras and most importantly were taught to see them as founded upon the *sūtra tradition. The Kadam school became renowned not only for its discipline (which involved four major abstentions—from marriage, intoxication, money, and travel) but also for the magical power of its ritual.

Kaddish (Aram., 'holy'). *Aramaic doxology recited at the end of the individual sections of Jewish services. There are four different types of kaddish (or five, if an expanded form recited by some after a burial, is included): (i) the whole kaddish which is said at the end of each *'Amidah except in the morning service and concludes worship; (ii) the half-kaddish which links the sections of the service together; (iii) the scholars' kaddish (which adds two prayers) after study; and (iv) the mourners' kaddish recited by mourners at the end of each service, and at the grave of parents or close relatives for eleven months after death, and on anniversaries of death (*yahrzeit).

The prayer is said standing, facing *Jerusalem. It is of ancient origin, being mentioned in the *Talmud as the concluding prayer at public *aggadic discourse. It was first prescribed as part of the *synagogue daily service in the 6th cent. CE. The practice of its recitation by mourners seems to date back to the 13th cent.—though according to a late aggadic tradition, R. *Akiva rescued a *soul from *hell by reciting one of its verses. The mourners' kaddish is a prayer of praise, conforming to the maxim, 'People should give praise for the evil that befalls them even as they give praise for the good' (*Ber.* 9. 5). According to *Orthodox, kaddish can only be recited by men, but *Conservative and *Reform allow women also. The point can be critical, since it is necessary (*Soferim* 10. 7) for ten to be present if kaddish is to be recited.

Kado (flower arranging): see IKEBANA.

Kāfir (Arab., *kafara*, 'conceal, be ungrateful'). One who does not believe in *Allāh, or in the content of *Qur'ān, or in the prophetic status of *Muḥammad. *Kufr*, unbelief, is thus fundamental opposition to God and Islam, and will be punished in *hell for ever.

Kagan, Israel Meir ha-Kohen: see ḤAFETS ḤAYYIM.

Kagawa Toyohiko (1888–1960). Japanese Christian evangelist and pioneer social worker. Kagawa was perhaps the greatest leader in the development of Japanese Christian social-welfare work and reform in the 20th cent. At the same time he preferred to describe himself primarily as an evangelist. This self-appraisal reveals how important to him were the numerous evangelistic activities in which he participated over the course of his life. Kagawa aimed, however, at the overall enlightenment of persons as well as their conversion to Christian faith. He frequently included data from natural science as well as the social sciences in his messages. The effect of his work was to inform the moral conscience of the whole nation probably more than any other of his countrymen in the 20th cent.

Kagawa was born in the city of Kōbe in central Japan on 10 July 1888. After the death of both parents, he was sent at the age of 4 to the ancestral home on the island of Shikoku to be raised by his father's neglected wife and mother. Here he spent his early youth amid hostile resentments expressed varyingly by beatings, verbal abuse, and studied indifference. Kagawa tasted in those years such a range of human sorrow that in later life there was hardly any suffering for which he did not have some affinity and understanding from his own experience.

Kagawa first encountered Christian faith in the middle school at Tokushima in Shikoku. He was befriended by a Japanese Christian teacher and by two *missionaries of the Presbyterian Church, USA. In the homes of these men the love-starved boy received a welcome, understanding, and sympathetic guidance such as he had never known. From them he learned of the God who cares, and was led to look up and out of his tortured condition. He read and reread the *New Testament until all the pent-up agony of his past burst forth in the prayer 'O God, make me like Christ'. From this developed a growing inner conviction that he had been given a divine commission to serve the poor.

Kagawa was able to enter Meiji Gakuin in Tokyo, the Presbyterian-Reformed Church-related school, where his genius flourished, reading almost all the important books in the library, both Eng. and Jap. In his second year at Meiji Gakuin Kagawa contracted tuberculosis and was compelled to leave school. He spent a year in an isolated seashore village where he came close to death and in the ordeal produced the first draft of a novel. Kagawa made only a partial recovery but gained enough strength to return to the Presbyterian seminary in Kōbe, and shortly after began his work in the Shinkawa slums of that city. On Christmas Day 1909, he carted his few belongings from the seminary dormitory to his one room in the slums. There Kagawa committed himself to service and love of the lowliest of persons, in whom he came to be convinced that God dwells, in the whole person and circumstance. For this reason he became a *Christian Socialist, a social seer and reformer as well as a Christian evangelist.

Kagawa revised the largely autobiographical novel which he had written earlier and added the story of his battle with death and of his experiences in the Shinkawa slums. The book, *Across the Death Line* (tr., *Before the Dawn*, 1925) became a best seller. With the royalties Kagawa was able in various concrete ways to improve the lot of Kōbe's poor. He helped to form the Japan Federation of Labor and to organize the labourers of Kōbe into a branch of this national body. He was perhaps the leading figure in the great strike of the shipyard workers in Kōbe in 1921. For the next forty years he was prominent in almost every movement for constructive social reform in Japan. In the movements for farmers' unions, co-operatives, credit unions, in campaigns against social evils of various kinds, in direct welfare work, he was not only an active pioneer but a spiritual guide. He organized relief work after the 1923 earthquake in Yokohama, and was imprisoned in 1940 as a pacifist.

Kagawa was always more concerned for persons than for organization; he saw the building of persons as the true work of God. He aimed more at the reconstruction of humanity than of the structures of society. In his methodology Kagawa was a thorough social evolutionist, a strict follower of the principle of non-violence. He tried to reach the conscience of all through every means open to him, and in no small measure because of his work the conscience of the larger Japanese public came to be aroused. In 1926 the Japanese government initiated a six-year programme designed to eliminate the slums in the six largest cities of the empire, one of the earliest and most far-reaching instances of national social reform in the 20th cent. Kagawa has been called one of the three greatest Christians of this century. His ideals were expounded in many books, e.g. *Love, the Law of Life* (tr. 1930) and *Christ and Japan* (Eng. tr., 1934).

C. M. Simon, *A Seed Shall Serve* . . . (1958).

Kagura (Jap., originally 'seat [or site] of the *kami', though now written with the Chin. ideograms for 'sacred music'). Dramatic ritual events performed during seasonal festivals in Japan. Thematically associated with mythological exploits in the **Kojiki* and **Nihongi*, the performances represent one form of ritual entertainment which constitutes an essential element of all *matsuri. Kagura is staged within *Shinto shrine precincts, either in front of the main hall or in a specially constructed structure nearby.

A nocturnal series of danced numbers, kagura typically begins with a formal purificatory rite, followed by several simply choreographed narratives recounting the exploits of sacred heroes. Structurally, kagura is important as a dramatic expression of the Japanese apprehension of the sacred as immanent and explicable. The variety of types and styles of kagura testifies to the diversity of Japanese religious expression, yet the essential integrity of its function within the matsuri structure remains consistent.

Kagyü (*bka'.brgyud*, 'oral transmission'). One of the four principal schools of Tibetan Buddhism, taking its name from the mode of transmission of its teachings before their proper systematization by *Gampopa (1079–1153). To it, or to some of its subdivisions, the name 'Red Hats' is often incorrectly given in the W. (for the use of that name, see RED HATS). Like the *Nyingma, the Kagyü have a strong identification with the Indian *siddha tradition, out of which they recognize two lineages culminating in *Marpa (1012–97) the 'great translator' who, like Rinchen Zangpo, made several journeys to India to enrich Tibet's resurgent faith with the 'new' cycles of Indian *tantras. Marpa's two principal teachers were the siddhas *Nāropa, disciple of *Tilopa, and Maitrīpa, whose lineage extends to the poet-siddha Saraha. From Nāropa, Marpa inherited the 'Six Doctrines of Nāropa', Tantric practices of mastery over self and phenomena which are now recognized by all schools, and which constitute the heart of a Kagyü *lama's training. Marpa was also instructed by Nāropa in the tantras of Guhyasamāja, Mahāmāyā, Srīcakrasaṃvara, and Hevajra. From Maitrīpa, Marpa inherited the philosophical doctrine of Mahāmudrā, in which the progression and culmination of the spiritual path are seen as the expression of a procreative *śūnyatā, in which bliss, luminosity, and wisdom are seen to coincide. The attribution of such predicates to emptiness in Mahāmudrā has inclined many Kagyü scholars towards a positive ontology of the ultimate status of things, in contrast to the *Geluk who adhere more closely to *Nāgārjuna's logical doctrines which define emptiness (śūnyatā) as the absence of all predicates. Nāgārjuna is none the less ascribed a position in the Kagyü tradition, but more importance is attached to his hymns.

From Marpa, the philosophy of Mahāmudrā and the practices of Nāropa passed to *Milarepa, and from Milarepa to Gampopa, who had also studied in the *Kadam tradition. It is only with Gampopa that one can begin to talk of a Kagyü 'school', and this immediately split into four subschools, the Tshal, Baram, Karma, and Druk. Today there are many Kagyü subschools, the two most important of which are the Druk ('brug) Kagyü, founded by Yeshe *Dorje (1161–1211), which became the dominant tradition in Bhutan, even giving its name to that country, and the Karma Kagyü, established by Düsum Chempa (1110–93), the first Gyalwa Karmapa hierarch, and which is generally today the dominant Kagyü school. The Karma Kagyü have always been headed by reincarnations within the office of the Gyalwa (rgyal.ba) Karmapa, the second, Karma Paksi (1206–83), being the first declared *tulku in Tibet. Traditionally, a letter has been left, indicating where the reincarnation will be found, but on the death of the sixteenth Gyalwa Karmapa (1924–81), no such letter was produced until 1992. It indicated an 8-year-old boy, Urgyen Thinley, who was enthroned in 1993, with the approval of the Chinese authorities. See Index, Kagyü.

Kahal (community leader): see MAʿAMAD.

Kai (Jap.). The Buddhist precepts: see ŚĪLA. Kai-gyō is the observance of the precepts ordered by the Buddha; and kai-dan is the platform from which the precepts are pronounced when an initiate takes them upon himself for the first time; kai-gi is the ritual for that purpose.

Kaibara Ekken (1630–1714). A Japanese *Confucian scholar of the early to mid-Tokugawa period. As an advocate of 'practical learning' (*jitsugaku*), Kaibara wrote many popular works encompassing a wide range of interests: philosophy, moral education, health and diet, and the natural sciences. Although originally a follower of the orthodox *Chu Hsi school of *Neo-Confucianism, he established his own independent, critical position, often compared to the school of Ancient Learning (*Kokugaku). For example, in his major work, the *Taigiroku* (Record of Grave Doubts), Kaibara attacks Chu Hsi's over-reliance on Buddhist and *Taoist teachings. He saw an inherent unity between the Confucian ethics of the early sages and Japanese *Shinto, while rejecting Buddhist ideas, such as the application of *honjisuijaku, in which Shinto deities were conceived as being merely manifestations of *buddhas and *bodhisattvas. He put great emphasis on the affinity of all natural appearance: humans and nature cannot be separated, and the great virtue of humanity lies in love and care for all things:

> Just as humans demonstrate filial obligation to parents in respectful service, so they should demonstrate to the utmost their benevolence (Chin., *jen., Jap., *jin*) toward nature. Jin means a sense of sympathy within oneself, and bringing active goodness to all things. For those who have been nurtured on the blessings of nature, the service of nature is the way to live.

Trs., Ken Yoshino (1913); Shingaro Takaishi (1905).

Kaidan. The ordination hall in a Zen monastery, where monks are initiated into an order and receive the ten precepts (*jujukai). The Kaidan-seki is a stone tablet set in front of the monastery, saying, 'Meat, fish, and alcohol are forbidden.'

Kaigen (Jap., 'opening the eye'). A general Zen expression for the awakening of a true insight into the nature of reality; thus the insight of a master (*roshi) is often referred to as his *dharma eye. More particularly, it is the ceremony whereby a representation of a *buddha or *bodhisattva (in sculpture or painting) is consecrated and brought to life, by giving it eyes. It thereby gives expression to the buddha-nature (*bussho) within it.

Kailāsa (Skt., 'ice/silver mountain'). 1. Mountain range in Himālayas, but also one mountain in particular sacred to both Hindus and Tibetan Buddhists. It is the paradise of the gods, especially *Śiva. Because Kailas is an isolated peak, it is possible for a pilgrim to make a *circumambulation of it. Ridges in the southern face resemble a *svastika, hence reference to it as 'the svastika mountain'.

2. A temple at *Ellorā, probably constructed by the king *Kṛṣṇa (d. *c.*773 CE), and dedicated to Śiva. The temple is constructed to translate the Himalayan mountain into architectural form—e.g. it is painted white.

C. Allen, *A Mountain in Tibet* (1982).

Kaimyō (Jap., 'precepts name'). The name Japanese Buddhist monks and nuns are given when 'taking the precepts', at the time of their ordination, which replaces their secular name. Occasionally, a 'precepts name' is given posthumously to recently deceased persons.

Kairos (time as opportunity): see TILLICH, P.

Kaisan (Jap., 'mountain founder'). The founder of a Zen monastery, or of a Buddhist school. The anniversary commemoration is called kaisan-ki.

Kaiten (turning of the heaven): see KAMIKAZE.

Kaivalya (Skt., 'alone, unique'). The state of the soul in Hindu *Rāja-yoga when it realizes that it is not dependent on such support systems as gods or material sustenance. Kaivalya-*mukti is thus freedom from all further rebirth; kaivalya-pada is the final part of *Patañjali's *Yoga Sūtra, which deals with liberation and release. In *Saṃkhya, it is the state of freedom finally obtained by *puruṣa.

Among Jains, kaivalya describes the *jiva (soul) emancipated from *karma, and regaining its original condition of isolation from *ajiva*: see KEVALA; KEVALIN.

Kaji (Jap.). The power of the *Buddha transferred to sentient beings, and the response to it. In particular, it is the transference of that power to those in need through prayer. Kaji-riki is the interaction between the Buddha and humans in activating this power.

Kakka food (acceptable from same or higher caste members): see FOOD AND RELIGION (HINDUISM).

Kakure Kirishitan (hidden Christians): see JAPANESE RELIGION.

Kakushin also **Shinchi Kakushin** (1207–98). Japanese Zen master who did much to establish *kōan practice in Japan, not least by introducing the *Wu-men-kuan* (see KŌAN). He began in the esoteric (*Mikkyō) form of the *Shingon school, and trained under several masters, including *Dogen, under whom he took the *bodhisattva vows. In 1249, he visited China and trained in (or perhaps established) the Fuke school (where playing the flute replaces *sūtra recitation), but settled with *Wu-men Hui-k'ai, of the Yōgi school of *Rinzai. Wu-men bestowed on him the seal of recognition (*inkashōmei) and made him dharma-successor (*hassu). He returned to Japan in 1254, and founded Saihō-ji (later called Kōkoku-ji). His teaching remained eclectic, but with concentration on kōans of the *Mumonkan* (*Wu-men kuan*) especially its opening kōan on 'nothingness'.

Kāla (Skt., 'time'). A general Hindu word for *time, displacing the Vedic *ṛtu*, which focused on the seasons. *Kal* means 'enumerate', or 'calculate' and moved the interest in time to the longer sequences of past, present, and future. Both *Viṣṇu and *Śiva are regarded as aspects of cosmic time, Śiva through his *śakti, *Kālī. Kāla-bhairava is thus Śiva in his terrible aspect of time devouring all things. In *Bhagavad-gītā 10. 32 *Kṛṣṇa states, 'I am all-devouring time'. But Kālaharamurti is a form (*murti) of Śiva as the conqueror of death. *Yama, death, is also associated with kāla (and is sometimes called Kāla), and the kāladaṇḍa, the staff of death, is one of Yama's emblems. Kāla is also the bringer of, in addition to death, destiny from the gods (*daiva); cf. PREDESTINATION.

Kalā (limit on efficacy): see KAÑCUKA.

Kālacakra (Tib., *dus.kyi.'khor.lo*, 'Wheel of Time'). Perhaps the most revered *tantra in Tibetan Buddhism, which in addition to yogic teachings involves an esoteric world history and *eschatology. According to Tibetan historians, the Kālacakra Tantra is variously said to have been taught by the *Buddha (in his eightieth year or the year of his *enlightenment) to Chandrabhadra, king of *Shambhala. The tantra was not disseminated in India, but was transmitted through the Shambhalic royal line for 1500 years until the time was deemed right to reintroduce it into India. The introduction of the tantra into Tibet is often ascribed to *Atiśa, but it is hard to substantiate this: Kālacakra is based on the Indian sexagenary calendar, which was adopted in Tibet in 1027; if, as is plausible, the calendar was adopted out of respect for the tantra, then this date does not square with the arrival of Atiśa in 1042. Moreover, the historian Golo Tsawa lists several Kālacakra lineages without once mentioning Atiśa. The Kālacakra teachings figured prominently in the old *Kadam and *Jonang schools due to its chief 14th-cent. promulgators, Butön and Dolpopa. The original 'root' text supposedly taught to Chandrabhadra, the *Paramādibuddha* (Supreme Primordial Buddha) *Tantra*, does not survive in Skt., though there is a Tibetan tr. Two texts which, according to tradition, were composed in Shambhala do survive in Skt. and date to early 11th-cent. India. These are the *Śri Kālacakra* (Holy Kālacakra), an abridgement of the *Paramādibuddha*, and the *Vimalaprabhā* (Stainless Light), a commentary on the *Śri Kālacakra*. These texts are the basic sources for the system.

The Kālacakra Tantra has three aspects, 'outer', 'inner', and 'other'. The 'outer' is lore concerning the environment: astrology, history, eschatology; the 'inner' concerns the esoteric physiology of the 'subtle body'; the 'other' consists of the 'generation' and 'completion' stages of yoga, and aims to purify the 'outer' and 'inner' aspects. Of these, the 'generation' (*utpattikrama*) involves the *visualization of the 722 deities of the Kālacakra *maṇḍala, which has at its centre the *Ādibuddha in the form of the sexual union (*yab-yum) of Kālacakra and Vishvamātā. The 'completion' (*sampannakrama*) stage involves the manipulation of one's subtle energies to produce a consciousness with the capacity for enlightenment. Kālacakra is a member of the Anuttara (unsurpassed) class of tantras, and as such offers buddhahood through its mastery.

It is possible in Tibetan Buddhism to take a tantric initiation as a blessing, without taking on the practice; in the past, Kālacakra initiations have been rare events but now, according to the *Dalai Lama (1985), 'because of past and future events, and in order to establish a strong karmic relationship with Kālacakra in the minds of the people, there is now a tradition of giving the initiation to large public gatherings'.

Sopa, Jackson, and Newman, *The Wheel of Time* (1985).

Kalām (Arab., *kalima*, 'word, discourse'). The science (*ʿilm) of theology in Islam, developed in parallel with ʿilm ul-*fiqh (and was originally called *al-fiqh al-akbar*, the greater fiqh). Its roots lie in early attempts to deal with rational questions prompted (or provoked) by *Qur'ān—e.g., how can the *qadar (determining power) of *Allāh be reconciled with the freedom and accountability of humans? Are the attributes of God in the Qur'ān real, unreal, or real but unlike human attributes? Is the Qur'ān created, uncreated, or uncreated in essence but created in the accidents of ink on paper? Is the Muslim who commits grave offence or sin punished forever, or is his/her fate uncertain until *Yaum al-Dīn, or is he/she placed in temporary punishment? The earliest group to bring reason to bear on such issues were the *Muʿtazilites, and in their tradition there developed the Islamic rescue of Greek philosophy and science which, in the Christian world, had fallen into abeyance (see e.g. IBN RUSHD; IBN SĪNĀ). But that inclination to give primacy to reason seemed to others to subordinate the Qur'ān. Kalām, therefore, for *al-Ashʿarī and *al-Māturīdī became the elucidation and application of the Qur'ān as the absolute (and uncreated) Word of God. The dangers of Kalām to the uninitiated were signalled by *al-Ghaz(z)ālī, whose reconciliation of philosophy, theology, and simple faith in effect put an end to theological exploration. Those who study theology are known as *mutakallimun*. See Index, Theologians (Muslim); Theology (Muslim).

A. S. Tritton, *Muslim Theology* (1947); W. M. Watt, *Islamic Philosophy and Theology* (rev. edn., 1984); H. A. Wolfson, *The Philosophy of the Kalam* (1976).

Kālāmukhas (Śaiva sect): see ŚAIVISM.

Kālarātri (Skt., 'the dark night'). One of a variety of names of *Devī. She is a Goddess of the night personifying Time, and at the end of each age assumes the form of Mahākālī, a dark destroyer born out of the wrath of *Śiva. She has tusks and wears a garland of skulls; also called Mahālaksmi, Mahāmāyā, Nidrā, Yoganidrā, etc.

In a *Skanda Purāṇa* legend Kālarātri is also a creation of Devī. When the Asura demon *Durgā had overcome the three worlds, rivers changed their course; fire lost its energy; the stars disappeared; earth yielded its crops out of season and the natural world was out of order. The lesser Gods who were forced to worship Durgā appealed to Śiva for help. He sent them to his consort Devī who agreed to destroy the demon. She first created a creature whom she called Kālarātri to battle against the Asuras. When Kālarātri failed, Devī herself engaged in a mighty combat with Durgā and upon succeeding, acquired his name.

Kālī or **Kālikā** (Skt. 'black'). A ferocious form of the Goddess (*Devī) in Hinduism, sharply contrasted with her benign aspects as *Śrī and *Lakṣmī.

Kālī, the devourer of time (*kāla), is depicted as having a terrifying appearance, naked or wearing a tiger skin, emaciated, with fang-like teeth and dishevelled hair, a lolling tongue, and eyes rolling with intoxication. She is garlanded with human heads, sometimes girdled with severed arms; laughing and howling, she dances, wild and frenzied, in the cremation grounds with a sword and noose or skull upon a staff.

As the terrifying aspect of divine creative energy, or *śakti, she is usually depicted as black, with four arms, two of which hold severed, bleeding heads, while the other two brandish a dagger and a sword. A necklace of skulls festoons her neck, and her tongue, dripping with the blood of those she has cannibalistically consumed, hangs from her mouth. She is even shown holding her own head and drinking her own blood as it spurts from the neck-wound. Kālī slew the demon Raktavīya, whose blood she afterwards drained since every drop that fell to earth would have created another demon.

Human *sacrifices were made to her in the past (cf. *Kālīkapurāṇa*, ch. 71), but now goats have to suffice, and such sacrifices are made at the main temple of her cult, Kālīghāṭa (*Calcutta). The Thugs were devotees of Kālī, to whom they offered worship before committing murderous theft. Many Hindus see Kālī as representing the realities of death and time; she stands for the frightening, painful side of life which all who desire to progress spiritually must face and overcome.

Although a precursor of her can be seen in the Vedic demon *Nirṛti, a personification of death and sorrow with a dark complexion (*Taittirīya Brāhmaṇa* I. 6. I. 4), and she is mentioned in the *Muṇḍaka Upaniṣad (II. 2. 4), Kālī is probably of non-Vedic origin from among tribal groups on the edges of Indian society. There are some references to her in the **Mahābhārata*, but it is in the *Purāṇas, specifically the *Devī Mahātmya*, that she fully enters the great tradition of Hinduism with her own cycle of mythology and consistent iconography (200 BCE–300 CE). In the *Devī Mahātmya*, Devī has been asked by the gods to defeat a host of demons. She becomes angry and Kālī, called Cāmuṇḍā, springs from her brow, crushing demons in her jaws and decapitating the demon heroes Caṇḍa and Muṇḍa, taking their heads back to Devī as a gift. Kālī also defeats Raktabīja, from the blood of whose wounds spring up exact replicas of him by swallowing them. Kālī becomes associated with *Śiva as his śakti and they dance madly together in the cremation ground, a dance which threatens to destroy the cosmos, though she is finally subdued by Śiva (**Liṅga-Purāṇa* 2. 100).

In *Tantrism Kālī is depicted as dancing upon the ithyphallic corpse of Śiva, a form expressing the passive consciousness (*puruṣa) and dynamic energy (*prakṛti) which comprise the universe. In the early Tantric Krama tradition (7th–9th cents. CE, see KASHMIR ŚAIVISM), Kālī as Kālasaṃkarṣini is the supreme deity who is absolute consciousness, from whom emanates twelve Kālīs representing successive stages in the projection and contraction of absolute consciousness. The ferocious, yet erotic, Kālī is the central deity of the Kālīkula tradition in contrast to the Śrīkula whose followers worship the gentle Śri. The Kālīkula adept or 'hero' (vīra) will follow the 'left-hand' path (*vāmācāra), worshipping Kālī in the cremation grounds by, for example, offering food to jackals who are regarded as her manifestations. In many tantras Kālī is equated with the absolute. The *Nirvāna Tantra* (tr. A. Avalon, *The Tantra of Great Liberation*) says that *Brahmā, *Viṣṇu, and Śiva arise from her like bubbles from the ocean and the *Kāmada Tantra* says that she is without qualities (*nirguṇa) and equates her with *sat-cit-ānanda.

In the 18th and 19th cents. Bengali poets such as Rāmprasād (1718–75) and *Ramakrishna (1836–86) wrote devotional poems to her as the supreme deity:

> O Kālī, my mother full of bliss. Enchantress of the almighty Śiva.
> In thy delirious joy Thou dancest clapping Thy hands together. Eternal one. Thou great first cause, clothed in the form of the void . . .
> Thou art the mover of all that move, and we are but Thy helpless toys.
> We move along as Thou movest us and speak as through us Thou speakest.
>
> (*The Gospel of Śri Rāmakrishna*, 1964, 159)

D. R. Kinsley, *The Sword and the Flute* (1975).

Kālidāsa. A Hindu poet and dramatist. Nothing certain is known about his life and family. It is possible that he lived during the Golden Age when the Gupta kings ruled in N. India, between 350 and 460 CE. This period is suggested from internal evidence found in his books *Meghadūta* and *Kumārasambhava*. His most celebrated works are the three plays **Śakuntalā* (*Abhijñanaśakuntala*, 'The Recognition of Śakuntalā'), *Vikramorvashīyam*, and *Mālavikāgnimitra*. His epic compositions, *Raghuvaṃsha* and *Kumārasambhava*, are unsurpassed in Skt. poetry, and his genius is equally evident in *Ṛtusamhāra*.

He was probably a devotee of Śiva, and was learned in the traditional lore of his times. His works display both his deep understanding of people and nature and his unsurpassed skill in the handling of Skt. According to L. Renou, his is 'the greatest name in the lyrical poetry of India'. A highly adapted version of *Śakuntalā* was prepared for the English stage by K. N. D. Gupta (ed. L. Binyon, 1920).

M. B. Emeneau, *Abhijñāna-śakuntala* (1962); K. Krishnamoorthy, *Kālidāsa* (1972); B. S. Miller (ed.), *Theater of Memory: The Plays of Kalidasa* (1984); A. W. Ryder (1912; 1959).

Kālikā-purāṇa. A Hindu ritual and mythological work in Skt., belonging to the genre of the upa-*purāṇas. It is a fairly amorphous compilation of material connected with the worship of the Hindu Goddess (see KĀLĪ). In its present form (which may well be as late as the 13th or 14th cent., put together in Assam or a neighbouring part of Bengal), the text has as its central figure the Goddess *Kāmākhyā. Her temple in Assam is one of the pīṭhas, and is said to derive from *Satī's *yoni. The *Kālikā-purāṇa* draws on many different traditions: orthodox temple-worship (*pūjā), local material connected with Kāmākhyā, tribal or *tantra-inspired heterodox cults, etc. But it was primarily due to its ch. 71 (tr. into Eng. already in 1799), with a description of human sacrifice, that the work acquired notoriety.

K. van Kooij, *Worship of the Goddess according to the Kālikāpurāṇa* (1972, contains the tr. of chs. 54–69).

Kali-yuga. The fourth and final of the *yugas, of increasing disorder and distress. The world is at present in a kali-yuga, which began in 3102 BCE.

Kalki. In Hindu mythology, the tenth and last in the standard list of *Viṣṇu's *avatāras, who is to come in the future. The earliest known description of Kalki is in **Mahābhārata*, but he is not identified with Viṣṇu until some uncertain later date. He is usually described as a warrior *brahman who will arise to punish evil-doers at the end of the *Kali-yuga and thus usher in a new Kṛta-yuga.

Kallah, months of. The months in the Jewish year when scholars gathered to study *Torah in the Babylonian *academies. The custom of Kallah dated back to the 3rd cent. CE. During the Kallah month, one particular tractate of the *Talmud was studied, and even ordinary people would come and listen to the debate. The custom has been revived in modern Israel.

Kallir, Eleazar (?6th cent. CE). Jewish liturgical poet. Kallir was one of the most prolific authors of liturgical *piyyutim. Little is known of his life, but he is thought to have lived in *Erez Israel and was described by *Saʿadiah Gaon as one of the old *paytanim* (liturgical poets). His poems were widely known, and today more than 200 are still extant in various rites. Although much is allusive and compressed, there is no mistaking his emotion for the suffering of Israel:

> The mother of children keens like a dove,
> In her heart she mourns and groans aloud;
> She laments bitterly, she cries out in despair,
> She pours forth tears, she is stunned and silent:
> 'My husband has forsaken me and turned away,
> He has forgotten my love as a bride . . .'.

Kalpa. In Hinduism, a day and a night in the life of *Brahmā, consisting of four *yugas, i.e. one *mahā* (great) *yuga*; or sometimes calculated as 1,000 yugas; in any case, an immense endurance of time.

In Buddhism (Pāli, *kappa*), the length of a kalpa is equally vast: through the four stages of a kalpa, a universe arises, continues, declines, persists in chaos. Within this mahākalpa, there are twenty small kalpas. The length of a kalpa is illustrated in many different ways, e.g. a person passes a cube of rock, 100 miles in its dimensions, once every 100 years, and brushes it with his cloak: a kalpa lasts as long as it takes to wear the rock away; or, a kalpa lasts as long as it takes to empty a city full of poppy-seeds by taking away one seed every three years. See also the discussion in *Calendar (Buddhist).

Kalpa Sūtras. Hindu texts which deal with details of life, especially ritual matters. Kalpa, dealing with ritual, is part of the *Vedāṅgas, i.e. the auxiliary disciplines which enable *brahmans to implement the Vedas in practice. Kalpa Sūtras are collectively the *sūtras which deal with public sacrifices (śrauta-sūtras), household rituals (gṛhyasūtras), and religious duties (*dharmasūtras). They do not contain new revelation (in addition to that in *śruti and *smṛti), but are important in the explication of revelation. The Jain *Kalpa Sutra* deals also with the life of Mahāvīra (tr. H. Jacobi, 1884).

Kal va-homer (Heb. 'light and heavy'). Principle of determining Jewish *halakhah: it means that what applies in a less important case will certainly apply in a more important one. The kal va-homer was the first principle of rabbinic *hermeneutics in the systems of *Hillel and *Ishmael ben Elisha. The phrase has come to mean an inescapable conclusion.

Kalyāṇa-mitta (Pāli, 'good friend', 'wise companion'; Skt., *kalyāna-mitra*). Teacher or mentor in *Theravāda Buddhism; one who advises and instructs in the choice and use of a meditation subject (*kammaṭṭhāna). In early canonical texts the word refers to one whose companionship was recommended because of his wisdom and moral example; for it is considered extremely difficult, if not impossible, for a person to develop spiritually without the assistance of a mentor (see PRATYEKA-BUDDHA). He is declared to be 'lovable, reverent and adorable; a counsellor, a patient listener, a speaker of deep discourses; and one who would not lead to a useless end' (*Anguttara Nikāya* 4. 32). In later, institutionalized, Buddhism the name came to refer to a monk who is adept in meditational instruction and therefore highly esteemed. The Buddha is regarded as the paradigmatic kalyāṇa-mitta. To him are ascribed the words: 'It is owing to my being a good friend to them that living beings subject to birth are freed from birth' (*Samyutta Nikāya* 3. 18). He gave each disciple a subject of meditation suited to his disposition and afterwards questioned him about it. In due course a tradition of persons grew up who followed this example.

Kalyāṇa-śraddha ('reliable faith'). One of the four perfections of the heart, developed in Integral Yoga by Śri *Aurobindo. The others are *prema-sāmarthya* (the power of love), *saumyatva* (gentleness), *tejas* (commitment).

Kāma (Skt., *kam*, 'desire'). Love, sexual pleasure, personified as the Hindu god of love. Kāma, erotic and aesthetic expression, is the third Hindu end of life (*artha), traditionally categorized as *preya* (pleasant) rather than *śreya* (good); but in *Mahābhārata* 12. 167, kāma is the source of both artha and *dharma, because without kāma, humans do not strive for anything.

In the *Vedas kāma denotes the primal germ of mind, the creative impulse (e.g. *Ṛg Veda* 10. 129). In Hindu mythology, Kāma and *Agni (fire) are often identified. In the *Purāṇas, Kāma is personified as a handsome youth riding on a cuckoo or parrot. He carries a bow of sugar-cane with a string of bees and a quiver of five flower-tipped arrows, and has the crocodile (*makara*) as his emblem. Kāma is often called the 'water-born' (*irā-ja*), the 'self-born' (*ātmabhū*), the 'mind-born' (*mano-ja*), or the 'unborn' (*aja*); or the son of Dharma (Justice) and *Śraddhā (Faith); or the son of *Lakṣmī (Wealth); or the son of *Brahmā, the Creator. Kāma is the husband of Ratī (Sexual Desire), and the father of Tṛṣṇā (Craving).

In one Hindu myth Kāma is sent to distract *Śiva from his meditation with erotic thoughts. He succeeds, but is reduced to ashes by Śiva's third eye. Kāma's widow, Ratī, persuades Śiva to restore Kāma to life, but only as a mental image of spiritual love. Hence a common epithet of Kāma is Anañga (Bodiless). See also KĀMAŚĀSTRA.

In Buddhism, kāma is a major obstacle to progress toward enlightenment. It belongs to the lowest of the three domains (triloka), the domain of desire (*kāmaloka*). It is one of the five hindrances (*nīvaraṇas) and one of the defilements, āsrava (see ĀSAVA).

Kāmākhyā or **Kāmākṣī** ('wanton-eyed'). Hindu goddess, a form of *Durgā. Her cult was associated with human sacrifice until 1832, when animal sacrifice was substituted. Details concerning her cult were gathered in **Kālikā-Purāṇa*.

Kamakura. Major centre in Japan of Shinto shrines, and of Buddhist temples and monasteries. Due south of Tokyo, it was a fishing village which became the effective capital in 1185, after the battle of Dannoura, for more than a century. The principal Shinto shrine, Tsurugaoka Hachiman-gu, is dedicated (as the name states) to *Hachiman. It is now a vast complex, including museums and open-air stages where Shinto dance is performed. Among the Zen monasteries, Kencho-ji is of particular importance, because Zen monks are still trained there. It was founded by Tao-lung in 1253, and is built, like the classic monasteries of *Kyōto, on the single-axis design. *Engaku-ji (also Enkaku-ji), founded thirty years later, contains a Relic Hall in which one of the *Buddha Śākyamuni's teeth is preserved; several of its buildings were destroyed in an earthquake in 1923. Also of note is Zuisenji, founded by Soshi in 1327, recently rebuilt and surrounded by gardens of great beauty. Kamakura contains the second largest *daibutsu (image of the Buddha, the largest being in Todaiji). Its original buddha-hall (daibutsuden) was carried away by a tidal wave in 1495, and has stood in the open since then. The *Jōdo school is represented by the Hasedera temple, which contains a massive image of Kannon (*Avalokiteśvara) carved from a single tree, and many shrines devoted to Jizō (see KṢITIGARBHA) by those who have lost infants.

Kamakura Period. The period in Japan of the Kamakura shoguns, 1192–*c*.1338 (when Ashikaga Takauji became shogun and the period of the Warring States began). It was a period when Buddhism flourished: see e.g. HŌNEN; DŌGEN; NICHIREN; SHINRAN; IPPEN; see also BUDDHISM IN JAPAN.

Kamakura Schools (of Japanese Buddhism): see TENDAI-SHŪ.

Kamalaśīla (*c*.740–95 CE). Indian Yogācāra-*Mādhyamaka pupil of *Śāntarakṣita, who significantly determined the form of Buddhism in Tibet during its 'first diffusion' (*snga.dar*) there. During Śāntarakṣita's time in Tibet, many Ch'an teachers were arriving from China, whose 'sudden attainment' (*ston.min.pa.*) understanding of enlightenment (together with their preaching of 'non-mentation', Skt., *amanasikāra*) contrasted with Śāntarakṣita's own 'gradualist' (*rtsen.min.pa*) approach to realization and teaching of the value of analytical insight (vipaśyanā). On Śāntarakṣita's recommendation, King Trisong Detsen invited Kamalaśīla from India to debate with the Chinese Hua Shang Mahāyāna at *Samyé (792–4 CE), on the understanding that the teachings of whichever school won the debate would be established as the religion of Tibet. Although there are Chinese accounts to the contrary, there is little doubt that Kamalaśīla won. In 795 CE, however, Kamalaśīla was murdered, though whether by his defeated opponents or by followers of the native *Bön religion is not clear. It has been suggested that Ch'an Buddhism did not completely leave Tibet as a result of the debate, and that elements of it remain in present *Nyingma and Bön teachings.

Kamalaśīla was an illustrious scholar who also influenced the development of Tibetan Buddhism by his writings. His most important work, *Madhyamakāloka* (Light on the Middle Way), presents the Madhyamaka doctrine of emptiness (*śūnyatā) and incorporates *Tathāgata-Garbha (Essence of Buddhahood) theory perhaps for the first time in the Madhyamaka school; his commentary (Skt., *pañjikā*) on Śāntarakṣita's *Madhyamakālankāra* (Ornament of the Middle Way) remains an important assessment of Buddhist philosophy (though a few Geluk scholars doubt its authenticity); his commentary on Śāntarakṣita's *Tattvasaṃgraha* (Compendium of Reality, tr. G. Jha, 1937–9) contains the first known Buddhist consideration of the Indian *Advaita school. In addition to this, Kamalaśīla's three texts on meditation, the *Bhavanakrama* (Stages on the

Meditative Path) represent his own position taken in the debate.

G. Tucci, *Minor Buddhist Texts* (1971, 1985).

Kāmaloka: see LOKA (BUDDHIST).

Kāmaśāstra (Skt., *kāma*, 'love', + *śāstra*, 'teaching'). Any of a class of Skt. texts concerned with *kāma—love, sexuality, and sensual enjoyment.

The Kāmaśāstra or science of erotics is attributed to the god *Prajāpati, who handed it down to Nandi, bull of *Śiva, after which it passed to Śvetaketu, Śaṅkha, and Bābhravya. The latter is said to have condensed the tradition of Kāmaśāstra into a work of 150 chapters in seven *adhikaraṇa* (sections), forming the basis of a school of sexology. The *adhikaraṇa* are: general principles; courtship; sexual union; marriage; how to steal other men's wives; prostitutes; and potions, spells, aphrodisiacs, *mantras, and devices.

The most influential Kāmaśāstra texts are the *Kāmasūtra* of Vātsyāyana (*c*.450 CE, tr. A. Daniélou), and the *Anaṅga-raṅga* (Theatre of the Love God), attributed to Kalyāṇamalla (?1460–1530 CE). The aim of the latter was not to encourage sensual indulgence but to promote marital harmony. Other classic Kāmaśāstra texts include Dāmodaragupta's *Kuṭṭanī-mata* (Lessons of a Bawd), Kṣemendra's *Samaya-mātṛikā* (The Harlot's Breviary), Koka's *Rati-rahasya* (Mysteries of Passion), and Jyotirīśa's *Pañcaśāyaka* (Five Arrows). Hundreds of popular Kāmaśāstra texts exist, in which the Hindu deities enact the various sexual postures as paradigms for human performance.

Kāmasūtra (Skt., *kāma* 'love', + *sūtra* 'aphorism'). A Sanskrit prose text concerning the art of love and sexual union. The *Kāmasūtra* of Vātsyāyana (*c*.450 CE) is the best-known Indian sexological manual, covering almost every aspect of human sexuality, with special attention to general principles. The work is encyclopaedic in format, in contrast to the specialized work of the Bābhravya school of *Kāmaśāstra. The *Kāmasūtra* attributed to Vātsyāyana includes later interpolations, and many later texts incorporate material from this text. The chief commentary on Vātsyāyana is the *Jaya-maṅgalā*, attributed to the 13th-cent. scholar Yaśodhara.

According to tradition, Vātsyāyana was an ascetic sage who remained celibate all his life, writing without personal experience, in contrast to most other Hindu sexological authorities.

Tr. A. Daniélou (1992).

Kami (Jap.). Sacred powers venerated by the Japanese, described in the *Shinto mythologies, and enshrined in Shinto shrines (*jinja*) as objects of worship. The etymology of kami is uncertain; the word is at once singular and plural, and while it often refers to personified beings, it also retains the sense of awesome sacred power. Shinto has no systematic theology analyzing the kami; they are rather worshipped and experienced as life-powers. The kami are numerous, even innumerable, according to the traditional phrase *yaoyorozu no kami* ('vast myriads of kami'), implying that the cosmos is replete with divine powers in which all forms of existence participate. The kami are commonly divided into heavenly kami (*amatsukami*) and earthly kami (*kunitsukami*). Many of the important kami are mentioned in the Shinto mythologies as recorded in the **Kojiki* and the **Nihongi* (*Nihon-shoki*), such as the two creator kami *Izanagi and Izanami, the sun kami *Amaterasu-ō-Mikami, the kami of Izumo *Ōkuninushi no Mikoto, and many others. But any form of existence that possesses some extraordinary, awe-inspiring quality could be called kami: mountains, seas, rivers, rocks, trees, birds, animals. Humans who have some extraordinary quality—people like emperors, family ancestors, heroes—could be referred to as kami. In the definition of the Shinto revivalist, *Motoori Norinaga:

> The word 'kami' refers in its most general sense to all divine beings on earth or in heaven which appear in the classic texts. More specifically, the kami are the spirits abiding in, and worshipped at, shrines. In principle, humans, birds, animals, trees, plants, mountains, oceans, can all be kami. In ancient usage, anything which was awe-inspiring or excellent or impressive was called kami.

The kami who are worshipped in the thousands of shrines in Japan are predominantly those mentioned in the Shinto mythologies. Also worshipped in shrines are ancestors of emperors and famous clans, kami of food and productivity, kami of land and professions, and historical figures who have made striking contributions to human society. Worshipping the kami includes rituals of purification, offerings of food (*shinsen), chanting prayers (*norito), offerings of dance and music, and the like, especially in shrine festivals (*matsuri). Not all kami are worshipped at shrines—though all kami need to be appeased and pacified with rites, such as the kami of fauna and flora, which can interfere in human existence. When work on a house is about to begin, a ceremony called *jichin-sai* is performed on the construction site to conciliate the kami of the area through offerings of rice, sake, lengths of cloth, or money.

The kami are sacred powers providing the benefits of life and happiness. They are not previously existent gods who create and thus transcend the world. And there is no absolute creator who stands beyond the creation and over all the other kami. Rather the kami are constituted from the nuclei of the world itself and are understood as the powers through whom life is generated and grows. They maintain harmony in the cosmos and in human existence. There are distinctions of rank between the kami, in terms of their contribution to human well-being and happiness; Amaterasu-ō-Mikami is usually recognized at the head of the kami, but her position is not absolute or exclusive, for she pays her respects to the other kami, and ordinary people worship other kami as well as Amaterasu. There are also, of course, kami with negative, destructive powers (e.g. *magatsuhi-no-kami) who are the source of sin and uncleanness and who inflict calamities. But ultimately they too are manifestations of a power of life which requires reverence and worship.

In Shinto, there is a significant continuity between the kami and human life, with humans as well as nature seen as children of the kami, blood relatives in an *oya-ko* ('parent–child') relationship. Thus in worshipping the kami, humans are brought into relation with life-power that is infinite and good, for the enhancing and promoting of life in this world.

It follows that kami have been decisive in creating Japanese attitudes to nature. There is no original Japanese word that corresponds to the modern concept of nature (*shizen*, meaning 'nature', is a loan word from China). Traditionally kami have been thought to be immanent in nature, manifesting themselves in and through natural objects (trees, rocks, rivers, mountains, etc.), but in some cases, natural objects themselves were taken to be intrinsically divine. The line of demarcation between natural objects themselves as kami and as the hierophanic media of kami was extremely thin and often blurred.

In the Nara and Heian periods, with the development of poetic tradition and with the refinement of aesthetic taste, there was an important shift in attitude toward nature. Though the traditional animistic view of nature did not disappear, the gentry looked at nature as pure and undefiled, as if it possessed a healing power, and this mode of feeling and apprehension has brought Japanese culture close to nature itself. See Index, Kami.

Sokyo Ono, *Shinto: The Kami Way* (1962).

Kamidana (Jap., 'kami-shelf'). In *Shinto, an altar or high shelf for enshrining a *kami in a quiet place in the house of a Shinto believer. A miniature shrine is placed on the shelf. The shrine is often decorated with sprigs of pine or the sacred *sasaki* tree, and a straw rope with paper pendants may be stretched above the shrine. Within the shrine there is usually a talisman of the Grand Shrine of Ise and others representing the local tutelary kami and other kami. Offerings such as rice, rice cakes, fish, seaweed, vegetables, fowl, or fruits are presented there morning and evening, and family members worship the kami by bowing, clapping the hands, and praying in front of the shrine.

Kamigakari (Jap.). A state of trance in which a spiritual being (*kami) possesses (*kakaru*) the human body by entering and speaking through it. Religious deities and animal, ancestral, and nature spirits are believed capable of possessing human beings. Kamigakari may be experienced spontaneously or induced through ascetic practices. Although it is often accompanied by violent physical symptoms, such as uncontrollable shaking and roaring, the experienced practitioner remains calm and relaxed. The possessed individual may or may not lose consciousness in the trance state or recall afterwards what was said. Women experience kamigakari more often than men. Kamigakari has been a common feature of Japanese folk religion since ancient times and has served as the initial source of inspiration for most founders of *new religious movements in 20th-cent. Japan. In cross-cultural perspective, it is most similar to the *altered states of consciousness experienced by Siberian and Polynesian *shamans.

Kamikaze (Jap., 'Divine Wind', so-called from the strong winds and storms which dispersed two Mughal invasions in 1274 and 1281). Japanese pilots during the Second World War who volunteered, from 1944 onward, to undertake missions against enemy targets in which they were 'flying bombs', and from which, therefore, they could not expect to return alive. They were first used at Leyte Gulf in Oct. 1944, and extensively at Okinawa. Related to kamikaze were the *kaiten* (turning of the heaven), human torpedoes. They wore white scarves and also round their foreheads a white cloth, taken from the *hachimaki*, the cloths worn by *samurai warriors. In a Zen perspective (often referred to by volunteers who survived), death is of no greater importance (or less) than any other event or manifestation. In a wider Japanese perspective, the spirits of warriors who die in obedience to the emperor return in any case to Japan, and in particular to the Shinto Yasukuni (Country of Peace) shrine in Tokyo (hence the ironic words of soldiers before battle, 'See you in Yasukuni'), where remembrance of them is made. This shrine was founded in 1879 as the Tokyo Shokon Jinja (shrine). Originally the spirits of all those who died in battle returned to Yakusuni, since all who died for the emperor were reckoned to be Shinto. Since 1945, only those who had themselves adhered to Shinto have been included, hence the strong resistance among some Japanese to formal state ceremonies in relation to the war dead being held at the shrine, since those of other religions (especially Buddhists and Christians) resist the post-mortem conversion of their ancestors; other countries (e.g. Korea) have objected to the enshrinement of war criminals.

Kamimukae, Kamiokuri (Jap., 'summoning *kami', 'sending off kami'). In *Shinto, ancient ceremonies of summoning kami to be present in a *himorogi and sending them off again. The himorogi or temporary dwelling-place is set up outside the shrine buildings for special celebrations. In the ceremony of kamimukae, the chief priest intones special verbal phrases summoning the kami, and other traditional ceremonies are performed, such as presenting *gohei*, offering *shinsen, and playing music. Kamiokuri follows the same pattern in sending off the kami from the special ceremonial place after the completion of the religious rites. The rituals of kamimukae and kamiokuri differ according to the traditions of the various shrines.

Kami no michi (Jap.), the native Japanese words meaning 'the Way of the *Kami', corresponding to the Chinese *shen-tao* (*Shinto) as the designation for the indigenous religion of Japan. This term is sometimes read as *kannagara no michi*, 'the way which accords to the kami'. This term was especially stressed by those in modern times who wanted to restore Shinto as the original, pure way of Japan.

Kamma: see KARMA.

Kammaṭṭhāna (Pāli, 'working-ground', i.e. 'support'). In Theravāda Buddhism, a subject of meditation; specifically, one of those which serves as the basis for the practice of mindfulness (*sati) and concentration (*samādhi). *Buddhaghosa's *Visuddhimagga* lists forty kammaṭṭhāna: (i) earth, (ii) water, (iii) fire, (iv) air, (v) blue, (vi) yellow, (vii) red, (viii) white, (ix) light, (x) enclosed space, (xi) swollen corpse, (xii) blueish corpse, (xiii) festering corpse, (xiv) fissured corpse, (xv) gnawed corpse, (xvi) scattered corpse, (xvii) hacked and scattered corpse, (xviii) bloody corpse, (xix) worm-eaten corpse, (xx) skeleton, (xxi) the Buddha, (xxii) the dharma, (xxiii) the *saṅgha, (xxiv) morality, (xxv) liberality, (xxvi) devas, (xxvii) death, (xxviii) what belongs to the body, (xxix) respiration, (xxx) peace, (xxxi) loving-kindness, (xxxii) compassion, (xxxiii) sympathetic joy, (xxxiv) equanimity, (xxxv) infinite space, (xxxvi) infinite consciousness, (xxxvii) nothingness, (xxxviii) neither perception nor non-perception, (xxxix) the disgusting aspect of food, (xl) the four elements. The meditator selects a topic or corpus of topics, on the grounds of their suitability to his own psychological disposition and character traits; in ideal circumstances he should be advised and guided in his choice by a teacher (*kalyāṇa-ṃitta). Nos. xxvii and xxxi are suitable for all persons, but the suitability of the others is governed by whether a person is primarily a 'greed' (**lobha*), 'hate' (**dosa*), or 'delusion' (**moha*) type. Some topics, for instance nos. xxxv–xxxviii, presuppose accomplishment in other forms of meditational attainment (see JHĀNA).

Kamo no Mabuchi (1697–1769). A Japanese *Kokugaku scholar and poet. Born the third son of Okabe Sadanobu, a *Shinto priest serving a branch of the Great Kamo Shrine (in *Kyōto) at the village of Okabe in Hamamatsu. He came into contact with Kokugaku and its foremost authority, *Kada no Azumaro, through a literary circle associated with Sugiura Kuniakira who married Azumaro's niece. In 1733, leaving his wife and child behind, he journeyed to Kyōto to master classical Japanese studies and ancient Japanese under Azumaro's tutelage. On the death of his master in 1736, he returned to Hamamatsu for a year and left home once again for Edo (modern Tokyo) to devote himself to the cause of Kokugaku. Succeeding to the tutorial post which Arimaro, the adopted son of Azumaro, had held, he went into the service of Tayasu Munetake, the second son of the Shōgun Yoshimune. He became a prolific writer on the themes of Shinto studies, court customs, linguistics, and poetics, especially when these made evident the superiority of the Japanese tradition, in contrast to China:

> Just as roads emerge naturally when people live in wild woods or on uncultivated land, so the way of the age of the gods took hold naturally in Japan . . . Japanese poetry takes for its subject-matter the human heart; and if it seems of no practical use and hardly worth writing, consider that when you know the poetry well, you know, without any need of further explanation, the reasons governing order and disorder in the world.

He grasped through the study of the *Kojiki* and *Manyōshū* the ethos of ancient Japan in terms of sincerity and virility. He advocated a return to the style of the *Manyōshū* as a poet, and his admiration for the ancient Japanese way of life became the main thrust of the Kokugaku Movement. His scholarship and thought attracted many able men such as *Motoori Norinaga, Kao Chikage, and Murata Harumi.

Kaṃsa. In Hindu mythology, *Kṛṣṇa's arch-enemy, identified with the demon Kālanemi. Having been warned by a heavenly voice that his kinswoman *Devakī's eighth child would slay him, Kaṃsa tried to avert his fate by demanding that all her children be handed over to him to be killed. When he realized that the eighth child, Kṛṣṇa, had escaped him and was living somewhere unknown, he ordered a massacre of all baby boys of the appropriate age. When that too failed he sent a succession of demons to kill Kṛṣṇa, who overcame them all. Kaṃsa's final plan, to lure Kṛṣṇa to his death in Mathurā, also failed, and he himself died at Kṛṣṇa's hands.

Kamuy (spiritual powers): see AINU.

Kaṇāda (*c.*2nd cent. BCE). Hindu philosopher who according to tradition founded the *Vaiśeṣika system (*darśana). The *Vaiśeṣika-sūtra* is attributed to him. He is also known as Kaṇabhuj, etc., 'atom delighter', because of the atomic nature of the theory.

Kanada Tokumitsu (founder of a Japanese religion): see MIKI TOKUHARU.

Kanah, Book of. Jewish *kabbalistic book. Modelled on the **Zohar*, the book is a commentary on the mitzvot (sing. *mitzvah) with additional mystical interpretations. Of unknown authorship, it was probably written in Spain in the 14th cent. It frequently reveals a negative attitude to the straightforward meaning of the text, and it was influential on the *Shabbatean movement.

Kan'ami Kiyotsugu (Nō writer): see NŌ.

Kāñcīpura (Conjeevaram). One of the seven Hindu holy cities, near Madras, a centre of pilgrimage, with mainly *Śaivite and *Vaiṣṇavite temples. It was once also an important Buddhist centre. *Hsüan-tsang (*c.*640 CE) mentions many *stūpas erected by *Aśoka, and also nearly 100 temples devoted to *Viṣṇu as Varadarāja, the royal giver of gifts or favours. See also DĀSANĀMĪ.

Kañcuka ('armour'). In *Kashmir Śaivism, the five ways in which *māyā covers over pure consciousness (*śuddha saṃvid*). The five are: *kalā*, limitation of efficacy; *vidyā, limited knowledge; *rāga, passion; *kāla, time; and *niyati*, fixed order or limitation relating to space and cause. The kañcukas are part of impure creation (*aśuddhādhvan*) occurring after the māyā *tattva, and can be regarded as limitations of the five *śaktis of pure creation (*śuddhādhvan*).

Kāṇḍa: see KARMA-KĀṆḌA.

Kangen (Japanese music not accompanying dance): see MUSIC.

Kaṅghā (comb): see FIVE KS.

Kangyur: see KANJUR.

K'ang Yu-wei (1858–1927). Leading figure in the Chinese Reform Movement which followed defeat in the Sino-Japanese war, 1894–5. His *Chronological Autobiography* shows that he was early dissatisfied with maintaining traditional ways and ideas: 'In searching for foundational truth in all the great names of the scholars ... to the present day, they were all empty and lacking in foundation.' He had an enlightenment experience of the one nature of all appearances (including his own), and withdrew into isolation where a sense of mission formed to offer a way of salvation to the world. He wrote **Ta t'ung shu* and *K'ung Tzu kai-chih k'ao* (Confucius as a Reformer). In 1898 he was invited to take charge of government by the emperor. He set about reform, but his twenty-seven reform edicts provoked a conservative *coup d'état* in favour of the empress dowager, Tzu Hsi. Forced overseas, he continued to oppose the Republic, but lived circumspectly when he returned to China. His major argument was that China could not be reformed simply by adding technology to Confucianism, but that Confucianism must change to validate change, as Confucius (he maintained) had himself advocated: 'The methods and institutions of Confucius aim at meeting particular times. If, in the age of Disorder, one attempted to establish the institutions of the age of Peace, the result would be great strain; but if, in the age of Order, we cling to the institutions of Disorder, this too will bring great harm.'

K.-c. Hsiao, *A Modern China and a New World: K'ang Yu-wei* ... (1975); L. G. Thompson, *Ta T'ung-shu* ... (1958).

K'an-hua ch'an (kōan-gazing Ch'an). Chin. for *Kanna Zen; see HUNG-CHIH; TA-HUI.

Kaniṣka. 1. A king of the Śaka-Kūṣāna period (*c.*78–144 CE), who ruled over the west of N. India, and some parts of Central Asia, about 78–102. Buddhist tradition celebrates him as a great patron of Buddhism, a view borne out by historical and archaeological evidence. He appears to have had two capitals, one in Mathura, the other in Puruṣapura (present-day Patna). His sympathies seem to have been with the *Sarvāstivadin school of Buddhism, and Chinese sources hold him to have presided over the fourth Buddhist *Council in Kashmir. Coins dating to the reign of Kaniṣka often contain images of the Buddha, although other deities, particularly Greek and brahmanical, are common. It is generally accepted that he erected a Buddhist temple in Puruṣapura, and one of the earliest references to the *Tripiṭaka is contained in an inscription of Kaniṣka. A famous headless statue is extant which confirms his Central Asian origin, since he is clad in a long quilted coat and trousers of a type common in that region. In his hand he carries a large, unsheathed broadsword.

Kaniṣka's reign was one of the most significant phases of Indian cultural development. Under his patronage, the Gāndhara school of art flourished. His court included such Buddhist luminaries as *Aśvaghoṣa, *Nāgārjuna, Pārśva, and Vasumitra, as well as the physician Caraka, the politician Māṭhara, and the Greek engineer Agesilaus, who designed and built a famous *stūpa in Kaniṣka's capital of Puruṣapura (Peshāwar). The accession of Kaniṣka to the throne is conventionally dated at 78 CE, which is the beginning of the so-called Śaka Era. A calendar based on the Śaka Era is used along with the Gregorian calendar by the contemporary government of India.

2. A class of Hindu deities of the fourteenth *manvantara* (cf. *Manu).

Kānji Svāmi Panth. Jain movement named after its founder. Kānji Svāmi was born in Gujarat of Śvetāmbara parents in 1889. He was initiated as a Sthānakvāsi ascetic at the age of 22, but tore his robe during the ceremony, an inauspicious sign. He never settled as a monk, although he gained great respect. When he was about 30, he read *Kundakunda's *Samayasāra* (Essence of Doctrine), which opened him to the possibility that the *Digambara way was the true one. Further reading convinced him of this, and although he remained in his Order, he increasingly adopted the Digambara viewpoint and expressed the ideas of Kundakunda in his preaching. Eventually this dual life proved unsustainable, and in 1934, he renounced his status as monk and became a Digambara layman. This took place at Songadh which remains the centre of the movement derived from him. He became an indefatigable preacher, mainly commenting on the works of Kundakunda and taking even further his stress on the primacy of the realization of the true soul (*paramātman) over all external observances, vows, and rituals. In 1937, he stated that in a previous incarnation, he had heard Kundakunda teaching, thereby validating the line of his own descent. The Panth is a mainly lay movement, though there are some *brahmacharis (ascetics), who live celibate but relatively free lives. The Panth is missionary and has adherents in many countries round the world.

Kanjur (*bka.'gyur*, 'translated word (of the Buddha)'). The primary part of the Tibetan Buddhist canon which comprises all *sūtras and *tantras attributed directly to the historical *Buddha *Śākyamuni, to his later revelation, or (in the case of some tantras) to another transcendent Buddha. The Kanjur numbers 100 or 108 vols. according to edn., and was largely systematized by the scholar and historian Butön, in the 14th cent. CE. See also TANJUR.

Kanna Zen (Jap.; Chin., K'an-huach'an). Zen based on the contemplation of words, a description of Zen in which the *kōan is pre-eminent. In time, it became virtually synonymous with *Rinzai, in contrast to *Sōtō, which was termed *mokushō zen. See also HUNG-CHIH; TA-HUI.

Kannen (Jap., 'meditation'). Meditation in Japanese Buddhism, especially on the *Pure Land of *Amida. Kannen jōza no tsutome is the practice of extended sitting in meditation.

Kannō-dōkō (Jap.). The direct and immediate connection and interaction between teacher and pupil in Zen (*dokusan, *mondō, *hossen).

Kannon (abbr. of Kanzeon, a bodhisattva): see AVALOKITEŚVARA.

Kannushi (Jap.). A Shinto priest, generally the guardian of a shrine. The position of kannushi was often hereditary, though adoption was a common remedy when no suitable heir to the teachings was available.

Kāṇphaṭa yogis (sect founded by Gorakhnāth): see GORAKHNĀTH.

Kan-shiketsu (Jap., 'dry shit stick'). Zen description of a person attached to the world of appearance. It is the *wato of *kōan 21 in the *Wu-men kuan*.

Kant, Immanuel (1724–1804). German philosopher. He was born in Königsberg of devoutly Pietist parents, and spent all his life there, becoming Professor of logic and metaphysics at the university in 1770.

Kant's earlier philosophical works, usually described as his 'Precritical' works, were in the tradition of Leibniz and Wolff. But he was, as he put it, aroused from his 'dogmatic slumber' in middle age by reading *Hume. He wrote his most important books in his later years, especially the three Critiques. The *Critique of Pure Reason* (1781) deals with fundamental questions about human knowledge, understanding, and reason, and has been one of the most influential works of modern philosophy. In it Kant sets out his programme for a 'Copernican Revolution' in metaphysics, whereby attention is devoted to the nature of the knower more than to the objects known. Although our knowledge derives from sense experience, Kant argues that it is only through our understanding that sense experience is ordered, and that certain concepts ('categories'), not derived from experience, are applied by the understanding. 'Transcendental' philosophy investigates the *a priori* conditions of the possibility of our experience of an objective world. It is a form of metaphysics, but a very chastened one, compared with traditional speculative metaphysics. Thus Kant's philosophy has a sceptical edge: the human mind is confined to the world of 'phenomena', and the 'noumenal' world of things-in-themselves is unknowable. Hence it is improper to infer the existence of a First Cause, God, because the term 'cause' is properly used only within our ordinary knowledge of phenomena. In the later part of the *Critique* Kant criticizes the *ontological, *cosmological, and *teleological arguments for God's existence. He allows, however, that the ideas of God, the soul, and the world may have what Kant calls a 'regulative' role: for example, the idea of a highest intelligence may inspire the scientist to find order in phenomena and help him to systematize his results. Thus, although Kant attacked traditional *metaphysics and *natural theology, he allowed for the possibility of a 'rational faith'. His preferred approach to this, however, was through ethics, as these words in the Conclusion of the *Critique* make unsurprising: 'Two things fill the mind with ever-increasing wonder and awe, the more often and the more intensely the mind of thought is drawn to them: the starry heavens above me and the moral law within me.'

Kant's *Groundwork of the Metaphysic of Morals* (1785) is a significant work on moral philosophy, famous for its discussion of the 'categorical imperative', a test whereby we judge our moral principles at the bar of reason, to see if they are indeed universal rules valid for all people: 'There is . . . but one categorical imperative: act only on that maxim whereby you can at the same time will that it should become a universal law.' The *Critique of Practical Reason* (1788) is also concerned with the nature of moral judgement. In an important section, Kant argues that beliefs in God, freedom, and the immortality of the soul are 'postulates of the practical reason', i.e. they are assumptions that have to be made in acknowledging the objectivity of the moral law. The role of these assumptions is also discussed towards the end of the *Critique of Judgement* (1790) which deals with the nature of aesthetic and teleological judgements.

Kant's last substantial discussion of religious questions was his *Religion within the Bounds of Reason Alone* (1793), in which he further developed his idea of a 'pure, rational religion', rejecting 'false worship'. He discussed questions concerning divine commands, grace, the nature of Christ's redemption, the atonement, and the Church, stressing the primacy of the rational moral judgement and often criticizing traditional doctrines.

Kant is sometimes described as 'the philosopher of Protestantism'. It is indeed true that he greatly affected much later Protestantism, especially in 19th-cent. Germany. His critique of traditional metaphysics and natural theology, his 'turn to the subject', and his stress on the primacy of ethics were deeply influential. Moreover, many of those who later investigated the nature of religious consciousness, e.g. Rudolf *Otto, did so in terms of Kant's transcendental philosophy (it has to be said, however, that Kant would not have sympathized with Otto's interest in mysticism). Many RC thinkers, especially neo-Thomists like *Maritain, have felt it necessary to attack Kant's critique of traditional metaphysics in order to reformulate and defend arguments for God's existence. On the other hand, later so-called 'transcendental Thomists' like Joseph Maréchal and Karl *Rahner sought to reconcile St Thomas *Aquinas and Kant by arguing that a transcendental analysis of the human subject may show that the latter is after all open to infinite being, i.e. God.

E. Cassirer, *Kant's Life and Thought* (tr. 1981); B. M. G. Reardon, *Kant as Philosophical Theologian* (1988); R. Walker, *Kant* (1978).

Kaṇva. 1. A Hindu *ṛṣi often referred to in the *Ṛg Veda*, to whom several of its hymns are attributed.

2. A demon of disease who destroys and devours embryos.

Kanzan: see HAN-SHAN.

Kanzeon: see AVALOKITEŚVARA.

Kao-Seng-Chuan (Biographies of Eminent Monks). Buddhist text compiled by Hui-chiao of the Liang dynasty (502–51 CE). It contains the biographies of 257 eminent Chinese and foreign Buddhist monks who lived in China from the 2nd cent. CE to the 6th cent. It exemplifies his distinction, 'If a man of real achievement keeps his brilliance concealed, he is eminent but not famous; if a man of slight virtue is in accord with his times, he is famous, but not eminent'.

Kāpāla (Skt., 'made of skulls'). Followers of *Śiva who worship him in his terrible (Bhairava) form: see KĀPĀLIKA.

Kāpālika (Skt., 'skull-wearer'). A sect of *Śaivism which flourished from the 7th to 14th cents. CE, also called the Somasiddhānta. The Kāpālikas were cremation-ground (*śmaśāna) dwellers who covered themselves with the ashes of corpses and carried a skull which they used as a bowl. The terrifying form of *Śiva as *Bhairava, *Mahākāla, or Kāpālabhṛt ('skull-carrier') was the central deity of the cult. Kāpālika practice aimed at a vision of, and possession (*aveśa*) by, a deity or power (*śakti), in order to achieve perfection (*siddhi). Practice included the consuming of corpse-flesh and scatalogical substances, meditation whilst seated on a corpse, sexual rites with low-caste women, and animal, human, and self-sacrifice. Orgiastic festivals occurred in the spring and autumn. Perhaps the earliest occurrence of the word *kāpālin* ('one who bears a skull') is in the *Yajñavalkya-smṛti* 3. 243 (2nd or 3rd cent. CE), in a description of one doing a penance for killing a *brahman. It says 'with a skull and a staff, living on alms, announcing his deed, and eating little food, the killer of a brāhmaṇa may be purified after twelve years'. It would seem that the Kāpālikas practised this penance known as the 'great vow' (mahāvrata), which they regarded as a re-enactment of Śiva's *asceticism after he had severed one of *Brahmā's five heads. Here we have the *Tantric notion of the conjunction of opposites, the lowest of criminals and the highest of ascetics. The Kāpālikas were scorned and feared by orthodox Brahmanism, and if a brahman saw one, he would stare into the sun to purify himself. The Kāpālikas were absorbed into the *Nāthas and *Aghorīs. See also PĀŚUPATA.

D. Lorenzen, *The Kāpālikas and Kālāmukhas* (1972).

Kapila. A legendary figure, traditionally recognized as the founder of *Sāṃkhya. He is said to have lived during the late 7th or early 6th cent. BCE though these dates precede his supposed authorship of the *Ṣaṣṭitantra* (*c.*100 BCE–200 CE) and other texts. The Buddhists connect him geographically to Kapilavastu, the birthplace of the *Buddha. He is a sage of antiquity surrounded by legend and contradiction, said to have been born since the beginning of creation, and held to be an incarnation (*avatāra) of *Viṣṇu, an incarnation of *Agni, and the son of *Brahmā.

In the **Rāmāyaṇa*, the sage Kapila becomes so angered when his meditation is disturbed by the 60,000 sons of the famous king Sagara that he turns them to ashes. The grieving king attempts to bring the life-restoring waters of the celestial Ganges (*Gaṅgā) to earth and thence to the ashes lying in the nether regions, but is unsuccessful. The task eventually falls to Bhagīratha who, after many labours, finally succeeds. Today, thousands of pilgrims gather at the point by the island Sagar where the river is said to have come to earth, and here they visit the hermitage (*āśrama) of the sage Kapila.

Kapilāvastu, Kapilavatthu (Skt.; Pāli). The early home of the *Buddha. It lies between the foothills of Nepal and the Rapti river, being at that time the capital of the domain of the Śākyas. It is one of the four major places of Buddhist *pilgrimage.

Kaplan, Mordelai Menachem (1881–1983). Founder of the Jewish *Reconstructionist movement. He was born in Lithuania, but was taken to the USA when he was 9. He studied at the *Jewish Theological Seminary, and was appointed *rabbi to an

*Orthodox congregation. But the erosive power of so many ideas around him (*Durkheim, Darwin, *Freud, *Marx, and *Wellhausen in particular) led him to leave his congregation and work as a teacher at the JTS. His radical views led to a further break with *Conservative Jews, and in 1922, he initiated the Jewish Reconstructionist movement, although at that stage not wishing it to be a separate organization. The laws remained important, but as a means to an end. Thus the *Sabbath has value because, just as an artist must stand back to see the picture he is painting, so we must stand back from life to see its meaning: the laws give context for that appraisal. He thought that Jewish élitism was a mistake, and argued that all reference to 'the *Chosen People' should be dropped from the liturgy. Yet after the Second World War, he appreciated that details of emancipation were trivial: 'Our emancipation will not be complete until we are free of the fear of being Jews.' Judaism was a preparation for a moral transformation of life and society, which to him was urgent: 'If you have a rendezvous with destiny, be sure to come on time.' He defined Judaism as an 'evolving religious civilization', maintaining that 'the past has a vote but no veto'. In his confrontation of the problems facing the Jewish tradition, he was a profound influence on generations of Conservative rabbis, although some extreme Orthodox repudiated him, excommunicating (*ḥerem) him and burning his revised Prayer Book. His views were expressed in his many books, the best known of which is *Judaism as a Civilization* (1934).

G. D. Cohen in *Mordelai M. Kaplan Jubilee Volume* (1953); R. Libowitz, *Mordecai M. Kaplan . . .* (1983).

Kappa (period of time): see KALPA.

Kapparot (Heb., 'atonements'). Folk custom in Judaism to secure atonement before the *Day of Atonement, so that an adverse judgement would not be reached on that day. On the day before Yom Kippur, a live fowl is taken (a cock for a man, a hen for a woman) and is swung by its neck round the head of the person who says: 'This is my atonement, this is in exchange for me, this is my substitute.' The fowl is then slaughtered and it (or its value) is given to the poor, while its disembowelled interior is given to the birds as a further act of charity. *Rabbis opposed the custom, but recognizing the power of *folk religion, they suggested that at least a monetary substitution for the fowl be made, of eighteen coins; and in that form the custom continues to the present. In Yiddish, a bad event is often met by the words, 'Oyf kapporos', may this be an atonement, i.e. a sufficient punishment to remove the need for any more.

Kaṛā (steel bangle): see FIVE KS.

Kaṛāh praśād (Pañjābī, *kaṛāh*, 'iron bowl', + *praśād* [= *prasadā]). Among Sikhs, sweet food offered to all attending worship in the *gurdwārā. To prepare the kaṛāh praśād as instructed in *Rahit Maryāda, men or women, who have bathed and put on clean clothes, fry wheat flour in clarified butter (ghi) until it is golden-brown, then add a syrup of sugar and water and cook until the mixture thickens. Meanwhile they recite hymns from the *Ādi Granth. The kaṛāh praśād is covered with a white cloth, sprinkled with water to symbolize cleanliness, and placed near the Ādi Granth. During the *Ardās it is marked with a kirpān. After the service the kaṛāh praśād is distributed to all present as a sign of their equality and unity and to ensure that no one leaves the Gurū's presence empty handed. It is received in both hands, held cupped, and eaten straight away. The first five portions are eaten in memory of the *pañj pyāre. See also GURŪ-KĀ-LAṄGAR.

Karaites (from Heb., 'readers', i.e. of scripture). Jewish sect basing itself on scripture, not subsequent interpretation. The name 'Karaite' was not used until 9th cent. CE. The sect is usually thought to have been founded by the ascetic *Anan b. David in the 8th cent., when his younger brother Hananiah was elected *exilarch. Anan insisted that the written scripture was the only authority: 'Search thoroughly in the *Torah and do not rely on my opinion'; and he taught his followers to disregard the rabbinic *oral law. The movement quickly splintered into various sects after Anan's death, but was consolidated from the 9th cent. as a result of the work of such eminent scholars as Benjamin b. Moses Nahawendi (*c.*830–60), Daniel b. Moses al-Qumisi (late 9th cent.), Abu Yusaf Yazub al-Kirkisani (10th cent.), Salmon b. Jeroham (10th cent.) who engaged in vigorous conflict with *Saʿadiah Gaon and Joseph b. Abraham ha-Kohen ha-Roeh al Basir (11th cent.). The Karaites themselves taught that their movement originated in the split between *Israel and *Judah in the 10th cent. BCE, and that they were the spiritual descendants of the *Sadducees. Their basic doctrine was that the Bible was the only source of law, and that scholars must study scripture for themselves and interpret it according to their own consciences. From the 12th cent., however, a process of systematization began under such scholars as Judah b. Elijah Hadassi (who summarized Karaite theology in his *Eshkol ha-Kofer*), Aaron b. Joseph ha-Rofe (who was an eminent biblical exegete and wrote *Sefer-Mivhar*, the classic Karaite commentary), and the codifier, Aaron b. Elijah the Younger, whose *Gan Eden* earned him the title of 'the Karaite *Maimonides'. Between 7th and 19th cents., Karaisim spread from Babylonia to Egypt, *Erez Israel, Turkey and the Ottoman Empire, and to Lithuania and the Crimea. Relations with the rabbinite Jews varied between extreme bitterness, as in the time of Saʿadiah Gaon, and reasonable harmony (as in the case of Maimonides who pronounced that they should be treated with 'respect, honour, kindness and humility'). They were perceived as Jews by their gentile rulers, and were in general subject to the same edicts. However, from 1795 in Russia, the

Karaites were permitted to pay less tax than the rabbinate Jews; from 1827, they were exempted from military service, and in 1863 they were given equal rights with the rest of the population while the rabbinates continued to suffer civil disabilities. During the Second World War, the German government pronounced that the Karaites were not Jews and they were thus spared the horrors of the *Holocaust. However, after the creation of the State of Israel, they were persecuted as Jews by the Arab states and were welcomed in Israel. There they have their own *bet din and they are not permitted either by *halakhah or by their own laws to intermarry with the rest of the population. See Index, Karaites.

J. Mann, *Texts and Studies in Jewish History and Literature*, ii. *Karaitica* (1935); L. Nemoy, *Karaite Anthology* (1952).

Karakashlar (sect): see DOENMEH.

Karāmat ʿAlī (d. 1873 (AH 1290)). Indian Muslim reformer, who contested the assimilation into Islam of Hindu customs, regarding them as *bidʿa: his book against them is entitled *Radd al-Bidʿa*. His differs from other conservative reform movements (e.g. *Wahhābīya) by accepting the value of spiritual guides (*pīr), and he could thus aim to reconcile *Sūfī movements with orthodox Islam.

Kāraṇa śarīra. The Hindu causal body which carries the effects of *karma into subsequent lives.

Karbalā'. The place where the Prophet *Muḥammad's grandson, *al-Ḥusain b. ʿAlī, was killed and his headless body buried. The tragedy at Karbalā' marks an important point in the development of *Shiʿism, and therefore the place attracts many pilgrims. The shrine of the third Shīʿa *Imām, al-Ḥusain, is enclosed in a beautiful sanctuary called Mashad al-Ḥusayn (tomb chapel of Ḥusain), and around it has grown a prosperous town that is the starting-point for Shīʿa pilgrim caravans to Najaf and *Mecca, as well as being a staging-post for trade with the Arabian interior. Amongst the Shīʿa, Imām Ḥusain's sanctuary has the reputation for securing paradise for those buried there; hence many people seek to be buried at this holy place, and the area to the west of Karbalā' has become a graveyard for devout Shiʿites.

Kardec, A. (spiritualist): see UMBANDA.

Karelitz, Avraham Yeshayahu (1878–1953). *Talmudic scholar. Karelitz was an enormous influence on his generation. He was the author of over forty books, including *Hazon Ish* (1911), by which name he is often known. After he settled in *Erez Israel, in 1933, his house was a centre for teaching and guidance.

K. Kahana, *Ha-Ish ve-Hazono* (1964).

Kare sansui (Zen dry gardens): see GARDEN.

Karet (Heb., 'cutting off'). Punishment from God. Karet is defined as premature death (*Sifra, Emor* 14. 4) and more particularly as 'death at the age of fifty' (*BMK* 28a). The *Mishnah lists the thirty-six sins for which karet is the penalty (e.g. *idolatry, eating *leaven at *Passover, incest, and *adultery). *Maimonides believed that suffering karet meant that one was excluded from the life of the world to come, but Nachmanides held that karet of the *soul did not mean total extinction.

Karma, kamma (Skt., Pāli: 'action', 'deed'; Chin., *yin-yuan*; Jap., *innen*; Korean, *inyon*). Karman, the law of consequence with regard to action, which is the driving force behind the cycle of reincarnation or rebirth (*saṃsāra) in Asian religions. According to karma theory, every action has a consequence which will come to fruition in either this or a future life; thus morally good acts will have positive consequences, whereas bad acts will produce negative results. An individual's present situation is thereby explained by reference to actions in his past history, in his present or in previous lifetimes. Karma is not itself 'reward and punishment', but the strict law producing consequence. The origin of the idea of karma is uncertain, but its beginnings could well be in non-*Vedic, heterodox groups such as the *Ājīvikas and *Jains (who have an extensive karma literature).

In Hinduism, the word karma first appears in the **Ṛg Veda*, where it means religious action, specifically sacrifice; there is no hint here of its later meaning as the force driving beings through saṃsāra. There is some hint of this in the *Brāhmaṇas, but only with the *Upaniṣads do we really find karma in the sense of causality of action—e.g. **Bṛhadāranyaka Upaniṣad* 4. 4. 5: 'As a man acts, as he behaves, so does he become. Whoso does good actions becomes good; whoso does evil actions becomes evil. Whatever action (karma) he does, that he attains.' Some schools of Indian thought, such as *Pāśupata Śaivism, believed karma to be transferable or transactional, that the results of action could pass from one person to another (see PĀŚUPATA), but *Vedānta and *Yoga had non-transactional karma theories. *Pūrva-Mīmāṁsā, which continued Vedic ways of thinking and emphasized *dharma, at first excluded karma from its literature, but later incorporated it in the notion of *apūrva, a store of efficacy of ritual. The early Mīmāṃsā rejection of karma points to its non-Vedic origin.

Action creates impressions (*saṃskāras) or tendencies (*vāsanās) in the mind which in time will come to fruition in further action. The *subtle body (*liṅga or śūkṣma śarīra), in which the individual soul (*jiva) transmigrates, carries the seeds of karma; and the gross body (*sthūla śarīra*) is the field (*kṣetra*) in which the fruit (*phala*) of action is experienced, and which also creates more karma.

Vedānta and Yoga speak of three kinds of karma: (i) *prārabdha*, karma to be experienced during the present lifetime, (ii) *sañcita*, latent karma, or the store of karma which has yet to reach fruition, and (iii) *āgamin* or *sañcīyama*, the karma sown in the present life which will be reaped in a future life. Liberation (*mokṣa) is freedom from karma. When mokṣa is attained, the great store of *sañcita karma* is burnt up, but the *prārabdha* remains to complete its course. The liberated person (jivanmukta) creates no more new karma and at death, having no more karma, is no longer reborn.

In Buddhism, much of the same basic sense of a law of consequence is retained, but there is no 'self' to be reborn. Stress is laid, not so much on the action as such, as on the intention which lies behind it. When an action cannot be performed, the intention will nevertheless produce the karmic consequence. Equally, intentions (and actions) which produce good karmic consequence are also a hindrance toward progress to enlightenment, because they form a rewarding future in the stream of reappearance (*punabbhāva)—i.e. they do not lead away from reappearance. Only intentions and actions free of desire, hate, and delusion are free of karmic consequence. Karma/kamma is neither fatalistic nor deterministic, since true insight enables one to direct the stream of continuity, or even to bring it to cessation.

Among Jains, karma is a kind of subtle matter which attaches itself to the *jīva and weighs it down in bondage and rebirth. All actions, good as well as evil, cause karmic matter to attach to the soul. Therefore, the abandoning of action, in complete ascetic renunciation (even to the extent of voluntary starvation), is necessary.

For Sikhs, karma (Pañjābi, *karamu*) is accepted as consequential action, but against it is set karma (Arab., *karam*, 'favour') meaning the grace of God. Instead of adjudicating on the issue of whether a soul is propelled by (bad) karma to rebirth, or whether it lives in one body only, Sikhs concentrate on bringing karma (*grace) to bear on karma, leading to union with God. See Index, Karma.

H. von Glasenapp, *The Doctrine of Karman in Jain Philosophy* (1942); R. Neufeldt (ed.), *Karma and Rebirth: Post-Classical Developments* (1986); W. D. O'Flaherty (ed.), *Karma and Rebirth in Classical Indian Traditions* (1980); S. S. R. Pappu, *The Dimensions of Karma* (1987); H. W. Tull, *The Vedic Origins of Karma . . .* (1989).

Karma Kagyü (Tib., *kar-ma bka'-brgyud*). One of the four main early subschools of *Kagyü (*bka'.brgyud*), founded by Düsum Chempa (Chos 'dzin dge 'phel Dus gsum mkhyen pa, 1110–93). Originally identified by Black Hats, made from the hair of *ḍākinīs who embody the good *karma of all the *buddhas, an early schism led to the Red Hats, with whom much conflict ensued. They contributed to *Rimé (*ris-med*), and have built up a considerable following in the West.

Karma-kāṇḍa (Skt.). The division, or practical part, of the *Vedas which refers to religious duties, *ritual, and actions; as opposed to the *jñānakāṇḍa of the *Vedānta which deals with philosophical knowledge. *Pūrva-mīmāṁsā is concerned with karma-kāṇḍa.

Karman: see KARMA.

Karma-pa. Title of the highest spiritual authority in the Tibetan Buddhist school of *Karma Kagyü who is an embodiment of compassion. His appearance was prophesied by the *Buddha Śākyamuni and by *Padmasambhava. There have been seventeen incarnations. For further details, see KAGYÜ.

Karma-yoga. One of the four main types of *yoga in Hinduism, leading to union with God. It consists of detachment, not from action as such, but from the fruits of all action, offering them instead as a sacrifice to God. It follows that karma-yoga is the opposite to abstention from works: it is the cultivation of the proper attitude to works, especially religious duties. *Bhagavad-gītā* 3 describes karma-yoga and the reasons for it:

> Not by abstaining from actions does anyone attain freedom from action, nor by renouncing actions does he attain the goal . . . But he who, having controlled his senses by his mind, follows the path of action without attachment, by means of the organs of action (*karmendriya), he excels.

Karmendriya (Skt., *karma + *driya*, 'organ'). The five organs or means of action, those of speech, hands, feet, excretion, and reproduction.

Karṇa. In the **Mahābhārata*, the half-brother of the *Pāṇḍavas, who serves as the third general on the side of the *Kauravas in the *Kurukṣetra war. Fathered by the sun god, of whom he is also a devotee and partial incarnation, Karṇa is born out of wedlock to *Kuntī before her marriage to Pāṇḍu. Set afloat in a basket by his embarrassed mother (an act which has warranted his inclusion in lists of heroes such as *Moses who were similarly endangered in childhood), Karṇa is found and raised by a charioteer and his wife. Having thus lost his rightful family name and class Karṇa is befriended and given a kingdom by *Duryodhana at the same time as he is ridiculed by the Pāṇḍavas; it is not surprising, therefore, that he opts for the Kaurava side in the war. He is paired particularly against the Pāṇḍava *Arjuna, whom he seems to match in strength and skill.

More than any other *Mahābhārata* character, Karṇa brings out the ambiguities of *dharma pivotal to the epic. Legally the oldest Pāṇḍava, and entitled to the throne, Karṇa is forced by circumstances to fight against his brothers. On the one hand, a mean and dreadful enemy, who must be defeated by the righteous Pāṇḍavas, Karṇa is, on the other hand, outstandingly loyal in his commitment to Duryodhana, and proverbially generous: he was born with earrings and armour, but cut them off to give to a *brahman (really *Indra in disguise). Again and again, throughout the *Mahābhārata*, Karṇa is shown to be caught up in a web of curses, oaths, and promises, which, in fact, make his cause hopeless. In the end, the 'righteous' Arjuna defeats the 'evil' Karṇa in battle, by the illegal expedient of shooting him while his chariot wheel is stuck in the ground.

Karo: see CARO.

Kār sevā (Pañjābī, *kār*, 'work', + *sevā*, 'service'). Voluntary work undertaken by Sikhs for the good of the community. In particular, it has come to be applied to the work undertaken each fifty years of clearing silt from the pool of the *Harimandir (Golden Temple). This was last undertaken according to schedule in 1973, but it was additionally undertaken after the assault on the Harimandir in 1985. It attracts many Sikhs from around the world, since ordinarily it occurs for most people only once in a lifetime.

Kartārpur (Pañjābī, 'abode of the Creator'). Name of two historic Sikh sites.

1. Town founded by Gurū *Nānak in 16th cent. CE. Kartārpur lies on the Rāvī river in Siālkoṭ district, Pakistan, 3 km. from Dehrā Bābā Nānak on the Indian bank. Despite chronological inconsistencies between the *janam-sākhīs Gurū Nānak probably founded the settlement on land bequeathed by a wealthy follower after returning from his major travels. He spent his final years here with his wife and sons. His teaching attracted numerous disciples, including his successor, *Aṅgad, who shared a life of religious discipline. Nānak died in Kartārpur, but his *samādhī* (tomb) was moved to Dehrā Bābā Nānak in the 17th cent. A *gurdwārā was built 1911–12.

2. Town founded by Gurū *Arjan Dev. Arjan founded Kartārpur in the Jalandhar (Jullundur) Doāb, *Pañjāb at the end of the 16th cent. CE. He sank a well, named Gaṅgsar. Kartārpur was subsequently the scene of fighting between Hargobind and Mughal forces. In the 18th cent., fighting between Dīp Siṅgh's Sikhs and the Afghans led to the gurdwārā being destroyed; it was rebuilt by Mahārājā *Rañjīt Siṅgh. The original copy of the *Ādi Granth, compiled by Gurū Arjan Dev, is housed in a gurdwārā called Śīś Mahal in Kartārpur. Thousands flock to Kartārpur for *Baisākhī and on every Amāvas (darkest night of the month).

Kārt(t)ikeya. Hindu god of war and pestilence, son of *Śiva from seed which was thrown into fire, the ashes of which were then cast into the *Gaṅgā, from which he emerged. He rides on a peacock. He is also called *Skanda, Kumāra, and Murugan—see TAMIL NĀDU.

Karuṇā (Skt., 'compassion').

1. In Hinduism, all actions that diminish the sufferings of others.

2. In Buddhism compassion is a virtue which is of importance in all schools but which is particularly emphasized by those of the *Mahāyāna persuasion. In early Buddhism, karuṇā figures as one of the four 'Sublime Attitudes', namely love or benevolence (*metta), compassion (karuṇā), sympathetic joy (*mudita), and equanimity (*upekkha). These qualities are cultivated especially through the practice of meditation and are directed towards other beings without restriction.

In the Mahāyāna, karuṇā is emphasized as the necessary complement to wisdom (*prajña) and as an essential ingredient in the perfection of the fully enlightened. In Mahāyāna sources, Wisdom and Compassion are compared to two wings with which one flies to the island of enlightenment. The followers of the *Hīnayāna are criticized for their lack of karuṇā and for seeking a purely personal enlightenment regardless of the needs of others. The *bodhisattva of the Mahāyāna, on the other hand, seeks to attain *nirvāna for the benefit of all, and vows that he will not cease from his efforts until all beings have attained liberation. Some sources go so far as to allow karuṇā to override all other considerations, and enjoin the commission of immoral actions if the bodhisattva sees that such an action would reduce suffering (see SKILFUL MEANS). In Mahāyāna iconography and art the embodiment of compassion is the great bodhisattva *Avalokiteśvara, 'the one who looks down from on high'. He is portrayed as having a thousand arms extended in all directions to minister to those in need. He is constantly appealed to for aid and intercession by those in difficult circumstances. In the course of time there appeared a doctrine of salvation by faith according to which the mere invocation of the name of a Buddha was sufficient, given the extent of the Buddha's compassion, to ensure rebirth in a *Pure Land or heaven.

Kasatkin, Ivan (personal name of Niolai): see NICOLAI, PÈRE.

Kaṣāya (earth-coloured dress): see HABIT, RELIGIOUS; MONASTICISM (BUDDHIST).

Kasb (acquisition): see QADAR.

Kasher, kashrut, kosher (foods pronounced fit): see DIETARY LAWS.

Kashf (Arab., 'unveiling'). Comprehension of facts, events, and truths (mundane and spiritual) by inner sight or light. A *Sūfī term, it is used for a revelation of any secret truth to the mind and heart by the grace and power of God. It is a gift of perception bestowed upon the individual by God without any conscious effort on the part of the seeker. It may be given to anyone regardless of state; therefore it is regarded as a divine mystery. Cf. ḤĀL.

Kashmir Śaivism. An esoteric *Śaivism prevalent in Kashmir, N. India, from the 8th to the 11th cents. CE. It comprises a number of related Śaiva and *Śākta systems, namely the *Kaula ('relating to the family'), Krama ('gradation'), and Trika ('threefold'), though the term often refers only to the latter school, which is the most important, in that it integrated the Kaula and the Krama.

The literature of the Trika school is divided into three stages: (i) *Āgama Śāstra, revealed truth as embodied in the sixty-four monistic Śaiva āgamas and the *Śiva Sūtras* (Eng. tr. Jaideva Singh, 1979) reputedly revealed by Śiva to Vasugupta (8th–9th cents. CE); (ii) Spanda Śāstra, a group of texts dealing with *spanda* ('vibration'), principally the *Spanda Kārikās* (Tr. Jaideva Singh, 1980), either by Vasugupta or his pupil Kallaṭa, which elaborate the *Śiva Sūtras*; and (iii) Pratyabhijñā śāstra, the philosophical systematization of the earlier material, which advocates a theology of the recognition (*pratyabhijñā*) of Śiva in all things. Somānanda's *Sivadṛṣti* first expounded this view, followed by Utpala's *Īśvarapratyabhijñā* (Tr. K. A. Subramaniya Aiyar and K. C. Pandey, *Bhāskarī* [1938]). The most famous Trika exponent was *Abhinavagupta who wrote the *Tantrāloka* (Ital. tr. R. Gnoli, 1972).

The absolute (*parama* Śiva) of which there is nothing higher (*anuttara*), is regarded as the union of Śiva and Śakti conceived as *prakāśa* (light) and *vimarśa* (awareness). Acting from absolute freedom (*svātantrya*) equated with Śakti, Śiva manifests the cosmos as Śakti in the form of the thirty-six pure and impure *tattvas. These are the gradual differentiation into a subject–object dichotomy. The pure tattvas comprise Śiva, Śakti, Sadāśiva, Īśvara, and Śuddha Vidya, whose śaktis are *cit (consciousness), *ānanda (joy), *icca* (will), *jñāna (knowledge), and kriyā (action), which indicate the function of each pure tattva. The impure tattvas are *māyā, the *kañcukas (coverings), *puruṣa (experient), and the *Sāṃkhyan tattvas from *prakṛti (nature) to earth.

There are four ways to liberation (*mukti) or recognition (*pratyabhijñā*) of *parama* Śiva: (i) *aṇu upāya, direct liberation through grace or the descent of śakti (śaktipāta); (ii) *śāmbhava upāya, the absorption of the self in divine consciousness by the upsurge of pre-cognitive emotion which shatters thought construction; (iii) *śākta upāya, realization through the development of pure thought, such as 'I am Śiva'; and (iv) āṇava upāya, meditation on the body, mantra, and chosen deity (*iṣṭadevatā). See Index, Kashmir Śaivism.

Kashmir Sufism: see SŪFĪS.

Kashrut (food ritually fit for consumption): see DIETARY LAWS.

Kāśi. One of the seven sacred cities of India, an earlier name for Vārāṇasī (Benares). A centre of pilgrimage with many temples, it is especially important for devotion to *Śiva, who is worshipped (in a temple of this name) as Viśvanātha, Lord of the universe. Anyone who dies here, murmuring the 'crossing over' *mantra, is assured of liberation by Śiva, thereby cancelling the consequences of *karma.

D. L. Eck, *Benares, City of Light.*

Kasiṇa (Pāli, derivation uncertain). A means in Buddhism of attaining *kammaṭṭhāna and *jhāna. According to Nyanatiloka, kasiṇa

> is the name for a purely external device to produce and develop concentration of mind and attain the 4 Absorptions (*jhāna*). It consists in concentrating one's full and undivided attention on one visible object as Preparatory Image (*parikamma-nimitta*), let us say a coloured spot or disc, or a piece of earth, or a pond at some distance, etc., until at last one perceives, even with the eyes closed, a mental reflex, the so-called Acquired Image (*uggaha-nimitta*). Now, while continuing to direct one's attention to this image, there may arise the spotless and immovable so-called Counter-Image (*paṭibhāga-nimitta*), and together with it the Neighbourhood Concentration (*upacāra-samādhi*) will have been reached. While still persevering in the concentration on the object, one finally will reach a state of mind where all sense-activity is suspended, where there is no more seeing and hearing, no more perception of bodily impression and feeling, i.e., the state of the 1st mental Absorption (*jhāna*) (*Buddhist Dictionary* (1956), 74).

Kasiṇa devices are ten in number and are as follows: *paṭhavi* (earth), *āpo* (water), *tejo* (fire), *vāyo* (air), *nīla* (blue), *pīta* (yellow), *lohita* (red), *odāta* (white), *ākāsa* (space), and *viññāṇa* (*vijñāna, consciousness). These ten form part of the forty objects of meditation, selection from which is recommended for each of the six temperament types. Out of the ten, the four colour kasiṇas point to adaption from a general Indian tradition of identifying human beings by their psychic colours, suggesting that it is most expedient to achieve *samādhi through the colour that is appropriate to one's psychic composition.

Thus, according to tradition, each of the following temperament types has a natural attraction to the colours relevant to it as follows: lustful temperaments (*rāga-carita*) for red, hateful temperaments (*dosa-carita*) for blue, delusive temperaments (*moha-carita*) for yellow, and faithful temperaments (*saddhā-carita*) for white. Hence, the kasiṇa of the relevant colour is recommended as the object of meditation. See also KAMMAṬṬHĀNA.

Kasogatan (local Javanese Buddhism): see WALUBI.

Kassapa (Pāli name): see MAHĀKĀŚYAPA.

Kaśyapa. In Hindu mythology, a divine seer, son of Marīci and grandson of *Brahmā. He married thirteen of Dakṣa's daughters, who bore him all kinds of living creatures. He is thus the common origin of opposing forces, e.g. gods and demons (from *Aditi, Danu, and *Diti), birds and serpents (from Vinatā and Kadru). Among the latter are the birds *Garuḍa and Aruṇa, and the serpents *Śeṣa, Vāsuki, and Takṣaka.

Kataku (school of Ch'an): see HO-TSE.

Kataphatic theology: see AFFIRMATIVE WAY.

Kathak (N. Indian dance): see DANCE.

Kathākali (S. Indian dance): see DANCE.

Katha Upaniṣad. An *Upaniṣad sometimes assigned to the **Atharva Veda*, but more often to the Black **Yajur Veda*. It contains *Yama's instruction of Naciketas, including the granting of three wishes, the third of which was to know the nature of life in the hereafter. For trs., see UPANIṢADS.

Kathāvatthu (Points of Controversy): see MOGGALLIPUTTA TISSA.

Kathenotheism. The worship of successive gods, treated for the moment as the only god: see HENOTHEISM.

Katsu: see HO.

Kattō (Jap., 'clinging vines'). Zen description of those who use too many words to describe buddhadharma, or of those who cling to the words of a teacher or *sūtra without penetrating their meaning. This is also known as *moji zen*.

Kaula (Skt.). Both an important school of *Tantrism whose adherents constitute the 'family' (*kula*) of *Śakti, and a theological term with many levels of meaning. According to *Abhinavagupta, the Kaula tradition was founded by Macchandra (5th cent. CE): he is identified with the legendary Matsyendranatha who, according to an early text, the *Kaulajñānanirṇaya*, is the founder of a subsect called the Yoginīkaula. The Kaula school reinterprets the teachings of the *Kula, rejecting the narrow sectarian bias of the Kula's *Kāpālika origins. The **Kulārṇava Tantra* represents the Kaula as a distinct system which maintains the union of *Śiva and Śakti as the absolute reality, and advocates the secret ritual of the *pañca-makāra. Emphasizing secrecy, the text defines a Kaula as one who is privately a Śākta, outwardly a Śaiva and among people a *Vaiṣṇava. The Kaula system must be distinguished from the Krama system of Kashmir whose absolute is the goddess Kālī. In *Kashmir Śaivism, the Kaula system is said to expound the *śambhāva upaya*, the direct means of realizing the absolute, whereas the Krama system is said to expound the *śakta upaya*, the gradual means of realization by the purification of thought construction (*vikalpa). Among the meanings of Kaula as a theological term are śakti (as opposed to Śiva who is *akula*), *Kuṇḍalinī, 'body', and 'universe'.

Kaur. Sikh woman's second name, usually translated 'princess'. Kaur is the female counterpart of *Siṅgh. It follows the forename and precedes the family name if this is used. It may serve as surname, so avoiding the *caste connotations inherent in the family name. See also NAMING.

Kauravas. In the **Mahābhārata*, the evil cousins of the *Pāṇḍavas, and their rivals for the throne; thus, the villains of the epic, whom the Pāṇḍavas eventually defeat in battle. Their name is a patronymic, referring to their descent from Kuru, an ancestor of Pāṇḍavas and Kauravas alike. They are also known patronymically as Dhārtarāṣṭras, sons of *Dhṛtarāṣṭra. The Kauravas are 100 in number, and were born out of an aborted 'lump of flesh' to Dhṛtarāṣṭra and his wife Gāndhārī. They are said to be incarnate *rākṣasas. Although all the Kauravas are listed by name in the epic, and their exploits and deaths in battle accounted for, the only ones with clearly delineated personalities and truly individual roles are *Duryodhana, Duḥśāsana, and Vikarṇa (who attempts to criticize his brothers, but is quickly silenced). The Pāṇḍava ally Yuyutsu, son of Dhṛtarāṣṭra by a serving woman, is not strictly one of the hundred, but tends to be included in the list. The Kauravas also have one sister, Duḥśalā.

Kauṣītāki Upaniṣad. A short *Upaniṣad of four chapters, dealing with several topics, but especially with *prāṇa as the first principle, and with the interpretation of dreams. Trs., see UPANIṢADS.

Kauṭilya (attributed author): see ARTHAŚĀSTRA; PUROHITA.

Kavvanah (Heb., 'directed intention'). Concentration in Jewish *prayer and when performing a *mitzvah. The prophet *Isaiah condemns those who 'with their mouths and with their lips do honour me, but have removed their heart far from me' (Isaiah 29. 13). R. *Simeon used to say, 'Do not regard your prayer as a fixed mechanical device, but as an appeal for mercy and *grace before the All-Present' (*Avot* 2. 13). *Maimonides taught that 'prayer without kavvanah is no prayer at all', and the **Shulḥān Arukh* insists, 'better a little supplication with kavvanah than a lot without it'. None the less, it was accepted that this was the counsel of perfection, 'since nowadays we do not pray with proper attention in any case' (*Sh. Ar*, OH 60. 3). Kavvanah is also required of those performing mitzvot, but here there was more controversy: while all agree that kavvanah is desirable in fulfilling an obligation, is it necessary? If, e.g., one hears the blowing of the *shofar on *Rosh ha-Shanah without giving one's attention to it, has the obligation been fulfilled? In Ḥasidism and devotional Judaism, kavvanah is of such importance that it is deliberately cultivated in preparations before religious duties and prayer—'Here I am: send me!' In *kabbalah, kavvanah is also a special concentration on words and letters in order to discern an inner meaning. Cf. *niyya in Islam.

Kawate Bunjiro (1814–83). Founder of *Konkōkyō, a Japanese new religion. He was born as Kandori Genshichi into a peasant family in the Okayāma prefecture, where popular religion was much concerned with warding off malevolent *kami, among whom Konjin was particularly feared. During a serious illness when he was 42, he encountered Konjin in a healing ceremony, and from that time pronounced him to be beneficent rather than the opposite. He began to call him Kane no Kami ('the kami of gold'), Tenchi Kane no Kami ('the golden kami of heaven and earth'), and Konkō Daijin ('the great kami of golden light'). He began to receive direct communications from Konkō Daijin, and in 1859 he retired from farming in order to mediate between the kami and human beings. This date is regarded by adherents as the founding date of Konkōkyō, although it was not organized until 1885, after his death, being recognized by the government in 1900. After 1859, Kawate took the name of Konkō Daijin and met individuals who came to him, to act as a direct link between themselves and the kami.

D. B. Schneider, *Konkōkyō* . . . (1962).

Kederi (Sūfī order): see QĀDIRĪYA.

Kedushah (Heb., 'holiness'). In Judaism, set apart through holiness. The *biblical commandment, 'you shall be *holy, for I the Lord your God am holy' (Leviticus 19. 2) has consistently been understood by the *rabbis as requiring that the *Jews must be a people 'set apart'. God's fearful holiness is associated with his moral purity (Psalms 24. 3–4) which will manifest itself in divine judgement (Isaiah 1. 4–9) and in mercy (Isaiah 29. 19–21). It is something to be feared as well as adored, and, by serving God, the individual can become sanctified. The ultimate hope is that not only the Jewish nation, but the entire universe will be filled with the divine glory (*kavod*), and the *prophet *Zechariah looked to a time when even the bells on horses will be inscribed with 'Holy to the Lord' (Zechariah 14. 20–1). In rabbinic literature, holiness is of God's essence ('The Holy One, Blessed be he'). *Israel can only share in God's holiness through the performance of the mitzvot (sing. *mitzvah) ('Blessed are you Lord God . . . who has sanctified us by your commandments'). This separates the Jewish people from the nations, and as *Abraham b. Hiyya put it, 'The people of Israel is holy, because it separated itself from worldly pursuits, and turned to the notion of God.' More specifically, kedushah is applied to parts of the liturgy, especially the doxologies based on Isaiah 6. 3 and Ezekiel 3. 12 which echo the praise of the *angels.

Kedushta (morning piyyut): see KEROVAH.

Keep Sunday Special: see LORD'S DAY.

Kegi (Jap., 'teaching method'). The four ways of teaching in Japanese Buddhism, especially as classified in *Tendai: (i) *tongyo*, sudden and abrupt; (ii) *zengyo*, gradual; (iii) *himitsukyō*, secret (meaning that pupils are attaining understanding without awareness of it); (iv) *fujōkyō*, discriminate (pupils attain understanding while aware of it).

Kegon School or **School of the Flower Garland.** One of six schools of Buddhism established in Japan during the *Nara period (710–84)—see BUDDHISM IN JAPAN. The school originated in China where it was known as *Hua-yen, and was based on the massive *Avataṃsaka-sūtra* (see AVATAMSAKA LITERATURE). In doctrine the school presented a totalistic view of the universe wherein the Absolute (*ri*) is immanent in every individual entity (*ji*) and each entity mirrors the Absolute. Kegon philosophy was first transmitted to Japan by Chinese and Korean priests (especially Shinjō who gave the first lecture at Nara, and is thus regarded as the founder in Japan), and the Tōdaiji temple in the ancient capital of Nara became its centre. Kegon never emerged as a popular movement of Buddhism in Japan, remaining an obscure school of philosophy studied only by erudite scholar-monks.

Keichu (scholar): see KOKUGAKU.

Keizan Jōkin (1268–1325). *Sōtō Zen master, the fourth patriarch (*soshigata) of the Sōtō-shu. He founded Sōji-ji, one of the two most important Sōtō monasteries (the other being *Eihei-ji), and after *Dōgen is regarded as one of the most important figures of the school. Among his writings, *Denkōroku* (a collection of biographies and teachings) has had the most extensive influence—see KEIZAN OSHO . . . He was born near Dōgen's Eihei-ji, and at the age of 13 become a monk under Ejō, the disciple of Dōgen. In 1295, he received the seal of recognition (*inka-shōmei) from Tettsū Gikai, abbot of Daijō-ji, whom he succeeded in 1302. From Tettsu he inherited the programme of popularizing Zen and making it accessible.

Keizan Oshō Denkō-Roko (The Account by the Monk Keizan of the Transmission of the Light). A Zen Buddhist collection of stories concerning the transmission of the buddha-*dharma in the *Sōtō school. The episodes have the enigmatic challenge of a *kōan.

Kekka-fusa (Jap., for Skt., *padmāsana). The lotus position in meditation. The legs are crossed, with right foot on left thigh, and left foot on right thigh, and hands, palms upward, on the heels of both feet. In *zazen, the left palm may rest on the right as a mark of the dominance of the passive over the active side of the body.

Kelal (Heb., 'surround, include'). A summary in rabbinic Judaism of the essential meaning of *Torah, or of a series of halakoth in the *Mishnah. One of the ideals in teaching is to follow *derek qezarah*, the short(est) way. Rabbis, therefore, used to search for a statement, preferably a verse from Torah, which would summarize the purpose and meaning of the covenant. Thus *Aqiba called Leviticus 19. 18 'the great kelal in Torah'; Simeon b. Azzai identified Genesis 5. 1. Perhaps the best known examples are those of *Hillel ('Whatever you would not have people do to you, do not do to them') and of *Jesus (combining Deuteronomy 6. 4 f. and Leviticus 19. 18, in Mark 12. 28 ff.; cf. Matthew 7. 12, Luke 6. 31 for the Golden Rule in positive form).

Kelal Yisrael (Heb., 'the whole Jewish community'). The kinship of the Jewish community. The *rabbis taught that 'All *Israel are sureties for one another' (*B.Shev.* 39a). It was believed that all *Jews, including *proselytes, were present when the *covenant was given on Mount *Sinai (*B.Shev.* 39a), and the whole community was personified in the notion of *Keneset Yisrael.

Kemal, Mustafa: see OTTOMAN EMPIRE.

Kempe, Margery (*c.*1373–after 1433). Author of the *Book of Margery Kempe*. Born in Lynn, Norfolk, she married young and had fourteen children, but was increasingly drawn to a deeper religious experience. In 1413 she and her husband took vows of chastity. Sharply critical of contemporary religious corruption, she went on *pilgrimage to Canterbury, the Holy Land, Compostela, and Norway, and also visited *Julian of Norwich. Her life, as revealed in her *Book*, became one of an imaginatively close relationship to Christ, her heavenly spouse, expressed in visions and highly emotional (some say disordered) devotion, and also in auditions:

> [She heard] a sort of sound as if it were a pair of bellows blowing in her ear: it was the sound of the Holy Ghost. And then our Lord turned that sound into the voice of a little bird which is called a red-breast, that sang full merrily in her right ear. And then she would ever have great grace after she heard such a token.

C. W. Atkinson, *Mystic and Pilgrim: The Book and the World of Margery Kempe* (1983).

Kempis: see THOMAS À KEMPIS.

Kena Upaniṣad also ***Talavakāra Upaniṣad.*** One of the thirteen principal *Upaniṣads, belonging to the **Sāma Veda*. It deals with the longing of all living beings to transcend reason and become one with *Brahman, and it speaks of the way in which Brahman cannot be attained by reason. For trs., see UPANIṢADS.

Kencho-ji (monastery): see KAMAKURA.

Kendo (Jap., 'way of the sword'). The Zen way of attaining mastery over emotions, by sword-play and fencing.

Keneset Yisrael (Heb., 'the community of Israel'). The totality of the Jewish community. In *aggadic literature, 'Keneset Yisrael' is used as the personification of the Jewish people in the dialogue with God. The term was also used by the Jewish community in *Erez Israel to describe itself between 1927 and 1948. The Keneset subsequently became the name for the Israeli parliament. Solomon *Schechter proposed the use of the term, translated as 'Catholic Israel', to pick out those elements on which the consensus of the Jewish people is agreed, as a kind of ecumenical rapprochement between the different kinds of Judaism which were developing in his time.

Kengyō (exoteric Buddhist teaching): see MIKKYŌ.

Kenite. A nomadic Middle Eastern tribe. The book of *Genesis lists the Kenites as one of the early tribes of *Canaan. Some scholars have maintained that the theology of *Moses was influenced by the Kenites through his father-in-law Jethro, and that this is the origin of the innovation of the god *Yahweh; this is the Kenite hypothesis.

Kenko, Yoshida (i.e., Yoshida Kenko): see YOSHIDA FAMILY.

Kenosis, kenotic theories. In Christian theology, formulas which seek to explain the *incarnation in terms of *Christ's self-'emptying' (Gk., *kenōsis*). The starting-point is Philippians 2. 5–11, though some scholars consider that the reference here is to *Jesus' death (cf. Isaiah 53. 12) rather than his becoming man. Kenotic *christologies first appeared at the Reformation (although the word *kenōsis* appears in the *patristic period), but became current in the 19th cent. as a way of understanding how Jesus could have shared the limitations of human beings while remaining the omniscient, omnipotent Son of God. The kenotic answer was: 'Remaining in unchanged personality, He abandoned certain prerogatives of the divine mode of existence, in order to assume the human' (C. Gore). The adequacy of kenosis to explain Jesus' human personality is doubtful, in the sense that any 'explanation' of a unique event is bound to be inadequate; but the kenotic emphasis on the reality of the human experiences of Jesus (his suffering, his temptations, his single, as opposed to double, consciousness) has persisted, and has affected the discussion of God's *impassibility. More broadly, however, the idea attaches to God; thus, 'God himself goes out of himself, God in his quality of the fulness which gives away itself' (K. *Rahner).

P. Dawe, *The Form of a Servant* . . . (1963); R. P. Martin, *Carmen Christi: Philippians 2. 5–11 in Recent Interpretation* (rev. edn., 1983).

Kensho (Jap., 'seeing nature'). The Zen experience of enlightenment, when one's own nature is seen for what it truly is, not to be differentiated from the buddha-nature which pervades all appearance. It is thus indistinguishable from *satori, but the latter is used of the experience of the *Buddha or of the Zen patriarchs, kensho of the initial experience of others which still needs to be deepened. The term also applies collectively to those who have attained this state, the wise.

Kenshō jōbutsu (realization of buddha-nature): see FUKASETSU.

Kensui (Jap., 'hammer and tongs'). The rigorous element in Zen training, the 'short, sharp, shock', much associated with *kōan method.

Kentan (Jap., 'looking at the *tan'). The morning survey by a Zen master of his pupils, to perceive their state of mind.

Kerbala (site of death of *al-Ḥusain): see KARBALĀ'.

Keriah. The rending of garments among the Jews as a sign of mourning. Keriah is a traditional Jewish response to grief. At the death of parent, child, sibling, or spouse, a tear is made in the lapel of an outer garment before the funeral takes place. The custom is based on Genesis 37. 34 and Job 1. 20.

Kerovah (pl. Ḳerovot). Jewish *piyyutim recited as part of the *'Amidah prayer. The kerovah recited in the morning service 'Amidah is known as the *kedushta*, while that said at the afternoon service is called the *shivata*. The piyyutim vary according to the week or the theme of the *festival.

Kerygma (Gk., 'preaching'). The basic Christian message of salvation through the death and resurrection of *Jesus, especially as preached by the earliest apostles (Acts 2. 14–39, 1 Corinthians 15. 3–11). It is contrasted to *didachē, 'instruction'. C. H. Dodd (*The Apostolic Preaching*, 1936) argued for an early kerygma underlying the diverse forms of the New Testament; but anything resembling an early *creed is unlikely. R. *Bultmann regarded the whole New Testament as kerygmatic, thus making futile a *quest for the historical Jesus as distinct from the *Christ of faith.

H. W. Bartsch (ed.), *Kerygma and Myth* (1953, 1962).

Keś (uncut *hair): see FIVE KS.

Keśadhārī (Pañjābī, 'one who keeps long *hair'). Sikh whose hair (and beard) are uncut. One of the *Five ks is the uncut hair (*keś*). See also AMRITDHĀRĪ; TURBAN.

Keshub Chandra Sen: see SEN, KESHUB.

Keśin (Skt., 'long-haired'). Solitary *ascetics in early Indian religion, as in *Ṛg Veda* 10. 136. They removed themselves from society, and were thus forerunners of the *śrāmaṇas, and important precursors of the ascetic emphasis among Jains.

Keswick Convention. An annual conference of *evangelical Christians. It began in 1875 with the conferences at Broadlands and Brighton. Its transference to the Lake District was due to the initiative of Canon T. D. Harford Battersby, vicar of St John's, Keswick. Although the full verbatim account of each convention is no longer published, a book containing the main Bible studies and selected addresses is edited annually, copies being sent to missionaries all over the world. 'Keswick' conferences may take place in other centres but will still have the purpose of trying to unify evangelical groups and teaching.

Ketav Rabbunat (letter of appointment): see RABBI.

Ket(h)er Malekuth (Heb., 'crown of royalty'). The mark of sovereignty of the Hebrew God. God's sovereignty is recognized by both humans and *angels in worship. *Kether malekuth* is also the name of Solomon ibn *Gabirol's poem which is recited after the evening service on the *Day of Atonement.

Ket(h)er Torah (Heb., 'crown of Torah'). Jewish metaphor for learning. According to *Avot* 4. 17: 'There are three crowns: the crown of Torah, of priesthood and of royalty, but the crown of a good name exceeds them all.' The term also refers to the ornament used to 'crown' the *Torah scroll in synagogues.

Ketubbah. Jewish *marriage document. The ketubbah sets out the financial obligations of the husband towards the wife. According to the Jewish law, a bridegroom may not cohabit with his wife until she has been given the ketubbah (*Sh. Ar.* EH 66). The document is intended to protect the wife 'so that he shall not regard it as easy to divorce her' (*B.Ket.* 11a); in the event of a divorce, it is stated that the woman will be given a certain amount of money. Many ketubbot are richly decorated and are works of art.

Kevala (Skt.). 1. In Jainism, the kevala(-*jñāna), the absolute knowledge of isolation, the attribute of a *kevalin. Kevala refers to the state of isolation of the *jīva from the *ajīva, attained through ascetic practices which burn off one's *karma residues, releasing one from bondage to the cycle of death and rebirth.

2. In *Sāṁkhya-Yoga, an adjective meaning both 'isolated, exclusive, pure, uncompounded' and 'whole, entire, absolute, and perfect', referring to the state of *kāivalya and one who has attained it.

Kevalin (Skt.). 1. In Jainism, a saint or *tīrthaṅkara, one possessing the *kevala(-*jñāna), an *arhat. The kevalin, having become cleansed of *karma-matter, and detached from bondage, ascends in complete isolation to the top of the universe, where he is omniscient and all-pervading. The kevalin, relieved of individualizing features, is absolutely separate from other beings yet absolutely unlimited and complete.

2. In the Hindu **Bhāgavata-purāṇa*, a meditative ascetic devoted to the doctrine of the unity of *ātman and *brahman.

Ke-yi. Matching the meanings, a reference to the practice of Chinese Buddhist translators who matched Buddhist technical terms with Chinese concepts so as to render the foreign ideas more easily understood by the Chinese. It was used extensively during the 4th cent. CE, when Buddhist philosophical texts were being translated into Chinese.

Khadīja. The first wife of *Muḥammad, and acknowledged as the first to believe in his message. She was a rich widow in *Mecca, who employed the young Muḥammad for several trading journeys, and subsequently married him, at which time it is said that she was about 40 and he 25. She bore him four female children, including *Fāṭima, and perhaps two sons, who, however, did not survive. When Muḥammad began to receive the messages of the *Qur'ān, Khadīja supported him, herself encouraged by a Christian cousin of hers, called Waraqa, to believe that Muḥammad was receiving a call like that of former *prophets. Until her death, possibly in the year 619 CE Muḥammad took no other wives. The *ḥadīth inform us that Muḥammad declared her to be one of the four best women of Paradise, along with Maryam, Fāṭima, and the wife of Pharaoh.

Khafd (female circumcision): see CIRCUMCISION.

Khajurāho. Group of eighty-five temples in Madhya Pradesh, built from about 850–1150, dedicated to both Hindu and Jain devotions. They cover about 8 square miles, and are notable for the graphic representation of *maithuna.

U. Agarwal, *Khajurāho Sculptures* . . . (1964).

Khalīfa (Arab., *khalafa*, 'succeed'). A successor or representative, often transliterated as 'Caliph'.

1. In the Qur'ān, frequently used of those who enter into the blessings enjoyed by their ancestors (e.g. 6. 165; 24. 55; 27. 62); and specifically of *Adam as khalīfat *Allāh on earth (2. 20).

2. The successor(s) of the Prophet *Muḥammad. When Muḥammad died, he had given no clear indication of his successor, beyond appointing *Abu Bakr to lead the *ṣalāt. Existing custom was to have hereditary leadership for general purposes, but designated leadership (i.e. of the man picked out by qualities) in crises or opportunities for action. Both methods were advocated by different groups among early Muslims, leading to the radical split between *Sunni and *Shī'a Muslims. Initially, the latter (designated leadership) prevailed, and the first three Khulafā' were Abu Bakr, *'Umar, and *'Uthmān. But those who espoused the former (hereditary), thought that *'Alī, Muḥammad's nearest male relative, should have succeeded. His claim prevailed briefly, and he was the fourth caliph; but other dynasties, 'Umayyad (661–750 CE), then 'Abbasid (750–1517) were established, and the Shī'a became minorities with their own rulers and successions (see IMĀM). On occasion, a Shi'ite caliphate could rival that of the Sunnis, as with the Fāṭimids in Egypt. The first four khulafā' are known as arRāshidūn, the upright or rightly guided. The Caliphate was assumed by the Ottoman Turkish rulers (sultāns) as a title, and it was abolished in the secularizing reforms of Kemal Atatürk in 1924. The Khalīfa is technically regarded as a necessary component of the Islamic state, and its absence is one reason why no Muslim state exists today, even though there are countries with Muslim majorities, ruled under Islamic law; in practice, there is little sign of any desire to return to the Caliphate.

For individual caliphs, see Index, Caliphs.

T. W. Arnold, *The Caliphate* (2nd edn., introd. S. G. Haim, 1965).

Khālistān ('the land where the *khālsā rules', or 'the land of the pure'). The name given to the territory which some Sikhs would like to see established as a Sikh homeland—either as an independent state, or as an autonomous province. There has been no agreement on its nature or extent. In some estimates, it would be greater than the present Pañjāb, and would include an outlet to the Indian Ocean.

Khālsā (Arab., 'khālis', 'pure'). Body of initiated Sikhs; also any true Sikh. The term denoted land in the Mughal emperor's direct possession, as opposed to lands owned by his lords. So, even before the time of Gurū *Gobind Siṅgh, khālsā could refer to groups of Sikhs whose loyalty was to the Gurū rather than to his *masands. However, according to tradition, the khālsā was instituted by Gobind Siṅgh on *Baisākhī (30 Mar.) 1699 CE, when the Gurū administered *khaṇḍe-dī-pāhul to the *pañj pyāre, followed by thousands more. He then enunciated a code of discipline (*rahit) to which all khālsā Sikhs must adhere. The khālsā was to be a casteless body of *Siṅghs and *Kaurs, outwardly distinguishable by the *five Ks. Khālsā Sikhs must be brave in battle and protect the needy. They must not commit adultery and must observe rules akin to those currently set down in the Rahit Maryādā. They must not worship Hindu deities, cemeteries, or cremation grounds, or go on *pilgrimage. They must refrain from *alcohol, *tobacco, narcotics, and halāl meat. Khālsā Sikhs must rise early, bathe, read the prescribed *hymns of the Gurūs (i.e. *nitnem) and meditate on the *Nām (name) of the one God.

Gobind Siṅgh declared that all who in future accepted this God-given form of initiation would be known as 'khālsa': 'Wherever there are five Sikhs assembled who abide by the guru's teaching, know that I am in the midst of them: henceforth, the guru is the khālsā and the khālsā is the guru.' Thus the Gurū was embodied in his khālsā, although subsequently the Gurūship of the *Ādi Granth has taken precedence, with the khālsā upholding the unique Gurūship of the scriptures.

Following the death of Gurū Gobind Siṅgh, the khālsā struggled militarily for survival. As an assembly (*sarbat khālsā*) it appointed *jathedārs* (leaders of *jathās) and passed *gurmatās. Later the Dal Khālsā (khālsā army) was divided into *misls. With Mahārājā *Rañjīt Siṅgh's reign came the nearest realization of khālsā rule. His court was the *darbār khālsājī*. In the late 19th cent. *Nāmdhārīs and *Akālīs reasserted the khālsā ideals which were challenged by moral degeneracy, Christian mission, and the

*Ārya Samāj. The khālsā remain the guardians of orthodox Sikh principles.

Khamr (Arab., 'fermented drink, wine'). Intoxicants forbidden (*haram) in Islam. In Qur'ān 5. 90–1/93–4, wine is linked with gambling and divination with arrows as an abominable creation of Satan. Khamr was extended by *Muḥammad to include every intoxicant (not just wine), and trading in khamr is forbidden, as is its exchange as a gift. Even assemblies at which khamr is consumed are forbidden. It cannot be taken for medicinal purposes: 'Allāh has sent down the disease and the cure, and for every disease there is a cure. So take medicine, but do not use anything which is haram as a medicine.' According to *'Umar, 'khamr is anything which confuses the mind', and on that principle, drugs are equally haram. It has been debated whether *tobacco is haram, but this is more in the category of the ban on ingesting anything which might harm health (2. 195; 4. 29): if it was proved that tobacco is always harmful, it would be prohibited; and many Muslims already regard it as in that category. In contrast, 47. 15/16 states that in the *Garden are 'rivers of wine, a joy to those who drink'. But in the Garden, those who are safe are beyond being diverted from their adoration of God. See also ALCOHOL; OMAR KHAYYAM.

Khanaqah (assembly place of derwishes; Fitzgerald's tavern): see OMAR KHAYYAM.

Khanḍ (Pañjābī, 'domain'). Stages of spiritual progress for a Sikh who is moving from *manmukh to *gurmukh: see SIKHISM.

Khanḍā (Pañjābī, 'sword'). Sikh symbol, two-edged sword. On *Baisākhī day 1699, Gurū *Gobind Siṅgh used a khanḍā to stir the baptismal water with which he initiated the *pañj pyāre, so instituting the *khālsā. The khanḍā is still used in this way in the *khanḍe-di-pāhul ceremony. The khanḍā, bisecting a circle (*chakkar*) and flanked by two kirpāns, symbolizes the khālsā, and appears on the *Niśān Sāhib.

Khandaka (division of Vinaya Piṭaka): see TRIPIṬAKA.

Khāṇḍava. In the **Mahābhārata*, the name of a forested tract of land given by *Dhṛtarāṣṭra to the *Pāṇḍavas; here the Pāṇḍavas built their splendid capital, Indraprastha. An important episode in the first book of the *Mahābhārata* is the burning down of the Khāṇḍava forest (against the wishes of its protector, *Indra) by *Agni, aided by *Arjuna and *Kṛṣṇa. An initiatory test for Arjuna, the burning of the Khāṇḍava forest is frequently cited later in the epic as proof of his outstanding heroism.

Khanḍe-dī-pāhul (Pañjābī, 'sword initiation'). Sikh incorporation or initiation ceremony. On *Baisākhī day 1699 (according to tradition), Gurū *Gobind Siṅgh instituted khanḍe-dī-pāhul or initiation by the double-edged sword (*khanḍā) to replace *charan pāhul. When the original *pañj pyāre had volunteered their lives, Gobind Siṅgh stirred water with a khanḍā in an iron bowl, while reciting certain prayers (see below). His wife added *patāse* (sugar sweets). The Gurū then gave each of the pañj pyāre in turn five palmfuls of the *amrit (sweetened water) to drink and sprinkled it five times in their eyes and on their hair. Each time the initiate repeated, '*Vāhigurū jī kā *khālsā; vāhigurū jī kī *fateh'. The Gurū himself then received amrit from them in the same manner. He gave them and himself the new surname Siṅgh (lion) and instructed them as his khālsā to maintain the *five Ks and observe certain rules and prohibitions.

Sikhs who wish to follow their faith more strictly, those who have lapsed since taking amrit, and those adopting Sikhism are still initiated in this way by the pañj pyāre. The candidates should have bathed and must wear the five Ks. Women often wear white and the men do not cover their *kachh* (drawers). Although children sometimes receive amrit, initiates are usually over 14 years of age. They must intend to keep the principles of the Sikh faith. Few apart from those involved may enter the hall where the ceremony is taking place.

The pañj pyāre kneel in a posture of military preparedness (i.e. with left knee raised) around a *bāṭā* (shallow iron bowl) filled with water and set on a pedestal. To make the amrit they add sugar or patāse, and each stirs in turn with a khanḍā while reciting the *Japjī, *Jāp, *Savayye, *Chaupaī, and *Anand. The *bāṭā* is lifted and the initiates are called by one of the pañj pyāre holding up a long sword. In succession the candidates receive amrit just as the first initiates received it from Gurū Gobind Siṅgh. Then each drinks the remaining amrit from the *bāṭā* in reverse order, demonstrating the equality of all.

The pañj pyāre and initiates next repeat the *Mul mantra five times. The senior member of the pañj pyāre bids them keep the five Ks, avoid haircutting, halāl meat, *adultery, and *tobacco, taking *alcohol or drugs. Those who receive amrit after a lapse must accept a *taṅkhāh (penalty). Initiates may take a new name. The khanḍe-dī-pāhul ceremony concludes with *Ardās, a *hukam, and the distribution of kaṛāh praśād. See also PATIT; RAHIT.

Khandha (aggregates of human composition): see SKANDHA.

Khaṇḍobā, Mallāri, Malhāri, Mārtaṇḍa, etc. A regional Hindu god, mainly worshipped in Mahārāṣtra and Karṇāṭaka. His central shrine is the hill-temple of Jejurī (near Puṇe), but there are many other temples scattered over the whole area. His worship is performed by non-*brahman priests (*guruvas*), and his devotees also are predominantly non-brahman. As a characteristic feature, the rites involve the lavish scattering of turmeric powder (Marāṭhī, *bhanḍār*). Traditionally children were dedicated to the god: the *vāghyas* (male) and *muraḷīs* (female). These act as religious folk-artists (and artistes) who sing, dance, and perform miniature plays in honour of the god, particularly during *jāghraṇs* in the houses of wealthier devotees on festive occasions. States of possession and feats of supernatural strength are demonstrated by the *vāghyas* on such occasions, while the *muraḷīs* act as 'dancing-girls'. Although institutionally and socially well defined in Mahārāṣṭra and Karṇāṭaka, the religion of Khaṇḍobā can be associated with other phenomena in two different ways. Quite apart from the fact that his name itself alludes to *Skanda, only minor and probably secondary features distinguish him, riding on a horse armed with sword and shield, from the similar figures of Pāpujī in Rājasthān or Aiyaṉār in Tamilnadu. We may well be dealing here with an ancient archetype, typical of W. India. On the other hand, there are many indications that today Khaṇḍobā is brought increasingly close to *Śiva. In Jejurī he is shown wielding a trident, and local temple legends make him into an *avatāra of Śiva, or even Śiva himself.

Kharatara Gaccha: see DĀDĀ GURŪS.

Kharijites (Arab., *kharaja*, 'go out'). Early schismatics in the Muslim community (*'umma). The details of their origin are obscure, but are connected by Muslim historians with the arbitration at the battle of Siffīn (see ʿALĪ B. ABĪ TĀLIB). Protesting that 'judgement belongs to God alone' (*lā ḥukma illā li-'llāhi*), they rejected both ʿAlī and *Muʿawīyya, and began a fierce and often brutal rebellion. Defeated by ʿAlī at Nahrawān in 658 (AH 38), they nevertheless persisted into the *ʿAbbāsid caliphate (and down to the present day as the ʿIbādiyya, a religious movement). Holding a strict view that a Muslim who sins grievously has become *murtadd (apostate), they reject all (so-called) caliphs (*khalīfa) except *Abu Bakr and *ʿUmar (and the first six years of *ʿUthmān), and believe that any Muslim recognized as irreproachable can become Imām, known as *Amīr al-Mu'minīn*, 'Leader of the Faithful'.

Khatm al-anbiyya/al-wilāyah: see SEAL OF THE PROPHETS.

Khatrī (cognate, 'Kshatriya'). A Pañjābī *zāt* (*caste). Gurū *Nānak was born to a Hindu Khatrī family and married a Khatrī wife according to caste practice. His nine successors and their wives were also Khatrī. Within a *zāt* are exogamous subdivisions called *gots*. Gurū Nānak, of the Bedī *got*, married a Choṇā. Gurū *Aṅgad was a Trehaṇ, Gurū *Amar Dās a Bhallā, and his daughter married a *Soḍhī, subsequently Gurū *Rām Dās. All succeeding Gurūs were of this Soḍhī line. From *Bhāī *Gurdās we see the early dominance of Khatrī Sikhs in the *Panth. The *masands were Khatrī, but Bhāī Dayā Rām was the only Khatrī among Gurū *Gobind Siṅgh's *pañj pyāre in 1699 CE. In traditional caste ranking the essentially urban, trading Khatrī is of superior status to the *Jaṭ. Despite the Jaṭs' later numerical superiority and influence on the Panth, respect is accorded to Khatrī Sikhs because of the Gurūs' Khatrī status. Khatrīs have contributed significantly to Sikh literature and reform movements. Many Khatrī Sikhs are *sahajdhārī, and *marriage with Hindu Khatrīs is common.

Khazars. National group, originally of S. Russia, who professed Judaism. The Khazars were an independent nation of E. Europe between the 7th and 10th cents. CE. They converted to Judaism *c.*740 CE, and in the 10th cent., Hasdai ibn Shaprut supposedly conducted a correspondence in Hebrew with the Khazar king, Joseph. The authenticity of these letters is much debated. The nation disappeared by the 11th cent., but as late as 1309, Hungarian Roman Catholics were forbidden to marry people described as Khazars. See also JUDAH HALEVI, who took the story of the conversion as the framework for his exposition of Judaism in *Sefer ha-Kuzari*.

Khemā (5th cent. BCE). The perfect or model Buddhist bhikhṣuni (nun; see BHIKHṢU) according to the Buddha. She was a queen of Bimbisāra, of great beauty; but through the Buddha's teaching, she realized the transience of the body and achieved the condition of *arhat. She became a wise teacher herself, giving answers to questions posed by the king Pasenadi which turned out to be identical to the Buddha's own answers when he was asked the same questions.

Khenpo (abbr. for *mkhan-po*): see ABBOT.

Khiḍr. In Islam, the mystical guide. He is at once human and angelic, mundane and celestial. Authorities such as *al-Tabarī and al-Nawawī consider him immortal. He is associated with the colour green, the highest of colours in Islamic cosmology. The starting-point for traditions about Khiḍr is the account in the Qur'ān (18. 60–82), in which the prophet *Moses meets Khiḍr and they set out on a journey. Khiḍr does many apparently absurd things that shock Moses into losing patience and demanding an explanation, whereupon Khiḍr replies, 'Did I not tell you that you would be lacking in patience with me?' He explains his actions, thereupon revealing his superior wisdom over Moses, and then departs. According to the *Sūfīs, Khiḍr is the immortal guide possessing wisdom and powers beyond human understanding. He can manifest himself at many places at the same time, become invisible at will, and fly through the air.

Khirqa (Arab., 'rag'). A distinctive woollen or sheepskin garment worn by the *Sūfīs. It is conferred by the spiritual guide in token of his approval for an initiate to enter the mystic path. It may take any form which serves to symbolize the Sūfī rejection of conventional dress. Many of the early Sūfīs, such as al-Hujwiri, objected to the khirqa on the grounds that 'it is the inner flame which makes the Sūfī, not the religious dress'. Others felt it useless, for only God knows what is best contained under the garment. Another school of thought said it was a symbol of ostentation, pretence, and hypocrisy. But in spite of influential censure, the khirqa came into general usage among the Sūfī orders as part of an investiture ceremony by the 10th cent.

Khitan (male circumcision): see CIRCUMCISION.

Khoja (Nizaris in India): see ISMAʿĪLĪYA.

Khomeini, Ayatollah (Shiʿite leader): see KHUMAYNI, RUḤ ALLAH.

Khomiakov, Alexis Stepanovich (1804–60). Russian lay theologian. Born in Moscow into a devout *Orthodox family, he studied literature and mathematics, and later art, after abortive attempts at a military career. He was at the centre of the Slavophil movement and was very influential, though his writings are mainly occasional. He saw the Orthodox Church as preserving the truest form of Christianity, finding its unity in *sobornost', a togetherness brought about in the Church by the *Holy Spirit, deeper than the authoritarian unity of the *Papacy or the individualist fragmentation of the *Protestants.

P. K. Christoff, *An Introduction to 19th Century Russian Slavophilism*, i. *A. S. Xomjakov* (1961).

Khrafstras (evil agents): see ANGRA MAINYU.

Khsathra (one of the Holy Immortals): see AMESA SPENTAS.

Khuddaka-nikāya (Pāli, 'short collection'). The fifth part of the Sutta-, or Sūtra-piṭaka, in the Buddhist Pāli *canon, containing fifteen 'short' sections: (i) *Khuddaka-pātha*, rules for ceremonies, etc.; (ii) **Dhammapada*, 426 verses on basic teaching; (iii) *Udāna*, 80 sayings of the *Buddha; (iv) *Itivuttaka*, on moral questions; (v) *Sutta-nipāta*; (vi) *Vimānavatthu*, 83 legends of devas to show how to attain reappearance as a *deva; (vii) *Petavatthu*, on reappearance as a hungry ghost; (viii) *Thera-gāthā*, 107 songs (*gāthā*) ascribed to the monks of old; (ix) *Therī-gāthā*, 73 ascribed to nuns of old; (x) *Jātaka*; (xi) *Niddesa*, commentary on (v); (xii) *Patisambhidāmagga*, analysis of philosophical issues; (xiii) *Apadāna*, stories of renowned monks and nuns in previous appearances; (xiv) *Buddhavamsa*, stories of previous Buddhas; (xv) *Cariya-piṭaka*, *jātaka stories showing how the Buddha reached the ten perfections (*pāramitā).

Eng. trs.: (i) Nanamoli (1960); (ii) C. A. F. Rhys Davids (1931); Rockhill (1892); (iii) Woodward (1935); (iv) Woodward (1935); parts of (v) Chalmers (1932); (vi and vii) Kennedy and Gehman (1942); (viii and ix) C. A. F. Rhys Davids (1909, 1913); (x) Cowell, Chalmers, *et al.* (1895–1907); (xii) Nanamoli (1971); (xiii) Feer (1891); (xiv) Law (1938); (xv) Law (1938).

Khulʿ (divorce initiated by woman): see MARRIAGE AND DIVORCE (ISLAM).

Khumayni, Ruḥ Allah (1902–89). Religious leader among *Ithna ʿAshariyya (Twelver) Shiʿite Muslims, and figurehead of the Islamic Revolution in Iran. He was born in Khumayn and followed a path of Islamic education in various centres including *Qom. He became both mujtāhid and *ayatollah. His first book, *Kashf al-Asrar* (The Unveiling of Secrets) was critical of the Pahlavi regime but in a comparatively muted style. The deaths of two ayatollahs in 1961 (Burujirdi) and 1962 (Abu'l Qasim Kashani) left him in an elevated position, and almost at once he dropped their quietist policies and began to oppose the so-called White Revolution in agriculture, which the Shah had initiated. He was briefly arrested, and on his release continued to oppose the government, especially for its links with the USA and (he claimed) with Israel. In 1964 he was exiled, settling until 1978 in Najaf, in Iraq, when he was again expelled, settling this time in France. Throughout this period he organized and sustained opposition to the regime, particularly through powerful speeches recorded on tape. His basic argument was consistently that Islam cannot be isolated from the whole of life—i.e. it cannot be relegated to 'the religious': it is to be applied to every aspect of life. He returned to Iran in triumph on 1 Feb. 1979, after the flight of the Shah. He assumed the position of leader of the revolution, a position formalized in the new constitution of the following Nov., and the Islamic Revolution had begun. His strong understanding of authority has deep roots in the Shiʿa understanding of the *Imām, and Khumayni pressed into new territory in his exercise of his powers (see AYATOLLAH). Despite the failures of the war with Iraq and his own disappointment at the ceasefire, his popularity remained to the end; and his *fatwā against Salman Rushdie and his book, *The Satanic Verses*, was accepted widely in the Muslim world.

A. Taheri, *The Spirit of Allah* . . . (1985).

Khurasani Sufism: see SŪFĪS.

Khuṭba (Arab., *khataba*, 'preach'). Sermon delivered in the *mosque during the Muslim weekly assembly (*jumʿa), in celebration of the two festivals (*ʿĪd), and on other special occasions. The *khātib* ('preacher') usually preaches in Arabic, and the sermon (or two sermons in the case of the jumʿa) precedes the *ṣalāt.

Khwāja Bāqī Bi'llah (Naqshbandi Shaykh): see AḤMAD SIRHINDĪ.

Khwarr (destiny): see FRAVASI.

Ki (Jap., 'potential'). One who is potentially able to receive the *Buddha's teaching; or to become a *bodhisattva or buddha; hence, 'a human being'.

Kibbutz. Voluntary agricultural collective in *Erez Israel. The first kibbutz to be founded was En Harol in 1921, and the founding of kibbutzim (pl.) has had an important part in the pioneering settlement of the land. Kibbutzim are run democratically, directed by a weekly general meeting and, in most cases, all assets are held in common. Different kibbutzim have different traditions and ideologies. Traditionally children lived apart from their parents in special houses, but this is now changing. The number of kibbutz members among army officers and in the Knesset is far above their proportion in the country at large.

B. Bettelheim, *The Children of the Dream* (1969); A. Fishman, *Judaism and Modernization on the Religious Kibbutz*; H. Near, *The Kibbutz Movement, Origin and Growth, 1909–39* (1992).

Kibbutz galuyyot: see GALUT.

Kiddush (Heb., 'sanctification'). *Prayer recited over a cup of wine to sanctify the *Sabbath or *festivals. It is forbidden to eat on a Sabbath or festival until the Kiddush has been recited. The prayer consists of an introductory paragraph from the book of Genesis (1. 31 and 2. 1–3), a *blessing over wine, and a blessing for the day. The custom has also evolved of reciting it at the end of *synagogue Sabbath evening services. In modern times, particularly in *progressive synagogues, a kiddush is recited after the Saturday morning service as part of a social hour. See also HAVDALAH.

Kiddush ha-Shem (Heb., 'sanctification of the divine name'). The glorification of the God of Israel, especially by remaining steadfast in faith. According to Leviticus 22. 32, the Israelites are commanded not to profane God's name: 'I will be hallowed among the Children of Israel; I am the Lord who hallows you.' The *rabbis taught that God's name could be sanctified in three specific ways: *prayer, excellent conduct, and *martyrdom. Prayer involved the readiness to accept martyrdom. When reciting the *Shemaʿ, a person should spiritually be offering himself for Kiddush ha-Shem. Excellent conduct sanctifies God's name, particularly when it provides an ethical example to the *gentiles. An example of such sanctification is Simeon b. Sheṭaḥ discovering a jewel hanging from the neck of a donkey he had bought from an Arab and immediately returning it. Martyrdom has always been seen as the ultimate expression of Kiddush ha-Shem. Martyrdom in the Jewish tradition is obligatory, rather than break the laws of *idolatry, unchastity, or murder. The history of Jewish martyrs goes back to the *Hellenistic era and includes persecution under the Romans (see AKIVA; ZEALOTS), in Christian Europe (see ANTISEMITISM), in E. European pogroms, and in the *Holocaust. The opposite is ḥillul ha-Shem, 'desecration of the Name', which involves consideration of how an action will be regarded in the gentile world. It includes the offence of erasing God's name following Deuteronomy 12. 3 f.). See Index, Martyrs (Jewish).

Kidō Chigu: see HSÜ-T'ANG CHIH-YÜ.

Kie (Jap. 'take refuge in'). The basic move of faith in Japanese Buddhism. It extends beyond *dharma (see THREE JEWELS), and may be a commitment to a teacher, *bodhisattva, etc.

Kierkegaard, Søren (1813–55). Denmark's best-known and widely influential contributor to modern religious thought. He studied under Hans Martensen (1808–84) at Copenhagen and, at first with enthusiasm and then with disappointment, heard Friedrich Schelling (1775–1854) lecture at Berlin. Schelling was a German idealist philosopher of wide interests who saw nature as a system with purpose (in which the Absolute realizes itself objectively) and history as a drama in which human freedom operates (and in which the Absolute reveals itself, especially in moral order translated into the rule of law). Kierkegaard had a troubled and guilt-ridden youth, which he managed to cope with in part through his highly imaginative literary productions, some of which were written under pseudonyms, and many of which show an acute awareness of the depths of the human psyche. For his psychological and philosophical writings he is widely regarded as the father of *existentialism. A prolific and playfully elusive writer, Kierkegaard indicates in *The Point of View for my Work as an Author* that all his work is dominated by the single issue of how to become a Christian in Christendom, where one automatically assumes oneself to be a good Christian if one is simply a good citizen. In all his writings on the topic, Kierkegaard stressed that to become a (true) Christian entails personal decision and individual commitment, born of risk in the face of 'objective uncertainty'. He attacked the idea of Christendom at first indirectly and then, in the last year or so of his life, increasingly directly and publicly. The centre of his own thought is regarded by many as his subtle analysis of the various modes of human existence or 'stages on life's way', which he termed the 'aesthetic', the 'ethical' and the 'religious', the last of which can be reached only by an extraordinary act of will, 'a leap of faith'. The 'stages' can be seen, from one point of view, as Kierkegaard's attempt to counter (dialectically) the *Hegelian dialectic, which he held to be untrue to the human condition ('I argue from existence, not to existence') and antithetical to Christian faith and its paradoxical foundation in *Christology.

J. Collins, *The Mind of Kierkegaard* (1965); L. Dupre, *Kierkegaard as Theologian* (1963); J. W. Elrod, *Kierkegaard and Christendom* (1981); G. Malantschuk, *Kierkegaard's Thought* (1963); P. Sponheim, *Kierkegaard on Christ ...* (1968); J. Walker, *To Will One Thing* (1972).

Kigen Kikō (Zen style of teaching): see MA-TSU.

Kikan-Kōan: see KŌAN.

Kilesa, Kleśa (Pāli, Skt., 'defilement'). In Buddhist doctrine, moral and intellectual faults. Triumph over the class of kilesas concerned with the intellectual side of human beings does not ensure triumph over those which refer to the emotions and passions, and vice versa. The former are expelled by insight (*vipassanā) and the latter by calm (*samatha). There is no formal list in the Suttas but the *Abhidharma lists ten: greed (*lobha), ill will (*dosa), delusion (*moha), conceit (*māna), speculative views (*diṭṭhi), sceptical doubt (vicikicchā), mental torpor (thīna), restlessness (uddhacca), lack of shame (ahirika), and lack of moral dread (anottappa).

Kill the Buddha: see LIN-CHI I-HSÜAN.

Kimbangu, Simon: see KIMBANGUISM.

Kimbanguism. The largest independent Christian movement in Black Africa. It derives from Simon Kimbangu (1889–1951), a *Baptist mission catechist, whose preaching and healing in the lower Congo started a mass movement in 1921. His subsequent death-sentence for alleged sedition was commuted to life imprisonment, after British Baptist missionaries had appealed to the Belgian king. The new movement continued underground, despite mass deportations by the colonial government. In 1957 it secured toleration and in 1959 legal recognition as Église de Jésus-Christ sur la Terre par le Prophète Simon Kimbangu (EJCSK, The Church of Jesus Christ through the Prophet Simon Kimbangu), under the leadership of Kimbangu's son, Joseph Diangienda (b. 1918). N'kamba, Kimbangu's birthplace and final burial place, is a pilgrimage centre and a 'New Jerusalem', and has a higher level theological college, largely staffed by sympathetic expatriates. There are about three million members and many branches in several Central African countries and in Europe; in 1969 the Church was the first of its kind to join the World Council of Churches. Its worship is non-*Pentecostal and Baptist in form (but without water baptism), and it rejects polygamy, alcohol, tobacco, dancing, magic, and violence. Its many social and modernizing activities include education, healing, agriculture, and co-operatives. There have been secessions and other Kimbanguist groups with different emphases, but all look to Simon Kimbangu as an idealized founder and martyr figure.

M.-L. Martin, *Kimbangu* . . . (1975).

Kimḥi, David, or **Radak** (*c*.1160–1235). Jewish grammarian and exegete. Kimhi was the son of the anti-Christian polemicist, Joseph Kimḥi (known as Rikam and author of *Sefer ha-Berit*, rejecting Christian interpretations of the Jewish Bible) and brother of the grammarian Moses Kimḥi (known as Remak) who was David's teacher. Kimḥi was the author of the grammatical treatise *Mikhlol* (1532); he wrote commentaries on the books of Chronicles, Genesis, the prophetic books, and the Psalms. He was a strong supporter of *Maimonides, and the correspondence between Kimḥi and Judah ibn Alfakhar on Maimonides' philosophy has been preserved.

F. T. Talmage, *David Kimhi* . . . (1975).

Kimō-tokaku (Jap., 'hair of a tortoise and horn of a hare'). Zen expression for belief in something that does not exist, especially in the existence of an independent self.

Kinah. Heb. mourning poem. Kinot (pl.) were traditionally spoken over the dead (e.g. Genesis 23.2) and at times of national calamity. Famous kinot include *David's lament for *Saul and Jonathan (2 Samuel 1. 19–27), and the entire book of Lamentations, which is read on the Ninth Day of *Av (Tishah be-Ab(v)). Outside the Bible, well-known kinot include Solomon ibn *Gabirol's lament on the death of Jekuthiel, and *Eleazar b. Judah's kinah on the murder of his wife and daughters. Kinot are particularly associated with the Ninth Day of Av, and many anthologies have been produced over the years.

King, Martin Luther, Jr. (1929–68). American *Baptist minister and leader of the civil rights movement. He was born in Atlanta, Georgia, and attended Moorhouse College and Crozier Theological Seminary where he was in search of a theology commensurate with his understanding of society through sociology. He gained a Ph.D. at Boston University School of Theology, where he became acquainted with the writings of *Gāndhī. In 1954 he became pastor of a Baptist church in Montgomery, Alabama, where he became involved in the boycott of the city's segregated buses, taking leadership of the campaign. In 1955, such segregation was declared unconstitutional. King founded the Southern Christian Leadership Conference to draw together campaigns against discrimination, emphasizing non-violence. He also endeavoured to draw in other Christians and their leaders. Somewhat disappointed at the general apathy, he wrote his 'Letter from Birmingham Jail' in 1963, when he was arrested during the massive demonstrations in Birmingham, Alabama. The letter was a reply to a public address to him signed by eight clergymen, but it became a defence of his campaign and a repudiation of Christian (and Jewish) apathy:

> Frankly, I have yet to engage in a direct action campaign that was 'well-timed' in the view of those who have not suffered unduly from the disease of segregation. . . . We have waited for more than 340 years for our constitutional and God-given rights. The nations of Asia and Africa are moving with jetlike speed toward gaining political independence, but we still creep at horse-and-buggy pace toward gaining a cup of coffee at a lunch counter.

King's campaigns culminated in the Washington march in 1963 and in his address—of which a reporter (James Reston) said, 'It will be a long time before we forget the melodious and melancholy voice of the Reverend Dr. Martin Luther King Jr. crying out his dreams to the multitude.' Drawing on the deep resonances of the *Authorized Version of the Bible, he spoke briefly, ending with his repeated, 'I have a dream': 'I have a dream that my four little children will one day live in a nation where they will not be judged by the colour of their skin but by the content of their character.' In 1964, he received the Nobel Peace Prize, again insisting that 'the choice today is not between violence and non-violence, it is either non-violence or non-existence'. He was assassinated in Memphis, Tennessee, in April 1968. The USA now observes 15 Jan. (his birthday) as a federal holiday.

D. L. Lewis, *King: A Biography* (1978).

Kingdom of God. A symbol or concept in ancient Judaism (though more usually 'kingdom of heaven') especially prominent in the preaching of Jesus. The term is rare in pre-Christian writings, although the *kingship and sovereignty of God is common in Ancient Near Eastern religions. When God's reign or kingdom is spoken of it may refer to his continuing rule over Israel or the world (e.g. Psalm 97; Daniel 4. 34) or to a future *apocalyptic state of affairs (e.g. Daniel 2. 44). In rabbinic literature the idea of keeping the *Torah was likened to taking upon oneself the 'yoke of the kingdom'. In Jesus' preaching the kingdom of God (or equivalent 'kingdom of heaven') was a central theme (Mark 1. 15; John 3. 5) but its meaning is elusive. Usually it is said to belong to the future (e.g. Matthew 6. 10; Mark 14. 25); sometimes it appears to be already present (Luke 11. 20); most often it is spoken of in *parables ('The kingdom of God is as if a man should scatter seed . . .', Mark 4. 26 ff.). The extent to which Jesus was wedded to the apocalyptic view of the kingdom (as urged strongly by A. *Schweitzer) is now a matter of dispute and depends on the genuineness of individual sayings. In any case Jesus seems to have avoided describing the kingdom concretely in propositions, in order to free it as a symbol for the proper response to his preaching, and thus for the recognition of the power and consequence of God.

The identification of the kingdom of God with the Church was made by *Augustine, who opposed it to 'the kingdom of the Devil'. Following him, medieval writers tended to equate it with the visible hierarchical church. Modern liberal theologians tend to speak of the kingdom of God generally as that state of human affairs in accord with God's will.

G. R. Beasley-Murray, *Jesus and the Kingdom of God* (1986); N. Perrin, *Jesus and the Language of the Kingdom* (1976); R. Schnackenburg, *God's Rule and Kingdom* (1963).

Kings, Books of. Two books belonging to the Former Prophets in the Hebrew Bible and to the historical books of the Christian Old Testament. In RC edns. of the Bible they are usually called 3 and 4 Kings, titles deriving from the *Septuagint where the books were grouped with *Samuel to form the four 'Books of Reigns'. The books were originally a single work, continuing the history of the Hebrew monarchy as far as the fall of Jerusalem in 586 BCE. The narrative includes the accession and reign of Solomon (1 Kings 1–11); the division of his kingdom into Judah and Israel, and the fortunes of each until the conquest of Israel by Assyria in 721 BCE (1 Kings 12–2 Kings 17); and the reigns of the last kings of Judah (2 Kings 18–25). Kings was compiled from several sources, three of which are even named (1 Kings 11. 41, 14. 19, 15. 7). The interest of the author is religious: Josiah's reform is described at length (2 Kings 22. 8–23. 25) while important political events are often passed over cursorily. Critics usually consider that these books were written or edited to form the final part of a *Deuteronomic history.

Kingship, Chinese. Traditional Chinese concepts of kingship were sacralized, the political, moral, and economic powers of the emperor all having a religious dimension. The emperor was seen as pivot and sustainer of the cosmic order, ruler of the four quarters of the world and mediator between *Heaven and earth. As the 'Son of Heaven', he lived in a palace complex called the Purple Forbidden City, modelled on the Purple Protected Enclosure, where the God of Heaven (*Shang-Ti) dwelt in the circumpolar region of the sky. Through a righteous emperor came the blessings of Heaven, while misrule might lead to various natural and social disasters, culminating in the withdrawing of his divine commission to rule, the so-called Mandate of Heaven. As 'Father and Mother of the People', the emperor was the summit of Chinese society and preserver of its sacred hierarchical order. As is the case with highly developed notions of divine kingship elsewhere, the Chinese emperor sought by his righteous rule to ensure the fertility of the crops. The occupations of agriculture and sericulture were chosen as paradigmatic, and each year the emperor performed a ritual ploughing in the spring to encourage farming. Less important but sometimes performed was a parallel ceremony in which the empress presided at the altar of silkworms.

Kingship, Sacral. In Judaism, the beliefs associated with the ruler chosen and supported by God. In the period of the *Exodus and *Judges, the Israelites did not have a king. Only when threatened by surrounding nations, was kingship reluctantly seen as a necessary institution (see Judges 8. 22–3 and 1 Samuel 8. 7). The initiation of the king involved *anointing with oil and him sitting on the throne in the royal palace. As well as the crown, the king was given the 'testimony' (see 2 Kings 11. 12)—probably a document listing the conditions of the king's *covenant with his people and with God. The king thus became God's chosen, his anointed one (*messiah), the man sanctified by God's spirit. He was expected to judge his people justly (see 1 Kings 3. 9), but in *Israel he was not the source of the law. As in other Middle Eastern cultures, the king was in some sense a *priest. He offered *sacrifices, he burned *incense, and he blessed the people. The relationship between God and the king was perceived as that of father and son (see Psalm 89. 27), but at the same time there was no suggestion that the king was anything but mortal. With the destruction of the Northern Kingdom in 721 BCE and the Southern Kingdom in 587 BCE, kingship came to an end, although it was briefly restored under the *Hasmoneans. The positions, rights, and limitations of the king are elaborated in the *Mishnah (*B.Sanh.* 2. 2–5).

The theory of sacral kingship suggests that, despite the limitations set in the biblical documents, the ideology of kingship drew heavily on Near Eastern ideas. These varied greatly, but often included the king as a representative of God in a New Year Festival, enacting the death and new life of fertility. *Sukkot in practice contained some of these 'rain-making' rites even though the biblical description has eliminated them; and the so-called messianic oracles may well have been derived from hopes vested in the present (in some instances, newborn) king, rather than in any future figure; future messianism was a development of the post-*Exile period, when no actual kings existed or were looked for.

A. R. Johnson, *Sacral Kingship in Ancient Israel* (1955); H. Ringgren, *The Messiah in the Old Testament* (1956).

Kinot (lamentations): see KINAH.

Kippah: see HEAD, COVERING OF (JUDAISM); YARMULKE.

Kirchenkampf (Germ., 'church struggle'). The conflict between German churches and the Nazi state. *Protestant opposition crystallized against the party of 'German-Christians', in control since 1933, who sought to assimilate both Christian doctrine to Nazi ideology and church organization to the state under the *Reichsbischof* ('state bishop'). The *Barmen Declaration of 1934 by the *Confessing Church rejected any outside control of the church, and succeeded in denying the government the docile collaboration of the church. The Confessing Church, however, was progressively weakened by disagreements in its own ranks about co-operation with the official Minister for Church Affairs; by tightening restrictions on church funds and paper for publishing and the conscription of pastors; and by the arrest of leaders like M. *Niemöller and D. *Bonhoeffer. Even so, the opposition mounted by the Protestant churches to Hitler seems small, a fact acknowledged in the 'Declaration of Guilt' made by Confessing Church leaders at Stuttgart in 1945.

The RC Church, seeing an ally against 'Bolshevism' in the Nazi government, quickly came to terms with it in a *Concordat of 1933. This was soon dishonoured (e.g. by the suppression of Catholic schools), and in 1937 Pope Pius XII issued a strongly anti-Nazi *encyclical *Mit brennender Sorge* (with burning anxiety). The Concordat was never rescinded, however, and no organized RC resistance emerged, although there were individual heroes. These included in different ways the outspoken bishop C. von Galen of Münster, and the Polish priest Maximilian Kolbe, canonized in 1982, who died at Auschwitz in another's place.

The silence of both Protestant and Catholic churches in the face of the Jewish *Holocaust (apologists still debate whether Pope Pius XII is specifically to be blamed for not speaking out against it) is widely recognized as a matter of particular guilt, which must be addressed by any statement on Jewish–Christian relations.

Kirpā (help from God): see SIKHISM.

Kirpān (dagger/sword): see FIVE KS.

Kīrtan (Hindī, Pañjābī, 'devotional singing', from *kīrat* = 'praise'). Hindu and Sikh corporate hymn-singing, often to instrumental accompaniment. This *Vaiṣṇava form of *worship, also central to Sikhism, is believed to purify those singing as it is a means of *nām simaran (remembrance of divine name). It is the second stage of *bhakti according to *Bhāgavata Purāṇa*. See also MARDĀNĀ; RĀG; RĀGĪ; SĀDH SAṄGAT; SOHILĀ.

Kīrtimukha. In Hinduism, the mask of a demon placed above the door of the temples of *Śiva to ward off intruders.

Kismet (Turkish from Arab., *qisma*, 'share, portion'). The allocation of whatever occurs, hence the acceptance in Islam that God determines all things: see QADAR.

Kissako (Jap., 'drink tea'). Zen saying, derived from *Chao-chou Ts'ung-shen, to emphasize that Zen is not divorced from the ordinary process of life.

Kiss of death: see DEATH, KISS OF.

Kiss of peace (Lat., *pax*). Mutual greeting during the Christian *eucharist, perhaps based on the command of Christ to make peace before bringing one's gift to the altar (Matthew 5. 23 f.), hence its association in E. and some W. *liturgies with the offertory. Often referred to now as 'the sign of peace', it goes back in sentiment to the earliest days (Romans 16. 16; 1 Corinthians 16. 20; 1 Peter 5. 14). Originally an actual kiss, its form has been modified in all rites, and nowadays varies. It may be observed ceremonially (e.g. with a formalized handshake and words like 'The peace of the Lord be always with you'—'And also with you') or, more usually, with an informal handshake and exchange of greetings.

Kiswa (Arab., 'clothing' or 'covering'). Curtain of cloth for the *Kaʿba, the central shrine of Islam, in *Mecca. It covers the four walls, except for the door for which there is a separate curtain. The kiswa is prepared each year in Egypt. It is generally of black brocade, with a gold band embroidered with *Quranic texts.

Kitabake Chikafusa (1293–1354). Leading advocate of Shinto revival. He lived during the confused period of conflict in Japan when there were two rival courts in the north and south (1336–92). He wrote to express his vision of a legitimate imperial line ruling over all Japan, and to reinforce the view of Ise Shinto (see HONJISUIJAKU) that Shinto is superior to the invading religions from China and India. *Jinnō Shōtōki* (Records of the Succession of the Divine Rulers) begins: 'Japan is the land of the *kami. Our heavenly ancestor, Kunitokotachi, laid its first foundations, and *Amaterasu, the sun goddess, left the land to her descendants to rule over it for ever. This is true only of our country. Nothing like it can be found in foreign lands.' He reinforced the argument with the claim that the succession of rulers is unbroken, even though it diverged into two streams on schismatic occasions: 'In our country alone the succession has remained unbroken, from the beginning of heaven and earth to the present. It has continued in a single line, and even when, as inevitably happens, the succession has split, it has always returned to the true line.'

Kitamura Sayo (founder of movement): see TENSHŌ KŌTAI JINGŪ KYŌ.

Kitawala. A widespread movement in Central Africa, especially 1908–30, based originally on contacts in S. Africa with *Jehovah's Witnesses, then known as the Watchtower Bible and Tract Society (hence *ki-tawala*, an Africanization of 'tower'). Elliot Kamwana Chirwa (1872–1956) brought the teachings to his native Malawi in 1908. His strong *millenarian and anti-colonial overtones soon led to his arrest and deportation. His followers took the movement to Zambia, where it was especially strong in the 1920s, with an emphasis on witch-hunting. Tomo Nyirenda, claiming to be Mwana Lesa (Son of God), was eventually hanged in 1925 for killing more than 100 so-called witches. The movement spread also into Zaïre and southern Tanzania. In all these areas it was regarded with much suspicion by the colonial authorities, but, in spite of persecution, it was never totally suppressed.

Kit(t)el (Yid., 'gown'). White garment worn by some *Ashkenazi Jews for special services. A kit(t)el may be worn during *Rosh ha-Shanah and *Day of Atonement services, by the person conducting the *Passover *seder, by the bridegroom at his *marriage, and by the dead for burial. White symbolizes purity, and at one time the kit(t)el was worn every *Sabbath. The kit(t)el is the clothing of angels, and on the Sabbath humans can be raised to the rank of angels.

Kiyomizu (temple): see KYŌTO.

Kleśas (Skt., 'pain', 'affliction'). In *Yoga philosophy, the five causes of human affliction. *Patañjali's **Yoga-sūtra* (ii. 3) enumerates the kleśas as: (i) *avidyā, 'ignorance', (ii) *asmitā*, 'egoism', (iii) *rāga, 'attachment', (iv) *dveṣa*, 'aversion', and (v) *abhiniveśa*, 'the fear of death'. These causes of human suffering are all rooted in the first kleśa, ignorance, which is defined (iii. 5) as 'seeing the impermanent as permanent, the impure as pure, the painful as joyful, and the not-Self as the Self'. The kleśas are not only the cause of all past and present suffering, but are also the basis of the latent impressions of our actions which bring future suffering in this life and in lives to come. The philosophy of the kleśas is not one of unmitigated pessimism, however. The kleśas can be minimized by the practice (2. 2, 28–9) of the eight 'limbs' of Yoga and finally overcome by the enlightening dawn of knowledge, *viveka-khyati*, the discriminative discernment of *puruṣa, pure consciousness, from *buddhi, intellect, a subtle form of unconscious matter (*prakṛti). This discrimination when held without attachment brings ignorance to an end and the path of Yoga to its goal.

For the Buddhist equivalent, see KILESA.

Klong-chen Rab-'byams-pa (often simplified to Longchenpa, 1308–63). Major Tibetan scholar of the *Nyingma-pa. He was of particular importance in the transmission of *dzogchen (Great Perfection). After a thorough education in the existing traditions, he became disillusioned with this and sought enlightenment as a pupil of Kumārarāja (1266–1343), a renowned wandering ascetic who was a noted exponent of dzogchen. For a time, Klong-chen Rab-'byams-pa was abbot of *Samyé, but he could not avoid the political conflicts of the time and spent a period as an exile in (modern) Bhutan. He wrote many works, especially *The Seven Treasures* (*mdzod-bdun*) and *Trilogy on Rest* (*ngal-gso skor-gsum*). His own teachings were reorganized and promulgated by Jigme Lingpa ('Jigs-med gling-pa, 1730–98), whence they became widely influential and were transmitted especially through the *Rimé movement.

Dudjon Rinpoche, *The Nyingma School* . . . (1990); S. G. Karmay, *Origins and Development of the Tibetan Religious Traditions of the Great Perfection* (1988).

Knights of Malta: see TEMPLARS.

Knowledge. A valued, but somewhat ambiguous, human competence in most religions. *Gnosis* (Gk., 'knowledge') as insight into the deepest mysteries flourished in the Hellenistic world, leading to both mystery religions (with initiates alone gaining access to healing or saving knowledge) and to *gnostic religions. But Judaism contrasted these with the revelations from God especially through *Torah and *prophets, and came to discern a distinction between knowledge and wisdom, in the sense that the latter is the source, and should be the control, of the former: the quest for knowing was the downfall of Adam and Eve, yet without that quest there would be no marriages, no houses, no inventions. Christianity inherited this sense that the knowledge of God is the beginning of wisdom, and *Paul issued stern warnings against trusting in wisdom in isolation from the power of God and the folly of the cross (1 Corinthians 1. 17–31). Christian history unfolds a tension between *fideism and the exploration of the universe as God's creation, out of which the natural sciences eventually emerged. There is a tension also between knowing about God, as in academic theology, and knowing God: 'With all their science, those people at Paris are not able to discern what God is in the least of his creatures, not even in a fly' (Eckhart). The tension was much reduced by attending to *The Degrees of Knowledge* (J. *Maritain, 1959: cf. B. *Lonergan, K. *Rahner). In Islam, knowledge receives the highest endorsement (see ʿILM); yet even here, knowledge in contrast to behaviour in conformity with *Qur'ān and *sharīʿa is suspect: 'The end reached by the *mutakallimun* [theologian] is the beginning of the way for the *derwīsh' (ʿAbd al-Wahhāb al-Shaʿrāni).

In Indian religions, the tension is equally evident. Ginyá is the all-important counter-availing value. Ignorance (*avidya) is the deepest fault and impediment which has to be dealt with if any progress is to be made toward a higher goal. Thus *jñāna-marga (the way of knowledge) is one of the three ways (*mārga) leading, in Hinduism, toward enlightenment and release (*mokṣa). Avidya is contrasted with six ways through which knowledge can be attained and secured (*pramāṇa)—though not all schools accept all six: perception (*pratyakṣa*), inference (anumāna), authority (*śabda), analogy (*upamāna*), implication (*arthāpatti*), and negation (*anupalabdhi*); all these are in themselves neutral in relation to religious or ethical progress. Avidya is countered by *vidyā, *samjña*, *prajña. Yet it is clearly recognized that there are different levels of knowledge, of which the earlier (e.g. knowledge of texts) is necessary, but comes to be seen as a kind of ignorance, compared with direct knowledge of *Brahman: 'Knowledge is the only means by which complete and absolute deliverance is obtained . . ., because knowledge disperses ignorance as light dispels darkness: once ignorance, the child of earthly desires, is removed, the true self [*ātman] shines forth with its own splendour, as the sun spreads light in all directions when the clouds have scattered' (*Śaṅkara). The high estimate of knowledge as a human excellence, however provisional its attainments are in relation to the final goal, make religions natural opponents of any kind of fundamentalism which questions the worth of human knowledge.

Knox, John (1505–72). Leader of the *Reformation in Scotland. As preacher at St Andrews he was captured by the French, and whilst serving as a galley slave, used the time to produce an edn. of Henry Balnave's *Treatise on Justification by Faith*. On his release (1549) he became preacher in Berwick and in 1551 chaplain to Edward VI, sharing in the revision of the Prayer Book. He refused the bishopric of Rochester, and on Mary's accession fled to the Continent where he met the Swiss *Reform leaders. His *First Blast of the Trumpet against the Monstrous Regiment of Women* (1558) argued that female sovereignty contravened natural and divine law: 'The nobility of England and Scotland are inferior to brute beasts, for they do that to women which no male among the common sort of beasts can be proved to do to their females: that is, they reverence them, and quake at their presence; they obey their commandments, and that is against God.' This was addressed originally against Mary Tudor, but shortly after it appeared, Elizabeth was crowned, which not surprisingly brought his name into disrepute at Elizabeth's court. In 1559 Knox returned to Scotland, devoting his time to preaching and writing. He drew up the *Scottish Confession*, shared in the compilation of *The First Book of Discipline*, and wrote his *Treatise on Predestination* (1560). He also took a major part in the compilation of the *Book of Common Order* (1556–64), the service book in use in Scotland until 1645. Constantly in conflict with Mary Stuart, he was fiercely outspoken in denouncing the *mass. Knox's memoirs are preserved in his *History of the Reformation of Religion with the realm of Scotland*, first published in 1587 and immediately suppressed. A ferocious controversialist, his firm conviction, integrity, and courage were matched by pastoral sensitivity, compassion, and evident spirituality. Inscribed on the Reformation monument in Geneva are the words: 'One man with God is always in the majority.'

J. S. McEwen, *The Faith of John Knox* (1961); J. Ridley, *John Knox* (1968).

Kō. Jap. for *kalpa.

Ko. Korean for *dukkha.

Kōan (Chin., *Kung-an*; 'public announcement', or 'precedent for public use'). A fundamental practice in Zen training, challenging the pupil through a question, or a phrase or answer to a question, which presents a paradox or puzzle. A kōan cannot be understood or answered in conventional terms: it requires a pupil to abandon reliance on ordinary ways of understanding in order to move into or towards enlightenment. The pupil must search for the answer to a kōan 'like a thirsty rat seeking for water, like a child thinking of its mother'. The answer lies outside logic, and enables the pupil to break through 'the skin and shell of things', to break down mundane ways of seeing. Thus an answer to perhaps the most famous kōan of all, 'What is the sound of one hand clapping?', is for the pupil, without a word, to thrust one hand forward: to be told the answer and to achieve it are two very different things indeed. The origins of kōan are uncertain, but predate Nan-yüan Hui-yung (d. 930 CE) to whom the first use is attributed. The earliest surviving collection is in the writings of Fen-yang Shan-chao (*Fen-yang lu*; Jap., *Fun'yōroku*), including a series of 100 kōan questions (*chieh-wen*; Jap., *kitsumon*). Fen-yang was of the *Rinzai school, and the use of kōans is particularly associated with Rinzai (*kanna zen), but is not exclusive to it. Under Fen-yang's successor, Shih-shuang, Li Tsu-hsü produced *Tenshō Kōtōroku*, one of the five foundation chronicles of Zen in the Sung period, containing many kōans. Among Shih-shuang's pupils, Wu-tsu Fa-yen extended the short, sharp kōan to its height ('*Śākyamuni and *Maitreya are simply his servants: so then, who is he?' (*Mumonkan* 45); 'It is like a buffalo going through a window: its head, horns and legs are through; why not its tail?' (ibid. 38); 'If you meet a man of *Tao on the road, greet him with neither words nor silence: so then, how will you greet him?' (ibid. 36)). Fa-yen's main pupil, *Yüan-wu K'o-ch'in (1036–1135) was a vital figure in developing kōan method in this period, completing the *Blue Cliff Record* (Chin., *Pi-yen-lu*; Jap., *Hekigan-roku*, for which see HSÜEH-TOU CH'UNG TSIEN).

The second largest collection of the Sung period is *Ts'ung-jung lu* (Jap., *Shōyōroku*, tr. T. Cleary, *The Book of Equanimity*, 1985), assembled by Wan-sung Hsing-hsiu (1166–1246). It was followed (1229) by the *Wu-men-kuan* (Jap., *Mumonkan*), edited by Wu-men Hui-k'ai (1183–1260)—many Eng. trs., e.g. S. Kudo (1974), K. Sekida, *Two Zen Classics* (1977). This originated from Wu-men's personal experience:

> The monks at Lung-hsiang asked me for instruction. I took the kōan of the masters as a club to knock at the gate in guiding them according to their characters and capabilities. Noting them down, they turned into a collection of 48 kōans, which I have not arranged in any order. I will call them *The Gateless Barrier* (see HSÜAN-SHA SHIH-PEI).

Kōan method continued in Japan, especially after the systematization of kōans in the school of *Hakuin (1685–1768). About 1,700 kōans survive, of which about 600 are in active use.

In Rinzai, five types of kōan are identified: (i) *hosshin-kōan*, to create awareness of identity with buddha-nature (*bussho); (ii) *kikan-kōan*, to create ability nevertheless to discern distinctions within non-distinction; (iii) *gonsen-kōan*, creating awareness of the deep meaning of the sayings of the masters; (iv) *nantō-kōan*, grappling with the hardest to solve; (v) *go-i-kōan*: when the other four have been worked through, the insight gained is tested once more. See Index, Kōans.

See also MU; WATO.

Y. Hoffmann, *The Sound of One Hand* (1977); I. Miura and R. Sasaki, *The Zen Koan* (1965) and *Zen Dust* . . . (1966).

Kobō-daishi (posthumous title of Kūkai): see KŪKAI.

Kobutsu (Jap., 'old buddha'). Originally a *buddha of an earlier age, but also a Zen term, like *kobusshin*, for a deeply enlightened master.

Kōchi Sanzō. Title of *Amoghavajra.

Kōfuku-ji (temple-complex): see NARA BUDDHISM.

Kogidō ('Hall of Ancient Meanings'): see ITŌ JINSAI.

Kogoshūi (Gleanings from Ancient Stories). An account of Japanese mythology and early history according to the Imbe clan, a hereditary *Shinto priestly family. It was composed and presented to Emperor Heizei in 807 CE, by Imbe no Hironari as a protest against a rival priestly family, the Nakatomi, who had increasingly eclipsed the Imbe. He requests that the Imbe be treated as favourably as the Nakatomi by referring to the precedents which, he claims, have been established in myths and historical traditions. He emphasizes especially the active role played by the ancestor of the Imbe in the ceremony, for luring the sun goddess *Amaterasu out of a rock cave, that was performed in the heavenly world; in the descent of Ninigi, the grandson of Amaterasu, from heaven to Mount Takachiho to rule the nation; and in the construction of the imperial palace for Emperor Jimmu, the great-grandson of Ninigi and Japan's legendary first emperor. The author's overall intention is to picture the ancestor of the Imbe as equal in dignity and importance with that of the Nakatomi. He concludes the account by calling His Majesty's attention to the 'eleven things' neglected by the government. While containing much the same material as the **Kojiki* and the **Nihongi*, the *Kogoshūi* preserves a number of interesting pieces of information that are not found elsewhere.

Tr. G. Kato and H. Hoshino.

Koheleth: see ECCLESIASTES.

Kohen (priest): see PRIEST.

Kohler, Kaufmann (1843–1926). Prominent US *Reform *rabbi. Born in Bavaria, in his youth Kohler came under the influence of the neo-Orthodox Samson Raphael *Hirsch. Recommended by Abraham *Geiger, he became rabbi of Temple Beth El in Detroit in 1869, and in 1879 he took over Temple Beth El of New York from his father-in-law, David *Einhorn. His collection of sermons *Backward or Forward* (1885) led to the convening of the Pittsburgh Conference of Reform rabbis, and in 1903, he was appointed President of the *Hebrew Union College. His best known book was *Jewish Theology* (1918).

He advocated a Judaism which made all things subordinate to moral law. 'On the last day of Judgement', as he put it, 'the only question that will be asked you is, Did you deal honestly with your fellow-man?' In his view, 'the real Torah is the unwritten moral law which underlies the precepts of both the written law and its oral interpretation [*halakhah]'.

R. J. Marx, *Kaufmann Kohler as Reformer* (1951).

Ko Hung (*c.*280–340 CE). Chinese *alchemist (according to J. Needham, the most outstanding in this field), best known as the author of *Pao-p'u tzu* ([Book of the] Master Who Embraces Simplicity). This consists of two parts: (i) tells of 'gods and genii, prescriptions and medicines, ghosts and marvels, transformations, maintenance of life, extension of years, exorcising evils, and banishing misfortune' (Ware tr., p. 17), and belongs to the Taoist tradition; (ii) gives 'an account of success and failure in human affairs and of good and evil in public affairs', and belongs to the Confucian school. He also wrote the *Shen hsien chuan* (Records of Gods and Immortals) and many other works.

In the *Pao-p'u tzu*, he sought to combine Taoist esoteric techniques with Confucian ethics. He described the procedures for attaining immortality on earth, the nature and practice of inner and outer alchemy, and a system of merit whereby actions increase or decrease one's days alive. Highly important for the development of popular and occult Taoism, he opposed the neo-Taoist (*hsüan-hsüeh) movement, *Ch'ing-t'an, because it lacked religious impetus and vision; it sought philosophical certainty before trusting what is probable but not certain—such as immortality:

> It is asked, 'Is it truly possible that immortals (*hsien) do not die?' Pao-p'u tzu said: 'Even with the most perfect vision, we cannot see everything; even with the sharpest hearing, we cannot hear every sound; . . . even if we knew all that [Ta-]yü, I and Ch'i-hsieh [legendary sages] knew, we would not know so much as we do not know. Innumerable things exist: what is there that could not exist? Why not the immortals . . .? Why not a way to immortality?'

Tr. (1st part) of *Pao-p'u tzu*: J. R. Ware, *Alchemy, Medicine and Religion in the China of A.D. 320* (1966).

Kojiki (Records of Ancient Matters). The earliest account of Japanese mythology and early history in three books. Compiled in 712 CE, it focuses on the origin of kingship in the sacred history as narrated in myths, and on the 'smooth' transition from myth to actual history. Emperor Temmu (672–86) initiated the process of compilation by making a master text of the 'genealogical record of the imperial family' (*teiki*) and of the 'collection of myths, legends, and song sequences' (*kyūji* or *honji*); Temmu issued in 681 a decree stating that the *teiki* and the *kyūji* handed down by the various families had ceased to be accurate and would have to be corrected. 'If these errors are not remedied at this time,' he said, 'their meaning will be lost before many years have passed.' His concern was expressed succinctly: 'This is the framework of the state, the great foundation of the imperial influence.' The master text was then recited and memorized at his command by Hiyeda no Are, an imperial scribe. However, it was not until 712 that the work was compiled into the *Kojiki* by another scribe in the imperial court, Ō no Yasumaro, and presented to Empress Gemmei (707–15).

Book i unfolds what is usually known as Japanese myths. It opens with the cosmogony and theogony through the marriage of the divine pair *Izanagi and Izanami; they engender Japan's eight islands and many deities until Izanami is killed by the god of fire. Izanagi descends in vain to the underworld to recover his wife. After returning to earth, Izanagi purifies himself; when he has washed his left eye, there comes into existence the sun goddess *Amaterasu, the primordial ancestress of the imperial family. Amaterasu is entrusted with the administration of the heavenly state. One of the major events in the heavenly world is her hiding in a rock cave, and in order to lure her out of it a ceremony is performed by the clan heads in charge of priestly functions. The climax of book i is the story narrating the descent of the heavenly state onto earth: Ninigi, the grandson of Amaterasu, descends from heaven to Mount Takachiho to rule the Japanese islands, holding the three items of the sacred regalia and accompanied by the five clan heads.

Book ii opens with the story narrating how Jimmu, the great-grandson of Ninigi and Japan's legendary first emperor, establishes the imperial dynasty at Yamato in central Japan; in the course of his eastward migration from Mount Takachiho in Kyushu, Jimmu searches for the centre of the world, defeats the forces of evil and, assisted by a giant crow, enters Yamato, the 'centre of the land', where he builds the imperial palace. The cycle of Jimmu is followed by the genealogies, myths, and legends of the thirteen fictitious emperors, and concluded with the story of Ōjin, the emperor of the early 5th cent. CE, whose historicity has been confirmed by current studies.

Book iii covers the period from the reign of Emperor Nintoku to that of Empress Suiko (593–628), presenting the genealogies of the emperors and their legendary stories. Cf. **Nihongi*.

Tr. D. L. Philippi, *Kojiki* (1968).

Kokka Shintō (Jap., 'state Shinto'). In Japan, the system of state-supported Shinto shrines, ceremonies, and education which the government administered from the early Meiji period until the end of the Second World War. The Meiji government attempted to provide a sense of national and cultural identity by restoring the ancient ideal of 'the unity of religious rites and government (*saisei itchi*)'. Shrine Shinto was separated from Buddhism and combined with the Shinto of the Imperial House. At the core of Kokka Shintō was the belief in the divinity of the emperor and the uniqueness of Japan's national polity (*kokutai). The main structure of Kokka Shintō was created in 1871 with a series of decrees declaring that Shinto shrines were places for 'national rites' (*kokka no sōshi*), priests were to be appointed by the government, all citizens must register as parishioners (*ujiko*) with the local shrines, and shrines would be assigned an official rank indicating the amount of support they would receive from the state. Since Kokka Shintō was legally considered a non-religious institution whose purpose was to foster patriotism and loyalty, all Japanese were expected to participate in it, regardless of their religious affiliation. Kokka Shintō was abolished by the Allied Powers in 1945 in their Shinto Directive which prohibited the control, support, and dissemination of Shinto by the government, making all Shinto shrines, personnel, and ceremonies private religious matters. This separation of government and religion was subsequently incorporated into the constitution of Japan.

Kokoro. Jap. reading of the Chin. character *hsin*, the fundamental and interior nature of a person, thus virtually equivalent to buddha-nature (*bussho, *buddhatā).

Kokorozashi (Jap.). The fundamental disposition of will and longing to find truth and enlightenment.

Kokugaku (Jap.), National Learning or Japanese Studies. Its foremost task was to study ancient Japanese literature by means of scrutinizing the exact meaning of ancient words, and for that reason, Kokugaku as an academic discipline can be defined as a school that relied on philology as its methodological tool to bring out the ethos of Japanese tradition freed from foreign ideas and thoughts.

The Hirata School in the late Tokugawa period reckoned *Kada no Azumaro (1669–1736), *Kamo no Mabuchi (1697–1769), *Motoori Norinaga (1730–1801), and Hirata Atsutane (1776–1843) as the four major exponents of the Kokugaku Movement. The honour as its founder, however, would go to Keichū, a Shingon priest and scholar, who introduced a new academic standard for the study of ancient Japanese literature. His method was to let the texts speak for themselves in the context of ancient words, and demanded that scholars suspend their own interpretations, infused as they were with Buddhist and Confucian ideas. Azumaro desired to establish a school for Kokugaku, but this was not realized.

The study of ancient Japanese literature in its own intrinsic value made Kokugaku scholars spirited contenders against Buddhism and Confucianism, especially the latter which dominated education in the Tokugawa period. The pursuit of Japanese antiquity also made them aware of the pristine form of Shinto, not contaminated with foreign elements, from which arose a passionate yearning for the ancient way of life believed to be natural and free of humanly based ethical demands. Norinaga articulated this ancient way through the study of the *Kojiki*, and Atsutane went beyond what his predecessors intended, turning it into an ideology in which an aspect of Christian theology was incorporated. See Index, Kokugaku.

M. Masao, *Studies in the Intellectual History of Tokugawa Japan* (1975).

Kokushi: see KOKUTAI.

Kokushittsū (Jap., 'can of black paint'). The condition in Zen meditation of total darkness before the light suddenly breaks through.

Kokutai (Jap., 'national polity'). Among nationalists of the late 19th and early 20th cents., a term referring to the Shinto-Confucian idealization of the Japanese nation-state. Japanese society was compared to a large family, with the emperor at the head as the benevolent guiding hand and patriarch. Imperial rule was advocated as an inviolable and uniquely Japanese institution because the line of emperors, unlike those of other nations, had been 'unbroken for ages eternal' (*bansei ikkei no kōtō*). As the living embodiment of national character and unity, the emperor was glorified as being a 'manifest god' (*akitsumikami*) and 'coeval with heaven and earth'. As such, the imperial throne served as the focus for the patriotic, nationalist fervour of the period prior to the Second World War. *Kokushi* (Chin., *Kuo-shih*) 'teacher of the nation' is the title of a Buddhist who teaches the emperor, because the nation is summarized in his person. *Ben'en was the first to receive the title in Japan (posthumously in 1312).

Kol Bo (Heb., 'everything within'). Jewish book of *halakhic rulings. *Kol Bo* was probably composed at the end of the 13th cent. CE. Its authorship is unknown, but it has been suggested that it is an abridgement of the *Orhot Ḥayyim* of *Aaron b. Jacob ha-Kohen of Lunel.

Kol Nidrei (Aram., 'all vows'). Prayer which begins the Jewish *Day of Atonement evening service. The prayer is customarily repeated three times, and declares that all personal vows made rashly to God which have not been fulfilled are now cancelled. The prayer has frequently been misunderstood by gentiles who have argued that it demonstrates that Jewish promises are worthless, but in fact the *halakhah imposes severe limitations on which vows can be cancelled. The German *Reform rabbis removed the prayer from the Reform liturgy in 1844, in consequence of this misunderstanding, but it has since (1961) been restored. So poignant and popular is the prayer, that the whole evening of the Day of Atonement is often referred to as Kol Nidrei. The traditional melody was given a well-known setting by Max Bruch in 1880.

Komagaku (Korean-derived music): see MUSIC.

Koma-inu (Jap., 'dog of Koguryŏ'). A legendary beast resembling a lion, said to have entered Japan from the ancient Korean kingdom of Koguryŏ (Koma). Statues of the animal, popularly conceived as a guardian figure, are commonly found in pairs at entrances to shrine and temple precincts and in front of or attached to buildings themselves to ward off evil. Representations vary, and they are not infrequently identified as *shishi*. Typically, the pair is seated, with one roaring while the other remains with mouth closed, though variations on this are not uncommon. Made of various materials including stone, wood, or metal, they are often distinguished by their decoration: when coloured, the one on the left (*shishi*) is painted gold with a turquoise mane, the other silver with a deep blue mane. They sometimes appear with horn(s) and an extended front paw, the latter frequently resting on a spherical jewel.

Kōmei-tō (party of clean government): see SŌKA GAKKAI.

Komusō (Jap., 'emptiness monk'). A monk of the Fuke School (see KAKUSHIN) who wanders through the countryside playing the flute. They wear large hats, shaped like beehives, to hide their faces and preserve their anonymity, pointing to truth beyond themselves. In self-disregarding attitude, they are often regarded as *holy fools.

Konārak (temple): see SŪRYA.

Konchok Gyalpo (founder of Sakya): see SAKYA.

Kong. Korean for *śūnyatā, the void, that which is empty of characteristics.

Kongō-kai Mandara (Diamond Maṇḍala): see TAIZO-KAI MANDARA; SHINGON.

Kōnin (Jap. name): see HUNG-JEN.

Konkōkyō (Golden Light). A movement founded in Japan in 1859 by *Kawate Bunjiro (1814–83). Although registered by the Japanese government as a Shinto sect, it represents in many respects a departure from Shintoism. Not only does it place the emphasis on individual as opposed to group salvation, but also, unlike Shintoism, it believes in the existence of a mediator, in the person of its leader, between God (known as Tenchi Kane no Kami, the parent Spirit of the Universe) and humans. Moreover, it rejects such Shinto practices as exorcism and divination, and attaches great importance to social welfare activities.

D. B. Schneider, *Konkokyo* . . . (1962).

Kontakion (hymn): see AKATHISTOS.

Kook, Abraham Isaac (1865–1935). First *Ashkenazi *Chief Rabbi of Israel. Kook emigrated to Israel in 1904 and became Ashkenazi Chief Rabbi in 1921. He maintained that the return to *Zion was a step towards the beginning of the divine redemption. He hoped that the creation of the office of Chief Rabbi would lead to the revival of the *Sanhedrin and, while identifying with the *Zionist movement, he taught that the Jews are chosen to 'work and toil with the utmost devotion' to pursue the goal of human perfection and universalism; he was, nevertheless, realistic about the conditions of life (not unlike Buddhists recognizing that the lotus depends on mud): 'If it were not for the leavening muck in the spirit of man, the ripe fruit, giving delight to God, could not have grown.' He believed that people are by nature mystical, and that they respond best to the world and to their circumstances when they see them as the unfolding of a divine poetry, in which God's will is written: 'The yearning for the dominion of God's will is our overriding desire'; 'Even as there are laws of poetry, so there is poetry in law.' *Torah remains primary. For that reason, he founded a *yeshivah in Jerusalem, the Merkaz ha-Rav, which presented an integrated programme of Jewish education, including *Bible as well as *Talmud. He was a prolific writer, and his books combine learning with mystical insight. Among his books are *Orot ha-Kodesh* (3 vols., 1963/4), *Iggerot ha-Re'ayah* (3 vols., 1962/5), and *Orot ha-Teshivah* (1955; Eng., 1968).

B. Z. Bokser, *Abraham Isaac Kook* . . . (1978); I. Epstein, *Abraham Yitzhak Hacohen Kook* (1951).

Koran: see QUR'ĀN.

Korban. Jewish practice of *sacrificing (or dedicating) property to God. The practice of pledging all possessions to the *Temple is mentioned in the New Testament. It died out with the destruction of the Temple in 70 CE.

Korean religion. Korea, lying as it does between China and Japan, was of such importance in the transmission of Chinese culture to Japan that its own contribution is easy to overlook. Even now, after many conversions to various forms of Christianity (and the production of its own religion under Sun Myung *Moon), elements of its own, *shaman-based, religion persist. *Mudangs* (female shamans) are most common, but there are also some males, often blind, known as *paksus*. The shamans map territory and make it safe for particular activities. The Buddhist predominance in Korea began in 372, when Sun-to, a monk from China, arrived in the kingdom of Koguryŏ and undertook the education of the king's sons. The second kingdom, that of Paekche (often in the later Japanese texts a synonym for Korea), sent to China for instructors, and in 545, the king sent the first missionary to Japan. The third kingdom, Silla, was the last to accept Buddhism but became the most stalwart. Of particular importance in the early centuries was *Wŏnhyo. The country was united by the Silla kingdom, and under the Koryŏ dynasty (935–1392), Buddhism attained its greatest influence, bringing Buddhism into a close relation with the state, including its defence. Buddhist festivals became national holidays, and those aspiring to government service had to take Buddhist-based exams modelled on the Confucian exams in China. The great endeavour of creating a Korean version of the major Buddhist texts was undertaken: see KOREAN TRIPIṬAKA. Although many temples were built of wood and have been burnt, some remains of the building activity of this period have survived. Notable is the cave, Sŏkkul-am, at the summit of Mount Pulguk-sa, containing an image of the Buddha illuminated by the rising sun. Yi Sŏng-gye overthrew the Koryŏ dynasty, establishing the Yi dynasty (1392–1910), and blaming the decay of the previous period on the excessive reliance on Buddhism (despite the efforts of such reformers as *Chinul). He and his successors endorsed Confucianism, especially as taught by *Chu Hsi, and reduced the status of Buddhism. In 1422, the many Buddhist sects were reduced to two schools, those of Sun (i.e. Ch'an or Zen) and Kyo (active in the world). Roman Catholicism entered Korea during the 18th cent., suffering considerable persecution. It was known as *Sŏhak* ('Western Learning') and evoked *Tonghak* ('Eastern Learning'). This was founded by Ch'oe Che-u (1824–66), who had a vision of Sangche (i.e. *Shang-ti) which led to a miraculous cure. Although Ch'oe Che-u was executed, the movement grew and became known as Ch'ŏndogyo/Ch'ŏndo-kyo ('Sect of the Way of Heaven', see Y.-C. Kim, *The Ch'ŏndogyo Concept of Man*, 1978). By 1893, the numbers were so great that they petitioned the king for official recognition. When no action was taken, they began campaigns for the removal of foreign influence; an appeal to the Chinese for help against them led to Japanese intervention against the Chinese, thus beginning the Sino-Japanese war (1894). Meanwhile, Protestant Christianity (especially *Presbyterians) had been growing even faster, and to some extent allied itself with Korean opposition to outside interference. Thus after the Japanese annexation of Korea in 1910, Protestant Christianity came under great pressure to conform to Shinto shrine worship; but this in turn was offset by a number of revivals which have left Protestant Christianity a major force in the country. Buddhism itself underwent a revival under Pak Chungbin who established *Won Buddhism. Despite the split of Korea and the pressures for each 'side' to outperform the other in secular terms, Korea remains a country in which religion plays a major part. See Index, Korean religion.

C. A. Clark, *Religions of Old Korea* (1924, 1961); J. H. Grayson, *Korea: A Religious History* (1989); H.-K. Kim (ed.), *Studies on Korea* (1980); S. J. Palmer (ed.), *The New Religions of Korea* (1967); F. Vos, *Die Religionen Koreas* (1977).

Korean Tripiṭaka or **Tripiṭaka Koreana.** A collection of Buddhist texts from the Koryŏ period (935–1392). Its first edition was completed during the reign of King Munjong (1047–82) but destroyed at the time of the Mongolian invasion of Korea in 1231. Under the patronage of King Kojong (1214–59) the wood-block carving of the second edition was undertaken in 1236 and completed in 1251; one of the most comprehensive collections of Buddhist texts up to that time, this is now stored at the Haein monastery on Mount Kaya.

L. R. Lancaster and Sung-bae Pak, *The Korean Buddhist Canon: A Descriptive Catalogue* (1979).

Kośa (Skt., 'covering'). The five coverings of the *ātman in Hinduism—see e.g. **Taittirīya Upaniṣad*: (i) the outer and furthest from ātman, annamaya-kośa, the material covering of food; (ii) prānamaya-kośa, the vital covering, manifest as breath; (iii) manomaya-kośa, the mental covering; (iv) vijñanamaya-kośa, the intelligence covering; (v) ānandamaya-kośa, the bliss covering, where the human is closest to ātman.

Kosher (*Ashkenazi pronunciation of Heb. *kasher*): see DIETARY LAWS.

Kōshin (Sino-Japanese pronunciation of the signs for 'metal' and 'monkey' in Chinese sexagesimal system of calendrical reckoning). A Japanese folk deity whose original impetus was Chinese folk belief (loosely, Taoist), but which by accretion has taken on both Shinto and Buddhist associations. The Chinese believed in three malevolent deities (literally 'three worms') who inhabit every human body, inflicting it with various ailments, and who on the nights of the six Kōshin days each year would escape to heaven to report to the gods the moral transgressions of their hosts, thus shortening their lives. This idea was spread in Japan in the Heian period by wandering *Onmyō-ji* ('*yin-yang masters'). It was thought that by keeping awake on Kōshin nights, the worms would be unable to escape to make their reports, hence the aristocratic custom of keeping Kōshin vigils and whiling away the hours in poetry-writing, musical entertainments, and games. In the popular mind the monkey association brought Kōshin into identification with Sarutahiko, the native monkey deity, and thereby also with *Dōsojin, both of whom had sexual overtones and functioned as guardians of travellers. Today the vigil is still kept to a degree, and Kōshin day is thought to be an inauspicious time for marriages or for cohabitation. The Buddhist association was with Shōmen Kongō (Vajrakumara), presumably because he was the messenger of *Indra, and because he, as a curer of diseases, offered a partial antidote to the depredations of the three worms.

Koshōgatsu (lesser New Year): see FESTIVALS AND FASTS, JAPANESE.

Kotani Kimi (co-founder): see REIYŪKAI.

[Ha-]Kotel ha-Ma'aravi: see WAILING WALL.

Koto-dama (Jap., 'word-spirit'). The traditional Shinto belief in spiritual power residing in spoken words. The ancient Japanese believed that beautifully phrased speech and correct words brought blessings from the *kami, while carelessly phrased speech and incorrectly uttered words brought evil. The use of *norito spoken in elegant ancient Japanese when praying to the kami is related to this belief.

Kotow or **kow-tow.** 'Knocking the head on the ground', the court ceremony of three kneelings and nine prostrations, which Chinese ritual of the Ch'ing period required of a foreign envoy when he was received by the emperor. Russians in general refused (and were not granted an audience), as did the British. Lord Macartney proposed in 1793 that a Chinese official should perform kotow before a portrait of George III, and as a result he was allowed to bend on one knee, as he would to the king; but this concession was not subsequently renewed. From 1873 onward, the kotow was not required.

Kotsu (Jap., 'bones'). Also known as *nyoi*, the staff bestowed on a Zen master (*roshi) on his attaining that rank. It has a slight curvature, like the human spine, and is used in teaching to emphasize a point or awaken a student.

K'ou Chien-chih (*c.*365–*c.*448 CE). Taoist successor of *Ko Hung who did much to organize that tradition in Taoism and to make it the official religion of the Northern Way dynasty. He received visions of *Lao-tzu in which he was urged to cleanse Taoism, especially of *Chang Chüeh's teachings. He saw Buddhist teachings and rituals as a competitive rival, and with the Confucianist Ts'ui Hao, influenced the emperor to declare Taoism the state religion, and in 438 to limit Buddhist ordination. Monasteries and temples were closed, and the killing of all monks began. K'ou protested against the extreme measures, but Ts'ui appealed to the principle, 'Kill the evil to help the good'. He became celestial master (*t'ien-shih) of the northern Wei court from 425–8. He introduced extravagant Taoist ritual to affirm the emperor as Perfect Ruler; but he was murdered by a palace eunuch, and his successor re-established Buddhism as the state religion.

R. B. Mather in H. Welch and A. Seidel (eds.), *Facets of Taoism* (1979).

Kovazim (collections): see RESPONSA.

Kow-tow (obeisance): see KOTOW.

Kōya (Japanese Buddhist): see KŪYA.

Kōya, Mount (Jap., Kōyasan). Site of a Buddhist monastic complex of the *Shingon sect in Wakayama Prefecture, Japan. Long considered by ascetics as a sacred mountain, Mount Kōya was selected in 816 by *Kūkai as a site for establishing a monastic community and is currently home to over 110 associated temples.

Kōzen Gokoku-ron: see EISAI.

Kraemer, Hendrik (1888–1965). Dutch Christian missionary and missiologist. Raised as an orphan, he experienced a conversion while reading the Bible at the age of 16. He took a doctorate in Oriental languages, and went as a missionary to the Netherlands East Indies (later Indonesia), where he advocated the indigenization of the Church. In 1928, he was part of the delegation to the Missionary Conference at Jerusalem which remained deeply critical of that Conference's attempt to find a new relation with non-Christian religions on the basis of shared values. In 1937, he became Professor of Comparative Religion at Leiden and prepared the discussion document for the successor Missionary Conference at Tambaram, in 1938. This 'document' is his classic work, *The Christian Message in a Non-Christian World*. Based strongly on the unequivocal theology of Karl *Barth, Kraemer argued that Christianity is a consequence of the act of God, issuing in biblical demand, whereas other religions are the consequence of the human religious quest. Between the two there is a radical discontinuity. His post-war books modified his approach somewhat, in the sense that he could see more elements of *praeparatio evangeliae* (preparation for the gospel) in other religions, but he remained a spokesman for an exclusivist interpretation of the Christian relation to other religions.

C. F. Hallencreutz, *Kraemer Towards Tambaram* (1966).

Kranz, Jacob, The Maggid of Dubno (1741–1804). Jewish preacher. Born in Lithuania, Kranz became famous as a preacher in the city of Dubno where he came in contact with *Elijah ben Solomon Zalman. Many of his sermons were printed posthumously in *Ohel Yā'akov* (The Tent of Jacob: 4 vols., 1830, 1837, 1859, 1863). He was a brilliant story-teller who was called by Moses *Mendelssohn 'the Jewish Aesop'—though few of his stories or parables involved animals. His habit was to collect stories and wait for an occasion to tell them—as illustrated by his story of an occasion when a young soldier found him standing before targets drawn on a wall, each of which had a bullet-hole through the centre of the bull. Asked how he could achieve such accuracy, he said that first he fired at the wall, then he drew the targets round the hole. His sayings often have a directness which lingers on: ' "Clean hands and a pure heart" [Psalm 24. 4] does not mean clean gloves and a white shirt.'

Kratophany (manifestation of power): see HIEROPHANY.

Krishna: see KṚṢṆA.

Krishnamurti, Jiddu (1895–1986). Indian religious figure and claimed *guru. The *Theosophists, Charles Leadbeater and Annie Besant, proclaimed him the 'World Teacher', the vehicle of the Lord *Maitreya, who showed himself in human form every 2,000 years. In 1911 Krishnamurti was made head of the newly founded 'Order of the Star in the East' (later shortened to 'Order of the Star'), and in the same year was brought to England by Mrs Besant to be educated there for his role as World Teacher. Unable to gain entry to Oxford, he turned this into an attack on intellectualism, and claimed it as evidence of his unfettered mind. In 1929 Krishnamurti, tired of the role assigned to him, dissolved the Order, renounced all claims to divinity, and declared that he no longer wanted disciples. Central to Krishnamurti's teaching is the notion that truth is what is and can only be attained by gaining complete self-awareness and self-knowledge through meditation. Today Krishnamurti Foundations are to be found in many parts of the world which aim to set people 'absolutely and unconditionally free'. Some of those close to him (e.g. M. Lutyens, *Krishnamurti: The Years of Awakening*, 1975; . . . *The Years of Fulfillment*, 1983) adulate him; others (e.g. R. R. Sloss, *Lives in the Shadow with Krishnamurti*, 1991) observed a more fraudulent and cynical character.

Kristallnacht (Germ., 'night of glass'). The night, 9 Nov. 1938, on which Nazi *anti-Semitism in Germany moved onto a new level of ferocity: *synagogues were burned down and Jewish-owned shops were looted and destroyed (hence the name, because the streets were covered in glass). From this point on, the mass deportations to concentration camps began. See also HOLOCAUST.

I. J. Borowsky (ed.), *Artists Confronting the Inconceivable* . . . (1992).

Kriyatantra (division of tantric texts): see TRIPIṬAKA.

Kriyā-yoga: see YOGA; YOGĀNANDA.

Krochmal, Nachman (ReNak; 1785–1840). A founder of the 'Science of Judaism' (Wissenschaft des Judentums): see also ZUNZ, LEOPOLD. As a leader of the *Haskalah movement, Krochmal's philosophy is summed up in his *Moreh Nevukhei ha-Zeman* (Guide to the Perplexed of Our Time, 1851). Influenced by the German idealistic philosophers, he identified God as 'a power equal to every latent and potential form within itself'. He believed that God created the world out of himself and that religion and philosophy are different ways of comprehending the absolute spirit. Krochmal maintained contact with all the prominent thinkers of the haskalah, and his main contribution was his attempt to study Hebrew literature, including the *halakhah, in terms of its history and development.

Krodha (Skt., 'anger, wrath'). In the **Mahābhārata*, one of the 'five sins' the *yogin must overcome: lust (*kāma), anger (krodha), greed (*lobha), fear (*bhaya*), and sleep (*svapna*).

In Hindu ethics, krodha is one of the six internal enemies against which all must be vigilant, the others being lust, greed, infatuation (*moha), pride (*mada*), and envy (*mātsarya*). The two basic sins from whence all others derive are kāma and krodha: in the **Bhagavad-gītā* (3. 37 f.), Arjuna asks *Kṛṣṇa,

> But under what coercion does a man, even against his will, commit sin, driven as it were, by force?

The Blessed Lord replied:

> Desire (kāma), this furious, wrathful passion (krodha), which is born of the *guṇa of violent action, is the great evil, the great hunger. Know that in this world this is the foul fiend.

Kṛṣṇā (heroine of Mahābhārata): see DRAUPADĪ.

Kṛṣṇa or **Krishna** (Skt., 'black', 'dark'). A composite figure in Hinduism, becoming eventually the eighth and most celebrated *avatāra (incarnation) of *Viṣṇu. In the **Ṛg Veda*, the name appears, but is not connected with divinity. He is the son of the Vedic Devakī and her husband Vasudeva (hence his patronymic Vāsudeva). He is also identified with the son of another Devakī, and is referred to in **Chandogya Upaniṣad* 3. 17. 6 as a scholar. The transformation of Kṛṣṇa appears to have been a part of a longing (expressed in **Bhāgavata Purāṇa*) for a more personal than philosophical focus for religious devotion and progress: according to 1. 3. 27, *Kṛṣṇas tu bhagavān svayam*, 'Kṛṣṇa is *Bhagavan himself.' He is prominent in the **Mahābhārata*, and it is he who instructs Arjuna in the **Bhagavad-gītā*. The many legends told about him make him one of the most popular and accessible figures of Hindu devotion (*bhakti).

Initially, Kṛṣṇa was closely associated with Viṣṇu, and may have been several different figures (in different parts of India), gradually drawn into one. Thus the Ghoṣuṇḍi pillar has been interpreted as linking Kṛṣṇa with *Nārāyana, who was eventually associated with Viṣṇu. As Vāsudeva, Kṛṣṇa is head of the Vṛṣṇi clan who liberates Mathura from the evil *Kaṃsa. As Gopāla, he is the cowherd, always distinct from Vāsudeva in sculpture and narrative. As a unified figure, Kṛṣṇa becomes the object of intense devotion (bhakti). His involvement with the *gopīs in amorous dance (*rasa līlā) becomes the model of passionate union with God; as the adviser to Arjuna in the *Bhagavad-gītā*, he transcends the action and evokes a comparable transcendence in those who attend to him. He is represented iconographically in sinuous dance, playing his irresistible flute to summon the gopīs (and his lovers); but he is also shown in images of power, raising Mount Govardhana above the floods unleashed by *Indra, or destroying the malevolent snake, Kāliya, who has poisoned the life-giving waters of the river *Yamunā. Kṛṣṇa is devoted especially to *Rādhā, and the two are often worshipped together.

See also VAIṢṆAVA; Index, Kṛṣṇa.

W. G. Archer (ed.), *The Loves of Krishna in Indian Painting and Poetry* (1957); F. E. Hardy, *Viraha Bhakti* . . . (1983); J. S. Hawley, *Krishna, the Butter Thief* (1983); B. Majumdar, *Krisna in History and Legend* (1969); W. Ruben, *Krishna: Konkordanz und Kommentar* . . . (1944); M. S. Singer (ed.), *Krishna* . . . (1966).

Kṛta-kṛtya (Skt.). The one in Hinduism who has fulfilled what has to be done, i.e. who has set his whole life to the realization of God and has attained liberation.

Kṛta-yuga: see YUGA.

Ks, Five: see FIVE KS.

Kṣanti (bodhisattva virtue): see PĀRAMITĀ.

Kṣatra (Skt., *ksi*, 'have power over'). Sovereignty (abstract or concrete ruling power) in the Vedic and Hindu traditions. Kṣatra was initially the power associated with sacrifice: '*Agni is *brahman, *soma is kṣatra'. Later, kṣatra, or princely power, complements and upholds *brahma, or priestly power, which helps to sustain the universe. The duty of kings and warriors (*rājadharma*) is to maintain kṣatra by means of *daṇḍanīti* or the science of punishment, treated in the *arthaśāstra.

The term kṣatra may also refer to the princely caste or *varna, in the Vedic tradition called *rājanyas*, and in later Hindu tradition called *kṣatriyas.

Kṣatriya. The second classification in the four *varnas of Hinduism. In its strict sense, it means 'a warrior', but it embraces all those involved in *kṣatra.

Kṣitigarbha (Skt., 'womb of the earth'; Korean, Chijang). In Buddhism a *bodhisattva who is believed to help children (especially deceased children) and to be a saviour from the torments of hell (*naraka). In China he is known as Ti-ts'ang and is represented as a monk holding a staff with six bells (to indicate his power in the six realms of the Kamaloka (see LOKA), and to open the entrance of hell), and also a wish-fulfilling jewel. In Japan, he is known as Jizō, and is of particular importance: statues and offerings are frequently to be seen, especially in graveyards as a supplication for the good reappearance of dead children.

Kṣudrakāgama (Indian division of Sūtrapiṭaka): see TRIPIṬAKA.

Kū. Jap. for *śūnyatā, the void, emptiness.

Ku, K'u. Jap. and Chin. for *dukkha.

Kuan (Chin., 'seeing'). Taoist monastery or nunnery, initially allowing celibates and married priests, but eventually insisting on celibacy.

Kuan-ti. Taoist god of war, who protects the kingdom from enemies, both internal and external. In folk religion he is also Fu-mo ta-ti, the great ruler who expels demons. Kuan-ti appears to have developed euhemeristically (*Euhemerus) from the 3rd-cent. CE warrior, Kuan Yü, whose life supplies many Chinese plays and stories. Devotion to Kuan-ti began relatively late (*c.*7th cent. CE), under Buddhist influence (he has even been regarded as a *bodhisattva who protects Buddhist monasteries). In the 19th cent., he was elevated to the level of Confucius and given the title of 'Military Emperor'.

Kuan-yin: see AVALOKITEŚVARA.

Kubera. An Indian earth spirit, mentioned in **Atharva Veda* 8. 10. 28, who becomes an increasingly important figure in Hindu myths and legends, especially in **Rāmāyaṇa*, where he becomes an ally of *Rāma after his defeat by *Rāvaṇa. He is one of the eight guardians of the world (*Loka-pālas), and, like *Śiva, is so associated with generative power that he is invoked at weddings. He is Yakṣapati, lord of the *yakṣas, and Guhyahapati, lord of the earth spirits; and he is associated particularly with wealth.

A. K. Coomaraswamy, *Yakshas* (1928, 1931).

Kubla Khan: see 'PHAGS-PA-BLO-GROS-RGYAL-MTSHAM

Kubo Kakutarō (founder): see REIYŪKAI.

Kubo Tsuginari (founder): see REIYŪKAI.

Kūdalasaṅgamadēva (Lord of the Meeting Rivers): see BASAVA.

Kuei (Chin., 'spirit'). Component of human being in Taoism and Chinese thought, associated with *p'o and thus with *yin, or the dark and physical side. In later systematization, kuei are the spirits of those who have been killed out of time (e.g. in war, murder, accident), or who have been wrongly executed or improperly buried, or for whom the proper remembrances (*tzu) have not been observed. The *li-kuei* return in vengeance, and must therefore be placated, for which purpose elaborate rituals, especially for the transfer of merit, developed. For further details, see SHEN.

J. W. Bowker, *The Meanings of Death* (1991).

K'uei-chi (pupil): see HSÜAN-TSANG.

Kuei-feng Tsung-mi: see FIVE WAYS OF CH'AN/ZEN.

Kuei-shan Ling-yu: see KUEI-YANG-TSUNG.

Kuei-yang-tsung (Jap., Igyō-shu). One of the *Goke-shichishū ('five houses, seven schools') of early (Tang period) Ch'an/Zen. Its name is derived from two mountains (Kuei and Yang) where the temples of its founders were located. Kuei-shan Ling-yu (771–853 CE) was appointed head of Ta-kuei monastery when *Pai-chang Huai-hai set a jug of water before his pupils: 'If you cannot call this a water-jug, what can you call it?' Kuei-shan kicked the jug over and walked away, demonstrating his enlightened state. His wordless action characterizes Kuei-yang-tsung, in which action and silence are connected to each other, to create the sudden and direct encounter with truth. It also placed emphasis on 'circle-figures' (Chin., *yüan-hsiang*; Jap., **ensō*). Circles and the full moon represent infinite, perfect enlightenment, the original face one had before one was born. In Kuei-yang-tsung, these were elaborated into the way of ninety-seven circles, or of ninety-seven symbols inscribed in circles. It was later contested as a reduction of Zen to artificial means. Among Kuei-shan's important successors were *Hsiang-yen Chih-hsien and *Yang-shan Hui-chi.

Kufr (unbelief): see KĀFIR.

Kuga Sorta (Cheremis, 'big candle'). Popular name for a *syncretist movement among the Cheremis people of the Mari Republic in the USSR from about the 1870s. Although nominally Christianized before this, the threat of Russian acculturation led to an attempt at cultural survival as 'true Cheremis' (their own term for the movement) through a synthesis of traditional and Christian elements. Ancient marriage ceremonies, the cult of the dead, and mythology of the spirit world were combined with belief in *Christ as the greatest of *prophets, and in guardian *angels assisting in the pleasing of the one righteous and merciful God without animal sacrifices. The worship featured a large central candle, but no images, and the pacifist and ascetic ethic rejected modern manufactures and medicine. They were persecuted by the *Orthodox Church and the Tsarist government, and were in conflict with the Soviet régime.

Kūkā (Sikh revivalist movement): see NĀMDHĀRĪ.

Kūkai (774–835). Known posthumously as Kōbō Daishi, the founder of the *Shingon school of Buddhism in Japan. Kūkai was born into a family of Confucian scholars, but in his youth he was attracted to Buddhist teachers. He gravitated toward esoteric Buddhism (Jap., *mikkyō), but the paucity of religious texts and the absence of a qualified teacher hampered his training. He therefore petitioned the imperial court for permission to study in China. In 804 Kūkai travelled to the Chinese capital of Ch'ang-an and sought out its foremost esoteric master, Hui-kuo (746–805). Under him Kūkai received instruction in the two fundamental esoteric scriptures and underwent initiation (Jap., *kanjō*; Skt., *abhiṣeka) into the two related *maṇḍalas—the Womb Maṇḍala (Jap., *taizōkai*) and the Diamond Maṇḍala (Jap., *kongōkai*). In esoteric Buddhism the goal is to 'Achieve Buddhahood in this very body' (*sokushin jōbutsu*). *Mudrā, *mantra, and maṇḍala are employed to attain this goal. Though Kūkai studied with Hui-kuo for only one year, he was introduced to all the texts, rituals, and initiations that his master had to offer. After Hui-kuo's untimely death in 805, Kūkai decided to return to Japan and to establish esoteric Buddhism there. He arrived back in 806 with over 200 religious objects from China, including scriptures, ritual implements, icons, and maṇḍala.

Kūkai gradually emerged as one of two eminent Buddhist masters in Japan. The other was *Saichō (767–822), the founder of the *Tendai school. Relations between the two were cordial at first. Kūkai inducted Saichō into esoteric initiations, lent him religious texts, and instructed his disciples. But when he realized that Saichō wanted to make esoteric Buddhism an appendage of Tendai, their friendship began to sour. Kūkai was convinced of the superiority of esoteric teachings over other forms of Buddhism, as indicated in his treatise *Jūjūshin ron* (Ten Stages of Religious Consciousness) written in 830. Kūkai's greatest benefactor was Emperor Saga (786–842) who, like Kūkai, was a master calligrapher. In 816 Saga granted Kūkai Mount *Kōya as a mountain retreat for the exclusive practice of esoteric Buddhism, and in 823 gave him jurisdiction over Tōji, an imperial temple in Kyōto. These became the centres of the Shingon school. Kūkai was skilful in introducing esoteric ceremonies into Japan's major institutions. In 822 he set up an esoteric altar at the magnificent Tōdaiji temple in *Nara, and he did the same at the imperial palace in 834. By the time of Kūkai's death, in 835, Shingon was a fully recognized school of Buddhism, and esoteric ritual pervaded Japan's religious establishment.

He was able to accommodate the other sects by working out a ten-stage understanding of religious consciousness:

> The mind like a goat or animal in its desires . . .; the mind infantile but temperate [Confucianism] . . .; the mind infantile but hopeful, like a calf following its mother [Brahmanism or popular Taoism, hoping for immortality] . . .; the mind recognising only the outside world but not its self [Śravaka Buddhism] . . .; the mind freed from *karma winning the fruits of *nirvana [Pratyeka Buddhism] . . .; the *Mahayana mind bringing about the salvation of others, . . . viewing distinctions between 'you' and 'me' as illusions [Hosso]; the mind aware of the negation of birth, . . . the mind empty and still, knowing peace and happiness that is beyond description [Sanron]; the mind which follows the one way of truth: the universe is transparent, knowledge and objects of knowledge are undifferentiated . . . [Tendai]; the mind without any characteristics of its own . . . [Kegon]; the mind filled with the splendour of the cosmic Buddha, when the medicine of exoteric teaching has done its work in clearing away the dust, the secret and true treasures are displayed [Shingon].

Tr. major works, Y. S. Hakeda (1972).

Kula (Skt., 'family'). 1. The family lineage and home in Hinduism, of importance (along with *jāti and gotra, the original ancestor) in determining the exact position of a person in society.

2. *Tantric school originating in the *Bhairava-Kālī cults and *Kāpālika cremation-ground (*śmaśāna) dwellers. The aim of Kula practice, which involved consuming scatological substances and corpse-flesh, was possession (*aveśa*) by a female deity to achieve perfection (siddhi). These forces were also manifested in human form as *yoginīs. Kula practice still continues in certain parts of India.

Kulacēkaraṉ (one of the Āḻvārs): see ĀḺVĀRS.

Kula-devatā. The god, or gods, chosen by a Hindu family for worship or for protection.

Kulārṇava Tantra (Skt., 'ocean of the family Tantra'). A text (1000–1400 CE) of the *Kaula tradition advocating various forms of *Tantric worship, including the five 'Ms' (*pañca-makāra). It advocates the ritual use of wine (though its 'drink and drink again' (7. 100) might refer to the drinking of inner nectar (*amṛta)). Wine and meat have symbolic meaning, of which the *sādhaka must be aware: alcohol is *Śiva, meat is *Śakti, and the consumer is *Bhairava. Indeed, to perform the left-hand rites, a sādhaka must possess a pure mind (2. 33). Other topics dealt with are *mantra, *dikṣa, devotion to the *guru, the seven stages of the spiritual journey (*ullāsa*), and worship of a woman as the incarnation of Śakti (śakti pūjā).

Eng. summary by M. P. Pandit (1973).

Kumāra (youthful offspring of Śiva): see SKANDA.

Kumārāja (Tibetan ascetic): see KLONG-CHEN RAB-'BYAMS-PA.

Kumārajīva (*c*.344–413 CE). One of the greatest of Buddhist translators. Kumārajīva was born in the Serindian town of Kuchat and studied first in N. India and then in Kashgar. His father was an ex-monk and his mother became a nun when he was 7 years old, taking him with her to India two years later. Returning in due course to Kuchat and Kashgar, Kumārajīva, who had grown up under the influence of the *Hīnayāna, became acquainted with the Mahāyāna teachings and was converted to them. He was ordained at the age of 20 and spent two years studying the Mahāyāna texts, being noted in a Chinese text of 379 CE as a brilliant devotee of Mahāyāna. Captured by Chinese in 383, he studied Chinese until he was liberated and welcomed to Chang-an in 401, where he spent the rest of his life teaching and translating. He rendered many of the most important Mahāyāna sūtras and treatises into elegant and accurate Chinese, in a style that has never been improved upon. A particularly important body of writings he translated consisted of the four central texts of the *Mādhyamaka school, which became the foundation of the *San-lun school of Mādhyamaka in China.

Kumārila Bhaṭṭa (7th cent. CE). A learned *brahman of Bihar and follower of the Mīmāṃsā school. He actively opposed the Buddhists and Jains. Tradition makes him a teacher of *Śaṅkara; he is also said to be an *incarnation of Kārttikeya, son of *Śiva. Author of the *Mīmāṃsā-vārttika* and also the *Śloka-vārttika* (the latter an extensive argument against the existence and the necessity of God), he adopted the principle of non-duality (*advaita). For Kumārila, liberation was not *mokṣa, but rather the state of the self free from pain.

Kumāri pūjā (Skt.). In *Tantrism, the worship of a 12-year-old virgin girl who represents the Goddess (*Devī) or *Śakti. She is installed on a seat (*pīṭha) and worshipped through *mantra repetition. The performance of this pūjā follows upon the completion of the daily Tantric pūjā, although alchohol and sexual intercourse (*maithuna) are prohibited. The rite is prevalent in Bengal, but is also found throughout India and Nepal.

Kumbha (Skt., 'pot'). The mark of a *sādhu's renunciation. The empty pot is also a symbol of the womb, and Kumbhamātā is the guardian deity of villages in Hinduism, especially prominent at marriages.

Kumbhaka. Suspension of breath between exhaling and inhaling, a part of Hindu *rāja- and *haṭha-yoga.

Kuṁbhamelā. Pilgrimage assembly of Hindu devotees, held every three years at four different places in turn. The places, *Hardwār, Nāsik, Prayāga, and Ujjain, are those where drops of *amṛta, the nectar of immortality, fell to earth during a heavenly conflict. Many millions of pilgrims are attracted to the kuṁbhamelās.

Kundakunda. Eminent *Digambara Jain teacher, writer, and philosopher of perhaps 2nd–3rd cents. CE. Details of his life are difficult to confirm, but his name may be a S. Indian village name, as he is sometimes referred to as 'Padmanandin muni of Konda-kunda'. His prolific Prakrit writings form the most authoritative source of Digambara Jain teaching. Sixteen works are attributed to him, but these attributions are not secure; at most, only parts of some works are likely to have been written by him. However, Digambara Jains regard all these works as coming from him and as having authority. Major works are *Niyamasāra* (Essence of Restraint, tr. U. Sain, 1931), *Pravacanasāra* (Essence of Scripture, tr. B. Faddegon, 1935), and *Pañcāstinikayasāra* (Essence of the Five Entities, tr. A. Chakravarti, 1920). His *Samayasāra* (Essence of Doctrine, tr. A. Chakravarti, 1930; R. B. Jain, 1931) is of great importance since it is devoted to a discussion of the real nature of the soul, a central preoccupation for Kundakunda. The soul is the absolute and foundational reality, known in its pure and free form as *paramātman. As a result of *karma, it becomes weighed down and impeded, though not in itself affected. It is like one who dreams that she is attempting to run but cannot move her limbs. So the soul only experiences the mental consequences of karma, while remaining what it is. It follows that the recovery of the unimpeded soul requires disciplined attention to the inner state, allowing the world and all external acts to fall away. This might seem to be heading in the direction of a repudiation of ritual, faith, and practice; and indeed, Kundakunda argued that such things only have validity in the world-perspective as a preliminary to direct soul-knowledge. Even the basic Jain virtues, including the *Three Jewels (Triratna), are at best servants to the knowledge of the soul: 'Mercy to living creatures, self-restraint, integrity, honesty, chastity, contentment, right faith, knowledge and austerity are but the entourage of truth.' Later commentators tried to reconcile the importance of Jain practices with this transcendental supremacy, using the image of a farmer who wishes to grow corn: without the preparation and the seed, there will be no harvest.

Kuṇḍalinī (Skt.). *Śakti (power) envisaged as a coiled snake at the base of the central channel (suṣumnā *nāḍī) in the mūlādhāra *cakra of *Tantric esoteric anatomy. Kuṇḍalinī *yoga is a means of attaining *samādhi and finally liberation in Tantric *sādhana. She is aroused by the arrest of breath and semen through *prāṇayāma and *mantra repetition (*japa). The left and right channels (*iḍā and *piṅgala nāḍīs) on either side of the central channel are emptied of *prāṇa (breath/energy) which is forced into the suṣumnā. This awakens Kuṇḍalinī coiled around a *liṅga in the *mūlādhāra*, and arouses an intense heat (*tapas). Kuṇḍalinī then ascends up the suṣumnā, piercing the cakras or 'knots' (*granthi*) until she reaches the thousand-petalled lotus (*sahasrāra padma) just above the top of the head where she unites with *Śiva. This is the union (*yāmala) of the male–female polarity within the body. In some systems Kuṇḍalinī descends back from the sahasrāra to the heart (hṛdaya) filling the body with the nectar (*amṛta) of bliss. Her ascent is associated with inner sound (*nāda) which reverberates in the suṣumnā. Kuṇḍalinī yoga is synonymous with *laya yoga, the dissolving of the universe (the macrocosm) within the body (the microcosm). This parallels the dissolution of the cosmos (*pralaya) in Hindu cosmology. It is thought to be highly dangerous to practise this yoga without the guidance of a *guru. A recent exponent of Kuṇḍalinī yoga was *Gopikrishna, who inadvertently aroused Kuṇḍalinī and gave an account of his experiences. His disciple, F. Dippong, founded the Kuṇḍalinī Research Institute in Canada in 1976. The Institute claims that Kuṇḍalinī is responsible for outstanding creativity, psychic powers, and mystical experiences. Kuṇḍalinī yoga is also used by contemporary religious sects such as the 3HO and the Rajneesh movement.

A. Avalon, *The Serpent Power* (7th edn., 1964); I. Bentov and L. Sannella, *Kundalini: Psychosis of Transcendence* (1976).

Kundalini Research Institute: see KUṆḌALINĪ.

K'ung. In Buddhism, the Chin. tr. of *śūnyatā (Skt., 'emptiness') which supplanted the earlier term **wu* ('non-existence'), which was misunderstood as implying *nihilism. K'ung literally means 'vacuity' or 'spaciousness' and was eventually considered more appropriate for expressing the *Mahāyāna teaching of no inherent existence.

Küng, Hans (b. 1928). Swiss RC theologian teaching at the University of Tübingen. His *The Council and Reunion* (1960; Eng. 1961) set out a programme of reforms for the Second *Vatican Council, many of which actually came about. After the council he wrote widely on *ecclesiology (especially *The Church*, 1967), *Christology, the existence of God, and many other topics. His questioning of some traditional RC doctrines in his *Infallible?* (1970; Eng. 1971) and *On Being a Christian* (1974; Eng. 1977) led to the intervention of the Sacred Congregation for the Doctrine of the Faith in Rome. In 1979 it was announced that he could no longer teach officially as a Catholic theologian. Although rarely a profound writer, Küng is amongst the most prolific and readable of contemporary theologians, and one whose works have achieved wide popularity.

Kung-an: see KŌAN.

K'ung-tzu: see CONFUCIUS.

Kunitokotachi (founding deity of Japan): see KITABAKE CHIKAFUSA.

K'un-lun. A mountain range in W. China, the abode of Hsi wang-mu and the immortals (*hsien), and thus the Taoist paradise.

Kuntī, also called **Pṛthā.** In the **Mahābhārata*, mother of the three oldest *Pāṇḍavas: Yudhiṣṭhira, *Bhīma, and *Arjuna. As a young girl, Kuntī is given a *mantra by the sage Durvāsas, whereby she may summon any god she chooses to engender a child upon her. She first used the mantra before her marriage, to call upon the sun god, an action which results in the illegitimate birth of *Karṇa (after which Kuntī's virginity is restored miraculously). Later, when Pāṇḍu is rendered virtually impotent by a curse, Kuntī uses the mantra again, and, having given birth to her three sons, passes it on to her co-wife Mādrī, who bears the two youngest Pāṇḍavas. Until the Pāṇḍavas' marriage to *Draupadī, Kuntī shares their adventures. During the Pāṇḍavas' exile, however, Kuntī remains at home, as an elder of the family. Just before the *Kurukṣetra war, she tries unsuccessfully to convince Karṇa, whom she had cast out at birth, to recognize the Pāṇḍavas as his brothers and allies. Some years after her sons' victory and reinstatement, Kuntī retires to the forest, and she later dies in a forest fire, along with *Dhṛtarāṣṭra and Gāndhārī.

Kuo Hsiang (early neo-Taoist): see HSÜAN-HSÜEH.

Kurahit (Pañjābī, 'misdeed'). Offences against the Sikh *rahit, the *khālsā code of discipline. They are removing or trimming *hair from any part of the body, eating halal meat, committing *adultery, and using tobacco. Transgressors have to be reinitiated.

Kūrma (Skt., 'tortoise'). In Hindu mythology an animal which is associated with *Viṣṇu in various ways. In the ancient fourfold cosmography of the *Purāṇas, it is said to be the form of Viṣṇu which supports Bhārata (India). In the earliest known versions of the myth of the Churning of the Ocean, the tortoise allows the gods and demons to use its back as a base for the mountain which serves as their churning-stick, and in later versions Viṣṇu himself takes the form of a tortoise in order to do this. Some ritual texts identify the tortoise with *Prajāpati, who is said to assume its form before creating living beings (kūrma is here linked with $\sqrt{kr}$, 'to make'), but later this identification is transferred to Viṣṇu, whose three strides propped apart earth and heaven, as the tortoise's body props apart its lower and upper shells. Kūrma is the second in the standard list of Viṣṇu's ten *avatāras.

Kurozumikyō: see KUROZUMI MUNETADA.

Kurozumi Munetada (1780–1850). Founder of Kurozumikyō, a Japanese new religion. He was a Shinto priest, the descendant of a line of priests at the Imamaura shrine. In 1812, both his parents died, and he contracted tuberculosis; as a result he was virtually bed-ridden for three years. Believing that his original goal of becoming a *kami in this life was now frustrated, he vowed that after death he would become a healing deity. However, in prayer to the sun goddess, *Amaterasu, he awoke both to healing and to the realization that the divine and the human are inseparable, and that consequently there is neither birth nor death but only movement in eternal life. This transformative vision occurred on 11 Nov. 1814, a date which is now commemorated as the beginning of Kurozumikyō. He extended his own healing through healing others, and his own vision through itinerant preaching. Kurozumikyō was given government authorization as an independent Shinto sect in 1876. Its leadership is held by direct descendants of Kurozumi and numbers about a quarter of a million adherents.

H. Hardacre, *Kurozumikyō and the New Religions of Japan* (1986).

Kursī (Arab., 'stool'). In Islam, the footstool of the throne (*al-ʿarsh*) of God, and often used as a synonym of 'throne'. It is thus central in debates about the literal or metaphorical sense of such terms in the *Qur'ān; metaphorically *al-ʿarsh* is the Being of God, al-kursī his non-formal manifestation. A kursī is also a support for a Qur'ān in a *mosque. For a translation of the Verse of the Throne, see THRONE OF GOD.

Kurukṣetra (Skt., 'field of the Kurus'). Site of a great war between the *Pāṇḍavas and the *Kauravas, the central action of the **Mahābhārata*. According to the epic, Kurukṣetra takes its name from the area's having been ploughed for many years by King Kuru, an ancestor of both the Pāṇḍava and Kaurava lines, in his effort to make of it an auspicious spot, a gateway to heaven for those who might die there. Kurukṣetra also seems to be so called from the fact that it is the core of the ancestral home of the Kuru race, that is, of Kuru's descendants. The **Bhagavadgītā* refers to Kurukṣetra as the *dharmakṣetra* ('field of *dharma'), for it is here, during the war, that dharma meets its ultimate test. More broadly, Kurukṣetra is known to the epic as an extremely potent sacred area, an altar of *Brahmā or *Prajāpati, of which it is said, for example, 'Merely by uttering the single statement, "I will go to Kurukṣetra, I will live in Kurukṣetra," one is released from all sins' (*Mahābhārata* 3. 81. 176; compare 3. 81. 2).

Identified as being in the area of Delhi, Kurukṣetra has also served as a battlefield in other contexts, mentioned in the epic itself, and elsewhere.

Kuśa. A species of grass regarded by Hindus as the most sacred of grasses (and often called, more popularly, *darbha*). It was spread over the whole sacred and sacrificial area during ritual celebrations. It was also used as a substitute for *soma.

Kusala (Pali; Skt., *kuśala*). In early Buddhist texts, the skilfulness which enables one to abstain from committing those actions which retard or obstruct spiritual development and to limit oneself to doing only those actions which help and bring about spiritual development. The operation of a kusala volition brings about a three-phased development. First, it provides the moral strength to abstain from those actions which are harmful to spiritual development; second, it prevents the reactivation of the harmful and undesirable emotions so suppressed; and third, the emotions which were rendered inactive by suppression are completely removed, resulting in total and lasting direction to spiritual development.

Kusala, when explained with reference to an individual's moral conduct is spelt out as consisting of ten actions. The *Sammādiṭṭhi Sutta* of the *Majjhima Nikāya* (1. 47 f.) explains these ten (*dasa kusala kammāni)* as follows: (i) abstinence from destruction of life (*pānātipātā veramaṇī kusalaṃ*), (ii) abstinence from theft (*adinnādānā veramaṇī kusalaṃ*), (iii) abstinence from unchastity (*kāmesumicchācārā veramaṇī kusalaṃ*), (iv) abstinence from lying (*musāvādā veramaṇī kusalaṃ*), (v) abstinence from slandering (*pisunāvācā veramaṇī kusalaṃ*), (vi) abstinence from rough speech (*pharusāvācā veramaṇī kusalaṃ*), (vii) abstinence from frivolous talk (*samphappalāpā veramaṇī kusalaṃ*), (viii) abstinence from covetousness (*anabhijjālū kusalaṃ*), (ix) abstinence from malice (*abyāpannacitto kusalaṃ*), and (x) right views (*sammādiṭṭhi kusalaṃ*).

In each instance, the abstinence indicated above constitutes only the initial step of the process of the relevant kusala action. The next and the more important step consists of deliberate involvement in the cultivation of the opposite positive qualities. For example, in the case of the first kusala, having abstained from causing harm or injury to creatures, the individual cultivates and develops kindness, sympathy, and friendliness towards all creatures (see ibid. 1. 179 f.).

Thus, a kusala action consists of these two essential components, the negative and the positive, either of which complements the other. A kusala is action born out of a moral volition rooted in either one or all of the following three: greedlessness (*alobha*), hatelessness (*adosa*), and undeludedness (*amoha*). The result which is generated by a kusala action is a *puṇya, but this subtle and important distinction between the cause and its effect has disappeared even in the later portions of the Pāli canon, with the two concepts being equated. For the opposite, see AKUŚALA.

Kuṣāṇa (period): see KANIṢKA.

Kusha (Buddhist sect): see NARA BUDDHISM.

Kuśinagara. Town (in Uttar-pradesh) where the *Buddha passed on (parinirvāna). Part of his remains were preserved as relics in a *stūpa in Kuśinagara, which thus became an important centre of *pilgrimage. When *Hsüan-tsang visited in 7th cent. CE, it had been destroyed. But it remains one of the four most holy places in Buddhism.

Kusti (sacred cord): see NAUJOTE.

Kūya or **Kōya** (903–72). Founder of the Kuya Sect of the Japanese *Tendai (Chinese, *T'ien-t'ai) school of Buddhism. Born in *Kyōto, he became a novice monk in his infancy. He was also one of the early advocates of *Pure Land Buddhist teaching and practice in Japan, spending his career as an itinerant teacher urging the common people to place faith in *Amida Buddha (the Buddha of Infinite Light) through the constant invocation of the Pure Land *nembutsu *mantra, *namu amida butsu*, 'I take refuge in the Buddha of Infinite Light.' For this reason, he was popularly regarded as a *nembutsu-hijiri* ('nembutsu holy man'). Kūya was also famous for his social work activities, such as building bridges, irrigation systems, centres for the care of the ill and the needy, and the repairing of roads in an effort to demonstrate in practice (and to inculcate) Amida Buddha's compassion among the people. In 938, after an extensive period of itinerant teaching in the northern provinces, he settled in Kyōto and began spreading Pure Land teaching and practice there. In Kyōto he was also popularly known as *ichi no shōnin* ('first of the saints'), *ichi hijiri* ('first of the holy men'), and *amida hijiri* ('Amida holy man').

Kuzari (text by Judah haLevi): see JUDAH HALEVI.

Kwannon: see AVALOKITEŚVARA.

Kwatsu (Jap. pronunciation): see HO (1).

Kyabdro. The Tibetan understanding and adaptation of 'taking refuge', the *Three Jewels (triratna) which constitute the fundamental Buddhist commitment and disposition. The Diamond Vehicle (*Vajrayāna) added a fourth refuge, the *lama; other schools added three, the lama, the *yidam (personal deity), and the *dākinī (sources of wisdom).

Kyō. Jap., for *sūtra.

Kyoge-betsuden (transmission outside formal teaching): see FUKASETSU.

Kyogen Chikan (Japanese name): see HSIANG-YEN CHIH-HSIEN.

Kyōha Shintō (Jap., 'sectarian *Shinto'). A group of independent Shinto sects which began their activities in the late Tokugawa and early Meiji periods. When the government created State Shinto (*kokka shintō), which embraced most of the Shinto shrines, it did not wish to incorporate these new groups but created the special category of Kyōha Shintō so that it could regard them as private religious organizations. These thirteen sects originated in close relation to peasant movements, devotional associations, magico-religious practices, and ideas about changing the world through religious practices. All but one of these movements, Shintō Taikyō, were founded by charismatic personalities, and they have their own unique sets of scriptures, either composed or revealed by the founder. All but *Konkōkyō and *Tenrikyo worship the traditional Shinto kami *Izanagi, Izanami, and *Amaterasu-o-Mikami. They all believe in the oneness of humanity and divinity, are more concerned with life in this world than in the next world, and advocate pure and selfless service for the advancement of human life. The thirteen traditional Shinto sects can be classified in several different groupings: pure Shinto sects (Shintō Taikyō, Shinrikyō, and Izumo Ōyashirokyō), Confucianistic Shinto sects (Shintō Shūseiha and Shintō Taiseikyō), purification sects (Shinshūkyō and Misogikyō), mountain-worship sects (Jikkōkyō, Fusōkyō, and Ontakekyō), and faith-healing sects (Kurozumikyō, Konkōkyō, and Tenrikyō). The Sect Shinto groups remain active with large numbers of adherents today. Most of the original thirteen sects, plus *Ōmoto (a similar movement which also began in the early Meiji period), belong to the Association of Sect Shinto (Kyōha Shintō Rengōkai). A large number of small splinter-sects which were subsumed under the thirteen main sects separated themselves after the Second World War and began independent activities. By 1979 there were some eighty-two sects with over 5 million followers claiming to stand in the Kyōha Shintō tradition. In addition, some forty-eight new Shinto sects that have sprung up since the war, with 2 million followers, are generally tabulated as 'New Sect Shinto' (*Shin Kyōha Shintō*).

Kyŏmik (fl. 6th cent. CE). Founder of the *Vinaya school of Buddhism in the kingdom of Paekche in Korea. Kyŏmik studied the Vinaya in India, returning home in 526 with the texts of the five-division Vinaya. Upon his return, he was commissioned by King Sŏngmyŏng (r. 523–53) to translate the Vinaya texts which, subsequently, became the foundation of Paekche Buddhism.

Kyōō-gokokuji (temple in Kyōto): see TŌJI.

Kyosaku also **Keisaku.** Zen 'wake-up stick', used by teachers to stimulate pupils and perhaps shock them into enlightenment. It represents the sword of *Mañjuśrī which cuts through all delusions.

Kyōto. Japanese city, of particular importance for its Buddhist temples and monasteries. Called originally Heian-kyo, the emperor attempted to restrict Buddhism to two sites, Saiji and Toji (which still survives, its pagoda being one of the highest in Japan). But the restriction disappeared, and virtually every school and sect in Buddhism had or has its location in Kyōto. Of particular early importance are the Hosso (*Dōshō) temple Kiyomizu, with its elaborate scaffolding construction (to throw oneself from the scaffold of Kiyomizu is to launch oneself into the unknown), and the Byōdō-in, temple of equality, the 'Phoenix Hall' of which survived the fire in 1483 which destroyed all else; it was beautifully restored in 1957. The arrival of Zen brought back the simpler style of a single axis leading from a southern entrance, through the triple gate (*sammon*), the buddha-hall (*butsuden), to the dharma-hall (*hatto*). Among the earliest are Nanzenji (13th cent., see MUKAN FUMON), and the smaller, but related Eikan-do. Of equal importance is *Daitoku-ji, whose original 14th-cent. buildings burned down in the 15th cent., but which remains a classic example of a Zen monastery. *Pure Land temples are also prominent in Kyōto, especially Chion-in of Jodo-shu, and *Honganji where *Shinran was buried. Also at Kyōto is the famous rock garden at the Ryoanji temple, fifteen rocks so placed in groups of seven, five, and three, that from any aspect, one rock is hidden. Of note also are the Gold and Silver Pavilions, constructed as palaces, but converted to temples on the death of their original owners.

D. Keene, *World Within Walls* (1976).

Kyoto School: see NISHIDA KITARŌ.

Kyōun-Shu: see IKKYŪ SŌJUN.

Kyōzan Ejaku (Jap. name): see YANG-SHAN HUI-CHI.

Kyrie (Gk., *Kyrie eleēson*, 'Lord, have mercy'). A brief prayer used in Christian liturgical worship. The Gk. words were kept untranslated in the Latin mass and often remain thus in English-language services.

Kyūdō (Jap., 'way of the bow'). The zen art of archery, in which control and mastery are cultivated.

E. Herrigel, *Zen in the Art of Archery* (1971).

L

Labarum. The military standard of the emperor *Constantine. According to *Eusebius's *Life of Constantine* it was adopted after Constantine saw a vision of the cross with the words 'by this (sign), conquer'. Its design was that of the Roman cavalry standard with the pagan emblems replaced by the *chi-rho monogram.

Lady, Our. Designation of the Blessed Virgin *Mary. Lady Day is the feast of the *Annunciation, 25 Mar. A Lady Chapel is one dedicated to Mary.

Laestadianism. A Christian revival movement in northern Scandinavia founded by Lars Levi Laestadius (1800–61). This Swedish pastor of the *Lutheran church in Karesuando, near the Finnish border in Lappland, was more interested in botany than in souls until a deep personal awakening in 1844 led to a new preaching of the gospel, with emphasis upon repentance and the absolute forgiveness of sins within the congregation as the body of *Christ and through his atoning death. This led to a general revival with ecstatic forms of worship from northern Norway across to Finland, and brought profound moral change, especially to the drunken and debauched Lapp (now Sami) community. Laestadianism continues as largely peasant and distinct communities within the state Lutheran Churches, numbering some 200,000 in the northern third of Finland, and also among some Sami groups. Emigrating Laestadianism Finns were responsible for the foundation of the Apostolic Lutheran Church in the USA in 1871.

Laetentur Coeli (Lat., 'let the heavens rejoice'). The title, taken from the opening words, of two unconnected Christian documents.

1. The Formulary of Reunion of 433 between the opposing parties after the Council of *Ephesus; it sets out an *Alexandrian christology, insisting on the *theotokos and both the unity of person and distinction of the natures in Christ.

2. The *bull of 1439 decreeing the union agreed at the Council of *Florence of the E. and W. churches, that the Orthodox accept the *filioque and the primacy of the see of Rome.

Lag Ba-Omer (Heb., 'thirty-third of Omer'). A Jewish holiday. Lag Ba-Omer is celebrated on the thirty-third day of counting the *Omer, i.e. 18 Iyyar. Mourning customs are lifted, weddings may be solemnized, and music enjoyed. In the Middle Ages it was seen as a scholar's festival and was first kept because a plague stopped on that day. In the *aggadic tradition, it was the first day of the giving of *manna (Exodus 16), and the *kabbalists regarded it as the anniversary of the *death of *Simeon b. Yoḥai. Customs associated with the festival include giving 3-year-old boys their first haircut, playing with bows and arrows, and lighting bonfires.

Laghiman (Skt., 'lightness'). Yogic ability in Hinduism to levitate. See also DARDURA-SIDDHI.

Laity (Gk., *laos*, 'people'). Baptized Christians who are not clergy or ordained to specific ministry (i.e. the majority). Since the New Testament envisages a priesthood of all believers, the place of the laity in the mission and life of the Church should be paramount. *Christifideles Laici*, a *Roman Catholic Apostolic Exhortation issued in 1989, appealed to the laity to 'overcome in themselves the separation of the Gospel from life' and to adopt 'an integrated approach to life that is fully brought about by the inspiration and strength of the Gospel'. In fact, virtually the whole of mainstream Christianity is dominated by the ordained clergy, so far as control and decision-making is concerned (but see CONGREGATIONAL CHURCHES), although *Anglicans have in recent years tried to give a more serious place to the laity. The term is now also applied to people in other religions who are not among the formally accredited personnel—e.g., in Buddhism, those who do not belong to the *saṅgha, the community of *bhikkhus, i.e. *upāsaka.

Lakṣaṇa (Skt., 'marks'). Marks on a body, auspicious for Hindus if they appear on the right (for a man) or the left (for a woman): see also ASHES. The term has also been used for the five characteristics of a complete *purāṇa: (i) creation of a cosmos; (ii) its dissolution and renewal; (iii) the origin and descent of gods and heroes; (iv) the work of the *Manus (lawgivers); (v) the work of their descendants.

For the thirty-two marks of a *Buddha, see DVĀTRIMŚADVARA-LAKṢANA.

Lakṣmaṇa. The half-brother of *Rāma and son of Daśaratha, king of *Ayodhyā. Lakṣmaṇa went voluntarily into exile with Rāma and his bride, *Sītā, when the couple were expelled from Ayodhyā so that another of Rāma's half-brothers, Bharata, might succeed to the throne through the machinations of his mother. A skilled archer, like Rāma, Lakṣmaṇa killed many threatening ogres during his exile, and sliced off the ears and nose of the monstrous

Śūrpanakhā. He accompanied Rāma in his search for Sītā after her abduction by *Rāvaṇa, king of Laṅkā, and fought bravely in the final battle to win her back, killing Rāvaṇa's son in the process. He was himself seriously wounded (some say killed) by Rāvaṇa, but was restored to health by the physician Sushena, using herbs brought specially by *Hanumān. After Lakṣmaṇa's return to Ayodhyā, he and his brother Śatrughna were defeated in conflict by Sītā's sons Lava and Kuśa, who thus showed the divine power they had inherited from their father Rāma. As Rāma's life-span was coming to an end, Lakṣmaṇa took upon himself the death-sentence that was Rāma's and committed suicide by drowning in the River Śarayū, whence his body was removed to heaven by the gods.

Lakṣmī (Skt., 'sign'). In the *Vedas a mark or indication, neither good nor bad unless so qualified (e.g. by *puṇya* if good). But at least from the time of **Mahābhārata*, Lakṣmī is personified as a Goddess of good fortune and the embodiment of beauty. As the former, she is depicted with four (generous) arms, but as the latter with two. According to **Ramāyāna*, she arose from the *Churning of the Ocean, hence her name Kṣīrābdhitanayā (daughter of the ocean of milk). She holds a lotus, or lies on a lotus leaf. She is the consort of *Indra and *Viṣṇu, and accompanies the latter on his incarnations (*avatāra). Thus when he appeared as Rāmacandra, she was *Sītā; and when as Paraśurāma, she was Dharaṇi (Earth). In all manifestations, she is associated with fertility and good fortune, and her image is often put on doorposts to ward off evil. In conjunction with *Nārāyaṇa (as Lakṣmī-Nārāyaṇa) the dual form signifies the perfect union between Viṣṇu and his *śakti, constituting the supreme *Brahman without distinction. Śrī Lakṣmī is often known simply as *Śrī.

Lakṣya (form of chosen deity): see IṢṬADEVATĀ.

Lal Ded: see LALLĀ.

Lalitā. Indian goddess, also known as Mahādevi (see DEVI), important in Tantric Hinduism. She is also the personification of *Līlā, and thus her form is the universe: she is *Pārvatī when dancing, and is the writhing which precedes birth and manifestation.

Lalitavistara (Skt., *lalita*, 'played', + *vistara*, 'details'). A Buddhist text of about 2nd cent. CE, highly valued in *Mahāyāna. The *Lalitavistara* gives a poetical account of the early life of the *Buddha up to the beginning of his ministry. It is probably based on a Pāli text of the *Sarvāstivadin school, subsequently elaborated into its present Skt. form of twenty-seven chapters in poetry and prose. It is now considered one of the earliest *sūtras of the Mahāyāna. Its mythological treatment of the life of the Buddha has been an important influence on Buddhist *iconography.

Tr. in G. Bays, *The Voice of the Buddha* (1983).

Lallā or **Lal Ded.** 14th-cent. *Kashmiri Śaivite poetess. Little is known of her life apart from an immense proliferation of stories, which attest to her popularity, but cannot be verified historically. She is said to have been born in a *brahman family and to have been married to a man whose mother treated her with great cruelty. She renounced married life and came under the instruction of a Śaivite yogi, Siddha Śrīkaṇṭha. From that point on she refused to wear clothes, as a mark of her detachment from this world. She composed verse sayings, known as *vakh*, which are often direct and simple—e.g. 'I, Lallā, wandered far in search of Śiva, the Lord who is everywhere, and after all this wandering, I, Lallā, found him at last within my own self, dwelling in his own home.' But many of them are in fact complex in their associations, so that translations cannot convey why they remain so deeply loved among Kashmiris, both Hindu and Muslim.

Trs., G. A. Grierson and L. D. Barnett (1920), R. C. Temple (1934); J. L. Kaul, *Lal Ded* (1973).

Lama (Tib., *bla.ma.*, 'Higher One'). An honorary title in Tibetan Buddhism conferred upon anyone accepted as a 'spiritual teacher' (corresponding to Skt., *guru), but generally only given to one who has completed particular scholastic and yogic training—a training which is still undertaken when someone has been recognized as a 're-incarnate lama' (*tulku), i.e. is understood to have already achieved lamahood in a previous life. It is possible to renounce one's monkhood without renouncing one's lama status, for purposes of marriage etc., which principles are within the keeping of the *Mahāyāna canon.

See also LAMAISM.

Lama dancing (Tib., *lha.'cham*, 'sacred dance'). Tibetan Buddhist *mystery play. A drama of great colour, costume, masks, and music, enacted predominantly by *lamas as a form of mime, in which every bodily movement carries a precise symbolic meaning. Such dances are normally performed at festivals, particularly those of the new year (*losar*) such as the Great Prayer held around the *jokhang, when they can double as *exorcism ceremonies, banishing evil from the community in order to begin the new year auspiciously. In such performances, the actors will dress particularly in the costumes of the wrathful protector divinities (the idea is that these divinities are truly invoked, which is probably why their parts are played by lamas) and overpower a human effigy onto which the negative influences of the community have been projected. Not all such dances have such purposive import, however; other favoured themes are the re-enactions of historical events, such as the killing of the evil King Langdarma (842 CE) and the Samyé debate (*c.*792–4 CE). Debate is a natural subject for Tibetan dancing, being a popular part of the monastic curriculum and itself invariably accompanied by theatrical gestures. Although lama dancing is a serious affair involving several days of preparation and propitiation, it is intended equally as entertainment, and being universally popular provides a valuable link between the monasteries and the community.

Lama dancing should not be confused with a popular form of dance called *A che lha mo* ('elder sister-goddess') which is performed by travelling theatrical troupes and where the subject-matter is more profane—the intricacies of love, perhaps—and the resolution of the plot is achieved by the intervention, in the role of an elder sister, of a 'goddess' such as the *bodhisattva *Tārā.

Lamaism. A now antiquated term used by early W. commentators (as L. A. Waddell, *The Buddhism of Tibet, or Lamaism*, 1895) to describe Tibetan Buddhism. Although the term is not accurate (because not all Tibetan monks are *lamas) and could be as misleading as, say, the term 'Priest-ism' to describe Christianity, it has been pointed out that 'Lamaism' does at least convey the great emphasis placed on the role of the spiritual teacher by this religion, and indeed it avoids the problem that not all followers of 'Tibetan Buddhism' are in fact Tibetan: the faith is followed in Bhutan, Sikkim, Ladakh, Nepal, parts of China and Mongolia, and now, of course, in increasing numbers in Europe and America.

Lamb. Christian symbol for *Christ. Its basis is the biblical *Passover lamb (Exodus 12. 1–13; 1 Corinthians 5. 7), the *suffering servant who was led as a lamb to slaughter (Isaiah 53. 7), and the words of *John the Baptist pointing out Jesus as 'the lamb of God' (John 1. 29–36). In the book of *Revelation, the lamb appears repeatedly as Christ, who stands next to the throne of God, in whose blood the saved wash their robes, and who will defeat his enemies and celebrate his marriage supper. In art, representations of Christ as lamb go back to the 4th cent. Before the *crucifixion was realistically depicted, the lamb was customarily substituted for the human figure of Christ; but this practice was forbidden by the Council of Trulla in 692. See also AGNUS DEI; AGNES, ST.

Lambeth Conferences. Assemblies of the bishops of the whole *Anglican Communion held about once every ten years under the presidency of the archbishop of *Canterbury (whose London residence is Lambeth Palace). The original idea of the conferences was that they should be councils to define doctrine, but this was abandoned before the first one was convened in 1867, and the bishops' resolutions have been expressions of opinion rather than binding rules. The eleventh conference was held in 1978; resolutions were made on social and economic injustice and violent 'liberation' movements, as well as doctrinal and ecumenical matters. The conference in 1988 was attended by twenty-seven primates, and a substantially larger number of bishops from Africa (175 in contrast to 80 in 1978). The Conference reflected the invitation, 'Bring your diocese with you', and placed emphasis on sharing local concerns. There was consequently a clear focus on the status of women (and on women's ordination), on AIDS, and on polygamy, as also on the relation of Christianity to non-Christian religions, especially Islam. A resolution on authority and decision-making endeavoured to make more systematic the process of consultation in the Anglican Communion.

The 'Lambeth Quadrilateral', approved at the conference of 1888, remains the Anglican statement of the fourfold essential basis for a reunited Church: (i) the Bible as the ultimate rule of faith, (ii) the *Apostles' and *Nicene creeds, (iii) the *sacraments of baptism and Lord's supper, and (iv) the 'historic episcopate'.

Lambeth Quadrilateral (basis for ecumenicism): see ANGLICANISM.

Lam Drey (siddha system): see SAKYA.

Lamed Vav Zaddikim (Heb., '36 righteous men', appearing in Yiddish as Lamedvovniks), according to Jewish legend, the minimum number of righteous men alive in any one generation required to prevent the destruction of the world. The *Talmud states, 'there are not less than thirty-six righteous men in the world who receive the divine presence' (*B.Sanh.* 97b). According to G. Scholem the belief draws on non-Jewish antecedents. Among the *Ashkenazim, there are various legends about the lamed-vovniks (Yid., '36 righteous men') who are responsible for the fate of the world and include the *messiah. For the novel, *The Last of the Just*, based on this legend, see HOLOCAUST.

Lamennais, Hugues Félicité Robert de (1782–1854). French religious and political writer. In the newspaper *L'Avenir* (1830–1) and elsewhere he advocated a policy of 'liberal *Ultramontanism': there should be complete separation of Church and State, with freedom of association, press, and religion, but with a strong *papacy to protect the rights of the Church. When his views were condemned by the pope, he retired to La Chênaie in Brittany (where he had established a centre for like-minded people) and wrote *Paroles d'un croyant* (1834). Condemned again, he left the Church and spent the rest of his working life in politics.

Lamentabili. Decree of the *Holy Office issued under Pius X in 1907, condemning sixty-five propositions drawn from the works of the RC *Modernists, especially A. F. *Loisy. They covered six main areas: *revelation, the interpretation of *scripture, *christology, doctrine, the *Church, and *sacraments.

Lamentations, Book of (in Heb., *Ekah* or *Kinot*). One of the five *scrolls of the Hebrew *Bible. The book consists of five chapters containing laments on the destruction of *Jerusalem by the Babylonians in 587 BCE. Supposedly written by the prophet *Jeremiah (perhaps from 2 Chronicles 35. 25), the book emphasizes the loneliness of Jerusalem and points to God's role in its destruction (chs. 1 and 2). Ch. 3 is concerned with the meaning of suffering; ch. 4 describes the suffering of the inhabitants and ch. 5 describes the distress of the remaining population. Most modern scholars deny Jeremiah's authorship, and it is possible that it is a composite work. Probably the author belonged to the upper classes; the book has close affinities with the other books of *wisdom literature. There are several parallels with other known Mesopotamian laments, and the book seems to have been written at the same time as the events it describes. It is read in Jewish liturgy on the Ninth of *Av.

Lammas Day. 1 Aug. in the calendar of the *Book of Common Prayer. By etymology it derives from 'loaf' and 'mass', and in the early English church it was customary to consecrate bread from the first-ripe corn at mass on this day, probably in thanksgiving for the harvest. Since the 19th cent., the unofficial Harvest thanksgiving has been more prominent.

Lamotte, Etienne (1903–83). A renowned Belgian scholar of Buddhism, who was an ordained priest and prelate of the pope's household. He studied under his great compatriot Louis de *la Vallée-Poussin, and specialized in the tr. of Buddhist texts from Tibetan and Chinese where the Sanskrit original was no longer extant, including *Mahāyānasaṃgraha*, the *Vimālakīrti-nirdésa-sūtra* (The Teachings of *Vimālakīrti), and the *Suraṃgama-samādhi-sūtra*. His greatest works were his *Histoire du bouddhisme indien* and his 5-vol. tr. of the 'Great Treatise on the Perfection of Wisdom' of *Nāgārjuna.

Lamrim (Tib., 'path stages'). Tibetan manuals describing stages on the spiritual path. Important examples are *Gampopa's *Jewel Ornament of Liberation*, *Tsong Khapa's *Graded Path to Enlightenment*, and (much later) Pältrül Rinpoche's *Instructions on All that Belongs to Good Teaching*.

Landau, Ezekiel (1713–93). Also known as Noda bi-Yehuda from the title of his book of *responsa, Jewish Talmudic scholar. He was born in Poland, where he served as a *rabbi, but he became well-known only when he became rabbi of Prague in 1755. His *yeshiva attracted students from all parts of Europe, drawn by his subtle knowledge of *Talmud. His book of 855 responsa (*Noda Biyhudah*, Known in Judah) shows a tendency to lenient interpretations (e.g. permitting shaving on intermediate days of festivals), some of which were reversed after his death. But the book was a subject of study and commentary for many generations. He strongly opposed *Shabbateanism and any kind of *messianic speculation, and was suspicious of the emerging *Ḥasidic movement. But he attempted to mediate in the bitter dispute between *Emden and *Eybeschuetz, even though he was not convinced that the latter was innocent of connection with Shabbateanism, because he felt that the damage to the Jewish community must be contained. His adherence to Talmud and tradition made him an equal opponent of the *Enlightenment and of Moses *Mendelssohn.

Laṅgar ('anchor'). Communal partaking of food when visiting a *gurdwārā. The practice was instituted by Gurū *Nānak and endorsed by his successors. It is fundamental among Sikhs because it demonstrates the abolition of *caste: all eat together, and any Sikh may provide or prepare the food. The food should be simple and vegetarian (in order to avoid giving offence). The laṅgar may be mainly symbolic, but it can still be the occasion for the distribution of food to the poor. For more detail, see GURŪ-KĀ-LAṄGAR.

Language-games: see WITTGENSTEIN, LUDWIG.

Laṅkāvatāra-sūtra (The Descent into Laṅkā). An important *sūtra in the *Mahāyāna Buddhist tradition which sets out the teachings of Idealism or *Vijñāna-vāda. The sūtra refers in an unsystematic way to the teachings of the Mahāyāna which were prominent at the time of its composition, with special emphasis on the doctrine of consciousness itself as the nature of ultimate reality: 'Consciousness alone is all that is: in the absence of subject and object, a self and whatever pertains to it cannot exist.' The text must have been in existence some time before 443 CE when the first Chin. tr. was made. Meditation based on the sūtra was emphasized by *Hui-k'o.

Tr. D. T. Suzuki (see also his *Studies in the Laṅkāvatāra Sūtra* (1930).

Lan Tsai-ho (one of eight immortals): see PA-HSIEN.

Lao-chun. The name of *Lao-tzu in his deified form, one of the highest deities in religious Taoism. As early as the Former Han dynasty (202 BCE–9 CE) he was regarded as the joint-founder (with Huang-ti: see HUANG-LAO CHÜN) and the source and foundation of Chinese civilization. He has been incarnated many times, and is deeply revered as the supreme focus of worship. The reverence of both Lao-tzu and the *Buddha ordered by the emperor Huan led to a belief that Lao-tzu actually was the Buddha, who assumed that guise in order to convert all people to the way of Tao.

Lao-Tzu also **Lao Tan** (Chin., 'old master'). A founding figure (though perhaps legendary) of Taoism, and according to tradition a contemporary (and teacher) of *Confucius. Many stories are told of him (e.g. his visit to India, where he taught the *Buddha

Śākyamuni—see HUA-HU CHING; or perhaps became the Buddha—see LAO-CHUN), but his main importance is the tradition that he is the author of **Tao-te ching*, which is consequently also known as *Lao-tzu*; though again that claim cannot be historically true. He was later deified in religious Taoism (*tao-chiao).

N. J. Giradot, *Myth and Meaning in Early Taoism* (1983); M. Kaltenmark, *Lao Tzu and Taoism* (1969).

Lapsi (Lat., 'the fallen'). Christians guilty in varying ways of *apostasy under persecution. Could such persons be readmitted to the Church? After the Decian persecution of 250–1, the Church, guided by the view of *Cyprian (expressed in his work *De Lapsis*), decided to do so after penance and a period of probation.

La-shanah ha-ba'ah bi-Yerushalayim: see NEXT YEAR IN JERUSALEM.

Last Gospel. A second *gospel reading which until 1964 came at the very end of *mass. It was usually John 1. 1–14.

Last of the Just: see HOLOCAUST.

Last Supper. The final meal of Jesus with his disciples before his death. In the *Synoptic gospels (Mark 14. 12–26 etc.) it is described as a *Passover meal at which Jesus interpreted the bread and wine as his body and blood and directed that the meal should be repeated in his memory (see EUCHARIST). John 13. 1–11 mentions only a supper at which Jesus washed his disciples' feet, and places the crucifixion before the time of the Passover meal—recording teaching relevant to an interpretation of the actions and intention of Jesus in ch. 6. Most scholars suppose John's chronology is faulty, but the discrepancy is hard to understand; it has the effect of relating the death of Jesus to the slaughter of the lambs for Passover.

Lateran Councils. A series of *councils of the Roman Catholic Church held at the Lateran Palace in Rome from the 7th to the 18th cents. Five are considered *ecumenical, of which the most important was the Fourth (1215), with a definition of the *eucharist in which the word 'transubstantiate' was used for the first time, and annual *confession for all Christians was prescribed.

Latihan (training, exercise): see SUBUD INTERNATIONAL BROTHERHOOD.

Latimer, Hugh (*c*.1485–1555). Bishop of Worcester and *Reformer. Ordained *priest in 1524, he was influenced by the conversion of Thomas Bilney and gradually became a zealous exponent of the reformed faith. In 1535 he was made bishop of Worcester, but in 1539 his convinced *Protestantism caused him to oppose Henry's Act of Six Articles. He was imprisoned in the Tower in 1546, but on the accession of Edward (1547) was released, becoming an increasingly popular preacher. Early in Mary's reign he was reimprisoned, excommunicated, and burnt along with *Ridley on 16 Oct. 1555. He was reported to have said to Ridley as the fire was kindled: 'Be of good comfort, master Ridley, and play the man. We shall this day light such a candle, by God's grace, in England, as I trust shall never be put out.'

Latitudinarianism. Anglican Christians who took a 'broad' view of the necessity for dogma and definition in matters of belief. In the 17th cent., they allowed reason a part (in addition to revelation and tradition) in the forming of judgement; in the 19th, they were *broad churchmen. They are naturally distinguished more by what they oppose than by what they propose as a consistent set of doctrines.

Latrocinium (Robber synod): see EPHESUS.

Latter-Day Saints: see MORMONS.

Lauds. The traditional morning *office of the W. Church, with the title *Ad Laudes Matutinas* (for morning praises). Before 1960, lauds was usually joined to *mattins and said overnight in anticipation (but not in religious orders which rose for the night office). In the 1971 Catholic *Breviary, lauds (also called morning prayer) and *vespers are enjoined as 'the two hinges on which the daily Office turns', and hence the 'chief Hours'. In the *Book of Common Prayer, *morning prayer embraces parts of lauds and mattins in a single service.

Laughing Buddha (Chin., *mi-lo-fo*). The depiction of the future buddha *Maitreya with stout belly, broad smile, and surrounded by children—symbolizing wealth and equanimity. He is identified with *Hotei (Chin., Pu-tai).

La Vallée-Poussin, Louis de (1869–1938). A renowned Belgian scholar of Buddhism who made a major contribution to the field, notably through the editing and translating of important Buddhist works in Sanskrit, Tibetan, and Chinese. Beginning in 1892 he published in serial form a tr. of *Śāntideva's 'Entering the Path of Enlightenment' (*Bodhicāryāvatāra*). At this early period his interest was drawn towards *Tantric Buddhism, and in 1898 he published a major work in this area entitled *Buddhisme: Études et matériaux*. During the First World War he continued his work in Cambridge, and his numerous publications established new standards for academic work. Towards the end of his life he was engaged upon two major works: the *Abhidharmakośa* of *Vasubandhu, and the *Siddhi* of Huan Tsang, which he completed before his death at the age of 69. The range of his knowledge was extensive, and he approached Buddhism as an organic whole rather than restricting his attention to specific topics, schools, or historical periods. His major contributions, however, were in the fields of *Mādhyamaka philosophy and *Abhidhamma scholasticism.

Lāvān (Pañjābī, 'reverent circumambulation of sacred fire or scriptures'). For Hindus this refers to the central *marriage rite in which bride and groom, linked by a scarf, walk clockwise around the sacred fire. For Sikhs it means circling the **Ādi Granth* four times. Before each round, the officiant reads one stanza of Gurū Rām Dās' hymn entitled Lavan (*Ādi Granth* 773). The ragis sing this again as the bridegroom precedes the bride around the scriptures. These stanzas affirm the *grahastī (householder) ideal, devotion to the true Gurū, detachment from the world in the company of the *saṅgat (congregation), and ultimate union of the soul with God.

Lavater, Johann (opponent): see MENDELSSOHN, MOSES.

Lavra (Gk., *laura*, 'street' or 'alley'). In the early Christian Church, a gathering of *anchorites who lived in separate dwellings or cells, and assembled only on Saturdays and Sundays. Lavras were established in Palestine in the 4th cent., the most famous being the Great Lavra or monastery of St Sabas (Mar Saba), SE of Jerusalem, established in 483. The term has also become the name of important *coenobitic monasteries and especially to the 'Great Lavra' or simply 'Lavra' on Mount *Athos founded by St Athanasios the Athonite in 962.

Law, William (1686–1781). Christian devotional writer. He was fellow of Emmanuel College, Cambridge, until deprived of his fellowship as a Nonjuror (see DIVINE RIGHT . . .) at the accession of George I. After a period as tutor to the father of the historian E. Gibbon, he retired in 1740 to his birthplace, Kings Cliffe, Northants., where he gave his remaining years to writing and local social concern, increasingly influenced by *Boehme and becoming much more idiosyncratic.

Law's early works include *Three Letters to the Bishop of Bangor* (1717; a reply to the *low churchman Benjamin Hoadly). His most famous work, published in 1728, was *A Serious Call to a Devout and Holy Life*. In this, Law recommends the exercise of moral virtues—temperance, humility, and self-denial—and meditation and ascetical practices; corporate worship, however, finds little place. The simplicity of its teaching and its vigorous style soon established the work as a classic, which has probably had more influence than any other *Protestant spiritual book except *Bunyan's *Pilgrim's Progress*, and which was appreciated by evangelicals such as the *Wesleys and G. *Whitefield. Law's later books *The Spirit of Prayer* and *The Spirit of Love* reflect the influence of Boehme: God is 'an eternal Will to all goodness'.

E. P. Rudolph, *William Law* (1980); A. K. Walker, *William Law . . .* (1973).

Law (Jewish): see HALAKHAH; TORAH.

Law Code of Manu: see DHARMA.

Law of Return. The Israeli law which gives every *Jew the right to settle in *Israel as an immigrant. The Law of Return was passed by the Israeli Knesset (Parliament) in 1950 and, according to David *Ben Gurion, 'this right is inherent in every Jew by virtue of his being a Jew'. Immigrant visas can only be denied to those who have actively worked against the Jewish people, and known criminals. Various legal problems have arisen concerning who counts as a true Jew, and although *Progressive converts are covered by the Law of Return, *apostates are not.

Law of the Fishes (political assumption): see ARTHAŚĀSTRA.

Laya (Skt., 'melting'). The merging of the soul with *Brahman in Hinduism; the dissolution of the cosmos at the end of a *kalpa.

Laylat al-Barā'ah (Muslim festival): see FESTIVALS AND FASTS.

Laylat al-Qadr (Arab., 'night of power'). One of the later nights—generally thought to be the 27th—of the month of *Ramaḍān. It is the title of sūra 97 of the *Qur'ān, which describes this night as 'better than a thousand months', since during it the *angels (*malā'ika*) and the spirit (rūḥ, see NAFS) descend to earth; it is 'peace until the rising of the dawn'. Many Muslims like to spend this night in prayer and retreat (*'Itikāf) in a *mosque.

Layman/person: see LAITY.

Leaven (Heb., *ḥamez*). Raising agent forbidden to Jews during the season of *Passover—hence this is sometimes called the festival of unleavened bread. Leaven must necessarily come from the preceding year's harvest, but the festival looks forward, in absolute trust in God, to the new year. The search for leaven (*bedikat ḥamez*) is based on the injunction in Exodus 12. 15 ff., to 'eliminate leaven from your houses'. The search is scrupulously conducted in silence, and all bread and crumbs are bundled together, ready for burning. An Aramaic formula of renunciation is pronounced, and on the next morning, before 10 a.m., the burning takes place, with the recitation of another renunciation. The search and burning has also been interpreted as the inner examination and burning out of moral offences.

In the New Testament, leaven is a likeness of the potential for growth in the kingdom (Matthew 13. 33); but equally it is an illustration of the speed with which evil and corruption spread (1 Corinthians 5. 8; Luke 12. 1). Leavened vs. unleavened bread for the *eucharist became a matter of dispute between the E. and the W. Churches: see AZYMITES.

Lectio Divina (Lat., 'divine/holy reading'). Attention to the scriptures (or occasionally to a spiritual text) in an attitude of prayer and devotion, leading to communion with God. It is thus in contrast to exegesis seeking meaning of the text (see HERMEN-

EUTICS). It is fundamental to the *Rule of St *Benedict* and to monastic life.

Lectionary. A book containing, or listing, passages from the Bible appointed to be read at public worship. The word may also refer to the whole system of apportioning the Bible to the calendar. By the 4th cent., the number of readings at the *eucharist was fixed as three (from the Old Testament, *apostolic writings, and the *gospels).

Lee, Ann (founder): see SHAKERS.

Lefebvre, Marcel (1905–91). Former archbishop of Dakar and leader of a traditionalist movement within *Roman Catholicism. He rejected the changes brought about by the second *Vatican Council, proclaiming that 'our future is the past', and he insisted on retaining the form of *mass established after the council of *Trent, rather than the revised rite instituted in 1969. The headquarters of his Priestly Fraternity of St Pius X, and the seminary belonging to it, are at Econe in Switzerland. After an unauthorized ordination of thirteen priests in June 1976, he was suspended from the exercise of his priestly ministry by the *pope. Cardinal Ratzinger, whose extreme conservatism recognized virtue in Lefebvre's position, negotiated a protocol of reconciliation, which Lefebvre signed in 1988; but he withdrew his signature when he realized that a Commission of Inquiry would have a Vatican majority on it. Although supporting, and supported by, right-wing political movements (e.g. C. Maurras and J.-M. Le Pen in France), his concern was basically eschatological: 'At the hour of my death, when our Lord asks me, "What have you done with your episcopate . . .?", I do not want to hear from His lips the terrible words, "You have helped to destroy the Church, along with the rest of them." ' (*Open Letter to Confused Catholics*, 1986, p. 166).

Left-hand Tantrism: see VĀMĀCĀRA.

Legate, Papal. A personal representative, in effect ambassador, of the *Holy See. Legates *a latere* are cardinals sent to deal with particular issues or events; nuncios represent the *pope in countries having full diplomatic relations with the Holy See, an internuncio in countries which do not; an apostolic delegate is the delegate of the pope to the RC Church in countries not having full diplomatic relations. A legate need not be a cleric, but is usually so, and is almost always a titular *archbishop. Apart from legates *a latere*, appointments are usually made through the career structure of the *Vatican diplomatic service.

Legio Maria (in distinction from the Legion of Mary, a Roman Catholic lay organization): see MARIA LEGIO.

Leibniz, Gottfried Wilhelm (1646–1716). German philosopher and mathematician. He studied law initially (at Leipzig), but turned to philosophy and mathematics, making an independent discovery of the infinitesimal calculus. In 1667, he became an ambassador for the Elector of Mainz, and although his missions to Paris and London were unsuccessful, he met distinguished scientists, and was elected to the Royal Society in 1673. He entered the service of the Brunswick family, staying in Rome for three years while writing a history of the family. From a Protestant background, he espoused the cause of reconciliation between Protestants and Roman Catholics—and was invited to supervise the Vatican Library. In *Essays on Theodicy* (1710), he argued that the law of continuity (based on the consistency of the universe) points to a perfect Being (i.e. God), who would necessarily create the best of all possible worlds (a view satirized by Voltaire, especially in *Candide*). In *The Monadology* (1714) he advanced the view that everything is made up of simple monads, without extension but endowed with force, or spiritual energy, able to achieve perfection, and therefore also known as entelechies. Arranged hierarchically, the soul is the ruling entechy of the body—offering an analogy of the relation of God to the world.

S. Brown, *Leibniz* (1984); R. Calinger, *Gottfried Wilhelm Leibniz* (1976); N. Rescher, *Leibniz . . .* (1979).

Lekhah dodi (Heb., 'Come, my friend'). Initial words and title of a Jewish *Sabbath hymn. *Lekhah dodi* is sung near the beginning of the Sabbath evening service to welcome the Sabbath. It contains nine verses, and the refrain can be translated, 'Come, my friend, to meet the bride; let us welcome the presence of the Sabbath.' The hymn may have been inspired by the accounts in the *Talmud of how scholars used to greet the Sabbath, and also by the practice of the *kabbalists of Safed who used to go out to the field to meet the 'Queen Sabbath': 'Come, let us greet the Queen Sabbath of grace, Source of all blessings in every place, Anointed and queen since time's earliest trace, Preceding in plan Creation's six days.' Many thousands of melodies have been composed for this hymn.

Lenshina, Alice (founder): see LUMPA CHURCH.

Lent (Old Eng., *lencten*; Germ., *Lenz*, 'spring'). The forty-day *fast before *Easter. The length was presumably suggested by the forty days' fasts of *Moses, *Elijah, and *Jesus himself. The actual fast days were differently reckoned, however, and did not amount to forty until the 7th cent., when the W. Church settled on the days from *Ash Wednesday to Easter, omitting Sundays. E. Churches begin Lent seven weeks before Easter, but omit Saturdays and Sundays. In the early centuries the fast (which may originally have been a preparation for *baptism) was strictly kept: toward evening one meal was allowed, and meat, fish, and in most places eggs and milky foods were forbidden. In E. Churches abstinence from these foods is still the rule. In the RC Church the obligation to fast has since 1966 been limited to the first day of Lent and Good Friday. Lent is observed as a time of penance by abstaining from festivities, by almsgiving, and by devoting time to prayer and religious study. In W. Churches these aspects of Lent are now more emphasized than physical fasting, as in Herrick: 'To starve thy sin, | Not bin; | And that's to keep thy Lent.'

H. Thurston, *Lent and Holy Week* (1904).

Leo I, St, known as **'the Great'** (d. 461). Pope from 440, who worked to enhance the pre-eminence of the see of Rome, claiming jurisdiction in Africa, Spain, and Gaul. Though this was not recognized in the E., his support was sought by all parties in the controversy over *Eutyches. In the course of this, Leo composed his *Tome*, expounding the *Christology of the Latin Church, according to which Jesus Christ is one person, the divine Word, in whom are two unconfused natures, the divine and human; each of these exercises its own particular faculties, but because of the *communicatio idiomatum it may be said that the Son of Man descended from heaven, and the Son of God was crucified. The *Tome* was given formal authority at the Council of Chalcedon in 451. Leo was declared a *Doctor of the Church by Benedict XIV.

T. G. Jalland, *The Life and Times of St Leo the Great* (1941).

Leo X (1475–1521). *Pope from 9 Mar. 1513. He was born Giovanni de Medici, a son of Lorenzo the Magnificent, and was a *cardinal by the age of 13. As pope he showed himself a patron of learning and of the arts, but wholly failed to appreciate the strength of *Luther's convictions (he issued the *bull *Exsurge Domine* in 1520) or the degree of hostility felt in Germany towards the taxes he had demanded to finance a *crusade against the Turks. His period of office plunged the papacy deeply into debt, through its extravagance. In the opinion of J. N. D. Kelly, he was 'a polished Renaissance prince who was also a devious and double-tongued politician and an inveterate nepotist' (*The Oxford Dictionary of the Popes*, 1986).

W. Roscoe, *The Life and Pontificate of Pope Leo X* (1973).

Leo XIII (1810–1903). *Pope from 20 Feb. 1878. Born Giocchino Vincenzo Pecci, he was educated by the *Jesuits at Viterbo and Rome, and after ordination entered the papal diplomatic service. After an unsuccessful, and brief, period of service as *nuncio in Brussels, he was sent to Perugia as *archbishop in 1845. He immediately set about improving the education of his clergy, and, with the assistance of his Jesuit brother Joseph, encouraged the study of Thomas *Aquinas in the diocesan seminary (Thomism was later to be strongly advocated in the *encyclical, *Aeterni Patris*). He carried his support of neo-*scholasticism into his pontificate, and one of his first acts was to write the encyclical commending the study of Aquinas's philosophy. He was a considerable patron of learning, insisting that the Church had nothing to fear from the truth. He failed to reach an accommodation with the new kingdom of Italy, and his encyclical **Rerum Novarum* gave support to those wishing to restore the *ancien régime*, though his endorsement of the workers' movement was of great psychological importance as the first such act by an authority of international standing. Leo also gave encouragement to the *ecumenical movement, both between the RC Church and the E. Churches, and, at first, with the *Anglican Communion, though his *bull **Apostolicae Curae* put an end for a time to hopes of reunion. In the end he accepted the legitimacy of secular political power, but encouraged the formation of RC political parties, thereby sowing the seeds of future conflicts.

E. T. Gargan (ed.), *Leo XIII and the Modern World* (1961); E. Soderini, *The Pontificate of Leo XIII* (1934–5).

Leontopolis. A 2nd-cent. BCE Jewish settlement in Egypt. As a reward to Jewish soldiers, the ruler Onias IV converted an Egyptian temple into a *temple for the God of Israel which survived until its closure by the Romans in 73 CE. During this period, the settlement seems to have been under independent Jewish rule, and at times it served as a refuge for right-wing protestors against innovations in the running of the Temple at Jerusalem.

Lessing, Gotthold Ephraim (1729–81). German poet, dramatist, and religious essayist who influenced theological and philosophical discussion both within Germany and beyond. Educated at Leipzig and Wittenberg, Lessing held various positions in Berlin, Breslau, and Hamburg before becoming librarian in Wolfenbüttel in 1770, a position he held for the rest of his life. There he used his position to arrange publication of some controversial essays by Hermann Samuel Reimarus (the *Wolfenbüttel Fragments*, 1774–8) in which then-novel methods of criticism were employed to undermine traditional aspects of Jewish and Christian scripture. Lessing's own religious views were broadly *deistic. Revelation was said to be simply a quicker way to learn what we could eventually discover through the use of reason alone. He advocated complete toleration in matters religious in his play *Nathan the Wise*, a work modelled loosely on his close friend Moses *Mendelssohn. His scepticism about the certainty of historical knowledge had implications for the relation of faith to history which much impressed and greatly influenced Søren *Kierkegaard, among others.

H. Allison, *Lessing and the Enlightenment* (1966); L. P. Wessell, *G. E. Lessing's Theology . . .* (1977).

Letter mysticism: see GEMATRIA.

Letter to Women (Apostolic Letter): see WOMEN.

Levi. Third son of *Jacob and Leah and ancestor of the Jewish tribe of Levi. According to Numbers 1. 48–53 and 3. 5–40, the Levites were singled out for the service of the *Tabernacle 'in place of all the *first-born among the Israelite people'. The changing role of the Levites in relation to the Temple reflects the consequence (and conflict) resulting from the building of the Temple, the centralization of the cult and the reordering of the Temple after the *Exile, through all of which the priesthoods of *Aaron and *Zadok had to be accommodated. Levi was the only tribe to lack fixed territory in the *Promised Land and in consequence of their religious duties received *tithes. The Levites seem to have been subject to the *priests, the descendants of Aaron, although, according to Deuteronomy 18. 6–9, all Levites are fit to serve in the *Sanctuary. During the period of the monarchy, the Levites became state officials in their administration of the cult; they became eventually the Temple singers. According to the *aggadah, when God purifies the *twelve tribes of *Israel, 'he will purify the tribe of Levi first' (*B.Kid.* 71a).

A. Cody, *A History of Old Testament Priesthood* (1969).

Leviathan. A large sea animal. In the Hebrew scriptures, the leviathan frequently represents the forces of chaos which are opposed to God. In Job 40. 15–24, Leviathan is associated with Behemoth, and in 2 Esdras 6. 49–52, both of them are said to have existed from the fifth day of creation. In *aggadah, they will be served at the messianic banquet, in a tent made from Leviathan's skin.

Levi ben Gershom, **Ralbag**, or **Gersonides** (1288–1344). Jewish philosopher and Bible commentator. Levi ben Gershom was born in France. His scientific work dealt with mathematics and astronomy. He was an eminent *Talmudist who wrote a commentary on *Berakhot* (now lost) and probably a commentary on the thirteen *hermeneutical rules of R. *Ishmael (publ. 1800). He wrote several commentaries on Averroes' paraphrases and commentaries on Aristotle; his biblical commentaries include works on Job, the Song of Songs, Ecclesiastes, Ruth, Esther, the former prophets, Proverbs, Daniel, Nehemiah, Chronicles, and the *Pentateuch. His major philosophical work was the *Sefer Milhamot Adonai* (The Book of the Wars of the Lord), written between 1317 and 1329. Divided into six parts, it deals with the immortality of the *soul, *prophecy, divine knowledge, providence, the celestial spheres, and creation. He gave priority to God-created reason: 'The law cannot prevent us from accepting as true what our reason compels us to believe.' For this reason (and its consequences), he was fiercely criticized by Hasdai *Crescas and Isaac *Abrabanel; and Shem Tov ibn Shem Tov described Levi's work as 'Wars against the Lord'. None the less his ideas were highly influential and he must be numbered as one of the greatest of the Jewish philosophers.

I. Weil, *Philosophie religieuse de Levi-ben-Gerson* (1868).

Levi Isaac [Yitsḥak] ben Meir of Berdichev (*c.*1740–1810). Jewish *Ḥasidic *zaddik. Levi Isaac was a pupil of *Dov Baer. He emerged as a Zaddik in the town of Zelechow, but was driven from there and from Pinsk by the *mitnaggedim. Finally he moved to Berdichev in 1785 where he lived until his death. He was recognized as a major Ḥasidic leader of his time and became a popular hero in Jewish fiction and poetry, in which he is regarded as an advocate for Israel before God: 'You, O God, are always making demands on your people: why do you not help them in their troubles?' He did not attempt to justify that suffering, advocating constancy, since 'here in exile, God is in exile': 'I do not wish to comprehend why I suffer, only whether it is for Your sake.' He wrote a two-part work, *Kedushat Levi*, which expounds Ḥasidic teaching in the form of a commentary mainly on *Torah. A constant theme is humility and practical love: 'You can only know if a person loves God from the love he exhibits to his neighbour.' Humility before God automatically fills a life with gentle reverence: 'The mind is the *Holy of Holies: to admit an evil thought is to set up an idol in the Temple.'

M. Buber, *Tales of the Hasidim: The Early Masters* (1947); S. H. Dresner, *Levi Yitzhaq of Berditchev* . . . (1974).

Levinsohn, Isaac Baer, or **Ribal** (1788–1860). Hebrew author. Levinsohn's literary output was mainly polemical. He was one of the founders of the *Haskalah movement in Russia, and he was concerned with the position of the Jews in E. Europe. His best-known work, *Te'udah be-Yisrael* (Testimony in Israel, 1828), described the Hebrew language as 'the bond of religion and national survival', and he argued against the use of *Yiddish. His book had considerable influence on Jewish life in Russia, although it was banned by the *Ḥasidim. He also wrote *Beit Yehudah* (House of Judah, 1838) which was an attempt to answer Christian questions about Judaism, and *Efes Damim* (No Blood, 1837) which was written to refute the *blood-libel.

L. S. Greenberg, *A Critical Investigation of the Works of Rabbi Isaac Baer Levinsohn* (1930).

Levirate marriage (*yibbum*). A Jewish custom which obliges a childless widow to marry her dead husband's brother. The obligation of levirate marriage is laid down in Deuteronomy 25. 5–6. If the brother-in-law does not want to marry the widow, the ceremony of *ḥalizah is performed which enables her to remarry someone else. In the course of time, it became accepted that the duty of ḥalizah took priority over levirate marriage, in order to avoid the *Levitical prohibition against marrying one's brother's wife (18. 16). In the State of *Israel ḥalizah is obligatory and levirate marriage forbidden; if a man refuses his sister-in-law ḥalizah, he can be imprisoned, and thus there is no danger that the woman will be placed in the position of an *agunah. *Reform Judaism has abolished Levirate marriage and, *ipso facto*, ḥalizah; *Conservative Judaism has invalidated levirate marriage but debate continues whether ḥalizah needs to be performed.

Lévi-Strauss, Claude (b. 1908). French anthropologist associated particularly with structuralism. Seeing himself as 'neolithic', Lévi-Strauss drew upon traditional societies, including their *myths and classificatory systems (taboos, etc.), to put the human imagination in its place: 'We are not therefore claiming to show how men think the myths, but rather how myths think themselves out in men and without men's knowledge' (*The Raw and the Cooked*, Eng. 1969). Bound up with cultural systems showing structural 'inertia', religious or artistic innovation is illusory: 'one never moves alone along the path of creation' (*The Way of the Masks*, 1982). Collective representations are the product of the human mind. They are 'thought out' in a way which reflects their virtual identity with fundamental mental structures of the mind, rather than their being autonomous creations. Although some have seen Lévi-Strauss as a 'culture hero', his emphasis on cognition to the virtual exclusion of emotion, his pessimistic view of imagination and progress, the excesses of his structuralism, and the apparently self-verifying nature of his approach, are drawbacks increasingly attended to by critics. So too are problems raised when collective representations are used as the basis of psychology.

See also MYTH.

R. A. Champagne, *Claude Lévi-Strauss* (1974); E. Leach, *Lévi-Strauss* (1970).

Levitation: see DARDURA-SIDDHI; LAGHIMAN.

Levite: see LEVI.

Levitical cities. Cities in *Erez Israel prescribed in the Hebrew scriptures for the tribe of *Levi. According to Numbers 35. 1–8, forty-eight towns were set aside for the *Levites, including the six *cities of refuge. Scholars do not agree on the historical accuracy of this provision.

Leviticus. The third book of the Hebrew Bible and Christian Old Testament. The Eng. title follows the Gk. and Lat. versions, the Heb. title *Vayyiqra* ('and he called') being the first word of the text. The book is essentially a manual for priests (the *tannaim called it *Torat Kohanim*, 'Guidance for Priests'). It consists almost wholly of legislation, the subjects of which are sacrifice (1–10), ritual purification and holiness (11–26), and vows and tithes (27). Ch. 16 contains the ritual for the *Day of Atonement. Nearly half of the *six hundred and thirteen commandments are found in Leviticus and a mass of *halakhah derives from it. Some Christian writers like the author of *Hebrews have used the language of Leviticus to describe *Christ's atoning death. Modern criticism of the *Pentateuch holds that the book is derived from the document P, except for chs. 17–26 known as the *Holiness Code, which seem older. In Judaism, Leviticus is, traditionally, the first book to be taught to school-children (Lev. R. 7. 3).

Lewis, Clive Staples (1898–1963). British scholar of English literature, writer and Christian apologist. As an Oxford don in the 1920s, C. S. Lewis moved from atheism to committed Christianity, specifically to an evangelical *Anglicanism. His most popular Christian works are *The Screwtape Letters* (1942), relating the advice given by a senior devil to his subordinate in luring a human subject away from salvation ('Readers are advised to remember that the devil is a liar: not everything that Screwtape says should be assumed to be true even from his own angle'); *Mere Christianity* (1952, but originally a series of radio talks begun in 1941); and his spiritual autobiography *Surprised by Joy* (1955: 'Joy is the serious business of heaven'). A science-fiction trilogy (1938–45) and the seven children's books known as the Chronicles of Narnia (1950–6) incorporate Christian themes allegorically. The death of his wife, Joy Davidson, evoked the searching record of his grief, *A Grief Observed* (first publ. under the name N. W. Clerk), and also the epitaph at Headington cemetery, summarizing much of his faith: 'Here the whole world (stars, water, air | And field and forest, as they were | Reflected in a single mind) | Like cast off clothes was left behind | In ashes; yet with hope that she, | Reborn from holy poverty | In Lenten lands, hereafter may | Resume them on her Easter Day.' Lewis's broadly traditional and orthodox position and clear, homely layman's style have made his religious books standard reading especially among evangelical Christians in the USA.

J. Beversluis, *C. S. Lewis and the Search for Rational Religion* (1984); R. L. Green and W. Hooper, *C. S. Lewis . . .* (1974); A. N. Wilson, *C. S. Lewis . . .* (1990).

Lex talionis (law of retaliation): see TALION.

Lhan.cig.skyes.pa (innate enlightenment indwelling the body): see SAHAJA.

Lhasa (*lha*, 'abode of the gods'). Sometimes known as 'the forbidden city', former home of the *Dalai Lama and centre of Tibetan Buddhist life. It was made capital city of Tibet in the 7th cent. CE, and it remains the capital of the autonomous Xizang region (Tibet), and contains the Potala, a fortress of a thousand rooms, in which are kept many images of the Buddha. The Jokhang temple in Lhasa was built in the 6th cent. CE, and contains a renowned Golden Buddha donated in 652 by a Chinese princess, who became the wife of the first Dalai Lama. Drepung monastery, 5 km. away, is an active centre of *lama life (though much reduced since 1959).

F. S. Chapman, *Lhasa, the Holy City* (1938).

Li. A Chinese word which 'on the most concrete level refers to all those "objective" prescriptions of behavior, whether involving rite, ceremony, manners, or general deportment, that bind human beings and the spirits together in networks of interacting roles within the family, within human society, and with the numinous realm beyond' (B. Schwartz, *The World of Thought in Ancient China*, 1985). The ideogram, thought to consist of a religious classifier and a vessel used in ritual offerings to the ancestors, suggests the cultic origins of the word.

Li was first developed as a moral and religious concept by *Confucius and his followers. Confucius claimed to be passing on a tradition of thought about li, and we find precedents for his own views in early works such as the *Book of Poetry* and the *Tso-chuan*. Confucius may have been the first, however, to speak of what we may call an 'inner' as well as an 'outer' meaning of li. In its 'outer' meaning, li consists of a pattern of behaviour which, when performed correctly, of itself effects and expresses harmony among the various hierarchically ordered elements of family, society, and the cosmos. Much attention is given in the *Analects* to the question of what ceremonial acts are appropriate to specific, concrete situations; book 10, for instance, lists exemplary cases in which Confucius acted properly. Li thus functions as a standard of behaviour to teach people their separate roles within hierarchical, interlocking spheres of relationships. But li also has an 'inner' meaning. Confucius repeatedly criticizes performances of li that are outwardly correct yet lacking in the right moral attitude or motivation. 'If a man is without *jen [humanheartedness], what can he have to do with li?' 'Li performed without reverence, the forms of mourning observed without grief—how can I bear to look on these things?' This 'inner' aspect of li is more fully developed by *Mencius, for whom li designated the sense of propriety and the disposition to do what is proper. Li had not the importance for Mencius that it carried for Confucius, however; it was subsumed under the broader concept of *i or 'righteousness'.

Hsün Tzu, a slightly later interpreter of the Confucian tradition, wrote what is perhaps the noblest treatise on li in all of Chinese literature. He stressed its power to educate and transform people, as well as to unite cultural and cosmic forms in harmonious correspondence: 'Through li Heaven and earth join in harmony, the sun and moon shine, the four seasons proceed in order, the stars and constellations march, the rivers flow, and all things flourish; human likes and dislikes are regulated and their joys and hates made appropriate. . . . Are they not wonderful indeed?' His treatise was incorporated into the canonical work on li established under the Han imperial system, the *Li Chi*; li remained a powerful concept in neo-Confucianism through the influential teaching of Ch'eng Yi (see CH'ENG HAO).

*Mo Tzu, in contrast, attacked the Confucian understanding of li. It has nothing to do with the training of people or the 'regulation of their likes and dislikes'. It has a certain limited value as an expression of gratitude to the spirits (belief in which Mo Tzu views as performing an essential social-moral function), but if performed extravagantly it wastes precious resources and distracts people from the more pressing tasks of ordering society. Taoists saw li as a prime example of the sort of contrived practice (*wei*) characteristic of the fall from primordial simplicity; it is therefore to be shunned by the sage, and its extravagances discouraged among the common people. Legalist writers such as Han Fei Tzu did not so much attack the Confucian concept of li as replace it with more practical advice to rulers on how to achieve their ends.

Despite these attacks, the concept of li remained central to the Confucian tradition in China down to recent times.

N. J. Girardot, *Myth and Meaning in Early Taoism* (1983); J. Legge (tr.), *The Li Ki* (1885); B. I. Schwartz, *The World of Thought in Ancient China* (1985).

Li (gold): see HUA-YEN.

Liberal Judaism: see REFORM JUDAISM.

Liberation Theology (perhaps more accurately in the plural, theologies), an understanding of the role of theology in moving from abstraction to praxis, in which the actual condition of the poor is the starting-point. It was defined by H. Assmann as 'teologia desde la praxis de la liberación' ('theology starting from the praxis of liberation'), and by G. Gutiérrez (b. 1928) as 'a critical reflection both from within, and upon, historical praxis, in confrontation with the word of the Lord as lived and experienced in faith'. Liberation theology arose in S. America out of 'an ethical indignation at the poverty and marginalisation of the great masses of our continent' (L. Boff), and it is theology both lived and written 'from the underside of history' (Gutiérrez). If it has a single point of departure, it is in the parable of judgement in Matthew 25. 31–46, with its criterion of evaluation, 'Inasmuch as you did it to the least of one of these . . .'. It is Christian community in action, arising from what Frantz Fanon called *The Wretched of the Earth* (his final work, publ. months before he died in 1961, which is a passionate refusal, in relation to Africa, of any 'shifting around of the chairs on the deck of the Titanic': liberation is to be achieved, not by a return to African culture, not by an enlightened middle-class, not by benevolent African dictators, not by 'a new negritude', but by a collective—and violent—catharsis).

Although liberation theology traces its origins to missionary protests on behalf of indigenous populations against colonialist exploiters (e.g. Antonio de Montesinos, d. 1545; Bartolomé de Las Casas), its first modern presentation was made by Gutiérrez in 1968 (publ. 1969, *Hacia una teologia de la liberación*, Towards a Theology of Liberation), leading to *Theology of Liberation* (1971). From the start, liberation theology saw itself as different from the social gospel programme of the turn of the century, epitomized in W. Rauschenbusch (1861–1919) and his saying, 'Christian *asceticism called the world evil and abandoned it: humanity is waiting for a Christian revolution which will call the world evil and change it.' Liberation theology saw itself facing a different agenda from that of Anglo-Saxon theology: for the latter, the agenda, set by unbelievers, is of how to speak of God in an unbelieving world. For liberation theology, the agenda is set by the question of the non-person: 'Our question is how to tell the non-person, the nonhuman, that God is love, and that this love makes us all brothers and sisters' (Gutiérrez). This immediately demands a priority, not so much for orthodoxy as for orthopraxis—hence H. Assman's preferred definition (above): experience of 'faith enacted' is a first act, theology as reflection comes after, as a second act. In *Theology and Praxis* (1978), Clodovis Boff emphasized the priority of the poor in actual political situations as the starting-point of theology. Scripture is interrogated, not for the location of abstract answers, but in order that the *hermeneutical circle may be closed: moving from a situation in the present, scripture is brought to that situation so that a new perspective on it is developed. From this arises (according to J. L. Segundo), not so much 'liberation theology' as the liberation of theology from its narrow abstraction from life.

Major themes of liberation theology can be discerned in the titles of some of the leading books. *Jesus Christ Liberator* (L. Boff, 1972) points out that in Christ, not words, but the Word was revealed in act, to make 'the utopia of absolute liberation' a *topia*, a place here and now. *Church: Charism and Power* (L. Boff, 1981) contests the 'institutional fossilisation' of the centuries which has produced a hierarchical Church, oppressive and clerical, which cannot be amended by minor reform; in its place, Boff (and others) propose *Iglesia popular*, the church arising from the people by the power of the Holy Spirit (*desde el pueblo por el Espiritu*)—in which connection, the importance of base (ecclesial) communities is paramount. *We Drink from Our Own Wells: The Spiritual Journey of a People* (G. Gutiérrez, 1984) took the phrase and argument of St *Bernard that in matters of the spirit, one must draw first on one's own experience: whereas this has usually, in the past, been a matter of individual process, aimed at an improved interior life, in S. America the experience is communal, and often of solidarity for survival: 'Spirituality is a community enterprise: it is the passage of a people through the solitude and dangers of the desert, as it carves out its own way in the following of Jesus Christ: this spiritual experience is the well from which we must drink'. *The Power of the Poor in History* (G. Gutiérrez, 1983) reflects 'the preferential option for the poor': by this is meant that 'the poor deserve preference, not because they are morally or religiously better than others, but because God is God, in whose eyes "the last are first" '—a mother with a sick child does not love her other children less just because she commits herself immediately to the child in need; it also allows the possibility that violence may be a necessary means of bringing about justice: 'We cannot say that violence is alright when the oppressor uses it to maintain or preserve order, but wrong when the oppressed use it to overthrow this same order.'

The response of the *Vatican to liberation theology was initially hostile, but became more circumspect. The second Latin American Episcopal Conference at Medellín (CELAM II) in 1968 condemned institutionalized violence and the alliance of the Church with it; CELAM III at Puebla in 1979 endorsed the preferential option for the poor, commended base communities, and made 'a serene affirmation of Medellín' (J. Sobrino, 'Puebla, serena afirmación de Medellín'), despite the presence of Pope *John Paul II warning them to sup with Marx only with a long spoon. In this was the heart of the original objections: it seemed that liberation theology was subordinating the Church and its teaching to the controlling categories of Marxism—of which the Pope had had first-hand experience in Poland. The *Congregation for the Doctrine of the Faith, ignoring the more reflective findings of the International Theological Commission's Dossier of 1976, issued its *Instruction on Certain Aspects of the Theology of Liberation* in 1984, and it summoned L. Boff to Rome for investigation, forbidding him, as a result, to lecture or publish—a ban that lasted for a year. The poverty of the analysis, thought by many to amount to a caricature, led to a second *Instruction on Christian Freedom and Liberation* (1986). This was to be read in conjunction with the first *Instruction*, and was not to be taken as contradicting it, but it is a far more positive document—which indeed scarcely mentions liberation theology at all, but sets the issues in a wider context; nevertheless, Gutiérrez was banned from lecturing in Rome in 1994.

Liberation theology has had extensive influence outside S. America. From the Detroit 'Theology in the Americas' Conference in 1975 (*Proceedings*, ed. S. Torres and J. Eagleson, 1976), the connections with black theology and with *feminist theology were so clear that the phrase 'liberation theologies' became preferred. In 1976, the Ecumenical Association of Third World Theologians (EATWOT) held its first meeting in Dar-es-Salaam, with a clear commitment to the struggle for a just society. Equally important has been the determination to require theology to arise from the context of experience (e.g. K. Koyama, *Waterbuffalo Theology*, 1974; C. S. Song, *Third-Eye Theology*, 1979; *minjung* theology in Korea, which takes the concept of people who are ruled and dominated, but who use the process of history to become free subjects).

P. Berryman, *Liberation Theology* (1987); L. and C. Boff, *Liberation Theology: From Confrontation to Dialogue* (1986); C. Cadorette *et al.* (eds.), *Liberation Theology: An Introductory Reader*; T. J. Davis, *Liberation Theology: A Bibliography . . .* (1985); R. Gibellini, *Il dibattito sulla Teologia della Liberazione* (1986); and *The Liberation Theology Debate*, (1987); M. Hebblethwaite, *Base Communities . . .* (1993).

Li Chi (Records of Rituals). One of the *Confucian Classics. Among the several collections of texts relating to secular and religious rituals, and the codes of behaviour for the privileged classes in general, the *Li Chi* is richest in material of a philosophical nature. Human life and well-being are entangled in a world of spirits, whose favour must be maintained through the ritual system. The Five Elements (*wu-hsing) constitute the universe, in association with *yin and yang. A wise life (as that of a wise ruler) is lived in harmony with these processes, discerned through divination. The *Li Chi* is a voluminous anthology, its component texts are undatable, but presumably mostly come from the last few cents. of the Chou dynasty (?1111–1256 BCE) and possibly in some cases from early Han (2nd cent. BCE).

Tr. J. Legge (1885).

Lieberman, Saul (1898–1983), Jewish *Talmudic scholar. Lieberman was born in Belorussia, but first settled in *Jerusalem, and then from 1940 taught in the *Jewish Theological Seminary. A prolific writer, he produced a series of studies on the text of the Jerusalem *Talmud, a commentary on the entire *tosefta, and two important books on *Hellenism, *Greek in Jewish Palestine* and *Hellenism in Jewish Palestine*. He was also an editor of the Yale University Judaica series and served as president of the American Academy for Jewish Research. The Lieberman Institute in Jerusalem (established in his memory) is making a computer edn. of the Babylonian Talmud.

Lieh-Tzu (The Classic of Complete Emptiness). Taoist text attributed to *Lieh Yü-k'au, whose personal name was Lieh-tzu; but in fact the text is much later (*c*.3rd cent. CE). It expresses the somewhat gloomy fatalism of the neo-Taoists:

> The longest life is only 100 years, and not one in a thousand live that long. But even if one does do so, half of that is lost in infancy and senility; of the other half, half is lost in sleep at night and dozing by day. And almost half of the rest is lost in pain, illness, sorrow and bereavement. Of the ten remaining years, about one hour is free from the slightest worry. So what is life for? Life is for beauty and wealth and sound and colour; and even those are often forbidden by law.

Along with **Lao Tzu* and **Chuang-Tzu*, it is the third of the old texts to form part of the Taoist canon. It contains stories, parables, and legends, and discussions on the nature of life. The *Tao is immanent and all-pervading: non-action and the way of emptiness are the surest ways to achieve union with the Tao.

Eng. trs., L. Giles (1912), A. C. Graham (1961). Germ. tr. R. Wilhelm (1981).

Lieh Yü-k'au (*c*.450–*c*.375 BCE). Taoist philosopher of whom little, if anything, is known, except for a tradition that he claimed that, after nine years of Taoist study, he was able to ride on the wind—'or is the wind riding on me?' The *Lieh-tzu* is attributed to him, but wrongly.

Lien-ch'i (Chin., 'melting the breath'). Taoist exercise in breathing, to allow the breath to flow to all parts of the body. It involves harmonizing the breath (*t'iao-chi) and swallowing it (*yen-ch'i), and then holding it as long as possible. It is an advanced exercise, and not to be attempted without careful and long preparation. See also CH'I.

Life after death: see DEATH.

Life as art: see MIKI TOKUHARU; LIEH-TZU.

Lifnim mi-shurat ha-din (beyond the boundary of what the law requires): see ETHICS.

Light: see NŪR.

Liguori, St Alphonsus (1696–1787). Christian moral theologian and founder of the Redemptorists. He was a Neapolitan nobleman and successful lawyer, who experienced an inner conversion when he won a law-suit on the basis of a document which he had wrongly interpreted. He intended to be a missionary in China, but was sent to the poor in Naples, where he soon built up a large following. He founded the Redemptorists with fellow-missionaries in 1732, stressing contemplation of the cross and the *eucharist. He was strongly opposed to the rigours of the *Jansenists, who, he felt, made the proper use of the sacrament of *penance impossible. His own views sought a middle way between Jansenist rigour and *Jesuit laxity—associated with *Probabilism, against which he set Equiprobabilism in discerning a course of action: this holds that a doubtful law does not oblige, and that a probable opinion may be followed, but that a law is doubtful only when the opinions for and against it are equally balanced. His views were set forth in *Annotationes* (1748) and more fully in *Theologia Moralis* (1753/5). He was the dominating influence in 19th-cent. R. Catholicism in the linking of morality to the confessional: he was beatified in 1813, made Doctor of the Church in 1871, and patron of confessors and moralists in 1950, when *Pius XII stated that he was 'a safe norm' in the Church.

Li-Hsüeh: see CHU HSI.

Li-kuei. The *kuei in Chinese popular belief who return after death as vengeful spirits. They return from those who were killed 'out of time'—in war or by murder or accident—or from those who were wrongly executed or improperly buried.

Līlā (Skt., 'play'). The 'joyous exercise of spontaneity involved [according to Hindus] in the art of creation' (S. *Radhakrishnan). Līlā is freedom of movement, as in the rush of water from a fountain. It represents an exuberance in creation, undertaken by the god(s) for sheer delight, and is thus the reason why there is something rather than nothing. Līlā is personified in *Lalitā. Because līlā arises from the creator's bliss (*ānanda(z)), the cosmos arises, continues, and dissolves in bliss. Sufferings and misery are then a consequence of *karma. Līlā is produced (in the **Brahma Sūtra* 2. 1. 32 f.) in response to the argument that creation (see COSMOLOGY (HINDU)) cannot come from the agency of a personal creator, since humans only strive to create that which they need or want; but the better *analogy is that of a king who engages in sport for its own intrinsic delight. Līlā then came also to refer to the acts of gods, so that dramatic re-enactments are called '-līlā', as e.g. *Ramalīlā* or *Kṛṣṇalīlā*.

D. R. Kinsley, *The Divine Player: A Study of Kṛṣṇalīlā* (1979).

Lilith. A female *demon in Jewish mythology. Isaiah lists Lilith among the beasts of prey which will devastate the land (34. 14). According to a *midrash, Lilith was the first *Eve who disputed with *Adam because she was unwilling to forgo her equality. Subsequently she gained the reputation of killing new-born babies. In the **Zohar*, she is described as Lilith the harlot, the wicked, the false, and the black.

L. Ginzberg, *Legends of the Jews* (1925).

Limbo (Lat., *limbus*, 'border', *sc.* of hell). In Catholic theology, the place for the dead who have deserved neither the beatific vision nor the punishment of hell. These include the righteous before the coming of Christ, and also unbaptized babies (and some children) held to be in *original sin but innocent of actual sins. The existence of limbo is a theological opinion on which the RC Church has never pronounced, and concerning which no official teaching is an advocate. It is distinct from *purgatory.

Liminality (rituals negotiating thresholds): see RITES OF PASSAGE.

Lin-chi I-hsüan (Jap. Rinzai Gigen, *d.* 867 CE). Chinese master who founded the Zen Buddhist Lin-chi line (*Rinzai-shū in Japanese). Lin-chi was noted for his emphasis on shouting (*ho) and striking (*kyosaku) as techniques for spurring on the spiritual progress of his students. He challenged his disciples to manifest in their actions the 'true person of no status', that is, the inherent enlightenment within every person. 'A type of Chinese Socrates' (Demiéville), he is one of the outstanding figures, not just of Buddhism, but of humanity.

The Lin-chi way is characterized by dialectical formulae, the three statements (*sanku*), three mysteries (*sangen*), and three essentials (*sanyō*); and the sets of four—four alternatives (*shiryōken*), four conversations, four types of shouting (*shikatsu*). The threefold formulae are dense and not explained. They perhaps arise from the three Buddha-bodies, dharmakāya, sambhogakāya, and nirmāṇakāya (*trikāya), or as the *Three Jewels. The *shiryōken* analyse four possible relations between subject and object to show how true insight transcends them all. The four conversations exhibit how teachers and pupils should *not* converse. The four *shikatsu* are: 'Like the jewelled sword of the Vajra king; like the crouching golden-haired lion; like the weed-tipped fishing-pole; not like a shout of any ordinary kind.' But the point is not dialectical skill. In his own words:

> The important thing in the study of Buddhism is to achieve a true understanding. If true understanding is achieved, one will not be defiled by birth and death, and wherever he may be, he will be free . . . He walks wherever he wants to walk, and sits wherever he wants to sit. He does not think for a single instant of attaining Buddhahood. Why? An old saying says, 'If one seeks after Buddhahood, the Buddha will become the cause of reappearance.'

His sayings and some biographical information are gathered in *Lin-chi lu* (tr. R. F. Sasaki, 1975; see also *Rinzairoku*), which includes the notable command: 'If you meet the Buddha, kill the Buddha; if you meet the patriarch, kill the patriarch', which summarizes the goal of independence from even the highest authority in the achieving of what they alone have the authority to teach.

P. Demiéville, *Entretiens de Lin-tsi* (1972).

Lindisfarne. 'Holy Island', off the coast of Northumberland in England. It became a missionary centre and episcopal see under St *Aidan in 635. St *Cuthbert's association with the monastery added to its celebrity. In 793 and 875 the monastery and church were pillaged by the Danes, and the monks fled. The see was eventually transferred to Durham in 995. There was again monastic life on the island from 1082 to the Dissolution. The Latin manuscript known as the Lindisfarne Gospels was written and decorated *c.*698–9 by Eadfrith (afterwards bishop of Lindisfarne) 'in honour of St Cuthbert'.

Lineages (Buddhist): see BUDDHIST SCHOOLS.

Ling (Chin.). A term used in Chinese religious, literary, philosophical, and medical texts to denote a wide variety of attributes and beings. The closest Eng. approximation is 'spiritual' or 'spirit'.

Liṅga(m) (Skt., 'symbol'). Hindu term for a mark or sign, especially the sign or symbol of generative energy. The liṅga and *yoni, the representations of the male and female sex organs, thus bring the issues of generation and fertility into a religious context. In *Śaiva temples, the liṅga stands on a pedestal (which represents the yoni), their union being the quintessential summary of creative energy. To call this 'phallic worship' is totally to misunderstand how representation in miniature, or in *symbolic form, creates and releases the power with which it is associated. Important examples can be found in the Liṅgarāj, in the temple dedicated to Śiva as the Lord of the Three Worlds (Tribhuvaneśvar) in *Bhubaneswar (hence the name of the city in Orissa, the site of many Hindu temples); at *Elephanta; and at Ellora in the Kailāsa temple, dedicated to Śiva. Among the most ancient (still a centre for worship) is that in Guḍimally in S. India. The twelve *Jyotirliṅga(m)s, made directly from light without human assistance, are each a centre of *pilgrimage. The *Liṅga Purāṇa is devoted to the honour of Śiva (e.g. promising the reward of Śiva's heaven to anyone who tears out the tongue of a reviler of Śiva, 1. 107. 41). See Index, Liṅga.

Liṅga-purāṇa. Long *purāṇa concerned with the four goals of life: *artha, *kāma, *dharma, *mokṣa. It has little connection with the *liṅga, although *Brahmā bestowed this name on the work.

Liṅga-śarīra or **Sūkṣma-śarīra.** The second, subtle sheath surrounding the *ātman. It supports the continuity from one life to another in rebirth, bearing the consequences of *karma.

Liṅgāyat (Skt., *liṅga, emblem of *Śiva). An ancient Indian *Śaivite sect believing in the One Undivided, or Non-dualistic, Being, *Brahmā, or Śiva-tattva, possessing latent creative energy in its aspect as pure 'existence' (sthala). Its adherents are also known as Vīraśaivas. Once the creative principle is activated, this Being becomes two: Śiva made manifest who is worshipped (liṅga-sthala), and each individual worshipping soul (*aṅga-sthala*).

Before the 12th cent. the Liṅgāyats, termed Ārādhya (devoted), maintained many traditional *brahmanic practices, but a reform movement was initiated by *Basava (*c.*1106–67/8), a S. Indian *brahman who carried out systematic attacks on Jains, Buddhists, and *Vaiṣṇavas, while sponsoring Śaivism and, in particular, the Liṅgāyat sect.

Vegetarianism and prohibition of alcohol, tobacco, and any form of drugs are the rule for Liṅgāyats, and it is noteworthy that they do not cremate, but bury, their dead. The Liṅgāyats adopted many socio-religious reforms, some of which were later to be promulgated throughout Hinduism, such as: denial of *caste distinctions; banning of child marriage; approval of widow remarriage; denial of brahmanical superiority and authority, rites, and rituals. Women and men came to be regarded as equal, and the former underwent no period of pollution monthly at menstruation.

Liṅgāyat priests (*jaṅgamas*) are highly regarded; while some are allowed to marry, those in the most prestigious category are *celibate. They have great influence in the community, and every Liṅgāyat, boy or girl, has to undergo initiation, at which the significance of the three types of liṅga is explained: the bhāva-linga of Śiva-tattva, the supreme, all-pervading, and eternal; the prāṇa-liṅga, that which a person may comprehend, the deity he worships; the ishṭa-liṅga, or 'desire'-liṅga, which may be seen and which fulfils all desire, and is therefore to be reverenced. All Liṅgāyats, after initiation, wear a stone liṅga in a silver casket; its loss is the equivalent of 'spiritual death': this is a reminder that the body is the true temple.

Liṅgāyats are found chiefly in Kanara, and much of the development of literary Kanarese is owed to them. The sect's teachings are enshrined in the thousands of scriptural texts, written in colloquial idiom, the liberal tenets of which may owe a great deal to Muslim influence in the area.

S. C. Nandimath, *A Handbook of Vīraśaivism* (1942); A. K. Ramanujan, *Speaking of Śiva* (1973).

Ling-chih (herb of immortality): see CH'ANG-SHENG PU-SSU.

Ling-pao Ching (Writings of the Magic Jewel). Chinese *Taoist texts underlying *Ling-pao p'ai, a religious Taoist (tao-chiao) movement. According to tradition, they came into being at the beginning of the world, though they appear to have been written between the 3rd and 5th cents. CE. They describe the Taoist pantheon and the rites by which they may be approached, and they contain instructions for rituals. See also SAN-CH'ING.

Ling-pao P'ai (Chin., 'School of the Magic Jewel'). A movement within religious *Taoism (tao-chiao), based on *Ling-pao Ching*. Influenced by Buddhist devotion to *bodhisattvas, it claimed that liberation or salvation depends on help from deities (*t'ien-tsun*). Of great importance is *chai (fasting) in projecting deities from within, and thus externalizing them for worship. The school is thus noted for its ritual.

Ling-pao t'ien-tsun (Taoist heavenly ruler): see SAN-CH'ING.

Li Po (Li Pai, Li T'ai-pai), (701–62). Chinese Taoist poet. Although he spent a short period in Ch'angan (*Sian/Xi'an) as a court writer (742–4), he spent most of his life wandering. He was so well-known for drinking that shops could carry the sign 'T'ai-pai yi-feng' ('the ways and habits of T'ai-pai') and it would be recognized that such shops sold wine. Tradition makes him one of the 'eight immortals of the wine cup', and he himself interpreted his wild behaviour as arising from the fact that he was 'a banished immortal': these are immortals who do some wrong in heaven and are banished to earth for a life-time. Whatever the source, his poems express a strong ecstasy, as well as sympathy with the misfortunes of others. He remains a very popular poet.

A. Waley, *The Poetry and Career of Li Po* (1950).

Litany (Gk., 'supplication'). A form of prayer, often addressed to God, but also to the Virgin *Mary or to *saints, made up of a series of petitions (in liturgical settings, these are often said or sung by a deacon, priest, or cantor), to which the people make set responses such as 'Lord, have mercy' or 'Grant this, O Lord'. Litanies said by the deacon are prominent, first in Byzantine liturgies (*c.*4th cent.), then commonly in E. liturgies, as an important congregational element. The *Kyrie in the Roman mass is the survival of a litany introduced by Pope Gelasius I

(492–6); Anglican service books also contain litanies.

Li T'ieh-kuai (one of eight immortals): see PA-HSIEN.

Li Tsu-hsu (Kōan collector): see KŌAN.

Little Brothers (order founded by): see DE FOUCAULD, CHARLES EUGÈNE.

Little Entrance. In the *Orthodox liturgy of the *eucharist, the procession with the book of the gospels at the beginning of the liturgy of the catechumens. The deacon, along with the priest and attendants, brings the book out from the sanctuary, and holds it up before the people, after which it is placed on the holy table.

See also GREAT ENTRANCE.

Little Flowers of St Francis: see FRANCIS, ST.

Little Gidding. The early 17th-cent. Huntingdonshire community of about forty members led by the *Anglican *deacon Nicholas Ferrar (1592–1637). Often critically referred to as 'the *Arminian Nunnery', from the title of a scurrilous pamphlet published in 1641, the household ordered its life by a set pattern of spiritual devotion with daily services, also paying attention to the study of theology and the practice of daily work. The community's life extended from its formation in 1625 until it was raided by Cromwell's soldiers in 1646. 'Little Gidding' is the title of one of T. S. *Eliot's *Four Quartets*, reflecting on time, eternity, and history: 'We shall not cease from exploration | And the end of all our exploring | Will be to arrive where we started.'

Little Office of Our Lady. A Christian devotion, modelled on a day of the daily *office, in honour of the Virgin *Mary. It was first used in the RC Church in the 10th cent. among the religious orders, and later became popular as a private devotion. It is the text of the many richly illuminated Books of Hours of the Middle Ages. Newer religious congregations have often adopted its use, which is also frequently enjoined upon tertiaries (*third orders). The desire of *Vatican II to make the official liturgy of the Hours more widely used was in some conflict with the 'Little Office'. Despite a Saturday memorial of Mary using texts from the 'Little Office', a new version was produced in 1986 and 1988 for those wishing a less complex observance.

Little Russians: see RUTHENIANS.

Little Spring Time: see TAIZÉ COMMUNITY.

Liturgical Colours. Christian practice, beginning to be regularized from about 12th cent., of specifying particular colours for vestments and altar hangings, according to the season in the W. Church's year, on the occasion of a particular day. Thus white is generally commended for the two festival periods, Christmas to the Sunday after Epiphany, and from Easter Day to Pentecost Week, for days celebrating saints, and for Trinity Sunday; red for Pentecost Week, Holy Week, days commemorating martyrs, and sometimes for *confirmation and *ordination; violet/purple during Advent and Lent, and (if black is not used) for funerals and the commemoration of All Souls; and green on other occasions.

Liturgical Movement. A 20th-cent. movement in W. Churches to revitalize liturgical worship and give the congregation a more active part in it. It began among RC religious communities (often dated from an address by *Benedictine L. Beauduin in 1909) with efforts to make assembly for worship the main place where people learn and grow in faith, and perhaps to recreate the worship of the Middle Ages; especially after the Second World War, pressure developed to reform the rite itself. The *encyclical *Mediator Dei* (1947) of *Pius XII cautiously encouraged the movement by insisting on the importance of the participation of the people, and from this time permission was given for the use of the vernacular except at the eucharist. The Second *Vatican Council in its *Constitution on the Sacred Liturgy* legislated for the use of the vernacular, and began a reform which produced a definitive *missal in 1970.

In Anglican churches the most notable effect of the liturgical movement has been to replace morning prayers as the main Sunday service by a *eucharist or 'parish communion'. In the eucharist there have been other ceremonial changes to stress the corporate nature of worship, e.g. the 'westward position' of the celebrant, facing the congregation. Anglican *Alternative Services and similar modern services in other churches are also the product of this movement.

A. Schmemann, *Introduction to Liturgical Theology* (1960; tr. 1966); C. Vagaggini, *Theological Dimensions of the Liturgy* (1965; tr. 1976).

Liturgy (Gk., *leitourgia*, from *laos*, 'people', + *ergon*, 'work'). Worship according to prescribed forms, as opposed to private devotions; hence 'the liturgy', the form of such worship. In Judaism, the pattern of liturgy developed from the practices in Palestine and Babylon in the Geonic (*Gaon) period. Out of the Palestinian rite, grew the Romanian rite (in use in Greece and Turkey until at least the 16th cent. CE), the Roman rite (in use in Italy), and the *Ashkenazi rite (followed in Germany, Switzerland, Holland, Belgium, N. France, Poland, Hungary, Russia, the Balkan countries, Scandinavia, and Britain). Out of Babylonia grew the *Sephardi rite (used in N. Africa, Spain, S. France, and the Yemen). In each, there are slight variations. The liturgy of the *Reform movement is shorter, includes less Hebrew, and removes prayers which are offensive to modern sensibilities, in particular omitting hope for the restoration of sacrifices, and changing the blessing offered by men to God 'who has not made me a woman' into 'who has made me in his own image'. See also PIYYUT; PRAYER BOOK (JEWISH); SYNAGOGUE.

In Christian use the word may refer to all the services of the Church (but not usually to those of Protestant churches). Most specifically, however, and especially in E. Churches, it is a title of the *eucharist or of a particular text of this service (e.g. the Liturgy of St John *Chrysostom, of St Basil, of St James, etc.). See Index, Liturgy.

A. Baumstark, *Liturgée comparée* (1939, 1953) and *Comparative Liturgy* (1958); I. Elborgen, *Jewish Liturgy*; C. Jones (ed.), *The Study of Liturgy* (1978); T. Klauser, *A Short History of the Western Liturgy* (1979); S. C. Reif, *Judaism and Hebrew Prayer* (1993).

Liturgy of the Presanctified. Ancient form of Christian *liturgy (sometimes called the Liturgy of St Gregory Dialogos, i.e. *Gregory the Great), which continues particularly in E. Christianity. It is celebrated on Wednesdays and Fridays in *Lent and on the first three days of *Holy Week. There is no prayer of consecration: the congregation may receive the *antidoron and perhaps the reserved sacrament.

Liu-tsu-ta-shih (Jap., Rokuso Daishi). Honorific title for *Hui-neng, often used instead of his name in works about him.

Liu-Tsu-Ta-Shih Fa-Pao-T'an-Ching/T'an-ching (Jap., *Rokuso daishi hōbōdan-gyo, Dan-gyo*). The Sūtra of the Sixth Patriarch from the High Seat of the Dharma Treasure, usually known as the *Platform Sūtra*, a key Zen work in which the biography and sayings of *Hui-neng are collected. However, it exists in longer and shorter forms, and may have been developed (as tradition affirms) from a lecture given by Hui-neng and recorded by Fa-hai; its longer form is thought by some to be a composition of Shen-hui (see SOUTHERN AND NORTHERN SCHOOLS). The sūtra is a practical guide to enlightenment: 'Learned friends, perfection is inherent in all people. If it were not for the delusions of the mind they could attain enlightenment on their own. As it is, they should seek help from the enlightened and thus be shown the way to see what is already their own nature.' The sūtra is offered as that help.

Trs. C. Luk, *Ch'an and Zen Teachings* (1962) and T.-c. Wing (1963); discussion in H. Dumoulin, *Zen Buddhism* . . ., i (1988).

Livingstone, David (1813–73). Christian medical *missionary and pioneer of Central and Southern African exploration. Influenced by Thomas Dick's writings, he professed personal faith: 'In the glow of love which Christianity inspires I soon resolved to devote my life to the alleviation of human misery.' Following medical training, he served in Africa with the London Missionary Society, inspired by Robert Moffatt, whose eldest daughter, Mary, he later married. His 30,000-mile missionary journeys, mostly under appalling conditions, gave him first-hand knowledge of slave-trade cruelties, and he constantly worked for its suppression. His work inspired many who later established dispensaries, clinics, and hospitals all over the African continent. He died in the village of Ilala; his body was buried in Westminster Abbey.

G. Seaver, *David Livingstone* . . . (1957).

Lobha (Skt.). Greed, or avarice, an impediment to enlightenment in Hinduism and Buddhism. Lobha is also one of the five sins (*akuśala) cited in the **Mahābhārata*, the others being *kāma (sexual desire), *krodha (wrath), *bhaya* (fear), and *svapna* (sleep). Lobha, like the other sins, must be 'cut off' by the practice of meditation. In Buddhism, it is one of the three vitiating roots (*hetu) of the human condition, which can be overcome by the practice of generosity (*dāna).

Locanā (goddess): see AKṢOBHYA.

Lo Ch'ing (1443–1527). Founder of an eclectic religion in China. From his writings, gathered in *Five Works in Six Volumes*, it seems clear that he attained enlightenment after a personal quest. His teaching attacks the vacuity of ritual and prayer, and stresses in contrast the importance of gratitude—for everything and everyone on whom one's being depends. His school has diversified into a number of different sects, including one, the Dragon Flower Way (Lung-hua) which has somewhat reversed his teaching and includes a ritual element.

Locke, John (1632–1704). English philosopher who became a major source for British empiricism and for liberal democracy, and who applied his thought to the support of Christian theistic belief. He was educated at Christ Church, Oxford, where he became a fellow in 1656. He worked with Robert Boyle, whose work in chemistry was grounded in empirical research. In 1667, he joined the household of Lord Ashley, later first earl of Shaftesbury, as physician and adviser. From 1675–9, he was in France, perhaps for political reasons, where he travelled and met many continental scientists. His return to England ended with the fall from power and death of Shaftesbury, and in 1683–9 he was in Holland, where he came in contact with the Remonstrants (see DUTCH REFORMED CHURCH), whose views reinforced his own. After the Glorious Revolution of 1688, Locke returned to England and published his *Essay Concerning Human Understanding* (1690). He had already written *The Letter on Toleration* and (anonymously) *Two Treatises on Government*, but it was his *Essay* which established his—controversial—reputation. He wrote *Thoughts on Education* (1693), *Reasonableness of Christianity* (1695), and works which appeared later, *The Conduct of the Understanding* (1706) and *Miracles* (1716).

He was concerned to mediate the implications of the new sciences and their methods, regarding the work of a philosopher to be the clearing away of 'some of the rubbish that lies in the way of knowledge'. In the *Essay*, Locke argued that humans are not born with a store of innate ideas, but are, rather, like a dark closet which needs to be furnished from without—or like a blank slate on which experience writes. The richness of mental life is built up from sensation and reflection, which build up experience. The world is not merely a matter of invention, since some of the ideas we develop stand for the original or primary qualities inseparable from the things observed (solidity, extension, figure, motion or rest, and number), while others stand for secondary qualities (colour, sound, taste, etc.) which are not in the objects themselves, but are discerned by us, being well-ordered to that end—thus Locke argued that if we were equipped with microscopes instead of eyes, we would not 'see' the secondary qualities of colour. That things are 'well-ordered' was important for Locke. Far from being 'a blind, fortuitous concourse of atoms', we are able to make sense, from our senses, of the universe, in which 'Nature never makes excellent things for mean or no uses'. From this, the existence of God is able to be demonstrated; and given that demonstrable truth, Locke was able to argue that certain rights which humans possess by nature are God-given and cannot be taken away: toleration becomes a primary virtue, to be exercised everywhere except where the rights of others are threatened. Locke's views were thus influential in forming the attitudes of the founders of the USA.

M. Ayers, *Locke* (1992); K. Dewhurst, *John Locke* (1984); J. Dunn, *John Locke* (1984); G. Parry, *John Locke* (1978); J. W. Yolton, *John Locke, . . . a Guide* (1985) and *Locke and the Compass of Human Understanding* (1970).

Logia (Gk., 'sayings'). Any of various collections of sayings of *Jesus in circulation in the early church. *Papias asserts that *Matthew compiled *ta logia* in Hebrew; if true the statement may have some reference to the source *Q. Other collections included one of which fragments have been found at Oxyrhynchus.

Logic. An activity both condemned and justified in the history of Buddhist thought. While the *Buddha discouraged vain philosophical speculation, there is no evidence that he disapproved of logic as such. The *Abhidhammic literature, with its listing of Buddhist concepts, is presented in a vaguely logical manner; and the *Theravādin *Kathāvatthu* is an attempt to refute logically more than 200 propositions held by opposing schools.

In the *Mahāyāna it has often been claimed that *Nāgārjuna used the *reductio ad absurdum* (*prasaṅga*), while both *Asaṅga and *Vasubandhu wrote on logic and the rules of debate. Asaṅga actually adopts the five-membered syllogism of the brahmanical Nyāya in his *Abhidharma-samuccaya*. It appears that in the early period of the Mahāyāna, Nāgārjuna's method held a stranglehold on the development of Buddhist logic, and only in the 4th and 5th cents. CE, with Dignāga and *Dharmakīrti was logic valued as an activity in its own right. The study of the logical writings of the Pramāṇa school is still an important element in the training of some Tibetan schools of Buddhism. See also TARKA.

Logos (Gk., 'word' or 'reason'). A term prominent especially in early Christian theology as a title or description of Christ. The Christian use depends on: (i) the popular Stoic idea (going back to Heraclitus, *c.*500 BCE) of a universal reason governing and permeating the world; and (ii) the Hebrew conception of God's word (as of his *wisdom) as having an almost independent existence (e.g. Isaiah 55. 11). In pre-Christian Judaism, *Philo to some extent already combined both concepts, speaking of the logos both as the divine pattern in the world and the intermediary between God and people. The prologue to the gospel of *John (1. 1–18) identifies the Logos as incarnate in Jesus. To the *apologists of the 2nd cent. the duality of the term was a welcome means of making *Christology compatible with popular philosophy. Later on (e.g. by *Athanasius), it was used to refer generally to the second person of the *Trinity.

Logos spermatikos ('innate word/wisdom'): see JUSTIN MARTYR, ST.

Lo-han. Chin. term (Jap., *rakan*) for the Theravādin Buddhist *arhat, though in Chinese Buddhism they have developed in the direction of minor deities, or (in the case of Ch'an) those who have obtained enlightenment by their effort. They resemble the *Hsien, the mountain-dwelling, cloud-riding immortals of Taoism. The Taoist word *chen-jen (immortals) was thus also used to translate arhat. In number eighteen (in early texts sixteen), they rule different regions assigned to them by the Buddha, and will not leave them until the advent of the next Buddha. In Ch'an/Zen they are found in groups of 500 (from the first Buddhist Council, at which 500 arhats were present), and they frequently appear in forms which make magical skill (*abhiññā) possible. Major cults and iconography developed.

W. Fong, *The Lohans and a Bridge to Heaven* (1958).

Lo-han Kuei-ch'en, also known as **Ti-ts'ang** (Jap., Rakan Keijin or Jizō; *c.*865–*c.*928 CE). Ch'an/Zen master, successor (*hassu) of Hsuan-sha Shih-pei and teacher of *Fa-yen Wen-i. He is particularly known for his exchanges (*mondō) with Fa-yen, e.g.: 'Ti-ts'ang asked Fa-yen: "Where are you going?" Fa-yen replied, "I'm wandering about." "What's the point of wandering about?" "I don't know." "Not knowing is closest." '

Loisy, Alfred Firmin (1857–1940). French biblical scholar and RC *Modernist. An enthusiastic exponent of the historico-critical study of the *Bible, he was dismissed from the Institut Catholique in Paris in 1893. In 1902 he wrote *L'Évangile et l'Église*, a defence of Catholicism against A. von *Harnack. He saw Catholicism's strength as lying in its ability to change continually and adapt itself under the impulse originally given by *Christ; but he denied that Christ founded the Church and established *sacraments; and he was sceptical about the possibility of recovering the words of Jesus, and about the traditional doctrines of the Church. His *Autour d'un petit livre* (1903) made his divergence from traditional Catholicism still clearer. Several of his books were put on the *Index in 1903, and Loisy was *excommunicated in 1908 after publishing a critique of **Lamentabili*. From 1909 to 1930 he was professor of the history of religions at the Collège de France.

Loka (Skt., 'world').

Hinduism The domains or regions which make up the cosmos. In origin there were three lokas (*triloka*), locations inhabited by beings appropriate to them: earth, atmosphere, and 'the yonder world' (of the gods, the sun, the moon, and the stars). But these were early related to domains pertaining to salvation (and its opposite). Thus *svar*, 'sky', is already synonymous in the *Vedas with *svarga, 'heaven', so that another triad was produced of svarga-loka, *bhūmi-* (earth), and *pātāla-* (underworld or hell). Later, these were elaborated into more detailed (especially soteriological) domains, as when it was assumed that gods of particular importance would have their own lokas—hence *Yāma-loka, Svar-loka (*Indra's paradise), *Brahma-loka. Cosmological analysis also produced longer lists, e.g. eight in *Saṃkhya and *Vedānta, fourteen in *bhakti, which embrace the soteriological.

Buddhism The primary sense is analytic, in which loka is the 'habitat' of gods and human beings. In these contexts, loka is explained as all the perceptible world, i.e. all that which comes within the spheres of the senses. Loka in its cosmographic sense includes the entire cosmos. A *lokadhātu* is a smaller unit within the loka, a unit which may be described as a solar system. Such a lokadhātu extends 'as far as the moon and the sun move in their course and light up the quarters with their radiance'. Such a unit consists of the following: the moon and the sun, mount Sineru, the four continents, the four great oceans, the four great Kings, and the sevenfold heavenly spheres. Each system of one thousand units of this, is the system of the thousandfold lesser world system (*sahassī cūlaṇikā lokadhātu*). A system which is a thousand times the size of this is the Twice-a-thousand Middling world system (*dvisahassī majjhimikā lokadhātu*). A system which is a thousand times the size of the foregoing (i.e. the *dvisahassī majjhimikā lokadhātu*) is the Thrice-a-thousand Mighty world system (*tisahassī mahāsahassī lokadhātu*) (M. M. J. Marasinghe, *Gods in Early Buddhism*, 1974, p. 44). Thus, the loka consists of myriads of such solar systems. Therefore, in its immensity, the loka is unlimited. It is not possible, therefore, to reach the end of the loka by travelling and its immensity cannot be grasped by thinking either. Hence, *lokacintā* is one of four unthinkables according to another *Anguttara Nikāya* discourse (2. 80).

The term *cakkavāḷa* in the post-Nikāya literature seems to have come into use in the same sense, but with more details of a cosmographic nature.

Buddhism also has its equivalent to the triloka of Hinduism (in Pāli, *trailokya* or *traidhātuka*). They are (i) kāmaloka, the domains of desire and attachment, including those of hell (*naraka), humans, animals, the *devas, and the *asuras; (ii) rūpaloka, the domain of form without desire, the gods in the *dhyāna heaven, attained through the four dhyānas; (iii) arūpaloka, the domain of formlessness. They may also be known as Kāmadhatu, etc.

Lokācārya (Skt., 'teacher of the people'). A theologian of *Śrīvaiṣṇavism and regarded as the figurehead of the *Teṉkaḷai. To distinguish him from an older teacher in the same tradition, he is called Piḷḷai, 'junior' (his personal name was Vāraṇādrīśa). He died during the earlier part of the 14th cent. CE. Eighteen treatises are ascribed to him, all in a highly Sanskritized form of Tamil, of which the *Mumukṣuppaṭi*, *Śrīvacaṉabhūṣaṇam*, and *Tattvatraya* are the most important. Lokācārya emphasized the commitment of God to those who seek him with devotion and love:

> The Lord's immanence [*vibhava*] is the remaining of the Lord with all sentient beings in all their conditions, in heaven or in hell, as a companion who is unable to leave them. It is the residing of the Lord in the *lotus of the heart, so that we may meditate on him in auspicious form, and that he, like closest family, may safeguard us.

See also PRAPATTI.

Lokadhatu: see LOKA (BUDDHISM).

Loka-pāla (Skt., 'world protector'). In both Hinduism and Buddhism, guardians of the whole world. In Buddhism, as protectors of the four quarters. In Hinduism, as protectors of the four quarters and the four intermediate positions (NE, etc.)—thus N., *Kubera; NE, *Soma; E., *Indra; SE, *Agni; S., *Yama; SW, *Sūrya; W., *Varuṇa; NW, *Vāyu.

Lokāyata. Hindu philosophy restricting truth and reality to this world (*loka) only, hence a name for the school of *Cārvāka.

Lokeśvararaja (a Buddha): see AMIDA.

Lokottara (Skt.; Pāli, *lokuttara*). The transcendental and supramundane in Jainism and Buddhism. In early Buddhism, it refers to all that leads beyond clinging (*taṇhā) and attachment to *nirvāna. In Mahāyāna, it applies especially to the Buddha conceived of as a transcendental being of limitless wisdom and power. The Lokottaravāda was a school maintaining that every utterance of the Buddha, even those which are apparently mundane, are in fact concerned with transcendental matters.

Lollards (etym. uncertain, poss. from Lat. 'tares', *sc.* growing amidst the good wheat, or 'one who mumbles'). Name (originally one of abuse) given to the followers of *Wycliffe, who took issue with the Church on a number of grounds, but especially the power of the papacy, *transubstantiation, and the privileges of the priesthood. Later the term was applied to those more generally dissatisfied with the Church. *Wycliffe's followers were less theologically informed than he was, and were apt to disagree with the Church about the place of the *pope, the efficacy of the prayer of the Blessed Virgin *Mary and of the *saints, transubstantiation, the necessity for auricular *confession, and the place of *scripture. Once seen as 'the morning star' of the *Reformation, they are now recognized as having had a more restricted influence; they were concentrated among people in the south of England, among cloth-workers and landowners of moderate means. They co-operated in the distribution of *Tyndale's New Testament, and were broadly in sympathy with the changes associated with the Henrician reformation. Their distinctive protest did not survive, but merged into the wider spectrum of Protestant views.

A. Hope, in P. Lake and M. Dowling (eds.), *Protestantism and the National Church* . . . (1987); A. Hudson, *The Premature Reformation: Wycliffe Texts and Lollard History* (1988).

Lonergan, Bernard (1904–84). Christian theologian of central importance in the development of *transcendental Thomism (see NEO-THOMISM) into new and daring territory. Born in Canada, he became a *Jesuit in 1922. He was ordained priest in 1936, and taught in both Canada and Rome. His major work is *Insight: A Study of Human Understanding* (1957), a detailed study of the conditions and levels of human understanding, leading (in the final chapter) to a paragraph beginning, 'In the thirty-first place . . .'. The work looks first at 'Insight as activity', answering the question, 'What is happening when we are knowing?'; and second at 'Insight as knowledge', answering the question, 'What is known when that is happening?' The book rejects the facile assumption of casual thought (and pervasive scientism) that 'what is obvious in knowing is what knowing is obviously about'; nothing could be more erroneous than the positivist assumption that 'knowing consists in simply taking a look'. In contrast, he argues that 'Insight' is *in*-sight, seeing into the observed object to discern it in various ways. Lonergan traced these ways through various levels of understanding, mathematical, scientific, aesthetic, moral, etc., leading up to the metaphysical. At each level, there is always left an 'empirical residue' which demands that the enquiring mind moves on further if it would become wise. There is thus created a relation between 'intelligent grasp and reasonable affirmation', which constantly pulls the intelligent mind to the realm of transcendent being: 'The immanent source of transcendence in man is his detached, disinterested, unrestricted desire to know.' This leads (in all religions, hence Lonergan's contribution to the wider *'ecumenism') to 'a grasp of the unconditioned', the realization that God is: if the real is intelligible, God exists; but the real is intelligible; therefore God exists. But such 'proof' is not coercive: it requires appropriation: 'Such, then, is the argument. As a set of signs printed in a book, it can do no more than indicate the materials for a reflective grasp of the virtually unconditioned. To elicit such an act is the work that the reader has to perform for himself.' His approach was elaborated in *Method in Theology* (1972).

H. A. Meynell, *An Introduction* . . . (1976); D. Tracy, *The Achievement of Bernard Lonergan* (1970).

Longchenpa (Tibetan scholar): see KLONG-CHEN RAB-'BYAMS-PA.

Longmen/Dragon Gate Caves or **Lungmen.** Large complex of caves occupied by Buddhists and containing, or supporting, carvings, and wall-paintings. There are about 1,300 caves, innumerable niches and a number of *pagodas. The caves are 9 miles south of Luoyang (cf. *Pai-ma-ssu) in Honan province. The earliest carvings are from the end of the 5th cent. and the latest from the 8th cent. Virtually every style from that period is represented, with, e.g., more than 100,000 carvings of the *Buddha. Other frequent representations are those of Amitābha (*Amida), *Avalokiteśvara, *Maitreya, and Ti-tsang (*Kṣitigarbha). Unusual is the Medical Prescription Cave, which has inscriptions offering remedies for a variety of illnesses. The caves have suffered little from natural causes, the major damage having been caused, first by the persecution of Buddhism by the emperor Wu, and second by Westerners looting—e.g. a superb mural depicting a royal procession was blasted away and is now in the Metropolitan Museum of Art in New York. Along with the caves at *Tun-huang and *Yun-kang, they are the most revered in China.

Loṅkā (Shah) (15th cent.). Jain reformer and influence on the Sthānakvāsi *Gaccha (sect). Virtually nothing is known for certain about his life beyond the fact that he was a Gujarati. He became convinced that the Jain scriptures (see AṄGA) gave no warrant for image worship. The claim has been made that in adopting this view, he was influenced by contact with Muslims, or even that he was persuaded by the *Qur'ān. Whatever the background reason, he set out on a path of rigorous reform, emphasizing personal asceticism. The term Sthānakvāsi means 'those who reside in preaching halls', emphasizing their avoidance of temples and images. Although few in number, they remain a part of Jain life to the present.

Lord of Misrule: see HOLY FOOLS.

Lord of the Dance: see DANCE.

Lord's Day. Christian name for *Sunday, based on Revelation 1. 10 (which however may refer to the day of judgement; cf. Amos 5. 18). It nowadays has *sabbatarian overtones, as in Lord's Day Observance Society, or in the more politically campaigning Keep Sunday Special.

Lord's Prayer. The prayer taught by Jesus in the *Sermon on the Mount (Matthew 6. 9–13) or privately to his disciples (Luke 11. 1–4). The two forms reflect different Aramaic versions no doubt already in liturgical use. Matthew's version is that universally used in public worship. In modern English liturgies it is:

Our Father in heaven,
hallowed be your name,
your kingdom come,
your will be done,
on earth as in heaven.
Give us today our daily bread.
Forgive us our sins
as we forgive those who sin against us.
Lead us not into temptation
but deliver us from evil.
For the kingdom, the power, and the glory are yours
now and for ever. Amen.

The doxology at the end was probably an early addition to Matthew's text: cf. Didache 8. A strongly *eschatological interpretation of the prayer is possible, e.g. taking 'temptation' to mean 'the time of trial'; but this is probably not necessary. In the ancient Church the prayer was taught to *catechumens at *baptism. It has a place in all *eucharistic liturgies, and in the divine *office.

J. Jermias, *The Prayers of Jesus* (1978); J. Petuchowski and M. Brocke, *The Lord's Prayer and Jewish Liturgy* (1978).

Lord's Supper. A title for the Christian *eucharist now used especially by Protestants. It is based on the term in 1 Corinthians 11. 20. Some scholars distinguish the 'mass' and 'lord's supper' as two different forms of eucharist in the earliest Church.

Loricae (breastplate prayers): see CELTIC CHURCH.

Lossky, Vladimir (1903–58). Russian lay theologian. He studied first at St Petersburg, then as an émigré (1922) at Prague and Paris, where he settled. One of the greatest 20th-cent. exponents of *Orthodox theology in the W., he was opposed to the sophiological theories of *Bulgakov, and championed a renewal of the thought of the fathers interpreted in the light of *hesychasm. Among W. thinkers he was drawn to Meister *Eckhart, on whom he wrote an important study. He combined a profoundly *apophatic theology with a doctrine of the mystery of the human person created in the image of God. His works include *The Mystical Theology of the Eastern Church* (1944, 1957); *In the Image and Likeness of God* (1967; 1975), and *Orthodox Theology* (1964, 1978).

Lotus (Skt., *padma*). Religious symbol in Eastern religions.

Hinduism The lotus represents beauty, and also non-attachment: as the lotus, rooted in mud, floats on water without becoming wet, so should the one seeking release live in the world without attachment. More specifically, it represents centres of consciousness (*cakra) in the body. It is equated with the tree of life springing from the navel of *Varuṇa (subsequently *Viṣṇu as *Nārāyaṇa), bearing the gods on its leaves.

Buddhism The lotus summarizes the true nature of those who float free of ignorance (*avidya) and attain enlightenment (*bodhi). It is therefore the throne or seat of a buddha; and in *Pure Land, it is the symbol of the Buddha's teaching.

See also PUṆḌARIKA.

F. D. K. Bosch, *The Golden Germ . . .* (1960).

Lotus Position: see PADMĀSANA.

Lotus School: see T'IEN-T'AI.

Lotus Sūtra (Skt., *Saddharmapuṇḍarikasūtra*, 'The *Sūtra on the True *Dharma [which resembles a] White Lotus'). An early (1st cent. BCE–2nd cent. CE) and most important *Mahāyāna sūtra. It is taught by *Śākyamuni *Buddha in his *Saṃbhoga-kaya (cf. *trikaya) form. The sūtra reveals a new interpretation of many traditional beliefs, particularly concerning the nature of the Buddha. In the *Lotus*, the Buddha is no longer regarded as a mere mortal but as a sublime being with supernatural powers who preaches in a mythological paradise surrounded by thousands upon thousands of followers. The Buddha is not described as God in the monotheistic sense but reveals that he has been enlightened 'from the beginning' and has watched over the welfare of beings like a father, even manifesting himself in human form as the Buddha Śākyamuni to show the way to liberation. The notion of the Buddha's great compassion (*mahākaruṇa*) is repeatedly emphasized, and parables illustrate how, through the use of skilful means (*upāya-kauśalya), the buddhas and *bodhisattvas appear in various guises to promote the welfare of beings. The goal of personal salvation or *'Arhatship' advocated by Hīnayāna is replaced by the new ideal of the bodhisattva path (*Bodhisattva-yāna) with its emphasis upon other-centred attitudes and actions. The sūtra thus distinguishes between the true dharma (Skt., *saddharma*) of compassion to all sentient beings and an inferior dharma (Hīnayāna) of personal liberation in *nirvāna. The nirvāna of personal liberation is explained as a resting-place created by the Buddha's *upāya for practitioners of small capacity, similar to an illusory city conjured up by a magician for weary travellers. The true dharma teaches that the buddhas pass into nirvāna after, not before, all sentient beings, and the true Buddhist unwearyingly labours along the bodhisattva path for the liberation of all beings. The sūtra contains many parables which have become very popular and it was selected by *Chih-I as the final teaching of the influential *T'ien-t'ai lineage.

Trs.: H. Kern, the Skt. version (1884); W. E. Soothill, the Chin. version of *Kumārajīva, the one used in the Far East (1930); L. Hurvitz (1976); Buddhist Text Translation Society, with extensive oral commentary by the contemporary Chinese Master Hsüan Hua, *Wonderful Dharma Lotus Flower Sutra*, in progress: chs. 1–13 currently available (1977–82, 10 vols.); members of the Japanese lineage Risshō Kōsei Kai (Bunnō Katō *et al.*), 'The Sutra of the Lotus Flower of the Wonderful Law' in *The Threefold Lotus Sutra* (1975).

Lourdes. In SW France, site of a shrine of the Virgin *Mary. In 1858 the 14-year-old peasant girl, *Bernadette Soubirous, had visions of the Virgin Mary who told her that she was the *Immaculate Conception (a dogma then recently defined). A spring appeared and miraculous healings began to be reported, with the result that increasing numbers began to visit Lourdes. In 1862, the pilgrimage was officially recognized, and the first of a succession of churches was begun. A recent building has been the vast underground basilica of St Pius X, dedicated by the future Pope John XXIII in 1958. Feast day of Our Lady of Lourdes, 11 Feb.

R. Laurentin, *Lourdes: Histoire authentique* (1961–6).

Love. The many facets of love have been given expression in religions in ways so diverse that they characterize priorities and attitudes. For examples of these characterizations, see AGAPE; KARUṆĀ; PREMA; RAḤMĀNĪYA; MO TZU; BHAKTI; KĀMA.

Love Feast: see AGAPE.

Low Churchmen. Christians who give a relatively 'low' place to the importance of the episcopate, priesthood, sacraments, and matters of ritual; specifically, the more Protestant (*evangelical) party in the Anglican Church.

Low Sunday. The first Sunday after *Easter, probably by contrast with the 'high' feast of Easter Sunday itself. It used to be called 'Sunday in White' (*Dominica in Albis*) because the newly baptized appeared in white clothes.

Loyola: see IGNATIUS (OF) LOYOLA.

Lu: see BUDDHISM IN CHINA.

Lubavi(t)ch. Movement within Jewish Ḥasidism, founded by *Shne'ur Zalman in the 18th cent. His descendants made Lubavici, in Russia, their main centre, hence the name. Their views are those of Ḥabad, so that the two are now synonymous (see ḤABAD for their beliefs), although there have been other and independent Ḥabad schools. As with other Ḥasidic groups, they revere the authority of the *zaddik. Since the headquarters of the Lubavich moved to New York, the zaddik, now known as Rebbe, has become much more than the one responsible for the spiritual well-being of the community. The sixth successor and seventh Lubavicher Rebbe, Rabbi Menahem Mendel Schneerson (1902–94), extended greatly the work and aims of the movement, establishing a network of educational institutions and a publishing firm, and encouraging the public presence of the movement to make known its views on orthodox observance. By some he was regarded as the *messiah, and by all, major decisions were referred to him on a battery of telephones in New York. The Lubavich regard the conversion of Jews to Judaism (i.e. to observant Judaism) as a matter of high priority, since otherwise the full return of the messiah cannot occur.

Lucar, Cyril (1572–1638). Patriarch of Constantinople from 1620. His earlier experiences in church politics had turned him against Rome, and in correspondence with Dutch theologians he expressed more and more sympathy with the *Reformed churches. His *Confession of Faith* published in Geneva in 1629 was an attempt to strengthen the Orthodox Church against Romanizing tendencies and bring it into dialogue with other Churches. It is strikingly *Calvinistic, and Cyril's letters imply that his personal views were even more so. His enemies, the dissident metropolitans and the Catholic ambassador in Constantinople, succeeded in having him put to death eight years later. His theology was finally condemned at the Synod of *Jerusalem (1672).

Lucifer (Lat., 'light-bringer'). In the *Vulgate and *Authorized Version of Isaiah 14. 12 ('How art thou fallen from heaven, O Lucifer'), an epithet for the king of Babylon. By some of the *fathers it was taken in conjunction with Luke 10. 18 as a name for the *devil, so that the whole passage Isaiah 14. 12–16 became one basis for the myth (developed in *Milton's *Paradise Lost*) that the devil is a rebellious *angel cast into *hell.

Luis of Granada (1504–88). Spanish spiritual writer. Born in Granada, he became a *Dominican in 1525. In 1555 he went to Portugal, was provincial for a while, and confessor to the great. He devoted his life to prayer, writing, and preaching. His spiritual writings, influenced by the *devotio moderna*, especially the **Imitation of Christ* and *Erasmus' *Encheiridion*, stress the importance of inward devotion. His books were condemned in 1559 but in revised form were widely influential, in particular on Francis *de Sales.

Luke, St. Travelling companion of *Paul, and (according to tradition) author of the third gospel and *Acts of the Apostles. Luke was a physician (Colossians 4. 11) who stayed with Paul in his imprisonment. If the 'we'-sections of Acts come from his journal, he was also with Paul on two earlier missionary journeys (Acts 16. 10–17, 20. 5–21. 18). Later tradition made him a painter, and in the Middle Ages a picture in Rome of the Virgin Mary was ascribed to him. He is the patron saint of doctors and artists. Feast day, 18 Oct.

The Gospel according to Luke is the third book of the New Testament. It forms a two-part work with the book of Acts. Questions of authorship and date turn mainly on the criticism of Acts. In the view of most critics, the gospel made use of the gospel of *Mark and a lost source *Q. The gospel contains: birth and infancy stories of Jesus (chs. 1–2); his baptism, genealogy, and temptation (3. 1–4. 13); his activities in Galilee (4. 14–9. 50); a 'travel narrative' of Jesus' doings and sayings on the way to Jerusalem (9. 51–19. 27, mostly independent of Mark); Jesus' last days in Jerusalem, death, and resurrection (19. 28–24. 53). Many well-known passages stressing Jesus' human kindness, e.g. the parable of the prodigal (15. 11–32), are peculiar to Luke. An interest in defending the political innocence of the Christian movement and in diverting attention from *eschatology is also apparent.

Lulav (Heb., 'a shoot'). A palm branch connected with the Jewish *festival of *Sukkot. The lulav is one of the *four species which are used in worship on the feast of Sukkot.

Lull, Raymond or **Ramón** (*c.*1233–1315). Christian missionary, mystic and philosopher. Born in Majorca soon after liberation from Islamic rule, he became a knight and married. At the age of 30, following a vision of the crucified Christ, he gave himself wholly to Christ's service as a *Franciscan tertiary, and he sought in particular the conversion of Islam. He studied Arabic, went on various missionary journeys, and wrote. His system of thought, by which he hoped (through the rigour of irrefutable arguments, as in *Ars Magna*) to persuade Islam and Judaism to Christianity, is *contemplative and *Neoplatonic, and may owe something to *Sufism. Among those he influenced was *Nicholas of Cusa. *The Book of the Lover and the Beloved* describes how the lover (the faithful Christian) cannot reach the Beloved (God), except *through* love. The end is then a union beyond surrender, in which 'their love mingles as water with wine: they are joined as heat with light, they agree and are united as Essence and Being'.

Tr. E. A. Peers; J. N. Hilgarth, *Ramón Lull* . . . (1971).

Lumbinī. One of four places especially sacred in Buddhism (with *Bodhgayā, *Kuśinagara, *Sārnāth), because it is believed to be the birthplace of the *Buddha. *Aśoka visited it in 249 BCE, and set up a pillar (rediscovered in 1896) to mark his visit and to exempt the inhabitants from taxes. Lumbinī is in the W. Terai of Nepal, just over 400 km. SW of Kathmandu; now known as Rumindei.

Lumpa Church. The most widely known independent church in Zambia. It was founded by a Bemba, Alice Mulenga Mubusha (1924–78), a *catechumen in the Church of Scotland mission, who experienced a mystic death and resurrection in 1953, and was commissioned to deliver Africans from witchcraft and sickness. A mass response led to the foundation of her Lumpa ('best of all') Church about 1954, which gathered some 60,000 members by 1960 under herself as Alice Lenshina (i.e. 'Regina' or Queen), with a new Sione ('Zion') as headquarters and a strict ethic forbidding magic, divorce, polygamy, inheritance of widows, and beer-drinking. After an initial alliance with Kaunda's National Independence Party, the attempt to withdraw from politics led to violent clashes with Kaunda's new government in 1964, in which some 600 lives were lost. The Church was banned in 1965, and Alice was detained until her death in 1978. Many of her followers had fled to neighbouring countries, but in the 1980s the Church was appearing again in many parts of Zambia.

Lung (Chin., 'dragon'). In Taoism, the dragon represents the *yang principle, and is thus often portrayed accompanied by representations of *yin—e.g. clouds or water. Dragons have important active roles in ruling and guarding the world. See also DRAGONS, CHINESE.

Lung-hua (sect): see LO CH'ING.

Lung-hu-shan ('Dragon Tiger Mountain'). Mountain in Chiang-shi province, regarded by Taoists as the home of the celestial masters (*t'ien-shih).

Lung-men ('Dragon Gate', Buddhist caves): see LONGMEN.

Lung-men (school): see CHÜAN-CHEN TAO.

Lung-t'an Chung-hsiu (Ch'an teacher): see TE-SHAN HSUAN-CHIEN.

Lung-wang ('dragon kings'). Taoist mythological figures who have immediate authority over life and death, in the sense that they are responsible for rain and funerals. Humans depend on them, but they in turn are accountable (annually) to the primordial lord who originates all things (Yüan-shih T'ien-tsun; see SAN-SH'ING). See also DRAGONS, CHINESE.

Lun Yü (Eng. rendering of the Dialogues or Conversations of Confucius): see ANALECTS.

L(u)oyang: see LONGMEN CAVES; PAI-MA-SSU (BAIMASI).

Luria, Isaac ben Solomon, Ha-Ari (1534–72). Jewish *kabbalist. Luria was brought up in Egypt and studied under *David b. Solomon ibn Abi Zimri. His early life is shrouded in legend, but he seems to have retired from communal life while a young man to study the **Zohar* and other mystical works, and during this time he wrote his commentary on the *Sifra Di-Zeniuta* (The Book of Concealment), a section of the *Zohar.* In *c.*1570 Luria settled in Safed and studied with Moses *Cordovero. In Safed, Luria drew round himself a group of disciples whom he instructed orally in the mysteries of the kabbalah. These teachings are preserved only in the descriptions of his students. He was said to have received 'the revelation of *Elijah'. The main legends about Luria's saintliness are contained in the *Ta 'alumot Hokhman*, a collection of letters written by Solomon Dresnitz (publ. 1629), and *Toledot Ha-Ari* (publ. 1720). His kabbalistic system is preserved in four different traditions: that of Moses Jonah of Safed, published as *Sefer Kanfei Yonah* (1786); that of Joseph ibn Tabul published in *Derush Hefzi-Bah* (1921); that of Luria's chief disciple Hayyim Vital in *Ez Hayyim* (1850–98); and that of Israel Sarug, author of *Sefer Luminudei Azilut* (1897). Luria was also the author of several hymns which reflect his mystical ideas.

For all these reasons, Luria's teaching is impressionistic and large-scale, rather than systematic and detailed. Addressing the issue confronting all religions which propose a transcendent creator (of how the absolutely transcendent moves into creation without diminution of that transcendence), he envisaged a 'contraction' (*tsimtsum*) in God to make space for creation in relation to himself. The term had formerly been used to account for God's presence in the *Holy of Holies, but Luria gave it a novel sense. There then followed, according to Luria, the process of emanation (*sefirot), but the vessels containing the emanation of light could not bear the weight of glory (or perhaps resisted: for surely, Luria's pupils asked, God could have created vessels strong enough for the task?) and disintegrated. This catastrophe is called *shevirah* or *shevirat ha-kelim*. Luria did not hesitate to accept that God is the source of both good and evil, since without his creative act, the manifestation of evil could not have occurred. However, set against *shevirah* is the work of repair, called *tikkun*, which was a particular responsibility for *Adam. His fall reinforced the powers of evil and weakened those of good. In consequence, God chose a people, the Jews, to shoulder the responsibility once more. Jewish history is the history of this struggle; and the detail of each biography is a contribution to it. In particular, the keeping of the law is essential, since even one failure delays the coming of the messiah when alone the final victory will have been won.

G. Scholem, *Major Trends in Jewish Mysticism* (1941).

Luria, Solomon ben Jehiel (Rashal/Maharshal) (*c*.1510–74). Jewish *Talmudic commentator. Luria served as *rabbi and rosh *yeshivah at Ostrog, Brisk, and Lublin. His *halakhic rulings were independent and avoided *pilpul and were generally accepted. Only a proportion of his work has been preserved, including his *Yam shel Shelomo* (The Seal of Solomon) on the *Talmud (1616–18) and his *Hokhmat Shelomo* (The Wisdom of Solomon, 1582), glosses on the text of the Talmud, printed subsequently in most edns. His *responsa (1574/5) give valuable insight into the culture of 16th-cent. Polish Jewry.

The Responsa of Solomon Luria, ed. S. Hurwitz (1938).

Lu-shan. Mount Lu. Buddhist centre from 4th cent. CE on, in Kiangsi province. Here *Hui-yüan founded *Pai-lien-tsung (the White Lotus school).

Lü-Shih Ch'un-Ch'iu (Spring and Autumn of Master Lū). A Confucian work produced under the supervision of Lü Pu-wei (*c*.3rd cent. BCE), which attempted to gather and systematize knowledge necessary for proper government, in matters of cosmology, ritual, politics, and morals: 'In all things one must not violate the way of heaven (*t'ien), nor destroy the principles of earth, nor bring confusion to the laws of humans.'

Luther, Martin (1483–1546). Founder of the German *Reformation. Born at Eisleben, a copperminer's son, Luther's early education at Mansfeld, Magdeburg, and Eisenach, was followed by his university arts course at Erfurt. In 1505 he entered an Augustinian monastery. Ordained *priest in 1507, he was sent for further study at the newly founded University at Wittenberg, later to Erfurt. In 1512 he was made Doctor of Theology and was appointed professor of scripture at Wittenberg, a post he held for the rest of his life.

Deeply troubled concerning personal guilt, he became convinced concerning *justification by faith alone, finding help in the study of the Bible, *Augustine's anti-Pelagian writings, John *Tauler's mysticism and the **Theologia Germanica*, as well as the sensitive counsel of his superior John Staupitz. In 1517, pastorally concerned about the propagation of the *indulgence traffic by the Dominican preacher J. *Tetzel, Luther protested in his famous ninety-five theses. In the inevitable controversy which followed their publication, Luther debated his views with Catholic opponents, and produced in 1520 some of his most influential writings, *On Good Works*, *The Babylonian Captivity of the Church*, *Address to the German Nobility*, and *The Freedom of a Christian*. In the same year the papal *bull, **Exsurge Domine*, censured his teaching as heretical, and the promulgation a few months later of *Decet Romanum Pontificem* declared him excommunicate. Luther was summoned to appear before the newly elected Emperor Charles V at an Imperial Diet (*Worms 1521), where he refused to recant his views unless persuaded by scripture. Concerned about Luther's safety, the Elector of Saxony gave him protection in the Wartburg Castle. This difficult period for Luther was put to great literary advantage as he worked on a translation of the New Testament into German as well as several devotional expositions. He returned to Wittenberg in 1522 in order to preach against the extreme views of Andrew *Carlstadt. During later years Luther was constantly engaged in controversy with either Catholics (e.g. James Latomus), *Zwinglians, *Erasmus, or the radicals. His fear of peasant revolution and ill-advised language caused many in the deprived classes to be disenchanted with his spiritual leadership, though he urged the nobles to give urgent attention to social justice.

In 1525 Luther married Catharine von Bora, a former nun; his secure family life was a constant source of strength to the Reformer, burdened as he was not only by controversy and divisions within the Reformation movement, but occasionally poor health, bubonic plague, bereavement, and the loss of colleagues through intense persecution. The *Augsburg Confession (1530), mainly the more diplomatic work of *Melanchthon, gave moderate expression to his leading ideas; and his prolific writings, on average a book a fortnight, circulated his teaching throughout Europe. His home offered hospitality to a constant stream of guests and visitors, students and preachers. A genuine pastor, whose care for souls is reflected in his letters, Luther's last act was that of journeying in winter conditions to his native territory in order to reconcile two estranged noblemen. Luther's teaching (see G. Ebeling, *Luther: An Introduction to His Thought*, 1970) was not arranged by him in any closely argued systematic way as, for example, in *Calvin's *Institutes*. His many writings were usually produced as a response to immediate pastoral needs and are often devotional or polemical in character, at times prophetic, impassioned outbursts, abounding in paradox. His leading ideas were treasured by the *Lutheran Churches who summarized Luther's essential message in their *Book of Concord* (1580). On major articles of faith (*Trinity, *Christology, *atonement, etc.) Luther adhered to the classic credal tradition. The distinctive Lutheran emphasis is on the authority of *scripture and *soteriology. Because scripture is the word of God, it is the truth of God, in relation to which innovations of the Church (esp. of the *papacy) must be judged defective. **Sola scriptura* (scripture alone) is the source of doctrine and practice. Scripture supremely reveals the obedience of Christ in his substitutionary work of atonement: *justification is God's effective, forensic act of forgiveness and of acquittal through Christ. Through 'faith alone' (*sola fide*), a sinful person receives (but does not create, as though faith is a work of merit) all that Christ has done for the world. Justification through faith is thus a central Lutheran theme. The whole of Christian life is derived from this theology of the *cross. See Index, Lutherans.

P. Althaus, *The Theology of Martin Luther* (1966); R. Bainton, *Here I Stand* (1950); C. Braaten, *Principles of Lutheran Theology* (1983); W. Elert, *The Structure of Lutheranism* (1962).

Lutheran Churches. Those churches formed in response to *Luther's teaching. Their doctrinal convictions are given expression in the *Book of Concord* (1580). Scripture is affirmed as the sole rule of *faith, and justification by grace alone is the principal tenet. There is a strongly Christocentric emphasis in all Lutheran theology, which also insists on the lost condition of human beings and their inability to please God by human effort or moral achievements. Solely by the initiative of divine grace, men and women are reconciled to God through faith in Christ by whose perfect righteousness they are accounted righteous in God's sight.

From its beginnings in Germany Lutheranism quickly spread throughout Europe, gaining dominance in Scandinavia, Iceland, Prussia, and the Baltic Provinces, but its energies were diverted in the late 16th cent. by internal conflicts. Its severe preoccupation with orthodox theological formulation led to widespread spiritual aridity in the 17th cent. Many of the Churches were quickened by the reactive *pietist movement (1670–1760) which emphasized the inwardness of religious experience; although world-renouncing in outlook, considerable advance was made in social work, education, and missions. Later pietism also challenged the rationalism of the 18th cent. with its depreciation of the supernatural elements in Christianity. The Lutheran Churches have produced outstanding theologians, philosophers, biblical scholars, composers, and musicians. They now have a worldwide membership of over 75 million. See Index, Lutherans.

C. Bergendoff, *The Church of the Lutheran Reformation* (1967); J. Bodensieck (ed.), *The Encyclopedia of the Lutheran Church* (1898–1906); A. Burgess (ed.), *Lutheran Churches in the Third World* (1970); E. Gritsch and R. Jenson, *Lutheranism* (1976); H. T. Neve and B. A. Johnson, *The Maturing of American Lutheranism* (1968).

Lutis (homosexuals): see HOMOSEXUALITY.

Lutron (ransom, to avoid strict interpretations of *tallion): see JESUS.

Lü-tsung (school of discipline): see TAO-HSÜAN.

Lu tung-pin (Taoist immortal): see HSIEN.

Luwum, Janani (1922–77). Christian archbishop of Uganda and *martyr. Son of a Christian convert, he became involved for a time with Balokole (see EAST AFRICAN REVIVAL), but moved away to mainstream Christianity, and was ordained Anglican priest in 1955. He became bishop of N. Uganda in 1969. After the Acholi massacres under Idi Amin in 1972, he became an increasingly outspoken opponent of Amin's excesses and cruelties, until he was himself arrested and shot.

Luzzatto, Moses Ḥayyim (Ramḥal) (1707–47). Jewish *kabbalist. Luzzatto lived in Padua and was the leader of a group of Jewish students. In 1727 (and subsequently) he believed he heard the voice of a *maggid who revealed secret doctrines. He was, however, attacked as a magician and a *Shabbatean and made to denounce the maggid's revelations. His most important kabbalistic works were the *Kelah Pithei Hokhmah*, an exposition of *Lurianic kabbalah, and his *Zohar Tunyana*, written under the influence of the maggid: in this work, he offered rules of conduct which, if observed, would hasten the coming of the *messiah. His highly influential ethical works include *Mesillat Yesharim* (The Path of the Righteous, 1936) which was studied in the E. European *yeshivot; and he also wrote poetry and verse dramas.

He summoned his readers (and followers) to a ceaseless energy on behalf of God—like a fire burning: 'Time wasted is a form of theft.' The guide to right conduct in ethical matters is always to allow oneself to be drawn to God, 'as iron to a magnet'. The sole purpose of human life is to be drawn nearer to God.

S. Ginzburg, *The Life and Work of M. H. Luzzatto* (1931).

Luzzatto, Samuel David, or **Shadal** (1800–65). Jewish *biblical scholar. In 1829 Luzzatto was appointed professor at the rabbinical college in Padua where he taught the Bible, philosophy, Jewish history, and philology. A prolific writer, he produced a Hebrew commentary on the *Pentateuch (5 vols., 1871–6) as well as commentaries on other biblical books. He conducted correspondence with many of the scholars of his day and his attitudes are best revealed in his letters (publ. 1881). He was a traditionalist who was critical of Jewish philosophy, *kabbalistic speculation, and secular European civilization, while firmly maintaining his belief in tradition, *revelation, and the *chosenness of the Jewish people: 'The basic principle of Judaism is simply this: belief in revelation and accepting the burden of *mitzvot [commandments].'

N. Rosenbloom, *Luzzatto's Ethico-Psychological Interpretation of Judaism* (1965).

LXX: see SEPTUAGINT.

M

Ms, Five (polluting acts): see PAÑCA-MAKĀRA.

Mā (Skt., 'mother'). Hindu mother goddess; also incorporated in names as a title of respect.

Maʿamad, mahamad (Heb., 'stand'). Jewish *Sephardi community leader, the equivalent of the *Ashkenazi *kahal*. Derived from the orders of priestly duties, they took decisions which were binding on those affected. They appointed their successors, and the appointment could not be refused.

Maʿamad har Sinai (revelation on Mount Sinai): see SINAI, MOUNT.

Maʿaravot. A series of *piyyutim (liturgical poems) which are added to the Jewish *maʿariv service on *festivals. The maʿaravot piyyutim are additional to the normal *prayers recited in the *synagogue service. Different communities follow different practices, but no maʿaravot are used among the *Sephardim.

Maʿarekhet ha-Elohut (Heb., 'The Order of God'). A Jewish *kabbalistic book. It was written in about the late 13th cent. and is of unknown authorship. It is an attempt to present the teachings of the kabbalah systematically.

Maʿariv (Heb., 'he [God] who causes the evening to come'). The Jewish order of evening *prayer. According to tradition, based on Genesis 28. 11, it was first ordained by the patriarch *Jacob, and the *Talmud relates a controversy as to whether or not it is mandatory. Unlike the morning and afternoon services, maʿariv does not replace a sacrifice from the original Temple, and was thus designated *reshut* ('voluntary') prayer. However, it was argued that it corresponded to the disposal of the remnants of sacrifices and should be regarded as obligatory. The service, which requires a *minyan, includes the *Shemaʿ and the *ʿAmidah.

Maʿaseh (Heb., 'story'). A Jewish legal source. Jewish legal principles are derived from various sources, e.g. *minhag (custom). A maʿaseh is a particular factual circumstance, such as a legal judgement or a specific act of an established *halakhic scholar. Because 'what has been done is no longer open to discussion' (*BRH* 29b), halakhah derived from a maʿaseh has particular force.

Maʿaseh Bereshit (Heb., 'work of creation'). Jewish mystical exploration of creation and of the power of the Word of God and of language. So great was the power released that instruction in this mysticism was restricted to individuals who had attained earlier levels of experience. Creation was tied to the letters of the alphabet (cf. *gematria), which corresponded with the *sefirot (emanations) from God, so that one could hope through this mysticism to reascend to the source of creation. An example of this can be found in *Sefer Yetzirah*. See also HEKHALOT AND MERKABAH.

Maʿaseh Book (Heb., 'Story Book'; Yid., *Mayse Bukh*). A collection of anonymous Jewish folk tales. The *Maʿaseh Book* was first publ. in *Yiddish in 1602 and contains 254 stories, including *Talmudic *aggadah, *midrash, legends, jokes, and oral traditions.

M. Gaster, *Maʿaseh Book* (1934).

Maʿaser(ot) (tithes): see TITHE(s).

Macarius, St, of Egypt (*c.*300–*c.*390). One of the *Desert Fathers, also known as 'the Great'. At about the age of 30 he founded a settlement of monks in the desert of Scetis (Wadi al-Natrun), which became an important centre of Egyptian monasticism.

The *Macarian Homilies* traditionally ascribed to him seem to come rather from a writer in N. Mesopotamia in the 4th–5th cents. They contain doctrines condemned as *Messalian, and perhaps needed the protection of an orthodox author's name in order to be preserved. In modern times the *Fifty Spiritual Homilies* have been an influential mystical text (e.g. on John *Wesley, who translated twenty-two of them into English). Among their themes are 'how one must withstand the spirits of evil, and be instructed how to seek help from the Lord and make war on our enemy, the Devil'.

Tr. A. J. Mason (1921).

Maccabees, Books of. Jewish *apocryphal and pseudepigraphical works containing the history of Simon the *Hasmonean and Judah Maccabee. *1 Maccabees*, originally written in Hebrew, covers the period of Jewish history from the accession of King Antiochus Epiphanes (*c.*175 BCE) to the death of Simon the Hasmonean in 135 BCE. It is the main historical source for the period and is thought to achieve a degree of accuracy and objectivity. *2 Maccabees* was originally written in Gk. and concentrates on the activities of Judas Maccabee until his victory over Nicanor in 164 BCE. It is in a completely different style from *1 Maccabees*, being far more literary and far less matter-of-fact. It is full of miraculous events, and the Jews are presented as brave and steadfast in contrast to the corrupt and barbarous *Hellenizers. It exemplifies developing beliefs in immortality (7. 9, 23, 37), expiatory suffering (7. 37 f.), and prayers for the dead (12. 43–5). *1 Maccabees* was almost certainly written by a single author who was an eyewitness to the events described. *2 Maccabees* is an abridgement of a larger work composed by Jason of Cyrene. *3 Maccabees* deals with the relations and decrees of Ptolemy IV affecting the Jews. *4 Maccabees* reviews episodes and issues in the historical period from the point of view of Greek philosophy. Thus where *2 Maccabees* records the story of the martyrdom of a mother and her seven sons and points to a reward after death through resurrection of the body, *4 Maccabees* tells the same story and points to reward through immortality of the soul. This dual Jewish exploration of the possibility of life after death had not been resolved by the time of Jesus and Paul, leading to a New Testament linking of the two.

Machpelah, Cave of. Burial place of the Jewish *patriarchs, *Abraham, *Isaac, and *Jacob. The site of the Cave of Machpelah is identified with Haram el-Khalil in Hebron. According to *Josephus, the ancient tombs were 'of really fine marble and exquisite workmanship'. A church was built over the site in the Byzantine period, which was later converted into a mosque. Jews were forbidden to pray at the tombs in 1267, but since the Six Day War, the cave has become a popular place of Jewish *pilgrimage.

Macumba: see AFRO-BRAZILIAN CULTS.

Mādhava (Skt., 'a descendant of Madhu'). 1. Any member of the tribe of Madhu, i.e. the Yādavas, whose kingdom and exploits are recounted in the **Mahābhārata* and the *Purāṇas. The most famous of the Yādavas was *Kṛṣṇa, regarded as a divine incarnation (*avatāra) of *Viṣṇu. Frequently in the **Bhagavad-gītā* and elsewhere, the term 'Mādhava' is used as an epithet for Kṛṣṇa. Various fictional characters in Skt. literature also bear the name Mādhava, and it is the name of several famous Hindu scholars.

2. According to tradition, Mādhavācārya, the 'learned Madhāva' (also called Vidyāraṇya), was the name of one celebrated author who, along with his famous brother Sāyaṇa, the commentator on the *Vedas, was associated with the court of the kingdom of Vijāyanagara in the latter half of the 14th cent. CE. This same Mādhavācārya is said to have composed the following works: *Sarvadarśana-saṁgraha*, a brilliant summary of the sixteen philosophical systems then current in India; *Jaiminīya-nyāya-mālā-vistara*, a commentary on *Nyāya philosophy; *Pañcadaśī*, an important summary of *Advaita Vedānta; *Jīvanmuktiviveka*, a work of Advaita Vedānta describing the life of a liberated sage; and *Śaṅkara-dig-vijaya*, a poetic biography of the great Advaita philosopher *Śaṅkara. In addition, Mādhava the brother of Sāyaṇa is also credited with having been the greatest teacher of Āyurvedic medicine since Vāgbhaṭa. It is highly unlikely that all these works were written by the same person. Quite possibly the first two works mentioned were written by the brother of Sāyaṇa at the court of Vijāyanagara, but judging from internal evidence within the works themselves, the last two were most likely composed by a second Mādhava during the first half of the 16th cent.

Madhhab (Arab., 'direction'). A Muslim system of thought, but more specifically (and usually), a *school of law: see SHARĪʿA.

Madhu 1. (Skt., 'honey'). The favourite drink of Hindu warriors. Honey was regarded in Vedic times as containing the essence of all plant life. It was thus a source of strength and remedy against illnesses—hence a little honey is often put in the mouth of a new-born infant. It features in *madhuvidya*, 'honey-knowledge', and thus on ritual occasions.

2. A demon killed by the Hindu god *Kṛṣṇa/*Viṣṇu, who thus is frequently called Madhusūdana. Generally, Madhu is mentioned along with Kaiṭabha; and the Jains in fact have a single figure Madhukaiṭabha as one of their prati-Vāsudevas (see ĀDI-PURĀṆA). In the *Devīmāhātmya* of the **Mārkaṇḍeya-Purāṇa*, the myth has the following form. At the time of creation, two demons (Madhu and Kaiṭabha) arose from the wax in the ears of Viṣṇu and tried to kill *Brahmā. But through the assistance of the Goddess (called here Mahāmāyā—see MĀYĀDEVĪ) Viṣṇu could kill them. Other texts add that from the marrow of these demons' bones the earth was formed. See also MAHIṢA.

Madhva or **Madhvacarya** (dates uncertain, ranging from 1199–1278 CE to 1238–1317). Founder of a Hindu *Vaiṣṇava school and philosophy whose adherents are known as Mādhvas. It is the third (with *Śaṅkara and *Rāmānuja) of three major related philosophical schools, and because it is opposed to the non-dualism of Śaṅkara and the qualified non-dualism of Rāmānuja, and because it maintains five irreducible dualities, it is known as *dvaita-vedānta. The five distinctions are between: God and the soul; God and matter; the individual soul and matter; between souls; between individual components of the material. The final union with God is not one of absorption, nor of a relation in which the constituent parts, while retaining identity, nevertheless constitute one reality, but rather of a distinction between lover and beloved which is eternal. Mythologically, Madhva is held to be an *avatāra of Vāyu, one of the *loka-pālas associated with the wind and with inspiration. This association may be because Madhva believed that God cannot be approached directly but only through Vāyu as mediator. The self is not an absolute agent, because, while remaining distinct, it is nevertheless dependent on God: 'As the carpenter is an agent under the employer who asks him to work, yet is also an agent of his own work, so with the self there is guidance from the Lord, as well as its own capacity for action.' He wrote many works, especially commentaries. He established his main temple (dedicated to *Kṛṣṇa) at Udipi, where his succession and school is still maintained.

Trs. E. B. Cowell and A. E. Gough, *Sarvadarśanasaṃgraha* (1904); C. M. Padmanabhacharya, *Life and Teachings* . . . (1970); B. N. K. Sharma, *A History of the Dvaita School* . . . (rev. edn., 1981); S. Subha Rao, *Vedanta-sutras* . . . (1936).

Madhyamāgama (Sanskrit name): see MAJJHIMA NIKĀYA; TRIPIṬAKA.

Mādhyamaka ('middle way'; Chin., *San-lun; Jap., *Sanron; Korean, Samnon). The 'Middle School', a system of Buddhist philosophy founded by *Nāgārjuna in the 1st cent. CE, extremely influential within the *Mahāyāna. The school claims to be faithful to the spirit of the Buddha's original teachings, which advocate a middle course between extreme practices and theories of all kinds, and it applies this principle to philosophical theories concerning the nature of phenomena. Thus the assertion that 'things exist' or that 'things do not exist' would be extreme views and should be rejected; the truth lies somewhere in-between and is to be arrived at through a process of dialectic, as opposing positions are revealed as self-negating. The adoption of any one position, it was argued, could immediately be challenged by taking up its opposite, and the Mādhyamaka therefore adopted a strategy of attacking their opponent's views rather than advancing claims of their own (which is not to deny that they might none the less hold their own philosophical views).

The scene for the appearance of the Mādhyamaka was set by the debates among the schools of the Theravāda over such basic doctrines as that all phenomena (*dharmas) are impermanent (*anicca) and without self (*anātman). This gave rise to philosophical difficulties concerning questions such as causation, temporality, and personal identity. The scholastic solution was to posit a theory of instantaneous serial continuity according to which phenomena (dharmas) constantly replicate themselves in a momentary sequence of change (*dharma-kṣaṇikatva*). Thus reality was conceived of as cinematic: like a filmstrip in which one frame constantly gives way to the next, each moment, none the less, being substantially existent in its own right.

The Mādhyamaka challenged this notion of the substantial reality of dharmas, arguing that if things truly existed in this way and were possessed of a real nature or 'self-essence' (*svabhāva), it would contradict the Buddha's teaching on no-self (anātman) and render change impossible. What already substantially exists, they argued, would not need to be produced; and what does not substantially exist already could never come into being from a state of non-existence. Thus real existence cannot be predicated of dharmas, but neither can non-existence, since they clearly present themselves as having a mode of being of some kind. The conclusion of the Mādhyamaka was that the true nature of phenomena can only be described as an 'emptiness' or 'voidness' (*dharma-śūnyatā*, i.e. 'emptiness of self'); and that this emptiness of self-nature is synonymous with the principle of dependent origination (see PATICCA-SAMUPPĀDA) as taught by the Buddha. This process of reasoning is fully set out in Nāgārjuna's concise verses in the **Mūla-Mādhyamaka-Kārikā*, the root text of the system.

There were implications also for *soteriology: since emptiness is the true nature of what exists there can be no *ontological basis for a differentiation between *nirvāna and *saṃsāra. Any difference which exists must be an epistemological one resulting from ignorance and misconception. Accordingly, the Mādhyamaka posits 'two levels of truth': the level of Ultimate Truth (*paramārthasatya*), i.e. the perception of emptiness of the true nature of phenomena (the view of the enlightened); and the level of 'relative' or veiled truth (*samvṛtisatya*), i.e. the misconception of dharmas as possessing a substantial self-existent nature (the view of the unenlightened). The gaining of enlightenment is the passage from the latter to the former.

After Nāgārjuna the work of the school was carried forward by his disciple Āryadeva, but subsequently two schools divided, the Svatantrika, led by *Bhāvaviveka; and the *Prāsaṅgika, championed by *Candrakīrti, which adhered to the negative dialectic of the founder. The Mādhyamaka system was transmitted from India to Tibet and China (where it flourished, particularly in Tibet, as a central school of Mahāyāna philosophy), and to Japan, where it is known as *Sanron. See also SAN-LUN.

T. R. V. Murti, *The Central Philosophy of Buddhism* (1955); R. H. Robinson, *Early Madhyamika in India and China* (1967); D. S. Ruegg, *The Literature of the Madhyamaka School* . . . (1981); F. Streng, *Emptiness: A Study in Religious Meaning* (1967).

Madhyamā-pratipad (Skt. for): see MIDDLE WAY.

Mādhyamika. An adherent of *Mādhyamaka.

Madīna, al-. Yathrib, 'the town' to which *Muḥammad made the *hijra at the invitation of its inhabitants. It is situated in the Ḥijāz, and is the place where the earliest organized forms of Islam could take root (hence the fact that the Madinan *suras of the *Qur'ān deal increasingly with practical issues of individual and social life). The so-called Constitution of Madīna gathers several different agreements drawn up with Jewish and other tribes. Muḥammad was buried in Madīna (as were *Abū Bakr and *'Umar, and also *'Uthmān, but in a place apart), so it has been a place of *pilgrimage for Muslims, although this was prevented when the *Wahhabīya had control of Madīna, since they were opposed to the veneration of humans.

Madonna (Ital., 'my lady'). A Christian designation of the Blessed Virgin *Mary, common especially in artistic representations.

Madrasa. Islamic school, for children, and for adult studies. The basis of education is learning and understanding the *Qur'ān, followed by the study of *ḥadīth. Closely associated with the *mosque, the madrasas often developed into extensive libraries, where *fiqh and *kalām were studied. The method of study was by lectures and memorizing.

Mae chii (buddhist nuns): see BUDDHISM IN SOUTH-EAST ASIA.

Ma-fa (in Buddhism, period of decline): see MAPPŌ.

Māgadhā or **Māgadhi.** An ancient Indian language. It is chiefly important as the language employed by the Mauryan court of *Aśoka and particularly in the rock edicts of that king. Māgadhī is a Prakrit, its most widespread script being Brāhmī.

It is often thought that Māgadhī was the main teaching language adopted by the *Buddha, and this has led some scholars to posit a lost Māgadhī canon. However, since the Buddha spent most of his life outside the lands later identified as Māgadhā, the belief in Māgadhī as the original language (*mūla-bhāṣa*) of Buddhism is unjustified, probably being related to the high regard shown to the Mauryan court in later times.

The kingdom of Māghadā was one of sixteen N. Indian states mentioned in Buddhist sources. It was in an area centred in what is now Bihar. Its kings included *Bimbisāra, a supporter of the Buddha. It was absorbed into the Mauryan Empire.

B. C. Law, *The Magadhas in Ancient India* (1946).

Magatsuhi-no-kami (Jap., '*kami of misfortune-force'). In Shinto, divine beings which bring about sin, pollution, disaster, and evil. They belong to the land of Yomi, the nether-world. Related terms are Ōmagatsuhi-no-kami which means 'Great Magatsuhi Kami' and Yaso-magatsuhi-no-kami which means 'Countless Magatsuhi Kami'. This type of kami is expressive of the ancient idea that evil comes to humans from without, caused by the magatsuhi-no-kami. In the Shinto mythology, immediately after the birth of the magatsuhi-no-kami there were born the *naobi-no-kami*, the 'rectifying kami'. When humans are affected by the attacks of the magatsuhi-no-kami, it is necessary to perform acts of purification (*harai).

Ma.gcig Lab.sgron (10th/11th cent. CE). Prominent Tibetan Buddhist yogin and teacher, who formalized the *Chöd (Gcod) meditational practice. She was early noted for her lack of regard for personal appearance, an attitude which she encouraged in practitioners of Gcod. When she explored Indian yogic methods, she was attacked for repudiating her vows, and after moving with her family, she then went into retreat for the rest of her life.

Gcod ('cutting') has the aim of cutting through the apparent dualities created by the process of thought: 'thinking' carries with it the impression of subject and object, and beyond that the impression that the objects of thought, or even the thinker, have real existence. The purpose of Gcod is to bring about the complete realization that nothing in reality exists. The path to this realization is one of making the five aggregations (*skandha) of one's appearance into a sacrificial offering to the best of one's hopes and the worst of one's fears in personified forms, passing in one of the rituals through four stages: (i) *dkar 'gyed*, 'white sharing', imagining one's body as sweet honey offered to the *Three Jewels; (ii) *khra 'gyed*, 'multicoloured offering', imagining one's body as desirable objects like gardens and gifts, offered to the Protectors who overcome hindrances to enlightenment; (iii) *dmar 'gyed*, 'red sharing', imagining the flesh and blood of oneself offered to the demons; (iv) *nag 'gyed*, 'black sharing', the gathering up of one's own faults and the faults of others into oneself and the offering of it to the demons as an act of reparation. Chöd/Gcod is best known for the offerings to the demons, but this process is watched over by a compassionate Goddess, *lus srog gzang du bor ba'ima*, 'she who rejects every process of life'. Hymns and prayers of great devotion and beauty are offered to this mother figure, who at the level of folk belief is often equated with Ma.gcig Lab.sgron (i.e. as her manifestation). Of course, neither she nor the demons have any reality outside the construction of the mind: the purpose of Gcod is to visualize the best and the worst in order to cut off one's belief that they have some reality: hence the importance of vivid pictures and rituals.

Magdalen (follower of Jesus): see MARY MAGDALENE.

Magen David (Heb., 'Shield of *David'). Six-pointed star which has become the symbol of Judaism. The oldest example of the magen David is on a seal dating from the 7th cent. BCE, found in Sidon. The sign was used as a magical sign and described as the 'seal of *Solomon', particularly in Arab sources, but it was not known as the 'Shield of David' until the 14th cent. CE. It was first used as a symbol of the Jewish community in Prague in 1354, and in the 17th cent. it was incorporated in the seal of Jewish communities (Vienna 1655, Amsterdam 1671). It only became the universally recognized symbol of Judaism in the 19th cent., and was taken over by the *Zionists at the 1st Congress in 1897 as a sign of hope. It was employed by the Nazis as a badge of shame and was the symbol chosen for the *Israeli flag. A red magen David is used as an equivalent of the Red Cross.

Maggid (Heb., 'one who relates'). Jewish popular preacher; or, a spirit which conveys supernatural teachings to Jewish scholars. A tradition of Jewish itinerant preachers grew up in the late Middle Ages. By the 17th cent., maggidim were common in E. Europe. Many of the early *ḥasidic leaders, such as *Dov Baer, were described as maggidim, as were some opponents of ḥasidism such as Jacob *Kranz, the maggid of Dubno. Their sermons were intended to be easily understood and were characterized by the use of *mashal (parable). In the *kabbalistic tradition, the term maggid was also used to describe a spirit who passes supernatural secrets to worthy students of the kabbalah. Descriptions of a maggid are to be found in the writings of Moses *Cordovero, Hayyim *Vital, and Joseph *Caro (whose diary was edited after his death as a commentary on the *Pentateuch, *Maggid Mesharim*: see H. L. Gordon, *The Maggid of Caro*, 1949). Maggidim also appeared to the followers of *Shabbetai Zevi, and a dispute was caused by the revelation of a maggid to Moses Hayyim *Luzzatto.

Maggid of Dubno (founder of Jewish sect): see KRANK, JACOB.

Maghreb (i.e. Arab., *al-maghrib al-ʿarabi*, the Arab West). The region comprising Libya, Tunisia, Algeria, Mauretania, and Morocco.

Magi. Originally a Median tribe (according to Herodotus, the Magoi were one of six Median tribes) responsible for all ritual activity regardless of religious boundaries, e.g. to which god a sacrifice was offered. As *Zoroastrianism spread across the Iranian plateau so it became part of their responsibility. In this way, it is thought, *Zoroaster's teachings were integrated into the general traditions of the region. Two examples of practices which it has been suggested were absorbed in this way are the exposure of the dead (*Daxma) and the idea of evil animals, *khrafstras* (*Angra Mainyu). It was the magi who thereafter carried Zoroastrianism through the Empire. During the Achaemenid era, Babylon was a major administrative centre, and it is likely that it was there that the magi became involved in the beliefs and practices subsequently named after them, *magic, and also astrology. It was this reputation which motivated the writer of Matthew's Gospel (see below) to relate a story about magi (the word used in the Gk. is *magoi*, and so the later Christian legend of kings does not do justice to the text). Some Syriac sources may perhaps indicate that the magi had a legend concerning the birth of the saviour, *Sōšyant* (*Frasokereti), in a cave and foretold by astrological signs. Since there was a community of magi in Antioch, the city where many commentators consider Matthew was written, it is possible that the gospel writer was incorporating a local legend.

The terms for priest vary throughout Zoroastrian history. Because of the fragmentary nature of the sources it is not always easy to define precisely the roles that went with the different titles. Zoroaster himself used two different terms to refer to a priest: *zaotar*, an officiating priest, and a *manthran*, who composes sacred *manthras*. The two terms may indicate different aspects of a priest's work, rather than different types of priests. As Zoroastrianism developed, the magi became ever more important in the work of the Zoroastrian 'church'. Naturally words change with time, *magus* (singular) became *mobed*, under a supreme head, the *Mobedan Mobed*. The *mobeds* were highly educated and held many senior secular offices in Sasanian Iran: advisers to the mighty King of Kings, judges, scholars. The term *rad* appears to denote a high-priestly official able to give judgements. *Herbad* was used probably to denote scholar priests. In post-Sasanian Iran, the high priest took the title *hudnan pesobay*, leader of the faithful, a title recalling Muslim titles. In modern times a high priest, *dastur*, is generally associated with a 'cathedral' fire temple (Atash Bahram, *Atas) whose liturgical life he oversees with a team of priests, *mobeds*, under him. The *dastur* is commonly sought for guidance and direction on religious matters. There is a strong tradition of learning among the dasturs, especially among the *Parsis in Bombay. The devotion of priestly duties in a number of temples in a locality (*panthak*) is overseen by a *panthaki*. There are two initiatory rites for priests, *navar* and *maratab*. A priest who has undertaken the first of these, and is therefore qualified to perform some of the minor rites, is known as an *ervad*. The *mobeds* and the *ervads* have essentially liturgical roles, with little sense of any teaching or pastoral duties. Until the 19th cent., Zoroastrian priests in practice had a tradition of scholarship, but this has declined in recent times as the able young priests have been attracted into better paid secular work. The priesthood is hereditary, through the line of the father. If more than two generations do not take up the priestly calling and undergo the necessary initiations, then that priestly line is extinguished.

Fundamentally, in Zoroastrianism, a priest is a man whose life is devoted to the preservation of the state of moral and physical purity necessary to perform the rituals. To perform the inner rituals he must preserve the state of purity achieved after a *baresnum* (*purity and pollution). Purity is necessary so that the duly empowered priest can, in devotion, through concentration on the ritual, generate ritual power (*amal*) so that the heavenly forces are present. Because of the centrality of the concept of purity, one term for priest is *yozdathrager*, 'Purifier'.

The Christian appropriation of the Magi reveals little knowledge of the above. According to Matthew 2. 1–12, they were guided by a star to Bethlehem, bearing gifts for the new-born *Jesus. Acts 13. 6 ff. uses the word to mean magic-workers, and *Ignatius of Antioch understood the word in that sense, arguing that magic yielded up its power when Jesus was born. *Origen inferred that they were three in number from the gifts, and *Tertullian suggested that they were kings. By the 6th cent., they were named Gaspar, Melchior, and Balthasar. What were claimed to be their *relics were taken to Europe and are now in Cologne Cathedral.

Magic. The production of effects in the world by actions, often ritualized, whose source of power is not open to observation; or by words, especially by incantation: chants of formulae, which may sound nonsensical to the outsider, may summon the relevant power, or may themselves effect the consequence: they may also be apotropaic. Attempts to define the relation of magic to religion have formed part of the modern study of religion since its inception at the end of the 19th cent. J. G. *Frazer argued for a complete separation of the two: religion is orientated toward transcendental beings (gods, spirits, etc.), but the magician 'supplicates no higher power: he sues the favour of no fickle and wayward being . . .. He can wield his power only as he strictly conforms to the rules of his art, or to what may be called the laws of nature as conceived by him'. Thus the worker of magic is a would-be scientist who misunderstood the true nature of causality. From Frazer derives the division of magic into major categories, of imitative magic (achieving results through mimicry), contagious magic (using materials which have been in contact with the object of the magic) and sympathetic magic (using items which symbolize the intended object).

E. *Durkheim accepted the radical distinction between magic and religion, claiming that religion is a communal matter (indeed, it is society being itself externalized in symbolic form), whereas magic is an affair between a practitioner and client: the magician has clients but no congregation. This division was contested by M. Mauss (*A General Theory of Magic*, 1902), who insisted that magic is a social phenomenon, making use of available power in a variety of different ways. In other words, he went behind the conduits through which this power flowed to identify the nature of that power. This he thought he had located in the Melanesian concept of *mana*, which R. H. Codrington (*The Melanesians*, 1891) had introduced: '*Mana* is power, *par excellence*, the genuine effectiveness of things which corroborates their practical actions without annihilating them. This is what causes the net to bring in a good catch, makes the house solid and keeps the canoe sailing smoothly: in the farms it is fertility, in medicine it is either health or death.'

This view of magic as pervasive power was the exact opposite of the view of Bronislav Malinowski (1884–1942), an anthropologist who based his arguments on his time in the Trobriand Islands. Since it is obvious that magic is not always or automatically successful, he maintained that magic must be understood primarily as a matter of psychology: magic operates in areas where knowledge or technology is wanting, and by isolating hidden forces at work, it thereby offers psychological relief—such-and-such a situation is beyond human competence. This was in strong contrast to the view of E. *Evans-Pritchard (*Witchcraft, Magic and Oracles among the Azande*, 1937), who held that magic belonged to an interactive world in which it is possible to ask questions which a Westerner would not ask. Thus the Azande are interested in 'cause-and-effect', but also ask why events have happened to one person rather than another: magic is a means of interrogation as well as of finding answers.

More recently, this view has been developed further, seeing magic as embedded in religion, where it acts as an organization of context and meaning. Thus for Mary Douglas (*Purity and Danger*, 1966), magic offers the framing of experience in a local context; and for Susanne Langer (*Philosophy in a New Key*, 1964) 'magic is not a method but a language: it is part and parcel of that greater phenomenon, ritual, which is the language of religion; ritual is a symbolic transformation of experiences that no other medium can adequately express'. In this perspective, magic offers the transformation of circumstances without guaranteeing effects: one consequence or its opposite will still be a demonstration that magic 'works', because it confirms the entire context in which a person lives. See Index, Magic.

A. C. Lehmann and J. E. Myers, *Magic, Witchcraft and Religion* . . . (1985).

Magic Jewel School (Taoist movement): see LING-PAO P'AI.

Magisterium, the teaching office of the RC Church, to which *infallibility attaches.

Magnificat. *Mary's song of praise in Luke 1. 46–55, from the Latin *Magnificat anima mea Dominum* ('My soul doth magnify the Lord'). It was early on the *canticle of vespers in the W. Church, now sung at Anglican *evening prayer, and in the Gk. Church morning office (*orthros*). It resembles that of the 'Song of Hannah' (1 Samuel 2. 1 ff.).

Mahābhārata. A great epic of India. It comprises 100,000 verses (in all, seven times the Iliad plus the Odyssey in length), divided into eighteen books, supplemented by a nineteenth, the **Harivaṃśa*. The epic recounts the events before, during, and after the great battle for kingship fought at *Kurukṣetra between the *Pāṇḍavas and *Kauravas, branches of the Kuru lineage and descendants of *Bharata (whence the Skt., *Mahābhārata*, 'the great [tale of] Bharata's descendants'). Also included is didactic material of encyclopaedic proportions (particularly in books 12 and 13, the **Śānti-* and *Anuśāsana-parvans*), along with elaborate genealogies and much myth and legend (especially in books 1 and 3). 'Any *brahman who should know the four *Vedas, along with the sciences based on them and the *Upaniṣads, but not know this tale [the *Mahābhārata*] would not be a truly wise man' (1. 2. 235; the *Mahābhārata* is considered to be the fifth Veda). 'No story is found on earth which does not depend upon this tale . . .' (1. 2. 240). '[W]hat is here is elsewhere; what is not here is nowhere' (1. 56. 34 and 18. 5. 38). The whole is attributed to the sage *Vyāsa (Kṛṣṇa Dvaipāyana), who is said to have composed the *Mahābhārata* and taught it to his student Vaiśampāyana; Vaiśampāyana, in turn, performed the first public recitation of the epic at a 'snake sacrifice' conducted by King Janamejaya, a descendant of the Pāṇḍavas, his purpose being to tell Janamejaya about the deeds of his ancestors. The epic was then carried by the bard Ugraśravas to the forest sacrifice of the brahman Śaunaka.

In truth, the *Mahābhārata* in its present form grew up over a long period of time, *c.*400 BCE–400 CE. In the course of its development, the work came under the influence of various groups, which it still reflects: warriors and their bards, brahmans, devotees. The action of the *Mahābhārata* proceeds at several levels at once. First is the typically Indo-European heroic tale of the battle of good against evil, modelled after the specifically Indo-*Āryan version of this theme, the *devas (gods, here incarnate in the Pāṇḍavas) against the *asuras (demons, reflected in the Kauravas, who incarnate *rākṣasas). From this point of view, the Kurukṣetra war is visualized as a gigantic sacrifice conducted by semi-divine epic heroes. Mixed with this semi-mythical material is consideration of the human-centred issue of the decline of *dharma at the onset of the *Kaliyuga, the present degenerate age of history, which the *Mahābhārata* conceives of as having begun at the time of the Kurukṣetra war. Dharma suffers a huge set-back at the Pāṇḍava–Kaurava dice game played early in the epic. Ever after, the lines of right and wrong are drawn less clearly than the Indo-European substructure of the epic might cause one to expect: for example, the 'good' Pāṇḍavas defeat the 'evil' Kauravas, but only by trickery and deceit. One high point of human uncertainty in the epic is the episode of the **Bhagavad-gītā*, in which the Pāṇḍava hero *Arjuna casts down his weapons before the war begins, dismayed at the prospect of having to fight against his relatives and elders on the other side. In the *Bhagavad-gītā* and throughout the *Mahābhārata*, it is a 'Hindu' element, revolving particularly around the character of the god *Viṣṇu, incarnate as *Kṛṣṇa, and his alliance with the Pāṇḍavas, which resolves the tension: 'Where Kṛṣṇa is, there is dharma . . . there is victory' (*Mahābhārata* 6. 62. 34, etc.). Orchestrated by Kṛṣṇa, the Kurukṣetra war is a cosmic event. Through its emphasis upon Kṛṣṇa, the *Mahābhārata* becomes the locus of a *bhakti (devotional) synthesis, which characterizes Hinduism from this time onward. The stage production by Peter Brook (1985) was filmed in 1989.

Trs. J. A. B. van Buitenen (bks. 1–5, 1973–8), P. C. Roy and K. M. Ganguli (1884–96, 1970), E. N. Dutt (1895–1905); A. Hiltebeitel, *The Ritual of Battle: Krishna in the Mahabharata* (1976); B. A. van Nooten, *The Mahābhārata* (1971).

Mahābhūta (Skt., 'great' + 'element'). The five elements in Hinduism: air, fire, water, earth, and aether; also a synonym for *dhātu.

Mahābodhi Society: see DHARMAPĀLA (2).

Mahābodhi-vaṃsa ('the great bodhi-tree chronicle'). Buddhist work which relates the story of the *bo(dhi) tree under which the *Buddha attained enlightenment. It is attributed to Upatissa, in *c.*11th cent. CE.

Mahābrahmā ('Great Brahmā'). Buddhist name for the creator deity of the Hindu religion, as known to the Buddhists of the 6th cent. BCE. According to the *brahmans, the world was created by the Great Brahmā, and he was conceived of as a personal, masculine deity: the 'Great Brahmā' (*Mahābrahmā*), the 'Supreme One' (*Abhibhū*), the 'Unconquered' (*Anabhibhūto*), the 'Ruler' (*Vasavatti*), the 'Overlord' (*Issaro*), the 'Maker' (*Kattā*), the 'Creator' (*Nimmātā*), the 'Greatest' (*Seṭṭho*), the 'Assigner' (*Sañjitā*), the 'most Ancient' (*Vasī*), the 'Father of all that are born and are to be born' (*Pitā-bhūtabhavyānaṃ*), the 'Steadfast' (*Nicco*), the 'Immutable' (*Dhuvo*), the 'Eternal' (*Sassato*), and the 'Unchangeable' (*Aviparināmadhammo*).

The belief in a creator deity of such or any other description was not acceptable to Buddhism, as the world according to Buddhism is not the product of such creative activity, but of an on-going evolutionary process. It is only the periodic beginnings and the periodic endings of the phases of this everlasting process which are identifiable. The space between each such periodic beginning and end is known as an aeon (*kappa* / *kalpa) which is an incalculably long period of time. According to the *Aggañña Sutta* of the *Dīgha Nikāya* (III. 80 f.) the brahmanic belief in a creator deity is founded on misunderstanding the beginning of one of these periodic beginnings of an aeon to be the first beginning of the world.

While there are eight realms of the Brahmas, rebirth into these is the result of higher spiritual attainments, the higher the attainment, the higher the realm of rebirth. Thus, those who die after attaining the First Jhāna are reborn into the First Brahma realm, while those who die after attaining the Second Jhāna are reborn into the Second Brahma realm, and so on, if they so desire. Although according to the *Kevaddha Sutta* of the *Dīgha Nikāya* (I. 221 f.) there is a Mahābrahmā who is the supreme god among the gods of the Brahmakāyika realms, this idea is not generally supported by other Nikāya evidence. In the post-canonical literature, the number of the Brahma realms has grown to twenty (G. P. Malalasekara, *Dictionary of Pali Proper Names*, 2. 336). The names of several Mahābrahmas are found in the Pāli canonical texts. Of these, Sahampati and Sanankumāra are more frequently referred to than others like Ghaṭīkāra, Baka, and Tudu.

Thus, the Buddhist reinterpretation of the current Hindu belief in the creator deity Mahābrahmā was designed not only to deny this belief, but also to build the case against it.

Mahādeva (Skt., 'great Lord'). 1. In Hinduism, a name of *Śiva. In the *Purāṇas, it is one of the seven names given to Śiva by *Brahmā, the creator-god, the others being Bhava, Śarva, Īśāna, Paśupati, Bhīma, and Ugra. Mahādeva is also one of the eight forms of Śiva/Rudra in the Tantras and Purāṇas.

2. In Buddhism, Mahādeva is associated with the first major schism in Buddhist history, the division into *Mahāsāṃghika and *Sthaviravāda which led to *Theravāda. Five theses are attributed to him concerning the exact attainments of the *arhat, which led to the dispute over them. Nothing certain is known of him or of his life.

Mahādevī (the Goddess in India): see DEVĪ.

Mahākāla (Skt., 'great-time'). A name of *Śiva in his destructive aspect; he also represents death. Mahākāla is one of the eight deities known as the Terrible Divinities, also venerated by the Mongols as 'protector of the tent' (*gur-gyi-mgnon-po*). In the Buddhist pantheon Mahākāla is reduced to being a doorkeeper of Buddha's temple. *Iconographically, he is represented in Hinduism in terrifying form with four, six, or eight arms: in the caves of *Elephanta he holds a human form, a sacrificial axe, a basin of blood, and a veil to extinguish the sun.

Mahākāśyapa (Skt.; Pāli, [Mahā]kassapa). Prominent follower of the *Buddha. He was rigorous in self-discipline, and took over the leadership of the *saṅgha (community of monks) after the Buddha's death. He summoned the first Buddhist *council because of his fears that *Ānanda (another prominent follower of the Buddha) was introducing innovations, and that discipline was growing lax. He is the first of the Zen patriarchs (Ānanda being the second), and his image usually stands beside that of the Buddha in Chin. monasteries.

Mahalā (from Skt., *mahilā*, 'woman', or Arab., *mahal*, 'place'). Followed by the appropriate numeral, this word is used in the *Ādi Granth to designate the compositions of the Sikh *Gurūs, e.g. Mahalā II or M. II = Gurū *Aṅgad.

Mahāmāyā. The great power of creating appearance in Hinduism. This power to make the universe appear as though it is real is exercised (in personified form) by Mahāmāyā, the goddess identified with *Durgā.

Mahāmudrā (Tib., *Phyag.rgya.chen.po*, 'Great Symbol'). Principal religious and philosophical teaching of the *Kagyü school (appearing also in Gelugpa, see GELUK) of Tibetan Buddhism, obtained by Marpa Lotsawa from the 11th-cent. yogins Maitrīpa and Nāropa Mahāmudrā has two aspects—*sūtra and *tantra. The sūtra aspects contain the teachings that the ultimate nature of reality is coincident wisdom and luminosity, bliss and emptiness (*śūnyatā), while the tantra aspects concern the active realization of this truth through spiritual practices—particularly the first of the Six Doctrines of Nāropa (*Nāro Chos Drug), where psychic wind (*rlung*; Skt., *prāṇa) is channelled into the central channel (*dbu.ma*) of the *subtle body. The term Mahāmudrā is deliberately ambiguous, since it also translates as 'Great Seal', conveying the sense of finality involved in the act of sealing or stamping. Ultimate reality is thus seen as a timeless 'ground' of which this world process is an illusory display, and by the nature of which the things of this world are marked. As a teaching, Mahāmudrā falls in the *zhen dong perspective of Tibetan thought, and is related also to *dzogchen, especially in the realization of the three kayas (*trikāya). Progress toward the condition of absolute attainment sometimes issued in 'people beyond convention', the equivalent of the *holy fool (see e.g. DRUGPA KÜNLEG).

Mahānāma: see MAHĀVAṂSA.

Mahānārāyaṇīya Upaniṣad. 1. An early work, not commented on by *Śaṅkara, which explains the hymns addressed to *Nārāyana. It is described by J. Varenne (*La Mahanarayaniya Upanisad*, 1960) as 'a breviary' for the Nārāyana cult.

2. A late work forming the tenth book of the *Taittirīya Āraṇyaka*. It celebrates *Prājāpati and an extensive pantheon, including *Durgā. It is concerned with ritual, and resembles the *Purāṇas more than the other *Upaniṣads.

Mahānavamī. Hindu *festival of nine days, celebrating the Goddess, usually as *Durgā.

Mahant (Hindī, Pañjābī, 'head of certain religious establishments'). Hereditary 'priests' who often appropriated the property of *gurdwārās under their control. During the 19th cent. CE, unscrupulous mahants (*Udāsī or Hindū) exploited gurdwārā revenues and often introduced idolatrous ritual contrary to Sikh tenets. Although their claims to possession were backed by the British authorities, the mahants were finally ousted by the *Akālīs of the early 20th-cent. Gurdwārā Reform movement, after clashes at e.g. *Rakāb Gañj, Delhi, and in *Amritsar.

Mahāparinibbāna-sutta (The Discourse on the Great Decease). The sixteenth discourse in the Long Collection of Discourses (*Dīgha Nikāya) of the Buddhist *Pāli canon. The text describes the events leading up to the Buddha's death and his travels during the last few months of his life, and records his final utterance: 'Decay is inherent in all composite things: work with diligence.' It contains a good deal of material which occurs in other canonical sources. In the course of the narrative the Buddha predicts the end of his life before partaking of the meal which finally causes his death. He also states that if he had been requested to do so it was within his power to prolong his life until the end of the aeon.

The narrative ends with the Buddha's cremation and the distribution of his relics. The account of the First Council, which followed, is then taken up in the *Vinaya-piṭaka (see COUNCILS, BUDDHIST).

Trs., many, e.g. T. W. and C. A. F. Rhys Davids (1910).

Mahāparinirvāna-sūtra. A Skt. rescension of the Pāli *Mahāparinibbāna-sutta. It is also a collection of Mahāyāna *sūtras, taking its name from the first of them, which has survived in Chin. tr.

Mahāpātaka. Great *sin in Hinduism, classified into five: (i) *brāhmaṇahatyā*, the killing of a *brahman—or of an unborn child or of a pregnant woman; (ii) *surāpāna*, drinking intoxicants (see ALCOHOL); (iii) *steyam*, theft, but the circumstances are limited; (iv) *guruvaṇganāgama*, relations with a *guru's wife, guru being variously understood; (v) *mahāpātakasaṁsārga*, associating in any way with one who has committed one of the great sins. Theoretically these sins are unforgiveable, although they may be expiated perhaps by death; but the *Purāṇas develop a system of penances which depend on the willingness of the Lord to forgive. Minor sins are known as *upapātaka*, and are not so formally classified.

Mahāprajāpati Gautami. Stepmother of the *Buddha, who brought him up after the early death of his mother. After the death of her husband, she secured the reluctant consent of the Buddha (persuaded by *Ānanda) to found the order of nuns (*bhikṣunī). He predicted that by this act, the period of the survival of his teaching would be reduced by at least 500, perhaps by 1,000, years.

Mahāprajñapāramitā-Hridaya-Sūtra: see HEART SŪTRA.

Mahāprajñapāramitā-Sūtra: see PERFECTION OF WISDOM LITERATURE.

Mahāpralaya (Skt., 'great' + 'dissolving'). The complete dissolution of a universe at the end of a *kalpa, when all the *lokas and everything within them, including *Brahmā, disappear.

Mahapurāṇa ('great purāṇa'): see PURĀṆA.

Maharaji (founder of movement): see DIVINE LIGHT MISSION.

Maharal (acronym): see JUDAH LOEW.

Maharam (acronym): see MEIR BEN BARUCH.

Mahāratnakūṭa (Sūtra collection): see RATNAKŪṬA.

Maharishi Mahesh Yogi. Proponent of *Transcendental Meditation. A disciple of Guru Dev, he held the office of Shankarcharya of Jyotir Math in Badarinath in the Himalayas, 1941–53. After leaving his place of seclusion in 1955, Maharishi began to tour India, Burma, Singapore, N. America, and Europe giving lectures on Transcendental Meditation, maintaining that both the ideas about and the practice of this ancient meditative technique, based on Vedic wisdom, had become confused.

According to Maharishi, the correct practice of Transcendental Meditation can only be taught by a qualified teacher, and to this end he established teacher-training centres in many parts of the world (e.g. Maharishi International University in Iowa, USA; Maharishi Univ. of Natural Law at Mentmore, UK). In Jan. 1975 Maharishi, from on board the flagship *Gotthard* on Lake Lucerne, Switzerland, inaugurated the dawn of the Age of Enlightenment, followed in Jan. 1976 by the inauguration of the World Government of the Age of Enlightenment.

Maharsha (Talmudic commentator): see EDELS, SAMUEL ELIEZER BEN JUDAH HALEVI.

Maharshal (acronym): see LURIA, SOLOMON BEN JEHIEL.

Mahārṣi: see ṚṢI; MAHARISHI MAHESH YOGI.

Mahāsāṃghikas (the 'Great Assembly'). A body which broke away from the Elder (*Sthavira) tradition of Buddhism after the Council of Pāṭaliputra in 350 BCE (see COUNCILS). According to tradition, the assembly gave rise to seven subschools, and it may be regarded as the forerunner of the *Mahāyāna movement in later centuries. The Mahāsāṃghikas distinguished themselves from the Sthaviras doctrinally in their conception of the Buddha as supramundane (*lokottara), and socially by their acceptance of popular religious beliefs and practices, allowing a greater role to the laity.

A. Bareau, *Les Sectes bouddhiques du petit véhicule* (1955).

Mahāsaṃnipāta (sūtra collection): see TRIPIṬAKA.

Mahāsatipaṭṭhāna-sutta. Section 22 of the Dialogues of the *Buddha (*Dīgha Nikāya* 2. 290 ff.), occurring also in *Majjhima Nikāya*, dealing with the cultivation of *sati (see also SATIPAṬṬHĀNA). It is a brief manual of basic Buddhist meditation, directed to four aspects of what might otherwise be impediments, body-awareness, body-feelings, consciousness, relation to *dharma/dhamma.

Tr. T. W. and C. A. F. Rhys Davids (1910).

Mahāsiddha (Skt., great masters of powers, *iddhis).

Hinduism Traditionally, there are eighty-four mahāsiddhas, mainly in the *Tantric tradition. Some are of legendary character, and are usually depicted in fearsome form, but others were teachers and prominent people.

Buddhism The eighty-four mahāsiddhas were adopted from Hinduism, and celebrated in stories and songs (*doha*). But the mahāsiddhas were then greatly extended in number, especially in *Vajrayāna, where a mahāsiddha is one who has acquired the teachings of the Tantras and demonstrates this through great powers (iddhis). Siddha biographies then become an important source of inspiration and technique: see e.g. J. B. Robinson, *Buddha's Lions* (1979), a tr. of Abhayadatta's *Caturśītisiddhapravṛtti* (History of the Eighty-four Siddhas).

Mahāsthāmaprāpta ('One of great power'). A Mahāyāna Buddhist *bodhisattva, who opens people's sight to their need for liberation. He is especially associated with Amitābha (*Amida); with *Avalokiteśvara, the two appear frequently in representations as the helpers of Amitābha, a kind of *trinity of compassionate grace and liberation.

Mahāśūnya (Skt., 'great' + 'emptiness'). Hindu *vedānta understanding of the complete emptying of duality when it is realized that there are no self-subsistent objects to create a dual relationship, e.g. of seer and seen. Cf. also the Buddhist development of *śūnyatā.

Mahat (Skt., 'the great one'). In *Sāṁkhya (and other non-theistic) philosophy, the first evolution of *mūlaprakṛti*, synonymous with *buddhi ('intellect'). Mahat contains all individual buddhis and all potential matter of the gross universe in its cosmic extent as the first manifest principle (*tattva). Mahat in turn produces *ahaṁkāra, the ego principle.

Mahātman or **Mahātma** (Skt., *mahā*, 'great', + *ātman*, 'soul').

1. In Hinduism, one having a great soul, any exceptionally distinguished, magnanimous, or wise person; also a particular group of deceased ancestors mentioned in the *Mārkaṇḍeya *Purāṇa*. Mohandas *Gāndhī was considered a Mahātma by many.

2. In the *Upaniṣadic tradition, the supreme principle or great soul of the universe.

Mahāvairocana-sūtra (Sūtra of the Great Radiant One). A *Tantric Mahāyāna Buddhist *sūtra, of importance in both China (e.g. *Mi-tsung) and Japan (e.g. *Shingon).

Mahāvākya (Skt., 'great saying'). Any one of several great sayings which occur in the *Upaniṣads and which are held to reveal the unity of the Self (*ātman) and Ultimate Reality (*Brahman). The number of these is generally said to be four, but five are commonly encountered in the later literature: **tat-tvam-asi* ('That Thou art'), *ahaṁ brahmāsmi* ('I am Brahman'), *sarvaṁ khalvidaṁ brahma* ('All this indeed is Brahman'), *ayam ātmā brahma* ('This Self is Brahman'), and *prajñānam brahma ('Pure Consciousness is Brahman').

Mahāvaṃsa (Pāli, 'great' + 'story'). Pāli Buddhist chronicle of Sinhalese history from the time of the *Buddha Śākyamuni to the 4th cent. CE. *Cūlavamsa* (Little Story) is an appendix which carries the story down to the 18th cent. The main chronicle was written *c.*5th cent. CE, and it is attributed to Mahānāma, though nothing certain is known of him.

Tr. W. Geiger (1912, 1930).

Mahāvastu (Skt., 'The Great Event'). A composite work of the *Lokottara(vāda) Buddhist school, dealing with previous existences (*jātaka) of the *Buddha. It describes *bhumi in a way that looks forward to the full elaboration in *bodhisattva belief, and the work is thus regarded as a transition from *Theravāda to *Mahāyāna—all the more so, since it appears to have been produced over several centuries. It describes the Buddha leaving the *Tuṣita heaven in a mind-created body. All the episodes of his life are designed to help those whom he meets at their own level; he himself is never other than transcendent.

Tr. J. J. Jones (1949–56).

Mahā-Vibhāṣā (Buddhist teaching commentary): see SARVASTIVĀDA.

Mahāvidyas (Skt., 'great' + 'knowledge'). Ten Hindu goddesses who represent the ten forms of transcendent knowledge and *tantric power, through the worship of whom one can gain knowledge of *Brahman, since they are all personifications of Brahman's *Śakti. They are *Kāli/*Lalitā; *Tārā (an emanation of Kāli); Soḍaśī (a girl of 16, the number of perfection, thus the perfection of the cosmic whole); Bhukaneśvari (the material world); *Bhairavi (the infinite variety of desires and the inevitability of death); *Chinnamastā/Vīrarātrī (eternal night, depicted naked drinking blood from her own self-severed head); Dhūmāvatī (the destruction, *pralaya, of the cosmos, when only smoke, *dhūma*, remains); Bagalā (emotional forces of hate, jealousy, etc.); Mātaṇgi (power and domination); Kamalā (the girl of the *lotus, pure consciousness). The Mahāvidya cult was prominent in medieval Bengal.

Mahāvīra (Skt., *mahat*, 'great', + *vīra*, 'hero'). In Jainism, the honorific title given to Vardhamāna Jnātṛputra, the 24th *tīrthaṅkara. The *Digambara and Śvetāmbara sects recount two divergent accounts of his life. Both agree that he was born the son of a *kṣatriya couple, Siddhārtha and *Triśalā, at Kuṇḍagrama just north of modern Patna (Bihar State, India) in 599 BCE. The Śvetāmbara Jains date his life 599–527 BCE (the Digambara hold that he died in 510), but some modern scholarship suggests 549–477 BCE. Śvetāmbara tradition claims that Mahāvīra married a princess Yośodā, who bore him a daughter, Priyadarśanā; but Digambara tradition rejects this. At the age of 30, Mahāvīra renounced family life to become a wandering ascetic in the tradition of *Pārśva—for a time in company with *Makkhali Gosala. After twelve years of severe fasting to cleanse his body, of silence to improve his speech, and of meditation to clear his mind, he gained omniscience (*kevala jñāna) and became a *jina. For the next thirty years he travelled throughout NE India, teaching by word and example the path of purification: 'Whoever conquers mind and passion, and acts with true austerity, shines like a fire into which the oblation has been poured' (*Isibhasiyaim* 29. 17). He gained a considerable following (the most notable disciple, *ganadhara*, being Indrabhuti Gautama) and he continued preaching in the *samavasarana*, the 'preaching arena' (see U. P. Shah, *Studies in Jaina Art*, 1955). Mahāvīra died and passed to *mokṣa at the age of 73 at Pāvāpurī, near Patna, leaving (tradition claims) 14,000 monks, 36,000 nuns, 159,000 laymen, and 318,000 laywomen to continue his teaching. Jains today look back on Mahāvīra as the greatest of all their teachers, preaching and demonstrating the way of salvation and laying stress on 'the pure unchanging, eternal law' that 'all things living, all things breathing, all things whatever, should not be slain or treated with violence or insulted or injured or tortured or driven away': the impediment of *karma does not affect the soul but weighs it down: austerity and *asceticism generate *tapas which burns away the impediment. The freed soul travels to the highest point of the universe to dwell with other liberated souls.

K. C. Jain, *Lord Mahāvīra and his Times* (1974); A. N. Upadhye, *Mahāvīra* . . . (1974).

Mahāvrata (a 'great vow'): see YAMA (2); for Jains, see FIVE GREAT VOWS.

Mahāyāna (Skt., 'Great Vehicle'; Chin., Ta-ch'eng; Jap., Daijō; Korean, Taesūng). The form of Buddhism prominent in Tibet, Mongolia, China, Korea, Vietnam, and Japan. It regards itself as a more adequate expression of the *dharma than what it calls *Hīnayāna (Skt., 'Lesser' or 'Inferior Vehicle'), a term it invented for forms of Buddhism superficially similar to but by no means identical with present-day *Theravāda, and elements of which it sometimes incorporates as preliminary teachings. Mahāyāna literature is unknown prior to the Common Era yet it claims to be the true teaching of the *Buddha Śākyamuni. This discrepancy is explained in various ways, e.g. Tibetan Buddhism ascribes, within the *Trikāya of the Buddha, the Hīnayāna to the historical Nirmāṇakāya and the Mahāyāna to the *Sambhoga-kāya; whereas *Zen claims a special wordless transmission that could not by its very nature have a literary witness. In any case, such teaching is now recorded in many *sūtras. The distinctive teaching of the Mahāyāna is that of compassion for all sentient beings such that the practitioner delays his own *nirvāna until all other beings shall have been liberated. This is called Great Compassion, while that of the Hīnayāna (which necessarily ceases with personal nirvāna), is called Small Compassion. The ideal practitioner is the *bodhisattva, i.e. one who has given birth to the *bodhicitta (Skt., 'enlightenment-mind') which strives to manifest Great Compassion. The two main philosophical schools of Mahāyāna are *Mādhyamaka and Yogācāra / *Vijñānavāda (for the lineages, see BUDDHIST SCHOOLS). Also of importance are the forms of devotion, e.g. to the Buddha Amitābha (*Amida) with the promise of rebirth in the paradise of *Sukhāvatī; the emphasis on sūtras containing the developed teaching of the Buddha (according to *upāya-kauśalya, his early teaching was adapted to the simple-minded); the recognition of the buddha-nature (*Tathāgata-garbha, *buddhatā) in all things.

P. Williams, *Mahāyāna Buddhism* . . . (1989).

Mahāyānaśraddhotpāda-śastra (Treatise on the Awakening of Faith in the Mahāyāna). A Mahāyāna Buddhist text, attributed to *Aśvaghoṣa, though it comes in fact from *c.*4th/5th cent. CE. It contains five sections: (i) its purpose, to liberate all sentient beings from suffering, and to teach the way to enlightenment, especially through devotion to Amitābha (*Amida); (ii) an explanation of Mahāyāna terms; (iii) an exposition of major items of belief; (iv) a description of Mahāyāna practice; (v) an account of the advantages accruing from Mahāyāna practice. It is a *sūtra which was also of importance in *Zen.

Mahdī (the awaited Imām): see AL-MAHDĪ.

Maḥdūd (finiteness of humans, in Islam): see ḤADD.

Mahendra ('Great Indra'). A name applied in Hinduism to *Indra, *Viṣṇu, and *Śiva. Offerings to Mahendra bring victory in conflict, and for that reason are restricted to leaders (i.e. *brahmans and *ksatriyas).

Maheśāna (Skt., 'great ruler'). In Hinduism, one of the older names of *Śiva; the sun as a form of Śiva.

Maheśvara (Skt., 'Great Lord'). Epithet of Śiva (also sometimes of *Viṣṇu). He is the source of knowledge (*jñāna), will (*iccha), and action (*kriya*). In *Kashmir Śaivism, the epithet points to an understanding of the cosmos and nature as an unfolding process within the universal mind.

Maheśvara-sūtra. A *Śaivite work, attributed to *Śiva. It deals with the four ways leading to ultimate insight—*yoga, *vedānta, language, and music.

Maheśvari (Skt.). A name of *Śakti; also one of the goddesses created by *Śiva who constitute the Divine Mothers (*Mātṛkās*); consort of *Maheśvara.

Mahfouz, Naguib (b. 1911). Egyptian author of novels, short stories, and film-scripts. He was born in Cairo and received his early education in a Quranic primary school, giving him a traditional faith. In his teens he suffered a religious crisis brought on by the reading of Darwin. After taking a degree in philosophy, he opted for a literary career, earning his living as a civil servant, first in the Ministry of Religious Endowments, later as film censor in the Ministry of Culture. His early works were set in Pharaonic Egypt; then followed novels of social realism, set in Cairo, culminating in the *Cairo Trilogy.* In 1959, after a long silence, his religious allegory, *Awlad Haratina* (tr. as *Children of Gebelaawi*), was serialized in the newspaper *Al-Ahram*. It caused offence to many readers by its familiar treatment of figures representing *Adam, *Moses, *Jesus, and *Muḥammad, and by allowing the death of the old man thought by many to stand for God. Publication in book form has never been permitted in Egypt, but the author has always claimed it to be a deeply religious work, affirming the humanity of the prophets and above all the absolute transcendence of the true God. Religious concerns continue to be prominent in the existentialist, stream-of-consciousness works of the 1960s and in the later works with their return to classical Arabic themes and forms. *Sūfī figures are frequently portrayed, though Mahfouz has never belonged to a Sūfī order. Controversy was revived by the award of the Nobel Prize for Literature in 1988 and, in the wake of the *fatwā against Salman Rushdie (see SATANIC VERSES), a hostile opinion was expressed in a Kuwaiti newspaper by Sheikh Omar Abdul-Rahman. Some interpreted this as a fatwā against the author, although the Sheikh himself has vigorously denied it. Mahfouz survived an attempted assassination in Oct. 1994.

Mahinda Festival. Buddhist (Śri Lankan) festival, better known as Poson, which celebrates the mission of the monk Mahinda who brought Buddhism to Śri Lankā. He was the son of *Aśoka, and pilgrimages are made to Mihintale where he converted the king of Śri Lankā.

Mahiṣa, Mahiṣāsura (Skt., 'water-buffalo'). 1. Name of a demon (*asura, thus also frequently Mahiṣāsura) in the shape of a buffalo, in Hindu mythology. The classical version of the myth about the Goddess killing the demon was told in the *Devīmāhātmya* of the **Mārkaṇḍeya-Purāṇa*, and from there acquired pan-Indian popularity. When the demon was creating chaos on a cosmic scale, the male gods were unable to defeat him, and the Goddess manifested herself by absorbing the total energies from all the gods. She rode into battle on a tiger, wielding many weapons in her eighteen hands, and emitted from herself other female warrior-companions (like *Cāmuṇḍā and the Seven Mothers, Sapta-Mātṛkās). When all the henchmen of Mahiṣa (like Raktabīja, whose every drop of spilled blood generated replicas of himself, so that Cāmuṇḍā swallowed it all up; or Caṇḍa and Muṇḍa from whose names Cāmuṇḍā's name is derived) had been killed, the Goddess fought a duel with Mahiṣa, cut his head off, and killed the person emerging from the buffalo's carcass. In the text itself, the Goddess is most frequently referred to as Ambikā ('little mother', see AMBĀ) or Caṇḍikā ('fierce woman'), but later iconographic traditions usually call her Mahiṣāsuramardini, 'she who crushed the Buffalo demon', while in religious contexts she is called Mahā-*Lakṣmī.

2. By no means all images depicting a female figure associated with a water-buffalo signify this Goddess or refer to this myth. A water-buffalo is the *vāhana, 'vehicle', of the Hindu god *Yama, the god of death, and in Mahārāṣṭra we find a goddess Yamāī riding on (or killing?) a buffalo. In Gujarāt a Goddess Vihat or Visat is depicted riding on this animal. In the same region, a goddess killing a buffalo (demon) may be Khoḍiār, Ambājī, Vihat, or Cavaṇḍ. Even more complex is the situation in Mahārāṣṭra where we find the male god Mhaskobā (Marāṭhī, *mhas/mhais*, 'water-buffalo') and the Pot-rāj (Dravidian, *pōt(t)u*, 'male buffalo', + Skt. *rāja*, 'King'). The latter appears either as a deity or a folk-religious priest and medium who whips himself in front of the Goddess Kaḍak-Lakṣmī ('Fierce Lakṣmī') and thus appears to personify Mahiṣāsura.

3. From ancient times until recently, when for economic reasons the custom became curtailed, buffaloes have been killed in Indian villages as part of sacrifices and for the sake of eating their meat. The myth about the Goddess killing Mahiṣa can at the most be regarded as a reflection of this custom, but not as a prescriptive rule.

See also MĀRIYAMNAM; MADHU; and CAṆḌĪ.

Mahr (dowry): see MARRIAGE.

Maḥzor (Heb., 'cycle'). Jewish festival prayer book. The term maḥzor distinguishes between the prayer book for festivals as opposed to the *siddur, which is the daily *prayer book. Both the *Ashkenazi and the *Sephardi versions are based on the 11th-cent. **Maḥzor Vitry* compiled by Simḥah ben Samuel of Vitry, a pupil of *Rashi. *Conservative and *Reconstructionist Judaism have produced their own maḥzorim more by way of amplification than by abandonment of the tradition.

Maḥzor Vitry. Jewish *halakhic-liturgical book. The *Maḥzor Vitry* was composed by Simḥah ben Samuel of Vitry, a pupil of *Rashi, in the late 11th cent. CE. The book gives the halakhic rulings of the *liturgy for the annual cycle of weekdays, *Sabbaths, and *Festivals.

Mai Chaza's Church. Church founded, among the Shona-speaking Manyinka in Zimbabwe, by Mai (Shona, 'mother') Chaza (d. 1960), after a mystical experience of death and resurrection while in a coma early in the 1950s. Initially remaining within *Methodism, development as a separate body began in 1955, based on her new village, Guta Ra *Jehovah ('city of Jehovah'), as the first of a series of holy cities which served as famous faith-healing centres, especially for barren women. She opposed ancestor veneration and the use of both Western and traditional medicine as well as magic, and enjoined a strict legalistic ethic supporting monogamy and banning *alcohol and tobacco. Infant *baptism, unusual in such bodies, was continued, but not the *Lord's Supper. Her works and teachings, as related to those of *Jesus, have been collected in a Guta Ra

Jehovah Bible. The movement's adherents have declined to no more than 3,000.

Maimon, Solomon (1753–1800). Jewish philosopher. Maimon studied philosophy in Posen, Berlin, Hamburg, Amsterdam, Attona, and Breslau. In a letter, the philosopher Immanuel *Kant remarked that no one understood his ideas as well as Maimon. He was the author of *Versuch ueber die Transzendentalphilosophie* (1790), *Streifereien im Gebiete der Philosophie* (1793), three works on the history of philosophy, a philosophical lexicon, and a commentary on *Maimonides' *Guide of the Perplexed*. He was condemned as a heretic and denied burial in a Jewish cemetery, mainly as a consequence of his evident subordination of revelation to reason: 'Whatever light I may receive, I shall always illumine it with the light of reason. My religion enjoins me to believe nothing, but to think the truth and to practise goodness.' To him is attributed the succinct comment: 'God knows what God is.'

S. H. Bergman, *The Philosophy of Solomon Maimon* (1967).

Maimonidean controversy. Jewish controversy (in fact, more than one) centring on the themes discussed by the philosopher *Maimonides. Maimonides himself initiated controversy against the authority of the geonim. He described the *gaon Samuel b. Ali as 'one whom people accustom from his youth to believe that there is none like him in his generation', and he sharply attacked the 'monetary demands' of the *academies. His own *Mishneh Torah* was fiercely condemned by such as *Abraham b. David of Posquières; and scholars such as Meir *Abulafia were appalled by Maimonides' apparent rejection of the doctrine of the *resurrection of the dead. A *ḥerem (excommunicatory ban) was pronounced on Maimonides' philosophical work. *Naḥmanides was aware that Maimonides' ideas were welcomed by the *assimilated and prosperous Jews of Spain and Provence, and argued that 'but for the fact that they live out of the mouth of his works . . . they would have slipped almost entirely'. None the less, he believed that Maimonides' ideas were heretical. In the West, the controversy was halted by the burning of Maimonides' books by the Christian *Dominicans in 1232. It was continued in the East by Maimonides' son, Abraham, although the desecration of Maimonides' tomb in Tiberias was a profound shock to all concerned. The controversy flared up again at the beginning of the 14th cent. when Solomon b. Abraham *Adret issued a ḥerem on 'any member of the community who, being under twenty-five years, shall study the works of the Greeks on natural science or metaphysics'. This tension between the anti-rationalists and the rationalists continued through the Middle Ages and is to be seen in such disputes as that between Moses *Isserles and Solomon b. Jehiel *Luria in the 16th cent.

Maimonides, Moses, Moses b. Maimon, or **Rambam** (1135–1204). Jewish philosopher and codifier. Maimonides grew up in Cordova, but as a result of persecution, the family eventually moved to Fez in N. Africa after years of wandering. During this period he wrote treatises on the Jewish calendar, logic, and *halakhah. In 1168, he completed his commentary on the *Mishnah. In 1170–80, he worked on his great code, the *Mishneh Torah* (The Repetition of the Law, sometimes known as 'The Strong Hand'). The purpose of this work was 'so that the entire *Oral Law might become systematically known to all without citing difficulties and solutions of differences of view . . ., but consisting of statements clear and convincing, that have appeared from the time of *Moses to the present, so that all rules shall be accessible to young and old'. This codification of the Law was fiercely criticized by such as *Abraham b. David of Posquières (see MAIMONIDEAN CONTROVERSY). His great philosophical work, The *Guide of the Perplexed* (Heb., *Moreh Nevukhim*) was influenced by Aristotle and the *Hellenistic commentators Alexander of Aphrodisias, Themistius, and Averroes, and also by the Muslim philosopher *al-Fārābī. The *Guide* shows 'the perplexed' how scripture can be interpreted spiritually as well as literally, and Maimonides aimed to reveal to his readers 'the science of the Law in its true sense'. To this end, he discussed God, creation, the nature of evil, divine providence, and morality. He also formulated his *thirteen principles of the Jewish faith which he believed every Jew was bound to accept. Many commentaries have been written on the *Guide*, the most famous being those of Profiat Duran, Shem Tov ben Joseph, Asher Crescas, Isaac *Abrabanel, and Solomon *Maimon. Maimonides' philosophical ideas have been enormously influential on the Jewish community, particularly in the period of the *Enlightenment. His work was also important for Christians such as Thomas *Aquinas, *Eckhart, and *Duns Scotus. He is also remembered as a significant physician and astronomer.

Central to Maimonides' position is his belief that a God-directed spirituality can be fully integrated with reason, an expression of the widespread medieval ideal of the love of God through reason: 'The foundation and support of all wisdom is the recognition that there is original Being, and that all else exists only through the reality of his Being.' He recognized the problem of predicating attributes to God so described. He argued that God is identical with his attributes, thus being the knower, the knowledge, and the known; but this precipitates him into analogical language, and he preferred to speak of the effects of God rather than his being: 'All attributes ascribed to God are attributes of his acts, and do not imply that God has any qualities.' It thus becomes possible to follow only the **via negativa* when speaking of God. He applied the same rationalizing process to all aspects of religion and became an uncompromising opponent of all that could not stand up to reason. Thus on *miracles he observed: 'A miracle cannot prove what is impossible; it is useful only to confirm what is possible.' He believed strongly in the tradition of the good and evil inclinations, which entails that every individual has the responsibility to become either 'righteous like Moses or evil like Jeroboam'. He saw his own work as a mediation of all that Judaism, as religion and philosophy, has to offer to help people to make a living conversion of behaviour in the direction of God. Somewhat like *Lonergan (where the medieval connection is thus no coincidence), he envisaged levels of human knowledge leading to God: 'When you understand physics, you have entered the hall; and when, after completing the study of natural philosophy, you master metaphysics, you have entered the innermost court and are with the king in the same palace.'

I. Epstein (ed.), *Moses Maimonides* (1935); D. Hartman, *Maimonides: Torah and Philosophic Quest* (1976); M. Kellner, *Maimonides on Judaism and the Jewish People* (1991); Y. Liebowitz, *The Faith of Maimonides* (1987). J. S. Minkin, *The World of Moses Maimonides* (1957); I. Twersky, *Introduction to the Code of Maimonides* (1980).

Maimuna. Celebration among some Jews (especially in or from N. Africa) of the last day of *Passover. Maimuna is celebrated in many eastern Jewish communities with special foods and picnics. Traditionally it is also the anniversary of the death of Moses *Maimonides' father.

Maithuna (Skt.). Sexual intercourse; in Indian religions, particularly *Tantrism, a vehicle for and metaphor of liberation (*mokṣa).

Although maithuna as a means of liberation is not found in the *Upaniṣads, the cosmic symbolism of the sexual act found there anticipates the *tantras. The **Bṛhadāranyaka Upaniṣad* (6. 4. 20) describes ritualized copulation for procuring a son during which the couple become identified with cosmic principles, the man with vital breath and heaven, the woman with speech and earth. Again in the same *Upaniṣad* (6. 4. 3) the woman becomes identified with the place of sacrifice: her lap becomes the sacrificial *alter (*vedi*), her hair the sacrificial grass, and her vulva the sacrificial fire (*agni). If a man copulates with her knowing this, then his world (*loka) becomes as great as one who performs the *vājapeya* sacrifice; that is, copulation becomes as efficacious in producing merit as ritual *sacrifice. In the same *Upaniṣad* we also find maithuna as a metaphor for union with the self (*ātman): 'As a man when in the embrace of a woman he loves knows nothing of the outside nor inside, so does the person (*puruṣa) know nothing of the outside nor inside when in the embrace of the wise self (ātman)' (*Bṛhadāranyaka Upaniṣad* 4. 3. 21).

The sexual act as a metaphor of divine union is found in the *Bhakti tradition, particularly the erotic (*sṛṇgāra*) bhakti to *Kṛṣṇa of the Gaudiya *Vaiṣṇavas, in which the bhakta identifies himself with the *gopīs, especially *Rādhā, and their adulterous love (*parākiya*) for Kṛṣṇa. Sexual love is here a symbol for the soul's love of God.

Maithuna as a means of liberation is found *par excellence* in Hindu and Buddhist *Tantrism, in the left-hand (*vāmācāra) traditions of the *Kaula-Kāpālika cults and the *Sahajīyās. Through ritual maithuna, sexual energy is transformed into spiritual energy, and desire is destroyed by desire. Human sexuality reflects the cosmic male–female polarity, and human copulation reflects the cosmic union (*yāmala, *yuganaddha*, *yab-yum) of *Śiva and *Śakti, in Hindu Tantra; and *Prajñā and *Upāya or *Śūnyatā and *Karuṇa in Buddhist Tantra. The rhythmical movement of maithuna also reflects the rhythmical vibration (*spanda*) of the cosmos.

The Tantras give details of rituals (*pūjā) involving maithuna (the *strī pūjā*), stressing their secrecy and the danger of *hell for one who performs these rites with desire. The adept (*sādhaka) must be a hero (*vīra*) or perfected one (*siddha). The female partner (*yoginī) is worshipped as a Goddess and should likewise be perfect. Abhinavagupta regards any female member of the yogin's family except his wife as suitable for ritual maithuna, whereas the **Kulārnava Tantra* (10. 11) stipulates it should be performed only with the yogin's initiated wife. Maithuna occurs as part of the Five Ms (*pañcamakāra).

Much Tantric literature stresses the need for seminal retention or the withdrawal of semen before emission (*vajroli *mudrā*), though this is not always the case as the deity is thought to be revealed during orgasm, and sexual fluids an offering to the deity. Some Tantric groups advocated uncontrolled use of maithuna in ritual 'orgies', as an extreme test of control and detachment.

Maitreya (Skt., 'loving one'; Pāli, Metteyya; Chin., Mile-fo; Korean, Mitūk; Jap., Miroku). One of the five earthly buddhas, the embodiment of all-embracing love, who is expected to come in the future as the fifth and last of the buddhas. In early Buddhism, Maitreya dwells in the *Tuṣita heaven (the realm of the fully delighted gods), waiting for the decline and eclipse of Buddhism, when he will become the next Buddha—in about 30,000 years time. This belief was further developed in all Mahāyāna countries, and above all in Tibet, where he is known as *byams pa* (*champa*). It is a particular commitment of *Gelugpa to prepare for his coming. He is depicted usually with feet placed firmly on the ground, ready to step into the world.

A. Sponberg and H. Hardacre (ed.), *Maitreya, the Future Buddha* (1988).

Maitreyanātha. Buddhist teacher of uncertain status. He is held to be a founder of Yogācāra/ *Vijñānavāda because of the statement that *Asaṅga was taught by Maitreyanātha. But this may be a reference to *Maitreya.

Maitri (Skt., 'kindness'; Pāli, *metta*). A major virtue in Buddhism. It is generous benevolence to all, which is free from attachment or calculation of reciprocal interests. Its cultivation is a specific *Theravādin meditation-practice, and its nature is explored in the *Metta-sutta*. That sutta is recited daily by monks, and often by laypeople. The sutta reads in part (tr. Conze):

This is what should be done by the man who is wise, who seeks the good, and knows the meaning of the place of peace. Let him be strenuous, upright and truly straight, without conceit of self, easily contented and joyous, free of cares; let him not take upon himself the burden of worldly goods; let his senses be controlled. . . . May all beings be happy and at their ease! May they be joyous and live in safety. . . . Even as a mother watches over and protects her child, her only child, so with a boundless mind should one cherish all living beings, radiating friendliness over the entire world, above, below, and all around, without limit. So let him cultivate a boundless good-will towards the entire world, uncramped, free from ill-will or enmity. Standing or walking, sitting or lying down, during all his waking hours, let him establish this mindfulness of good-will, which men call the highest state! Abandoning vain discussions, having a clear vision, free from sense appetites, he who is made perfect will never again know rebirth.

Maitrī-karunā. Kindness and compassion linked in Buddhism as the supreme characteristic of a *bodhisattva.

***Maitri Upaniṣad*.** A late work written in the prose style of a *brāhmaṇa. Its contents are varied, but it is valued particularly for its discussion of the distinction between the two forms of *ātman: the eternal ātman 'abiding in its own greatness', and the bhutātman, the elemental self entangled in change, as a bird is caught in a snare.

Trs.: see UPANIṢAD.

Majjhima nikāya (Skt., Madhyamāgama). The Middle Length (second) Collection (*nikāya) of the Sutta/*Sūtra-*piṭaka of the *Pāli (Buddhist) canon (see also BUDDHIST SCRIPTURES). The Pāli canon contains 150 sūtras, the Chin. tr. of the (lost) Skt. 222; 97 are found in both.

Eng. trs. of parts are found in many places, e.g. Chalmers, *Further Dialogues of the Buddha* (Sac. Books of the Buddhists, 6; 1927); I. B. Horner, *Middle Length Sayings* (1954–9); H. C. Warren, *Buddhism in Translations* (1915).

Majjhimapātipadā (way taught and practised by the Buddha): see MIDDLE WAY.

Majlisī (Shiʿite theologian): see AL-MAJLISĪ, MUḤAMMAD BĀQIR.

Makara. A sea-beast, resembling a crocodile, on which the Hindu god *Varuṇa rides. A makara is believed to increase fertility, and is the emblem of *Kāma.

Makāra. The performance in *Tantra of the Five Ms—see PAÑCA-MAKĀRA.

Makiguchi Tsunesaburō (founder): see SŌKA GAKKAI.

Makkhali Gosala or **Maskarin Gosala** (Pāli, Skt.). Sectarian teacher and leader of the *Ājīvaka sect who was criticized by the Buddha for his doctrine of determinism. A synopsis of his teaching is preserved in Buddhist sources:

There is no cause, either ultimate or remote, for the depravity of beings; they become depraved without reason and without cause. There is no cause, either proximate or remote, for the rectitude of beings, they become pure without reason and without cause (. . .) There is no such thing as power or energy, or human strength or human vigour. All animals . . . are without force and power of their own. They are bent this way and that by their fate. (*Dialogues of the Buddha*, i. 71, tr. T. W. and C. A. F. Rhys Davids).

Makyō (Jap., 'devil' + 'phenomenal appearance'). The deceptive appearances which arise for a Zen Buddhist in *zazen. They may be of any kind, from sweet sounds and smells to hallucinations and levitation. They amount to the experience of an unenlightened person. Provided they are ignored or put aside, they are harmless.

Māl (name of god): see TAMILNADU.

Mālā (also **japamālā**). A *'rosary' for Hindus, Buddhists, and Sikhs.

Hinduism Basically, mālā is a garland made of beads and/or berries, presented to honoured guests, and to symbolize victory. They consist (usually) of 108 berries, and are then used in the practice of *japa. 108 is the number of evil passions to which humans are subject.

Buddhism The number of beads is the same, and they are used to count repetitions in the recitation of *dhāraṇīs, *mantras, and the name of a buddha (*nembutsu).

Sikhism It is usually made of wool, and has 108 knots, though smaller ones of twenty-nine knots are also used. They are used to aid concentration on the name (*nām) of God.

Malabar Christians. The Christians of the state of Kerala on the Malabar (SW) coast of India. They number over 2 million, now divided into several communities (see SYRIAN CHURCHES). They are known as 'Thomas Christians' from their claim—taken seriously by some W. scholars too—that their ancestors were evangelized by St *Thomas. In any case, by the 6th cent. there was a Church in the region using Syriac in its liturgy and dependent for bishops on the (*Nestorian) catholikos of Baghdad. After heavy-handed missionary work by the Portuguese, the Church was formally purged of Nestorianism, brought under Roman obedience, and thoroughly Latinized at the synod of Diamper

(Udayamperur, near Cochin) in 1599. Latin government of the Church continued as a source of tension down to the 20th cent. There was a defection of a large body eventually to the Syrian Orthodox in the 17th cent.; this schism gave rise to another in the 19th cent. with the creation of the *Mar Thoma Church. The Catholics are now styled the 'Syro-Malabar Church', having been granted their own metropolitanate of Ernakulam with Indian bishops in 1923.

L. W. Brown, *The Indian Christians of St. Thomas* (1956).

Malabar rites. The customs and rites adopted from Hindu customs by *de Nobili in India, to enable converts to Christianity not to feel estranged from their culture. Although he took up customs he regarded as civil and not religious, he was opposed by *Dominicans and *Franciscans for confusing the disjunctive nature of Christianity. Rome upheld de Nobili in 1623, but ruled against most of the adaptations in 1712, in a process parallel to the controversy over *Chinese rites.

Malachi, Book of. Last of the books of the Jewish *minor prophets. Malachi is of anonymous authorship, but was probably written early in the post-exilic period, possibly before the writing of *Ezra and *Nehemiah. The book falls into six clear sections dealing with God's love for Israel (1. 2–5), the neglect of the sacrificial cult (1. 6–2. 9), a reproach against mixed marriages (2. 10–16), God as the Lord of Judgement (2. 17–3. 5), the duty of giving *tithes (3. 6–12), and reward and punishment on the *Day of the Lord (3. 13–21). The book ends with the promise that the prophet *Elijah will return before the coming judgement (3. 22–4/4. 5 f.). This was highly influential on future *messianic expectation and was seen by Christians as fulfilled in *John the Baptist. In the *aggadah, Malachi is considered to be the last of the prophets and, after his death, prophecy departed from Israel (*B.Yoma* 9b).

Malāḥidah (heresy in Islam): see HERESY.

Malak/malā'ika ('messengers with wings' in Islam): see ANGEL.

Malankara Church: see UNIAT(E) CHURCHES; SYRIAN CHURCHES.

Malcolm X (1925–65). Leading figure in the Nation of Islam (see ELIJAH MUHAMMAD) and civil rights activist in the USA. He was born in Nebraska as Malcolm Little, and after an early life of petty crime (somewhat exaggerated later), he was converted through the Nation of Islam programme. His prominent part in fund-raising led Elijah Muhammad to appoint him National Representative of the Nation of Islam, and its deputy head. His appearance on the TV programme, 'The Hate that Produced Hate', projected him into national prominence, leading to a rift with Elijah Muhammad. He opposed civil rights movements, looking for direct action, and he contrasted 'true' with 'compromise' Islam. He left the movement, and, while on pilgrimage (*ḥajj) to *Mecca, he was converted to *Sunni Islam. He took the new name of el-Hajji Malik el-Shab(b)az(z). He failed to establish himself as an independent leader, and was assassinated by black Muslim loyalists in 1965. A popularizing film led to a revival of his influence in the 1990s.

B. Perry, *Malcolm . . .* (1992).

Mālik b. Anas (d. 795 (AH 179)). Author of *Kitāb al-Muwaṭṭa*, one of the earliest surviving Muslim lawbooks. It records Islam as practised in *Madīna, addressing issues on that basis which had not already been settled by *sunna and *ijmāʿ. From his work derives the *Mālikite school of law, one of the four classic *schools of law (*sharīʿa), which is prevalent in the *Maghreb. Mālik was sensitive to the untrustworthy ways in which sunna was being produced, and for that reason allowed *istiṣlāh to overrule a deduction from *Qur'ān and sunna. Mālikites are therefore intermediate between Hanifites and Shāfiʿites.

Mālikites. Muslim school (*schools) of law, deriving its name from *Mālik b. Anas, though not established in a formal sense by him. Its tendency was to control exegesis by reference to *ijmaʿ and the practices in *Madīna; only if these failed to specify did they allow *ijtihād; *ḥadīth were also supplementary. Its main strength is in N. and W. Africa (i.e. the Muslim West).

Malines Conversations. Meetings of Anglican and Roman Catholic theologians held at Malines (Mechelen) in Belgium between 1921 and 1925. Agreement was reached in particular on matters of *eucharistic doctrine and acceptance of the primacy of Rome in honour. The Protestant constituency in the Church of England was uneasy, and from the Catholic side further progress was hindered by Pius XI's anti-*ecumenical encyclical *Mortalium animos* (1928). However, the conversations stimulated the movement for co-operation between the two Churches. See also ARCIC.

Malinowski, B.: see MAGIC.

Malka or **Malca** (Heb., *melek*, 'king'). The 'royal' or holy leaven, used by *Nestorians in the preparation of bread for the *liturgy. It goes back in an unbroken line to the bread used by *Jesus at the *Last Supper, since, according to tradition, St *John took some of that bread and mixed it with water that came from the side of Jesus at the *crucifixion: a part of that bread was mixed with the preparation of the next loaf, and so on down to the present day.

Malkhuyyot (Heb., 'kingships', i.e. 'sovereignty'). The first part of the *musaf prayer for the Jewish *festival for *Rosh ha-Shanah (New Year). The *prayer is composed of verses taken from the

*Psalms, the *Pentateuch, and the *prophets, all asserting God's sovereignty. After the prayer, the *shofar is sounded.

Mamlukes (dynasty): see SLAVERY (ISLAM).

Mamzer (Heb., 'bastard'). Jewish person conceived as the result of an illicit union. A mamzer is a child conceived by a married woman with a man other than her husband, or as the result of incest. Illegitimate children in the usual sense are not mamzerim. A mamzer may not marry a legitimate Jew and only the marriage between two mamzerim or a mamzer and a *proselyte is permitted. However, a mamzer has equal rights of inheritance, can hold public office, and 'a mamzer who is a scholar takes precedence over a *high priest who is an ignoramus' (*Hor.* 3. 8). Foundlings are only considered to be mamzerim if they have been abandoned with no care whatsoever for their survival (*B.Kid.* 73b).

Man. A primordial and cosmic figure, occurring in several religions, but with different emphases. In Hinduism, see NARA.

Man (Hindī, Pañjābī, 'one's total being'). Mind, heart, and soul. In Sikhism this bears the connotation of human capriciousness. A Sikh's aim must be to overcome this waywardness and achieve spiritual equilibrium: *'Mani jītai jagu jītu'* (Ādi Granth, p. 6), i.e. conquest of inclination is conquest of the world.

Māna (Pāli, Skt.). Pride, conceit; a moral fault in Buddhism. It takes three forms: thinking of oneself as inferior to, equal to, or better than others.

Mana (inherent power): see MAGIC.

Manas (Skt., 'mind'). In Skt. literature, the mind, the co-ordinating organ of intelligence, thought, understanding, perception, and will. In Vedic times manas meant the individual spirit and the basis of speech (*vāc). In the Upaniṣadic period manas is variously treated: sometimes it is closely associated with speech and *breath as a triple entity, sometimes considered more as the intermediate link between the Self, *ātman, and the senses. **Kaṭha Upaniṣad* pictures manas as the bridle and reins by which the intellect (*buddhi), as the driver of the chariot, guides the horses of the senses.

In the *darśanas, manas is seen as a special additional sense organ by which thoughts and sensations have access to the ātman. In *Sāṃkhya philosophy, the principle (*tattva) of manas together with intellect (buddhi) and ego (*ahaṃkāra) makes up a threefold 'inner instrument' (*antaḥkarana*). Here manas is an evolute of buddhi-principle and a special kind of sense organ and organ of action which can bridge the internal and external realms. In general, manas is of philosophical importance as the organ of ordinary waking consciousness, the proper handling of which may facilitate higher consciousness and liberation.

In Buddhist psychology, manas is the rational or intellectual faculty of the mind. Manas has both an active and a passive function: in its passive mode it is responsible for the reception, ordering, and interpretation of data received through the five senses, its operation being triggered off by the input of sense-data. The manner in which manas performs this function is the result of conditioning and habit and can be modified through the exercise of self-awareness. In its active mode manas is responsible for the production of feelings and wishes. In the Pāli canon it is said to be synonymous with *citta and *vijñāna (2).

Manasā. A Goddess of folk Hinduism worshipped in Bengal and neighbouring areas by middle and lower strata of society. From *c.*14th cent. onward, she played an important role in Bengali literature, but failed to reach the same level of popular veneration as *Caṇḍī, *Durgā, and *Kālī in this region. In both the oral legends connected with her *vrata (special rites performed by women) and the sizeable Manasā-maṅgal literature, she is depicted as wilful, unpredictable, and potentially very malicious. She is often associated with snakes, is envisaged as one-eyed and limping, and as usually manifesting herself as an old *brahman woman. On the other hand, she is capable of offering grace and fortune to those who venerate her—a veneration that sometimes she is ready to enforce through considerable violence. The Manasā-maṅgal literature (more than fifty individual works belonging to this genre are known) has in many variations dealt with one particular story, and could be regarded as the attempt of the more educated Bengalis to come to terms with this (probably in origin tribal) Goddess. Against the antagonism of Caṇḍī or Durgā, Manasā intends to establish her worship on earth. Real success can only come about, if the merchant Chando (variously seen as worshipper of Śiva, Caṇḍī, or as a *tantrika) accepts her. Only through a long series of tribulations and Job-like disasters can she break this man's obstinacy.

E. Dimock, *The Thief of Love: Bengali Tales from Court and Village* (1963), 197–294, tr. of the latter part of Ketakadāsa's *Manasā-maṅgal*.

Manasseh ben Israel (1604–57). Jewish scholar. He founded the first Hebrew printing-press in Amsterdam. He himself was the author of several theological works, including *Piedra Gloriosa* which was illustrated with engravings by Rembrandt who also painted his portrait. He dedicated his *Esperanca De Israel* to the English Parliament in 1650 and was closely involved in the negotiations to readmit Jews to England in the Commonwealth period, using for his argument the belief that Jews must be dispersed through all the nations of the world before the *messiah can come. In his view, the Jews have an existence necessary for the good of the world: 'The Israelites are a distinct people and must remain so, having the essential duty of sanctifying life.'

He viewed with contempt the endeavour of the *Inquisition to coerce Jews into Christianity: 'Unreasoning animals are instructed by blows, but humans are persuaded by reason.'

C. Roth, *Life of Menasseh Ben Israel* (1934).

Manasseh, Prayer of. Jewish *psalm included in the *Apocrypha. According to 2 Chronicles 33, King Manasseh (2 Kings 21. 1–18) was taken by his captors to Babylon, repenting of his *sins. The Prayer of Manasseh was probably written at the end of the 1st cent. BCE, and is put forward as Manasseh's supposed words. The prayer invokes *God's mercy for past sins. In the E. Church, it is recited in Great *Compline during *Lent and on the eve of some feasts.

Mānava-dharmaśāstra (laws of Hindu lawgiver Manu): see MANUSMṚTI.

Mandaeans: see MANDEANS.

Maṇḍala (Skt., 'circle'; Chin., *man-ta-lao*; Jap. and Korean, *mandara*; Tib., *dkyil.'khor*). A symbolic pictorial representation of the universe, originating in India but especially prominent in *Tibetan Buddhism, and which is *visualized in the context of *Tantric ritual. Although maṇḍalas are commonly found on scrolls or as wall-paintings, for important rituals the practice is to trace the maṇḍala onto consecrated ground using coloured powders which may be erased upon termination of the ritual. In meditation, they can be visualized without external representation.

All maṇḍalas follow a precise symbolic format. Their circular shape, indicating an all-including pervasion, consists first of an outer ring of flames. This lends the area a protective nature, and as the *yogin visualizes his entry into the maṇḍala, his impurities are symbolically burned. A second circle consists of a ring of *vajras, symbolizing the indestructible quality of *enlightenment. Especially in maṇḍalas of *wrathful divinities, there is a third circle of eight cemeteries, in which die the eight superficial modes of consciousness which would distract the yogin from his required concentration. A final ring of lotus petals signifies the purity of the land the yogin now enters. Having in his visualization crossed these borders, the yogin stands outside a 'pure palace' (*vimāna*) which, by representing the four directions in its four walls adorned with auspicious symbols, and its four open gateways (*dvāra*), is understood to include within itself the whole external world; and its own centre is seen as the *axis mundi. Around the divinity inhabiting this central spot as 'Lord of the World', whose nature is pure *śūnyatā and with whom it is the goal of the yogin to identify, various other deities represent the emanating tendency of the centre, and thus also represent the relationship of *saṃsāra to *nirvāna as the insubstantial display of an a-spatial, a-temporal 'basis'. By visualizing his physical body as the maṇḍala, the yogin sees the universe contained within himself as microcosm; and by identifying with the central deity the yogin places himself in the ultimate state where the co-incidence of nirvāna and saṃsāra is seen. In absorbing the compassion, wisdom, and skilful means (see UPĀYA-KAUŚALYA) of that deity, the yogin effects a transmutation of his own mundane personality which will outlast the duration of the ritual itself.

In Hinduism, maṇḍalas are described in great detail in the Tantras and *Āgamas. For example, the *Pañcarātra text, **Lakṣmi Tantra* (37. 3–19), describes a maṇḍala of nine lotuses. This is made up of a series of squares with nine lotuses within the central square, upon which various deities are situated; namely, *Nārāyana with Lakṣmi in the central lotus, surrounded by the divine emanations (*vyūhas) and other deities on the petals. Further emanations of *Śakti are located upon the other lotuses. Thus we have a model of cosmogony, the source of manifestation symbolized by the central deities from whom emanate the cosmos and other deities.

In liturgy (*pūjā) a maṇḍala is the place where a deity is invoked by *mantra. The placing of mantras upon the maṇḍala (*nyāsa) gives it life, and the maṇḍala is then regarded, like mantra, as the deity itself (and not a mere representation of the deity). A maṇḍala is also visualized (*dhyāna) by the yogin who aims at merging with the deity. Visualization is accompanied by mantra repetition and the practice of mudrā for the control of mind, speech, and body. The maṇḍala is sometimes identified with the yogin's subtle body (*liṅga/sūkṣma śarīra), thereby identifying the individual subject with the cosmos.

In the West, the psychologist C. G. *Jung developed a theory that the maṇḍala is a symbol of psychic reintegration or individuation which arises from the unconscious. See also CAKRA; YANTRA; Index, Mandala.

G. Tucci, *The Theory and Practice of the Maṇḍala* (1969).

Mandalah. Islamic derivation from the Hindu *maṇḍala, consisting in the drawing of an inkspot surrounded by verses of the *Qur'ān (one of which is always 50. 22) on the hand of a boy. After incantations, he is enabled to see the answer to questions about things unknown.

Maṇḍala-nṛtya. An Indian *dance performed in a circle. It is based on the dance of *Kṛṣṇa with the *gopīs, in which he moved so rapidly around them that they did not notice a moment when he was absent from any one of them. In the same way, God is available for full union with any one of his devotees in *bhakti at any time.

Maṇḍala of the Five Jinas or **Tathāgatas.** A basic type for Buddhist maṇḍalas, the maṇḍala of the five jinas (Tib., *rgyal.ba*, 'eminent ones') is a representation of the psyche and the world in fivefold symbolism, appearing perhaps for the first time in the *Sarvatathāgata tattvasamgraha* (Compendium of Reality in all the *Tathāgatas) *tantra (*c.*7th cent.

CE?), and also in the *Guhyasamāja* tantra where the jinas appear with their consorts.

The basic form of this maṇḍala consists in the five jinas who have each become assigned a series of qualities as follows: (i) *Vairocana, white, in the centre, represents the element ether, the *skandha of consciousness, the ignorance of delusion, and the wisdom of the *dharmadhātu; his consort is Ākāśadhātvīśvarī and his associated *bodhisattva is Samantabhadra; (ii) Akṣobhya, blue, in the east, represents the element water, the skandha of form, the ignorance of hatred and the mirror-like wisdom; his consort is Locanā and his associated bodhisattva is Vajrapāṇi; (iii) Ratnasambhava, yellow, in the south, represents the element earth, the skandha of feeling, the ignorance of arrogance and the wisdom of equality; his consort is Māmakī and his associated bodhisattva is Ratnapāṇi; (iv) Amitābha, red, in the west, represents the element fire, the skandha of perception, the ignorance of craving and the wisdom of all-knowing; his consort is Pāṇḍarā and his associated bodhisattva is Padmapāṇi; (v) Amoghasiddhi, green, in the north, represents the element air, the skandha of volition, the ignorance of jealousy and the wisdom of all-accomplishing; his consort is Samayatārā and his associated bodhisattva is Viśvapāṇi. In addition, each jina has a particular sound, *mudrā, symbol, and animal-vehicle. The intention is of a schema in which all aspects of existence are somewhere comprehended.

Of particular interest are the five ignorances and wisdoms, which may be said to represent an early form of psychological typology. The jina governing his respective ignorance and wisdom presides over a 'family' (*kula*) of all sentient beings who are preponderantly motivated by that particular ignorance, and by ascertaining to which family an aspiring yogin belongs (this is generally achieved by casting a flower, blindfolded, into the maṇḍala), appropriate practices can be prescribed centred on that governing deity, in order to transmute that ignorance into its respective wisdom. Whether the maṇḍala or other forms of intentional meditation are used, it is never *simply* a symbolic representation, but a blueprint accompanying Tantric instructions for the effective transmutation of the mundane personality into Buddhahood.

Maṇḍapa. Any kind of canopy or tent, a ceremonial building, but especially the main area of a Hindu temple. It is transferred into Buddhism in relation to *paritta ritual.

Mandara. Jap. and Korean for *maṇḍala.

Mandara. The mountain on which, according to Hindus, the gods and giants stood for the *Churning of the Ocean. It was supported by the *Kūrma *avatāra (incarnation) of *Viṣṇu.

Mandāra. The coral tree (*erythrina indica*) which stands in *Indra's heaven, and which, when someone smells it, summons up remembrance of times past.

Mandate of Heaven (transcendent order in China): see T'IEN MING.

Mandeans. Religious group in S. Iraq and the Iranian province of Ḥuzistan, and the only surviving representative of *gnosticism.

Mandean literature, written in a dialect of Aramaic and in a distinctive script, is quite extensive. The major books are the *Ginza* ('treasure') and *Book of John*, both compilations of mythology and theological discourses; and the large 'canonical prayerbook'. These display a typically gnostic system, including a myth of creation, redemption by a series of messengers beginning with one called 'Gnosis of Life', and ascent of the soul after death.

The age of this literature and the early history of the sect are obscure. They are also very controversial, especially among interpreters of the New Testament, for whom it is crucial to know what elements if any may be treated as contemporary or antecedent to Christianity. The fact that *John the Baptist appears in Mandean texts as a 'priest' suggested to 18th-cent. Christian missionaries that the Mandeans were descendants of John's own disciples, and they called them 'Christians of St John'. Although these references to John now seem to be secondary, many scholars none the less hold that the Mandeans began as a Jewish baptising sect of the Transjordan in the 1st cent. CE or earlier. In this case, their marginal status in Judaism will have opened them up to gnostic influence. By the 2nd cent. they will have emigrated eastward into Persian territory. They are probably the Sabeans (?'baptizers') mentioned in the *Qur'ān with Jews and Christians as 'peoples of the book' (*Ahl al-kitāb), and so were tolerated by Islam. By Muslims they are today known as Subbas.

The Mandeans have a hierarchy of priests, bishops, and a 'head of the people'. The chief liturgical act is *baptism (*maswetta*) by a priest which is by immersion in flowing water, traditionally a special pool within a sanctuary next to a river, accompanied by other ritual acts including anointing. Baptism is seen as purifying from sin and may be often repeated. Baptisms take place on Sunday. The other ceremony is the funeral *massechtha* ('ascent'), consisting of readings and ceremonial meals at intervals for forty-five days after a death.

Mandeans number 15,000–25,000, and are traditionally skilled silversmiths. There are, however, few priests and among the urban young people religious life is weak.

E. S. Drower, *The Mandaeans of Iraq and Iran* (1937); W. Foerster (ed.), *Gnosis* . . ., ii (1974); K. Rudolph, *Die Mandäer* (1960, 1961).

Mandir(a) (Skt., 'dwelling'). Hindu temple. Because the divine pervades appearance and can be realized in any place or object, temples were not prominent in early Indian religion, and are not an obligation (as is, e.g., assembly in the *mosque for Muslim men). Yet they are important because they are supremely the place where the image (*murti) of God is housed and can be brought to life, and are therefore known also as *devagṛha* ('house of God') and *devālaya* ('abode of God'). The image is only alive when appropriate rituals make it so. The 'awakening' of God is a part of the daily ritual: in the morning, there are chants (*bhajana*) and washings, as well as offerings of food in worship (*pūjā). After a restful afternoon, the deity is welcomed in the evening with *music, *dance, and lamps (*ārati). But worshippers may come to the temple at any time, usually making a circumambulation (*pradakṣina) before entering, and often sounding a bell or gong to begin the process of arousing the God. Temples are built according to strict rules of design and measurement: the ground-plan is a *yantra (cosmic diagram), with the central square dedicated to *Brahmā or some other prominent deity, at the centre of the universe. The image is housed in the *garbhagṛha, the 'womb-chamber', symbolizing a dark cave. Above it rises the structure of the temple leading up to the summit of the symbolic mountain which it is: the line is the *axis mundi, up which the worshipper ascends. Temples are protected by many other deities, spirits, and signs, beautifully and elaborately carved. They may also have protective walls which are pierced by cow-gates (*gopuram*). See ART (HINDUISM).

S. Kramisch, *The Hindu Temple* (1976); G. Michell, *The Hindu Temple . . .* (1977).

Mandorla (almond-shaped aureole): see HALO.

Māndūkya Upaniṣad. An *Upaniṣad belonging to the **Atharva Veda*. It deals with the sound *Oṃ and the four states of consciousness: waking, dreaming, deep sleep, and *turīya, which alone is real: 'Oṃ! this syllable is the whole world. . . . The past, the present, the future, everything is just the sound Oṃ. And whatever else that transcends threefold time, that too is just the word Oṃ. For truly everything here is *Brahman, this self is Brahman. . . . He who knows this, with his self enters the Self—he indeed who knows this.'

Many trs., e.g. R. E. Hume (1931), Nikhilananda (1949–59), S. Radhakrishnan (1953).

Maṇi (Skt.). Jewel in the shape of a tear-drop, powerful in removing the causes of sorrow or of evil.

Manichaeism. Religion founded by Mani in 3rd-cent. Iran and later very widely established.

Mani was born in 216 near Seleucia-Ktesiphon, the Iranian capital. The best source of information about his background and early life is now a biography (in a tiny codex first edited in 1975) stemming from early Manichaean circles. According to this, he was reared in a community of Jewish Christian *Elkesaites. At the age of 12 he had his first vision of his heavenly twin (identified later with the *Paraclete), who instructed him. Thereafter he disputed with the community, and after a second vision, calling him to be an 'apostle', he separated from them, with his father and two disciples, sometime after the age of 25. Mani's later life is not well known. After preaching in India he returned to Iran *c.*242 where his patron was the new Sassanid ruler Shapur I. His religion prospered until the accession of Bahram I (274–7), who at the instigation of Kartir imprisoned and executed him in 276.

Although suppressed in Persia, Manichaeism spread west and east. It had reached Egypt already in the 3rd cent., and from there N. Africa, Spain, and Gaul. *Augustine was an adherent before his conversion to Christianity. It was, however, opposed by the Roman state (as shown in an edict of Diocletian in 297) and the Christian Church, and was in decline by the 6th cent. Its influence may perhaps be detected in later groups like the *Bogomils. In the Middle East under Islam, Manichaeism was again tolerated for a time, then persecuted by the *ʿAbbāsids. In central Asia it had more lasting success, even being made the state religion of the Turkish Uigur Empire in 762. It also reached China in 694 where, known as the 'religion of light', it seems to have persisted, in spite of official opposition at various periods, almost down to modern times.

Sources for Manichaean doctrine and practices are principally documents found only in the 20th cent. in central Asia and Egypt (notably Coptic hymns and Mani's lectures known as *Kephalaia*), plus Christian reports and polemic. Mani's teaching was fundamentally *gnostic and *dualistic, positing an opposition between God and matter. There was an elaborate cosmological myth: this included the defeat of a primal man by the powers of darkness, who devoured and thus imprisoned particles of light. The cosmic process of salvation goes on as the light is delivered back to its original state. Saving knowledge of this process comes through 'apostles of light', among whom Mani, a self-conscious syncretist, included various biblical figures, *Buddha, *Zoroaster, and *Jesus. He himself was the final one.

The Manichaean 'church' was divided into the 'elect' (or 'righteous') and 'auditors' ('hearers'). The burden of Manichaean ethics, to do nothing to impede the reassembly of particles of light, was on the elect. According to Augustine, they submitted to 'three seals': on the mouth, hands, and sexual organs. The first meant abstaining from wine and meat: the elect had to eat only vegetable products (melons and fruit juice being highly prized). The second meant not harming plants or animals, and the third, renouncing all sexual relations. Obviously the elect, not even able to harvest their own vegetables, could only survive with the support of the auditors. These could apparently lead quite unrestricted lives. They were responsible for the

Church's considerable wealth, evidenced for example in the sumptuousness of many Manichaean manuscripts. The calendar contained one major festival, the Bema feast on the anniversary of Mani's 'passion'. Fasting was enjoined on two days each week, plus a whole month before the Bema feast.

S. N. C. Lieu, *Manichaeism in the Later Roman Empire and Medieval China* (1985); M. Tardieu, *Le Manichéisme* (1981); G. Widengren, *Mani and Manichaeism* (1965).

Māṇik(k)avācakar ('the ruby-worded saint', 8th or 9th cent.). Tamil poet and holy man, a *Saivite devotee, one of the *Nāyaṇmārs. At one time he was a chief minister at the Pandyan court of Mathurai. Repelled by the impersonality of Buddhism, he took up residence at the temple of *Naṭarāja in Chidambaram, and became one of the greatest of the poets of devotion to *Śiva. His most celebrated work, *Tiruvācakam* (Sacred Utterances, tr. G. V. Pope, 1903, 1970; R. Navaratnam, 1963), is included in *Tirumuṟai*, a virtual *'canon' of *Tamil Śaivism. Śiva is the one who has gone to every length to find and rescue even the gods who 'drank the poison in order to save them: how much more do I need your mercy expressed in love?' In response, 'I will clasp your holy feet and call on your name; I will melt like wax in the flame, crying out without ceasing, "My beloved Father". . . . In joyful bliss I will come into the communion of your saints, and I will look up and hear you say from your lips of great beauty, "Fear not".'

G. E. Yocum, *Hymns to the Dancing Śiva* . . . (1982).

Maniple. A Christian *eucharistic *vestment, worn over the left arm, or carried. The corresponding Orthodox vestment is the *epigonation*.

Manī Siṅgh, Bhāī (d. 1738 CE). Sikh scholar and *martyr. Bhāī Manī Siṅgh was born in Karbovāl village, District Paṭiālā, *Pañjāb. Manī visited Gurū *Gobind Siṅgh, remained with him, and was later initiated by him. He remained celibate, devoting his life to the Gurū's service. In Dec. 1704, Manī Siṅgh left *Anandpur with the Gurū's wives, Sāhib *Kaur and Sundarī, accompanying them first to Delhi and then to *Damdamā Sāhib. He wrote the verses of the *Ādi Granth at Gobind Siṅgh's dictation and accompanied him to *Nandeṛ.

After the death of Gurū Gobind Siṅgh, Manī Siṅgh remained as *granthī in *Amritsar. By casting lots, he prevented fighting between the rival Sikh factions of the Tat *Khālsā and the Bandeīs, the followers of *Bandā Siṅgh. He was a learned exponent of the Ādi Granth, and to him are attributed *Gyān Ratanāvalī*, a *janam-sākhī, and *Bhagat Ratanāvalī*, a list of famous Sikhs up to the time of Gurū *Hargobind. These two works were probably based respectively on Vār I and Var XI of Bhāī *Gurdās. In 1734 he compiled the *Dasam Granth* from the writings of Gobind Siṅgh and his court poets. He also prepared a revision of the Ādi Granth in which the *hymns of each contributor were grouped together, rather than being divided between the *rāgs, but this was not approved.

In 1738, Manī Siṅgh obtained permission from the Governor of Lahore, Zakariā Khān, for a *Divālī celebration in the *Harimandir on condition that he paid a large sum. This he was unable to pay from the anticipated offerings, as the Sikhs were prevented from coming. Consequently, as he refused the option of accepting Islam, he was tortured to death and cremated in Lahore.

Mañjī (Pañjābī, 'string bed'). 1. Sikh area of jurisdiction. Gurū *Amar Dās designated twenty-two mañjīs, each of which was later assigned to a *masand who gave spiritual instruction seated on a mañjī and collected contributions on the Gurū's behalf.

2. The small 'bed' on which the Ādi Granth is installed in the *gurdwārā is called the Mañjī Sāhib.

Manjushri Institute. Religious and educational foundation established at Conishead Priory in Britain in 1976 by students of the *Geluk Tibetan Buddhist tradition. Housing a small community of monks, nuns, and laypeople, the Foundation, with its headquarters at a monastery in Nepal, has for its primary purpose the preservation and dissemination of teaching according to the lineage transmitted through Lama Thubten Yeshe (1935–84).

Mañjuśrī (Jap., Monju, Tib., 'Jam.pa'i.dbyangs). A great *bodhisattva of the *Mahāyāna tradition of Buddhism closely associated with learning, knowledge, and transcendental wisdom (*prajñā). His origins are obscure, but he figures in the *Lotus Sūtra* and many later Mahāyāna *sūtras. Legend associates him with the *Perfection of Wisdom (Prajñāpāramitā) treatises which reveal the profound truth of the emptiness (*śūnyatā) of all phenomena. Mañjuśrī is prominent in Buddhist *Tantra and is frequently invoked in ritual and depicted in mystic diagrams and *maṇḍalas. In iconography he is portrayed with the sword of wisdom in his right hand and a book to his left-hand side. In Tibet, great teachers are often regarded as incarnations of Mañjuśrī, e.g. *Tsong Khapa. He also appears in angry form, and as a *yidam of that sort, is especially important in *Gelugpa.

In Tibet traditions, Mañjuśrī is the chosen subject of invocation in morning *pūjās of many monasteries; the text for this worship is taken from the *Ārya Mañjuśrī nāma saṅgīti* (Reciting the names of Noble Mañjuśrī) which identifies him as an emanation of Buddha *Akṣobhya, who often appears above his head. His most common iconographic representation is seated, *'lotus position' (*padmāsana), on a lotus-moon throne carrying the Prajñāpāramitā scriptures in his left hand; his raised right hand holds the sword of discriminating awareness, ready to strike down ignorance. Mañjuśrī's name means Gentle Holy One, yet he has a terrifyingly wrathful form as the bull-headed Yamāntaka (Slayer of Death), who as Vajrabhairava has been chief protector of the *Geluk since his *sādhana (ritual practice) was institutionalized by Tsong Khapa. Vajrabhairava—the most common form of Yamāntaka—is blue-black in colour with eight wrathful heads surmounted by a ninth, peacefully smiling Mañjuśrī. That Mañjuśrī as the wisdom-overcoming-death should be wrathful is understandable by the nature of the task, but that a certain amount of wrathfulness is necessary in simply dealing with one's own ignorance is also suggested by the symbolism of the sword in his peaceful aspect. Mañjuśrī is not known to have been iconographically represented before the 5th cent. CE, and he does not figure in the Prajñāpāramitā literature which he holds. He was elevated to his present position by later *sūtras such as the *Lotus*, *Śūraṅgamasamādhi*, *Vimalakīrti*, and *Gaṇḍavyūha*. Mañjuśrī is sometimes referred to as Mañjughoṣa (Gentle Voice) or Vāgīśvara (Lord of Speech), the latter also being a title of *Brahmā whose concerns include wisdom and study; on the strength of this a link has been suggested between the two deities.

R. Birnbaum, *Studies on the Mysteries of Mañjuśrī* (1983).

Manmukh (Pañjābī, 'person guided by inclination'). According to Sikhs, a self-willed, perverse individual who, in contrast to the *gurmukh, is controlled by the impulses of *man, rather than by the dictates of the *Gurū. According to the *Ādi Granth, the manmukh is ignorant of the Name of God (*Nām), is engrossed in worldly desires, and suffers the penalties of sin. Involved in *māyā, the manmukh cannot achieve union with God. See also FIVE EVIL PASSIONS; HAUMAI.

Manna. Food from *heaven described in the Jewish book of *Exodus. During the period of wandering in the wilderness after the exodus from Egypt, the Israelites were fed on manna (16. 26–36). Differing suggestions have been made as to the exact nature of this substance, the most probable being that it is the secretion of insects on tamarisk trees which has a sweet taste. In the *aggadah, manna was ground by the *angels in heaven (*Tanḥ.B.*, *Ex.* 67), and receiving it daily encouraged the Israelites to turn their hearts to God (*B.Yoma* 76a).

Mannheimer, Isaac Noah (1793–1865). Rabbi and author of a *Reform Jewish *liturgy. Mannheimer served as leader of Reform Jewish communities in Copenhagen, Berlin, Leipzig, and Vienna. He was a renowned preacher, and followed a moderate form of liturgy. In contrast to the move of some congregations to other languages, his prayers continued to be in Hebrew, the prayer for *Zion was retained, and no organ music was permitted. His books include a German tr. of the *prayer book. He also worked for Jewish civil liberties, and, as an elected member of the Reichstag, he succeeded in abolishing the 'Jews' Tax'. For him, the 'messianic dogma' meant national recovery, and he did not believe that this would involve the restoration of the Temple and 'its bloody sacrificial ritual'. Despite his moderation and efforts on behalf of the entire community, he was bitterly attacked by the *Orthodox.

Manning, Henry Edward (1808–92). Roman Catholic *cardinal. Initially an Anglican and *archdeacon of Chichester, he became attracted to the *Oxford Movement and wrote Tract 78 of *Tracts for the Times*. Following the Gorham Judgement in 1851, he became a convert to Roman Catholicism, and (his wife having died in 1837) he was ordained priest. He founded the Oblates of St Charles Borromeo, and became archbishop of Westminster in 1865. He was *ultramontane in his sympathies and a strong defender of papal *infallibility. In 1889, he mediated successfully in a dock strike, and did much through that action to establish a more sympathetic attitude to Roman Catholicism in the country at large. On his deathbed, he entrusted to Cardinal Vaughan his wife's hand-written prayer book, saying, 'All the good I may have done, all the good I may have been, I owe to her'; but he did not waver on the necessity for clergy celibacy. He was buried in Kensal Green cemetery, but was reburied in Westminster Cathedral which he had helped to found.

V. A. McClelland, *Cardinal Manning* . . . (1962); D. Newsome, *The Convert Cardinals*.

Manseren and Koreri. Millennial *cargo cults in N. Irian Jaya. These derive from the myth of Manseren. In a typical version, an ugly culture hero, Manamakerei, secured a wife and son by magical means, called himself Manseren Manggundi ('the Lord himself') and created the local peoples. They rebelled against him so he departed westwards but will return to begin a golden age or Koreri ('we replace our old skins by new ones'). Since the arrival of Dutch missionaries in 1855, there have been scores of Konoors ('prophets') announcing the Koreri so that people abandoned ordinary customs and work, and engaged in ritual dances to hasten the arrival of Manseren, sometimes assimilated to *Jesus. As one example, there was Angganita, a woman in the Schouten Islands, who had visions and trances in 1939, renamed local places with biblical names, and called herself Queen of Judea; she was imprisoned by the Japanese and was probably executed with other cult leaders in 1942.

Mansukh (abrogation): see NASKH.

Man-ta-lao. Chin. for *maṇḍala.

Manthra (sacred chant): see MAGI.

Manthran (composer of sacred chants): see MAGI.

Mantra (Skt., 'instrument of thought'; Chin., *chou*; Jap., *ju*; Korean *chu*). A verse, syllable, or series of syllables believed to be of divine origin, used in a ritual or meditative context in Indian religions. Mantras are used for the propitiation of the gods, the attainment of power (*siddha), and identification with a deity or the absolute, which leads to liberation from *saṃsāra. First appearing in the *Vedic *Saṃhitās (2nd millennium BCE), mantras take on a central role in sectarian Hinduism, and Buddhist and Hindu *Tantrism, especially in the Buddhist Mantrayāna school (7th/8th cents. CE).

There are three kinds of mantra: linguistically meaningful, such as namaḥ śivāya, 'homage to Śiva'; linguistically meaningless, the *bīja or 'seed' mantras, such as oṃ aḥ huṃ; and combined, such as the Buddhist *oṃ mani padme huṃ, 'om jewel in the lotus huṃ'. Bījas have esoteric significance, and are often the compacted forms of the names of gods or texts. For example, the bīja *praṃ* is said to be the essence of the voluminous *Aṣṭasāhasrikā Prajñāpāramitā*; or *kriṃ* is the essence of *Kṛṣṇa.

There is an underlying assumption in Tantrism of the *Mīmāṃsaka (see PŪRVA-MĪMĀṂSĀ) idea that sound (*śabda) is eternal and the sound of a word is part of its nature. Thus there is no distinction between bīja and *devatā, between sound and object. Tantrism also accepts the idea of phonic evolution, that the cosmos evolves from the highest sound (para*vāc) through levels of subtle sound (*paśyanti* and *madhyama*) to gross sound (*vaikhari*); thus mantras are expressions of, and derive their power from, absolute sound, the source of all creation. By repeating a mantra the vibrational frequency of the *sādhaka's consciousness is transformed to that of the deity. Through concentration on the mantra or *dhāraṇī his consciousness takes on the form of the mantra which corresponds to the form of the deity; thus the sādhaka becomes the deity. Mantra repetition (*japa) leads to transcendent experience through the destruction of language.

Mantras, however, are only endowed with transformative power if given in initiation (*dīkṣa) from the mouth of a *guru. It is not so much correct pronunciation, but rather the power with which the mantra is endowed that gives it transforming capability. Through continued repetition, the sādhaka realizes the identity of mantra, devatā, guru, and himself. In Tantric *pūjā, mantras are connected with the divinization of the sādhaka through *bhūtaśuddhi and *nyāsa. Buddhist Tantra (*Vajrayāna) emphasizes the purity of body, speech, and mind through *mudrā, mantra, and *maṇḍala. See also manthra under MAGI. See Index, Mantra.

Mantrayāna (Skt., 'path of mantra'). A term used synonymously with *Vajrayāna or *Tantric Buddhism, but which perhaps misleadingly suggests that incantation is the fundamental Tantric practice; in fact, practices of body (*yoga) and practices of mind (*visualization) are equally as important as practices of speech (*mantra), although in some early forms of Vajrayāna, mantra may well have been the dominant practice.

Mantra Yoga. The practice of *mantra repetition (*japa) as a means of liberation (*mokṣa), especially in *Tantrism. By this, the *sādhaka's consciousness is transformed from the level of gross sound (*vaikhari*) through levels of subtle sound (*madhyama* and *paśyanti*) to the absolute, the unmanifest origin of sound (Śabdabrahman or Nādabrahman). This process takes place within the body. Prāṇāyāma and the *yoni bandha āsama* (covering the nostrils, eyes, and ears with the hands) block the outer senses and consciousness enters the suṣumṇā *nāḍī, conceived as raising the *Kuṇḍalinī. Subtle sound is heard by an inner ear which pulls the consciousness up to its source through the various levels, to merge with the Śabdabrahman.

Manu. Hindu lawgiver to whom is attributed **Manusmṛti* (The Laws of Manu). If historical, he may have been of the *Kṣatriya *varṇa, and was probably the compiler of legal traditions antecedent to him. The name Manu may have been given to the anonymous compiler(s) in order to give the collection the sanctity and authority of the mythological personage Manu Svāyaṁbhuva. If the *Manusmṛti* is a metrical recasting of a *dharmasūtra of the Mānava *brahmans, the hypothetical compiler may have deliberately situated his compilation in the tradition of the Mānavas in order to give it the authority of the Vedic Manu.

Manu (Skt., √*man*, 'think'). In Hindu mythology, a semi-divine patriarch who is progenitor of humanity and ruler of the earth. Each Manu rules over an aeon, or *manvantara*, each of which is shorter than the preceding. Accounts of the number and length of *manvantaras* vary greatly, but the Manus are generally numbered fourteen (the last six being probably a later addition to the list), perhaps a dynasty of *ṛṣi kings. They are (i) Svāyaṁbhuva, or Manu the lawgiver; (ii) Svārochiṣa; (iii) Uttama (or Āuttami); (iv) Tāmasa; (v) Rāivata; (vi) Cākṣuṣa; (vii) Vāivasvata, the Manu of the present age; (viii) Sāvarṇa (or Sāvarṇī); (ix) Dakṣa-Sāvarṇa; (x) Brahmā-Sāvarṇa; (xi) Dharma-Sāvarṇa; (xii) Rudra-Sāvarṇa; (xiii) Rāuchya; and (xiv) Bhāutya.

Manual of Discipline: see DEAD SEA SCROLLS.

Manusmṛti (Skt.). The Laws of Manu, a Hindu *dharmaśāstra attributed to the mythical lawgiver *Manu; also known as *Mānava-dharmaśāstra* or *Manu-saṃhitā*. *Manusmṛti* is the most authoritative of Sanskrit legal texts. Its social, moral, and ethical precepts, and its ceremonial rules, are considered binding on Hindus, although apparent contradictions in the text sometimes make literal interpretation difficult for the orthodox Hindu. *Manusmṛti* consists of 2,685 śloka verses divided into twelve books. It describes: creation; the source of law; *varṇāśramadharma; the role of women in society; dietary obligations; political maxims and the *dharma of kings; civil, criminal, and domestic law;

the origins of *caste and caste-mixing; the nature of good and evil; expiation for sins, especially sins against caste; and the doctrine of *karma and rebirth. *Manusmṛti* is chiefly devoted to caste ideology. The institution of caste (*varṇa) is given divine sanction, and the supremacy of the *brahman caste is maintained. Although having the authority of *smṛti, this authority is rejected by some lower-caste Hindus who regard the *Laws of Manu* as brahman propaganda. *Manusmṛti* may be a metrical recasting of an earlier *dharmasūtra, perhaps that of the Mānava brahmans, one of the schools of the *Black *Yajur Veda*. The present compilation is no older than 100–300 CE.

G. Bühler (tr.), *The Laws of Manu* (1866, 1967); P. V. Kane, *History of Dharmaśāstra* (1930–46); W. D. O'Flaherty (1992).

Mao-shan (religious movement): see TAOISM.

Mao Tzu-yuan (developer of school of Buddhism): see PAI-LIEN-TSUNG.

Mappō (Jap.; Chin., *mo-fa*, 'last *dharma'). In Buddhism, especially *Pure Land, the period of decadence and decline at the end of a time-cycle. According to Tao-ch'o, 2nd patriarch (562–645 CE), the year 549 was 1,500 years after the *Buddha's death and marked the beginning of mappo-ji, the period of 'latter-day dharma' predicted in the *Lotus Sūtra*, when no one can achieve enlightenment by their own effort, but must rely on Amitābha/ *Amida. It is the third of three periods after the Buddha's death, for which see SHŌZŌMATSU.

Maqām (unintentioned but stable states of emotion, etc.): see ḤĀL.

Māra. A Hindu god of pestilence and mortal disease, lord of the *kāma-dhātu: it is the attraction of sensual pleasure which makes humans reckless in what they do. Māra is better known in Buddhism, where he is the opponent of the *Buddha. His attempts to terrify or seduce the Buddha ended in futility. He is the lord of the sixth heaven in the kāma*loka, and is often represented with 100 arms, riding an elephant. He is also known as Namuci, the tempter. According to the Buddha, 'I reckon that there is no power so hard to subdue as the power of Māra' (*Digha Nikāya* 3. 77). A collection of stories about Māra is in the *Māra-Saṃyutta* of *Saṃyutta Nikāya.

J. W. Boyd, *Satan and Māra* ... (1975); T. O. Ling, *Buddhism and the Mythology of Evil* (1962).

Marabout (Arab., *murābit*). Name given (especially in N. Africa) to holy Muslims, or to their descendants. The acquisition of holiness may be by any of many different paths—i.e. there is no formal school, nor restricted process of beatification.

Maraṇa. Death in Buddhism, not of the bodily aggregation, which is *cuti*, but of all phenomena as they rise into appearance and pass away. Cf. MĀRA.

Maranant'a or **Mālānanda.** A Serindian Buddhist missionary to Paekche (Korea). Maranant'a travelled from Eastern China to Paekche in 384, during the first year of the reign of King Ch'imnyu (384–5); this event is traditionally regarded as the official introduction of Buddhism to the kingdom of Paekche. Through the court's patronage, a *monastery was erected in Hansan (modern Kwangju) during the second year (385) and ten monks were ordained in honour of Maranant'a.

Maranatha. An Aramaic Christian formula in 1 Corinthians 16. 22, probably to be translated 'O Lord, come!' (cf. Revelations 22. 20). It seems to reflect the urgent expectation of the *parousia in the earliest Church.

Maranke, Johane (founder of Christian movement in Africa): see AFRICAN APOSTLES.

Maranke Apostles (independent Christian movement in Africa): see AFRICAN APOSTLES.

Marāṭhī. A language which is a direct descendant of the literary Prākrit language called Mahārāshtrī. The other Prākrit languages are Pāli, Ardha-Māgadhī, Shaurasénī, and Paishācchī.

Marāṭhī became the court and literary language of W. India from about 800–1000 CE onwards. *Bhāvārtha-Dīpikā*, a commentary on the *Bhagavadgītā* by *Jñāneśvar is the earliest celebrated work in Marāṭhī, having been completed in 1290. *Vivekasindhū* of Mukundarāj and *Ratnamālā*, a book on astronomy by Shrīpatī, were composed in Old Marāṭhī a hundred years before Jnāneshva. The Maratha confederacy at its height (at the end of the 18th cent.) covered most of central India.

Marburg, Colloquy of. The meeting of *Protestant leaders in October 1529 at the Castle of Marburg-on-the-Lahn to discuss theological differences. Initiated by Philip of Hesse under political pressure and encouraged by the eirenic ambitions of Martin *Bucer, the Colloquy failed to achieve the unity desired. Fourteen articles were formulated expressing basic agreement on major doctrines, but in the debate concerning the fifteenth article it proved impossible fully to reconcile the divergent eucharistic views of *Luther and *Zwingli. See also REFORMATION.

March of a Million Men (rally in Washington): see ELIJAH MUHAMMAD.

Marcion (d. *c*.160). Founder of a Christian movement which was a rival to *Catholic Christianity in the 2nd and 3rd cents.: he was excommunicated in 144. However, he organized ascetic communities extensively, and at Edessa the name 'Christian' was at one point assumed to mean 'Marcionite'. Many anti-heretical writers, notably *Irenaeus and *Tertullian, attacked him. By the end of the 3rd cent. most Marcionite communities had been absorbed by *Manichaeism.

Notable in his teaching (e.g. in his (lost) *Antitheses*) was the absolute opposition between the Old Testament with its wicked God and the God of Love revealed by Jesus. He therefore rejected the Old Testament, and from the New Testament admitted to his canon only the letters of Paul and an edited version of the gospel of Luke. His orthodox opponents reckoned him among the *gnostics, but his system lacks typical gnostic mythology. Marcion was sympathetically studied by A. von *Harnack who saw him as a kind of ancient *Protestant.

The Marcionite Prologues precede each of the Pauline Epistles in early manuscripts of the *Vulgate.

E. C. Blackman, *Marcion and his Influence* (1948); R. J. Hoffman, *Marcion and the Restitution of Christianity* (1984).

Mardānā (d. *c.*1535 CE). Companion of Gurū *Nānak. Mardānā was a Dom (Dum or Mirāsī), i.e. a musician of low-*caste Muslim background. His closeness to Gurū Nānak is attested by all the *janam-sākhīs and by *Bhāī *Gurdās, although his presence in particular episodes cannot be proven. According to tradition Mardānā played the *rabāb*, a stringed instrument, to accompany Gurū Nānak's spiritual teaching, travelling with him to Indian centres of pilgrimage and to Arabia. One popular *sakhi relates Mardānā's magical transformation into a ram in a country ruled by women and his subsequent restoration to human form by Nānak. According to one tradition he died in Afghanistan; according to another, in *Kartārpur. Three *śaloks of the *Ādi Granth are attributed to Mardānā, one of the five Muslim contributors. His Muslim descendants are still honoured musicians in *gurdwārās. See also BĀLĀ SANDHŪ; ICONOGRAPHY.

Maréchal, J. (neo-Thomist philosopher): see RAHNER, KARL.

Mārga (Skt., 'path'; Pāli, *magga*). In Hinduism and Buddhism, the way or path to release or enlightenment. It thus occurs in *aṣṭangika-mārga, the eightfold path advocated by the *Buddha; *bhakti-, *jñāna-, and *karma-marga in *Bhagavad-gītā* (and elsewhere).

Mari. A Mesopotamian centre of the 3rd millennium BCE. Important documentary finds at Mari have added extensively to our understanding of the organization of early Israelite society, including indications of functionaries resembling *prophets, who may have been the antecedent of the cultic prophets of Israel (though this is doubted by E. Noort, *Untersuchungen zum Gottesbescheid in Mari* . . . (1977).

A. Malamat, *Mari and the Bible* (1980); A. Parrot (ed.), *Mari* (1953).

Maria Legio or **Legio Maria.** The largest independent church with *Roman Catholic origins in Africa. It arose in Kenya from a heavenly visit experienced in 1962 by a Luo farmer and Roman Catholic catechist, Simeon Ondeto. In 1963, he was joined by a 20-year-old Roman Catholic Luo woman, Gaudencia Aoko after an experience of death and resurrection. Called at first 'Legion of Mary', it grew rapidly to over 50,000 members, with several thousands more among Luo migrants in Uganda and Tanzania. *Pentecostal features, *exorcism, and healing by prayer have been added to Roman Catholic rituals, symbols, and hierarchical organization, although it is anti-Catholic. The ethic accepts polygamy but rejects all medicines, *alcohol, tobacco, and dancing. Gaudencia Aoko left it, and the movement has gone into decline.

Maria Lionza. A complex of informally organized spirit-possession cults in Venezuela. Beginning among rural Indians of Yaracuy in the 18th cent., it has expanded in this cent. across Venezuela, especially among the urban poor of all racial origins, and by adding African spirits from immigrant Cubans and Trinidadians, it has come to resemble *Shango, etc. Maria Lionza was a legendary Indian princess in the Sorte mountains of Yaracuy, who is now often assimilated to the Virgin [*Mary] of Coromoto, patroness of Venezuela, honoured with Roman Catholic rites and besought by practising Roman Catholics. She is now surrounded by a pantheon of lesser spirits who may include Simon Bolivar, Pope *John XXIII, Hitler, and astral and occult powers. These spirits speak through mediums, mostly women, during a possession trance, and after magical rites have been strictly observed at meetings in private houses. Healing incorporates traditional curing rituals and magical 'operations'. There is a pilgrimage centre in the Sorte mountains and the movement is still developing many new forms.

Mariology. The study of the Blessed Virgin *Mary in Christianity. It is based on New Testament texts having reference to Mary (Matthew 1. 16–2. 23; 12. 46 ff.; 13. 55; Mark 3. 31–5; 6. 3; Luke 1. 26–2. 52; 8. 19–21; 11. 27 f.; John 1. 14; 2. 1–12; 19. 25–7; Acts 1. 14; Romans 1. 3; Galatians 4. 4) and embraces (at least for *Roman Catholics) defined dogmas which have at best ambiguous status in scripture: her perpetual virginity, the *immaculate conception and her *assumption into heaven. In *Vatican II, *The Dogmatic Constitution on the Church*, ch. 8, offers a summary of the basic constituents of Mariology.

Maritain, Jacques (1882–1973). French neo-Thomist philosopher. After he and his wife Raïssa became Roman Catholics in 1906, he devoted most of his life to studying and writing about the works of St Thomas *Aquinas and their application to life, society, art, and politics. His achievements include his elucidation of the different forms of knowledge (*The Degrees of Knowledge*, 1932; Eng. 1937), outlining a new form of Christian humanism (*True Humanism*, 1936; Eng. 1938) and developing a philosophy of art

(*Art and Scholasticism*, 1920; Eng. 1923). He also helped to foster interest in Christian democracy. Shortly before he died, he exemplified that simplicity which he believed to be at the heart of a good life by becoming a Little Brother (see DE FOUCAULD) in Toulouse.

Maritain believed that the contemporary world, in all its aspects, had fallen into a narrow-mindedness which has produced a deep malaise. This is rooted in a loss of confidence in finding truth in any of the major questions concerning reality, aesthetics, morality, or politics. This in turn goes back to *Descartes and his quest for an absolute foundation for all knowledge which in effect left science and positivism as the only claimants to being able to determine what is the ultimate nature of what is real. In that situation, science deals with what is real and philosophy tidies up the ways we talk about it; metaphysics becomes the endeavour, not to say anything factual about the world, but to describe the actual structure of our thought about the world. In strong contrast, Maritain argued that confusion has arisen because *'knowledge' and 'empirical knowledge' have been regarded as synonyms: empirical knowledge is one way of knowing amongst many others (including perhaps *mysticism); consequently, there is a hierarchy of ways of knowing, each of which arises from, and opens up, a different perspective on what is real. Empirical knowledge deals with whatever presents itself materially; mathematical knowledge deals primarily with quantity, shape, and order; metaphysics builds on these to explore the being of whatever is. These do not have separate subject-matters, but rather examine the same 'world' through different means. Metaphysics is concerned fundamentally with existence, with the fact that things are, not simply with the exploration of what they are. In his view, to predicate 'existence' of something is to say something additional about it—though many philosophers have contested whether existence is a predicate. Nevertheless, on this basis Maritain was able to argue that human beings, as ensouled essences, depend constantly on the creative work of God for their existence, with the 'gap' between humans and God to be closed by grace: 'Grace, while leaving us infinitely distant from pure Act [i.e. God] in the order of being, is still, in the order of spiritual operation and relation to its object, a formal participation in the Divine Nature.' This is 'knowledge by connaturality', and can only be attained by the very act of knowing in this mode:

> As we confront God, there is no way of going beyond knowledge through concepts except by making use, in order to know him, of our very connaturality. . . . What is it that makes us radically connatural with God? It is sanctifying grace, whereby we are made *consortes divinae naturae*. And what makes this flower into the actuality of operation? Charity.

That is why Maritain ended his days as a Little Brother.

D. and I. Gallagher, *The Achievement of Jacques and Raissa Maritain: A Bibliography, 1906–61* (1962).

Māriyamnam (in Tamil, etc.; in Marāthī she is Māri-ai; and there are other forms). A Goddess of folk Hinduism worshipped by the lower *castes in a wide area, from Mahārāṣṭra down to *Tamilnadu. Her name consists of 'mother, goddess' (*ammaṉ, āī) and the doubtful 'killing' (from Skt., *mārī*?). She appears very frequently associated with epidemic diseases like smallpox or cholera, and simple shrines of her are found all over the region. In Mahārāṣṭra, she is more often called 'kaḍak Lakṣmī', 'fierce Lakṣmī' (although the nature of this Goddess is as different from *Lakṣmī as that of *Jyeṣṭhā, the goddess of evil and misfortune). She is envisaged as violent, bloodthirsty, and creating havoc (outbreaks of epidemics), if not properly worshipped. This worship includes animal sacrifice, rites of possession, and sometimes fire-walking. A particular group of devotees, the *pōt-rājs* (a mixed word, from Dravidian, *pōtu*, 'buffalo', and Skt., *rāja*, 'king') perform special rituals. While his female partner, carrying the image of the Goddess on her head and dancing, enters into a state of possession by Māri-āī, the *pōtrāj* draws his own blood in front of her by whipping himself. Some connection with, or interference from, the mythology of *Mahiṣa is possible here.

Mark, St. One of the four *Evangelists. He is traditionally identified with the cousin of *Barnabas who accompanied him and *Paul (Colossians 4. 10; Acts 12–15). According to *Papias he was the 'interpreter' of *Peter in Rome (cf. 1 Peter 5. 13). By the 4th cent. he was credited with founding the church of Alexandria. His relics were removed from there to Venice in the 9th cent. Feast day, 25 Apr.

The Gospel according to Mark is the second book in the New Testament. It contains: the preaching of *John the Baptist (1. 1–8); Jesus' baptism and temptation (1. 8–13); his appearance and career in Galilee (1. 14–5. 43); his journeys in and out of Galilee (6. 1–9. 50); his move to Jerusalem (10), last week there (11–13), death (14–15), and resurrection (16). Most scholars hold that Mark is the earliest of the *Synoptic gospels; his crude Greek, paucity of sayings of Jesus, and theological roughness (e.g. 4. 38) were remedied by the Gospels of Luke and Matthew. His main purpose may have been to insist on the importance of Jesus' suffering and death over and above his reputation as a wonder-worker. There is no reason to discount the traditions linking the gospel with Rome. A date in the 60s is most likely. In the best manuscripts the gospel ends abruptly at 16. 8, perhaps intentionally or perhaps because an original end has been lost.

Markan Apocalypse: see APOCALYPSE.

Mārkaṇḍeya-Purāṇa. A Hindu mythological text in Skt., belonging to the genre of the *purāṇas. It is included in all lists of the eighteen mahā-purāṇas (major purāṇas) and can be regarded as an old representative of that tradition, since it contains material adopted in fairly unaltered form from the *Purāṇa-pañcalakṣaṇa* (an archetype reconstructed by W. Kirfel). The sage Mārkaṇḍeya figures in the frame-story as the narrator, and this explains the title. The bulk of the work deals with ancient Indian cosmography and cosmology, with the structure of the world, and the history of its ancient kings (the descendants of *Manu) during past and future manvantaras. This core may well belong to the 3rd cent. CE. But almost half of the extant text consists of various later additions, among which two are particularly interesting. One is an early work on the *antinomian sage *Dattātreya and his teachings. The second, known generally as the *Devī-māhātmya* (Glorification of the Goddess) or *Caṇḍī, is the classical text for the mythology of the Goddess, and narrates in three sections the myths of *Madhu-Kaiṭabha, *Mahiṣāsura, and Śumbha/Niśumbha. These additions may belong to the 6th or 7th cent. CE. The text does not provide us with any indication of its place of origin, but Mahārāṣṭra (in the widest sense of this term) might have been the provenance of the interpolations.

Tr. F. E. Pargiter (1904).

Marks of perfection, thirty-two (of a great man or Buddha): see DVĀTRIṂŚADVARA-LAKṢANA.

Maronites. *Uniat *Syrian Christian body whose homeland is Lebanon. Maronite scholars trace their origin to a monastery founded by the disciples of a 4th-cent. Syrian *anchorite, called Maro. It seems certain, however, that they became a separate body only in the 7th cent., with their adoption of *Monothelite doctrines and subsequent excommunication in 680. Following the Arab conquest, their monastery on Mount Lebanon was destroyed. They formally united with Rome at the time of the Crusades (1182), and since then have maintained relations with the West In the 19th cent. they suffered severe treatment at the hands of the Turks and *Druzes (some were beatified as martyrs in 1926). Today, although a minority in Lebanon, they outnumber the other communities (*Sunni, *Shīʿa, and Druzes) individually. By tacit agreement in 1934, the president of Lebanon is to be a Maronite; however, all such balances in the Lebanon because unsustainable following the Israeli invasion and internal conflict.

As a Uniat body they have their own liturgy (mostly Syriac) and their own hierarchy of patriarch and ten bishops. Outside Lebanon and Syria there are also churches in Cyprus, Egypt, and N. and S. America.

A. S. Atiya, *History of Eastern Christianity* (1968).

Maror (Heb., 'bitter herb'). The bitter herb the Jews eat at the *Passover festival. According to Exodus 12. 8, the Israelites were commanded to eat maror with unleavened bread (*mazzah) and the Passover offering, and it is one of the *foods displayed and eaten at the *seder table. According to *Mishnah (*Pesaḥim* 2. 5), five plants are permissible.

Mar-pa (Mar-pa Chos kyi blo gros) (*c*.1012–*c*.1098). Tibetan *yogi, who journeyed three times to India and returned with the teachings of *mahāmudrā and *Nāro Chos Drug. He taught *Milarepa, and was the key link in the transmission lineage of *Kagyupa. According to his biography, he was tempestuous in character: he 'reared a family, quarrelled with his colleagues, and preoccupied himself with building and agriculture'. Nevertheless, his demanding teaching produced many pupils, including 'the Four Pillars'.

Nalanda Translation Committee, *The Life of Marpa the Translator* (1982).

Marranos (from Span., 'swine'). Baptized Jews of Spain and Portugal, i.e. *anusim, or forced converts. Jews in Spain were forced to convert to Christianity in 1391 and in Portugal in 1497. These 'new Christians' were always suspected of harbouring their original faith and were renowned for their reluctance to eat pork. Particularly after the introduction of the *Inquisition into Spain in 1481 and into Portugal in 1536, many Marranos fled abroad, although, for economic reasons, the authorities tried to prevent this. Morocco and the Ottoman Empire, with their Muslim rulers, became a natural refuge. Marranos also lived undisturbed in many *Protestant states, particularly in the German cities and, in the 17th cent., in Holland, where Amsterdam became known as 'the Dutch Jerusalem'. In *Roman Catholic countries, their situation was far more precarious, and in most places they had to maintain the semblance of Catholicism. None the less, many Marrano families rose to great prominence in trade and banking, and, with their international connections, could establish large companies. Many became completely *assimilated into the dominant *gentile culture, but even today, groups can be found who have retained various Jewish practices, sometimes without even being aware of their Jewish ancestry.

See also ANTI-SEMITISM; APOSTASY.

A. Farinelli, *Marrano: Storia di un vituperio* (1925).

Marriage and divorce. Marriage is the union between at least two people (in *polygamy it may be more), in which commitment is made and responsibility undertaken. It is recognized and controlled in society, because of its obvious relation to the procreation and nurture of the next generation. Because of the profound consequences of the institution of marriage (yielding experience including, but going far beyond, the pleasure of sexual satisfaction), marriage is a frequent metaphor in religions for union with God. But it is recognized that not all marriages are realized in relation to the goals, however described. Divorce is regarded in general as at least a matter of regret, more often as a matter of defeat and fault. The facilities for divorce therefore differ between religions.

Judaism According to the Hebrew scriptures, marriage is a state instituted by God because 'it is not good that the man should be alone' (Genesis 2. 18). Although various biblical figures (such as *Jacob, *Saul, *David, etc.) had more than one wife, monogamy seems to have been the general rule, and the prophets used marriage as an illustration of God's relationship with Israel. Certain marriages, particularly between close relatives, were forbidden, and marriage between Jew and *idolater was strongly condemned (see EZRA). Although a continuing marriage was much to be desired, divorce was permitted (Deuteronomy 24. 1–4). The *rabbis strongly advocated marriage, arguing, 'He who has no wife is not a proper man' (*B.Yeb.* 62b); it is so important that a man may even sell a *Torah *scroll in order to marry. Having children is also a positive duty, and if a man refuses to produce children, 'it is as if he shed blood, diminished the image of God and made the *Shekhinah depart from Israel' (*Sh.Ar.*, EH 111). The actual marriage ceremony was in two parts, the *kiddushin* or *erusin* (betrothal) and the *nissuin* (marriage proper). In the Middle Ages, the two parts were combined. The ceremony is performed under a *huppah. The bridegroom has previously undertaken the obligations of the *ketubbah (marriage contract) and is led to the bride. *Blessings are recited over wine and the couple drink from the same cup. The bridegroom places a ring on the bride's finger and recites in Hebrew the formula, 'Behold you are consecrated to me with this ring according to the Law of Moses and Israel'. The ketubbah is read out; seven *benedictions over wine are recited; and, in most communities, the bridegroom crushes a glass with his foot. It is a time of great rejoicing, in which, in detail, different communities follow different practices.

Although divorce is a matter of great regret ('If a man divorces his first wife, the altar weeps', *B.Gittin* 90b), it is possible. According to Jewish law, if both husband and wife agree, a husband may give a get ('bill of divorce') to his wife. The role of the *bet din (Jewish religious court) is to decide on the terms of the divorce, and, when one party does not agree, whether the husband can be compelled to give or the wife to receive a get. Both husband and wife can demand a divorce if the spouse has a physical defect, such as being 'afflicted with boils or leprosy', or because of unsatisfactory conduct. It is, however, in a post-ghetto society notoriously difficult for the community to compel a husband to give a divorce, and if he refuses, the wife is tied; she cannot marry again, and any subsequent children will be *mamzerim. There is provision, however, under Jewish law for a man to take another wife if the woman refuses to accept the get.

Despite modifications of the law through the centuries, basic problems remain: since the husband is the one who must give the get, he must, necessarily, be found; otherwise, the wife remains *agunah ('tied woman') and cannot remarry. Again, rabbis cannot compel husbands to comply, outside Israel; and the wife remains agunah. In *Conservative Judaism, a *takkanah (1953) allows a clause to be inserted in the ketubbah whereby both parties agree to abide by a decision of the bet din if there is conflict. Reform Judaism has dropped the practice of the get. The law of divorce is covered in *B.Gittin*.

P. Elman, *Jewish Marriage* (1967); M. Lamm, *The Jewish Way in Love and Marriage* (1980).

Christianity Marriage, in the words of the **Book of Common Prayer*, 'is an honourable estate, instituted of God in the time of man's innocency [Genesis 1 and 2], signifying unto us the mystical union that is betwixt Christ and his Church [Ephesians 5. 21 ff.]; which holy estate Christ adorned and beautified with his presence, and first miracle that he wrought, at Cana of Galilee [John 2. 1–12]'. The causes of marriage are three (for the procreation of children and their nurture, for a remedy against sin and to avoid fornication, and for the mutual society, help, and comfort that the one ought to have of the other, both in prosperity and adversity). In the *Alternative Service Book*, the order of the three is inverted (and the second expressed positively), a revision which reflects changing understandings of the nature of marriage, and which is also the order of the Eastern *Orthodox. In *Roman Catholic understanding, marriage is a *sacrament which creates a *vinculum*, an unbreakable (metaphysical) bond; it can only be brought to an end by a recognition, on various specific grounds, that it never happened in the first place, i.e. by annulment. Among other Christians, there is a more serious wrestling with the vision of Jesus Christ that marriage recreates the lost and disturbed conditions of the Garden of Eden (see *Marriage, Divorce and the Church*, below): in those circumstances, any setting apart or divorce is to go against the intended conditions of creation. But what if those circumstances do not obtain? Jesus is reported to have allowed the possibility of the ending of a marriage if it had indeed already 'ended' through *porneia* (Matthew 19. 3, 9), though no exception is recorded in Mark 10. 2–12. What is also not recorded is what Jesus would have said to a woman who had been divorced and abandoned by her husband: would he, as a matter of principle, have said that she could never be married again? Uncertainty about the texts has led to a divergence of practice among Christians, some allowing remarriage after divorce (with a previous partner still living) in some circumstances, while others do not. The Eastern Orthodox position, which allows divorce and remarriage in some circumstances, is summarized in *Marriage, Divorce and the Church* (Root Report, 1971), which was followed by a second report, *Marriage and the Church's Task* (1978);

together, they offer a survey of the Christian understanding of marriage, starting from the human fact of marriage.

Islam Marriage in Islam does not have to take place in a specifically religious context. It is thus a civil matter (so far as such distinctions can be drawn in Islam). Nevertheless, it is one of the signs (*ayā) of God: 'Among his signs is this, that he created for you mates from among yourselves, that you may dwell in tranquillity with them . . .' (Qur'ān 30. 31). The word for a pair or a mate is *zawj*, which is a term used for marriage (*al-zawaj*), as also is *nikāḥ*, the marriage contract. There is debate in the schools of *sharīʿa about whether marriage is a compulsory obligation. In general it is for those who can pay the dowry (*mahr*), who can support a wife and children, who is healthy, and who fears that otherwise he will commit fornication (*zinā'); for women it is compulsory for those who have no other means of maintaining themselves and who fear zinā'. For *Muḥammad, marriage is 'half of his religion', because it is a shield against sexual license and builds up the family as the context of *ʿibadat, service of God. Conversely, *celibacy is rejected. Marriage is a contract between the two parties, often under the initiative of fathers or guardians. According to 2. 228, men have a degree or rank (*darajah*) over their wives, and in 4. 38 are 'standing over them' (*qawwumun*, which *may* mean 'standing beside in support'). Marriage with non-Muslims, who might be suspected of *shirk, is forbidden, but Muslim men are allowed to marry women who belong to *ahl al-Kitāb (the people of the Book). The mahr is given by the groom to the bride, and it remains hers even in the event of a divorce (half of it if the marriage is dissolved before consummation). The amount of mahr is not stipulated in sharīʿa. Polygamy (up to four wives) is allowed in Qur'ān 4. 3, provided they can be treated equitably (some believe that this condition can never be attained, and that in practice monogamy is required); Muḥammad himself married eleven wives. Divorce (*ṭalāq*, 'to set an animal free') is permitted, but 'of all things that are permitted, divorce is the most hated by God'. A statement of divorce should be followed by a waiting period (*'idda*) of three menstrual cycles, to ensure that no child has been conceived, and to offer the chance of reconciliation. *Talāq ḥasan* requires three successive pronouncements of divorce to be made, during three consecutive periods of purity (*ṭuhur*); it is not permissible to pronounce the three repudiations all at one time. Divorce may be initiated by the wife (*khulʿ*); if there is a cause (lying in the behaviour of the husband), provision and her dowry must be allocated to her, but if she does so without identifiable cause, she must abandon the dowry. For the early (and disputed) temporary marriage, see MUTʿA.

M. A. Rauf, *The Islamic View of Women and the Family* (1977).

Hinduism Marriage is an expected norm for all Hindus except those who become renouncers and adopt a community or *ascetic life. For a woman, the ritual of marriage (*vivāha*) is in itself a route to *mokṣa. Marriages are generally a matter of arrangement between families, attempting to ensure compatibility of (obviously) *caste, but also of such things as education and wealth. A woman makes a complete transition to the family of her new husband and is expected to show some signs of grief at the change from her old family and friends. The ritual is one of the most important of the *saṃskāras (rites of passage), and involves great expense, with gifts passing between the families. The details of the ritual differ from place to place, but some elements are constant. Although celebrations may last for several days, the actual ceremony is simple. It begins with the formal giving away, by the father, of the bride—the greatest gift a man can give, for which much good *karma is received in return. Songs of blessing are then sung, followed by oblations to the sacred fire, *homa, before which the couple are sitting. They then take seven steps (*satapadi*) round the fire, with the groom leading the bride. If evening has fallen by this time, the couple will go out to see the star Dhruva (the Pole Star), and the bride vows to be as constant as that star. The festivities then continue.

According to classic theory (e.g. *Arthaśastra), a marriage brought into being by the proper rituals cannot be dissolved. It follows that a widow should not remarry—and in a case of absolute devotion, a widow should follow her late husband into death (*satī). Nevertheless, before death mokṣa (release) is possible on various grounds (the exact grounds are debated). Defects in bride or groom (especially lack of virginity and absence of virility) are usually accepted as sufficient grounds, as may be prolonged absence, or desertion, or cruelty. The Hindu Marriage Act, 1955, allows divorce, but for traditional Hindus it is still, in general, unacceptable.

Buddhism In the long process which leads eventually to enlightenment, the Buddha espoused the wisdom of addressing teaching and practice to the levels attained by different people (*upāya-kauśalya). In this perspective, marriage properly undertaken is a legitimate step, even though sexuality will be transcended in due course. In the *Sigālovāda Sutta*, the Buddha laid out the responsibilities of lay Buddhists which embrace the duties involved in a householder's life. Paramount (and one of the Five Precepts, *śīla) is the avoidance of sexual impropriety. If a marriage fails, there may be a contribution of *karma to the failure, but in any case the dismantling of the marriage must attempt to avoid hurt to either of those involved.

Sikhism The 1909 Anand Marriage Act legalized the Sikhs' Anand Karaj ceremony, following pressure from reformers—though many weddings are still influenced by Hindu practice. Although, according to *Rahat Maryādā, *caste is immaterial, marriages are usually arranged within caste. Astrological considerations should not decide the date. There is no formal engagement: the girl's parents may visit the boy's, and, after *Ardās, present a *kirpān*, *kaṛā* (see FIVE KS), *praśād*, and sweetmeats. Often betrothal (Pañjābī, *maṅgaṇī*, *kūrmāī*) is more elaborate, with the bestowal of more gifts. Subsequently a *chunni* (scarf) and other gifts are presented to the bride-to-be. The marriage ceremony takes place on a mutually convenient day, and (outside India) usually occurs after the civil marriage on a weekend morning after *Āsā kī Vār. The bridegroom, his family, and friends come to the *gurdwārā as guests of the bride's family who make the arrangements. In front of the congregation, the couple sit before the *Ādi Granth, the bride to the groom's left. She generally wears red and his turban is often pink. *Ardās is said. The officiant (any approved Sikh) explains the ceremony's significance, reminding them to show love and loyalty. Bride and groom bow in assent to the Ādi Granth. A pink scarf (*pallā*) now links them. Four times the bride follows the groom clockwise around the Ādi Granth. Before each circumambulation, one stanza of the *Lāvān is read and the *rāgīs sing it as the couple walk around. They are garlanded and given money. The service concludes with six verses of *Anand *Sāhib, the Ardās, and distribution of *kaṛāh praśād. A reception follows. The bride accompanies her husband to his parents' home, often briefly returning after a night to her parents before rejoining him. This custom is called *muklāvā*. *Nāmdhārīs practise a different and simpler form of marriage.

Chinese The married state, one of the five relationships, is essential in this life and afterlife for the purposes of uniting families and assuring descendants. Traditionally, marriage is arranged by a matchmaker and based on the eight character horoscopes. While keeping her family's surname, the wife is bodily, spiritually, ritually, and juridically transferred to the husband's family, subordinate first to the husband then to the eldest son, and remains in that family after death. By marriage, a husband assures his place in the ritual continuity of generations by assuming responsibility for his wife. Imagined marriages exist between divine figures such as 'Niu Kua and Fu Hsi', expressed in the rainbow nuptials of nature, or between the Weaving Maid and Herd Boy over their bridge of magpies; between divine and human figures, as in the *shaman visits to the 'clouds and rain' of Mount Wu, and in spirit marriages; or between human and animal figures such as in fox–woman marriages.

See Index, Marriage, divorce.

Marsiglio (Marsilius) of Padua (*c*.1275–1342). Political philosopher who called in question the primacy of Church over State in the political order. His *Defensor Pacis* (1324) was held to be antipapal and led to his expulsion from Paris. He argued that the State, not the Church, is the unifying bond in society, and that the task of a ruler is to maintain peace. The Church has the higher goal or end, but this cannot be identified with goals in this life. The State must serve the purpose of supporting fulfilment and the good life, but it reigns supreme in resisting evil and threats to society. Both papacy and priesthood are subordinate, and the role of priests is confined to teaching and sacraments. It is people who are the source of political power, since it is they who constitute a State. The papacy, in contrast, has introduced strife by its attempts to control the temporal and the secular; its power was, in any case, derived from rulers ordained by God (Romans 13). For these reasons, he is seen as a forerunner of *Reformation political thought.

A. Gerwith, *Marsilius of Padua: The Defender of Rome* (1951, 1956).

Mārtāṇḍa (misshapen foetus who is shaped as the sun): see ĀDITYAS.

Martel, Charles: see UMAYYADS.

Martha, St. The sister of Mary and Lazarus who according to Luke 10. 38–42 received, and cooked a meal for, Jesus in her house. She is commonly regarded as typifying the active Christian life as contrasted with Mary, who typifies the contemplative. In John 11 she affirms confidence that God will grant to Jesus whatever he asks. Feast day in E., 4 June; in W., 29 July.

Mar Thoma Church. Christian body of *c*.300,000 in Kerala, S. India. It originated from a party of *Syrian Orthodox who came under the influence of the *CMS in the mid-19th cent. and were known as 'Reformed Jacobites'. Their leader Matthew Mar Athanasius was excommunicated in 1875 and a separate 'Mar Thomite' hierarchy was the result. The Mar Thomites maintain the liturgical externals of a Syrian church, but are broadly Protestant in doctrine and have links with the Church of S. India. See also MALABAR.

Martial arts in Japan. They were formerly called *bugei* (martial arts) or *bujutsu* (martial skills), but the word *budō* (martial ways) is commonly used today, though they are not identical in details. The budō, which evolved from bugei, aim at the self-realization of aspirants through discipline and training. To all intents and purposes, the bugei were for mastering the skills and forms of fighting, with or without weapons, in actual combat. The *dō* (way) type of martial arts had become a means of spiritual training based on religio-philosophical ideas which are, more or less, in affinity with the goal of other dō oriented activities such as *chadō (tea ceremony) and kadō (flower discipline, see IKEBANA).

There is no standard list of martial arts. An expert enumerates thirty-four *bugei*, whereas the traditional list counts eighteen (*bugei juhappan*, the eighteen martial arts). In the Tokugawa period warriors had to master sword-play, spear, archery, horsemanship, *jujutsu* (proto-judō), and firearms, together with academic subjects.

Even though there were no standard warrior codes stipulated by the state, the unwritten principles dictated the warriors' life. Buddhism, Taoism, and Confucianism provided the basic rationale by which warriors resolved the question of death as well as improved their skill in handling weapons. The principle, '*Bushido means the determined will to die' (*Hagakure*), was fundamental to every generation of warriors, and in this regard, the *Zen doctrine of No-mind (*mushin*) or No-thought (*munen*) had an important role to play in martial arts, summarizing indifference to, or transcendence of, the events or accidents of life, including death.

D. F. Draeger, *Classical Bujutsu* (1973), *Classical Budo* (1974), and *Modern Bujutsu and Budo* (1974).

Martyr (Gk., *martus*, 'witness'). One who suffers death on behalf of his or her faith, often for refusing to renounce it. See Index, Martyrs.

Judaism See KIDDUSH HA-SHEM.

Christianity The Gk. word was only gradually restricted to those whose witness to their faith had led to their death in persecutions. From the 2nd cent. martyrs were specially honoured in churches, and the anniversaries of their deaths, as (heavenly) 'birthdays', were kept as feasts. They were venerated as intercessors in heaven, and their relics sought after. Accounts ('Acts') of martyrdom form an important class of *hagiography (see H. Musurillo (ed.), *The Acts of the Christian Martyrs*, 1972). A few such early accounts consist of eyewitness reports, and fewer still of court records; the rest are largely, or wholly, imaginative. Official lists of martyrs (martyrologies) began as calendars listing the martyrs and their place of martyrdom. The local Roman calendar dates from 354. Later 'historical' martyrologies add stories of varying value. In the Roman liturgy martyrs are ranked above other *saints, and (until 1969) their relics had to be contained in every consecrated altar.

T. Baumeister, *Die Anfänge der Theologie des Martyriums* (1980); D. W. Riddle, *The Martyrs: A Study in Social Control* (1931).

Islam See SHAHĪD.

Sikhism Many Sikhs have died for their faith, particularly under the Mughal emperor, Auraṅgzeb, and during the conflicts of the 18th cent. During the 20th cent., Sikhs have died at British hands and in claiming greater freedom from the Indian government. Martyrs (Pañjābī, Hindī *śahīd*) are remembered daily in *Ardās, and pictures of martyrdoms are displayed in the *gurdwārās. *Gurūs *Arjan Dev and *Tegh Bahādur were martyred. Other śahīds, who chose torture rather than acceptance of Islam, were Mati Dās, imprisoned with Tegh Bahādur and sawed in half in his presence in Delhi, 1675; Diāl (Dayāl) Dās, boiled to death before Tegh Bahādur's eyes, 1675; Sati Dās, roasted alive in oil-soaked cloth in front of Tegh Bahādur, 1675; the *Sāhibzāde; the 'forty immortals' of *Muktsar; *Bandā *Siṅgh; Tārā Siṅgh, who died fighting in 1725; *Manī Siṅgh; Botā Siṅgh and Garjā Siṅgh, who died fighting; Mahtāb Siṅgh, tortured to death on a wheel in 1745; Tārū Siṅgh, who was scalped and died in 1745; the victims of the Chhotā Ghallūghārā (Lesser Massacre), many of whom were executed in Lahore in June 1746; Subeg Siṅgh, tortured on a wheel with knives, Lahore 1748, and Śāhbāz Siṅgh, his son, similarly tortured; Dīp Siṅgh, who died fighting in 1757, reputedly continuing after his head had been severed until he reached the *Harimandir, *Amritsar; the many victims of the Vadā Ghallūghārā (Great Massacre) of Feb. 1762.

Ma'rūf al-Karkhī (d. 815–16 (AH 200)). A *Sūfī master of the Baghdād school, who emphasized sobriety in life and religion. He emphasized that Sūfī attainment cannot be achieved by effort, but only by God's gift: 'Love is not to be learned from humans, it is a gift of God and comes from his grace.' Ma'rūf was venerated as a saint. His tomb, on the west bank of the Tigris in Baghdad, is still a centre of pilgrimage.

Maruts (etym. uncertain: perhaps *mṛ* + *ut*, 'immortal'; or *mā rud*, 'do not weep'). A collection (*gaṇa*) of *Vedic storm gods, who work in the service of *Rudra, and who are therefore also known as Rudriyas (though in some accounts the Rudriyas are separate and different). They appear in lightning, ride on the wind, and are the bearers of rain. 'They have iron teeth, they go about roaring like lions and drive in chariots of gold' (*Ṛg Veda* 1. 133. 6). Their numbers vary from 21 to 180. They are the allies of *Indra, who is known as the leader of the Maruts, Marutvat.

Marx, Karl (1818–83). German social and political theorist. As a student at Berlin he was attracted to but then later repudiated aspects of *Hegel's thought as mediated through 'the young Hegelians', especially Bruno Bauer and Ludwig *Feuerbach. He advocated a form of humanism and is widely regarded as an important critic of religion, although he himself attached little importance to this aspect of his thought. He criticized (but also adapted) much of Feuerbach's critique of *theism, a critique which he regarded as too narrow in its scope and as too individualistic in its understanding of human nature. Marx was primarily interested in religious life as a symptom of a more general self-estranged and unfulfilled human existence. Humans attempt through religion to have in fantasy what has been denied them in reality. The determinants of religious behaviour are ultimately extra-religious: 'Since the existence of religion is the existence of a defect, the source of this defect must be looked for in the nature of the state itself.' Remedy the conditions which are expressed in them and religions will of themselves wither away. Marx thus extended the Feuerbachian critique of religion into a more general critique of society by extending analogically the idea that God is alienated human nature into a general theory of social alienation: 'As it is in religion, so it is in the rest of society' is a recurring sentence in Marx's writings from the mid-1840s. Finally, Marx defended a sort of historical dialectic which owed much to Hegel, but he repudiated the philosopher's alleged idealism and replaced it with a variety of materialism. According to Marx, history is propelled by the dialectical opposition of material forces, namely the economic conditions of human existence in society. The history of ideas is merely an overlay of the real forces at work in history. The critique of religious ideas is thus subsumed under a more general critique of ideology.

I. Berlin, *Karl Marx* (1948); D. McLellan, *Karl Marx* . . . (1973); J. Siegel, *Marx's Fate* . . . (1993).

Mary, Blessed Virgin. The mother of *Jesus, counted pre-eminent among the *saints. She is prominent in the 'infancy stories' in Matthew 1–2 and especially Luke 1–2. According to both gospels, she conceived Jesus while a virgin (see VIRGIN BIRTH OF CHRIST). She appears in the background during his career (Mark 3. 31; Luke 11. 27–8; John 2. 1–11), then at the foot of the cross (John 19. 25), and with the apostles after Easter (Acts 1. 14).

By the earliest *Church fathers Mary is mentioned rarely and usually in contrast with *Eve. *Mariology (devotion to Mary) probably owed much of its impetus to two currents of early and medieval Christian thought: (i) the predilection for celibacy and virginity as a style of life superior to marriage; and (ii) the removal of Jesus from the human level, particularly in breaking the entail of sin (see ORIGINAL SIN). The first of these was congenial to the tradition of Mary's 'perpetual virginity' (i.e. even after giving birth to Jesus), which was current by the time of *Athanasius, and later to the doctrine of the *immaculate conception, according to which Mary was without stain of original sin from the moment of her being conceived. The second current of thought may be observed in the canonization of the title *Theotokos ('Mother of God') for Mary at the council of *Ephesus (431): this was a title favoured in *Alexandria, where just such a *Christology was developing. Broadly speaking, as Christ became a more austere and distant figure in medieval theology, Mary took his place as the representative of humanity in heaven and the figure to whom popular piety looked. She eventually became known in the W. Church as 'co-redemptress' and 'mediator of all graces', the latter title being popularized by St Alphonsus *Liguori. The doctrine of her bodily *assumption into heaven was first formulated in orthodox circles by Gregory of Tours (d. 594), and was defined as Catholic dogma in 1950.

At the Reformation there was a strong reaction against Marian devotion, partly owing to the rejection of the cult of saints, and partly in keeping with a more positive view of sex and of the married state. Hostility to Mariolatry ('worship of Mary') is still a touchstone of *Protestantism, although signs of moderation can be seen, e.g. in the foundation of the Ecumenical Society of the Blessed Virgin Mary (1967), and in some theology (indebted to psychologists like C. G. *Jung) which expounds the need for a feminine element in God. It is, on the other hand, the contention of some feminists that Mary has been held up by a male-dominated Church as a model of harmless feminine passivity.

In the Roman Catholic Church Marian devotions include the *'little office of *Our Lady', as well as the Saturday mass and office, and the popular *Hail Mary, *rosary, *Angelus, and May and October devotions (some of these being retained by some *Anglicans). Since *Vatican II, however, these practices have been less prominent. Among pilgrimage places associated with Mary are *Lourdes, *Fatima, and Walsingham. In Orthodox worship Marian devotion is expressed in the *Akathistos hymn and the *Theotokia* or short prayers to the Theotokos. The main feasts of Mary are the Assumption (15 Aug.), Nativity (8 Sept.), Annunciation (25 Mar.), Purification (2 Feb.; *Candlemas), and Visitation (2 July; in the RC Church now 31 May).

In Islam, Maryam is the mother of 'Īsā (*Jesus); the name is probably derived from Syriac-Christian usage. Sūra 19 of the *Qur'ān, 'Maryam', relates a version of the *annunciation, followed by an account of Maryam's giving birth, alone, at the foot of a date palm (19. 17–33; cf. 3. 45–51, a slightly different version of the annunciation). The Qur'ān here confirms the virgin birth, and calls Maryam 'chosen and purified' by God (3. 42). But she and her son are only human beings (5. 78), and 'Īsā denies having told the people to worship him and his mother 'as gods' (5. 119). The *ḥadīth relate that Maryam and 'Īsā were preserved from the 'touch of Satan' which affects all children at birth, i.e. were free from sin; further, she is considered one of the four best women of Paradise, along with *Fāṭima, Āsiyā (Pharaoh's wife), and *Khadīja.

See Index, Mary.

R. E. Brown (ed.), *Mary in the New Testament* (1978); H. Graef, *Mary: A History of Doctrine and Devotion* (1963–5); R. Radford Ruether, *Mary: The Feminine Face of the Church* (1979); M. Warner, *Alone of All Her Sex* (1979).

Maryam: see MARY, BLESSED VIRGIN.

Mary Magdalen(e). A follower of Jesus out of whom he cast seven devils, who ministered to him in Galilee (Luke 8. 2). She remained close to the *Cross (Mark 15. 40) with other women (when the male disciples had fled), and she was the first to meet the risen Christ, being charged to proclaim the resurrection to the eleven. For that reason, she was called (first by Hippolytus of Rome, early 3rd cent.) 'the apostle to the apostles'. However, *Gregory I merged Mary Magdalene with two other Marys, the sinner who anointed Jesus (Luke 7. 37) and Mary of Bethany who also anointed him (John 12. 3), thus producing the composite figure of the sexually aberrant penitent. From this, 'Magdalens' became a term for prostitutes who had turned to Christ, and for the Houses which took them in, sometimes as specific religious orders. There is, however, no ground for Gregory's identifications, and they have been abandoned even by the *Roman Catholic Church where they had great emotional importance. Mary Magdalene is now recognized as a pioneering representative of women's ministry, for which there is much evidence in the New Testament, but which was rapidly suppressed by men in the Church until its spasmodic but accumulating recovery in the 20th cent.

S. Haskins, *Mary Magdalen* (1993).

Mar Zutra (Jewish exilarch of 5th cent.): see ZUTRA, MAR.

Masada (site of last Jewish stand at end of First Revolt): see SUICIDE.

Masand (Hindī and *Pañjābī corruption of Persian *masnad-ī-ālā*, lofty throne, title of courtiers). Agent of Sikh *Gurūs. Gurū *Amar Dās divided Sikhs into twenty *mañjīs, and Gurū *Rām Dās continued the system. Gurū *Arjan Dev's projects, notably the construction of the *Harimandīr and tank at *Amritsar, required a central financial reserve. To ensure this he appointed for each of these administrative areas a masand, i.e. steward-cum-missionary to organize the worship of the *sangats and to collect their offerings. The masands were instructed to come annually on *Baisākhī day to present the Sikhs' contributions. The masands appointed were devout, informed men who could instruct the increasing saṅgats. As the number of devotees increased, Gurū *Hargobind appointed more masands.

Unfortunately, the system degenerated as individual masands supported rival claimants to Gurūship, such as *Rām Rāi and *Dhīr Mal; set themselves up as gurus locally, nominating successors; extorted money from poor peasants with whom they traded, instead of forwarding all offerings to the Gurū. Consequently Gurū *Gobind Siṅgh dismissed the masands and in successive *hukamnāmās bade the Sikhs to ignore them and bring their offerings direct to the Gurū.

Mashal (Heb., 'likeness, fable'). Short Jewish moral tale normally with animal characters. Such fables can be found in *midrash and the *Talmud; in the Middle Ages, popular collections were produced by Jewish authors. Many of these fables can be traced to Arab sources. In their earliest form, among the *rabbis, they resemble the *parables of *Jesus, including many of the form, 'To what can the kingdom of God be likened?'

Mashhad or **Meshed.** Capital of the Iranian province of Khurāsān and the most important place of pilgrimage for Persian Shiʿites. It is here that the eighth Imām of the *Ithna ʿAsharīīyya (Twelvers) ʿAlī al-Riḍā b. Mūsa (d. 818 (AH 203)) is buried. Around his tomb grew a large town. Mashhad contains a sacred area, called *Bast, which can only be entered through two gates, and is strictly forbidden to non-Muslims. Strict discipline is maintained there by its own police. The Bast has a *mosque, *madrasas, courts, sanctuaries, etc., and thus forms a town in itself. Mashhad is famous for its large cemeteries, it being the wish of every Shiʿite to be buried near one of the beloved Imāms. Every year thousands of corpses from all over the world are brought to be laid here for a fee that brings revenue to the authorities for the maintenance of the Sanctuary. Mashhad is also a centre of Muslim theological and legal studies, and is rivalled in Iran only by Qum. Recently the town has acquired fame as the birthplace and home town of ʿAlī *Sharīʿatī. For Mashad ʿAlī, see NAJAF, AL-.

Since mashhad means 'a place where one has borne witness', i.e. died as a *martyr, the word may be used of any place where this has occurred. Notable examples are *Karbalā', *Najaf, Kazimain (near Baghdad, with the tombs of the 7th and 9th Imams of the Twelvers, Ithnā ʿAsharīyya, namely Musa al-Kazim and Muḥammad al-Jaurad), and Samarra (10th and 12th, ʿAli al-Hadi and Hasan al-Askari).

Masjid (Muslim place of assembly): see MOSQUE.

Masjid al-Aqsa, al- ('the furthest mosque'). The Muslim *mosque built in the 7th cent. CE, on the Temple Mount in *Jerusalem (al-Quds). It is the mosque associated with the Night Journey (*isrā') and the Ascent (*miʿrāj) of *Muḥammad, based on Qur'ān 17. 1: 'Praise be to him who took his servant on a journey during the night from the sacred mosque to the furthest mosque, whose precincts are blessed.' It is a building distinct from the *Dome of the Rock.

Masjid al-Ḥarām, al-. The *mosque at *Mecca, closely associated with the *Kaʿba and *Zamzam.

Maskilim (proponents of the Haskalah, enlightenment): see HASKALAH.

Maslow, Abraham Harold (1908–70). Psychologist and theorist of human personality. Maslow was educated during the 1930s, when behaviourism was dominant. He began to doubt the wisdom of applying the behavioural study of animals to humans as though this will 'explain' human behaviours. He allowed that there are animal inheritances ('instinctoids'), but that human behaviour in culture and in individual appropriations of culture and inheritance demand a *sui generis* understanding. He insisted that this should be based, not on disease or psychopathology, but on the study of what men and women aspire to and achieve at their best. He proposed 'a hierarchical prepotency of basic needs', goals to which we address ourselves in roughly the same order, with one desire rapidly succeeding another when the first is satisfied: physiological, safety, love, esteem, self-actualization. The self-actualized person exhibits unusual degrees of detachment and self-dependence. S/he also achieves peak-experiences in greater number, which take the individual far beyond the ordinary levels of striving to achieve more proximate goals. He argued that religions derive from founders who have sustained extended peak-experiences: the organization of religions is intended to share those peak-experiences with a wider population, but the routinization which is required soon leads in the opposite direction, not to self-actualizations, but to repression and restrictive dogma.

R. J. Lowry, *A. H. Maslow* . . . (1973).

Masorah. The rules and practices of reading certain books of the Hebrew Bible in Jewish public worship. Among *Ashkenazi Jews, a tradition of cantillated reading of the *Torah and *liturgy developed which was recorded by special accents and marks placed in the texts. These conventions were developed in the 6th–9th cents. CE by scholars known as the masoretes whose aim was to preserve the authentic Hebrew text. They added vowel signs to the individual words, as well as cantillation accents, and indicated where the written form of the word differed from the pronunciation. The accepted text is that determined by Aaron ben Asher of the Tiberias School of Masoretes.

Masoret (tradition): see TRADITION (JUDAISM).

Masowe Apostles (Independent Christian movement in Africa): see AFRICAN APOSTLES.

Mass (Lat. *missa*, from the words *Ite, missa est*, 'Go, you are dismissed' at the end). In the *Roman Catholic Church, and among *Anglo-Catholics, the usual title for the *eucharist. Outside Catholic circles, the word has come to be associated in theological contexts with the doctrine of the eucharistic *sacrifice.

Among special kinds of masses may be noted: the nuptial mass, the wedding mass including the celebration of the marriage and nuptial blessing; votive masses, since 1970 limited to fifteen (e.g. to the Trinity, Holy Spirit, Blessed Sacrament) which may be said, e.g. at the request of donors of a mass offering, when there is no other observance in the calendar; and the *requiem mass.

Parts of the mass may be sung or chanted, in simple (e.g., plainchant) form, or in very elaborate musical settings (as e.g. of Mozart), until, in the 19th cent., they became virtually works for the concert hall (e.g. the Requiems of Verdi, Berlioz, Dvořák).

Massacre of St Bartholomew's Day (massacre of French Calvinists): see HUGUENOTS.

Massekhet (Heb., 'a web' and 'a tractate'). A subdivision of one of the six orders (*sedarim) of the Jewish *Mishnah. Each order of the Mishnah is divided into a number of massekhtot, which, in their turn, are divided into chapters. By convention since the 16th cent. each massekhet has a fixed number of pages. After a person completes the study of a massekhet, it is a custom for him to hold a *siyyum* (celebration).

Mastema. The *devil's name in the Jewish *Book of *Jubilees*. Mastema is portrayed as the chief of the evil spirits and the enemy of righteousness. According to *Jubilees*, it was Mastema rather than God who tested *Abraham and slew the *firstborn in the land of Egypt. In Hosea, 'mastema' means enmity (Hosea 9. 7), and the *Book of Jubilees* uses the term 'the Prince of Mastema' ('the Prince of Enmity') as well as Mastema as a proper name.

***Mater et Magistra*.** An *encyclical issued by *John XXIII on 15 May 1961 to mark the 70th anniversary of **Rerum Novarum*. It began to break the ties between the Roman Catholic Church and socially conservative groups, approving a greater role for the State in national life than earlier papal statements had countenanced (it was the first major discussion by a *pope of development aid). Nevertheless, the freedom of individuals remains paramount: 'This principle must always be retained: that State activity in the economic field, no matter what its reach or extent may be, ought not to be exercised in such a way as to curtail an individual's freedom of action, but rather to increase it, provided the essential rights of each individual person are duly safeguarded.'

Maṭha (Jain centres): see BHATTARAKA.

Mathurā, Mattra, or **Muttra.** Ancient city on the river Yamunā in Uttar-Pradesh. As the birthplace of *Kṛṣṇa, it is one of the seven *sacred cities of India. It is a major centre of pilgrimage, and the site for the enactment of *Rāslīlā*, a series of plays based on the life of Kṛṣṇa. It became also (*c.*2nd/3rd cents. CE) an important centre of Buddhist art and iconography, with the *Buddha portrayed, not in withdrawal or meditation, but as the active teacher of *dharma; and it was a holy place for Jains from the time of their first diffusion.

N. Hein, *The Miracle Plays of Mathurā* (1972); N. P. Joshi, *Mathurā Sculptures* . . . (1966); D. M. Srinivasan, *Mathura, the Cultural Heritage* (1989).

Mātikā (heading in Abhidhammapiṭaka): see TRIPIṬAKA.

Matriarch: see PATRIARCHS AND MATRIARCHS.

Mātṛkas (divine mothers): see MAHEŚVARI.

Matsah (unleavened bread): see MAZZAH.

Ma-tsu (Chinese Goddess): see T'IEN-SHANG SHENG-MU.

Matsuo Bashō (Japanese poet): see HAIKU.

Matsuri. Japanese festivals. Derived from a verb meaning 'to attend to', 'to entertain', or 'to serve the *kami', the souls of the deceased, or a person of higher status, matsuri implies 'the mental attitude of respect, reverence, and the willingness to listen, serve, and obey' (J. M. Kitagawa). Always there is an element of revelation, whereby sacred beings manifest their wills to the human community, which responds in matsuri.

Given the immanental Japanese world-view, every act can be considered an act of matsuri, which in this sense is a ritualization of everyday life. Since the function of government under the imperial system was to actualize the sacred will, the ancient word for government was *matsurigoto* or 'matsuri affairs'. Matsuri, or its sinocized pronunciation (*-sai*), came to refer to special ceremonies at court or at Shinto shrines which involve formal procedures, from the invocation and arrival of kami, through the phase of festive communion (*naorai*), to their final dispatch. Some form of sacred entertainment always accompanies the communal feast.

In modern Japan, as in the West, the essential context of the festival is often disregarded, resulting in strictly commercial or civil celebrations also known as matsuri.

Ma-tsu Tao-i (Jap., Baso Dōitsu; 709–88). Third-generation leader of the Ch'an/Zen school of *Hui-neng, who, with Shih-t'ou, established the two main characteristics of Ch'an, issuing eventually in *Rinzai and *Sōtō. He was the immediate successor (*hassu) of *Nan-yüeh Huai-jang. The details of his life are hazy (the earliest biographies are in *Sodōshu* and *Sō Kōsōden*, about 200 years later). He is the first known to use the abrupt methods of Ch'an/Zen, e.g. the shout (*ho) and the stick (*kyosaku). He concluded one exchange with *Pai-chang by twisting Pai-chang's nose so hard that he yelled in pain—and attained enlightenment. *Keitoku dentōroku* summarizes Ma-tsu's teaching:

> Apart from the mind there is no Buddha, apart from the Buddha, there is no mind. Do not cling to good, do not reject evil. If you cling to neither purity nor defilement, you come to know the nature of the emptiness of sin. At no moment can you grasp it, since it possesses no self-nature. Therefore the three worlds (*trikaya) are only mind. The universe and all phenomena bear the seal of the one *dharma (tr. Dumoulin).

Since there is only one undifferentiated nature of all appearance, it has to be realized as already being the only truth that there is; it cannot be attained as something not yet realized. So when his teacher, Nan-yüeh, asked Ma-tsu why he was meditating, he replied, 'I wish to become a buddha'. Nan-yüeh rubbed a tile on stone. Ma-tsu asked why. He replied: 'I am polishing it to make a mirror.' 'How can you make a mirror by polishing a tile?' 'How can you make a buddha by practising *zazen?' Hence his famous answers to the same question in **Wu-men-kuan* (30. 33), 'What is the Buddha?' He answered, 'The mind is the Buddha'; and 'Neither mind nor Buddha.' According to *Keitoku dentōroku*, 'His appearance was memorable. He walked like a bull and glared like a tiger. When he put out his tongue it reached over his nose, and on his feet were two circular marks.' His style is summarized in the phrase *kigen kikō*, 'strange words and extraordinary actions', which became a model for other Zen masters.

Matsya (Skt., 'fish'). The leading character in an important Hindu myth. In the earliest known version, *Manu, the ancestor of humanity, finds in the water for his morning ablutions a tiny fish, which asks for his protection and promises in return to save him from a flood which will destroy all other life. Manu puts the fish into ever larger receptacles as it grows to such an enormous size that only the sea can contain it. When the flood comes the fish tows Manu's ship to the safety of the northern mountain. In the **Mahābhārata* the story ends with the fish revealing itself as *Brahmā. In the *Purāṇas it is regarded as *Viṣṇu, and in the **Bhāgavata-Purāṇa* version, it not only saves Manu, the Seven Seers (Saptarṣi, see ṚSI), and all kinds of animals and plants, but also rescues the *Vedas from the demon Hayagrīva who has stolen them from Brahmā. Matsya is the first *avatāra of Viṣṇu in the standard list of ten.

Matthā ṭekṇā (Pañjābī, 'to bow the forehead'). Upon entering the *gurdwārā, Sikhs kneel before the *Ādi Granth, touching the floor with their foreheads as a sign of respect to it as *Gurū. This is also the custom when greeting an elderly relative.

Matthew, St. One of the twelve *Apostles and of the four *Evangelists. In Matthew 10. 3 he is described as a tax collector. According to *Papias he made a collection in Hebrew of the sayings of Jesus, and since the time of *Irenaeus he has been credited with the authorship of the gospel bearing his name. In art he is depicted with a sword, a money-bag, or a carpenter's square. Feast day in the E., 16 Nov.; in the W., 21 Sept.

The Gospel according to Matthew is the opening book of the New Testament. It contains: a genealogy and 'infancy narrative' (1–2); the preaching of *John the Baptist (3. 1–12); Jesus' baptism and temptation (3. 13–4. 17); his mission in Galilee (4. 18–15. 20); his work further afield including the confession of messiahship to Peter (15. 21–18. 35); his journey to Jerusalem (19–20), death, and resurrection (21–8). Most critics hold that the writer of Matthew used the gospel of *Mark and a lost source '*Q'; in this case the ascription to Jesus' disciple Matthew is untenable. The gospel is notable for its tendency to assimilate Jesus' teaching to that of the *rabbis; this and other Jewish colouring suggests its origin in a Jewish Christian Church. The destruction of the *Temple in 70 CE is perhaps assumed in 22. 7;

otherwise any date between *c*.65 and 100 is possible.

Matthias, St. The *apostle chosen to fill the vacancy in the twelve left by the treachery of *Judas, according to Acts 1. 15–26. *Eusebius makes him one of the seventy disciples of Luke 10. 1. He was early equated with St *Matthew, and then with Zacchaeus (Luke 19. 1–10). The *Acts of Andrew and Matthias* relate missionary adventures among the man-eaters. His supposed *relics were brought to Rome and thence to Trèves in the 11th cent. Feast day in W., 14 May (24 Feb. in Anglican churches); in the E., 9 Aug.

Mattins or **Matins.** The West Christian *office for the night, derived from the *vigils of the primitive church and so called until the 11th cent. In the *Rule* of St *Benedict it was prescribed for 2 a.m. The usual practice, however, became to 'anticipate', i.e. to say mattins on the evening before. Mattins was replaced in the 1971 Catholic *Breviary by the office of readings. 'Mattins' is also an unofficial name for Anglican *morning prayer.

Māturīdī, Maturidites: see AL-MĀTURĪDĪ.

Matzah, Matzo (unleavened bread): see MAZZAH.

Maudūdī: see MAWDŪDĪ.

Maundy Thursday. The Thursday before *Easter. It celebrates Jesus' institution of the *eucharist at the *Last Supper on that day. The English name 'Maundy' derives from a Latin *antiphon *Mandatum novum* ('a new commandment', John 13. 34) sung on this day. In the Western Church mass is celebrated in the evening, with a general communion. The liturgy includes the ceremony of the washing of the feet (*Pedilavium*, formerly a separate ceremony) in which the celebrant solemnly washes and dries the feet of twelve men in memory of Jesus' action at supper (John 13. 2–11); and the chrism mass is also held in every diocese on this day. The washing of the feet of only men (since the apostles were male) has become controversial in recent years, since it implies a tradition-literalism which seems (not only to women) to continue the patriarchal character of the Church. Many churches no longer retain the custom. The royal Maundy Ceremony in the UK, in which the reigning sovereign distributes Maundy money to twelve deserving and (relatively) poor people, has lost all contact with the original commemoration.

Maurice, Frederick Denison (1805–72). Christian clergyman and social reformer. He was the son of a *Unitarian minister, and was unable to graduate from Cambridge University because he could not subscribe to the *Thirty-Nine Articles. Influenced by the writings of *Coleridge and by a profound conversion experience, he became an *Anglican and was ordained in 1834. After a curacy, he became chaplain to Guy's Hospital in London in 1836, when he published *The Kingdom of Christ*. In this he argued that since Christ is the head of every person, all people are bound in a universal fellowship which life in all its aspects should make manifest. In a letter in 1843 he wrote: 'The great principle of social faith [is] the principle that we exist in a permanent communion which was not created by human hands, and cannot be destroyed by them.' In this spirit, he committed himself to the cause of education, especially for those who traditionally had no access to it—e.g. workers and women; and in 1848 he was one of the founders of Christian Socialism. Meanwhile, he had been appointed professor of English literature and history at King's College, London. In 1853, he published *Theological Essays*, which included a rejection of eternal punishment determined at the moment of death. He had 'no faith in man's theory of a Universal Restitution' (i.e. *universalism), but maintained that the quest for the return of the prodigal would have no end. Yet equally he recognized that the rebellion of sin might also continue:

> I dare not pronounce what are the possibilities of resistance in a human will to the loving will of God. There are times when they seem to me (thinking of myself more than others) almost infinite. But I know there is something which must be infinite in the abyss of love beyond the abyss of death. More than that I cannot know, but God knows—I leave myself and all to him.

This cautious view was nevertheless taken to be a subversion of the necessary foundation for moral life, and he was therefore dismissed from the College (although the real animus against him lay in his connection with Christian Socialism: see B. M. G. Reardon, *From Coleridge to Gore . . .*, 1971). He went on to become (1866) Knightsbridge Professor of Moral Philosophy at Cambridge and incumbent of St Peter's, Vere St., and later of St Edward's, Cambridge.

A. R. Vidler, *The Theology of F. D. Maurice* (1948) and *F. D. Maurice and Company* (1966).

Maurya dynasty. The first unifying, imperial dynasty in India, *c*.321–180 BCE. Its founder was Chandragupta (d. *c*.297); his grandson was *Aśoka.

K. A. N. Sastri, *The Age of the Nandas and Mauryas* (1967); R. Thapar, *Aśoka and the Decline of the Mauryas* (1961).

Mauss, M. (sociologist of religion): see SACRIFICE.

Mawdūdī, Sayyid Abū al-Aʿlā, usually known as **Mawlānā Mawdūdī** (1903–79). Founder of the political party Jamaat-al-Islam (i.e. *Jamāʿat-i Islāmī) in India and Pakistan. He wrote 138 major works in Urdu (much translated), the most influential being *al-Jihād fi'l-Islam* (1927), and *Tafhīm al-Qur'ān* (Urdu version of the Qur'ān, 1947–72). He advocated a return to pure Islam, considering Islam to be a total system and rejecting anything extraneous: 'If anybody wants to reorient or reconstruct Islam, let him do so . . . , but after these improvements, amendments, substitutions, additions . . . , for an ordinary Muslim there would be not any other way to greet it than with a flat rejection.' Mawdūdī's confident, no-compromise approach found support among a section of college- and university-educated Pakistanis, but aroused bitter opposition from the *Barelvi and *Deobandi *ʿulamā, and from the modernists over his refusal to allow any exegetical interpretation of the Qur'ān other than his own. Furthermore, Mawdudi's espousal of the *Wahhābī and anti-*Sūfī attitude alienated him from the mainstream Sunni masses. Mawdūdī's failure to gain a broad base of support in Pakistan contrasted strangely with his influence abroad.

K. Ahmad and Z. I. Ansari (eds.), *Islamic Perspectives* . . . (1979); K. Bahadur, *The Jamāʿat-i Islāmī of Pakistan* (1980).

Mawla (Arab.). In early Islam, a 'client' or protected person, who was a convert to Islam and by this procedure was integrated into the existing Arab tribal and family system. Mawla also means 'master', and al-Mawla is a term for God.

Mawlawīy(y)a. A Derwīsh order, known colloquially as 'whirling dervishes'. The name is derived from *mawlānā* ('our master'), a title of *Jalāl al-Dīn al-Rūmī. The dance induces trance- and ecstatic-states, and is undertaken by pivoting on the right foot, while engaging in *dhikr (concentration on God). The Mawlawīy(y)a Order embraces a wider constituency and range of practices than this (although the two are often identified). The Order was of great importance in the Ottoman Empire, not least in the development of *music and *calligraphy. The name of the Order is often transliterated as Mevlevi.

Mawlid, Mawlūd (Arab., *walada*, 'give birth'). The celebration of a birthday, but especially of the Prophet *Muḥammad, 12 Rabīʿ I. The mawlid al-nabi is the place where the Prophet was born in *Mecca. A mawlid may also be a poem celebrating a birthday of this kind.

G. E. von Grunebaum, *Muhammadan Festivals* (1951).

Maximus the Confessor (*c*.580–662). Greek theologian, mystic, and ascetical writer. After a distinguished secular career, he became a monk *c*.612 in Chrysopolis, fleeing to Africa before the Persian advance in 626. A strong opponent of *monothelitism, he secured its condemnation in Africa and Rome (649). In 653 and again in 661 he was brought to Constantinople, where he refused to submit to monothelitism, was condemned as a *heretic, mutilated, and died shortly afterwards in exile. He was vindicated at the third Council of *Constantinople (680). A prolific writer, he was the great synthesist of Byzantine theology, fusing the ascetic teaching of *Evagrius, *Dionysius the Areopagite's *Neoplatonism, and the *Alexandrine/Cappadocian theological tradition. Within this context the incarnation of the Son of God and the responding movement of deification (*theōsis*) on the part of humans is given a cosmic setting and a detailed ascetic programme. The saints are those who express the Trinity in themselves, so that 'God and those who are worthy of God have the same energy.'

G. Berthold, *Maximos Confessor* . . . (1985); L. Thunberg, *Man and the Cosmos* . . . (1985).

Māyā. 1. The mother of Gotama who became the *Buddha. She died within a few days of his birth. Later accounts (e.g. *Buddhacarita*) recount many miracles, including a virgin birth.

2. (Skt., 'supernatural power'). In the early Vedic literature, māyā generally means supernatural power or magic. It also carries the connotation of deceit or trickery. In the *Bhagavad-gītā*, *Kṛṣṇa declares that, although he is the unborn, changeless Lord of all beings, he assumes human birth through his own māyā in every age for the protection of the good and the destruction of the wicked whenever there is a decline of virtue; so here, māyā is the power to bring things into apparent form.

In *Mahāyāna Buddhism, māyā means a delusion or an illusion such as that produced by a magician. According to the earlier *Theravāda analysis, the phenomenal world is composed of transitory *dharmas and is therefore insubstantial and impermanent. The later Mahāyāna schools go further, viewing the phenomenal world as illusory, māyā, with the *Mādhyamaka arguing that the separate dharmas themselves are conditioned and have no being of their own, and the Yogācāra/*Vijñānavāda school regarding the dharmas as merely ideas or representations.

In *Advaita Vedānta philosophy, *Gauḍapāda used the term māyā for the power of the apparent creation of the world as well as the world so created. *Śaṅkara extended the term by associating it with *avidyā (ignorance). For Śaṅkara, avidyā, ignorance of the Ultimate Reality (*Brahman) produces the illusory world of name and form, or māyā, through superimposition. Later Vedāntins develop this line of thought further by describing māyā as the power both of concealing Reality (*āvaraṇa-śakti*) and of misrepresenting it as the phenomenal world (*vikṣepa-śakti*). In contrast to the sense developed in Mahāyāna (above), it is usually misleading to translate māyā as 'illusion'. Nevertheless, soteriologically the power of māyā is wisely treated as such; and in later Hinduism, māyā as Cosmic Illusion is sometimes personified and identified with the great goddess *Durgā.

Among Sikhs, the teaching of the *Gurūs is that māyā is a real part of God's creation. However, the attractions of māyā (i.e., wealth, physical love, etc.) are also, in the end, delusory and cannot accompany a person beyond death. Preoccupation with māyā leads to separation from God and to continual rebirth. If attracted by māyā one's predicament resembles that of a fish caught on a hook (Ādi Granth 1187) or iron which must be melted in the furnace and recast (Ādi Granth 752). See also HAUMAI; MANMUKH; FIVE EVIL PASSIONS.

P. D. Devanandan, *The Concept of Māyā* (1950); T. Goudriaan, *Māyā Divine and Human* (1978); R. Reyna, *The Concept of Māyā* (1962).

Māyādevī. Name of the Hindu Goddess as personified delusion. Other names include Mahāmāyā, Yogamāyā, Viṣṇumāyā. She plays an important role (e.g. in the **Bhāgavata-Purāṇa*, where she is presented as Yaśodā's daughter who was exchanged for *Kṛṣṇa). See VINDHYAVĀSINĪ.

Maybaum, I.: see HOLOCAUST.

Mayoi (Jap., 'error'). Zen understanding of delusion, whenever the phenomenal world wrongly understood appears to be real and substantial. Seen rightly, there is only one undifferentiated nature empty of self (*śūnyatā), so that even *saṃsāra and *nirvāna are one.

Māyōṉ. S. Indian name of the Hindu god *Kṛṣṇa/ *Viṣṇu. The name derives from a Tamil adjective meaning 'a person of black complexion'; synonyms are: Māyaṉ, Māyavaṉ, Māl, Mālavaṉ, and Tirumāl. Some sporadic references in the Tamil *caṅkam* literature (1st cent. BCE to 3rd cent. CE?) indicate a knowledge and veneration of the N. Indian god Kṛṣṇa also in the extreme South. There is no evidence here for the assumption that Māyōṉ was originally an autonomous (Dravidian) god similar to Murukaṉ (see TAMILNADU) who only eventually became identified with the Sanskritic *Skanda/ *Kārtikeya. During the next centuries, more extensive sources allow us to catch glimpses of a folk religion in which Māyōṉ is mainly the cowherd Kṛṣṇa, and—in a different milieu—of a developed temple culture which envisages Māyōṉ predominantly as *Nārāyaṇa/Viṣṇu. Furthermore, in literary circles a strong association of Māyōṉ with 'love-in-separation' evolved. Thus (in contrast to the **Bhagavad-gītā*) Māyōṉ = Kṛṣṇa is not envisaged as an *avatāra of Viṣṇu; and the South synthesized features of the latter god with those typical of Kṛṣṇa in the one figure of Māyōṉ. Even with the *Āḻvārs (6th–9th cents.) who drew on these different strands of Māyōṉ religion and developed a new religious system with them, 'Kṛṣṇa' remained the real centre of their devotion. Only with the *Śrīvaiṣṇavism institutionalized by *Rāmānuja in the 12th cent. does Viṣṇu emerge as the central god-figure.

Mayse Bukh: see MAʿASEH BOOK.

Mazal tōv (Heb., 'good planetary influences'). Traditional Jewish greeting, wishing someone 'Good luck!' The greeting is derived from a belief in the planets influencing human behaviour: see ASTROLOGY.

Mazhabī (Pañjābī, 'religious'). Sikh of sweeper *caste. Members of the *Harijan Hindu Chuhṛā caste who became Sikh were frequently termed Mazhabī. See also BĀLMĪKI; RĀMDĀSĪ; RAṄGHṚETĀ; RAVIDĀSĪ.

Mazzah. Unleavened bread eaten by Jews during the *Passover Festival. When the Israelites left Egypt, they took mazzah with them because they could not wait for the dough to rise (Exodus 12. 39). There are many laws concerning the baking of Passover mazzah so that any form of rising is avoided. There was enormous resistance to machine-made mazzah when it was introduced in the 19th cent., because it was believed that the machine process must cause fermentation. It is forbidden to have any form of leaven (*ḥamez) in the house during the whole Passover season, but the positive duty of eating mazzah only applies to the first night of the festival. This is based on the Exodus verse, 'In the evening you shall eat mazzot' (12. 18). Mazzah is described in the Passover *seder as 'the bread of affliction', based on Deuteronomy 16. 3. See also AFIKOMEN; PASSOVER; SEDER.

MBTI (Myers Briggs Type Indicator): see JUNG, CARL GUSTAV.

Mean, doctrine of the (book in Confucian Classics): see DOCTRINE OF THE MEAN.

Mecca (Makka). The birthplace of the Prophet *Muḥammad. It was already, before his birth, an important trading and religious centre, with very little other means of life-support: set amid rocky hills, there is little rain or fertile soil. Muḥammad's initial preaching made little impression, and indeed evoked increasing opposition, esp. from the ruling clan, the Quraish. He therefore made the *hijra to *Madīna, only recapturing Mecca near the end of his life. He immediately established the *ḥajj practices, thus ensuring the centrality of Mecca to Muslim life, even when the centres of political power under different *dynasties of caliphs (*khalīfa) moved far away. The *mosque at Mecca is al-*Masjid al-Ḥarām; and the two towns, Mecca and Madīna, are known as *al-Haramain* (Arab. dual, 'the two holy places'). Muslims turn toward Mecca in prayer (*ṣalāt, *qibla), and make the obligatory pilgrimage (ḥajj) to it.

E. Rutter, *The Holy Cities of Arabia* (1928); W. M. Watt, *Muhammad at Mecca* (1953).

Mechtild of Magdeburg (Beguine nun): see RHENO-FLEMISH SPIRITUALITY.

Meddlesome Friar: see SAVONAROLA, GIROLAMO.

Medellín: see LIBERATION THEOLOGY.

Medical Prescription Cave: see LONGMEN/ DRAGON GATE CAVES.

Medicine: see HEALING.

Medicine Buddha: see BHAIṢAJYAGURU.

Medīna: see MADĪNA, AL-.

Meditation. A form of mental prayer. In Christianity, the term has been used since 16th cent., in distinction from *contemplation, as a discursive activity, which involves thinking about passages from scripture and mysteries of the faith with a view to deeper understanding and a loving response. Many methods of meditation were taught, especially by the *Jesuits. Outside this historical context, the term meditation is used more widely, embracing contemplation; and in this wider sense, is applied to practices of many different kinds in virtually all religions: see Index, Meditation.

Judaism The Heb. terms *hitbonenut*, *kavvanah, and *devekut all refer to concentration on the spiritual world; they were much used by the *kabbalists. The *merkabah mystics strove for a contemplative vision of the merkabah, and the later kabbalists attempted to commune with the world of the *sefirot (emanations from God). *Moses b. Shem Tov de León gives a description of the third sefirah flashing in his mind through meditation. Instructions on methods of meditation were widespread—e.g. Abraham *Abulafia taught meditation in his *Hokhmat ha-Zaruf*; and the most detailed textbook is the 16th-cent. *Evan ha-Shoham* by Joseph ibn Sayah of Damascus. The meditative practices of the *ḥasidim were influenced by the kabbalists of Safed, whose doctrines were largely handed down orally.

Hinduism See DHYĀNA.

Buddhism Meditation in Buddhism is the process of training, developing, and purifying the mind, which is likened to an animal (especially an elephant or an ox) which is dangerously destructive when wild, but supremely useful when tamed. It is the third element in the triple training (Skt., *triśikṣā*) along with conduct or ethics (Skt., *śīla) and knowledge or wisdom (Skt., *prajñā), and as such is essential to Buddhist practice. General terms for it include *dhyāna/*jhāna (Skt., Pāli, 'thinking'), concentration (Skt., *samādhi), and mindfulness (Skt., *smṛti). There are two aspects, calming the mind (Skt., *śamatha) and using the calm mind to see reality clearly (*vipassanā). These are distinguishable but not distinct. Śamatha is attained principally by observing the breathing. Similar methods are found in many traditions and śamatha broadly corresponds to 'meditation' in everyday English. Vipassanā uses the śamatha methods for distinctly Buddhist ends. A variety of altered states is recognized, usually called jhāna, in *Theravāda and samādhi in *Mahāyāna. Concentration on a particular object (Skt., *ālambana*, 'basis') may be prescribed as an antidote (Skt., *pratipakṣa*, 'opposite wing') to a particular delusion (Skt., *kleśa, 'affliction'), e.g. on the decomposition of a corpse for one addicted to physical beauty. Tibetan Buddhism, especially in its *Tantric forms, recommends elaborate *visualizations of deities, *maṇḍalas, etc., as methods of focusing on purified mind. Formless meditation, i.e. holding the mind in the present moment or observing the mind directly, is found in *Zen (which derives its name from a transliteration of dhyāna) and in some advanced Tantric practices such as *dzogchen. 'Blanking' the mind is not a Buddhist practice. The triple training is structurally similar to the *Benedictine practice of balancing the three elements of liturgy (Lat., **opus dei*, 'work of God'), labour (Lat., *opus manuum*, 'manual work'), and study (Lat., *lectio divina*, 'spiritual reading').

See also MENPEKI; ZAZEN; Index, Meditation.

G. C. Chang, *The Practice of Tibetan Meditation* (1963); E. Conze, *Buddhist Meditation* (1956); P. J. Griffiths, *On Being Mindless: Buddhist Meditation and the Mind-Body Problem* (1986); W. L. King, *Theravada Meditation* . . . (1980).

Medujigore: see PILGRIMAGE.

Meera (Hindu devotional poetess): see MĪRĀBĀĪ.

Megasthenes. Greek ambassador at the court of Chandragupta Maurya at *Pāṭaliputra, *c.*302 BCE. His account of his travels throughout N. India, *Indica*, is an important historical resource on *Mauryan India, and, although the original is lost, valuable excerpts are to be found in the writings of later classical historians such as Arrian and Diodoras.

Megillah (Heb., 'scroll'). Each of the 'five scrolls' in the Hebrew Bible. The books of *Ruth, Song of Songs, *Lamentations, *Ecclesiastes, and *Esther are all referred to as 'megillot' (pl.), but later, Megillah came to refer to Esther alone. The term also refers to the tenth tractate in the Order *Mo'ed* in the *Mishnah.

Megillat Ta'anit (Heb., 'Scroll of Fasting'). An Aramaic 1st/2nd cent. CE work listing days prohibited for fasting for the Jews. According to *B.Shab.* 13b, it was written by Hananiah b. Hezekiah, but in an appendix, Eliezer b. Hananiah is named as the author. The list contains thirty-six days on which victories or happy events occurred, and the document is thus a valuable addition to *Josephus for the history of the second Temple period.

Meher Baba ('compassionate father', 1894–1969). An Indian spiritual master and founder of the Meher Baba movement. Baba claimed to be the final *avatāra or manifestation of God, who unfolded his truth in the form of three fundamental precepts—good thoughts, good words, good deeds—through *Zoroaster, *Rāma, *Kṛṣṇa, *Buddha, *Jesus, and *Muḥammad, all of whom were avatāras of a previous age. Baba declared, and his disciples or 'Baba lovers' believe, that his love sustains the universe. In 1924, he established a community at Meherabad, near Ahmednegar, with shelter and health care for the poor. In 1925, he announced that he was entering 'the Silence'; by 1954, all communication had been reduced to gestures.

The Baba's tomb at Meherabad is now a centre of pilgrimage. While it has attracted several thousand people in the West since the 1950s, the overwhelming majority of 'Baba lovers' are still to be found in India.

C. B. Purdom, *The God-Man* (1964).

Mehizah (Heb., 'partition'). Partition screen between men's and women's seating in Jewish *synagogues. According to the *Talmud, men and women were allocated separate spaces in the Court of Women of the Jerusalem Temple on the Festival of *Tabernacles (*B.Suk.* 51b–52a). In synagogues, either women sit in a separate gallery which is screened off, or a partition is placed between the front seats and the back seats. The *Progressive movement has abolished the mehizah on the grounds that nowhere in the Bible is it stated that men and women must sit separately. *Orthodox authorities, such as Moses *Sofer in the 19th cent., strongly argue for the retention of separation.

Meiji. Throne-name of the Japanese emperor under whom imperial rule was restored in 1868, after the overthrow of the Tokugawa shogunate; hence the name of the era, 1868–1912 (when Meiji died). The era is characterized by the slogan, 'Enrich the nation and strengthen its arms'. The leaders pursued a policy of ambitious innovation combined with vigorous adherence to the traditions and values of the past. In fact, the two were effectively combined, since the past to which appeal was made was to a great extent a creation of the present, building especially on the initiative of *Fukko Shintō. The sentiment is found in the Imperial Rescript on Education (1890), distributed to all schools in Japan and hung beside the emperor's portrait, to both of which obeisance was made: 'The Way set forth here is the very teaching handed down from our imperial ancestors, to be observed, both by their descendants, and by their subjects: it is infallible for all ages and true in all places.' Among the military leaders of the overthrow of the Tokugawa shogunate was Saigō Takamori (1827–77), who advocated aggressive policies (especially against Korea), and who revived the *samurai ideals—in ways that led eventually to the *kamikaze (winds of the *kami) pilots of the Second World War, who, like Saigō, were prepared to die without hesitation. To Saigō is attributed the verse: 'I am a boat | Given to my country. | If the winds blow, let them; | If the waves rise, let them.' During this period, the *kokutai model of the nation developed; and the vigour of *new religious movements was harnessed by classifying them, where feasible, as Shinto sects—e.g. as *Konkōkyō and *Tenrikyō. Meiji is venerated at a shrine in Tokyo.

W. G. Beasley, *The Meiji Restoration* (1972).

Meir, Rabbi (2nd cent. CE). Jewish *tanna. R. Meir was a student of *Akiva, *Ishmael, and *Elisha b. Abuyah. It was said that he was given the name Meir ('illuminator') because 'he enlightened the eyes of the *sages of the *halakhah' (*B.Erubin.* 13b). After the renewal of the *Sanhedrin, Meir was appointed *ḥakham, but, as a result of a conflict with the *nasi, *Simeon b. Gamaliel, it was decreed that all Meir's later statements quoted in the *Mishnah should be introduced anonymously. None the less, Meir made considerable contributions to the halakhah, and the *Talmud maintains that 'an anonymous mishnah represents the view of Meir following that of Akiva' (*B.Sanh.* 86a). He was described by his contemporary, Yose b. Halafta, as 'a great man, a holy man, a modest man' (*TJ. Ber.* 2. 7. 5b).

Meir ben Baruch of Rothenburg (Maharam) (*c.*1215–93). Jewish scholar and community leader. Meir was born into a prominent scholarly family. As a young man, he witnessed a public burning of the *Talmud in France which prompted him to write a poem of mourning that is included in the *Ashkenazi *liturgy for 9 *Av. Reputed as the greatest scholar of his generation, he acted as supreme arbiter in community disputes in Germany. His *responsa were sent throughout W. Europe, and about a thousand still survive. Despite his reputation, he seems to have held no national position, although he was head of the *yeshivah at Rothenburg. Besides his responsa, his activities were described in detail by his students who carried his influence to communities throughout Germany, Austria, and Bohemia. He was a particular inspiration to his pupil *Asher b. Jehiel and to Asher's son Jacob. At the end of his life, he was imprisoned by the forces of the emperor while he was trying to flee Germany, a fate which he accepted philosophically: 'Imprisonment is made sweeter to a man if truth is in prison with him.' As well as his responsa, he wrote *tosafot to eighteen tractates of the Talmud, commentaries on two orders of the *Mishnah, and compendia of laws for special purposes.

I. A. Agus, *Rabbi Meir of Rothenburg* (1947).

Meister Eckhart: see ECKHART, MEISTER.

Mekhilta of R. Ishmael (*mekhilta*, Aram., 'a measure'). Jewish *halakhic *midrash on *Exodus. The *Mekhilta of R. *Ishmael* interprets much of the Book of Exodus verse by verse and is a compilation of halakhic midrash. Almost certainly it was the product of Ishmael's school, with the final redaction taking place in *Israel at the end of the 4th cent. CE.

Tr. J. Z. Lauterbach (1933–5).

Mekhilta of R. Simeon ben Yohai. Jewish *halakhic *midrash on *Exodus. Like that of R. *Ishmael, the *Mekhilta of R. *Simeon ben Yohai* interprets much of the Book of Exodus verse by verse and is a compilation of halakhic midrash. It probably dates from the beginning of the 5th cent. CE. Although known and quoted in the Middle Ages, it was lost but rediscovered from fragments in the *Cairo Genizah and from the *Midrash ha-Gadol* of David b. Amram Adani.

J. N. Epstein and E. Z. Melamed (eds.), *Mekhilta de-Rabbi Shimon ben Yohai* (1955).

Melā (Hindī). 'Fair', particularly one held in India to celebrate a local Hindu *festival or, among Sikhs, a *Gurpurb. See also BAISĀKHĪ; GOINDVĀL; HOLĀ MAHALLĀ; MUKTSAR; KUṂBHAMELĀ.

Melanchthon, Philipp (1497–1560). German Reformer. Born in Bretten, Baden, Philipp Schwarzerd was given the name 'Melanchthon' (Gk. equivalent of the underlying German 'black earth') by his great-uncle, Johannes Reuchlin, because of his outstanding ability in linguistic and humanist studies. After studying at Heidelberg, Tübingen, and Wittenberg, he was appointed Wittenberg's Professor of Greek at the age of 21, becoming *Luther's keen follower and closest friend. In 1519 he participated in the Leipzig Disputation and also defended in his Wittenberg BD thesis the conviction that the *Bible alone is authoritative, not papal decrees or conciliar decisions (see COUNCILS). During Luther's 1521 confinement in the Wartburg he led the *Reformation movement and in the same year published his *Loci Communes*, the first systematic exposition of Reformed doctrine and its repudiation of *scholasticism. His energies were devoted to teaching and writing, especially the translation and exegesis of scripture. He was a leading figure at important theological debates amongst the Reformers and with Catholics, notably at the Diet of *Augsburg (1530) where he was mainly responsible for its famous Confession. Occasionally too hesitant for Luther, he was a man of conciliatory spirit whose skill as a negotiator and influential writings were an outstanding contribution to the Reformation.

Trs. O. Clemen; C. L. Hill; H. Lietzmann; C. L. Manschreck; C. L. Manschreck, *Melanchthon* . . . (1965); M. Rogness, *Philipp Melanchthon* . . . (1969).

Melchites: see MELKITES.

Melchizedek (Heb., 'my king is Zedek/righteous'). Biblical king of Salem. According to Genesis 14. 18–20, Melchizedek welcomed the *patriarch *Abraham after he defeated the four kings, and he is described as 'a priest of God Most High'. In Psalm 110. 4, it is written, 'the Lord has sworn and will not repent, you are priest for ever after the manner of Melchizedek'. It seems likely, therefore, that David adopted a sacral *kingship when he captured *Jerusalem, and that these passages reflect a positive assessment of this move against those who protested against it as innovation. The exact nature of Melchizedek's priesthood has, nevertheless, been the cause of much speculation. He is mentioned in the *Qumran texts, in the Slavonic *Book of *Enoch*, and in several other *rabbinic texts where he is identified as having *messianic functions. He features also in the New Testament, i.e. in *Hebrews where Christ's priesthood is prefigured by that of Melchizedek, and is superior to that of *Aaron and the *Levites.

Melek Taus (name for Satan amongst Yezīdīs): see YEZĪDĪS.

Melito, St (d. *c*.190). Christian *father. He was bishop of Sardis in Asia Minor. The most important of his few surviving works is a sermon 'On the *Pasch' in rhythmic prose, which expounds the Passover as a *type of the work of Christ.

Gk. text with Eng. tr. by S. G. Hall (1979).

Melkites or **Melchites** ('Emperor's men', from Syriac *malkaya*, 'imperial'). Christians of Syria and Egypt who accepted the Council of *Chalcedon and remained in communion with *Constantinople. After the rise of Islam their liturgical language became Arabic. Today the term embraces all Arabic-speaking Christians of the Byzantine *rite, whether *Orthodox or *Uniat, in the patriarchates of Antioch, Jerusalem, and Alexandria. The Orthodox number about 750,000, while the Uniats (for whom there has been a separate hierarchy since 1684) number *c*.400,000.

Melville, Andrew (1545–1622). Scottish Reformer and theologian, concerned especially with educational reform. Entrusted in 1575 with the responsibility of compiling the *Second Book of Discipline*, he vigorously opposed *episcopacy and so incurred the displeasure of James VI of Scotland (I of England). Imprisoned in the Tower of London for four years, he was released in 1611 to become professor of biblical theology at the University of Sedan.

Memento mori (Christian remembrance of death): see FOUR LAST THINGS.

Memra (Aram., 'word'). The Word of God by which the universe was created. The term 'memra' occurs in the *Targum literature with similar connotations to the Gk. term *logos*, understood by *Philo to mean the mind of God as revealed in creation.

A. Chester, *Divine Revelation and Divine Titles* (1986).

Menander: see MILINDAPAÑHA.

Mencius (Chin., *Meng Tzu/Mengzi*; *c*.391–*c*.308 BCE). Early *Confucian thinker. Mencius' ideas appear in a book bearing his name that contains sections, often unconnected, which range from brief aphorisms to long dialogues. Perhaps written by Mencius and his disciples, it was edited, with parts discarded, in the 2nd cent. The book became extraordinarily influential: *Chu Hsi (1130–1200) declared it one of the *Four Books, and the Mongol court in 1315 included it in the civil-service exams; from that time forward its impact continued to grow.

*Neo-Confucians read Mencius in terms of their own pursuit of the 'enlightenment' that occurs through contact with a moral and omniscient mind. But Mencius's own concern is to show Confucianism's superiority to (especially) two positions: one, the proto-utilitarianism of *Mohism, aiming to replace traditional norms with rational judgements about what will benefit most people; the other, exemplified by *Yang Chu, counselling people to reject social responsibility and pursue individual satisfaction. Against these ideas, Mencius argues that Heaven (*T'ien) produces in human beings four potentials that define human nature, making it good, giving birth to four central virtues when actualized: benevolence (*jen), propriety (*li), practical wisdom (*chih*), and *i, 'duty' or 'proper behaviour'. The cultivation of these potentials is a person's most significant task. Such cultivation brings great aid to other people, helps realize Heaven's purposes, and produces profound satisfaction within a person; indeed, evocative but cryptic hints exist that such cultivation allows people to make contact with transhuman forces. Mencius also enters the political debates of his time. Much of the book covers topics in political or social thought, and Mencius combines conservative and radical strains. He insists on strict adherence to traditional institutions and practices, but he also thinks rulers and their counsellors must observe the highest ethical standards. Obligation and love cannot be given indiscriminately to all (as in *Mo Tzu), but depend on the nature of the relationship: 'When left to follow its natural feeling, human nature will do good. That is why I say it is good. If it becomes evil, it is not the fault of the original capability' (*Meng Tzu* VI. A. 6). After his death, he was dubbed the Second Sage, and his spirit tablet (*ancestral cult) was placed next to that of Confucius in the Confucian temples.

Trs. J. Legge, D. C. Lau; A. Verwilghen, *Mencius* . . . (1967).

Mendelssohn, Moses (RaMbeMaN) (1729–86). Jewish Enlightenment philosopher. Mendelssohn had initially a traditional Jewish education. He moved to Berlin in 1743 where he worked as a merchant, while pursuing literary activities and conducting a huge correspondence. His original interest was in the development and spread of German culture—the Christian writer, G. E. *Lessing, was a close personal friend; but after 1769, when he became involved in a dispute on the Jewish religion, he confined his writing to Jewish matters. His early philosophical works dealt with aesthetics and human psychology. In 1763, his *Abhandlung ueber die Evidenz in Metaphysischen Wissenschaften*, on the philosophy of religion, won the first prize of the Prussian Royal Academy of Science, but as a Jew, he was rejected for membership of the Academy. He became involved in a religious dispute with the Swiss clergyman, Johann Lavater, somewhat against his will, because, as he said, 'I wanted to refute the world's derogatory opinion of the Jew by righteous living, not by pamphleteering.' His response to Lavater's attack was published as *Schreiben an den Herrn Diaconus Lavater zu Zuerich* (1770). This prompted widespread debate and caused Mendelssohn to concentrate his activities on improving the civic status of the Jews and on devising a philosophical justification for his belief in Judaism. His *Jerusalem: Oder, verber religioese Macht und Judenthum* (1783) summarized his thoughts. In it he discussed his attitude to Church and State (arguing for separation, since the role of the State is social, not religious) and the place of Judaism. He argued, 'Let every man who does not disturb the public welfare, who obeys the law, acts righteously towards you and his fellow men be allowed to speak as he thinks, to pray to God after his own fashion or after that of his fathers, and to seek eternal salvation where he thinks he may find it.' In that spirit, he prepared Jews to live in the midst of German life, translating the *Pentateuch into German (transliterated into Hebrew letters) and adding to it a rationalizing Hebrew commentary. Mendelssohn, as a young man, had also produced works of literary criticism, and through his relationship with Lessing, he participated fully in German intellectual life. It is generally thought that the character of Nathan in Lessing's *Nathan the Wise* is a portrait of Mendelssohn. His death was widely mourned, and a Hebrew biography was published by his student Isaac Euchel less than three years after his death. He is regarded as the forerunner of *Reform Judaism. Despite his own loyalty to the *halakhic tradition, by subjecting Judaism to the test of rationalism, the gulf between the world of the 18th-cent. Enlightenment and *Orthodox belief and practice was emphasized. Of his six children, four subsequently converted to Christianity, either from conviction or to improve their social opportunities.

A. Altman, *Moses Mendelssohn* . . . (1973). H. M. Z. Meyer, *Moses Mendelssohn Bibliographie* (1965).

Mendicant friars (literally, 'begging' brothers). *Religious orders which renounced the right to own income-producing properties. The *Dominicans adopted begging as part of their programme of itinerant preaching in imitation of the *Apostles, and extended it to a general refusal of revenues, though they retained ownership of their houses. The *Franciscans repudiated legal possession even of their houses. Later, other orders, particularly the *Carmelites and *Augustinian hermits became mendicant. The term is now largely meaningless, since most if not all of the originally mendicant orders have been given the right to own capital.

Meng Tzu: see MENCIUS.

Mengzi: see MENCIUS.

Mennonites. Christian denomination. It derives from followers of the 16th-cent. *radical Reformer Menno Simons (1496–1561), a Dutch *Roman Catholic priest who joined the *Anabaptists in 1536. Simons's leadership was an inspiration to them during a period when, after the failure of the attempted Kingdom of the Saints at Münster (1535–6), they were understandably exposed to fierce opposition. His teaching about believers' *baptism, Church discipline, pacificism, and the non-participation of Christians in the magistracy gained wide support in many congregations, amongst whom he exercised an itinerant leadership ministry for twenty-five years. His followers greatly increased in the 17th and 18th cents., especially in Holland, later migrating to various parts of Europe and the Ukraine. They made a significant contribution to agricultural and industrial development. In the late 19th and early 20th cents. Russian Mennonites were driven by persecution to Canada and the USA, and some settlements were established in S. America. Today there are about 700,000 Mennonites in various parts of the world, mostly in America where their ranks have been occasionally fragmented by division. *Congregational autonomy continues to be an important principle. There is no common doctrinal basis for their united life, but a World Mennonite Conference successfully incorporates most groups. Recognized American colleges and journals provide a frequent interchange of ideas, and their historians have made an outstanding contribution to the study of the 16th-cent. radical Reformers.

H. S. Bender and C. H. Smith (eds.), *The Mennonite Encyclopedia* (1954–9); C. J. Dyck, *An Introduction to Mennonite History* (1981); N. P. Springer and A. J. Klassen, *Mennonite Bibliography, 1631–1961* (1977).

Menorah (Heb., 'candelabrum'). Jewish seven-branch candlestick, which from early times became a symbol of Jewish identity. According to the Hebrew scriptures, the menorah was an important furnishing of the *tabernacle in the wilderness and of the *Temple in *Jerusalem. According to Exodus 25. 40, a pattern of the menorah was given by God to *Moses on Mount *Sinai; and in *Solomon's temple there were ten menorot (pl.) of gold (1 Kings 7. 49). A menorah is clearly visible on the Arch of Titus in Rome which represents the sack of the Temple in 70 CE. In the *kabbalah, the menorah is portrayed as a pattern of the structure of the *sefirot (emanations), and in the Jewish community of the *diaspora it became the most common emblem of the Jewish religion. In 1948 it became the official symbol of the State of *Israel. See also MAGEN DAVID.

S. S. Kayser and G. Schoenberger, *Jewish Ceremonial Art* (1959).

Menpeki or **Mempeki** (Jap., 'facing the wall'). Zen description of the nine years which *Bodhidharma spent 'facing the wall', i.e. in profound meditation at Shao-lin. It became a virtual synonym for *zazen. In Chinese it is known as *pi-kuan* meditation and it is markedly different from Hindu *dhyāna, or from *T'ien-t'ai 'steady-gazing' (*chih-kuan*, Jap., *shikan*), according to the early chroniclers; however, the exact nature of the 'wall-gazing' has not survived. *Sōtō continues the practice of zazen facing the wall.

Men-shen (Chin., 'gods of the doorway'). Deities in Chinese folk religion who protect the doorways of public or private buildings. They appear to have been promoted *euhemeristically from two generals of the T'ang dynasty, Ch'in Shu-pao and Hu Ching-te. Their fearsome figures are painted on door-posts.

Menstruation. The periodic loss of blood from the womb: as such, it has evoked in all religions responses of caution, since blood, connected as it is with life and death, is regarded as potentially threatening, and therefore polluting. Yet at the same time the connection of the recurrent period with fertility is almost universally recognized. Nevertheless, K. E. Paige and J. M. Paige (*The Politics of Reproductive Ritual*, 1981) comment:

> Perhaps no other event in the female reproductive cycle evokes as negative an emotional response as the periodic appearance of menstrual bleeding. . . . Despite the importance of menstruation as proof of a wife's continued fertility, throughout world societies menstruating women are subject to numerous taboos and social restrictions. The menstrual taboos of the ancient Hebrews, described in the Old Testament, are often cited to illustrate extreme contempt for women [for continuing Jewish practice, see NIDDAH]; but similar menstrual taboos and postmenstrual purification rituals are the norm in world societies rather than the exception . . . : men are supposed to refuse to sleep with a menstruating wife, refuse to eat the food she has cooked, and prohibit her from coming near their property, animals, or gardens during this dangerous period.

Even in a religion, Christianity, which is supposed to have transcended the detail of the law, the tenacity of this fear has persisted, especially in those parts of the Church dominated by male celibates (e.g. the *Roman Catholic refusal until very recently, 1992, to allow girl servers into the sanctuary). The fact remains that the onset of menstruation, especially in the absence of knowledge and modern sanitary towels, is a disturbing event. The dissonance now set up, in law- or custom-based religions, between modern knowledge and religious requirement is an increasing point of stress.

Me'or ha-Golah: see GERSHOM BEN JUDAH.

Mercersburg theology. Movement in American theology in the 19th cent. Its principal figures were John W. Nevin (1803–86) and Philip Schaff (1819–93), colleagues at the German Reformed seminary in Mercersburg, Pennsylvania, from 1844 to 1851. Opposing what Nevin called 'Puritanic' in American Protestantism, the movement decried *revivalism, accorded Christian *tradition an importance complementary to that of *scripture, affirmed the *Church as an article of faith, asserted a *Calvinist sacramental view of the *eucharist, and championed *liturgical worship. Although its contemporary influence beyond the German Reformed denomination was small, Mercersburg theology, especially in its liturgical aspects, now elicits wide interest within Reformed Churches in the USA.

Merit. In Christian thought, the recognition by God that certain works are worthy of reward. In Catholic teaching—deriving ultimately from statements about reward in the New Testament (e.g. Matthew 5. 46; Romans 2. 6; 1 Corinthians 3. 8)—merit has a central place, although it is emphasized that merit *de condigno* ('of worthiness') must be acquired in a state of *grace and with the assistance of actual grace. Protestant theology denies or limits merit as efficacious in salvation: created beings can never establish any claim upon God or earn any reward from him; otherwise salvation is a matter of works and not God's grace. Merit *de congruo* is merit based on equity.

A consequence of the Catholic doctrine is the existence of a 'treasury of merits', consisting of the superabundance of the merits of Christ, the Virgin *Mary, and the *saints. The Church is empowered to draw on this through the granting of *indulgences to those deficient in merit. See also SUPEREROGATION.

In Buddhism, merit and its transfer form one of the most important parts of the dynamic of society. The acquiring of merit and its transfer to others is an important way in which monks and laypeople interact. For details, see DĀNA; PUṆYA (Pāli, puñña); KUŚALA (kusala).

Among Jains, there are seven types of activity which are conducive to progress in rebirth (*puṇyakṣetra*): donating an image, or a building to house an image, paying for the copying of holy texts, giving alms to monks, or to nuns, assisting laymen, or laywomen, in their religious activities or other needs: see P. S. Jaini, *The Jaina Path of Purification* (1979).

Merits of the Fathers (Heb., *zekut aboth*). Jewish doctrine of benefits secured for children by the good deeds of their ancestors. According to Jewish teaching, good deeds can secure future blessings for one's descendants. In particular the merits of the *patriarchs, *Abraham, *Isaac, and *Jacob, are believed to have obtained benefits for future generations of the Jewish people.

A. Marmorstein, *The Doctrine of Merits in Old Rabbinical Literature* (1920).

Merkabah mysticism (Heb., 'Chariot' mysticism). Jewish speculations on God's throne. Later Jewish mystics speculated on the prophet *Ezekiel's vision of God's chariot, and such study was recognized to have particular dangers to untutored minds. In the Babylonian *Talmud, merkabah mysticism was described as a major subject while rabbinic casuistry was assessed as minor (*B.Suk*. 28a); and fragments of merkabah traditions have been found in the *Dead Sea Scrolls and in rabbinic *midrash. *Johanan ben Zakkai was a practitioner of merkabah mysticism, and early accounts of his experience (e.g. in a *Cairo Genizah fragment) so closely resemble the accounts of Saul/*Paul's *Damascus road experience (with the obvious exception of the perception of Jesus) that it seems virtually certain that Saul had been an adept also. Merkabah mysticism spread to Christian gnostics, and the traditions were preserved among the *kabbalists. See further HEKHALOT AND MERKABAH.

G. Scholem, *Jewish Gnosticism, Merkabah Mysticism and Talmudic Tradition* (1965).

Merton, Thomas (1915–68). *Trappist monk and writer. Born in France, he went to school in England and university in the USA, where, after a confused adolescence, he became a *Roman Catholic and in 1941 joined the Trappists at Gethsemani Abbey in Kentucky. His autobiography, *The Seven Storey Mountain* (1946), portrayed a traditional conversion story to traditional Catholicism. But Merton's way, recorded in his immense literary output, echoed the changes in modern Catholicism, leading to a greater openness to other traditions, and a deep concern for the moral dilemmas of the contemporary world, though he himself sought greater and greater solitude. Becoming increasingly interested in the spirituality of Eastern religions, he was killed accidentally in Bangkok.

M. Furlong, *Merton: A Biography* (1980); M. Mott, *The Seven Mountains of Thomas Merton* (1984); A. Padovano, *The Human Journey . . .* (1982); G. Woodcock, *Thomas Merton: Monk and Poet* (1978).

Meru, also **Sumeru.** Mythological golden mountain, axis or centre of the world, recognized in both Hinduism and Buddhism. In Hinduism, it appears in many myths in the *purāṇas, where it is placed in the *Himālayas. *Brahma's city of gold is on its summit, and its suburbs are the eight cities of the *loka-pālas. The *lokas of *Kṛṣṇa and *Viṣṇu are located on it. *Gaṅgā (Ganges) springs from it. In Buddhism, Meru is surrounded by seas and continents, beneath which are the hells (*naraka) and domains of the *pretas. Above are the devalokas and rūpaloka (*loka) and, for *Pure Land, the buddhafields. The part played by Meru in this diagrammatic visualization of the process toward (or away from) enlightenment is discussed in M. Tatz and J. Kent, *Rebirth: The Tibetan Game of Liberation* (1977).

Meshed: see MASHHAD.

Meshullaḥ (emissary): see SHALI'AḤ.

Mesrob, St (361–439). Armenian Christian *father. He succeeded Sahak as patriarch in 440 but died in less than six months. He invented the Armenian alphabet *c*.406. Thereafter, gathering around him a band of scholars, he directed a programme of theological translations into Armenian, starting with the Bible (*c*.410–44). This activity succeeded in starting a national literature, and helped free the Armenian Church from dependence on Greek and Syriac institutions.

Messalians. A Christian sect of the 4th–7th cents. Their name derives from Syriac *mṣallyane*, 'praying people'; they were also known by the cognate Gk. name *Euchites*. They lived ascetically and by begging, in order to give themselves entirely to prayer. Their practice was probably a survival of the earliest

Christian *asceticism, which was reserved in its attitude to a public church and sacraments. Their book, the *Asceticon*, has correspondences with the *Macarian homilies. The Messalians were attacked by *Orthodox writers including *Epiphanius, and were condemned finally at the Council of *Ephesus in 431.

Messiah (adaptation of Heb., *ha-mashiaḥ*, 'the anointed one', also transliterated *haMashiach*).

Judaism Anointed descendant of the Jewish king *David who will restore the Jewish kingdom. The idea of the messiah did not exist before the second *Temple period, but grew out of the biblical hope that the House of David would again rule over the Jewish people. The so-called 'Messianic oracles' in the *Prophets (e.g. Isaiah 7. 14; 9. 1–6) do not look for a distantly future king, but express the hopes vested in the new-born royal child. The kings (see KINGSHIP, SACRAL) played a role in the cult, representing the people before God—a role vividly expressed in the many royal psalms. The failure of the kings historically led to a reassessment during the *Exile, when the future hope replaced present kingship. In the intertestamental period, messianic speculation included three messianic figures (the righteous *priest, the *anointed king, and the prophet of the last days). These can be found in the literature of the *Dead Sea Sect. In the **Psalms of Solomon*, *4 *Ezra*, and in the *Apocalypse of *Baruch*, the Davidic messiah has become central. As a result of the Roman occupation of *Erez Israel, various messiahs emerged, including Jesus (as interpreted after his death by his followers), Judas the Galilean (mentioned in *Josephus), and Simeon *Bar Kokhba (see MESSIANIC MOVEMENTS). The *rabbis taught that, with the coming of the messiah, the climax of human history would be achieved and God's *kingdom would be established on earth. The Davidic messiah would be preceded by a secondary figure, Messiah ben *Joseph, whose symbolic function is unclear. The pseudepigraphical *Book of *Zerubbabel* appeared in the 6th cent. CE. It describes how the Messiah ben Joseph would tackle the final satanic emperor of Rome; all the Jews would gather in Jerusalem; Messiah ben Joseph would be killed; but the city would be saved by Hephzibah, and it would be Hephzibah's son, Messiah ben David, who would institute the messianic age. The book was immensely influential and spawned a vast literature which had universal appeal in the Jewish community. Messianic speculation thus became a constant feature of Jewish culture. Belief in the coming of the messiah is included in *Maimonides' *Thirteen Principles of the Jewish faith, even though Maimonides himself discouraged speculation. From the 13th cent., messianic expectations were centred on *kabbalistic thought and culminated in the *Shabbatean movement (see MESSIANIC MOVEMENTS). The *Reform movement substituted a belief in the golden messianic age for belief in a personal messiah. Because of their attachment to their *diaspora countries, the early Reform leaders rejected the hope of the return of the *exiles to *Zion. When the Reform movement adopted *Zionism after the *Holocaust, the return to Erez Israel was still separated from the messianic hope. The *Orthodox, on the other hand, still maintain the belief that a Davidic messiah will reign in Jerusalem and rebuild the Temple. The establishment of the State of *Israel has been seen as the beginning of the redemption, and messianic speculation still exists in some circles.

See further MESSIANIC MOVEMENTS.

J. Klausner, *The Messianic Idea in Israel* (1955); G. Scholem, *The Messianic Idea in Judaism* . . . (1971); A. H. Silver, *A History of Messianic Speculation in Israel* (rev. edn., 1959).

Christianity Although at an early date the followers of *Jesus were marked out as those who believed that Jesus was the promised messiah/christ (Acts 11. 26, 'It was at Antioch that the disciples were first called Christians'), Jesus appears to have resisted any attempt to interpret what he was doing and saying in his God-derived way through that category—to such an extent that it gave rise to the theory of the messianic secret—see SCHWEITZER, ALBERT. Jesus in fact interpreted himself through the phrase (it was not even a title), 'the *son of man', as the one who is *not* a supernatural figure, like an angel or a messiah, but who is subject to death (son of *Adam), yet demonstrates the 'power' (*dunamis*) of God to change life through himself. Some aspects of his life (e.g. the entry into Jerusalem) were clearly open to the interpretation that he was acting as the descendant of David, but it was only after his death and resurrection that the appropriateness of interpreting him as messiah was developed (e.g. Matthew 1. 1; Luke 1. 27, 2. 4; Acts 2. 29 f.; Romans 1. 3). The term *christos* (Gk., 'anointed one' = Heb., *ha-Mashiaḥ*, i.e. messiah) then became virtually a proper name. The New Testament reveals a certain amount of scripture-searching to find ways in which Jesus fulfilled messianic prophecies in *Tanach (Jewish scripture), but it remains a Jewish objection to Jesus as Christ that few of the biblical signs of the messiah were fulfilled.

Islam In Islam, al-Masiḥ is a description (almost a name, except that the Arabic article is never dropped) for 'Isā/*Jesus: 'O *Maryam, see, Allāh promises you a word from him whose name is al-Masiḥ, 'Isā b. Maryam' (Qur'ān 3. 45). In modern Arabic, Christians are often called Masīḥiy(y)un, rather than the older *Naṣārā. Less exactly, Muslim beliefs about *al-Mahdī are sometimes referred to as 'messianism'. See Index, Messianic speculation.

A. A. Sachedina, *Islamic Messianism* (1980).

Messianic movements. Movements centred on the Jewish hope for the coming of the *messiah. Throughout later Jewish history, the community in *exile has yearned for a charismatic king of the house of *David and for political independence in

*Erez Israel. These aspirations have been centred on particular figures. Jesus of Nazareth was believed by his Christian followers to be the messiah. According to Josephus, at the end of the 1st cent. BCE, Judas the Galilean condemned the people for 'consenting to pay tribute to the Romans and tolerating mortal masters after having God for their Lord'. Slightly later, other claimants came forward, e.g. Theudas and a Jew from Egypt 'who gained for himself the reputation of a *prophet'. The revolt against Rome in 66 CE must be seen in the context of messianic aspiration, and in the uprising of 132 CE, the great Rabbi *Akiva recognized Simeon *Bar Kokhba as the king–messiah. Further claimants arose, both in Muslim lands (such as the 7th-cent. Abu Isa), and in Christian Europe (e.g. the *Karaite Kohen Solomon in the 12th cent.). The 12th cent. in particular saw many messianic movements, possibly induced by Crusader violence. One claimant, Moses Al-Dari, was even admired by *Maimonides, and David Alroy persuaded the sophisticated Jews of Baghdad of his authenticity. Abraham b. Samuel *Abulafia saw himself as the forerunner of the messiah in the 13th cent. and Hasdai *Crescas believed that the messiah had been born in Castile. Messianic expectations continued to be aroused in the late Middle Ages until the time of the great *kabbalistic claimant, *Shabbetai Zevi, in the 17th cent. With the *Haskalah, the messianic hope tended to be transformed into a desire for social reform or secularized into modern *Zionism.

A. H. Silver, *A History of Messianic Speculation in Israel* (1959); see also MESSIAH; Index, Messianic speculation.

Messianic secret: see MESSIAH (CHRISTIANITY); SCHWEITZER, ALBERT.

Metaphysical movements. Groups that share a common definition of metaphysics as a practical religious philosophy and that seek to relate spiritual and psychic phenomena to everyday life. Among the groups classified as metaphysical are the older ones—*Spiritualism, *Theosophy, and *Anthroposophy—and a number of newer ones such as the Spiritual Frontiers Fellowship. The majority of the metaphysical movements today in the USA, for example, were established between 1950 and 1970, and are loosely organized into the International New Thought Alliance. Their ideas, like those of the older groups, bear remote relations to the *gnostics of the early Christian period. They tend to blend an occult with a metaphysical stream of thought. All, both old and new, hold to a monistic view of God and adhere to the belief that the inner, real self of humans is divine. Salvation is equated with the discovery of this divinity within.

J. Stillson Judah, *The History and Philosophy of Metaphysical Movements in America* (1967).

Metaphysical(s) Poets. Term applied by Samuel Johnson to a group of 17th-cent. Christian poets (especially J. *Donne, G. *Herbert, T. *Traherne, H. *Vaughan). He intended it as a term of dismissal, but they have come to be recognized as, collectively, one of the finest expressions of Christian poetry. Their intricate style explored the paradoxes and mysteries of Christianity, such as *grace and human response, the *incarnation ('Immensity cloystered in thy dear womb') and the *Trinity.

Metaphysics. The study of the most fundamental constituents of reality. The term was given by a later editor to a series of treatises by *Aristotle, because the topics covered came after (*meta*) the philosophy of nature (*physics*). In those treatises Aristotle dealt with topics which do not belong to any particular science, both the analysis of fundamental concepts like 'substance', 'cause', 'form', and 'matter', and theological questions, especially that of the 'Unmoved Mover'. He also dealt with 'First Philosophy', which he defined as the theory of being *qua* being.

Later philosophers questioned the scope, and sometimes even the possibility, of metaphysics. *Kant likened much of it to a series of futile mock battles, and condemned attempts to transcend the world of ordinary experience by speculating about the supra-sensible (*Critique of Pure Reason*, 2nd edn., 1787). The Logical Positivists dismissed metaphysical claims as meaningless, because unverifiable (A. J. Ayer, *Language, Truth and Logic*, 1936). Yet Kant himself, in his 'critical philosophy', attempted a chastened but scientific form of metaphysics, which restricted itself to laying bare the fundamental structure of our conceptual framework. Similarly, more recently, P. F. Strawson has distinguished between 'descriptive' metaphysics, which is content to describe the actual structure of our thought about the world, and 'revisionary' metaphysics, which aims to produce a better structure (*Individuals*, 1959). The former at least remains a lively and respected branch of philosophy today.

Metatron. *Angel mentioned in Jewish *apocalyptic literature. Metatron is frequently referred to as 'the Prince of the countenance'. In the *Talmud he is described as being seen seated by *Elisha b. Abuyah, as having 'a name like that of his master', and even, in some manuscripts, as 'the lesser *YHWH'. He is to be identified with Jahoel, mentioned in the *Apocalypse of *Abraham*, who was responsible for the highest tasks in heaven and performs many of the duties traditionally ascribed to the Archangel *Michael. At the same time he is associated with *Enoch who 'walked with God' (Genesis 5. 22). The *kabbalists noted that his name could be spelt (in Hebrew) either with seven letters or with six. They identified the seven-letter Metatron with the supreme emanation from the *Shekhinah, while the six-letter Metatron was Enoch.

G. Scholem, *Jewish Gnosticism* (1965).

Metempsychosis. The passing of some quintessential part or consequence of a person (e.g. soul or spirit) from one body to another through the process of death. It is frequently known as 'rebirth', especially in Indian religions, but in Buddhism there is no 'self' being reborn, only the process of caused and causal change.

Methodism. A Christian denomination, itself made up of several parts, deriving from the preaching and ministry of John and Charles *Wesley, and initially of George *Whitefield. The term 'methodist' was in origin used derisively by opponents of the Holy Club at Oxford, but Wesley used it from 1729 to mean the methodical pursuit of biblical holiness: 'A Methodist is one who lives according to the method laid down in the Bible.' Wesley sought renewal in the Church (of England, in which he was ordained), not a new denomination: he set up classes under itinerant pastors whose members were to live a life of prayer and discipline in the fellowship of the Holy Spirit: he resisted the extremes of *Calvinist predestination (thus all can be redeemed) and of reliance on 'faith alone', insisting that conversion must be followed by a life of personal holiness. The rapid success of Methodism, reaching places and people that the established Church did not, soon set up a tension, since the class system seemed to be setting up a 'parish' within a parish, especially when those converted wanted no connection with the parish church. In any case, Wesley was compelled by the shortage of ordained preachers in America (after the war of Independence) to ordain his fellow presbyter, Thomas Coke (1747–1814), as Superintendent over 'the brethren in America', who became the Methodist Episcopal Church; the title of Superintendent became that of Bishop in 1787. Wesley insisted that only those preachers who were episcopally ordained should administer Holy Communion, but after his death a non-sacramental understanding of the ordained ministry prevailed, not least in reaction against the hostility of the Anglican *Tractarians. Many divisions occurred in the 19th cent.: the Methodist Episcopal Church divided in 1844 over the issue of slavery; before that, two black Churches had been established, the *African Methodist Episcopal (1816) and the African Methodist Episcopal Zion (1820), which now number over 4 million. Among many groups in Britain, the Wesleyan, Primitive, and United Methodists came together in the Methodist Church of Great Britain and Ireland, in 1932. In the USA, a similar process brought into being the United Methodist Church in 1968. Attempts to reunite with the Church of England in 1969 and 1972 were approved by Methodists and promoted in the Church of England, but in the latter the majority failed to reach the required two-thirds. The World Methodist Council was set up in 1951, not only to draw Methodists together, but to seek transconfessional actions and unions. Methodists number about 60 million in 100 countries.

F. Baker, *From Wesley to Asbury* (1976); E. S. Bucke (ed.), *The History of American Methodism* (1964); R. E. Davies, *Methodism* (1976); R. E. Davies, A. R. George, and E. G. Rupp, *A History of the Methodist Church in Great Britain* (1965–88); N. B. Hamon, *Encyclopedia of World Methodism* (1974).

Methodius: see CYRIL AND METHODIUS.

Metrical psalms: see PSALMS, LITURGICAL USE OF.

Metropolitan. Christian *bishop of a province, who presides over all the other bishops in the province. The title comes from the organization of the Church in the Roman Empire, in which each city in a province had a bishop, and the bishop of the civil capital (or metropolis) normally came to have authority over the others. In the *Roman Catholic Church most *archbishops are metropolitans. Most *Anglican Churches, though not the *Episcopal Church of the USA, are organized into provinces (in England: Canterbury and York) with a metropolitan, also styled archbishop, at the head. In many Eastern and *Oriental Churches (but not in Russia) nearly all bishops have the title metropolitan.

Metta (Pāli). Buddhist virtue of generous kindness and goodwill. It is one of the four *brahmavihāras.

Metta(-sutta): see MAITRI.

Metteyya (future Buddha): see MAITREYA.

Metz, J. B.: see POLITICAL THEOLOGY.

Mevlevis (Sūfī order): see DERWĪSH; MAWLAWĪY(Y)A.

Mezuzah (Heb., 'doorpost'). Parchment scroll attached to the doorposts in Jewish houses. According to Deuteronomy 6. 9, Jews are commanded to write the words of God upon the doorposts of their houses. This commandment is fulfilled by fixing a small container, with the words of Deuteronomy 6. 4–9 and 11. 13–21 written on parchment inside, to the right-hand doorpost of every room or gate in the house. A mezuzah parchment has been found at *Qumran. According to the *Talmud, the mezuzah commandment is one of seven precepts by which God, in his love, singled out Israel.

Mīān Mīr, Hazrat. *Sūfī who, according to one tradition, laid the foundation-stone of *Harimandir Sāhib, *Amritsar. The Muslim Mīān Mīr was a friend of the Sikhs' fifth Gurū, *Arjan Dev.

Micah. Sixth book in the collection of *Minor Prophets in the Hebrew Bible and the Christian Old Testament. It consists of three main sections. The first three chapters are concerned with the condemnation of Israel, in particular the secular leaders who ignore the laws of God. This is followed in chs. 4 and 5 with the promise of consolation, victory, and an *ingathering of the tribes; the final section, chs. 6 and 7, are a mixture of condemnation and consolation, preceded by a truncated historical recital, thus suggesting a derivation from secular *covenant forms. The prophet was a native of the Southern Kingdom and is probably referring to the political events occurring in the reign of King Hezekiah. Like *Isaiah, Micah emphasized that God has chosen a descendant of *David to bring salvation to the people. His verse, 'what does the Lord require of you, but to do justly and to love mercy and to walk humbly with your God' (6. 8) was understood by the *rabbis to be a summary of all the *Commandments (*B.Mak.* 24a).

Michael. Archangel mentioned in the Hebrew scriptures. With *Gabriel, he is the only *angel mentioned by name in the Bible (Daniel 10. 13), where he is seen as a divine messenger. In the *aggadic literature, he is the guardian angel of Israel, the chief opponent of *Satan and the keeper of the heavenly keys.

Michi (spiritual path): see DŌ.

Mida. Abbr. of *Amida.

Middle Way 1. (Skt., *madhyamā-pratipada*; Pāli, *majjhimapātipadā*). General term for the way taught and practised by the *Buddha, which avoids extremes—e.g. the apparent choice between having an eternal soul (*ātman) or not having one (and therefore going to oblivion at death). In developments of Buddhism, the middle way is specified between other and different extremes, e.g. in *Nāgārjuna, whose analytic philosophy exposes the constant futility of opposing views, hence the system derived from him being known as *Mādhyamaka.

2. In the Latin form, *via media*, it is used to describe the *Anglican Church, which is both Catholic and Reformed; neither papalist nor dissenting.

Midnight Vigil. The practice of observing a special time of prayer during the night. Among Jews, Isaac *Luria introduced *tikkun ḥatzot* as a time for mourning the destruction of the *Temple, and for praying for the return of the *shekhinah to the world. Among Christians, midnight mass particularly anticipates *Christmas day, commemorating the birth of *Jesus at night. It is also customary to 'watch with Christ' (in contrast to the disciples who slept) on the night before *Good Friday, accompanying Christ in *Gethsemane.

Midrash (Heb., 'interpretation'). Type of Jewish literature mainly concerned with the interpretation of *biblical texts. Arguably the earliest surviving midrash is in the *Passover *Haggadah which includes an interpretation of Deuteronomy 26. 5–8. The *aggadic midrashim seeks to derive a moral principle or theological concept from scriptures, while the *halakhic midrashim aim to explain the full meaning of a biblical law. The *rabbis formulated various rules to deduce hidden or new meaning, and midrash was produced from the *tannaitic period until the 12th cent. CE. The best known example is the collection *Midrash Rabbah* on the *Pentateuch and five *megillot (Eng. tr., ed. H. Freedman and M. Simon). **Tanḥuma* contains discourses on the weekly portion of the Torah which is read in the *synagogue. The *pesiktot contain midrashim for special *sabbaths and festivals. Collections of midrashic ethical teachings include *Derekh Eretz Rabbati*, *Derekh Eretz Zuta*, and *Tanna de-ve-Elyahu*. *Avot de-Rabbi Natan* is an expansion of the tractate **Avot*, and *Pirke de-Rabbi Eliezer* contains stories about biblical events. From the 12th cent., various anthologies of midrashim were compiled, drawing from the earlier sources. Examples include the *Yalkut Shimeoni* and the *Midrash ha-Gadol*.

J. Bowker, *The Targums and Rabbinic Literature* (1969); A. G. Wright, *The Literary Genre Midrash* (1967).

Miḥna (Arab., *maḥana*, 'prove, examine'). Examination in Islam of those whose religious orthodoxy is suspect. The earliest organized miḥna was instituted by the caliph (*khalīfa) al-Ma'mūn, who held the *Muʿtazilite position, especially on the createdness of the *Qur'ān, and required *qāḍīs (judges) to make formal attestation of agreement. The test of theologians followed, some submitting, others refusing—notably *ibn Ḥanbal, who was imprisoned. The miḥna is sometimes referred to as a Muslim *inquisition.

Miḥrāb (directional niche): see MOSQUE.

Mikagura (Shinto music): see MUSIC.

Miki Tokuharu (1871–1938). Founder of the Japanese religion Hito-no-michi, and indirectly of PL Kyōdan. He was a Zen Buddhist priest who joined a movement called Tokumitsukyō. This had been founded by Kanada Tokumitsukyō (1863–1924), who had identified the sun as the source of all appearance. The sun is both *Vairocana and *Amaterasu and, as the source of all being, holds all beings in a universal bond. Through ascetic exercising, including the climbing of mountains, it is possible to attain the buddha-nature. He introduced a form of faith-healing called *ofurikae*, through which he would take on himself, like a *bodhisattva, the afflictions of all who came for help. When Kanada died in 1924, it looked as though the movement would disappear. But Miki Tokuharu followed the instructions of Kanada and planted a memorial tree at which he worshipped for five years, experiencing the presence of Kanada. As a result, he and his son, Tokuchika, re-established the movement with the name Hito-no-michi Kyōdan ('The Way of Man Society'), which was renamed again after the Second World War as P(erfect) L(ife) Kyōdan. During the 1930s, Miki adapted to the requirements of the imperial government to some extent (e.g. recognizing Amaterasu as the supreme deity), but both father and son were arrested for teaching that Amaterasu is the sun and not the sun Goddess, and for violating the Peace Preservation Law. The father died the following year while on bail, but the son survived to re-establish PL

Kyōdan after the War. The twenty-one precepts revealed by Kanada remained the basis of belief, but the central practice of life now became summarized in the words, *jinsei wa gejutsu de aru*, 'living life as art', or 'life is art', which means that any activity honestly undertaken can be converted into a work of art and beauty. PL Kyōdan not only sponsors art extensively, but also encourages a wide range of activities, from sports to medicine, all of which exemplify the human possibility of converting life into art.

Mikkyō (Jap., 'secret teaching'). Esoteric Buddhism (as opposed to *kengyō*, 'exoteric teaching', all other forms of Buddhist teaching), a Japanese term also for *Vajrayāna and *Tantric Buddhism. This form of Buddhism came to Japan in the 9th cent. CE, with *Saichō (founder of *Tendai) and *Kūkai (founder of *Shingon). Both established monasteries in *Kyōto, which became the main centres.

Miko, more fully **Kamiko.** Women in Shinto who are dedicated to the service of the *kami. When the shrine system broke down in the Middle Ages, the miko became merged with the *ichiko*, who are mediums working closely with *shamans, mediating connection with spirits not normally found in shrines.

Mikoshi (Jap., *mi* (honorific) + *koshi* ('palanquin'), homophonously, *mi* ('sacred') + *koshi*). A large portable shrine used in festive processions in Japan. It resembles an aristocratic palanquin, and can vary greatly in shape and size. Traditionally made of black lacquered wood with gilded bronze or gold fixtures, it is secured to a platform with two long poles attached, which are used to lift and carry the shrine. Often so heavy that twenty or more men are required to transport it through the streets, it is said that the erratic movement of the entourage is dictated by the will of the shrine's *kami passenger.

Mikveh (Heb., 'a collection', i.e., of water). Jewish ritual bath. A mikveh is used for ritual cleansing after contact with the dead or after menstruation (see NIDDAH). It can also be used for immersing vessels and as part of the *initiation ceremony for *proselytes. The water in a mikveh should be of sufficient quantity as that which is contained in a square cubit up to the height of three cubits (i.e. 250–1,000 litres), and only water which has not been drawn previously into a receptacle is suitable. There must be no leakage, but provided there is the minimum quantity of water which fulfils the above criteria, extra drawn water may be added to it. The regulations are contained in the *Talmudic tractate *Mikva'ot*. The laws of *purity are ancient: in the days of the second *Temple, *Josephus described the obligation of purification in a mikveh before visiting the Temple area, and archaeological remains of mikvaot (e.g. at Masada) can be found throughout *Erez Israel, with medieval examples existent throughout Europe.

Milam (*rmi-lam*, 'dream'). One of the six teachings of Nāropa (*Nāro chos drug), also known as 'dream yoga'. By the cultivation of particular dreams, awareness grows that the waking state is equally a constructed dream.

Milan, Edict of. A declaration made in 313 by the emperors *Constantine and Licinius to tolerate all religions and give legal status to Christianity. The text given by *Eusebius and Lactantius cannot be that of a formal edict, however.

Milarepa (Mi-la Ras-pa) (1043–1123). Tibetan Buddhist who remains exemplary to many Tibetans, and who was instrumental in founding *Kagyü. The earliest biographies are from a period about four cents. after his death. According to these accounts, he was reduced to poverty after the death of his father by unjust means. Seeking revenge, he brought about the death of many of those responsible, mainly through *magic. But realizing the evil of what he had done, he sought out the renowned teacher, *Mar-pa, who subjected him to a fiercely disciplined instruction. Eventually he acquired the teachings and was recognized by Mar-pa as his chief disciple. He entered on a mainly isolated life, often walled up in caves for months or years at a time. Nevertheless, disciples came to be near him from many parts, and the lineage of *yogins derived from him continues to the present, well-adapted to the persecutions inflicted by the Chinese on Tibetan religious practitioners. Two collections of songs (through which he expressed his realization) are attributed to him; for these, see *A Hundred Thousand Songs of Milarepa* (G. C. Chang, 1962), and *Drinking the Mountain Stream* and *Miraculous Journey* (L. Kunga and B. Cutillo, 1978, 1986).

W. Y. Evans-Wentz, *Tibet's Great Yogi Milarepa* (1951); L. Lhalungpa, *The Life of Milarepa* (1977).

Mile-fo. Chin. for *Maitreya, the future Buddha.

Milindapañha (Pāli, Milinda + *pañha*, 'question'). A Pāli Buddhist text (also in Chin. tr.) concerning a debate between a Buddhist monk, *Nāgasena, and a disputatious king, Milinda. Milinda is probably Menander, a Yavana king of Śākala (Siālkot, E. Puñjab) who ruled in the 2nd/1st cent. BCE; he is mentioned by Plutarch and Strabo. The text itself probably originated in 1st-cent. CE India as a Skt. *Sarvāstivādin work. While not generally regarded as canonical, it is often quoted by *Buddhaghoṣa as an authoritative source and has been accorded canonical status in Burma.

During the dialogue the king puts eighty-two separate dilemmas to Nāgasena which are successfully countered. At the conclusion of the contest, Milinda becomes a Buddhist lay disciple. Among the topics treated are the concept of personal identity (*pudgala), the limb of existence (bhavaṅga), and a rudimentary form of the teaching-body (see TRIKĀYA) doctrine. Sea travel between India, Alexandria, and China is also mentioned in passing.

The *Milindapañha* makes frequent use of canonical materials and often introduces *Abhidhammic terminology. Because of an overall lack of cohesion it is often claimed to be the work of various authors from different periods of Buddhist history.

Its most often quoted sequence is the question of the identity of a chariot. We are entitled to identify an appearance as a chariot rather than a cloud, but what 'is' the chariot? Its constituent parts are not 'the chariot', but the chariot is simply the sum of its constituent parts, aggregated (*skandha) in that way and not another. So also with humans: we are our aggregates, identifiable by particular names (e.g. Nāgasena), 'but in the absolute sense, there is no ego here to be found', i.e. *anātman.

Trs. I. B. Horner (1963); T. W. Rhys-Davids (1890–4; 1963).

Millennialism or **Millenarianism.** In the narrowest sense, the belief in a future millennium, or thousand-year reign of *Christ. The main source of the belief is Revelation 20. Its adherents are pre- or post-millennialists, according to whether they conceive Christ's second coming (*parousia) as coming before or after the millennium. Post-millennialists are accordingly the more optimistic about the progress of history toward the millennium. In the early Church, millenarian expectations were held by such writers as *Justin, *Irenaeus, and *Hippolytus (all pre-millennialists). In so far as such expectations came to stress the pleasures to be enjoyed by the *saints in the thousand years of their reign, a reaction against these views set in (e.g. in *Origen, culminating in *Augustine). Millenarian groups since the Reformation include *Anabaptists, Bohemian and *Moravian Brethren, early *Independents, 17th–18th cent. *Pietists, *Catholic Apostolic Church, *Plymouth Brethren, and *Adventists.

From its place in the theology of *fundamentalist groups (who are specifically pre-millennialist), millennialism has acquired a slightly wider reference, to the whole *apocalyptic view of the future resulting from the interpretation of biblical books like *Daniel and Revelation as explicit and detailed prophecy still to be fulfilled. It is characterized by interest in apocalyptic motifs in the Bible such as the *rapture, *Armageddon, and *Gog and Magog. Popular books like H. Lindsey, *The Late Great Planet Earth* (1970), show how millennialism can shade into science fiction. See also DISPENSATIONALISM.

In a still more general sense, millenarian movements are those which envisage a coming age (usually imminent) in which a faithful group will be particularly rewarded on this earth. Such movements are extremely common. Some are derived from Christianity (e.g. some elements of *T'ai-ping, *Adventists), but others have no such connection.

P. Worsley, *The Trumpet Shall Sound* (1957); E. R. Sandeen, *The Roots of Fundamentalism* (1970).

Millet (non-Muslims): see DHIMMA.

Mi-lo-fo: see LAUGHING BUDDHA.

Milton, John (1608–74). Poet and controversialist. Hostile to Archbishop W. Laud's *high churchmanship and the 'hireling shepherds', he supported the parliamentarians in the Civil War and served as Latin Secretary under the Commonwealth. Favouring the disestablishment of all Churches, he came to disagree with Cromwell's later ecclesiastical policy. Difficult relationships with his first wife probably occasioned his sympathetic approach to marriage problems in *The Doctrine and Discipline of Divorce* (1643). A prolific writer, he published works against *episcopacy and wrote vigorously in support of the freedom of the press (*Areopagitica*, 1644). He became totally blind in 1651. His monumental *Paradise Lost* (1667) undertakes to 'justify the ways of God to man' and to show the cause of evil and injustice in the world:

> Of Man's first disobedience, and the fruit
> Of that forbidden tree, whose mortal taste
> Brought death into the world, and all our woe,
> With loss of Eden . . .

It is often observed that the devil gets, if not the best, then many of the best of the lines:

> The strongest and the fiercest Spirit
> That fought in Heav'n; now fiercer by despair.
> His trust was with th' Eternal to be deemed
> Equal in strength, and rather than be less
> Cared not to be at all.

Its sequel *Paradise Regained*, and *Samson Agonistes*, appeared in 1671. His treatise *De Doctrina Christiana*, published posthumously, contains much that was thought to be unorthodox.

R. Parker, *Milton* . . . (1968).

Mīmāṃsā: see PŪRVA-MĪMĀṂSĀ.

Mīmāṃsā-paribhāṣa (Clear Presentation of Mīmāṃsā). Exposition of Mīmāṃsā by Krishna Yajvan.

***Mīmāṃsā-sūtra*.** Work attributed to *Jaimini, which forms the basis of *Pūrva-mīmāṃsā. The interpretations of Vedic rituals are summarized, and the sources of Vedic knowledge are assessed. Against the objection that not all that is in the *Vedas can be regarded as equally valuable—'The purpose of the Veda lying in the enjoining of actions, those parts of the Veda which do not serve that purpose are useless. In these, therefore, the Veda is declared to be non-eternal (unreliable)'—Jaimini replies, 'Being construed along with injunction, those passages will reinforce by commending the injunctions.'

Tr. (with commentary of Śabara), Ganganatha Jha (1933–6); N. V. Thadani (1952).

Mimi shehui (Jap.): see SECRET SOCIETIES.

Min (Heb., 'heretic'). Hebrew term for *heretic or sectarian. A min can be a Jewish heretic (as in *B.Horayot* 11a, where a Jew who eats forbidden food in a flaunting fashion is a min) or a *gentile (as in *B.Pesaḥim* 87b, where a Roman nationalist is described as a min). Some scholars have tried to show that the minim are one particular sectarian group, but the evidence is against this. Meat slaughtered by a min is not kosher, and *scrolls, *tefillin, and *mezuzot written by minim cannot be used (*Hul.* 2. 20). It was Samuel ha-Katan in the late 1st cent. CE who composed the '*benediction' (i.e. imprecation) against the minim found in the *ʿAmidah, and this seems originally to have been directed against the Judaeo-Christians: see BIRKAT HA-MINIM.

Mīṇā (Pañjābī, 'a bull with horns inclined down along its face', 'deceitful'). Name given by *Bhāī *Gurdās to followers of *Prithī Chand, *Soḍhī Miharbān, and the latter's son, Harijī. The Mīṇās, whose significance faded in the late 18th cent. CE, disputed the succession of Gurū *Arjan Dev. See JANAM-SĀKHĪ.

Minaret (tower): see MOSQUE.

Minbar (pulpit): see MOSQUE.

Mindfulness of death. Buddhist meditative practice to reinforce the sense of impermanence (*anicca) in all things, including one's own brief appearance. It is usually combined with meditation on the transient nature of the body, and both are summarized in *Buddhaghosa's *Vissudhimagga* 8. 1–144. The mindfulness of death is undertaken in solitary retreat, concentrating on the ways in which death (*maraṇa) is approaching me personally: as appearing like a murderer, sword in hand, the invariable companion of birth ('as budding toadstools always come up lifting dust on their tops, so beings are born along with aging and death'); as the ruin of success ('all health ends in sickness, all youth ends in ageing, all life ends in death'); by comparison with those who have been great in the world, but who nevertheless are all equally dead; by reflecting on the deaths which are already occurring in the body, inhabited as it is by many short-lived parasites ('here they are born, grow old and die, evacuate and make water: the body is their maternity home, their hospital, their charnel ground, their lavatory and their urinal; through the upsetting of these worms the body itself can be brought to death'); as always close because of the vulnerability and weakness of the body; as being usually unpredictable; as putting an inevitable limit on even the longest of lives; as in any case being related to the fact that a human does not exist for longer than a single instant (there being no self, *anātman), as when the rim of a turning wheel touches the ground only for an instant. Mindfulness of the body dwells on 'the repulsiveness and foulness of the body', in thirty-two stages, from the soles of the feet to the top of the hair, in order to realize that there is nothing in the body to which one would wish to cling, if one understands its true nature and composition.

Mind-only (Buddhist school): see VIJÑĀNAVĀDA.

Ming 1. (Chin., 'light-bearing'). Taoist enlightenment. According to Lao-tzu, it is attained by realization and acceptance of the return of all things to their proper root (*fu). It is to live according to *Tao, as rhythm and return. *Tao te-ching* 16 says:

> Attain complete emptiness; be at peace. A myriad things rise and fall while the self sees only their return. As much as they flourish, they all return to their source. Returning to the source is peace; it is nature's way. The way of nature is unchanging (*ch'ang), to know the unchanging is enlightenment (*ming*). . . . Being at one with the Tao is eternal; for such a one, though the body dies, the Tao will never disappear.

2. The celestial mandate in Confucianism, the will of heaven (*t'ien). Subsequently it came to mean the constraints in the universe which set limits on human action because they are non-negotiable (e.g. what might be called 'natural laws'). To know ming and to act according to it, without attachment to the success or failure of the action, is an ideal of Confucianism.

Ming chi (sustenance): see FUNERAL RITES (CHINESE).

Ming-tao: see CH'ENG HAO.

Ming-ti (58–75 CE). Chinese emperor of the Han dynasty, who, according to legend, was instrumental, as a consequence of a dream, in establishing Buddhism in China.

Minhag (Heb., 'custom'). Customs which have become binding on various Jewish communities. Minhag is an important ingredient of *halakhah. Some have taken the force of commandment and have become part of the written law for the entire Jewish community, while others have only local force (e.g. 'the custom in *Jerusalem', *BBB* 93b). Some customs even override the halakhah, and of these it was said, 'The minhag annuls the halakhah' (*TJ Yev.* 12. 1). To justify their reliance on custom, the *sages used to quote such biblical verses as, 'Remove not the ancient landmarks which your fathers have set' (Proverbs 22. 28). In cases of halakhic dispute, the *amoraim said, 'Go and see what is the practice of the people' (*B.Ber.* 45a). The principle *minhag mevattel halakhah* ('custom overrides the law') applies in general to civil, not to ritual, law, and for a custom to be valid, it must be widespread, common, and unequivocal. However, custom can be disregarded if it is based on error or if it is contradictory to the basic principles of Jewish law. Over the years, collections of minhagim have been drawn up, the earliest being the 8th-cent. CE *Sefer ha-Hillukim bein Mizrah ve-Erez Yisrael* (Variations in Customs of the People of the East and *Israel).

Minḥah. Jewish afternoon *prayer service. Traditionally the Minḥah service dates back to the days of the *patriarch *Isaac who 'went out to meditate in the field at eventide' (Genesis 24. 26). It is regarded as a substitute for the afternoon *sacrifice in the *Temple. The *synagogue service includes the *Ashrei, the *ʿAmidah, the Tahanun prayer, and the *Aleinu. The Minḥah can be recited up until sunset and, in modern times, the *Maʿariv service is recited shortly afterwards.

Minim (pl.): see MIN.

Minjung theology: see LIBERATION THEOLOGY.

Minor Prophets (Aram., *terei asar*, 'twelve'). The collection of twelve shorter *prophetic books in the Hebrew scriptures. The collection of minor prophets is counted as a single book in the Palestinian *canon of scripture and in the *Septuagint. It includes the books of *Hosea, *Joel, *Amos, *Obadiah, *Jonah, *Micah, *Nahum, *Habbakuk, *Zephariah, *Haggai, *Zechariah, and *Malachi. The twelve books were probably assembled together in the 4th cent. BCE. *Augustine called them *minor* in comparison with *Isaiah, *Jeremiah, *Ezekiel, and *Daniel (though in the Hebrew Bible Daniel is assigned to the *Writings).

Minucius Felix. Christian *apologist of the 3rd (or perhaps 2nd) cent. He is known as the author of the *Octavius*, a Latin treatise refuting the common pagan charges against Christianity, arguing for monotheism and providence, and attacking mythology. It probably depends on *Tertullian's work.

Minyan (Heb., 'number'). Quorum necessary for public Jewish services. According to the Talmud, if ten men pray together, the divine preserve is with them (*B.Ber.* 6a). The *ʿAmidah, the *Torah and *haftarah readings, the *priestly *benediction, and the *kaddish cannot be recited in the *synagogue without the presence of ten adult (i.e. over 13) men. Outside the synagogue, a minyan is required for the seven benedictions at a wedding, for the redemption of the first-born, and for grace after the meal following a *circumcision. R. *Johanan said, 'When God comes to a synagogue and does not find a minyan there, he is angry . . .' (*B.Ber.* 6b). Occasionally a 'minyan man' is paid to make up the quorum, and in the *Reform movement, women as well as men are counted as part of the minyan.

Mi-p'nei ḥata'einu ('on account of our sins'): see HOLOCAUST, SHOʾAH.

Mīqāt (times of Muslim worship): see ṢALĀT.

Mīrābāī. Hindu saint-poetess (a Rajasthani princess) in the *bhakti tradition of perhaps 15th–16th cent. CE. It is difficult to construct any accurate biography from the many stories which relate, e.g., how she flouted all convention by refusing to accept her Rajput husband, acknowledging only Lord *Kṛṣṇa as her true bridegroom. After refusing to commit *satī on the early death of her husband, she was persecuted by his family and became a wandering mendicant singing *bhajans* (chants) to Kṛṣṇa until finally being absorbed into his image in the Kṛṣṇa temple in Dvārakā.

The grace, melody, and simplicity of her songs have been preserved in Hindī and Gujarati, and her songs are still popular in many parts of India. They give expression to a constant, powerful devotion to Kṛṣṇa in the face of all criticism, and some project a deep pathos as she pines at her sense of separation from him: 'Deep is my agony in this night of separation | When will the streaks of golden dawn appear? | The moonlight is no comfort to me. | If I sleep, I wake as if startled by a dream. | O merciful One, deprived of You I lie in anguish, | Bless me, then, with a vision of Your face.' The anthology *Padāvalī* consists of hundreds of songs and poems of great devotion:

> My only consort is Giridhar Gopāl [Kṛṣṇa as the lifter of a mountain, and as a cowherd], none else in the whole world, which I have seen through and through. . . . With the water of my tears I have raised up the vine of divine love. . . . The king sent me poison which I drank with delight; for since all people know that Mīrā is attached inseparably by love to God, nothing beside it matters: what was destined has simply happened.

A. J. Alston, *The Devotional Poems of Mīrābāī* (1980); A. P. Chaturvedi, *Mirabai ki Padavali* (1976); S. Futehally, *In the Dark of the Heart* . . . (1994); H. Goetz, *Mira Bai, Her Life and Times* (1966).

Miracle. A striking event brought about (usually by God) for a religious purpose, against the usual course of nature; for example, the *resurrection or the instantaneous healings recorded in the Christian gospels. Reports of miracles raise two main *phenomenological questions: did they really happen; and, if so, what do they show? In recent centuries more attention has been devoted to the former question. David *Hume defined miracles as violations of laws of nature and argued that, since the accumulated evidence for laws of nature always outweighs any evidence from testimony for a breach of such laws, it is unlikely that a claimed miracle has occurred (*Enquiry Concerning Human Understanding*, 1748). Others have claimed that such violations are impossible, or that naturalistic explanations could be found for apparent violations. Respondents to these objections have queried the initial definition of miracles or the rigid determinism presupposed; and have pointed out that Hume's argument ignores the possibility that one might behold a miracle or else encounter the traces of one, e.g. a healed person. The second question asks about the moral or religious point of miracles: they are usually regarded as signs of God's power, or as vouching for the authority of a revelation, prophet, or holy person.

Among Jews, belief in miracles rests on the biblical descriptions of the interventions of God, beginning with creation itself. In the Hebrew Bible, such events as the Ten Plagues and the parting of the Red Sea are understood as interventions by God. In the *Talmud, miracles were understood as part of God's foreordained creation: 'Ten things were created on the *Sabbath eve of creation . . . , including the mouth of the ass of *Balaam which spoke' (*Avot* 5. 6). However, the *rabbis did not regard miracles as definite evidence of religious truth, and, on the other hand, they emphasized that daily life was a normal series of miracles ('Come and consider how many miracles the Holy One, blessed be He, performs for humans and they are unaware of it' (*Ex.R.* 24. 1)). The medieval Jewish philosophers found it difficult to accept the supernatural element in the biblical understanding of miracles, but this way of thinking has been condemned as *'Hellenism' by such thinkers as S. D. *Luzzatto. See also MAIMONIDES, MOSES.

In Islam the *Qur'ān speaks of the 'signs' of Allāh (*āyāt*, singular **āyā*) as proofs of the divine power: natural phenomena, and extraordinary events. The term used in Islam for 'miracle', though not occurring in the Qur'ān, is *mu'jiza* (that which could not normally be achieved; cf. **i'jāz*, from the same root). This is a sign given by Allāh to prove the authenticity and truthfulness of a *prophet, in particular *Muḥammad. Although the sole 'miracle' of Muḥammad is said to be the Qur'ān, yet in the *sīra, *ḥadīth, and legend many miracles are attributed to him, some of which are reminiscent of New Testament narratives. Within *Shī'a Islam, miracles are attributed to *'Alī and the *Imāms. The term *'ajība*, plural *'ajā'ib*, is also used to denote marvellous events, 'wonders'. A *karāma* is a 'favour', often of a minor nature, granted to a *walī (holy person) or a marvel which such a person can perform, generally with no publicity. Both *mu'jiza* and *karāma* count as *khāriq al-'āda*, 'breaking of (divine) custom' or of the natural order.

In E. religions, miracles are extremely common—so much so that they almost cease to be objects of wonder (Lat., *miraculum*). They surround the births of teachers or holy people, and are particularly associated with *siddha and *iddhi powers. Such powers would be expected of a living manifestation of the divine (*avatāra), as, e.g., in the contemporary case of Satya *Sai Baba. The Sikh Gurūs condemned appeal to miracles, mainly because they saw them as exploitation of the credulous. Nevertheless, many miracles are told of the Gurūs themselves.

See Index, Miracles.

C. Brown, *Miracles and the Critical Mind* (1984); R. Swinburne, *The Concept of Miracle* (1971); T. C. Williams, *The Idea of the Miraculous* (1991).

Miracle Plays: see THEATRE AND DRAMA.

Mi'rāj (Arab., 'ascend'). The ascension of *Muḥammad to heaven on a night journey, which becomes connected to the night journey to Jerusalem (see ISRA'), so that the ascension takes place, not from *Mecca (as perhaps in some early *ḥadīth), but from Jerusalem. The mi'rāj is not described in *Qur'ān (see 17. 1 for a possible allusion), but is extensively so in ḥadīth. Muḥammad travelled on *Burāq, and, accompanied by *angels, visited the seven *heavens, finding paradise in the seventh. Before the throne of *Allāh, he conversed with God about *ṣalāt. Despite some discussion about whether these events were in a dream, or in a spiritual experience (and *Sūfīs often take them as symbols of the soul's ascent to God), Muslims in general regard them as matters of fact.

G. Widengren, *Muhammad the Apostle of God and his Ascension* (1955).

Mirghadab (Shi'ite policing force): see BIHBAHĀNĪ, VAHID.

Mīrī and pīrī (Pañjābī, 'temporal' + 'spiritual'). Sikh affirmation that belief and commitment relates to all aspects of life: there can be no distinction between secular and religious, or between spiritual and political; all aspects of life must be governed by the teaching of the Gurū Granth Sāhib (*Ādi Granth).

Miroku. Jap. for *Maitreya.

Mīrzā Ghulām Aḥmad Qādiyānī (founder): see AḤMADĪY(Y)A.

Miserere (Nobis) (Lat., 'have mercy on us'). A prayer in common use in Christianity, derived from such *Psalms as 51. 1, and often used as a response (*Kyrie eleison).

Mishnah (Heb., 'teaching'). The Jewish *oral law, and in particular, the collection of oral law compiled by *Judah ha-Nasi. Originally all oral law was designated as 'mishnah' and it was accepted that the mishnah of one *tanna was different from that of another. After Judah ha-Nasi had redacted and arranged his six orders of mishnah at about the beginning of the 3rd cent. CE, it was initially described as 'Our Mishnah'. The Mishnah is divided into six *sedarim* (Heb., 'Orders') known as *Zeraim* (Seeds), *Mo'ed* (Festivals), *Nashim* (Women), *Nezikin* (Damages), *Kodashim* (Holy Things), and *Tohorot* (Purities): the *Talmuds are based on these sedarim. Judah ha-Nasi embodied in his collection many earlier collections: he 'systematised the mishnayot; they had previously been systematised, but he stated the *halakhah both anonymously and according to the views of a score of disciples of the *sages. . . . Thus the final text contains many different styles as well as an enormous variety of opinion' (Samson of Chinon). At the same time, Judah ha-Nasi did lay down his own rulings which is why the *amoraim could on occasion assert, 'The Mishnah represents an individual opinion' (*B.Suk.* 19b). By combining and selecting from existing collections, Judah ha-Nasi's Mishnah became representative of the entire community and thus authoritative, although other collections were attempted, e.g. *Tosefta. Later commentators disagreed as to whether the early mishnah collections had been in writing, and it is sometimes argued that even Judah ha-Nasi's Mishnah was only taught orally. Different sequences of the six sedarim are given by Resh Lakish and R. Tanḥuma which argues for an oral transmission. Each seder was divided into **massekhtot* ('tractates'). The sequence of tractates differs within the orders in the different manuscripts. The text was also emended by later teachers; the most important early manuscripts are the Kaufman manuscript in Budapest, the Parma manuscript, the Oxford manuscript which contains *Maimonides' commentary, and the Cambridge manuscript. It was first printed in Spain in 1485, but the first surviving whole printed edn. is that printed in Naples in 1492. See also TALMUD; ORAL LAW.

Text and Eng. tr. P. Blackman (1951–6); J. Neusner, *The Modern Study of the Mishnah* (1973) and *Judaism: The Evidence of the Mishnah* (1981).

Mishneh Torah (Heb., 'repetition of *Torah'). A name for *Deuteronomy; but more usually, the collective name for the code of *Maimonides.

Mishpat ivri (Heb., 'Hebrew law'). That portion of the Jewish *halakhah which parallels the legal systems of secular nations. The notion of mishpat ivri first appeared in the early 20th cent. in response to the desire for a Jewish homeland. In the State of *Israel, the *rabbinical courts have jurisdiction in matters of *marriage, divorce, and ḥaliza. The general courts are compelled to decide matters of personal status in accordance with rabbinical law unless State law has already dealt with the matter. According to Article 46 of the Israeli constitution, in the event of a lacuna in the existing law, Jewish sources of law must be explored, and thus the heritage of the Jewish legal tradition is preserved in a modern, largely secular, state.

Misl (Arab., 'alike', 'file', 'record'). Late 18th-cent. band of Sikh fighters. Traditionally twelve misls emerged in the mid-18th-cent., following the confusion after *Bandā Siṅgh's death, to defend *Pañjāb from Afghan attacks. Apart from the Phūlkiā misl, the misls consisted of *jathās of the Sikhs' army, the Dal *Khālsā. A record (misl) of each jathā's exploits was kept. Although theoretically equal, they varied from a few hundred men to the over 10,000-strong Bhaṅgī misl. The other misls were *Rāmgaṛhīā, Āhlūwālīā, Siṅghpurīā, Sukarchakīā, Kannhiā, Niśānvālā, Nakaiīā, Karoṛīā, Ḍalevālīā, and Śahīd. Jassā Siṅgh Āhlūwālīā was the overall commander. With the ending of the Afghan threat, 1769, the misls degenerated into internecine strife, finally disappearing with the rise of Mahārājā *Rañjīt Siṅgh. See also SARDĀR.

Misogi (Jap., 'pouring water [over] the body'). An act of ritual purification. A form of *harae, misogi is technically a ritual performed at a river or seashore for the purpose of cleansing pollution from the body, often as part of preparations for a larger religious ceremony. Though not restricted to these occasions, seasonal misogi rituals are performed in the spring (for three days beginning on the sixth day of the third month of the lunar calendar) and autumn (on the fourteenth day of the seventh lunar month).

Misrule, Lord of (medieval subversive): see HOLY FOOLS.

Missal. The book (in full *Missale Romanum*) containing introductory documents and everything to be said at the celebration of the *mass (Lat., *missa*), together with the major ceremonial directions. The missal of the pre-*Vatican II rite (the Tridentine missal, or missal of Pope St Pius V) was replaced by the Roman Missal of Pope Paul VI in 1970. By an indult in 1984, extended through the apostolic letter, *Ecclesia Dei* (1988), permission to use the 1962 edn. of the former missal has been allowed in some circumstances.

Mission (Lat., *missio*, 'sending'). The sense of obligation in all religions to share their faith and practice with others, generally by persuasion, occasionally by coercion (see e.g. MARRANOS). The emphasis on mission varies from religion to religion. Thus in the case of Judaism, there was a strong practice of mission in the period of the second *Temple, anticipating the fulfilment of the prophecy that the knowledge of God would one day cover the earth as the waters cover the sea. There were even anxieties expressed by Romans that the brightest young people were becoming *proselytes, since they found in Judaism a rational monotheism which was attractive in comparison with state or popular religion. But after the failure of the two Jewish revolts, Judaism reconceived its vocation, and understood it to be the development of a holy community which is preparing the way for the coming of the *messiah. Thus converts (who mainly come through marriage) are almost discouraged by being reminded of the burden of *Torah-observation which they will have to carry.

Christianity, in contrast, believes that the messiah has come, that he is *Jesus Christ, and that he has commanded his disciples to go out into all the world, proclaiming the good news (i.e. *gospel), and baptizing all who believe. When this was united with a belief that those who are not baptized will be condemned to hell for ever, there developed a missionary zeal which Pearl Buck described in the case of her father (a missionary in China) as 'a madness of necessity, an urgency of salvation'. The 19th cent. was one of immense missionary expansion, culminating in John *Mott's visionary slogan for the Student Volunteer Movement, 'the evangelisation of the world in this generation' (*not*, as it is often misquoted, 'the world for Christ in our generation', since he intended only that every person should have the opportunity of hearing the gospel). The Christian mission, characterized by the founding of many missionary societies, was somewhat contradicted by its own multiple divisions, often conducted with extreme rivalry and animosity. To overcome this, the Edinburgh Conference was convened in 1910, which became the origin of the modern *ecumenical movement. Further Conferences were convened by the new International Missionary Council (IMC, 1921), which itself amalgamated with the World Council of Churches in 1961. The two emphases in Christian mission are those of, on the one hand, sharing and receiving (often taking the model of the *Magi bringing their treasures to Christ as the appropriate one for the relation to non-Christian religions see also DIALOGUE), and on the other, the necessity to bring unbelievers formally into relationship with Christ through repentance and baptism. The two were summarized by Mott at the second IMC Conference at Jerusalem in 1928, looking back to Edinburgh: 'Our fathers could not bear to think of people dying without Christ; we cannot bear to think of people living without Christ.'

Islam is necessarily missionary (see DAʿWA) because it is derived from *Muḥammad's absolute and unequivocal realization that for God to be God, there cannot be other than what he is. Thus other religions are assessed in terms of their description of God and attitude to him: on the one hand, there are 'peoples of the Book' (*ahl al-Kitab), who have received their own *Qur'ān, even though they have not preserved it without corruption, and they are the closest to God; on the other, there are those who are far from God, above all those who continue in any form of idolatry. There is to be 'no compulsion in religion' (Qur'ān 2. 257/6), but there is to be zeal in defending the honour of God. It is sometimes held that Muslims are required to fight for God and convert by force, but *jihād is strictly controlled by rules, and is in any case defensive. Short of that, Muslims believe that all humanity belongs to a single *'umma (community), a belief that derives from *tawhīd, the unity of God. Consequently, missionary activity is simply the realization of that community, and is vigorously pursued, making Islam (with Christianity) the fastest growing religion at the present time.

It is sometimes felt that Eastern religions are less inclined to mission than Christianity and Islam, but that is only partially true. Hindus traditionally have regarded India as the centre of the world in which the practice of *dharma (appropriate ways of life) is possible, with the outside world being a chaotic waste. It has therefore been regarded as a fault for a *brahman to travel beyond the borders of India. After all, the process of rebirth will eventually bring all to the opportunity of *mokṣa (release) without a necessity being imposed on Hindus to go out and accelerate the process. Nevertheless, in the 19th cent. societies were formed to propagate Hinduism (or rather, movements within the Hindu way); and in the 20th cent. some of the fastest growing *new religious movements have been Hindu-based, attracting many converts.

In the case of Buddhism, the same consideration of rebirth obtains, but there was originally a far greater emphasis on making disciples. Within a few centuries, through the work of such figures as *Bodhidharma and *Kumārajīva, Buddhism had spread through China to Korea, and thence eventually to Japan. In contrast to Christianity (with exceptions, e.g. *Ricci and *de Nobili), Buddhism did not try to replace the cultures it encountered. Buddhism integrated the religions and cultures it met, being in turn profoundly affected by them. The missionary goal for Buddhism is not salvation from sin, but the overcoming of ignorance (*avidya). Within the bracket of the *enlightenment which the *Buddha received, there may be innumerable 'wisdoms' to reinforce the way which he opened up. There have been a few societies formed with the intention of winning others to the Buddha's way, but these have not been so influential as have individuals in the West. See further, Index, Missionaries.

R. Bulliet, *Conversion to Islam in the Medieval Period* (1979); K. Ch'en, *The Chinese Transformation of Buddhism* (1973); K. S. Latourette, *A History of the Expansion of Christianity* (1937–45) and *Christianity in a Revolutionary Age* . . . (1958–63); S. Neill, *A History of Christian Missions* (1964).

Mitama-shiro (Shinto spirit symbol): see SHINTAI.

Mithra. God worshipped in four different religions: in Hinduism (as *Mitra); in Zoroastrianism (Mithra); in Manichaeism (Mithra), and in the Roman Mithraic mysteries (Mithras). Why this Zoroastrianized Indo-Iranian deity was the focus of a cult in the enemy empire of Rome remains something of a historical puzzle. The first evidence for the cult comes from the end of the 1st cent. CE. It was popular mainly among the military and was therefore commonly found in the frontier regions along the Danube, the Rhine, and Hadrian's Wall in N. England. There were, however, civilian temples, notably in Italy, above all in Ostia, the port of Rome. The cult was eclipsed in the 5th cent. by the rise of Christianity. The reconstruction of Mithraic belief and practice is difficult, because no specifically Mithraic texts have survived, only inscriptions and accounts by outsiders, notably *Porphyry. The main source of evidence is hundreds of excavated temples (Mithraea) and their statuary. The cult explicitly claimed to have been founded by *Zoroaster and became known as the Persian mysteries. There were seven grades of initiation, each under the protection of a planet: Raven (Mercury), Bride (Venus), Soldier (Mars), Lion (Jupiter), Persian (moon), Runner of the Sun (sun), Father (Saturn). Progression through the grades was thought to reflect the soul's progress through the planetary spheres, and it probably reflected ever deeper esoteric knowledge. The main cult relief (tauroctony) depicted Mithras slaying the bull, a scene thought to have soteriological significance, understood at least in part in astrological terms. Other scenes depicted Mithras and Sol banqueting in what was probably the mythic prototype of the community ritual meals of bread and wine. The death of the bull and the ritual meal were both depicted taking place in a cave, for the universe was thought of as a cosmic cave, and the temple structures were commonly made cave-like to emphasize the cosmological significance of the acts within. Side scenes in the temple showed the birth of Mithras from a rock (he was known as Mithras Petrogenes). Some older popular books state that the cult included the rite of the taurobolium in which an initiate descended into a pit over which a bull was slain and in whose blood the initiate bathed. This could not have been practised in Mithraism, because virtually all known temples were too small for a bull to enter. The death of the bull, therefore, appears to have been thought of as a unique inimitable act of the god himself, who is described in one inscription as having saved the initiates by the shedding of the eternal blood. Mithraism appears from the inscriptions to have been a very respectable cult, inculcating a disciplined, ascetic, and arduous life. It is interesting both in its own right and as a mystery cult whose growth, and some of whose ideas, paralleled emerging Christianity.

J. R. Hinnells (ed.), *Mithraic Studies* (1975) and *Studies in Mithraism* (1994).

Mithuna (ritual sexual intercourse in Indian religions): see MAITHUNA.

Mithyā (Skt., 'false'). According to the philosophy of *Advaita Vedānta, the phenomenal world perceived by the senses, which is 'false' (*mithyā*). The world cannot be determined as either existent or non-existent. The well-known example of the snake and the rope illustrates this: a rope lying across a path at dusk may be mistaken for a snake but when seen under better light is found to be a rope. That which is sublated by a later perception cannot be non-existent since it was originally perceived. That which is absolutely non-existent cannot be perceived. On the other hand, that which was originally perceived is later sublated and therefore cannot fully exist. That which exists cannot be destroyed by mere perception. According to Advaita Vedānta, the illumined sage sees the world as the Absolute, *Brahman, undifferentiated consciousness, existence, and bliss. Yet the world, *qua* world, is perceived by the unillumined. Hence the phenomenal world is 'false', and its ontological status is indeterminable (*sadasadbhyām anirvacanīya*).

Mitnaggedim (Heb., 'opponents'). Designation of the Jewish opponents to *ḥasidism. *Elijah b. Solomon Zalman, the Vilna *Gaon, led the opposition to ḥasidism and created an alternative pattern of Judaism which rested on intellectual discipline, study, and *Orthodox practice. His followers, the mitnaggedim, were determined in their disapproval of Ḥasidim, but, in the late 19th cent., they supported each other in their stand against the *Haskalah (Enlightenment). The two groups still differ in their religious worship: the Mitnaggedim retain the traditional *Ashkenazi Polish rite, while the Ḥasidim follow the largely *Sephardi *Prayer Book of Isaac *Luria.

Mito school. A school (of Tokugawa period, 17th–19th cent.), of neo-Confucian and neo-Shinto thought in Japan. Initially inspired by the writings of the Chinese neo-Confucianist *Chu Hsi (1130–1200 CE), and associated with the Mito family in Japan, this group of thinkers and writers were later influenced by the National Learning (*kokugaku) movement of the Tokugawa period. The school produced an influential book called *The History of Great Japan* (*Dai nihon shi*) which stressed the divine origins of the nation and Japan's history as a sacred tradition, and helped provide a theoretical basis for the Shinto nationalistic and imperial restoration movements of the late 19th cent.

Mitra. Hindu Vedic god, one of the *Ādityas, 'he who awakens people at daybreak and prompts them to work' (*Ṛg Veda* 3. 59. 1). Because *mitra* means 'friend', Mitra is usually associated with another god in partnership, especially *Varuṇa. Mitra-Varuṇa are handsome, shining, and young. They are appointed kings by the *devas, and *soma is pressed for them. Since Mitra rules over day, Varuṇa rules over night.

J. Gonda, *Mitra* (1972).

Mitre (Gk., *mitra*, 'turban'). The head-dress of a Christian bishop, worn on liturgical or ceremonial occasions. It is worn at all solemn functions, but removed during the prayers and the *canon of the *mass.

Mi-tsung. 'School of Secrets', *Tantric school of Chinese Buddhism. It was brought to China from India in the 8th cent. CE, by three masters, including Śubhākarasimha who translated the **Mahāvairocana-sūtra*, which became the basic text. The teaching was transmitted orally, to protect it, and was taken to Japan by *Kukai, where it is known as *Shingon.

Mitūk. Korean for *Maitreya, the future Buddha.

Mitzvah (Heb., 'commandment'). Jewish commandment, ritual duty, or good deed. The *rabbis categorized the mitzvot (pl.) into *mitzvot de-oraita* ('the *biblical commandments') and the *mitzvot de-rabbanan* ('the rabbinic commandments'). All male Jews are expected to keep the mitzvot from the age of 13, while females are exempted from time-bound affirmative commandments. Before performing a mitzvah, it is usual to recite a *blessing ('Blessed art thou Lord God, King of the Universe, who has sanctified us through your commandments and commanded us to . . .'). The reward for performing mitzvot will be in the hereafter (*B.Kid.* 39b), but through observing them, true sanctity will be found (*B.Shab.* 30b). It was debated whether *kavvanah (intention) is necessary for the fulfilment of a command. In general, it was accepted that fulfilment was acceptable for an ulterior motive (e.g. for the healing of a child, *BRH* 4b), but that this was only a stage toward the goal of undertaking to obey the mitzvot for their own sake (*B.Pes.* 50b). There are 613 mitzvot in *Torah (*taryag mitzvot*), of which 365 are prohibitions (one for each day of a solar year), and 248 are positive (one for each limb of the human body). To these E. Fackenheim added a 614th: see HOLOCAUST.

Mitzvot (de-oraita/de-rabbanan): see MITZVAH.

Mixed marriage. In Judaism, a *marriage between a *Jew and a *gentile. Mixed marriage is forbidden under Jewish law; Deuteronomy (7. 3) states, 'Neither shall you make marriages with them.' Therefore, in Jewish law, a mixed marriage has no legal validity. In the case of *divorce, no *get is required and the wife has no right of maintenance. No mixed marriage can be celebrated in the State of *Israel, because marriage is in the control of the *rabbinic courts (see MISHPAT IVRI). However, the children of a Jewish woman are regarded as Jewish even if their father is a gentile. The children of Jewish men are not accepted as Jews unless their mother is Jewish (an exception has been made to this in the *Reform movement). Mixed marriage is seen as a very real threat to the Jewish people. Since the *Haskalah, Jews have largely been accepted into gentile society, with the result that there is greater opportunity for mixed marriage. With the disappearance of arranged marriages and the greater value in society of romantic love, mixed marriage also becomes increasingly likely, and in some communities is reputed to run as high as 75 per cent. Statistically, Jewish men are more likely to marry out than Jewish women; and divorced people have a very high rate of mixed marriage. Despite much discussion of the issue in the communities and greater efforts to produce more effective Jewish education, the rate of mixed marriage shows no sign of diminution. See also PROSELYTES.

W. J. Cahnman (ed.), *Intermarriage and Jewish Life* (1963).

Mizrachi movement (from Heb., *merkaz ruhani*, 'spiritual centre'). A Jewish movement which emphasizes that *Zionism and the establishment of the State of Israel must be spiritual as well as political. Its maxim is 'The land of Israel for the people of Israel in accordance with the *Torah of Israel'. The Mizrachi movement underlies the National Religious Party of Israel, i.e. Mafdal.

Mizraḥ (Heb., 'East'). Direction to be faced by Jews during prayer; also, ornament on *synagogue or house wall to mark the easterly direction. According to the *Mishnah, the Jew who prays in the *diaspora should turn towards *Erez Israel. If he prays in Israel, he should turn to Jerusalem; if in Jerusalem towards the *Temple and if in the Temple towards the *Holy of Holies (*Ber.* 4. 5). In *Orthodox households a mizraḥ is often placed to mark the east, and this is often a highly artistic object.

Mizugo (unborn child in Japan): see ABORTION.

Mkhan-po (senior Tibetan Buddhist): see ABBOT.

Mleccha (foreigner): see HERESY (E. RELIGIONS).

Mobed (Zoroastrian priest): see MAGI.

Mo-chao ch'an (Chinese Ch'an/Zen master): see HUNG-CHIH CHENG-CHÜEH.

Mo-chia (Chin.): see MOHISM.

Modalism. The more important kind of *monarchian doctrine in Christianity of the 2nd–3rd cents. Its most sophisticated form was *Sabellianism. See also PATRIPASSIANISM.

Modernism. The attempt, especially in the *Roman Catholic Church at the beginning of the 20th cent., to reformulate doctrine in the light of contemporary philosophical and scientific research. It began in France under the influence of neo-*Kantianism and evolutionary theory, and led to the rejection of the notion of unchangeable *dogma. Exegetes, the most distinguished of whom was Alfred *Loisy, argued that the scriptures had to be treated simply as historical documents, and studied without reference to tradition or to the *magisterium of the Church. The English Jesuit George *Tyrrell, influenced both by Loisy and by von *Hügel, went on to suggest that dogmas were simply attempts to give expression to the divine force which individuals experience. In Italy a social and political modernism led by Romolo Murri espoused action within the political realm freed from any hierarchical constraint. Modernism was condemned by the *Holy Office in the decree *Lamentabili* of July 1907, and by Pius X's *encyclical *Pascendi* the following Sept. Pius reduced its errors to the denial of the validity of rational (*scholastic) argument in religion, and to the derivation of religious truth from human need. The ensuing purge in the Church has been known as 'the anti-modernist terror', requiring as it did the anti-Modernist oath. Outside the RC Church modernism may be generally identified with theologically liberal Protestantism; and with the movement in *Anglicanism which issued in the Modern Churchmen's Union.

B. M. G. Reardon, *Roman Catholic Modernism* (1970); A. M. G. Stephenson, *The Rise and Decline of English Modernism* (1984); A. R. Vidler, *The Modernist Movement . . .* (1934).

Mo'ed (Heb., 'season'). One of the orders of the Jewish *Mishnah. According to Simeon b. Lakish, it is the second order, but according to R. Tanḥum, it is the fourth. *Mo'ed* is composed of twelve tractates dealing with *Sabbaths, *Festivals, and *Fasts.

Moggallāna (Pāli, Maudgalyāyana). Second (after *Sāriputta) of the *Buddha's two leading disciples. In early life, they both agreed to follow any teacher who could bring them release. It was Sāriputta who found the Buddha, but Moggallāna soon followed him and became the disciple with most prowess in visiting the heavens and in defeating demons. Despite this, he died a violent death as a consequence of *karma from a previous life. He is represented iconographically as standing at the left hand of the Buddha.

Moggalliputta, Tissa (3rd cent. BCE). Leading Buddhist monk and scholar. He is said to have presided over the 3rd *Council in the reign of *Aśoka, when the final part of the Buddhist *canon, the *Abhidhamma, was closed. At the end of the Council, Moggalliputta composed the *Kathavatthu* (The Book of Controversies, tr. S. Z. Aung and C. A. F. Rhys-Davids, 1979). The existence of the Council and of this account has been doubted since it is not well-attested. The work is nevertheless of importance in reviewing the Vibhajjavādin/Theravādin objections to other schools of early Buddhism.

W. Rahula, *History of Buddhism in Ceylon: The Anuradhapura Period* (1956).

Mog(h)ila, Peter/Petr (1596–1646). Russian Orthodox theologian and *metropolitan of Kiev. He was born in Moldavia and was educated in Poland (and possibly also in Paris). He became metropolitan (in 1633) at a time when many Ukrainians were attracted by Roman Catholicism. In some respects (e.g. allowing the term *'transubstantiation', and agreeing that the transaction occurs, not at the moment of *epiclesis but at the words of institution) he seemed to concede ground to Roman Catholicism. But overall he defended Orthodoxy against both Catholicism and Protestantism. He wrote the *Orthodox Confession of the Catholic and Apostolic Eastern Church*, which was amended before it was endorsed in 1643 and at the Synod of Jerusalem in 1672. His own teaching he maintained in the *Little Catechism*.

J. J. Overbeck and J. N. W. B. Robertson, *The Orthodox Confession* . . . (1898).

Moha (Pāli, Skt.). 'Delusion', which prevents discernment of truth in Hinduism and Buddhism. In the latter, it is one of the three 'unwholesome roots' (*akuśalamūla*) which, together with craving (*lobha)—or attachment (*raga)—and hatred (*dosa) leads to rebirth and suffering in cyclic existence (*saṃsāra). Moha is synonymous with ignorance (*avijjā), which is the first link in the series of *Paticca-samuppāda and which must be removed if suffering (*dukkha) is to cease. Most fundamentally moha and avijjā relate to ignorance about the true nature of things as summarized in the *Four Noble Truths of Buddhism. This includes ignorance of one's own nature and that of the world at large, and manifests itself in the belief that phenomena are permanent and stable, and that a self or soul underlies personal identity. The way to cleanse the mind of these misconceptions is through the practice of the Eightfold Path (see AṢṬANGIKA-MĀRGA) which destroys delusion (moha) and replaces it with wisdom (*paññā*), and by systematic and methodical attentiveness (*yoniso manasikāra*).

Mohel. The one who carries out the operation at the Jewish ceremony of *circumcision.

Mohinī. In Hinduism, *Viṣṇu's female form. He assumed this beautiful form in order to entice the *asuras and get from them their share of *amṛta (the nectar of immortality) after the *Churning of the Ocean. He also assumed this form in order to test *Śiva when Śiva was in his *ascetic mode.

Mo(h)ism. W. term for the teaching associated with *Mo Tzu. The Chinese equivalent is mo-chia.

Moji Zen (word-dependants): see KATTŌ.

Mo-kao/Mogao Caves (Buddhist shrines): see TUN-HUANG.

Mokṣa (Skt., from *muc* or *mokṣ*, 'release', 'liberation'). The fourth and ultimate *artha ('goal') of Hinduism, release from the round of death and rebirth (*saṃsāra). This is attained when one has overcome ignorance (*avidyā) and desires. The routes leading toward mokṣa are, in effect, a map of 'Hinduism': the **Bhagavad-gītā* tries to reconcile the different forms of *yoga, *jñāna, *karma, and *bhakti, as all having their place. Although mokṣa is the soteriological goal of Hinduism, it is paradoxically not a goal at all, since its attainment depends upon one's abandonment of all desire and attachment, including the desire for mokṣa. Mokṣa is the transcendence of all goals (arthas). Its attainment while alive (*jīvan-mukti) or discarnate (*videha-mukti) marks the end of rebirth and suffering. Mokṣa is not personified or localized in the Hindu tradition.

For Jains, mokṣa is emancipation from the impediment of karma, and this lies beyond enlightenment (which provides the means for rooting out the remaining traces of karma): see also KEVALA.

W. D. O'Flaherty (ed.), *Karma and Rebirth in Classical Indian Traditions* (1980).

Mokṣa Dharma. A text which forms part of the **Mahābhārata*, dealing with philosophical issues.

Moku-funi (Jap., 'silent not two'). Zen belief that the realization of the one, undifferentiated buddha-nature (*bussho) in all appearances can only be expressed in silence. This is the 'thundering silence' of Vimalakīrti, a lay Buddhist praised by *Mañjuśrī in the *sūtra bearing Vimalakīrti's name.

Mokusa (part of Buddhist ordination): see MOXA.

Mokushō Zen (silent illumination Zen): see HUNG-CHIH CHENG-CHÜEH.

Molcho, Solomon (1500–32). Jewish *kabbalist and pseudo-*messiah. Of *Marrano stock, Molcho converted to Judaism. Fulfilling the Talmudic legend that the messiah would suffer, Molcho fasted in Rome dressed in rags. He secured the protection of the Pope, but was eventually burnt at the stake by the Emperor Charles V for his refusal to convert to Christianity. Many of his followers did not believe he had really died, and messianic legends grew up round his name.

J. H. Greenstone, *The Messiah Idea in Jewish History* (1906).

Molinos, Miguel de (Christian quietist): see QUIETISM.

Moloch Worship. Ancient Middle-Eastern cult. The *Canaanites seem to have sacrificed first-born children to Moloch by passing them through fire. According to Jeremiah 7. 31, an altar was built to Moloch near Jerusalem even though passing sons and daughters through fire was forbidden specifically in the law of Moses (Deuteronomy 18. 10).

Monarchianism. A Christian understanding of God, of the 2nd–3rd cents. Concerned to uphold monotheism and the unity ('monarchy') of God, it was condemned as heretical for threatening the independence of the Son. The *modalist monarchians held that within the Godhead there was no difference of persons, only a succession of transitory modes of operation. Modern scholars also speak of those *adoptianists who held that Christ was a mere man, endued with God's power at his baptism, as 'dynamic' monarchians.

Monasticism

Christianity The Gk., *monachos*, underlying 'monk', points to someone being 'on their own'. It may originally have meant *'celibate' and only later 'solitary'; but monasticism came to refer to those who withdraw from society (in a celibate state) in order to devote themselves with greater intensity to God through prayer, austerity, and discipline. In its extreme form, it is *anchorite (living alone), but it may also be *coenobitic (living in community). Monasticism began to emerge in Egypt in the 3rd cent.; St *Antony is regarded as the 'father' of Christian monasticism, although *Pachomius had begun to organize communities before him. *The Sayings of the Fathers* (*Apothegmata Patrum*), brought together by *Evagrius of Pontus, did much to popularize the 'spirituality of the desert', affecting especially *Palladius and John *Cassian. A separate and even more extreme form of monasticism developed separately in Syria, including *Stylites (pillar-dwellers) and 'browsers', who lived as animals, depending for everything on God. Monasticism filtered to the West, where it was promoted by *Jerome and *Augustine; but it received its major impetus and order from St *Benedict. Monasticism subsequently divided into a myriad of different orders and styles, among which the Benedictines, *Dominicans, *Cistercians, and *Carthusians have been prominent. In the Eastern Church, the influence of *Basil the Great has been acknowledged as supreme, along with the desert fathers. Monasticism has not divided into orders, but has adopted different styles, the coenobitic and the grouping of individuals, who pursue either a communal life on a smaller scale (see LAVRA) or an individual life (*idiorrhythmic, allowing considerable individual freedoms). Of particular importance is Mount *Athos, where monks from many different parts of *Orthodox Christianity live.

D. J. Chitty, *The Desert a City* (1966); C. G. Constable, *Medieval Monasticism: A Select Bibliography* (1976); M. D. Knowles, *Christian Monasticism* (1969); J. Leclerq, *The Love of Learning and the Desire for God* (1961); R. Panikkar *et al.*, *Blessed Simplicity: The Monk as Universal Archetype* (1982); M. B. Pennington, *Monastic Life: A Short History* . . . (1989); H. Waddell, *The Desert Fathers* (1936).

Islam Rahbānīya (monasticism, derived from *rāhib*, 'monk') is taken to be opposed in Qur'ān 57. 27 ('We put in the hearts of those who followed 'Isā/*Jesus compassion and mercy; monasticism they instituted (but we did not prescribe it to them) only out of a desire to please God. But they did not observe truly, and we gave to those of them who believed their reward, but many of them were evil-doers.' But 'monasticism' may also (grammatically) be a third object of the verb 'we put'; in which case it is a divine institution. However, the exegesis with only two objects of 'we put' has prevailed, and the Muslim opposition to monasticism is strong, not least because it seems to denigrate (by vows of poverty and celibacy) the good things of God's creation. That did not preclude the widespread adoption of asceticism, often communal, among *Sūfīs—but they too were sometimes suspect in this regard to the orthodox.

Buddhism The monastic lifestyle arises quite naturally out of the general Indian tradition of the homeless wanderer as a private option on the periphery of society, and develops into an institution at the heart of the religion so much so that to take refuge in the *saṅgha (the Buddhist community, but also the community of monks) is one of the *Three Jewels. Śākyamuni Buddha is taken as the model monk. He is said to have composed the monastic regulations (Skt., Pāli: *Vināya) and ideally a monk can trace his ordination lineage back to the Buddha. Renunciation (see ASCETICISM) is moderate by Indian standards: clothing is worn, the hair and beard are shaved, nails are trimmed, and the body is kept clean. Again contrary to general Indian practice, women have from the beginning been accepted as nuns (see BHIKṢU/BHIKṢUṆĪ). The original habit was made up of discarded material, yellowed (Skt., *kaśāya*, 'earth-coloured') with age, and pieced together. The modern habit in *Theravāda is three strips of yellow, brown, or orange cloth, normally cotton, wound around the body so as to cover it for reasons of modesty and protection against the weather. The upper toga-like robe (Pāli, *cīvara*) has a patchwork pattern which is a formalization of the primitive piecing-together of rags. The clothing of all ranks, and of nuns, is indistinguishable. The *Mahāyāna habit is of two types: Tibeto-Mongol and Sino-Japanese. The former is dominated by maroon woollen components and the latter by a tailored garment resembling a Christian cassock, and grey or black in colour. Some form of yellow or brown patchwork garment is always present but its form varies between a full *cīvara* for formal occasions, a vest (especially in Tibet) and a kind of apron (especially in Japan; Jap., *kesa*, from *kaśāya*). This garment may be treated with special reverence like the scapular of Christian monks. Mahāyāna monks commonly possess elaborate ceremonial robes, especially in connection with *Tantric liturgies, but again there is no distinctive habit for nuns or distinguishing marks of rank in the informal (non-liturgical) attire. Theravāda has two levels of initiation, novitiate (Pāli, *pabbajjā*, 'going out', i.e. from one's natural family in order to enter the Buddha's family); and full ordination (Pāli, *upasampadā*, 'completion'), leading respectively to the states of novice (Pāli, *sāmaṇera, fem. *sāmaṇeri*, 'striver') and monk (*bhikṣu, 'mendicant'). The Mahāyāna levels are similar but are complicated by the blending of the monastic life as such with the *bodhisattva vows, academic degrees (especially in Tibet), and administrative functions (especially in Japan). Monastic buildings were at first simple shelters for the retreat (Pāli, *vassa) conducted during the monsoon, and have developed into elaborate centres of culture, sometimes resembling universities (especially in Tibet) or walled cities (especially in Japan) and containing notable temples and perhaps famous orchards (e.g. in Tibet) or gardens (e.g. in Japan). Since the monk functions in relation to the wider community, monasteries are rarely located in unpopulated areas, although there is an eremitical tradition. Generally, monasticism is more central to Buddhism than it is to Christianity, and there is often a lively spirit of co-operation between monks and laypeople, which is the social dynamic of many Buddhist communities.

Because of the general resemblances of community and at least partial separation from society, the term 'monk' is widely used in English with reference to Buddhism: thus any male Buddhist official is liable to be called a monk or priest and any female Buddhist official a nun. This common English practice obscures the complexity of Buddhist hierarchies of which there are two major forms (Theravādin and Mahāyānist), two sub-forms of the Mahāyānist (Tibeto-Mongol and Sino-Japanese), and many other varieties depending on local custom. In its purest form, 'monk' refers to one who has taken the full vows of a bhikkhu or bhikṣu, and 'nun' to a bhikkhunī or bhikṣuṇī. However, bhikkhus, although celibate, perform ceremonies for the laity in the manner of priests, and indeed the ritual of *upasampadā*, by which they become bhikkhus, is commonly called 'ordination' rather than 'profession'. In some forms of Mahāyāna, e.g. Tibetan *Nyingma and Japanese *Zen, trainees may maintain celibacy but marry subsequent to 'ordination'. In other forms of Mahāyāna, e.g. Tibetan *Gelugpa and Korean Chogye, continued celibacy is strictly required. In Japanese *Jōdo Shinshū, celibacy is explicitly abandoned and temple duties are passed down from father to son, yet the habit and tonsure of a 'monk' are maintained. It seems best to abandon the English term monk and use terms such as bhikkhu, *lama, *sensei, and *rōshi as appropriate.

See Index, Monasticism; Monks.

S. Dutt, *Early Buddhist Monachism* . . . (1924) and *Buddhist Monks and Monasteries of India* (1962); J. Prip-Møller, *Chinese Buddhist Monasteries* (1967); W. Rahula, *The Heritage of the Bhikkhu* (1974).

Mondō (Jap.; Chin., *wen-ta*). 'Question and answer', the exchange between teacher and pupil in Zen Buddhism, which evokes from a pupil, not so much an answer as an expression of the pupil's deepest disposition (*kokoro). Many mondōs were recorded later as *kōans. See also HOSSEN.

Monica, St (*c.*331–87). Mother of St *Augustine of Hippo. Concerned about her son's lifestyle, she followed him from N. Africa to Rome and then Milan, praying for, and eventually in 386 witnessing, his conversion. She died on their return journey to Africa. A cult of St Monica began in the Middle Ages. In 1430 her relics were transferred to Rome, to the church of S. Agostino. She is frequently patron saint of associations of Christian mothers. Feast day, 27 Aug.

Monism. The belief that only one substance exists, in contrast to pluralism. Monistic religions are therefore those which maintain that there is only one underlying substance (Lat., *substantia*, standing under) despite the multiplicity of appearances. *Advaita Vedanata is thus monistic, in contrast to *Dvaita. Philosophically, the term was first applied (by Christian Wolff, 1679–1754), and may apply either to the kinds of substances there are, or to their individual instances.

D. W. Hamlyn, *Metaphysics*, (1984).

Monji-hōshi (Jap., 'dharma master of scriptures'). Zen teacher who adheres to the literal sense of the

Buddha's teaching in the *sūtras. As such, he is unlikely to develop wisdom or insight.

Monju (Japanese): see MAÑJUŚRĪ.

Monk: see MONASTICISM.

Monkey king, the (Chinese immortal): see HSIEN.

Monna (Jap., 'question word'). The question posed by a Zen student to his teacher in a *mondō (exchange).

Monomyth: see MYTH.

Mono no aware (sensitivity, a key Shinto virtue): see MOTOORI NORINAGA.

Monophysites. The party who maintained, against the definition of *Chalcedon (451) that in *Christ there was but one (Gk., *monos*) nature (*physis*). The Monophysites' doctrine derived from the *Alexandrian christology and especially *Cyril of Alexandria to whose writings they constantly appealed. They flourished in Syria and Egypt under leaders like Severus of Antioch and were alternately conciliated and persecuted by the imperial government until the Arab invasions of the 7th cent. Their direct modern descendants are the *Oriental Orthodox churches.

According to Monophysite doctrine, the union of God the Word (*Logos) with the flesh at the *Incarnation was such that to speak of distinct divine and human natures thereafter is wrongly to separate what was united. They did not, however (as some modern treatments suggest), speak of Christ's single nature as a 'divine' nature: modern Monophysites repudiate such a view as identical to that of *Eutyches. From the Chalcedonian point of view it might have seemed that the Monophysite position was either subtly *docetic or merely different in expression. However, in 1984 the Syrian Orthodox *patriarch (Mar Ignatius Zakka II) and the *pope (John Paul II) signed a declaration affirming agreement, and declaring that the apparent differences arose from cultural and linguistic inadequacies.

Monotheism (Gk., 'only' + 'God'). Belief that there is one God (and only one), in contrast to *henotheism or polytheism.

Monotheletes or **Monothelites.** Adherents of the doctrine that in Christ there were two natures but only one (Gk., *monos*) will (*thelēma*). This doctrine was promulgated by the *Ekthesis* (Gk., 'statement of faith') of the Roman Emperor Heraclius in 638, in an effort to reconcile the *Monophysite party without repudiating the definition of *Chalcedon. It was the work of Sergius, patriarch of Constantinople, in consultation with Pope Honorius. But the formula 'one will' was soon disowned by Honorius' successors, and in the wake of continued controversy by the emperors also. The matter was settled by the second Council of *Constantinople (680) which condemned the Monothelete formulas and affirmed the existence of two wills in Christ. The *Maronite Church appears to have begun as Monothelete, but renounced its heresy at the time of the *Crusades.

Monsignor (abbr. Mgr., from Ital., *monsignore*, 'my lord'). In the *Roman Catholic Church, a title given to members of the 'papal household'. In most cases, however, the holder is a 'supernumerary' and the title is only honorary. All *archbishops and *bishops are entitled to it.

Monstrance (Lat., *monstrare*, 'to show'). A vessel used for containing and displaying the *sacrament at *exposition and *benediction. It developed alongside these eucharistic devotions in the late Middle Ages. It is also called an *ostensorium* (Lat., *ostendo*, 'I show'). At the centre is a round glass (or crystal) container in which the *host is placed (the *luna*). Around it is a frame, often with gold or silver rays spreading outward. Some monstrances for processions are so large that they can be moved only on a wheeled conveyance.

Montanism. An early Christian *heresy. In the latter half of the 2nd cent., *Montanus, claiming the inspiration of the *Holy Spirit (or *Paraclete), prophesied that the Heavenly Jerusalem would soon descend near Pepuza in Phrygia. His followers were led by *prophets and prophetesses, through whom the Paraclete spoke, and embraced a severe *asceticism, marked by fasting, forbidding of second marriages, and an enthusiastic attitude to *martyrdom. The movement spread from Phrygia to Rome and beyond, and *c.*206 won the allegiance of *Tertullian in N. Africa. There was much anti-Montanist literature, but little of it has survived. It was formally condemned before 200 CE by Asiatic synods, and later by Rome. Whether it was a resurgence of primitive fervour in the face of the growing institutionalism of the Church, or (more likely) an early instance of recurrent *apocalyptic movements which have marked Christian history, is disputed.

Montanus (2nd cent. CE). A self-proclaimed *prophet, who attracted followers to his message that the end of the world was imminent. He proclaimed the advent of the New Jerusalem, evidenced by the outpouring of the *Holy Spirit. He demanded an austere life which was not afraid of persecution, so that a purified church would be ready as a bride for the bridegroom, Christ. Initially the movement had the support of *Tertullian, but it came to be vigorously opposed, until, at the Synod of Iconium, its baptisms were held to be invalid.

P. de Labriolle, *Les Sources* . . . (1913).

Montefiore, Claude (1858–1938). English leader of *Progressive Judaism. Claude Montefiore was a great-nephew of Sir Moses *Montefiore and a student of Solomon *Schechter. He founded in England a radical form of *Reform Judaism, known as

Liberal Judaism, which was centred on the Liberal Jewish *Synagogue in London. He espoused the 'many paths, one goal' view of religions ('Many pathways may all lead Godward, and the world is richer for that the paths are not few') and also the view that *Paul was the source of the Christian hatred of the Jew: 'No one misunderstood Judaism more profoundly than Paul.' An opponent of *Zionism, he was very involved in Jewish education and Christian–Jewish relations. The major difference between the two religions lay, in his view, in the Christian belief that it is not possible to approach God directly, but only through a mediator and redeemer. Applying his 'many paths' principle, he wrote: 'We are richer for possessing both the ethical teaching of the *Rabbis and the lofty enthusiasm and paradoxes of the *Sermon on the Mount.' He did much to mediate that teaching through his *Rabbinic Anthology* (ed. with H. Loewe, 1938).

E. Kessler, *An English Jew* . . . (1989); W. R. Matthews, *Claude Montefiore, the Man and his Thought* (1956).

Montefiore, Sir Moses (1784–1885). Anglo-Jewish leader. Montefiore was sheriff of London in 1837–8 and was knighted by Queen Victoria. He received a baronetcy in 1846 for his humanitarian efforts for the Jewish community, taking as his motto, 'Think and thank'. He was president of the Board of Deputies of British Jews, 1835–74, and was active in his support of Jewish projects in *Israel and on behalf of oppressed Jews abroad. He said strongly, and as early as 1885, 'Palestine must belong to the Jews, and *Jerusalem is destined to become the seat of a Jewish commonwealth.'

S. U. Nahon, *Sir Moses Montefiore* (1965).

Months of Kallah (Jewish months for study of Torah): see KALLAH, MONTHS OF.

Moody, Dwight Lyman (1837–99). American *revivalist preacher. He left a promising shoe business in Chicago in 1860 for evangelistic work with the YMCA. A tour of Britain in 1873 met an enthusiastic response, and Moody, along with his organist and song leader Ira D. *Sankey, became internationally famous. Moody's meetings were characterized by respectability and lack of hell-fire sensationalism. His preaching concentrated on God's love and on individual salvation and holiness. Although in the mainstream of pre-*millennialist, *fundamentalist thought, he avoided theological controversy. Moody was a *Congregationalist, but like other evangelists to follow, he worked mainly outside denominational boundaries.

J. F. Findlay, *Dwight L. Moody* . . . (1969).

Moon (emblem of Islam): see CRESCENT MOON.

Moon, Blessing of the. Jewish prayer recited at the time of the New Moon. According to the *Talmud, 'Whoever pronounces the *benediction over the new moon in its due time, welcomes, as it were, the presence of the *Shekhinah' (*B.Sanh.* 42a). In the *mishnaic period, the proclamation of a new month (Rosh Hodesh) was made by the *rabbinic court and it was celebrated with rejoicing. The Jewish *calendar is lunar and the moon is understood as a symbol of nature's renewal as well as of Israel's redemption.

Moon, Sun Myung (b. 1920). Founder of the Unification Church, whose members are popularly known as Moonies. He was born in N. Korea, and when he was 10, his family converted to Christianity. On Easter Day 1936, Moon experienced a vision of *Jesus Christ who commissioned him to particular work. For the next nine years, he prepared for this, communicating with other religious leaders, such as the *Buddha and *Moses. The revelations which he received form the basis of Unification theology. He founded his Church after the Second World War, and after much opposition and persecution from the Communists, he established the Holy Spirit Association for the Unification of World Christianity in 1954. His business interests multiplied rapidly—in 1984 he was imprisoned for tax evasion—and his Church took an increasing part in the sponsorship of interreligious and intercultural meetings and activities. The Church has been controversial for two reasons: (i) it has been accused of *brain-washing (the *Daily Mail* newspaper successfully defended a libel action on this point); (ii) because of its beliefs. Central to these is the teaching (in *The Divine Principle*) that the *Fall was the result of Eve having a spiritual relationship with Lucifer before a sexual one with Adam, with the result that their children and descendants have been born with defective natures. God has attempted to remedy this through key individuals, but because Jesus was killed before he could marry, he could effect only spiritual redemption. By his own marriage in 1960, Moon has begun to effect a more complete redemption, transmitted through mass wedding ceremonies, as a consequence of which the children of participants are born without fallen natures. The Unification Church has become a test-case of rights to freedom of religious belief, because of accusations of illegitimate means of conversion. Defenders of the Church (by no means all of them members) suggest that conversion may be more a consequence of need for acceptance and love than of manipulation.

F. Sontag, *Sun Myung Moon* . . . (1977).

Moral argument for God's existence. A type of theistic argument which became common in the 19th and early 20th cents. An important influence on many such arguments is *Kant's claim that the existence of God is a 'postulate of the practical reason', i.e. a necessary presupposition of moral reasoning (*Critique of Practical Reason*, 1788), although Kant himself did not describe this claim as a proof of God's existence. Typically, such arguments contend that the binding character of moral obligation can only be explained in terms of God's will. For example, J. H. *Newman argued that as a knock on the door implies that someone is knocking, so the demand made by conscience implies that some person is making the demand (*Grammar of Assent*, 1870). Critics of such arguments either deny that morality has any such absolute sanction (e.g. by pointing to the relativity of moral judgements), or else claim that whatever sanction it has can be accounted for without appealing to God.

Morality plays: see THEATRE AND DRAMA.

Moral Majority. Organization in the USA which aims to exert political pressure in favour of traditional 'moral' values (family life, free enterprise, strong national defence) and against such causes as homosexual rights and freer abortion. Moral Majority, Inc. was founded in 1979 by the Baptist pastor and television evangelist Jerry Falwell (b. 1933), and rose to prominence in the presidential election campaign of 1980. Although it is 'pluralistic' and 'not based on theological considerations', the organization's support comes mainly from conservative Protestant Christians. Falwell identifies himself as a *Fundamentalist, and argues e.g. that free-enterprise is a biblical doctrine. Appealing to the principle of 'separation of church and state', opponents of Moral Majority exist within the US evangelical churches, as well as outside.

J. Falwell, *Listen, America!* (1980); P. L. Shriver, *The Bible Vote: Religion and the New Right* (1981).

Moral Re-Armament (i.e., MRA). Before 1938 the Oxford Group Movement, founded by Frank *Buchman. Its largest organizations are now in the USA, Britain, Japan, and Switzerland. Its message, at home among conservative evangelical Christians, is the need for a moral awakening to reconvert the world.

Moravian Brethren. The Church of the United Brethren, a Christian body which renewed the declining Bohemian Brethren, after refugees from the Thirty Years' War took refuge on the estates of Count Zinzendorf (1700–60), who presided over a great spiritual revival. As a 'unity of brethren' (*Unitas Fratrum*), they did not seek to become a separate church, but saw themselves as a leaven in existing churches. Nevertheless, survival dictated organization (it was recognized as a church, e.g. in Britain in 1749), and it was vigorously missionary throughout the world. It is strongly *evangelical, regarding the Bible as the sole rule of faith and conduct.

J. T. and K. G. Hamilton, *A History of the Moravian Church* (1900, rev. 1967); J. Weinlick, *Count Zinzendorf* (1956).

More, Henry: see CAMBRIDGE PLATONISTS.

More, Thomas, St (1478–1535). Chancellor of England and *martyr. Born in London, he went to Oxford University but was called home and sent to Lincoln's Inn in 1496, being called to the bar in 1501. Three years later he entered parliament. Despite long consideration of a priestly vocation he married in 1505, and had four children by his first wife. He was a man of notable learning, and a friend of scholars such as *Fisher and *Erasmus. He wrote what is perhaps his best-known book, *Utopia*, in 1516. He strongly opposed the rise of *Protestantism in England, and Henry's divorce from Catherine of Aragon. He was Lord Chancellor from 1529, but resigned in 1532 over the king's opposition to the *papacy. Like Fisher he refused to take the oath attached to the Act of Succession, though ready to accept the succession itself, and was imprisoned in the Tower of London, where he wrote his best spiritual work, *Dialogue of Comfort against Tribulation*. He was put on trial in 1535 for opposing the Act of Supremacy, and was executed on 6 July. He was canonized in May 1935. Feast day, 22 June.

Moreh Nevukhim (philosophical work): see MAIMONIDES, MOSES.

Moriscos. Muslims who remained in Spain after the fall of Granada in 1492. Although many outwardly conformed to Christianity, under pressure of persecution, the majority maintained Muslim practice and belief in private. Most were expelled from Spain in 1619.

Mormons or **The Church of Jesus Christ of Latter-Day Saints.** Religious movement derived from Joseph Smith (1805–44) and the *Book of Mormon*. In 1822, the angel Moroni revealed to Smith where gold tablets were to be found, on which were written God's words. He published a translation of them in 1830. The book tells of the lost tribes of Israel, the Jaredites and the Lamanites, who came to America. The Jaredites soon perished, and the Lamanites turned against the fraternal and faithful Nephites. Only Mormon and his son Moroni survived: Mormon wrote the text on the tablets, and Moroni buried them near Palmyra, New York, in 438 CE. The texts tell of a post-resurrection appearance of Christ in America to establish religious order and truth. The authenticity of the text has been called in question because of its grammatical errors, its reminiscences of the *Authorized Version, its resemblance to an unpublished novel, etc., but for Mormons, its authenticity is not in doubt. Under persecution and opposition, the Mormons made several moves, until Joseph Smith was arrested in Carthage, Illinois, and was killed by a mob. Schisms resulted, partly over leadership, partly over doubts about polygamy. Plural marriage after the order of Abraham had been introduced by a special revelation in 1843. Most Mormons followed Brigham Young (1801–77), who led the movement to the Salt Lake area of Utah, where Zion in the Wilderness was constructed. Central to Mormon belief is the Restoration: the Churches have apostasized, but true Christianity has been restored by Joseph Smith. According to Smith, God is self-made—only matter being eternal. Entrance to Christ's kingdom is by repentance and baptism by immersion. The dead can be baptized and thus share in the *millennial age. The movement spreads under a strong missionary imperative.

Morning Prayer. The morning *office of the *Anglican Church. It was composed, for the Prayer Book of 1549, on the basis of medieval *mattins with supplements from *prime. Its structure is similar to that of *evening prayer. In the two offices together, the Psalter is read through once every month. The *Alternative Service Book* 1980 contains a modern English version, with a larger repertory of *canticles and thirteen-week cycle for the Psalter. See also MATTINS; LAUDS.

Moroni (Mormon angel): see MORMONS.

Mortal sin. According to Christian (mainly Catholic) teaching, a deliberate act of rejecting God as one's final end in favour of some lesser desire. It is held to involve both the loss of sanctifying *grace and eternal damnation. If feasible, every mortal sin must be confessed to a priest; but if that is impossible, the desire to do so, together with an act of contrition, will be met by God's forgiveness. For a sin to be mortal, the matter must be grave (e.g. murder, adultery), there must be conscious awareness of the contemplated sin, and there must be full consent of the will. However, what counts as 'grave sin' (e.g. non-attendance at Sunday *mass) may change at least as a matter of emphasis. 'Grave matter' is fundamentally 'specified by the Ten Commandments' (*Catechism of the Catholic Church*, §1858). See also VENIAL SIN.

Mortification (Lat., *mortificare*, 'to kill'). The 'killing' or subduing, especially through *ascetic practices, of unruly or disordered appetites which militate against spiritual advance: 'If by the Spirit you put to death the habits originating in the body, you will have life' (Romans 8. 13). The term is then applied to ascetic rigour in other religions.

Moses (*c.*13th cent. BCE). Jewish leader and lawgiver. According to the Book of Exodus, Moses was born in Egypt to Amram and Jochabel, who hid him in the reeds of the river Nile to escape Pharaoh's order to slaughter all Jewish male babies. He was rescued by Pharaoh's daughter: 'From the water I drew him' (Exodus 2. 10), *meshitihu*, hence the name Mosheh (Eng. Moses). She adopted him and he grew up in the royal palace. As a young man, he killed an Egyptian whom he found beating a Jew. He fled to Midian where he married the daughter of a local priest. While keeping his father-in-law's sheep on Mount Horeb, he encountered God in a *burning bush. He was commanded to liberate the Hebrew slaves in Egypt and lead them to the *Promised Land. After ten plagues had struck Egypt, Pharaoh agreed to let the slaves leave. Moses led them across the Red or Reed Sea which miraculously parted to let them through. He guided them for forty years in the wilderness, and, on Mount *Sinai, he received God's revelation of *Torah, including the *Ten Commandments. Before his death, he appointed *Joshua as his successor. In the Jewish tradition, Moses has a unique status. He is said to have spoken to God 'face to face' (Exodus 33. 11) and is described as 'God's servant' (Numbers 12. 7–8). In the narrative, he is perceived as a *prophet (Deuteronomy 33. 1), as a political leader, as a founder of the cult, as a lawgiver, and as 'the meekest man on earth' (Numbers 12. 3). The *rabbis taught that the whole world exists only on account of the merit of Moses and *Aaron (*B.Hul.* 89a), and he is generally spoken of as 'Mosheh Rabbenu' (Moses, our master). He was given not only the written law, but the entire *oral law in the encounter on Mount Sinai (*TJ Pe'ah* 2. 6). At the same time, the rabbis were anxious that there should be no personality cult, and his faults, such as his quick temper, were recognized (*B.Pes.* 66b). Many *aggadic stories were told of him, and in medieval Jewish thought it was accepted that the revelation through Moses was superior to that of all the prophets. His personality and role in the Jewish religion have continued to engage such diverse commentators as *Aḥad Ha-'Am, Martin *Buber, and Sigmund *Freud. In Christianity, he appears with *Jesus at his transfiguration (Mark 9. 2–8) and, according to the Qur'ān, where he is known as Mūsā, he prophesied the coming of Muḥammad (7. 140). The biblical stories have provided inspiration for writers, artists, and musicians.

Moses, Assumption of. Jewish *apocryphal text. The *Assumption of *Moses* probably dates from the 1st cent. CE. It consists of a prophecy by Moses for his successor *Joshua, concerning the future of the Israelites and the last days. It finishes abruptly and it is likely that the original ending was lost. The Latin version was discovered in 1861, but the lost original was in Greek.

J. H. Charlesworth (ed.), *The Old Testament Pseudepigrapha* (1983).

Moses, blessing of. *Moses' blessing of the Israelite tribes as described in Deuteronomy 33. The *benediction consists of descriptions of each of the Hebrew tribes except Simeon, with a prayer for their well-being. It probably dates from the 11th cent. BCE, although some scholars put it later.

Moses ben Joshua of Narbonne (1300–62). French Jewish philosopher. Among other works, his commentary on *Maimonides' *Guide to the Perplexed* was well known and was printed with the original text (ed. I. Euchel, 1791). He does not seem to have known the works of the Christian *scholastics, but was influenced by the Muslim philosopher, Averroes (i.e. *Ibn Rushd), whose work he knew in Hebrew translation.

M.-R. Hayoun, *La Philosophie et la théologie de Moïse de Narbonne* (1989) and *Moshe Narboni* (1986).

Moses ben Maimon (Jewish philosopher): see MAIMONIDES, MOSES.

Moses ben Shem Tov de León (*c.*1240–1305). Jewish *kabbalist. Moses Ben Shem Tov taught his version of the kabbalah in his *Midrash ha-Neʿelam* (Mystical *Midrash) which became the foundation of the **Zohar*. From 1292 he led the life of a wandering scholar and, according to Abraham b. Solomon of Torrutiel, was the author of twenty-three other books, most of which are now lost. Following his death, a controversy broke out about the role of Moses de León in the composition of the *Zohar*. Since the *Zohar* was ascribed to R. Simeon b. Yoḥai of the 2nd cent. CE, the issue initially was whether Moses de León had been copying from the original manuscript which was now lost, or whether, as his widow maintained, he had composed the work. Modern scholars (e.g. G. Scholem) tend to the view that he composed the work making use of earlier material.

G. Scholem, *Major Trends in Jewish Mysticism* (1946).

Moses of Narbonne (French Jewish philosopher): see MOSES BEN JOSHUA OF NARBONNE.

Mosheh (Hebrew form): see MOSES.

Mosque or **Masjid** (Arab., *masjid*, from *sajada*, 'he bowed down', Egypt. dial., *masgid* > Fr., *mosquée*). The Muslim place of assembly (*jumʿa) for *ṣalāt. While a special place is not necessary for ṣalāt (*Muḥammad built the first masjid in *Madīna, not in Mecca), it is certainly desirable, and should be attended where possible. Masjids (masājid) are 'houses which God has allowed to be built, that his name may be spoken in them' (Qur'ān 24. 36). Masjids in general have a minaret from which the call to prayer (*ādhān) can be made by the *muezzin (*mu'adhdhīn*), a large hall or halls for the assembly, in which a niche (*miḥrāb*) is placed in a wall indicating the direction of *Mecca (the *qibla), and in which there is a pulpit (*minbar*). There may also be a platform (*dakka*) from which further calls to ṣalāt are made, and a stand (*kursī*) for the Qur'ān. The principal officers of a masjid are the *imām, the *mu'adhdhīn*, and the *khātib* (preacher, see KHUṬBA). Because of the prohibition in Islam on art which mimics creation (especially portraits of humans), the decoration of mosques is simple, and mainly achieved through the carving of texts from the Qur'ān. However, relics may be kept and revered, though these are suspect to Muslims who think that reverence should be addressed only to God—e.g. *ibn Taiymīyya condemned reverence of the Prophet's *footprint in Jerusalem and Damascus.

The masjid soon became associated with education (see MADRASA), and it also became the centre for administration and justice. Masjids could also be built in relation to the tombs of prominent Muslims, especially of martyrs (*shahīd), caliphs (*khalīfa), and *Sūfī saints. To build (or pay for) a masjid is itself an act which puts one in the category of shahīd.

The Mosque of the Prophet (Masjīd al-Nabī) is a mosque in Madīna, the second most venerated in Islam (after Masjīd al-Ḥarām in Mecca). It contains the tomb of Muḥammad, as also of *Abū Bakr and *ʿUmar. The Mosque of the Two Qiblas (Masjīd al-Qiblatayn) is also in Madīna: it is the mosque where Muḥammad turned for the first time from facing Jerusalem for prayer, and faced Mecca instead.

J. D. Hoag, *Islamic Architecture* (1977); A. Papadopoulo, *Islam and Muslim Art* (1979).

Mosshōryō (Jap., 'unsayable'). The true nature of reality according to Zen Buddhism, which cannot be described or spoken of. Cf. *fukasetsu, *mokufuni.

Mosshōseki (Jap., 'leaving no trace'). The condition, according to Zen Buddhism, in which one who has experienced enlightenment should live. As a fish leaves no trace in water, nor a bird in the air, so the enlightened one should live naturally with no evidence of his enlightenment. This is the second natural state, the first being that of an infant (who soon falls from it). One who lives showing traces of enlightenment (*goseki) still 'stinks of enlightenment'.

Mother Earth: see PṚTHIVI (Hindu).

Mothering Sunday. A derivative from Refreshment or Laetare Sunday, during *Lent. On this day, the fasting rules were relaxed (the *gospel reading in the **Book of Common Prayer* is the feeding of the 5,000); the first words of the opening prayer of the *mass are 'Laetare Jerusalem', 'Rejoice Jerusalem . . .', and honour is given to Mother Church. The extension to actual mothers was gradual, and much influenced Anna Jarvis who (*c.*1900) proposed a day (in May) of thanks to mothers. The two have now merged, and have become a single commercial exploitation.

Mo Ti (Chinese philosopher): see MO TZU.

Motoori Norinaga (1730–1801). Leading scholar of the New Learning (*Kokugaku) movement in the Shinto revival (*Fukko Shintō). Motoori was a pupil of *Kamo no Mabuchi, who had insisted that the Manyōshū poetry of the 8th cent. (and earlier) had been free of foreign influence and thus expressed the genuine Japanese spirit without adulteration. Motoori pushed this quest for the genuine Japanese spirit into other areas, especially in rescuing the **Kojiki* from relative neglect in comparison with the **Nihongi* (*Nihonshoki*). The *Kojiki* is at first reading an unpromising source of religious and national renewal. But Motoori argued that all language about ultimates (e.g. gods and goddesses) is necessarily limited and approximate, but that in the *Kojiki* there were to be found primal, utterly sincere expressions of genuine emotion. These pure and spontaneous emotions precede, and are more important than, rational reflections on them. The adoration of the Sun (*Amaterasu) indicates that Japan gave birth to the Sun (Nippon means 'origin of sun'), from which it follows that Japan and its people are 'closer to God' than any other people: 'The true way is one and the same in every country, in heaven as on earth. But this way has been transmitted rightly in our Imperial Land only.' On this basis, Motoori was able to take other classic Japanese works and set them in the foundation of the true and pure spirit which should inform life—e.g. *Shinkokinshū* (The New Collection of Poetry Ancient and Modern, compiled *c.*1205) and Murasaki Shikibu's *Tale of Genji* (the story of Prince Genji, already recognized as the supreme work of Japanese literature, whose integration, therefore, was essential to Motoori's programme; tr. A. Waley, 1935; E. Seidensticker, 1976). He took the latter to be portraying the sensitivity of a good life—what he called *mono no aware*, which becomes the key virtue in the Shinto revival:

> The purpose of the *Tale of Genji* is like a man who greatly desires the lotus flower: in order to plant and cultivate it, he must gather muddy and manure-saturated water. The impure mud of the illicit affairs of the *Tale* is not there to be admired, but to nurture the flower of awareness of the sorrow of human existence.

Matsumoto Shigeru, *Motoori Norinaga* . . . (1970).

Mott, John Raleigh (1865–1955). American *Methodist layman and *ecumenical pioneer. Born in New York, he studied at Upper Iowa, then at Cornell University, where he was converted through the ministry of J. E. K. Studd. Mott travelled widely sharing his passionate concern for Christian *missions and the need for ecumenical co-operation to achieve 'the evangelization of the world in our generation'. He was instrumental in convening the first International Missionary Conference at Edinburgh in 1910, devoting himself tirelessly to the *ecumenical movement through the International Missionary Council, 'Life and Work', and the World Council of Churches, of which he became co-president in 1948.

Motu Proprio (Lat., 'on his own initiative'). A papal ordinance emanating from the *pope himself (rather than the *curia) and bearing his signature. It deals with matters of discipline less important than in an 'apostolic constitution'.

Mo Tzu (honorific title, 'Teacher Mo', given to Mo Ti, *c.*470–*c.*380 BCE). Leading philosopher among the 'hundred philosophers' of early China. He was educated in the classic texts, and may for a time have followed *Confucius; but he strongly opposed Confucianism for its agnosticism about heaven (*t'ien) and spiritual beings, and its preoccupation with ritual. He advocated an attitude of love (*ai) to all beings, not just toward family or those from whom reciprocal favours can be expected. This love, which is central to Mo Tzu's teaching, means regarding all as equally deserving of it. Extravagant activities, and above all warfare, should be abandoned. All this is in accord with the will of T'ien, now personified as actively seeking the practice of love. Mo Tzu took part in quests for peace and reconciliation, once walking for ten days over rough tracks and cutting his clothes gradually to pieces in order to bind his bleeding feet. But if efforts at conciliation failed, he advocated vigour in defence of the vulnerable—and he and his followers were skilled at defensive warfare. The work known as *Mo Tzu* contains his teaching, but was probably compiled by his later followers. After about two centuries, his way declined in relation to Confucianism, but he and his teaching remain as an impressive protest on behalf of a better way in the conflicts of human nature and society: 'As regards universal love and mutual help, they are immeasurably beneficial and not difficult. The problem is that no ruler endorses them. If a ruler endorsed them with rewards and punishments, I believe people would tend toward universal love and mutual help as fire tends upward and water down: nothing in the world could stop them.'

Trs. Mei Yi-pao (1929), B. Watson (selections, 1967); Mei Yi-pao, *Motse* . . . (1973).

Mount Athos (centre of Orthodox monasticism): see ATHOS, MOUNT.

Mount Hiei. The site in Japan, north of Kyōto, where *Saichō established his first *Tendai (Chin., *T'ien-t'ai, hence the alternative name for Mount Hiei, Tairei) temple, Enryaku-ji. The early buildings were destroyed in 1572. The Hall of Study (Daikodo) and the Main Hall (Konpo-chudo) were rebuilt in the 17th cent.

Mount Sinai (mountain where Moses was given Torah): see SINAI, MOUNT.

Mourides or **Muridiyya** (Arab., *murīd*, 'aspirant' or 'disciple'). An innovative Muslim brotherhood in Senegal. It derives from Amadu Bamba (*c.*1850–1927), a saintly, scholarly *marabout within the *Sūfī and *Qadariy(y)a tradition, and Ibra Fall (1858–1930), an aristocratic Wolof. Ibra Fall submitted to Amadu Bamba as a disciple, not for the usual prayer and study, but as a leader of manual work groups. Together they founded new agricultural villages and a new holy city, Touba, which became the centre for the Magal, an annual pilgrimage which attracted half a million pilgrims by 1975. Ibra Fall became the wealthy leader of a deviationist section, the Bay Fall, mainly among the urban Wolof. A hierarchical organization is headed by the *Khalīfa-General; then several hundred marabouts each have voluntary followers or *talibes* working their own and their marabout's land, and engaging in the simple religious exercises drawn up by Amadu Bamba; finally, young men form a voluntary labour force as novices. Deviations from orthodox Islam include rejection of the duty of holy war (*jihād) and of the Meccan pilgrimage (*ḥajj), reduction of almsgiving to tithes to the marabout, and giving more attention to the latter than to Islamic law, and to Amadu Bamba than to *Muḥammad. The Mourides dominated Senegal's main export crop, groundnuts, and hence became a political power. From 1968 Amadu Bamba's third successor, another son, Abdu Lahette, attacked corruption and luxury within the order and introduced economic and modernizing reforms. Mouridism catered for the landless masses and Wolof warriors untouched by the older brotherhoods, but represents only a rudimentary understanding of Islam.

Mourners of Zion (Jewish group): see AVELEI ZION.

Mourning rites. One among several kinds of rites performed by a community (or an individual) upon the death of one of its members. Mourning rites characteristically function initially to separate those related (in various ways) to the deceased from the rest of the living community. They also constitute a process of transition through which the mourners are finally reintegrated into their community. Mourning rites are thus a kind of *rite of passage undergone in almost all societies by those in some way connected to one who has died. They are to be distinguished from funeral rites, which concern the disposition of the remains of deceased. Through them, the living in many cultures express a mixture of affection for the deceased, fear of the corpse, and self-protection against the return of a malicious ghost or spirit.

Particular mourning rites vary greatly by culture, but typically they may be divided into three phases: an initial separation of the bereaved from others; a more or less lengthy period of transition, or the mourning period proper; and reintegration, or rites for the lifting of mourning. The initial imposition of rites of separation marks off those who were related by kinship or other ties to the deceased. Their effect is often to isolate mourners from normal social intercourse and daily activity. Aside from the very common custom of wailing and weeping, particular practices by mourners in various societies also include special diet, often fasting; concealment or other physical separation from others; self-inflicted wounds; strict silence, sometimes for a year or more; and, in general, cessation of whatever activities are routine. In particular, a special garb may identify mourners, and it is often the reverse of whatever garb is normal. People who usually wear their hair long will often cut or shave it in mourning; those who wear clothing will often go naked, or wear coarse, scanty, or worn-out clothes. Sometimes clothing is worn inside out; in some societies the sexes exchange garb. It has been suggested that such reversals of routine activity and dress are generally, or were originally, for the purpose of deceiving the potentially malevolent spirit of the deceased. But this interpretation is disputed and, as a claim about the remote origins of these practices, cannot be demonstrated.

The duration of mourning varies widely, from several days to several years. It often varies according to degree of kinship: spouses of the deceased commonly mourn the longest, others by lesser degrees. Generally, the higher the social station of the deceased, the greater the number of survivors who fall under mourning restrictions: in the case of a chief or king, a whole society may mourn for an extended period, interrupting normal life patterns. The transitional period of mourning, especially when long, is often punctuated by ritual events (feasts, gradual stages of the lifting of mourning, etc.) at fixed intervals.

At the successful completion of the transitional process of mourning, rites of the lifting of mourning generally express the reintegration of mourners into normal patterns of life. These often include dancing, singing, and feasting, and are occasions for joy. Mourning garb is exchanged for normal dress, all exceptional practices and prohibitions cease, the state of pollution and taboo ends, and mourners rejoin society.

Mourning is practised by and for the living, but in fact the mourners and the dead often constitute a group, and move simultaneously through structurally similar phases. The rite of passage of the living through the mourning corresponds, in many societies, to that of the deceased. For the latter, death itself marks the initial separation from the living community. It is often followed by a transitional journey to another world or state, sometimes culminating in an ordeal or trial. If successful, the one who has died is thought to be reintegrated into a 'society' of the dead and/or of deities; he or she finds again a place to belong. Evidence from many cultures shows that the temporal and ritual markers of progress through these phases—of the living mourners, and of the one whom they mourn—often correspond exactly. The point at which mourning is lifted and survivors rejoin society, therefore, is often also the point at which the soul of the dead has successfully passed through the dangerous zone and liminal period of transition and reached the place of rest or of bliss.

During the biblical period, Jewish mourning customs included the rending of garments (Genesis 37. 34), wearing sackcloth (Psalm 30. 12), sitting on the ground (Jonah 3. 6), placing dust on the head (Jeremiah 6. 26), fasting (Ezekiel 10. 6), and abstaining from washing (2 Samuel 12. 20). In contemporary practice, the mourning period begins after the *funeral. The bereaved put on special clothes, stay at home for seven days (shivah), receive visitors sitting on a low stool, and only attend *synagogue on the *Sabbath. No work may be done and sexual relations are forbidden. Parents and children should be mourned for thirty days (*sheloshim*) during which time the hair is left uncut and no weddings may take place. Modified mourning continues for a year after the burial. A *yahrzeit lamp is kindled during the mourning period and *kaddish is said every day. Subsequently the lamp is lit and kaddish recited on the anniversary of the death. See also M. Lamm, *Jewish Way in Death and Mourning* (1969). In Christianity, mourning adapts itself to the customs of the country or community, while bringing them under the control of belief in the efficacy of Christ's atoning death and of the resurrection. The former has made prayers for the dead controversial, when or if it implies that the prayers of the living can add to the benefits of the *atonement. However, some Christians (especially Catholics) maintain that after death those who have not wholly alienated themselves from God but who fall short of perfection enter *purgatory. Here they may be aided by the prayers of the faithful, so that mourning may include such prayers, including requiem masses. These are made annually on All Souls' Day.

In Islam, death belongs to the order and will of God, so that mourning should not be excessive. According to Jabir b. Atik, *Muḥammad allowed lamentation for the sick until the moment of death, but not after. Tears and weeping are believed traditionally to disturb the dead during 'the period in the grave'. Yet in fact *niyaha* ('lamentation') occurs throughout the Muslim world (see e.g. H. Granqvist, *Muslim Death and Burial* . . ., 1965), an instance of local custom and human sentiment overcoming doctrinal correctness and religious injunction.

In Indian religions, the understanding of death is controlled by the understanding of rebirth (or of release). Thus mourning is made practical by rituals which sustain the dead, bring merit to them, and ward off evil. The extreme of these is *satī on the part of a Hindu widow, but short of that, there are obligations on the part of the living to the dead which convert mourning into action. In Japan, this is also the case, though set in the context of different beliefs about the status of *ancestors. On the seventh day after death, the dead soul may receive a posthumous name (*kaimyō), in a ceremony which draws a line on this world and gives the soul new identity in the next.This name is inscribed on two (temporary) wooden mortuary tablets (*ihai): one is placed by the grave, the other in the *butsudan. After forty-nine days, a permanent ihai, embellished in gold, is placed in the butsudan, and it is to that ihai that members of the family come and address their prayers and conversations. The dead remain a part of the family (receiving meals and any new bride entering the family): rituals and commemorations continue, especially at *o-bon*, through which the grief of parting is muted, and through which the human instinct to do (usually) the best one can for those who have died is expressed. See also DEATH; FUNERAL RITES.

Movement of the Wondrous Law of the Lotus Sūtra (Japanese Buddhist movement): see NIPPONZAN MYŌHŌJI.

Moxa (*mokusa*). Part of Buddhist ordination ceremony, especially in China. It involves burning marks on to the head of the monk or nun. This became a more general practice for developing reliance on the help of a *bodhisattva, in overcoming pain.

Mozarabic rite. The form of Christian liturgy (*rite) which was in use in Spain before the Islamic conquest of the 8th cent. It is the only non-Roman rite still in use in the *Roman Catholic Church, though it survives in regular use only in one chapel in the cathedral of Toledo. A number of features distinguish the Mozarabic mass, e.g. an extra reading (the Prophecy), and a dismissal of the *catechumens.

Mṛtyu. Death, the Hindu personification of death. In the Vedic period, there was no belief in an immortal life beyond death. The most that could be hoped for was the restoration of life again on this earth. Death was thus seen as the opponent to be defeated, and the *Vedas contain *mantras to keep death at bay. Originally, the gods were not exempt from death. They resisted death through the reception of sacrifices, and therefore rewarded those who offered them. *Prajāpati made his body 'undecaying' through sacrifice and by practising *tapas (austerities), and he then taught the remaining gods how to do the same (*Śatapatha Brāhmaṇa* 10. 4). Mṛtyu complained that he would have no food if this skill was passed on to humans, and he pointed out that heaven would become overcrowded. The gods decreed that only those humans who surrender to Mṛtyu voluntarily will attain immortality; the rest will remain 'the food of death'.

J. Bowker, *The Meanings of Death* (1991).

Mṛtyuñjaya-siddhi (Skt., 'death' + 'conquest' + 'power'). One of the Hindu powers (*iddhi) which lead to supernatural attainment, in this case, victory over death.

Ms, Five (ritual ingredients): see PAÑCA-MAKĀRA.

Mu (Jap.; Chin., *wu*). Zen emptiness of content, nothingness, closely related to *śūnyatā. *Dogen explored ways of illuminating the buddha-nature (*busshō), which is empty of self, but which produces apparent form. In the central exchange between Dogen and his successor, Koun Ejo, Dogen asked: 'What is your name?' He replied: 'There is a name, but not an everyday name'. He asked: 'What name is it?' He replied, 'Buddha-nature'. Dogen said: 'You have no Buddha-nature.' He said: 'You say I do not *have* it because Buddha-nature is emptiness.' From this arises the first *kōan of the *Wu-men-kuan* (*Mumonkan*), which introduces the Zen student to 'the world of mu': 'A monk asked master *Chaochou respectfully: "Does a dog actually have a

Buddha-nature or not?" He replied: "Mu" '. The opposite is *U.

Mu'adhīn (caller of Muslims to prayer): see MUEZZIN.

Mu'āwiyya(h) ibn Abi-Sufyān (d. 680 (AH 80)). Founder of the *Umayyad dynasty. He was a late convert to Islam, but was immediately appointed as 'personal secretary' by the Prophet *Muḥammad. *Abū Bakr sent the talented Mu'āwiyya as an army officer to Syria, and he was later appointed governor of that province by *'Umar and confirmed in it by *'Uthmān. In this office he distinguished himself as a leader and administrator. Upon 'Uthmān's murder, he posed not only as an avenger of a relative but as a champion of the legitimacy of the Caliphate (*Khalīfa). He put 'Alī on the horns of a dilemma: 'produce 'Uthmān's assassins or accept the responsibility of an accomplice'. Moreover, he was supported by reliable and loyal Syrians in the conflict with 'Alī and this was an important factor in Mu'āwiyya's favour. He politically outmanœuvred 'Alī in the truce after the claim for the Caliphate. After 'Alī's death in 661 (AH 61), Mu'āwiyya easily persuaded *Hasan, the Prophet's eldest grandson, with a grant of a large sum, to step down in his favour.

As khalīfa, Mu'āwiyya pursued a policy of pragmatism: 'I apply not my lash where my tongue suffices, nor my sword where my whip is enough. And if there be one hair binding me to my fellow men, I let it not break. If they pull I loosen, and if they loosen I pull.' In politics he insisted on rapprochement. His approach to dissidents was through persuasion and monetary gifts. Arab historians credit Mu'āwiyya with possessing *hilm* ('self-control') and *duha* ('political fitness'): qualities which enabled him to cope with the problems which baffled 'Uthmān and 'Alī, and to secure the services of three exceptional politicians of the time: 'Amr ibn al-Ās (Egypt), al-Mughira ibn Shuba (Kufa), and Ziyad (Basra and S. Iran). It was Mu'āwiyya who changed the character of the Caliphate to one of hereditary monarchy (*mulk*).

Mu'āwiyya's twenty years of rule were characterized by internal peace, stability, and foreign conquests. He built the first navy and began the first system of postal service in Islam. His tolerant policy towards Christians and Jews secured their loyalty and services (in important posts as administrators, physicians, finance officers, and courtiers) for the Empire. On the question of succession Mu'āwiyya tried to secure a peaceful transfer of power to his son Yazīd. Upon his death, however, these plans backfired and led to the beginning of the Second Civil War in Islam.

M. Hodgson, *The Venture of Islam* (1974).

Mu-chou Ch'en-tsun-su (Jap., Bokushū Chinsonshuku; *c.*780–877). Ch'an dharma-successor (*hassu) of *Huang-po Hsi-yün, whose abrupt methods he developed even further. Thus *Yun-men attained enlightenment when he went to Mu-chou, who followed his practice of listening to the footsteps of approaching students, and of admitting them only if their steps expressed a prepared state of mind. If he admitted them, he would shake them hard, saying, 'Speak, speak!' If unable to do so, they would be thrown out and the door would be slammed behind them. This happened to Yün-men (after he had asked Mu-chou three times for truth), but the door caught his leg and broke it. He attained instant enlightenment. Mu-chou's teaching was short and abrupt, and he appears in example 10 of *Pi-yen-lu* (see KŌAN).

Mudalavan (name of god): see TAMILNADU.

Mudangs (female shamans): see KOREAN RELIGION.

Muditā (Skt., Pāli, 'empathy'). One of the Buddhist *brahma-vihāras, a state of joy over the rescue and liberation of others from *dukkha. It is aspired to as a practice, by entering into the joys of others, and refusing to take pleasure in their misfortunes. See also UPEKKHA.

Mudra (Skt., 'seal', 'sign'). In both Hinduism and Buddhism, a sign of power, through the body, especially the hands.

In Hinduism, the mudras of ritual worship (*pūjā) are an outward and visible sign of spiritual reality which they bring into being. Thus mudras frequently appear in Hindu sculpture (as they do in Jain and Buddhist), especially *dhyāna (meditation, hands linked in front of body with palms upward), abhaya, cf. *abhaya-vacana (fear-repelling, hand lifted, palm outward), and *varada* (hand held out, palm upward, bestowing bounty). The *añjali* mudra is the best-known to the outsider, since it is the 'palms together', at the level of the chest, greeting in India. As a mudra, it expresses the truth underlying all appearance. Cf. also HASTA.

In Buddhism (Chin., *yin-hsiang*; Jap., *in-zō*; Korean, *insang*), a mudra is a particular configuration of the hands accompanying a *mantra and associated with a *visualization or other mental act, the three elements together (called by *Kukai 'the union of the three mysteries', Jap., *sammitsu kaji*) possessing sacramental efficacy in regard to a particular deity or liturgical action. Also, it refers to iconographically determinate gestures. *Mahāmudrā* ('great mudrā') is the special form of *Tantric practice followed by the Tibetan Kagyudpa lineage (*Kagyü).

See Index, Mudra.

E. D. Saunders, *Mudra: A Study of Symbolic Gestures in Japanese Buddhist Sculpture* (1960).

Muezzin (Arab., *mu'adhdhin*). The one who gives the *ādhān (call to prayer) to the Muslim community before the five daily times of *ṣalāt. The ādhān is generally given from the minaret of the *mosque. The office of mu'adhdhin was instituted in the first or second year of the *hijra, and is sometimes hereditary. The first mu'adhdhin was *Bilāl, an

Abyssinian slave. In the earliest days of the Muslim community there was no formal summons, but the ādhān became a necessary component of the ritual worship; and this call of the human voice was developed into a chant, which can carry for some considerable distance.

Muftī (Arab.). In Islamic law, one qualified to give a *fatwā, legal opinion on a disputed point of law. Such a person had to be a Muslim, of upright character, with appropriate knowledge and experience in legal matters. A muftī could act in a private capacity, or might be a public office holder, with special responsibility for advising magistrates and other officials. A muftī might sometimes himself be a magistrate, but was then debarred from exercising his function of muftī concerning any case brought before him in the court. The office of muftī was elaborated in the Ottoman Empire.

Mughal or **Mogul empire.** A Muslim dominion in India, lasting from 1526 to 1857. It was founded by Babur (d. 1530), and reached its height of power under *Akbar, Jehangir (1605–27), Shah Jehān, who built the Taj Mahal (1627–58), and *Auraṅgzéb. By the time of the Indian mutiny, it had diminished to a small area around Delhi.

S. R. Sharma, *The Religious Policy of the Mughal Emperors* (1962).

Muhajirun (followers of Muḥammad in the hijra): see EMIGRANTS.

Muḥammad 'Abduh: see 'ABDUH, MUḤAMMAD.

Muḥammad Aḥmad b. 'Abd Allāh (*c.*1834–85 (AH 1258–1302)). *Al-Mahdī of the Sudan. After early religious experience, he believed himself called to cleanse the world from corruption and wanton behaviour. His first target was the Turkish Empire. He made his first public appearance as Mahdī in 1881, and resisted all attempts of the Sudanese and Egyptians to defeat him. The extension of his campaigns took him to Khartoum, where, in 1885, General Gordon was killed. He himself died not long after, and the incipient Mahdīya movement was ended by Kitchener in 1898 at the battle of Omdurman.

His Islam was austere in practice, and he substituted his own teaching for much of the accumulated tradition and commentary. To the *shahāda he added the words, 'and I bear witness that Muḥammad Aḥmad is the Mahdī of God and successor (*khalīfa) of his prophet'. His popular appeal rested on his abolition of class and status, with opportunity for the lowest in origin to rise to the highest office.

P. M. Holt, *The Mahdist State* . . . (1970).

Muḥammad al-Mahdī (12th Imām): see AL-MAHDĪ.

Muhammadans, Mohammedans, Mahotmetans. Westernized terms for Muslims, both inaccurate and offensive, because they suggest that Muslims are followers of *Muḥammad, rather than worshippers of God; and also because *al-Muḥammadīya* ('Muhammadians') are members of sects regarded as heretical by mainstream Islam (though in Indonesia it is the name of an orthodox reforming movement, which has adapted Western institutions, e.g. Boy Scouts, to Muslim ends).

Muhammad b. Ismāʿīl (Shīʿite Imam): see ISMĀʿĪLIYA.

Muḥammad ibn 'Abd Allah (570–632). The last of the *Prophets, from whose proclamation of *Qur'ān Islam derives. Muḥammad was born in *Mecca in the 'Year of the Elephant' (i.e. when an Abyssinian army attacked Mecca). He was of the family Banu Hāshim in the tribe of the Quraysh. He was born after the death of his father and became the ward of his grandfather, *'Abd al-Muttalib. At an early age, he had an experience of a visitation by two figures (later identified as angels) who 'opened his chest and stirred their hands inside'. It was the first of several unusual experiences which led Muḥammad increasingly to search for the truth of God and religion on his own. This quest was reinforced when he was employed by a widow, *Khadījah, to take trading caravans north to Syria, where he met Christians and Jews, especially the monk Bahīra who recognized in him the signs of the promised *messiah. By now he was under the protection of his uncle, *Abu Tālib, and at the age of 25 he married Khadījah; they had two sons who died and four daughters. Muḥammad was increasingly influenced by the *Ḥanīfs (pl., *ḥunafā'*), those who were seeking to preserve a monotheism which they traced back to *Abraham (Ibrāhīm); Arabia was an important refuge for Jews and unorthodox Christians when they came under persecution, and their beliefs are clearly reflected in the Qur'ān. Mecca was polytheistic, with revered idols, and Muḥammad recognized the contrast as extreme. He went with increasing frequency into isolation in a cave on Mount Hira in order to struggle with the truth of God lying behind the bewildering conflict of idols and religions. On one occasion, he had the strong sense of a presence (later identified with *Gabriel/ Jibrīl) pressing on him and insisting three times, ' 'Iqra', read (or recite). He resisted, but then felt words being impelled through him, the first words of what became many revelations, collected eventually in the Qur'ān: 'Recite, in the name of your Lord who creates, who creates man from a drop: Recite; for your Lord is the most generous, who teaches by the pen, teaches man what he knows not'—the opening words of *sūra 96.

At first Muḥammad believed that he had gone insane and thought of killing himself. But Khadījah found him and told him to test the truth of what he was certain he had experienced. There followed some further revelations, but then a break which was equally testing. He began preaching, but encountered great hostility. From his initiating vision he saw with absolute clarity that if God is God, then there can only be what God is: there cannot be a God of the Christians, a God of the Jews, still less can there be the many deities of Mecca. It followed that the idolatry of Mecca was deeply wrong about God and must be abolished. In a sense, the whole of Islam is a footnote to this simple observation: there is only one God and all creation is derived from him. Therefore all humans should live in a corresponding unity (i.e. community, *'umma); and Islam is the quest for the realization of 'umma, under God. Not surprisingly this message was violently resisted by the Meccans. After Khadījah, ʿAli (Muḥammad's cousin) and his servant Zayd were the first to believe, followed by the first non-family member, *Abū Bakr. They were called *al-muslimūn*, i.e. Muslims, those who enter into a condition of safety because of their commitment to God. As the crisis and persecution grew worse, Muḥammad was invited to Yathrib to make his way of unity a practical reconciliation between the two contesting ruling families there. He made this move, the *Hijra, in 622 (to become later the first year of the Muslim *calendar) and began to establish the first community under the rule of God's revelations as they continued to be given. The revelations were clearly distinguished from the words which Muḥammad spoke as a man, both through his changed appearance, and through the entirely different style of the utterance—rhythmic and tied loosely by rhyme, and without exact precedent in the Arabian context.

At Yathrib, now to be known as al-*Madīna ('The City'), Muḥammad was joined by some seventy other emigrants, the Muhājirūn (see EMIGRANTS). The opposition from Mecca did not cease, partly because Muḥammad took to raiding their caravans. At the battle of *Badr, in 624, a small army of Muslims defeated a much larger army of Meccans; but in 625, the Meccans reversed this defeat at the battle of Uhud: both battles remain epitomes of faith and lack of trust. In 627, the Quraysh failed to win a siege with numbers overwhelmingly in their favour (the battle of the Trench), and subsequently Muḥammad took the fight to his enemies, capturing Mecca in 630 and purifying it from idols. Meanwhile he had been organizing not only life in Madina, but also the relations of the new community with surrounding tribes: some of these endeavours are gathered together in the so-called Constitution of Madīna, a kind of 'anthology' of early treaties with different surrounding tribes. When Muḥammad died in 632, there was no obvious successor. He had at various times eleven wives and at least two concubines, but no son had survived—his nearest male blood relative was his cousin *ʿAli who had married one of his daughters. In any case, Arab communities recognized two forms of leadership, one hereditary, the other by selecting the best man for an occasion (e.g. in a crisis). The Muslim community selected a successor, *khalīfa (caliph), by the second procedure, and chose Abū Bakr. But there remained those who believed it should have been the nearest member of Muḥammad's family, ʿAli; and from this uncertainty the division of Islam between *Sunni and *Shīʿa became an embittered fact within a generation of Muḥammad's death.

As the Seal of the Prophets, Muḥammad has brought the revelation of God which is the same as that mediated through previous prophets, but before Muḥammad, all communities had corrupted revelation for their own purposes. After Muḥammad, there can be no further prophet or revelation, because now the pure and uncorrupted revelation exists in the world. Muḥammad himself is not regarded as superhuman: he is not without sin. Nevertheless, he is the first living commentary on the meaning of the Qur'ān in the practice of life. Consequently, the first biographical fragments are in *ḥadīth. The first connected life of Muḥammad is that of Ibn Ishaq, edited by Ibn Hisham (tr. A. Guillaume, 1955). See Index, Muḥammad's life.

T. Andrae, *Die person Muhammeds in lehre und glauben seiner gemeinde* (1918); M. H. Haykal, *The Life of Muhammad* (1938); A. Schimmel, *And Muhammad is His Messenger . . .* (1985); M. Watt, *Muhammad at Mecca* (1953) and *Muhammad at Medina* (1956).

Muḥammadīya, al- (Muslim sectarians): see MUHAMMADANS.

Muḥarram. First month of the Muslim calendar, the first ten days of which are observed by *Shīʿa Muslims as a period of mourning for the death of *Al-Husain. For *Sunni Muslims, 10 Muḥarram is celebrated as a day of blessing.

Muḥāsibī (Shāfiʿite theologian): see AL-MUḤĀSIBĪ.

Mu-ichimotsu (Jap., 'not one thing'). A Zen extension of *mu, emphasizing that no phenomenon has any substantial, underlying, permanent foundation—as *śūnyatā also affirms.

Muʿjiza (Islamic): see MIRACLE.

Mujōdō-no-taigen (Jap., 'the embodiment of the unsurpassable way'). The embodiment of Zen enlightenment (*satori, *kensho) in the midst of everyday life. It is the realization of the buddha-nature (*busshō), with no residue of worldly attachment left. It is a continuous state of *samādhi. It does not occur *with* satori, but can only be attained on its foundation, probably after many further appearances.

Mujtāhid (judge of Islamic law): see IJTIHĀD; ʿULAMĀ; QĀḌI.

Muju (Zen monk): see ICHIEN, DŌKYŌ.

Mukan Fumon (1212–91). Zen pupil of [Enni] *Ben'en, who was summoned by the emperor

Kameyama to exorcise the ghosts who were disturbing his new palace in *Kyōto, the traditional priests having failed. Mukan and his monks sat in silent meditation and the spirits disappeared. The emperor converted the palace to a Zen monastery, Nanzen-ji, and Mukan became the first abbot. However, he died before taking up this post.

Mukasa, Reuben (founder): see AFRICAN GREEK ORTHODOX CHURCH.

Mukhaliṅga. A *liṅga in Hinduism on which faces are depicted, the number depending on the purpose of the ritual; thus the two-faced liṅga is used in rituals for the destruction of enemies.

Mukta (Skt., *muc*, 'release', 'liberation'). In Hinduism, one who has attained *mokṣa or *mukti. One whose liberation from attachment and desire occurs during one's life is a *jivanmukta; one whose liberation occurs in the discarnate state after death is a videha-mukta. Attainment of *jivanmukta is the *dharma of the *saṁnyāsa *āśrama (see VARṆĀŚRAMADHARMA). A jivanmukta, though released, remains in this world due to unripened karmic residues (*karmāśayas*), as a potter's wheel continues to turn once the potter's hand is removed.

Mukte (Hindī, Pañjābī, 'liberated ones'). 1. Those who have achieved salvation (cf. MUKTA).

2. Five Sikhs who received *initiation immediately after the *Pañj Pyāre.

3. Forty Sikhs who died fighting at Chamkaur.

4. See MUKTSAR.

Mukti (Skt., from *muc*, 'release', 'liberation'). In Vedic Skt., mukti meant release from the limitations of the body and mind, effected by ritual action. Later the term became identified with *mokṣa. This is the term used by Sikhs for liberation from successive rebirths.

A. G. K. Warrier, *The Concept of Mukti in Advaita Vedānta* (1961).

Muktsar (Pañjābī, 'lake of *salvation'). Historic Sikh site in Ferozepur District, Pañjāb. Originally called Khidrāṇā, the place was renamed after forty Sikhs, who had earlier deserted Gurū *Gobind Siṅgh, but who returned to die fighting against the men of the local governor, Wazīr Khān. The Gurū forgave their perfidy, pronouncing them liberated ones (mukte). They are commemorated daily in *ardās and by an annual *melā on 1 Māgha (Jan.–Feb.).

Mukyokai (Japanese Non-Church movement): see UCHIMURA KANZŌ.

Mūla-Mādhyamaka-Kārikā (*The Root Verses* on the Mādhyamaka). The major work of *Nāgārjuna in which he laid the foundation for the development of Mādhyamaka philosophy. In the 445 short verses which comprise the treatise, Nāgārjuna applies a rigorous dialectical logic to the basic teachings of the Buddha, such as causation, the aggregates (*skandhas), *karma, *duḥkha, the *tathāgata, and *nirvāna. In all he examines twenty-seven topics and demonstrates that the concepts and categories with which the intellect normally operates are inadequate to grasp the true nature of phenomena and the manner in which they are related. The breakdown of reason at this point means that reality can only be described as inexpressible or 'void' (*śūnyatā), and the crisis of logic-failure which is precipitated through this reasoning brings about the intellectual purification which is enlightenment. For the philosophical standpoint, see *MĀDHYAMAKA.

The Root Verses were extensively commented upon in India, Tibet, and China, notably by *Buddhapālita (400–50 CE), *Candrakírti (600–50), *Bhāvaviveka (500–70), Piṅgala (4th cent.), *Kumārajīva (344–413), *Chi-tsang (548–623), and *Tsong Khapa (1357–1419).

Tr. K. Inada (1970); F. J. Streng, *Emptiness . . .* (1967).

Mula Saṅgha (The Root Assembly). The central organization of *Digambara Jain ascetics. In Digambara estimation, the succession from *Mahāvīra was organized in the Nirgrantha *saṁpradāya, but in order to pre-empt the inevitable dissensions of the *Kāli-Yuga, the Mula Sangha was broken up into four groups, the Deva, Nandin, Sena, and Simha. In fact, the Jains developed into innumerable sects and groups, maintaining lineage, but splitting like the delta of a river.

Mūla-sarvāstivāda. Name adopted by the Buddhist *Sarvāstivāda school some time in the 7th cent. CE, to distinguish it from three subschools which had detached themselves. The three subschools, of the Dharmagupta, Mahīśāsaka, and Kāśyapīya, became established in Central Asia, whereas the Sarvāstivāda was prominent in NW India in Kashmir and Gandhāra. The term *mūla* ('root') indicates that the Sarvāstivāda was the parent school from which the others were descended.

Mūlavijñāna (Skt., *mūla*, 'root', + *vijñāna*, 'consciousness'). A doctrine characteristic of the *Mahāsāṃghika school of early Indian Buddhism. As a consequence of the centrality of the teachings on impermanence (*anicca), and not-self (*anātman), it was felt necessary in the developing Buddhist systems to account for mental continuity in individuals, particularly between one existence and another, and after deep meditational trances, without committing the essentialist fallacy of *Upaniṣadic teachers who posited a permanent soul (*ātman). The notion of a basic consciousness (*mūlavijñāna) is the solution arrived at by the Mahāsāṃghikas. This doctrine has much in common with the limb of existence (*bhavāṅga*) of the *Theravāda and the subtle mind (*sūkṣmacitta*) of the *Sautrāntika school. Many modern commentators have seen in the mūlavijñāna an anticipation of the distinctive Yogācāra/*Vijñānavāda idea of a 'store-consciousness' (*Ālaya-Vijñāna).

Mulla (Arab., *mawla*, 'master'). A Muslim (man or woman) who has studied the basic disciplines. In *Ithna ʿAshariyya Shiʿism, a mulla is a teacher and preacher, who leads the congregational prayer; Persian *akhun(d)* is the equivalent.

Mulla Nasruddin. Character in Muslim folktales, also known as Juha and Nasruddin Khoja. He views the whole world (especially its officialdom) with humour.

Mullā Ṣadr al-Dīn Muḥammad ibn Ibrāhīm Shīrāzi (known as **Mullā Ṣadrā**) (1571–1640 (AH 979–1050)). Shiʿite philosopher. He was born in the province of Ṣadrā in Iran, and began his work in Isfahān. During his life, there was contest between those who did and did not want a philosophized account of *Shiʿa Islam. Mullā Ṣadra was clearly of the former, achieving a profound reconciliation of Islam with *Aristotelianism and *gnostic systems—though as a result he underwent periods of forced and voluntary exile. In his thought he confronted the fundamental problem of how the absolute and transcendent creator can create without diminution, and how creatures can in turn be related to God without affecting that absolute nature of Being. He argued that there are gradations of being, some drawing nearer to the source of all being, who is Being in essence, without affecting that Being. Thus some might call the sunlight and the warmth of the sun 'the sun'; yet the rays and the warmth are gradations of being, derived from the sun without being identical with the sun. In ... *al-Asfār al-Arbaʿah* (The Four Journeys), he described the process by which a spiritual journey can be made back to the source without becoming fused with it: (i) detachment from the world and the body; (ii) penetration of the divine names (and attributes) of the *Qur'ān; (iii) *fanā' (annihilation of one's own attributes as a self-possessed individual); and (iv) the return in utter independence (because wholly dependent on God) to bring guidance to others (*jalwah*).

S. H. Nasr, *Mullā Ṣadrā* ... (1978); F. Rahman, *The Philosophy of Mulla Sadra* (1975).

Müller, Max (1823–1900). Historian of religions and pioneer of the comparative study of religions. His main interest was in Indian religions, and after translations of *Hitopadeśa* (see PAÑCATANTRA) and *Kalidasa's *Meghaduta*, he moved to Oxford where he became professor of comparative philology, and where he remained for the rest of his life. He was a prolific author, with interests ranging from the production of both editions and translations of Eastern religious texts (he edited the series *Sacred Books of the East*, 1879–94, and began the series *Sacred Books of the Buddhists* in 1895) to arguments about the origins of religion and *mythology. In his view, mythology began in the human sense of the overpowering might of natural phenomena (hence the name for those who followed his views, 'nature mythology'), with these powers early being personified and deified. In particular he argued for the fundamental importance of solar mythology, arguing that heroes and gods were in origin solar metaphors. From what he called his Copernican revolution (the discovery that the Sanskrit Dyaus equals, philologically, the Greek Zeus), he concluded that India was the original home of humanity, and that people diffused from that centre with connected languages, beliefs, and myths. Although his views were much satirized (e.g. the demonstration by H. Gaidoz that Müller himself had never existed but was a corrupted solar myth), he was also a much admired figure in his own time. He held (on his own understanding of what was implied by *Kant, whose *Critique of Pure Reason* he translated in 1881) that religion is the human capacity to perceive the infinite, and that all religions consequently contain to some degree the eternal truths of belief in God, in the immortality of the soul, and in a future retribution.

J. H. Voigt, *Max Müller* ... (1967).

Mul Mantra (Pañjābī, 'basic sacred formula'). Concentrated and essential Sikh teaching, one of the first compositions of Gurū *Nānak, which is placed at the head of the Gurū Granth Sāhib (*Ādi Granth), preceding even the *Japjī. It contains the essence of Sikh theology, and is beyond translation: 'Ik onkār satnām kartā purukh, nirbhau, nirvair, akāl murat, ajuni, saibham, Gurprasād.' It is paraphrased by Jodh Singh (*Guramati Niranay*, n.d.) as:

> This Being is One. He is eternal. He is immanent in all things and the sustainer of all things. He is the creator of all things. He is immanent in his creation. He is without fear and without enmity. This Being is not subject to time. He is beyond birth and death. He is himself responsible for his own manifestation. (He is known) by the Gurū's grace.

Mumonkan (Zen text): see KŌAN.

Mumukṣutva (Skt., 'serious for liberation'). One of the four prerequisites in Hindus for those who aspire to *mokṣa (liberation). *Śaṅkara describes the others as the power to discriminate between what is real and unreal (*viveka), natural capacity and willingness to grow away from worldly things (*vairāgya), and the six great virtues (*ṣatkasampatti).

Munāfiqūn, al- (Arab.). Term in the *Qur'ān denoting those who pretended allegiance to Muḥammad's cause but in bad faith. Sūra 63 is named for them, and there are evidences elsewhere of their 'hypocrisy'. It is not clear how far they were an organized party. But the element of force in Muḥammad's mission, especially as it prospered, required increasing vigilance against those whose accession was merely prudential and devious. The fact that success engenders in some a feigned adherence, masking conspiracy, is seen in Islam as a necessary hazard which resolution can overcome.

Muṇḍaka Upaniṣad. One of the eighteen principal *Upaniṣads, considered the most poetical. The name means 'shaven', and perhaps reflects the emphasis on the life of *saṁnyāsa. It argues that there are two kinds of knowledge, higher (*parā*) and lower (*aparā*), and describes the way to the former, which is knowledge of *Brahman as the unproduced Producer of all that is: 'As a spider emits and draws in its thread, . . . as hairs of the head and body arise from a living person, so from that which is imperishable arises everything that appears' (1. 1. 7). This Upaniṣad also includes the famous illustration of the relation of *jīva to *ātman: 'Two birds, inseparable companions, sit on the same tree, the one eating the sweet fruit, the other looking on without eating' (3. 1. 1). When jīva, attached to the world, realizes that it is not other than ātman, which is in the world but not of it, it leaves the sweet fruit, 'becomes' the other bird, and becomes freed from sorrow.

For trs., see UPANIṢADS.

Mundāvaṇi (Pañjābi, 'seal', some suggest 'riddle'). The passage at the end of the Sikh *Ādi Granth which indicates that nothing further is to be added. The whole is likened to the offering dish of the Hindu sacrifices: it contains the three treasures of truth, wisdom, and satisfaction.

Muni (Skt., etym. uncertain; perhaps from √*man*, 'think', 'be silent'; or *mud*, 'intoxicated ecstasy'; or *muka*, 'dumb'). In Hinduism, Jainism, and Buddhism, one who has progressed far on the way to enlightenment. In Hinduism, a muni in the Vedic period is one who possesses magical powers (*Ṛg Veda* 136. 2), a wise *ascetic, especially one who has taken a vow of silence. In the *Upaniṣads (e.g. **Katha Upaniṣad* 1. 4), a muni is one who has transcended attachment to this world and life by the realization of *ātman.

In Buddhism, the early use of the term is suggested by a usage mostly confined to the oldest poetical portions (for example, **Sutta-nipāta*) of the Pāli canon, and as an epithet of the Buddha and of *paccekabuddhas but rarely of *arhats. It is used of one who has achieved tranquillity (*santi*; cf. ŚANTI) as a result of emancipating himself from views (see DIṬṬHI) and passions (*rāgā) and who therefore advocates the doctrine of tranquillity (santivāda—*Sutta Nipāta* 5. 845). The term probably referred to that aspect of the *Śramaṇa tradition which lay at the origins of Buddhism, and possibly Jainism as well, and denoted those who claimed to have 'silenced' the passions, including the propensity to argue contentiously. In later canonical and post-canonical Buddhist literature the word is used to mean one who practises restraint in the triple activity of thought, word, and deed. In Jainism, it has become the common word to denote the avowed *ascetic.

Munkar and **Nakīr.** The two *angels, in Islam, who examine the dead in their graves, asking their opinion of *Muḥammad. Those who answer that he is *rasūl Allāh*, the 'apostle of God', will be left in peace until the *yaum al-Qiyāma (day of resurrection). *Kāfirs and other sinners, who cannot thus answer, will begin their punishment forthwith. The names of the angels, and details of punishment in the grave, are not given in *Qur'ān, but they are, with much elaboration, in *ḥadīth. Martyrs (*shahīd) are exempted from this interrogation.

Münzer, Thomas (*c.*1490–1525). German *radical Reformer. He was born in Saxony and was educated at Leipzig and Frankfurt. He was ordained and spent four years (1516–20) as an itinerant priest. At the Leipzig Disputation (1519) he met *Luther and created a good impression, but later developed revolutionary views, asserting as authority for his radical message a form of Spirit-inspired direct revelation. Under the influence of *Hus, he became a Protestant. For the furtherance of his aims he encouraged participation in active conflict and endeavoured to involve his followers in the Peasants' Revolt. When he could see that Luther was opposed to such activities, he turned fiercely against him calling him 'Dr Liar' and 'Brother Soft Life'. Some continental historians have taken a keen interest in him, regarding Münzer as a prototype of later social revolutionaries. He was in repeated conflict, and after the defeat of the peasants, he was captured and executed: according to Luther, it was 'a just and terrible judgement of God'.

W. Elliger, *Thomas Müntzer* (1975); E. W. Gritsch, *Reformer without a Church* (1967).

Muratorian canon. The oldest surviving list of New Testament books, discovered by L. A. Muratori (1672–1750) in an 8th-cent. Latin manuscript at Milan. It mentions all the books except Hebrews, James, and 1–2 Peter, and includes (though cautiously) the Apocalypse of *Peter and *Wisdom of Solomon. It rejects a series of other writings including the Shepherd of *Hermas. It may be a translation from the Greek; perhaps it is the work of *Hippolytus; but in any case it comes from the late 2nd cent.

Murji'a (Murji'ite; Muslim movement): see ĪMĀN.

Murtadd (Arab., 'one who turns away', hence *ridda). An apostate from Islam. The ultimate punishment for an apostate, according to Qur'an 3. 86–9/80–3; cf. 2. 161–2/155–6, lies in the next world after death. There are, however penalties in this world, including restrictions on inheritance and annulment of marriage. In accord with the fundamental principle, 'There is no compulsion in religion' (2. 257/6), no physical pressure may be put on those who seek to change their religion, though in practice this happens, even to the extent of death. The penalty of death is not mentioned in the Qur'an, but comes from a *ḥadīth transmitted through *al-'Abbās, 'Whoever changes [*badala*] his religion [*dīn], kill him.' But even here the issue is debated. According to some Muslims, the hadith includes the provision that the one who changes religion must also subsequently attack Islam, so that the death penalty is then an act of *jihād, in defence of Islam (see SATANIC VERSES); othewise, those who are over-zealous are themselves liable to account for their actions on the Day of Judgement (for varying opinions, see J. W. Bowker, *Voices of Islam*, 1995, 100–5). It is also a matter of dispute whether a murtadd should be given time to repent or reconvert.

Mūrti (Skt., 'embodiment'). In Hinduism, the embodied form of the infinite deity, the Indian way of bringing the all-pervasive divine into particular focus and concentration (see ICONOGRAPHY (HINDUISM)). The making of a divine image is controlled by extremely detailed rules, but remains inert until it is consecrated through the installation ceremony of *pratiṣthāpana*. The image may be consecrated *sine die* (unless it suffers injury), i.e. *nitya-abhiṣeka*; or it may be consecrated only for the specific duration of the worship (as e.g. with the images of Mahādevī in *Durgā-pūjā: see DEVĪ). The image usually bears iconographic resemblance to the god or goddess imagined, but, in the case of Śaivites, it is the *liṅga. Mūrti-pūjā is of great importance, not just in the temple, but also in the home.

J. P. Waghorne and N. Cutler (eds.), *Gods of Flesh/Gods of Stone: The Embodiment of Divinity in India* (1985).

Murtipujaka (image-worshipper): see TEMPLE (JAINISM).

Murugan (name of Tamil god): see TAMILNADU.

Murukaṉ (name of Tamil god): see TAMILNADU.

Mūsā (Muslim form of Moses): see MOSES.

Musaf. Additional Jewish service for *Sabbaths and *Festivals. In the *Jerusalem Temple, extra *sacrifices were made on Sabbaths and Festivals after the regular morning offering (*B.Yoma* 33a). After the destruction of the Temple, the Musaf prayer was formalized into the *synagogue service and was considered by the *rabbis to be as important as the normal morning service (*B.Ber.* 30b). It is customarily recited after the *Torah and *haftarah readings and consists of the half *kaddish, the Musaf *ʿAmidah (which changes according to the festival), and various changing *piyyutim.

Musalmān. Turkish and Persian form of Muslim, from which derive the Fr. *musulmane* (for Muslim) and the (now rare) Eng. Mussulman.

Musama Disco Christo (Fanti, 'Army of the Cross of Christ'). An independent Ghanaian Church, founded by a highly *charismatic Fanti *Methodist teacher, Joseph Appiah (1893–1948). In 1923, he formed his own Church after dismissal from the Methodists for *pentecostal-like deviations, changed his name by revelation to Jehu-Appiah, and established a holy city, Mozano ('God's own town'), which was moved to New Mozano near Gomoa Eshiem after his death. The polity draws on both the Akan state system and some Methodist structures, and further Methodist influences are seen in orthodox and biblical doctrinal beliefs, the layout of churches, infant *baptism, *holy communion (held before dawn), a strict ethic, and the Fanti hymnal. Further developments represent an African version of the religion of Israel, with an inner Holy Place containing an *ark for the recorded vows and prophecies of Jehu-Appiah, and drumming, dancing, and acceptance of polygamy. All members receive new, divinely given names, and the Church has a strong sense of a distinctive identity as divinely founded.

Musar (Heb., 'ethics'). Jewish moral instruction. In biblical Hebrew, the term 'musar' was used variously to mean 'punishment' or 'instruction'. Later, in *Talmudic times, it came to mean ethics or moral instruction. A distinct branch of Musar literature grew up in the Middle Ages which dealt with ethical matters; and in the 19th cent., a movement for ethical education arose particularly among the *mitnaggedim of Lithuania. Threatened by the *Haskalah, the leaders of the movement concentrated their efforts on the students of the *yeshivot. It became the practice to study ethical literature by intoning it in unison, thus creating an intense religious mood. In addition students were required to subdue their natural instincts by a series of disciplinary activities.

Z. F. Ury, *Musar Movement* (1970).

Mushrik (offender, by association of less-than-God with God): see SHIRK; DHIMMA.

Music. Since music has charms to do much more than soothe the savage breast, it has been a major part of all religions. It has powers to alter and match moods, to sustain and evoke emotion, to induce trance or *ecstasy states, to express worship, and to entertain. At the same time, it is supremely a corporate activity: it not only binds together performers and audience, it is an activity in which many people can be engaged at once—people, for example, can chant together (not necessarily in unison) in a way which would become noise and babble in ordinary speech—facts which were much developed and exploited in oratorio and opera. At moments of despair and of triumph, humans sing, and sing together. Of the experience of prisoners building the bridge over the River Kwai, E. Gordon wrote, 'Man need never be so defeated that he cannot do anything. Weak, sick, broken in body, far from home, and alone in a strange land, he can sing! He can worship!'

In India, sound itself (*śabda, *Om) is the sacred source of all appearance: music therefore has the capacity to articulate the order and ordering of the cosmos. The characteristic musical form of the *rāga is said to resemble in its gradual construction the building of a temple (see ART). In the *Vedas, which are believed to be eternal and not simply a matter of contingent revelation, music is embedded in the chants of the *Sāma Veda. While many of the sacrifices, of which the chants (*sāman*) once formed a part, are no longer practised, the protection of the chants themselves still continues, even in the degeneracy of this stage of the *Kāli yuga. Music is also integrated into the religious occasions and purposes of *dance, as classically formulated in the *Nātyśāstra*, which pays particular attention to the ways in which religious and other sensation (*rasa) can be produced. Although Indian music divided into two major traditions (the Hindustani and Carnatic), the underlying religious perceptions remain the same. As with other religious wisdom, the transmission of skills and content is more through formal traditions of teacher to pupil (*saṁpradāya) than through textual means.

In China, music received official recognition and support at an early date (at least by 1000 BCE) as an instrument of education and court ceremony. Ritual music of this kind was later called *ya-yüeh* (*yayue*, 'elegant music'), in distinction from 'popular music', *su-yüeh* (*suyue*). When *Confucius emphasized ethics and education as the basis of government and society, music formed a natural part in sustaining appropriate rituals and attitudes. *Shih Ching* (*Shijing*, The Book of Odes) became one of the *Confucian Classics, but no music from it survives. Music was equally central in Taoism: poetry-writing and the playing of the *ch'in* (*qin*, a kind of zither-like instrument) were regarded as avenues to the realization of the *Tao: Hsi K'ang, for example, one of the Seven Sages of the Bamboo Grove (see TAOISM) wrote *A Poetical Essay on the Ch'in*, in which he stressed the evocative power of music to create appropriate moods for contemplation. Buddhism not only introduced Indian musical forms and instruments, but also encouraged the didactic music which sang of the life and accomplishments of the Buddha.

In Japan, music was early connected with *shamanistic rituals, but later music was much affected by 'imports' from Korea, China, and Central Asia. Thus *gagaku* (elegant music; cf. China above) is the traditional court music developed during the *Nara period, and codified during the Heian period (794–1185), which includes *mikagura* (music for the Shinto cult in relation to the court). *Mikagura* is divided formally between *komagaku* derived from Korea, and *tōgaku*, derived from China. If *gagaku* is music for the purpose of accompanying *dance, it is known as *bugaku, if not, as *kangen*. In 701, a department of court music (Gagaku-ryō) was established employing hundreds of musicians, often for specific state rituals and occasions: in 749, for example, more than 400 musicians were involved in the celebration of the completion of the great *daibutsu at Tōdai-ji; some of the instruments used on that occasion are preserved in the Imperial Treasury at Nāra. During the Heian period, the Buddhist practice of chanting *sūtras, known as *shōmyō*, became widespread, and was of particular importance for *Shingon and *Tendai. Music is also important in *theatre, with its continuing religious connections, as e.g. in Kabuki and *Nō.

Buddhist music has undergone a comparable transformation in Tibet. Ritual chanting of myths and formulae seems to have been a part of *Bön religion (and in music a greater degree of the continuity from the indigenous religion can be discerned), with drums playing an important part. But the advent of Buddhism led to the development of music, both vocal and instrumental, partly to accompany the rituals, but even more to prepare those present for *visualization and *meditation. Ritual drama (e.g. *'cham*) was also an important occasion of public music.

Jewish music is clearly rooted in the biblical traditions which speak of the Temple music and of the powerful music of *David. But none of this has survived, and the most important continuity of Jewish music is secured in the *synagogue. From the earliest period, synagogue music included the sung recitation of *Psalms (psalmody, extremely simple in style so as not to distract attention from the words), *cantillation (recitation of the *masoretic text of *scripture according to accent marks written in the text, led by the ḥazzan or *cantor, or by a member of the congregation, in cadences indicated by gestures of the hand—hence 'chironomy', the traditional instruction of these techniques), and the chanting of prayers. To these were added a large number of hymns and *piyyutim, and among the Ḥasidim *niggunim*, sung to nonsensical words, or to no words at all, in order to induce the desired state of ecstatic joy.

Christians from the outset were enjoined to 'sing psalms and hymns and spiritual songs' (Colossians 3. 16; Ephesians 5. 19), and they have not stopped doing so since: as early as the letter of Pliny to Trajan (early 2nd cent.), the practice is noticed of Christians 'singing hymns to Christ, addressing him as God'. The biblical text underlay the development of Christian music, with especial emphasis on the Psalter. Plainchant (*plainsong) is a monophonic chant in free rhythm, which developed in various traditions (e.g. Ambrosian, Gallican, Gregorian, Mozarabic, Armenian, Byzantine, etc.). But plainchant led into polyphony, introduced in about the 11th cent., but coming to maturity from the 14th cent. on. The recovery of pagan *myths during the Renaissance allowed the possibility of telling stories through music, i.e. of opera (early examples of opera are two settings of *Euridice* and *Dafne*). The opportunity they afforded to the Reformation of telling the biblical story (thereby reinforcing the claim of 'all that is necessary for salvation' being known *sola scriptura*, by scripture alone) led to the astonishing achievements of Heinrich Schütz (1585–1672), whose major works, *Cantiones Sacrae*, *Symphoniae Sacrae*, *Psalmen Davids*, *The Resurrection History*, *The Christmas History*, and *The Seven Last Words from the Cross*, indicate how important the biblical text was. Even more spectacular was the development of the oratorio by J. S. Bach (1685–1750): although written for church settings, his Passions according to St Matthew and St John can still convey a religious sense of occasion, even in concert performances: 'Bach almost persuades me to be a Christian' (Roger Fry). Although music became increasingly decoupled from the Church from this period on, there still remained and remain many composers who write specifically Christian music. But in the Church, during this whole period, there had been developing the early Greek custom of singing *hymns, some early examples of which are still in use. Hymns have also spread their skirts a little into the related forms of motet, canticle, anthem, and cantata. Many other forms of music have emerged in relation to church services and evangelism (see Index, Hymns; also AFRICAN-AMERICAN RELIGION).

In Islam, music is related to the chanting of the Qur'ān which is highly technical and stylized, and to the *mosque, where the *ādhān (call to prayer) is taught and adjudged musically. The power of music to affect moods has led to its extensive use in *Sūfī movements. Although no body of religious music has been developed in Islam, Muslims have taken a great interest in music as a part of God's creation, and early works on music (especially that of *al-Fārābī) were translated into Latin, thereby extending their influence into Europe.

See Index, Music.

F. Blume *et al.*, *Geschichte der evangelischen Kirchenmusik* (1965; tr. 1974); P. Crossley-Holland, 'The Religious Music of Tibet . . .', in Crossley-Holland (ed.), *Centennial Workshop on Ethnomusicology* (1967); B. C. Deva, *Indian Music* (1974); K. J. De Woskin, *A Song for One or Two: Music and the Concept of Art in Early China* (1982); W. Douglas, *Church Music in History and Practice* (1963); *Encyclopédie des musiques sacrées* (1968); K. G. Fellerer (ed.), *Geschichte der katholischen Kirchenmusik* (1972–6); E. Harich-Schneider, *A History of Japanese Music* (1974); A. Z. Idelsohn, *Jewish Music in its Historical Development* (1929); A. Lewis (ed.), *Opera and Church Music, 1630–1750* (1975); F. Lieberman, *Chinese Music: An Annotated Bibliography* (rev. edn., 1979); W. P. Malm, *Japanese Music and Musical Instruments* (1959) and *Nagauta: The Heart of Kabuki Music* (1963); M. Nulman, *Concise Encyclopedia of Jewish Music* (1975); S. Prajnananda, *A Historical Study of Indian Music* (1965); A. Shiloah, *The Theory of Music in Arabic Writings, c.900–1900* (1979); B. Smallman, *The Background of Passion Music: J. S. Bach and his Predecessors* (1957, 1970); N. Sorrell and R. Narayan, *Indian Music in Performance . . .* (1980); R. H. van Gulik, *Hsi K'ang and his Poetical Essay on the Lute* (1941); B. C. Wade, *Music in India: The Classical Traditions* (1979); A. Weisser, *Bibliography . . . on Jewish Music* (1969).

Music of the Spheres. The perfect harmonies created by the friction between the moving spheres of Greek (and later Christian) cosmology. It was originally a Pythagorean theory, expounded by Plato (*Republic* 10. 11) but rejected by Aristotle (*On the Heavens* 2. 9. 12). Nevertheless, it was extended by Macrobius (*Commentary* 2. 3) and was eventually fused with Aristotle's attribution of an intelligence for each sphere. Where it had been supposed that the nine muses sung the notes, these became the nine orders of angels, so that the angelic choirs became identified with the celestial harmonies and intelligences of the Greeks. *Boethius (*On the Principles of Music*) laid out the relations between the music of the spheres which is inaudible to human ears (*musica mundana*), the harmonies of a correspondingly well-ordered human life (*musica humana*), and the music of instruments (*musica instrumenta constituta*): humans mediate between the perfect harmonies of the heavenly spheres and the potential chaos and disorder of the lower worlds. Although the Copernican revolution destroyed the cosmology, the underlying idea of attainable harmonies persisted, as can be seen, e.g., in Thomas Browne (1605–82), *Religio Medici*:

> There is a music wherever there is a harmony, order or proportion; and thus far we may maintain the music of the spheres; . . . for even that vulgar and tavern music, which makes one man merry, another mad, strikes in me a deep fit of devotion, and a profound contemplation of the First Composer, there is something in it of divinity more than the ear discovers.

A distant shadow of this aesthetic can be discerned in the theology of H. U. von *Balthasar.

Muslim: see ISLAM.

Muslim b. al-Ḥajjāj al-Qushayri (817–75 (AH c.202–61)). Muslim scholar. His collection of *ḥadīth is, with *al-Bukhārī's *Ṣaḥīḥ*, the most highly esteemed amongst Muslim holy books. He was born at Nishāpūr in Persia, and after completing his formal education, travelled widely to collect the traditions of the Prophet *Muḥammad. His Ṣaḥīḥ (Sound) collection was composed out of 300,000 traditions. It consists of fifty-two books dealing with the *five pillars of faith, also marriage, slavery, barter, hereditary law, war, sacrifice, manners and customs of the Prophet and the Companions, and eschatological subjects. It differs from other ḥadīth collections in two ways: the books are not subdivided into chapters, and he pays special attention to the *isnād (chain of authorities) for the sake of accuracy. It is believed that he wrote many other books on *fiqh, traditions, and biography, but none have survived.

Tr. 'Abdul Ḥamīd Siddīqī (1978).

Muslim Brotherhood: see AL-IKHWĀN AL-MUSLIMŪN; ḤASAN AL-BANNĀ'.

Musō Soseki, also known as **Shōkaku Kokushi** and as **Musō Kokushi** (1275–1351). A leading Zen monk of the *Rinzai school during the Five Mountain, Ten Temple period, based on *Kyōto and

*Kamakura. In a time of conflict, seven emperors bestowed the title of *kokushi* on him, and he did much to integrate Buddhism into Japanese culture, especially in Kyōto. Nevertheless, much about his own life is obscure. He was educated in a *Shingon temple, but when his teacher died and he realized that the real problems of human existence (how to live and how to die) cannot be solved by education, he converted to Zen: during a period of 100-day prayer before the image of the Buddha, he saw in a dream two Zen monks, and he realized that 'dreams are a conversation with what one truly is and desires'. He travelled widely, until, in 1305, he was walking on a dark night, and stopped to think: he leant against a wall that was not there, and as he fell, so did his darkness:

> For many years I dug in the earth and searched in the blue sky | And always, always my heart grew heavier, grew heavier | One night, in the dark, I took stone and brick | And without mindful thought | I struck the bones of the empty heavens.

He received the seal of recognition (*inka-shōmei) from Koho Ken'ichi, and still continued to move from hermitage to hermitage. Eventually (and reluctantly) he was appointed abbot of Nanzen-ji in Kyōto, and although he still moved on several occasions, he remained close to the reform and rebuilding of Rinzai Zen, a legacy from which remains in his rules for monasteries, *Rinsen kakun* (tr. in M. Collcutt, *Five Mountains*, 1981), *San'e-in yuikai*, and *Saihō yuikai*.

In his teaching, he refused to endorse the growing division between *sūtra and *kōan methods, believing the means are determined by the capacity of the student. He employed the term *shōgyoku* as a virtual equivalent to *upāya. In the same way, progress in Zen is not limited to *zazen: any and all circumstances can be the occasion of Zen practice. For that reason, he made vital contributions to the development of the arts and of garden design as ways of Zen. He was also inclusive in his attitude to other Buddhist schools, arguing that 'the Buddha taught *dharma to save all sentient beings'; any school which serves that purpose authenticates itself:

> Masters of Zen with clear sight do not have fixed teachings to be adhered to, come what may. They teach as the situation requires and preach as the spirit takes them. . . . They may swing their stick or shout, Katsu! (see HO), or raise a finger. All such methods may be used, and are known as 'the vigorous treatment of the Zen Buddhist.' They are unintelligible to those who have not entered into this domain.

Among many works, his *Muchū-mondō shū* (Dialogue in a Dream) explains Zen Buddhism in response to questions from the Shogun.

M. Collcutt, *Five Mountains* . . . (1981).

Mussulman (archaic name for Muslims): see MUSALMĀN.

Musubi (Jap., from *musu*, 'to produce', + *bi*, 'spiritual power'). The mysterious power and source of creativity producing all things in the universe. The word appears originally in the 'Age of Gods' section of the **Nihongi* (720). But it is also found in other early works, such as the **Kojiki* and **Kogoshūi*, as part of the names of the creative gods (*kami); for example, Takami-musubi no kami and Kamimusubi no kami. In the Shinto revival of the 18th cent., *Motoori Norinaga and other scholars of national learning (*kokugaku) emphasized the uniquely Japanese character of the idea. The creativity of the cosmogonic gods in early Japanese literature revealed a miraculous power of divinity beyond human understanding, a power that, by divine descent, was also transmitted through *Amaterasu, the Sun Goddess, to the imperial line. With the concept of musubi, these scholars rejected as foreign accretions all rationalistic cosmological speculations, such as the Chinese theory of *yin and yang, which were interspersed throughout the ancient Japanese writings. Buddhism, Confucianism, and yin/yang thought only served to obscure the uniquely Japanese insight into the mysterious creativity of the gods, and in the ever-present beauty and bounty of the world of nature.

Mutʿa (Arab., *mattaʿa*, (of God) 'let one enjoy something'). Temporary marriage in Islam, a contracted marriage for a limited period. Based on Qur'ān 4. 24 ('You are permitted to seek out wives with your wealth, in proper conduct, and not in fornication. But give them their recompense [*ujūr*] for what you have enjoyed of them'), this became a divisive issue between *Sunni and *Shīʿa Muslims. Sunnis take this to refer to marriage in the ordinary sense, Shiʿites that it authorizes mutʿa. The latter hold that the original text (suppressed by Sunnis) added, *ilā ajalin musamman*, 'for a definite period'. Both parties agree that the Prophet *Muḥammad allowed mutʿa in the early days, when Muslim men were engaged in campaigns which took them far from home for long periods. Sunnis then refer to *ḥadīth in which Muḥammad makes it *harām, appealing to the principle of 'gradualism' through which the true *sunna became established (cf., *badā'); and *ʿUmar was explicit in forbidding it. However, the Shiʿites do not accept that ʿUmar had authority to prohibit what Muḥammad allowed.

Mutakallimūn. Those who engage in *kalām (theology in Islam).

Mutawwiʿūn (enforcers of obedience): see WAHHĀBĪYA.

Muʿtazilites (Arab., *ʿitazala*, 'separate from'). An early theological school in Islam, which espoused the use of reason in finding a middle way between unbelief and naïve *fideism. The 'intermediate state' may have political origins, neutrality in the conflict between *ʿAlī and his opponents, and separation from it. The founding of the theological school is attributed to *Wāṣil b. ʿAṭā' and ʿAmr b. ʿUbaid,

AH *c*.105–30. The issue raised by the murder of *ʿUthmān (what is the status of a Muslim who has committed a grave sin?), which divided *Kharijites from Murji'ites (see ĪMĀN), left the Muʿtazilites holding that the Quranic descriptions of *kāfir, hypocrite and believer clearly do not apply. Such a person must be in a different category, in an intermediate state between the two extremes. Theologically, the Muʿtazilites were characterized by five principles (*uṣūl*): (i) *Aṣl al-*tawḥīd*, strict monotheism and repudiation of anthropomorphism; (ii) *Aṣl al-ʿadl*, the absolute justice of God, which led to emphasis on the freedom and accountability of humans, and to the reality of God's 'promise and threat' of heaven and hell (which, on a strong view of *qadar, could have no effect on human decisions, because God knows and determines the outcome); hence (iii) *Aṣl al-waʿd waʾ l-waʿīd*, the promise and the threat, which have real consequence in the forming of belief (*īmān); (iv) *Aṣl al-manzila baina 'l-manzilatain*, the state between the states (of Sunnis and Shiʿites) in relation to the caliphate (*khalīfa); (v) *Aṣl al-amr bi 'l-maʿrūf*, commanding the good and forbidding the evil, appropriate action in spreading the faith, and in establishing a Muslim society. The Muʿtazilites were opposed by those who gave primacy to the Qur'ān over reason, especially *al-Ashʿarī and *al-Māturīdī.

R. T. M. Peters, *God's Created Speech* (1976); W. M. Watt, *The Formative Period of Islamic Thought* (1973).

Myers Briggs Type Indicator: see JUNG, CARL GUSTAV.

Myōchō Shūhō (Zen master): see SHŪHŌ MYŌCHŌ.

Myōgō-renga (Jap.). A Japanese linked verse in which each line contains the name of a *buddha or *bodhisattva. They were often composed as a memorial for a dead person to accrue merit to him.

Myōkōnin (Jap.). One who practises Shin Buddhism (*Jōdo Shinshū) in exemplary fashion, and who is likened to a lotus flower. According to Shantao (613–81, see PURE LAND SCHOOLS) just as the lotus (Skt., *puṇḍarīka) is the most wonderful, superior, rare, and unexcelled among flowers, growing out of muddy waters, so too is the person who manifests the working of *Amida Buddha's true compassion in the midst of a passion-laden world. Biographies of myōkōnin were first compiled by Gōsei (1720–94) and followed by others of Jōdo Shinshū tradition. They were relatively unknown until D. T. *Suzuki (1870–1965), the *Zen scholar, drew attention to them as exemplifying Japanese spirituality.

Myōō (protective deities): see FUDŌ.

Mysterium Tremendum: see OTTO, RUDOLF.

Mystery plays (Christian): see THEATRE AND DRAMA.

Mysticism. The practices and often systems of thought which arise from and conduce toward mystical experience. Mystical systems are distinguished from other metaphysical systems by their intimate connection to a quest for salvation, union, or liberation realized through distinct forms of mental, physical, and spiritual exercise. Because 'mystical experience' lies far beyond description, it is sometimes assumed that all such experiences, in whatever context they occur, must be the same—a unity at the heart of all religions; but that remains an assumption: it clearly cannot be demonstrated. Mysticism occurs in all major religious traditions. Its degree of affinity with the religion to which it is related is proportionate to the mystical ambience of the tradition. In a classic definition:

> Mysticism, according to its historical and psychological definitions, is the direct intuition or experience of God; and a mystic is a person who has, to a greater or lesser degree, such a direct experience—one whose religion and life are centred not merely on an accepted belief or practice, but on that which he regards as first-hand personal knowledge (E. Underhill, *The Mystics of the Church*).

But mysticism need not even be theistic. *Theravāda Buddhism, for example, is more conducive to mystical thought, experiences, and practices than Islam in general; yet *Sufism emerged in Islam giving priority to the mystical apprehension of God. Mystical experiences tend to reflect the doctrinal and ritual context in which they occur. Generally, though, those that follow upon spiritual techniques involve the apprehension of a transcendent (of some entity, state, or person) that lies 'beyond' the spatio-temporal realm or 'within' the self which bears a reality and value greater than the realm of everyday consciousness. They thus bring a serenity or bliss to the mystic. Such experiences may have some relation to the spontaneous experience of the unity of the world ('panenhenic' experience) and with certain kinds of chemical- and drug-induced experiences; but the connections are much disputed (see, e.g., J. W. Bowker, *The Sense of God . . .*, 1973). See also BIOGENETIC STRUCTURALISM; Index, Mysticism.

E. A. Bowman, *Western Mysticism: A Guide to the Basic Works* (1978); E. O'Brien, *Varieties of Mystical Experience* (1964); B.-A. Scharfstein, *Mystical Experience* (1973); S. Spencer, *Mysticism in World Religion* (1963); E. Underhill, *Mysticism* (1911).

Mysticism (Jewish): see KABBALAH.

Myth (Gk., *muthos*, 'story'). Narrations through which (amongst much else) religious affirmations and beliefs are expressed. In popular usage, especially in the media, myth has become synonymous with falsehood, as e.g. J. M. Brown: 'Even when the facts are available, most people seem to prefer the legend and refuse to believe the truth when it in any way dislodges the myth.' Yet in religions, myths are simply the means whereby individual biographies are located in stories of a more extensive kind—e.g. concerning the nature of time, space, and place.

Because many myths appear to be about putative matters of fact (e.g. about the origins of the cosmos, or of death) and are often aetiological (giving an account of the reasons why events or objects, etc., came into being), it has seemed obvious to the modern mind that, if the explanations are shown to be false, so also myths have been shown to be in error. Thus Lord Samuel: 'Without doubt the greatest injury of all was done by basing morals on myth, for, sooner or later, myth is recognised for what it is, and disappears: then morality loses the foundation on which it has been built.' Slightly more wise was Gilbert Ryle at the opening of *Concept of Mind*: 'A myth is, of course, not a fairy story. It is the presentation of facts belonging to one category in the idioms appropriate to another. To explode a myth is accordingly not to deny the facts but to reallocate them. And this is what I am trying to do.' Yet still the basic error is being made, that myths are defective (category-mistaken) accounts of putative matters of fact which can now be improved upon.

The truth is far more complex. Myths are frequently distinguished from legends and folk-tales by the way in which they offer explanations. But while myths *may* be both intended and understood as factual, it is clear that more often they are stories which point to truths of a kind that cannot be told in other ways, and which are not disturbed if the apparent 'facts' of the supposed case are shown to be otherwise (so that the purported explanation strictly fails: but the value of the story does not fail with it). That is why a religion may, for example, have many myths of creation which are strictly incompatible with each other (see COSMOLOGY), without seeking to reconcile them. No matter how remote from history myths may be (though some are clearly rooted in historical events; and historical events can take on the heightened characteristics of mythology—e.g. the myth of the Kennedy era), they supply the means through which the meaning of experience can be affirmed, and through which history is converted from threat of unpredictable chaos and change to stability. In particular, myth places individual biographies and local events in a larger context which supplies them with meaning and significance. Myth endures because it engages human attention at the extremes of terror and delight; and also because it illuminates, and is illuminated by, *ritual.

Myth is so pervasive and recurrent that it is clearly a human universal. In what way it is a universal and is thus able to bear, as it does, the weight of human biography, is open to widely different interpretations—of which only some examples can be given here. Perhaps most obviously, *Jung was fascinated by the recurrence of stories, symbols, etc., in all ages and places. He concluded (see *Aion*, 1951; *Mysterium Conjunctionis*, 1955/6; *Essays on a Science of Mythology*, 1949; and *Man and His Symbols*, 1964) that myths arise from the universal and underlying collective unconscious, biologically inherited and born anew in each individual. These profound, brain-stored archetypes are dynamic, not passive, manifesting timeless patterns and dramas of human existence in individual experience. Examples of archetypes are the hero, the self, the number four, the anima and the animus (the contrasexual part of the psyche in each individual), the shadow (cf. also *Four Archetypes: Mother, Rebirth, Spirit, Trickster*, 1970). Myths personify the archetypes and give them accessible life, making it possible for individuals to deal with these primordial constituents of life and to grow toward a mature expression of them—or, toward individuation:

> The sum of the archetypes signifies for Jung the sum of all the latent potentialities of the human psyche—an enormous, inexhaustible store of ancient knowledge concerning the most profound relations between God, man and the cosmos. To open this store . . . means nothing less than to take the individual out of his isolation and to incorporate him in the eternal cosmic process (J. Jacobi, *The Psychology of C. G. Jung*, 1942).

*Freud equally set myth in the formation of the psyche, but related it to the recapitulation of those primordial situations of conflict which made sexuality so dominant in his theory. Beyond that, he regarded myth as related to dream: in dreams, we can escape the constraints of hard reality, and become as poets or artists, for whom all things are possible. Art is a public dream, and myth is verbalized art.

*Lévi-Strauss (see *Introduction to a Science of Mythology*, 1969–81, including in vol. iv a response to criticisms; *Myth and Meaning*, 1978) also maintained that the meaning of myth must be sought behind the level of surface-content in the universal structure of the human mind: while different circumstances may have evoked different developments and applications, everywhere particular motifs reappear in myth. To him this suggests that, although the contents of myth may seem to us to be absurd or fanciful or arbitrary, nevertheless they represent a quest for order and logic—the logic of the concrete, 'which is constructed out of observed contrasts in the sensory qualities of concrete objects, e.g., the difference between the raw and the cooked, wet and dry, male and female' (E. Leach, *Lévi-Strauss*, 1970). Drawing on the work of de Saussure and Jakobson in linguistics (arguing that the enormous variety of sounds becomes intelligible through a few contrasting features, so that we hear phonetic variety at the etic level, but interpret this through a phonemic system at the *emic level, so that intelligibility arises from systems which can be studied synchronically and a-historically), Lévi-Strauss maintained that the elements of myth (mythemes) are chaotically meaningless if taken in isolation. They become meaningful only in relation to other elements. Structure reveals itself at many different levels, but Lévi-Strauss was particularly interested in the ways in which myths mediate the binary oppositions which arise in experience (as above): 'The real question is not whether the touch of a woodpecker's beak does in fact cure toothache. It is rather whether there is a point of view from which a woodpecker's beak and a man's tooth can be seen as "going together", . . . and whether some initial order can be introduced into the universe by means of these groupings' (*The Savage Mind*, 1962, 1966).

Others, however, have felt that it is the content of myth, not some underlying structure, which reveals universal human preoccupations. For *Eliade, myth places events *illo tempore*, 'in that (great) time' of primordial origins, a sacred and ideal time radically separated from the present. Myths make connection with this real and sacred time: myths are themselves sacred for that reason; they are exemplary, offering models of approved (and disapproved) behaviour; and they are significant, pointing out similarities in existential situations and exhibiting the meaning of otherwise random events. Joseph Campbell (1904–87, in e.g. *The Hero with a Thousand Faces*, 1968; *The Masks of God*, 1959–68; *Myths to Live By*, 1973) also emphasized the importance of content in understanding myth. He argued that myth serves four functions: mystical (evoking awe and gratitude), cosmological (providing models of the cosmos which are coherent with the sense of the *numinous), sociological (supporting the existing social order), and psychological (initiating individuals into their own potentialities, especially in the domain of the spirit). Myth, far from returning to the past, transforms the present. Campbell also sought to discern a central 'monomyth' associated with the fortunes of the primordial hero which recurs in all mythologies and is available for recapitulation in subsequent lives.

The ambivalent character of myths (combining popularity with, often, amorality, and literal narrative with improbable explanation) has led to their constant re-evaluation (see e.g. *demythologization). Thus Xenophanes (6th cent. BCE) was already regarding the gods as anthropomorphic inventions. Euhemerus (3rd cent. BCE) argued that the gods were originally human beings of great prowess who had been 'promoted' into gods by the tales told about them (hence the term *'euhemerism'). Plato (3rd/4th cent. BCE) distinguished between *logos* and *muthos*, and while he allowed a limited value to myth for the ill-educated, Socrates in *The Republic* (2. 37789) argued that myths should be eradicated from education since 'a child cannot distinguish the allegorical sense from the literal, and first ideas are likely to become indelibly fixed'. The reference to allegory indicates an early major attempt to re-evaluate myths. When Rome absorbed Greek mythology, myths came to be applied by some as allegories of several different types—often combined in a single myth—for example, physical (myths pointing to features of natural phenomena); historical (pointing to historical events or people); and moral (pointing to virtues and vices). The ascendancy of Christianity led to a reinforcement of allegorization, although attempts were made to remythologize the myths by regarding the gods as fallen angels or demons, or as planets or stars. In the Renaissance, mythology reasserted itself as a resource of imagination, not only by way of allusion ('When Oeta and Alcides are forgot | Our English youth shall sing the valiant Scot', Marvell), but also as narrative subjects—e.g. Venus and Adonis, Hero and Leander. In the 19th cent., the knowledge of mythology, especially Norse and Indian, was greatly extended (the term 'myth' was itself coined), and for some it offered a way of telling truth which lay outside the boundary and ambition of post-Newtonian science and technology. Myth was thus a positive term for *Strauss; and, as the culmination of this process, Wagner sought to create (especially in *Parsifal*) a myth which would bear the weight of human questions beyond those which physics can answer, and beyond (though incorporating) the impoverished or inadequate myths of existing religions. Theologians can consequently talk of 'the myth of God incarnate' and imagine that they are giving a positive evaluation of *Jesus; but to the popular mind, myth is now irredeemably associated with falsehood, so that such claims suggest a subversion of historical truth.

See Index, Mythology.

A. M. Birrell, *Chinese Mythology* (1994); Y. Bonnefoy, *Mythologies* (Eng. 1991); R. Carlyou, *A Guide to the Gods: An Essential Guide to World Mythology* (1989); A. Dundes (ed.), *Sacred Narratives* (1984); L. H. Grey and J. A. MacCulloch (eds.), *The Mythology of All Races* (1916–22); G. S. Kirk, *The Nature of Greek Myths* (1974); *New Larousse Encyclopedia of Mythology* (1974); W. D. O'Flaherty, *Other People's Myths* (1989); I. Okpewho, *Myth in Africa* (1983).

Mythemes (elements of myth): see MYTH.

Myth of secularization: see SECULARIZATION.

N

Naasenes (Heb., *naḥash*; a gnostic sect): see OPHITES.

Nabī (Arab., 'prophet', cf. Heb., *nabhi*). A *prophet, the basic description, with *rasūl (apostle), of *Muḥammad's role and status. According to the *Qur'ān, prophets have been sent to all peoples, conveying the same guidance and warning from God. Thus *Moses, *Jesus, *Ḥūd (to give only three examples) are recognized equally as prophets in the Qur'ān. But Muḥammad is the *khātam*, 'seal', of the prophets, because, whereas previous communities have distorted the Qur'ān entrusted to them, Muḥammad and his community have preserved the Qur'ān without corruption. He is, therefore, the last of the prophets (hence the Muslim opposition to e.g. *Bābīs, *Ahmadīyya, who seem to be claiming an extension of prophecy). Prophets are characteristically persecuted by the people to whom they come, and Muḥammad was no exception; but 'Īsā/Jesus alone was exempted from death. In later Islam, considerable effort was made to relate the work of the prophet (whose word by definition comes from God) to that of the philosopher (who relies on intellect, and may therefore be unnecessary to the discovery of the truth that matters).

W. A. Graham, *Divine Word and Prophetic Word in Early Islam* (1977); F. Rahman, *Prophecy in Islam* . . . (1958).

Nachi sennichi no gyōja. An *ascetic in Japanese religion (usually Buddhist) who completes the practice of standing naked for a thousand days beneath the Nachi falls, near Katsu-ura. The falls drop in a narrow band of water for about 130 m. At the base of the falls is the Hirō-ō (Flying Dragon) shrine. The Nachi shrine is above the falls, an ancient site, but the present buildings are recent (1848).

Nachmanides (Spanish Jewish philosopher): see NAḤMANIDES.

Naciketas. Son of Vājaśravas, who appears in *Taittrīya Brāhmana* and in **Katha Upaniṣad*, where he learns from *Yama the secret of immortality:

> Realise the self (*ātman) as riding in a chariot: the body is the chariot, the intellect (*buddhi) is the driver, the mind is the harness, the senses are the horses. . . . He who does not understand does not reach the goal, but goes to rebirth (*saṃsāra), but he who does understand reaches the goal: . . . That which has no sound, no touch, no form, no life-span, no taste, no variation, no odour, no beginning, no end, . . . by discerning That (*Brahman) one is liberated from the jaws of death.

Nāda (Skt., 'sound'). In Hinduism (especially *Tantrism) cosmic sound: *Brahman conceived as sound underlying all phenomena. This sound is 'unstruck' (*anahata*) and reverberates at all times. Through *yoga, especially *mantra yoga, the senses are withdrawn (*pratyahāra) and the yogin becomes aware of the nāda within him reverberating in the central channel (*suṣumna *nādī*) of his subtle body (*liṅga/sūkṣma śarīra). Thus the vocalized sound of mantra becomes the unvocalized, inner sound of God. The *Vijñānabhairava* (38), a text of *Kashmir Śaivism, says: 'One who is steeped in the sound of God (*śabdabrahman)—the unstruck sound [nāda] vibrating without impact which can be heard by the ear made competent by the guidance of the *guru, the unbroken sound rushing like a river—attains to supreme Brahman.' The *Tantras describe various levels of this inner sound as resembling a bell, a kettledrum, a village drum, and finally a *vīna*. One classification divides the sound into nine levels associated with different centres (*cakras) of the body. At the eighth level self-realization (*ātmavyāpti*) is achieved, and at the ninth God-realization (*śiva-vyāpti*). Nāda is also equated with *Kuṇḍalinī. See further Ṃ; ŚABDA; VARṆA; VĀC; and Index, Sound.

Nadar (help from God): see SIKHISM.

Nāḍī (Skt., 'channel' or 'vein'). A channel of the subtle body (*sūkṣma śarīra) connecting the *cakras, along which life-energy (*prāṇa) flows to regulate bodily functions. There are said to be 72,000 nāḍīs, though some texts, such as the *Śiva Saṃhita* (2. 13), say that there are 350,000. There are innumerable minor nāḍīs (upanāḍī). The *suṣumṇā* (the Buddhist *avadhūtī*) is the most important, rising from the base of the spine to the *brahmarandra* ('hole of Brahma') and the *sahasrāra padma at the top of the head. Within the *suṣumṇā* are three other nāḍīs, the *vajra*, the *citriṇī*, and the *brahma*. The *suṣumṇā* is red, associated with *tamas, the *vajra* is lustrous, associated with *rasa, and the *citriṇī* is pale, associated with *sattva. The *iḍā* and *piṅgalā* (the Buddhist *lalanā* and *rasanā*) flank the *suṣumṇā* on the left and right. They either run parallel to it or are entwined about it in a spiral movement. Opening at the nostrils, they meet the suṣumṇā at the *ājña* and *mūlādhāra* cakras. The *kaṇda* is the root of all nāḍīs, commonly placed at the *mūlādhāra*.

Nāfila (Arab.). A work of *supererogation in Islam, based on *Qur'ān 17. 79: 'Perform vigils during a part of the night, reciting the Qur'ān, as a nāfila for yourself.' The most obvious nawāfil (pl.) are additional *ṣalāts; see also ROSARY.

Nafs (Arab.; cf. Heb., *nephesh*). The individual self or soul in Islam, which exists in conjunction with *rūḥ* (see below). In the *Qur'ān, nafs is sometimes nothing more than a reflexive pronoun ('you yourself'). But it also has stronger content as 'living person' (21. 35 f.), and as the self or soul removed by God at death (39. 43). It is the subject of accountability at the Day of Judgement (*Yaum al-Dīn) (2. 281). *Rūḥ* (cf. Heb., *ruaḥ*) is the breath breathed into humans by God to create living beings, and is thus less individualized, but it carries the consequential meaning of a speaking being, hence something like 'spirit'. Nafs is frequently the lower self, the self with appetites and passions, 'the soul which incites to evil' (12. 53). *Rūḥ* is the humanizing spirit, the active intellect which (for the classic Muslim philosophers) is continuous with the primordial or First Intellect, and thus raises humans above the level of animals and even angels. *Rūḥ Allah* is the name of *Jesus/ʿĪsā in Qur'ān 4. 169, and by implication of *Adam (15. 29), perhaps reflecting the first Adam/second Adam symmetry of *Paul.

Nāga (Skt., 'snake'; the *Nāgās are derived from a different root). 1. In Indian mythology nāga is both snake and elephant, but especially mythical serpents. Sometimes nāgas are half-human and half-snake.

2. Devotees of an Indian snake cult, especially in the south, Bengal and Assam. In addition, *Śaiva *Liṅgayats worship snakes, in association with *Śiva; and *Viṣṇu rests on the snake *Śeṣa in the period between two creations.

3. In Buddhism, Nāga is a half-human, half-divine figure. Mahānāga (Great Nāga) is an epithet of the *Buddha and all who have passed beyond rebirth. In Tibetan Buddhism, nāgas are water deities who protect Buddhist scriptures until humans are ready to receive them.

4. A people and their country, in E. Assam, never fully assimilated into Hindu culture.

J. P. Vogel, *Indian Serpent Lore* (1926).

Naganuma Myōkō (co-founder): see RISSHŌ KŌSEI KAI.

Nāgapañcami (Hindu festival): see FESTIVALS AND FASTS.

Nāgārjuna (*c*.150–250). The founder of the *Mādhyamaka school of Buddhism and author of the **Mūla-Mādhyamaka-Kārikā* and other important works. As a philosopher he has few equals in the history of Buddhism, yet the details of his life are obscure and surrounded by mythological accretions.

All the accounts of his life agree that he was born as a *brahman in S. India and entered the Buddhist Order as a young man. It is reported that he was presented with the texts of the *Prajñāpāramitā-sūtras* (*Perfection of Wisdom) by the king of the *Nāgas, a mythical race of serpents with magic powers. He brought these texts back to India and studied them deeply, finding them far more profound than the teachings he had met previously.

Nāgārjuna is reputed to have been friendly with a Śatavāhana ruler who built a monastery for him in Śrīparvata. This was probably King Gautamīputra for whom Nāgārjuna composed his 'Friendly Epistle' (*Suhṛllekha*). The details of his death are obscure: he is reported to have either ended his own life or allowed himself to meet death at the hands of another. He is regarded by many Buddhists of the *Mahāyāna tradition as a 'Second Buddha', and his philosophy of emptiness (*śūnyatā) was of enduring significance for later Buddhist thought.

Nāgārjuna reached this position through a dialectic of oppositions. The initiating recognition of *anātman (no Self in the human appearance) still left an awareness that the human appearance sustains activities with characteristic natures (*dharma natures). Nāgārjuna argued that these too are empty of self (*dharma-nairātmya*), and are not independent constituents of appearance: they depend on each other and have no more reality than their interdependence. If, then, there is nothing with its own (substantial) nature, there is nothing with 'other-nature' (*para-bhāva*); and if there is no persistent reality, there cannot be non-existent reality either. *Abhava can then only be the passing away of appearance, like a mist at dawn, or like dawn at day, or like day at dusk, etc. All dharmas are *māyā (dreamlike appearance).

However, appearances have at least that much existence—they appear to be. Thus Nāgārjuna charts the Middle Way between substance and solipsism. Although conventional language is right to speak of appearances according to their characteristics ('the sun is hot'), in fact all appearances, since they are 'empty of self' (śūnyatā), have the same nature. Teaching by skilful means (*upāya-kauśalya) starts where people are, but leads to the point where even the language of śūnyatā is abandoned: 'The emptiness of all dharmas is empty of that emptiness.' The 'thusness' (*tathatā) of what is cannot be described but only realized, as undifferentiated in nature. Therefore even *nirvāna and *saṃsāra have the same nature ('there is not the slightest difference between the two')—they are not other than each other, since all is empty of self. For that reason, a *bodhisattva is not giving up a reward in order to return to help those still bound in saṃsāra, for he remains in the same realization. In that sense, all oppositions between nirvāna and saṃsāra, heaven and earth, icon and index, disappear.

The purpose of a wise life, therefore, is not to strive to attain some goal or target (heaven, enlightenment), but to uncover and discover what one already is, and has been all the time: the buddha-nature which is the same nature of oneself and all appearance (see BUDDHATĀ; BUSSHO; TATHĀGATA; Index, Nāgārjuna.).

K. K. Inada, *Nagarjuna* . . . (1970); C. Lindtner, *Nagarjuniana* (Budd. Trad. Ser. 2; 1987); V. K. Ramanan, *Nagarjuna's Philosophy* . . . (1966); F. J. Streng, *Emptiness* . . . (1967); M. Walleser, *The Life of Nāgārjuna from Tibetan and Chinese Sources* (1979).

Nāgās (from Skt., *nagna*, 'naked'). A Hindu sect of naked *ascetics. They were recruited mainly from non-*brahman *castes, and became well-known for their belligerence in defending their tradition. At times (e.g. of the Muslim invasion) they were employed by other Hindus, who were committed to non-violence, to defend the community.

Nāgasena. A Buddhist sage who lived probably in the present-day Pañjāb, in the early 2nd cent. BCE. He appears in a 1st-cent. CE Pāli text, **Milinda-pañha*, where after lengthy debate he succeeds in converting his opponent, King Milinda, to Buddhism. In a *Sarvāstivādin version of the same text, he is given the name Dhītika.

Nag Hammadi library. A collection of thirteen texts, written on papyrus, found in 1945 buried near Chenoboskion (Nag Hammadi) near the Nile, in Egypt. The books contain fifty-two short tractates in Coptic, of which most are *gnostic works translated from Greek. All but one of the volumes are now in the Coptic Museum in Cairo. They were probably hidden by Christian monks during a hunt for unorthodox literature in the 5th cent. The gnostic texts are practically the only surviving documents of gnosticism apart from quotations in anti-heretical writers. They have titles such as the **Gospel of Truth*, the *Apocalypse of Adam*, *Gospel of *Thomas*, and *Trimorphic Protennoia*.

Tr. in J. M. Robinson (ed.), *The Nag Hammadi Library in English* (1977).

Nagid. The head of the Jewish community in a Muslim country. In Islamic countries, a head of the community was appointed by the head of the state. He was frequently a physician, or else he held some high office at court. His duties consisted in representing the community, ensuring the payment of taxes, appointing *dayyanim and other officials, and overseeing the community's religious and state duties. The Babylonian *exilarch performed the functions of the nagid, but differed in that he was appointed by virtue of his *Davidic descent rather than through his own merits. In the Middle Ages, there were negadim (pl.) in Yemen, Egypt, Kairourian, and Spain, and in the 16th–19th cents., there were negadim in Algeria, Morocco, and Tunisia. The authority of the nagid was reinforced by his power to flog or imprison anyone who opposed him, and he could also *excommunicate members of the community. The office was discontinued in the 19th cent.

Naḥmanides, Moses ben Naḥman, or **Ramban** (1194–1270). Spanish Jewish philosopher and Talmudic scholar. Naḥmanides earned his living as a physician. He founded a *yeshivah in Gerona and among his students was Solomon ben Abraham *Adret. He had enormous prestige during his lifetime and was referred to as *ha-rav ha-ne'eman* (the trustworthy *rabbi). In the *Maimonidean controversy, he tried to reach a compromise, on the one hand condemning the way *Maimonides' writings had been used; on the other, arguing against the *ḥerem that the French rabbis had declared. In 1263, he was compelled to participate in a religious disputation with the *apostate Pablo Christiani, in which he was so successful that the *Dominicans instituted proceedings against him for blasphemy. Forced to leave Spain, he finally settled in *Erez Israel. About fifty of his works survive, including prayers, *piyyutim, theological works, biblical commentaries, and novellae on the *Talmud and *halakhah. His *Commentary on the *Torah* (publ. 1480) was written 'to appease the minds of the students, weary through *exile and trouble'.

His feelings for *Jerusalem were powerfully expressed: 'The loss of all that delighted my eyes is as nothing compared to my present joy in a single day in your courts, O Jerusalem [Psalm 84. 10], where it is granted to me to caress your stones, to run my fingers through your dust and to weep over your ruins.' His halakhic works were influenced by the French *tosafists, the Spanish authorities and the rabbis of Provence. He was strongly committed to respect for earlier authorities; nevertheless, 'I do not regard myself as "a donkey carrying books", because, having explained their value, I plead, with due modesty, my right to judge according to my own perspective: the Lord gives wisdom in every time and every age.'

Until the expulsion of the Jews from Spain in 1492, Naḥmanides' novellae were as much studied as *Rashi's commentary, and his halakhic writings were particularly influential on Solomon b. Abraham Adret, whose glosses on the Talmud clearly derive from his work. He produced no exposition of the *kabbalah, but there are frequent kabbalistic references in his prolific writings; and until the 14th cent., his works were much studied in this light.

H. Chone, *Nachmanides* (1930); Y. Unna, *R. Moses ben Nahman* (Heb., 1954).

Naḥman of Bratslav (1772–1811). Jewish *ḥasidic leader. A direct descendant of *Israel b. Eliezer (Baʿal Shem Tov), he emerged as a *zaddik in Podolia and the Ukraine. Naḥman believed he was destined to be at the centre of controversy, by his vocation to contest insincere leaders among the Ḥasidim: 'It was too hard work for Satan to subvert the whole world on his own, so he appointed prominent rabbis in many different places; it was too hard work for the Angel of Death to kill everyone in the whole world on his own, so he appointed doctors to help him.' Between 1800 and 1802, he was in dispute with Aryeh Leib, a popular ḥasidic leader who accused him of *Shabbatean and *Frankist leanings. Subsequently, in Bratslav, where he lived between 1802 and 1810, he came into conflict with all the local zaddikim. He left Bratslav for Uman, in the Ukraine, and died there of TB. His followers subsequently obeyed his instruction to dance around his grave on his *yahrzeit (anniversary): 'Melody and song lead our hearts to God.'

His disciple, Nathan Sternhartz, wrote his biography, *Hayyei Moharan* (1875), and organized his followers after his death. Groups of Bratslav Ḥasidim still follow Naḥman's teachings in Israel and elsewhere. Naḥman maintained he was the final link in the chain stretching back through *Simeon b. Yoḥai, Isaac *Luria, and Israel b. Eliezer, but he introduced many innovations. In particular, he taught that there is only one true zaddik, implying himself, who is destined to be the *messiah. It is the duty of every ḥasid to travel to the zaddik because 'the main thing is what he hears from the mouth of the zaddik' and 'through his teachings, the zaddik teaches the Holy One, blessed be he, how to deal with us'.

Naḥman placed great emphasis on daily conversation with God in which the ḥasid pours out his feelings to God (*hitbodedut*). He promised that he would continue to lead his Ḥasidim after his death—hence his followers are called by other Ḥasidim 'the dead Ḥasidim', because they have no living rebbe. He was a strong opponent of philosophical religion (with *Maimonides as a particular example of error), stating that 'where reason ends, faith begins'. He extended the Lurianic doctrine of *tsimtsum* (see LURIA) to demonstrate the literal vacuity of reason: it operates in the vacuum left by God's withdrawal to make space for creation (i.e. it deals only with the created order). What is required for a true relation with God is a 'leap of faith', which takes one across the void: 'Better a superstitious believer than a rationalistic unbeliever'; 'Since God is Infinite and humans are finite, we are bound to have religious doubts. But, like Moses, we should go into the dark, and we will find God.'

Sternhartz, as well as writing his biography, collected many of Naḥman's words and works in several volumes, of which the best-known is *Sippurei Ma'asiyyot* (Tales of Rabbi Naḥman, tr. A. J. Band, 1978). At the heart of his vision was the sense of all things coming from God as creator; thus everything—even the worst criminal—has its good side. The world is a kind of living whole before God: 'If a person kills a tree before its time, it is as though he has committed murder'; 'In the winter, the earth is pregnant, bearing within itself a great secret; in the spring, the secret is revealed.' In religious life, he valued the simplicity of the soul before God: at least one hour of solitude is necessary every day: 'The test of sincerity in the service of God is when a person does not want it to be noticed.' He lived by his own principle in teaching: 'To send children to sleep, tell them a story; to wake up the souls of human beings, tell them a story.'

M. Buber, *Tales of Rabbi Nachman* (1956); A. J. Band, *Nahman of Bratslav: The Tales* (1978); A. Green, *Tormented Master: A Life . . .* (1979).

Naḥman of Horodenka. Jewish *ḥasid. Naḥman was a disciple of *Israel b. Eliezer (Ba'al Shem Tov) and the grandfather of *Naḥman of Bratslav. His encounter with Israel b. Eliezer changed his life: 'When I was a great pietist, I immersed myself in a *mikveh so cold that nobody else could bear it . . . Even so I could not rid myself of impure thoughts until I was compelled to seek the wisdom of the Ba'al Shem Tov'. In 1764, Naḥman led a group of ḥasidim to *Israel and settled in Tiberias.

Nahn (purification): see PURITY.

Nahum, Book of. One of the *Minor Prophets of the Hebrew Bible and Christian Old Testament. Nahum seems to have been active in the late 7th cent. BCE, probably just before the final destruction of Nineveh. The book contains an acrostic hymn of theophany (ch. 1) and an oracle addressed to the Assyrian capital, Nineveh (chs. 2 and 3), 'Woe to the bloody city . . .'. He describes the tumult in the city and rejoices that the Assyrian Empire has been destroyed. God is praised as the avenger of wrongdoing and the salvation of all who put their trust in him.

Naigoma (interiorized fire ritual): see GOMA.

Naiṣkarmya-Siddhi. A work of four chapters expounding *Advaita Vedanta, by one of Śaṅkara's pupils, Sureśvara. It warns against reliance on prayer or meditation (since these imply duality) and expounds the meaning of *Tat tvam asi.

Tr.: *The Realisation of the Absolute* (1957).

Najaf, al-. Town of pilgrimage in Iraq, 6 miles west of al-Kūfa, the traditional burial-place of *Adam and *Noah, and site of the tomb of Imām *'Alī b. Abī Ṭālib. However, the place of 'Alī's burial is not known (cf. KARBALĀ'). According to the *Shī'a, his body was placed (as he had instructed) on a camel, and the body was buried at the spot where the camel first knelt down. The caliph Hārūn arRashīd (d. 809 (AH 194)) recognized the spot while hunting, and built a shrine, now known (after many rebuildings) as Mashhad Gharwah (awesome place of martyrdom).

Najah (salvation): see SALVATION (ISLAM).

Nakagawa Sōen, also **Sōen Roshi** (1908–83). A leading Zen master of the *Rinzai school, dharma-successor (*hassu) of Yamamoto Gempo. He was abbot of Ryūtaku-ji, and was much concerned to spread understanding and practice of Zen in the West. He was characterized by his ability to convert everyday occasions into Zen practice (e.g. a coffee-break could be as much an occasion as the traditional tea-ceremony). In this, he extended the example of a revered predecessor, *Musō Soseki.

Nakayama Miki (Japanese visionary): see TENRIKYŌ.

Nālandā. The site of a ruined Buddhist monastery and *stūpa in Bihar, N. India. Founded in the Gupta period (4th–5th cents. CE.), in the land of *Māgadhā, the monastery became the largest and most prestigious university and teaching centre of medieval Buddhism. The site seems to have derived its sanctity from the fact that *Śāriputra resided in Nālandā. Buddhist tradition holds it to have been the seat of most important teachers, such as *Nāgārjuna, *Asaṇga, *Dignāga, and *Padmasaṃbhāva. Nālandā is also claimed to have been the locus for the rise of the *Mahāyāna itself.

The Chinese traveller *Hsuan-Tsang described Nālandā during the 7th cent., when it was visited by pilgrims from all over the Buddhist world. It supported (he claimed) 10,000 students (archaeological evidence suggests fewer), and taught Buddhist novices and non-Buddhists alike a curriculum of grammar, logic, medicine, and Buddhist and Hindu philosophy. The library was a three-storied building, and during Hsuan-Tsang's time 100 different lectures were given every day. Despite being fortified, it was destroyed, probably by Muslim armies, sometime in the late 12th cent.

Nālandā is also a significant holy site for Jains since it is associated with the life of *Mahāvīra.

Nāl-āyira-divya-prabandham, Nāl-āyira-ttiviya-ppirapantam, or ***divya-prabandham.*** A collection of hymns and poems in Tamil by the S. Indian *Āḻvārs. The title (mixed Tamil and Sanskrit.) means 'the Sacred Composition in 4,000 [stanzas]'. This collection was compiled around 900 CE, allegedly by the *Vaiṣṇava *brahman (Śrī-Raṅga-)Nāthamuni who is also said to have composed the music for the hymns. As in the case of the roughly contemporary *Śaivite *Tirumuṟai*, this is a codification of vernacular *bhakti literature which began in the 6th cent. CE. Although the figure 4,000 is precise, the corpus was enlarged in the 12th cent. through the inclusion of a further poem in praise of *Rāmānuja. The original work consists of four books of roughly equal length. The first contains possibly the latest material, by poets like Periyâḻvār, Āṇṭāḷ, Kulacēkaraṉ, and other minor poets. The main theme here is the early life of *Kṛṣṇa, and the (by now) central religious role of the temple of Śrī-Raṅgam. The second book consists of poems by Parakālaṉ (Tirumaṅkai-Āḻvār) (8th cent.) the majority of which are dedicated to individual temples in S. India and are arranged in the form of a pilgrimage. Archaic bardic poetry on *Viṣṇu/*Kṛṣṇa religion generally makes up the bulk of the third book. The last quarter is taken up entirely by the *Tiruvāymoḻi* of *Nammāḻvār (7th/8th cent.). These 'Sacred Utterances' (implying an allusion to the *Vedas) explore, in a grand fusion of theological speculation, mysticism, and sophisticated poetry, Vaiṣṇava religion in a typical S. Indian setting. *Śrī-Vaiṣṇavism, to which Rāmānuja gave definite theological form, accepted the Āḻvārs in its lineage of teachers, and the *Divya-prabandham* as a Tamil parallel to the Vedas. A very large commentarial literature on the corpus, in Maṇipravāḷa (a scholastic language of mixed Skt. and Tamil), has been cultivated in this movement up to the present day. The *Īṭu* on the *Tiruvāymoḻi* (by Vaṭakku ttiru vīti Piḷḷai, 13th cent.) is perhaps the most important work in this genre. Independently from Śrī-Vaiṣṇavism, the poems of the Āḻvārs had considerable influence on the **Bhāgavata-purāṇa* and thereby, indirectly, also on the rest of India.

See also TEṈKAḶAI.

Tr. of a selection, A. K. Ramanujan, *Hymns for the Drowning* (1981). A detailed analysis of the *Divya-prabandham* will be found in F. Hardy, *Viraha-bhakti* (1983).

Nām (Hindī, Pañjābī, 'name'). Name of God. For Hindus and Sikhs, God's name is a formula (*mantra) encapsulating divine reality. Through meditation (*nām simaran), this takes root in the devotee, whose thoughts, words, and deeds become its expression (cf. *dhikr). 'Nāam' recurs frequently in the *Ādi Granth—e.g. 'Meditate on God's name and through the Name enter the state of supreme bliss' (Ādi Granth 26). It should be repeated in the ear of a dying person. For an example of its centrality, see KABĪR.

Beyond the devotional, the sense of Nām takes on for Sikhs a profound theological importance. It is the means of God's self-manifestation ('God, who is Being in himself, became manifest in Nām; beyond that came the creation of the universe', Ādi Granth 463). Names of God (*Allāh, *Brahmā) are approximate characterizations of some aspect of his nature, but Nām lies behind these approximations: 'How can Nām be known? Nām is within us, yet how can Nām be reached? Nām is at work everywhere, permeating the whole of space. The perfect Gurū [Granth Sāhib] awakens you to the vision of Nām. It is by the grace of God that one comes to this enlightenment' (Ādi Granth 1242).

Nāmajapa: see NĀMAKĪRTANA.

Nāmakīrtana. The constant repetition of the name of a god, which may lead to a trance or ecstatic state. More modestly, the repetition is a means of adoration and of identifying oneself with the god. As *nāmajapa* (see JAPA), the repetition becomes a *mantra, encapsulating the nature of the god.

Nāmarūpa (Skt., 'name' + 'form'). 1. In Hinduism, the way in which *māyā, the power of all appearance to become apparent, achieves characteristic and identifiable properties.

2. In Buddhism, the description of the characteristic form of appearance, able to be named (even though there is no Self conferring persistent or subsistent identity). It thus summarizes the aggregation of the five *skandhas (components of human

appearance), with nāma standing for the last four, and rūpa for the first. Nāmarūpa is the fourth link in the chain of the conditioned arising of appearance (*paticca-samuppāda).

Namaskār, namaskāra mudrā (Hindu and Buddhist hand signs): see MUDRA.

Namaskāra-mantra. In Jainism, a much-repeated, reverent salutation of the five holy beings. Its repetition is often the first and the last act of the day, and it is chanted in the final hours of life especially of those who have taken the rite of *sallekhanā. Much used in Jain worship, this great *mantra can be translated:

> Homage to the *Jinas!
> Homage to the souls that have attained *mokṣa!
> Homage to the ascetic leaders of the Jain order!
> Homage to the preceptors!
> Homage to all the mendicants in the world!
> This fivefold salutation, which destroys all sin,
> Is of all auspicious things the most auspicious!

Nāmdev. A Hindu poet from Mahārāṣṭra, to whom at least 2,000 *abhaṅgs* in Marāṭhī are attributed; in Hindī a smaller corpus of poems is included in the Sikh *Granth Sāhib. It is undecided (i) whether we are dealing with one man (who 'converted' to the *iconoclastic religion of the Hindī *sants), or with more than one Nāmdev; and (ii) which can be regarded as genuine *abhaṅgs* by him and which are anonymous (later) creations attached to his name. For such a 'Marāṭhī' Nāmdev, the 14th or 15th cent. would be a likely date. This material is closely related to the temple tradition of Paṇḍharpur in Mahārāṣṭra where Viṭhobā (Viṭṭhala) is worshipped: 'From all my foolish fondness let me loose: in Viṭṭhala, in Viṭṭhala alone, is found my peace.' Many of these *abhaṅgs* deal with legends about the saints associated with this cult.

According to such traditions, Nāmdev met his *guru when he entered a temple and came upon an old man with leprosy, resting his feet upon an image of *Śiva. Nāmdev was shocked by such irreverent behaviour and told the man to remove his feet from the idol. The old man replied that Nāmdev should remove them and place them where God was not. Nāmdev then realized that God was omnipresent and the old man, Visoba Khecar, became his guru.

The poems attributed to Nāmdev proclaim the oneness and omnipresence of God and the need to realize this *nirguṇa God by 'dying' to the world. His poems speak of longing for union with God and devotion to the guru. But above all he stressed the repetition of God's name as the means of liberation. Only through meditation upon his name can sin (*pāpa) be destroyed and *karma uprooted: 'If there were a cessation to the utterance of the name of God in my mouth my tongue would split a thousand-fold' (*Abhaṅga* 49).

P. Machwe, *Namdev* (1968).

Nāmdhārī or **Kūkā** (Pañjābī, 'adherent of divine name'). A Sikh movement which others regard as a sect, although Nāmdhārīs regard themselves as a revival of Sikh orthodoxy. The Nāmdhārī movement was founded in the 19th cent. by *Bālak Siṅgh's disciple, *Rām Siṅgh, who based himself at Bhaiṇī Sāhib, Pañjāb. Bālak Siṅgh's insistence on the importance of repeating God's name (*Nām) gave his followers their title. The alternative name, Kūkā, resulted from the ecstatic cries (Pañjābī, *kūk*) of Rām Siṅgh's followers during worship.

Nāmdhārīs regard their belief in an indispensable, ever-living *Gurū, apart from the scriptures, as consonant with the *Ādi Granth, but this tenet is rejected by other Sikhs. According to Nāmdhārīs, Gurū *Gobind Siṅgh did not die at *Nandeṛ, but continued to travel, finally bestowing the Guruship on Bālak Siṅgh. While awaiting the return from exile of Rām Siṅgh, Nāmdhārīs look upon *Jagjīt Siṅgh as their Gurū, in succession to Rām Siṅgh's brother, Hari Siṅgh, and nephew, Partāp Siṅgh.

Under Rām Siṅgh's leadership the movement aimed at social uplift, particularly of *women, at ending British rule, and protecting the cow from Muslim butchers. The Nāmdhārīs' life is strictly disciplined. They must rise early, bath, then meditate upon a *mantra confided to each by the Gurū. A woollen *rosary of 108 beads is used. Their diet is vegetarian and dress must be simple, with the *turban tied flat across the forehead as in portraits of Gurū *Nānak. Ostentation in the *gurdwārā is avoided. Nāmdhārīs preserve the most traditional style of *kīrtan, valuing music highly. Srī Jīwan Nagar is now the Nāmdhārīs' centre in India. The Gurū resides at Bhaiṇī Sāhib. In Britain there are important centres at East Ham and Birmingham.

Nāmdhārīs have simple corporate marriages during *melās (e.g. *Divālī). The ceremony should cost only a nominal sum. Receptions and engagement ceremonies are forbidden. The couples must dress in white, the groom wearing *kachh* (see FIVE KS) the bride leaving her face uncovered. They receive *amrit and each bride puts a woollen rosary around her groom's neck. In succession couples circle a sacred fire while the *lāvān are read.

F. S. Bajwa, *The Kuka Movement* (1965); S. K. Jolly, *Sikh Revivalist Movements . . .* (1988).

Name of Jesus. A subject of Catholic devotion. Reflection on the Holy Name derives ultimately from the New Testament (e.g. 1 Corinthians 6. 11), but the devotion was popularized by the *Franciscans in the 15th cent. The feast, the second Sunday after *Epiphany, was prescribed for the whole Church in 1721, but suppressed in 1969. A feast day on 7 Aug. is found in Anglican calendars.

Names of God (in Islam): see NINETY-NINE BEAUTIFUL NAMES OF GOD.

Naming. Although many Sikhs do not name their children in this way, the distinctive religious practice is as follows. About forty days after birth, the parents take the baby to the *gurdwārā, where the *granthī prepares *amrit and puts some on the baby's tongue with the tip of a *kirpān, the mother drinking the remainder. The *Ādi Granth is opened at random and usually the first word of the *śabad which ends at the top of the left-hand page is read. The parents choose a name beginning with the same initial or commencing with another letter from that word. The granthī announces this to the congregation, adding *Siṅgh for a boy and *Kaur for a girl. His cry of 'Jo bole so nihāl' is answered by the congregation's '*Sat Srī Akāl'. The first five and last *paurīs of the *Anand *Sāhib are read, and after *Ardās and a *hukam, *kaṛāh praśād is distributed. The child's parents pay for this and may also offer a *rumālā and take one home.

Most Sikh forenames have a religious meaning and are common to both sexes. Common endings are -bīr, -dīp, -inder, -jīt, -pāl, and -wānt. Frequently Siṅgh and Kaur serve as a surname, rather than the family name which indicates *caste.

Nammāḻvār (Tamil, 'Our Saint'). The most important among the twelve Hindu *Āḻvārs. His real name was Caṭakōpaṉ, and he may have lived during the 7th or earlier 8th cent. Mystic and theologian, he created a novel poetic style of *bhakti poetry of great sophistication, and contributed almost one-third of the **Nāl-āyira-divya-prabandham*. A large commentarial literature on his works, called the *Bhagavadviṣayam*, constitutes one of the fundamental scriptures of *Śrīvaiṣṇavism, particularly of the *Teṉkaḷai.

His poems exhibit a profound devotion to *Viṣṇu and his *avatāras, especially *Kṛṣṇa:

> Be gracious, Lord of all the heavenly ones,
> Born in all births to save all lives, and hear
> Your servant's prayer: grant that I may not
> Regain a nature such as this, a body gross,
> A mind unsound, a character defiled.

Nampo Jōmyō (also Shōmyō, also **Daio Kokushi)** (1235–1308). Major figure in establishing *Rinzai Zen in Japan. He started training under Lan-hsi in Kamakura, and in 1259 travelled to China where he studied under *Hsü-t'ang Chih-yü, from whom he received the seal of recognition (*inka-shōmei) in 1265. He returned to Lan-hsi, and then took charge of Kōtoku-ji, followed three years later by Sōfuku-ji. His teachings in this period are gathered in *Kōtoku-ji goroku* and *Sōfuku-ji goroku*, and emphasize that Zen is not a 'foreign' import: it is timeless and not confined to one place, since *Bodhidharma is constantly 'coming from the west'. In 1304, he became abbot of Manju-ji in *Kyōto, where he insisted on the purity of Zen and resisted syncretistic tendencies to assimilate ideas from *Shingon or *Tendai. His best known dharma-successor (*hassu) was *Myōchō Shūhō; and in the lineage derived from him, the major figure is *Hakuin Zenji. His last poems read: 'Buddhas and Fathers cut to pieces— | The sword is ever kept sharpened | Where the wheel [of *dharma] turns, | The void gnashes its teeth'; 'I scorn the wind and scoff at the rain; | I know nothing of Buddhas and Fathers; | My single-pointedness penetrates as the blink of an eye, | Swifter than a lightning flash'.

Nām Simaran, Nām Japan (Pañjābī, 'remembrance of the name', 'repetition of the name'). Remembrance of God, a term common to Hindu and Sikh devotion. Whether silently or aloud, through singing *hymns or with the help of a *rosary, God's name must be consciously repeated. Sikhs focus their mind in *meditation on the word *Vāhiguru. By continuous concentration upon the Nām, one absorbs God's qualities.

Namu (Jap., 'praise'). Adoration and homage in Japanese Buddhism, hence equivalent to, 'I take refuge in' (see THREE JEWELS). It is therefore found in many combinations, e.g. the *nembutsu, namu-*Butsu, namu-Kanzeon, namu-Miroku, etc.

Namuci (the tempter): see MĀRA.

Ñāna: see JÑĀNA (Budhism).

Ñāṇadassana ('knowledge and insight'). Buddhist *knowledge as an act of 'seeing'. *Dassana* indicates 'seeing or sight'. When combined with *ñāṇa* it gives the special meaning, 'insight arising from knowledge'. Thus the *Buddha is described as one who 'knows and sees' (*tam ahaṃ jānāmi passāmi, Majjhima Nikāya* 1. 329). The central truths of Buddhism are 'seen' (*Saṃyutta Nikāya* 229). Even nirvāna is 'seen' (*Majjhima Nikāya* 1. 511). According to the Nikāyas this 'knowledge and insight' is a result of mental concentration (*samādhi), and it is said that there is a causal relation between the attainment of mental concentration and the emergence of this knowledge and insight (*Dīgha Nikāya* 1.75).

The five impediments (*pañcanīvaraṇā*) are the obstructions to 'knowledge and insight', and the elimination of these five impediments will clear the way to a meditative state of mind and to the attaining of the Fourth *Jhāna. It is at this stage that a yogi turns his mind to 'knowing and seeing'. A specific activity of ñāṇadassana is mentioned as the realization of the nature of the body (*sarīra*) as it is composed of four great elements (*cātummahābhūtiko*), and consciousness is associated with the body (*Dīgha Nikāya* 1. 75). This kind of analytical knowledge is called *yathābhūtañāṇadassana* (insight into the real nature of things), and is called *paññā* (wisdom). The arising of aversion (*nibbidā*) and dispassionateness (*virāgo*) which is necessary for emancipation (*vimutti) are the results of this 'insight into the real nature of things' (*Anguttara Nikāya* 3. 19). This emancipation itself is called 'the knowledge and insight of emancipation' (*vimuttiñāṇadassaṇa, Majjhima Nikāya* 1. 167, 3. 162). Thus ñāṇadassana plays a very important part in the process of the path of liberation.

Apart from that, in the Nikāyas ñāṇadassana refers also to extrasensory perception. When the Buddha said that 'there arose in him the knowledge and insight that Uddakarāmaputta had died the previous night' (*Majjhima Nikāya* I. 170), this knowledge and insight was obtained by means of extrasensory perception.

The phrase *apariśesa ñāṇadassana* ('infinite knowledge and insight') which is synonymous with 'omniscience' is used in the Nikāyas in relation to the claim of the Jaina leader Nigaṇṭha Nātaputta (*Anguttara Nikāya* I. 220).

Nānak, Gurū (1469–1539 CE). First *Sikh *Gurū, and founder of the Sikh religion. The sources of his life are limited: there are some hints in the *Ādi Granth, otherwise the first *vār of *Bhai Gurdas and the hagiographic *janam-sākhīs contain information. His father was Mehtā Kālū, a Bedī *Khatrī by *caste, an accountant in the village of *Talvaṇḍī Rāi Bhoi dī, Pañjāb. Nānak's elder sister was Nānakī.

Nānak was educated in Sanskrit, Persian, and Arabic, but showed more interest in religion than in his schooling. Aged 12 he was married to Sulakhaṇī who subsequently bore him two sons, *Srī Chand and Lakhmī Dās. Despite his father's efforts to interest him in earning a living by minding their cattle or conducting business, Nānak was preoccupied with his spiritual quest. However, thanks to Jai Rām, Nānakī's husband, he obtained the post of accountant to the Nawāb, Daulat Khān Lodī, in Sultānpur (Lodī) where he worked conscientiously. He spent many hours singing hymns to *Mardānā's accompaniment.

At Sultānpur, probably in 1499, Nānak experienced God's call while bathing in the River Bein. After a mystical experience, reputedly of three days' duration, he reappeared, gave away his possessions and repeated, 'There is neither Hindu nor Muslim', probably meaning that the majority were not truly religious. He then devoted his life to preaching.

Nānak set out with Mardānā on a series of travels to many places (*udāsī), including notable *pilgrimage centres. His first itinerary was probably to the east as far as Āssām; then he travelled around Pañjāb before journeying south, reputedly to Srī Lankā. He next travelled north to Ladākh and, lastly, west to *Mecca, *Madīna—and even to Baghdad, according to tradition. In each place he taught the people, sang his hymns, discussed religion with Hindu and Muslim divines, and established a *dharmsālā* as a centre of worship.

Eventually Nānak settled in *Kartārpur where followers gathered and observed a daily regimen of bathing, hymn-singing, and eating together in the *Gurū-kā-laṅgar. Among these devotees was Lehṇā, later Gurū *Aṅgad, whom Nānak designated his successor as Gurū, in preference to his sons. Thus the Sikh movement continued with a succession of human Gurūs beyond his death, which probably occurred in Sept. 1539.

Gurū Nānak's teachings, as recorded in the *Ādi Granth, form the basis of Sikh theology. The *Mūl mantra encapsulates Nānak's assurance that God is one, the creator of all, and immune from death and *rebirth. He is formless and immanent as realized in the mystical union to which human *bhakti (devotion) is directed. To refer to God, Nānak used many Hindu and Muslim names (e.g. *Hari, *Rām, Khudā, *Sāhib), but especially *Sat(i)nām, i.e. his Name is Truth, as opposed to illusion.

By meditating upon God's name (nām japan, *nām simaran) the individual can master the wayward impulses of the *man (mind) and so conquer *haumai (egoism) and the *five evil passions. But above all one must trust to the Gurū—the guide to salvation from the *karmic cycle of rebirth—who discloses the *śabad (word of divine manifestation). Nānak stressed the irrelevance of *caste. Inner purity was what counted—not *asceticism but purity amid impurity, spiritual detachment while shouldering the family responsibility of a *grihasth (householder).

The Ādi Granth contains 974 hymns (including *pauṛīs and *śaloks) composed by Gurū Nānak. Of these, the most famous compositions are *Japjī, *Āsā kī Vār, Sodar, *Āratī, and *Sohilā, all repeated daily, and the *bārah-māhā* (in Tukharī, *rāg). All are in the vernacular, blending Old Pañjābī with Old Western Hindī (Khaṛī Bolī) and words from other contemporary languages. All are metrical. The style is terse but rich in imagery: e.g. 'If a hundred moons and a thousand suns rise . . . there is terrible darkness without the Gurū'; 'The world is diseased, the Name is the medicine'; 'As is the staff in a blind person's hand so is the name of Hari to us.' In the teaching and hymns, the main influences can be found in the Hinduism and Islam of the religious background. In particular, from *Vaiṣṇava bhakti, influenced by the *Nāth *yogīs and elements of *Sufism, emerged such *sants as *Nāmdev, *Ravidās, and *Kabīr, and the Sūfī Farīd. In this sant teaching is rooted Nānak's powerful religious message.

From the janam-sākhīs come the traditional stories of Nānak's life current in gurdwārā teaching and popular belief—e.g. when, as a boy, he was sent to trade with his father's money, he used it to feed religious mendicants, claiming that this was a 'true bargain'. During his travels, on reaching *Hardwār, he observed pilgrims throwing water towards the east. Nānak proceeded to throw water westward, answering their protests by saying that if their water could reach their ancestors in heaven, his water could reach his crops in Pañjāb. Similar perception of the futility of outward ritual and of God's omnipresence is illustrated by the account of Nānak's visit to Mecca where he lay with his feet towards a mihrāb (see MOSQUE). When rebuked by a *qāzī, Nānak asked him to drag his feet towards a place where God was not. As the qāzī moved Nānak's legs round so the mihrāb followed them.

The miraculous deeds ascribed to Nānak are scarcely compatible with his recorded emphasis on inner religion.

Gurū Nānak's birthday is celebrated annually on the full moon of Kārttika (Oct.–Nov.) in accordance with the *Bālā janam-sākhī, although scholarly opinion, based on the other janam-sākhīs, sets his birth in Baisākh (Apr.–May).

In popular iconography Nānak is represented as a robed figure with radiant face and flowing white beard, wearing a *turban, and holding a *rosary. He is often portrayed seated, singing to Mardānā's *rabāb*, while fanned by Bhāī Bālā. He is respected by Hindus, Muslims, and Sikhs: 'Bābā Nānak śāh fakīr | Hindū kā gurū, musalmān kā pīr.' He is regarded as the father of Pañjābī literature and as a pioneer of a casteless social order. His personal piety and profoundly formative influence upon religion in Pañjāb have gained steadily increasing recognition.

See Index, Gurū Nānak's life.

J. S. Grewal, *Guru Nanak in History* (1969); W. H. McLeod, *Guru Nanak and the Sikh Religion* (1968).

Nan-ch'uan P'u-yuan (Jap., Nansen Fugan; 748–835). Ch'an/Zen master, dharma-successor (*hassu) of *Ma-tsu Tao-i. From a study of Buddhist philosophy, Ma-tsu pointed him to enlightenment. In 795, he retired to a hut on Mount Nan-ch'uan (hence his name), but after thirty years he was persuaded to settle in a monastery and to teach students who never numbered less than a hundred. His *kōans and sayings became particularly famous in Zen, often seeming contradictory even of his own teacher—e.g. 'Consciousness is not Buddha, knowledge is not the way.'

Nanderṛ. Sikh place of pilgrimage, *c*.320 km. NW of Hyderabad, India. In July or Aug., 1707 CE, Gurū *Gobind Siṅgh arrived in Nanderṛ, now in the S. Indian state of Mahārāṣṭra, on the banks of the river Godāvarī. Here he met the *bairāgī (Hindu renunciant) Madho Dās, who became his follower, taking the name *Bandā Siṅgh. At Nanderṛ, Gurū Gobind Siṅgh was stabbed by a Pathān, and, although at first the wound apparently healed, he died on 7 Oct. 1708. In Nanderṛ there are several sites revered by Sikhs, e.g. *Saṅgat *Sāhib where Gobind Siṅgh instructed his disciples, and Hīrā Ghāt where he reputedly threw away a diamond ring given to him by the emperor Bahādur Shāh. The most important shrine is the *gurdwārā built 1832–7 by Mahārājā *Rañjīt Siṅgh. This gurdwārā, a *takht known as Hazūr Sāhib or Sachkhaṇḍ Śrī Hazūr Abchalnagar Sāhib, is a two-storeyed building reminiscent of the *Harimandir, *Amritsar. The weapons inside emphasize the military aspect of Gobind Siṅgh's leadership. The Sikh heroine, Māī *Bhāgo, is also believed to have died at Nanderṛ.

Nandi. The bull vehicle of the god *Śiva. His image often has a shrine of its own at the entrance to temples dedicated to Śiva. The bull image is usually shown kneeling, facing the temple entrance, implying that Nandi gazes always at his Lord. Because of this his expression is gentle and smiling, full of joy at being in the presence of Śiva.

Even small Śiva-*liṅga shrines may have an image of the guardian Nandi facing them.

Nand Lāl 'Goyā' ('one who speaks', *c*.1630–1712). Eminent contemporary of Gurū *Gobind Siṅgh. Nand Lāl 'Goyā' composed predominantly philosophical works in Persian, notably *Dīvān* and *Zindagī-nāmā*. These were omitted from the *Dasam Granth, but, like the compositions of *Bhāī *Gurdās, they are approved for recitation in *gurdwārās. Their influence has been limited by language to a small élite. See also RAHIT.

Nan-hua chen-ching (name of Chuang-tzu): see CHUANG-TZU.

Nan'in Egyō (Jap., for Nan-yuan Hui-yung): see KŌAN.

Nanjiō (Nanjō) Bunyū (1849–1927). Japanese Buddhist scholar who was one of the first to study in Europe and introduce W. methodologies in Buddhist studies to Japan. He studied under Max *Müller (1823–1900) for nine years from 1876 to 1885 and returned to Japan to become lecturer in Sanskrit at the Tokyo Imperial University. Later he moved to the Buddhist University established by Higashi Hongwanji of *Jōdo Shinshū (later known as Ōtani University) and eventually became its president in 1914. He edited the Skt. texts of *Pure Land *sūtras, the *Lotus Sūtra*, and compiled *A Catalogue of the Chinese Translation of the Buddhist Tripiṭaka* (1883).

Nansen Fugan (Ch'an/Zen master): see NAN-CH'UAN P'U-YUAN.

Nantes, Edict of: see HUGUENOTS.

Nanto (Jap., 'the southern capital'). The Japanese city and its environment of Nara, associated with *Nara Buddhism. Nanto Rokushu are thus the Six Sects (for list, see NARA BUDDHISM), and Nanto no shichidaiji are the seven great temples of Nara.

Nanto-kōan: see KŌAN.

Nanto Rokushu (six sects): see NANTO.

Nan-yang Hui-chung (Jap., Nan'yō Echū; 8th cent. CE). Prominent Ch'an/Zen master, one of the 'five great masters' of the school of *Hui-neng, whose pupil he was. According to tradition, he did not speak before he was 16, and refused to cross the bridge in front of his parents' house. One day, when he saw a Ch'an teacher approaching, he ran across and asked to be ordained as a monk. The teacher sent him to Hui-neng, who told him that he would be 'a buddha standing alone in the world'. After training, he retired to Mount Pai-ya in Nan-yang (hence his name) for about forty years. When about 85, he responded to the emperor's invitation to become his instructor (as also of Tai-tsung, his successor). As a result, he was called 'National Teacher of Two Emperors', the beginning of the tradition of the honorific titles *kuo-shih* (Jap., *kokushi*: see KOKUTAI). Thus Nan-yang is also known as Chung-kuo-shih (Jap., Chū Kokushi). Several *kōans of his survive, but he is more usually associated with 'the seamless pagoda'. The emperor asked Nan-yang how he could honour him on his 100th birthday. Nan-yang replied, 'Build the old monk a seamless pagoda'. When the emperor asked for advice about the construction, Nan-yang told him that his pupil, Tan-yüan, would lead him out of his ignorance. Tan-yüan supplied the 'explanation':

> South of Hsiang, north of Tang
> Between, abundant gold
> The ferry beneath the tree without shadow
> In the emerald palace you see no holy person.

Nan'yō Echū (Ch'an/Zen master): see NAN-YANG.

Nan-yuan Hui-yung (originator of kōans): see KŌAN.

Nan-yüeh Huai-jang (Jap., Nangaku Ejō; 677–744). Ch'an/Zen master, pupil and dharma-successor (*hassu) of *Hui-neng. From him, the second main lineage of the Ch'an tradition in China developed, and he remains best-known as the teacher of *Ma-tsu Tao-i.

Nanzenji (Buddhist temple): see KYŌTO.

Naorai (communion with kami): see MATSURI.

Naqshbandiy(y)a. *Sūfī order (*tarīqa) named after Khwāja Muḥammad Bahā' al-Dīn Naqshband (1317–89 (AH 717–91)). It originated in Central Asia, but soon spread to India, and eventually to China and Egypt. It adhered strictly to *sunna and *sharīʿa, and sought to 'Islamicize' the state through its influence on rulers: 'The ruler is the soul, the people the body; as the ruler is, so also are the people.' It was equally detailed in laying out the map of spiritual progress through particular stages, and it saw itself as commissioned to bring others to the truth, perhaps if necessary recognizing their own religions as preliminary stages. Thus the *Vedas could be regarded as revealed scripture (thereby making Hindus 'people of the book', *ahl al-Kitāb), with the many gods understood as childish pictures of the attributes of *Allāh—though this attitude was itself disputed. Outstanding among later members of the order were *Jāmī and Shaykh Aḥmad Sirhindī, in the Pañjāb. The latter reorientated the order by dropping the doctrine of *waḥdat al-wujūd*, the unitary nature of all being, so important to *Ibn ʿArabi, and replacing it with *waḥdat al-shuhūd*, the unitary nature of consciousness. He also rejected any seeming accommodation between Islam and other religions if that compromised the absolute supremacy of Allāh, and he repudiated *Akbar's eclectic explorations. The order remains active in Afghanistan, Turkey, and Russia, resistant to all political or secularizing erosions of Islam, and it has established a number of centres in Europe and the USA.

Nara. In Vedic Hinduism a general word for 'man', but in later texts, primordial *Man, the agent through whom the creation of humanity is effected. Nara and *Nārāyana are also depicted as *ṛṣis, the sons of *Dharma and *Ahiṁsā, of great ascetic holiness. They are also regarded as emanations of *Viṣṇu, and for that reason the **Mahābhārata* can regard *Arjuna and Kṛṣṇa as incarnations of Nara and Nārāyana.

Nara Buddhism. The place and period (709–84) in which Buddhism was introduced into Japan. Earlier attempts (as when, in 552, the king of Paekche (see KOREAN RELIGION) had persuaded the emperor Kimmei to accept Buddhism) had been frustrated by disasters which had enabled the Shinto authorities to re-establish control. The prince-regent Shōtoku Taishi (574–622) became a devout follower of Buddhism, accepting Korean emissaries and sending to China for further support and instruction. In 604 he promulgated the 'Seventeen Article Constitution' which included (Art. 2) the instruction to reverence the *Three Jewels (*Buddha, *dharma, and *saṅgha). He is also said to have delivered addresses (later formed into commentaries) on three major *sūtras, the **Lotus*, the *Vimalakīrti*, and the *Śrīmālādevī*, which became thenceforth fundamental in Japanese Buddhism. Most of the emperors and empresses in the 8th cent. were Buddhist, and the court patronage led to a profusion of sects and building, especially in the capital, Nara, founded by the emperor Shōmu (701–56) in 710. The proliferation of sects was such that an alternative title for the period is that of 'The Six Sects' (Nanto Rokushu), of which the most important and enduring were *Sanron, Hossō, and *Kegon, the others being *Ritsu, Kusha, and Jojitsu, all *Hīnayāna-based. The Buddhism which flourished as a state religion was concerned with the 'nation-protecting' qualities of sūtras, *bodhisattvas, and other guardians. To the sūtras above were added the *Sūtra of Golden Light* (*Survarṇaprabhāsa*; Jap., *Konkōmyōkyō*) and *Sūtra of the Virtuous King* (*Jen-wang-ching*; Jap., *Ninnōkyō*), both of which brought protection down to the individual level of cures for disease, etc. The emperor *Shōmu gave particular impetus to the building of many temples, particularly in Nara. He founded Temples of Golden Light and of the Four *Devas in all the provinces, and he planned and built the *daibutsu (large image of Birushan/*Vairocana) in Tōdai-ji, so that the power of Birushan would emanate to the local temples from the centre. The Great Buddha Hall, said to be the largest wooden structure in the world, was restored in 1980. Other important temple complexes are Jōruri-ji (*Shingon Ritsu), founded 1047, with *Amida images from the Heian period;

Kōfuku-ji, founded *c*.670 (Hossō); Shinyakushi-ji (Shingon Ritsu), founded 745; Tōshōdai-ji (Ritsu), founded 759, notable for the Fan Festival (Uchiwa-maki), held on 16 May; Yakushi-ji (Hossō), founded in 680, notable for the portrait on hemp of Kichijoten, on view once a year from the end of Oct. to the beginning of Nov. Hōryū-ji, founded by Shōtoku Taishi in 607, is the oldest temple complex surviving and is 12 km from Nara.

P. Popham, *Wooden Temples of Japan* (1990); Shiro Usui, *A Pilgrim's Guide to Forty-Six Temples* (1990).

Nārada. One of the seven great *ṛṣis in Hinduism, to whom a number of hymns in the Veda are ascribed (e.g. *Atharva Veda*, 5. 19. 9, 12. 4. 16). The Purāṇas contain many stories about him, especially in relation to his musical prowess and his invention of the lute.

Naraka (Skt.; Pāli, *niraya*). In both Hinduism and Buddhism, states of punishment and torment, the equivalent of 'hell'. In neither case can the torment be 'everlasting', since rebirth or reappearance is always continuing. In Hinduism, there are many narakas—the number varying in different works, ranging from six to twenty-eight—but all with many subdivisions. In Buddhism, the equally many and varied narakas constitute one of the three negative modes of existence (*gati).

Nara period (709–84): see NARA BUDDHISM; BUDDHISM IN JAPAN.

Narasiṃha (Skt., 'man-lion'). In Hindu mythology, the fourth in the standard list of *Viṣṇu's *avatāras. The *Daitya *Hiraṇyakaśipu usurped the sovereignty of the triple world, having obtained from *Brahmā the boon of being virtually indestructible. In some versions of the story it is said that he could be killed only by an enemy who could strike him down single-handed in the presence of all his armed followers. In others, the conditions under which he can be killed appear to be even more unlikely: his assailant can be neither human nor animal, and his death can come neither by day nor by night, neither indoors nor outside. These seemingly impossible conditions are fulfilled, however, by Viṣṇu's appearance in man-lion form, at twilight, on the veranda of Hiraṇyakaśipu's palace. Some versions say that Narasiṃha destroyed Hiraṇyakaśipu in order to prevent the latter from killing his son Prahlāda, who was Viṣṇu's devotee. In other versions, the demon's usurpation of world sovereignty and his withholding the sacrifice from the gods are enough to bring his death upon him. Although the figure of Narasiṃha is the most bloodthirsty of Viṣṇu's avatāras, he is often portrayed in yogic posture, and in some *Pāñcarātra contexts he is associated with the tranquillity of meditation.

Nārāyana. The personification, in Hinduism, of the creative energy of *Viṣṇu, associated, therefore, with the sun. It is Nārāyana, as the solar energy, moving on the face of the waters, which produces creation. At the end of the cycle of this particular universe, Nārāyana/Viṣṇu rests on the coiled form of *Śeṣa-nāga, the endless serpent, and when, in due course, he wakes again, the creative process is renewed. This myth of cosmic origins was then widely applied to the spiritual awakening which occurs to one who meditates on Viṣṇu in his different aspects, but especially on that of Nārāyana. Eventually, both *Vaiṣṇavites and *Śaivites identified Nārāyana with *Brahmā and regarded him as the *ātman which is present in all manifestation. He is also closely associated with *Nara, so that nara-nārāyana constitute the union man–god, i.e. ātman is *brahman.

Narmadā, Nerbuddha. Sacred river to Hindus, second only to the *Gaṅgā. Its pebbles which resemble the symbol of *Śiva (*liṅga svayambhū) are especially treasured.

Nāro chos drug, Chödrug. Six Doctrines of Nāropa. One of the principal bodies of teaching of the *Kagyü school of Tibetan Buddhism, so-called because they passed from Nāropa (1016–1100) to the Kagyü founder, Marpa Lotsawa. Nāropa had received them from his *guru *Ti-lo-pa (988–1069), who in turn had obtained them from their ultimate source Vajradhara, a *dharmakāya* (see TRIKĀYA) form of Buddhahood itself. Nāropa became abbot of the monastic university of *Nālandā in 1049, but, following a vision of his guru-to-be, resigned his post after eight years to search for him. The twelve arduous years spent with Ti-lo-pa before attaining enlightenment establish Nāropa as a paradigm of the *siddha tradition, belittling any intellectual attainment that does not produce inner changes.

The Six Doctrines are standard practice in the three-year, three-month, and three-day retreat undergone by trainee Kagyü *lamas. They consist of:

1. *Tummo* (*gtum.mo*, Heat Yoga), by which the indivisibility of bliss (*bde.ba*) and emptiness (*stong.pa.-nyid*) are realized. The effect is of unusual body heat, sufficient to allow the *yogin to meditate comfortably in the lowest temperatures.

2. *Gyulü* (*sgyu.lus*, Illusory Body), by which the insubstantiality of all phenomena is realized.

3. *Milam* (*rmi.lam*, Dream Yoga), where the knowledge gained in gyulü is extended into the maintenance of consciousness in the dream state.

4. *Osal* (*'od.gsal*, Clear Light), by which the natural luminosity of emptiness is apprehended.

5. *Phowa* (*'pho.ba*, Ejection), in which the ability to separate the consciousness from the body is attained. A form of phowa often mentioned separately (making seven yogas) is Transference (*grong.-'jug*—sometimes called 'resurrection'). This enables the yogin to transfer his consciousness, in the event of premature death, into the body of a fresh corpse, so that he may continue his meditation without the

interruption involved in being reborn as a baby. The ability to transfer the consciousness of another, usually to a *pure land, is included.

6. *Bardo* (*bar.do*, Intermediate State between death and rebirth), in which the yogin re-enacts his experiences in that state and obtains control over his bardo passage and rebirth.

It should be noted that all the doctrines relate to phenomenal insubstantiality and concomitance with mind, so that through their practice a 'kingship' or control over the external world and personal destiny within it is reached.

Nā-ro-pa/Nāropa or **Nāḍapāda/Nāroṭapa** (1016–1100). Pupil of *Ti-lo-pa, and teacher of *Marpa, through whom his teachings (and Six Doctrines, *Nāro chos drug) passed into Tibet. Nā-ro-pa was born in Bengal, but received a Buddhist education in Kashmir and at *Nālandā. In 1057, he set out in search of a teacher whose name, Ti-lo-pa, had been given to him in a dream. His search was constantly impeded by repellent people (an old beggar frying live fish, a man who had impaled his father on a stake and asked Nā-ro-pa's help in finishing him off, and many others). Always Nā-ro-pa recognized these as Ti-lo-pa, but too late to consult him. Eventually he decided to kill himself and try again in another life: 'This body is the result of *karma. Since it impedes me, I will discard it with the resolve to meet the *guru in another life.' He heard a voice saying: 'If you kill the buddha-nature (*buddhatā), how will you find the guru? Is it not me whom your resolve intends?' Ti-lo-pa then appeared, and the great instruction began. In this, the great severity of discipline continued, but Ti-lo-pa passed on the (mainly) yogic practices which were in turn passed on to Nā-ro-pa's followers. His teaching is contained in a number of works attributed to him.

H. V. Guenther, *The Life and Teachings* . . . (1972).

Nāsadāsīya. Skt. title of the Hymn of Creation, *Ṛg Veda* 10. 129:

Neither not-being nor being was, at that time. There was no air-permeated space, nor sky beyond. What enfolded all? Where? Under whose protection? Was there deep, unfathomable water? . . . Who knows for certain? Who can state it, when was it born, and whence came this creation? The gods appeared later, after this world's creation, so who can know whence it has evolved? . . . He who surveys it in the highest heaven, He only knows—or perhaps even He does not know.

Nasā'ī (Muslim collector of ḥadīth): see AL-NASĀ'Ī.

Naṣārā (Arab., Christians (singular Naṣrānī), possibly derived from al-Nāṣira (Nazareth) but most likely from Syriac *naṣrāyā* (Nazaraioi of Acts 24. 5)). In modern Arabic, Christians are generally called Masīḥiyyūn, i.e. followers of the Masīḥ (Messiah). The name Naṣārā is used in the *Qur'ān for the various Christian communities at the time of *Muḥammad. The Byzantine and Abyssinian territories were both officially Christian, whether *Orthodox or *Monophysite, and had frequent contact with Arabia for purposes of trade. To the east, the Sassanian Empire was the home of numerous *Nestorian Christians.

The doctrinal and political differences within the Christian community are clearly reflected in the Qur'ān, though there is little knowledge of actual Christian teachings, and later Islam has seldom been concerned to investigate them. There is 'enmity and hatred between them, till the day of Resurrection' (Qur'ān 5. 15), and they are known to dispute with the Jews (2. 113). The Naṣārā are considered to be recipients of a revelation, the *Injīl, and thus among the *Ahl al-Kitāb, people possessing a genuine scripture, and of *dhimma (protected) status. Together with the Jews, they are held responsible for some form of *taḥrīf (corruption) of their own scripture which is thus considered unreliable, incomplete, and anyway replaced by the Qur'ān.

When the Naṣārā would not accept the teachings of Muḥammad, the Qur'ān began to declare the independence of the Muslims: Allāh is 'our Lord and your Lord' (2. 139), and to reject any sense of superiority on the part of the Naṣārā: 'Say: do you know better than Allāh?' (2. 140). An ambivalent attitude is shown towards them: they are appreciated as devout, for 'nearest . . . in love to the Believers (are) those who say: we are Naṣārā; for among them are priests and monks, and they are not arrogant' (5. 85), they are eligible for the reward of Paradise (5. 88), and will be judged by Allāh (22. 17). They show compassion and mercy; but their *monasticism was not ordered by Allāh (57. 27). On the other hand, Muslims are warned: 'Take not Jews and Naṣārā for your friends' (5. 54); there is even the command to fight against those who would not accept Muḥammad, even the People of the Book, 'until they pay the *jizya' (9. 29).

With the fairly sizeable community of Christians in Najrān, a treaty was made, in which Muḥammad allowed them freedom to practise their religion and to keep their property; treaties were similarly made with Christian tribes in the Arabian peninsula. Later, however, *'Umar had the majority of the Najrān Christians exiled to Iraq.

Both the *ḥadīth and the *tafsīr (Qur'ān commentary) elaborate on the history and status of the Naṣārā, often referring to apocryphal gospels and to legend. For their legal and social status in later periods, see DHIMMA.

Nashim (Heb., 'women'). The third order of the Jewish *Mishnah. *Nashim* deals with matrimonial law and sexual morality, and also includes the tractates *Nedar* (*Vows) and *Nazir* (The *Nazirite).

Nasi (Heb., 'ruler'). Jewish leader. The failure of kings (*kingship) led to their 'demotion' in the restoration after the *Exile. The term 'king' was largely reserved for a future *messiah, and Jewish rulers from the second *Temple period used the term 'nasi'. Simeon *Bar Kokhba, for example, described himself as 'Shimon Nasi Yisrael' on his coins. Authorities disagree as to whether the title was in use by *rabbinic leaders before *Judah ha-Nasi (*c.*190 CE). The last nasi was Rabban *Gamaliel IV (d. 425 CE), but in the 3rd and 4th cents., the nasi was recognized as the secular head of the Jewish community by their Roman rulers. He presided over the *Sanhedrin, fixed the *Calendar, led prayer, and kept in touch with the *diaspora communities. The title persisted in different communities through the post-*geonic period, and the *Karaites described their leader as 'nasi' until the 18th cent.

Nāsik. The main city (pop. *c.*80,000) of the district by the same name in Mahārāṣtra state and 20 miles from the famous Trymbakéshver temple built by the Peshwās. About sixty different temples, dedicated to various deities, were built by the Peshwās and prominent families of the former Marāṭhā state, including Peṭhé, Oak, Chandrachooḍ Vinchūrker, and Hoḷker. In the *Purāṇas the town is called Padmanagar, and in the **Rāmāyaṇa* it is known as Janasthāna.

It is a holy city where one of the four Hindu orthodox Dharmagurus has a seat, the other three places being Shṛṅgeri, Purī, and Dwārakā; it is also one of the four cities where a *kuṁbha-mela is held once every twelve years. The pious consider Nāsik as the *Kāśī of the South. In the nearby hills, there are ancient caves with rock sculpture dating from the Sātavāhana period, and the city is renowned for Sanskrit scholarship.

Naskh (Arab., 'deletion'). The Muslim procedure whereby certain verses of the *Qur'ān modify or abrogate others. The verses so modified are known as *mansukh*. The general principle is that the Qur'ān remains absolute and unqualified, but *Allāh in his mercy makes its application bearable in particular situations. Naskh in this sense is referred to in 2. 106 and 16. 101, and possibly 13. 39, 17. 41/3, 17. 86/8. The abrogated verses remain as part of the Qur'ān. A second sense refers to the cancellation of verses insinuated by *Satan/Shaitān: see 22. 52/1 f. The best-known example is that of the *Satanic Verses. The doctrine of abrogation is known as *al-nasikh wa'l-mansukh*.

Nasruddin (character in folktales): see MULLA NASRUDDIN.

Nāstika (Skt., 'atheistic'). Hindu term for heterodox systems of Indian religion and thought, which deny the authority of the *Vedas. They include *Carvaka, Jainism, and Buddhism. In other religions, those regarded as nāstika are defined in relation to those different systems: thus for a Jain, the Carvakas were so designated.

Nāṭarāja (Skt., 'Lord of the dance'). Śiva, the cosmic dancer, especially in the Tāṇḍava *dance. His dance manifests creation, sustenance, destruction, balance, and liberation. Śiva as Nāṭarāja appears in his familiar dancing form from the 5th cent. CE onwards, at e.g. *Ellora and *Elephanta.

C. Sivaramamurti, *Nataraja in Art, Thought and Literature* (1974).

Nāth or **Nātha** (Skt., 'Lord'). A medieval *yoga tradition of India, influenced by *Tantrism, *Śaivism, and Buddhism. The tradition traces its origin to Matsyendranāth, one of the eighty-four *siddhas, who is regarded as its *adiguru*, and his pupil *Gorakhnāth (*c.*1200 CE). Originating in N. and NE India, the tradition became pan-Indian, tending to adopt the religious forms of a particular region. Thus most Nāths follow Śaiva practices, though in W. India Nāths tend towards *Vaiṣṇavism, and in Nepal towards Buddhism.

The aim of Nāth yoga is liberation in this life (*jīvanmukti) which is attained in a perfected or divine body (siddha/*divya deha*). The practice of developing the body (*kāyā* *sādhanā) under the guidance of a *guru, involves a long process of purification, *Haṭha, and *Kuṇḍalinī yoga which creates a ripe (*pakva*) body out of an unripe (*apakva*) one. The yogin is then a perfected one (siddha) or lord (nātha). In this perfection, the nāth realizes the correspondence between macrocosm and microcosm, that the hierarchy of the universe is contained within the hierarchy of the body. Furthermore he has united within him the masculine–feminine polarity symbolized by the sun (*sūrya) and the moon (*candra*).

An oral tradition of songs in the vernaculars, especially Bengali and Hindī, praises the Nāth saints, and a written literature in Skt. describes yoga practice. Gorakhnāth is credited with writing the *Haṭha Yoga*, now lost, and the *Gorakṣa Sataka*. Other important texts of the Nāths are the **Śiva Saṃhitā*, the *Gheranda Samhitā*, the *Haṭhayogapradīpika*, and the *Siddha Siddhānta Paddhati*, which deal with yoga and the attaining of perfection in a perfected body.

The Nāth tradition still exists in India and has influenced other forms of Hinduism such as the *Sant tradition, the *Sahajīyās, and Indian *alchemy (*rasayāna*).

Nāthamuni or **Nātamuni** (10th cent. CE). Collector of the important *Vaiṣṇava anthology of hymns and poems, **Nāl-āriya-divya-prabandham*. He is said also to have composed music to them. Nothing certain is known of his life.

Nathan. Hebrew biblical *prophet. According to 2 Samuel 7, Nathan prophesied the postponement of building the *Temple; he rebuked *David for his behaviour with Bathsheba (2 Samuel 12); and with *Zadok the *priest, anointed David and Bathsheba's son, *Solomon, king. The 'Book of Nathan the Prophet' which supposedly contained the histories of the reigns of King David and Solomon is mentioned in the first Book of *Chronicles (29. 9).

Nathan of Gaza (1643–80). A leader of the Jewish *Shabbatean movement and *kabbalist. Nathan studied the kabbalah of Isaac *Luria and in 1665 had a vision of the divine world. As a result of this, he was convinced that Shabbetai Zevi was the *messiah and that he was his *prophet. He wrote letters to the *diaspora communities announcing that redemption was at hand. Even when Shabbetai Zevi converted to Islam, Nathan never wavered in his faith and defended the *apostasy on kabbalistic grounds. He travelled throughout Turkey, Italy, Macedonia, and Bulgaria, despite the extreme hostility of many of the Jewish leaders of the time. Many legends were told of him, and his grave became a place of *pilgrimage. His letters were much copied and circulated, and his kabbalistic system was explained in his *Sefer ha-Beriah*, written in 1670. His students believed he was a reincarnation of Isaac Luria and circulated descriptions of his customs and behaviour.

National Covenant (Scottish Presbyterian commitment): see COVENANTERS.

National Learning School/Movement (School studying antiquity in Japan): see KOKUGAKU.

Nation of Islam (African-American movement): see ELIJAH MUHAMMAD.

Nats. Spirit beings (often to be propitiated) originally so-called in Burma, though the term has now spread. There are two sets of thirty-seven overlords among them, the Inner Nats (so-called because they were allowed inside sacred buildings as Hindu or Buddhist deities) and the Outer Nats, more variously listed, but also more significant, because they represent the spirits of figures in Burmese history or legend, and appear frequently in Burmese art, dance, music, and sculpture. Attempts by Buddhists to reduce the attention paid to the Outer Nats (by emphasizing the Inner Nats, whom they could control) have always (so far) failed. Offerings must be made to them in order to placate them and perhaps to secure them as guards. They resemble *Yakkhas, and permeate the world as lived and experienced.

M. H. Aung, *Folk Elements in Burmese Buddhism* (1962); R. C. Temple, *The Thirty-Seven Nats* (1906).

Natural law (Lat., *lex naturae, ius naturale*). The view that there is an intelligible and consistent order which exists independently of human opinion or construction, and that this order is a source of moral constraint and command for human beings. It is particularly prominent in E. religions, as, for example, in the understanding of the *Tao, or in the Indian understanding of *ṛta and *dharma. In the W., the Stoics conceived of a universal reason ordering and providing law for the cosmos and for human beings (and this was expressed in Roman law as a distinction between *ius gentium* and *ius naturale*); and, for the Christian tradition, there is an allusion to the natural discernment of right and wrong in Paul's Letter to the Romans. But the first major elaboration occurs in *Aquinas. The eternal law of God is conveyed to humans, partly through revelation (especially the Decalogue (see TEN COMMANDMENTS) of the *lex vetus* and the *gospel ordinances of the *lex nova*) and partly through what is open to human discernment in natural law. By obedience to natural law, humans put into effect their responsibility to be secondary causes in the action of God in relation to the universe. The appropriation of 'natural law' by the sciences has made its continuing use in relation to human behaviour ambiguous (although appeal is made to it in such *encyclicals as **Rerum Novarum*, 1891, and *Humani Generis*, 1950): its relation to the fallen state of human discernment and will, and to the searching issue of how values are related to facts, has raised questions about competence, and about the priority of virtue-*ethics over law-ethics. It remains important, however, in the continuing quest for ethics based on notions of 'human flourishing' or eudaimonism (see ETHICS).

A. P. d'Entreves, *Natural Law* (1951); J. Finnis, *Natural Law and Natural Rights* (1980); D. J. O'Connor, *Aquinas and Natural Law* (1967).

Natural theology. Knowledge of God obtainable by human reason alone without the aid of *revelation. Exponents of such theology claim that God's existence and at least some of his attributes can be known through reason (e.g. by philosophical argument), and often cite Romans 1. 18–20 in support of their position. The traditional arguments for God's existence are a central part of such theology (see COSMOLOGICAL; MORAL; ONTOLOGICAL; PHYSICO-THEOLOGICAL; and TELEOLOGICAL ARGUMENTS).

The 16th-cent. Reformers rejected the enterprise of natural theology, as also did Karl *Barth in the 20th cent.; and *Hume, *Kant, and other later philosophers raised objections to the traditional theistic arguments. The Roaman Catholic Church, however, following St Thomas *Aquinas affirmed the possibility of natural theology at the First *Vatican Council in 1870. Natural theology continues to be an important part of the philosophy of religion; and the traditional theistic arguments are still vigorously debated.

A. Farrer, *Finite and Infinite* (1943); E. L. Mascall, *He Who Is* (1966); R. Swinburne, *The Coherence of Theism* (1977) and *The Existence of God* (1979).

Natura naturans/naturata (the relation of God to creation when both are held to be eternal): see IBN RUSHD.

Nāṭya Śastra (text relating to Hindu dance): see DANCE.

Naujote (generally interpreted as 'new birth'). The *Zoroastrian initiation ceremony. The central conviction behind Zoroastrian ethics is the emphasis on human free will. Initiation, therefore, cannot take place until a child is old enough to choose for him/

herself, usually seen as just before the age of puberty. The rite is seen as initiation into the responsibilities of the religion, into the army of *Ahura Mazda. There is no concept of saving grace, or of initiation aiding salvation. The religious responsibilities, and therefore the initiation, are the same for male and female (although women have additional responsibilities because of the purity laws). Prior to the ceremony, the initiate has a ritual bath (*nahn*) inwardly cleansed by a sip of *nirang* (consecrated cow's urine). Initiations may take place in the home, made especially clean for the occasion, in a public place (*baag*), or in a temple (*atas). The child enters the appointed place clad in white trousers and a shawl over the upper body. Fundamentally the rite consists of the investiture by the priest (*magi) with the sacred shirt and cord, the *sudre* and *kusti* (sometimes referred to as the 'armour of faith') and the first ritual recital of the associated prayers which the initiate should henceforth offer five times daily. The rite has retained its significance among *Parsis, but is not as important to Iranian Zoroastrians.

The Naujote raises the question of who can be a Zoroastrian. There is surprisingly little evidence for early belief and practice, but certainly in recent centuries, and especially among Parsis, there has been a strong conviction that only the offspring of Zoroastrian parents can be initiated. This was confirmed in law in a test case in 1906 in Bombay, in which it was decreed that the line was through the father. Conversion was not simply made difficult, but seen as forbidden, even to the offspring of a woman who had married out of the community. The arguments are that since there is truth in all religions, conversion is not necessary for salvation. Because religion is part of a person's conditioning from infancy (indeed many Parsis would say it is in the hereditary 'make up' of each individual), conversion, by alienating people from their roots, causes psychological damage. Mixed marriages, it is argued, have a higher rate of breakdown, and the children tend to be brought up in a religious vacuum. Zoroastrians associate conversion with religious persecution, intolerance, and oppression. They often argue that more people have been killed for religion than for any other cause. However, intermarriage is a growing phenomenon in the *diaspora Zoroastrian communities, so that the children of mixed marriages are being accepted into the religion by groups outside India. In Iran there is less hostility to conversion, but there is no element of proselytizing.

The *sudre/kusti* prayers are one of only two compulsory religious duties in Zoroastrianism. The other is observance of the *gahambar* (*festivals). The *sudre* is made of cotton and is worn at all times next to the skin, like a vest. It is white to symbolize purity and has a small pocket at the front of the 'V' neckline in which the faithful are exhorted to store up good thoughts, words, and deeds. The *kusti* is a long lamb's wool cord, tied around the waist (unlike the brahman cord, both of which presumably originated in Indo-Iranian religion). The prayers start with the untied *kusti* being held in both hands in front of the worshipper who faces the divine creation of light. As the prayers rejecting the evil *Angra Mainyu and affirming allegiance to Ahura Mazda are recited, the initiate ties knots at the back and in front vowing to practice good thoughts, words, and deeds. There is, therefore, a repeated daily affirmation of commitment to work for God.

K. Mistree Hinnells, *Persian Mythology* (1973); J. J. Modi, *The Religious Ceremonies and Customs of the Parsees* (1937).

Nautch dancers (Hindu): see DANCE.

Navarātri (nine days of Hindu observance): see FESTIVALS AND FASTS.

Nava Vidhāna (New Dispensation proclaimed by K. C. Sen to supplant Christianity): see SEN, K. C.

Nāyaṇmār (sing., *nāyaṇār*, 'leader'). Title bestowed on a claimed sixty-three saints in the Tamil *Śaivite tradition. The hymns (especially of Ñāṉacampantar, Cuntaramūrti, and *Appar) are regarded by Tamil Śaivas as equal in worth to the *Vedas. They are gathered in the *Tēvāram*, part of the Tamil Śaiva canon. Their lives (in *hagiographical style) are contained in Cekkilār's *Periya Purāṇam* (12th cent. CE), building on earlier works, especially that of Suntarar (Nampiyārūrar). Cekkilār includes an account of Suntarar in his own work, tracing his life from his abode with *Śiva to his earthly manifestation, which he undertook, with Śiva's permission, in order to marry—provided he worshipped Śiva on earth. He proceeded to the former and forgot the latter. Śiva appeared and stopped the wedding, and Suntarar took off at speed to the nearest temple and in penitence began the poems which now stand as book vii of the eleven books of the *Tirumurai*. *Periya Purāṇam* was added as book xii. See also MĀṆIKKAVĀCAKAR.

F. Kingsbury and G. E. Phillips, *Hymns of the Tamil Śaivite Saints* (1921); K. Zvelebil, *The Smile of Murugan* . . . (1973).

Nayavāda (Skt., *naya*, 'viewpoints'). In Jain philosophy, the doctrine of viewpoints, sometimes called the doctrine of relative pluralism. This doctrine is a unique instrument of analysis which asserts that all viewpoints are only partial expressions of the truth. No statement can be absolutely true because it is a view arrived at from only one angle or one particular standpoint. When combined with the kindred teaching of *syādvāda, this doctrine results in the distinctive Jain teaching of *anekāntavāda, in which Jain philosophers delineate seven *nayas*. The seven possible points of view (*saptabhaṅgī*) are figurative, general, distributive, actual, descriptive, specific, active (see e.g. **Tattvārthasūtra* I. 31 f.), and they are abstracted from what a thing may be in itself (*pramāṇa*). These doctrines have helped the Jains avoid extreme and dogmatic views, and have bred an intellectual toleration and a breadth and realism to their thinking which acknowledges a complex and subtle world.

Nazarene. Term used in various senses.

1. It is an epithet for Jesus, usually understood to mean 'of Nazareth' (e.g. Acts 10. 38). This is how Matthew interprets the prophecy 'He shall be called a Nazarene' (Matthew 2. 23), but its origin and meaning are obscure.

2. 'Nazarenes' (or Heb., *Noṣerim*) appears as a Jewish term for Christians in early times.

3. Jewish Christian groups called 'Nazarenes', perhaps related to the *Ebionites, are mentioned by some 4th-cent. writers.

4. The *Mandeans are described as 'Nasoreans' in some of their early writings.

Nazarene, Church of the. An international holiness denomination which, in the early 20th cent., united various American groups which taught John *Wesley's doctrine of 'perfect love'. Influenced while in the USA by these churches, the Lanarkshire preacher George Sharpe began the Church of the Nazarene work in Glasgow (1906), its first introduction to the British Isles. Committed to Wesley's teaching concerning 'entire sanctification', the denomination also has keen missionary interests and emphasizes the importance of Christian education in the local church, *tithing, and separation from the world. In the British Isles the churches formerly associated with the International Holiness Mission were united with the Church of the Nazarene in 1952, whilst in 1955 a further union took place with the Calvary Holiness Church.

Nazarite Church (Zulu, *ama-Nazaretha*) or **Shembe's Church.** The largest independent movement among the Zulu, later including other peoples. It is named from the biblical *Nazirites, and represents an Old Testament form of religion—sabbatarian, and with two main festivals, Tabernacles (see SUKKOT) and the *New Year, focused on their holy city Ekuphakameni, near Durban, and their holy mountain Nhlangakazi, 130 km north. The founder, Isaiah Shembe (1870–1935), a black *Baptist church member, was a *charismatic prophet-healer who composed a great corpus of hymns in Zulu. Healing is stressed, and polygamy and anti-white or anti-government attitudes are discouraged. John Galilee Shembe (1904–76), succeeded his father, and his followers grew to some 10,000 by 1965. His death led to a long leadership dispute, with violence and litigation, between his brother Amos and his son Londa.

J. L. Dube, *uShembe* (1936); G. C. Oosthuizen, *The Theology of a South African Messiah* and *An Analysis of the Hymnal* (1967); A. Vilakazi, *Shembe . . .* (1986).

Nazirite (Heb., *nazar*, 'dedicate'). A Jewish ascetic who vows to abstain from grape products, from cutting hair, and from touching a corpse. The rules for Nazirites are described in Numbers 6. 1–21 and in the tractate 'Nazir' in the order **Nāshim* of the *Mishnah. A Nazirite is described as 'holy to the Lord' (Leviticus 21. 6). Both *Samson and *Samuel were lifelong Nazirites, but the vow normally was only kept for thirty days and was discouraged by the *rabbis as being against the spirit of Judaism. The Nazirite laws could only be kept in *Erez Israel and, although they have been renewed in recent years, there are no references to Nazirites in the Middle Ages.

Neale, John Mason (1818–66). *Anglican *high churchman and *hymn-writer. He was one of the founders (1839) of the Cambridge Camden Society, which stimulated interest in church architecture and Catholic worship, thus contributing to the *Ritualist movement in the Church of England. From 1846 until his early death he was Warden of Sackville College, E. Grinstead, dividing his time between the Sisterhood of St Margaret, which he founded in 1855, and literary work. His love of the *Orthodox Church is shown in his many translations of Greek hymns and his *History of the Holy Eastern Church* (1847–73). Besides his own hymns he also produced fine translations from the Latin (e.g. 'Jerusalem the golden').

L. Litvack, *J. M. Neale and the Quest for Sobornost* (1994).

Neasden temple (Hindu temple in London): see SVAMINARAYAN.

Nedavah (vow): see VOWS (JUDAISM).

Neder (vow): see VOWS (JUDAISM).

Negative way: see APOPHATIC THEOLOGY; VIA NEGATIVA.

Nehan. Jap., for *nirvāna.

Nehemiah. Governor of *Judah after the Babylonian *exile. Nehemiah restored the walls of *Jerusalem and established order within the community. In the *aggadah he is identified with *Zerubbabel. The Book of Nehemiah in the Hebrew scriptures was referred to as the second part of the Book of *Ezra by the *sages because Nehemiah spoke disparagingly of his predecessors (Nehemiah 5. 15; *B.Sanh.* 93b). None the less he appears to have been highly religious in his concern for the *Levites (13. 10–14), his appreciation of the *Sabbath (13. 15–21), and his provision for the *Temple (10. 33–40). The book consists of an account of his commission (1. 1–10); the rebuilding of the Jerusalem walls (1. 11–7); the law read by Ezra and the *covenant renewed (8–12); and Nehemiah's reforms (13). See also EZRA.

Nei-ch'i: see NEI-TAN.

Nei-kuan or **Nei-shih** (Chin., 'inner viewing'). A Taoist practice of visualizing the interior of the body, in order to facilitate the distribution of vitality (*ch'i) and to contact the inner powers/deities. It also produces great mental calm.

Nei-tan. Interior *alchemy or inner elixir. Contrasted with Wai-tan (exterior alchemy), or techniques of concocting the elixir of immortal transcendency by cooking certain substances in a cauldron. In Nei-tan the 'substances' are the basic elements of life—*ch'i (vital breath), *ching (generative essence), and *shen (spirit)—and the 'cauldron' is the practitioner's own body. The techniques involve circulating these life-elements throughout the body in accordance with Taoist notions of physiology, and the process is thus a form of yogic concentration. Important in the development of Nei-tan was Chang Po-tuan (984–1082), who shifted the emphasis away from chemical transmutation to interior achievement of immortality (see his *Wu-chen p'ien*, Essay on the Awakening to the Truth).

Nembutsu (Jap.; Chin., *nien-fo*). The foremost religious practice in the *Pure Land Schools of Buddhism. Nembutsu literally means 'Mindfulness of the Buddha'. It was thus originally a meditational practice with the Buddha and his innumerable merits 'kept in mind', i.e. as an object of contemplation. In the earliest period of Pure Land development it was interpreted as a form of meditation in which the Buddha *Amida (Jap.; Chin., O-mi-t'o; Skt., Amitābha/Amitāyus) and his transcendent Pure Land are visualized. In China and Japan it was reinterpreted to mean invoking the name of the Buddha in the form *Namu Amida Butsu* (Jap.; Chin., *Na-mo O-mi-to fo*), 'I take refuge in the Buddha Amida'. This interpretation was most forcefully enunciated by Shan-tao in China, and by *Honen in Japan. The invocation was considered a sacred practice which Amida created and bestowed on sentient beings. By invoking Amida's name one would be assured of birth in Pure Land and, ultimately, of Buddhist enlightenment during one's next lifetime. Chanting the nembutsu became the most widespread religious practice in China and Japan, especially among the common people.

Neminātha or **Ariṣṭanemi.** The 22nd of the Jain *tīrthaṅkaras, who ruled over Dvaraka, the place where *Kṛṣṇa ended his days on earth. Consequently, popular stories are told about the contests between the two which presumably reflect contests between the two communities. Thus, for example, after Neminātha had prevailed in a trial of strength, Kṛṣṇa tried to entice Neminātha into marriage, thinking that this would dissipate his strength. Neminātha got so far as to set out on his wedding procession, but then he heard the sounds of the animals who were to be slaughtered or sacrificed for the celebration of the wedding. He immediately withdrew, gave away all his possessions, undertook the ascetic way, and achieved enlightenment on Mount Girnar.

Nenbutsu (Jap., 'thought' + 'Buddha'). The deliberate recollection of the *Buddha, and meditation on the Buddha. It is more often transliterated *nembutsu.

Nenge mishō (Jap.). The wordless transmission of the truth from *Buddha Śākyamuni to *Mahākāśyapa. From this paradigmatic interaction, *Zen developed the key notions of transmission from heart to heart or mind to mind (*ishin-denshin) and the special transmission outside the scriptures (*kyoge-betsuden*; (see FUKASETSU). The phrase means 'lifting the flower and smiling'. It refers to the incident when the Buddha was with a company of followers on the Vulture Peak, and he lifted up a garland of flowers offered to him by a god. Only Mahākāśyapa understood the meaning of what had happened, indicating this with a smile. The Buddha then proclaimed that he would transmit the essence of his teaching to him. Hence, this is taken to be the origin of Zen Buddhism.

Nenju or **juzu** (Jap., 'thought beads'). A Japanese Buddhist *rosary. The name of a *Buddha, especially *Amida, is recited with each bead.

Nenjū gyōgi (annual festivals): see FESTIVALS AND FASTS.

Neo-Catechumenate. *Roman Catholic movement for the renewal of traditional faith. The movement was founded in 1964 by K. Arguello, in order to resist the increasing *secularization of society and the erosion of traditional understandings of faith and practice. Reverting to the practice of the early Church of training *catechumens before *baptism, the Neo-Catechumenate, more simply called 'The Way', establishes teams of trained people who are dispersed into parishes in order to train others. They in turn move into other parishes to continue the movement. While some (including the pope, *John Paul II) welcome this as a renewal of informed commitment, others see it as destructive of parish community, because it creates an élite with its own structure (including separate activities and *masses) in the midst of what might otherwise be regarded as a united church.

Neo-Confucianism. The revived form of *Confucianism which became dominant in China especially after the 10th cent. CE, under the leadership of a succession of great philosophers of the 11th cent., including Chou Tun-yi, *Ch'eng Hao, Ch'eng Yi (see CH'ENG HAO), and Chang Tsai, as well as the later synthesizer *Chu Hsi (1130–1200), all of the Sung dynasty. It is a Confucianism which developed in response to Buddhist metaphysical challenges, and did so by partially incorporating certain Buddhist insights, while returning mainly to the source of Confucian inspiration in the selected *Four Books (*Analects*, *Book of Mencius*, *Great Learning*, and *Doctrine of the Mean*). Neo-Confucianism attempted to offer certain explanations of the problems of the universe and of human existence, developing a cosmology of the Great Ultimate (*T'ai-chi, Chou Tun-yi), a doctrine explaining the rise of evil in human nature (Chang Tsai and Ch'eng Yi), grounded in the metaphysics of *li (principle) and *ch'i (matter-energy), and a practical teaching of cultivation which regards as important intellectual pursuit as well as moral progress (Ch'eng Yi and Chu Hsi). It also criticized what it considered as Buddhist indifference to family virtues and to the improvement of society, as well as a sense of 'cosmic pessimism' which Buddhist presuppositions were thought to bring with them. Neo-Confucian philosophy became accepted as orthodox interpretation of Confucian teachings when the commentaries of Ch'eng Yi and Chu Hsi, together with the Four Books, became the basis for the examination syllabus (1313). But Neo-Confucianism itself is hardly monolithic. As a philosophical movement, it is usually described as having at least two principal branches, the 'realist' school of Chu Hsi with its emphasis on li or principle, and the 'idealist' school of *Wang Yang-ming (1472–1529), with its preference for the subjective *hsin* (mind-and-heart). Neo-Confucianism spread from China to Yi Korea and Tokugawa Japan, which also witnessed local developments of the Chu Hsi schools (and, in the case of Japan, of the Yang-ming school also).

C. Chang, *The Development of Neo-Confucian Thought* (1957); W. T. de Bary and J. K. Haboush (eds.), *The Rise of Neo-Confucianism in Korea* (1985); Tu Wei-ming, *Neo-Confucian Thought in Action* (1976).

Neo-Orthodoxy. 1. A modernist faction among the *Orthodox Jewish community. As a movement, Neo-Orthodoxy was established in the late 19th cent. under the leadership of Samson Raphael *Hirsch. He taught the principle of **Torah 'im derekh erez* ('Torah [in harmony] with the way of life') i.e. careful observance of *mitzvot (commandments) and customs combined with a positive attitude to secular life where no conflict obtained. From the *Reform movement, the aim of respect for worthwhile aspects of modern society was accepted as was the *Haskalah programme of education. Practical *halakhah was emphasized rather than the traditional Torah learning of the *yeshivot, while an insistence on the traditional faith of the *rabbis (*emunat hakhamim*) was maintained. Azriel Hildesheimer founded a *rabbinic seminary in 1873 and established contact between the German Neo-Orthodox establishment and the communities of E. Europe.

H. Schwab, *History of Orthodox Jewry in Germany* (1950).

2. A Protestant Christian reaction against 19th-cent. liberalism in theology. The reaction was not organized, and is particularly associated with K. *Barth: the beginning of the reaction is usually dated to the publication of his commentary on Paul's letter to the Romans (1919). Quintessentially, Neo-Orthodoxy rejected the liberal belief that it is possible to argue from experience to God, or, more extremely, that theology is disguised anthropology. For Neo-Orthodoxy, the word and revelation of God constitute a disjunctive act which cannot be subordinated to human judgement: this self-revelation is uniquely embodied in *Jesus Christ, the Word of God made flesh.

Neo-Paganism. A variety of *witchcraft and other movements such as the *Pagan Pathfinders that have emerged in recent times to revive and spread what is called the pagan way of being, to protect pagan sacred places and more generally Mother Earth. Use is made of herbal medicines, and sometimes of electronic equipment to induce alpha (brain) rhythms, auto-suggestion, and various occult rituals for the purpose of developing the powers latent within the human mind with a view to approaching the earth with heightened awareness and sensitivity. For the Pagan, the divine is immanent, and it is this belief which motivates and sustains the individual. Neo-Paganism often sees itself as belonging to the *New Age movement.

Neoplatonism. The philosophy of *Plotinus and his followers, derived (remotely) from Plato. After Plotinus, its most outstanding proponents were *Porphyry, Iamblichus (3rd/4th cent. CE), Eunapius of Sardis, and *Proclus. The major aim of Neoplatonism was to provide a satisfactory account of the relationship of the One to the many. Between the One at the summit of the hierarchy of beings and the material world, it proposed a series of intermediaries. The main distinction between Plotinus and later Neoplatonism is the tendency to increase the number of intermediaries between Plotinus' three (the One, Intelligence, the World-Soul) and to classify these into further triads. The various members of the hierarchy are related by a timeless process of *emanation. The One, as a consequence of its perfection, flows out of itself without thereby diminishing itself. The progressively less perfect intermediaries are constituted by procession from their respective sources. Through abstractive thought, the soul can return to its source and be mystically united with it.

In this way, God is abstracted into absolute transcendence, and is protected from involvement in the material and evil; and human beings (who have in them some aspect of the divine) can return upwards to God, the 'flight of the alone to the Alone'. Ammonius Saccas, the teacher of Plotinus, is sometimes regarded as the founder of Neoplatonism, but Plotinus was of greatest importance, followed by his own pupil, Porphyry. The later School of Athens (including Proclus) sought unity in Plato, Aristotle, and Plotinus, but was closed by Justin in 529 because of its hostility to Christianity. Many of the Latin Neoplatonists (probably including *Boethius) were Christians, and interpreted the *Trinity in Neoplatonic ways. The next major influence was Pseudo-*Dionysius (the Areopagite), extending to *Erigena and *Eckhart. Much later, in the 17th cent., the *Cambridge Platonists drew on Proclus and Plotinus to emphasize the importance of reason in religion, and the indwelling of God in the mind ('The spirit of man is the candle of the Lord': B. Whichcote).

In Judaism, the original Platonic influence exhibited in *Philo had no lasting consequence. Neoplatonism entered into Jewish philosophy largely as a consequence of contacts with Islam, where both Plato and Aristotle were drawn on to create a new resource for theological language and reflection. In general, the Platonic forms were identified with the creative 'thoughts' of God, the means through which the Absolute and uncompromised One could create and remain in relation to his creation. Levels of being derive (or emanate) from the Source: the human soul is a particle from a higher realm, often called in Judaism 'the Throne of Glory', thereby making connection with biblical imagery. Among early Jewish Neoplatonists were Isaac Israeli (*c.* 9th/10th cent.) and ibn *Gabirol. Both stressed the unknowability of God's essence: only his existence can be known, but this is enough to set the soul on the upward quest to the source of being. The highest attainment possible is known as *devekut. Although Aristotelianism became philosophically more important, a Neoplatonic approach continued to dominate spiritual Judaism, e.g. in *kabbalah and *Ḥasidism.

In Islam, *falsafah* (philosophy) made no particular distinction between Plato, Aristotle, and Neoplatonism, since it was concerned only with the opportunity of philosophy, not its history. The translation of what was taken to be Aristotle began in the reign of al-Ma'mūn (d. 833 (AH 218)), and through these endeavours, Greek philosophy and its texts were effectively rescued for the world, with many texts surviving only because of this Muslim interest. Neoplatonism entered Muslim thought in this way, though often attributed to Aristotle (e.g. when books iv and vi of Plotinus' *Enneads* were translated); al-Kindī and *al-Farābī were key figures in the establishing of this way of thought, though the major figures were *ibn Sīnā and *ibn Rushd, and *ibn 'Arabī on the mystical side.

H. J. Blumenthal and R. A. Markus (eds.), *Neoplatonism and Early Christian Thought* (1981); R. T. Wallis, *Neoplatonism* (1972).

Neo-Taoism: see HSÜAN-HSÜEH.

Neo-Thomism. The application and development of the work of Thomas *Aquinas. Somewhat improperly, 'Neo-Thomism' is used to refer to the revival of interest in Aquinas in the 16th and 17th cents., which was inspired by the writings of *Cajetan (see also THOMISM). More accurately, Neo-Thomism refers to the revival after *Vatican I reinforced by *Leo XIII. One approach has been to emphasize the opinions of Aquinas' commentators, explicating and systematizing these. Another (and more influential) has been to abandon *scholastic method in favour of reformulating Aquinas' thought in more discursive and historical ways. Notable exponents of this latter approach have been J. *Maritain and E. *Gilson. Both approaches have shared Aquinas' point of departure that reason can know *that* God is, but that revelation is needed to know *what* God is. The term 'neo-Thomism' is also sometimes applied to those who develop philosophical themes from Aquinas in ways which they intend to meet the challenge of *Kant to develop a self-critical awareness of the limits of reason and the ways of knowing—hence they are more usually known as Transcendental Thomists. Notable exponents of neo-Thomism in this sense have been B. *Lonergan and K. *Rahner.

V. J. Bourke, *Thomistic Bibliography, 1920–40* (1945) and *1940–78* (1980).

Ner tamid (light burning before the Ark in synagogues): see ARK (3); ETERNAL LIGHT.

Neshāmah yeterah (Heb., 'additional soul'). Popular Jewish belief that each Jew is given an additional soul for the duration of the *Sabbath. The belief is found in the *Talmud (*B.Bezah* 16a), and also in *kabbalistic literature. One reason for the use of spices at the *Havdalah service is to rejuvenate the remaining soul after the departure of the neshāmah yeterah.

Nestorianism. The Christian *heresy that within the incarnate *Christ there were two separate persons, the one divine, the other human. It is named for Nestorius (d. *c.*451), patriarch of Constantinople from 428, who rejected the title *Theotokos ('God-bearer') for the Virgin *Mary as suggesting *Apollinarianism. Opposed by *Cyril of Alexandria, he was deposed at the Council of *Ephesus in 431. In 436 he was banished to Upper Egypt, where he died. Whether Nestorius actually taught 'Nestorianism' is open to doubt. Many scholars consider that his *Christology was of a straightforward *Antiochene type, and his condemnation was due in part to ecclesiastical rivalries. The major source is *The Bazaar of Heraclides*, tr. G. R. Driver and L. Hodgson (1925).

The so-called Nestorian Church is the ancient church of the Persian empire, now most properly called the *Church of the East. From the 5th cent. it embraced a strongly anti-*Monophysite Christology. By the 7th cent. this had hardened into the dogma (contradicting the definition of *Chalcedon) of 'two *hypostases' in Christ; at the same period Nestorius was canonized. The Nestorian Church expanded away from the dominating West, establishing itself in India and China: see A-LO-PEN.

A. Grillmeier, *Christ in Christian Tradition*, i (1975).

Neti, neti (Skt., 'not this, not this'). The phrase (*Brihadāranyaka Upaniṣad* 4. 2. 4) through which, in Hinduism, the reality of appearances in the universe is rejected. Instead (ibid. 4. 5. 15) appearance is superimposed on *Brahman, giving the appearance of duality. But *ātman, which *is* Brahman, is not to be identified with appearance: 'That Self (ātman) is not this, not this. It is uncontainable, because it cannot be contained; indestructible, because it cannot be destroyed; unattached, because it does not attach itself. It is unlimited, intangible, incapable of being injured.'

Neturei Karta (Aram., 'guardians of the city'). Ultra-religious Jews who, for religious reasons, do not recognize the State of *Israel. The group consists of a few dozen families centred in Mea Shearim in *Jerusalem. They do not accept an Israeli identity card, recognize Israeli courts, or vote in elections.

New Age movement. A diverse set of organizations united by their enthusiasm for the creation of a new era of enlightenment and harmony in the 'Aquarian Age' (in *astrology the era or cycle of *c.*2,150 years when the constellation and zodiacal sign of Aquarius will coincide, following on from the 'Piscean Age' during which the same is true for Pisces). For some, this has already begun, but for others it has not yet arrived. Believing it to constitute a new stage in the development of human history, enthusiasts are convinced that the evolution this time will be primarily spiritual and psychological, rather than structural. The end result in this Aquarian Age will be the emergence of a new mind: consciousness will be all in all.

New Age 'teachings' are characterized by an emphasis on monism, relativism, individual autonomy, and the rejection of the Judaeo-Christian emphasis on sin as the ultimate cause of evil in the world. Instead, New Age posits lack of knowledge and awareness as the root of humanity's problems. It is eclectic in style, gathering in a wide range of people and teachings if they reinforce the central concern.

M. Ferguson, *The Aquarian Conspiracy* (1980).

New Apostolic Church. Christian denomination deriving from the *Catholic Apostolic ('Old Apostolic') Church in Germany. It began in 1860 with the ordination of three apostles to succeed those who had died and thus perpetuate the apostolate. New Apostolics number *c.*2 million, including a sizeable branch in the USA.

New Christians (forced Jewish converts): see MARRANOS.

New (Jerusalem) Church: see SWEDENBORG, E.

Newman, John Henry (1801–90). Christian theologian and leader of the *Oxford Movement, also a writer, poet, and historian, whose genius lay in the combination of these talents. He rose to prominence in the 1830s when, as vicar of the university church in Oxford, he urged the *Church of England to become in practice the *'via media' it had always claimed to be in theory. Arguing against the extremes both of *Roman Catholicism and *nonconformity, he appealed to *Anglicans to pursue a middle way and return to the heritage of an undivided Christendom. He placed special emphasis on the traditions of the Fathers of the Church, and wished to see greater awe and mystery in worship. He was opposed to the rise of liberalism and rationalism.

Increasingly attracted to the mystery and authority in religion that Catholicism seemed to offer, Newman's heart, and then his mind, were drawn towards Rome. In 1841 he published *Tract XC* (one of a series of tracts published by the Oxford Movement), which attempted to show that the *Thirty-Nine Articles could be read in a manner consistent with Catholic teaching. In the early 1840s he withdrew from leadership of the Oxford Movement and, in 1845, converted to Roman Catholicism. For Newman, Rome offered that assurance Anglicanism seemed to lack and for which he longed. Of allegiance to the Church and acceptance of its teaching he wrote 'ten thousand difficulties do not make one doubt'. *Dogma becomes 'the fundamental principle of any religion: I know no other religion . . .; religion, as a mere sentiment, is to me a mockery'. Undergirding all is the sense of judgement and accountability: 'We can believe what we choose, but we are answerable for what we choose to believe'. In 1848 he founded the Birmingham *Oratory. He spent the rest of his life there, save for a period in Dublin, between 1854 to 1858, to which he went as rector of the new Catholic university. He also helped to found the London Oratory, and was made a *cardinal in 1879.

His published works are substantial. They include his autobiography, *Apologia pro vita sua*, published in 1864 in response to an attack from Charles Kingsley; a treatise on education *The Idea of a University* (1852); numerous theological texts, including *An Essay on Development of Christian Doctrine* (1845); *An Essay in Aid of a Grammar of Assent* (1870); the novel *Loss and Gain*, and *The Dream of Gerontius* (1865).

V. F. Blehl, . . . *A Bibliographical Catalogue* (1978); S. Gilley, *Newman and His Age* (1990); D. Newsome, *The Convert Cardinals* . . . (1993); D. Nicholls and F. Herr (eds.), *John Henry Newman* (1991); B. M. G. Reardon, *From Coleridge to Gore* (1971).

New Moon: see MOON, BLESSING OF THE.

New quest for the historical Jesus: see QUEST FOR THE HISTORICAL JESUS.

New religions in Japan (Jap., *shinkō shūkyō*). While *new religious movements are a common and recurrent phenomenon, the strength and importance of new religions in Japan is such that it makes them distinct. They are made up of movements which have emerged during the last two cents., and which may have connections with Buddhism, Shinto, or Christianity, or may be entirely independent. They are 'new' in relation to shrine Shinto and temple Buddhism, both of which carried with them the control of vital rituals. With only a few exceptions, they are far from being marginal; and at the same time, they are rarely radical in political (or even religious) terms (but see AUM SHINRIKYO for an exception). They usually integrate veneration of ancestors, and discourage (if not prohibit) the ritual function of women (because of traditional feelings about pollution); but the participation of women in other ways is markedly encouraged, and the new religions have strong female membership, and sometimes leadership.

Early examples of new religions in the 19th cent. are Nyoraikyō (cf. *nyorai), Kurozumikyō (see KUROZŪMĪ MUNETADA), *Tenrikyō, *Konkōkyō, and *Ōmotokyō. All of these emphasized the importance of lay members (over against the exclusive role of the priests in traditional religions), and made healing available outside the traditional rituals. In the 20th cent., important examples are *Reiyūkai, *Sōka Gakkai, and *Seichō no Ie. Quite apart from the deliberate involvement of Sōka Gakkai in politics, the Union of New Religious Organizations was established in 1951 (with nearly 100 member groups) with a view to putting forward agreed candidates for elections.

Hori Ichiro *et al.* (eds.), *Japanese Religion* (1972); see also NEW RELIGIOUS MOVEMENTS.

New religious movements. A generic term referring to the literally thousands of religious movements (and occasionally secular alternatives to religion) that have emerged world-wide, but especially in Africa, Japan, and the West during this cent. Their adherents are to be estimated in millions. While for the most part highly syncretistic, the ritual and content of many of these new religions have been influenced, to a greater or lesser degree, by Buddhist, Christian, and Hindu spiritual techniques and perspectives. There is also a sizeable number of Islamic- and Jewish-oriented new religions, and numerous esoteric, *metaphysical, and *neo-pagan movements.

In the developing world, Africa has seen the greatest explosion of new religious movements, with some 5,000 emerging during the era of colonial rule (*c.*1885–*c.*1960), and others coming into existence since. Those with Christian connections are often referred to collectively as 'independent churches' (see AFRICAN INDEPENDENT CHURCHES) partly because some of the earlier African new religious movements, known as *Ethiopian or African churches, emphasized above all else the necessity for independence from the control and support of the Christian mission churches. Others, equally concerned with independence but stressing also the central importance in Christian life and worship of charismatic or spiritual gifts (such as prophecy, faith healing, and prayer) are referred to as charismatic, spiritual, prophet, *Zionist, or *Aladura (praying) churches. A more refined classification (J. W. Fernandez), based on the origins of a movement's symbols and how these are used, locates four types of African new religions: separatist, nativist, reformative, and messianic.

Although, as in Africa, their very number and great diversity of style and function, determined in large measure by the specific socio-cultural context of their origin, makes classification exceedingly difficult, there have been several attempts at constructing a typology of new religions of the post-Second-World-War era, as found in the West. One of the more successful of these (R. Wallis), using 'response to the world' as the principal distinguishing criterion, separates two main types: world-denying and world-affirming movements—and a third, relatively minor category, the world-accommodating type. The first type emerged as participants of the *counterculture, somewhat disillusioned with its approach and objectives, began to turn to religions such as Hare Krishna (see INTERNATIONAL SOCIETY . . .), the *Divine Light Mission, the Unification Church (see MOON, SUN MYUNG), and the *Children of God, which shunned the world and stressed the importance of the expressive, experiential approach to religious truth over against reason and reflection.

For a time these movements, highly authoritarian, rigid, demanding, and communalistic, exercised most appeal, sometimes rivalled by the world-affirming *Scientology and *Transcendental Meditation. More recently, however, world-affirming movements as a whole (embracing among others *metaphysical movements such as the *Spiritual Frontiers Fellowship, such 'self-religions' as *Exegesis and *Silva Mind Control, African and Japanese new religions, for example the Aladura churches and *Sōka Gakkai respectively) have experienced considerable growth. However, too fine a distinction should not be drawn between this type of movement and the world-denying type, since there has developed a tendency among the latter to readjust and take a more positive view of the world.

The world-affirming movements (or self- or psycho-religions) aim to transform the individual by providing the means for complete self-realization, in the sense of becoming fully aware that the real or inner self is divine and that the ultimate goal of the religious quest is not to know but to become God. Once 'self realized' then all things are possible, including the transformation of the world. Less explicitly religious than the world-denying type, these movements, often grounded in various forms of lay psychotherapy and underpinned by religious concepts, reflect a desire to be a better person in order to improve the quality of life as a whole. Little or no distinction is made between the sacred and profane, and (as in the world-denying type) personal experience is exalted above reason and scripture as the most appropriate means of validating religious truth.

Other common characteristics include a strong

*millennial dimension (most pronounced in movements such as the Worldwide Church of God (see ARMSTRONG, H. W.)), the use made of contemporary language and symbols, eclecticism, and an egalitarian emphasis which in theory permits all to attain the highest levels of spiritual growth. The world-accommodating movements (such as the growth of Christian house churches, and the various restoration and renewal groups) are more concerned with personal holiness and the revitalization of the established religions than with the wider society.

The impact of these movements has been uneven. Profound in Japan and Africa, they have been of somewhat less significance to date in the N. American and W. European context. The response of the wider society has also been uneven. The methods of recruitment of certain movements and their spiritual techniques, doctrines, and lifestyle have aroused the concern of, among others, psychiatrists, psychologists, politicians, and journalists. Moreover an *anti-cult movement has grown up to counter what are considered to be the mercenary motives and the damaging effects for individuals and society at large. Others, however, have pointed to the important questions that these movements raise for the wider society and to the actual or potential contribution certain of them may have at both of these levels.

Rapid social change, the decline in some societies of established religions, increased culture contact, and awareness of other religious traditions, the search for a spirituality appropriate to the modern, industrialized world, the problems posed for many by the loss or absence of community, and the deinstitutionalization of identity have all contributed to the widespread emergence of new religions in recent history.

E. Barker (ed.), *New Religious Movements: A Perspective for Understanding Society* (1982); J. A. Beckford (ed.), *New Religious Movements* (1986); H. B. Earhart, *The New Religions of Japan: A Bibliography* (1983); C. Y. Glock and R. N. Bellah (eds.), *The New Religious Consciousness* (1976); Kiomi Morioka, *Religion in Changing Japanese Society* (1975); J. A. Saliba, *Perspectives on New Religious Movements* (1995); R. Stark and W. S. Bainbridge, *The Future of Religion* . . . (1985); H. W. Turner, *Religious Innovation in Africa* . . . (1979); R. Wallis, *The Elementary Forms of the New Religious Life* (1984); B. R. Wilson, *Contemporary Transformations of Religion* (1976).

New Sect Shinto: see SECT SHINTO.

New Testament. The collection of books which in addition to the Jewish scriptures make up the Christian Bible. The Greek word *diathēkē*, 'covenant, testament', in the sense of writings goes back to *Paul (2 Corinthians 3. 14). See BIBLE; CANON.

New Thought. A loosely structured movement that emerged in the USA in the last quarter of the 19th cent., which includes a variety of *metaphysical, occult, healing sects, schools, and groups such as *Christian Science, Divine Science, The Unity School of Christianity, and Science of Mind. It was strongly influenced by Phineas Parkhurst Quimby, who practised a form of mesmeric healing with the aid of a medium and advanced the idea that by positive or right thinking it is possible to realize one's highest ideals in the here and now, especially in the realm of healing where prayer is a central part of the process. However, healing, which covers all forms of sickness and difficulties, is not an end in itself, but a way of demonstrating the power of the Mind of God and of directing people beyond the material side of life to spiritual reality which constitutes the true human nature. While they do not in general regard themselves as sectarian or unorthodox, some of these movements have developed their own particular styles, procedures, institutional forms, and doctrinal positions with regard to certain Christian teachings, rejecting such beliefs as eternal punishment. Since the 1950s there has been a revival of interest in these movements in the USA and W. Europe.

New Year. There are four dates for New Year in the Jewish tradition: 1 Nisan is reckoned as New Year for the religious *calendar and for calculating the reigns of Jewish kings; 1 Elul is the New Year for *tithing; 1 Tishri: see ROSH HA-SHANAH; 1 Shevat is the New Year for trees (according to Bet Shammai): see TU BI-SHEVAT.

Next Year in Jerusalem (Heb., *la-shanah ha-ba'ah bi-Yerushalayim*). Traditional phrase expressing the Jewish hope for the coming of the *messiah and for their return to Jerusalem. Because there was a dispute between R. Joshua and R. Eliezer about whether the messiah would return during Nisan (when *Passover occurs) or Tishri (when the *Day of Atonement occurs), the phrase is especially used towards the end of the Passover *seder and after the blowing of the *shofar on the Day of Atonement. For those in Jerusalem or in *Erez Israel, the word *ha-benuyah*, 'rebuilt', is added.

Nezifah (rebuke): see ḤEREM.

Nezikin (Heb., 'damages'). Fourth order of the Jewish *Mishnah. Nezikin is concerned with civil law and legal procedure, especially in cases of damage. It also includes the tractate **Avot*.

Neziv (Jewish Talmudic scholar): see BERLIN, N. Z. J.

NGK (Nederduitse Gereformeerde Kerk): see DUTCH REFORMED CHURCH.

Ngor (sect of Sakya): see SAKYA.

Nibbāna: see NIRVĀNA.

Nibbuta (Pāli). 'He who is cooled', i.e. from the fever of attachment, clinging, and desire (*taṇhā, thirst).

Nicaea, Council of. The first *ecumenical council of the Christian Church, held in 325. The site is modern Iznik in NW Turkey. It was an assembly of bishops called by the emperor *Constantine to deal with the *Arian controversy and secure the unity of the church in the East. It is traditionally known as 'the synod of the 318 fathers', but probably the number in attendance was between 220 and 250, with only six from the West. The proceedings are not known in detail, but the Arian party was defeated: a creed was promulgated by the council which contained the *homoousion formula and to which anti-Arian *anathemas were attached. The council also promulgated canons and reached decisions on the Melitian schism in Egypt, the calculation of the date of *Easter, and the precedence of the major Christian sees. See also NICENE CREED.

W. H. Bright (ed.), *The Definitions of the Catholic Faith and Canons of Discipline* . . . (1874).

Nicene Creed. A Christian statement of faith used in both E. and W. It runs:

We believe in one God, the Father, the almighty, maker of heaven and earth, of all that is, seen and unseen. We believe in one Lord, Jesus Christ, the only Son of God, eternally begotten of the Father, God from God, Light from Light, true God from true God, begotten not made, of one Being with the Father. Through him all things were made. For us men and for our salvation he came down from heaven; by the power of the Holy Spirit he became incarnate of the Virgin Mary, and was made man. For our sake he was crucified under Pontius Pilate; he suffered death and was buried. On the third day he rose again in accordance with the Scriptures; he ascended into heaven and is seated at the right hand of the Father. He will come again in glory to judge the living and the dead, and his kingdom will have no end. We believe in the Holy Spirit, the Lord, the giver of life, who proceeds from the Father (and the Son). With the Father and the Son he is worshipped and glorified. He has spoken through the Prophets. We believe in one holy, catholic and apostolic Church. We acknowledge one baptism for the forgiveness of sins. We look for the resurrection of the dead, and the life of the world to come. Amen.

Although it contains the *homoousion, the creed does not originate from the council of *Nicaea, nor probably from the later council of Constantinople (381) as traditionally held. It was, however, current as part of the *eucharist by the 5th cent. All liturgical churches now use it: Rome was the last Christian centre to adopt it, in 1014. The phrase in parentheses (the *filioque) was added to it in the W. in the early Middle Ages. In the E. Church the creed is also used at baptism. In modern times it has sometimes been proposed as a basis for Christian unity.

Nichikō (Japanese Buddhist movemnet): see NICHIREN SHŌSHŪ.

Nichiren (1222–82). Japanese Buddhist monk who was the founder of *Nichiren Shū, and whose name literally means 'Sun Lotus', 'sun' standing for Japan and 'lotus' for the **Lotus Sūtra*. Nichiren was born the son of a fisherman in Kominato Village in present-day Chiba Prefecture. His given name was Zennichimaro. At the age of 12 his family placed him in the care of a local *Tendai Buddhist temple in his village known as Seichōji. There he was given his 'precepts name' (*kaimyō*), Zenshōbō, at the age of 16. For the next ten years he travelled to various temples in search of a form of religious teaching and practice which he could regard as 'true Buddhism'. In Kamakura, he studied the teachings of *Pure Land school (Jōdo Shū) and *Zen. Later, after a brief return visit to Seichōji in his home village, he enrolled in the monasteries of Mount Hiei and began an intensive study of Tendai teaching and practice. Because of his radical ideas, he was driven out of Mount Hiei, and so he moved on to Mount Kōya to study the esoteric teachings and practice of the *Shingon ('True Word') school of Buddhism. It was during his study on Mount Kōya that he finally concluded that the only true form of Buddhism was that taught by *Saichō (Dengyō Daishi, 'great teacher Dengyō'), who had established the Tendai (Chin., **T'ien-t'ai*) School of Buddhism in Japan in the 8th cent. Saichō taught the superiority of the *Lotus Sūtra* over all Buddhist sūtras. Nichiren, after discovering the *Lotus Sūtra* for himself, returned to his home village and began preaching to the common people that enlightenment was available to every human being through simple trust in the truth (*dharma) expressed in this sūtra:

If you wish to attain Buddhahood immediately, lay down the banner of pride, cast away the club of resentment and trust yourselves to the dharma of the *daimoku* . . . When you fall in an abyss, and someone lowers a rope to pull you out, will you hesitate to grab the rope because you doubt the competence of the helper? Has not the Buddha declared, 'I alone am the protector and saviour'? Here is the power! Here is the rope! . . . Our hearts ache, our sleeves are soaked with tears until we see face to face the gentle figure of the One who says to us, 'I am your Father'.

The act of faith which Nichiren taught was the invocation of a specific *mantra which he called *daimoku*, 'sacred title': *namu myōhō renge kyō*, 'I take refuge in the Lotus of the Wonderful Law Sūtra.'

In Feb. 1260, Nichiren wrote his well-known essay, *Risshō ankoku-ron* (Treatise on the Establishment of Righteousness to Secure the Peace of the State), in which he criticized and denounced the government of the Hōjō regents who controlled the country from Kamakura. He also condemned all forms of religious teaching and practice other than his own understanding of Buddhism as false and demonic, proclaiming that unless the entire country was converted to his understanding of Buddhism, Japan would suffer terrible disasters. In fact, during the period 1256–60, the country had experienced a number of natural calamities: earthquakes, storms, droughts, famines, and epidemics. Nichiren interpreted these events as signs of the advent of the final period of the Dharma, *mappō. He also predicted that Japan would suffer an invasion by a foreign army, a prediction which was realized in 1268 when a Mongol military force invaded Kyushu: 'Even if all the soldiers were gathered (from every part), how could they repel the invasion? It is decreed that all in Japan will suffer from the invaders. Whether this comes to pass or not will prove whether Nichiren is the true propagator of the Lotus of Truth.'

Because of the radicalness and outspokenness of his criticism of the government and his attacks against other schools of Buddhism, Nichiren was arrested in 1261 and exiled to the Izu Peninsula for two years. He was pardoned in 1264. However, Nichiren did not recant. He returned to Kamakura and began publicly denouncing the government in sermons he preached on the streets of the city. The previous regent, Saimyōji, was in hell, he said, and the current regent, Tokimuni, was soon to follow him. Nichiren was again arrested, this time receiving the death sentence. According to tradition, the executioner's sword was struck by lightning just at the moment he began to strike at Nichiren's neck. Whatever happened, the execution was stayed, and he was again sentenced to exile, this time on the isolated island of Sado in the Sea of Japan.

During the three years of his second exile on Sado Island (1271–4), Nichiren wrote *Kaimokushō* (Treatise on Opening the Eyes) and *Kanjin Honzonshō* (Treatise on Contemplating the True Object of Worship):

> This spot among the mountains is cut off from the life of the world. There is no human habitation anywhere around ... I am living now in loneliest isolation. Yet in my heart, in Nichiren's body of flesh, is hidden the great mystery which the Lord Śākyamuni (*Buddha) revealed on Vulture Peak and has entrusted to me. My heart is the place where all Buddhas are immersed in contemplation, turning the wheel of truth on my tongue, being born from my throat, attaining Enlightenment in my mouth.

Together with *Risshō Ankokuron* and two later works, *Senjishō* (Selection of the Time) and *Hōonshō* (Repaying Kindness), these two treatises comprise Nichiren's major writings. Along with 230 letters collected in his *Gosho* (Sacred Writings) these serve as scripture for Nichiren Buddhism. Nichiren is also believed to have created the original Object of Worship, the *gohonzon*, a calligraphic inscription on wood of the invocation, *namu myōhō renge kyō*. The Nichiren Shū claims it is enshrined at their headquarters temple at Mount Minobu, while the Nichiren Shōshu claims it for theirs at Taisekiji.

Again Nichiren was pardoned on 13 Mar. 1274. He still had not recanted his teachings, but instead of returning to active teaching in Kamakura, he retired from public life, leaving the more active expressions of his attempt to reform Buddhism to his younger disciples. During this final stage of his career, he set out to establish 'Vulture Peak', the mythical mountain where the historical Buddha, Śākyamuni, is said to have delivered the teachings of the *Lotus Sūtra*. Nichiren believed the earthly form of Vulture Peak was in Japan, and he selected Mount Fuji (*Fujisan) as the site, and established a temple, Kuonji, nearby on Mount Minobu.

Nichiren died on 13 Oct. 1282, at the home of a patron named Uemondayū Munenaka Ikegami. According to Nichiren Shū teaching, Nichiren's remains are now enshrined at Mount Minobu. For subsequent history, see NICHIREN SHŪ. See also Index, Nichiren.

Anesaki Masaharu, *Nicheren* ... (1916); L. R. Rodd, *Selected Writings* (1980); P. Yampolsky, *Selected Writings* ... (1990).

Nichiren Shōshū. Japanese Buddhist religious movement. When *Nichiren died, his followers agreed that the guardianship of his tomb should circulate among his six senior disciples. When the turn came of Nikō (1253–1314, priest of the Kuonji temple) he declared that he and his successors would take the responsibility permanently. Nichikō (1246–1332) broke away and founded the Daisekiji temple at the foot of Mount Fuji to defend the true teaching of Nichiren. Against the other five, he maintained that the two halves of the **Lotus Sūtra* are not equal in importance: the second half (the Honmon, fourteen chapters which reveal the eternal nature of the *Buddha) are a superior wisdom to the first half (the Jakumon, fourteen chapters which deal with the form taken by the Buddha in order to accommodate himself to human understanding). The Nichiren Shōshū reveres Nichiren as the religious founder (*shūso*) but Nichikō as the true sect founder (*haso*). It believes that in the *mappō (degenerate age), only Nichiren can provide any help (thus relegating the historical Buddha to second place), and that the government should endorse Nichiren Shōshū and establish it as the state religion—a principle known as 'politics united with Buddhism', *ōbutsu myōgō*. As with other Nichiren movements, the *nembutsu is central and of paramount importance.

Nichiren Shū. A collection of Japanese Buddhist sects in the *Mahāyāna tradition which trace their origins to the 13th-cent. *Tendai monk *Nichiren, who sought to restore what he considered to be the orthodox teachings of the historical *Buddha, *Śākyamuni. Next to the *Jōdo Shū (Pure Land Schools), the Nichiren tradition has the largest numbers of devotees of all religions in Japan today. There are currently, according to the *Shūkyō Nenkan* (Yearbook of Religions), eighteen Nichiren Buddhist sects and nineteen Nichiren-related 'new religions' such as *Reiyūkai, *Risshō Kōseikai, Myōshikai Kyōdan, *Sōka Gakkai, *Nichiren Shōshū.

Mochizuki Kanko, *The Nichiren Sect* (Eng., 1958).

Nicholas (Nikolaos) Cavasilas (Greek Orthodox theologian): see CAVASILAS.

Nicholas of Cusa or **Cusanus** (*c.*1400–64). German Christian philosopher. Born in Kues on the River Mosel, he studied at Heidelberg, Padua, and Cologne. He was present at the council of *Basle (1433) and worked for unity within the Church, initially allying himself with the Conciliar movement but later supporting the papal cause. He was made a *cardinal and was briefly *vicar-general of Rome. As a philosopher he was a late *Neoplatonist, indebted to Meister *Eckhart. The two fundamental principles of his thought are *docta ignorantia* ('learned ignorance'—the furthest the human mind can reach) and the *coincidentia oppositorum* ('coincidence of opposites'), which is found in God who is at once transcendent and immanent, the centre and circumference of the universe, the infinite and the infinitesimal, and therefore beyond the grasp of the human intellect. This position was defended in his most famous work, *De Docta Ignorantia*. He is often regarded as a precursor of the Renaissance.

Trs. G. Heron (1954), J. Hopkins (1981), C. L. Miller (1979); J. E. Biechler, *The Religious Language of Nicholas of Cusa* (1975); J. Hopkins, *A Concise Introduction* . . . (1978); P. E. Sigmund, *Nicholas of Cusa and Medieval Political Thought* (1963); P. M. Watt, *Nicolaus Cusanus* . . . (1982).

Nicodemus of the Holy Mountain, the Hagiorite (*c*.1749–1809). Greek monk and spiritual writer. Born in Naxos, he became a monk on Mount *Athos in 1775. He was immensely prolific in editing and publishing traditional monastic texts on spiritual, ascetic, and liturgical subjects, and a great advocate of the *Jesus prayer and frequent *communion. His most important work, with Macarius of Corinth, was the **Philokalia* (1782), an anthology of spiritual texts treasured by the *hesychasts. Tr. into Slavonic by Paissy Velichkovsky (1722–94) and Russian by Theophan the Recluse (1815–94), it has profoundly influenced the revival of Russian Orthodoxy.

The Philokalia: The Complete Text, tr. and ed. G. E. H. Palmer, P. Sherrard, and K. Ware (1979–).

Nicolai, Père (1836–1912). Russian *Orthodox pioneer *missionary to Japan, raised to *archbishop in 1906. Nicolai, whose personal name was Ivan Kasatkin, was the pioneer leader in what has been called the most spectacular achievement in the long history of Russian missionary work. The unique aspect of this work lay in Nicolai's making an almost complete separation from Russian political aims or interests its basic working principle.

Nicolai arrived in Japan on 2 June 1861 to serve as chaplain of the Russian consulate in Hakodate. His proficiency in Japanese and growing understanding of the people and their culture enabled the Orthodox Mission to become indigenized quickly and to raise up Japanese leaders of distinction. Nicolai returned to Russia over 1869–70 in order to secure from the Holy Synod the formal establishment of a Japan Mission, based on his rules for mission which came to constitute the principles of operation for the next half-century and more, stressing the learning of languages and training of catechists.

The spirit and methodology of Nicolai were later summed up by Sergius Tichomorov, who became his coadjutor bishop in 1908. The primary means of evangelism was teaching in families. The mode of apostolate was always positive, never 'apologetic'. It was without polemics, without criticism of other Christian confessions or attack upon Buddhism or Shinto. Nicolai's primary conviction was that the *Christ himself, full of Truth, would win hearts by the methods of peace. By these methods Nicolai and his colleagues, Russian and Japanese, were able to hold together the growing Japanese Orthodox Church even through the intense strains of the Russo-Japanese War of 1904–5.

Nidāna (link in chain): see PATICCA-SAMUPĀDA.

Niddah (Heb., 'menstruating woman'). The Jewish laws relating to menstruating women. Seventh tractate of the order Tohorot of the *Mishnah. According to Jewish law, sexual intercourse is forbidden from the time menstruation begins until seven days after it has finished. Similarly, after giving birth, a woman is unclean for seven days if she has a boy and fourteen days if she has a girl. At the end of the periods of uncleanness, the woman must immerse herself in a *mikveh. These laws are numerous and complicated, but are considered essential to a pure family life. They are justified on the grounds of *Eve's *sin (*Gen.R.* 17. 13) and for maintaining the excitement of the marital relationship (*B.Nid.* 31b). The *Reform movement has rejected the laws of Niddah in their entirety.

Niddesa (part of Buddhist Pāli canon): see KHUDDAKA-NIKĀYA.

Niddui (Separation): see ḤEREM.

Nidi dhyāsana (Skt., 'contemplate'). Third and culminating component of meditation in *Vedānta, leading to spiritual knowledge. The first is *śravaṇa*, hearing and reading scripture; second is *manana*, reflection and assimilation of the first; third is the integration of both through meditation.

Niebuhr, Reinhold (1892–1971). Christian theologian, reflecting especially on social and political issues. After twenty-three years in a Detroit working-class church, he moved to Union Theological Seminary in New York, where he became professor of Christian ethics, remaining there until his retirement. *Moral Man and Immoral Society* (1932) already anticipated his Gifford Lectures, *The Nature and Destiny of Man* (1941–3). Human nature has an awareness of and desire for transcendental goals and goodness, but sin vitiates the attempts of human institutions and language to achieve them: 'Man's capacity for justice makes democracy possible, but man's inclination to injustice makes democracy necessary.' What he looked for was 'a combination of moral resoluteness about the immediate issues with a religious awareness of another dimension of meaning and judgement', thereby grounding politics in realism about human frailty. His attitude is epitomized in the prayer: 'God, give us the serenity to accept what cannot be changed; give us the courage to change what should be changed; give us the wisdom to distinguish one from the other.'

D. E. Fecher, *The Responsible God* (1975); R. W. Fox, *Reinhold Niebuhr* (1985); R. W. Lovin, *Reinhold Niebuhr and Christian Realism*, (1995).

Nieh-pan. Chin. for *nirvāna.

Niemöller, Martin (1892–1984). German pastor and *Confessing Church leader. He was a submarine commander in the First World War, and later a pastor in Dahlem, a suburb of Berlin. (His 1934 book *From U-Boat to Pulpit* was a best-seller.) He formed the Pastors' Emergency League to resist the Nazi takeover of church life, and this formed one basis for the Confessing Church. As an outspoken preacher against the regime, Niemöller was arrested by the Gestapo in 1937 and only freed from concentration camps in 1945. He did much to restore the German church after the war and bring it into the *ecumenical movement, later (1961–8) serving as a president of the World Council of Churches. He had meanwhile become a pacifist, and was an early exponent of reconciliation with the east and of nuclear disarmament. Into his 80s he remained an active leader of the Christian peace movement.

D. Schmidt, *Pastor Niemöller* (1959).

Nien-fo (Chin.; Jap., *nembutsu*). The foremost religious practice in the *Pure Land schools of Buddhism: see NEMBUTSU.

Nietzsche, Friedrich Wilhelm (1844–1900). Philosopher and literary figure who, although German, preferred to be called a 'European'. He was reared in an atmosphere of narrow Lutheran *pietism, against which he struggled for most of his productive life. He indicted Christianity as 'the one great curse, the one intrinsic depravity, the one immortal blemish upon humankind'. He attacked on several fronts: (i) like all religions, it is a narcotic to protect people from fear of unknown forces; (ii) theistic explanation has been made unnecessary by the rise of science, and theistic belief has become 'unbelievable'; (iii) Christian values are anti-human and hostile to life, being fit only for slaves or the weak and inadequate. His most positive thoughts about what could be expected to replace Christianity are found in his strangely magical book, *Thus Spoke Zarathustra* (1883), in which is unfolded his enigmatic doctrine of 'eternal recurrence'. We are encouraged by Nietzsche to will categorically our already determined future, to love unreservedly our already certain fate: ' "So *that* was life?", I will say to Death, "Right on! The same again!" ' His major works are *The Birth of Tragedy* (1872), *Human, All Too Human* (1878), and *Beyond Good and Evil* (1886).

R. J. Hollingdale, *Nietzsche* . . . (1973); R. Schacht, *Nietzsche* (1983).

Nigama (dialogue in Tantra): see TANTRA.

Niggunim (Ḥasidic chants): see MUSIC.

Night Journey (of Muḥammad): see MIʿRĀJ.

Night of power (night in month of Ramaḍān): see LAYLAT AL-QADR.

Nigoda. Minute, single-celled, living beings which, according to Jains, pervade the universe. Their presence makes the Jain commitment to *ahiṁsā (non-violence) even more scrupulous than in other Indian religions.

Nihaṅg (Pañjābī, 'without anxiety'). Militant core of Sikh *Khālsā. Nihaṅg *Siṅghs arose in the time of Gurū *Gobind Siṅgh whose *Dasam Granth they particularly revere. Nihaṅgs are distinguishable by their dark blue shirt and tall, tightly tied *turban, surrounded by a steel ring. As well as the *Five Ks they carry steel weapons. For Nihaṅgs iron/steel symbolizes God's might. Cannabis is used to aid meditation. Nihaṅgs belong to four *dals* (armies) and, whether married or celibate, observe a strict daily routine. Groups of Nihaṅgs, preceded by the *Ādi Granth, travel through *Pañjāb on horseback, participating in religious events such as *Hola Mahallā. See also AKĀLĪ.

Nihilism (Lat., *nihil*, 'nothing'). The view that positive claims (in metaphysics, ethics, epistemology, religion, etc.) are false; or (in its own way more positively) that oblivion awaits humans after death and the cosmos in due course. The term was applied by Turgenev (in *Fathers and Children*, 1862) to a Russian revolutionary movement which engaged in assassinations, but with no programme or goal in mind. However, the attitude is much more ancient (among the Greeks, e.g., the scepticism of Pyrrho). 'Nihilism' is used of a belief refuted by Buddhism. In *Theravāda, it is the false belief that the self is identical with the body-mind continuum and therefore perishes completely at death (Pāli, *uccheda-diṭṭhi*). In *Mahāyāna it is the false belief that nothing exists at all (Skt., *uccheda-dṛṣṭi*) or that reality is an illusion (Skt., **māyā*). The opposite is *Eternalism.

Nihil obstat (Lat., 'nothing obstructs'). The approval in *Roman Catholicism granted by the officially appointed censor to books requiring permission before being published. The nihil obstat precedes and is required for the *imprimatur.

Nihongi or ***Nihonshoki*** (Jap.). Chronicle of Japan, the first of the six histories (*rikkokushi*). In 681 the emperor Temmu appointed Prince Kawashima, his nephew, and eleven men to compile an official version of the imperial genealogy and ancient records, and it is commonly believed that this was the initial stage of the making of the *Nihongi*. The work, written in Chinese, was compiled in 720, consisting of thirty volumes and one book on genealogy which was lost. The first two volumes cover the age of *kami, from the creation of the Japanese archipelago (not the creation of the world) to the birth of the emperor Jimmu, the first (mythological) emperor, of the imperial lineage. The following twenty-eight volumes document the imperial reigns from the emperor Jimmu to the empress Jito (r. 686–97).

The compilers made use of various source materials ranging from the Korean chronicles to native oral tradition, which includes myths, rituals, beliefs, tales, songs, various traditions of clans, priestly tradition, the origin of temples, *Confucian ideas, reference to religious *Taoism, Buddhist *sūtras, and diaries. In this respect, the *Nihongi*, as compared with the **Kojiki* (712), is more useful for the study of ancient Japan. The sections of mythology contain different versions of the same episode, which the *Kojiki* lacks, and this difference seems to suggest that these two books were compiled with different purposes in mind.

The *Nihongi* seems to have been written in response to the need for an official chronicle equal to the Chinese historical records. The Chinese view of the sage king became a model for instituting the Japanese monarchic system with a major modification. The Japanese monarchic system was based on the continuance of the imperial lineage, which excluded the Chinese view of changing rulership by means of revolution. The unbroken imperial lineage was extended far into the mythological age by historicizing myth.

Tr. W. G. Aston, *Nihongi* . . . (1896; 1956).

Nihon Jōka Ryōhō (early form of *Sekai Kyūseikyō).

Niiname-sai (Jap., 'festival of new food'). In *Shinto, an important annual rite celebrated by the emperor in the eleventh month in which he makes an offering of the newly harvested rice to the *kami of heaven and earth and partakes of the rice offering in communion with the kami. The **Nihongi* records that the niiname-sai was first performed by the divine imperial ancestress *Amaterasu Ōmikami, using newly harvested rice from the divine fields in heaven. The emperor performs the niiname-sai as an annual repetition of the *daijō-sai, a similar ritual celebrated by a new emperor at his enthronement. In recent times the day on which the niiname-sai is held, 23 Nov., has been designated as a new national holiday, Labour Thanksgiving Day (*Kinrō Kansha no Hi*). A popular expression of the imperial niiname-sai is the widely celebrated autumn festival (*aki matsuri*) in which the people gather at the shrines to offer thanks to the kami for an abundant harvest.

Nijūshi-ryu (Jap., '24 currents'). The twenty-four Zen schools or traditions in Japan. They include the three major divisions, *Rinzai, *Sōtō, and *Obaku, and also the divisions of Rinzai usually named after the monastery where they began.

Nikāḥ (marriage contract): see MARRIAGE.

Nikāya (Pāli, 'body'). A collection of works within the 'baskets' (*pitaka*) of the Buddhist Pāli canon. Thus the *Sūtra-piṭaka contains five nikāyas: Dīgha, Majjhima, Saṃyutta, Anguttara, and Khuddaka. It may also be a 'body' of *bhikṣus (monks), and is so used of sects or schools in the *saṅgha.

Nikō (Japanese leader of sect): see NICHIREN SHŌSHŪ.

Nikodemos of the Holy Mountain: see NICODEMUS.

Nikolai (Kasatkin), Père (Russian Orthodox missionary): see NICOLAI, PÈRE.

Nikon or **Nikita Minin** (1605–81). Orthodox patriarch of Moscow, 1652–8. He was a married parish priest, with three children. But when the children died, he went, with the agreement of his wife, into monastic solitude. He was drawn back into ecclesiastical life by the support of the Tsar, but continued the pursuit of reform when he was made patriarch, thereby creating the fierce resistance of the *Old Believers. He fell out of favour with the Tsar and resigned. He made an attempt to return to office, but was imprisoned. When at last he was invited to return to Moscow, he died before he could get there. He remains deeply respected (except by descendants of the Old Believers) as one of the greatest of the patriarchs for his reforms.

Nil(us) Sorsky, St (leader of Non-Possessors movement): see POSSESSORS.

Niʿmat Allāh Walī, Shāh Nūr al-Dīn (*c*.1331–1431 (AH 731–834)). Founder of the Niʿmatullahi *Sūfī order, one of the few *Shīʿite Muslim orders which has had a continuing history. He was born in Aleppo, the son of a Sūfī master. He said later, 'What a man on a forty-day retreat has failed to realize at the age of thirty was revealed to me when I was three.' He was dissatisfied with his traditional education and set off in search of an enlightened teacher, whom he found in Shaykh Yāfiʿī. He remained with him for seven years. He then set out on extensive travels, recognized as the *qutb (spiritual centre) of his age. He met Tamerlane, but without ameliorating effect. He was married, and his son, Burhān al-Dīn Khalīl Allāh (b. 1373 (AH 885)) became his spiritual successor. He settled in Kirman in Iran, where he died and where his tomb is a centre of pilgrimage. At the heart of his way was his instruction to keep the name of God constantly in mind, since this would lead to actions imitative of God, especially mercy and generosity. This leads to the expansion (*bast) of the heart instead of contraction (*qabd). He forbade his followers to wear any distinctive religious dress (to show that they were Sūfīs), and he insisted that the Sūfī experience was open to all, not just to an élite: the only condition of 'entry' was an unqualified desire for love—the love of God and of all others. In this spirit, he wrote much memorable poetry. In the words of J. Nurbakhsh, 'His poetry is the chant of the ode of life, it is a tune of the flute of being, a melody of the music of God.'

The Niʿmatullahi Order has houses in the USA, and in London. It continues to see contemplation as a basis for ethical action and reconciliation in the world.

J. Nurbakhsh, *Masters of the Path* . . . (1980).

Niʿmatullāhi (Sūfī order): see NIʿMAT ALLĀH WALĪ, SHĀH NŪR AL-DĪN.

Nimbārka (11th/12th cent. CE). Indian philosopher of the near-*dvaita (Bhedābheda) Vedānta tradition, and founder of the *Vaiṣṇava sect devoted to Rādhā-Kṛṣṇa; followers are known as Nimbārkas. In the pattern of *Kṛṣṇa with *Rādhā, they seek, not union (still less absorption) in God, but rather the proximity of everlasting mutual joy. Nimbārka's own views are preserved mainly in his commentary on the *Vedānta Sūtra*, *Vedānta-Parijāta-Saurabha*. It is possible that Jayadeva's **Gitāgovinda* was influenced by Nimbārka.

Nimbus: see HALO.

Nimitta (Pāli, Skt.). In Buddhism, variously translated as 'outward aspect', 'general appearance', 'perceived object', 'mark', 'image', 'sign', 'omen'. Its five most significant usages are as follows.

1. In canonical Buddhism, the outward aspect or general appearance of an object; that aspect which we find attractive (*abhijjhā*) or repulsive (*domanassa*) when our senses perceive things. We can react to these perceptions in either of two ways: remain alert, restraining the senses from paying attention to the demands the nimitta makes upon them; or give full rein to the activity of our senses by allowing them to indulge and feed off our perceptions of the nimitta. In the latter case, the nimittas will serve as the seed-bed for the unwholesome states of greed (*lobha), hate (*dosa), and delusion (*moha) to germinate and thrive. In this context, therefore, the idea of nimitta represents an important concept. First, it explains how the negative psychological condition of attachment to the world occurs, by providing an account of the perceptual mechanism through which this happens. Secondly, it shows that unwholesome karmic states are rooted in our (misplaced) perceptions of the world.

2. In meditation, the perceptual objects used for contemplation (*kammaṭṭhāna) are referred to as nimitta because they function as a mark, sign, or image on which the eye and mind focus their attention. There are three recognized stages to the process of contemplation: (i) the contemplation of the physical object itself which is called the preparatory image (*parikamma-nimitta*); (ii) a mental or acquired image (*uggaha-nimitta*) arises as a result of prolonged concentration upon the physical object, and this is next contemplated; (iii) finally, the mental image is succeeded by the emergence of an even more abstract idea or concept called the sublimated or counterpart image (*paṭibhāga-nimitta*); this is free of all the faults and phenomenal characteristics of the original object (see JHĀNA). Unlike the desultory manner of general perception described above, the meditator is seeing into the nature of the object (*ārammana*) by a process of deep contemplation.

3. According to the Pāli Commentaries (*Aṭṭhakathā*), at the last moment of consciousness before death the sign of previous *karma (*kamma-nimitta*) together with the sign of future destiny (*gati-nimitta*) arise as mental objects, as an indication of that person's impending rebirth.

4. It is the term for the 'signs' or 'omens' of old age, sickness, death, and the wandering mendicant which, according to legend, convinced the Buddha to leave home and lead the ascetic life (see FOUR SIGNS).

5. In the Yogacārya (*Vijñānavāda) branch of Buddhism, it is the term for the perceived object, which has no existence independently of the perceiver but is merely a representation of his inner consciousness.

Ninety-nine beautiful names of God. The names of *Allāh in Islam, most of which are taken or derived from the *Qur'ān. There are several different lists, and while each list contains ninety-nine names, there are variations in the lists. The names are called *al-asmā' al-ḥusnā*, from 7. 179, 'To him belong the most beautiful names'. The names are divided into two categories, those of essence (*al-dhat*) and those of quality (*al-ṣifāt*). They are also divided into the names of mercy and the names of majesty (or judgement), *al-jamāl wa'l-jalāl*. The names are recited on the Muslim *rosary (*subḥa*), which consists of a *yad* (for the unity of God) and ninety-nine beads (or thirty-three, to be repeated three times). According to a *ḥadīth, anyone who repeats the names of God will be sure of *paradise. For an example, see A. Jeffery, *A Reader on Islam* (1962), pp. 553 ff.

Ninigi. The grandson of the *Shinto deity *Amaterasu, and an important figure in the mythologies of the founding of Japan. In Shinto myth, Ninigi is charged by his grandmother, the sun-goddess Amaterasu, to descend from the heavenly realms to earth (i.e. Japan) in order to extend the rule of the heavenly *kami (gods) to earth. In doing so, Ninigi brings to earth the sword, jewels, and beads symbolic of divine authority, and sets in motion the processes by which humanity, history, and culture come into being—most importantly the divine institutions of the imperial line and rule. Not unlike *Adam and *Eve, Ninigi is the bridge between myth and history, the age of the gods and the age of humanity, heaven and earth, the gods and human beings. He also represents an important motif of descent in Shinto: throughout Shinto, the kami are thought to descend from high places (sky, mountains, etc.) in order to bring their power, authority, and benefits.

Ninomiya Sontoku (founder of Japanese religious movement): see HŌTOKU.

Ninth of Av (Heb., *Tishah be-Av*). Jewish fast day, which commemorates the destruction of the first and second *Temples in 586 BCE and 70 CE. In the *synagogue, the book of *Lamentations is read and dirges are recited. Pious Jews abstain from meat and wine for nine days before the fast; and for three weeks before, no festivities or marriages can take place.

Nippon (origin of the sun): see MOTOORI NORINAGA.

Nipponzan Myōhōji. A Japanese Buddhist revival movement, founded in 1917 by Fujii Nichidatsu (1884–1985), based on the teachings of *Nichiren. It is therefore also known as the Movement of the Wondrous Law of the Lotus Sūtra. Its basic practice is the repetition of the name of the **Lotus Sūtra*. It organizes marches for peace, and builds peace *pagodas throughout the world (in the UK at Milton Keynes and in Battersea Park), and thus became separated from some other movements derived from Nichiren, whose policies are more aggressive. Fujii's book, *Beating Celestial Drums*, reflects the practice of beating the drum of heaven to extend the reverberations of peace.

Nirang (ritual cow's urine): see NAUJOTE.

Nirañjan (Pañjābī, 'without darkness, untinged'). Sikh epithet for God. The *Gurūs so describe God to show his total purity and freedom from *māyā. The original meaning of *añjan* was black collyrium applied to the eyes.

Niraṅkār (Pañjābī, 'formless one'). Sikh name for God. Gurū *Nānak described God as without form, Niraṅkār, thirteen times in the *Ādi Granth. This is emphasized in stanzas 16–19 of *Japjī Sāhib, each of which ends with the word Niraṅkār. In Sikh thought, Niraṅkār remains an important name for God. See also NĀM; NIRAṄKĀRĪ; AKĀL PURUKH.

Niraṅkārī. Sikh reform movement, regarded as a sect by mainstream Sikhs. Niraṅkārīs emphasize reliance on the will of God, *Niraṅkār. Despite the injunctions of their founder, Dayāl Dās (1783–1855), he and his successors, Darbārā Siṅgh, Hārā Siṅgh, and Gurbakhsh Siṅgh, are venerated as *Gurūs in succession to *Gobind Siṅgh. Niraṅkārīs have a distinctive flag, greeting ('dhan niraṅkār'), and a modified *Ardās in which 'Niraṅkār' replaces the divine titles, Bhagautī, *Vāhigurū, and *Satgurū. The Niraṅkārīs' headquarters have moved from Dayālsar, near Rawalpindi, Pakistan, to Chandigaṛh (*Pañjāb). Like the *Nāmdhārīs, the Niraṅkārīs originated as a 19th-cent. renewal of true Sikhism. Dayāl Dās called Sikhs to worship Niraṅkār, rejecting idol-worship, *brahmanical birth- and death-ritual, and pilgrimage to *Hardwār. Despite opposition, he is said to have pioneered the *Anand marriage rite. He urged abstention from meat and intoxicants. His sandals are venerated by Niraṅkārīs. Sant Niraṅkārīs are a separate movement often confused with Niraṅkārīs. In 1978, following clashes between Sant Niraṅkārīs and followers of Jarnail Siṅgh *Bhindrānawāle, a *hukamnāmā was issued from the *Akāl Takht, bidding all Sikhs to boycott the Sant Niraṅkārīs.

S. K. Jolly, *Sikh Revivalist Movements* ... (1988); J. C. B. Webster, *The Nirankari Sikhs* (1969).

Niraya (state of punishment and torment): see NARAKA.

Nirbīja (without seed, a stage in samādhi): see ASAMPRAJÑĀTA.

Nirguṇ (Pañjābī, 'without qualities'). In the *Ādi Granth, *Brahman (God) is described as nirguṇ, i.e. abstract, lacking attributes. However, as creator, the immanent source of all qualities, he is also *saguṇ, endowed with attributes. Nirguṅ is interchangeable with *niraṅkār. See also VIA NEGATIVA.

Nirguṇa-Brahman (Skt., 'Brahman without qualities'). The term in Vedānta Hinduism for the Absolute and indescribable nature of *Brahman, in contrast to *saguṇa Brahman. For explication, see ŚAṄKARA.

Nirmalā (Pañjābī, 'spotless, pure'). A learned, *quietist Sikh group. In the *Ādi Granth the word describes God and those who meditate on his *Nām. Gurū *Gobind Siṅgh sent the five original Nirmalās to Banāras to study Hindu theology. Nirmalās observe the *Five Ks, wear saffron robes (see MONASTICISM (BUDDHIST)), and expound the Ādi Granth. They are *celibate, follow distinctive rules, and live in *monasteries called *akhāṛās* (literally, 'wrestling arenas').

Nirmāna-kāya (Buddha in human form): see TRIKĀYA.

Nirodha (Skt., *ni* + *rodha*, 'obstruction'). 1. In Hinduism, the state of intense concentration in which the distinction of subject and object is destroyed, so that the mind attains realization of non-duality. For *Patañjali (1. 2), it is the bringing to a halt of *citta as it pursues choices (*vṛtti).

2. In Buddhism, the cessation of *dukkha (the third of the Four Noble Truths); it is thus also equated with *nirvāna.

Nirodha-samāpatti. In Buddhism, the cessation of mental activity as a consequence of *meditation practices of specific and well-tested kinds. Since all mental activity is brought into a state of cessation, the condition cannot be described—and it is sometimes held to be virtually equivalent to *nirvāna, although in fact bodily states are continuing. The philosophical issues which this raises—of the relation between mind and body, and of how mental activity is initiated again from a state of cessation—are reviewed in P. J. Griffiths, *On Being Mindless* . . . (1986).

Nirṛti. Evil, misery, dissolution and decay, personified in Hinduism as a Goddess. Dark in appearance, she seeks those who fail to offer appropriate sacrifices; hence three black bricks are incorporated in the fire-altar of the home, as her portion. She knows 'everyone who is born', but pursues obvious offenders. According to *Manusmṛti* 11. 105, a man who seduces the wife of his *guru must cut off his genitals, and, carrying them in his hands, walk towards the domain of Nirṛti (in the SW) until he dies.

Nirupadhiśeṣa-nirvāṇa (Skt.; Pāli, *anupadisesa-nibbāna*). *Nirvāna with no lingering conditions remaining—as opposed to nirvāna which is attained, but with residual shadows of previous existence still continuing. The latter condition means that the *Buddha can be completely enlightened, but his bodily appearance continues, so that he can, for example, teach others. *Parinirvāṇa* is then the attainment of complete nirvāna at death (though *parinirvāṇa* can also mean nirvāna before death, hence the present term). Cf., but contrast, the *Mahāyāna *pratiṣṭhita-nirvāna.

Nirvāna (Skt., 'extinction'; Chin., *nieh-pan*; Jap., *nehan*; Korean, *yŭlban*). The final goal and attainment in Indian religions.

In Hinduism, nirvāna is the extinguishing of worldly desires and attachments, so that the union with God or the Absolute is possible. According to S. K. Belvalkar, the term originated in Kāla philosophy before the advent of Buddhism. In *Mahābhārata*, nirvāna is serene peace (*śānti*, 12. 196. 6, 341. 8) and satisfaction (*susukhi*, 3. 126. 15). In *Anugītā* 4. 11, it is described as 'a fire devoid of fuel'. In *Bhagavad-gītā*, it seems to be contrasted deliberately with the Buddhist understanding, because it is described as the attainment of *Brahman ('He who forsakes all objects of desire and goes about without cravings, desires or self-centredness attains serene peace. . . . Staying in this state, even in his last hour, he attains *brahmanirvāṇa*', 2. 71 f.), and the yogin is described, not (as in Buddhism) as a candle blown out, but as 'a candle flame away from a draught which does not flicker' (6. 19). The attainment of nirvāna is thus *mokṣa.

In Buddhism there is no Self or soul to attain any state or union after death. Nirvāna (Pāli, *nibbāna*) therefore represents the realization that that is so. It is the condition of absolute cessation of entanglement or attachment, in which there is, so to speak, that state of cessation, but no interaction or involvement. Thus *nibbuta* (past participle) is 'he who is cooled', i.e. from the fever of clinging and thirst (*tanhā). It does not mean 'extinction', a view which the Buddha repudiated (*nihilism). That is why nirvāna can receive both negative (what it is not) and positive (what it is like) descriptions, though it cannot in fact be described. In *Theravāda, only the Buddha can realize the condition of nirvāna absolutely, but *arhats realize it with lingering conditions until the end of this life-cycle. In *Mahāyāna, the development of *śūnyatā (*Nāgārjuna) led to the realization that all things must share the same nature (since everything is empty of self and of separate individuation). Consequently, nirvāna and *saṃsāra (the world of entanglement) share the same buddha-nature. It was this perception which opened the way to the *bodhisattva ideal, and to the goal of nirvāna being identified with the realization of the buddha-nature (*buddhatā, *bussho, *tathāgata) in, or through, all appearance, as all there is—if 'is' is not too strong a word. While accepting that analysis, the so-called 'Nirvāna School' of early (5th-cent.) Chinese Buddhism, stressed the positive aspects of nirvāna, and regarded it as an eternal and blissful condition. The final attainment of the state of nirvāna, with no residues remaining (of involvement in the appearance of this world) is pari (complete) nirvāna.

See also APRATIṢṬHITA-NIRVĀNA; SOPADHIŚEṢA-NIRVĀṆA; NIRUPADHIŚEṢA-NIRVĀṆA; Index, Nirvāna.

J. W. Bowker, *The Problems of Suffering* . . . (1970) and *The Meanings of Death* (1991); W. L. King, *In the Hope of Nibbāna* (1964); V. Nyanaponika, *Pathways of Buddhist Thought* (1971); A. K. Warrier, *The Concept of Mukti in Advaita Vedanta* (1961).

Nirvāna school: see NIRVĀNA.

Nirvikalpa-samādhi: see SAMĀDHI.

Niśān Sāhib (Pañjābī, 'flag' + 'respected'). Flag indicating a Sikh *gurdwārā. The Niśān Sāhib is triangular and usually saffron-coloured, bearing a black *khaṇḍā in the centre. It is flown all year at full mast from a tall flag-pole draped in saffron-coloured cloths. Each year, beginning generally on *Baisākhī, a new flag is flown. Devout Sikhs show respect to the Niśān Sāhib before entering the gurdwārā.

Nishida Kitarō (1870–1945). Leading Japanese Buddhist philosopher and founder of the Kyōto school of philosophy. He assimilated W. philosophy and created his own distinctive philosophical system based largely upon Buddhist religious thought. Nishida studied at Tokyo University and became a middle-school teacher, and in 1910 went to Kyōto University. He taught philosophy there until 1928, and he continued to publish his philosophy through lectures and books. In 1911 he published his first work, *A Study of Good* (*Zen no kenkyū*), which was to become the most widely read philosophical book written by a Japanese and which began his creation of a modern system of philosophy permeated with the Japanese tradition. This work formulated the concept of 'pure experience', prior to and underlying all oppositions such as subject and object or body and mind. He next developed his mystical concept of 'absolute free will'. Then with his work, *Hataraku mono kara miru mono e* (From the Acting to the Seeing, 1927), Nishida began systematically building up his concept of 'place' (*basho*), the self-identity of 'absolute Nothingness' from which the individual reality of everything could be derived. In this concept he emphasized the *Mahāyāna Buddhist idea of the contradictory aspect of phenomenological reality, which is finally 'nothingness' or 'voidness'—the attitude of seeing the form of the formless and hearing the voice of the voiceless (see ŚŪNYATĀ). While such Buddhist ideas defy analytical examination, Nishida tried with the help of W. philosophy to find a new logic to incorporate them. In the world of human reality, through religious experience we enter into 'absolute nothingness', the final determination and field of everything.

Nishkam Sēwak Jathā. Sikh reform movement. It was founded by Sant Puran Siṅgh (who lived at Kericho in Kenya, hence his other name, Kerichowale Bābā, d. 1983). He encouraged a return to the elementary conditions of *gurmat, especially the avoidance of alcohol and the practice of *nām simaran. Its members are vegetarian, although Sikhs are not strictly required to be so.

Nīti-śāstras. Indian *śāstras that concern *ethics and wise or prudent behaviour. They are told mainly through stories and narratives, but particularly important maxims are encapsulated in verse: 'Niti is the art of surviving in a world of enemies, thriving on the folly of others, and making the best out of a given situation' (Klostermaier).

Nitnem (Pañjābī, 'daily rule, prayer'). Sikh daily prayer. Nitnem may consist of *Japjī, *Jāp, *Savayye, Sodar, *Rahirās, *Chaupaī, *Anand, *Ardās, and *Sohilā. These prayers are repeated by devout Sikhs, some in the early morning, others in the evening. All except Ardās occur in the *Ādi Granth or *Dasam Granth. They are available in *guṭkās (manuals).

Nitya (Skt., 'enduring'). In Hinduism, the Absolute. One united with the Absolute is known as nitya-*mukta; one who is thus united but returns to birth for the sake of others (cf. *bodhisattva) is called nitya-siddha (an example is *Nārada). Nitya is the Absolute at rest, in contrast to *līlā, through which manifestation occurs.

Nīvaraṇas (Pāli, 'hindrances'). In Buddhism, mental and emotional factors which hinder the acquisition of knowledge and insight. There are five: (i) sensuous desire (*kāmacchanda*); (ii) anger (*vyācada*); (iii) sloth and torpor (*thīna-middha*); (iv) excitability and anxiety (*uddhacca-kukkucca*); (v) doubt (*vicikicchā*). In the Buddhist *Suttas they are likened to water or a pool in which one cannot see one's own reflection: sensuous desire is as though the water has been coloured with dye; anger, as if the water is boiling; sloth and torpor, as if the water is covered with algae; excitability and anxiety, as if the water is agitated by the wind; and doubt, as if the water is muddy and turbid. They primarily interfere with memory and concentration, so that attainment of meditative absorption (*jhāna) is not possible until they have all been at least temporarily suspended. Their complete eradication is a sign of having achieved a supramundane state. Eliminating doubt leads to the state of *sotāpanna*; eliminating sensuous desire, anger, and anxiety to the state of *anāgamin; and sloth, torpor, and excitability to the state of *arhat.

Nivedita, Sister (1867–1911). Hindu nationalist and nun, originally Miss Margaret Noble. As Sister Nivedita, she became a disciple of Swami *Vivekānanda after meeting him in London. On moving to India, she joined the Ramakrishna Mission, and devoted herself to social work, notably in Calcutta, where she established a girls' school in the most orthodox Hindu area of the city. She strongly supported the campaign for Indian independence, and wrote extensively in English on the nobility of ancient Hindu ideals. Immediately after the death of Swami Vivekānanda she left the Ramakrishna Mission, in order to be free to devote herself to the service of India.

L. Reymond, *The Dedicated: A Biography . . .* (1953).

Nivṛtti (Skt.). Return, rest, especially in Hinduism the return of manifestation to its source in *Brahman. Nivṛttidharma/marga is thus the spiritual exercise which involves withdrawal from the world and from all activity (including religious activity) in order to return to the source.

Niwano Nikkyō (co-founder of RKK): see RISSHŌ KŌSEI KAI.

Niyama (Skt., 'restraint'). 1. In Hinduism, the second 'limb' of 'eight-limbed' (*aṣṭanga) or *rāja *yoga concerning self-discipline to help purify the mind of impediments (*kleśa). Five rules are given in the **Yoga Sūtra* (2. 32): (i) purity (*śauca*), (ii) contentment (*samtoṣa*), (iii) austerity (*tapas), (iv) own-study (*svādhyāya*), the recitation of sacred scriptures, and (v) devotion to the Lord (*Īśvara *praṇidhāna*).

2. In Buddhism, the constraints which control eventualities into their outcomes: (i) *bīja-niyama, biological or hereditary constraints; (ii) mano- or *citta-niyama, unwilled operations of the mental order; (iii) *karma-niyama, the consequences of volitional dispositions; (iv) uti-niyama, constraints in the physical environment; (v) *dharma-niyama, constraints derived from the transcendental order. From these, it will be seen that events cannot be construed as the simple working out of karma, as though all eventualities must have a preceding karmic cause.

Thus if a bus crashes and kills all the passengers, it is not the bad karma of each individual which has put them on the bus and then caused his or her death. It may be (following the above categories): (i) a genetic defect leading to the sudden death of the driver; or (ii) an unwilled error on his part caused by being dazzled by the sun; or (iii) by his deliberately drinking while driving, or (iv) by a failure of the braking system, or (v) by the malice of *Māra distracting the driver's attention.

Niyya (Arab., 'intention'). The 'intention' which must be pronounced before carrying out a religious observance, in order to make it valid in Islamic religious law. Merit is attributed in accordance with the intention. Set forms exist for *ḥajj, *ṣawm, and *ṣalāt. *al-Bukhāri's collection of *ḥadīth begins with the statement that 'actions will be judged only by their intention', so that if one made the *hijra for God and for his Prophet, it would be rewarded, but if for the sake of gaining a wife, it would not.

Niẓām al-Mulk (ruling Muslim adviser): see WAZĪR.

Nizārī (Ismāʿīlī sect): see ISMĀʿĪLĪYA; ASSASSINS.

Noachide laws. The seven laws believed by Jews to be obligatory for everyone. The Noachide laws are based on those given to *Adam (Genesis 2. 16) and *Noah (*Gen.R.* 34). They are prohibitions against *idolatry, *blasphemy, sexual sins, murder, theft, and eating from a living animal, as well as the injunction to formulate a legal system. According to the *sages, a Jew is obliged to keep the whole *Torah, while every *gentile who keeps the Noachide laws is a *ger-toshav* ('resident stranger'). Maimonides taught that such a *ḥasid (righteous person) has a share in the world to come. Because of their Trinitarian beliefs, Christians were not always regarded as Noachides, but Muslims, with their strict monotheism, invariably were.

D. Novak, *The Image of the Non-Jew in Judaism: An Historical and Constructive Study of the Noachide Laws* (1983).

Noah. Survivor of the great flood in the Hebrew scriptures. According to Genesis, Noah was commanded to save himself, his family, and a breeding pair of each animal species in a wooden *ark. After surviving the flood, Noah offered sacrifices to God who blessed him and made a *covenant (see NOACHIDE LAWS) with him (Genesis 6. 9–9. 17). In the *aggadah, the *rabbis filled out the tradition that Noah was a righteous man (Genesis 6. 9) by providing instances of his goodness. After the flood, he planted the first vineyard (9. 22). Similar flood traditions occur in other Mesopotamian sources.

A. Heidel, *The Gilgamesh Epic and Old Testament Parallels* (1946).

Nobili, Roberto de (Christian Jesuit missionary): see DE NOBILI, ROBERTO.

Noble savage (Rousseau's concept of 'primitive simplicity'): see IBN TUFAYL.

Nō drama (Jap., *nōgaku, nohgaku*; 'skill music' or 'skill entertainment'). A highly sophisticated dance, music, dramatic form with important religious connections to all the religions of pre-modern Japan (from *c.*14th cent. when most plays in the classical repertoire were written). Although Nō is not exclusively related to any one religion and is often performed in a non-religious context, historically and still today it has overtones of religious ritual, while the content of the plays reflects a generalized religious world-view of traditional Japan. *Shinto and popular forms of Buddhism are particularly evident in the plays, while *Zen Buddhism and *Confucian ceremony have influenced its style of performance.

Nō attained its classical form through the work of Kan'ami Kiyotsugu (1333–84) and his son, Zeami Motokiyo (1363–1443), who also wrote a number of treatises concerning the art of Nō. Many of Zeami's aesthetic categories and his conception of artistic discipline are linked with Buddhist notions and practices. Plays are roughly classified into five categories: (i) god plays, (ii) warrior plays, (iii) woman plays, (iv) madness plays, and (v) demon plays. The plays are typically dramatizations of pilgrimages or journeys to temples, shrines, and other sacred places. The plays frequently centre on the encounter of wandering monks and other figures with *kami, *bodhisattvas, demons, or spirits of the dead in search of enlightenment. In many of the more famous plays, Buddhist monks encounter spirits of the dead, hear a narration of their life story, and perform rites to aid the ghost in its search for enlightenment.

Y. Inoura and T. Kawatake, *The Traditional Theatre of Japan* (1981); D. Keene, *No* . . . (1966), (ed.), *Twenty Plays of the No Theatre* (1970), and *No and Bunraku* (1990); Komparu, Kunio *The Noh Theatre* . . . (1983); Y. Nakamura, *Noh* . . . (1971); L. C. Pronko, *Guide to Japanese Drama* (1973); J. T. Rimer and Yamazaki Masakazu, *On the Art of the No Drama: The Major Treatises of Zeami* (1984); M. Zeami, *The Secret of No Plays: Zeami's Kadensho* (1968).

Noh (type of Japanese drama): see NŌ DRAMA.

Nominalism and realism. A philosophical debate with implications both for theology and religion. In the West, the debate goes back to Greek philosophy: what is truly real, individuals or universals? Nominalism argued that individuals are real (this particular book before me) and that universals (the idea of 'books') are concepts abstracted from our experience of individuals. Realists held that particular books come and go, but that the idea of 'books' endures while particular individuals do not; thus the idea is more real than the items illustrating it. Theological nominalism (see e.g. WILLIAM OF OCKHAM) held that the pure Being of God is real, and that attributes are equivalent to universals, being conceptual abstractions which organize our limited apprehension of God (enabling us to say *something*, however inadequate), but having no corresponding reality in God. This position reinforces *apophatic theology. Theological realism accepts the approximate and limited nature of human language, but argues that the perfections of God are revealed in the ways in which God is related to the universe of his creation, and to humans in particular. But for that revealed relatedness not itself to be simply a human construction, the inference must be drawn that the ground for the possibility of God being revealed in that way lies in the nature of God *a se* (in himself, i.e. in his aseity): the perfections endure even when the creatures who dimly apprehend them come and go. In E. religions, the issue arises out of *avidyā, ignorance. Is the appearance of reality something which humans superimpose on that which is the cloak of what alone is truly real, or do the particulars have some enduring reality (see e.g. ŚANKARA; RĀMĀNUJA; MADHVA)? Is there some reality in the particulars of this (albeit transitory) cosmos, or is every manifestation devoid of characteristics, being simply a manifestation of the only nature that there is, i.e. the buddha-nature (see ŚŪNYATĀ)?

M. H. Carré, *Realists and Nominalists* (1961); R. R. Dravid, *The Problem of Universals in Indian Philosophy* (1972); H. Veatch, *Realism and Nominalism Revisited* (1954).

Nomothetic ambition. The attempt (characteristic of work in the 19th cent.) to find laws, comparable to those of the natural sciences, governing social and individual behaviour, including religion. See further SOCIOLOGY OF RELIGION.

Non-Church movement (Japanese Protestant movement): see UCHIMURA.

Nonconformists. Members of *Protestant churches in England outside the *Church of England. The term alludes to the separation of these denominations from the established church in the 17th cent.; they are otherwise known as *Free Churches.

Non-Jurors: see DIVINE RIGHT OF KINGS.

Non-official religion: see FOLK RELIGION.

Non-violence (in Indian religions): see AHIṀSĀ.

Norito (Jap., probably 'words stated with awe'). In *Shinto, sacred words and prayers expressed in elegant ancient Japanese and addressed to the *kami in Shinto worship. The use of norito is related to the traditional belief in spiritual power residing in beautiful and correctly spoken words (*koto-dama). The **Kojiki* (712) relates that norito were recited before the cave in which the imperial ancestress, *Amaterasu Ōmikami, had secluded herself, to induce her to rejoin the heavenly kami. The earliest norito texts are in **Engi-shiki*, a law book compiled in the 10th cent. CE. Among these twenty-seven norito are the norito for the annual harvest festival (*toshigoi no matsuri*) and for the ritual of the 'Great Exorcism' (*oharae*) celebrated on the last day of the sixth month. Until the Meiji period, norito to be used in worship of the kami were freely composed by priests of each shrine as appropriate, but during the period of government-controlled State Shinto (*kokka shintō) the wording of the norito was determined by the government in accordance with the *Engi-shiki*. At present, prayers drafted by the Association of Shrine Shinto are in general use, but priests are free to compose their own according to individual needs. Usually the chief priest of a shrine chants the norito on behalf of the worshippers. Typical norito give praise of the kami, make reference to the origin of the specific rite or festival, express thanksgiving to the kami, report to or petition the kami, enumerate the offerings presented, identify the persons on whose behalf the prayers are recited and the priests who are reciting them, and finally add some parting words of respect and awe.

Tr. D. L. Philippi, *Norito* (1959).

North end. The end of the communion table from which in some Anglican churches the priest celebrates the *eucharist. Advocates of this practice, now only found in the aggressively *Protestant wing of the Church, say it eliminates any hint that the celebrant is a sacrificing *priest.

Northern Kingdom: see ISRAEL.

Northern school (of Zen Buddhism): see SOUTHERN AND NORTHERN SCHOOLS.

Notarikon. System of exegetical abbreviation used by Jews. Notarikon is used as a system of interpreting the *Pentateuch. Either each letter in a word is thought to stand for a whole word, or a word is divided into shorter components with separate meanings. See also HERMENEUTICS, RABBINIC.

Not-returner (Buddhist on third stage of path to attainment): see ANĀGĀMIN.

Novatian (d. 257/8). Leader of a *schism in the Latin Church. He was a Roman presbyter and author of an important work *On the Trinity*. He joined the rigorists who rejected concessions to the *lapsi, and was consecrated rival bishop of Rome. He was martyred in the persecution under Valerian. The Novatianists were excommunicated, even though their doctrine was orthodox. A Novatianist Church continued into the 5th cent., and in smaller communities to an even later date.

Novena. In the *Roman Catholic Church, continuous prayer, private or public, either on nine consecutive days, or once a week for nine weeks. The purpose is for a particular intention, or in honour of a *saint or virtue of *Christ (e.g. the *sacred heart). The observance of novenas dates only from the 17th cent., though it has a biblical model (Acts 1. 13 f.).

Nubūwah (Arab.). The office of prophecy (i.e. of being a *nabī) in Islam.

Nü-kua. Chinese female deity, who created human figures from yellow earth, but when she grew bored with this activity, she dipped a rope in the mud, swung it about and thus produced the poor (in contrast to the rich and well-endowed). She also instituted marriage.

Numbers (hidden meanings): see GEMATRIA; Index, Numbers.

Numbers, Book of. Fourth book of the *Pentateuch in the Hebrew scriptures and in the Christian Old Testament. Numbers is known in Hebrew from its first word *Be-Midbar*, 'in the wilderness'. It contains the story of the Israelites' sojourn in the wilderness from their departure from *Sinai until their stay in Shittim. The first section, the nineteen days at Sinai (1–10. 10) includes a census of the twelve *tribes, the *Nazirite laws, and the protection of the *Tabernacle (6), the presents offered by the tribal leaders to the Tabernacle (7), and the final preparations for the march. The second section, the journey from Sinai to the plains of Moab (10. 11–22. 1), describes the moral degeneration of the people, the giving of *manna and quails (11), the initiation of the seventy elders, the loss of faith of *Aaron and Miriam and the failure of the Israelites to invade *Canaan from the south (13–14). This is followed by particular regulations (15), the rebellion of Korah (16–17), the laws of the *Levites and the *red heifer, and *Balaam's mission to Balak (22–4), another census (26), other laws, and a tribal division of the *Promised Land. The book is traditionally believed to have been written by *Moses although scholars put it considerably later; source criticism assigns most of it to the priestly source P.

Numinous (derived by R. *Otto from Lat., *numen*, 'divinity'). The non-rational elements in what is experienced in religions as the 'Holy'. Experience of the numinous is of a *mysterium tremendum fascinans et augustum*. As *mysterium*, the *numen* is revealed as a 'wholly other'; here lies the source of the religious **via negativa*. The numen, although 'wholly other' is experienced as possessing a bipolar character. As *tremendum*, it generates boundless awe and wonder in the person who experiences it. As *fascinans*, it entrances and captivates the individual. It is of supreme subjective value for humans and possesses in itself objective value (*augustum*).

The effects of the experience of the numinous are the sense of the sacred, the consciousness of creatureliness, nothingness, sin, and guilt, the assurance of redemption and salvation. Such effects are permeated by the apprehension of a meaning and value that is uniquely and irreducibly religious. For Otto, the whole course of the history of religions is determined by an evolving apprehension of the fundamental elements of the numinous. It is therefore held to be the core of all religion.

Nun. A member of a religious order of women. The term is technically used of Christian women who belong to a religious order with solemn vows, but it is used more loosely in practice, and is applied at times to women in orders in other religions—e.g. to bhikṣunīs in Buddhism (see BHIKṢU; MONASTICISM).

Nunc Dimittis. The song of the old man Simeon (Luke 2. 29–32) who greeted the baby Jesus in the Temple. It begins 'Lord, now lettest thou thy servant depart in peace'; the name comes from the opening words in Latin.

Nuncio or **apostolic nuncio.** A representative (with status of ambassador) of the *pope, appointed initially to the countries which were signatories to the Convention of Vienna in 1815. He ia usually a titular archbishop.

Nūr (Arab.). Light, and especially *Allāh as the source of light: 'Allāh is the light of the heavens and of the earth. His light is like a niche in which there is a lamp . . . Allāh leads to his light whom he will . . .' (Qur'ān 24. 35). The cultivation of the vision of God through the contemplation of light became a widespread practice, particularly among *Sūfīs. Among philosophers, especially *al-Fārābī and *ibn Sīnā, nūr is the light bestowed by God through which God who is nūr can be discerned: 'In thy light I see light.' Thus nūr Muḥammad associates Muḥammad closely with God as the mediator of light, on the basis of 33. 45 (where Muḥammad is called *sirāj munīr*, 'a shining lamp') and 5. 15 which states, 'There came to you from God a light and a clear book'; and at least from the time of Muqatil (8th cent.) 24. 35 was applied to Muḥammad. Among the Sūfīs, the luminous, light-bestowing, nature of Muḥammad was increasingly extolled.

W. H. T. Gairdner, *Al-Ghazzali's Mishkāt al-Anwār* (1924), a tr. of 'The Niche of Lights', also tr. by R. Deladrière, *Le Tabernacle des Lumières* (1981); A. Schimmel, *And Muḥammad is His Messenger* (1985).

Nūrbakhshīy(y)a. Religious movement in Islam, named after its founder, Muḥammad b. Muḥammad b. 'Abd Allāh, who was known as Nūrbakhsh ('gift of light'), and who lived 1393–1465 (AH 795–869). He was proclaimed caliph (*khalīfa) and *al-Mahdī by his followers, and was (not surprisingly) persecuted by the Sultan Shāh-rukh. He maintained a *Sūfī understanding of the world as manifestation of God, and a *Shiʿite insistence on the necessity for the true *Imām to be a descendant of *ʿAlī.

Nūr Muḥammadī (Pers. abbr. of Arab., 'light of Muḥammad'). The essential nature of *Muḥammad which was created before the creation of the world, and is thus something akin to 'the pre-existent prophet'. For the Shiʿites, the belief lent itself to the continuing inspiration of the *Imāms, who share in the nature of the Prophet through the dispensation of his illumination. Among the Sunnis, it was more modestly interpreted as the nature of the *rasūl once called by God. The origins may perhaps be *Manichaean.

Nusaḥ or **nosaḥ** (Heb., 'arrangement'). Musical term in Jewish *liturgy. The term is used both in the sense of 'traditional tunes', and as signifying a particular musical mode.

Nuṣairī or **Alawī.** An extreme *Shī'a sect, strongly influenced by *Ismā'īlīs and Christianity. Mainly found in N. Lebanon, Syria, and S. Turkey, they number over a million, maintaining a tribe-like lineage system. The Nuṣairī believe that *'Alī is the supreme manifestation of God, that the *Qur'ān is an initiation to devotion to 'Alī, and that 'Alī, *Muḥammad, and *Salmān al-Farsī (identified with the archangel *Gabriel) are a trinity. Their tenets are mostly secret, for they practice an initiatory rite which lays importance on *ta'wīl (allegorical interpretation) of Qur'ān. The Nuṣairī employ *taqīya (dissimulation), but in most cases are renowned for their deep devotion to 'Alī and hatred of their adversaries. They have no *mosques, partake of wine during religious ceremonies, and exclude *women altogether from formal religion. They also believe in *tanāsukh (rebirth) of an elaborate kind. Since the 1980s the Nuṣairī have become powerful in Syrian politics. Hafez Assad, a Nuṣairī, rose to become leader of Syria over a *Sunnī majority.

Nyāntiloka (1878–1957). A German Buddhist scholar and translator. Born Walter Florus Gueth, he encountered Buddhism while travelling in Śri Lankā (Ceylon). He was ordained in Rangoon in 1910/11, but attempted to settle in Śri Lankā (where he was interned and expelled in both World Wars). Apart from editions and translations, his most influential works were a *Buddhist Dictionary*, *The Word of the Buddha*, and *Path to Deliverance*.

Nyāsa. The ritual placing of *mantras or letters on the body through touch and visualization, thereby making the body divine and filling it with power (*śakti). Although a non-*Vedic practice, *Ṛg Veda* mentions nyāsa with reference to fixing the mantras of the *Puruṣa sūkta onto the body, a theme taken up in the pre-*Tantric *Ṛgvidhāna*. But it is in the *Āgamas and *Tantras that nyāsa assumes a central role in ritual. After the symbolic destruction of the mundane body in the *bhūtaśuddhi ritual, the *sādhaka constructs a divine body by replacing his old one with that of his chosen deity (*iṣṭadevatā). Thus through the ritual homology of profane with sacred, human limitation is transcended.

Nyāya (Skt., argumentation, that by which the mind is led to a conclusion). Logical proof or demonstration, the third (in addition to *śruti and *smṛti) means of religious *knowledge in Hinduism. More particularly, Nyāya is one of the six philosophical systems (*darśana) of Hinduism, based on logical argument and analysis. It is therefore also known as Hetuvidyā (the knowledge of causes), Vādavidyā (the knowledge of ways of demonstration), Pramāṇaśastra (discipline of logic and epistemology), etc. Its founder is held to be Gautama (known also as Gotama and Akṣapāda) to whom is attributed the major work of the school, *Nyāya-Sūtra* (*c.*3rd cent. BCE; Eng. trs. G. Jha and S. C. Vidyabhusana); this is usually studied in conjunction with Vātsyāyana's commentary, *Nyāya-bhāṣya* (5th cent. CE), itself the subject of further commentaries by, e.g., Uddyotakara and Vācaspati. Also important are *Udayana's *Nyāya-Kusumāñjali* and Jayanta's *Nyāya-Mañjarī*. Nyāya extends and develops *Vaiśeṣika (producing the form Nyāya-Vaiśeṣika), which is classed as *samānatantra*, a similar philosophy. Both accept that life is burdensome and full of pain and suffering, and that the true goal is liberation (*mokṣa) which can only be gained through right understanding—hence the stress on valid argument and demonstration. But Nyāya extended these with great sophistication, producing sixteen categories within which all seven of Vaiśeṣika are subsumed in one (*prameya*, the knowable); and whereas Vaiśeṣika recognized two valid routes to true knowledge (*pramāṇa), perception and inference, Nyāya disentangles comparison and verbal authority from inference. The purpose remains unequivocally religious: logic serves to lead to truth and thus to mokṣa, since the major impediment is *avidyā (ignorance). In the 12th cent., Nyāya was developed further into Navyanyāya (New Logic), especially in the 14th-cent. *Tattvacintāmaṇi* of Gaṅgeśa. He reinforced the means of valid cognition (pramāṇa), resting on the four means of ascertaining truth: (i) *pratyakṣa*, sense perception; (ii) *anumāna*, inference, from cause to effect, from effect to cause and from common characteristics; (iii) *upamāna*, analogy; (iv) *śabda, verbal testimony from a reliable authority. Nyāya maintained a critique of Buddhism, and insisted especially on the legitimacy of its proofs for the existence of *Īśvara (personal deity). From the experience of contingency, diversity, change, activity, and individual existence, an unseen cause (*adṛṣta*) must be inferred, but from purposive arts and authority, that cause must have the character of personal agency.

S. C. Chatterjee, *The Nyaya Theory of Knowledge* (1965); S. C. Vidyabhusana, *A History of Indian Logic* (1920).

Nyingma (rnying.ma, 'ancient'). One of the four major schools of Tibetan Buddhism, so-called because its adherents trace their tradition to the first diffusion of Buddhism in Tibet, and particularly to the figure of *Padmasambhava, whom they consider their founder. The Nyingma have always been the least politically or philosophically inclined of all the schools, and in their practical orientation are held to be the closest to the *Bön tradition. This latter fact has been thought due to the days when Buddhism survived in Tibet by synthesis with the native culture, but we know little of the early nature of Bön, and that Bön today is more coloured by Nyingma than the other way around. The Nyingma identification with Padmasambhava also reveals the Indian *Siddha tradition as a primary influence.

The Nyingma are noted for their separate canon, consisting of *terma literature and the *Compendium of Old *Tantras* (rnying.ma'i.rgyud.'bum) which was preserved between the two diffusions (9th–11th cents.), and which was noticed by *Atiśa at Samyé to contain much material which by the 11th cent. had already become extinct in India. While the **Tibetan Book of the Dead* is the best known, the most important Nyingma text is the *Heart-Drop* (snying.thig); a terma text discovered in the 12th cent. by Zhangtön and commentated upon by Longchenpa, it contains teachings on Dzogchen (rdzogs.chen; 'Great Perfection'), the primary Nyingma system of meditation. It is sometimes considered that the Great Perfection, which teaches 'sudden enlightenment', resulted from the attempted introduction of Ch'an Buddhism from China in the 8th cent.; however the Nyingmas themselves attribute the *Heart-Drop* to the Indian master Vimalamitra, a companion of Padmasambhava.

Although they have influenced the Bön into adopting a similar classification, the Nyingma are unique amongst Buddhist schools in dividing their practices into nine 'vehicles' (*yānas*). The first three are the *Śrāvaka-, *Pratyekabuddha-, and *Bodhisattva- (i.e. practice of the Six Perfections) vehicles. The Kriyā-, Upāya-, and *Yoga-vehicles form the lower tantras, after which come the higher tantras of the Mahāyoga-, Anuyoga-, and Atiyoga- (which comprises Dzogchen) vehicles. Although it is desirable to progress gradually through these, there is a claim, unique in Tibetan Buddhism, that it is possible to obtain enlightenment through Dzogchen without having trained in the *Mahāyāna in this life; it is stressed however that this can only occur if the correct predispositions have been acquired in previous lives.

The Nyingma has produced several great scholars, such as Longchenpa (1308–63) and Mipham (d. 1912), who was influential in the 19th-cent. *Rimé movement. A recent supreme head of the order, Dujom Rinpoche (1904–87) was considered an incarnation of Dujom Lingpa. He founded two centres in France, and visited London, but Nyingma has not become extensively established in Europe. In the USA, there is a meditation centre in Berkeley, California. See Index, Nyingma.

Nyorai (Jap.; Skt., *tathāgata*). Synonym of *Buddha and one of his ten titles. The original Skt., *Tathāgata, can be analysed as 'coming' (*āgata*) from 'suchness' (*tathā*) or 'going' (*gata*) to 'suchness', suchness referring to truth or reality. Nyorai is the translation for the former, literally meaning 'coming from suchness', and, because of its dynamic connotation, it is preferred over its synonym, Buddha. Thus, in Japan people make reference to *Amida Nyorai, *Dainichi Nyorai, Shaka Nyorai, and so forth. Nyoraikyo is a Japanese *new religion, founded in 1802.

Nyūdō (home-living Buddhist under rule): see SHŌMU TENNŌ.

O

Oaths. A self-curse in Judaism which would be fulfilled if certain conditions were not met. Oath-taking was common in Ancient Israel over both serious and trivial matters (e.g. Judith 21. 1; 1 Samuel 14. 28; Genesis 21. 23; Joshua 9. 18). A false oath would be punished by God, 'who will not hold guiltless one who swears falsely by his name'. In *Talmudic law, oaths were used as a means of judicial proof in civil cases and could not be sworn by known liars, minors, the deaf and dumb, or the insane. Taking an oath involved holding the *Scroll of the Law and swearing by God or one of his attributes (*B.Shevu.* 38b). From the 14th cent., it became customary to 'swear in' witnesses, although some authorities maintained that if a witness cannot be believed without first swearing an oath, he cannot be believed at all. See also CURSING.

In Christianity, Matthew 5. 33–7 has been taken by some (e.g. *Baptists, *Mennonites, *Quakers, *Waldensians) to preclude any kind of oath-taking; but more generally it has been understood as a prohibition on swearing.

Obadiah, Book of. *Minor Prophet of the Hebrew scriptures and Christian Old Testament, the shortest book therein. Scholars disagree whether the book is a single prophetic speech. It includes five oracles of woe against Edom and announces salvation to *Zion: Edom would be punished for its support of Babylon in the siege of *Jerusalem of 587 (although some authorities date the book earlier). The final section, which is often regarded as a later appendix, contains the promise of the establishment of God's kingdom and the triumph of the Israelites. The rabbis identified Obadiah with King Ahab's servant (1 Kings 18. 3–4), but this is unlikely in view of the similarity between the oracles of Obadiah and those of *Jeremiah (see Obadiah 1–4, 5–6, 8, and Jeremiah 49. 14–16, 9–10, 7).

Ōbaku Kiun (Ch'an/Zen master): see HUANG-PO HSI-YÜN.

Ōbaku-shū (Jap. pronunciation of 'Huang-po', a religious mountain in China where the school originated + *shū*, 'tradition', 'school', or 'teachings'). One of the three major schools of Japanese Zen Buddhism originating in China. Unlike the more influential *Rinzai and *Sōtō schools brought to Japan from Sung China in the 13th cent., Ōbaku-shū was introduced in the 17th cent. by Yin-yüan (1592–1673, Ingen in Japanese) and reflects the syncretism between the Zen and *Pure Land *nembutsu traditions characteristic of Ming China. Although not popular religiously, Ōbaku-shū has influenced Japanese culture by introducing late Ming artistic forms.

Oberammergau (Passion play): see PASSION.

Ōbutsu myōgō (politics united with Buddhism): see NICHIREN SHŌSHŪ.

Occam/Ockham (Ockham's Razor): see WILLIAM OF OCKHAM.

Occasionalism. The view that God is the direct creator by way of cause of all occasions; or that God is the occasioning intermediary between soul and body. For the former, see CREATION (Islam). The latter arose because of the extreme disjunction in Cartesian dualism (*Descartes): if mind and body are *so* unlike, how can they interact? God as intermediary was proposed by Malebranche, Geulincx, Clauberg, and others: when the soul consents to an action, God moves the body, and when the body makes a demand of any sort, God makes the soul aware of it.

Occultation: see HIDDEN IMĀM.

Oceanic experience. The experience, usually brief and completely unexpected, of being at one with the entire universe, and of feeling a deep meaning and purpose to every part of existence. It is often accompanied by feelings of compassion and love for all beings. The experience is relatively common, and generally does not occur more than once or twice in a lifetime—though for a few people (e.g. the poet Lord Tennyson) it is recurrent. Since the experience does not carry with it any account of what has given rise to it, it is open to various interpretations, ranging from dismissal as an aberration in brain-behaviour to the foundation for the conversion of life. Some who remained sceptical about religious claims (e.g. Bertrand Russell) have not regarded the experience as evidential, and yet have regarded the experience as profound and unforgettable. Others have extended the experience through religious practice. For examples of all these, see J. W. Bowker, *Beyond Words: Religions and the Poetry of Presence* (1997). See also BIOGENETIC STRUCTURALISM.

Oceanic religion. The religion of the Pacific region. The term is imprecise, but at least draws attention to the fact that migration and trade have produced some common features in the life and culture of the Pacific region, the main part of which is water, in which is set a large number of widely scattered islands. The whole region was subdivided by explorers and colonizers into three major areas: Polynesia ('many islands', to the E., and including the Hawaiian Islands, Samoa, Tahiti, New Zealand, and at the furthest eastern extreme Easter Island); Micronesia ('small islands', to the NW, and including Palau, the Carolines, and Kiribati); and Melanesia ('black islands', SW, and including New Guinea, the Solomon Islands, and New Caledonia). Obviously, none of these areas has been sealed off in isolation, so that the distinctions are more or less artificial (thus Fiji is on the border of Polynesia and Melanesia, and exhibits characteristics of both). The study of the religions of the area now includes also the relation between these areas and the countries of the Pacific Rim and of the Pacific Basin. Generalizations about religion in so vast an area, with so many cultural variations, are impossible. G. W. Trompf observed of Melanesia: 'Melanesia has been revealed as the home of about one-third of mankind's languages, and that means—considering how languages are so crucial in defining discrete cultures—just as many religions' (*Melanesian Religion*, 1991; see also his *Payback: The Logic of Retribution in Melanesian Religions*, 1994). Nevertheless, the area has thrown up concepts which have been mediated via the *anthropology of religion into the study of religion in general: see e.g. MAGIC (for *mana*); TABOO.

P. Bellwood, *Man's Conquest of the Pacific: The Pre-history of Southeast Asia and Oceania* (1978) and *The Polynesians* (1978); P. Crawford, *Nomads of the Wind: A Natural History of Polynesia* (1993); A. C. Moore, *Arts in the Religions of the Pacific* (1995); R. Poignant, *Oceanic Mythology* (1967).

Ocean of breath (location of human life energy according to Chinese religion): see CH'I.

Ockham (Christian philosopher): see WILLIAM OF OCKHAM.

Octave. The period of eight days beginning with a Christian feast (i.e. until the same day of the next week), during which it may continue to be celebrated.

Odium theologicum (Lat., 'theological hatred'). Phrase drawing attention to ill-tempered passions to which theological argument frequently gives rise.

Oecumenical. Archaic spelling of *ecumenical, now used almost exclusively in the title of the Oecumenical *Patriarch of Constantinople. The distinction is valuable, as more conservative members of the *Orthodox churches consider all aspects of the ecumenical movement as unorthodox, or even heretical.

Offertory. In the Christian *eucharist the worshippers' offering of the bread and wine to be consecrated; also of gifts, especially of money. In E. rites the offertory takes place at the *prothesis outside the liturgy itself, the elements being brought to the altar at the *Great Entrance. In non-liturgical churches, 'offertory' refers to the collection of money made during the service while a hymn is sung.

Office, Divine (Lat., *Officium Divinum*). The daily prayers prescribed in liturgical churches in Christianity. In its modern form, the office contains some elements from the earliest morning and evening prayer in *cathedrals and parish churches, and other elements from the scheme of worship first devised among the early monks of Palestine, Egypt, and Gaul. All the fixed *hours of prayer consist of *psalms, hymns, lessons, *antiphons, responses and *versicles, and prayers.

In the W., the arrangement of the monastic office goes back to St *Benedict, who named it the 'work of God' (*opus Dei*): in his Rule the offices comprise the 'day hours' (*lauds, *prime, terce, sext, none, *vespers, and *compline) and the 'night office' (*mattins); the whole Psalter was recited each week. In the Middle Ages this office became obligatory for secular clergy as well. In the revised *Breviary of 1971 the offices, also called the 'Liturgy of the Hours', were reduced in number and now are: lauds (or morning prayer), vespers (or evening prayer), the *office of readings, prayer during the day, and *compline. Religious orders 'in choir' say the whole office every day, and lauds and vespers in particular are also prescribed for all priests. In *Anglican churches, the office consists of *morning and *evening prayer. Under the influence of the *ecumenical movement, some *Protestant churches have also produced service-books for daily worship along the lines of the office, of which the Anglican (*Franciscan-based) *Celebrating Common Prayer* (1992) is a notable and widely used example.

In the E., there is a similar sequence of hours to that of the W., of which the most familiar is Orthros (lauds). The whole office is of great length, and is abbreviated by all except monks in choir.

Office of Readings. An *office prescribed for Roman Catholics which may be said at any hour of the day. It includes two readings, one from the Bible and a second from the *fathers or from some other Christian writing. It replaced *mattins in the 1971 revision of the *Breviary.

Ofurikae (transference of affliction): see MIKI TOKUHARU.

Ogyū Sorai (1666–1728). Japanese Confucian scholar who laid, indirectly, the foundations for the School of National Learning (*Kokugaku). When 25, he started to give free lectures in Edo, in front of the temple of Zōjō-jī. These drew increasingly wide attention, eventually leading to the Shogun commending him and thus securing his position—necessary, because of his critical attitudes to *neo-Confucianism. *Itō Jinsai (1627–1705) had already argued for a return to the classic Confucian sources, in a school known as *Kogidō*, 'School for the Study of Ancient Meaning'. Ogyū followed him at first, but concluded that Itō had not gone far enough in making his study of the past serve the needs of society: he was right in criticizing the neo-Confucians, but he had remained, like them, too concerned with individual ethics and self-improvement. In his view, *Hsun Tzu was a better guide, because his realism about the intrinsic evil in human nature pointed to the need for strong social institutions: rites and political institutions are indispensable. It was precisely the political institution, the Shogunate, which protected him from the opposition of the neo-Confucianists, who saw his position as a betrayal of the human responsibility to cultivate a better life for oneself. By appealing to the proper study of antiquity in order to contradict them, Ogyū had a profound effect, because it was realized by his pupils that the antiquity of Japan could equally be studied and established as a court of appeal against the domination of Chinese thought.

O. G. Lindin, *The Life of Ogyū Sorai* . . . (1973); J. R. MacEwan, *The Political Writings of Ogyū Sorai* (1962); Yoshikawa Kojiro, *Jinsai, Sorai, Norinaga* . . . (tr. Kikuchi Yuji, 1983).

Ōjo (Jap., 'birth'). Rebirth, especially in the *Pure Land of *Amida, but found also in many combinations, for example, ōjo-ko, a prayer-meeting for the practice of *nembutsu, with a view to attaining rebirth in Amida's Pure Land; ōjo-nin, one who has been thus reborn; ōjo-no-gō, an act leading to such rebirth.

Ōjōyōshū. A collection of scriptural quotations outlining religious practices that lead to birth in *Pure Land. It was compiled in 985 by the Japanese Buddhist priest *Genshin (942–1017) of the *Tendai school. The primary practice that he advocated was the *nembutsu (invoking the name of the Buddha *Amida). Genshin considered the nembutsu best used in conjunction with meditation on Amida and his Pure Land, but for believers untrained in meditative techniques he recommended simple chanting of the name. The *Ōjōyōshū* made a strong impression on Pure Land Buddhists because of its graphic descriptions of the splendours of Pure Land and the terrors of hells. It became popular as a religious handbook on ways of performing the nembutsu, including a deathbed ceremony involving nembutsu chanting and meditation. See also EMAKI.

Tr. A. K. Reischauer, *Trans. Asiatic Soc. of Jap.* 7 (1930), 16–98; see also A. A. Andrews, *The Teachings Essential for Rebirth* (1973).

Okada Mokichi (founder of a Japanese religion): see SEKAI KYŪSEIKYŌ.

Oker Harim (uprooter of mountains): see RABBAH BAR NAḤMĀNĪ.

Ōkuninushi no Mikoto (Jap., 'great lord of the land'). An important *Shinto *kami. Originally a major local kami of Izumo Province (now Shimane Prefecture), he was incorporated into the national Shinto mythology by the time of the compilation of **Kojiki* (712), in which he plays a prominent part. Said to be either the son of Susanoo no Mikoto or a sixth-generation descendant of Susanoo, he is portrayed as a heroic, benevolent, and civilizing kami who carries through his noble tasks in spite of adversity. After he demonstrated kindness to a hare tormented by his brothers, he was persecuted by them but was saved through divine intervention. He was designated the possessor of the *utsushi-yo* ('actual world'), and he punished evil spirits, developed the land, cured illnesses, and removed disasters caused by birds and insects. Later he presented the land to the emissaries of *Amaterasu Omikami, the sun kami and divine imperial ancestress. The *Izumo no Kuni fudoki* (Gazetteer of Izumo Province, 733) shows that he was viewed in Izumo as the creator of the world and as an agricultural kami. The chief shrine to Ōkuninushi is the Izumo Taisha in Taisha-machi, Shimane Prefecture, one of the oldest shrines in Japan.

'Olam ha-Ba (Heb., 'the coming world'). In Judaism, the hereafter, in contrast to *'olam ha-zeh*, 'this world'. According to R. Jacob, 'One moment of repentance and good deeds in this world is better than the entire life of the world to come' (Avot 4. 7). 'Olam ha-ba is to be distinguished from the days of the *messiah which will precede it. The hereafter will begin with a general *resurrection of the dead and the final judgement. The righteous will receive their full reward and 'enjoy the effulgence of the divine presence' (*B.Ber.* 17a). The 'pious of the nations' will also have a portion in the world to come. See also AFTERLIFE.

Olcott, Henry Steel (co-founder of Theosophical Society): see THEOSOPHICAL SOCIETY.

Old Believers. Dissident groups of Russian Orthodox Christians. Because they have been in *schism (*raskol*) since 1666, they are known also as Raskolniki. The schism began when Nikon, patriarch of Moscow, introduced reforms of ritual (e.g. blessing with three fingers, not two) which were practised among Orthodox elsewhere, but which the Council of 1551 had declared heretical. Those who adhered to the older rites called themselves *staroveri*, misrendered Old Believers. Their leader, *Avvakum, had already been in exile. He returned on the death of Nikon in 1664, but was soon in exile again. The Old Believers were fiercely pursued and persecuted, finding refuge only in remote parts. This persecution was interpreted by them as the work of *Antichrist. The persecution was alleviated under Peter III and Catherine II, but was renewed under Nicholas I (1825–55). Penal laws remained in force until 1903. Under such continuing pressure, there were several divisions, but two main groups: the *popovtsy* (those with priests) and the *pezpopovtsy* (those without priests who resorted to less formal organization).

R. O. Crummey, *The Old Believers and the World of Antichrist* (1970).

Old Catholics. Christians who adhere (according to the declaration of their *bishops in 1889) to the *Vincentian Canon, not in order to resist all change, but in order to guard against unwarranted innovation. The roots of the separation of Old Catholic Churches go back to the post-Reformation debates in the Netherlands: the *Jansenist Church of Utrecht retained the *apostolic succession after its separation from Rome in 1724 and was later able to supply valid consecration of bishops. The major breach occurred as a consequence of the *Vatican I proclamation of papal *infallibility. Protest arose within *Roman Catholicism especially in Germany, Switzerland, Bohemia, and Moravia. In 1889, the newly called Old Catholic Churches united in the Union of Utrecht. Later accessions include the Polish National Catholic Church of the USA and Canada, and the Polish Catholic Church (in Poland). *Ecumenical contacts have led to intercommunion with the *Anglican Church, established by the Bonn agreement in 1931 (becoming full communion in 1958). Old Catholics recognize the seven ecumenical *Councils and the teachings of the undivided Church before the *Great Schism of 1054. Clergy may be married, and women have been admitted to the diaconate (i.e. have been made *deacons); in 1996, the first moves to the ordination of women as priests were made.

C. B. Moss, *The Old Catholic Movement* . . . (1948).

Old Man of the Mountain (name for ruler of Syrian sect): see ASSASSINS.

Old Testament. Christian name for the Jewish scriptures (see TANACH) which form the first part of the *Bible. In Roman Catholic usage the *deuterocanonical books are included.

Olympian religion: see CHTHONIAN RELIGION.

Oṃ or **Auṃ.** The most sacred syllable in Hinduism, which first appears in the *Upaniṣads. It is often regarded as the *bija (seed) of all *mantras, containing, as it does, all origination and dissolution. It is known as *praṇava* ('reverberation'), and it is the supreme *akṣara* (syllable). Although it is made up of three (pointing to *Brahma, *Viṣṇu, and *Śiva) connected but distinct elements (as sounded), the silence at its conclusion is regarded as a fourth, expressing the attainment of *Brahman/ātman: see *Māṇḍūkya Upaniṣad*, which is devoted to Oṃ. See also ŚABDA.

OM.AH.HUM (Buddhist chant): see ĀDI BUDDHA.

O-mamori (Jap., *o* (honorific) + 'protection'). A Japanese amulet (*charms). The o-mamori is an object, often a small placard, emblem, or card in a talismanic case, obtained from shrines and temples for protection from evil and misfortune. These amulets are worn on the person or affixed to vehicles or buildings, and by virtue of the sacred power of their source afford safety and prosperity to the believer.

Omar Khayyam. Anglicized version of ʿUmar al-Khayyām (1048–1125 (AH 439–c.519)). Muslim mathematician and astronomer who made important contributions to the development of algebra, but who is perhaps best known as a poet. He composed four-line verses (i.e. *rubāʿiyyāt*, 'quatrains') which became known through the Eng. version of Edward Fitzgerald as *The Rubaiyat of Omar Khayyam*. Yet very little of what ʿUmar wrote has in any case survived (though much is attributed to him); and Fitzgerald does not appear to have realized that the terms of the original verses are *Sūfī. Thus 'wine', far from being the one compensation which God has allowed in a hard world, is a common symbol of the recollection (*dhikr) of God (the most spectacular example is *al-Khamriyya*, the Wine Ode of the Sūfī, Ibn al-Fāriḍ, 'We drank in, so deeply, the remembrance of the Beloved that we were drunk indeed—before the vine was even created'); the tavern (*khanaqah*) is the assembly place of *derwishes. Fitzgerald claimed to have taken the poem at face value, and his version of 'eat, drink, and be merry' seems to be exactly that, not least because it brings God into judgement: 'Oh, Thou who man of baser Earth didst make, | And who with Eden didst devise the snake: | For all the Sin wherewith the face of Man | Is blacken'd, Man's Forgiveness give—and take!' But this is far removed from the philosophy of ʿUmar al-khayyām.

Omega point: see TEILHARD DE CHARDIN; PROCESS THEOLOGY.

O-mei, Mount: see SAMANTABHADRA.

Omer (Heb., 'sheaf'). An offering brought to the *Temple on 16 Nisan in the Jewish religion. By extension 'Omer' became the name of the period between *Passover and *Shavuʿot. The *rabbis defined the omer as one-tenth of an ephah of barley. On 16 Nisan, the ephah was reaped and the omer was waved by the priest (*Men.* 10. 1) and burnt on the altar. The ceremony was intended as a prayer for a safe harvest. Forty-nine days were then counted from the presentation of the omer, and it was common practice to have an omer calendar in the house to aid the counting. Traditionally the days of the omer are ones of semi-mourning which is associated with a plague that struck the disciples of R. *Akiva (*B.Yev.* 62b). *Lag Ba-Omer is celebrated on the thirty-third day, but the origins of this minor festival are obscure.

O-mi-t'o (Chin. for Amitābha): see AMIDA.

Oṃ maṇi padme hum (Tib. pron.: *Om maṇi pehme hung*). The *mantra of *Avalokiteśvara (Tib.,

Chenrezig). In spite of being the most well-known and commonly recited mantra of Tibet, where it is to be found inscribed everywhere, from homes to mountain passes and roadside rocks, it has been greatly misunderstood. Usual translations, such as 'Oh, the jewel is in the lotus' or 'hail to the jewel in the lotus', are misconceived. *Oṃ and hum are invocation syllables which require no translation; *maṇi ('jewel') is not a word but a stem, and therefore joins *padme* ('lotus') to make a single word, *maṇipadme* ('jewel-lotus') which is feminine and locative. This suggests a female deity being invoked, called Maṇipadmā, the problem being that no such deity is recorded anywhere. Bharati (1965), however, noting that the *Tantric consorts of Buddhas often have the same name as their respective Buddha in feminine form, is happy to accept Maṇipadmā as the consort of Buddha Maṇipadmā Lokeśvara, or as the feminine form of this Buddha himself. In spite of this logical rationale, it still remains to be explained how *om maṇi padme hum* managed to become so ubiquitous when no text mentioning Maṇipadmā can be found, and indeed how it became attributed to Avalokiteśvara. The usual translations may have no linguistic accuracy but they do closely express through the separation of the words jewel (male, form) and lotus (female, emptiness) a sense of the symbolism of opposites at the heart of manifestation in *Mahāyāna Buddhism; the explanation is then advanced that between the two 'seed syllables' the enlightenment consciousness (*bodhicitta) arises within the lotus of ordinary (but trained) consciousness; but this is clearly a paraphrase at best. The possibility of the present form of the mantra being a corruption of its original Sanskrit cannot be dismissed.

Omnipotence. A characteristic of God in all theistic religions. It is especially prominent in Islam, where the power of God cannot be frustrated and where everything that is or that happens can only be or do so because he wills it. This led to fierce debates in early Islam about the accountability of humans if their free will is not genuine (see QADAR; ALLĀH). In Jewish and Christian scripture, omnipotence is implied, rather than asserted as a doctrine. Thus the Bible describes God as able to do all things (e.g. in Job 42. 2; Jeremiah 32. 17, 27), a characteristic which is to be connected both to his being creator and to his being an adequate object of worship, for this power ensures that God's wisdom, love, and good purposes are not thwarted. Theologians have introduced some qualifications in their attempts to define the extent of God's power: nearly all would rule out God's being able to do something self-contradictory, whilst many would say that God not only does not but also *cannot* do evil. God's omnipotence does not preclude his limiting or abdicating from his power on occasion: *kenotic christologies see the incarnation as such a self-emptying of divine power (cf. Philippians 2. 6–8). Similarly, one common argument in *theodicy (the 'Free Will Defence') contends that in making free creatures, God voluntarily relinquished his control over them, even to the extent of permitting evil. The so-called 'paradoxes of omnipotence' concern whether God can make a stone so heavy that he cannot lift it, can make a creature which he cannot subsequently control, and so on.

Ōmoto-kyō or **Omoto** (Teaching of the Great Origin and/or Foundation). A Japanese 'new religion'. The group traces its history from 1892 when its foundress, *Deguchi Nao (1837–1918), was possessed by the folk deity Ushitora-no-Konjin. Through this and later experiences of *kamigakari, she articulated a radical *millennarian world-view centred on this god. Following the failure of her *eschatological prophecies in 1905, her cult was reorganized by her son-in-law and co-founder, Deguchi Onisaburō (1871–1948). Onisaburō rejected Nao's more radical teachings in favour of his own nationalistic Shinto doctrines, modernization theories, and spiritualistic practices. The group expanded rapidly, attracting a large national membership, but Onisaburō's increasing popularity eventually incurred government persecution. In the early 1920s and again in the 1930s, the group's facilities were destroyed and its activities suppressed. In 1935, Onisaburō was imprisoned on charges of *lèse majesté* and not released until 1942. Ōmoto-kyō has never recaptured its pre-war prominence. After Onisaburō's death in 1948, his wife, Sumi, re-established the group on a much smaller scale. Under her leadership, and later that of her children and grandchildren, the focus of Ōmoto-kyō doctrine and practice was consciously shifted from the political to the cultural sphere. Today, the group maintains headquarters at Kameoka and Ayabe in W. Kyoto prefecture and claims a national membership of 163,000. Ōmoto-kyō ordains its own priests and performs rituals in the Shinto manner; however, the group also conducts funerals and encourages ancestor worship. Special emphasis is placed on the practice of various traditional Japanese art-forms as a source of religious understanding and a means to spiritual purity. Although non-proselytizing, Ōmoto-kyō supports charitable activities abroad and participates in the international ecumenical and peace movements.

H. Iwao (ed.), *The Outline of Oomoto* (1970).

Oṃ tat sat (Skt., 'Oṃ That Being'). Hindu sacred formula (*mantra) often uttered at the beginning and the conclusion of prayers, or the recitation of a passage from the *Vedas and other religious literature. The sacred syllable Oṃ, by itself originally an auspicious particle implying consent, is regarded in the *Upanisadic and later Hindu thought as a manifestation in sound of Ultimate Reality (*Brahman) or of the Lord (*īśvara). *Tat* and *sat* in this context both signify Brahman. Since the Skt. 'o' is made up of the contraction of 'a' and 'u', the sacred syllable is also written Aum.

Onanism. Coitus interruptus, unnatural sexual intercourse or masturbation. In the Jewish tradition, onanism is associated with the biblical figure Onan who was condemned by God for spilling his seed 'on the ground' (Genesis 38. 7–10). Many rabbinic authorities regard Onan's sin as a special case—that the whole purpose of his marriage to his brother's widow was to produce children—and that in some instances, sexual relations with no reproductive consequences are permissible. However, most *responsa recommend contraception only for medical reasons and, if possible, only methods (such as the contraceptive pill) which are not onanistic.

D. M. Feldman, *Birth Control in Jewish Law* (1968).

Once-returner (Buddhist close to enlightenment): see SAKADĀGĀMIN.

One hand clapping: see HAKUIN.

One-pointedness (of mind): see EKĀGRATA.

One word barriers (single-word answers): see YÜN-MEN WEN-YEN.

Onias. Four Jewish *high priests of the second *Temple period. Onias I (4th cent. BCE) is mentioned in 1 *Maccabees* 12. 20–3; Onias II (late 3rd cent. BCE) was involved in the war between Ptolemy III and Queen Leodice; Onias III (2nd cent. BCE) was deposed by Antiochus IV; and Onias IV, son of Onias III, erected a temple in *Leontopolis.

Onkelos. Translator of the Hebrew *Bible into *Aramaic. Onkelos was a *proselyte to Judaism. He had a close relationship with R. *Gamaliel and was regarded as even more assiduous in keeping the law. He is often associated with Aquila who translated the Bible into Greek and it may be that the legends refer to the same person. According to the Babylonian Talmud, Onkelos did his translation under the guidance of R. *Eliezer and R. Joshua, but the parallel passage in the Jerusalem Talmud refers to Aquila and the Greek translation. Onkelos stays close to the Hebrew text, but its choice of words etc., shows that it is related to the Palestinian targum tradition with its incorporation of exegesis: see J. W. Bowker, *The Targums and Rabbinic Literature* (2nd edn., 1979).

Onmyō-ji (yin-yang masters): see KOSHIN.

Ontic theories: see ONTOLOGY.

Ontological argument. An argument for God's existence, first formulated by *Anselm (1033–1109) in his *Proslogion*, chs. 2–3. Anselm argued that since anyone can think of 'a being than which no greater can be conceived', such a being must exist at least in the understanding; but if it existed only in the understanding, we could conceive of an even greater being, namely one existing both in the understanding and in reality; therefore, the being than which no greater can be conceived must exist both in the understanding and in reality. In ch. 3 he went on to argue that this being must exist necessarily.

This argument was criticized by St Thomas *Aquinas, but further versions were put forward by *Descartes, *Spinoza, and *Leibniz. *Kant objected that existence is not a real predicate, and that the concept of necessary existence is illegitimate since all existential judgements are synthetic (*Critique of Pure Reason*, 1781). Despite these objections, the argument was defended by *Hegel and, more recently by C. *Hartshorne (e.g. in *Anselm's Discovery*, 1965); whilst N. Malcolm claims that the argument in *Proslogion*, ch. 3 is immune to Kant's critique (*Philosophical Review*, 1960).

Ontology (Gk., *ōn*, 'being', + *logos*, 'reflection'). Reflection in philosophy and metaphysics on what truly exists, or on what underlies appearance by way of existent reality. The issue of ontology was robustly summarized by W. V. O. Quine in a paper 'On What There Is' (in *From a Logical Point of View*, 1961):

> A curious thing about the ontological problem is its simplicity. It can be put in three Anglo-Saxon monosyllables: 'What is there?' It can be answered, moreover, in a word—'Everything'—and everyone will accept this answer as true. However, this is merely to say that there is what there is. There remains room for disagreement over cases; and so the issue has stayed alive down the centuries.

The issues are clearly important for religious since religions claims include claims to the existent reality of such putative realities as ghosts and gods, buddhas and bodhisattvas, souls and saviours; whether claims to the true reality of God fall into that category depends on a concursive debate about whether existence can be predicated of God. But even the scope of ontological reflection is debated. The term was introduced in the 17th cent., when the study of being as being was also called *ontosophia*. In the continuity of *scholasticism, ontology was the term applied to the study of the properties of being as such, in contrast to special metaphysics which studied aspects of being open to experience. In *phenomenology, the question of existence is initially 'bracketed out': all that we can be sure of are *cogitationes*, appearances in consciousness. However, Husserl was prepared to return those degrees of ontological reality which appearances in consciousness allow or require one to infer (in order to account for the appearances having the consistency which they do). He therefore allowed 'regional ontologies' in the characteristic areas of human discourse (e.g. natural sciences, mathematics, common sense—and, at the end of his life, theology), calling them also 'material ontologies'; formal ontology then deals with essences which are the ultimate basis of science. Quine himself made a distinction between *ideology and ontology, and between meaning and reference: he argued that what one takes to be existing depends on the values required or allowed by the variables of the language in use, so that there is a necessary relation between language and ontic commitments—hence his claim that 'to be is to be the value of a variable'. While this might seem to allow virtually any belief to have an ontological correspondent, in fact metaphysical systems (which he called 'ontic theories') are tested by their compatibility with science which interacts publicly (and by various other criteria) with the world and universe around us. It then becomes obvious that ontology is intricately related to epistemology (roughly, how do we know what we know?).

Ontologism was a system of philosophy which, applied to theology, claimed that humans know God immediately and directly through natural cognitive abilities: the first act of human cognitive powers is the intuition of God. It was condemned (on the grounds that our knowledge of God can only be *analogical) in 1861 and again by *Vatican I.

Ontosophia: see ONTOLOGY.

Oomoto (Japanese new religion): see ŌMOTO-KYŌ.

Ophites (Gk., *ophis*, 'serpent'). A group of *gnostic sects. According to them the wise serpent (Genesis 3. 14 f.) symbolized a higher god, who acts to liberate humanity and give illumination. The sinuous form may have been taken as a mark and source of the cyclic nature of the universe. Some sects worshipped the serpent, regarding the *fall as God's denying of promised wisdom. They were also known as Naasenes.

Oppenheimer, Samuel: see COURT JEWS.

Option for Options: see SECULARIZATION.

Option for the Poor: see LIBERATION THEOLOGY.

Opus Dei (Lat., 'work of God'). Either the divine *office, especially as sung in choir; or (and now more commonly) a *Roman Catholic religious association founded in Madrid in 1928 by José Maria Escrivá de Balaguer, known more fully as the Priestly Society of the Holy Cross and the Work of God. Its status since 1982 has been that of a personal prelature, its superior exercising over members a similar authority to that of a *bishop, though not on a territorial basis. Some 1,000 of its 70,000 members are priests, and it has houses in over eighty countries. The spiritual formation of members is based upon the speeches and writings of its founder, especially his collection of 999 maxims, *The Way*. There are several levels of membership, the highest being that of *numerarii*, who take the equivalent of permanent vows and live in communities. Married members living at home are called *supernumerarii*. Its main purpose is to foster a life of prayer, sacrifice, humility and *asceticism *in medio mundo*, 'in the midst of the world', and to mediate into the world a Christian (i.e. RC) perspective. It has evoked criticism of its authoritarian style and control. Its founder was declared blessed by Pope John Paul II in 1992, despite widespread criticism in the Church of the style and speed with which this was done.

G. Rocca, *L' 'Opus Dei': Appunti e documenti per una storia* (1985).

Oracle bones. Usually the scapula and split leg bones of cattle which the Chinese of the Shang dynasty used for divination purposes. Priests wrote out on the bones questions which the king or aristocrats wished to have put to the gods. This is but the oldest of several methods of divination which the Chinese have employed; possibly as old is divination using *tortoise shells, while the casting of the yarrow stalks in conjunction with the **I Ching* (Book of Changes) has been known from the late Chou period. The oracle bones, once used, clearly retained a sacred aura both for the ancient Shang people who carefully preserved them, and for later Chinese who, thinking them to be dragon bones, used them in powdered form as a medicine. To scholars, the hundreds of bones uncovered so far constitute an antiquarian treasure: they are by far the oldest examples of the Chinese writing system and furnish the only reliable information on the religion and social culture of the first Chinese *dynasty known to archaeology. The written questions were of a type which could be answered by a simple 'yes' or 'no' (or 'auspicious' or 'inauspicious'); these words were scattered about the bone's surface, which was then heated to induce cracking. The cracks passing through or near a 'yes' or a 'no' indicated the answer. Questions indicated anxiety and curiosity about success in hunting and war, the abundance of crops, the adequacy of rainfall, as well as auspicious days for ceremonies, the advisability of marriage, etc. A number of gods are mentioned, most notably the high god *Shang-ti and the gods of wind and of millet, of various heavenly bodies, of mountains and rivers. But the most important personages questioned in the Shang oracle bones were the *ancestors, for they were powerful spiritual forces capable of granting favours or inflicting punishments. Many questions asked whether or not the ancestral rites as performed had been satisfactory, and the divination itself apparently took place in the ancestral temples.

Oral law (Heb., *torah she-be'al-peh*). The (in origin) orally transmitted interpretation of the Jewish written *law. According to the *rabbis, there are two parts of *Torah 'one written and one oral' (*ARN* 15. 61). Traditionally both Torahs were given to *Moses on Mount *Sinai. During the second *Temple period, the oral law was upheld by the *Ḥakhamim (sages) against the *Sadducees who rejected it. The sages maintained that 'the Holy One made a *covenant with *Israel only for the sake of that transmitted orally' (*B.Git.* 60b), and it is through the oral law that the written law was preserved, invested with authority and explained anew to each generation. It also had the advantage of being Israel's 'mystery'—that which outsiders could not get hold of for themselves, as Christians had appropriated scripture and interpreted it for their own purposes (see J. W. Bowker, *The Targums and Rabbinic Literature*). It was studied in the *academies and eventually collected together and written down by *Judah ha-Nasi in the 2nd cent. CE (see MISHNAH). Subsequently, commentary and interpretation of the Mishnah were recorded in the *Talmud (6th cent.). After the redaction of the Talmud, it remained the main object of study in the *yeshivot (rabbinic schools). During the *geonic period, the *Karaites rejected the authority of the oral law and interpreted the written Torah by their own standards. In the modern era, the *Progressive movements have largely rejected the belief in the divine origin of Jewish law and are therefore ready to disregard any *halakhic provisions which conflict with modern secular values.

B. Martin (ed.), *Contemporary Jewish Thought* (1968).

Oral tradition (in Islam): see ḤADĪTH.

Orangemen. Members of the *Protestant fraternal Orange Order, prominent in N. Ireland, concerned to defend Protestant ascendancy. The order was founded in 1795, named from William III, William of Orange. (Orange is a town on the river Rhône, once capital of a small principality from which William's ancestors took their name.) The marches of the Orangemen in N. Ireland are a public manifestation of what the *Roman Catholic population perceives as a determination of at least some Protestants to remain dominant and a part of the United Kingdom.

Orange People (Indian-based religious movement): see RAJNEESH, BHAGWAN SHREE.

Orange/saffron robes: see MONASTICISM (Buddhist).

Oratorio. The setting of a religious (usually Christian) text to music; the setting is extensive, with soloists, chorus, and instruments. It is not, however, like opera, in that it is not staged or acted out. Oratorio developed gradually, receiving particular emphasis from the dramatic services of St Philip Neri (d. 1595) at the Oratory in Rome. It was cultivated especially in the 17th–18th cents. English oratorio was the creation of G. F. Handel, with works such as *Saul* (1738), *Israel in Egypt* (1739), *Samson* (1741), and *Messiah* (1742). English choral festivals have maintained the popularity of oratorios and have produced new and sometimes secularized works (e.g. M. Tippett, *A Child of Our Time*, 1939–41).

Oratory, Oratorians (Lat., *oratorium*, 'place of prayer'). *Roman Catholic place of worship other than a parish church, and the name of those belonging to a community based on an Oratory. From the oratory of S. Girolamo in Rome came the Oratory of St Philip Neri, a community of priests whose constitution was ratified by Pope Paul V in 1612. Oratories spread rapidly: they are congregations of secular priests living in community without vows, the more wealthy, therefore, being expected to support themselves. Each Oratory is independent (there is no central organization, though there is a Visitor), with the aim of developing powerful liturgy (hence *oratorio) and converting through prayer and preaching. J. H. *Newman founded the Birmingham Oratory in 1848; tensions with F. W. Faber led to a split and to the establishing of the London (Brompton) Oratory. The French Oratory was founded by P. de Bérulle in 1611, called Oratoire de Jésus-Christ from 1613. It has a central organization.

Order of Ethiopia. A semi-independent, mainly Xhosa, section within the *Anglican Church in S. Africa. James M. Dwane (1851–1916), an ordained *Methodist minister, seceded in 1894 to the Ethiopian Church (see ETHIOPIANISM) and drew this Church into the orbit of the black African Methodist Episcopal Church in the USA, through which he became ordained as 'vicar-bishop'. This uncertain status led him and many of the Ethiopian members to become the Order of Ethiopia within the Anglican Church in 1900, in the hope of his becoming a *bishop within the *apostolic succession. He was ordained deacon in 1900 and priest in 1909. The Order retained a peculiar extra-parochial position, with its own synod and finance, and a provincial, but no bishop. Periodic negotiations failed to find a solution until 1983, when Siggibo Dwana, principal of an Anglican theological college, was consecrated as bishop, and he and the Order, now with some 50,000 members, have full diocesan rights within the Church.

Order of the Cross. A religious movement or fellowship founded in England in 1904 by J. Todd Ferrier. The movement proclaims 'the brotherhood of man', the essential unity of all religious quests and the unity of all living beings in the divine. It opposes anything which it sees as violating the teachings of 'the Christ', and (above all) anything that involves the shedding of *blood; hence the adoption of a bloodless diet and the opposition to blood sports. The movement has spread from the United Kingdom to France, North America, Australia, New Zealand, and elsewhere.

Orders. The various grades of Christian ministers. In the W. Church until 1972 these were *bishop, *priest, *deacon, *subdeacon, *acolyte, exorcist, reader, and doorkeeper (though sometimes 'bishop' was not considered a distinct order from 'priest'). Those of bishop, priest, deacon, and (since the 13th cent.) subdeacon, were the 'major orders', or 'holy orders', the others being the 'minor orders'. The

Anglican Church ordains only bishops, priests, and deacons.

In 1972 the Roman Catholic orders of subdeacon, exorcist, and doorkeeper were suppressed; the other two minor orders which had formerly been nominal steps to the priesthood, were called 'ministeria' and allowed to be conferred on laymen. In most E. churches the major orders are bishop, priest, and deacon, and the minor orders subdeacon and reader. (Other titles like *chorepiscopus and *archpriest are not usually considered separate orders.)

In traditional Catholic theology the gift of order is a *sacrament which imparts an indelible character. Hence a clergyman once ordained cannot lose the gift or be reordained. But where there is doubt about the validity of an ordination it may be repeated 'conditionally'. W. churches, following *Augustine, hold that even a *schismatic or *heretical bishop may validly ordain; hence e.g. an Orthodox priest is not reordained if he becomes a Catholic. However, since the *bull *Apostolicae Curae* (1896) of Pope Leo XIII the RC Church has not recognized the validity of *Anglican orders. See also ORDINATION.

Ordinal (Lat., *ordinale*). Originally a Christian manual giving details of the variations in the *office according to changes in the ecclesiastical year. From the 17th cent., the Ordinal in the Church of England has been 'The Form and Manner of Making, Ordaining and Consecrating of Bishops, Priests and Deacons' (*Book of Common Prayer), whose content forms part of the doctrine of that Church.

Ordinary. In *canon law, an ecclesiastic having the spiritual jurisdiction over a particular area as part of his office. Thus the ordinary of a diocese is the *bishop, etc.

Ordinary of the Mass (Lat., *ordo missae*). The (almost) invariable parts of the *mass, comprising the preparatory prayers, *Kyrie, *Gloria and *Creed, the *Preface and *Sanctus, the *canon, *Lord's Prayer, *fraction and *Agnus Dei, and part of the communion and post-communion devotions. It is distinguished from the *proper.

Ordination. The conferral of office in a formal, often ritualized manner. For Judaism, see SEMIKHAH. Among Christians, in Catholic and Orthodox practice, priests and deacons are ordained by a bishop, acting as minister of Christ and successor of the apostles (for the doctrine see APOSTOLIC SUCCESSION). A bishop is ordained (or 'consecrated') by his *metropolitan and two other bishops. The ordination service usually takes place within a *eucharist, with a central act of the laying on of hands on the candidates. Symbols of office, e.g. a Bible or a New Testament for priests, a mitre, ring and staff for bishops, may be presented.

In Protestant churches ordination is generally conceived as an appointment by the church to carry out the functions of celebrating the Lord's Supper and preaching, rather than as a sacramental gift. Somewhat various ideas are displayed in Baptist practice, for example, where an ordinand is examined by an association of churches, but actually ordained by a local congregation to be its pastor.

The term 'ordination' has then been applied to the formal and ritualized admission procedures in other religions, especially of the admission of women and men to the Buddhist *saṅgha, whereby they become 'nuns' (*bhikṣunī) and 'monks' (*bhikṣu/bhikkhus). Such terms are inevitable in translation, but they are misleading if they obscure differences—e.g. Buddhist 'ordination' is not necessarily for life. See also HASSU.

Oriental Orthodox Churches. The *Syrian, *Coptic, *Ethiopian and *Armenian Orthodox churches. They have in common their historic rejection of the Council of *Chalcedon and its *christology of two natures in Christ. They are therefore sometimes called the 'non-Chalcedonian' Churches (although properly this term includes the *Church of the East also) or the *monophysite churches (though the term is sometimes considered misleading). They should not be confused with the ('Eastern') *Orthodox churches, which are Chalcedonian. Since the 1960s the Oriental Orthodox have held conferences together, and, aiming at theological reconciliation, with the Orthodox and *Roman Catholic Churches.

Oriental Rite Catholics: see EASTERN RITE CATHOLICS.

Origen (*c*.185–*c*.254). Christian scholar and theologian. He was brought up in Egypt by Christian parents, and became head of the catechetical school in Alexandria after *Clement. He led a strictly ascetical life and even (according to *Eusebius, and on the basis of Matthew 19. 12) castrated himself. He travelled to Rome, Arabia, and in 215 and 230 to Palestine. On the latter visit he was ordained priest by bishops there, and in consequence of this breach of discipline (and no doubt other disagreements) his own bishop Demetrius sent him into exile. He took refuge in 231 at Caesarea in Palestine where he established a famous school. He was tortured in the persecution of Decius in 250. Origen's works are mostly preserved in fragments and translations, owing to their great length (e.g. his **Hexapla*) and the later condemnations of his views. Origen wrote commentaries and homilies on much of the Bible; theological treatises, nearly all of which are lost except *On First Principles*; a defence of Christianity *Against *Celsus* (tr. H. Chadwick); and *On Prayer* and *Exhortation to Martyrdom*.

Origen's method of interpreting the Bible may be classed as *Alexandrian. He justified his liking for *allegory by contending that everything has both a bodily aspect, accessible to all, and a spiritual aspect, known only to the perfect. He was led to distinguish two classes of Christians, the simple and the perfect. Origen affirmed both the unity of God and the threefold nature of the Godhead. The Son was God, but only in a lesser sense than the Father. In his work *On Prayer* he claimed that prayer should be addressed only *to* the Father, *through* the Son. Some of his other speculations were idiosyncratic (e.g. that creation is eternal; that through free will all spirits have developed into a hierarchy, some falling into sin and becoming either souls or demons; and that the ascent and descent of souls goes on even after death, continually, so that at the end even the devil may be saved).

The term Origenism refers to the views of (or at least attributed to) Origen which gave rise to two later controversies. These include the pre-existence of souls and the distinction between the mortal and the resurrection body. In the 4th cent. the controversy also concerned his doctrine of the *Trinity; and he was accused of teaching *metempsychosis and a purely allegorical reading of the Bible. Among his defenders were *Athanasius and *Basil, but *Epiphanius and *Jerome attacked him, and Theophilus of Alexandria called him the 'hydra of heresies'. In the 6th cent. controversy flared up again, especially among monks in Palestine. The anti-Origenists were victorious at a synod convened by the emperor Justinian in 543, and Origenism was finally condemned at the 2nd Council of *Constantinople (553).

H. Chadwick, *Christian Thought and the Classical Tradition* (1966); J. Daniélou, *Origen* (1955); C. Kannengiesser (ed.), *Origen of Alexandria* (1988).

Original sin. In Christian theology the state of sin into which everyone is born as a result of the *fall of Adam. The basis of this in the Bible is *Paul's teaching that 'through one man [Adam] sin entered the world', so that 'by the trespass of the one the many died' (Romans 5. 12). It was developed by the early Greek *fathers, but became most precise in Latin writers of the 2nd–5th cents., culminating in *Augustine's formulation. According to this, Adam's sin has been transmitted from parent to child ever since, through 'concupiscence', in this case the sinful sexual excitement which accompanies procreation. The human race has thus become a 'lump of sin' (*massa damnata*), as shown e.g. by the practice of baptizing even new-born babies with exorcisms. In the *Pelagian controversy Augustine's view prevailed, although his extreme views were not adopted in the East. In the Middle Ages the doctrine was newly treated by St. Thomas *Aquinas. He distinguished Adam's ordinary nature from the supernatural gifts he possessed before the fall. Original sin is the loss of these gifts, leaving Adam's successors to the natural operation of their wills and passions. The instrument of transmission is procreation, but independently of 'concupiscence'. This was a more optimistic view of human nature than Augustine's, and was restated at the Council of *Trent, in opposition to the pessimistic views of *Luther and *Calvin. According to present Catholic teaching, original sin is the loss of sanctifying grace; 'concupiscence' is its result, not its essence. Since the 18th cent. the influence of Old Testament criticism, combined with natural science, has either attenuated the dogma, especially in Protestantism (although it is strongly affirmed in conservative and *neo-orthodox (2) circles), or changed the emphasis to one of describing human inability to rescue itself from its condition out of its own strength or resources: genetic endowments, combined with social, cultural and historical circumstances, precede the birth of all individuals and are not chosen by them; yet they form both character and action in ways that are inevitably disordered.

Orthodox Church. Major grouping of Christian churches, constituting, by full communion with each other, a single Church. The Orthodox Church claims direct descent from the Church of the *apostles and of the seven ecumenical *councils. The name 'Eastern Orthodox' (to be distinguished from *'Oriental Orthodox') arose from accidents of history and geography which led to a separation from 'the West'; but Orthodoxy has in fact spread throughout the world.

The Orthodox Church comprises a number of *autocephalous bodies in communion with one another: the ancient *patriarchates of *Constantinople, *Alexandria, *Antioch, and *Jerusalem, and the Orthodox Churches of *Russia, Serbia, Romania, Bulgaria, *Georgia, *Greece, Czechoslovakia, Poland, Cyprus, and Albania. In addition, there are autonomous churches (whose *primate is under the aegis of one of the autocephalous churches) in Finland, Crete, Japan, and China, and missions yet to become autonomous in Korea and Africa. The tiny Orthodox Church of Sinai, comprising only the Monastery of St Catherine and its dependencies, is also autocephalous. The Orthodox Church in America was declared autocephalous by the patriarchate of Moscow in 1970, but this has not yet been confirmed by the *oecumenical patriarch of Constantinople. Rivalry for jurisdiction is a major structural problem for Orthodoxy, which a council in preparation will attempt to solve. The oecumenical patriarch of Constantinople has a primacy of honour, but no universal jurisdiction to correspond to that of the *pope.

In 1966, the disputes over jurisdiction (which the break-up of the former Soviet Union precipitated) broke out seriously, threatening schism, when the Patriarch of Constantinople (Bartholomew) asserted his authority in Estonia and appointed Archbishop Johannes as temporary head of the Church in Estonia. Patriarch Aleksi II of Moscow and All Russia dropped reference to Bartholomew in the liturgy and ordered Russian Orthodox priests not to celebrate the liturgy with those under the jurisdiction of Constantinople. Beyond Estonia, the 'pull' toward Constantinople in former territories of the Soviet Union is fuelled by desire for independence and memories of the Russian Orthodox association with the Soviet government.

The ancient church of the Byzantine Empire was weakened in Syria and Egypt by the separation of the *monophysites in the 5th–7th cents., so that only small *Melkite churches remained in those lands under *Islam. In the W. there was a progressive estrangement between Rome and Constantinople, partly on account of divergent liturgical usages (see below) and also because of the claims of the Roman *papacy. There was a temporary schism under patriarch *Photius, then a final one under Michael Cerularius in 1054. Attempts at reunion, notably at the Council of *Florence (1439), have been ineffective.

The Orthodox Church traces its history back to the missionary work of *Paul, and itself became missionary, achieving notably the conversion of the Slavs through the 'apostles of the Slavs', *Cyril and Methodius. Russia became a Christian kingdom under St *Vladimir in 988.

After the fall of Constantinople (1453), the Church came under Muslim rule. The principal Christian churches were each treated as one nation (*millet*: see DHIMMA), with their patriarch responsible for them and their behaviour as *millet-bashi*, 'head of the nation'. Moscow then declared itself to be the 'Third Rome', and became an autocephalous patriarchate in 1589. In 1985, out of some 140 million baptized Orthodox in the world, more than 85 per cent lived in the USSR and Communist E. Europe.

Orthodox doctrine proceeds from the Bible, the formulae of the seven *ecumenical councils, and broadly from the writings of the Greek *fathers. Many doctrines of more recent definition in the W., e.g. the nature of *sacraments and the *Immaculate Conception, are not laid down. On the other hand, constant and exclusive appeal to ancient authorities makes Orthodox theology inherently conservative. The best-known difference between E. and W. theology is often seen to lie in the view of the *Trinity, epitomized by the Orthodox rejection of the *filioque, though many modern theologians in the W. would see this difference as principally semantic. The spiritual and ascetical theology of the Orthodox Church (e.g. that associated with *hesychasm) is often reckoned to be that from which most can be learnt by the W.

The Orthodox liturgy (*eucharist) is longer than the Western, and typically celebrated with greater ceremonial. The congregation stand throughout. Since much takes place behind the *iconostasis, the high points of the service for them become the two *Entrances: the Lesser Entrance with the Gospel book and the *Great Entrance with the Holy Gifts, the bread and wine to be consecrated. The faithful receive *communion after *confession, and usually only infrequently: it is given in both kinds, together in a spoon. Leavened bread is always used. The church year contains a number of fasts, and *Lent is kept particularly strictly. Some Orthodox churches retain the Julian *calendar. *Baptism is by immersion, and is followed by *chrismation; the latter alone is the rite administered to converts from other churches, provided that their baptism is seen to have been valid. *Icons are an essential part of the furnishing of a church building, and in houses are a focus of private prayers.

Parish priests are usually married, but may not marry after their ordination as *deacon. Bishops, however, are always celibate, and therefore do not come from the parish clergy but from the ranks of monks. Occasionally widowers are consecrated to the episcopate. Besides providing bishops, monasticism has also provided the intellectual and spiritual centre of Orthodoxy, specifically in modern times at Mount *Athos, but many theologians today are laypeople. See Index, Orthodox Church.

D. Attwater, *The Christian Churches of the East* (rev. edn., 1962); D. Constantelos, *Understanding the Greek Orthodox Church* (1982); D. Drillock and J. Erickson (eds.), *The Divine Liturgy* (1982); G. A. Maloney, *A History of Orthodox Theology since 1453* (1974); J. Meyendorff, *The Orthodox Church . . .* (1981); N. Zernov, *Eastern Christendom* (1961).

Orthodox Judaism. Traditional Judaism. The term 'Orthodoxy' was first applied in Judaism in 1795 as a distinction between those who accepted the written and *oral law as divinely inspired and those who identified with the *Reform movement. The Orthodox believe that they are the sole practitioners of the Jewish religious tradition and regard non-Orthodox *rabbis as laypeople and non-Orthodox *proselytes as *gentiles. Orthodoxy involves submission to the demands of *halakhah as enshrined in the written and oral law and in the subsequent codes (see CODIFICATIONS OF LAW) and *responsa. Within Orthodoxy, some authorities have retained a position of isolation, detaching their followers from the temptations and perils of the modern secular world (see ḤASIDISM), while others (see NEO-ORTHODOXY (1)) have tried to espouse openness to modern culture while insisting on the binding character of the halakhah. The traditional Orthodox way of life has been under threat in W. Europe since the *haskalah, and in E. Europe it was undermined by emigration and *Zionism in the early 20th cent. and ultimately destroyed by the *Holocaust. None the less, Orthodox communities continue to exist, particularly in *Israel, the USA, W. Europe and the British Commonwealth.

In the USA, the Orthodox community seemed likely to establish itself in numbers during the immigrations between 1880 and 1920. But in fact, much *assimilation or adaptation took place, and the Orthodox revival really began with the influx of refugees from Europe before and after the Second World War, which set up a degree of tension between Orthodoxy as exemplified in the style of the influential Joseph *Soloveichik and the more traditional, 'Torah-true', Orthodoxy. It is not possible, therefore, to categorize all institutions, etc., as having the same character, even though they would be regarded as 'Orthodox'. Nevertheless, notable institutions and organizations are or have been: Torah Umesorah, which organized schools and yeshivot from 1944 onward; the Union of Orthodox Jewish Congregations of America (which certifies, internationally, reliable kosher *food); Yeshiva University and the Hebrew Theological College in Chicago; the Union of Orthodox Rabbis and the Rabbinical Alliance.

H. H. Donin, *To Be a Jew* (1972); R. P. Bulka (ed.), *Dimensions of Orthodox Judaism* (1983); S. Heilman, *Defenders of the Faith* . . . (1992).

Orthopraxy (Gk., *orthos*, 'correct', + *praxis*, 'action'). Right action, in addition to (or sometimes in contrast to) orthodoxy, 'right belief'. Many religions are characterized by an emphasis on orthopraxy—e.g. 'Hinduism', whose concern is with *sanātana dharma (everlasting dharma, with dharma meaning, roughly, appropriate ways to live) or Islam, where the account to be rendered on the day of judgement (*yaum al-Din) is one of works. Of course, beliefs underlie both concerns, but the contrast is with Christianity, where *creeds, *confessions, and correct belief are central. Yet even in Christianity, where the relation between faith and works in relation to salvation has been a battleground (see e.g. JUSTIFICATION, PREDESTINATION), the emphasis on orthopraxy has been returned to the centre in *liberation theology and *political theology.

Ōryō E'nan (Japanese name of Ch'an master): see HUANG-LUNG HUI-NAN.

Ösal (Clear Light): see NĀRO CHOS DRUG.

Ostrich eggs. Often found in E. Christian churches where they are regarded as a symbol of the *resurrection, as a breaking open of the tomb. They are also a symbol of faith, since it was believed that ostriches hatch their eggs by gazing fixedly on them.

Otto, Rudolf (1869–1937). Philosophical theologian and professor of systematic theology at the University of Marburg, 1917–29. He is most renowned for *Das Heilige* (1917, The Idea of the Holy), a *Kantian analysis of the non-rational core of religion—the *numinous experience—and its relation to the rational. This work synthesized the philosophical, phenomenological, and theological concerns evident in his earlier works and influenced his later comparative analyses of Hinduism and Christianity (*India's Religion of Grace and Christianity*, 1930; *Mysticism East and West*, 1932).

P. C. Almond, *Rudolf Otto* . . . (1984).

Ottoman empire (13th cent. CE–1924 (AH 7th cent.–1342)). Extensive Muslim empire, whose disintegration has contributed greatly to the complexities of Middle East politics, not least through the demise of the office of caliph (*khalīfa). 'Uthman (also spelt Othman, hence the name) founded a principality in Asia Minor which, in 758, began to expand into Macedonia, Serbia, and Bulgaria (where Muslim populations remain strong). By 1453 (AH 857) they were strong enough to take *Constantinople. In 1517 (AH 923) Selim I (Yavuz, 'the Grim') conquered Egypt, claiming that the last *'Abbāsid caliph, al-Mutawakkil III, had relinquished the caliphate to his family. This claim, however, may be a later (18th-cent.) fiction in response to Russian expansion, when the sultans wished to mobilize Muslim religious resistance. Nevertheless, the early success of the Ottomans made the claim in any case acceptable to the Muslim world—success epitomized in *Sulaimān the Magnificent, whose empire extended from the Atlantic to the steppes of Russia. The first signs of decline came in 1571 (AH 979) at the battle of Lepanto, when the Ottomans lost control of the W. Mediterranean. They besieged Vienna (for a second time) in 1683 (AH 1094), but were driven back by the king of Poland. The 19th-cent. attempts at revival by the assimilation of W. ideas and technology in fact hastened the move to a secular state, established under Mustafa Kemal, Atatürk ('father of the Turks'): the sultanate was abolished in 1922, the caliphate in 1924.

M. A. Cook, *The History of the Ottoman Empire* (1976); H. Inalcik, *The Ottoman Empire . . . 1300–1600* (1973); N. Itzkovitz, *The Ottoman Empire and Islamic Tradition* (1972); B. Lewis, *The Emergence of Modern Turkey* (1968).

Ōuchi Seiran (supporter of Sōtō): see SŌJĪ-JI.

Our Lady. Christian reference to Mary, the mother of Jesus, equally familiar in French, Notre Dame, as in *Basilica of Notre Dame de Paix.

Outcastes. The gravest punishment for a member of any one of the four *varṇa* was to be declared an outcaste, and, in former times, this outcasting would be ritually performed against anyone who seriously offended against caste laws. This effectively cut the offender off from social intercourse, religious ritual, economic gain, even home and family. This almost amounted to a sentence of death in some cases. Usually the outcaste would remain so for a specified period, before being ritually cleansed and returned to caste, but for this privilege he would be dependent on the tolerance and regard of fellow caste-members. For other categories of outcaste, and for Harijans, see UNTOUCHABLES. For those sometimes called 'the untouchables of Japan', see BURAKU-(MIN).

Outer elixir (*wai-tan*, techniques in quest of immortality): see NEI-TAN.

Outer Shrine Shinto: see ISE.

Oxford Movement. A movement in the *Church of England, beginning in the 19th cent., which had a profound impact on the theology, piety, and liturgy of *Anglicanism. Its acknowledged leaders, John

Keble, J. H. *Newman, and E. B. *Pusey, were all Oxford dons, and it is Keble's 1833 sermon on 'National Apostasy' (attacking the government's plan to suppress, without proper reference to the Church, ten Irish bishoprics) which is conventionally seen as the moment when the movement came to birth. It owed a debt to the teaching of the Anglican Divines of the 16th and 17th cents., but differed from them in its attitude to the *Reformation and Church-State relations, where it was more negative, and towards *Roman Catholicism, where it was more positive.

The movement reacted against decline in church life, the threat posed by liberal theology and rationalism, and the fear that the government was, in the words of Keble, intent on making the Church of England 'as one sect among many'. In consequence the movement emphasized the Catholic inheritance of Anglicanism, both as a source of historical legitimacy and supremacy, and as an inspiration for a deeper spirituality and the restoration of awe and majesty in worship. This was reflected in an interest in the history and liturgy of the early church, an emphasis on Catholic continuity rather than *Protestant reformation, and a desire to use what they learnt from the early and pre-Reformation church as a model for reinvigorating 19th-cent. worship.

The organ of the movement was the series of Tracts for the Times (1–90; 1833–41) from which its supporters derived the name *Tractarians. Although aimed against both 'Popery and Dissent', they were viewed with increasing alarm by those outside the movement who saw in them evidence of creeping Romanism. Newman's *Tract Ninety,* which attempted to square the *Thirty-Nine Articles with Roman Catholicism, was condemned by many bishops, and a crisis was reached in 1845 when Newman and some of his supporters converted to Rome.

Despite this set-back, and continued hostility from other Anglicans, the movement grew. Its most obvious consequence was the rise of *Ritualism, but the fathers of the movement were wary of this particular development lest it promote a superficial holiness. They were not interested in greater ceremonial, private confession, or more regular Communion as ends in themselves, but saw them as means to promoting a more profound spirituality. The heart of the movement's renewal of Anglicanism lay not so much in the ritual of worship, as in the impetus it gave to more godly living worked out through the revival of religious communities and a deep commitment to parish and mission work, especially among the poor and deprived.

O. Chadwick (ed.), *The Mind of the Oxford Movement* (1960); R. W. Church, *The Oxford Movement* (1891); P. B. Nockles, *The Oxford Movement in Context* (1994); G. Rowell, *The Vision Glorious* (1983).

Ox-herding pictures (depicting stages of Zen progress): see JŪGYŪ-(NO)-ZEN.

Oyf kapporos ('may this be an atonement'): see KAPPOROT.

P

Pabbājita or **paribbājaka** (Pāli; Skt., *parivrājaka*, 'homeless one'). One who has left home for religious purposes. In early Buddhism, it is a name for one who has joined the *saṅgha (community). See also AÑÑATTITHIYA PARIBBĀJAKA.

Pacceka-buddha (solitary Buddha): see PRATYEKA-BUDDHA.

Pacem in Terris. An *encyclical letter of Pope *John XXIII, dated 11 Apr. 1963, on the achievement of peace through the establishment of justice. Not as original as John's earlier social encyclical **Mater et Magistra*, it attracted greater attention because it appeared in the course of *Vatican II, which had drawn a large number of journalists to Rome to cover the Council. It argues that peace can be established in the world only if the moral order 'imprinted by God on the heart' is obeyed. It falls into four parts: (i) the rights and duties of human beings; (ii) the relations between citizens and states; (iii) the relations between states; (iv) the relations between states and the world community.

J. Newman, *Principles of Peace: A Commentary* . . . (1964).

Pa-chiao Hui-ch'ing (Jap., Bashō Esei; *c.*10th cent. CE). A Korean Zen master of the Igyō school (see KUEI-YANG-TSUNG), who travelled to China and became the dharma-successor (*hassu) of Nan-t'a Kuang-jun. He is best remembered for his *kōan (*Wu-men-kuan* 44): 'If you have a staff, I will give you a staff. If you do not have a staff, I will take your staff away.'

Pachomius, St (Coptic, Pakhom; *c.*290–346). Founder of *coenobitic Christian monasticism. It is difficult to disentangle the details of his life from hagiographical legends. It seems that he was converted after meeting Christian monks while in the army. On his discharge in 313 he became a disciple of the hermit Palamun, and in 320 founded a monastery at Tabennisi on the Upper Nile. Other foundations followed, and at his death he was head of nine monasteries for men and two for women. The monks worshipped, worked, slept (three to a cell), and ate together; literacy was required at least after a three-year novitiate; severe ascetical practices were discouraged. The *Rule of Pachomius* influenced *Basil, *Cassian, and *Benedict.

Tr. A. Veilleux, *Pachomian Koinonia* (3 vols., 1980–2).

Pactum Callixtinum (agreement between Papacy and Holy Roman Emperors): see CONCORDAT.

Padma (symbol in E. religions): see LOTUS.

Padma-purāṇa. One of the eighteen Vaiṣṇavite Mahāpurānas, telling of the earliest times when the world was a golden *lotus (*padma*). It is exclusivist in tendency, especially at the end where *Śiva tells *Pārvatī, his consort, the qualities of *Viṣṇu, and they worship him. Other teachings (e.g. the Śaivite) are heretical in the sense that they lead to rebirth in *naraka (hell). Even the so-called *māyā doctrine (Śaṅkara's *Advaita) is dismissed as Buddhism in another guise (4. 263).

Padmasambhava ('Lotus-born'; Tib., Padma-'byuṅ-gnas). Prominent member of the Indian *siddha tradition associated with the introduction of Buddhism to Tibet and founder of the *Nyingma school. He is more commonly known by Nyingmapas as Gurū Rinpoche (Precious Teacher) and sometimes as the 'second Buddha'. Beyond the fact that he was invited to Tibet by King Trisong Detsen in the 8th cent. CE on the strength of his reputation for subduing demons and in order to assist *Śāntarakṣita (who was having difficulties establishing Buddhism there and completing the *Samyé monastery), it is as difficult to separate legend from fact in his life as it is in that of the Buddha. According to legend, Padmasambhava was born in Oḍḍiyana (possibly the Swat Valley in Pakistan) eight years after the Buddha's death, which would make him over a thousand years old when he visited Tibet. Followers of the legend, who believe him still to be alive, point to the **Mahāparinibbāna Sutta* where the Buddha tells *Ānanda that if only he had asked him three times to stay alive for the rest of this world cycle he would have done so, for such is within the power of a Buddha. Padmasambhava had an early life similar to that of *Śākyamuni in that, following a miraculous birth (from a lotus in the Milk-Ocean), he was found by a king who brought him up as a prince and would not allow him to leave the kingdom. Padmasambhava, however, killed the son of one of the king's ministers, thus getting himself sent into exile. He took up the practice of *Tantra, studied with many teachers including Ānanda, was ordained as a monk and achieved many *siddhis (superpowers). Two kings attempted to burn him alive, but each time he turned the fire into a lake. The first time, the king was so amazed he gave Padmasambhava his daughter. Padmasambhava instructed her in Tantric yoga and together they achieved the siddhi of deathlessness. The second time it was his stepfather, who now converted to Buddhism and took teachings from him. For several hundred years Padmasambhava wandered, giving teachings and performing miracles, until receiving the invitation to Tibet. His intervention there successfully cleared the way for the introduction of Buddhism, and he even contributed to the scholastic side of things, though most of this was done in a paranormal way: he established the *terma tradition of burying texts because Tibet was not yet ready for his more advanced teachings, and magically manifested Tantric texts from India, ready for translation. When *Atiśa visited Samyé in 1042 CE and noticed many tantras he had been unaware of in India, he remarked that they 'may have been brought from the land of the *ḍākinīs by the power of Gurū Rinpoche'. Padmasambhava did join the Samyé translation team, translating several tantras himself, but accounts vary as to how long he stayed in Tibet. Some say he left soon after Samyé was completed, others that he stayed for fifty-five years. All accounts say that Trisong Detsen's ministers conspired against him, and whenever he did leave, he did so in appropriate fashion by riding his horse through the air. He is believed by many to have predicted the present Tibetan diaspora and the introduction of Buddhism to the West (and the aeroplane) with this saying: 'When the Iron Bird flies in the sky, then the *Dharma will go to the land of the red man'. Although Śāntarakṣita got to Tibet first and was responsible for training its first monks, it is to Padmasambhava that the Nyingma school traces its lineage, thus showing the importance to Tibet of the Indian siddha tradition.

K. Douglas and G. Bays (trs.), *The Life and Liberation of Padmasambhava* (1978).

Padmāsana. The Lotus position, adopted for meditation, in which Hindu and Buddhist gods, *bodhisattvas, etc., are often depicted. For details, see ĀSANA.

Padyab (purification): see PURITY.

Paekche (Korean kingdom): see KOREAN RELIGION.

Pagan Pathfinders. A *neo-pagan movement, established in Britain in the 1970s. Combining pagan and occult techniques with practical psychology, it aims to achieve altered states of consciousness and quicken the pace of personal growth. Emphasis is placed on the technique of 'God-casting' whereby a particular pagan god or goddess is assigned to each member of the group and in response to evocations transmits divine powers and qualities to the individual.

Pagoda (poss. from *dāgaba*, 'relic-container', via Portugese). Buddhist structure, developed from the Indian *stūpa, and often a name for a stūpa. Its many variations contain characteristic features in common: they are usually raised and narrow structures, with four or eight sides, with several levels and prominent eaves. On the top is a post with many rings encircling it. Pagodas, like stūpas, contain *relics (*śarīra) of a/the Buddha, or of a famous teacher/master. They express the Buddhist cosmos in symbolic form: the central truth of the Buddha and his *dharma is expressed in the central pillar. The central axis is the centre of the cosmos (*axis mundi), and the four quarters radiate to the protectors (in *Mahāyāna) of particular Buddhas. The levels are the different worlds (*triloka*) and stages (in Mahāyāna) of the bodhisattva path, or (in *Theravāda) of the eightfold-path. The latter is also expressed in the eight-sided ground plan where it occurs (especially in China). A pagoda is thus a *maṇḍala in its own right.

In the history of Buddhist architecture, the placing of the pagoda is the issue which then dominates the overall layout and design of Buddhist temple areas and monasteries. When the Chinese adapted the pagoda from the stūpa, they recognized it as the holiest place (because it contained the relics). But the Buddha Hall, containing images which continued Chinese religious priorities, was equally vital. The Chinese love of (geomantic) symmetry suggested two pagodas, off the central axis leading to the Buddha Hall. But that would convert the pagodas into decorations. The geographical solutions to the problem are diverse, but always provide a clue to the religious priorities of the community and age involved.

Pahlavi ('Parthian'). Term used in Islamic times to debate earlier Iranian (*Zoroastrian) material. It is also referred to as 'Middle Persian' to distinguish it from the Old Persian (cuneiform) of the royal inscriptions and the New Persian of modern times. It was a language used between approximately 300 BCE–10th cent. CE. It encompasses secular work, poetic, historical, and epic material, but most extant works are religious and include the books from which Western scholars reconstruct 'traditional' Zoroastrian teaching (though most modern Zoroastrians consider this literature with the same hesitations many modern Christians view their medieval literature). Most Pahlavi Zoroastrian texts were written in the 9th–10th cents. to translate, summarize, and expound the ancient religion so as to support the faithful at a time of fierce Islamic persecution. It therefore includes a wide variety of texts. This entry can only point to a few which students of other religions are most likely to encounter (see also BUNDAHISN and Zand in *Avesta). The largest work is the *Denkard* which in six books is a compendium of Zoroastrian knowledge from many epochs and of diverse types (e.g. book vi is an anthology of wise sayings); other books include summaries of the original Avesta and collections of apocalyptic texts. Two brothers, Zadspram and Manuscihr produced a number of important works in the 9th cent., the *Wizidagiha i Zadspram* (Selections) and the *Dadistan i denig* (Religious Judgements—in response to ninety-two questions) being among the most important for the reconstruction of Zoroastrian (and *Zurvan) teaching. An intellectual justification of Zoroastrianism in contrast to other religions of the day was offered by the (late) 9th-cent. writer Mardanfarrox in his *Skand-Gumanig Wizar* (Doubt-Destroying Exposition). Two important eschatological texts are *Arda Viraf Namag* (The Visions of the Righteous Viraf) in which a holy man has visions of the fate befalling souls in heaven and hell and *Zand-i Vohuman Yasn* (Commentary on the Bahman Yast) which contains details on the apocalyptic scene paralleling those in the *Bundahisn* and found in parts of the *Denkard*). Since each of these texts is evidently based on older materials, where they support each other we can be reasonably confident that we are dealing with ancient ideas.

A central issue of academic debate concerning the Pahlavi literature is the extent to which it can be used to interpret the earlier and above all the Gathic (see GATHAS) texts. Generally scholars have assumed that it represents later priestly speculation, mythological in nature, polytheistic in doctrine, and therefore at a distance from the teaching of Zoroaster, albeit including some pre-Zoroastrian mythology. This has been fundamentally questioned by M. Boyce (see her 1978 article) who, as in her approach to the Avesta, argues that the Zoroastrian priestly tradition is characterized by continuity rather than change, and that Zoroastrian priests are more likely to be reliable interpreters of their ancient texts than modern Western scholars. Further, she argues that an oral tradition, preserved in a priestly/ritual setting, in areas cut off from outside influences, is more likely to remain unchanged than a literary tradition which is subject to interpretation and speculation as it is disseminated beyond the ritual context. Although some scholars may consider that she has carried her arguments to extremes at times, her work has brought the Pahlavi literature into the centre of discussions regarding the history, including the early history, of Zoroastrian doctrine. It is in the Pahlavi texts that the detailed apocalyptic material (*Frasokereti) occurs which most closely parallels Judaeo-Christian thought. The fact that they are 9th-cent. productions does not preclude the theory of Zoroastrian influence on the Judaeo-Christian tradition, because (i) the roots of most doctrines can be seen to be ancient, and (ii) the Pahlavi texts are so often, as noted above, compilations, summaries, even translations of earlier materials.

The term 'Pahlavi' was adopted by the 20th-cent. Iranian royal dynasty of Reza Shah as a marker of the importance it attached to the pre-Islamic culture of Iran.

M. Boyce, 'Middle Persian Literature', in B. Spuler, *Handbuch der Orientalistik* (1968), 31–66, and 'The Continuity of the Zoroastrian Quest', in W. Foy (ed.), *Man's Religious Quest* (1978), 603–24; S. Shaked, *Wisdom of the Sasanian Sages* (1979); A. V. Williams, *The Pahlavi Rivayat Accompanying the Dadestan i Denig* (1990).

Pa-hsien (Chin., 'eight immortals'). Taoist figures ('perfected persons', *chen jen) associated symbolically with good fortune. They are also associated with the 'eight conditions of life': youth, age, poverty, wealth, high rank, *hoi polloi* (general population), feminine, masculine. They are frequently portrayed in art and literature: (i) Li T'ieh-kuai (also known as Ti Kuai-li), Li with the iron crutch, a bad-tempered eccentric who nevertheless carries a gourd containing magic and healing potions; (ii) Chang Kuo-lao, a historical figure of the T'ang dynasty, but better known through legends—e.g. of his donkey capable of travelling 1,000 miles a day, who could be folded up and carried in a pocket; his symbol is a fish drum; (iii) Ts'ao Kuo-chiu (d. 1097 CE), usually symbolized through a pair of castanets; (iv) *Han Hsiang-tzu, the epitome of the peaceful mountain-dweller, the patron of music, portrayed with a flute, flowers, and a peach; (v) Lü Tung-pen (b. 798 CE), who received from a fire dragon a sword which enabled him to hide from death; (vi) *Ho Hsien-ku, the only female immortal (but see vii); she was told in a dream to grind a stone known as the 'mother of clouds' and to consume it. She did so, and became so light that she could fly from mountain to mountain until one day she disappeared and became an immortal; (vii) Lan Ts'ai-ho appears in rags, with a boot on only one foot, carrying a basket of flowers: he is a type of 'holy fool'; he is sometimes portrayed with female features; (viii) Chung-li Ch'üan (also Han Chung-li), a stout man with only wisps of remaining hair, but with a beard reaching his waist; his symbol is a fan, indicating power to raise the dead. His stoutness is an indication of his mastery of breathing (*ch'i); when identified as Han Chung-li, he was a governor during the Han dynasty, *c.*207 BCE–220 CE.

Kwok Man *et al.* (eds.), *The Eight Immortals of Taoism* (1990).

Pai-Chang-Ch'ing-Kuei (Jap., *Hyakujō Shingi*). A manual of rules governing Ch'an/Zen monasteries (*tera), associated with *Pai-chang Huai-hai, but subsequently reworked at least by Te-hui. The surviving text contains, e.g., prayer formulae which come from Tantric sources, whereas Pai-chang claimed that he made no innovations or deviations from the existing *Vinaya tradition.

Yi T'ao-t'ien, 'Records of the Life of Ch'an Master Pai-chang . . .', *The E. Buddhist*, 8 (1975).

Pai-chang Huai-hai (Jap., Hyakujō Ekai; 720–814). Ch'an/Zen master, dharma-successor (*hassu) of *Ma-tsu Tao-i. His major achievement was to establish a rule of life for Ch'an monasteries, thereby securing their independence and self-identity in relation to other Buddhist schools—hence his title, 'The patriarch who created the forest' (i.e. the communities of many monks). His rule was first practised in the monastery he founded, Ta-chih shou-sheng ch'an-ssu (Jap., Daichijushō-zenji), where the vital addition of a monks' hall (*sōdō*) was first made, allowing the Zen monk's 'life on a straw mat' during periods of ascetic training—i.e. the mat on which he would sleep, eat, and meditate. He stressed manual labour ('A day without work, a day without food'), and the day was carefully divided between meditation, worship, and labour, until body and mind are abandoned, whatever 'they' are doing: 'When the mind is like wood or stone, there is nothing to discriminate.'

Pai-chang Huai-hai is sometimes identified with another pupil of Ma-tsu, *Ta-chu Hui-hai, which leads to the attribution to Pai-chang of a major *Mahāyāna work. This identification seems to be a simple confusion.

Pai-lien-tsung. 'White Lotus School', a school of *Pure Land Buddhism, founded by *Hui-yüan in 402 CE, and developed by Mao Tzu-yuan, of the T'ien-t'ai school, in the 12th cent. CE. It was devoted to Amitābha (*Amida) but regarded the Pure Land as the attainment of a mental construct and state. Toward that purification, the school was vegetarian and practised daily penance. Associated with rural unrest and rebellion in the 15th cent., it was accused of becoming a secret society, not a Pure Land school: see WHITE LOTUS SOCIETY.

D. L. Overmyer, *Folk Buddhist Religion* . . . (1976).

Pai-ma-ssu/Baimasi. White Horse Monastery/Temple, Buddhist monastery and temple near Luoyang in China. It was founded in 75 CE by two Indian monks, Matanga and Chu-fa-len, who arrived on a white horse. They were the first to translate *sūtras into Chin., on the so-called 'Cool Terrace'. The existing buildings date from the Ming dynasty, and were restored during the 1950s. It remains a working centre for Ch'an Buddhists.

Pai-yün Kuan (Baiyun Guan). Monastery of the White Clouds, a Taoist 8th-cent. monastery (*kuan) in Beijing, rebuilt in 1167. It is the only surviving Taoist temple on this scale in Beijing. The complex contains six major halls, which show evidence of the fusion of Taoist and Buddhist symbols.

Pakka food (i.e. acceptable from a wide range of people): see FOOD (HINDUISM).

Pak Subuh (founder): see SUBUD.

Pa-kua. Eight trigrams, the eight signs which form the basis of **I Ching*, and from which the sixty-four hexagrams are constructed.

Palamas (Greek theologian): see GREGORY PALAMAS, ST.

Palestinian Talmud: see TALMUD.

Paliau Maloat (*b.* 1907). Leader of a development and religious movement on Manus (Admiralty Islands), Papua New Guinea. As an orphan without education, but highly intelligent and able, he joined the police in 1928 and learnt to write. Stimulated by his experiences in the war with Japan, he returned to his native village in 1946, believing he was sponsored by *Jesus to set up a New Way that would unite the area, with co-operatives and new villages, a fund for development, and a Western lifestyle. His version of Christianity was expressed in the Baluan Native Christian Church, modelled on the Roman Catholic mission, where he as leader recited the 'Long Story of God', his account of the history of the world, of the biblical period, and of Christianity. In 1950 he was imprisoned by a hostile administration. He became, however, president of the first local government council, 1951–66. The expectations he aroused led to two *cargo-cult outbreaks, the first called 'The Noise' in 1946–7, which he repudiated at the time, and the second in 1953–4; in effect these opened the way for Paliau's changes. He was twice elected to the national House of Assembly, 1964–72, but in 1980, he retired to his home village, still leading the remnant of his Baluan Church.

Pāli Canon. The earliest collections of Buddhist authoritative texts, more usually known as Tipiṭaka (*Tripiṭaka), 'Three Baskets', because the palm-leaf manuscripts were traditionally kept in three different baskets: Vinaya, (Monastic) Discipline; Sutta, Discourses; Abhidhamma, Further Teachings. The Sutta-pitaka consists of five *Nikāyas (Collections): **Dīgha* (thirty-four 'long' discourses/dialogues); **Majjhima* (150 'middle length' discourses); *Saṃyutta* (7,762 'connected' discourses, grouped according to subject-matter); **Aṅguttara* (9,550 'single item' discourses); *Khuddaka* (fifteen 'little texts', listed under *Khuddaka). Much has been tr. by the Pali Text Society.

See also BUDDHIST SCRIPTURES; and for further detail, TRIPIṬAKA.

K. Warrier, *Indian Buddhism* (1970); R. Webb, *Analysis of the Pali Canon* (1975).

Palladius (*c.*365–425). Historian of Christian *monasticism. His *Lausiac History* (*c.*419) is of great importance for the history of early monasticism in Egypt, Palestine, Syria, and Asia Minor. Palladius spent several years with monks in Egypt, where he was a pupil of *Evagrius, and his account of the movement includes his own reminiscences as well as information somewhat credulously set down from pious hearsay. His intention (expressed in the dedication to Lausus—hence the name—*praepositus*, or chamberlain, to Theodosius II) was 'that you may have for the benefit of your soul a solemn reminder, an unfailing cure for forgetfulness, and that you may drive away . . . the excitements of the world, and may, with unfailing desire, make progress in the purpose of piety'.

Trs. H. Moore (1921), W. K. Lowther Clarke (1918).

Pallium. The symbol of the *archbishop's office in the *Roman Catholic and *Uniat Churches. It is a circular band of white wool with two hanging pieces, front and back, and is now marked with six black crosses. It is worn over the *chasuble. The wool comes from sheep blessed on St *Agnes' day in Rome. Since the 9th cent. all R. Catholic *metropolitans have been required to petition to the pope for it. A *motu proprio of *Paul VI, *Inter Eximia Episcopalis*, restricted privileges associated with it.

Palm Sunday. The Sunday before *Easter which thus commences *Holy Week. Palms are blessed and carried in procession, representing Jesus' 'triumphal entry' into Jerusalem in the last week of his life. The procession dates back to the 4th-cent. church of Jerusalem, and in the Middle Ages usually went from one church to another. In Roman and Anglican churches palm leaves made into crosses are blessed. The service may also include the chanting of the passion story from one of the gospels, and for that reason is also known as Passion Sunday (a name which is also given to the preceding Sunday: *Vatican II attempted to combine the two).

Pañcadaśi ('the fifteen'). A major Hindu work so-called from its fifteen chapters. It was written by *Vidyāranya, a follower of *Śaṅkara. It is an *advaita exploration, of great complexity, of the elements surrounding *ātman (*śarīra), the great precepts (Mahāvākyas), and the nature of bliss.

Text and tr. S. Swahananda (1967).

Pañca-makāra or **pañca-tattva.** Five ritual ingredients whose first letter is 'm': *madya* (wine or alcoholic beverage), *maṃsa* (meat), *matsya (fish), *mudrā* (parched grain), and *maithuna (sexual intercourse). The five Ms are central to *Tantric liturgy, and are interpreted, either literally by left-hand (*vāmācāra) sects such as the *Kaulas and *Kāpālikas, or symbolically by right-hand (*dakṣinācāra) sects. The left-hand groups seek perfection and power (*siddhi) through the use of prohibited substances such as meat and alcohol which are also regarded as aphrodisiacs. A Tantric text, *Jñānasiddhi*, says, 'by the same acts that cause some men to be born in hell for a thousand years, the *yogin gains his eternal salvation'. Cannabis (*vijāya*) is also used before the pañca-makāra. Right-hand groups use substitute ingredients (*pratinidhi*): a non-alcoholic drink for the wine, vegetables and cereals for the meat and fish, and meditation on the union of opposites—the union of *Kuṇḍalinī with *Śiva in the thousand-petalled lotus (*sahasrara padma)—for sexual intercourse.

Pañca-mārga (Skt., 'five paths'). Five stages in Buddhist progress (cf. *bhūmi): (i) sambhāra-marga, path of accumulation; (ii) prayoga-marga, path of preparation; (iii) darśana-marga, path of seeing; (iv) bhāvanā-marga, path of meditation; (v) aśaikṣa-marga, path of not-learning any further.

Panca namaskāra (five Jain homages): see FIVE SUPREME BEINGS.

Pañcānana (Skt., 'five-faced'). A Hindu epithet of *Śiva, representing any of the fivefold characteristics of his nature—e.g. the elements; the four quarters + Sadaśiva—the most complex of the faces, invisible even to the advanced yogin. The contemplation of the five faces is a central focus for meditation.

Pañcanīvaraṇa (five kinds of higher knowledge): see JÑĀNA (BUDDHISM); NĪVARANA.

Pañca parameṣthin (five exemplary modes of being for Jains): see FIVE SUPREME BEINGS.

Pañcarātra. An early *Vaiṣṇava tradition and sect with a large number of texts called *Saṃhitās, of which the 'three gems' (the *Pauṣkara*, *Sāttvata*, and *Jayākhya Saṃhitās*) are the most important and earliest (5th–6th cents. CE). These texts are almost identical in structure to the Śaiva *Āgamas. Pañcarātra literally means 'five-night', and may refer to the five-night sacrifice in *Śatapatha Brāhmaṇa* (13. 6. 1). Before the Saṃhitās, the earliest source for the tradition is the Nārāyanīya section of the *Mahābhārata*. Creation occurs in three stages for the Pañcarātra: pure, mixed, and impure. Pure creation consists of the emanations (*vyuha*) from *Vasudeva (or *Viṣṇu united with *Lakṣmi) to Śankarṣana, Pradyumna, and Aniruddha. Mixed and impure creation follows the order of the Sāṃkhya tattvas, though time (*kāla) and fixed order (*niyati*) are added. Through creation Śakti or Lakṣmi manifests Viṣṇu's six attributes (*gunas) of knowledge (*jñāna), lordship (*aiśvarya*), power (*śakti), strength (*bala*), virility (*vīrya), and splendour (*tejas). Souls (*jīvas) are distinct from Viṣṇu and classified as eternally free, liberated through grace, or fettered. The *Jayākhya Saṃhitā* is the *locus classicus* of Pañcarātra religious practice, which consists of the divinization of the body through the assimilation of a divine *mantra body by *nyasa and *visualization. *Bhakti and grace are also important. Other topics dealt with are outer worship (*bāhya yoga*), temple building, initiation, *śraddha, and funeral rites.

F. O. Schrader, *Introduction to the Pancaratra, and Ahirbudhnya Samhita* (1916).

Pañca-śila (Buddhist obligations): see ŚĪLA.

Pañcatantra. A collection of stories and legends, in five (*pañca*) books (*tantra*), compiled by Viṣnuśaram in the early cents. CE. The original is lost, but it continues in at least three different lineages, and in many adaptations or imitations, of which *Hitopadeśa* is the best-known. The stories may have been intended to teach moral and other lessons, but they extend beyond that into the realms of entertainment. As a 'story-book', it passed into many other cultures and languages (see especially J. Hertel, *Das Pañcatantra . . .*, 1914).

Germ. tr. G. L. Chandiramani (1971); Eng. trs. F. Edgerton (1924), A. W. Ryder (1925).

Pañca-tattva: see PAÑCA-MAKĀRA.

Pañchama (lowest category of Hindu society): see UNTOUCHABLES.

Panchen Lama (abbr. *Pandita Chen.po*, 'Great Teacher'). Holder of the Tibetan Buddhist monastic throne of Tashilhunpo in Shigatse, the religious nature of which has become inseparable from Sino-Tibetan political history. The office had been established by the third *Dalai Lama as a position attainable by merit, until the Great Fifth Dalai Lama—who had become close to his contemporary Panchen Lama (Chokyi Gyaltsen, 1570–1662) who was also his tutor—predicted that the throne would be retained by reincarnation, from which time Chokyi Gyaltsen has been considered the 'first' Panchen Lama. When the Great Fifth Dalai Lama—himself an *emanation of *Avalokiteśvara—made this prediction, he also recognized the Panchen Lama as an emanation of the Buddha Amitābha (*Amida) of whom Avalokiteśvara is also an emanation. Richardson (1962) explains this as an acknowledgement of the Panchen Lamas' more abstract, spiritual nature, which should have kept them above the temporal concerns with which the Dalai Lamas had to contend; in view of which, the fate of the Panchen throne is most ironic.

In 1728, when the seventh Dalai Lama had been forced into exile by the Chinese, who had themselves felt obliged to interfere in Tibetan affairs by the earlier Tibetan patronage of their enemies, the Dzongar Mongols (see 'PHAGS-PA), the emperor of China conferred upon the second Panchen Lama Lobsang Yeshe (1662–1737) sovereignty of Gtsang (Tsang) and W. Tibet, in an attempt to dilute the power of the Dalai Lama and to split the *Geluk hierarchy. Since Lobsang Yeshe (like his successors) wished nothing other than to be subordinate to the exiled Dalai Lama, he carefully accepted only a part of the offer (although even this has been retrospectively viewed as a mistake, legitimizing Chinese power to direct Tibetan affairs). When, however, the ninth, tenth, eleventh, and twelfth Dalai Lamas all died before the age of 21, it was inevitable that the importance and responsibility attached to the Panchen Lama's office should grow, to the annoyance of the Lhasa regents and creating conflict not between the Dalai and Panchen Lamas but between the two courts of Shigatse and Lhasa. Thus, when the Great Thirteenth Dalai Lama survived his majority, his court took the opportunity of asserting the new supremacy of Lhasa by attempting a large tax on Tashilhunpo for maintenance of the Tibetan army; fearing that the Dalai Lama was being misled by machinating officials, the sixth Panchen Lama, Chokyi Drakpa, in 1927 fled to China, where he became the hostage of the Chinese who would only return him with a military escort. In 1937 he died, thus dissolving the excuse to invade, but the Chinese had clearly recognized the value of a Panchen Lama in their hands; and in 1944 the seventh Panchen Lama, Chokyi Gyaltsen (whom the Chinese reckon as the tenth, thus increasing his status), was declared by the Chinese to have been discovered in China. It was not until 1951 that Chokyi Gyaltsen was recognized by the Tibetans, and only then as part of the seventeen-point agreement (signed with false Tibetan seals by a deserter and collaborator, Ngapo Ngawang Jigne, who held office in the Chinese government) forced on them after the 1950 invasion while the Dalai Lama was in exile. 'Discovered' by the Chinese, brought up in China, and given a Chinese education, Chokyi Gyaltsen toed the Chinese line until, in 1960, his seat at Tashilhunpo was ransacked and his entire corpus of 4,000 monks was either executed or sent to labour camps. In 1961 he witnessed the mass starvation which followed the attempt to replace barley with wheat and the diversion of meat to Chinese troops, and pleaded unsuccessfully with Mao for a reversal of those policies. In 1964, in a speech to 10,000 citizens of Lhasa, he asserted Tibet's right to independence. He was imprisoned, released in 1978, and in 1979 accounts of his tortures appeared on the 'Democracy Wall'. For ten years he pressed for improvements in health and education and for the preservation of Tibetan culture while remaining within the constraints of his role set by the Chinese, until, in 1988, at a speech in Tashilhunpo, he declared that 'the detriments of Chinese rule in Tibet outweighed the benefits'. Three days later he suffered a fatal heart attack. His wife, a nurse, was denied access to him, and a doctor was called from Chengdu, several days' journey away. In 1990 his embalmed body was enshrined in a *chorten at Tashilhunpo. The search for the Panchen Lama's reincarnation was then set in motion, and in 1995 the Dalai Lama recognized him in a 6-year-old boy, Gedhun Choekyi Nyima. The Chinese authorities refused to recognize him, ostensibly on the grounds that he was morally unworthy (it was claimed that he had once drowned a dog), and they removed him and his family to Beijing. They then insisted on their traditional right (see above) to supervise the appointment, following procedures which, it was claimed, the Dalai Lama had ignored—in particular the designation of three candidates, all of whom have passed the tests of authenticity, one of whom is then selected by the drawing of lots from a golden urn (used in earlier choices, e.g. in the selection of the Panchen Lama in 1822). This procedure was conducted at *Jokhang at the end of 1995, producing a 5-year-old boy, Gyancain/Gyaltsen Norbu.

H. E. Richardson, *Tibet and its History* (1962).

Pāṇḍavas. Five *kṣatriya 'brothers' of the Kuru lineage, Yudhiṣṭhira, *Bhīma, *Arjuna, and the twins, Nakula and Sahadeva, the heroes of the epic *Mahābhārata*, which recounts their battle for sovereignty against their cousins, the *Kauravas. Their name is a patronymic, derived from the name of Pāṇḍu, their ostensible father, but in truth each is the son and incarnation of a god: *Dharma, *Vāyu, *Indra, and the twin *Aśvins, respectively. Such double fathering (human and divine) is typical of epic heroes. *Kuntī is the mother of the three oldest

Pāṇḍavas; Mādrī, of the twins. The Pāṇḍava family is an extremely harmonious unit, seen, not least, in the common marriage of all five brothers to a single wife, *Draupadī (though each Pāṇḍava also has at least one wife of his own).

Indo-Europeanists of the school of Georges *Dumézil have interpreted the Pāṇḍava family structure as a reflection of Indo-European tri-functional ideology: Yudhiṣṭhira represents the priests, Bhīma and Arjuna represent the warriors, and the twins represent the farmer/artisan function. This interpretation is just one attempt to characterize the individual Pāṇḍavas, and explain their interconnection.

Paṇḍita, paṇḍit, or **pundit** (Skt.). A Hindu scholar, learned man, teacher, or philosopher. Paṇḍitas are those who conserve the Sanskrit tradition, specialists in memorization of the classical traditions of Indian philosophy and literature. Each paṇḍita specializes in a particular group of classical texts along with the appropriate commentaries. Sanskrit paṇḍitas are trained to index particular words from the texts, providing the contexts by which the meanings of words may be determined, and are necessarily adept at the subtleties of Sanskrit grammar and syntax.

In the villages of India the function of the paṇḍita may be performed by the temple priest, who may also recite sacred texts, sing devotional songs, and serve as village astrologer. In urban areas the function of the paṇḍita is usually separate from that of priest. Paṇḍitas are often associated with particular philosophical schools, and attempt to live as a separate community of literati, cultivating the Sanskrit language as a *lingua franca* for communication with paṇḍitas from all of India.

Panentheism: see PANTHEISM.

P'ang Yün or **P'ang-chu-shih** (Jap., Hō Un/Hō Koji; 740–808). A lay Ch'an/Zen Buddhist, regarded in his time as 'a second *Vimalakīrti'. He sought instruction from several Zen masters, including *Ma-tsu, under whom he attained the great enlightenment. He remains a model of how Zen attainment is possible to laypeople, and not just to monks. His last words were: 'Everything is shadow and echo.' His sayings were collected after his death in *P'ang chü-shih yü-lu* (Jap., *Hō Koji goroku*).

Tr. R. F. Sasaki *et al.*, *The Recorded Sayings of Layman P'ang* (1971).

Pāṇini. Author of *Aṣṭādhyāyi*, the earliest surviving work on Sanskrit grammar, written at some time between the 7th and 4th cents. BCE. The religious importance of grammar lay in the necessity to transmit and interpret sacred and ritual texts correctly, in order to relate adequately to *śabda. Grammar, as a consequence of Pāṇini, assumed a controlling position in Hindu science, and is highly analytic. His own work was considered divinely inspired, like the *Vedas, and to have come directly from *Vac.

Eng. tr. S. C. Vasu (1891–8); Fr. tr. L. Renou (1847–54); Germ. tr. O. Böhtlingk (1887); V. S. Agrawala, *India as known to Pāṇini* (1963); G. Cardona, *Pāṇini: A Survey of Research* (1976).

Pan-Islam. Movements to unify the Muslim world, particularly in reaction against Western threats of encroachment. In the 19th cent. these movements were small and ineffective, though Western imperial powers were aware that Muslim loyalty was worth securing in their contests against each other. After the Second World War, Pan-Islam has had more substance, but has so far always broken down in the face of the self-interest of newly independent nation-states. Theoretically, Pan-Islam is a natural expression of the fundamental and necessary Muslim concept of *'umma, but its realization in practice is elusive.

J. M. Landau, *The Politics of Pan-Islam* (1990).

Pañjāb (Pers., 'five, water', i.e. land of five rivers). Punjāb, homeland of the Sikhs. The present NW Indian state of Punjāb was created in 1966, excluding former areas which now comprise Himachal Pradesh and Haryana. The state language is *Pañjābī, and Sikhs outnumber Hindus. In 1947 the much larger British Punjāb had been partitioned between Pakistan and India, with the boundary dividing *Amritsar from, e.g., Nānkāṇā *Sāhib (*Talvaṇḍī Rāi Bhoī dī). Thousands of Sikhs moved from east to west but remain anxious for free access to holy places in a relatively (or completely) autonomous homeland: see KHĀLISTĀN. Pañjāb's geographical position, as a gateway to successive invasions of India from further west, and its extremes of climate and relative fertility, have moulded a people noted for enterprise.

Pañjābī or **Punjābī.** 1. Person whose family originates from *Pañjāb, often referring to its pre-1947 boundaries.

2. Mother tongue of Pañjābīs, regardless of their religion. Pañjābī, in *Gurmukhī script, is the official language of Indian Pañjāb, and has been especially respected by Sikhs.

Pañj kakke (five marks of a khālsā Sikh): see FIVE KS.

Pañj Piāre: see PAÑJ PYĀRE.

Pānj Pīr (Pañjābī, 'five guides'). Popular Hindu cult of Five Saints, who may be *any* five the devotee may remember or worship. The cult includes Muslim figures, such as the Prophet *Muḥammad, *'Alī, *Fāṭima, *al-Ḥasan, and *al-Ḥusain. Another popular 'quintet' is Ghazi Miyan, Baba Barahna, Palihar, Amina Sati, and Bibi Fāṭima (the last two being most obviously Hindu–Muslim hybrids). The Panj Pir cult is followed by some fifty-three Hindu castes. Since the Hindus have elevated the quintet to deities, they hold celebrations where offerings are made in order to fulfil certain needs: Ghazi Miyan is worshipped after marriage with an offering of boiled rice, curds, and fowl. This cult may be an adaptation of Muslim ideas into Hindu epics over a thousand years of Hindu–Muslim coexistence in India.

Pañj pyāre (Pañjābī, 'five beloved ones'). 1. Five men who volunteered their heads for Gurū *Gobind Siṅgh on *Baisākhī 1699. According to tradition Gobind Siṅgh invited his followers to the Baisākhī *melā at *Anandpur 1699. He demanded if anyone would give his life for him. Eventually Dayā Rām rose, entered the Gurū's tent, and the crowd saw blood trickle out. Four more times the Gurū demanded a Sikh's head, and four men who chanced to be of different *castes, Dharam Dās, Mukham Chānd, Sāhib Chānd, and Himmat Rāi, volunteered. Each time blood flowed. The Gurū then revealed them unharmed to the astonished onlookers, for the blood had come from slaughtered goats. Some believe that the Gurū did indeed sever their heads, miraculously restoring each head to different shoulders. Gobind Siṅgh proclaimed the pañj pyāre to be the nucleus of the *khālsā and initiated them with *amrit (sweetened water) before himself receiving the same from them. All were renamed Siṅgh. They subsequently fought bravely for the Gurū. The pañj pyāre are remembered daily in *Ardās, and a portion of *kaṛāh praśād is taken out in their memory before general distribution.

2. Five baptized Sikhs who administer *khaṇḍe-di-pahul. They are normally men and must be *amritdhārī, physically whole, and known to observe the Sikh code of conduct (*rahit). They stir the amrit, reciting prayers, give it to the initiates, and one of the five proclaims the requirements of Sikh religion. For the ceremony they are barefoot, usually wearing a saffron-coloured tunic, blue or white *turban, a sash around the waist, and, on their left side, a *kirpān* (dagger) attached to a sash tied over the right shoulder.

3. The central and final authority for all Sikhs, located at *Amritsar.

P'an-ku. Taoist creator of the world, and also the first human. From the original chaos in the form of an egg, P'an-ku emerged. The constituent parts of the egg separated into the heavy (*yin) and the light (*yang), and P'an-ku grew at the same rate until he filled the space between the two. At his death, his body was allocated to the creation of different parts of the world.

Pañña (wisdom): see PRAJÑA (2).

Pannikar, Raimundo (1918–). Christian promotor of Hindu–Christian dialogue. He was born in Barcelona of a Hindu father and Roman Catholic mother, and from an early age was brought up to read the *Veda as well as the *Bible. He gained a D.Sc. as well as a DD and Ph.D., and was ordained priest in 1946. He worked first in Mysore and then in Varānasi (Benares), and in 1968 he published, on the basis of his experience of *dialogue, *The Unknown Christ of Hinduism*. Along the lines that led to the formulation of the concept of anonymous Christians (see RAHNER), he argued that Christ is universal and that his presence and reality can be articulated in Hindu terms. Furthermore, a faithful Hindu achieves salvation through Hindu faith and sacraments. In a revised edition in 1981, he went further in maintaining that Hinduism and other religions are not 'preparatory' in relation to Christianity, but can be the means to salvation in their own right. This book led to the correction by M. M. Thomas that Christ has already been acknowledged in Hinduism by various people in various ways, which he proceeded to review, in *The Acknowledged Christ of the Indian Renaissance*. Pannikar also wrote *The Trinity and the Religious Experience of Man* (1973), and *The Vedic Experience* (1977).

Pansil. Abbreviation of pañca-sila (*sīla), the five precepts which should be expressed in the life of every Buddhist.

Panth (Pañjābī, 'way, sect'). Religious community in E. religions, but especially among Jains (see e.g. KĀNJĪ SVĀMI PANTH) and Sikhs. Among the latter, Panth denotes the whole Sikh community. The term 'panth' is more flexible than 'sect', although often used to mean the Sikhs as distinct from Hindu society. Panth refers to those following a particular religious teacher or doctrines. Thus Nānak-panthī refers to *Gurū *Nānak's disciples, and Kabīr-panthī to *Kabīr's disciples. Sometimes the adjective, Panthic, is used to refer to the Sikh community. See also KHĀLSĀ.

Pantheism, panentheism. A family of views dealing with the relation between God and the world. In contrast to *theism's stress on the total transcendence of God, both terms reflect an emphasis on divine *immanence. In pantheistic views, God and the world are essentially identical; the divine is totally immanent. In panentheistic views, the world exists in God (all reality is part of the being of God), but God is not exhausted by the world; the divine is both transcendent and immanent. Such views are often closely related to *mysticism.

In Hinduism, the roots of such views lie in later parts of the **Ṛg Veda*. In the *Upaniṣads, the doctrine of *Brahman reflects a number of theistic, pantheistic, and panentheistic views. *Śaṅkara's *Advaita Vedānta synthesized these in its assertion of the sole reality of Brahman and the corresponding unreality of the world. Rāmānuja also emphasized Brahman's transcendence but reasserted the reality of the world as the body of Brahman. In *Mahāyāna Buddhism, especially in *Aśvaghosa and *Nāgārjuna, there is a trend towards the assertion of the ultimate unreality of ordinary existence and the sole reality of what might, in other traditions, be called the Absolute (*tathatā, *śūnya).

The major source of W. pantheism and panentheism is *Neoplatonism. The Neoplatonic doctrine of emanation became the cornerstone of Arabic philosophy, coming to full prominence in *al-Fārābī, *Ibn Sīnā, and *Ibn Rushd. Panentheistic themes in interplay with Islamic monotheism played a central role in the *Sufism of *al-Bistāmī, *al-Junayd, *al-Hallaj, *al-Ghazzālī, and *Ibn ʿArabī. In Judaism, panentheistic elements are central to the medieval *kabbalah and *Ḥasidism. Via *Augustine and *Dionysius the Pseudo-Areopagite, Neoplatonic panentheism formed the framework of much Christian mysticism. 17th-cent. pantheism is exemplified in the works of Jakob *Boehme and *Spinoza. The 19th-cent. German Idealism of J. G. Fichte, F. W. J. Schelling, and G. W. F. *Hegel was in essence a quest for a rational panentheism. And similar themes permeated the Romantic F. D. E. *Schleiermacher. Characteristic expressions of 20th-cent. panentheism may be found in N. *Berdyaev, A. N. Whitehead, and C. *Hartshorne.

Pantisocracy (egalitarian society): see COLERIDGE, S. T.

Pāpa (Skt.). In Hinduism, evil, *sin, misfortune. Like its synonym, *adharma, pāpa includes both moral and natural evil, which are considered aspects of the same phenomenon. An absolute distinction between moral evil (or evil willed by humans) and natural evil (or an 'act of God'), is not present in Hindu thought. One can sin unintentionally by unknowingly eating a prohibited food or making an error in ritual. One's sin, whether intentional or unintentional, may have consequences, not only for oneself, but for others, so that one must pray for deliverance from the sins of others as well as from one's own sins. In Hindu mythology humans, nature, and even the gods partake of evil, which is complementary to good. Pāpa consists in striving against nature, against *dharma.

In Buddhism, the connotation of evil and immorality is applied particularly to states of mind and actions. Pāpa is considered evil because it takes one away from the path of spiritual development, the path of *nirvāna. Pāpa, like its opposite *punya, prolongs one's cycle of births and deaths. While punya leads to birth in pleasant and happy states and conditions of life, pāpa leads to birth in unpleasant and unhappy states and conditions of life. Pāpa is never considered to be inherent in human nature, nor is it an offence against any external or other authority. The idea of pāpa as defilement or pollution seems a parallel development with the incorporation of the concept of the holy and is much later than the period of the Pāli canonical texts. Therefore, the concept of *kilesa (defilement) as synonymous with pāpa belongs to post-canonical growth in Buddhism.

Pāpa is what ensues from an *akuśala action. However, this important cause and effect relationship between akuśala and pāpa seems to have receded in the later portions of the Pāli canon. According to an *Anguttara Nikāya Sutta*, the commission of the ten akuśala actions constitutes commission of pāpa (II. 222). See also KARMA/KAMMA.

Papacy. The office of the *bishop of Rome as leader of the *Roman Catholic Church. Claims to some form of leadership over the churches seem to be implicit in Roman documents from the end of the 1st cent. onwards, but were made more explicit in the century between popes Damasus and Leo. They depend upon *Christ's words to *Peter, 'You are Peter and on this rock I will build my church' (Matthew 16. 18), upon Peter's leading role among the *apostles, and upon the historical links between Peter, and to some extent *Paul also, and the church of Rome. Acceptance of the papal fullness of authority ('plenitudo potestatis') over other churches has varied with the personal standing of the bishops of Rome and other historical circumstances, but is generally held to have been at its height during the pontificate of *Innocent III, whose skill as a lawgiver and arbitrator neatly coincided with the expectations of a feudal society. During the Napoleonic era, the sufferings of Pius VI and Pius VII earned the papacy support even from non-RC governments and, together with the loss of the papal states, gave impetus to papal claims to spiritual leadership. At *Vatican I the bishops asserted the pope's 'ordinary and immediate' authority over all churches and members of churches, and his *infallibility when defining matters of faith or morals to be held by the whole church. Despite a statement in 1875 by the German bishops that the definitions of *primacy and infallibility were not intended to exalt the papal office at the expense of the local bishops (a statement endorsed by *Pius IX), this was indeed the outcome of Vatican I, at least until the pontificate of *John XXIII, when an attempt was made to reinstate the collegiality of bishops and their consequent joint responsibilities. See Index, Papacy.

P. C. Empie and T. A. Murphy, *Papal Primacy and the Universal Church* (1974); J. Haller, *Das Papsttum* ... (1950–3); J. N. D. Kelly, *The Oxford Dictionary of Popes* (1986); F. X. Seppett, *Geschichte der Päpste* (1954–9).

Papal aggression. Popular name for the action of Pope *Pius IX in 1850 making England and Wales an ecclesiastical province of the *Roman Catholic Church (with an archbishop and twelve *suffragans with territorial titles), referring with evidently calculated contempt to the Church of England as 'the *Anglican schism'.

Papias (*c*.60–130 CE). Christian bishop of Hierapolis in Asia Minor. His work *Exposition of the Sayings of the Lord*, known only from quotations in *Irenaeus and *Eusebius, contained oral traditions and legends. The most important of these concern the writing of the *gospels: *Matthew 'composed the sayings (*logia*) in Hebrew, and everyone translated them as best he could'; *Mark was 'the interpreter of Peter' who set down 'accurately though not in order' Peter's memories of Jesus' words and activities.

Para. Skt., 'supreme, highest', found in conjunction with many Hindu words to express the superlative state—e.g. *para-*bhakti* and see under VIṢṆU. Unless some special sense is created, the meaning will be carried within the basic word, and will not be listed separately here.

Parable (Gk., *parabolē*). A story or illustration of important teaching, used by *rabbis and by *Jesus, more direct than *allegories, and, in the case of Jesus, usually making a demand on the hearers. As such, some modern scholars insist the parables cannot be understood apart from the particular audiences to whom they were addressed and perhaps also the particular occasions in Jesus' life on which they were spoken. Since the gospels do not usually preserve this information—and indeed sometimes apply a parable to a Christian readership—the original sense of Jesus' parables is hard to recover. Jesus' insistence on teaching in parables, however, implies something about the nature of the *kingdom of God. Most of the thirty to forty gospel parables are found in Matthew (e.g. the clusters in chs. 13, 25) and Luke (among the best-known, 10. 25–42, 15. 11–32). For Jewish parables, see MĀSHAL.

J. Jeremias, *The Parables of Jesus* (Eng. tr. of 6th German edn., 1963).

Paracelsus (Theophrastus Baumastus von Hohenheim, 1493–1541). *Alchemist and physician. He was born in Switzerland and travelled extensively throughout Europe, gaining a reputation as the leading figure in the Renaissance quest for interior meanings and transformations of nature. He drew on *kabbalah as well as alchemy, working out an elaborate scheme of Man as the microcosmic reflection of the macrocosm. Medicine formed a part of this as the exploration of the disturbance of the natural order.

W. Pagel, *Paracelsus* (1958).

Paraclete. A figure mentioned by Jesus in the gospel of John (chs. 14–16), as coming after his own departure, to be with his disciples. The Gk. word *paraklētos* may mean 'comforter', 'counsellor', 'advocate', but none of these translations entirely matches the range of functions ascribed to him. He is once identified with the *Holy Spirit (14. 26), and it is easy to see why Christian tradition took up this identification. This being so, however, the Johannine church had a distinctive view of the Spirit bound up with its own self-understanding as a minority Christian group in a hostile world. In Islam, the (Arab.) *faraqlīt* is identified with Muḥammad as the one who was promised (John 16. 7).

Paradise (Gk., possibly from Pers. *pardes/pairidaeza*, 'enclosure, park', hence 'garden'). Idyllic state in the presence of God, especially after death, hence often a synonym for heaven. The *Septuagint uses the word of a literal *garden (Ecclesiastes 2. 5; Song of Songs 4. 12), but the reference is more often the Garden of Eden (Paradise Lost) or the restored Garden (e.g. Ezekiel 36. 35, 47. 12; Isaiah 51. 3—Paradise Regained). In ordinary Christian usage, it is more likely to mean simply 'heaven', as in the funeral liturgy, *In paradisum deducant te angeli* . . ., 'May the angels lead you into paradise'. By application, paradise is used of other religions, especially al-Janna (the Garden) of Islam: see EDEN; HEAVEN; GARDEN; and Index, Heavens, paradises.

J. H. S. Armstrong, *The Paradise Myth* (1969); E. B. Moynihan, *Paradise as a Garden* . . . (1979); G. H. Williams, *Wilderness and Paradise in Christian Thought* (1962).

Parah adummah (red heifer): see RED HEIFER.

Pārājika-dhamma. The four most serious offences against the Buddhist monastic code of discipline (*prātimokṣa), the penalty for which is lifelong expulsion from the Order (*saṅgha). They are (i) sexual intercourse, (ii) serious theft, (iii) murder, and (iv) falsely claiming to have attained supernatural powers. A monk who commits a pārājika offence is compared to 'a person whose head is cut off, or a withered leaf dropped from the tree, or a stone slab split in two, or a palm tree cut from the top'. Such a one has been 'defeated' (the traditional etymology of pārājika) and cannot be readmitted to the Order.

Parakīya (woman, one outside ordinary bounds): see SAHAJĪYĀ.

Paramahaṃsa (Skt., 'highest flyer'). The highest of four categories of Hindu ascetics seeking *mokṣa; also the followers of a school derived from Śaṅkara.

Paramātman (Skt., 'Supreme Self'). The Supreme Spirit, i.e. *Brahman. In the *Pañcadaśī, the paramātman is defined as 'the substratum on which the individual souls (*jīvas) are superimposed'.

Among Jains, paramātman takes on a comparable significance, especially after the work of *Kundakunda. The self, freed from all impediment of *karma, in its unconditioned and absolute state, is realized by liberated *jīvas. Since this paramātman pre-exists all manifestations and is unaffected (however much impeded) by them, the paramātman becomes an object of reverence for Jains: it can be revered in all beings, but especially in the *tīrthaṅkaras (ford-makers). This foundational and absolute reality is described, on occasion, as 'god'. Thus although Jainism is 'atheistic' (in the sense that it believes the entire cosmic appearance to be cyclical and eternal, and not the product of a Creator), it has quasi-theistic attitudes, not least in its poets (e.g. *Banārsīdās).

Parameśvara (Skt., 'the highest god'). In *Kashmir Śaivism, the highest Reality, conceived to be either beyond all thirty-six *tattvas or as the thirty-seventh. All reality, both mystical and material, emanates from Parameśvara, also called Paramaśiva, through a process of 'shining forth' (*ābhāsa*). This process involves successive divisions or limitations (*kala*) of Parameśvara, dividing the Absolute into the various limited realities of creation.

Parameśvara shares most qualities attributed to the Absolute in other Indian systems, thus he is totally transcendent without thought or desire. Unique to the Kashmir Śaiva tradition is the paradox that he is also with division (*sakala*). This concept is necessary to explain the most basic principle of this tradition: although Parameśvara is totally transcendent he exists in his full nature in every aspect of the manifested universe; he is both creator and creation. All things have Parameśvara as their ultimate nature.

Pāramitā (Skt., 'that which has crossed over'). In Mahāyāna Buddhism, the six (or later ten) virtues developed by *bodhisattvas: (i) *dāna-paramitā, generosity; (ii) *śīla-paramitā, correct conduct; (iii) kṣānti-paramitā, patient acceptance of injuries received; (iv) *vīrya-paramitā, exertion; (v) *dhyāna-paramitā, meditation; (vi) *prajña-paramitā, wisdom; (vii) *upāya-kauśalya-paramitā, skill-in-means; (viii) pranidhāna-paramitā, the bodhisattva vow; (ix) bala-paramitā, manifestation of the ten powers of knowledge; (x) *jñana-paramitā, true wisdom. Of these, (vi) is often considered paramount, the others relating more to means than to the end. Consequently, there developed the *Perfection of Wisdom literature and school (Prajñāparāmitā).

H. Dayal, *The Bodhisattva Doctrine* . . . (1932).

Paramparā (Skt., 'succession'). A lineage of spiritual teachers (*guru/*acārya) in Hinduism. The paramparā is thought to be the means of channelling spiritual power through time, passed on from one guru to his successor. The guru's teaching is thus authenticated by the lineage (hence the frequent form, *guruparamparā*). Each paramparā has a founder (*ādiguru) who is often thought to have received teachings directly from a divine source. For example, the *Nāths trace their lineage back to Matsyendranāth who in the form of a fish overheard a conversation between *Śiva and *Devī.

The lineage of teachers is important in the *Upaniṣads, the **Bṛhadaranyaka* giving a list of teachers going back to *Brahmā (4. 6. 1–3). Traditions whose focus of practice is the guru, such as *Tantrism and the *Sant tradition, emphasize the paramparā and the direct transmission of divine power, hence the importance of establishing the legitimacy of the successor. In Tantrism the paramparā is often invoked at the beginning of ritual (*pūjā). Each student is expected to learn the succession of previous gurus in order to be able to legitimate his claim to knowledge.

Parapsychology. Literally the scientific study of what lies beyond (Gk., *para*) those properties of the mind which are accepted by current scientific research. However, since there is very considerable debate as to whether or not paranormal (or 'psi') phenomena actually exist, it is better defined as the scientific investigation of a possibility. The main psi candidates which have been advanced for research purposes can be classed under two headings: ESP (extrasensory perception) which covers paranormal cognition, as with telepathy, clairvoyance, and precognition, and PK (psychokinesis) which covers paranormal action, such as influencing electronic and atomic randomizers. PK phenomena also include physical mediumship, paranormal healing, poltergeist manifestations, out-of-the-body experiences, survival after death, reincarnation, and the like, but these are much harder to study scientifically.

Recent research, involving sophisticated technologies and strategies (such as using animals) for ruling out reinterpretation and fraud, suggest that it is increasingly difficult to reject at least some psi phenomena. If they are accepted, either physics must be revised (hence the interest of a number of physicists), or there must be more than physics (hence the long-standing interest of *spiritualists). If, on the other hand, they are not accepted, parapsychology will have to be reformulated to become the psychological study of erroneous beliefs.

M. L. Albertson *et al.* (eds.), *Paranormal Research* (1988); J. E. Alcock, *Science and Supernature: Critiques of Parapsychology* (1989); J. Beloff, *Psychological Sciences* (1973); H. J. Irwin, *An Introduction to Parapsychology* (1989); P. Kurtz (ed.), *A Skeptics Handbook* . . . (1985); M. A. A. Thalbourne, *A Glossary of Terms Used in Parapsychology* (1983).

Parāśara. A *ṛṣi who is said to have been one of the four law-givers. *Ṛg Veda* 1. 65–75 and 9. 97 are attributed to him.

Paraśurāma (Skt., 'Rāma with the axe'). In Hindu mythology, a *brahman of the *Bhṛgu clan, destined from birth to lead a warrior's life. He is chiefly known as the hero of two myths. In one he beheads his mother Reṇukā at the request of his father Jamadagni, and then restores her to life again. In the other he takes vengeance upon the sons of Arjuna Kārtavīrya for the death of his father, not only killing them but destroying all male *kṣatriyas twenty-one times over, so that the earth has to be repopulated by the union of brahmans with the kṣatriyas' widows. After this slaughter he performs a great sacrifice and grants the whole earth to *Kaśyapa, leaving no room for himself so that he has to request a narrow strip of land from the ocean. He is thus credited in several legends and folk stories with having reclaimed from the sea various portions of the west coast of India. In many ways Paraśurāma is a puzzling figure: although the *Purāṇas identify him with *Viṣṇu and he becomes the sixth *avatāra in the standard list, he is also presented as a protégé of *Śiva, who gives him his celebrated axe. Moreover, he has no definite place in mythical chronology, being contemporaneous with the heroes of both epics, even though they belong to different times. In *Rāmāyaṇa he is outshone by the youthful Prince *Rāma, who succeeds in bending the great bow of Viṣṇu which Paraśurāma carries. In *Mahābhārata he is said to have been defeated by *Bhīṣma in a combat which lasted for twenty-one days, and is visited by the *Pāṇḍava brothers during their exile.

Parāvṛtti (Skt., *parā* + √*vrt*, 'turn away'). A revolution, according to Buddhists, in one's understanding of reality. The term is not found in the Pāli *Tripiṭaka but is used frequently in the writings of the Yogācāra (*Vijñānavāda) and of Buddhist *Tantrism. *Laṅkāvatārasūtra* talks of a fundamental change in the operation of the store-consciousness (*ālaya-vijñāna) through which a person's understanding of reality is purified. This process is called a revolution at the basis (*āśrayaparāvṛtti*). Such a revolution takes place when one is far advanced on the Buddhist path and has eliminated the hindrances of defilement (*kleśāvaraṇa*) and the knowable (*jneyāvaraṇa*). The *Laṅkāvatārasūtra* goes on to say that parāvṛtti is associated with the eighth stage (*bhūmi) in the progress of a *bodhisattva. Through parāvṛtti the bodhisattva attains the body of a *Tathāgata (*tathāgatakāya*) and is beyond the reach of the illusory world. This is *nirvāna.

Pardes (Pers., 'garden', perhaps underlying Gk., *paradeisos*). It appears in scripture three times (see PARADISE, plus Nehemiah 2. 8). In *B.Ḥag.* 14b, it is used of the Divine Wisdom; and in medieval Judaism, it was taken to be an acrostic of the four major styles of biblical interpretation: *Peshat (literal); Remez (allusive); Derash (homiletical); Sodh (esoteric or mystical).

Pardon. Forgiveness; hence a name for an *indulgence. The attempt to sell such pardons by 'pardoners' was attacked by Chaucer and Langland, long before the *Reformation and its own attack on indulgences.

Paribbājaka (one who joins a community): see AÑÑATITTHIYA PARIBBĀJAKA; PABBĀJITA; PARIVRĀJAKA.

Pariṇāmavāda. The Hindu *Saṃkhya teaching of evolution: effects exist latently within causes (since otherwise eventualities would be random and inconsistent in relation to similar causes); all that is required is the appropriate 'trigger' to release the latent effect. However, such latency may mean that the direction of unfolding (*udbhāva*) can run backwards with equal consistency (*anudbhāva*).

Parinirvāṇa or **parinibbāna** (passing into nirvāna at death): see NIRUPADHIŚEṢA-NIRVĀṆA; MAHĀPARINIBBĀNA SUTTA.

Parish (Gk., dwelling near). A geographically designated area having its own church and minister; hence the people and work of that area. From this derives the (usually pejorative) sense of 'parochial', being too narrowly or locally concerned.

Paris worth a Mass: see HUGUENOTS.

Paritta (Pāli, Sinhalese, *pirit*, from Skt., *pari* + √*trā* to protect). A formula which is to be recited for protection or blessing; the non-canonical collection of such formulae; and the *ritual at which the collection of this formulae or specific portions thereof are recited. Paritta is a Buddhist healing and blessing rite. Originally adopted to cater to the extrareligious needs of the new converts to Buddhism, both from the *brahmanic and the non-brahmanic religious followings, it has absorbed into itself many features of the protective, healing, and blessing rites of those religions.

From an original simple substitution for the non-Buddhist religious rites ensuring protection from evil spirits, natural disasters, and circumstances of private distress, by affirming the truth of the *Dhamma, it has grown into a complex religious rite with individual formulae answering to the diverse needs of the Buddhist community such as fear, ill health, natural calamity, etc., each with its own attendant ritual components to be complied with for efficacy.

The Pāli texts used in the paritta rites form a separate text consisting of twenty-nine *sūtras of mixed length. While all these belong to different texts of the five *Nikāya collections, the majority are associated with individual instances of healing or blessing. All such texts may have been incorporated into a single text after the paritta attained ritual significance.

In the parittas, there is neither placation, *exorcism, nor anathematization of spirits. Instead, it is by the expression of unbounded love and kindness that both spirits and the elements are tamed to behave in conformity with the aspirations and welfare of humans. However, in later Buddhist use, there is profuse intrusion of *magical elements into all aspects of the paritta rite. The monks who chant the parittas do so inside a ritually perfected *maṇḍapa. Not only is the maṇḍapa constructed according to ritual specifications, it is decorated also with ritually acceptable ingredients such as special kinds of green leaves, flowers, cereals, etc. The monks hold a ritual string in their hands while chanting. This string is tied to connect the casket of *relics, the Paritta text (usually made of ola leaves), the pot of water (usually a new clay pot), and the ritual post (*indakhīla*), and passes through the special rings made for the purpose, thus covering the entire maṇḍapa in a clockwise direction before reaching the monks, after passing through whose hands it is finally placed back on the table. A smaller string made of three strands of thread which takes off from this at some point near the 'roof' of the maṇḍapa and continues to the assembled people and is held by them, transmits the blessings of the chanting to them. At the conclusion of the ceremony, the ritually pure water is sprinkled and drunk while pieces of the thread are tied either round the neck or (right) wrist. In this form, it is the magical power of the chanting, fuelled by the magical power of the ritual, that is expected to bring the desired result.

Parivāra (division of Vinayapiṭaka): see TRIPIṬAKA.

Parivrājaka (Skt., *pari* + √*vraj*, 'to wander about'). A wandering religious mendicant. Although this term occurs in the early Brahmanic tradition of the *Upaniṣads, it is also applicable to *Buddhist and *Jain monks, as well as to Hindu *saṁnyāsins. The Pāli equivalent is *paribbājaka*.

Pariyatti. The entire teaching of the *Buddha: it is thus one of the Buddhist meanings of *dharma.

Parker, Matthew (1504–75). Archbishop of Canterbury from 1559. His main objective as archbishop was to preserve the Elizabethan religious settlement which sought to safeguard Protestantism while retaining some of the moderation placed on it by the experience of the past; hence his involvement with the issue of the *Thirty-Nine Articles and of the 'Bishops' Bible' (1568) as well as his own *Advertisements* on what he believed were matters of order. These provoked the *Puritans into opposition, but Parker did not seek controversy. He sought to find the proper doctrinal and historical basis for the Church of England, and to this end he accumulated a library with many Anglo-Saxon and medieval manuscripts (which can be seen in Corpus Christi College, Cambridge).

Parliament of Religions: see WORLD'S PARLIAMENT OF RELIGIONS.

Parochet or **parokhet.** The curtain that separated the 'holy place' in the sanctuary from the *Holy of Holies (Exodus 26. 31–3) and later in Solomon's *Temple (during the years in the wilderness, the tabernacle served as a temple for the Israelites). Parochet was made by *Bezalel of scarlet, purple, and fine linen with a woven design (Exodus 26. 31). Nowadays the term is used by the *Ashkenazim to refer to the curtain hanging before the *Ark in the *synagogue.

Parousia (Gk., 'presence' or 'arrival'). The future return of Christ in glory (the 'Second Coming') to judge the living and the dead. Belief in an imminent parousia was widespread in the earliest church (cf. 1 Corinthians 16. 22) but quickly faded (2 Peter 3. 3–10). It has been revived from time to time in various Christian and *extra*-Christian circles (*Adventists), often accompanied by belief in a *millennium, or thousand-year reign of Christ on earth. Prevailing Christian tradition, however, while maintaining the certainty of a final judgement, has been opposed to any focus of thought on its time and manner.

Parsis. *Zoroastrians who (in the 8th cent. CE), in unknown numbers, decided to leave their Iranian homeland in the face of ever greater Muslim oppression and seek a new land of religious freedom. The story of that migration is contained in the text the *Qissa* (or *Tale*) *of Sanjan* (see S. H. Hodivala, *Studies in Parsi History*, 1920). The *Qissa* was written in 1600 by a Parsi priest on the basis of oral tradition. How reliable that tradition was is unknown, and the *Qissa* may best be understood as the *myth (in the technical sense of the word) relating to the foundation of the community. It is a good reflection of Parsi perceptions of their experiences in India. The *Qissa* relates that the migrating Zoroastrians acted under the guidance of a wise astrologer priest, who advised them on the propitious time to move and where they should go. After crossing the great Iranian desert they embarked on ship and sailed towards India. A great storm blew and threatened their lives, so the priests prayed and vowed that if they were delivered safely then they would consecrate a major fire (*Atash Bahram*) as an act of thanksgiving. The storm abated and they landed safely. They approached the local Hindu ruler, Jadi Ranah, and sought permission to settle and consecrate their fire. In response to his questions they affirmed that they shared many values and ideals, such as reverence for the cow (*gō), for the sacred creations, and the purity laws. The prince granted them permission and required of them only that they should not carry any weapons, should speak the local language, and should observe marriage customs. In short, Parsis consider that their settlement was written in the stars, that it was an answer to prayers, and a refuge, that they share much in common with Hindus, and have not been required to compromise any of their important community traditions. It is a perception which contrasts strongly with Zoroastrian memories of their relations with Muslims in Iran.

The generally accepted date of the Parsi settlement on the western coast of India is 937 CE. Little is known of their history for the next 700 years. Basically they appear to have lived in peace and gradually spread throughout Gujarat as they prospered in trade and textiles. When the Muslim armies invaded the region in the 16th cent. the Parsis fought valiantly but in vain alongside the Hindus. Muslim rule in India was not as harsh as it had been in Iran, and the Parsis continued to flourish. With the arrival of the European trading powers in the 17th cent., especially the British, they prospered as middle men in trade. When the British made their base in Bombay, Parsis began to migrate there. In 1736, a Parsi master shipbuilder, Lowji Wadia, was brought from Surat to organize the building of Bombay dockyard. His family retained control of the shipbuilding industry until the late 19th cent. Not only did they control this foundation of Bombay's commercial success, the Wadia family diversified their interests and became a leading wealthy family in the city. Many other Parsis followed their example. In the 19th cent., though still representing only 6 per cent of the island's population, they became extremely influential in the growing business world, the commerce, banking, industrial, and above all educational institutions of W. India. As a result they grew also in political importance; e.g. they were at the heart of the Indian National Congress from its inception in 1885 until the radical takeover in 1907.

One part of this growth in Parsi fortunes was due to their involvement in overseas trade. Parsi firms and associations were established in the China Seas, in E. Africa, in Sind, and in Britain. This global Parsi *diaspora injected much wealth into the 'old country', which has led to self-sufficiency and much charitable work (not restricted to Parsis). Their influence in politics and industry has been extensive. The transformation of the community from a tiny obscure group into a major force in W. Indian life has inevitably had its effect on their religion. Until the 19th cent., religion was mainly practised in the home, with worship offered before the household fire. But with the growth in wealth and the employment of servants (usually non-Parsis), the home was no longer the pure centre necessary for worship. The wealth provided the solution, for the community was able to build many temples. Although daily prayers are still said at home, many of the important moments of worship are now located in a place set apart for that purpose. Large *baugs*, public places, were set up for splendid functions for initiations, weddings, and public religious feasts (*gahambars*). There was, in short, a considerable degree of institutionalization of community religion.

There were also significant developments in faith. Parsis pursued Western education with such fervour and success that they internalized many of the principles associated with it. In particular they studied Western scholarly works on Zoroastrianism, written, as it happened, mostly by *Protestants. The consequence was that many educated, Westernized Parsis reinterpreted much of the teaching and practice in Protestant terms. Reformers called for prayers in the vernacular instead of the use of the sacred language of *Avesta; they urged the simplification of rituals; the abandonment of many of the purity laws and the interpretation of others in terms of modern Western views on hygiene. The priests were expected to be able to articulate their religion in logical, rational terms. Inevitably a reaction set in. At the end of the 19th cent., many Parsis, like a number of Westernized Hindus, sought to legitimate traditional practices in terms of *Theosophy and the occult interpretations that the Western-originated movement propounded. When Theosophy became more closely associated with Hinduism and the Independence movement, then a Zoroastrian occult movement grew, Ilm-i Kshnoom (Path of Knowledge). Instead of turning to the Tibetan Masters invoked by Theosophists, Khshnoomists follow the teaching of Behramshah Shroff who claimed to have been given his esoteric message by a secret race of Zoroastrian masters in Iran. This movement shares the Theosophical ideals of vegetarianism and teetotalism, the doctrine of rebirth, the belief in the occult power of prayers recited in the sacred language, and in a personal aura. Thus in the 19th cent. Parsi doctrine became polarized between the Liberal Protestants and the Orthodox who have inclined more towards the occult. Since Independence and the departure of the British the occult emphasis has grown, as has interest in Indian holy men, for example the Babas. There is, nevertheless, a continuing interest in Western scholarship, and there have been various teaching initiatives to encourage an informed concern with traditional teaching and practice.

There are regional differences within the Parsi religious world. Bombay is home to more Parsis than any other city and is the centre of the educational initiatives; it also houses most of the major institutional organizations, notably the Bombay Parsi Punchayet, which is mainly a charitable institution but often claims to speak on behalf of traditional Parsis. The Bombay community is the most diverse. Although no centre has a uniform nature, broadly speaking the towns and villages of Gujarat house traditional Orthodox Parsis, the bigger cities, especially Delhi, are more reforming in nature. Karachi, the commercial capital of Pakistan, has a substantial and wealthy Parsi community which has again made extensive provision for its poor with hospitals, schools, housing, temples, social clubs, and other help. Centred in a Muslim environment, the Parsis here are typically more distanced emotionally from the general public than their co-religionists in India, and as a result they have acculturated less. The numbers in the subcontinent are decreasing dramatically. In India they decreased by 10 per cent in 1961–71 and by 20 per cent in the following decade. There are now *c.*60,000 Parsis in India. Numbers in Karachi have dropped from *c.*5,000 in the 1950s to 2,000 in the 1990s. The main cause appears to be that Parsis have come to expect such a high standard of living and thus to pursue education and their careers so determinedly, that marriage is delayed (the average age for men is around 30, for women around 27) and many avoid marriage altogether (some 30 per cent of Parsi women of marriageable age remain single). Even when they marry they typically have very small families. The community is therefore ageing and diminishing.

An unknown number, but a substantial proportion, of the Parsi population has migrated, first to Britain (initially in the 19th cent., but more particularly from the 1960s, *c.*3,000), then America and Canada, also from the 1960s (*c.*7,000), and from the 1980s to Australia (*c.*1,000). Because these diaspora communities consist mainly of young and middle-aged people there is a low death rate, so numbers are increasing, unlike the old country. They are also dominated by highly educated professionals (one survey found 92 per cent of Zoroastrians in New York and Chicago had been to university). There is, therefore, a general air of confidence in their capacity to organize and develop their potential. Many diaspora Parsis consider the future of the religion lies with them and not in the old country. Since the fall of the Shah in 1979, they have been joined by many Iranian Zoroastrians, so the two branches of the religion have come together (not always easily) especially on the west coast of America and Canada. In the W. centres the impact of scholarship has gone hand in hand with the common trend towards Protestantisation that many such diaspora groups experience. Consequently, there is a sense of a divide between the old and the new centres in religious attitudes. The late 20th cent. has, therefore, seen dramatic changes in the geographical dispersal, the social standing, and religious traditions of the Parsis.

M. Boyce, *Zoroastrians: Their Beliefs and Practices* (1979); J. R. Hinnells, *Zoroastrians in Britain* (1995); E. Kulke, *Parsees in British India* (1974); P. Nanavutty, *The Parsis* (1977).

Pārśva. Twenty-third *tīrthaṅkara in Jainism. Accepted now as a historical figure, born in the 9th cent BCE (*c*.250 years before *Mahāvīra), tradition claims that he was born the son of a queen of Benares. After living for thirty years as a householder, he became a wandering ascetic for seventy years, teaching the law of fourfold restraint: *ahiṃsā (non-injury); *asatya* (not lying); *asteya* (not taking anything not given); *aparigraha (non-attachment to people, places, or things). According to 11th-cent. Jain commentators, this latter restraint included *brahmacharya (chastity), the fifth vow in Mahāvīra's *mahāvratas* (see FIVE GREAT VOWS). Jain scriptures describe him as 'the Best', 'the Awakened', and 'the Omniscient', and claim that he gained a large following in his travels through Bihar and W. Bengal, where Jains today give him special honour, particularly on Mount Sammeta where he attained *nirvāna and died. He is said to have systematized the Jain religion by dividing its followers into four groups: *śramaṇa, monks; *śramaṇi*, nuns; *śravaka*, male laity; *śravika*, female laity; and by appointing chief disciples (*gaṇadharas) in charge of the *saṅgha. Mahāvīra's parents were followers of Pārśva's teaching which seems, like Mahāvīra's, to have been a revival and restatement of ancient tradition rather than a new religion. Numerous excavations in N. India have uncovered images of Pārśva seated under a canopy of cobras, the symbol associated with this *jina.

Particular Baptists. Those *Baptists committed to the *Calvinistic doctrine of 'particular' redemption for the elect only. The term distinguishes them from the other main group of English Baptists with 17th-cent. origins, the *General Baptists, who adhered to an *Arminian theology.

Pārvatī (Skt., 'daughter of the mountain'). Also called *Umā or Gaurī. A beautiful benign Goddess in Hinduism, the wife of *Śiva and daughter of the mountain *Himālaya whose mythology is found in the **Mahābhārata* and the *Purāṇas. In grief over the death of his immolated wife *Satī, of whom Pārvatī is a reincarnation, Śiva returns to his meditation at Mount Kailāsa. During this time, however, the demon Tāraka begins to terrorize the cosmos, so *Brahmā sends the god of love, *Kāma, to awaken in Śiva love for Pārvatī in order that a son might be born to them to destroy the demon. Śiva, however, destroys Kāma with a ray from his third eye and scorns the dark complexion of Pārvatī. She then performs austerity (*tapas) to win his love and succeeds (*Matsya Purāṇa* 154. 289–92). They have a son *Kārttikeya or Skanda who destroys Tāraka and later the elephant-headed god *Ganeśa is born to them. Their marriage is a model of male dominance with Pārvatī docilely serving her husband, though this is also a model of the way a mortal should serve the god. Although at one level subservient, there is behind Pārvatī the power of the Goddess (*Devī) who is thought to be beyond the gods.

Parveh or **pareveh** (Yid., 'neutral'). Food which is classified by the Jewish authorities as neutral. It is neither milk nor meat and therefore under the rules of *kashrut* can be eaten with either. See DIETARY LAWS (JUDAISM).

Paryūsana. Jain *festival of repentance, fasting, self-discipline, and universal goodwill, held over an eight (*Śvetāmbara) or ten (*Digambara) day period in the months of Shrāvana / Bhādrapada (Aug. / Sept.) when Jain monks and nuns are in retreat for the monsoon season. It is the most distinctive and important of Jain festivals, when the laity seek forgiveness for any misdeeds of the previous year and spend time with their ascetic leaders performing *sāmāyikas, listening to regular sermons and attending rituals in the temple. Some Jains fast for the whole period, whilst others take only one meal each day, fasting completely on the final day which is called Saṃvatsarī. On Saṃvatsarī the homes of friends and relatives are visited, so that faults can be openly admitted and forgiveness sought, and letters are dispatched to those away from home with a similar intent. Every effort is made to ensure that no animal is injured during the festival period, and food is offered to the pigeons and animals. It is a time of universal friendship and goodwill, when a famous verse is much repeated: 'I ask pardon of all living creatures: may I have a friendly relationship with all beings and be unfriendly with none.'

Pascal, Blaise (1623–62). French mathematician and philosopher. Born in Clermont-Ferrand, he was brought up in Paris, and privately educated. He showed great precocity in mathematics and physics. From 1646 he was closely involved with the *Jansenists and the convent of Port-Royal. On 23 Nov. 1654 he experienced a conversion, recorded in his *Mémorial* (but found stitched into his coat, known as Pascal's amulet), in which he discovered 'the God of Abraham, God of Isaac, God of Jacob, not of the philosophers and the men of science'. When the Jansenist, Arnauld, was condemned in 1655, he wrote his *Lettres provinciales* in which he satirized the laxity implicit in *Jesuit theories of grace and moral theology. In his *Pensées*, published posthumously from his notes, Pascal saw Christianity as lying beyond exact reason and apprehended by the heart which dares to risk: 'The heart has its reasons of which reason knows nothing . . . It is the heart which apprehends God, and not the reason.' The argument is informed by his mathematics and turns to account the new scientific awareness of the vastness of the universe. He is associated also with his 'wager': if we believe God exists and he does, the reward is eternal happiness; if he does not exist, we lose nothing; and the same is true if we disbelieve and he does not exist; whereas if we disbelieve and he does exist, we have lost eternal life. On the mathematics of probability (see further, G. Schlesinger, *Religion and Scientific Method*, 1977), the wager should be taken up *unless* the existence of God can be conclusively disproved—which it cannot.

H. M. Davidson, *Blaise Pascal* (1983); A. Kraishaimer, *Pascal* (1980); J. Mesnard, *Pascal, l'homme et l'œuvre* (1951, tr. G. S. Fraser, *Pascal, His Life and Works*, 1952).

Paschal (Aramaic, *pasḥa*, 'Passover'). Of or relating to the Jewish *Passover or more usually the Christian *Easter. 'Paschaltide', or Eastertide, is the period in the Christian year from Easter to *Pentecost. It is traditionally a joyful season with no penitential observances. In the liturgy there are frequent *Alleluias. The 'paschal candle' is a large candle used in W. churches during Paschaltide. It is first lit from the new fire in the Easter vigil service, after being marked with the sign of the cross, alpha and omega (Revelation 1. 8, 21. 6, 22. 13), and the year. Thereafter it is lit during liturgical functions until *Ascension Day when it is extinguished after the gospel reading.

Paschal lamb. The lamb sacrificed in the Temple as part of the Jewish *Passover festival. The paschal lamb was sacrificed on 14 Nisan, roasted whole and eaten by the community (Exodus 12. 1–28; Deuteronomy 16. 1–8). In Christianity, *Jesus became identified with the paschal Lamb, which was then converted (often) into a sacrificial offering—e.g. in the hymn, 'Paschal Lamb, by God appointed, All our sins on thee were laid'; on which H. A. Hodges commented (*The Pattern of Atonement*, 1955): 'The effect is impressive, and one does not stop to remember that the sins of Israel were never laid on the Paschal Lamb, and that the beast on which they were laid, the scapegoat, was not sacrificed.'

Paschal mystery. The Christian understanding of human salvation concentrated in Christ, dead, risen from the dead, and ascended to heaven, who is the *paschal Lamb of the new Passover: hence the Pentecost Preface: 'Today you sent the Holy Spirit on those marked out to be your children by sharing the life of your only Son, and so you brought the paschal mystery to its completion.'

Pasha. Turkish military and civil title denoting someone of high rank. The title persists in some Arab countries for more local authorities.

Passion (Lat., *passio*, 'suffering'). The events of *Jesus' last days as recounted in the *gospels, culminating in his crucifixion. From at least the 4th cent. the passion was recited with musical settings in churches during *Holy Week; by the Middle Ages, the chant was *plainsong, with motet choruses added in the 15th cent.; *c.*1525 Johann Walter translated a passion into German. Heinrich Schütz (1585–1672) added texture by assigning to different soloists the various characters in the text. Further extensions were made by the addition of poems, hymns, and chorales, some of which were to be sung by the congregation. The *St John Passion* (1723) and *St Matthew Passion* (1729) of J. S. Bach are among the most familiar of these Passions.

Passion Sunday is the 5th Sunday in Lent, a week before *Palm Sunday. It begins the two-week season of Passiontide. Before 1969 in Roman Catholic churches it was the practice to veil all crucifixes and images in the church in purple during this time, but this is now confined to Holy Week, and Passion Sunday is now fused with Palm Sunday.

Passion plays are enactments of the suffering, death, and resurrection of Jesus which served, originally, important didactic purposes. The best known of these is a late example, the play at Oberammergau in Bavaria. According to tradition, the village was spared from plague in 1633, and vowed, in gratitude, to perform a passion play once every ten years. From 1680, the performance was moved to the decennial year, being cancelled only in 1870 and 1940. The text has been open to charges of *anti-Semitism (it was admired by Hitler), and amidst controversy has been changed from the version written in 1860 by J. A. Daisenberger. It is now a major tourist attraction. The term 'passion play' is also used of dramatic reenactments, by Shīʿa Muslims, of the martyrdom of *al-Husain (and *al-Hasan): see TAʿZIYA. For a text, see L. Pelly, *The Miracle Play of Hasan and Husain* (1879).

Passion plays (in Shīʿa Islam): see TAʿZIYA.

Passion Sunday: see PALM SUNDAY.

Passover (Heb., *pesaḥ*). Jewish Festival of Unleavened Bread (*mazzah), one of the *Pilgrim Festivals.

Originally, there were two separate festivals at the same time of year, Passover which had reference to the protection of flocks, and Unleavened Bread which made a commitment of trust in God for the next year's harvest. When *Josiah attempted to centralize the cult in *Jerusalem, the two had to be amalgamated, and they were made together into a pilgrimage feast. The festival begins on 15 Nisan and lasts seven days in *Israel and eight in the *diaspora. During this time, the *exodus from Egypt is commemorated. It is so called because God 'passed over' the houses of the Israelites during the tenth plague of Egypt (Exodus 12). Traditionally the *paschal lamb was sacrificed in the *Temple on Passover eve (14 Nisan), and both *Josephus and the *Talmud record Passover celebrations in the second Temple period. After the destruction of the Temple, the celebrations of the festival reverted to being home-based and the Passover *seder is based on the biblical command, 'You shall tell your son in that day, saying: It is because of that which the Lord did for me when I came forth out of Egypt' (Exodus 13. 8). The special order of service was formulated in the Middle Ages and set down in the Passover *Haggadah. During the Passover season, no *ḥamez* (*leaven) must be found in the house, and mazzah must be eaten instead of bread. The seder ceremony includes reflections on the final redemption and a place is laid for *Elijah, the herald of the *messiah. In the diaspora, a seder is held on both the first and second night of Passover, and on the second night the counting of the *omer is begun. Passover is a major festival which is celebrated even by secularized Jews. See also LEAVEN; SEDER; FESTIVAL; FIRST-BORN.

P. Goodman, *The Passover Anthology* (1961); C. Raphael, *A Feast of History* . . ., (1972); J. B. Segal, *The Hebrew Passover: From the Earliest Times to A.D. 70* (1963).

Pastoral Epistles. The three letters, 1–2 *Timothy and *Titus in the New Testament, so-called because they contain instructions for church officers and organization. The letters all claim to be from *Paul to his assistants, but their weaker theology, differences in style and terminology, and supposed place in Paul's life (after the end of the story in *Acts?) make the claim more or less doubtful. Of interest in the letters is the term *episkopos*, later *'bishop', but here (e.g. Titus 1. 7) not distinguished from *presbyteros*, *'elder'.

Pāśupata (Skt., *paśu*, 'beast', + *pati*, 'lord'). An early *Śaiva sect worshipping *Śiva as Pāśupati. Their name is derived from the threefold Śaiva doctrine of Lord (*pati*), soul (*paśu*, 'beast'), and bondage (*pāśa*). Accounts of them are given in the **Mahābhārata*, the *Vayu *Purāṇa* and the *Atharvaśiras *Upaniṣad*. Their doctrines are known from the later *Pāśupata Sūtra* and the commentary by Kauṇḍīnya (5th or 6th cent. CE; tr. H. Chakraborti, 1970). The Pāśupatas maintained that Śiva is transcendent, and is the instrumental, not the material, cause of the world. The aim of Pāśupata practice, which comprised *yoga, *asceticism, and *mantra repetition, was freedom from suffering, which comes about only through grace (*prasāda). There are five main categories in the Pāśupata system: (i) *dukhānta*, the 'end of suffering'; (ii) *karya*, 'effect', i.e. created souls (*paśu*); (iii) *karaṇa*, 'cause', i.e. the Lord Paśupati; (iv) *yoga; and (v) *vidhi*, 'behavioural injunction', one of the most important features of which was bathing in *ashes thrice a day. The Pāśupatas were celibate (*urdhvā retas*, ones who 'keep their semen up'), and ascetic (*tapasvin). They also practised anti-social behaviour, such as snoring in public, acting as if mad, and talking nonsensically, in order to court abuse, whereby the *karma merit of the abuser would be transferred to the abused. A subsect of the Pāśupatas were the Lakulīśa Pāśupatas who regarded their founder Lakulī as an incarnation of Śiva. They went naked, with matted hair, covered in ashes, and frequented cremation grounds. See also KĀPĀLIKA; INDUS VALLEY CIVILIZATION.

D. N. Lorenzen, *The Kāpālikas and Kālāmukhas* . . . (1972).

Paśupati (lord of cattle). *Śiva as the lord of all creatures.

Pāṭaliputra. The capital of the ancient kingdom of Magadha (near present-day Patna in N. India), was founded in the 5th cent. BCE, and reached its peak (with 570 towers on its battlements and 64 guarded gateways) during the *Mauryan Empire. After the reign of *Aśoka, who expanded the city and held the third Buddhist *Council there (247 BCE), Pāṭaliputra fell into decline.

Patañjali. 1. The reputed author of the **Yoga Sūtra* (2nd–3rd cents. CE), in which classical yoga is given systematic presentation. Patañjali seems to have synthesized various yoga traditions, moulding yoga into a system of philosophy (*darśana) based upon *Saṃkhya and developing eight-limbed (*aṣṭanga) or *rāja yoga. The final chapter is now believed to be later (*c.*400 CE). For trs. see YOGA SŪTRA.

2. An Indian grammarian of the 2nd cent. BCE who wrote *The Great Commentary* (*Mahābhāṣya*, tr. S. D. Joshi and J. A. F. Roodbergen, 1968–80), an explanation of grammar based on the *Aṣṭadhyāya* of *Pāṇini. His text is concerned with various philosophical and grammatical problems such as the relation of word to meaning. He has sometimes been collated with Patañjali (1), but whether the two are really one person is still uncertain.

The name Patañjali denotes no particular caste, and according to legend implies being an incarnation of *Śeṣa, the cosmic serpent, who descended (*pata*) in the form of a small snake into the palm (*añjali*) of the grammarian Pāṇini. Patañjali is also known as Gonardīya and Gonikāputra.

R. S. Mishra, *The Textbook of Yoga Psychology* . . . (1963).

Paten. The dish on which the bread is placed at the Christian *eucharist. Usually of precious metal (gold or silver), they may now be of hard materials 'that do not easily break or deteriorate'.

Pater noster. Lat. for 'Our Father'. See LORD'S PRAYER.

Pāṭh (Hindī, Pañjābī, 'reading'). For Sikhs, a reading of the entire *Ādi Granth. This may be an uninterrupted reading (*akhaṇḍ pāṭh) or may take about ten days or longer (sahaj pāṭh, sadhāran pāṭh). A saptāhik pāṭh is completed within one week. Sikhs are enjoined to read the complete scriptures frequently, always commencing with six verses of *Anand *Sāhib, the *Ardās, and a *hukam.

Paticca-samuppāda (Pāli; Skt., *pratītya-samutpāda*). A key concept in Buddhism, variously translated—e.g. 'dependent origination', 'conditioned genesis', 'interconnected arising', 'causal nexus'. It states that all physical and mental manifestations which constitute individual appearances are interdependent and condition or affect one another, in a constant process of arising (*samudaya*) and ceasing to be (*nirodha). The analysis is laid out in, e.g., **Saṃyutta Nikāya* 2. 1–133 and **Dīgha Nikāya* 2. 55–71: 'This being, that comes to be; from this arising, that arises; this being absent, that is not; this ceasing, that ceases' (*Saṃyutta Nikāya* 2. 28). Every appearance is connected to (and depends on) some other appearance: nothing, except the absolute, non-interactive state of *nirvāna, can escape its connectedness to some other manifestation, so that all unravels as surely as it is knitted together. There is no Self or substance which is independent of paticca-samuppāda (*anātman). The 'knitting-together' which constructs appearances and activities in the realm of *samsāra is the twelve-link (*nidāna*) chain of paticca-samuppāda, which leads inevitably to entanglement and *dukkha (the cessation of dukkha being the unravelling of the chain in reverse order): (i) ignorance, *avidyā leads to (ii) constructing activities, *samskāra, to (iii) consciousness leading into another appearance/birth, *vijñāna, to (iv) *nāma-rūpa, name and form of a new appearance, to (v) the sense awareness of the six object realms, to (vi) contact with those environments, to (vii) sensation and feeling, *vedanā* (see SKANDHA), to (viii) craving, *tṛṣṇa, to (ix) clinging on to life and further life in a new womb, *upādāna, to (x) further becoming and appearance, *bhāva, to (xi) birth, *jāti*, to (xii) old age, senility, and death.

D. J. Kalupahana, *Causality: The Central Philosophy of Buddhism* (1975).

Pāṭihāriya (Pāli, 'wonder', 'marvel', 'phenomenon'). A device that could be put to use in winning converts to Buddhism. Canonical Buddhism acknowledges three: the wonder of magic power (*iddhi-pāṭihāriya), of mind-reading (*ādesanā-pāṭihāriya*), and of instruction (*anusāsana-pāṭihāriya*). The use of displays of the first two to impress and convert laypersons was severely criticized by the Buddha, because they were feats which non-Buddhist ascetics could also perform and because they played upon people's credulity. He stressed the absolute sovereignty of the third device, instruction in the *dharma, because it was a means of communicating truths that were intelligible and beneficial to its audience and not a form of exhibitionism like the others.

Pātimokkha (Buddhist moral code): see PRĀTIMOKṢA.

Paṭipatti. The practice of Buddhist truth, and thus one of the many meanings of *dharma.

Patisambhidāmagga (part of Buddhist Pāli canon): see KHUDDAKA-NIKĀYA.

Patit (Pañjābī, 'fallen'). Lapsed Sikh. Any *amritdhārī Sikh who breaks the *khālsā's code of discipline (*rahit), most often by hair-cutting and removal of *turban, is termed 'patit'. Patit Sikhs cannot be elected to the *S(hi)romaṇī Gurdwārā Parbandhak Committee. Apostates may renew their commitment by receiving *amrit at the *khaṇḍe-dī-pāhul ceremony and discharging a *taṅkhāh (penalty). See also MANMUKH; SAHAJDHĀRĪ.

Paṭivedha. The realization of Buddhist truth through stages, leading up to *nirvāna, and thus one of the many meanings of *dharma.

Patriarch. 1. Title from the 6th cent. for the presiding *bishops of the five main sees of Christendom (Rome, Alexandria, Antioch, Constantinople, and Jerusalem), corresponding to provinces of the Roman Empire, who had authority over the *metropolitans in their territories. In addition to these, the heads of some *autocephalous Orthodox churches, the heads of *Uniat Churches, and the heads of the *Oriental Orthodox and *Assyrian Churches also have the title of patriarch. The patriarch of Constantinople is seen as 'first among equals' of the Orthodox patriarchs, and is given the title *Oecumenical Patriarch. The patriarchate of Moscow was established in 1589, and abolished by Peter the Great in 1720: it was restored by the Holy Synod in 1917, but was vacant between 1925 and 1943.

2. The term is also used as an English equivalent of *soshigata, the founder of a Buddhist, especially Zen, school, together with his lineage successors.

Patriarchs and matriarchs. The ancestors of the Jewish people. The *rabbis designated *Abraham, *Isaac, and *Jacob and their wives Sarah, Rebekah, Leah, and Rachel as the patriarchs and matriarchs of Israel. The book of *Genesis portrays the patriarchs and matriarchs as tent-dwellers, leading a nomadic life in the hill-country and semi-desert of *Erez Israel. They were buried in the Cave of Machpelah. According to the *aggadic tradition, it was through the *merits of the fathers, that God hastened the redemption of the Israelites from Egypt (*BRH* 11a); and it was they who introduced the daily prayers. The opening *blessing of the *ʿAmidah, the heart of every prayer service, begins, 'God of Abraham, God of Isaac and God of Jacob . . .'; in recent years, non-*Orthodox congregations have added the names of the matriarchs.

S. Teubal, *Sarah, the Priestess* . . . (1984).

Patrick, St (*c*.390–*c*.460). Christian missionary bishop of Ireland. He was born in Britain and after being abducted by pirates at the age of 16 and kept in semi-slavery in Ireland for six years, he escaped and returned to his family. There he trained for the ministry, learning it seems a rather conservative rule of faith and a knowledge of the Latin Bible. At some point he was sent from Britain as 'bishop in Ireland', and he spent the rest of his life there.

The only certain information about St Patrick's life comes from his one surviving letter and from his autobiographical *Confession*. His authorship of the ancient Irish hymn 'The Breastplate of St Patrick' is unlikely. In later legends, he becomes a miracle-worker who drove the snakes out of Ireland. The same legends, concerned to make him the sole 'apostle of the Irish', exaggerate the scope of his missionary work. His place of burial was not known, allowing *Glastonbury to claim possession of his relics. Feast day, 17 Mar.

R. P. C. Hanson, *Saint Patrick* . . . (1968).

Patripassianism (Lat., *pater*, 'father', + *passus*, 'suffered'). The Christian doctrine, usually held to be *heretical, that God the Father was the subject of Jesus' sufferings. It is inherent in *modalism. Somewhat differently, among modern theologians, J. Moltmann has spoken of the Father's suffering in giving up the Son to death. See also IMPASSIBILITY OF GOD.

Patristics. The study of Christian writers, specifically the *Church Fathers, in the period from the end of New Testament times to *Isidore of Seville (d. 636) in the W. and *John of Damascus (d. *c*.749) in the E. The term 'patrology', synonymous in older books, now usually refers to a handbook on the patristic literature.

Patrology: see PATRISTICS.

Patronage (nominating to a benefice): see ADVOWSON.

Patron saint. A *saint who is recognized, or has been chosen as the special protector or advocate in heaven of a particular place, church, organization, trade, etc. The building of churches over the tombs of martyrs associated churches with saints. The 'patronal festival' is the patron saint's feast day.

Pa-tuan-chin. A series of eight Taoist physical exercises, dating from the 12th cent. CE, to which others were added at a later date. They exist in two forms, northern (harder) and southern (easier). See further S. Pálos, *Atem und Meditation* (1980).

Paul, St (d. *c*.65 CE). The most important early Christian *missionary *apostle and theologian.

The main source for Paul's biography is *Acts, which however must be tested against the sparse data in Paul's own letters. Paul (originally 'Saul') was a Jewish native of Tarsus in Cilicia. He was brought up as a *Pharisee and probably studied in Jerusalem. He opposed the Christian movement, but while on a mission to Damascus (*c*.33 CE) to arrest Christians he was converted by an encounter with the risen *Christ (described in Acts 9. 1–19), probably while practising *merkabah mysticism. Paul's main missionary work appears to have begun fourteen or seventeen years later (Galatians 1–2). According to Acts it took the form of three missionary journeys beginning and ending at *Antioch: 13–14, 15. 36–18. 23, 18. 23–21. He thus established congregations in south and central Asia Minor, Ephesus, and Greece. These were largely Gentile congregations, although he continued to preach in *synagogues. He was constantly harassed by local authorities and Jewish communities (2 Corinthians 11. 24–7). He was at last arrested in Jerusalem, and sent for trial to Caesarea, and then (on his appealing to Caesar) to Rome (Acts 21–8). An early tradition holds that Paul was acquitted, and then preached in Spain before being re-arrested and put to death by the sword under Nero. The church of St Paul Outside the Walls in Rome was built over the site of his burial. Feast days: with Peter, 29 June; conversion, 25 Jan.

Of the thirteen letters in Paul's name in the New Testament (*Hebrews makes no claim to be by Paul), scholars generally, but not unanimously, distinguish seven as certainly genuine (*Romans, 1–2 *Corinthians, *Galatians, *Philippians, 1 *Thessalonians, *Philemon) and six as 'deutero-Pauline'. The latter (*Ephesians, *Colossians, 2 *Thessalonians, 1–2 *Timothy, *Titus) reflect Paul's thought more or less weakly, but are by no means certainly not written by Paul. The genuine letters date from the period from *c*.51 (1 Thessalonians) to *c*.58 (Romans). Philippians, Colossians, Philemon, and Ephesians, known as 'captivity epistles', if from Paul, may have been written later in Rome, or from an earlier time in prison in Ephesus or Caesarea.

Although they are not systematic writings, Paul's letters laid the foundations for much of later Christian theology. Paul's doctrine, starting from the traditions he 'received' (1 Corinthians 15. 3–11), was further worked out in controversy with right-wing Jewish Christians, against whom Paul held that sinful humanity is redeemed and justified by God's *grace through *faith in Jesus Christ, independently of keeping the Jewish *law. Christ's death had abrogated the Law and ushered in the new era of the *Holy Spirit. Christians therefore form a new *'Israel of God' (Galatians 6. 16) and inherit the promises of God to Israel (see especially Galatians and Romans). The local congregation is likened to a body by Paul, and in Colossians 1. 24 the whole church is called the body of Christ. Paul expected a speedy return of Christ to judge the world (e.g. 1 Thessalonians 4) but this theme recedes in the later letters.

Paul's doctrine of grace, *predestination, and free will was developed and expanded by *Augustine in his struggle with *Pelagius, and has figured in the controversies between *Thomism and *Molinism, and between *Calvinism and *Arminianism. His doctrine of *justification by faith also was fundamental to the *Lutheran reformation. In modern times the unsettling prophetic side of Paul's preaching has been re-emphasized by K. *Barth (see especially *The Epistle to the Romans*, tr. 1935).

C. K. Barrett, *Paul: An Introduction* . . . (1994); J. C. Beker, *Paul the Apostle* . . . (1980); G. Bornkamm, *Paul* (tr. 1969); F. F. Bruce, *Paul* . . . (1977); R. Scroggs, *Paul for a New Day* (1977); D. E. H. Whiteley, *The Theology of Saint Paul* (1964).

Paul III (1468–1549). *Pope, 1534–49. He received a humanist education and was made cardinal deacon by pope Alexander VI in 1493 (his nickname was 'cardinal petticoat', because his sister was the pope's mistress). He was not ordained priest until 1519, but he nevertheless held benefices and bishoprics. As bishop of Parma (1509), he put the reforms of the Fifth Lateran Council into effect, and began to reform his own life. Elected pope unanimously, he became 'a renaissance pope', encouraging artists and architects (e.g. commissioning Michelangelo to complete the 'Last Judgement' in the Sistine Chapel and to supervise work on the new St Peter's), and engaging in nepotism (two grandsons were made cardinals at the ages of 14 and 16, and given important posts). He also undertook reform of the Church (he is sometimes called 'the first pope of Catholic reform') to meet the threat of *Protestantism. The report he commissioned (*Consilium de Emendenda Ecclesia*, 1537) became the basis of the work of the Council of *Trent. In 1540, the *bull, *Regimini Militantis Ecclesiae*, gave approval to the Society of Jesus (*Jesuits), and in 1542 the Congregation of the Roman *Inquisition or the Holy Office was established with strong powers of censorship to combat heresy. Politically, he sought a balance between Francis I of France and the emperor Charles V, seeing far greater threats from the *Ottoman Turks and from Protestants. He supported Charles in his campaign to destroy the alliance of Protestants known as the Schmalkaldic League, and he excommunicated Henry VIII in 1538.

Paul VI (1897–1978). *Pope from 21 June 1963. Born Giovanni Battista Montini near Brescia, he entered the papal secretariat of state in 1924 and served there until appointed archbishop of Milan in 1955. As pope he pledged himself to continue the policies of *John XXIII: he continued the Second *Vatican Council, instituted a regular *synod of bishops to assist in governing the church, reformed the *curia and the diplomatic service, legislated for revised *liturgical rites, and abolished the *Index. He visited the World Council of Churches, and twice travelled to see the *patriarch of Constantinople in pursuit of better *ecumenical relations. He also travelled widely outside Europe—including once to the United Nations—and drew upon his experiences in the *encyclical *Populorum Progressio*, in which he discussed problems of development in the Third World. In 1967 he published **Humanae Vitae* which reiterated the traditional RC rejection of artificial means of birth control, and this overshadowed his more progressive actions, such as the 1975 Apostolic Exhortation *Evangelii Nuntiandi* with its implicit endorsement of some elements of *liberation theology.

Paulus P. P. Elenchus Bibliographicus (1981); P. Hebblethwaite, *Paul VI* (1993).

Paulicians. Christian sect prominent in the 7th–11th cents. in Armenia and the east of the Byzantine Empire. According to Gk. sources they were *Manicheans, and by modern scholars they have often been considered a link in the chain between the early *gnostics and the Manichees of the Middle Ages in the West Armenian sources, however, indicate that gnostic doctrines (dualism, *docetism, etc.) may have been a secondary development. In Armenia, where the sect originated, its *Christology appears to have been of an *adoptionist type, perhaps akin to that of *Paul of Samosata or perhaps a survival of a very archaic native form of Christianity left behind by the Orthodox Church in the 4th–5th cents. Apart from a period of favour under the *Iconoclast emperors of the 8th–9th cents., the Paulicians were persecuted in the Empire, and allied themselves with the Muslim power.

Paul of Samosata (3rd cent.). Christian *heretic. He became bishop of Antioch *c.*260 but was deposed by a synod there in 268 on account of his *Christological teaching, little of which has survived. The best-attested accusation against Paul is that he taught that Christ was a mere man. It appears he denied Christ's real pre-existence, his 'descent' to redeem humanity, and his actual metaphysical status as God. Such language was permanently ruled out in orthodox Christian circles after Paul's condemnation.

Pauṛī (Pañjābī, 'ladder'). Sikh verse. The *padās* (sections) of longer poems in the *Ādi Granth are called pauṛīs. For example, the *Japjī contains thirty-eight pauṛīs. The metre and structure of pauṛīs vary, although they are consistent within each *vār. Pauṛīs by a single author are interspersed with *ślaloks of varied authorship.

Paytanim. Jewish liturgical poets (e.g. Eleazar *Kallir): see PIYYUT.

Peace (exchange of greetings): see KISS OF PEACE.

Peacock Angel (Yezīdī term for Satan): see YEZĪDĪS.

Peak-experiences: see MASLOW, A. H.

Peculiar People. A small *Free Church denomination taking its title from the description in 1 Peter 2. 9. They were initially called the 'Plumstead Peculiars' from the place of their origin in 1838. Founded by William Bridges, churches with a strong emphasis on *faith-healing and *anointing with oil (James 5. 14) developed in various parts of Kent and Essex, but only rarely beyond those counties. Most of these congregations no longer use their original title and have now become affiliated to the Fellowship of Independent Evangelical Churches.

P'ei Hsiu (Jap., Haikyu): see HUANG-PO HSI-YÜN.

Pelagianism. The Christian *heresy which holds that a person can come to salvation by her or his own efforts apart from God's grace; or in co-operation with grace. It is named from the British theologian Pelagius, who taught in Rome in the 4th–5th cents. Pelagius' teaching was ascetic and moral, arguing that human nature is created by God in such a way that individuals are free to choose good or evil. He was critical of *Augustine's prayer 'Give what you command, and command what you will', which seemed to deny any scope to human freedom or will. However, much of the controversy with Augustine was brought on by Pelagius' rationalizing disciples, who pressed the denial of the effects of *original sin in an Augustinian sense. Pelagianism was finally condemned at the Council of *Ephesus in 431. Its influence continued, especially in the S. of France in the form of a movement now called 'semi-Pelagianism'. First expounded by John *Cassian, this was a doctrine midway between Augustine and Pelagius, mainly in opposition to Augustine's extreme views of predestination. It held that the first steps toward the Christian life were taken by the human will, God's grace supervening only later. After its condemnation in 529, Augustine's teaching on grace and free will prevailed everywhere in the Christian West.

R. F. Evans, *Pelagius* . . . (1968).

Pelican. A bird, employed as Christian symbol. Because of the false belief that the pelican feeds her young with her blood by piercing her breast with her beak, the pelican became a popular medieval symbol for Christ's redemptive work, especially as mediated through the *eucharist.

Penance. In Christianity, punishment (Lat., *poena*) for sin. In the early church, it appears to have emerged in connection with the issue of whether sins after baptism can be forgiven: penance accepted that such sins can be forgiven, but deserve some punishment; such punishment, via penance, is better accepted in this world than in the next. By the 3rd cent. the system had emerged in which the sinner, after public confession, was placed, once only in his or her life, in an order of 'penitents', excluded from communion and committed to a severe course of prayer, fasting, and almsgiving for a specified time. This scarcely workable system gave place to another, originally *Celtic, in which confession was made privately. In the beginning, penance was severe, and absolution withheld until it was completed. Gradually, however, it began to be possible to commute long penances, e.g. with the payment of money, and from this idea perhaps developed the practice of *indulgences. In the 11th cent. absolution also came to be granted on confession before penance was begun. Public penance continued for notorious offences. From all this developed the Catholic practice of *confession, *absolution, and light penance. After *Vatican II, greater emphasis was placed on communal acts of confession, diminishing thereby individual penance; but the present code of *Canon Law still requires Roman Catholics to confess all *mortal sins by number and species at least once a year—and commends confession of *venial sins as well. Formally, 'penance' refers to the whole *sacrament in which the guilt of post-baptismal sin, both mortal and venial, is remitted through confession and absolution, and its punishment is remitted through the penance (or 'satisfaction') itself.

J. Dallen, *The Reconciling Community: The Rite of Penance* (1986).

P'eng Lai. Taoist 'isle of the immortals' (*hsien), first referred to in **Lieh-tzu*. Many stories are told of expeditions to reach it and find the mushroom of immortality. All fail, because if the hazards of shipwreck, etc., are overcome, the island sinks beneath the sea as the sailors approach. The story becomes in later Taoism an allegory of the spiritual quest. See also FANG-SHIH; HSIEN.

P'eng-tzu. Mythological figure in China, representing long life. In religious Taoism, he is said to have introduced *fang-chung shu (sexual exchange of power) for that purpose. *Ko Hung included his biography in *Pao-p'u-tzu*.

Penitence, Ten Days of. The period of ten days from *Rosh ha-Shanah to Yom Kippur in the Jewish *Calendar. According to tradition, individuals are judged at the *New Year (1 Tishri) and the judgement is announced on the *Day of Atonement. Clemency can be obtained through sincere repentance during the Ten Days of Penitence. *Seliḥot are said daily, and a particular *liturgy is followed.

Penitential prayers (Jewish): see SELIḤOT.

Penn, William (1644–1718). *Quaker leader and founder of Pennsylvania. He was influenced as an undergraduate by the Quaker teaching of the Oxford tradesman, Thomas Loe. On hearing Loe again in Ireland, Penn committed himself wholeheartedly to the Quaker cause. Frequently imprisoned for his writings, he used his confinements to produce further apologetic works, notably *No Cross No Crown* (1669), and assisted the Quaker pursuit of religious and political freedom by obtaining from

Charles II a charter for Pennsylvania. His later years were saddened by ill health, poverty, and imprisonment.

M. B. Endy, *William Penn and Early Quakerism* (1973).

Pentateuch (Gk., *penta*, 'five', + *teuchos*, 'book'). The first five books of the Hebrew *Bible, also known as *Torah (for Hebrew names see each book): *Genesis, *Exodus, *Leviticus, *Numbers, and *Deuteronomy. The Pentateuch contains the history of the Jewish people from the creation of the world until the death of *Moses. Traditionally it was believed to be a single document revealed by God to Moses and written down by him. As Exodus 33. 11 puts it, the revelation to Moses was unique in that 'the Lord spoke to Moses face to face as a man speaks to his friend'. The belief in the divine origin of the Pentateuch is fundamental to *Orthodox Judaism and is formulated in the eighth of *Maimonides' *Articles of the Jewish Faith ('I believe with perfect faith that the whole Torah now in our possession is the same as that which was given to Moses our teacher'). However, most biblical scholars now date the Pentateuch no earlier than the time of the monarchy. According to the 'documentary hypothesis', it is composed of four major sources: J (Jahwistic) which uses the *tetragrammaton as the divine name; E (Elohistic) which refers to God as *Elohim; P, the *Priestly source; and D, the *Deuteronomic. J and E, which have been combined by a later editor are thought to have been written during the period of the united kingdom (i.e. 10th cent. BCE), while Deuteronomy was produced in the 7th cent., and the Priestly source is dated to the time of *Ezra and *Nehemiah. However, the precision of these claims has more recently come under attack. Greater emphasis is placed on kinship and sanctuary traditions which have been more deliberately and creatively drawn together. Despite the differences between the sources, a common tradition can be detected, including such themes as the promises to the *patriarchs, the *exodus from Egypt, the giving of the *law and the making of the *Covenant at Mount *Sinai, and the inheritance of the *Promised Land. These themes were recapitulated and recited at sacred ceremonies (see Deuteronomy 25. 5–9). The entire Pentateuch is divided into fifty-four sections (*Sedarot) and one section is read each week in the *synagogue, concluding on Shemini Atzeret. The text is written on a *Scroll which is dressed and kept in the Synagogue *Ark. The Pentateuch, as the written law of the Jewish people and the ultimate source of the *oral Law, is often known as the Torah, and thus the Scroll as the Torah Scroll.

J. H. Hertz (ed.), *The Pentateuch and Haftorah* (1929–36); R. N. Whybray, *The Making of the Pentateuch* . . . (1987).

Pentecost. The Jewish feast of Weeks, i.e. *Shavu'ot, held fifty days (hence the name) after *Passover. The Greek name occurs in (e.g.) Tobit 2. 1; *Josephus, *Antiquities*, 17. 10. 2. In Christian use, 'Pentecost' refers specifically to the occasion at the conclusion of the Jewish festival when, according to the account in Acts 2, the *Holy Spirit descended on the *apostles 'with the noise of a strong driving wind' in the form of tongues of fire, so that they began to speak in foreign languages. The name is also applied to the feast celebrating this event (also known as Whitsunday) on the fiftieth day of Eastertide. In early times the vigil of Pentecost became a secondary date for *baptisms. In the church year the following Sundays until Advent are numbered 1st, 2nd, etc. after Pentecost.

Pentecostals/Pentecostalism. Groups of Christians who emphasize the descent of the *Holy Spirit on the *apostles at the first (Christian) Pentecost (Acts 2) and the continuing post-conversion work of the Holy Spirit. The modern movements date from the ministry of Charles Parham (1873–1929) in the USA, in 1900/1901. He linked baptism in the Spirit with *glossolalia (speaking with tongues), and saw the revival as a restoration of the gifts promised in the latter days. There is thus a strong *eschatological emphasis, exalting spiritual experience over intellectual reflection. It is characterized by participatory forms of worship—hand-clapping, dance, raised arms, prophecy—and has had a strong appeal to the poor and less-educated (hence the title of the study by R. M. Anderson, *Vision of the Disinherited*, 1979). Because experience outweighs formal ministry, there have been many Pentecostal churches; and although the first Pentecostal world conference was held at Zurich in 1947 (the second was in Paris in 1949), there has been strong opposition to the forming of a representative body which might 'speak for' Pentecostals. There has been equal resistance to the *ecumenical movement, since the churches involved are almost entirely in an apostate condition. There are at least 130 million Pentecostals worldwide, with particularly rapid expansion in S. America. See also CHARISMATIC (MOVEMENT).

N. Bloch-Hoell, *The Pentecostal Movement* . . . (1964); M. Burgess and G. B. McGee, *Dictionary of Pentecostal and Charismatic Movements* (1989); D. Dayton, *Theological Roots of Pentecostalism* (1972); W. J. Hollenweger, *The Pentecostals* . . . (1972); C. E. Jones, *A Guide to the Study of the Pentecostal Movement* (1983); J. T. Nicol, *Pentecostalism* (1966); V. Synan, *The Holiness/Pentecostal Movement in the U.S.* (1971).

People of God (Russian sect): see DOUKHOBHORS.

People of the Book (those whom Muslims accept have received revelation from God): see AHL AL-KITĀB.

Peoples' Temple. Movement founded by the Reverend Jim Jones, a Christian socialist, in Indianapolis during the early 1950s. Having moved to California in 1965, Jones then established Jonestown, Guyana (1977). The Jonestown tragedy occurred in Nov. 1978, when 913 followers and Jones himself died, a sizeable number by drinking cyanide-laced

'Flavor-Aid' (the remainder were murdered). The great majority of those who died were black, generally from lower-class backgrounds. Jonestown was to be the promised land, allowing freedom from Satanic repression and racism. Jones, who had become increasingly dictatorial and *fundamentalistic, took the theme of world-rejection to its extreme. One way of explaining the tragedy is in terms of the logic, 'better die for heaven above than allow Satan to take over here'. The tragedy was in fact triggered by an investigation by Congressman Les Ryan and a party of journalists, seen as demonic agents.

Peot (Heb., 'corners'). The growth of *hair by Jews in accordance with the command of Leviticus 19. 27, 'You shall not cut around the corners of the head.' The reason for the original command is unknown—perhaps it was to make distinction from a pagan or idolatrous rite. By the *Talmudic period, it was interpreted to mean that some hair must be left between the back of the ears and the forehead, and for many Jews in the present the command is obeyed by taking care not to remove all the hair by the ear. For *Orthodox Jews and for Ḥasidim, the command has been reinforced by *kabbalistic interpretations, which see in the long strands of uncut hair the stream of mercy from God or the providential channels to draw off wild imagination. Hence Ḥasidim encourage the long twisting locks which mark them off from gentiles (and from other Jews), although there is no specific commandment for them. In some families, young boys have their first haircut after their third birthday on the day *Lag ba-Omer, when all hair is removed except for the hair beside the ear.

Perek Shirah (Heb., 'Chapter of a Song'). An anonymous Jewish tract containing hymns of praise. The hymns are placed in the mouths of all creation (except for humanity) and set in a *midrashic framework. It is preserved in different versions in various manuscripts and dates from as early as the 10th cent. CE. It is sometimes recited as a private prayer after the morning service.

L. Ginzberg, *Legends of the Jews* (1909).

Perennial philosophy: see PHILOSOPHIA PERENNIS.

Perfection. A term meaning 'completeness', in which sense it is only absolutely appropriate to God, though the Gk. term (*teleiosis*) can also mean 'consecration'. Matthew 5. 48 suggests that the Christian goal is divine perfection, so perfection is frequently synonymous with the *unitive way. Often a twofold perfection has been envisaged, the one, more complete, found in the religious life (cf. Matthew 19. 21), the latter available to all Christians through grace. Whether perfection is possible in this life, even through grace, has been disputed amongst Christians, *Protestants being mainly doubtful, though *pietists and *Methodists see it as the normal consequence of conversion. For the ten Buddhist perfections see BHŪMI.

R. N. Flew, *The Idea of Perfection in Christian Theology* (1934).

Perfection of Wisdom literature (Prajñāpāramitā). This Buddhist literature was composed over a long period, the nucleus of the material appearing from 100 BCE to 100 CE, with additions for perhaps two cents. later. There followed a period of summary and restatement in the form of short sūtras such as the **Diamond* and **Heart Sūtras*, *c.*300–500 CE, followed by a period of *Tantric influence, 600–1200 CE. The oldest text is *Aṣṭasāhasrikā-prajñāpāramitā-sūtra* (Perfection of Wisdom in 8,000 Lines, tr. E. Conze). The place of origin of the Prajñāpāramitā literature is disputed: the traditionally accepted area is S. India, but there is evidence of its presence also in the NW.

The Prajñāpāramitā literature was innovative in two principal ways: (i) it advocated the *bodhisattva ideal as the highest form of the religious life; and (ii) the 'wisdom' it teaches is that of the emptiness (*śūnyatā) and non-production of phenomena (*dharmas), rather than their substantial, albeit impermanent, mode of being. The scholar who pioneered research in this field, E. Conze, summarized it as follows:

> The thousands of lines of the *Prajñāpāramitā* can be summed up in the following two sentences: 1) One should become a bodhisattva (or, Buddha-to-be), i.e., one who is content with nothing less than all-knowledge attained through the perfection of wisdom for the sake of all beings. 2) There is no such thing as a Bodhisattva, or as all-knowledge, or as a 'being', or as the perfection of wisdom, or as an attainment. To accept both these contradictory facts is to be perfect. (*The Prajñāpāramitā Literature*, 1978, pp. 7–8.)

Other important developments in the Perfection of Wisdom literature are the concept of 'skilful means' (**upāya-kauśalya*) and the practice of dedicating one's religious merit to others so that they are assisted in realizing śūnyatā in their own case. The major exponent of the Perfection of Wisdom school was *Nāgārjuna.

Trs. E. Conze, 1974, 1975.

Perfect Life Society/Kyōdan (Japanese religious movement): see MIKI TOKUHARU.

Pericope (Gk., 'section'). A passage of scripture; specifically, one that is a self-contained product of oral tradition, or one prescribed for liturgical reading.

Periyâḻvār (one of the Āḻvārs, group of Hindu poets): see ĀḺVĀR.

Persecution. Adherents of virtually all religions have suffered persecution for their faith at some point in their history, and such persecution has generally been held to forge a more resilient faith. Thus the pressure on *Muḥammad during the Meccan period made him more determined, so that *martyrs (*shahīd) became highly favoured and revered in Islam. That 'the blood of the martyrs is the seed of the church' (see TERTULLIAN) arose as a belief from the early cents. of Christianity, when Christians were sporadically persecuted as a non-conformist minority: there was only formal imperial persecution under the Emperors Decius (250), Valerian (257–8), and Diocletian (304–11). Nevertheless, the period before 312 holds the Christian imagination as the 'age of the martyrs', martyrdom becoming the archetype of sanctity. With Constantine's conversion in 312 persecution of those regarded as orthodox ceased, though persecution of heretics continued, Priscillian being the first to be executed (386). In the W. persecution has been reserved for heretics; E. Christians, however, have known persecution, by Muslims (despite their status as a 'people of the book', *ahl al-Kitāb) and by Western Christians, notably during the Crusades. In the West, the *Reformation led to an increase in persecution of Christians by Christians which continued until the Enlightenment. The 20th cent. has seen persecution of Christians on an unprecedented scale—by atheistic communism, by fascism, and by militant Islam in certain countries. See also ANTI-SEMITISM; HOLOCAUST.

Perushim: see PHARISEES.

Pesaḥ (Jewish festival): see PASSOVER.

Peshāt. The literal meaning of a Jewish text. Peshāt is generally contrasted with *derāsh, the non-literal interpretation. This distinction was possibly first drawn by *Abbaye in the 4th cent. CE (*B.Sanh.* 100b), but came into common use after it was employed by *Rashi in his *biblical commentary. See also PARDES.

D. W. Halivni, *Peshat and Derash* . . . (1991).

Pesher (Heb., 'interpretation'). An inspired application of the Hebrew *prophecies to the historical events of the end of time. The term is used with that implication in Daniel 4. 16 (cf. Ecclesiastes 8. 1). In the *Dead Sea Scrolls it designates the interpretative gifts which will explain God's mysteries. These gifts will be displayed by the *Teacher of Righteousness 'to whom God made known all the mysteries of the words of his servants the prophets' (*1 Qp.Hab.* 7. 5). Thus in the *Habbakuk Commentary*, the description of the Chaldeans of Habbakuk 1. 6–17 is applied to the Kittim (probably the Romans).

Pesikta (Aram., 'section'). Jewish *midrashic homilies. The best-known pesikta are *Pesikta de-Rav Kahana* and *Pesikta Rabbati* (tr. W. G. Brande, 1968). The former contains homilies on the *Torah and *haftarah readings for festivals and special *sabbaths. It probably originated in Palestine in the 5th cent. CE. The latter is a later (7th cent. onward?) collection of midrashim on festival readings. It is partly based on the *Pesikta de-Rav Kahana* and was much used by *Eleazar ben Judah of Worms.

Peta (form of the dead): see PRETA.

Petavatthu (part of Buddhist Pāli canon): see KHUDDAKA-NIKĀYA.

Peter, St. In Christianity, foremost of the *apostles. His name was Simon but according to the gospels *Jesus called him from his work as fisherman and gave him the name 'Cephas', the Aramaic equivalent of Greek 'Peter' (*petra*, 'rock'). He usually takes the lead among Jesus' disciples and is their mouthpiece, as in his confession of faith in Matthew 16. 13–20. Here Jesus says, 'You are Peter, and on this rock I will build my church.' Peter is recorded during Jesus' trial as having denied any knowledge of him (Mark 14. 66–72), but in one account he was the first to whom Jesus appeared after his death (Luke 24. 34). Thereafter he became the first missionary preacher, and leader of the Jerusalem church (Acts 1–12. 17). According to a unanimous and early tradition Peter visited Rome where he was martyred (*1 Clement* 5, etc.); but the claim that he was its *bishop is an anachronism. According to the 2nd-cent. *Acts of Peter*, the apostle, while fleeing from Nero's persecution, met Jesus on the road. Peter asked, 'Domine, quo vadis?' ('Lord, where are you going?'). When Jesus answered 'I am coming to be crucified again', Peter turned back to the city to face his *martyrdom. His tomb in St Peter's basilica may be authentic. Feast day, 29 June.

The two Letters of Peter are found among the *Catholic Epistles of the New Testament. 1 Peter is written from Rome (if 'Babylon' in 5. 13 = Rome) to communities in Asia Minor to encourage them in enduring persecution. The author emphasizes Christ's example to those in suffering and the need to lead a godly life in heathen surroundings. Peter's authorship is often questioned, especially because persecution in Asia Minor is unattested in his lifetime. 2 Peter is a warning against false and corrupt teachers; 2. 1–3. 3 seems to be borrowed from *Jude; features such as the treatment of Paul in 4. 15–16 suggest a date well after Peter's death.

Other 2nd-cent. books attributed to Peter include the *Gospel of Peter* (a *docetic retelling of Jesus' death and *resurrection based on the four New Testament gospels) and the Apocalypse of Peter (a description of heaven and hell put into the mouth of Christ after his resurrection).

O. Cullmann, *Peter* . . . (1962).

Peter Damian, St (1007–72). *Monk and *cardinal. Born at Ravenna of poor parents, he attracted attention by his intelligence and received an education. In 1035 he entered on an ascetic life in the *Benedictine hermitage at Fonte Avella. About 1043 he became prior and was active in monastic reform (regarding a monastery as a piece of heaven on earth) and as a preacher against the worldliness of the *clergy. Made cardinal bishop of Ostia (against his will) in 1057, he played a prominent part in the reform movement that heralded the Hildebrandine

Reform. He was influential too as theologian and spiritual writer. In 1828, he was pronounced Doctor of the Church.

O. J. Blum, *Saint Peter Damian* (1947).

Peter Lombard (*c.*1100–60). Christian theologian. Born in Lombardy, after studying in Italy, he went to Reims, and then to Paris where he taught from *c.*1134. In 1159 he became bishop of Paris. His chief work, the *Sentences*, was written 1155–8. Its four books treat of (i) the *Trinity, (ii) creation and *sin, (iii) the *incarnation and the virtues, and (iv) the *sacraments and *eschatology. Theology is presented as a series of doctrines ('sentences') supported by a wealth of *patristic references. It became the standard textbook of theology during the Middle Ages, commented on by nearly every theologian of repute.

Peter (Petr) Moghila (Russian Orthodox theologian): see MOGHILA, PETER.

Petiḥah (Heb., 'opening'). The Jewish ritual of opening the *Ark of the *synagogue. Petiḥah is performed during the course of services to take out the *Torah scrolls or to recite prayers of particular importance. It is customary for the congregation to stand whenever the Ark is opened.

Petits Frères. French (and proper) name for the Little Brothers, a *Roman Catholic order derived from *de Foucauld, characterized by long training, especially in prayer, and by absolute commitment to the places (usually poor) where they are sent. Notable among them have been René Voilleaume (see especially his *Seeds of the Desert*) and J. *Maritain.

Petrine texts. Those New Testament texts which are held by *Catholics (mainly, but not exclusively, *Roman Catholics) to establish the supreme authority of *Peter over the *Church, whose foundation, after *Christ, he is. The major text is Matthew 16. 18 f., but others are Mark 3. 16, Luke 24. 34, 1 Corinthians 15. 5. On these texts, the *papacy in fact and theory is founded.

Peyote. A hallucinogenic cactus and the basis of an inter-tribal religion among N. American Indians. It grows only in the Rio Grande valley and N. Mexico, and has long been central in local rites. By the 1880s it had become the basis of a new religion that repudiated the old faiths and offered an Indian alternative to Christianity. It has since spread across some fifty tribes in the USA and Canada, and involves perhaps 100,000 Indians. The buttons growing on top of the root-like cactus are prepared for eating, smoking, or drinking and used as the sacramental element in the Saturday all-night ritual of prayers and songs around an earth altar and sacred fire. This occurs in a tepee or peyote house, and is followed by a communal breakfast on Sunday morning. Peyote brings peace and healing, resists alcoholism, and gives visions of the Peyote Spirit who is regarded either as *Jesus or an Indian equivalent. It has been misunderstood as a narcotic, and the religion has been attacked by missionaries, state and federal governments, and tribal councils. Since 1918 religious freedom has slowly been gained by incorporation in various states as the 'Native American Church', but incorporation may still be contested.

Pezpopovtsy ('without priests' group among Old Believers): see OLD BELIEVERS.

'Phags-pa Blo-gros-rgyal-mtshan (*c.*1235–80). One of the five leading figures of the Sa-skya order of Tibetan Buddhism. He was a prolific author who addressed a wide range of topics, engaging also in correspondence with Mongol princes in which he summarized Buddhist teaching. In 1244, when his uncle, Sa-skya Paṇḍita, was summoned to serve in the Mongol court, 'Phags-pa went with him. As a result of this, the Sa-skya order was delegated to rule over Tibet, but 'Phags-pa was kept by the emperor of China, Kubla (Qubilai) Khan, to ensure Tibet's submission to Mongol rule. He so impressed the emperor with his *Tantric skills (which eclipsed those of the court *shamans) that he was made instructor of the court and ruler (in absence) of Tibet. The pattern of relationship between China and Tibet was thus established which is known as *yon mchod*, 'patron and priest', and which was overthrown by the Chinese annexation of Tibet. The emperor is protector of the *lama and through him, by extension, of the land, and the leading lama of Tibet (in due course, the succession of *Dalai Lamas) is the spiritual advisor and guarantor of rites to the emperor. For the complexity of this relationship, see also PANCHEN LAMA.

'Phags-pa-lha (leading exponent of Buddhist Mādhyamaka): see ĀRYADEVA.

Pharisees (Heb., *perushim*, 'separatists' or 'interpreters'). Members of a Jewish religious sect of the second *Temple period. The Pharisees emerged *c.*160 BCE, after the *Hasmonean revolt. They believed themselves to be the inheritors of the traditions of *Ezra and were scrupulous in their obedience to the *oral law as well as to the written *Torah. In some sense, they were the predecessors of the *rabbis; yet rabbinic texts attack *perushim* as extremists, in terms as rigorous as in the Christian *gospels. It may be that originally they were called *perushim* derisively by the Sadducees—they cut themselves off from the good things of this life in the deluded hope that they will be rewarded in a (non-existent) future life (*ARN* 5); but they seized the name and converted it to mean 'interpreters' of scripture. Later, the name was isolated to mean 'extremists' in the rigour of their interpretations. Literally their name means 'the Separated Ones' (*B.Kid.* 66a); they were separated from the *gentiles and from those who compromised with heathenism (e.g. the *Sadducees). As they became more powerful, they came into increased controversy with the Sadducees and, under John Hyrcarnus, were even excluded from the *Sanhedrin. None the less, through teaching the law of God in the synagogues and by encouraging the hope of the *resurrection of the dead and the coming of the *messiah, they affected the religious beliefs and practices of the entire Jewish people. Despite the strong anti-Pharisaic bias of the New Testament, there is no doubt that the Pharisees set high moral standards for themselves and through their devotion sustained the people through the trauma of the destruction of the Jerusalem Temple and the loss of the sacrificial cult. Relevant texts are translated in J. Bowker, *Jesus and the Pharisees* (1973).

E. F. Rivkin, *A Hidden Revolution* . . . (1977).

Phenomenology (Gk., *phainomenon*, 'that which appears', + *logos*, 'reflection'). The study of the ways in which appearances manifest themselves. The phenomenology of religion is thus the study of religious appearances; it may also embrace reflection on the nature of what gives rise to them. The term is used of endeavours to study religion, without commitment to the truth or otherwise of what is being studied, and with the suspension of value-judgements about the worth or otherwise of what is being studied. Such a wide understanding of the term allows many different styles of the study of religion to be called 'phenomenological'. Whether any such value-free study is possible remains a matter of doubt—or at best of dispute.

The term was first used by J. H. Lambert in 1764, but with the completely different sense of the theory of appearance as one of four philosophical disciplines. As a term it appears e.g. in *Kant and *Hegel. In its more modern sense, it is particularly associated with the work of Edmund Husserl (1859–1938). He was a pupil of Franz Brentano, and therefore began his work on the foundations of mathematics. In particular, in *The Philosophy of Arithmetic* (1891), he sought to identify the essences of the concepts of numbering which occur in consciousness. This led him to the consideration of the independence of logical forms, the essences of which, he claimed, can be discerned through phenomenological method (*Logical Investigations*, 1900). Initially that method was understood as being the description of the subjective processes involved (i.e. nothing more than a branch of psychology). However, in the 2nd edn. Husserl began to articulate the possibility of an eidetic science (one in which subjective processes are analysed, both for their essential character, or essences, and for their ideal possibilities). Husserl began to realize not only that philosophers had failed to resolve the issue between solipsists and realists, but that it would make no practical difference to the lived and experienced world if they did so. Clearly, philosophical doubt must be driven further back: *Descartes had thought that he had secured a foundation of certain knowledge in his *cogito, ergo sum* ('I think, therefore I am'); but Husserl pointed out that the conclusion is not entailed; therefore he proposed that the only secure foundation of knowledge lies in the cogito: all that we can be sure of (and from this it is clear that Husserl remained a foundationalist despite some interpretations of his thought to the contrary) are *cogitationes*, appearances in consciousness.

In his later works (the most accessible of which are *Cartesian Meditations*, 1931, tr. D. Cairns, 1970, and *The Paris Lectures*, 1950, tr. P. Koestenbaum, 1967), he argued that transcendental phenomenology 'brackets out' (*epoche*) all assumptions about existence, truth, and value, and analyses the *cogitationes* in terms of the stream of consciousness. But since consciousness is directed to what it takes to be an external world (or to its own past and future, etc.) through its *Intentionalität* (intentionality), it is legitimate to consider, perhaps even to infer, what may be a ground, in independence from consciousness, sufficient to give rise to the particular appearances in consciousness which happen to arise—especially when these arise with consistency. In this way, Husserl was able to return those degrees of reality to the world which the consistency of the data in consciousness seemed to require. Thus 'you' may appear in my consciousness with the consistency of a person whom I can label and name; I do not have to resolve the argument about solipsism before extending the intentionality of my consciousness toward 'you' as a consistent appearance in my own consciousness (i.e. I can bracket out the issue of whether you are truly there or not, or in what sense). Moreover, 'you' appear in my consciousness with the characteristic of marking off other appearances with an equal consistency, so that together we can label a world of appearances and name it—that is why Husserl called people 'walking object indices'.

Through this process, it is possible to build up a world of intersubjective reliability without solving first the contentious philosophical issues of existence—though Husserl persisted in his quest for essences, which would thus have priority over existence. By this method of *epoche* and eidetic reduction, Husserl returned those degrees of reliability to the world which the consistency of particular appearances seemed to demand, and in this way he built up what he called 'regional ontologies'. An obvious candidate was the world of the natural sciences (though even then he retained a distinction between the inferred world as it must be in order to give rise to the appearances in consciousness as they happen to occur, and the *Lebenswelt*, 'lived world' which is derivative from it). At the very end of his life, Husserl realized that there is an extensive reliability in the world of theology (or more exactly of *prayer and *worship, etc.), and that his method required him to return a corresponding degree of reality to God.

Husserl's thought proved immensely fertile, both in philosophy (leading directly into *existentialism) and in the study of religion. Virtually no phenomenologist of religion has ever followed a strictly Husserlian programme: words and indications are picked up from his thought, and are brought to bear in largely novel ways. Thus the early phenomenologists of religion were attracted by the prospect of identifying essences (understood loosely as identifying essential characteristics in religions or in religious beliefs and practices). This proved largely unilluminating, since it tended to squeeze an ocean into a thimble. Others seized on *epoche* and understood phenomenology to be description on the basis of which one might be able to enter empathetically into the phenomena being described. The most sophisticated attempt was made by Gerardus van der Leeuw (1890–1950), in *Phänomenologie der Religion* (1933, tr. as *Religion in Essence and Manifestation*); he achieved brilliant insights, especially in the relation of religion to power, but in fact he made little attempt to bracket out his own assumptions.

Thus phenomenology has been a powerful influence, but the phenomenology of religion remains to be undertaken. As matters stand, phenomenology has transformed the study of religion in schools, colleges, and universities *at the first level*: it has ushered in the dispassionate (as opposed to confessional) teaching of religion, in a way which brackets out questions of whether e.g. God or gods 'exist': religions are studied as an important expression of human life. But the second level (as Husserl envisaged it, albeit in dense language) is always demanded by the first: given that these are the phenomena, what in reality has given rise to them, or brought them into being? The integration of the two levels has not yet been achieved.

D. Bell, *Husserl* (1990), E. Kohak, *Idea and Experience . . .* (1978); *The Embers and the Stars* (1984); R. C. Solomon (ed.), *Phenomenology and Existentialism* (1972).

Philaret (Theodore Nikitich Romanov, *c.*1553–1633). *Patriarch of Moscow and founder of the Romanov dynasty. A cousin of Tsar Theodore I, he was banished to a *monastery by Boris Godunov after Theodore's death in 1598. Released by the pretender Dimitri in 1605 he became *metropolitan of Rostov. Imprisoned by the Poles in 1610, he was only freed in 1619, by which time his son, Michael, was Tsar. He became patriarch and was virtual ruler of Russia until his death. A zealous reformer, he encouraged the study of theology and the establishment of seminaries in each diocese.

Philaret Drozdov (1782–1867). Russian theologian. Educated at the *monastery of the Holy Trinity near Moscow, he became a lecturer there in 1803 and a *monk in 1808. In that year he went to St Petersburg as professor of philosophy. In 1818 he became a member of the *Holy Synod, and in 1821 *archbishop of Moscow, receiving the title *metropolitan in 1826. He was an exemplary *bishop—a wise administrator and popular preacher. Among his many theological works, his *Christian Catechism* (1823) was most influential, despite the alleged influence in it of *Lutheran ideas.

Philemon, Letter to. An *epistle of *Paul. It is a private letter carried by Onesimus (a runaway slave who had met Paul) back to his owner. It is a tactful plea for Philemon's forgiveness. It is to be dated at the same time as *Colossians.

Philip, Gospel of. A *gnostic treatise preserved in the *Nag Hammadi Library. It contains reflections on the quest for salvation, understood in a *Valentinian way, with no narrative and only a few sayings attributed to Christ: '. . . come into the house of the Father, but do not receive [anything] in the house of the Father and do not take [anything] away'. 'When a blind man and one who sees are in the dark, they do not differ, but when the light comes, he who sees will see the light, and he who is blind will remain in darkness.'

R. M. Wilson, *The Gospel of Philip* (1962).

Philippians, Letter to the. An epistle of *Paul and book of the New Testament. The addressees are Paul's first congregation in Europe, at Philippi in Macedonia. It was written from prison, either in Rome *c.*60–2, Caesarea *c.*56–8, or Ephesus *c.*53–5. Paul sees himself balanced between life and death (1. 19–26). Among the ringing exhortations in ch. 2 is the important passage verses 5–11, a hymn which speaks of *Christ's 'self-emptying' (*kenōsis). This has traditionally been taken as a basic statement of incarnational *christology, though some argue that it refers to Jesus' willingness to accept a shameful death.

Philippine Independent Church. This stems from Gregorio Aglipay (1860–1940), a Filipino *Roman Catholic priest, who first formed the Filipino National Catholic Church after the revolution; this languished for lack of papal recognition, and in 1902, Isabelo de los Reyes proclaimed a new Philippine Independent Church with Aglipay as Supreme Bishop. This soon acquired nearly half the RC population, but after the Supreme Court returned its properties to the RC Church it gradually declined and affiliated with *Unitarians in 1931. Since then there has been a remarkable renewal by division between unitarian and conservative groups, with the latter securing consecration of *bishops in 1948 from the Protestant Episcopal Church in the USA, entering into an intercommunion *concordat in 1961, and securing training for its priests in the Episcopal seminary in Manila until 1980, when an independent seminary was developed. It makes up about 5 per cent of the Philippine population.

Philistines. The people occupying S. Palestine who were in conflict with the Israelites at the time of the *Judges. The Philistines occupied the cities of Ashdod, Ekron, Gath, Ashkelon, and Gaza; and, according to 1 Samuel, it was because of the Philistine threat that the Israelites felt it necessary to have a king. Contrary to the colloquial English usage, whereby 'Philistine' means 'antagonistic to culture', the Philistines had a sophisticated culture. Matthew Arnold adopted the term from the German *philister* used by townspeople to refer to the depredations of university students: 'We are imperilled by what I call the "Philistinism" of our middle class. On the side of beauty and taste, vulgarity; on the side of morals and feeling, coarseness; on the side of mind and spirit, unintelligence,—this is Philistinism' (*On the Study of Celtic Literature*).

E. Noort, *Die Seevölker in Palästina* (1993).

Philo (*c*.20 BCE–50 CE). *Hellenistic Jewish philosopher. Very little is known about Philo's life except that he came from a noble family of Alexandria, and that his brother is mentioned by *Josephus. His writings were preserved by the Christian Church in their original Gk. Mainly dealing with the *Pentateuch, they include *De Opificio Mundi* (On the Creation), *De Vita Mosis* (On the Life of *Moses), *Legum Allegoriae* (*Allegorical Interpretation), *De Somniis* (On Dreams), *Quaestiones et Solutiones in Genesin* (Questions and Answers on *Genesis). In addition, he produced various philosophical treatises on such subjects as providence and the eternity of the world. He also wrote works (of great historical importance for understanding the situation of the Jews in Alexandria) against the oppression of Jews by Flaccus, and concerning the cruelty of the Roman emperor Gaius. Philo's philosophy was strongly influenced by Stoicism and Platonism. He described God as 'transcending virtue, transcending knowledge, transcending the good itself and the beautiful itself', and he made a clear distinction between the world of opinion and the world of truth. The only ultimate realities for Philo were God and the *soul, and it is the soul that connects humanity with God. Philo saw the three Jewish *patriarchs as archetypes for reaching union with God through learning (*Abraham), nature (*Isaac), and training (*Jacob), and he argued that the Jewish law was not only superior on an earthly level, but carried an ultimate symbolic meaning. Philo had greater influence on Christianity than on Judaism. The early Church *Fathers such as *Ambrose, *Origen, and *Clement of Alexandria adopted many of his ideas and drew on his allegorical interpretations. There are traces, however, of Philo's influence in the *Midrash.

Tr. F. H. Colson and G. H. Whitaker (1953–63); E. R. Goodenough, *An Introduction to Philo Judaeus* (1940); H. A. Wolfson, *Philo: Foundations of Religious Philosophy in Judaism, Christianity and Islam* (1940).

Philocalia (Gk., 'love of what is beautiful'). The title of two Christian works: (i) the *Philocalia* of *Origen, an anthology from his writings compiled by *Basil and *Gregory of Nazianzus; and (ii) the *Philocalia* of Sts Macarius Notaras and *Nicodemus of the Holy Mountain, first publ. in Venice in 1782, a collection of ascetic and mystical writings of the 4th–15th cents. Through a Russian tr. by Bishop Theophan the Recluse (5 vols., 1876–90) it has exercised an important influence throughout the modern Orthodox world.

Eng. tr. of parts of (ii) E. Kadloubovsky and G. E. H. Palmer (1951, 1954); and G. E. H. Palmer *et al.* (1979–).

Philosophia perennis (Lat., 'perennial philosophy'). Originally introduced as a term (by Steuchen) in 1540 to describe what the school of Padua and *scholasticism had in common. The term since then has had various technical applications, e.g. to what Greek and medieval philosophy have in common, or to *Thomism as a whole. But a looser sense was introduced by *Leibniz (1646–1716) to pick out those elements of philosophy which had endured through time—his own philosophy being, in his own view, the proper continuation and development of it. Even more loosely, the term has come to refer to a fundamental core of truth to be found at the heart of all religions, no matter how diverse their external appearance and practices may be. Thus Aldous Huxley began his book, *The Perennial Philosophy* (1946) with these words:

> Philosophia perennis—the phrase was coined by Leibniz [but see above]; but the thing—the metaphysic that recognises a divine Reality substantial to the world of things and lives and minds; the psychology that finds in the soul something similar to, or even identical with, divine Reality; the ethic that places man's final end in the knowledge of the immanent and transcendent Ground of all being—the thing is immemorial and universal.

Philosophical Taoism: see TAOISM.

Philosophicus Autodidactus (text by Ibn Tufayl): see IBN TUFAYL.

Philosophy, six schools of (Indian): see DARŚANA.

Philosophy of religion. Philosophical thought about religion. The term was first used in Germany in the late 18th cent., for the philosophical investigation of the origin, essence, and content of religion, and for the critique of its value and truth. Although the question of the relation between philosophy and religion remains a lively one, more attention has been given in recent decades to the critical role of the subject. Modern philosophy of religion is much concerned with assessing the reasons for religious belief, especially arguments for God's existence (see NATURAL THEOLOGY), investigating the nature of religious language, and considering the philosophical problems raised by religion. These problems include the coherence of the concept of God, the problem of *evil, *miracles, *prayer, immortality, and the nature of religious truth. It is likely that increasing attention will be given to issues raised by the comparison of the major religions, especially with regard to the apparent contradictions between their beliefs. For philosophy in Islam, see FALSAFA. See also Index, Philosophers, Philosophy.

W. J. Abraham, *Introduction* . . . (1985); S. C. Brown (ed.), *Reason and Religion* . . . (1977); V. Brunner, *Theology and Philosophical Inquiry* (1981); S. L. R. Clark, *The Mysteries of Religion* . . . (1986); M. L. Diamond, *Contemporary Philosophy and Religious Thought* (1974); M. Gardner, *The Whys of a Philosophical Scrivener* (1983); E. Kohak, *The Embers and the Stars* (1984); G. I. Mavrodes and S. C. Hackett, *Problems and Perspectives* . . . (1967); L. P. Pojman (ed.), *Philosophy of Religion: An Anthology* (1987); P. J. Sherry, *Religion, Truth and Language-Games* (1977); R. Swinburne, *The Coherence of Theism* (1977) and *The Existence of God* (1979).

'pho ba (one of Six Doctrines of Nāropa): see NĀRO CHOS DRUG.

Phoenix. A mythical bird of great splendour, which after a long life was said to burn itself to ashes and then rise to life again. From *Clement of Rome and *Tertullian onwards, it was regarded by Christian writers, and occasionally by Christian artists, as a symbol of the *resurrection.

Photius (sometimes called 'The Great', *c.*810–*c.*895). Patriarch of *Constantinople. A high official at the Byzantine court, Photius succeeded the patriarch Ignatius who was deposed by the emperor in 858. His election, at first endorsed by the legates of Pope Nicholas I, was then (863) annulled by the pope and a schism ensued. Divisions were sharpened by an encyclical of 867 in which Photius attacked the *filioque in the W. creed, and by the rival claims of Rome and Constantinople to the newly evangelized territory of Bulgaria. The pope was declared excommunicated in 867. In the same year Photius was deposed by a new emperor Basil I, but regained his see in 877, this time with the support of the pope. The schism was renewed at some time soon after, and lasted until Photius was banished by a new emperor in 886. The Photian schism anticipated the final East–West schism of the 11th cent., and Photius is remembered in the E. Church as a champion against Rome.

Photius' learning was amazing. His most important work, his *Biblioteca*, describes several hundred books and is a mine of information. In the W., 'Had he not given his name to the great schism, he would always be remembered as the greatest scholar of his time, and as, in every way, the greatest man in the Byzantine Church' (A. Fortescue).

F. Dvornik, *The Photian Schism* (1948).

phowa (one of Six Doctrines of Nāropa): see NĀRO CHOS DRUG.

phyagchen. Short form of Tib., *phyag-rgya-chen-po*, i.e. *mahāmudrā.

phyag-rgya chen-po (teaching of Kagyü school of Buddhism): see MAHĀMUDRĀ.

Phylacteries (containers for Jewish commands): see TEFILLIN.

Physico-theological Argument. Type of argument for God's existence, from determinate experience of the natural world, especially of its order, purposiveness, and beauty. It is the third kind of theistic argument discussed by *Kant, after the *ontological and *cosmological arguments, in his *Critique of Pure Reason* (1781). The phrase 'physico-theology' was current in the 18th and 19th cents., but nowadays such arguments are referred to as '*teleological'. Kant said the argument should be mentioned with respect, as being the oldest, clearest, and most in accordance with the common reason of humanity, of the traditional theistic proofs. But he considered that the utmost that it could prove was the existence of an architect, not a creator, of the world: to prove the existence of a more religiously adequate being it would be necessary to fall back on the cosmological and ontological arguments, which he had already criticized.

The argument has been revived in the 20th cent., but it is often presented as an argument from analogy which seeks to establish the probability rather than the certainty of divine existence.

Pi-ch'iu. Chin. for *bhikṣu.

Pico della Mirandola, Giovanni (1463–94). Christian mystical and humanistic writer. A considerable linguist, he regarded *kabbalah as illuminating Christianity. The created order emerges in hierarchies of emanation, with humans mediating between the spiritual and the material, able to know God as a friend rather than a fact (cf. *I–Thou): 'Philosophy seeks the truth, theology finds it, religion possesses it.' Kabbalah thus exceeds *hermeticism in excellence because it invokes the name of the true God and points even more clearly to the central dignity of humanity: humans alone can occupy a middle place in the hierarchy of beings—an assertion of Christian humanism which he argued in *De Hominis Dignitate* . . . (1492).

Pietà (Ital., 'pity'). Representation (often in sculpture) of the Blessed Virgin *Mary lamenting over the dead and recently deposed body of *Christ, after the *crucifixion.

Pietism. A movement in Protestant Christianity which reacted against too rigid a confessional orthodoxy, and emphasized good works and a holy life. It began soon after the Thirty Years War (1618–48), led by Jakob Spener (1635–1705). Invited to write a preface to a book of sermons, he wrote a short tract, *Pia Desideria* (1675; tr. T. G. Tappert, 1964), which became a kind of 'manifesto', laying down six 'simple proposals' (*einfältige Vorschläge*) for a more godly life: individual study of the Bible; the exercise of the priesthood of all believers (i.e. including the laity); the importance of good works; the control of charity in controversy; the better training of ministers, with training conforming to life; and the reformation of preaching to serve all these purposes. Spener was widely influential (though also opposed, as all reformers are), affecting especially A. H. Francke (1663–1727), who committed himself to the poor of Halle (see E. Beyreuther, *August Hermann Francke*, 1956). Foreign missions were established; and among many influenced by Pietism were Count Zinzendorf (who brought together the *Moravian Church) and John *Wesley.

D. Brown, *Understanding Pietism* (1970); F. E. Stoeffler, *The Rise of Evangelical Pietism* (1965), *German Pietism during the 18th Century* (1973), and *Continental Pietism and Early American Christianity* (1976); H. Weigelt, *Pietismus-Studien* (1965).

Pigu (Buddhist monk). Korean for *bhikṣu.

Pikku'aḥ nefesh (Heb., 'regard for human life'). The Jewish obligation to save human life in situations of danger, if necessary overriding the law. According to the *Talmud, pikku'aḥ nefesh supersedes even *Sabbath law (*Yoma* 85a). The principle is derived from the commandment in Leviticus 19. 16, 'Neither shall you stand idly by the *blood of your neighbour.' Only when facing a choice between death and *idolatry, murder, or incest (sexual crimes) should martyrdom be chosen. Setting aside Sabbath law to protect life should also include possible danger, as in the case of illness (*Yoma* 8. 6) or childbirth. Thus it is permitted to light a fire on the Sabbath to keep a sick person warm or extinguish a light to help them sleep (*Shab.* 2. 5).

Pi-ku. Taoist practice of abstaining from eating grain, in order to attain immortality: as the five types of grain are the staple diet of life, so they are the food of worms which threaten life and consume the body. Detachment from the former signals escape from the latter.

Pilate, Pontius. The governor ('prefect') of Judaea under whom *Jesus was crucified. The gospels may show him in an unduly favourable light in their insistence on blaming the Jewish mob for Jesus' death.

The apocryphal text known as the *Acts of Pilate* (4th cent. at the earliest) can hardly derive from any official records of Jesus' trial, although *Justin and *Tertullian mention such documents. It describes the trial, death, and *resurrection of Jesus, and in some manuscripts is coupled with a text describing the *descent into Hell. The work forms a basis of the medieval play-cycle on the Harrowing of Hell, and the legends of *Joseph of Arimathea and the Holy *Grail.

Pilgrimage. The literal or metaphorical movement to a condition or place of holiness or healing. Pilgrimage may be interior or exterior. Interior pilgrimage is the movement of a life from a relatively abject condition to the goal (ultimate or proximate) in a particular religion: John *Bunyan's *The Pilgrim's Progress* is a classic Christian expression of this theme, particularly as expressed in its full title, . . . *from this World to That which is to Come: Delivered under the Similitude of a Dream, wherein is Discovered the Manner of his Setting Out, his Dangerous Journey, and Safe Arrival at the Desired Country.* Life becomes metaphorically a pilgrimage ('Ere the days of his pilgrimage vanish, How pleasant to know Mr. Lear'), with the sentiment being that of *Tolstoy: 'What does it profit me to go across the sea to *Christ, if all the time I lose the Christ that is within me here?' Interior pilgrimage is stressed by Sikhs, bearing in mind the comment of Gurū *Nānak (aware of the vast number of actual pilgrimages undertaken in India—see below): 'There is no place of pilgrimage like the guru who alone is a well of compassion and contentment.' Although Sikhs do have places of actual pilgrimage, especially *Amritsar and the Golden Temple, and the bathing place (*baoli*) at *Goindval, Gurū Nānak reminds them that 'pilgrimages, penances and almsgiving bring no more merit than the size of a sesame seed'. Exterior pilgrimage is a journey to some place which is either itself associated with the resources or goals of a religion, or which is the location of objects which may assist the pilgrim—e.g. *relics. The reasons for pilgrimage are extremely varied. They may, for example, be for healing, holiness, cleansing, penance, education, gratitude, in response to a vow, to recapitulate an event which occurred at the pilgrimage centre (as, for example, to see for oneself a reported vision; or, somewhat differently, to re-enact events in the past, as in the Muslim *ḥajj, or in the Christian retracing of the *Via Dolorosa in Jerusalem). Pilgrimage frequently, and not surprisingly, takes on the character of a *rite of passage; and as such, the stage of liminality exhibits the inversion of values and status; pilgrimages may then take on the character of a holiday, in which everyday life and its values are suspended—as in Chaucer's *Canterbury Tales*. The festive and holiday atmosphere of pilgrimages led (at least as early as the 15th cent.) to the proverb which was common in Europe, 'Dieu sait qui est bon pelerin' (John Ray, *English Proverbs*, 1678, 'God knows who are the best pilgrims'). See Index, Pilgrimage.

V. Turner, *Dramas, Fields and Metaphors* (1974); V. and E. Turner, *Image and Pilgrimage in Christian Culture* (1978).

Judaism The major practice is that of making *ʿaliyah to *Jerusalem, as required in Deuteronomy 16. 16 (even though originally the command may have applied to a more local centre). According to the *Torah, all male Jews should go up to Jerusalem three times a year, on *Passover, *Shavuʿot, and *Sukkot (Exodus 34. 23). In the days of the *Temple, thousands of Jews from *Israel and the *diaspora converged on Jerusalem for the festivals to 'sojourn in the Temple courts', to offer *sacrifices, and to 'prompt him to study Torah' (*TJSuk*. 5. 1). After the destruction of the Temple in 70 CE pilgrimage continued, but now they were times of sorrow when the verse, 'Our holy and our beautiful house . . . is burned with fire and all our pleasant things are laid waste' (Isaiah 64. 10) was recited. Nevertheless, the longing to be in Jerusalem endures as a continuing theme in Jewish life (see e.g. JUDAH HA-LEVI), epitomized in the phrase, 'Next year in Jerusalem!' (see LA-SHANAH HA-BA'AH BI YERUSHĀLAYIM). Since the Six Day War and the reunification of the city, the remaining wall of the Temple (*Wailing Wall) has become the centre of Jewish pilgrimage. The tradition of going up to Jerusalem for the pilgrim festivals has been, to some extent, resumed, particularly during the intermediate days of Sukkot. Because there is no temple, no sacrifices are performed.

Christianity There is no record of the earliest Christian pilgrimages, but the practice of journeying to the Holy Land received much impetus from the visit of the empress Helena, mother of *Constantine, in 326. *Peregrinatio Etheriae* (The Pilgrimage of Etheria, tr. M. L. McClure and C. L. Feltoe, 1919; J. Wilkinson, 1971) is a vivid account of a pilgrimage to the Holy Land at the end of the 4th cent. Rome became a centre of pilgrimage because of its connection with Sts *Peter and *Paul; and other centres proliferated through the connection with other saints. Notable was the supposed burial place of St *James, Santiago at Compostela in NW Spain: it became the goal of the famous 'pilgrims' route' to Compostela (see J. S. Stone, *The Cult of Santiago* . . ., 1927). The association of pilgrimage with *indulgences and credulity (especially in relation to relics) made pilgrimage highly suspect to the *Reformation; but it has revived in the 20th cent., not least as a consequence of the lucrative tourist trade. Devotion to *Mary has led to increasing claims of visions of Mary, with consequent pilgrimages, e.g. to *Lourdes, *Fatima, and Medjugorje.

Z. Aradi, *Shrines of Our Lady Around the World*, (1954); J. Sumption, *Pilgrimage: An Image of Medieval Religion* (1972); V. and E. Turner, *Image and Pilgrimage in Christian Culture* (1978).

Islam See ḤAJJ; ZIYARA.

Hinduism See TĪRATH; TĪRTHA. Pilgrimage is supremely important in Hinduism, both in an interior and exterior sense. The interior pilgrimage is epitomized in the *yogi who 'visits' the seven *sacred cities while remaining motionless in a specific kind of meditation. The exterior pilgrimage is dramatically obvious in the constant movement of people in every part of India, but especially to the seven cities. Prayāga (renamed by the Muslims Allahābad), Gāyā (i.e. *Bodhgāyā to Buddhists), and *Kāśi are the major sites on the Gaṅgā (Ganges); and of these, Kāśi exceeds all. Indeed, to make pilgrimage and die in Kāśi means that the burden of karma and the necessity for rebirth are removed by *Śiva himself. It was a question much discussed in the law codes, and still relevant today, whether to commit suicide in other places of pilgrimage might have the same effect, making such a place a literal 'final goal'. Places of pilgrimage are called in India tīrthas ('fords'), and the pilgrimage is tīrtha-yatra. There are so many tīrthas that they cannot be counted, let alone be named and described (though P. V. Kane, *History of Dharmasastra*, iv. 552–827 gives many). In a sense, the whole of India is a place of pilgrimage, because the divine power is present in all places; pilgrimage evokes the divine. In the *Tīrtha-yatra* section of *Mahābhārata*, a description is given of the whole of India as a place of pilgrimage, mapping out an itinerary in a clockwise direction. In one of the earliest references to pilgrimage, *Āitareya Brāhmaṇa* 7. 15, the pilgrim is likened to a flower growing who rises above the dirt: 'All his sins fall away, slain by the labour of his journeying'.

S. M. Bhardwaj, *Hindu Places of Pilgrimage in India* . . . (1973); E. A. Morinis, *Pilgrimage in the Hindu Tradition* (1984).

Buddhism and **Jainism** Buddhist pilgrimage is common, in both Theravāda and Mahāyāna forms. Of particular importance are sites where relics are held, e.g. of the Buddha's tooth at Kandy (in Śri Lankā); or where there are associations with the Buddha, especially the places of his birth, first sermon, enlightenment, and *parinibbāna, and of his presence, e.g. of his footprint (notably in Śri Lankā on Mount Siripāda, 'Adam's Mount', since Muslims revere the footprint as that of *Adam, though for Hindus it is that of Śiva). Equally important are sites where cuttings derived from the *bo tree (the tree under which the Buddha attained enlightenment) are growing. In China and Japan, mountains are extensively sites of pilgrimage. In China, the Five Peaks are thought to be important for the protection of the country. One, Mount Tai, is Taoist, the other four are associated with four *bodhisattvas: Emei is linked with *Samantabhadra, Wūtai with *Mañjuśrī, Putuo with *Avalokiteśvara, and Chiu-hua with *Kṣitigarbha. A new emperor was required to make pilgrimage to Mount Tai; to the other four mountains (remote though they are) both monks and laypeople make pilgrimage, known as 'journeying to a mountain and offering incense'. In Japan, the major Buddhist centres are Saikōkū, dedicated to Kannon (Avalokiteśvara) and Shikōkū. For Japan, see also ISE and FUJISĀN (Fujiyama).

Among Jains, pilgrimage cannot possibly be undertaken in order to visit a site containing relics, since there are no relics of the *tīrthaṅkaras: the relics of *Mahāvīra were collected after his funeral by *Indra and taken to heaven where the gods worship them while working for the liberation of their own *jīvas. However, places associated with tīrthaṅkaras or other holy *ascetics, or with images of the tīrthaṅkaras, are places of pilgrimage—as indeed may be a living and revered ascetic: particularly revered are places where someone has undertaken *sallekhanā (death by fasting). Some places which are identified by Jains are also Hindu holy places, and this may represent an attempt to integrate with the dominant population (as in the case of Kāśi and *Ayodhyā); others may be shared with Hindus (e.g. Mount *Abu). For the *Digambaras, the White Lake of the Ascetics (Śravana Belgola), in the state of Karnataka, is of great importance, with its hill on which stands the image of Bahubali, the first person of this world cycle to attain liberation. Of corresponding importance for the Śvetāmbara (see DIGAMBARA) is Mount Śatrunjāya ('The conqueror of enemies'). It is one of five holy mountains, standing near Palitana in Gujarat. To organize a pilgrimage is an act of great merit for Jain laymen—the equivalent, according to some, of undertaking initiation as a monk. The organizer is called *saṅghapati*, 'the lord of the community' (cf. *saṅgha).

Pilgrimage for Jains is thus basically an act of commemoration and gratitude. While some early Śvetāmbara texts condemn the Hindu practice of pilgrimage, both their texts and those of the Digambara begin to speak of pilgrimage sites by at least the 5th cent. CE. It became customary to expect that a Jain layperson would go on at least one major pilgrimage before the age of 50, and monks and laypeople combined in pilgrimages which, by the Middle Ages, had often become huge expeditions. Jain pilgrimage sites suffered severely at the hands of the Muslim invaders of N. India, but even the shattered remnants and ruins were believed to continue to work good effects and remained, therefore, the centres of pilgrimage, albeit on a reduced scale.

Pilgrim Fathers. English Christian Dissenters who set sail in 1620 to cross the Atlantic (in the *Mayflower*) and who established Plymouth Colony. They numbered 102, though a baby was born at sea. The name was based on Hebrews 11. 13.

Pillars of Islam: see FIVE PILLARS OF ISLAM.

Pilpul (derived from *pilpel*, 'pepper'). A method of Jewish *Talmudic study. Traditionally pilpul meant the logical distinctions by which contradictions in the texts could be explained. Pilpul was distinguished from *girsah* (the cursory straightforward meaning of the words) and it served the functions of resolving contradictions, making the text relevant to changing circumstances, and providing a constant changing intellectual challenge. From the 15th cent., however, pilpul became more casuistic and dependent on sharper and sharper differentiations. Some Talmudic scholars such as Judah Loew criticized the new pilpul as being hairsplitting and not conducive to serious conscientious study.

L. Jacobs, *Studies in Talmudic Logic and Methodology* (1961), and *The Talmudic Argument* (1984).

Piṇḍa. A ball of rice offered, in Hindu funeral rites, to the *pitṛs (ancestors). Five piṇḍas are placed on the corpse with the words (*Ṛg Veda* 10. 17. 3), 'May the protecting god Pūṣan guide you on your long journey and deliver you safely to the pitṛs.'

Piṅgalā. In Hinduism, the solar channel which runs through the body, through which (in conjunction with its counterpart *iḍā) connection is made with *kuṇḍalinī energy. See also PRĀṆA.

Pippalāda (wise man): see PRAŚNA UPANIṢAD.

Pīr (Sūfī spiritual guide): see IMĀM.

Pīr-i-Anṣār (Sūfī poet): see SŪFĪS.

Pirit (Buddhist healing rite): see PARITTA.

Pirke de Rabbi Eleazar or ***Eliezer*** (8th cent. CE). Jewish *aggadic work. The book consists of an aggadic narrative about Eliezer b. Hyrcanus, the creation of the world, the early history of the Jews, and the blessings of the *'Amidah prayer. The surviving text is incomplete, and the book clearly reflects the *halakhic customs prevalent in *Israel at the start of the *geonic period. First published in 1514, it has been reprinted many times.

Tr. G. Friedlander (1916).

Pirqe Avot (treatise of Jewish Mishnah): see AVOT.

Piśācas. Demons in Hinduism who eat flesh and are ranked even lower than *rākṣasas. They dwell in cremation grounds, and can assume any form—even that of invisibility. They can enter into (and possess) anyone who yawns without covering the mouth.

Piṭaka (Pali, 'basket'), gathered collection of Buddhist texts. The 'three baskets', i.e. *Tripiṭaka, form a fundamental collection, equivalent to a *canon of scriptures.

Pitha (post-Vedic, possibly from *pi sad*, 'sit on', hence seat or throne), an important centre, especially for pilgrimage. Four major pithas became associated with the points of the compass, and represented the presence of *Devi (the Goddess). Many other pithas were established associated with Devi. The more general association of deities with the cardinal points is discussed in B. K. Smith, *Classifying the Universe* . . . (1994).

Pitṛ (Skt., 'father'). The ancestors (pl., pitaras), who dwell in the pitṛ-loka, which is sometimes identified with heaven (*svarga). Funeral rituals (*śrāddha) are essential to maintain the pitṛs in their proper state—and for that purpose, a son is necessary. If the proper rituals and sacrifices are not observed, the deceased might stay in the transitional state of *preta, and suffer torment as a hungry ghost. In Vedic religion, the pitṛ travels, after cremation of the body, along the pitṛyāna, the way of the fathers/ancestors, to recover his or her body in order to dwell with the gods (sustained, like them, by offerings). In the *Brāhmaṇas, the pitṛyāna becomes a place of judgement.

Pittsburgh Platform (statement of principles): see REFORM JUDAISM.

Pius IX (1792–1878). *Pope from 16 June 1846. Born Giovanni Maria Mastai-Ferretti, he served briefly in the papal diplomatic service after ordination, but then held a number of pastoral offices. As Bishop of Imola he instituted a series of reforms, but he was no liberal in temperament, and his refusal, after his elevation to the *papacy, to accept a leading role in Italian politics turned many away from him. In 1848, revolution in Rome occasioned his flight from the city, and he only returned after his safety was guaranteed by French troops. It was the withdrawal of these troops in 1870 which brought about the fall of Rome and Pius' retreat into a largely self-imposed 'captivity' in the *Vatican. In 1854 he had, on his own authority, defined the *dogma of the *immaculate conception of Mary. Other aspects of his pontificate bolstered his authority—superiors of religious orders were encouraged to move to Rome, even the clerical dress customary in Rome was adopted elsewhere—and the First *Vatican Council defined the dogma of papal *infallibility without having the opportunity to situate it within a wider decree on the church. Pius' rejection of many of the changes in the modern world were listed in his **Syllabus Errorum* of 1864.

R. Aubert, *Le Pontificat de Pie IX, 1846–1878* (1962).

Pius XII (1876–1958). *Pope from 2 Mar. 1939. Born Eugenio Pacelli he came from a family with a long history of service to the *papacy, and after *ordination entered the secretariat of state. In 1917 he went to Bavaria as papal *nuncio, and three years later moved to Berlin. He became secretary of state in 1930, and negotiated a number of *concordats, most notably that with Hitler in 1933. As pope he used his diplomatic skills without success first to prevent and then to limit the Second World War. He has been accused of being insufficiently active in opposition to Nazi policy towards the Jews, and this inactivity may have sprung from his search for a diplomatic settlement of the war. In the later part of his pontificate he vigorously opposed the spread of communist régimes in E. Europe. Within Roman Catholicism he did much to encourage scholarship, and instituted a number of *liturgical reforms. He spoke frequently on major topics of the day, in a manner which reflected his elevated view of the papal office. In the definition of the *dogma of the *assumption of Mary he was the last pope (to date) explicitly to invoke papal *infallibility.

C. C. Clump (ed.), *The Social Teaching of Pope Pius XII* (1956); C. Falconi, *The Silence of Pius XII* (1970); S. Friedlander, *Pius XII and the Third Reich* (1966).

Pi-yen-lu (Chinese verses): see HSÜEH-TOU CH'UNG-HSIEN.

Piyyut (perhaps from Gk., *poiētēs*). A Jewish poem intended to embellish community or private prayer. Originally piyyutim (pl.) were composed as substitutes for the established *liturgy. Texts of piyyutim can be found in *Talmudic sources, but the earliest known composer of piyyutim was Yose b. Yose who worked in *Erez Israel in the 6th cent. CE. Piyyutim continued to be produced up to the time of the *Haskalah, but it is generally acknowledged that the great period of composition was 9th–13th cents. Different types of piyyutim include the *kerovot*, which were designed to be included in the *'Amidah prayer, and the *yozerot* which were said with the *shema' *benedictions at the morning service. Later piyyutim were composed for private religious occasions such as *Sabbath meals and *havdalot, and also to accompany private prayer. The *paytanim* ('poets') employed different systems of rhyme and rhythm. The earliest piyyutim did not use rhyme, but later paytanim followed different poetic conventions. Initially there were no fixed collections and each cantor followed his own choice, but over the years, anthologies were compiled for the various occasions.

A. Musky, *Reshit ha-Piyyut*.

Plainsong or **Plainchant.** The traditional *music of the Latin Christian *rite. It is generally known as 'Gregorian' chant, though its exact connection with St *Gregory the Great is debated. Plainsong is monodic and does not need instrumental accompaniment (though this may be provided). In so far as it has time values, they follow the patterns of spoken speech. See also MUSIC.

Platform Sūtra (key Zen work): see LIU-TSU-TA-SHIH FA-PAO-T'AN-CHING.

Platonism. The philosophical system found in Plato's writings or derived therefrom. In Plato's writings, which take the form of dialogues, it is usual to see a development from a presentation of the thought of Plato's master, Socrates, through systematization of that thought in the 'middle' dialogues, to the more technical later dialogues, in which Socrates seems subordinate to some of his great predecessors (e.g. Parmenides). Fundamental to Platonism is the conviction that truth cannot be found in everyday life and sensible reality, but in a (more real) ideal realm (of the 'Forms'). To attain that, purification, both moral and intellectual (through dialectic and becoming accustomed to abstract thought), is necessary. Much variety is found in later Platonism: Middle Platonism (1st cent. BCE–2nd cent. CE) developed a religious cosmology from the *Timaeus*, whereas *Plotinus found inspiration for his doctrine of the One in the *Parmenides*. In addition to the ideal realm (of intellect) and the realm of ordinary life (of soul), Plotinus posited the One from which all else proceeds, which is unknowable except in ecstatic union. Such *Neoplatonism was developed in particular by *Porphyry, Iamblichus, and

*Proclus and had a great influence on later thought, Christian, Jewish, and Muslim.

PL Kyōdan (Japanese religious movement): see MIKI TOKUHARU.

Plotinus (*c*.205–70). Founder of *Neoplatonism and mystic. His works were published after his death by his pupil *Porphyry in six 'Enneads' (Groups of Nine, tr. S. MacKenna, rev. B. S. Page, 1969). The major theme of Plotinus' thought is the relation of the One (*to hen*) or the Good at the summit of the chain of beings to the realm of multiplicity. Beneath the undifferentiated One is the intelligible world of ideas (*nous*) and, beneath it, the World Soul (*psyche*). This latter is the creator and orderer of the material world. The various members of the hierarchy are related by a process of *emanation that descends from the One. The emanating entity is both transcendent to its product and immanent within it. The aim of the Plotinian scheme is to attain knowledge of the One by a return to it through *contemplation. Through ascetic practices, the soul turns progressively from the sensuous and intellectual realm and 'ascends' to unite with the One. In such union, the soul becomes identical with its source. Plotinus' thought decisively influenced the development of Judaic, Christian, and Islamic mysticism. He died with the words to a friend, 'I was waiting for you before the divine in me joins the divine in the universe.'

E. Bréhier, *The Philosophy of Plotinus* (1958); J. M. Rist, *Plotinus . . .* (1967); R. T. Wallis, *Neoplatonism* (1972).

Plumstead Peculiars (Free Church sect): see PECULIAR PEOPLE.

Plymouth Brethren. A Christian sect which has divided into more than one group since its foundation, which is derived from the first congregation being formed in Plymouth in 1831 (though the group started in Dublin in 1829). Brethren, regarding themselves as the true Christians, reject the name 'Plymouth', though many accept the name Brethren or Christian Brethren, so long as these do not convey the impression of a denomination (one among many). After many disputes in the early years, two major groups emerged, the Open and the Exclusive Brethren (the latter of which have themselves divided several times).

F. R. Coad, *A History of the Brethren Movement* (1968).

P'o. Component in Chinese anthropology, one of two spiritual elements in the human (the other being *hun). P'o is associated with the dark and passive side, i.e. *yin; and at death, the p'o returns to the earth. With the p'o is associated the *kuei, which represents the unsettled and vengeful element of p'o in some circumstances of death: for details see SHEN.

Pocomania or **Pukkumina** (possibly from Span., 'a little madness'). Afro-Jamaican cults descended from surviving forms of African religion mixed with *Protestant elements from the time of the Great Revival in Jamaica in 1860–2. They take the form of small local 'bands' led by a 'Captain', 'Mother', or 'Shepherd/ess' who lives at and rules over the band's Yard. This usually consists of a ritual bathhouse, a meeting building, and a holy 'Seal' area, with pole and flag around which ritual dances serve to induce trance and possession (especially through a *breathing technique) by the spirits of Africans, former slaves, or the recent dead. Healing occurs through washings, herbs, or patent medicines. Pocomania passes over into ancestor-spirit cults on one side, and into *Revival Zion on the other, and some adherents belong to the Christian churches.

Pogrom (Russ., *gromit*, 'destroy'). An attack involving looting, murder, and rape by one sector of the population on another. More precisely, the term pogrom has been used to describe attacks against the Jews, specifically between 1880 and 1920 in Russia and Poland. These pogroms spurred both the desire for emigration to the USA at the end of the 19th cent. and the desire for a Jewish homeland. The frequency of these attacks opened the way directly to the *Holocaust. See also ANTI-SEMITISM; ZIONISM.

Pole, Reginald (1500–58). *Cardinal and last *archbishop of *Canterbury (to date) in communion with Rome. He was studying abroad at the time of the break between Henry VIII and the *Holy See, and after he had been created cardinal in 1536, he attempted to rally the Catholic princes of Europe against Henry. He identified himself with those seeking reform of church government, and was one of the three cardinals appointed by *Paul III to preside over the opening of the council of *Trent. On Paul's death in 1549 he was very close to being elected *pope. After the accession of Mary Tudor to the English throne, Pole was sent as papal legate. He arrived in 1554, received the country back into communion with Rome, and instituted a number of reforms, though his desire to restore church lands aroused great hostility. In 1556 he was appointed to Canterbury. He died just twelve hours after the death of Queen Mary.

Political theology. A Christian concern to explore the implications of theology for political life and thought. The term has an uneasy history, being associated, for example, with the endorsement by Carl Schmitt of Hitler and the rise of German nationalism. However, the term is now usually associated with the work of Johann Baptist Metz (who sometimes uses the phrase 'the new political theology') and Dorothee Sölle. In contrast to what it takes to be the traditional concentration of theology on the individual and on personal holiness, allowing the support of virtually any political system or party (or none), Metz sees 'the deprivatising of theology as the primary critical task of political theology'. The promises of the New Testament in relation to the kingdom (involving justice, reconciliation, peace) cannot be private matters, but 'make the individual free with regard to the political society around him, in the sense of committing him to it in a free critique of it'. *Orthopraxy becomes the mark of true discipleship more than the traditional orthodoxy. The connections with *liberation theology are clear, although liberation theologians regard themselves as differently rooted in the experience of the poor.

A. Kee, *Reader in Political Theology* (1974).

Polycarp, St (*c*.69–*c*.155). Christian bishop of Smyrna in Asia Minor. According to his pupil *Irenaeus he associated with 'John and with the rest of those who had seen the Lord'; he is thus a link between the apostles and the orthodox writers of the 2nd cent. His *Letter to the Philippians* is preserved, as well as one of *Ignatius' letters addressed to him. According to the contemporary *Martyrdom of Polycarp* he was arrested during a pagan festival and, on his refusing to recant his faith, burnt to death. Feast day, 23 Feb.

Polygamy. Marriage in which a person may have more than one spouse at the same time (in contrast to monogamy). Polygyny is the marriage of a man to more than one wife, polyandry the marriage of a woman to more than one husband. Polyandry is relatively rare (e.g. the Nayar and Toda of India), polygyny more common, especially in Africa. In Islam, marriage to more than one wife is allowed (see MARRIAGE), but in general, religions have moved toward monogamy or have endorsed it from the start. Thus in India, some polygyny was practised and permitted in the *Vedic period, even if only for the wealthy; by the time of the *śastras, it is recognised in some circumstances (e.g., if the first wife is barren). But the ideal is undoubtedly monogamy. This was inherited by the Sikhs: Gurū *Nānak and Gurū *Gobind Siṅgh both advocated fidelity in marriage, and monogamy is the norm. Nevertheless, both Gurū *Hargobind and Gobind Siṅgh had three wives, probably because some devout Sikhs dedicated their daughters at birth exclusively to the Gurū or his relations. A comparable process is clear in Judaism: early biblical society was polygynous, although some passages, e.g. Proverbs 31, seem to reflect the values of monogamy. However, monogamy was seen to be an appropriate reflection of the marriage between God and the Jewish people (Hosea 2. 21–2; Song of Songs), and it became the norm. The *takkānah of *Gershom b. Judah (*c*.1000 BCE) forbade polygamy, thereby giving formal sanction to the existing practice of *Ashkenazi Jews. Among the *Sephardim, polygyny continued to be recognized in religious law, although it was not in fact practised. Christianity inherited the attitude of Judaism (the 'marriage between Christ and his Church' being a powerful metaphor) and practised monogamy. This was reinforced from Roman law, so that *Augustine (*The Advantage of Marriage*, 7) could write: 'In our time, and in keeping with Roman customs, it is no longer allowed to have more than one wife living.' The prohibition on polygamy was taken into the world through missionary expansion, where it often came into conflict with existing practice. Although Pope Gregory II advised *Boniface in 726 to tolerate polygamy until the Germanic people could be weaned gradually from their old ways, the later attitudes were more adamant. *Roman Catholics, on the basis of the constitution of *Paul III, *Altitudo* (1537), insisted that all but one wife must be divorced (despite the protest of missionaries against the extreme hardship which this produced), and *Pius XII went even further in establishing the canonical regulation whereby the pope has power to dissolve valid marriages between non-Christians, neither of whom intended to be baptized. Protestant attitudes (and actions) range from the insistence on divorce of all but one wife, to baptism of the whole family, provided no further (polygynous) marriage is entered into. The *Lambeth Conference of 1888 declared polygamy to be 'inconsistent with the law of Christians', but the Conference of 1988 allowed baptism to those who undertook not to enter into further (polygynous) marriages, and it asked that the consent of the local Anglican community should be sought (resolution 26). *African Instituted Churches are divided on the issue.

E. Hilman, *Polygamy Reconsidered* (1975).

Pŏmnang (fl. 632–46). The Korean monk credited with introducing Sŏn (Ch'an/Zen) to Korea. Pŏmnang studied Sŏn under Tao-hsin (580–651), fourth patriarch of the Ch'an sect in China, during the reign of King Sŏndŏk (632–46), and transmitted his lineage to the kingdom of Silla. Among his disciples was Sinhaeng (d. 779) who introduced Northern Ch'an to Korea.

Pongyi (Burmese Buddhist monk): see BUDDHISM IN SOUTH-EAST ASIA.

Pontifex Maximus (Lat., *pontifex*, 'bridge-maker', of uncertain significance). Title of the *pope. It was originally the title of the chief pagan priest at Rome. In Christian usage from the 5th cent., it was occasionally used of other bishops as well, but was later confined to the pope alone. In English it is rendered 'supreme pontiff'.

Pontifical. The liturgical book in the *Roman Catholic Church which contains the prayers and ceremonies for rites involving a bishop. It is divided into three parts: (i) relating to persons, e.g. *confirmation, *ordination; (ii) relating to things: consecration of churches, altars, etc.; and (iii) rites for special functions.

Pontificals are the particular vestments etc. worn by a bishop when celebrating a pontifical mass, and also the functions themselves.

Poor Clares. The 'Second Order' of St *Francis, founded by him and St Clare some time between

1212 and 1214. Clare was moved by the preaching of Francis to abandon her possessions and to join a Benedictine house. In 1215, she became abbess of a new and separate community, living under a severe rule—later ameliorated for some convents. Nevertheless, Poor Clares are regarded as the most austere religious order in the *Roman Catholic Church.

Poor men of Lyons (followers of Waldenses): see WALDENSES.

Pōp. Korean for *dharma.

Pope (Gk., *pappas*, 'father'). In the *Roman Catholic Church a title applied exclusively to the *bishop of Rome since the 11th cent., though used earlier of all bishops. The *Coptic patriarch of *Alexandria is also known as the pope, and in the Greek *Orthodox Church the title is commonly used of all priests. For examples, see Index, Popes.

Pope of Taoism: see T'IEN-SHIH.

Popovtsy ('with priests' group of Old Believers): see OLD BELIEVERS.

Popular religion: see FOLK RELIGION.

Pormalim. A *messianic religion among the Batak of Sumatra. It derived from the tradition of Singa Mangaradjas (Skt., 'Lion King'), legendary priest-kings, the last of whom, Ompu Pulo Batu, was killed in 1907. He allegedly founded the Pormalim (Batak, *malim*, 'be independent') religion, after which it was developed by a *guru, Somailung, in resistance to Christian missions and Dutch control. There are no Islamic but many Christian influences, including belief in a miracle-working son born of a virgin, and a weekly service in a special temple with a sermon. Fermented lemon juice is used to induce trance, during which the Singa Mangaradja speaks; a goat sacrifice usually ends the service. Pormalim was at its height between 1910 and 1920 but still exists, scattered across the Toba highlands.

Porphyry (*c*.232–*c*.303). *Neoplatonist philosopher and anti-Christian writer. His philosophical works include an *Introduction to the* Categories *of Aristotle* which became a standard medieval textbook; he wrote a *Life* of his teacher *Plotinus, and the treatise *Against the Christians*. This was condemned to be burnt in 448 and survives only in quotations in works of refutation. Porphyry considered the apparent failure of Jesus' life to be proof that he was not divine, and he condemned the apostles and leaders of the Church for treachery, especially in resisting the religious revival of the emperors Decius and Aurelian. He also attacked the inconsistencies in the gospels and the traditional date of *Daniel.

Port Royal Logic (writing of Antoine Arnauld): see ARNAULD, ANTOINE.

Porvoo Declaration (ecumenical agreement between some Anglican and some Lutheran Churches): see ANGLICANISM.

Posal. Korean for *bodhisattva.

Posek. A Jewish scholar who is concerned with practical *halakhah. Originally the posekim (pl.) included the heads of the *yeshivot, the *rabbis, and the *avot battei din. Their rulings were laid down in accordance with their own community practice and therefore were only binding on that community. After the Codes of Jewish law were widely disseminated, the role of the posekim changed. Through extensive practical experience of interpreting the Codes, they maintained their position as local sources of authority. For an example of a much revered 20th-cent. posek, see FEINSTEIN, MOSHEH.

Poson (Buddhist festival): see FESTIVALS AND FASTS.

Possessors. Party in a monastic controversy in *Russian Orthodoxy. St Joseph of Volokalamsk (1439–1515) argued that monks should live lives of poverty and *asceticism, but that monasteries should accumulate wealth in order to serve and support the Church. His followers were enthusiastic patrons of musicians, builders, and *icon-painters. He and they were also severe against *heretics. In contrast, the Non-Possessors, led by St Nil(us) Sorsky (*c*.1433–1508) believed that the whole Church is called to poverty, and that heretics should be treated with understanding and patience. Both were canonized by the Council of 1551, but the position of St Joseph was endorsed. However, the view of St Nil was kept alive, first by the 'holy fool' tradition (*salos/yurodivy*), along with mystical teachers and hermits, and then by the *Old Believers: as Church and State grew closer together, the Old Believers withdrew increasingly into a spiritual and sometimes apocalyptic vision of Christianity.

Potala (Tibetan Buddhist fortress): see LHASA.

Potlatch (N. American Kwakiutl ceremony): see ALMSGIVING.

Prabhākara (*c*.7th cent. CE). Philosopher in the Hindu *Pūrva-Mīmāṁsā system; but whereas Mīmāṁsā in general holds that *mokṣa leads to life in heaven, Prabhākara remained closer to most other systems, defining mokṣa as 'the absolute cessation of the body brought about by the exhaustion of all *dharma and *adharma* [merit and its opposite]'. His major work was a commentary on *Sābara-bhāṣya* (itself a commentary on the *Mīmāṁsā Sūtras* attributed to *Jaimini) entitled *Bṛhati* (ed. S. K. R. Sastri, 1931).

Prabhavana. The Jain custom of offering a sweetmeat to those who have participated in a religious ceremony. In origin, it refers to the eight ways in which the Jain way is commended and exalted: through knowledge of the scriptures; through debating; through preaching; through mastery of *astrology; of *magic; of invocation; through writing; through *asceticism. Prabhacandra's *Prabhavakacarita* tells the stories of twenty-two performers of prabhavana who are seen as protectors of the community.

Prabhupada, Bhaktivedanta Svami (1896–1977). Founder (i.e. *ācārya) of the *International Society for Krishna Consciousness. He was born Abhay Charan De in Calcutta, and followed a successful career as a business manager until 1933, when he was entrusted (by Bhaktisiddhanta Thakura of the Gaudiya Vaishnava Mission) with the work of carrying Krishna Consciousness to the West. He undertook translation work until he retired in 1959, when he took the *saṃnyasin vow which set him free for his mission. In 1965 he went to Boston and established ISKCON. In 1967 he moved to California where the movement began to grow rapidly. In contrast to some other Hindu-based new religions, he discouraged his followers from regarding him as an *avatāra, but rather presented himself as one who, like them, was endeavouring to be a servant of God.

Practical kabbalah: see KABBALAH.

Pradakṣina. Hindu rite of circumambulation, to express reverence to an object (or to the deity or Brahman within it), or to protect it, or to secure safety if it contains potential for evil.

Pradhāna (Skt.). Nature in its undeveloped state, the equivalent in Hindu Sāṃkhya of *prakṛti.

Pradyumna (manifest power of Viṣṇu): see VIṢṆU.

Praemunire. The title of statutes (first passed in 1353, 1365, and 1393) which were designed to resist papal encroachment on the rights claimed by the English crown. In later times, Elizabeth I used Praemunire to deal with civil offences and Catholic *recusants. The Criminal Law Act of 1967 repealed all the statutes.

Prajāpati (Skt., 'Lord of creatures/creation'). A conceptual development in the late Vedic period of Hinduism drawing together the many manifested forces of nature into a single source of creation, and often, therefore, made synonymous with *Indra and *Sāvitrī. Prajāpati also subsumed other views of creation represented through *Puruṣa and *Hiraṇyagarbha, and was eventually merged with *Brahmā. Prajāpati is linked to the sacrificial root of creation, either by continually creating living creatures out of the sacrifices to the gods (*Taittirīya Brāhmaṇa* 1. 6. 2. 1), or as being himself the sacrifice from which life is sustained: 'Prajāpati is sacrifice, for he created it as his own self-expression' (*Śatapatha Brāhmaṇa* 11. 1. 8. 2). In relation to the thirty-three gods of the classical system, Prajāpati was reckoned the thirty-fourth, embracing and including the others:

> In the beginning, he arose as Hiraṇyagarbha. When born, he was the one Lord of all that exists. He supported the earth and this heaven. What God with our offering shall we worship? . . . O Prajāpati, you alone have encompassed all these created things: may that for which with longing we have called upon you be ours; may we become lords of wealth (Hymn to Prajāpati, *Ṛg Veda* 10. 121).

Prajña (Skt., 'wisdom', 'consciousness'). 1. In Hinduism, the competence of *ātman to realize itself for what it is, and thus to abide in this state as in a dreamless sleep.

2. In Buddhism (Pāli, *pañña*; Jap., *hannya*), prajña is the third heading of the three into which the eightfold path is divided (see AṢṬANGIKA-MĀRGA)—i.e. right thought and right view constitute wisdom. Although *Mahāyāna initially criticized the setting of pañña at the apex, and balanced it with *karuṇā, compassion, prajña became central to Mahāyāna as the awareness that cannot be achieved by propositions, arguments, or concepts. Supremely, it is the direct awareness of *śūnyatā (emptiness of self) in the case of all appearance. See further PERFECTION OF WISDOM LITERATURE; NĀGĀRJUNA.

Prajñānam Brahma (Skt., 'consciousness is *Brahman'). One of the five Hindu *mahāvākyas (great precepts): 'All that is is guided by prajñānam, is founded on prajñānam. Prajñānam is Brahman' (*Aitareya Upaniṣad* 3. 5. 3).

Prajñāpāramitā (Buddhist literature): see PERFECTION OF WISDOM LITERATURE.

Prajñaptivāda (Skt., *prajñapti*, 'designation', + *vāda*, 'way'). An early school of Buddhism. Having originated in the late 3rd cent. BCE as an offshoot of the *Mahāsaṃghikas, the Prajñaptivāda claims a line of descent from one of the Buddha's disciples, Mahākātyāyana. No texts of the school are extant but both Paramārtha and Vasumitra claim that the Prajñaptivāda had a special *Abhidharmic text which differentiated between two levels of statement in the *Buddha's teachings; those acceptable for non-initiates and therefore requiring further elaboration, and those aimed at adepts. Such a distinction closely corresponds to the *Mahāyānist doctrine concerning conventional (*saṃvṛti*) and ultimate (*paramārtha*) *sūtra utterances; and for this reason the Prajñaptivāda is sometimes held to be a proto-Mahāyānist school. The most characteristic doctrine of the school is its differentiation between designations (*prajñapti*) and the things they signify, the latter being ultimately existent, the former being only conventionally so.

There is no indication that the Prajñaptivāda spread beyond its original territory in E. India, but it does seem to have flourished there until the time of the Muslim invasions.

Prajñāvimukta (arhat who has attained supreme wisdom): see ARHAT.

Prakṛti (Skt., 'making first'). In Sanskrit. literature, primordial material nature. In mythology prakṛti is personified as a goddess of cosmic creative energy, *Śakti, the female counterpart of every god. In *Vedānta, prakṛti is synonymous with cosmic manifestation, hence as appearance, *māyā. In *Sāṃkhya-yoga prakṛti plays an important role as the ultimate material reality juxtaposed with *puruṣa, the ultimate spiritual reality. Here prakṛti is the matrix of the universe, the material cause of all manifest matter and energy. As such, prakṛti is composed of three balanced *guṇas (Skt., 'strands') or constituent modes which, in disequilibrium, combine to generate all other material principles (*tattvas): intellect (*buddhi), ego (*ahaṁkāra), mind (*manas), the five sense capacities, the five action capacities, the five subtle elements, and the five gross elements. This creative display of prakṛti is unconscious. Puruṣa, as pure consciousness, illumines prakṛti and inspires by his sheer presence her evolutionary dance, the manifestation and continuous transformation of the universe.

Pralaya or **laya** (Skt., 'dissolution'). The Hindu understanding that all appearance is subject, not to destruction, but dissolution—leading to re-creation. It is especially used of the ending of a *kalpa (cosmic cycle), which then, via *pravṛtti, leads to the beginning of a new creation. But there may also be lesser pralayas, as e.g. in the great flood of Manu (see *Mahābhārata, Vana-parva* 187; *Śatapatha Brāhmaṇa* 1. 8. 1. 1–10), which occurred when all creation was submerged under a deluge; but Manu had rescued a tiny fish which was thus enabled to grow large: the fish told him to build a large boat and to take into it seeds and animals, and the fish towed the boat to safety by anchoring it on the highest of the *Himālayas.

Pramāṇa (Skt., 'measure', 'authority'). 1. In Hinduism, proof, the means for attaining true knowledge, as by logic, sensory perception (within the limits of *māyā), the *Vedas. See further NYĀYA; KNOWLEDGE (for the six ways).

2. In Buddhism generally, a school of thought established by Dignāga. In its more technical sense, however, pramāṇa refers to differing means of knowledge. Classical Brahmanism accepts four pramāṇas. i.e. perception (*pratyakṣa*), inference (*anumāṇa*), scripture (*smṛti), and tradition (*aitihya*). The situation in Buddhism is more confused. In the early period it was held that neither inference nor the authority of scripture or tradition could be relied on to provide truth, a stance which was widened by the *Madhyamikas who seem to have rejected all pramāṇas. *Vasubandhu oscillated between accepting two or three pramāṇas and finally in the Pramāṇa school itself only direct perception and inference were considered to furnish indisputable knowledge of particulars and universals respectively.

The Pramāṇa school appears to have centred on Nālandā; its other important exponent, a pupil of Dignāga, was *Dharmakīrti. The works of both authors are still studied by Tibetan Buddhists. See also JÑĀNA.

Prāṇa (Skt., 'breath'). In Hinduism, the vital force which differentiates the living from the dead. By the *breath from his mouth, *Prajāpati created the gods. In *Atharva Veda*, Prāṇa is personified, and one hymn is addressed to him. There are five different 'life-winds', i.e. types of prāṇas, of which the first, prāṇa itself, the essential characteristic of breath as life-bestowing, was eventually identified with *Brahman present as *ātman: 'He is your ātman, which is in all things' (*Bṛhadāraṇyaka Upaniṣad* 3. 4. 1). The cultivation of prāṇa-control is an important part of yoga—see PRĀṆĀYĀMA.

Prāṇapratiṣṭhā (Skt., 'endowing with breath'). The ritual acts in Hinduism through which life is endowed on a representation of God, so that the divine reality becomes active in and through the image.

Prāṇāyāma (Skt.). Breath (*prāṇa) control in *yoga; the fourth limb of *Patañjali's eight-limbed (aṣṭāṅga) or *rāja yoga. In the **Yoga Sūtra* (2. 49) Patañjali defines it as the 'cutting off (*viccheda*) of the flow of inhalation and exhalation' which is achieved after the attaining of 'posture' (*āsana) and prepares the mind for concentration (*dhāraṇā). The yogin makes his breathing rhythmical and slower by equalizing the three moments of breath, namely inhalation (*pūraka*), exhalation (*recaka*), and retention (*kumbhaka*). Eventually the breath ceases altogether or becomes so minimal as to be undetectable. Due to the connection between breath (prāṇa) and consciousness (*citta), it is thought that through arresting the breath the yogin is thereby arresting and calming consciousness and so achieving one-pointed (*ekāgratā) concentration.

*Haṭha Yoga texts connect prāṇāyāma with the physiology of the subtle body (*sūkṣma-śarīra, *liṅga-śarīra). The yogin should breath in through the right nostril, thought to be the entrance to the *iḍā *nāḍī, and out through the left, thought to be the entrance to the *piṅgalā nāḍī. This practice results in perspiration and trembling. Through constant practice the nāḍīs are purified and the yogin achieves the ability to hear inner sound (*nāda).

Physiological studies have shown that the reduction of breathing is accompanied by reduction of heart-beat in yogins, a condition which resembles the state before death. The restriction of breathing in yogins can be so great that they can be buried alive for some time without danger.

Praṇava (reverberation): see OṂ.

Praṇidhāna (Buddhist vow): see BODHISATTVA VOW.

Prapatti (Skt., 'seeking refuge'). A key-concept of *Śrīvaiṣṇava theology. Synonyms are the Skt. *śaraṇāgati* ('arriving for protection'), *nyāsa* ('placing down [one's responsibilities]' and the Tamil *aṭaikkalam* ('resorting [for protection]'). As a technical term, prapatti does not yet occur in the theological works of *Rāmānuja, although its existence in the related traditions of the *Pāñcarātra and Vaikhānasas is earlier. Post-Rāmānuja theologians, belonging both to the *Teṉ- and Vaṭa-kalai, employ it as a central term in their discussion. It now denotes the acceptance of *Viṣṇu's grace which has been made available universally through the scriptures, his temple incarnations (see AVATĀRA), the hymns of the *Āḻvārs, the teaching of Rāmānuja, etc. Thus it is *the* 'means' of achieving salvation. Of primary importance in the discussion is the contrastive term *bhakti. As defined here, it denotes the bhakti-yoga expounded in works like the **Bhagavad-gītā* and the **Viṣṇu-Purāṇa*, and implies structured meditation exercises. Many Śrīvaiṣṇava teachers (of the Teṉ-kaḷai) claimed that only prapatti yields *mokṣa; others (like *Vedāntadeśika) allowed also for bhakti, at least in the case of outstanding sages of the past. Moreover, the Teṉ-kaḷai assumed that grace was mediated via *Lakṣmī, who was regarded by them as inferior to Viṣṇu, while the Vaṭa-kaḷai, by holding that Lakṣmī was co-natural with Viṣṇu, had no need for such mediation. But the centre of the theological dispute within the Śrīvaiṣṇava movement became the question of to what extent grace operates independently of human co-operation. In the extreme case (with some Teṉ-kaḷai teachers), even a ritual performance of prapatti during youth (as the Vaṭa-kaḷai have it) was rejected as interfering with the free working of grace. The Vaṭa-kaḷai insisted that at least a token of human co-operation is required, for otherwise the workings of grace would be totally random and arbitrary.

Prapatti itself has been divided into five *aṅgas* or aspects: (i) to concern oneself with what gives pleasure to Viṣṇu; (ii) to avoid what is unpleasant to him; (iii) absolute faith and confidence in him; (iv) to choose him as one's sole protector; (v) to be aware of oneself as totally powerless. Yet this is not meant as a long, structured spiritual programme. Ultimately prapatti is the realization (in both senses of the word) of a factually given situation—total human dependence on Viṣṇu—which has been obscured by a separate self-awareness (ignorance) due to past *karma.

Prasāda or **prasad.** 1. In Hinduism, the sense (especially in the *Upaniṣads) of the free action of favour or *grace, coming to the assistance of individuals and helping them toward *mokṣa (release): 'When favoured by *Brahman, the self (*ātman) attains immortality' (*Śvetāśvatara Upaniṣad* 1. 6). *Kaṭha Upaniṣad* puts it even more strongly: 'This ātman [i.e. the recognition *tat tvam asi] cannot be attained by instruction, or by intellect, or by learning. He can be attained only by the one whom he chooses: to such a one that ātman reveals his own nature' (2. 23). 'Grace' is thus opposed to 'works' (i.e. the strict working out of *karma). See further, S. Kulandran, *Grace in Christianity and Hinduism* (1964); and for its importance among Sikhs see SIKHISM.

2. Food offerings, which are then shared among worshippers, carrying with them spiritual effect.

3. Peace of mind received, without effort, as a gift.

Prāsaṅgika. A branch of the *Mādhyamaka school of Buddhist philosophy which regards itself as adhering most faithfully to the methodology of *Nāgārjuna, the founder of the Mādhyamaka system. It adopts the strategy of criticizing the views of its opponents by deriving undesired consequences (*prasaṅga*) from them, rather than setting out a positive thesis of its own. The other main branch of the school, the Svatantrika-Mādhyamaka, adopted a contrary view and argued that a purely destructive, negative critique was inadequate and must be followed by a positive statement in which one's own position is established. Main proponents of the Prāsaṅgika method were *Buddhapālita and *Candrakīrti, while the Svatantrika cause was championed by *Bhāvaviveka.

Praśna Upaniṣad. An Upaniṣad belonging to the **Atharva-Veda*. It deals with six questions posed to the wise man, Pippalāda: (i) how matter and life derive from *Prajāpati; (ii) why *prāna precedes other vital elements; (iii) how prāna is dispersed in the body; (iv) the nature of dreaming and sleeping states; (v) the meaning of *OṂ; (vi) the sixteen radiating divisions of the human appearance.

Trs.: see UPANIṢAD.

Praśnavyākarana-aṅga (Jain text): see AṄGA.

Praśnottara (Skt.). In Hinduism, the process of 'question and answer', through which teaching proceeds.

Prasthānatraya (Skt., 'system' + 'threefold'). The three authoritative sources, in *Advaita Hinduism, of *Vedānta, the *Upaniṣads, the **Bhagavad-gītā*, the **Brahma-sūtras*.

Prātimokṣa (Skt.; Pāli, *pātimokkha*). Part of the Buddhist *Vinaya-pitaka, containing the rules for *bhikṣus (monks) and for bhikṣunis (nuns). It is recited at every *uposatha ceremony. Originally, public confession of fault against the code was made, but this became an individual confession prior to the ceremony, with a silent assent at its conclusion. Three codes survive: *Theravādin (227 rules for bhikṣus, 311 for bhikṣunis), Mula-*Sarvastivādin (258 and 366), and Dharmaguptaka (250 and 348).

The rules are arranged in order of severity of the offences. Attitudes to the importance of the rules have varied in Buddhist history: there have been Vināya schools (e.g. *Geluk, Lu (*Buddhism in China), and *Ritsu), but there have been others who have been cautious about rule-based enlightenment (e.g. *Saicho, *Shinran).

C. S. Prebish, *Buddhist Monastic Discipline* (1974).

Pratiṣṭhita-nirvāna. In Mahāyāna Buddhism, the attainment of final *nirvāna, with no remaining connection with the world of appearance. A *bodhisattva postpones this attainment to help others (*pranidhāna*), though in fact, since all is of the same nature, empty of self (*śūnyatā), he is in the condition of nirvāna while helping still in the domain of appearance (*saṃsāra). Thus although the concept seems the equivalent of the *Theravāda *nirupadhiśeṣa-nirvāna, the two are radically different.

Pratītya-samutpāda (the causal nexus of interconnected appearance): see PATICCA-SAMUPPĀDA.

Pratyāhāra (Skt., 'withdrawal'). 1. In Hinduism, sense-withdrawal, the fifth 'limb' of 'eight-limbed' (*aṣṭaṅga*) or *rāja yoga, referring to the contraction of consciousness from the external world and senses, as a tortoise contracts its limbs. In order to concentrate his mind inwards and so achieve higher states of consciousness (*samādhi), the yogin's mind should become completely cut off from his outer environment. *Vyāsa, in his commentary on the **Yoga Sūtra* (2. 54), says that as a swarm of bees flies up when the queen bee flies and settles when she settles, so the senses are restrained when consciousness is restrained or withdrawn.

2. A technical sense in Sanskrit grammar meaning the compression to one syllable of a series of letters or affixes, by combining the initial letter with the final. For example, *a*, the first letter of the *devanāgarī* alphabet, combines with *ha*, the last letter, to make *aha*, which thus denotes the entire Skt. alphabet. Furthermore, *aha* suggests the totality of cosmic emanation which in Hinduism is regarded as a manifestation of sound (*varṇa, śabda *vāc). Add an anusvara or *bindu, and the word becomes *ahaṃ, 'I', a term indicating the absolute *Parameśvara in *Kashmir Śaivism.

Pratyekabuddha (Skt.; Pāli Pacceka). In Buddhism, one who attains the condition next to that of *arhat entirely on his own. He has no teacher and does not belong to the *saṅgha, and he makes no attempt to communicate his way or his attainment to anyone else. He is therefore known as the Solitary or Silent Buddha, and is described as 'a lonely rhinoceros'. Such buddhas belonged originally to the *śramaṇa tradition, and supplied the context for *Gautāma's vocation.

M. Wiltshire, *Ascetic Figures Before and in Early Buddhism* . . . (1990).

Pratykṣa (perception): see RĀMĀNUJA.

Pravrajya. 'Going forth' from home, the determination to renounce the world and undertake an *ascetic way. It is characteristic of Jains, but applies also to Hindus.

Pravṛtti (Skt., 'origin, arising'). The unfolding or emergence of a new cosmos, after its dissolution (*pralaya).

Praxis (Gk., 'activity'). Action which arises from true belief, the manifestation of religion in practice. In Aristotle, praxis is the competence of humans to live together in a *polis* ('city', i.e. community), and this was adapted in Christianity to form a contrast with the higher virtue of the *contemplation of God: the former has to do with life in this world, the latter with life in *eternity. However, the post-*Marx return of attention to realized *eschatology (the view, associated especially with the *New Testament, that the final state is already beginning to be realized and anticipated in the present) and to this world and life as bearing the responsibilities of God's creation, has led also to a renewed emphasis on *orthopraxis in conjunction with orthodoxy (right belief or opinion). This is of particular importance in *liberation theology.

R. Bernstein, *Praxis and Action* . . . (1971); R. Chopp, *The Praxis of Suffering* . . . (1986); N. Lobkowicz, *Theory and Practice: The History of a Concept from Aristotle to Marx* (1967).

Prayāga or **Prag.** 'Place of sacrifice'. Hindu place of *pilgrimage (*tīrtha), later called by Muslims Allāhābād, at the meeting point of *Gaṅgā and Yamunā rivers, and the subterranean Sarasvatī. It is therefore called *triveṇī*, 'triple-thread'. Even its soil is so sacred that a small part of it can cleanse from sin. It is one of the seven *sacred cities, and one of the four sites of the *kuṁbha-mela, which takes place every twelve years. To avoid the Muslim name, Hindus usually call it Ilāhābād, the abode of Ilā, the mother of a solar dynasty king.

Prāyaścitta. In Jainism, the practice of making vows in repentance for sins committed. Although sometimes imposed by ascetics on the laity after confession, more often these vows are self-imposed and untold. They may involve long periods of silence, not speaking until a wrong has been righted, fasting, giving up some pleasure or luxury, and restrictions on movement especially at night.

Prayer (from Lat., *precare*, 'to beg, entreat'). The relating of the self or soul to God in trust, penitence, praise, petition, and purpose, either individually or corporately. Some of these aspects of prayer have been isolated (e.g. petition as intercession), as have some of the ways of being before God (e.g. *contemplation, *meditation, recollection), so that the term 'prayer' may cover more, or less, in each tradition. In Eastern religions, prayer falls more naturally into the domain of worship (*pūjā) and devotion (e.g. *bhakti), as in *nām simaran, the calling to mind of God among both Hindus and Sikhs: see e.g. PREMA-BHAKTI, as the highest form of devotion among Hindus. See Index, Prayer.

Judaism See TEFILLAH; PRAYER BOOK (JUDAISM).

Christianity Prayer is the acknowledgement of God as the source of all goodness and therefore the One who can meet human need and longing. It is thus an expression of wonder and a cry for help. A. Tanquerey (*The Spiritual Life . . .*, 1930) defined prayer as 'an elevation of our soul to God to offer Him our homage and ask for His favours, in order to grow in holiness for His glory'. Christian prayer is prayer in Christ, sharing in the prayer of the Son to the Father through the Spirit, who in prayer exposes our deepest need (cf. Romans 8. 14–27). Awe and intimacy, knowing God both as ineffable and as One whose face is turned towards us in fatherly love: such paradox lies at the heart of Christian prayer. The model then is Jesus' prayer to his Father, joyful, intimate, trusting, and obedient; the pattern is the prayer he gave to his disciples, the *Lord's Prayer, which moves from adoration of the Father, through surrender to his will, to petition for sustenance, recognition of the need for forgiveness in the darkness of the world, and a cry for deliverance. The prayer of Christ is the fulfilment of the prayer of God's chosen people, *Israel, and so the *Psalms, which express the joy and thankfulness, the longing and need for forgiveness of those who live within God's *covenant of love, become a fundamental expression of Christian prayer, especially in the development of the daily round of prayer, sanctifying time, called the divine *office. Outside the liturgy, individual prayer is realized by short, repeated prayer, or by the cherishing of a 'still centre' through *contemplation which then unconsciously suffuses life. The supreme expression of Christian prayer, the prayer of the children of God united in the Son of God, is the eucharist, an act of thanksgiving, adoration, penitence, and pleading, in which all the longing and concern of the people of God is caught up in Christ's sacrifice of love to his Father.

Islam Prayer in Islam is a practical expression of the ash *Shahāda, the witness that there is no God but God. Since all life comes from him, its appropriate response is thanksgiving and praise, along with penitence and supplication. There are three major forms of prayer in Islam: *ṣalāt, the obligatory prayer five times a day; *dhikr, remembrance of God, developed especially in *Sūfī Islam; and *du'ā', a more personal calling on God, of which the prayers based on *yā Laṭīf*, 'O Gracious One', are an example, based on Qur'ān 42. 19: 'O Gracious One, . . . as you were generously kind in creating the heavens and the earth, and to me in the darkness of the womb, so be generously kind in your unswerving decree [*qadar], and in your decisions concerning me.' Prayers, or blessings, on the Prophet are also important, following Qur'ān 33. 56, 'You who believe, call blessings on him and peace.' From this derives the blessing on the Prophet whenever a believer speaks or writes his name—Muḥammad, *ṣalla-llāhu 'alayhi wa sallam*, 'may God bless him and give him peace'—a formula followed also for other prophets (including *Jesus/'Īsā) and *Gabriel. For popular prayer in Islam, see C. E. Padwick, *Muslim Devotions* (1961).

Hinduism Prayer permeates Hindu life, but not in so formal or detached a style as it does e.g. for Muslims. Great merit (*puṇya) is accrued from the saying of prayers, many of which are derived from the Vedic hymns. Prayer is highly devotional, especially in *bhakti, and often merges into *mantra.

Sikhism Prayer is rooted in *nām simaraṇ, the calling to mind of God, brought about by meditation. Formal and informal prayer both begin and end with *ardas. Praise is expressed through *kirtan. Out of all this, petition flows, as encouraged by *Guru Nānak, 'Whoever cries and begs at the door of God will be heard and blessed.' See also NITNEM.

Zoroastrianism The prophet *Zoroaster probably thought of prayer (if he had ever used such a word) as conversation with God (*Ahura Mazda), since most of his extant words (the *Gāthās, composed in hymnic form, see AVESTA) are in a very direct and personal style, expressing questions and doubts, affirmations of faith and devotion, in what was for the prophet the vernacular. However, he was a practising priest steeped in Indo-Iranian religious practice (cf. the *Ṛg Veda*). That tradition, and later Zoroastrian practice, especially that of the *Parsis, has a different perspective on prayer, namely, that the recitation of the sacred words in the powerful holy language, provided they are offered in both moral and physical *purity and with devotion, links people directly to God and thereby generates ritual power (*amal*). Understanding the meaning of the words, it is thought, can inhibit the mystical experience because by thinking about the meaning the worshippers limit themselves to human conceptual thought.

There are two main types of Zoroastrian prayer: private and more public liturgies. Every Zoroastrian is expected to recite the *kusti* prayers (*naujote) at least five times daily having first cleansed himself or herself physically (by washing). The duty of prayer is common to all, high or low, male or female. Prayers are offered on many other occasions, at meal times, before major undertakings, in the temple, and at major turning-points of life (birth, marriage, or death). There are a series of Avestan prayers which each Zoroastrian is expected to learn by heart, the *Yatha Ahu Vairyo* (Pahlavi, *Ahunavar*), thought to have been composed by Zoroaster himself: as the greatest of all Zoroastrian prayers, it can, where necessary, replace all other acts of devotion; *Asem*

Vohu in praise of truth or righteousness; the *Yenhe hatam*, in praise of holy beings which is recited at the end of litanies; and the *Airyema ishyo* especially recited at weddings and which will be recited by the saviours at *Frasokereti. These prayers are almost untranslatable, because of the antiquity of their language and the poetic allusions. Also important, for example, as part of the *Kusti* prayers, are the *Kem na Mazda* (seeking divine protection and repudiating evil); *Hormazd Khodae* (again rejecting evil, and seeking forgiveness for all sins and ending with a vow to work for truth and to promote the world of Ahura Mazda); the *Fravarane*, almost a creed, affirming commitment to the Zoroastrian religion, so also the *Din-no Kalmo*.

There are also the formal liturgies performed mainly in a temple, though some are still performed in the home. These are divided into the 'Higher or Inner' and 'Lower or Outer' ceremonies. The former can only be performed in a pure place apart, generally a fire temple, by a pure priest. The latter may be performed in a temple (*Atas), or in any private house and require less strict observance of the higher purity laws (e.g. the priest does not have to be observing the *Baresnum*, Purity). The obvious example of the Inner ceremonies is the *Yasna* (cf. Vedic *yajña*, sacrifice), developed in Zoroastrianism as the *Yasna Haptaghaiti*, the worship of the even sections, the liturgy enshrined within the two blocks of the Gāthās in the *Avesta. The *yasna*, like other acts of worship, is concerned to make present the spiritual forces, notably the *Amesa Spentas, whose creations are physically present in the act of worship. In earlier times, animal sacrifice was part of the *yasna*, but in modern times this has been, not simply dropped, but even denied by Parsis, though the practice continued in Iran (where Islam also practices animal sacrifice). The ancient rite, including the pounding and consecration of the haoma plant, is thought to strengthen the material world by making the divine forces present. Inevitably, such a powerful ritual requires the strictest purity in the location for its performance and in the priests offering it. The laity may be present, though it is common for them simply to 'commission' its performance on their behalf, e.g. as part of the ceremonies for the dead. There are, of course, many other temple-based ceremonies, notably the *baresnum*, investitures for priests (*Magi), the *Nirangdin* when the urine (*gomez*) from the sacred bull (*vaisya*) is consecrated and thereafter known as *nirang*, believed to cleanse not just physically (the urine has a high ammonia content and thus can be used as an antiseptic on cuts) but also spiritually.

Although the layperson may in practice seek the spiritual succour provided by the higher liturgies, and offer worship in temples, the holy life can be lived without involvement in them, simply by the worship before the household fire (*Atas), through the prayers and practices of the *Sudre/Kusti*, and through the duties involved in the feasts (*gahambars*), as well, of course, by living up to the high ethical ideals of Zoroastrianism (*Bundahisn).

M. Boyce, *Zoroastrianism* (1992), and *Sources for the Study of Zoroastrianism*; K. Mistree, *Zoroastrianism: An Ethnic Perspective* (1982); J. J. Modi, *Religious Ceremonies and Customs of the Parsis* (1922).

Prayer Book

Judaism These are books containing the texts of daily and festival prayers. In *tannaitic and *amoraic times, prayer books did not exist, and all prayers were known by heart (*Ber.* 5. 3–5). However, by the *geonic era, prayer books began to be produced. The book containing regular prayers is known as the *Siddur*. The earliest known Jewish prayer book is the 9th-cent. *Seder Rav Amram* **Gaon*. Other famous *siddurim* include the 10th-cent. *Siddur* **Sa'adiah Gaon* and the 11th-cent. **Maḥzor Vitry* compiled by Simḥah b. Samuel, a pupil of *Rashi. The *Ashkenazim use four types of prayer book: *Ha-Maḥzor ha-Gadol* (*Kol Bo) containing all the yearly prayers, the *Maḥzor* which contains the prayers for each particular festival, the small *Siddur* for individual use, and the fuller *Ha-Siddur ha-Shalem*. The *Sephardim use the *Tefillat ha-Hadesh* which contain daily and *Sabbath prayers, *Mo'adim* which contain the prayers for the pilgrim festivals *Rosh ha-Shanah* containing *New Year prayers, *Kippur* for the *Day of Atonement, and *Ta'aniyyot* which has prayers for *Av 9. The *Ḥasidim and the *Progressive movements have produced their own prayer books reflecting their own customs.

J. H. Hertz (ed.), *The Authorised Daily Prayer Book* (1941).

Christianity See BOOK OF COMMON PRAYER; BREVIARY; MISSAL.

Prayer Book society: see BOOK OF COMMON PRAYER.

Prayer mat (Muslim): see SAJJĀDA.

Prayer of the heart: see JESUS PRAYER.

Prayer shawl (Jewish): see TALLIT.

Prayer wheel. A cylinder, used in Tibetan Buddhism, inscribed on the outside with a *mantra (often *Oṃ mani padme hum), and containing scrolls on which this and other mantras, as well as sacred texts, are written. Turning the wheel (clockwise, never anti-clockwise, except among adherents of *Bön) releases the power inherent in the texts and prayers. The origins may lie in the power gained from *circumambulation in general, since until recently the use of the wheel in Tibet to bear burdens was regarded as wrong. Prayer wheels may be small (from 3 inches in height) to large (at least 20 feet), and may be set in rows. Some may be turned by water power and, among Tibetans outside Tibet, may now be turned by electric motors.

W. Simpson, *The Buddhist Praying Wheel* (1896).

Prayopaveśana. The Hindu devotion of lying prostrate before a representation of the divine/god, fasting and praying for some particular goal.

Preaching: see Index, *ad loc*.

Prebendary. A member of a cathedral *chapter whose living came from a share ('prebend', Lat., *praebere*, 'furnish') of its endowment. In the Church of England it became an honorary title in the 19th cent. and since then has been replaced in general use by *canon.

Precatory (form of absolution): see ABSOLUTION.

Precentor. The cleric responsible for the direction of the choral services of a *cathedral or chapel.

Precepts, Ten/Five (undertaken by Buddhists): see ŚĪLA.

Precious blood. The *blood of *Jesus as an object of Catholic devotion. Apart from the veneration of particles of Christ's blood as *relics, devotion to the precious blood was most of all a product of the medieval spirituality of the *passion. The period of its greatest cultivation was the 19th cent., when Pope *Pius IX proclaimed its *feast day as part of the calendar of the whole Church (1859). *John XXIII promoted the devotion, along with that of the *Sacred Heart and *Name of Jesus, in an apostolic letter as late as 1960. The feast day, formerly 1 July, was suppressed in 1969. Among *Evangelical Christians, the phrase carries with it praise and thanksgiving for the death of Jesus on the cross, through which salvation becomes possible—hence Vachel Lindsay's 'General William *Booth Enters into Heaven': 'Booth led boldly with his big brass drum— | (Are you washed in the blood of the Lamb?) | The Saints smiled gravely and they said: "He's come." | (Are you washed in the blood of the Lamb?)'

Predestination. The theological view that God foreknows and predetermines the outcome of all things, including an individual's life and eternal destiny; predestination is sometimes used of foreknowledge alone; and in Christianity it may apply to salvation alone or to condemnation as well (single and double predestination). Predestination is usually discussed in relation to the fierce and unending controversies in Christianity, but the term is also applied to similar doctrines in other religions, especially to *qadar in Islam, but also to *kāla, *karma, *daiva, and *astrology in Hinduism, and to the (heavenly) mandate (*ming) in China. The Christian understanding rests on New Testament texts, especially Romans 8. 28 f., 9. 6–24; Ephesians 1. 3–14, 2 Timothy 1. 9 (and on the Old Testament texts taken to imply this). The doctrine became associated particularly with *Augustine, who held that humans are so subverted by *sin that they do not have the capacity even to seek for salvation, let alone find it: he thus doubted the ability of humans to produce works of worth in the sight of God. If any are saved, it can only be because the sovereign will of God so decrees it—although even so, it remains the case that all are still justly condemned. *Pelagius, in contrast, held that humans had the freedom to choose or deny God (semi-Pelagians held that God's *grace was a necessary initiative, but that works had status thereafter), but Augustine maintained that the will is enslaved to sin, that grace is needed to make the choice for God, and that this grace is given to those whom God has predestined to receive it. To say less than this is to limit the omniscience and omnipotence of God. The Augustinian view was upheld at the Council of Carthage (418) when Pelagius was condemned, and at the 2nd Council of Orange (529) which rejected semi-Pelagianism. However, the Augustinian position, while it gave adequate emphasis to the grace of God, raised problems about the responsibility of humans in their decisions, and about the justice and severity of God in predestining so many to damnation—the doctrine of reprobation. The issues were much debated by the Scholastics. *Aquinas and many medieval theologians followed Augustine, but in contrast to the majority opinion, *William of Ockham confined predestination to foreknowledge. Both *Wycliffe and *Hus had emphasized the importance of election, since this meant that predestination has to do with the formation of the community of the elect, rather than with individual acts which might or might not be worthy of salvation. The *Reformers agreed that acts are not the basis of salvation, which must be by grace (and election) alone. But this led to a renewed stress on the Augustinian position, that since the will is wholly enslaved (as *Luther held against *Erasmus), even the assent of faith which admits to the community of the elect must be enabled by the grace of God, wholly and completely unearned and unmerited. But if the gift is entirely gracious, it can of course lie within God's predestined intention. *Melanchthon attempted to rescue a place for the worth and validity of the human will, in the so-called 'Synergistic' ('working together with') controversy; and in *Calvinism, which held strongly to predestination, comparable controversies broke out (and continue) over the scope of what God willed (and foresaw) in relation to the *Fall. In general, the human situation was taken to be one in which all deserve to be damned, not necessarily because of actual sins, but because of the human solidarity with the *original sin of *Adam. If any are saved, it is only because God elects to do so, not as a reward for any good deeds; and in that case it is irrelevant whether God foreknows who will be saved, or what particularly they will do. But the argument then ensued between those who were later called sublapsarians (or infralapsarians) and supralapsarians: did God always know, when he created, that some would be saved and some not, so that he allowed the Fall (*lapsus*) in order to bring this about (as the supralapsarians held); or (since, as the sublapsarians held, this seemed to make God the author of sin), did he create with a foreknowledge of the possibility of the fall, and, when it happened, then elect some to salvation, leaving the rest in a condition of enmity (but that seemed to suggest a lack of control on the part of God, and also that Christ's *atonement had reference only to a few)? The Synod of Dort (1618–19) upheld the sublapsarians, whose position is expressed in the Westminster Confession (1647). Various attempts (see e.g. ARMINIUS; SUAREZ for Congruism) were made to ameliorate the most severe forms of the doctrine, attributing, as it seems to do, a character to God which would be prosecuted if exhibited by a human father to his children. Among *Roman Catholics, the debates were equally fierce, concentrating much more on the role of the human will in the process of salvation (see e.g. JANSENISM). From the 18th cent. onward, the issues became entangled in the scientific world-view derived from Newtonian mechanics, in which it seemed that the movement of everything in the universe is governed by such strict law that nothing has genuine freedom. Applied to theology, this might seem congenial to those who favour predestination, but in fact it seemed to put restriction on God's own freedom, especially to perform miracles. A more general solution has seemed to lie in the understanding that the general outcome of events may indeed be predestined, but not the entire detail of the route to the end, much as in contemporary science, events at a macroscopic level are (at least in theory) predictable, but the events at the level of constituent particles are not; human free will is not then to be defended at the particle level, which is necessary but irrelevant, but rather in terms of the interaction between consciousness and behaviour. In that case, there is space for both grace and freedom. More recently, therefore, *Barth shifted the emphasis by taking *Paul's argument to be pointing to the absolute centrality of Christ as the one who experienced in himself both election and reprobation for the sake of all humanity.

G. C. Berkouwer, *Divine Election* (1960); J. Farrelly, *Predestination, Grace and Freewill* (1964); W. M. Watt, *Freewill and Predestination in Early Islam* (1948).

Preface. In Christian liturgies the words introducing the *eucharistic prayer, in between the *Sursum Corda and *Sanctus. The preface is an ascription of praise to God, e.g. in the **Book of Common Prayer* beginning 'It is very meet, right, and our bounden duty, that we should at all times, and in all places, give thanks unto thee, O Lord, Holy Father, Almighty, Everlasting God.' The *BCP* has a few *proper prefaces (for particular feasts); more have been added in the *Alternative services; in the Roman *missal the preface varies with the season of the year and festival.

Preferential option for options: see SECULARIZATION.

Preferential option for the poor: see LIBERATION THEOLOGY.

Prelate. A church official of high rank. In the Church of England the term is used only of bishops. In the Roman Catholic Church it is also applied to a variety of officers attached to the Roman *curia who may have only an honorary dignity. The evident delight of such dignitaries in hierarchy, authority, and self-adornment led to the adjective 'prelatical', a style which many bishops now try to avoid, not all with equal success.

Prema(-bhakti). The highest form of the love of God in Hinduism, comparable to para-*bhakti, described as the desperate longing as of a drowning person for air. However, this condition is permanent and cannot be taken away: 'In pure love, the *bhakta* discards all desire, all ritual, all *jñāna and all *karma, and is attached to *Kṛṣṇa with every capacity. Such a *bhakta* desires nothing from the Lord, but rests content with loving him' (*Caitanya-caritāmṛta* 19).

Presanctified, liturgy of: see LITURGY OF THE PRESANCTIFIED.

Presbyter. In the Church from the 2nd cent. on, a Christian minister of the second rank in the hierarchy of *bishop–presbyter–*deacon. It corresponds to the modern office of *priest. Before that time, presbyters and bishops were not distinguished. The word (Gk., 'elder') and office were taken over from the practice of *synagogues which were administered by a board of senior men. See also ELDER.

Presbyterianism (Gk., *presbuteros*, 'elder'). Forms of Christian Church order and doctrine which emerged from the *Reformation (although in their own estimate they are in direct continuity from the New Testament), relying on the ministry and governance of elders. Although the term 'Reformed' is often used of all Churches derived from the Reformation, there is in fact a distinction between the *Lutheran and others. Zwinglians and Calvinists had achieved reconciliation at Zurich (1548), which led into Reformed/Presbyterian Churches, and into *Congregationalism. When the Swiss reformation reached Scotland, the quest for a Church order which would be both scriptural and open to constant reformation (the principle of *semper reformanda*, 'always to be reformed') led to Presbyterianism (the government by *presbyters, parity of ministers and the participation of all church members) and beyond Scotland to Congregationalism (the autonomy of congregations). Presbyterians did not intend to found a new Church, and laid much stress on the early *creeds explicated in *Confessions—though even there disputes have arisen about the use of these in testing the orthodoxy of ministers. Presbyterians characteristically hold that the glory of God is the supreme end and purpose of human life. Yet humans stand as sinners before God, so that salvation is as much the work of God as creation. It is achieved through the free gift of his Son, Jesus Christ, who died on the cross in perfect obedience, thereby restoring those whom God elects to save (cf. *predestination). The Holy Spirit brings this salvation to those whom the Father wills, regenerating them so that they are enabled to accept the salvation offered: sinners choose Christ only because Christ has chosen them. Reformed/Presbyterian Christianity has been characterized by constant division, to such an extent that the myriad Churches cannot be listed here. In the opposite direction, various alliances have been made, culminating in the formation in 1970 of the World Alliance of Reformed Churches (Presbyterian and Congregational).

G. D. Henderson, *Presbyterianism* (1954); D. McKim (ed.), *Encyclopedia of the Reformed Faith* (1992); L. Vischer (ed.), *Reformed Witness Today . . .* (1982).

Prester John. Legendary king of the orient. Stories of a Christian king who had defeated the Muslim powers in central Asia (possibly based on a real victory of a Turkish or Mongol chief) were known in Europe in the middle of the 12th cent. In 1165 a letter from 'Prester [i.e. Presbyter] John', who ruled 'from the Tower of Babel to the sunrise' began to circulate. It was an obvious fabrication of Western origin, but was wishfully believed at a time of ebbing Christian fortunes in the Holy Land. In the 13th cent. a more exact knowledge of the Mongols, e.g. from *Franciscan missionaries, made it clear that there could be no such Christian prince in Asia. The idea, however, persisted, and accordingly Prester John was relocated in India, or—as the latest form of the legend—Ethiopia.

Preta (Skt., 'deceased'; Pāli, *peta*). In Hinduism, the condition of the dead between death and joining the ancestors (*pitṛ). Their state is that of a kind of *purgatory; and the correct funeral rites (*śrāddha) are essential if the transition is to be effected, since otherwise the preta may threaten the living. The pretaloka is the sphere where they remain until the rites are completed.

In Buddhism, their domain constitutes one of the three undesirable forms of existence (*gati). Their *karma is good enough to keep them from the hells (*naraka) but not sufficient to project them to *asura. If they do not receive appropriate support from the living, they can become vengeful. Their condition is described in *Petavatthu* (*Khuddakanikāya).

Priest

Judaism The *kohanim* (sing., *kohen*) are a hereditary class whose special responsibility was the performance of the cultic ceremonies of the Jerusalem *Temple. The Hebrew scriptures indicate in some places that only the descendants of *Aaron have the right to priesthood (Leviticus 8) and in others that the entire tribe of *Levi has a priestly role (Deuteronomy 33. 8–10); to these were added the Zadokites (perhaps predecessors of *Sadducees) when *David captured Jerusalem and assimilated the cult of Zadok. In the Temple, the functions of the priests were to offer *sacrifice, bless the people in the name of God, sound the *shofar, and prepare the ritual objects for the ceremonies. In addition, the *high priest consulted the *Urim and Thummim (Numbers 27. 21) and cast lots for the making of public decisions. The priests also were expected to conduct ceremonies to purge disease or ritual impurity in both humans and animals, and to participate in judging and teaching the people. In the time of the second Temple, the priests were divided into twenty-four divisions and each division was on duty for two weeks each year. After the destruction of the Temple in 70 CE, the sacrificial system came to an end. Knowledge of priestly descent can no longer be proved. None the less supposed Kohanim enjoy certain privileges: they should be called up first to read the *Torah; they may invoke the priestly blessing in the *synagogue; and they may have no contact with the dead. According to the *halakhah, they may not marry a divorced woman, a harlot, or a *proselyte; if they disregard these prohibitions, their marriages are valid, but their children are *halalim* ('non-Kohanim'). Because of the doubt entailed in priestly ancestry, the *Progressive movements disregard all the laws applying to Kohanim. See also HIGH PRIEST; LEVI; SACRIFICE; TITHES.

Christianity In Roman Catholic, Orthodox, and Anglican Churches, the priest is the minister who is typically in charge of a *parish. The English word is ultimately derived from Gk. *presbyteros*, as the office is derived from that of the early Christian *presbyter. The idea of 'priesthood', in the sacrificial sense continuous with the Jewish office, only gradually attached to this order of minister. At first, the *sacrifice of the *eucharist was the function of *bishops only, but with the spread of Christianity to country districts priests were allowed to consecrate the eucharist themselves. This opened the way for a doctrine that priestly powers were conferred in *ordination, especially when in the 11th cent. the practice spread of ordaining priests who had no benefice. The priest thus became the normal celebrant of the eucharist and after 1215 the one who heard *confessions. He remained, however, subordinate to the bishop, who alone could ordain and *confirm.

The tendency of medieval theology to see the priesthood of the clergy in terms of the *mass led to its rejection by the *Reformers. Protestant Christians thus take the view that priesthood belongs only to Christ (following the New Testament theme in e.g. Hebrews 5. 10; John 17; Ephesians 2. 18), and, derivatively, to 'all believers' (1 Peter 2. 5, 9). As a term for a minister in the Church of England 'priest' appears in the **Book of Common Prayer*, but has only come back into currency (at the expense of 'clergyman') since the *Oxford Movement.

The term 'priest' is then sometimes applied to functionaries in other religions, as e.g. to *mullahs in Islam, or to *granthi or *mahant among Sikhs, to *hotṛ and *brahmans among Hindus, to *tao-shih among Taoists, to *magi among *Zoroastrians, but the differences in order, duties, appointment, and role are extreme. See Index, Priests.

Primate. The *metropolitan of the 'first see' (Lat., *prima sedes*) of a whole nation or people. In the Roman Catholic Church the title is controlled by the Holy See; it is honorary in the case of the archbishops of Westminster and Baltimore (for England and the USA). Anomalously, the archbishop of *Canterbury is 'Primate of All England' and the archbishop of York 'Primate of England'.

Prime, terce, sext, none. The 'little hours' of the divine *office of the W. Church, appointed to be read at the first, third, sixth, and ninth hours (i.e. 6, 8, 11 a.m., and 2 p.m.) respectively. In the 1971 Roman Catholic *Breviary prime has no place; terce, sext, and none are combined into a form of 'prayer during the day' which may be used for a single office or (by religious orders in choir) for the traditional three.

Primitive Methodist Church. A branch of early 19th-cent. *Methodism. In N. Staffordshire Hugh Bourne and William Clowes engaged in open-air preaching at revivalist 'Camp Meetings' similar to those conducted by the American itinerant evangelist Lorenzo Dow. Concerned lest such activities should become disorderly, uncontrolled, or subversive, the Liverpool *Wesleyan Conference (1807) condemned their 'highly improper' meetings as 'likely to be productive of considerable mischief'. Once expelled by the parent body, Bourne and Clowes officially formed the Primitive Methodist Connexion in 1811. Within a few decades Primitive Methodism spread not only throughout England but also to the USA and Canada, maintaining a vigorous evangelistic outreach especially within working-class communities. In 1932 the denomination joined with the Wesleyan and United Methodists to form the Methodist Church of Great Britain and Ireland.

Primordial Shinto (Yuiitsu Shinto): see HONJI SUIJAKU.

Primus. The presiding bishop in the Scottish Episcopal Church. He is elected by the bishops in Scotland to preside over the synod, but does not have the powers of a *metropolitan.

Principles of Faith (Ikkarim): see ARTICLES OF FAITH.

Priscillianism. Christian *heresy of the 4th–5th cents., so-named from Priscillian, bishop of Avila in Spain. Priscillian was exiled for a time in 381, and executed for sorcery together with several of his adherents in 386. The movement continued in Spain until after its condemnation by the Council of Braga in 563. The Priscillianists were understandably called *Manicheans by their Catholic opponents: they taught a *modalist doctrine of the Trinity and denied the pre-existence of Christ as well as his real humanity; they condemned marriage, the procreation of children, and eating meat. How much of this was taught by Priscillian himself is uncertain.

Prithī Chand (16th cent. CE). Claimant to succession as Sikh *Gurū. Prithī Chand (or Prithīā) was Gurū *Rām Dās' eldest son. He opposed the succession of his younger brother, *Arjan Dev, turned Emperor Jahāṅgir further against him, and unsuccessfully attempted to kill the young *Hargobind. His son was Soḍhī Miharbān, and their followers were the Mīṇās. See also JANAM-SĀKHĪ.

Probabilism. A moral theory conceding to the individual the right to act in accordance with a probable opinion about the rectitude of that act, even though there may be a more probable opinion, apparently supported by law, against the action. The theory which insists that the more probable opinion must be followed is probabiliorism (Lat., *probabilior*, 'more probable'). Probabilism favours freedom, asserting that where a law, or the application of a law, is unclear, the law cannot bind. This basically common-sense position is now generally accepted by moral theologians, but its espousal by the *Jesuits in the 17th and 18th cents. led to attacks upon them for laxity, especially by *Jansenists.

The term also refers to the position, held by Sceptics, that certainty, in matters of judgement, cannot be attained.

Procession of the Holy Spirit. A disputed issue between E. and W. Churches. See FILIOQUE.

Process theology. A Christian theological system emphasizing the fluid rather than static nature of the universe, and finding God within the process of becoming, rather than as the transcendent source of being. Process theology owes much to the metaphysical thought of A. N. Whitehead (1861–1947) which culminated in *Process and Reality* (1929). Whitehead regarded *metaphysics as presupposed in natural science; his task he saw as one of supplying an adequate metaphysic in relation to modern science. The universe is constituted by events (which Whitehead called 'actual occasions'), not by static objects. The occasions of experience are not permanently existing 'things', but are self-creating strivings toward the realization of some value. Hence each is dipolar, made up of a physical pole (the past) and a mental pole (the achievable future). Yet the coherence of this process makes it inconceivable that the process is random; which suggests that there is an initial aim; and this aim is the occasion of God, who supplies the aim and is also the totality of all occasions: when an occasion arises, it immediately passes away, but it is not lost: it becomes embedded in the experience (to which it has necessarily contributed) of God forever—a form of objective immortality. Everything is thus 'in God', but God is more than the sum of the parts (panentheism; see PANTHEISM)—just as I am my body, and yet I am more than the sum of the parts of my body. God is not apart from the universe, but is the comprehension of the whole process: 'Each temporal occasion embodies God, and is embodied in God.' God is in the process of becoming, and thus shares the same characteristic of dipolarity: at the non-temporal, mental pole, God envisages the immense variety of eternal objects, contributes the novel aims and primordial valuation of all possibilities and supplies 'the lure' to the actual entities in the process of becoming. But in this primordial nature of possibility, God lacks actualization. Therefore at the other temporal or physical pole, God in his consequent nature prehends the temporal world (i.e. is the location of all passing entities in such a manner that they are not lost and are interrelated), and in this growing and changing nature, experiences the process, knowing and loving it. This entire cosmic process is God, and God works like an artist attempting to win order and beauty out of opportunity. God is thus 'the great companion—the fellow-sufferer who understands'. This metaphysic was developed in a theological direction by Charles Hartshorne (e.g. *Man's Vision of God and the Logic of Theism*, 1941), and in a *Christological (and applied) direction by John Cobb (e.g. *Christ in a Pluralistic Age*, 1975; *Process Theology as Political Theology*, 1982; *The Liberation of Life*, 1981). Christ is interpreted as the one who embodied the most perfectly obedient response to the 'lure' of God. Not surprisingly, therefore, his teaching can be translated directly into the pattern of modern science, displaying God as 'the One who calls'. Because Christ is the source of value-directing novelty in the world, he can be regarded as 'creative transformation'. Salvation is the redemptive activity of God in accepting the occasions of evil, transforming them (like the artist who works on a mistake) into good, and continuing to lure people into a self-authenticating acceptance of value. The whole process moves along undetermined lines to a *telos* (goal or end), somewhat like *Teilhard de Chardin's Omega point, but not involving a necessary end to the cosmos. The possible connections with Buddhist thought have not been overlooked: see e.g. J. B. Cobb, *Beyond Dialogue: Towards a Mutual Transformation of Christianity and Buddhism* (1982).

J. B. Cobb and D. R. Griffin, *Process Theology . . .* (1976); L. S. Ford, *The Lure of God* (1978); S. Sia, *God in Process Thought* (1985).

Proclus (*c*.410–85). *Neoplatonic philosopher. Born in Lycia, as a young man he went to Athens, where he spent the rest of his life, latterly as head of the School of Athens. His many works expound a systematization of the form of Neoplatonism derived from *Plotinus via Iamblichus and Syrianus. In line with this tradition, he set considerable store by *theurgy ('divine action'), a kind of white magic that exploited the sympathy between elements and processes underlying the unity of the cosmos, to further the ascent of the soul to the One.

The Elements of Theology, tr. E. R. Dodds (1963); L. J. Rosan, *The Philosophy of Proclus* (1949); R. T. Wallis, *Neoplatonism* (1972).

Progressive Judaism. A collective term to refer to non-*Orthodox movements within Judaism. Although usually applied to *Reform or Liberal Judaism, it may sometimes be used to include the very different *Conservative and *Reconstructionist movements. See Index, Progressive Judaism.

Projection. The theory that God and gods are merely objectifications of human needs, ideals, or desires. With few exceptions, the theory in modern Western thought forms part of reductionistic accounts of *theistic belief. These accounts are in general built on the thought of L. *Feuerbach and K. *Marx, on the one hand, or of S. *Freud and the psychoanalytic school, on the other. Some other theories of projection build on aspects of *Kant's thought as interpreted and extended by Hans Vaihinger (1852–1933) in *The Philosophy of 'As If'*. However great their differences in detail, most theories of projection are reflexive in character: some subjective desire or need is projected upon some other object (real or imaginary), which in turn is believed to act upon the original subject as if it were an external agent.

In Eastern religions, projection takes on a different and more fundamental significance. In Hinduism, it implies the basic ignorance (*avidyā) which superimposes reality on to *Brahman, as though appearances have independent existence.

In Buddhism, the projection of reality on to the unreal world of appearance arises equally from ignorance; and in *Mahāyāna, especially Ch'an/ *Zen, it involves a failure to realize that all appearances are equally empty of self (*śūnyatā).

Promise and threat (Islamic philosophical issue): see MUʿTAZILITES.

Promised Land. The land promised to the Jewish *patriarch, Abraham. The phrase does not appear in scripture, though 'land of promise' refers in Hebrews 11. 9 to the faith of Abraham. The concept of the promised land underlies the ambition among some Israelis to establish, so far as possible, the intended biblical boundaries. In Christianity, it is transferred to heaven, and thence to any desirable goal, secular as well as religious—e.g. sexual union in Lawrence Durrell's 'Ballad of the Good Lord Nelson'. See also CANAAN; EREZ ISRAEL; ISRAEL.

Promotor fidei: see DEVIL'S ADVOCATE.

Proofs of the existence of God: see QUINQUE VIAE.

Propaganda. The 'Sacred *Congregation for the Evangelization of Peoples or for the Propagation of the Faith'. It is concerned with Roman Catholic missions in non-Christian territories and the administration of the Church where there is no established hierarchy.

Proper. The part of the Christian *eucharist and *offices which changes with the season of the *calendar or festival. For example, in Anglican service-books the proper consists of the *collect and biblical lections for all the services, and the *prefaces in the communion service.

Prophet, Prophecy

Judaism In the Jewish Bible, a prophet (*nabi*; pl., *nebi'im*) is one who speaks on behalf of God. In origin, they were a part of a Near Eastern phenomenon (e.g. at *Mari), cultic functionaries who make known the unknown. Among these functionaries were also the *ḥozeh* ('seer') and *ro'eh* ('seer'), and *'ish ha-Elohim* ('the man of God'). The relationship between these is unclear, 1 Samuel 9. 9 simply affirming that he who is now called a prophet was in former times called a seer. It seems probable that the so-called classical prophets (whose oracles have been gathered in the prophetic books) come from a background of cultic prophecy, and in some instances remained connected to the cult (*Amos, Michaiah ben Imlah, and *Isaiah all had visions of God in connection with the altar). All these prophets had visible signs of God-possession (going into trances and speaking ecstatically on occasion), but the classical prophets became distinct because their authenticity was to be judged by the content of their message (was it loyal to *Yahweh?), whether or not the external signs were present. This shift is clear in the attempts to distinguish between the true and false prophets in Deuteronomy 13 and 18. In the early period, *Samuel is described as a *ro'eh* and had the ability to find *Saul's lost asses (1 Samuel 9). As an *'ish ha-Elohim*, he anointed Saul as king of *Israel. The term *ḥozeh* tended to be used only of court seers (1 Chronicles 25. 5). Mention is also made of groups of prophets 'coming down from the high place with harp, tambourine and lyre before them' (1 Samuel 10); these groups were connected with ecstatic seizures, and when Saul met them 'the spirit of the Lord came mightily upon him and he spoke in ecstasy among them' (1 Samuel 10). Prominent among the pre-classical prophets were Samuel, *Nathan, *Elijah, and *Elisha. Elisha in particular was connected with a prophetic group (e.g. 2 Kings 4. 38), one of whom he sent to anoint King Jehu (2 Kings 9). These prophets seem to have been consulted for advice (e.g. 2 Kings 3. 4 ff.), they were paid for their services (e.g. 2 Kings 8. 9), and were intimately involved in the political life of the time (e.g. 1 Kings 22): Nathan served in King *David's court, did not hesitate to reprove the king (2 Samuel 12), and was involved with the choice of *Solomon as his successor (1 Kings 1). The pre-classical prophets were believed to be able to foretell future events (e.g. 1 Kings 17. 1); they performed symbolic actions to bring their words into effect (e.g. 2 Kings 13. 14 ff.) and could perform *miracles (e.g. 1 Kings 17. 17–24).

The classical or literary prophets are those whose oracles were preserved in writing, i.e. Isaiah, *Jeremiah, *Ezekiel, and the twelve *Minor Prophets. Like the pre-classical prophets, the classical prophets spoke in the name of God ('Thus says the Lord . . .'), but they tended to put greater emphasis on the importance of ethical monotheism rather than on the performance of the cult and foretelling the future. Like the pre-classical prophets, some at least were subject to ecstatic seizures (e.g. Hosea 9. 7), they performed symbolic acts (e.g. Isaiah 20. 2 ff.), and they were intimately involved in the current affairs of the nation. Several of the classical prophets were called to their mission (e.g. Isaiah 6) and one at least, Jeremiah, expressed extreme reluctance (Jeremiah 1. 6). The life of the prophet was perceived by him to be frightening and lonely ('Why did I come forth from the womb to experience trouble and grief and waste my days in chagrin?': Jeremiah 20. 18), and yet the call was irresistible ('If I say I will not mention him or speak any more in his name, there is in my heart as it were a burning fire shut up in my bones and I am not able to hold it in': Jeremiah 20. 9).

According to Deuteronomy 18. 22, the criterion of a true prophet was whether his words came true, but through his role of intercessor, he could try to avert the doom he pronounced. Thus Jeremiah unsuccessfully attempted to turn God's anger (Jeremiah 18. 20) as did Ezekiel (Ezekiel 9. 8–10). The prophets constantly pleaded with Israel to repent (e.g. Amos 5. 4). The later classical prophets realized that humanity could not by its own efforts return to God and they looked forward to a time when God would initiate a 'new *covenant' when 'I will write my law upon their hearts . . .' and 'I will remember their *sin no more' (Jeremiah 31. 33–4). In that day, the faithful *remnant of Israel would live in peace and God's glory would again be manifest through all the earth (Isaiah 40. 5). It was generally agreed that prophecy had ceased in the time of the second *Temple: after the *Exile, authority was transferred to the Temple and its priests, interpreting *Torah (to ensure holy behaviour and thus no repetition of the Exile); but who could control or countermand someone claiming direct authority from God ('thus says the Lord')? The *rabbis taught that *Moses was the greatest of the prophets (*B.Yev.* 49b) and that prophecy added nothing new to the Jewish religion ('A prophet may make no innovations': *B.Shab.* 104a). However, some modern Jewish thinkers have seized on Hebrew prophecy as an inspiring model of *progressive revelation and identify the prophets as the thinkers who transformed Judaism from a tribal superstition to a universal system of ethical monotheism (see KOHLER, KAUFMANN).

J. Blenkinsopp, *A History of Prophecy in Israel* (1983); M. Buber, *The Prophetic Faith* (1949); R. Coggins *et al.*, *Israel's Prophetic Tradition* (1982); C. F. Whitley, *The Prophetic Achievement* (1963).

Christianity Early Christians experienced the consequences of the *Holy Spirit, and believed that this 'return' of the Holy Spirit in visible gifts was a mark of the redemptive will of God. Thus in addition to accepting the earlier Jewish prophets (who were seen to have been foretelling the coming of Christ and events surrounding and arising from that advent), prophets returned as functionaries in the early Church. However, the same problem recurred: what control could Church leaders have over the inspired (or claimed-to-be inspired) utterances of an individual? The problem became acute in relation to *Montanism; and prophets ceased to have a major role, until the revival of their importance in African Christianity: see AFRICAN INSTITUTED CHURCHES.

Islam See NABĪ; RASŪL.

See also Index, Prophets.

Prosbul (from Gk.). Jewish legal formula for reclaiming debts after the *Sabbatical Year. A prosbul was signed by witnesses before a *bet din and would entitle the creditor to collect his debts despite the intervention of the Sabbatical Year (*Shev.* 10. 2). The prosbul was introduced by *Hillel and was seen to benefit the rich (in that it secured loans) and the poor (since it enabled them to obtain loans, *B.Git.* 37a). By the Middle Ages, the practice was largely abandoned because it was felt that the provisions of the Sabbatical Year were no longer operative. *Conservative and *Reform *rabbis take the prosbul as a key example of the ability of Judaism to nullify an explicit command of *Torah; for the *Orthodox, the principle is inherent in Torah.

Proselytes. Converts to a religion, and especially (because formally defined and controlled) to Judaism. Proselytism was widespread in the second *Temple period. According to *Josephus, the inhabitants of both Greek and foreign cities displayed great zeal for Judaism. The *tannaim laid down the procedure for the acceptance of proselytes. Non-Jews who sought admittance should be warned of the disadvantages *Jews face and if the *gentile responded, 'I know of this and I am not worthy', he should be accepted immediately (*B.Yev.* 47a) and should be informed of the Commandments. A proselyte had to offer a *sacrifice although this provision was abolished by R. *Johanan b. Zakkai after the destruction of the Temple (*B.Ket.* 9a), and only *circumcision (for males) and immersion in a *mikveh was required. These acts must take place before a *bet din of three members. Once converted, the proselyte is given a new name and is described as 'Ben' or 'Bat' Avraham (son or daughter of *Abraham). He is cut off from his previous family and must observe all the precepts which bind Jews. A female proselyte may not marry a *priest (*B.Yev.* 60b), but may marry a *mamzer (*B.Kid.* 4. 7); and a male proselyte may not be appointed to any Jewish public office (*B.Yev.* 45b). Attitudes towards proselytes have changed throughout history. In *Talmudic times, the attitude was generally positive ('Proselytes are beloved; in every place they are considered part of *Israel', *Mekhitta Va-Yehi* 2), although there are some negative sayings ('Proselytes are as hard for Israel as a sore' (*B.Yev.* 47b). Such scholars as R. *Meir, R. *Akiva and Shemaiah were said to be descended from proselytes. However, once the canons of the Christian Church had forbidden 'Judaizing', proselytism became increasingly negative, although the **Shulḥan Arukh* listed the conversion laws. Because Christians could be regarded as followers of the *Noachide laws, there was no incentive to proselytize, and the penalties from the Christian majority for doing so were frequently severe. However, in modern times, with the increase of *intermarriage, conversion to Judaism has become more common, particularly in the *Progressive movement.

D. Eichorn (ed.), *Conversion to Judaism: A History and Analysis* (1965).

Prostitution, sacred. The sense of union in the sexual act became in many religions a powerful expression of religious union. This is most familiar in Indian practice (see DEVDĀSĪ), but it was clearly a common practice elsewhere. The *hierodouloi* were not confined to the Greek and Roman world: the practice of what was then regarded as religious prostitution is fiercely contested in Jewish scripture (e.g. Deuteronomy 23. 18 f.), which indicates how common the practice was. It was equated by the *prophets with *idolatry (e.g. Ezekiel 23. 27).

Protestant ethic: see WEBER, MAX.

Protestantism. Generic term for manifestations or expressions of Christianity arising from the *Reformation. Although the Lat., *protestari*, means 'to protest' (sc., against the errors of Roman Catholicism), it also means 'to avow' or 'to affirm'. Thus Protestants were, and are, not simply negative, but seek to return to a faith and order based on scripture, and in continuity from the early apostolic Church. They stress the sovereign majesty of God, who as Father entrusts Lordship over creation to his Son. They hold strongly to *justification by faith and the *priesthood of all believers. They reject the claims of papal supremacy, at least as so far practised and expressed, and also the seven *sacraments of Catholicism, adhering to the two which have dominical (i.e. from the Lord) warrant, *baptism and the *Lord's Supper. The latter is, generally, a memorial meal, not a repeated sacrifice (against the *mass), but it may include a commemoration of the sacrificial death of Christ. Protestantism has proved highly fissiparous, and embraces extremes of conservatism and radicalism. There are, in extremely approximate terms, about 500 million Protestants in the world.

J. Dillenberger and C. Welch, *Protestant Christianity* . . . (1954); E. G. Léonard, *Histoire générale du protestantisme* (1961–4; tr. 1965–8); F. Senn (ed.), *Protestant Spiritual Traditions* (1986); J. S. Whale, *The Protestant Tradition* (1955).

Prothesis or **proskomide.** The ceremonial preparation of the bread and wine which takes place at a table apart within the sanctuary before the beginning of the *Orthodox *eucharist. The priest cuts the bread into pieces with the 'lance' (a small knife) and arranges it on the *diskos* (plate); then the *deacon pours wine and warm water into the chalice; and the whole is afterwards veiled. Historically, the prothesis is the *offertory moved back to the beginning of the service.

***Protocols of the Elders of Zion*.** An *anti-Semitic forgery of the 19th cent., written to demonstrate a Jewish conspiracy to achieve financial and political power world-wide. Despite their evident falsity, they were used by the Nazis, and have resurfaced as anti-Jewish propaganda during the conflict over Palestine/Israel.

N. Cohn, *Warrant for Genocide* (1967).

Proverbs, Book of. One of the three *wisdom books in the Hebrew scriptures. The Book of Proverbs is a collection of riddles, old sayings of the *sages, warnings, and proverbs. It reads as a manual of instruction, guided by the principle, 'The fear of the Lord is the beginning of Wisdom' (1. 7). The book consists of four parts: the first includes five wisdom poems surrounded by instructional discourses (1. 8–9); the second part (10–22. 16) contains the first collection of Solomonic proverbs; the third part (22. 17–24. 22) includes precepts of the sages; the fourth part (25–9) is the second collection of Solomonic proverbs which is followed by four short appendices. Traditionally ascribed to '*Solomon, son of *David, King of *Israel', it is generally dated in the post-*exilic period, but obviously contains much earlier material. See also WISDOM.

Providence (Lat., *providere*, 'to foresee'). The belief that all things are ordered and regulated by God towards his purpose. A distinction is usually made between general providence (which occurs through the laws of nature) and special providence (which is related to individuals).

Providence Industrial Mission. The first independent church related to *Ethiopianism in Malawi (formerly Nyasaland), founded in 1900 by John Chilembwe (*c.*1870–1915). Chilembwe was educated in the USA, and supported then and later by the National *Baptist Convention. Growing disillusionment with colonial government, local land conditions, and forced recruitment for the First World War led Chilembwe to organize an abortive rising in 1915. Chilembwe was killed and the rising easily suppressed, but he remains a national hero in Malawi today. His 'New Jerusalem' church, built in 1913 at Chiradzulu, was demolished by the authorities. His followers were allowed to reorganize in 1926, under the leadership of Dr Daniel S. Malekebu (also educated in the USA). The Church split in the 1970s. One branch, the Independent Baptist Convention, claims a following of 25,000–30,000, and is a member of the Christian Council of Malawi.

Proximate salvation (attainment of immediate, not ultimate, goals): see GREAT TRADITION, LITTLE TRADITION.

Pṛthivi ('the extended one'). The Hindu manifestation of the earth, the womb of *Agni (*Śatapatha Brāhmana* 7. 4. 1. 8), the Mother in whose womb the embryonic earth is formed. She could not sustain the increasing population, and begged *Brahmā for relief. He created Death as a beautiful woman who wept at her task, her tears becoming fatal diseases. She is sometimes joined with the sky as Dyāvā-Pṛthivi, and remains associated with agriculture. In later Hinduism, she is Bhūdevī, the consort of *Viṣṇu.

Psalms, Book of (Gk., *psalmoi*, 'songs accompanied by string music'). The first of the *Writings in the Hebrew Bible and nineteenth book in the Christian Old Testament. The Hebrew title is *Tehillim* ('songs of praise'), from the same root as the common refrain *Alleluia. The 150 Psalms are numbered differently in Protestant (following the Hebrew) and Roman Catholic (following the *Septuagint/Greek and *Vulgate) Bibles. Here the Hebrew numbering is given first, with the Greek in parentheses: 1–8 (1–8), 9–10 (9), 11–113 (10–112), 114–15 (113), 116. 1–9 (114), 116. 10–19 (115), 117–46 (116–45), 147. 1–11 (146), 147. 12–20 (147), 148–50 (148–50).

The Psalms are traditionally divided into five books: 1–41, 42–72, 73–89, 90–106, 107–50, each except the last ending with a doxology. There are indications of earlier collections, e.g. in 72. 20, 'The prayers of David, the son of Jesse, are ended', and in the common titles 'Of David', 'Of Asaph', etc. Some titles, like that to Psalm 88, with now unintelligible directions for rendition, make it clear that the book of Psalms is a liturgical book: hymns, laments, and songs of thanksgiving are predominant. It has often been described as the 'hymnbook of the Second *Temple'. Special classes of psalm are the *Hallel (Psalms 113–18), 'royal psalms' (e.g. 2, 18, 20, 21, 45, 72, 110—important for Christian theology), psalms reflecting the *wisdom literature (e.g. 1, 37, 128), and alphabetical psalms (e.g. 119 with sections of eight verses each beginning with successive letters). The attribution of the entire book to *David is found first in rabbinic literature ('Moses gave the five books of *Torah to Israel, and David gave the five books of Psalms', *Midr.Ps.* 101) and then in many of the Latin *Fathers. Most modern scholars believe that the Psalms are of widely differing date, and are only associated with David because he was a musician (e.g. 1 Samuel 16. 16–23) who established Jerusalem as the cultic centre where the Temple would be built.

Psalms, liturgical use of. Use of *Psalms in the Jewish and Christian *liturgical services. In the *Talmudic period, the set prayers contained no psalms and the *Hallel was only recited on the pilgrim festivals and *Ḥanukkah. However, the modern Jewish liturgy contains many of the psalms because 'the people have adopted the custom' (*Tam.* 18. 1). In addition, the practice of reciting the entire Book of Psalms is widespread as an act of piety. The daily Psalms, beginning on Sunday, are 24, 48, 82, 94, 81, 93, 92, and are also recited as an act of piety.

In Christianity, texts from the Psalms were already being used as 'proof-texts' in the New Testament, some attributed to *Jesus. Their regular use in liturgy is at least as early as the 4th cent. (though in fact probably as early as Christianity itself), when they were commended by St John *Chrysostom in the E. and by St *Ambrose in the W.—Ambrose wrote that they embrace the whole of human life. The introduction of Gregorian chant (see GREGORY I) universalized the style of their use; and St *Benedict made it a requirement in his *Rule* that the whole *psalter should be said or sung each week—an observance still followed by many religious orders. Anglican chant was a developed simplification of Gregorian chant which, when an agreed system of 'pointing' (dividing the words and phrases) was introduced in the 19th cent., extended the chanting of psalms to virtually every parish church and took the phrases and spirituality of the psalms deep into English/American culture. The increasing disappearance of morning and evening prayer as liturgical services has led to a marked decline in the use of the psalter, though metrical psalms (psalms translated into metrical hymns) remain popular; and some modern forms of chant (e.g., Gelineau and *Taizé) have kept parts of psalms in use.

Psalter. The book of *Psalms in a form for use in devotion or worship. The psalter in the **Book of Common Prayer* derives from the 'Gallican Psalter' of *Jerome's *Vulgate, so (unlike the *Authorized Version) contains readings of the *Septuagint Old Testament at variance with the Hebrew. Metrical versions of the psalter were produced at the Reformation as a more biblical alternative in *Reformed churches to *Lutheran hymns. They were popular in England until the 19th cent. (the best known being that of N. Tate and N. Brady (1696)). Metrical psalms remain a characteristic feature of worship in the *Church of Scotland and some other *Presbyterian churches.

Pseudepigrapha. Jewish and Christian books whose purported origin or authorship is not as claimed by themselves. Thus books are attributed to Moses, Baruch, Solomon, Peter, Thomas, etc. In the case of Jewish books they date mainly from the second *Temple period onward and are not reckoned among the *canon of scripture. The exact number of pseudepigraphical books is not known; famous examples include the *Book of *Enoch*, **Jubilees*, *The Ascension of *Isaiah*, *The Assumption of *Moses*, *The Book of *Adam and Eve*, and *The *Testament of the Twelve Patriarchs*. See also APOCRYPHA.

J. H. Charlesworth (ed.), *The Old Testament Pseudepigrapha* (1983).

Pseudo-Dionysius (author of corpus of spiritual and theological writings): see DIONYSIUS.

Psychodynamic theory. A dynamic model of the self which concentrates in particular on emotions and drives. This is perhaps the most widely used theory in the *psychological study of religion, and has also been frequently employed by anthropologists, sociologists, and historians. Developed most forcefully by *Freud, the theory has since been modified. In Freud's view, instincts (belonging to the id) demand satisfaction (catharsis). When satisfaction is prevented by internalized social standards (the superego), instinctual needs find surrogate means of satisfaction (the related processes of displacement and *scapegoating). One important way in which this 'hydraulic', self-regulating model has been modified has involved speaking of emotions, rather than instincts, and accepting that emotions are also under cultural control—and so are not entirely governed from within.

Good examples of psychodynamic theory applied to religious phenomena are provided by the study of *witchcraft (the witch providing an outlet for repressed emotions), the study of rituals of rebellion (providing cathartic release), and those studies which hold that religious institutions serve to compensate for social or other deprivations. Victor *Turner's *The Forest of Symbols* (1967) contains good illustrations of modified psychodynamic theorizing.

J. Jones, *Contemporary Psychoanalysis and Religion* . . . (1991); J. McDargh, *Psychoanalytic Object-Relations Theory and the Study of Religion* . . . (1983); W. Meissner, *Psychoanalysis and Religious Experience* (1984).

Psychology of religion. The field of study which employs psychological techniques and theories to explore and explain religious phenomena. In the W., various schools of psychology have given birth to different treatments of religion. Theories have been taken from associational psychology (J. G. *Frazer's *The Golden Bough*, 1890–1937), from psychoanalysis (S. *Freud, C. G. *Jung), from social psychology (as surveyed by M. Argyle and B. Beit-Hallahmi in *The Social Psychology of Religion*, 1975), and from cognitive psychology (see L. Festinger, *When Prophecy Fails*, 1956, and D. Sperber's *Rethinking Symbolism*, 1975). The most influential of these approaches has been psychoanalytic theory, specifically in the *psychodynamic form.

In most cultures, however, psychologies are less 'of' religious life than they are integral to it. Since religions must address participants as well as whatever is taken to be ultimate, they contain their own psychologies. The most sophisticated, and, it appears, efficacious indigenous psychologies appear in the great Eastern traditions (see e.g. Rama *et al.*, *Yoga and Psychotherapy*, 1976), but there are countless other examples (e.g. V. *Turner on rites of passage and curing rituals).

The most frequently met aim of indigenous psychologies 'of' religion is transformative. The aim of Western, supposedly more scientific psychologies of religion is explanatory. Psychological techniques are employed to measure what has to be explained (e.g. incidence of reported religious experiences). Theories are then employed to address a wide range of questions, including such matters as how religious activities result in psychological changes, what motivates people to engage in religious activities, and, most grandly of all, how psychological processes result in religious phenomena, including frequently encountered symbols and experiences.

Although the psychology of religion is often regarded as an impoverished discipline, few theories—whether sociological or anthropological—are devoid of psychological assumptions and theories. The approach is of vital, indeed necessary, importance, and it is unfortunate that it has not been institutionalized to any significant extent.

M. Argyle and R. Beit-Hallahmi, *The Social Psychology of Religion* (1975); C. D. Batson and W. L. Ventis, *The Religious Experience* (1982); L. Brown (ed.), *Psychology and Religion* (1973); L. B. Brown (ed.), *Advances in the Psychology of Religion* (1988); D. Capps *et al.*, *Psychology of Religion: A Guide to Information Sources* (1976); B. Spilka *et al.*, *The Psychology of Religious Knowing* (1988).

P'u (Chin., 'rough block'). Taoist understanding of the original innocence and simplicity of human nature, like that of raw silk or a new-born child. It acts spontaneously (*wu-wei) in accord with *Tao, and it is the state to which the wise aspire to return: 'Discern the unadorned (*su*), embrace p'u, reduce the self, decrease desires, forego learning and vexation will cease' (*Tao-te Ching* 19).

Pudgala (person): see PUDGALAVĀDINS.

Pudgalavādins (Skt., *pudgala*; Pāli, *puggala*). 'Personalists', a school of Buddhist philosophy which began 3rd cent. CE, and which posited the existence of a self or soul over and above the five aggregates (*skandhas). This school, also known as the Vātsiputrīya, regarded the pudgala or 'person' as an entity which continued through each life in the cycle of rebirths, carried along in some manner by the skandhas, but which disappeared when liberation was gained. It was thus a kind of impermanent or temporary soul, unlike the Hindu *ātman which was thought of as eternal. The relationship between the pudgala and the skandhas was obscure, but was said to be like that between fire (the pudgala) and its fuel (the skandhas), the pudgala being neither the same as the skandhas nor different from them.

The doctrine of the pudgala was accepted by no other school and was actively criticized, with the result that it died out in the medieval period. An extract from Buddhist sources setting out the controversy in the form of a debate between opponents and supporters of the doctrine is in E. Conze, *Buddhist Scriptures*. See also ANĀTMAN.

Puebla: see LIBERATION THEOLOGY.

Puggala: see PUDGALAVĀDINS.

Pugio Fidei (text by Adret): see ADRET, SOLOMON BEN ABRAHAM.

P'u-hsien (Bodhisattva): see SAMANTABHADRA.

P'u-Hua (Jap., Fuke; d. 860). Ch'an/Zen master, dharma-successor (*hassu) of P'an-shan Pao-chi. Well-known for his unconventional style (he represented the nature of the dying P'an-shan by turning a somersault), he was important in the founding of the Fuke school which made non-*sūtra activities important, e.g. flute-playing: see KAKUSHIN; KOMUSŌ. P'u-hua remains a model of the *holy fool style of Zen.

Pūjā (Skt., Pāli, 'respect, homage, worship', perhaps early Dravidian 'flower' + 'offer'). Immensely varied acts, in Eastern religions, of offering, devotion, propitiation, etc., but often including the offering of flowers. In early (Vedic) Hinduism, pūjā began to replace yajña (*sacrifice) as 'invocation, reception and entertainment of God as a royal guest' (Gonda). According to S. K. Chatterji, pūjā developed in the non-Aryan culture: *homa was exclusively Aryan, requiring animal *sacrifice (*paśu-karma*), but pūjā was open to all and required flowers (*puspa-karma*). Certainly in later Buddhism the offering of flowers (*puppha-pūjā*) has become the main pūjā ritual.

For Hindus, pūjā relates humans to the domain and action of the deities in all their many ways of sustaining or threatening the cosmos and life within it, and thus it takes a vast number of different ritual forms, of which the simplest is *darśan, looking on the image of the deity (or in the case of Jains, on the image of a *tīrthaṅkara; among the Jains, an ascetic can only look at an image, never act toward it; such interior devotion is known as *caityavandana*, and is one of the six obligations). Pūjā is mentioned in the early *Gṛhya Sūtras*, with focus on home rituals (which remain central). In the *Sūtras, the reception of, and hospitality for, *brahmans in the home to preside over rites for ancestors is called pūjā, and it may be that *devapūjā* (worship of deities) developed from this: *devapūjā* is described in the *Purāṇas only in sections added later; but it then becomes fundamental in *bhakti. Important in such pūjā is the distribution and eating of the food that has been offered to the god and which the god has 'consumed', an act known as *prasad (attaining the 'goodwill' of the deity).

Among Jains, that understanding of prasad is impossible (the tīrthaṅkaras cannot consume anything). Instead, the offering of food is understood as a gesture of renunciation. Equally, pūjā addressed to the tīrthaṅkaras with expectation of response is inappropriate, because they have given all that they can, 'instruction in faith, knowledge and behaviour' (Vattakera); but expressions of gratitude and love are natural, and increase merit. In general, the *Digambaras do not touch images themselves, but employ a priest (*upadhye*) to do so, whereas the Śvetāmbaras perform the rituals and employ temple servants (*pujārī*) to clear up after them. The 'pūjā of the eight elements' is a rite of transition for Jains from the profane to the sacred world, though the exact meaning of this central ritual varies.

In Buddhism, pūjā may be offered to the deities (as Buddhism understands them), but it is also translated in a non-theistic direction (as in the case of *dāna). It then becomes a basic form of religious observance, through recitation of the threefold 'Refuge Formula' (*triśarana), etc., but even more through offerings of thanksgiving, food, and flowers to the *Buddha: each such offering has its own ritual formula, the reciting of which makes it acceptable.

P. V. Kane, *History of Dharmaśāstra*, ii (1941).

Pujārī: see PŪJĀ.

Pu-k'ung Chin-kang (teacher of Buddhism, 8th cent.): see AMOGHAVAJRA.

Pul. Korean for *buddha.

Pulgyo (Korean). Buddhism. See BUDDHISM IN KOREA.

Pumbedita. Centre of Jewish learning, 2nd–4th cents. CE. The *academy at Pumbedita and the academy at *Sura were together the centres of Jewish scholarship in Babylon. *Rabbah b. Naḥmāni, *Abbaye, and *Rava were among the heads of the Pumbedita academy.

Puṃsavana. A Hindu ritual to ensure the birth of a male child—vital for the proper performance of funeral (*śraddha) rites. It is usually performed in the third month of pregnancy: see *Atharva Veda* 6. 11. 1–3.

Punabbhava (Pāli 'again-becoming'), the Buddhist understanding of rebirth. Sicne there is no self or soul being reborn, 'rebirth' suggests too strong an understanding of what continues. Re-becoming simply affirms that there are continuities of consequence, in which a consciousness of what is happening (as in the case of humans) is a part of the process.

Punarājāti (Skt., 'rebirth'). Hindu belief that the process toward release (*mokṣa) requires many rebirths—perhaps as many as 84 million. For this central belief, other terms are also used, especially *punarijīvātu*: see REBIRTH.

Punarāvritti (Sanskrit term): see REBIRTH.

Punarjanman (Sanskrit term): see REBIRTH.

Punarmṛtyu. Repeated death, the predicament for Hindus which is brought about by *karma through the process of *saṃsāra. The *trimārga offer the routes to escape: 'He who understands overcomes repeated death: death cannot get hold of him, death becomes his body, and he becomes one with the *devas' (*Bṛhadāraṇyaka Upaniṣad* 1. 2. 7).

Punarutpatti (Sanskrit term): see REBIRTH.

Puṇḍarika ('white lotus'). Water plant unfolding above the surface, symbolizing attainment of purity, and also the appearance of a manifest world. It is also the symbol (especially in Tantra) of the *yoni. See also LOTUS; MYŌKŌNIN.

Pundit (Hindu learned man): see PAṆḌITA.

Puṇḍra (marks in Hinduism made on the body): see TILAKA.

Punjāb: see PAÑJĀB.

Puñña (merit): see PUṆYA.

Puṇya (Skt.; Pāli, *puñña*). The accumulation of beneficial consequence (loosely, *merit) in Eastern religions, through the process of *karma. In Buddhism, it is acquired through cultivating the right dispositions, acting on them through *dāna and other forms of almsgiving, reciting *sūtras, etc. It is a major goal of a Buddhist layperson. Mahāyāna criticizes any self-centred understanding of puṇya, encouraging its acquisition on behalf of others, especially the deceased. The transfer of puṇya to the dead is an important function of *saṅgha and other monastic rituals. See also KUŚALA.

Punyaksetra (Jain acts of merit): see MERIT.

Purāṇa (Skt., 'ancient'). Any of a class of Sanskrit verse texts which contain mythological accounts of ancient days. Purāṇas are considered *smṛti or non-*Vedic Hindu scripture. They were probably compiled between 500 and 1500 CE, although they contain much earlier material from the *itihāsa (epics) and other sources.

The Purāṇas have their origin in texts for the Vedic edification of lower *castes and women. Later the Purāṇas became associated with the *Trimūrti, and in the medieval period with the rival *bhakti cults of *Viṣṇu and *Śiva. The earlier Vedic material is reworked to serve sectarian interests, and earlier material on medicine, astrology, chronology, geography, military tactics, and grammar is incorporated in these popular devotional texts.

A proper Purāṇa should expound the *pañcalakṣaṇa* (five subjects): *sarga* (creation), *vaṁśa* (genealogy of gods and *ṛṣis), *manvantara* (the reigns of the *Manus), *pratisarga* (destruction and recreation, together with the history of humanity), and *vaṁśānucarita* (legendary history of the Solar and Lunar dynasties). Very few Purāṇas conform to this scheme, the **Viṣṇu Purāṇa* being one that does. Purāṇas are generally revealed by ṛṣis or animals, are cast in dialogue form, and sometimes have prophetic purport.

The Purāṇas are divided into two categories, Mahāpurāṇas (major) and Upapurāṇas (minor), each category having eighteen members. The Mahāpurāṇas are divided into three categories: those of *Brahmā (Rājasa Purāṇas, *rajas *guṇa prevailing); those of Viṣṇu (Sāttvika Purāṇas, *sattva guṇa prevailing); and those of Śiva (Tāmasa Purāṇas, *tamas guṇa prevailing). The Rājasa Purāṇas are: (i) *Brahmā* (or *Ādi*, or *Saura*); (ii) *Brahmāṇḍa*; (iii) *Brahma-vāivarta*; (iv) *Mārkaṇḍeya*; (v) *Bhaviṣya*; (vi) *Vāmana*. The Sāttvika Purāṇas are: (i) *Viṣṇu*; (ii) **Bhāgavata* (or *Śrīmad Bhāgavatam*, the best-known Purāṇa); (iii) *Nārada* (or *Nāradīya*); (iv) *Garuḍa*; (v) *Padma*; (vi) *Vārāha*. The Tāmasa Purāṇas are: (i) *Śiva*; (ii) *Liṅga*; (iii) *Skanda*; (iv) *Agni*; (v) *Matsya*; (vi) *Kūrma*. In addition to the Mahāpurāṇas and Upapurāṇas, there are extant many recent puranic texts of archaic language and attribution.

Purāṇas stress bhakti (devotion) and miraculous manifestations of divine grace. Although many Hindu reformers such as *Dayānanda have attacked puranic religiosity, it remains the dominant form of Hinduism.

Trs. are in the series *Ancient Indian Tradition and Mythology* (in progress); C. Dimmitt and J. A. B. van Buitenen, *Classical Hindu Mythology* . . . (1978); W. D. O'Flaherty, *Hindu Myths* (1975); L. Rocher, *The Purāṇas*, ii and iii in J. Gonda (ed.), *A History of Indian Literature* (1986).

Purandaradāsa (Hindu musician): see HARIDĀS, SVĀMĪ.

Puran Siṅgh, Sant (founder of Sikh reform movement): see NISHKAM SĒWAK JATHĀ.

Puraścaraṇa (Skt., 'preparation'). Preparing the way in Hinduism for meditation by repeating a *mantra, and by performing the appropriate rituals. The repetition of a mantra may extend over many days (often from new moon to new moon) and thus produce a large number of repetitions.

Purdah (Pers., *pardah*, 'curtain'). The Muslim seclusion of women from strangers, related to *hijāb (the veil). The basis is in Qur'ān 33. 53, 'When you ask anything of them [the wives of *Muḥammad], ask it of them from behind a curtain [hijāb].' Purdah led to special quarters for women and thence to the harem (see ḤARAM).

Pure Gate of the East Mountain (group of followers of Hung-jen): see HUNG-JEN.

Pure Land (Skt., *sukhāvatī*; Chin., *ching-t'u*; Jap., *jōdo*). An untainted transcendent realm created by the *Buddha Amitābha (*Amida), to which his devotees aspire to be born in their next lifetime. Since all the conditions in Pure Land propel one toward enlightenment, anyone born there will attain *nirvāna quickly and easily. Pure Land provides a religious alternative for ordinary believers who are incapable of meditation and other stringent practices that are conducive to nirvāna in this world. According to *Mahāyāna doctrine, there are countless Pure Lands or Buddha Lands (Skt., *buddhakṣetra*; Chin., *fo-t'u*; Jap., *butsudo*), each produced by a different Buddha. In addition to Amitābha's, the one created by the Buddha *Akṣobhya is frequently mentioned in Buddhist writings. None the less, only the Pure Land of Amitābha ever achieved widespread popularity in E. Asian Buddhism. Hence, in China, Korea, and Japan the expression 'Pure Land' came to be used as a proper noun signifying Amitābha's transcendent realm rather than as a generic term for any Buddha Land.

Detailed descriptions of the Pure Land are contained in three Pure Land sūtras (*Sukhāvatīvyuha Sūtras*) revered by E. Asian Buddhists: *Wu-liang-shou ching* (Jap., *Muryojukyo*; Larger Pure Land Sūtra); *O-mi-t'o ching* (Jap., *Amidakyo*; Smaller Pure Land Sūtra); *Kuan wu-liang-shou-fo ching* (Jap., *Kanmuryōjukyō*; Pure Land Meditation Sūtra): trs. *Buddhist Mahāyāna Texts*, Sacred Books of the East, 49. According to them, Amitābha's realm is located in the western direction, and it is known by the name *Sukhāvati (Skt.; Chin., *chi-lo*; Jap., *gokuraku*), meaning 'Utmost Bliss'. In that realm there is no sickness or suffering. Everyone born there is endowed with miraculous powers and is assured of attaining enlightenment without retrogression. The Pure Land is adorned with jewelled trees, giant lotus ponds, panoramic terraces, splendid thrones, and chiming bells. The singing of exquisite birds and the playing of heavenly musicians fill the air with melodious strains that are transformed into the teachings of the *dharma in the ears of those who hear them. The persons born in Pure Land range from *Bodhisattvas of considerable religious advancement to lowly wrongdoers who, upon their deathbed in their previous lifetime, simply invoked Amitābha's name and placed their faith in him. The ability of people of such low religious standing to achieve birth in Pure Land is what inspired a popular devotional movement centring on Amitābha and his Pure Land. The chanting of Amitābha's name, known in Japan as the *nembutsu, emerged as the most common practice in this movement. These devotions eventually resulted in the formation of organized *Pure Land Schools in E. Asian Buddhism. See Index, Pure Land.

Trs. in Sacred Books of the East 49; *The Shinsu Seiten* (1955); *Kuan wu-liang-shou Ching* (1984).

Pure Land schools. A devotional form of Buddhism centring on the Buddha Amitābha (Skt.; Chin., O-mi-t'o; Jap., *Amida) and his transcendent realm known as *Pure Land. Everything in Pure

Land is conducive to Buddhist enlightenment; hence, persons born there in their next lifetime will attain *nirvāna without fail. Pure Land Buddhism originated in India, but it gained its largest following in E. Asia once Pure Land scriptures were translated into Chinese. One of China's early Pure Land adherents was *Hui-yuan (334–416), an eminent Buddhist master who established a monastic community on Mount Lu. In 402 he organized a society of 123 believers who performed devotions to Amitābha and jointly vowed to be born in Pure Land. The spread of Pure Land Buddhism to the general populace occurred a century or two later as a result of the evangelistic efforts of several Pure Land masters. The first of these was T'an-luan (476–?560). He embraced the Pure Land teachings at the urging of the Indian priest Bodhiruci, a famous transmitter and translator of Buddhist scriptures. T'an-luan spent his life popularizing such devotional practices as meditating on the Pure Land and chanting Amitābha's name. Tao-ch'o (562–645), who carried on T'an-luan's work, added a historical dimension to the Pure Land teachings. He maintained that the world has passed into a period of decline, the age of the Latter-day Dharma (Chin., *mo-fa*; Jap., *mappō) during which the earlier teachings of Buddhism no longer have efficacy. Only Amitābha's Pure Land offers hope of salvation and enlightenment to sentient beings. Tao-ch'o's successor, Shan-tao (613–81), was the great systematizer of Pure Land thought (see Fujiwara Ryosetsu, *The Way to Nirvana*, 1974). He encouraged believers in five types of religious practice: reciting scripture, meditating on Amitābha and his Pure Land, worshipping Amitābha, chanting his name, and making praises and offerings to him. Among these he emphasized the invocation of Amitābha's name as the paramount act leading to birth in Pure Land. The simplicity of this practice, known as the *nien-fo (Chin.; Jap., *nembutsu), made Pure Land an appealing form of Buddhism to those unable to perform more rigorous religious devotions. In Shan-tao's wake, a burgeoning Pure Land movement arose that pervaded all levels of Chinese society. The lineage of Buddhist masters that coalesced around these teachings and the temples that they founded became the backbone of the Pure Land School in China.

Pure Land Buddhism passed into Japan as one of many cultural imports from China. It first existed as an ancillary form of devotion within other schools of Buddhism. From *c.*10th cent., Pure Land increased in popularity with the publication of a handbook on Pure Land practice by the *Tendai priest *Genshin (942–1017), entitled the **Ōjōyōshū*. He presented the nembutsu as most efficacious when practised during meditation on the Buddha and his Pure Land. Although strong at the aristocratic level of society, Pure Land did not emerge as an independent school of Japanese Buddhism until *Hōnen (1133–1212). He propagated the nembutsu as a simple verbal expression of reliance on Amitābha, whether performed in meditation or in any other context. Under Hōnen's leadership a formal Pure Land school known as the *Jōdo school came into existence. Hōnen's many disciples carried his message to all levels of Japanese society. Among them *Shinran (1173–1262) stressed faith in Amitābha as the essence of the nembutsu and as the true cause of salvation. His followers, drawn primarily from the peasant class, went on to establish the *Jōdo Shinshū school of Buddhism. The other major Pure Land school to arise in Japan was the Ji school founded by *Ippen (1239–89). He also inherited Hōnen's teachings, but he advocated simple repetition of Amitābha's name whether undergirded by faith or not. He considered the syllables of the nembutsu to embody special religious power that unites the believer with the Buddha. Ippen spent his career travelling throughout the country, advocating nembutsu chanting and distributing amulets inscribed with it. All of these schools made Pure Land one of the dominant forms of Buddhism in Japan. See Index, Pure Land.

J. Foard and M. Solomon (eds.), *The Pure Land Tradition* (1994); D. and A. Matsunaga, *Foundations of Japanese Buddhism* (1974, 1976); P. Williams, *Mahayana Buddhism* (1989).

Pure Land sūtras: see PURE LAND.

Pure Yang (form of Taoism): see CH'ÜAN-CHEN TAO.

Purgative Way. The first of the *Three Ways of the mystical life. This triadic division, popularized by *Dionysius the Areopagite, begins with the necessity of purification: in the Christian tradition, it is primarily purification from sin by forgiveness and the practice of virtue, though Dionysius, following *Platonism, envisaged intellectual purification as well. See also ILLUMINATIVE and UNITIVE.

B. Groeschel, *Spiritual Passages* . . . (1983).

Purgatory. According to Catholic teaching, the place or state in which those who have died in the grace of God expiate their unforgiven *venial sins, by undergoing due punishment before being admitted to the *beatific vision. The doctrine of purgatory evolved alongside the ancient Christian practice of praying and offering the eucharist for the dead, and more specifically as a clarification concerning the state of souls between death and the general *judgement. Scriptural warrant is claimed in 2 Maccabees 12. 39–45; Matthew 12. 31 f.; 1 Corinthians 3. 11–15. The foundation of the Catholic doctrine of expiatory suffering after death is found in *Augustine (*City of God*, 21. 13, 24); it was amplified by Thomas *Aquinas, and eventually defined at the councils of Lyons (1274) and *Florence (1439; here with a view to reconciling the Orthodox). The Roman Catholic Church is, however, reserved about descriptions of purgatory, the most credited being those of St *Catherine of Genoa. The doctrine of purgatory was openly rejected at the *Reformation, and Protestants deny it as unscriptural and a denial of the complete forgiveness of sins through faith in Christ's saving work: 'In the bitter disputes that pitted Protestants against Catholics in the 16th cent., the former severely reproached the latter for their belief in Purgatory, to which Luther referred as "the third place" ' (J. Le Goff, *The Birth of Purgatory*, 1984).

For a Buddhist equivalent, see YAMA.

Puri. Hindu pilgrimage centre in Bengal, site of the *Jagannātha temple, and one of the seven particularly holy places of India (see SACRED CITIES, SEVEN).

Puril Pojo (Zen reformer): see CHINUL.

Purim (Heb., 'lots'). Jewish feast commemorating the deliverance of Jews, as recorded in the book of *Esther. The *festival of Purim celebrates the deliverance of the Jews by Mordecai and Esther from Haman's plot to kill them. It derives its name from the lots cast to determine the month of the massacre. The feast is celebrated on 14 Adar; it was established by the 2nd cent. CE, and the *Mishnah tractate **Megillah* discusses its observance. The *Scroll of Esther* (see SCROLLS, FIVE) is read in the *synagogue, and *Rava taught that a man should get so drunk in celebration that he cannot distinguish between the names of Haman and Mordecai (*B.Meg.* 7b: see ADLOYADA). In modern times, it is customary to dress up, and a carnival atmosphere prevails. Purim plays (Yiddish, *purimshpiln*) are dramatic representations of religious themes (derived from Purim, but not restricted to that festival or the story underlying it), which, at the level of folk religion, represent many features of a liminal rite (see RITES OF PASSAGE).

N. S. Doniach, *Purim* . . . (1933).

Puritans. Those members of the late 16th-cent. church in England who were dissatisfied with the Elizabethan Settlement of Religion. The term was one of abuse coined in the 1560s to describe 'a hotter sort of *Protestant'. These included people who had returned to England after exile under Queen Mary (1553–8), some of whom refused to be *bishops, and who held strong views about worship, as well as others who pressed vigorously for the purification of the Church. They attacked what they regarded as unscriptural practices, such as the wearing of *vestments (M. Parker's *Advertisements*, 1564/6), repetition in the **Book of Common Prayer*, and the sign of the cross at *baptism. The term 'Puritan' thus describes attitudes to the Church of England which changed through time. Among those called by their opponents 'Puritan', there were those radical pamphleteers who opposed *episcopacy (the Marprelate Tracts), and those who held local conferences under the patronage of influential laymen ('prophesyings'), providing regular opportunity for biblical exposition and the discussion of controversial ecclesiastical issues. Thomas Cartwright's Cambridge lectures on Acts, and the *Admonition to Parliament* (1572) of John Field and Thomas Wilcox, advocated a *Presbyterian form of church government, but these views were strenuously opposed by Archbishop John Whitgift, whose Articles of 1583 and the 1593 Act against 'seditious sectaries' represent a debate on the more contentious issues raised by some Puritans. Richard *Hooker's *Laws of Ecclesiastical Polity* (1594–7) is a voluminous apologia for *Anglican church life on the basis of scripture and reason. In the early 17th cent., the lines separating Puritans and English Protestants became more blurred as they continued, in the main, to worship in the same churches and espouse the same basic theology. Certain issues proved contentious: the *Book of Sports* (1618), which allowed certain forms of recreation on Sundays (understood as the *Sabbath), was one such; the growing popularity of plays and masques was another. The appointment by Charles I of a number of bishops who were *Arminian in much of their theology, together with the seeming alliance of court and church in promoting *high church practices, alienated many: it raised questions about the *episcopate, the *liturgy, and the proper way of life for the elect (cf. *election), which had largely lain dormant for half a century. Not so by 1642, when these issues figured in the English Civil War, the so-called Puritan Revolution. In its wake, the privileged and monopolistic position of the *Church of England was abolished, and Puritans and some English Protestants tended to become adherents of sects such as *Baptists, *Congregationalists, and, eventually, *Quakers. This situation was not wholly changed with the restoration of the Church of England in 1662 and the imposition of penalties on those who could not belong to it. But whereas at the beginning of the 17th cent. most Puritans were Anglicans, by the end of it the positions they potentially stood for had taken many of them away from that allegiance. Some Puritans, like Robert Browne (*A Treatise of Reformation without Tarrying for Any*), John Greenwood, Henry Barrow, and John Penry, frustrated that their radical ideals were not likely to materialize, became Separatists, believing in a *Congregational form of church government. Several of these Separatist leaders were executed, whilst others were compelled to leave the country (e.g. the Pilgrim Fathers) in order to enjoy religious liberty.

The English Puritans were mainly *Calvinists in theological allegiance, though there were some exceptions, like John Goodwin, who preferred *Arminianism. Others, like Richard *Baxter, expounded a *via media* between these two divergent theological positions. The Puritans' extensive biblical expositions, devotional and pastoral homilies provide a rich example of a spirituality which emphasizes election, self-examination, corporate discipline, pilgrimage, conflict, and the sanctification of all life.

The Puritans played a major part in the forming of the immigrant communities in the European settlements in America which began with the *Pilgrim Fathers. Under the auspices of the Massachusetts Bay Company, Puritans settled in all the new colonies, but especially in New England and Virginia. Prominent leaders were Richard Mather, John Cotton, and Roger Williams. Until the end of the 17th cent., the strong Puritan sense of holding authority under God (as God's elect) created a kind of 'holy commonwealth', with strong religious control. In 1630, John Winthrop preached to the Puritan settlers while still on their way to America: 'We must consider that we shall be as a City upon a Hill, the eyes of all people are upon us, so that if we shall deal falsely with our God in this work we have undertaken and so cause him to withdraw his present help from us, we shall be made a story and a by-word through the world.' One consequence of this *zeal was the detection and eradication of deviance, in the form of witches and of the possessed: on this, see K. T. Erikson, *Wayward Puritans . . .* (1986).

See Index, Puritans.

S. Bercovitch, *The Puritan Origins of the American Self* (1975); C. Cohen, *God's Caress . . .* (1986); P. Collinson, *The Elizabethan Puritan Movement* (1967); P. Lake, *Moderate Puritans and the Elizabethan Church* (1982); G. F. Nuttall, *The Puritan Spirit* (1957); D. Wallace (ed.), *The Spirituality of the Later English Puritans: An Anthology* (1988); O. C. Watkins, *The Puritan Experience*, (1972), L. Ziff, *Puritanism in America* (1973).

Purity

Judaism Purity (Heb., *tohorah*) involves the state of being ritually acceptable. According to Leviticus 11–17 and Numbers 19, the three major causes of ritual impurity are leprosy, sexual emissions, and contact with the dead. According to Leviticus 13. 45–6, a leper is unclean, and complicated provisions are laid down for his purification. However, these laws are no longer observed since the disease now called leprosty is not deemed to be the same as biblical leprosy. For the laws concerning emissions from the sexual organs, see MENSTRUATION. The carcasses of all creatures, particularly the corpses of human beings, are regarded as impure, and those who have come into contact with the dead are unclean for seven days (Numbers 19). In the *halakhah, the laws of ritual purity and impurity are laid out in twelve tractates of the *Mishnah and the *Tosefta. Human beings, utensils, and food can all become impure, and purification involves the performance of particular rituals, although many have fallen into disuse in modern times. However, the laws of *niddah are still observed, and *kohanim* (see PRIEST) still avoid contact with dead bodies. See also MIKVEH; NIDDAH; TOHORAH.

Islam See ABLUTION.

Hinduism See ŚODHANA.

Zoroastrianism Purity and pollution are central concerns in *Zoroastrian thought and practice. In Zoroastrian theology (**Bundahisn*) *Ahura Mazda is wholly good and all that leads to death and decay is the work of the evil *Angra Mainyu. The ultimate pollution is a corpse, especially that of a righteous person, for their death represents a greater triumph for evil than that of a sinner. But anything leaving the body (urine, spittle, blood, cut hair, etc.) is also thought of as dead, and therefore polluting. Thus a woman during menstruation is thought of as a locus of pollution. Just as Angra Mainyu sought to destroy the Good Creation at the beginning, so he also seeks to destroy new life at birth. As the womb is where the holy event of birth takes place, so inevitably it is where Angra Mainyu seeks to perpetrate his foul deeds. The menstruating woman is, therefore, not sinful but the hapless victim of evil assault. But since death is associated with her, it is important that she should not approach that which is particularly holy, the sacred fire, waters, or a serving priest (*magi). Indeed, in times past she was kept in isolation from all other people. Similarly, mothers were kept in isolation after birth, which is intelligible in ancient society where death in childbirth was common. Although the ancient myth and theology are no longer strong among Zoroastrians, the associated practices are, either as matters of custom, or (sometimes in India) by interpretation according to occult ideas of the individual aura which may be affected during menstruation, etc.

The purity laws affect most aspects of life for all Zoroastrians, from the obligation to clean the home; to observing laws which are nowadays seen as hygienic; to acts of worship (*Atas); funerals (*daxma); even to rules against intermarriage or in strict priestly homes against commensality with anyone who does not observe the purity laws, especially non-Zoroastrians (*juddins*).

There are various rites of purification. For minor pollutions, the *padyab*, washing and saying the *kusti* prayers (*Naujote), is all that is necessary. On special occasions, for example before initiations or weddings, the *Nahn* is necessary. This begins with the *Padyab-kusti*; the symbolic eating of a pomegranate leaf and drinking of *nirang* to cleanse spiritually; the recital of the *Patet*, the prayer of repentance, and finally a bath. For serious pollution, for example after contact with a corpse, or in order to acquire the highest state of purity (e.g. for a priest to perform the higher liturgies) then the nine-day *baresnum* ceremony is necessary. This takes place in the temple precincts, involves periods of prayer and washing and the aid of two priests. It is also important to note that moral as well as physical purity is expected. The concept of 'pure' is essentially that the Good Creation of Ahura Mazda is in the ideal state in which he created it. The impure is that which is tainted by evil forces. *Juddins* are necessarily impure since they do not observe the purity laws.

It is of course entirely logical that in a religion which emphasizes the holiness not only of the spiritual side of life, but also of the material, there should be strict theological directives for the care of that Good Creation. The purity laws have been described as 'essentially a series of battle orders' in the war against evil.

M. Boyce, *A Persian Stronghold of Zoroastrianism* (1977); J. J. Modi, *Religious Ceremonies and Customs of the Parsees* (1937).

Pūrṇa-yoga. The Integral Yoga of Śri *Aurobindo.

Purohita. Early functionary in Aryan India, who counselled the ruler, especially through ritual techniques. Purohitas became increasingly central (e.g. *Aitareya Brāhmaṇa* 8. 24 lays down that a king's offerings depend on a purohita for validity). The best-known purohita in post-Vedic times was Kauṭilya, to whom **Arthaśastra* is attributed. See also VASIṢṬHA. In the Vedic period, the purohita was also an advisor at all levels of sacrifice, and could be the officiant.

Puruṣa (Skt., 'man', 'person'). A spiritual concept variously understood in Hindu religion and philosophy. The earliest references in the **Atharva Veda* and *Kāthaka-Saṁhita*, may, according to J. W. Hauer, link puruṣa with the *Vrātya tradition and identity with the Vedic god *Rudra. The famous **Puruṣa-sūkta* (*Ṛg Veda* 10. 90) celebrates puruṣa as a cosmic demiurge, the material and efficient cause of the universe, whose sacrifice and division gave rise to the *Veda and all of creation. The early *Upaniṣads and the **Bhagavad-gītā* use the term to mean an individual's spirit, psychic essence, or immortal Self. In *Sāṃkhya philosophy, puruṣa is the first principle (*tattva), pure contentless consciousness, passive, unchanging, and witness to the unconscious dynamism of *Prakṛti, primordial materiality. Salvation here, as in *Yoga philosophy, results from the discrimination of the two independent ultimate realities.

Puruṣārtha. The four legitimate goals of life for high-caste Hindus. The first is *dharma, which controls the others, since it embraces appropriate belief and behaviour. The second is *artha, material goods and wealth. The third is *kāma, which is enjoyment of the senses. The fourth transcends the others, since it is *mokṣa, liberation.

A. Sharma, *The Puruṣārthas: A Study in Hindu Axiology* (1982).

Puruṣa-sūkta. The famous creation hymn of *Ṛg Veda* 10. 90, attributed to *Nārāyaṇa. This hymn celebrates *puruṣa (Skt., 'person') as the primordial Cosmic Man, a giant who is both the material and the efficient cause of the universe, a symbol of the totality of the world. Puruṣa as depicted has a thousand eyes and a thousand feet and pervades the world in all directions. The hymn represents the earliest myth of secondary creation. The sacrifice of Puruṣa by the gods becomes a model for all Vedic sacrifice, generating the metres and hymns of the *Veda, animal life, and the socio-economic divisions of humankind. As a sacrificial victim, Puruṣa's body was immolated and divided such that:

> The *brāhman was his mouth, his two arms were made the *rājanya (warrior), his two thighs the *vaiśya (trader and agriculturalist), from his feet the *śudra (servile class) was born.
>
> The moon was born from his spirit (*manas), from his eye was born the sun, from his mouth *Indra and *Agni, from his breath *Vāyu was born.
>
> From his navel arose the middle sky, from his head the heaven originated, from his feet the earth, the quarters from his ear. Thus did they fashion the worlds. (10. 90. 12–14)

The *sūkta* gives a basis in Veda for the divisions of Vedic society and the later *caste system as detailed in **Manu-smṛti*. *Sūkta* 10. 90 was used ritually for people desiring a son, for purificatory purposes, and for consecrating temples built in the image of Puruṣa.

Trs. many, incl. trs. of *Ṛg Veda*.

Puruṣottama (Skt., 'the highest person'). A perfected soul, the nearest Indian equivalent to a *saint. Puruṣottama is the supreme Lord, i.e. God.

Purva (Skt., 'aboriginal'). 1. Hindu term, in combination with other words, to express chronological priority, but also greater depth, profundity, etc. It contrasts with *uttara* to express later and higher realities.

2. Jain texts of great authority, now lost (but their 'resonance' continues through oral teaching: see DIGAMBARA).

Pūrva-mīmāṁsā (Skt., *pūrva*, 'earlier' + *mīmāṁsā*, 'investigation'). One of the six orthodox systems of Indian philosophy, usually referred to simply as Mīmāṁsā. It is concerned with the interpretation of the ritualistic and ceremonial portion (*karma-kāṇḍa) of the *Vedas. It is to be distinguished from the later *Uttara Mīmāṁsā, also called *Vedānta, which deals with the teachings of the *Upaniṣads.

Mīmāṁsā, extant perhaps as early as the 3rd cent. BCE, was later formulated by *Jaimini in the **Mīmāṁsā-sūtra* (*Mīmāṁsādarśana*) which is the oldest and basic text of the Mīmāṁsā school. The Vedas are held to be eternal, uncreated, and need no further authority; any discrepancy within them, therefore, is only apparent. Sound (*śabda) is also eternal, so meaning is naturally inherent in the word itself. The idea of periodic creation and dissolution is rejected. Emphasis is on duty (*dharma), with life in heaven a reward for correct works (i.e. attending to details in rituals, sacrifices, offerings, etc.). Liberation (*mokṣa) was rejected, though later Mīmāṁsākas introduced God and *mukti into the philosophy.

The infallibility of the Vedas is upheld through a process of logical reasoning: (i) the subject is proposed; (ii) doubts are stated; (iii) objections are stated; (iv) refutation is given; (v) the result is decided. Jaimini's *Sūtra* contains 915 of these propositions (*adhikaraṇas*) organized into twelve books.

After the 8th cent., two schools developed as a result of disputes over the interpretations of the commentaries of *Kumārila and *Prabhākara, noted teachers of Mīmāṁsā.

Tr. of Jaimini, Ganganatha Jha (1933–6); tr. of Kumārila, Ganganatha Jha (1909). Ganganatha Jha, *Purva-mīmāṃsa in its Sources* (1942); P. Shastri, *Introduction to Pūrva Mīmāṃsa* (rev. G. Sastri, 1980).

P'u-sa. Chin. for *bodhisattva.

Pūṣan (prosperity): see ĀDITYAS.

Pusey, Edward Bouverie (1800–82). Leader of the *Oxford Movement. As Regius Professor of Hebrew he lent his prestige and erudition to the Tractarian cause, which even became known, to its opponents, as 'Puseyism'. His most influential activities were preaching and polemical writing, as well as spiritual counselling and acting as confessor to a wide range of people. After the death of his wife in 1839 he started to practise many austerities. His advocacy of the *real presence in the *eucharist, of private *confession, and of the monastic life were influential in the *Anglo-Catholic revival in the Church of England.

Pu-tai (popular figure in Zen iconography): see HOTEI.

P'u-t'i-ta-mo (Chinese name): see BODHIDHARMA.

P'u-t'o-shan. A mountain island in the E. China Sea, the holy place of Kuan-yin (*Avalokiteśvara), and a place of particular importance for Chinese Buddhism.

Pyx (Gk.). A box used for holding the *reserved sacrament, and specifically a small silver box used for carrying the sacrament to the sick, when the pyx is wrapped in a small corporal (linen cloth) and carried in a pyx-bag around the priest's neck.

Q

Q (prob. an abbreviation of Germ. *Quelle*, source). A symbol denoting a (hypothetical) document used by the authors of the *gospels of *Matthew and *Luke. Its existence is inferred from parallel passages in those gospels, containing substantially the same material, which do not come from *Mark (see SYNOPTIC GOSPELS). Thus the Q hypothesis proposes a second written source beside the gospel of Mark for Matthew and Luke. It normally envisages that Luke did not use Matthew, and is therefore the main rival to the view that Luke knew and used Matthew (within either a Mark–Matthew–Luke or a Matthew–Luke–Mark sequence).

The genre and setting of this predominantly, though not exclusively, 'sayings source', as well as the number of recoverable stages in its development, are disputed. Given the presence of wisdom and prophetic material within Q, some writers classify it as wisdom discourse, while others see it as an essentially prophetic text. The latter seems preferable in view of the emphasis on John the Baptist and *Jesus as *prophets (Luke 7. 24–8, 11. 47–51, 13. 34–5), the use of wisdom motifs for prophetic purposes (Luke 12. 22–31), and Jesus' charismatic prophetic stance in dispute with Pharisees (Luke 11. 42). The rejection of the demand for a sign (Luke 11. 29) and of the potential call for journeys to sacred sites (Luke 17. 23), suggests the period of, and a critical stance towards, the Palestinian 'sign prophets' described by *Josephus. An approximate date in the 50s CE would also allow sufficient time for the delay of the *parousia to have become an acute problem (Luke 12. 42–6).

The horizon of Q is the Jewish people, who are called to repentance and renewal. Gentile persons are mentioned, not as recipients of a Christian mission, but as paradigms of the response which should be, but often has not been, forthcoming in Israel (Luke 7. 2–10, 10. 12, 11. 31–2). Jewish hearers are being stirred, even shamed, into a response. A fierce insistence on the timeless authority of the whole law (Luke 16. 17), coupled with the absence of any extended reflection on its content or status, suggests that those who prize this tradition are aware of, but theologically distanced from, that (Pauline?) mission to the gentiles which undercuts traditional legal definitions of the identity of the people of God.

While the presupposition of Q seems to be the obligation to continue Jesus' own mission to Israel (Luke 10. 2–16), most particularly to the poor (Luke 6. 20–1, 7. 22), there is unmistakable evidence of post-Easter *christological cognition. The beleaguered community legitimates itself by appeal to the revelation of the exalted Son (Luke 10. 22). It meets the challenge of the 'sign prophets' with an insistence on the coming of the heavenly *Son of man (Luke 11. 30, 17. 24). This 'coming one', announced by John the Baptist (Luke 3. 16), has already been encountered in the person of Jesus (Luke 7. 18–23), and is now the focus of the commitment, the obedience (Luke 6. 46), and the traumas (Luke 6. 22) of the Q followers of Jesus. Although currently repulsed in Israel as a whole, most painfully in Jerusalem where the violent rejection of prophetic missions (including that of Jesus) has led to the withdrawal of the divine presence from the *Temple (Luke 13. 34–5a), he will finally be recognized and welcomed (Luke 13. 35b). Meanwhile, the interval between his original and his final comings remains a time for loving conciliation with fellow Jews (Luke 6. 27–35), strenuous missionary activity (Luke 10. 2), obedient service (Luke 19. 12–27), and confident hope.

D. R. Catchpole, *The Quest for Q* (1993); A. D. Jacobson, *The First Gospel* (1992); J. Kloppenborg, *The Formation of Q* (1987); E. P. Meadows, *Jesus, the Messianic Herald of Salvation: A Study of Q and Mark* (1995).

Qabbalah (Jewish mystical exploration): see KABBALAH.

Qabd (Arab. 'contract'). In *Ṣūfī Islam, a technical term (in contrast to *basṭ) describing fear and desolation, akin to 'spiritual dryness': 'When God gives, he shows you his generosity, and when he takes away, he shows you his power (*qadar), and in both he is making himself known to you' (ibn 'Aṭā' Allah).

Qadar (Arab., *qadara*, 'have strength for, gain mastery over'). The decree of *Allāh which, in Muslim belief, determines all eventualities. The *Qur'ān reiterates constantly the power of God, who is the sole creator of all that is, and the One who knows all that is to be. Nothing can happen unless God wills it—hence the popular recognition of this in the phrase, *insh'Allah*, 'if God wills it'. How strong is this determinism? If God determines everything that happens, how can humans be held responsible on the Day of Judgement (*yaum al-Dīn)? This was a major and divisive issue in early Islam. According to M. S. Seale (*Muslim Theology*, 1964), *qadar* (and *qada'*) do not have in the Qur'ān the strongly deterministic senses given to them in later debates. *Qada'* means 'to command, legislate, order, decide'; *qaddara* 'to fashion, arrange, ordain, plan'. Both words convey the power of God to fashion and order things according to his plan. However, at one extreme (eventually excluded from orthodox Islam), the Jabriy(y)a (Jabariy(y)a) emphasized the power and authority of God to such an extent that it implied absolute predestination. At the other extreme, the Qadariy(y)a, who became identified with the *Muʿtazilites, held that humans, as the caliphs (*khalīfa) of God on earth, have the delegated power to create their actions. The mediating positions of the Maturidites (*al-Māturīdī) and the Ashʿarites (*al-Ashʿarī) held that all possibilities are created by God, but that humans have the responsibility to 'acquire' (*kasb, iktisāb*) actions out of the possibilities, thus becoming accountable (hence 'the doctrine of acquisition'). However, they gave a slightly different focus: Maturidites believed that acquisition operates at the moment of intending or willing to do something, whereas Ashʿarites believed that the acquisition applies to the capacity to act at the time of the action.

W. M. Watt, *Freewill and Predestination in Early Islam* (1948).

Qadariy(y)a (Muslim school of thought defending free will, not to be confused with *Qādiriy(y)a): see QADAR.

Qaddish (sanctifying doxology): see KADDISH.

Qadhaffi, Muʿammar (b. 1938). Libyan leader, founding his revolution (and *Green Book*) on Islamic principles. Having received a religious primary education, he came to believe that only the army could be the instrument for reviving Libya. He led a *coup d'état* in 1969. In 1975, he began to publish the *Green Book*. His basic aim was to return to the original Islam of the 7th cent., with direct, not representative, democracy, 'partners, not wage-earners', and respect for natural ways of life. Because the *Qur'ān alone is the control, he rejected the *sunna, including accretions which, e.g., subordinated women to men: 'It is not written in the Qur'ān that women should be slaves, submissive and despised .... Oppression is the result of a social process.' Fundamental is the opposition to all that opposes *Allāh, by all means—hence the initiatives which the West finds erratic and which it fails to comprehend. Thus it fails to recognize that the sing., *jumhūriya*, 'republic', becomes for Qadhaffi the pl., *jamāhīriya*, to reflect the Quranic emphasis on the equalities of access implied in *'umma.

Qāḍi. 1. A Muslim judge appointed by a ruler or government because of his knowledge of Muslim law. For *Sunnis, the decisions are in accord with one of the schools of *sharīʿa, controlled by precedent, since the route to new decisions via personal opinion (*ijtihād) is effectively closed.

2. A name sometimes given to an adherent of *Ahmadīy(y)a.

Qādiriy(y)a. A *Sūfī order (*ṭarīqa) founded in the 12th cent. by *ʿAbd al-Qādir al-Jīlī, who was revered as a teacher and also as a worker of miracles. Given the Sūfī tendency to see the manifestation of Being in the particulars of creation, but especially in Sūfī adepts, it is not surprising that al-Jīlī was regarded as Lord of creation after and under God, and reverenced as such. His tomb in Baghdad is a place of *pilgrimage. The order makes use of music and dance, particularly to encourage trance states. It is widespread from Morocco to India.

Qajars (Persian dynasty): see AL-MAJLISĪ.

Qalandar. Eastern name for holy beggars, perhaps *derwishes. The name occurs in the *Thousand and One Nights*, as though the Qalandars are a particular sect; but although they have been associated with the *Bektāshīy(y)a, it seems more probable that they were unorganized and simply took to begging as a way of life.

Qal va-homer ('light and heavy' principle of exegesis): see KAL VA-HOMER.

Qarmatians (Arab., *al-Qarāmiṭah*). Members of a broad, often revolutionary, movement in Islam, which sought social reform and justice during the 9th–12th cents. CE, in Khurāsān, Syria, Yemen, and Egypt. Egalitarian in emphasis (a communal meal, sharing the 'bread of heaven' is attributed to them), they regarded evil as having an independent reality which had to be contested. The Qarmatians were named after their 9th-cent. leader, Hamdān al-Qarmaṭ. They emerged from the *Ismāʿīli *Seveners, accepting Muḥammad b. Ismāʿīl as the final *Imām. They were thus in some sympathy with the branch of the Ismāʿīli family which established the *Fāṭimid dynasty, and conversely the Fāṭimids exercised some control over them. But the Qarmatians believed that the office of Imām is not a hereditary monopoly transmitted in a dynasty, but an imperative mandate passed on to a person from among the initiates by a sudden illumination of his intellect, making him a spiritual son of his predecessor. Their teaching was kept as a secret *'gnosticism' among initiates.

Their most notorious act was the abduction, in 930 (AH 317), of the *Black Stone, refusing offers to ransom it. They threw it back into the mosque in Kufah in 951 (AH 340), saying, 'By command we took it, and by command we return it'—now in seven pieces, perhaps to affirm the seven Imāms? Although they disappeared as a sect, their influence continued in other movements, e.g. perhaps the Alawis (see NUṢAIRI).

B. Lewis, *The Origins of Ismāʿīlism* (1940).

Qawwāli (Indian Sūfī singers): see CHISHTI.

Qaynuqa. An ancient Jewish tribe of the city of *Madīna. The Banu Qaynuqa (a tribe of metal-workers) was the first Jewish group to be persecuted by Muḥammad. From the Jewish point of view, they opposed his teaching (and were expelled from the city in 622/3 CE) because it was an adaptation of Judaism which did not preserve what was important in it; from the Muslim point of view, they were one among several tribes who sought to subvert and get rid of Muḥammad.

Qedushah (holiness): see KEDUSHAH.

Qibla. Direction of *Mecca, more specifically the *Kaʿba, towards which each Muslim must turn in order to perform the *ṣalāt validly. In a *mosque, the qibla is marked by the *miḥrāb*. On a journey, a compass may be used to ascertain the correct qibla; in case of necessity the individual may use his own judgement, or the general direction may be observed.

During the early period of Islam in Mecca, the Muslims would pray facing the Kaʿba, or, according to an alternative account, towards *Jerusalem; after the *Hijra, for a while Muḥammad directed that prayers should be said facing Jerusalem, the qibla of the Jews. After about sixteen months, Muḥammad ordered the Muslims to pray facing Mecca. This is made authoritative in the *Qurʾān: 'The foolish will say: What has led them to abandon their former Qibla? Say: The East and the West belong to Allāh .... Turn then your face towards the holy *Masjid ...' (Qurʾān 2. 142–4). It is said that these words were revealed to Muḥammad during morning ṣalāt at a place called Qubāʾ, or, alternatively, during noon ṣalāt in a mosque of the Banū Salima, which thereafter was known as Masjid al-Qiblatayn (Mosque of the two Qiblas).

The word 'qibla' is then also used more loosely for a fixed direction of prayer in any religion.

Qin Shihuangdi: Ch'in Shih Huang Ti. See BURNING OF BOOKS.

Qiṣāṣ (Arab., 'retaliation'). The principle, in Islam, of limited retaliation for harm inflicted. In contrast to the blood-feuds of pre-Islamic Arabia (often lasting for years and generations), the *Qurʾān commends a substitutionary compensation (5. 45)—though where victim and perpetrator are of equal status, *talion is admitted in strict relationship to the perpetrator alone. Where a life has been taken, the life of the killer may be taken (2. 179), but no further revenge-killing is allowed: in effect, retribution replaced revenge.

Qissa-i-Sanjan (story of Zoroastrian migration): see PARSIS.

Qiyāma (resurrection): see YAUM AL-QIYĀMA.

Qiyās (Arab., 'measure'). 'Deduction by analogy' whereby *Qurʾān and *Sunna can be brought to bear on novel issues or circumstances. Qiyās has served an important function in *usul-i-*fiqh* (principles of law) in all the Islamic law schools. Qiyās is used in the cases which are not dealt with by the Qurʾān, Sunna, or *ijmāʿ. Wine-drinking, for example, is prohibited by the Quranic text. The reason for the prohibition is the intoxicating effect and the ensuing social evils, hence in whatever these effects predominate, prohibition will be enforced. Thus by use of analogy (qiyās) the law can be extended to all cases of a similar nature. It is a reasoned opinion, based on the similitude of circumstances with basic reference to the Qurʾān and Sunna, and must not run contrary to an established law. Moreover, the analogical reasoning and deduction must not be such that its reason cannot be understood by human intelligence, nor may it be an exception to some shared human experience.

Qizil Bash (Turkish Ṣafavis): see ṢAFAVIDS.

Qodashini (set apart through holiness): see KEDUSHAH.

Qoheleth (alternative name for Biblical book): see ECCLESIASTES.

Qom. Iranian town, south of Teheran, a major centre for the training of Shīʿa Muslim teachers and leaders. The tomb of Hazrat-i-Fātima, the sister of the eighth *Imam, ʿAli al-Rida, is located here, and it is the most important place of *pilgrimage after his own tomb at *Mashhad. It became a place of sanctuary where a person could take refuge until a legal issue had been resolved. Qom had lapsed as a centre of training until 1920, when it was re-established by Shiʿite leaders who feared that their position in controlling the shrine towns of Iran might be lost in the transition from *Ottoman to British interest. In 1978 the first outbreak of protest against the Pahlavi rulers occurred in Qom.

Qorbān, qurbān: see SACRIFICE (JEWISH); VOWS.

Quadragesima (Lat., 'fortieth [day]'). Another name for the forty days of *Lent, or for the first Sunday in Lent, six weeks before *Easter.

Quadragesimo Anno. An *encyclical issued on 15 May 1931 by *Pius XI on the fortieth anniversary of *Leo XIII's **Rerum Novarum*, an encyclical concerned with the ordering of society and of economic relations, giving rise to 'a true Catholic social science'. *Quadragesimo Anno* addresses, more than its predecessor, questions of ownership and of wages.

Tr. *Two Basic Social Encyclicals* (1943).

Quakers. Usual name for the Society of *Friends. It was first given in the mid-17th cent. to the followers of George *Fox. Its derivation is uncertain: it may be derived from an occasion when, in 1650, Fox told a judge in Derby to 'tremble at the Word of the Lord'; or from an existing women's sect; or from the 'spiritual trembling' experienced at meetings.

Quartodecimans. Early Christians who observed *Easter on 14 Nisan, the same day as the Jewish *Passover, rather than the following Sunday. The practice was strong in Asia Minor where it was believed to derive from St John. Efforts by Pope Victor (*c.*190) to suppress it were not immediately successful, and Quartodecimans survived as a separate sect down to the 5th cent.

Qubbat al-Ṣakhra: see DOME OF THE ROCK.

Quds, al- ('the Sanctuary'). Muslim name for Jerusalem; by extension it may also refer to Palestine as a whole.

Queen Anne's Bounty. A fund established by Queen Anne of England in 1704 to receive *tithes and other payments formerly diverted to the crown by Henry VIII, so as to improve the endowments of poorer parishes. The fund was subsequently enriched by grants from Parliament and various private benefactions. In 1948 it was subsumed by the *Church Commissioners.

Quest for the historical Jesus. The attempt to recover from the New Testament, especially the *gospels, an account of *Jesus disentangled from the confessional presentation of him in those documents of faith. The 'Quest' is associated with A. *Schweitzer and his review of previous attempts (mainly of the 19th cent.) to write 'lives of Jesus'; its impossibility was strongly argued by R. *Bultmann (see also KERYGMA). *A New Quest of the Historical Jesus* (1959) was initiated by J. M. Robinson, who accepted that Bultmann's negative critique was correct, and that the rescue of historical items from the mass of confessional material was impossible; even if it could be achieved, ' "the historical Jesus" comes really to mean no more than "the historian's Jesus" '. In contrast, he argued that 'Jesus' understanding of his existence, his selfhood, and thus in the higher sense his life, is a possible subject of historical research.'

Questions of King Milinda (title tr. of Pāli Buddhist text): see MILINDAPAÑHA.

Quicunque Vult (Christian statement of faith): see ATHANASIAN CREED.

Quietism. Used broadly of any spirituality that minimizes human activity and initiative, leaving all to the will of God. More strictly, it is applied in Christianity to the teaching of certain 17th-cent. writers, especially Miguel de Molinos (condemned in 1687), but also Mme. Guyon and Archbishop *Fénelon. In its essence, it takes teaching about the importance of simple surrender to God's will (characteristic of *contemplation) out of its context as the end-result of a life of moral discipline and participation in the sacraments. The stress, found in, e.g., *John of the Cross, on inactivity, *nada* ('nothing'), becomes a principle of the whole spiritual life, leading to neglect of the sacraments and even of resistance to temptation, since even actions that would be sinful in others are held not to matter so long as the state of annihilation of one's will, 'mystic death', once achieved, is not disturbed. Christian perfection is attained by *contemplatio passiva infusa*, in which the powers of the self are suspended, to be replaced by God himself: thus any striving (e.g. for moral perfection) is bound to be frustrated.

Quinquagesima (Lat., 'fiftieth [day]'). The Sunday before *Lent, seven weeks before *Easter. In earlier times a stage in pre-Lenten discipline, e.g. the abstinence from meat, began on this day. The previous two Sundays, known by analogy as Sexagesima ('60th': third before Lent) and Septuagesima ('70th': fourth before Lent) marked still earlier stages. All three names were suppressed in the Roman Catholic Church in 1969, but are still in use in Anglican churches.

Quinque Viae (Lat., Five Ways). Five classical arguments pointing to the existence of God, summarized by *Aquinas at the opening of the **Summa Theologica*:

> The first way is the argument from motion [which requires a first Mover] . . . The second is from the nature of efficient cause [the chain of causation requires an uncaused Cause] . . . The third way is taken from possibility and necessity [roughly, 'why there is something rather than nothing' requires a necessary being] . . . The fourth way is taken from the gradation to be found in things [comparisons, e.g. 'hotter', relate to a perfect standard, 'hottest', so overall to God as the cause of perfection] . . . The fifth way is taken from the governance of the world [that things are evidently designed to an end, requiring a Designer]. (*ST* I, qu. 2, art. 3).

The first four are related to the *Cosmological Argument, the fourth remotely to the *Ontological Argument, the fifth to the *Teleological Argument. Related to the *affirmative way, the Five Ways are not so much proofs as preliminaries to the human engagement with God in love, prayer, and action, in response to the action and love of God disclosed in *revelation.

L. Velecky, *Aquinas' Five Arguments* . . . (1994).

Quires: see CHOIR.

Qumran community. Jewish monastic community which lived near the shores of the Dead Sea. Major archaeological excavations have taken place in the area. Khirbet Qumran is the site of a building complex which includes a large cemetery. It has been suggested that it was the site of the *Essene community described by Pliny the Elder (but see further DEAD SEA SCROLLS). The occupants of the site clearly aimed at self-sufficiency with large storerooms and an elaborate system of customs. These have been connected to the elaborate cleansing prescriptions laid down in the *Manual of Discipline* in the *Dead Sea Scrolls. The buildings were destroyed and burnt *c.*70 CE, presumably by the Romans during the Jewish war (see JOSEPHUS). Near the site are the caves where the Dead Sea Scrolls were found. These give a remarkable picture of the daily life and religious aspirations of a monastic community which presumably was the same as the community living in Khirbet Qumran. See also ESSENES; DEAD SEA SCROLLS; YAHAD.

M. A. Knibb, *The Qumran Community* (1987); R. de Vaux, *L'Archéologie et les Manuscrits de la Mer Morte* (1961). G. Vermes, *The Dead Sea Scrolls in English* (3rd edn., 1987).

Quo vadis? (whither are you going?): see PETER, ST.

Qur'ān. The scripture of Islam, believed by Muslims to be the word of *Allāh, revealed to *Muḥammad between the years 610 and 632 CE, recited by him, and subsequently recorded in written form.

The word itself is probably derived from the Syriac *qeryānā*, 'scripture reading', though the root *qara'a* is also found in the Qur'ān (e.g. 96. 1: 'recite!'). In the Qur'ān itself, the word *qur'ān* means primarily the action of reciting; it can also in some places indicate an actual passage of scripture, or a part of the whole revelation, or the book; it is also mentioned together with the *Tawrāt and *Injīl (3. 3; 9. 111). The word *kitāb* (book) is also used as a synonym (e.g. 4. 105). The Qur'ān is thought to 'confirm', but also supersede, former scriptures (10. 37). It is taken from *umm al-kitāb, the pre-existent scripture preserved in heaven.

The Qur'ān in its present form consists of 114 chapters (*sūras) composed of varying numbers of verses (*ayāt*; sing., **ayā*), and roughly arranged in decreasing order of length. The first sūra, of only seven verses, is the *Fātiḥa. In general, the earlier sūras are the shorter ones, and thus are found towards the end of the book. First in chronological order are said to have been the first verses of sūra 96: 'Recite! in the Name of your Lord, who created . . .'. It was about the year 610 that Muḥammad began to receive messages, of whose origin he was at first uncertain but later defined as coming from Allāh through the intermediary of the angel Jibrā'īl (*Gabriel; named in 2. 99). Many sūras reflect events, and others contain *ad hoc* judgements—for example, there is reference to the battle of *Badr in 3. 123; directions for *ḥajj (pilgrimage) rituals are given in 2. 158, 196–200, 5. 98–100. These passages raise questions, which have been much debated in Islam, about the relation of the eternal Qur'ān to the contingent circumstances of its revelation.

The generally accepted belief among Muslims, although there has been criticism of the details (see the critical analysis by J. Burton, *The Collection of the Qur'ān*, 1977), is that during Muḥammad's lifetime portions of the Qur'ān were written down, at his dictation, but that the first collection was made during the caliphate of *Abū Bakr (632–4 (AH 11–13)), by Muḥammad's scribe Zayd b. Thābit. These sheets of paper became the property of Abū Bakr, and in 634 (AH 13) passed to *'Umar, then on his death (644 (AH 23)) to his daughter Ḥafṣa, a widow of Muḥammad. Subsequently, under *'Uthmān, a recension was made by Zayd and a few others, on the basis of the copy owned by Ḥafṣa. Any other written versions of single parts were ordered to be destroyed. Thus within some thirty years of Muḥammad's death a definitive text was established, which has remained virtually unchanged down to the present day.

The Qur'ān is divided into the sūras revealed in *Mecca, and those revealed in *Madīna. Western studies have grouped sūras (taken as wholes, while allowing that some are composite) into four periods: (i) early Meccan: mainly short, with oaths and eloquent appeals to the hearers, summoning them to belief in one God, to worship, to social justice; (ii) middle Meccan: referring especially to signs of God in nature and creation; Allāh is often named al-Raḥmān (the Merciful), while stories of punishment of former disobedient and unbelieving peoples are prominent; (iii) late Meccan: longer and less poetic, containing sermons and stories; (iv) Medinan: far more legislative and narrative, reflecting the situation of the Muslims and the growth and development of the new community. A more elaborate chronological arrangement was proposed by Richard Bell, in *The Qur'ān, Translated, with a Critical Re-arrangement of the Surahs* (2 vols., 1937, 1939).

Although the Qur'ān describes itself as a 'clear book' (2. 2), and a clear 'Arabic Qur'ān' (12. 2), some of its passages are acknowledged to be obscure and in need of interpretation. The science of commentary and interpretation (*tafsīr and *ta'wīl) has given rise to a large body of literature. There are parables, similes, and borrowed words. The Qur'ān is the main source of Islamic legislation, on matters ranging from divorce, times of worship, fasting, and inheritance, to warfare and the division of booty. In many cases Quranic verses are explained or amplified by the *ḥadīth.

As the speech (*kalām*) of Allāh, the Qur'ān is considered one of His attributes (*ṣifāt*), and also as co-eternal with him. The Qur'ān was, in general, held to be uncreated, but the school of theological thought known as the *Mu'tazila held that there could be no other uncreated being beside Allāh, so the Qur'ān must be created. Although this school was politically influential for a time during the 9th cent., Muslim teaching in general has been that the Qur'ān is eternal, uncreated, and perfect. Its inimitability (*i'jāz) is an article of faith (10. 38, 11. 13) and a proof of its divine origin. The earthly manifestation of its words, on the tongue or the printed page, is, however, created. The intense respect for the words of the Qur'ān has led to an eagerness to recite portions frequently, and to learn the whole book by heart, one who has so learnt being known as a *ḥāfiẓ*. There has also been some reluctance to translate it into other languages. Any version other than *Arabic is considered as, at best, an 'interpretation', a sentiment respected in the translation by A. J. Arberry, *The Koran Interpreted*, which aims to convey the poetical nature of many sūras, and the more literal one by M. M. Pickthall, *The Meaning of the Glorious Koran*. See also Index, Qur'ān.

K. Cragg, *The Event of the Qur'an* (1971); E. Ihsanoglu (ed.), *World Bibliography of Translations of the Meaning of the Holy Qur'an* (1986); H. E. Kassis, *A Concordance to the Qur'an* (1982); Fazlur Rahman, *Major Themes of the Qur'an* (1980); A. Rippin (ed.), *Approaches to the History of the Interpretation of the Quran* (1988); W. M. Watt, *Bell's Introduction to the Qur'an* (1970).

Qurayza, Banu. Ancient Jewish tribe in the city of *Madīna. The Banu Qurayza believed themselves to be of priestly descent and were primarily engaged in agriculture. By order of Muḥammad, the men were massacred and the women and children sold into slavery in 627 CE.

Qutb (Arab., 'pole, axis'). In Islam, especially among *Sūfīs, the idea of a central axis around which the interests of the world revolve. The centrality is that of God's will and word, manifested through a great saint or caliph (e.g. the first four). Thus it is not held that the individual is without fault or flaw, but rather that at certain moments the qutb is manifest through him.

R

Ra'av: see BERTINORO, O.

Rabad (acronym): see IBN DAUD, ABRAHAM . . .

Rabbah bar Naḥmānī (*c.*270–330 CE). Babylonian Jewish *amora. Rabbah was head of the *Pumbedita academy for twenty-two years during its time of greatest influence. He was famous for his interpretation of the *Mishnah and when he died a heavenly voice is said to have pronounced, 'Happy are you, O Rabbah b. Naḥmānī, whose body is pure and whose soul has departed in purity' (*BBM* 86a). Because of his skill in argument, he was known as Oker Harim, 'uprooter of mountains'. His death was described as 'being summoned to the heavenly academy', thenceforth a synonym for the death of a learned person. He died saying, 'Pure, pure', a reflection of his expertise on leprosy.

J. Neusner, *A History of the Jews in Babylonia, ad loc.* (1966–70).

Rabbanites. Name used to designate the opponents of the *Karaites in the Jewish religion. From *c.*10th cent., the Rabbanites were those Jews who accepted the *oral law in contrast to the Karaites who rejected it.

Rabbi, Rabbinate (Heb., 'my master'). Hence 'Rabbinic Judaism'. Jewish learned man who has received ordination (see SEMIKHAH). The term rabbi was not used as a title until the time of *Hillel. In *Talmudic times, this was not granted outside *Erez Israel, so that the Babylonian sages bore the title of 'Rav'. During this period rabbis were interpreters and expounders of the scriptures and *oral law. It was not until the Middle Ages that a rabbi became the spiritual leader of a particular Jewish community, with teaching, preaching, and administrative functions. Rabbis, however, were not *priests. They had no sacramental role, and *blessing the people was not an integral part of their duties. Originally rabbis were not paid. The *Torah was to be taught free of charge, and it was customary for rabbis to have another occupation. By the 14th cent. there is evidence of payment, not for teaching the law, but as compensation for loss of time taken up with rabbinical duties. In order to serve, the *Ashkenazim in particular insisted that rabbis should have a diploma of *Semikhah; and his duties were laid down in a letter of appointment (*ketav rabbanut*). As community leader, he was asked to give *responsa on legal problems and ambiguities, and to serve in Jewish courts; later, in E. Europe, the office was frequently combined with that of 'rosh *yeshivah' (head of the yeshivah). Since the Enlightenment, the function of the rabbi has undergone substantial change. In the *diaspora, national governments have abolished most Jewish rights of jurisdiction in civil law, and, with the growth of secular education, the traditional yeshivah training was felt to be less than adequate for the modern rabbi (see RABBINICAL SEMINARIES). Nowadays the role of the rabbi varies from community to community. Among *Reform congregations, he (and since 1972 possibly she) performs a function analogous to that of a Christian minister. He is regarded as spiritual leader of the community; he is involved in preaching, leading services, educating, and counselling. The *Orthodox rabbi has also taken on these duties, but has retained his role as legal consultant and interpreter of the written and oral law. In *Israel the rabbi has a unique role, since the Orthodox rabbinic courts have jurisdiction over matters of personal status. See also BET DIN; CHIEF RABBI; HAKHAM; SEMIKHAH. For individual rabbis, see Index, Rabbis, Teachers etc.

R. Hertz, *The Rabbi Yesterday and Today.*

Rabbinical conferences. Synods held by Jewish *rabbis to provide authoritative guidance. From the mid-19th cent., the need was felt for rabbinical conferences to give definite rulings. This was firmly attacked by the *Orthodox, who argued that no one could abrogate the least of the religious laws. None the less, *Reform conferences were held at Wiesbaden in 1837, Brunswick in 1844, Frankfurt-am-Main in 1845, Breslau in 1846, Leipzig in 1869, and Augsburg in 1871. In the USA, the Reform movement adopted its Pittsburgh platform in 1887, which was partly reversed in 1937 at Columbus at its annual convention. In 1961, the Federation of *Reconstructionist Congregations laid down its guidelines at a conference. Among the Orthodox, there has been some agitation for the restoral of the *Sanhedrin.

Rabbinical seminaries. Seminaries for the training of Jewish *rabbis. Traditionally, rabbis were trained in *yeshivot, but under the influence of the *Haskalah, it was felt that the old *Talmudic curriculum was not adequate for the modern professional rabbi. The first seminary to be established was the Istituto Convitto Rabbinico in Padua in 1829. The École Centrale Rabbinque was founded in 1830, the Juedisch-Theologisches Seminar of Breslau in 1854, London's *Jews' College in 1855, the Berlin Juedische Hochschule in 1872, and the Orthodox Hildesheimer's Seminar in 1873. Seminaries were less successful in E. Europe because of the attachment to traditional yeshivah training. In the USA, the *Conservative Jewish Theological Seminary was founded in 1886, the Reform *Hebrew Union College in 1875, and the Elchanan Theological Seminary (later a unit of *Yeshiva University) in 1897.

Rābiʿa al-ʿAdawiyya (*c.*713–801 (AH 95–185)). An outstanding *Sūfī and one of the few women in Islam to be considered the actual equal of men. Her name Rābiʿa means 'fourth'; she was the fourth daughter of a poor family, and while still a child sold into slavery, but later freed. She devoted herself to a life of prayer, poverty, and seclusion. She combined extreme asceticism with a purely disinterested love of God, and is generally acknowledged as the first Sūfī to teach this aspect of piety which later became prominent in Sufism. She said that her love for God left no place for any other love, nor even for hate of his enemies. She once saw Muḥammad in a dream, who asked her, 'Do you love me?' She replied, 'O Prophet of God, who is there who does not love you? But my love of God has so possessed me that no space is left for loving—or hating—any but him.' She often declared that one should not worship from desire of paradise or fear of hell, but for love of God alone: 'O my Lord, if I worship you from fear of hell, burn me in it; if I worship you in hope of paradise, exclude me from it. But if I worship you for your own sake, then do not hold me back from your eternal beauty.' Miracles were attributed to her, and her sayings and teachings were handed down from one generation to another of Sūfīs.

M. Smith, *Rabiʿa the Mystic and her Fellow Saints in Islam* (1928).

Rachel. Wife of *Jacob and one of the matriarchs of Israel. She was the younger daughter of Jacob's uncle, Laban, who tricked Jacob before Jacob eventually acquired her as wife. She was the mother of *Joseph and Benjamin—it was in giving birth to Benjamin outside Bethlehem that Rachel died. Her tomb is a place of *pilgrimage, especially for barren women, since Rachel was barren for many years. The Jews passed her tomb on the way into the *Exile, and, in heaven, she wept and prayed for their return: hence Jeremiah 31. 15–17.

Racovian Catechism (statement of faith of rationalist Christian movement): see SOCINIANISM.

Radak (acronym): see KIMḤI, DAVID.

Radbaz (acronym): see DAVID BEN SOLOMON.

Radcliffe-Brown, A. R. (British social anthropologist): see EVANS-PRITCHARD, E.

Radewijns, F. (fellow-worker): see GROOTE, G.

Rādhā, Rādhikā. A consort of the Hindu god *Kṛṣṇa, one of the *gopīs. A common girl's name, it derives from the lunar mansion more frequently called *viśākhā* (which indeed is found as a synonym for the gopī Rādhā in some older texts). Allusions to the legends about Kṛṣṇa as a cowherd in the forest of Vṛndāvana near Mathurā and his amorous affairs with the gopīs, the 'milkmaids' or 'cowgirls', can be found in Indian sources from almost the beginning of the Common Era. But it is only in secular poetic sources, not religious ones, that we hear also about Rādhikā (later mostly Rādhā) as Kṛṣṇa's favourite gopī and mistress. Apart from conventional episodes dealing with infatuation, love-making, jealousy, and quarrels of the lovers, nothing further is said about Rādhā till 12th cent. CE. The *purāṇas ignore her till an even later date, and a variety of Kṛṣṇaite traditions knows of a different favourite or female associate of Kṛṣṇa (e.g. in the Tamil-speaking South it is Piṉṉai (in Skt. texts called Nīlā or Satyā), a cowherd's daughter whom Kṛṣṇa/*Māyōṉ won as wife by defeating one—or seven—bull(s); in the cult of the temple of *Jagannātha it is Subhadrā; in the religion of Viṭhobā found in Mahārāṣṭra and Karṇāṭaka, it is (the princess) Rukmiṇī (in Marathi: Rakhumāī)). Yet from the 14th or 15th cent., the figure of Rādhā begins to dominate Kṛṣṇaite literature and religion. Since the *Bhāgavata-purāṇa*—the single most important religious work influencing Kṛṣṇa religion in N. India—does not mention her, some other popular source must be assumed to account for her ubiquitous popularity. This may well have been Jayadeva's *Gītagovinda*, a highly erotic poem written in Bengal *c.*1185 CE. Although it deals with Kṛṣṇa's and Rādhā's love-making in terms of the secular poetic conventions, later mystics and religious movements have treated it as a religious, mystical work.

A second factor in the evolution of Rādhā as central religious figure was evidently the teaching of the theologian *Nimbārka (14th/15th cent.?). By him Kṛṣṇa is regarded as identical with *Brahman, and Rādhā as co-natural with him. Similar ideas are expressed by many subsequent theologies. Thus in the teaching of Rūpa and Jīva Gosvāmī, the disciples of the Kṛṣṇaite mystic *Caitanya (*c.*1486–1533), Rādhā is conceived of as Kṛṣṇa's (= Brahman's) *hlādinī-śakti*, the embodiment of 'the bliss' into which the old Vedantic idea of Brahman as *saccidānanda has been subsumed. The relationship between Kṛṣṇa and his *hlādinī-śakti* is seen as *a-dvaita, 'non-dual'. Another theologian contemporary with Caitanya, Vallabha (*c.*1480–1533; see VAIṢṆAVA), seems to have ignored Rādhā, but through his son and successor Viṭṭhaladeva (*c.*1518–86) Rādhā gained theological centrality also in this tradition. Vernacular religious poetry on Kṛṣṇa from the 15th cent. onwards places Rādhā into a similar prominent position. As somewhat outside the mainstream may be mentioned here *Caṇḍidāsa (1400?) who wrote in Bengali and influenced Caitanya. Of far wider influence was a group of poets who lived during the 16th cent. and wrote in Braj-bhāṣā, the language of Vṛndāvana. *Sūrdās and Kumbhanadās are associated with the school of Vallabha; Hit Harivaṃś became the founder of a separate tradition, that of the Rādhāvallabhīs, and from Haridās derives the *Hāridāsī-sampradāya*. They all share an intense interest in the *nikuñj-līlā*, the love-making of Rādhā and Kṛṣṇa during the night—the 'sport in the bower'. This feature distinguishes them from the Caitanyites who emphasize Kṛṣṇa's and Rādhā's *viraha*, 'separation'. Whether theological-Sanskrit, or vernacular-poetic, all these traditions agree on these amorous sports possessing three dimensions: historical (a discrete event in the past, during Rādhā's physical life on earth); eternal (Rādhā and Kṛṣṇa making love continuously in the highest heaven of Goloka, an eternal counterpart to the earthly Vṛndāvana); and geographical (the locality of Vṛndāvana where even today the heavenly love-games, invisibly, take place). Not surprisingly, most personalities mentioned above actually lived in Bṛndāvan (the modern place believed to correspond to the mythical Vṛndāvana). With the followers of Vallabha, Kṛṣṇa's eternal consort is usually referred to as Svāminī-jī, 'the Mistress', and 'Rādhā' is reserved for her earthly manifestation. With some Caitanyites, Caitanya himself is regarded as an *avatāra of Rādhā and Kṛṣṇa together.

The poetry about Kṛṣṇa's love for Rādhā (to which must be added the late *Brahmavaivarta-purāṇa* and late strata in the **Padma-purāṇa*, both in Skt.) cannot avoid describing Kṛṣṇa as totally devoted and subservient to Rādhā, due to his love and passion for her. At least in the case of the Rādhāvallabhīs, this is not just seen as denoting an ultimate unity of Kṛṣṇa and Rādhā as Brahman, but has been developed into a form of 'Rādhāism': theologically speaking, Kṛṣṇa is dependent on Rādhā as the Absolute. (A parallel process can be observed in the case of *Rāma and *Sītā; the *Adbhuta-Rāmāyaṇa* attempts to establish a 'Sītāite' theology.)

J. S. Hawley and D. M. Wulff (eds.), *The Divine Consort* (1983); B. S. Miller, *The Love Song of the Dark Lord* (1977).

Radhakrishnan, Sarvepalli (1888–1975). Hindu philosopher and President of the Indian Republic. He was born in S. India, and was educated at a Lutheran Mission school, and at Madras Christian College. After various professorial posts in India, he became the first Spalding Professor of Eastern Religions and Ethics at Oxford, 1936–52. He served as Ambassador for India in countries which included the Soviet Union. He was Vice-President of India, 1952–62, and President, 1962–7. Radhakrishnan held strongly that all religions are different paths leading to the same goal, and that beyond the differences of credal formulations and practices there is an essential unity, since 'the signpost is not to be confused with that to which it points'. His own position was a blend of *Advaita Vedānta (in relation to which he corrected the mistaken impression that *māyā means 'illusion') and idealism. Religion is the highest state of human being, requiring not less than total commitment:

> We seek the religious object by the totality of our faculties and energies. Such functioning of the whole man may be called spiritual life, as distinct from a merely intellectual or moral or aesthetic activity or a combination of them. The spiritual sense, the instinct for the real, is not satisfied with anything less than the absolute and the eternal. It shows an incurable dissatisfaction with the finiteness of the finite, the transiency of the transient. Such integral intuitions are our authority for religion. They reveal a Being who makes himself known to us through them and produces revolt and discontent with anything short of the eternal.

He wrote many books, including *Indian Philosophy, The Hindu View of Life, Eastern Religions and Western Thought*, and translations with commentary of the *Upaniṣads and of the **Bhagavad-gītā*.

R. A. McDermott, *Radhakrishnan: Selected Writings* . . . (1970); P. A. Schlipp (ed.), *The Philosophy of Sarvepalli Radhakrishnan* (1952).

Rādhāsoāmī Satsaṅg (Hindī, 'pious congregation of the supreme being, Lord of Rādhā'). Religious movement originating in N. India. Since Soāmījī Mahārāj (Shiv Dayāl Siṅgh) of Āgrā (1818–78) founded this movement in 1861, it has divided into two main groups, each with its own succession of Masters and organization, and many smaller followings. One *āśram has continued in Dayālbāgh (Garden of the Merciful) near Āgrā, UP, India, with Satgurūs Rai Saligram, known as Hazūr Mahārāj (1829–98), Mahārāj Sāhab (1861–1907), Sarkār Sāhab, Sāhabjī Mahārāj, and Mehtājī Sāhab. The other centre is Beās, near *Amritsar, *Pañjāb, founded in 1891 by Soāmījī Mahārāj's follower, Jaimal Siṅgh, whose successors were Sawan Siṅgh (1858–1948), Jagat Siṅgh, Charan Siṅgh (d. 1990), and Gurinder Siṅgh Dhillon. There are now branches throughout India and in other countries. Devotees are from different countries and religious backgrounds, but from Hindu tradition spring the name Rādhāsoāmī, the universalist attitude to religions, and such fundamental concepts as liberation from *karma by the *Satgurū—i.e. the Ultimate in human form for his redemptive purposes. Rādhāsoāmī is the Supreme Being. Each person, a composite of physical, subtle, and causal bodies, mind and soul, is a microcosm of the totality which is likewise graduated from the coarse, physical universe to the perfect Sat Desh (Realm of Truth). Through the Master's gift of knowledge, the *Gurmukh may practise *surat-śabad-yoga* and so hear the audible lifestream (equated with *śabad, *nām, *logos, Word) and be drawn to its divine source. Followers must avoid meat and intoxicants. Their special celebration commemorating former Satgurūs is called *bhaṇḍārā*.

M. Juergensmeyer, *Radhasoami Reality* . . . (1986); A. P. Mathur, *Radhasoami Faith* . . . (1974).

Radical Reformation. In Christianity, the 'left wing' of the 16th-cent. *Reformation, whose leaders maintained that the 'magisterial' Reformers were not sufficiently radical in their quest for a renewed Church life. *Luther, *Calvin, *Zwingli, and *Bucer asserted that reformation must be effected either under the direction, or at least with the approval, of the secular rulers or civil authorities, whereas more radical Reformers were persuaded that the implementation of necessary changes in doctrine and practice were matters for the Church and did not require the co-operation of the State.

The Radical Reforming groups defy neat classification and include revolutionaries claiming direct inspiration of the *Holy Spirit (*Carlstadt, *Münzer, and the Zwickau prophets), evangelical *Anabaptists, *adventists, mystics, and anti-trinitarian rationalists. Fiercely attacked by Luther, Zwingli, and Calvin, most of the radicals opposed infant *baptism, insisting on the necessity of repentance and personal commitment to Christ which was given expression in believers' baptism. Local 'gathered' churches, organized on the separatist principle, were committed to biblical teaching, rigorous discipline, the forbidding of oaths, and evangelistic zeal. Christ became the proto-*martyr of these persecuted minorities, who expounded not only the *sin of humans, but the 'fall' of the Church since the days of Constantine. All this was clearly in direct opposition to the Lutheran concept of the Godly Prince. Although some radicals took up arms, most were committed to non-resistance; purity within the church was to be maintained by 'the Ban', not the sword, and religious liberty was considered the rightful inheritance of everyone. In the 20th cent. the research work of American *Mennonite historians greatly contributed to renewed appreciation of the origin and nature of their teaching (*The Mennonite Encyclopaedia*, 4 vols., 1955–9), whilst from an entirely different perspective some German historians have regarded the Radical Reformation as a faintly disguised expression of an economic and social protest against the oppressive class system of their day. Recent research (C. P. Clasen, *Anabaptism: A Social History*, 1972) suggests that their numerical strength may have been exaggerated.

G. H. Williams, *The Radical Reformation* (1962).

Rāfiḍites (Arab., *al-Rāfiḍah* or *al-Rawāfiḍ*, 'the repudiators'). A name given by *Sunni Muslims to the *Shīʿa in general, as a term of disapproval or abuse. They are called 'repudiators' because they reject the first three of the four al-Rāshidūn, the first four caliphs (*Khalīfa) after *Muḥammad, holding that the fourth of them, *ʿAlī, should (as Muḥammad's son-in-law) have succeeded in the first place.

Rāg, rāga (Skt., 'colour', a melodic sequence). In Indian music, combinations of notes associated with certain moods and times. The division of the Sikhs' *Ādi Granth is by rāg. Thus within each section appear compositions of diverse authorship to be sung to a particular melodic setting. The thirty-one rāgs of the Ādi Granth are Sirī, Mājh, Gaurī, Āsā, Gūjarī, Devgandhārī, Bihāgṛā, Vaḍhans, Soraṭh, Dhanāsarī, Jaitsrī, Toḍī, Bairāṛī, Tilaṅg, Sūhī, Bilāval, Gauḍ, Rāmkalī, Natnārāin, Mālī Gauṛā, Mārū, Tukhārī, Kedārā, Bhairo, Basant, Sāraṅg, Malhār, Kānaṛā, Kaliān, Prabhātī, Jaijāvantī. Neither the saddest nor the most exuberant rāgs are included. The Ādi Granth concludes with a Rāgamālā (garland of rāgs)—which, however, does not completely correspond with the rāgs used. The rāgs can be found in Western notation in M. A. Macauliffe, *The Sikh Religion*, v (1909), 333–51. See also RĀGĪ.

Rāga (Pāli, Skt.). In Eastern religions (for Hinduism, see ASMITA), the form of attachment identified with lust, greed, and passion. According to Buddhists, it is one of the most basic characteristics of human nature, having the pleasures of the senses as its object; but it also exists as attachment to more subtle pleasures at higher levels of spirituality (*saññojanā*) and is not finally disposed of until *nirvāna is reached. It is personified as one of the daughters of the evil deity, *Māra, who tempts and seduces human beings with the pleasures of the flesh. It is countered by the practice of dwelling upon the ugly or unlovely (*asubha*) rather than the attractive aspect of things. Rāga is often linked with ill will (*dosa) and delusion (*moha) as the three states of mind collectively at the root (*mūla) of all immoral behaviour; according to Buddhist psychological theory, any one of these three may also be the predominant feature of a person's temperament. They are symbolized respectively as the cockerel, snake, and pig as depicted on the Buddhist wheel of life (*bhavacakra).

Rāgī (Pañjābī, 'musician'). Sikh devotional music (*kīrtan), sung in *gurdwārās by amateur or professional rāgīs, usually accompanied by harmonium and drums (*tablā*, *dhaḍḍ*), *saurangī* (a bowed, stringed instrument), and *chimṭā* (tongs-shaped percussion instrument). See also RĀG.

Rahirās or **Sodar Rahirās.** Sikh early evening prayer. The Rahirās, repeated daily by devout Sikhs, consists of *Gurū *Nānak's 'sodar' *hymn, followed by eight more *śabads by Gurūs Nānak, *Rām Dās, and *Arjan Dev, three compositions by *Gobind Siṅgh (a *chaupaī, *savayye, and *dohrā*), the first five and last stanzas of *Anand *Sāhib, plus five hymns by Arjan Dev. *Ardās is performed at the conclusion of Rahirās. See also NITNEM; SOHILĀ.

Rahit, Rahat (Pañjābī, 'code'). Rahit Maryādā, Sikhs' code of discipline. Following the institution of the *khālsā, 18th-cent. rahitnāmās (written codes) were recorded, providing a cohesive factor in maintaining *Panth identity. Early rahitnāmās are the *Chaupā Siṅgh Rahitnāmā*, the *Prem Sumārag*, and others attributed to such associates of Gurū *Gobind Siṅgh as *Nand Lāl 'Goyā'. In 1945 the *Shiromaṇi Gurdwārā Parbandhak Committee approved the Rahit Maryādā (Code of practice), published 1950 (*Rehat Maryādā*).

After defining a Sikh, the Rahit Maryādā prescribes conduct expected of the individual and the Panth. A Sikh should study the scriptures and meditate on God, live according to the Gurū's teachings, and serve all humanity. First come instructions for *nitnem (daily prayer) and *Ardās, and for respectful behaviour towards the *Ādi Granth and within the *gurdwārā, including *kīrtan, *pāṭh, preparation of *kaṛāh praśād, and scriptural exposition.

Sikhs must worship one God and believe in the oneness of the ten Gurūs. They must avoid superstitions, respect other faiths, and bring up their children as Sikhs. *Tobacco, intoxicants, and narcotics are prohibited. So are infanticide, gambling, theft, and *adultery. *Birth, *naming, *marriage, and *funeral rites are detailed. All should willingly perform *sevā (service) e.g. in serving *Gurū-kā-laṅgar. Regulations for *khaṇḍe-dī-pāhul (baptism) are specified followed by *taṅkhāh (penance) and *gurmatā (religious decision). See also HUKAMNĀMĀ.

W. H. McLeod, *The Chaupa Singh Rahit Nama* (1987).

Raḥmānīya. Muslim religious order (*ṭarīqa), mainly in Algeria, named after its founder Muḥammad b. ʿAbd al-Raḥmān (d. 1793 (AH 1208)). Originally a missionary in India for another order (Khalwatī), he received visions of the Prophet *Muḥammad, which prompted him to claim immunity from *hell for those who adhered to him and his way. Much opposed by the *marabouts, he eventually retired into semi-seclusion.

Rahner, Karl (1904–84). Christian philosopher and theologian. He was born in Freiburg im Breisgau and entered the N. German province of the Society of Jesus (the *Jesuits) in 1922. He studied philosophy and then theology, and was ordained priest in 1932. From 1934 he undertook research at Freiburg. His dissertation on *Aquinas' metaphysic of judgement was rejected for its explorations away from traditional interpretation into the direction of transcendental Thomism. He moved to Innsbruck where his dissertation was accepted, later published as *Geist im Welt* (Spirit in the World). During 1939–45, he was engaged in pastoral work and some lecturing. After the War, he held various academic appointments, retiring to Munich in 1971, and to Innsbruck in his last year. His work dominates 20th-cent. philosophical theology, made up of densely laid foundations and sparkling raids on many different problems (some gathered in the long series, *Theological Investigations*), dominated by his pastoral concern that Christian truth must not be divorced from human living. He was influenced early on by the agenda set by *Kant, by his teacher Heidegger, and by Joseph Maréchal, who laid the foundations of neo-Thomism. Maréchal drew out the implications of the Thomist epistemology: knowledge is based on sense-data; the mind directs itself to sensory images; the mind therefore penetrates reality in the sense that it enters into the ontological nature of other things in its movement toward them of comprehension. These were summarized in three medieval aphorisms: *nihil in intellectu quod non fuit prius in sensu* ('there is nothing in the intellect which was not first in a sense'); *mens convertit se ad phantasmata* ('the mind turns itself toward sensory images'); *mens quodammodo fit omnia, non entitative sed intentionaliter* ('the mind can in a particular way become all things, not by being what they are, but by stretching out into them'). Maréchal argued that the unity of sense and intellect, in the act of a unitary human subject *knowing*, required necessary conditions for its possibility, namely, that the knower and the sensible objects of knowledge be composed of matter, form, and existence, since otherwise the act of knowing (as it *is* known) could not occur.

In this way, Maréchal set the stage for neo-Thomism as the working out of its detail. Rahner set out to establish what he called 'a transcendental Thomism' and 'theology taking a transcendental turn'. Rahner grasped that philosophy and theology must start with the human subject as the one who constitutes the world of possible knowledge: 'The enquiring subject becomes the subject of enquiry.' But this subject (i.e. the human subject) transcends itself by its outreach to other subjects and to other objects. 'Intellect' is characterized by its outreach or projection, not just to 'an object' as an item, but to an object 'in being', and hence to being as such. But the horizon of being cannot be limited to the being of one object after another, but to the absolute fact of being, hence to being itself. Similarly, 'conversion to the phantasm' (i.e. sense knowledge, see above) was understood by Rahner in terms of Heidegger's insistence that this reveals the 'situatedness' of human beings at particular moments and occasions. Thus the unity of this otherwise dual reference, towards the infinite (Absolute Being) and towards the finite (situatedness in the world) is the human subject as it constantly seeks to transcend itself and its existing points of departure, aspiring to the infinite while rendering the world intelligible. The latter is only possible because humans have a prehension (*Vorgriff*) of the former—a genuine 'pre-grasp' of Infinite Being as the true horizon of the world as lived.

On this philosophical foundation, Rahner insisted that theology must begin 'at the human end', not with *a priori* dogmas handed out as though self-evidently true. This 'theological anthropology' investigates human being in so far as it is turned toward God—which is, at once, on the basis of his previous argument, transcendental anthropology. In this way, the otherwise largely remote doctrines of Christianity are firmly located in the actual conditions of human knowing and living. Life experienced as spiritual and full of grace leads to the proposition that the world is exactly that (notwithstanding the human experience of fallenness as well). In that case, all human beings are participants in the grace of God which seeks to redeem the fallen, and thus all are 'Anonymous Christians', and within the salvific purpose of God, whether they are baptized or not. Humans come to know God, not by trying to solve doctrinal puzzles, but by truly experiencing themselves as what they are, subjects questing for knowledge and understanding (cf. *Lonergan) in a necessary process of constant self-transcendence. This is in fact the process of revelation, a process which needed, certainly, to be made historical and an object of possible knowledge outside itself, hence the Jewish covenant and the *incarnation. But even here Rahner works from the human upward, not from God downward: it is the analysis of human existence which throws up the need for just such a manifestation of the process and of the goal of self-transcendence. At the centre of all Rahner's thought remains the unequivocal pastoral demand, how can we help each other to attain the unlimited horizon of God?

The 'spiritual life' is life with God and toward God. We are leading this life when we forget ourselves for God, when we love him, praise him, thank him. 'Spiritual life' in grace means that we realise the inner divine life in ourselves; it means waiting for eternity in faith, hope and love, bearing the darkness of human existence; it means not identifying oneself with this world, living according to the prayer in the *Didache*: 'Let this world pass away, and let the grace of God come.' All that, certainly, is an unforced gift of the free grace of God.

He wrote many articles and also edited lexicons and encyclopaedias to diffuse his ideas more widely.

R. Bleistein and E. Klinger (eds.), *Bibliographie Karl Rahner, 1924–69* (1969; suppl. 1974); W. Dych, *Karl Rahner* (1992); L. J. O'Donovan (ed.), *A World of Grace . . .* (1980); H. Vorgrimler, *Understanding Karl Rahner* (1986).

Rāhula. The son of Gautama, the *Buddha. He was born at about the time that Gautama decided to leave his home in search of enlightenment. The Buddha later visited his son who was ordained as a novice (*sāmaṇera), and who received teaching from the Buddha. A number of *Sutras(z) and *Jātaka stories are thought to have been transmitted via Rāhula—even though he is said to have died before his father.

Raidās (Indian saint-poet): see RAVI DĀS.

Raigō (also raikō) **Raikō** (Jap., 'welcome'). The welcome given by *Amida and the attendant company of the *bodhisattvas to those who enter the *Pure Land. Raigo-in is the manual sign of welcome.

Rain (Heb., *geshem*). A recurrent theme in Jewish liturgy (see esp. the tractate **Taʿanit*), perhaps reflecting the agricultural base of life in the biblical period. It was a mark of the *messiah's connection with God that he would mediate rain to the land: this arises directly from the way in which the kings in Judah were involved in rain-making rituals in the cult; these persisted in *Sukkot as practised in the *Hasmonean period, even though there is no hint of them in the *Torah regulations—one of the major conflicts between Sadducees (who wished to follow Torah alone) and Pharisees (who wished to continue custom).

For the rainy season in Buddhism, see VASSA.

Rai Saligram (Hazūr Mahāraj, guru): see RĀDHĀSOĀMĪ.

Rāja (Skt.). A ruler or revered (because authoritative) figure. In the former case, the term became common during the British period in India (itself referred to often as 'the Raj') to refer to lesser authority figures in relation to the overriding rulers, Mahā (Great) rājas. In the latter case, it is used of a dancer, musician, sculptor, etc., who is skilled in his art or craft.

Rāja- (Skt., 'royal') or **aṣṭāṅga-** (Skt., 'eight-limbed') **yoga.** Classical yoga as developed in *Patañjali's **Yoga Sūtra* and in the commentarial literature. Rāja yoga assumes the *Sāṃkhya distinction between the conscious subject (*puruṣa) and manifested nature (*prakṛti). The aim of this yoga is isolation (*kaivalya) or freedom of the puruṣa from entanglement in prakṛti and the covering of the three *guṇas, which is the cause of suffering (*dukha*). However, classical yoga differs from Sāṃkhya in that it is theistic, accepting the 'lord' (*Īśvara), not as the creator, but as a special kind of puruṣa who has never been entangled in prakṛti, and who is an object of meditation.

Patañjali defines yoga as the 'cessation of mental fluctuations' (*cittavṛtti *nirodha) (Yoga Sūtra I. 2). This cessation is the distinguishing of ordinary awareness (*citta) from the real conscious self (puruṣa). This is achieved by practising the 'eight limbs' (aṣṭāṅga) of yoga: restraint (*yama), discipline (*niyama), posture (*āsana), breath-control (*prāṇāyāma), sense-withdrawal (*pratyāhāra), concentration (*dhāraṇā), meditation (*dhyāna), and enstasy (*samādhi). Yama and niyama are concerned with moral development and purification as a basis for developing higher states of consciousness through withdrawal of the senses from the outside world. Once the senses are withdrawn one-pointedness (*ekāgrata) is achieved and the yogin's attention is fixed entirely within. The last three stages, dhāraṇā, dhyāna, and samādhi, collectively termed *saṃyama, are stages of concentration very closely connected. Samādhi itself is categorized into samādhi 'with support' (*samprajñāta) and 'without support' (asamprajñāta), the latter being the stage at which Īśvara is revealed. Beyond this stage the yogin achieves liberation or isolation (*kaivalya). Through practising saṃyama the yogin also develops various magical powers (*vibhūti or *siddha) such as knowledge of his own previous births (*Yoga Sūtra* 3. 18), telepathy (3. 19), knowledge of the past and future (3. 16), and levitation (3. 39) etc., though these are regarded as distractions from the main goal of kaivalya.

P. Y. Deshpande, *The Authentic Yoga* . . . (1978); K. Werner, *Yoga and Indian Philosophy* (1977).

Rājacandra, Śrīmad (1867–1901). Jain spiritual reformer. He was born Raichandbhai Mehta, his later name being a title bestowed on him by his followers. In his youth, he reviewed all religions and came to the conclusion that Jainism was the truest, given that all religions contain corruptions and imperfections. He became a jeweller and was married—worldly preoccupations which he put down to the working out of *karma from previous lives, some of which he claimed to remember as a consequence of an experience at a cremation. He continued to study texts more closely, especially those of the *Digambaras, and came to believe that his vocation was to found a new religion as a reformed version of Jainism. He particularly mistrusted sectarian divisions and ritualism, and focused instead on the indispensable importance of understanding and exercising the nature and purpose of the *ātman (soul). In *Atmasiddhi* (Self-Realization, 1896; tr. D. C. Mehta, 1976), he maintained that true religion consists of six principles: (i) the soul exists; (ii) the soul is eternal; (iii) the soul is the agent of its own acts; (iv) the soul experiences what it enacts; (v) the state of deliverance exists; and (vi) the means to attain deliverance exists. Once ātman is properly realized, deliverance is already real. Rājacandra held that *ascetic withdrawal from the world is not a necessary condition of attainment, and that (as his own life demonstrated) the harder way of a householder does not preclude progress—though toward the end of his life he did become more monastic and ascetic.

Rājacandra is well-known for the influence he had on *Gāndhī, not least for his emphasis on *ahiṁsā and for persuading him not to go any further on the path toward Christianity. Only three of Rājacandra's letters to him survive (one urges him to observe the duties of *caste as a constraint on moral behaviour). Gandhi himself said that he was his refuge in moments of spiritual crisis, but that he held back from absolute commitment: 'In spite of this regard for him, I could not enthrone him in my heart as my *Guru. The throne has remained vacant and my search still continues' (*An Autobiography*).

S. R. Mehta and B. G. Seth, *Shrimad Rajacandra* . . . (1971).

Rājagriha, Council of: see COUNCILS, BUDDHIST.

Rajas (Skt.). In *Sāṃkhya one of the three strands (*guṇas) of material nature (*prakṛti). It is present in varying degrees in all things except pure consciousness (*puruṣa). In the external world, rajas is manifested as force or movement: that which moves has a predominance of rajas. In the individual, it is ambition, effort, and activity; it is also anxiety, passion, wickedness, and all forms of suffering. Through interaction with the other guṇas all varieties of creation arise.

Rāj karegā Khālsā (Pañjābī, 'the Khālsā shall rule'). Rallying cry of the Sikhs, introduced during the 18th cent. The verse in full states, 'The *Khālsā shall rule. No hostile enemy will endure: frustrated in their aims, they will submit, while those who come in for shelter will be protected.' The first line concludes the *Ardās at the end of communal worship.

Rajm (Arab., 'to stone', 'to curse'). 1. The punishment of stoning to death for adultery or sexual intercourse outside the permitted relationships (*zinā'). The punishment appears in *ḥadīth, not in *Qur'ān, and is surrounded by careful conditions, e.g. four competent male witnesses must report the incident in detail, and if their evidence breaks down, they are themselves liable to severe punishment.

2. The casting of seven small stones during al-*ḥajj. The original meaning is obscure (the rite is not mentioned in the Qur'ān). Traditionally, it is associated with the driving away of *Satan (Shaitan, known as *rajīm* in Qur'ān). It is, or may be, accompanied by the prayer (*du'ā'), 'O God, make this ḥajj a devoted one, forgive our sins, and reward our endeavours.'

Rajneesh, Bhagwan Shree (1931–90). Founder of an Indian-based movement known variously as the Orange People (from their dress), Sannyasins or neo-Sannyasins, Rajneeshees, or followers of Bhagwan. He was born Mohan Chandra Rajneesh of a Jain father. He became enlightened, by his own account, in 1953. He started an academic career, but resigned in 1966 to start full-time spiritual teaching. He moved to Pune (Poona) in 1974, attracting visitors from around the world. In 1981, having temporarily disappeared, he moved to Oregon in the USA, where a new city was planned, called Rajneeshpuram. Rajneesh took a vow of silence until 1984, so the foundation was run (increasingly autocratically) by his personal assistant, Ma Anand Sheela. In 1985, she absconded (and was later arrested), and Rajneesh was expelled from the USA. He resettled in Poona, where he became known as Osho. After his death, his followers continued to offer courses in his teaching. At one time, the movement was one of the fastest growing of the *new religions, and, largely on account of its views on sexuality, one of the more controversial. It has clients as well as believers, and while the former attend the centres for therapeutic and other purposes, the latter regard the founder as one of humanity's greatest enlightened ones.

In the Bhagwan's monistic interpretation of the world, there is only one source of energy and that is bio-energy, called 'life' or 'love' or 'light'. Most of the practices of Rajneeshism, including elements of *Tantra yoga, meditations derived from *Gurdjieff, and rituals such as the energy darshan (*shaktipat*, whereby power is transmitted by touch or glance), are designed to make it possible for individuals to resolve 'unresolved conflicts', unblock 'blocked energies', and most of all become aware of the 'bio-energy' or 'life force'. Awareness of one's inner life enables one to stand at a distance from it, and eventually to become an impartial observer and witness—the *sashi* of classical Indian *yoga. Awareness in this sense is the key to Rajneesh's thought: whatever one does, provided it is done with awareness, leads to the same goal. Thus, for example, if one is 'aware', then whether one enters into or renounces sexual relationships, the end result is the same.

J. Thompson and P. Heelas, *The Way of the Heart* . . . (1986).

Rajputs. Rulers in Rājputana (now Rājasthan) in India. They were *Kṣatriyas who rose to prominence before and during the *Gupta dynasty. They claimed *Aryan origin, and became fervent defenders of the Hindu way, especially against the Muslim invaders—though some later co-operated with Muslim rulers.

Rak'a. Unit of movements during the Muslim *ṣalāt (obligatory worship). These are: *rukū'*, bending forward; *sujūd*, prostration; *julūs* (half-sitting, half-kneeling); a second *sujūd*.

A set number of rak'as is ordered for each time of worship: *ṣalāt al-fajr*, two; *ẓuhr*, four; *'aṣr*, four; *maghrib*, three; *'ishā'*, four. More rak'as may be added voluntarily by the worshipper at any of these times, but do not constitute part of the obligatory ṣalāt.

Rakāb Gañj Gurdwārā. Sikh shrine in New Delhi. In 1675 Gurū *Tegh Bahādur was beheaded in Chāndnī Chauk, Delhi. According to tradition, a follower, Lakhī Shāh, who lived in the stirrup-makers' colony (*rikāb*, 'stirrup'), carried away the body and cremated it by burning down his house. The present *gurdwārā, opposite Parliament House, is a two-storeyed marble building with several domes and similar frontage on all four sides. See also ŚĪŚ GAÑJ GURDWĀRĀ; ANAṆḌPUR SĀHIB.

Rakan (Jap. for Theravādin Buddhist arhat): see LO-HAN.

Rakan Keijin (Ch'an/Zen master): see LO-HAN KUEI-CH'EN.

Rakhi Bandhan (Hindu festival): see FESTIVALS AND FASTS.

Rākṣasa. A class of demons or evil spirits in India, hostile to humans. They can appear in many forms, including those of animals, and they operate mainly at night.

Ralbag (acronym): see LEVI BEN GERSHOM.

Rāma, also **Rāmacandra.** The hero of the major Hindu epic, *Rāmāyaṇa. The initial core of the epic portrays Rāma as a courageous prince following the example of his ancestor Raghu (hence his epithet Rāghava). But in the full epic and the *Purāṇas, Rāma is an *avatāra (manifestation) of *Viṣṇu, the seventh and almost equal in importance to *Kṛṣṇa. Rāma and his wife *Sītā are the model spouses for Hindus. *Vālmīki traces the spiritual path of Rāma in *Yoga-vasiṣtha*, and to him also is ascribed the central part of *Rāmāyaṇa*. The present work is in seven *kāndas*, sections, of which (ii)–(vi) tell of Rāma's birth (celebrated in the festival Rāma Navami) and childhood; his life in *Ayodhyā and his banishment; his life in the forest and Sītā's abduction by *Rāvaṇa; Rāma's life with his monkey allies; his crossing over the bridge to Śri Lankā; the battle, the defeat of Rāvaṇa (celebrated in the *festival of Daśarā) and the rescue of Sītā; his life in Ayodhyā, Sītā's banishment and return, their death and ascent to heaven. (i) and (vii) contextualize the narrative by glorifying Rāma as an avatāra of Viṣṇu. To read the epic is to be associated with Rāma: 'Whoever reads and recites the holy, life-giving *Ramāyāna* is freed from sin and attains heaven.' The same is effected by repeating Rāma's name in the ear of a dying person. Rām as a *mantra is held, especially by *Vaiṣṇavites, to contain the universe, and from that mantra all languages have emerged. See also Index, Rāma.

Trs. M. N. Dutt (1892–4); W. Buck (1973); R. P. Goldman (1984) and S. I. Pollock (1986, 1990); R. T. H. Griffith (1870–4); S. Mazumdar (1974); N. Raghunathan (1981); H. P. Shastri (1952–9, complete); K. Subramaniam (1981).

Ramabai, Pandita (1858–1922). Indian Christian reformer. Born into a *brahman family, she lost both her parents during a pilgrimage in 1874. Because her parents had encouraged her in a classical education, she was able to support herself and her brother by becoming a wandering reciter of Hindu scriptures. She so impressed *pandits in Calcutta that she was given the title 'pandita'. She became increasingly active in work for women's education, and for overcoming the *caste system—which she embodied in her own case by marrying into a lower caste in 1880. Her husband died two years later. She met Christians in Bengal, and was helped by the Wantage Sisters (an *Anglican religious order) to go to England for further education. There she and her young daughter were baptized. She went to America and secured financial support for her work, then returned to India, where she established a school especially for child widows. She remained deliberately free from religious identity, but after a conversion experience in 1891, her work was increasingly evangelistic. She founded the Mukti (salvation) Mission, which continued after her death as a community.

S. M. Adhav, *Pandita Ramabai* (1979).

Ramaḍān. The ninth month of the Islamic year, and the period of *ṣawm (fasting). It is mentioned in the *Qur'ān as a blessed month, 'in which the Qur'ān was revealed' (2. 185). It is a time also of greater prayer and devotion, and during the last ten days and nights many of the pious practise retreat (*iʿtikāf) in a *mosque. One of these nights, generally believed to be the 27th, is *Laylat al-Qadr (the 'Night of Power'), holiest in all the year. The month of Ramaḍān ends with *Īd al-Fiṭr, feast of the breaking of the fast. Like all Islamic (lunar) months, Ramaḍān moves forward gradually each solar year. See also FESTIVALS AND FASTS.

Ramah (acronym of Rabbi Meʿir ha-Levi): see ABULAFIA, MEʿIR.

Ramakrishna (Gadādhar Chattopādhyāya; 1836–86). Hindu *ascetic and mystic. Born in a Bengali village, he displayed from an early age an eagerness for various kinds of religious experience and a tendency to fall suddenly into the state of *samādhi. At 19 he became the priest of *Kālī at Dakshineśwar, near Calcutta, and lived there for almost all the rest of his life, exploring a wide range of religious experiences—not only various types of *sādhana within the Hindu tradition, but also (albeit in a somewhat simplistic fashion) some Muslim and Christian devotional disciplines. Ramakrishna drew around himself a band of English-educated young Bengalis, who saw in him a living symbol of their ancient religious tradition and a sign of its renewed vitality in the modern world. He came to be regarded by some as an *avatāra (manifestation) of God. To these disciples he expounded his teaching, mainly in stories and short sayings. For Ramakrishna himself the central point seems to have been his exposition of the state of consciousness which he called *vijñāna, but today he is chiefly remembered for saying that all religious paths lead to the same goal. After Ramakrishna's death, his disciple, *Vivekānanda, drew together many of his other followers in a movement which is now world-wide, the Ramakrishna Mission, basing it upon his own interpretation of his master's teaching. It regards all religions as to some degree approximating to the truth. The most reliable guide to Ramakrishna's ideas, however, is *The Gospel of Śrī Ramakrishna*, the record kept by Mahendranath Gupta ('M') of his master's conversations between 1882 and 1886:

> Everything is in the mind. Bondage and freedom are in the mind. You can dye the mind with any colour you wish: it is like a piece of clean white linen: dip it in red and it will be red, in blue and it will be blue . . . If you keep your mind in evil company, it will be coloured with evil; but keep in the company of Bhaktas, and your thoughts, ideas and words will be of God. The mind is everything.

Tr. Swami Nikhilananda, *The Gospel of Sri Ramakrishna* (1942); R. R. Diwakar, *Sri Ramakrishna* (1956); C. Olson, *The Mysterious Play of Kali: An Interpretive Study of Ramakrishna* (1989).

Ramakrishna Mission: see RAMAKRISHNA.

Rāmana Maharishi (*māhā-ṛṣi*; 1879–1950). Hindu *ṛṣi who attained union with *Brahman at the age of 17, without the help of instruction or a *guru. His experience was triggered by a sense of his own death, which led to the realization that at death a body dies, but this cannot affect the identity which was manifest through the body. That Self is unaffected by the passing of momentary states. This realization of *ātman as Brahman remained with him as a constant condition, first in absolute silence on a hill in Tiruvannāmalai, later in dialogue with seekers, concentrating on the question, 'Who are you?' An *āśrama developed around him at Tiruvannāmalai, which remains a place of pilgrimage.

A. Osborne, *The Collected Works of Ramana Maharishi* (1959).

Rāmānanda (?1360–?1470). Founder of the *Vaiṣṇavite Rāmānandī sect. A *saṁnyāsin who was originally a devotee of *Rāmānuja, he was offended by his fellow-disciples when, after years of preaching throughout India, they forced him to sit apart at meals for fear of the pollution he might have acquired through eating with others during his journeys. As a result of this he established his own sect, preaching against *caste and urging the equality of all people in the sight of God (thereby admitting *women to his order). His first twelve disciples were of varied castes, and included the Muslim *Kabīr, and a woman. Although he did not condemn the polytheistic beliefs of popular Hinduism, Rāmānanda urged worship of one deity, *Rāma, with *Sītā, his consort, through *bhakti, personal devotion to one God. His teachings, in the common language of Hindī, influenced by Rāmānuja, spread widely and gave rise to a religious fervour which is still alive today. Later disciples of note were *Mīrābāi and *Tulsīdās, as well as the poets Malukdās and Nābhāji. His followers (in the *saṁpradāya which continues to this day) are devoted to Sītā and Rāma, sometimes wearing women's clothes and jewellery to indicate the indifference of gender. When they become members, they may burn the name of Rāma into their skin, and often add *dāsa* ('slave') to their names. Their main centre is *Ayodhyā, where their devotion to Rāma is intense.

G. N. Mallik, *The Philosophy of the Vaishnava Religion* (1927); T. A. G. Rao, *History of Sri-Vaishnavas* (1923); H. V. Sreenivasa Murthy, *Vaisnavism of Samkaradeva and Ramanuja* (1973).

Rāmānuja (11th/12th cent.). Hindu philosopher, theologian, and source of the school known as *Viśiṣṭādvaita-vedānta. He was born in the village of Bhūtapuri (in Tamil, Perumbundur), of a *brahman family. He was married, but later renounced married life and became *saṁnyāsin. He studied under many *gurus (e.g. Kāñcīpūrṇa, Mahāpūrṇa and Gosthipūrṇa), but is said to have revered *Yāmunamuni—though other accounts say that Yāmuna sent for Rāmānuja when he heard that he was being persecuted but died before Rāmānuja could reach him: the biographies of Rāmānuja are at least a hundred years later than his death and contain many inconsistencies. Initially, he lived as a temple-based *ascetic, and then travelled all over India, engaging in disputation especially with *Advaitins. He retired eventually to Śrīrangam in S. India where he died, traditionally in 1137. He was a *Śrivaiṣṇavite, who sought to give the devotional attitude implicit in that allegiance a more reflective and philosophical foundation. He accepted three means of knowledge: *pratykṣa* (perception), *anumāna* (inference), and *śabda or *śāstra* (verbal testimony). He accepted the basic texts of *Vedanta philosophy (the *Upaniṣads, the **Brahmasūtra*, and the **Bhagavad-gītā*), but he also allowed the authority of the hymns of the *Āḻvārs, the Pāñcarātra-Āgamas, and the *Viṣṇu-* and *Bhāgavata-purāṇas*.

The major works attributed to him are *Śrībhāsyam*, *Vedāntadīpah*, and *Vedāntaśarah* (all commentaries on the Vedanta Sūtras), a commentary on the *Gīta*, *Vedārthasamgrahah* (an exposition of his viewpoint), *Śaraṇāgatigadyam* (on self-surrender to God), *Śrīrangagadyam* (on the devotions and praise evoked by the Śrīrangam temple and its presiding deity), *Vaikuṇṭhagadyam* (on the nature of the liberated state), and *Nithyagranthah* (on worship).

Rāmānuja agreed with *Śaṅkara that *Brahman is that which truly is, without distinction (*advaita), but did not agree that there is nothing else that is real, and that all else is *māyā (appearance), the projection of *avidyā (ignorance). He held that individual selves and the world of matter (described in terms derived from *Sāṃkhya) are real, but that they are always dependent on Brahman for their existence and functions—hence his view is known as qualified non-duality, viśiṣtādvaita. Selves and matter are the instruments of Brahman in a relationship like that of souls and bodies (*śarīra-śarīrī-bhāva*); the relationship is described in many terms, e.g. as part to whole, as supported to supporter. Since Rāmānuja also differed from Śaṅkara in regarding Brahman, not as without characteristics (*nirguṇa), but as *Viṣṇu/Nārāyaṇa (i.e. as God), he could understand God as the material cause (*upādāna-kāraṇa*) and as the efficient cause (*nimitta-kāraṇa*) of the dependent realities. Although God is beyond description, nevertheless much can be inferred and attributed analogously to God from his manifestations in the world as *avatāra (incarnation). He is thus the source of grace (*anugraha*), seeking the salvation of those who turn to him, in a general way through revelation (*Veda), and in particular to his devotees. There are two means to *mokṣa (liberation): (i) *bhakti, devotion to God, which requires (*a*) discernment in matters of food purity, *viveka*; (*b*) non-attachment, *vimoka*; (*c*) constant meditation, *abhyāsa*; (*d*) performance of religious duties such as the five great sacrifices, *kriyā*; (*e*) performance of auspicious moral duties such as openness, truthfulness, *kalyāṇa*; (*f*) equanimity in the sense of transcending sorrow, and (*g*) joy, *anuddharṣa*; and (ii) *prapatti, as it was later called, self-surrender to God. The state attained through mokṣa is not, as for Śaṅkara, a union of total absorption in Brahman: selves remain distinct (though still dependent on Viṣṇu), and they remain in the service of Viṣṇu (*kaimkarya*) in his eternal abode (*Vaikuṇṭha).

J. B. Carman, *The Theology of Ramanuja* (1974); E. J. Lott, *God and the Universe in the Vedantic Theology of Ramanuja . . .* (1976); J. A. B. van Buitenen, *Rāmānuja on the Bhagavad-gītā* (1968).

Rām(a)prasād (18th cent.). Bengali Hindu saint and poet. He was devoted to *Kālī:

> O my mind, worship Kālī in any way you desire: repeat day and night the *mantra given to you by your *guru. When you lie down, think that you are prostrating yourself before her. . . . When you eat, think that you are making offerings to her . . . Rāmaprasād declares in joy that the Mother pervades all things.

It is said that when he was working as a bookkeeper, he was so preoccupied with Kālī that he entered, not figures, but poems in her honour. His employer provided him with a pension so that he would no longer need to work.

Rāmāyaṇa (The Exploits of Rāma). One of two major Hindu epics (the other being **Mahābhārata*), ascribed to *Vālmīki. For further details, see RĀMA.

Rambam (acronym): see MAIMONIDES.

Ramban (acronym): see NAḤMANIDES.

Ramcaritamānasa (work by Indian poet Tulsīdās): see TULSĪDĀS.

Rām Dās, Gurū (1534–81 CE). Fourth Sikh *Gurū. Rām Dās ('God's servant') was the name assumed by Jeṭhā ('first-born') on becoming Gurū in 1574.

Born to a *Soḍhī family in Lahore he later married Bībī Bhānī, daughter of Gurū *Amar Dās. Of their three sons, *Prithī Chand, Mahāndev, and *Arjan Dev, he chose the latter to succeed him. Rām Dās died in *Goindvāl.

As Śrī Jeṭhā, he served faithfully in Amar Dās' *Gurū-kā-laṅgar at Goindvāl. According to tradition, Amar Dās tested the suitability of his sons-in-law, Śrī Rāmā and Śrī Jeṭhā, for Gurūship by asking each to build and pull down a platform repeatedly. Jeṭhā's outstanding patience was rewarded.

As Gurū, Rām Dās is best remembered for founding *Amritsar, variously known as Gurū kā Chak, Chak Rām Dās, and Rāmdāspur. Reputedly the land was granted by emperor *Akbar to Bībī Bhānī. Rām Dās organized preaching through a network of *masands based in *mañjīs*. The *Ādi Granth contains 679 of his hymns (including *pauṛīs and *śaloks). His *Lāvān is central to Anand marriage.

Rāmdāsī or **Rāmdāsiā.** Sikh of the leatherworker *caste. People of *Chamār caste who became Sikhs were frequently called Rāmdāsī. The name may result from confusion between the names of Gurū *Rām Dās and *Ra(v)i Dās. The Rāmdāsīs were often *keśadhārī and abandoned the traditional occupation of tanning and cobbling. See also RAVIDĀSĪ.

Rāmgaṛhīā or **tarkhāṇ.** Sikh *caste (*zāt*, *jati). Many *gurdwārās bear this name, indicating their establishment by members of the local Rāmgaṛhīā community, although open to all, regardless of caste. In Britain, Rāmgaṛhīā Sikh families arrived mainly between 1960 and 1975, having had to leave E. Africa. A large proportion of the men are *keśadhārī, frequently wearing white *turbans.

Rāmgaṛhīā Sikhs take their name from the 18th-cent. *misl leader, Jassā Siṅgh Rāmgaṛhīā. His original name, Thokā, indicated his Tarkhāṇ (i.e. carpenter) caste. After playing a key role in relieving the besieged Rām Raunī fort near *Amritsar, he was appointed its governor. The fort was renamed Rāmgaṛh and from this he took his new title. Other tarkhāṇs and Sikh members of certain other artisan castes, especially masons and blacksmiths, also assumed the more prestigious name of Rāmgaṛhīā. A relatively large number of Rāmgaṛhīā Sikhs settled in E. Africa since the British needed skilled workers to construct the railway. They subsequently entered many professions. See also CASTE.

Ramḥal (acronym): see LUZMATTO, MOSES ḤAYYI.

Rāmlīlā (the playful delight of *Rāma). The dramatic exposition of the story of Rāma's exploits. It is enacted during the *Daśahrā festival, and is based on the work of *Tulsīdās.

Rām Mohan Roy (Hindu apologist and reformer): see ROY, RĀM MOHAN.

Rām Rāi (17th cent. CE). Son of Sikh Gurū *Har Rāi. Rām Rāi is regarded as an apostate. He incurred his father's displeasure by changing one of Gurū *Nānak's lines in the *Ādi Granth to satisfy emperor Auraṅgzeb at whose court he was detained. He substituted *beīmān* ('faithless') for *Mussalmān* ('Muslim') in the line 'The Muslim's clay comes under the potter's power'. Rām Rāi disputed the succession of his younger brother Har Krishan and great-uncle *Tegh Bahādur. His followers, the Rāmrāiyās, were hostile to subsequent Gurūs and their disciples. *Amritdhārī Sikhs are forbidden to associate with them, as with *Dhīr Mal's followers.

Rām Siṅgh (b. 1816). Founder of *Nāmdhārī Sikh movement. Rām Siṅgh, a carpenter from Bhainī *Sāhib, Pañjāb, was a disciple of *Bālak Siṅgh. He made Nāmdhārīs distinguishable from other Sikhs by their white turbans, tied in the manner of Gurū *Nānak's, their woollen *rosaries, style of worship, and greeting. He led resistance to the British authorities, prophesying a Sikh revival. In 1872, following the murder by Nāmdhārīs of Muslim cow butchers, he was exiled to Rangoon. Nāmdhārīs await his return to herald a new age, and thus, although non-Nāmdhārīs believe he died in 1885, Nāmdhārīs do not believe he has died.

Rānadé, Mahādev Govind (1842–1901). Indian lawyer and judge, who because of his keen powers of perception and analysis, became the leader of many social, political, industrial, and religious movements in Mahārāṣṭra. He regarded much in traditional Hinduism as destructive and enervating. He was the first to introduce the idea of *svadeshī* (home-produced goods) which was later used by *Tilak and others with some effect against the British Government in India. He supported the Hindu widow's remarriage movement and started Prārthanā Samāj at Bombay (Prayer Society, modelled on *Brahmo Samāj). He was a pioneer of reforming Hinduism, and of finding the inspiration within Hinduism for the reform of itself: 'Revival is impossible; as impossible as mass-conversion into other faiths. But even if it were possible, its only use to us would be if the reforms elevated us and our surroundings.' Thus, in his own case, he allowed himself to be cajoled into a second marriage (after his first wife died) with a girl of 12; but he then made sure that she became highly educated.

J. Kellock, *Mahadev Govind Ranade* (1926); R. P. Tucker, *Ranade and the Roots of Indian Nationalism* (1976).

Rang dong (*rang.stong*, 'Emptiness of Self'). The central doctrine of *Prāsaṅgika *Mādhyamaka. Rang dong is frequently misunderstood as meaning 'an object is empty of being itself'; Hopkins (1983) points out the error of this: 'If a table were empty of itself there would be no tables and, by extension, no phenomena'. In fact, rang dong is strictly the doctrine that all objects are empty of inherent existence, and is a statement about ultimate truth (*paramārtha satya*) from which standpoint the folly of conventional truth (*saṃvṛti satya*—that objects do have inherent existence) is realized. According to rang dong, the two levels of truth are themselves a convenient designation for the errors of consciousness—conventional truth is not true at all, it only appears to be. When the **Heart Sūtra* says: 'form is emptiness, emptiness is form', the implication is that there is only one true way of seeing things, by which form and emptiness are in some sense co-extensive. A difficulty arises in that when we are immersed through meditation in the perception of emptiness, the objects which are the basis for the imputation of that emptiness do not appear; similarly, when we perceive objects in everyday consciousness, their emptinesses do not appear. This no doubt contributed to the *zhen dong heresy, which sees form and emptiness as separate. The doctrine of rang dong, held chiefly by the *Geluk who assert it to be the teaching of *Nāgārjuna, requires that only Prāsaṅgika logic can cut through the apparent distinction, and that only in Buddhahood can form and emptiness be simultaneously comprehended.

J. Hopkins, *Meditation on Emptiness* (1983).

Raṅghṛetā (Raṅghar kā beṭā, i.e. child of a Raṅghar, Muslim outcaste group). Any *Mazhabī Sikh, who traces family association with Sikhism to Gurū *Gobind Siṅgh's period. According to tradition, emphasized by *Bālmīkis, a Raṅghṛetā brought *Tegh Bahādur's severed head to *Anaṇḍpur Sāhib for cremation by his son Gurū Gobind Siṅgh—who declared, 'Raṅghṛetās are the Gurū's children.'

Rañjīt Siṅgh, Mahārājā (1780–1839). Sikh ruler of *Pañjāb, 1799–1839. Rañjīt Siṅgh, son of Mahān Siṅgh, headed the Śukerchakīā *misl. He eventually gained overall supremacy between the Sutlej River and the Khyber Pass, ending Afghan influence in Pañjāb. After recapturing *Amritsar, he had the *Harimandir rebuilt and covered with gold leaf. Ranjīt Siṅgh's reign was the only period of *khālsā political sovereignty in Pañjāb. After his death, the kingdom disintegrated and was annexed by the British. His son, Duleep Siṅgh, the first Sikh to live in Britain, has achieved a symbolic importance in the community.

M. Alexander and S. Anand, *Queen Victoria's Maharajah* (1980).

Ransom. It is recognized in Judaism that compensation can be paid to avoid punishment, slavery, or death. In ancient Israel, it was common to pay ransom as an alternative to corporal punishment except in the case of murder (Numbers 35. 31–4). In general, compensation was assessed on a 'measure for measure' basis (Leviticus 24. 18), and later, set amounts were established (Deuteronomy 22. 29). It was also a religious duty to ransom Jewish captives, and it is said that a river parted to enable R. Phileas b. Jair to fulfil this obligation (*B.Hul.* 7a). The issue of whether a ransom is possible, or whether exact retribution must be made, was disputed between *Sadducees (who maintained that no ransom by way of payment is possible) and their opponents (who held that substitution by way of payment is possible except in cases of wilful murder). This means that the remark attributed to Jesus in Mark 10. 45 is more likely to be authentic than not, since there are other instances of Jesus using the current debates to make his own creative interpretation. For details see J. Bowker, *Jesus and the Pharisees* (1973).

Ranters. A loosely organized mid-17th-cent. radical group with *antinomian tendencies. Its leaders substantiated their individualistic teaching by appealing to revelatory experiences of the *Spirit or the indwelling *Christ. Jacob Bauthumley's *The Light and Darker Sides of God* expounds their *'inner light' teaching, whilst Joseph Salmon's writings represent the *pantheistic views of many Ranters. Accusations of immorality and popular confusion with the Quakers caused George *Fox to write vigorously against them and win converts from their ranks. The movement died out in the 17th cent., but the term was later used colloquially to describe the *Primitive Methodists.

Rantō (Jap., 'egg-shaped tower'). The tower which surmounts the tomb of a Zen monk.

Raphael (Heb., 'God is healing'). An angel recognized in Judaism and Christianity. Raphael appears in the *Apocrypha (*Tobit* 12. 15 and 1 *Enoch* 20. 3). He is one of the four archangels who defeats the *demon *Asmodeus and binds *Azazel. According to the *Talmud, he was one of the three angels who visited *Abraham after his *circumcision (*B.Yoma* 37a), and in *kabbalistic literature, he represents the earthly element, the green of the rainbow, and he brings relief to the sick: his name is often inscribed on amulets (*charms).

Rapture (Lat., *raptus*, 'seized'). The action in which believers will be 'caught up' (1 Thessalonians 4. 17; *Vulgate, *rapiemur*) to meet Christ in the air at his second coming (*parousia). Among *millennialists, it is a matter of dispute whether the Church will be thus removed from the earth before, during, or after the period of tribulation which is mentioned, e.g., in Revelation 7. 14. In mystical Christianity, rapture is the carrying away of the believer by the overwhelming power of God, a 'flight of the spirit'. Classic descriptions occur in *Teresa of Avila, *Life*, chs. 18 and 20, and *Interior Castle*, 6th Mansion, 4–6.

Rasa (Skt., 'relish', 'passion'). Hindu state of spiritual ecstasy in union with the divine. In a more general way, it then refers to the eight different sentiments or emotions, e.g. *raudra (see also ART). Rasa is analysed into its levels and constituent characteristics in the Gauḍīya-Vaiṣṇavism (*Caitanya) of Bengal (see S. K. De, *Early History of the Vaiṣṇava Faith . . . in Bengal*, 1961).

Rashal (acronym): see LURIA, SOLOMON.

Rashba (acronym): see ADRET, SOLOMON BEN ABRAHAM.

Rashbam (acronym): see SAMUEL BEN MEIR.

Rashi (acronym of Rabbi Solomon ben Isaac; 1040–1105). Jewish biblical and *Talmudic commentator. Miraculous stories are told of Rashi's birth. He grew up in Troyes in France and, having studied in Mainz and Worms, he returned to France where his school became one of the most famous in Europe. He wrote commentaries on all the books of the

Bible with the exception of *Ezra, *Nehemiah, *Chronicles, and the final chapters of *Job. The commentaries as they have been handed down include annotations by his students. They are largely based on *midrashic sources which he rewrote for greater clarity. He himself stated, 'As for me, I am only concerned with the literal meaning of the Scriptures and with such *aggadot as explain the biblical passages in a fitting manner.' His most important source was the *Targums, particularly Targum *Onkelos and Targum Jonathan, but on one occasion he declared, 'I have had no one to help me, nor a teacher, in all this edifice, but it is as revealed to me from Heaven.' He was a meticulous grammarian, and scattered through his work are remarks on grammar and syntax. His biblical commentaries were enormously popular, and he was influential on Christian as well as Jewish scholars. His commentary on the *Pentateuch was the first Hebrew book to be printed (1475). He also produced a commentary on the Babylonian Talmud, and this was published with the first printed edition of the Talmud. Again, with its realistic, comprehensible, and colourful explanations, it was extraordinarily popular. He was regarded as an *halakhic authority throughout France and Germany. According to legend, Rashi moved his school to Worms at the end of his life and, before the Second World War, his putative *bet ha-midrash could be visited adjoining the Worms Old *Synagogue.

Tr. M. Rosenbaum and A. M. Sitbermann, *Rashi's Commentary on the Pentateuch* (1929–34); H. Hailperin, *Rashi and His World* (1957).

Rashīd Riḍā (d. 1933). A Syrian Muslim, supporter of reform and an influential Muslim scholar. He championed *al-Afghānī and *ʿAbduh's vision of a dynamic Islam. Whereas the early reformers had dealt with the problem of Muslim weakness and backwardness in a general way, Riḍā was much more systematic. He saw the important need for modification of the existing *sharīʿa: Islamic law had to face the realities of the modern world. In this matter Riḍā adopted a very controversial position. He refused to admit that the four recognized law schools, *Mālikite, *Hanafite, *Shāfiʿite, and *Hanbalite, were binding upon the modern *'umma. Instead, Riḍā advocated that Islamic law be redrafted, based on the Qur'ān and sound *ḥadīth, in accordance with the light of changing times. The Prophet *Muḥammad 'acted according to circumstance'—adaptability was the key. Therefore, it was right for the religious scholar to act according to circumstances. Riḍā proposed that a council of Islamic experts be set up to reformulate a new sharīʿa for the needs of the 20th-cent. Muslim world, and thus obtain *ijmaʿ (consensus) of the Muslim community for the proposed reforms. Riḍā exerted a strong influence throughout the Muslim world through his journal *al-Manār* (The Lighthouse). In 1920, he was elected President of the Syrian National Congress, and in 1923 he published his views in *al-Khilafa* (The Caliphate).

Rāshidūn (first four successors of Prophet Muḥammad): see KHALĪFA (2).

Rashtriya Svayamsevak Sangh (Indian political militia): see BHARATYA JANATA PARTY.

Raskolniki (dissenting groups of Russian Orthodox Christians): see OLD BELIEVERS.

Ras Shamra. Site of the ancient city of Ugarit. Archaeological discoveries at Ras Shamra have added greatly to our knowledge of ancient *Canaanite customs and beliefs, especially through the Ugaritic texts. These relate myths which, although fragmentary and difficult to translate, suggest something of the context in which the faith of the bene Jacob (Israel) was formed.

G. R. Driver, *Canaanite Myths and Legends* (1956).

Rastafarians. Members of a *messianic religio-political movement originating among unemployed, landless, young men in Jamaica in the 1930s. It began under the influence of the Jamaican black nationalist, Marcus Garvey, and his 'Back to Africa' movement, which identified blacks as the true biblical *Jews, superior to whites, and surviving either in Ethiopia (see ETHIOPIANISM) or in Jamaica, where they had been exiled as a divine punishment. When Crown Prince (Ras) Tafari was crowned Ethiopian emperor in 1930 as Haile Sellasie, this was a sign that the sentence was completed, the *millennium was at hand, and the return to Africa would begin. Haile Sellasie was regarded as either a messiah or God. In 1955 he gave 500 acres of land for black people wishing to return, but in 1970 there were only twenty people living there. His dethronement in 1974 and death in 1975 had little effect on Rastafarians. Deputations touring Africa in the early 1960s, seeking acceptance, were unsuccessful, and more recent tendencies have been to find 'Africa' in Jamaica and replace repatriation by rehabilitation.

The movement first became visible in the 1930s when members formed peaceful communities living on the Kingston garbage dumps, and established distinctive modes of language, music, dress, 'dreadlock' hair forms, crafts, and lifestyle. European culture and Christian churches were rejected as 'Babylon'. They made their own selections from the Bible, eliminating the distortions introduced by its white translators, and adopted ganja (marijuana) as the sacramental herb for healing and meditation experiences. This, together with their fierce appearance and infiltration by violent or criminal elements, brought police persecution, but by the 1970s they were being courted for political support by the government party. By this time middle-class youth had begun to identify with the Rastafarian ideology and with the reggae music that carried this around the world, especially through singer Bob Marley and his band; for example, a visit to New Zealand resulted in the conversion of incorrigible Maori youth gangs to the Rastafarian ideology of love and peace, but devoid of the 'return to Africa' element. Emigrants carried the movement to other Caribbean islands, the USA, and Britain, but confusion with 'Black Power' or criminal groups has led to many difficulties. Emigrant Rastafarians often still regard themselves as only in transit to Ethiopia, and some have begun learning Amharic. Despite its wider influence, it is essentially a Jamaican movement.

In Jamaica it has never been centralized but has presented a great variety of forms (peaceful or violent, political or apolitical, using or rejecting ganja, 'dreadlocks' and 'clippies', unemployed or developing economic self-help enterprises) and has divided into many sections or new organizations with different names; some have joined the branch of the *Ethiopian Orthodox Church that was established in 1970 after encouragement both by government and the Christian churches. The total membership of what has been called the most dynamic religious movement in Jamaica may be as high as 100,000.

L. E. Barrett, *The Rastafarian Movement* . . . (1977); H. Campbell, *Rasta and Resistance* (1987); P. B. Clarke, *Black Paradise* (1988); T. C. Myers, *The Essence of Rastafari Nationalism and Black Economic Development* (1986); J. Owens, *Dread: The Rastafarians of Jamaica* (1976).

Rasūl (Arab., *rasala*, 'send'). One whom God sends, a messenger or apostle, and supremely, in Islam, the Prophet *Muḥammad (cf. *nabī). Each *'umma has received its rasūl (Qur'ān 10. 47; 16. 36), but Muḥammad was sent to a people who had not yet received a rasūl. Previous rasūls (*rusul*) in Qur'ān are Nūḥ (Noah), Lūt (Lot), Ismā'īl (Ishmael), Mūsa (Moses), Shu'aib, Hūd, Ṣāliḥ, and 'Īsā (*Jesus). They are regarded as being free from sin.

Ratana Church. The largest independent movement and the third largest religious group among the Maoris of New Zealand, with headquarters at Ratana Pa ('village') near Marton. It was founded by Tahupotiki Wiremu Ratana (1873–1939), a *Methodist farmer who in 1918 received a visionary call to destroy Maori religion and return to *Jehovah. In the 1918 world epidemic of influenza, he discovered his healing powers, and by 1919 crowds sought healing at Ratana Pa which developed into a model village. After initial co-operation with the churches, he formed the Ratana Church in 1925 which had some 25,000 members by the 1973 census, including about 1,000 whites. Ratana preached moral reform (no *alcohol or gambling) and promised the assistance of the holy angels in obeying the one God of the Bible who was revealed through the *Mangai* ('mouth-piece'), interpreted variously as Ratana himself or as the Spirit of God. Ratana members have held up to all four Maori seats in New Zealand's parliament and have exercised considerable political power. A secession, less political and with a strict ethic, formed in North Island in 1941 as the Absolute Established Maori Church of Aotearoa, and has remained very small.

Ratnākaraśānti. A Buddhist philosopher of the 11th–12th cents. CE. He was a member of the *Pramāṇa school of *Dignāga and *Dharmakīrti, and a pupil of Ratnakīrti. Ratnākaraśānti is also known as Śānti. His important works include commentaries on the 8,000- and 25,000-line *Prajñāpāramitā Sūtras* (*Perfection of Wisdom), the *Hevajratantra*, and the work of *Śāntarakṣita. The Tibetan doxographer Tāranātha believed there to be two separate 11th-cent. authors of the same name, but this has not been proved. Ratnākaraśānti is now chiefly notable as one of the final Indian systematizers of the *Mādhyamaka-Mantrayāna synthesis.

Ratnakūṭa or **Mahāratnakūṭa** (Skt., *ratna*, 'jewel' + *kūṭa*, 'mountain'). Collection of Buddhist *Mahāyāna scriptures. Although only four works are now extant in the original Skt. (*Ratnakūṭasūtra*, *Rāṣṭrapālaparipṛcchā*, *Sukhāvatīvyūha*, and *Aṣṭasahāsrikāprajñāpāramitā*), both Tibetan and Chinese sources assign forty-nine short titles to this collection. Thought to include the earliest of Mahāyāna *sūtras, Sinhalese tradition has it that the Ratnakūṭa originated amongst the Āndhras. Mahāyāna mythology states that the texts remained hidden in various non-human worlds from the time of the Buddha until their introduction into this world. It is known for certain that some of the collection was tr. into Chinese in the late 2nd cent. CE.

Ratnasaṃbhava (Skt., 'jewel-born one'). One of the five transcendent *Buddhas. He is linked to the earthly Buddha Kaśyapa and to the *bodhisattva Ratnapani. He is usually represented with the *mudra (hand gesture) of granting wishes.

Raudra (Skt., 'furious'). In Indian literature one of eight prevailing sentiments, *rasas. Raudra is based in turn on the complementary 'emotion' (*bhāva) of anger, *krodha*. The term raudra may also denote a follower of the god *Rudra or a class of evil spirits.

Rauschenbusch, W. (19th-cent. exponent of social gospel programme): see LIBERATION THEOLOGY.

Rav (Babylonian equivalent to Rabbi): see RABBI.

Rav (3rd cent. CE). Abba b. Arikha (i.e. 'the tall'). Jewish Babylonian *amora. Rav was the founder of the *academy at *Sura. He was called Rav (see RABBI) because he was 'the rav of the entire *diaspora' (*B.Bezah* 9a). Ordained by *Judah ha-Nasi in *Erez Israel, he was so respected that his independent authority was universally accepted: 'From the time Rav arrived in Babylonia, we in Babylonia have put ourselves on the same footing as Erez Israel with regard to . . .' (*BBK* 80a). He taught that study was 'more important than the offering of daily sacrifices' (*B.Er.* 63b), and that 'it is superior to building the *temple' (*B.Meg.* 16b). He defined 'the true Jew' as one who has compassion on all people, since those lacking in mercy have not inherited the compassion of *Abraham: 'God himself prays, "May my mercy overcome my anger."' He affirmed very strongly the goodness of God's creation (contrast *asceticism): 'All will be called to account in the world to come (*ʿOlam ha-Ba) for every enjoyment they refused in this world without sufficient cause.' The discussions of Rav are an important element in the Babylonian *Talmud.

J. Neusner, *A History of the Jews in Babylonia* (1966–70), *ad loc.*

Rava (4th cent. CE). R. Abba b. Joseph b. Ḥama. Jewish Babylonian *amora. The discussions of Rava and his companion *Abbaye are found throughout the Babylonian *Talmud. In general, the *halakhah follows Rava's opinion. His *academy at Mahoza attracted many students and his pupils took no satisfaction in the teachings of other sages (*B.Taʿan.* 9a). Despite his emphasis on the study of *Torah (he taught that study was an antidote to the evil *inclination), he maintained that 'the goal of wisdom is repentance and good deeds, so that a man should not study the Torah and *Mishnah, and then despise his father and mother' (*B.Ber.* 17a). He was insistent that religion can only be known in practice, in a kind of living exegesis of Torah based on constant study of Talmud (more important than prayer, because prayer is concerned with affairs of this world, but the study of Torah with one's eternal destiny); e.g. he stated that anyone who causes shame for another in public cannot have a share in the world to come.

J. Neusner, *A History of the Jews in Babylonia* (1966–70), *ad loc.*

Rāvaṇa. The demon king of Lanka and leader of the *rākṣasas. He is the antagonist of *Rāma, and is represented in *Ramāyāṇa* as the embodiment of evil. He is described as having ten heads and twenty hands. Through his severe *ascetic practices (*tapas) in early life, he obtained from *Brahmā exemption from death. His ensuing pride and arrogant behaviour led to the incarnation of *Viṣṇu as Rāma to destroy him.

Ra(v)i Dās or **Raidas** (14th–15th cent.). Indian saint-poet. Ravi Dās was a bhagat of *chamār *caste in the N. Indian *Sant tradition. Nothing is known of his life except that he was a Banāras leatherworker and reputedly, but implausibly, a disciple of *Rāmānanda. Legends abound, showing his miraculous powers and often linking him with the *brahman caste: e.g. jealous priests slashed his chest and found inside the thread (*janeu*) from his previous life. The *Ādi Granth contains forty of his *hymns, including an *Āratī hymn, all written down in the composite dialect of contemporary N. Indian Sants (Sādhukhaṛī or Santbhāṣā). These poems express his humble devotion to God, repetition of whose name saves one from rebirth. Caste is irrelevant to salvation. For the 20th-cent. Ād *Dharm or *Ravidāsī movement, Ravi Dās, venerated as *Gurū, is a focal, cohesive symbol.

Ravi Dās' poetry advocates total surrender to an absolute God beyond all attributes (*nirguna), whose grace and love save all kinds of beings, not just those who practise austerities (*tapas) and repetition (*japa). This grace comes through the guru or saint. The soul (*jīva) is attached to the world and because of this attachment is reborn. But with the grace of the guru and through remembering God's name (*nām) or sound, it becomes attached to God. Ravi Dās' poetry is characterized by a sense of helplessness before God and of great longing for union with God.

> O Lord Rām, life of creation, do not forget me
> I am your slave.
> Remove my calamity, bestow love on your servant.
> I do not let go your feet
> Though my body be consumed.

(Ādi Granth, Rāg Gaurī, Ravi Dās 1)

W. M. Callewaert and P. Friedlander, *The Life and Works of Raidas* (1992). Darshan Singh, *A Study of Bhakta Ravidāsa* (1981).

Ravidāsī. Religious movement among Pañjābīs of the leatherworker *caste. The memory of *Ra(v)i Dās survived with a loose network of shrines (*dehrās*) serving as focal points for *chamār devotion. However, the Ravidāsī movement only took shape in the early 20th cent., as members of lower castes, especially urban, educated chamārs, sought religious and political identity. They called their religion Ād *Dharm (the original religion). In 1907 *Sant Hirān Das established a Ravi Dās Sabhā, soon followed by other *dehrās* in *Pañjāb.

Many scheduled-caste Pañjābīs migrated to Britain between 1950 and 1968. Local Ravi Dās associations were formed to establish temples, e.g. in Wolverhampton and Coventry. Pictures of Ravi Dās, their *Gurū, are prominently displayed, and his *śabad (*hymns) from the *Ādi Granth are sung in congregational worship resembling Sikh *dīvān. At the close of *Ardās, Gurū Ravi Dās' name is coupled with Gurū *Nānak's.

Despite affinity to Sikhism, Ravidāsīs frequently have Hindu names and are clean-shaven. Their major festival is Gurū Ravi Dās' birthday. See also AMBEDKAR; BĀLMĪKI; GURPURB; MAZHABĪ; RĀMDĀSĪ.

M. Juergensmeyer, *Religion as Social Vision* (1982).

Rawḍa khānī or **rawẓah-khvānī.** Ritual recitation in Iran by Shiʿites of the sufferings and martyrdoms of *Imāms, and especially of *al-Ḥusain. These are particularly prominent on 10 Muḥarram, when public processions take place with many emulating the sufferings of the Imāms with self-laceration and beatings. See also TAʿZIYA.

Raychandbhai Mehta: see RĀJACANDRA, ŚRĪMAD.

Rāzī: see AL-RĀZĪ (Abū Bakr; and Fakhr al-Dīn).

Raziel, Book of. Jewish mystical collection, which, on its own account, was conveyed to *Adam by the angel, Raziel. The *Book of Raziel* was first printed in 1701, and ownership of it was believed to protect the owner's house from danger. It consists of works on *merkabah mysticism and other literature dating from the *Talmudic and *geonic period, as well as works dating from the 13th cent. which originated in the *Ḥasidei Ashkenaz movement. Some manuscripts of parts of the *Book of Raziel* date back to the 16th cent. *Sefer ha-Razin* is a related book, conveyed to *Noah, which contains comparable material on mysticism and magic.

Ṛddhipāda (four components of power in Buddhism): see IDDHI-PĀDA.

rDzogs-chen (Atiyoga): see DZOGCHEN.

Reading of the Law: see TORAH, READING OF.

Realism: see NOMINALISM.

Real presence. In Catholic and some *Protestant teaching, the presence of the body and blood of Christ in the *eucharist. According to the Council of *Trent (1551): 'After the *consecration of the bread and wine, our Lord Jesus Christ . . . is truly, really and substantially contained under the perceptible species of bread and wine.' This formulation was intended to refute the more radical Protestant positions, that the eucharist was a memorial celebration. The specifically Catholic aspects of the doctrine are: (i) its understanding in terms of *transubstantiation, and (ii) its consequences for eucharistic devotions such as the *exposition of the sacrament.

Rebbe (Yid., 'teacher'). Jewish teacher. It is the title given by the *Ḥasidim to their spiritual leader. See also LUBAVI(T)CH; ZADDIK.

Rebecca (Rebekah). Wife of Isaac and one of the matriarchs of Israel. She was chosen by God to be Isaac's wife, because of her kindness to Eliezer, *Abraham's servant. She was the mother of the twins, *Jacob and Esau, the root of the schism between worshippers of God and idolaters. According to *aggadah, while she was pregnant, whenever she passed a house of *Torah study, Jacob struggled to get out, but when she passed a temple containing idols, Esau struggled to get out. She was buried in the cave of *Machpelah.

Rebellious elder (Heb., *zaqen mamre*). A stubborn, qualified teacher in Judaism who insists on his own opinion, even though the majority opinion is against him. Such a person, according to Deuteronomy 17. 8–13, must be taken through the whole range of available courts, culminating in whatever is the highest authority, 'the judge who shall be in those days'. If the teacher persists in his own opinion, he must be executed, because, as the *rabbis later put it, he is creating two *Torahs (*toroth*) in Israel, which destroys the *raison d'être* of Israel. In a graphic incident, R. Eliezer once claimed that his view on the purity of a type of oven was correct, but the other *ḥakhamim disagreed. R. Eliezer called on miracles to demonstrate that he was correct, culminating in an appeal to God himself: the *bath qol (the echo of God's voice) said that 'the law is according to R. Eliezer in all matters'. Even then the ḥakhamim refused, saying that God had entrusted the interpretation of Torah to his people, and that the majority must be correct: 'It is not in heaven.' Since *Jesus was investigated for a threat to the *Temple authority (cf. also Stephen, Acts 6. 13), and since he was eventually taken before the highest judge of the time, it is likely that Jesus was being investigated to see whether he came within the category of *zaqen mamre*, which would unquestionably have been an offence deserving the death penalty.

Rebellious son (Heb., *ben sorer u-moreh*). Jewish Commandment which was not counted in the 613 commands of *Torah, on the ground that it could never be applied. It is the command in Deuteronomy 21. 18–21, which requires that 'a stubborn and rebellious son who will not listen to the voice either of his father or of his mother and, even when they punish him, will not pay attention to them', must, after due process, be stoned to death. However, *Talmud places such conditions that the law is impracticable: the son must be within three months of his *bar mitzvah, must have stolen in order to buy a prodigious amount of food and drink, must have already been disciplined by his parents, and must have been warned in front of three witnesses. *B.Sanhedrin* 71a comments: 'There never was and never will be a rebellious son. So why was the law given? For us to receive the reward of studying it.'

Rebirth. The belief (also transmigration, *metempsychosis, reincarnation, etc.) common in Eastern religions, that there is a continuity from one life to a next, either of a self or soul (see e.g. ĀTMAN), or, in the case of Buddhism, of the process itself. Buddhism teaches a *karmically controlled continuity of consciousnesses between lives but denies that there is an ātman or inherently existing self which is the bearer of these consciousnesses (see *punabhāva). The feeling of self at any given moment is valid but this self is a dynamic coherence (Skt., *santāna*, 'continuum') which changes constantly throughout a lifetime and changes profoundly between lifetimes. Thus, it is more accurate to say that there is rebirth but not transmigration. There are six realms of rebirth: three are pleasant (peaceful deities (*deva), wrathful deities (*asura), and humans), and three are unpleasant (animals, hungry ghosts (*preta), and hell-beings). The human realm is the most fortunate since in it the path to *nirvāna can be most easily discerned and followed.

In Hinduism also, rebirth may be in many forms, including those of animals, and on many levels of heavens and hells (see e.g. NARAKA); in fact, rebirth as a human is rare, and is an opportunity to bring the process of 'wandering' (*saṃsāra) to an end in *mokṣa (release) or nirvāna. Short of such attainment, the outcome of each new birth is governed by *karma, an exact law of consequence. Terms for rebirth in Skt. include *punarājātī, *punarāvritti*, *punarutpatti*, *punarjanman*, *punarjīvātu*. Among Jains, for whom karma is an accumulated impediment, rebirth of the *jīva is immediate and instantaneous, 'leaping like a monkey' (*Viyahapannatti Bhagavai*), which eradicated the need for *ancestor rituals, and for speculation about what supports the soul or process as it awaits rebirth (as in Hinduism and Buddhism). All these religions emphasize the importance of the right mental and spiritual formation at the moment of death in order to secure a good rebirth. Ideas of rebirth have appeared in Western religions, but have remained marginal: see DIBBUK; GILGUL; ORIGEN; TANĀSUKH. See also TIBETAN BOOK OF THE DEAD; Index, Rebirth.

S. G. F. Brandon, *Man and His Destiny in the Great Religions* (1962); J. Head and S. L. Cranston, *Reincarnation* . . . (1977).

Recapitulation (Lat. *recapitulatio*; Gk., *anakephalaiōsis*, 'summing up, summary'). In the writings of the Christian *fathers, the restoration of fallen humanity to communion with God through the obedience of Christ. The concept derives from Ephesians 1. 10, where God is said to sum up all things in Christ, and was first elaborated by *Irenaeus. The term is also used in patristic literature to refer to the summing-up of the previous revelations of God in the *incarnation.

Rechabites. A Jewish religious sect mentioned by *Jeremiah. The Rechabites claimed descent from Jonadab, a contemporary of King Jehu. They seem to have been related to the *Kenites (1 Chronicles 2. 55), they were tent-dwellers and abstained from wine (Jeremiah 35. 19). According to the *Mishnah, 'the children of Jonadab' had a fixed day each year for bringing wood to the *Temple (*Ta'an.* 4. 5), and the *Midrash traces 'water-drinking sacrificers' to Jonadab (*Sif. Num.* 78, 81). It seems clear that they are an early instance of 'tradition-fundamentalists', who adhered to what had been established in the Wilderness period of the *Exodus, and who refused innovations (e.g. wine, since vines could not be planted and harvested in that period).

Recollection. The concentration of one's mental powers, especially the will, on the presence of God, perhaps best known as one of *Teresa of Avila's states of prayer. More generally a state of composedness in one's everyday life as a result of which one's sense of the presence of God is only barely subconscious. It requires the deliberate 'gathering together within oneself of the vagabond mind'.

Reconstructionism. A modern movement within Judaism. Reconstructionism was inspired by Mordecai *Kaplan who argued that Judaism was an evolving religious civilization. The movement became formal with the founding of the Society for the Advancement of Judaism in 1922, in New York. In 1935, the *Reconstructionist* magazine was founded to disseminate his ideas, and in 1945 the Reconstructionist **Sabbath* **Prayer Book* appeared. It included neither the idea of *Chosenness of the Jewish people, nor that of God's revelation to *Moses on Mount *Sinai, nor that of a personal *messiah. In 1968, a *rabbinical college was established in Philadelphia. Although there are few Reconstructionist congregations, Reconstructionist ideas have been highly influential in the American Jewish community. See also CONSERVATIVE JUDAISM; Index, Reconstructionist Judaism.

M. Ben Horin, *Common Faith—Uncommon People: Essays in Reconstructionist Judaism* (1970); M. Kaplan, *Judaism as a Civilization* (1934).

Rector. The title of certain Christian priests: (i) in the Church of England, an incumbent of a parish whose *tithes were in the past not appropriated by anyone else (cf. VICAR); (ii) in the Roman Catholic Church a priest serving certain churches other than parish churches; (iii) the head of a Catholic seminary or university.

Recusancy (Lat., *recusare*). Refusal to attend *Church of England services as required by the 1559 Act of Uniformity. *Nonconformists were therefore also recusants, but the term is more usually reserved for *Roman Catholics. The penalty for non-attendance was originally fixed at 12d. for each offence. It was later heavily increased, though the full weight of fines and other penalties was rarely imposed. Many RCs had at first conformed, but the incidence of 'church papists' declined after the *excommunication of Elizabeth and the arrival of *Jesuits and other newly trained clergy. From 1592 to 1691 convicted recusants, including *Protestants, were listed on special Recusancy Rolls. The offence of recusancy was abolished by the Catholic Relief Act of 1791.

Redeemer liveth (mistranslation): see REDEMPTION.

Redemption

Judaism The Heb. words *padah* and *ga'al* were used originally of commercial transactions, implying the existence of prior obligations (for examples, see Leviticus 25, 27). *Ga'al* is also used of the brothers of someone who has died childless: they are under obligation to 'redeem' the name of the deceased (Ruth 4. 1–10; Deuteronomy 25. 5–10). The *go'el* is the blood-avenger of Numbers 35. 12–29; in Job 19. 25 (translated, of old, 'I know that my redeemer (*go'el*) liveth') it is a legal term: 'I know that my advocate is active'. These basic meanings were all transferred as metaphors of God's activity, nature, and commitment.

According to the biblical *prophets and the *Psalmist, God will redeem his people from oppression (Isaiah 1. 27) and death (Hosea 13. 14), and he is described as 'the father of orphans, defender of widows' (Psalm 68. 6). It was God who redeemed his chosen people from slavery in Egypt and ultimately would restore them and establish an everlasting *covenant. The *Dead Sea sect seem to have believed in redemption at the end of time, 'when God with his truth will clarify the deeds of humanity' (*Manual of Discipline* 2. 20), and the *Talmud taught that such redemption is dependent on good deeds and repentance (*B.Yoma* 86b). The *messiah would bring about these eschatological events and all the righteous *gentiles as well as Jews would be brought 'beneath the wings of the *Shekhinah' (*Tanḥ.B., Gen.* 108). The medieval philosophers continued to emphasize that final redemption involves both the restoration of the land of *Israel to the Jewish people and a final judgement by which those righteous in thought and deed will be saved. The *kabbalists understood redemption as a process by which the Shekhinah returns to God and the unity of the Godhead is fully restored. In modern times, the emphasis has become more 'this-worldly', and redemption tends to be understood as the triumph of good over evil in human history or in the individual's personal life. See also ZIONISM.

Christianity In Christian theology the term is inherited from the New Testament, where it is associated with the death of Christ (e.g. Ephesians 1. 7). For this conception and its later developments see ATONEMENT. The actual metaphor of 'redeeming' or 'ransoming' has been more prominent in some formulations than others, and has caused well-known problems when pressed: e.g. whether the price or *ransom is thought of as paid to *Satan or to God himself (see also SALVATION). More generally and loosely, the term is now used of the process whereby the human race is restored to that communion with God, for which it was created, through the salvific work of *Christ.

More loosely still, redemption is then applied to salvific processes and achievements in other religions—e.g. the work of *bodhisattvas in Mahāyāna Buddhism.

Redemptorists (Christian missionary order): see LIGUORI, ALPHONSUS.

Red Hats. A loose term used by early W. commentators on Tibetan Buddhism to refer sometimes to the *Nyingma school, sometimes to the students of the Zhamar ('Red Hat') *Rinpoche as if these constituted a subschool within the Karma *Kagyü, and sometimes to refer to all Tibetan Buddhist schools collectively, in contradistinction to the *Geluk school who are colloquially called *Yellow Hats. The term 'Red Hats' is not used among Tibetans themselves.

Red Hats (Turkish adherents of the Ṣafavis): see ṢAFAVIDS.

Red Hats (rebels in China): see RED TURBANS.

Red heifer (Heb., *parah adummah*). The animal used in Jewish ritual purification of persons or objects defiled by contact with a dead body (Numbers 19. 1–22). According to Numbers 19. 3, the heifer had to be slaughtered outside the camp and the carcass burned. The ashes were combined with spring water and used for purification on the third and seventh day after defilement. The tractate *Parah* in the *Talmud discusses the laws of the red heifer. Although no more heifers could be sacrificed after the destruction of the *Temple, because some ashes still remained, the rituals continued until late into the *amoraic period (*B.Nid.* 6b). It is believed that nine animals have been utilized in this way, and that the *messiah will supervise the burning of the tenth.

Red letter day. Important feast or saint's day (in Christianity), printed in *calendars in red.

Red Sea, crossing of (Heb., *keriyat yam suf*; possibly 'reed' rather than 'red'). The miraculous event which enabled the Israelites to escape from the pursuing armies of the Egyptians at the beginning of the *Exodus. The parting of the waters was a reward for the faith of the first Israelite who put his sandal in the water (or also because of the faith of the *patriarchs; see MERITS OF THE FATHERS). The angels wanted to sing a hymn of praise but were prevented by God who refused exultation when his creatures had been drowned; nevertheless, the Israelites were permitted the song in Exodus 15.

Red Turbans. Rebel and millenarian bands, associated with the *White Lotus, which appeared during the Yuan dynasty (1260–1367) in China. The 'turbans' were in fact sashes, but were sometimes worn round the head. They believed in the imminent return of *Maitreya, and went before him to prepare his way.

Reformation, the. Movements for reform in the Christian Church in the West, which took place in the early 16th cent. This was arguably the greatest crisis in Christendom before the challenges of the present time. Modern scholarship no longer seeks to spell out the causes of a reformation movement in simplistic terms, and it is very important to think of *reformations* in the plural. There was a near-infinite variety of protest among factions and groups of Christian people in Western Europe concerned to question traditional religion, its theory and practice. In some quarters these critiques of Roman *papal orthodoxy and the Catholic *status quo* were referred to as the search for 'a new divinity'; and when the original protestors gained a following, they were known eventually as 'protestants'. The differences between the reformations owed much to the interaction between innovative theologians and the interests of rulers and ruled in allowing varying ideas to flourish while avoiding war, either civil or international. It is, therefore, helpful to see the reformations in terms of their common intellectual background and of the varying interpretations to which this was put.

Universities in the West had long sought to contain the revival of *Aristotle. The problems he posed for the Christian creed spawned centuries of *scholastic debate, and endless ideological controversies. Remote from such high-level reasoning, medieval families were caught up in a lay piety which sought to highlight practice and not to look to its reasoned defence. Orthodoxy in the late medieval parish was dominated by what has aptly been described as 'the mechanics of ritualised religion', which put faith into non-verbal language. Worship was focused on the celebration of the *Mass. The *priests who regularly offered the sacrifice, and irregularly communicated the people, possessed few books apart from the *Missal and the *Breviary. The rhythms of the *Liturgy thus became the rhythms of life itself, and medieval people, revering the sheer spectacle of the Mass, were encouraged to find a spirituality of devotion to the Virgin *Mary and to *saints, which made Christianity very much 'a cult of the living in the service of the dead'.

In the critical appraisal of academic debate, with its distance from pastoral involvement, was Desiderius *Erasmus (*c.*1466–1536). He sought a textual basis for faith. Combining linguistic competence from the world of antiquity with knowledge of sacred literature in a widely varied church tradition, he forwarded what he held to be the authentic philosophy of Jesus Christ (*philosophia Christi*). His *Enchiridion* (1503) set out, in sensitive spiritual writing, a vision of undogmatic Christianity, with a piety open to all, and by no means limited to those, under vows, who were priests or members of religious orders. His cry that 'Monkery is not piety', but merely *one* among many vocations, resonated around Europe, just as, in skits for the schoolroom intended to improve his pupils' written style, his *Colloquies* popularized the need for Church reform 'in head and members'. In his aim to secure religious, moral, and social reform, he anticipated much of the programme later adopted by *Luther (1483–1546), and by the Swiss and other 'protestant' theologians. His influence was also felt throughout the Catholic Church, not least in his work on the *New Testament, writing a critical exposition of the received text. Taking a lead from the Italian humanist, Lorenzo Valla (*c.*1406–57), and his critique (*The Annotations*) of the Latin Bible (*Vulgate), Erasmus aspired to be the new *Jerome. His *magnum opus* and crowning achievement was his edition of the Greek New Testament, *Novum instrumentum omne* . . . (1516), showing how the Vulgate had embraced inaccuracies from the Greek, and had thus distorted the meaning of Scripture. Erasmus avoided the fire of those who could have sent him to the stake as an heretic, and survived instead to become the darling of Europe for the wit and learning of a New Testament scholarship set out in a whole series of *Annotations* and *Paraphrases*. He had no desire simply to excite the universities. He wanted lay people to read the Bible. In this he was helped by the recent invention of printing. But it was for others to work out what the pastoral and theological consequences would be of accurate, widely available Bibles, especially when translated into the vernacular.

The lead from university to parish was made by Luther. He is usually remembered for his outburst against the selling of *indulgences, and for his challenge to Johann *Tetzel (*c.*1465–1519), with the wild claim that 'So soon as coin in coffer rings| The soul from Purgatory springs'. Luther was principally concerned with the biblical issues which scholastic theology obscured. While still an Augustinian friar, he struggled spiritually (in his Tower experience in his cell at Wittenberg) to know how he, a sinner, could be saved. Directed to search the Scriptures by Johann von Staupitz (?1469–1524; 'If Dr. Staupitz had not helped me . . . I should have been swallowed up and left in Hell'), he resolved his crisis of conscience in an understanding of *justification by faith *alone* (*justificatio sola fide*), which he held out as a 're-discovery' of the gospel. Moving away from *Augustine, he understood justification as the instantaneous realization that sinners are forgiven and made righteous by the work of the crucified Christ. By imputation, fallen humanity had been reconciled in Christ to God the Creator. Thus salvation is not a gradual process or accumulation of *intrinsic* righteousness. It is altogether *extrinsic*, accomplished, not by 'a passive righteousness' (i.e. 'not by pieces but in a heap'). The unmerited grace of the Almighty is conveyed to sinners because of the atoning work of Christ on the Cross (*Sermon of the Threefold Righteousness*, 1518). Luther's stand as a reformer is far clearer in the *Christocentric* emphasis of the Heidelberg Disputation (Apr. 1518), with its theology of the Cross, its contrast of 'law' and 'gospel', and its departure from scholasticism, than in the notoriety he gained by circulating *Ninety-Five Theses* (Oct. 1517) in order to debate the indulgence controversy.

Nothing in W. Christendom was quite the same again. Although Luther's teaching remained uncondemned in the university of Paris, he was summoned to appear before a panoply of secular and ecclesiastical power at the next Imperial Diet (the parliament of the Holy Roman Empire). Already threatened with excommunication (**Exsurge Domine* gave him sixty days to recant), the Edict of Worms (May 1521) outlawed him and placed him under ban for seeking to 'disseminate errors and depart from the Christian way'. He was saved by another of the key factors in the reformations: the lay ruler of his country, Friedrich, Elector of Ernestine Saxony (from 1486 to 1525), smuggled him into exile. Kidnapped, he was taken to Wartburg, and there, in a seclusion which he called 'my Patmos', he worked out the full implications of his stand, with profound consequences. In two tracts of 1520, he had already sought to recruit both secular authority and sympathetic clergy. A third, the celebrated *Treatise of the Liberty of a Christian Man* (1520), commended the new faith to those who would know Christ. He now pondered the principles of a pastoral reformation, and was able (brilliantly) to retranslate the New Testament into German 'which so many people are anxious to have'. Trouble in Wittenberg led him to return. As the professor in the pulpit, it was his style to lay down ground rules for reformation in a revival of the teaching and preaching of Christ, deploring the exclusive and mediatory power of the priesthood. But he was conservative when contrasted with the radicalism of the Peasants' Revolt which so nearly ruined the whole cause. With the aid of *Melanchthon (1497–1560), he masterminded a visitation of Saxon churches, and by his *Catechisms* (1529) he sought to instruct 'common people', who 'especially in the villages' knew 'nothing at all of Christian doctrine'. His ministry has hardly been paralleled. Embattled in controversy with *both* radicals *and* 'holy Rome', he proved a natural leader and pastor, whose spiritual perception guided him through decaying ecclesiastical structures to found in 'protestantism' a new kind of Church for a rapidly changing world. His output was immense, whether in Bible commentary and translation (*Die Deutsche Bibel* was complete in 1534), hymns (mainly written in 1523–4), lectures, liturgy (*Deutsche Messe und Ordnung Gottes diensts*, 1526), innumerable polemical tracts against countless opponents (the break with Erasmus came with *On the Bondage of the Will* in 1525), key confessional treatises (especially *Das diese Worte Christi*, 1527, and *Vom Abendmahl . . . Bekenntnis*, 1528, maintaining the 'real presence' in the Lord's Supper), or the collected *Table Talk* gossip which still brings him alive as raconteur and critic on the issues of his day.

Luther was protected in his 'reformation' by a prince. Another reformer, Ulrich *Zwingli (1484–1531), addressed himself to a very different task in his Swiss City State, with different results: Zwingli in Zurich illustrates the way a people's priest (*Leutpriester*) might work with the civic authorities and, by public disputation, defeat the bishop and his representative in debate. The argument that popular demand could legitimately accomplish the will of God (*vox populi* being accounted *vox Dei*) enabled Zwingli to abolish the Mass in Zurich (1525) and to secularise convents and monasteries to fund the common chest. Similar disputation soon secured support for reformers in other cities and cantons, notably Constance, Berne, St Gallen, Biel, Muhlhausen, and Basle. But the Swiss reformation did not help Luther. As he and Zwingli were largely working independently in different circumstances, so differences between them emerged. Thus Zwingli repudiated the presence of Christ in the *elements, and attempts to heal the divisions at the Colloquy of Marburg (Oct. 1529) failed, despite the efforts of Landgraf Philipp of Hesse (1504–67).

Again distinct but of huge consequence for the W. Church was the work and ministry of John *Calvin (1509–64), who promoted John *Knox (the reformer in Scotland, *c.*1505–72) to proclaim *Geneva 'the most perfect school of Christ that ever was in earth since the days of the apostles'. Calvin, just after he had published *The Institutes* (*Christianae Religionis Institutae*, 1536), was diverted to Geneva because of troop movements in the Italian Wars. Recognized by the fiery Farel (1489–1565), he was prevailed on to help those who had only 'a little while before expelled the papacy' from their midst. By 1538, when the authorities reacted again and repudiated the reform party, he reached Strasburg, enjoying an influential three-year stay with Martin *Bucer (1491–1551), writing the brilliant *Reply to Sadolet* (Jacopo Sadoleto, the cardinal who had been attempting to win back Geneva). The pause was not to last. In 1541 the Magistracy of Geneva invited him to fill a preaching role at the Cathedral of St Pierre. For the next twenty-five years he became a prophet of Christian order, denouncing the religion of Rome as a legal tyranny and as entirely false by the standards of The *Acts of the Apostles and of the organization of the primitive Church. His *Ecclesiastical Ordinances* (1514) repudiated the role of bishops and priests, arguing instead for the oversight of ordained 'pastors' and 'doctors' (teachers), and the new lay offices of 'elder' and 'deacon'. He was never fully accepted in Geneva (because of his Picard origins) and was regularly tried almost beyond endurance as Consistory vied with Magistracy for civic supremacy and care of the godly. But his preaching and teaching were profoundly influential, with a wide missionary outreach propagating the principles of reformation as he conceived them. Luther's faith, in contrast, had spread only indirectly as students returned from Wittenberg to their native land. The Petri brothers, for instance, did much to reform the Swedish Church, Laurentius securing appointment as Archbishop of Upsala in 1531; and in Denmark, Hans Tausen consolidated the work he had begun there by persuading the king, Christian III (1533–59), to invite Bugenhagen (1485–1558) to set to work on a Danish Church Order, aided by the Wittenberg parish pastor, Justus Jonas (1493–1555). The influence of Calvin was far more direct through his College of Geneva, founded in 1559 to prepare pastors to promote biblical theology throughout Europe (and later, via England, Scotland, and Holland, to evangelize the New World). The definitive edition of *The Institutes* was published in that year and adopted as a training text. Calvin succeeded in reaching a measure of agreement with Zwingli in 1549 (*Consensus Tigurinus*) and thus did something to correct the divisive effects of the number of different Protestant reformations.

Unlike the Protestant reformation in Europe, the reformation in England focused first on the needs of the ruler and only secondly on a desire to change theological formulae and lay piety. Movements to reform the universities were flourishing, with Greek scholars and influential theologians at both Oxford and Cambridge. Such reforms were a development, rather than a protest against the domination of pope and priest. The earlier protests of John *Wycliffe and of the Lollards, and the movement toward vernacular Scripture, tended to be confined to an area and to be successfully persecuted as 'heresy'. The desire of Henry VIII (1491–1547, r. 1509–47) to annul his marriage with Catherine of Aragon obliged him to repudiate the restrictions of Roman canon law and ultimately the papacy itself. He used the Parliament of England to help him, and he put in positions of strategic importance Thomas Cromwell (*c.*1485–1540) and Thomas *Cranmer, the former as Secretary and Vicegerent, the latter as Archbishop of Canterbury. They steered a largely reluctant king toward the dissolution of the monasteries, a number of restatements of doctrine, and (most importantly) the order that a Bible in English should be put in every church (1539).

By the time Henry died a *Litany in English had been produced, but under his son, Edward VI, liturgical reform began in earnest, with the **Book of Common Prayer* of 1549, revised in 1552. An archiepiscopal coup (often overlooked in its importance) was Cranmer's success in persuading Martin *Bucer, exiled from the Imperial city of Strasburg by the Interim of the Diet of Augsburg (1548), to come to England. The presence at Lambeth of such a significant first-generation reformer, and his appointment as Regius Professor of Divinity at Cambridge, strengthened the impact of Swiss and South German theology. It was balanced by the humanist Oecolampadius (1484–1531) whose use of the *fathers was formative in the debate about the Eucharist. Had the boy-king lived, reformation in England would have been different: his death in 1553 illustrates the crucial importance of supportive secular authority.

Edward was succeeded by the daughter of Catherine of Aragon, Mary. She reinstated the power of the papacy and a medieval liturgy in Latin, which again raised questions about the place of Scripture and lay involvement. Cranmer was burned, and the stage was set for the restoration of Catholicism. It was not to be. In 1558 Mary was succeeded in England by Elizabeth (1533–1603, r. 1558–1603). Elizabeth owed her birth to her father's repudiation of Rome, and she knew the pain that religious upheaval caused. She has been imprisoned by Mary and narrowly escaped death. Her cousins had been less fortunate. Under her, with the help of Parliament and of Matthew *Parker, her able Archbishop of Canterbury, a Protestant settlement of religion was established by law. The *Book of Common Prayer* of 1552 was adopted with emendations; the Church was to be episcopally governed under the Queen and Parliament. The theological enquiry and defence of the settlement resumed, notably at the hands of John Jewel (1522–71) and Richard *Hooker (1553–1600). Gradually parishes in England came into step.

Most Protestant reformations had an extremist fringe. *Anabaptism developed from Zwinglianism ('They have sprung from us', Zwingli recorded). At Munster in 1535 starry-eyed zealots established a community for the millennium under Bockelson as *King John*. Besieged for almost a year, it was a sectarian regime that withstood combined Catholic and 'protestant' troops until the violent wing of such *radicalism was discredited, and lawful authority was restored. Henceforth extremists were hard-pressed, with their principled protest that 'infant *baptism is no baptism' taking them into a wilderness of dissent. Persecution was answered with non-resistance, and in such men as Denck (whom Bucer called 'the Anabaptist Pope'), Franck (1499–1542), and Schwenkfeld (1490–1561), mysticism, liberalism, pacifism, and above all toleration were prized as, not merely a vital agenda, but an altogether new emphasis which characterized 'root-and-branch' reformation.

Throughout the 16th cent., the Catholic Church also underwent reformation. This spontaneous movement to reform the religious life, to re-evangelize Protestant countries, and to convert the newly discovered peoples of America and of the East, was associated with the emergence of the new religious Order of *Jesuits, under *Ignatius of Loyola. His deep spiritual vision and stern understanding of discipline gave Catholic Europe a task-force undeterred by the threat of persecution or the lonely deprivation involved in seeking the soul of China or Japan. Other Orders were reformed, especially in Spain with St *Teresa of Avila and St *John of the Cross, with an influence still felt today. The attempts by the Council of Trent (1545–7, 1551–2, 1562) to heal the rifts in Christian unity were a failure, but the Council achieved new definitions of justification and a revised liturgy. Papal sovereignty became more firmly entrenched, with permanent status being given to Congregations (committees of *cardinals) such as those which formed the *Inquisition (1542) and *Index (1566) to safeguard Catholic faith and practice.

The resulting transformation of Europe at the hands of different reformers was the rending of the seamless robe (not regretted by the 19th–cent. historian von Ranke, who argued that the progress of European culture 'had taken the place of ecclesiastical unity'). This was the price paid for a Catholic Church no longer as corrupt in its head and members as it had been when Erasmus surveyed it. The Protestants also contributed a much more informed and individually aware acceptance of faith which was manifest in family life and prayers, in a certain gravity of dress, and in diligent responsibility in work and play. All the reformations, Protestant or Catholic, needed to use education to their own advantage: schools were founded and refounded, and the advance of literacy meant that reason ultimately replaced indoctrination. The Reformation also did much to awaken social conscience, although not with immediate effect. Even so, it was not only the early *Franciscans who served 'Christ's poor'. The words of the English Hugh *Latimer deserve attention: 'If you list to gild and paint Christ in your churches and honour him in vestments, see that before your eyes the poor people die not for lack of meat, drink and clothing.' Philanthropy was on both sides of a great divide—no mean harvest yielded by those whose new-found commitment resulted in lives of thank-offering after the assurance of salvation.

Cultural achievement is more difficult to estimate, and it is not only the aesthetes who deplore the *iconoclasm of radical protest, as when church interiors were vandalized to make the pulpit dominate the discarded altar. Protestant churches were not noteworthy for architecture. But there were advances in portraiture and *music, as with Cranach (1472–1533) and the Bach family. Above all else, the revolution in printing, a process updated with moveable type and new paper, promoted a quite different spirituality, to give heart and transforming faith that must ultimately symbolize the magnitude of this significant crisis in Christendom. The 16th-cent. reformations may thus be likened to a series of relay stations: the faith that *Paul had proclaimed to the Corinthians, a creed reinforced and re-echoed by St Augustine of Hippo, was 'rediscovered' by Luther, Calvin, Ignatius and their contemporaries, and was relayed on to crown and complement Christian values in new and testing times.

See Index, Reformation; for individual figures, see bibliography, *ad loc.*

L. G. Abray, *The People's Reformation: Magistrates, Clergy and Commons in Strasburg, 1500–1598* (1985); E. Cameron, *The European Reformation* (1991); H. O. Evennett, *The Spirit of the Counter-Reformation* (1968); R. W. Scribner, *The German Reformation* (1986); M. Rubin, *Corpus Christi: The Eucharist in Late Medieval Culture* (1991).

Reformed Churches. Term loosely applied to *Protestant churches, but specifically those which hold *Calvinistic, as opposed to *Lutheran, theology. See further PRESBYTERIANISM for the distinctions among Reformed Churches.

Reformed Ogboni Fraternity. A Nigerian equivalent to a Masonic lodge, deriving mainly from the efforts of an educated Yoruba *Anglican clergyman, J. A. T. Ogunbiyi, who had been chaplain to the Masonic lodges in Lagos. In 1914 he established a Christian Ogboni Society, both as a Yoruba version of Christianity modelled on the traditional Ogboni secret society, and as an alternative to imported freemasonry. This was opposed both by Muslims and by some churches, but after Ogunbiyi had lost his ministerial status in the early 1930s, he changed the name to Reformed Ogboni Society; since then it has grown into a widespread fraternity embracing upper-class members of all faiths and operating much like Western lodges.

Reformed Scholasticism (Calvinistic movement): see BEZA, THEODORE.

Reform Judaism. A modern post-Enlightenment interpretation of Judaism. Initially there was an attempt to make Judaism more relevant by abbreviating the traditional *liturgy and introducing choral singing and prayers in the vernacular (see JACOBSON, I.). As a result of various *rabbinical conferences in the middle years of the 19th cent., many aspects of the liturgy were reformed, but these changes were justified by reference to the *Talmud and the Codes (see CODIFICATIONS OF LAW). In Great Britain, the Reform movement initially distinguished between the Bible and the Talmud, regarding only the former as authoritative. Subsequently it became more traditional, and a more radical movement, entitled 'Liberal Judaism', was founded in 1901. In Germany, reform liturgies became widespread, but the congregations generally remained theologically conservative. In the USA, the reform platform was established at Pittsburgh in 1885, where the *rabbis declared,

> We recognise in the modern era of universal culture of heart and intellect the approach of the realisation of Israel's great Messianic hope for the establishment of the kingdom of truth, justice and peace among all men . . . We recognise in Judaism a progressive religion, ever striving to be in accord with the postulates of reason . . . We accept as binding only the moral laws and maintain only such ceremonies as elevate and sanctify our lives, but reject all such as are not adapted to the views and habits of modern civilization . . .

This position was modified in Columbus in 1937, and the Reform movement has since abandoned its anti-*Zionist stance. Reform congregations are united in the World Union for Progressive Judaism, and rabbis are trained at the *Hebrew Union College in the USA and the Leo Baeck College in the UK. Reform Judaism has no official status in Israel (though it has a few congregations and *kibbutzim), because only *Orthodox rabbis are recognized; and the Orthodox repudiate such Reform innovations as the ordination (*semikhah) of women as rabbis. See also CONSERVATIVE JUDAISM; RECONSTRUCTIONISM; Index, Reform Judaism.

M. A. Meyer, *Response to Modernity: A History of the Reform Movement* . . . (1988); D. Philipson, *The Reform Movement in Judaism* (1967); W. G. Plant, *The Rise of Reform Judaism* (1963) and *The Growth of Reform Judaism* (1965).

Refuge. Characteristic attitude of Buddhists, summarized in the Three Refuges, a formula repeated three times: *Buddhaṃ saraṇaṃ gacchāmi, Dhammaṃ saraṇaṃ gacchāmi, Saṅgham saraṇaṃ gacchāmi*: I take refuge in the *Buddha, the *dharma, and the *saṅgha. See THREE JEWELS (*triratna*).

Regensberg Colloquy (meeting in 1541 between Roman Catholics and Protestants to reunify the Church): see CONTARINI, GASPARO.

Reigenki (Japanese stories): see DENSETSU.

Reincarnation: see REBIRTH.

Reiyūkai (Jap., 'friends of the spirit association'). A movement within *Nichiren Buddhism, founded in Tōkyō in 1925 by Kubo Kakutarō (1890–1944) and his sister-in-law Kotani Kimi (1901–71). It came into being *c.*1925 as an informal association. It stresses the importance of the **Lotus Sūtra* and of reverence for *ancestors. The spirit of any individual is linked with all spirits in the universe at one of three stages, of natural desire (*yokukai*), of freedom from desire with wonder at the nature of things still remaining (*shikikai*), and of transcending all attachment (*mushikikai*). To offer food and worship to ancestors is therefore to offer it to every spirit, including *kami and buddhas. To neglect such worship is to neglect all spirits, hence the urgency in Reiyūkai to gather as many ancestral mortuary tablets (*ihai) as possible in order to reverence them. It was the most successful of the 'new religions' (*shinshū kyō*) after the Second World War, when, unlike most other *new religious movements, it was freed from governmental supervision. But because Reiyūkai was always prone to schism, it has been weakened by frequent defections. Thus Reiyūkai's significance lies in its being the source of numerous Nichiren-related new religious movements, the most important of which is *Risshō Kōsei Kai, the 'Society for the Establishment of Righteousness and Friendly Relations'. Under the presidency of the founder's son, Kubo Tsuginari, Reiyūkai has been modernized and has experienced a regeneration by an influx of young people. A training centre has been established on the Izu Peninsula, and a sophisticated periodical entitled *Inner Trip* now attracts a fairly wide readership. The headquarters is located in Tōkyō.

H. Hardacre, *Lay Buddhism in Contemporary Japan: Reiyokai Kyodan* (1984); Kotani Kimi, *A Guide to Reiyu-kai* (1958).

Relaxati (party in Franciscan controversy): see ZELANTI.

Release of the burning mouths (Chinese Buddhist ceremony): see FANG YEN-KOU.

Relics

Christianity The word is applied to material remains of a *saint after death, and to sacred objects associated with Christ or with saints. The earliest witness to the veneration of relics comes from the *Martyrdom of *Polycarp* (*c.*156–7) where the saint's remains are described as 'more valuable than precious stones and finer than refined gold', therefore to be revered. *Jerome and *Augustine defended this attitude to relics, and the second Council of Nicaea (787) laid down that no church should be consecrated without them. In the W. Church the cult of relics increased enormously, especially during the *Crusades when quantities of spurious relics were brought to Europe. They were kept in reliquaries (often elaborate, decorated vessels of formalized shape), carried in procession, and believed to have miraculous powers. Relics of martyrs were placed under the altar stones of all Roman Catholic churches until 1969. The Council of *Trent upheld the cult of relics against the *Reformers. Owing to fewer canonizations and the role of *icons in *Orthodox churches, the cult of relics has never had the same place in the East as in the West.

Buddhism The earliest Buddhist relic (*śarīra) was the *bo tree (of enlightenment): trees grown from cuttings or seeds (taken from the original tree under which *Gotāma achieved enlightenment) became objects of veneration. This reverence involves *circumambulation (indicating the centre of one's life) and the offering of flowers or water. The development of the *stūpa included the placing of relics (indeed, if developed from earlier forms of burial mounds, may have been designed for the placing of relics) in their interior. Since there is no part of a person (e.g. a soul) which has used the body as a vehicle, any part of the body is equally infused with lingering power for goodness. Relics may thus be from the Buddha, or of a past Buddha, or of an *arhat. Stūpas have become widely known as *pagodas, possibly itself a corruption of the word *dāgaba, the mound where relics are contained, hence a 'relic-container'.

See Index, Relics.

Religion: see INTRODUCTION.

Religion as story: see INTRODUCTION.

Religionless Christianity: see BONHOEFFER, DIETRICH.

Religions: for individual religions, see Index, Religions.

Religionsgeschichtliche Schule (History of Religions School). A method developed originally at Göttingen (hence sometimes called 'the little Göttingen faculty') for attempting the study of religions as part of an unfolding historical development. Its main focus was to set the study of early Christianity firmly in the context of Jewish and Hellenistic religion, making it in effect 'one among many'; but the method was applied to the Old Testament, and eventually, more ambitiously, to a general history of religions.

Religious habit: see HABIT, RELIGIOUS.

Religious Orders. The organization of groups of men or women living in accordance with a common rule, and owing obedience to a single superior. In W. Christianity such orders are distinct from monastic congregations, which are associations of independent monasteries, although the earliest orders were those of Cluny and Citeaux (the *Cistercians), groups of monks living a particular interpretation of the Rule of St *Benedict, who recognized a common abbot general and met in general congregations to determine matters of common policy. Unlike the monastic orders, the orders of *friars (13th cent. onwards) did not promise stability to an individual house, though they retained many monastic practices, in particular the recitation of divine *office in common. The clerks regular (16th cent. onwards) abandoned even this custom. In the *Roman Catholic Church, religious orders, whether male or female, are to be distinguished from religious congregations: the former take solemn *vows, the latter do not. Although outside the RC Church religious orders disappeared at the *Reformation, they were revived to some extent in *Anglicanism in the 19th cent., especially under the influence of the *Oxford Movement. In the *Orthodox Church, religious orders are not differentiated and the religious are mainly monastic.

The phrase is also used, by application, for organized communities in other religions, e.g. *tarīqa among *Sūfīs, *saṃpradāya among Hindus, *saṅgha among Buddhists. The need for organized communities basically reflects what is required for the transmission of information in a formal sense.

For examples, see Index, Christian Orders.

E. A. Wynn, *Traditional Catholic Religious Orders* (1987).

Religious Taoism: see TAOISM.

Rema (acronym): see ISSERLES.

Remak (acronym): see KIMḤI, DAVID.

Remey, C. M. (Claimant to as Bahā'ī guardianship): see SHOGHI EFFENDI RABBĀNĪ.

Remnant (of Israel; Heb., *she'erit Israel*). The few faithful Jews who are believed to survive calamitous punishment. The biblical *prophets taught that as a result of its unfaithfulness, *Israel would be driven into *exile and destruction. At the same time, a faithful remnant would be saved (or, nothing but a few would be saved). The prophet *Isaiah in particular developed this theme; his son was called Shear-Jashub ('a remnant shall return'), and in ch. 6 it is promised that, despite the complete devastation of the land, a 'holy seed' shall remain. Similar doctrines can be found in *Micah, *Jeremiah, and *Joel. To this day in the daily prayers are included the words, 'Guardian of Israel, guard the Remnant of Israel and suffer not Israel to perish.'

Remonstrants: see DUTCH REFORMED CHURCH.

Renan, Joseph-Ernest (1823–92). Historian of Jewish and Christian religion. He prepared for the *priesthood in France, but felt unable to proceed to ordination. His work in Semitic languages led to his appointment as professor at the Collège de France. After an expedition to Syria and the Holy Land, he published, in 1863, *Vie de Jésus*, which won immediate fame (or notoriety). Renan attempted to rescue Jesus from the later impositions on his story made by enthusiastic disciples. *Miracles, in particular, were either legends or embellishments of natural events: 'No miracle has ever taken place under conditions which science can accept. Experience shows, without exception, that miracles occur only in times and in countries in which miracles are believed in, and in the presence of persons who are disposed to believe in them.' Yet the power of Jesus' teaching and high idealism remains as necessary as ever: 'All history is incomprehensible without Christ.' Renan was expelled from his post, not to be reinstated until the fall of the Second Empire in 1870. He continued to work on *Histoire des origines du christianisme* (1863–82, tr. 1897–1904), culminating in a study of Marcus Aurelius through which he expressed much of his own feeling about life in the midst of disintegrating certainties. He then embarked on an unfinished history of the Jewish people, with Jesus seen as the connecting link (and thus source of Western civilization) between the Semitic and Hellenistic worlds.

R. M. Chadbourne, *Ernest Renan* (1968); H. W. Wardman, *Ernest Renan* . . . (1964).

Rending of garments: see KERIAH.

Rennyo (Japanese Buddhist): see JŌDŌ-SHINSHŪ.

Repentance: see PENANCE; PENITENCE; TESHUVA.

Reproaches (Lat., *improperia*). A set of responses sung at the *veneration of the cross on *Good Friday. They contrast God's loving acts for his people and their treatment of Christ. The response to each item is 'O my people, what have I done to you? How have I hurt you? Answer me.'

Reprobation: see PREDESTINATION.

Requiem (Lat., 'rest'). A *mass offered for the dead. The opening words of the *introit, which until recently began all such masses in the Roman rite, are: Requiem aeternam dona eis, Domine ('Lord, grant them eternal rest'). The 1970 *missal embodies a complete revision of these masses, and many of their previously distinctive characteristics, e.g. the requirement of black *vestments, have disappeared. Requiems have evoked great and moving music (Mozart, Verdi, Berlioz, Dvořák), even from *agnostic composers (e.g. Fauré); and some corresponding Protestant works, biblically based, e.g. Brahms's *German Requiem*.

Rerum Novarum. Papal *encyclical issued on 15 May 1891, 'On the Condition of the Working

Classes'. It represents the response of *Leo XIII to problems created by the Industrial Revolution, and formulates a doctrine of work, profit, industrial relationships, social justice, and the necessity of a proper wage. Fearful of revolutionary activity in the late 19th cent., it asserted both the rights of private ownership and the *Church's responsibility to speak out on contemporary social and moral issues. It affirms the principle of the just wage (endorsed strongly in *Quadragesimo Anno*, 1931) and the right to the private ownership of property. A principal aim was 'to keep under all strife and all its causes'.

P. Furlong and D. Curtis (eds.), *The Church Faces the Modern World: Rerum Novarum and its Impact* (1994).

Reserved sacrament. Bread (occasionally wine) consecrated at the Christian *eucharist and kept for devotion (see BENEDICTION) and for *communion, especially for the sick. In the earliest times the faithful kept the blessed sacrament in their homes or carried it on their persons; but from the time of Constantine, churches have been the ordinary places for reservation. In modern Catholic practice the reserved *hosts are kept in a *tabernacle on an *altar, or in an aumbry (in *Anglicanism). Reservation is marked by a continuously burning light. The practice is similar in the *Orthodox Church, except that the reserved sacrament consists of the host with a drop of consecrated wine on it, and there are no extra-liturgical devotions.

Resh Kallah. Title of leading Jewish sages of the Babylonian *academies. The reshei Kallah were expected to preach publicly in the academies, and there were seven of them at any one time. Only two are mentioned by name in the *Talmud, R. Naḥman b. Isaac (*BBB* 22a) and R. *Abbahu (*B.Hul.* 49a).

Responsa (Heb., *she'elot u-teshuvot*, 'questions and answers'). Exchanges of letters primarily on Jewish *halakhic matters. The practice of sending responsa is mentioned in the *Talmud, when letters were exchanged between Johanan in *Israel and *Rav in Babylon (*B.Hul.* 95b). From the *geonic period, the *oral law was largely disseminated throughout the *diaspora by means of responsa—the earliest surviving examples being those of Yehudai Gaon. Responsa covered every aspect of Jewish life and were usually sent to Babylon from the *yeshivot of Spain, N. Africa, and the Middle Eastern countries. The queries were first discussed in the yeshivah during the months of *Kallah, and the final letters were signed by all the senior members of the yeshivah. The geonic responsa were copied and sometimes collected into *kovazim* ('collections'). In the period of the *rishonim, responsa were increasingly restricted to halakhic queries, and the surviving collections were generally made by pupils of the authorities (e.g. *Sefer ha-Yasher* of Jacob Tarn). Unlike the geonim, the rishonim sometimes indicated doubt and used such expressions as 'in my humble opinion' or 'requires further thought'. *Orthodox rabbinic authorities have continued to give responsa to this day (*aharonim*), and the responsa literature provides an important source for the social history of the various Jewish communities through the ages. Modern-day responsa deal in particular with problems arising out of modern technology (e.g. artificial insemination, the use of refrigerators on the *Sabbath, etc.), the establishment of the State of *Israel (e.g. whether there is an obligation to make pilgrimage on the three *pilgrim festivals), and the *Holocaust (e.g. whether a Jew may save his life by converting to Christianity).

S. B. Freehof, *The Responsa Literature* . . . (1955).

Restoration movements. A tendency, in Christianity, to turn away from established churches and to seek to 'restore' what is taken to be primitive or original Christianity. Frequently associated with *charismatic gifts and *millennial expectations, examples are the Church of the *Latter Day Saints, or the House Church movement (see ECCLESIOLOGY).

Resurrection (Lat., *resurgo*, 'I arise'). The destiny of the dead in the restoration to them of bodies through which their continuing identity can be expressed. The belief occurs especially in Judaism, Christianity, and Islam. In Judaism, the belief that people will ultimately be raised from the dead is not found in the Hebrew scriptures until the end of the biblical period. As the book of Job puts it, 'A cloud dissolves and is gone; so is one who descends to *Sheol; he will not ascend' (7. 8). However, by the *rabbinic period, the doctrine had become a central tenet of the Jewish religion. According to the *Mishnah, 'The following have no position in the World to come: one who says "There is no resurrection of the dead" . . .' (*Sanh.* 10). Belief in the doctrine was a central difference in the theologies of the *Pharisees and the *Sadducees, but it was incorporated early into the *liturgy (e.g. the second *benediction of the *'Amidah). In rabbinic thought the doctrine involved reward and punishment for the whole nation, and a belief that body and *soul are indivisible and both will be resurrected. Connected with the idea of resurrection is the notion of the 'Days of the *Messiah', but the chronological stages of these events and their relationship to the final end are not always clear. Later Jewish philosophers continued to disagree on the details; in his *Mishneh Torah*, for example, *Maimonides (who included resurrection in his Principles of Faith; see ARTICLES OF FAITH) taught, 'In the world to come there is no body, rather the souls of the righteous are alone without a body, like the ministering *angels', and was taken to task by *Abraham b. David of Posquières, who pointed out, 'The words of this man seem to us to be close to one who says there is no resurrection for bodies'. In general, *Progressive Judaism has abandoned the doctrine of the resurrection of the body in favour of belief in the immortality of the soul, but it remains a basic tenet of *Orthodoxy.

In Christianity, the belief in resurrection rests partly in the teaching attributed to *Jesus and in the debates in the Jewish context of the time, but much more in the *resurrection of Christ. This produced the traditional teaching that at the *parousia of Christ departed souls will be restored to a bodily life, and the saved will enter in this renewed form upon the life of heaven. The doctrine is of a resurrection 'of the body' (*Apostles' creed) at 'the last trumpet' on the day of *judgement (1 Thessalonians 4–5); in both respects it differs from, although it complements, a doctrine of the immortality of the soul. It is usual to say that the resurrection body will be 'spiritual' (1 Corinthians 15. 35–53), raised above the limitations of the earthly body, with which it will be identical only in the sense that it will be the recognizable organism of the same personality.

For Resurrection in Islam (Arab., *baʿth, nushūr*), see YAUM AL-QIYĀMA; YAUM AL-DIN.

J. W. Bowker, *The Meanings of Death* (1992); P. Carnley, *The Structure of Resurrection Belief* (1987); L. Jacobs, *Principles of the Jewish Faith* (1964); M. Harris, *Raised Immortal*.

Resurrection of Christ. Fundamental tenet of Christianity, that *Jesus was raised from the dead by God 'on the third day' after his crucifixion. It was part of the earliest Christian preaching (the *kerygma), as may be seen in *Paul's summary statements in Romans 1. 1–3 and especially 1 Corinthians 15. 1–17, as well as in the speeches recorded in Acts, e.g. 2. 24. The source of this 'Easter belief' is a deep question. All four gospels record that Jesus' tomb was found empty on Easter Sunday morning, but no one would have come to believe that he had been raised from the dead on that basis alone. In any case, the empty tomb is not explicitly mentioned by Paul. According to Paul and the gospel writers (except *Mark?) the cause of the belief was Jesus' appearances to his followers (beginning with *Peter: Luke 24. 34). The stories of these appearances are confused, and only Luke says that they stopped after forty days. Some scholars accordingly consider that they originated later, alongside claims of various people to authority in the church; other scholars take the confusion to be a sign of very primitive traditions—so much so that the resurrection as an event is necessary to account for the nature of the accounts and for the way they have been transmitted. Scholars who discount the appearances of Jesus as the cause of the Easter belief usually hold a 'theological theory' instead: the disciples, reflecting on Jesus' death, believed that it could not have been the end, and came to faith that God had raised him up; but in the Jewish context, and in the context of the fact of the crucifixion, there is no serious possibility that theological theories of this kind are correct.

Already in the New Testament the theological significance of the resurrection is variously expressed: as God's vindicating Jesus and raising him to his right hand in heaven (Acts 2. 34–6); as an anticipation of the general *resurrection (1 Thessalonians 4. 14); as Christ's victory over death (1 Corinthians 15. 57); and as the basis of the new life of Christians (Romans 4. 24).

Muslims deny the resurrection of Christ, believing that he did not die on the cross at all; and the *Aḥmadīyya maintain that he went on to preach in India, and believe that they can identify his tomb.

Retreat. A period of days spent apart from the world, in pursuit of religious ends. In Christianity, its origins are lost in history, though *Christ's forty days in the desert are often regarded as lending the practice Christian authority. Retreats are formally part of the life of *Jesuits (*Ignatius' *Spiritual Exercises* being a retreat plan), and it was the Jesuits who promoted the retreat as a formal practice. In the 17th cent. retreats became popular, and retreat houses were set up. The practice (usually with the guidance of a 'conductor') spread to *Anglicanism and beyond in the wake of the *Oxford Movement.

The term is used, in application, in other religions for withdrawal from the world, e.g. the time spent by *Muḥammad in isolation on Mt. Hira (which led to the revelation of the first words of the *Qur'ān); *vassa in Buddhism.

Retrogressive rituals. *Rituals which enable people to bring the past into the present, or to 'visit' the past in order to deal with events that lie in the past. The former bring into effect past events so that they are of consequence in the present (as in recapitulating dramatic moments of salvation, e.g. *Passover, *Good Friday); the latter are particularly important in enabling people to deal with offences or sins in the past which might otherwise seem to be literally 'past redemption'—hence rituals of *penance, *confession, *atonement, *absolution, etc. In commemoration of the holy or wise, they enable a conversation with the past which acts as a constraint over life in the present.

Reuben. One of the twelve sons of *Jacob and forefather of one of the *tribes of *Israel. Reuben was the first-born of Jacob and Leah. According to tradition, the tribe of Reuben settled east of the Jordan river (Numbers 32). In the *aggadah, Reuben is frequently contrasted with *Esau who also lost his first-born hegemony to his younger brother (e.g. *B.Ber.* 7b).

Reuchlin, Johannes (1455–1522). *Gentile defender of Jewish scholarship. Reuchlin's *De Rudimentis Hebraicis* (1506) was a pioneering attempt at an understanding of Judaism by a Christian scholar. He battled against Johannes Pfefferkorn in his attempt to condemn the *Talmud: 'The Talmud was not composed for every blackguard to trample with unwashed feet and then to say he knew all of it.' He also studied the *kabbalah, and his *De Arte Cabalistica* (1517), which was dedicated to the pope, did much to spread knowledge of Jewish mysticism to Christian readers.

M. Brod, *Johannes Reuchlin und sein Kampf* (1965).

Reuveni, David (d. 1583). Jewish adventurer who evoked *messianic expectation. Reuveni is mentioned in letters and produced his own diary. He claimed to be of royal descent from one of the lost *tribes of *Israel. At the age of about 40, he appeared in Venice in 1523 and was received by the pope in 1524. He visited Portugal in 1525, where he was greeted as the herald of the messianic age by the *Marranos, but was subsequently imprisoned. After shipwreck off the coast of France, he returned to Italy where he was again imprisoned in 1532. Although inspiring messianic fervour, he himself stressed he was merely a military commander trying to raise an alliance against the Muslims and recapture *Erez Israel for the Jews.

A. S. Aescoly, *Sippur David ha-Reuveni* (1940).

Revelation (Lat., *revelare*, 'to unveil'). The disclosure or communication of truths which would not otherwise be known, at least in the same way. A distinction is often made between, on the one hand, 'natural revelation' or 'general revelation', whereby such truths are discerned within the natural order (either by reason or by conviction that absolute value, especially beauty, has invaded a contingent moment or object or circumstance); and on the other hand, special or supernatural revelation, which comes from a source other than that of the human recipient, usually God. Natural revelation was also understood by some Christians (e.g. *Justin, Ficino) to underlie, via the pervasive work of the *Logos, the wisdom in pagan philosophers. The method of supernatural revelation is variously understood, ranging from direct dictation (in which the limitations of a human author are overridden) to concursive activity (in which the source is God, or the *Holy Spirit, working with the human author—a view which, in the Jewish and Christian case, recognizes the contingency of the words produced, but raises difficulties for traditional claims of inerrancy in revealed words). Jews, in particular, believe that God reveals himself in words in the *Pentateuch and *Prophetic books of the Hebrew scriptures. The *Talmudic sages identified the *Torah as being the instrument by which the world was created (*Avot* 3. 14) and they taught that no Jew who denied that the Torah came from heaven had a place in the world to come (*B.Sanh.* 10. 1). *Orthodox theologians are still committed to this view, but *Progressive Jews hold a variety of different opinions—see e.g. Franz *Rosenzweig. Orthodox rabbis such as *Kook and J. B. *Soloveichik maintain that the continuing revelatory action of God can still be encountered in the study of Torah.

Muslims hold a strong doctrine of revelation, believing that 'the mother of the book' (*umm al-Kitāb) is with God in heaven. The *Qur'ān, therefore, is sent down to prophets as they and their circumstances can bear it—and consummately so through *Muḥammad, whose recipient community preserved it without corruption or loss. The major terms for 'revelation' are tanzīl and *waḥy.

Whereas in W. religions revelation is usually related to particular persons and occasions, in Hinduism the concept is more subtle and diffused. The *Veda is believed to have no human author, and in some sense is revealed—the exact sense is not agreed. *Śabda (sound) is a source of knowledge with many different aspects. Within the context of sound, *anubhūti* (direct experience of *Brahman) arises from meditation on texts from the *Upaniṣads as they are *heard*—not simply as they are read in silence. But this experience is possible only because the Upaniṣads themselves arise from the Vedas which are the constant (or in some views eternal) revelation of the truth about *dharma and Brahman. In *Mīmāṁsā, the Vedas are eternal, without beginning or end, as the cycles of time are eternal; the Vedas have the authority of simply 'being there', like the cosmos: they contain no empirical information (so cannot be falsified): they display what is involved in living in accord with the cosmic process (*ṛta), so that their imperatives must be obeyed. Other schools see God as the source of the Veda, but not necessarily as author (in the sense that Shakespeare wrote *Hamlet*): God manifests the Vedas at the start of each new cycle of time exactly as they were in the previous cycle, as part of his creative function; and when humanity begins to fall into disarray and disorder, he incarnates himself (*avatāra) to restore Vedic order. In *Vedānta, the Vedas are no more real than anything else (*māyā), but they serve to point beyond themselves to what is real, much as a picture points to that which it endeavours to portray.

See Index, Revelation.

J. Baillie, *The Idea of Revelation in Recent Thought* (1956); A. Dulles, *Models of Revelation* (1978); *Revelation Theology: A History* (1970); K. S. Murty, *Revelation and Reason in Advaita Vedanta* (1959).

Revelation, Book of. The last book and the only *apocalypse in the *New Testament. The book is a series of visions, prefaced (chs. 1–3) by letters to seven churches in Asia Minor. The visions include the opening of a book with seven seals (chs. 5–9); the 144,000 faithful of Israel (7); the destruction of the harlot Babylon (clearly Rome; 17–18); the marriage supper of the Lamb and binding of *Satan for a thousand years (19–20); and the New Jerusalem (21–2). The author, 'John the Divine' according to the title, is traditionally identified with the *apostle *John, but the common authorship of this book and the gospel of John is very doubtful. The hostile attitude to Rome suggests a date during Nero's persecution, *c.*64, or later under Domitian (81–96). In

Christian history the book has become important in times of persecution and in the context of *millenarian movements.

Revival Zion or **Revivalism.** Afro-Jamaican cults resembling *Pocomania in their hierarchical and authoritarian organization, in their Yards, and in their concern with healing by diverse means and with spirit possession. A more Christian content is seen in the words used from *Protestant hymns (but not the mode of singing), in reliance on God and the *angels (without identifying African spirits with *Catholic saints), in preaching and a biblical (usually *Old Testament) emphasis, and in testimonies and confession of sins. There is, however, no demand for personal holiness or moral behaviour as in the newer *Pentecostal churches, which since the 1950s have been replacing declining Revivalism.

Revivalism may also be a more general description of movements within Christianity which lead to a renewal of fervour and commitment. Examples are *Pietism, the *Great Awakening in N. America, the *Wesleys and the origins of *Methodism, 19th-cent. *mission meetings.

Revolutionary Guards (Shiʿite religious police): see BIHBAHĀNĪ.

Reza, Imām Ahmad (founder): see BARELVI.

Ṛg Veda (Skt., 'knowledge in verse'). The oldest of the *Veda collections of hymns (*c*.13th cent. BCE) and the most important for its scope and originality. It consists of sung strophes (*ṛc*) arranged into hymns (*sukta*) by the *hotṛ priests. Altogether the collection includes 1,028 hymns (or 1,017 excluding Vālakhilya hymns attached to the 8th *maṇḍala) divided into ten maṇḍalas (circles or schools). Maṇḍalas 2 to 7 are family collections, and are the oldest core of the *Ṛg Veda*. These are arranged according to the gods they address and according to decreasing length. Maṇḍala 8 collects hymns from a number of families. Maṇḍala 9 is devoted exclusively to the god *Soma. Maṇḍalas 1 and 10 preserve late hymns for the most part, including the more speculative hymns and those to figures otherwise unmentioned in the *Ṛg Veda*. In tone the *Ṛg Veda* is generally devotional and laudatory. The sacrificer calls upon the gods through his singing and asks for some blessing. The first hymn of the *Ṛg Veda* begins:

*Agni I pray to, the household priest who is the god of the sacrifice,
the one who chants and invokes and brings most treasure.

Eng. trs. R. T. H. Griffith (1920–6), H. H. Wilson (1850–8); selections, A. A. Macdonell (1922), H. Oldenberg (1897), W. O'Flaherty (1981); German (with commentary), K. F. Geldner (1951).

rgyal tshab: see GSHEN RAB MI-BO-CHE.

Rhazes (Muslim philosopher and physician): see AL-RĀZĪ, ABŪ BAKR MUḤAMMAD.

Rheno-Flemish spirituality. A style of Christian mystical devotion of the 13th cent., which developed in Belgium and the Rhineland. The Rhineland mystics emphasized the seeking and finding of God within, rather than in outward devotions. They were rooted in the practice and experience of the Beguines (and their male counterparts, the Beghards), who were lay religious groups seeking the simplicity of the early Church in communal association with each other (they were condemned, especially for their use of the vernacular Bible and private interpretation of scripture, but their descendants survive to the present). One major figure was Mechtild of Magdeburg (1210–*c*.1290), who lived most of her life as a Beguine, but retired to a convent when her writings were attacked; her main work, *Das fliessende Licht der Gottheit* (The Flowing Light of the Godhead), is a compendium of her own experiences and of medieval mysticism:

Lord God, I am now a naked soul, and you are clothed in glory: we are two in One, now that we have reached the goal, immortal *rapture that cannot die; a blissful silence flows over us: both have willed it. He is given to her and she to him: what happens next the soul knows well, and therefore I am full of comfort.

Gertrude of Helfta (1256–1301/2), often called 'the Great', experienced, at the age of 25, a bond of love with Jesus, a kind of 'nuptial mysticism' (*Brautmystik*), and from that time entered a life of contemplation; she wrote the much-admired *Legatus Divinae Pietatis* (The Herald of Divine Love, parts of which were written later from her notes), and was one of the first to develop devotion to the *Sacred Heart. Hadewijch of Antwerp (early 13th cent.), whose *Visions* develop the same theme of a union with God of ecstatic love (*minnemystiek*), Jan van *Ruysbroeck, and *Hildegard of Bingen are often associated with this group; and the *devotio moderna* of Gerard *Groote is usually regarded as a direct successor.

E. Z. Brunn and G. Epiney-Burgar, *Women Mystics in Medieval Europe* (tr. 1989); C. W. Bynum, *Jesus as Mother* . . . (1982); E. W. McDonnell, *The Beguines and Beghards in Medieval Culture* (1954).

Rhineland mysticism: see RHENO-FLEMISH SPIRITUALITY.

Rhys Davids, C. A. F. (née Foley, 1857–1942). An important editor, translator, and commentator on Pāli Buddhist texts. After her marriage to T. W. *Rhys Davids in 1894, she worked as Honorary Secretary to the Pāli Text Society until her husband's death in 1922, when she became President. Academically she promoted the cause of Pāli studies as Lecturer on Indian Philosophy at Manchester (1910–13), and, on the establishment of the School of Oriental and African Studies in London, as Lecturer in the History of Buddhism (1917–33). Much of her spare time was devoted to the welfare of children and working women. She was an ardent advocate of women's suffrage, and a writer of poetry.

Her major writings include translations of the *Saṃyutta Nikāya* (2 vols.), *Dhammasaṅgaṇi*, *Therīgāthā*, and an important early study of the Buddhist conception of mind, *Buddhist Psychology* (1914).

Rhys Davids, T. W. (1843–1922). Influential promoter of Pāli Buddhist studies in England. After studying Sanskrit in Germany, he entered the Ceylon Civil Service in 1864, soon becoming fluent in Tamil and Sinhalese. Disillusioned with the injustices of colonial rule, he left Ceylon in 1877.

Though not the first scholar of Pāli, he did much to introduce Buddhist ideas to the British public, and in his Hibbert Lectures of 1881 announced the foundation of the Pāli Text Society, of which he was the first chairman. After his time as Professor of Pāli at University College, London, he was (1904–15) Professor of Comparative Religion in the Victoria University, Manchester.

His vast output of work can be conveniently classified under the three headings of translation, history, and philology. The principal translations include *Vinaya Texts*, with H. Oldenberg (1881–5), *Dialogues of the Buddha*, with his wife C. A. F. Rhys Davids (1899–1921), and *Questions of King Milinda* (1890–4). His historical works include *Buddhism* (1878) and *Early Buddhism* (1908), while the great labour of his final years was the compilation of a Pāli–English Dictionary, completed by W. Stede.

Ri. This may be spelt Ṛ or ṛ; check at appropriate alphabetical order.

Ribā (Arab., 'increase'). The taking of interest on capital investment, which is prohibited in Islam (e.g. Qur'ān 2. 278 f.). The Qur'ān allows profit through trade, but if there is investment, it must be on a profit-sharing basis. Thus some risk-taking is permissible, but money cannot be traded as a commodity. The attempt to recover a pan-Islamic banking and commercial practice is undertaken through such institutions as the International Association of Islamic Banks, and such banks as the Islamic Development Bank.

Ribal (acronym): see LEVINSOHN, ISAAC BAER.

Ribusshō (Jap.). The buddha-nature (*busshō) as the inherent and only constituent of all living beings, especially in Hossō (see DŌSHŌ).

Ricci, Matteo (1552–1610). *Jesuit missionary in China. He gained the attention of Chinese intellectuals by displaying and explaining to them European clocks, a map of the world, etc., planning thereby to bridge the difference in cultures and convert the country from the official classes downwards. His missionary success also owed much to his accommodation of Christianity to Chinese religion (cf. *de Nobili). In 1603, he prescribed the observance of traditional honours to *Confucius and the cult of *ancestors in Jesuit churches in China. These rites, however, gave rise to a protracted controversy after his death, and were pronounced by the *Holy See in 1704 and 1715 to be incompatible with Christianity.

V. Cronin, *The Wise Man from the West* (1955); L. J. Gallagher (tr.), *China in the Sixteenth Century: The Journals . . .* (1953).

Ridda (Arab., *'irtadda*, 'retrace one's steps'). Apostasy from Muslim belief (cf. MURTADD), especially al-Ridda, the wars of apostasy which immediately followed the death of *Muḥammad, when many tribes who had given allegiance to his personal leadership simply reverted to their traditional tribal ways. The penalty is death if the apostate (murtadd) speaks against Islam (see also BLASPHEMY). The penalty is not stated in the Qur'ān, and is based on *ḥadīth.

Ridley, Nicholas (*c.*1500–55). English *Reformation *bishop. Born in Northumberland, Ridley was educated at Cambridge, the Sorbonne, and Louvain, before returning to Cambridge (about 1530) as Fellow of Pembroke. He was later *Cranmer's chaplain, and vicar of Herne, Kent, before becoming Master of Pembroke in 1540. Consecrated bishop of Rochester in 1547, he was, on Bonner's deprivation, made bishop of London (1550). A memorable preacher, he gave forceful publicity in his diocese to his revised *eucharistic views by replacing the stone altar with a wooden *Communion table. On Mary's accession he was arrested and later burnt with *Latimer at Oxford. He exerted a great influence on Cranmer who always regarded him as of superior ability, especially in controversy.

Riḍvān (Paradise). Place outside Baghdād of great holiness to Bahā'īs. In 1863, *Bahā'u'llāh was summoned (at the instigation of the Persian government) to Constantinople. Bahā'u'llāh moved to the garden of Najīb Pāsha to prepare for the journey, and on 21 Apr. announced that he was the one whose coming had been foretold by the Bāb (see BĀBĪS). The garden was named Riḍvān, and the twelve days spent there are commemorated in the feast of Riḍvān.

Rif (acronym): see ALFASI.

Righteous gentiles (Heb., *ḥasidei 'umōt ha-'olām*). Gentiles who keep the *Noachide laws. They will have a share in the world to come (*'Olam ha-Ba) when the *messiah comes. More specifically, the term is used of those gentiles who risked their lives to save Jews during the *Holocaust. There is an Avenue of the Righteous Gentiles in the Holocaust Memorial, Yad Vashem, in *Jerusalem.

Right-hand tantrism: see DAKṢINĀCĀRA.

Right mindfulness (Pāli, *sati*). Part of the Buddhist eightfold path (*aṣṭangika-marga), which consciously endeavours to look on all things in the true perspective—including aspects of the body of which usually one is not conscious, e.g. breathing. This brings insight into the equally transitory (*anicca) nature of all phenomena. These are the four awakenings of mindfulness, *satipaṭṭhāna. See in more detail SATI.

Rig-Veda (collection of hymns): see ṚG VEDA.

Rikam (acronym): see KIMḤI, DAVID.

Rimé (*ris.med*, 'without partiality'). 19th-cent. Tibetan eclectic movement, initiated in 1864 by the publication of the first of Jamgon Kongtrul's 'five treasuries', the *Treasury of All Knowledge* (*Shes.bya. mdzod*). Eclecticism was by no means new to Tibet—many great *lamas had studied in all the major schools, such as the Nyingmapa Longchen Rabjampa, and the *Geluk founder *Tsong Khapa who even included the later proscribed *Jonang—but this was the first time a movement had been launched with the intention of unifying all teachings. It was a peace-making movement, and it has to be understood in the context of the political rivalries that had characterized the previous centuries. Kongtrul himself, brought up as a *Bön priest, was a somewhat reluctant politician involved with all four schools when, encouraged by Khyentse (1820–92) he began writing, and resurrected Jonang texts from their incarceration in Tāranātha's monastery, Phuntsho Ling. In this way what had been a heresy—the *zhen dong doctrine—became the bedrock of a major national movement, which sought to harmonize all teachings in the light of an ontologically positive ultimate reality which is essentially beyond definition. Rimé received a strong *Nyingma emphasis from the vision of all *Vajrayāna as culminating in the *atiyoga* of Dzogchen (Khyentse was an incarnation of Jigme Lingpa, a master of it), something further developed by Mipham (1846–1912). Rimé was at its strongest in its own province of Khams and its effects were felt strongly everywhere but, perhaps because of the importance attached by all schools to their respective lineages, it never looked like dissolving the distinctions fully. The Geluk indeed stayed well apart from it as a school, unflinching in their condemnation of the zhen dong heresy.

Rimpoche (precious one): see RINPOCHE.

Ringatu (Maori, *Ringa-tua*, 'upraised hand'). The oldest continuing prophet movement in New Zealand. It was founded by Te Kooti Rikirangi (?1830–93) among prisoners captured during the Anglo-Maori wars, with whom he had been unjustly deported to the Chatham Islands in 1866. His earnest Bible study established a new Maori religion which spread after their escape home in 1868. He is now revered as *saint and *martyr, and creator of the Ringatu *liturgy, which embraces five services for different purposes, each with a cycle of prayers, hymns, and panuis (*Old Testament verses), and ending with the sign of the upraised hand. These are held on the *Kaumaru* ('Twelfth') day of each month, circulating round the meeting-houses of different communities, and all committed to memory and in classic Maori. More recent changes include the printing of the liturgy in the 1960s, a greater emphasis on the *New Testament and on *Christ, the constitution of the Ringatu Church in 1938 (about 5,000 members in the 1970s), and closer relations with the main Christian community.

Rinka monasticism (style of Zen monasticism): see JAKUHITSU GENKŌ.

Rinpoche (Tib., *Rin po che*, 'Precious One'). A title of respect given to all *lamas in Tibetan Buddhism. A monk who becomes a lama for the first time (i.e. in this incarnation) will be accorded the title equally with a 'reincarnate lama' (*tulku). The *Dalai Lama, for example, may also be called 'Gyalwa Rinpoche' (Precious Eminence).

Rinzai Gigen (founder of Zen Buddhist Lin-Chi line): see LIN-CHI I-HSÜAN.

Rinzairoku. Abbreviated title of *Chinjū Rinzai Eshō zenji goroku*, Chin., *Chen-chou Lin-chi Hui-chao ch'an-shih yü-lu*, a major and classic work of Zen Buddhism. Its present form dates from the 12th cent. CE, and it is in three parts: (i) Discourses (*goroku*); (ii) Dialectic (*kamben*), questions and answers addressed to true existence; (iii) record of pilgrimages (*anroku*), which includes an account of Lin-chi's enlightenment, and a memorial inscription.

Trs. R. F. Sasaki (1975), I. Schlogel (1976); Fr. tr. P. Demiéville (1972).

Rinzai-shū (Jap. pronunciation of 'Lin-chi', the Chinese founder of the line, + *shū*, Jap., 'tradition', 'school', or 'teachings'). With *Sōtō-shū, one of the two dominant forms of *Zen Buddhism widely practised in Japan. This tradition, founded by the Chinese master, *Lin-chi I-hsüan (d. 867), is usually considered to have been introduced into Japan by Yōsai, also known as *Eisai (1141–1215). In fact, however, it did not crystalize as an independent Japanese school until two or three decades after his death. The modern Japanese tradition owes much of its spiritual development to the revitalization of the practice brought about by *Hakuin Ekaku (1685–1768).

Rinzai-shū is noted for its emphasis on the more audacious forms of Zen training, including shouting, striking, and the dynamic exchanges between master and disciple centring on the *kōan. According to Hakuin, the master's role is to bring about a crisis in the student called the 'Great Doubt' or the 'Great Death' so that, in a moment of realization (*satori), the student makes a spiritual breakthrough. The *enlightenment will then be manifest in the student's every activity, whatever form it may take.

When the Rinzai school was officially recognized by the state, it was organized in a tripartite system of *gozan* (Five Mountains), *jissetsu* (Ten Temples), and *shozan* (the remaining larger temples). This was based on the Chinese system of *wu-shan*, *shih-ch'a*, and *chia-ch'a*. The list of Five Mountain temples changed many times (though it remained based on *Kyōto and Kamakura), but this structured and state-recognized form of Rinzai is often called Gozan Zen.

H. Dumoulin, *Zen Buddhism, a History: Japan*, ii (1990).

Rishi (Indian seer): see ṚṢI.

Rishis (Sūfī order): see SŪFĪS.

Rishonim (Heb., 'first ones', i.e. early authorities). Jewish scholars of an earlier period. The notion of 'rishonim' appears in the *Talmud: 'If the rishonim were as *angels, we are as men, and if the rishonim are as men, we are as donkeys' (*B.Shab.* 112b). However, in *geonic times it was accepted that 'the law is in accordance with the later authority' (*Seder Tanna'im ve-Amora'im* 25). Nowadays, the term is used to indicate the authorities that succeeded the geonim until those of the mid-15th cent. after rabbinic *semikhah was revived.

M. Kasher and J. D. Mandel, *Sarei ha-Elef* (1959): a bibliography of the printed writings of the rishonim.

Rishon le-Zion (Heb., 'First of Zion'). Hebrew title of the *Sephardi head of the *rabbis of *Israel. The first Rishon le-Zion was Moses b. Jonathan Galante (1620–89). From 1920, the Rishon le-Zion was given the additional title of *hakham bashi* (*Chief Rabbi) of *Erez Israel.

Risshō Kōsei Kai ('Establishment of Righteousness and Friendly Intercourse'). New religion, derived from *Nichiren, started in Japan in 1938 by Naganuma Myōkō (1889–1957) and Niwano Nikkyō (b. 1906). Placing its own version of the *bodhisattva ideal at the centre of its teachings, this movement stresses that everyone can travel the road to Buddhahood by leading a life of moral and spiritual wisdom and by foregoing *nirvāna in order to be of service to weak and suffering humanity. It is by leading such a life that one conquers the laws of *karma and reappearance. Recitation of the name of the **Lotus Sūtra* is a central meditation practice.

The word *risshō* alludes to Nichiren's injunction in 1260, *risshō ankoku ron*, 'establish authentic Buddhism to secure peace in our land'; *kōsei* points to a faith-oriented fellowship of those seeking the Buddha's goal; *kai* means 'association' or 'society'. RKK is highly organized, from the network of districts throughout Japan, down to the most local level, where people gather for *hōza*, i.e. seated (*za*) to share problems and solutions related to Buddhist principles (*ho*).

K. J. Dale, *Circle of Harmony* (1975).

Rita (cosmic order): see ṚTA(M).

Rite: see RITUAL.

Rite. Term in Christian use. 1. A form of liturgical worship, e.g. *Anglican Rites A and B for the eucharist in the **Alternative Service Book* 1980. (For the Catholic Congregation of Rites, see CONGREGATIONS, ROMAN.)

2. Any of the major local types or families of ancient *liturgies, e.g. the Latin, Byzantine, and *Mozarabic rites, and the churches where these were practised and their modern descendants.

3. In *Catholic use, a division of Catholic Christendom. Non-technically this sense corresponds with the previous one, e.g. with reference to *Uniat 'Byzantine-rite' churches. More narrowly, in canon law it denotes a particular Catholic Church with its own discipline (e.g. the Bulgarian and Greek rites, both descendants of the Byzantine Church).

Rites controversy. A conflict among *Roman Catholic missionary orders in China in the 17th and 18th cents. It centred on the issue of whether Chinese converts could continue with some pre-Christian practices (especially *ancestor rituals), and whether *T'ien could be regarded as the equivalent of God. The *Jesuits were in favour, the *Dominicans and *Franciscans against (on grounds of syncretism and dilution of the faith). On appeal to the *pope, the Jesuits were overruled in 1704; the order against integration was repeated in 1715 and 1742. The Chinese court regarded this as interference in internal religious matters, and issued countermeasures, banning missionary preaching unless it accepted the so-called Matteo *Ricci regulations—i.e. following his example in approving the rites. The virtual eclipse of Christianity in China was the result of the papal ruling.

Rites of passage. Rituals which mark major transitions in human life (and death). A. van Gennep (*The Rites of Passage*, Eng. tr., 1960) drew attention to a recurrent pattern in such rituals of one distinction, two categories, and three stages: for example,

death; dead/alive; alive → dying → dead
marriage; married/single; single → engaged → married

Van Gennep noted that the most important rituals are not those dealing with the first and last stages, but those dealing with the transition, which 'have a duration and complexity so great that they must be granted a sort of autonomy'. This hint was much developed by R. Hertz (*Année Sociologique*, 10 (1907)), who argued that these rituals move the person in question over a *limen*, 'a threshold', so that they are in a condition that society can know and cope with. The central importance of liminality in rites of passage was taken even further by Victor *Turner, who recognized many more rites of passage than those which have to do with obvious transitions (indeed, nearly all rituals have this characteristic of moving those involved from one state to another); and in these rituals, he stressed 'the autonomy of the liminal': it is the liminal state which is both threatening and at the same time the only route to change—hence the centrality of focus on liminality in religious life.

For examples, see BAPTISM; CIRCUMCISION; FUNERAL RITES; MARRIAGE; PILGRIMAGE; SAṂSKĀRA.

Ritroma (Tib., *ri khrod ma*, 'the lady of the mountain ranges'). A Tibetan female deity, who is an object of meditation. She is associated with healing, since she brings from the forests particular remedies. She is usually depicted wearing a skirt of leaves, indicating a forest-dweller. She is one of the *wrathful deities.

Ritsu (Jap.; Skt., *vināya*). Codes of discipline which govern the Buddhist monastic life. The *vinaya were compiled about 100 years after *Śākyamuni Buddha's death and transmitted orally until they were put down in writing in the 1st cent. BCE, forming the Vinaya-piṭaka of the *Tripiṭaka. Each of the various *Hīnayāna schools that flourished during the schisms following the Buddha's death and before the rise of *Mahāyāna Buddhism had its own version. The one that prevailed in E. Asia was the *Ssu-fen lü* (Vinaya in Four Parts), translated into Chinese between 410 and 412 by Buddhayaśas (no Sanskrit original or Tibetan translation exists). Said to be a transmission of the Dharmaguptaka school, its contents fall into two categories: those that govern the communal life (100 rules) and those that cover the personal life (250 rules for monks and 348 rules for nuns). The latter includes a detailed listing of infractions that would justify expulsion or suspension from the order, confession and absolution, forfeiture, minor violations, and those that are indefinite. The former contains rules governing ordination, bi-weekly convocations, summer retreats, completion ceremonies, and rules covering dwelling, food, clothing, medicine, disputes, council meetings, decision-making, and owning property. There were several other vinaya texts translated and utilized, all of Hīnayāna origin, but the *Ssu-fen lü* became standard, primarily due to the efforts of Tao-hsüan (596–667) of the Southern Mountain tradition. This became the basis of the Ritsu school in Japan, one of the six schools of the Nara period, based on Lu-tsung (see BUDDHISM IN CHINA), and introduced by *Ganjin. Attempts were also made to establish similar codes based on Mahāyāna *sūtras, focusing on the *bodhisattva ideal, in contrast to the Hīnayāna monastic disciplines, but they never took deep roots to become accepted universally. When the compound, kai-ritsu is used, ritsu (vinaya) refers to an objective code of disciplines, and kai (*śīla) denotes precepts to be undertaken voluntarily, such as the Five Precepts. Thus monks and nuns observe both kai-ritsu, whereas lay believers take on only the kai. Two main schools survive: Ritsu, whose centre is the Tōshōdaiji; and Shingon-ritsu, whose centre is the Saidaiji.

Ritsu and **ryō.** The written criminal and civil codes that were the foundation for the imperial bureaucracy of Japan from the early 7th to the 12th cents. Prior to this period of extensive cultural influence from China, the Japanese archipelago was under the political hegemony of the Yamato court. Rule was based mainly on early tribal law accentuating ceremonial purity, divining the will of the gods (*kami), and dispensing justice, usually by the hand of the sovereign who acted as chief priest and political authority.

With the regency of Prince Shōtoku (593–622), and the subsequent Taika reform measures (645), the ritsu-ryō system of rule, adapted from T'ang Chinese models, was gradually instituted in a bold attempt to centralize power around the imperial throne. Several compilations of penal and civil codes were drafted, most notably the Taihō codes of 701, and the Yōrō codes of 718.

The ritsu were essentially disciplinary sanctions of a penal character. The ryō were prescriptive regulations for the organization of governmental administration. A distinctive feature of the Japanese bureaucracy, however, was the establishment of a second branch with prestige superior to that of the Department of State. This was the *Jingikan or 'Department of Shinto' with jurisdiction over the cult of the national gods (kami). The ritsu-ryō government dissolved in the 12th cent., being replaced by shogun military rule.

In Japanese *music, ritsu and ryō are scales drawn from Buddhist chant.

Ritual (Lat., *ritus*, 'structure', 'ceremony'). Actions repeated in regular and predictable ways, both in religious and secular contexts, serving so many purposes that summary is impossible. Ritual is clearly an integral part of religious life, but it is common and persistent outside the domain of religion: consider the ordered expectations in different kinds of parties, for New Year's Eve, retirements, pre-wedding nights, etc. Religious ritual is usually thought to comprise repetition, commitment, intention, pattern (especially of movements), tradition (often by linkage with *myth which is regarded by some as supplying the meaning of the ritual), purpose, and performance. At the very least, public ritual is social drama, which makes unsurprising the origin of *theatre in religious ritual, for example in Greece, India (where ritual and drama are still closely linked), and Japan (see NŌ DRAMA). Beyond that elementary point, definitions and explanations of ritual proliferate. Thus to indicate some major examples, ritual emerges: from play (J. Huizinga, *Homo Ludens*); or from work, to bring the uncontrollable, such as rainfall, into relation with the controlled, such as ploughing and sowing (J. G. *Frazer); as a culturally shared obsessional neurosis (S. *Freud); or as a consequence of the demand for redundancy in the transmission of culturally vital information (V. P. Gay); as a means of expressing the collective consciousness of a group through the enacted reinforcement of social structure (E. *Durkheim); or as a means of doing the same, but by allowing the normal social structure to be inverted and broken out of temporarily, so that the return to everyday structure is enhanced in value (V. *Turner, *The Ritual Process*, 1969; *The Forest of Symbols*, 1967)—or by doing that, but in rituals of rebellion which remove anxiety and resentment through catharsis (M. Gluckman, *Order and Rebellion*, 1963); in order to 'fuse, under the agency of a single set of symbolic forms, the world as lived and the world as imagined' (C. *Geertz); or in order to contradict the world as lived by immersing the body in a larger process of Becoming (E. M. Zuesse, *Ritual Cosmos*, 1979); to mediate, beneath the level of surface meaning, oppositions at the level of deep structure (C. *Lévi-Strauss); or to construct surface-level meaning by the procedures of an internally coherent life-world (P. Ricœur). This list of the antinomies of ritual could be extended almost indefinitely. Some have gone back further to establish, or suggest, the biogenetic conditions which are satisfied by ritual—R. A. Rappaport (*Pigs for Ancestors*, 1968) in terms of ecology and natural selection, E. d'Aquili (*The Spectrum of Ritual*, 1979) in terms of the underlying biogenetic structures of the brain (see BIOGENETIC STRUCTURALISM). These approaches are reinforced by the study of animal behaviour where repetitive actions directed to goals are frequently referred to as 'rituals'. While some such gene-based structuralism is clearly a *sine qua non* for so universal and pervasive a behaviour, it is clearly also necessary to observe what ritual achieves in transforming (through the ritualization of) space, time, objects, persons, actions, identity, sound, in order to understand why human ritual transcends repetitive, naturally selected animal behaviours. Both meaning and action are connected. Thus while ritual may seek to be causative (or may be understood by some or all participants to be so), it is also expressive (e.g. of human need or solidarity); and by being expressive, it may then in different ways become causative of those many consequences which underlie the diverse definitions above. On this basis, A. F. C. Wallace (*Religion: An Anthropological View*, 1966) suggested five main categories of ritual: (i) technological, including rites of divination, of intensification (to obtain such things as food or alcohol), and of protection; (ii) therapeutic (and anti-therapeutic); (iii) ideological (for the sake of the community as a whole), including rites of passage, of intensification (to ensure adherence to values), of taboos, ceremonies, and courtesies, and of rebellion (leading to catharsis); (iv) soteriological, aimed at repair of communal and individual damage, including rites of possession and exorcism, of new identity, and of ecstasy; and (v) revitalizing. From this it can be seen that ritual is at least the recognition in the midst of time of the ways in which the sequential passage of time affords the possibility of reassertive and significant action.

See also RITES OF PASSAGE; PSYCHODYNAMIC THEORY; JUNG, C. G.; Index, Rituals.

C. Bell, *Ritual Theory, Ritual Practice* (1991); *Research in Ritual Studies: A Programmatic Essay and Bibliography* (1985); R. L. Grimes, *Beginning Ritual Studies* (1982); J. S. la Fontaine, *The Interpretation of Ritual* (1985).

Ritual bronzes: see BRONZE VESSELS.

Ritualism. A movement in the Church of England in the late 19th cent., to adopt the ritual and Gothic ornament of the Roman Catholic Church. It was 'an aesthetic expression, the tangible poetry of the *Oxford Movement' (P. T. Marsh), though it was equally or more a visual translation of *Gothic romanticism. It flourished most notably in some slum parishes, and among priests of saintly reputation, but it was distrusted by those who regarded it as crypto- (or manifest) papalism. Attempts to repress it in the secular or church courts (on the basis of the Ornaments rubric) from 1869, and through an act of Parliament (1874), were not ultimately successful. Temporary restrictions were secured against e.g. Edward King, bishop of Lincoln, through the Lincoln Judgement in 1890.

Ritual slaughter: see SHEḤITAH; AL-HALAL.

Rituals of retrogression: see RETROGRESSIVE RITUALS.

Rivers: see SACRED RIVERS, SEVEN.

Rizalistas. Members of religious movements in the Philippines which honour José Rizal y Mercado (1861–96) as divine, as the power of the *Holy Spirit, as a second *Christ, or as a new *messiah who will return. Rizal was an intellectual, physician, novelist, and nationalist who was shot by the Spanish after the Philippines revolution broke out. Although not himself especially religious, he has become a national *martyr and symbol of Philippine independence. By 1970, there were some 300,000 adherents of these rurally oriented Rizalist movements, looking to Rizal to remove their poverty and exploitation. Among the larger movements are Bathalismo (*Bathala*, 'God') claiming to antedate the arrival of the Spanish; Banner of the Race Church (Watawat ng Lahi) which resembles *Roman Catholicism and awaits the return of Rizal; Sacred Church of the Race (Iglesia Sagrada ng Lahi) with its own ancient 'bible' kept secret until Rizal appeared as God on earth; Philippine Church or Adarnistas (after 'Mother Adarna' the founder) for whom Rizal was not executed but lives as true God and man; Patriotic Church of our Lord Jesus Christ. Rituals range from Catholic forms to simple house-prayer gatherings, and many have a New Jerusalem, actual or ideal.

Rmi.Lam (dream yoga): see MILAM; NĀRO CHOS DRUG.

Rnying-ma-pa: see NYINGMA.

Rōba Zen. 'Grandmother Zen', so-called because it adopts a gentle method of training. This arises from the character of either the pupil or teacher or both.

Robinson, John A. T. (1919–83). *Anglican theologian. Formerly a New Testament scholar at Cambridge, it was as bishop of Woolwich in SE London (1959–69) that he became a public figure. His book *Honest to God* (1963), which admitted difficulties in traditional understandings of God and prayer, sold 3½ million copies, but also brought accusations of *heresy and atheism. To the controversy his writings provoked he replied that 'the Church has a greater investment in integrity than in orthodoxy. Not without reason, men find this hard to believe.' Without expectation, but with some hope, of further preferment in the Church of England, Robinson returned to Cambridge, where the Faculty of Divinity also largely ignored him. His occasional writings ranged over such subjects as law reform, the *Shroud of Turin, and disarmament. His scholarly work was also controversial, particularly that which defended the earliness (pre-66 CE) date of the New Testament documents, particularly the gospel of John.

Rock garden: see KYŌTO.

Rogation days. In W. churches, days of prayer and fasting in the early summer, associated with *intercession (Lat., *rogare*, 'ask'), especially for the harvest. For Roman Catholics, rogation days were replaced in 1969 by periods of prayer at different times of the year (fixed locally) for the needs of humanity and for the work of human hands.

Roger (Schutz), Brother (founder of Christian community): see TAIZÉ.

Rokkakudō (Jap., hexagonal hall). The common name for a *Tendai temple in Kyōto, otherwise known as Chōhōji. It was built by Shotoku to enshrine an image of Nyorin Kannon, and it became the emperor's prayer hall in 822. It was the site of *Shinran's fast which led to his conversion to *Pure Land teaching. Successive buildings have been destroyed by fire; the present building was built in 1877.

Rokudō. Jap. for the six realms of existence (*gati); see also SHŌBŌ-NENJO-GYŌ.

Rokusō (Jap., 'six aspects'). The six features which, according to *Kegon teaching, can be found in all appearances: (i) *sōsō*, able to undertake a variety of functions; (ii) *bessō*, able to focus on one particular function; (iii) *dōsō*, possessing a function which is also held in general by other appearances; (iv) *isō*, having a distinctive feature of its own; (v) *jōsō*, having the power to form or construct in combination with other appearances; (vi) *esō*, persistence through destruction. *Rokuso en'yu* is the ability of those trained in Kegon to see the six elements as being undifferentiated, whereas the untrained see these features as disparate.

Rokuso daishi hōbōdan-gyo (key Zen work): see LIU-TSU-TA-SHIH FA-PAO-T'AN-CHING.

Rolle, Richard (*c*.1300–49). Christian hermit and mystic. Born near Pickering in Yorkshire, he became a hermit as a young man, latterly near the convent of Cistercian nuns at Hampole, where he died, perhaps of the Black Death. His writings, both in Latin and English, give expression to a highly affective mystical experience of 'heat', 'sweetness', and 'song'.

> Be it known to all manner of people in this wretched dwelling-place of exile abiding, that no man may be embued with love of endless life, nor be anointed with heavenly sweetness, unless he truly be turned to God. It behoves truly he be turned to him . . . before he may be expert in the sweetness of God's love.

He was very influential in medieval England, especially through his lyrics and vernacular writings, though his emphasis on experience was regarded as suspect in his own time, notably by the author of the **Cloud of Unknowing*.

F. M. M. Comper, *The Life* . . . (1928).

Roman Catholic Church. Those churches in communion with the Church of Rome, recognizing the leadership of the *pope. The word '*Catholic' means 'universal', and thus the addition of 'Roman' seems to some contradictory, since they regard the Church under the successor of *Peter (see PETRINE TEXTS) as the one, universal Church; other Christians (i.e. those who are baptized and 'honoured by the name of Christian', *Lumen Gentium*, 15) are held to be 'in a certain, although imperfect, communion with the Catholic Church' (*Unitatis redintegratio*, 3). To be in complete communion with the Church of Rome is to belong to the Catholic Church. However, the addition of 'Roman' has become more common during the recent decades of *ecumenicism, not least in recognition of the status of *uniate Churches and of other uses of the world 'Catholic'; 'Roman Catholic' is therefore used in this article and throughout the *Dictionary*.

Roman Catholics for the most part share a common *liturgy based upon vernacular translations of the Roman *rite, but there are a number of *uniate churches with distinctive liturgies, hierarchical structure, and *canon law. The canon law of the Roman-rite churches was first codified in 1917, and a revised edn. was published in 1983. Central government is exercised by the pope and *curia (usually referred to as 'the *Vatican), assisted at three-yearly intervals by a *synod of *bishops elected by episcopal conferences. The development of episcopal conferences at both national and regional level has, since *Vatican II, allowed, at least in theory, greater autonomy to the local churches. However, bishops are still appointed by the Vatican, with due consideration of the names sent in to them.

It is by far the largest of the Christian denominations, with approaching a billion members. About half of these are in Europe or N. America, but it is calculated that by the end of the century nearly three-quarters of Roman Catholics will live in the Third World. Serving the Church's members are just over 400,000 priests, 68,000 male religious, and just short of one million female religious. There are rather more than 2,000 *dioceses or equivalent administrative areas, but a quarter of these are in Europe.

The Roman Catholic Church insists on its continuity of belief, liturgy, and structure from the pre-*Reformation church, and upon its right, as (in its own view) the one church founded by *Christ, to hold *councils of its own bishops which are regarded as *ecumenical and, doctrinally, of the same standing as the councils of the early church. It has held three since the Reformation, those of *Trent, Vatican I, and Vatican II. On some theological issues Trent sharply distinguished RC doctrine from that of the Reformers, rejecting, for example, the *Lutheran teaching on *justification, the manner of Christ's presence in the *eucharist, and *indulgences. At Vatican I the bishops asserted the primacy and *infallibility of the pope, but at Vatican II the RC Church made an effort to come closer to other Christian churches, and formulated no firm doctrinal statements—setting, for example, Mariological (see MARY) devotion (so typical of Catholicism) firmly within its ecclesial framework. In the subsequent years, *Paul VI did much to put into effect the programme of Vatican II, but began also to express a caution which became also a marked feature of the policy of John Paul II—culminating in *Catechism of the Catholic Church* (1993/4): in this, for example, the Bible is used as though a-historical, as though its embeddedness in history has no effect on the application of the text to current issues. Whether the attempt of John Paul II to reorganize the Church on the basis of its achievements in the past is regarded as 'a conservative winter' or as 'an overdue return to the immoveable foundations' depends on prior attitudes and experience: for the tension, see e.g. LIBERATION THEOLOGY. Many would say that it is neither of these, but an attempt to hold in balance the progressive currents in the Church with a rigid notion of truth combined with a centralizing of authority in the magisterium.

Throughout its history, the Roman Catholic Church has placed great emphasis on the offering of life, through the Church, to God in obedience and holiness. It has thus given special importance to the *monastic life, which epitomizes the choice of God rather than the world. However numerous the reforms of monastic and religious orders and the foundation of new ones may have been (for examples, see Index, 'Christian Orders'), they have consistently focused all the faithful on the necessity for prayer: the development of different approaches to the formation of spiritual life is a characteristic consequence. At the same time, the radical choice for God has led to a constant acceptance of *martyrdom, which the outreach of evangelism (not least in the 20th cent.) has repeatedly brought about; the strong emphasis on being the only Church has equally led Roman Catholics to be zealous in their persecution of others, and evangelism often accompanied conquest, as in the policy of Spain (between the 16th and 18th cents.). In this context, the prayer of the faithful was, until the 15th cent., apt to be of a verbal and repetitive nature. The Latin liturgy and Bible (*Vulgate) increased the problems for the laity in understanding the faith. Since Vatican II, the change to vernacular liturgies and Bibles, together with the transformation of the penitential rites (*confession) and the move of the altar to the centre of the church, has increased the active participation of all in worship. It remains the case that strict rules govern membership of the Church, e.g. concerning who may communicate at *Mass, or the status of divorced people; celibacy is a requirement for priests (even though in some parts of the world this means that the celebration of the Mass is infrequent); and the laity are under obligation not to use artificial contraception (see HUMANAE VITAE). The latter arises from definitions of the meaning of 'the person', and of when the life of any particular person begins. The same consideration underlies the absolute opposition to *abortion. Control (through licensing) is also exercised over those teaching in Catholic schools and universities, and while many such institutions are now under the direction of lay professionals, publications and lectures may still occasion discipline, which many include the silencing of so-called progressive theologians. Conformity has not in the past meant a repetitive *theology: theology and philosophy have had a high place in Roman Catholicism, by no means confined to *scholasticism.

The central place, both of the Mass in worship, and of the Church in the community, has contributed to the inspiration of enduring *art, architecture, and *music, as well as many kinds of literature. The Church as patron has had immense consequences for civilization as a whole. So also has the absolute requirement to be generous to those in need (a requirement which goes back to Christ). As a result, schools, hospitals, places where the needy and dying can find refuge, and a wide range of aid programmes have multiplied. This tradition is also expressed in 100 years of teaching on social justice issues, from **Rerum Novarum* to the *Constitution of the Church in the Modern World* (*Gaudium et Spes*) in 1965, and subsequent encyclicals. The financial cost of the Vatican is great and falls heavily on the Church in the USA, where the majority have a vision of the Church in the service of the world which has been increasingly at variance from the official Vatican line (though, they would say, in line with the vision of Vatican II). The resulting tension can be seen particularly in the radical divide over the opportunities open to women to have a voice comparable to that of men in the Church. Roman Catholicism is highly clericalized, and the refusal to allow the possibility that women can be ordained means that they can never be a serious part of the leadership or decision-making of the Church.

See Index, Roman Catholicism and further references there.

T. Bokenkotter, *A Concise History* . . . (1990) and *Essential Catholicism* (1986); L. S. Cunningham, *The Catholic Heritage* (1983); C. Carlen, *The Papal Encyclicals, 1740–1981*; D. Dorr, *Option for the Poor: One Hundred Years of Catholic Social Teaching* (1985); P. E. Fink (ed.), *A New Dictionary of Sacramental Worship* (1990); A. Hastings, *Modern Catholicism* (1990); M. Downey (ed.), *The New Dictionary of Catholic Spirituality* (1993); R. P. McBrien, *Catholicism* (1980).

Romanos the Melodist, St. (d. ?556). The greatest of Greek hymn-writers (although only a few—80 out of 1,000—of his hymns survive). A Syrian by birth, after a time as deacon at Berytus, he found his way to Constantinople under Patriarch Anastasius I (d. 518). The subjects of his hymns include events from the life of *Christ and the Virgin *Mary, and figures from the *Old Testament: they manifest brilliant dramatic characterization and great theological insight. Hardly any of his hymns are still used in the liturgy, though the famous *Akathistos hymn is widely regarded as his. Feast day, 1 Oct.

Tr. E. Lash, *On the Life of Christ: Kontakia*, (1995).

Romans, Letter to the. A book of the *New Testament and the longest of *Paul's epistles. It was written *c.*58 CE from Corinth. Paul had not founded the church in Rome but hoped to visit it. Chs. 1–8 deal with the universality of *sin, *justification apart from the law through *faith, *Christ as a second *Adam, and life according to the *(Holy) Spirit. In chs. 9–11 Paul attempted to understand God's purpose in evidently displacing the Jews. Chs. 12–15 are more practical, including the admonition to obey the 'powers that be' (13. 1–7). Romans is the most systematic of Paul's letters, and since the 4th cent. it has stood first among them in the Bible. It has powerfully affected Christian doctrine on such questions as *original sin, *merit, and justification.

Rome. 'The eternal city', capital of modern Italy (embracing the Vatican City since the Lateran Treaty in 1929 between the *pope and the Italian government of Mussolini), and major centre of Christianity since the arrival of *Paul and *Peter (the presence of the latter having sometimes been disputed). Both *apostles are believed to have been martyred in Rome: St Peter's Basilica stands on the traditional site of Peter's burial. The gradual Christian domination of Rome is epitomized in the Church of San Clemente, where layers of different sacred buildings (all still accessible) are built above each other, the lowest being a temple dedicated to *Mithras. The city is replete with churches and Christian art, including early examples in the *catacombs. It is a centre of *pilgrimage and (in the Vatican City) of *Roman Catholicism.

Romero, Oscar Arnulfo (1917–80). Christian archbishop of El Salvador, assassinated in 1980. He studied theology in Rome, 1937–43, became a parish priest and bishop of Santiago de Maria in 1974. Thought to be a conservative bishop (not least because of his support of *Opus Dei), he was appointed archbishop in Feb. 1977, in the expectation that he would not disturb the political *status quo*. Three weeks later, the *Jesuit Rutilio Grande, together with two others, was gunned down in his jeep. The event was, for Romero, a conversion. He began a ministry of outspoken commitment to those who had no voice of their own. *Paul VI gave him encouragement, but the accession of *John Paul II, with its cult of the pope and movement away from the vision of *Vatican II, led to an increasing campaign against Romero in Rome. The details of this are disputed. It appears that John Paul asked him not to deal with specifics but to talk only of general principles; Romero tried to explain that specific murders in El Salvador were not adequately dealt with by stating general principles. The Vatican response was to appoint an apostolic administrator to oversee his work, but Romero was killed before this could be put into effect. He returned from his last visit to Rome to the slogan painted on walls, 'Be a patriot, kill a priest'. He was killed as he said mass in the chapel of the Divine Providence Hospital where he lived.

O. Romero, *A Shepherd's Diary* (1993).

Romuald (Christian monk): see CAMALDOLESE.

Rosary. In Christianity, a *Catholic devotion which consists in reciting fifteen 'decades' (groups of ten) of Hail Marys (*Ave Maria), each decade preceded by the *Lord's Prayer and followed by the *Gloria Patri. A string of variously numbered (e.g. 55 or 165 'beads', Med. Eng., *beda*, 'prayer') are used to count the individual prayers. Each decade represents one of the 'fifteen mysteries' (five 'joyful', five 'sorrowful', five 'glorious'), each an event in the life of *Jesus or his mother. Ordinarily only one-third of the rosary, one 'chaplet' of five decades, is said at a time. Devotion to the rosary seems to have developed gradually since the 15th cent. under Dominican and Cistercian influence.

Prayer beads are also used in other religions (e.g. Hinduism and Buddhism: see MĀLĀ; Jap. Buddhism: see NENJU), and are referred to in English as 'rosaries'. Thus, many Sikhs use a rosary (*mālā*) to assist meditation. Rosaries consist of 108 (the number of evil passions to which humans are subject) beads or 27 (quarter size). In Sikh iconography Gurū *Nānak is frequently depicted holding a rosary. For *Nāmdhārīs it must be of white wool. On each bead devotees utter, *'Vāhigurū'. See also NĀM SIMARAN. In Islam, the *subḥa* (Arab., *sabbaḥa*, 'praise God', cf. *subḥān Allāh*, 'Glory to God!') is the Muslim string of prayer beads, in three groups, divided by two larger beads (*imām*), with a larger piece serving as a handle. By different reckonings, the total is always 100—Allāh + his *Ninety-nine Beautiful Names. The beads are both a means of counting and also an act of supererogatory *ṣalāt (prayer): see *NĀFILA.

Rosenzweig, Franz (1886–1929). German Jewish theologian. He was born into an *assimilated family, and, as a young man, he was much influenced by a relative, E. Rosenstock-Huessy, with whom he conducted a correspondence, later published in part. Under this influence, Rosenzweig contemplated converting to Christianity, but in 1913, after attending a *High Holy Day Service, he resolved to remain faithful to Judaism. Influenced by Herman *Cohen and Martin *Buber, and while still a soldier in the First World War, he wrote *Der Stern der Erloesung* (1921; tr. W. W. Hallo, *The Star of Redemption*, 1971). This monumental work is in three parts. In part (i) he argued that truth is subjective and is arrived at and tested through personal experience. In part (ii) he maintained that *revelation is God's continuous initiation of a relationship with humanity and that this relationship demands a particular kind of interaction between human beings. The commandments of *halakhah must be seen as expressions of the love-relationship. In part (iii), he argued that Jews from their very biological descent have entered into a relationship with God which finds its expression in the *calendar and the *liturgy. In contrast, Christians must be converted into their *covenant which has been superimposed on its pagan origins. However, Rosenzweig believed that both Judaism and Christianity would be superseded at the end of time. After the War, Rosenzweig founded the Freies Juedisches Lehrhaus ('The Free Jewish House of Learning') for assimilated Jews to study the Jewish classics. From 1921, he was afflicted with progressive paralysis, but he continued to work translating *Judah Halevi's poems, and, with Martin Buber, he started translating the Hebrew scriptures. This project was completed by Buber after the Second World War.

N. N. Glatzer (ed.), *Franz Rosenzweig: His Life and Thought* (1953); S. S. Schwarzschild, *Franz Rosenzweig . . .* (1961).

Rosh (acronym): see ASHER BEN JEHIEL.

Rosh ha-Shanah (Heb., 'New Year'). The Jewish *New Year. Rosh ha-Shanah is celebrated on 1 Tishri (and 2 in the *diaspora). According to R. *Eliezer, the world was *created in the month of Tishri (*RH* 27a), and Rosh ha-Shanah is the day on which all humanity is judged (*RH* 1. 2). The four names of the festival in the Jewish tradition reflect the various themes of the day: Rosh ha-Shanah, Yom Teru'ah ('Day of Blowing the Horn'), Yom ha-Din ('Day of Judgement'), and Yom ha-Zikkaron ('Day of Remembrance'). According to tradition, the completely wicked are inscribed in the Book of Death on Rosh ha-Shanah, the completely virtuous in the Book of Life, while for the in-betweens judgement is suspended until Yom Kippur (*Day of Atonement). A variety of reasons is given for the blowing of the *shofar, and it is blown in a particular way. According to *Maimonides, its purpose is to say, 'Awake from your slumbers, you who have fallen asleep, and reflect on your deeds' (*Yad. Teshuvah* 3. 4). During the festival, the *Ashkenazim greet each other with the phrase, 'May you be inscribed [in the Book of Life] for a good year', and it is customary to eat something sweet as a token of a sweet year ahead. On the first afternoon, the *Tashlikh ceremony is often performed, although there is no reference to this in the *Talmud.

P. Goodman, *The Rosh Hashanah Anthology* (1971).

Rosh ha-Shanah. A tractate of the Jewish *Talmud. The tractate deals with the laws and customs of the various *New Years in the Jewish *Calendar.

Rosh Ḥodesh (new month): see MOON, BLESSING OF THE.

Roshi (Jap., 'old master'). Title of a Zen master. Initially, the title was hard-earned, being bestowed by people at large on one who was recognized as having realized the *dharma of the Buddha by direct experience, and as having sustained it in everyday life (*mujōdō-no-taigen). The title was confirmed in years of further training, leading to the seal of recognition (*inka-shōmei) and success in dharma contests (*hossen). 'Roshi' has now become a more general title of a Zen teacher, who may be monk or lay, man or woman; and it has degenerated even further into a term of respect for any old or venerated monk.

Rossi, Azariah ben Moses Dei (1511–78). Jewish scholar. Rossi was born into an eminent Jewish family. He was the author of *Me'or Einayim* (Enlightenment to the Eyes, 1573–5), which shows his familiarity with Greek and Latin authors, the Church Fathers, and *Philo. It was the source of some controversy, as he questioned the historicity of *Talmudic legends. The work consists of three chapters: the first discusses earthquakes, the second is a Heb. tr. of the *Letter of *Aristeas*, and the third is a study of the development of Jewish history. He envisaged an interaction of mutual good between Jews and gentiles: 'We who have been scattered to the four winds of heaven should pray to God the Almighty for the peace of all the inhabitants of the world, for in their peace is our peace.'

Rota Sacra Romana. The 'Sacred Roman Rota', the usual tribunal for judging cases brought before the *Holy See. Its jurisdiction in civil matters ended along with the temporal power of the papacy in 1870. It is the court to which appeals in nullity and other matrimonial cases are referred.

Roy, Rām Mohan (1772–1833). Hindu apologist and reformer. Born in Hughli District, West Bengal, of a well-placed brahman family, Rām Mohan Roy was a fine linguist, knowing not only Bengali and English but also the classical languages of Sanskrit, Arabic, and Persian. He was employed as Revenue Officer in Rangpur for the East India Company until 1814, when he retired from this work to settle in Calcutta. He was widely read in both religious and political philosophy, and from his knowledge of Muslim, Hindu, and Christian religious writings he developed into one of the foremost reformist intellectuals of early 19th-cent. India. In 1828 he founded the Brāhmo Sabha, a monotheistic form of Hinduism with no images, which stressed the One True Formless God who alone was worthy of worship. It led to the forming of the *Brahmo Samāj. Rām Mohan Roy denied the role of prophets and the exclusivist concept of Son of God, and so drew upon himself attacks not only from traditionalist Hindus but Muslims and Christians as well. He was opposed to caste, polygamy, suttee (see SATĪ), the prohibition of widow remarriage, the lack of education for ordinary people, and the seclusion of and institutionalized discrimination against women. He worked actively and unceasingly for the relief of social evils, and achieved a great deal, especially in the field of education, for he urged the study of W. science, philosophy, and languages so that Indians might develop a synthesis of the best of W. and E. thought. He always affirmed that he was a Hindu, and sought to reform Hinduism from within, without breaking down the whole structure.

Politically Rām Mohan Roy was a nationalist, and a strong campaigner against prevalent injustices against Indians in their own land, for example the heavy land tax imposed on peasant farmers and the prohibition against Hindus and Muslims sitting on the Grand Jury. He urged the industrialization of India, and was a firm believer in his nation's right to govern itself. He was thus one of the first to sow the seeds that flowered in the Indian National Congress.

Rām Mohan Roy, invested with the title of *Rāja* by the titular Moghul emperor Akbar II, visited Britain in 1830 to present the emperor's grievances to the British king and parliament. In Britain he interpreted India through publications and speeches and took an active interest in British politics of the time, e.g. the Reform Movement, 1830–2. He died at Bristol on 27 Sept. 1833, but his influence lived on in the many subsequent Hindu progressive movements, and he held a high position among Bengali intellectuals.

S. Chakravarti, *Rammohan Roy: Father of Modern India* (1935); S. Collett, *Life and Letters of Raja Rammohan Roy* (1914); B. N. Dasgupta, *The Life and Times . . .* (1980); M. C. Kotnala, *Raja Ram Mohun Roy . . .* (1975); K. Nag and D. Burman (eds.), *The English Works . . .* (1945–51); A. K. Ray, *The Religious Ideas . . .* (1976).

Ṛṣabha (Skt., 'bull'). In Jainism, the first *tīrthaṅkara of our present *avasarpiṇī*, who is also given the title *Ādinātha. An extremely popular figure in Jainism, he is credited by Jains with having founded the organization of human society, establishing *caste, law, monarchy, and agriculture. Many legends are associated with his name, attributing to him a vast life-span. Some scholars have linked him with finds from the Indus Valley civilization, through the bull motif which is Ṛṣabha's symbol, and through the find of standing male nudes which are depicted in the *kāyotsarga* posture of *yoga, a characteristically Jain posture, particularly associated with Ṛṣabha. Ṛṣabha is mentioned in the Hindu **Bhāgavata-purāṇa* as a minor incarnation of *Viṣṇu, which probably reflects the popularity of his cult in the medieval period.

Ṛṣi (Skt., 'seer'). In Skt. literature, a patriarchal poet-sage. The ṛṣis are the visionary authors of the Vedic hymns (and other sacred literature) 'heard' within the silent depths of the heart and preserved in the orthodox *brahman *gotras of which they are the founders. This élite group of primary ancestors of the major priestly families is recorded in the *Veda, whose ritual use is made effectual by the solemn recitation of their names. Such ṛṣis were known as maharṣis, 'great seers', or brahmarṣis, 'priestly seers'. Of these the saptarṣis, 'the seven seers', identified with the constellation Ursa Major (their wives with the Pleiades), are particularly prominent. However, there is much variation in the different lists of these 'mind-born sons of *Brahmā' in the Vedas, Epics, and *Purāṇas. The lists include: Agastya, Aṅgiras, Atri, Bharadvāja, Bhṛgu, Jamadagni, Kaṇva, Kaśyapa, Vasiṣṭha, Marīci, Pulastya, Pulaha, Kratu, and Gautama. Other ṛṣis include the *devarṣis*, 'divine seers', such as Mārkaṇḍeya, and *rājarṣis*, 'royal sages', *kṣatriya kings honoured for their wisdom, such as Janaka and Gṛtsamada.

According to legend the ṛṣis were men of extraordinary creativity and magical power. Much of Skt. literature is devoted to accounts of their supernatural powers (e.g. flying, creating celestial worlds) and command over nature. Even the gods stood in awe of the wisdom and irresistible power of their austerity and wrath. The term ṛṣi or maharṣi survives today in contemporary usage as a title for certain 'holy men', such as Ramana Maharṣi and Maharṣi Mahesh Yogi.

RSS (Indian political party): see BHARATYA JANATA PARTY.

Ṛta(m) (Skt., 'fixed order, rule'). In Hinduism, the sense of fundamental order and balance which obtains in the universe and must be observed and sustained through appropriate sacrifices, rituals, and behaviours. Ṛta as a word is related to *ṛtu*, the seasons, which recur with regularity out of the control of humans—or for that matter, of gods. *Mitra and *Varuṇa are invoked in the *Vedas as guardians of ṛta, but they are never regarded or described as its creator or controller. Ṛta is deeper and more fundamental than the gods, and anticipates the impersonal law of *karma, and the pervasive rule of *dharma.

H. Lüder, *Varuṇa*, ii. *Varuṇa und das Ṛta* (1959).

Ṛtu (Skt.). A point in time: in Hinduism, it is the time appointed for ritual occasions which is determined by *astrological calculations.

Ṛtvij. The Hindu priests employed in sacrificial rituals. In origin four, they extended to seven: Hotar, Potar, Neṣṭar, Agnīdh, Praśāstar, Adhvaryu, and Brahman. By the time of **Śatapatha Brāhmaṇa* (3. 6. 2. 1), they are called 'seven *Hotṛs', Hotṛ having become the chief.

Ruaḥ ha-Qodesh (the Holy Spirit): see HOLY SPIRIT.

Rubā'iyyat (quatrains): see OMAR KHAYYAM.

Rubenstein, R. L. (Jewish commentator and writer): see HOLOCAUST.

Rublev, A. (icon-painter): see ICON.

Rubric (Lat., 'red'). A directive in printed forms of Christian *liturgy (for an example, see CHOIR). The name derives from the fact that these instructions and guides were printed in red in the *Missal, to distinguish them from the text of the liturgy.

Ru-chia: see CONFUCIANISM.

Rudra (Skt., 'roarer', or 'the ruddy one'). A Vedic storm god. Rudra is sometimes identified with *Agni or *Indra, especially in connection with the monsoon rains. Like rainstorms, he has two aspects, one associated with fertility, healing, and welfare, the other associated with destruction, rage, and fear. Since no fire oblation was offered to Rudra, and other offerings were made at ill-omened places, it seems likely that his fearful aspect dominated.

Rudra manifests the destructive power of lightning and thunder. His form is described as brilliant and dazzling, copper-coloured and ruddy. He is armed with lightning bolts and arrows. His sons are the *Maruts, shining storm gods, sometimes called Rudras or Rudriyas. Rudra himself is followed by howling dogs and the hosts of the dead. His female attendants, Ghoṣinīs ('Noisy Ones') may indicate that he was originally a pre-Vedic god.

In post-Vedic times Rudra gradually becomes identified with the great god *Śiva. In the *Veda, *śiva*, 'the auspicious one', is one of Rudra's epithets. In later times, *rudra* is an epithet of Śiva, referring to his destructive aspect.

E. Arbman, *Rudra* (1922).

Rudra Cakrin (final king of Shambhala): see SHAMBHALA.

Ruether, Rosemary Radford. A *Roman Catholic theologian at the forefront of *feminist theology. Ruether has written extensively on the question of Christian credibility, addressing issues of *ecclesiology and its engagement with Church–world conflicts; Jewish–Christian relations; *christology; politics and religion in America; feminism and feminist theology; and God and creation. Her approach is holistic, interdependent, and inclusive: 'Women, as the denigrated half of the human species, must reach for a continually expanding definition of inclusive humanity—inclusive of both genders, inclusive of all social groups and races.' Two of her books, *Sexism and God-Talk* (1983), and *Womanguides: Readings Towards Feminist Theology* (1985) have served as key texts in her own teaching, as together with her students she seeks, 'to analyse the patterns of gender construction that had ratified patriarchy in the dominant tradition and to begin a tentative construction of alternative patterns that might be transformative and healing'. Ruether's work draws on a wide range of theological sources, including mainstream Orthodox, Protestant, and Catholic traditions; *gnosticism, *Montanism, *Quakerism, and the Shakers, and non-Christian traditions, while always questioning sexism within any tradition. Praxis, 'our on-going work of transforming ourselves and our societies in response to this whole process of reflection, and about our communities of praxis' is integral to the working out of Ruether's theology. She has been involved in writing over twenty-two books and at least 500 articles. Her other most notable works are *Gaia and God* (1992); *Women-Church* . . . (1986); *New Woman, New Earth* . . . (1975).

Rūḥ (spirit): see NAFS.

Rumālā (Pañjābī 'cloth'). The cloth which covers the Sikh scriptures. A rumālā is usually brightly coloured with a decorative border. It measures about 1 metre by 1.25 metres, and covers the open *Ādi Granth when it is not being read. Sikhs offer a rumālā at the *gurdwārā on occasions of thanksgiving or of sorrow, when a *pāṭh (reading) is completed.

Rūmī (mystic poet of Islam): see JALĀL AD-DĪN RŪMĪ.

Rūpa (Skt., 'form'). The means in Eastern religions through which the accidental and transitory flux of appearance achieves identifiable shape. By means of rūpa, appearance becomes an object of perception. But the term applies in Hinduism especially to representations of gods, which are then contrasted with lesser objects of perception, stones, trees, etc.; the latter have form, nevertheless they are called *arūpa*—literally 'formless', but clearly something 'aniconic', not bearing the divine form.

In Buddhism, rūpa is associated with nāma, as in *nāma-rūpa, in the analysis of human appearance, to denote corporeality; see also KHANDHA.

Rūpa Gosvāmī (disciple of Caitanya): see CAITANYA.

Rūpaloka: see LOKA (BUDDHISM).

Rural Dean. The head of a group of parishes (rural deanery).

Rushdie, Salman: see SATANIC VERSES.

Russian Orthodox Church. The *Orthodox *Patriarchate of Moscow. Although Christianity spread into Russia early (1st cent.), it was insignificant until the 10th cent. St *Vladimir of Kiev proclaimed Greek Christianity the faith of his realm in 988, and *baptism was ordered. In the 14th cent., leadership moved from Kiev to Moscow, and independence from *Greek Orthodoxy was established. *Monasticism played a key role during the Mughal invasion and rule (13th–15th cents.) especially notable being St *Sergius of Radonezh, whose Monastery of the Holy Trinity became particularly famous. After the fall of Constantinople (1453) and the defeat of the Mongols (1480), the powerful Russian state under Ivan IV ('the Terrible') enhanced Moscow's claim to be the 'Third Rome'. A close alliance (eventually subservience) between Church and State ensued, reinforced by the *Possessors controversy: thus while Filaret governed the church from 1613 to 1633, his son Michael ruled as Tsar. The patriarchate itself had been established in 1589, when Patriarch Jeremias II of *Constantinople officiated at the first enthronement.

In 1727, Peter the Great abolished the patriarchate, and set up a Holy Synod of twelve members nominated by the Tsar, so that the church became a department of state. Its institutional subservience was counteracted by the religious renewal initiated by a monk, Paissy, who emphasized continual prayer and obedience to a *staretz (elder). In the period of the startsi, St Seraphim of Sarov (1759–1833) was especially revered.

The Patriarchate of Moscow was re-established in 1917 by a Council which met between the February and October Revolutions: however, after the October Revolution, the Church's status in the USSR became very precarious. The document which determined Church–State relations was the Declaration of Loyalty of Metropolitan Sergius (head of the church after the death of Patriarch *Tikhon) in 1927, according to which the church would support the aims of the Soviet state in exchange for the legalization of its organization. The wisdom of this declaration is still debated—the Declaration itself was certainly obtained after the metropolitan had spent several weeks in detention: the institutional church was saved by his action, but undoubtedly at great cost to its own integrity. The benefits to the church were, furthermore, eclipsed by persecutions under Stalin, especially in 1929–30 and 1937–8, but the election of Metropolitan Sergius to the still-vacant patriarchate was permitted in 1943. After an easier period during the Second World War, in which the church was encouraged to promote the patriotic efforts of the people, a determined programme of closing churches and seminaries followed under Khruschev between 1959 and 1964. The church had been guaranteed its freedom to worship by art. 124 of the Constitution of 1936, but activities and 'propaganda' outside regular worship were forbidden. After earlier hostility, the Russian church joined the World Council of Churches in 1961: but as a pro-government voice it did not contribute to criticism of religious persecution in Communist countries. *Glasnost* and *perestroika* led to a remarkable resurgence of Christian confidence, allied to the role of other Christian churches (notably the *Roman Catholic) in overthrowing Communist regimes in E. Europe.

The largest body of Russian Orthodox in America, the 'Orthodox Church in America' was declared autocephalous and independent of Moscow in 1970. A synod of Russian bishops who had left during the Revolution, and met at Serbskiy Karlova in Yugoslavia in 1921, organized what has become the Russian Church in Exile: this was very hostile to the Moscow patriarchate, though signs of some relationship are now apparent. There is also an independent 'Paris jurisdiction' in W. Europe, under the direct control of the *Oecumenical Patriarch.

J. Ellis, *The Russian Orthodox Church* (1986); G. P. A. Fedotov, *A Treasury of Russian Spirituality* (1950); N. Zernov, *Moscow, the Third Rome* (1937) and *The Russians and their Church* (1964).

Rustenburg Declaration (against apartheid): see DUTCH REFORMED CHURCH.

Ruten (Jap., 'drifting'). The process of rebirth or reappearance (*saṃsāra). Ruten-no-go is the *karma which brings about rebirth.

Ruth, Book of. One of the Five Scrolls of the Hebrew *Bible. Ruth tells the story of the Moabite Ruth who stays with Naomi, her Israelite mother-in-law, and subsequently meets the prosperous farmer Boaz, a kinsman of her former husband. They make a *levirate marriage and become the ancestors of King *David. The aim of the book seems to be to illustrate the ancestry of the Davidic kings (to demonstrate, like the later *Jonah, a positive relationship to the non-Jewish), and although it is set in the days of the *Judges (which explains its position in the English Bible), it was written in the days of the monarchy. There is no definite evidence to link it with *Ezra's edict against foreign wives. In the *aggadah, Ruth is regarded as the prototype of the righteous *proselyte. When Naomi told her that Jewish women do not go to circuses, she replied, 'Where you go I will go'; when told the Israelites live in houses with *mezuzot, she said, 'Where you lodge, I will lodge'; her words, 'your people will be my people' imply 'I will destroy all *idolatry within me' (*Ruth R.* 2. 22). In the New Testament, Ruth is specifically mentioned in the genealogy of *Christ (Matthew 1. 5).

Ruthenians or **Little Russians** (in distinction from Great Russians, those based on Moscow). Catholic Slavs. They come from SW Russia, Poland, the old Czechoslovakia, and Hungary, but are dispersed now throughout the world, especially in the USA.

Ruysbroek (Ruusbroec), Jan van, St (1293–1381). Flemish Christian mystic. Born in Ruysbroek and educated in Brussels, in 1343 he retired with two others to a hermitage at Groenendael, near Brussels, later an important centre of the *devotio moderna* (see THOMAS À KEMPIS). In the growing controversy over mysticism, he was critical of the 'Brethren of the Free Spirit', but his principal work, *The Spiritual Espousals*, was itself attacked by Gerson. His many, mainly short, writings in Flemish betray the influence of *Eckhart in particular, but develop within a clearly defined trinitarian framework, at their summit exploring the 'waylessness' of the soul's encounter with God. Nevertheless, in the approach to the summit, he discerned three stages: (i) active (the purification of moral life), (ii) interior, seeking pure simplicity ('nudity', freedom from sense images), (iii) union. He is known as the Ecstatic Doctor; feast day, 2 Dec.

P. Mommaers and N. de Paepe (eds.), *Jan van Ruusbroec* . . . (1984); J. A. Wiseman (ed.), *John Ruusbroec: The Spiritual Espousals and Other Works* (1985).

Ruzhin, Israel (1797–1850). Jewish *ḥasidic leader. A great-grandson of *Dov Baer, he succeeded to ḥasidic leadership at the age of 16. He set up court in Ruzhin, but in 1838 he was imprisoned for being instrumental in the deaths of two Jewish informers. Subsequently, he moved from town to town until he finally settled near Sadgora. Thousands of ḥasidim streamed to his court, and after his death, six of his sons established ḥasidic dynasties.

Ryō: see RITSU AND RYŌ.

Ryōbu Shintō (Jap., 'dual Shinto'). The pattern of *Shinto-Buddhist coexistence which developed in Japan. As a general term, it refers to the various forms Shinto took in the course of Shinto-Buddhist syncretism. More specifically, Ryōbu Shintō refers to the Shingon Shinto tradition under the influence of *Shingon Buddhism. The *Tendai Buddhist amalgamation with Shinto is called Sannō Ichijitsu ('Mountain-king one-truth'). In the early period of Buddhist influence on Shinto, the *kami were considered to be protectors of the Buddha's law and were enshrined in Buddhist temples. Later, the kami were felt to be in need of salvation through the help of the Buddha, and Buddhist scriptures were chanted before altars of the kami. After the middle of the Heian period, the idea developed that the kami's original nature was really the Buddha essence, and thus the kami were regarded as worthy objects of worship and adoration as manifestations of the Buddhas. It was asserted that *Amaterasu Ōmikami, enshrined at Ise, was a Japanese manifestation of *Mahavairocana, the Great Sun Buddha who was the chief divinity in Shingon Buddhism. Ryōbu Shintō adopted the Shingon notion that the whole world can be understood through two *maṇḍala, symbolic cosmic pictures representing the bipolar character of reality. Kami could be co-ordinated with Buddhist divinities by placing some kami in the Womb Realm maṇḍala and others in the Diamond Realm maṇḍala, giving rise to the designation of 'Dual (*ryōbu*) Shintō'. The influence of Ryōbu Shintō is still seen in some Shinto torii or gates, in which each of the two upright poles has attached to it two smaller poles, indicating the dual character of the world transcended by an overarching unity. The Tendai Buddhist theory that all Buddhas are really only 'one reality' (*ichi-jitsu*) was used to support the view of Tendai Shinto that the various kami are Japanese historical appearances that correspond to Buddhas—all subsumed in the 'one reality'.

Ryōkan Daigu (1758–1831). Monk of the *Sōtō school, and one of the greatest Zen poets. The name given by his master, Kokusen, means 'abundant goodness'. His self-bestowed name, Daigu, means 'big fool'. He sought simplicity, rejecting 'poems by poets, calligraphy by calligraphers and cooking by cooks', and preferring to play with children—the highest form of Zen was playing ball with children. Much influenced by the works of *Dōgen, he travelled after the death of Kokusen (1791), eventually settling in Gogō-an, where he lived as a hermit. It was here that most of his poetry was written, with about 1,400 poems surviving. Many express his way of acceptance which obliterates anxiety or distress: 'When you meet with misfortune | It is good to meet with misfortune. | When you die, it is good to die. | This is the wonderful way | To escape misfortune.' Everything is of the same nature (*śūnyatā), so every occurrence is an intriguing exploration into that nature. In his last years, Teishin became his pupil, and they communicated in poems written to and for each other. When he died, she collected his poems in an anthology, *Dew-drops on a Lotus Leaf.* Koji Nakano, *Philosophy of Honest Poverty,* made Ryōkan a cult hero in Japan in the early 1990s.

B. Watson, *Ryōkan: Zen Monk-Poet of Japan* (1977); N. Yuasa, *The Zen Poems of Ryōkan* (1981).

Ryū (Jap., 'dragon'). A deity which protects Buddhism. It is the equivalent of *nāga, a snake-like creature with power to cause rain.

S

Sa'adiah Gaon (882–942). Leader of Babylonian Jewry in the *geonic period. Sa'adiah grew up in Egypt, but eventually settled in Baghdād. From 921, he became involved in a struggle between the *Jerusalem *academy and the Babylonian authorities on the dating of the *festivals—in his *Sefer ha-Mo'adim*, he gives an account of the affair. In 928, he became head of the academy at *Sura. At the time he was described as 'a great scholar', 'not afraid of any man and not showing favour to anyone because of his great knowledge, eloquence and piety'. With extraordinary energy he revived the academy, but he quickly came into conflict with the *exilarch David b. Zakkai, who deposed him. Sa'adiah in his turn appointed an alternative exilarch. Ultimately the two were reconciled, but not until a bitter and long-drawn-out quarrel had taken place. Sa'adiah is remembered as a *halakhist, a philosopher, a grammarian, and a *liturgist. He wrote several halakhic books, most of which are still in manuscript. Those in print were collected and edited by J. Mueller (1897). His major philosophic work was his *Kitab al-Amanat w'al-I'tiqadat* (tr. S. Rosenblatt, *The Book of Beliefs and Opinions*, 1948). The Hebrew translation by Judah ibn Tibbon, *Sefer ha-Emunot ve-ha-De'ot* (1562) was extremely influential and was drawn on by the opponents of *Maimonides. It was written to give guidance to the people in the face of the religious disputes and conflicts of the 10th cent., and Sa'adiah was the first medieval philosopher to try and reconcile biblical revelation with philosophy: 'We have two foundations of our religion, after the Bible: the first and earlier is the fountain of reason, the second and later is tradition.' Thus the arbiter in disputed matters is reason: 'Any interpretation that conforms to reason must be correct.'

As a grammarian, he wrote three books: *Sefer ha-Agron* (which attempted to provide a rhyming dictionary of Hebrew); *Pitron Shivim Millim* (a polemical work designed to prove to the *Karaites that the *oral law was indispensable since without it the biblical text was incomprehensible); *Sefer Zahut ha-Lashon ha-Ivrit* (dealing with various grammatical problems). Sa'adiah also produced the first Arabic translation of the Heb. scriptures with popular commentary. As a liturgist, he made a collection of prayers for the whole year in Arab. and was the composer of many *piyyutim. Abraham *ibn Ezra described Sa'adiah as 'the ultimate gaon'. According to Maimonides, who did not always agree with Sa'adiah's philosophy, 'Were it not for Sa'adiah, the *Torah would have well-nigh disappeared from the midst of *Israel.'

I. Efros, *Studies in Medieval Jewish Philosophy* (1974); H. Malter, *Life and Work of Saadiah Gaon* (1970).

Śabad (Pañjābī from Skt., **śabda*, 'word'). The divine word. Sikhs generally use this term for the *hymns of the *Ādi Granth. For *Nānak, it was the Satgurū's revelatory Word. Śabad also signifies the mystical 'sound' experienced at the climax of *Nāth *Yoga and the authoritative Word in the *Vedic tradition.

See also ŚABDA.

Sabaeans (a people of the Book in Islam): see MANDEANS.

Sabaoth (Heb.). 'Hosts' or 'armies', as in the biblical title 'Lord of Hosts'. It is often retained untranslated, e.g. in the *Septuagint and in the Greek New Testament in Romans 9. 29 and James 5. 4. It also appears in the traditional Eng. version of the *Te Deum.

Sabbatai Z(e)vi (Jewish messianic claimant): see SHABBETAI ZEVI.

Sabbath (Heb., *shabbat*; Yid., *shabbas*). The seventh day of the week, on which Jews abstain from work. According to the Bible, God worked for six days in creating the world and on the seventh day he rested. Therefore he blessed the seventh day and made it holy (Genesis 2. 1–3). In the decalogue (*ten commandements), work is forbidden on the Sabbath for this reason (Exodus 20. 8–11) and also to give *slaves and animals rest because the Israelites themselves had been slaves in Egypt (Deuteronomy 5. 14–16). The *prophets emphasized that the Sabbath was a sign of Israel's consecration (e.g. Ezekiel 20. 12), and after the *exile, *Nehemiah forbade all commerce on the Sabbath (10. 32). This tradition was maintained in the teaching of the *rabbis who laid great stress on sabbath observance: 'If Israel keeps one Sabbath as it should be kept, the *Messiah will come. The Sabbath is equal to all other precepts in the *Torah' (*Ex.R.* 25. 12). They classified thirty-nine main classes of work to be avoided (*B.Shab.* 7. 2), and required that, as it is a festive day, three meals should be eaten (*B.Shab.* 119a). It is the custom for the mother of the household to light two candles before the start of the Sabbath, and, before the special Sabbath *Kiddush is recited (*B.Pes.* 106a), the parents bless the children. The reason for two Sabbath lights is to fulfil the two commandments, 'Remember the

Sabbath day' (Exodus 20. 8) and 'Observe the Sabbath day' (Deuteronomy 5. 12); and there are generally two loaves of bread to commemorate the double portion of *manna (Exodus 16. 22–6). Where possible, guests should be invited to the Sabbath meals. In the *synagogues, there is a special *liturgy for the services, and the Sabbath concludes with the *havdalah ceremony. Modern technology has produced new Sabbath problems: electrical devices, for example, have to be put on time switches to avoid the prohibition of kindling on the Sabbath. The articles used for Sabbath ritual (candlesticks, Kiddush cups etc.) are frequently extremely artistic. Certain Sabbaths are regarded as 'Special Sabbaths', either because of the readings allocated to them, or because of their place in the calendar, especially when a Sabbath falls during a festival. Three are associated with the beginning of a month: Shabbat Mevarekhim, 'The Sabbath of Blessing', founded on prayer for a good month; S. Maḥar Ḥodesh, on the eve of the New Moon; S. Rosh Ḥodesh, on the New Moon. Four occur in the spring: S. Shekalim, 'The Sabbath of the Shekel Tax', which used to be paid to the Temple (sometimes associated now with appeals for the support of religious institutions in Israel); S. Zakhor, 'The Sabbath of Remembrance', the Sabbath before *Purim: the remembrance is of the attacks of the Amalekites, Haman being considered a descendant of the Amalekites; S. Parah, 'The Sabbath of the [*Red] Heifer', looking toward *Passover, and preceding S. ha-Ḥodesh in the month of Passover. Other Special Sabbaths of importance (at least in the past) are: S. Shuvah, 'The Sabbath of Return', also known as the Sabbath of Repentance (S. Teshuvah) because it falls during the ten days of penitence; S. Ḥol ha-Moʿed Sukkot, on an intermediate day during *Sukkot; S. Bereshith, 'The Sabbath of Genesis', from the opening of the reading of Torah on the Sabbath after *Simḥat Torah; S. Ḥanukkah falls during *Ḥanukkah; S. Shirah, 'The Sabbath of the Song', i.e. when Exodus 15. 1–18 is read; S. ha-Gadol, 'The Great Sabbath', immediately before Passover; S. Ḥol ha-Moʿed Pesaḥ, occurs during Passover; S. Ḥazon, 'The Sabbath of Prophecy', immediately preceding 9 *Av; S. Naḥamu, 'The Sabbath of Comfort', immediately after 9 Av. These Sabbaths have different liturgies and customs. They are no longer all observed in *Reform communities.

The Sabbath has been of paramount importance for Jews and Judaism: 'More than the Jews have kept the Sabbath, the Sabbath has kept the Jews' (*Aḥad ha-ʿAm). The Sabbath takes Jews back to the condition which God originally intended in the Garden of *Eden, but even more it anticipates the final state. According to R. Ḥanina b. Isaac, 'The Sabbath is the incomplete form of the world to come'; according to the *Zohar, 'The Sabbath is a mirror of the world to come.' See S. Goldman, *Guide to the Sabbath* (1961).

Since Christianity emerged as an interpretation of Judaism with Jesus accepted as messiah, many early 'Christians' (the name first appeared at Antioch, according to Acts 11. 26) observed the Sabbath and attended synagogue. However, with an increasing number of gentile converts, the observance of the Sabbath fell away in importance: its observance is not one of the *Noachide laws (so that it was not included in the Jerusalem decision on minimal observances, Acts 15. 28 f.); and eventually (after the failure of the first Jewish revolt in 70 CE), rabbinic Judaism dissociated itself clearly from the new religion. The Lord's Supper moved to the beginning of *Sunday (i.e. to Saturday evening) and eventually to early Sunday morning. The transfer of 'rest' from the Sabbath to Sunday began from about the 4th cent., but the reason given was to enable people to worship God, rather than to revive the abstention from work in imitation of the sabbath rest. The phrase 'the Christian sabbath' dates from about the 12th cent. The early Reformers (e.g. *Luther, *Calvin, *Cranmer, *Knox), insisted on the day of rest, though not in imitation of the Sabbath. The *Puritans in England tried to enforce a more rigorous understanding of the Sabbath (see N. Bownde/Bound, *Sabbathum Veteris et Novi Testamenti, or The True Doctrine of the Sabbath*, 1595, enlarged 1606), which was taken with them to the New World. The *Evangelical Revival reinforced strict sabbath observance in 19th cent. Britain (the Lord's Day Observance Society was founded in 1831), but the influence of Sabbatarian movements on the Continent was more limited. The erosion of 'sabbath observance' is now extensive. Seventh-Day *Adventists believe that the churches have been in error in abandoning the observance of the Sabbath on the original day and have reverted to that practice.

Sabbatical Year (Heb., *shemittah*). The year in which, according to Jewish law, the land lies fallow. According to Exodus 23. 10–11 and Deuteronomy 15. 1–11 on the Sabbatical Year, all agricultural work must be suspended and all debts remitted. Leviticus 25. 1–7 refers to this time as a '*Sabbath for the Lord'. The seventh Sabbatical Year (or possibly the year after the close of seven Sabbatical cycles) was designated the *Jubilee Year. There is disagreement among scholars about how these provisions worked in practice in ancient Israelite society. The *rabbis taught that the laws concerning the Sabbatical remission of debt were still operative, but the obligation of letting the land lie fallow was only necessary in *Erez Israel. However, when R. *Hillel noticed that people had stopped lending because of the Sabbatical Year, he instituted the *prosbul (*B.Git.* 36a). 2000–1 is a Sabbatical year, followed by 2007–8, and so on, running from one *Rosh ha-Shanah to the next.

Sabbatthivādins (school of early Buddhism): see SARVĀSTIVĀDA.

Śabda (Skt., 'sound'). Indian, and especially Hindu, recognition that 'sound' has levels of meaning, and is not mere noise: (i) *sphoṭa, arising from the eternal, unmoving principle with illuminating power (*śakti); (ii) *nāda, perceptible only to a poet or *ṛṣi; (iii) *anāhata*, potential (e.g. a thought) but not expressed; (iv) *āhata*, sound of all kinds, whether humans can hear it or not. Śabda has power in its own right, not just in speech, especially in *mantras or in bells and drums: *Śiva's drum (*ḍamaru) manifests creation. *Vāc channels sound into speech, and the spoken word (*dhavani*), conversely, reconnects, when properly controlled, with the source of creation, and can lead to direct illumination. Śabda-brahman is then the ultimacy of sound devoid of attributes, the realization of *Brahman. Initially, this was equated with the *Vedas, but in the *Upaniṣads it is Brahman. It is one of the three sources of knowledge for, e.g. *Rāmānuja and Gaṅgeśa (see NYĀYA).

For the particular Sikh understanding of śabda, see ŚABAD.

Sabellianism. Christian *heresy according to which the Godhead consists of a single person, only expressing itself in three different operations. It belongs to the school of *modalist *monarchianism. Of the Sabellius to whom the view is attributed, nothing is known, but he was excommunicated by Pope Callistus (217–22).

Sabīja (state of suppressed cosciousness in Rājā yoga): see SAMPRAJÑĀTA.

Sabʿiy(y)a (Seveners, a Muslim, Shīʿa-related movement): see ISMĀʿĪLIY(Y)A; SEVENERS.

Ṣabr (Arab.). Characteristic Muslim virtue of patient acceptance, often linked with *shukr* ('thanksgiving'), e.g. by *al-Ghaz(z)ālī, 'Belief consists of two parts, one ṣabr, the other *shukr*'; cf. Qur'ān 14. 5. Ṣabūr is one of the *Ninety-nine Beautiful Names of *Allāh.

Saccidānanda or **sat-cit-ānanda** (Skt., 'being', + 'consciousness' + 'bliss'). In *Vedānta, a threefold characterization of *Brahman, the Absolute, as that which is pure being, consciousness, and bliss. Sat-cit-ānanda characterizes the essence of brahman as it is grasped in human experience (*anubhava). Sat, 'being' or 'truth', emphasizes the unchanging nature of Brahman as pure unqualified existence with ontological priority over all other experience. Cit, 'consciousness', emphasizes the conscious nature of Brahman experience: Brahman is the epistemological ultimate, the self-luminous essence of knowing which is the witness of all other experience. Ānanda, 'bliss', emphasizes the sublime value of the experience of Brahman. Brahman is the axiological ultimate, the highest and most fulfilling human experience, the goal of human experience. However, sat, cit, and ānanda are not to be understood as qualities attributed to brahman which is *nirguṇa, beyond all relative qualification. Rather sat, cit, and ānanda are each the very essence of Brahman known through the experience of ecstasy.

Sach Khaṇḍ. The Sikh 'realm of truth', the fifth and final stage of spiritual ascent. It is the abode of the One without form, where the believer enters into union with God, and as such, the term can sometimes be a synonym for 'heaven'.

Sacrament. Any of certain solemn religious acts, usually associated with Christianity. The Lat., *sacramentum* (in secular usage, 'oath'), acquired this technical sense by its use to translate the Gk., *mystērion*, in the Latin New Testament. The exact reference has varied. *Augustine defined it as the 'visible form of invisible *grace', picked up in the *Anglican *catechism as 'an outward and visible sign of an inward and spiritual grace . . . ordained by *Christ himself'. He applied it to formulae such as the *creed and *Lord's Prayer; and this wide application was maintained into the Middle Ages. However, by the time of *Peter Lombard, seven particular sacraments have become traditional and are enumerated: *baptism, *confirmation, the *eucharist, *penance, extreme *unction, *orders, and *marriage; in E. Christianity, they retain their Gk. names, i.e. *baptisma*, *chrism*, *koinōnia* (as well as *eucharistia*), *metanoia*, *euchelaion*, *hierosunē*, *gamos*. This list was accepted by Thomas *Aquinas and affirmed at the councils of *Florence and *Trent. According to the latter *council, all seven were instituted by Christ, but in the case of some (notably confirmation, extreme unction, and marriage) there is no identifiable occasion of their institution. The sevenfold enumeration of the sacraments is also accepted in E. churches, where sacraments, as *mustēria*, are much more than signs: they are the saving action of God expressed through sacred actions.

The traditional Catholic theology of the sacraments holds that they are channels of God's grace to the recipient. The right 'matter' (bread and wine for the eucharist, etc.), the right 'form', and the right *intention are essential for the sacrament to be 'valid'. In addition, the recipient must be in a proper state of faith and repentance for it to be 'efficacious'. Baptism, confirmation, and orders imprint an indelible 'character' and therefore cannot be repeated. In recent theology, Christ himself as the expression of the eternal *Word in human nature, and the church as his body, have been described as the primordial sacraments on which all others depend. This notion finds expression in the documents of *Vatican II.

In Anglican tradition (Art. 25 of the *Thirty-Nine Articles) baptism and the eucharist are distinguished as having been ordained by Christ (i.e. Dominical sacraments), from the other five so-called sacraments. *Protestant theology generally speaks of these two sacraments only, usually seeing them not as conveying grace but only as being of paramount importance on account of Christ's command.

Churches in the *Puritan tradition (notably *Baptists) use the word 'ordinance' instead of sacrament. The *Quakers and the *Salvation Army make no use of sacraments at all.

'Blessed Sacrament' (or 'sacrament of the altar') refers specifically to the eucharist, or the bread and wine consecrated at it.

The term 'sacrament' is then applied to actions and substances in other religions where fundamental meaning is expressed through non-verbal languages (even if accompanied by words). The term is thus commonly applied to the Hindu *saṃskāras.

See Index, Sacraments.

J. D. Crichton, *Christian Celebration: The Sacraments* (1973); R. Duffy, *Real Presence . . .* (1982); M. Lawler, *Symbol and Sacrament . . .* (1987); J. Martos, *Doors to the Sacred* (1981); A. Schmemann, *For the Life of the World: Sacraments and Orthodoxy* (1973); J. F. White, *Sacraments as God's Self Giving* (1983).

Sacramentals. In Christianity, acts or objects resembling (but less important than) the *sacraments. Their number is not agreed, but they include the sign of the cross, grace at meals, *stations of the cross, *litanies, the *angelus, *rosary, etc.

Sacrament of the present moment (realization of God in all circumstances): see CAUSSADE, J. P. DE.

Sacred and profane. A distinction in human experience of the world which to *Durkheim seemed to be the essence of religion:

> All known religious beliefs, whether simple or complex, present one common characteristic: they presuppose a classification of all things, real and ideal, of which men think, into two classes or opposed groups, generally designated by two distinct terms which are translated well enough by the words *profane* and *sacred*. This division of the world into two domains . . . is the distinctive trait of religious thought; the beliefs, myths, dogmas and legends are either representations or systems of representations which express the nature of sacred things, the virtues and powers which are attributed to them, or their relations with each other and with profane things.

From this derives his definition of religion:

> A religion is a unified system of beliefs and practices relative to sacred things, that is to say, things set apart and forbidden—beliefs and practices which unite into one single moral community called a Church, all those who adhere to them. The second element which thus finds a place in our definition is no less essential than the first; for by showing that the idea of religion is inseparable from that of the Church, it makes it clear that religion should be an eminently collective thing. (*The Elementary Forms of the Religious Life* (1912; tr. 1961), 52, 62 f.)

The human inclination to organize the experienced world in terms of this distinction (between sacred and profane) was taken much further in the development of structuralism, especially by *Lévi-Strauss, since it was argued that the human mind is under an innate and universal obligation to perceive binary oppositions (up/down, male/female, night/day, etc.), not just in the case of the sacred and the profane, but in general. However, these classifications are bound to leave anomalous or ambiguous cases, so that religion is better understood by attending, not only to the classification systems, but also to the ways in which the anomalous is dealt with, since this will disclose why communities find some things abhorrent and others acceptable. This methodology was applied influentially by Mary Douglas (*Purity and Danger*, 1966), showing that 'dirt' as a concept leads to pollution rules which are not primarily concerned with hygiene. The binary opposition between wholeness (holiness) and imperfection (uncleanness) underlies the biblical laws concerning holiness: to be wholly attached to God brings blessing, to be removed from God brings a curse. Creatures designated as unclean according to the food laws are those which are anomalous or on a borderline between categories (e.g. if they are not clearly domesticated or wild, or belonging to air or sea). In *Implicit Meanings* (1975) she argued further that pollution beliefs (understood in this way) serve a social function, because they protect society at its most vulnerable points, where ambiguity would erode or undermine social structure. For *Eliade's understanding, see HIEROPHANY.

B. Lang (ed.), *Anthropological Approaches to the Old Testament* (1985); B. J. Malina, *The New Testament World: Insights from Cultural Anthropology* (1981); J. Neusner, *The Idea of Purity in Ancient Judaism with a Critique and Commentary by Mary Douglas* (1973).

Sacred cities, seven. Places where Hindus can attain *ānanda (bliss): (i) *Ayodhyā; (ii) *Mathurā; (iii) Gayā (*Bodhgaya); (iv) *Kāśī (Vārānasī, Benares); (v) *Kāñci; (vi) Avantikā (Ujjain); (vii) Dvārakā.

Sacred cow (in Hinduism): see GO.

Sacred Heart. The physical heart of Jesus as a subject of Catholic devotion. The devotion has been officially defined only since the 18th cent., though it can be traced back to the mystics of the Middle Ages (e.g. *Bonaventura) and ultimately to meditation on Jesus' wounds at his crucifixion. St John Eudes (1601–80) worked to provide a theological foundation for the devotion, and to establish a feast. But its great popularity dates from the visions (1673–5) of the French Visitandine nun, St Margaret Mary Alacoque, in which the form of the devotion was revealed to her. A mass and office for the feast were authorized by Clement XIII in 1765; *Pius IX and *Leo XIII increased its importance, and the latter solemnly consecrated all humanity to the Sacred Heart (1899). The feast is observed on the Friday of the week after *Corpus Christi.

Devotion to the Sacred Heart derives from its natural symbolism for the redemptive love of Christ, and emphasizes 'reparation' for the outrages committed against this love. Since the 17th cent. the Sacred Heart has been a subject of popular, often highly sentimental, art; it is typically shown enflamed and surmounted by a small cross and crown of thorns. Under Popes Pius X–Pius XII there was a campaign to encourage the display, or 'enthronement', of the Sacred Heart in the home.

J. Stierli (ed.), *Heart of the Saviour* (1957).

Sacred rivers, seven. Among Hindus, all water is sacred, and rivers especially so; but seven rivers are particularly revered: *Gaṅgā (Ganges), Yamuna, Godavari, Sarasvatī, Narmada, Sindhu, Kaveri.

Sacred thread (rite in Hinduism through which a boy makes the transition to student life, i.e. brahmacarya): see UPANAYANA.

Sacrifice (Lat., 'that which is made sacred'). The offering of something, animate or inanimate, in a *ritual procedure which establishes, or mobilizes, a relationship of mutuality between the one who sacrifices (whether individual or group) and the recipient—who may be human but more often is of another order, e.g. God or spirit. Sacrifice pervades virtually all religions, but it is extremely difficult to say precisely what the meanings of sacrifice are—perhaps because the meanings are so many. Sacrifice is clearly much more than technique: it involves drama, ritual, and action, transforming whatever it is that is sacrificed beyond its mundane role: in general, nothing that is sacrificed has intrinsic worth or holiness before it is set apart; it is the sacrifice that gives it added value. Sacrifice has been understood as expiation of fault or sin; as propitiation of an angry deity; as apotropaic (turning away punishment, disaster, etc.); as purgation; as an expression of gratitude; as substitutionary (offering to God a substitute for what is rightly his, e.g. the first-born); as commensal, establishing union with God or with others in a community; as *do ut des* ('I give in order that you may give', an offering in order to evoke a gift in return); as maintaining cosmic order (especially in Hindu sacrifices); as celebration; as a means of coping with violence in a community; as catharsis; as a surrogate offering at the level of power and its distribution. Sacrifice seems rarely to be spontaneous; it seems more often to be evoked as a standard obligation, or in response to a command or demand, frequently expressing degrees of dependency.

Amongst many particular theories, that of H. Hubert and M. Mauss, *Sacrifice, Its Nature and Function* (1898; Eng. tr. 1964), has been influential. *Durkheim's insistence on the primacy of the social in explaining religious phenomena is applied to the wide diversity of sacrificial practices and beliefs: the purpose of sacrifice can be discerned, not in the analysis of beliefs, but in the social function served by sacrifice, i.e. the connection made between the *sacred and profane worlds. Through sacrifice they interpenetrate and yet remain distinct, thereby allowing (or requiring) self-interest to be subordinated to the service of the social group. The methodology was extended by Mauss in the even more influential *The Gift* (1924; Eng. tr. 1954): gift-giving practices (especially potlatch: see ALMSGIVING), including extravagant feasts, seem at first to work against self-interest, but they establish social bonding and stability:

> All these institutions reveal the same kind of social and psychological pattern. Food, women, children, possessions, charms, land, labour, services, religious offices, rank—everything is stuff to be given away and repaid. In perpetual interchange of what we may call spiritual matter, comprising men and things, these elements pass and repass between clans and individuals, ranks, sexes and generations.

See Index, Sacrifice.

M. F. C. Bourdillon and M. Fortes (eds.), *Sacrifice* (1980).

Judaism The general Heb. term, *qorbān*, has been taken to mean 'bringing close', sc., of humans and God. In ancient Israel, sacrifices were of various kinds. *Sin-offerings (*ḥatat*) could be made by individuals, or collectively at the sacred festivals, and were offered in propitiation for sin; guilt offerings (*asham*) were a particular kind of sin-offering, to be made when, e.g., someone had defrauded another or when lepers were cleansed. Dedicatory offerings expressed dedication to God. Burnt offerings (*'olah*) were offered twice daily in the *Jerusalem *Temple as part of the regular ritual, with two additional lambs offered each *Sabbath. Besides animal sacrifices, offerings of grain or loaves (meal offerings) accompanied burnt offerings and a libation was also poured out. In addition there were extra free-will offerings and peace offerings at *Shavu'ot, when the *Nazirite vow was completed, and at the installation of *priests. The *patriarchs and the *judges made offerings at various *altars, but the Temple, after it was built in the time of King *Solomon, became the centre of sacrifice. However, the *high places of *Judah continued to function, and the shrines of the Northern Kingdom were at Bethel and Dan. After the *Exile, the Temple was acknowledged as the only legitimate sanctuary (Ezra 6. 17), with the *Elephantiné temple being the only possible exception. Full details of the Temple ritual are preserved in the *Talmud, tractates *Tamid* and *Zevaḥim*. After the Temple was destroyed by the Romans on 9 *Av, 70 CE, the sacrificial system came to an end. Prayer took its place. The *Shaḥarit service stood for the morning sacrifice, the *Minḥah service for the afternoon sacrifice and the *Musaf prayers for additional offerings. None the less, the *rabbis looked forward to the restoration of the Temple services in the days of the *messiah, and the *'Amidah contains the petition that 'the Temple be speedily rebuilt in our days'. The *Progressive movements have no reference to sacrifice in their liturgy.

Christianity Ideas of sacrifice are attached primarily to Jesus' death, probably going back to his own words at least at the *Last Supper. As a practical consequence, the more liberal elements in the earliest Jewish church seem to have repudiated sacrifice in the Temple (Acts 6. 13–14; 7. 48) as something superseded by Jesus' death. The writer to the *Hebrews gives an elaborate treatment of Christ's once-for-all sacrifice as superior to the Old Testament cult. The *fathers took up the biblical theme, stressing that Christ was a voluntary victim; a victim of infinite value; and also himself the *priest. (See also ATONEMENT.) From early times, the *eucharist was also called a sacrifice, in virtue of its immediate relation to the sacrifice of Christ. It was therefore possible to say that in the mass Christ was sacrificed 'again', although e.g. Thomas *Aquinas insisted that the mass was itself an 'immolation' only so far as it was an image of Christ's own *passion. The Reformers, however, rejected all talk of the eucharistic sacrifice as a denial of the unique sacrifice of Christ's death. In the Anglican communion service the prayer that God will accept 'this our sacrifice of thanks and praise' suggests a notion of sacrifice as an individual's conscious obedience, active or passive, to God's will. The *ARCIC agreement accepted that there is only the one, original, sacrifice of Christ, 'made once, for all': the sacrament is not a repetition of that sacrifice, but 'enters into the movement of the self-offering'.

Islam The Arabic words *aḍḥā*, *dhabaḥa*, and *naḥara* refer to the slaughter of animals; *qurbān* (cf. Heb., *qorbān*) comes from the verb meaning 'to draw near' and implies an offering without slaughter. The major Muslim sacrifice occurs at al-*ʿĪd al-Aḍḥā ('the feast of the sacrifice', also known as ʿĪd al-Kabīr, 'the great feast') which commemorates the offering by Ibrāhīm (*Abraham) of a ram instead of his son. In addition, sacrifice may be performed at any time with the intention of drawing closer to God, and is particularly expected when a child is born (*al-ʿaqīqah*).

Hinduism Sacrifice (*yajña*) is deeply involved among Hindus in the maintenance of cosmic order, and although it obviously has reference to the gods, it is distinct from the approach to God in *pūjā (worship). In the early *Vedic age, sacrifice was relatively simple: sacrifices were based on the home, bringing the relevant power of natural phenomena to bear on such events as birth, marriage, death, house- and fire-building, agriculture, etc. Since the *devas were not regarded as the personifications of natural phenomena, but rather as manifestations of them, sacrifice was a way of bringing the power inherent in the natural order to bear in relevant ways. Hence there were also sacrifices at regular moments, such as morning and evening, new and full moon, etc. For these ceremonies, the *gṛhapati* (householder) is usually the officiant, though he could call on a *purohita if necessary. These offerings are known as *gṛhyakarmāṇi*, and are usually performed by the casting of milk, *ghī* (*ghṛta), grain, etc., into the fire. In the later Vedic period, sacrifices became elaborately detailed, and a distinction was made between *gṛhya* sacrifices (which rested on *smārta, i.e. oral tradition and memory) and śrauta sacrifices (those based on *śruti). The **Sāma Veda* and **Yajur Veda* were composed for the purposes of sacrifice, and the *Brāhmaṇas were compiled with a major purpose of explaining the meaning of the sacrifices. Whereas in the earlier sacrifices there had been a strong element of *do ut des* (see introductory paragraph), there now developed a sense that the gods were dependent on sacrifices and to an extent under the control of humans (or more specifically, of priests). The śrauta sacrifices are traditionally divided into two groups of seven, Haviryajñas (including *Agnihotra, animal sacrifices, and *Piṇḍapitṛyajña) and Somayajñas. In general, these sacrifices were on a large scale, with the instigator of the sacrifice (*yajamāna*) doing little more than distribute generous payments (*dakṣinā) to the priests. Four groups of priests were required (headed by four chief priests): (i) Hotṛ, who invokes the gods by reciting verses from the **Ṛg Veda*; (ii) Udgātṛ, the chanter of *sāmans*; (iii) Adhvaryu, the performer of the sacrifice; (iv) the *brahman, who supervises the whole procedure, making sure that no errors are made. The intricacy of detail put the priestly classes in a position of great power, since only they could bring the gods into action. Sacrifice became the fundamental principle of cosmic process: 'Sacrifice is *Viṣṇu, sacrifice is *Prajāpati, sacrifice is the source of sustenance [the navel] for the universe: it is essential for creation, and even the gods depend on it.' Yet śrauta sacrifices also became prohibitively expensive, and only vestigial remains of them survive in practice, confined to symbolic acts like the pouring of a glass of water or the giving of a handful of rice. Occasionally, a larger sacrifice is organized (e.g. against the menace of nuclear war in 1957), but only a few brahmans now maintain the daily ritual and study which underlie the larger occasions.

P. V. Kane, *History of Dharmasastra* (1930–62); F. Staal, *Agni* . . . (1983) and *The Science of Ritual* (1982).

Sacrilege (Lat., the theft of sacred objects). The violent, contemptuous, or disrespectful treatment of persons or objects associated with religious reverence or dedicated to God. In Judaism, the violation of sacred things is a deep offence, as can be seen, e.g., in the biblical story of Nadab and Abihu who were burnt to death for offering 'strange fire' (Leviticus 10. 1–2). The *Talmudic tractate *Meʿilah* is concerned with the subject, and today *Torah *Scrolls, *tefillin, holy books, *synagogues with their furnishings, and cemeteries must all be treated with respect. In Christianity, the notion of sacrilege is extended to include receiving the *sacraments unworthily or in a state of *mortal sin.

Sadācāra (right behaviour in Hinduism): see HERESY (E. religions).

Ṣadaqa (Arab.). Almsgiving, voluntary charity. The word is sometimes used as a synonym of *zakāt, the official alms tax (as in Qur'ān 9. 58, 104); but ṣadaqa (pl. ṣadaqāt) is considered a pious duty, the details of which are not laid down. It may be substituted for a religious obligation which has been omitted due to no deliberate fault or negligence. The Qur'ān specifies the recipients of alms, but although the word ṣadaqa is here used, the verses refer to the zakāt, whose collection and distribution are regulated by the Muslim community (9. 58).

Saddhā (faith): see ŚRADDHĀ.

Saddharmapuṇḍarīka sūtra (early Mahāyāna sūtra): see LOTUS SŪTRA.

Sadducees. Jewish sect of the second *Temple period. The Sadducees were made up of the more affluent members of the population. As Temple *priests, they dominated Temple worship and formed a large proportion of *Sanhedrin members. The name Sadducee is perhaps derived from King *Solomon's *high priest *Zadok. The *Talmud uses the term interchangeably with *Boethusian, both being groups that denied *resurrection and *afterlife. They stood in opposition to the *Pharisees in that they rejected the *oral law and only accepted the supreme authority of the written *Torah. They are mentioned in the New Testament and in *Josephus' *Antiquities*. After the destruction of the Temple in 70 CE, the Sadducees ceased to exist.

Sādhaka (Skt.). In a general sense the practitioner of a spiritual path (*sādhana), though the term has a more precise technical meaning in the *Āgamas and *Tantras as one who has undergone a certain kind of initiation (*dīkṣa) and who follows a certain path. The Āgamas distinguish between those desirous of liberation (*muṃukṣu*) and those desirous of pleasure (*bubhukṣu*); the sādhaka follows the latter path. After the *nirvāna dīkṣa (initiation which gives access to the absolute), the adept becomes a *putraka* ('son' of the *guru or of *Śiva) on the path to liberation (*mokṣa), but he can undergo a further consecration, the sādhaka *abhiṣeka, and so become a sādhaka on the path to liberation by way of pleasure (*bhukti*) and power (*siddhi). The sādhaka certainly wants liberation, but this goal is a long way off, and his immediate concerns are more mundane. The sādhaka's practice comprises *mantra repetition (*japa), *visualization (*dhyāna) of his chosen deity (*iṣṭadevatā), and observance of certain daily rites. He should dwell in an isolated place (such as a cremation ground, cave, or wood), eating little, and should be pure, energetic, and courageous—purity being the best defence against malevolent supernatural forces. After repeated practice he becomes one with his *mantra and deity, and so gains power. This power is of three types: the lowest, black magic; the middle, white magic; and the highest, the ability to travel through different planes of existence and to become a universal Lord (*cakravartin). The *Śaiva texts, *Mṛgendra-Āgama* and *Svacchanda Tantra*, make a distinction between two types of sādhaka, the *lokadharmin* (following the way of the world, whose practice includes sacrifices and doing good works) and the *Śiva-dharmin* (who gives himself up to mantra). This latter way leads to the pleasures of the earth (*bhoga *bhūmi) which the sādhaka will enjoy until the dissolution (*pralaya) of the cosmos, when he will be merged into Śiva and so liberated.

Sādhana (Skt., √*sādh*, 'complete'). The spiritual practice of Hindu and Buddhist *Tantrism; a path to liberation (*mokṣa) and power (siddhi/*iddhi) distinct from orthodox Vedic practice, which aims to unite the male–female polarity within the body, or to merge the individual self (*jivātman) with the highest self (*paramātman). Tantric sādhana consists of worship (*pūjā) and *yoga. Pūjā can involve various preliminary purifications such as the ritual bath followed by *bhūtaśuddhi and *nyāsa, during which the adept is identified with his chosen deity (*iṣṭadevatā). Pūjā of left-hand schools (*vāmacāra) involves the use of the five Ms (*pañca-makāra). Tantric yoga includes *mantra repetition and *Kuṇḍalinī yoga. Mantra is the most important constituent of sādhana, and through its constant repetition, the *sādhaka merges into the mantra and thereby into the deity. *Visualization of a deity (*dhyāna) with whom the sādhaka must identify himself, is also an important aspect which accompanies mantra. Beyond this precise meaning, sādhana has been applied to a large number of directed practices aimed especially at *tapas. The term has also been linked to God-devoted practices, not much more austere or *ascetic than self-denial and voluntary suffering. In general, to perform sādhana, initiation (*dīkṣā) is needed from a *guru who will give the mantra and specify the appropriate practice in accordance with the disciple's personality, the lineage of his guru (*paramparā), and his desired goal. Sādhana is practised by both householders and renouncers (see ĀŚRAMA).

Sādhāran Brahmo Samāj (reforming Hindu movement): see SEN, KESHUB CHUNDER; BRAHMO SAMĀJ.

Sādh saṅgat (Pañjābī, 'saintly association'). Sikh congregation. The term refers generally to the congregation gathered for worship in the *gurdwārā, and strictly speaking to those who meditate upon God's name (*nām). The injunction, 'Join the society of godly persons (sādh saṅgat) and meditate upon the Name' recurs in the *Ādi Granth (e.g. p. 26).

Sādhu (Skt., √*sādh*, 'accomplish'). One who has controlled his senses, a Hindu holy person who has renounced the world, and seeks Brahman or God. The female equivalent is sādhvī. They are also known as *sant or 'saint'. They may be formally initiated into an order (*saṁpradāya), or they may be svatantra sādhus who follow the life and dress (if any: naked sādhus are known as nāga sādhus) without formal initiation by a *guru. The extreme diversity of sādhus is effectively summarized by K. Narayan in *Storytellers, Saints and Scoundrels* (1989):

> There is no overarching structure to monitor all the different kinds of *ascetics . . ., and even within the same sect or monastery sādhus may display a marked individuality. There are naked sādhus and ochre-coloured sādhus; sādhus with matted *hair, and those with shining bare scalps; poor, wandering sādhus and jet-set, Rolls-Royce-transported sādhus; sādhus who interact with a handful of Indian villagers, and sādhus who hold forth to audiences of thousands in New York or Switzerland.

In its most general sense, a sādhu is one who follows a *sādhana (path): while he is still on the path, he is known as sādhaka; when he reaches the goal, he becomes a *siddha.

G. S. Ghurye, *Indian Sādhus* (1964).

Sadmaya-kośa. The sheath of *sat (Being) which surrounds and sustains *ātman. In Hinduism, the approach to the realization of *Brahman requires this sheath, since otherwise it could not be imagined. But without this sheath, ātman is one with Brahman.

Ṣafavids. Persian dynasty which ruled 1501–1732 (AH 907–1145). It derived from Shaykh Isḥāq Ṣafī al-Dīn (d. 1334 (AH 735)), who was the leader of a *Sūfī order named after him, the Ṣafavis—hence the name of the dynasty. The order became associated with the *Ithnā 'Ashariy(y)a Shī'as (Twelvers), and for that reason the Turkish adherents wore a red hat with twelve tassles on it, and became known as Qizīl Bash, 'red hats'. By making this form of Shi'ism the state religion, the Ṣafavids isolated Persia to a great extent from the more widely spread *Sunni Muslims—though Ṣafavid-derived dynasties were established in India. Even after the cessation of their effective power, the emphasis on the *Hidden Imām made Persia a fruitful ground for individuals (and their followers) claiming to be the representative or reality of that figure—e.g. BĀBĪS; BAHĀ'Ī FAITH.

Saffron robe (of Buddhist bhikṣus): see HABIT, RELIGIOUS; MONASTICISM (Buddhism).

Sagdid (Zoroastrian death ritual): see DAXMA.

Sages (Heb., *hakhamim*, sing., *hakham*). Jewish scholars and biblical interpreters, often translated as 'the Wise'. The sages were the active leaders and teachers of the Jewish religion from the beginning of the second *Temple period until the Arabian conquest of the East. *Ben Sira described a sage as one who 'gives his mind to the law of the Most High' (Ecclesiasticus 39. 1–5). They valued and upheld the *oral law and, after the destruction of the Temple, they maintained their influence firstly through *Bet Hillel and Bet Shammai and then through the *nesi'im and the *academies. The *Mishnah gives innumerable examples of sages acting as judges, as expositors of the *Torah, and as builders of the *halakhah. The ideal sage was guided by principles of saintliness (*ḥasidūt*), and their ultimate ideal was the conquest of the *evil inclination (*Avot* 4. 1). They are also known as Ḥazal, an acronym for *Ḥakhameynu zikhronam li-berakhah*, 'our sages of blessed memory'.

Sagga (Pāli, derived from Skt., *svarga*, 'heaven, the next world'). In Buddhism, the pleasant conditions of reappearance (*punnabhāva) which result from a life of moral, religious living.

According to the Pāli canonical texts, sagga is not 'heaven' in spatial terms, in keeping with the early Buddhist non-cosmographical conceptions. It is described as a condition or state of birth: the beings reborn into heavenly conditions are described as *devas (gods) and they are in the same spatial dimension as are human beings. The names of the different heavens, given as fourteen (consisting of the six lower heavens and the eight higher heavens) do not describe separate mini-worlds or compartments in space, but only different conditions of spiritual attainments by which alone they come to be distinguished.

In the post-canonical Buddhist literature, Buddhist cosmological thinking seems to have assimilated the cosmographical world-views of non-Buddhist Indian religions (especially Jainism) and hence we find cosmographical readings made into these early textual contexts.

According to the *Mahāsīhanāda Sutta* of *Majjhima Nikāya* (I. 76) the beings reborn into the heavenly realms experience feelings which are exclusively pleasant (*ekantasukhā vedanā*). But unlike the Brahmanic (i.e. early Hindu) conception of heaven, the happiness in the heavenly realms is merely temporary and can last only as long as the power of the good deeds which conditioned such rebirths lasts (see KARMA). Reappearance in the heavenly existences is neither automatic, accidental, nor compulsory, but is the result of express wish and aspiration directed thereto. The direction of effort for such a proximate salvation (though regarded as a possibility) has never been considered as quite adhering to the true spirit of seeking the ultimate goals of *arhat, *nirvāna. In popular Buddhism, however, heavenly existence has been retained as an occasional resting place on the long, long journey through the cycle of births (*saṃsāra) until maturity to Nibbanic attainment: see proximate salvation in GREAT TRADITION.

Sagi Nahor (Kabbalist): see ISAAC THE BLIND.

Saguṇa-Brahman. 'Brahman with qualities', in contrast to *nirguṇa-Brahman. In the perspective of *Advaita, the latter is the highest, essential nature of Brahman, but in order that Brahman may become knowable, it manifests itself with qualities (*guṇa, upādhi), though these are always superimposed on Brahman and do not have ontological independence. In personified form, saguṇa-Brahman becomes *Īśvara, God, and by application *iṣṭa-devatā, the personal god of a devotee, and thus outside Advaita, saguṇa-Brahman is not devalued or made preliminary.

Ṣahāba. The Companions of the Prophet *Muḥammad. They have high status in Islam, because of their role in establishing *ḥadīth—in two senses: (i) their own sayings and actions are recorded; and (ii) they were the witnesses of what Muḥammad said and did. Originally, therefore, they were confined to those who knew him well, but eventually the term applied to all who encountered him. Thus the last of the ṣahāba was ʿAmīr b. Wāthil, who died *c.*AH 100, so that he could only at best have seen Muḥammad as a child.

Sahaj (Pañjābī, 'easy'). Ultimate, blissful state experienced by the spiritually disciplined. Gurū *Nānak frequently used 'sahaj', a term employed by the *Nāth yogīs, for the inexpressible mystical union reached through devoted *nām simaran.

Sahaja (Skt., 'innate'). In Buddhist *Tantrism and the *Vaiṣṇava *Sahajīyā cult, the absolute which exists within the body. The term is used in the *Tantras, such as the *Hevajra Tantra*, and also by the Buddhist *Siddhas such as *Ti-lo-pa and Saraha in their poems (*dohas* and *caryāpadas*), where it means the essence of everything, the unmoving, ineffable state beyond thought construction (*vikalpa) and beyond sin (*pāpa) and merit (*puṇya). It is therefore a synonym for *nirvāna, *mahā sukha (great bliss), and the perfected essential body (*svabhāvika kāyā*). The *Hevajra Tantra* says: 'The whole world is of the nature of sahaja—for sahaja is the quintessence of all (*svarūpa*); this quintessence is nirvāna for those who possess the perfectly pure mind (*citta).' The Vaiṣṇava Sahajīyās retain the meaning of sahaja as the innate enlightenment indwelling in the body, but for them it also becomes equated with pure love which is the union of *Rādhā and *Kṛṣṇa. The Tibetan is *Lhan.cig.skyes.pa*.

Sahajdhārī (Pañjābī, 'gradual adopter'). A Sikh who accepts the *Gurūs' teachings without observing the *five Ks or taking amrit (as an *amritdhārī). The term originally may simply have indicated an acceptance of Gurū *Nānak's teaching of *sahaj attained through *nām simaran.

Sahajīyā (Skt., from *sahaja). A sect of *Tantrism preponderant in Bengal, whose practice involved ritual sexual intercourse (*maithuna). The origins of the sect are in the Sahaja-*yāna of the Buddhist *Siddhas (8th–12th cents. CE), whose poems, the *dohas* and *caryāpadas*, speak of sahaja as the highest state. The Sahajīyās became integrated into *Vaiṣṇavism. There are no Vaiṣṇava Sahajīyā writings until after *Caitanya (1486–1533 CE) and most texts are dated to the 18th cent., though possibly a Sahajīyā cult did exist before Caitanya and may have influenced him and the Gosvāmins (see ABHINAVAGUPTA).

The Vaiṣṇava Sahajiyas adopted the theology of the Gauḍiya Vaiṣṇavas who maintained that the soul is both identical with and distinct from *Kṛṣṇa or *Rādhā-Kṛṣṇa. This doctrine is known as unthinkable difference-in-identity (*acintya bedhābheda*). There is a distinction in Kṛṣṇa *bhakti between *aiśvarya* ('majestic', worship of Kṛṣṇa in a majestic form) and *madhura* ('sweet') or *śṛngāra* ('erotic') bhakti (worship of Kṛṣṇa as a lover). Erotic bhakti is regarded as superior, but is interpreted differently, by the Gauḍiya Vaiṣṇavas as sexuality sublimated to a devotional end, but by the Sahajīyās as literal use of sex, with the sexual act between man and woman recapitulating the divine union of Rādhā and Kṛṣṇa. The purpose of Sahajīyā ritual sex is to transform desire (*kāma) into pure love (*prema). Ritual sex was performed with a *parakīya* woman, unmarried or 'belonging to another'. As in other *Tantric sexual rites, semen is not ejaculated but directed 'upwards' through the suṣumṇa *nāḍī to the *sahasrāra padma where the bliss of Rādhā and Kṛṣṇa is enjoyed. Another component of Sahajīyā practice is the union of polarities within the body by meditation on the *cakras and the transformation of the profane body (*sādhaka deha) into a pure, perfected body (*siddha deha). For a further development, see BĀUL.

Sahasrāra (Skt., 'thousand'). The *lotus (*padma*) or circle (*cakra) which exists at or above the crown of the head, at the top of the suṣumnā *nādī in the *Tantric esoteric anatomy of the *subtle body. It is the place where *Śiva and *Śakti are united enjoying perpetual bliss. The *guru is also thought to dwell there, at one with the divine. The sahasrāra is envisaged as lotus, a symbol of purity, with innumerable petals on which are inscribed the letters of the Skt. alphabet and all their possible combinations. In the centre of the lotus is the nectar of immortality (*amṛta). The sahasrāra is attained through the yoga of *Kuṇḍalinī.

Sāhib (Pañjābī, 'sir', from Arabic, 'lord, master'). A title appended to names of religious significance for Sikhs. In the *Ādi Granth, God is called Sāhib. As it is regarded as the living voice of the *Gurū, the Ādi Granth is usually called the Gurū Granth Sāhib. Individual compositions, such as *Japjī and *Anand, are also given this title, as are famous *gurdwārās and places of religious importance (e.g. *Harimandir Sāhib, *Anaṇḍpur Sāhib). See also TAKHT.

Sāhibzāde (Urdū, Pañjābī, 'Master's sons'). Gurū *Gobind Siṅgh's four sons, Ajīt, Jujhār, Zorāwar, and Fateh. Ranging in age from 18 to 7 years, all died at Mughal hands in Dec. 1704 CE. Ajīt and Jujhār were killed defending the Gurū at Chamkaur, Pañjāb. Zorāwar and Fateh escaped with their grandmother, Gūjarī, only to be betrayed by a *brahman to Wazīr Khān, ruler of Sirhind. According to current tradition, he bricked them up alive in a wall because they refused to accept Islam, and Gūjarī died of shock. See also MARTYR.

Ṣaḥīḥ (Arab., 'sound'). Title (al-Ṣaḥīḥ) given to the two major collections of *ḥadīth, of *al-Bukhārī and *Muslim.

Sahl al-Tustarī, Abū Muḥammad (818–96 (AH 203–83)). *Sunnī theologian and mystic, of strict and ascetic standards. He wrote nothing, but his 'thousand sayings' were collected and edited by his pupil, Muḥammad ibn Sālim, and formed the basis for a theological school, the Sālimīya. An eclectic in his views, he agreed with *al-Ashʿarī that a Muslim is anyone who prays facing the *qibla (see IMĀN), but he accepted the Shīʿa claim of *jafr. Faith must nevertheless be demonstrated in works ('to love is to obey'), while the true lover of God is constantly detaching himself from the world. The demonstration of God is in the life of the saint—hence his claim, in a *shaṭḥ, 'I am the proof of God.'

Sai Baba. 1. Hindu spiritual guide and miracle (*siddha/*iddhi) worker. He died in 1918, and was recognized as one who had direct experience of reality and truth—so much so that many regard him as a manifestation (*avatāra) of God. He lived by paradox—e.g. neither writing nor reading, yet displaying mastery of texts—and exhibited the character of a *holy fool. He is known as Sai Baba of Shirdi to differentiate him from the following.

2. Sai Baba (b. 1926) of the *āśrama Prasanti Nilayam, who is believed by his followers (now worldwide) to be a reincarnation of the first Sai Baba. He too is well-known for his miraculous powers.

H. Murphet, *Sai Baba* . . . (1971); A. Osborne, *The Incredible Saibaba* (1958).

Saichō (also known from his posthumous name as Dengyō Daishi, 767–822). Japanese Buddhist monk and founder of *Tendai. Together with *Kūkai, he was one of the two leading figures in the Heian ('peace and tranquillity') period in Japan. He studied under *Tao-hsüan and was much affected by *Kegon. In 788, soon after he was ordained, he sought a more simple life in a hut on the slopes of Mount Hiei. In 784, the emperor Kammu decided to move his capital from *Nara, home of the Six Sects, because he was disillusioned by the worldliness of the religious life there. He chose Nagaoka and then *Kyōto, which was in an inauspicious direction, but this was counterbalanced by the fact that it was close to Saichō. Kammu became suspicious of the rivalries and political ambitions of Buddhism, yet he needed Buddhist support for the reforms he wished to bring about. Saichō met Kammu's needs exactly. In 804, he went to China, to study *T'ien-t'ai, and to gain sanction for the new foundation on Mount Hiei. He did not intend to introduce, still less found, a new school, and for some time he applied himself to esoteric Buddhism as much as to T'ien-t'ai. When he returned to Japan in 805, he endorsed both as a kind of middle way between the Nara sects, *Sanron and *Hossō. His endeavours to incorporate esoteric Buddhism were overshadowed by the brilliance of *Kūkai, and after an early friendship, relations between the two deteriorated. The incorporation of esoteric Buddhism was accomplished by Saichō's disciples, Enchin and *Ennin. As a result, Saichō realized that he would have to be more deliberate in training and retaining his own disciples, so that, in consequence, Tendai-shū in Japan began to be established on the basis of T'ien-t'ai. Saichō spent the last six years of his life trying to establish Tendai as the true *Mahāyāna, and as the 'protector of the nation':

> What is the treasure of a nation? The religious nature is the treasure. Whoever has cultivated this nature is the treasure of the nation. It was said of old that ten pearls as big as pigeon's eggs are not the treasure of a nation: only when someone illuminates a part of the nation from his nature can one speak of the nation's treasure.

Because he hoped that the monastery would produce the leaders of the nation, the training (of twelve years duration) was severe—'the training of a *bodhisattva', with emphasis on the **Lotus Sūtra* and on *shikan* (contemplation, *chih-kuan). When Kammu died in 806, the pre-eminence of Saichō was threatened, and it was only in 822 that the line of ordinations was emancipated from Nara. During this last period, Saichō composed his major works (including *Shugo-kokkai-shō* (Treatise on the Protection of the State), *Hokke-shūku* (Superlative Passages of the Lotus Sūtra), and *Kenkai-ron* (Treatise on the Precepts), in which he argued that Tendai was superior to other forms of Buddhism. He regarded his time as the period of Spurious Dharma (*zōmatsu*), and that only in Tendai would the people find guidance. A complex of many temples was established on Mount Hiei, but most (along with the major temple) were destroyed in 1571/2. Enryaku-ji was rebuilt on the mountain-top in the 17th cent. The main hall (Konpo-Chudo, 1643) is the third largest wood building in Japan.

P. Groner, *Saicho* . . . (1984).

Said Nursi (1873–1960). An influential religious scholar who led the defence of orthodox Islam against the forces of secularism in Turkey. Born in the village of Nurs in E. Anatolia into a Kurdish family, he was early attracted to *Sufism though he felt that its method of teaching was out of touch with the modern age. He therefore set out to adjust *ʿilm al-kalām, regarding modern science not as a threat but as a supplement to faith. His ambitious project for establishing an Islamic University to reconcile the religious sciences with modern science was thwarted by the government and never realized.

Despite official opposition (continual harassment and imprisonment), he produced his greatest work *Risāla-i-Nūr* (The Treatise of Light), said to have been written after his Divine Illumination, an attempt to demonstrate the spiritual dimension of the *Qur'ān to an age under the sway of scepticism and materialism. Since the recent resurgence of Islam in Turkey, Said Nursi's *Risāla-i-Nūr* has played a prominent role in the Islamic revival.

Saigō Takamori (Japanese military leader): see MEIJI.

Saikōkū (Japanese centre): see PILGRIMAGE.

Sain Sāhib (Sikh reformer): see SIKHISM.

Saint (Lat., *sanctus*, 'holy'). The title is given to exemplary Christians who are venerated and invoked in prayer—as also to the *angels *Raphael, *Gabriel, and *Michael. (For individual saints, see under name, and see also the Index under Saints.) In the New Testament the word 'saint' is synonymous with 'Christian' (e.g. Ephesians 1. 1). The doctrine that those with places of honour can intercede for those on earth is grounded instead in a variety of biblical allusions (e.g. 2 Maccabees 15. 12; Matthew 19. 28; Revelation 6. 9 f.). The first Christians to receive special veneration were *martyrs, beginning with *Polycarp whose followers treasured his *relics and celebrated the 'birthday' of his martyrdom. From the 4th cent., devotion to the saints increased and included 'confessors' (those who suffered but did not die in persecutions) and ascetics. From the 6th cent. onward, *diptychs of martyrs and confessors began to have a place in the liturgy, and from the 8th cent. the lives of saints were read at *matins. At an early date saints were also believed to effect *miracles after their death; in the West these could include the incorruption of the saint's own body. The relics of saints were also associated with healing. From the 9th cent. the stories of saints' lives, often with little or no historical basis, were increasingly popular. *Synods frequently tried to control the excesses and superstitions of popular devotion. At the *Reformation the cult of saints was rejected, especially by the *Zwinglians and *Calvinists. It is debated whether Art. 22 of the Anglican *Thirty-Nine Articles condemns the invocation of saints altogether, or only the excesses of the time.

The modern cult of the saints in the Roman Catholic Church is regulated by *canon law, which recommends the veneration of the saints and especially of *Mary. The attitude of Eastern churches is akin to that of Rome. In 1969 a reform of the Roman liturgical year reduced the number of saints' days to be observed by the whole church, and eliminated some saints with dubious historical credentials. See also CANONIZATION; PATRON SAINT. Major saints are commemorated on particular feast days; the commemoration of All Saints occurs on 1 Nov.

In Christian art the depiction of saints probably first attended the veneration of their relics. By the end of the Middle Ages in the West, a complex system had evolved for representing them. Besides their known or traditional personal characteristics (e.g. St Paul's baldness) they were shown with attributes. Common to all, from the 5th cent., was a *halo around the head, but each saint had individual attributes as well. These were usually an emblem (e.g. keys for St *Peter, the symbols for the *Evangelists), or an instrument of martyrdom (e.g. St *Andrew's cross), a building (e.g. a bishop's cathedral), a book (for teachers), or an allusion to patronage (e.g. an organ for St *Cecilia). See also ICON.

In Islam, there is a veneration of holy people who are often referred to in English as 'saints'. The 'friends of God' (*walī) are important (cf. Qur'ān 10. 63), as are the pure and blessed ones (*ṭāhir*) and many *Sūfī teachers. The veneration of saints and of their tombs, while widely popular, is resisted by conservative Muslims. For a remote resemblance in Judaism, see ZADDIK. 'Saint' is then used widely of holy and revered persons in all religions: see e.g. NĀYAṆMĀRS; SANT TRADITION.

G. D. Bond and R. Kieckhefer, *Sainthood: Its Manifestations in World Religions* (1988); L. Cunningham, *The Meaning of Saints* (1980).

Saint-Cyran, Abbé de (French Augustinian monk): see JANSENISM.

Śaiva: see ŚAIVISM.

Śaiva-Āgama. Authoritative texts of *Śaivism, the earliest being written between 400–800 CE. The texts deal with Śaiva liturgy which involves *nyāsa, *mudrā, *mantra, the construction of *yantras or *maṇḍalas and *visualization (*dhyāna), the construction of shrines and *temples, and *festivals. Interest in philosophy is somewhat limited and is mainly concerned with speculation on the power of speech and the *tattvas. Initiation (*dīkṣā) is important in the texts. There are three kinds of Śaiva initiation, the first two, *samaya* and *viśeṣa*, allowing the disciple access to Śaiva teachings and liturgy, the third, *nirvāna dīkṣā, giving access to liberation (*mokṣa).

The *Āgamas and Upāgamas are the authority for a number of Śaiva schools. They are traditionally divided into four classes: śaiva, *paśupata, *soma* (whose doctrines are unknown), and *lakulīśa*. The śaiva is subdivided into three groups: left-hand (*vāma) Āgamas, of left-hand sects such as the *Kāpālikas; right-hand (*dakṣina) texts of *Kashmir or Trika Śaivism; and *siddhānta* texts of dualistic Śaiva Siddhānta. There are held to be sixty-four monistic Āgamas in the Kashmir Śaiva canon and twenty-eight in the Śaiva Siddhānta canon. The Āgamas theoretically follow a fourfold structure of *jñāna, *yoga, *kriya*, and *carya padas*, though this pattern is seldom strictly adhered to.

Śaiva Siddhānta. A dualistic school of *Śaivism prevalent in S. India. The canon of this school is made up of the twenty-eight *dualist *Śaiva-Āgamas and Upāgamas, though, unlike in *Kashmir Śaivism, the authority of the *Vedas is also acknowledged. Two currents can be discerned in the school, the one gnostic, the other devotional.

The gnostic tradition emphasized knowledge (*jñāna) and used Skt. as its medium of expression. Its dualist theology is summarized in the *Tattvaprakāśa* (Light on the Tattvas) of Bhojadeva (*c*.11th cent.) and expounded in *Aghorasiva's commentaries on dualist Āgamas. The *paddhati* (ritual manual) of Somaśambhu (11th cent.) gives a full account of Śaiva Siddhānta liturgy. This gnostic school of thought may have developed from the dualistic Śaiva tradition of Kashmir.

The devotional tradition, which used Tamil as a medium of expression, emphasized *bhakti and surrender to the Lord *Śiva. Although the Tamil Śaiva Siddhānta adhered to the metaphysics of the gnostic school and revered the twenty-eight dualist Āgamas, equally important if not more so was the devotional Tamil poetry of the *Nāyaṇmārs (4th–9th cents. CE). This poetry was collected by Nampi Āṇṭār Nampi in the *Tirumuṛai* (1080–1100 CE) and included Māṇikkavacakar's *Tiruvācakam* (5th cent. CE) which is sung daily in temples and homes. In it the poet sings of God's love for humankind and its dependence upon God:

> If you leave, I perish. None but you upholds your devotee,
> Source of my life, indwelling in me. (6. 23)

The most important theological text of the school is the Tamil *Civañāṉapotam* (Skt., *Śivajñānabodha*) by Meykaṇṭatēvar (Skt., Meykaṇḍadeva) (*c*.1220 CE) which is said to be the quintessence of the Vedas and Āgamas.

There are three eternal realities in Śaiva Siddhānta theology: the Lord (*pati*), souls (*paśu*, literally 'beast'), and world (*pāśa*, literally 'bond'). Souls and world are dependent upon God who is both immanent and transcendent. Through his grace (Skt., *prasāda; Tamil, *anpu*) souls are delivered from bondage, but even in liberation (*mokṣa) they remain distinct from the Lord.

M. Dhavamony, *Love of God according to Śaiva Siddhānta* . . . (1971); J. M. N. Pillai, *Studies in Śaiva Siddhānta* (1962).

Śaivism. One of the major theistic traditions of medieval Hinduism, worshipping *Śiva or one of his forms or symbols such as the *liṅga. Although difficult to generalize about, because of its diversity, Śaivism tends to be more ascetic than *Vaiṣṇavism. The origins of Śaivism are probably non-Vedic and its roots may lie in the pre-Aryan culture of the Indus Valley, where seals have been found depicting an ithyphallic, horned god, in a yogic posture and surrounded by animals. This may be a precursor of Śiva who is lord of yogis and animals. The earliest textual references to *Rudra-Śiva are minor ones in *Ṛg Veda*. The Śatarudriya of the *Yajur Veda* (2nd–1st millenium BCE) lists a hundred names and attributes of Rudra, and in **Śvetāśvatara Upaniṣad* (*c*.400 BCE) we find Rudra-Śiva as the absolute. However, Śaiva literature only flourished with the Śaiva Purāṇas (4th–9th cents. CE) which are mainly concerned with mythology, and the *Śaiva-Āgamas, which are primarily concerned with initiation, ritual, *yoga, *mantra, and temple-building. The *Īśvara Gīta* of the Kūrma Purāṇa and the *Śivajñānabodham* of the Raura Āgama are particularly influential texts. Śaivism became closely allied to *Tantrism.

Various Śaiva sects developed, ranging from those who adhered to *Smārta orthodoxy to those who flouted it. The following sects can be distinguished: (i) *Pāśupatas, the earliest Śaiva sect, along with a subsect, the Lakulīśa Pāśupata, who took an 'animal' vow (*vrata) of asceticism, bathing in ashes, and engaging in anti-social behaviour; (ii) *Kāpālikas, cremation-ground dwellers who carried a skull and performed antinomian practices; (iii) Kālāmukhas, ascetics closely associated with the Pāśupata; (iv) Vīraśaivas or *Liṅgāyats, who may have developed out of the Kālāmukhas, and who worshipped Śiva in the form of the liṅga; (v) *Kashmir Śaivism or *Trika, so called because of its threefold category of God (Śiva), energy (*śakti), and individual (*aṇu); (vi) *Śaiva Siddhānta, a dualist system which became *bhakti-oriented with the Tamil bhakti poets, the *Nāyanṃārs; (vii) Smārta, orthodox Śaivism which adhered to the *varnāśrama-dharma advocated in the *smṛti literature, such as the law books of *Manu and Kalpa Sūtras, and regarded Śiva as one of the five central deities to be worshipped (*pañcayatana-pūja*); and (viii) *Nātha or Kanphata yogis, a sect traditionally founded by *Gorakhnātha, combining Pāśupata Śaivism with Tantric and *Hatha yoga.

Of these, the most theologically developed are the monistic Trika or Kashmir Śaivism; Śaiva Siddhānta, a dualist system developed in the south; and Vīraśaivism (Liṅgāyat), also in the south. The Śaiva-Āgamas were the authoritative texts for these systems, and there is a common body of doctrine, though differently interpreted, concerning the evolution of the *tattvas as manifestations of śakti; the three categories of Lord (*pati*), beast (*pasu*, i.e. souls), and bondage (*pasa*); the five faces of Śiva (*pancavakira*); ritual; *dīkṣā; and *mantra.

Śaivism spread throughout India: Trika in Kashmir, Śaiva Siddhānta in the Tamil-speaking south, Vīraśaiva in the Kannada-speaking south, and Pāśupata in Gujarat. Today Śaivism is especially prevalent in Madras State. Śaiva ascetics are distinguished by their long matted hair, sometimes piled on top of their heads, three horizontal marks smeared on the forehead, the trident which they carry, and the ashes in which they are often covered. Śaiva temples and pilgrimage sites are found throughout India from the Amarnāth cave in Kashmir where there is an ice liṅga, to the Viśvanāth temple at Vārānasi and the Rauleswaram temple at the southernmost tip of India.

R. G. Bhandarkar, *Vaiṣṇavism, Śaivism and Minor Religious Systems* (1913, 2nd edn., 1980); J. Gonda, *Viṣṇuism and Śivaism* (1970); A. K. Ramanujan, *Speaking of Śiva* (1973).

Saiyid (Arab., 'Lord, owner'). A title of respect, and in particular, the title/name of a direct descendant of *Muḥammad through his daughter *Fāṭima and *ʿAlī ibn Abī Ṭālib.

Sajjāda (Arab., *sajada*, 'bow down', 'worship'). The prayer mat on which *ṣalāt is performed. *Muḥammad is said to have preferred ṣalāt on the earth, as some *faqīhs still prefer. The design in the carpet is not symmetrical, but leads to a point on one of the short sides which is placed in the direction of the *qibla. Sajdah is the point of prostration in prayer when the forehead touches the ground. The word underlies *masjid*, mosque, the place of prostration.

Sakadāgāmin (Pāli; Skt., *sakṛdāgāmin*). A 'Once-Returner': in Buddhism, one of the Four Noble Persons (*ariya-puggala*), who is distinguished by having only one more rebirth to experience before gaining enlightenment.

Śākhā (Skt., 'branch'). A branch or school of the *Veda, especially any one of the particular recensions of one of the four *Vedic collections (*saṁhitās) as represented by a brahmanic lineage (*caraṇa*) entrusted with its preservation. According to Śaunaka there are five śākhās of the Ṛg Veda Saṁhitā (namely, Śākala, Bāśkala, Āśvalāyana, Śānkhāyana, and Māṇḍukāyana). Of these five, only the Śākala śākhā is extant.

Sākhī (Pañjābī, 'witness'). A section of a *janam-sākhī narrative. The term is also used for the couplets (otherwise called *dohā* or *śalok) of *Kabīr.

Sakīna (peace from God): see SHEKHINAH.

Sakka. Buddhist form of *Indra, who dwells in the Tāvatiṃsa heaven: see COSMOLOGY (Buddhist).

Sakkāya-diṭṭhi. 'Personality Belief': in Buddhism a basic misconception concerning the nature of personal identity in relation to the five aggregates (*skandhas). There are twenty possible permutations of this wrong view: (i)–(v) that one's self is identical with any one of the five aggregates; (vi)–(x) that it is contained in them; (xi)–(xv) that it is independent of them; and (xvi)–(xx) that it is the owner of them. Sakkāya-diṭṭhi is the first of the 'Ten Fetters' (*saṃyojana), and is only abandoned when one reaches the stage of 'Entering the Stream' (*sotāpatti-magga*). For the error, see also PUDGALAVĀDINS.

Śakra (courage): see ĀDITYAS.

Sakṛdāgāmin: see SAKADĀGĀMIN.

Śakti (Skt., 'power'). Creative power in Hinduism manifested as Goddess and consort of *Śiva. She is venerated under many aspects (e.g. each *cakra is governed by a particularization of Śakti) and many names (e.g. *Durgā, *Kālī, *Ambā). Devotion to Śakti is thus extremely diverse: see ŚĀKTISM. As the creative power, able to bring things into appearance, Śakti resembles *māyā; for that reason, goddesses in their role as śakti are often referred to as Māyā.

See Index, Śakti.

Śāktism (Skt., *śakti*, 'power'). A Hindu tradition or current of thought with *śakti, divine female power, as the focus of its worship. This power is either the supreme being conceived as female or a consort of one of the Hindu gods.

The origins of Śaktism as Goddess worship can probably be traced to the Indus Valley culture, and iconographical evidence dates back to the pre-Christian era. The goddess *Durgā appears as a powerful deity in the sixth book of the **Mahābhārata* and the fifth book of the **Viṣṇu* **Purāṇa* (5th cent. CE), but it is in the Devīmāhātmya portion of **Mārkaṇḍeya Purāṇa* (7th cent. CE) that the Goddess (*Devī) is worshipped as supreme. In texts called *Tantras and Śākta *Upaniṣads we find a developed Tantric form of worship of the Goddess as Śakti.

The Śākta Tantras are closely allied to monistic or *Kashmir Śaivism and adhere to a non-dual theology with either Śakti or the union of Śiva and Śakti as absolute. Most Śākta Tantras declare themselves to be of the *Kaula or *Kula school and can be divided into two main categories: (i) the *Śrī Kula*, which advocates worship of the benign and beautiful goddess *Śrī/Lakṣmī as Tripurāsundarī; and (ii) the *Kālī Kula*, which advocates worship of the fierce goddess *Kālī. A smaller third category advocates worship of the Goddess *Tārā. The Śākta *sādhaka (practitioner) will follow one or other cult prescribed for him by the *guru according to his personality. Two kinds of worship comprise the *Śrī Kula*: *Śrī Cakra*, worship of the *yantra, a geometrical design of nine intersecting triangles, as identical with the sādhaka's own body, and *Śrī Vidyā*, the worship of Śakti as a number of Skt. syllables. The sādhaka must realize the identity between the Goddess, the yantra, the Śrī Vidyā, the guru, and himself. The *Kālī Kula* advocates *antinomian practices such as the ritual involving the five Ms (*pañca makāra). Some Tantras such as the *Kulārṇava are not specific to either the Śrī or Kālī cults.

The Śākta sādhaka is classified in three ways which are also regarded as stages on the spiritual path: the beast (*paśu*), dominated by the quality of inertia (*tamas guṇa), must worship the Goddess externally with *mudra and *nyāsa; the hero (*vīra*), dominated by passion (*rajas guṇa), must worship in the *cakra pūjā and with the five Ms which he must practice without attachment; and the divine (*divya*), dominated by light (*sattva guṇa), can practice *Kuṇḍalinī yoga, the most advanced *sādhana.

Śaktism developed, and is still practised principally, in Bengal and Assam, though worship of the goddesses at village level is found throughout India, especially in the south. Theoretically Śaktic sādhana is open to all *castes, and during the śakta pūjā there is equality: 'all *varnas (classes) become Brahmans', says the **Kulārṇava Tantra*. Indeed, even a Caṇḍāla (*untouchable) can become a guru. Śaktism exalts the position of women by regarding them as incarnations of the Goddess; it is a mistake, however, to regard Śaktism as a force for improving the social conditions of women or low castes. Equality is only in ritual, and the role of woman is to act as a partner (śakti or *dūtī*) for the male sādhaka. A low-caste woman is said to be best suited for the role of the *dūtī*, probably because on her there are fewer social restrictions. Equality, then, is only ritual equality and not equality in everyday life. Indeed, it has been argued that, far from being revolutionary, śākta practices are caste-confirming.

See Index, Śakti.

S. G. Gupta and T. Goudriaan, *Hindu Tantric and Sakta Literature* (1981).

Śakuni. In the **Mahābhārata*, the evil maternal uncle of the *Kauravas, a master gambler, said to be an incarnation of the demon Dvāpara, named for a throw of dice. On behalf of Duryodhana, he plays a dice game against Yudhiṣṭhira, which he wins by trickery. The game leads to the great *Kurukṣetra war, in which Śakuni fights on the Kaurava side, and is killed by the *Pāṇḍava Sahadeva.

Śakuntalā. The title character of the play *Abhijñānaśakuntala* (Śakuntalā Recognized), by the Indian poet and playwright *Kālidāsa, probably of the Gupta period (3rd cent. CE). The play is often called simply *Śakuntalā*. Śakuntalā marries King Duṣyanta by the gāndharva form of marriage (simple consent between the two), but is forgotten and repudiated by him due to a curse of the sage Durvasas. The confusion is resolved when Duṣyanta's recognition of a ring he had given her mitigates the curse, as Durvasas had promised. The story is taken from the first book of the **Mahābhārata*. It became well-known in Europe after the Orientalist, Sir W. Jones, translated it.

Sakya (Sa.skya, 'Grey Earth'). One of the four principal schools of Tibetan Buddhism, taking its name from the Grey Earth monastery founded by Konchok Gyalpo in 1073 CE. Konchok Gyalpo had been a *Nyingma follower until meeting the traveller, translator, and *yogin Drokmi, from whom he learnt the Hevajra cycle of *tantras and the system known as Lam Drey (lam.'bras, 'The Way and its Fruit'), which is attributed to the Indian *Siddha Virupa. Konchok Gyalpo's son Kunga Nyingpo formally systematized the Sakya teachings from the writings of Drokmi, with Lam Drey at the centre relating tantra to *sūtra and offering enlightenment in a single lifetime. The Sakya school has always hosted a wide variety of views: *Tsong Khapa's teacher Ren Da Wa (Red.mda'.ba; 1349–1412) was strongly *Prāsaṅgika, for instance, while the great Shākya Choden (Shākya.mchog.ldan; 1428–1507) accepted the view of the *Jonang.

The situation of the Grey Earth monastery on a trade route ensured the Sakyas an early growth in wealth, and a succession of learned *lamas gave them a reputation for erudition. The Sakya Paṇḍiṭa Kunga Gyaltsen (1182–1251), author of perhaps the oldest of Tibetan histories and whose logical treatises were translated into Skt. for use in India and Nepal, also showed political acumen in establishing relations with the Mughals. His nephew Phakpa ('Phags.pa; 1235–80) was subsequently given the title 'Ti Sri' (Viceroy) by Kublai Khan in 1260 and with it temporal rule over most of Tibet. This political dominance was short-lived, however, declining as Mughal strength diminished in the 13th cent.

The Sakya produced two subsects, the Ngor (15th cent.) and the Tshar (16th cent.). Headship of the school alternates between two 'palaces' (*phodrang*) within the surviving Dunchod branch of the founding Khön dynasty, to which the Ngor and the Tshar are subordinate. The present head is Sakya Trizin (b. 1945) of the Drolma Phodrang, who resides chiefly in India, while Sakya Dakchen (b. 1929) of the Phuntsok Phodrang resides in America. The Ngor and the Tshar appoint their own heads on a merit basis. A *tulku system is recognized in the Sakya, but it is not always connected with the transmission of major posts.

Sākyamuni (Pāli), **Śākyamuni** (Skt., '*muni of the Sākyas'). A title of the *Buddha denoting that he stemmed from the Śākya tribe which inhabited a region of present-day Nepal. He is also accorded the title Śākyasiṁha ('lion among the Śākyas').

Sakyapa (an order in Tibetan Buddhism): see 'PHAGS-PA.

Saladin: see SALĀḤ UD-DĪN.

Salaf al-Ṣāliḥīn (virtuous/exemplary ancestors): see SALAFIY(Y)A.

Salafiy(y)a. Movement founded by Jamal al-Din *al-Afghānī and Muḥammad *'Abduh, which sought to reconcile Islam with the advances of Western science and rationality. It received its name from the phrase *salaf al-ṣāliḥīn*, 'the virtuous ancestors', but it was not regarded by its opponents as preserving the essence of the past, but rather as subverting it. It provoked the now widespread Islamic response of 'not subordinating revelation to reason', but of finding the achievements of modern science anticipated in the *Qur'ān. The movement gave rise to the first extensive movement for the emancipation of women from the controls of *sharī'a.

In contrast, the same word is now used to translate *'fundamentalism'.

Salāḥ ud-Dīn or **Saladin** (1138–93 (AH 532–89)). A Kurdish soldier who recaptured *Jerusalem from the *crusaders. When his uncle was killed leading an army against the *Fāṭimids, he took command. Since the Fāṭimids received support from the crusaders, it was natural for the defeat of the Fāṭimids to lead to further campaigns against their allies. By 1187 (AH 583) he had captured Jerusalem, but he did not succeed in expelling them from their last stronghold in Tyre. They received reinforcement, and in 1191 (AH 589) Richard Cœur de Lion retook Acre. In the ensuing conflicts, Salāḥ ud-Dīn earned a reputation for chivalry which long outlasted his political empire.

Salām (Arab.). Peace, used in greeting. The Hebrew equivalent is *shālōm.

Ṣalāt. The ritual worship of the Muslim community; as worship through prayer, it is to be distinguished from *duʿā', personal prayer or supplication by the individual or group. The words of ṣalāt are always in Arabic. Derived from Syriac, or from Aramaic, where the root *ṣl'* means to bow or bend, the Arabic verb *ṣallā*, to perform the ṣalāt, is derived from the noun.

One of the *five pillars of the faith, it is frequently mentioned in the *Qur'ān as a duty. Believers are 'those who perform the Ṣalāt and give the *Zakāt (alms)'. Times (*mīqāt*) and regulations for ṣalāt are given in detail in the *ḥadīth, and were eventually fixed at five times: Ṣalāt al-Ṣubḥ or Ṣalāt al-Fajr (Dawn), Ṣalāt al-Ẓuhr (Noon), Ṣalāt al-ʿAṣr (Afternoon), Ṣalāt al-Maghrib (Sunset), Ṣalāt al-ʿIshā' (Night). According to tradition, Muḥammad was given these instructions by Allāh on the occasion of his *Isrā' (Night Journey) to heaven.

Ṣalāt should be performed in common, in a *mosque, especially the Noon prayer on Friday (*Jumʿa). But the Muslim may pray individually or in small groups, when one member is chosen as the *Imām, and this may be in any ritually clean area, marked off by *sutra. A prayer mat, *sajjāda, is commonly used. Ṣalāt must be performed facing the *qibla, the direction of *Mecca, which in a mosque is indicated by the *miḥrāb* (see MOSQUE).

Ṣalāt is preceded by ritual ablution (*wuḍū'*, *ghusl, or *tayammum*) as appropriate. It is divided into distinct movements, accompanied by formulae. First, in a standing position facing the qibla, is the pronouncement of the *niy(y)a (intention) to perform the ṣalāt; then the *takbīr (Allāhu Akbar), followed by the *Fātiḥa and a verse or two from the Qur'ān. The movements then are: *rukūʿ*, bending till the palms are level with the knees; kneeling; a prostration, *sujūd*; back again into *julūs* (between sitting and standing); another sujūd. At most movements, the takbīr is repeated. This set of movements, from the standing position to the end of the second *sujūd*, constitutes one *rakʿa, the number of which is fixed for each prayer time. After the final rakʿa, in a sitting position, the worshipper pronounces the *tashahhud* (profession of faith, *shahāda); the prayer upon the Prophet Muḥammad; finally the *taslima*, greeting, 'Al-Salām ʿalaykum' ('Peace be upon you'), even when he is alone. Extra rakʿas may be added by the individual. The ritual may vary slightly according to the *madhhab.

In a mosque, worshippers stand in rows (*ṣaff*), but *women pray separately, at the back, or in a special enclosure, or often in a women's gallery above and to the rear of the main hall. Ṣalāt may be held for special purposes, as in prayer for rain (*istisqā'*) or in time of danger. Rituals exist for the two *ʿids, and for *jināza* (funeral rites).

Ṣalāt, as an obligation upon all Muslims and a sign of submission and humility, and of adherence to the Islamic community, is held to be the sign of the true believer, who thus, for his devout and conscientious regular worship, will gain admittance to *paradise.

Sales/Salesian (Christian spiritual director/style): see DE SALES, FRANCIS.

Salih. *Prophet and *rasūl who, according to the *Qur'ān, was sent to the Thamūd. Nothing is known of him apart from the Qur'ān, where he appears, like other prophets, as a warner, who was rejected by most of his people. His camel was made lame by the people of Thamūd, instead of being given water, thus making the treatment of camels an epitome of the human relation to the gifts of God in creation. For the punishment of the people of Thamūd, see 7. 73 ff.

Sālimīya (Muslim theological school): see SAHL AL-TUSTARĪ.

Sallekhanā. In Jainism, ritual death by fasting. This 'holy death' in a state of meditation is recommended for Jain mendicants (and is often seen as an important goal by the laity also) as a wise, righteous, and planned preparation for the inevitable, and also as a powerful final act of renunciation. Through gradual fasting in accordance with detailed prescription and under close supervision of mendicant teachers, Jains can meet their death in a controlled and peaceful manner. Jains insist that this is a noble act, and not common suicide, because the vow to take sallekhanā is made publicly and the consent of the *ācarya or family must first be given. The final hours are spent repeating the *namaskāra-mantra, or listening to others chanting it. Throughout Indian history the Jains have been noted for this unusual approach to death. It is still practised today and stands as an extraordinary sign to the world of the Jain ideal of conquering the material world through renunciation.

Salmān al-Fār(i)sī ('the Persian'). Close companion of the Prophet *Muḥammad and a central figure of many Muslim legends. He embraced Islam in *Madīna after long experience with other religions, e.g., Zoroastrianism and Christianity. According to early sources, it was Salmān who advised the Prophet to dig ditches and trenches before the siege of Madīna by the Meccans (the Battle of the Ditch, *khandaq*). *ʿUmar appointed him as governor of al-*Madāʾin and he is said to have died there during *ʿUthmān's reign. Salmān's tomb at al-Madāʾin is a place of pilgrimage for *Shiʿites returning from *Karbalāʾ. According to many *Sūfī orders, Salmān is a leading mystic and teacher in their *silsilah (chain of transmission). The *Nuṣairī raise him to their trinity of ʿAlī, Muḥammad, and Salmān, in which he is considered to be the figure who, under the name of *Gabriel, taught the Qurʾān to Muḥammad.

Śalok (Pañjābī, from Skt., 'śloka', 'verse'). Short verse of two or more lines interspersing longer verses in the *Ādi Granth. Śalok refers to the distich form used by the Bhagats, e.g. *Kabīr and the *Gurūs.

Salvation (Lat., *salus*, 'sound, safe'). The act or state of being safe in ultimate terms. Although all religions have some sense of a condition which might appropriately be called by this name, the state and the way to it are very differently understood. Thus in Judaism, there is concern to achieve deliverance from sin and for a final *messianic victory, but no word or phrase in general use that summarizes the idea of 'salvation'. Again, in Islam, there is much concern with the day of judgement (*yaum al-Din) and with the mercy of God, who is constantly invoked *b'ismi-Llāhi rahmāni warahīm*, 'in the name of God, merciful and compassionate'. But the most common word for 'salvation', *najah*, is used only once in the *Qurʾān ('O my people, how is it that I invite you to salvation, but you invite me to the fire?', 40. 44), and salvation is seen as a practical matter, lying within the individual's competence to follow the guidance of the Qurʾān. Again, in Buddhism, there is strong emphasis from the Buddha that he is only a physician who can diagnose ills and suggest the path to a cure, but that each person must be his or her own saviour. It is only in Mahāyāna Buddhism that figures akin to saviours (especially *bodhisattvas) enter in. Otherwise, there is certainly a strong sense of safety in the three refuges (*saraṇa*: see THREE JEWELS); but while intermediate salvation is possible in the *devaloka, it is only temporary and not to be compared to the attainment of *nirvāna. In Hinduism, the notion is more clearly expressed through terms derived from *muc*, 'release from pains or penalties', such as *mukti (mukta) and *mokṣa. The mukta is one who has attained release from *avidya (ignorance) and thus from *saṃsāra (rebirth). While this may be by effort of an appropriate kind, help from a 'saviour', especially an *avatāra of Viṣṇu, and above all from *Kṛṣṇa, is acknowledged. On India, see A. G. K. Warrier, *The Concept of Mukti in Advaita Vedanta* (1961). It is in Christianity that great emphasis is laid on salvation, deriving from the centrality of Christ. The Christian doctrine has several aspects: (i) the work of Christ in the *atonement (and, broadly, in the *incarnation generally); (ii) the *justification and sanctification of men and women by God's *grace; and (iii) the outcome of death and of history (see JUDGEMENT; ESCHATOLOGY). The word itself (Gk., *sōtēria*) and its cognates are frequent in the New Testament, but their meanings often overlap this classification with such apparent deliberation that it is often said that salvation is characteristically both 'already' and 'not yet'.

S. G. F. Brandon, *Man and his Destiny in the Great Religions* (1962).

Salvation Army. Christian denomination. Founded in 1865 by W. *Booth for evangelism, and for social work, it is now established in about 100 countries. From the beginning, its organization has been along military lines: members sign the 'Articles of War'; meeting places are called citadels. Booth and his son Bramwell were the first two Generals, but since 1931 the election of the General has been the responsibility of the Army's High Council, comprising its leading officers from various parts of the world. The Army's international structure divides its many 'territories' into 'provinces' and 'divisions'. Its *Arminian doctrinal convictions, embodied in its *Orders and Regulations* (1878), reflect the *Wesleyan background of its founder, particularly in universal *redemption, human free will, and a post-conversion sanctification experience. Salvationists do not observe the *sacraments, and attempt to work closely with other denominations. Music has always played an important role in the Army's worship and witness. Since publication of Booth's *In Darkest England* their commitment to social work has also earned worldwide admiration. Membership: *c.*1 million; 75,000 in Britain (1980).

F. Coutts, *No Discharge in this War: The History of the Salvation Army* (1947–68); R. Sandall, *History of the Salvation Army* (1947).

Salvation history (Germ., *Heilsgeschichte*). In Christian theology, the history of God's saving work among men and women. Some scholars (e.g. K. *Barth) have used the term to call attention to the special supra-historical character of the biblical narrative. More usually it is supposed to denote a distinctive concept in the Bible itself, according to which God is essentially one who acts in history, and Christ is the midpoint of a continuum from creation to consummation (O. Cullmann, *Heil als Geschichte*; Eng. tr., *Salvation in History*, 1967).

Sāma (chant): see SĀMA VEDA.

Śama (the six virtues according to Śaṅkara): see ṢATKASAMPATTI.

Samā' (Arab., 'hearing', 'listening'). *Sūfī practice of making and listening to music to encourage attention to God, and the states ensuing therefrom. Music in general has been discouraged in Islam if it distracts from awareness of God, or if it is simply an idle amusement, or if it excites the passions. According to ibn Majah, *Muḥammad said: 'Some people of my *'umma will drink wine, calling it by another name, while they listen to singers accompanied by musical instruments. God will cause the earth to swallow them, and he will turn some among them into monkeys and pigs.' But it is not absolutely forbidden, and has been important for some groups. The common human experience of mood alteration through music, leading at an extreme to trance and other ecstatic states, was developed among Sūfīs (see IBN 'ARABĪ), especially in association with *dance, and both music and dance may now be referred to through the term *ḥaḍra* ('presence'; see GHAIBA), i.e. that which brings one into the presence of God. The more general practice of music received extensive classical analysis: for details, see A. Shiloah, *The Theory of Music in Arabic Writings, c.900–1900* (1979).

H. G. Farmer, *History of Arabian Music to the XIIIth Century* (1929); E. Zonis, *Classical Persian Music* (1973).

Samādhi (Skt., 'putting together', 'union'). Enstasis, intense concentration or absorption of consciousness in a variety of higher mental states in Hindu, Buddhist, and Jain *yoga, in which distinction between subject and object is eliminated; the eighth 'limb' of 'eight-limbed' (*aṣṭāṅga*) or *rāja yoga. Samādhi is the consequence of meditation rather than the state of meditation itself.

In Hinduism, samādhi is achieved through yoga in which the yogin's consciousness (*citta) is absorbed in the object of meditation and there is no awareness of the physical or material world. Magical powers (*siddha) are a consequence of this condition. Samādhi is attested throughout Indian religious literature (in the *Upaniṣads, **Mahābhārata*, *Purāṇas, and *Tantras). Classical yoga as explained in the **Yoga Sūtra* should be particularly noted. Here samādhi is a culmination of rāja yoga, and a terminology of different stages of samādhi prior to liberation (*kaivalya) is employed. During samādhi, consciousness becomes like a transparent jewel (*Yoga Sūtra* I. 41), contentless and free from impurity (*kleśa). According to Bhoja, a commentator on the *Yoga Sūtra*, there can be three objects of samādhi with which the yogin's consciousness unites: God, the self (*ātman) or nature (*prakṛti). *Patañjali in the *Yoga Sūtra* makes a distinction between samādhi 'with support' (*saṁprajñāta) or 'with seed' (*sabīja*) and 'without support' (*asaṁprajñāta*) or 'without seed' (*nirbīja*). Saṁprajñāta samādhi, subdivided into four stages is a condition in which consciousness is still supported by an object, whereas in *asaṁprajñāta* consciousness becomes contentless, without object or support. At this stage karmic impressions (*saṃskāras, *vāsanās) are uprooted and consciousness becomes self-absorbed, the yogin realizes his true self (*puruṣa). God (*Īśvara) can also be revealed at this stage. Total liberation conceived as the isolation (kaivalya) of the *puruṣa from nature (prakṛti) follows from *asaṁprajñāta* samādhi, though the two states are mediated by a further samādhi called the 'cloud of *dharma' (*dharma megha*).

Other Hindu traditions such as *Vedānta, *Śaivism, *Vaiṣṇavism, and *Tantrism accept the idea of samādhi as a consequence of yoga practice, while adhering to a diversity of metaphysical systems and practices. For example, Vedānta accepts yoga practice but rejects the *Sāṃkhya conception of liberation as kaivalya. Tantrism accepts samādhi as found in classical yoga, but emphasizes the attainment of samādhi and liberation (*mokṣa) through *Kuṇḍalinī and *mantra yoga.

Samādhi is still integral to yoga and some modern Hindu religious figures are thought to have entered it. For example, *Rāmakrishna frequently entered samādhi. Some yogins have displayed their powers of samādhi by being buried alive for varying periods of time (cf. PRĀṆĀYĀMA).

In Buddhism, samādhi is produced through the practice of that aspect of Buddhist meditation concerned with mind-development (*citta-*bhāvanā), involving tranquillity (*samatha) and the absorptions (*jhāna), as distinct from insight-development (*vipassanā-bhāvanā). It is therefore used as a synonym for these meditations. According to the Pāli Commentary tradition, there are three stages involved in the production of samādhi: preparatory concentration (parikamma-samādhi), with the fixing of one's attention on the meditational object (*kaṣina); neighbourhood concentration (upacāra-samādhi), associated with the appearance of a sublimated image (patibhaga-*nimitta) of the meditational object, signifying, as the word 'neighbourhood' suggests, the meditator's close proximity to the attainment of absorption; and full concentration (appanā-samādhi), which characterizes the mental state during any of the absorptions.

Unlike insight (vipassanā), samādhi can be realized by non-Buddhist as well as Buddhist ascetics, and it is through its practice that supernormal powers (*iddhi) are achieved. However, traditional Buddhism sees its principal function as facilitating insight by ridding the mind of those distractions and hindrances (*nīvaraṇa) which impede clear vision: 'he who is concentrated knows, sees what really is' (*Samyutta Nikāya* 3. 13). For this reason samādhi is generally regarded as an indispensable component of Buddhist practice and forms one of the links of the Eightfold Path (*aṣṭangika-marga) as well as part of the threefold dimension of the Path, together with *śīla (morality) and *prajñā (wisdom). It is listed as one of the seven factors of enlightenment (*bojjhanga), the five spiritual powers (*bala), and six perfections (*pāramitas).

Many *Mahāyāna scriptures contain long lists of what are referred to as particular samādhis, specific meditational attainments of various buddhas and *bodhisattvas. The most common way of depicting the Buddha in the images of Theravada Buddhist countries is in the state of samādhi. He is shown with legs crossed, hands folded in the lap, and eyes half-closed signifying the intensity of his concentration. One of the most famous examples, and possibly the oldest extant, is the giant stone image at Anuradhapura, Śri Lankā.

In Zen Buddhism, samādhi (Jap., *sanmai, zenmai*) is the overcoming of a dualistic, subject–object, awareness, through concentration on a single object and experiencing unity with it.

Among Jains, samādhi is a virtual equivalent of *dhyāna or *bhāvanā, the meditation which seeks to destroy the accumulation of *karma in order to release the *jīva. It is the interior preparation for, and exercise of, increasingly severe *asceticism (*tapas).

G. Feuerstein, *The Philosophy of Classical Yoga* (1980); G. Oberhammer, *Strukturen yogischer Meditation* (1977).

Samael. The name of *Satan in Judaism from the *amoraic period. It first appears in the Ethiopic *Book of *Enoch*. In the *Ascension of *Isaiah*, Samael is portrayed as the counterpart to *Belial, and in certain gnostic works, he is described as the 'blind god'. The **Targum Jonathan* of Genesis 3. 6 identifies Samael with the angel of death, and in *Deuteronomy Rabbah* he is described as 'Samael the wicked, the head of all *devils'; in *Enoch* 14. 2, he is 'the chief of all tempters'. He appears in later sources as the consort of *Lilith, and he is a prominent character in the **Zohar* and in *kabbalistic literature.

Samān (chant): see MUSIC.

Samaṇas. Hindu wandering philosophers of the Upaniṣadic period, who rejected Vedic tradition and family ties, and depended on alms for sustenance. Jain and Buddhist ascetics were in origin akin to samaṇas; Buddhist assessment of them occurs in *Sāmañña-phala Sutta*, part of **Dīgha Nikāya*.

Sāmaṇera (Pāli; Skt., Śrāmaṇera). One who is making a first approach to full membership of the Buddhist saṅgha (community)—i.e. the equivalent, in Western terms, of a novice monk.

Samantabhadra (Skt., 'he who is all-pervadingly good'; Chin., P'u-hsien; Jap., Fugen; Tib., Ādi Buddha). A *bodhisattva of great importance in Mahāyāna Buddhism. He is the protector of all who teach *dharma, and he is the embodiment of the realization that sameness and difference are a unity. He rides a six-tusked elephant, the tusks representing the conquest of attachment to the six senses. He rode on the elephant to China, settling on Mount O-mei, where he is venerated as one of the four great bodhisattvas. He is also closely associated with *Vairocāna. For the Tibetan development, see ĀDI BUDDHA.

Samaritans. A tribe descended from Israelites who were regarded as heretics by Jews. The Samaritans themselves believe they are descended from the tribes of *Ephraim and Manasseh and, until the 17th cent. CE, their *high priest was a direct descendant of *Aaron. According to the Hebrew scriptures, they intermarried with non-Israelite colonists after they had been defeated by the Assyrians in 721 BCE (2 Kings 17. 24–41). After they were rejected by the returning *exiles in the Persian period, Sanballat, the Samaritan ruler, built a rival *temple on Mount *Gerizim (Nehemiah 13). This was destroyed by John Hyrcanus in 128 BCE, but it was said to have been rebuilt by the Romans as a reward for Samaritan help against the *Bar Kokhba revolt. The animosity between Jews and Samaritans is illustrated on several occasions in the New Testament (e.g. John 4). The Samaritans were persecuted throughout their history by the Romans, the Christians, and the Muslims in turn. The last Aaronite High Priest died in 1624, leaving no sons, and the office passed to the descendants of Uzziel b. Kehat, the uncle of Aaron. By the 19th cent. only a very small community remained in Shechem. In 1842, they were recognized by the *Jerusalem *Chief Rabbi as 'a branch of the Jewish people that confess to the truth of the *Torah', and, after the establishment of the State of *Israel, they were recognized as citizens under the *Law of Return. In 1963, the first Samaritan *synagogue in Israel was established, and by 1970 the community numbered 430. The Samaritans have their own version of the *Pentateuch, and they claim that their most ancient *scroll dates back to the thirteenth year of the Israelite settlement of *Canaan. They have their own *liturgy and various expositions and commentaries on the Pentateuch. Their *priests are the interpreters of the law and the keepers of the *Calendar; *Moses, and possibly *Joshua, are their sole *prophets. They believe in *resurrection based on their understanding of their version of Genesis 3. 19. They have developed a *code of law by direct interpretation of the Pentateuchal text, and there are a few Samaritan compendia of laws. They keep all the *festivals mentioned in the Torah. *Passover, *Shavu'ot, and *Sukkot involve *pilgrimage to Mount Gerizim, and *sacrifices are made at Passover. The *Sabbath is kept very strictly, in absolute accord with the biblical laws, and they do not light fires or travel on the seventh day. They *circumcise their sons and they keep all the laws of ritual *purity and impurity as laid down in Leviticus. Boys and girls are expected to read and understand the entire Pentateuch before becoming full members of the community, and Samaritan marriage follows the three stages of *kiddushin*, *erusin*, and *nissu'in* (for these terms see MARRIAGE AND DIVORCE). Intermarriage with Jews is only permitted if the Jew is willing to conform to all the Samaritan *customs. Their dead are buried on Mount Gerizim and, like *Joseph, they mourn for seven days. Hebrew has been retained as the language of the liturgy, although it is a Hebrew influenced by Aramaic and Arabic.

A. D. Crown (ed.), *The Samaritans* (1989) and *Companion to Samaritan Studies* (1993); J. A. Montgomery, *The Samaritans* (1968); J. D. Purvis, *The Samaritan Pentateuch and Origin of the Samaritan Sect* (1968).

Samaritans (organization): see SUICIDE.

Samatha (Skt., Pāli śamatha, 'tranquillity', 'calming-down'). The form of Buddhist *meditation whose purpose is mind-development (*citta-*bhāvanā) and which is defined in terms of the end that it achieves—mental tranquillity. It is to be distinguished from the other form of Buddhist meditation, *vipassanā, whose purpose is insight into Buddhist doctrinal truth. It is thus an alternative designation for concentration (*samādhi), the system of meditation based on the forty *kammaṭṭhāṅa. In normal consciousness the mind is in a constant state of flux owing to the distraction of the senses, the desires, and discursive reflection. By providing the mind with a single focus of attention these objects of meditation free it of those hindrances (see NĪVARAṆAS) and bring it to a condition of tranquillity. The recurrent practice of this form of meditation leads, in the longer term, to increased non-attachment (*virāga*) by allaying unwholesome mental activities (see SANKHĀRA); this is what is meant by mind-development. Samatha is highly valued in Buddhism because some degree of mental tranquillity is needed to make vipassanā possible.

Sāmavasarāna (Jain assembly hall): see ART (Jainism).

Samavāya-aṅga (Jain text): see AṄGA.

Sāma Veda (Skt.). The Vedic collection of chants (sāman) used by the Udgātṛ priests in the sacrificial rites with the belief that proper tone and pitch gave creative power to the singer of the chant. The sāman differs from the ṛc of the **Ṛg Veda* primarily in the addition of melody and the rearrangement of verses. All but seventy-five of the verses of the *Sāma Veda* are found in the *Ṛg Veda*. The melody and employment of the sāmans were at first passed on orally, then recorded in songbooks (*gaṇas*) corresponding to the two divisions of the text: the Pūrvārcika and Uttarārcika. The former contains single verses used as aids in memorizing and recollecting the various melodies. The latter contains texts of the complete chants.

Tr. R. Griffith (1963).

Sāmāyika (Skt., 'attaining equanimity'). In Jainism, a 48-minute period of *yogic meditation and restraint practised by both ascetics and the Jain laity, and (according to Jain texts), the highest form of spiritual discipline. It can be observed at any time, but is often practised at dawn or sunset (before or after the day's activities) when the Jain can sit unmoved and undisturbed, forgiving and seeking forgiveness. The ritual is commended as the highest form of spiritual discipline, and seems to have had ancient origins. The significance of the 48 minutes is that it is a *mahūrta*, a standard Indian unit of time often employed for ritual purposes. It is one-thirtieth of a day, just as a day is one-thirtieth of a month. It is accompanied by the prayer: 'Friendship to all beings, delight in the qualities of the virtuous ones, unlimited compassion for all suffering beings, equanimity to those who wish me harm, may my soul have these dispositions now and for ever.'

Sambatyon. A river in Jewish legend. After the Assyrian conquest of 721 BCE, the ten Northern *tribes were said to have been *exiled across the river Sambatyon. It was said to flow with a huge current six days of the week, but to rest on the *Sabbath (*Gen.R.* 11. 5). *Naḥmanides identified the river with the biblical river Gozan (2 Kings 17. 6). It is mentioned by Pliny in his *Natural History*, and also by *Josephus. The legend persisted through the Middle Ages.

Śambhala (semi-mythical kingdom in Tibetan Buddhist cosmology): see SHAMBHALA.

Sambhoga-kāya. 'Enjoyment Body', one of the Buddha's 'Three Bodies' (*Trikāya), and the intermediate form in which he manifests himself in the heavens or celestial paradises.

Sambō. Jap., Mahāyāna, and Zen term for the *Three Jewels (*triratna*), i.e. 'three treasures', the foundation for all Buddhist life. In Mahāyāna, the significance of the three is greatly extended by exploring (i) how the three are nevertheless one, ittai-sambō; (ii) how they manifest themselves, genzen-sambō; (iii) how they are verifiable and verified. Ittai-sambō is often expressed through the conjunction of *Vairocana, representing the sameness of all buddha-nature (*busshō) empty of self (*śūnyatā), with *dharma as the true understanding of how all appearance occurs: the two together lead to the transcendent state of enlightenment. Genzen-sambō is, specifically, the historical Buddha and his disciples; verification is through *sūtras, iconography, and the actual practice of professed disciples. The three treasures are, in Japanese, *butsu (the *Buddha), *hō (*dharma), and *sō* (the *saṅgha).

Sambō-ekotoba. Three scrolls of paintings and explanations of *Sambō, composed by Minamoto Tamenori (d. 1011). They contain, in addition, outline biographies of famous Buddhists.

Sambō-ji (Buddhist monastery): see DAINICHI NŌNIN.

Saṃcita-karma. In Hinduism, the accumulation of *saṃskāras (acquired characteristics) which have been created and transmitted via *karma from previous lives.

Saṃdhinirmocana-sūtra (The Explanation of Mysteries, or The Unravelling of the Hidden Meaning). An important text in the Buddhist school of *Vijñānavāda (Yogācāra), and the source upon which many of the exponents of the school based their teachings. The *sūtra consists of an introduction and ten chapters arranged in an unsystematic form, being evidently a composite of three separate sections placed together during the course of the 2nd cent. CE, and reaching its final form early in the 3rd cent. The work forms a bridge between the speculative *Perfection of Wisdom (Prajñāpāramitā) literature and the mind-only philosophy of the Vijñānavāda which was developed in the treatises it inspired.

Fr. tr. from the Tibetan, E. Lamotte (1935).

Saṃdhyā (Skt., 'juncture'). The interval between light and dark (dawn, evening), manifested in Hinduism as a wife of *Śiva and daughter of *Brahmā. It is the moment of daily devotion, often meditation, for every *caste-born Hindu, centred on the *Gāyatrī mantra. It is the term also for the beginning of a *yuga (world-age).

Saṃgha (religious communities in India): see SAṄGHA.

Saṃghabeda (divisions in Buddhism): see SCHISM.

Saṃhitā (Skt., 'joined', 'collected'). The collected arrangements of hymns, chants, etc., constituting the *Vedas, and thus the basis of Hindu scripture. In origin, the term referred to the connected and continuous style of recitation, and was then applied to the collections of the hymns and chants thus recited.

Śaṃkara (Indian religious philosopher): see ŚAṄKARA.

Saṁkarṣana (manifest power of Viṣṇu): see VIṢṆU.

Sāṃkhya. One of the six orthodox schools of interpretation (*darśana) in Hinduism. Its founder is said to have been *Kapila. Sāṃkhya posits a fundamental contrast between *puruṣa and *prakṛti. Puruṣa is the conscious, intelligent self or essence, prakṛti the eternal, unconscious potentiality of all being or appearance. In itself, prakṛti rests in a state of perfect equilibrium, composed of three strands (*guṇas), *sattva (the subtle principle of potential consciousness), *rajas (the principle of activity), and *tamas (the principle of passivity). The unfolding or evolution of prakṛti from its state of equilibrium occurs when puruṣa becomes present to it, creating the duality of subject and object. The union of the two is compared to a lame man with good sight being carried on the shoulders of a blind man with sound legs. The 'blindness' of prakṛti means that it is not conscious of the process of evolution, while nevertheless producing all appearances: their variety is a consequence of the different proportions of the guṇas: e.g. if sattva predominates, mind (*manas) is produced; but this is not the self. The self is puruṣa, still in association with the products of prakṛti, but unmoved, unchanging, imperturbable. By the light of the consciousness of puruṣa, humans are able to become aware of prakṛti. If puruṣa forgets its true nature and regards the body or mind as the true self, then it remains attached to prakṛti. Salvation or release is simply to recognize what is already the case, namely, that the true self (puruṣa) was always independent and free. Freedom is obtained by discriminatory knowledge (sāṃkhya), which is practical as well as theoretical; and that is why yoga became attached to Sāṃkhya, producing the so-called Sāṃkhya-yoga of *Patañjali, although the distinctions make the proposed union an unhappy one. Potentially, and often actually, Sāṃkhya is a non-theistic system. Thus, it argued that every effect or manifestation is inherently present in the preceding cause, since otherwise causes might produce, not stable or predictable effects, but random ones. However, gods are easily incorporated as products of prakṛti; or God as Puruṣa.

Īśvarakṛṣna's *Sāṃkhya-kārika* is the earliest surviving text (*c*.3rd cent. CE), Eng. tr. S. S. Suryanarayana Sastri (1935); G. J. Larson, *Classical Sāṃkhya* . . . (1979).

Sammana (members of male communities in E. religions): see ŚRĀMAṆA.

Sammā-padhāna (Pāli; Skt., *samyak-prahānāni*). The four perfect efforts in Buddhism, designed to eliminate obstacles in the present and future: (i) the effort to avoid obstacles; (ii) the effort to overcome them; (iii) the effort to cultivate the seven contributions to enlightenment (*bojjhanga); (iv) the effort to maintain them. They are the sixth step on the Eightfold Path (*aṣṭangika-marga).

Sammāsambuddha (Pāli), **Samyaksaṃbuddha** (Skt.). Perfectly Enlightened One, Supremely Awakened One; the proper title of *Gotāma the Buddha, marking him out from all other beings, including the other variety of enlightened person, the *paccekabuddha* (*prateyaka-buddha). Gotāma is one of a series of sammāsambuddhas (see FORMER BUDDHAS) who arise in the world at various times but never simultaneously (see SĀSANA). According to traditional Buddhist teaching, their principal distinguishing features are: having the marks of a Universal Monarch (*cakravartin) on the body at birth; having the past history of one who is destined for enlightenment, the *bodhisattva; subsequent to attaining enlightenment, causing the wheel of the doctrine (*dhamma-cakka) to revolve, that is, teaching others the way to enlightenment and founding a community of followers (*saṅgha) who put that teaching into practice; possessing omniscience (*sabbaññutā*).

Sammeta, Mount (Jain centre): see PĀRŚVA.

Sammon (triple gate entrance to Buddhist temples and monasteries): see KYŌTO.

Samnon. Korean for *Mādhyamaka.

Saṁnyāsa (Skt., 'putting or throwing down', 'renunciation'). In Hinduism, the formal and final renunciation of all ties to family, caste, and property. It is a way of life outside the normal duties and rewards of society, dedicated solely to the goal of liberation (*mokṣa). According to the Hindu law books, saṁnyāsa is the fourth and last stage in life (*āśrama) of twice-born Hindus, and may be entered upon when one has seen the birth 'of the eldest son's son'. One must give up the sacred fires, the sacred thread, any permanent abode (and all possessions except loin-cloth, water-pot, and begging bowl), and spend the remaining span of one's life wandering about, subsisting on alms, with the mind fixed on the highest ideal. Later texts state that one may formally renounce the world when moved by a burning spirit of renunciation, no matter what one's formal stage of life.

The full ritual process by which one formally renounces may extend over two or more days. The main elements may be listed as follows: penance, the performance of *śrāddha ceremonies including an offering to one's self, the performance of a sacrifice to *Brahman, fasting and the keeping of an all-night vigil, a ritual bath, the further offering of sacrifices to various deities, the mental rite of placing the sacrificial fires within one's self, the performing of purificatory oblations (*virajā homa*), the casting off of the sacrificial thread and the plucking out of the remaining tuft of hair (the *śikhā), the formal utterance of the *praiṣa mantra* (the sacred declaration of renunciation), and the gift of safety to all creatures. Following these rites it is customary for the newly initiated saṁnyasin to make his first round of begging alms (*bikṣā*).

Besides the normative description of the life of renunciation found in the Dharmaśāstras and their later commentaries, there exists a whole class of minor *Upaniṣads, the Saṁnyāsa Upaniṣads, which extol the ideals of renunciation. There is also a body of literature, dating from the medieval period and as yet largely untranslated, of independent treatises devoted to the subject of saṁnyāsa. Vasudevāśrama's *Yatidharmaprakāśa* has been translated (A Treatise on World Renunciation) by P. Olivelle (1977).

The status of saṁnyāsi was open to all *castes, and although women were not encouraged to enter this āśrama, some did so. To his family, the saṁnyāsi was as dead, and every year at the śrāddha ceremonies, *piṇḍa would be offered in commemoration of him. On death he would be buried; no sons could be present to perform the required cremation rituals, as no one would know the saṁnyāsi's family origins; in any case, even when alive, his earthly form would be regarded as merely a dry, empty shell from which the life-giving energy, the soul, had already departed to the Infinite. His goal is the highest *dharma, knowledge of, and unity with, the divine. Saṁnyāsins are often associated with the doctrines and practices relating to *Śiva, and many saṁnyasins are members of the *Daśanāmī order. See also ASCETICISM.

P. Olivelle, *Saṁnyāsa Upaniṣads: Hindu Scriptures on Renunciation* (1992); J. F. Sprockhoff, *Saṁnyāsa: Quellenstudien* . . . (1976).

Sampai (Jap., 'three' + 'prostration'). Threefold prostration in Zen Buddhism, probably in honour of the Three Jewels (*sambō).

Saṁpradāya (Skt., from *saṁ-pra da*, 'to give completely up', 'to hand down by tradition'). In Indian religions, any established doctrine and set of practices transmitted from one teacher to another. From this it has come to mean any sectarian religious teaching or a religious sect. In the **Mahābhārata* (*Anuśāsanaparvan* 141), the four (supposedly) original saṁpradāyas are listed more as styles of increasing *asceticism through which *tapas is generated: *kuṭicakas*, who remained near and supported by their families; *bahūdakas*, who lived near settlements and received support only from *brahman families; *haṁsas* (swans), wandering from place to place; *paramahaṁsas*, wandering and with no support or clothes. For Jains, see MULA SANGHA.

Samprajñāta (Skt., 'differentiated') or **sabīja** (Skt., 'with seed'). A stage of *samādhi in *rāja *yoga following from *dhyāna and preliminary to *asamprajñāta samādhi. It is a state of suppressed or controlled consciousness made up of four stages: (i) *savitarka*, the state in which consciousness (*citta) is accompanied by thought (*savitarka*) and is identified with the gross (*sthūla*) aspect of an object of concentration; (ii) *nirvitarka*, a state in which consciousness is identified with the gross aspect of an object without thought (*nirvitarka*), in which memory and logical associations cease to function; (iii) *savicāra*, the identification of consciousness with the subtle (*sūkṣma) aspect of an object accompanied by reflective thought (*savicāra*); and (iv) *nirvicāra*, the non-reflective identification of consciousness with the subtle aspects of an object of concentration.

Saṃsāra (Skt., Pāli, Prkt., 'wandering'). Transmigration or rebirth; in Asian religions, the cycle of birth and death as a consequence of action (*karma). Liberation (*mokṣa, *nirvāna, *kaivalya) is release from samsāra, conceived as either going beyond samsāra or realizing it to be an illusion (*māyā). The idea of samsāra, like karma, is possibly of non-Vedic or heterodox origin, though the matter is contentious.

The word *samsāra* does not appear in the *Vedas, but the idea of redeath (*punarmṛtyu) does, and the *śrāddha and *sapindakarana* rites may have been to prevent the dissolution of the deceased in the next world, which is contrary to later Hindu views of the need to prevent rebirth. In the *Upaniṣads the soul (*ātman) takes one of two paths after death, either the way of the fathers (*pitṛ-yāna), the southern path which leads back to earth, or the way of the gods (*deva-yāna), the northern path which leads to liberation. Taking the southern path, the soul passes into the smoke of the funeral pyre, from there into the night, then into the waxing half of the moon, then, in the six months when the sun is moving south, to the world of the fathers (pitṛ-*loka); from there it goes to space (*ākāśa) and then to the moon. After remaining there for as long as its merit allows, the soul returns again into space, wind, smoke, mist, cloud, rain, and then into a plant. When eaten by a man, the soul goes into his semen and thence into a womb and the cycle begins again. Those who follow the northern path go into the flames of the pyre, then into light, day, the waxing half of the moon, then to the six months when the sun is going north, the year, the sun, the moon, and then into lightning. From there the soul is led by a non-human being (*amānava*) to *Brahmā (*Chandogya Upaniṣad* 5. 10. 1–10).

This basic pattern of release or continued transmigration is found in later Hinduism, transmigration being regarded as undesirable. Indian theism such as *Śaiva Siddhānta, regards samsāra as a means for the dispensation of grace (*anugraha*), the ultimate reason for samsāra being the liberation of souls: thus *Śiva both conceals himself (*tirobhāva*) and reveals himself (*anugraha*).

In Buddhism, samsāra is the cycle of continuing appearances through the domains of existence (*gati), but with no Self (*anātman) being reborn: there is only the continuity of consequence, governed by karma.

Among Jains, the whole universe depends on the conscious and unconscious (*jīva, ajīva) elements. Saṁsāra is the process through which souls are able to be disentangled from the material.

W. D. O'Flaherty (ed.), *Karma and Rebirth in Classical Indian Traditions* (1980); P. Yevtić, *Karma and Reincarnation in Hindu Religion and Philosophy* (1927).

Samsin. Korean for *trikāya.

Saṃskāra (Skt., *saṃ*, 'together', + *kr*, 'make'). 1. The saṃskāras are the rituals through which high-*caste or twice-born Hindus mark their transitions through life (and death), and may thus be regarded as *rites of passage. In Pandey's summary, the saṃskāras are 'for sanctifying the body, mind and intellect of an individual, so that he may become a full-fledged member of the community'. The saṃskāras differ in number, depending on how many of the lesser moments which are marked by ritual (e.g. a child's first outing) are included. However, a fairly standard list of sixteen rites includes (i) *Garbhādhāna*, the securing of conception; (ii) *Puṃsavāna*, the securing of the birth of a male child; (iii) *Sīmantonnayana*, parting the hair of the pregnant woman to secure her from evil spirits (this again has reference to the birth of a male child; in W. India it is known as *Dohada*, and men cannot be present); (iv) *Jātakarma*, the securing and celebration of safe delivery; (v) *Nāmakaraṇa*, the giving of the name to the child on the twelfth day after birth; (vi) *Niṣkramana*, the making auspicious, by seeing the sun and going to a temple, of the child's first outing; (vii) *Annaprāśana*, the first feeding with solid food; (viii) *Caudakaraṇa*, shaving of the head during the first or third year; (ix) *Karṇavedha*, the piercing of the ear or nose between 3 and 5; (x) *Vidyārambha*, the learning of the alphabet; (xi) *Upanayana, the sacred thread; (xii) on the day following, for those deemed competent, *Vedārambha*, the beginning of the study of the *Vedas; (xiii) *Keśānta*, the first shaving of the beard; (xiv) *Samāvartana*, the end of student life; (xv) *Vivāha*, *marriage; (xvi) *Antyeṣṭi, funeral rites.

V. Kane, *History of Dharmaśāstra*, ii (1978); V. P. Kanitkar, *Hindu Festivals and Sacraments* (1984); R. Pandey, *Hindu Samskaras* (1969).

2. In Hinduism the formations in consciousness which accumulate from thoughts and actions in earlier lives, and which constitute individual character. In Buddhism, see SANKHARA.

Samson (Heb. Shimshon). An Israelite *Judge. The story of Samson is to be found in Judges 13–16. He was a *Nazirite from birth and possessed of superhuman strength. As an adult, he fulfilled his destiny of beginning 'to save *Israel from the hand of the *Philistines'. Eventually he was deprived of his strength by the Philistine Delilah who cut his hair while he was asleep. He was blinded by his enemies, but, when his hair had grown back, he pulled down the temple of Dagon, 'so the dead he slew at his death were more than those whom he had slain during his life' (Judges 16. 30).

Samu (Jap., 'work-service'). The Zen practice of physical work, at set times, in monasteries. It is understood as work in service of the Three Jewels (*sambō), and was stressed by *Pai-chang.

Samudramathana (Hindu myth): see CHURNING OF THE OCEAN.

Samuel (*c*.11th cent. BCE). Israelite *prophet and *judge. Samuel's activities are to be found in 1 Samuel 1–16. His mother dedicated him to God from his birth, and he grew up in the shrine at Shiloh. He is depicted as a judge of Israel (1 Samuel 7), and he was instrumental in the founding of the monarchy. Despite a certain ambiguity towards the institution (cf. 8. 7 and 10. 6), Samuel anointed the first king, *Saul (ch. 11). Later, Samuel broke with Saul (ch. 15) and anointed *David. According to the *aggadic tradition, Samuel was the author of the books of *Judges and *Ruth (*BBB* 15a), and the father of the prophet *Joel (*Mid.Sam.* 1. 6). His (traditional) tomb on Mount al-Nabi Samwīl, overlooking *Jerusalem, was a place of *pilgrimage in the Middle Ages.

Samuel, Book of. The eighth book of the Hebrew scriptures. Originally a single work, it was subdivided in the *Septuagint and *Vulgate (which has four Books of Kings). 1 Samuel 1–7 describe the activities of the last *Judge, *Samuel; chs. 8–15 are concerned with the relationship between Samuel and the first king of *Israel, *Saul; chs. 16–31 deal with the growing rivalry between King Saul and the young *David. 2 Samuel 1–8 describe David's rise to power; chs. 9–20 cover the history of David's court and chs. 21–4 are an appendix. Thus the book describes how *kingship became the established form of government in Israel. It contains units of narrative, poetry (three poems are regarded as ancient, 1 Samuel 2. 1–10; 2 Samuel 1. 19–27; 22), oracles (e.g. 1 Samuel 2. 27–36), and lists (e.g. 2 Samuel 3. 2–5). The 'Court History' of David is of high historical and literary value, the anonymous author of which is sometimes regarded as 'the father of history', as opposed to Herodotus. The book's final form was produced by the *Deuteronomist in the 6th cent. BCE, but it contains both pro- and anti-monarchical material.

Samuel ben Hophni (d. 1013). Jewish *gaon of *Sura. Samuel was descended from generations of scholars. He was a prolific writer, although most of his works are now lost. Among his writings mentioned by later authorities were an introduction to the *Talmud, a book of precepts, and an Arabic translation and commentary on the *Pentateuch. From *Kimḥi's quotations from him, he seems to have been an early rationalist: 'The account of the witch of Endor cannot be accepted as a literal account, rabbinic opinion notwithstanding, since it is contrary to reason.' In his view, 'God worked miracles, but only for the *prophets.'

Samuel ben Meir (Rashbam, *c*.1080–*c*.1174). Jewish biblical and *Talmudic commentator. A grandson and student of *Rashi, Samuel lived in France. He produced a commentary on the Bible which is notable for its preference for the literal meaning of the text (*peshāt), even when this opposes *halakhah. He also supplemented Rashi's commentary on the Talmud and wrote *tosafot on various tractates. He was a noted composer of *piyyutim and wrote a grammatical work, *Sefer Daikut*.

Samuel ha-Nagid (Isma'īl ibn Nagrel'a, 993–1055). Jewish vizier (*wazīr) of Granada. Samuel had a distinguished career as a public servant to King Habbus and King Badis of Granada which included commanding the army. His victory against the army of Almeria was the origin of a special *Purim among the Granadan Jews. He was a poet as well as a soldier, and three collections survive: *Ben Tehillim*, *Ben Mishlei*, and *Ben Kohelet*. His works display a kind of practical shrewdness—e.g. 'A humble man keeps his feet on the ground, but his thoughts can search the sky'; 'Better to eat wayside weeds in safety than meat in danger'; 'A wise man, before he climbs down into a hole, fixes a ladder to climb out'; 'Prepare your proof before you argue'. He also concerned himself with Jewish communal affairs and was a noted *halakhist. Although he acknowledged his supremacy of the *gaonate in legal matters, he is described by Abraham *ibn David as 'the first of the generation of the *rabbinate'.

D. Jarden, *Divan Shemu'el ha-Nagid* (1966).

Samurai (Jap., derived from *saburau*, 'to serve'). Warriors. Originally the word was applied only to noble warriors with good family lineage, but this became the common designation for warriors in the Tokugawa period. The appearance of warriors as a distinct class coincided with the development of the *shōen* system dealing with private proprietary land management. The inability of the central government to control the various provinces and districts allowed them to develop their own defence force, from which the warrior class evolved. The revolt of Taira no Masakado in 935 was a sign foretelling the dawn of a new era, and the founding of the Kamakura shogunate in 1192 firmly established the military rule which dominated subsequent Japanese history until the Meiji Restoration of 1868.

The *shōen* system fostered the paternalistic bond between the lord and his retainers. The medieval tales of warriors, though highly idealized, glorified heroism, courage, honour, and loyalty to one's lord, which became the core of *bushidō, the ethical code of the samurai class. Early bushidō was less articulated than the Confucianized version of the Tokugawa period. Instructions written for the families (*kakun*) in the 15th cent. emphasized the importance of religious faith. Religion helped warriors resolve the question of life and death; see further MARTIAL ARTS; and for further reading, BUSHIDŌ.

Samyak-prahānāni (four perfect efforts in Buddhism): see SAMMĀ-PADHĀNA.

Samyaksaṃbuddha (perfectly enlightened one): see SAMMĀSAMBUDDHA.

Saṃyama (Skt., 'restraint'). Inner discipline, the three final stages in Hindu *rāja yoga, as analysed by *Patañjali: *dhāraṇā, *dhyāna, *samādhi. See *Yoga-Sūtra*, ch. 3. Among Jains, it is the key practice in the ascetic way, along with the generation (in counter-balance) of *tapas.

Samyé (*bsam.yas*). The first monastery in Tibet and scene of the great debate in which *Kamalaśīla defeated the Chinese emissary Mahāyāna, thus ensuring that Indian rather than Chinese Buddhism would be the model for the development of religion in Tibet. The Samyé monastery was commissioned by King Trisong Detsen (790–858) and its building begun by *Śāntarakṣita, formerly abbot of Nālandā, and completed with the assistance of *Padmasambhava. The building itself, said to have taken seven years before Padmasambhava's arrival and five years after, was architecturally important for having set the pattern for all future monasteries in Tibet. Modelled after Odantapurī in Bihar (itself destroyed by Muslims in 1193), it contained one large and twelve small temples, four large and 108 smaller *chörtens, all surrounded by a high wall, thus representing in *maṇḍala form the ideographic Buddhist universe. The central temple, representing our own continent (i.e. occupied by humans) of Jambudvīpa, used the architectural styles of India, China, and Tibet in its three storeys. To the monastery was attributed (through its design) the power of having consecrated Tibet as a 'new world' of Buddhism, following the old world of *Bön and *animism. On its completion, Trisong Detsen requested Śāntarakṣita to train seven monks only as a trial; it was a success, many more enrolled, and a school for the study of Sanskrit was opened. In one small temple alone 100 great Indian and Tibetan scholars worked on the translation of *sūtras and *tantras. When *Atiśa visited Tibet in 1042 he announced that he had never seen so complete a system of translation. Samyé was for most of its life a *Nyingma monastery, but later passed into *Sakya control. During the cultural revolution it was completely destroyed by the Chinese. The name Samyé continues in Samyé Ling (see TRUNGPA, RINPOCHE), the first Tibetan centre in Scotland, founded in 1975.

Samyé-Ling Centre (Tibetan Buddhist centre in Scotland): see TRUNGPA, RINPOCHE.

Saṃyojanas (Pāli, *sam-yuj*, 'to bind to'). In Buddhism, bonds or fetters that tie a being to the Wheel of Becoming. Traditionally there are ten: belief in self (*sakkāya-diṭṭhi), doubt (*vicikicchā*), attachment to works and ceremonial observances (*sīlabbata-parāmāsa), attachment to sense-desire (*kāma-rāga*), anger (*vyāpāda*), attachment to the world of form (*rūpa-rāga*), attachment to the formless world (*arūpa-rāga*), pride (*māna), excitability (*uddhacca*), and ignorance (*avijjā). The first five are named the 'lower fetters' (*orambhāgiya-samyojana*) as they bind a person to rebirth in the world of desire (*kama-loka*), the last five are named the 'higher fetters' (*uddhambhāgiya-samyojana*) because they tie a person that has escaped the world (*loka) of desire to the upper regions of the Wheel of Becoming. Therefore a being must escape all the fetters to achieve *nirvāna.

Saṃyuktāgama (Indian division of Sūtrapiṭaka): see TRIPIṬAKA.

Saṃyutta Nikāya. The 'unified collection', the third collection (*nikāya) of the *Sūtra/Sutta-pitaka, containing more than 7,000 discourses: the name Saṃyutta derives from an attempt to 'yoke' together suttas dealing with similar topics.

Eng. tr., C. A. F. *Rhys Davids and F. L. Woodward, *The Book of Kindred Sayings* (1917–30); Germ. tr., W. Geiger (1925, 1930).

Sanātana dharma (Skt., *sanātana*, 'eternal', + *dharma*, 'law'). In Hinduism, the absolute and eternal law (*dharma) as opposed to relative duty (*svadharma). Sanātana dharma applies to everyone, including *outcastes. According to *Yājñavalkvasmṛti*, absolute dharma includes purity, good will, mercy, and patience. Later texts such as *Vāmana* **Purāṇa* list the ten limbs of the eternal dharma as non-injury, truth, purity, not stealing, charity, forbearance, self-restraint, tranquillity, generosity, and asceticism. Sanātana dharma frequently conflicts with svadharma, and attempts to resolve these conflicts are found in the Purāṇas and **Bhagavad-Gītā*.

In modern Indian usage, sanātana dharma is often equated with 'Hinduism' as a name, stressing the eternal foundation of it.

B. K. Tirtha, *Sanātana Dharma* (1964).

Sāñchī. A Buddhist religious centre in Central India, consisting of a number of *stūpas, *vihāras, and temples. It is also known as Caityagiri. The most important building in terms of size and artistic merit is the Great Stūpa, the core of which dates from the time of *Aśoka. It was however greatly enlarged in the Early Āndhra period (72–25 BCE), with additional alterations until about 10 BCE. The four stone gateways (*toraṇa*) in particular are richly carved with scenes from the life of the *Buddha, animals, vegetation, and female deities (*yakṣīs), and are regarded as masterpieces of Buddhist sculpture. The oldest building in the complex is stūpa 2, thought to date from the Śunga period (185–72 BCE). Excavation of stūpa 3 has revealed two caskets possibly containing relics of Śāriputra and Maudgalyayāna, who were contemporaries and followers of the Buddha. The remains of an unusual free-standing *caitya hall dating from Gupta times (320–630 CE) has recently been found at Sāñchī.

Buddhist chronicles hold that Mahendra, the son of Aśoka, began his journey to convert Śri Lankā to Buddhism from Sāñchī which was, at that time, a stronghold of the *Theravādins.

J. Marshall *et al.*, *The Monuments of Sañchi* (1940).

San-chiao (Chin., 'three ways'). The three major religions/philosophies of China: Confucian, Taoist, and Buddhist. There is no obligation to choose, or live by, only one of these ways: they can be lived and practised in combination, according to the particular moments and needs of life.

San-chieh-chiao ('School of Three Stages'). School of Chinese Buddhism during the Sui and T'ang periods, founded by Hsin-hsing (540–94). It portrayed the process of Buddhism as one of degeneration through three stages: (i) the period of true *dharma, which lasted for 500 years after the *Buddha Śākyamuni's translation from earth, during which the teaching was observed; (ii) 1,000 years of corrupted dharma, with many innovations; (iii) 10,000 years, most yet to come (beginning 550 CE), of increasing disintegration. Against this, Hsin-hsing set a rule of radical observance of *śīla, *dāna, and asceticism, eschewing monasteries, although willing to support them.

San-ch'ing (Chin., 'the three pure ones'). The three Taoist heavens (*t'ien) and those who inhabit them.

1. Yü-ching, the heaven of pure jade, inhabited by Yüan-shih t'ien-tsun, one of the highest deities of religious Taoism (*tao-chiao*). He created heaven and earth, and at the start of each new age, he gives **Ling-pao ching* to subordinates who instruct humans from it in the way of Tao. He is without beginning, and entrusts the administration of heaven to *Yü-huang, who was later regarded as more important.

2. Shang-ch'ing, the heaven of purity, ruled by Ling-pao t'ien-tsun. He is the guardian of *Ling-pao ching*, and regulates time and the balance of *yin and yang.

3. T'ai-ch'ing, the heaven of highest purity, ruled by Tao-te T'ien-tsun, the guardian of *tao and *te. He is identified with *Lao-tzu.

For the offerings made to them, see CHIAO.

Sañci (Buddhist centre in Central India): see SĀÑCHĪ.

Sancita-karma (transmitted characteristics): see SAṂCITA-KARMA.

Sancta Sophia (church, later mosque): see HAGIA SOFIA.

Sanctification: see HOLINESS.

Sanctuary (Lat., *sanctuarium*). A holy place, especially in Christianity the part of a church containing the altar (or high altar). It was preserved for the clergy and their attendants, in a degree of greater holiness (hence the Roman Catholic refusal to allow girl or women servers until 1992, perpetuating the view which regards them as potentially contaminating). From this derives the right (or benefit) of sanctuary: this was recognized in Roman law, limited by Justinian in 535 to more serious crimes. *Canon law allowed sanctuary for a limited period so that compensation might be agreed (sacrilege and treason were excepted), but in England, one who had taken sanctuary was obliged either to submit to trial or to leave the country. In 1540, Henry VIII limited refuge to Derby, Launceston, Manchester (transferred to Chester), Northampton, Wells, Westminster, and York. Criminal sanctuary was abolished in 1623, though it persisted for another century in civil cases.

The term 'sanctuary' is then applied to the sacred parts of buildings in other religions, especially in Judaism (Heb., *bet ha-miqdash*) for the most holy part of a Jewish place of worship. The term is applied to the ancient shrines at Shiloh, *Bethel, and elsewhere that contained the *Ark. In the Jerusalem *Temple, the sanctuary was the *Holy of Holies. In a modern *synagogue, the area around the Ark is described as the Sanctuary. The term is also applied to the place of refuge for accidental killers. See CITY OF REFUGE.

J. C. Cox, *Sanctuaries and Sanctuary Seekers of Medieval England* (1911); H. W. Turner, *From Temple to Meeting House* (1979).

Sanctus (Lat., 'holy'). A hymn of adoration based on Isaiah 6. 3 and used in Christian liturgies near the beginning of the *eucharistic prayer. In modern Anglican and Roman Catholic rites it is:

> Holy, holy, holy Lord, God of power and might,
> heaven and earth are full of your glory.
> Hosanna in the highest.
> Blessed is he who comes in the name of the Lord.
> Hosanna in the highest.

The last two lines, based on Matthew 21. 9, are separately called the 'Benedictus [qui Venit]'.

Sandak. The one who holds the baby on his knee at a Jewish *circumcision ceremony. It is considered a great honour to be the sandak at the rite and it is customarily bestowed on the grandfather of the child.

Sandhya (time of Hindu daily devotion): see SAṂDHYĀ.

Sangai. Jap., for *triloka* (*loka), the realm of desire (Skt., *kāmadhatu*, Jap., *yokkai*), of form (*rūpadhātu*, *shikkai*), of non-form (*ārūpyadhātu*, *mushikikai*).

Sangai(-yui)-isshin (Jap., 'three worlds, (only) one mind'). Zen belief that the three worlds of desire, form, and no-form arise from unenlightened awareness (*kokoro, heart–mind), and have no objective reality: all is projection.

Sangat, Satsang, or **Sadhsaṅgat.** A Sikh group or association, often the local congregation of a *gurdwārā. The whole Sikh community is known as Sikh Panth. The strong stress on the communal nature of Sikhism means that an individual *ascetic Sikh who leaves the sangat to pursue the goal of God on his own is virtually unheard of: Gurū *Gobind Siṅgh called the *khālsā 'his other self'.

Sangen (three mysteries in Lin-chi Zen Buddhism): see LIN-CHI.

Saṅgha or **saṃgha** (Skt./Pāli, 'gathering, community'). Religious communities in India, e.g. the Jains, but most often used of Buddhists. In general, it means 'those who follow the teachings of the *Buddha', i.e. the four groups of Buddhists (Skt., *pariṣad*; Pāli, *parisā*), monks and nuns (*bhikṣus, bhikṣunīs), laymen and laywomen (*upāsaka, upāsikā); but again, the reference is usually more precise, to the community of monks and nuns alone, or to those of advanced spiritual attainment as distinguished from beginners (Skt., *aryasaṃgha* or *savaka-saṃgha*, 'holy community'), or to the entire Buddhist community at a particular place. To take refuge in the saṅgha is one of the *Three Jewels (*trīratna*) of Buddhism.

In so far as saṅgha refers to monastic Buddhism as opposed to lay Buddhism, the dynamic interplay between the two is fundamental to Buddhist societies. The Buddha required Buddhism to be *missionary, 'for the benefit of many, for the support of many'. The saṅgha therefore developed with two emphases, one being the pursuit of enlightenment through contemplation (*vipassanā *dhura*), the other being 'the bearing of books' (*gantha dhura*), undertaking work on behalf of society at large, in teaching, performing rituals, reading apotropaic texts, etc., and also through involvement in politics. Conversely, laypeople support the saṅgha and earn *merit thereby, either for themselves or on behalf of others. The rules governing the life and organization of the saṅgha (in the restricted sense) are found in *Vinayapiṭaka. The saṅgha is basically mendicant, and it has no hierarchical organization (apart from a senior monk, Skt., *sthavira*; Pāli, *thera). The development of *Mahāyāna did not diminish the importance of the saṅgha, even though routes to enlightenment/salvation were opened up outside the saṅgha. The vinaya traditions persisted, and only in Japan did the organization of schools diminish the importance of the monastic saṅgha. In 1966, the World Buddhist Saṅgha Council was established.

M. Wijayaratna, *Buddhist Monastic Life* (1991).

Saṅghapati (organizer of pilgrimage): see PILGRIMAGE (Jain).

Sangjwabu. Korean for *Theravāda.

Saṅgrānd or **sankranti** (Pañjābī, 'first day of Hindu month'). The saṅgrānd is the day when the sun enters a new zodiac sign. Every saṅgrānd is marked in *gurdwārās with a service including Gurū *Arjan Dev's hymn, Bārah-Māhā (Twelve Months), symbolizing the human spiritual journey. See also ASTROLOGY; BAISĀKHĪ; CALENDAR; FESTIVALS AND FASTS; GURPURB; SABBATH.

Sanhedrin (Heb. loan from Gk., *sunhedrion*). When or if it existed, the supreme political, religious and judicial body in *Erez Israel during the Roman period. *Josephus portrays the Sanhedrin as a political council, an assembly of the leading people of Jerusalem (*Life*, 28). The *tannaitic sources, however, describe it as a permanent assembly of *sages who met daily between the first and second *sacrifice. It was the place 'where the Law went forth to all *Israel' (*B.Sanh.* 11. 2). It is frequently referred to as the 'court of seventy-one' and, according to the tannaim, was composed of *Pharisaic scholars and presided over by the *nasi or av *bet din. Other sources indicate that the *high priest was the president; and rabbinic sources would certainly minimize or eliminate the presence of *Sadducees. There is much scholarly discussion therefore as to the composition and function of the Sanhedrin, especially whether there were two 'sanhedrins', or councils, from which the impression of a single Sanhedrin was formed—in other words, the assimilation of councils into Sanhedrin would mean that *the* Sanhedrin as such never existed in the period of the second *Temple. After the destruction of the Temple, the Sanhedrin met first at Jabneh and subsequently in Galilee. The Romans seem to have withdrawn their recognition of the institution *c.*425 CE. See also BET DIN.

S. B. Hoenig, *The Great Sanhedrin* (1953); H. Mantel, *Studies in the History of the Sanhedrin* (1961).

San-hsing (Chin., 'three stars'). Three Chinese figures (variously identified in each case) who became gods because of their virtues: (i) Fu-hsing, Lucky Star, portrayed usually with a child, or as a bat; (ii) Lü-hsing, Highly Honoured Star, often portrayed as a stag; (iii) Shou-hsing, Star of Long Life, usually holding the staff or support of life in one hand, and the peach of immortality in the other. All are important in folk religion.

San-i (Chin., 'the three ones'). Threefold action of the one *Tao, derived from **Lao-tzu* 42: 'Tao gave birth to one, one gave birth to two, two gave birth to three, three gave birth to all the myriad things.' The creative three may be personified as the guardians of the inner fields of human life and energy; or they may be the Supreme One (*T'ai-i), the Earthly One (Ti-i), and the Heavenly One (T'ien-i); or they may be mind (*shen), vitality (*ch'i), essence (*ching). There is some correspondence to the Hindu and Christian recognition that manifestation requires a relational nature in the unproduced Producer: see TRINITY.

Sañjaya Belaṭṭhiputta (Pāli). The leader of a sect of sceptics (*Amarāvikkhepikas), and one of the six heretical teachers whose doctrines are described in the *Sāmañña-phala Sutta* (see SAMAṆAS). As a way of indicating his total scepticism, he is said to have used the method of denying truth-claims in any logical form they could be presented. There is a canonical tradition which says that among the Buddha's earliest converts were all or most of the followers of Sañjaya, including *Sāriputta and *Moggallāna. In Skt. texts he is known as Sañjayī-Vairaṭiputra or Sañjayī-Vairaṭṭīputra.

Sankan ('three barriers' of Zen Rinzai teaching): see HUANG-LUNG HUI-NAN.

Śaṅkara or **Śaṅkarācārya** (trad., 788–820, but perhaps earlier). The pre-eminent philosopher and proponent of *Advaita Vedānta, and one of the most influential thinkers in the entire history of Indian religion. Apart from the traditional biographies written long after his time and embellished with legends of miraculous deeds, there is little known of his life. Even the dates are guesswork. Western scholars have generally accepted the above dates, but there is considerable evidence suggesting that he lived at least a century earlier.

Although the traditional biographies disagree in

many details, the main outlines of the saintly life portrayed in them are clear. He was born of a *brahman family in S. India, probably at Kālaḍi in the modern state of Kerala. His father died while Śaṅkara was a child, and while still a boy, Śaṅkara left his mother in the care of some relatives, and set out on the life of a wandering mendicant. At a cave on the banks of the Narmadā River he met the sage *Govindapāda, the disciple of *Gauḍapāda, and remained there long enough to become his pupil, to study *Vedānta philosophy with him, and receive from him formal initiation into the life of a renunciant (*saṁnyāsa).

Leaving Govindapāda, Śaṅkara walked to Vārāṇasī (Benares) where he began to write, teach, and attract disciples of his own. From Vārāṇasī he journeyed north to Badarīnātha near the source of the Ganges in the foothills of the Himālayas. There, he composed his famous commentary on the **Brahmasūtra*. The last years of his short life were spent wandering the length and breadth of India proclaiming the philosophy of Advaita Vedānta and taking on all rivals in debate. This period is called the 'Tour of Victory' (*digvijaya*), during which Śaṅkara defeated Maṇḍana Miśra and many other worthy proponents of rival schools of religious philosophy, including Buddhists, Jains, and various sectarian *Śaivas.

During his wanderings Śaṅkara is credited with the establishment and renovation of many temples and the founding of monastic centres situated near the borders of the subcontinent in the four cardinal directions. The abbots in charge of these monastic 'seats' (*pīṭhas*) bear the title of 'Śaṅkarācārya' and today still enjoy positions of great veneration and authority among traditionally observant Hindus. In addition, Śaṅkara, or his immediate disciples, founded the Order of *Daśanāmī Saṁnyāsins, a loose federation of monks who have been widespread, highly visible, and influential advocates of Advaita philosophy.

Near the end of his life Śaṅkara is said to have visited Kashmir and there at the Śāradā temple to have ascended the throne of all-knowledge. One of the most widely accepted accounts of the end of his life is that at the age of 32 he left Kedārnāth in the Himālayas travelling northward toward Mount Kailāsa, the abode of *Śiva, and was seen no more.

For a description of his religious teaching see ADVAITA VEDĀNTA; ṢATKASAMPATTI.

W. Cenkner, *A Tradition of Teachers: Śaṅkara and the Jadagurus Today* (1983); K. H. Potter, *Advaita Vedānta up to Śaṅkara and his Pupils* (1981).

Śaṅkarācārya (teachers in the tradition of Śaṅkara): see DAŚANĀMĪ.

Śaṅkaradeva (*c*.1449–1569). Hindu religious leader who was primarily responsible for the spread of the *Vaiṣṇava movement in Assam. The details of his early life are uncertain. He may have been a *Śūdra, who received a classical education, and who set out on the pilgrimage tour of India in 1541. Certainly he seems to have come in contact with several Vaiṣṇava leaders, and to have developed an eclectic system of devotion (*bhakti) from them. He emphasized the recitation of the name *Hari, and set up a formal structure for the spread of devotion to God. The *sattras* were monasteries in which attention was paid to the ancilliaries of *music, *dance, and drama (*theatre); the *nāmagharas* were set up in villages to co-ordinate religious life, but eventually became centres of social and economic life as well. Śaṅkaradeva composed many songs, narrative poems, and dramas to encourage participation in bhakti, and to bring the presence of God immediately before the participants:

> Save me, O *Rāma, Hari without fault or form: you are the source and cause of all that is, the moving and the motionless, as an earring is inseparable from the gold of which it is made. You are the animals and the birds, the gods and the demons, the trees and the plants. Only the ignorant suppose that you are other and remote.

B. K. Barua, *Sankaradeva* . . . (1960).

Sankey, Ira D. (1840–1908). Singer and composer of gospel *hymns. He joined Dwight L. *Moody in 1870 and became his regular organist, singer, and musical director. His voice was not exceptional but his solo renditions of gospel songs had a powerful appeal. He composed a number of tunes, most to be found in his compilation *Sacred Songs and Solos* (many edns. since 1873), which remains probably the best-known collection of revivalist hymns.

Sankhara (Pāli; cf. Skt., *saṃskāra). In Buddhism, the fourth of the *skandhas/khandhas, the aggregations which constitute human appearance. Sankharas are the constructing initiatives and activities, which set life forward and give individual character to a life.

Sankhya (philosophical school in Hinduism): see SĀṂKHYA.

Sanki (Jap., 'the three refuges'): see THREE JEWELS.

Sanku (three statements, of Zen Buddhist Lin-chi line): see LIN-CHI.

San-kuan (Chin., three rulers). Three Taoist deities, rulers of heaven, earth, and water. They are prominent in folk religion, bestowing fortune and forgiveness, but also keeping a record of faults that need such forgiveness.

San-lun. School of the Three Treatises, established in China by *Kumārajīva (344–413 CE), the Kuchean monk who translated the three treatises—Treatise on the Middle, Treatise on the Twelve Gates, Treatise in One Hundred Verses—into Chinese. The school was instrumental in introducing the teachings of the Indian philosopher *Nāgārjuna (2nd cent. CE) concerning the concept of emptiness (*śūnyatā) to the Chinese. Chinese *Mādhyamaka was thus able to resolve the traditional tensions between *wu (non-being) and *yu* (being), *ching (potential), and *tung* (action). A major exponent of San-lun was *Chi-tsang.

H. Robinson, *Early Madhyamika in India and China* (1967).

Sanmai (state of attainment through meditation in E. religions): see SAMĀDHI (Zen); ZANMAI.

Sanmotsu (Jap., 'three things'). The Zen ceremony of recognition of a *rōshi who has also attained the rank of *shōshi. On three strips of paper, the names of the lineage from the *Buddha Śākyamuni are written and conferred on the master, usually in his own *zendō.

Sanne (Jap., 'three robes'). The three robes used by a Japanese Buddhist monk: (i) *sōgyari*, made of nine to twenty-five pieces of cloth, worn for appearance in public, e.g. for begging; (ii) *uttarasō*, made of seven pieces and worn at ceremonies, lectures, etc.; (iii) *andae*, for ordinary use. See HABIT, RELIGIOUS.

Sannyāsa (renunciation of all ties with family etc. in Hinduism): see SAṀNYĀSA.

San-pao (Chin., 'three treasures'). Taoist virtues derived from **Tao-te ching* 67: 'Here are my three treasures, guard and cherish them: the first is mercy/love; the second is no excess/frugality; the third is, never be ahead of the pack/modesty.' The three then nurture and reinforce each other.

Sanron-shū. 'Three treatises' (Jap.) of *San-lun, brought to Japan by the Korean monk Ekwan in 625. From his followers derived Jōjitsu. Sanron was not an independently organized school, but its teachings, mediating *Mādhyamaka and *Nāgārjuna, were much studied. They were influential on Shōtoku (574–622) who unified Japan, in conjunction with *Confucianism. See NARA BUDDHISM.

San-Shen. Chin. for *trikāya.

San-sheng Hui-jan (Jap. Sanshō Enen), *c.*9th cent. CE, dharma-successor (*hassu) of *Lin-chi I-hsuan, to whom the compilation of **Rinzairoku* (*Lin-chi-lu*) is ascribed; but this is uncertain. To him, Lin-chi's last words were spoken, 'This blind donkey!'.

Sanshin. Jap. for *trikāya.

Sant: see SANT TRADITION.

Śāntarakṣita (Skt.; Tib., Zhi.ba.tsho; *c.*705–88 CE). Indian philosopher and chief exponent of the *Vijñavāda-*Mādhyamaka synthesis, who played a significant role in the 'first diffusion' (*snga.dar*) of Buddhism in Tibet (see TIBETAN RELIGION). A central feature of Śāntarakṣita's system is his doctrine that the mind's capability of self-awareness (Skt., *svasaṃvedana*) is the primary differentiation to be made between the mind and the objects of its awareness, which are said to be 'inert' (*jaḍa*). Having adopted the idealism of *Dharmakīrti, by which external objects are seen as being of the same nature or 'stuff' as mind (because the mind cannot 'know' something which is of a different order from itself), Śāntarakṣita believed that the apprehension of external phenomena is an act of self-perception by the mind, and that our perception of 'subject' and 'object' is an erroneous bifurcation produced by original ignorance. Having thus used Vijñanavādin idealism to ascribe to the mind a conventional self-existence, Śāntarakṣita then invoked Mādhyamaka *śūnya-vāda to describe the mind as being non-self-existent ultimately; he believed that the doctrine of 'mind only' (*cittamatra*, see VIJÑĀNAVĀDA) was helpful in leading students towards the insubstantiality of phenomena, at which point the mind itself should be regarded as empty of own-being (*svabhāva-śūnya*).

Śāntarakṣita first visited Tibet in 763 CE and a second time in 775, staying until his death. It was he who, according to *Padma.ka'i.thang.yig* (The Clear Decree of Padma; a 15th-cent. *terma), advised King Trisong Detsen (Khri.srong.lde.brtsan) to invite *Padmasambhāva to Tibet on the basis of the latter's supernatural powers, because of magical opposition to Buddhist teaching from the native *Bön religion. Śāntarakṣita also recommended the invitation of *Kamalaśīla to defend the teachings against the Chinese Buddhists in the debate at *Samyé (bsam. yas). Formerly a professor at *Nālanda, Śāntarakṣita became abbot of Tibet's first monastery at Samyé, which he co-founded with Padmasambhāva in 775 CE. Śāntarakṣita's major works are *Madhyamakālaṅkāra* (Ornament of the Middle Way) with his own commentary, and *Tattvasaṃgraha* (Compendium of Reality), an assessment of the Indian schools.

Santa Sophia (church, later mosque): see HAGIA SOFIA.

Santería (Cuban, 'the way of the saints'). A complex of religious cults in the Afro-Cuban population, combining Yoruba African and Spanish Catholic traditions, especially concerning the *saints (*santos*) who are identified with the spirits (*orisha*) of the Yoruba pantheon. Each worshipper may have a personal patron spirit and belong to a cult group or congregation under a priest, with great variety among the groups. Where Santería closely follows Roman Catholic rites it is hard to distinguish from folk Catholicism; other forms emphasize trance possession by the spirits. Worship features prayers and songs in Yoruba, drumming which may speak for the spirits, and sacred stones of power, associated with the spirits, kept under the altar, and 'baptized' and fed annually with herbs and blood. These cults endeavour to control and use the spirits for practical benefits, but lack any ethical requirements; their main growth since the Castro revolution has been among Cuban exiles, especially in the USA.

M. González-Wippler, *The Santería Experience* (1982) and *Rituals and Spells of Santería* (1984); R. F. Thompson, *Flash of the Spirit* . . . (1981).

Śanti (Skt., 'tranquillity'). Interior peace, personified in Hinduism as a daughter of Śraddha (faith); also a ritual for averting curses, adverse stellar or planetary influences, and bad *karma.

Śānti (Buddhist philosopher): see RATNĀKARAŚĀNTI.

Santiago (pilgrimage centre): see PILGRIMAGE (CHRISTIAN).

Śāntideva (8th cent. CE). Buddhist poet and adherent of the *Prāsaṅgika branch of the *Mādhyamaka school. He composed two important works, the 'Compendium of Discipline' (*Śikṣā-samuccaya*), and 'Entering the Path of Enlightenment' (*Bodhicāryāvatāra*). The former is basically a collection of extracts from *Mahāyāna *sūtras grouped together around twenty-seven verses on the theme of conduct and behaviour, while the second deserves to be ranked as a classic in the world's religious literature. In 'Entering the Path', Śāntideva describes the various steps to be taken by one pursuing the *bodhisattva path to enlightenment from the production of the thought of enlightenment (*bodhicitta) through the practice of the Perfections (*pāramitās) to full enlightenment. He lays special emphasis on placing oneself in the position of others (*parātma-parivartana*) in order to promote selflessness and compassion: 'Whoever wishes to rescue himself and another quickly, he should practise the supreme mystery: the exchanging of himself and the other' (8. 120). The work culminates in the penultimate chapter (ch. 9) with an explanation of transcendental wisdom (*prajñā), its realization of emptiness (*śūnyatā), and the doctrine of the Two Truths, i.e. reality as seen in its ultimate and relative aspects.

Eng. tr. with a long introduction to Śāntideva's thought, M. Matics, *Entering the Path of Enlightenment* (1971).

Sant Niraṅkārī (Sikh movement): see NIRAṄKĀRĪ.

Sant tradition. In Indian religions, a sant is a holy or dedicated religious person. He or she is thus equivalent to a *sādhū (fem., *sadhvī*). More specifically, Sant traditions are those in which a succession of styles and teachings have been developed and transmitted. Of these, one is the Vārkarī movement of Paṇḍharpur in Maharaṣtra. But more usually the Sant tradition refers to a succession of religious teachers and devotees in N. India whose influence was extensive from the 15th to 17th cents., and persists to the present day. The Sant tradition also refers to itself as Nirguṇa Saṁpradāya (see NIRGUṆA; SAṀPRADĀYA), or Nirguṇa Pantha. This Sant tradition was a coalescence of different religious strands, of which *Vaiṣṇava bhakti, especially as associated with *Ramananda, was particularly important—although ultimately contradicted, since the Sant tradition directed its devotion to God without the intermediary of any incarnation (*avatāra). Also important as a source was *Nāth yoga, and to a lesser (and disputed) extent, *Sūfī Islām. The Sants stressed that the way to union with God is open to all (and thus they included low-*caste people and women among their members), provided that the teaching of the guru (who might be a human figure or might be the inner voice and demand of God) is adhered to, and that the necessary effort and discipline is undertaken. *Ritual, *pilgrimage, *sacrifice, *asceticism, and *celibacy are all equally useless in leading to God, who indwells his creation and unfolds the assurance of his presence by *grace. Because the Sants were close to ordinary people, they abandoned Skt. for their hymns and prayers, and composed them instead in a language known as Sādhukkaṛi, a composite dialect based on Khaṛī Bolī. Major figures among the Sants include *Nāmdev, *Ravi Dās, and *Kabīr; but the most dramatic influence was exercised on Gurū *Nānak, and thus on the formation of the Sikh tradition. See NIRAṄKĀRĪ.

The term 'sant' is also an honorific title given to revered teachers (cf. *sādhu). See Index, Sants.

A. Eschmann *et al.* (eds.), *The Cult of Jagannath* . . . (1978); D. Gold, *The Lord as Guru: Hindi Sants in the N. Indian Tradition* (1987); K. Schomer and W. H. McLeod (eds.), *The Sants* (1987).

Sanusis/Senusis (Sūfī movement): see AL-SANŪSĪ.

Sanyo (three essentials of Zen Buddhist Lin-chi line): see LIN-CHI.

Sanzen (Jap., 'going to Zen'). Going to a Zen master (*rōshi) to receive instruction. For *Dōgen, it means the correct practice of Zen. For *Rinzai, it is a synonym of *dokusan.

Sapir–Whorf hypothesis (role of language in creating cultural diversity): see CULTURAL RELATIVITY AND RELIGION.

Saptarṣi (visionary authors of Vedic hymns): see ṚṢI.

Sarah (wife of Abraham, ancestress of the Jewish people): see PATRIARCHS AND MATRIARCHS.

Saraṇa (refuge): see THREE JEWELS.

Sarasvatī. 1. In Hinduism, consort of Brahmā, and patron of learning and the arts. Sarasvatī is widely revered, and particularly attracts the worship of *brahmans and students. She is depicted as very fair-skinned, beautiful, and elegant, and usually holds the *vīna* (a musical instrument); her *vāhana, or vehicle, is the peacock. Sanskrit, the sacred language, is said to have been created by Sarasvatī, and in the *Ṛg Veda* she appears as *Vāc (speech), sacred utterance personified, and mother of the Vedas, or God-given knowledge.

2. The legendary river of NW India, personified as Sarasvatī.

Sardār (Pañjābī, 'chief'). Usual form of address for Sikh men, corresponding to 'Mr'. Sardārjī conveys more respect. The chieftains of the Sikh *misls were termed sardār or *misldār*.

Sari. The traditional dress of Hindu women, now frequently worn by women of other religious groups in India as well. It consists of a 4-foot-wide length of cloth, generally varying in length, 5–9 yards, though for daily wear a 6-yard length is favoured. The sari often has a colourful border, especially on the *pallu*, the end which is draped over the right or left shoulder after the cloth has been wound round the body from waist to ankle, with generous pleats at the front to allow freedom of movement. The *pallu* may be drawn up over the hair as a modest head-covering when required. The style of tying the sari varies from region to region. In Maharaṣṭra a 9-yard sari for daily wear used to be common; this allowed for the material to be drawn up between the legs and tucked into the waist at the back, forming a divided skirt, very practical for work. Saris of longer lengths are usually reserved for ceremonial occasions, such as for brides at weddings, when not much walking or hard work is to be done, as their weight and size inhibit movement. Saris for daily wear are generally of cotton or, these days, nylon, but beautiful silken ones are worn for festivals or religious ceremonies. The sari is usually worn with a brief blouse, leaving a bare midriff.

Sāriputta or **Sāripūtra.** 1. One of the two principal followers of the *Buddha (with *Moggallāna). He was regarded as the wisest of all the adherents, but in later texts is somewhat criticized for severity and overattention to minute details. He is represented iconographically on the Buddha's right hand.

2. A 12th-cent. leader of the Buddhist *saṅgha (monastic communities), and a highly revered commentator on the *Pāli canon. His work is marked by a quest for inclusion and reconciliation, and he was called 'the ocean of wisdom'.

Śarīra (Skt., 'husk'). 1. In Hinduism, the three surrounding protections or supports for the *ātman (undying self): (i) sthūla-śarīra, the apparent body; (ii) sūksma-śarīra, also liṅga-śarīra, the subtle body, not evident to direct sight; (iii) kārana-śarīra, the body that supports the possibility of the attainment of bliss (*ānanda). Because the ātman is thus protected, it can be carried from death to rebirth.

2. In Buddhism, the relics of the *Buddha Śākyamuni, or of any other prominent Buddhist, usually preserved in a *stūpa or *pagoda.

Sārnāth. North of the Ganges (*Gaṅgā), near Vārāṇasī (*Kāśi), the place where the *Buddha delivered his first sermon. The Buddhist texts are in some disagreement as to the exact nature of this sermon, but agree that it was given to his five former companions and included reference to the avoidance of extremes, the consequent acceptance of a middle path (*madhyamā pratipad*), and the Āryan Eightfold Path (*aṣṭangika-marga). The exact spot in Sārnāth where this took place is known as the Deer Park (Iṣipatana) and the event is called 'the turning of the Wheel of Dharma' (*dharmacakra-pravartana*).

Sārnāth has continued to be an important *pilgrimage site. The 7th-cent. CE Chinese pilgrim *Hsuan Tsang describes the presence of a polished stone pillar, fragments of which are still preserved at the Sārnāth museum. The ruins of the Dhāmeka *stūpa, dating from the Gupta period (320–630 CE), are still standing. A number of important statues of the Buddha have also been found in the area. Though never as prominent as *Nālandā, a monastic complex flourished here until the Muslim era. During the last hundred years numerous *vihāras have been re-established, and the whole impressive site excavated and extensively restored.

D. R. Sahni, *Catalogue of the Museum of Archaeology at Sarnath* (1972).

Sarum Use. The plainchant and ritual developed in Salisbury Cathedral from the 13th cent. to the *Reformation. It was increasingly followed in other dioceses. In 1559, it was abolished, but its influence remained in the revisions leading to the **Book of Common Prayer*.

F. Proctor and C. Wordsworth, *Breviarum ad Usum Sarum* (1879–86); J. Wickham Legge, *The Sarum Missal* (1916; 1969).

Sarvamedha. Hindu sacrifice of universal or power-creating efficacy. It is described in **Śatapatha Brāhmaṇa* 13. 7. 1 ff. It lasts ten days, and consists in the self-offering of the creator Svayambhu on behalf of his creation.

Sarvaṅ khalvidam Brahma. 'All this is truly *Brahman', one of the Hindu *mahāvākyas (great sayings). It appears in *Chandogya Upaniṣad* 3. 14. 1.

Sarvāstivāda (Pāli, Sabbatthivāda, from *sabbam atthi*, 'everything exists'). One of three systematic schools of early Buddhism which derived from the *Sthaviravāda of the first schism, the others being *Pudgalavādins and *Vibhajjavādins. They became the most prominent non-Mahāyāna school in N. India, whence they moved into China. Their main works on *Abhidharma survive in Chinese and Tibetan. They are distinguished, in their teaching, by their view that *dharmas have real existence, not only in the present but in the past, since they must exist as causes of *karma. Thus they made dharmas into reified entities, indivisible constituents of reality. Each has its own nature (*svadharma), and they are bound together in forms of appearance without constituting a self. Conflicts among Sarvastivādins led to a Council, *c.*100 CE, under Kaniṣka I, which produced a commentary of agreed teaching, *Mahāvibhāṣā*. Mainstream Sarvāstivādins, following this, were also called Vaibhāṣikas; dissenters split off to form the *Sautrāntika school.

In the 4th cent. CE, *Vasubandhu produced a survey of Sarvāstivāda, *Abhidharma-kośa*; but he also developed a critique from the point of view of Sautrāntika, who had already broken away. They regarded *sūtras/suttas as having authority, and rejected the reality of dharmas. It is consciousness (cf. VIJÑANA) which carries consequence from one life to another, but nothing 'exists' for longer than a moment. Ultimate reality cannot be described, but theories of being, appearance, etc., can act as provisional devices leading toward enlightenment. Both groups together can be regarded as a transition between *Hīnayāna and *Mahāyāna.

A. Bareau, *Les Sectes bouddhiques du petit véhicule* (1955).

Sarvodaya ('The Awakening and Welfare of All'). Buddhist-based rural self-development movement, initiated in Śri Lankā and mainly found there. The movement is based on *śramadāna*, community work projects, and is sometimes known as Sarvodaya Shramadana. The concept was endorsed by *Gāndhī, but the specifically Buddhist movement began in 1958, when a young teacher, A. T. Ariyaratne, encouraged his pupils to engage in a fortnight's holiday work camp, starting from the needs as perceived by the destitute villagers themselves. Many other schools and colleges followed this example, and before long *bhikṣus were involved: Ariyaratne saw his idea of self-help as being an extension of the traditional dynamic between village and *saṅgha; and he saw it also as an extension, (i) of the emphasis of *Aśoka on the establishing of a just relation between village communities and the saṅgha, and (ii) of the basic Buddhist values. Above all, he stressed that 'the chief objective of Sarvodaya is personality awakening'. All problems in the environment must be tackled by attending first to problems in oneself: 'It is one's own doing that reacts on one's own self [*karma], so it is possible to divert the course of our lives.' Sarvodaya translates Buddhist virtues (e.g. *metta, *karuṇā) into their immediate social implications. As the movement grew and became formalized, it took care to keep decision-making decentralized, establishing Village Awakening Councils (*samhiti*) which administered their own budgets and decided their own programmes. About a third of all Śri Lankā's villages became involved; and in 1981, Sarvodaya Shramadana International was instituted, with a concern, not only for Third World development, but for errors in developed societies as well.

J. R. Macy, *Dharma and Development* ... (1985).

Sāsana (Pāli) or **śāsana** (Skt.). Teaching, instruction, message of the *Buddha; however, the term by custom has come to mean the Buddhist religion (Buddha-sāsana) or tradition itself, especially with respect to the period of its duration as a historical phenomenon. So sāsana refers to the 'dispensation' of the teaching. When a *sammāsambuddha discovers and imparts the *dharma, his message and its impact on society and the world endures for a limited period of time only. The circumstances or fortunes of the dharma change, being subject, like all things, to the law of impermanence (*anicca), although the dharma itself, of course, never changes. Gradually Buddhist tradition wanes until it eventually disappears from the earth altogether. It remains lost until the next sammāsambuddha appears and introduces dharma to the world again. In this intervening period, which may last for many millennia, between the sāsana of one sammāsambuddha and the next, the possibility of *nirvāna ceases except for an exceptional few; such persons are dubbed *pratyekabuddhas. The idea of cosmic or historical cycles of relative good or bad is a belief which Buddhism shares in common with Hinduism (see COSMOLOGY).

Predictions of the life-span of the present sāsana of *Gotāma Buddha are found in both *Hīnayāna and *Mahāyāna tradition. The *Pāli canon maintains that the Buddha's decision to allow ordination of women meant the duration of true doctrine (*saddhamma*) would be reduced from 1,000 to 500 years. Predictions for the survival of the sāsana in later traditions range from between 1,000 and 5,000 years. These traditions too assign stages to the gradual decline of sāsana: **Milinda-Pañha*, for example, states that (i) the capability of spiritual attainment will vanish, then (ii) the practice underlying it, and lastly (iii) the superstructure or externals (e.g. *saṅgha and *relics of the Buddha) will also vanish.

In Sinhalese Buddhist tradition, it is believed that the final eclipse of the sāsana will happen in a dramatic (equivalent to *apocalyptic in other religions) manner: those relics of the Buddha still remaining in the world—the last vestiges of tradition—together with those in the various heavens, will gather and reassemble themselves into the form of a Buddha-image at the very spot where Gotāma became enlightened. This image will emit rays illuminating all the world-systems (*loka-dhātu*), and then, in an instant, vanish from sight for ever. The doctrine of the disappearance of the teaching (*sāsana-antaradhāna*) has made a profound impression on the religious consciousness of the Theravāda Buddhists of SE Asia. Generally, monks (taking the canonical prediction at face value) no longer consider feasible the attainment of nirvāna in their present life, and therefore train themselves with a view to reaching that attainment in some future existence, notably during the sāsana of the next Buddha, *Maitreya.

Śāsanadevatā. Jain spiritual beings who serve the *jinas but who also respond as gods, at a popular level, to the devotion and prayers of humans. Frequently they are Hindu deities, and thus have afforded a way in which not only the natural human desire for God is satisfied, but also respect for those deities is made manifest in a Hindu context. Of particular importance are Śri *Lakṣmī, *Sarasvatī, and *Amba, the guardian of the jina *Neminātha.

Under the name of Sachika, *Durgā, the slayer of *Mahiṣa, is revered (mainly in Rājasthān). Yakṣadampati, pairs of attendant *yakṣas and yakṣis, are often found in carvings without any further identity beyond that of the jina whom they serve.

Sa-skya (order of Tibetan Buddhism): see 'PHAGS-PA.

Sassatavāda (Pāli) or **śāśvatavāda** (Skt.). Eternalism, the doctrine of an immutable soul or self which survives death and continues everlastingly. Both eternalism and its opposite view, annihilationism, are versions of the so-called soul heresy (*sakkāya-diṭṭhi) and represent, according to Buddhism, the two alternative directions which misrepresentations of reality take. Buddhism regards as by implication eternalist any theory which rests on the premiss of the separateness of the self from matter. It was in opposition to these polarizing extremes that the Buddha came to formulate his teaching on causality (*paticca-samuppāda) and to affirm the pre-eminence of the Middle Way. According to the *Brahmajāla Sutra*, there are eternalists who infer the existence of an eternal self on the basis of remembering some of their former lives, and others who argue that, in spite of the sense-organs being impermanent, an unchanging self is to be found in the mind (*manas), thought (*citta), and understanding (*vijñāna). The Buddha opposed eternalism, not only on theoretical grounds, but also because of what he considered to be the harmful moral consequences of the doctrine. The belief that the self was an unchanging reality that survived death was seen as providing no incentive for self-improvement or for alleviating the plight of others and of the world in general. For this reason it is classed as an evil belief (*pāpakaṃ diṭṭhigatam*) as well as a false one (*micchadiṭṭhi*).

Śāstra(s) (Skt., 'command, rule'). 1. Hindu treatise or treatises on particular topics, amounting to law books or codes. The *sūtra manuals of the priests are extended and better organized. The best known examples are the *Dharmaśāstras (e.g. *Manusmṛti*, *Yajñavalkyasmṛti*), *Arthaśāstra, and Kāmaśāstras (e.g. of Vātsyāyana).

2. In Buddhism, Mahāyāna commentaries on philosophical issues in the *sūtras.

P. V. Kane, *History of Dharmasastra* (1930–62); L. Sternbach, *Bibliography on Dharma and Artha in Ancient and Medieval India* (1973).

Sat (Skt., 'being', 'essence', 'right'). Absolute, unqualified Being in Hinduism, and thus identical with *Brahman. In ethics it means 'good', in epistemology 'true'. It is combined with *cit and *ānanda in the basic formula *saccidānanda.

Satan (Heb., 'adversary'; Arab., *al-Shaytan*). In Jewish, Christian, and Islamic tradition, the chief enemy of God.

Judaism In the older books of the Hebrew Bible, the word *sātān* is a common noun (e.g. 1 Samuel 29. 4), and is a human adversary (1 Kings 11. 14, 23, 25). Apart from the figure of the serpent in Genesis 3, there is no figure to correspond to the later tradition. This begins to emerge after the *Exile, perhaps under *Zoroastrian influence. In *Job, 'the Satan' is a heavenly figure who tests Job, but always with God's permission (e.g. chs. 1 and 2). In 1 Chronicles 21. 1 David's decision to number Israel is attributed to Satan, here a proper name for the first time. Similar references to Satan, as personifying the forces opposed to God, occur in the **Testaments of the Twelve Patriarchs* and other *pseudepigrapha: thus 'Manasseh forsook the service of the God of his fathers and he served Satan and his angels ...' (*Martyrdom of Isaiah*, 2. 2). However, in the *amoraic period, he becomes a significant individual. He is said to have been responsible for all the sins in the Bible (*PdRE* 13. 1), and the reason for blowing the *shofar on *Rosh ha-Shanah is 'to confuse Satan' (*BRH* 16b). The Christian Church has frequently identified the Jews as the children of Satan, based on Jesus' words in the Fourth Gospel, 'You are of your father the devil' (8. 44). In later Judaism (especially *kabbalah) he becomes known by other names, e.g. *Samael.

J. Trachtenberg, *The Devil and the Jews* (1943).

Christianity The cognate term 'the devil' (Gk., *diabolos*), which has become the usual word in Christian tradition, alternates with 'Satan' in the New Testament (see also BEELZEBUB). Here the Jewish picture is elaborated: the devil is master of the world (Matthew 4. 8–9) and the opponent of the *Kingdom of God (Matthew 13. 24–30) whom Jesus has seen to fall from heaven (Luke 10. 18). He has no power over Christ (John 14. 30) for he is already judged (John 16. 11) and with his angels will depart to eternal fire at the last *judgement (Matthew 25. 41); yet he must be always resisted (1 Peter 5. 8–9).

The identity of Satan as a fallen angel is asserted by Revelation 12. 7–9. Under the influence of the book of *Enoch (interpreting Genesis 6. 1–4), many of the early fathers held that the angels' fall was the result of their desiring human women, and that demons are the offspring of their unions. The view which prevailed, however, was that the devil, *'Lucifer', fell through pride, because he would not submit to God. Satan's defeat by Christ on the cross led to 'Christus Victor' theories of *atonement, revived and made important in the 20th cent., by G. Aulén: the conquest of personified evil reinforced many Christians in their resistance to totalitarian dictators.

The majority of Christians perhaps accept the traditional teaching about Satan, if not in all its elaborations. The issue among critical theologians is whether the idea of a personal demonic being is to be rejected as pre-scientific or whether such a myth is required to do justice to the nature of evil.

J. W. Boyd, *Satan and Māra* . . . (1975); J. B. Russell, *The Devil* (1977).

Islam Al-Shaytān is, in the *Qur'ān, the adversary. The term describes Iblīs (Gk., *diabolos*, 'devil') and his descendants as they cease to be simply rebellious *jinn, and become subverters or tempters of humans (eighty-eight times in thirty-six chapters: see e.g. 7. 11, 27; 20. 120). Al-Shaytān has no authority over those who take refuge in God (41. 36): they become 'God's party' (58. 22), while those who follow al-Shaytān become his party (58. 19) and end in *jahannam* (the fire of *hell, 19. 68).

Satanic Verses. Verses insinuated into the *Qur'ān by al-Shaytān (Satan), when *Muḥammad was uttering authentic verses. According to *al-Tabari, Muḥammad was anxious to make it easy for the Meccans to accept the truth of his message; indeed, he was approached by the Meccans who said that if he would only make some mention of their traditional goddesses, al-Lāt, al-ʿUzza, and Manāt, they would be glad to sit beside him. At this point, the *sūra al-Najm (53) was revealed. When Muḥammad came to the verses (19 f.), 'Have you considered al-Lāt and al-ʿUzza, | And Manat, the third, the other?', 'Satan caused to come upon his tongue, "These are the swans exalted whose intercession is to be hoped for. Such as they do not forget [*or* are not forgotten]." ' The Meccans immediately followed Muḥammad when he prostrated himself before God. It may be that a compromise was being proposed, whereby the Meccans could consider their goddesses to be like winged *angels, carrying messages (and prayers) between earth and heaven. But the compromise was not at all as the Meccans understood it, as they assumed that their goddesses had been endorsed. Consequently, a further verse was revealed (22. 51): 'We [God] never sent an apostle (*rasūl) or a prophet (*nabī) before you without it happening that when he formed a desire, Satan threw something into his desire. But God will cancel (*naskh) anything that Satan throws in.'

The phrase has become notorious as the title of a novel by Salman Rushdie (1988), which elicited a *fatwā from the Ayatollah *Khumayni, placing the author under sentence of death—in effect for *apostasy, followed by the bringing of Islam into ridicule—though more colloquially for blasphemy. Ironically, the whole novel can be read as an extended ambiguity, which is a consequence of what happens if the devil is still allowed to insinuate his voice into the modern world of the novel: 'Which was the miracle worker? Of what type—angelic, satanic—was Farishta's song? Who am I? Let's put it this way: who has the best tunes [see BOOTH, WILLIAM]?' In the reaction to the novel, the question of who is doing the devil's work most effectively is sharply posed: liberals in the West who defend freedom of speech no matter what is said are not innocent of offence from any point of view, not just in relation to religious sensitivities.

Satapadi (seven steps): see MARRIAGE (Hinduism).

Śatapatha Brāhmaṇa. The 'Brāhmaṇa of a Hundred Paths', is the longest and fullest *brāhmaṇa. It is attached to the White **Yajur Veda*, and its *āraṇyaka is the *Bṛhadāranyaka Upaniṣad*. It describes the five great sacrificial ceremonies, *vājapeya*, *rājasūya*, *aśvamedha, *puruṣamedha*, and *sarvamedha*, and it reveals much of the political and religious condition of late Vedic times. It exists now in different textual traditions.

Eng. tr. J. Eggeling, *Sacred Books of the East*, 5 vols.

Sat cakra bheda (Skt., 'piercing the six wheels'). In *Tantrism, the movement of the *Kuṇḍalinī up the suṣumṇā *nāḍī, passing through the six *cakras to the thousand-petalled lotus (*sahasrāra). This is also called *laya yoga. Tantric texts usually speak of the piercing of three knots (*granthi*) accompanied by the manifestation of different kinds of subtle sounds. The *arambha* ('preliminary') stage is when the Kuṇḍalinī has pierced the first knot, the *Brahma granthi, in the *mūlādhāra*, and the yogin becomes aware of a ringing sound, having arrested the movement of breath (*prāṇa), semen (*vīrya*), and mind. Next the *ghaṭa* (*jar*) stage is when the Kuṇḍalinī has pierced the *Viṣṇu *granthi* at the *anāhata* cakra, experienced as the sound of a kettle-drum. At the *paricaya* (introduction) stage, the sound is like a tom-tom; and finally the *Rudra *granthi* is pierced at the *ājña* cakra accompanied by a sound like a *vīṇā*. From here the Kuṇḍalinī can rise to the thousand-petalled lotus without hindrance.

Sat-cit-ānanda (three-fold characterization of Brahman): see SACCIDĀNANDA.

Sat Gurū. For Sikhs, the supreme *Gurū, i.e. God. God is called by other names, e.g. *Akal Purukh, *Vāhigurū, but Gurū *Nānak used the term Sat Gurū more than 300 times in the *Ādi Granth, as the only source of true guidance. The term may also be used as an honorific title for gurus.

Satī. The wife of *Śiva who committed suicide when her father insulted Śiva.

The term (anglicized as 'suttee') was used for the self-immolation of Hindu widows, either by joining the dead husband on his funeral pyre, or by committing suicide later on a pyre lit by embers from that pyre. Not even pregnancy could save a woman from this fate; the ceremony was merely postponed until two months after her child's birth. The origins of the custom are mysterious; there is no reference to it in the *Vedas, except for a hint in the rituals for the *antyeshṭi (funeral) rite which describes how a widow might lie beside her dead husband on the unlit pyre, his bow in her hand; she was then formally recalled to life and might marry his brother, or beget children by *niyoga*. The **Mahābhārata* and **Ramāyana*, however, both contain references to extensive satī practices. The first historical instance of satī is found in Gk. records of 316 BCE, when the wife of an Indian general who was killed in battle is said to have been burnt. One of the last was the sister of Dr A. S. Altekar, who joined her husband on his funeral pyre in 1946, in spite of impassioned pleas by her relatives, imploring her not to do so. The custom continues, but infrequently and illegally.

Hindu law books of the 1st and 2nd cents. CE see the act as gaining spiritual merit; 400 years later it was considered that for a woman to survive her husband was sinful. Originally it was reserved for widows of rulers and military leaders, but, as it gained prestige, it spread even to the lower castes. The proper procedures for the ceremony are recorded in the *Padma-Purāṇa* of the early 12th cent. Originally a N. Indian custom, especially prevalent among Rajputs, it had spread to S. India by the 10th cent. As polygyny was usual among rulers and the nobility throughout India, literally hundreds of widows and concubines would be called upon to face self-immolation on their husband's death. Among Rajputs the practice of *jauhar* was a variant.

It is unlikely that many widows went voluntarily to the flames, though it is certain that some did. Many were forcibly burnt; even sons would be deaf to their mothers' pleas, in order to protect family honour.

Satī was opposed by several Hindu lawyers and writers over the centuries, but until *Tantric scholars condemned it as positively sinful, there was no concerted opposition. The *Mughals, in their efforts to abolish it, instituted a permit system by which a woman stated she was committing satī by her own choice, but this scheme was widely open to abuse. Not until 1829, under Lord Bentinck's Regulation, did satī become legally homicide, after pressure was brought to bear on the British authorities by Christian missionaries and Hindu reformers, notably Rām Mohan *Roy.

Sati (Pāli) or **smṛti** (Skt., 'mindfulness'). A form of mental application which lies at the very heart of Buddhist meditational practice, whose object is awareness, lucidity, true recognition. It is concerned with the bare registering of the objects of our senses and minds as they are presented to us in our experience, without reacting to them in terms of the behaviour of the ego—i.e. in terms of our likes and dislikes, passions and prejudices. Only then can the true nature of things become illumined. Sati combines both attention and memory—through attention solely to the bare facts of experience a true knowledge or proper memory occurs: 'Thus must you train yourself . . .: in the seen there will be to you just the seen, in the heard just the heard, in the imagined just the imagined, in the cognized just the cognized' (*Udāna* 8). It conduces both to the calming (*samatha) of the emotions and to insight (*vipassanā) into the *Three Marks of Existence. Right mindfulness (*sammā-sati*) is part of the Eightfold Path (*aṣṭangika-marga). The exercises composing sati are described as the setting-up of mindfulness (*satipaṭṭhāna).

Satipaṭṭhāna (Pāli, *sati-upaṭṭhāna*, 'the establishing or setting up of mindfulness'; Skt., *smṛti-upasthāna*). The system of meditation based on mindfulness (*sati), set forth by the Buddha in a discourse (*sutta*) of that name (*Dīgha Nikāya* 2. 290–315; *Majjhima Nikāya* 1. 55–63), and regarded as the one scheme of practice indispensable to the realization of *nirvāna. It consists of mindfulness directed successively upon the four objects which together represent the total range of the individual's experience of himself: his body (*kāya*), feelings (*vedanā*), mind (*citta), and mental concepts (*dhamma). Clear comprehension (*sampajañña*) of the body occurs when the meditator lives contemplating the bodily process of breathing in and out (*ānāpānasati), the external and internal parts of the body, the body as composed of the four elements (*mahābhūta), his bodily actions as they are being performed, and the mortality of his body. Clear comprehension of feelings occurs when he lives contemplating their occurrence and identifying them for what they are: as pleasant, painful, or neutral. Of the mind, this occurs when he lives contemplating whether states such as attachment (*rāga), ill will (*dosa), and delusion (*moha) are present or absent, whether the mind is in a developed or undeveloped stage of consciousness (*jhāna), and whether it is composed or uncomposed, attached or freed. Of mental concepts, it occurs when he lives contemplating whether any of the five hindrances (*nīvaraṇa) to mental concentration are present within him, and when they arise and disappear. Finally he cultivates an awareness of those mental concepts which comprise fundamental Buddhist truths: the five components of separate individuality (*skandhas), the twelve sense-bases (*āyatana), the seven factors of enlightenment (*bojjhanga), and the *Four Noble Truths. These meditations are throughout accompanied by the consciousness that body, feelings, mind, and mental concepts are subject to the law of impermanence (*anicca).

The practice of satipaṭṭhāna counteracts the tendency to confuse the ego with the body, feelings, mind and mental concepts by disclosing just 'the body in the body, feelings in feelings, mind in mind, and mental concepts in mental concepts'. Consequently, traits of the ego's behaviour resulting from this confusion, such as discontent (*domanassa*), dissolve away. They are replaced by a correct comprehension (*jñāṇa) and recollection (*paṭissati*) of the way things are.

An indication of the importance of satipaṭṭhāna to the Buddhist tradition is provided by the Buddha's own words: 'This is the only way (*ekayāna*) for the purification of beings, for the overcoming of sorrow and lamentation, for the destruction of suffering and grief, for reaching the right path, for the attainment of nirvāna, namely the fourfold setting-up of mindfulness.' Elsewhere the Buddha is also reported to have said that it will be the lapse in the practice of satipaṭṭhāna that will occasion the decline of the Buddhist religion.

Maha-Satipatthana Sutta, tr. T. W. and C. A. F. Rhys-Davids (1910).

Sati Srī Akāl: see SAT SRĪ AKĀL.

Sat-kārya-vāda (Skt., 'theory of existent effect'), in *Sāṁkhya, the concept that any effect pre-exists in its cause; there is no creation of a thing previously nonexistent. According to Saṁkhyakārikā 9 (trsl. G. Larson), the effect exists (before the operation of cause) (*satkārya*) (a) because of the non-productivity of non-being; (b) because of the need for an (appropriate) material cause; (c) because of the impossibility of all things coming from all things; (d) because something can only produce what it is capable of producing; (e) because of the nature of the cause (or, because the effect is non-different from the cause).

Everything that occurs exists potentially in its cause. Creation is produced simply through a recombination of the constituents of the uncreated (*avyakta*). By analogy, a statue pre-exists in the stone; curds in milk. Specifically, creation involves a reorganizing of the three *guṇas which exist in perfect equilibrium in the primal 'stuff' (*mūlaprakṛti*) of creation. All change occurs through the interaction of these three guṇas.

Ṣatkasampatti (Skt., 'six attainments'). The six great virtues which, in *Śaṅkara's Hindu system, must be fulfilled as one of the four prerequisites by a student of *Vedānta—the others being *mumukṣutva* (striving for liberation), *viveka (discrimination), and *vairagya (detachment). The six virtues are (i) *śama*, concentration and control of the mind, directed towards an object of meditation; (ii) *dama*, control of the organs of sense; (iii) *uparama*, quieting of the mind, especially by the fulfilment of one's duty of *dharma; (iv) *titikṣa*, the patient balance between opposing dualities; (v) *śraddhā, faith, trust in what scriptures teach; (vi) *samādhāna* (cf. SAMĀDHI), the concentration which enables one also to transmit truth to others.

Satnām (Pañjābī, 'whose name is true'). Distinctively Sikh appellation for God. Sikhs frequently invoke God with the words 'Satnām Śrī *Vāhigurū'.

Satori (Jap.; Chin., *wu). Zen term for the experience of awakening or enlightenment. It is derived from *satoru*, 'know', but it has no connection with knowledge in any ordinary sense. Retrospectively, satori is the enlightenment experience of the *Buddha (Chin., *wu*; Skt., *bodhi), but in Zen it is more often used prospectively, of the enlightenment to which the disciple or pupil is now aspiring. A first enlightenment experience is known as *kenshō, which may be followed by a small, then great, satori. The essence of satori remains the same, but the one who attains it gains in profundity within it.

Śatrunjāya, Mount (holy mountain): see PILGRIMAGE (JAINISM).

Satsaṃga (Skt., 'good' + 'company'). The virtue in Hinduism of seeking the company of good people so that the 'spark' of wisdom can pass from one life to another. Hence satsangis, those who are 'companions of the truth', those who have been initiated into a way or tradition, e.g. a *saṁpradāya.

Satsang (Sikh association): see SANGAT.

Sat Srī Akāl (Pañjābī, 'True is immortal God'). Sikh greeting. This replaced the earlier 'sat kartār'. In battle 'Sat Srī Akāl' was the Sikhs' war-cry. The followers of *Bandā Siṅgh used an alternative greeting, as do *Nāmdhārīs and *Niraṅkārīs: see FATEH.

Sattva (Skt.). In *Sāṁkhya, one of the three strands (*guṇas) of material nature (*prakṛti). It is present in varying degrees in all things except pure consciousness (*puruṣa); it is luminosity. In the material world sattva is manifested as buoyancy or lightness: bright colours, air, light foods, etc. In the individual psyche it is expressed through intelligence, virtue, cheerfulness, etc. It is a predominance of sattva over the other guṇas which begins the creation process in prakṛti. Through sattva, puruṣa is most accurately reflected in prakṛti.

Sattva predominates at the subtler levels of the evolutionary scheme, the subtlest in the individual being intelligence (*buddhi), and it is to this level that the *yogin strives. The yogin, after purifying first his body and then his mind, attains a pure sattva state, reflecting most clearly the light of puruṣa. From this state he passes over completely to puruṣa which is beyond all guṇas.

Sattyasiddhi: see SAUTRĀNTIKAS.

Satyāgraha (Skt., 'truth force'). The power of truth without force or violence to change political and other circumstances. It was developed by M. K. *Gāndhī, drawing on an association of *sat with *satya* ('truth'), and *agrah* ('grasp firmly'). It puts together the power associated with *tapas and the tradition of *ahiṃsā, and is often equated with nonviolence as such.

J. Bondurant, *Conquest of Violence* (1958); D. Dalton, *Mahatma Gandhi* (1993); G. Sharp, *The Politics of Non-Violent Action* (1973).

Satya Sai Baba (Hindu spiritual guide and miracle worker): see SAI BABA.

Saul. The first king of the Israelites. Saul was anointed king by the seer *Samuel in response to pressure from the people. They were harassed by the *Philistines and other surrounding nations and they wanted a king 'to govern us like all the nations' (1 Samuel 8. 5). 1 Samuel contains several stories about Saul's accession (see 9. 1–10. 16; 10. 17–27; 11), some indicating conflict about the propriety of so great an innovation. Saul's reign was occupied by campaigns against the Philistines, the Moabites, the Aminorites, the Edomites, and the Gibeonites. He fell out with Samuel over a sacrifice (1 Samuel 13) and over his failure to exterminate the Amalekites (15. 34–5). He was threatened by the growing military success of the young *David, and gradually he descended into periods of gloom and despair (e.g. 16. 14–23). He died by his own hand after his army was defeated by the Philistines on Mount Gilboa 'lest these uncircumcised come and make sport with me' (31. 4). Saul is dealt with sympathetically in the *aggadic tradition (e.g. *Yoma* 22).

Sautrāntikas. Members of a Buddhist school seceding from the *Sarvāstivādins (*c.*200 CE) on the grounds that only *sūtra and not *abhidharma is the authoritative word of the Buddha—hence their name, Sautrāntika (*sūtrānta* + *ika*). Their doctrines anticipated developments in the *Vijñāpti-mātra school. In China, they were continued by Ch'eng-shih (Jap., *Jōjitsu*), the Sattyasiddhi school.

H. V. Guenther, *Buddhist Philosophy* . . . (1971, 1972).

Savayye or **Swayyā** (Pañjābī, 'type of verse'). Panegyric; Sikh hymn. Savayyās of varied metrical form, composed by bards in praise of the first five *Gurūs, occur near the end of the *Ādi Granth. Gurū *Gobind Siṅgh's Savayyās, incorporated in *Nitnem, are recited after *Japjī and *Jāp by devout Sikhs each morning. The Gurū emphasizes worship of one God and the futility of ritual.

Savitar (Vedic sun god): see SURYA.

Savitṛ (one of the Ādityas, the power of words): see ĀDITYAS; SŪRYA.

Sāvitrī. Hindu Goddess, daughter of the Sun (Savitar). She is known as the mother of the *Vedas, and is often identified with *Gāyatrī (thus seen as a personification of *Ṛg Veda* 3. 62. 10, the Gāyatrī *mantra, addressed to Savitar). Epic legend, particularly *Mahābhārata* 3. 277–83, tells of a princess Sāvitrī, named after the Goddess, who marries Satyavān, a man fated to die in a year, and then, by her unswerving loyalty to her husband, persuades *Yāma (Death) to give up his claim. In India, Sāvitrī is often idealized as the perfect wife, and the festival of Sāvitrī *pūjā is celebrated by women as a fast day to ensure the long lives of their husbands and the birth of many sons. A lengthy poetic reworking of the Sāvitrī legend by Śri *Aurobindo Ghose follows the careers of the various characters in the story as an allegory of the divinization of human life, a concept central to Aurobindo's philosophy. In the West, the composer Gustav Holst (1874–1934), having learnt Sanskrit in order to write *Choral Hymns from the Rig Veda* (1908–12), composed the chamber opera *Savitri* (1908, first staged 1916).

Savonarola, Girolamo (1452–98). Christian reformer and preacher. He was born at Ferrara in Italy, and entered the *Dominican Order in 1475. In 1482, he went to Florence, where he began to develop his programme of *ascetic morality. This he based on *apocalyptic preaching, emphasizing the final judgement and the possibility of eternal damnation. After three years in Bologna, he returned to Florence, where he preached against corruption in high places, and gave prophetic warnings, some of which appeared to come true. When Charles VIII invaded Italy, Savonarola averted the threat to the city, and the people made him their ruler. He attempted to establish a theocratic state with severe standards of behaviour: in the 'bonfire of vanities', the people burnt frivolous or lewd items. He denounced Pope Alexander VI and his corrupt court, and was summoned to Rome to account for his actions as 'a meddlesome friar': he refused to go and was excommunicated. A *Franciscan challenged him to ordeal by fire, which he refused. He was seized, tortured, and executed.

R. Ridolfi, *The Life* . . . (1959); D. Weinstein, *Savonarola and Florence* (1970).

Savoraim (Aram., 'explainers'). Jewish Babylonian scholars between the time of the *amoraim and the *geonim. Traditionally the era of the amoraim ends in 499 CE, and the era of the Savoraim ends either in 540 CE or, according to Abraham *ibn Daud, in 689 CE. In the Jerusalem *Talmud, a savora is a scholar competent to render decisions (*P.Kid.* 2. 63d), and *Sherira ben Ḥanina Gaon indicates that a number of savoraic decisions are included in the Talmud.

Savupadisesa-nibbāna (in Buddhism, nirvāna while still in the condition of this life): see SOPADHI-ŚEṢA-NIRVĀṆA.

Ṣawm or **ṣiyām.** Fasting, the fourth *pillar of Islam. Fasting is obligatory on Muslims, during the whole month of *Ramaḍān, and at other times in compensation for days then missed; it can also be practised in fulfilment of a personal vow, or as a pious action. Ṣawm must be preceded by the *niy(y)a, 'intention', whether this is pronounced before each dawn during the month, or once to cover the whole period. The first Muslims in *Madīna observed the fast of *'Āshūrā', together with the Jews, until the second year of the *hijra, when the general regulations for the Ramaḍān fast were given (Qur'ān 2. 183 ff.).

During Ramaḍān, any adult Muslim of sound mind and in good health must abstain from food, drink, smoking, and sexual relations during daylight hours, which are estimated as beginning when 'the white thread becomes distinct to you from the black thread' at dawn (Qur'ān 2. 187). Those on a journey, the sick, and women during their monthly periods or in pregnancy or when suckling a child, are exempt while these conditions prevail, but should make up the time later, or give *alms in lieu. It is customary, and recommended, for the Muslim to have a final meal (*saḥūr*) shortly before daybreak; in the evening the first food (*fuṭūr*) should be of water or dates, with a large meal following.

While the *ḥadīth give details of a practical nature for ṣawm, they also stress its spiritual aspects and the special blessings and privileges in the next life which it brings. *Al-Ghazālī emphasized the real purpose of fasting: 'to purify the heart and to concentrate all its attention upon God' (*The Mysteries of Fasting*, tr. N. A. Faris of the *Kitāb asrār al-ṣawm* of al-Ghazālī's *Iḥyā' ʿulūm al-dīn*, repr. 1974).

Saʿy. The part of the Muslim *ḥajj which comes after the circumambulation of the *Kaʿba. The pilgrim leaves the *masjid, left foot first, ascends the steps of al-Ṣafā and makes an invocation, looking toward the Kaʿba. He then descends and crosses the valley at a run until he reaches al-Marwa where again he prays. Tradition says that *Ibrāhīm first did this after prayer in order to escape *Satan who was waiting for him in the valley. But the custom is based on the anxiety of *Hagar, who ran between the two hills when the last of her water was used up and she despaired of the life of Ismāʿīl (*Ishmael). It was then that water started to flow from the well *Zamzam.

Sayadaw (Burm., 'teacher'). Burmese title for a Buddhist monk. Strictly it applies to the head of a monastery, but it is used as a general honorific.

Sayers, Dorothy L. (1893–1957). British writer and Christian lay theologian. Her religious writings date from 1937 on, when her fame was already established by her detective novels (1926–37), and were at their most vigorous during the Second World War. Her radio plays on the life of *Jesus, *The Man Born to be King* (broadcast 1941–2) were remarkable for their character study, especially of *Judas. In *The Mind of the Maker* (1941) she expounded the doctrine of the *Trinity by analogy with a creative artist's Idea, Energy, and Power.

B. Reynolds, *Dorothy L. Sayers . . .*, (1993).

Sayings of the Fathers (text commending the spirituality of the desert): see MONASTICISM (CHRISTIANITY).

Sayyid (title of descendant of Muḥammad): see SAIYID.

Sayyid al-Shuhadā' (leader of martyrs): see AL-ḤUSAIN B. ʿALI.

Scapegoat. Jewish *sin-offering let loose on the *Day of Atonement. The Day of Atonement Temple ritual included casting lots between two goats. One was *sacrificed to God, while the other was dedicated to *Azazel. It was released into the wilderness and cast over a cliff: see Leviticus 16.

Scapular (Lat., *scapulae*, 'shoulder blades'). Part of the Christian religious *habit consisting of a piece of cloth worn over the shoulders and hanging down in front and behind. It represents the yoke of Christ (Matthew 11. 29 f.).

Schechter, Solomon (1847–1915). Jewish scholar. Schechter came from an *ḥasidic background. After studying at the Berlin Hochschule, he came to England at the invitation of Claude *Montefiore and taught rabbinics at Cambridge University (1890–8). Through his efforts, the manuscripts and fragments of the *Cairo Geniza were recovered and brought to England. From 1902, he was President of the *Jewish Theological Seminary, and his *Studies in Judaism* (1896–1924) and *Some Aspects of Rabbinic Theology* (1909) are classics of *Conservative Judaism. He defended traditional ways and values against what he took to be *assimilationist tendencies in *Reform Judaism, but accepted that change and development in *halakhah are still desirable, especially when voiced by the faithful in some degree of consensus: he referred to the faithful in this sense as 'catholic Israel', or 'the catholic conscience of Israel'. At the same time, he did not seek consistency: 'It was said by a great writer that the best theology is that which is not consistent, and this advantage the theology of the synagogue possesses to its utmost extent.' He believed that 'the "sea of the *Talmud" has also its gulf stream of mysticism', and that the great gift of the Jewish people to the world was not that they invented printing or discovered America, but that 'we gave to the world the Word of God'.

N. Bentwich, *Solomon Schechter* (1948).

Schism (Gk., *schisma*, 'tear, rent'). A formal division of a religious body into separate parties. In Christian usage the word refers to sects or churches separating from communion with one another where *heresy is not involved. Early schismatic bodies (i.e. from the *Catholic Church) included the *Novatianists and *Donatists. The Orthodox and Catholic churches have been divided by schism (the 'East–West schism') since 1054. See also GREAT SCHISM. Roman Catholic theologians hold that all those out of communion with the pope are in a state of material schism, although *Vatican II stated that those in other Christian communions were in 'a certain, albeit imperfect, communion with the Catholic Church'. Schism is held to contradict the prayer of *Jesus, that 'they may all be one'. See also ECUMENISM.

Divisions and separations in other religions may be equally profound, but the use of the term 'schism' appears to be more a matter of chance than of intrinsic characteristics. Thus the divisions in Judaism (between Orthodox, Conservative, Reconstructionist, Reform, etc.), in Islam (between Sunni and Shīʿa, and among Shiʿites) and in Jainism are not usually so described—still less among Hindus, where a vast number of different traditions (cf. *saṁpradāya) coexist; yet it often is used of divisions among Sikhs (e.g. Niraṅkārīs and Nāmdhārīs) and of early Buddhism. While having none of the specific constituents of the Christian understanding, nevertheless Buddhist 'schism' (*saṃghabeda*) has its own formality: schism appeared early in the history of Buddhism, due in part to the Buddha's refusal to appoint a successor as leader of the Order and his reluctance to impose a rigid discipline in matters of monastic practice. He counselled his followers to be 'lamps to themselves', and Buddhism has never recognized a supreme source of authority in matters of doctrine or practice.

A schism (*saṃghabheda*) is defined as occurring when nine fully ordained monks leave a community together, as a result of dissent, and perform their own communal services apart. If the number is less than nine, there is 'dissent' rather than schism. To cause a schism maliciously or from selfish motives is considered a grave offence and one destined for swift retribution (*anantārya*). On the effects of schism in Buddhism see EIGHTEEN SCHOOLS OF EARLY BUDDHISM.

Schleiermacher, Friedrich (1768–1834). Christian *Protestant theologian, sometimes called 'the father of modern protestantism'. He followed his father into the *Moravian Brethren in 1783, and attended a Moravian school. He went to the university at Halle, and in 1794 was ordained into the ministry of the Reformed Church, and became a chaplain at the Charité Hospital in Berlin. Here he associated with an intellectual circle which included the two von Schlegel brothers, and in which there was much criticism of prevailing religion. In response, he wrote *Über die Religion: Reden an die Gebildeten unter ihren Verachtern* (On Religion: Speeches to its Cultured Despisers, 1798). He shared the distaste of the cultured despisers for the arid philosophy of religion which issued in *Deism, and even more for the petty and futile divisions of the Church over dogma and outward form. But this, he argued, is not truly 'religion', which is 'the immediate consciousness of the universal existence of all finite things in and through the infinite, and of all temporal things in and through the eternal'. Religion cannot be found as the conclusion of an argument: it is the direct and unmediated sense of the totality of all there is bearing upon the individual. Thus 'true religion is sense and taste for the Infinite'. This sense of the Whole, not (as in Newtonian physics) as a passive arena of inert forces, but as an active movement toward the human, evoking a certain feeling (*Gefühl*), is the origin of religion, 'raised above all error' because it is primordial and inescapable—it precedes the organization of church and doctrine. But a feeling of what? Schleiermacher here pointed to its relation to the commonly experienced human feeling of dependence (*Abhangigkeit*), but in the religious case, this is a feeling of absolute dependence ('das Gefühl der schlechthinigen Abhangigkeit'). The fundamental intuition (*Auschauung*) through which the *Weltgeist* (spirit of the world) is apprehended, is not a mere emotion: it is a response of the whole person to what is God.

In 1800, he applied his understanding to ethics in *Monologen* (Soliloquies), and after some years of pastoral work, he became Professor of Theology at Halle. The disruption caused by the Napoleonic wars sent him to pastoral work in Berlin (from which came his 'Dialogue on the Incarnation'), until he returned to the reconstituted Humboldt University of Berlin. There he produced *Der Christliche Glaube* . . . (The Christian Faith), in which every religion is seen as the consequence of the feeling of absolute dependence, but Christianity derives from 'the Ideal Representative of Religion', i.e. from Jesus of Nazareth whose consciousness was entirely taken up with this awareness of God. Christians (in the true sense) are those whose feeling of absolute dependence has been renewed through the work of Christ.

K. W. Clements, *Schleiermacher* (1987); R. R. Niebuhr, *Schleiermacher on Christ and Religion* (1965); M. Redeker, *Schleiermacher* . . . (1973).

Schneur Zalman of Lyady (founder of movement in Judaism): see SHNE'UR, ZALMAN.

Scholasticism. A Christian intellectual movement which endeavoured to penetrate, and perhaps to bring into a single system, the fundamental (especially revealed) articles of faith by use of reason. It flourished in the 13th cent., and is characterized by the production of *Summae* (i.e. summations) of theology and philosophy. The best known of these are the *Summae* of Thomas *Aquinas. The method of scholasticism was that of disputation, in which problems were divided into parts, objections were raised and answered, and a conclusion was reached. Scholasticism was thus an assertion of the responsibility of reason in relation to revelation. *Augustine (*De Doctrina Christiana*) had urged the use of dialectics in the study of doctrine, and John Scotus *Eriugena had distinguished between authority (in scripture) and reason, whose task it is to investigate data supplied by authority. When Greek philosophy, especially Aristotle, permeated the West (mediated through Islam), scholasticism developed in major (and often conflicting) branches—e.g. Augustinians, Latin Averroists, Dominicans. Scholasticism as a programme in the relation between faith and reason, and with controlling constraint from Aquinas, was revived in the 19th and early 20th cents. in *neo-Thomism. In the *encyclical, *Aeterni Patris* (1879), *Leo XIII encouraged the study of Aquinas.

M.-D. Chenu, *Nature, Man and Society in the Twelfth Century* (1968) and *Toward Understanding of St Thomas* (1964); F. C. Copleston, *A History of Medieval Philosophy* (1990); M. D. Jordan (ed.), *Medieval Philosophy and Theology* (1991); N. Kretzman *et al.*, *The Cambridge History of*

Later Medieval Philosophy (1982); P. E. Persson, *Sacra Doctrina: Reason and Revelation in Aquinas* (tr. 1970); J. Pieper, *Scholastik . . .* (Eng. tr., *Scholasticism*, 1961).

School of the Three Stages. A Chinese Buddhist school founded by Hsin-hsing (540–94 CE) during the Sui dynasty (581–618). The three stages were based on the idea that the teachings of the *Buddha may be divided into three periods; pure *dharma, duration 500 years; counterfeit dharma, duration 1,000 years; decay of the dharma, said to last 10,000 years. Hsin-hsing taught that his age was already the third stage, and pointed out the signs of decay then existing, such as non-conformity with the rules of monastic discipline, prevalence of heresies, failure to distinguish between right and wrong, etc. For this age, he prescribed strict adherence to the monastic rules and considered all living beings to be possessors of the *buddha-nature. As such, they were all worthy of respect. The school also advocated the performance of altruistic deeds and almsgiving. To carry out these deeds, the school relied mainly on the income of the Inexhaustible Treasury established in the Hua-tu Monastery in Ch'ang-an. The emphasis on almsgiving encouraged donations and contributions from faithful followers to the Treasury, resulting in a situation that no matter how much was spent on social welfare services, the Treasury was always replenished by donations, hence the designation Inexhaustible Treasury. It was said that the donors brought their gifts by the cartload and then disappeared without leaving their names. The income of the Treasury was divided into three portions, one for the repair of the temples and monasteries, one for social welfare, and one for ceremonies to the Buddha. Because the school insisted that it taught the sole formula for salvation during the age of decay, it met with opposition from other schools of Buddhism. Again, its contention that the contemporary age was one of depravity and lawlessness, and that the ruling government was not worthy of respect, was unacceptable to the ruling dynasty. The T'ang emperors therefore condemned the school as heretical and ordered the Inexhaustible Treasury dissolved in 721, with its enormous wealth seized and distributed to other monasteries. Its scriptures were also proscribed. These actions on the part of the rulers sealed the fate of the school.

Schools of Law, Muslim (Arab., *madhab*, pl., *madhāhib*, 'direction'). Muslim life is founded on *Qur'ān, which itself was first expressed in the lives and words of the Prophet *Muḥammad and his *Companions. Their words and actions were collected in aḥādith (*ḥadīth), and these become exemplary in Muslim life. Even so, not every circumstance was covered, so application of these sources to life became necessary. These eventually issued in (among *Sunni Muslims) four major schools of law (*sharīʿa), named after their founders: (i) Mālikite (*Mālik ibn Anas), which relies on the customary interpretations of *Madīna, and puts less reliance on methods of exegesis such as *ijmāʿ (consensus) or *ra'y* (informed opinion); (ii) *Hanīfite (*Abū Ḥanīfa), seeking consensus, and prepared to use methods of exegesis to make sharīʿa readily applicable; (iii) Shāfiʿite (Muḥammad b. Idrīs *al-Shāfiʿī), seeking rules to govern the methods of exegesis, which is thus kept under control, the school mediating between innovative and conservative; (iv) *Hanbalite (Aḥmad *ibn Ḥanbal), conservative and defensive of early patterns of observation. In the Muslim world, (i) is strong in W. Africa and the Arab west, (ii) in the former *Ottoman Empire and the Indian subcontinent, (iii) in the far East, (iv) in Saudi Arabia and Qatar. Each school regards the others as legitimate, but a Muslim is expected to live within the pattern of one of them: eclecticism (*talfiq*) is discouraged. There is also a number of *Shīʿa schools, though by its nature, Shīʿa Islam is less strongly organized in a centralized sense.

Schopenhauer, Arthur (1788–1860). German essayist and philosopher who developed a closely knit system in which was emphasized the primacy of the will over both reason and sensation. The world as a whole and every individual in it are said to be governed by blind, unconscious striving, which cannot be successfully overcome by wilful opposition (since that, too, is a striving), but only through resignation and detachment leading to serenity. Much indebted to *Kant (regarding himself as the 'only true Kantian'), Schopenhauer was also greatly influenced by Indian thought, which he held paralleled Kant in every key respect. He attributed this parallelism to the indirect influence of ancient Eastern thought on modern Western thought through the mediation of Christianity, whose founder—he deduced—must have been familiar with Hindu and Buddhist ideas, so that from its inception 'Christianity has had Indian blood in its veins'. Schopenhauer had little time for Judaism or Islam and used every opportunity to emphasize that Christianity is nearer in essence to Buddhism than it is to either of its radically monotheistic cousins. Not surprisingly, a favourite saying of his was, *Simplicitas sigillum veritatis* (simplicity is a sign of truth). His major work was *Die Welt als Wille und Vorstellung* (1819; tr. 1883, *The World as Will and Idea*).

P. L. Gardiner, *Schopenhauer* (1963); D. W. Hamlyn, *Schopenhauer* (1985); B. Magee, *The Philosophy of Pessimism* (1988).

Schütz, H. (composer of Christian works): see MUSIC.

Schweitzer, Albert (1875–1965). Christian theologian and mission doctor. A superb musician and organist, he made a name in academic circles when he published *Das Messianitats- und Leidensgeheimnis* (1901; *The Mystery of the Kingdom of God*, 1925). In this he argued that 'Jesus' is embedded in the interests and presuppositions of the *gospel writers, and to an extent, therefore, remains to us as 'One unknown'. What at least can be said is that Jesus shared the *apocalyptic expectations of his contemporaries, and that he saw himself as the one who was to inaugurate the Final Kingdom, not least through his sacrificial suffering. This 'messianic secret' was not divulged to any until the so-called 'Confession at Caesarea Philippi'. His extreme call for moral perfection was unrealistic if understood as a programme for life and history, but not if it was intended as an 'interim ethic', to be maintained in the short interval before the inauguration of the kingdom. Despite this misconception, Jesus still makes the demand of absolute love upon us in his own example:

> He comes to us as One unknown, without a name, as of old, by the lakeside, he came to those men who knew him not. He speaks to us the same words: 'Follow thou me!' and sets us to the tasks which he has to fulfil for our time. He commands. And to those who obey him, whether they be wise or simple, he will reveal himself in the toils, the conflicts, the sufferings, which they shall pass through in his fellowship, and, as an ineffable mystery, they shall learn in their own experience who he is.

Schweitzer developed this perspective further in *Von Reimarus zu Wrede* . . . (1906; *The Quest for the Historical Jesus*, 1910), and in *Geschichte der Paulinischen Forschung* . . . (1911; *Paul and his Interpreters*, 1912). These works set an inescapable agenda for subsequent work on the New Testament; yet his most enduring work was *Die Mystik des Apostels Paulus* (1930; The Mysticism of Paul the Apostle). Meanwhile a profound experience of the unity of all life, evoking reverence for life, led him to establish a mission hospital at Lambaréné in Gabon, where he based himself for the rest of his life. Although criticized for his stern paternalism, his commitment and his work for reconciliation were recognized with the award of the Nobel Peace Prize in 1964.

J. Brabazon, *Albert Schweitzer* . . . (1975); N. S. Griffith and L. Person, *Albert Schweitzer: An International Bibliography* (1981).

Science and religion. The relationship between science and religion has been described in various ways, falling between two extremes. At one extreme, the relationship is seen as one of warfare, as in the titles of two 19th cent. books, J. W. Draper, *History of the Conflict Between Religion and Science* (1874), and A. D. White, *A History of the Warfare of Science with Theology* (1896). Influential examples of the warfare model include R. Dawkins, in, for example, *The Selfish Gene* (1989), *The Extended Phenotype* (1982), *The Blind Watchmaker* (1986), and *Viruses of the Mind* (1992)—but see J. W. Bowker, *Is God a Virus?: Genes, Culture and Religion* (1995) for a critique. At the other extreme, the relationship is seen as one of convergence and confirmation, in which the insights of religion (albeit expressed in prescientific languages) are seen to point to the same truths as those claimed in contemporary sciences, as in A. de Riencourt, *The Eye of Shiva* . . . (1980): 'The new picture of the universe disclosed by contemporary physics appears to be largely in accord with Eastern metaphysics'. Wide-selling examples of the latter approach include F. Capra, *The Tao of Physics* (1975), G. Zukav, *The Dancing Wu Li Masters* (1979); for a critique, see R. H. Jones, *Science and Mysticism: A Comparative Study of Western Natural Science, Theravada Buddhism and Advaita Vedanta* (1986). Between the extremes are many different ways of evaluating the possible relationship between science and religion. Ian Barbour (*Religion in an Age of Science*, 1990) classified them in four groups: conflict, independence (as enterprises they are so different that there is no connection between them), dialogue, and integration. All these can be exemplified in any religion. There may indeed be conflict (especially if revelation is understood to require particular propositional allegiance in matters where scientific claims are different), but equally religions have been the resource and inspiration of much science: obvious examples are in China (see J. Needham, *Science and Civilisation in China*, 1954–86), India (see D. P. Singhal, *India and World Civilization*, 1972), Islam (words beginning with the Arabic definite pronoun *al-* are a trace of this, al-gebra, al-kali, al-gorithm, al-chemy, al-embic, etc.; see S. H. Nasr, *Science and Civilisation in Islam*, 1968; *Islamic Science: An Illustrated Study*, 1976) and Christianity: where religions in general and Christianity in particular are often accused of idle speculation, summarized in the accusation that they are preoccupied with counting the angels on the head of a pin, in fact that issue was a precise way of raising a crucial matter in the history of mathematics: 'So complex was the issue underlying that discussion (concerning potential or actual infinities) that it was not until the end of the nineteenth century that it was resolved by Cantor in favour of actual infinities' (J. W. Bowker, *Licensed Insanities: Religions and Belief in God in the Contemporary World*, 1987).

In the field of science and religion, a weakness of much work is its assumption that there is some 'thing' called science and some 'thing' called religion whose relationship can be discussed. Science changes, both in content and in methodologies, and religions have changed greatly through the course of time (for the consequent problem of defining religion, see Introduction). Furthermore, in most discussion, religion and theology are subsumed, whereas in fact theology would be better considered in the domain of theory-construction, and religion in the domain of human explorations of its own nature and environment (i.e. somatic exploration and exegesis: see Introduction). Religions are systems for the protection and transmission of human achievements and discoveries. For the most part, they arise from goals, methods, and objectives which are very different from those of the sciences, hence the impossibility of reducing the one to the other. But this means that religions can hardly be in competition with the sciences as comparable *systems*, even though the sciences will frequently challenge the content and methodologies of religious exploration, and religions will challenge the dehumanizing applications of science where they occur. For that reason particular issues will constantly arise, as notoriously in the case of Galileo and Darwin. But there neither was, nor is, only one way in which religions respond to such challenges. There are, and have been in the past, many different ways in which achievements in the sciences have been evaluated, ranging from denial to appropriation. Leaving aside individual responses, the responses of those who control or operate religious systems (i.e. the officials or authorities of the system) are almost invariably *strategic*. They are strategies adopted by control-figures to maintain the integrity of the system and their own authority. There is nothing *within religion itself* which dictates which strategy must be adopted. Thus there can be major changes in attitude and strategy, as well as different, even competing, strategies at any one time. It is instructive to compare the reinstatement of Galileo by the Vatican in 1983 (see P. Poupard (ed.), *Galileo Galilei: Toward a Resolution of 350 Years of Debate, 1633–1983*, 1987) with the maintaining of literalism in the relating of death to Adam and Eve, in *The Catechism of the Catholic Church* (1994). Different (and strictly speaking incompatible) strategies have been adopted in order to maintain authority and control. Thus while there will always be propositional and conceptual issues between science and religion, and while they are often both interesting and important, they are second-order issues. Of primary concern are the issues of power, authority and control.

M. A. Arbib and M. B. Hesse, *The Construction of Reality* (1986); I. G. Barbour, *Religion in an Age of Science* (1990); H. Rolston, *Science and Religion . . .* (1987); N. Murphey, *Theology in an Age of Scientific Reasoning* (1990).

Science of hearts (Sūfī description of the work of one of the earliest Sūfīs): see ḤASAN AL-BAṢRĪ.

Scientology. The creation of L. Ron *Hubbard, who in the early 1950s, using his theory of lay psychotherapy (Dianetics) as its basis, developed a religious philosophy which was then incorporated into the Church of Scientology. While Dianetics deals in the main with the 'reactive mind' (the subconscious), Scientology is concerned with the 'Thetan' or everlasting spirit.

Scientology holds that human beings, in essence spiritual beings, are overwhelmed by guilt feelings accumulated during countless reincarnations. However, through 'auditing' (counselling) sessions the Thetan or spirit is released from this 'pre-clear' state and the individual, now in a state of 'clear', can contribute to making this planet 'clear', and to building a paradise of happy, fulfilled people. The movement has been accused of aggressive and on occasion unlawful methods in its ways of recruitment and its methods of defence against critics, so that its short history has been surrounded by controversy.

R. Wallis, *Road to Total Freedom* (1976).

Scillitan Martyrs. Seven men and five women of Scillium in N. Africa who were put to death in 180 when they refused to renounce Christianity and swear by the 'genius' of the Roman emperor. The contemporary account of their martyrdom shows that the officials sought a recantation, but that the martyrs refused any compromise.

Lat. text with Eng. tr. in H. Musurillo (ed.), *The Acts of the Christian Martyrs* (1972), 86–9.

Scofield, Cyrus I. (1843–1921). American biblical scholar, and editor of the *Scofield Reference Bible* (1909; new edns. 1919, 1967). Its good typography and tacit rejection of all 'higher criticism' made it enormously popular in conservative Protestantism, and so secured an audience for its *dispensationalist teaching. Scofield's views appear in his notes and cross-references and in headings within the text which give the impression that dispensationalism is inherent in the biblical text itself.

Scopes trial (for teaching of Darwinism): see CREATIONISM.

Scotus (medieval Christian philosopher): see DUNS SCOTUS.

Scotus Eriugena (neoplatonic philosopher): see ERIUGENA.

Scribe (Heb., *sofer*). Copier of Jewish documents, also a recognized transmitter and scholar of Jewish law. In the biblical period, scribes (pl. *soferim*) were attached to all government and *temple offices—the highest position being that of royal scribe. It has been suggested that '*Ezra the scribe' as a title indicates his position in the Persian court (Ezra 7. 6). In the *rabbinic period and subsequently, scribes were professional inscribers of *Torah *Scrolls, *tefillin, *mezuzot, and *gittim* (bills of divorce: see MARRIAGE). *Masseketh* or *Hilkoth Soferim* is one of the Minor Tractates in the *Talmud dealing with scribal matters. A scribe should be in a state of ritual *purity before writing a Torah Scroll, and it is customary for him to visit a *mikveh. So important is his work that a scholar is forbidden to live in a town without a scribe (*B.Sanh.* 17b). The decrees transmitted by scribes are known as *dibre soferim* ('words of the scribes'), *tikkune soferim* ('corrections of the scribes'), and *dikduke soferim* ('minutiae of the scribes').

Scripture. Texts regarded as sacred (usually revealed: see REVELATION), having authority and often collected into an accepted *canon. Despite the origin of the word (Lat., *scripto*, 'I write'), most religious scriptures began as recited texts, being preserved in orally transmitted forms: the *Vedas of the Hindus were written down only because the world moved into the degenerate *Kāli yuga; *oral law (*Torah she beʿal peh*) was as much revealed on *Sinai as was written Torah; the *Qur'ān was not written down until after the death of *Muḥammad; and the Pāli canon was not committed to writing until (theoretically) the First *Council, though in fact much later. Christianity is an apparent exception only because it originated as an interpretation of what the Jewish covenant should be, and thus shared Jewish scripture (so far as it was established at that time); yet even here there is a connection, since the teaching of Jesus was initially passed on orally (see B. Gerhardsson, *Memory and Manuscript*, 1961; *Tradition and Transmission in Early Christianity*, 1964). When scriptures were eventually written down, it often remained a primary religious act to recite (rather than read) scripture, and to do so correctly: in the case of the Qur'ān (*tajwīd), the recitation of the Arabic text may be made by a reciter who does not understand Arabic. The definition of scripture may be a long (and sometimes contested) process: thus the canons of Jewish and Christian scripture took many centuries to achieve; and in the Christian case, agreement has not yet been reached. Despite the possible haze at the edges of a canon, scripture, once achieved, becomes a major constraint over outcomes in the lives of believers, although the ways in which scripture is related to life are themselves also disputed (see HERMENEUTICS): the historical embeddedness of scripture (i.e. the fact that however eternal the Word may be, it is manifested in a language in the midst of time) gives a natural bias to at least a species of *fundamentalism, since it relates present-day life to a supreme moment of revelation.

For different scriptures, see Index, Canonical Collections.

H. Coward, *Sacred Word and Sacred Text: Scripture in World Religions* (1988); F. M. Denny and R. L. Taylor (eds.), *The Holy Book in Comparative Perspective* (1985); G. Lanczkowski, *Sacred Writings* (1966).

Scroll of the Law (Heb., *sefer torah*). The scroll on which the Jewish *Pentateuch is inscribed. The Scroll of the law is always used for public reading in the *synagogue. It is composed of strips of vellum or parchment, which are sewn together to form a roll, each end of which is attached to a wooden stave and rolled towards the middle. It is written by a qualified *scribe and, when not in use, it is kept in the *synagogue *Ark. It is the most revered of ritual objects: it is customary to stand when a Scroll is in human sight. If it has to be removed from the synagogue, it is wrapped in a *tallit (prayer shawl). The last of the 613 commandments is that each Jew should write a scroll, or, if (as often) this is impracticable, should contribute to the writing of at least one letter. *Sefer Torah* is the title of a Minor Tractate in the Talmud, concerned mainly with guidance for scribes.

Scrolls, Five (Heb., *Ḥamesh Megillot*). The five shortest books of the Hebrew scriptures. The Five Scrolls are the Books of *Ecclesiastes, *Esther, *Lamentations, *Ruth, and the *Song of Songs. The Song of Songs is read on the intermediate *Sabbath of *Passover; Ruth is read on *Shavuʿot; Lamentations on 9 *Av; Ecclesiastes on the intermediate Sabbath of *Sukkot; and Esther on *Purim.

Seal of Confession. The obligation and commitment that nothing said in *confession will be revealed to any other person.

Seal of recognition (mark of succession in Zen Buddhism): see INKA-SHŌMEI.

Seal of the Fathers (Patriarch of Alexandria and Church Father): see CYRIL, ST.

Seal of the Prophets/prophecy (Arab., *khatm al-anbiyya, khatm al-nubuwwah*). Title of the prophet *Muḥammad, indicating that he is the last prophet whose message supersedes that of earlier prophets (e.g. *Moses, *Jesus). Whereas the message of earlier prophets, which in content was the same, had been corrupted by those who heard it for their own ends, the Qur'ān remains as God revealed it through Muḥammad. No further prophet, therefore, will appear. Jesus (i.e. ʿĪsā) is known as *khatm al-wilāyah*, 'the seal of sanctity', because he expressed his inner holiness to the highest degree in outward word and action.

Seamless pagoda, the (part of a kōan): see NAN-YANG.

Sebastian, St. Roman Christian martyr who is believed to have died in the persecution of Diocletian (late 3rd cent.). According to a legend of the 5th cent. he was sentenced by Diocletian to be shot by archers, but recovered from his wounds and reappeared before the emperor, who then caused him to be clubbed to death. As a young man transfixed by arrows he was an extremely popular subject for Renaissance artists. Feast day, 20 Jan.

Second Coming (of Christ to earth): see PAROUSIA.

Second days. Additional holy day or days observed by Jews living in the *diaspora at the *festivals of *Passover, *Shavuʿot and *Sukkot. The need for them arose from the problem of securing the observation of the New Moon, on which the date of the festivals (and subsequent festivals or fasts) depend. Of old, eye-witnesses reported to the *Sanhedrin, who then sent messengers to convey the information. During the last days of the Second Temple, the system broke down, and Jews in the diaspora began to keep two holy days (both at the beginning and at the end) of the three festivals. When a fixed *calendar was introduced in the 4th cent. CE, Jews in Babylon asked the authorities in the land of Israel whether these 'two festivals of the Exile' (*yom tov sheni shel galuyyot*) should be discontinued. They were told that so long-standing a custom should be continued even though the reason for it had disappeared.

Second diffusion (of Buddhism in Tibet): see TIBETAN RELIGION.

Second Rome. *Constantinople, which, after the sack of *Rome in 476, became the capital of the Christian world. When Constantinople fell to the Turks in 1453, Moscow claimed to be the Third Rome, as in the letter of Philotheus of Pskov to the Tsar, Basil III, 'Two Romes have fallen, but the third stands, and there will not be a fourth.'

Secret societies, Chinese. Unlawful associations in China were of two main kinds, the brotherhoods (*hui*) of sworn association, pursuing secular ends, often of a criminal kind, and the religious (*chiao*) associations pursuing healing and salvation by unorthodox means. Membership could often overlap, and the current term, *mimi shehui* (adopted from Japanese) covers both. The Triads are not a single society, but a number of branches, each of which shares a common system of signs, initiation rites, etc., engaging in activities outside the law, and often characterized by anti-government activities. See Index, Secret Societies.

J. Chesneaux (ed.), *Popular Movements and Secret Societies in China, 1840–1950* (1972); F. Davis, *Primitive Revolutionaries of China* (1971).

Secrets of Enoch (apocalyptic text): see ENOCH.

Sects. Groups, usually religious, which are set up with their own organization in distinction from, and often in protest against, established religions. Sects featured in *Troeltsch's *Church–Sect typology, but it is clear that a much wider understanding of sects is required. Thus H. R. *Niebuhr (*The Social Sources of Denominationalism*, 1929) regarded the dichotomy as too simple, and argued that it needed to be supplemented by 'denomination': sects are necessarily short-lived and transient, either disappearing or becoming a denomination with more stable structure and organization. Sects are characterized by: depending on volunteers (to be born into a sect indicates that it is on the way to stability); *charismatic authority; strict discipline with clear rules of conduct; sense of élite privilege (of being the only ones in a true, or enlightened, or saved state); restriction on individuality. In addition, R. Wallis (*Salvation and Protest*, 1979) suggested that sects are either world-affirming (seeing power, value, etc., emerging from within the universe) or world-denying (seeing the world as evil and requiring rescue by God). Attempts to map sects on to particular social strata (e.g. the underprivileged) have been defeated by the recognition that sects can emerge at almost any social level. For examples, see Index, Sects, movements, etc.

M. Hill, *A Sociology of Religion* (1973).

Sect Shinto. Official (i.e. registered with the Ministry of Education) Shinto organizations in Japan. They are assigned (chronologically) to one of three categories: jinja Shinto (Shrine Shinto, founded before the modern era), *kyōha Shinto (Sect Shinto, autonomous organizations authorized between 1868 and 1945—i.e. *Meiji to end of the Second World War), and shin kyōha Shinto (New Sect Shinto, post-1945). All of these very many movements have been discussed academically as *new religions, but some are clearly newer than others. For lists, addresses, and some brief descriptions, see *Japanese Religion*, a survey issued by the Agency for Cultural Affairs.

Secular clergy. Christian priests who live in the world (Lat., *saeculum*), as distinguished from members of religious communities who live according to a rule ('regular clergy'). They are not bound by vows and may possess property, and they owe obedience to their bishops.

Secular institutes. Organizations among *Roman Catholics whose members, lay or ordained, are committed to common rules while living in the world, without making public vows or wearing distinctive dress (*habit). They received papal approval in 1947.

G. Reidy, *Secular Institutes* (1962).

Secularization (Lat., *saeculum*, 'age' or 'world', i.e. this world). The (supposed) process whereby people, losing confidence in otherworldly or supernatural accounts of the cosmos and its destiny, abandon religious beliefs and practices, or whereby religion loses its influence on society. Secularization is an elusive and much-debated concept. In origin, the term referred to the alienation of Church property to the State, and thence to the loss of temporal power by the Church. It referred also to the process whereby ordained clergy reverted to the lay state. It then came more loosely to refer to the transition from the religious to the non-religious world. At this preliminary level, it is possible to treat religion and the secular at the level of *ideology (despite the fact that ideology is itself a complex concept), and to understand the process as one in which one ideology is compelled to give way to another. This is the account offered by D. Cupitt in a widely read book, *The Sea of Faith* (1984):

> To secularise something means to transfer it from the sacred to the secular realm . . .. However, that implies that the sacred is being methodically stripped and in the end completely swallowed by a confident, well-organised and self-conscious secular power . . .. The shift, then, is from myths to maths, from animism to mechanism, and from explanation down from above to explanation up from below.

The weakness of this account is that it fails to recognize the fact that religions in novel circumstances react in vastly different ways, ranging from adaptation to resistance, but more frequently by failing to act as ideology at all, and by doing complementary, not competitive things. More responsibly, therefore, Bryan Wilson proposed the 'secularization thesis' (e.g. *Religion in Secular Society*, 1966). Defining secularization as 'the process whereby religious thinking, practices and institutions lose social significance', he argued, not that people have necessarily lost interest in religion, nor that they have adopted a new ideology, but more restrictedly that religion has ceased to have any significance for the working of the social system. Many problems in this position have been exposed, ranging from the measures and methods of social significance (in the past as much as in the present) to the relevance of a contingent observation about the distribution of power to the understanding of religion. After all, the experiment of secularization in the sense of this thesis has been deliberately made in different societies, with extremely diverse consequences in the religious domain—suggesting that there are far too many variables for single, simple correlations to be established in the name of 'secularization': Communist countries attempted to enforce the predicted 'withering away' of religion under the dictatorship of the proletariat (and the persistence of religion in those countries took many different forms, not least in China); India was established, formally and legally, as a secular state following Independence (see D. E. Smith, *India as a Secular State*, 1963); the separation of Church and State was very carefully attempted in the American Constitution. Religions clearly duck and weave through the vicissitudes of history, and are not in some single and invariant conflict with a reality which can be defined as 'secularization'.

For these (and other) reasons, T. Luckmann argued that 'the notion of secularisation offers a largely fictitious account of the transformations of religion in Western society during the past centuries' (*Life-World and Social Realities*, 1983), and called this spurious account 'the myth of secularisation': its basic mistake is to tie religion to the institutional forms it has happened to take, and then to measure religion by the fortunes (or misfortunes) of those institutions. In so far as there is a biogenetic base for religious behaviours in the human brain (see BIOGENETIC STRUCTURALISM), then clearly Luckmann's insistence on a more careful attention to what humans do with their religious preparedness (in the brain) is necessary. The explanation of the occurrence of *new religious movements in an age of claimed secularization has been central to the secularization debate, but it is only a minor aspect of that to which Luckmann is calling attention. Nevertheless, there have clearly been major changes in human knowledge and technology, and equally major changes in the exercise of power in political and other systems. Certainly these have had their effect on religions, as changes of such magnitude always do. It may be, therefore, that the phenomena which have evoked the term 'secularization' would be much better considered as a consequence of roughly three centuries of often bitter struggle to maximize the autonomy of individuals and (increasingly in contradiction) of markets. In political terms, the consequence of the struggle is referred to as 'democracy'. It is a commitment to the maximum freedom of choice for individuals and groups within the boundary of law. It is, in brief, a preferential option for options. But quite apart from its pressure to disentangle Church from State, it also has had the consequence of making religion optional, where once it was less so. But this understanding of secularization, while it does indeed raise problems for institutions, and may drive them to 'market' themselves as though a commodity, does not threaten the basic 'religiousness' of humanity; for the supposition that *Weber's 'shift to rationalisation' will leave religions behind has proved already to be false.

R. K. Fenn, *Towards a Theory of Secularisation* (1978); P. E. Hammond (ed.), *The Sacred in a Secular Age* (1985); N. Luhmann, *Funktion der Religion* (1977); D. Martin, *A General Theory of Secularisation* (1978).

Secularization Thesis: see SECULARIZATION.

Sedarim. The six orders (or divisions) of the Jewish *Mishnah.

Sedarot. Portions of the *Pentateuch read in the Jewish *synagogue on the *Sabbath. Each sidrah (sing.) has a distinctive name taken from the first important word in the text. The Pentateuch is divided into fifty-four sedarot so that the entire work is read each year.

Seder (Heb., 'Order'). The order of a Jewish service, especially the home ceremony normally used at the festival of *Passover. In the *diaspora, the Seder takes place on two consecutive nights; in *Erez Israel, it is celebrated on the first night of Passover (see SECOND DAYS). The structure of the ritual is laid down in the *Mishnah *Pesaḥim* 10. Its essential features include the recitation of the *Kiddush prayer, the reading of the *Haggadah, the sharing of special foods (e.g. *mazzah, *maror), the eating of a festive meal, the drinking of four cups of wine at specified intervals, the recitation of the *Hallel, the singing of Passover songs, and the concluding cry, 'La-shanah ha-ba'ah bi-Yerushalayim' (*Next year in Jerusalem).

Seder 'Olam (Order of the World). Two Jewish chronicles. Written in Hebrew, the *Seder 'Olam Rabbah* is mentioned in the *Talmud and is a *midrashic chronology from the Creation of the world to the *Bar Kokhba revolt. It is said to have been written by R. Johanan (3rd cent.) and Yose b. Ḥalafta (2nd cent.), and was the first book to establish the era AM (*anno mundi*, in the year of the world) which was adopted in the Jewish community *c.*9th cent. The *Seder 'Olam Zuta*, written in a mixture of Heb. and Aramaic, traces the chronology of the generations from *Adam until the end of the Babylonian *exilarchate. Scholars disagree on its date of composition.

See. The seat (Lat., *sedes*) of a Christian *bishop; hence the town or district surrounding the cathedral (where the bishop has his *cathedra*, or throne), is known as the see. See also HOLY SEE.

Seed mantra/syllable (power underlying appearance in Indian religions): see BĪJA.

Sefer ha-Aggadah (Book of Aggadah): see AGGADAH.

Sefer ha-Bahir (Jewish Kabbalistic work): see BAHIR, SEFER HA-.

Sefer ha-Ḥayyim (Jewish heavenly book containing names of the righteous): see BOOK OF LIFE.

Sefer Ḥasidim (The Book of the Holy Ones). A popular Jewish text describing the way of the *Ḥasid. It is attributed to Judah the Ḥasid of Regensburg of the 13th cent., but it is a compilation of stories, maxims, and expositions coming from different hands. It contains much popular and folk-belief, in addition to its moral teaching. There is strong insistence on charity and on scrupulously honest dealings with gentiles.

Sefer ha-Jashar (Israelite book of poetry): see BOOK OF JASHAR.

Sefer Torah (scroll on which Pentateuch is inscribed): see SCROLL OF THE LAW.

Sefirot. Jewish *kabbalistic term meaning God's emanations. There are ten sefirot that emerge from *Ein Sof. Each one points to a different aspect of God's creative nature, and together they compose the world of divine light in the chain of being. All ten together form a dynamic unit, sometimes portrayed as a tree, by which God's activity is revealed. The three highest sefirot are the Supreme Crown, *Wisdom, and Intelligence. The seven lower are Love, Power, Beauty, Endurance, Majesty, Foundation, and Kingdom. The whole concept is influenced by *gnostic thought and is an attempt to explain how a transcendent God can interact with the world.

Seichō no Ie (Jap., 'House of Growth'). A Japanese religion founded by Taniguchi Masaharu (1893–1985) in 1930. Central to the teachings of this movement, an offshoot from *Ōmotokyō, is the belief that all human beings are divine and equal in that they are all children of God. This is the 'liberating truth' which when perceived and acted upon not only gives rise to good, but leads to the conquest of disease and other such 'evils', which are the result of personal sin. What he called (and experienced as) 'the life of reality' (*jisso*) involves the realization that sin and illness have no reality in themselves. The movement is eclectic, drawing on many religions and regarding them as preparatory to itself.

Seigan (vows in Zen Buddhism): see SHIGUSEIGAN.

Seirai-no-i (Jap.). The coming of meaning from the west, the arrival of *Bodhidharma from India to China, and thus of the buddha-dharma with him.

Seiza (Jap., 'sitting in silence'). Zen position of meditation, kneeling on one's heels with straight back. In *zazen, it is an alternative to the lotus position (*padmāsana).

Sekai Kyūseikyō (Jap., 'The Religion for World Salvation'). Japanese religion founded by Okada Mokichi (1882–1955). Okada originally belonged to Ōmotokyō, until in 1926, it was revealed to him in a state of divine possession that he was the *messiah of the present age. He established Dainihon Kannonkai, focused on the *bodhisattva Kannon (see AVALOKITEŚVARA), with the purposes of establishing communion with Kannon and of healing. Required by the government to choose one or the other, he chose healing, and the movement was renamed Nihon Jōka Ryōhō. After the Second World War, he reverted to the two goals, calling the movement Nihon Kannon Kyōdan, but after a schism, he arrived at the present name. Faith-healing is central in the movement, under the name and technique of *jōrei*: this involves transmitting healing divine light through cupped hands. Equally important is *shizen nōhō*, agriculture that follows the way of nature. Just as *jōrei* carries with it the view that medicine is poisonous, so *shizen nōhō* carries with it the view that artificial fertilizers are harmful. Sekai Kyuseikyo believes that heaven on earth (*chijō tengoku*) can be established on earth at its centre at Atami. Museums and gardens exhibit the importance of harmony and beauty.

Sekishu (name for the koān, 'what is the sound of one hand clapping?'): see HAKUIN.

Sekisō Soen (Jap., for Shih-shuang Ch'u-yuan): see KŌAN.

Self-Realization Fellowship. Founded by the Indian *guru Paramhansa Yogananda (1893–1953) in Boston, Mass., in 1920. Yogananda taught specific yoga techniques to develop soul awareness and a form of meditation which heightens consciousness to the point where it becomes one with that of the guru. According to the founder and his disciples, Christianity and Hinduism are basically in harmony, in that the *yoga taught by *Christ and *Kṛṣṇa were the same. Moreover, all true religions share the same principles of truth. Only on completion of the second course in meditation can students be initiated by a minister and become formal members of the Fellowship, which is administered by monks and nuns who have taken monastic vows.

Seliḥot. Penitential prayers seeking forgiveness (Heb., *seliḥah*), forming in effect an additional Jewish prayer-service for fast days and the penitential season. The *Mishnah gives six additional blessings to be recited with the *ʿAmidah on fast days, and the *tannaim taught that the order of Seliḥot was revealed by God to *Moses in the thirteen attributes revealed in Exodus 34. 6 f. (see e.g. *BRH* 17b). Different communities have produced different rites. The *Sephardim usually recite seliḥot for forty days from Rosh Ḥodesh Elul (see NEW YEAR) to *Yom Kippur, while the *Ashkenazim begin on the Sunday before *Rosh ha-Shanah. Seliḥot are also recited on all official fast days.

A. Rosenfeld, *The Authorised Selichot for the Whole Year* (1957).

Semikhah (Heb., 'laying on' (of hands)). The Jewish rite of *ordination. In biblical times, leaders were ordained by the laying on of hands (e.g. Numbers 27. 22; 11. 16–17). Membership of the Great *Sanhedrin required ordination, and it was agreed by the time of *Judah ha-Nasi that religious decisions could only be made by those qualified (*B.Sanh.* 5b). The formula for Semikhah was 'Yoreh Yoreh. Yaddin Yaddin' ('May he decide? He may decide! May he judge? He may judge!'); and in the early days any ordained teacher could ordain his students, although the rite was restricted to *Erez Israel (see RABBI). From the 5th cent., license to judge was often accompanied by an official document, and from the 12th cent., there was a tendency, particularly among the Ashkenazim, to call the document 'semikhah'. There have been various attempts over the centuries to restore the Sanhedrin and thus restore semikhah in its original sense. This has been opposed on the grounds that it is anticipating the *messianic era. None the less, by the 13th cent. neo-semikhah documents began to contain the old formula which continues to this day.

J. Newman, *Semikhah* (1950).

Semiotics (study of signs): see SYMBOLS.

Semi-Pelagians (Christians who believe that God's grace is a necessary precondition, but that works have status thereafter): see PREDESTINATION.

Semper reformanda (always to be reformed): see PRESBYTERIANISM.

Sen, Keshub (Keshab) Chunder (Chandra) (1838–84). Indian reformer, and third leader of *Brahmo Samāj. He came from a wealthy Calcutta family, related to the Sena kings of Bengal. He joined the Brahmo Samāj in 1857, working with Debendranāth *Tagore to promote its aims, and lecturing widely in English on theistic doctrine and Brahmo philosophy, establishing branches of the Samāj in Bombay, Madras, and other centres.

Throughout his life Sen claimed to have had mystical experiences, and to have received direct messages from God, whom he perceived as an ever-present Reality, brought near to the worshipper by contemplative prayer and repentance. He believed only God's power, invoked by prayer, could result in effective action. The influence of Christian missionaries is strong in Sen's teaching, not least in the addition to Brahmo *dharma of *baptism, the doctrine of the *Trinity, and the *Lord's Supper. He almost became a Christian in 1866, the only obstacle being an inability to accept the uniqueness of *Christ, though he turned against the philosophical system of Hinduism, including *Vedānta, supporting widow remarriage and repudiating the wearing of the sacred thread (*upanayana), finally breaking with Debendranāth Tagore in 1865. In 1866 he established the Bhāratvarshīya Brahmo Samāj, which preached the brotherhood of all under the Fatherhood of God, a teaching enshrined in the *Śloka-saṁgraha* scriptures.

Sen later adopted still more social reforms, such as the banning of child-marriage, the encouragement of the education and emancipation of Indian women, inter-caste marriage, temperance, literary programmes, and the establishment of schools and colleges for young men and workers. In 1872 the government legalized Brahmo marriages. He relied increasingly on direct inspiration, which enabled him, despite his previous opposition to child-marriage, to marry his 13-year-old daughter to a Hindu prince. Many of his followers abandoned him for this, setting up in 1878 Sādhāran (General) Brahmo Samāj. In 1879 he proclaimed a New Dispensation (Nava Vidhāna) to supplant Christianity: 'When I gathered truths from one set of scriptures, I have longed for others, and before finishing these I have looked out for others again, lest anything should become old or cold to me. This is my life.' He chose twelve disciples, promulgated the Motherhood of God, revived the *āratī* and *homa ceremonies, the *Durgā Pūjā festival, and the religious dance of *Caitanya, while urging that *idolatry and polytheism were forms of *theism. Although he became less influential the older he grew, he remained honoured and respected until his death, regarded as Brahmāṛishi by his fellow-countrymen.

M. Borthwick, *Keshub Chander Sen* . . . (1977); P. C. Mazoomdar, *The Life and Teachings of* . . . (1887).

Sengai Gibon (1751–1837). Outstanding Zen artist and calligrapher. He became a monk at 11, and went on wandering pilgrimage (*angya) when 19. He became dharma-successor (*hassu) of Gessen Zenji, and was appointed abbot of Shōfuku-ji in 1790. He was noted also for his humorous instruction.

D. T. Suzuki, *Sengai, the Zen Master.*

Senge (Jap., 'entering transformation'). Zen Buddhist term for death which stresses its transition-nature, and its inherent unimportance.

Seng-ts'an (Jap., Sōsan). Third patriarch (*soshigata) in the Ch'an Buddhist lineage in China, and dharma-successor (*hassu) of *Hui-k'o. He died in 606 CE, but nothing certain is otherwise known of him. He is said to have been attracted by *Laṅkāvatāra Sūtra*, which he received from Hui-k'o, and also to have written the poem *Hsin-hsin-ming* (Jap., *Shinjimei*, 'Inscribed on the Believing Mind'), but its union of Taoist and Mahāyāna ideas make this unlikely. It (especially its opening) is much quoted in Zen writings: 'The Perfect Way is not difficult | It only refuses to express preferences | Only when freed from hate and love | It reveals itself fully and without concealment.'

Eng. tr., D. T. Suzuki, *Essays in Zen Buddhism*, i. 196–201.

Sengyo (Jap., 'fish-run'). Zen expression derived from **Chuang-tzu* 31: 'A fish-run is constructed to catch fish: we should keep the fish and forget the run. A snare is to catch rabbits: we should keep the rabbits and forget the snare. Words are to transmit meaning: we should keep the meaning and forget the words.' *Sūtras, methods of *zazen, etc., are necessary, but only helpful if they are transcended and 'forgotten'.

Senju-Kannon (Skt., *Sahasrabhuja-sahasra-netra*, 'a thousand arms and a thousand eyes'). Kannon (see AVALOKITEŚVARA) with a thousand arms growing from the palm of each hand, each arm having an eye: this enables him to see all distress and act to alleviate it.

Senkō Kokushi. Posthumous title of *Eisai.

Sennin (Jap.). Immortal beings. The idea is of Chinese origin (*hsien-jen), associated with religious *Taoism and *alchemy. In the Ch'in and Han periods of China they were called *ch'ien-jen*, loosely rendered as 'man who ascends aloft', of whom the historian Ssu-ma Ch'ien spoke as the dwellers in the sacred mountains who sought for the medicine of immortality. When Taoism reached Japan is uncertain. Together with the spread of knowledge in religious Taoism among the Japanese gentry in the Nara period, the legends of Japanese sennin, like Kume no Sennin, possessing supernatural powers and riding clouds, began to appear. In Buddhism, the word sennin is one of the translations for the Sanskrit *ṛṣi. En no Gyōja, the supposed founder of *Shugendō, was also called a sennin.

Sen no Rikyū (formulator of tea ceremony): see CHADŌ.

Sensei (Jap., 'teacher'). In the Japanese tradition, a general term of respect accorded to, amongst others, university lecturers, instructors in the martial arts, priests of *Jōdo Shinshū Buddhism, and priests of *Zen Buddhism below the rank of *Rōshi.

Senshō-fuden (Jap., 'unable to be told by a thousand of the wise'). Zen insistence that truth cannot be carried or conveyed by words, but has to be recognized by an individual awareness or enlightenment. See also FUKASETSU.

Senusis (members of the Sanūsiya order): see AL-SANŪSĪ, SĪDĪ MUḤAMMAD.

Sephardim. Jews descended from those who lived in the Iberian Peninsula before 1492 (hence the name, Heb., *Sefarad*, Spain). However, the term 'Sephardim' is often also used to indicate all non-*Ashkenazi Jews. After the expulsion of the Jews from Spain in 1492, Jews settled in N. Africa, Italy, and the Turkish Empire. A century later, the *Marranos were also expelled; many reverted to Judaism and settled in Holland, England, America, France, and Germany. The Sephardi language is Ladino, a type of archaic Spanish; and Sephardic literature includes works in Hebrew and Spanish as well. The Sephardim, like the Ashkenazim, base their religious practice on the tenets of the *Talmud. However, they follow Joseph *Caro's **Shulḥān Arukh* without the amendments of Moses *Isserles, and thus their interpretation of the law tends to be more liberal (e.g. rice can be eaten at *Passover). Customs vary (e.g. phylacteries, *tefillin, are wound outwards rather than inwards), and there are considerable differences in *liturgy, Hebrew pronunciation, and nomenclature. From the 17th cent., the Sephardim declined in number relative to the Ashkenazim. Before the *holocaust, 90 per cent of Jewry was Ashkenazic. Today, there are just over thirty Sephardi *synagogues in the USA, fairly vibrant congregations in Central and S. America, and small congregations in W. Europe. As a result of worsening conditions, there have been large-scale emigrations from the communities in Muslim countries to *Israel since 1948, where there is a dual *Chief Rabbinate. In general, Sephardim have felt themselves to be put in second place by Ashkenazim, and only slowly have come to positions of authority in government. A Sephardi, Leon Tamman (1927–95) founded Taʿali, the World Movement for a United Israel, to reconcile the two communities, and progress was made as a result.

H. J. Zimmels, *Ashkenazim and Sephardim* (1958); L. Gubbay and A. Levy, *The Sephardim* (1992).

Seppō Gison (Japanese name): see HSÜEH-FENG I-TS'UN.

Seppuku (ritual suicide): see HARA-KIRI.

Septuagesima. The third Sunday before *Lent, nine weeks before *Easter. See also QUINQUAGESIMA.

Septuagint (often written LXX, the Latin numerals). The early Greek translation of the Hebrew scriptures inherited by the Christian Church. It is so-called because it was supposed to have been translated by seventy scholars (according to the *Letter of *Aristeas*, it was 72). The *Pentateuch was probably first translated in the early 3rd cent. in Alexandria, and the other books during the following two cents. The manuscripts comprise the Great Codices (the Alexandranicus, the Sinaiticus, and the Vaticanus), and numerous minor codices still survive. It differs from the Heb. text in having extra books (the *Apocrypha) and variant readings in many places, and in abandoning the divisions into 'Law', 'Prophets', and 'Writings'.

Sequence. A hymn, usually in couplets, sung in the *mass on certain days after the *epistle. In medieval times a large number of sequences (*c.*150 melodies and 400 texts, with at least 5,000 having been written) were in regular use, but in the *missal only five are now printed: the *Victimae paschali* (at *Easter), *Veni, Sancte Spiritus* (at *Pentecost), *Lauda Sion* (at *Corpus Christi), *Dies irae* (at All Souls', see ALL SAINTS), and **Stabat mater* (on the feast of the *Seven Sorrows of the Virgin Mary).

Seraph. Either a species of serpent mentioned in the Hebrew scriptures, or a type of *angelic being. In Numbers 21, God sends 'seraph-snakes' to punish the *Israelites, and *Moses makes a copper serpent when the Lord tells him to make a seraph. In *Isaiah's vision in the *Temple he sees seraphim with three pairs of wings (ch. 6). These are clearly semi-divine beings and are reminiscent of *Ezekiel's *cherubim (ch. 1). See also ANGEL.

Seraphim of Sarov (1759–1833). Russian monk and *staretz. Born in Kursk, he entered the monastery at Sarov *c.*1779. From 1794 he lived as a hermit, first in the nearby forest, later in a cell in the monastery. From 1825 he engaged in spiritual direction of his many visitors. He also founded a community of nuns. Severe in his personal asceticism, he was gentle with others, his spiritual teaching focusing on the joyful transfiguring power of the *Holy Spirit—expressed especially in a conversation with Nicolas Motovilov—though full of foreboding about the future of Russia.

V. Zander, *St Seraphim of Sarov* (1975).

Serendib. An old name for *Śri Lankā. It was derived from the Arab. version of the Skt. name Sinhala-dvipa (Pāli, Sihala-dvipa). The name was used during the Roman Empire. From it, Horace Walpole coined the word, 'serendipity', in *The Three Princes of Serendib* (1754).

Sergius (Sergii) of Radonezh, St (*c.*1314–92). Russian monastic reformer. Born at Rostov, as a boy he fled with his family to Radonezh near Moscow, where he founded with his brother the monastery of the Holy Trinity (and afterwards many others), thus reviving monasticism which had collapsed during the Tatar aggression. He was a great influence for peace, supporting Prince Dmitri in resisting the Tatars, thereby saving Russia. In 1378 he refused to become metropolitan of Moscow. He is regarded as one of the founders of Russia and the greatest of Russian saints. Feast day, 25 Sept.

M. Klimenko, *The 'Vita' of St Sergii of Radonezh* (1980); P. Kovalevsky, *Saint Sergius and Russian Spirituality* (1976).

Sermon on the Mount. A collection of sayings of *Jesus presented in Matthew 5–7 as a single discourse given 'on the mountain' (5. 1). It includes the *Beatitudes, *Lord's Prayer, *Golden Rule, and other ethical sayings. The 'sermon on the plain' in Luke 6. 20–49 is somewhat parallel though shorter.

W. D. Davies, *The Setting of the Sermon on the Mount* (1964).

Servant songs. Poems about a faithful servant of the Lord found in the Hebrew Book of *Isaiah. The Servant songs are located in Isaiah 42. 1–4; 49. 1–6; 50. 4–9; 52. 13–53. 12. The songs either have been interpreted collectively (see 49. 3)—the servant represents the Jewish people, the ideal *Israel, or the faithful *remnant—or have been understood to refer to a particular individual (e.g. the writer of the songs, Hezekiah, *Josiah, Zerubbabel, Cyrus, *Ezekiel, *Moses, *Job, etc.). In the Christian tradition, the songs are thought to point forward to the sufferings of Jesus. The question has been raised more recently whether it is correct to think of a group of Servant Songs at all.

C. R. North, *The Suffering Servant in Deutero-Isaiah*; T. N. D. Mettinger, *A Farewell to the Servant Songs* (1983).

Servetus, Michael, or **Miguel Serveto** (1511–53). Christian theologian. He was born in Spain and studied at Saragossa, Toulouse, and Paris. He turned from law to medicine which he practised intermittently throughout his life. During his travels he met *Bucer and perhaps some other *Anabaptist leaders. His interest in theology led him to produce *De Trinitatis Erroribus* (1531, On the Erroneous Understanding of the Trinity), in which he argued that the Son and the Holy Spirit are modes in which God manifests himself in creation, redemption, and sanctification, and that the Trinity is not made up of 'persons'. He reiterated these arguments in *Christianismi Restitutio* (1546, The Restoration of Christianity), by which time he had also argued against *predestination and infant baptism. He was arrested, first by the *Inquisition, and then (when he escaped to Geneva) by the Protestants. He was convicted and burnt to death, his death provoking debate about the bounds of tolerance.

R. H. Bainton, *Hunted Heretic . . .* (1953).

Śeṣa (Skt., 'remainder'). In Hindu mythology, the serpent which forms *Viṣṇu's couch and canopy during the periods between destruction and creation. Śeṣa is also called Ananta (Skt., 'endless'), and can be represented as supporting the earth and the regions which lie below it. *Kṛṣṇa's brother *Balarāma (or Saṃkarṣaṇa, as he is often called in this context) and *Rāma's brother *Lakṣmaṇa are both said to be human manifestations of Śeṣa.

Sesshin (Jap., 'collecting the heart-mind'). Days in Zen monasteries of particularly concentrated practice: long periods of *zazen are interrupted by only brief interludes of sleep, work, etc.

Sesshu Tōyō (1420–1506). A major Japanese Zen painter, considered by many the greatest master. He entered a Zen monastery when 12 and was trained at Shōkokuji in *Kyōto. He visited China, 1467–9, acquiring technical skills, returned to Japan, and after a period of wandering, settled near Yamaguchi. The control of his brush and line are a perfect expression of Zen control. 'The Four Seasons' is usually singled out as his masterpiece (see e.g. T. Hoover, *Zen Culture* (1977), p. 127), but 'Landscape in the Broken Ink Style' (ibid. 129) is an equally superb achievement.

Sesson Yubai (1288–1346). Japanese Zen master of the *Rinzai school. He was a pupil and dharma-successor (*hassu) of I-shan I-ning. In 1306/7 he went to China, where he was imprisoned for ten years, but also sought instruction from different masters, before returning to become abbot of Engaku-ji and Nanzen-ji. He was a writer of considerable care and style who is considered one of the founders of the *gosan-bungaku.

Setsubun (Jap.), the day before the beginning of spring, now celebrated on the 3 or 4 February. Setsubun, which means 'seasonal division', originally referred to the day before the beginning of the 24 divisions of the calendrical year, but it has become synonymous with the last day of the last division called *daikan* (great cold) which starts on the 20 or 21 January. On the eve of the beginning of spring (*risshun*) the evil spirits are expelled by the bean-throwing rite. This *exorcism is called *tsuina* (Chinese, *chui-no*), whose origin reaches as far back as Chou China. This Chinese custom of exorcizing evil spirits was adopted by the Japanese, probably in the 8th cent., and initially performed on New Year's Eve. The bean-throwing rite on the eve of the beginning of spring (*risshun*) began in the Muromachi period.

Setsuwa (Jap., 'explanatory stories'). Japanese stories of miraculous happenings which carry a moral message. They are frequently Buddhist, and exemplify the powers of Buddhism and the consequences of good or of bad behaviour (i.e. the working out of *karma). Important collections are *Nihon Ryoiki* (9th cent., written by a Buddhist monk, Kyokai, tr. K. M. Nakamura, 1973), *Konjaku Monogatari* (12th cent.), and *Uji Shui Monogatari* (13th cent., tr. D. E. Mills, 1970). See also DENSETSU and SHINWA for other kinds of Japanese story.

Se'udah (Heb., 'meal'). A Jewish festive meal. According to the *Talmud, there are two sorts of festive meals. *Se'udah shel reshut* has nothing to do with religion, and scholars are discouraged from participating (*B.Pes.* 49a); *se'udah shel *mitzvah*, on the other hand, is a meal held in conjunction with religious rejoicing, as at a *circumcision, a wedding, the *Sabbath, the *Passover *seder, etc. It is a religious duty to share in and to enjoy such feasts. Appropriate customs must be observed: hands must be washed before eating bread (see ABLUTIONS); *benedictions must be recited and *grace after the meal must be said. Those who discuss the *Torah while eating 'are as though they had eaten of the table of God', while those who do not 'are as though they had eaten of sacrifices of the dead' (*Avot* 3. 3). In the *aggadic tradition, at the end of time there will be an eschatological se'udah at which God will be the host. The meat of *leviathan will be eaten, and wine stored since the time of the creation will be drunk (*BBB* 74b–75a).

Sevā (Pañjābī, 'service'). Sikh ideal of service. Service rendered in accordance with God's will and without expectation of reward counteracts *haumai (egoism). Sevā denotes attention to duty in all spheres of life and, in particular, service in the *gurdwārā, such as preparing and serving *Gurū-kā-laṅgar, fanning the congregation, or minding their shoes. *Kār sevā means such voluntary labour as constructing or cleaning the gurdwārā pool. A sevā panthi is a Sikh who has spent a life in service to the *panth; or more specifically, a member of a group which serves others, founded in memory of Bhāī Kanayhā who tended the wounded in battle on both sides.

Seven Churches. The recipients of seven letters incorporated into chs. 1–3 of the New Testament book of *Revelation. They are all local churches in Asia Minor: Ephesus, Smyrna, Pergamum, Thyatira, Sardis, Philadelphia, and Laodicea.

Seven deadly sins. In Christianity: pride, covetousness, lust, envy, gluttony, anger, and sloth (*accidie). The traditional number is first found in *Gregory the Great (although with *tristitia*, 'gloom', instead of *accidie*). For five deadly sins, see GOGYAKU-ZAI.

Seven dimensions of religion: see Introduction.

Seveners. *Ismāʿīlī sect (or sects; from Arab., *sabʿīya*) which holds that the legitimate line of *Imāms ended with the seventh (hence the name). The sixth Imām was Jaʿfar al-Ṣādiq: his eldest son, Ismāʿīl, died before his father, leading to a complex contest of claims to legitimate succession. The Seveners held that Ismāʿīl was the true (and perhaps, because of the significance of the number 'seven', the final) successor, but they then held that he transmitted his own authority in diverse ways, thus producing a number of different Sevener sects. Two of these became prominent, the *Fāṭimids, whose rulers were Imāms of the sect, and the *Qarmatians (who may have accepted that the Fāṭimids were the authentic Imāms, or may have held that each member of the sect was an Imām). All groups placed emphasis on esoteric teaching, and were therefore known as *Batinis (*bāṭinī*). There is a tendency to reject the outward observances of religion, including schools of *sharīʿa, in favour of reliance on the instructions and authority of a divinely guided leader. The *Qur'ān was interpreted in increasingly allegorical ways, leading to a realization of inner truth. Thus 15. 99 ('Serve your Lord until *al-yaqīn* [the irresistible, usually understood as death] comes upon you') was taken to mean 'the perfect knowledge of God'.

Seven false views (wrong seeing in Buddhism): see DIṬṬHI.

Seven gods of luck (Japanese deities): see DAIKOKU.

Seven holy cities (Hindu): see SACRED CITIES, SEVEN.

Seven holy rivers (Hindu): see SACRED RIVERS, SEVEN.

Seven precepts (basic rules of Druze life): see DRUZES.

Seven Sacred Cities (Hindu): see SACRED CITIES, SEVEN.

Seven Sages of the Bamboo Grove (Taoist philosophers): see TAOISM.

Seven Sleepers of Ephesus. The heroes of a romance which was popular among both Christians and Muslims in the Middle Ages. In the story, seven Christian young men take refuge from the persecution of the emperor Decius (249–51) in a cave near Ephesus, fall asleep and reawaken under the Christian emperor Theodosius II (408–50). They become proof of the *resurrection of the dead. Behind the legend lie: the Rip Van Winkle theme, which occurs widely in folklore, e.g. the ancient Greek story of Epimenides; a polemical motive within the *Origenist controversy over the resurrection of bodies; and perhaps a real episode in Ephesus in the 5th cent. in which some men claimed to have survived from the time of persecution. The story may have been written by the bishop of Ephesus in the period 448–51; it was in any case widely known by the 6th cent. in both East and West. It appears briefly in the Qur'ān (18. 9), where the sleepers (3, 5, or 7) are called *aṣḥāb al-kahf*, 'companions of the cave', and it is further elaborated in Islamic tradition. The grotto of the Seven Sleepers in Ephesus was an important Christian pilgrimage place until the Islamic conquest of Asia Minor in the 15th cent. Muslims located the story and tomb in various places, including a different Ephesus (Afsūs) which was within Arab territory from the 7th cent.

Seven Sorrows of the Virgin Mary. According to the Roman *Breviary: (i) at the prophecy of *Simeon (Luke 2. 34–5); (ii) at the flight into Egypt (Matthew 2. 13–15); (iii) at the loss of the holy child (Luke 2. 41–52); (iv) on meeting *Jesus on the way to *Calvary (Luke 23. 27–31); (v) at standing at the foot of the cross (John 19. 25); (vi) at the taking down of Christ from the cross (Luke 23. 53); (vii) at his burial (Matthew 27. 59–60, etc.). The seven sorrows are commemorated on 15 Sept., the feast of Our Lady of Sorrow.

Seventeen Article Constitution (Shōtoku's reform which gave support to Buddhism): see NARA BUDDHISM.

Seventeenth of Tammuz (Jewish fast day): see TAMMUZ, FAST OF.

Seventh Day Adventists (members of Christian sect who believe in the literal Second Coming of Christ): see ADVENTISTS.

Seventh Heaven. The highest of all the spheres in the created order, hence the nearest that humans can approach to God. The theory of seven heavens/spheres is widespread in religions, e.g. in *kabbalah.

Seven Virtues. In Christian tradition: faith, hope, charity, prudence, temperance, fortitude, justice. The first three are the 'theological virtues', grouped together by Paul in 1 Corinthians 13. 13. The last four are the 'cardinal virtues', a classification taken over by the chief Christian *moral theologians, e.g. *Ambrose, *Augustine, and Thomas *Aquinas, from Plato and Aristotle.

Seven Words from the Cross. Sayings of Jesus on the cross used as subjects of Christian meditation, especially on *Good Friday. They are: (i) 'Father forgive them; for they know not what they do' (Luke 23. 34); (ii) 'Today you will be with me in paradise' (Luke 23. 43); (iii) 'Woman, behold your son! . . . Behold your mother' (John 19. 26 f.); (iv) 'Eli, Eli, lama sabachthani: My God, my God, why have you forsaken me?' (Matthew 27. 46; Mark 15. 34); (v) 'I thirst' (John 19. 28); (vi) 'It is finished' (John 19. 30); (vii) 'Father, into your hands I commend my spirit' (Luke 23. 46). A musical interpretation was written by Haydn in his Sonatas on the Seven Last Words.

Sevorah (Jewish Babylonian scholars): see SAVORAIM.

Sexagesima. The second Sunday before *Lent, eight weeks before *Easter. See also QUINQUAGESIMA.

Sex and religion. Since both sex and reproduction are fundamental in human and other life, it is not surprising that religions give central importance to both (the two are not synonymous, as will be seen). At the most basic level, religions have been in the past, and to a great extent still aspire to be, systems which protect gene replication and the nurture of children. It was not possible in the past to have any knowledge of genetics, but that, from an evolutionary point of view, is irrelevant. Natural selection operates on the heritable differences which occur between individuals. Those which are better adapted to the environments they inhabit, and to the contingencies within them, will survive and will have better opportunity to reproduce. It follows that all organisms are shaped by natural selection operating through differential reproduction. Reproduction does not depend on sex, since asexual reproduction is not only possible but common (e.g. in algae, strawberries, protists, corals). The evolution of sex is in some ways odd, because it carries with it a high cost in terms of energy and time: in contrast to asexual reproduction of single-celled species, which involves duplication of chromosomes followed by division, sexual reproduction involves a sequence of processes (meosis, recombination, two reduction divisions, and fusion). While this introduces the possibility of far greater variation (on which natural selection can operate), it also *may* involve for the female the possibility of long periods of gestation and care of offspring (there are costs also for males; for refs. see H. Bernstein *et al.*, 'The Evolution of Sex: DNA Repair Hypothesis', in A. E. Rasa *et al.*, 1989). The evolution of sex has therefore carried with it a vast range of different strategies through which the chances of successful reproduction are maximized (e.g. a mating pair might produce the maximum offspring in the minimum time with no nurture, so that a few individuals survive, e.g. herrings; or they might produce few offspring with long gestation and maximum nurture so that the few individuals survive, e.g. elephants—or humans). There is no suggestion that organisms make conscious decisions about the strategies they adopt; rather, the strategies adopted are winnowed impersonally by the test of whether they produce fit individuals to continue the process.

In the human case, however, consciousness *is* introduced. Thus although humans are carried by the same process of natural selection, they can also enhance the process by the creation of cultural defences and controls. It is in this sense that gene replication in the human case is protected by *both* the body *and* culture. Until the present century, this could not have been consciousness of genetics. But it was consciousness of what were taken to be the conditions for the successful production of children and their growth of maturity. Within that general bracket, human communities have devised a vast diversity of strategies which have then been winnowed by the same basic test of whether they have 'worked'. Have the communities survived and flourished, or have they gone to extinction?

It is here that religions have been so important: they are the earliest cultural creations of which we have evidence which supply contexts of security and controls over human behaviours and evaluations of them. They have extended the unit of selection beyond the family and the kinship group, by bonding strangers to each other and by thus extending the virtues of kinship altruism into a metaphor and reality of social co-operation and coercion. Sexual variance may thus be harnessed—or prohibited (e.g. *celibacy or *homosexuality may serve the community, or they may be regarded as aberrant): as always, religions produce a bewildering variety of different strategies. The resulting religious control has produced high degrees of stability: it has produced moral codes, designations of who may mate with whom (including prohibited relationships), techniques and rituals for producing offspring (often of a desired gender), education, protection of women, assurance of paternity (by restricting access to women) and thus of heredity and continuity in society. The consequence has been strong male control of women, in which have been combined reverence for women and subordination of them (see further WOMEN).

At the same time, religions have made much, in different ways, of the distinction between sex and reproduction. Even before the relation between sexual acts and reproduction was better understood, the potential of sex for pleasure and power was well-recognized. This, in itself, reinforced the male control of women, since promiscuous or unlicensed sexual activity would clearly subvert that ordering of families in particular and of society in general which was rewarded in natural selection (i.e., in continuity, from the limited perspective of the participants). Thus whereas male sexual activity, outside the reproductive boundary, might not be disruptive, it would clearly affect the family as the unit of selection; and in any case, female sexual activity of that kind would certainly be subversive. There is, therefore, a context of restriction which is necessary form the point of view of natural selection and evolution. Within that context of restriction, the nature of sexuality and sexual feelings have evoked widely differing responses in religions, ranging from a fear of being enslaved to the passions (leading to a dualistic subordination of sexuality, as in *Manichaeism) to a delight in sexuality as a proper end in life, as among Hindus: see *puruṣārtha, *kāma. In any case, the exploration of sexuality has been religiously important. In Eastern religions, in particular, the nature of sexual energy was explored in many directions. Since sexual arousal seems to make its own demands, what might be the consequence if that energy is brought under human control? In China this lent itself to the quest for immortality and the gaining of strength (see e.g. *breath, *ch'i, *fang-chung shu, *hsien, *Taoism), in India to the acquisition of power (see *Cakra Pūjā, *Dūtī Pūjā, *kālacakra, *Kāpālika, *maithuna, *pañca-makāra, *Sahajīyā, *Śaktism, *Tantrika, *Tantrism). In Christianity, the issue of control led in a different direction. In so far as human sex transcends both reproduction and biological imperatives, it is no longer an end of that kind in itself. How, then, does it relate to the end of salvation and the vision of God? One answer is to say, Extremely well: the union of a man and a woman, transcending the union of male and female in a biological sense, has seemed religiously to be the nearest one can come on earth to the final union with God (for many examples of this in different religions, see J. Bowker,

Beyond Words: Religions and the Poetry of Presence, 1997). But another answer has been to say that sex is of lesser value than the final end of God, and is among those things which may have to be given up if the unqualified love of God is to flourish. This *ascetic option gives the highest value to *celibacy, chastity, and virginity, and it became the dominant voice of the official Church, especially in the West. That means it became the voice of men, since only men have control and authority in the Church (since women, until recently, and still in *Roman Catholicism and *Orthodoxy, cannot be ordained). Thus the subordination of sex, and the attempt to make it in effect synonymous either with sin or with reproduction, became, within Christianity, a particular strategy through which men kept control and gave to control a new meaning.

But this has been only a part of the story. The experience of sex and the better understanding of reproduction have also brought gradual changes to the contextualization of sex in relationships of an enduring kind. In the West, polygyny (see POYGAMY), but not polyandry, was accepted well into the Biblical period, and remains permissible for Muslims (see MARRIAGE AND DIVORCE). Yet beyond polygamy, there began to develop a recognition, first of the obligations of 'sharing bread together' (the underlying Latin of 'companionship'), then of friendship enduring through time, then of emotions translated into delight (the introduction of romantic love), and now of fundamental choice in those societies which have espoused (and can afford) the preferential option for options (see SECULARIZATION). Male resistance to the erosion of male control has produced in all religions vigorous defences of the status quo, along with a deriding, as 'political correctness', of attempts to implement the recognition that women are no longer at the disposal of men. The *Vatican resistance to the courtesy of gender-inclusive language is an obvious example of this, but in all religions a comparable resistance is evident. This arises, not simply out of self-interest (often on the part of women, some of whom have much to lose in the changes at present taking place), but much more because of the breaking of the link between sex and reproduction. In the past, and for millennia, religions have been brilliant and effective systems for the protection of gene-replication and the nurture of children. They have enhanced this effectiveness by endorsing the values of loyalty and love, albeit expressed in different cultural ways in different religions. But sex and reproduction were in practice, and especially for women, close to being synonymous. Contraception (see BIRTH AND POPULATION CONTROL) has been known to all religions and has been differently evaluated, but in general it has always been linked to the priority of reproduction, especially of male children who will continue the line of descent. In the last century, the development of simpler and more effective contraception has broken the link: sex and reproduction are no longer synonymous. What is the value of sex detached from reproduction, and from the necessity for the family unit to provide protection for the nurture of children? Religions have been *so* effective as systems in the old order that they are, in general, finding it difficult to relate their transcendent values to the new circumstance (see also the concluding paragraph of *sociology of religion). The simplest option is to insist on maintaining the old order, and this is, at present, the majority voice in official religion. The price to be paid is an increasing schism in the human community between the religious wisdoms, values, and experiences acquired through millennia of testing, and the practices (by no means devoid of wisdoms and values) of those who have realized and accepted the distinction between sex and reproduction.

See Index, Sexuality.

J. W. Bowker, *Is God a Virus? Genes, Culture and Religion* (1995); V. L. Bullough, *Sexual Variance in Society and History* (1976); P. J. Greenwood and J. Adams, *The Ecology of Sex* (1987); J. B. Nelson and S. P. Longfellow (ed.), *Sexuality and the Sacred* (1994); K. E. and J. M. Paige, *The Politics of Reproductive Ritual* (1981); G. Parrinder, *Sexual Morality in the World's Religions* (1996); M. H. Phayer, *Sexual Liberation and Religion in the Nineteenth Century* (1977); A. E. Rasa *et al.* (ed.), *The Sociobiology of Sexual and Reproductive Strategies* (1989); J. R. Wegner, *Chattel or Person: The Status of Women in the Mishnah* (1993).

Sforno, Obadiah ben Jacob (*c*.1470–1550). Italian Jewish biblical commentator. After settling in Bologna, he practised medicine and set up a *bet-midrash* ('house of study'). He wrote commentaries on the *Pentateuch, the *Song of Songs, and *Ecclesiastes (1567), on the *Psalms (1586), on *Job (1589), and on *Jonah, *Habakkuk, and *Zechariah (1724). In general, he kept to the literal meaning of the text; although he sometimes used *allegory, he avoided *kabbalistic interpretation. He also produced a work of philosophy, the *'Or Ammim* (Light of Nations, 1537), the Lat. tr. of which was dedicated to Henri II of France.

C. Roth, *Jews of the Renaissance* (1959).

SGPC (authoritative elected Sikh body): see SHIROMAṆĪ GURDWĀRĀ PARBANDHAK COMMITTEE.

sgyu lus ('Illusory Body' in Buddhist doctrine): see NĀRO CHOS DRUG.

Sh. May be spelt ś; check in appropriate alphabetical order.

Shabbat. The first tractate of the Jewish *Mishnah, *Tosefta, and the two *Talmuds of the order of *Mo'ed*. *Shabbat* deals with the laws of the *Sabbath and consists of twenty-four chapters. It discusses such questions as kindling the Sabbath lights, keeping food warm, the thirty-nine categories of work, *circumcision on the Sabbath, and rest for domestic animals.

Shabbat (seventh day of the week for Jews when they abstain from work): see SABBATH.

Shabbateanism: see SHABBETAI ZEVI.

Shabbat ha-Gadol (Heb., 'The Great Sabbath'). The Sabbath preceding the Jewish *Passover. On this Sabbath, in the afternoon service, it is customary to read the greater part of the *Haggadah, and in the sermon the Passover laws of *leaven are discussed. It is possibly called the 'great Sabbath' because the *haftarah reading is from *Malachi and refers to the 'great and terrible day of the Lord' (3. 23).

Shabbetai Zevi (1626–76). Jewish *messianic leader. Shabbetai Zevi was *ordained as a *ḥakham after a thorough *Talmudic and *kabbalistic education. Throughout his life he was subject to periods of alternating depression and elation; as a result of his erratic behaviour, he was banished from his native Smyrna. In 1665, he travelled to Gaza to meet *Nathan of Gaza 'in order to find *tikkun and peace for his soul'. Nathan was convinced that *Shabbetai was the *messiah and on 17 Sivan, Shabbetai so declared himself. He appointed representatives of the twelve tribes and circled *Jerusalem on horseback like a king. As the *prophet of the messiah, Nathan called the people to repentance and sent out letters to the *diaspora communities announcing the great event. He predicted that Shabbetai would take the crown of the Turkish Sultan and in a few years would bring back the *ten lost tribes from beyond the River *Sambatyon. Rumour spread throughout Europe. Shabbetai was *excommunicated in Jerusalem and returned to Smyrna, and the entire community was thrown into a state of messianic fervour. A division arose between the believers (the *ma'aminim*) and the 'infidels' (the *koferim*), but so hysterical was the excitement that many of the infidels were forced to flee from the city. After appointing counterparts to the ancient kings of *Israel, Shabbetai sailed for Constantinople, where he was arrested and held in moderately comfortable imprisonment. Meanwhile, news of the advent of the messiah produced enormous excitement throughout the diaspora, and broadsheets and pamphlets were circulated throughout Europe. In some instances support was given to the movement by Christian millenarians who believed that the world would come to an end in 1666. Ascetic practices coupled with hysterical rejoicing became commonplace, and a new era ('the first year of the renewal of prophecy and the Kingdom') was instituted. From prison Shabbetai continued his activities, abolishing the fasts of 17 *Tammuz and 9 *Av, and signing his letters as 'the firstborn son of God' and even 'the Lord your God Shabbetai Zevi'. In Sept. 1666, he was taken to the Sultan's court where he was given the choice of death or conversion to Islam. Shabbetai agreed to *apostasy, took the name of Aziz Mehmed Effendi, and accepted a royal pension. His conversion was a profound shock to the whole Jewish world. Nathan of Gaza defended it on the grounds that the messiah had to behave in this scandalous manner before the process of *tikkun could be accomplished, and he remained loyal to Shabbetai. Shabbetai himself continued to act as before among his secret followers in Adrianople and was finally exiled to Albania where he died in 1676. Although repressed by the *rabbis, Shabbatean ideas, particularly in the realm of the kabbalah, continued to circulate, especially in Turkey, Italy, and Poland, and continued to inspire popular movements such as the *ʿaliyah of 'the holy society of Rabbi Judah Ḥasid' to Jerusalem in 1700. Such scholars as Moses *Luzzatto, Jonathan *Eybeschuetz, and Nehemiah Hiyya *Hayon provoked controversy because of their continued Shabbatean ideas. For later developments see DOENMEH; FRANK, JACOB.

G. Scholem, *Sabbatai Sevi: Mystical Messiah* (tr. 1973).

Shadal (acronym): see LUZZATTO, SAMUEL DAVID.

Shādhiliy(y)a. A Sūfī order founded by al-Shādhilī (1196–1258 (AH 593–656)) who left, not written works, but many sayings and chants. The best-known collection is *Ḥizb al-Baḥr* (Incantation of the Sea), which effected many *miracles. He strongly emphasized *ṣabr (acceptance) and *shukr* (thanksgiving), as well as complete detachment in attitude to all people, whether they are in distress or in prosperity. Nevertheless, his followers must work, even attain high office, but with detachment directed toward al-*Fanā'. He insisted on observance of *Sunnī orthodoxy, hence avoiding conflict as the movement spread, mainly into N. Africa. From the Shādhiliy(y)a derived many other orders, e.g. the ʿAlawiy(y)a, the Darqawiy(y)a. The influence of the Shādhiliy(y)a was extended in the 20th cent. beyond the Muslim world through the writings of René Guénon, also known as Shaykh ʿAbd al-Wāḥid Yaḥyā, who sought to identify comparable spiritual and cosmological principles underlying all the great religions; and through the work of Frithjof Schuon.

S. H. Nasr (ed.), *Islamic Spirituality: Manifestations* (1991).

Shadkhan. Jewish *marriage broker. Traditionally all marriages were arranged in Judaism. It was said that '*Rav punished any man . . . who betrothed a woman without previous *shiddukhin' (*B.Kid.* 12b). The term 'shadkhan' first appeared in the 13th cent. The shadkhan was normally awarded 2 or 3 per cent of the dowry; it was a respected profession, and was even embarked upon by *rabbis. In Jewish folklore, the shadkhan was regarded as liable to exaggeration, but generally good-natured and loquacious.

P. and H. Goodman, *The Jewish Marriage Anthology* (1965).

Shadow-boxing: see T'AI CHI CH'ÜAN.

Shadow theatre: see THEATRE AND DRAMA.

Shadrach, Meshach, and Abednego. Babylonian names for Hananiah, Mishael, and Azariah, the three Jewish exiles who were cast into the fiery furnace for their refusal to worship idols (Daniel 3). According to tradition, they were enabled to come out alive because *Gabriel received permission to cool the fire at the centre, driving the heat to the extremity. During their ordeal, the three sang 'The Song of the Three Children', in the Gk. version (*Septuagint): the Prayer of Azariah and the Song (also known as the Song of the Three Jews/Young Men) are added between 3. 23 and 24.

Shafāʿa (Arab., *shafaʿa*, 'double, repeat a prayer'). *Intercession in Islam. The *Qur'ān insists that no intercession will be possible on the Day of *Judgement, which will evaluate a strict balance of good and evil works. However, the Qur'ān allows an exception, either *to* whomsoever God allows it, or *for* whomsoever God allows it—the Arabic preposition can mean either. The latter is then a matter of God's *qadar (power to dispose) and opens the scope and practice of intercession widely; the former is supremely identified with *Muḥammad, the efficacy of whose intercession becomes a matter of *ijmaʿ (agreed belief by consensus), making him something much closer to a redeemer. To Muḥammad were then added many other intercessors, e.g. angels and martyrs (*shahīd), and, among the *Shīʿa, *Imāms (especially for *Ithna ʿAshariy(y)a, *al-Mahdī), and *Fāṭima.

J. W. Bowker, 'Intercession in the Qur'ān . . .', *Journ. of Sem. Studies* (1966).

Shāfiʿites. School of Muslim law derived from *al-Shāfiʿī. The school was founded by his pupils and followers. It is characterized by his own adherence to *Qur'ān and *ḥadīth as the absolute sources of law. Great importance is therefore attached to the methodology of exegesis. Ḥadīth and *sunna supply the first principles of exegesis, followed by *qiyās (analogy) and *ijmaʿ (consensus): qiyās can only be applied provided that there is no solution to be found in Qur'ān and ḥadīth; together these form the principles of Islam (*uṣūl al-Fiqh), of which al-Shāfiʿī is traditionally regarded as the founder.The school is therefore characterized by its continuing openness to interpretation and application on this basis. Al-Shāfiʿī said of himself, 'My opinion is correct within the possibility of its being in error, whereas an opinion differing from mine is in error, but within the possibility of its being correct.' It was dominant in the central Muslim territories, but made less impact in India and C. Asia. It is strong in SE Asia. His *Risāla* (Epistle), in which, toward the end of his life, he expounded his views, has been translated by M. Khadduri, *Islamic Jurisprudence* (1961).

Shahāda. Profession of faith in *Allāh and his messenger; the first *Pillar of Islam, proclaiming the uniqueness of Allāh, and the centrality of *Muḥammad as his prophet. Pronouncing the shahāda implies acceptance of Islam in its totality, and is the only formal requirement for entry into the *'umma (community).

(Ashhadu aina) lā ilāha illā Allāh
wa-Muḥammad rasūl Allāh
(I bear witness that) there is no god but God
and Muḥammad is the messenger of God.

The shahāda is included in the *ādhān (call to prayer) and is pronounced during the *ṣalāt, as part of the tashahhud, which, however, contains extra phrases. In a wider sense, giving witness to Islamic belief can imply fighting and death in the service of Allāh, and the cognate term, *shahīd, has come to signify *martyr.

Shaḥarit. The Jewish daily morning service. Traditionally believed to have been instituted by *Abraham (Genesis 19. 27), it replaces the *Temple morning *sacrifice (*B.Ber.* 26b). The service consists of the morning *benedictions, the *Shemaʿ and its benedictions, the *ʿAmidah with its appropriate blessings, and the *Torah reading (on specific mornings), as well as various other prayers, quotations, and sometimes *piyyutim. It must be recited between daybreak and before a quarter of the day has passed (*Ber.* 1. 2). On weekdays, both *tallit and *tefillin are worn (on the *Sabbath, only the tallit), and a *minyan must be present if the full service is to be recited.

Shaheed (Sikh martyr): see SHAHĪD.

Shahīd (Arab., 'a witness'). In the *Qur'ān, one who bears witness, as God bears witness to human deeds. Its subsequent use for one who bears witness to God by dying in his cause—i.e. as a *martyr—is based on the Qur'ān (e.g. 3. 156, 166; 4. 69; 47. 4–6), although the word is not found in the Qur'ān. In *ḥadīth, the martyr who dies in battle against the *kafirun (infidels) is promised great rewards: he passes through the *barzakh, is exempted from the examination in the grave by *Munkar and Nakīr, and goes to the highest rank in *paradise, nearest to the throne of God. Because they are already pure, they alone are not washed before burial, and may be buried in their blood-stained clothes—though those last points have been disputed. The shahīd eventually makes effective intercession (*shafāʿa).

The concept was subsequently extended to include those who die during the performance of a godly action (e.g. during al-*ḥajj, or while building a mosque), or while fulfilling one's God-given obligation (e.g. during childbirth). It could also include violent death (e.g. in a shipwreck or a storm) when accompanied by *islam* or trust in God.

Martyrdom is of particular importance in *Shīʿa Islam. *al-Ḥusain is *shāhi shuhadā*, king of the martyrs. Ritual participation in his sufferings includes self-flagellation, often of a severe kind, and also the performance of *taʿzīya (condolence, expressed through re-enactments of the life and death of al-Ḥusain). Clearly, too strong an emphasis on shahīd might lead to a rapid depopulation of the

Muslim world. It is, therefore, moderated by *ṭaqīya, the concealment of faith under persecution or pressure—perhaps even as an obligation.

The word and the concept of martyrdom were adopted by the Sikhs (though usually transliterated as 'shaheed'). Those who 'dedicate their bodies to God will attain glory both here and hereafter' (Ādi Granth, 698).

Shahrastānī, Abu-'l-Fath Muḥammad ibn 'Abd al-Karīm (1076–1153 (AH 469–548)). Muslim scholar, especially of the relation of religions to Islam. He was a *Sunni and an Ashʿarite (*al-Ashʿari), who wrote a work on the limitations of philosophy in relation to theology (*Nihāyat al-Iqdām fi 'Ilm al-Kalām*, tr. A. Guillaume, 1931–4), but he is remembered particularly for *Kitāb al-Milal wʿal-Nihal* (The Book of Religions and Systems, Germ. tr. T. Haarbrücker, 1850–1). Islam is placed at the centre, as the recipient of the uncorrupted *Qur'ān, and other religions (including Islamic sects) are then placed in varying degrees of positive or negative relation to Islam. Thus the closest are *ahl al-Kitāb, the People of the Book (those who received revelation and did not wholly lose it); next are those who have only traces of the revealed book left (e.g. *Manichaeans); then those who have transcribed the equivalent of *natural law into codes and behaviours, although without the benefit of revelation; and finally those who live according to their own ideas, worshipping the stars and idols. He was among the first to put forward the idea that *Paul had corrupted the original religion of ʿĪsā/*Jesus, which he called the 'religion of Peter'.

Shah Waliullah (1702–62). An Indian Islamic reformer, who was a *Sunni and a leading *Naqshbandī *Sūfī. He lived at a time when the Indian Muslims were bitterly divided and were suffering a decline in political power. He wrote fifty-one major works in Arabic and Persian. His *magnum opus, Hujjatullah-ul-Balaghah* (covering *Qur'ān, *sharīʿa, *tasawwuf, politics, and philosophy), is a restatement of Islam allowing rational and empirical arguments on a much broader basis than the traditional line. He argued for a return to the spirit of Islam, but recognized that 18th-cent. India was different from *Muḥammad's Arabia. His practical attitude provoked opposition from the traditional *ʿulamā, but since he upheld the supremacy of revelation over reason, he attracted many Muslims to his cause. His vast influence can still be perceived in such reform movements as *Jamaat-al-Islam, Tableeghi Jamaat, *Iqbal's neo-modernism, the *Ahl-al-Hadith, the *Barelvi, and *Deoband, all of which invoke Shah Waliullah's authority in support of their views.

Waliullah's Persian version of the Qur'ān was the first popular version in the history of India. He believed that concentration on the Qur'ān itself would promote the emergence of new ideas and meanings, relevant to the times of the reader, and that the Qur'ān could be studied independently without exclusive reference to traditional commentaries. Waliullah opened an academy, Dar-ul-Hadith, the first of its kind in the subcontinent to conduct research on the classical *ḥadīth collections. Against the consensus of the ʿulamā, he declared most of the ḥadīth literature unreliable, except for the *Muwatta* of Imām *Mālik.

In the field of Islamic law, Waliullah subordinated jurisprudence to the discipline of ḥadīth. He argued that the formulations of the classical jurists had a relative rather than an absolute value, and cannot be a substitute for the unquestionable authority of the Qur'ān and the genuine tradition: 'The time has come that the religious laws of Islam should be brought into the open fully dressed in reason and argument'; 'Growth and change in Muslim society demand the use of *ijtihād [reasoned reconstruction], for the religious laws are based on *maslaha* [the general good].'

Waliullah, an eminent Sūfī himself, also began the task of reforming Sufism which had declined extensively into a commercial exploitation of superstition. He declared, 'Those mystics who do not possess efficient knowledge of the Qur'ān and fail to practise the *Sunna of the Prophet, are in reality the thieves and robbers of religion.' Waliullah acknowledged the positive attributes of Sufism and harmonized the useful innovations into orthodox Sunni Islam.

On political and socio-economic matters, Waliullah upheld the principle of unity and toleration, condemning sectarianism and Sunni/Shīʿa polemics.

G. N. Jalbani, *Teachings of Shah Waliullah of Delhi* (1967); S. A. A. Rizvi, *Shāh Walī-Allāh and his Times* (1980).

Shaikh al-Islām or **shaykh.** Honorific title for Muslims who achieve eminence in various ways, but especially in *kalām or *fiqh. It became, under the *Ottomans, a formal institution, associated with the *muftī of Constantinople, who acquired authority over the *ʿulamā of the empire, represented through his issuing of *fatwas. The office disappeared with the dissolution of the Ottoman Empire, 1922–4. Among *Sūfīs, a shaikh is one who has attained spiritual mastery (Pers., *pir*) by submitting to the discipline and instruction of another shaikh. It is thus a title given to one who can trace his lineage back to the foundation of the order (*ṭarīqa) in question: see SILSILAH.

Shaikhī. Followers of *Shaykh Aḥmad Aḥsā'ī (1753–1826), a *Shīʿa Muslim who lived in Persia. They reject what they regard as the excesses of *Sufism, especially the view that the essence of God becomes manifest in all that he creates (because essence cannot be divided into parts), but equally they are more rationalistic than many Shiʿites would allow. Thus they reject the resurrection of *this* body, saying that it goes to dust, but affirm a subtle body which subsists and is resurrected; and they interpret such miracles as the *miʿrāj (ascension) metaphorically. The *Imāms are regarded as the agents of God's creativity, so that without them there would have been no creation.

Shaitān (the devil in Islam): see DEVIL.

Shaiva, Shaivism, etc. (major tradition of Hindu practise and devotion to Śiva): see ŚAIVISM.

Shakers. Popular name for the United Society for Believers in Christ's Second Appearing. The *sect was founded by Ann Lee (1736–84). She was converted to the Shaking Quakers (so-called because of their trembling and ritualistic dancing) in 1758. She then, as Mother Ann, received revelations that she was the female counterpart of Christ, and that she was to take the small group that had begun to form around her to the New World to await the millennium (see MILLENNIALISM). The community was to be strictly *celibate and was to hold all things in common. By about 1840, they had reached around 6,000 in number, in twenty communities, but have now virtually disappeared: the 'Mother Church' at Mount Lebanon in New York was sold in 1947, and membership was declared closed in 1965. Nevertheless, there is a small continuing community in Maine.

E. D. Andrews, *The People Called Shakers* (1953); S. J. Stein, *The Shaker Experience in America: A History* (1992).

Shakkyo (Jap., 'the teaching of Śāk(yamuni)'). A term for what in the West is called 'Buddhism'. Other such terms include *Shakumon*, 'Buddha's gate', and *Shakushi no oshie*, 'Śākyamuni's teaching'.

Shakti (creative power in Hinduism): see ŚAKTI.

Shakubuku (breaking and subduing): see SŌKA GAKKAI.

Shakumon (Buddha's gate): see SHAKKYO.

Shali'aḥ (Heb., 'messenger'). Jewish emissary. The term is a synonym for Meshullaḥ. In the *rabbinic period emissaries were sent from *Erez Israel to communities in the *diaspora, often to raise funds for charitable institutions. Because they travelled widely, these emissaries performed the useful function of keeping communities in touch, and their accounts of their travels serve as important historical sources.

Shālōm (Heb., 'peace'). Common Hebrew greeting. 'Shālōm' indicates security, contentment, good health, prosperity, friendship, and tranquillity of heart and mind. The Arabic equivalent, also used in greeting, is *salām.

Shamans. Inspired, ecstatic, and *charismatic individuals, male and female, with the power to control spirits, often by incarnating them, and able to make journeys out of the body, both to 'heaven' and 'hell'. The word is traced to the Tungu in Siberia (where shamanism is common), though the claim is also made (but not universally accepted) that the origin is in the Skt. *śrāmaṇa, reaching China in the form of *shamen* and Japan of **shamon*. The word is now used of a wide variety of people who enter trance and ecstatic states, and make 'out of the body' journeys. In so far as Tungu shamanism acts as a control on usage, the careful description of S. M. Shirokogoroff (*The Psychomental Complex of the Tungus*, 1935) indicates that a potential shaman is marked out by a traumatic episode or illness. If she or he can bring the spirit causing this under control, and can demonstrate ecstatic states, then s/he is recognized as a shaman. The inducing of ecstatic states is accomplished in many ways, including exclusion of general sensory stimuli through drumming, concentration on a mirror, etc., and through tobacco, alcohol, and hallucinogens (see M. J. Harner (ed.), *Hallucinogens and Shamanism*, 1973). The spirits involved are not regarded as inherently either good or evil: the outcome depends on context and on whether they are controlled. The shaman removes threat to an individual or community by incorporating potentially destructive spirits into his or her own body and thereby neutralizing them. The ability to make journeys to upper or (more often) lower worlds is a part of the protective role of the shaman extended from its main focus on this earth. This, as C. Blacker points out in relation to Japanese shamanism (*The Catalpa Bow*, 1975), is different from the medium (*miko) who passes on messages from the spirits, although the two work closely together. In general, according to Shirokogoroff,

> the term shaman, in all the Tungu languages, refers to persons of both sexes who have mastered spirits, who at their will can introduce these spirits into themselves and use their power over their spirits in their own interests, particularly helping other people who suffer from the spirits; in such a capacity they may possess a complex of special methods for dealing with the spirits.

This and other careful observations of shamanism make the analysis of M. *Eliade (*Le Chamanisme et les techniques archaiques de l'extase*, 1951) improbable, although it has had wide influence. Eliade argued (against observation) that 'the specific element of shamanism is not the incorporation of spirits by the shamans but the ecstasy provoked by the ascension to the sky or by the descent to hell: the incorporation of spirits and possession by them are universally distributed phenomena, but they do not necessarily belong to shamanism in the strict sense'. He further attempted to separate the two historically, regarding the ascent as a survival of archaic religion, to be called 'pure shamanism' (but by other writers 'white shamanism'), with the descent and contest against malevolent spirits as innovations ('black shamanism'). There is no serious warrant for these distinctions in the practice of shamanism as observed; the imposition of them is more likely to be a creation of the modern mind than a distinction in the origins of shamanism.

See Index, Shamanism.

J. Dow, *Shamanism* (1990); J. Halifax, *Shamanic Voices* (1979); G. Samuel, *Civilized Shamans: Buddhism in Tibetan Society* (1993); A.-L. Siikala, *The Technique of the Siberian Shaman* (1978); R. N. Walsh, *The Spirit of Shamanism* (1990).

Shambhala (Skt., obscure: 'happiness giving'? Tib., bde.'byung, 'source of happiness'). A semi-mythical kingdom in Tibetan Buddhist cosmology; 'the only *Pure Land which exists on earth' (Birnbaum). While playing an important part in the *Kālacakra cycle of *tantras, Shambhala is also a popular myth in its own right. Located 'somewhere north of Tibet', Shambhala is governed by a line of thirty-two wise and powerful kings—of whom the present king is generally reckoned as the twenty-eighth—who guard the true doctrine of Buddhism through a period of world history which sees a decline in religious values. When this decline is at its lowest depth, the final king of Shambhala, Rudra Cakrin, will emerge from his kingdom with a great army, subdue the forces of evil, and establish a golden age. It is supposedly possible for those with the appropriate spiritual predisposition (*karma) to locate Shambhala, where they will find teachings specifically concerned with attaining enlightenment through the understanding of Time. This learning is also available through mastery of the Kālacakra. Paradoxically, the division of the world into 'forces of good' and 'forces of evil' is neither a typically Buddhist nor Tibetan viewpoint. The lore associated with the Kālacakra teachings states that, having originally been taught by the Buddha, they were reintroduced into India from the north at a later time. Hoffmann (1969) has made a good case for the origins of the myth in Central Asia, where Buddhism coexisted with *Manichaeism, Islam, and Christianity in Turfan. One early Kālacakra text, mentioning these three religions, identifies Islam as the force provoking the apocalypse. If the Shambhala myth had its origins in such inter-religious conflict, it is also possible that 'Shambhala was once a real area but has become mythical' (Hoffmann). See also SHANGRI-LA.

E. Birnbaum, *The Way to Shambhala* (1980).

Shamen: see SHAMANS; ŚRĀMAṆA.

Shammai (*c.*50 BCE–*c.*30 CE). Jewish rabbinic leader. Shammai was a contemporary of *Hillel and together they were the last of the *zugot (pairs). He was the founder of the great school of Bet Shammai which was known for its stringent attitude towards the law. Shammai himself does not always seem to have taken a hard line in the *halakhot transmitted in his name, and he is remembered for his dictum, 'Make your study of the *Torah a matter of established regularity, say little and do much, and receive all people with a friendly countenance' (*Avot* 1. 15).

Shammash. Jewish salaried official attached to a *synagogue or *bet din. The duties of a Shammash vary according to the institution. He may act as secretary, messenger, tax collector, bailiff, notary, handyman, almoner, and grave-digger. With the *rabbi and *cantor, he is one of three salaried officials, and his supervision is essential for the smooth running of communal activities.

Shamon. Jap. for *śrāmaṇa, a world-renouncer; a Buddhist monk; sometimes (dubiously) linked to *shaman.

Shams al-Dīn Tabrīzī (Sūfī): see JALĀL AL-DĪN RŪMĪ.

Shang-Ch'ing (Taoist heaven): see SAN-CH'ING.

Shang Ch'ing (writings revealed through Wei Huatsun): see TAOISM.

Shango. Yoruba god of thunder and focus of a cult mainly in Trinidad and Granada, which is primarily of 19th-cent. African origin, and resembles Jamaican *Pocomania, Cuban *Santería, and the *Afro-Brazilian cults. Shrine areas have small shrines for many deities besides Shango, and these are sometimes equated with *Roman Catholic saints. There is also a cult house with altar and a great collection of Catholic and African ritual paraphernalia. Animal sacrifices may be made to the particular deity whose practical help is sought through possession of his devotee or through simple forms of divination or by dreams and prophecy; healing and *exorcism of evil spirits are also prominent. There are probably several thousand devotees; some of these also belong to the *Spiritual Baptists and others are clients drawn from the Christian churches.

Shangri-la. A fictional hidden valley created by James Hilton in his novel *Lost Horizon* (1933). Sited in the Kunlun mountains of N. Tibet (not the Himālayas), Hilton's Shangri-la is a paradisal place where people live without ageing, in the continual enjoyment of art, music, science, and the exercise of wisdom. The centre of Shangri-la is a Buddhist monastery, where all that is precious in E. and W. culture is to be preserved in order to serve the re-education of the world in a post-apocalyptic recovery. As such, Hilton's image of Shangri-la has some parallels with the Tibetan myth of *Shambhala, of which he had at least a little knowledge from sources such as the missionary Abbé Huc and possibly the author-explorer Nicholas Roerich.

Shang-ti (Lord of Heaven). In China, a collective name for gods, perhaps representing one supreme god or overlord. Ti were worshipped as deified ancestors of the Shang *dynasty, and the Shang rulers worshipped Shang-ti—but the absence of a plural form makes it uncertain whether Shang-ti was one or many. He or they had overarching functions of control (e.g. over natural phenomena and plagues). Shang-ti was regarded as the Ancestor of the royal house of the Chou dynasty (*c*.1123–1221). According to the imperial tradition, Hou-chi, founder of the Chou dynasty, was conceived by his mother when she stepped accidentally on the footprint of Shang-ti. This supernatural conception makes Hou-chi son of Shang-ti; consequently the successive Chou kings all claimed him as their First Ancestor to whom seasonal sacrifices were solemnly offered. His chief attribute was control of the seasons for auspicious sowing and good harvest. However, he was also a moral deity who expected his descendants to obey his laws: he would send down natural disasters to punish the kings when they committed serious wrongs. Thus there is a reciprocity between him and his descendants. In later history Shang-ti or *T'ien (Heaven) became semi-monotheistic; the worship of him was primarily an imperial cult confined to the royal houses and their supporters—the *Confucian official class.

Shang-ti in later times was often referred to, in abbreviation, as Ti (Lord). But Ti was also commonly used in later history to refer to an emperor; his origin is divine because his First Ancestor is Shang-ti. Christian missionaries adopted Shang-ti as the name of God, though T'ien-chu (Lord of Heaven) was also used.

Shang-tso-pu. Chin. for *Theravāda.

Shankara (pre-eminent Indian philosopher): see ŚAṄKARA.

Shan-tao (founding master): see PURE LAND SCHOOLS.

Shao-lin-ssu (Jap., Shōrin-ji). Chinese Buddhist monastery, built in 477 CE, by the emperor Hsiao-wen. It was to here that *Bodhidharma moved from S. China when he saw that the time was not ripe for the reception of *dharma there. In this monastery, he spent nine years 'facing the wall' (*menpeki) in silent meditation (*zazen), until his dharma-successor (*Hui-k'o) found him there. Shao-lin-ssu is associated with the development of *kung-fu*, an aspect initially of ch'i-kung (see CH'I). *Kung-fu* was initially concerned with control of interior fears and thoughts, but developed in different directions in Japan in association with other *martial arts.

Sharīʿa (Arab., 'the path worn by camels to the water'). The path to be followed in Muslim life. The term goes back to Qur'ān (e.g. 45. 18, 'We gave you a sharīʿa in religion, so follow it, and do not follow the passions of those who do not know'), but it became the description of the systematic organization of how Muslims should live, wherever there is no permitted freedom (see AL-HALAL WA'L-ḤARĀM). This especially applies to the four classic *schools, *Ḥanafite, *Ḥanbalite, *Mālikite, and *Shāfiʿite. They are rooted in Qur'ān and *ḥadīth, the *sunna of the Prophet, but with different attitudes to what else is legitimizing. To put the relations between them oversimply (see further SCHOOLS OF LAW): Ḥanafites recognize that Qur'ān and ḥadīth do not decide every issue, so they allow *qiyās and ra'y (opinion and judgement, based on a committed knowledge of Qur'ān); Mālikites are cautious about ḥadīth and control its use by *istiṣhah; Shāfiʿites sifted out authentic ḥadīth and regard Qur'ān and ḥadīth as superior to human opinions and considerations; Ḥanbalites are even more insistent on the control of Qur'ān and ḥadīth alone. Since those do not define every detail of life in the relevant areas (nor do they define the methodology of relating the past to the present), the differences between the schools are regarded as a blessing from God (endorsing Muslim diversity within limits). This also makes necessary the constant extension of sharīʿa in the present, since Islam cannot be a reproduction of life in 6th-cent. Arabia. The extension of sharīʿa is made particularly by *ijmaʿ, qiyās and *ijtihād, and in practice through *fatwā. It is also modified by local custom (*adat).

Actions are classified in sharīʿa into five categories (with detailed sub-divisions in each case: (i) obligatory (*fard or *wājib*); (ii) meritorious; (iii) indifferent; (iv) reprehensible; (v) forbidden (*ḥarām*: see AL-HALAL WA'L-ḤARĀM). Fundamental to all are the *Five Pillars.

N. J. Coulson, *A History of Islamic Law* (1964); A. Hasan, *The Early Development of Islamic Jurisprudence* (1970); J. Schacht, *An Introduction to Islamic Law* (1964).

Sharīʿatī, ʿAlī (1933–77). Iranian thinker whose writings and lectures represent the ideology that precipitated the 1979 Islamic revolution in Iran. Sharīʿatī went to Paris in 1959, where he earned a doctorate in sociology at the Sorbonne and became involved in Third-World anti-colonial movements. From his return to Iran in 1964 until his death, he was ceaselessly harassed by the authorities. Forced to relinquish his post as lecturer at Meshed (*Mashhad) University, he began to attract vast audiences, mainly university and college students, at the Husayniya-i-Irshad, a religious centre in Tehran. During this time he produced his greatest work, *The Desert* (Pers., *Kavir*): 'Seeking refuge in history out of fear of loneliness, I immediately sought out my brother Ayn al-Quzat [12th-cent. Persian Sūfī] who was burned to death in the very blossoming of his youth for the crime of awareness and sensitivity, for the boldness of his thought. For in an age of ignorance, awareness is itself a crime.' The government closed the centre and imprisoned Sharīʿatī for eighteen months, during which time he was tortured. Upon his release he was allowed to go to England, where shortly after his arrival he died in mysterious circumstances.

Sharīʿatī's appeal for Iranians rests on his skill in blending traditionalism and modernism and on a fiery style of expression that reached the hearts of Iranians searching for an alternative ideology to that of the Shah's programme of rapid westernization superimposed upon traditional society.

Eng. trs., *The Islamic View of Man* (1978); *Marxism and Other Western Fallacies* (1980); *On the Sociology of Islam* (1979).

Sharīf (Arab., 'noble'). Title of honour, but in Islam especially of those descended from the Prophet *Muḥammad's family, among the banu Hāshim. The most prominent in the post-Second-World-War years has been King Hussein of Jordan, hence the Hashimite dynasty.

Shas. Acronym of Heb., *shishah sedarim*, i.e. the six *seders (orders) of the *Mishnah or *Talmud.

Shaṭḥ (Arab.). An ecstatic or divinely inspired utterance, especially among *Sūfīs. Since they often express extreme claims, the *Sunnīs rapidly contested their validity and authority. For examples see AL-BISTĀMI; AL-HALLĀJ; SAHL AL-TUSTARĪ.

Shavu'ot (Heb., 'weeks'). The Jewish festival of Pentecost. The festival is celebrated on 6 Sivan (and 7 in the *diaspora) and is one of the three pilgrim festivals (see Deuteronomy 16. 16). It falls fifty days after the first day of *Passover, and it originally marked the end of the barley and the beginning of the wheat harvest. The *first fruits were brought to the *Temple (Deuteronomy 26. 1–11), and in *rabbinic times the festival also became the anniversary of the giving of the *Torah to *Moses on Mount *Sinai. In the Middle Ages, young children first went to Hebrew school on Shavu'ot, and in *Reform congregations, confirmation takes place on the festival. It is customary to read *Ruth in the *synagogue, and the Torah reading includes the *Ten Commandments. The synagogue is decorated with green plants (*BRH* 1. 2), and in *Israel there have been some attempts to revive the harvest connotations of the festival. It is also customary to eat dairy products because *Song of Songs compares the Torah with milk (4. 11).

P. Goodman, *A Shavu'ot Anthology* (1975); C. Pearl, *A Guide to Shavuoth* (1959).

Shaybānī (influential figure in development of one of the schools of sharī'a): see ḤANAFITES.

Shaykh (Arab.). Old man, chief, or elder; a title of respect in Islam, especially for religious leaders, usually transliterated *shaikh.

Shaykh Aḥmad Ibn Zayn al-Dīn al-Aḥsā'ī (1753–1826). Shī'a Muslim who founded the Shaykhīs. He was born in Arabia, but moved to Iran, where he became a teacher and prolific writer. His belief that he received, in dreams and visions, direct and infallible communications from the *Imāms, combined with suspect teaching on other matters, led to his condemnation in 1822. He died on pilgrimage to *Mecca, but his teaching was continued by Sayyid Karīm Rashtī (d. 1843 (AH 1259)) who organized the Shaykhīya/Shaikhīya order more formally. Many Shaykhīs/*Shaikhīs became followers of the Bāb (see BĀBĪS).

M. Bayat, *Mysticism and Dissent* (1982); H. Corbin, *L'École shaykhie en théologie shi'ite* (1967).

Shaytan (the devil in Islam): see SATAN (ISLAM).

Shaytl: see HEAD, COVERING OF (Judaism).

Shebu'ah (vow): see VOWS (Judaism).

Sheḥitah. Jewish method of slaughter for food. According to Deuteronomy 12. 21, 'You shall kill of your herd and of your flock which the Lord has given you, as I have commanded you'. The principle behind sheḥitah is that the animal must be killed as swiftly and painlessly as possible by cutting horizontally across the throat in a firm uninterrupted movement. From *c.*1220, no one could act as a *shoḥet* ('slaughterer') without having passed an examination on the theory and practice of sheḥitah, and certificates are not issued to minors, women (except in the Yemen), the handicapped, and those who are lax in performing religious duties. The knife must be perfectly clean and smooth, and the act of slaughter must be preceded by a *benediction. According to *Maimonides, since 'the desire to procure good food necessitates the slaying of animals, the law enjoins that the death of the animal should be as easy and painless as possible'.

J. J. Berman, *Shehitah* . . . (1941).

Shekalim. A tractate in the order of Mo'ed in the Jewish *Talmud. *Shekalim* deals with the laws concerning the half shekel *Temple tax.

Shekhinah (Heb., 'dwelling'). The divine presence as described in Jewish literature. The Shekhinah is sometimes used to refer to God himself ('Is it possible for a man to walk after the Shekhinah? . . . Rather this means one should emulate the virtues of the Holy One', *B.Sof.* 14a), but generally it signifies God's presence in this world. It is frequently associated with light ('The angels in heaven and the righteous are sustained by the radiance of the Shekhinah', *Ex.R.* 32. 4). In the *Talmud, the Shekhinah is said to radiate the world (*B.Sanh.* 39a), but rests predominantly on *Israel rather than the *gentiles (*B.Shab.* 22b). It supports the sick (*B.Shab.* 12b); it rests on a worthy married couple (*B.Sof.* 17a), and *proselytes are said to be taken under its wings (*B.Shab.* 31a). Later Jewish philosophers were concerned to avoid *anthropomorphism and therefore tended to maintain that the Shekhinah does not refer to God himself, but is an independent created intermediary. Thus *Sa'adiah Gaon argued that the Shekhinah is the same as the glory of God which was seen by the *prophets in visions. He identified it with the 'created splendour of light', and this view was accepted by *Maimonides. The *kabbalists argued that the Shekhinah was the tenth and final of the *sefirot and represents the feminine principle. Everything that happens to Israel is reflected in the Shekhinah, and she is the first goal of the mystic in his attempt to achieve *devekut.

In Islam, *sakīna* is supreme peace sent by God to dwell in human lives (e.g. Qur'ān 48. 4). In 2. 248, it refers to the Ark of the Covenant: 'Their [the children of Israel] Prophet said to them, "A sign of his sovereignty is that there shall come to you the Ark in which is a *sakīna* from your Lord".' But in general Islam resisted any localization of the transcendent power of God.

J. Abelson, *The Immanence of God in Rabbinic Literature* (1912).

Sheli'aḥ Zibbur (Heb., 'messenger of the community'). Leader of communal worship in a Jewish congregation. The Sheli'aḥ Zibbur repeats the *benedictions of particular prayers, reads certain doxologies, leads the *ʿAmidah, and recites the intermediary *Kaddish prayers. See also CANTOR (*ḥazzan*).

Shem, ha- (Heb., 'The Name'). Hebrew term for God. When reading, or speaking, the term 'ha-Shem' is used to avoid pronouncing the *Tetragrammaton. It is found in such phrases as *Barukh ha-Shem* ('Blessed be the name') and *'Im yirtze ha-Shem* ('God willing').

Shemaʿ (Heb., 'hear'). Declaration of God's unity in the Jewish *liturgy. The Shemaʿ consists of three *Pentateuchal passages: Deuteronomy 6. 4–9, 11. 13–21, and Numbers 15. 37–41. They read:

Hear, O Israel, the Lord [is] our God, the Lord is one. You shall love the Lord your God with all your heart, with all your soul and with all your might. These words which I command you this day you shall take to heart. You shall teach them diligently to your children. You shall recite them when you are at home and when you are away, morning and night. You shall bind them as a sign on your hand, they shall be a reminder above your eyes, and you shall inscribe them on the doorposts of your home and on your gates.

It is recited twice daily in the evening and the morning, and the practice dates back at least to the 2nd cent. CE. There was much debate among the *tannaim as to the correct time for the recitations, and the final decision was that the evening Shemaʿ must be said between nightfall and dawn, and the morning Shemaʿ between dawn and the end of the first quarter of the day. It should be recited with full concentration and in a voice loud enough to be heard. R. *Akiva is said to have recited it just before his death, and his example has been followed by later Jewish *martyrs. After the first sentence ('Hear, O *Israel . . .), it has been customary since rabbinic times to insert a short doxology ('Blessed be the name of his glorious kingdom for ever and ever').

Shembe, Isaiah (founder): see NAZARITE CHURCH.

Shembe's Church (Zulu movement): see NAZARITE CHURCH.

Shemini Azeret (Jewish festival): see SIMḤAT TORAH.

Shemoneh Esreh (Heb., 'eighteen'): see ʿAMIDAH.

Shen. Chinese word for spirits. In antiquity, it refers to the spirit of the *ancestor who enjoys an afterlife because of the continuing and periodical sacrifices offered to him by the members of his offspring. At one time, ancestor-worship was confined to the noble families, and the commoner did not have the privilege of being a shen. It was during the Han times (206 BCE–220 CE) that the ancestor cult was extended to include commoners. But because ancient China did not have a concept of *soul in the Greco-Christian sense, shen is not immortal; it is contingent upon the continuing offering of the sacrifices. Ancient China had a composite concept of the 'soul' in the body composed of *hun and *p'o. After death, hun becomes shen and partakes of the ancestral offerings. P'o, after death, becomes *kuei and goes to the Yellow Spring—the underworld. But in later times, shen and kuei refer to the two alternative designations of the spirit of the deceased: it is called shen when continuing sacrifices are offered to it, and it is called kuei when such sacrifices are denied to it. Shen blesses and kuei harms the family.

Shen, later on, was also used as the common term to refer to a god or goddess. But its root meaning is the ancestral spirit. Like the ancestral spirit which ceases to exist when sacrifices are discontinued, a god or goddess also ceases to function when offerings are no longer performed. In *Ch'eng Hao, shen is a pervasive and controlling spiritual attitude which it is the purpose of a good life to develop.

Sheng(-jen). In China, one who hears the way of Heaven (*T'ien) and develops understanding, often translated as 'sage'. Sheng-*jen is therefore the ideal wise person who penetrates the hidden meaning of all things and lives accordingly. In *Confucius, the reference is to rulers (exemplified in the past) who are capable of transforming an empire in the direction of virtue. In *Mencius, there is more hope that the sheng may appear in the present, on the basis of rigorous effort. For *neo-Confucianists, sheng is related to a basic moral order which can be learnt in ordered stages, but which is inherent in human nature: sheng is more to be realized than created from nothing. In this way, sheng enters deeply into Chinese anthropology.

Shen-hsiang (teacher of Huo-yen who took the school to Japan): see HUA-YEN.

Shen-hsiu (Ch'an/Zen Buddhist teacher): see SOUTHERN AND NORTHERN SCHOOLS.

Shen-hui (responsible for establishing Ch'an/Zen Buddhist school in China): see SOUTHERN AND NORTHERN SCHOOLS.

Sheol. The dwelling place of the dead in Jewish thought. Mention is made in the Bible of the dead going down to Sheol which was thought to have been located somewhere below the earth (Isaiah 57. 9). It was neither heaven nor hell, but something like 'the primitive grave' (Pedersen). It was abhorrent (as frequently in the Psalms and Job) because all connection with God and the living was cut off.

J. W. Bowker, *The Meanings of Death* (1992).

Sherira ben Ḥanina Gaon (*c.*906–1006). Jewish *gaon of *Pumbedita. Sherira claimed descent from King *David, and both his father and grandfather preceded him as gaon. Under Sherira, for a short time, the Pumbedita *academy regained its prestige. He was a prolific writer of *responsa, and he produced his epistle, *Iggeret Rav Sherira Gaon*, on the compilation of the *Mishnah and *Talmud. He also wrote commentaries (now lost) on certain *Talmudic tractates and biblical books. He died at the age of 100, having already resigned in favour of his son who succeeded him as gaon.

Shevirah (destruction): see LURIA, ISAAC BEN SOLOMON.

Shevirat ha-kelim (destruction of the vessels): see LURIA, ISAAC BEN SOLOMON.

Shewbread. The bread laid out in the Jerusalem *Temple. According to Leviticus 24. 5–9, twelve loaves were laid out on the *altar, and frankincense was placed on top of them. They were changed every *Sabbath and eaten by the priests. As with other *sacrifices, after the destruction of the Temple, no more shewbread was offered.

Shīʿa (Arab., 'party'). Those Muslims who believe that *ʿAlī was the legitimate successor (*khalīfa) to *Muḥammad and that ʿAlī, *al-Ḥasan, and *al-Ḥusain were cheated of their right to succeed and fell (as *martyrs) victims to tyranny. Close to the *Sunni majority in most respects, their most important differences are: the Shīʿa community's suffering is consecrated by the suffering (regarded as martyrdom) of the founding *Imāms; the office of Imām is bestowed by God on a chosen person from Muḥammad's family; these Imāms are a spiritually perfect élite and are therefore infallible; the *hidden Imām's return will bring victory over an unjust political order, against which true believers have always been in opposition; meanwhile, the Shīʿa community is guided by the *mujtāhids* (religious specialists in the Shīʿa context). The importance of the *mujtāhid* (e.g. Imām *Khumayni) produces a radical notion of personal authority and a model of action; the *Karbalāʾ paradigm asserts a correspondence between the struggles of ʿAlī and al-Ḥusain and the Shīʿa community's contemporary situation. It thus forms a model and ground for Shīʿa individual and group consciousness. The idea of suffering, divine leadership, and of personal involvement come together in the re-enactment in passion plays (*taʿziya) of the tragic drama of Imām Ḥusain at Karbalāʾ, and also appears in the custom of self-beating in the mosque and public processions that occur on 10 Muḥarram. In addition, the Shiʿites identify as issues between themselves and the Sunnis: *mutʿa (temporary marriage), *taqīya (dissimulation in face of danger), *rawḍa khānī (recitation and memorial of Imāms), *ziyāra (pilgrimage to tombs), and above all the nature and identity of the Imām. Because of their strict allegiance to Imāms, Shiʿites have divided into many sects, of which the following are or have been important: *Ithnā-ʿAsharīya (Twelvers), Zaydis (*Seveners, see ISMAʿĪLĪS), *Bātinites, Nizāris (now called *Aga Khanids), and the *Druzes. Shīʿa communities are found as majorities in Iran and parts of Iraq, and as sizeable minorities in India, Pakistan, Lebanon, Yemen, Persian Gulf States, and E. Africa.

See Index, Shiʿa beliefs; Shiʿa Muslims.

S. H. M. Jafri, *The Origins and Early Development of Shiʿa Islam* (1976); M. M. Momen, *An Introduction to Shiʿism* (1985); S. H. Nasr *et al.* (eds.), *Shiʿism . . .* (1988); M. H. Tabatabai, *Shiʿa* (Eng. tr. 1979).

Shibli (Sūfī mystic of Baghdād): see AL-SHIBLI.

Shichi-fuku-shin (Japanese seven gods of luck): see DAIKOKU.

Shiddukhin (Aram., tranquillity). A formal promise, in Judaism, to marry at some future date. The promise is generally confirmed in writing, and the date of the *marriage and the size of the dowry would be specified. If the agreement is broken, all gifts have to be returned, and compensation may have to be paid unless there are legitimate grounds for breaking the contract. The betrothal is an important stage in marriage, and some authorities, such as *Elijah b. Solomon, consider that it is better to marry and divorce immediately than to break a betrothal. The betrothal is divided into two stages, a word (Yid., *vort*) of agreement sealed by the taking of an object (Ruth 4. 7), followed later by a written agreement stating the terms (*tenaʾim*) and the date of the marriage ceremony: this is concluded by the breaking of a dish to symbolize that the agreement cannot be revoked (i.e. the prior state cannot be reassembled). The betrothal ceremony, which used to be known as *erusin*, is now called *kiddushin*, i.e. the consecration of the woman who is now bound to her husband alone. See also SHADKHAN.

Shiguseigan (Jap.). 'Four great vows' in Zen Buddhism. They are part of the *bodhisattva vow as recited three times at the end of *zazen: (i) *shujō muhen seigando*, 'beings are countless, I vow to save them all'; (ii) *bonnō mujin seigandan*, 'passions are countless, I vow to eradicate them'; (iii) *homon muryo seigangaku*, '*dharma gates are many, I vow to enter them all'; (iv) *butsudō mujō seiganjo*, 'the way of the Buddha is unsurpassable, I vow to actualize it'.

Shih. 1. Phenomenal world: see HUA-YEN. 2. Song Lyrics: see SHIH CHING.

Shih Chi (Records of the Historian): see HISTORIES IN CHINA.

Shih-chieh (Chin.). 'Separation from the corpse', Taoist explanation of how an immortal (*hsien) appears to have died before ascending to heaven (*fei-sheng). When the coffin is opened, it is found to be empty, or to contain some emblem of an immortal.

Shih Ching. *Scripture of Song Lyrics* (also rendered as *Odes*, *Poems*, or *Songs*), one of the three pre-*Confucian Classics. *The Lyrics* are songs of court and countryside, some dating back perhaps as far as the 8th or 9th cent. BCE. They were invested by traditional Confucian literati (*ju) with allegorical moral significance. However interpreted, they were the fountainhead of all Chinese poetry in the form called *shih* (poems to be sung). Beyond their intrinsic value, they are of importance in understanding archaic Chinese society and its religion.

Eng. trs., B. Karlgren (1950), J. Legge (1871, 1895), A. Waley (1937); see also M. Granet, *Festivals and Songs of Ancient China* (1932).

Shih-i (Chin., 'ten wings'). The commentaries (*i-chuan*) on the Taoist **I-Ching*, Book of Changes: (i) *Tuan-chuan* (2 parts); (ii) *Hsiang-chuan* (2 parts); (iii) *Ta-chuan* or *Hsi-tz'u* (2 parts); (iv) *Wen-yen*; (v) *Shokua*; (vi) *Hsü-kua*; (vii) *Tsa-kua*. The Ten Wings are utilized and parts translated by R. Wilhelm (1968).

Shihō (Jap.). Dharma transmission in Zen Buddhism: see HASSU; INKA-SHŌMEI; SOUTHERN AND NORTHERN SCHOOLS.

Shih-shuang Ch'u-yuan (chronicler of Zen and collector of kōans): see KŌAN.

Shih-te (lay Ch'an Buddhist and poet): see HAN-SHAN.

Shi'ism, Shi'ite: see SHĪ'A.

Shikan (T'ien-t'ai meditation methods): see CHIH-KUAN.

Shikantaza (Jap., 'nothing but simply sitting'). A form of the practice of *zazen in Zen Buddhism, in which none of the supports (e.g. attention to breathing) are used. It was advocated by *Dōgen as the purest form of zazen.

Shikatsu (Zen shouting): see LIN-CHI I-HSÜAN.

Shiko (Jap., 'four kalpas'). The four periods of change in Japanese Buddhism: (i) *jōkō*, *kalpa of creation; (ii) *jūkō*, kalpa of continuing existence; (iii) *ekō*, kalpa of destruction; (iv) *kūgō*, kalpa of destruction.

Shimenawa (Jap., etymology uncertain; perhaps 'forbid-rope'), in *Shinto, a sacred rope stretched before the presence of a *kami or around a sacred area. It is made of new rice straw twisted into a rope, from which hang zigzag-cut paper strips (*shide*). It is often stretched between the pillars of the *torii at the entrance to shrines, but it is also found within and without the main buildings. It is often used to mark off sacred areas for special rites, and it encircles sacred objects such as trees or rocks. It may be used also in private homes, especially at festival times. It is believed to bind the power of the kami to the devotee.

Shim'on: see SIMEON.

Shinbutsu-shugō or **Shinbutsu-konkō** (Jap.). Syncretism of *Shinto and Buddhism. The *Tendai school formulated Sannō-ichijitsu Shinto and the Shingon school, *Ryōbu Shintō, approximately at the end of the Heian period. The merger of Buddhism with Shinto, however, goes back to the Nara period. The earliest appearance of *jinguji*, a Buddhist temple associated with a Shinto shrine, was in the early part of the 8th cent. When the great image of the *Buddha (*Daibutsu) was made, the Buddhist priest Gyōki visited the *Ise shrine, and the *kami of the Usa Hachiman in Kyushu was enshrined in the compound of the Todaiji Temple. In 781 the Buddhist title of *bosatsu (*bodhisattva) was conferred on the kami of the *Hachiman, and since then, this kami has been known as Hachiman Daibosatsu.

The union of Buddhism and Shinto was done on the basis of a *Mahāyāna doctrine, *honji-suijaku, which explains the relation of the Absolute Buddha to the Historical Buddha. Aided by this doctrine, the theory assumes that the Japanese kami are Buddhas/Bodhisattvas who reveal themselves for the sake of sentient beings. Buddhas/Bodhisattvas are said to be the true nature (honji) of Japanese kami, and conversely the Japanese kami are the revealed forms (suijaku) of Buddhas/Bodhisattvas. In the early stage of theoretical development the Japanese kami were regarded as sentient beings in need of salvation, but their position was steadily elevated, and by the 11th cent. their status became equal to their Buddhist counterparts. Furthermore, with the rising tide of nationalistic sentiment in the 13th cent., Shinto scholars made use of the same Buddhist logic to elevate the position of Japanese kami and made them superior to Buddhas/Bodhisattvas.

Shingaku. A popular religious movement, sometimes known as 'Education of the Heart', started in 1729 in Japan by *Ishida Baigan (1685–1744), a self-taught scholar and chief clerk for a Kyōto commercial house. Shingaku appealed mainly to the urban merchants, but it also attracted devotees from the peasant and *samurai classes who listened to Baigan's public lectures or were acquainted with the movement's many popular tracts and house codes (*kakun*). The teachings of Shingaku were an eclectic blend of *Confucian moral precepts, Buddhist meditational practices, and worship of the national gods (*kami). Self-cultivation, after the fashion of the Confucian sages, was considered to be a twofold process of attaining enlightenment (*kenshō), or 'knowing the heart', and ethical practice. To know the human heart was to realize spiritually its identity with the heart of heaven and earth. This religious insight liberated one from deluding selfish desires and reinforced the key virtues of loyalty to superiors, filial piety, and devotion to hard work. Shingaku was one of the great influences on the morality of the common people in the Tokugawa period (1600–1868).

Shingon (Jap. pronunciation of Chin., *chen-yen*, 'true word', which represents Skt., **mantra*). A school of esoteric Buddhism established in Japan by *Kūkai after his learning experience in China, especially from Hui-kuo. The 'School of the True Words' (Skt., *mantrayāna*, Jap., *shingon*) emphasizes three mysteries or secrets which all possess, and through which the buddha-nature can be realized: body, speech, and mind. The secrets of the body include *mudrās and the handling of the *lotus and the thunderbolt (*vajra). The secrets of speech include *mantras and *dhāraṇīs. The secrets of mind are the five wise ways of perceiving truth. These skills are transmitted orally from teacher to pupil, never in writing, and not as public teaching. The *Buddha Śākyamuni had taught publicly because the aptitude of his audience required it. The esoteric mysteries were expounded by the cosmic buddha, *Vairocana/ Dainichi Nyorai, for his own delight. In so far as its truth can be expressed at all, it can only be done in representational, above all *maṇḍala, form: 'The esoteric teachings are too profound to be expressed in writing, but with painting their obscurities may be understood. The attitudes and mudrās of the revered images arise from the Buddha's love, and one may attain the buddha-nature simply by looking at them. . . . Art is what reveals to us the state of perfection' (Kūkai). Music and literature, as well as the implements of religion and civilization, are equally important, but central are the two maṇḍalas, Vajra (Diamond) and Garbha (Womb). The first is active, with Vairocana seated on a white lotus surrounded by four transcendent Buddhas; the second is passive, with Vairocana on a red lotus, surrounded by eight buddhas and bodhisattvas. An initiate throws a flower on to the maṇḍalas and becomes the devotee of the buddha on which the flower falls. In Kūkai's case, it fell on Vairocana in both the Diamond and the Womb maṇḍalas.

Some access was given to Shingon when the emperor Junna, in 830, commanded the six existing Buddhist schools to give an account of their teaching. Kūkai produced *The Ten Stages of Religious Consciousness*, tracing the evolution of true religion/ insight from 'the deep, dim, most distant past' of animal awareness, through Confucianism and Taoism, into the stages of Buddhism, culminating in Shingon.

Shingon affirmed the transcendent power of Vairocana and other buddhas, but when this was translated into an apparatus for securing material benefits, other schools, such as *Jodo, arose in protest. But Shingon remains a large Buddhist school in Japan, in six main branches, with more than 10,000 temples.

Minoru Kiyota, *Shingon Buddhism* . . . (1978).

Shinje (Tibetan Lord of Death): see TIBETAN WHEEL OF LIFE.

Shinjimei (Ch'an Buddhist poem): see SENG-TS'AN.

Shinkokinshū (Collected Poetry, Ancient and Modern): see MOTOORI NORINAGA.

Shinkō Shūkyō (new religions): see NEW RELIGIONS IN JAPAN.

Shin Kyōha Shinto (Shinto organization in Japan): see SECT SHINTO.

Shinnyo. Japanese pronunciation of the Chinese character for the Skt., *tathatā. It is the true nature within or underlying all appearance, which cannot be perceived or sensed but simply realized for what it is. Since 'what is' is the buddha-nature (*bussho), shinnyo is effectively a synonym.

Shinran (Shōnin Shinran; 1173–1262). Founder of *Jōdo-shin-shū, a major school of Japanese Buddhism. He became a *Tendai monk at the age of 9. Twenty years later, a period of malaise led him to meditate for 100 days in *Kyōto, which led him to become a pupil of *Hōnen. When Hōnen was exiled in 1207, Shinran rejected the necessity of monastic rules and residence. He married and fathered children. He was pardoned in 1211, and began to establish a community of followers. His belief that the buddhas and bodhisattvas fulfil their commitments and vows to help all in need led him to reject all 'ways of effort' (*jiriki) and to rely on 'the power of the other' (*tariki*; see JIRIKI), concentrated on the Buddha *Amida. Not even repeated calling on Amida's name (*nembutsu) was strictly necessary: one plea sincerely meant will bring Amida's help: 'If there is aroused even once in us one thought of joy and love through Amida's vow, we turn, just as we are, with our sins and lusts upon us, toward *nirvāna.' But having attained rebirth in the *Pure Land (*ōsō*), we return to help others (*gensō*). Even in his afflictions, he made no attempt to justify himself, relying always on Amida alone. He spent the remainder of his life working on his *Kyogyo-Shinshō* (True Teaching, Practice and Realization of the Way).

A. Bloom, *Shinran's Gospel* . . . (1965) and *The Life of Shinran* . . . (1968); A. Lloyd, *Shinran and his Work* (1910).

Shinrikyo (Japanese religious movement): see AUM SHINRIKYO.

Shinsei (founder of Tendai Shinsei-shu): see TENDAI SHŪ.

Shinsen (Jap.). In *Shinto, the food offerings made to the *kami as part of a worship festival (*matsuri). These food offerings vary at different shrines, but generally they consist of food like rice, sake wine, rice cakes, fish, fowl, vegetables, seaweed, fruit, salt, and water. They are ceremonially prepared with great care in the kitchen building, and then they are brought to be placed on tables before the worship building (*haiden) and offered to the kami as tokens of gratitude. Afterwards they are consumed by priests and laypeople in a divine feast (*naorai*).

Shin-shu (true school): see JŌDO-SHIN-SHŪ.

Shintai (Jap., 'kami body'). In *Shinto, the symbol of the *kami or object in which the spirit of the kami is believed to reside, used as the object of worship in a shrine. Also called *mitama-shiro* ('august spirit symbol'), it is housed within the innermost chamber (*honden*) of the shrine sanctuary. When the sacred symbol is present, the inner sanctuary is inviolable and the doors at the front of the inner compartment are kept locked or, when they are opened, a curtain hangs in the entrance-way. The sacred symbol varies from shrine to shrine. Often it is a mirror, but other symbols are sacred wands, jewels, combs, wooden images, and swords; even natural objects such as a mountain or waterfall can be shintai.

Shinto (Jap., 'the way of the kami'). The indigenous Japanese religious tradition. The term Shinto was coined in the 6th cent. CE, using the Chin. characters *shen* ('divine being') and *tao* ('way'); in the native Japanese reading it is *kami no michi or *kannagara no michi*. The origins of Shinto are clouded in the mists of the prehistory of Japan, and it has no founder, no official sacred scriptures, and no fixed system of doctrine. In a real sense, Shinto is the underlying value orientation of the Japanese people, forming the basis of the divergent and yet uniquely Japanese sensitivities, religious beliefs, and attitudes.

By the early historical period (*c*.3rd cent. CE) the Japanese people had attained a degree of self-consciousness as one people sharing a common culture based on the *uji* (clan) system centred around the various tutelary kami (*ujigami*) of the clans. There were of course not only clan kami but also other spiritual powers and beings which had the kami nature—some were connected with geographical regions, others were believed to reside in mountains, trees, rivers, etc. To deal with these kami, *shamans and diviners were important. As the imperial (Tennō) clan gained supremacy, its myths also gained ascendancy, providing the dominant motifs into which the myths of the other clans were integrated to some extent. These myths were collected in the two 8th-cent. collections of mythology and early history, the **Kojiki* of 712 (Records of Ancient Matters) and the **Nihongi*/*Nihonshoki* of 720 (Chronicles of Japan), and they established the basic themes of Shinto, such as the cosmological outlook consisting of a three-level universe, the Plain of High Heaven (*takama-no-hara*), the Manifested World (*utsushi-yo*), and the Nether World (*yomotsu-kuni*); the creation of the world by *Izanagi and Izanami; the forces of life and fertility, as also of pollution and purification; the dominance of the sun kami *Amaterasu Ōmikami; and the descent of the imperial line from Amaterasu. The mythology also established the basic Shinto worship practices, dances, and chanting of *norito.

In the history of Japan, Shinto has gone through many transformations: the imperial edicts prescribing the national rituals in the 7th cent.; the stratification of the Shinto priesthood; the Institutes of the Engi Era (**Engi-shiki*) regulating Shinto in the 10th cent.; Buddhist influence which resulted in the Shinto-Buddhist amalgamation (*Ryōbu-shintō and Sannō ichijitsu); the influence of *neo-Confucianism on Shinto; and finally the resurgence of Shinto stimulated by the 'National Learning' (*kokugaku) movement in the 18th and 19th cents. which returned Shinto to its former position as the guiding principle of Japan and provided a theoretical framework for Shinto thought. There still exist in modern Japan several different types of Shinto. The Shinto of the Imperial Household (kōshitsu shintō) focuses on rites for the spirits of imperial ancestors performed by the emperor. Shrine Shinto (jinja shintō) is presently the form of Shinto which embraces the vast majority of Shinto shrines and adherents in Japan, administered by the Association of Shinto Shrines (jinja honchō), which continues to emphasize the traditionally close relationship between Shinto and Japanese life and the need for national regeneration. Shrine Shinto is free from government control and financially independent now, but to understand this situation it is necessary to mention State Shinto (*kokka shintō) which was created by the Meiji government and continued until the end of the Second World War to control most Shinto shrines and rituals in accordance with the ideological aims of the government. New Shinto movements which arose in the social and economic distress toward the end of the Tokugawa period and in the beginning of the Meiji period, founded by charismatic personalities and promising worldly benefits such as cures for sickness, wealth, and success, were designated by the government as Sect Shinto (*kyōha shintō). Sect Shinto groups continue today, joined by a group of 'New Sect Shinto' (shin kyōha shintō) movements which have developed in the post-war period. Folk Shinto (minkan shintō) is a designation for the extremely wide-ranging group of superstitious, magico-religious rites and practices of the common people, embracing conceptions of the spirits and souls, good and evil kami, geomantic directional taboos, and unlucky days. Folk Shinto does not stand in opposition to Shrine Shinto or Sect Shinto but might be considered as the substratum of those more organized forms.

Shinto has no carefully articulated system of doctrine and ethics; rather, it is a religion of participation in traditional rites and festivals in the shrine setting and, by extension, in the household. The typical setting for the practice of Shinto is the shrine (*jinja*) precinct, which is an enclosed sacred area with a gate (*torii), ablution area, and sacred buildings including the main sanctuary (*honden*) which houses the symbol of the kami (*shintai) and a worship area (*haiden). The natural surroundings are also regarded as permeated with the kami presence; in fact, occasionally a mountain or sacred forest may take the place of the sanctuary. Important in worship at the shrine are rituals which bring about purification from defilements and which foster an integration of human life with the life-bearing power of the kami. Other rituals centre around rites of dedication such as offerings of sprigs of the sacred sasaki tree or offerings of foods (*shinsen) to the kami. Priests (*shinshoku*) chant special prayers (*norito) for the worshippers expressing gratitude to the kami. At special times through the year, shrines become the focal point for community *festivals (*matsuri), held according to the tradition of each shrine at stated times in honour of its own kami, although there are many common festivals, such as the Spring Festival (haru-matsuri), Autumn Festival (aki-matsuri), and the like. For the devout Shintoist, daily life itself is matsuri or service to the kami, and one worships before the home altar (*kamidana). The family is the focal point of individual rites of passage, which often involve participation in the local shrine. After birth (*tanjō*), for example, an infant is taken to the local shrine to be dedicated to the tutelary kami. Further celebrations include the Seven, Five, and Three Festival (*shichigosan*), at which boys of 5 and girls of 3 and 7 are brought to the shrine; Coming of Age celebrations (*seijin shiki*) for those who turn 20; and marriage rites involving the ritual exchange of nuptial cups of sake in the presence of the kami. Interestingly, mortuary rites are usually conducted by Buddhist priests, even though Shinto lays great emphasis on veneration of the ancestral spirits.

Shinto stresses the importance of gratefulness for the blessings of the kami and the benefits of the ancestors. Humans, like nature, are children of the kami and thus inherently good when defilements are removed and the original purity is restored. Humans receive their sacred life from the kami and from the ancestors, together with all the blessings life involves. Their purpose in life is to contribute to the vital development of existence as it is entrusted to them and to realize the will of the kami and the ancestors as this pertains to the family, the community, and the nation. Shinto is thus a 'this-worldly' religion, in the sense that it is interested in tangible benefits which will promote life in this human world.

See Index, Shinto.

H. Hardacre, *Shinto and the State, 1868–1988* (1989); D. C. Holtom, *The National Faith of Japan* (1938, 1965); Hori Ichiro *et al.* (eds.), *Japanese Religion* (1972); G. Kato, *A Historical Study of the Religious Development of Shinto* (1988); J. M. Kitagawa, *Religion in Japanese History* (1966); A. Schwade, *Shinto: A Bibliography in Western Languages* (1986).

Shinwa (Jap., 'stories of the kami'). Japanese stories about the actions of the *kami, more closely resembling *myth than *densetsu or *setsuwa. The most important collections are **Kojiki* and **Nihongi* or *Nihonshoki*.

Shinyakushi-ji (temple-complex): see NARA BUDDHISM.

Shiqquz shomen (idolatrous object set up in the Jerusalem temple): see ABOMINATION OF DESOLATION.

Shirk (Arab.). The most heinous of sins in Islamic reckoning, the alienation from God, to some pseudo-deity, of what only and properly is God's. Shirk is the antithesis of *tawḥīd. The root verb has to do with 'sharing' or 'association': the latter word picks up the offence of associating anything/one with God as God; but it is unsatisfactory if it implies a total dissociation of God from the world, since that would preclude the meaning of creation and the possibility of prophets. Shirk violates the exclusive sovereignty of God, as idolatry does. To worship what is not divine is shirk al-ʿIbāda. But there is also shirk al-maʿrifa when knowledge, possessed only by God, is attributed to another. To commit shirk is to be a mushrik, one who is not *muslim (submitted) to God.

Shiromaṇī Gurdwārā Parbandhak Committee (Pañjābī, 'Chief Temple Management Committee'). Authoritative, elected Sikh body. The SGPC was established in 1920 during the *Akālī movement for reform of *gurdwārā management, and was legally recognized in 1925 by the Sikh Gurdwārās Act. Apart from controlling historic gurdwārās in *Pañjāb, Haryānā, and Himāchal Pradesh, the committee, consisting of 140 elected members and 20 ex-officio members, gives rulings on religious affairs, patronizes education and the training of Sikh preachers, and publishes Sikh literature.

Shiryōken (four alternatives of the Buddhist Lin-chi line): see LIN-CHI.

Shishōtai. Jap. for the *Four Noble Truths.

Shi-tennō (four world protectors in Buddhism): see CELESTIAL KINGS.

Shiva (major Hindu deity): see ŚIVA.

Shivah (Jewish rite): see MOURNING RITES (JUDAISM).

S(h)ivānanda (1887–1963). Indian spiritual leader, influential in establishing the World's Parliament of Religions. He worked as a doctor before abandoning his possessions and wandering through India as a beggar. He founded the Divine life Society and the Yoga-Vedānta Forest Academy, both of which were dedicated to extending spiritual truth without reference to the boundaries of religion, and to offering all seekers food, medicine, and knowledge. Among many works, *Yoga for the West* (1951) and *Self-Realisation* (1954) express his developed views.

Shiva Sharan (musician and scholar of Indian religions): see DANIÉLOU, ALAIN.

Shivata (afternoon Piyyut): see KEROVAH.

Shiv Dayal Siṅgh: see RĀDHĀSOĀMĪ SATSAṆG.

Shizen nōhō (agriculture following nature): see SEKAI KYŪSEIKYŌ.

Shne'ur Zalman of Lyady (1745–1813). Founder of the *Ḥabad *Ḥasidism movement in Judaism. A student of *Dov Baer, he was set to compose an up-to-date **Shulḥān Arukh* (publ. 1814). He became the Ḥasidic leader of Reisen in 1788. He was arrested twice by the Russian government, but was fully acquitted. By 1801 he was settled in Lyady and known as the '*Rav of Lyady'. His *Likkutei Amarim* (Collected Sayings) is the principal text of the movement. The work is also known as *Tanya* and is, unlike most Ḥasidic works, a systematic exposition. It is often referred to as the 'written law of the Ḥabad'; and Shne'ur Zalman is known as Ba'al ha-Tanya. He lived with a single-minded devotion to God: 'Lord of the universe, I want neither your Garden of *Eden nor your rewards in the life to come: I desire only yourself.' See further, ḤABAD.

N. Mindel, *Rabbi Shneur Zalman . . .* (1969).

Sho (Jap., 'nature'). Fundamental or essential character. It appears usually with other terms, as *kensho, realizing one's own nature, or *bussho, buddha-nature.

Sho'ah (calamity): see HOLOCAUST.

Shōbō (Jap., 'true *dharma'). 1. The teaching of the *Buddha, hence *shōbō-shū*, 'Buddhism' in Eng.; and *shōbō-rin*, 'the wheel of true dharma', which is compared to a flying wheel that attacks enemies and destroys wrong views.

2. 'Appropriate reward', main reward for *karma in previous lives, i.e. this body and life—in contrast to *ehō*, 'dependent reward', i.e. secondary consequences such as house, place, and possessions.

Shōbō-genzō (Treasure Chamber of the Eye of True Dharma). A major work of *Dōgen, and one of the supreme works of Japanese Zen. It is a vast and difficult work, written and compiled during the last decade of his life. Dogen intended 100 books but completed only 92—75 unrevised, 12 revised, and an appendix of 5. Much of it, including the title, is untranslatable. Eng. versions are paraphrases—e.g. K. Nishiyama and J. Stevens (1975–83), Y. Yūhō (1986, 75 books).

Shōbōgenzō Zuimonki. A record of brief talks, comments, and exhortations of *Dōgen. It was compiled between 1235 and 1237, and was first published in 1651. The standard (*rufubon*) text was established in 1769. It contains basic instruction (e.g. comment on the old advice on starting as a monk, 'Take one step off the top of a hundred foot pole'; 'If you must be bothered by criticism, be bothered by the criticism of an enlightened man'; 'Unless he behaves as one who is deaf and dumb, a man cannot succeed as the head of a house').

Tr. Reihō Masunaga, *A Primer of Sōtō Zen* (1971).

Shōbō-nenjo-gyō. Sūtra of the Mindfulness of True Dharma, tr. by Pajñaruci, *c.*540 CE. It expounds the causes leading to the six lower domains of appearance (*rokudō): hell, hungry spirits, animals, *asuras, humans, heavenly beings. It encourages escape from them.

Shodō (calligraphy): see ART (Ch'an/Zen).

Shofar. An animal horn (now traditionally a ram's horn) blown during Jewish rituals. The shofar is first mentioned in Exodus 19. 16 at Mount *Sinai. It was used to proclaim the *Jubilee year (Leviticus 25. 9) and sounded on *Rosh ha-Shanah. According to the *Talmud, R. Judah stated that 'the Shofar of Rosh ha-Shanah must be of the horn of the ram, to indicate submission', and that a cow's horn may not be used because of the *golden calf (*BRH* 3. 2). Today, it is blown daily from 2 Elul until the end of Rosh ha-Shanah and again at the end of the last service on Yom Kippur (*Day of Atonement). According to *Maimonides, the reason for sounding the shofar is to 'arouse you from your slumbers, to examine your deeds, to return in repentance and to remember your Creator'.

Shōgatsu (Japanese New Year): see FESTIVALS AND FASTS.

Shoghi Effendi Rabbānī (1897–1957). Guardian (*valī*) of the *Bahā'ī Faith (1922–57), eldest grandson of *'Abdu'l-Bahā, and his appointed successor. He effectively established the modern system of Bahā'ī administration with its locally and nationally elected Spiritual Assemblies (1922–3) and its separate branch of advisory leaders (from 1951). He instituted a series of plans for the expansion of the religion which eventually extended to most parts of the world. He constructed or expanded the Bahā'ī shrines and gardens in Haifa and Akka, and he translated several volumes of *Bahā'u'llāh's writings into English. By his own voluminous writings, he provided authoritative interpretations of Bahā'ī scripture and doctrine. His main writings include his early letters on *Bahā'ī Administration* (1922–9), his delineation of the goals and characteristics of the *World Order of Bahā'u'llāh* (1929–36), and his interpretative history of *Bābī and Bahā'ī history, *God Passes By* (1944). He died unexpectedly, 4 Nov. 1957, in London. Although he had not appointed a successor, the interim leadership of a group of leading believers was readily accepted by nearly all Bahā'īs, despite a challenge by the American, Charles Mason Remey, who claimed to be the second guardian. In 1963, in accordance with references in the Bahā'ī writings, the *Universal House of Justice was elected. No new guardian was appointed, and only a tiny minority of Bahā'īs followed Remey.

For a biography of Shoghi Effendi by his widow, Ruhiyyih Rabbānī (née Mary Maxwell), see *The Priceless Pearl* (1969).

Shōgyoku (leading Zen monk): see MUSŌ SOSEKI.

Shōji. 1. (Jap., 'birth and death'). The cycle of birth and death in Japanese Buddhism: transmigration and reappearance, often referred to as *shōji no rōgoku*, 'the prison of birth and death'.

2. (Jap., 'superior person'). A person of outstanding virtue and wisdom.

Shōjō. Jap. for *Hīnayāna.

Shōjō Daibosatsu. The great *bodhisattva worshipped at the Shōjō shrine at Kumano in Japan. He is an incarnation of *Amida (*gongen), who demonstrates (*shōjō*, 'prove and bear witness') the effectiveness of Amida's route to salvation.

Shokaku Kokushi (leading Zen monk): see MUSŌ SOSEKI.

Shōkan or **Shōken** (Jap., 'seeing one another'). The meeting (*dokusan) of a Zen student with his teacher (*rōshi), when he is accepted as pupil; hence, attaining the same spiritual level as one's teacher.

Shōken. Jap., for 'right view', one of the steps on the Eightfold Path (*aṣtangika-marga).

Shoko Asahara (i.e., Asahara Shoko, Japanese cult leader): see AUM SHINRIKYO.

Shokon Jinja Shrine (Shinto shrine to those who died in battle): see KAMIKAZE.

Shōmu Tenno (701–56). Japanese emperor and patron of Buddhism in the *Nara period. He reigned 724–49, and sought to make Buddhism a foundation for the peace and order of the state. In 728 he ordered that *Konkōmyō-kyō* (The Golden Splendour Sūtra, Skt., *Suvarṇa-prabhāsa-uttama-sūtra*) should be distributed and recited for the protection of the nation. In 741, he ordered the building of a temple in each province to be occupied by nuns (*kokubunji*) to work for the overcoming of those impediments to enlightenment experienced by women. In 745, he ordered the setting up of the *daigedatsu in Tōdai-ji. He inaugurated and dedicated the image, making a personal commitment to the *Three Jewels (*sambō). After his abdication, he became a home-living religious (*nyūdō*), i.e. one who shaves his head and wears the Buddhist religious *habit, but does not join a community.

Shōmyō (chanting sūtras): see MUSIC.

Shōmyō (major figure in establishing Rinzai Zen in Japan): see NAMPO JŌMYŌ.

Shōrin-ji (Chinese Buddhist monastery): see SHAO-LIN-SSU.

Shoshi (Jap., 'true master'). The recognition which a Zen student (who has already received the seal of recognition, *inka-shōmei) receives from his master that he too is competent to train others. Usually, he is already running his own meditation hall (*zendō).

Shōshū (Jap., 'small school'). Jap. name for *Hīnayāna.

Shōtoku Taishi (Japanese prince): see NARA BUDDHISM.

Shou (Chin., 'Long life'). The extension of life via Taoist practices, as a preliminary to immortality (*ch'ang-sheng pu-ssu).

Shou-i (Chin., 'preserving the One'). Taoist meditation practice, in which the deities (*shen) within the body are *visualized, and thus prevented from leaving the body. The controlling or supreme One is visualized in such a way that it may lead to union.

Shou-lao. Popular name of Taoist god of long life, Shou-hsing: see SAN-HSING.

Shou-shan Sheng-nien (Jap., Shuzan Shōnen; 926–93). Ch'an/Zen master of the *Lin-chi succession of the *Rinzai school. He was dharma-successor (*hassu) of Feng-hsueh Yen-chao who regarded him as the saviour of the line. Shou-shan was the master of Fen-yang through whom the revival of Rinzai began. Shou-shan is the originator of the 'stick' *kōan: 'He held up a stick, and said to his pupils: "If you call that a stick, it is an error; if you call it 'not a stick', it is senseless. What, then, will you call it?" '

Showbread (bread laid out in Jerusalem Temple): see SHEWBREAD.

Shōyōroku (Japanese title of collection of kōans): see KŌAN.

Shōzōmatsu (Jap., *shōbō + *zōbō* + *mappō). The three periods, especially in *Pure Land Buddhism, following the *Buddha's death, of true *dharma, semblance dharma, last dharma. In the first, of 500 (or for some 1,000) years, dharma can be followed and enlightenment attained; in the second, of 1,000 (or 500) years, dharma, but not enlightenment, is possible; in the third, dharma exists, but reliance on Amitābha (*Amida) is the only true hope.

Shraddha (supplementary funeral rite): see ŚRĀDDHA.

Shri Chinmoy Centre. Founded by Shri Chinmoy Kumar Ghose (b. 1931), a Hindu *guru from Bengal who arrived in the USA in 1964 to teach his 'path of the heart' towards union with God. Appointed Director of the United Nations Meditation Group in 1970, Shri Chinmoy's New York Center (the main one of many that now exist in the West) received accreditation as a non-governmental organization in 1975. This much-travelled guru has attracted many disciples whom he is said to lead to higher states of consciousness. He himself is believed to have attained that state of consciousness where, following a *Vedic notion of God, the individual has become united with the divine.

Shrine Shinto (Shinto classification): see SECT SHINTO.

Shromaṇī . . . (authoritative Sikh body): see SHIROMAṆĪ.

Shroud of Turin. Christian *relic venerated as the burial shroud of *Jesus (mentioned e.g. in Matthew 27. 59). It is a strip of linen, 4.3 × 1.1 m., bearing the shadowy image of the front and back of a man's body, as if it had been folded over him at the head and the image somehow transferred. The shroud has reposed since 1578 in Turin cathedral. It seems likely that it came to Europe from Constantinople at the time of the Fourth *Crusade, but the theory which attempts to trace its history further back, by identifying it with the image of Christ known as the mandylion of Edessa, has not won acceptance.

The shroud began to attract scientific interest in the 20th cent. mainly as a result of observations of the wounds depicted on the man's body, which correspond to Roman practices of execution in ways unlikely to have occurred to a medieval forger (e.g. nail-marks in the wrists, not the palms of the hands). A team of American scientists tested the shroud intensively in 1978. They seem to have established that it contains actual bloodstains, and that the image of the body cannot have been painted on. However, by 1988 tests on the material had made it clear that the shroud itself (i.e. the material) could not be dated earlier than 1260. The way in which the image was produced is still unknown: some who considered the shroud authentic speculated that it happened as a result of some sort of radiation at Jesus' *resurrection. In 1995, Dr N. Allen produced the same kind of image by using a camera obscura and materials available in the 14th cent. If so, it would be the world's earliest photographic image.

Shrove Tuesday. The day before *Ash Wednesday, so named from the 'shriving', i.e. *confession and *absolution, of the Christian faithful on that day; it is also a day of celebration before the fasting of Lent begins—of which pancake-making and races are vestigial remains.

Shtetl (Yid., 'small town'). Jewish communities in E. Europe, 16th–early 20th cents. The life of the Jewish community centred round home, *synagogue (*shul), and market. The values of *Yiddishkeyt* ('Jewishness') and *menshlikhkeyt* ('humanness') were all-important. Life in the shtetl is now well-known in the West through the paintings of Marc Chagall and the stories of Sholom Aleichem. The pattern of life was eroded in the 20th cent. through pogroms, economic depression, emigration, and ultimately the *Holocaust.

M. Samuel, *The World of Sholom Aleichem* (1943).

Shtibl (Yid., 'little room'). Ḥasidic *synagogue; developed as a centre of prayer, study, and social life when Ḥasidim were excluded by *mitnaggedim (their opponents) from their own synagogues.

Shtible (Yid.). Small Jewish village in E. Europe; see also SHTETL.

Shu (reciprocity): see ETHICS (Confucian).

Shu Ching. Scripture of Historical Documents of Archaic Times, or Book of History, one of the three pre-*Confucian Classics. Collection of both genuine and spurious documents, some purporting to date back to 18th cent. BCE, but some, according to sceptical scholarship, being products of the Han dynasty (206 BCE–220 CE). All were regarded as scripture by most traditional literati (*ju). Among many important ideas given religious sanction by this collection, that of the Mandate of Heaven (*T'ien ming) was perhaps most influential.

Trs. B. Karlgren (1950); J. Legge (1865).

Shugendō. Japanese Buddhist mountain devotion. The sect was founded by En-no-Ozunu (born *c.*635 CE), hence it is also known as En-no-gyōja. From the age of 32, he devoted himself for thirty years to esoteric Buddhism on Mount Katsuragi until he attained miraculous powers. He developed ascetic mountain Buddhism by teaching ways of entering into the strength of mountains. He was exiled in 699, pardoned two years later, and died shortly after. Mountain Buddhists develop esoteric powers, and are known as *yamabushi* or *shugenja*.

Shūhō Myōchō, also known as **Daito Kokushi** (1282–1338). A Zen master of the *Rinzai school, dharma-successor (*hassu) of *Shōmyō, and one of the founders of the Ō-tō-kan lineage. He was the founder and first abbot of Daitoku-ji in *Kyōto, where he insisted on strict and rigorous observance. In his early days, he was taught by *Nampo Jōmyō, who recognized his breakthrough to enlightenment: 'You have cast off brightness and embraced darkness. I am not like you, but now that my line has reached you, it is soundly established.' When he knew that his death was near, he struggled to attain the *lotus position; his brittle leg broke and blood soaked his robe, but he composed his farewell poem in the perfect position: 'I have cut off Buddhas and Patriarchs | The sword is clean | When the wheel of dharma turns | The emptiness rages in vain.'

Shūjō (Jap., 'teaching of a school'). The teaching of a Buddhist school or movement, and in particular that of *Zen.

Shul (Yid., 'School'). Yiddish term for *synagogue, common among *Ashkenazi Jews in Europe. It was a community meeting-place, in which local politics were as prominent as prayer.

Shulḥān Arukh (Heb., 'the prepared table'). Code of Jewish *halakhah (law) written by Joseph *Caro. The *Shulḥān Arukh* is a synopsis of *Jacob b. Asher's *Arbaʿah Turim*. Its four parts deal with the daily and *Sabbath *Commandments, laws governing everyday life (e.g. *dietary laws, *purity, *mourning), laws of *marriage and divorce and, finally, civil and criminal law. It was first printed in 1565, and after amendments for the *Ashkenazim had been added by Moses *Isserles, it became accepted as the most authoritative code of Jewish law. Initially there was considerable opposition from Solomon *Luria, on the grounds that Codes simply give rise to further commentaries and complications, and that the last state is worse than the first. The *Shulḥān Arukh* has in fact been subject to a whole series of commentaries (e.g. the 17th-cent. *Turei Zahav* of David b. Samuel ha-Levi and the *Siftei Kohen* of Shabbetai b. Meir ha-Kohen), but these served to make the Code acceptable to every sector of the Jewish community.

Shushi-gaku. Japanese term for the orthodox *neo-Confucian teachings of *Chu Hsi (1130–1200) and his followers. Although these teachings were known in Japan centuries earlier, they did not find a following until the 17th cent. when they benefited from a measure of recognition by the government (*bakufu*) of the time. The major advocates of Shushi-gaku in Japan were Hayashi Razan (1583–1657), who served the shōgun and established a school staffed throughout the Tokugawa (1600–1868) period by his descendants, and Yamazaki Ansai (1618–82), who stressed the more religious aspects of neo-Confucianism. The teachings contributed substantially to the rationalism, humanism, and historical-mindedness that characterize Tokugawa thought as a whole.

Shushogi (text summarizing Sōtō): see SŌJI-JI.

Shūso (religious founder): see NICHIREN SHŌSHŪ.

Shusse (Jap.). One who has transcended an existing state. The application is various, e.g. to one who has renounced the world to become a Buddhist monk, to a *bodhisattva who appears in this world to save sentient beings, to a *Zen monk who undertakes the headship of a community or temple, etc.

Shuzan Shōnen (Ch'an/Zen master): see SHOU-SHAN SHENG-NIEN.

Shwedagon Pagoda. Major *pagoda in Burma. It is set on a hill in Rangoon, and its present form is a consequence of many extensions and rebuildings after earthquakes. Many of the additional buildings, and the elaborate gold decoration, are a result of *merit-seeking gifts, especially from the rulers of Burma.

Shylock (Jewish character in Shakespeare): see USURY.

Sian (Xi'an, 'Western Peace'). Major Chinese city (capital of Shaanxi province), frequently the capital of China, near which (30 km. to the east) the vaults of the Terracotta Warriors were discovered in 1974. When the Emperor Qin Shi Huangdi unified China in 221 BCE, he established his capital to the east of Sian and began to build a magnificent palace on the site of present-day Sian: it was then known as Chang'an. The warriors were discovered in his tomb—more than 8,000 in number. The first vault revealed the infantry of his army, the second and third vaults the charioteers. Sian also contains the Big Wild Goose Pagoda, in imitation of a pagoda of the same name in India: the name is derived from a time when some starving Buddhist monks prayed for food and a wild goose fell out of the sky. In gratitude, they buried the goose instead of eating it, and built a temple on the spot. It is one of the oldest (originally built in 652) buildings in China (restored during the 1950s). The Little Goose Pagoda (707–9) was early destroyed in war; the rebuilt Pagoda was damaged by earthquake in the 16th cent., but was repaired and reopened in 1977.

Sibylline Oracles. A collection of prophetic oracles in fourteen books by Jewish and Christian authors. The prologue claims that the work comprises the utterances of pagan Sibyls (female ecstatic prophets described, e.g., by Virgil, *Aeneid* 6. 77–102) of various periods. Modern critics, however, recognize them as religious propaganda to gain the pagan world to Judaism or Christianity. Books 3–5 are probably mainly Jewish, of which 3 is the oldest (*c.*140 BCE) and 4–5 later than 70 CE. The other books are either of Christian origin or with heavy Christian interpolations. Their dates are disputed, but probably range from the late 2nd to the 4th cents.

Tr. J. H. Charlesworth, *The Old Testament Pseudepigrapha*, i (1983), 317–472.

Sicarii (Lat., 'men armed with curved daggers'). Jewish resistance fighters against the Romans in the 1st cent. CE. According to *Josephus, the Sicarii assassinated the *high priest, Jonathan, and held the fortress of Masada in 70 CE. He seems to have avoided the term *'Zealot' and preferred 'sicarii', since it was more derogatory. The Sicarii carried out guerrilla war against the Romans and their allies, and the 'sikarim' are mentioned in the *Talmud in connection with the siege of Jerusalem (*Makhsh* 1. 6).

Sicilian Vespers. A massacre of 3,000–4,000 French in Sicily, 30 Mar. 1282, initiated when the bell for *vespers was rung. It marked the end of the plans of Pope Martin IV and Charles of Anjou to reconquer Constantinople, and led indirectly to the decline of papal power. The theme supplied (remotely) the libretto for Verdi's *I vespri siciliani*.

S. Runciman, *The Sicilian Vespers* (1958).

Siddha (Skt., 'perfect, complete'). In E. religions, one who has attained the supreme goal, who may also have acquired the siddhi powers. The siddhi powers of a *yogi include becoming invisible, leaving the body and re-entering it at will, reducing the size of one's body to that of a seed, or increasing it to that of a mountain. Despite the warning of great teachers (e.g. *Patañjali) that these powers should not be pursued as an end in themselves, many yogis have deliberately cultivated siddhi powers. For Śaivites, *Śiva is the supreme Siddha, Ādi-nātha, of whom all other siddhas are incarnations. In Buddhism the *iddhi powers are comparable. For Tantric Buddhism, see SIDDHA TRADITION. In the *Sāṁkhya tradition the eight powers are translated into interior attitudes: the use of reason, study, accepting instruction, rational discussion, generosity, detachment from suffering, either from that arising from personal circumstances, or from chance or fate. Among Jains, siddhas are souls (*jīva) which have attained release from *karma and attained the goal. See also FIVE SUPREME BEINGS.

Siddharta (personal name of the Buddha): see SIDDHATTA.

Siddhasena Divakara ('The Sun', *c*.4th/5th cent. CE). Jain logician. Since the earliest biography is many centuries after his death, the details of his life are uncertain. It is not even clear whether he was a *Digambara (his work shows traces of their position) or Śvetāmbara. He appears to have been a *brahman who was converted after losing a debate with a Jain monk, Vṛddhavādin, who then performed many miracles disclosing the truth of his new faith. The major works attributed to him are *Nyāyāvatāra* (The Descent of Logic) and *Sammatitarka* (The Examination of True Doctrine, tr. S. Sanghavi and B. J. Doshi). He also wrote verse compositions of a more devotional kind, e.g. *Dvātriṃśika*.

Siddha tradition (Skt.; Tib., *grub.thob*, 'person of achievement'). A tradition in Indian Tantric Buddhism which had great influence on the development of Buddhism in Tibet. While *siddha generally signifies a *yogin (Hindu or Buddhist) who has achieved psychic powers (siddhi/*iddhi), Tibetan Buddhism recognizes a canon of eighty-four principal siddhas whose achievement is enlightenment itself: their magical powers are a display of the achievement. Eminent in the tradition are Virūpa, who prevented the sun from moving for two days and a night in order to continue drinking wine, and who originated the *Sakya *Lam Dré* system of relating *sūtras and *tantras; *Padmasambhava, who as Sakara ended a twelve-year famine by causing rains of food, water, and jewels, and who founded the *Nyingma school; Bhusuku, the Nālandā monk who levitated, cured blindness, and as *Śāntideva wrote the *Bodhicaryāvatāra* (Entering the Path of Enlightenment), a seminal *Geluk text; and *Nāropa, whose Six Doctrines (*Nāro Chos Drug) embody the very nature of siddhahood and still delineate the training of a *Kagyü *lama.

The siddha tradition is primarily important to Tibetan Buddhism because the Indian siddhas were progenitors of Tibetan lineages. Yet this process is also evidence that many qualities mistakenly characterized as Tibetan developments of Buddhism are actually of Indian origin, such as the importance of a teacher (*guru), the so-called 'crazy-wisdom' (denoting the liberation from conventional behaviour sometimes demonstrated by holy people, see HOLY FOOL); the stress on the possibility of enlightenment in this lifetime (often declared a Chinese influence) and, of course, *Vajrayāna itself.

J. B. Robinson, *Buddha's Lions* (1979).

Siddhattha (Pāli) or **Siddhartha** (Skt.). Personal name of the *Buddha. It means 'he whose aim is accomplished'.

Siddha Yoga Dham. A movement founded by Swami Muktananda which practises a form of *Kuṇḍalinī yoga. In this, a force referred to as *śaktipat* ('descent of power') is said to activate the spiritual energy within the central nervous system.

Muktananda arrived in the USA at the invitation of Werner Erhard, founder of *EST, in 1976 and established a centre there. Today there are centres in over fifty countries and an estimated 40,000 devotees. There are few strict rules apart from daily meditation and vegetarianism.

Siddh Goṣṭ (Pañjābī, 'discourse with siddhs'). Gurū *Nānak's discourse with *siddhs* (*Nāth *yogīs). The *janam-sākhīs provide a context of religious debate for the unified composition attributed to Nānak in the *Ādi Granth (938–46). The Siddh Goṣṭ summarizes Nānak's teaching in answer to wide-ranging questions.

Siddhi (yogic powers): see SIDDHA.

Siddur (Jewish prayer book): see PRAYER BOOK.

Sidrah (part of the Jewish Pentauteuch read in synagogue): see SEDAROT.

Siffin (battle): see ʿALĪ B. ABĪ ṬĀLIB.

Sifra (Aram., 'a book'). *Halakhic midrash to *Leviticus. *Sifra* was probably compiled in *Erez Israel in the 4th cent. CE. It may have originated in the school of *Akiva. It is quoted in the Palestinian *Talmud, but in the Babylonian only in a form that does not agree with the surviving text. It interprets Leviticus verse by verse, and was known by the *geonim as the *Torat Kohanim* (The Law of Priests).

Sifre(i) (Aram., 'books'). *Halakhic midrash on *Numbers and *Deuteronomy. *Sifrei* was probably compiled in *Erez Israel in the 4th cent. CE. Although the two parts have traditionally been printed together, they belong to different *tannaitic schools. The *Sifrei to Numbers* probably originated in the school of *Ishmael, while the *Sifrei to Deuteronomy* originated mainly in the school of *Akiva. Both provide verse-by-verse commentaries to the text.

Sifrei Zuta. A *halakhic midrash to *Numbers. *Sifrei Zuta* was extensively quoted, but the original text was lost until it was rediscovered in the *Cairo Genizah. It should be dated in the 4th cent. CE, and it contains the names of several *tannaim who are not mentioned in the *Mishnah.

Sigālovāda (discourse from Pāli canon): see DĪGHA NIKĀYA.

Siger of Brabant (Averroist philosopher): see AVERROISM.

Signs: see SYMBOLS.

Sikh (Pañjābī, 'learner, disciple'). One who believes in one God (*Ik Onkar) and is a disciple of the *Gurū. For further detail see SIKHISM.

Śikhā. The tuft of hair, also called *choṭī*, left unshaven by orthodox Hindus at the place (*brahmārandra) where the *ātman leaves the body at death or cremation. It is cut off, or plucked out, by anyone becoming a *saṁnyāsin.

Śikhaṇḍin. In the *Mahābhārata, a Pāñcāla prince, son of Drupada, and brother of *Draupadī and Dhṛṣṭadyumna, whose character is determined by his previous incarnation as a princess of *Kāśi named Ambā. Years before, Ambā, having been gravely offended by *Bhīṣma, had performed austerities and then committed suicide, with the promise of rebirth as a man to avenge the insult. She was, however, reborn as a woman, but after some confusion, managed to trade away her femininity for the masculinity of a generous *yakṣa, thus becoming a man at last. This man, Śikhaṇḍin, like the other Pāñcālas, joins the *Pāṇḍava side in the *Kurukṣetra war, where he is paired against Bhīṣma, who is serving as the first general for the *Kauravas. The Pāṇḍavas having determined that Bhīṣma will not defend himself against Śikhaṇḍin, because he has taken an oath never to fight a woman, *Arjuna succeeds in killing Bhīṣma by shooting from behind Śikhaṇḍin. Śikhaṇḍin later dies, along with other Pāñcālas, in a night raid staged by *Droṇa's son Aśvatthāman. In *Mahābhārata* legend, Śikhaṇḍin is best remembered for his transsexuality. He/she is also said to be the incarnation of a *rākṣasa.

Śikhara (symbolic mountain): see ART (Hinduism).

Sikhism. The religion and life-way of those who are Sikhs. The word *sikh* (Pañjābī; cf. Skt., *śikṣya*) means 'a learner', 'a disciple'. Sikhs are those who believe in one God (*Ik Onkar) and are disciples of the *Gurū. In Indian usage, *gurū* can apply to any religious teacher or guide, but for Sikhs it is restricted to God as *Sat Gurū (true teacher), the ten Gurūs (listed under *Gurū) from Gurū *Nānak (b. 1469 CE) to Gurū *Gobind Siṅgh (d. 1708), and to the *Ādi Granth (Sikh scripture), known as Gurū Granth Sāhib and revered as such. Sikhs accept *initiation with *amrit, according to the *rahit maryādā which gives detailed requirements. Together Sikhs make up the *panth in which it is believed that the guidance of the Gurū is also present, but in a more limited way. Fully committed and initiated Sikhs belong to the *khālsā. There are *c.*14 million Sikhs in India, four-fifths in *Pañjāb. In a wide *diaspora, the largest community (*c.*300,000) is in the UK.

Sikhism began in the context of the Muslim–Hindu confrontation in N. India, when some (e.g. *Kabīr) were seeking reconciling truth. It was a time also of vivid and moving devotion to God (*bhakti), all of which (especially the *Vaiṣṇavites) was influential on Gurū Nānak, though even more so was his own profound experience of God. But whereas others like Kabīr and *Dādū Dāyal left no organized movement to perpetuate their vision of God, Gurū Nānak did, not least because of his decision to appoint a succeeding gurū. He did not attempt to merge Hinduism and Islam, but simply insisted on the worship of the True Name (*Nām), God who can be found within and does not require the rituals and doctrinal controversies of existing religions: 'There is no Hindu or Muslim, so whose path shall I follow? I shall follow the path of God.'

Gurū Nānak thus emphasized the absolute unity and sovereignty of God, creator of all that is: everything is dependent on his will (*hukam). He does not become present in the world (in contrast to Hindu understandings of *avatāra), but makes his will and his way known. In discerning this, *meditation (*nām simaran) on *śabda ('sound') is of paramount importance, especially through repetition of the Name, or on the hymns of the Gurū Granth Sāhib. *Karma and *saṃsāra are accepted: the way to release or liberation is to move one's life against one's own wilful and disordered inclination (*haumai) into alignment with the will (hukam) of God. This is only possible because of the help of God, the equivalent of *grace, described in many words, e.g. *kirpā, nadar*, *praśād: 'Karma determines the nature of our birth, but the door of salvation is found only through grace' (Ādi Granth, p. 2). A Sikh therefore moves from being a wayward wrong-doer (*manmukh) to being one who is devoted to and absorbed in the Gurū (*gurmukh). The manmukh gives way to the *five evil passions and is lost in *māyā (understood by Sikhs as the error which attributes higher value to the material world than to the spiritual). Those who move from manmukh to gurmukh pass through stages (*khaṇḍ): dharam khaṇḍ (living appropriately; cf. *dharma); giāñ khaṇḍ (deeper knowledge); saram khaṇḍ (effort or joy); karam khaṇḍ (effort or joy); *sach khaṇḍ (bliss beyond words and beyond rebirth, merging with the divine as a drop in an ocean or as a spark in a flame). The attainment of sach khaṇḍ does not depend on an *ascetic renunciation of this world, but on finding and following the will of God in everyday life. Thus Sikhs remain *grihasth* ('householders'), in contrast to the four *āśramas of the Hindus, for whom *gṛhastha is only one stage, to be followed by progressive renunciation.

Gurū Nānak did not hold that other religions are untrue or worthless, but he believed that their attention to the details of ritual and outward observance are likely to be an impediment: 'Humans are led astray by the reading of words; performers of ritual are vain and proud. How can it help to bathe in a place of *pilgrimage, if the uncleanness of pride is in the heart?' Under the first four Gurūs, there was no conflict with the surrounding majority religions, but marks of identity were further developed—e.g. Sikh days in the religious calendar. Under *Rām Dās, 'the tank of nectar', *Amritsar, was built, leading to the *Harimandīr (Golden Temple), the centre of Sikh identity. Always more at ease in general with Hindus, Sikhs found tensions with Muslims and the Mughal emperors increasing; this led to the forming of the *khālsā under the tenth Gurū, Gobind Siṅgh. The khālsā is the community of Sikhs who have received *khaṇḍe-dī-pāhul, and are distinguished by the *Five Ks. Driven increasingly into co-operation with the Hindus against the continuing ambitions of Muslim conquest, Sikhs began to revert to customs abhorred by the first Gurūs, e.g. *caste, the sacred cow (*gō), *satī. Various reform movements emerged, notably that of Dyāl Dās (1783–1855) whose *Niraṅkārīs (the formless) resisted the use of images, even of the Gurūs; Sain Sahib (d. 1862) whose *Namdhāris attacked all reversion to Hinduism and held that a continuing Gurū is necessary; and Sant Niraṅkārī Maṇḍal (the Universal Brotherhood, not to be confused with the Niraṅkārīs), which has modified traditional practices and was banned or boycotted by the *Akal Takht in 1978. In response to Christian missionaries, the *Siṅgh Sabhā was formed. The British (having conquered the last Sikh empire in the Sikh Wars), recognized with some gratitude Sikh assistance during the Mutiny, and reinforced their spiritual independence. Partly from this encouragement, the *Akāli movement emerged, which secured the return of *gurdwārās to Sikh control and remains committed to Sikh autonomy in the Puñjāb (*Khālistān).

The communal nature of the Sikh religion is greatly emphasized by its institutions, with *sevā (community service) being highly valued. Gurū Nānak had established the *dharmsālā* as a place of assembly, in distinction from Hindu temples, not least by including the *langar as a basis for communal meals. The *dharmsālā* led to the gurdwārā (though Namdhāris retain the older name). Sikhs are expected to rise early, bathe, and recite the *Japji, which begins with the *Mul Mantra. Sikhs share some *festivals with Hindus (though adapted in a Sikh direction) and have others of their own celebrating the Gurūs. Worship is simple compared with Hindu ritual; and *kīrtan is prominent.

N. G. Barrier, *The Sikhs and Their Literature: A Guide to Tracts, Books and Periodicals, 1849–1919* (1970); W. O. Cole and P. S. Sambhi, *The Sikhs* . . . (1985); Gopal Singh, *The Religion of the Sikhs* (1971); C. M. Joshi (ed.), *Sikhism* (1980); Khushwant Singh, *A History of the Sikhs* (1963–6); M. A. Macauliffe, *The Sikh Religion* . . . (1909); W. H. McLeod, *Guru Nanak and the Sikh Religion* (1968), *The Sikhs* (1989), and *Textual Sources for the Study of Sikhism* (1984); J. T. O'Connell, *Sikh History and Religion in the Twentieth Century* (1988); Ganda Singh, *A Select Bibliography of the Sikhs and Sikhism* (1965); Hakam Singh, *Sikh Studies: A Classified Bibliography* . . . (1982); Rajwant Singh, *The Sikhs* . . . (1989).

Śīla (Skt.; Pāli, *sīla*). 'Precepts', the basic obligations which Buddhists undertake, ten for *bhikṣu/bhikṣunis, five for laypeople (or the first eight on *uposatha days): the undertaking, in the rule of training, is to abstain from (i) harming any living being, (ii) taking anything not given, (iii) misconduct involving sense-pleasure, (iv) false speech, (v) losing control of mind through alcohol or drugs, (vi) solid food after midday, (vii) frivolous entertainments, (viii) perfumes and jewellery, (ix) raised, soft beds, (x) involvement with money or other valuables. These are understood, not so much as 'ten commandments', as promises that Buddhists make to themselves at the start of each day.

H. Saddhatissa, *Buddhist Ethics* . . . (1970).

Sīlabbata-parāmāsa (Pāli) or **śīlavrata-parāmārśa** (Skt., 'cleaving to rules and rites'). According to Buddhism, the mistaken view that adherence to rules and rites is sufficient to bring about holiness and purity. The view is rejected as one of the four kinds of clinging (*upādāna) to existence and one of the ten fetters (*saṃyojanas) that bind a person to continued rebirth. Criticism was chiefly directed at the *brahmans who stressed adherence to tradition and externals as an essential component of religion.

Silsilah (Arab., *salsala*, 'make a chain'). The chain of transmission in *Sūfī Islam from the initial blessing (*baraka) of God, running down in succession to the present *shaykh. Most silsilahs are traced back to *Muḥammad, one (the *Tijāniy(y)a) claiming to be derived from a direct vision of Muḥammad to the founder. The Khāḍiriy(y)a claim to be founded directly by *Khiḍr. It is an initial obligation on joining an order to learn the silsilah in order to understand how the baraka has been transmitted.

Silva Mind Control. Established by Jose Silva in Mexico and the USA in 1966, this is a method for increasing the powers of the mind. The claim is to provide 'the science of tomorrow—today'. 'Dynamic meditation' is held to provide contact with the 'Alpha dimension', a level of consciousness belonging to the spiritual world. It is claimed that contact with this god-like realm has far-reaching effects: improving memory, problem-solving, and creative learning abilities, and developing willpower; freeing psychic powers to heal, to obtain goals, to help others, and to practice ESP.

J. Silva and P. Miele, *The Silva Mind Control Method* (1980).

Silver-tongued Smith (Christian preacher): see CHRYSOSTOM.

Sīmā (bounded space in Buddhism): see VINAYA.

Simeon, Charles (1759–1836). Second-generation leader of the *Evangelical Revival. Appointed Vicar of Holy Trinity Church, Cambridge, in 1782, he gave himself to expository preaching, and to a long ministry to undergraduates. A zealous promoter of overseas *missions, he also encouraged the work of the British and Foreign *Bible Society. A. W. Brown's *Recollections of Simeon's Conversation Parties* (1863) illustrates this occasionally eccentric bachelor's teaching methods and influence on undergraduate life for over fifty years. His favourite gesture in the pulpit, much imitated by undergraduates, resembled that of catching a fly between finger and thumb. His Simeon Trust was formed to purchase livings for evangelicals. His loyalty to the Church of England never wavered and he insisted on the primacy of parish work over itinerancy.

C. H. Smyth, *Simeon and Church Order* (1940).

Simeon Bar Kokhba (leader of Jewish revolt): see BAR KOKHBA, SIMEON.

Simeon Bar Yoḥai (2nd cent. CE). Jewish *tanna. Simeon bar Yoḥai was a student of R. *Akiva, and was vigorous in his opposition to the Romans. Surviving the *Bar Kokhba revolt, he 'revived the *Torah at that time' (*B.Yev.* 62b). According to the *Mishnah, 'Every anonymous statement is by Simeon in accordance with the rules of Akiva' (*B.Sanh.* 86a). He was betrayed to the Romans and was forced to live in hiding for twelve years. After he emerged, he established a *yeshivah in Tekoa. He is remembered for many sayings, including, 'If *Israel were to keep two *Sabbaths according to the laws, they would be immediately redeemed' (*B.Shab.* 118b); 'To honour your parents is more important than to honour God'; 'God is angry with anyone who does not leave a son as his heir'; 'It is forbidden to observe a *mitzvah [commandment] by doing something forbidden.' He edited a collection of *halakhic *midrashim on Exodus, of which only fragments survive, and he is traditionally credited with the authorship of the **Zohar*. *Kabbalists remember his death on the festival of *Lag Ba-Omer.

I. Konowitz, *Rabbi Shimon b. Yohai* (1966).

Simeon ben Gamaliel I (1st cent. CE). *Nasi of the Jewish *Sanhedrin. According to *Josephus, he was 'a man highly gifted with intelligence and judgment'. He presided over the Sanhedrin during the period of the Roman destruction of Jerusalem, and is remembered for his moderate leadership. He is traditionally included among the *Ten Martyrs.

Simeon ben Gamaliel II (early 2nd cent. CE). Jewish *nasi. Simeon ben Gamaliel II was the son of Rabbi *Gamaliel II and father of *Judah ha-Nasi. After the *Bar Kokhba revolt, he went into hiding, but was appointed nasi at the second meeting of the *Sanhedrin after the revolt. He was known for his humility (*BBM* 84b), and many *halakhot are preserved in his name in the *Mishnah. According to R. *Johanan, 'Wherever Simeon b. Gamaliel taught in our Mishnah, the halakhah follows him' (*B.Ket.* 77a).

Simeon the New Theologian (Byzantine mystic): see SYMEON.

Simeon the Stylite, St (*c.*390–459). First of the Christian *stylites. He began as a monk in the monastery of Eusebona near Antioch, then moved to Telanissos, where after several years as an *anchorite, he mounted a pillar; this was at first close to the ground, but the height was eventually raised to 18 m. He lived there until he died, occupied in prayer and worship. Many pilgrims came to see him, from as far as W. Europe, and this new *asceticism began to be imitated (e.g. by Simeon the Younger and Daniel). His influence was extensive, as can be inferred from the remains of the church and monastery built around his pillar (modern Qalʿat Simʿān). Feast day, 1 Sept. in the E., 5 Jan. in the W.

Siṃhabhadra (Indian Buddhist philosopher): see HARIBHADRA.

Simḥat Torah (Heb., 'rejoicing in the *Torah'). The last day of the Jewish *festival of *Sukkot. This is the day on which the cycle of Torah readings is completed and a new beginning made. In *Israel, it is celebrated on the same day as Shemini Azeret, but in the *diaspora it is the following day. The readings are accompanied by festivities (see BRIDEGROOMS OF THE LAW) and children participate in the rejoicing. There are Torah processions, hymns of praise are sung, and the *bimah is circled seven times.

Similitudes of Enoch (part of pseudepigraphical book): see ENOCH.

Simon, St. One of the twelve *apostles; 'the Less', called 'the Cananean' or 'the Zealot' (Mark 3. 18; Luke 6. 15). He need not be identified with Jesus' brother Simon (Mark 6. 3). In W. churches he is traditionally paired with St *Jude in the ecclesiastical calendars and in dedications of churches. Feast day, 10 May in the E.; 28 Oct. in the W.

Simon Magus. An opponent of St *Peter, later identified as a heresiarch (see HERESY). According to Acts 8. 9–24 he was a sorcerer known as 'that Power of God which is called Great', who practised in Samaria. After being baptized he was rebuked by Peter for trying to buy spiritual powers with money (hence the term *simony). Later Christian writers (*Justin, *Irenaeus) knew of a *gnostic sect of Simonians and appear to have accepted that Simon was its founder; he thus became 'the prime author of every kind of heresy' (*Eusebius). His career is also elaborated in the **Clementine Homilies* and *Recognitions*, and also in other legends from which, perhaps, that of *Faust evolved.

Simons, Menno (Dutch priest and radical reformer): see MENNONITES.

Simony. From the action of *Simon Magus in Acts 8. 18–24, the purchase or sale of spiritual things, and specifically of an ecclesiastical benefice or preferment.

Sin

Judaism In the Hebrew scriptures there are three main categories of sin. *Ḥet* indicates a failure of mutual relations—so *Jacob asks, 'What is my *ḥet* that you have so hotly pursued after me?' (Genesis 31. 36). *Pesha* indicates a breach in the relationship between two parties—so the Northern Kingdom is described as creating *pesha* against the House of *David (1 Kings 12. 19), and God's forgiveness is asked when his people have made *pesha* against him (1 Kings 8. 50). The verb *awah* (*avah*) expresses the notion of crookedness—so the prophet *Isaiah (59. 2) declares that, as a result of human *awonot*, a wall has been set up between God and the sinner; *avon* is usually a more deliberate sin, more in the social and ethical domain than the ritual. The *rabbis used the term *averah* (passing over), so sin is a passing over or rejection of the will of God. In general, sins of commission are regarded more seriously than sins of omission (*B.Yoma* 85b, 86a), and the primary cause of sin is the *evil inclination. R. Simeon b. Lakish pronounced, '*Satan, the evil inclination and the *angel of death are one and the same' (*BBB* 16a). The antidote for sin is the study of *Torah: 'If you occupy yourself with Torah, you will not be delivered into the inclination's hand' (*B.Kid.* 30b). See also SACRIFICE; TESHUVA; FORGIVENESS.

S. Schechter, *Aspects of Rabbinic Theology* (1909).

Christianity In the New Testament there are distinctive treatments of sin in (i) Paul, for whom sin is a ruling power in the world (Romans 5. 12; Galatians 3. 22) and in people (Romans 6. 6, 7. 14–20); (ii) the *Johannine writings, where 'sin' is the opposite of 'truth' and is related to disbelief in *Christ (John 9. 41, 15. 24); and (iii) *Hebrews, where it is a disorder atoned for by sacrifices (2. 17, 5. 1). Otherwise the word and its cognates are used without great precision, particularly in expounding the saving work of Christ (e.g. 1 Timothy 1. 15; see ATONEMENT): 'sin' is whatever has separated humans from God (Romans 3. 23), and Christ is necessary to restore the new *covenant relationship.

Of later elaborations of the understanding of sin, the most important is probably the concept of *original sin, the hereditary sinful state of human beings (ab-original sin, because it is derived *ab origine*, from the condition of human life). On this *Augustine, in opposition to *Pelagius, largely determined the medieval teaching. Also important was the development of the penitential system, which offered a practical way of dealing with the reality of the post-baptismal sins of Christians: see PENANCE. This development gave rise to a distinct corpus of *moral theology in Thomas *Aquinas and other writers. Since the 16th cent. this has in turn produced such precise distinctions as those now drawn between *mortal and *venial sin.

The medieval practice could also foster an external and mechanical view of sin: for each sin, due satisfaction was to be paid in a measurable quantity of penance or the equivalent. The *Reformers were largely concerned to reject such ideas of sin. The doctrine of *justification by faith only was held by M. *Luther to be the one solvent for every external view of sin. The *Calvinistic teaching on *predestination brought vividly before the imagination the terrifying consequences of sin. In the 17th cent. the *Jansenist movement in the Roman Catholic Church had affinities with the Reformers' teaching, while in Protestant churches, certain *Arminian tenets had much in common with Catholic teaching.

Under the secularizing influences of the *Enlightenment attempts were made to remove sin from its religious setting and interpret it as moral evil ('philosophic sin'). More recently dialectical theology has again emphasized the gravity of sin as part of the human situation; and social sin has been increasingly recognized as amounting to far more than the sum of individual sins and sinners, as e.g. in *Liberation Theology. See also SEVEN DEADLY SINS.

Islam There are more than ninety words in the *Qur'ān for sin or offence against God or one's fellow human beings; it is therefore impossible to summarize the many nuances of sin in Islam. But from that fact alone, it is obvious that the mission of *Muḥammad was addressed to humans who are in grave danger because of their propensity to sin. There is no trace of an ab-original fault which affects all subsequent humans. Nevertheless, there are many ways in which humans fall into sin or error, and the Qur'ān offers guidance so that there can be no doubt what behaviour God requires. The Day of Judgement (*yaum al-Din) is decided on an exact balance between good and evil acts—though evaluation takes account of *niy(y)a (intention). But God is merciful and compassionate, and the way of repentance (*tawbah*) is always open. Even so, there were those in early Islam who held that a Muslim who sins has become an apostate and therefore no longer belongs to the community (see KHARIJITES).

Hinduism As in other E. religions, the most radical fault which has to be overcome is not so much sin as ignorance (*avidyā). Nevertheless, it is perfectly well recognized that there are behaviours (and thoughts) which are wrong and which might well be called sin, for which the most usual word is *pāpa. The foremost of these (pāpātama) is *moha. Closely associated are *lobha and *krodha* (anger). The classic texts of *dharmaśastra develop an elaborate casuistry, dividing sins into *mahāpātakas (great offences) and upapātakas (lesser offences). There are five greater offences: killing a *brahman (*brāhmaṇahatyā*; killing an *outcaste is a lesser offence than killing a cow, since there is no *dharma of religious consequence in relation to those without caste); drinking intoxicants (*surāpāna*); stealing (*steyam*, not in general, but in specified ways); sexual relations with the wife of a *guru (*guruvaṅganāgama*; sometimes interpreted as 'father', i.e. against incest); associating with a known sinner (*mahāpātakasaṁsārga*). The lesser offences are far more varied and differently listed. The way to deal with offences is to undertake penance and make atonement. Penance may range from *prāṇāyāma and *tapas (to burn out offence) to gifts to brahmans and pilgrimage.

Buddhism Buddhism does not accept the existence of an omnipotent deity and has no concept of sin as the offence against such a being by the contravention of his will as expressed through revelation or deduced by reason. It does, however (in terms of the doctrine of *karma), distinguish clearly between good and evil deeds. The doctrine of karma states the implications for ethics of the basic universal law, or *dharma, one aspect of which is that moral acts inevitably entail consequences (karma-*niyama). It is impossible to escape these consequences, and no one, not even the *Buddha, has the power to forgive evil deeds and short-circuit the retribution which is to follow.

A wrongful thought, word, or deed is one which is committed under the influence of the 'Three Roots of Evil' (*akusalamūla), namely greed (*lobha), hatred (*dosa), and delusion (*moha). Good deeds, on the other hand, stem from their opposites, namely the 'virtuous roots' (*kusalamūla) of generosity (alobha), love (adosa), and understanding (amoha). These good or evil roots, nourished over the course of many lives, become ingrained dispositions which predispose the individual towards virtue or vice. Wrongful actions are designated in various ways: as evil (*pāpa), bad (*akusala*), demeritorious (*apuñña*), or corrupt (*sankiliṭṭha*), and all such deeds lead inevitably to a deeper entanglement in the process of suffering and rebirth (*saṃsāra) and away from the fulfilment and enlightenment of *nirvāna.

According to Buddhist thought the involvement of the individual in saṃsāra is not the result of a 'fall' or due to an 'original sin' through which human nature became flawed. Each person, accordingly, has the final responsibility for his or her own salvation and the power of free will with which to choose for good or evil.

See Index, Sin, offence, etc.

Sinai, Mount. The mountain on which *Moses was given the Jewish *Torah. Mount Sinai is also referred to as Mount Horeb (Exodus 33. 6). According to Exodus, Moses was given the *Ten Commandments on Mount Sinai; he also received the tablets of the law after remaining there for forty days. In the *aggadic tradition, the mountains quarrelled for the honour of receiving the Torah, and God declared that 'Sinai is the only mountain on which no *idolatry has been practised; therefore it alone is fit for the honour.' In recent times the acceptance of the doctrine of *Torah mi Sinai* ('Torah from Sinai') is the primary criterion of *orthodox belief. Jews have not been much concerned to identify the mountain, since it adds nothing to the revelation which occurred there (*maʿamad har Sinai*) by which they are required to live. Jubal or Jebel Musa, the mount of Moses, in southern Sinai is an old (Christian) identification: the Monastery of St *Catherine was built on orders of the emperor Justinian in the 6th cent. at the foot of Jubal Musa, at the traditional site of the burning bush. In Islamic territory already during the *iconoclast period, its rich collection of mosaics and *icons escaped destruction. Its famous library contains some 3,000 manuscripts, chief of which was the 4th-cent. Codex Sinaiticus of the Bible (most of which, however, was removed to Russia in 1859 and to the British Museum in 1933). The monastery is, anomalously, *autocephalous, the archbishop of Sinai residing in Cairo. It was in Israeli-held territory from 1967 to 1982. There are few monks.

B. Bernstein, *Sinai* (1979).

Sīnān (Ottoman architect): see SULAIMĀN THE MAGNIFICENT.

Siṅgh (Skt., *simha*, 'lion'). Second name of male Sikhs. It is a common surname also among *Kṣatriya Hindus, e.g. Rajputs and Gurkhās. According to tradition, Gurū *Gobind Siṅgh (hitherto Gobind Rāi) took this surname on *Baisākhī Day 1699 CE. He gave to the *pañj pyāre and to all males subsequently initiated into the *khālsā the name Siṅgh, to emphasize their equality, regardless of *caste, and their courage in battle. See also KAUR.

Siṅgh Sabhā (Hindī, Pañjābī, '*Siṅgh Assembly'). Sikh movement to defend the *panth against incursions by missionaries. Initially it was thought that Christian missionaries were the main threat, but it came to be recognized that *Ārya Samāj (at first regarded as a potential ally) was equally a threat. The Siṅgh Sabhā was formed in 1873, with the intention of extending education, publishing, and reforming the management of the *gurdwārās. The first president was Thakur Siṅgh Sandwalia, and the first secretary Giana Gian Siṅgh. The leading writer was Vīr Siṅgh, who also founded the first Pañjābī newspaper, *Khālsā Samāchār.* Khalsa College in *Amritsar was established in 1892, followed by a proliferation of other Khalsa Colleges. As awareness of political oppression grew, the movement gave rise to the *Akali Party.

H. S. Oberoi, *The Construction of Religious Boundaries* (1994).

Sion (hill given sacral significance in Jerusalem): see ZION.

Sīra. 'Life', in Islam of the Prophet *Muḥammad. No connected biography of the Prophet was written, but *ḥadīth (traditions) of what he said and did were already being collected during his lifetime. The earliest work on the biography of Muḥammad was by ʿUrwa b. al-Zubayr, but the dominant work became that of Muḥammad ibn Isḥāq whose Sīra survives in a recension by ibn Hishām. The life of Muḥammad is given in connected, chronological order, with attention to the pre-Islamic prelude. Also of importance are the works of al-Wāqidī, especially his *Kitāb al-Maghāzī*.

The Life of Muhammad, tr. A. Guilleaume (1955); M. A. Anees and A. N. Athar, *Guide to Sira and Hadith Literature* (1986).

Sirach (book of the Apocrypha): see BEN SIRA.

Sirhindī, al- (Indian Sūfī teacher): see SŪFĪS.

Śīś Gañj Gurdwārā (*śīś*, Pañjābī, 'head'). Sikh shrine. 1. This *gurdwārā marks the place in Chandnī Chauk, Delhi, where Gurū *Tegh Bahādur was beheaded in 1675 CE, on the orders of the Mughal emperor, Auraṅgzeb. According to tradition, a *Raṅghretā Sikh, *Bhāī Jaitā, carried the Gurū's head to *Anaṇḍpur Sāhib for cremation. The present, golden-domed gurdwārā, dating from 1930, houses the trunk of the tree under which, reputedly, Gurū Tegh Bahādur was executed.

2. Shrine in Anaṇḍpur Sāhib. See RAKĀB GAÑJ GURDWĀRĀ.

Śiśupāla. In the *Mahābhārata* and *Purāṇas, *Kṛṣṇa's evil cousin, king of the Cedis, destined to be killed by Kṛṣṇa. The story of the killing of Śiśupāla, later turned into a classical poem by Māgha, is told in full in book ii of the *Mahābhārata*. Śiśupāla was born with three eyes and four arms, of which it was prophesied that the extras would disappear when he should come into contact with his future killer; this happened when the child was set upon Kṛṣṇa's lap. Kṛṣṇa promised Śiśupāla's mother that he would allow Śiśupāla to offend him 100 times with impunity, and so he did, enduring even the destruction of his city, Dvārakā, by Śiśupāla. Finally, however, Śiśupāla went too far: what was evidently his hundred-and-first insult to Kṛṣṇa occurred when he objected violently to Kṛṣṇa's being honoured at Yudhiṣṭhira's royal consecration, and Kṛṣṇa killed Śiśupāla on the spot, cutting off his head with his discus. Śiśupāla's radiance then returned to Kṛṣṇa, whence, as *Bhīṣma had explained, it had emerged. The **Viṣṇu* and **Bhāgavata Purāṇas* see Śiśupāla as a reincarnation of the earlier demons *Hiraṇyakaśipu and *Rāvaṇa, both of whom were pitted against incarnations of Viṣṇu.

Sītā (Skt., 'furrow'). Consort of *Rāma and considered therefore to be an incarnation of the Goddess *Lakṣmī. She is the heroine of the epic poem **Rāmāyaṇa*. She was born as a result of her father's prayers, and is said to have sprung from a furrow ploughed by him; she is thus closely associated with the 'mother-earth' concept and is the Vedic patron of agriculture.

Sītā was captured by the demon-king *Rāvaṇa during the absence of Rāma and his brother *Lakshmaṇa from the home of their exile in the forest, and carried off to his kingdom of Laṅkā. From here she was rescued eventually by her husband and his brother after they had undergone many hazards and adventures, described in detail in the *Rāmāyaṇa*. Rāma, however, refused to accept Sītā once again as his consort, believing her to be polluted by contact with Rāvaṇa, in spite of the fact that she had firmly retained her chastity throughout her time in Laṅkā. Crushed by Rāma's attitude, Sītā asked Lakshmaṇa to build a funeral pyre, on which she threw herself, but was rescued by the gods, thus proving her innocence. Still Rāma did not accept her as his wife, though she returned with him to his kingdom, Ayodhyā, where he was crowned. Still Rāma was troubled by jealousy, and, becoming further vexed by reported comments of his subjects on Sītā's supposed inconstancy, he ordered Lakshmaṇa to take her to the forest and kill her, though she was pregnant at the time. Instead of killing Sītā, Lakshmaṇa left her in the forest, where she was protected by the sage *Vālmīki and bore twin sons. When they were 15 years old Rāma, who did not know of their existence, ordered a horse-sacrifice, and the boys captured the animal when it reached their forest-home. This represented a challenge to Rāma, who, when the boys defeated his army, came in person against them; he was astonished at their likeness to himself, and Vālmīki told him he was their father.

At last, Rāma accepted Sītā's innocence, and proclaimed it publicly, but her heart was broken, and, calling on her mother-earth to receive her and thus show beyond doubt to everyone how devoted to her husband and how chaste she was, she fell to the ground, which opened to receive her, and so passed from Ayodhyā for ever.

Śītalā. Goddess of pustular diseases, dominant in Bengal. Her *līlā (play) is to sweep through the countryside with her companion Jvarāsura, the fever demon. Śītalā means 'cool one', perhaps a euphemism to ward off her fury. Worship of her, and writing poems to her, tend to follow upon an epidemic, thus belonging to the cults of *affliction.

Situation ethics (ethics which arise from evaluation of particular circumstances): see ETHICS (CHRISTIANITY).

Sitz im Leben (Germ., 'place' or 'setting in life'). In historical criticism of religious traditions, the supposed circumstances in which a particular story, saying, etc., either originated, or was preserved and transmitted. See also FORM CRITICISM.

Śiva (Skt., 'auspicious'). Major deity in Hinduism, the third in the Hindu trinity (*trimūrti), along with *Brahmā and *Viṣṇu. In the *Vedas, *śiva* appears as an epithet of *Rudra, not as separate manifestation of divine power. The joint form, Rudra-Śiva appears in the *gṛhya* (household) rites, which suggests that there was a gradual process of assimilation, and that Śiva has roots and origins in the pre-Vedic period. Thus one of the *Harappā seals depicts a three-faced figure sitting cross-legged and surrounded by animals; and this has suggested an anticipation of Śiva as the supreme *yogi and lord of the animals, who is possessed of a diverse nature. By the 2nd cent. BCE, Rudra was waning in significance, and Śiva began to obtain a powerful separate identity. In **Rāmāyaṇa*, he is a mighty and personal god, and in **Mahābhārata* he is at times the equal of Viṣṇu, perhaps even the creator of Viṣṇu and Brahmā, worshipped by other gods. He became associated with generation and destruction, especially in conjunction with *Śakti, and is therefore worshipped through the power of the *liṅga. The liṅga is sometimes depicted with four or five faces as the face of Śiva, thereby representing his multifaceted nature. The Mahādeva image in the *Elephanta caves already depicts Śiva in the threefold guise of creator, destroyer, and preserver: in this and other such images, the two faces on either side represent (apparent) opposites—male and female (*ardhanārī); terrifying destroyer (*bhairava) and active giver of repose; mahāyogi and *gṛhasta—while the third, serene and peaceful, reconciles the two, the Supreme as the One who transcends all contradictions. The three horizontal marks which Śaivites put on their foreheads represent the triple aspect of *Śiva. To some extent, this development of the trimurti aspect may be an attempt also to reconcile *Vaiṣṇavites and *Śaivites (see J. Gonda, *Viṣṇuism and Śivaism* . . ., 1970); the same can also be seen in the representation of Śiva as Harihara, e.g. in the Sangameṣvara temple in Mysore, Hari being a title of Viṣṇu, and *Hara one of Śiva. As a personal god (*iṣta-deva), he is worshipped in many forms of manifestation, important examples being *Nāṭarāja (lord of the *dance) and Dakṣiṇāmūrti, spiritual teacher: he may be *jñāna-Dakṣiṇāmūrti (teacher of knowledge), *yoga-Dakṣiṇāmūrti, vīṇādhara-Dakṣiṇāmūrti (teacher of music). In this guise, he is depicted facing south (*dakṣiṇā*), his right foot resting on the demon of ignorance and his right hand in a *mudra of explanation. Otherwise, Śiva is usually represented with the *abhaya mudra (hand in upright position indicating protection) and with downward-pointing hand indicating liberation for all who trust in him. His *mantra is 'sivo 'ham'. Śiva is particularly associated with the river *Gaṅgā (Ganges) which flows through his hair (his matted hair is wild and loose in his role of destroyer; it is tied up with a moon or with the figure of Gaṅgā surmounting it in his role of creator), and with Mount *Kailāsa in the *Himālayas.

See Index, Siva.

A. M. Gaston, *Śiva in Dance, Myth and Iconography* (1982); J. Gonda, *Viṣṇuism and Śivaism* (1970); W. D. O'Flaherty, *Siva, The Erotic Ascetic* (1981); A. K. Ramanujan, *Speaking of Siva* (1973).

Śivabhuti. A Jain who, according to the Śvetāmbara, caused the eighth, and major, schism among Jains. He believed that he could emulate the *tīrthaṅkaras, especially in discarding clothes as a mark of true asceticism. Hence the *Digambaras endorse nudity for true ascetics. The Digambaras have a different version of this schism, for which see DIGAMBARA.

Śiva-Jñāna-Bodha (Skt.; Tamil, *Śivañāṉapōtam*, 'realization of the knowledge of Śiva'). An important theological text of *Śaiva Siddhānta written by Meykaṇḍadeva (Tamil, Meykaṇṭartēvar; 13th cent. CE). Scholars are uncertain whether it was originally written in Skt. or Tamil. Possibly it was taken from the *Raurāva* **Āgama*, although manuscripts of that text do not contain it. The *Śiva-Jñāna-Bodha* is a concise, systematic exposition of Śaiva theology, which maintains that God (*Śiva) is transcendent and immanent, and souls are wholly dependent on him. To attain union with Śiva through his grace, one should offer devotion (*bhakti) to him.

Śivananda (1887–1963). Hindu founder of the Divine Life Mission. He was born Kuppuswami Iyer in Tamil Nadu. He trained and initially practised as a doctor, both in India and in Singapore. In 1923, he entered on the path of renunciation, becoming a *saṁnyāsin in 1924. After twelve years of *ascetic preparation, he founded the Śivananda *āśram and the Divine Life Society. This is basically *advaitin, involves a form of *Hatha yoga, and aims to be non-sectarian. The Mission now has branches worldwide.

Svami Krishnananda, *The Divine Life Society* (1967).

Śivarātri (Hindu festival): see FESTIVALS AND FASTS.

Śiva Saṃhita. A Sanskrit text of the *Nātha yoga school (13th–15th cents.), a mixture of *advaita philosophy, *Hatha and *Tantric yoga. The first chapter advocates a doctrine of non-duality (advaita), that in reality there is only the one universal absolute characterized by knowledge: 'the one knowledge (*ekam jñānam*) is eternal' (1. 1). Ch. 2 concerns the macrocosm contained in the microcosm of the body, and the *cakras and *nāḍīs of the subtle body. The body exists as a result of *karma which binds the soul (*jīva), but the body can become the means of liberation: 'when the karma-born body becomes the means (*sādhana) to *nirvāna, (only) then bearing a body becomes fruitful, not otherwise' (2. 49). Ch. 3 concerns yoga, the different winds (*vayus) in the body, *prāṇāyāma, *āsanas, and the importance of the *guru. The fourth chapter describes the awakening of *Kuṇḍalinī and various positions (*mudrā) to control the forces of the body. These include the *vajroli mudrā, the withdrawal of semen back into the penis after its discharge during sexual intercourse (*maithuna). The last chapter enumerates obstacles to yoga, and also the four kinds of yoga which are, in ascending order, *mantra, *hatha, *laya, and *kriya*. The latter involves closing off the senses and listening to inner mystical sound (*hāda).

Śiva-tattva (the supreme being in Indian sect): see LIṄGĀYAT.

Six Doctrines of Nāropa (body of teaching in school of Tibetan Buddhism): see NĀRO CHOS DRUG.

Six Gosvāmīs (disciples of Caitanya): see CAITANYA.

Six heretical teachers. The six sectarian teachers who were contemporaries of the Buddha and who were castigated by him for their false teachings, principally their denial of the doctrine of *karma. The fullest exposition of their views is to be found in an early discourse entitled 'The Fruits of the Religious Life' (*Sāmaññaphala-Sutta*), the second discourse of the *Dīgha Nikāya*.

The views of the six, briefly, were as follows. Pūraṇa Kassapa denied that the religious life had any purpose whatsoever, good and evil deeds being equally devoid of religious significance. *Makkhali Gosāla was a determinist who taught that human destiny was preordained by fate, while *Ajita Kesakambala held a materialist view according to which an individual is utterly annihilated at death. Pakudha Kaccāyana espoused a doctrine of fatalistic pluralism according to which the individual was a compound of elemental substances which dispersed at death, in the light of which the religious life was futile. All of the above four were ethical nihilists (*natthikavāda*) and denied the existence of moral causation (*ahetuvāda*).

Sañjāya Belaṭṭhaputta was described as an 'eel wriggler' in that he refused to take a stand on any position, and the Jain leader Nigantha Nataputta, while accepting the doctrine of moral retribution (*kiriyavāda*) reduced the life of religious endeavour to physical discipline and mortification. In view of their failure to appreciate the true purpose of the religious life and its goal all six teachers were roundly condemned by the Buddha.

Six hundred and thirteen commandments. The laws found in the Jewish *Pentateuch. There are 248 positive commandments and 365 negative ones. The first classification was made by Simeon Kayyara, and *Maimonides later set them out in his *Sefer ha-*Mitzvot*. They are known as Taryag Mitzvot, because *taryag* has the numerical value in Hebrew of 613. For the 614th, see HOLOCAUST.

Six principles of Nāropa (six doctrines of Nāropa): see NĀRO CHOS DRUG.

Six realms (six states of possible rebirth): see TIBETAN WHEEL OF LIFE.

Six schools of philosophy (Indian): see DARŚANA.

Six sects (of Buddhism): see NARA BUDDHISM.

Six ways (classification of Chinese religions/philosophies): see CHINESE RELIGION.

Six yogas of Nāropa (six doctrines of Nāropa): see NĀRO CHOS DRUG.

Ṣiyām (fasting in Islam): see ṢAWM.

Skaṁbha (Skt., 'pillar, support'). Vedic Hindu term for a pillar, known in post-Vedic times as staṁbha. In the *Vedas, it is the scaffolding (metaphorically understood) supporting creation—e.g. *Atharva Veda* 10. 7 and 8. It is also the *axis mundi. In practice, skaṁbhas were set up for many reasons, and with elaborate decoration. Central are those associated with the *liṅga, but others are devoted to virtually any god. The classic work on architecture, *Mānāsara* 15, analyses the types of skaṁbhas.

Skanda. Hindu deity, offspring of *Śiva (conceived without the assistance of a female being), who became a notable warrior. He was suckled by the six Kṛttikas (Pleiades) and developed six faces for this purpose. From this derives the name Kārttikeya by which he is commonly known and worshipped. He was made head of the army of the gods and (according to *Mahābhārata*) defeated *Mahiṣa and

Tāraka who, through *tapas, were threatening the gods. He is depicted as young and chaste (i.e. as Kumāra), clothed in red, with a spear (which always hits its target and returns to his hand). His cult, of great antiquity, used to cover India, but is now mainly in the south: in *Tamilnadu, he has merged with Murukan̄/Murugan. *Skanda Purāṇa* is one of the eighteen classical Purāṇas (the longest of them) and contains what purports to be his teaching.

Skandha (Skt., 'group'; Pāli, *khandha*). In Buddhism, the five aggregations which compose or constitute human appearance (*nāma-rūpa): (i) *rūpa, material composition; (ii) *vedanā*, sensing, including sensing through the sixth sense of mental impressions; (iii) *saṃjña* (Pāli, *sañña*), perception; (iv) *saṃskāra (Pāli, *sankhāra*), mental formations producing character; (v) *vijñāna (Pāli, *viññāna*), consciousness. They are constantly in the process of change, and do not constitute a self (*anātman). The five skandhas are also grouped into three: rūpa, *cetasika* (conditioning factors of consciousness, (ii), (iii), and (iv) above), and *citta (state of consciousness); or even simply as rūpa + nāma, i.e. rūpanāma. These alternative organizations are a reminder that there is nothing fixed or substantial in the skandhas, such that 'it' can be named.

Skete (Gk., 'dwelling'). A small monastic community, especially associated with Mount *Athos.

Skilful means, skill in means (skill in adapting teaching to the aptitude of those who are taught): see UPĀYA-KAUŚALYA.

Slaughter, ritual (Jewish): see SHEḤITAH.

Slavery

Judaism The institution of masters owning their servants is accepted in the Hebrew scriptures. A Hebrew could become a slave to redeem his debts (Leviticus 25. 35) or to make restitution for theft (Exodus 22. 2). According to Leviticus 25. 44–5, it was permissible to take slaves of 'the nations that are round about you'. Slaves were members of the household; they kept the *Sabbath (Deuteronomy 5. 14, 15), were *circumcised (Genesis 17. 12–13) and were not to be ill-treated (Deuteronomy 23. 17). Hebrew slaves had to be freed after six years (Deuteronomy 15. 12), but *gentile slaves could be kept for their lifetime (Leviticus 25. 46). The extent of the practice of slavery among the Jews in the *Talmudic period is debatable. After the cessation of the *Jubilee Year, it is possible that the keeping of Hebrew slaves ceased (*B.Kid.* 69a), although Tebi, the slave of Rabban Gamaliel, is mentioned in the sources (e.g. *Pes.* 7. 2). Alien slaves continued to be kept, although the practice slowly died out in the *diaspora (persisting in Muslim countries). *Maimonides summed up the *rabbinic laws of slavery by saying, 'It is permissible to work the slave hard; but while this is the law, the ways of ethics and prudence are that the master should be just and merciful.'

Christianity Slavery in the New Testament period is not questioned as an institution. A slave can fulfil his duty as a Christian by serving his master as Christ (Ephesians 6. 5–8), though the owner must realize that the slave is his brother in Christ and must treat him accordingly. Perhaps, even, he should set him free (Philemon 14–21). The more important point is that the age is being inaugurated when all divisions of this kind will be abolished, when there will be 'neither Jew nor Greek, slave nor free, male and female' (Galatians 3. 28), because all are one in Christ. Nevertheless, inequalities continued to be regarded as a consequence of the *Fall (e.g., by *Augustine), even though slavery gradually gave way in Europe to serfdom. The biblical warrant for slavery was appealed to in the development of the slave-trade (which, after fierce struggle, was formally ended at the Congress of Vienna, 1814–15) and in the perpetuation of slavery in America. But equally the logic of love in the New Testament made it obvious to most that slavery was incompatible with Christianity. Slavery ended in America after the Civil War through the Emancipation Proclamation (1863) and the Thirteenth Amendment (1865).

Islam Slavery is taken for granted in the *Qur'ān and in *ḥadīth—where the subject of slavery is mainly a concern with manumission and its consequences. The word *'abd ('slave') is used also of the human relation to God: it implies a condition of absolute dependence and obedience. Nevertheless, various rules were also given which ameliorated the situation of slaves, not least the fact that the liberation of slaves is regarded as extremely meritorious. Legally, slaves could only be obtained as a consequence of war, or as the children of existing slaves. Slaves were able to rise to positions of considerable responsibility, even seizing power in the case of the Mamlukes (the word means 'owned one', and refers to a dynasty derived from Turkish and Circassian slave soldiers, which held power in Egypt, 1250–1517 (AH 648–922)). Since Qur'ān and ḥadīth cannot be abrogated, it is not possible for slavery to be abolished, at least as a theoretical possibility, in Islam.

Hinduism Slavery appears to have existed in early India (Dev Raj, *L'Esclavage dans l'Inde ancienne*, 1957), but it did not continue as an institution extensively. Instead, forms of obligatory service developed through *dharma and the *caste system.

See Index, Slavery.

Śloka (epic metre): see VĀLMĪKI.

Sloka-saṁgraha (collected teachings): see SEN, KESHUB CHUNDER.

Smārta Sūtra. Any Hindu sūtra based on *smṛti, understood as traditional law. They include those concerned with family and household rituals (*gṛhya*) and the Dharma Sūtras. Smārtas are also those who compose such texts, and those *brahmans who integrate devotional theism into *dharma. The smārta movement was a syncretistic movement connected in origin with *Śaṅkara, who recognized five deities in particular (*Viṣṇu, *Śiva, *Pārvatī, *Gaṇeśa, and *Sūrya) as the guarantors of dharma and social order in harmony with the order of the cosmos.

Śmaśāna. Hindu cremation ground. Normally (i.e. according to the norms of *dharma) abhorrent and defiling, for Tantric cults of the left hand they are important as the place of testing detachment in the domain of the repellent. Śmaśāna *sādhana also includes rituals to control malevolent spirits.

Smith, Joseph (founder): see MORMONS.

Smṛti (Skt., 'recollection'). In Hinduism, the second part of 'scripture', less than *śruti, but possessing authority. Smṛti, passed on orally by tradition, gains validity by being derived from śruti. It extends to a wide range of works, including *Vedāṅgas, *Smārta Sūtras, *Purāṇas, *Itihāsa, including **Mahābhārata* and **Rāmāyaṇa*, Nīti-śastras.

In Buddhism, smṛti is the Skt. equivalent of *sati, 'mindfulness': it is the meditational practice which observes closely and continuously what is going on in the interior life of the practitioner. 'The four mindfulnesses [i.e. the foci] are the path which leads to the goal . . ., the attainment of the way and the realisation of *nirvāna' (*Dīgha Nikāya* 2. 290). The four are the body (*kaya*), sensation (*vedanā*), mind (*citta), and the Buddha's way (*dharma).

Smṛti-upasthāna (system of mediation in Buddhism): see SATIPAṬṬHĀNA.

Snake-handling. A practice in certain *Pentecostal churches mostly in the mountains of the SE USA. It is inspired by the words in Mark 16. 17–18 that 'these signs will follow those who believe: in my name they will cast out demons; they will speak in new tongues; they will pick up serpents, and if they drink any deadly thing, it will not hurt them'. Handling snakes while in an ecstatic state thus becomes a sign of one's faith and possession of the *Holy Spirit. Snake-handling is first documented in 1909, as part of the ministry of George Hensley, of Grasshopper, in Tennessee. Since 1949 laws have been passed against it. This fact makes information on snake-handling churches hard to get; they come to public attention occasionally, when fatal bites are reported (these are apparently rare, but often are regarded as desirable, as a proof that the snakes used are deadly). The American Civil Liberties Union has defended snake-handling religion as a test case of the constitutional right to freedom of religious belief.

T. Burton, *Serpent-Handling Believers* (1993); W. La Barre, *They Shall Take Up Serpents* (1962).

Sober Sufism (style of Sūfī practice): see ʿABD AL-QADIR AL-JĪLĪ; AL-JUNAID; SŪFĪS.

Sobornost'. A Russian word derived from the Slavonic *soborny*, which translates 'catholic' in the *creed, and related to the word for a council (*sobor*). Its etymological root is the verb *sbrat'*, 'to gather together', and since its use in *Khomiakov's *The One Church* (1850), the term, understood to mean 'togetherness', has been used to characterize the *Orthodox understanding of the unity of the *Church, an organic unity of free persons brought about by the *Holy Spirit, in contrast to the authoritarianism of *Roman Catholicism and the individualism of *Protestantism.

Societies, Chinese religious. An important feature of the Chinese religious tradition. In a society whose foundation traditionally has been the family-centred cult of *ancestors, supported by the state, various intermediate organizations—ranging from local fraternal or sororal pseudo-kinship groups to large-scale societies—have, throughout most of Chinese history, provided an alternative focus of loyalty and network of support for Chinese of both sexes and all ages. They have been particularly important for those without a secure place in the family and clan system. Such communities have usually been organized around religious ideals and symbols, sometimes including special revelations, in writing or through oral media. They have often been constituted by rites of initiation and maintained by oaths of loyalty. Most have been protected by tutelary deities, and led by a sometimes elaborate hierarchy of religious leadership. The state has often been suspicious of them because of their liminal social position and deviant loyalties, and sometimes with good reason, since many rebellions were inspired and led by such groups. The Taoist-led Yellow Turban rebellion in the Han (see CHANG CHÜEH), the nationalistic White Lotus revolt (see WHITE LOTUS SOCIETY) which helped to overthrow Mongolian rule and restore a Chinese ruler to the throne at the outset of the Ming, the millenarian *Eight Trigrams uprising in N. China in 1813, and the *T'ai-p'ing rebellion later in the same century, are only four of the most prominent examples. The Societies may be Taoist or Buddhist, but most are deliberately syncretistic.

Many Chinese religious societies, however, have been smaller than these, and without explicit political goals or reformist militancy. Their membership has varied widely, reaching into most classes and sections of Chinese society. There have been sororities for single women and widows, diverse occupational guilds for both sexes, small fraternities of adventurous youths bound to each other by sacred oaths, Buddhist lay societies, confraternities devoted to the practice of martial or other arts, and many other types. Many societies have remained locally organized at the village level; others have joined in regional and national federations, though in most cases the degree of central control is minimal.

Society of Jesus (RC religious order founded by Ignatius of Loyola): see JESUITS.

Socinianism. A rationalist movement within Christianity, leading in a *Unitarian direction. It developed from the ideas of Lelio Sozzini (1525–62) and his nephew Fausto (1539–1604). Followers of the Sozzinis, i.e. Socinians, hoped to restore a primitive Christianity, rejecting the accretions of Rome. Scripture was subject to the analysis of reason, and while Jesus was accepted as the revelation of God, he was regarded as only a man. The separation of Church and State was urged, along with a non-resistant attitude. Only those who obeyed the commands of Jesus would survive death. A basic statement of faith was drawn up in Fausto's revision of the Catechism of Racov (i.e. the Racovian Catechism), and more generally in his *De Jesu Christo Servatore* (1578). Persecution in Poland led to a wide diffusion throughout Europe. The influence of Socinianism can be seen in such figures as Isaac Newton and John Locke, and among the *Cambridge Platonists. The lead into Unitarianism can be seen in the title of Stephen Nye's work, *A History of Unitarianism, Commonly Called Socinianism* (1687).

G. H. Williams, *The Radical Reformation* (1962).

Sociobiology and religion: see Introduction; SEX AND RELIGION.

Sociology of religion. The study of religion in its social aspects and consequences, undertaken in all parts of the world. Emerging as part of the 19th-cent. *nomothetic ambition (i.e. the belief that accounts of social behaviour can be given which conform to laws like those of the natural sciences: see J. Bowker, *The Sense of God*, 2nd edn. 1995), sociologists of religion have in general been committed to a would-be scientific analysis of the role played by religion in the emergence, persistence, and evolution of social and cultural systems. In the main, they subscribe to two fundamental propositions: (i) that the study of religion is absolutely essential to the understanding of society and (ii) that the investigation of society is an indispensable prerequisite to the comprehension of religion.

Though the sociology of religion has never been among the largest subdisciplinary ventures, its practitioners remain steadfast in their conviction of its central theoretical significance for the discipline as a whole. Remembering that religion was a paramount concern of the founders of sociology (August Comte and Henri de Saint-Simon both established secular scientistic religions of their own devising), they regard the current relative neglect of the topic as a misguided capitulation to the secular spirit of the age and a serious flaw in the mainstream sociological agenda. The decline and possible demise of their subject-matter has infused research with a sense of urgency and dedication.

The sociology of religion reflects the main theoretical and methodological divisions among professional sociologists, including functionalism, *Marxism, *Freudianism, symbolic-interactionism, *phenomenology, structuralism, and post-modernism, together with rational-choice, market, world-systems, and globalization theories, all coexisting more or less peacefully. In a similar manner, research utilizing such quantitative (or neo-positivist) methods as large-scale social surveys, mailed questionnaires, structured interviews, and statistical analysis is conducted simultaneously with inquiries using such qualitative (or interpretive) procedures as participant-observation, unstructured interviews, and textual or discourse analysis. Ironically, in the one area where more diversity would be an undeniable asset, the subdiscipline has been slow in transforming itself. As a creation of the Enlightenment, sociology has characteristically conceptualized religion in Judaeo-Christian terms, and has largely restricted its investigations to a Christian (mostly Protestant) context. For a long time, it appeared unwilling or unable to engage in genuinely comparative research involving other major world religious traditions, although enthusiastically commemorating the monumental comparative initiative of Max *Weber. In recent years, however, energetic attempts have been made to transcend such inappropriate eurocentrism and increasing attention has been devoted to non-Western forms of religious belief and practice.

Although usage of the term tends to follow a number of basic formulae, there is no explicit or universal consensus among sociologists of religion regarding what 'religion' *is*. The problem of defining religion (see further, Introduction), and of doing so in a manner which adequately addresses its profoundly social character, is one which still periodically surfaces to challenge scholars anew regarding the fundamentals of their enterprise. Substantive definitions of religion are now less popular than in the 19th-cent. heyday of social evolution when Sir Edward *Tylor's succinct 'belief in Spiritual Beings' attained wide currency. Contemporary formulations of this kind tend to focus on somewhat elusive phenomena such as the sacred, the transcendent, the supernatural, or the super-empirical. While functionalism no longer represents theoretical orthodoxy within the realm of sociology, broadly conceived functional definitions (which assert that religion is what religion does in a social context) continue to dominate subdisciplinary discussion. Drawing on the classic accounts of Weber and *Durkheim, these definitions conceive religion in terms of the fulfilment of a range of social and psychological functions, from the specific to the extremely diffuse. They depict religion as an indispensable source of social consensus and cohesion which aids human adaptation to the environment and ensures societal survival by explaining the meaning of existence and providing answers to questions of ultimate human concern. In the most inclusive definitions of this sort, society itself assumes a religious quality; an insight confirmed by T. Luckmann's conception of 'the transcendence of biological nature by the human organism' as a religious phenomenon (see INVISIBLE RELIGION). As this example suggests, sociological employment of 'religion' may sometimes differ dramatically from everyday societal usage.

Durkheim and Weber may justifiably be regarded as the founding fathers whose divergent approaches still supply the main axes of intellectual tension within subdisciplinary theoretical discourse. Durkheim's primary concern with religion's role in social cohesion, group stability, and the reproduction of socio-cultural forms is strategically complemented by Weber's preoccupation with its part in radical, large-scale social and cultural transformation. Thus, for a broad range of current research topics (including *sectarianism, *millennialism/millenarianism, *civil religion, *invisible religion, *new religious movements, and *secularization), they remain influential. While many sociologists of religion are content to accept the continuing relevance of the classics, others are impatient to break their intellectual spell. Convinced, like A. N. Whitehead that 'a science which hesitates to forget its founders is lost', they anxiously seek to demonstrate that their subdiscipline is no longer in thrall to its illustrious progenitors. No decisive *coup de grâce* nor overall armistice is to be expected in this debate. None the less, such scholarly stock-taking is a useful means of assessing subdisciplinary progress (in various senses) and of evaluating the adequacy of existing theoretical models for the description and explanation of the most recent findings of empirical research.

The issue of whether modern religious (or irreligious) reality can still be analysed within a classic framework or whether, on the contrary, it requires radical reconceptualization is nowhere more pertinent than in the perennial 'secularization debate', for which see SECULARIZATION. Whatever the ultimate fate of the concept of secularization, the richness of current research cannot be denied. A new generation of sociologists of religion is profitably engaged in a wide variety of investigations into topics as diverse as Latin American *Pentecostalism, *New Age ideology, early Christianity, spiritual *healing practices, Islamic *fundamentalism, and the prospects of religion in former iron-curtain countries. For more than twenty years, considerable empirical and theoretical attention has been devoted to the beliefs, practices, composition, organization, and influence of so-called *new religious movements (NRMs), more popularly known to the mass media as *'cults' (obvious examples are the Moonies (*Moon), *Rajneeshis, *Scientologists, *Transcendental-Meditationists, Hare Krishnas (see INTERNATIONAL SOCIETY FOR KRISHNA CONSCIOUSNESS), and Wiccans (see WITCHCRAFT)). Despite their own exaggerations and the moral panic on the part of outsiders which so often accompanies their activities, such groups represent a minuscule proportion of religious believers in their host societies. Sociological rationales for their study thus tend to stress their embryonic character, evolutionary potential, and capacity for revealing, in microcosm, wider truths about religion and society.

Concerned that a preoccupation with NRMs is sustained by the lure of the exotic, some scholars suggest that social-scientific energies are better expended in investigations of either 'mainline' religious traditions or other more socially significant manifestations of radical religiosity. Countless mainline denominational studies continue to address such issues as falling church attendance, declining ministerial vocations, and the changing ecclesiastical role of women. Meanwhile, numerous other projects probe the revival and growth of conservative (evangelical) churches, the global impact of *fundamentalism, the role of religion in national ideology, and the intensified use of mass communications in religious proselytization and mobilization.

In *fin de siècle* mood, sociologists of religion can now look back on a century of scholarly achievement while simultaneously anticipating the intellectual challenges which lie ahead. Continuing their examination of religion's myriad mutual relationships with other social institutions (e.g. the family, the economy, the polity, and the law), they are increasingly alert to its elusive, problematic, and precarious contemporary character. In circumstances where commitment appears to have acquired the fragmentary, syncretic, consumerist qualities of *bricolage, belief is increasingly divorced from belonging and religion becomes less a social institution than a broad, pliant cultural resource at the disposal of autonomized individuals. Whether religion's heightened privatization or individualization will continue or whether its old capacity as a source of authoritative meaning will inspire new, lasting, and significant forms of collective and public spiritual expression remains to be seen.

J. A. Beckford, *Religion and Advanced Industrial Society* (1992); M. B. Hamilton, *The Sociology of Religion* (1995); R. Homan, *The Sociology of Religion: A Bibliographical Survey* (1986); R. L. Johnstone, *Religion in Society* (3rd edn. 1988); M. B. McGuire, *Religion: The Social Context* (3rd edn., 1992); R. O'Toole, *Religion: Classic Sociological Approaches* (1984); K. A. Roberts, *Religion in Sociological Perspective* (3rd edn. 1995).

Söderblom, Nathan (1866–1931). Christian *archbishop of Sweden and pioneer of the Christian *ecumenical movement. He was the son of a *Lutheran pastor and followed his father into the ministry. While chaplain in Paris, he completed a doctorate in Persian religion, and then was professor of the history of religion in Uppsala, 1901–14. He was appointed archbishop in 1914, and he committed himself to the task of reconciliation between nations that had been at war, involving the Churches in working for peace and justice. This led to a necessary quest for common ground in this 'work of the Kingdom'. This work was recognized by the award of the Nobel peace prize in 1930.

B. Sundkler, *Nathan Söderblom* . . . (1968).

Sodh (Heb., 'secret'). A Jewish esoteric method of exegesis, based on the biblical understanding that prophets enter into the sodh of God. Sodh extends the belief that the *Torah has more than one level of meaning. It was used particularly to interpret the Creation account in *Genesis and *Ezekiel's vision of the chariot (see MAʿASEH).

Śodhana. Hindu purification. Cleansing from impurity may be necessary on different levels, and for different reasons. Physical purification is a part of daily ritual, which may, in the case of *sādhus, be very elaborate. It is necessary also if *caste rules have been broken, and before *pūjā. Interior purification is an important part of *Hatha yoga. Spiritual purification involves setting the self free, as through the exercise of the restraints (*niyama).

Soḍhī. Pañjābī family to which belonged most of the Sikh *Gurūs. Like Bedī, Soḍhī is a *Khatrī 'got' (exogamous subdivision of *caste) whose legendary origins are traced in Gurū *Gobind Siṅgh's Bachitra Nāṭak (*Dasam Granth). According to this Lav, *Rāma's son, was the ancestor of Gurū *Rām Dās and so of Gurūs *Arjan Dev, *Hargobind, *Har Rāi, *Har Krishan, *Tegh Bahādur, and Gobind Siṅgh. Such rival claimants to Gurūship as *Prithī Chand, *Dhīr Mal, and *Rām Rāi were also Soḍhī. Because of their enmity, Gurū Tegh Bahādur moved to *Anaṇḍpur. To Prithī Chand's son, Soḍhī Miharbān, is attributed the Miharbān *janam-sākhī. Present-day Soḍhīs of *Kartārpur own the Kartārpur *Ādi Granth.

Sodom and Gomorrah. Two cities near the Jordan river. According to Genesis 18 and 19, Sodom and Gomorrah were destroyed by God despite the pleas of the *patriarch *Abraham because of their extreme wickedness. In later biblical books, they are cited as a warning of the extent of God's anger (e.g. Amos 4. 11). The biblical understanding of the offence of the cities seems to have been that it is one of disregarding the obligations of hospitality. There are many tales in the *aggadah of the evils of the city, e.g. because a young girl gave food to a beggar, the citizens daubed her with honey and left her to be stung to death by bees (*B.Sanh.* 109b) and the names of the four judges of Sodom were said to be Liar, Awful Liar, Forger, and Perverter of Justice.

J. A. Loader, *A Tale of Two Cities* . . . (1993).

Soelle, D. (Christian theologian): see POLITICAL THEOLOGY.

Sōen Roshi (Zen master): see NAKAGAWA SŌEN.

Sofer, R. Moses of Pressburg (Ḥatam Sofer, 1762–1839). Jewish *halakhic authority and *orthodox community leader. Sofer served as *rabbi of Pressburg, Hungary, for the last thirty-three years of his life. He founded a large and successful *yeshivah, and he firmly opposed the *maskilim* (see HASKALAH) in their attempts to adjust Judaism to the spirit of the times. 'Even if there were no hope for our redemption,' he argued, 'We would still owe allegiance to *Torah.' Since God is unchanging, there cannot be need to change what he commanded: 'Never say, "Times have changed". We have an eternal Father, blessed be his name, who has not changed and will not change.' He was the founder of the Sofer dynasty who remained leaders of Pressburg and elsewhere. After his death, his *responsa (in 7 vols., *Ḥiddushei Teshuvot Mosheh Sofer*, known from the initials as *Ḥatam Sofer*), sermons, and letters were published, all of which reflect his devotion to the orthodox cause and his encouragement of Jewish settlement in *Erez Israel.

S. Ehrmann in L. Jung (ed.), *Jewish Leaders* (1953).

Soferim (transmitter of Jewish documents): see SCRIBE.

Sōgō. Those in authority in Japanese Buddhism who have responsibility for maintaining the rules (*gō*) of a community. There is a considerable hierarchy, from forms of Sōjō at the top, through forms of *sōzu*, to forms of *risshi*.

Sŏhak (Western learning): see KOREAN RELIGION.

Sōhei (warrior-monks): see AKUSŌ.

Sohilā (Pañjābī, 'hymn of joy'). Sikhs' late evening prayer, taking its name from a word in the second line. The Sohilā, also called *Āratī Sohilā and *Kīrtan Sohilā, follows the *Japjī and *Rahirās hymns, *Sodar* and *So purakh*, at the beginning of the *Ādi Granth, and is included in *Nitnem. Devout Sikhs recite Sohilā before going to bed, and it is recited in the *gurdwārā as the Ādi Granth is laid to rest. The Sohilā is repeated during *cremation of the deceased. It consists of five hymns, Gurū *Nānak's Gauṛī Dīpakī, Āsā, and Dhanāsri (or Āratī, as he here reinterprets the Hindu ritual), and the Gauṛī Pūrbī of Gurūs *Rām Dās and *Arjan Dev.

Sōji-ji. One of the two major *Sōtō Zen monasteries in Japan (along with *Eihei-ji). It was founded in the 8th cent. CE, by Gyōgi as a *Hossō monastery, but it became Zen under Keizan Jōkin in 1321. When it was destroyed by fire in 1898, it was moved to Yokohāma, its present location. Sōji-ji was distinguished by its periodic system of appointing abbots, which spread the feeling of responsibility through the community. It also fostered the dissemination of *Sōtō in rural areas, in some rivalry with Eihei-ji. By the religious laws promulgated at the outset of the Edo period (1615), the two were accorded exactly equal status, and other Sōtō temples were made subordinate to them. Nevertheless, Sōji-ji had, by the 18th cent., 16,179 branch temples, compared with 1,370 of Eihei-ji. When an imperial decree pronounced Eihei-ji head of the Sōtō school, bitter and continuing conflicts broke out. Not until 1879 was a formal agreement (*kyōwa meiyaku*) reached that both were to have equal say in Sōtō. The establishing of a central office (Sōtōshūmu-kyoku) and the determination to re-establish monastic training on the foundations of *Dōgen led to the revival of the 20th cent., assisted by lay well-wishers (e.g. the journalist and publisher, Ōuchi Seiran, 1845–1919, who promulgated the summary of Sōtō, *Shushōgi*, Germ. tr. K. Ishimoto and E. Naberfeld, *Nipponica*, vi; Eng. tr. N. Kaiten, 1896).

Sōka Gakkai (Jap., 'Association for Creating Values'). Religious movement deriving from *Nichiren Shōshū and closely related to it. In 1930, Makiguchi Tsunesaburō (1871–1944) and Toda Jōsei (1900–58) founded the Sōka Kyōiku Gakkai. It became Sōka Gakkai (and a specifically religious movement) in 1937. Through aggressive proselytization and through its journal, *Kachi Sōzō* (The Creation of Value), the group disseminated Makiguchi's philosophy. This argued that the traditional triad of absolute values, the true, the beautiful, and the good, needs amending, because the true does not necessarily lead to what is itself of value—it is as likely to lead to unhappiness as to the opposite. Consequently he argued that what is worth pursuing is happiness and that this may include material success and all that goes with it.

In 1943, the government tried to unify all Nichiren sects, but this was resisted by Makiguchi and Toda. They were arrested, ostensibly on the charge of advising their followers not to purchase amulets from the national *Ise Shrine. Makiguchi died in prison, but Toda deepened his faith greatly through his reading in prison. When released, he reconstructed the organization, and in 1952 it was incorporated as an independent religious institution. It rapidly became a multi-million-member organization, extending beyond Japan to other parts of the world, especially the USA and France. It possessed what was at the time of its building the largest temple on earth, on the slopes of Mount Fuji. Under *Ikeda Daisaku, Sōka Gakkai established a political party, Komei-to, the party of clean government. Initially, Sōka Gakkai had strongly exclusivist attitudes, following Nichiren in regarding other religions as false and other Buddhist sects as heretical. It was accused of forced conversions through its technique of *shakubuku*, breaking and subduing. However, since the 1970s, there has been a moderation of its extreme views.

N. S. Brannen, *Sōka Gakkai* . . . (1968); J. A. Dator, *Sōka Gakkai* . . . (1969).

Sōka Kyōiku Gakkai: see SŌKA GAKKAI.

Sŏkkul-am (cave): see KOREAN RELIGION.

Sokushin jobutsu (Jap., 'becoming a Buddha in one's existing body'). The *Shingon Buddhist belief that the buddha-nature can be realized now, and in this present appearance. It rests on the view that all sentient beings already are the buddha-nature (*rigu*), but it mobilizes the actual realization of this through connection with the power of the Buddha (*kaji*) until it becomes a manifest and realized fact (*kentoku*).

Sola Scriptura (Lat., 'by *scripture alone'). The belief that the truths of Christian faith and practice can and must be established from scripture alone, without additions from, e.g., tradition or development. It is thus in contrast to *Roman Catholicism and *papal definitions of truth in matters of faith and morals (see INFALLIBILITY), although theoretically such definitions are said to be rooted in scripture.

Solemn League and Covenant (in defence of Scottish Presbyterianism): see COVENANTERS.

Sölle, D. (Christian theologian): see POLITICAL THEOLOGY.

Solomon (Heb., Shelomoh, 10th cent. BCE). King of *Israel. Solomon was the son of King *David and Bathsheba. According to the biblical account, he was anointed king by *Nathan the *prophet and *Zadok the *priest, he reigned *c.*967–*c.*928 BCE and his kingdom stretched from the borders of Egypt to the Euphrates (1 Kings 5. 1). He embarked on massive building projects, including the *Temple in Jerusalem. He made alliances with the nations round about which were cemented by extensive foreign marriages, including an alliance with the daughter of Pharaoh. His wealth and splendour were renowned, and the peace and prosperity of the country were attributed to the *wisdom of the king. He was, however, condemned in the *aggadic tradition for his toleration of the *idolatry of his wives.

Solomon, Ibn Gabirol (Jewish Spanish poet and philosopher): see GABIROL, SOLOMON.

Solomon, Odes of. A collection of forty-two short hymns in *Syriac linked in manuscripts to the Psalms. Their date must be earlier than the time of Lactantius (3rd–4th cents.) who quotes them, but their unorthodox imagery and indirect reference to Christ make them difficult to place. It is even uncertain whether the Syriac text is a translation from Greek. Suggestions of a *gnostic or sectarian Jewish background for the *Odes* are tenuous; more probably they were hymns used on the days of *Lent as part of the final preparation of catechumens for baptism.

Syriac text, ed. and tr. by J. H. Charlesworth (1973).

Solomon, Psalms of. A collection of *pseudepigraphical psalms ascribed to the Israelite King *Solomon. Originally written in Hebrew, the eighteen psalms now exist only in Gk. and Syriac versions. They probably date from the 1st cent. BCE, and are thought to refer to Pompey's conquest of *Erez Israel in 63 BCE. They also look forward to the coming of a *messiah descended from King *David. They divide the nation into 'the righteous' (mostly the *Pharisees, to whom the author evidently belongs) and 'the sinners' (the *Sadducees).

Eng. tr. in R. H. Charles, *The Apocrypha and Pseudepigrapha . . .*, ii (1913).

Solomon, Song of (part of Hebrew scripture): see SONG OF SONGS.

Solomon, Wisdom of (book of the Apocrypha): see WISDOM OF SOLOMON.

Soloveichik, Joseph Baer of Volozhin (1820–92). Jewish *Talmudic expert. Joseph was the son of Isaac Ze'ev, the *rabbi of Kovno, who was himself the descendant of a line of eminent rabbis. He was the head of the *yeshivah at Volozhin from 1849, although he fell out with his co-head, Naphtali *Berlin. His grandson, Isaac Ze'ev ha-Levi Soloveichik (1886–1959), was regarded as a supreme *halakhic authority in Jerusalem. Another grandson, Moses (1876–1914), was rosh-yeshivah at *Yeshiva University; his eldest son, also Joseph Baer (Joseph *Solovei(t)chik), was a leading figure in the interpretation and application of *halakhah in the USA. Although various *responsa of the Soloveichiks have been preserved, there was a family tradition against publication.

Solovei(t)chik, Joseph (1903–93). Jewish *Orthodox *rabbi and *Talmudic expert. He was born at Pruzhan, in Poland, received both a Talmudic and a secular education, gaining a doctorate in philosophy from Berlin University. He emigrated to the USA in 1932, and became Orthodox rabbi in Boston. He established an institute for advanced Talmudic studies, meeting the needs of the flow of refugees from Europe; but he became widely known and revered when he began to teach at Yeshiva University in New York. He believed strongly that the Jewish vocation is to make all things holy, as God had commanded, not to accept that they are holy because God has made them so. This commitment to holiness requires scrupulous attention to the detail of *halakhah, and he made no accommodation with the changes in modern life. He believed personally that the defence of the Western Wall (*Wailing Wall) in Jerusalem was not worth a single life, and that the Jewish vocation of holiness was of paramount importance; but he did not argue publicly for such views. His commitment to teaching was in line with his view on the importance of halakhah and its oral transmission, and in consequence he did not put his interpretations into published form.

Soloviev, Vladimir (1853–1900). Russian poet and philosopher. A brilliant student of both philosophy and theology at Moscow, after lecturing there briefly, he held a post at St Petersburg and travelled and wrote. From 1873 he was a friend of *Dostoevsky. As a poet, he was a leader of the Symbolists; as a philosopher, he was influenced by German idealism and *gnostic occultism; as a theologian, he was a proponent of visible unity with Rome, after initial sympathy with the Slavophils. Underlying all was a vision of Sophia (Wisdom), the creative and redemptive feminine principle, providing a fragile coherence increasingly threatened by apocalyptic disaster.

E. Munzer, *Vladimir Solovyev* (1956).

Solzhenitsyn, Alexander Isayevich (b. 1918). Russian novelist. Born in Rostov-on-Don, he studied mathematics at Rostov University. During the Second World War he served in the army. In 1945 he was arrested and spent the next eight years in labour camps. Released on Stalin's death in 1953, he was exiled for three years. On his return he taught and began to write. His first novel, *One Day in the Life of Ivan Denisovich* (1962), was an immediate success. After increasing tension with the Soviet authorities, he was expelled in 1974, having received the Nobel Prize for Literature in 1970. His voice is a voice from the Gulags, the labour camps, where he was converted to Christianity: the voice of profound faith in God and in his image in human beings, equally critical of Soviet inhumanity, Western lack of values, and ecclesiastical frailty. He returned to Russia in 1994.

Soma (Skt., *su*, 'to press'). 1. Intoxicating or hallucinogenic juice or substance, offered in Hinduism to the gods, and ingested by the *brahmans and other participants in sacrificial rituals. The identification of the plant is uncertain and contested, though R. G. Wasson (*Soma*, 1968) persuaded many that it was *amanita muscaria*, the fly agaric mushroom; others suggest *Sarcostemma viminale* or *Asclepias acida*. Because of its power, it was regarded as the 'food of immortality', i.e. of resisting death, *amṛta*. The power of soma is manifested in the *Vedas in the god Soma, who is associated with *Agni; all 114 hymns of *Ṛg Veda* 9 are addressed to Soma. The ways of preparing and drinking soma are carefully described, and it is said to make one acquire the eight powers of the god.

2. Hindu moon god who protects herbs and rides in a chariot drawn by white horses or antelopes. The moon is the cup of soma (above).

S. S. Bhavve, *The Soma-hymns of the Ṛg veda* (1957–62); W. D. O'Flaherty, *Soma* (1968).

Sōma Sēma (the body a tomb): see CREMATION; SOUL (Christianity).

Somatic exegesis: see CULTURAL RELATIVITY AND RELIGION; Introduction.

Somayajña (group of sacrifices): see SACRIFICE (Hinduism).

Sŏn (Korean). Ch'an/Zen in Korea. During the latter half of the Silla dynasty (668–935), the nine Sŏn traditions ('Nine Mountains'), which comprise Sŏn Buddhism, were founded, seven of them being derived from the lineage of Ma-tsu Tao-i (709–88) of the southern school of Chinese Ch'an. These nine traditions were integrated into the Chogye sect by *Chinul (1158–1210), and it is this Chogye tradition that became dominant at the end of the 16th cent. and continues to this day to be the most influential Buddhist sect in Korea.

Song of Songs. One of the five *scrolls of the Hebrew scriptures. In the hagiographa (*Writings), it follows Job and precedes *Ruth. Song of Songs consists of a series of love songs of an entirely secular nature. It has, however, been interpreted as an *allegory of the love of God for his people, either the Israelites or the Christian soul. R. *Akiva declared, 'He who trills his voice in the chanting of the Song of Songs in the banquet-halls and makes it a secular song has no share in the world to come' (*M.Sanh.* 12. 10). He vociferously defended the work's *canonical status, insisting, 'All the *writings are holy, but the Song of Songs is the Holy of the Holies' (*M.Yad.* 3. 5). Although it was traditionally composed by *Solomon, the book is unlikely to have reached its present form before 400 BCE. It is included in the *liturgy of *Passover, and is a voluntary reading before the *Sabbath evening service.

Song of the Three Children. An *apocryphal addition to *Daniel in the Hebrew scriptures. The *Song of the Three Children* was inserted between Daniel 3. 23 and 3. 24. It dates back to the 2nd or 1st cent. BCE, and consists of the *prayer of Azariah, a description of the fiery furnace and the song of *Shadrach, Meshach, and Abed-nego. In Roman Catholic bibles it forms 3. 24–90; the Christian canticle known as the *Benedicite comes from vv. 35–66.

Son of man, a (Heb., *ben Adam*). Phrase used in Jewish scripture (especially Psalms and once in Job) in parallel to other words for 'man'. Since it is literally 'son of Adam' (i.e. descendant of the one who, with his descendants, is subject to the penalty of death, Genesis 3. 1–19), the phrase is used most often in contexts where it means 'humans subject to death' (a point already noticed and understood by the *Targums, early translations of scripture). It carries with it the association of 'humans subject to frailty and death'. In Daniel 7 (in an Aramaic passage), the phrase 'a son of man' is used of a figure seen in a vision as vindicated before a heavenly tribunal and awarded an everlasting kingdom. This probably epitomizes Jewish martyrs, vindicated by their obedience (which they have taken to the point of death), as the true kingdom of Israel. The phrase does not occur in scripture as a title.

Son of man, the (Gk., *ho huios tou anthropou*). A phrase (not title) used in the New Testament which occurs exclusively in the sayings of *Jesus (and once elsewhere, Acts 7. 56), the anarthrous (i.e. without the definite article *the*) form in John 5. 27 being the only exception. The definite form in the singular (otherwise found only in the plural, 'the sons of men') has not yet been found in any pre-Christian Hebrew literature, except once in the *Dead Sea Scrolls (*1QS* 11. 20, and there apparently as an afterthought, since the article is added above the line). On the other hand, the definite form is found in Aramaic, so that if Jesus spoke Aramaic it is a natural expression (the view that there would be no difference in meaning between the two forms in Aramaic has been contested). The widespread opinion that the Greek phrase with the definite article is bad or awkward or unusual Gk. is nonsense: it is idiomatic Gk. for the phrase (however unusual the phrase may be), *the* son of man. The conclusion is inescapable that the phrase was used deliberately and with specific intent by Jesus to convey 'the son of man, the one you all know about'. The regular use of the definite article in the Gk. tradition is hard to account for unless in the Aramaic sayings some formula of definite reference was made (cf. the Ethiopic of *1 Enoch* 37–71).

It seems probable, therefore, that Jesus used the phrase to draw together the two major uses in what was already becoming scripture by his time, namely, that he was teaching and acting among them with direct authority from God, not as a superhuman figure (e.g. an *angel or a *messiah or a *prophet) but as one who is as much subject to death as anyone else, who believes nevertheless that he will be vindicated by God despite death. When it seemed on the cross that the vindication had not happened, the cry of dereliction ('My God, my God, why have you forsaken me?') was real indeed; which makes the actual vindication in the resurrection all the more compelling, since it appears to have taken his followers very much by surprise. The allusion to Daniel 7 (and *Josephus, *Antiquities* 10. 267 implies that the passage might have been widely known) would also have carried with it a sense of his own obedience constituting the true vocation of Israel and the only ultimate basis for kingship—an obedience to which he called his followers also (however little they comprehended it at the time).

Other views have been put forward (summarized in J. W. Bowker, 'The Son of Man', *Journ. of Theol. Studies*, 38 (1977), 1–30). For example, it has been argued that the phrase is an overliteral translation into Gk. of an Aramaic expression for 'a man' or 'someone' or 'I'. In that case, some general statements of Jesus (e.g. 'man is lord of the sabbath', Mark 2. 28) were only later applied to him alone. However, extremely few unequivocal (i.e. that could not be interpreted with equal probability in other ways) examples of the Aramaic usage meaning 'I' have been found—perhaps only one. And it remains a problem how 'the son of man' came to have those double-reference associations of suffering and future glory which characterize the gospel sayings (Mark 8. 31, 14. 62; John 8. 28, etc.), unless they do come from the two major senses in scripture, Daniel 7 and the more pervasive 'humans subject to death'.

C. C. Caragounis, *The Son of Man* . . . (1986); C. F. D. Moule, *The Origin of Christology* (1977).

Sons of Light. Hebrew phrase used in the *Dead Sea Scrolls. The 'sons of light' are contrasted with the 'sons of darkness', and are presumably to be identified with members of the *Qumran community. New initiates to the community swore to 'love all the sons of light' (*1QS* 1. 9), and *apostates were 'cut off from the midst of the sons of light' (*1QS* 2. 16).

Sopadhiśeṣa-nirvāṇa (Skt.; Pāli, *savupadisesa-nibbāna*). In Buddhism, *nirvāna while still in the condition of this life: the *kleśas are extinguished, but the *skandhas, the aggregations which constitute appearance, continue. At death, the condition of nirvāna is obtained. In Mahāyāna, the complete awareness, which must necessarily precede this, leads in the direction of *bodhisattva.

Sorskii/Sorsky, Nil(us) (leader of Non-Possessors Russian monastic group): see POSSESSORS.

Sōsai. Japanese Shinto funeral services. Uncommon since 17th cent., due to over two centuries of government proscription, these rites are now chiefly performed for shrine priests and their families. Nowadays based on the teachings of Hirata Atsutane, the ceremony is distinctive in that ritual offerings are made to the departed soul and, in contrast with Buddhist cremation, the corpse itself is buried.

Sōsan (patriarch in Ch'an Buddhist line): see SENG-TS'AN.

Soshi. The Elder or Patriarch, Zen Buddhist title of *Bodhidharma.

Soshigata. The elders or patriarchs in Ch'an/Zen Buddhism, the great masters, practitioners, and teachers who stand in lines of direct transmission of *dharma—ultimately, from the *Buddha Śākyamuni, though some early links in the chain are doubtful historically. In India there were twenty-eight successors, in China six. *Hui-neng, the sixth, made no formal transmission, but the subsequent schools derive from his five chief pupils.

Sōšyant (expected saviour): see ZOROASTER; FRASOKERETI.

Sotāpanna (stream-enterer, one who has entered the Buddha's path): see ŚROTĀPANNA.

Sotaranzō. Jap. for *sūtra/sutta piṭaka.

Soteriology. The doctrine of *salvation (Gk., *sōtēria*). In Christian theology this means the saving work of God in the *incarnation and especially the *atonement, and through *grace. The doctrines of the *Fall and of *sin are presuppositions. See also REDEMPTION; Index, Soteriology.

More widely, the term is used of any discussion of salvation or its equivalent in other religions.

Sotoba. Jap. for *stūpa; also the tablet set up on the grave of a dead person, bearing the name and a sacred formula to assist the spirit of the deceased.

Sōtō Shū (Chin., *Ts'ao-tung*). One of the two major schools of *Zen (Chin., *ch'an* or 'meditation') Buddhism and one of the thirteen traditional Japanese Buddhist schools. The name *sōtō* is derived from the names of two places in China: Ts'ao (Jap., Sōkei), where the Sixth Patriarch, *Hui-neng (Jap., Enō) lived; and Tung-shan (Jap., Tōzan), where Liang-chieh (Jap., Ryōkai), the Chinese founder of the Sōtō school lived. Among the Japanese schools of Zen, only the *Rinzai (Chin., Lin-chi) and the Sōtō schools have prospered.

The Sōtō school was brought to Japan from China by *Dōgen Kigen (1200–53). Doctrinally, the Sōtō and Rinzai schools maintain quite similar interpretations of Buddhism. The major areas of difference between them occur in the matter of practice. Whereas Rinzai Zen teaches *kanna zen* (*'kōan introspection'), emphasizing 'seated meditation' (*zazen) focused on a kōan in order to achieve a first enlightenment experience (*kenshō), the Sōtō school refers to itself as *mokushō zen*, 'silent illumination Zen', because of its sparing use of the kōan and its identification of zazen itself with enlightenment (*shikan taza*, 'zazen only').

In Japan, the history of Sōtō is bound up with the two major monasteries, *Eihei-ji and *Sōji-ji.

See Index, Soto.

Soul

Judaism In the Hebrew scriptures, the soul and the body are not sharply distinguished. The words *ru'aḥ* ('breath', 'wind'), *nefesh* (that which locates the animate as opposed to the dead—as e.g. 'the waters have come up to my *nefesh*', i.e. neck), and *neshāmah* ('vitality') have no independent, ontological status: they refer to that which gives life and which, if it is absent, leads to death. The *rabbis of the *Talmudic period recognized some separation: God was said to breathe the soul into the life of *Adam (*B.Ta'an* 22b), and after death the soul would leave the body until it was finally reunited at the *resurrection (*B.Sanh.* 90b). The soul was understood as the guest of the body during the body's earthly life (*Lev.R.* 34. 3), and human beings protect the purity of their souls by walking in the way of *Torah (*B.Nid.* 31a). Jewish philosophers, such as *Philo, *Sa'adiah Gaon, and Solomon ibn *Gabirol, were influenced by Platonism in their teachings on the immortality of the soul, while the *kabbalists taught that the soul was a divine entity that evolved downwards to enter the body. It has its origins in the divine emanation and its ultimate goal is its return to the world of *sefirot.

Despite the biblical emphasis on the unitary nature of the animated body (and thus on the resurrection of the body as a necessary condition if there is to be any continuing life after death—itself a belief which only appears very tentatively at the end of the biblical period), many Jews have preferred 'immortality of the soul' to 'resurrection of the body' in thinking of eternal life. Thus the Pittsburgh Platform (see REFORM JUDAISM) declared: 'We re-assert the doctrine of Judaism that the soul of man is immortal, grounding this belief on the Divine nature of the human spirit . . . We reject as ideas not rooted in Judaism the belief both in bodily resurrection and in *Gehenna and *Eden.' The *Orthodox retain the traditional beliefs.

J. W. Bowker, *The Meanings of Death* (1992); H. W. Wolff, *Anthropologie des Alten Testaments* (1973; Eng., 1974).

Christianity The New Testament writers inherited the biblical terminology (though in Greek), together with the undecided contest about the basic human composition and about whether any part of it might continue after death. Roughly, *nephesh* became *psyche* and *ruaḥ* became *pneuma*; but both these were transformed by the resurrection of Jesus and by the experience of the *Holy Spirit in the early Church. Thus early Christianity came to believe that the *psyche* must be surrendered to God with complete commitment and trust, even to the extent of, so to speak, losing it (Matthew 6. 25, 16. 25; Mark 8. 35; Luke 9. 24; John 12. 25) and thus securing it. The soul was then associated with a belief that there will be an embodied resurrection. In the Hellenistic world, an application of the *dualism of Plato nevertheless seemed spiritually attractive, since the sense of a soul imprisoned in a body (*sōma sēma*, 'the body a tomb') led to a heroic spirituality in which *ascetic efforts might be made to ensure the soul's escape and safety. Aristotle had argued against Plato that the soul is the form of the body—i.e., roughly, that the soul is the human, being human in its characteristically appropriate way; in this sense, the 'knifeness of a knife' means that here too the soul is the form of the body: the soul of a knife is potential while it is lying in a drawer, and actualized when it is being used in its characteristically appropriate way. Applied religiously, the human soul is potential until it is actualized in humanly appropriate ways, of which the most characteristically appropriate is the adoration of God in the communion of all the saints. Thus whereas Aristotle could (probably, the point is disputed) see no room for individual immortality, but only the endurance of a kind of supra-individual world-soul, *Aquinas could see individual immortality of the soul as a natural conclusion to be drawn about the particular form of the human body (*Summa Theol.* 1, qu. 76). At the same time, it seemed obvious that the 'soulness' of the human body (i.e. ensoulment) could only be bestowed by God at the appropriate point in the development of the human embryo, at the point when the relation to God became a possibility. In this way, Aristotelian animation and medical morphology remained coherent with each other and with Christian anthropology. However, in 1869 the *Roman Catholic position was changed and it was stated that the soul is conferred at the moment of conception, so that the embryo is *personne à devenir*, 'a person in the process of becoming such'. This is strictly inaccurate, since the fertilized egg may be committed to a non-human development (e.g. a hydatidiform mole) and is not *personne à devenir* at all. However, the matter has passed into the arena of church politics, and despite the clear innovation in 1869 is now treated in institutional Roman Catholicism as an inviolable truth.

A. Pegis, *Saint Thomas and the Problem of the Soul* . . . (1983).

Islam See NAFS.

Indian Religions See ĀTMAN; ANĀTMAN; JĪVA.

Soul-friend (counsel in the spiritual life): see CELTIC CHURCH.

Sound: see Index, Sound.

Sounding brass (emptiness of life without agape): see CHARITY.

South-East Asian Buddhism: see BUDDHISM *ad loc*.

Southern and Northern Schools. An early division of Ch'an/Zen Buddhism in China. Both schools agree in accepting the first four successors or patriarchs after *Bodhidharma: *Hui-K'o, *Seng-ts'an, *Tao-hsin, and *Hung-jen. They divide over the next successor. The division is reinforced by basic issues concerning the way to enlightenment. Thus, contrary to the titles, the division was not so much one of geography as of emphasis. Roughly, South is associated with sudden enlightenment, North with gradual approaches—hence the summary formula, *nan-tun pei-chien* (Jap., *nanton hokuzen*), 'suddenness of south, gradualness of north'. The history of the schism is obscured by the fact that it is mainly told by the eventual 'winners', the South. But the North had a central part in the transmission from Bodhidharma via Fa-ju (638–89), who addressed his teacher, Hung-jen, as 'patriarch' (indicating for the first time formal transmission), and who is regarded as the founder of the North. He was succeeded by Shen-hsiu (667–730), although Southern accounts replace him with *Hui-neng. But Shen-hsiu received the seal of recognition from Hung-jen (*inka-shōmei), and was widely recognized for his wisdom and powers of meditation. He systematized the earlier teachings which he had received, in *Kuan-hsin lun*, harmonizing *sūtras and meditation practices, and transmitting the foundations laid by Bodhidharma into China. According to his epitaph, 'he cut off the flow of ideas and put a stop to the rush of imagination, and with all his energy concentrated his mind', and he was able to go 'to that domain where there is no longer any distinction between sacred and profane'.

All that is far removed from the dominant Southern accounts, which in their tendentiousness are like Roman Catholic histories of Protestantism (or *vice versa*). The South was established by Shen-hui, a disciple of Hui-neng, at the Great Dharma Assembly on 15 Jan. 732, in Hua-t'ai. Of Shen-hui's earlier life, little is known apart from his disputes with pupils of Shen-hsiu, P'u-chi and I-fu. According to the Tun-huang text, Shen-hui argued that Bodhidharma is the authentic source of Zen: he stopped the futile activity of building temples, carving images of the Buddha, and copying sūtras. The dharma seal of recognition and the robe were transmitted to Hui-K'o, from whom they were transmitted in unbroken line to Hui-neng. The Northern protagonist refused to confine transmission to one line, via the robe. Shen-hui replied: 'The robe authenticates dharma, and the dharma is the doctrine [confirmed by] the robe . . . There is no other transmission.' Nor can North and South be regarded as complementary: Shen-hsiu seeks a gradual progress, via stilling of the mind through study and exercises, to enlightenment; but true enlightenment, according to Shen-hui, is a sudden breakthrough to no-mind: 'Our masters have all grasped enlightenment at a single stroke [Jap., *tantō jikinyū*], with no concession to steps or progressions.'

North persisted for several more generations, but the Southern view prevailed and became what is now recognized as Zen. But the different emphases between *Sōtō and *Rinzai indicate that the issue was never wholly resolved.

J. Gernet, *Entretiens* . . . (1949); I. Miura and R. F. Sasaki, *Zen Dust* (1966).

Southern Baptist Convention. The largest organization of *Baptist churches in the USA. It was formed in 1845 following serious division among US Baptists over slavery. Since the 1940s, however, it has spread to all the states (partly on account of its membership among US military families) and has lost a little of its regional identity. Its 36,000 member churches (1983) join the Convention entirely on the basis of voluntary association, knowing that it exerts no authority over them. *Conservative evangelical in theology, Southern Baptists maintain a vigorous commitment to evangelism, missionary work, and Christian education. In view of its numerical strength (13.9 million members in 1983) and resources, the Convention has considerable influence among Baptists, especially through the Baptist World Alliance.

Southern Kingdom (of Israel): see ISRAEL (3).

Sōzan Honjaku (co-founder of Ch'an school): see TS'AO-SHAN PEN-CHI.

Sozzini, Lelio, and Fausto (source of Socinianism): see SOCINIANISM.

Spartas (founder): see AFRICAN GREEK ORTHODOX CHURCH.

SPCK (Society for Promoting Christian Knowledge). British missionary society and publisher, founded in 1698. Its main work outside the UK is now through grants to churches to publish and distribute their own literature.

Special providence (God's action in relation to particular circumstances and individuals): see PROVIDENCE.

Special sabbaths (particular sabbaths in the Jewish calendar): see SABBATH.

Spector/Spektor Isaac Elchanan (1817–96). Lithuanian Jewish religious leader. Spektor served as the *rabbi of a number of communities, ultimately of Kovno. He founded a *yeshivah for rabbinical training. He was the only rabbi invited to the 1881 St Petersburg Conference for Jewish leaders. Because of the deteriorating situation of Jews in Russia, he supported the Hovevei *Zion (Lovers of Zion) movement, and publicly proclaimed the religious duty of settling in *Erez Israel. Many of his letters and *responsa have been published. Two yeshivot were founded in his memory in 1897, one of them in New York—the Rabbi Isaac Elchanan Theological Seminary. This developed into Yeshiva University, one of the largest Jewish institutions of higher education in the USA.

E. Shimoff, *Rabbi Isaac Elchanan Spektor* (1961).

Spener, Jakob (leader of Protestant movement): see PIETISM.

Spheres, Music of (perfect harmonies in the moving spheres of cosmology): see MUSIC OF THE SPHERES.

Sphoṭa (Skt., 'a boil'). In Hindu understanding, the capacity of meaning to burst forth (as from a lanced boil) from the sound (*śabda) of words, because all sound has the potential to manifest the source of sound, namely, *Brahman: 'The eternal word, called sphoṭa, without division is the cause of the world, and is in truth Brahman. . . . Brahman, without beginning or end, is the indestructible essence of all speech: it shines out in the meaning of all things, and it is the source of the whole world' (*Sarvadarśana-saṁgraha* 13. 6).

H. G. Coward, *The Sphoṭa Theory of Language* (1980).

Spinoza, Baruch (1632–77). Jewish philosopher. Despite his traditional education in Amsterdam, he associated with free-thinkers in his youth, and was *excommunicated from the community in 1656 for 'the abominable heresies practised and taught by him' and 'the monstrous acts committed by him'. He was reported as denying the law of *Moses and the immortality of the soul. His *Tractatus Theologico-Politicus* (1670, published anonymously) was a work of biblical criticism which questioned revealed religion, opposed persecuting churches (including *Calvinism), and argued for religious freedom. His major work, *Ethics*, was not published until after his death and presented his ideas in geometrical order, arguing from definitions to demonstrations of propositions: its Latin title, *Ethica Ordine Geometrico Demonstrata*, indicates how influenced he was by the success of mathematical demonstration in the Newtonian physical world-view. However, his *pantheistic, impersonal God was completely alien to the Jewish community and he remained under a ban (*ḥerem) for the rest of his life, once the edict had been issued.

In contrast, Novalis called him *Gott-trunckener Mensch* ('God-intoxicated man'), and there is no doubt of the centrality of God in his understanding of all things. Book i of the *Ethics* lays out the necessary conditions of appearance, leading to the demonstration of the existence of God. In his own summary:

> In these propositions, I have explained the nature and the properties of God: that he necessarily exists: that he is one alone: that he exists and acts merely from the necessity of his nature: that he is the free cause of all things, and in what manner: that all things are in God, and so depend on him that without him they could neither exist nor be conceived: and finally, that all things were predetermined by God, not through his free or good will, but through his absolute nature or infinite power.

Spinoza began with axioms which had to be true because they could not logically be denied. But looking at it, so to speak, backwards, and tracing the chain of propositions back to deductions back to axioms, everything is logically and actually dependent on an absolutely infinite Being whose existence cannot be denied, and this is what Spinoza called God, though equally it is Nature—understood in this way; hence his saying, *Deus sive Natura*. Clearly this is far from the personal creator outside and apart from his creation; or as his contemporary, *Pascal, might have put it, far from the God of Abraham, Isaac, and Jacob. If the infinite substance is God, then all things are, in a sense, in God (hence his being described as a pantheist), who is the ultimate ground and explanation of all things; and it follows equally that 'all things are determined by the necessity of the divine nature'. Spinoza allowed a small space for human endeavour (*conatus*) within the strictly determined, and that was in the human effort to raise its life above all that seeks to destroy it, including passions and emotions. This effort to become 'the captain of one's soul' and to rise above passion through reason is called 'the concept of positive freedom', and has been an important goal in other systems of ethics. The free person has emotions, but they rise from rational control and understanding.

S. Hampshire, *Spinoza* (1951); H. A. Wolfson, *The Philosophy of Spinoza* (1934).

Spirit: see HOLY SPIRIT.

Spiritual. A type of American folk hymn of the 18th–19th cent. 'White' spirituals appeared on the American frontier, in the forms of religious ballads and camp-meeting choruses, characterized by repetitions and refrains. 'Black' spirituals, the religious songs of slaves, are better known, partly on account of their musical idiom, and partly because of the intensity of feeling shown in songs like 'Nobody knows the trouble I seen', and 'Were you there when they crucified my Lord?' In the late 19th cent. spirituals were ousted from most black churches by urbanization and by gospel hymns, but they survive in concert performances.

Songs of Zion (1981); G. P. Jackson, *White and Negro Spirituals* (1943); J. Lovell, *Black Song . . .* (1972).

Spiritual Baptists. A group, known as 'Shouters' in Trinidad and Granada, and as 'Shakers' in St Vincent, representing an Afro-Protestant *syncretism within autonomous congregations mainly of African descent. This started on St Vincent in the late 19th cent. Although outlawed 1912–65, it survived underground and is now publicly accepted. Worship begins with *Methodist forms and may end with mild trances and possession by the *Holy Spirit; healing is not prominent. After spreading to Trinidad, where it was banned from 1917 till 1951, it became less orthodox and closer to *Shango, combining ecstatic worship with *Protestant fundamental beliefs. Immersion *baptism is preceded by biblical and moral instruction, and spiritual development is sought by 'mourning', being shut up in a small structure for days awaiting a 'gift' from the Spirit. Promotion to a hierarchy of offices depends on further development through 'building', a disciplinary period of prayer and fasting. Churches combine Christian features with a central ritual post of African origin.

Split-ear yogis (Kānpaṭha yogis, derived from Gorakhnāth): see GORAKHNĀTH.

Spurgeon, Charles Haddon (1834–92). Christian *Baptist minister. He was born in Essex, in England, and underwent a conversion experience in 1850—'I looked at God and he looked at me and we were one for ever.' In 1851, he became a Baptist. He began preaching, and was appointed to a chapel at Waterbeach, near Cambridge. In 1854 he moved to New Park Street Chapel in London, where the crowds who came to hear him were so great that the Metropolitan Tabernacle was built for him in Newington Causeway, completed in 1861: he ministered there to the end of his life. The printed sermons (in the end amounting to 63 vols.) enabled him to reach an even wider audience. He was firmly *Calvinistic in doctrine, and he withdrew from both the Evangelical Alliance and from the Baptist Union. In this, he was true to his word, that 'controversy for the truth against the errors of the age is the peculiar duty of the preacher'.

G. H. Pike, *The Life and Work . . .* (1894).

sPyan-ras-gzigs (Tibetan name of Avalokiteśvara): see AVALOKITEŚVARA.

Śrāddha (Skt.). In Hinduism, a supplementary funeral rite involving daily offering of water and occasional offerings of food (*piṇḍa) to the three immediately preceding generations of paternal and maternal ancestors. These offerings nourish the deceased, enabling the subtle bodies (*liṅga-śarīras) of one's ancestors to accumulate merit and to pass along the path of *saṃsāra (rebirth) to *mokṣa (release). Hence one needs sons to feed one after one's death.

The śrāddha rite is a source of merit for those who perform it with faith (*śraddhā). It should be performed in a secluded place away from the sight of women, outcastes, and eunuchs. Only offerings of pure water and foods are accepted by the ancestors.

Śraddhā (Skt.). 'Faith', personified as a goddess in Hinduism. She kindles in worshippers the faith to approach *Agni (and other gods) without which offerings are in vain.

In Buddhism (Pāli, *saddhā*), śraddhā is devoted commitment to the *Buddha and his *dharma: it underlies as a prerequisite the first two stages of the Eightfold Path (*aṣṭangika-mārga). In Mahāyāna, it is a fundamental trust, especially in the help of *bodhisattvas. From its devotion to Amitābha (*Amida), *Pure Land is sometimes known as 'The Way of Faith'.

Śrāmaṇa (Skt.; Pāli, *sammana*; Chin., *shamen*). In Eastern religions, the name given to members of male communities (usually translated as 'monks') or *ascetics; the feminine ('nuns') is śrāmani—see e.g. PĀRŚVA. Perhaps preceded by *keśins, the śrāmaṇas were numerous at the time of the *Upaniṣads, and may have been precursors of Jains and Buddhists.

G. C. Pande, *Śramana Tradition* (1978).

Śrāmaṇera (fem., *śramaṇerika*). Buddhist novices who have undertaken, through preliminary ordination, to observe the ten precepts (*śīla). The minimum age is 7 (the age of Rahula, the *Buddha Śākyamuni's son, when he entered the *saṅgha, and became thereby the patron-protector of all novices).

Śrauta sacrifices: see SACRIFICE (HINDUISM).

Śrautasūtras (texts detailing sacrificial procedures): See SŪTRA.

Śrāvaka (Skt., 'one who hears'). In Eastern religions, a layperson with religious commitment (see e.g. PĀRŚVA). In Buddhism, it referred originally to personal disciples of the *Buddha, or to students in general, but in *Mahāyāna, it refers to those who, in contrast to *bodhisattvas, seek personal enlightenment to the level of *arhat.

Śrāvakayāna (the way of the disciple, a less derogatory name for Hīnayāna): see HĪNAYĀNA.

Śrī (Skt., 'prosperity, splendour'). An honorific title in Hinduism, but also personified as a goddess, emerging from *Prajāpati after his creation of all other beings. The other gods were jealous and sought to kill her, but Prajāpati reminded them that men do not kill women, and that Śrī would be generous. Taking no chances, the gods plundered her gifts, *Indra her power, *Soma her royal attributes, etc. Prajāpati insisted that they were only loans, to be restored constantly through sacrifice. The association of Śrī with good fortune led to her assimilation with *Lakṣmi.

Sri Aurobindo (Hindu teacher): see AUROBINDO.

Srī Chand (1494–1612 CE). Elder son of Gurū *Nānak, founder of *Udāsīs. Gurū Nānak disappointed his celibate son by appointing *Aṅgad as successor. *Hargobind's son, Gurdittā, was born after the aged Srī Chand had blessed Dāmodarī.

Srid.pa'i 'khor.lo (pictorial representation of saṃsāra cycle in Tibetan art): see TIBETAN WHEEL OF LIFE.

Śrī Harṣa (1125–80 CE). A Hindu philosopher of the *Vedānta tradition and arguably the greatest Indian logician. His main work is the *Khaṇḍanakhaṇḍakhādya*, in which he rejects the *pramāṇa (means of knowing) system as a way of gaining knowledge. To refute his opponents—such as the *Nyāya-*Vaiśeṣika theologian *Udayana, the Mimāmsa *Kumārila and Prābhākara, and the Buddhist *Dharmakīrti—he employed the *vitaṇda* method of argument which refutes a thesis (*pratijñā*) by *reductio ad absurdum*, but offers no positive counter-thesis. By this method he showed that all propositions are illogical, for what follows from any proposition either contradicts that proposition or runs counter to experience. This parallels the *prasaṅga* method of the Buddhist *Nagārjuna.

Tr. in P. E. Granoff, *Philosophy and Argument in Late Vedanta* (1978).

Srī Pada (sacred mountain): see ADAM'S PEAK.

Śrī-Vaiṣṇavism. Hindu devotion to *Viṣṇu with his consort Śrī, one of the six major movements devoted to Viṣṇu. In early sources, there is no mention of Śrī as the consort of Viṣṇu, and indeed it seems clear that there was originally an independent cult of Śrī, which was absorbed into the worship of Viṣṇu. Once the cults were united, Śrī became inseparable from Viṣṇu, who now wears on his body the mark of Śrī (*śrīvatsa*). Not surprisingly, Śrī became identified with *Rādhā. The particular cult of Śrī-Vaiṣṇavism is strong in S. India, where it draws on the traditions of the *Āḻvārs. Thus they adhere to 'the theology of the two scriptures', i.e. *Vedānta and the Āḻvār hymns, especially *Tiruvāmoḻi*, which is held to be equal to the *Upaniṣads. It is characteristic of Śrī-Vaiṣṇavas that having made a ritual act of total surrender to God, they ask for nothing more.

They practise *darśana, the 'seeing' of the Lord through or in his image. Among major teachers, Puruṣottamācārya emphasized the ethical consequences of this *bhakti.

E. T. Hardy, *Emotional Kṛṣṇa Bhakti* (1978); K. Rangachari, *The Sri Vaishnava Brahmans* (1931).

Śrīvatsa (mark of Śrī): see ŚRĪ-VAIṢṆAVISM.

Śrī Yantra or **Śrī Cakra** (Skt.). In Hinduism, especially *Tantrism, the best known sacred diagram (*yantra) charged with power. It commonly comprises nine intersecting triangles, five 'female' triangles representing *Śakti pointing downwards and four 'male' triangles pointing upwards representing *Śiva, though in some forms the order is reversed. These triangles are surrounded by five circles, the innermost circle embellished with eight lotus petals, the next with sixteen. Beyond the circles are three concentric rectangles with four gates. A dot (*bindu) in the centre represents the source of manifestation, often equated with the Goddess Tripurāsundarī, while the intersecting triangles represent the interpenetration of Śiva and Śakti, the male–female polarity of the cosmos. Thus the Śrī Yantra is a representation of the universe which emanates from and contracts into a single source. See also SVASTIKA.

Within the Śrī Kula tradition of Tantrism, the Śrī Yantra is the visual equivalent of the Śrī Vidyā, a *mantra of fifteen syllables. Each syllable represents a goddess who is located within the Śrī Yantra. The Śrī Yantra is drawn or inscribed on wood, stone, animal skin, or on the ground and is used in worship (*pūjā) and meditation (*dhyāna). The adept (*sādhaka) will homologize the yantra and its mantra with the *cakras of his body through the practice of *nyāsa, thereby creating a correspondence between the cosmos and himself, by which he hopes to gain eventual liberation (*mokṣa).

Śrotāpanna (Skt.; Pāli, *sotāpanna*). 'One who has entered the stream', the beginning of the Buddhist way. A 'stream-enterer' is free from the three fetters (*saṃyojana), but not yet from the passions (*kleśa). He will have to be born in a new appearance at least seven more times, but these will always be in the higher domains (*gati), and not in *hell, or as an animal, etc.

Sṛṣṭi (Skt., 'sending forth'). Hindu understanding of creation as an emanation or re-emergence of the cosmos after its period of rest.

Śrutapañcami (Jain festival): see FESTIVALS AND FASTS.

Śruti (Skt., 'that which is heard'). In Hinduism, sacred and eternal truth, now in the form of revelation. As the word implies, this revelation was 'heard' (or alternatively 'seen') by seers (*ṛṣis) in a mythical past and transmitted orally, now by *brahmans. It is completely authoritative because śruti is believed to be eternal, unmarked by human redaction, and only written down in the age of disorder. Thus it is distinguished from *smṛti, 'that which is remembered', this latter being sacred and of divine origin, but imperfect because it is an indirect form of revelation. Śruti is synonymous with the *Veda. Smṛti in its widest application includes the *Vedāṅga, the ritual *sūtras, the lawbooks, the *itihāsas, the *Purāṇas, and the Nītiśāstras.

Ssu-hsiang (combinations of heaven and earth in Chinese philosophy): see T'AI-CHI.

Ssu-ma Ch'ien (son of Ssu-ma T'an, both historians): see HISTORIES IN CHINA.

Ssu-ming (Chin., 'Lord of fate'). A Taoist version of Tsao-chün, the 'lord of the hearth'. Tsao-chün watches over a household from his vantage-point, and is therefore of great importance in folk religion. A picture of him above the hearth is venerated on days of new and full moon, and on New Year's eve, when honey is smeared on his lips, so that his report on the family will be sweet. As Ssu-ming, he keeps the books of death and of the immortals (*hsien), according to the behaviours he observes.

Ssu Shu (group of Confucian texts): see FOUR BOOKS.

Stabat Mater Dolorosa. Opening words of a Latin hymn describing the sorrows of the Virgin *Mary at the cross of Jesus. Its author and date are unknown, though it is sometimes attributed to Jacapone da Todi (d. 1306). It was popularized in the 14th cent. by the flagellants who sang it in processions, but it was not printed in the Roman service-books until 1727. In the 1970 *missal it is kept as a *sequence for optional use on 15 Sept. (see SEVEN SORROWS OF THE VIRGIN MARY). Its beauty and popularity are reflected in the many English translations (e.g. 'At the Cross her station keeping') and musical settings, some of which are performed at concerts rather than in *liturgy (e.g. Rossini, Liszt, Dvořák, Verdi).

Stages of life (Hindu): see ĀŚRAMA.

Staṁbha (Hindu pillar): see SKAṀBHA.

Staniloae, Dumitru (1903–93). Romanian Orthodox theologian and guide to the Church during decades of political turmoil—leading to his book on Church–State relations in the particular setting of Romania. After study in Romania, he worked for his doctorate in Athens. He engaged in further studies in Germany and Paris, before taking up a post at the Theological Academy in Sibiu. He became editor of a church paper, and then moved in 1949 to Bucharest. He began his long task of translating the **Philocalia*, which was interrupted when he was arrested, in 1958, during a clamp-down on the Orthodox Church. He was pardoned in 1964, and continued his work in Bucharest until his retirement in 1973. He supported opponents of Ceaucescu, as he did also Metropolitan Balan in his takeover of the remnants of the Eastern Rite Catholic Church (see UNIAT(E) CHURCHES) after its suppression in 1948. His writing was direct and simple (*Theology and the Church* appeared in Eng. in 1980), and (somewhat like *al-Ghaz(z)ālī's concern to 'trust the religion of the old women') he controlled his thought by the consideration, 'What would the people of my old village make of this?'

Stanisław or **Stanislaus, St** (1030–79). Patron *saint of Poland. As *bishop of Cracow he came into conflict with King Bolesław II and was put to death. According to hagiographical sources, in particular a biography of the 15th cent., Stanisław rebuked the king's cruelty and oppression and specifically the abduction of a nobleman's wife, and finally *excommunicated him. Bolesław ordered his guards to kill the bishop, and when they would not, did the deed with his own sword. Most modern historians, however, hold that Stanisław was implicated in a plot to oust the king in favour of his brother, and that his execution was ordered, with whatever admixture of other motives, for treason. His remains were buried under the main altar of Cracow cathedral in 1088, and he was canonized in 1253. Feast day, 11 Apr.

Staretz (Russ. tr. of Gk., *geron*, 'an old man'). A spiritual father in Russian Orthodoxy. The *geron* was originally a senior monk, priest or lay, to whom other monks (and others) turned for spiritual direction. Such people are found throughout the history of monasticism. The monastic revival in the Slav countries under Paissy Velichkovsky (1722–94) was accompanied by rediscovery of the role of the staretz, and famous startsi (pl.), such as Amvrosy of Optina (1812–91), were eagerly sought out. One of Amvrosy's visitors was *Dostoevsky, and the staretz Zossima, in *Brothers Karamazov*, is a partial reminiscence of him.

Starhawk (proponent of Wicca): see WITCHCRAFT.

Star of David (symbol of Judaism): see MAGEN DAVID.

Station days. Certain days on which the pope formerly celebrated mass in the 'stational' churches (Lat., *statio*, 'assembly') in Rome. They became a part of *Lent devotion, with processions headed by a *relic of the True Cross. Today, a list of stational churches is published at the beginning of Lent, with the day of observance. Outside Lent, important 'stations' are St John Lateran for *Easter, and St Mary Major for the Christmas midnight mass.

Stations of the Cross. A series of fourteen incidents in the *passion of Jesus. They are: (i) he is condemned to death; (ii) he receives the cross; (iii) he falls; (iv) he meets his mother; (v) Simon of Cyrene is made to carry his cross; (vi) his face is wiped by *Veronica; (vii) he falls a second time; (viii) he meets the women of Jerusalem; (ix) he falls a third time; (x) he is stripped of his garments; (xi) he is nailed to the cross; (xii) he dies on the cross; (xiii) his body is taken down; (xiv) it is laid in the tomb.

In Roman Catholic and some Anglican churches, pictures or carvings of these incidents are arranged around the walls, and are the subject of public and private devotions in *Lent and Passiontide. The devotion probably arose as a substitute for the pilgrims' practice of walking the route in Jerusalem. It was popularized in the late Middle Ages by the *Franciscans.

Stcherbatsky, F. I., later **Theodore** (1866–1942). Russian scholar of Buddhist philosophy. Born in Poland of Russian aristocratic parents, he studied philology at St Petersburg University before turning his attention to Sanskrit poetics. He read Indian philosophy with Jacobi in Bonn (1900) and soon after made the first of a number of journeys to Mongolia to study Buddhism at close quarters under the guidance of Buriat Lamas. Between 1910 and 1911 he took lessons in Skt. and Tibetan from Indian pandits in Poona and in 1918 was elected full member of the St Petersburg Academy. Little is known of his life after the 1917 revolution, although he did visit Europe twice, being made an Honorary Member of the Royal Asiatic Society in 1923, and continued with his visits to Central Asia.

He is chiefly remembered today for his work on *Mahāyāna Buddhist philosophy, and in particular the first detailed treatment of the Logical or *Pramāṇa school of *Dignāga and *Dharmakīrti. His most influential writings are *The Central Conception of Buddhism* (1923), an examination of the *Abhidharma notion of *dharma; an exposition of the thought of *Nāgārjuna, *The Conception of Buddhist Nirvana*; and his magisterial *Buddhist Logic*, 2 vols. (1932). Stcherbatsky was instrumental in introducing, for the first time, the complexities of Mahāyāna philosophy to a wide European audience and this is his primary importance, although today many of his translations, particularly of technical Skt. terms, may appear curious. Much of this may be accounted for by the importance he placed on the Kantian philosophy as a tool in the interpretation of Buddhist thought. In later life he was a Professor of the Universities of Petrograd and Leningrad, and was a Member of the Academy of Sciences of the USSR.

Steiner, Rudolf (founder): see ANTHROPOSOPHICAL SOCIETY.

Steinheim, Salomon Ludwig (1789–1866). German Jewish poet and philosopher, Steinheim argued that religious *revelation is of its very nature nonrational. He alienated the advocates of *Reform Judaism by his supra-naturalism, and the *Orthodox by not identifying revelation with the Jewish holy books. His major work was *Die Offenbarung nachdem Lehrbegriffe der Synagoge* (4 vols.), but it had little influence on his contemporaries. He is now regarded as a forerunner of existentialism.

Stephen, St (d. *c*.35). The first Christian martyr. He was one of 'the seven' appointed 'to serve tables' (traditionally the first *deacons) in the Jerusalem church. On account of his preaching and miracles he was brought before the *Sanhedrin, and after making a defence denouncing Israel's perennial hardness of heart, was put to death by stoning (Acts 6. 1–8. 2). As with *Jesus, the basic offence appears to have been a refusal to accept the final authority of the *high priest and Temple (cf. Deuteronomy 17, and see REBELLIOUS ELDER). Feast day, in the W. 26 Dec., in the E. 27 Dec.

Sthāna-aṅga (part of Jain text): see AṄGA (2).

Sthaviravāda. One of two early Buddhist schools into which the community split at the Buddhist Council of *Pātaliputra, the other being *Mahāsāṅghika. The cause of the split is uncertain, but probably concerned proposals to extend the *vinaya rules, so that traditional practices could be formalized as obligatory. The conservative majority, Mahāsāṃghikas, resisted innovation. Traditionally, the split was over the exact status of *arhat. According to the Mahāsāṃghika, he is still subject to temptation, can still make progress, has not overcome all ignorance; according to Sthaviravāda, he is no longer 'human' in those ways. But this account seems to reflect later debates.

Sthūla-śarīra (in Hinduism one of three protections for the undying self): see ŚARĪRA.

Sticharion (Gk.). A liturgical *vestment worn by *Orthodox priests and bishops. It corresponds to the Western *alb, but may be coloured (especially dark red) as well as white. There are slight differences according to the clerical status of the person wearing it. It is at least as early as the 4th cent., when it is mentioned by John *Chrysostom.

Stigmata. The wounds of *Jesus at his crucifixion reproduced on the body of a Christian. In some cases they have been invisible (i.e. the 'stigmatized' person feels only the pain), in others, they are visible, in the form of wounds or blood blisters which resist treatment but are liable to bleeding at times such as Fridays, Lent, and Passiontide. The phenomenon dates from the 13th cent., a time of growing devotion to the suffering of Christ. The first saint known to have received the stigmata is St *Francis of Assisi, but the official attitude of the Roman Catholic Church has been guarded. More than 400 cases are known, and some instances have occurred outside Roman Catholicism.

H. Thurston, *The Physical Phenomena of Mysticism* (1952); I. Wilson, *Stigmata* (1988).

Stole. A Christian eucharistic *vestment, hung round the neck (or, by a deacon, over the left shoulder). It is coloured according to season. The equivalents for the *Orthodox are *epitrachelion* (for priests) and *orarion* for deacons.

Storefront Church: see AFRICAN-AMERICAN RELIGION.

Storehouse consciousness (the continuum of subjective consciousness in Buddhism): see ĀLAYA-VIJÑĀNA.

Story-telling in religions: see Introduction.

Strange words, extraordinary actions (style of Zen teaching): see MA-TSU TAO-I.

Strauss, David Friedrich (1808–74). German Protestant theologian and biblical critic. He was a pupil of F. C. *Baur and had hoped to be of *Hegel—but Hegel died shortly after Strauss arrived in Berlin. He was profoundly influenced by both. He was a lecturer at Tubingen, 1832–5, mainly teaching philosophy from a Hegelian standpoint. In 1835 he produced *Das Leben Jesu Kritisch Bearbeitet* (The Life of Jesus Critically Examined, tr. 1846). This, it has been said, produced both fame and ruin: its radical ideas prevented any future employment (he was appointed to a chair at Zurich but could not actually exercise the post). His *Christliche Glaubenslehre* (1840, Christian Faith) was a hostile account of the unfolding of Christian doctrine; and *Der alte und der neue Glaube* (1872, The Old Faith and the New) expressed more of his disillusion and unhappiness, rejecting, for example, any hope of immortality. When he died, he was buried according to the instructions of his will, without any religious ceremony. Strauss addressed the deep schism in the 19th cent. between the materialism which rested on the success of Newtonian mechanism and the Romantic protest that there is more to human nature and experience than a Newtonian scheme can account for. Applied to the biblical narrative, this resulted in, on the one side, an *a priori* dismissal of all that was irreconcilable with the scientific outlook, and on the other, a supernaturalism which insisted that, if Jesus was uniquely God incarnate, it becomes impossible to say what he can and cannot do. In his *Life of Jesus*, Strauss exploited Hegel's distinction between 'idea' and 'fact', with 'idea' being the significance which transcends mere occurrence. Religions are communities of 'meaning-making', or, to use Strauss' own term, of myth-making. *Myth did not mean (as it has come to mean colloquially) something false, but rather a way in which significance and meaning can be shared. Pure myth may have no connection with any event, though equally, myth may arise from events in order to draw out their meaning. Thus when Strauss called attention to the primary role of myth in relation to Jesus, he was not denying that there were facts and events which had happened. He was rejecting the approach which tries to sort out the facts first and dismisses the rest as invention. *Whatever* happened in the case of Jesus, incomparably more important than his biography is the way in which his followers used the mythological opportunities in the Bible to expound his significance. As factual history, Strauss could concede that such items as the Virgin Birth, walking on water, and even the resurrection and ascension, were improbable. But they remain of essential importance as the means through which the significance of Jesus is conveyed. Thus he was not 'explaining away' the supernatural, as he is often accused of doing; he was trying to show how the life of Jesus is embedded in the mythological codes of the time as a language of explication.

H. Harris, *David Friedrich Strauss . . .* (1973).

Stream-enterer (one at the start of the Buddhist way): see ŚROTĀPANNA.

Street called Straight: see DAMASCUS.

Stūpa (Skt.; Pāli, *thūpa*). A reliquary (*relics) monument ubiquitous throughout the Buddhist world and which, as an object of formal devotion and as a symbol of Buddhahood itself, has been compared in role to the *cross in Christianity. The stūpa originated in India from the earlier *caitya, a funeral mound commemorating regional kings. Instructions from the *Buddha that he himself should be so commemorated—in order to remind people of the possibility of *nirvāna—are contained in the *Hīnayāna **Mahāparinirvāṇa Sūtra*. It became the practice, however, to house the remains of any saintly person in this way, and as the building of a stūpa became associated with the acquisition of merit, it came to be built for its own sake, often containing only religious images.

The earliest form of the stūpa (e.g. from the 1st cent. CE, at Sañci, C. India) consisted of a simple base supporting an egg-shaped dome (*aṇḍa*) which contained the relics, and a spire with three rings—a combination in meaning of the ceremonial parasol and the *Three Jewels. The whole was surrounded by railings which circumscribed the stūpa as a sanctified area. From this basic form eight theoretical types were developed of which only two were commonly built. These were the Enlightenment Stūpa, which follows the above description, and the Descending Divinity Stūpa, commemorating the descent of the Buddha to teach his mother (after a *Jātaka tale), which has steps leading to a raised walkway around the dome. *Mahāyāna variations of these types could have five or seven 'umbrellas' to represent stages on the path to Buddhahood, and a multiple base to represent the five elements, thus greatly aligning the stūpa with the *maṇḍala as a cosmogrammatic representation. The stūpa continued to evolve outside India, producing the *pagoda in E. Asia, and reaching the height of its symbolic richness in the Tibetan *chorten.

See Index, Stupas.

T. Bhattacharya, *The Canons of Indian Art* (1963); A. L. Dallapiccola (ed.), *The Stūpa: Its Religious, Historical and Architectural Significance* (1980); S. Paranavitana, *The Stupa in Ceylon* (1946).

Stylite (Gk., *stulos*, 'pillar'). An early Christian *ascetic living on top of a pillar. They were mainly located in the Middle East. These pillars varied in height and size—some of them having a small shelter. Their main preoccupation was prayer, but they also gave instruction, and participated in theological controversy. The first stylite, *Simeon, was regarded as their founder. There were many stylites from the 5th to the 10th cents., after which they have become infrequent.

Suárez, Francisco de (1548–1617). Christian theologian and philosopher. He was born in Granada, in Spain, and became a *Jesuit in 1564. He was ordained in 1572, and, apart from five years in Rome, spent his life teaching in Spanish universities. He published many works, often linking papal power with *natural law. Thus he argued for a natural community of nations governed by *ius gentium* ('law of nations'), in which individuals coinhere whose acceptance of authority is based on natural rights. All these are interpreted by the *pope and mediated through the Church. Thus there is no divine right of kings standing over against the people (or for that matter the pope): the pope may depose for *heresy, but may not violate a nation's natural rights. In philosophical theology, he developed a position (especially in *Disputationes Metaphysicae*, 1597, Disputed Issues in Metaphysics), which is sometimes called after him 'Suarism' or 'Suarezianism'. He maintained, with the Jesuits against the *Dominicans, that God does not create the acts of individuals, but rather gives them the special graces (*gratia congrua*, from which this position is known as 'congruism') which, by his foreknowledge, he knows they will need. He was called by Paul V 'doctor eximius et pius'.

R. de Scorraille, *François Suarez de la compagnie de Jésus* (1912–13).

Subbas (Mandeans): see MANDEANS.

Subdeacon. An *order of Christian minister below *deacon. It was originally a minor order, and remains so in Eastern churches; in the Roman Catholic Church it became a major order in the 13th cent., but was suppressed altogether in 1972. The subdeacon was one of the three ministers at *high mass, with the function of attending to the sacred vessels and reading the *epistle. A priest or deacon now usually takes this part.

Subḥa (prayer beads in Islam): see ROSARY.

Sublapsarians (relation of election to fall): see PREDESTINATION.

Subordinationism. View in Christianity of the Triune Godhead which regards either the Son as subordinate to the Father, or the *Holy Spirit as subordinate to both, in contrast to the co-equality of all three Persons. It was condemned at the Council of *Constantinople in 381.

Subtle body (Skt., *liṅga śarīra* or *sūkṣma śarīra*). In Indian religions, a non-physical body. It is also called *puryaṣṭaka* ('city of eight'). This latter term refers to a classification of the subtle body in accordance with the *tattvas, namely the five *tanmatras* or subtle elements (sound, touch, form, taste, and smell) and the *antah kāraṇa* or inner instrument (comprising *buddhi, *ahaṃkāra, and *manas). A Vedantic classification, however, says that the subtle body comprises seventeen parts, namely the five *prāṇas, ten organs of action and knowledge, manas, and buddhi.

The subtle body is the vehicle in which the soul (*jīva) transmigrates through *saṃsāra, and the repository of karmic seeds (*saṃskāras) which determine the physical body and individual destiny. Beyond the subtle body is the causal (*kāraṇa*) or highest (*parā*) body. The causal, subtle, and gross bodies correspond to the states (*avasthā) of deep sleep, dreaming, and waking.

The structure of the subtle body as elaborated in Tantrism comprises energy centres (*cakras) connected by channels or veins (*nāḍīs) through which life-energy (*prāṇa) flows, maintaining bodily functions. Most representations show the central suṣumṇā nāḍī (the Buddhist *avadhūtī*) piercing the cakras, but according to the *Sat cakra nirupana* (Eng. tr. J. Woodroffe, *The Serpent Power*), the cakras are contained within the suṣumṇā and pierced by a further nāḍī within it. On either side of the suṣumṇā run the two nāḍīs, *iḍā and *piṅgalā (the Buddhist *lalanā* and *rasanā*), which represent the rivers *Gaṅgā and Sarasvatī as well as the moon and the sun. There are three 'knots' (*granthi*) or blocking points along the suṣumṇā at the *múlādhāra* (the *Brahma *granthi*), the *anāhata* (the *Viṣṇu *granthi*), and the *ājña* (the *Rudra *granthi*) where the yogin encounters obstruction in his spiritual journey, but through *Kuṇḍalinī yoga these knots are broken and the consciousness rises up to the thousand-petalled lotus (*sahasrāra padma*).

Subud International Brotherhood. A *new religious movement started in Indonesia in 1933 by Muhammad Subuh Sumohadiwidjojo (1901–87), Pak Subuh, called Bapak ('father') by his followers. It claims to be a spiritual experience rather than a religion or belief system. The name Subud is an abbreviation of the Skt. terms *suśīla*, *buddhi*, and *dharma*, which are given the meanings: 'living according to the will of God', 'the force of the inner self within humanity', and 'surrender and submission to God', respectively. The whole (Subud) means 'right living, with all one's parts awakened'.

Pak Subud is regarded as a spiritual guide, and it is he (and the 'helpers' appointed by him) who alone can transmit what is described as contact with the power of God, or Subud contact, to others. At the heart of the movement is *latihan* (or *latihan kejiwaan*), an Indonesian term meaning 'training' or 'exercise'. Latihan cannot be taught or acquired through imitation; it is said to arise spontaneously from within the individual after contact has been transmitted. Latihan, practised twice weekly in half-hour sessions, can take several forms, including that of outward physical movements and sounds expressive of a deep, inward action, which lead to purification and growth. It is held that physical improvement may be the first sign that inward purification has begun.

This movement, with members in some seventy countries, is responsible for many large enterprises, including banks and schools.

Suchness or **thusness** (*tathatā). Commonly used in Mahāyāna Buddhism to denote the essential nature of reality and the quiddity or true mode of being of phenomena. It is synonymous with 'emptiness' (*śūnyatā), but has more positive overtones which make it preferable to those schools with an absolutist bias. It is used interchangeably with 'true suchness' (*bhūtatathatā*) and is said to be the essence of the 'true reality' (*dharmakāya*).

Sudden enlightenment (belief that enlightenment does not need many years or lives of preparation): see HO-TSE; SOUTHERN AND NORTHERN SCHOOLS.

Śuddhādvaita (Skt., 'pure non-dualism'). The philosophical position of Vallabha (1473–1531 CE) and his successors. This school of *Vedānta accepts the *Vedas, the **Bhagavad-gītā*, the **Brahmasūtra*, and the **Bhāgavata Purāṇa* as authoritative, and teaches that both the cause (*Brahman) and the effect (the phenomenal world) are 'pure' (i.e. real) and one. Śaṅkara's doctrine of *māyā is rejected, and Parabrahman (conceived of as *sat, cit, ānanda, and *rasa—being, consciousness, bliss, and 'sentiment' or love) is affirmed as both the material and efficient cause of the universe. The purpose of creation is described as 'divine play' (*līlā). This highest entity, Parabrahman, is personal, described as both 'perfect' (*purṇa*) and 'the best of beings' (*puruṣottama*) and having qualities such as knowledge (*jñāna) and activity (*kriyā*).

The three traditional paths toward liberation, *karma (ritual action, i.e. Vedic rituals), jñāna (knowledge that everything is Brahman), and *bhakti (devotion to the Lord), are recognized as valid, ranked in that order of ascending spiritual attainment. Bhakti *mārga, the highest path, is in turn divided into *maryādā-mārga* and *puṣṭi-mārga*. The former involves following the dictates of the Vedas, leading to love of the Lord and ultimately to absorption in his body (*sāyujya-mukti*). *Puṣṭi-mārga* (the path of pure love) is bestowed on the devotee by divine grace alone and leads to participation with the Lord in his eternal play (*nitya-līlā*) and divine bliss (*bhajanānanda*), as exemplified in the divine play of the cowherd girls (*gopīs) with their beloved Lord *Kṛṣṇa (the rāsa-līlā).

There is a lower Brahman called the 'immutable' (*akṣara Brahman*) whose bliss is limited and who appears in various aspects as divine incarnations (*avatāras) and as the 'inner controller of the soul' (*antaryāmin*). The individual souls were created out of this lower *akṣara Brahman* like sparks from fire, and although minute or 'atomic', they experience the body and the outside world through the quality of intelligence (*caitanya) which is borrowed from *akṣara Brahman* and which 'pervades' the body.

Śūdra. Fourth social, or occupational, division (*varna) in Hinduism. The origin of the word is uncertain. From *Ṛg Veda* 10. 90. 12, where the hierarchy is *rājanya* (rulers), *brāhmaṇas, *vaiśyas, and śūdras, it is assumed that they were already menials, though at least included in the Vedic community, even if, as not being 'twice-born', not wholly integrated. Their emergence in creation from under the feet of Puruṣa summarizes their position in society. **Manusmṛti* states that a śūdra's name should combine a note of his low status with a description of his work, and that when dead, his body should be carried out of the south gate—the bodies of the 'twice-born' out of any of the others. See also CASTE.

Suffering: see THEODICY.

Suffering servant. The figure in Deutro-*Isaiah who bears suffering in hope of redemption, perhaps an individual, but understood as Israel in *exile. It was applied to *Jesus.

Suffragan. A Christian *bishop, who gives his suffrage (help). It may be any bishop, subordinate to his *metropolitan or *archbishop. In the Church of England, it is a bishop appointed as an assistant to the bishop of a diocese. He has no diocese and takes his name from a fixed list of places; e.g. the bishop of Lancaster is a suffragan bishop in the diocese of Blackburn. His public duties are mainly to take the place of the diocesan at *confirmations and other occasions requiring a bishop. The relative triviality of the work of a suffragan has led to moves to make suffragans into area bishops.

Sufi Order in the West. Established in London in 1910 by Hazrat Inyat Khan (1882–1927), from Baroda, India. He was succeeded by Pir Vilayat Inayat Khan (b. 1916), eldest son of the founder. The stated aims of the Order are to provide a vehicle for the transmission of spiritual truth in a manner that is consistent with modern, Western culture, and generally to act as a bridge between East and West. This form of the *Sūfī way focuses on the evolution of consciousness by realizing the common ground on which all things rest. This is referred to as the state of 'the one', the reality of the absolute which people strive to attain and which is found in God, *Buddha, and *Christ. The Order holds services of universal worship and provides what are called alchemical retreats, drawing on practices from several religious esoteric and mystical traditions.

Sūfīs (for suggested etymologies, see TAṢAWWUF). Muslims who seek close, direct, and personal experience of God, and who are often, therefore, described as mystics. Sufism is usually treated as a single phenomenon, although it is made up of different strands and styles. Sufism is a major part of Islam, and Sūfīs have been particularly important in the spread of Islam. By the 18th/19th cent. CE, at least a half (perhaps as many as three-quarters) of the male Muslim population was attached in some sense to a Sūfī *ṭarīqa (order). Thus although Sufism has often been contrasted with the forms of Islam concerned with *fīqh and *sharīʿa (i.e. with the lawful ordering of Muslim life), and although there have historically been clashes between the two, there is no inherent or necessary conflict: Sūfīs in general have been insistent on the necessity for the proper observance of Islam (examples are *al-Muḥāsibī and his pupil *al-Junaid, who is known as 'the father of sober Sufism') and have themselves been critical of *antinomian tendencies or individuals in Sūfī movements—associated e.g. with Khurasān, or with the *Qalandars. The union between Sūfī devotion and sharīʿa is associated particularly with *al-Ghaz(z)ālī and the great Indian teacher, Aḥmad Sirhindī (d. 1625 (AH 1034)): he was a Sūfī of the *Naqshbandī order who affirmed that while the experience of the unity of all being in God is real, it is neither the whole nor the end of religion: moral and virtuous life are as important—and to enforce this he wrote letters to his many followers throughout India. The Sūfī experience of absolute reality (*ḥaqīqa*) is not opposed to sharīʿa but is its foundation.

The early history of Sufism is not yet clear. It seems to have emerged from a determination among some early Muslims not to be distracted by the rapid Muslim expansion over vast territories from the vision and practice of *Muḥammad in realizing the absolute sovereignty of God in life. The contrast was extreme between the simplicity of the old desert life and the comfort of the new order. Their determination to remain close to the original simplicity was perhaps reinforced by their encounter with Syriac Christian *monasticism (despite the warnings of the *Qur'ān against the blasphemous implications of the *asceticism implied by monasticism). Of this early attitude, al-*Ḥasan al-Baṣrī (Basra being an important centre of it) is a major example, and later Sūfī orders look back to him as a key link in the connection back to the Prophet. Also from Basra was the notable *Rabiʿa al-ʿAdawiyya; but Sūfī devotion took root in many different places, often absorbing in each place something of its different atmosphere. Thus Khurasāni Sufism reflected its parched surroundings in an austere asceticism, producing such remembered figures as

Fudayl ibn ʿIyad, Ḥātim al-Aṣamm (who left behind the four principles of Sūfī life, to remember that no one eats your daily bread for you, that no one performs your acts except yourself, that as death is hurrying toward you so address your life now to meet it, and that every moment of your life is under the eye and judgement of God), and Ibrāhīm ibn Adham. The latter was a prince who experienced a dramatic conversion when, out hunting,

> I heard a voice three times, speaking (from the horn of my saddle, I swear by God!), saying, 'It was not for this that you were created, it was not this that you were commanded to do'; at once I dismounted and, coming across one of my father's shepherds, I took from him his woollen garment and put it on; I gave him my horse and set out at once on foot for *Mecca (Farid al-Dīn ʿAṭṭar, *Tadhkirat al-Awliya'*).

Or again Kashmiri Sufism, from the 14th cent. onward, drew on Hindu asceticism, even producing an order, the Rishis, whose name was derived from the word *ṛṣi (understood as 'a singer of sacred songs').

Since Sufism was a commitment to God in absolute trust and obedience, it (unsurprisingly) gave rise to intense experience of that relationship. Techniques were developed (e.g. *dhikr, *samaʿ) which were capable of producing trance states of ecstasy. In general, Sūfīs were careful to warn against the pursuit of ecstatic experience for its own sake (as opposed to attention to God for the sake of God alone). Nevertheless, the realized condition of union with God produced such a sense of the absolute truth of God, and of the bliss of union with him, that poetry and teaching began to emerge in which the distinction between God and the self seemed to be blurred—or even obliterated: the disturbance this caused for those sensitive to the absolute transcendence of God can be seen in the fate of *al-Ḥallāj, although far more threatening in effect was the mystically monistic system of *ibn al-ʿArabī, for whom, not only is there no God but God (*shahāda), but in fact there is nothing but God, with the world being his outward manifestation; yet he was insistent on the transcendent otherness of God. Any potential conflict between the *ʿulamā and the Sufis was largely overcome by the work of al-Ghaz(z)ālī, who knew both positions at first hand, and demonstrated the part that both play in Islam.

From the experience of devotion to God, the Sūfī poets, especially in Persia, produced works of enduring beauty and power. Among the earliest was Pīr-i-Anṣār (ʿAbdullah al-Anṣārī, d. 1088 (AH 481)), of Herat in Khurasān:

> 'Poor but proud' your lovers sigh,
> This to heaven their battle-cry,
> Shrugging off the fool's derision,
> Letting all the world go by;
> Pīr-i-Anṣār, drinking deeply,
> Such a fire of passion feels,
> That, like Laila's lover smitten,
> Through a ruined world he reels.

Other memorable poets were Farīd al-Dīn *ʿAṭṭār, ibn al-Fāriḍ, *Jāmī, and perhaps consummately *Jalāl al-Dīn Rūmī.

The wide extent and influence of Sufism (together with the fact that, despite the warnings mentioned above, many charlatans and stuntmen of the spirit appeared) led to attempts being made to give systematic order to its teachings and techniques—a notable example being Ali Hujwīrī (d. 1702). But even more important was the organization of Sūfī traditions into formal orders (*tarīqa, pl. turūq; *silsilah). For examples, see CHISHTI; MAWLAWIY(Y)A; NAQSHBANDIY(Y)A; QĀDIRIY(Y)A; SHĀDHILIY(Y)A; and Index, Sūfī orders. An adherent is known (in general terms, though these words also have a wider use) as *derwīsh, *faqīr, *marabout.

A leader is known as *shaykh. The greatest of these became possessed of *baraka. Common practices among Sūfīs, designed to draw them away from the world and closer to God, in addition to dhikr and samāʿ, are the assembly to celebrate the anniversary of a shaykh (and on other occasions), and *wird. Modern attempts to present Sufism as a gnostic wisdom for a materialistic age have misrepresented the deeply Muslim character of Sufism. It arises from the direct call and invitation of God to give one's devotion wholly and happily to him alone, not from an invitation to enhance one's spirituality in a programme of self-improvement.

See Index, Sūfī beliefs; Sūfī orders; Sūfīs.

A. J. Arberry, *Sufism* (1972); T. Burckhardt, *Introduction to Sufi Doctrine* (1976); N. R. Keddie (ed.), *Scholars, Saints and Sufis* (1972); M. Lings, *What is Sufism?* (1976); S. H. Nasr (ed.), *Islamic Spirituality: Foundations; . . . Manifestations* (1991); J. Nurbaksh, *Sufi Symbolism . . .* (1984–90); P. Nwyia, *Exégèse coranique et langage mystique* (1970); S. A. A. Rizwi, *A History of Sufism in India* (1978, 1983); A. Schimmel, *Mystical Dimensions of Islam* (1975) and *As Through a Veil* (1982); J. S. Trimingham, *The Sufi Orders in Islam* (1971).

Suhrawardī, Shihāb al-Dīn Yaḥyā, Shaykh al-Ishrāq (1154–91 (AH 549–87)). Muslim eclectic who established the *ishraqi* (Illuminationist) school of philosophy. He was born in Iran, and after years of wandering, settled in Aleppo. However, his unorthodox views led to his imprisonment and death, probably by execution—for which reason his followers called him al-Shaykh al-Maqtul (murdered) to distinguish him from two other famous *Sūfīs of the same family. He produced many works expounding the philosophy of Illumination, of which the best-known is *Kitab Hikmat al-Ishraq* (The Book of the Illuminationist Wisdom). In this he shows how humans can travel from darkness to light, not only metaphorically. He believed that the centre of light is in the point where the *Qur'ān was revealed, and that those living far away are in the position of those who are yearning to return. His influence continued particularly among *Shiʿites.

Œuvres philosophiques . . ., ed. H. Corbin (1976–7); *L'Archange empourpré . . .*, tr. H. Corbin (1976); W. M. Thackston, *The Mystical and Visionary Treatises . . .* (1982).

Suicide. The deliberate taking of one's own life is condemned in all religions, although exceptions on the margins (death accepted or embraced for religious reasons) are usually made. In Judaism, there is no explicit condemnation in the Bible, but it came to be prohibited, partly on the basis of the sixth commandment ('Thou shalt not kill') and partly on the basis of life being received as a direct result of God's creation: it is his to determine when life shall begin and end. However, suicide to avoid even greater offence (e.g. to avoid murder or idolatry) was regarded as praiseworthy: the reported suicides at Masada, to avoid falling into the hands of the Romans at the end of the Jewish revolt, 66–70, remained a model of martyrdom—see *kiddush ha-Shem. In any case, people who commit suicide are usually regarded as having been 'out of their minds' and therefore not culpable, and can, therefore, receive burial. Christians have, until recently, been less charitable: martyrdom is commended in the pattern of Christ who laid down his life for others, but the deliberate taking of one's own life is condemned on much the same grounds as those of the Jews, but with an added sense of the wrong done to family and society at large. Suicides could not, until recently, receive Christian burial, and suicide was a crime (it ceased to be a felony in the UK in 1961, though it remained an offence to aid or abet a suicide). The sense of compassion and support needed for those tempted to commit suicide led to the founding of the Samaritans by Chad Varah in 1953. Islam shares the same kind of attitude: martyrs (*shahīd) are highly commended, but suicide (although barely mentioned in the *Qur'ān: see 4. 29) is strongly condemned in *ḥadīth: 'Whoever throws himself from a cliff and commits suicide is throwing himself into the fires of hell. Whoever drinks poison and commits suicide will drink that poison forever in the fire of hell. Whoever kills himself with a weapon will hold that weapon stabbing himself forever in the fire of hell.'

In Eastern religions, the ambiguous border is not so much between martyrdom and suicide as between suicide and sacrifice. The *Brāhmaṇas envisage a religiously motivated suicide, as this body is relinquished; and *satī (the self-immolation of a widow) was seen, at least by some, to be highly advantageous in relation to rebirth. Among Jains, the religious relinquishing of the body is taken to a marked extreme in *sallekhanā. In Buddhism, the propriety of suicide to benefit another is recognized (e.g. in the *Jātaka stories, where the Buddha-to-be fed himself to a starving tigress who was thus enabled to feed her young). But the consideration of *ahiṁsā (of doing no harm to a sentient being) makes suicide generally forbidden. Japanese *harakiri (*seppuku*) was originally a social rather than specifically religious act, but its endorsement by Zen Buddhism gave it a religious support.

M. P. Battin, *Ethical Issues in Suicide* (1982); N. L. Farberow, *Suicide in Different Cultures* (1975), and (ed.), *The Many Faces of Suicide* (1980); U. Thakur, *The History of Suicide in India* (1963); S. Goldstein, *Suicide in Rabbinic Literature* (1989).

Suiga Shintō or **Suika Shintō** (Jap., 'Shinto of grace and protection'). An eclectic school of *Shinto which was influenced by *neo-Confucianism. It was founded by Yamazaki Ansai (1619–82), a Buddhist priest turned Confucian scholar who attempted a grand synthesis of neo-Confucian metaphysical and ethical concepts with the traditions of the various Shinto schools of the early Tokugawa period. Yamazaki appropriated the neo-Confucian notion of *li (Jap., *ri*), 'the unifying principle', to affirm the unity of humans and the *kami; and he taught the virtue of *tsutsushimi*, a circumspect attitude of reverence, as the basis of human behaviour. This school stressed the uniqueness and divinity of the imperial line and taught supreme reverence for the emperor.

Suigatsu (Jap., 'moon-reflected image'). A common summary in Japanese Buddhism of the transitory and non-substantial nature of all appearance.

Suijin matsuri (festivals of the water kami): see FESTIVALS AND FASTS.

Suika Shintō: see SUIGA SHINTŌ.

Sukh Asan (Pañjābī, 'sit at ease'). The Sikh ceremony during which the Gurū Granth Sāhib (*Ādi Granth) is formally closed for the night. The *Ardās is read and a reading is taken at random from the book. It may be carried in procession, with signs of reverence (bowed head) being shown.

Sukhāvatī. The Western Paradise, ruled over by the Buddha Amitābha (*Amida). For *Pure Land Buddhism, it is the goal attainable by devotion to Amitābha, from which one cannot fall back into rebirth in other domains.

Sukhāvatīvyūha (Skt., *sukhāvatī*, 'place of happiness', + *vyūha*, 'description'). A Buddhist *Mahāyāna scripture. A *sūtra of the early *Ratnakūṭa collection, it is also known as *Amitābhavyūha*, *Amitābhaparivarta*, or *Aparimitāyur-Sūtra*, 'Sūtra of Unending Life'. On being questioned by Ānanda, the *Buddha recounts the story of a monk named Dharmākara who takes a vow to achieve Buddhahood during the time of the Buddha Lokeśvararāja. Finally completing his task, the monk becomes the Buddha Amitābha (*Amida) living in a marvellous world, Sukhāvatī, an inconceivable distance in a westerly direction from our own. The text includes a detailed description of Sukhāvatī and makes the point that whoever sincerely desires *enlightenment, with a mind fixed on Amitābha, will be reborn in that wonderful world. Doctrinally important is its treatment of the *bodhisattva's vow of enlightenment and the conception of the Buddhafield (*buddhakṣetra). The *Sukhāvatīvyūha* is the textual base of the Japanese *Pure Land school of Buddhism, along with *Amityāyurdhyāna-Sūtra*. In Japanese, it is known as *Amida-Kyō*.

Sukhmanī (Pañjābī, 'hymn of peace'). Composition by Sikh Gurū *Arjan Dev. The Sukhmanī, *Ādi Granth pp. 262–96, is read daily in morning worship. It brings comfort, especially to the dying. According to Sukhmanī, spiritual peace comes from constant recollection of God's name (*nām). The Sukhmanī consists of twenty-four *aṣṭapadīs, each introduced by a *śalok: 'The Name of God is sweet sustenance, source of peace and joy within; the Name of God brings perfect peace to those who are truly devout.'

Sukkah, Sukkot (Heb., 'Booth', 'Festival of Booths'). The Jewish autumn festival. According to Leviticus 23. 42, 'You shall dwell in booths seven days that your generations may know that I made the children of *Israel to dwell in booths when I brought them out of the land of Egypt.' The construction of the booth is discussed in the *Talmudic tractate *Sukkah*: through the days of the festival, it must be regarded as one's principal residence. Sukkot is one of the three *pilgrim festivals. It begins on 15 Tishri, and work is forbidden on the first day (and second in the *diaspora). The festival concludes with Shemini Atzeret and *Simḥat Torah. In biblical times, it was clearly connected with the agricultural year (Deuteronomy 16. 13–15), and, based on Leviticus 23. 40, the *four species are to be held during the worship services. In the days of the *Temple, a special ceremony of water libation was held, and the light of the candlesticks used to be reflected in the poured-out water. Nowadays, it is customary to build a sukkah both at home and at the *synagogue, although in colder climates there is no obligation to sleep in it. On the first day, in the synagogue, as part of the *liturgy, the *lulav is waved in every direction and the congregation walks in procession around the *bimah as a reminder of the procession round the *altar of the Temple in *Jerusalem. The seventh day is known as *Hoshana Rabba; prayers are recited for a good harvest in the coming year and the Book of *Deuteronomy is studied. In Israel, Shemini Atzeret and Simḥat Torah are celebrated on the same day, but in the diaspora they are celebrated separately.

J. Fabricant, *A Guide to Succoth* (1958).

Sūkṣma (Skt., 'subtle'). Usually in combination with *śarīra, the subtle body, especially in *Kuṇḍalinī and *Tantric yoga, the support of the *cakras.

Sulaimān (the Magnificent), al-Qānūnī ('the law-giver', 1494–1566 (AH 900–74)). *Ottoman caliph (*khalīfa) who led the empire to its highest points of achievement. Committed to good administration, he issued in 1530 (AH 937) the Kānūnnāmeh, a corpus of law to bring greater uniformity to the immense empire. He initiated public buildings and municipal works, encouraging the great architect Sīnān (1488–1587 (AH 895–996)), who built many of the best-known *mosques in Istanbul and Turkey, and rebuilt the Great Mosque in *Mecca. He also campaigned extensively, annexing Hungary and besieging Vienna. After his death, intrigue and rivalry among his descendants (from different wives) led to steady and continuing decline in the empire.

Sulūk (Arab., 'journey'). Among the *Sūfīs, the mystic's progress on the way to God. It is a deliberate quest, beginning with one's initiation into a Sūfī order, followed, under the guidance of a *shaikh, by the methodical purification of the self through stages or stations (*maqāmat*). The Sūfī orders have their own individual programmes of stations for the sālik, the one who pursues this journey. For example, the *Qādirīya have: repentance, poverty, *dhikr, trust in God, love and knowledge, and so on. It is an endless journey for it leads to the Infinite Being, *Allāh. It should be noted, however, that the journey does not lead to a union of God and the human, but merely a union of will. Furthermore, all Sūfī orders consider love of God to be the dynamic force that propels the sālik during the course of sulūk, and it is the power of love that attracts and leads humans to knowledge. Since Allāh's knowledge is infinite, the sālik is forever gaining an infinite series of illuminations that have neither end nor limit.

Sumeru (sacred mountain in Indian religions): see MERU.

Summa. 'Total' or 'totality', used by medieval writers to denote a compendium of theology, philosophy, or canon law. They became handbooks for the *Scholastics, succeeding *Peter Lombard's *Sentences*, and consisted of 'questions' systematically arranged. The most famous are *Aquinas' *Summa Theologiae* and *Summa contra Gentiles*.

Sumohadiwidjojo, Muhammad Subuh (founder): see SUBUD.

Sundar Singh, Sadhu (1889–*c*.1929). Indian Christian teacher and mystic. Born of wealthy Sikh parents (though describing himself as a seeker, not a Sikh), he was converted to Christianity by a vision, and in 1905 was baptized into the Anglican Church. He wore the robe of a *sādhu to point to the possibility of Christianity in a Hindu context. He travelled extensively in Asia, and made trips to the West in 1920 and 1922. His Eastern connections aroused great interest in Europe (shown in the writings of B. H. Streeter and N. *Söderblom among others), but in Germany also some accusations that he was a charlatan or a victim of his own fantasies. He was last heard of in Apr. 1929.

C. J. Davey, *The Yellow Robe* . . . (1950).

Sunday. As the Christian weekly day of worship it may perhaps be attested in the New Testament (Acts 20. 7; Revelations 1. 10: see LORD'S DAY), but emerges clearly in Rome in the 2nd cent. It was early understood as a weekly commemoration of Christ's resurrection on the first day of the week, but it may also owe something to the early Christians' desire to distance themselves from Jewish customs and worship on a day other than the *Sabbath. The coincidence with the pagan 'day of the sun' (*dies solis*) was rationalized by referring it to Christ 'the Sun of Righteousness' (Malachi 4. 2). The observance of Sunday as a day of rest began to be enforced in the 4th cent., e.g. by *Constantine in a law of 321 which prohibited work for townspeople. Present-day Catholic practice in the West requires the faithful to hear mass and abstain from defined kinds of work on Sundays. For the transfer to Sunday of the 'day of rest', see SABBATH.

Sundo (Chin., Shun-tao). The first Buddhist missionary to Koguryŏ, in Korea. Sundo travelled to Koguryŏ in 372, the second year of King Sosurim's reign (371–84), with an envoy dispatched by King Fu Chien (r. 357–85) of the Former Ch'in dynasty (351–94), presenting Buddhist images and scriptures to the Koguryŏ court. (Another tradition holds that Sundo came from the Eastern Ch'in (317–420) rather than the Former Ch'in.) In either case, this event is regarded as the first introduction of Buddhism to Korea.

Sunna (Arab., 'custom'). Customary practice which, in Islam, may refer to both bad and good examples in the past. Thus in the *Qur'ān the sunna of the people of old is usually the way in which they rejected the *prophets who were sent to them (e.g. 8. 38; 15. 13). But supremely the sunna refers to the way in which the Prophet *Muḥammad and his Companions (*Ṣahāba) lived, and to what they said and did (attending also to that concerning which they were silent). Thus Qur'ān is the fundamental authority, but the sunna forms the first living commentary on what Qur'ān means, and thus becomes equally the foundation for Muslim life: the *sunnat al-nabī*, the 'example of the prophet', controls Muslim life even in small details. Non-Shīʿite Muslims are therefore known as *Ahl al-Sunna wa'l-jamāʿa*, the people of the sunna and of the gathered assembly, i.e. Sunnis. According to Muḥammad, 'He who wearies of my sunna does not belong to me.' The sunna is thus one of the foundation principles or sources (*uṣūl) of *fiqh, and those who adhere to the Qur'ān and sunna are known as *Sunnis. Shīʿites (*Shīʿa) share most of the sunna with them, but place emphasis on the role of the Imām in guiding the community, and they also accuse Sunnis of suppressing *ḥadīth which support Shīʿa beliefs and practices.

W. A. Graham, *Divine Word and Prophetic Word in Early Islam* (1977); A. Hasan, *The Early Development of Islamic Jurisprudence* (1970); S. H. M. Jafri, *The Origins and Development of Shīʿa Islam* (1979); J. Schacht, *An Introduction to Islamic Law* (1979).

Suññattā: see ŚŪNYATĀ.

Suntarar (Tamil Śaivite): see NĀYAṆMĀR.

Sun Wu-k'ung. The monkey king, one of the Chinese *hsien (immortals).

Śūnyam. In Indian mathematics, the sign for 'nought' or zero. Its decimal potential, in combination with integers, enabled the Hindu imagination to create vast numbers—simply by adding to 1, 2, etc., an indefinite series of zeros. Equally, the emptiness of zero opened up the conceptualization of *Brahman without attributes (*nirguṇa), and pointed towards *śūnyatā in Buddhism. Among *Bāuls, the *guru is sometimes called śūnya.

Śūnyatā or **Suññattā** (Skt., Pāli, 'emptiness'; Chin., *k'ung*; Jap., *kū*; Korean, *kong*). In early Buddhism, the term suññatā is used primarily in connection with the 'no-self' (*anatman) doctrine to denote that the Five Aggregates (*skandhas) are 'empty' of the permanent self or soul which is erroneously imputed to them. By extension the term came to be applied to reality as a whole: just as the individual is 'void' of a self, in the sense of an unchanging controlling agency, so too is the whole universe 'void of a self or anything belonging to a self' (*suññam attena vā attaniyena va*).

The doctrine of emptiness, however, received its fullest elaboration at the hands of *Nāgārjuna, who wielded it skilfully to destroy the substantialist conceptions of the *Abhidharma schools of the *Hīnayāna. The latter considered the emptiness of phenomena to lie in their impermanency, and maintained that, while entities are subject to a process of almost instantaneous change, they are none the less substantial and possessed of a true 'self-nature' (*svabhāva) in their moment of being. Nāgārjuna took the doctrine of emptiness to its logical conclusion and argued that this notion of a 'self-nature', albeit momentary, was at variance with the *Buddha's teaching of no-self. The true nature of phenomena, he concluded, was to be empty of a self or self-essence of any kind. The doctrine of emptiness is the central tenet of the *Mādhyamaka school, and a statement of Nāgārjuna's views in support of it may be found in his **Mūla-Mādhyamaka-Nārikā*.

Emptiness thus becomes a fundamental characteristic of *Mahāyāna Buddhism. The teaching is subtle and its precise formulation a matter of sophisticated debate, since the slightest misunderstanding is said to obstruct progress towards final liberation. Emptiness is never a generalized vacuity, like an empty room, but always relates to a specific entity whose emptiness is being asserted. In this way up to twenty kinds of emptiness are recognized, including the emptiness of emptiness. To the untrained mind, reality appears to consist of subjects, objects, and their relationships, all existing in their own right (Skt., svabhāva, 'own-being' or 'essence'), which are therefore clung to or avoided as the real sources of happiness or misery. When these entities are seen as space-like rather than particle-like, clinging and avoidance ceases and liberation results. The basis of the teaching is found in Hīnayāna which, somewhat like *Theravāda, views the sense of self (Skt., *ātmagraha*, 'grasping at "me" ') as empty (Pāli, *suñña*), i.e. as not implying a single, inviolable, and eternal entity without which 'I' would not exist, just as a river exists but does not have an eternal 'self' by means of which it exists. On this basis, Mādhyamaka shows that the method of analysis which fails to uncover an eternal 'I' (Skt., anātman, 'not-"I" ') similarly fails to uncover eternal essences in external objects and processes. For example, if something is said to go by means of a 'going', this going cannot be the same as the goer, for then it would just be a synonym, nor different from it, for then it could never reach the goer to make it go. Thus it is shown that, although something definitely goes, the essence by which it goes is *not discoverable*. The necessary indiscoverability of essences is the Mādhyamakan emptiness. It is important to distinguish this from *nihilism. In Yogācāra (*Vijñānavāda), emptiness is taught as the inability to think of an object apart from the consciousness which thinks of that object, i.e. the necessary indissolubility of subject and object in the process of knowing is the Yogācārin emptiness. It is important to distinguish this from idealism and solipsism.

Śūnyatāvādin (Skt., *śūnyatā*, 'emptiness', + *vādin*, 'teacher of'). Loosely used to denote a follower of the philosophy of *Nāgārjuna. The term first occurs in the *Vijñānakāya*, an *Abhidharma text of the *Sarvāstivādins where a śūnyatāvādin is described as someone who holds that the concept of person (*pudgala) is empty (*śūnya*). A śūnyatāvādin, then, is opposed to the doctrine of the pudgalavāda. Since one of the central tenets of the system of Nāgārjuna is the emptiness (*śūnyatā) of all phenomena, the term has been more generally applied to any adherent of his school, the *Mādhyamaka. In this context the term is rather imprecise, partly because many non-Mādhyamakas recognize the centrality of emptiness, but also because the Mādhyamakas themselves split into various subsects after the time of Nāgārjuna. Nevertheless the word śūnyatāvādin in this generalized sense is still widely employed.

Supercommentaries. Jewish commentaries on the chief commentators on the *Pentateuch. Commentaries have been produced on the works of *Rashi, Abraham *ibn Ezra, and *Naḥmanides.

Supererogation, work of. A work which is not required as a matter of obligation in morality, but which is beneficial for the good of others or for the strengthening of spiritual or moral life. They include works done purely for the love of God.

The *counsels of perfection (poverty, chastity, obedience) are typically considered works of supererogation. The concept was precisely defined by the Scholastics, for whom works of supererogation contributed to the treasury of *merits, transferable to others through the Church's granting of *indulgences. It was repudiated by the Reformers, e.g. in Art. 14 of the Anglican *Thirty-Nine Articles. For an example in Islam, see NĀFILA.

Supralapsarians (relation of election to fall): see PREDESTINATION.

Supremacy, Act of. An Act of 1559 declaring the Queen of England (Elizabeth I) to be 'the only supreme governor of this realm . . . as well in all spiritual or ecclesiastical things or causes as temporal'. The act was a revised form of Henry VIII's Act of 1534 repealed by Mary. It is intrinsic to the 'establishment' of the *Church of England.

Sura. Site of one of the Babylonian Jewish *academies. Sura was an important centre of *Torah study. It was established by *Rav in 219 CE. Among the important heads of the academy were Rav Huna, Rav Ashi (367–427), Mar Samuel (8th cent.), and R. *Yehudai b. Naḥman (8th cent.). It was known as the '*yeshivah of the right', because its head sat on the right hand of the *exilarch at his induction ceremony. At the beginning of the 10th cent., the academy moved to Baghdād. *Sa'adiah Gaon became its head in 928. By the 12th cent. the town was in ruins.

Sura. One of a class of Hindu deities. They inhabit *Indra's heaven, but they have no strong role or identity—indeed, they may be derived from a mistaken view that the 'a' in *asuras is a negative, producing 'gods' (suras) and anti-gods (asuras). Hence arises the further play on words (with *surā*, 'wine'), in **Rāmāyaṇa* 1. 45: 'Those who drank the wine [*surā*, which appeared at the *Churning of the Ocean] are known as gods [suras], while the sons of *Diti who did not, are known as anti-gods [asuras].'

Sūra. A division of the *Qur'ān (roughly equivalent to a 'chapter'). The term originally referred to a single portion of scripture, in this sense equivalent to *qur'ān*, a recitation. The word may come from the Syriac *ṣūrtā* (or *sūrthā*), a 'writing'. In the Qur'ān itself, it has the sense of a text of scripture. The Qur'ān is composed of 114 sūras in all, each one with a name, by which it is known to Muslims. Each sūra is classified as Meccan or Madinan according to whether it was first recited before or after the *Hijra, though it is accepted that some sūras contain verses from both periods. They are not classed in chronological order but, apart from the first sūra, the *Fātiḥa, in approximate order of length starting with the longest; thus some of the earliest sūras are towards the end of the Qur'ān.

Each Sūra is composed of a number of *ayāt (singular, *āya*), a word which really means 'sign' (especially of *Allāh's power), but came to be used for the units of the Quranic sūras. Each sūra except the ninth is preceded by the 'bismillah', the formula 'in the name of Allāh, the merciful, the compassionate', considered to be part of the sūra in its original form and thus dating back to the time of *Muḥammad.

W. M. Watt, *Bell's Introduction to the Qur'an* (1970), 57–61.

Sūrdās (15th/16th cent., b. *c.*1478). Hindu poet renowned for his devotion to *Kṛṣṇa as well as for his musical abilities. Little is known for certain of his life. He was blind (possibly, but not certainly, from birth). He met Vallabhacarya (see VAIṢṆAVA) and became a member of his movement. Of six works attributed to him, and *Sūrsārāvalī* is based on the *avatāra of Kṛṣṇa, *Sāhityalaharī* deals with the *līlā of Kṛṣṇa. His most famous work is *Sūrsāgar*, based loosely on **Bhagavata Purāṇa*. Of this work, book x is the most outstanding and revered, a collection of poems dealing with the childhood of Kṛṣṇa, his līlā, and his dance with the *gopīs.

J. S. Hawley, *Sur Das* . . . (1984); S. M. Pandey and N. Zide, in M. Singer (ed.), *Krishna: Myths, Rites, and Attitudes* (1966); V. Varma, *Surdas* (1957).

Suri (Jain teachers): see DĀDĀ GURŪS.

Surplice (Lat., *superpelliceum*, 'over-fur garment'). A Christian *vestment. It is a wide-sleeved loose linen garment reaching to the knees (or lower), worn over the cassock in the course of worship. In the Roman Catholic Church surplices are usually trimmed with lace, and are often of a shorter form called a cotta. In Anglican churches the surplice is worn by the ministers at morning and evening prayer, and may be worn in lieu of alb and chasuble at the *eucharist.

Sursum Corda (Lat.). The words 'Lift up your hearts' addressed to the congregation at the beginning of the *eucharistic prayer. The reply is 'We lift them up to the Lord'.

Sūrya, Savitar, or **Savitṛ** (nourisher). In Hinduism, the sun. As the source of heat and life, Sūrya is supreme among the *Ādityas, and one of the three chief gods of the *Vedas—indeed, since Āditya means 'son of the primordial vastness' and thus also 'the source', Āditya may be a synonym for Sūrya. He is ruler of the domain of life, and the gateway to immortality (*Chandogya Upaniṣad* 8. 6. 5). As illumination, he resides within as the source of wisdom (*Maitri Upaniṣad* 6. 34). Later, he was superseded by *Viṣṇu. Sūryā is the daughter of Sūrya, who appears in *Ṛg Veda* 10. 6 ff. The Konārak, or 'Black Pagoda', was built at Orissa, in N. India, in the 13th cent. CE, as a temple to Sūrya. The surviving Great Hall is built as a replica of Sūrya's chariot.

Susanna and the Elders. Jewish *apocryphal work. It tells the story of the virtuous Susanna who was wrongly accused of *adultery and was acquitted after an interrogation conducted by *Daniel. Scholars do not agree on the book's original language (Heb. or Gk.). It was added to the Roman Catholic canonical Book of Daniel as ch. 13 (following the *Septuagint), and was highly popular in the Middle Ages. In early Christian art, the story epitomized the salvation of souls.

Suso (German mystic): see HENRY SUSO.

Susoku-kan. Zen Buddhist practices of 'contemplation by counting the breath'. It is a group of practices in the early stages of *zazen, to help collectedness of mind and avoidance of distraction: (i) *shutsu-nyosoku-kan*, counting breaths in and out; (ii) *shussoku-kan*, counting out; (iii) *nissoku-kan*, counting in; (iv) *zuisoku-kan*, following the breath.

Sutra (Arab., 'to conceal, veil'). In Islam, an object (often a *rosary) which a worshipper places before him during *ṣalāt, in the direction of the *qibla, making a protected place, free from human (or demonic spiritual) interference (cf. *capella*—cloak pulled over one in prayer—chapel). From the example of *Muḥammad, almost any object may serve for a sutra.

Sūtra (Skt., 'thread'). 1. In Hinduism, sūtras seem to have originated as manuals for those concerned with household and other rituals. Sūtra literature is written in a condensed prose. The *Kalpasūtras are concerned with ritual, and fall into three major categories: Śrautasūtras, Gṛhyasūtras, and *Dharmasūtras. As the names imply, the first deal with the performance of sacrifices (in complex detail), the second with home rituals including *saṃskāras, and the third with these and with other duties belonging to the *āśramas. They were extended in the verse-form *śastra literature. Sūtras are also sharp and elliptical works which are commented on in the *darśana (philosophical) works: e.g. *Jaimini, *Bādarāyaṇa, *Kaṇāda, *Patañjali.

2. In Buddhism, sūtras (Pāli, *sutta*) are the collections of the discourses or teachings of the *Buddha. In *Theravāda, they are gathered in the second part of the Pāli canon (*tripiṭaka), the Sūtra-(Sutta-) piṭaka. They are then divided into five collections, *nikāyas (Skt., *āgama). In Mahāyāna, many additional sūtras have been preserved, some of which become foundational for particular schools of Buddhism (e.g. the **Lotus Sūtra*, **Sukhāvatīvyūha*, **Laṅkāvatāra-Sūtra*). Virtually all were composed in Sanskrit, but have usually survived only in Chinese or Tibetan translations. Sūtras may be grouped (e.g. Vaipulya-Sūtras) or stand independently.

3. For Jain sūtras, see AṄGA.

J. Gonda, *The Ritual Sūtras* (1977).

Sūtrakṛta-aṅga (part of Jain scripture): see AṄGA.

Sūtra of the Garland of Buddhas (extensive and foundational Buddhist text): see AVATAMSAKA LITERATURE.

Sutta: see SŪTRA.

Sutta-nipāta (part of Buddhist Pāli canon): see KHUDDAKA-NIKĀYA.

Sutta-piṭaka (collection of suttas): see SŪTRA.

Suttavibhanga (division of Vinayapiṭaka): see TRIPIṬAKA.

Suttee (devotion through self-immolation of a widow): see SATĪ.

Su-yüeh (popular music): see MUSIC.

Suzuki, Daisetz Taitaro (1870–1966). Professor of Buddhist Philosophy at Ōtani University, Kyōto, from 1921, and an important scholar of *Mahāyāna Buddhism and *Japanese religion in general. From a poor family, he abandoned university before graduating, and spent the next thirteen years studying in the USA, where he translated *Aśvaghoṣa's (attr.) *Awakening of Faith in the Mahāyāna* (1900), and wrote his *Outline of Mahāyāna Buddhism* (1907). Returning to Japan as an English teacher in 1909, he did not take up a full-time university post until he was 52. Having started *Zen training under two separate masters at the age of 22, his academic work was always informed by a deep spiritual insight. He is chiefly known in the West for his popularization of Zen Buddhism; his scholarly writings in Japanese and European languages concern the exposition of the Buddhist thought of *Bodhidharma, *Bankei, and *Rinzai, the Zen doctrine of No-Mind, the *Pure Land school, and an examination of the basis of Japanese spirituality.

Svabhāva. 'Self-nature' or 'Own-being': a property which, according to the *Mādhyamaka, is falsely ascribed to *dharmas, or the world of phenomenal reality. According to the *Abhidharma, however, it constituted the unique and inalienable 'mark' or characteristic by means of which phenomena could be differentiated and classified. Thus the schools of the *Hīnayāna, while denying a self of persons (*pudgala-nairātmya*), and explaining personal identity by recourse to the teaching of the Five Aggregates (*skandhas), nevertheless accepted the substantial reality of those elements (dharmas) which composed the aggregates and the world at large.

*Nāgārjuna was more radical and undercut this teaching by applying the no-self doctrine to reality as a whole: thus in addition to denying a self of persons (*pudgala-nairātmya*) he also denied a self of phenomena (*dharmanairātmya*). All entities were therefore alike in lacking a discrete mode of being or self-essence (svabhāva) and in sharing the common attribute or 'mark' of emptiness (*śūnyatā).

Svabhāvikakāya (the unity of the three manifestation forms of the Buddha): see TRIKĀYA.

Svadharma (Skt., *sva*, 'own', + *dharma*, 'duty, right'). In Hinduism, one's own right, duty, or nature; one's own role in the social and cosmic order. Svadharma is relative to one's *caste and stage of life (cf. *varṇāśramadharma), and to one's situation (cf. *āpaddharma). Svadharma or relative *dharma often conflicts with sādhāraṇa dharma, universal dharma, or *sanātana dharma, absolute or eternal dharma. For example, to kill is a violation of eternal dharma, yet a warrior's *svadharma (own duty, nature) is to kill. Likewise, to oppose the gods is the svadharma of a demon, which (except in *bhakti or devotional texts) is considered binding upon a demon although contrary to absolute dharma.

The code of svadharma is one reaction of orthodox Hinduism against the ascetic ideal of the *Upaniṣadic traditions, which held that one can free oneself from the evil of one's caste or time and attain release through transcendent knowledge (*jñāna). The code of svadharma holds that some individuals are doomed to evil roles, which must be borne out patiently for the greater good of the society and cosmos and for one's own ultimate salvation.

Svāmi or **Swāmi** (Skt., 'owner', 'master'). Title of respect for a holy man or teacher.

Svaminarayan Movement. Founded by a high-caste *brahmaṇ, Sahajānanda Swami, known as Lord Svaminarayan, in Gujarat, India, in the early 19th cent. Since then there has been considerable segmentation. A follower of the *Vaiṣṇava teacher *Rāmānuja, Svaminarayan made qualified monism a fundamental precept and developed his movement in the *bhakti tradition of devotional worship. Disciples were drawn from all *castes with the exception of certain unclean untouchables, and for the monks strict rules of celibacy were laid down. Svaminarayan is regarded as an *avatāra of *Viṣṇu who took on an earthly, human form in order to bring salvation to his followers. Successive leaders have also been regarded in a similar light. The movement spread from India to Britain in the 1950s, to become one of the largest Indian religions in that country. In 1995, it opened a large temple in Neasden (London), to be a centre for pilgrimage. Built at great expense, it revived skills of temple-carving and traditional decoration.

R. B. Williams, *A New Face of Hinduism* . . . (1984).

Svarga. In Hinduism, heaven, and especially the heaven of Indra, situated on one of the *Himālayas, usually Mt. *Meru. By proper performance of sacrifice, the good can hope to attain svarga, and in later texts (e.g. *Viṣṇu Purāṇa* 2. 2) may attain the form of *devas.

Svastika (Skt., *su*, 'well', + *asti*, 'is': i.e. 'all is well'). A cross with each extremity bent at right-angles to the right, an auspicious sign in Indian religions (found also in many other religions, e.g. as a sign of the infinite and of the sun among American Indians). Among Hindus it is associated with the sun who constantly returns things to life. In the *Śrīyantra, the triangles are sometimes framed within two svastikas, one breaking to the left, the other to the right, summarizing dissolution and creation: they close concentric circles which surround the triangles. For the svastika mountain, see KAILĀSA.

In Buddhism, the svastika is a symbol of the wheel of dharma (*dharma-cakra), or in Zen, the seal of the buddha-mind (*busshin-in*) transmitted from patriarch (*soshigata) to patriarch.

In the 20th cent., the svastika/swastika was adopted by the Nazis in Germany as the party emblem. It was mistakenly understood as an Aryan symbol, indicating racial purity and superiority.

S. A. Freed and S. Ruth, 'The Origin of the Swastika', *Natural History* (1980).

Svatantrika-mādhyamaka (Buddhist philosophical School): see CANDRAKIRTI.

Svayambhū (Skt., 'unoriginated'). The capacity of objects to be self-existent, not dependent on the causal agency of another, and thus perhaps to sustain themselves from the idea concealed within them. It also represented an early attempt in Hinduism to recognize an unproduced Producer of all that is, an originator such as *Puruṣa, *Prajāpati or *Brahmā. In the *Purāṇas, it becomes the principle of indefinite cosmic elaboration, but in *Advaita and in the *Upaniṣads, it expresses the self-existent nature of *Brahman. *Vaiṣṇavites and *Śaivites apply it to *Viṣṇu and *Śiva respectively. In Buddhism, it is applied to the *Buddha as the one who is utterly independent of support in the apparent cosmos, and in Mahāyāna it is comparably applied to all buddhas, e.g. *Ādi Buddha.

Svedaja (Skt., 'born of sweat'). The fecundity in Hinduism of moist and humid conditions. It was linked to *tapas, so that the sweat of, e.g., a priest during rituals could be regarded as a sign of efficacious power.

Śvetāmbara ('white-clothed'). One of two major divisions among Jains, the other being *Digambara. For details of the issues between them, see DIGAMBARA. For their sacred texts, see AṄGA.

Śvetāśvatara Upaniṣad. One of the principal *Upaniṣads, belonging to the Black *Yajur Veda*, and one of the most profound and frequently referred to. It does not present a single philosophy, but draws out the implications of various positions—e.g. of *Sāṃkhya and *Yoga as well as *Advaita. Its tendency, though, is towards a theistic account:

> The One who, himself without colour, by the manifold application of his power distributes many colours in his hidden purpose, and into whom, its end and its beginning, the whole world dissolves—He is God [*deva] . . . His form is not to be beheld. No one soever sees him with the eye. They who thus know him with heart and mind as abiding in the heart become immortal (4. 1, 20).

Trs.: see UPANIṢAD.

Swāmi: see SVĀMI.

Swaminarayan (manifestation of God and Hindu movement): see SVAMINARAYAN.

Sweat: see SVEDAJA.

Swedenborg, Emanuel (1688–1772). Speculative religious reformer and visionary. He was the son of a Lutheran *bishop, who became interested, after his university education at Uppsala, in the natural sciences. He sought further education in England and France, and returned to Sweden to become an assessor in the royal mines—a post he held until 1747. His early works explain the origin of the universe in mechanistic terms, and explore the nature of soul and body on the basis of anatomical studies. A severe religious crisis in 1743–5, accompanied by increasing dreams and visions, made him turn his attention to more religious matters; and when a vision of *Jesus Christ resolved his crisis, he spent the rest of his life expounding his understanding of Christianity in *Neoplatonic terms. Among many works, the 8-vol. *Arcana Caelestia* (Heavenly Secrets) and *The True Christian Religion* (1771) give vivid descriptions of his spiritual experiences. He did not seek to found a new Church or new religion, but rather hoped that his vision and teaching would lead to the conversion of existing Churches to the truth. Nevertheless, his followers, after his death, organized, in 1787, the New (Jerusalem) Church, though this, too, is meant to parallel, not supplant, existing Churches.

I. Jonsson, *Emanuel Swedenborg* (1971).

Swiss Brethren (Protestant group): see ANABAPTISTS.

Sword of the Spirit. A *Roman Catholic lay organization founded in London in 1940 to defend and propagate Christian principles in national and international affairs. Originally intended to be *ecumenical in membership, the Catholic hierarchy insisted that it become a strictly Catholic organization, though considerable co-operation with Anglicans was retained throughout the war years. After the war, Sword developed research into issues of justice and human rights, and started a volunteer programme. In 1965 its name was changed to the Catholic Institute for International Relations.

Syādvāda (Skt., *syāt*, 'perhaps'). Jain theory of knowledge which emphasizes the relativity and multifaceted nature of human judgement: it is therefore also known as *sapta-bhaṅgi-naya*, the 'dialectic of the seven steps'; and leads to *anekāntavāda. The Jains characteristically value the story of the blind men and the elephant, who feel only one part of the elephant and infer from that limited information what the elephant is like—a water pot (from the head), a winnowing basket (from the ears), a plough (from the tusks), a snake (from the trunk), a tree (from the legs), a rope (from the tail). The blind men then fall into furious argument, each one convinced that he alone possesses the whole truth. In contrast to the Western endorsement of the law of the excluded middle (either p or not-p), the Jains emphasize the provisionality of human judgements which allow several to coexist as contributions to truth, including some which appear to be mutually exclusive. See also NAYAVĀDA.

Syag (fence around Torah): see HOLINESS.

Śyāmā (Skt., 'black'). A form of the Hindu Goddess *Durgā / *Kālī.

Syllabus Errorum. A summary in eighty theses published in 1864 by *Pius IX of a number of papal pronouncements on a variety of issues, philosophical, theological, and political. The last of the theses rejected the belief that 'the Roman Pontiff can and ought to reconcile and harmonize himself with progress, liberalism and recent civilization'. It was well understood in Italy that these words were directed at the *anti-clericalism of the Piedmontese, but outside Italy they were taken at face value, doing considerable damage to Pius' reputation.

Symbolists: see SYMBOLS.

Symbols, symbolism (Gk., *sumbolon*, 'sign, token, pledge'; *sumballein*, 'cast together'). The representation in visible form of ideas, beliefs, actions, persons, events, etc., frequently (in the religious case) of transcendent realities, which bring the observer into connection and participation. So pervasive is the human use of symbols that E. Cassirer (*An Essay on Man*, 1944) called the human species *animal symbolicum*. He distinguished signs and signals (which are widely used by other species) from symbols, the former being operators within the physical world, the latter being designators and part of the human world of meaning. Signs, in order to work, must relate to their referent in a fixed and unique way (since otherwise confusion is inevitable), whereas symbols are flexible and fluid in their reference, while nevertheless making apparent the field of their reference. S. K. Langer (*Philosophy in a New Key*, 1942) developed these distinctions further: signs are proxies for their objects which they announce to the subjects, indicating the existence (past, present, or future) of a thing, event, or condition; thus the sign-relation is triadic, consisting of subject, sign, and object. Symbols are vehicles for the conception of objects, so that symbols 'mean', not the thing but the conception. The symbol-relation is thus fourfold: subject, symbol, conception, and object. Humans are 'symbolific animals', and there is an experienced difference between representational symbols which can be defined, and unconsummated symbols in art. It is a mark of modernism (and one might add, of post-modernism also) that attention has turned from what people say to the symbolic modes through which they say it. Thus, although it might seem obvious to define a symbol as that which stands for something which it represents (as a flag might be said to 'stand for' the country which it represents), in fact a symbol involves far more complex conditions of meaning—to be seen not least in the fact that symbols frequently stand for themselves, especially in the religious case (see R. Wagner, *Symbols that Stand for Themselves*, 1986): the symbolic actions of the Hebrew *prophets, for example, do not stand for (i.e. summarize in advance) a future event, but rather bring the reality of that event into being in the present. Beyond that, symbols may be non-referential and of effect in creating community and meaning (see A. P. Cohen, *The Symbolic Construction of Community*, 1985).

Since religions in that way are often evocative in their use of language, it is not surprising that the religious use of symbols can be paralleled in the turn to symbolism in arts and literature at the end of the 19th cent. The Symbolists were a loose association of artists and writers who turned strongly against the realist (and referential) ambitions of, for example, the Pre-Raphaelites or the neo-Impressionists, or of such writers as Flaubert and Zola (see J. Bowker, *Licensed Insanities* (1987), ch. 2). In a succinct definition, Jean Moréas proclaimed in the Symbolist Manifesto: 'Opposed to "teaching, declamation, false sensibility, objective description", symbolic poetry seeks to clothe the Idea in a perceptible form.' Baudelaire's poem *Correspondances* articulated the theory that a work of art should be so expressive of basic feelings and evocative of ideas and emotion that all the arts would interrelate in such a way that sounds would suggest colours, colours sounds. For him 'the whole visible universe is only a storehouse of images and signs to which the imagination assigns a place and a relative value; it is a kind of nourishment that the imagination must digest and transform'. It is only a blind humanity ('the imbecile human flock') that stumbles 'through forests of symbols, | Which watch them with familiar glances'. These ideas were more formally organized by G.-A. Aurier ('Les Peintres symbolistes', 1892, in *Œuvres posthumes*, 1893), who also argued that 'objects cannot have value more than the objects as they are. But to the artist, they appear only as signs. They are the letters of an enormous alphabet which only the man of genius knows how to spell'. In his view, a work of art will be (i) ideist, aiming simply for the expression of the Idea; (ii) symbolist, expressing the Idea through many forms; (iii) synthesist, presenting these forms according to whatever methods will be intelligible; (iv) subjectivist, the object only being considered, not as an object, but as the sign of an idea as perceived by the subject; (v) decorative, since this is nothing other than the manifestation of art which is subjective, synthetic, symbolic, and ideist. The importance of decoration in this sense is profoundly important in religious symbolism, though largely overlooked: there is an aesthetic satisfaction no matter what other purposes are being served. Most accounts of religious symbolism look at their function, especially as codes. However, R. Firth (*Symbols Public and Private*, 1973), argued that

> symbolic concepts merit respect as a framework for organising experience, as a way of apprehending the world around one, especially the world of human relations. Whether or not the assertion that symbolism constitutes a unique and verifiable mode of perception is justified (a claim I myself am not prepared to concede), symbolism surely yields results that are aesthetically satisfying and often operationally viable.

For him, it is the very imprecision of symbols which gives them value in the creation of meaning and action: 'Because of the allusiveness and indefiniteness of symbols, possibly their ambiguity, they allow some greater understanding of complex entities and action within them.'

On this basis, M. *Eliade's understanding of the study of religion as the development of 'a competent *hermeneutics', deciphering the messages waiting to be understood (*The Quest*, 1969) would be a frustrating task (a cryptological view of symbols strongly criticized by D. Sperber, *Rethinking Symbolism*, 1975). But in any case, religious symbols have a high degree of stability, however much they remain open to varying appropriations in life. In other words, religions in the use of symbols did *not* take the step of modern art from 'Idea in perceptible form' toward complete abstraction: an early meaning of *sumbolon* in Christianity is that of *creed, where the function of symbols in compressing (Gk., *sumballein*, 'to throw together') meaning and making it publicly available is emphasized. As C. S. Peirce realized, humans use different kinds of signs and symbols, each bearing some of the characteristics of the others. As a consequence of his work, the study of symbolism is firmly embedded in semiotics (Gk., *sēma*, 'a sign'). Peirce drew a distinction between three types of sign: icon, index, and symbol. An icon is a sign containing some of the qualities associated with the thing signified (e.g. maps and diagrams); an index is a sign which is in a dynamic relation with the thing signified and calls attention to what is signified (e.g. the column of mercury in a thermometer measuring temperature and indicating health or illness); a symbol is a conventional sign with an agreed connotation. Thus (to follow the example of M. Spiro, 'Religious Symbol Systems', in J. Maquet (ed.), *On Symbols in Anthropology*, 1982), a statue of the Buddha is an icon of him; a relic of the Buddha is an index of him; and the word 'Buddha' is a symbol of him. Because Peirce is correct in saying that each of the three participates in the characteristics of the other two, immense confusion has arisen from accounts of religious symbolism which imply that there are no legitimate distinctions. Symbols are economies of statement and feeling which conserve successful accounts of context (success being measured crudely by persistence) and which evoke coherence by their power to unite immense diversities of human being and experience. But equally they set forward new opportunities of exegesis and action. For examples, see Index, Symbols. See also FEMININE SYMBOLS AND RELIGION; ICONOGRAPHY.

P. Boyer (ed.), *Cognitive Aspects of Religious Symbolism* (1993); J. E. Circlot, *A Dictionary of Symbolism* (1962, 1971); B. Cooke, *The Distancing of God: The Ambiguity of Symbol in History and Theology* (1990); W. Eberhard, *A Dictionary of Chinese Symbols* . . . (1986); A. Grabar, *Christian Iconography: A Study of its Origins* (1968); J. Hall, *Dictionary of Subjects and Symbols in Art* (1974); J. Maquet, *The Aesthetic Experience* (1986); J. Skorupski, *Symbol and Theory* (1976).

Symeon the New Theologian (949–1022). Byzantine mystic and spiritual writer. After entering the imperial service, he became a monk, first at Studios, then at St Mamas in Constantinople, where he became abbot. In 1005 he was forced to resign because of opposition to his teaching, and he was exiled. Though this was revoked, he remained in voluntary exile. Much influenced by the **Macarian Homilies*, he was a formative influence on *hesychasm. He laid great stress on 'felt devotion', the gift of tears, and the vision of the Divine Light, while being strongly Christocentric and eucharistic. He is known as the 'new' or 'second' theologian, second only to *Gregory Nazianzen.

H. J. M. Turner, *St Symeon the New Theologian* . . . (1990).

Symmachus ben Joseph (late 2nd cent. CE). Jewish *tanna. Symmachus was a disciple of Meir. He was the author of the principle, 'Money, the ownership of which cannot be decided, has to be equally divided' (*BBK* 46a), but is not to be identified with the Symmachus who translated the Bible into Greek (see also ONKELOS).

Synagogue (Heb., *bet *keneset*). Jewish meeting house and place of worship. The synagogue, in embryonic form, may perhaps date back to the period of the Babylonian *exile. *Ezekiel wrote, 'Thus says the Lord God, "Although I have removed them far off among the nations . . . yet I have been to them a little *sanctuary" ' (II. 6). According to the *Talmud, the 'little sanctuary' was the synagogue (*B.Meg.* 29a). The earliest archaeological remains of synagogues have been found in the *diaspora, but by the 1st cent. CE, the synagogue emerges as a well-established institution. It is mentioned by *Philo, *Josephus, and in the New Testament. The Talmud enumerates 480 synagogues in Jerusalem before the destruction of the *Temple (*TJMeg.* 3. 1). With the calamity of 70 CE, the synagogue became the main focus of Jewish religious life. Many of the rituals and customs of the

Temple were adopted in the synagogue (e.g. the times of the Temple *sacrifices became the times of the synagogue prayers), and the synagogue also performed the function of a community centre. According to the *halakhah, a synagogue must have windows (*B.Ber.* 34b) and should be oriented towards Jerusalem (*B.Ber.* 30a). The *Torah *Scrolls are housed in the *aron kodesh* (holy *Ark), a reader's desk is placed in front of the Ark, and the *bimah is located traditionally in the middle of the building. Men and women are seated separately, the women either in a gallery or separated behind a *meḥizah. The **Shulḥān Arukh* forbids gossiping, frivolity, transacting business, sleeping, or entering to escape bad weather. Different patterns of architecture have been followed in synagogue buildings. Many modern *Orthodox synagogues have a small synagogue nearby, known as a *bet ha-midrash, which is used for weekday services. In addition there are community halls and facilities for synagogue schools. The *Reform movement has built impressive synagogues (known as Temples in the USA); they have no special section for women; the bimah is generally placed in front of the Ark (so there is more room for seating) and there is often an organ and choir loft. *Ḥasidic synagogues, on the other hand, tend to be small and undecorated; the atmosphere is informal and communal meals are held there. Generally, the salaried officials comprise the *rabbi, the *cantor, and the *shammash, but prayers are often led by laymen. Synagogues are grouped into organizations (e.g. The United Synagogue, The Federation of Synagogues, and the Union of Orthodox Hebrew Congregations (all British Orthodox organizations)) and rabbinic training is controlled by the organizations who sponsor the *rabbinical seminaries. Attendance at synagogue is encouraged; the rabbis taught that 'a man who usually attends synagogue and misses a day causes God to inquire after him', and 'God becomes angry when he comes to synagogue and does not find a *minyan' (*B.Ber.* 6b).

See Index, Synagogue.

J. Gutmann, *The Synagogue: Studies in Origins, Archaeology and Architecture* (1975); I. Levy, *The Synagogue . . .* (1963).

Synagogue, The Great. Jewish institution mentioned in the *Mishnah. According to **Avot*, 'the men of the Great Synagogue' lived between the time of the *prophets and the time of the *rabbis. Most scholars date the period from the time of *Ezra, and the Great Synagogue was probably a representative body which met from time to time to pass resolutions. The men of the Great Synagogue are credited with instituting 'the *benedictions and prayers as well as the benedictions for *Kiddush and *Havdalah' (*B.Ber.* 33a). They are said to have instituted the festival of *Purim and various fasts, and to have included the books of *Ezekiel, *Daniel, *Ezra, and the *Minor Prophets in the *canon.

Synanon Foundation. A *new religious movement. It was established in California in 1958 by Charles E. Dederich as a voluntary association of reforming alcoholics, soon developing into a therapeutic community for the treatment of narcotic addicts, and then into Social Movement and Alternative Society, a commune, with successful business operations and substantial real-estate holdings. In 1977 the Board of Directors proclaimed the Synanon Religion, with the so-called reconciliatory principle as its central tenet: dichotomies such as good and evil exist in the everyday world and must be acknowledged, but in a sense do not really matter since the underlying unity of the universe ensures their ultimate resolution. Another important proposition is that individuals evolve by contributing to the community.

Synaxarion (Gk.). In E. Churches, a brief account of, or homily on, the life of a saint or the significance of a feast. The Greater Synaxarion is a liturgical book used in those churches, which contains short accounts of saints or feasts appointed to be read in the daily *office.

Synaxis (Gk., 'assembly'). In the early church, the service consisting of lessons, psalms, prayers, and sermon, probably derived from the worship of the *synagogue. It was later joined to the *eucharist, and may now be identified in the Mass of the *Catechumens or Antecommunion. In the Orthodox Church the term 'synaxis' may be used to refer to the whole liturgy including the eucharist, although technically it refers to a collection of prayers. It may also mean 'a gathering of the faithful', e.g. to celebrate saints who are associated with another festival celebrated the previous day; or of monks.

Syncretism (Gk., explained by Plutarch with reference to the Cretans who, while habitually at odds with each other, closed ranks in the face of a common enemy). The amalgamation of religious beliefs and practices in such a way that the original features of the religions in question become obscured. The word has thus taken on a pejorative sense, derived from H. Usener who translated it (1898) as *religionsmischerei*, not so much a mixing as a confusing. The term is now usually used of those who are accused of abandoning a historic faith and practice in pursuit of some ecumenical religion which transcends the boundaries of existing religions. Despite this dismissive sense, all religions are syncretistic in the sense of absorbing and incorporating elements of other religions and cultures as they encounter them. Thus Islam was described by Hampeté Ba as being like water flowing over the ground and taking on the colour of the earth it flows over. Some religions are deeply suspicious of syncretism (e.g. Judaism, which is inclined to see it as bowing down before gods other than Yahweh), while others set out to incorporate the virtues of existing experience (e.g. Sikhs, *Bahā'īs). The belief that one can recover a pristine form of a religion exempted from its syncretizing history (e.g. New Testament Christianity) is an illusion. Nevertheless, what remains at issue is the control and limitation of syncretism, by reference to the received traditions, so that disruptive novelty is kept in check.

Synderesis (Gk., perhaps from *synteresis*, 'spark of conscience'). In Christianity, human knowledge (innate) of the first principles of moral behaviour. It is distinguished from conscience (although the two are sometimes used interchangeably) because the latter involves, not a basic intuition, but a judgement. *Jerome, commenting on Ezekiel 1. 4–15, took the man to be the rational part of the soul, the lion the irascible, the ox the appetitive, and the eagle to be the spark of conscience (*scintilla conscientiae*) which remained in *Adam when he was expelled from *Eden. In mystical theology, synderesis is the centre of the soul where mystical union occurs.

Synergistic controversy (on the relation between God's will and human freedom): see PREDESTINATION.

Synod (Gk.). A Christian church gathering for doctrinal and administrative purposes. In the *Roman Catholic Church, there are (under the revised *canon law) two types, the synod of *bishops and the diocesan. The Synod of Bishops assembles representatives of the episcopal conferences from around the world. It is held approximately once every three years, usually with a topic selected by the *pope (e.g. 1980 the role of the family, 1983 reconciliation, 1987 the laity). The diocesan synod dates from the 4th cent., the first perhaps being that of Sircius in Rome in 387. Like the Synod of Bishops, it is consultative only, and is held when the diocesan bishop thinks it necessary. In other Churches, synods have varying status and function. Among Presbyterians, it is a review court above the presbytery. In the Church of England, it replaced the Convocations and Church Assembly in 1969/70, in an endeavour to bring laypeople more effectively into the counsels and decision-making of the Church.

Synod of Dort (conference to prepare doctrine for Protestant Church): see DUTCH REFORMED CHURCH.

Synoptic Gospels. The three *gospels of Matthew, Mark, and Luke, so-called because their texts can be printed for comparison in a three-column 'synopsis'. The gospels share much of their subject-matter, and tell their stories in the same order and in many of the same words. The 'synoptic problem' is solved when these facts are accounted for. The most widely accepted solution (the 'two-document hypothesis') is that Mark is the earliest of the three and was used by both Matthew and Luke and that the additional matter common to Matthew and Luke was taken by them from a source *Q. Material peculiar to Matthew or to Luke is usually called 'M' and 'L' respectively. For the classic statement of this, see B. H. Streeter, *The Four Gospels* (1924). It was queried by W. R. Farmer, *The Synoptic Problem* (1964), who followed the much earlier (so-called Griesbach, from the 18th-cent. advocate) hypothesis, that Matthew was the earliest, Luke drew on Matthew, and that Mark, the latest, drew on both. For a brief review of the issues involved, see G. M. Styler, 'The Priority of Mark', in C. F. D. Moule, *The Birth of the New Testament* (3rd edn., 1981).

Syrian churches. The churches whose traditional liturgical language is Syriac. The Syriac-speaking area in the ancient world included 'Syria', but its earliest and most important ecclesiastical centres were N. Mesopotamia (modern SE Turkey and N. Iraq) and Persia. Recently there has been a movement among these Syrian Christians to call themselves 'Assyrians' (but see ASSYRIAN CHURCH). All these churches share the heritage of Syriac literature before the 5th cent., e.g. the *Peshitta Bible and works of *Ephrem. After *Chalcedon their traditions gradually diverged.

The Syrian Orthodox Church descends from the *Monophysite movement in the patriarchate of *Antioch. The name *Jacobites is sometimes used in the West. Their numbers have been reduced by poverty and gradual losses to Islam, in the 14th cent. by the Mughal invasions, and at the turn of this century by massacres in Turkish territory. They now number *c*.300,000 in the Middle East, and 50,000 in N. and S. America. The patriarch ('of Antioch') now resides in Damascus. In the 17th cent. a large body of Syrian Christians in *Malabar (India) transferred their allegiance to the Syrian Orthodox patriarch; their descendants now exceed 1 million (although their submission to the Syrian Orthodox patriarch has been a matter of continuing controversy and *schism). The doctrinal position of the Syrian Orthodox is the same as that of the other *Oriental Orthodox churches.

The Syrian Catholic Church is the *Uniat body which came into existence from Roman Catholic conversions among the Syrian Orthodox. The hierarchy dates back to 1738. The present seat of the patriarch is Beirut. Their membership in the Middle East is *c*.80,000, with further churches in N. and S. America.

The *Maronite Church, a Catholic body, has had a separate existence from the Syrian Orthodox since the Middle Ages.

The Syro-Malankara Church is the product of a union with Rome among a group of Syrian Orthodox in India. They number *c*.200,000, with their own metropolitan of Trivandrum.

The *Church of the East is the descendant of the ancient Syriac-speaking church of Persia. It is more commonly known as the *Nestorian or *Assyrian Church; but none of these names is without its drawbacks. Total membership does not exceed *c*.50,000.

The Syro-Malabar Church is the largest body of *Malabar Christians. They have been Catholic since the time of Portuguese rule in India in the 16th cent. Relations with Rome were, however, often troubled until the church obtained its own hierarchy of native bishops in 1923. The liturgy is a slightly revised form of *Addai and Mari, now celebrated in the vernacular Malayalam.

The Chaldean Church is the Uniat body deriving from the Church of the East. Its numbers are also probably less than 50,000.

A. S. Atiya, *A History of Eastern Christianity* (1980).

T

Ta'anit. Tractate of the Jewish *Mishnah and *Talmud. *Ta'anit* is concerned with the *halakhah related to fasts (see FESTIVALS AND FASTS).

Tabarī: (Muslim scholar): see AL-TABARĪ.

Tabernacle (Heb., *mishkan*). The portable *sanctuary constructed by the Hebrew people in the wilderness. Exodus 25–31 and 35–40 describe the construction of the tabernacle, and Numbers 3. 25 ff. and 4. 4 ff. discuss its furnishings and the duties of the Levites (see LEVI). It was surrounded by curtains and divided in two parts by a screen. The inner part, the *Holy of Holies, contained the *Ark of the Covenant. The tabernacle stood in the centre of the Israelite camp and was transported from place to place. The divine presence was thought to dwell on the throne of the *cherubim in the Holy of Holies. According to the *aggadah, the tabernacle symbolically resembles God's heavenly abode (*Ex.R.* 35. 6).

In Christianity the word was originally applied to a variety of canopied structures in a church building, but most usually refers to an ornamental receptacle or cupboard for the *reserved sacrament. It stands, covered with a veil, in the centre of the back of an altar, or to one side of the sanctuary, often in a side chapel.

Tabernacles, Feast of (Jewish festival): see SUKKAH.

Tablet in Heaven (source of the Qur'ān): see UMM AL-KITĀB.

Tablets of the Law/Covenant. The stones on which the Jewish decalogue (*ten commandments) were first inscribed. According to Exodus 24. 12, *Moses received 'the tablets of stone and the *Torah and the commandments'. He subsequently smashed them in his anger over the *golden calf, and they had to be inscribed again. Subsequently they were kept in the *Ark of the Covenant in the *Tabernacle. In the *aggadic tradition, the tablets of the law were created on the eve of the *Sabbath of the *Creation (*Avot* 5. 6) and they also contained the *oral law (*Ex.R.* 46. 1).

Tablīghī Jamā'at (Urdu, 'Party which Propagates'). An Islamic movement which originated in India in 1923, and became a major international force for Islamic revival. It differs from other Muslim religious movements in that its founder, Mawlānā Ilyās (1885–1944), kept it free initially from political influences and zealously guarded it from being utilized for political purposes. He believed that spiritual regeneration of the individual should be the primary objective of any religious movement engaged in improving the condition of the Muslim community. In his view the problem in the community was that 'the desire for reward and salvation was fast disappearing from their hearts; Muslims had begun to take their faith for granted at a time when the very foundation of that faith had become shaky'. He thus disagreed with other, more politically oriented, modernists such as *Iqbal, Jinnah, and Sir Sayyid Ahmad Khan. Mawlānā Ilyās adopted seven basic principles for his movement: the 'Article of Faith' (*shahāda); prayers; knowledge of Islam and *dhikr (remembrance of God); respect for Muslims; sincerity of purpose; donation of time for the movement; and abstention from useless and worldly talk.

The movement has grown in popularity and strength, and has established many centres in African and Asian countries. In the 1960s Tablīghī Jamā'at reached Japan, Britain, the USA, France, Belgium, Holland, and W. Germany, and won over numerous converts to Islam. Its European headquarters were situated at Dewsbury, Yorks., a large complex containing mosque, school, residence halls, and kitchen. Implicated, probably wrongly, in the 1979 siege of *Mecca, the Tablīghī Jamā'at has since faced government disapproval in many Arab countries, especially Saudi Arabia where all its centres were closed. Official censure has, however, increased its prestige and swelled its ranks at the popular level.

M. A. Haq, *Tablighi Jamaat: The Faith Movement of Mawlana Ilyas* (1972).

Taboo or **tabu** (Polynesian, *tapu*, 'marked off'). A power in relation to particular people, places, or objects which, if it is negative, marks them off as dangerous; it is thus related to *mana* (see MAGIC). More colloquially, the word has come to mean a prohibition against conduct which would invade the marked-off areas and thus disrupt the prevailing and desirable structures of life and society; hence the expression, 'taboos against . . .'. The understanding of taboo was side-tracked by the speculations of S. *Freud in *Totem and Taboo* (1913), in which he argued that humans began their cultural history in a social organization in which a single patriarch held sexual rights over women including sisters and daughters. The sexually deprived sons killed their father and ate him. Overcome with guilt, they repressed their desire to engage in sex with their mothers, sisters, or daughters. To facilitate expiation, they created the *totem as the animal symbol of the father, henceforth taboo as food except on ritual occasions. So came into being the Oedipus complex, incest taboo, group exogamy, and totemism. Preferring to deal with what can be observed of ritual avoidance in surviving practice, A. R. Radcliffe-Brown (*Structure and Function in Primitive Society*, 1952) regarded taboo as being a system of assigning social value; though why some items and not others should be given negative value is not clear. In *Purity and Danger: An Analysis of Concepts of Pollution and Taboo* (1966), M. Douglas made an attempt to meet that problem by locating taboo in the requirement in any society for the maintenance of order (and boundaries).

R. B. Browne, *Forbidden Fruits* (1984); H. Webster, *Taboo: A Sociological Study* (1942).

Tabrīzī (Islamic Sūfī): see JALĀL AL-DĪN RŪMĪ.

Tabu: see TABOO.

Ta-ch'eng. Chin. for *Mahāyāna.

Tachikawa-ryū. A sect derived from *Shingon, accused by its opponents of *antinomian and immoral practices. It was founded (according to most accounts) by Ninkan in the 12th cent. While he was in exile during the civil wars of the Hōgen era, he both taught and studied with an adept (from Tachikawa) in the *Yin-yang school, and from this a kind of *Tantric system was developed, in which sexual union realized the unity of all appearance.

Ta-chu Hui-hai (8th cent. CE). Pupil of *Ma-tsu Tao-i, who cared for his teacher in his old age. While doing so, he produced the manuscript of a work on sudden enlightenment, which Ma-tsu read. He exclaimed, 'Here is a great pearl, the perfect and bright illumination which penetrates everywhere without impediment.' For that reason Hui-hai became known as Ta-chu, great pearl. His work was edited by Miao-hsieh and appeared as *Tun-wu ju-tao yao-men lun*, in which the southern school of Ch'an is integrated with the *Mahāyāna *sūtras.

Tr. J. Blofeld, *The Zen Teaching of Hua Hai . . .*, 1962.

Taesūng. Korean for *Mahāyāna.

Tafsīr (Arab.). Explanatory commentary on the *Qur'ān, generally a straightforward continuous comment on the text. At first, the term *ta'wīl was synonymous with tafsīr, but came later to designate more allegorical interpretation, while tafsīr was concerned more with philological explanation.

In tafsīr, reference is made to the *ḥadīth for interpretation and elaboration, in particular of any legal or ritual commands, to grammar, to pre-Islamic poetry, to Bedouin usage, and to what was known of biblical or apocryphal narrative: fundamental is a knowledge of Arabic. A branch of tafsīr was concerned with *asbāb al-tanzīl*, the precise circumstances and reasons for the 'sending down' of particular verses of the Qur'ān, although this did not give rise to a sense that the relevance of any text was limited to the occasion of its revelation.

One who pursued the study of tafsīr was known as a *mufassir*: among the most famous are *al-Ṭabarī, the historian (d. 929/310); *al-Zama-khsharī (d. 1144/538); *al-Baiḍāwī (d. 1286/685); and in more modern times, the Egyptian scholar Muḥammad *'Abduh (1849–1905), whose commentary was edited by his follower *Rashīd Riḍā' as *Tafsīr al-Manār*.

See Index, Tafsir.

J. M. S. Baljon, *Modern Muslim Koran interpretation, 1880–1960* (1968); H. Gatje, *Koran und Koranexegese* (1971; tr. A. T. Welch, *The Qur'an and its Exegesis*, 1976); J. Wansborough, *Quranic Studies . . .* (1977).

Tagore, Debendranath (1817–1905). Hindu reformer and leader of *Brahmo Samāj. He was primarily interested throughout his life in religion and education, especially in the role both can play in social reform and national development. He thus helped to lay the foundations of modern Indian society and political structure. From 1843, he successfully led the *Brahmo Samāj and founded *Tattvabodhini Patrika*, a journal of serious discussion, emphasizing the importance of maintaining the mother tongue, the need for the study of both science and religion, and the acceptance of both the best of Western culture and whatever was admirable in traditional Indian culture. Hostility to Christian proselytization, as well as Hindu superstition and social evils, was a recurring theme of the journal. His conservation of the worthwhile in traditional Hinduism led ultimately to a break with Keshab Chandra *Sen, and with more radical thinkers who formed the breakaway *Sadharan Brahmo Samaj*. Nevertheless, he continued to enjoy high regard until the end of his days. His autobiography was translated by S. Tagore and I. Devi (1914).

Tagore, Rabindranath (1861–1941). Probably the greatest modern Indian poet, and certainly the one most widely known internationally. He was the son of Debendranath *Tagore, and achieved recognition as a national poet when only in his twenties. The Eng. version of his lyrics, *Gitanjali*, won him the Nobel Prize for Literature in 1913. In addition to poetry, he excelled as a dramatist, essayist, and novelist. In 1912 he received an honorary doctorate from Calcutta University, and in 1913 a British knighthood; the latter he subsequently resigned in protest at the Jallianwala Bagh massacre. He was a confirmed internationalist, travelling extensively (and seeking a revival of Eastern wisdom to counteract Western materialism), but this did not make him any the less an Indian, concerned for the prestige of his country. He encouraged indigenous industries, and traditional songs, dances, arts, and crafts, establishing the centre of Visva-Bharati at Śantiniketan in 1901 (it is now financed by the Indian Government as a university). He was a close friend of Mohandas *Gāndhī, who, like so many others, honoured him with the title *Gurudeva*, and derived from him the inspiration to stand against the seemingly invincible strength of the British presence:

Be not ashamed, my brothers, to stand before the proud and the powerful
With your white robe of simpleness.
Let your crown be of humility, your freedom the freedom of the soul.
Build God's throne daily upon the ample bareness of your poverty
And know that what is huge is not great, and pride is not everlasting.

V. Bhattacharya, *Tagore, Citizen of the World* (1961); S. Hay, *Asian Ideas of East and West . . .* (1970); K. Henn, *Rabindranath Tagore: A Bibliography* (1985); K. Kripalani, *Rabindranath Tagore: A Biography* (1962); S. Radhakrishnan, *Rabindranath Tagore, a Centenary Volume* (1961); R. Tagore, *The Religion of Man* (1931); E. Thompson, *Rabindranath Tagore* (1948).

Ṭahāra (Arab., 'cleanliness'). Ritual purification in Islam. Purification is required before actions which are not lawful without ablutions—especially *ṣalāt, *circumambulation of the *Kaʿba, touching the *Qur'ān. The general requirement is given in Qur'ān 5. 7/8: 'O you who believe, when you prepare for prayer, wash your faces and your hands to the elbows; rub your heads and your feet to the ankles.' These instructions have been precisely elaborated in great detail in the *sunna. Impurity is mainly brought about by emissions from anus or genitals, and is dealt with by wudu' and *ghusl: see ABLUTIONS (Islam). Details (following the *Ḥanafite school) are given in M. A. Quasem, *Salvation of the Soul and Islamic Devotions* (1983).

Taḥrīf (Arab., 'corruption'). In Islam, an alteration of the written words, alteration when reading aloud, omission from or addition to the text, or wrong interpretation of an unaltered text. The charge, originally made against the Jews, was extended to the Christians also, of having somehow changed their scriptures (*Tawrāt and *Injīl respectively). The cognate verb *ḥarrafa* is used in Qur'ān 2. 75, and in 4. 46 and 5. 14, where it seems to imply 'displace words from their right places'. Although later Muslim opinion has diverged between a charge of falsification of written texts, and one of faulty interpretation (maybe only on specific occasions), the general uncertainty and the Quranic accusations have had the effect of making most Muslims consider that the Christian scriptures are unreliable and incomplete. For Muslims, the entire revelation is contained in the Qur'ān and anything not in accord with it must be rejected without argument.

Ta Hsüeh (The Great Learning): see GREAT LEARNING.

Ta-hui Tsung-kao (Jap., Daie Soko, 1089–1163), Ch'an/Zen teacher in the *Rinzai school. He was the dharma-successor (*hassu) of Yüan-wu K'o-ch'in, and was a major advocate of training by use of *kōans. In this he opposed his friend, Hung-chih Cheng-chüeh, who accepted kōans, but put emphasis on quiet meditation, as in his brief text, *Mo-chao ming*, Jap., *Mokushomei* (The Seal of Silent Illumination). Ta-hui called this *jazen*, unwise Zen, dismissing those who practice it: 'They insist, obstinately, that empty silence and hazy unconsciousness are the original state of the absolute. Eating rice twice a day and sitting with thoughts eliminated in meditation is what they call total peace.' Ta-hui gave to this position the name *mokushu zen*, i.e., 'silent-illumination zen'. Hung-chih called the way of Ta-hui *k'an-hua ch'an*, Japanese *kanna zen, 'Kōan-gazing zen', and these two names were adopted as the names of these two positions. Despite the choice that has to be made, each position regards the other as a legitimate part of Zen. The effect of kōans, according to Ta-hui, is to create doubt, and doubt dislodges certainties: only then can enlightenment break through.

T'ai-chi (Chin., 'ridge-beam'). The supreme ultimate in Chinese philosophy and religion. It is the source of order and appearance in the **I-Ching*: 'In the changes, t'ai-chi produces the two energies [*yin-yang], which produce the four images [*ssu-hsiang*, the four possible combinations of Heaven and Earth, which give rise to the four seasons], from which arise the eight trigrams.' In *neo-Confucianism, t'ai-chi combines *li (structure) and *ch'i (primordial materiality), in an alternation of rest (yin) and activity (yang): from these arise the five elements (*wu-hsing) which constitute all existence.

T'ai-chi-ch'üan (Chin., 'power of the Great Ultimate'). An old form of physical and mental discipline in China. It consists of a sequence of stylized, graceful, slowly executed movements. In China it is commonly used as a daily exercise routine, but its roots lie in the great *martial arts tradition. It has sometimes been called 'shadow-boxing' in the West. See also GYMNASTICS, TAOIST.

T'ai-ch'ing (Taoist heaven of highest purity): see SAN-CH'ING.

T'ai-chi-t'u (Chin., 'diagram of the supreme ultimate'). The *yin-yang diagram, central to *Chou Tun-(y)i's explanation of how diversity arises from a single and unproduced source; hence *T'ai-chi Tu Shou*, the title of his work explaining the oscillation between activity and rest: 'The supreme ultimate through movement produces the yang. This movement, when it reaches its limit, is followed by rest, and by this produces *yin. When rest has reached its limit, there is a return to movement.' In so far as T'ai-chi is the unproduced producer of all that is, T'ai-chi has been regarded as the nearest equivalent to God (in the classic Judaeo-Christian-Muslim understanding of theism).

T'ai-hsi (embryo breathing): see CH'I.

T'ai-hsu (1889–1947). Chinese Buddhist monk, who did much to restore and revive Buddhism in China. He reorganized the *saṅgha, and founded the Buddhist Society of China (1929) and the Institute for Buddhist Studies. He argued that *Fa-hsiang is compatible with modern science, especially when combined eclectically with *Hua-yen and *T'ien-t'ai. His collected works were published in 64 vols.

T'ai-i (Chin., 'the supreme one'). The ultimate source of all appearance in *Taoism, which has received very different characterization in the many different forms of Taoism. In religious Taoism, he is personified as the supreme God; in philosophical Taoism, it is the unproduced source of all appearance; in interior Taoism, he is the controlling deity within the human system. T'ai-i is also equated, at times, with *t'ai-chi.

T'ai-I Chin-hua Tsung-chih (Teaching of the Golden Flower of the Supreme One). 17th-cent. Taoist text of the *ch'üan-chen tao (school of religious Taoism). It is a manual for circulating illumination through the body by breathing exercises, until the 'golden-flower' is formed. From this, the embryo of the immortal being can be produced. A Germ. tr. by R. Wilhelm (1938; Eng. version 1962) attracted the attention of C. G. *Jung, who saw in it confirmation of his views on *symbols.

T'ai-i Tao (Chin., 'way of the supreme one'). A school of religious Taoism (*tao-chiao), founded in 12th cent. CE, by Hsiao Pao-chen. From strict obedience to rules, the power to cure diseases, etc., is derived.

Tai-mitsu (Tendai esotericism): see ENNIN.

T'ai-p'ing Ching (Book of Supreme Peace). An early Taoist text, ascribed to *Yü Chi, which survives in differing forms, some only fragmentary. It was a basic text for *T'ai-ping tao.

Taiping Rebellion (1850–64). A major Chinese uprising which threatened to overthrow the Ch'ing dynasty. The Taiping's 'Heavenly Kingdom of Great Peace' (*T'ai-p'ing t'ien-kuo*) was a theocracy established and ruled by Hung Hsiu-ch'uan (1814–64). Influenced by Confucian utopianism and Protestant Christianity, Hung came to understand himself through dramatic visionary experiences to be the brother of *Christ Jesus and God's second holy son. Christian doctrine and practice, as interpreted by Hung, therefore, provided the basic religious ideology for the new kingdom. The religio-political movement stressed the equality of the sexes, Christian education, and social welfare. It prohibited *ancestor-worship, opium-smoking, foot-binding, prostitution, and slavery. It also eliminated the private ownership of land and property in favour of a communal economy. As Hung Hsiu-ch'uan promised his followers reward in *heaven for *martyrdom on earth, zealous Taiping forces fought Ch'ing government troops with remarkable success. Hung soon came to rule, from his capital in Nanking, a kingdom which encompassed most of Kiangsi, Anhwei, and Hupeh provinces. At the zenith of its wealth and power, however, the Taiping kingdom was shaken by internecine strife, and the religious community slowly began to disintegrate. Realizing the end was near, Hung Hsiu-ch'uan committed suicide in 1864. Shortly thereafter, Ch'ing troops overran Nanking and massacred its defenders. The Taiping Rebellion lasted for fourteen years and inspired many later anti-Ch'ing revolutionaries such as Sun Yat-sen and *Chiang Kai-shek. Indeed, it has been considered by some Chinese Marxist historians as the first true peasant revolution in modern China.

The basic 'programme' of the rebellion is contained in *T'ien-t'iao shu* (Eng. tr., *North China Herald*, 14 May 1853), including a reapplied Ten Commandments.

Extracts from Taiping documents appear in W. T. de Bary (ed.), *Sources of Chinese Tradition*, ii. 24–42; Jen Yu-wen, *The Taiping Revolutionary Movement* (1973); V. Y. C. Shih, *The Taiping Ideology* . . . (1967).

T'ai-p'ing Tao (Chin., 'Way of Supreme Peace'). Early *Taoist school founded by *Chang Chüeh *c.*175 CE. It was a revolutionary, utopian movement, based on healing and confession of fault. For its alternative name, the Yellow Turbans, see CHANG CHÜEH.

Tairei (Mount Hiei): see MOUNT HIEI.

T'ai-shan. Sacred mountain in China. It is in Shantung province, and is therefore known as the 'sacred mountain of the east'. Its god, T'ai-yüeh ta-ti, is the ruler of the earth, and inferior only to the Jade Emperor (*Yü-huang). He regulates birth and death, and the attainments of humans in the interval between the two. His daughter Sheng-mu is the protector of women and children. From T'ai-shan souls were sent out for birth and returned at death. The mountain is ascended by about 7,000 steps, the Stairway to Heaven, lined by shrines and temples to other Taoist deities. It is one of the four sacred mountains (standing at the corners of China) which were visited by the emperors to mark out their territory.

T'ai-shang Kan-ying P'ien (Treatise on Action and Recompense). A text on Taoist morality. Life is lengthened or shortened according to one's conformity to the rules and advice offered.

Eng. tr. in J. Legge, *The Texts of Taoism* (1962).

T'ai-shang Tao-chün (Chin., 'supreme master of the Tao'). One of the highest deities of religious *Taoism. He is considered (as is *Lao-tzu) an incarnation of the *Tao, to make manifest the Tao in heaven, as Lao-tzu was to make it manifest on earth.

T'ai shih. 1. Taoist breathing exercises at a preliminary level, distributing saliva to other parts of the body.

2. The 'great beginning', the form of the world before it received form—i.e. formless, but with potential within it.

Taishō Issaikyō. Jap. edn. of the Chinese *tripiṭaka, ed. Takakusu in 100 vols. (1924–34).

Taittirīya Upaniṣad. *Upaniṣad belonging to the Black *Yajur Veda. It contains an ethical discourse, sometimes known as the 'Convocation Address', an exposition of the five sheaths of the Self, and the scale, or ladder, of perfections, leading up to the bliss of *Brahman: '*Oṃ! He who knows Brahman attains the highest. As to That, this has been stated: he who knows Brahman as the real [*sat], as knowledge [*jñāna], as the infinite, gathered into the most inner place and in the highest heaven, he obtains all his desires, together with realised Brahman' (2. 1).

Trs.: see UPANIṢAD.

T'ai-yüeh ta-ti (Chinese mountain God): see T'AI-SHAN.

Taizé Community. Christian Community, Roman Catholic in foundation, in the village of Taizé in France, engaged in reconciliation in the world and in the Church. It was founded by Brother Roger (Roger Schutz-Marsauche, b. 1915, known also as Roger Schutz) in 1940, but was closed down in 1942 by the Gestapo. In 1944 he returned with three brothers, and in 1949, seven brothers took monastic vows of celibacy, respect for authority, and common property (cf. the traditional vows under HABIT, RELIGIOUS). The community now numbers about 100, drawn from all parts of the Church, some living in poor parts of the world. The whole tries to fulfil the initial vision that it should be 'a parable of communion'. In 1982, the 'pilgrimage of trust' was inaugurated, to make apparent especially the yearnings and hopes of young people. Taizé has become a major place of pilgrimage and renewal. Each year thousands of people (especially the young) assemble and follow different programmes, but always participating in the thrice-daily prayer of the community. The Taizé chant has traditional roots, but its emotional power has led to its being adopted widely in the Church. Pope *John XXIII spoke of the community as a sign of hope in the world—'Ah! That little spring time'.

J. L. Balado, *The Story of Taizé* (1988); Brother Roger's own works include *The Dynamic of the Provisional* (1981), *Afire with Love* (1982), *And Your Deserts Shall Flower* (1984).

Taizo-kai Mandara. Jap. for *garbha-dhātu maṇḍala*, the Womb. Maṇḍala, one of two (with *vajradhātu maṇḍala*, the Diamond Maṇḍala) *maṇḍalas of central importance in esoteric (*mikkyō) Buddhism in Japan. The first has more than 200 deities contained within it, in thirteen divisions, the second has nearly 1,500 in nine. See also *SHINGON.

Taj Mahal. A monument and tomb, built at Agra in India by the Mughal emperor, Shah Jehān (1592–1666), for his favourite wife Mumtaz-i-Māhāl. Shah Jehān was also buried within it, their tombs being surrounded by a marble screen bearing the *ninety-nine beautiful names of Allāh. It was built between 1632 and 1647, and is now seriously threatened by air pollution.

R. Nath, *The Immortal Taj Mahal: The Evolution of the Tomb in Mughal Architecture* (1972).

Tajwīd (Arab.). The art of *Qur'ān recitation, though it might better be called 'science' than 'art'. The precise classifications and orders are more like the ordering of a musical score. To recite the Qur'ān is to participate in the word of God in a way that in certain other religions might be regarded as *sacramental. There are three major styles of tajwīd: (i) *tartīl*, slow and deliberate, in order to reflect on the meaning (73. 4); (ii) *ḥadr*, rapidly, in order to cover as much text as possible (e.g. in fulfilment of a vow, for merit, etc.); (iii) *tadwīr*, intermediate. The extreme detail of tajwīd can only be learnt from an acknowledged master of the skill. The major treatise is Ibn al-Jazarī's *Al-Nashr fi'l-Qirā'āt al-'Ashr* (15th cent.; 2 vols., 1926).

Takbīr (Arab., the verbal noun from the reflexive verb *kabbara*, 'to magnify', 'to confess the greatness of'). A technical term, denoting the saying, by the Muslim, of *Allāhu akbar*, 'greater is God', in the prayer ritual, in the *ādhān, or call to prayer, and in personal devotion. Qur'ān 17. 111 says: *kabbirhu takbīran*, 'make him (God) greatly great'. As in the Christian *Magnificat, the 'making' means 'the acknowledging to be great'.

Takht (Pañjābī, 'throne'). 1. Five historical Sikh shrines where decisions taken by the *saṅgat are authoritative. The takhts are *Akāl Takht, *Amritsar; Harimandir *Sāhib, Paṭnā; Kesgaṛh Sāhib, *Anandpur; Hazūr Sāhib, *Nandeṛ; Damdama Sāhib, near Batinda in the Pañjab. See also GURDWĀRĀ; GURMATĀ.

2. Wooden frame on which *Ādi Granth is installed in the *gurdwārā.

Takkanot (Heb., sing., *takkanah*). Directives enacted by Jewish scholars which have the force of law. The authority to enact takkanot is derived from Deuteronomy 17. 11, 'According to the law which they shall teach you and according to the judgement which they shall tell you, you shall not turn aside from the sentence which they shall declare to you, to the right hand or to the left.' The difference between a takkanah and a *minhag is that a minhag is anonymous while a takkanah is deliberately made. The purpose of the takkanot is to deal with problems that emerged and which were not dealt with by the existing *halakhah; and a number of rules and guidelines governing takkanot were laid down by the *amoraim. The *rabbis taught that takkanot had been enacted from the time of the *patriarchs (e.g. their institution of prayers, *B.Ber.* 26b), and one of the main tasks of the men of the Great *Synagogue was to make a fence around the *Torah (*Avot* 1. 1). Most takkanot which have come down from *tannaitic times are anonymous. Later takkanot continued to be enacted until the Enlightenment, particularly in such areas as personal status, inheritance, *ḥalizah, and the *agunah. Subsequently, with the increased role of national government, there was a sharp decline in the resort to takkanot until the foundation of the State of *Israel. To be distinguished from the takkanot in general are the takkanot ha-kahal, which is Jewish legislation enacted not by halakhic authorities but by the communal leaders for members of their particular community. Examples of takkanot are: Jews must not breed pigs; litigation between Jews must be resolved by Jewish courts; every community must have an elementary school teacher; bigamy is forbidden (cf. POLYGAMY).

Takuan Sōhō. Japanese Zen master of the *Rinzai school, Sōhō (1573–1645). He became a monk as a boy, and received the seal of recognition (*inka-shōmei) from Mindō Kokyō. He became abbot of Daitoku-ji in *Kyōto under orders in 1609, but retired after three days. Much later he was first abbot of Takai-ji in 1638. Famous for his skill in the ways of *calligraphy (*shōdō*) and tea ceremony (*chadō), he also, in *Fudochi Shimmyō-roku*, explored the relation between the way of the sword (*kendō) and the mental disposition of a Zen practitioner. Takuan attempted to retire to Sugyō-ji, but the *shie jiken* ('purple robe') episode drew him back into activity: in 1615 the shōgun government insisted on its right to bestow the purple robe on any abbot of Daitoku-ji (and Myōshin-ji), and required that any abbot must have thirty years Zen experience and the mastery of 1,700 *kōans. Takuan drew up a remonstrance (*bemmeiron*) and was promptly exiled to Uzen—where he returned gladly to retirement. He became known as 'the naked monk', since he had only one robe, and when he washed it, he remained in his room. Later he was required to live in Edo, where argument persisted. Facing death, he determined on the simplicity that had been denied him in life. Instead of his self-portrait, he painted a circle with a tiny ink-point in the centre, and he left his last instructions: 'Bury my body on the mountain behind the temple, throw earth on it and go away—no *sūtras, no offerings . . . go on with your meals; no *pagoda, no monument, no posthumous name; and no biography full of dates!'

His writings were many, including poetry, but little has been translated. He explored in particular the meaning of Confucian thought in relation to Zen.

Matsuda Bugyo, *Takuan* (1978).

Takuhatsu (Jap.; Skt., *piṇḍapātika*). The practice of alms-begging, one of the disciplines undertaken by Buddhist monks. In India alms-begging before the noon hour was a daily practice, as it still is in some SE Asian Buddhist countries. In China, the rounds of alms-begging were seasonal and on special occasions; and in Japan it is undertaken periodically by monks, mainly of the *Zen school. The monks learn humility in alms-begging, receiving the minimal amount necessary for survival, while ascertaining that they do not cause unnecessary hardship to the laity; the laypeople practise charity and non-attachment, and they accumulate religious merit.

Tala (Skt.). Darkness, either self-imposed by way of ignorance and evil behaviour; or as a group of seven 'places of darkness', i.e. hells.

Ṭalāq (Islamic divorce): see MARRIAGE AND DIVORCE.

Talbīyah (Arab.), ritual formula recited repeatedly by Muslims during *hajj (pilgrimage). They are the words attributed to Ibrahīm (*Abraham) when he summoned all people to the pilgrimage to *Mecca:

> Labbayka-'Llāhumma labbayk
> labbayka-'Llāhumma labbyk
> lā sharika laka, labbayk
> inna-'l-ḥamda wa-'l-ni'mata laka wa-'l-mulk
> lā sharika laka labbayka-'Llāhumma labbayk.

Here am I, O God, here am I, here am I, O God, here am I, I associate nothing with you, here am I: surely praise and blessing are yours, and dominion, I associate nothing with you, here am I, O God.

Tale of Genji (Japanese text): see MOTOORI NORINAGA.

Talfīq (eclecticism): see SCHOOLS OF LAW, MUSLIM.

Talion (i.e. *lex talionis*, 'law of retaliation'). A punishment which is equivalent to the offence. Thus according to Genesis 9. 6, 'Whoever sheds a man's blood, by man shall his blood be shed.' Most talions were abolished in *Talmudic times, and monetary payments were substituted (*BK* 8. 1) on the grounds that 'an eye for an eye' is only superficial justice—one eye may be stronger or more effective than the other. None the less, ultimately it was accepted that 'the measure by which a man measures is the measure by which he will be measured' (*Sot.* 1. 7).

Tallis, Thomas (*c.*1505–85). Church composer, often associated with *Byrd for their formative effect on composition. He was organist of Waltham Abbey until its dissolution in 1540. Subsequently he joined Byrd as organist at the Chapel Royal. His skill is shown at its height in a motet, *Spem in alium nunquam habui*, written for eight choirs in five parts, in which all forty parts combine at the climax. His epitaph, at St Alphege, Greenwich, read: 'As he did live, so also did he die, In mild and quiet sort, O happy man.'

P. Doe, *Tallis* (1976).

Tallit, tallit katan. Jewish prayer shawl. On the four corners of the tallit, *zitzit (fringes) are attached. It is normally white, frequently with black or blue stripes, and is made of wool or silk. It is worn by men at the morning service and all day on the *Day of Atonement. Before putting it on, a *blessing is pronounced. The tallit katan is a garment with fringes on the corners which is worn by strictly *Orthodox Jews all day under their clothes. Again it is worn to fulfil the commandment of zitzit, and the fringes themselves are visible (*Shulḥān Arukh*, OH 8. 11). Outside Orthodoxy, tallit are increasingly worn by women.

Talmid ḥakham (Heb., 'a disciple of the wise'). A Jewish rabbinical scholar. According to the *Talmud, a talmid ḥakham is the ideal type of *Jew, and even though a *mamzer, a talid ḥakham takes precedence 'over a *high priest who is an ignoramus' (*Hor.* 3. 8). In order to qualify, a scholar must be familiar with the Bible and the *oral law, he must have come under the influence of a great teacher, and he must be personally pious. According to the *rabbis, a talmid ḥakham was exempted from many civic duties, he had to be impeccable in dress and be 'externally as he is internally' (*B.Yoma* 72a).

Talmud (from Heb., *lmd*, learn, study, teach). The body of teaching, commentary and discussion of the Jewish *amoraim on the *Mishnah. There are two Talmuds: the Jerusalem (or Palestinian) Talmud which originated in *Erez Israel in *c.*500 CE, and the Babylonian Talmud which was completed in *c.*600 CE. Both works are commentaries on some or all of the Mishnaic orders of **Zera'im*, **Mo'ed*, **Nashim*, and **Nezikin*. The Babylonian Talmud also includes commentaries on *Kodashim* and *Tohorot*. The commentaries on the Mishnah are known as *gemāra. The language of the Jerusalem Talmud is Western Aramaic, and, in general, discussion is concise. By the 11th cent. the supremacy of the Babylonian Talmud was finally established; as Isaac *Alfasi put it, 'we rely upon our Talmud since it is later in time, and they were more versed in Talmud than we are'. Traditionally Rav Ashi and Ravina brought the editing process of the Babylonian Talmud to an end, but there is evidence that the *Savoraim continued this work until the end of the 6th cent. It consists largely of the oral discussions as they were held in the *academies, and frequently the discussions are discursive. The entire Talmud text contains *c.*2½ million words, one-third *halakhah and two-thirds *aggadah. Because it is so varied, and because discussions arose from particular problems and situations, it is an extraordinary historical source, including folklore, manners, customs, popular proverbs, prayers, ceremonial, and medical remedies. Once it became an authoritative text, commentaries on it began to be produced, the most popular and influential being that of *Rashi which was completed in the 12th and 13th cents. by the *tosafists. As it was preserved in manuscript, there are numerous readings of the text. Individual treatises were printed from the end of the 15th cent.; the first complete edition was printed in Venice in 1520–3 by the Christian Daniel Bomberg. It is printed with the gemara following each Mishnah; Rashi's commentary is printed on the inside margin and that of the tosafot on the outside. Study of the Talmud remains a religious duty, and the text was seen as subversive and dangerous by the Christian Church, which, from the 13th to 18th cents., frequently gave the order to burn it. It was included on the first Index Expurgatorius of 1559.

See Index, Talmud.

Tr. ed. I. Epstein (1935–52); M. Adler, *The World of the Talmud* (1958); Z. H. Chajes, *Student's Guide Through the Talmud* (1960); M. Mielziner, *Introduction to the Talmud* (1968); M. Hengel *et al.* (eds.), *Übersetzung des Talmud Yerushalmi* (1975–); J. Neusner (ed.), *The Study of Ancient Judaism*, ii (1981) and *The Talmud of the Land of Israel* . . . (1990); A. Steinsaltz, *The Talmud: A Reference Guide* (1989); I. Unterman, *The Talmud: An Analytical Guide* (1985).

Talvaṇḍī Rāi Bhoi Dī. Birthplace of *Gurū *Nānak. According to the *janam-sākhīs, Gurū Nānak was born in the village of his father, Kālū. Rāi Bhoi, the name of the founder, distinguishes it from many other villages called Talvaṇḍī. It is situated in Shekhpurā tehsīl, about 65 km. west of Lahore. Now known as Nānkāṇā or Nānakiāṇā *Sāhib, this is the most important Sikh shrine in Pakistan. It is mentioned daily in the *Ardās.

In 1921 the shrine marking Gurū Nānak's birthplace was the scene of bloodshed during conflict between the resident *Udāsī *mahant and *jathās of Akālī Sikhs, enraged at his abuse of the premises. Other shrines in Talvaṇḍī commemorate events from Nānak's early life as narrated in the janam-sākhīs. For example, Maljī Sāhib is where he slept while grazing cattle and was shaded by a cobra; Kiārā Sāhib is where a farmer complained that Nānak's cattle had destroyed his crops, which were subsequently revealed to be miraculously intact; and Tambū Sāhib signifies the tent-like tree beneath which Kālū rebuked Nānak for using his 20 rupees to feed *ascetics instead of conducting business.

Tam, Rabbenu (Jacob ben Meir, *c.*1100–71). French Jew and one of the leading *tosafists. His name *tam* ('perfect man') derived from Genesis 25. 27, 'Jacob was a *tam* dwelling in tents.' He was the son of *Rashi's daughter and studied under his father and his brother, *Samuel ben Meir (Rashbam). He was almost killed by passing crusaders during the Second Crusade, but was rescued by a nobleman who promised to convert him to Christianity. He headed the *yeshivah at Ramerupt, his birthplace, and became recognized as the greatest halakhic authority in his day. He issued many *responsa, generally taking a lenient line, and so far as possible he adhered to the text of *Talmud, preferring to wrestle with a difficult text rather than rush into amendment. His best-known work is *Sefer ha-Yashar* (Book of the Upright), in which he affirmed, 'I can always reconcile two contradictory texts', and he also wrote poetry—which led him to approve the introduction of *piyyutim into the liturgy. He was cautious about innovation, even when an appeal was made to tradition, observing that '*minhag [custom] when spelt backwards makes *Gehenna'.

Tamas (Skt.). In *Sāṁkhya, one of the three strands (*guṇas) of material nature (*prakṛti). It is present in varying degrees in all things except pure consciousness (*puruṣa); it predominates in the five subtle and gross elements (*tanmātra* and *mahābhūta).

In the external world, tamas is manifested as heaviness, darkness, and rigidity. In the individual it is reflected as fear, sloth, stupidity, indifference, etc., and is considered a negative force in humans. As the quality of inertia, tamas interacts with the guṇas, *rajas, and *sattva, giving rise to creation.

Tambiah, Stanley Jeyaraja (b. 1929). Anthropologist of SE Asian Buddhist societies. Tambiah's *Buddhism and the Spirit Cults in Northeast Thailand* (1970), based on fieldwork in a north-eastern Thai village, is still the most thorough and detailed of its kind. For Tambiah, Buddhism is a shorthand expression for a total social phenomenon which encompasses the lives of monks and lay Buddhists, and which cannot be broken up, in a facile way, into its religious, political, and economic realms, as these are currently understood in the West. *World Conqueror and World Renouncer* (1976) is a more historically based account of Thai society as a whole, with particular reference to the institution of kingship, which plays such a central role in SE Asian Buddhist societies. *The Buddhist Saints of the Forest and the Cult of Amulets* (1984) is a study of individual Buddhist leaders and sects in contemporary Thailand.

Tambo, Oliver Reginald (1917–93). Christian leader, known as OR, who led the struggle for a free and democratic S. Africa. He was educated at mission schools in the Transkei, and was sponsored by the Anglican Province of S. Africa at St Peter's school, Rosettenville, and at the University of Fort Hare. He was dismissed from Fort Hare for 'subversive activities', and became a teacher. He retained the support of the Anglican Church as he translated his deep religious convictions into the political struggle for freedom. Recognizing that the white minority government was determined to retain power over the black majority, he looked for international support (especially in the United Nations, when that organization was founded, and in the Anti-Apartheid Movement), and he also valued the support of the Communist Party, the only political party committed to ending apartheid (see DUTCH REFORMED CHURCH): the African National Congress did not become a political party until it contested S. Africa's first non-racial democratic elections in 1994. He was President of the ANC, 1967–90, and was accused by the S. African regime of being a communist and a terrorist. A close friend of Nelson Mandela, he was, with Walter Sisulu, one of the outstanding leaders in S. Africa who put *liberation theology into a practice that was widely regarded as exemplary.

Tamid (Heb., 'Continuous Offering'). A tractate of the order of *Kodashim* in the Jewish *Mishnah. *Tamid* describes the work of the *priests in the *Temple of Jerusalem.

Tamilnadu or **Tamil Nadu.** A state forming the southern area of India, at one time covering the areas where the Dravidian languages are prevalent (including Andhra Pradesh, Karnāṭaka, and Keralā). Its sense of separate identity is so strong that there have been movements for independence from the Indian republic. Although Aryan Hinduism from the north spread over Tamil areas, there has always been active interchange, with influence flowing in both directions. Thus although Tamilnadu is associated with devotional Hinduism (see ĀḺVĀRS) and especially devotion to *Śiva, in fact the name of Śiva occurs fairly late in Tamil texts, and is identified with the indigenous Mudalvan, with adaptation occurring in the transition (see D. D. Shulman, *Tamil Temple Myths*, 1980). Again, Viṣṇu is known as Māl ('great one') and became associated with Tirumāl. One Tamil deity, Murukaṉ/Murugan, who is worshipped in a particularly frenzied sacred *dance, resisted assimilation altogether. This independence of Tamil religion is epitomized in *Tiruvaḷḷuvar's *Tirukkural*. Tamil religion is most usually associated with *bhakti poetry in which caste and ritual are reduced in importance, and the path to *mokṣa through devotion rather than knowledge (*jñāna) is prominent. Indeed, *Nammāḻvār's *Tiruvaymoei* is regarded as the Tamil *Veda, and is chanted by some alongside the Vedas. In addition to many devotional poets (see NĀYAṈMĀR), the Tamil area has produced major philosophers, including *Śaṅkara, *Rāmānuja, and *Radhakrishnan. The vigorous independence of the Tamils has given much to, while it has necessarily received much from, the north. See Index, Tamil religion.

F. W. Clothey, *The Many Faces of Murukaṉ* . . . (1978); V. Dehejia, *Slaves of the Lord: The Path of the Tamil Saints* (1988); K. K. Pillai, *A Short History of the Tamils* (1973); K. A. N. Sastri, *The Culture and History of the Tamils* (1964); B. Stein, *South Indian Temples* (1978); G. Welbon and G. E. Yocum, *Religious Festivals in S. India and Sri Lanka* (1982); K. V. Zvelebil, *The Smile of Murugan* . . . (1973).

Tammuz, fast of (17 Tammuz). A Jewish fast day (see FESTIVALS AND FASTS). The fast of Tammuz commemorates the breaching of the walls of *Jerusalem by the Babylonian Nebuchadnezzar in 586 BCE, and the Roman Titus in 70 CE. According to the *Mishnah, 17 Tammuz was also the day when *Moses broke the *tablets of the law, when the daily sacrifice ceased in the First Temple, and when the heathen Apostomos set up an idol in the *sanctuary. The *liturgy for the Fast of Tammuz is similar to that of the other fast days.

Tammuz/Dumuzi (deities associated with death and the return of life): see DYING AND RISING GODS.

Tan. 1. Chin., 'cinnabar', the most important element in religious *Taoism, in the pursuit of immortality. In Outer *Alchemy, *wai-tan*, effort was devoted to purifying tan and converting it to gold, to prolong life. In Inner Alchemy, tan is understood to be the interactive energy of *yin-yang produced by appropriate breathing.

2. The slip of paper which designates the sitting-place of a Zen monk for *zazen.

3. Earth-bound component of the body in Zoroastrianism: see FRAVASI.

Tanabata (Jap. star festival): see FESTIVALS AND FASTS.

Tanach or **Tanakh.** Hebrew scriptures. Tanakh is an acronym for *Torah (*Pentateuch), Nevi'im (*Prophets), and Ketuvim (*Writings, Hagiographa). An Eng. tr., *Tanakh*, was begun in 1955 and completed in 1982 (rev. 1985) by the Jewish Publication Society, which comes as close as Judaism allows to an 'authorized version'.

Tanāsukh. Islamic word for rebirth of souls. Although it would apparently contradict the orthodox description of the *afterlife, it was nevertheless held to be true by some *Shīʿa sects. Some *Ismāʿīlīs believe in rebirth until the *Imām is recognized. More elaborately, the *Nuṣairīs have seven levels of rebirth: a sinner among them will be reborn as a Sunnī (or Jew or Christian), a *kāfir will be reborn as an animal. These beliefs can be reconciled (theoretically) with orthodox views, by pointing out that God bestows the soul (*nafs, *ruḥ*) to, and takes it away from, the body; in principle this could happen several or many times. But, in fact, it is rejected in mainstream Islam. On the other hand, the pre-existence of souls accords with the power of God to create and bestow them (though *ibn Sīnā denied the truth of pre-existence). According to one *ḥadīth, 'Souls were like assembled armies before they were united with bodies'; thus, they already know *Allāh (or that Allāh is) from the moment of birth or embodiment.

T'an-ching (Zen work): see LIU-TSU-TA-SHIH FA-PAO-T'AN-CHING.

Taṇḍava. In Hinduism, *Śiva's cosmic dance of creation and destruction. The name is said to come from the *ṛṣi Taṇḍi, who received *Śaivite teaching from the *Rudras. It is the turning of the wheel of life, through which Śiva goes out, through *līlā, to veil himself in the *māyā (appearance) of creation, and then withdraws, carrying with him his devotees into union with himself and escape from *saṃsāra (rebirth).

Tango no Sekku (Japanese boys' festival): see FESTIVALS AND FASTS.

Taṇhā (Pāli) or **tṛṣṇā** (Skt., 'thirst'). Thirsting or craving after the objects of the senses and the mind; according to the second Noble Truth (see FOUR NOBLE TRUTHS) in Buddhism, the root cause of all suffering. In the doctrine of the links of causation (*paticca-samuppāda), taṇhā is caused by sensation (*vedanā*) and causes grasping (*upādāna). It takes three specific forms: thirsting for pleasures, for rebirth (especially for rebirth in heaven), and for no rebirth. It is personified as *Māra's army and as one of his daughters. *Nirvāna is synonymous with the extinction of all thirsting.

Tan-hsia T'ien-jan (Jap., Tanka Tennen; 739–834). Chinese Ch'an/Zen master, dharma-successor (*hassu) of Shih-t'ou Hsi-chien. Nothing is known of his early life, beyond the fact that he studied *Confucianism and planned to be a state official, but on his way was diverted by a Ch'an monk who advised him that it would be wiser to seek to be a buddha, and sent him to *Ma-tsu. After his training with Shih-t'ou, he returned to Ma-tsu, and when asked what he had learnt, he sat on the shoulders of an image of *Mañjuśrī. The monks were outraged, but Ma-tsu said, 'My son, you are entirely natural'—hence his monastic name T'ien-jan, 'the natural'. He remained well-known for his unconventional behaviour. During his wandering years, he stopped, one freezing night, in a Ch'an temple, and chopped up a buddha-image to make a fire. The temple-priest abused him for sacrilege, but Tan-hsia said, 'I'll get relic bones of the Buddha out of the ashes.' 'How can you find relic bones in wood?' 'Why, then, are you abusing me for burning wood?'

Tan-huang. The oasis town in NW China, near which the caves of Mo-kao-k'u were found. These are the largest complex of Buddhist cultic caves, dating from about 5th cent. CE. They were abandoned before the spread of Islam, and the caves filled with sand. They were discovered by a farmer in 1900, but were then invaded by Europeans, who removed vast quantities of texts, images, and frescoes, many of which remain unseen and even uncatalogued in Western museums. The remaining frescos have often been damaged by Muslim iconoclasts, but the caves are still a spectacular legacy of Buddhist devotion and its consequences in art.

Tanḥuma. A group of Jewish *aggadic *midrashim. *Tanḥuma* was first published in Constantinople in 1522 and contains many midrashim attributed to Rabbi Tanḥuma Bar Abba (late 4th cent. CE). It survives in several fragmented manuscripts, and there is scholarly disagreement over its origins. It contains anti-*Karaite polemic, so the original collection cannot be dated before *c*.800 CE; but parts of it are clearly much older. *Tanḥuma* is based on the triennial cycle of *Torah reading observed in *Erez Israel.

Taniguchi Masaharu (founder): see SEICHŌ NO IE.

Tanjur (bstan.'gyur, 'translated doctrine'). The secondary part of the Tibetan Buddhist canon complementing the *Kanjur, and which comprises all treatises (Skt., *śāstra*) and commentaries on Buddhist doctrine available in Tibet prior to the 1959 Chinese invasion. The collection numbers many hundreds of volumes (varying according to edition), and was almost entirely systematized for the first time by the prodigious Butön (1290–1364). See further TRIPIṬAKA.

Tanka Tennen (Chinese Ch'an/Zen master): see TAN-HSIA T'IEN-JAN.

Taṅkhāh (Pañjābī, 'a fine'). Penalty imposed on lapsed Sikhs. A *pātit Sikh may repent publicly, taking *amrit again, after offending against Sikh discipline (e.g. by hair-cutting). The taṅkhāh imposed is normally *sevā (service) of the *saṅgat (congregation), e.g. minding shoes, sweeping the *gurdwārā, or else additional daily recitation of *nitnem (prayers from the *Ādi Granth). During the 1990s several eminent Sikhs have carried out taṅkhāh at *Amritsar for offences including critical study of the Sikh tradition.

T'an-luan (*c*.488–554). Chinese Buddhist monk generally considered to be the founder of the *Pure Land School in China. According to the teachings of this school, rebirth is attained in the Pure Land or Western Paradise by faithfully repeating the formula, Homage to Amitābha (*Amida), the presiding *Buddha of the Western Paradise. He was the author of the first known Chinese systematic work on Pure Land Buddhism, known as *Lun chu*, an abbreviation from *Wu-liang-shou ching yu-p'o-t'i-shê yüan sheng chi chu*. He taught the 'Easy Path' to enlightenment, by reliance on the power of Amitābha Buddha rather than the 'Difficult Path' or 'Holy Path' of the traditional practices. The Easy Path has five 'gates': worship, praise, resolve to be born in Amitābha's Pure Land, *visualization of the Pure Land, and compassionate outreach towards all sentient beings. He taught that the Pure Land 'exists extra-phenomenally' (Chin. *ch'u yu êrh yu*), i.e. outside of *saṃsāra, so that when one is reborn there, one takes on its 'unborn' nature: the apparently sensuous delights of the Pure Land are actually a sacrament of *śūnyatā. Also, the Name of Amitābha ('He of Immeasurable Light') is a sacrament of his essence (immeasurable wisdom), hence the repetition of his Name (see NEMBUTSU) disperses the practitioner's ignorance. Practically ignored by later Chinese Buddhism, in Japan T'an-luan was treated as a major authority by *Shinran and is thus regarded as a patriarch of *Jōdo Shinshū.

R. J. Corless, 'T'an Luan . . .', in J. Foard and M. Solomon (eds.), *The Pure Land Tradition* . . . (1994).

Tanmātra (five elements): see AHAṂKĀRA.

Tanna. A Jewish *sage of the 1st and 2nd cents. CE. The tannaim (pl.) were teachers who handed down the *oral law and *midrashim and were distinguished in the *Talmud from the later scholars, the *amoraim. Notable among the tannaim were *Johanan b. Zakkai, *Akiva, *Ishmael, *Meir, and *Judah ha-Nasi. During the period of the tannaim, the Jews suffered the two calamities of the destruction of *Jerusalem in 70 CE and the failure of the *Bar Kokhba revolt in 135. Despite these disasters, the tannaim succeeded in maintaining the authority of the Great *Sanhedrin, establishing *yeshivot, and finally codifying the oral tradition in the *Mishnah.

Tan-t'ien (Chin., 'cinnabar fields'). In religious *Taoism, three regions of the body through which *ch'i flows and is to be directed.

Tantra (beliefs, practices, etc.): see TANTRISM.

Tantra (Skt., 'extension', 'warp on a loom'). A text of *Tantrism. The word is also sometimes used as a synonym for *āgama and in a general sense for Tantric doctrine. Tantra denotes specifically *Śaiva and especially *Śākta texts, though a clear distinction is often difficult to make. Some *Vaiṣṇava texts are also called Tantras, such as the *Lakṣmi Tantra* (tr. S. Gupta, 1972) of the *Pañcarātra. The teachings of the Tantras are esoteric, concerning macro-microcosmic correspondence, phonic evolution (see MANTRA), esoteric anatomy, and *Kuṇḍalinī *yoga. Central place is given to the transformation of desire (*kāma) to a spiritual end; the metaphor used is of removing a thorn by a thorn.

Tantras take the form of a dialogue between *Śiva and the Goddess (*Devī). Either the Goddess asks questions and Śiva replies (*āgama*), or vice versa (*nigama*). The distinction between *āgama* and *nigama* can also refer to that between Tantra and *Veda. The Tantras claim to be of transcendent origin, being transmitted through divine emanations, divine beings (such as the *vidyeśvaras*), and sages (*ṛṣis) to humanity. Often they are written in bad Skt. and are obscure on account of secret or 'intentional' language (*sandhābhāṣā*).

The Tantras are difficult to date, though Buddhist Tantras such as the *Hevajra* (tr. D. Snellgrove, 1959) are probably earlier (400–700 CE) than the Hindu. The most important Śākta Tantras are the *Nityaṣoḍaśikārṇava*, the *Yoginīhṛdaya*, the *Tantrarāja* (summary J. Woodroffe, 1971), the **Kulārṇava*, all written between 1000 and 1400 CE, and the 18th-cent. *Mahānirvāṇa Tantra* (tr. J. Woodroffe, 1971). See also TANTRIKA; TANTRISM.

D. L. Snellgrove, *The Hevajra Tantra* (1959).

Tantra-yoga (yoga associated with tantric analysis of the body): see KUṆḌALINĪ.

Tantrika (Skt., 'relating to Tantra'). A Hindu classification of ritual (*pūjā) in opposition to Vaidika (relating to *Veda). Tantric ritual follows the basic Vedic pattern of daily rites (*nitya), occasional rites (*naimittika*), and rites for the attainment of desires (*kāma), but differs in content. Tantric pūjā involves *mantra repetition (*japa), *nyāsa, and *visualization of one's own deity (*iṣṭadevatā). Tantric pūjā may also involve the consumption of alcohol, meat, and fish and the performance of sexual intercourse (see PAÑCAMAKĀRA). These latter are anathema to Vaidika thought and practice. Tantrika worship implies monotheism in the sense of devotion to one God or Goddess only, whereas orthodox Vaidika worship is polytheistic, adhering to worship of the five gods of the *pañcāyatana. *Śakti plays a central role in Tantrika pūjā, but does not in Vaidika. See also TANTRA; TANTRISM.

Tantrism (Skt., *tantra*, 'extension', 'warp on a loom'). A major current in Indian religious thought, in tension with the orthodox *Vedic tradition. It emphasizes the feminine aspect of a bipolar reality and advocates a practice (*sādhana) to unite these polarities and so attain freedom (*mokṣa). Tantrism is said to be the appropriate means of liberation for the degenerate modern age, the *Kālī Yuga.

The origins of Tantrism are obscure. Its roots may go back to autochthonous magic and fertility cults of pre- or non-*Aryan India, and certainly Tantrism arose on the edges of Aryan influence in N. India, Bengal, and Assam. On the other hand, a continuity can be traced between the *Vedas and the *Tantras. The dating of the Tantras and *Āgamas, the texts of Tantrism, is problematic, though Buddhist Tantric literature (the pre-Tantric *dhārāṇīs and the *Guyasamaja Tantra*) is probably earlier than the Hindu (being written between 300 and 600 CE). In Hinduism, Tantra pervades the theistic traditions of *Śaivism, *Śaktism, and *Vaiṣṇavism. Other Tantric literature includes commentaries on the Āgamas, ritual manuals (*paddhati*), texts on magic, and Yoga *Upaniṣads. Tantrism also exerted considerable influence on Jainism. In a narrower sense Tantrism refers to doctrines and practices embodied in specific Śaiva and Śākta texts called Tantras. The distinctions between the terms śākta, *kaula, and tantra are imprecise, but it would seem that Tantrism is a wider category encompassing Śaktism. There are no Śākta texts which are not Tantric, whereas Tantra refers to Śaiva, Vaiṣṇava, and Jain texts as well. Oral tradition is also important for the transmission of secret teachings, access to which can only occur through initiation (*dīkṣa) from a Tantric *guru.

Tantrism is multilevelled and Tantric texts range from crude magic to the sophisticated metaphysics of theologians such as *Abhinavagupta. There are *dualist and non-dualist Śaiva *Tantras, though philosophical differences might not be reflected in practice. For example, dualist and monist Śaiva ritual is structurally very similar in the texts and does not seem to reflect differences of superstructure found in the philosophical portions (*jñāna pada*; see ĀGAMA) of the Tantras. Certain concepts, however, are common in Tantrism, for instance, the male–female polarity in which Śiva is passive and Śakti active. (Tantric Buddhism reverses this polarity with passive female *prajñā and active male *upaya*.) Tantrism maintains that the cosmos is hierarchical, created through a transformation of Śakti who manifests herself in the form of the *tattvas. From a state of union (*yāmala) with the Lord she evolves through various subtle levels to impure, gross creation. This cosmic hierarchy is recapitulated in the body which is regarded as a microcosm.

In Tantric sādhana the body is of central importance. It binds the soul (*jīva) yet can also be the means of human perfection. Reality is both revealed and concealed in the body. The idea of bodily perfection in order to achieve liberation and/or power (*siddhi) was especially developed by the *Nātha yogins with their 'body practice' (*kāya sādhana*). For this reason, *maithuna is of central importance, especially in left-handed Tantra (see below), leading to the Indian definitions of Tantra: *mukti is *bhukti* ('enjoyment'), *yoga is *bhoga* ('sensual pleasure'). But clearly, maithuna requires ritual context, since otherwise everyone would be enlightened.

Tantric sādhana consists of *pūjā (worship) and yoga. Different Tantric sects, such as the *Kāpālikas, Kaulas, or Sahajīyās, followed different texts, but a similar pattern of sādhana is found in the most important Śākta Tantras such as the *Nityāṣodaśikārṇava*, the *Yoginīhṛdaya*, the **Kulārnava*, and *Tantrarāja Tantra*. In many ways Tantric pūjā follows Vedic pūjā and is of three kinds: *nitya*, to be performed daily; *naimittika*, to be performed on special occasions; and *kāma*, to affect a particular desire. *Nitya pūjā* follows a specific pattern although all elements of the ritual, such as *cakra pūjā, would not be performed every day. Rites in this pūjā include consecration of the ritual area, the seat (*āsana), and worship of the line of gurus. Then a geometrical design (*yantra, *cakra, or *maṇḍala) which symbolizes the divine abode is drawn and meditated upon, followed by purification of the sādhaka's own body through *bhūtaśuddhi (dissolving the mundane body), replacing the mundane self with the divine self, *nyāsa (divinization of the body), *dhyāna (visualization of the chosen deity or *iṣṭadevatā), and inner worship (*antara yāga*). This is followed by outer worship (*bahiya yāga*) of the deity and perhaps animal sacrifice. Among the Kaulas the *dūtī pūjā* (woman worship) then occurs which entails the use of the five Ms (*pañcamakāra). These are the consuming of fish (*matsya*), meat (*mamsa*), alcohol (*madya*), parched grain (*mudra*), and sexual intercourse (maithuna) with a woman who has been transformed into Śakti by *nyāsa*. Collective or 'circle' worship (*cakra pūjā*) can take the place of dūtī pūjā. This involves ecstasy (*ullāsa*). Finally a young girl can be worshipped (*kumārī pūjā). Drugs such as hashish (*vijaya*) were also used, along with the five Ms.

Tantrism has developed a sophisticated esoteric anatomy comprising of energy centres (*cakras) connected by channels (*nadis). This anatomy is visualized in Tantric yoga of which there are two important kinds, *mantra and *laya or *Kuṇḍalinī. Mantra yoga is meditation on manifest forms of sound (*vaikharī*) to take the sādhaka back to the origin of sound (*śabdabrahman* or *nādabrahman*). Kuṇḍalinī yoga arouses Śakti to unite with Śiva within the body.

An important classification in Tantra is between the right-hand path (*daksināċāra) which interprets the five Ms symbolically, and the left-hand path (*vāmācāra) which interprets them literally. Some left-hand sects such as the Śaiva Kāpālikas and the *Aghoris live in charnel grounds and are said to have consumed the flesh of corpses and scatological substances in order to achieve perfection and power (siddhi). By breaking *taboos they hope to transcend human limitation and become Śiva. Animal and human sacrifice, self-sacrifice, and consuming human flesh (*mahamamsa*) were also performed by left-hand sects. It is these *antinomian practices of the left hand that orthodoxy has reacted against.

There are no caste restrictions for initiation into Tantrism. Ritually there is equality, though this equality is not practised outside the ritual context (for the status of women and low castes see ŚĀAKTISM). Though the development of Tantrism reached its peak about 1000 CE, it has never died out and has exerted considerable influence on modern religious movements such as the *Ananda Marga and Bhagavan Sri *Rajneesh movement.

For Buddhist tantrism, see also VAJRAYĀNA.

See Index, Tantrism.

A. Bharati, *The Tantric Tradition* (1975); N. N. Bhattacharya, *History of the Tantric Religion* (1982); C. Chakravarti, *Tantras . . .* (1963); S. Dasgupta, *Obscure Religious Cults* (1969); H. V. Guenther, *The Tantric View of Life* (1977); S. Gupta, D. J. Hoens, and T. Goudriaan, *Hindu Tantrism* (1979); S. G. Gupta and T. Goudriaan, *Hindu Tantric and Śakta Literature* (1981); D. I. Lauf, *Tibetan Sacred Art: The Heritage of Tantra* (1976); P. Rawson, *Tantric Art* (1973).

Tanzīh (Arab., 'remove'). The insistence in Muslim theology on the way in which the attributes of God are not to be identified with the being of God. While it must be possible to have some idea of God (since otherwise he would be unknowable), the ideas and epithets are approximate and limited. Thus if he is called 'merciful', it is somewhat like what is recognized as merciful among human beings, but 'removed from' an exact and literal identification. Cf. ANALOGY; see also TASHBĪH; TA'WĪL; and see *bilā kaif* in *Allāh.

Tanzīl (sending down of revelation in Islam): see WAḤY; REVELATION.

Tao (Chin., 'way'). Central concept of *Taoism, supplying the name of this philosophical and religious system. In *Confucian usage, tao is (as the pictogram suggests) 'teaching', and 'the way humans should follow'. In *Lao-tzu (*Tao-te ching*), Tao becomes the source from which all appearance derives, the unproduced Producer of all that is, and the guarantor of its stability and regularity. In its manifestation, it appears as *Te, and human virtue is to live with discernment in accordance with Te expressing Tao:

The Tao that can be spoken of
Is not the eternal Tao.
The name that can be named
Is not the eternal name.
Unnameable, it is the origin of heaven and earth;
Able to be named, it is the mother of all things:
Always nonexistent
That we may penetrate its inner secret;
Always existent,
That we may comprehend its outer manifestations:
These two are the same;
Only as it manifests itself do they receive different names
. . . The expression of Te
Is derived from Tao alone.
As for Tao itself,
It is hidden, concealed,
Hidden, concealed,
Yet within it there are suggestive hints.
Within it, vital power, real and true . . .
The Tao in the world is like the flow of streams through valleys into a river into the sea (1, 2, 21, 32).

All things return into the Tao, humans by pursuit of Te, which is the realization of Tao in the midst of the flux of phenomena, especially through *wu-wei.

M. Chin, *The Tao of the Chinese Religion* (1985); H. G. Creel, *What is Taoism?* (1970); M. Saso, *Taoism and the Rite of Cosmic Renewal* (1972).

Tao-an or **Shih Tao-an** (312–85). Chinese Buddhist monk, of key importance in the Chinese assimilation of Buddhism, and in the transition from *Theravāda to *Mahāyāna. Trained in both, he was also a pupil of Fo-t'u-teng, under whom he studied *Perfection of Wisdom texts and the *sūtras and practices of *dhyāna. He rejected syncretistic methods (*ko-i*) and insisted on disciplined life—though he replaced *Vinaya rules somewhat with his own. This was balanced by devotion, especially to *Maitreya. In all these organized practices, the purpose was the penetration to the realization of the fundamental 'non-beingness' (*pen-wu*; Jap., *honmu*) as the absolute truth. In that way, he was pointing to the elaboration of *śūnyatā in Chinese terms. He wrote a commentary on *Sūtra on the Perfection of Wisdom*.

K. S. Chen, *Buddhism in China* (1964), 94–103.

Tao-chia (philosophical Taoism, one of the two main streams of Taoism, along with tao-chiao): see TAOISM.

Tao-chiao (religious Taoism, one of the two main streams of Taoism, with tao-chia): see TAOISM.

Tao-ch'o (Buddhist patriarch): see MAPPŌ.

Tao-hsin (Jap., Dōshin; 580–651). Fourth patriarch in the Ch'an/Zen succession through *Bodhidharma: he was dharma-successor (*hassu) of *Seng-ts'an and master of Hung-jen. He instructed students in *Laṅkāvatāra Sūtra*, with emphasis on *zazen, and, settling on Mount Shuang-feng, gathered many students who formed a settled monastic community, a founding model for later Zen monasteries. He emphasized that 'the Buddha is the mind', which allows the possibility of sudden realization of this truth, yet he also emphasized disciplined and gradual progress—the tension that divided Southern and Northern schools. He exhorted his students (the oldest text advocating *zazengi*, 'seated meditation'):

> Sit eagerly in meditation: sitting in meditation is basic to everything else—preferably for 35 years, resisting hunger with a little food and closing the doors [of the senses]. Do not read *sūtras, do not engage in discussion. When you practice like that, the fruit is sweet—as for a monkey who gets the nut from the shell. Such people are few indeed!

Tao-hsüan (596–667 CE). Chinese Buddhist who founded the Lü-tsung, School of Discipline. This was based on strict observance of Vinaya rules. It was transmitted to Japan in 754 by Chien-chen (*Ganjin) and became the foundation of the *Ritsu school. Tao-hsüan was also one of the earliest historian/biographers, producing the vast *Hsü kao-seng chuan* (Jap., *Zoku Kōsōden*), 30 vols. of biographies, including (book xvi) the first biography of *Bodhidharma: 'Bodhidharma, of S. Indian *brahman descent, was a man of wonderful wisdom and penetrating clarity who understood everything that he heard. . . . He understood small things as well as matters of great moment. He deepened *samādhi. He took pity on this remote corner and guided us with the help of *dharma.' The general view is that Tao-hsüan provides reliable historical accounts, within the obvious limits of the period.

T'ao Hung-ching (452–536). Taoist mediator of Mao Shan (see TAOISM), and follower of *Ko Hung who did much to consolidate Ko Hung's great achievements in systematizing Taoism and making it widely acceptable. T'ao Hung-ching worked out the corresponding relations (in a way of which *Durkheim would have approved) between the state/imperial hierarchy and the domains of the immortals (*hsien) and deities (*shen). His use of religious Taoist techniques to predict the future was sufficiently accurate for the emperor to invite him to live in the imperial court, but he refused to leave Mount Mao, where the emperor used to consult him—for which reason he became known as 'the prime minister of the mountains'. His major work was *Chen-kao* (Declarations of the Perfected), which gathered the Supreme Purity scriptures and gave an account of their revelation.

Tao-i (leader of Ch'an/Zen school of Hui-neng): see MA-TSU TAO-I.

Taoism or **Daoism.** Chinese religious and philosophical system, taking many different forms, and influencing other religions greatly, especially Buddhism. The two major forms of Taoism are philosophical, *tao-chia (daojia), and religious, *tao-chiao (daojiao); but both are intertwined (and not, as was once thought, incompatible alternatives).

Tao-chia goes back traditionally to *Lao-tzu and **Tao-te ching* (*Daode jing*). Although that work has usually been seen as a mystical and personal work, it is addressed to the issues of human nature and the proper functioning of society. However, where Confucians proposed a system of identifiable values, through observance of which a good society might be obtained, *Tao-te ching* proposes a transformation of character within, from which good society and behaviour will flow. Where a Confucian asks, 'What should I do?', a Taoist asks, 'What kind of person should I be?' This involves discerning the *Tao, the primordial source of order and the guarantor of the stability of all appearance. Tao is the unproduced Producer of all that is. Through the energetic initiative of creativity, i.e. through *Te, the inner and inexpressible nature of Tao nevertheless appears in manifest forms. To live in accord with Tao is to realize this order and nature and stability in one's own life and society. Te is then the virtue of the person who achieves that goal, and who lives in the peace that comes from understanding the 'grain of the universe', and living accordingly. That produces the characteristic Taoist virtue, active inaction, *wu-wei: 'Tao invariably does nothing [wu-wei], and yet there is nothing that is not done. . . . Simplicity, which has no name, lies in the absence of desires. Being free of desires, it is tranquil, and the world will then, of its own accord, find equilibrium' (*Tao-te ching* 37). Finding oneself within the spontaneity of nature without anxiety requires close attention to it, hence the powerful impetus from Taoism to Chinese art.

The political philosophy of Taoism requires the ruler to be equally 'invisible'. But since the ideal is never realized, the ruler has responsibility to enforce virtue; and this (especially *Tao-te ching* 6, 36, 65) has been criticized as encouraging despotism. This was reinforced indirectly by the second major figure/text of tao-chia, *Chuang-tzu, where the pursuit of absolute self-command and of the 'usefulness of the useless' is taken even further. In contrast, neo-Taoism, e.g. *Hsüan-hsüeh, rehabilitated Confucianism as an illustration of what wu-wei, properly understood, would mean in practice. By a different sort of contrast, the Seven Sages of the Bamboo Grove maintained that being in command of oneself and going with the grain of Tao allowed one to eat, drink, and be merry, since, as Liu Ling put it, 'I take the whole universe as my house and my own room as my clothing.' The Seven Sages belonged to that part of the neo-Taoist revival known as *Ch'ing T'an, 'The School of Pure Conversations'.

Tao-chiao has had a far more diverse history, with many schools and teachings, and constant interaction with popular Chinese religion. The unifying thread is the search for the Way (Tao) of Great Equilibrium and the quest for immortality, though this may be understood literally, metaphorically, or as a temporary (quest for longevity) postponement of death. Because all nature is united in Tao, immortality cannot be achieved by emancipating some aspect of nature (e.g. a soul or spirit) in order to escape from nature; rather, it must be sought in the proper directing of the forces of nature within one's own body. The major areas of concern, emphasized in different ways in the different schools, are (i) inner hygiene, attention, especially through diet and gymnastic exercises, to the conditions of life; in the Inner Deity Hygiene School, the endeavour is to visualize and work with the deities who control the functions of the body, by making offerings to them of appropriate food and behaviour; (ii) breathing, attention to *ch'i (breath), not simply as the necessary condition of life, but because it can bring with it the forces of the cosmos properly understood; (iii) circulation of the breath within the body, bringing its power deliberately to every part; (iv) sexuality, attention to the techniques leading to the retention of energy by retaining semen or controlling orgasm, and by sending this retained power through the body; (v) *alchemy, see especially KO HUNG; (vi) behaviour, attention to the kinds of moral behaviour which will be in harmony with the Tao; (vii) the search for the Isles of the Blessed where the immortals (*hsien) might be found who would reveal the secrets of their immortality.

While Tao-chiao rests on the same basic texts as Tao-chia, it rapidly produced many more (for the canon, see TAO-TSANG), and began to produce a proliferation of different schools. The first of these (in the sense that it produced deliberate organization and continuity) was *Wu-tou-mi tao, of *Chang Tao-ling and *Chang Lu. A different note was introduced by Wei Hua-ts'un (251–334): she had risen in the Celestial Master hierarchy, but then married and raised a family. After her family was grown up, she returned to her studies and received visions of the Immortals who entrusted to her the first sections of *Shang ch'ing*, writings which were to become the scripture of the new movement. When she died, her place was taken by her son and an official, Yang Hsi. In 364, Yang Hsi was commanded to go to Mount Mao, where Wei Hua-ts'un visited him with many of the Immortals, and began the dictation to him of the remainder of the scripture. From the connection with Mount Mao, the movement is known as Mao-shan. Although the scripture was rapidly dissipated and much of it was lost, *T'ao Hung-ching recovered much of it for the first Taoist canon. Religious Taoism is made up of many schools or sects: at least eighty-six major movements have been listed. At one extreme, the excessive (especially sexual) rituals of popular Taoism are opposed, and much emphasis is placed on quiet meditation, and on inner hygiene techniques and asceticism. At the other are the practitioners of rites and divination, who pass on hereditary skills. Among these many schools, of early importance were *Ling-pao and T'ai-ping Tao (an early example of the revolutionary and somewhat *millennarian strand in religious Taoism, familiar in the *Boxer rebellion). Later schools of importance include *Cheng-i Tao and *Ch'üan-chen Tao.

Chang Chung-yuan, *Creativity and Taoism* (1963); H. J. Creel, *What is Taoism?* (1970); M. Kaltenmark, *Lao tseu et le taoisme* (1965; tr. R. Greaves, 1969); J. Lagerway, *Taoist Ritual in Chinese Society and History* (1987); S. Little, *Realm of the Immortals: Daoism in the Arts of China* (1988); H. Maspero, *Taoism and Chinese Religion* (1981); K. Schipper, *Le Corps taoiste* (1982); M. Strickmann, *Le Taoisme de Mao-Chan* (1981); H. Welch, *The Parting of the Way* (1957) and with A. Seidel (eds.), *Facets of Taoism* (1977); K. Wolf, *Westliche Taoismus-Bibliographie* (1986).

Taoist canon (authoritative Taoist texts): see TAO-TSANG.

Tao-sheng or **Chu Tao-sheng** (355–434). Chinese Buddhist who founded the Nirvāna school (*nirvāna). Recognized early as a man of great insight, he went to Ch'ang-an in 405 and collaborated with *Kumārajīva. There he developed the arguments later accepted extensively, but at the time so revolutionary that he was expelled from the monastery—especially that all beings possess the buddha-nature (*buddhatā), and can realize this through sudden enlightenment. Nevertheless, it can and should be prepared for through meditation and study. Because even nirvāna is empty of self (*śūnyatā), he rejected *Pure Land tendencies to think of 'heavenly' rewards, but he insisted that the state of nirvāna has to be regarded as the highest, because undisturbed, bliss.

Tao-shih. The scholars and ritual functionaries of religious *Taoism (*tao-chiao*). In addition to local congregations, they came to take charge of organized communities, eventually developing monastic rules. See CHANG LU.

Tao-te Ching (The Book of the Way and its Power). A work attributed to *Lao-tzu (hence reference to it as *Lao-tzu*), foundation text of *Taoism. It is made up of 5,000 pictograms, hence the title, *Text of the Five Thousand Signs*. Trad. dated to 6th cent. BCE, it is more likely to come from 4th/3rd cent.; the oldest existing copy is *c.*200 BCE. The text expounds the *Tao as the unproduced and inexpressible source of all appearance, which nevertheless becomes manifest through *Te, through proper understanding of which the return to, and union with, Tao becomes possible.

Many trs., e.g. W.-t. Chan (1963), C.-y. Chang (1975), G.-f. Feng and J. English (1972), D. C. Lau (1963); poetic tr. J. C. H. Wu (1961); but note H. Welch, *The Parting of the Ways* (1957): 'No translation can be satisfactory, because no translation can be as ambiguous as the Chinese original'.

Tao-te t'ien-tsun (ruler of Taoist heaven of highest purity): see SAN-CH'ING.

T'ao-t'ieh ('ogre masks'): see BRONZE VESSELS.

Tao-tsang. The *Taoist *'canon' of authoritative texts. After a list in Pan Ku's *Han Shu* (1st cent. CE), an early attempt to list such texts was made by *Ko Hung in *Pao Pu Tzu*. Lu Hsu Ching (5th cent.) was the first to divide Taoist writings into Three Caves (*tung/dung*); later Four Supplements were added. The first edition supported by the emperor appeared in the Tang dynasty, and contained anything (according to different accounts) between 3,000 and 8,000 rolls (texts), but it was lost or destroyed in the ensuing wars and rebellions. Further editions appeared until the Ming dynasty (1368–1644), when the Tao-tsang included nearly 8,000 rolls. There is no organizing principle, and many of the texts are concerned with immortality—with the foundations in Tao and *ch'i, with the cosmological support in *myths and *rituals, and with techniques for attaining immortality. The First Cave (*Tung-chen*) has as its basis the Shang-ch'ing texts; the Second (*Tung-hsuan*) has as its basis the Ling-pao texts, revealing Buddhist influence; the Third (*Tung-shen*) has as its basis the San-huang texts.

J. Holm and J. Bowker (eds.), *Sacred Writings* (1994).

Tao-yin (Taoist exercise for guiding the breath to different parts of the body): see GYMNASTICS, TAOIST.

Tapa Gaccha (Jain sect): see GACCHA.

Tapas (Skt., 'heat'). *Asceticism conceived as a force of creative heat in Indian religions. This force is instrumental in the acquisition of spiritual power (*siddhi) and in gaining liberation (*mokṣa).

In the *Vedas, tapas has both a cosmic and a human aspect.

1. As a cosmic force it is the power underlying manifestation. Indeed, the *Ṛg Veda* (10. 129. 3) says that the one universal being was created by tapas and likewise cosmic order (*ṛta) and truth (*satya) were born from it (10. 190). Tapas is thus a force which is not created by the gods but used by them. For example, *Prajāpati creates the universe by heating himself (*Śatapatha Brāhmaṇa* 7. 1. 2, 13).

2. At a human level, tapas could be created in the fire sacrifice (*agnihotra) and in the sacrificial priest (*hotṛ) who manifested tapas by sweating. Ascetic practices, such as fasting and celibacy, were gradually adopted by priests to build up their 'heat' for the performance of rituals. Thus tapas in the Vedas and *Brāhmaṇas is a preparation for the fire sacrifice, though a trend towards a total ascetic life is certainly found in the *Āranyakas.

With the *Upaniṣads and the development of *yoga, tapas becomes not a preparation for ritual but a means of realizing the self (*ātman) and gaining release (mokṣa) (*Muṇḍaka Upaniṣad* 1. 2. 11). The outer fire sacrifice becomes the inner sacrifice of the breath (*prāṇa) (*Kauśītaki Brahmaṇa Upaniṣad* 2. 5); the external fire becomes the fire produced by austerity. In the **Yoga Sūtra* (2. 32) tapas is one of the practices of *niyāma, the second part of *rāja yoga, though according to **Bhagavad-gītā* (6. 46), yoga is beyond tapas. The practice of austerity produces inner heat; for example, in Buddhism the *Majjhima Nikāya* (1. 244) speaks of the heat obtained by holding the breath; and in Hinduism, the rise of *Kuṇḍalinī is associated with the arousal of heat.

One of the central characteristics of asceticism is chastity (*Śatapatha Brāhmaṇa* 11. 5. 4. 16), and the ascetic's store of tapas is threatened by sexual arousal (*kāma), as many stories illustrate. For example, the asceticism of Ṛṣyaśṛṅga was so great that the god *Indra felt threatened and sent a heavenly nymph (*apsarā) to seduce him. She succeeded and thereby destroyed his tapas. This idea also applies to non-human beings. An apsaras, for instance, fell from heaven because her tapas was destroyed when she desired a mortal man (*Matsya Purāṇa* 14. 4–6). Although kāma destroys tapas, sexual fulfilment with an apsaras is yet regarded as a reward of tapas (*Skanda Purāṇa* 6. 257) for the ascetic who has become very potent through its practice. Paradoxically, tapas is associated both with chastity and liberation as well as with desire and fecundity. This paradox is expressed in the god *Śiva who is both ascetic, amassing tapas through yoga, and erotic, making love to *Pārvatī for thousands of years.

Asceticism in some form is common to all yoga schools, though actual practices vary in intensity from mere celibacy to more extreme forms of asceticism such as never lying down, piercing the skin with a sharp instrument, bearing extremes of heat and cold, or, in Jainism, even slowly starving to death as a means of withdrawal from the world (*sallekhanā): see also ASCETICISM.

D. M. Knipe, *In the Image of Fire: Vedic Experiences of Heat* (1975).

Taqīy(y)a (Arab., 'fear, guard against'). The dispensation for Muslims which allows them to conceal their faith when under persecution or threat or compulsion: 'God gave the believers freedom of movement by taqīya, so hide yourself!' The importance of *nīy(y)a is related to taqīya because 'God takes his servants as their hearts believe, not as the tongue may profess' (*al-Tabari, *Tafsir*, on Qur'ān,

16. 106). There is much discussion of details (is it allowed or is it an obligation? can it be for private reasons, or for the good of the community?), and of the proviso that it does not conflict with the virtues of *shahīd if that occurs.

Among the *Shīʿa, taqīya is equally, if not more, prominent, despite the redemptive beliefs focused on the death of *al-Ḥusain. One should not seek a martyrdom which serves no purpose: the prior obligation is to preserve oneself for the faith and for the community. In a situation of *jihād, taqīya no longer has the same priority.

Taqlīd (Arab., *qallada*, 'put a rope on the neck of an animal'). A word, in Islam, for authority in matters of religion, and particularly for the obligation to recognize established positions in *fiqh. Taqlīd should be an intelligent recognition of authority, not a blind and unquestioning obedience; but it is in contrast to *ijtihād.

Tārā (Skt. 'Star', Tib. *sgrol.ma* or *drolma* 'She who saves'; possibly from Skt., *tārayati*, 'crossing, transcending'). Tibet's most important deity. She is a *bodhisattva who for many Tibetans has already become a *Buddha, having vowed—on being advised of the spiritual advantages of male rebirth—never to relinquish her female form. Tārā has the epithet 'mother of all the Buddhas', and is viewed with great affection by Tibetans who in one myth (*Red Annals*, 14th cent.) trace their own origins to her and Chenrezi (*Avalokiteśvara) in the respective forms of a rock-ogress and monkey. Her association with Chenrezi is repeated in another myth, of her own origin, where she sprang from the tears shed by Chenrezi as, about to enter his final *nirvāna, he looked back at all the beings he was leaving behind. Chenrezi stayed with the world as bodhisattva of compassion, and Tārā embodies much of his nature.

It is generally accepted that Tārā was a Buddhist deity assimilated into Hinduism (and Jainism). Common in Hinduism as 'the Star', as the esoteric form of *Devī, and as a manifestation of *Kālī, her name has served as an epithet for many goddesses, most notably *Pārvatī; and the Tibetan statues of Tārā, recently ubiquitous in Hindu homes, are considered forms of Pārvatī. Originally she was a *Tantric deity, prominent in 7th-cent. *tantras, though stone carvings of her (i.e. at *Ellorā) have been dated to the 6th cent. By the 8th cent. her cult was established at *Borobodur in Java, in itself showing the early extent of Tantric influence. Although her appearance in Tibet has been noted as 8th cent., it was not until the arrival of *Atiśa in 1042 that worship of Tārā became widespread. Atiśa's own life was significantly dominated by devotion to Tārā—it was she who instructed him to visit Tibet—yet of the 117 texts Atiśa wrote, only four pertain to Tārā, and of the seventy-seven texts Atiśa helped translate, only six pertain to her. Of these, three were from the cycle *Cheating Death* by Vāgīśvarakīrti, the first mention of White Tārā. Thus it was the tradition of White Tārā that initially spread in Tibet. The more Tantric texts based on Green Tārā were, due to the pervading moral climate, not promulgated (some attribute this decision to Atiśa's disciple Dromdon) until the *Jonang Tāranātha, 500 years later.

Tibetan Buddhism recognizes twenty-one Tārās, according to the definitive text on her worship, *Homages to the Twenty One Tārās*, brought from India by Darmadra in the 11th cent. Each Tārā has a different function (averting disasters, wish-fulfilling, increasing wisdom, healing, etc.), each has a particular colour, *mudrā, and *mantra, and each emanates from Green Tārā as source. Each school has a preference for a different Tārā—Sakya for Red Tārā (Kurukullā), Nyingma for Blue Tārā (Ekajaṭā), Kagyü for White Tārā, Geluk for Green Tārā. After the mantra of Chenrezi (**om maṇi padme hum*), the mantra of Tārā (*om tāre tuttāre ture svāhā*) is the most commonly heard on the lips of the Tibetan people.

S. Beyer, *The Cult of Tara* . . . (1973).

Targum (Heb., 'translation'). A translation of the Hebrew scriptures into *Aramaic. The best-known Targum is *Targum *Onkelos* which was regarded as so authoritative that the pious were instructed to read the weekly *Torah portion 'twice in the original and once in the Targum' (*B.Ber.* 8a). *Targum Jonathan* is the Targum to the *prophetic books, and *Targum Yerushalmi* is a largely *midrashic translation (or interpretation) of the *Hagiographa. *Targum Pseudo-Jonathan* is a late targum on the whole Pentateuch (Genesis 15. 14 mentions the wives of *Muḥammad as the wives of *Ishmael), but preserving the earlier interpretations. Several fragmentary targumim (pl.) have survived, together with an early form of the Palestinian targum tradition in Neofiti I (a manuscript of a targum to the whole of the Pentateuch). From all this it is clear that there was a relatively stable, though developing, targum tradition, which is unsurprising, given the connection between targumim and *synagogues. Few people, in the period of the Second Temple and after, knew Hebrew: the reading of scripture was always in Hebrew, the language of revelation, but this was accompanied by an Aramaic targum which incorporated exegesis of difficult passages, or of passages used by Christians in their own interest. The targumim, therefore, offer vital insight into the early, and relatively standard, Jewish understanding of scripture.

M. Aberbach and B. Grossfeld, *Targum Onkelos to Genesis* (1982); J. W. Bowker, *Targums and Rabbinic Literature* . . . (1969); B. Grossfield, *A Bibliography of Targum Literature* (1972, 1977); G. J. Kuiper, *The Pseudo-Jonathan Targum and its Relationship to Targum Onkelos* (1972); M. McNamara (ed.), *The Aramaic Bible* (1987–); *The New Testament and the Palestinian Targum* . . . (1966); *Targum and Testament* . . . (1972); L. Smolar and M. Aberbach, *Studies in Targum Jonathan to the Prophets* (1983).

Tariki (Jap., 'power of the other'). Liberation in Buddhism received through the help or power of another, especially *Amida/Amitābha. Liberation depending on one's own effort is *jiriki. The two are often called 'cat and monkey': a cat carries its kitten to safety, whereas a young monkey clings to its mother.

Ṭarīqa (Arab., 'path, way'; pl. *ṭuruq*). Originally (9th/10th cent. CE) a way of classifying the rules and methods by which a mystical approach to God might be sustained, it became a term for the different Sūfī systems themselves, along with their rules and rituals. Often contested on grounds of *bid'a (innovation), ṭuruq nevertheless claimed lineages going back through a *shaykh to the *Companions of the Prophet and to *Muḥammad himself. For examples, see BEKTĀSHĪ(Y)YA; NAQSHBANDI(Y)YA; QĀDIRI(Y)YA.

A. Schimmels, *Mystical Dimensions of Islam* (1975); J. A. Subhan, *Sufism, its Saints and Shrines* (1960); J. S. Trimingham, *The Sufi Orders in Islam* (1971).

Tarka (Skt., 'reason', 'philosophy'). An activity of mind usually condemned by Buddhists. In the *Upaniṣads, tarka is held to be a preliminary, but inadequate, means for understanding the ultimate. The Buddhist canon generally speaks of tarka in the pejorative sense of vain speculation, a sense well brought out by the Buddha's refusal to answer questions of a philosophical nature, since these will not be conducive to *enlightenment (see AVYĀKATA). In some instances, however, the Buddha seems to adopt the Upaniṣadic position, particularly in a conversation with Ānanda when he ascribes a limited value to reasoning (*Saṃyutta Nikāya* 1. 56).

Some scholars have pointed out that when the Buddha condemns tarka, he may not in fact be condemning all philosophy but simply sophistry and destructive criticism. He may not have been so opposed to more systematic forms of thought. This dichotomy is reflected in the history of Buddhist thought, the *Mādhyamaka, for instance, going along with the wholesale critique of tarka, while the Pramāṇa school adopts a more sympathetic attitude towards reason.

Tarn Tāran (Pañjābī, 'means of crossing ocean of life to salvation'). A Sikh shrine. Tarn Tāran lies 20 km. south of *Amritsar. Here Gurū *Arjan Dev constructed a *gurdwārā in honour of Gurū *Rām Dās and a pool whose water reputedly cures leprosy. The town dates from 1590 CE, and the present gurdwārā building from 1830, when it was rebuilt by Mahārājā *Rañjīt Siṅgh. In 1921 a violent clash erupted there between the lax *mahants and *Akālī reformists. On the *amāvas* ('darkest night') of each month many devotees visit Tarn Tāran. See also HEALING; RAKĀB GAÑJ; TALVAṆḌĪ RĀI BHOI DĪ; TĪRATH.

Tarpaṇa. Part of Hindu morning *ablutions. The morning cleansing with water is a basic obligation. Tarpaṇa is the point at which the worshipper makes a cup with his hands and pours the water back into the river while reciting *mantras. After sipping some water, he may then apply the distinguishing mark of his *saṃpradāya (tradition), e.g. three vertical lines (*tripuṇḍra*) for a Śaivite, three horizontal lines for a Vaiṣṇavite. It is followed by *saṁdhyā (morning prayer).

Taryag Mitzvot (the total of commands and prohibitions in Torah): see SIX HUNDRED AND THIRTEEN COMMANDMENTS.

Taṣawwuf (Arab., prob. form V *masdar* from √*ṣūf*, 'wool'). Muslim name for the commitment of those known as the *Sūfīs. If this etymology is correct, it may derive from the characteristic woollen garment worn by many early Sūfīs. Other etymologies have been proposed (e.g. *ahl al-ṣuffa*, those regularly sitting on 'the bench' of the *mosque in *Madīna; *ṣūfiyya*, those who have been purified; Banū Ṣūfa; Gk., *sophos*, 'wise', i.e. Sophists—although otherwise the Gk. letter sigma in transliteration becomes sīn not ṣād); but none seems convincing. By *abjad (numerical values to letters), taṣawwuf equals the Arabic for 'divine wisdom', but this is fanciful. A number of Muslim understandings of taṣawwuf were assembled by R. A. Nicholson, *Journ. of the Royal Asiatic Society* (1906). For the nature of Sufism, see SŪFĪS.

Tashahhud (Muslim profession of faith): see SHAHĀDA; ṢALĀT.

Tashbīh (Arab., *shabaha*, 'liken, compare'). The issue raised in Islam by statements in the *Qur'ān which attribute to God human likenesses—e.g. a face, hands, and eyes—and which describe him talking and sitting. A fierce battleground in early Islam (see ALLĀH), it led to an avoidance of literal anthropomorphism by affirming *tanzīh (keeping God free from such reductions to human size), along with an agnostic acceptance of the language *bilā kaif* (see ALLĀH), without knowing how it is to be taken. The opposite view was to accept that nothing can be said of God beyond the extremely approximate and corrigible, and that God should be emptied of all attributes (*ta'ṭīl*): they cannot belong literally to his own nature or being, and simply reflect our perception of his dealings with us. An intermediate (but often suspect) position (*ta'wīl) took the statements of the Qur'ān to be allegorical. The issue has remained central to the major and continuing divisions of Islam. See also TANZĪH.

Tashlikh. Jewish *New Year ceremony. *Micah declares, 'You will cast (*tashlikh*) all their sins into the sea.' On the first day of *Rosh ha-Shanah (or on the second if the first day falls on the *Sabbath), the ceremony of symbolically casting sin into the sea is performed by running water. The tradition is not mentioned in the *Talmud and may have a pagan origin. Micah 7. 18–20, Psalms 118. 5–9, 33, and 130, and Isaiah 11. 9 are recited, and *kabbalists include passages from the *Zohar. The earliest mention is in the 15th cent., though *Tertullian mentions 'prayers at the seashore': see J. Z. Lauterbach, *Heb. Union College Annual*, 11 (1936).

A. C. Feuer, *Tashlich* (1989).

Tassels (on prayer shawl): see ZITZIT.

Tathāgata (Pāli, Skt.; Chin., *ju-lai*; Jap., *nyorai*; Korean, *yotae*: usually left untranslated; if translated then as 'Thus-Gone' or 'Truthfinder'). According to Buddhist tradition, the title chosen by the Buddha for himself. The title was intended to convey his identity as a perfect being, though the precise meaning of the word remains problematic. Etymologically it can be read as (i) 'thus-gone' (*tathā gata*) or 'thus-come' (*tathā āgata*), generally taken to mean 'one who has gone (or come)' i.e. attained emancipation; (ii) 'one come (*āgata*) to the truth (*tatha*)'. The etymology may itself be suspect, however, since it is not certain whether the word is Skt. or vernacular in origin.

Further interpretations of the meaning based on textual considerations are: 'a master and teacher *come* from the Tusita Heaven' (*satthā Tusita gaṇim-āgata*), *Sutta Nipāta* 5. 955, as *Former Buddhas have come, thus indicating the fulfilment of popular expectations; 'a teacher *come*' (*gaṇiṃ āgato*), *Sutta Nipāta* 5. 957, meaning one who makes a perfect teacher, because there is absolute accord between what he says and does (see *Digha Nikāya* 3. 135); and 'thus-gone', meaning one who has 'gone before', 'trodden the path first', that is, a 'way-maker' (*magga-uppādetā*) as distinct from his disciples who are called 'way-followers' (*maggānugā*). A verse from the *Mahābhārata* says: 'Just as the foot-prints of birds flying in the sky and of fish swimming in the water may not be seen, *so is the going* of those who have realized the truth' (*tathā jñānavidām gatiḥ*), *Śāntiparva* 181. 12. The idea here of traceless foot-prints or tracks connects up with the representation of the Buddha *qua* Tathāgata as 'untraceable' (*ananuvejja*) and 'trackless' (*apada*) according to Buddhist canonical writings. Hence 'tathāgata' seems to have been used to refer to one who has realized the Truth and therefore is trackless, i.e. transcendent.

See also CAKRAVARTIN; TATHĀGATA-GARBHA.

Tathāgata-garbha. The 'Embryonic Tathāgata', a concept which emerges in *Mahāyāna Buddhism and in terms of which all living beings are regarded as potential *Buddhas by virtue of their participation in a universal 'buddha-nature'. In the course of time this embryonic seed or potency which exists in each creature will flower into full enlightenment, and since the potency is shared by all, the enlightenment will be a universal one. The embryonic latent buddha-nature is conceived of as the personal reflection of the Absolute which itself engenders the drive for liberation and is at the same time the transcendent goal of the spiritual life. The sources which expound this teaching, such as the *Ratnagotravibhāga* and the *Tathāgatagarbhasūtra*, regard it as a third and final cycle in the development of Buddhist thought, being the culmination of both the Buddha's early teaching and its philosophical elaboration by the Mahāyāna. Its critics, on the other hand, saw it as dangerously close to the monistic doctrines of Hinduism as expounded by the *Advaita Vedānta school of *Śaṅkara. See Index, Buddha-nature.

D. S. Ruegg, *La Théorie du Tathagatagārbha et du Gotra* (1969); tr. of the *Ratnagotravibhāga* in J. Takasaki, *A Study of the Ratnagotravibhāga-Uttaratantra* (1966).

Tathatā (Skt., 'suchness'; Chin., *chen-ju*; Jap., **shinnyo*). Mahāyāna Buddhist attempt to express the absolute and true nature inherent in all appearance, and obviously contrasted with it *qua* appearance. It has no 'own nature' (*svabhāva), and is not other than the buddha-nature (*buddhatā, *bussho, *tathāgata-garbha), except of course that the 'two' cannot be compared or equated, because they have no characterized nature to be so compared. For that reason, the Buddha as *tathāgata is necessarily synonymous with tathatā (e.g. as argued in the **Diamond Sūtra*). See Index, Buddha-nature.

Tatian. Christian *apologist and ascetic. He was a pupil of *Justin Martyr in Rome between 150 and 165, but *c*.172 he returned to his home in 'Assyria' where he is said to have founded the sect of *Encratites. His *Oratio ad Graecos* attacks Greek civilization as too evil to be reconciled with Christianity. In the Greek and Latin Churches he is traditionally considered a heretic. But in the Syriac Church he was venerated as the author of the **Diatessaron*, which remained in use until the 5th cent.

Taʿṭīl (emptying God of attributes): see TASHBĪH.

Tattva (Skt., 'that-ness'). 1. In *Saṁkhya philosophy, in Hinduism, tattvas are the constituent subtle elements of *prakṛti; in Jainism, tattva is the categorical (i.e. true) constituent of appearance and release: 'Tattva (the categories of truth) are sentient selves [*jīva], not-sentient selves, inflow of karmic particles into the self, binding of the karmic particles to the self, blocking its inflow, shedding it, liberation [*mokṣa]' (*Tattvārthā(dhigama)-Sūtra* 1. 4).

2. In Buddhism, tattva does not have the same technical philosophical sense. The proto-Mahāyānist *Prajñaptivādins defined tattva as the real phenomenon which underlies concept (*prajñapti*). In the *Vijñanāvāda (Yogācāra) this meaning is substantially retained, though now extended to take in the totality of entities. The *Ratnagotravibhāga* of *Asaṅga talks of reality (tattva) being devoid of the subject–object dichotomy, and other texts by the same author state that, since words and concepts do not partake of the nature of the things they denote, tattva is ultimately inexpressible.

Authors representing the Mādhyamaka tendency are careful not to use tattva in the Yogācārin sense in their effort to avoid all terms which may be taken as absolutes. *Nāgārjuna does, however, talk of the reality or truth (tattva) of the Buddha's teaching.

Tattvabodha (The Knowledge of the Truth). Short work of *Advaita Hinduism by *Śaṅkara, exploring the competence of *jīva—its relation to *Īśvara, its knowledge of its own relation to *ātman, hence to *Brahman.

Tattvabodhini Patrika (Indian journal): see TAGORE, D.

Tat-tvam-asi (Skt., 'That thou art'). One of the great sayings (*mahāvākya) which appears in **Chāndogya Upaniṣad* (6. 8. 7, 6. 9. 4, 6. 14. 3): the sage Uddālaka instructs his son Śvetaketu concerning Ultimate Reality (*Brahman) immanent as the Self (*ātman) in all beings: 'That which is the finest essence—this whole world has that as its self. That is Reality (satyam). That is the Self (ātman). That thou art, Śvetaketu.'

Tattvārtha Sūtra or ***Tattvārthadhigamasūtra.*** Jain text revered by both Śvetāmbaras and *Digambaras. It is attributed to *Umāsvāmi (also Umāsvāti, *c.*2nd cent. CE?), and consists of ten chs. of 357 sutras, expounding the seven *tattvas (principles). It is said that 'there is no Jaina doctrine or dogma which is not expressed or implied in these aphorisms' (K. B. Jindal), and it is recited daily in many temples. According to tradition, the work came into being because a devoted layman, Dvaipāyaka, had made a vow to complete a work of aphorisms, epitomizing Jaina teaching. His first aphorism was 'Belief, knowledge, conduct, the path to liberation'. Fearing that he might forget it as he went to work, he wrote it on the side of his house. Umāsvāmi came by, and, being received hospitably by Dvaipāyaka's wife, noticed the aphorism and added to each of the three words the all-important word 'right' or 'enlightened' (*samyag*), thus forming the foundational triad of Jainism, the *Three Jewels. Dvaipāyaka sought out Umāsvāmi and begged him to complete the book, which became the *Tattvārtha Sūtra*.

S. Ohira, *A Study of Tattvarthasutra with Bhasya* (1982); tr. N. Tatia, *That Which Is . . .* (1994).

Ta T'ung Shu (The Book of Great Unity/Commonwealth). Major text written by *K'ang Yu-wei while in seclusion on Mount Hsi Chao Shan, 1884–5, though not published until 1901. It is an eclectic work, drawing on all resources which point to the abolition of social and labour divisions, so that (echoing Confucius), 'the world may become a common state'.

Tauler, Johann (*c.*1300–61). German Christian mystic. He became a *Dominican at Strasbourg in 1315 where he probably came under the influence of Meister *Eckhart and *Henry Suso. Famous as a preacher and director, especially of nuns, he became still more popular because of his devotion to the sick during the Black Death. His mystical doctrine, found mainly in his sermons, is firmly grounded in *Thomism, and concentrates on the practical consequences of God's indwelling, manifest particularly in humility and abandonment to the will of God: 'God illumines his true friends, and shines within them with power, purity and truth, so that such people become divine and supernatural persons.' Such experience is not for its own sake, but for 'nourishment and support to help us in our active work.' Hence, 'one can spin, another make shoes, and all these are gifts of the *Holy Spirit. I tell you, if I were not a priest, I would think it a great gift to make shoes, and I would try to make them so well as to be a pattern to all.'

Trs. S. Winkworth, E. Colledge; E. Filthant, *Johannes Tauler . . .* (1961); I. Weilner, *Johannes Taulers Bekehrungsweg* (1961).

Tāvatiṃsa Gods (33 Vedic gods): see COSMOLOGY (Buddhist).

Ṭawāf (Arab.). Ritual circuit of a sacred place or object, especially in Islam the circumambulation of the *Kaʿba during the *ḥajj.

Tawbah (repentance): see SIN.

Tawḥīd (Arab., verb. noun of *waḥḥada*, 'make one'). Asserting the oneness of God, the supreme duty, and passion, of Islamic theology. There is an antiseptic quality to the expression. It is not merely that God is believed to be One, but that his unity must be affirmed, in strenuous negation of all *dualism, idolatry, and superstition—i.e. of *shirk. Qur'ān 112, the Sūra of Unity, is the classic statement: 'Say: "He is God, One, the ever self-sufficing, God, the Eternal [*al-Ṣamad*]. He does not beget and he was not begotten, and there is not any one like him." ' This emphasis on the Oneness of God, from whom all life and all creation is derived, was the central thrust of Muḥammad's mission. In *Sūfī thought and poetry, tawḥīd means, not the unitariness of God as affirmed, but the unitive state in which the devotee transcends individuation in *fanā' and enters the unitive state in which distinction between God and the self no longer obtains, although 'the Lord remains the Lord, and the servant the servant'.

Tawḥīd-i Ilāhī (Divine Faith of Akbar): see AKBAR.

Ta'wīl (Arab.). In Islam a term for commentary on the *Qur'ān. It was originally synonymous with *tafsīr, but it became associated later with commentary on the content of the Qur'ān, and eventually with allegorical interpretation, often in support of particular schools or parties of Islam: e.g. see ISMĀʿĪLĪYA. It was a method held in some suspicion because of the danger of 'explaining away' the uncongenial, and it came to be held that ta'wīl could never contradict the plain sense.

Tawrāt (Arab.; Heb., *Torah). The Quranic term for the scripture of the Jews, who thus qualify as *Ahl al-Kitāb, 'People of the Book' (scripture). The Tawrāt was 'sent down' (Qur'ān 3. 3), to *Moses, and contains 'guidance and light' (5. 47). The Jews, however, are accused of having 'distorted' it (2. 75; 5. 14), or of 'concealing' what the scripture contained (3. 71; 5. 16; 6. 91), or of 'corruption' (*taḥrīf) of their scripture. The Qur'ān itself is considered a continuation, correction, and confirmation of the message already received; and even claims that *Muḥammad is 'mentioned in their own scriptures, Tawrāt and *Injīl' (7. 157)—here referring also to the *Naṣārā (Christians).

Taylor, Jeremy (1613–67). *Anglican *bishop and writer, 'the Shakespeare of the divines' (Emerson). He was chaplain to Charles I, and rector of Uppingham (1638–42). When the king's cause failed, he used his exile in Carmarthenshire to write his plea for toleration, *The Liberty of Prophesying* (1647), his influential devotional works, *The Life of Christ* (1649), *Holy Living* (1650), *Holy Dying* (1651), *Unum Necessarium* (1655), and various sermons. He was appointed bishop of Down and Connor in 1660. He regarded his *Ductor Dubitantium*, a comprehensive study of *moral theology, as his most important work. Opposed by *Presbyterians, he defended *episcopacy, whilst his *The Real Presence . . . Proved* (1654) attacks the doctrine of *transubstantiation. His emphasis is on the constant presence of God, with whom one can therefore converse at any time: 'We can no more be removed from the presence of God than from our own being.' In advocating toleration, he went beyond *Milton (for whom adherence to scripture was a sufficient bond) in regarding the *Apostles' Creed as the ground of Church union; but beyond that 'they were excellent words which St. *Ambrose said in attestation of this great truth, that the civil authority has no right to interdict the liberty of speaking, nor the sacerdotal to prevent speaking what you think.' In practical matters his advice was prudent:

> Let man and wife be sure to abstain from all those things which by experience and observation they find to be contrary to each other: they that govern elephants never appear before them in white; and the masters of bulls keep from them all garments of blood and scarlet, and as knowing that they will be impatient of civil usages and discipline when their natures are provoked by their proper antipathies.

H. T. Hughes, *The Piety of Jeremy Taylor* (1960); C. J. Stranks, *The Life and Writings* (1952).

Taz (Jewish halakhic authority): see DAVID BEN SAMUEL.

Taʿziya (Arab.). An expression of condolence, but particularly the 'passion plays' of Shīʿa Muslims. The plays focus on the death of *al-Ḥusain at *Karbalā', but they include figures from the earlier (biblical) history who bear witness that the sufferings of Ḥusain are greater than their own. The redemptive power of his martyrdom is effected through his intercession. At the end of one version of the play, *Jibrīl gives to Ḥusain, through Muḥammad, the key of *paradise by means of intercession. Muḥammad says: 'I hand you this key of intercession: go and deliver from the flames every one who has shed but a single tear for your suffering.' The rescued sinners give thanks as they enter paradise: 'We were thorns and thistles, but are now made cedars, owing to his merciful intercession.'

M. Ayoub, *Redemptive Suffering in Islam* (1978); P. Chelkowski (ed.), *Taʿziyeh: Ritual and Drama in Iran* (1979); L. Pelly, *The Miracle Play of Hasan and Husain* (1879, 1970).

Te (Chin., 'power', 'virtue'). The means in Chinese thought, and especially in Taoism, through which the *Tao becomes manifest and actualized. The underlying character is made up of three elements, moving ahead, the eye, and 'heart-and-mind'. Philologically this suggests an underlying sense of a self-aware arising and disposition in a particular direction; but it may also include the sense of going in a straight direction. Te is thus the making particular of the potency of Tao, and is the inherent nature or quality which makes a thing what it is and what it ought to be: 'Tao is the opening out and arraying of Te: the process of living and growing is the radiating of Te' (*Chuang Tzu*); 'Tao engenders them, Te nourishes and rears them' (*Tao-te-ching*). If Te applies Tao consistently, any distinction between the two disappears, since Te *is* Tao as it unfolds. The 'good person' (*chen jen) is thus one who understands Tao and works to transform things in that true direction. In Confucianism, Te is the quality possessed by wise and civilized people who are a model to their fellow-citizens. For Confucius, it was the moral power on which he relied in times of personal threat or political danger.

Tea ceremony (Zen ceremony to overcome ordinary consciousness): see CHADŌ.

Teacher of Righteousness. The title given to the organizer of a Jewish sect in some of the documents of *Qumran. The name appears in the **Zadokite Fragments* and in various Qumran commentaries on books of the Bible. According to the *Zadokite Fragments*, God raised up for the *remnant of the people 'a Teacher of Righteousness to direct them in the way of his heart', and he is distinguished from a future *messiah who 'stands up from *Aaron and from *Israel'. The biblical commentaries indicate that the Teacher was a *priest who 'suffered iniquity' from the hand of 'a wicked priest'. Attempts have been made to identify the Teacher, and possible candidates have included *Ezra, Onias III (the last Zadokite *high priest), Judah b. Jedidiah (a *sage martyred by Alexander Jannai), or Menaḥem b. Judah (killed by the captain of the *Temple in 66 CE).

F. F. Bruce, *The Teacher of Righteousness in the Qumran Texts* (1957).

Tebah (reading platform in Jewish synagogue): see ALMEMAR.

Te Deum. A Latin hymn to the Father and the Son, in rhythmical prose, beginning *Te Deum laudamus* ('We praise thee, O God'). The Te Deum has often been set to music for use at public occasions of thanksgiving, and it forms a central part of *mattins and morning prayer in *Roman Catholicism and *Anglicanism. According to tradition, it was a spontaneous composition of *Ambrose and *Augustine, who sang it antiphonally on the occasion of the baptism of Augustine by Ambrose. In fact, it is evidently a composition of at least three parts, only loosely connected.

Tefillah (Heb., prayer). The Jewish *'Amidah prayer; also (for the *Sephardim), the *Prayer Book. Tefillah is also one of many terms (but the most common in the Bible) for prayer in general. The Hebrew root means 'to think, entreat, judge, intercede', and the reflexive means 'to judge oneself', and 'to pray'. Prayer in the Bible is both individual and corporate, with the *Psalms containing both as well as being embedded in *Temple and sanctuary ritual (S. Mowinckel, *The Psalms in Israel's Worship*, 1951; tr. 1962, offered a pioneering study). The destruction of the second Temple accelerated the development of regular liturgical prayer, as a counterpart to the vanished Temple worship and sacrifices—it was known as *avodah she-ba-lev*, 'the service/ worship of the heart' (*B.Ta'an*. 2a). With a strong emphasis on *blessings and *benedictions, Jewish prayer eventually (*c*.8th/9th cent. CE) led to the compilation of prayer books. The risk of formalism (despite reiterated reminders that prayer, if it is not to be empty, must be accompanied by devotion and right intention, *iyyun tefillah*, *B.Shab*. 127a) led to the more emotional and freer styles of prayer returning, especially among the Ḥasidim (see L. Jacobs, *Hasidic Prayer*, 1993). If possible, Jews should pray facing in the direction of Jerusalem (as King *Solomon anticipated, 1 Kings 8. 30, 35; 2 Chronicles 6. 21, 26). Muḥammad initially followed this custom as well (see QIBLA).

Tefillat tal (Jewish prayer): see DEW, PRAYER FOR.

Tefillin. Jewish phylacteries. According to Exodus 13. 1–10, 11–16; Deuteronomy 6. 4–9 and 11. 13–21, a *Jew must bind 'these words for a sign upon your hand and a frontlet between your eyes'. This commandment is fulfilled by binding two small leather boxes containing these scriptural passages around the head and left arm by means of leather straps. This practice is first mentioned in the *Letter of *Aristeas*; it is alluded to in the New Testament (Matthew 23. 5) and the *rabbis believed the custom was of ancient origin (*B.Sanh*. 92b); fragments of tefillin were found at *Qumran, but with variations in the order and addition to the four paragraphs. Although ancient, however, the wearing of tefillin is not specified (although it forms one of the Minor Tractates of the Talmud) as a literal commandment in the *written law and is not observed by the *Samaritans. The order and manner of laying tefillin is precisely laid down, although the *Ashkenazim wind the arm straps anticlockwise while the *Sephardim wind clockwise. The *Talmud stresses the importance of the duty—even God puts on phylacteries (*B.Ber*. 6a). The duty begins at the age of 13 and should be performed every weekday. As a positive time-bound commandment, women are exempt, though the rabbis taught that 'Michal the daughter of *Saul wore tefillin and the *sages did not protest' (*B.Er*. 96a); consequently, the wearing of tefillin has been made a mark of Jewish feminism.

A. Cowen, *Tefillin* (1960).

Teg(h) Bahādur, Gurū (1621–75 CE). Ninth Sikh *Gurū, poet and *martyr. Tyāg Mal, youngest son of Gurū *Hargobind and Nānakī, was born in *Amritsar and earned the name Tegh Bahādur, meaning 'hero of the sworḍ'. He married Gūjarī and, on his father's death went with his wife and mother to Bakālā where he lived quietly.

Since the dying Gurū *Har Krishan had indicated that his successor would be an older man from Bakālā, twenty-two local *Soḍhīs claimed the succession. According to tradition, Tegh Bahādur's gurūship was discovered and proclaimed by Makhaṇ Shāh Labāṇā, a merchant, who had vowed 500 gold coins to the Gurū if he escaped shipwreck. On reaching Bakālā he gave a few coins to each claimant. When finally he met Tegh Bahādur and made a similar offering to him, the latter remonstrated, 'You promised 500 coins', so revealing his supernatural insight.

*Dhīr Mal, *Rām Rāi, and other Soḍhīs and their supporters harassed the Gurū, and the *masands refused him admission to the *Harimandir, Amritsar. Tegh Bahādur showed no resentment. In 1665 he founded *Ananḍpur, but, when harassment continued, he travelled eastward with his wife and mother, via Āgrā, Allāhabād, Banāras, and Gāyā, to Paṭnā. Here he left Nānakī and Gūjarī who later gave birth to Gobind Rāi, the future Gurū *Gobind Siṅgh. Meanwhile Tegh Bahādur travelled through Bengal to Āssām where he achieved a peaceful settlement between Auraṅgzeb's emissary and the rebel king of Kāmrūp.

The Gurū returned to Paṭnā, and then went to the *Pañjāb, which was troubled by Auraṅgzeb's persecution of non-Muslims. His family subsequently rejoined him in Ananḍpur. Here Kashmīrī *panḍits, prime targets of the imperial campaign of conversion, begged the Gurū to protect their Hindu faith. Encouraged, reputedly, by his young son, he told the panḍits to assure Auraṅgzeb that if Tegh Bahādur became a Muslim all would follow suit. The Gurū journeyed slowly towards Delhi and was arrested in Āgrā. With five Sikhs he was escorted to Delhi, where he chose torture and death rather than

Islam or the performance of miracles. He symbolically appointed the absent Gobind Rāi his successor.

On 11 Nov. 1675 he was beheaded on the site of the present *Sīs Gañj *gurdwārā. A follower rescued his body for cremation in *Rakāb Gañj. His head was cremated in Anaṇḍpur. During his captivity Tegh Bahādur composed over fifty *hymns and *śaloks, all included in the *Ādi Granth by Gurū Gobind Siṅgh. These verses exhort freedom from bondage to the transitory world and praise of God, the only support in trouble.

Teheran (founding of as capital): see AL-MAJLISĪ.

Teilhard de Chardin, Pierre (1881–1955). French *Jesuit palaeontologist and theologian. He entered the Society of Jesus in 1899 and was ordained in 1911. He began his doctoral thesis in 1912, but did not present it at the Sorbonne until 1922. He briefly taught geology in Paris before going to China in 1923, where he collaborated in the discovery of Sinanthropus, and from where he travelled widely in Asia. In 1946 he returned to France, but in 1951 became a fellow of the Wenner-Gren Foundation for Anthropological Research, went to New York, and remained there, apart from two expeditions to Africa, until his death. His theories on the origin and development of humanity, first privately circulated among his fellow Jesuits, but later published, attracted a good deal of attention, especially *The Phenomenon of Man* and *Le Milieu divin*. He argued that the stuff of which the universe is formed increases in complexity as it evolves, and likewise increases in consciousness. Humanity is one peak in this process, which moves through ever more closely knit social relationships and integration of consciousness towards the Omega Point. This, theologically, he identified with *Christ. Some of his theory especially as it related to the problem of *evil and *original sin, gave rise to anxiety in the *Roman Catholic Church, and in 1962 the *Holy Office gave a warning that his works had to be read with caution; they were never formally condemned.

C. Cuénot, *Teilhard de Chardin* (1965).

Teishin (Zen poet): see RYŌKAN DAIGU.

Teisho (Jap., 'presentation'). The presentation of Zen realization by a Zen master (*rōshi) during a period of *sesshin. The offering, usually based on a *kōan or *sūtra passage, is made to the *buddha. It is not an address to the assembled company, but a return of insight to its source.

Tejas (Skt.). Fire, energy, majesty, authority, in Hinduism. It may be of the gods, but can also be a visible aura surrounding a spiritual master, or one who is meditating.

Tekiden (Jap.). 'Authorized transmission' in Zen Buddhism of the *buddha-dharma from a master to his pupil (cf. HASSU), confirmed by the seal of recognition (*inka-shōmei).

Telakhon (Karen, 'fruit of wisdom'). A Buddhist-influenced *millennial movement among the Karen of Burma, founded in the mid-19th cent. by Con Yu. Their mythology speaks of a withdrawn high god, Ywa, whose offer of a Golden Book of knowledge and power was ignored by their ancestors; the millennium, with freedom from British and later Burmese oppression, would arrive when the Book was restored by the Karen's white younger brothers, and in preparation animal sacrifice was banned and a strict ethic adopted. In the early 1960s American missionaries brought vernacular *Bibles from W. Thailand, expectations ran high on both sides, and membership increased to some 10,000, but the Bible was rejected as not unveiling the mysteries of Western knowledge or being the true Golden Book. There have since been armed clashes with the Burmese government but some *rapprochement* with Christian missions.

Teleological argument. A type of argument for God's existence starting from signs of order or purpose in the world; also known as the Argument from Design and the Physico-Theological Argument. St Thomas *Aquinas' Fifth Way (*Summa Theologiae*, 1a, ii. 3) is an example of such an argument: he notes that things lacking knowledge, e.g. natural bodies, act for an end, since they act in the same way to obtain the best result; but things lacking knowledge cannot move towards an end unless directed by some being endowed with knowledge and intelligence, as an arrow is directed by an archer. Therefore, he concludes, natural beings are directed to their end by an intelligent being, God.

David Hume criticized such arguments in his *Dialogues on Natural Religion* (1779), contending that they depend on drawing an analogy between the universe and human artefacts; but such an analogy is at best partial, and in any case other analogies (e.g. that of a vegetable) are available. Despite his criticisms, and those of Kant and later philosophers, other versions of the argument have been propounded subsequently, e.g. by W. Paley (*Natural Theology*, 1802), F. R. Tennant (*Philosophical Theology*, 1928, 1930), and R. Swinburne (*The Existence of God*, 1979).

Templars or **Knights Templar.** The Poor Knights of Christ and of the Temple of Solomon. They were founded in 1118 by Hugh de Payens to protect pilgrims in the Holy Land. They were housed originally near the site of Solomon's Temple in Jerusalem, and were given a formal 'rule' in 1128. Their property (especially in the form of castles) and wealth grew rapidly—which led to their downfall after the loss of the Holy Land. They resisted an attempt to merge them with the Hospitallers (known from 1530 as the Knights of Malta, founded to provide hospitality for pilgrims, but adding to this the care of the sick), but could not withstand an assault from the king of France (and the *Inquisition), and they were suppressed in 1312.

Temple

Judaism (also Temple Mount) The central place of Jewish worship in ancient times. The first Temple was built in *Jerusalem by King *Solomon. The construction involved 30,000 Israelites and 150,000 *Canaanites (1 Kings 5. 27, 32; 2 Chronicles 2. 16) and it was dedicated in a ceremony lasting fourteen days (1 Kings 8. 65). By, or during, the time of King *Josiah, the Temple was established as the only *sanctuary for the Jewish people. It was destroyed by King Nebuchadnezzar of Babylon in 586 BCE, and the fast of 9 *Av was instituted to commemorate the event. Solomon's Temple performed the same function as the *Tabernacle: it was primarily built to house the *Ark of the Covenant in the inmost room, the *Holy of Holies. It was the only legitimate place for *sacrifice but (see SAMARITANS); it was the site of public assembly, particularly at the *pilgrim festivals, and there the *Levites sang regular praise to God. It was rebuilt after the return from *exile under the leadership of *Zerubbabel (Haggai 2) and was greatly enlarged and improved by King Herod the Great (1st cent. BCE). The *Mishnah describes the structure ('He who has not seen the Temple of Herod has never in his life seen a beautiful building', *BBB* 4a); the account of *Josephus, in his *Antiquities* and *Jewish Wars*, and archaeological excavations have added to our knowledge. Within the walls lay the Temple Court open even to *gentiles; at the east end beyond the Gate Beautiful was the Court of Women which lay inside the consecrated area. Beyond this lay the Court of the Israelites, open to all male Jews, from which the sacrifices performed on the *altar in the Court of Priests could be viewed. Up further steps was the Temple proper, consisting of the porch, the *sanctuary which was furnished with the altar of incense, the table of *shewbread, and the golden *menorah, and finally the Holy of Holies. Temple ritual is described in the Mishnaic tractates, *Tamid*, *Middot*, and *Yoma*. The building was destroyed by the Romans (again on 9 Av) in the siege of Jerusalem in 70 CE, and reliefs of soldiers plundering the sacred vessels can be seen on the Arch of Titus in Rome. The only remaining part was the Western Wall on the edge of Temple Mount (*Wailing Wall). The Mount is traditionally identified as the site of the *'Akeda and has a special status in the *halakhah. Because only the ritually pure may enter the area and there are no ashes of the *red heifer remaining to effect purification, entrance is forbidden to the observant Jew. When Jerusalem was made a single city once more, in 1967, the Israeli government decided to ban Jewish worship in any case on the Temple Mount, and its administration was undertaken by a Muslim religious council (*waqf). This was in recognition of the fact that two major religious buildings had been constructed (and in part taken over) by Muslims, the al-Aqṣa mosque and the Dome of the Rock (see further JERUSALEM). The Temple Mount is known in Islam as al-Ḥaram ash-Sharīf (the noble sanctuary).

T. A. Busink, *Der Tempel von Jerusalem* ... (1970–80); M. Haran, *Temples and Temple Service in Ancient Israel* (1978).

Hinduism See ART.

Jainism Although there has been occasional dissent among Jains (e.g. the Terapanth), the majority of Jains have regarded the building of temples and the revering of the fordmakers in them as meritorious; and they would describe themselves as *murtipujakas*, 'image-worshippers'. Jain temples are a reflection of the fifty-two temples on the island of Nandiśvara, which have always been in existence, which house the perfect images of the fordmakers, and which are available to the gods for them to pay homage. Jain temples reflect early descriptions of the first preaching hall of *Mahāvīra, and usually include a tower said to represent Jain *cosmography, but perhaps absorbed from Mount *Meru as the *axis mundi.

Japanese Religion (Jap., *tera, ji*) Centres for institutionalized Buddhist practice in Japan. Japanese Buddhist temples, both architecturally and religiously, were heavily influenced initially (6th–8th cents. CE) by the Chinese and Korean temple systems. Later, Japan adopted these systems to their own practices and developing sectarian movements. Temples are often connected to monasteries, and thus the distinction between temple and monastery in Japan is not always clear—though in conjunction with monasteries, temples serve additional functions.

Temples generally belong to one or another of the many sects of Japanese Buddhism, including some of the Buddhist '*new religions' of Japan. As such, they represent Japanese Buddhism in its sectarian and institutionalized form. At the heart of most temples is the enshrined figure of some particular *buddha, *bodhisattva, saint, or historical founder which gives that temple its unique religious character and/or establishes its connection to some particular sect. The primary function of the vast majority of these temples, however, is to serve various religious needs of the laity connected to that temple—especially, but certainly not exclusively, in the area of funeral and memorial rituals.

Temple, William (1881–1944). Christian *archbishop of Canterbury, prominent worker for social and ecumenical ends. He was the son of Frederick Temple, archbishop of Canterbury, 1896–1902. He was fellow of Queen's College, Oxford, 1904–10, and headmaster of Repton (an English public school), 1910–14. He was ordained in 1910, retaining reflective doubts which he explored in subsequent works, *Mens Creatrix* (1917), *Christus Veritas* (1924), and *Nature, Man and God* (1934). His thought was imbued with the Oxford neo-Hegelianism of his youth, seeing the purposeful process of the universe leading to the central event of the *incarnation, where the highest possibility of the union of matter, life, mind, and spirit is displayed—and enacted: 'We have been led by the argument to a view of the universe which requires for its confirmation a divine act in the midst of history. We have found that God is such as to act in a special way if occasion demand; we have found an occasion which demands such an act.' He envisaged in the universe a series of 'superventions', whereby the emergent condition depends on that which it supervenes and does not destroy it, yet passes beyond it:

> When Life supervenes upon Matter, it does not indeed lead to any contradiction of the 'laws' of physical chemistry, but it takes direction of the physico-chemical system. . . . So when Mind supervenes upon the living organism, it takes direction and becomes the cause of the agent's conduct. We shall expect, therefore, to find that when God supervenes upon humanity, we do not find a human being taken into fellowship with God, but God acting through the conditions supplied by humanity. And this is the Christian experience of Jesus Christ.

Yet his academic reflection fell away in importance compared to his commitment to the application of his strongly incarnational belief. His progress in the Church (canon of Westminster, bishop of Manchester 1921, archbishop of York 1929, archbishop of Canterbury 1942) enabled him to set in motion or influence organizations in the direction of a gospel applied to society—e.g. COPEC (the Conference on Christian Politics, Economics and Citizenship), the Workers' Educational Association, Faith and Order. He sought 'middle axioms', i.e. statements derived from theology, taking seriously the complexities of human situations, which would nevertheless offer working guidelines. His death registered as a national and indeed international shock, beyond the boundaries of the Church; and although his views have (inevitably) come to seem simplistic, they nevertheless showed a practical commitment to the command of Christ to give priority to the poor. In an establishment style, he was one of the first of the *liberation theologians.

F. A. Iremonger, *William Temple . . .* (1948).

Temple of Heaven. The Hall of Annual Prayers in Bei-jing (Peking), where the 'Sons of Heaven', the Chinese emperors, received the Mandate of Heaven (*t'ien-ming) to rule. It contains surrounding halls of prayer for good harvests, peace, etc. It goes back to the Ming dynasty (1368–1661), and is built in a spacious park outside the (former) Forbidden City. An annual sacrifice of burnt offerings was performed here by the emperor, at the time of the winter solstice.

Temple Scroll. Scroll of the Jewish *Qumran sect. The *Temple Scroll* was among those found in the *Dead Sea collection and dates from the end of the 2nd cent. BCE. It includes *halakhot on ritual *purity and impurity, rules for the celebration of the *festivals, the commandment to build the *Temple (this supposedly is the missing instruction mentioned in 1 Chronicles 28. 11 ff.) and statutes concerning the king's bodyguard. It is now housed in the Shrine of the Book in Jerusalem.

Y. Yadin in D. N. Freedman and J. C. Greenfield (eds.), *New Directions in Biblical Archaeology* (1969).

Temptation of Christ. An episode in the gospels (Mark 1. 13; Matthew 4. 1–11; Luke 4. 1–13) in which Jesus after his *baptism is tempted by the *devil in the wilderness. Matthew and Luke describe these temptations: to use his power as Son of God to satisfy his hunger (turn stones into bread); to perform a spectacular miracle (cast himself down from a pinnacle of the Temple); and to obtain from the devil power over the whole world. It is a matter of Christian faith that Christ was tempted 'as we are, yet without sin' (Hebrews 4. 15). The *fathers understood the story as a recapitulation by *typology of *Adam's temptation, and as a link to Jesus' coming *passion. The story is a usual subject of meditation in *Lent.

Tenchi kane no kami (parent Spirit of the Universe): see KONKŌ-KYŌ.

Ten Commandments. The Decalogue, the ten laws proclaimed by God to *Moses as the representative of the Jewish people. The Ten Commandments are recorded in Exodus 20. 2–14 and Deuteronomy 5. 6–18. They were recorded on the *tablets of stone which were later broken when Moses found the Israelites worshipping the *golden calf. After returning up Mount *Sinai, he inscribed a second set which were kept in the *Ark of the Covenant. The Commandments enjoin worshipping one God only, keeping the *Sabbath day and honouring parents, and they forbid *idolatry, making graven images, theft, murder, adultery, false witness, and covetousness.

W. Harrelson, *The Ten Commandments and Human Rights* (1980); A. Phillips, *Ancient Israel's Criminal Law: A New Approach to the Decalogue* (1970); J. J. Stamm and M. E. Andrew, *The Ten Commandments in Recent Research* (1967).

Tendai Shū (Chin., *t'ien-t'ai*). An academic school of Buddhism established in the 6th cent. CE, in China by *Chih-i on T'ian-t'ai Shan ('Heavenly Terrace Mountain'), and introduced to Japan in the 9th cent. by the Japanese monk *Saichō.

Sometimes called the Lotus school (i.e. Hokke-shū, from the Jap. for *Lotus Sūtra*, *Hokekyo*), Tendai evolved as a distinctively Chinese interpretation of the enormous variety of Indian Buddhist *sūtras available in Chinese translation by the 6th cent. Chih-i developed a comprehensive synthesis of this literature by arranging them chronologically into five periods of the *Buddha's career, four methods of teaching, and four types of doctrine. Although eclectic in his interpretation of Buddhist teaching and practice, Chih-i placed the **Lotus Sūtra* at the apex of the Buddha's *dharma, emphasized the unity of relative truth and absolute truth in his doctrine of 'threefold truth', and elaborated the doctrine of interdependence in 'three thousand realms in one instant of consciousness'.

In 788 a Japanese Buddhist monk named *Saichō (Dengyō Daishi, 766–822) established a small temple NW of *Kyōto on Mount Hiei. When the capital was moved to Kyōto by Emperor Kammu, Saichō was commissioned to study in China and return with a form of Buddhism suitable for the location of the new capital. Saichō studied Tendai in China during the year 804, and after his return to Japan introduced it in his temple, Enryaku-ji, on Mount Hiei. With the emperor's approval he ordained 100 disciples in 807. The traditional Tendai synthesis of Buddhist teaching and practice was maintained by Saichō, but he also widened this tradition by introducing a number of doctrines and practices of the esoteric tradition of Buddhism, known in Japanese as *Shingon or 'True Word', which was being taught by his contemporary *Kūkai on Mount Kōya. Later, especially under his successor *Ennin, the esoteric tradition of Buddhism came to dominate Japanese Tendai even though Chinese T'ien-t'ai maintained its distance from it. A further synthesis of Japanese Tendai occurred when attempts were made to include Shinto beliefs and practices under the name *ichijitsu shintō* ('One-truth Shinto').

The Tendai school is also of major historical importance since it was, because of its synthesis of the major forms of Buddhist teaching and practice, the source of the four 12th-cent. 'Kamakura schools' of Japanese Buddhism. *Hōnen (1133–1212) the founder of Jōdo Shū (*Pure Land school), *Shinran (1173–1262) the founder of *Jōdo Shinshū (True Pure Land school), *Eisai (1141–1215) the founder of Japanese *Rinzai Zen, *Dōgen (1200–53) the founder of Japanese *Sōtō Zen, and *Nichiren (1222–82) the founder of the Nichiren school were all trained at Enryaku-ji. In the 10th cent., disputes between successors of Ennin and Enchin (814–91) led to two rival Tendai centres on Mount Hiei, with the Jimon-shū eventually setting up the Onjoji temple as its centre. A further schism in the 15th cent. was produced by Shinsei (1443–95), who introduced Pure Land elements and founded Tendai Shinsei-shū as a result. In recent years Tendai has looked for a revival through the *Ichigū o terasu undō* ('Brighten a corner') movement, which has sought to popularize Saichō's teaching, but Tendai remains small in comparison with other sects such as Nichiren or *Zen.

See Index, Tendai.

Ten Days of Penitence (period of repentance; Jewish Calendar): see PENITENCE.

Tenebrae. The special form of *mattins and *lauds for the last three days of *Holy Week. Until 1955 it was said by anticipation on the preceding evenings, and the name (Lat., 'darkness') comes from the practice of extinguishing fifteen candles, one at a time, during the service. The 1971 *Breviary retains some of the texts in the offices for the mornings of *Good Friday and Holy Saturday.

Tenjō tenge yuiga dokuson (Jap.). 'Above heaven, under heaven, I alone am worthy of honour', a statement which Zen Buddhists believe was made by the *Buddha Śākyamuni after his enlightenment. Far from being self-aggrandizing, it is a subtle statement of the realization that all appearances in the universe share the same buddha-nature (*busshō) and are equally empty of self (*śunyatā).

Teṉkaḷai and **Vaṭakaḷai.** The two rival religious movements within *Śrī-Vaiṣṇavism. In origin, this division goes back to different theological positions, taken by *Vedāntadeśika in relation to the teachings of Piḷḷai *Lokācārya, about the nature of *prapatti, *Lakṣmī, and divine grace. The former argued that the traditions inherited from the *Āḻvārs and *Rāmānuja had to be regarded together (as the *ubhaya-*Vedānta*, 'the twofold Vedic heritage') and as fulfilling orthodoxy, not as cancelling it. He implicitly objected to a one-sided emphasis on a locally restricted, vernacular tradition (namely, the *Āḻvārs, as interpreted by the Lokācārya). Grace had to be 'earned' through at least a minimum of human co-operation, which must include orthodox behaviour. His opponents viewed things differently. They regarded the Āḻvār heritage as supreme and produced a vast commentarial literature on the **Nālāyira-divyaprabandham* in Tamil. Not only did they read Rāmānuja's theology into the poems, but their exegesis derived from them also the blueprint of a totally novel form of religion. The novelty lay in the assumption of the unconditional availability of grace, with two important corollaries. First, no restrictions (as through *caste, etc.) must be imposed on it; and secondly, 'orthodox behaviour' was seen as creating the delusion of being able to merit divine grace. Through the teaching and organizing of Maṇavāḷa mā-muṉi (15th cent.) the obvious social, institutional, and cultural implications of all this were actualized and given a further economic and political dimension. Central in this was the question of control over temples (and their endowments). Later developments widened the rift further. The names teṉ- and vaṭa-kaḷai themselves are significant here. Originally they may have suggested no more than a purely geographic distribution. *Teṉ*, 'south', would refer to such centres of theological learning as Kurukūr and Śrīraṅgam, and *vaṭa*, 'north', to Kāñcīpuram, Kaṭikai, Ahobilam, etc. (*kaḷai*, from Skt. *kalā*, means here 'school tradition'). This got distorted to mean that the Teṉkaḷai cultivated Tamil and the Vaṭakaḷai only Sanskrit. A scholasticism that moved even further away from the original discussion evolved during the colonial period. Primarily for legal and administrative reasons, treatises were produced in which eighteen differences between the two branches were proclaimed, in partisan manner. R. *Otto derived from this an interpretation that saw a parallel here to the Protestant–Catholic division. Less distorting is perhaps the characterization of the two movements as *marjāra-* and *kapi-mārga*, the path towards salvation symbolized by the behaviour of a cat and a monkey respectively. While the mother cat simply carries the kitten in her mouth to safety, the young monkey must hold on to the mother's neck—the human co-operation with grace. (The distinction is known more generally as jiriki/*tariki.)

The characteristic signs are a U containing a single vertical line for the Vaṭakaḷai (central line usually yellow) and the same supported on a stem for the Teṉkaḷai (central line red). Control over temples goes by *kaḷai*; similarly, there are separate monastic institutions (*maṭams*, from Skt. *maṭha*). There is no intermarriage between the followers of the two *kaḷais*.

Ten lost tribes. The Jewish tribes who disappeared from history after the Assyrian conquest of 722 BCE. According to 2 Kings 17. 6 and 18. 11, all the Jewish tribes, with the exception of Judah and Benjamin, were exiled to 'Halah and Habor by the river Gozan'. The belief in the continued existence of the tribes continued, so that *Josephus, in the 1st cent. CE, could maintain that 'the ten tribes are beyond the Euphrates till now'. The *rabbis believed they were in *exile beyond the river *Sambatyon. Various identifications have been made: David *Reuveni claimed to be connected to the tribes of Reuben, Gad, and Manasseh. The *Falashas were said to be a lost tribe, as have been the British (i.e. the British Israelites), the Japanese, the Afghans, and certain Red Indian tribes.

H. Godbey, *The Lost Tribes, a Myth* (1930).

Ten martyrs. Ten Jewish *sages martyred by the Romans. The first list of ten martyrs appears in the *midrash *Lamentations Rabbah*, and the legend was circulated particularly in mystical circles. The sources differ as to the names of the ten and it has proved impossible to match the legend to historical fact. The legend was a frequent theme for *piyyutim and was an encouragement to the Jews in times of persecution. See also KIDDUSH HA-SHEM.

Ten Ox-Herding pictures (depiction of stages of Zen progress): see JŪGYŪ(-NO)-ZU.

Ten powers of a Buddha: see DAŚABALA.

Ten precepts (undertaken by Buddhist bhikṣus): see ŚĪLA.

Tenrikyo ('Religion of Heavenly Truth'). Japanese *new religious movement, eventually classified (1908) as a Shinto sect. It derives from the revelatory experiences of Nakayama Miki (1798–1887), especially in 1838. Adherents believe in Tenri-Ō-no-Mikoto, the creator of the universe. On one plot of land, man was created. The plot, *jiba*, is the centre of the main temple, with a pillar, the axis mundi, set up on it (*kanrodai*). Adherents live in the pattern of Nakayama's life and receive special help (*fushigi na tasuke*) as they do so. In 1970, Tenrikyo withdrew from the Association of Shinto Sects, and asked to be classified by the government under 'Other Religions', on the basis of its belief that it is a world religion with a universal mission, in which activity it is vigorous. Its expectations have moved more from a materialistic to a spiritual advent.

Fukaya Tadamasa, *Fundamental Doctrines of Tenrikyo* (1973).

Tenshō Kōtai Jingūkyō, Japanese *new religious movement, founded by Kitamura Sayo (1900–67). She received a revelation that the world was about to end, and in 1945 proclaimed herself universal saviour. Her followers believed her to be the successor of the *Buddha and *Jesus. The movement is known as 'the dancing faith', because of its use of dance to induce ecstatic and trance states.

Tenshō Kōtōroku (Zen text): see KŌAN.

Ten Wings (added commentary): see I CHING; SHIH-I.

Tenzin Gyatso (current Dalai Lama): see DALAI LAMA.

Tephillin (Jewish phylacteries): see TEFILLIN.

Tera or **O-tera** (Jap.). A temple or monastery. After a name, it appears as -dera, or -ji, the Sino-Japanese way of reading the character for tera—thus, *Sōji-ji. See TEMPLE, JAPANESE.

Terapanth (Jain reforming sect): see BHIKṢU; ĀCĀRYA.

Teraphim. Household gods mentioned in the Hebrew scriptures. The teraphim appear in the story of *Jacob and Rachel (Genesis 31. 34) and of Michal and *David (1 Samuel 19. 13). Despite the prohibition against *idolatry, the household gods seem to have persisted. Teraphim were also used for divination in Judges 17. 5 and seem to have been placed in the *Temple. They were condemned and removed by *Josiah in his reform of the cult (2 Kings 23. 24).

Terefah (unfit food): see FOOD; DIETARY LAWS.

Teresa, Mother (b. 1910). Founder of the Missionaries of Charity, winner of the Templeton Prize and of the Nobel Peace Prize (1979). Born Agnes Gonxha Boyaxhiu she joined the Sisters of Loreto to work in India, where she went after a brief period in Ireland. Upon completing her noviceship in Darjeeling, she was sent to teach in Calcutta. In her spare time she worked among the very poor and the sick, and in

1948 she left the Sisters of Loreto, gained some medical knowledge, and returned to Calcutta to found her order. Her first postulant, a former pupil, entered the order in 1949. Her nuns, in their distinctive sari-like habit, are now to be found all over the world, working with the poorest in society. Mother Teresa became also a constant campaigner against both artificial birth control and abortion.

Teresa of Avila (1515–82). Spanish *Carmelite nun and mystic, canonized in 1622 and made a Doctor of the Church in 1970. She entered the Carmelite convent of the Incarnation at Avila in 1535. After years of a fairly lax discipline, she was drawn to a stricter life, encouraged by her extraordinary mystical experiences. In 1562 she founded the convent of St Joseph at Avila, the first of the houses of the Carmelite Reform (called 'discalced', i.e. without shoes). Her reform met with much opposition but she found support from, amongst others, St *John of the Cross. Alongside her reform, she wrote for her nuns several books on the spiritual life, especially her *Autobiography*, the *Way of Perfection*, and the *Interior Castle*. In these she traces the spiritual life from its beginnings to union with God in the 'spiritual marriage' and illustrates its stages from her own experience. Her classification of the various stages of prayer—*recollection, quiet, union—has been enormously influential. The 'interior castle' is of access especially to those in religious orders ('I think it will be a great consolation for you, in some of your convents, to take your delight in this Interior Castle, for you can enter it and walk about in it at any time without asking leave from your superiors'), but she affirmed, in letters of spiritual encouragement, that it can be a refuge even for those in the midst of a busy life. The test of spirituality is in practice ('The Lord is among the saucepans', *Book of Foundations*).

J. Beever, *Saint Teresa of Avila* (1961); D. Green, *Gold in the Crucible* . . . (1989); E. A. Peers, *Handbook to the Life and Times of Saint Teresa* . . . (1954).

Teresa of Lisieux (1873–97). *Carmelite nun. Born into a devout middle-class family she entered the Carmel at Lisieux when only 15. Within ten years she had died of tuberculosis. Under obedience she wrote her autobiography, and fame came to Teresa through the decision of the prioress (her sister) to publish an edited version of it. She was canonized in 1925. But Teresa's real importance lies less in the 'saint' propagated by her convent, than in the extraordinarily honest following of Christ in little things—the 'little way'—revealed more clearly in the original form of her writings published in recent times. Through her honesty with herself and her refusal to put conventional limits to her love, she shows how a Christian life can share in the darkness and despair of the modern world, share even its faithlessness, and yet just there manifest love for God and the world.

Autobiography of a Saint (tr. 1958).

Terma (Tib., *gter.ma*, 'Treasure'). A class of texts in Tibetan Buddhism, of which the **Tibetan Book of the Dead* is an example, which were concealed rather than revealed upon their creation, thus requiring a discoverer (*terton* or *gter.ston*, 'treasure-finder') at a later date. The practice of burying texts was initiated during the first diffusion of Buddhism in Tibet by *Padmasambhava, who saw that the country was not then ready for his more advanced teachings. The first terma discoverer was the *Nyingma Sangye Lama (*c*.1000–80 CE), and although the practice has spread to other schools it has remained a predominantly *Nyingma activity. The timing of the first terma discovery (1040 CE), when the newer schools were ascendant during the second diffusion, may suggest a Nyingma need to affirm their links with the earlier period. Termas may be discovered as a result of either personal insight or divine assistance, and because they may be concealed in the psychic as well as the physical dimension it is also possible to discover a terma in meditation.

Terracotta Warriors (Chinese tomb figures): see SIAN.

Tertiaries (lay Christians living under a rule associated with a religious order): see THIRD ORDERS.

Terton (discoverer of text): see TERMA.

Tertullian (*c*.160–*c*.225), Christian *father. He was born in Carthage and became a Christian before 197. He was the first important Christian writer in Latin, with a long and various list of works (the chronology of which is disputed). He eventually left the *Catholic Church in favour of *Montanism. His *Apology* (*c*.197) has the typical concerns of the *apologists of the time, resting on the view that there is a natural basis for the recognition of God's action in Christ—i.e. the argument that there is 'anima naturaliter Christiana': *O testimonium animae naturaliter Christianae*, 'O witness of the soul naturally Christian'. In his *Apology* there already appears the rigorous commitment to the faith summarized as 'The blood of the martyrs is the seed of the Church'—though he wrote, 'We grow just as much as we are mown down by you, the seed is the blood of the Christians.' His moral and disciplinary works (e.g. *The Soldier's Crown*, *On Penitence*) are rigorous in their insistence on separation from pagan society. The corresponding rigour in his adherence to the faith is epitomized in his sentence, *Certum est quia impossibile est*, 'It is certain because it is impossible', (*De Carne Christi*). He considered military service to be wrong, and accepted that martyrdom might have to be embraced. His theological works are mainly polemical. The most important are *De praescriptione haereticorum* (Against Heretics, following the model of *Irenaeus), *Against *Marcion*, and *Against Praxeas* (attacking *modalism and formulating a doctrine of the *Trinity). His work *On the Soul* prepared the way for the pessimistic doctrine of the *Fall which through *Augustine came to dominate Latin theology. Tertullian's Montanist works clearly show his uncompromising rigour, e.g. *On Modesty*, written in the 220s against Pope Callistus' leniency in disciplining sexual sin.

T. D. Barnes, *Tertullian* . . . (1971).

Terumah or **terumot** (heave-offering): see TITHES.

Te-shan Hsüan-chien (Jap., Tokusan Senkan; 782–865). Ch'an/Zen master, dharma-successor (*hassu) of Lung-t'an Chung-hsin. Originally trained in the Northern school (see SOUTHERN AND NORTHERN SCHOOLS), and learned in the **Diamond Sūtra*, he was in some despair at its teaching that it may take thousands of *kalpas to attain buddhahood. Hearing of the Southern school, he set out to learn more of it, meeting an old woman on the way who sent him to Lung-t'an. Lung-t'an handed him a paper torch, and as he took it, Lung-t'an blew it out. He received immediate enlightenment. Next day, he took his commentaries on the *Diamond Sūtra* and set fire to them, saying, 'Even if we have mastered the profound teachings, we have placed only a single hair in the vastness of space.' After years of seclusion, he became abbot of Te-shan (hence his name), and taught many disciples in the style of *Ma-tsu, with much use of sticks (*shippei*, *kyosaku) and shouts (*katsu*: see HO). 'If you can speak, 30 blows. If you cannot speak, 30 blows.' He described the enlightened person much as a Taoist might: 'He has no fear of death or rebirth. He has no compulsion to attain *nirvāna or to prove enlightenment. He is just an ordinary person, who has nothing further to do.'

Teshuva (Heb., 'repentance'). The renunciation of sin, appeal for forgiveness and return to righteous living in Judaism. Repentance is an important theme in the Hebrew scriptures and is the theme of the Ten Days of *Penitence. Forgiveness depends on true repentance, and, if another person is involved, restitution must be made. Medieval Jewish writers dealt extensively with this subject, and during the modern period there have been various movements within Judaism (e.g. the *Musar movement) to encourage repentance. It is central to Jewish anthropology, which sees the two *inclinations (for good and for evil) in contest for the informed and educated decision of Jews under the guidance of *Torah. But since the inclination to evil is in itself necessary to the formation of the human world, it follows that error, fault, and sin are inevitable (quite apart from human weakness). Repentance is the constantly available 'way back': 'Great is repentance, since it turns sins into incentives to do right' (Simeon b. Lakish). This sense of *felix culpa ('happy fault') recurs often—e.g. in the **Zohar*: 'Happy are the penitent who in a flash can draw as near to the Holy One as do the righteous in many years.' But the costliness of true repentance is not overlooked: 'Repentance is pain, accompanied by the idea of oneself as cause' (Spinoza).

Testaments of the Twelve Patriarchs. A *pseudepigraphical writing relating in twelve books the message that each of the twelve sons of *Jacob gave to his descendants on his deathbed. These messages are a mixture of prophecy and ethical instruction. It is a matter of dispute whether the work was Christian in origin or Jewish (in which case the Christian passages are interpolations). If Christian it may be dated *c.*200 CE; if pre-Christian it has important links with the *Qumran community (e.g. in dualistic language), and in ethical matters is 'one of the most important sources for the understanding of Jesus' message' (D. Flusser).

Tr. in J. H. Charlesworth (ed.), *The Old Testament Pseudepigrapha*, i (1983).

Tetragrammaton (Gk., 'four lettered'). The four letters, YHWH/JHWH, of the Hebrew name for God. Traditionally the tetragrammaton is not pronounced, and in the biblical text, YHWH is read as *'Adonai' (my Lord) or 'Ha-*Shem' (the Name). The English 'Jehovah' is a vocalization of JHWH, inserting the vowels from Adonai.

Tetzel, John or **Johann** (1465–1519). *Dominican friar. Renowned as a preacher of *indulgences, he collected money for the building of St Peter's, Rome, and the purchase of Albert of Magdeburg's archbishopric. His money-raising activities at Jüterbock, claiming that appropriate payments would deliver *souls from *purgatory, were brought to the attention of *Luther who, in nearby Wittenberg, on 31 Oct. 1517, published his famous ninety-five theses attacking the indulgence traffic. In 1519 the papal *nuncio von Miltitz endeavoured to restrain Tetzel in an attempt to reconcile those who were scandalized by his eloquent commercialism.

Tevah (raised platform for Torah reading): see BIMAH.

Ṭhag (Prakrit, *ṭhagga*; Sindhī, *ṭhagu*). The anglicized Thugs or Thugees. They were devotees of the Goddess *Kālī in the form of *Bhavānī, to whom they offered the victims of their attacks, plus a third of the proceeds. Known especially for strangling victims, any method was acceptable provided blood was not shed. The date of origin is unknown, but *Hsüan-tsang reported their activity in the 7th cent. CE. Muslim Thugs developed in imitation. The British largely eliminated the Thugs by 1861, but the cult, with its affinities with left-handed *Tantra, persists. There is still a temple devoted to Bhavānī at Mirzāpur, near Varāṇasī.

Thakur Siṅgh Sandwalia (president of Sikh movement): see SIṄGH SABHĀ.

Thanawīya (Arab., *thanā*, 'reiterate, double'). Dualism, suspect in Islam because of its necessary *shirk (association of anything as equal with God). Thanawīya was linked by Muslims with Mānī (Manichaeism), Mazdak (Zoroastrianism), and ibn Daiṣān. The threat arose with the conquest of Persia.

Thanksgiving Day. A national holiday in the USA on the fourth Thursday of Nov., to give thanks for the blessings of the past year. It is traditionally derived from the settlers in Plymouth, Mass. who observed a day of thanksgiving for their first harvest in the autumn of 1621. It became a national holiday in 1863 when President Lincoln proclaimed it 'as a day of thanksgiving and praise to our beneficent Father'. The religious nature of Thanksgiving is still discernible in the language of the president's annual proclamation, and in church services on the day (though not necessarily in the dinner with turkey and pumpkin pie which is its most traditional observance). There is a similar holiday in Canada on the second Monday in Oct.

Thanksgiving Psalms. Designation of one of the *Dead Sea Scrolls. The Scroll was first published in 1955 and is now housed in the Shrine of the Book in Jerusalem. It contains a number of poems, all of which begin, 'I thank thee, O Lord', or 'Blessed be thou, O Lord'. The theology of the psalms is similar to that of the *Manual of *Discipline*, and they are reminiscent of many biblical passages. The manuscript dates from the 1st cent. BCE.

E. L. Sukenik, *Dead Sea Scrolls of the Hebrew University* (1955).

Thaumaturgy (Gk., 'wonder-working'). The power to work miracles, hence 'thaumaturgical', religions endorsing the working of miracles, especially healing. The term 'thaumaturgus' is applied in Christianity to saints who have worked many miracles, e.g. St Gregory Thaumaturgus (213–68), who was made bishop of Neocaesarea and converted virtually the whole city—the first of many miracles; he is the first person on record to whom the Virgin *Mary appeared, with St *John the Evangelist, in order to communicate a statement of doctrine on the *Trinity.

Theatre and drama. Theatre, both East and West, has been, and often still is, closely connected to religious *ritual: the development of theatre and dramatic form is equally connected to liturgy. Conversely, liturgy and ritual share much in common with theatre and drama (see e.g. R. Schechner, *Between Theater and Anthropology*, 1985; E. Barba and N. Savarese, *The Secret Art of the Performer: A Dictionary of Theatre Anthropology*, 1991). In religious theatre, as in ritual and liturgy, meaning is expressed through the body, especially through the hands, often in coded and non-verbal languages, at least as much as it is through text—indeed, frequently there is no spoken text at all—hence the links with ballet: see DANCE. These connections remain particularly obvious in E. religions. In India, there is a continuing tradition of dance, which is not simply derived from ritual but is still an expression of it. In the dance-dramas, especially those articulating the life and deeds of *Kṛṣṇa, members of the audience approach the dancer-deities with gifts in a manner approaching *bhakti. The spread of Hinduism into SE Asia led to an integration with indigenous rituals, leading to many characteristic forms of ritual drama—e.g. in Bali and in Java in the 'shadow theatre' (a type of puppet theatre, *wayang kulit* or *wayang purwa*).

In Christianity, theatre remained closely connected to ritual through liturgical drama which issued eventually in the miracle plays (dramatizations setting forth the life, miracles, and/or martyrdom of a saint), the mysteries (cycles of plays in which the story of humanity was set forth from the fall of *Lucifer to the Last Judgement; these were early connected with the feast and procession of *Corpus Christi, as at Chester by the early 14th cent., and at Beverley: the cycles of Chester, Coventry, Wakefield, and York have survived), and the moralities (dramatized allegories; early examples are *The Castle of Perseverance* and *The Summoning of Everyman*, more usually known simply as *Everyman*). In so far as these dramas elaborated on scripture and went far beyond the text, they were opposed in the Reformation (although biblically based plays were written as a substitute). One consequence was to accelerate the development of a secular theatre. Even so, religious themes continued to be important (e.g. *Faust), and a specifically Christian theatre was developed by the *Jesuits (partly in reaction to Protestant productions, but even more as a natural development of the Ignatian emphasis on the imagination of place and circumstance; the introduction of music, e.g. di Lasso's choruses for *Samson*, contributed to the development of opera and oratorio). In Spain, the *auto sacramental* was an even more direct development from the medieval morality plays, and led to the powerful transformations of the form effected by Calderón (1600–81). He wrote more than seventy *autos*, which expounded the meaning of faith, but which were devotional as well. A. A. Parker (*The Allegorical Drama of Calderón*, 1943) has called Calderón 'the dramatist of *Scholasticism in general, as *Dante was the poet of *Thomism in particular'. As theatre has become increasingly detached from its location in liturgy and ritual, so its connection with religion has depended on the outlook of the dramatist. Thus Corneille and Racine could not have written as they did without a Christian context and rootage (as Péguy observed, 'In Racine we discover our wounds, in Corneille we discover ourselves'; and R. Speaight (*The Christian Theatre*, 1960) regarded Corneille's *Polyeucte* as 'among the rare masterpieces of the Christian theatre, . . . standing on a lonely eminence'). In the 20th cent., there have been notable attempts in the theatre to explore Christian faith by dramatists who have strongly held Christian beliefs themselves, notably T. S. *Eliot and Charles Williams, and less successfully (because more obviously) Graham Greene.

See also RITUAL and DANCE; for Japan see NO DRAMA; for Shīʿa passion plays see TAʿZIYA.

I. M. Bandem and F. de Boer, *Kaja and Kelod: Balinese Dance in Transition* (1981); J. R. Brandon (ed.), *On Thrones of Gold: Three Javanese Shadow Plays* (1970); B. de Zoete and W. Spies, *Dance and Drama in Bali* (1938, 1973); O. B. Hardison, *Christian Rite and Christian Drama in the Middle Ages* (1965); C. Hooykaas, *Kama and Kala: Materials of the Shadow Theatre in Bali* (1973); I. Shekhar, *Sanskrit Drama* (1960); K. Young, *The Drama of the Medieval Church* (1933; 1967).

The Family (new religious movement): see CHILDREN OF GOD.

Theism. The doctrine that there is one transcendent, personal God who freely created all that exists out of nothing, and who preserves and governs it. He is believed to be self-existent, present everywhere, all-powerful, all-knowing, and perfectly good, and therefore worthy of human worship. His governance of the world is said to be manifested in divine providence and also, according to most theists, in occasional miraculous interventions and in revelations of his nature and purposes. Christianity, Judaism, and Islam are examples of theistic religions. Theism is nowadays distinguished from *Deism: the latter denies God's personal governance of the world, usually by ruling out the possibility of providence, miracles, and revelation. Theological and philosophical debate about theism has centred around certain divine attributes, especially omnipotence, immutability, necessary being, and eternity; and also round the status of the claimed sources of the knowledge of God, namely *natural theology, religious experience, and revelation.

The Noise (cargo-cult): see PALIAU MALOAT.

Theodicy. The justification of God, in response to the charge that the evils of the world are incompatible with his omnipotence and perfect goodness. The word was coined by *Leibniz in his *Theodicy* (1710), in which he argued that this world is the best of all possible worlds. John Hick, in his *Evil and the God of Love* (1966) claimed to discern two traditions of Christian theodicy: the *Augustinian, which stresses the role of the *Fall, seeing evil as either sin or the result of sin; and the *Irenaean, which regards evil more as a feature of an evolving universe and the result of human immaturity: the world, with its tests, becomes 'a vale of soul-making'. Both positions (though without the specific appeal to the Fall) can be found in all theistic religions. Thus in Judaism an early (biblical) understanding of suffering as a consequence of *sin ('Where you see suffering, there you see sin') gave way to views less in obvious conflict with the facts of experience. While it is accepted that the facts of suffering call in question the belief that God is both all-powerful and benevolent, the Hebrew scriptures none the less teach that suffering is an inevitable part of human existence (Genesis 3. 19). The primary explanation for this is that suffering is a punishment for sin: 'When a man sees he is being chastised let him examine his ways' (*B.Sanh.* 27b). Yet both *Abraham and *Job reproached God for inflicting undeserved suffering. Such affliction can only be justified either by a doctrine of reward and punishment in the world to come or by understanding suffering as a means of *purification. Both positions can be found in Jewish sources. The problem is particularly acute in view of the *Holocaust.

In Christianity, the understanding of theodicy is set in the new context of the cross. The cross clearly does not answer questions, but rather affirms the involvement of God in the conditions of his creation (a sufficient independence to make secondary acts of causality genuinely free and responsible), creating proleptically an ultimate victory in which people can participate now. In Islam, the control of God in creation is even more strongly affirmed. Suffering is therefore described in the *Qur'ān as a punishment for sin (e.g. 4. 80, 7. 92–4, 43. 55 f.) and as a test of faith (e.g. 2. 150 f., 3. 134, 21. 36), and is thus instrumental in the purposes of God.

In Eastern religions, the issue of theodicy is not so acute, either because the understandings of cosmogony are diffused, or because there is no belief in a God who is responsible for creation (Jains and Buddhists). For Indian religions, the understanding of *karma in any case gives more direct answers to the questions of the occurrence and distribution of suffering. For Hindus, the sense of God participating in the conquest of evil is strong (e.g. *Kṛṣṇa in **Bhagavad-gītā*).

The term 'theodicy' has received a different analysis in the work of *Weber, for whom theodicy is central in his understanding of religions. In his view, religions offer theodicies, not simply as abstract solutions to intellectual puzzles, but as programmes for action. Weber recognized the nature of the classical problem (if God is both omnipotent and all-loving, how can there be suffering in the world?), but he focused on the rather wider issue of the human experience of so much inequality—some rich, some poor, some healthy, some sick, some male, some female, etc. In *The Sociology of Religion*, he first described the classical issue ('the more the development tends toward the conception of a transcendental unitary god who is universal, the more there arises the problem of how the extraordinary power of such a god may be reconciled with the imperfection of the world that he has created and rules over'), but then moved on at once to the human experience of inequalities as the problem 'which belongs everywhere among the factors determining religious evolution and the need for salvation'. Referring to 'a questionnaire submitted to thousands of German workers', it 'disclosed the fact that their rejection of the god-idea was motivated, not by scientific arguments, but by their difficulty in reconciling the idea of providence with the injustice and imperfection of the social order'. Thus all humans experience great inequalities which carry with them much suffering, unequally distributed. Religions pour into the gaps meaning and explanation (i.e. theodicies) of which Weber discerned three pure types (in Weber's analysis, pure types are rarely found in unadulterated form, but can be discerned as characteristic, nevertheless): 'These three gave rationally satisfactory answers to the questioning for the basis of the incongruity between destiny and merit: the Indian doctrine of karma, *Zoroastrian *dualism and the *predestination decree of the *deus absconditus. These solutions are rationally closed; in pure form they are found only as exceptions.'

From the adopted theodicy of a particular religion flow social consequences which give to different societies their characteristic forms and actions (or lack of them). Thus he concluded of 'the pious Hindu and the Asiatic Buddhist':

> That these religions lack virtually any kind of social-revolutionary ethics can be explained by reference to their theodicy of rebirth, according to which the *caste system itself is eternal and absolutely just. The virtues or sins of a former life determine birth into a particular caste, and one's behaviour in the present life determines one's chances of improvement in the next rebirth.

It is an obvious defect of Weber that he had only an impressionistic knowledge of the religions with which he was dealing. Nevertheless, his extension of the concept of theodicy drew admirable attention to the dynamic consequences of theodicy and the quest for salvation (or its equivalent) in the forming of religious societies. See also EVIL.

J. W. Bowker, *Problems of Suffering in Religions of the World* (1970); J. Hick, *Evil and the God of Love* (1977); A. Plantinga, *God, Freedom and Evil* (1974); K. Surin, *Theology and the Problem of Evil* (1986); T. W. Tilley, *The Evils of Theodicy* (1991).

Theodore of Mopsuestia (*c.*350–428). Christian theologian and biblical commentator. He became bishop of Mopsuestia (in Cilicia, modern SE Turkey) in 392 and remained there the rest of his life. His writings include commentaries on most of the Bible, and a number of theological works (homilies, *On the Incarnation*, etc.). He is the chief representative of *Antiochene biblical exegesis and *Christology, avoiding allegorical interpretation. On account of his Christology, identified with *Nestorianism, he was condemned at the Council of *Constantinople in 553; as a consequence his works have mostly been lost in Greek. In the church of Persia, however, his works were preserved (in Syriac trs.) and studied, and he was venerated as 'the Interpreter'. On the basis of these Syriac versions, modern W. scholars have usually allowed that Theodore's thought is not unorthodox.

R. A. Greer, *Theodore of Mopsuestia* (1961); L. Patterson, *Theodore of Mopsuestia and Modern Thought* (1926).

Theodore of Studios, St (759–826). Christian monastic reformer. In 799 the community of which he was abbot at Saccudium, moved to the monastery of Studios at Constantinople. This monastery, founded in 463, had followed the rule of the *Acoemetae, but had become almost extinct under the *Iconoclast emperor Constantine V. Under Theodore, however, it became the centre and model of E. monasticism. It became especially famous for its school of copyists and artists, and very many of its ancient hymns are still in use in the Greek Church. During the second *Iconoclastic controversy, Theodore was exiled (813–20), but still managed to organize an effective opposition to the government's policy. He was a man of personal sanctity and strong determination, and is widely venerated in the Orthodox Church. Feast day, 11 Nov.

Theodoret (*c.*393–*c.*466). Christian bishop of Cyrrhus near *Antioch, and theologian. He was a friend and admirer of *Nestorius and became a defender of the *Antiochene Christology against *Cyril of Alexandria. He continued to oppose Cyril even after Nestorius was deposed in 431; he was himself deposed at the 'Robber Synod' of *Ephesus in 449, and reinstated at *Chalcedon only when he reluctantly anathematized Nestorius. His writings against Cyril were later condemned at the second Council of *Constantinople (553). Theodoret's other works include erudite biblical commentaries, a *Religious History* giving an account of monks and *ascetics in Syria, a church history continuing that of *Eusebius to 428, an apology *The Cure of Pagan Maladies*, and an anti-*Monophysite work *The Beggar* (i.e. his opponent, who has 'begged' his various absurd doctrines).

Theogonies. Births of gods used to give an account of the origin of the cosmos—e.g. in Hesiod, or in the primordial sacrifice of *Puruṣha in *Ṛg Veda* 10. 90. Theogonies are thus a specialized form of cosmogony.

Theologia Germanica. Anonymous 14th cent. Christian treatise on mysticism. It greatly influenced *Luther, who edited it in 1518; though *Calvin rejected it (as 'a poison from the *devil'), and Pope Paul V placed it on the *Index. Of a tendency later known as *Quietism, the work advocates absolute acceptance of God's will, looking for union for its own sake, and (as the hymn, 'My God, I love thee', puts it) 'not because | I hope for heaven thereby, | Nor yet because who love thee not | Are lost eternally'. Through the Eng. tr. of S. Winkworth (1854) it exercised a wide influence in the Eng.-speaking world. Its purpose is summarized in its conclusion: 'That we may thus deny ourselves, and forsake and renounce all things for God's sake, and give up our own wills, and die to ourselves, and live to God alone and to his will, may he help us, who gave up his will to his heavenly Father,—Jesus Christ our Lord . . .'.

Theology (Gk., *theos*, 'god', + *logos*, 'discourse'). Reflection on the nature and being of God. Initially, in Greek, the word was reserved for poets such as Hesiod and Homer who wrote about the gods. A distinction was then made between their *myth-based theology and the kind of philosophical enquiry undertaken by *Aristotle. The term is not natural to the Jewish understanding of God unfolded in scripture (though *Philo, with his Greek leanings, called *Moses *theologos*, the spokesman of God). The term was introduced by the Church fathers, but not yet as a separate discipline of human enquiry and reflection. *Theologia* means more naturally 'speaking of God', i.e. praise. The systematic organization of theology began especially with the *scholastics, as with the concern of *Aquinas to show that revealed truths were not believed unreasonably, and was taken in different (more Bible-controlled) directions by the *Protestant reformers. Theology, especially as a university discipline, and systematic theologies became increasingly valued, being, in time, broken up into different disciplines, e.g. dogmatic, doctrinal, systematic, pastoral, historical, biblical, etc. Theology thus developed as a highly coded and formal system, in which rules of appropriateness are generated within the system. Attempts to break out of the circularity (some have said sterility) of such a strongly coded system (e.g. in *liberation theology, or plural 'theologies of . . .') are unlikely to return theology to the human community of knowledge, since they themselves are evaluated from within the circle.

The same is (so far) true of individual attempts to reconnect theology with life, e.g. of K. *Rahner, or of T. F. Torrance, who saw in modern science an exemplary way in which truth is achieved or attempted, not by detachment from reality, but by a relationship to reality which evokes new attempts; thus both theology and science begin with faith, understood as a rational, intuitive, but nevertheless cognitive apprehension of what is real. 'What is real' in the case of theology is God, who gave himself in an act of grace to be known in the Word made flesh. Theology develops the methods and constructs (e.g. *creeds) appropriate to its subject-matter, but it remains integrated to the whole endeavour of human enquiry and wisdom. Outside Christianity, 'theology' is not isolated from life in the same way, though *kalām in Islam came under suspicion of leading in that direction.

See Index, Theologians, philosophers; Theology.

A. E. McGrath, *Christian Theology: An Introduction* (1994) and (ed.), *Blackwell Encyclopedia of Modern Christian Thought* (1993).

Theophany (manifestation of divinity): see HIEROPHANY.

Theosophical Society. Organization founded in New York by Mrs H. P. Blavatsky and Colonel H. S. Olcott in 1875, to derive from ancient wisdom and from the insights of evolution a world ethical code. In 1882, it moved its headquarters to India, and became the Adyar Theosophical Society. Although intended to be eclectic, it drew increasingly on Hindu resources. An important advocate of the Society was Annie Besant.

B. F. Campbell, *Ancient Wisdom Revised: A History of the Theosophical Movement* (1980).

Theotokos (Gk., 'God-bearer'). Title of the Virgin *Mary. It was used from *Origen onwards, and became both a term of devotion and a mark of accepting the divinity of Christ. In 429 it was attacked by *Nestorius and his supporters as incompatible with the full humanity of Christ, and the word *Christotokos* was proposed in its place. It was, however, upheld at the councils of *Ephesus (431) and *Chalcedon (451) and has remained an orthodox term ever since (except in the *Church of the East). The usual Latin equivalent is *Dei Genitrix*, 'Mother of God', or less usually, *Deipara*, as in Bacon's *Confession of Faith*, 'The blessed Virgin may be truly and catholicly called *Deipara*' (*c*.1600).

Thera (Pāli, 'elders'). Senior monks (*bhikṣu) in Buddhism, determined either by age or accomplishment. Therī is the female equivalent, but here determination is more often by date of entry to the community.

Thera- and ***Therī-gāthā*** (part of Buddhist Pāli canon): see KHUDDAKA NIKĀYA.

Therapeutae (Gk., 'healers'). Jewish ascetic sect. The Therapeutae are described by *Philo in his *De Vita Contemplativa*. They are believed to have lived near Alexandria, and their lifestyle resembled that of the *Essenes. Philo (who in fact contrasted them with the Essenes, since the Essenes 'pursued an active life') described them as 'the citizens of heaven and of the universe', and many scholars believe that their way of life was copied by the early monks of the Christian Church.

Theravāda (Pāli, 'teaching of the elders (of the order)'; Chin., Shang-tso-pu; Jap., Jōzabu; Korean, Sangjwabu). An early school of Buddhism, derived from *Vibhajjavādins and associated with *Sthaviras. As the major survivor of this line, the term became synonymous with Buddhism derived from, and defensive of, the *Pāli canon—in contrast to *Mahāyāna. Theravāda is the form of Buddhism in Śri Lankā and SE Asia. Mahāyāna ('Large Vehicle') calls Theravāda '*Hīnayāna', 'Small Vehicle', and this term, despite its contemptuous associations, still persists. Theravāda, though strictly inaccurate, is preferable, even though Theravāda was simply one among many early Buddhist schools.

A. Bareau, *Les Sectes bouddhiques du petit véhicule* (1955); K. L. Hazra, *History of Theravāda Buddhism in South-East Asia* (1982); R. C. Lester, *Theravada Buddhism in Southeast Asia* (1973).

Thérèse of Lisieux (Carmelite nun): see TERESA OF LISIEUX.

Therī: see THERA.

Thessalonians, Letters to the. Two epistles of *Paul and books of the New Testament. They were probably written from Corinth *c.*51 and are thus the earliest of Paul's letters (possibly excepting *Galatians). Both are concerned mainly with the *parousia of Christ. In 1 Thessalonians Paul says that the dead will rise first to meet him (4. 16). In 2 Thessalonians Paul tries to cool the Christians' feverish expectation. The genuineness of 2 Thessalonians is often denied, in which case 2. 2 and 3. 17 are seen as attempts to get the letter accepted as Paul's.

Theurgy (Gk., 'divine action'). The inducement of the direct action of God through a human agent. In contrast to black magic, which invokes power from forces opposed to God, theurgy utilizes help from angels or saints, as mediators of God's power. In *Neoplatonism, divine powers enter the soul of the mystic to make him or her superhuman, though *Plotinus himself opposed theurgists, and *Augustine accused them of 'criminal curiosity'. *Shamanism is an example of theurgy in a very general sense.

Thich Quang Duc (Vietnamese Buddhist monk): see BUDDHISM IN SOUTH-EAST ASIA.

Third eye (divine-seeing eye in Hinduism): see DYOYA-DṚṢṬI.

Third Orders. Associations of (mainly) lay Christians, who are known as tertiaries, who live under an approved rule in association with a First (male) or Second (female) religious Order. They began to emerge in about the 12th cent., but the best-known was that of St *Francis, who wrote his own Rule for a Third Order (subsequently lost), which was approved in 1221. Subsequently, some Third Order members began to live vowed lives in common, and were given the status of religious institutes, and were known as Third Orders Regular.

P. Foley, *Three Dimensional Living: A Study of Third Orders Secular* (1962).

Third Rome (Moscow): see SECOND ROME.

Thirteen principles of the faith. Principles of the Jewish faith drawn together by *Maimonides. They include the existence of God, the unity of God, the incorporality of God, the eternity of God, that God is the only hearer of prayer, that the *prophets were inspired by God, that *Moses is the supreme prophet, that the *Pentateuch was given in its entirety to Moses, that the *Torah is immutable, that God is omniscient, the reality of divine reward and punishment, that the *messiah will come and that the *dead will be raised (see RESURRECTION). These principles are printed in most editions of the Jewish *Prayer Book.

Thirty-Nine Articles. The articles of faith, designed in the 16th cent., to elucidate the particular tenets of the *Church of England, in contrast to the Catholic and reformed churches of the Continent. They were curtailed by Convocation in 1563 from the Forty-Two Articles of 1553, and were approved finally in 1571 'for the avoiding of diversities of opinions and for the establishing of consent touching true religion'. They are commonly printed at the end of the **Book of Common Prayer.* The Articles are in no sense a creed, but only statements of the *Anglican position on dogmatic questions of the 16th cent., and are expressed, generally, in broad terms. Art. 28, for example, excludes both *transubstantiation (in the sense there defined) and the *Zwinglian doctrine of the eucharist, but does not specify the sense in which the body and blood of Christ are received; cf. also Art. 17 on *predestination. Subscription to the Articles was required of all clergy, but the affirmation, that the doctrine of the Church of England as set forth in the *Book of Common Prayer* and Articles is agreeable to the Word of God, was reviewed in 1975, and the new Declaration of Assent treats them as historically significant in the development of Anglicanism.

Thirty-two marks (of a Buddha): see DVĀTRIṂŚADVARA-LAKṢANA.

Thomas, St. One of the twelve *apostles. According to John 20. 25–8 he doubted *Jesus' resurrection until Jesus appeared to him and invited him to touch his wounds. In later tradition, the *Acts of Thomas*, a 3rd-cent., ascetical, and probably *gnostic work, recounts Thomas's missionary work in India. The *Syrian 'Christians of St Thomas' in Kerala, S. India (along with some Western scholars) strongly defend this tradition as explaining the origin of their church. Feast day: 3 July in the Roman Catholic and Syrian Churches; 21 Dec. in the Church of England; 6 Oct. in the Greek Church.

The *Gospel of Thomas* is a Coptic document consisting of 114 secret sayings of Jesus to his disciples. It was among the papyri discovered at *Nag Hammadi in 1945–6, and was published in 1959. The Gk. original dates from *c.*150. The sayings are gnostic and depend mostly on the New Testament gospels, but they may include some genuine words of Jesus preserved nowhere else, e.g. 'Love your brother as your soul [i.e. self], guard him as the apple of your eye' (§ 25); 'Woe to the flesh which depends upon the soul; woe to the soul which depends upon the flesh' (§ 112; cf. § 87). This work is not to be confused with the *Infancy Gospel of Thomas*, a collection of miracle stories about the child Jesus.

Tr. of the Acts and Gospel in E. Hennecke, *New Testament Apocrypha* (1963), ii. 425–531 and (1965), i.

278–307; A. E. Medlycott, *India and the Apostle Thomas* (1905); A. C. Perumalil, *The Apostles in India* (1971).

Thomas à Kempis (*c.*1380–1471). Christian ascetical writer. Thomas Hemerken was born at Kempen, near Cologne, was educated at Deventer by the Brethren of the Common Life, and in 1399 joined the Canons Regular at Agnietenberg, near Zwolle, where he spent the rest of his life, writing, preaching, and much in demand as a spiritual director. His teaching, which was deeply influenced by the *devotio moderna* (see GROOTE, GEERT), stresses the importance of an inward devotion of love and obedience to Christ, which finds classic expression in the **Imitation of Christ*, of which he is probably the author:

> Lord, in simplicity of heart I offer myself to you this day to be your servant for ever, for obedience and for a sacrifice of perpetual praise: receive me with this holy oblation of your precious body, which I offer to you this day in the presence of angels invisibly attending, that it may be for the salvation of myself and of all your people (3. 9. 1).

Thomas Aquinas (Dominican philosopher and theologian): see AQUINAS.

Thomas Christians (Christians in India): see THOMAS, ST; UNIAT(E) CHURCHES.

Thomism. Christian philosophical theology based on the writings of St Thomas *Aquinas. Although some propositions of Aquinas were initially condemned, his system was established in the 16th cent. onwards (known as Second Thomism, but also, confusingly, as *Neo-Thomism/Neo-*Scholasticism) as the basis of Roman Catholic theology and education. This was powerfully reinforced by *Leo XIII in his *encyclical *Aeterni Patris* (1879) which gave rise to what is more properly known as Neo-Thomism. More recent writing on Aquinas has rejected the distorting lenses of the various Thomistic schools, and by returning to the text of Aquinas' works has emphasized the significant divergences between Aquinas and his commentators. (For transcendental Thomism, see RAHNER, K.)

D. Burrell, *Aquinas, God and Action* (1979) and *Knowing the Unknowable God* (1986); M.-D. Chenu, *Toward Understanding St Thomas* (1950; tr. 1964); B. Davies, *The Thought of Thomas Aquinas* (1992); E. Gilson, *The Christian Philosophy of St Thomas Aquinas* (1956).

Thread ceremony (Hindu ritual and one of the most important of the saṃskāras): see UPANAYANA.

Thread-cross (Tib., *mdos*). Implement used in the magical rites of *Tibetan religions, principally to deflect negative influences away from a person or community. The simplest form consists of two sticks bound together in the form of a cross with threads of five colours stretched over it to resemble a cobweb, but complex forms can be as much as eleven feet in height, resembling the *stūpa in shape and symbolism. The thread-cross can serve as a temporary residence for a deity in rites of 'creating good' (such as protection for travellers), but more commonly in rites of 'dispelling evil' (such as assisting a person bothered by demons); images, hair, spittle, and so forth of the person concerned are placed inside the thread-cross in the form of a *torma, and the demons are 'enticed' into the thread-cross to accept these images as a substitute, or '*scapegoat', for that person. This being achieved, the thread-cross containing the demons is carried outside the community to be abandoned or destroyed, while purification rites within the community prevent the demons' re-entry. While thread-cross rituals are used in Tibetan Buddhism, their practice in Tibet has been thought to be pre-Buddhist, and is notably prominent in *Bön funeral ceremonies (although this need not imply their origination in Bön). R. de Nebesky-Wojkowitz (*Oracles and Demons in Tibet*, 1956), has drawn attention to the finding of thread-crosses in S. Africa, S. America, Australia, and Scandinavia, as well as in several areas of India.

Three barriers kōan: see TOU-SHUAI TS'UNG-YUEH.

Three bodies (the ways in which the buddha-nature becomes apparant): see TRIKĀYA.

Three Children, Song of (apocryphal addition to Hebrew scriptures): see SONG OF THE THREE CHILDREN.

Three gems (three Vaiṣṇava texts): see PAÑCARĀTRA.

3HO (Sikh-derived movement): see HEALTHY, HAPPY, HOLY ORGANIZATION.

Three Hours' service. A Christian non-liturgical service held on *Good Friday from noon to 3 p.m., the time of Jesus' crucifixion. It usually takes the form of meditations on the *seven words from the cross. The service was instituted by the *Jesuits in 1687, and became popular in Anglican and Roman Catholic circles in the 19th cent. in Britain.

Three Jewels (Skt., *triratna*; Pāli, *tiratana*). In Buddhism, the three most precious things, *Buddha, *dharma, and *saṅgha. Taking refuge in them is the hallmark of all Buddhist practice. Since they are considered to be a unit, the translation 'Triple Jewel', though uncommon, is more appropriate.

In Taoism, see SAN-PAO. In Jainism, they are Right belief, Right knowledge, Right conduct, the path to liberation: see TATTVĀRTHA SŪTRA.

Three liberations (Skt., *vimokṣa*; Pāli, *vimokka*). A Buddhist meditation practice which concentrates on the realization that all appearances are empty of self (*śūnyatā), are without essential characteristics (*animitta*), and should be, in one's own case, detached from passion. To achieve this is to realize *nirvāna.

Three marks of existence (Pāli, *ti-lakkhaṇa*; Skt., *tri-lakṣaṇa*). In Buddhism the collective term for *anicca (impermanence), *dukkha (suffering), and *anattā (no-self). Although each comprises a topic of meditation in its own right conceptually they are interrelated: there is 'no-self' because there is 'impermanence', and because there is 'impermanence' there is 'suffering'. Reflection on the 'marks' serves to dispel illusions about the character of the world and of life. See also VIPASSANĀ.

Three Pillars of Zen. A term usually taken to refer to *dai-funshi, *dai-gidan*, and *dai-shinkon*. But it is also used more generally to refer to 'teaching, practice, and enlightenment', as in P. Kaplean's book, *The Three Pillars of Zen* (1980).

Three poisons (one of ten powers of a Buddha): see DAŚABALA.

Three refuges (basic Buddhist orientation of life): see TRIŚARAṆA.

Three-self policy (indigenizing commitment of Christian mission): see VENN, HENRY.

Three Stages School (School of Chinese Buddhism): see SAN-CHIEH-CHIAO.

Three steps (cosmic control of one of Viṣṇu's avataras): see VĀMANA.

Three vehicles (Mahāyāna account of the three stages of Buddhism): see TRIYĀNA.

Three ways. Three constitutive elements of spiritual and prayer life, associated especially with Christianity, but applied less systematically to other religions. The ways are *purgative, *illuminative, and *unitive. Although perhaps anticipated in *Origen, the Three Ways became explicit and normative from the work of *Dionysius. For *Bernard of Clairvaux, they become the threefold kiss of the Beloved; for *Catherine, they become the threefold stair of ascent to the crucified Christ.

Three weeks. Period between the Jewish fasts of 17 *Tammuz and 9 *Av (hence the Heb. name *ben ha-metsarim*, 'between the straits', from Lamentations 1. 3). The three weeks are a time of *mourning in which no music, entertainment, bathing for pleasure, new clothes, new fruit, or cutting hair should be enjoyed. Very pious Jews also abstain from meat and wine except on the *Sabbath.

Three Worlds (the constitutive levels of manifestation in the cosmos, in Indian religions): see LOKA.

Three worms (malevolent Japanese folk deities): see KŌSHIN.

Throne of God. Jewish vision of the transcendent power of God. God is described as sitting on a throne by the *prophets Micaiah (1 Kings 22. 19), *Isaiah (Isaiah 6), *Ezekiel (Ezekiel 1) and *Daniel (Daniel 7. 9). The imagery is also to be found in *Talmudic and *midrashic sources. Some mystical tracts speak of God's throne as his *'merkavah' (chariot). In the *Pentateuch, the *Ark of the Covenant is understood as the throne of God, (and in his *mercy seat). Many Jewish philosophers, such as *Saʿadiah Gaon and *Maimonides, interpreted all talk of God's throne as *allegory; e.g. Maimonides: ' "The *Heaven is my throne" means "the Heaven indicates my existence, grandeur and power." '

In Islam, the throne of God became a subject of controversy in the early years: how literally was it to be taken? The *Qur'ān speaks frequently of al-ʿArsh (e.g. 7. 54, 9. 129) and of al-Kursi (the footstool, but often taken to be a synonym of al-ʿArsh), notably in *āyat al-Kursi*, the verse of the Throne, 2. 256:

> God, there is no God but he, the living, the eternal: no slumber can seize him, nor sleep. His are all things in the heavens and the earth. Who is there that can intercede with him except by his leave? He knows what is before them and what is after them, nor shall they comprehend anything of his knowledge except what he wills. His *kursi* extends over [comprises?] the heavens and the earth, and preserving them does not weary him: he is the exalted, the mighty.

This verse is supremely one of commitment in trust to God, and is frequently written on amulets (*charms). Conflict arose because to take these verses literally would imply extreme anthropomorphism; to take them metaphorically might seem to impugn the direct meaning of the Qur'ān.

Thugs (devotees of the Goddess Kāli): see ṬHAG.

Thurible or **censer.** A metal vessel for the ceremonial burning of *incense, carried by a thurifer.

Ti (Chin.). Lord, God, especially in China as in *Shang-ti.

T'iao-ch'i (Chin., 'harmonizing the breaths'). A Taoist exercise in breathing. It is a preliminary to other exercises, e.g. *fu-ch'i, *hsing-ch'i*, *lien-ch'i, *t'ai-hsi*, *yen-ch'i. It consists in assuming the lotus position (*padmāsana), and breathing deeply, expelling contamination and calming the mind. See also CH'I.

Tibetan Book of the Dead. The name given by its first editor, W. Y. *Evans-Wentz, to the principal one of several Tibetan works referring to the afterdeath state, and which is properly called the *Bardo Todrol* (*bar.do'i.thos.grol*), Liberation by Hearing in the Intermediate State (*bardo). The *Bardo Todrol* is designed to be spoken to a person in the bardo as a guide towards enlightenment or, for one less able, as an aid to negotiating the experiences thrown up by mental construction in the journey towards rebirth. The text is an example of the *Nyingma *terma literature, supposedly written by *Padmasambhava in the 8th cent. CE, and concealed until its rediscovery by Karma Lingpa. Because Karma Lingpa had *Kagyü students, and because of ties between the Nyingma and *Sakya lineages, the *Bardo Todrol* has also passed into the Kagyü and Sakya traditions.

The doctrine of the *Bardo Todrol* does not seem to be consistent with the idea found in some Eastern traditions that there is a strongly determining connection between the nature of one's last thought and one's future birth; rather, one's last thought-moment, appearing in the Time of Death bardo, 'determines' one's future birth by offering an excellent opportunity to attain liberation, by presenting to the mind the 'clear light' (*'od.gsal*) of the Dharmakāya (see TRIKĀYA). However, if this opportunity is unrealized, as it generally is by all but the highest of yogins, then the dead person, realizing he is dead only by the pain of seeing and talking to relatives who are unaware of his presence, after three or four days will enter a second Reality bardo, but still under the delusion that he possesses a body. In this bardo the dead person confronts the world of his own mind in the form of peaceful and wrathful deities, and his experience is predominantly hallucinogenic, in terms of piercing light and sound. At this time, liberation is still possible if the dead person can recognize the nature of the brighter lights as emanations of his innate wisdom, but if this fails, the delusion of possessing a body being finally dispelled and the desire for a new body being generated, after fifteen days he follows the smoky lights into the third bardo of Seeking Rebirth.

In this bardo, the disembodied consciousness looks back over his past life and assesses it, making resolutions for achievements in the next. The symbol is given of a 'Lord of Death' who weighs one's good deeds as white pebbles, against the black pebbles of one's bad deeds, and holds up a 'mirror of karma'. Again the dead person looks back at his family, tries to comfort them yet gets no reply, and feels the pain of 'a fish threshing about on red-hot sand'. Following this, he is propelled by the winds of his previous karma towards an appropriate womb, and as the womb nears he sees visions of men and women (and animals if animal birth is signified) in copulation. Attraction to the father and jealousy of the mother will indicate female birth, while attraction to the mother and jealousy of the father will indicate male birth. Different landscapes rise up, signifying which of the six realms (see TIBETAN WHEEL OF LIFE) is being entered, but even up to the last moment the possibility, though dwindling, of liberation is present.

Because Buddhism interprets the changing states of this life as a continual succession of minor births and deaths, so that at any moment we are in an intermediate state between our past actions and our future evolution, Tibetan teachers always stress that the *Tibetan Book of the Dead* is as valuable a guide for this life as it is for the bardo.

Tr. F. Fremantle and C. Trungpa (1975).

Tibetan religion. Covering 1½ million square miles between Ladakh in the west, India, Nepal, Bhutan, and Burma in the south, Mongolia in the north and China in the east, Tibet forms the highest country in the world. It is necessary to distinguish between Tibet geographical (population six million) and Tibet political (in Chinese terms the Tibet Autonomous Region, population two million), since large parts of Amdo and Kham were assimilated into the provinces of Xinjiang, Qinghai, Gansu, Sichuan, and Yunnan following the 1950 annexation of Tibet by China. The number of Tibetan refugees in India and the West is around 150,000.

In its known history Tibet has been host to two principal religions: *Mahāyāna Buddhism (in its *Vajrayāna aspect), which is now represented by the four major schools of *Nyingma, *Sakya, *Kagyu, *Geluk, and the indigenous *Bön religion, also now divided into different schools, which has come to resemble Tibetan Buddhism in most respects.

Tibetan history separates itself from legend with King Songsten Gampo (*c.*609–50). At this time Tibet was already the centre of a powerful empire, as shown by his acceptance of a Chinese and a Nepalese wife as military dues. To these women the introduction of Buddhism is credited. Although Gampo built the *Jokhang and other temples and is said to have commissioned the creation of a Tibetan alphabet for the purpose of translating Indian Buddhist texts, it is uncertain how much he was personally touched by his wives' faith, for Tibet continued to further its empire, later capturing the Chinese capital Ch'ang-an and reaching as far west as Samarkand, forcing the Baghdad Caliph Hārūn al-Rashid (see ʿABBĀSID) to ally with China to counter Tibetan expansionism. The first Tibetan king truly to adopt Buddhism was Trisong Detsen (*c.*741–97), the 'Tibetan *Aśoka'. He built the first Tibetan monastery at *Samyé, invited the Indian missionaries *Śāntarakṣita, *Kamalaśīla, and *Padmasambhava, and ensured Tibetan Buddhism would develop along Indian rather than Chinese lines. Following his espousal of Buddhism, the Tibetan empire soon evaporated. Perhaps in response to this as much as in defence of the native Bön, King Langdarma (*c.*803–42) seized power from King Ralpacan (*c.*805–36), and began a programme of persecution of Buddhism so ruthless that historians now isolate 'first and second diffusions' of Buddhism in Tibet. Langdarma was himself assassinated by a Buddhist monk, propelling the country into two centuries of anarchy.

The 'second diffusion' began in the 11th cent. In 1012 the heirs of those monks who had escaped to the east moved into central Tibet and founded the Gyal Lukle monastery. Simultaneously, sympathetic descendants of the broken royal line which had escaped to the west encouraged translators such as Rinchen Zangpo (*c.*958–1055) to study with Indian teachers and bring back *sūtras and *tantras. The instruction to his nephew from the kidnapped King of Guge, Yeshe Öd, to spend his ransom money on inviting a *pandit from India instead of saving his life, led to the arrival in 1042 of *Atiśa, whose effect on Tibetan Buddhism has lasted to the present day. For the next nine centuries Tibetan Buddhism developed its own character, although many of its particular characteristics (the harnessing of art for religious expression, the rigorous monastic education which made it arguably the most intellectual branch of Buddhism, the tradition of unconventional *yogins developing strange powers, the importance given to oral teacher-disciple transmission) have their roots in the India of Atiśa's time. Tibetan Buddhism may have assimilated something of the native Bön tradition, but it owes far more to Indian Vajrayāna.

As can be seen from the biographies of the *Dalai and *Panchen Lamas, Tibet has paid for its own pre-Buddhist imperialism by relentless cycles of Mongolian and Chinese invasion. It had survived with its independence and religion unscathed until the 1950 annexation by China and the driving into exile of the present Dalai Lama. After that, the systematic dismantling of Tibetan religion and culture began. With upwards of 6,000 monasteries and a monkhood comprising nearly a quarter of the male population, Tibet had been dubbed the most religious society on earth. After 1959 virtually all its monasteries were destroyed, and most of its monks executed or sent to labour camps. The accusation of genocide against China by the International Commission of Jurists in 1960 had no effect in obstructing the policy, and by the time Mao died in 1976, 1.2 million Tibetans are estimated to have died as a result of the occupation.

Today, religious activity (banned completely 1966–79 along with the use of Tibetan clothing and even food bowls) remains subject to strict controls, and evidence of religious sympathy still prevents employment. A few monasteries (on tourist routes) have been renovated, and a limited a number of monks (who must be vetted by the Communist Party committees governing each monastery) are now permitted, yet monks and nuns are estimated by western human rights groups to comprise the majority of China's Tibetan political prisoners. Though monastic education is reappearing, the use of *tantric imagery remains subject to stringent restrictions (this has been likened to a ban on representing Mary in Catholicism), and it is outside Tibet that Tibetan religious currently flourish, with a particular growing appeal for Tibetan Buddhism in the West.

See Index, Tibetan religion.

J. Hopkin *et al.*, *The Buddhism of Tibet* (1984) and *The Tantric Distinction: An Introduction to Tibetan Buddhism* (1984); D. L. Snellgrove and H. E. Richardson, *A Cultural History of Tibet* (1980); G. Tucci, *The Religions of Tibet* (1980).

Tibetan Wheel of Life (*Srid.pa'i.'khor.lo*). Pictorial representation of the cycle of *saṃsāra and the single most common example of Tibetan art, valued for its clear embodiment of much Buddhist teaching. The wheel itself is held by Shinje (Skt., *Yāma), Lord of Death, to whom all life is subject, and is made to turn by the *three poisons at the centre—ignorance, desire, and hatred in the form of a pig, cockerel, and snake, usually shown chasing each other's tails. Clockwise on the outer rim are symbolized the twelve causes of existence of the *patīcca-samuppāda, and between the centre and the outer rim is the main body of the picture—the six realms of existence depicting all possibilities of birth: gods (*lha*), semi-gods (*lha.ma.yin*), animals (*byal.sang*), hell (*dmyal.ba*), hungry ghosts (*yi.dvags*), and humans (*mi*). These are to be understood as psychological as much as physical states, and we pass through them as our mental states and physical situations change. The attribution of a particular emotion to each realm reveals the wheel as a form of character typology.

The god-realm is shown at the top as a place of maximum luxury and minimal suffering, where selfish pride and unremitting sensual delights keep away any thoughts of mortality or philosophy—a hedonistic millionaire with a yacht on the Riviera may exemplify a god-realm inhabitant. To the right, the realm of the semi-gods is shown as a place of relative luxury but great discontent, due to jealousy of the gods. For semi-gods life is a continual striving for more possessions motivated by envy. Below, the animal-realm is a place of confusion due to ignorance, where beings act according to instinct and are apathetic to anything except basic needs. The hell-realm at the foot of the wheel divides into hot and cold hells, with tortures as horrific as in any other cultural depiction. It is said that the hot hells are inhabited by beings who committed crimes 'in the heat of the moment', and cold hells by more calculating criminals. Freezing to death or emotional isolation may be forms of a cold hell, while dying of dehydration in the desert or being the victim of intense anger are forms of a hot hell. The hells are essentially places of hatred, of one's situation and one's fellows. The realm of the hungry ghosts depicts beings with enormous appetites shown by their large stomachs and surrounded by food, but with mouths so small they can never get satisfaction. The dominant mood here is of greed. The final realm, the human, is marked by old age, sickness, and death, where suffering largely results from desire. Each realm is shown as under the influence of a Buddha because the *dharma can be heard in any situation, but only in the human realm can the mind be balanced enough to practise it. The wheel thus accentuates the preciousness of human birth as the only realm where one can bring to fruition the motivation to become a Buddha (*bodhicitta), which is the only way of leading beings to escape the dominion of Shinje. For the additional representations in Buddhism, see BHAVACAKRA.

T'ien. Chinese supreme source of power and order, usually translated as Heaven. Initially associated with *Shang-ti (see HEAVEN AND EARTH, SACRIFICES TO), T'ien achieved independent importance during the Chou *dynasty. T'ien was early associated with a moral life: 'When the capital of Shang was full of crime, the ruler was not distressed that Yin was ruined. . . . So T'ien determined to destroy Yin. It is not that T'ien is cruel: it is people who bring ruin on themselves' (*Chiu Kao* 11). So to live according to the way of Heaven (and for an emperor according to *T'ien-ming, the Mandate of Heaven) becomes a summary of the goal of the appropriate life, however defined. The arrival of Buddhism led to T'ien being divided into different realms (along Buddhist lines), and led also to T'ien becoming the impersonal power of nature which brings things into appearance. This was congenial to Taoists, who could relate T'ien to *Tao. It follows that T'ien bears many different meanings: it is a place where gods, spirits, and immortal beings live; it is a supreme order, or a personal Lord, governing the cosmos in all its manifestations; or it is the unity of that cosmos as a single system.

A. Lubke, *Der Himmel der Chinesen* (1931).

T'ien-chih (will of heaven): see T'UNG CHUNG-SHU.

T'ien Fang (Chin., 'cube of heaven'). Chinese Muslim name for the *kaʿba.

T'ien-ku (Chin., 'heaven's drum'). *Taoist exercise to drive off harmful influences/spirits before breathing exercises. The drumming noise is produced by finger motions on the back of the head.

T'ien-ming (Chin.). The Heavenly Mandate, a concept developed in Chou philosophy (*c.* 8th cent. BCE) to define legitimate rulers. The concept is attributed to *Mencius. It holds that an emperor lacking in virtue has forfeited the right to rule. This right is then granted from *T'ien to the conqueror who establishes the next dynasty. T'ien-ming was developed further during the Han dynasty, and thereafter it was received by emperors in the *Temple of Heaven. It could be recalled by heavenly disapproval (expressed through portents and signs), and rulers would then have to amend their rule. When Wang Mang seized power from the failing Han dynasty (9 CE), he could appeal conversely to signs of fortune: 'When an emperor receives the t'ien-ming, there must be auspicious signs . . . : he must bring into effect the five elements/agents (*wu-hsing), that he may be rewarded with good fortune. . . . So when the house of Hsin [Wang Mang] arose, its virtue and blessing were manifest . . . The spirits of earth and heaven were pleased and happy.' (*Han Shu*).

T'ien-shang Sheng-mu ('Holy Mother in Heaven'). A Chinese Goddess of seas, protector of seafarers, and patron saint of fishermen and boatpeople. She is one of the most popular divinities on the SE coast of China and its adjacent islands. Due to her efficaciousness, the Ming emperor in 1409 honoured her with the title of T'ien-fei ('Princess of Heaven'). In appreciation for her assistance for the conquest of Taiwan by the Ch'ing dynasty, its emperor in 1683 raised her to the title of T'ien-hou ('Queen of Heaven'). The common people, however, call her affectionately Ma-tsu (Lord Mother). Numerous legends developed around her which attributed her origin to a human being born in the founding year of the Sung dynasty, 960 CE, in the island of Meichou off the coastal province of Fukien. As a maiden, she was gifted with supernatural power which once enabled her to save her father and two elder brothers from being drowned at sea. She died at the age of 28 and was immediately transformed into a deity.

T'ien-shih (Chin., 'celestial master'). Title of Taoist masters, descendants of *Chang Tao-ling, of the *wu-tou-mi tao, and of its successor, *cheng-i tao. A t'ien-shih has little actual authority, though he may formally recognize the head of Taoist congregations or communities. The Western equation of t'ien-shih with 'the pope' of Taoism is wide of the mark.

T'ien-t'ai, Tiantai, or **Fa-hua-tsung** (Chin., 'School of the Celestial Platform'). School of Chinese Buddhism derived from *Chih-i (538–97), who lived on Mount T'ien-t'ai. Because of its veneration of the **Lotus Sūtra* it is also known as the Lotus school. T'ien-t'ai looked back on previous Buddhist history and sought a way of giving status to its diverse teachings, classifying the Buddha's teaching into *'five periods and eight schools', and allowing that his teaching was adapted, in successive periods of his life, to different levels of attainment (*upāya-kauśalya). The *Lotus Sūtra* contains the consummation and highest level of teaching. T'ien-t'ai approximates to the teaching of *Nāgārjuna, whom it sees as its patriarch, with three levels of truth: (i) *śūnyatā (all appearances equally devoid of characteristics and empty of self); (ii) temporary appearance of a kind sufficient to create identification; the transcendent connection of (i) and (ii) by realizing that consequently all appearance is equally constituted by the buddha-nature (*buddhatā). Thus all are capable of realizing the buddha-nature, which is enlightenment. The major practice towards that realization is *chih-kuan. T'ien-t'ai was taken to Japan by *Saichō, where it is known as *Tendai. See Index, Tendai.

D. W. Chappell (ed.), *T'ien-t'ai Buddhism* . . . (1983); L. Hurvitz, *Chih-i (538–597)* . . . (1960–2).

T'ien-t'iao shu (T'ai-p'ing text): see BOOK OF HEAVENLY COMMANDMENTS.

T'ien wang (four world protectors in Buddhism): see CELESTIAL KINGS.

Tijāniy(y)a. Muslim *Sūfī order (*ṭarīqa) founded by Abu'l-ʿAbbās Aḥmad al-Tijānī (1737–1815 (AH 1150–1230)). He was admitted to the *Qādiriy(y)a (and other orders) before founding his own order, based on Fez, having received a direct commission from a vision of the Prophet *Muḥammad in the desert. Members of the order are called *aḥbāb* ('friends'), and are forbidden to join any other *ṭarīqa (order), because their line of descent is directly from Muḥammad, and not via other teachers/guides. They use two special prayers ('Of Victory' and the 'Jewels of Perfection'), the latter of which they claim was taught by Muḥammad to their founder. They adjusted to W. rule, especially to the French, and are therefore strong in parts of Africa which were formerly French colonies.

Tikhon of Zadonsk, St (1724–83). Russian *bishop and writer on religious and spiritual matters. Born of poor parents, he studied at the seminary in Novgorod, where he later became professor, taking monastic vows in 1758. In 1761 he was consecrated bishop and in 1763 became bishop of Voronezh. He resigned in 1767 and retired to the monastery of Zadonsk from 1769. Both as bishop and recluse he displayed deep pastoral concern and devoted himself to those in need. He was an influential and prolific writer, and like many Russians in the 18th cent., was open to Western thought, especially the writings of the *Lutheran Arndt and the *Anglican bishop, Joseph Hall. He is unusual in *Orthodox spirituality in his experience and understanding of the *dark night of the soul, though otherwise he is deeply rooted in the ascetic and mystical traditions of *Russian Orthodoxy. He is believed to be the model for Zosima in Dostoevsky's *The Brothers Karamazov.*

N. Gorodetzky, *Saint Tikhon of Zadonsk* (1951).

Tikkun. Jewish *kabbalistic term for cosmic repair. Tikkun is particularly associated with the thought of Isaac *Luria.

Tikkun Ḥatsot. Jewish ceremony, mainly among *kabbalists, held at midnight in order to make repair and restitution by means of penitence (see TESHUVAH) in response to the exile (*galut) of God's presence following the destruction of the *Temple. The custom is based on an old opinion that God himself laments through the night for the destruction of the Temple and the exile of his people.

Tikkun Soferim (Heb., 'repair of the *Scribes'). Changes in the text of the Heb. *Bible. The *rabbis attribute eighteen tikkunim (pl.) to the men of the Great *Synagogue, who changed the text because it showed lack of respect to God. Thus, 'He that touches you touches the apple of my eye' (Zechariah 2. 2) was changed to 'his eye' in order to avoid it referring to God.

Tikkun tal: see DEW, PRAYER FOR.

Tilak, Bāl Gangādhar (1856–1920). Indian politician and patriot, who perceived the importance of religion in political matters, especially in relation to self-government. Thus when all political assemblies were banned by the government, Tilak started the public celebration of the festival of *Gaṇesha throughout Bombay Province, so that people could assemble in large numbers ostensibly for religious reasons, and he could preach his political philosophy with impunity.

The partition of Bengal in 1905 enabled Tilak to express his philosophy through Swarāj, Swadeshī, Boycott, and National Education. For his forthright articles in 1908, he was deported to Mandalay for six years. In prison in Mandalay he wrote his famous book *Srimad *Bhagavad Gītā Rahasya* (The True Import of the Gītā), which saw 'the religion of the Gītā, combining spiritual knowledge, devotion and action' as the foundation of India's revival. After his release in 1914 he became active in the Congress Party, and in 1916 at the Lucknow Congress, he brought about Hindu–Muslim unity in politics. Starting the Home Rule movement, he was once again in the limelight. On his sixtieth birthday the Indian people gave him a lac of rupees as a gift, which he promptly donated to the national cause.

His rigid insistence that political reforms must precede social reforms and self-government before anything else, led him to be described by Sir Valentine Chirol as 'the Father of Indian unrest'. Tilak died on 1 Aug. 1920, and because the people came in such large numbers to pay their last respects to the national hero, the cremation took place at Chowpati Beach, Bombay.

D. V. Tahmankar, *Lokamanya Tilak* (1956).

Tilaka or **puṇḍra.** Marks in Hinduism, made on the body, usually the forehead, to indicate caste or sect membership. The single spot of red, white, or yellow in the middle of the forehead is the sign of marriage. Lines of *ash (puṇḍra) are worn by male ascetics, three vertical lines in V formation for devotees of *Viṣṇu, three horizontal lines for those of *Śiva, twelve to different parts of the body for those of Śrī-*Kṛṣṇa.

Tillich, Paul Johannes Oskar (1886–1965). Christian Protestant theologian. He was born in Prussia, and after education at Berlin and Tübingen, and ordination in 1912, he served as a chaplain in the First World War, receiving the Iron Cross. After several university appointments, he was expelled by the Nazis from the University of Frankfurt and emigrated to the USA in 1933. He became professor at Union Theological Seminary until he retired in 1955. He then became professor, first at Harvard, then at Chicago. He was a major and innovative theologian, taking his point of departure from Schelling: symbols, as human creations of meaning (participating in the reality to which they point) mediate between bare objects and conventional signs. But humans are always involved existentially in questions (arising from limitation and above all from awareness of the personal ending which is to come) and predicaments (situations which seem to lead to self-defeat). These questions and predicaments have no solution (and are thus empty symbols in quest of meaning) until they are brought into relation with religious symbols which offer the meaning sought. This is the basis for the principle of correlation (J. P. Clayton, *The Concept of Correlation*, 1980) which led him to explore the theology of culture. In so far as forms of cultural expression set forth something of unconditional importance, they are expressing that which is religious. Unconditional meaning (*Gehalt*) breaks into the form of a cultural work in such a way that the content of the work can be seen to be a matter of indifference in relation to it. Tillich was later to call the unconditional meaning 'ultimate concern'. Religion then becomes the state of being unconditionally concerned about that which concerns one unconditionally. Thus 'God' is in no way a synonym for 'ultimate concern'. Indeed, that which is truly God, the God above God, cannot be spoken of except as being-itself: 'God does not exist. He is being itself beyond essence and existence. Therefore to argue that God exists is to deny him.' But 'God' enters our vocabulary because the ground of being enters our lives as the answer to the question implied by human finitude, the 'metaphysical shock' involved in realizing the existential threat of non-being. In contrast to that, finitude also brings home to us the fact that being as such is independent of us, and that the ground of the symbol (in the above sense) that God is, is the deepest possible demand for ontological concern. Theology should thus be a constant interaction with the real concerns of any particular age, since the method of correlation is otherwise a total impossibility. Tillich thus attempted to find a middle way between the two extremes which offer 'answers' with great assurance but only by ignoring the realities of the human situation—revelation combined with supernaturalism, and science combined with materialism. Theologians are handicapped by the fact that they already participate in the world of religious symbols. But they must all the more make the conscious effort to incarnate themselves in the ways in which the questions and predicaments present themselves at any time; for time is thereby not simply transition but *kairos*, opportunity: she or he must

> participate in the human predicament not only actually—as he always does—but in conscious identification. He must participate in man's finitude, which is also his own, and in its anxiety as though he had never received the revelatory answer of 'eternity'. He must participate in man's estrangement, which is also his own, and show the anxiety of guilt as though he had never received the revelatory answer of 'forgiveness'.

Not surprisingly, Tillich's ideas are communicated, not simply in technical works (e.g. *Systematic Theology*, 3 vols., 1953–63), but also in sermons (e.g. *The Shaking of the Foundations*, 1948; *The Eternal Now*, 1963) and lectures (e.g. *The Courage to Be*, 1952).

J. L. Adams, W. Pauck, and R. L. Shinn (eds.), *The Thought of Paul Tillich* (1985); C. W. Kegley (ed.), *The Theology of Paul Tillich* (1982); W. and M. Pauck, *Paul Tillich . . .* (1976).

Ti-lo-pa (989–1069). One of the eighty-four *mahāsiddhas of Indian Tantric Buddhism, and the first human teacher in the *mahāmudrā tradition. He passed on his powers and teachings to Nā-ro-pa, through whom they were transmitted into the *Kagyü school in Tibet. According to much later biographies, he was born in India as a *brahman. He was taught by the siddha Nagarjuna (not the philosopher of that name), and he became a wandering Buddhist. He eventually withdrew into meditation on the banks of the Ganges, where he encountered the celestial buddha, *Vajradhara. As a result of this, he began teaching and established his lineage.

Time. Religious understandings of time rest on human awareness of transition in daily activities, in the movement from birth to death, and in the unfailing periodicity of the sun, moon, stars, and seasons. Much of the religious understanding of time seeks to find connections between these, and to interpret their significance. Therefore, a primary source for a religion's perception of time is to be found in its *cosmology, which is generally replete with time-related characteristics. The cosmologies, though often theological in purpose, may incorporate some rather specific physical features, and provide a world-view or setting for the abiding spiritual guidance and sustenance needed by worshippers in dealing with themselves, others, nature, and time. The cosmology of the natural world is often endowed with a *soteriological meaning by using it as a metaphorical milieu for the spiritual path through time, leading to an eternal goal of enlightenment or salvation.

The cosmologies of some archaic cultures were centred on the worship of heavenly bodies such as the sun, moon, planets. The Egyptians were prototypical in finding help in dealing with lived time by worshipping the sun god, Reʿ (Ra), who rose from chaos to generate a race including the gods Isis and Osiris, and their son Horus. The myth of Isis and Osiris symbolized the renewal and continuity of the life beyond, especially for the royalty, nobility, and their train. Other pyramid-builders, for example the Mayans of Mesoamerica worshipped the planet Venus as a male god. Their intricate and remarkably accurate calendric system intermeshed the 584-day orbital cycle of Venus, the 365-day solar cycle, and the 260-day human pregnancy period. Although their calendar dates the world's beginning at 3113 BCE, the Mayan calculations can be projected back 400 million years.

While the solar year as a unit of time is of Egyptian origin, the majority of other cultures of recorded history (including Egypt itself for a certain period) observed a year that was both lunar and solar, that is 360 (twelve thirty-day months) plus five intercalary days. However, the solar year for many archaic peoples was the primary basis for the contrast between the cyclical and sequential view of time, a contrast which is evident in the studies of M. *Eliade (e.g. *The Myth of the Eternal Return*, 1971). Based on common features found in many (but not all) ancient religions throughout the world, a pattern of cyclical religious behaviour is noted among these traditions in which there is a regularly recurring need to return to some mythical beginning.

Eliade associated what is termed 'sacred' time with such cyclically governed religious times and 'profane' time with ordinary daily temporal existence. Sacred time was experienced in a ritualistic yearly repetition of some mythical creation act, often involving an hero-god who brought about creation and order by fighting and overcoming the forces of darkness, evil, and chaos.

The power of the *ritual lay in the belief of the participants that they were in reality reliving the creation act. A coincidence of the mythical event with the present moment was realized, so that profane time, regarded as essentially unreal, was erased. The result was a total sense of renewal because the accumulation of all sins, miseries, and tragedies of the past year were also erased. Thus in effect time itself was regenerated. In this way these early peoples dealt with what Eliade called the 'terror of history'.

This primitive cyclical experience can be compared with that of the early Israelites, suggesting that they began to deal with this terror from a considerably different spiritual viewpoint, namely that of faith. It was this faith that was the undercurrent nourishing the seeds for the gradual growth over many centuries of a sense of time as progressive and non-cyclical, i.e. with events related significantly to each other (e.g. *Abraham's willingness to sacrifice his only son, *Isaac, the *Exodus from Egypt). Thus they adapted the *Canaanite festivals (which celebrated gods of fertility and nature in a yearly cyclical fashion reminiscent of the archaic cultures described above) to celebrations of some of the major past events in their interaction with *Yahweh, especially those occasions on which Yahweh intervened on their behalf. The account of this succession of divine events of which none could be omitted developed into a sequential history. It spanned the entire period starting with Abraham and the succeeding *patriarchs, through the period of the *Judges, and into the period of the *Kings. The organization of this into the *Deuteronomic history was an important step in distinguishing 'times' as revealing the purposes of God.

This biblical view of time, or 'times', was later expressed primarily in terms of two Gk. words, *kairos* and *chronos*, endowing time roughly with quality and extensiveness, respectively. *Kairos* had the general purport of 'decisive moment', or 'opportunity', with powerful elements of fate and crisis. It was believed that God governed and dispensed these crucial moments, a prototype for which would be the 'Time of *Judgement'. On the other hand, chronos could mean time in general, duration, lifetime, or age. The periods of time characterizing *chronos* lacked the precision of modern time increments. Since the Bible was written as narrated history of the spiritual interaction of men and women with God, time tended to be 'measured' in humanly graspable intervals, such as a person's lifetime.

The early Christians quite naturally continued the Israelite tradition of 'event-oriented' time. With the Christians, in addition to the biblical events, there were further decisive sacred events, compressed, of course, into a much shorter period of time. By far the most crucial of these were the crucifixion and resurrection of *Jesus, but continuing with 'the *acts of the *apostles' and other early Christians, especially *Paul. Although it was not viewed so in biblical times, for Christians in later centuries and today Jesus as *Christ stands at the centre of history, BC (before Christ) and AD (*anno Domini*, in the year of the Lord) years being numbered from this time. In general, therefore, in the biblical period, time seems to have been experienced and viewed on three different levels. The first is that of human subjectivity, time as realized in the worldly and religious life of persons and communities. The second is the cosmic level based on the understanding of the order of the natural world, which exhibits a manifold diversity of temporal aspects. The third level is that realized by the divine encounter with God; it is God's eternal time.

It is the interplay of these last two levels that provides the fabric of the Judaeo-Christian, as well as the Islamic, cosmologies. They are 'one-time' cosmologies characterized by one unrepeatable beginning and evolving redemptively to a specified end, involving an *eschatology of final salvation and judgement. The eschatologies feature *inter alia* the coming of the *messiah, the second coming of Christ as described in *Revelation, and the Day of Judgement (also depicted in the *Qur'ān, e.g. sūras 73, 75, 82, and 99). Therefore, in addition to a sense of the sequential advance of time inherited from the dialogue of the early Israelites with God, these cosmologies clearly establish a sweeping spiritual view of time's progression.

It should be noted that the Israelites and early Christians saw time as embedded in an *eternity that was essentially everlasting time brought to a 'fullness of time' with God's Judgement. In contrast, *Augustine interpreted the beginning of the world as also the beginning of time. God created the natural world and time along with it. Questions as to what happened 'before' this beginning are meaningless; there was no 'before': the only antecedence is a non-temporal God.

In later centuries, the Western association of time with progress was supported by many Islamic thinkers. For example, the Shīʿa Muslim philosopher, *Mullā Ṣadrā, saw movement as the only reality in the world, and superimposed on the concept of advancing time the belief in irreversible progress to ever greater excellence or perfection; a movement backward, from the more perfect to the less perfect, is impossible. But in any case, and in general, the Muslim sense of God's purpose, in persisting with *prophets until Muḥammad, contributed to the irrepressible belief in progress, which still prevails today. For the individual, time is the arena of test and opportunity in relation to judgement: how one acts now leads to eternal consequence.

In contrast to the Western religious view of sequential and progressive time, set in a cosmology with an unrepeatable beginning and ending, the Eastern view of time exhibits a cohesive interrelation of both cyclical and non-cyclical characteristics. The cyclical is evident in Hinduism in the earliest times when the *Vedic altar was considered to be time itself, with 360 bricks for the days and 360 stones for the nights. However, the usual diversity of thought in Indian religion is already apparent in the *Sūtras and the religious philosophy of the six major schools (*darśana) of Hindu thought. All six schools do adhere to some common time-related views, perhaps because the problem of time was a central concern in the historical development of these positions. Thus the concept of repeated creation and dissolution of the universe is accepted by all schools, except the *Pūrva-Mīmāṁsā; and all, with the Upaniṣads, maintain that being cannot arise from nothing; it is uncaused, indestructible, beginningless, and endless. However, notwithstanding these common beliefs, there is much more that distinguishes the schools. For example, in the *Nyāya-Vaiśeṣika pluralistic system, time and space are but two of nine equally fundamental realities. As one of the transcendent realities, time is conceived as static; it does not flow as described by Isaac Newton. As such it cannot be directly perceived, only inferred from motion and change. Nevertheless, time is regarded as a necessary condition for change and movement. In other words changes are in time; time itself cannot change.

For the dualistic *Saṁkhya-Yoga, with two irreducible realities, *puruṣa and *prakṛti, time is considered absolutely inseparable from change and motion, which are essential characteristics of prakṛti. For the *Advaita Vedānta of *Śaṅkara, the sole source of all appearance is Brahman: beginningless, endless, changeless, ineffable, and beyond good and evil, time, space, the universe, and causation. In particular, since only the timeless Brahman is real, time itself has no absolute reality. Time, space, and the universe are seen as but transient manifestations which arise from, and return to, Brahman repetitively. In this way, Advaita Vedānta was able to integrate the vast scale of this periodic creation and destruction of the universe as described e.g. in the *Purāṇas. The smallest period of this cosmic process is the *yuga, of which there are four of progressively shorter duration, but which total 4,320,000 years, a mahāyuga. This in turn is but an increment in a succession of periods of larger and larger scale, the largest of which is the '100-year' life of *Brahmā, 311,040 billion years. Brahmā, the creator, is one of the trinity of gods, along with *Viṣṇu, the preserver, and *Śiva, the destroyer, who drive the periodicity (see also KĀLA). Linked to it are beliefs in reincarnation (*saṃsāra) and *karma: the endless periodicity of creations and annihilations is presented deliberately as a metaphor for the painful monotony of continuous deaths and rebirths if mokṣa is not achieved. With mokṣa, one is released from the ensnarements of the natural world, from the bonds of karma, and from saṃsāra.

The awesome periodicity of the Indian cosmology is often cited by Western writers as the basis for a general claim that a strictly cyclical view of time characterizes this tradition. This claim has only very limited validity. First, the yugas are not equal in duration, nor in moral content, and even if they were, it is the karmic growth and progression of the soul through this periodicity that is the essential soteriological feature. Secondly, there is a voluminous scriptural literature in the tradition that meticulously expounds an incredibly broad spectrum of time concepts, most of which are not cyclical.

Nevertheless, the concept of rhythmic repetition, but in altered form, also found its way into the cosmologies of most Buddhist schools. Again the cosmologies provide a milieu for the path to salvation. In this case it means transcending the samsaric cycle of births, deaths, and all attendant suffering, and escaping time with achievement of *nirvāna. However, the concept of time differs fundamentally in Buddhism from Brahmanism. For the Buddhist, flux and change (*anicca) characterize the world, so that change is the ultimate reality; nothing is exempt from change. The position on this doctrine is so fundamental that the world is seen not as matter undergoing change, but as change bringing about 'matter'. Inseparable from this doctrine is the equally fundamental conviction concerning the reality of the moment. All being is essentially instantaneous. Each moment is a creation entirely new, never seen in the same way before: 'The moment is change manifested' (L. Kawamura). Consistent with this is the understanding of *anātman (no-self).

However, this discussion of the reality of change and the moment must be considered as valid only in broad and general terms. Among the manifold Buddhist sects, there is a plethora of differing views involving a spectrum of subtleties and nuances concerning how cause and effect, being and non-being, and contingency and non-contingency affect the nature and reality of the moment. No one theory of cosmic time or the duration of its divisions is accepted by all schools of Buddhism, and speculation on such matters was discouraged by the Buddha as not directly relevant to the quest for liberation. Such speculation as did occur was based upon Hindu notions of endlessly recurring cycles of time, and it is from this procession of saṃsāra that the Buddhist seeks release. Thus time in itself has no eschatological significance and there is no doctrine of an apocalypse.

In Buddhism the most common theory of cosmic time takes the 'Great Aeon' (*mahākalpa*) as the largest standard unit of measurement. This extends over a complete cycle of cosmic decline and renewal, and is said to last as long as it would take to erode a great mountain by brushing against it with a piece of silken cloth once every hundred years. The Great Aeon is divided into four 'Immeasurable Aeons' (*asaṅkhyeyakalpa*) which are each in turn subdivided into twenty 'Intermediate Aeons' (*antarakalpa*). The first Immeasurable Aeon is characterized by decline and destruction, the second by chaos or emptiness, the third by renovation and renewal, and the fourth by comparative stability involving regular smaller cycles or ages (yuga) of growth and decay. We are now in the first Intermediate Aeon of the fourth Immeasurable Aeon; the remaining nineteen will each undergo a phase of increase and decrease through four ages (yuga). There will be increase through the Iron, Bronze, Silver, and Golden Ages followed by decrease in the reverse order. The twentieth and final Intermediate Aeon will be of increase only, after which a new Great Aeon will commence with an Immeasurable Aeon of destruction.

Among the Jains, time is understood as an ongoing series of revolutions of a wheel, rising up from the lowest point, and turning over the top into descent. The downward half is known as *avasarpini*, starting from the apex of a golden age, and descending through six spokes or ages to the *kaliyuga (*duhsama*) in which Jain teaching and practice disappears. The uprising is known as *utsarpini*. The cycle is driven by itself, not by the intervention of any god or other agent. During each cycle of the wheel, the *tīrthaṅkaras appear in order.

The importance of the spontaneous and the quality of the moment, as well as adherence to a cyclical cosmology, can also be found in the Taoist tradition of China, but in a generally more softened and less philosophically rigorous way. The *Tao-te Ching* conveys the sense of serene, passive rhythm in all of nature, including men and women and their interactions. The Tao is the mysterious quiet that pervades all nature. This is reflected in the Taoist cosmology, which reveals two aspects of Tao. There is an apparent aspect manifested by the order and plenitude of the universe and an absolute aspect which is the Essence from which the order arises. This Essence or Absolute Tao is often referred to as the Nameless or Non-Being.

The world and all its creatures emerge from and return to the Absolute Tao, which is ineffable and timeless. Taoist rituals involve a complex system of cosmological models in which all beings are classified according to some periodic time measure and which are metaphorical expressions of natural processes. In keeping with the general Chinese conviction that time is real, Taoist practice has as its purpose the use of time for a healing reversion to one's original natural wholeness. Salvation involves a gracious transcendence of all that is not natural and instinctive and an ultimate return to the Absolute Tao.

In this survey of the time-related views of major world religions there are two general features that are common: (i) the value placed on the living moment; (ii) the attempt to relate and reconcile lived time with some form of divine eternity, whether it is endless time, the totality of all time, or absolute timelessness. The general scientific or philosophic view of time as a chain of mathematical instants, an unrepeatable succession of experienced moments, or an irreversible continuous flow, is enriched by the religions which bestow a sacredness to each living moment; thus it is value-endowed time. Furthermore it is a goal-directed time that is set in a context of divine eternity or against a timeless transcendent background of reality with which the believer strives to find unity.

A. Aveni, *Empires of Time* (1989); J. Barr, *Biblical Words for Time* (1962); A. N. Balslev, *Time in Indian Philosophy* (1985) and with J. N. Mohanty (eds.), *Religion and Time* (1994); L. W. Fagg, *The Becoming of Time: Integrating Physical and Religious Time* (1995); J. T. Fraser (ed.), *The Voices of Time* (1981); J. T. Fraser, N. Lawrence, and D. Park (eds.), *The Study of Time III* (1978); J. Marsh, *The Fulness of Time* (1952).

Time of ignorance (period in Arabian society prior to Islam): see JĀHILĪYYA.

Timothy, St. Companion of *Paul. According to *Acts he was circumcised by Paul and accompanied him on his second missionary journey. His name is joined to Paul's at the head of seven of his letters. By tradition he was the first bishop of Ephesus and was martyred there on 22 Jan. 97.

The two Letters to Timothy are two of the *Pastoral Epistles in the New Testament, professedly by Paul to his deputy Timothy in Ephesus. In 1 Timothy, he is told to deal firmly with teachers of false doctrine, probably an incipient *gnosticism (6. 20), and is instructed in church organization and moral teaching. 2 Timothy is a more personal encouragement from Paul to Timothy. The authenticity of these letters is a matter of continuing debate.

Tinkling cymbal (allusion in Christian scripture): see CHARITY.

Tipiṭaka (Pāli, 'Triple Basket'): see BUDDHIST SCRIPTURES; TRIPIṬAKA.

Tiracchāna-kathā (Pāli, 'animal talk'). Worldly chatter or gossip, regarded by Buddhists as unseemly, especially for *bhikṣus (monks). Canonical writings define it as 'talk about kings and robbers, ministers and armies, danger and war, eating and drinking, clothes and dwellings, garlands and scents, relations, vehicles, women and heroes, street talks, talks by the well, talk about ghosts, tittle-tattle, the telling of fabulous tales about the land and sea, talk about gain and loss' (AV 128). In its place the following subjects of conversation are recommended: 'on wanting little, about contentment, seclusion, solitude, energetic striving, virtue, concentration, insight, release, and release through seeing and knowing' (ibid. 129).

Tīrath (Hindī, Pañjābī), 'Pilgrims' bathing place'. Gurū *Nānak rejected the Hindu practice of ritual bathing at tīraths (see TĪRTHA) as irrelevant to salvation. He used the imagery of tīrath to describe the nature of true, interior religion. This message is clearly expressed in his verses, e.g. Ādi Granth 687 and 789, 'The true tīrath is the divine *Nām.'

According to the *janam-sākhīs, Nānak visited the sixty-eight Hindu tīraths and *Mecca, showing pilgrims the absurdity of localizing God. Despite Nānak's insistence on inner devotion, his followers honour numerous shrines associated with the lives of the Gurūs, particularly the *Harimandir and *takhts (see DAMDAMĀ SĀHIB; HEMKUNT; KARTĀRPUR; MUKTSAR; RAKĀB GAÑJ; ŚĪŚ GAÑJ; TALVAṆḌĪ; TARN TĀRAN; AMAR DĀS), without denying Nānak's emphasis, and established a Sikh tīrath at *Goindvāl. See also ABLUTIONS.

Tirmidhī (Muslim collector of Ḥadīth): see AL-TIRMIDHĪ.

Tīrtha (Skt., 'ford', 'crossing place'). In Indian religions, a recurrent metaphor for a sacred place where one can cross over easily and safely to the far shore of liberation (*mokṣa): a *limen* or threshold. Tīrthas are the focus of devotion and *pilgrimage (tīrthayātrā) throughout India and can be found at actual fords across rivers and by tanks, lakes, and the seashore, as well as up mountains, in forests, and in cities. These thresholds between heaven and earth are charged with a power and purity which afford a spiritual crossing and are often associated with great events relating to the heroes of myth and legend or the appearances of the gods. Tīrtha can also refer to a holy person or path which affords access to the sacred. Hence the twenty-four great Jain teachers are referred to as *tīrthaṅkaras, 'builders of the ford'; see also TĪRATH.

Tīrthaṅkara (Skt., 'builders of the ford'). In Jainism, the title given to the twenty-four omniscient spiritual teachers who have displayed the way of salvation across the ocean of suffering and existence, thus a synonym for *jina. With the exception of *Ṛṣabha (first), *Pārśva (twenty-third), and *Mahāvīra (twenty-fourth), the Jain canon gives a highly stereotyped description of their lives, all coming from *kṣatrya families and most of them being born in Ayodhyā and attaining *nirvāna on Mount Sammeda. Nemi (twenty-second) is claimed to have been a contemporary and relative of *Kṛṣṇa. In the Śvetāmbara tradition (*Digambara), Malli (nineteenth) was a woman. Jain teaching stresses the fact that these were human teachers who achieved omniscience (*kevala jñāna) and subsequently *mokṣa, and that when Jains pay homage to their images, they are adoring the qualities which they are striving to acquire. Nevertheless, the Jain laity often credit them with god-like status. Jain temples today house identical images of all twenty-four tīrthaṅkaras, which are distinctively identifiable only from the totem which is commonly associated with each: (1) Ṛṣabha (bull), (2) Ajita (elephant), (3) Sambhava (horse), (4) Abhinandana (ape), (5) Sumati (heron), (6) Padmaprabha, (7) Supārśva, (8) Candraprabha, (9) Suvidhi (crocodile), (10) Śītala (wishing tree), (11) Śreyamsa (rhinoceros), (12) Vasupujya (male buffalo), (13) Vimala (boar), (14) Ananta (hawk/bear), (15) Dharma (thunderbolt), (16) Śānti (deer), (17) Kunthu (goat), (18) Ara (diagram), (19) Malli (water jar), (20) Manisuvrata (tortoise), (21) Nami (blue lotus), (22) Nemi (conch shell), (23) Pārśva (snake), (24) Mahāvīra (lion). See Index, Tirthankaras.

Tirukkuraḷ: see TIRUVAḶḶUVAR.

Tirumaṅkai-Āḻvār (Hindu poet): see ĀḺVĀRS.

Tirumuṟai ('canon' of Tamil Śaivism): see MAṆIK(K)AVACAKAR.

Tiruvaḷḷuvar (*c*.5th cent. CE). Author of a major work in Tamil, *Kuraḷ* or *Tirukkuraḷ*. The work reviews three of the four ends of human life (*puruṣhartha): *aram* (*dharma), *porul* (*artha), and *inpam* (*kāma), but not the final end of *mokṣa. The ends are not treated with the detail of the classic Indian codes (although he was clearly acquainted with Kautilya's **Artha Śastra*), and it is uncertain to which religion the author actually belonged: he has been claimed by Jains and Christians as well as Hindus. Its ethical stress and openness of manner have led to its being translated many times. It is regarded by Hindus in S. India as a sacred text, and for that reason is often called Tamilveda.

G. U. Pope, *The Sacred Kural of Tiruvalluvar-Nayanar* (1886).

Tisarana (the three fundamental Buddhist commitments): see TRIŚARAṆA; THREE JEWELS.

Tishah be-Ab(v) (day of mourning in Jewish calendar): see AV, NINTH OF.

Tithes

Judaism (Heb., *maʿaser*). Money or goods levied for the maintaining of sacral institutions. Several types of tithe are mentioned in the Hebrew scriptures. According to Numbers 18. 24, the 'first tithe' was given to the *Levites after the 'heave-offering' (*ter-*

umah) had been separated from it for the *priest. The 'second tithe' (Leviticus 27. 30–1; Deuteronomy 14. 22–6) was a tenth part of the 'first tithe'. The laws of tithes are compiled in the tractate *Ma'aserot* in the *Mishnah. During the second *Temple period, the whole of the 'first tithe' was given to the priests and the 'second tithe' was consumed by the owner himself in *Jerusalem in the first, second, fourth, and fifth year of the *Sabbatical year cycle. In the third and sixth years, a 'poor tithe' was levied instead of the 'second tithe' and this was given to the poor. 'Animal tithes' are mentioned in Leviticus 17. 32 and discussed in the tractate *Bekhorot*; they were levied three times a year and the selected animal was sacrificed. The tractate *Terumot* deals with the laws of heave-offering; *terumot* and *ma'aserot* continued to be set aside after the destruction of the Temple, but according to the *halakhah, these duties do not apply outside *Erez Israel.

Christianity In Europe a system of tithes came into legal force in the early Middle Ages (e.g. in England in 900), as a tax for the support of the Church and relief of the poor. The levy consisted of a tenth part, originally of the produce of lands ('praedial' tithes) and later of the profits of labour also ('personal' tithes). The system did not survive the secularization of continental European states after the *Reformation. In England the Tithe Acts of 1936 and 1951 have commuted all tithes to payments to the Crown, the last of which was made in 1996. The word 'tithe' is now heard mostly in churches in which voluntary contributions are called for on the basis of the *Old Testament concept.

For regulated giving in other religions, see ZAKĀT; DASWANDH.

Ti-ts'ang. Chin. for *Kṣitigarbha, a *bodhisattva who helps children and has power over the six realms of rebirth.

Titus, Letter to. One of the *Pastoral Epistles of the New Testament, professedly by Paul to his assistant Titus in Crete. It deals with the duties of *presbyters (ch. 1), the duties of various classes in society (2), and the Christian virtues (3). Its authenticity is disputed.

TM: see TRANSCENDENTAL MEDITATION.

Tobacco. Prohibited for Sikhs. The use of tobacco is specifically prohibited in the *khaṇḍe-dī-pāhul (initiation) ceremony of *khālsā Sikhs, and is avoided by Sikhs, both *sahajdhārī and *keśadhārī. Gurū *Tegh Bahādur condemned the recently introduced habit of smoking, as did his son, Gurū *Gobind Siṅgh, who reputedly declared that wine was bad, cannabis destroyed one generation, but tobacco destroyed all generations. On *Baisākhī day 1699, he forbade association with smokers. No tobacco is allowed in a *gurdwārā, as laid down in the *Rahit Maryādā.

For its possible prohibition for Muslims, see KHAMR.

Tobit, Book of. Book of the Jewish *apocrypha. Tobit contains the story of the righteous Tobit whose sight was restored after his son Tobias had been guided by an *angel. Tobit was righteous because, against a government decree, he buried abandoned corpses, and Tobias fulfilled his obligation of marrying a kinswoman. The book dates from the Persian period; Tobit was a member of one of the *ten lost tribes who were still believed to exist in Media. The story may well have connections with the widespread folklore of the young man who was rescued from mortal peril by the spirit of a poor man whom he has, out of charity, buried. The merit of marrying a kinswoman is another common motif. It became a favourite subject in Christian art, often with Tobit's dog (5. 16), the only one mentioned favourably in the Bible.

Todai-ji (temple-complex): see NARA BUDDHISM; BODHISENA.

Toda Jōsei (co-founder): see SŌKA GAKKAI.

Tōgaku (China-derived music): see MUSIC.

Tohorah (Heb., 'purification'). The Jewish ceremony of washing the dead before burial. The justification for tohorah is the Ecclesiastes verse, 'As he came, so shall he go' (5. 15). The dead are laid on a special tohorah board; they are thoroughly washed with lukewarm water while particular biblical verses are recited (i.e. Zechariah 3. 4; Ezekiel 36. 25 etc.). The nine measures (four and a half gallons) of water are poured over the body while it is held upright, and, after it is dried, it is dressed in shrouds. The ceremony for great scholars is even more elaborate. *Progressive Jews have abandoned the practice. See also PURITY.

M. Lamm, *The Jewish Way in Death and Mourning* (1969).

Tōji. A temple in *Kyōto, built in 796 by the emperor Kanmu when the capital was relocated there. In *c.*830, it was given to *Kūkai to serve as the centre of *Shingon, after which it was called Konkōmyō-shitennō-kyōō-gokokuji, or Kyōō-gokokuji for short. The beautiful five-storey *pagoda was reconstructed in the 17th cent.

Tokudo (Jap., 'attainment of going beyond'). The ceremony in Zen Buddhism through which a layperson is initiated into Buddhism, or a monk is ordained.

Tokugawa period. The period in Japan between 1600 and 1868 when power was held by the Tokugawa clan. Because of a strong emphasis on the worth of the traditions and past glories of Japan, it led to a revived interest in *Shinto, and laid the foundations for *Kokugaku (the School of National Learning).

Maruyama Masao, *Studies in the Intellectual History of Tokugawa Japan* (1974).

Tokumitsukyō (Zen Buddhist movement): see MIKI TOKUHARU.

Tokusan Senkan (Ch'an/Zen master): see TE-SHAN HSUAN-CHIEN.

Toledot Yeshu (Heb., 'The Life of Jesus'). A Jewish life of Jesus. *Toledot Yeshu* was compiled, from more ancient sources, in the 10th cent. It claims that Jesus' mother was raped. Jesus himself had supernatural powers, but his magic was exorcised by the *sages. Some of his *miracles, such as the resurrection, are given a natural explanation. Several versions of the work have been preserved.

H. G. Enelow, *A Jewish View of Jesus* (1931); M. Goldstein, *Jesus in the Jewish Tradition* (1950).

Tolstoy, Leo (1828–1910). Russian novelist and advocate of reform. Scion of an ancient Russian family, he studied briefly at Kazan and, influenced by Rousseau, became an enthusiast for social reform. He spent a period in the army and a further period travelling in Europe, studying educational and social reform. On his return in 1862 he married and wrote his greatest novels, *War and Peace* and *Anna Karenina*. The rest of his vast literary output was on moral and religious subjects, directly through essays, and indirectly through short stories and his novel, *Resurrection*. He became increasingly critical of the formalism of the *Orthodox Church ('Christ certainly could not have established the Church, that is, the institution we now call by that name, for nothing resembling our present conception of the Church—with its sacraments, its hierarchy, and especially its claim to infallibility—is to be found in Christ's words or in the conception of people of his time'). He was eventually excommunicated—to which he replied (1901): 'I believe in God, whom I understand as Spirit, as Love, as the Source of all.' He made huge demands of God in pursuit of an anguished humility, which made Gorky observe that the relationship of Tolstoy with God reminded him of 'two bears in one den'. He preached a gospel of love and moral goodness, and dispensed with dogma and ritual, though occasionally (e.g. in *The Death of Ivan Ilych*) he suggests that humans discern truth in an act of absolute renunciation, even of their achievement through good works.

I. Berlin, *The Hedgehog and the Fox* (1953); T. G. S. Cain, *Tolstoy* (1977); H. Troyat, *Tolstoy* (1968).

Tomurai. Japanese funeral rites. At the approach of death, people plead with the soul not to depart, but when it is clear that it has nevertheless gone, a bowl of rice is placed by the head of the deceased for sustenance in the spirit world, with a sword or sharp knife on the other side for protection against evil spirits. The body is washed and dressed in white before being placed in the coffin. Words of comfort may be spoken (e.g. by Buddhist functionaries), and the body is then buried or cremated. A week later, on *shonanuka* ('seventh day'), a posthumous name is bestowed. Mourning continues for seven weeks. Commemorations are made, especially at Bon (see ULLAMBANA; FESTIVALS AND FASTS). When these are complete, the last being called exactly that, *tomurai age*, 'completion of the rites', the spirit has become one with the ancestral *kami.

Tonghak (Eastern learning): see KOREAN RELIGION.

Tongyō (Jap., 'sudden enlightenment'). The attainment of sudden or immediate enlightenment in Zen Buddhism, in contrast with the gradual progress (*zengyō) through long training, meditation practice, etc. Tongyō-tonshu is 'sudden enlightenment and sudden practice' (i.e. all meritorious acts are performed in a short time), tongyō-zenshu is 'sudden enlightenment and long practice'.

Tonsei or **tonzei** (Jap.). Retreating from the world, the Buddhist practice of world-renunciation; tonsei-sha is one who has renounced (and eventually an adherent of *Jishū who became an artistic adviser). After the Kamakura period, tonsei became a more formal group of those who simply wished to live in seclusion.

Tonsure (shaving of the top of the head): see HAIR.

Tooth Relic Temple. More accurately known as Dalada Maligawa, the shrine in Śri Lankā in which the relic of the Buddha's tooth is kept. It is now in Kandy, but there were several earlier shrines after the tooth was brought to Śri Lankā in the 4th cent. CE. It is an object of constantly maintained devotion, and it is brought out in procession once each year.

A. M. Hocart, *The Temple of the Tooth* (1931).

Torah (Heb., 'teaching'). The teachings of the Jewish religion. In the *Pentateuch, the term 'Torah' can mean all the laws on a particular subject (e.g. Leviticus 7. 2) or the summation of all laws (e.g. Deuteronomy 4. 44). It is also used to refer to the Pentateuch in contrast to the *Prophets and *Hagiography (as in *Tanach), and later a distinction was made between the *written and the *oral law. Although the *rabbis taught that '*Moses received the Torah from *Sinai', they also taught that it was in existence before the *creation of the world, and R. *Akiva declared it to have been 'the precious instrument by which the world was created'. *Rav Hoshaiah equated it with *Wisdom described in the Book of *Proverbs, and *Philo, in his discussion of the *logos (word of God), identified the logos with Torah. These conjectures were the source of much discussion among such later Jewish philosophers as *Saʿadiah Gaon, Abraham *ibn Ezra and *Maimonides. The purpose of Torah is to make *Israel 'a kingdom of *priests, a holy nation' (Deuteronomy

33. 4), and much Hebrew poetry is concerned with the sweetness and joy entailed in keeping it (e.g. Psalms 19 and 119). None the less, the message of the Torah is for all humanity, and 'a pagan who studies the Torah is like a *High Priest'. In a famous exchange *Hillel summarized Torah in the maxim, 'What is hateful to you, do not to your fellow' (*B.Shab.* 31a), and Akiva maintained that its overriding principle was 'Love your neighbour as yourself' (Leviticus 19. 18). *Maimonides laid down in his *thirteen principles of the Jewish faith that Torah is immutable and that it was given in its entirety to Moses. The belief in the divine origin of both the written and oral Torah remains the touchstone of *Orthodox Judaism. The *Karaites accepted the written, but not the oral law, while the *Progressive movements tend to distinguish between the moral and ritual law. See Index, Torah.

W. D. Davies, *Torah in the Messianic and/or Age to Come* (1952).

Torah, reading of. The practice of reading the Jewish *Torah publicly. In Deuteronomy 31. 10–13, the Jewish community is commanded to assemble to hear the reading of the law, and the *scribe *Ezra read the Torah to all the people on the first day of the seventh month. Both *Josephus and *Philo refer to public readings, while the *Septuagint seems to have been compiled partly for reading in the *synagogue. The Babylonian *Talmud refers to a fixed cycle of readings (*B.Meg.* 29a), with the entire *Pentateuch being read over the course of three years. By the 12th cent., it became the universal practice to read it over an annual cycle. It is divided into fifty-four portions beginning on the *Sabbath after *Sukkot and ending on Shemini Atzeret/ *Simḥat Torah. The reading is 'completed' with a set passage from one of the *prophetic books—the *haftarah. Before and after the reading the Torah *scroll is carried in procession around the synagogue. It can only be read if a *minyan is present, and at least seven men are called up to read (*ʿaliyah). Either before the reading (among the *Sephardim) or after (among the *Ashkenazim) the scroll is raised (*hagbahah) to show the congregation. When the portion is finished, the scroll is rolled and returned to the *Ark. The readers recite particular *benedictions before and after their reading which is normally chanted (see CANTILLATION).

Torah ornaments. The coverings of the Jewish *Torah *Scrolls. The scrolls are rolled on two staves known as *azei ḥayyim* ('trees of life'). On the top of the staves are two finials, the *rimmonim*, and these are covered with an open crown (*keter*). The *Sephardim encase the scrolls in a double-hinged wooden box decorated with leather or metal. The *Ashkenazim cover their scrolls with a decorative mantle, often richly embroidered, on which a breastplate is suspended. The breastplate is reminiscent of the costume of the *high priest. In order to avoid touching the parchment of the scroll, a pointer, the *yad* ('hand'), is used.

A. Kanof, *Jewish Ceremonial Art* (1971).

Torah she-beʿal peh (Torah transmitted by mouth): see HALAKHAH.

Torah she-bi-khetav (Torah which is written): see HALAKHAH.

Torii. The gateway into *Shinto temples, standing also before sacred rocks, bridges, etc. They are made generally of two posts supporting two horizontal lintels. Worshippers bow to the gods as they pass through them. Their shapes and design vary greatly.

Torma (*gtor.ma*, 'scattered (oblation)'; Skt., *bali*, 'offering'). Sacrificial cake-offering in Tibetan Buddhism, made of barley flour, brightly decorated with coloured butter and shaped according to ritual requirements. It is so called because almost invariably it is scattered for eating by birds and animals after the ceremony, though occasionally it may be consumed during the ritual. Tormas may be offered to *bodhisattvas, *ḍākinīs, local spirits, even as bribes to satisfy demons. There are many different purposes, and according to Beyer a head *lama should know how to make about fifty different types. Beyer reports that there are three aspects of a torma: 'as an *offering* it is presented to the deity; as an *evocation* the deity is generated within it, and the power thereof may be transmitted to a recipient through physical contact; and as a *substance of magical attainment* it may be eaten by the participants at the end of a ritual, to absorb the empowerment it contains'. Tormas often play a part in empowerment (Skt., *abhiṣekha; Tib., *dbang.bskur*) rituals, where the empowerment to perform the practice of a particular deity is given by the lama first projecting the deity into the torma, and then anointing the disciple with it.

S. Beyer, *The Cult of Tara* (1973).

Toronto Blessing. The term was first coined by British churches for the claimed experience of a new wave of the Holy Spirit beginning in 1994. At the end of Jan. 1994 a small *charismatic church in Toronto, of the Vineyard denomination (the 'Airport Vineyard') experienced what they believed to be a new and concentrated outpouring of the Spirit night after night. The Airport Vineyard church has since been recognized as 'a worldwide renewal centre'. Various manifestations deemed to be evidence of the presence of the Spirit have become synonymous with 'Toronto': they include falling or resting in the Spirit, laughter, shaking, and crying. From the outset, the highly publicized nightly 'renewal meetings' regularly attracted between 1,500 and 5,000. Many give testimony to great spiritual refreshment, a deep encounter with God, a new sense of the joy of the Lord, and a new love for *Jesus, the *Bible and the *mission of the *Church. The effect of the Toronto Blessing has been felt around the world, not least in the mainline denominations in the UK, South Africa, East Asia, and North America. Many other centres of renewal have begun around the world after an initial visit to Toronto. The Toronto Blessing has not been without criticism, not only from non-charismatic churches but from within. *Pentecostal churches have by no means endorsed the movement, especially as the emphasis has been on renewal and refreshment rather than *baptism in the Spirit, a characteristic Pentecostal emphasis. In Dec. 1995, the founder and overseer of the Vineyard churches, John Wimber, released the Airport Vineyard from the Vineyard denomination for reasons of growing unhappiness with the emphasis on the extraordinary manifestations of the Spirit, and because he no longer felt able to exercise oversight over the Church and its activities. After Jan. 1996, the church continued to exist as an independent church. By the end of 1995 the church had received more than 700,000 visitors and continued to meet six nights a week. Despite the controversy, testimony continued strongly of those claiming to have been greatly blessed by God.

G. Chevrau, *Catch the Fire* (1994); M. Mitton, *The Heart of Toronto* (1995).

Torquemada, Tomas de (1420–98). Grand Inquisitor in Spain. A *Dominican, he joined the *Inquisition in 1482, and was responsible for about 2,000 executions and for the expulsion of those Jews from Spain (in 1492) who refused *baptism. His methods were summarized in the handbook, *Instrucciones de la santa Inquisición* (1484).

T. Hope, *Torquemada . . .* (1939).

Torrance, T. F. (Christian theologian): see THEOLOGY.

Tortoise oracle. Ancient Chinese method of divination, similar in antiquity and use to the *oracle bones. Unlike the latter, however, the tortoise oracle was not forgotten to later Chinese history and in fact enjoyed considerable fame in art, literature, and philosophy. The cosmic tortoise is known from ancient myths as the foundation of the world, but it is from traditions which coalesced around the **I Ching* (Book of Changes) that the sacred and mysterious significance of the tortoise is largely derived. According to the Great Appendix of that work, the eight trigrams (building-blocks for the sixty-four hexagrams around which the divination text is organized) were discovered by the legendary emperor Fu Shi, who took as models the patterns of heaven and earth, and of birds and animals (*Ta Chuan*, ii). Other legends specifically mention the markings on the tortoise shell as the origin of both the trigrams and the Chinese writing system, given by the same culture-hero, Fu Shi. The legend that the earth is supported by a tortoise is apparently attributable to the **Lieh-Tzu*; other legends explain the symbolism of the tortoise as more fully cosmic, since the round and vaulted shell represents the heavens, the flat underside the square earth with the four legs denoting the four quarters of earth.

Tortosa, Disputation of. A Jewish–Christian disputation held in Tortosa in 1413–14. The disputation was the longest of the medieval disputations. It was presided over by the *pope and was predominantly a missionary exercise on the part of the Christians. The Christian side was led by the *apostate, Geronimo de Santa Fé, who was always allowed to conclude the discussion. Jewish participants included Zerahiah ha-Levi, Astruc ha-Levi, Joseph *Albo, and Mattathias ha-Yizhari. Many Jews were baptized as a consequence.

A. Pacios Lopez, *La Disputa de Tortosa* (1957).

Tosafot (Heb., 'additions'). Collections of comments on the Jewish *Talmud. The tosafot grew out of the French and German schools which aimed to develop and enlarge the Talmudic commentaries of *Rashi. The tosafot are records of discussions between teachers and pupils in the *yeshivot. Important practitioners include Isaac b. Nathan (Rashi's son-in-law), *Samuel b. Meir, Jacob *Tam, Isaac b. Meir (his grandsons), Eliezer of Metz, Moses of Coucy, Isaac of Corbeil, Baruch of Worms, and Eliezer b. Judah of Worms. The tosafot literature is vast: it extended to commentary on *Pentateuch commentary and even on the *halakhot of *Alfasi. It is normally included in editions of the Talmud so 'a page of *gemāra' means the text, Rashi's commentary (known as *perush*), and tosafot (collectively described by the acronym GaPaT). *Pilpul was particularly associated with the study of tosafot in Germany and Poland.

E. E. Urbach, *Baʿalei ha-Tosafot* (1955).

Tosefta. A collection of works by the Jewish *tannaim. The Tosefta parallels and supplements the *Mishnah. It dates from *c.*2nd cent. CE, and has the same six orders as the Mishnah. Some paragraphs (known as *beraitot*) are alternative versions of mishnaic paragraphs (e.g. the tractate *Yoma*) while others contain completely new material and include subjects not discussed in the Mishnah. The question of the exact relationship of the two works has produced no conclusive scholarly answer. The Tosefta was written in Mishnaic Hebrew in *Erez Israel, and presumably the aim of the anonymous compiler was to produce some sort of supplement or alternative to the Mishnah. The latest critical edition with a detailed commentary is by S. Lieberman.

Tōshōdai-Ji (temple-complex): see NARA BUDDHISM.

Totemism. The practices and beliefs relating to the identification of a totem object. The word totem is taken from the Ojibwa of Canada, the word *dotem/oteman* signifying, 'he is a relative of mine'. Ojibwa clans are named after animal species, so that the totem idea expresses membership of the same exogamic group. However, the word 'totem' was applied, far more loosely, to animals, plants, or other objects associated with a social or kinship group, often regarded by the group as sacred. Totemism thus became the cornerstone of far-reaching theories of religion, especially in the case of *Durkheim and *Freud (see TABOO). C. Lévi-Strauss (*Totemism*, 1962) set himself against these uses of totemism to explain early (and by evolutionary assumptions, all subsequent) religion, and suggested that totemism does not properly belong in the domain of religion, *sensu stricto*, at all. Totemism is neither an institution nor a religion, but is rather a classificatory device which mediates between conceptions of the natural world and social categories and relations. It is a mode of thought in which relations are established through totemic emblems of such a kind that a single, unified cosmos is envisaged and established.

Totum simul (Lat., 'everything' + 'at the same time'), a synonym for *eternity, derived from *Boethius.

Tour of Victory (journeys of pre-eminent Indian philosopher): see ŚAṄKARA.

Tou-shuai Ts'ung-yueh (1044–92). Ch'an/Zen master of the Ōryō lineage of *Rinzai, and dharma-successor (*hassu) of Pao-feng K'o-wen. He is remembered for the 'three barriers' *kōan (*Mumonkan* 47):

> To go to isolated places to practise *zazen is to seek your true nature: so where now, at this moment, is your true nature? When you have experienced your true nature, can you liberate yourself from birth and death—how can you do so when your eyesight fails? When you have freed yourself from birth and death, you know where you are going: when your body breaks down into the four elements, where do you go then?

Tower of Silence (place where Zoroastrians and Parsis dispose of dead bodies): see DAXMA.

Toyouke Okami (Ise shrine deity): see ISE.

Tōzan Ryōkai (co-founder of school of Buddhism): see TUNG-SHAN LIANG-CHIEH.

Tractarians. The early leaders of the *Oxford Movement, so-named from the series of *Tracts for the Times* (1833–41) in which their ideals were expounded. The name is therefore also used for those of a *high church tendency.

Tradition. The formal transmission of information (both verbal and non-verbal) in religions. In non-text religions, the process of tradition is all the more vital since there is no independent repository of information in written form, whether designated as *scripture or not—hence the foundational importance of *myth and *ritual in all religions. In text-related religions, scripture may (theoretically) precede tradition, as in the case of the *Vedas among Hindus or of the *Bible among Christians, but even there tradition is instrumental in delivering the texts which become recognized or designated as 'scripture'. In Judaism, tradition became the authoritative interpretation and application of *Torah, handed down, initially in oral form, from teacher (*rabbi) to pupil. This tradition became of such importance that it was designated 'second Torah', *Torah she be'al peh* ('Torah transmitted by word of mouth'; see HALAKHAH). More widely, tradition in Judaism is referred to as *masoret*, which in the *Talmud includes custom, law, history, and folklore. Tradition (see ḤADĪTH) is equally formal in Islam, since *Muḥammad and his companions were the first living commentators on *Qur'ān. In Christianity, the status of tradition is more complex (and controversial), since one part of the Church (the *Roman Catholic) has given to tradition (as the unfolding of scripture) a defining role in some matters of salvation: that which is at best dimly alluded to in scripture, or only to be inferred (e.g. *purgatory, the *Assumption of the Blessed Virgin Mary) can be defined by the pope *ex cathedra: such definitions are *infallible and irreformable—i.e. tradition has become equivalent to scripture. The formality of transmission in other religions can be seen in the importance of the *saṃpradāyas among Hindus (see also VEDA), and the succession lists and transmission procedures and rituals among some Buddhists.

R. Lingat, *The Classical Law of India* (1973); K. Narayan, *Storytellers, Saints and Scoundrels* . . . (1992); J. Pelikan, *The Vindication of Tradition* (1984); E. Shils, *Tradition* (1981); J. Vansina, *Oral Tradition* . . . (1965).

Traducianism (the generation of souls): see CREATIONISM.

Traherne, Thomas (*c.*1636–74). *Anglican clergyman, and *Metaphysical poet. His main work remained unpublished until the beginning of the 20th cent., when his *Poems* and *Centuries of Meditation* appeared. Trusting the divine intuitions of childhood ('The corn was orient and immortal wheat which never should be reaped nor was ever sown . . . The green trees when I saw them first . . . transported and ravished me [and made me] almost mad with ecstasy'), he expresses a strong sense of the mystical embrace.

Trailokya (regions of the cosmos in Buddhism): see LOKA (BUDDHISM).

Transcendental anthropology: see RAHNER, KARL.

Transcendentalists, New England: see EMERSON, R. W.

Transcendental meditation. Taught by *Maharishi Mahesh Yogi and comprising 'a specific and systematic mental technique which can be easily learnt and enjoyed by anyone, whatever his opinions or beliefs'. The Indian-based philosophy holds that this (*mantra) technique leads practitioners to 'the field of pure consciousness'. This alone 'is the self-sufficient reality of life'. Physical and psychological life is held to be greatly enhanced when people function in accord with 'natural law'. What is more important is that they move beyond the usual superficial 'thought ruts' governing life to encounter the deeper level of transcendental creative intelligence. Transcendental meditation is widely used, especially in America where it enters into the worlds of education, business, and welfare. This is in accord with Maharishi's aim of transforming society, especially through the World Government of the Age of Enlightment. In 1995, the movement attempted to purchase a redundant UK air base (Bentwaters) in order to establish a university.

M. Yogi, *The Science of Belief and the Art of Loving* (1966).

Transcendental Thomism see RAHNER, KARL; NEO-THOMISM.

Transfiguration of Christ. The story recorded in the first three gospels (Mark 9. 2–13, etc.) according to which Jesus took his disciples Peter, James, and John to a mountain where he took on a glorious appearance alongside Moses and Elijah. The Feast of the Transfiguration on 6 Aug. has been observed in the East since before 1000 CE, and in the West since 1456.

Transmigration: see REBIRTH.

Transmission outside the scriptures (transmission of teaching and truth directly from teacher to pupil): see FUKASETSU.

Transubstantiation. In Catholic theology of the *eucharist, the change of the substance (underlying reality) of the bread and wine into the substance of the body and blood of Christ, leaving the 'accidents' (i.e. the appearances of the bread and wine) intact, so that the faithful do not literally touch Christ's body. The term was recognized at the Lateran Council of 1215, and was formally defined at *Trent in 1551. Depending on Aristotelian categories, especially as formulated by St Thomas *Aquinas, recent (R.) Catholic theology has sought to express the change in other terms (e.g. transignification, which points to the change in the relation of the individual to God through Christ in this self-giving action). The E. Church entertains an essentially identical doctrine to transubstantiation, but many modern Orthodox theologians avoid the term because of its associations with Latin *scholasticism.

Trapeza (Greek altar): see ALTAR.

Trappists. Popular name (from La Trappe) for *Cistercians derived from the reform instituted by the abbot Armand de Rancé in 1664. Its rule is particularly severe (hence they are known as Cistercians of the more strict observance).

Trent, Council of (1545–63). A council of *Roman Catholic *bishops and superiors of *religious orders, reckoned by that church to be the 19th *ecumenical *council. It was convoked only after pressure from the Emperor Charles V, who hoped for reconciliation between Catholics and *Protestants in his German dominions. It was agreed that the council would discuss, *pari passu*, both doctrinal issues and ecclesiastical reform. It met in three sessions at Triento in N. Italy, 1545–9, 1551–2, and 1562–3. Protestant representatives attended only the second of these sessions, with no lasting effect. The fathers of the council rejected Protestant sacramental theory and *Luther's doctrine of *consubstantiation, in the latter case endorsing the theory of *transubstantiation. The council stopped short of making transubstantiation a *dogma, and, while refuting Luther's theory of *justification, it did not put any other theory in its place. Among the ecclesiastical reforms there was an attempt to abolish pluralism, an insistence that bishops must reside in their sees, a provision of better education for, and closer control over, the clergy, and a reform of the Roman *curia. A new *missal and *office book were produced shortly after the council closed. As well as defining Catholic positions on disputed questions against Protestant ones, it also reasserted the traditional teaching on a number of issues such as *indulgences, the existence of *purgatory, and the veneration of *saints. Despite the hesitation of successive popes (through fear of conciliarism, see ANTIPOPE) about summoning the council, its outcome strengthened the papal office. It was, perhaps, the single most significant element in the *Counter-Reformation.

H. Jedin, *A History of the Council of Trent* (1957–61, vols. i–ii of *Geschichte des Konzils von Trient*, 1949–75).

Tretā-yuga. The second of the four *yugas, or divisions of *time, in Hinduism. It lasts 1,296,000 years: sacrifice begins, but righteousness declines; it is the yuga during which *Rāma appears as *avatāra (incarnation).

Tribes, the twelve. The traditional composition and division of the Jewish people. The twelve tribes were supposedly descended from the sons and grandsons of the patriarch *Jacob. They include Reuben, Simeon (Levi), Judah, Issachar, Zebulun, Benjamin, Dan, Naphtali, Gad, Asher, Ephraim, and Manasseh. After the Israelites were settled in the land of *Canaan, each tribe (except Levi) had a particular territory. Ten of the tribes (see TEN LOST TRIBES) disappeared from history with the Assyrian conquest of 722 BCE. Most modern scholars do not accept the biblical account of the origins of the tribes, but the consciousness of the twelve tribes was fundamental to Israelite self-understanding.

W. Duffy, *The Tribal History Theory on the Origin of the Hebrews*; N. K. Gottwald, *The Tribes of Yahweh* (1979); J. D. Martin, in R. E. Clements (ed.), *The World of Ancient Israel* (1989).

Tricivara (wearing a robe made of three pieces, in Buddhism): see DHŪTA.

Trickster (term introduced by D. G. Brinton, *Myths of the New World*, 1868). A hero, and also anti-hero, in many religions and cultures. Although the Trickster was identified particularly in the stories of N. American Indians, the recognition of similar characteristics in a wide range of stories has led to the emergence of a kind of composite figure, of one who subverts and satirizes the norms of society, and yet who emerges as hero: Brer Rabbit is a familiar example. In the N. American stories, the Trickster often begins as an inept, amoral creature who gains control over his own anatomy, ceases to oscillate between male and female and becomes male, secures his own identity and learns to live skilfully and appropriately in his own environment. Thus in many respects he recapitulates the process from infancy to maturity: he creates chaos, inverts social order, and breaks *taboos, and yet he gains great advantages in the process. P. Radin (*The Trickster*, 1955) traced an evolutionary development, but the wide scatter of characteristics in different cultures and religions has made a 'family-resemblance' analysis more convincing.

W. J. Hynes and W. G. Doty, *Mythical Trickster Figures* (1993); R. D. Pelton, *The Trickster in West Africa* ... (1980).

Tridharma (Skt., 'three teachings'). An Indonesian group which bases its beliefs on a combination of those of *Buddha, *Confucius, and *Lao-Tzu. It was founded in Jakarta in 1938 by Kwee Tekhoay, a Chinese writer. Tridharma is affiliated to the All Indonesia Federation of Buddhist Organizations (WALUBI) and currently comprises not more than a few thousand members.

Trika(śāsana). *Kashmir *Śaiva system which postulates three fundamental sources of all appearance: *Śiva, who creates from his imagination the world as though independent of himself, whereas it is always an expression of his will; *Śakti as the energy through which this is achieved; and Aṇu as the individualized *ātman who takes local initiatives. Through Śiva's aid or *grace the individual can realize that s/he was and is always the expression of Śiva, and by attaining this (re)union, can then lead others to the same truth. The system was elaborated by Vasugupta (770–830), whose main works are *Śiva-Sūtra* and *Spanda-Kārikā*.

Trikāya (Skt., 'three bodies'; Chin., *san-shen*; Jap., *sanshin*; Korean, *samsin*). A doctrine which came to prominence in *Mahāyāna Buddhism according to which the *Buddha manifests himself in three bodies (trikāya), modes, or dimensions. Even in early Buddhism, the precise nature of the Buddha had been ambiguous: on the one hand he was born and lived as a human being, on the other hand he transcended human nature through his enlightenment, by virtue of which he participated in the supramundane condition attained by all Buddhas past and future. To have realized the *dharma, the ultimate truth or way of things, meant that he had become transformed in accordance with it and to a large extent identified with it. The Buddha himself had stated, 'He who sees the Buddha sees the Dharma, he who sees the Dharma sees the Buddha.' In addition to the transcendent aspect of his nature on the one hand, and his earthly physical form and activity on the other, the Buddha, as a great *yogin, possessed supernatural powers by means of which he could travel at will through the heavens and manifest himself in the form of a magical body to preach the doctrine to the gods.

Several centuries after his death, these three facets of the Buddha's nature were articulated in the form of a doctrine developed initially by the *Sarvāstivāda school, but quickly taken up and elaborated by the Mahāyāna. According to this development, the Buddha, and all Buddhas were, in their essential nature, identical with the ultimate truth or absolute reality. This is their first 'body'. At the same time, Buddhas have the power to manifest themselves in a sublime celestial form in splendid paradises where they teach the doctrine surrounded by hosts of *bodhisattvas and supernatural beings. This is their second body. Furthermore, motivated by boundless compassion, they project themselves into the world of suffering beings (e.g. the human world) disguised in an appropriate manner through the use of skilful means (*upāya-kauśalya) so as not to frighten and alarm, but instead to provide that which is most necessary and useful. This is their third body.

Applied in more detail, the Trikāya is the system or *upāya by which Buddhas manifest their presence and activity. A Buddha in human form is called a Nirmāṇakāya (Skt., 'transformation body') and one in celestial form is called a *Saṃbhogakāya (Skt., 'enjoyment body'); the identification of these two bodies with particular figures varies with the lineage (see BUDDHIST SCHOOLS). The unmanifest form is the Dharmakāya (Skt., 'dharma body') which is synonymous with *Tathatā (Skt., 'Thus-ness') and *Tathāgatagarbha (Skt., 'womb *or* embryo of the Buddhas'). In the Tantric tradition, the Dharmakāya is said to be manifest as an *Ādi-Buddha (Skt., 'Original Buddha')—identified in different lineages as *Vajradhara, *Vairocana, *Samantabhadra, etc.—who is non-dual with his unmanifest ultimate nature. Buddhists sharply distinguish the Dharmakāya from the Hindu *Brahman and do not regard it as a 'ground of Being'. The Saṃbhogakāya always manifests the bodily marks of a hero (Skt., *mahāpuruṣa*) such as the protruberance on the head (Skt., *uṣṇīṣa*) and may be, as in the **Lotus Sūtra*, gigantic. The Nirmāṇakāya is of normal human appearance like, for example, the *Dalai Lama, who is a Nirmāṇakāya of the Bodhisattva *Avalokiteśvara. A simile of the Trikāya is that of the three mental states of waking, dreaming, and dreamless sleep. The waking state corresponds to the physical limitations of the Nirmāṇakāya; dreaming to the relative freedom from space and time of the Saṃbhogakāya, and dreamless sleep to the total freedom of the Dharmakāya. That these three states are experienced by the same person and yet are different symbolizes that the three bodies are neither the same nor different. The unity of the Trikāya is sometimes taught as a fourth aspect, *Svabhāvikakāya* (Skt., 'essential body').

Trikona yantra (Skt., 'triangle'). Hindu diagram of two intersecting triangles. The downward-pointing triangle represents masculinity and God, the upward femininity and *śakti.

Trilocana (Skt., 'three-eyed'). Epithet of *Śiva in Hinduism. According to **Mahābhārata*, *Pārvatī, his consort, covered his eyes in play, and a burning third eye burst forth in his forehead. Śiva is often portrayed with a third eye, surmounted by a crescent moon, and he uses it destructively—e.g. of *Kāma, for evoking amorous thoughts in Pārvatī. The 'third eye' is also claimed by adepts, especially in Tibet, to give spiritual vision: see ŪRṆĀ.

Triloka (three constituent domains in the cosmos): see LOKA.

Trimārga (Skt., 'three ways'). The three major ways through which Hindus can approach *mokṣa (release). They are *karma-mārga (the way of action, especially of sacrificial ritual), *jñāna-mārga (the way of knowledge, especially associated with *Upaniṣads and *Vedānta), and bhakti-mārga (the way of devotion to God).

Trimūrti (Skt., 'of three forms'). The Hindu recognition of threefold interaction being necessary for creation and dissolution, hence especially the three interrelated manifestations of the divine: *Brahmā, *Viṣṇu, and *Śiva. Brahmā embodies *rajas (see GUṆA), the passion which creates; Viṣṇu embodies *sattva, the goodness which maintains balance; and Śiva, *tamas, the fire which destroys. In other analyses, Viṣṇu creates and Brahmā maintains equilibrium. As Brahmā diminished in importance, the 'social' necessity of being (cf. TRINITY) led to Viṣṇu or especially Śiva being represented in threefold activity.

Trinity, The. A predominantly Christian understanding of the inner nature of the Godhead. Trinitarian understandings of God may arise primarily from revelation, as Christians affirm, but they are more widely embedded in a belief that there is an analogical relationship between God and the created or manifest world (see ANALOGY): since in this world it is only possible to be a self in a field of selves, the inference is drawn that the interior nature of God must be relational, and not monistically abstract. Among Hindus, the relational character of God may be dipolar, with opposites united in a single character and action, but equally, as in the *Trimūrti emphasis, it may be of far greater complexity. None of this contradicts the insistence in Islam (though many Muslims suppose that it does) on *tawḥīd, the absolute unity of God, since whatever God may turn out to be, it can only be God that God turns out to be—though it so happens that that nature is relational: see also SAN-I in Taoism; TRIKĀYA in Buddhism.

It is, however, in Christianity that the Trinitarian nature of God has been most complexly explored, affirming that there is the one God, who exists in three persons: Father, Son, and *Holy Spirit. The basis for this doctrine in the Bible consists of threefold formulae like Matthew 28. 19; 1 Peter 1. 2, and Isaiah 6. 3. These passages in no way predicate a God who is eternally three in one, but they set the terms for later thinking toward that end. In the 3rd and early 4th cents., against *Sabellianism and *Arianism, the Son and Father were defined as distinct yet coequal and coeternal. In the late 4th cent. the *Cappadocian Fathers took the final step by understanding the Holy Spirit as of the same status. God was then to be spoken of as one *ousia* (being) in three *hypostases (persons), and this has remained the orthodox formulation.

Eastern Christian thought starts in general with this evident distinction of persons in the Trinity and tries to understand their mysterious unity in one 'God'. As an analogy: 'We may be confronted by many who individually share in human nature, such as Peter, James, and John, yet the "man" in them is one' (*Gregory of Nyssa, *On Not Three Gods*). It also holds that the Father is the single focus of unity in the Godhead, and the source of the other two persons. Western thought, on the other hand, starts with the unity of the Godhead and tries to understand its threeness. *Augustine's contribution, elaborated by the *scholastics, was to conceive this in terms of relations: in his best-known analogy, the Father is the lover, the Son the loved one, and the Holy Spirit the love between them. Also, in traditionally heated disagreement with the E., the W. dogma is that the Holy Spirit proceeds from the Father *and the Son* (*filioque), in order to insist on the equality of the Persons.

It may be said that whereas E. conceptions of the Trinity tend to sound 'tritheistic', W. ones have tended to sound abstract and, until recently, have removed the Trinity to the periphery of practical theology. Many modern scholars have said that, given the essential mystery of the doctrine, the two kinds of conceptions need not be considered incompatible: the doctrine of the Trinity is a necessary consequence of *Christology, and takes seriously the necessity for interrelation in the formation of all appearance or reality. The *patristic concept of *circumincessio* (Gk., *(em)perichoresis*), the inner involvement of the Three Persons, anticipates the current social model of the Trinity, of three distinct realities, inseparably requiring each other to be the sort of reality they are, and therefore also only one reality.

C. M. La Cugna, *God for Us: The Trinity and Christian Life* (1991); G. L. Prestige, *God in Patristic Thought* (1952).

Trinity Sunday. In W. Christian churches, the first Sunday after *Pentecost. Its observance was made binding on the Church by Pope John XXII in 1334. To the objection that through its *doxologies, etc., the Church celebrates the Trinity on *every* Sunday, the reply was made (e.g. here by Anthony Sparrow, bishop of Norwich, 1676)

> that such a Mystery as this, though part of the meditation of each day, should be the chief subject of one, . . . for no sooner had our Lord ascended into heaven, and God's Holy Spirit descended upon the Church, but there ensued the notice of the glorious and incomprehensible Trinity, which before that time was not so clearly known.

In the **Book of Common Prayer* the Sundays until Advent are numbered 'after Trinity'.

Tripiṭaka (Skt., 'Triple Basket'; Chin., *San-ts'ang*; Jap., *Sanzō*; Korean, *Samjang*). The threefold collection of authoritative texts in Buddhism. It is used more loosely in *Mahāyāna Buddhism to mean the entire body of the Buddhist scriptures, corresponding to the Pāli Tripiṭaka in its general meaning, although the content and arrangement of the Mahāyāna canons, of which the chief are the Chinese Tripiṭaka and the Tibetan canon, are significantly different.

The Pali Tripiṭaka is the most fundamental collection extant, though it is believed that each of the original eighteen schools of Buddhism had tripiṭakas of their own. Tradition has it that, before the schisms, all Buddhists held a canon in common which had its origin in a Council of 500 *arhats held at Rājagṛha after the cremation of the *Buddha. At that council, under the supervision of Kāśyapa, the discourses of the Buddha were recited by Ānanda and committed to memory by the rest of the congregation. In a similar manner, the regulations for monastic discipline and behaviour were recalled by Upāli. These two elements of the Buddha's teaching became the Sūtra piṭaka and the Vinaya piṭaka respectively. There is disagreement about the origin of the third member of the tripiṭaka, the *Abhidharma. In the tradition of the Theravāda and *Mahāsaṃghika, only the first two Piṭakas were recited at Rājagṛha. The *Sarvastivadins hold that the Abhidharma was recited by Ānanda together with the sūtra material. Since it is in the Abhidharma section that there is the most discrepancy between schools, it seems likely that this was composed at a later date. Each of the three piṭakas is further subdivided, probably as an aid to memory before the corpus was written down. The Sūtra piṭaka, for instance, is divided into five traditions (*āgama) or collections (*nikāya), on the basis of a number of criteria such as length, structure, subject-matter, and authenticity. These divisions were probably also related to how much individual monks were capable of learning.

At the beginning, any language seems to have been regarded as suitable for transmitting the canon, and this gave rise to controversy. As a result, a council at *Vaiśālī in 386 BCE of 700 monks rehearsed and reauthorized the Vinaya, while at *Pāṭaliputra in 349 BCE, the whole tripiṭaka was revised in line with the doctrinal stance of the *Mahāsaṃghikas. By the end of the 1st cent. CE, the canons of all the original schools had been committed to writing in a variety of Indian languages, expounding a variety of doctrinal viewpoints.

The Pāli tripiṭaka, being by far the most complete, has attracted the most scholarly attention. It contains material of varying authorship and age, but attempts at stratification, on the basis of structure and doctrinal content, are at an early stage. During the Mahāyāna period, new texts were added to the canon, both Mahāyāna sūtras and *śāstra material, written by influential thinkers such as *Nāgārjuna. At a later date still, *Tantric material was introduced. This explains why the old threefold division is obscured in the Chinese and Tibetan tripiṭakas (the Tib. tripiṭaka is divided between *bka-'gyur*, containing works attributed to the Buddha himself, amounting to more than 100 vols., and *bstan-'gyur*, 220 vols. of mainly commentaries). Further, the doctrinal standpoint of both collections is often confused, since they comprise material collected from more than one Indian source. See also KOREAN TRIPIṬAKA.

*Buddhaghosa records the early fivefold division of the Sutta piṭaka into *Dīgha Nikāya, *Majjhima Nikāya, *Saṃyutta Nikāya, *Aṅguttara Nikāya, and *Khuddaka Nikāya (not all of which is recognized as canonical by all schools). In the Indian (Skt.) canon (little of which has survived outside translation), the corresponding divisions of the Sūtra piṭaka are Dīrghāgama, Madyamāgama, Saṃyuktāgama, Ekottarāgama, and Kṣudrakāgama: more is included in the āgamas than in the nikāyas, the arrangement is often different, and the texts also may be different in details of expression; the differences do not affect the overall content of teaching.

The *Vinaya piṭaka is divided into three parts: Suttavibhaṅga, containing the Pātimokkha casuistic rules; the Khandhaka, containing complementary rules which address communal life and ceremonies, and seek to avert schism; and the Parivāra, ancillary works which amount to an appendix making the earlier parts more manageable.

The Abhidhamma piṭaka is made up of logical and philosophical analysis gathered under headings (*mātikā*) which give brief notes on the doctrine in question. In the *Theravāda tradition, there are seven books; other schools have different collections, but all undertaken in the same style.

The development of the sūtra tradition led to four major collections: Prajñāpāramitā (*Perfection of Wisdom), (Mahā)ratnakūṭa (found mainly in 5th-cent. Chinese translations, sūtras which seem to be a compendium of Mahāyāna teaching), Buddhāvataṃsaka (see AVATAṂSAKA for an example), and

Mahāsaṃnipāta (a diverse collection showing an interest in *magic).

The addition of Tantric texts represents the last stage of the Buddhist canon. The earliest Tantric texts are short formulae (*dhāraṇī) attached to sūtras, but from the 4th cent. CE they began to be developed into longer treatises. They are now divided into four groups: (i) Kriyātantra, describing relatively obvious and accessible rituals; (ii) Caryātantra, more advanced 'outer ritual' and the beginnings of 'inner yoga'; (iii) Yogatantra, the workings of 'inner yoga' in meditation and trance; (iv) Anuttarayogatantra, esoteric rituals, often concerned with the workings of sexual symbolism, accessible only to the initiated.

J. Holm and J. Bowker (eds.), *Sacred Writings* (1994).

Triple Body (of the Buddha): see TRIKĀYA.

Tripuṇḍra (three marks indicating allegiance): see TARPAṆA.

Tripuṭi (Skt., 'threefold sheath'). The Hindu analysis of appearance in terms of a metaphysic of relationships. If there is one field of reality, nevertheless it exists or appears in the relationship of subject, object, and the relation between the two—as lover, beloved, and love created between them. In Hinduism, such a metaphysic of perception contributes to illusion and has to be transcended.

Triratna (three fundamental commitments of a Buddhist): see THREE JEWELS.

Trisagion or **Trisyatoe.** Christian *hymn beginning 'Agios O Theos' ('holy God'), of great antiquity, and now embedded in the *liturgy. It is reputed to be the hymn of praise sung by the *angels in heaven. It appears in slightly variant forms, notably through the addition of a clause, 'who was crucified for us', which converts the hymn from an address to the *Trinity into an address to the *Son—a change which belongs to the controversies about the divinity of Christ. In the Byzantine rite, the hymn is sung at the *Little Entrance, repeating thrice: 'O Holy God, Holy Mighty, Holy Immortal One, have mercy upon us.'

Triśalā. Mother of Vardhamāna *Mahāvirā. Jain tradition records her as the sister of the Vaisali ruler, Ceṭaka. Triśalā married Siddhārtha, a chieftain of the Jnatr clan, and both were followers of *Pārśva. Śvetāmbara sources recount how Triśalā experienced fourteen dreams (the *Digambaras claim sixteen) before Mahāvirā's birth, which were portents of the birth of a great teacher. These dreams are recalled today by Jains when they celebrate the five auspicious moments (*kalyāṇakas*) in Mahāvirā's life, of which the first is conception. The dreams are also popular subjects of Jain sculpture and painting. Śvetāmbara tradition has a further strange story, rejected by Digambaras, that originally Mahāvirā was conceived by a brahman couple, Ṛṣabhadatta and Devānandā, but that on the eighty-third day after conception, the god *Indra transferred the embryo to the womb of the *kṣatrya woman, Triśalā. This story probably reflects the Jain regard for the kṣatrya caste. Other prebirth stories describe how Mahāvirā lay perfectly still in the womb never kicking his mother, thus reflecting his prenatal sense of *ahiṃsā. Śvetāmbara tradition also claims that Mahāvirā refused to become an ascetic until after his parents' death because he did not wish to hurt them, but this too is denied by the Digambaras.

Triśaraṇa (Skt.; Pāli, *tisaraṇa*, 'threefold refuge'). Basic Buddhist orientation of life, taking refuge in the *Three Jewels (*triratna*): the *Buddha, the *dharma, and the *saṅgha.

Triśula (Skt., 'trident'). *Śiva's emblem in Hinduism, denoting his threefold role (*trimūrti) in creating, sustaining, and destroying; or his use of the three *guṇas. Śaivites frequently set up a triśula before worship (*pūjā).

Trisvabhāva (three aspects, central teaching of Vijñānavāda): see VIJÑĀNAVĀDA.

'Trito-Isaiah' (chapters in biblical book): see ISAIAH.

Trivikrama (cosmic version of Hindu god): see VĀMANA.

Triyāna (Skt., 'three vehicles'). The *Mahāyāna Buddhist analysis of the three vehicles that bring one toward *nirvāna: (i) *śravaka-yāna = *Hīnayāna; (ii) *pratyeka-yāna; (iii) *bodhisattva-yāna = Mahāyāna. In the *Lotus Sūtra* these are unified as reinforcing parts of a single vehicle (*ekayāna*), to be taught according to the abilities of students (*upaya-kauśalya), and they are likened to carts drawn by goats, reindeer, and oxen.

Troeltsch, Ernst (1865–1923). Christian historian of culture and religion. He was born in Bavaria and studied Protestant theology at Erlangen before transferring to Berlin and Göttingen, where he was much influenced by Ritschl. He became professor of systematic theology at Heidelberg in 1894, and professor of 'religious, social and historical philosophy and the history of the Christian religion' at Berlin in 1915. The latter title points effectively to Troeltsch's general position. Historical relativism (or 'historicism') suggests that cultural values are embedded in history and change over time. No religions (including Christianity) express absolute values which are exempt from this process; and the recognition that this is so is the consequence of the modern historical consciousness—and that is why Troeltsch maintained that the modern age began with the Enlightenment, not with the Reformation, which he regarded as a medieval phenomenon. But in that case, is there anything about religion which persists and endures through the vicissitudes of time? Here, Troeltsch, like R. *Otto, took a *Kantian line, and argued that there is an *a priori* religious mode of consciousness, which brings religions, in all their variety and relativity, into being. In *Die Absolutheit des Christentums* . . . (1902; The Absoluteness of Christianity . . .) he claimed that Christianity is 'relatively absolute' (*relativer absolutismus*) as a religion because it, more than any other religion, affirms the value of personal and ethical beings, locating this character in God and exhibiting it in Christ. His work was wide-ranging, and was much influenced by Max *Weber as he used sociological ideas to analyse the unfolding of Christian forms and institutions. His development of the *Church–Sect (and mysticism) typology has remained influential. In his major work, *Die Soziallehren der christlichen Kirchen und Gruppen* (1912; The Social Teaching of the Christian Churches), he argued that underprivileged and less educated populations are the driving force in religious creativity, since they feel more and ask less: 'It is the lower classes which do the really creative work, forming communities on a genuinely religious basis. They alone unite imagination and simplicity of feeling with a non-reflective habit of mind, a primitive energy and an urgent sense of need.'

S. Coakley, *Christ Without Absolutes* (1988); H.-G. Drescher, *Ernst Troeltsch* (tr. 1993); F. W. Graf and H. Ruddies, *Ernst Troeltsch Bibliographie* (1982); B. A. Reist, *Towards a Theory of Involvement* . . . (1966).

Tṛṣṇa (Skt., 'thirst'). 1. In Hinduism, tṛṣṇa is the longing for life which keeps one bound to *saṃsāra (continuing rebirth); it must be contested by deliberate exercise (*sādhana).

2. In Buddhism, it is more closely analysed. See under its Pāli form, *taṇhā.

Trungpa, Rinpoche Vidyadhara Chögyam (1939–87). Tibetan Buddhist of Kagyü and Nyingma schools. He was recognized as the eleventh Trungpa Tulku when 1 year old and began training, including *Vajrayāna. He escaped to India when the Chinese invaded Tibet, and in 1963 received a Spalding award to study at Oxford. In 1967, he co-founded Samyé-Ling Tibetan Centre in Scotland, and married. Conflict in Scotland meant that in 1970 he left for N. America, where he founded several centres. He also established the Vajradhātu Association of Buddhist Churches. His autobiography (co-authored) is *Born in Tibet* (1977), and he wrote many other works mediating Tibetan Buddhism to the West.

Tsaddik (Ḥasidic leader): see ZADDIK.

Ts'ai-shen. *Taoist god of prosperity, one of the most important gods of religious Taoism (*tao-chiao*), and of folk religion. He is usually portrayed with a dark face and heavy moustache.

Ts'ao Kuo-chiu (one of eight immortals): see PA-HSIEN.

Ts'ao-shan Pen-chi (Jap., Sōzan Honjaku; 840–901). Co-founder, with his teacher (of whom he was dharma-successor, *hassu) *Tung-shan Liang-chieh, of *Ts'ao-tung. He stayed with him only three years or so, but perfectly understood what Tung-shan was attempting to say, eventually expressed in the Five Ranks (see also GO-I). The histories list nineteen disciples, but within four generations his line ended. His true succession lies in *Sōtō.

Ts'ao-tung (Jap., Sōtō). Ch'an/Zen school of Buddhism, the name being derived from the graphs of the two founders, *Tung-shan Liang-chieh and Ts'ao-shan Pen-chi, who in turn received their names from the mountains of their monasteries. In its Chinese form, it is also known as 'The Five Ranks', from its fivefold approach to recognizing the identity of the absolute and the relative, the one and the many. The subtle stanzas appear, with *Hakuin's commentary, in Muira and Sasaki, *Zen Dust*. In reflection of *Taoism, the apparent polarizations can be represented by black and white circles. The Five Ranks encourage the recognition of the movement of each into other, the bent within the straight, the straight within the bent, the emergence from within the straight, the convergence at the middle of the bent, the unity attained. The stanzas of the Five Ranks are now regarded as the consummation of the *kōan process. See further GO-I. Ts'ao-tung is one of the Five Houses of Ch'an Buddhism in the period of the Five Dynasties; but its future lay in Japan as *Sōtō.

Tseng-tzu (supposed author of *Hsiao Ching*): see HSIAO.

Tshar (sect of Sakya): see SAKYA.

Tsha-tshas. Small clay or dough images of holy persons, *chörtens, symbols etc., in Tibetan Buddhism, which may be made with herbs, ground relics, or the ashes of a dead *lama mixed in. They are used as amulets, tied or carried about the person (even to dream of one auspiciously suggests averted disaster), or as votive offerings they may be placed on home or temple shrines, in chörtens, and other holy places. Tsha-tshas are often an art form all of their own, containing carefully wrought designs in just a few square inches or less.

Tsimtsum (contraction in Godhead): see LURIA, ISAAC BEN SOLOMON.

Tsitsit (fringes on a prayer shawl): see ZITZIT.

Tso-ch'an. Chinese for *zazen.

Tsong Khapa (Lobsang Drakpa, *blo.bzang.sgrags. pa*; 1357–1419). Eminent Tibetan scholar and founder of the *Geluk school of Tibetan Buddhism. Having begun his spiritual education at the age of 2 when, already famous for the supernatural portents around him, he received the layman's (*upāsaka) vows from the fourth Karmapa Rolpé Dorje, Tsong Khapa devoted his life to studying *sūtra and *tantra in many different schools, including the later proscribed *Jonang (where he studied Kālacakra) and especially the *Sakya.

At the age of 40, and as probably the most learned man of his era, Tsong Khapa joined the *Kadam monastery of Radreng (*rva.sgreng*), which had been founded in 1056 on *Atiśa's principles of monastic discipline, celibacy, and of only teaching tantra in the context of a 'graduated path' which took sūtra as its basis. Here, in 1402, Tsong Khapa completed his *magnum opus*, *The Great Graduated Path* (*lam.rim.chen.mo*), which was principally based on *Atiśa's *Bodhipathapradīpa*, and has become the root text of the Geluk school. As elsewhere in his voluminous writings, Tsong Khapa emphasizes *Prāsaṅgīka-madhyāmaka as the highest form of reasoning and stresses the correct understanding of relative reality as that which, while not possessing even a conventional own-being, can nevertheless be demonstrated by reasoning to be not non-existent. At the heart of *The Great Graduated Path* is the thesis that, while tantra may be necessary in order to become a fully enlightened Buddha, a prior study of sūtra is absolutely necessary for a preliminary development of wisdom and compassion. In another important work, *The Great Graduated Path of Mantra* (*sngags.rim.chen.mo*), which discusses the four classes of tantra, Tsong Khapa defines the relationship of tantra to sūtra as that between method and wisdom.

In 1408, Tsong Khapa established the Great Prayer (*smon.lam.chen.mo*), a New Year festival held in the *Jokhang, which won him much devotional support. In 1409, Tsong Khapa had enough followers to found his own monastery of Riwo Ganden ('Joyous Mountain'), and although initially calling his order the 'New Kadam', they soon became known as the Geluk. Tsong Khapa's views were similar to those of Atiśa, and it is unclear whether Tsong Khapa had reformed a Kadam tradition which had become lax, or whether the Geluk simply grew out of the Kadam under the impetus of his own personal renown. The founding of Drepung (*'bras.sprungs*) followed in 1416, and of Sera in 1419, the year of Tsong Khapa's death when his body was embalmed and placed inside a *chörten at Ganden.

During his life Tsong Khapa had many visions of *Mañjuśrī, with whom he was said to have a 'teacher–pupil' relationship, yet he is considered to have been *emanations of *Avalokiteśvara and Vajrapāni, as well as of Mañjuśrī, in one body. A popular legend says that Tsong Khapa achieved Buddhahood at death, having postponed it while alive on the grounds that the necessary taking of a Tantric consort may have created misapprehensions among his followers.

Trs. R. A. F. Thurman, *The Life and Teachings of Tsong Khapa* (1982) and *Tsong Khapa's Speech of Gold* . . . (1984); R. Kaschewsky (ed.), *Das Leben* . . . (1971).

Tsou Yen (4th/3rd cent. BCE). One of the earliest Chinese philosophers to systematize a naturalism based on *yin-yang—hence the Yin-yang school (or more fully Yin-yang Wu-hsing-chia, Yin-yang Five Phases School). Through the interaction of male–female, light–dark, heavy–light, heaven–earth, and other opposites, the *T'ai-chi, the primordial foundation, works its way into manifestation by use of the five elements (*wu-hsing*). Change, whether in nature or in history, is a consequence of the distribution of the elements; and Tsou Yen analysed previous history from this point of view. He also held the 'nine continents' view of cosmography, seeing the cosmos as made up of nine continents separated by oceans.

Tso-wang (Chin., 'sitting forgetting'). *Taoist technique of meditation in which the mind floats completely free from content and association and is at one with Tao. It is therefore the highest point of Taoist achievement, requiring much training and discipline. It is the complete realization of *wu-wei. Its attainment is described in *Chuang-tzu* 6. 7.

Tsukimi (moon festival): see FESTIVALS AND FASTS.

Tsung (ancestral): see CHINESE RELIGION.

Tsung-chiao (religion): see CHINESE RELIGION.

Ts'ung-jung Lu (collection of kōans): see KŌAN.

Tsung-mi (5th patriarch): see FIVE WAYS OF CH'AN/ZEN; HUA-YEN.

Ts'un-ssu (Chin., 'sustaining the thought'). *Taoist method of meditation, concentrating on a particular object. This may be literal or conceptual (e.g. the three treasures, *san-pao), or it may be the visualization of the inner deities.

Tsuya (Jap., 'all night'). The Japanese practice of keeping vigil over the dead; the relatives, friends, and acquaintances of the dead keep a watch over his or her soul all night before the day of the funeral ceremony.

Tübingen School. A group of scholars of early Christianity who were influential in the mid-19th cent. They were led by F. C. *Baur and included E. Zeller, A. Hilgenfeld, A. Schwegler, and (for a time) A. Ritschl. In their view, influenced by *Hegel's conception of history, the early church was divided into a Jewish party led by Peter and a gentile party led by Paul. The opposition of the two parties was resolved only in the *'catholic' synthesis of the 2nd cent., at which time the bulk of the New Testament was written. Baur's influence declined after the 1840s, and the work of A. *Harnack and J. B. Lightfoot is usually said to have led to the abandonment of its positions.

Tu bi-Shevat. Jewish *festival of *New Year for trees. This festival is celebrated on 15 Shevat. Among the *Ashkenazim, it was customary to eat fifteen types of fruit. A special order of service was supposedly compiled by *Nathan of Gaza for the *kabbalists. Since the establishment of the State of

*Israel, the festival has become one of thanksgiving for the revival of the land, accompanied, often, by ceremonial tree-plantings by children.

C. Pearl, *Guide to the Minor Festivals and Feasts* (1962).

Tucci, G. (1894–1984). Italian explorer and orientalist, the most influential scholar of Indian and Tibetan *Mahāyāna Buddhism of recent times. After studies in Europe he made his first visit to India in 1925 where his knowledge of Skt. and Tibetan was said to have dazzled the *paṇḍits. He organized a total of eight expeditions to Tibet, and in 1948 he stayed in Lhasa as a personal guest of the fourteenth Dalai Lama and was the only W. Buddhist scholar to spend time at the monastic citadel of *bSam-yas*. His interests covered all things oriental. In his twenties, as a professor of Chinese history, he translated the *Book of Mencius* (1921) into Italian, but his attention soon turned towards Indian Buddhism and the thought and culture of Tibet and its neighbouring regions. Tucci was the founder of the Instituto Italiano per il Medio ed Estremo Oriente in Rome and was a prolific writer of travel books as well as more technical literature. The latter writings cover Tantricism, iconography, Indian logic, folk music, and archaeology, and among his more important publications are *Tibetan Painted Scrolls* (1949), *The Religions of Tibet* (1980), *The Theory and Practice of the Mandala* (1949), and *Storia della filosofia indiana* (1957). On his travels he collected an enormous number of Skt. and Tibetan manuscripts, including over 2,000 Bon-po texts. This in itself was immensely important since many of these works were thought to be no longer extant. Throughout his career Tucci published a great number of scholarly editions of these texts.

Tukārām (*c.*1607–1649). Hindu poet, who, after an unhappy second marriage, turned to religion, starting with the worship of Viṭhobā at Paṇḍherpur. He studied the **Bhāgavata* of *Eknāth, and after a period of study and meditation, began composing verses in Abhaṅga metre. His Abhaṅgas number 6,000–8,000 and are devotional in character, with practical advice for the ordinary man and woman. He banished all *caste barriers from his mind and treated all people alike, putting into effect the equality of all people before God as expounded in the *Bhāgavata*. He practised the presence of God in every detail of life, including his own (anticipated) death: 'I saw my death with my own eyes—superbly glorious it was: the whole universe shook with joy . . . Death and birth are now no more, and I am free from the pettiness of "me" and "mine". God has set me in his place to live, and in his world I am setting him forth.'

J. Nelson-Fraser, *The Poems of Tukārām* (1909–15).

'Tukutendereza' (revivialist chorus: 'We praise thee, Jesus'): see EAST AFRICAN REVIVAL.

Tulasīdās: see TULSĪDĀS.

Tulku (Tib., *sprul.sku.*, 'Transformation Body'). A title applied in Tibetan Buddhism to a reincarnate *lama, i.e. to one who is understood to have already attained lamahood in a previous life. Thus the present fourteenth *Dalai Lama, for example, is considered to be the same 'person' as the first Dalai Lama, successively reincarnating within the same office. Although probably originating for reasons of statecraft, the system of reincarnating lamas coincides well with the *Mahāyāna doctrine of the *bodhisattva, who through wisdom achieves control over his births and deaths, and through compassion exercises that control for the benefit of all beings. The first declared tulku in Tibet was the second *Karmapa Lama, Karma Pakshi (1206–83), of the *Kagyü school.

Tulsi (leader of Jain sect, the Terapanth): see BHIKṢU; ĀCĀRYA.

Tulsīdās or **Tulasīdās** (1532–1623). Indian poet and devotee of *Rāma. He was the son of a *brahman, born in N. India, but because of a bad conjunction of stars, he was abandoned and brought up by a *sādhu. He married a wife to whom he was devoted, but her words ('If you loved Rāma half as much as you love this perishable body, your sorrows would be over') turned him to devotion to Rāma. He retold the **Rāmāyaṇa* in Hindi. His *Ramcaritamānasa* (The Holy Lake of the Deeds of Rāma) is far from being a translation, and remains a profoundly influential spiritual encouragement (sometimes called 'the Bible of North India'): 'Those who regard other men's wives as mothers, and the wealth of others as more lethal than poison, who rejoice when others flourish and are deeply pained when they are afflicted, those to whom you, O Rāma, are dearer than life, in them is your abode full of blessing.' Later, he wrote *Kavitāvali* (tr. R. Allchin, 1964), poems (of that metre) to Rāma, and *Vinayapatrikā*, the petition to Rāma, and at least seven other works.

Trs. A. G. Atkins (1954), W. D. P. Hill (1952), F. S. Growse (1889, 1937); R. Allchin, *Tulsi Das . . .* (1964).

Tummo (one of the Six Doctrines of Naropa): see NĀRO CHOS DRUG.

T'ung Chung-shu (*c.*180–*c.*105 BCE). Confucian philosopher who effected the connection between the assumptions underlying the Yin-yang school (*Tsou Yen) and the state, thus opening the way for *Confucianism to become the state religion. His major work is *Ch'un-ch'iu fan-lu* (Profound Meaning of the Spring and Autumn Annals):

> Those who, in ancient times, invented writing, drew 3 lines and connected them through the middle [王]: the 3 are heaven, earth and humans; that which passes through the centre of each unifies them: possessing the centre of heaven, earth and humans, passing through and unifying them, if that is not the king, who else can do this?

Through this work and three memorials submitted to the imperial court on the relationship between heaven and humans, he exercised great influence on the thought of Han China. For him, *T'ien (Heaven) is both the presiding power and the cosmos as directed to its proper end and purposes. T'ien has a will and creates all things for a purpose: for humans, that purpose is to sustain order. For this reason, *t'ien-ming (Mandate of Heaven) is conferred on the emperor who must respond to this trust with moral excellence. In this way, *t'ien-chih* (the will of heaven) is expressed in the world. It is manifest especially in the Three Bonds of yang and yin which hold society together: ruler (yang) and subject (yin), father and son, husband and wife. Because the cosmos is teleological (addressed to a purpose), dynasties are not stable, but succeed each other according to natural laws.

Tung-shan Liang-chieh (Jap., Tōzan Ryōkai; 807–69). Co-founder, with his pupil Ts'ao-shan, of *Tsao-tung. He began his temple education when young, and was soon recognized as exceptional, and was sent, eventually, to Yün-yen T'an-sheng, through whom he acquired power to 'understand the sermons of inanimate things', i.e. to hear them silently eloquent of their undifferentiated nature. He became dharma-successor (*hassu) of *Yün-yen, and asked him, 'If someone asks me to portray you truly in 100 years time, what shall I say?' Yün-yen replied, 'Say, Just that it is.' Tung-shan did not wholly understand, but later, crossing a stream, he saw his reflection and completely understood.

Tun-huang (Dunhuang). Town in NW of Kansu province in China, a major staging post on the Silk Road trading route. Because it was the point of access to China for Buddhist *missionaries travelling on the overland route from India, it became an important Buddhist centre. The major remains of this presence are in the Mo-kao (Mogao) Caves, also known as the Caves of a Thousand Buddhas, the oldest Buddhist shrines in China. Hundreds of caves contained carvings, decorative paintings, and scrolls. The caves were abandoned in the 14th cent., and rediscovered by accident in 1900. The Manchu government took no interest, and vast quantities of material were sold mainly to Western collectors and museums. In 1961, the Caves were declared national treasures, and much work has been done to prevent flood and other natural damage.

V. H. Mair, *Tan-huang Popular Narratives* (1983); I. V. Vincent, *The Sacred Oasis* (1953).

Tun-wu ju-tao yao-men lun (Zen text on enlightenment): see TA-CHU HUI-HAI.

Turban (Pañjābī, 'pagg', 'pagrī'). Headdress of male *keśadhārī Sikhs from boyhood. Although not one of the *Five Ks, the turban distinguishes male *khālsā Sikhs as the *keś* (uncut hair) must be covered in this way. Turbans are not exclusive to Sikhs, and among Sikhs vary in style and colour. Usually a 5 m. × 1 m. length of starched muslin is used. To receive a turban is an honour. At death, a father's turban is conferred on his eldest son. For many Sikhs the turban is a powerful symbol of their faith. See also AKĀLĪ; DRESS; HEALTHY, HAPPY, HOLY ORGANIZATION; NĀMDHĀRĪ; NIHAṄG.

Turbulent priest: see BECKET, THOMAS À.

Turin Shroud (Christian relic): see SHROUD OF TURIN.

Turīya (Skt., 'the fourth'). The accomplished state of absolute consciousness in Hinduism, beyond waking, dreaming, and deep sleep. It is the realization of the *ātman as *Brahman. The four states are described and analysed in **Māṇḍūkya Upaniṣad* 12, starting from *Oṃ: 'The fourth is without an element, with which there can be no interaction: it is the ceasing of further development, peaceful, without a second. Thus Oṃ is ātman indeed. He who knows this enters the Self with his self—he who knows this indeed'.

Turner, Victor (1920–83). British social and cultural anthropologist latterly working in the USA, best known for his investigations of the meaning, nature, grounds, and functions of Ndembu (Zambia) rituals and symbols. Having treated *rituals as an important component of the social process, Turner came to emphasize their role as mediating between human nature and culture. Influenced by *Freud, he argued that ritual 'brings the ethical and jural norms of society into close contact with strong emotional stimuli' and thereby 'converts the obligatory into the desirable' (*The Forest of Symbols*, 1967). Turner has also contributed to the understanding of the nature of symbolism, how to interpret (decode) *symbols, and, for example, the nature of curing rites. His interest in Ndembu *rites of passage, where liminal periods are important, encouraged Turner to advance the theory of communitas: as well as structured interaction, all societies require contexts of anti-structure; contexts in which bare, and so equal, individuals can recognize their 'humankindness' (see *The Ritual Process*, 1969 and subsequent works on pilgrimage; cf. M. *Buber's *das Zwischenmenschliche*). At the end of his life, he came to realize that the emphasis in his work (and his teaching of other anthropologists) had been wrong, and that he should have recognized that *biogenetic structuralism was correct in returning a genetic contribution to human (and thus religious) behaviours: see his 'Body, Brain and Culture', *Zygon* (1983), 221 ff.

V. Turner (ed.), *Celebration* ... (1982); *Ritual in Human Adaptation*, *Zygon*, 18 (1983).

Tu-shun or **Fa-shun** (557–640). First patriarch of the Chinese Buddhist *Hua-yen school. Beginning life in the army, he became a monk at 18 and originated the theory of the 'ten gates', which were reworked by *Fa-tsang, the founder of the school.

Tu-shun, *Tract on the Meditation of Dharmadhātu* appears in G. G. C. Chang, *The Buddhist Teaching of Totality* (1971).

Tuṣita (Skt., 'contented ones'). Buddhist heaven inhabited by the 'contented gods' (*deva). It is the domain of all *buddhas who need to reappear only once more on earth to work out the last remnants of *karma. It is the domain also of *Maitreya.

T'u-t'an chai (Tao ritual): see CHAI.

T'u-ti. A Chinese deity, the 'earth god', an ubiquitous deity worshipped in almost every village or district of China. His dwelling is the sacred space of the community, whether it is a simple mark or a modest roadside shrine. T'u-ti Kung (Elder Earth) is the protector and benefactor of the locality, who oversees its harvest, health, morality, and other needs. In antiquity, he was mainly god of the dead and fertility, for the earth not only receives the dead but also gives life to the seeds. As China advanced, T'u-ti took on other responsibilities, although these two attributes are still his primary function even to this day.

Hou-t'u is an earlier name for Earth God. In antiquity, there was God Hou-chi (Prince of Millet), progenitor of the Chou dynasty (*c.*1122–256 BCE). 'Hou' denotes fertility or the generative force in Chou times. 'Hou-t'u' therefore denotes the generative force of the earth.

Fu-teh Chen-shen (God of Prosperity and Virtue) is a later name for Earth God. It was given by religious *Taoism in the Sung dynasty (960–1279). 'Chen-shen' is a Taoist designation for divinity, connoting immortality. As Fu-teh Chen-shen, Earth God has become a member of the Taoist pantheon.

Tutu, Desmond Mpilo (b. 1931). Archbishop of Cape Town, and determined opponent of apartheid (see DUTCH REFORMED CHURCH). He was ordained Anglican priest in 1961, and after work in chaplaincy and as a lecturer in theology, he worked for the *World Council of Churches and as general secretary of the South African Council of Churches, 1978–85. He became bishop of Johannesburg (1985–6) and archbishop in 1986. His opposition to apartheid, conducted with dignity and non-violence, earned him the Nobel Peace Prize in 1984. His ebullient and enthusiastic faith earned him the even more important support of a wide diversity of people in S. Africa. He is the author of *Crying in the Wilderness* (1982) and *Hope and Suffering* (1984).

Tvaṣṭṛ. The craftsman of the gods in Hinduism. The ability to create new forms from formless stone, wood, etc., is a manifestation of divine power embodied in Tvaṣṭṛ (*Atharva Veda* 12. 3. 33), and only animals with testicles (i.e. begetters) can be offered to him in sacrifice. He is one of the *Ādityas.

Twelfth Night. A Christian observance, the evening preceding *Epiphany (twelve days after *Christmas). It was the evening of the New Year in the Alexandrian calendar, from which the observance may have derived. It commemorated the different epiphanies of *Christ, e.g. to the shepherds, to the *magi, to the world when he changed water to wine. When the feast was adopted in the West, it became an occasion for festivity and games.

Twelvers, The (Shiʿa movement): see ITHNĀ ʿASHARĪYA.

Twelve Tribes (division of the Jewish people): see TRIBES, TWELVE.

Twice-born. An epithet of the first three *varnas, *brahmans, *kṣatriyas, and *vaiśyas, since the males of these three groups are seen as achieving a second, spiritual, birth (*dvija, 'twice-born') at the investiture of the sacred thread (*upanayana). *Śūdras and *pañchamas* do not share in this ceremony, and are therefore termed 'once-born'.

'Twice-born' is also used of those who have undergone a 'born-again' experience in religion. Although it is usually used of Christians who have undergone a reconversion experience, William *James recognized it as a category in all religions.

Tyāgarāja (1767–1847). Born Tyāgabrahmam, the *primus inter pares* of three S. Indian composers, the others being Muttusvami Dīkṣitar (1777–1835) and Śyāmā Śāstri (1762–1821). Tyāgarāja was a devotee of *Rāma, who resisted invitations to become a court musician—many of his compositions were spontaneous reactions to places of pilgrimage. He believed profoundly that music rested in the primordial creativity of sound (see MANTRA), and that music combined with *bhakti would lead more directly to *mokṣa (release) than any other route, including *yoga:

> To understand and realise the nature of sound as it originates in the six centres of the body is already bliss (*ānanda) and mokṣa, as is the knowledge of the resonant capacities of the body which give rise to the seven resplendent notes of music. Through knowledge (*jñāna) one may indeed attain mokṣa, but only after further births; he who knows music, combined with bhakti, becomes a freed soul (*jīvanmukti) now and here.

Tylor, Sir Edward Burnett (1832–1917). The 'father' of cultural anthropology, whose most influential work was *Primitive Culture* (2 vols., 1871). Although Tylor's evolutionary and psychologistic theorizing as to the origins of language, myth, magic, representations of the self, *animism, and religion as a whole are no longer accepted, he was the first, systematically and carefully, to identify and attend to the problem of explaining apparently irrational or erroneous beliefs and activities. In general terms, his theorizing has a remarkably modern tone: C. *Lévi-Strauss and C. G. *Jung have also seen religious phenomena, to use Tylor's phrase, as 'direct products of the human mind'. In his view (first expressed in 1866), animism is the earliest form of religion, to be studied through 'survivals'.

Tyndale, William, or **Huchens** (*c.*1494–1536). Biblical translator and religious reformer. He was born in Gloucestershire, and worked for his BA and MA at Magdalen Hall, Oxford, 1506–15, at a time when the serious study of Greek was made possible by William Grocyn and Thomas Linacre, and when the lectures of John Colet on *Romans in 1497 had begun to change the way in which the Bible was expounded. From Oxford, he may have gone to Cambridge before becoming tutor to the children of Sir John Walsh in Gloucestershire (important for *Lollardy) in 1522. He preached in Bristol and had to defend himself against charges of *heresy. He translated *Erasmus' *Enchiridion Militis Christiani* for Sir John. But his linguistic skills and his desire to see the Bible translated into English took him to London where he tried to gain the necessary patronage for this from Cuthbert Tunstall, then bishop of London. He discovered that 'not only was there no room in my Lord of London's palace to translate the New Testament but also that there was no room in all England'. Tyndale accordingly went probably to Wittenberg, but then to Cologne and to Worms (all connected with the Protestant *Reformation). His translation of the New Testament was published in Worms in 1526 and was smuggled to England. The Pentateuch came next (Antwerp, 1530), the first translation ever made of Hebrew into English; *Joshua* and *II Chronicles* followed. His New Testament was ceremoniously burnt in London in 1526, and his own life was in danger from English spies and Henry VIII's allies. In 1535 he was imprisoned in the castle of Volvorde, and after trial for heresy he was strangled and burnt at the stake, 6 Oct. 1536, praying that God would 'open the King of England's eyes'. His translations were not immediately used in England (when the Great Bible, see COVERDALE, was finally printed), but they underlie some 80 per cent of the *Authorized Bible (1611). His skill and achievement as a translator left an enduring mark, including many now commonplace phrases: 'the salt of the earth', 'clothed in his right mind', 'the patience of Job'. He preferred to work from the original languages, not from the Latin *Vulgate which perpetuated errors (e.g. Matthew 6. 33, 'kingdom of heaven', not 'of God'). His work outlived his critics, and his intention 'to prepare this pathway into Scripture' by translation was achieved for his day and for the Eng.-speaking world for centuries after. Modern spelling versions have been produced by D. Daniell in 1989, 1992. Other works include *The Obedience of a Christian Man* (1528, a discussion of obedience under God to the secular powers), *The Practice of Prelates* (1530, an attack on the English episcopate), and tracts in answer to Thomas *More's criticism of his translation.

D. Daniell, *William Tyndale, A Biography* (1994); G. E. Duffield (ed.), *The Work of William Tyndale* (1964).

Typology (Gk., *typos*, 'example, figure'). A method of exegesis which takes a text as having a symbolic or anticipatory reference in addition to its apparent historical sense. It is characteristic of traditional Christian readings of the Old Testament, which e.g. finds a 'type' of baptism in the Israelites' crossing of the Red Sea (cf. 1 Corinthians 10. 1–6) or of *Christ in *Adam, *Joshua, or *Melchizedek. It is sometimes said to be more legitimate than *allegory, which loses sight of the plain sense of the text.

Tyrrell, George (1861–1909). *Modernist theologian. An Irish *Protestant by birth, he became a *Roman Catholic and joined the *Jesuits in England. His friendship with F. von *Hügel led to an interest in the historico-critical study of the Bible, and to acquaintance with German scholarship and the works of *Loisy and *Blondel. He became increasingly dissatisfied with *scholasticism, and stressed the experiential aspects of religion and the relativity of theology and doctrinal formulations (e.g. in *Through Scylla and Charybdis*, 1907, and more radically in *Christianity at the Crossroads*, 1909). Expelled from the Jesuits in 1906, he suffered minor excommunication in 1907, and was refused Roman Catholic burial.

D. G. Schultenover, *George Tyrrell . . .* (1981).

Tzitzit (fringes on a prayer shawl): see ZITZIT.

Tzu (Chin., 'ancestor'). Respect for, and sustenance of, ancestors is as central in Chinese religion as in any other. They are commemorated on plaques, before which food and offerings are left, and with which conversations are held, so that ancestors remain a part of the family. For the importance of sustaining ancestors in appropriate ways, see HUN; KUEI.

Tzu Ssu (author of Confucian text): see CHUNG YUNG.

U

U (Jap., 'being'). Existent appearance, in Japanese Buddhism, in contrast to *mu. It is therefore the constituent cause of appearance, as well as the state produced by the working out of *karma.

UAHC: see UNION OF AMERICAN HEBREW CONGREGATIONS.

Ubiquity (Lat., *ubique*, 'everywhere'). The claim, in general, that God is present to all events and circumstances, i.e. is omnipresent. In *Luther, ubiquity is the presence of Christ to each enactment of the *Lord's Supper.

Ucceda-diṭṭhi (nihilism): see UCCHEDAVĀDA; NIHILISM.

Ucchedavāda (Pāli, Skt., 'the doctrine of the cutting-off (of the soul and the body)'). Annihilationism (*nihilism), the doctrine of no afterlife in any form whatsoever, the belief that personal identity perishes with the body at death. It and its antithesis, *eternalism, occur in the Buddhist *Nikāyas as the two most common forms of misrepresenting reality. The *Buddha is reported to have raised two principal objections to this doctrine: it is shown to be false by the ability to remember previous lives; and it is a viewpoint which precludes the possibility of *karma, because the annihilation of self at death implies the identity of self and body. Charged, himself, with being an annihilationist owing to his teaching of no-self (*anatta), the Buddha replied that he believed only in the annihilation of attachment (*rāga), hate (*dosa), and delusion (*moha). According to the *Pāyāsi Sutta* (*Dīgha Nikāya* 2. 332–9), criminals were put to death in various gruesome ways as part of experiments intended to show there was no survival of a soul at death.

Ucchiṣṭa (Skt., 'left over'). The remnants/remainders of a sacrifice in Hinduism. The continuing power within them helps to sustain the world (*Atharva Veda* 11. 7).

Uchimura Kanzō (1861–1930). Pioneer Japanese *Protestant leader and founder of the Non-Church (Mukyōkai) movement. Like many of the first generation of Japanese Protestant leaders, Uchimura was born into a *samurai family. He joined the initial class of the agricultural academy in Sapporo founded by the national government, under William S. Clark, president of Massachusetts Agricultural College. Clark stayed in Japan only eight months but influenced many young Japanese and introduced Uchimura to Christianity. Before Clark left, all the class signed the 'Covenant of Believers in Jesus', which Clark himself had written; and even after Clark's departure they succeeded in winning the entire next class to sign the same covenant.

They were baptized by M. C. Harris, an American *Methodist missionary who now became their pastor. Seven members of this group, however, became dissatisfied with the structure of their church and with the methods of their pastor. They decided to form a fellowship according to their own understanding of the New Testament. All seven were held to be equal in authority and took turns in assuming the responsibilities of leadership, including preaching. Harris was sympathetic, but with the coming of missionaries of other denominations, misunderstanding arose, and the young men became angry over what they felt were the evils and folly of denominational rivalry. In addition, an unfortunate incident in the use of money from Western churches impressed upon them the necessity of financial independence from W. missionaries. From this modest beginning grew the great Mukyōkai movement in Japan, of which Uchimura Kanzō became the most influential leader.

Uchimura spent four years studying in the USA at Amherst College and Hartford Seminary, returning in 1888. Two years later, he became a teacher in the new government academy to prepare students for the Imperial University. On 9 Jan. 1891, the teachers were compelled to participate in a ceremony that became standard procedure for all schools in the Japanese empire until the end of the Second World War. This was to make a low bow of obeisance before a personally signed copy of the Imperial Rescript on Education, which had been promulgated the previous autumn. Some Christian teachers absented themselves from school to avoid the issue of possible idolatry. Uchimura refused to do this, and in the presence of sixty professors and over 1,000 students he went forward but did not bow.

Uchimura was assured by Christian friends that bowing in this case was not an act of worship, and after reflection he decided to conform. The incident, however, became a *cause célèbre*, and Uchimura was forced to resign his post. He continued to support himself by teaching, but from 1892 he turned seriously to writing. Uchimura was deeply patriotic, but uncritical affirmation of the socio-political *status quo* appeared to him a perversion of patriotism. As a result he used his pen in the boldest criticism of contemporary 'feudalism, corruption and chauvinism'. His public criticism of both the Sino-Japanese War (1894–5) and the Russo-Japanese War (1904–5) emerged from these convictions.

Uchimura wrote at first for secular periodicals, but his posture in considering socio-political issues was consistently that of a moral prophet. He began publication in 1900 of his own magazine, *Seisho no Kenkyū* (Biblical Research), which had increasing popularity over the years and printed much of his best work. In 1918 Uchimura began a programme of Sunday public lectures which affirmed the concept and practice of the Church as a relatively unorganized *ecclesia, over against the tendency in almost all the major confessions or denominations in the West to give high theological value to specific structures of church organization.

Uchimura was primarily concerned for Christian freedom, and in the context of his own time and place this meant the spiritual independence of Japanese Christians *vis-à-vis* the almost overwhelming cultural influence of W. forms of Christianity. For this reason Uchimura was able to speak with telling power to members of Japanese churches as well as to those of Mukyōkai, to non-Christians as to Christians. He affirmed *both* Japan *and* Jesus, and was often attacked from each side. He wrote as the inscription for his tomb: 'I for Japan; | Japan for the world; | The world for Christ; | And all for God.'

Diary of a Japanese Convert (1895); Masaike Megumu, *Uchimura Kanzo den* (Jap., 1950; 1977); R. Moore, *Culture and Religion in Japanese-American Relations: Essays on Uchimura Kanzo, 1861–1930* (1981).

Uchiwamaki (fan festival): see NARA BUDDHISM.

Udāna. 1. In Hinduism, 'breathing upwards', the *prāṇa which unites the physical and metaphysical aspects of human form.

2. In Buddhism (solemn utterances): see KHUDDAKA NIKĀYA.

Udāsī (Pañjābī, 'withdrawn, dejected', from Skt., *udas*, 'grief'). 1. Ascetic Sikh order. The Udāsīs revere Gurū *Nānak and the *Ādi Granth, claiming as their founder Srī Chand, Gurū Nānak's unmarried elder son. They emphasize celibacy (*brahmacarya) in contrast to the mainstream Sikh ideal of *grahastī, and so perpetuate *Nāth principles within Sikhism.

When Gurū Nānak appointed *Aṅgad as successor instead of Srī Chand, the latter displayed his grief by throwing ashes on his own head and body. Consequently Udāsīs use *ashes for ceremonial purposes. They generally wear salmon-coloured clothing and are clean-shaven, although some have long, matted hair. They are forbidden to consume flesh, spirits, and *tobacco.

The four principal sub-orders (*dhūans*, 'hearths') were established by the four disciples of Srī Chand's chosen successor Gurdittā, a son of Gurū *Hargobind. During the period of persecution by the Mughals, Sikhs entrusted the care of many important shrines to Udāsī *granthīs and *mahants, who could save their lives by denying association with Sikhism. Udāsī mahants installed Hindu deities, and in some cases abused *gurdwārā premises by misconduct. (See TALVAṆḌĪ RĀI BHOI DĪ). By the 1925 Sikh Gurdwārās Act, Udāsī shrines could not be classed as gurdwārās.

2. Gurū Nānak described the true udāsī or renunciant in *Vār Rāmkalī, Ādi Granth, p. 952.

3. In the *janam-sākhīs, udāsī refers to the travels of Gurū Nānak, perhaps because during these he assumed the appearance of travelling mendicants.

Udayana (1025–1100 CE). A Hindu theologian of the *Nyāya-Vaiśeṣika tradition who established arguments for the existence of God (*Īśvara) by means of the Indian syllogism. The main argument in his 'Handful of the Flowers of Logic' (*Nyāyakusumāñjali*) is a form of the *cosmological argument that the universe must have a maker as its cause because it has the nature of an effect. Udayana argues that the maker, Īśvara, has intentionality (*icchā*), cognition (*jñāna), and effort (*prayatna*), and through these qualities (*guṇa) he moves the eternal atoms (*aṇu) into the various combinations which constitute the cosmos. The particular soul (*ātman) is eternally distinct from Īśvara, who arranges the cosmos in order that the soul can experience the results of its past actions (*apūrva). Through all this, the analysis is itself an act of worship: 'Logical investigation may be well called the contemplation of God, and this is really worship when it is attached to the hearing of *śruti [scripture].'

Tr. of *Kusumāñjali* by E. B. Cowell (1864).

Uddālaka Āruni (character in the Chandogya Upaniṣad): see CHANDOGYA UPANIṢAD.

Udgātṛ or **Udgātar.** One of four chief priests in a Hindu *sacrificial ritual. He chants the hymns of the *Sāma Veda*, the chant being called udgītha.

Uemura Masahisa (1858–1925). Pioneer Japanese *Protestant Christian leader. Uemura was a member of the original Yokohama Band. A characteristic of early Japanese Protestantism was the formation of 'bands' of young Christians, the best-known other bands being the Sapporo Band, from which came *Uchimura Kanzō, and the Kumamoto Band, from which came Niijima Jō. Enduring great privation in order to continue his education under American missionaries, Uemura never graduated formally from any school but read widely.

He was baptized in 1873 and almost at once committed himself to the life of a Christian evangelist. In 1877 he entered the new theological seminary at Tsukiji in Tokyo, starting to preach in the city, and seeking to find meaning in the 'history of salvation' for his own pre-Christian religious experience and that of his people.

Uemura remained in Tokyo after leaving the

seminary, and finally as pastor of what became the great citadel of *Presbyterian-Reformed faith in Japan, Fujimichō church, he found the base for his increasingly extensive and influential Christian service. He began early to show unusual talent as a writer. In 1890 he began publication of the bimonthly magazine *Nihon Hyōron*. His first important theological work, *Shinri Ippan* (Universal Truth), was published in 1884. He also became a member of the Old Testament Translation Committee (Protestant) and co-operated in the preparation of the first joint Protestant hymnal. After the founding of Meiji Gakuin by James Hepburn, Uemura became a professor in its theological department, without relinquishing his pastoral responsibilities or broader literary work. He participated as a leader of growing importance in the organizational development of the *Nihon Kirisuto Kyōkai* (The United Church of Christ in Japan).

Uemura showed his independence of spirit when he published a statement in support of Uchimura Kanzō, leader of the independent Non-Church movement, after the famous disloyalty incident in 1891 (see UCHIMURA KANZŌ), and in conducting a memorial service for Ōishi Seinosuke, executed after the high treason incident of 1910. One of the most illuminating aspects of his career was his attitude toward women: married in 1880, he both loved and respected his wife in a way unusual in Japan at the time. He once sharply reproved a younger pastor who referred to his own wife by the old-fashioned Sino-Japanese term *gusai* (presumably suggesting humility but literally 'foolish wife'). In correspondence with his own wife, Uemura on occasion employed the word *kensai* ('wise wife'), and in the context of contemporary views of women, the practice constituted a veritable revolution in literary usage. Uemura was the first to propose the ordination of women as elders in the *Nihon Kirisuto Kyōkai* and in spite of opposition was able to secure the adoption of this policy, perhaps the first instance of the ordination of women as elders in the history of the Presbyterian-Reformed tradition anywhere in the world.

Ugarit (*Ras Shamra). Ancient city of the Middle East. Archaeological excavations, especially of the Ugaritic texts, at Ugarit have had an important effect on biblical studies: the city is not mentioned in the Bible, but its social structure in the Late Bronze Age casts light on *Canaanite culture and religion.

G. R. Driver, *Canaanite Myths and Legends* (1956); C. F. A. Schaeffer (ed.), *Ugaritica*, i–vi (1939–69).

Ŭich'ŏn (1055–1101). Korean Buddhist monk. Ŭich'ŏn founded the Ch'ŏnt'ae (*T'ien-t'ai) sect in Korea in the year 1097 and, in addition, laboured to bring about a reconciliation between the 'doctrinal school' (*kyojong*) and the 'meditational school' (*sŏnjong*). He compiled a catalogue of scriptural commentaries and treatises, altogether 1,010 titles in 4,740 fascicles, and, on the basis of this work, endeavoured to publish supplements to the Korean Buddhist canon existing at that time.

Ŭisang or **Master Taesŏng Wŏn'gyo** (625–702). Korean Buddhist monk, who studied *Hua-yen Buddhism under Chih-yen (602–68). The second patriarch of the Hwaŏm (Chinese Hua-yen) sect, he founded the Pusŏk subsect of Hwaŏm in Korea, and established Hwaŏm as the ideological foundation of the Silla dynasty (668–935). His *Diagram of the Hwaŏm One-Vehicle World*, a *mandalic, meditational device of 210 Chinese characters, has been highly acclaimed by E. Asian Buddhists as a superb compendium of Hua-yen thought. He had ten Hwaŏm monasteries built, convertible to forts in the event of foreign invasion.

For illustration of the *Diagram*, see S. Odin, *Process Metaphysics and Hua-yen Buddhism* (1982).

Uji (equivalence of being and time): see DOGEN.

Ujigami. Japanese *kami of the kinship group, eventually personified as the ancestor god. Ujigami protected the family, and in later times becomes the kami of one's birthplace. At the New Year celebrations, those who cannot return home have some earth from their home Ujigami shrine sent to them. An ujiko is a child of the Ujigami, so the word is also used of Shinto worshippers.

Ujiko: see UJIGAMI.

Ujjayini (Ujjain, originally Avanti). One of the four sacred Hindu cities where a *kuṃbha-mela is held once every twelve years.

ʿUlamā (Arab., pl. of *ʿalīm*, one who possesses *ʿ*ilm*, 'knowledge'). The learned and qualified in Islam, in matters of law, constitution, and theology. Through them the *ijmaʿ (consensus) of the community is expressed, and they are the guardians of tradition, both in a general and technical (*ḥadīth) sense. In Shīʿa Islam, the nearest equivalent in practice is the *mujtāhid*, though the term ʿulamā is applied.

Ullambana (from Skt., *avalambana*, 'hanging down'). Rituals performed to save deceased people from torments after death—such as being suspended upside down. According to *Ullambana Sūtra*, the first performance of the ritual was by Maudgalyāyana (3rd cent. CE) on behalf of his mother. In China, Ullambana is held on the fifteenth day of the seventh month to help hungry ghosts (*preta): offerings of food and wealth (often in paper or representational form) are made to succour them. In Japan, Urabon (or more simply Bon) is held on 15 July or 15 Aug.

Ultimate concern: see TILLICH, PAUL.

Ultimate salvation (in contrast to proximate): see GREAT TRADITION, LITTLE TRADITION.

Ultramontanism (Lat., *ultra montes*, 'beyond the mountains', i.e. the Alps). A movement emphasizing the pre-eminence of *Roman authority in the Church. It was opposed from the 17th cent. onwards to *Gallicanism in France, Josephinism in Austria, and similar attempts elsewhere to promote the development of national churches independent of Roman, but under state, control. In the 19th cent., ultramontanism was closely associated with support for the *papacy's temporal power, and for the doctrine of papal *infallibility.

Umā. Non-Vedic Hindu goddess, first mentioned in *Kena Upaniṣad*, where she mediates between Brahmā and other gods. She is the daughter of Himavat, ruler of the *Himālayas, so she is the highest point of being. As the spouse of *Śiva (hence his name Umāpati, Umā's spouse), she became identified with many goddesses, *Pārvatī, *Durgā, etc.

ʿUmar al-Khayyām (Muslim mathematician and poet): see OMAR KHAYYAM.

ʿUmar ibn al-Khattāb (d. 644 (AH 23)). Second caliph (*khalīfa) and main architect of the Arab Islamic empire. Originally he was an enemy of Islam, but had a sudden conversion four years before the *hijra. In *Madīna, ʿUmar's energy of will, piety, wisdom, and organizing ability made him second to the Prophet *Muḥammad in authority and prestige. The Prophet nicknamed him *faruq*, 'distinguisher' (between truth and falsehood). According to tradition, Muḥammad said, 'If God had willed that there should have been another prophet after me, ʿUmar would have been he.' ʿUmar successfully championed Abu Bakr's nomination as caliph upon the prophet's death. ʿUmar emerged as a natural leader, a fact recognized by his contemporaries. As second caliph he organized the Islamic conquests and the administration of the empire. Traditions reveal, however, that he was feared rather than loved, and at the height of his power he was assassinated at Madīna.

In his inauguration speech ʿUmar declared, 'The Arabians are truly an unruly camel, and, by God, I am he who can keep them on the right path.' He recognized that tribal identification was too deep-rooted in Arabian society to be abolished by a decree, and that the allegiance and co-operation of the tribal leaders was essential for the smooth running of his administration. Also, tribal identification provided a means by which ʿUmar classified individuals for pay, military organization, tax, and settlement. ʿUmar secured the loyalty of the tribal leaders, first by persuasion on a purely religious ground (unity of the *'umma), and secondly by resorting to a policy of 'conciliation of hearts', services in return for a promise of extra booty.

It was during ʿUmar's caliphate that Muslim religious and political institutions arose which were to be the model for future generations. Among these were: the *dīwān* ('stipend register'), a form of welfare state by which annual stipends were paid to all Muslims from the public treasury; regulations for non-Muslim subjects (*dhimmi); military garrisons which later became the great cities of Islam, e.g. Kūfā and Fustat; the office of *qāḍi (judge); religious ordinances such as obligatory nightly prayers in the month of *Ramaḍān; civil and penal codes; the hijra *calendar; and the standardization of the text of the *Qur'ān.

Orthodox *Sunni sources praise ʿUmar for piety, justice, and make him a model for all the virtues of Islam. In contrast, *Shīʿa sources retain an animus against the man who blocked the claims of *ʿAlī.

Umāsvāmi or **Umāsvāti** (*c.*2nd cent. CE). Jain disciple of the revered *Kundakunda. To him is attributed the **Tattvārtha Sūtra*. He and his *Sūtra* are claimed by both of the two major divisions among the Jains, *Digambara and Śvetāmbara, the former calling him Umāsvāmi, the latter Umāsvāti.

Umayyads (Arab., *al-dawlah al-Umawiyyah*). The first hereditary dynasty of caliphs (*khalīfa) in Sunni Islam. The founder of the dynasty was *Muʿāwiyya, the son of *Abu Sufyān, of the Umayyah (hence the name) clan of the *Quraysh of *Mecca. Muʿāwiyya was the governor of Syria who led the opposition to the claims of *ʿAlī. He established his capital at Damascus in 661 (AH 41) and ruled until 680 (AH 60). He was succeeded by his son, Yazid I, who continued to resist *Shīʿa uprisings, winning the battle of *Karbalā' and putting to death the son of *ʿAlī, *al-Ḥusain. Under the Umayyads, the Muslim Empire increased at a rapid rate, stretching by 732 from the Atlantic and the borders between Spain and France in the West, to the borders of China and India in the East—in that year Charles Martel halted the Arab advance at Poitiers and Tours. In Spain, the foundations were laid for a great flourishing of trade, crafts, architecture, and learning—the final expulsion of the Muslims did not take place until the 17th cent. But elsewhere the Umayyads ruled more severely and autocratically, introducing a client system (*mawla) which, with the taxation necessary to sustain the caliphs, produced inevitable resentment. The Shiʿites (i.e. *Ithna ʿAsharites) remained a focus for the increasing unrest; the ʿAbbāsids sought their support and adopted or adapted some points of their doctrine. The last Umayyad caliph, Marwan II, 'the wild ass of Mesopotamia', was beheaded in Egypt in 750 (AH 132). The ʿAbbāsids succeeded, although an Umayyad dynasty continued in Spain, known as the Western Caliphate.

Umbanda. A Brazilian cult which, because of its syncretizing tendencies, has also become a general term for all forms of a new eclectic and *syncretist religious complex in urban Brazil. The spiritual world is composed of many spirit powers drawn from sources such as the following: (i) *caboclos*, spirits of great Amerindian leaders or of spiritualized natural forces; (ii) *pretos velhos*, spirits of the old or wise among Negro slaves, (iii) *crianças*, spirits of children who died young; (iv) *orixas*, spirits of African ancestors or deities, especially Yoruba; (v) spirits of *Jesus, the Virgin *Mary, or the saints of Portuguese folk Catholicism, often equated with the previous group; and (vi) other spirits and occult powers as understood in the sophisticated French spiritualism articulated by Alan Kardec (1804–69), which attracts the higher social classes. Communication with these spirits through mediums brings knowledge or power to overcome life's difficulties, and those who begin as clients at a séance may end by identifying with some local cult centre and its beliefs. Estimates of adherents vary from 20 to 30 million, and suggest that Umbanda has been sampled by up to 80 per cent of the population. Although expanding into Uruguay and Argentina, it is essentially a Brazilian religion that fuses the three main races and cultures (Indian, African, and European); replaces folk Catholicism as this is eroded by Catholic reform and modernization; and has a religious system of patron *saints that matches the social system of political patronage.

H. F. Figge, *Geisterkult, Besessenheit und Magie in der Umbanda-Religion* . . . (1973).

'Umma (Arab., pl. *umam*). People, community, a powerful and sometimes visionary concept in Islam. The word has various uses in the *Qur'ān, but it is used especially in contrast to the social divisions of humanity: 'Humanity was a single 'umma. Then they fell into divisions. If a word had not previously gone out from your Lord, the matter between them would have been decided, concerning which they disagreed' (10. 19). Such division is in disobedient conflict with the unity which is a necessary consequence of the unity of God from whom all creation comes (*tawhīd). To each 'umma in separation (i.e. nation), therefore, a prophet has been sent to recall it to Islam—with little success until the coming of *Muḥammad. While the Qur'ān required Muḥammad to establish an Arab 'umma out of the disunited tribes, it also envisaged the creation of a single 'umma transcending the continuing divisions in the world. The first implementation of this in practice can be seen in the Constitution of *Madīna. The early disintegration of the Muslim community into *Sunni and *Shiʿa Islam (despite much that is held and done in common by them), and the relatively ineffective efforts to establish *pan-Islam, show how far the vision is from being realized: this fact has given much impetus to resurgent Islam in the 20th cent., not least in its critique of governments in what are ostensibly Muslim states (i.e. those in which Muslims are a majority of the population, but in which Islamic principles do not constrain government).

'Umm al-Kitāb (Arab., 'Mother of the Book'). The 'heavenly pattern' of the *Qur'ān itself. This original is thought of as pre-existent 'in a tablet preserved' in heaven (85. 21). From it, the revelations of the Qur'ān were sent down gradually to the Prophet *Muḥammad. The term 'Umm al-Kitāb is also used for the *Fātiḥa, which is said to contain the essentials of the whole Qur'ān. The tablet is known as al-Lawḥ.

Ummī (Arab.). A term used in Qur'ān 7. 157 and 158, *al-rasūl al-nabī al-ummī* ('the prophet, messenger, the unlettered one'), denoting Muḥammad. It is traditionally (and generally by Muslims) understood as meaning that Muḥammad was totally unable to read or write, so emphasizing the miracle (*iʿjāz) of the *Qur'ān, with its surpassing eloquence coming into being via a complete illiterate. If, however, ummī is read as expressing a distinction from the Jews (who were 'people with a book'), then it must mean 'scriptureless', i.e. 'illiterate' in being, as yet, without an Arabic scripture. Ummī has also been translated 'gentile', or 'of the common folk'; but this is to miss the real clue. The sense suggested tallies with the Qur'ān's own insistence that it is 'an Arabic Qur'ān'. It seems doubtful that Muḥammad could have been a successful merchant if totally unable to read or write, though in respect of the Qur'ān, he may well have used amanuenses.

Ummon School. One of the *'five houses' (*goke-shichi-shu*) of Ch'an Buddhism, founded by *Yun-men Wen-yen (Jap., Ummon Bun'en), hence known as Yun-men-tsung (Ummon-shu). The best-known representative of the school in China is *Hsüeh-tou Ch'ung-hsien; eventually the school was absorbed into *Rinzai.

'Umra. Muslim *pilgrimage, specifically the 'lesser pilgrimage' within the boundaries of the *Masjid al-Ḥarām in *Mecca. These rites can be performed at any time by the individual, who thus gains merit; but they constitute part of the *ḥajj, and as such are carried out in common in the month of *Dhū'l-hijja. The rites of 'Umra consist of: *ṭawāf ('circumambulation' of the *Kaʿba); kissing the *Black Stone; *saʿy (running) between the two elevations of al-Ṣafā' and al-Marwa. 'Umra, along with the ḥajj itself, has origins in the pagan period, but the rites were given an Islamic character by the *Qur'ān and by Muslim practice.

Unam Sanctum (bull): see EXTRA ECCLESIAM . . .

Unction. The religious use of oil for *anointing; and in Christian use specifically the rite of anointing of the sick. The practice has its authority in the New Testament (Mark 6. 13, James 5. 14 f.), and in the Middle Ages came to be numbered among the seven *sacraments. In the early cents., it was connected with recovery from illness, but thereafter the rite became so closely connected with repentance and the whole *penitential system that it was commonly postponed until death was approaching. Thus the name 'extreme unction' by which the rite was long known probably derives from its reception *in extremis*. The 1972 Catholic rite uses only the title

'Anointing of the Sick', and lays much greater emphasis on healing. In the Greek Orthodox Church the rite is called *euchelaion* ('oil of prayer'). It should, if possible, be administered by seven priests, but one is permitted. A brush is used, and the oil is mixed with wine (from the parable of the Good Samaritan). The anointing ends with the *gospel being laid on the head of the sick person, to signify that the same *dunamis* ('power') is being transferred.

Underhill, Evelyn (1875–1941). Christian spiritual writer. Born into an unreligious upper middle-class family, she quickly showed an interest in the religious capacities of the human soul, culminating in her great work, *Mysticism* (1911). Her own personal religion developed erratically: drawn to Rome but repelled by anti-Modernism, she found her eventual home in Anglicanism only in 1921 (under the influence of von *Hügel). Her understanding of the spiritual life became more sacramental and Christocentric. As an Anglican, she exercised an enormous influence through her books (among them, *Worship*, 1936) and spiritual direction, both with individuals and in the giving of retreats. All gardeners know the importance of good root development before we force the leaves and flowers. So our life in God should be deeply rooted . . . before we presume to expect to produce flowers or fruits; otherwise we risk shooting up into one of those lanky plants which never do without a stick.

C. J. R. Armstrong, *Evelyn Underhill* . . . (1976).

Underworld. Domain in which the dead are (or were) believed to have continued existence—'life' would be too strong a word (see SHEOL). Whereas it was once thought that all the dead ended up in the same place somewhere beneath the earth, it was later believed that the evil were separated from the good, and that only the evil were in the underworld, which then became a place of punishment. In this way *hell developed from the underworld.

S. G. F. Brandon, *Man and his Destiny in the Great Religions* and *The Judgement of the Dead* (1967).

U-Netanneh Tokef (Heb., 'let us declare the importance'). Jewish *piyyut recited on *Rosh ha-Shanah and Yom Kippur (*Day of Atonement). It was written *c.*8th cent. CE, and announces that God is full of forgiveness, and that 'repentance, prayer and charity avert the severe judgement'. According to tradition, the piyyut was first recited by R. Amnon of Mainz whose hands and feet had been cut off on the orders of the local *archbishop when he refused to become a Christian. Carried into a synagogue, he chanted this prayer with his dying breath. However, the discovery of a manuscript of the piyyut in the *Cairo Genizah means that it antedates R. Amnon by at least three centuries.

P. Birnbaum, *High Holiday Prayer Book* (1951).

Ungan Donjō (Ch'an/Zen master): see YUN-YEN T'AN-SHENG.

Uniat(e) Churches. More properly Eastern Catholic or Eastern-rite Catholic Churches. Churches in union with *Rome, but retaining their own language, customs, and *canon law—e.g. allowing marriage of the clergy and communion in both kinds. The name 'Uniates' is a disparaging term used by the *Orthodox Church with unhappy memories of what this form of association with Rome has implied. The Council of *Florence (1438–45) had set forward the principle that in reunion between E. and W. there should be diversity of traditions in unity of faith. But this gave way to an encouragement of piecemeal reunion, often under political constraints, especially when boundaries changed, altering the predominant religious group—as with the union with Ukraine, Ruthenia, and Romania. In the Middle East, the situation of Christians under Islam was in any case different. Apart from the several different rites (Antiochene, Alexandrian, Chaldean, Armenian, *Melkite) which entered into union mainly because of the assistance the connection might bring, the *Maronite Church has a history distinct from Orthodoxy. In India, the attempt of the Portuguese to impose W. discipline on the St Thomas Christians created various divisions. Two groups entered into union with Rome, the *Malabar Christians and the Malankara Church. In fact, far from reinforcing local tradition, all of these unions led to a process of Latinization, which demonstrated to Orthodoxy at large that this was a process of proselytization, not of seeking a union of equals. The Eastern Catholic Churches rapidly became an obstacle to union, rather than a step towards it. *Vatican II emphasized their ecumenical role, and the revised canon law has jurisdiction only in the West: all regulations for the Eastern Catholic Churches are said to be provisional until reunion with Eastern Orthodoxy is achieved. The Uniat Church in Ukraine was forcibly joined to the Orthodox Church by the Soviet government in 1946, and the Uniat Church in Romania was compelled to join the Romanian Orthodox Church in 1948: since the liberalization of the political regimes in Ukraine and Romania, Uniat groups are working for the return of their church buildings, and look again to union with Rome. The collapse of Communist regimes has again reopened the issue of proselytization, particularly in view of Pope *John Paul II's vision of a newly Christianized Europe. For the Orthodox, the question of 'whose Christianity?' is inevitable.

V. Pospishik, *Ex Occidente Lex* . . . (1970); R. G. Robertson, *The Eastern Catholic Churches* (1990).

Unification Church: see MOON, SUN MYUNG.

Uniformity, Acts of. Four acts of Parliament (1549, 1552, 1559, 1662) which regulated the worship of the Church of England and the use of the *Book of Common Prayer*. The 1662 Act, part of the Restoration settlement, contained as an annex the *BCP* still in use, and required all ministers to assent to it. This Act remains on the statute-book, but has been radically amended by 1974 legislation allowing *alternative services.

Union of American Hebrew Congregations (UAHC). Association of *Reform Jewish congregations in the USA and Canada. The organization, founded in 1873, was responsible for the foundation of the *Hebrew Union College. It is concerned with religious education, congregational organization, brother- and sisterhoods, youth work, *synagogue administration, and social action. Its headquarters are in New York.

Union of Orthodox Jewish Congregations of America (UOJCA). Association of *Orthodox Jewish congregations in the USA. The organization was founded in 1898 and is responsible for *kashrut* supervision, sponsors a women's and a youth division, and provides administrative advice to Orthodox congregations.

Unitarianism. A religious movement connected with Christianity. Unitarians are those who reject the Trinitarian understanding of God. Although there are many antecedents, the specific point of origin for the movement is usually taken to be the work of *Servetus, and of the Sozzinis (i.e. *Socinianism). The first Unitarian congregation in England was formed in 1774, and in the USA in 1782, but the movement did not become fully organized until the Baltimore sermon of W. E. Channing in 1819, on 'Unitarian Christianity'. The American Unitarian Association was founded in 1825. In 1961, the Unitarians merged with the *Universalists, the joint movement becoming known as the Unitarian Universalist Association. It is characterized by an emphasis on members seeking truth out of human experience, not out of allegiance to creeds or doctrines. There is no hierarchical control, each congregation being self-governing. There are more than a thousand congregations, mainly in the USA and Canada.

D. Robinson, *The Unitarians and the Universalists* (1985); E. M. Wilbur, *A History of Unitarianism* (1945, 1952).

Unitarians. Arab. *al-Muwaḥḥidūn* can be translated as 'the Unitarians', and it occurs particularly, in Islam, in *Ismāʿīlī and *Sūfī movements, where the unity of Being is stressed, with human (or sometimes all) appearances being manifestations of that one Being. See also Almohads in *Ibn Tumart; Druzes.

Unitas Fratrum: see MORAVIAN BRETHREN.

United Church of Christ. The body formed in the USA by the union of the Congregational Christian churches with the Evangelical and Reformed in 1961.

D. Horton, *The United Church of Christ* (1962).

United Reformed Church. The body formed by the union of the *Congregational Church of England with the *Presbyterian Church of England, which came into being in Oct. 1972. The URC's work is distributed throughout twelve provinces, each with its own moderator. In 1983 it had a membership of over 140,000 with 1,943 churches. Negotiations with the *Churches of Christ resulted in the majority of its churches joining the URC in 1981.

United Synagogue. Association of *Ashkenazi Jewish congregations in Great Britain. The organization was established by Act of Parliament in 1870. It supports the British *Chief Rabbinate, the London *Bet Din, and all the *synagogues which accept the authority of the Chief Rabbi.

United Synagogue of America. Association of *Conservative Jewish *synagogues in the USA and Canada. The organization was founded by Solomon *Schechter in 1913. It seeks to strengthen 'historical Judaism' through such agencies as the United Synagogue Commission on Jewish education, the National Academy for Adult Jewish Studies, the National Women's League of the United Synagogue, the Rabbinical Assembly, the United Synagogue Youth, the National Federation of Jewish Men's Clubs, and the Commission on Social Action.

Unitive Way. Third and last of the *Three Ways in prayer. In this, after experiencing the *purgative and *illuminative ways, the soul is united with God by love: hence the imagery of spiritual betrothal and marriage, which itself suggests the indefectible state of cleaving to God characteristic of this way.

Universal Church of the Kingdom of God. An evangelistic church founded in Brazil in 1977 by Edir Macedo, called *bishop. The church emphasizes faith healing, and evokes generous giving on the part of the faithful (estimated in 1995 at about $15 million a week). As a result, the church has bought television and radio stations and other media businesses. The church spread rapidly in Brazil (and in at least thirty other countries), adopting a critical attitude to *Roman Catholicism, the dominant religion of Brazil. The church became publicly controversial in 1995 when, after a television attack was made on the Virgin *Mary, the attorney-general in Brazil ordered an investigation of the church for alleged tax fraud and for alleged links with drug cartels. The accusations were reinforced by videos of Macedo and other church leaders discussing how to extract more donations from their followers.

Universal House of Justice (*Baytu'l-adl-i aʿẓam*). The Supreme ruling body of the *Bahā'ī Faith. Formulated in the writings of *Bahā'u'llāh and his successors, the House of Justice was first elected in 1963 by ballot vote by the members of all national Bahā'ī Assemblies. At present, the House of Justice is re-elected every five years and comprises nine members. Bahā'īs regard its judgements as divinely guided and authoritative.

Universalism

Judaism The claim, in contrast to particularism, that a religion is true for all humanity. Judaism is universalistic in that it recognizes the absolute sovereignty of God and that *messianic redemption is for all humankind. It is particularist in that it perpetuates the survival of the Jewish people as a separate entity.

D. Cohn-Sherbok, *Judaism and Other Faiths* (1993).

Christianity The doctrine that all beings will in the end be saved. It starts from the conviction that a loving God cannot impose eternal punishment (in *hell), and that eternal bliss cannot be complete while any are excluded (contrary to e.g. *Aquinas who held that the joys of the redeemed include observing the punishments of the damned). Universalist views may be detected in Christian writers from *Origen onward, becoming controversial in the *Church of England with F. D. *Maurice's *Eternal Life and Eternal Death*. A separate movement/denomination had begun in the 18th cent. (especially in N. America), receiving impetus from Hosea Ballou, *Treatise of the Atonement* (1805). It merged in 1961 with the *Unitarians, to become the Unitarian Universalist Association.

R. E. Miller, *The Larger Hope . . .* (1979, 1986); D. Robinson, *The Unitarians and the Universalists* (1985).

Universal love (*chien ai*, of Mo Tzu): see JEN.

Unknowability of God: see APOPHATIC THEOLOGY.

Unknown Christ of Hinduism: see PANNIKAR, RAIMUNDO.

Unleavened bread: see MAZZAH.

Unnō (Jap., 'cloud robe'). A Zen term, comparable to *unsui, for the cloudlike detachment of the Zen life.

Unsui (Jap., *un*, 'cloud', + *sui*, 'water'). *Zen monks who exemplify the homeless life, drifting like clouds and forever moving like water. It is descriptive of a monk's life on several levels: his renunciation of family and society, his travels from monastery to monastery testing himself, and his alms-begging which takes him from household to household. A Zen saying sums up the life of Unsui: 'Ordinary people are always at home but are forever wandering, while the monks are forever wandering but always at home.'

Untouchables. The fifth, and lowest, category (*pañchama*) of Hindu society. To it belonged the offspring of mixed-caste unions, tribals, and foreigners, and those with defiling occupations, such as the *Chāmar (leather-workers), Dom (scavengers and funerary specialists), Bhaṅgi, Mahār, Ḍheḍ, Chūhra (sweepers), Paraiyan (scavengers), Koraga (basket-makers), and many others. Some, such as the Paraiyan, would carry a small drum to warn others of their approach; others, such as the Pulayan, only moved about at night, and even then would have to call out to warn anyone they might meet of their presence. Some castes were so polluting they were not only untouchable but unseeable, such as the Vannān of S. India whose job was to wash the clothes of other untouchables, and who might leave their homes only during darkness since even the sight of one of them was enough to pollute a higher caste person.

Untouchables lived outside village boundaries, and were not allowed to draw water from wells used by higher castes. Education was prohibited; they were not allowed to read the sacred texts, and only by patiently accepting their humble lot was salvation possible for them. Orthodox Hindus will not eat with, marry, or work with untouchables. The *Laws of *Manu* define their social position thus: 'Their dwelling place shall be outside the village, and their wealth shall consist of dogs and donkeys. Their clothing shall be the garments of corpses, their food eaten from broken dishes. Their ornaments shall be of black iron, and they are condemned to wandering from place to place.'

Untouchables represented various forms of threat to the wellbeing of mainstream Hindu society, and thus were physically cut off from it. Dirty occupations carried the danger of infection and disease; mixed marriages and their offspring threatened accepted cultural norms and social stability; foreigners represented a challenge to established values and customs.

The Constitution of modern independent India has abolished untouchability in theory, but in practice, especially in rural areas, the concept still survives. Reform movements, or individuals (see e.g. AMBEDKAR, B. R.), have tried to eradicate it, so far without success. *Gāndhī attempted to improve the image of untouchables by giving them the name 'Harijans' (Children of God); officially they are termed 'Scheduled Castes', but terminological change does not necessarily effect status change. The Scheduled Castes now enjoy a number of privileges—scholarships and college places reserved for them, Civil Service jobs allocated to them, etc.—and this has given rise to a backlash of resentment from higher castes in several areas of India. Socially untouchables still suffer discrimination, in spite of the State's efforts to integrate them into the modern Indian nation.

B. R. Ambedkar, *The Untouchables* (1948); D. Hiro, *The Untouchables of India* (1982); J. M. Mahar (ed.), *The Untouchables in Contemporary India* (1972).

UOJCA: see UNION OF ORTHODOX JEWISH CONGREGATIONS OF AMERICA.

Upādāna (Pāli, Skt.; lit., 'that which fuels a process' or 'keeps it going'). Grasping, clinging, attachment; according to Buddhism the mark of human behaviour generally. There are four types: grasping after sense objects, speculative philosophies (*diṭṭhi-vāda), rules and rituals (see SĪLABBATA-PARĀMĀSA), and theories of a soul (*atta-vāda*). According to the Buddhist doctrine of causation (*paticca-samuppāda), grasping results from craving (*taṇhā) and itself fuels the process of becoming (*bhava) or continued rebirth. The source of grasping lies in the five groups of individuality, the *skandhas, whose fundamental nature it is 'to grasp'; consequently grasping is eliminated by developing non-attachment toward the skandhas. It can and does persist in subtle ways throughout the highest forms of Buddhist meditation, so that the meditator can become ensnared in the pleasantness of his temporary attainment and lose the incentive for *nirvāna.

Upadhye (ritual officiant in Jain worship): see PŪJĀ.

Upāgama (a supplementary text to an Āgama): see ĀGAMA.

Upanayana. Sometimes called 'the thread ceremony', or 'sacred thread' ceremony, this is one of the most important rites of passage in Hinduism. It is a ceremony that marks a boy's transition from childhood to his student life, when traditionally he would come under the authority of his guru, or teacher, and be instructed in sacred lore and Skt. He becomes *dvija ('twice-born') and assumes the duties and responsibilities of his caste. He eats for the last time with his mother; he will now join the men of the family, eat with them, and be served by the womenfolk. Brahman boys receive the thread, which is usually of cotton, though it may vary from caste to caste, at the age of 8, *Kṣatriyas at 11, and Vaiśyas at 14. *Śūdras do not go through the ceremony. It is thought that formerly girls also went through this rite but later it was restricted to boys only.

The ceremony has fifteen stages: the boy, wearing a loin-cloth, is brought before his guru; his father requests the guru to accept the boy as his pupil; the guru places the boy under the care of the gods; he asks the boy's name and other details; then he touches the boy's thumb, hand, shoulder in acceptance; the guru offers the boy upper and lower garments; he ties round his pupil's waist the triple-corded girdle (*mekhalā*); the boy receives a staff, then water in his cupped hands from the guru's cupped hands, all this to the accompaniment of appropriate *mantras. The pupil now stands on a stone, symbolizing steadfastness; he eats some curds, symbolizing absorption of the knowledge he will receive; he is shown the sun, as the ideal light to show the way to learning; then the *Gāyatrī mantra is told him, and he is taught how to recite it. He places wood on the sacred fire, symbolizing his ritual maturity as a sacrificer, and finally he *circumambulates the fire, and receives alms from those present.

Nowadays the receiving of the thread (*yajñopavītā*) is the most important part of this ceremony; its connection with the commencement of religious education is usually forgotten. On receiving the thread, which must have at least three strands, be woven by a virgin, and have as many knots as there are noteworthies among the pupil's ancestors, the boy picks up his staff and pretends to leave home for Benāres or Kashmir for his education. He is begged to return, which, of course, he does. In Maharaṣṭra a boy's maternal uncle offers him his daughter in marriage if he will come home, an arrangement which would be incestuous elsewhere. The thread runs over the left shoulder and under the right arm, except during funerary rites, when it is reversed. It is renewed annually, and the old thread is burnt on the sacred fire.

Upāṅga (auxiliary aids): see VEDĀṄGA.

Upaniṣad (Skt.). In Hinduism, the genre of texts which end or complete the Vedic corpus. For this reason they are also called *Vedānta, 'the end of the Veda'. The word 'upaniṣad' itself is usually understood to mean 'esoteric teaching', the preferred etymology (*upa* + *ni* + *ṣad*, 'to sit close by') referring to the proximity necessary for the transmission of such teachings. *Śaṅkara in his commentary on the *Kaṭhopaniṣad* gives an equally interesting etymology based on the verbal root *śad*, 'to destroy'. Thus the word 'upaniṣad' is taken to mean the teaching that 'destroys' *avidyā or untruth. The Upaniṣads, as texts, developed out of the earlier speculations on the Vedic ritual contained in the *Brāhmaṇas and *Āraṇyakas. In number they are counted by some as being over 200; traditionally, there are 108, listed at the beginning of *Muktika Upaniṣad*. Most of these, however, are from a post-Vedic period. The authentically Vedic upaniṣads (*c*.600–400 BCE) are much fewer in number. Nine show a clear relationship to preceding brāhmaṇas or āraṇyakas. Six more are commented on or mentioned by Śaṅkara. *Radhakrishnan, in his work *The Principal Upaniṣads* (1953), included eighteen. The central teaching of these early upaniṣads is that the Self (*ātman) is identical to the ultimate ground of reality (*Brahman). He who realizes this finds liberation (*mokṣa) from the cycle of suffering (*saṃsāra) embodied in birth, death and rebirth. This speculative perspective, extolling the way of knowledge (*jñānamārga), became a point of departure for much of Indian philosophy, particularly the various schools of Vedānta. The later Upaniṣads, composed under Purāṇic, *Tantric, or devotional influences, are less philosophical and more sectarian. Their importance is not so much for the history of philosophy in India as for an understanding of its popular religion.

The major Upaniṣads are **Aitareya*, **Bṛhadāranyaka*, **Chandogya*, *Īśa*, **Katha*, **Kauṣītaki*, **Kena*, **Mahānārāyaṇīya* **Maitri*, **Māṇḍūkya*, **Muṇḍaka*, **Praśna*, **Śvetāśvatara*, **Taittirīya*. See Index, Upaniṣad.

Many trs.: see e.g. R. E. Hume (1931), Nikhilananda (1949), S. Radhakrishnan (1953), V. L. Shastri (1948); S. Bhattacharji, *Literature in the Vedic Age*, ii (1986);

P. Deussen, *Philosophy of the Upanishads*; K. Klostermaier, *A Survey of Hinduism*; R. D. Ranade, *A Constructive Survey of Upanishadic Philosophy* . . . (1926, 1968); N. S. Subrahmanian, *Encyclopedia of the Upanishads* (1985).

Upapātaka (minor sin): see MAHĀPĀTAKA.

Uparama (one of six great Hindu virtues): see ṢATKASAMPATTI.

Upāsaka (fem., *upāsikā*; Pāli, 'one who sits close by'). Buddhist layperson, who has taken refuge in the *Three Jewels (*triratna*) and undertaken the five precepts (*śīla). Although far from the goal of *arhat, they can acquire merit (*puṇya), especially through support of the *Saṅgha ((see DĀNA) *DĀNA), and can hope to reappear as a monk (*bhikkhu).

Upāsakādhyana-aṅga (Jain text): see AṄGA.

Upāsana (Skt., 'act of sitting'). A word of varied though related meanings in Indian religious thought. It can mean ritual worship, devotional worship, and meditation. In his commentary on the **Vedānta Sūtra*, *Rāmānuja equates upāsana with devotional meditation and knowledge of *Brahman (5. 1. 1). This is a higher kind of knowledge which has the character of devotion (*bhakti) and consists in direct intuition of Brahman. Rāmānuja also says (4. 1. 3) that upāsana is continued remembrance of God which is meditation (*dhyāna).

Upa Veda. Secondary *Veda in Hinduism, attached to, but having no other connection with, revealed Veda. They are (i) *Āyur Veda*, on medicine; (ii) *Ghāndharva Veda*, on music and dance; (iii) *Dhanur Veda*, on archery and military skills; (iv) *Sthāpatya Veda*, on architecture (sometimes referred to as *Śilpa Śastra*).

Upāya-kauśalya ('skill in means'). Adaptation of teaching in Buddhism to the level of the audience's existing attainment. The concept of 'skilful means' is of considerable importance in *Mahāyāna Buddhism and is expounded at an early date in texts such as the **Lotus Sūtra* and the teachings of **Vimalakīrti Sūtra*. At the root of the idea is the notion that the *Buddha's teaching is essentially a provisional means to bring beings to *enlightenment, and that the teachings which he gives may therefore vary: what may be appropriate at one time may not be so at another. The concept is used by the Mahāyāna to justify what appear to be its innovations in doctrine, and to portray the Buddha's early teachings as limited and restricted in accordance with the spiritual potential of his early followers. In the Mahāyāna, skilful means comes to be a legitimate method to be employed by buddhas and *bodhisattvas whenever the benefit of beings would seem to warrant it. Spurred on by their great compassion (*karuṇā), the bodhisattvas are given a licence (in many sources) to break the precepts and commit actions which would otherwise attract moral censure. The assumption underlying the doctrine is that all teachings are in any case provisional, and that once liberation is attained it will be seen that Buddhism, as a body of philosophical doctrines and moral precepts, was only of use as a means to reach the final goal, and that its teachings do not have ultimate validity.

In *Lotus Sūtra*, ch. 2, the Buddha introduces the doctrine of skilful means and demonstrates through the use of parables throughout the text why it is necessary for him to make use of stratagems and devices. He is portrayed as a wise man or kindly father whose words his foolish children refuse to heed. To encourage them to take his advice he has recourse to 'skilful means', realizing that this is the only way to bring the ignorant and deluded into the path to liberation. Although this involves a certain degree of duplicity, such as telling lies, the Buddha is exonerated from all blame, since his only motivation is compassionate concern for all beings.

M. Pye, *Skilful Means: A Concept in Mahayana Buddhism* (1978).

Upekkha (Pāli, 'equanimity'). Fundamental Buddhist state of equilibrium in the mind. It is one of the seven constituents of enlightenment, and one of the four cardinal virtues (with *metta, *karuṇā, *muditā), which controls the other three.

Uposatha (Pāli, 'fasting'; Skt., *upavasatha*; Jap., *fusatsu*). Buddhist observance on the days of (initially) new and full moon, now of the quarter moons. For laypeople (*upāsaka) it involves a day of more careful observance, sometimes by undertaking an additional three rules (*śīla), and by assembling at the local monastery, for worship, instruction, and renewal of vows to keep the precepts (śīla). Monks are under obligation to attend a ceremony in which (or before which) acknowledgement of fault against the *pratimokṣa is made. The pratimokṣa is recited at this ceremony.

Uppalavaṇṇā or **Utpalavarṇā** (5th cent. BCE). One of the best-known (with *Khemā) women *arhats who attained enlightenment through the teaching of the Buddha. Although she was born into a wealthy family, she chose not to marry; instead she joined the order of *bhikkhunīs (women religious). While sweeping a floor by lamplight, she concentrated on the flame and attained the condition of arhat. She was named by the Buddha, with Khemā, as the ideal model of bhikkhunī.

Ur. Ancient city of the Middle East. The city of Ur is referred to in the Hebrew scriptures as the place of origin of the *patriarchs (Genesis 11. 28, 31), although originally it was not realized that Ur was a place. Since the letters form the Hebrew word for 'fire', it was believed that Abram/*Abraham came from the fire of the Chaldaeans. This was taken to be the fire of persecution, hence the elaboration of many stories concerning Abram's refusal of idolatry.

Although resting on a mistake, these stories persist into Islam.

Urabe family (Shinto family of diviners): see YOSHIDA SHINTŌ.

Urabe Shintō (Shinto school): see YOSHIDA SHINTŌ.

Urabon (rituals for the dead): see ULLAMBANA.

Urbi et Orbi (Lat., 'to the city and to the world'). The blessing given by the *pope on solemn occasions, initially from any one of the basilicas in Rome, but now from St Peter's. The custom was revived in 1922 after an interval of fifty years, becoming increasingly an occasion of adulation of the pope.

Uriel. An *angel mentioned in the Jewish book of *1* **Enoch*. Uriel serves as a guide to Enoch in the Upper *Heavens and governs the angelic army. In *4* **Ezra* he reveals visions of the future to Ezra. In the *midrash, Uriel is one of the four angels placed around God's throne (*Num.R.* 2. 10).

Urim and Thummim. A priestly device for telling oracles in the ancient Israelite religion. The *high priest wore the Urim and Thummim on his breastplate. It was used for questioning God on behalf of the ruler (Numbers 27. 21) and it seems to have given a 'yes-or-no' answer (1 Samuel 23. 10–12). The practice had ended by the post-*exilic period and hard questions were put on one side 'until a priest would appear with Urim and Thummim' (Ezra 2. 63). The underlying meaning of the two words is not known.

Ūrṇā (Skt., 'wool'). A circle of hair between the eyebrows. In both Hindu and Jain understanding, this is, or conceals, the jewel or ornament of the 'third eye', which is derived from *Śiva's production of his third, burning, eye: see TRILOCANA.

ʿUrs (Arab.). Bride and bridegroom, hence marriage. From this, it is also the collective name for ceremonies observed at the anniversary of the death of a *Sūfī saint or *murshid*. The death of a saint is regarded as a time of reunion with his Lord and therefore considered a happy occasion. For example, the death anniversary of Shaykh *ʿAbd al-Qadīr al-Jīlānī is popularly celebrated as an ʿurs on 11 Rabiʿ al-'akhir (the fourth Muslim month). Each Sūfī order celebrates its particular annual ʿurs programme. Ideally, the ʿurs should take place at the shrine of the saint, but it can be celebrated anywhere. In England, ʿurs dates have become an important social event in Muslim communities. Men, women, and children travel to other cities in order to participate and share the *baraka (blessing) of the ʿurs (such as the healing of sickness and the fulfilment of wishes). The ʿurs ceremony generally has three stages: (i) Qur'ān recital, prayers, and a sermon on the saint; (ii) *samāʿ (musical audition), when the whole congregation listens to qawwals (singers and musicians) reciting Sūfī poems (when some devotees may lapse into ecstatic states, *wajd). At the conclusion of samāʿ, the Sūfī order's litany is recited, and this leads to (iii) a feast. Though the ʿurs has been condemned as a negative innovation by the puritanical *Wahhābīs and the *Ahl-al-Hadith, it still has strong support amongst orthodox believers.

Urvan (soul): see FRAVASI.

Uṣas (Skt., 'dawn'). Hindu goddess of the dawn, restorer of life and bounty: 'The divine Uṣas lights up with her beams the quarters of the heavens. . . . Bringing with her life-sustaining blessings, and giving consciousness to the unconscious, she imparts to the world her superb radiance' (*Ṛg Veda* 1. 16. 8).

Use. A local modification of the prevailing Christian *rite (especially the Roman rite). These uses, which differed from the parent rite only in details, came to be standardized and employed over wide areas. The **Book of Common Prayer* of 1549 superseded five local uses in England, the most important being that of Sarum (Salisbury). The Council of *Trent abolished all uses except those which could prove an existence of two centuries.

Usha, synod of. 2nd-cent. CE convention of Jewish *sages. After the persecutions at the close of the *Bar Kokhba revolt, a synod met at Usha to reactivate the *Sanhedrin. Rabban *Simeon b. Gamaliel was appointed *nasi, R. Nathan ha-Bavli av *bet din, and R. *Meir *ḥakham. Several *takkanot are described as 'takkanot of Usha' in *Talmudic literature, and the *tannaim of the period were involved in the establishment and compilation of the *halakhah.

ʿUshr (Arab., 'tenth part'). The tithe on property owned by Muslims, often levied for public assistance, in distinction from *kharāj*, which was levied on property owned by non-Muslims. The word does not occur in the *Qur'ān, and the practice was clearly inherited. Eventually it became virtually synonymous with *zakāt, even though zakāt is not one-tenth.

USPG (United Society for the Propagation of the Gospel). Christian missionary society formed in 1965 by the amalgamation of the SPG and the Universities' Mission to Central Africa. The former was founded in 1701 to assist in the work of the *SPCK in British territories abroad; the latter was formed in response to an appeal by D. *Livingstone in Cambridge in 1857. The USPG now supports churches in forty countries, especially in the work of training nationals as clergy, and also sponsors mission work in Britain. Its theology is closer to that of the *high church than that of the *CMS, though both are seeking ways of closer integration. It shares the weakness of many church organizations of having been overdominated by clergy control.

Ussher, James (1581–1656). Anglican *archbishop of Armagh, Ireland. A scholar of vast learning, he was an authority on such diverse subjects as the letters of *Ignatius (of which he distinguished the seven genuine ones) and the early history of Ireland. After the Irish revolution of 1641 he remained in England, endeavouring to bring about a reconciliation between Churchmen and Dissenters. He is probably best remembered today in connection with the dates for biblical chronology printed in many English Bibles since 1701; these derive from his scheme based on the genealogies, according to which, e.g. the world was created in 4004 BCE.

Uṣūl (Arab. pl. of *aṣl*). Root or principle. In Islam, the word is used for a branch of learning, especially uṣūl al-*hadīth, uṣūl al-*fiqh, and uṣūl al-*kalām (earlier uṣūl al-dīn); and also for the sources of those disciplines, *Qur'ān, ḥadīth (together, *sunna), *ijmaʿ, and *qiyās at least: claims to further sources would be disputed. Uṣūliy(y)a is used for what in English might be called *fundamentalism.

N. J. Coulson, *A History of Islamic Law* (1971).

Uṣūlī (school of Shiʿite law): see BIHBAHĀNĪ.

Usury. The lending of money at interest. The exacting of interest on loans to a fellow-Jew is forbidden in the Hebrew scriptures (Exodus 22. 24), including loans to a resident alien (Leviticus 25. 35–7) but it is permitted on loans to a 'foreigner' (Deuteronomy 23. 20 f.). In the Middle Ages, Jews were excluded from trade and craft guilds, and money-lending became a common Jewish activity. The Christian Church forbade usury to Christians in 1179, but the canon law did not apply to Jews. The *Talmud only allowed the taking of interest from *gentiles, if no other means of subsistence were available. The *tosafists argued that 'because there is no end to the yoke and the burden king and ministers impose on us', that condition was fulfilled. The stereotype of the Jew in the late Middle Ages was thus of an avaricious usurer (e.g. Shakespeare's Shylock, Marlowe's Barabbas).

For usury in Islam, see RIBĀ.

ʿUthmān b. Affān (d. 655 (AH 35)). Third caliph (*khalīfa), who was an early convert to Islam. He married the Prophet *Muḥammad's daughters, Rukaiya and (after her death) Umm Kulthum. He was a close companion of the Prophet, and assisted the early *Madīna community through his wealth and business expertise. Upon election as caliph he promised to follow and develop *ʿUmar's policies of uniformity in religion and government. It was during his time that Islamic conquests reached their peak, bringing with them novel problems of the relation between the original community and the newly acquired territories. ʿUthmān, already old, was unequal to these difficulties. He began to rely on his ʿUmayyah family, and was consequently accused of nepotism and corruption. Opposition to ʿUthmān came to be represented in the figures of *ʿĀ'isha (Prophet Muḥammad's favourite wife) and *ʿAlī, with the introduction of a religious accusation that ʿUthmān was not following the precepts of the Qur'ān and the Prophet. ʿUthmān's circulation of the official edition of the Qur'ān, to preserve uniformity in religion, precipitated a chain of events that led to his assassination: the *Qurra* ('Qur'ān-reciters') had been the expositors of the sacred text and had exercised great influence over the new converts, which gave them religious prestige and authority in the provinces. ʿUthmān's official Qur'ān deprived these monopolists of control over divine revelation. The religious grievance over the Qur'ān now became allied to social, economic, and political discontent; anti-ʿUthmān feeling spilled over into open rebellion. Rebel forces from Egypt, Kūfā, and Basra advanced on Madīna, declared ʿUthmān unfit to rule, and murdered him. The bloody end to ʿUthmān's rule marks a turning point in Islamic history: political and religious unity was at an end and the period of schisms and civil wars had begun. The murder of ʿUthmān raised the complex issue of just murder and unjust killing, and this too created further division amongst the Muslim community: had ʿUthmān acted in ways that contravened Islam, and, if so, had he so ceased to be a Muslim that he could be treated accordingly and be legitimately killed? For the main parties to this dispute, see ĪMĀN.

Utpalavarṇā (woman arhat): see UPPALAVAṆṆĀ.

Uttara-Mīmāṃsā (Skt., 'latter discussion/revered thought'). One of the six philosophical systems (*darśana) of early Hinduism. Generally related to *Vedānta, it is linked to *Bādarāyaṇa and the *Vedānta-* or *Brahma-Sūtra.* Where *Jaimini's *Pūrva-Mīmāṁsā deals with karmakāṇḍa, or the duties required by the *Veda, Uttara-Mīmāṁsā explores the religious and philosophical speculations of the Upaniṣads. The *Vedānta Sūtra* then becomes the major text on which subsequent commentaries are made, delineating the diverse interpretations of the nature of Brahman and Brahman's relation to the created order; the three best-known are those of *Śaṅkara (*advaita, non-dualism), *Rāmānuja (*viśiṣtadvaita, qualified non-dualism), and *Madhva (*dvaita, dualism). Because of its subject-matter, Uttara-Mīmāṁsā is also known as Jñāna- or as Brahma-Mīmāṁsā.

V

Vāc (Skt., from *vac*, 'speech'). The Hindu goddess of speech, the manifestation of. From early Vedic times, reliance on the sacred oral teachings 'heard' by the *ṛṣis, properly intoned and accented, thrust the folk-divinity Vāc into prominence. Since effective sacrifice depended on effective speech, the supreme vehicle of knowledge and ritual power (*Ṛg Veda* 10. 71), Vāc even gained precedence over *Agni. As the 'Word', Vāc is somewhat like the Neoplatonic *'logos': Vāc is the source of creation and the mother of the *Veda. In the *Tantric tradition she is also celebrated as Para-vāc, Transcendental Speech, the mother of all sacred *mantras. Vāc was also identified with the river goddess Sarasvatī, the banks of whose sacred river were fertile soil for the growth of brahmanical culture.

Vāc is variously assigned as the daughter of *Brahmā (their incestuous union produced humanity) or of Dakśa. She is known as the wife of *Kaśyapa or *Indra and the mother of the *Gandharvas and Apsarasas. According to the *Ṛg Veda, Vāc is to be invoked like a muse of wisdom and eloquence, making whom she loves powerful and intelligent.

Vacanam (form of religious verse): see BASAVA.

Vāhana (Skt., 'vehicle'). The bird or animal on which a Hindu, Jain, or Buddhist deity is conveyed. In post-Vedic Hinduism, the vehicles are associated iconographically with the deities in question and are linked to their attributes, e.g. *Agni, a ram; *Bhairava, a dog; *Brahmā, a swan (*haṃsa); *Durgā, a tiger (or lion); *Gaṇeśa, a rat; *Garuḍa, a bird; *Indra, an elephant; *Kāma, a parrot; *Śiva, a bull; *Varuna, a fish; *Yama, a buffalo.

Vāhigurū or **Wāhegurū** (Pañjābī, 'praise to the Gurū'). Used by Sikhs as name for God. Vāhigurū is frequently heard in the proclamation *Srī Vāhigurūjī kā *khālsā: Srī Vāhigurūjī kī *fateh* (The khālsā is God's: God's is the victory). In the early *janam-sākhīs, however, Vāhigurū was not a name for God but an ascription of praise either to God or to the Gurū (i.e. *Nānak). From its repetition in meditation (see NĀM SIMARAN) Vāhigurū naturally came to be regarded as God's name. The *Ardās repeatedly enjoins the congregation to utter 'Vāhigurū'.

Vaibhāṣika. An influential Buddhist school of the Hīnayāna, closely related to the *Sarvāstivāda, which flourished in NW India principally in Gandhāra and Kashmir. Their name derives from a great treatise known as the *Vibhāṣā*, compiled in the early centuries of the Christian era as a commentary on a fundamental work of the *Abhidharma tradition, the *Jñānaprasthāna* (Basis of Knowledge) of Katyāyanaputra, a Sarvāstivādin philosopher. The commentary is an encyclopaedia of Vaibhāṣika philosophy, and records the views of distinguished teachers of different schools on technical points of Buddhist doctrine. The *Vibhāṣā*, which survives only in Chin. translation, formed the basis of debate between the schools of the Hīnayāna for many centuries, and many shorter treatises, such as *Vasubandhu's *Abhidharmakośa*, were composed to summarize and supplement it.

H. V. Guenther, *Buddhist Philosophy* . . . (1971).

Vaikuṇṭha. *Viṣṇu's paradise (and thus also an epithet/name), variously located, e.g. on Mount *Meru, or in the depths of the ocean. Unlike the heavens entered and vacated through the process of *saṃsāra, Vaikuṇṭha is eternal. As Baikunth, 'heaven' enters into the teaching of Gurū *Nānak, but only in a demythologized form: Baikunth is the bliss of union with God.

Vailala Madness. The best-known of the early *cargo movements, in the Gulf division of Papua. In 1919, an old man, Evara, had trance experiences and prophesied that a steamer would come with the spirits of their ancestors and a cargo of European goods; others had similar visions depicting a coming *millennium and sometimes featuring God or *Christ. Traditional rituals and objects were attacked, gardens and trade were abandoned, and a new *ascetic ethic enjoined *Sunday observance, cleanliness, and rejection of personal adornment. New cult temples similar to churches were built, a new type of ritual feast for the returning dead reflected European customs of combining men and women and sitting around tables, flagpoles were erected for communication with the ancestors, and there were new forms of ritual dancing and military drilling. It spread rapidly and did not die out till about 1931, but is still remembered as an idealized time of wonders. It was much more than mere anti-white hysteria, for it arose from resentment at the inadequacy of the old ways in comparison with those of the whites.

Vairāgya (Skt., 'absence of passion'). An attitude of genuine dispassion and freedom from worldly desires. It is considered a primary requisite for aspirants in most systems of Indian spiritual discipline. The *Yoga Sūtra* (1. 12) states that the goal of *Yoga, namely the restraint of the fluctuations of the mind so that the See-er (Pure Consciousness) may rest in its true form, can be attained by dispassion and repeated practice (vairāgya and *abhyāsa). In the *Advaita *Vedānta of *Śaṅkarācārya, dispassion is one of the four requisites of one who seeks liberating knowledge: 'dispassion with regard to all enjoyments in this life or the next' (*Brahmasūtrabhāṣya* 1. 1).

Vairocana (Skt., 'the illuminator', 'he who is like the sun'). 1. In Hinduism (as Virocana), an *asura who attempted, with Indra, to find the self (*ātman): see *Chandogya Upaniṣad* 8. 7.

2. In Buddhism, one of the five transcendent Buddhas, associated with the *bodhisattva *Samantabhadra and the earthly buddha Krakuccanda. He is often depicted making the hand-clasped sign (*mudra) of supreme wisdom. His symbols are the sun and thus the wheel of teaching (*dharma-cakra). When *Mahāyāna developed the idea of the supreme Buddha (*Ādi-buddha) expressed through 'three bodies' (*trikaya), Vairocana became identified with the Ādi-buddha as the personification of *dharma-kāya. Vairocana is no longer an epitome of the absolute and undifferentiated nature of all appearance, to be approached only through aeons of insight-meditation, but becomes Mahāvairocana, accessible through cult and ritual. Devotion to Mahāvairocana, described especially in **Mahāvairocana Sūtra* and *Tattvasaṃgraha*, spread throughout Mahāyāna Asia and Tibet. The disciple replicates the significations of Mahāvairocana, through mudra and *mantra, but especially through *maṇḍalas derived from the above two texts, the Womb Maṇḍala (Garbhakośadhātu) and the Diamond Maṇḍala (Vajradhatu). In the Womb Maṇḍala, he is golden as the sun, seated in meditation on the moon which rests on a red *lotus blossom; he is surrounded by other cosmic figures who represent and embody his attributes (particularly his intention to illuminate all beings). In the complex Diamond Maṇḍala, he is white, or sometimes blue, seated on a lotus blossom which rests on the moon. These two maṇḍalas allow all phenomena to be interpreted and decoded in their relation to Mahāvairocana. In Japan, Birushana is central in *Shingon.

Vaiśākhi (Indian spring festival): see BAISĀKHĪ.

Vaiśālī (Skt.; Pāli, Vesālī). City north of the *Gaṅgā (Ganges), location of the Second Buddhist *Council (for which see also M. Hofinger, *Étude sur le Concile de Vaiśālī*, 1946).

Vaiśaradya (Skt.), four certainties, the mark of a *Buddha. He is certain that: (i) his enlightenment is irreversible; (ii) all defilements (*āsava) are exhausted; (iii) all obstacles are overcome; (iv) the way of overcoming reappearance (*saṃsāra) has been proclaimed.

Vaiśeṣika (Skt., 'referring to the distinctions', *viśeṣa*). The oldest of the six early Hindu philosophical systems (*darśana) related to *Nyāya. Founded by Kaṇāda, to whom *Vaiśeṣika Sūtra* is attributed, it begins with *dharma and the authority of the *Veda. But it then proceeds to the analysis of the six categories or objects of experience (*padārthas*) and makes no mention of God or gods. The six are: (i) *guṇa, quality; (ii) *dravya, substance; (iii) *karma, activity; (iv) *sāmānya*, generality; (v) *viśeṣa*, distinguishable particularity; (vi) *samavāya*, coinherence. To these Vaiśeṣika later added a seventh, ceasing to be, non-existence. (i)–(iii) have observable, real existence, (iv)–(vi) depend on intellectual discrimination and judgement. The self as soul is inferred, because consciousness is not a possessed property of body or mentality. Plurality of souls is inferred from the varieties in status and condition, and each soul experiences the consequences of its deeds. Later Vaiśeṣika could not regard all this as coming together from nowhere, and therefore postulated an unproduced Producer of all that is, i.e. God. Vaiśeṣika led on to the multiple systems of Nyāya, often known as Nyāya-Vaiśeṣika.

Tr. N. Sinha (Sacred Books of the East 6); G. Bhattacharya, *Tarkasaṃgrahadīpikā* (1976); K. H. Potter (ed.), *Indian Metaphysics and Epistemology: The Tradition of the Nyāya-Vaiśeṣika up to Gaṅgeśa* (1977).

Vaiṣṇava. An adherent of Vaiṣṇavism, one of three major forms of Hindu devotion (*bhakti), along with *Śaivas and *Śaktas. Vaiṣṇavism is the cult of *Viṣṇu, initially connected with Viṣṇu as the sun, pervading all things with light and spiritual enlightenment (*Ṛg Veda* 3. 62. 10). He was assimilated with *Nārāyana, cosmic energy, and was later associated with *Kṛṣna-Vāsudeva, until the relation between all three became one of dynamic manifestation. Viṣṇu came to be regarded as *Īśvara, Supreme Being, and also as *Brahman theistically conceived. He becomes manifest in incarnate forms (for the list of these see AVATĀRA), especially in times of crisis or need, and it is mainly in these forms that he is worshipped. The two major instances are those of Kṛṣṇa and *Rāma, which are usually (though not always) exclusive of each other where cult is concerned. The primary text for those devoted to Rāma is the **Rāmāyaṇa*, an epic which was often retold in forms lending themselves to devotion—e.g. *Tulsīdās in Hindi, Kamban in Tamil, and Kṛttivas in Bengali. The primary text for those devoted to Kṛṣṇa is the **Bhagavad-gītā* in the **Mahābhārata* (and the **Harivaṃśa*, which is attached to it), and the **Bhāgavata Purāṇa*. But the cult of Kṛṣṇa evoked also a wealth of devotional poetry and prayer (e.g. among the *Āḻvārs), which remains formative. Vaiṣṇavism has divided into many schools and sects. Of enduring importance have been *Caitanya and his contemporary Vallabha (*c.*1479–1531). Vallabha's

*Śuddhādvaita Vedānta (pure non-duality vedānta) mediates between *Śaṅkara and *Rāmānuja, by maintaining the goodness and purity of both world and self as parts of what truly is, namely Kṛṣṇa, so that while appearances are an expression of *māyā, the bliss-relation of the parts to the whole, and thus of *ātman to *Brahman, is not: thus bhakti (devotion) is the realization of this, and is the true path to *mokṣa (release). Philosophically, Vaiṣṇava devotion also underlies the work of *Rāmānuja and *Madhva. Devotionally, the relation to Kṛṣṇa may take several different forms, of which the five most common are: Kṛṣṇa as transcendent, the worshipper abased; Kṛṣṇa as master, worshipper as servant or slave; Kṛṣṇa as child, worshipper as guardian or parent; both as friends; Kṛṣṇa as lover, worshipper as beloved (cf. GOPĪ). For face markings, see TILAKA. See also NIMBĀRKA; RĀMĀNANDA; ŚRĪ-VAIṢṆAVISM.

R. G. Bhandarkar, *Vaiṣṇavism, Śaivism and Minor Religious Systems* (1913); S. K. De, *Early History of the Vaiṣṇava Faith and Movement* (1961); J. Gonda, *Aspects of Early Viṣṇuism* (1954); *Viṣṇuism and Śivaism* . . . (1970); S. Jaiswal, *The Origin and Development of Vaiṣṇavism* (1967).

Vaiśvadeva. A Hindu household ritual, offering homage to the gods, especially *Agni who bears offerings to the heavens. Fire is fed with consecrated fuel, and offerings are thrown into it, accompanied by *mantras. In the *bali-haraṇa* which ends the ritual, the food-offering is arranged in a circle with each part assigned to a particular deity. The ashes of the fire are applied to the body with a prayer to Rudra to refrain from harming the family or its cattle. See *Manusmṛti* 3. 84.

Vaiśvānara (Skt., 'relating to all people'). An epithet of *Agni (fire). Agni Vaiśvānara is regarded as the author of *Ṛg Veda* 10. 79 and 80. He represents the fire of digestion, as in *Bhagavad-gītā* 15. 14: 'In the form of fire of digestion, I reside in all beings and digest the four kinds of food.' According to *Ṛg Veda* 1. 59. 2, Vaiśvānara was produced by the gods for the Aryans, to be a light for them.

The term is then applied in *Vedānta to the waking state of human beings, one of the four states, the others being deep sleep, dreaming, and sublimity (*turīya).

Vaiśya. The third of the four Hindu social categories, or *varna. Traditionally the Vaiśyas were traders and businessmen, or peasant farmers. They were expected to be specialists in their particular branch of trade, whether jewellery and precious metals, spices, cloth, furnishings, or, indeed, any kind of merchandise. Vaiśyas are often vegetarian, and zealous in religious observance; they have a particular devotion to *Lakṣmī, goddess of wealth.

Vajra (Skt.; Tib., *rdo.rje*, 'diamond', 'thunderbolt'). 1. In Hinduism, the weapon of *Indra. Although often described as his 'thunderbolt', the adamantine ('diamond') connections of vajra mean that it is equally described as hard and sharp—the splitter. The association may simply be in the connection between lightning and thunder.

2. Double-headed ritual implement in *Tibetan Buddhism, used in conjunction with a bell (Skt., *ghaṇṭā*; Tib., *dril.bu*). The bell is always held in the left hand where it represents wisdom, emptiness (*śūnyatā) *nirvāna, and the feminine principle; the vajra is always held in the right hand where it represents skilful means (*upāya-kauśalya), compassion, *saṃsāra, and the masculine principle. The two meanings of vajra suggest unbreakability, preciousness, and power, and in these senses it has lent itself as a term not only to the *Tantric tradition of Tibet as the way of the vajra (*Vajrayāna), but also to many of the *Buddhas, *bodhisattvas, *ḍākinīs, and other sacred beings. Thus *Vajradhara (*rdo.rje-.'chang*), the blue *Ādi Buddha or *dharmakāya aspect of Buddhahood and source of many esoteric teachings such as *Kālacakra and *Mahāmudrā; Vajrasattva (*rdo.rje.sems.dpa'*), the white *sambhogakāya aspect of Buddhahood and revealer of *maṇḍalas; Vajrapāṇi (*phyag.na.rdo.rje*), the indigo bodhisattva, one of the most important *'wrathful deities' or protectors (*dharmapāla*); Vajravārāhī (*rdo.rje.phag.mo*), the red ḍākinī with a sow's as well as a human head, revealer of secret teachings, embodiment of emptiness, and consort of Cakrasaṃvara; Vajrayoginī (*rdo.rje.rnal 'byor.ma*), the semi-wrathful *yidam important in many Tantric practices; and many others.

Vajracchedika-[Prajñapāramitā-]Sūtra: See DIAMOND SŪTRA.

Vajradhara. In Tantric Buddhism, the source of the Five Jīnas or *Dhyāni-Buddhas. He is identified with the Absolute or primordial reality which is the source of all enlightenment. In iconography he is portrayed holding a thunderbolt (*vajra) in his right hand, symbolizing the power of compassion and skilful means (*upāya-kauśalya) and a bell in his left, symbolizing the pure clear sound of transcendental wisdom (*prajñā) which penetrates everywhere without obstruction.

Vajrayāna (Skt., 'thunderbolt-' or 'diamond-vehicle'). The *Tantric aspect of *Mahāyāna Buddhism, which sees itself as a succession built upon the preliminary stages of Hīnayāna (where an initial understanding of the relationship between suffering and *saṃsāra produces an aversion from saṃsāra and a desire for personal liberation), and of Sūtrayāna (the *sūtra aspect of Mahāyāna Buddhism where the feeling of the suffering of others as being one's own impels one to desire the liberation of all beings and to enter the *bodhisattva path). Followers of Vajrayāna see the Sūtrayāna as a long path, developing only compassion and wisdom; the Vajrayāna, however, is seen as a swift path (Tib., *myur.lam*) offering enlightenment in the present lifetime by the development of method. The term Vajrayāna is often (mistakenly) used synonymously with Tibetan Buddhism; in fact, Tibetan Buddhism teaches all three vehicles according to personal advancement, and stresses that while Sūtrayāna may be taught separately from Vajrayāna, Vajrayāna may not be taught separately from Sūtrayāna, but rather as an extension of it.

V. Guenther, *The Origin and Spirit of Vajrayana* (1959).

Vajrayoginī (a Tantric form of Durgā): See CHINNAMASTA.

Vajroli mudra (Skt.). A Tantric practice of reabsorbing, into the penis, semen discharged during intercourse. Semen (*bindu), breath (*prāṇa), and thought (*citta) correspond in *Tantrism, and through reabsorbing the semen, the Tantric adept seeks to arrest breath and thought. This practice is advocated in *Natha yoga texts such as the *Śiva Samhita* (4. 59) and *Hathayogapradipika* (3. 83–7), which describes how to perfect this *mudra by blowing into the penis through a fine tube to clear impurities, and practising with water. The loss of semen leads to death, but its retention leads to the conquest of death (*Hathayogapradipika* 3. 88).

Vāk (goddess of speech/sound): see VĀC.

Vakh (verse sayings): see LALLĀ.

Vāk laina. The way in which Sikhs get advice from the Gurū Granth Sāhib (*Ādi Granth), by prayer, followed by opening the book 'at random'. The book is held between the hands, the hands are moved slowly outward, and the reading begins at the first line of the first complete hymn on the left-hand page. A vāk commences the installation of the Gurū Granth Sāhib each day.

Valabhī, Assembly of. A Jain Assembly at which an attempt was made to formalize something approaching a canon of sacred texts. It was held in 453 CE (though by some reckonings in 466). Since there is no record of the unclad (i.e. *Digambaras) attending, it seems to have been a Śvetāmbara endeavour. The main works accepted are described under *aṅga.

Valentine, St. Roman Christian martyr of the 3rd cent. The commemoration on 14 Feb. of two Valentines (whose *acts are legendary) may, according to the *Bollandists, be reduced to a single person. The association of St Valentine's Day with lovers and choosing of a 'Valentine' has nothing to do with the martyr, but probably derives from customs of the Roman festival of Lupercalia in honour of the goddess Februata Juno, when boys drew by lot the names of unmarried girls (mid-February), or just the season of the year, when birds traditionally are thought to choose their mates. The suggestion of Francis *de Sales that the names of saints to be emulated should be drawn as Valentines has not caught on.

Valentinus (2nd cent. CE). *Gnostic theologian. According to his orthodox opponents (*Irenaeus, *Tertullian, *et al.*) he lived at Rome, *c.*136–*c.*165, and only left the Catholic Church after failing to be elected bishop. His sect, the Valentinians, was the largest of the gnostic bodies, and some of his disciples (through whom his own system is best known) founded schools of their own. He produced a variety of writings, including the earliest commentary on the gospel of *John and perhaps the **Gospel of Truth*.

Vallabhā (exponent of Vaiṣṇava): see VAIṢṆAVA.

Vālmīki. Legendary author of the epic **Rāmāyaṇa*, which he claimed to have visualized in the *Vedas; in fact, *Rāmāyaṇa* bears signs of different layers of composition, but Vālmīki may have been a *kuśīlava* ('bard') who introduced the *śloka*, the epic metre of two lines, each of two parts with eight syllables in each, which was used also for much of **Mahābhārata*. To him is attributed another epic work, **Yoga-Vaisiṣtha*, but there is no real historical evidence for him. For the community revering Vālmīki, see BĀLMĪKĪ.

Vāmācāra (Skt., 'left-handed conduct'). A spiritual path, especially in *Tantrism, which is counter to established social ways. Since the present age (*Kaliyuga) is the most decadent, ascetic spiritual practices are no longer effective. In this age a Tantric must 'rise with the aid of those things which make most men fall'. For many this includes deriving power from meat, liquor, sex, and other normally restricted things. In its 'pure' form, however, vāmācāra does *not* involve any abandonment to the senses. The practitioners are *yogins adept at meditation; their 'indulgence' is ritualized in the *pañcatattva*, or the taking of the five essentials. This is an elaborate rite preceded often by months of meditation. The participants consume four substances thought to be aphrodisiac: wine, meat, fish, and parched grain. This is followed by ritualistic sexual intercourse (*maithuna), which is held to be most efficacious with a low-caste woman or prostitute: she symbolizes both the highest reality of *Śakti and the lowest of the material world. Uniting thus with both extremes of the cosmos, the yogin builds up his sexual energy which is nothing but Śakti herself, and then, instead of releasing it through semen, forces it to the six *cakras, creating a mystical experience of *Śiva-Śakti.

An underlying tenet of the left-handed path is that the world is itself a manifestation of Śiva-Śakti. The process of creation is an act of enjoyment, not suffering; hence to fully realize this ultimate reality, the yogin must not only attain transcendent realization of Śiva-Śakti (*mokṣa), but must also participate in creation, enjoying it with the full realization, 'I am Śiva.'

Vāmana (Skt., 'dwarf'). In Hindu mythology, the form (the fifth) *avatāra which *Viṣṇu adopted in order to trick the demon king *Bali into restoring the world to the gods. When Bali agreed to give him three paces of land, the dwarf grew to an enormous size so that his first two steps covered earth and heaven, and Bali had to offer his own head for the third step. (This cosmic version of Vāmana is known as *Trivikrama*, Skt., 'three steps'.) Vāmana is the fifth *avatāra in the standard list, and his is the only avatāra story which has a clear connection with the Viṣṇu of the **Ṛg Veda*, where many passages describe the three great strides with which he measured out earth, air, and sky. A passage in the **Śatapatha Brāhmaṇa* identifies Viṣṇu in dwarf form with the sacrifice, and foreshadows the later Vāmana-Bali myth with a reference to the demons letting the gods have as much land as the dwarf can cover when lying down. Since the power of the sacrifice, however limited its outward form may be, is of cosmic dimensions, the dwarf takes up the whole earth.

Vānaprastha. The third of the four *āśramas, or stages of life, of the Hindu. The term meant literally 'forest departure', a time of retirement when a householder, having raised his children and made them independent, devoted himself, with or without his wife's company, to preparing for death and the next stage of his existence. He was supposed to withdraw from the active concerns of life, both physically and spiritually, and live apart, cared for by his sons and their families. The time at which he should do this varies: some say at 50 years old, others when a grandson is born, or at the appearance of grey hair. Nowadays few people withdraw from their homes in old age, but many elderly folk devote themselves to prayer and ritual observances, while helping with, and teaching, their grandchildren.

van der Leeuw, G.: see PHENOMENOLOGY.

Vanity of vanities: see ECCLESIASTES.

Va Postori (followers): see AFRICAN APOSTLES.

Vār (Pañjābī, 'ballad'). Any of a set of twenty-two hymns of praise in the *Ādi Granth. They have several stanzas (see PAUṚĪ), each with associated *śaloks, which may be of different authorship from the vār concerned. Vārs are grouped within each *rāg between the *chhants and the hymns of the *bhagats. Examples are Vār Rāmkalī and *Āsā kī Vār. The forty vārs bearing the name of *Bhāī *Gurdās, though not canonical, may be recited in *gurdwārās.

Varāha (Skt., 'boar'). In Hindu mythology, the form which *Viṣṇu assumed in order to raise the earth from the cosmic ocean. In its earliest forms this story is a creation myth, and the boar is identified with the creator god *Prajāpati. Later it is identified with *Brahmā and then with Viṣṇu, eventually being regarded as the third *avatāra of the standard list. Once it becomes an avatāra myth, the story's character changes, and Varāha is seen as having rescued the Earth from the demon *Hiraṇyākṣa who had drawn her down to the nether regions. Varāha is also regarded as symbolizing the sacrifice, and many Purāṇic versions of this myth work out a detailed correspondence between various elements of the *Vedic ritual and parts of his body.

Vārāṇasī (Indian sacred city): see KĀŚĪ.

Vardapets (unmarried clergy): see ARMENIAN CHURCH.

Varna (Skt., perhaps from *vṛ*, 'veil', hence 'colour'). 1. The four social orders, or categories, of Hindu society, *Brahmans, *Kṣatriyas, *Vaiśyas, and *Śūdras. These divisions date from the time of the early *Aryan settlement in N. India, and, according to the **Ṛg Veda*, were created by the gods from the body of *Puruṣa, the first man. From his head sprang the Brahmans, from his arms the Kṣatriyas, from his thighs the Vaiśyas, and from his feet the Śūdras. Into these four major divisions the castes (*jāti) later fitted. Some maintain there is a fifth category, the Harijans, or *untouchables, while others place them within the Śudra division, dividing this into two segments, 'clean' and 'unclean'. The three upper varṇa are termed *'twice-born', since the male family members go through a thread ceremony (*upanayana) which implies a spiritual rebirth, marking the transition into adulthood, and the student stage (*āśrama) of life. Reading, writing, and the pursuit of knowledge were regarded as irrelevant for the Śūdra way of life, so that varna was excluded from the thread ceremonies.

The word varna means 'colour', hence the hypothesis that the system reflects an observed difference in appearance between the fair-skinned Aryan ('noble') invaders from the north and the darker skinned indigenous inhabitants (*dāsas*, 'slaves'). Certainly a passage in the *Ṛg Veda* discourages marriages between fair and dark individuals; and the ancient Indian scholar *Patañjali finds blond hair to be a brahmanic attribute, though this must have been extremely rare even in his lifetime.

The individual's varna, and, within it, his caste, gives his ascribed status in society; he is born into it and remains in it throughout life, unless (in former times) he was made outcaste for some offence. Even in modern India the varna provide a hierarchical framework for the castes, although an individual is no longer compelled to undertake the designated occupation of his varna.

2. See BINDU.

J. H. Hutton, *Caste in India* . . . (1963); M. Klass, *Caste* . . . (1980).

Varṇāśramadharma. The code of conduct by which a Hindu should live, according to his ascribed status by birth (*varna), his stage of life (*āśrama), and the *dharma, or appropriate duty laid down for each of these. Thus what is right for a *Brahman will not be right for, say, a *Vaiśya; what is right for a young man will not be so for his grandfather. Interpretation of the four aims of life—dharma (moral righteousness), *artha (prosperity), *kama (pleasure), and *mokṣa (release from the cycle of existence)—will be influenced by varna and āśrama. Conformity to varṇāśramadharma provides the ideal Hindu social order, one which subsumes the duty of the believer to society, to family, and to himself, both socially and spiritually. Underlying it is the concept that if an individual does his duty, his rights are automatically safeguarded by the performance by others of their responsibilities. Though Hinduism is often represented as group-oriented, with the individual counting for little *socially, spiritual* advancement is the responsibility of each person to himself, with or without the help of society. No man can win mokṣa for another; the individual's quest for salvation is his alone.

The most authoritative formulation is in the **Manusmṛti*. *Manu describes the *svadharma or specific duties of the four varṇas (varṇadharma), as well as those of the four āśramas or life-stages (āśramadharma). For example, the svadharma of a Brāhman (priest) is to study the *Vedas, and that of a Kṣatriya (prince) is to fight and rule. Members of a twice-born caste (*dvijāti varṇa) must ideally pass through four twenty-five year stages: the *brahmācarya āśrama, in which one studies the Vedas under a *guru; the *gṛhastha āśrama, in which one establishes a household; the *vānaprastha āśrama, in which one retires to the forest as a hermit; and the *saṁnyāsa āśrama, in which one performs one's own funeral and lives the life of a wandering ascetic. Varṇāśramadharma is the dharma of a particular varna in a particular āśrama. It remains the orthodox Hindu ideal, although it is seldom if ever followed exactly according to *Manusmṛti*.

Varuṇa. Early Hindu god, prominent in the Vedic period. Possibly connected with *vṛ* ('veil'), he was associated with the all-covering sky, but in the *Vedas his activities resemble those of *Indra and *Agni. As a ruler of the *Ādityas, he maintains celestial order, especially seasons, sunrise and sunset, rainfall (*Ṛg Veda* 6. 48. 14, 10. 99. 10). As Lord of *ṛta, he watches over humanity with a thousand eyes, and he shares responsibility for sacrificial order. He is also connected with the emergent and related concept of *dharma. He remains particularly connected with oceans and rivers, though in later mythology Indra has taken precedence over him, and he has been reduced to the god of death. The connections with the Gk. Ouranos have been explored by G. *Dumézil, *Ouranos-Varuṇa* (1934).

H. Lüders, *Varuṇa* (1951, 1959).

Vāsanās (Skt., 'underlying desire'). 1. In Hinduism, the underlying desires, memories, ambitions, etc., which form character, and which can surface at any moment. They are thus close to (sometimes synonymous with) *saṃskāras(z).

2. In Buddhism, they contribute to the storehouse consciousness, *ālaya-vijñāna.

Vaṣaṭ or **Vauṣat.** Ritual exclamation in Hinduism uttered by the hotṛ (see ṚTVIJ) priest at the end of the sacrificial offering verse. Once it is uttered, the oblation is cast in the fire. Vaṣaṭ summons the gods and unifies the cosmos in the offering.

Vasiṣtha. Prominent *ṛṣi of the Vedic Hindu period. To him is attributed *Ṛg Veda* 7. 18; and to him also the victory of the *Brahmanas over the *Kṣatriyas is ascribed, leaving the former dominant in society because of their control of ritual, especially *purohita.

Vassa. Three-month rain period (sometimes referred to as a 'Buddhist *Lent') when Buddhist *bhikkhus remain in their monasteries for more intense meditation, and when laymen may join the community for a brief period. Vassa begins with the *festival of Poson. See also MONASTICISM.

Vasu (sphere of existence): see ĀDITYAS.

Vasubandhu (4th/5th cent. CE). Buddhist philosopher, said to be a younger brother of *Asaṅga. According to tradition, Vasubandhu was originally a follower of *Sarvastivāda (in *Hīnayāna), but was converted to *Mahāyāna when his brother feigned illness and blamed his condition upon grief and anxiety at Vasubandhu's adherence to the inferior doctrine. When the teachings of the Mahāyāna were revealed to him, Vasubandhu quickly came to see its superiority and embraced the *Vijñānavāda school which his brother had established. Vasubandhu's major works include the *Abhidharmakośa*, a scholastic compendium, and the extensive *Vijñapti-mātratāsiddhi*, a work on idealism. Shorter works are the *Triṃśikā* and the *Viṃśatikā*, which summarize the essence of the Vijñānavāda system. Scholars have debated inconclusively the suggestion that there were two Vasubandhus rather than one (see E. Frauwallner, *On the Date of the Buddhist Master of the Law Vasubandhu*, 1951).

S. Anacker, *Seven Works of Vasubandhu* . . . (1984); L. de La Vallée Poussin, *L'Abhidharmakośa* . . . (1923–31) and *Vijñaptimātratāsiddhi* . . . (1928–9).

Vasudeva. In Hindu mythology, a prince of the Vṛṣṇi clan, son of Śura, and father of *Kṛṣṇa and *Balarāma. His sister *Kuntī was the mother of the three elder Pāṇḍavas, thus making a link between them and Kṛṣṇa. To save the life of his wife *Devakī,

Vasudeva was prepared to hand over their children at birth to her kinsman *Kaṃsa, but rescued their eighth son Kṛṣṇa by secretly exchanging him for the infant daughter of the cowherd Nanda.

Vāsudeva. Manifestation of *Viṣṇu in power, worshipped as such by *Vaiṣṇavas. It is often regarded, both within the Vaiṣṇava tradition and by W. scholars, as a patronymic from Vasudeva, and thus another name for *Kṛṣṇa, but this derivation is by no means certain. In Purāṇic texts, the word vāsudeva is often said to mean 'dwelling in all things', and as such may have been the name of a tribal god who became identified with Kṛṣṇa and with the all-pervading *Viṣṇu. There are also some epic and Purāṇic passages where Vāsudeva appears to be a title, to which other princes unsuccessfully challenge Kṛṣṇa's right. In the *Pāñcarātra system Vāsudeva is the highest of the four *vyūhas* (see VIṢṆU), from whom the other three proceed.

Vasumitra. Teacher of the *Sarvāstivāda school of Buddhism who put forward a thesis to defend the school's basic tenet that entities (*dharma) exist in the past and future as well as in the present. According to Vasumitra, dharmas exist in a noumenal or latent condition in the future until they attain their moment of causal efficacy (*karitra*) in the present. This marks their entry into a functional relationship with other phenomena. When this moment is past they once again enter into a noumenal mode which is now described as 'past'. Vasumitra's theory of temporality was accepted by the school in preference to the contending views of three other philosophers, Dharmatrāta, Ghoṣaka, and Buddhadeva.

Vaṭakaḷai (religious movement within Śrī-Vaiṣṇavism): see TEṈKAḶAI.

Vatican. A city-state of some 109 acres, occupying the Vatican hill on the west bank of the Tiber in *Rome. Created by the Lateran Treaty of 1929 between the kingdom of Italy and the *Holy See, it now provides a base for the *pope and the *curia. Though papal territory outside the Vatican proper amounts to another 160 acres, it is the world's smallest state, and in it papal authority, exercised through a commission of *cardinals, is absolute. The Vatican has many of the trappings of a full nation-state: its own security services (including the Swiss Guard, a small body of mercenary soldiers), coinage, and postage stamps. It houses an important library and museums. Only those resident may have citizenship, which they lose when they move elsewhere. 'The Vatican' may also refer to the central, hierarchical organization of *Roman Catholicism, hence Vatican Catholicism.

G. Bull, *Inside the Vatican* (1983); P. Hebblethwaite, *The Vatican* (1980); P. Letarouilly, *The Vatican and the Basilica of St Peter* (1966); E. Pucci, *The Vatican City* (1971).

Vatican Council, First, or **Vatican I** (1869–70). A *Roman Catholic *council. Called by *Pope *Pius IX. This council adopted only two constitutions, despite the advance preparation of fifty-one *schemata*. The constitution on *faith, *Dei Filius*, dealt with God as creator, *revelation, faith, and faith's relationship to reason, adopting positions similar to those of St Thomas *Aquinas. It endorsed *natural theology in its statement that God's existence can be known through the light of reason from created things without revelation. The *schema* on the *Church was not voted on; instead, the question of the *papacy was brought forward, although many (e.g. J. H. *Newman) regarded this as inopportune. The constitution *Pastor Aeternus* defined the primacy of the pope and also his *infallibility when he speaks **ex cathedra*, i.e. when as chief pastor of the Church he defines a doctrine on faith or morals to be held by the whole Church.

After Italian troops occupied Rome, the Council was suspended in Oct. 1870. It never reconvened, and the incompleteness of its work led to a serious imbalance in RC Church teaching. It was left to *Vatican II to complement its predecessor's definitions on the papacy with teaching on the *bishops, the laity, and indeed the whole church.

C. Butler, *The Vatican Council, 1869–70* (1962).

Vatican Council, Second, or **Vatican II** (1962–5). A *Roman Catholic *council. In calling for an *ecumenical council, *Pope *John XXIII spoke of his desire for *aggiornamento in the RC Church, for 'a new *Pentecost'. He lived to see only the first session: the Council's work was concluded under his successor, *Paul VI (pope 1963–78). The debates showed deep disagreements on many issues, sometimes leading to the rejection of draft *schemata* prepared before the Council. Sixteen documents were eventually produced, five of which are particularly important. The Constitution on the Church (*Lumen Gentium*) gave a deep theological analysis of the nature of the Church, and defined the authority of *bishops and the position of the laity. The Constitution on Revelation (*Dei Verbum*) outlined the nature of *revelation, *scripture, and *tradition; it laid down canons for biblical interpretation and encouraged greater use of the Bible in *theology, *liturgy, and private devotion. The Pastoral Constitution on the Church in the Modern World (*Gaudium et Spes*) dealt with the Church's attitude to human life and culture, and to marriage, economic development, war, and other contemporary issues. The Constitution on the Liturgy set out a theology of the liturgy and principles for reform (e.g. through wider use of the vernacular; see LITURGICAL MOVEMENT). The Decree on Ecumenism explained the RC Church's attitude to other Christians, and outlined a programme for reunion.

Despite the ensuing period of great turbulence, the Council succeeded in producing the greatest changes in the RC Church since the Council of *Trent in the 16th cent.

W. M. Abbott (ed.), *The Documents of Vatican II* (1966); C. Dollen, *Vatican II: A Bibliography* (1969); H. Vorgrimler (ed.), *Commentary on the Documents of Vatican II* (1967–9).

Vātsīputrīya (Skt., followers of Vātsīputra). A school of early Buddhism. According to tradition Vātsīputra was a *Mahāsaṁghika who claimed to have supernaturally received an *Abhidharmic text in nine sections from *Śāriputra and *Rāhula. This is known as the *Śāriputra-Abhidharma*. Vātsīputra probably lived in the early 3rd cent. BCE in Kośala (E. India) and it seems that the Vātsīputrīyas flourished in that region until the 11th cent. CE.

Their texts, which do not survive, were written in Apabhraṃśa and treat positively the notion of personal identity (*pudgala*). The Vātsīputrīyas were therefore *Pudgalavādins. Since they also distinguished between the existence of things in the past, present, and future, as opposed to the *Sarvāstivādins who did not, they are often referred to as Distinctionists (Vibhajyavādins). The school itself gave rise to four subsects of whom the Sammitīya are the most important. The Tibetan historians consider *Dignāga originally to have been a Vātsīputrīya.

Vaudois (adherents of Christian reform movement): see WALDENSES.

Vaughan, Henry (1622–95). Welsh doctor and *Metaphysical poet, known as the Silurist. His main work, *Silex Scintillans* (The Flashing Flint) was influenced by G. *Herbert. Aware of the restlessness of human nature ('Lord! what a busie restless thing | Hast thou made man!') and of the experience of the absence of God ('Thy anger I could kiss, and will: | But O! thy grief, thy grief doth kill!'), he is especially remembered for vivid images of mystical vision ('I saw Eternity the other night, | Like a great ring of pure and endless light'; or: 'There is in God, some say, | A deep but dazzling darkness . . . | O for that night! Where I in him | Might live invisible and dim').

Vāyu (Skt., *va*, 'blow'). Indian god of wind and warfare. He was born from the breath of *Puruṣa and was the first to drink *soma. He is the subtle pervader of all space and one of the guardians (see LOKAPĀLA) of the quarters. He came to be seen as the vital guarantor of *prāṇa. According to *Bhāgavata Purāṇa*, he assisted *Nārada in the attempt to purloin the summit of Mount *Meru. He eventually succeeded and threw the summit into the sea where it became Śri Lankā. He is the father of both *Bhīma and *Hanumān.

Veda (Skt., 'knowledge'). The body of sacred knowledge held to be the basis of true belief and practice among Hindus. Through it the knower contacts the divinities, or discovers the universal foundation of things, thereby attaining to his desires and overcoming all that is undesirable. The Veda is *śruti, and is thus authoritative, in that it is held to be eternal (*sanātana) and of non-human origin (*apauruṣeya*). Various traditions exist as to its creation—out of *puruṣa (*Ṛg Veda* 10. 90. 9), from the god *Brahman (*Śatapatha Brāhmaṇa* 6. 1. 1. 8), out of the threefold universe represented by *Agni, *Vāyu, and *Āditya (*Chandogya Upaniṣad* 4. 7. 1). In ancient times, it is held, the Veda was 'heard' (śruti) or 'seen' by priestly seers (*ṛṣis), and it is the families descended from these seers who have preserved it through oral transmission. Originally the Veda consisted of two parts: *mantras (verses of invocation and praise) and *Brāhmaṇas (discussions of the proper use of mantras in ritual settings, and explanation of the mythic background of the verses). Later the Veda was extended to include two further groups: *Āraṇyakas and *Upaniṣads. These grew out of the speculative tendencies of the Brāhmaṇas. The mantra portions were organized into collections (*samhitās) associated with particular aspects of the *Vedic *sacrifice and with particular priests. Of these, three were at first recognized as Veda: the *Ṛg Veda*, *Sāma Veda*, and *Yajur Veda*. Later a fourth was included, the *Atharva Veda*. To each of these four collections Brāhmaṇas, Āraṇyakas, and Upaniṣads were appended. In addition to these strictly Vedic compositions a number of other texts became associated with the Veda, including the *Vedāṅga, the Upavedas, and the ritual sūtras. Finally the sanctity of the Veda was extended by some to include the *Itihāsa and the *Purāṇas as the 'fifth veda'. Estimates of the age of the Veda have varied. Max Müller's guess that the earliest hymns or mantra portions originated in the 13th cent. BCE is still generally accepted, though the composition period may well have ranged 18th–4th cents. BCE. The Veda was discovered by Europe in the early 19th cent. From that time it has proved to be essential, not only for the study of Hinduism, but also for Indo-European studies, linguistics, and comparative religion.

S. Bhattacharji, *Literature in the Vedic Age* (1986); J. Gonda, *Vedic Literature* (1975); S. R. Goyal, *A Religious History of Ancient India* (1984); L. Renou, *Vedic India* (tr. 1971); J. Santucci, *An Outline of Vedic Literature* (1976).

Vedanā (Hindu deity): see SKANDHA.

Vedāṅga (Skt., 'the limbs of the *Veda'). The group of auxiliary texts in Hinduism developed over many centuries to preserve and explicate the Veda, especially in relation to ritual. They are sometimes considered part of the Veda, but strictly lie outside and are reckoned as *smṛti, not *śruti. The Vedāṅga are written mostly in *sūtra style and are traditionally six in number: *śikṣa* (phonetics); *chandas* (metre); *vyākaraṇa* (grammar); *nirukta* (etymology); *jyotiṣa* (astronomy and calendar); *kalpa* (ceremonial). The additional 'limbs' are the Upāṅgas, four in number: *purāṇa, *nyāya, *mīmāṃsā, and *dharmaśāstra.

Vedānta (Skt., 'Veda' + 'end'). The end, i.e. culmination, of the *Vedas, especially as contained in the last section of the *Veda, the *Upaniṣads. However, Vedānta understood as the culmination of the Vedas in ordered reflection (i.e. as a philosophical and religious tradition) rests also on the **Bhagavad-gītā* and on the **Brahma Sūtra* of *Bādarāyaṇa (also known as *Vedānta Sūtra*) which attempted to bring order and harmony to the scattered reflections in the Upaniṣads on the nature of *Brahman and the relation of Brahman to the created order, in particular the continuing presence of Brahman within it as *ātman. These three works became the basis of the philosophy of Vedānta, and became the subject of commentaries leading to the diverse interpretations of Vedānta, of e.g. *Śaṅkara, *Rāmānuja, and *Madhva. Cf. also *Uttara-mīmāṃsā See Index, Vedanta.

E. Deutsch, *Advaita Vedānta* . . . (1969); B. N. K. Sharma, *A History of the Dvaita School of Vedānta* . . . (1981).

Vedāntadeśika (Skt., 'teacher of the *Vedānta'). One of the most outstanding figures in post-*Rāmānuja *Śrīvaiṣṇavism. His real name was Veṅkaṭeśa or Veṅkaṭanātha, and he died *c.*1370 CE, aged nearly 100. He became regarded as the figure-head of the Vaṭakaḷai (see TEṈKAḶAI). More than a hundred works in Tamil and Skt., on every aspect of Śrīvaiṣṇava thought and practice, were written by him. These include not only theological treatises like the *Rahasyatrayasāram* or *Tattvaṭīkā* (a commentary on the *Śrī-Bhāṣya*) or philosophical works like the *Nyāyasiddhāñjana* and *Nyāyapariśuddhi*, but also poetic works (including a drama, two *mahakāvyas*, and thirty devotional poems in *kāvya*-style).

Vedanta Society. A Hindu movement formed in New York in 1896 by Swami Vivekananda, a disciple of Sri *Ramakrishna. It is the W. branch of the Ramakrishna Math (monastery), based at Belur near Calcutta, and was established for the purpose of acquainting the West with the spiritual heritage of India in return for the scientific, educational, and other material benefits of the West.

Organized along W. lines and combining W. and Hindu methods of instruction, the Vedanta Society teaches a philosophy derived from the *Upaniṣads. According to the Society, human nature is essentially divine, and the purpose of human life consists in revealing this nature. This is done principally through the practice of *yoga and the Vedanta ethical code, which is centred on the maxim that to injure another is to injure oneself, while to do good to another is to do good to oneself.

Today the Vedanta Society has many centres in the West, and, while some Vedantists dedicate themselves entirely to spiritual advancement, others—lay members—are encouraged to work in the world for its social as well as spiritual improvement.

Vedānta Sūtra (Hindu text): see BRAHMASŪTRA.

Vedas (more comprehensively, *Veda). The four collections which lie at the foundation of Hindu scripture, **Ṛg Veda*, **Sāma Veda*, **Yajur Veda*, **Atharva Veda*. They constitute the foundation of revealed (*śruti) scripture.

Vedi (Hindu altar): see ALTAR.

Vedic. Adjective applied to the language, literature, religion, mythology and ritual pertaining to the *Veda. Generally it indicates the archaic period in Indian culture preceding the classical. Vedic language encompasses the Skt. composed prior to its codification in *Pāṇini's Grammar which set the rules for classical Skt. For Vedic literature, see VEDA. Vedic religion (sometimes called *Brahmanism) can be distinguished from the religion which grew out of it, now usually referred to as Hinduism. Some of the more notable differences between the two religions are seen in their mythology and ritual. Vedic mythology presents a pantheon of deities many of which are solar or meteorological in some of their aspects. These deities are summoned to the human plane in the Vedic rituals (*yajñas*, see *sacrifice). Of the many deities of the Vedic pantheon, few survive into Hinduism and those that do are transformed in character. Similarly, the Vedic ritual, though preserved among some *Brahmans to this day, gives way to a ritual centred not in yajña but in *pūjā.

J. Gonda, *Die Religionen Indiens*, i (1960, 1963) and *Vedic Literature* (1975); P. V. Kane, *History of Dharmasastra* (1930–62); A. A. Macdonell, *Vedic Mythology* (1897); R. C. Majundar (ed.), *The History and Culture of the Indian People*, i. *The Vedic Age* (1965); R. Panikkar (ed.), *The Vedic Experience* . . . (1977); L. Renou, *Bibliographie védique* (1931), continued in R. N. Dandekar, *Vedic Bibliography* (1946–85), and *Vedic India* (1957).

Vegetarianism. The conscious avoidance of eating animal flesh, frequently extended to fish, and sometimes to animal products. In the West, health and ethical reasons predominate, although 'spiritual' explanations have also been influential: these emphasize the purity of the diet and its conduciveness to higher spiritual states. Vegetarianism in the West is often associated with an interest in Indian spirituality and with movements concerned with self-actualization. It has an older tradition in monastic observance, as well as roots in Pythagoreanism and *Manichaeism. In the East, it is most closely associated with Hindu, Jain, and Buddhist traditions: see FOOD.

Veil (in Islam): see ḤIJĀB.

Veneration of the Cross. A ceremony of the Latin *rite for *Good Friday, in which clergy and people solemnly kiss the foot of a crucifix at the entrance to the sanctuary. In the Middle Ages it was called 'creeping to the cross'. A comparable ceremony in the Orthodox Church takes place on the feast of the *Exaltation of the Cross.

Venial sin. In Christian *moral theology, a sin which is less grave or deliberate than *mortal sin and so does not deprive the soul of sanctifying *grace. On the basis of John 5. 16 the *fathers posited two classes of sins, but the modern distinction goes back to the *scholastics, especially Thomas *Aquinas. According to the theology of *penance, there is no obligation to confess venial sins. For the Hindu distinction between major and minor offences, see MAHĀPĀTAKA.

Venite. Psalm 95, so-called from its first words in Lat.: *Venite exultemus* ('O come, Let us worship'). It is most familiar to English-speakers from its place at the beginning of Anglican *morning prayers.

Venn, Henry (1796–1873). Christian organizer of missionary work, and one of the founders of the *CMS (Church Missionary Society). After a conventional start to his career as fellow of Queen's College, Cambridge, and incumbent of two parishes, he became increasingly involved in the Society, first as part-time (from 1841), then as full-time (from 1846) secretary. On the basis of Matthew 28. 19, he envisaged the emergence of national churches with their own indigenous characteristics. This vision is summarized in the 'three-self' policy—though that concept and phrase may have originated from Rufus Anderson: the churches should be self-governing, self-supporting, self-propagating. Despite his securing a great increase in native clergy and the consecration of Samuel Crowther, the increasing sense, especially among young missionaries, of imperial responsibility for 'lesser' races led to great opposition. Nevertheless, important foundations were laid.

W. R. Shenk, *Henry Venn* . . . (1983).

Veronica, St. A woman of Jerusalem who, according to legend, offered her head-cloth to Jesus to wipe his face on the way to his crucifixion. When he gave it back, his features were impressed on it. A 'veil of Veronica' seems to have been at Rome since the 8th cent. It was greatly venerated throughout the Middle Ages, especially after its translation to St Peter's in 1297. The legend was probably written in its present form in the 14th cent. to explain the relic. The incident is now devotionally important as the sixth of the *stations of the cross. Feast day, 12 July.

Versicle. In Christian worship, a short sentence, often taken from the Psalms, which is said or sung and answered by a 'response', e.g. between priest and congregation. Versicle and response are often denoted by the symbols ℣ and ℟:

℣ O Lord, open thou our lips.
℟ And our mouth shall show forth thy praise.

Verstehen (understanding): see HERMENEUTICS.

Vesak or **Vesākha Pūjā** (Skt., Vaiśākha). Major *Theravādin Buddhist *festival, celebrated at full moon in May. It commemorates the birth, enlightenment, and parinibbāna (*nirupadhiśeṣa-nirvāṇa) of the *Buddha.

Vespers. The evening *office of the W. Church.

Vestments. The liturgical dress of the Christian clergy. It derives not, as formerly believed, from the vestments of the ancient Jewish priesthood, but mainly from the secular dress of Roman antiquity retained inside the Church.

In the W., the principal liturgical vestments and their use had been established by the 10th cent. In the 10th–13th cents. the *surplice was introduced as a substitute for the *alb, the *chasuble came to be almost reserved for the celebration of mass, the tunicle became the vestment of the *subdeacon, and *bishops assumed extra vestments such as sandals, *mitre, and gloves. In the 19th cent. vestments imitated the 'gothic' style, but now generally follow earlier, more flowing models. See also LITURGICAL COLOURS.

In the Orthodox E., the vestments evolved in a parallel way, and correspond mostly to those of the W. The vestments of the priest are the *sticharion, epitrachelion, girdle, epimanikia, and phainolion. Bishops wear the sakkos, omophorion, and epigonation. There are no special liturgical colours.

VHP (Indian political party): see BHARATYA JANATA PARTY.

Via Dolorosa. The route in Jerusalem which Jesus is supposed to have followed from the judgement-hall of *Pilate to his crucifixion on Mount *Calvary. It is marked by fourteen *stations of the cross.

Via eminentiae (Lat., 'the way of eminence'). The way in which one may arrive positively at the discernment that God is, and to some extent what God is; contrast *via negativa.

Via media (Lat., 'the middle way'). The *Anglican Church in so far as it holds within itself both Catholic and Reformed beliefs and practices (and people), and in so far as it mediates between the two extremes of Christendom. Via media is then used of other central (and often reconciling) positions, e.g. Buddhism as a *middle way.

Via negativa or **Via negationis** (Lat., 'way of negation'). Realization that since God is not a universe or an object in a universe, 'he' is not open to observation or description. It follows that God can only be spoken of *analogically or poetically; and that it is easier to say 'what God is not' rather than what God is. This awareness occurs, in different forms, in all theistic religions, e.g. in *ein-sof, *bilā kaifa, *neti neti, *nirguṇa-brahman. This is *apophatic, as opposed to kataphatic theology.

Vianney, Jean-Baptiste Marie, St (1786–1859). French priest, better known as the Curé d'Ars, because of his pastoral ministry in that village. He was born near Lyons and received little formal education. He was dismissed from two seminaries in his attempt to become a priest, but was eventually ordained at Grenoble in 1815. In 1818 he began his ministry in Ars-en-Dombes, a village of about 230 of those whom he regarded as souls, not people. The life of the village was transformed, and soon penitents came to him in vast numbers: during his last years, he spent up to eighteen hours a day in the confessional. He was made patron of parish priests in 1929.

Viaticum (Lat., 'provision for a journey'). Holy *communion given to those close to death, to give them strength and grace for the next stage of their history.

Vibhajjavādin (Pāli, 'Distinctionist'). A school of early Buddhism belonging to the Elder (*Sthavira) tradition which at the Buddhist Council of Pāṭaliputra in 250 BCE was adjudged to embody the orthodox teachings of the *Buddha. The appellation thus seems to be an alternative designation for the *Theravāda school, and may be derived from the Buddha's basic methodological practice of making a 'distinction' between extreme views of all kinds in his teachings. It is unclear, however, whether the Vibhajjavādins comprised one sect or a group of sects, and the precise nature of the movement, its doctrines, and duration remain obscure. See also VĀTSĪPUTRĪYA.

Vibhaṅga (Skt., 'distribution', 'division', 'classification'). A Buddhist commentarial work. In the Pāli *Tripiṭaka, a vibhaṅga consists of a detailed exposition of any short section of scripture (*uddesa*). In this sense many discourses of the Sutta Piṭaka (e.g. Dhātuvibhaṅga and Saccavibhaṅga: *Majjhima Nikāya* 3. 202–57) may be considered to be vibhaṅgas in their own right. The second book of the Abhidhamma Piṭaka has the straightforward title Vibhaṅga, since it comprises a classification and definition of the various elements of existence (*dharma (2)) posited by Abhidharmic *ontology, under eighteen separate headings. The *Vibhaṅga* of the *Sthaviravāda shows surprising similarities to both the *Dharmaskandha* of the *Sarvāstivādins and the *Śāriputrābhidharmaśāstra* of the Dharmaguptakas, and this fact has led some scholars to suppose that all three texts have their roots in an identical tabulated summary (*mātikā*) of the doctrine. If this is so, the Vibhaṅga may represent part of the most original Abhidharmic system common to all schools.

Vibhāṣā (Vaibhāṣika text): see VAIBHĀṢIKA.

Vibhūti. 1. In Hinduism, superhuman powers, especially associated with *Śiva, but also listed by *Patañjali in *Yoga Sūtra* 3. 16–55. Since they include knowledge of past and future, previous births, hour of death, etc., they are virtually identical with siddhis/*iddhis. More generally, they are the inspirations of musicians, artists, etc.

2. The ashes with which *Śiva smeared his body (as do his devotees), having the power to restore the dead to life.

Vicar (Lat., *vicarius*, 'substitute'). Title of certain Christian priests. In the Church of England a vicar is the priest of a parish whose *tithes were the property of a monastery in medieval times and thereafter of a 'lay rector'. As parish priests, a vicar and a *rector have exactly the same status. In the Roman Catholic Church, a vicar is a priest appointed as a substitute for a parish pastor. Since the time of Pope Innocent III (1198–1216) the title 'Vicar of Christ' based on John 21. 15 ff., has been a title reserved to the pope.

Vicar-General. In the Roman Catholic Church a priest appointed by a *bishop to assist in administering his diocese. The office developed in the 12th cent. to curb the *archdeacons who could act independently of the bishop's authority. The Vicar-General can carry out most of the functions of the bishop, and has precedence over the other clergy of the diocese. A Vicar Apostolic is a titular bishop, overseeing the church in a territory without a normal hierarchy, as in England before 1850 (see PAPAL AGGRESSION).

Victory, Tour of (period in life of Indian philosopher Śaṅkara): see ŚAṄKARA.

Videhamukti (Skt., 'bodiless' + 'liberation'). *Mokṣa through knowledge that one is not one's body but rather *ātman. One becomes in consequence disembodied or discarnate.

Vidyā (Skt.) or **vijja** (Pāli). 'Knowledge', the total and integral knowledge which precedes and comes after the incomplete non-knowledge (*avidyā) or ignorance which binds people to the wheel of transmigration (*saṃsāra). Vidyā penetrates *māyā and thus enables us to apprehend all things (however apparently different) as they really are. In Hinduism, it is of two types: (i) apara-vidyā, lower knowledge, acquired through intellect; (ii) para-vidyā, higher, spiritual knowledge, leading to enlightenment and liberation (*mokṣa).

Vidyā is defined more precisely than *jñāna, which also means knowledge. There were originally four branches of vidyā: trayī-vidyā, knowledge of the triple *Veda; *ānvīkṣikī*, metaphysics and logic; *daṇḍa-nīti*, the art of government; and *vārttā*, or agriculture, trade, and medicine. A fifth, ātma-vidyā, the knowledge of the *ātman, was added later. Various sources (e.g. *Manu) give lists of vidyās. One such mentions fourteen: the four Vedas, six *Vedāṅgas, the *Purāṇas, *Nyāya, *Mīmāṃsā, and *Dharma. Longer lists include astronomy, architecture, and music. Skill in magic and the ability to use hallucinogenic drugs have been called vidyās, and the concept has also been personified and identified with *Durgā.

In view of the close classical association between spiritual and empirical knowledge, it is not surprising that 19th-cent. Indian reformers and philosophers used vidyā as the natural term to denote the drawing together via comprehensive scientific theories of what at the beginning of the century had been separate scientific disciplines. The Bharatiya Vidyā Bhawan ('House of the Nation's Knowledge/Science') in Bombay publishes popular scientific paperbacks and *Bhawan's Journal*, which has been described as the 'Reader's Digest of Hindu India'.

Vidyāraṇya or **Madhāvācarya** (14th cent. CE). Hindu philosopher who expounded the *Advaita Vedānta of *Śaṅkara. His *Pañcadaśi* became a basic work of this school, and continues to be used in Indian universities: ed. with Eng. tr. Swami Swahananda, 1967.

Vigil. A night service before a Christian festival. Vigils may have been introduced in accordance with the belief that the Second Coming (*Parousia) would take place at midnight. The earliest and most important was the *Easter vigil, which lasted throughout the night. Night-long vigils are now more common on the night of *Maundy Thursday, being related to *Jesus in *Gethsemane and to his question to his disciples, 'Could you not watch with me . . .?' In the West, vigils developed into fast days, kept before certain feasts (sixteen in the *Book of Common Prayer). Among Russian Orthodox, vigils are kept in both parishes and monasteries, among Greek Orthodox in monasteries only.

Vigraha (Skt., 'form'). The divine represented in Hinduism through a manifest form. An image is consecrated by *mantras and other rituals, but does not 'become' God: it becomes the mediating vehicle through which the divine becomes real to the worshipper.

Vihāra (Skt., 'dwelling'). Originally a Buddhist monastic retreat during the rainy season, later becoming a permanent monastic establishment. The rock-carved vihāras of the Western Ghats, usually associated with a *caitya hall, are among the earliest surviving examples of Buddhist architecture, though Jain vihāras (1st and 2nd cents. BCE) are found in Orissa. In the early period, monks of differing doctrinal affiliations lived side by side, with vihāras only being organized on sectarian lines from about the beginning of the CE. In the *Mahāyāna period, the situation reverted to the original arrangement. Of the rock-carved variety, Bhājā, dating from the early Śunga period (2nd cent. BCE) is a good example, consisting of a central rectangular chamber surrounded by individual cells. Later vihāras are simply an elaboration on this basic theme, in which a central courtyard (very often enclosing a railed *Bo Tree, shrine room, and ambulatory) is encompassed by monks' cells, sometimes reaching several storeys with veranda attached. The kitchen, bathroom, etc., are generally placed behind one of these rows of cells.

The vihāra is a fundamental feature of all Buddhist cultures: many may be found in close proximity to Buddhist pilgrimage sites. In the classical period, large vihāras sometimes became the headquarters of a particular school (such as the Mahāvihāra at *Anurādhapura which became the centre for Sinhalese *Theravāda, *c.*256 BCE) or developed into universities, as was the case at *Nālandā. The Indian state of Bihar is so called because of the large number of vihāras which at one time covered the landscape.

S. Dutt, *Buddhist Monks and Monasteries of India* (1962).

Vijñāna (Skt., 'knowing'). 1. In Hinduism, knowledge which penetrates ritual and sacrifice, and understands its meaning (e.g. *Chandogya Upaniṣad* 7. 7. 1; *Taittiriya Upaniṣad* 2. 5. 1). It is therefore the highest state of consciousness in which the meditator sees *Brahman, not just in the condition of *samādhi, but in the whole of everything. In *Vedānta, this is 'seeing Brahman with open eyes'.

2. In Buddhism (Pāli, *viññāna*), the fifth of the five *skandhas. As 'perception', it is contrasted with *jñāna ('understanding'). Its importance was enhanced in *Vijñanavāda (Yogācāra), because it is the basis of the 'storehouse consciousness' (*ālaya-vijñāna), which contains the seeds of all *dharmas (constituents of manifestation).

Vijñānavāda. Buddhist school of idealism, also known as Yogācāra ('yoga-practice') or the doctrine of 'Mind-Only' (*citta-mātra*). The school developed in the 4th cent. CE, and its leading exponents were Maitreyanātha, *Asaṅga, and his brother *Vasubandhu. Its literature is extensive and includes the **Laṅkāvatāra Sūtra*, **Samdhinirmocana Sūtra*, and the **Avataṃsaka Sūtra*, as well as many treatises composed by its followers.

The basic postulate of the school is that consciousness itself is the fundamental and only reality, and that the apparent diversity of the empirical world is the product of instability and obscuration in the individual field of consciousness. The standard form of the doctrine distinguishes eight functions or aspects of consciousness, the most fundamental being the *ālaya-vijñāna ('Receptacle Consciousness', or storehouse consciousness) which is the foundation of personal identity. Due to the effect of previous actions (*karma) the ālaya becomes tainted and unstable, and proceeds to manifest itself in a dualistic form whereby the notions of 'self' and 'other' arise. This is the second aspect, the 'defiled consciousness' (*kliṣṭa-mano-vijñāna*). The division of consciousness is carried further through its operation in the six sense-modalities (touch, taste, smell, hearing, sight, and thought) which completes the list of eight functions. An image commonly used to describe this scheme is that of the ocean: its depths are like the ālaya, and the operation of the six senses are compared to the waves which disturb its surface stirred by the wind of *karma. For the Vijñānavāda enlightenment is achieved through the recognition of the ālaya as the only reality and the consequent cessation of dualistic imaginings.

The Vijñānavada introduced a doctrine of 'three aspects' (*trisvabhava*) to describe the ways in which the ālaya manifests itself. The level of ultimate truth or perfection (*parinispanna*) is the nature of the ālaya when perceived non-dualistically in its natural unitary state. The level of 'dependent' or 'relative' (*paratantra*) truth corresponds to the dualistic perception of self and other, while the lowest level, that of the imagined or misconceived (*parakalpita*), relates to misapprehensions and illusions which have no real status even at the level of relative truth (e.g. unicorns or dream-images).

The doctrine of 'Mind-Only' had a profound influence in all *Mahāyāna Buddhist countries and became especially popular in the Far East.

J. P. Keenan, 'A Study of the Buddhabhūmyupadeśa: The Doctrinal Development of the Notion of Wisdom in Yogacāra Thought' (Ph.D., Wisconsin, 1980); P. Williams, *Mahāyāna Buddhism* (1989); J. D. Willis, *On Knowing Reality* (1979).

Vijñapti-mātra. The doctrine of 'mere imagining' or 'thought only' associated with the *Vijñānavāda school of Buddhist idealism. According to this teaching the empirical world of objects is regarded as the product of pure ideation, with no reality beyond the consciousness of the perceiving subject. Despite the denial of the external world, the problem of bondage and liberation is similar to that envisaged by early Buddhism, which had itself placed considerable emphasis on right views, correct perception and understanding, and had described the world as 'led by the mind' (*Saṃyutta Nikāya* I. 39). In terms of the doctrine of Vijñapti-mātra, enlightenment is the realization of the imaginary status of phenomena and the non-substantiality of the self and external objects. As before, this comes about through the eradication of the craving for appropriation (*taṇhā) with the result that the mind ceases to project the illusion of duality between self and other and abides in a state of undifferentiated awareness.

Vikalpa (Skt., *vi* + *kḷrp*, 'variation', 'diversity'). In Buddhist philosophy, the imaginative tendency of unenlightened minds. The Pāli term *vikappa* is not used in a technical sense in the *Tripiṭaka of the *Sthaviravādins, but it is common in *Mahāyāna philosophical works, particularly of the Yogācāra (*Vijñānavāda) variety. The *Abhisamayālaṅkāra* considers both 'subjectivity' (*grāhaka*) and 'objectivity' (*grāhya*) to be the result of imagining (vikalpa). Since another technical term, 'mental discrimination' (*prapañca*), also conveys the idea of consciousness developing in a dichotomous mode, and since vikalpa and *prapañca* often occur in the same text, there is some reason to take them as virtually synonymous. Vikalpa is said to come to an end in the enlightened state, when one comes to understand reality freed from all thought-construction. A common synonym for this state is 'gnosis devoid of imagining' (*nirvikalpajñāna*). In a doctrine peculiar to the *Laṅkāvatāra-Sūtra*, vikalpa is said to be the third of the five dharmas (*nāma*, 'name'; *nimitta*, 'sign'; *vikalpa*; *samyagjñāna*, 'right knowledge'; *tathatā, 'suchness'). As such it corresponds with the second of the three 'own-natures' (*trisvabhāvāḥ*), the 'dependent' (*paratantra*).

Vikāra (Skt., 'transformation'). The means, in Hinduism, especially in *Sāṁkhya, whereby one substance is changed into another, as cream into butter, etc. Thus *prakṛti is able to manifest all forms of appearance.

Village Awakening Councils (Buddhist self-development organizations): see SARVODAYA.

Vilna Gaon (Jewish spiritual leader): see ELIJAH BEN SOLOMON ZALMAN; MITNAGGEDIM.

Vimalakirti (bodhisattva): see BODHISATTVA.

Vimalakīrti Sūtra or ***Vimalakirti-nirdeśa-sūtra*** (Teachings of the *Bodhisattva Unstained-Glory). Major *Mahāyāna text—according to its translator, É. Lamotte, it 'is perhaps the crowning jewel of the Buddhist literature of the Great Vehicle'. He describes it as 'vibrating with life and full of humour', avoiding the prolixity of other Mahāyāna works while equalling them in the profundity of its teachings. A measure of its popularity is the number of translations: into Chinese (eight times), Tibetan (three times), Sogdian, and Khotanese. The Skt. original has not survived.

The Sūtra is divided into twelve chapters, and tells the story of the householder-bodhisattva Vimalakīrti who feigns illness and is visited at his house by the saints of early Buddhism whom he proceeds to confuse with his profound knowledge of the doctrine of emptiness (*śūnyatā). He disconcerts his audience by performing miracles of all kinds and ridicules their dualistic conceptions by constantly undermining the basis for ontological dualism of any kind.

The Sūtra, which was composed not later than 2nd cent. CE, has been especially popular with the laity, since the protagonist is himself a lay householder. Thus the world-renouncing monastic ethos of the Hīnayāna is rejected, and the status of the laity legitimized as part of the broad re-evaluation of religious ideals undertaken by the Mahāyāna.

Tr. *Sacred Books of the Buddhists*, 32; R. A. F. Thurman (1976); K. Y. Lu (1972).

Vimānavatthu (part of Buddhist Pāli canon): see KHUDDAKA NIKĀYA.

Vimokkha (Pāli), **vimokṣa** (Skt., 'liberation', 'deliverance'). A term occurring in early Buddhism in connection with two classificatory lists. First: the Eight Liberations or Stages of Liberation. These form a slight variant on the eight *jhānas as a system of classifying stages of attainment in developing concentration meditation (*samādhi). They are (i) awareness of oneself and of forms outside oneself, (ii) awareness of forms outside oneself only, (iii) awareness of one's meditation subject only, (iv)–(vii) identical to the four higher jhānas, (viii) the state of cessation of perception and feeling.

Second: the Three Doors to Deliverance (vimokkha-mukha). When a person resolves to attain *nirvāna, he cannot make nirvāna itself a subject of meditation, for it is 'inconceivable', not an object of thought. He therefore makes his way towards nirvāna through its aspects of the 'signless' or 'conditionless' (*animitta), the 'desireless' or 'wishless' (*appaṇihita*) and 'emptiness' (*śūnyatā); that is, by making impermanence (*anicca), suffering (*dukkha), and no-self (*anatman), respectively, his subjects of meditation. During the course of his meditations he will, at some point, acquire 'insight-understanding' (*vipassanā-paññā*) into those truths, and so be said to have gained entrance upon the path that leads to liberation. If this happens whilst he is contemplating impermanence, he is said to have entered through the door of the signless deliverance; if whilst contemplating suffering, through the door of the desireless deliverance; and if whilst contemplating no-self, through the door of the emptiness deliverance.

Vimokṣa: see VIMOKKHA.

Vimutti (Pāli, 'freedom', 'release', 'deliverance'). Freedom from suffering (*dukkha), the goal of the Buddhist path. Canonical Buddhism distinguishes two kinds: freedom through understanding (paññavimutti) and freedom of mind (ceto-vimutti). The former means final release from suffering, the ending of rebirth, *nirvāna, and is so named because it is brought about by understanding (*prajña) which develops out of the practice of insight meditation (*vipassanā). The latter represents the qualified freedom from suffering which arises out of the practice of concentration meditation (*samādhi), specifically those meditations which produce states of consciousness emancipated from the impingement of sense-stimuli upon the mind, for example the divine abidings (*brahma-vihāras), meditation on the signless (*animittā), on emptiness (*śūnyatā), on nothingness (*ākiñcaññā*), and the eight liberations (*vimokkha). Since this represents a freedom tied to mind-states which are by their very nature impermanent, according to Buddhist doctrine (see ANICCA), then the freedom is only of a temporary (*sāmāyika*) kind; sooner or later the meditator must return to normal consciousness and the world of suffering again. Ceto-vimutti can only become permanent and unshakeable (*akuppa*), synonymous with final release, if it is combined with paññā-vimutti, that is, if the meditator cultivates insight as well as concentration. A person may, therefore, become enlightened in either of two ways: by way of insight alone (he is then known as 'one freed through understanding', *paññā-vimutto*), or by concentration and insight (he is known as 'one freed-both-ways', *ubhato-bhāga-vimutto*).

The term *saddhā-vimutti* ('released by faith') is also found in canonical Buddhism. It there applies to someone who comes to an unalterable confidence (*saddhā) in the Buddha and the truth of his doctrine, but has not yet realized that truth for himself. If such a person does not go on to achieve final release during the remainder of his life, he is assured, nevertheless, of reaching that goal in some future existence.

Vinaya ('that which separates'). The rules which govern the *saṅgha, and thus lives of Buddhist *bhikkhus and bhikkunīs. It is one of the three parts ('baskets') of the *Tripiṭaka. It is divided into three parts: *Sutta Vibhaṅga* (*Sūtravibhaṅga*, also known as *Vinayavibhaṅga*), which has incorporated an earlier disciplinary text, *Pratimokṣa Sūtra*: it thus becomes a statement and explication of the *pratimokṣa rules; it also gives a context for the rules by explaining when and in what circumstances each of the rules was formulated, and it gives case illustrations of the rules. The second part is *Skandhaka* (*Khandhaka*, 'Chapters', also called *Vinayavastu*), of more diverse materials, and itself divided into *Mahāvagga* ('Greater Section') and *Cūlavagga* ('Smaller Section'): in addition to rules governing rituals and communal occasions, e.g. *uposatha, *vassa, admission to the order, *schism, it contains a partial biography of the *Buddha and an account of the first two *Councils; it also establishes the importance of *sīmā*, 'boundary', which establishes much more than territory: it designates a sacred space in which all new members of the community are ordained, thus securing the continuity of the community. The third part is *Parivāra*, a kind of appendix which organizes the material of the other parts in ways which make it easier to learn. See also TAO-HSÜAN; RITSU.

Tr. I. B. Horner, *The Book of the Discipline* (1938–66); E. Frauwallner, *The Earliest Vinaya* . . . (1956); J. C. Holt, *Discipline: The Canonical Buddhism of the Vinayapiṭaka* (1981).

Vincent de Paul (founder): see VINCENTIANS.

Vincentian Canon. A threefold (but never realized) criterion of *Catholic doctrine: *quod ubique, quod semper, quod ab omnibus creditum est* ('what has been believed everywhere, always, and by all'). It was formulated by St Vincent of Lérins (d. before 450) in his *Commonitorium*, a guide to *heresy and to determining the true faith.

Vincentians. The most usual name for the Congregation of the Mission (CM), a Roman Catholic religious order founded by St Vincent de Paul in 1625. He had been moved by the plight of a poor woman in 1617, and established Les Dames de Charité, an early expression of organized charity. From this developed Les Filles de la Charité, who, in addition to collecting money, committed themselves to service. The underlying principle was expressed by Fléchier, 'God's purpose in creating the rich is that they may be disposed to charity, . . . as channels through which the external marks of his goodness can flow.' As dispensers of charity and as missionaries, they are also known as Lazarists, from the priory of St. Lazare, Vincent's headquarters in Paris. The original work of the congregation was missionary work and *retreats in France. Later they became very active in foreign missions and established seminaries. They began work in the USA with the Louisiana Purchase of 1803. More recently Irish Vincentians established the order in Britain.

Vinculum (bond in marriage): see MARRIAGE.

Vindhyācalavāsini. 'Dweller on the Vindhya', perhaps originally a tribal goddess of the Vindhya hills, but later a form of *Kālī, worshipped by the *Ṭhags.

Vindhyavāsinī (Skt., 'she who lives on the Vindhya mountains'). Name of a goddess in a well-known Hindu temple. The shrine stands near Mirzapur, E. Uttar Pradesh, and has been famous since at least the 7th cent. CE, even with N. Indian court poets. In the *Purāṇas and with the Jains, this goddess is often associated with *Māyādevī, the girl exchanged for Kṛṣṇa and dashed by Kaṃsa on to an execution stone. Of tribal origin, the cult was supposed to be associated with human sacrifice and the *Ṭhags.

Viññāna (consciousness): see VIJÑĀNA (2).

Vinobā Bhāve, Ācārya (1895–1982). Hindu reformer who succeeded, and developed the ideas of, *Gāndhī. Drawn to an ascetic life, he burnt his school certificates and eventually joined Gandhi's *āśrama at Sabarmati. In 1921, Gandhi sent him to start a new āśrama at Wardha, and in 1941 he was the first *satyāgrahi to be arrested in the civil disobedience movement. In 1951, the idea came to him of a middle way between Communist insurrection and landholding aggrandisement by asking large landholders to donate surplus land to the landless. The principle of *sarvodaya, 'welfare for all', was not in fact far from Communism:

When the first offer of land came at Pochampalli, I began to think deeply that night over the significance of this incident. I thought there must be some divine indication in this. With some faith in arithmetic as in God, I began to calculate: I thought that 5 crores of acres got in this way would solve the land problem . . . If this sarvodaya method is not possible, it will have to be accepted that communism alone can achieve the objective. Thus we came close to each other. Two points at the end of a circle are close to each other.

He began a long progress on foot through India, securing the gift of much land—though not, as he hoped, the supplanting of the coercions of the state by disinterested love.

S. Narayan, *Vinoba* . . . (1970).

Violence. An aspect of human behaviour often bound up with emotions (especially anger), which religions cannot ignore—and often express. Opinion is divided as to where violence should be located along the nature–nurture spectrum. Those favouring natural processes or *psychodynamic theory hold that religious activities reduce violence if they function cathartically, but increase violence if they result in frustration (see M. Spiro, *Burmese Supernaturalism*, 1978). Those favouring cultural processes hold that religions function as learning systems. It is pointed out that apparently non-aggressive societies are informed by religions which function to instil peace by presenting the adverse consequences of violence. Aggressive peoples, on the other hand, often live with aggressive religious ideologies. An additional consideration is that religions often put 'violence'—if that is what it is—to religious ends, examples here being *sacrifice, head-hunting, many male rites of *initiation, and the justification of war (*just war) on religious grounds.

J. W. Bowker, *Licensed Insanities* (1987) and (ed.), *Origins, Functions and Management of Aggression in Biocultural Evolution, Zygon* (1983).

Vipāka (Pāli, Skt., 'ripen'). The coming to fruition, in Buddhism, of an act—the consequence of the law of *karma.

Vipāka-sūtra-aṅga (Jain text): see AṄGA.

Vipassanā (Pāli), **vipaśyanā** (Skt., 'see clearly', 'penetrate an object thoroughly'). Insight into the truths of impermanence (*anicca), suffering (*dukkha), and no-self (*anātman); the form of *meditation which has the personal apprehension of these specific truths of Buddhism as its object. Together with tranquillity (*samatha) it represents the two-fold dimension to Buddhist meditational practice. But it is superior to the latter because it is concerned with that aspect of meditation which is distinctively Buddhist, and because it alone produces the form of understanding, prajña, through which liberation takes place. It is the central focus of meditational training in *Theravāda Buddhist centres.

Vipaśyanā: see VIPASSANĀ.

Virabhadra. A fearsome manifestation of *Śiva, created to threaten Dakṣa and wreck his great sacrifice when he forgot to invite Śiva to it.

Viraśaivas ('heroic Śaivas'): see LIṄGĀYAT.

Virgin Birth of Christ. The Christian doctrine that *Jesus was conceived by the Virgin *Mary by the operation of the *Holy Spirit and without sexual relations with a man (one should strictly speak of 'virginal *conception*'; that Mary remained a virgin even in giving birth is a later idea). It is congruent with the belief that God took radical action to redeem humanity; but the New Testament evidence, critically considered, is not strong. It is not mentioned by Paul, Mark, or John (if Galatians 4. 4–5; Mark 6. 3; John 1. 13 are discounted, as they should be); and it plays no part in the gospel story outside Matthew 1. 18–25 and Luke 1. 26–38. Scholars usually explain its currency, if not its origin, as a rebuttal of charges that Jesus was conceived out of wedlock (cf. John 8. 41). Parallels with Graeco-Roman stories in which children are fathered by gods are not close, though they may be significant in establishing the belief. Likewise the prophecy of Isaiah 7. 14, though used as a proof-text already by Matthew, cannot have given rise to the belief.

Among modern Christians belief in the virgin birth is often taken as a touchstone of orthodoxy, both by *Catholics, for whom it is involved with *mariology, and *Protestants (see FUNDAMENTALISM). Some liberal theologians have criticized the doctrine as setting Christ's humanity apart from ours. They have also drawn attention to the widespread claim of virgin births in many religions (e.g. Mahāmāyā and the *Buddha, *Kuntī/Pṛtha and Karna, *Zoroaster and the saviour, Saoshyant), and have suggested that this is a reverential theme introduced for apologetic reasons. Even stronger criticisms have been made by feminist writers and theologians, who point out that Mary is not even accorded the participation of parthenogenesis if perpetual virginity (see above) is affirmed: 'In the myth of the Virgin Birth, Mary does nothing, whereas in parthenogenesis the female accomplishes everything herself' (M. Daly, *Gyn/Ecology*, 1979).

R. E. Brown, *The Virginal Conception and Bodily Resurrection of Jesus* (1974); D. A. Leeming, *Mythology . . .* (1980).

Vīr Siṅgh (Sikh writer): see SIṄGH SABHĀ.

Virūpa (Tibetan siddha): see SIDDHA TRADITION.

Virya (Skt.; Pāli, *viriya*). Effort and exertion of will in Buddhism; it appears in the eightfold path (*aṣtangika-marga), as one of the four perfect exertions, of the five powers (*bala), and of the seven factors of enlightenment.

Vishishtadvaita (qualified non-duality): see VIŚIṢṬĀDVAITA-VEDĀNTA.

Vishnu (Hindu god): see VIṢṆU.

Viśiṣṭādvaita-vedānta. The teaching and school, in Hinduism, of qualified non-duality, in contrast to *Advaita. The name is derived from *viśiṣṭa* ('distinct', 'particular to') and *advaita* ('not-dual'). Although introduced by the *Vaiṣṇava writer, Yamunācārya, the school is usually associated with *Rāmānuja. The world, selves, and God are all real, but the world and self depend on God, since God creates the cosmos out of his *subtle body by transforming it into a gross one—though he does not prevent faults or blemishes occurring. Selves depend in such a way that they are sustained in continuing, independent existence, even after liberation (*mokṣa). But they remain part of the whole body of *Brahman as attributes, Brahman being 'all that is'. Since the highest mode of being is personal (i.e. higher than inanimate, or non-relational being), Brahman is personal, i.e. containing the relational within his being 'all that is'. In this respect, though not in its detail or application, the argument resembles the Christian conclusion of the Trinitarian nature of God.

P. N. Srinivasachari, *The Philosophy of Viśiṣṭādvaita* (1946).

Visiting the sick (Heb., *bikkur holim*). A major commandment in Judaism. In *midrash, God visited *Abraham when he was recovering from circumcision, setting the example. According to the *Talmud, a visit to a sick person removes one-sixtieth of the illness, while failure to do so may result in the death of the sick person so that 'whoever does not visit the sick is as a murderer' (*B.Ned.* 39b–40a). The way in which this should be done is carefully described, including the wise advice never to sit on the bed. From this general requirement (at least as old as Ecclesiasticus 7. 35) it passed into the fundamental teaching associated with *Jesus in the parable of the separation between the sheep and the goats (Matthew 25).

Viṣṇu. The 'pervader', or perhaps, the 'one taking different forms', a Hindu god of little importance in the *Vedas, but subsequently a major deity, and a member of the Hindu 'trinity' (*trimūrti). He is the preserver of the universe and embodiment of goodness and mercy. For *Vaiṣṇavites, he is the supreme deity, *Īśvara, from whom all created things emanate. As Īśvara, he becomes incarnate (*avatāra) at moments of great crisis (for list, see AVATĀRA). Īśvara is the material cause of the universe, omnipresent to it, and sustaining it in life. Through his presence, he is the refuge of all who need his help. Īśvara exists in five forms, *para*, *vyūha*, *vibhava*, *antaryāmin*, and *ārcāvatāra*. In his transcendent being, he is called *para, as in Parabrahman, Paravāsudeva. He manifests his power through four *vyūhas*—*Vāsudeva, Saṁkarṣana, Pradyumna, and Aniruddha—thereby being able to create and being available for worship. Viṣṇu is usually depicted standing, holding weapons, or reclining on *Seṣa, the serpent. Because of his pervasive presence, images of Viṣṇu are extremely important, whether in the home or in temples—some of which have consequently evoked magnificent architecture. According to *Rāmānuja, Viṣṇu underlies both Vedas and *Upaniṣads (despite the apparent scant mention of Viṣṇu), since words like power, body, form, splendour in the former denote Viṣṇu, as do, in the latter, mentions of Brahman, the soul of all, etc. Vaiṣṇavites are thus able to regard *Advaita as profoundly false: 'Viṣṇu alone is the instructor of the whole world: what else should anyone teach or learn except him, the supreme Spirit?' (*Viṣṇu Purāṇa* 1. 17). See Index, Viṣṇu.

S. Bhattacharji, *Indian Theogony* . . . (1970); J. Gonda, *Aspects of Early Viṣṇuism* (1954).

Viṣṇu Purāṇa. In Hinduism one of the eighteen *Mahāpurāṇas. It may have been compiled towards the end of the 3rd cent. CE, or near the beginning of the 4th. Unlike most *purāṇas, it is a unified and clearly structured composition, with a consistent theological viewpoint discernible throughout. *Viṣṇu is identified with *Brahman, and his omnipresence and omnipotence are constantly emphasized. Book i deals mainly with the world's origin, ultimately from Viṣṇu, although various other creator figures play subordinate roles. Book ii sets out the geography of the universe, with Viṣṇu at the centre, in the lowest depths, and in the utmost heights. Book iii deals mainly with the *Vedas and *varṇāśramadharma, and stresses that Viṣṇu is pleased with those who keep the latter. Book iv presents a pageant of kings and heroes, including many through whom Viṣṇu has been active, while book v deals with the central point of that pageant, when Viṣṇu himself lived on earth in the form of *Kṛṣṇa. Finally book vi describes the future destruction of the universe and its reabsorption into Viṣṇu. The *Viṣṇu Purāṇa* has been influential in the development of *Vaiṣṇava theology, being frequently quoted by *Rāmānuja and serving as a model, to some extent, for the **Bhāgavata Purāṇa*. It was the first purāṇa to be translated into Eng., by H. H. Wilson in 1840 (3rd edn., 1961).

Viṣṇuśaram (compiler of *Pañcatantra*, collection of legends): see PAÑCATANTRA.

Viṣṇuyaśas. A prominent Hindu *brahman. One of his descendants will be born at the end of the *Kali-yuga, as *Kalki(n), the *avatāra, of the future, of *Viṣṇu. His coming will restore peace and innocence to the earth (*Viṣṇu Purāṇa* 4. 24).

Visualization (*dmigs.pa*). An essential component of *meditation in Tibetan Buddhism. Though it has been linked with *Theravādin *nimitta practice, and even by Beyer (*The Cult of Tara*, 1973) to *soma-taking in early *Vedic ritual, visualization does characterize *Vajrayāna as a step away from *Hīnayāna and other forms of *Mahāyāna meditation which rely to a great extent on awareness (*samatha) and insight (*vipassanā). Indeed, as Beyer says of Tibetan ritual: 'If contemplation is the heart of the ritual, then visualization is its living soul'. Principal subjects for visualization are *maṇḍalas and deities, and to be able to visualize them well means to be able to see their every detail as indistinguishable from common reality—a feat said to require at least one lifetime of total devotion to the skill. Visualization has four stages: projection, which is the creation of the appearance; pride, which is the identification of the self with that which is visualized; recollection of purity, which is the contemplation of the meaning of the practice and the nature of the deity; absorption, which is the reintegration of the deity into the *yogin. It will normally be accompanied by *mudrā and *mantra, so that the energies of body and speech are harmonized along with the mind (*Body, Speech, and Mind). In addition to the benefits peculiar to the practice, the yogin is reminded by it that preconceptions of the solidity and permanence of the external world are misplaced, and that the true nature of all things is as the nature of the visualized.

Visuddhimagga ('Path of Purification'): see BUDDHAGHOSA.

Viśva-devās (Skt., 'all gods'). In the *Ṛg Veda*, all the gods together. But the concept is more subtle than that of a collective polytheism: it expresses the way in which one god can incorporate the powers and characters of all others. Thus attributes which might logically belong to only one (e.g. sole creator) can belong to any and many gods. Such unity is expressed in *Ṛg Veda* 1. 164 and 10. 129 (Hymn of Creation, *Nāsadāsīya).

Viśva Hindu Paraśad (Indian political group): see BHARATYA JANATA PARTY.

Viśvakarman (Skt., 'all-creating'). The Hindu *Vedic creative power, the personified divine architect of the universe. In *Ṛg Veda* 10. 81. 2–3, 82. 2, he binds heaven and earth together. In *Śatapatha Brāhmaṇa* 13. 7. 7 he sacrifices himself in the universal sacrifice (*sarvamedha), which is then replicated in every sacrifice, thereby sustaining the cosmos. He is also the patron and inspirer of architects: he is worshipped on the day when the sun enters the constellation of Bhādrapada, and on that day no architectural tool or implement may be used.

Viśvāmitra. Famous Hindu *ṛṣi, said to be composer of the third maṇḍala of the *Ṛg Veda* which contains the most sacred *mantra, *Gāyatrī (3. 62. 10). Originally *purohita of King Sudas, he lost the conflict with *Vasiṣtha.

Viśvanātha (Skt., 'lord of the universe'). In Hinduism:

1. Manifestation of *Śiva at Kāśī, where a temple bears his name.

2. Author of *Rāghava-Vilāsa*, a life of *Rāma, and *Sāhita-darpana*, a treatise on poetry.

Viśvarūpa-darśana. The vision in Hinduism of the universal divine form, celebrated especially in *Bhagavad-gītā* 11, when it is manifested to *Arjuna: 'This form of mine, which is indeed very hard to see, you have seen. Gods long to see me in this form. But in this form I cannot be seen either by *Vedas, or by asceticisms, or by offerings, or by sacrifices. Only by undeviating devotion to me can I thus be known, seen, entered into.'

T. S. Maxwell, *Visvarupa* (1988).

Vitakka or **vitarka** (Pāli, Skt., 'thought-conception'). In Buddhist psychology the initial application of the mind to its object. It is defined as laying hold of the object of thought and directing attention towards it. Closely associated with vitakka and usually following it is *vicāra* ('discursive thought'). The relationship between the two is said to be like taking hold of a bowl in one hand and scrubbing it with the other, to the striking of a bell and its resounding, or to the fixed point of a compass and the revolving point which moves around it. Both vitakka and vicāra are eliminated from the mind in the early stages of meditation (*jhāna/dhyāna).

Vital, Ḥayyim ben Joseph (1542–1620). Jewish *kabbalist. Vital was the principal student of Isaac *Luria in Safed and arranged and elaborated on his teachings. *Ez ha-Ḥayyim* (Tree of life) is a record of these teachings, and this was re-edited by his son and circulated under the title *Shemonah She'arim* (Eight Gates). Vital also produced an autobiography (*Sefer ha-Hezyonot*, Book of Visions), commentaries on the *Talmud, volumes of sermons, a commentary on the **Zohar*, and various *halakhic *responsa. As the chief formulator of the Lurianic kabbalah, he was an important influence on the development of later Jewish *mysticism. He held the view that the dispersion of the Jews among the nations was necessary to recover and kindle such sparks of goodness as there might be among them. The separation of good from evil is the necessary precondition of the coming of the *messiah—'therefore it was necessary that Israel should be scattered to the four winds'.

Vitarka: see VITAKKA.

Viṭhobā (Mahārāṣtra deity): see NĀMDEV.

Viṭṭhala (Mahārāṣṭra deity): see NĀMDEV.

Vivāha (marriage): see MARRIAGE.

Vivasvat (social law): see ĀDITYAS.

Viveka (Skt., 'discrimination'). In *Sāṁkhya philosophy, the direct intuitive discrimination between *puruṣa (pure consciousness) and *prakṛti (materiality), and the goal of the Sāṁkhya system. In *Advaita Vedānta viveka is considered one of the four requisites of a seeker after knowledge of Brahman and is defined by *Śaṅkara as: 'an (intellectual) discrimination between what is eternal and what is non-eternal' (*Brahmasūtrabhāṣya* I. I).

Viveka-cūḍāmaṇi (The Crest Jewel of Discrimination). A work on the distinction between reality and appearance by *Śaṅkara.

Tr. Prabhavananda and C. Isherwood (1947).

Vivekānanda (1863–1902). A devout follower of *Ramakrishna, and founder of the Ramakrishna Mission which now has more than a hundred centres throughout the world. Swami Vivekānanda was born in Calcutta, of Kāyastha *caste. His original name was Narendranāth Datta. Educated at a Christian missionary college, he absorbed the radical ideals of such Western social reformers as John Stuart Mill. After a meeting with Keshab Chandra *Sen, he joined the *Brahmo Samāj. All his life he acted on the principle that all people hold within themselves the means to achieve their full potential.

It was after becoming a disciple of Ramakrishna that Vivekānanda received his new name, and the honourable title of 'swāmi'. After six years of contemplation in the Himālayan region he carried out, with missionary zeal, tours of S. and W. India, becoming the most noteworthy teacher of modern *Vedānta. In 1893 a *World's Parliament of Religions was held in Chicago. Swami Vivekānanda represented Hinduism with outstanding success, and, through the power of his oratory and his impressive appearance, became known worldwide. In Britain he made several converts, notably Sister *Nivedita. After repeated world missionary tours Vivekānanda founded his *maṭha* in Bengal, from where he travelled round India preaching his reformed Hinduism.

Vivekānanda opposed *brāhman oppression of lower castes and child marriage, and urged opportunities for women to exploit their abilities. His philosophy was one of social action, with emphasis on service, and although he accepted that renunciation is a way to salvation, he stressed that 'the *ātman cannot be known by the weak'; thus he deplored the ideology of non-violence. He had regard for the leaders of all major religions, seeing them all, whether *Kṛṣṇa, *Buddha, or *Christ, as *incarnations of God.

Though preaching that there is no polytheism in India, he nevertheless defended the use of images, while urging the existence of one divine power as the source and motivation of all that is. Vivekānanda stood for the universalism of Vedānta, accepting *Śaṅkara's teaching that creation represents the sport, or amusement (*līlā), of God.

Though Vivekānanda was hostile to Christian missionary endeavours in India, he seems to have been influenced by such methods in the pursuance of much of his policy of social reform. His was an active doctrine of practical, applied Vedānta, and it is perhaps that aspect of his teaching which gave it such success and appeal in the West.

Complete Works (7 vols., 1919–22); R. Rolland, *The Life of Vivekananda and the Universal Gospel* (1953); Swami Virajananda, *Life of Swami Vivekananda* (1924–8); E. M. Williams, *The Quest for Meaning of Svāmī Vivekānanda* (1974).

Vizier (Muslim government minister): see WAZĪR.

Vladimir, St (d. 1015). Prince of Kiev and 'apostle of Russia'. Brought up a pagan, he invited Greek missionaries to his realm and became a Christian in 988. His motives cannot have been unconnected with the desire for an alliance with Byzantium, and he married Anne, sister of the emperor Basil II, shortly after. Vladimir set about the conversion of his people by enforcing *baptism by law. He is remembered as pious and even scrupulous, wondering whether the death penalty could be used by a Christian prince. Feast day, 15 July.

N. de Baumgarten, *Saint Vladimir et la conversion de la Russie* (1932).

Vodou, vodum, vodun, voodoo, or **voudou** (Fon, in Benin, *vodu*, 'deity' or 'spirit'). The name given to the folk religion of Haiti, developing since the 18th cent. among the rural and urban poor, but despised by the other classes until intellectuals began to defend it in the 1930s as the Haitian national religion. French *Roman Catholic elements are synthesized with African religious and magical elements derived from slaves of Dahomean origin. In 1996, the African origins of Vodou were reaffirmed when the ban on Vodou was lifted in Benin, and its validity as an indigenous religion was recognized. The effective divinities are the capricious *loa*, representing ancestors, African deities, or Catholic *saints. They communicate through dreams or descend during the cult ritual and 'ride' their devotees while in a trance state; to encourage this, the *loa's* own symbolic patterns (*veves*) are laid out in flour on the ground. Autonomous local groups have their own initiations, sanctuaries, and priests (male 'houngans', female 'mambos') who serve as cult leaders, healers, and protectors. For the first half of this century the RC Church launched ineffective anti-vodou campaigns, aided in 1941 by the government forces destroying vodou temples. After 1957, the ruling Duvalier family both courted vodou for political reasons, and encouraged the growth of *pentecostalism as against R. Catholicism. Pentecostalism, however, joined with the breakup of the large extended family (which supported major vodou centres) and other modernizing influences (such as tourism) to produce a decline in vodou. It nevertheless persists, not least in the diaspora.

A. Metraux, *Voodoo in Haiti* (1959); R. F. Thompson, *Flash of the Spirit: African and Afro-American Art and Philosophy* (1981).

Vohu Manah (the Good Mind): see AMESA SPENTAS.

Void (in Buddhism): see ŚŪNYATĀ.

Von Hügel, F.: see HÜGEL, F. VON.

Voodoo: see VODOU.

Vorgriff (pre-hension): see RAHNER, KARL.

Voudou: see VODOU.

Vows. Promises or commitments to undertake, or abstain from, particular actions, lifestyles, etc. All religions offer the opportunity to formalize one's intentions in this way, to such an extent that there can be uncertainty about whether a vow once made can be revoked. Thus in Judaism vows are not required of Jews in the Bible, but once made they have to be carried out with precision (Deuteronomy 23. 22–4). Vows are thus inviolable (1 Samuel 14. 24 ff.; Judges 11. 30 ff.), and there is no mechanism for absolving oneself from one's vow (see Numbers 30. 1–16). In later books, reservations are expressed about making vows (e.g. Ecclesiastes 5. 3 f.), reservations which are reiterated in the *Talmud (e.g. *B.Ned.* 22a), where the problems of vows made in haste and then not fulfilled are recognized. Perhaps for that reason, the *rabbis evolved an elaborate system for the annulment of vows in the tractate *Nedarim*. Jewish law uses three terms for vows, *neder* (general), *nedavah* (freewill offering), and *shebu'ah* (to pursue or not to pursue a course of action)—see also KOL NIDREI; NAZIRITE; OATHS.

Some early Christians followed the practice of taking vows (Paul, e.g., taking the temporary vow of a Nazirite, Acts 21. 22–6), although *Jesus had warned against letting a dedication of something to God through *qorban* take precedence over more fundamental obligations (Mark 7. 11). Vows came to be understood as a social act through which a person donates himself or herself to another (marriage vows), or to God in a religious community. Thus vows are a voluntary dedication of the future, and an undertaking of more than the moral law requires. A vow is called 'solemn', as opposed to 'simple' if it is recognized by the Church, and may be perpetual or temporary. Members of religious orders take vows to observe the evangelical counsels of poverty, chastity, and obedience.

For examples of vows in other religions, see BODHISATTVA VOW; FIVE GREAT VOWS (among Jains); SHIGUSEIGAN (the four great vows in Zen); VRATA; see also Index, Vows.

Vrata (Skt., 'will'). The Indian religious commitment of the will to some religious end—e.g. pilgrimage, chastity, devotion. Vows are fundamental to Jains, in the sense that they constitute the Jain commitment: see FIVE GREAT VOWS. For vrata in the sense of celebration, see FESTIVALS AND FASTS.

Vratya. One bound by a vow. Vratyas appeared as groups of people (bound perhaps by common vows) in NE India, perhaps the first of the *Aryan invaders. They had their own distinct beliefs and customs which they took with them as they migrated east to Magadha. Their religion was assimilated into the **Atharva Veda*. They persisted as groups of religious functionaries.

Vṛndāvana (Skt., 'grove of a multitude'). A sacred forest in India by the river Yamunā, near Mathurā, the birthplace of *Kṛṣṇa. Here he spent his youth, in delight with the *gopīs, especially *Rādhā. As the summary of the divine play of the soul with its Lord, it is a place particularly sacred to *Vaiṣṇavas. The modern town is also known as Brindavan.

K. Klostermaier, *Hindu and Christian in Vrindavan* (1969).

Vṛtra (Skt., 'storm-cloud'). In Hinduism, the dark cloud of ignorance and sloth, personified as a demon-serpent, vanquished by *Indra. The story is the subject of several *Vedic hymns, e.g. *Ṛg Veda* 1. 32; 10. 124.

Vṛtti (Skt., 'wave'). In Hinduism, the thoughts of the waking and dream states which wash over consciousness like waves, and prevent the seeing of truth. Vṛtti may also mean 'the means of subsistence', 'the support of meaning', and as such is a commentary on a commentary, i.e. on *bhāṣya.

Vulgate (Lat., *versio vulgata*, 'popular version'). The Lat. version of the Christian *Bible of widest circulation where Latin continued to be used. Mainly the work of *Jerome, it was intended to end the confusion of varying readings in the existing 'Old Latin' MSS of the Bible. In the New Testament, Jerome probably revised only the gospels; of the Old Testament he revised all the Hebrew books plus Tobit and Judith. He made two versions of the Psalms, the 'Gallican Psalter' (*c.*392) based on the *Septuagint, and much later the 'Hebrew Psalter' based on the Hebrew text only. The Vulgate as we now have it was compiled probably in the 6th cent. The Council of *Trent (1546) pronounced the Vulgate the only authentic Lat. text of the scriptures. A full critical edition by the *Benedictines was begun at the direction of Pope Pius X in 1907.

Vulture Peak (mythical mountain): see NICHIREN.

Vyāhṛti. The Hindu utterance of sacred sounds, *mantras, etc., especially the sacrificial utterances of *Prajāpati, *bhūr, bhuvar, svar*, 'the three clear ones'. *Manusmṛti* 2. 76 calls them 'the great vyāhṛtis', and they are recited by *brahmans after *Om at the beginning of each day's prayer. With four more—*mahar, janar, tapar, satya*—they epitomize the seven worlds, and are personified as the daughters of *Savitṛ. The three clear ones are the opening words of the *Gāyatrī mantra.

Vyākhyā-prajñapti-aṅga (Jain text): see AṄGA.

Vyāsa (Skt., 'collector'). Collectors and compilers of Hindu works, especially Veda-vyāsa, the compiler of the *Vedas. Traditionally, this is said to be Śaṣvata, though clearly many were involved. In the *Purāṇas, eighteen are sent to the earth to compile the Vedas and disseminate them.

Vyūha (manifest power of Viṣṇu): see VIṢṆU.

W

Waco, Texas: see BRANCH DAVIDIANS.

Wager, Pascal's: see PASCAL.

Waḥdat al-shuhūd; Waḥdat al-wujūd (unity of consciousness, unity of being): see AḤMAD SIRHINDĪ.

Wahhābīya. An ultra-conservative, puritanical Muslim movement adhering to the *Ḥanbalite law, although it regards itself as *ghair muqallidīn*, non-adherent to parties, but defending truth. It arose in Najd in the Arabian peninsula during the 18th cent. Its founder, Muḥammad ibn ʿAbd al-Wahhāb (1703–87 (AH 1115–1201)) found a champion in the tribal leader Muḥammad ibn Saʿūd of the Darʿiya region, and from then on the Saudis became the main supporters of the movement. They believe that the Muslims have abandoned their faith in One God (*tawhid) and have distorted Islam through innovations (*bidʿa) which run counter to pure Islam: 'All objects of worship other than *Allāh are false, and all who worship such are deserving of death' (Abd al-Wahhāb). The Wahhābīs accept only the *Qur'ān and the authentic *Sunna, and reject 1,400 years of development and interpretation in Islamic theology and mysticism. They oppose any veneration of saints and tombs, prohibit the decoration of mosques, ban luxury, and forbid any importation of *kāfir culture in their society. Furthermore, all Muslims who do not accept their creed are regarded as heretics, especially the *Shīʿa, who are considered as archenemies of Islam.

During the 19th cent., the Wahhābīs in alliance with the Saʿūd family began to expand territorially, and to threaten the interests of the *Ottoman Empire. In 1802 they captured *Karbalā', and in 1803 *Mecca. Thrown back by a long campaign, they were not politically strong until ʿAbd al-ʿAziz Āl Saʿūd captured Riyādh and established a new kingdom. The Hejaz was taken, but attempts to expand northward were blocked. Within the new kingdom of Saudi Arabia, the Wahhābīs became dominant in conservative control, introducing *mutawwiʿūn*, 'enforcers of obedience', a kind of private religious police, monitoring not only public but also private conformity to Islam (since before Allāh there is no distinction between private and public).

Wāhigurū (Sikh acclamative name of God): see VĀHIGURŪ.

Waḥy (Arab., 'to suggest, put something in someone's mind'). The idea of 'revelation' in Islam: in general, communication, verbal or non-verbal, of divine origin, generally to prophets, inspiring action or giving a correct article of belief (e.g. that *Allāh is One: Qur'ān 21. 108; 41. 6). The term waḥy is used especially for the giving of the *Qur'ān, itself described as a 'revelation revealed' (*waḥy yūḥā*, 53. 4). The corresponding verb is *awḥā*: Allāh reveals his will to *Muḥammad, or to another *prophet (17. 39; 34. 49; 53. 10). The theory of revelation developed from an early stage in which Muḥammad perhaps thought that he had seen or heard Allāh directly, to the belief that the message was conveyed by a mediator, later personified as the angel Jibrīl/*Gabriel (2. 97). The content of waḥy was that portion of the entire scripture (*umm al-kitāb, preserved in heaven) which was appropriate to the occasion. Muḥammad received the message and then recited the words: 'I follow what is revealed (*yūḥā*) to me from my Lord' (7. 203; cf. 43. 43). Waḥy refers also to revelation given to former prophets, as to *Moses (20. 13), and is indirect, for humans cannot see Allāh (42. 50). The *ḥadīth give details as to the manner of revelation, and the way in which Muḥammad himself was affected physically by the force of the message he received.

The more common term for the giving of the Qur'ān is 'sending down', from the verbal root *n-z-l*: (i) *nazzala*, 'cause to descend' (2. 97; 17. 106; 3. 3); the verbal noun *tanzīl* is one of the names for the whole process: *tanzīl al-kitāb* (45. 2); (ii) *anzala*, 'cause to descend' (3. 3, 7; 5. 50, 52; 17. 105; 6. 91, 92; 97. 1).

W. M. Watt, *Bell's Introduction to the Qur'ān*, 20–2, 144.

Wahyguru (Sikh acclamation): see VAHIGURU.

Wai-ch'i (breathing in Chinese religion and medicine): see CH'I.

Wailing Wall (*ha-Kotel ha-Maʿaravi*). Western Wall of the Jewish *Temple in *Jerusalem. The Wailing Wall was all that remained of the Temple after its destruction by the Romans in 70 CE. It is a place of *pilgrimage and the most holy place in the Jewish world. Since 1967, when it came into *Israeli hands, the area in front of the wall has been cleared and converted into a large paved area where Jews can gather and pray. The original wall was 485 m. long; the surviving part which is the focus of prayer is 60 m. long, toward the southern end of the original. It is not known when prayer began to be offered there. According to *midrash (e.g. *Exod.R.* 2. 2; *Num.R.* 11. 2) the Western Wall was not destroyed because the *Shekhinah (divine presence) rests there. Prayer thus reaches God through the wall, and for that reason, prayers are often written on slips of paper and inserted in the wall. In Muslim tradition, it was at the Western Wall that Muḥammad tethered his miraculous mount (al-*Buraq) when he made his Night Journey (*miʿrāj) and ascent to heaven.

Wai-tan (external alchemy): see ALCHEMY.

Wajd (Arab., *wajada*, 'find, know by experience'). Ecstasy or rapture, a *Sūfī term for a state of mental and physical excitement that manifests itself when the heart of the devotee is undergoing divine illumination. Poetry, music, or speech, especially *Qur'ān recital, may spontaneously trigger off such a condition. It is considered a major sin to simulate wajd, and when wajd occurs, one should attempt to control oneself as much as possible. Classical Sūfī literature prizes wajd highly: 'Sometimes in the veil of human existence appears an opening through which a ray from God shines . . . It promotes a state wherein all sensible qualities have been cut off, and turns the heart to great grief or to great joy.' Often the wajd lasts only for a few minutes, but it leaves an impression never to be forgotten. However, it is reported, conversely, that a Sūfī master, Bakthīyar-Kaki Chistī, expired during wajd which had lasted for several days.

Wājib (duty in Islam): see FARḌ.

Waka (Japanese verse form): see HAIKU.

Waldenses/Waldensians or **Vaudois.** Adherents of a reforming movement which began in the 12th cent., in the *Roman Catholic Church and became a *Protestant Church. It originated with a Frenchman, Pierre Valdès (Peter Waldo), when he obeyed the command of Christ to sell all that he had and give it to the poor (Matthew 19. 21), and set out (much as, in different ways, did *Francis and *Dominic) to recover the Church as Christ intended. When the small group who gathered around him ('the poor men of Lyons') were banned by Pope Lucius III (at the Council of Verona) from unauthorized preaching in 1184, they organized an alternative Church. It adhered closely to Catholic orthodoxy, though it rejected *purgatory and *indulgences, and allowed *women to preach. As with Jan *Hus, they raised a protest against a Constantinian Church (see A. Molnar, *A Challenge to Constantinianism*, 1976). The antagonism of the RC Church issued in oppression and massacres. Their return to a biblical Christianity made them, in a sense, precursors of the *Reformers, and in 1532 they made common cause with them. They continued to be victims of persecution (including the massacre in 1655 which evoked Milton's Sonnet, 'On the Late Massacre in Piedmont'), but survived long enough to be granted religious freedom in 1848. They number now about 20,000.

G. Tourn, *The Waldensians* . . . (1980).

Waldo, Peter (founder of Waldenses): see WALDENSES.

Walī (Arab., *waliya*, 'protect'). A benefactor or protector in Islam. In the *Qur'ān it is used especially of God ('God is the walī of those who believe', 2. 257), and it is a title of *Muḥammad. Conversely, a walī is a friend of God, and is the title of one particularly devoted to God: 'He loves them and they love him' (5. 59; cf. 10. 63). A walī is capable of performing *karāmāt* (*miracles), including levitation and control of the weather. According to Hujwīrī, walīs are entrusted with the governing of the universe. Their effect on the faithful (e.g. healing) is known as *baraka (blessing). The *Muʿtazilites naturally rejected this (incipient) extravagance and called all faithful Muslims walīs of God. Nevertheless, the veneration of walīs became a highly popular part of Islam, particularly focused on their tombs. Thus Baghdād has been called 'the city of the walīs', because so many are venerated there—e.g. *al-Junaid, Sīdī *ʿAbd al-Qādir al-Jili, Shihāb al-Dīn al-Suhrawardī. Among the *Sūfīs, elaborate hierarchies of awliyā' (pl.) were produced, along with levels or stages, in the progress towards wilayat, becoming a walī.

Wali Allah or **Waliullah** (Indian Islamic reformer): see SHAH WALIULLAH.

Walking object indices (apparent people providing cross-reference to the world): see PHENOMENOLOGY.

WALUBI. Acronym for Per-*WAL*-ian *U*mat *B*uddha *I*ndonesia, or All-Indonesia Federation of Buddhist Organizations. It was founded in Jogyakarta in 1978 to promote union among Indonesia's 3 million Buddhists. The Federation includes both *Theravāda and *Mahāyāna Buddhist groups (the former having strong links with Dhammayutika temples in Thailand via the Phra Dhamma-Dūta missionary programme) and Buddhayana, a syncretistic combination of both these branches of Buddhism plus Kasogatan, a local type of Javanese Buddhism. Monks and lay Buddhists are strongly represented in most branches of WALUBI. See also TRIDHARMA.

Wandering Jew. Figure in a Christian legend of a Jew who, as a consequence of rejecting *Jesus, is condemned never to die, but to wander homeless through the world until the Second Coming (*Parousia) of Christ, or until his last descendant shall have died. The legend lent itself to *anti-Semitism and to constant repetition in different forms—notably in Eugène Sue's novel with that title. The novel tells the story of the last seven members of the family, who get involved in the Society of Jesus (*Jesuits), against which the novel displays its strongest animus. When the last descendant dies, the Wandering Jew 'attains the happiness of eternal sleep'.

Wang An-shih (reformer): see CH'ENG HAO.

Wang-pi (important figure in neo-Taoism): see HSÜAN-HSÜEH.

Wang Yang-ming (Jap., Ō Yōmei; 1472–1529). Chinese philosopher, soldier, and statesman, of the Ming dynasty. He was a follower of the Confucian school who incorporated into his own teachings Buddhist and Taoist insights. His principal tenets include the unity of knowledge and action (cf. Socrates' identification of knowledge and virtue), and the paradoxical identity between mind and heart (*hsin*) and *li ('principle', referring to being, and to virtue). 'The great man regards Heaven and earth and the myriad existent things as one body: the world is one family and the country one person. . . . Even when he sees a tile shattered or a stone crushed, he cannot help feeling sorrow or regret.' His efforts were made as a response and reaction to the orthodox school of *Chu Hsi (Jap., Shu Shi; 1130–1200), with its intellectualist biases, implicit in its interpretation of the teaching of the Great Learning that the 'extension of knowledge' lies in the exhaustive pursuit of li through the investigation of things. Yang-ming attempted to make the goal of sagehood accessible to all, including the uneducated, and said instead that the only knowledge worth extending is that of the innate moral intuition (*liang-chih*). For him, however, this refers also to a mystical 'divine spark' within all, a kind of universal seed of sagehood. The Yang-ming school became very popular in late Ming China (16th cent.), and spread as well to Japan, as Yōmei-gaku, where it gained adherents among the lower *samurais, many of whom worked actively for the success of the Meiji restoration in the 19th cent.

J. Ching, *To Acquire Wisdom: The Way of Wang Yang-ming* (1976).

Wanshi Shōgaku (Chinese Ch'an/Zen master): see HUNG-CHIH CHENG-CHUEH.

Waqf (pl., *awqāf*). Legal term in Islam, to prevent something (by dedication) falling into the possession of another, hence especially the dedication of land, buildings, etc., to religious purposes, or for family endowments. In either case, the object must be pleasing (*qurba*) to God, and that is particularly the case when it benefits the poor. The alienation of waqf land in Israel/Palestine has been a particular source of grievance to Palestinian Muslims.

War: see JUST WAR.

Ward, Mary (founder): see INSTITUTE OF THE BLESSED VIRGIN MARY.

Warrior-monks (Japanese): see AKUSŌ.

Warsaw Ghetto: see GHETTO.

War Scroll. One of the *Dead Sea scrolls found near *Qumran. The *War Scroll* is an *apocalyptic work describing the conflict at the end of time between the Sons of Light and the Sons of Darkness.

Tr. G. Vermes.

Wasan (Jap., 'song of praise'). In Buddhism, a song/hymn celebrating a *buddha, *bodhisattva, *soshigata, etc., or some Buddhist theme. Especially famous is *Hakuin's *Zazen wasan*: 'Sentient beings are in themselves Buddha | It is the relation of water and ice: | With no water, no ice | With no sentient beings, no Buddha.'

Tr. I. Miura, R. F. Sasaki, *Zen Dust* (1966).

Wāṣil B. ʿAṭā', Abū Hudhaifa (699–748 (AH 80–131)). Leading *Muʿtazilite theologian in Islam. He belonged to the associates of *Ḥasan al-Baṣrī, though he separated from his views enough to start the school of the Muʿtazilites (a separation once thought to be the origin of the name). He held four distinctive views: (i) the qualities/attributes of *Allāh are not eternal; (ii) humans possess free will (cf. *Qadarites); (iii) a Muslim who sins is in an intermediate state between that of a Muslim and that of a *kāfir; (iv) it is possible to judge that one of the parties in the murder of *ʿUthmān, and in the battles of the Camel and Siffīn (see ʿALĪ) was wrong.

Watarai Nobuyoshi (1615–90). A Shinto scholar and religious leader of the early Tokugawa period in Japan. As a descendant of the famous Watarai line of priests, who were the hereditary officiants at the outer shrine of *Ise, Nobuyoshi reversed the flagging fortunes of his school of Shinto. Since the 13th cent., Watarai Shinto had developed a complex syncretic system synthesizing *Confucian and Buddhist ideas within a Shinto framework. This religious outlook elevated the food deity enshrined at the outer shrine, Toyouke no Ōkami, to a position above all the other deities of the Shinto pantheon, including *Amaterasu, the sun goddess of the inner shrine of Ise, venerated by the imperial house. Through his research and lectures, as well as his establishment of a library of Shinto works, the Toyomiyasaki Bunko, Nobuyoshi reversed his school's decline. His major work, the *Yōfukuji*, is the most important source of his own religious ruminations, which largely follow the traditional doctrines originally set forth in the Five Books of Shinto (*Shintō gobusho*).

Watarai Shinto: see ISE; WATARAI NOBUYOSHI.

Watcher. A heavenly being in the biblical book of *Daniel. The watcher delivers a strange dream to King Nebuchadnezzar of Babylon which is interpreted by Daniel. The *Septuagint translates the term as *angel. Watchers also appear in *pseudepigraphic and later *mystical books.

Watchman Nee (Ni To Shang/Duo Sheng, 1903–72). Founder of the Christian-based Little Flock Movement in China. He was converted while a student at Trinity College, Foochow (Fuzhou), and having been baptized, he began preaching. His *fundamentalist approach insisted on the necessity for the human spirit to be broken in order to be released into union with the Spirit of God, so that soul and body can be kept in subjection and obedience. He established Assemblies, which by 1949 had reached *c.*500 in number. He was arrested in 1952 and remained in captivity for the rest of his life. The Little Flock Movement now numbers nearly a million.

N. H. Cliff, *The Life and Theology of Watchman Nee* . . . (1993).

Watch-night. A dedication service held on New Year's Eve. Derived from early Christian *vigils, it came, by way of *Moravianism, into 18th-cent. *Methodism. J. *Wesley encouraged monthly watch-nights, but the more frequent practice gave way to a New Year's Eve service which was gradually adopted by other churches.

Watchtower, The (magazine of Jehovah's Witnesses): see JEHOVAH'S WITNESSES.

Wato (Jap., 'word-head'). The key point, line, or word in a *kōan.

Watts, Alan (1915–73). Comparative religionist, theologian, philosopher, and student of mysticism. This Californian *'guru' greatly influenced the counter-culture of the 1960s. Connected with the Esalen Institute, Watts also helped formulate that persisting aspect of the counter-culture, the Human Potential Movement. Writing with particular public success in *The Way of Zen* (1957) and *Psychotherapy East and West* (1961), he argued that people in the West are in a state of confusion, seeking solace in satisfying their egos. The solution is to change consciousness, to realize that everything is interrelated as necessary components of one process. Whether his own life exemplified the confusion or the solution is the question raised by M. Furlong's biography, *Genuine Fake* (1984).

Watts, Isaac (1674–1748). English hymn-writer. He was for a time pastor of a prestigious *Independent congregation in London, but was forced into a long retirement by ill health. Watts's *hymns include many still in common use, e.g. 'Jesus shall reign where'er the sun'; 'When I survey the wondrous cross'; and 'Our [now, O] God, our help in ages past'. The power and wide appeal of his hymns was instrumental in breaking down the resistance to hymn-singing (other than metrical Psalms), first in Nonconformity and ultimately in the established church.

Wayang kulit/purwa (Javanese theatre): see THEATRE AND DRAMA.

Way of Supreme Peace (early Taoist school): see T'AI-PING TAO.

Wazīr (Arab., *wazara*, 'he carried a burden'). Minister in Muslim governments, anglicized as vizier. Under the Caliphs (*khalīfa), wazīrs were advisers who on occasion ran the entire government—e.g. the Barmecides, until they were eradicated by Harūn al-Rashīd; or Niẓam al-Mulk under the Saljuqs.

Weber, Max (1864–1920). Major scholar and sociologist, who is regarded, alongside E. *Durkheim, as a founder of the *sociology of religion. Although his work has often been regarded as a dialogue with the ghost of *Marx, recent scholarship stresses his intellectual debt to the incendiary legacy of *Nietszche. Despite (or perhaps because of) his self-confessed tone-deafness to the 'music of religion', Weber's encyclopaedic comparative investigations of a vast range of cross-cultural religious phenomena remain unsurpassed in sociological literature. Indeed, his application of a distinctive version of social-scientific methodology in the analysis of such topics as Chinese Confucianism, the Hindu *caste system, ancient Israel, early Christianity, and 17th-cent. *puritanism remains challenging and influential.

Weber's essay *The Protestant Ethic and the Spirit of Capitalism* (1904–5) generated one of the longest-running and most intellectually provocative controversies of the 20th cent. and thus understandably dominates discussion of his achievement, especially in more popular accounts. Often misunderstood and even more frequently severed from the main theme of his research enterprise, this work encapsulates the central tenets of Weber's sociological approach to religion. Popular accounts notwithstanding, Weber did not claim that *Protestantism caused capitalism. Rather, by postulating an 'elective affinity' between the ethic of Protestantism and the spirit of modern rational capitalism he articulated one specific link in a complex causal chain of socio-cultural elements. Rejecting the determinism of both *Hegelian idealism and Marxian materialism, Weber saw religion as a potential independent variable in a multivariate formula: a proactive as well as a reactive element in social life. Thus, while he acknowledged and documented its conservative and reactionary aspect, Weber was primarily concerned with religion's crucial role as a dynamic and even revolutionary ingredient in the process of major social change.

For Weber, the study of religion is not an end in itself but simply an indispensable means of understanding human society. Though he steadfastly refused (in contrast to Durkheim) to formulate an explicit definition, his implicit conception of religion was clearly grounded in an assessment of its universal social and psychological functions. From this perspective, religion represents humanity's continuous effort to impose intellectual and moral order on the chaos of existence and, in the process, to discover the ultimate meaning of the cosmos for both individuals and collectivities. Contributing their own distinctive solutions to the problem of meaning (for example, in *theodicies which explain the existence of suffering and evil), the great world religions provide the main focus of Weber's vast comparative-historical analysis of civilizations and constitute the essential background to his penetrating account of the emergence of the modern world.

Recognizing the quest for salvation as a momentous driving force in world history, Weber explored its dimensions through the method of empathic understanding (*Verstehen*: see also HERMENEUTICS). Distinguishing an attitude of resigned accommodation to the world from a compulsion to control or alter conditions imposed by it, he utilized the resultant *ideal-type concepts of *mysticism and *asceticism in investigations of the ways in which salvation religions (inner-worldly and other-worldly) significantly affect the conduct of ordinary life. Alert to the social tensions it engenders, Weber examined the social contexts in which the hope of salvation emerges and thrives. Devoting special attention to the 'carriers' of *new religious movements, he scrutinized the propensities of various privileged and disprivileged classes, status groups, and occupational formations (for example, in recruitment to Roman Mithraism, early Christianity, and European puritanism). In this respect, Weber's meditations on the respective roles of women and intellectuals are particularly noteworthy.

The transformation of a collective desire for salvation from a diffuse sentiment to a new religious dispensation is, according to Weber, the achievement of the *prophet. By claiming a special gift of divine grace (*charisma), this type of religious leader (whether in exemplary or ethical guise) challenges the legitimacy of the established religious and social order and attempts a breakthrough into a realm of new values. In decisively breaking with tradition, the prophet initiates a more systematized cultural order and is thus a prime mover in the process of rationalization which dominates Weber's broad vision of social dynamics and underlies his dark ruminations on the fate of the world.

Though originally an outcome of a religious ethic of inner-worldly asceticism, the precise sequence of accelerating rationalization (see further IDEAL TYPE) to which Weber attributed the emergence of a genuine modernity is, paradoxically, the basis for an unprecedented demystification or disenchantment of the world. *Secularization is, therefore, the inevitable accompaniment to life in an iron cage of scientific calculation, economic acquisition, bureaucratic administration, and interpersonal instrumentalism. Whether disenchantment now constitutes a permanent feature of society is, in Weber's opinion, impossible to decide at the present time. Certainly, his image of the foreseeable future is bleak: a 'polar night of icy darkness and hardness' unthawed by the warmth of community. None the less, he left open the possibility, however remote, that a world of 'mechanized petrefaction embellished with a sort of convulsive self-importance' may be undermined by the rise of new prophets or the rebirth of old ideals. Religious escape routes from the iron cage are at least conceivable in Weber's own prophetic vision of the world to come.

Fervently committed to the development and expansion of social science, Max Weber still exerts a significant influence on its practice as scholars continue to grapple with his insights three-quarters of a century after his death. This is nowhere more evident than in the sociology of religion where his conviction that the study of religion requires the analysis of society, while the study of society demands the investigation of religion, is now the first article of subdisciplinary faith.

The Protestant Ethic and the Spirit of Capitalism, tr. T. Parsons (1930) and *The Sociology of Religion*, tr. E. Fischoff (1963); R. Bendix, *Max Weber: An Intellectual Portrait* (1960); M. M. W. Lemmen, *Max Weber's Sociology of Religion* (1990); D. G. MacRae, *Weber* (1974); R. O'Toole, *Religion: Classic Sociological Approaches* (1984).

Wee Frees (Scottish Free Church): see FREE CHURCHES.

Weeks, Feast of (Jewish festival): see SHAVU'OT.

Weeping Sūfīs. *Sūfīs who seek to stay close to God by constant weeping, or who do not resist weeping when they hear of the mercy of God. The worth of this practice is derived from Qur'ān 17. 107–9: 'They prostrate themselves, weeping, and it increases humility in them.'

Wei (learning and effort): see HSÜN TZU.

Wei Cheng (guardian of the emperor, and of temples): see DOOR GODS.

Wei Hua-tsun (founder of Tao-chiao movement): see TAOISM.

Weil, Simone (1909–43). Religious philosopher of intense personal commitment. Born into a non-practising Jewish family, she taught in various French schools between 1931 and 1937, while at the same time being politically active on behalf of the humiliated—all whom she identified as exploited, such as factory-workers, peasants, and the colonized, or, historically, the Provençal *Cathars. In 1934–5 she worked in a factory, and in 1936 worked in the front line in the Spanish Civil War as a cook. Out of these experiences came her early appeals, not simply for greater justice in the distribution of power in relation to work, but for the transformation of the process of work in the direction of its humanization (e.g. *La Condition ouvrière*, essays published in 1951). In 1942, she left France to join the Free French in England. Here she became deeply and dialectically involved in Catholic Christianity. She was never baptized (for that reason she has been called 'a Saint outside the Church') and remained fiercely critical of the hierarchical organization of Christianity. But she became increasingly insistent on the necessity to attend to 'God' (i.e. to what *Tillich might have called 'the God above God') through a contemplative perfection which separated itself from the gross elements of this world (including sex and food), and which involved the willing participation in 'the gift of affliction': 'Religion insofar as it is a source of consolation is a hindrance to true faith.' This fierce refusal of day-dreaming (the root of evil, as she thought it), carrying with it in an unequivocal immersement in the seriousness of evil in pursuit of a goodness which transcends it, led to her early death from virtual self-starvation in a tuberculosis sanitarium. For her, the nature of God cannot be unravelled and laid out before us:

> There is a God. There is no God. Where is the problem? I am quite sure that there is a God in the sense that I am sure that my love is no illusion. I am quite sure there is no God in the sense that I am sure there is nothing which resembles what I can conceive when I say that word.

Thus in all religions (and outside them) the awareness of God is possible and has left its mark. The mark of truth is goodness: 'The essential thing to know about God is that God is good. All the rest is secondary.' For that reason, she was prepared to make what she regarded as a better wager than that of *Pascal, because hers did not have reference to a supposed *afterlife:

> If we put obedience to God above everything else, unreservedly, with the following thought, 'Suppose God is real', then our gain is total . . . If one follows this rule of life, then no revelation at the moment of death can cause any regrets, because if chance or the devil governs all worlds we would still have no regrets for having lived this way. This is greatly preferable to Pascal's wager.

J. Hellman, *Simone Weil* . . . (1982); S. Petrément, *Simone Weil* . . . (1976); G. A. White, *Simone Weil* . . . (1981).

Wei P'o-yang or **Pai-yang** (2nd cent. CE). Foundation figure in religious *Taoism (*tao-chiao*), who attempted to unify the practices of *alchemy with Taoist philosophy and *I Ching*. His major work, *Chou-i ts'an-t'ung-ch'i* (very roughly, the unifying and harmonizing of the three ways, Lao-Tzu, and *I Ching*) became the subject of subsequent commentaries (e.g. of *Chu Hsi, Yü Yen), and the basis of other works which came to be regarded as authoritative. The aim of the book is to show how life can be prolonged and the cosmic forces brought into harmony and balance.

Wei-t'o. Chinese general, regarded by Buddhists as the guardian of the South. He wears a helmet and holds a *vajra, with which he destroys opponents of the *Buddha's teaching. When the Buddha entrusted the *dharma to him, he saw him face to face. Thus their statues/images are usually placed facing each other. In some monasteries, when a new abbot is selected lots are drawn before Wei-t'o, who makes the selection.

Wellhausen, Julius (1844–1918). German *biblical critic. Wellhausen put forward the theory in his *Die Composition des Hexateuchs* (1887) that the *Pentateuch was compiled from four separate sources. Although his views were to a great extent accepted by most modern biblical scholars, they remained anathema to *Orthodox Jews and to those Christians who maintain the Mosaic authorship of the Pentateuch.

Wenceslas, St (*c*.907–29). Bohemian prince and *martyr. The son of Duke Wratislaw and Drahomira, he was brought up a Christian by his grandmother, St Ludmilla. After his father's death, he took over the government from his mother in *c*.922. In pursuit of the religious and cultural improvement of his people he formed friendly links with Germany. This, and pagan opposition to him, led to his murder by his brother Boleslav. He was soon venerated as a martyr, and by the end of the century had come to be regarded as the patron *saint of Bohemia. The connection with the carol is one of imagination, not fact.

Wen-ch'ang. Taoist god of writing and literature. He is invoked by those taking exams. Chinese aspiring to education put up a plaque representing him with the wish-fulfilling sceptre (*ju-i*).

Wen-shu-shih-li. Chin. for Mañjuśrī, bodhisattva associated with wisdom and the conquest of ignorance.

Wesley, Charles (1707–88). Brother of John *Wesley and hymn-writer. In 1738 he experienced a conversion like that of his brother, and became an itinerant preacher until 1756, settling finally in London in 1771. He never approved of his brother John's Methodist ordinations. Charles Wesley is generally considered the most gifted of Anglican writers of hymns. The first collection, *Hymns and Sacred Poems*, appeared in 1739, to be quickly followed by others, all professedly the joint work of the two brothers. Of his more than 5,500 hymns, some of the best known are 'Hark! the herald angels sing', 'Lo, he comes with clouds descending', 'Jesu, lover of my soul', 'O for a thousand tongues to sing', and 'Love divine, all loves excelling'. He is recognized in the Church of England Lesser Festivals, 24 May.

See J. Wesley for bibliography.

Wesley, John (1703–91). Founder of *Methodism. After ordination in 1725 and a brief curacy, Wesley became fellow of Lincoln College, Oxford (1726), where he was a member of a small religious society nicknamed the 'Holy Club' and also dubbed 'Methodists' because of their emphasis on discipline and self-examination. In 1735 he undertook missionary work in Georgia, but, burdened by disappointment and a sense of personal need, he returned home in 1738, writing 'I went to America to convert the Indians, but oh who shall convert me?' Influenced by

*Moravians, he experienced conversion at a meeting in Aldersgate St, London ('I felt my heart strangely warmed'), and thereafter became a passionate evangelist, constantly preaching in the open air throughout England, Scotland, and Ireland, as well as sending preachers to N. America. Travelling on horseback approximately 8,000 miles a year, he recorded his experiences and frequently hostile receptions in his *Journal* which was published by instalments in his lifetime. With considerable organizational skill, he planned an annual conference for preachers appointed to care for his converts. A prolific letter-writer, he also published tracts, expositions, translations, and abridgements of important devotional works, as well as his famous sermons. An autocratic figure, he was noted not only for outstanding powers of leadership, but also for practical holiness, social concern, and immense courage. He had no wish to secede from the *Church of England; but opposition, and the necessities of the mission field in America (which caused him to ordain Thomas Coke as Superintendent or *bishop) led to increasing separation. He and Charles *Wesley are recognized in the Lesser Festivals of the Church of England, 24 May.

H. H. Green, *John Wesley* (1964); A. C. Outler, *John Wesley* (1964); M. Schmidt, *John Wesley* . . . (1962–73); F. Whaling (ed.), *John and Charles Wesley* (1982).

Westcott, Brooke Foss (1825–1901). Anglican scholar and bishop. He became Regius Professor of Divinity at Cambridge in 1870, and with F. J. A. Hort prepared their widely-used edition of the Gk. New Testament (published 1881). His commentaries on the gospel and epistles of John (1881, 1883) and Hebrews (1889) are best known for their sensitivity to shades of meaning and their 'mystical' style of exegesis. As bishop of Durham from 1890 he somewhat surprisingly made social problems his special concern, and was long remembered (cf. *Manning) for his mediation in the coal strike of 1892.

Western Buddhist Order or **Friends of the Western Buddhist Order.** An eclectic movement established in London, England, in 1967 by Venerable Sangharakshita, an Englishman who had studied extensively in India, writing prolifically (e.g. *A Survey of Buddhism*, 1957).

There is no exclusively monastic membership of this Order, which attempts to make known the Buddhist path by using a language appropriate to the contemporary Western world. All who participate are known as 'friends', and *saṅgha refers to the whole community, but those who advance with commitment can be ordained as mitras, and then as Order Members. Order Members may also commit themselves to periods of celibacy. Activities include meditation courses, study groups, retreats, yoga classes, and courses in human communication. There is some argument among Buddhists whether this eclecticism represents the true Westernization of Buddhism (cf. the diffusions into Tibet), or whether it is an erosion of tradition.

Western Paradise (ruled over by the Buddha Amitābha): see SUKHĀVATĪ.

Western schism: see ANTIPOPE.

Western Wall: see WAILING WALL.

Westminster Confession. A credal statement of *Calvinistic Christianity, drawn up for Presbyterian Churches, 1643–6. In the context of the English Civil War (which began in 1642) and of the strong Scottish statement, in the National Covenant (1638), of Calvinism, Parliament sought a deliberate reconciliation. Doctrinal points were rapidly agreed (partly by avoiding divisive issues such as supralapsarianism: see PREDESTINATION), but the statement on Church and State relations was more difficult. In the end its compromise was overtaken by events, with the restoration of Charles II in 1660, and the re-establishment of the Anglican Church. But it remained a credal foundation for the Presbyterian Church in Scotland.

G. S. Hendry, *The Westminster Confession for Today* (1960).

Wheel of Life (symbol of the cycle of rebirth): see TIBETAN WHEEL OF LIFE.

Whichcote, B. (philosopher): see CAMBRIDGE PLATONISTS.

Whirling dervishes (ecstatic Muslims): see DERWĪSH.

White Eagle Lodge. Spiritualist movement whose teachings are based on communications from White Eagle, a Native American, who spoke through Grace Cooke. The movement teaches that God the eternal spirit is both Father and Mother, and that the divine Son, or Cosmic Christ, dwells in every living thing, giving unity and harmony to the Cosmos. There is also a belief in reincarnation, in the Hindu law of *karma, in the doctrine of correspondence which holds that the microcosm is part of the macrocosm, and in spiritual healing.

While some devotees have been initiated into the Outer Brotherhood for the work of projecting the Christ Star, a method of healing the soul of the world, others have progressed to the higher Inner Brotherhood where great devotion and obedience to White Eagle is demanded in preparation for the coming Golden Age.

Whitefield, George (1714–70). *Calvinistic preacher and leader in the *Evangelical Revival. Born in Gloucester, Whitefield was educated at Oxford, where he associated with the *Wesley brothers. His skill as a communicator was at its best in his outdoor evangelistic preaching to vast crowds, having learnt much from the marketing skills of the commercial world. A man with a compassionate social outlook, his preaching tours were also used to raise substantial funds for his orphanage in Georgia. His ardent Calvinism brought him into conflict with J. Wesley, but the two men retained their friendship, Wesley preaching the sermon at Whitefield's funeral. He visited America for extended preaching tours on seven different occasions, eventually dying there.

A. A. Dallimore, *George Whitefield* . . . (1970); S. C. Henry, *George Whitefield* . . . (1957); F. Lambert, *'Pedlar in Divinity': George Whitefield and the Transatlantic Revivals, 1737–70* (1994).

Whitehead, A. N. (philosopher): see PROCESS THEOLOGY.

White Horse Monastery/Temple (Buddhist monastery in China): see PAI-MA-SSU.

White Lake of the Ascetics: see PILGRIMAGE (Jain).

White Lotus School (school of Buddhism): see PAI-LIEN-TSUNG; T'IEN-T'AI.

White Lotus Society. Chinese folk movement, with strong millenarian beliefs. It consisted of a number of organizations, developing from (11th cent.) a relatively simple devotion to *Amida under lay leadership into the practice of magic, healing, and exorcism. In the 14th cent., its eclectic tendency absorbed Taoist elements and expectation of the imminent advent of *Maitreya. The preparatory conflict with the evil rulers of their day (e.g. among *Red Turbans) led to their prohibition and persecution. The White Lotus Rebellion of 1796–1805 and the *Boxer Rebellion illustrate the continuing power of the movement.

S. Naquin, *Millenarian Rebellion in China: The Eight Trigrams Uprising of 1813* (1976) and *Shantung Rebellion* (1981); D. L. Overmyer, *Folk Buddhist Religion* (1976).

White shamanism: see SHAMANS.

Wicca (witchcraft): see WITCHCRAFT.

Wiesel, E. (Jewish writer): see HOLOCAUST.

Wig, wearing of: see HEAD, COVERING OF.

Wilberforce, William (1759–1833). *Evangelical *Anglican and reformer. Born in Hull, he became MP for the city in 1780. He later took the county seat for Yorkshire and worked tirelessly in Parliament for the abolition of the slave-trade. His *Practical View of the Prevailing Religious System of Professed Christians* (1797) exposed the nominal Christianity of many in 'the Higher and Middle Classes' and became a religious best-seller for forty years. Concerned about declining moral standards, he founded the Society for the Reformation of Manners (1787), whilst his missionary and educational concern was given expression in the part he played in the formation of the Church Missionary Society (*CMS) (1795) and the British and Foreign *Bible Society (1804). He is recognized in the Lesser Festivals of the Church of England, 29 July.

Wild ass of Mesopotamia (name for last Umayyad caliph): see UMAYYADS.

Wilfrid, St (634–709). English *bishop. As abbot of Ripon, he introduced the *Benedictine rule, and at the Synod of Whitby (664) he helped to secure the Roman (against the *Celtic) dating of *Easter (see also HILDA). His career as bishop of York was troubled, and he twice appealed to Rome against his treatment by archbishops of Canterbury. He ended his life in the more modest see of Hexham. He also did successful missionary work at various times in Sussex and Frisia. He is remembered as a cosmopolitan churchman and proponent of closer relations between the English Church and Rome. Feast day, 12 Oct.

William of Ockham or **Occam** (14th cent.). Christian philosopher. He studied at Oxford but, since he did not complete his master's degree, he remained an inceptor, hence his nickname, Inceptor Venerabilis. He began to write logic and commentaries, especially on Aristotle's *Physics*. Here he argued against prevalent views which allowed the intellect to constitute individuals as universals, never perceiving them directly as such, but knowing them to be so by reflection. To Ockham, individuals alone are real, as they are and as they can be observed; and what can be known is the individual, not some unperceivable universal: 'Every universal is one singular thing and is universal only by the signification of many things.' In this insistence on observation, he has been regarded as the forerunner of Bacon, Newton, and *Descartes. His argument went further: matter and form cannot be known in abstraction, but only in the relations (and oppositions) that they have with each other. But if we cannot know an apparent object *propter sibi* (for what it is in itself), but only in its contingent manifestation, still less can we know God 'in himself'. Ockham allowed that 'God' as the first conserving cause of the world can be demonstrated by argument, but not that 'God exists' by any of the classic proofs (see in contrast AQUINAS). Consequently, reason unaided by revelation cannot arrive at a knowledge of God, so that our only possible relation to God is one of faith; but (by definition as well as by his own argument) there is no necessity in faith. For a time, Ockham believed that the Church, through the pope, exercised legitimate authority in matters of faith, but after he was summoned to defend himself before the pope in Avignon and fifty-one of his propositions were found to be heretical, he restricted legitimate authority to scripture. He was forced to flee to Bavaria and was excommunicated from the Franciscan order. In 1348, he asked to be reinstated, and in 1349, the pope gave authority for his absolution, but it is uncertain whether news of this reached him before his death—probably from the Black Death. His name has been given to the principle of ontological economy (popularly known as 'Occam's razor'), *entia non sunt multiplicanda praeter necessitatem* ('entities ought not to be multiplied beyond necessity'), i.e. that in accounting for phenomena, one should not posit more (especially by way of cause or reality) than is necessary to give a satisfactory or true explanation; and as such it might seem to call in question the propriety of invoking God to account for anything. The principle is derived from Aristotle, and is referred to by Grosseteste as *lex parsimoniae*, but the words do not occur in the surviving works of Ockham.

G. Leff, *William of Ockham* . . . (1975).

William of St-Thierry (*c*.1085–1148). Christian theologian and mystical writer. Born at Liège and probably educated at Laon, he became a *Benedictine and *c*.1120 was appointed Abbot of St-Thierry, near Reims. He had long been a friend of St *Bernard of Clairvaux, whose life he wrote, but did not join the *Cistercians until 1135, owing to Bernard's resistance. In his writings he shows wide reading of the Fathers, Greek as well as Latin, and (especially in his *Golden Letter*) develops an understanding of the soul's knowledge of God through love which lays bare and fosters a kind of kinship with God: through an assent of the will to Christ's love, a person can begin to recover the lost kinship with God, which constantly reflects the *Trinity. It follows that the image of God in humanity was not wholly destroyed by the *fall: there remains a natural tendency to love God ('Love itself is knowing, love itself is understanding') which can be developed by *asceticism controlled by reason—*a ratio fidei*, 'by reason of faith'. It is faith which carries a person from sin to God.

D. N. Bell, *The Image and Likeness* (1984).

Williams, Roger (*c*.1604–83). Advocate of religious toleration, and an American colonist. After ordination (probably in 1629) he became chaplain to Sir William Masham, but separatist views compelled him to seek religious freedom in N. America (1630). He established a settlement which he named 'Providence' (1636), and founded Rhode Island where he formed the first *Baptist church in the colonies. A vigorous campaigner for religious liberty, he wrote his controversial pamphlet *The Bloody Tenet of Persecution* (published anonymously 1644) while visiting England to obtain a charter for the new colony. His principles extended naturally to friendship with the indigenous people (the Naragansett tribe).

Wine: see ALCOHOL; KHAMR.

Wine Ode, The: see OMAR KHAYYAM.

Wird (Arab.). A time of private prayer (cf. *duʿāʾ) in Islam (in addition to *ṣalāt), and also the formula of prayers recited on these occasions (also known as *ḥizb*). Awrād (pl.) are usually made up of passages from the *Qurʾān, and among Sūfīs are recited at least seventy times morning and evening.

Wisdom (Heb., *ḥokhmah*, *binah*, 'discrimination'). An ethical and religious quality of life as advocated by the Hebrew scriptures. Wisdom is sometimes used in the sense of 'intelligence' (e.g. Ecclesiastes 2. 3), but it came to symbolize a particular cultural tradition within Judaism. The wisdom books of the *Bible are *Proverbs, *Job, and *Ecclesiastes. The *Apocrypha includes *Ecclesiasticus* (**Ben Sira*) and the **Wisdom of Solomon*. Wisdom was perceived as a divine gift (Proverbs 2), but it could be acquired through education and counsel. Proverbs 8 speaks of wisdom as being a co-worker with God in the process of creation, and the philosopher *Philo equated wisdom and *Torah with the divine *logos. Many of the Psalms are in the wisdom tradition; they are addressed to fellow human beings and recommend a life of piety (e.g. Psalm 37). Wisdom literature also was produced in other ancient Middle Eastern cultures.

J. L. Crenshaw, *Old Testament Wisdom* . . . (1981); J. G. Gammie (ed.), *Israelite Wisdom* . . . (1978); D. F. Morgan, *Wisdom in the Old Testament Traditions* (1981).

Wisdom (in Mahāyāna Buddhism): see PERFECTION OF WISDOM LITERATURE; PARĀMITĀ.

***Wisdom of Solomon*.** One of the books of the *Apocrypha. It contains: a description of the destinies awaiting the righteous and the wicked (chs. 1–5); a meditation on wisdom, including Solomon's prayer for wisdom (6–9); and a review of Israel's history down to the *Exodus, emphasizing rewards and punishments and the evil of *idolatry (10–19). The first-person references to Solomon (e.g. 7. 1) are a literary device; the author's familiarity with Gk. philosophy places him as a Jew of Alexandria in the period 2nd cent. BCE–1st cent. CE. The terms used of Wisdom in ch. 7 passed into Christian theology as applied to Christ.

Wise, Isaac Meyer (1819–1900). Pioneer of *Reform Judaism. He was born in Bohemia and emigrated to the USA in 1846. From 1854, he was *rabbi of the Cincinnati congregation of B'nai Jeshuran. He founded the periodical, *The Israelite*, in 1854, organized the 1855 *Rabbinical Conference in Cleveland, and was a key figure in the founding of the *Hebrew Union College in 1875. Although he was initially cautious in introducing change, he ended up making great endeavours to ensure that the practice of Judaism was possible in a new land. He agreed that *Torah was the source of authority, but only the Decalogue (see TEN COMMANDMENTS) was absolutely obligatory—all else was open to interpretation. The criterion of judgement is truth—

'Truth, the redeemer, the savior, the *messiah!' His major aim in making practice possible was to strengthen the *synagogue—for 'Israel lives in its congregations.'

J. G. Heller, *Isaac Mayer Wise* (1965); S. D. Temkin, *Isaac Meyer Wise* . . . (1992).

Witchcraft (from *wicca*). The belief that human affairs and features of the environment can be ordered, controlled, and changed by skilled practitioners whose powers are usually believed to be innate. Witchcraft is closely associated with *magic, but its techniques are derived from within or given by a supernatural agent, rather than (as often with magic) learnt. The belief that the agent was the *devil led to ferocious persecution of witches in medieval Christian Europe (see B. Levack, *The Witch-Hunt in Early Modern Europe*, 1989), an antagonism reinforced by the fact that since the activity of witches frequently lies outside the boundaries of customary social behaviour, they are often feared. Although witchcraft thus has had, in the past, a strongly negative connotation, it has been reassessed more recently in increasingly positive terms, in two main ways. First, anthropologists have described its positive role in small-scale societies, in healing, reducing hostilities and social tensions, reinforcing social order (e.g. the belief that the old, if not looked after, may mobilize their latent potential to become witches leads to care for the aged), supplying plausible meanings to inexplicable events, providing surrogate action in crises (e.g. the *evil eye). Second, the increasing emancipation of women from the control of men in religions has led to a re-evaluation of the role of women as witches (since women have always far outnumbered men as witches), and to the postulation that 'witchcraft' represents an unbroken religious tradition which men opposed because it empowered women. This tradition is often known as Wicca (or Wicce, from the Old English, the root of which means 'to bend' or 'shape'), but it is embedded in a wider neo-Paganism. According to Starhawk, a leader of the recovery of Wicca, 'Followers of Wicca seek their inspiration in pre-Christian sources, European folklore, and mythology. They consider themselves priests and priestesses of an ancient European *shamanistic nature religion that worships a goddess who is related to the ancient Mother Goddess in her three aspects of Maiden, Mother and Crone.' She protests against the caricature of witches as 'members of a kooky cult', and claims that Wicca has 'the depth, dignity and seriousness of purpose of a true religion' (*The Spiral Dance* . . ., 1979). The emphasis is on the application of power to change existing circumstances, especially by interior transformation ('the power within oneself to create artistically and change one's life', M. Adler, *Drawing Down the Moon*, 1987).

J. C. Baroja, *The World of Witches* (1964); E. W. Gadon, *The Once and Future Goddess* (1989); R. Guiley, *The Encyclopedia of Witches and Witchcraft* (1990); Starhawk, *Dreaming the Dark* (1982) and *Truth or Dare* (1987).

Wittgenstein, Ludwig (1889–1951). Austrian philosopher. He studied mathematical logic with Bertrand Russell in Cambridge in 1912–13, fought in the Austrian army in the First World War, and wrote his *Tractatus Logico-Philosophicus* (1921; tr. 1922) whilst a prisoner of war in Italy. He gave up philosophy for several years, but resumed work in it in the late 1920s. He returned to Cambridge, and became Professor of Philosophy there in 1939. Apart from a single article, he published nothing further in his own lifetime: his later works were all published posthumously, starting with the *Philosophical Investigations* (1953).

Wittgenstein's later philosophy took a different direction from that of the *Tractatus*, and was critical of it in many respects. But in both cases he was concerned with the relation between language and the world. The *Tractatus* sees meaningful language as ultimately analysable into basic propositions, which picture the world. Since *ethics, aesthetics, and religious language do not picture anything, they are relegated to the realm of the mystical and inexpressible. In his later work, however, Wittgenstein disclaimed any attempt to give a unitary account of the nature of language. Instead, he saw language as composed of many different 'language-games', a term used to indicate that uses of language are rule-governed and go with activities and practices; he also compared language to a set of tools, each having its own use.

Wittgenstein wrote little about religion as such, though interesting observations about it are scattered throughout his works. In 1938 he gave some lectures on religious belief, in which he presented the distinctiveness of such beliefs as lying in the ways in which they express certain reactions and regulate our lives: he compared, for instance, belief in the Last Judgement to living with a certain picture before us which influences all our actions. These lectures were reconstructed later from the notes of his students and published (in *Lectures on Aesthetics, Psychology, and Religious Belief*, 1966). Similarly, some remarks which he wrote about *Frazer's *Golden Bough* were published in *Synthese* in 1967. Otherwise, his most substantial remarks on religion and theology are to be found in a collection of miscellaneous writings, *Culture and Value* (1977; tr. 1980).

It is Wittgenstein's later philosophy in general, however, that has had more influence on the philosophy of religion and theology than his few writings on religion as such. Sometimes relatively short treatments of single topics have been influential: John Hick, for example, used the discussion of the difference between 'seeing' and 'seeing as', in which Wittgenstein makes use of Jastrow's ambiguous drawing of the 'duck-rabbit' (*Philosophical Investigations*, II. xi) in his construal of theistic faith as a way of 'seeing as' or, better, 'experiencing as' (in *Faith and Knowledge*, 1957). But it was Wittgenstein's later view of language which particularly attracted the attention of philosophers of religious language.

Whereas the Logical Positivists (who were much influenced by the *Tractatus*, though it can be argued that they misunderstood it) dismissed religious language as meaningless because unverifiable in empirical terms, Wittgenstein's later philosophy seemed to offer a more tolerant approach which would permit the inclusion of religious language amongst meaningful uses of language. For religious language-games are just as much parts of human life as other uses of language, and indeed Wittgenstein includes 'praying' in his list of common language-games, in *Philosophical Investigations* § 23; and there is no superior vantage point from which this, or any, language can be assessed.

More recent work on Wittgenstein's significance for religion has ranged further afield. Fergus Kerr's *Theology after Wittgenstein* (1986) sees his work as a remedy for the Cartesianism which has infected much religious thinking, especially the tendency to think of religion in terms of private mental processes, or of a disembodied ego communicating with God, cut off from body, society, and a cultural context. Other writers regard his work as a remedy for what they see as misguided attempts to justify or attack religion in rational terms. Much philosophy of religion has been concerned to provide a rational foundation for religious belief, especially by seeking evidence in *natural theology or, more recently, in religious experience, or else to criticize such attempts. But it may be the case that religion neither can, nor needs to be, provided with such foundations. Rather, religion is rooted in certain common human reactions like wonder, gratitude, pity, and repentance, which are 'forms of life' and part of the 'natural history' of humanity (to use two favourite phrases of the later Wittgenstein). Such reactions need no intellectual justification in general (though particular exemplifications of them may be justified or criticized).

If this account is correct, the philosophy of religion and much theology should be concerned more with coming to understand the distinctive nature of religious beliefs and practices, through a perspicuous description and analysis of them, than with shoring them up with intellectual defences. We are, however, left with the questions of what kind of truth religion and theology might have, and how it is discerned.

D. Z. Phillips, *Wittgenstein and Religion* (1993); P. J. Sherry, *Religion, Truth and Language-Games* (1977).

Woking Mosque: see AḤMADĪYYA.

Wolff, Joseph (1795–1862). Christian missionary to the Jews (and others) of the orient. Although the son of a *rabbi, Wolff converted to Christianity and devoted the latter part of his life to bringing the Christian message to the Jews of Palestine, Mesopotamia, Turkey, Persia, Kurdistan, Khurasan, Bukhara, India, and the Yemen. He wrote several accounts of his travels which provide lively and interesting details about the eastern communities.

H. P. Palmer, *Joseph Wolff* . . . (1935).

Womb Mandala (maṇḍala in exoteric Buddhism): see TAIZO-KAI MANDARA; SHINGON.

Women. The status of women in religions has, in the past, been tied closely to the reproductive cycle, both that of humans, and that of crops and herds. The controls of evolution and of natural selection (of course not known or understood) established boundaries within which, either the replication of genes and the nurture of children succeeded, or the family / group / community / village went to extinction. Religions, as the earliest cultural systems of which we know, have created strong protections for replication and nurture, often by way of controls over behaviour—hence the preoccupation of religions with sexual behaviours and food. Characteristically, societies developed a necessary division of labour, based on biology but extended symbolically, with women responsible for the upbringing of the family and for related activities in preparation of food (both in cooking and in the fields), and with men relating to a wider environment, e.g. in hunting, warfare, political relations. The feminine is thus often celebrated in religions as the source of life and gift of fertility. There is some (disputed) evidence that the feminine, as Mother Goddess, was the primordial focus of worship: at a time when the male contribution to reproduction was not realized, this is unsurprising. Equally unsurprising (from a genetic point of view) is the way in which men consequently took control of the reproductive cycle. That control is mirrored in the increasing dominance of patriarchal religion. Even in India, where the feminine has remained central in worship, and where the Goddess may still be the single focus of devotion for many Hindus, the Goddess on her own is usually destructive and fierce, and only fruitful in relation to a consort, such as *Śiva. The subordination of women to men became widespread in all religions: exceptions are very much exceptions to the rule, because the rule is biogenetically based; it does not follow from that observation that there is some natural and innate 'character of women' which legitimizes that subordination, though men in religions frequently pervert the argument in that way. It is, more simply, that religions are the (unconscious) expression of genetic strategies. Thus the religious subordination of women to the authority of men is not usually one of status (since women, and their role in the family, may be very highly revered); it is, more often, one of control and protection. Combined with profound fears about the dangers surrounding sexuality (elaborated in complex ritual customs to deal with 'purity and danger', the title of a relevant study by Mary Douglas), this led to literal separations of women from men, especially in worship (for example, in *synagogue or *mosque or in the *Roman Catholic refusal of the *ordination of women, or, until 1992, of girl servers near the altar), and to religiously sanctioned restrictions on the opportunities afforded to women to dispose of their own lives (and bodies and property) according to their own decisions. Yet women have repeatedly secured their own religious identity on the terms allowed to them, as many studies have shown: see e.g. C. W. Bynum, *Holy Feast and Holy Fast* (1982) and R. S. Kraemer, *Her Share of the Blessings: Women's Religions Among Pagans, Jews and Christians* . . . (1994). In so far as this led to a domain of competence and control in *witchcraft, it is unsurprising (in view of the continuing control of religions by men) that witchcraft has been given a high status in recent times by those concerned to re-evaluate the role of women in religion in distinction from patriarchy (see e.g. M. Adler, *Drawing Down the Moon*, 1986; Starhawk, *The Spiral Dance* . . ., 1979).

While it is true that the increasing emancipation of women in many parts of the world has led to major adjustments in the place accorded to women in most religions, the phrase 'place accorded to' reveals the continuing truth: men remain predominantly in control and allow some women some greater access to authority and decision-making. A classic example was the 'Letter to All Women' issued by Pope John Paul II in 1995. While it was remarkable in apologizing for the oppressive record of the Church in relation to women ('if objective blame [*for the prevention of women* from truly being themselves], especially in particular historical contexts, has belonged to not just a few members of the Church, for this I am truly sorry'), the document as a whole adopted the usual male strategy of congratulating women on the gifts of their characteristic natures, while at the same time making it clear that those natures prohibited women from undertaking certain roles reserved for men—the kind of argument which in the past perpetuated slavery and prevented women from being educated. For the spurious nature of this strategy in relation to the ordination of women, see J. Bowker, *Is God a Virus*? . . . (1995).

See Index, Women.

J. Holm and J. Bowker, *Women in Religion* (1994); U. King (ed.), *Women in the World's Religions* (1987); A. Sharma, *Women in World Religions* (1987); S. Young, *An Anthology of Sacred Texts By and About Women* (1993).

Judaism The Hebrew scriptures teach that woman was created as a 'helper' to men (Genesis 2. 23–4). Her chief duty was to be childbearing (Genesis 3. 16), and a good wife and mother was cause for praise (Proverbs 31. 28). Women were regarded as full human beings in that both men and women suffered the same penalty for adultery or *apostasy, but they were none the less clearly lesser in status. A wife is inferior to her husband who will 'rule over her' (Genesis 3. 16); she has no right to *divorce, and a man could sell his daughter as a payment for debt (Exodus 21. 7). The *rabbis exempted women from all time-bound positive commandments (see SIX HUNDRED AND THIRTEEN COMMANDMENTS) (*Kid.* 1. 7), and female education was not encouraged ('Whosoever teaches his daughter *Torah teaches her lasciviousness'). The daily service still contains the *benediction, 'Blessed are you, O Lord our God, who has not created me a woman'. None the less, many of the rabbis seem to have loved their wives and taught that 'an unmarried man lives without joy, blessing and good' (*B.Yev.* 62b). It was the *kabbalists who introduced the practice of reciting Proverbs 31. 10–13 on the *Sabbath, and they stressed the importance of the female as well as the male principle in the *Shekhinah. In 1994, a Commission, convened by the Chief Rabbi of the UK, issued a far-ranging report on the status of women in Orthodox Judaism, recommending that the exclusion of women from *kaddish, the separation of women from men in synagogue by *mechitzah* ('partition') should be ended or modified, and that a pre-nuptial covenant, guaranteeing the supply of the *get* (bill of divorce: see MARRIAGE AND DIVORCE, JUDAISM) in the case of divorce, should be supplied. *Progressive Jews stress the absolute equality of men and women and have female as well as male rabbis, *cantors, and *synagogue leaders. See also NIDDAH.

R. Biale, *Women and Jewish Law* (1984); M. M. Brayer, *The Jewish Woman in Rabbinic Literature* (1986); R. Loewe, *The Position of Women in Judaism* (1966); I. M. Ruud, *Women and Judaism: A . . . Bibliography* (1988); J. R. Wegner, *Chattel or Person? . . . Women in the Midrash* (1988).

Christianity Early Christianity was an egalitarian movement in which women played a prominent part. Not only did *Jesus give and receive much in ministry to and from women (with an openness which went against the norms of his day), but women clearly played an important part in the life and running of the early Church. Yet at the same time, Jesus did not offer new context-dependent interpretations of existing Jewish law, but rather offered context-independent principles, sometimes in the form of *kelal ('love God and your neighbour as yourself'). The New Testament writings, especially the letters, are constantly attempting to make those principles context-dependent, by suggesting (often in forms that resemble law) what they mean in practice and in particular situations. There is thus a reaffirmation of traditional and cultural attitudes, leading to the continuing subordination of women to the authority of their husbands, and to men in the Church (e.g. 1 Corinthians 14. 34; Ephesians 5. 22 f.; Colossians 3. 18; 1 Timothy 2. 11 f.; Titus 2. 4 f.). The Church subsequently has endeavoured (generally speaking) to confirm that subordinate status of women by turning the context-dependent applications of the New Testament into context-independent commands. The Church has thus, historically, admired women from a distance, insisting on their special and higher vocations, while at the same time regarding them as inherently the source of sin, because of their descent from *Eve, and certainly not to be admitted to the male preserves of decision-making and priesthood. The Virgin *Mary became the role model, calling sexuality into question and exhibiting the way to salvation through perfect obedience. The greatest opportunities for women outside marriage were therefore either in martyrdom or in the religious life, where they could become *saints—though only on the terms defined and controlled by men. Nevertheless, within these constricting boundaries, women achieved degrees of independence in religious life on their own terms (see e.g. RHENO-FLEMISH SPIRITUALITY), and even achieved positions of authority. Although initially the *Reformation made matters worse for women (by removing the religious orders in which they could exercise degrees of autonomy, and confining them to *Kinder, Küche, Kirche* under the authority of their husbands), the post-Reformation Churches have divided along familiar lines, some insisting on the subordination which the New Testament is taken to require, but others returning to the context-independent principles and liberating the gifts and spiritualities and leadership of women for the Church and the world. The issue has come to focus on the ordination of women: increasingly, outside the boundaries of the *Orthodox Churches and the *Roman Catholic Church, women are being ordained. In the latter two, the majority of church leaders (male) oppose change in what they regard as an unbroken tradition (though some possible exceptions have been claimed); and in 1994, Pope *John Paul II tried to make all further debate about the matter impossible. Nevertheless, the preceding document, *Inter Insigniores*, is barren of any argument beside that of such ordination never having been done before, being reduced to citing authorities whose remarks, if they had been more fully quoted, exhibit the familiar misogyny of the male-dominated Church. Yet clearly there are many RC and Orthodox Christians who are, despite discouragement, committed to the realization within time of that final vision, in which the Christian attitude to all oppressed groups is summarized, when there shall be 'neither Jew nor Greek, slave nor free, male and female' (Galatians 3. 28).

C. W. Bynum, *Holy Feast and Holy Fast* (1987) and *Jesus as Mother* . . . (1982); E. Clark and H. Richardson, *Women and Religion: A Feminist Sourcebook of Christian Thought* (1977); E. S. Fiorenza, *In Memory of Her* . . . (1983); S. Marshall (ed.), *Women in Reformation and Counter-Reformation Thought* (1989); M. Warner, *Alone of All Her Sex: The Myth and Cult of the Virgin Mary* (1976).

Islam In Islam, it is believed that women and men are different but equal. The advent of Islam brought great advantages to the status and protection of women, and women, especially *ʿĀisha, played an important part in the early years of Islam, as they have continued to do. Women are not the source of sin (Eve, Ḥawwā, is not named in the *Qurʾān, which makes it clear that both Adam and Eve were equally at fault: see e.g. 2. 36 f.), though they may be the source of particular impurity after childbirth and menstruation. Women, and mothers in particular, are deeply honoured (when Muḥammad was asked whom one should most honour, he replied three times, 'Your mother', and only then added, 'Your father'). Women have access to education and retain control of their own property. At the same time, certain inequalities between women and men, together with the fact that some customs have become virtual obligations in some parts of the Muslim world, have raised questions about the implementation of Qurʾān and *ḥadīth in this area. Thus the veil (*ḥijāb), or more total covering of *chaddor*, is not required by Qurʾān, which only commands modesty in dress (24. 31); the widespread practice of female circumcision is not required at all; polygamy is envisaged in the Qurʾān, but not polyandry; men may marry women of the *ahl al-Kitāb, but women may not marry such men. In any case, the authority of men over women remains, derived from two verses in particular: having affirmed mutual rights for women, 2. 228 states, 'But men have *darajah* over women.' *Darajah* means 'rank' or 'degree' or 'precedence', and may simply be restricted to the different ways in which men and women can initiate divorce, but it is often taken in a more general sense. In another verse (4. 34/8), it is said that men are *qawwumūn* over women (because they have to support them) and that women suspected of ill-conduct must be admonished, banished to their beds, and beaten. *Qawwamūn* is usually taken to mean 'standing over', i.e. having authority; but the meanings of the Qurʾān are not fixed, and the word may legitimately mean 'standing in attendance'; and in any case, the beating cannot be painful and is largely symbolic. Even so, for many Muslim women these particular aspects of the assymetry between men and women raise searching questions about the (theoretically possible) rethinking of the meaning of *sharīʿa in the spirit of Muḥammad's own support for the worth and dignity of women. As matters stand, the experience of many Muslim women, as they report it, is one of which Muḥammad could scarcely have approved, and which the Qurʾān did not intend.

L. Ahmed, *Women and Gender in Islam* . . . (1992); L. Beck and N. Keddie (eds.), *Women in the Muslim World* (1978); J. W. Bowker, *Voices of Islam* (1995); N. El Saadawi, *The Hidden Face of Eve: Women in the Arab World* (1980); F. Husain (ed.), *Muslim Women* (1984); S. R. Meghdessian, *The Status of the Arab Woman: A Select Bibliography* (1980); F. Mernissi, *Women and Islam* (1991); J. Minces, *The House of Obedience: Women in Arab Society* (1980); A. Al-Qazzaz, *Women in the Middle East and N. Africa: A Bibliography* . . . (1977); A. Schleifer, *Motherhood in Islam* (1986); J. I. Smith (ed.), *Women in Contemporary Muslim Societies* (1980); J. Brijbushan, *Muslim Women* (1980).

Hinduism The status and role of women in Hinduism are complex. At the level of home and society, they are revered, yet at the same time they are dependent on men and are to be guarded by them. In the *Dharmaśāstras, they are ritually impure and a source of impurity (and therefore, e.g., not to study or recite *mantras): their husbands are their *gurus, and their domestic duties are their rituals. Their devotion to their husbands is their highest good (especially if consummated in *satī), and yet, according to *Manusmṛti 2. 213 f., they are incapable of achieving absolute devotion. Nevertheless, at the same time, feminine images of the divine are more obvious in Hinduism than in other religions (with the possible, but limited, exception of devotion to *Mary in Christianity, where she is only associated with the divine). Even then, goddesses usually appear as consorts with male gods, and are beneficial in co-operation with them, otherwise being, in general, destructive. Women are prominent in myths, and in life they have been even more prominent in *bhakti (devotion to God). Women are recognized by Hindus as a source of immense power, but they remain, nevertheless, firmly under patriarchal control.

A. S. Altekar, *The Position of Women in Hindu Civilisation from Prehistoric Times to the Present Day* (1938); N. A. Falk (ed.), *Unspoken Worlds: Women's Religious Lives in Non-Western Cultures* (1980); J. S. Hawley and D. M. Wulff (eds.), *The Divine Consort: Radha and the Goddesses of India* (1982, 1986); P. Mukherjee, *Hindu Women: Normative Models* (1978); C. Sakala, *Women of South Asia* (1980).

Buddhism The *Buddha's attitude towards women was not radically different from that of his contemporaries: for those pursuing the religious life, women are a temptation and a snare; but in the context of lay society, the role of women as wives and mothers was crucial to the stability of the social order. The Buddha frequently cautioned monks to be on their guard when dealing with women lest they be overcome by lust and craving. The following interchange, taken from the **Mahā-parinibbāna-sutta*, between the Buddha and Ānanda, his attendant, may be taken as typical in this respect:

—Lord, how should we conduct ourselves with regard to women?
—Don't see them, Ānanda.
—But if we should see them?
—Don't talk to them.
—But if they should talk to us?
—Keep wide awake, Ānanda.

However, from the outset women were allowed to become nuns, although with more severe rules imposed on them. Regarding the role of women in lay life the Buddha upheld the traditional values of his time, describing the relationship between husband and wife in the following terms:

In five ways should a wife ... be ministered to by her husband: by respect, by courtesy, by faithfulness, by handing over authority to her, by providing her with adornments. In these five ways does the wife, ministered to by her husband ... love him: her duties are well performed, by hospitality to the kin of both, by faithfulness, by watching over the goods he brings, and by skill and industry in discharging all her business (*Sigālovāda-suttanta*).

I. B. Horner, *Women Under Primitive Buddhism* (1930); D. Y. Paul, *Women in Buddhism: Images of the Feminine in Mahāyāna* (1979); C. Sakala, *Women of South Asia: A Guide to Resources* (1980).

Jainism The status of women in relation to enlightenment is a specific issue between *Digambaras and Śvetāmbaras, with the latter regarding gender as usually irrelevant: see DIGAMBARA.

Sikhism The recurring image in the *Ādi Granth of the soul offering itself to God as a chaste woman surrenders to her husband reveals the traditional relationship. In accordance with the ideal of *grahastī, Sikhs are expected to marry, and motherhood is an honoured role. Sikh teaching condemned the once-prevalent practices of female infanticide and *satī. Women participate in *gurdwārā *worship and are prominent in preparing *Gurū-kā-laṅgar. They may read the scriptures publicly or sing, and serve as management committee members.

N.-G. K. Singh, *The Feminine Principle in the Sikh Vision of the Transcendent* (1993).

Won Buddhism (Korean, *won*, 'circular'). Korean Buddhist movement, founded by Soe-tae San (1891–1943). He spent his early years in ascetic practice until achieving enlightenment in 1915. In 1924, he founded the Association for the Study of Buddha-Dharma, though under the Japanese occupation, it was relatively unknown. After 1946, the school gained many adherents. Its teaching combines the goal of seeing the *Buddha in all things (and living consistently with this perception), with 'timeless and placeless' Zen, i.e. Zen meditation does not depend on allocated places and times. Thus its only object of meditation is a black circle (hence the name) on a white field, representing the dharmakāya (*trikāya) of the Buddha. Won is not dominated by a monastic wing—indeed, monks may marry: and much emphasis is placed on Zen permeating lay life.

Wŏnhyo (618–86). Korean Buddhist scholar-monk. Wŏnhyo founded the Punhwang (or Haedong) subsect of the Hwaŏm (*Hua-yen) sect, integrated various Buddhist thoughts through his notion of the 'harmony of disputes' (*hwajaeng*), and popularized Buddhism through dance and song. A prolific writer, his works include *Kisillonso* ('Commentary on *Awakening Mahāyāna* Faith') which had a profound influence on Buddhists in E. Asian countries.

S. B. Park, diss., *Wŏnhyo's Commentaries* (1979).

Woolman, John (Quaker committed to abolition of slavery): see FRIENDS, THE SOCIETY OF.

World-affirming, World-denying (categorization of sects): see SECTS.

World Alliance of Reformed Churches: see PRESBYTERIANISM.

World Buddhist Sangha Council: see SAṄGHA.

World Council of Churches: see ECUMENISM.

World Fellowship of Buddhists. Founded in 1950 by a Sinhalese Buddhist, Malalasekera. Its objective is to spread understanding of Buddhism and to reconcile the divergent styles and teachings of Buddhism.

World protectors (in Buddhism): see CELESTIAL KINGS.

Worlds, The four. Jewish *kabbalistic doctrine. The kabbalists identified four stages in the creation process which correspond to the four letters of the *tetragrammaton: the world of Azilut (the source of all being), Beriah (creation), Yezirah (formation), and Asiyyah (angelic world). These four worlds expressed a declining order of being, and were discussed by such scholars as Moses *Cordovero and Ḥayyim *Vital.

World's Parliament of Religions. A meeting of representatives of the major world religions at Chicago in 1893. The meeting was sponsored by the League of Liberal Clergymen, who saw the encounter of religions as an opportunity of extending religious vision and morality by co-operation rather than by proselytizing conflict. Although little was achieved directly, indirectly a major consequence was the recognition and status which it gave to world religions and their representatives: the spread in the West began of religions other than Christianity and Judaism. A less expected consequence was the impetus it gave to the endeavour among Christians to find common ground in their own *missionary endeavour, culminating in the Edinburgh Conference of 1910. A further World Parliament of Religions was held in 1993, to mark the centenary of the first, also in Chicago. Attempts to establish a World Council of Religions were coolly received. Instead, the possibility of Centres for Interfaith Study were envisaged, which might then form networks of consultation. A Global Ethic was proposed, drawing together the common elements in the *ethics of different religions: based on the *Golden Rule, it hoped to establish a new human consciousness from which a culture of non-violence would emerge.

J. H. Barrows (ed.), *The World's Parliament of Religions* (1893).

Worldwide Church of God: see ARMSTRONG, H. W.

Worms, Concordat of: see CONCORDAT.

Worms, Diet of. The imperial diet of 1521 at which M. *Luther defended his teaching before the emperor Charles V. The *papal legate, Aleander, opposed Luther's doctrines and the Reformer was required to answer charges concerning his 'teachings and books' which he refused to recant. According to an early tradition he concluded his answer with the famous words 'Here I stand. I can do no other. God help me. Amen.' A few weeks later he was declared an 'outlaw' by the papacy and his teachings formally condemned.

Documents in P. Balan, extracts in H. J. Kidd.

Worship. The offering of devotion, praise, and adoration to that which is deemed worthy of such offering, usually God. Worship of that which is less than God as though it is equivalent to God, especially if it is addressed to particular images, is *idolatry. Worship is such a major part and practice of all religions that it is impossible to summarize all that belongs to it. Even in the case of religions which demote theistic forms of appearance from transcendence to being a manifestation (albeit an exalted manifestation) within the universe, the practice of worship is still important. Thus in Buddhism, even *Theravādins express gratitude to the *Buddha and revere the traces of his presence (see RELICS; STŪPA); and although it cannot be stated whether the Buddha is accessible to that gratitude (see AVYĀKATA), it is still appropriate to express it—a reminder that an important component of worship is the sense of dependence (on others as much as on the Other) for the possibility and process of life, as in the Christian marriage commitment, 'With my body I thee worship.' Many Buddhist homes contain a shrine to the Buddha, and Buddhist *festivals celebrate events in his life. In *Mahāyāna, the practice of worship is taken very much further in devotion to *Buddhas and *bodhisattvas (see e.g. AMIDA; AVALOKITEŚVARA; BHAIṢAJYA-GURU; TĀRĀ; among many); devotion and worship may equally be offered to a text which carries within it the words which lead to deliverance and *enlightenment, as with the *Nichiren devotion to the *Lotus Sūtra* (Sikhs also reverence the text of the *Ādi Granth as though it is the living presence of God, but their worship is clearly directed to God from whom the revelation comes). Jains (who have a comparable assessment to that of Buddhists of the limited status of the gods) express grateful devotion to the *tīrthaṅkaras, though the iconography of their representations remains an issue between *Digambara and Śvetāmbara.

More often, however, worship is associated with the adoration of the supreme Being, the unproduced Producer of all that is, from whom all things and all events ultimately come, and to whom all things return. This sense of the transcendence of God necessarily evokes worship. The interior pressure to speak and act more worthily in the presence of the One on whom all things depend and from whom they derive can be seen most clearly in the biblical period of Jewish history: from a circumstance in which *Yahweh was simply one god among many, under the general oversight of *El, the Jews arrived at a realization that there can only be what there is in the case of God, not a kind of committee of gods: Yahweh no longer sits in the council of El: he *is* whatever El is. From this sense of the absolute majesty, holiness, and supremacy of God derives Israel's life of worship, of the constant recognition of God in *Temple, *sacrifice, *Psalms, *pilgrimage, and eventually *synagogue, *liturgy, and *Prayer

Book—epitomized in *kiddush ha-Shem. By wearing the *tefillin, an observant Jew bears on his body a constant worship of God.

Christians inherited this sense of God's independence from, and yet concern for, the universe which he has created—and in particular they inherited the Psalms, which from the start informed their religious intelligence and became the backbone of prayer and devotion. But Christianity recognizes in *Jesus the *incarnate presence of God, through whom praise and worship is offered to the Father—in other (less contingent) words, transcendence and immanence are held together in the reality of Jesus' own prayer. At the same time, God had been truly present to the life and ministry of Jesus, in such a way that the Holy Spirit was early recognized as being God already and always at work in prayer and worship—so much so that Christian prayer and worship were understood, as early as the time of *Paul, as being the activity of God himself (i.e. of the Holy Spirit) within human life, so that humans in prayer and worship are caught up into the natural life or activity of God. Prayer and worship are thus inevitably Trinitarian, as the *Athanasian creed defines 'the *catholic faith': *Fides autem catholica haec est, ut unum Deum in Trinitate et Trinitatem in Unitate veneremur.* On the human side, the body becomes the Temple, to be made holy as God is holy; and worship particularly celebrates the actions of God in Christ (above all in the *eucharist) by which all this becomes possible. Festivals follow the life of Christ. It is characteristic, therefore, of Christian worship that *hymns are sung and that people should feel the truth of their salvation—manifestly so in *charismatic worship.

Islam shares the Jewish sense of the absolute uniqueness and oneness (*tawhīd) of God. Since this and its consequences (not least in belief and behaviour) are made known in the *Qur'ān, the very chanting of the Qur'ān (even without a knowledge of what it means) becomes an act of worship. But the acknowledgement of God is so fundamental that it becomes a daily obligation in *ṣalāt, and an annual obligation in *ṣawm, the month-long fast in *Ramaḍān—both of these being among the *Five Pillars of Islam. But Muslim devotion goes far beyond obligation, spectacularly so in the case of the *Sūfīs, whose attitudes were mediated so extensively into the whole of Islam that informal prayer and worship become for many Muslims the atmosphere in which they live (see e.g. C. E. Padwick, *Muslim Devotions*, 1961).

An attitude of worship and devotion is equally characteristic of Hindus and it defies brief description. Worship (*pūjā) is held and sustained in the home (where there is likely to be a small shrine devoted to a particular deity), but it readily flows out into temples and shrines, and into many practices of particular devotion. Since Hindus in general believe that *Brahman becomes manifest in many different ways, there are many different forms of the deity: their representations in image or carving are evidently worshipped, but in fact they themselves are only pointing the worshipper to the truth of God which lies behind them. An important part of Hindu worship involves bringing the presence of God into the focal object of devotion, whether temple or image. There is no formal pattern that all Hindus must follow. Hindus are likely to choose, or be given, their own focal image and representation of God (*iṣṭadevatā), but they will join in the festivals of other gods and goddesses, because there cannot be an ultimate schism of the divine. More formal communal worship may be expressed through *dance and drama, or through the singing in groups of *kīrtana and *bhajana* ('songs of praise'). These are usually associated with *bhakti, a particularly powerful tradition of devotion and praise. But for the Hindu, the human relation to the divine is possible at all times: every circumstance can be an occasion of the divine. It is this which underlies the importance in worship of *mantra, *maṇḍala, and *yantra. For the Hindu, worship is as natural as birth and death: it is the bridge which connects the one to the other.

See Index, Worship.

J. Holm and J. W. Bowker (eds.), *Worship* (1994).

Wrathful deities. Deities who, in Buddhist *tantra, convey the transcendence of *dosa (hate), itself one of the three major impediments to the attainment of enlightenment. Wrath is thus the purified form of hate, turned against the self in its emotional indulgence. Wrathful deities are depicted in fierce and fearsome guises, but this is intended to represent the attitude necessary to transform hate into wrath against itself (and the other 'poisons' of the mind). The *maṇḍala of wrathful deities conveys the power of the peaceful deities into this specific campaign against dosa.

In W. religions, the wrath of God is the righteous anger of God against wrong-doing, which in the Bible often carries with it punishment of wrongdoers, combined (in Christianity and Islam) with the threat of eternal punishment. God is described as 'one who expresses his wrath every day' (Psalm 7. 11), as 'a consuming fire' (Hebrews 12. 29), and as one whose wrath is part of his supreme plan (Qur'ān 7. 97–9). While this may well express a morally necessary abhorrence of evil, it has also raised questions about the character of God thus described: if parents treated their children comparably, they would be prosecuted. Against the wrath of God is therefore set the love of God and the mercy of God. Consequence nevertheless remains a necessary condition of moral order and freedom, and in that context, the wrath of God, described as it is in contingent language, becomes an invitation to moral seriousness.

A. T. Hanson, *The Wrath of the Lamb* (1957); R. V. G. Tasker, *The Biblical Doctrine of the Wrath of God* (1951).

Wrekin Trust. A *New Age movement established in Britain by Sir George Trevelyan (1906–96), who became an advocate of 'alternative spirituality' after hearing a lecture on Rudolph Steiner's anthroposophy in 1942. The Trust was established to encourage the exploration of the spiritual nature of humans and of their universe through residential courses, conferences at New Age centres and elsewhere, and through publications. Trevelyan regarded much of the New Age movement as being exploited by charlatans, and the purpose of the Trust was to sift the true from the fraudulent. The interests of the Trust were thus cast as widely as Trevelyan's own (he remained president until 1986) which ranged from astrology and Arthurian legend to the healing of the planet and transpersonal psychology.

Writings or **Hagiographa.** The third section of the Hebrew scriptures (see TANAKH). The Writings contain: *Psalms, *Proverbs, *Job, the *Song of Songs, *Ruth, *Lamentations, *Ecclesiastes, *Esther, *Daniel, *Ezra, *Nehemiah, and 1 and 2 *Chronicles.

Wu (Chin., 'not/non-being'). Key concept in *Taoism, denoting the absence of qualities perceivable by the senses, but not 'non-existent'. It is the basic characteristic of *Tao, whose emptiness of attributes does not deprive it of character and effect, as *Tao-te ching* (11) tries to explain: 'Shape clay into a pot: it is the space in the hollow that makes it useful; open doors and windows for a room: it is the opening which illuminates and gives access'. To understand the emptiness of character in the Tao which nevertheless is its truth is to be drawn into becoming an expression of the same in one's own life, through active inactivity (*wu-wei). Thus wu may also be the word through which the state of that realization is expressed.

Wu-ch'ang (Chin., 'five constants'). The five cardinal virtues in *Confucianism: (i) *jen, empathy; (ii) *i, propriety; (iii) *li, rights and customs observed; (iv) *chih*, insight, wisdom; (v) *hsin*, mutual trust. They have their corresponding types of relationship (*wu-lun*), which form the basis of society: (i) parent and child; (ii) ruler and subject; (iii) husband and wife; (iv) older and younger children; (v) friend and friend.

Wu-chen Pien (Treatise on Awakening to Truth). Work of Cheng Po-tuan of the inner elixir school (see NEI-TAN). He rejected the outer elixir (*wai-tan*) quest for external means to immortality, contending that all humans contain what is necessary within. This work sets out the ways of mobilizing these interior resources. The work became an important text for *Ch'üan-chen tao.

Wu-chi (Chin., 'summit of nothingness'). According to Taoists, the primordial, unconfined, limitless source to which all manifestation returns; cf. FU.

Wu-ch'in-hsi (Chin., 'movement of the five animals'). *Taoist exercises, developed by Hua T'o (2nd/3rd cent. CE), to resist ageing, by adapting the different means through which animals distribute *ch'i within the body. The five are bear, bird, monkey, stag, tiger.

J. Zöller, *Das Tao der Selbstheilung* (1984).

Wu-chi-t'u (diagram of emptiness): see CH'EN T'UAN.

Wudū' (minor ablution in Islam): see ABLUTIONS.

Wu-hsing, also known as **wu-te** (Chin., 'five movers'). Five virtues, the five elements which work as agents, fundamental in Chinese and Taoist understanding of the cosmos and history. The five are not physical substances, but the metaphysical forces associated with the nature of the substances. The five are wood, fire; earth; metal, water. The basic identifications are obvious, connected with the seasons and the cycle of life: spring, summer—autumn, winter. Earth mediates between the four, sustaining and being sustained by them. The correspondences derived by analogy from the basic identifications produced a comprehensive symbolic code applying to every aspect of life and the cosmos. In particular, it was worked into the theory of dynasties, identifiable from the colour of the controlling agent. Important in the Yin-yang school (*Tsou Yen), wu-hsing received its most complex application in the work of *Tung Chung-shu. In combination with *yin-yang, wu-hsing remains important in divination.

Wu-lun: see WU-CH'ANG.

Wu-men Hui-k'ai (1183–1260). Chinese Buddhist. Successor of Wu-tsu Fa-yen in the Yang-ch'i line of *Rinzai, although in an offshoot represented in the teacher Yüeh-an Shan-kuo (whose eyes were like meteors and acts like lightning), whose dharma-successor (*hassu) he became. He was also taught by Yueh-lin, who set him the *mu* *kōan; after six years he had not progressed through it, and he resolved not to sleep until he did so. In a desperate state, he heard the midday drum, and reached enlightenment—reflected in his verse, 'In a clear blue sky a thunderclap | All sentient beings have opened their eyes | Everything under the sun has swayed at once | Mount Semeru has jumped up and danced the people's dance.' In 1228 he assembled the kōan collection named after him *Wu-men-kuan* or *Mumonkoan*—see KŌAN. His death poem is: 'Emptiness is not born | Emptiness does not pass away | When you know emptiness | You are not other than it.'

Wu-men-kuan (collection of Zen kōans): see KŌAN.

Wu-shan (federation of Ch'an/Zen monasteries): see GOSAN.

Wu-shih Ch'i-hou (Chin., 'five periods, seven stages'). *Taoist analysis of progress to the goal. First: (i) the mind is always on the move; (ii) the mind calms down; (iii) calm and movement are in balance; (iv) calm predominates by concentration on an object of meditation; (v) the mind rests and is not 'kept going' by external inputs. Next: (i) anxiety then subsides; (ii) the appearance reverts to that of a child at rest, but supernatural powers develop; (iii) the condition of immortal (*hsien) is attained; (iv) *ch'i is perfected, and the perfect being (*chen-jen) emerges; (v) *shen-jen is attained; (vi) harmony with all forms is attained; (vii) perfect harmony with *Tao is realized in the practice of life.

Wūtai (mountain): see PILGRIMAGE.

Wu-t'ai-shan ('Five Terrace Mountain'). Place of pilgrimage for Chinese Buddhists who venerate *Mañjuśri (Chin., Wen-shu). It is in Shansi province. Nearly sixty of the monasteries survive from the more than 200 of its heyday (6th cent. CE).

Wu-te (five virtues): see WU-HSING.

Wu-tou-mi Tao ('five pecks of rice Taoism'). School of religious *Taoism (*tao-chiao*), founded by *Chang Tao-ling (2nd cent. CE) and his grandson, *Chang Lu. Those wishing to join paid five pecks of rice to the functionaries (*tao-shih), hence the name. The leaders were called *tien-shih, celestial masters, and this is another name for the school, the Celestial Master, or Heavenly Master, School. Based on *Lao-tzu, it interprets **Tao-te ching* in both an esoteric and a practical direction, especially in eliminating fault (by fasting and confession) to eradicate impediments in realizing *Tao. It also practised *ho ch'i* (see FANG-CHU SHU), the sexual ritual, 'the union of vital breaths'. It has continued to the present day, more respectfully known as *cheng-yi*, 'the Orthodox way'.

Wu-tsu Fa-yen (exponent of kōans): see KŌAN.

Wu-tsung (814–46). Chinese emperor (841–6) of the T'ang dynasty, who espoused the claims of religious *Taoism (*tao-chiao*) for the attainment of immortality. The Taoist hierarchy (*tao-shih) urged the suppression of their rivals, the Buddhists, and edicts were issued which led to the virtual destruction of institutional Buddhism:

> If even one man fails to work the fields, someone goes hungry; if only one woman neglects her silk-worms, someone goes cold. There are now innumerable monks and nuns in the empire waiting for farmers to feed them and silkworms to clothe them. . . . If Buddhism is completely abolished now, who will argue that this is not appropriate? Already over a hundred thousand idle Buddhists have been expelled, and countless of their gaudy, useless buildings destroyed. (845)

The principle from this was established that a religion in China will only be allowed if the state permits it; and that 'foreign' religions are suspect. This principle (and often specific appeal to Wu-tsung) remains to the present day.

Wu-wei (Chin., 'not/non-doing'). The mode of being and action in *Taoism which 'goes with the grain' of the way of Tao in bringing manifest forms into appearance. It is not total lack of activity, but, rather, active inactivity which allows the way of Tao to be expressed. It is described in **Tao-te ching* 48: 'The world is ruled by letting things run their course, not by interfering.' See also HSÜAN-HSÜEH. Wu-wei was adapted into Buddhism (especially Ch'an/Zen), where it approximates more closely to 'the unconditioned'.

Wyclif(fe), John (*c*.1329–84). English philosopher, theologian, and proponent of reform. Born at Wycliffe-on-Tees, he studied at Oxford and attained a D.Th. in 1372/3. He was resident in Oxford for most of his life, but in accordance with contemporary practice he was also appointed to the living of Fillingham, was made canon of Westbury-on-Trym, was appointed to Ludgershall, and to the rectory of Lutterworth (1374). His skills as a philosopher and controversialist were quickly recognized in Oxford and beyond, especially by John of Gaunt and later the king. He was present at Parliament in 1371, and his doctrinal views were vigorously opposed by his ecclesiastical contemporaries. His views were not wholly original, and were somewhat protected by the fact that they were normally expressed within the university. However, he engendered controversy by stressing the importance of civil powers within the Church, which scandalized the *pope and leading clergy. He is chiefly remembered for his opposition to *transubstantiation and his support for vernacular scripture. Some of his ideas were preserved in Wycliffe's *Wicket*, but his major achievements were to provide a translation of the Bible in English, and to put forward views on the Church which were later promoted by the *Lollards—few of whom shared his high theological aspirations. His influence on, and contacts with, the *Hussites in Bohemia are still a matter of academic dispute. He died in his bed before *heresy was an issue in England (many of his followers did not), but his bones and books were subsequently burnt and scattered (hence the common metaphor, from Fuller to Wordsworth, of the flow from Avon to Severn to sea, standing for the dissemination of his beliefs): 'Though they digged up his body, burned his bones and drowned his ashes, yet the word of God and the truth of his doctrine, with the fruit and success thereof, they could not burn' (John *Foxe). He is recognized in the Church of England Lesser Festivals, 6 Oct.

K. B. MacFarlane, *John Wycliffe* . . . (1952).

X

Xavier, Francis (Jesuit priest and missionary): see FRANCIS XAVIER.

Xenoglossolalia (speaking in a language unknown to the speaker but known to the hearer): see GLOSSOLALIA.

Xerophagia (Gk., dry nourishment). An intensification, in E. Churches, of the *Lenten fast during the beginning (Monday to Thursday) of *Holy Week. Water is allowed, but otherwise only bread, onions, and salt, with herbs and garlic.

Xi'an: see SIAN.

Xizang Autonomous Region. Chinese name for Tibet (see TIBETAN RELIGION; DALAI LAMA).

Y

Yab-Yum (Father-Mother). The iconographical representation of two deities in ritualized intercourse (Skt., *maithuna) in Tibetan Buddhism. Although such Tantric representations have a long Indian history, the Yab-Yum, with an active female astride and facing a passive male, is a peculiarly Tibetan style. Equally germane to Tibet is the deviation from Hinduism in the attribution of symbolic qualities—the female consort (*mudrā*) is not a *śakti (power) but a *prajñā (Tib., *shes.rab*, 'wisdom') who also represents *śūnyatā (Tib., *stong.pa.-nyid*, 'emptiness'). The qualities of the male consort are *upāya (Tib., *thabs*, 'skilful means') and *karuṇā (Tib., *snying.rje*, 'compassion'). The two are said to make one *ontological whole, and also to represent the indivisibility of the two truths—ultimate truth and relative truth. While the function of the Yab-Yum is primarily as an instructive *symbolism that may also serve as a basis for *visualization, its actual enactment through the taking of Tantric consorts is not unknown.

Yad (pointer): see TORAH ORNAMENTS.

Yad Fāṭima (symbol/charm of power): see HAND OF FĀṬIMA.

Yad Vashem (memorial to victims of the *Holocaust): see ḤASIDEI UMMOT HA-ʿOLAM.

Yahad (Heb., 'Unity'). A term used in the *Dead Sea Scrolls to express the unifying spirit of the sect. The members of the group are described as 'men of the yahad'.

Yahrzeit (lit., 'year's time'). The anniversary of a death in Judaism. Yahrzeit is observed on the anniversary of the death of parents, spouse, siblings, and children, and also for great individuals (see LAG BA-OMER). *Kaddish is recited, and a twenty-four-hour memorial candle is lit. Among the *Sephardim, the practice is called *naḥalah* ('inheritance'), and it is widely observed throughout the Jewish community.

H. Rabinowicz, *A Guide to Life* (1964).

Yahweh. The God of Judaism as the *tetragrammaton, YHWH, *may* have been pronounced. By Orthodox and many other Jews, God's name is never articulated, least of all in the Jewish liturgy; for alternatives to the attempts to guess at the pronunciation, see TETRAGRAMMATON.

Yahwist. The supposed editor of one of the hypothetical sources of the Jewish *Pentateuch. According to *Wellhausen, the Pentateuch was compiled from four separate sources. The oldest source, known as J because it uses the *tetragrammaton to refer to God, was composed by the Yahwist, and is thought to date from the 9th cent. BCE. However, in recent years the documentary hypothesis has come under question once more.

R. N. Whybray, *The Making of the Pentateuch* (1987).

Yahya. Islamic form of *John the Baptist.

Yajamāna (instigator of sacrifice): see SACRIFICE.

Yajña (Hindu sacrifice): see SACRIFICE.

Yajñavalkya. Hindu sage at the court of King *Janaka, to whom *Vājasaneyi-saṁhitā*, known also as *White *Yajur Veda*, is attributed. This work was said to have been revealed to him by the sun in the form of a horse (*vājin*), from which he came to be called Vājasaneya. The adherents of the school which he founded were then called Vājasaneyins. Other works attributed to him include **Śatapatha Brāhmaṇa*, to which *Bṛhadāranyaka Upaniṣad* is attached. This includes his dispute with *brahman philosophers, and his instruction to Maitreyī, one of his two wives (2. 4. 1 ff., including 2. 4. 12):

> It is as salt in water which dissolves in it: there is no longer salt to be gathered from it, as it were, but wherever one takes from it, it is salty: so this being of ours [*bhūta] . . . is just a complex of knowledge: arising out of the elements of being [bhūta], into them one vanishes away. After death, there is no consciousness.

Yajñopavītā (receiving of the thread in Hindu 'sacred thread' ceremony): see UPANAYANA.

Yajur Veda (Skt.). The *Vedic collection of sacrificial prayers (*yajus*) used by the Adhvaryu priest. Of the four *Vedas, it most reflects the Vedic sacrifice in its ritual character and full scope, concerning itself with the Full and New Moon sacrifice, the *Soma sacrifice, and the *Agnicayana. Many of the prayers are taken from the **Ṛg Veda*. Nevertheless, the *yajus* is distinct from the *ṛc* of the *Ṛg Veda* and the *sāman* of the *Sāma Veda in being a prose unit. The *Yajur Veda* has two major divisions: the *Black Yajur Veda* existing in four versions and the *White Yajur Veda* existing in two versions. The recensions of the *Black Yajur Veda* are probably older, showing less corruption in the *mantra portions of the text. The titles appear to have arisen as polemical terms used by the followers of the White school to characterize the purity of their tradition. Unlike the *Black Yajur Veda*, which interwove mantra and *brāhmaṇa, the *White*

Yajur Veda arranged these as wholly separate. Keith estimated the recension of the *Black Yajur Veda* at not later than 600 BCE.

R. Griffith, *The Texts of the White Yajurveda* (1957); A. B. Keith, *The Veda of the Black Yajus School* (1967).

Yakkha (Pāli; Skt., *Yakṣa). 1. In Buddhism, historical and legendary communities. References to Yakkhas belong to three main types or classes: (i) the records of Buddhist contact with individual Yakkhas or communities of Yakkhas: either those whose tribal territories were brought to the very borders of the Empires by the fast expansion of the latter or those who were actually living within the domains of the Empires, having been dislocated from their tribal lands; (ii) the records showing the actual process of amalgamation of the Yakkha tribes with the 'cultured peoples'; (iii) the records which preserve the myths and legends of the Yakkhas as they persisted in society long after the Yakkhas lost their tribal identities. Discourses such as the *Ālavaka Sutta* (1. 213), the *Suciloma Sutta* (1. 207), and the *Indaka Sutta* (1. 206) of the *Saṃyutta Nikāya* belong to the first type. These are examples of Buddhist contact with the Yakkha tribal groups whose homelands came within the range of influence of the contemporary monarchical powers. These contacts resulted in winning many converts from the Yakkha tribes to Buddhism. The Buddha persuaded some of these Yakkha tribal chieftains to accept items of food in place of raw flesh for their ritual offerings.

The *Ālavaka Sutta* and the *Suciloma Sutta* are excellent examples also of the second type as in these we witness the actual process of winning over the Yakkha tribal peoples taking place. The *Sānu Sutta* (1. 208), the *Piyankaramātā Sutta* (1. 209) and the *Punabbasumātā Sutta* (1. 209) belong also to this second type. It was this merging with the cultured peoples which cost the Yakkhas their separate identity as a tribe, thus leaving only the myths and legends, especially of the Yakkhas as comprising the retinue of Vessavaṇa, one of the four Great Kings of the gods (*cattāro mahārājāno*). Two important discourses coming under this third type are the *Janavasabha Sutta* (2. 200 f.) and the *Āṭānāṭiya Sutta* (3. 194 f.) of the *Dīgha Nikāya*. Of the two, the *Āṭānāṭiya Sutta* is also important in that it contains a post-early Buddhistic concession made to tribal beliefs and ritual which is characteristic only of the post-Mauryan religio-ritualistic syncretism in India.

2. Supernatural beings in Buddhism (cf. Hindu *yakṣa) who may be neutral in their relations to humans, but who more often are malevolent. Deriving the name from *yaj*, 'sacrifice', they came to be regarded as beings to whom sacrifices have been offered, and were thus thought of as 'flesh-devourers'. They are the opponents especially of the *saṅgha.

Yakṣa. Collective name for supernatural beings in Hinduism, who inhabit the countryside and forests, but became especially associated with the sacred trees in villages. They can assume any form, and often appear as the servants of *Kubera, the god of wealth. They can be beneficent or malevolent, but are usually known as *punyajana*, 'good beings', to propitiate them in advance.

In Jainism, they are attendants on each of the twenty-four *tīrthaṅkaras.

A. K. Coomaraswamy, *Yakshas* (1928, 1931).

Yakushi. Jap. for *Bhaisajya-guru Buddha.

Yakushi-ji (temple-complex): see NARA BUDDHISM.

Yā Latīf (Islamic prayer): see PRAYER.

Yali Movement. A *cargo cult on the Rai coast of New Guinea, especially among the Tangu people. Yali Singina was a well-travelled and able ex-sergeant-major from the war with the Japanese, who enjoyed enormous prestige. He at first opposed the Letub cargo cult, when it was revived in 1946 and sought to adopt him as a leader who had returned from the dead; instead, he supported the government development programme. After disillusionment with Christianity and European ways, he became violently anti-mission and joined the Letub leaders in reviving traditional mythology and developing a mass movement; this led to clashes with the government and to Yali's imprisonment, 1950–5. Support for Yali increased in the 1960s, although by 1974 he had again repudiated cargoism. After his death in 1975 the movement was reorganized as the Lo-Bos ('law-boss') movement based on the town of Madang, with weekly meetings for confessions of law-breaking, moral and social discipline, and messages from Yali or the spirits.

Yalkut (Heb., 'compilation'). Title of several Jewish *midrashic anthologies. The best-known Yalkut are the *Yalkut Shimoni* (13th cent.) which covers the whole Bible, the *Yalkut ha-Makhiri* (14th cent.), and the *Yalkut Reuveni* (17th cent.) which has been arranged to correspond to the weekly readings of the *Torah *Scroll.

Yama (Skt., 'restraint'). 1. The god of death in Hinduism and Buddhism, also called *Dharma Rāja, possibly connected with the Iranian *Yima. In the **Ṛg Veda* he appears in books 1 and 10 presiding over the ancestors or 'fathers' (*pitṛ) in the third (highest) heaven of the sky (*svarga) realm (above atmosphere, *bhuvah*, and earth, *bhūr*). In the **Kaṭha* **Upaniṣad*, Yama bestows highest knowledge. *Naciketas has been banished to the realm of Yama, but has to wait three days for his return, upon which Yama grants Naciketas three wishes. His first wish is to return to his father, the second is knowledge of the Naciketa fire sacrifice to gain immortality (*amṛta) in heaven (svarga *loka), and the third is knowledge about death and the soul. To this last wish Yama replies that the soul (*ātman) is eternal and that God (*deva) is realized through meditating on one's own self (ādhyātma *yoga). Post-Vedic mythology in contrast portrays Yama as a judge and punisher of the dead in a lower world where the soul (ātman, *jīva, *puruṣa) goes after death and receives its sentence after an account of its actions (*karma) is read out by Citragupta the recorder. In the *Mahābhārata*, however, a good warrior goes to *Indra's realm and not Yama's. The *Mahābhārata* depicts Yama as clothed in red with glaring eyes, holding a noose with which to bind the souls of the dead. This image is embellished in later mythology where he is a terrible deity inflicting torture upon souls. Yama is associated with the south, the realm of the dead.

In Buddhism, Yama is the Lord of the Underworld. In some respects, he is replaced by *Māra. The canonical account of Yama is contained mainly in the two almost identical *Devadūta Suttas* in *Majjhima Nikāya* 3. 179 ff., and *Anguttara Nikāya* 1. 138 ff. In this account, although Yama is still (after his pre-Buddhist image) retained as the Lord of a kind of *purgatory system, he does not function as the judge who decides on the type, nature, place, or duration of the punishment that beings must undergo in expiation of their karmic misdeeds. Such determination is made by the self-operative law of kamma/karma which does not need the mediation of a god like Yama for its operation.

According to the accounts of the two suttas referred to above, when beings who are born into the purgatory system are led before Yama, he enquires whether they have seen the divine messengers (which are birth, old age, illness, punishment for crime, and death) and have taken due heed. When the reply is in the negative, he reminds them that it is they themselves who have committed the misdeeds and therefore must suffer the consequences. After this, Yama keeps silent and the subjects are taken away by the administrators of the purgatory system (*nirayapālā*) who see them through the painful process of expiatory suffering.

According to the commentaries, the torturers themselves are born in that capacity due to their previous bad karma. Even the role of purgatorial administrator is not therefore an advantage under any circumstances. Quite in keeping with the general pattern of the initial adoption and the subsequent adaptation of the other gods, Yama too has been relieved of his essential functions. Thus he performs neither an essential nor an indispensable function in Buddhism.

In the post-canonical Buddhist literature, Yama is depicted as the overlord of the purgatory system who assigns to beings the punishments they must undergo in expiation of their karmic misdeeds. In *Tantric Buddhism, Yama is a fierce deity. Tibetan iconography and the **Tibetan Book of the Dead* (*Bardo Thodol*) portray Yama, who appears at death, as standing in a halo of flames, adorned with human skulls and heads, holding in his left hand the mirror of karma (which reflects the good and bad deeds of the deceased) and in his right hand the sword of wisdom (*prajña).

S. Bhattacharji, *The Indian Theogony* . . . (1970); M. M. J. Marasinghe, *Gods in Early Buddhism* (1974).

2. The first limb of eight-limbed (*aṣṭaṅga*) or *rāja *yoga comprising five ethical rules: (i) non-injury (*ahiṁsā), (ii) truthfulness (*satya), (iii) non-stealing (*asteya*), (iv) celibacy (*brahmacarya), and (v) greedlessness (*aparigraha*). Commitment to these is the Great Vow (Mahāvrata).

Yamabushi (mountain ascetics): see FUJISAN; SHUGENDŌ.

Yāmala (Skt., 'pair'). 1. The goal of the *sādhaka's spiritual practice (*sādhana) conceived as the union of *Śiva and *Śakti.

2. An old group of texts in *Tantrism such as the *Brahma-yāmala*, *Rudra-yāmala*, and *Jayadratha-yāmala*. These are Śaiva texts with *Bhairava as the central deity but with strong Śākta tendencies. Dating from the 6th to the 9th cents. CE, they are a source of Śaiva and *Kaula developments in Kashmir (see KASHMIR ŚAIVISM), and can be regarded as the articulation of a cremation-ground tradition. The subject-matter of these texts is typically Tantric, concerning the quest for perfection by erotic and horrific means. Subjects discussed include *bindu, various śaktis, spiritual success (*siddhi), deities who are forms of *Kali, the mystical nature of speech (*vāc), and rituals involving the use of alchohol, corpses, and sexual intercourse with a menstruating woman (śakti).

Yamamoto Gempō (1866–1961). Prominent Zen Buddhist of his time, sometimes called 'the 20th-cent. *Hakuin'. A foundling, with poor eyesight, he was virtually illiterate. He abandoned his wife and home to seek Zen training, receiving the seal of recognition (*inka-shōmei) from Sōhan. He specialized in the way of writing (*shōdō*: see ART (CH'AN/ZEN)), and the Zen of indifference—remaining fond of wine and women.

Yama no Kami (mountain deities): see FESTIVALS AND FASTS.

Yamaoka Tesshu (1836–88). Zen layman who became the major exponent of the way of the sword (*kendō). He was also an outstanding calligrapher and painter.

J. Stevens, *The Sword of No-Sword* (1989).

Yamazaki Ansai (1618–82). A leading Japanese advocate of *Shushigaku during the Tokugawa (1600–1868) period. His school stressed *Chu Hsi's moral and ethical teachings, with an emphasis on memorization and moral rigour. Eager to reconcile *neo-Confucian metaphysics with *Shinto theology, Yamazaki Ansai also formulated his own school of Shinto called Suika Shintō; in the end, Shinto is in control:

Yamazaki Ansai once asked his students, 'If China were to attack our country, with *Confucius as general and *Mencius as second-in-command, what do you think we, as students of Confucius and Mencius, should do?' The students were unable to answer. 'If that were to happen,' Yamazaki told them, 'I would put on armour, take up a spear and fight until I brought them captive to the service of my country; for that is what Confucius and Mencius teach us to do.'

Yamoussoukro (site of basilica in the Ivory Coast): see BASILICA OF NOTRE DAME DE PAIX.

Yāmuna (known in Tamil as Āḷavandār; 10th/11th cent.). One of the early leaders of the *Śrīvaiṣṇava movement in S. India. Little is known of him beyond the story that after a life in some authority (perhaps as a local ruler), he was converted to the service of God by reading the *Bhagavad-gītā*. Six works are attributed to him in which the foundations of the Śrīvaiṣṇavite devotion and of *Viśiṣṭādvaita can be found. He is said by one biography to have been *Rāmānuja's most revered teacher, but by others to have indicated Rāmānuja as his successor, but to have died before they could meet. His *Āgama-prāmāṇya* (tr. J. A. B. van Buitenen, 1971) argues that temple worship (*pūjā) has displaced Vedic ritual.

M. Narasimhachari, *The Contribution of Yāmuna* . . . (1971); W. G. Neevel, *Yāmuna's Vedānta and Pāñcarātra* . . . (1971).

Yamunā or **Jumna.** One of the seven Hindu *sacred rivers.

Yāna ('path, course', 'journey', 'vehicle, carriage'). A 'way' of progress, especially in Buddhism. The term is best known in *Mahāyāna Buddhism, but it occurs in early Buddhism as well. Texts in the *Pāli canon refer to the eightfold path as yāna (*Therīgāthā* 389) and say that 'by that yāna shall men and women be in the presence of *Nirvāna' (*Samyutta Nikāya* 1. 33). In *Samyutta Nikāya* 5. 5, man has a cart (*ratha*) drawn by pure white mares and people say it is the best of vehicles (brahma-yāna). The *Buddha is asked: Can one point to the best of vehicles in this teaching (*dhamma-vinaya*)? He replies that one can call the noble eightfold path the best of vehicles, the vehicle of the *dharma (*dhamma-yāna*): 'This cart (*ratha*) rolls on to complete security (*yogakkhema*; a synonym of nibbāna) . . . in this best of vehicles, the wise get out of the world.' Similarly, the post-canonical *Milinda-pañha* (276) says that mounting the vehicle of accomplishment (iddhi-yāna; perhaps 'vehicle of (extraordinary) transformation'), one arrives at the city of Nirvāna.

Much of the Mahāyāna understanding of yāna is adumbrated in these passages. The *locus classicus* for the later use of the term is ch. 3 of the *Lotus Sūtra* (*Saddharmapuṇḍarīka Sūtra*), which relates the parable of the burning house. In order to entice his sons (all beings) out of an old and decaying house (*saṃsāra) that is engulfed by fire (suffering), the father (the Buddha) offers three kinds of cart (*ratha*) pulled by goats, deer, and bullocks. Wishing to have these toys, the children rush out of the house. But the father gives them all the third and best kind of cart, the one drawn by great (mahā) white bullocks. This cart is the great vehicle (mahā-yāna). (The other two are vehicles suited to people of lesser spiritual aspirations.) It is explicitly stated in this chapter that the Buddha's action is skill-in-means (*upāya-kauśalya). He offers three kinds of yāna but only actually gives one—the mahā-yāna or buddha-yāna or eka-yāna ('single vehicle')—which leads all beings to become Buddhas (*Lotus Sūtra* 3. 89–91).

This running together of the terms *upāya and yāna is crucial to understanding the meaning of yāna in Mahāyāna texts, and it has a number of far-reaching consequences that totally transform its usage (compared with early Buddhism). First, yāna refers to the various means (upāya) that are used by the Buddha to bring beings to enlightenment.

Secondly, because these devices are really only modifications of the one truth, yāna also means that one truth or liberation itself. *Laṅkāvatāra Sūtra* (286) says that the yāna is known within oneself (*pratyātma-vedya*). According to the *Śrīmālā Sūtra*, the two lesser vehicles are included in the great vehicle, mahā-yāna; the mahā-yāna is the buddha-yāna; the three vehicles are counted as one vehicle (eka-yāna). This one vehicle is synonymous with enlightenment, with nirvāna and with the dharma-body (dharma-kāya: see TRIKĀYA) of the Buddha. 'The ultimate realization of the Dharmakāya is the one vehicle' (*The Lion's Roar of Queen Śrīmālā*, tr. A. & H. Wayman, 1974, p. 92).

Thirdly, because this eka-yāna is the same as the Buddha, it can never be limited or defined or even pointed to. Here we enter the paradoxes of Mahāyāna metaphysics. One cannot get at the beginning, middle, or end of this one great vehicle (*Aṣṭasāhasrikā-Prajñāpāramitā Sūtra* 23); hence in the last analysis, there is no yāna and no one who rides it (*Laṅka* 135). It is just like space, which contains all forms but itself has no form and can never be got hold of. In typical Mahāyāna style, therefore, we are offered everything and nothing at the same time.

Yang (constituent energy in the universe): see YIN-YANG.

Yang-ch'i Fang-hui (school of Ch'an/Zen Buddhism): see YŌGI SCHOOL.

Yang-ch'i-tsung (the Chinese name): see YŌGI SCHOOL.

Yang Chu (fl. *c.*450 BCE). Early Chinese philosopher. He seems to have taught a doctrine of self-preservation in opposition to hedonism. No complete work of his survives, but he is often referred to in later works such as *Lü-shih ch'un ch'iu* (Mr Lü's Springs and Autumns), which may preserve authentic fragments from his writings or sayings, and *Huai-nan tzu*. He is perhaps best known for constantly being labelled by the early Confucian thinker *Mencius as one of his key philosophical opponents.

Yang-hsing (Chin., 'nourishing the life principle'). Collective term for Taoist exercises to prolong life and attain immortality, whether addressed to body (*yang-sheng) or mind (*yang-shen).

Yang-shan Hui-chi (Jap., Kyōzan Ejaku; *c*.810–*c*.887). Ch'an/Zen master, dharma-successor (*hassu) of Kuei-shan Ling-yu (see KUEI-YANG TSUNG), and so renowned that he became known as 'the little Śākyamuni'. His parents opposed his early inclination to become a monk until he presented them with two of his chopped-off fingers as a mark of his determination. He visited many masters, including *Ma-tsu and *Pai-chang, but found perfect connection with Kuei-shan. The two are regarded as co-founders of the Igyo school, with its emphasis on the ninety-seven circles of contemplation.

Yang-shen (Chin., 'nourishing the mind'). Taoist practice, especially of the inner deity hygiene school (see TAOISM), to prevent the inner deities from leaving the body.

Yang-sheng (Chin., 'nourishing the body'). Taoist practices, especially through breathing and directing the breath (*ch'i) to prolong life and attain immortality.

Yannai (3rd cent. CE). Jewish *amora. Yannai was of *priestly descent and a pupil of R. Ḥiyya. Yannai established an academy, and his rulings are frequently quoted in the *Talmud. He was the originator of the principle that danger may not be incurred in the expectation of a *miracle (*B.Shab.* 32a), offering the wise advice, 'Never depend on a miracle.' He explained the involvement of the name of God (*El) in Israel by saying that 'God attached his name to that of Isra-el, as a king secures a key to his chain, in order that it may not be lost.'

Yantra (Skt., 'instrument for supporting'). A geometrical design representing the cosmos used in Hindu liturgy (*pūjā) and meditation (*dhyāna), especially in *Tantrism. Though akin to *maṇḍala, yantra differs in that it can be a three-dimensional object of worship made of stone or metal plates. Like maṇḍala, the yantra is a symbol of cosmogonic development from the absolute in the centre to the material world at the outer edges, and like maṇḍala is the visual equivalent of *mantra. Yantras often have a seed (*bīja) mantra inscribed upon them. In Tantric pūjā, the yantra, if made of stone or metal, is invested with power and meditated upon as the deity. There are various yantras for different magical purposes, such as protection, fulfilling desires, controlling others, or killing an enemy. The most famous yantra is the *Śrīyantra.

M. Khanna, *Yantra: The Tantric Symbol of Cosmic Unity* (1979).

Yaʿqūb. Islamic form of *Jacob.

Yaqui Church. A body in N. Mexico and Arizona. It derives from *Jesuit missions among the Yaqui people in Mexico from 1617 until the Jesuits were suppressed in 1767. Left on their own, with Yaqui religion now defunct, they integrated the new *Roman Catholic form with community life, and resisted Mexican government efforts to assimilate them. Many Yaqui migrated to Arizona in the late 19th cent. and now there are community villages centred upon the church at Guadalupe, Old Pascua, New Pascua, and Barrio Libre, with a total of some 5,500 members, and up to 3,000 scattered elsewhere. The great cycle of open-air ritual dramas features the biblical events in *Holy Week.

Yarmulke (Yid., etym. uncertain; the tradition that it is a corruption of the Heb. for 'in fear of God' is unlikely). Skull cap worn by *Orthodox Jewish men. The yarmulke is worn by the observant at all times as a sign of humility (*yirat Shama'im*, 'fear of the Heavenly One') before God. The less orthodox only cover their heads for prayer. The *custom is of relatively recent origin (*c*.17th cent.) and its religious basis lies in the proscription of *gentile practices (i.e. of uncovering the head as a sign of respect). See also HEAD, COVERING OF; HAIR.

Yasna (from *yaz*, 'sacrifice, worship'). Worship among Zoroastrians (the word is akin to *yajña). Yasna is an obligation in general, originally undertaken in close proximity to the creations of *Ahura Mazda, in conditions of great purity, and only later in temples. Yasna is also the daily ritual of Zoroastrians, with offerings to fire and water (*zaothra). The offering is made by a zaotar/zot, and is not congregational. The offering to fire, which initially involved blood sacrifice, creates a sense of bonding between animals and humans, in which the souls of humans, and of domestic and wild animals, are equally reverenced. It came to be believed that the souls of animals which had died in sacrifice, or consecrated, were absorbed into Geush Urvan, the Bull Soul. The involvement of that which has given life by way of food was recognized in the scattering of grass. The offering to water was made from milk, the pressed leaves of one plant, and stem of another. The last of these was called *haoma* (Avestan = Skt., *soma), and from its importance derived the divine priest, Haoma, the recipient of a share of each sacrifice. These elements continue to the present day. Yasna is also the name of the liturgical text recited during the ritual, the central section of which, Staota yesna, is believed to be the most powerful *manthra* (cf. Skt., *mantra). Of central importance are the *Gāthās.

J. J. Modi, *Religious Ceremonies and Customs of the Parsees* (2nd edn., 1937).

Yaśovijaya (1624–88). Jain logician who set himself the task of reconciling conflicting sects. He was born in Gujarat and belonged initially to the Tapa *Gaccha, tracing his lineage back to *Hīravijaya. He studied at *Kāśi (Benares), concentrating especially on logic. He endeavoured to show the interior correspondences and meanings of external religious acts, e.g. in *Jñānasāra* (tr. A. S. Gopani, 1986). His attempt to heal divisions among the Jains had as much success as such endeavours generally have, i.e. very little.

Yasukuni shrine (Shinto shrine in Tokyo): see KAMIKAZE.

Yathrib. Original name of al-*Madīna.

Yati (Skt.). One who practises a discipline in Indian religions, an *ascetic.

Yaum al-Dīn. The Day of Judgement in Islam, succeeding immediately the day of resurrection (*yaum al-Qiyāma), so that the two can be regarded as parts of the same event, and are often virtually synonymous. It is the day when each person's deeds will be weighed on an exact balance (Qur'ān 7. 8 f.; 21. 47; 23. 103 f.; 101. 6–9), and the book of record for each person will be opened (10. 61; 17. 13 f., etc.). No one can help another; but the possibility of intercession (*shafā'a), as it was accepted in Islam, modified the strict accounting.

Yaum al-Qiyāma. The day of resurrection in Islam. Referred to frequently in the *Qur'ān as a matter of certainty (against the scepticism of *Muḥammad's opponents), it is likened to the power of God to bring new life from the dead earth. The descriptions of what it will be like are frequent and detailed. It is preceded by signs of the End, especially the appearance of *al-Dajjāl (Antichrist) and of 'Īsā/*Jesus who will destroy him (and/or of *al-Mahdī to the same effect). There will then be a period of order and faith. At the first blast of the final trumpet, all will die; at the second, after an interval, all, including the previously dead, will be brought to life again. After a period of standing (and sweating) in the presence of *Allāh, the day of judgement (*yaum al-dīn) begins. The division into *heaven (*janna*) and *hell (*jahannam*) follows.

J. W. Bowker, *The Meanings of Death* (1991).

Yavez (pen-name): see EMDEN, JACOB.

Yavneh (centre of early rabbinic Judaism): see JABNEH; ACADEMIES.

Ya-yüeh (elegant music): see MUSIC.

Yazatas (worshipful beings): see AHURA MAZDA.

Yazīdīs (religious movement): see YEZĪDĪS.

Yazrain ('two inclinations'): see INCLINATION, GOOD AND EVIL.

Year (religious): see CALENDAR.

Yehuda (common Jewish name derived from the son of the Jewish patriarch, Jacob): see JUDAH.

Yehudai ben Naḥman or **Yehudai Gaon** (8th cent.). Head of the Jewish *academy of *Sura. Yehudai was described by the *exilarch as having 'no equal in knowledge'. He was the first *gaon to write a book, the *Halakhot Pesukot*, and the first to compile *responsa. He rested his decisions entirely on the Babylonian *Talmud, and through his influence the Babylonian rather than the Palestinian Talmud became the basis of halakhic decisions. He and his pupils defended the *oral law against the *Karaites, and it was said by *Sherira ben Ḥanina that 'we may not do what Yehudai refrained from doing'. See also CODIFICATIONS OF LAW.

Yelammedenu (Aram., 'let him pronounce'). The opening word of each sermon in the 4th-cent. **Tanḥuma*. It thus has become an alternative title for *Tanḥuma*.

Yellammā (Ellammaṉ, Eḷammā, Yēlū, and many further forms). A goddess of folk Hinduism, venerated particularly in Mahārāṣṭra, Karṇāṭaka, and further south, by the lower *castes. The most likely etymology of her name is from a Dravidian *ēḻ*, 'seven', and *ammaṉ*, 'mother, goddess', and thus alludes to a belief, found all over W. India, in the 'seven sisters' or 'seven mothers'. However, folk religion treats Yellammā as a single goddess and may at the most refer to *her* other sisters as minor figures. The main ritual centres of her worship are the temples of Mahūr (E. Mahārāṣṭra) and Saundattī (Karṇāṭaka), but in simpler form her worship is performed all over the area in the villages. A special group of devotees (deriving from children offered to her)—the *jogtī* (male) and *jogtīṇ* (female)—provides a connecting link between these two levels. They carry images of the goddess in a basket from door to door and recite songs in her honour, sometimes of considerable sophistication. Such songs narrate myths and legends about Yellammā who tends to manifest herself in order to make some, usually small, demand, or whose appearance is seen as a challenge by established authorities. She has to suffer tribulations and humiliation, and seemingly impossible tasks are imposed on her. But inevitably she succeeds in revealing her supreme power, taking her revenge on those who rejected her and granting her grace to those who accepted her. The antagonists range as widely as from gods, demons, farmers, to British Colonial officers and her own son whom she bore without the help of a male. This son, now, tends to get identified with the Sanskritic figure of *Paraśu-Rāma, and thereby Yellammā turns into his mother Reṇukā whose head he cuts off in obedience to his irascible father Jamadagni, Reṇukā's husband. Thus by being drawn into the purāṇic, Sanskrit tradition Yellammā loses her autonomous role as regional goddess.

Yellow Hats. In early Western writers on Tibetan Buddhism, the *Geluk school, who distinguish themselves from other schools by their wearing of yellow hats. See also RED HATS.

Yellow Turban rebellion (Taoist rebellion): see CHANG CHÜEH.

Yen-ch'i (Chin., 'swallowing breath'). A Taoist exercise in embryonic breathing (*tai-hsi*), which controls the level from which breath is exhaled. It is usually linked to *lien-ch'i.

Yen-t'ou Ch'uan-huo (Jap., Gantō Zenkatsu; 828–87). Ch'an/Zen master, dharma-successor (*hassu) of Te-shan Hsuan-chien. His death, murdered by robbers, caused the problem of 'Yen-tou's cry': far from accepting death with equanimity, he uttered a cry heard for miles around. *Hakuin solved the problem when he attained enlightenment and said, 'Indeed, Gantō is alive, strong, and well'.

Yeshivah (pl. yeshivot). Institute of Jewish *Talmudic learning. The term 'yeshiva' is applied to the *academies of Jewish learning in Babylonia and *Erez Israel in which the *amoraim studied the *Mishnah (see TALMUD), to the academies of *Sura and *Pumbedita in the *geonic period, and to later local Talmudic institutions. The earliest yeshivot to be established away from Babylonia or Erez Israel were those of the 8th cent. in Spain and N. Africa. From there the institution spread to Italy (9th cent.), France (10th cent.), Germany (11th cent.), Bohemia (12th cent.), and Austria (13th cent.); see TOSAFOT. In the 16th and 17th cents., there were several famous yeshivot in Poland, Russia, and Lithuania. Yeshivot were organized by prominent scholars who were supported by rich student and communal charities. By the mid-16th cent., many yeshivot were supported and governed by local community councils. The curriculum centred on the Talmud and its commentaries, although *minhagim, *posekim, and *responsa were also studied. By the 14th cent. (in *Ashkenazi communities) the requirements for *semikhah were formalized and the title of *rabbi was awarded on graduation. By the 20th cent., it was accepted in many areas that the curriculum should be broadened (see MUSAR; RABBINICAL SEMINARIES). The *Holocaust destroyed the yeshivot of E. Europe, but important yeshivot still exist in *Israel, the USA, and the British Commonwealth, many of which are connected with the *Habad movement. See Index, Yeshivot.

W. B. Helmreich, *The World of the Yeshiva* (1982).

Yeshivah of the right (academy for Torah study): see SURA (1).

Yeshiva University. Jewish *Orthodox institution of higher education. Yeshiva University was founded in 1897 in New York as the Rabbi Isaac Elhanan Theological Seminary for advanced *Talmudic study. The *rabbinical programme follows a traditional *yeshivah curriculum, but the university has absorbed other institutions and now includes a high school, a teachers' institute, an undergraduate college, a graduate school of secular studies, a college of medicine, and a school of social work.

Yeẓer ha-raʿ/ha-tov (evil/good inclination in Judaism): see INCLINATION, GOOD AND EVIL.

Yezīdīs, also **Yazīdī.** A religious community found among the Kurds of Iraq, Turkey, Syria, Germany, Armenia, and Georgia. Its nucleus was a Muslim *Sūfī brotherhood founded in Iraq by the Arab sheikh Adi b. Musafir (*c*.1075–1162 CE), a descendant of the *Umayyad caliphs (*khalīfa). In the 14th–15th cents., a distinct religion emerged and was adopted by a number of the semi-independent Kurdish tribes. Expansion of the Ottoman Empire and subsequent persecutions caused massive defections to Islam. But the religion survived in the Sheikhan district N. of Mosul (Iraq), and in the Jebel Sinjar mountains to the West. Yezidis are also found in SE Turkey (many of them now in Germany), the Jebel Siman mountains west of Aleppo (Syria), and in Armenia and Georgia. The total number of Yezīdīs is around 200,000, of whom half live in Iraq.

The distinctive feature of the religion—a monotheistic faith incorporating many Jewish, Christian, and Muslim traditions—is the belief that the fallen angel *Lucifer has been pardoned by God for his disobedience and that those who venerate him are the elect of humankind. This concept was thought to have been proclaimed by the Sūfī *al-Hallāj, but may be traceable to pre-Islamic religions. Some scholars suggest Manichaean or Zoroastrian origins, although dualism is not part of the Yezīdī religion. Belief in the transmigration of souls (into animals in the case of wicked people) may also reflect extraneous elements.

Yezīdīs are forbidden to use the term *Satan, whom they call Melek Taus ('Peacock Angel'). A large bronze image of a peacock is paraded at important festivals and for many years replicas were carried by alms-gatherers among Yezīdī villages. The Yezīdīs are not, however, devil-worshippers, as they have sometimes been called.

Illiterate until recently, the Yezīdīs derive their religious heritage from oral traditions. They have two 'sacred books', both written in Arabic. The *Jelwa* (Book of Revelation) is a short homily attributed to Sheikh Adi. The *Meshaf Resh* (Black Book), attributed to his great-grandnephew Sheikh Hassan (d. 1246), contains the Yezīdī version of *Genesis. A more recent document attached to the *Meshaf Resh* details the religious ceremonies and feasts.

The tomb of Sheikh Adi at Lalish (a mountain valley north of Mosul, often itself called 'Sheikh Adi') is the principal shrine of the Yezīdī religion. A five-day festival there in mid-Oct., attended by many pilgrims, includes ritual dancing, singing, and feasting, as well as secret ceremonies associated with the great peacock and with a spring of water called

Zemzem that gushes out of the rock beneath Sheikh Adi's tomb. Pellets made from local dust moistened with holy water are used as amulets by returning pilgrims. A spring festival in mid-Apr. is celebrated in every Yezīdī village.

The religious hierarchy consists of six categories, largely derived from Sūfī traditions: (i) sheikhs (cf. *shaykh): a hereditary caste of priests who preside at religious functions, the Baba Sheikh (chief sheikh) is in charge of the Lalish sanctuary and sometimes plays an important role in Yezīdī affairs; (ii) *pirs*: a secondary caste of priests, in attendance at religious functions but more concerned with meditation than with administrative matters; (iii) *kawals* (chanters): a caste of itinerant priests who preach and conduct services wherever Yezīdīs live, and also collect alms to support the Lalish sanctuary; (iv) *faqīrs: a category open to all but largely hereditary, whose function is to minister to Yezīdīs in the absence of a sheikh; (v) kocheks: a category open to anyone gifted with ecstatic powers, often employed as soothsayers; (vi) *murids*: the laymen of the community who support the religious hierarchy with regular and special contributions. The secular arm of the community is represented by the Mir of Sheikhan, who lives at Baadri, immediately south of Lalish. The Chol dynasty was established in the 17th cent., and was accorded semi-divine status. But the Mir's civil authority was curtailed by the extension of Ottoman bureaucracy in the 19th cent., followed by the British occupation of Iraq (1918–32, 1941–5). The most notable member of the Chol family was Mayan Khatun, who held a dominant position among the Yezīdīs, 1899–1957, as wife, mother, and grandmother of successive Mirs. The present (1995) Mir of Sheikhan, Tahsin Beg, succeeded in 1944.

J. S. Guest, *The Yezidis: A Study in Survival* (1987), reissued as *Survival among the Kurds* (1993); P. G. Kreyenbroek, *Yezidism: Its Background, Observances and Textual Tradition* (1995).

Yezirah, Sefer (Heb., 'Book of Creation'). An early Jewish mystical work. There is no scholarly consensus as to the date or place of origin of *Sefer Yezirah*. It was certainly in existence by the 10th cent. It is divided into six chapters and it discusses such matters as the derivation of the cosmos from the Hebrew alphabet and the ten *sefirot, but there is no clear explanation as to the relationship between the two. Knowledge of the mysteries of creation, including particular combinations of letters, supposedly confers magical powers on the initiated. *Sefer Yezirah* was an immensely influential text in the development of *kabbalistic thought and early Jewish philosophy. It was the subject of many commentaries, including those of *Saʿadiah Gaon, Abraham *ibn Ezra, Eleazar b. Judah of Worms, *Isaac the Blind, *Naḥmanides, Abraham *Abulafia, Moses b. Jacob *Cordovero, and *Elijah b. Solomon of Vilna.

G. Scholem, *On the Kabbalah and its Symbolism* (1966).

YHWH. Name of the Jewish God: see TETRAGRAMMATON.

Yibbum (Jewish obligation to ensure male descent): see LEVIRATE MARRIAGE.

Yidam (Tib., *yi.dam.*, 'bound in thought'). A class of tutelary deities in Tibetan Buddhism corresponding to the Indian *Iṣṭadevatā. It also parallels the Western concept of the *guardian angel, in that the yidam inspires, guides, and protects, although restricted in role to the context of *Tantric practice. The yidam selected by the *yogin may be that of his school or monastery, but often the choice is determined by personal feeling; having made his selection—which may be for life or for the duration of a particular practice—the yogin seeks to become 'bound in thought', i.e. identified, with the deity, who then assists the yogin towards *enlightenment. Yidams are classified in appearance as *wrathful, semi-wrathful, and peaceful, and are often considered as 'aspects' of well-known *bodhisattvas. For example, the wrathful yidam Yamāntaka is an aspect of *Mañjuśrī.

Yiddish (contracted from *Yidish-daytsh*, i.e. Jewish-German). Language used by *Ashkenazi Jews. Yiddish is related to German, but has many Slavic, Hebrew, and *Aramaic words, and it is written in the Hebrew script. From the time of the *Haskalah, it largely died out in W. Europe, but continued to be widespread among the communities of Poland, Lithuania, Hungary, the Ukraine, and Russia. Before the *Holocaust, there were estimated to be approximately eleven million Yiddish speakers.

E. Markowitz, *The Encyclopedia Yiddishicana* (1980); M. Weinreich, *A History of the Yiddish Language* (1979); U. Weinreich, *Modern English–Yiddish, Yiddish–English Dictionary* (1968).

Yigdal (Heb., 'May he be magnified'). Jewish *liturgical hymn. The hymn is based on *Maimonides' *Thirteen Principles of the Jewish faith. It is printed in the *Ashkenazi Siddur at the beginning of the daily *Shaḥarit service, and among the *Sephardim it is recited at the end of the *Sabbath and *Festival evening services. A Christian version (made by T. Olivers, 18th cent.) is sung as 'The God of Abraham praise . . .'.

Yi Li. *Ceremonials and Rituals*, one of the collections of ritual texts included in the *Confucian Classics (Tr. J. Steele (1917)). While undated, they are probably from late Chou times (roughly 5th–3rd cents. BCE), although they may contain much earlier material.

Yima. Iranian mythological king, who presided over a perfect place (known as *var*) where neither death nor winter were able to enter until someone sinned. When a *taboo was broken, Yima saved his people by taking death upon himself, and thus became the first mortal.

Ying-chou (island of the immortals, China): see FANG-SHIH.

Yin-Hsiang. Chin. for *mudra.

Yin-yang. The two opposite energies in Chinese thought, from whose interaction and fluctuation the universe and its diverse forms emerge. They are the polar extremes of the unbounded *Tao of the supreme and ultimate source (*t'ai-chi), and from their intermingling arise the five elements (*wu-hsing), which give rise to the myriads of forms, and to history and time. The yin-yang symbol expresses this interaction, with the two spots (white in the dark, dark in the white) indicating that each of the two contains the seed of the other and is about to produce the replication of its opposite in interaction. All oppositions can be mapped onto yin and yang, yin representing e.g. the feminine, yielding, receptive, moon, water, clouds, even numbers, and the yang the masculine, hard, active, red, the sun, and odd numbers. Combined with wu-hsing (five phases), these represent the organizing categories of the Chinese world-view.

Yin-yüan (introduced Ōbaku-shū to China in 17th cent.): see ŌBAKU-SHŪ.

Yishtabbaḥ (Heb., 'praised shall be [your name]'). A Jewish *benediction. The Yishtabbaḥ concludes one section of the *Shaḥarit service. It contains thirteen individual praises which, according to the *Zohar*, activate the thirteen attributes of God. It is recited standing.

Yizkor (Heb., 'he shall remember'). Jewish memorial *prayer. The Yizkor is said for close relatives on the last day of *Passover, on the second day of *Shavu'ot, on Shemini Atzeret (see SUKKOT), and on the *Day of Atonement.

Yoga (Skt., 'yoking', 'joining'). The means or techniques for transforming consciousness and attaining liberation (*mokṣa) from *karma and rebirth (*saṃsāra) in Indian religions. The mind (*manas, *citta) is thought to be constantly fluctuating, but through yoga it can be focused, one-pointedness (*ekāgrata) developed, and higher states of consciousness (*samādhi) experienced. Such control of consciousness, which is taught by a *guru, also results in the attainment of paranormal powers (*siddhi).

It is probable (though not agreed) that yoga is of non-*Vedic origin. This is indicated by seals of the *Indus Valley Civilization (2500–1500 BCE) depicting a horned, sometimes ithyphallic, figure sitting in a posture resembling a yoga *āsana. A further indication of non-Vedic origin is found in the *Keśin hymn of the *Ṛg Veda* (10. 136) which describes a figure resembling a yogin—long-haired, naked, silent (*muni)—in contrast to the Vedic *ṛṣi. There is, however, also evidence of Vedic influence, as there is clear documentation of *tapas in the *Ṛg Veda* (8. 59. 6), a force which is later thought to be generated by yoga. Also the *Atharva Veda* describes an *Aryan group called the *Vrātyas who practised austerities and breathing exercises suggestive of yogic breath-control (*prāṇayāma).

Techniques of meditative absoption (*dhyāna, samādhi) were developed in the *Śramana tradition which constrained Jainism and Buddhism, emphasizing control of consciousness as the means of liberation. Although the early *Upaniṣads speak of the interiorization of the sacrifice, the actual term 'yoga' and technical terms such as āsana do not appear until the late Upaniṣads (500 BCE onwards). For example, the *Śvetāśvatara Upaniṣad* (II. 8–9) clearly states the idea of controlling the mind through the control of body and breath (*prāṇa): 'Suppressing the breaths, with controlled movement, he should breathe through his nostrils with diminished breath. Let the wise man vigilantly restrain his mind as he would a chariot yoked to bad horses.' The text goes on to describe the kind of place conducive to yoga and describes the forms or visions which appear in the yogin's mind prior to the realization of *Brahman. One who practises yoga achieves a transformed body, 'made in the fire of yoga', which is beyond old age, sickness, and death (*Śvetāśvatara Upaniṣad* 2. 12). Yoga becomes systematized into various stages. **Maitrī Upaniṣad* (6. 18–19) describes a sixfold yoga comprising the stages of breath control (prāṇayāma), sense-withdrawal (*pratyāhāra), meditation (dhyāna), concentration (*dhāraṇa), contemplative enquiry (*tarka), and absorption (samādhi).

Classical yoga is referred to as one of the six systems of Indian philosophy (*darśana). Expressed in *Patañjali's **Yoga Sūtra* (2nd–3rd cents. CE) it represents a refinement of ideas and practices found in the Upaniṣads. Patañjali states the goal of yoga to be quite simply the 'cessation of mental fluctuation' (*cittavṛtti *nirodha) which results in higher levels of consciousness or absorptions (samādhi) and the purification of the self (*ātman). The *Yoga Sūtra* advocates *rāja or eightfold (aṣṭaṅga) yoga which comprises the same stages as in the *Maitrī Upaniṣad*, only adding restraint (*yama), discipline (*niyama), and posture (*āsana), and dropping tarka. Classical yoga is closely allied with *Sāṃkhya which provides its theoretical underpinning, though Yoga differs from Sāṃkhya in that it is theistic, that is, it accepts God (*Īśvara) as an object of consciousness; and Patañjali uses such terms as *puruṣa and *prakṛti in ways different from Sāṃkhya.

The **Bhagavad-gītā* addresses yoga specifically, in that here *Kṛṣṇa is the object of the yogin's meditation. The *Gītā* advocates three kinds of yoga, *karma yoga, the performance of action without attachment to its result, *jñāna yoga, knowledge of God, and *bhakti yoga, devotion to God (which the *Gītā* evidently regards as the highest).

Yoga became associated with the theistic traditions of *Vaiṣṇavism, *Śaivism, and *Śaktism, the object of meditation becoming the deities of those traditions. During this period (900–1600 CE) various yoga techniques were developed along with ideas about the physiology of the subtle body (*liṅga/ *sūkṣma śarīra)—for example in the Yoga Upaniṣads. The *Nāth tradition developed *Haṭha yoga, though the latter is not confined to this one tradition. Nāth texts such as the *Haṭhayogapradīpika*, *Gheranda Samhitā*, and *Siddha Siddhānta Paddhati* are syncretistic, dealing with subtle physiology, prāṇayāma, samādhi, *Kuṇḍalinī yoga, siddhi, and the attaining of a divine (*divya*) or perfected body (*siddha deha*), not subject to decay and death. The yoga of *Tantrism includes these ideas, but places particular emphasis on practices involving sound and vision, that is the *visualization of *maṇḍalas, *yantras, and deities (*devatā), *mantra, and kuṇḍalinī yoga. Tantrism also uses sexual intercourse (*maithuna) as a form of yoga.

Today yoga is an integral part of Hinduism. Important modern Hindus have advocated various kinds of yoga. For example, *Aurobindo advocated a form of Tantric yoga, calling it Integral Yoga, *Rāmakrishna practised bhakti yoga, and *Ramana Maharṣhi the yoga of knowing the identity of the self and God. Many of the new religions encourage the practice of some kind of yoga. For example, the *Vedānta Society practices jñāna yoga, ISCKON/ Hare Krishna (*International Society . . .), bhakti yoga, and the 3HO (*Healthy, Happy, Holy Organization) a form of Tantric yoga. Haṭha yoga has become very popular in the West, though more as an aid to health than as a soteriology.

See Index, Yoga.

G. Feuerstein and J. Miller, *A Reappraisal of Yoga* . . . (1971); G. Oberhammer, *Strukturen yogischer Meditation* (1977); J. Varenne, *Yoga and the Hindu Tradition* (1973); K. Werner, *Yoga and Indian Philosophy* (1977).

Yogācāra (Buddhist school of idealism): see VIJÑĀNAVĀDA.

Yogānanda, Paramahamsa (1893–1952). Founder of the Hindu Self-Realization Fellowship. Taking Yukteśvar as his *guru, he went to lecture in the USA in 1920 and stayed there, founding a Yoga Institute in Los Angeles in 1925. He travelled extensively, extending the Fellowship, and advocating Kriyā-yoga, *yoga based on practical efforts. His own account is in *Autobiography of a Yogi* (1946).

Yoga Sūtra. The text of classical *yoga attributed to *Patañjali and composed during the 2nd or 3rd cents. CE. The text comprises 195 aphorisms (*sūtras) and is divided into four sections (*pada*) on (i) *samādhi or concentration, (ii) *sādhana or practice, (iii) *vibhūti or magical powers, and (iv) *kaivalya, the condition of isolation or freedom. The *Sūtra* is a systematic exposition of the theory and practice of eight-limbed (*aṣṭāṅga) or *rāja yoga, using a highly developed technical vocabulary and assuming *Sāṃkhya metaphysics. There are many commentaries on the text though these may not be of the same school as Patañjali. The oldest commentary is the *Yoga Sūtra-bhāṣya* of *Vyāsa (5th cent.) which throws light on many obscure sūtras; Vācaspatimiśra wrote a subcommentary, *Tattvavaiśāradi* (*c.*850–*c.*950); the Śaiva king Bhoja wrote a commentary, *Rājamārtaṇḍa* (1000–50); and the Persian scholar *al-Bīrūnī (11th cent.) translated the sūtra into Arab. which may have influenced Persian mysticism. Finally Vijñānabhikṣu annotated Vyāsa in the *Yogavārttika* (*c.*1550) from a Vedāntic viewpoint.

Trs. many, e.g. M. N. Dvivedi (1980), G. Feuerstein (1979), P. N. Mukerji (1981), R. Prasada (1978), I. K. Taimni (1961), M. R. Yardi (1979).

Yogatantra (division of Tantric texts): see TRIPIṬAKA.

Yogi (Skt., 'one who is joined'). A participant in one of the schools of *Yoga. More casually, the word is used of Hindu *ascetics in general.

Yoginī. An initiated female partner in Hindu *Tantric *maithuna; female deities in the service of *Durgā; adepts possessed of *magic powers.

Yōgi school (Chin., Yang-ch'i-tsung/p'ai; Jap., Yōgi-shu). School of Ch'an/Zen Buddhism, originating with Yang-ch'i Fang-hui. In the phrase 'five houses and seven schools' (*goke-shichishu), the latter indicates a twofold derivation from *Lin-chi, Yōgi and Ōryū, the two lines of *Rinzai. Its best-known representative was *Wu-men Hui-k'ai.

Yohanan (form of Jewish name): see JOHANAN.

Yōka-genkaku (Ch'an/Zen master): see YUNG-CHIA HSÜAN-CHÜEH.

Yŏlban. Korean for *nirvāna.

Yoma (Heb., 'the day'). Fifth tractate of the order *Mo'ed* in the Jewish *Mishnah (and *Talmuds). *The* day is the *Day of Atonement, with which the tractate deals.

Yōmei-gaku. Jap. term for the heterodox *neo-Confucian teachings of *Wang Yang-ming (Jap., Ō Yōmei, 1472–1529), also known as the School of Mind or Intuition. Nakae Tōju (1608–48) is considered the school's founder in Japan, which also included the *samurai reformer Kumazawa Banzan (1619–91). The school's politically activist teachings attracted numerous followers during the Tokugawa (1600–1868) period's final decades, including figures like Ōshio Chūsai (Heihachirō), Sakuma Shōzan, and Yoshida Shōin, whose students became leaders of the Meiji Restoration of 1868.

Yom Haatzma'ut (Independence Day). The anniversary of the State of *Israel's Declaration of Independence. It is observed as an annual public holiday on 5 Iyyar.

Yomi (death): see IZANAGI AND IZANAMI.

Yom Kippur (Jewish festival): see DAY OF ATONEMENT.

Yom Kippur war. So-called because on this day in 1973 (6 Oct.) Egypt and Syria attacked Israeli positions in the Sinai peninsula and on the Golan heights.

Yom tov (Heb., 'a good day'). General term for a Jewish *festival.

Yom tov sheni galuyyot (second days of festivals): see SECOND DAYS.

Yoni (Skt., 'source'). In Hinduism, the female origin of all appearance. In particular, it is the female sexual organ, symbolized as a triangle. By *śaktas, it is venerated, either on its own, or in conjunction with the *liṅga.

Yon mchod (patron and priest, pattern of relationship between China and Tibet): see 'PHAGS-PA BLO-GROS-RGYAL-MTSHAN.

Yōsai (Tendai monk): see EISAI.

Yose b. Yose (early composer of piyyutim): see PIYYUT.

Yoshida family (Jap.). In *Shinto, a family of diviners serving in the emperor's court in ancient times, later serving as hereditary priests in the Yoshida Shrine and Hirano Shrine of *Kyōto. Before 1387, they were known as the Urabe family. The members of this family were recognized as scholars of classical and Shinto studies. Urabe Kanekata was a 13th-cent. scholar who compiled *Shaku nihongi*, an important commentary on the **Nihon-shoki*; and his son Kanefumi wrote the earliest extant commentary on the **Kojiki*. The famous writer Yoshida Kenkō (*c*.1283–*c*.1352), author of the *Tsurezuregusa* (Essays in Idleness), was also of this family. Their greatest Shinto scholar was Yoshida Kanetomo (1435–1511), who organized and systematized the Yoshida traditions and founded the school known as *Yoshida Shintō, through which the Yoshida family played a prominent role within Shinto up until the Meiji Restoration in 1868.

Yoshida Shintō (Jap.). A school of *Shinto which draws on Confucianism, Taoism, and *Shingon Buddhism, but considers Shinto as the central root or foundation. The Shinto learning passed on in the *Yoshida priestly family since the Heian period was summarized and systematized by Yoshida Kanetomo (1435–1511), restoring the ideological independence of Shinto. This school of Shinto called itself 'Shinto of the Original Source' (*Gempon Sōgen Shintō*) because of its belief in a supreme primordial *kami, Daigen Sonshin (Venerable Kami of the Great Origin), who preceded heaven and earth and was the source of the myriad kami. Kanetomo held that a special Shinto teaching had been transmitted within the Yoshida family, involving esoteric rituals such as the *goma* (kindling a sacred fire to burn away defilements) and the *kanjō* (anointing the head with sacred water). He also taught that, since the kami are immanent in all living creatures, the soul is the proper place to worship the kami through discipline and purity. Yoshida Shintō was widely spread in Japan from the later medieval period until the Meiji Restoration and was influential in appointments to the priesthood, decisions about religious ceremonies, and the like. It was also called Yui-itsu Shinto ('unique Shinto') and Urabe Shinto.

Yotae. Korean for *tathāgata.

Yotzer (Heb., 'He creates'). The Jewish *benedictions which frame the *Shemaʿ. Yotzer can be used to refer to the whole *Shaḥarit service, to the hymn that precedes the Shemaʿ, or all the special hymns added to the Shemaʿ on *Sabbaths and *Festivals. In the plural (Yotzerot) it stands for all the liturgical hymns (*piyyutim) chanted during the morning service.

Young, Brigham (Mormon leader in 19th cent.): see MORMONS.

Yüan-ch'i (Chin., 'primordial breath'). The fundamental energy in which *yin and yang are still closely interactive in producing the universe. The yüan-chi is now dispersed, but can be summoned together again in the *Taoist breathing exercises which distribute it to the whole body.

Yuan-chueh-ching (Skt., *Purṇa-buddha Sūtra*; Jap., *Engaku-kyo*). 'The Sūtra of Perfect Enlightenment', a Ch'an/Zen sūtra supposedly translated into Chinese by Buddhatrāta in 693 (but it is not certain that there was a Skt. original). The *Sūtra* tells how twelve *bodhisattvas (including *Mañjuśri and *Samantabhadra) are instructed on the nature of perfect enlightenment. It was a text of wide influence in Ch'an—e.g. Kuei-feng Tsung-mi (see FIVE WAYS OF CH'AN/ZEN) read it when he was already a *Vinaya master and was reduced to tears: 'Because it displays the essence and brings people to surrender to the invitation of Buddhism, no text is comparable to this.'

Yüan-shih t'ien-tsun (Taoist deity): see SAN-CH'ING.

Yüan-wu K'o-ch'in (Jap., Engo Kokugon; 1063–1135). Master of the *Yōgi lineage of *Rinzai, dharma-successor of Wu-tsu Fa-yen, and major figure in the development of *kōan-based Zen. He received a Confucian education, but was intrigued by Buddhist scriptures and entered a monastery. There he studied *sūtras, but after a near fatal illness, became convinced that study of that kind could not lead to enlightenment. Wu-tsu led him to enlightenment. He was head of different monasteries, and was favoured by the northern emperor, Hui-tsung, who called him Fo-kuo Ch'an-shih, 'Zen master of the buddha fruit'. When the northern kingdom fell, he escaped to the south, where the emperor Kao-tsung also favoured him, calling him Yüan-wu Ch'an-shih, 'Zen master of full enlightenment'. His major work was the joint-compilation of *Hekiganroku*, the *Blue Cliff Record*—see KŌAN. On the approach of death, he wrote: 'My work slips off into the dark | For you no song remains to sing | The hour is here, I am far gone | Look to yourselves with proper care.'

Yü Chi or **Kan Chi** (d. 197 CE). *Taoist scholar and practitioner of the skills of religious Taoism in effecting cures, etc. He wrote *T'ai-p'ing ching-ling shu* (The Book of Supreme Peace and Purity), which became foundational for *T'ai-p'ing Tao—though according to tradition, he received the book miraculously, rather than writing it.

Yuga (Skt.). An 'age' in Hinduism, one of the four periods into which a world cycle is divided: (i) kṛta (or satya)-yuga, the golden age when there is unity (one god, one *veda, one ritual), in which the *varnas perform their roles without oppression or envy; (ii) tretā-yuga when righteousness begins to decline by a quarter and sacrifice begins; (iii) dvāpara-yuga, when righteousness again declines by a quarter, the Vedas split into four, and few study them; (iv) kali-yuga, further decline by a quarter, when disease, despair, and conflict dominate. At present, we are in (iv), which began 3102 BCE, so that one should not be optimistic about the general prospect for the world. The duration of each yuga (with each in succession reducing by a quarter to reflect the decline in righteousness) is: (i) 1,728,000 human years; (ii) 1,296,000; (iii) 864,000; (iv) 432,000. The total, 4,320,000 = one *mahā-yuga*, or 'great age': 2,000 *mahā-yugas* = one day and one night in the life of *Brahmā (*kalpa).

Yugyō-ha (school of wanderers): see JISHŪ.

Yü-huang (Chin., 'Jade Emperor'). Deity of wide importance in Chinese folk religion and religious *Taoism (*tao-chiao*). He is one of the three Pure Ones (*san-ch'ing), who determines all that happens in heaven and on earth. For that purpose, in a manner of which *Durkheim would have approved, he controls a vast administration which reflects the administration of the Chinese empire. Each year the deities report on their performance, and are promoted or demoted accordingly. His earthly deputies are T'ai-yüeh ta-ti (mountain deity who rules the earth and all people, deciding the moments of birth and death), Cheng-huang (guardians of cities who guide the souls of the dead), Tsao-chün (the lord of the hearth, who observes all that happens in the home), and T'u-ti (guardians of particular parts of cities or towns). He is portrayed usually on a throne in a robe decorated with *dragons, holding a string of thirteen pearls and a ceremonial plaque. His feast day is the ninth day of the first lunar month.

Yuige (Jap., 'poem left behind'). A verse left by a Zen teacher for his pupils, when he knows that death is near. In it, he expresses his quintessential understanding of Zen, gathered in a lifetime. For examples, see YÜAN-WU K'O-CH'IN; WU-MEN HUI-K'AI.

Yui-itsu Shinto (school of Shinto): see HONJI SUIJAKU; YOSHIDA SHINTŌ.

Yukta (Skt.). In Hinduism, one who has attained realization of, and union with, *Brahman permeating all appearance, and lives in that condition of freedom from all appearance.

Yün-chi Ch'i-ch'ien (11th cent. CE). Taoist encyclopaedia, containing, in many vols., a survey of all the works and practices addressed to the prolonging of life and attaining of immortality up to that time. It contains much early Taoist work that no longer survives in any other form.

Yung-chia Hsüan-chüeh (Jap., Yōka Genkaku; 665–713). Last of the great masters of the school of *Hui-neng. He combined the philosophy of *T'ien-t'ai with Ch'an practice, and related both to *Mādhyamaka. These views are reflected in a poem attributed to him, *Shōdōka*, 'Hymn on the Experience of *Tao/truth': 'One who follows the Buddha admits his poverty, because surely in the body he is poor—but not in his Tao. All can see his poverty with his body in rags, but his Tao is his mind which possesses a priceless jewel.'

Tr. C. Luk, *Ch'an and Zen Teaching*, iii (1962).

Yun-kang/Yungang (Chin., 'Cloud Hill'). Complex of caves 16 km. west of the N. China town of Ta-t'ung (Datong), with cave temples containing among the greatest expressions of Chinese Buddhist art. Begun in the 5th cent. CE, as an act of reparation for the Buddhist persecution under Emperor Wu, the endeavour of the first caves, under T'an-yao, was to express the indestructible endurance of Buddhist *dharma. The latest caves are from the Sui dynasty period, 589–618.

Yün-men Wen-yen (Jap., Ummon Bun'en; 864–949). Founder of the Ch'an/Zen *Ummon school. He was dharma-successor (*hassu) of *Hsueh-feng I-ts'un. His early training was in *Vinaya, but he became restless for deeper truth and started to wander. He attained enlightenment under the rigorous Mu-chou, when, on his third request for the highest truth, Mu-chou threw him out, slammed the door on him, and broke his leg. A ruler from the Liu family built a monastery for him on Mount Yün-men (hence his name), where many disciples gathered. Yün-men used the stick-and-shout method (*katsu* see HO, *kyosaku), but is better known for his careful use of word structures in dialogue, leading into *kōans—e.g. he would offer different answers, or answer for the student, or make the answer a question. He is particularly renowned for introducing 'one-word barriers', single-word, challenging answers (though in fact they may be of more than one character), thus: 'What are the words of the revered Buddhas and great patriarchs?' 'Dumplings'; 'What is Zen?' 'It'; 'What is the eye of the true *Dharma?' 'Everywhere'.

Yunus. *Jonah in the *Qur'ān.

Yun-yen T'an-sheng (Jap., Ungan Donjō; *c*.780–841). Ch'an/Zen master, dharma-successor (*hassu) of Yueh-shan Wei-yen, and master of *Tung-shan Liang-chieh, co-founder of *Ts'ao-tung. Several formative exchanges (*mondō) between the two have been recorded—for an example see TUNG-SHAN.

Yūpa (Skt., 'post'). Stake to which, in Hinduism, a sacrificial victim is tied. It is regarded as the tree of life, uniting earth and heaven (cf. SKAMBHA), and was clearly associated with *liṅga power. It is often eight-sided, and when anointed, it was addressed as 'the tree of divine sweetness'. In early rituals, husband and wife participated: to his invitation, 'Let us ascend to heaven', she replied, 'Let us ascend'. He would then climb a ladder to the top of the yūpa, saying, 'We have become immortal'.

Yūsuf. Islamic form of *Joseph.

Z

Zabuton (Jap., 'sitting mat'). The mat on which *zazen is practised; cf. ZAFU.

Zacuto, Moses ben Mordecai (1620–97), Jewish *kabbalist. For much of his life Zacuto lived in Italy and was a member of the Venetian *yeshivah. Although initially drawn to the *Shabbatean movement, he rejected it after the *apostasy of *Shabbetai Zevi. He edited the kabbalistic *Zohar Ḥadash* (1658) and annotated the work of *Luria and *Vital under the acronym of ReMeZ (Rabbi Moses Zacuto). He was the author of the first Hebrew biblical verse drama, *Yesed ʿOlam* and arranged special kabbalistic prayers for several religious ceremonies. His poems have been collected in various anthologies, and his great dramatic poem, *Tofteh Arukh* (1715), attained great popularity.

A. Apfelbaum, *Moshe Zacut* (1926).

Zaddik (Heb., 'righteous man'). A model of Jewish behaviour who is much praised in biblical literature. He will be rewarded with riches and his merit will endure for ever (Proverbs 11. 31). The *rabbis taught that it was because of the merit of the zaddikim that the world exists (*B.Yoma* 38b), and it will never be destroyed while fifty righteous men are still alive (*PdRE* 25). The zaddik is the name given to the *ḥasidic leader whose charismatic personality is devoutly admired among his followers. He is believed to have attained mystical union with God, and employs his powers for the benefit of his community. He keeps court to which the individual Ḥasid makes *pilgrimage, and he is perceived as the ladder between Heaven and earth.

M. Buber, *Hasidism* (1949); S. H. Dresner, *The Zaddik* (1960); H. M. Rabinowicz, *World of Hasidism* (1970).

Zaddik, Joseph ben Jacob Ibn (d. 1149). Spanish poet and philosopher. Zaddik was the author of *Sefer ha-ʿOlam ha-Katan* (ed. 1854), which was praised by *Maimonides. It explores what constitutes 'everlasting good' and comes to the conclusion that 'knowing God and doing his will' leads to the greatest happiness. He corresponded and exchanged verses with *Judah Halevi and served as *dayyan in Cordoba.

Zadok (11th cent. BCE). Israelite *priest. Zadok was a descendant of *Aaron and together with Abiathar was King *David's chief priest. At David's behest, he anointed *Solomon the next king of Israel, and Solomon appointed Zadok's son as the *high priest of the *Temple. From then on, the high priesthood remained in the Zadokite family until the *Maccabean era.

Zadokites (Heb., 'Benei Ẓadok', 'Sons of Zadok'). Members of the ascetic community at *Qumran. According to the *Dead Sea Scrolls, 'the sons of Zadok are the elect of *Israel, called by name, who arise in the latter days'. In the *Manual of Discipline*, new initiates into the community place themselves 'under the authority of the sons of Zadok'. Since the *high priesthood had ceased to be held by descendants of *Zadok from 171 BCE, the Qumran community saw itself as the true faithful of Israel.

Zaehner, Robert Charles (1913–74). Spalding Professor of Eastern Religions and Ethics at Oxford from 1953. Although a specialist in Persian, from 1953 he became absorbed in the textual traditions of India. He expounded and criticized the Hindu classics 'from inside' and correlated them with the Catholicism to which he had been converted in 1936. His major works are *Mysticism, Sacred and Profane* (1957), *At Sundry Times* (1958), *Hindu and Muslim Mysticism* (1960), *Dawn and Twilight of Zoroastrianism* (1961), *Hinduism* (1962), *The Bhagavad-Gītā* (1969), *Concordant Discord* (1970). Towards the end of his life, he became increasingly preoccupied with the problems of rationality and unreason, good and evil, the latter given full rein in his last book *Our Savage God* (1974).

Zafarnāmā (Pers., 'epistle of victory'). Guru *Gobind Siṅgh's reply to *Auraṅgzeb *c.*1705, included in the *Dasam Granth. Gobind Singh wrote the Zafarnāmā in Dīnā, S. Pañjāb, after leaving *Anaṇḍpur and suffering defeat. Like the Hikāyat the *Zafarnāmā* is in Persian verse in *Gurmukhī script. It was dispatched by special messengers to the emperor Auraṅgzeb in Ahmednagar. After invoking God at length, Gobind Siṅgh calls the emperor totally faithless, referring to the broken promise not to harm the *Gurū. After vivid description of the unequal fighting, he suggests they meet at Kaṅgar, and exhorts the emperor to fear God.

Zafu (Jap., 'sitting cushion'). Round, black cushion, on which *zazen is practised: cf. ZABUTON.

Ẓāhiriy(y)a, al. Those who derive law governing Muslim life from the direct text (ẓāhir) of the *Qur'ān and *Sunna. Their view rejected *hermeneutical methods of relating Qur'ān and Sunna to life—not only *ray'y*, *istiṣḥāb*, *istiḥsān, but also *qiyās; and *ijmaʿ could only be accepted as the consensus of the *Companions. While this was likely to freeze Muslim life in the 1st cent. AH, it could in fact be more liberal, because if something was not explicitly commanded or prohibited, it fell into the domain of the permitted (see AL-HALAL WA'L-HARĀM). The leading figure in this school was *ibn Ḥazm, who epitomized the Ẓāhiriy(y)a claim, 'We describe God as God describes himself.'

Zaidīy(y)a, al-, Zaidis, or **Zaydis** (sometimes called 'Fivers' because they seceded over the fifth *Imām), a sect of *Shīʿa Muslims, in contrast to the *Ithna ʿAsharīy(y)a (Twelvers) and the *Seveners (see also ISMĀʿĪLIY(Y)A). When the fourth Shiʿite Imām, ʿAli Zayn al-ʿĀbidīn, died in 713 (AH 95), the Zaidis followed Zaid rather than his brother, Muḥammad al-Baqīr, as Imām. Zaid al-Shahīd rebelled against the *Umayyad caliph in 737 (AH 121), but was killed in battle. He left a guide to *fīqh (which has not survived), and the movement began to be organized by al-Qāsim al-Rassī ibn Ibrāhīm. A long period of conflict ended when Nāṣir al-Uṭrūsh (a descendant of Zaid's brother) led a conquering exodus into Mazandaran and became Imām. They have subsequently lived mainly in the Yemen. Strict in their observance, they reject *mutʿa and *Sūfī claims. The Imām is not a matter of succession (hence there can be periods without an Imām) but of recognition: any descendant of *Fāṭima who is learned in religion and exemplary in behaviour and who is able to defend the truth, if necessary by force, can be an Imām. It is possible for one with only some of the required characteristics to be recognized as Imām in relation to those features.

Zakāt. The third *Pillar of Islam, the official alms tax levied on certain types of property and payable by every adult Muslim of sufficient means. The word is borrowed from the Heb. *zakūt*, and the Arab. root *zakā* is itself connected with the meaning of purity. This is elaborated by some commentators: the believer gives a portion of his wealth to Allāh, and so can 'purify' the rest and use it with a good conscience. In the *Qur'ān, almsgiving is often cited along with prayer as a duty of the Muslim: 'Perform the prayer, and give the alms' (2. 43, 110, 277).

Zakāt is the formal poor tax, whereas *ṣadaqa signifies voluntary almsgiving; however, the two terms are sometimes used as synonyms. Recipients of zakāt are listed in the Qur'ān (where the word used is ṣadaqa): for 'the poor and needy, those who work for the alms fund, those whose hearts have been reconciled, prisoners and debtors, in the cause of Allāh, and for the wayfarer' (9. 60).

The institution of zakāt was introduced in *Madīna, when the community needed funds to support its more indigent members, and, as the Quranic verse implies, sometimes had to 'reconcile' or win over formerly hostile persons. The percentage to be paid on property varies for different classes of goods, and interpretations differ between the schools of law. Zakāt al-Fiṭr is an obligatory alms consisting of provisions to be given to the needy on the occasion of *ʿĪd al-Fiṭr.

Zakkai, Johanan ben (leading Jewish sage): see JOHANAN BEN ZAKKAI.

Zalman, Schneur (founder of movemnet in Judaism): see SHNE'UR ZALMAN OF LYADY.

Zamakhsharī (Muslim grammarian): see AL-ZAMAKHSHARĪ.

Zammai, also **Sanmai.** Japanese pronunciation of *samādhi. Beyond the *Mahāyāna understanding, Zen added the collectedness of the mind into itself, especially by one-pointedness of mind. While zammai can be a temporary attainment, it can also be synonymous with complete enlightenment. Sanmai is also the practice of meditation by concentration on a single object, either physical or metaphysical, often leading to visualization. Sanmai-do is a meditation hall; in particular, it is a shrine built near a graveyard for the performance of hokke-zanmai rituals for the benefit of ancestors, and thus also any hokke-zanmai-in temple of *Tendai.

Zamzam. The sacred well of *Mecca, also called the well of *Ismāʿīl, because, according to tradition, Jibrīl (*Gabriel) opened it to save Hargar and her son in the desert. Important in the *ḥajj, pilgrims hope to dip in, or touch with, its waters the clothes in which they will be buried.

Zanāna (often transliterated as 'Zenāna', as in the Zenana Missionary Society). The women's quarters in Muslim homes in India.

Zaotar (officiating priest): see MAGI; YASNA.

Zaothra (offerings): see YASNA.

Zaqen mamre (contumacious and obstinate teacher): see REBELLIOUS ELDER.

Zarathustra (founding prophet): see ZOROASTER.

Zasu (Jap., 'master of the seat'). The ruling functionary in a Buddhist institution (school, temple, etc.). As a title, it is especially associated with Enryaku-ji on Mount Hiei.

Zat Sikh form of *jāti, *caste.

Zawj or **al-zawaj** (marriage): see MARRIAGE (ISLAM).

Zaydiy(y)a (sect of Shīʿa Muslims): see ZAIDĪY(Y)A.

Zazen (Jap., 'sitting' + 'absorption'; Chin., *tso-ch'an*). Basic meditation practice in Ch'an/Zen, the gateway to enlightenment. Associated above all with *Dōgen (his way of Zen is sometimes called *shikan taza*, 'zazen alone'), it is described in his classic work *Fukanzazengi*:

If you wish to attain enlightenment, begin at once to practise zazen. For this meditation you need a quiet room; food and drink should be taken in moderation. Free yourself from all attachments and bring to rest the ten thousand things. Think not of good or evil; judge not on right or wrong; maintain the flow of mind, will, and consciousness; bring to an end all desire, all concepts and judgments!

To sit properly, first lay down a thick pillow and on top of this a second (round) one. One may sit either in the full or half cross-legged position. In the full position one places the right foot on the left thigh and the left foot on the right thigh. In the half position, only the left foot is placed upon the right thigh. Robe and belt should be worn loosely, but in order. The right hand rests on the left foot, while the back of the left hand rests on the palm of the right. The two thumbs are placed in juxtaposition. Let the body be kept upright, leaning neither to the left nor to the right, neither forward nor backward. Ears and shoulders, nose and navel must be aligned to one another. The tongue is to be kept against the palate, lips and teeth firmly closed, while the eyes should always be left open.

Now that the bodily position is in order, regulate your breathing. If a wish arises, take note of it and then dismiss it! If you practise in this way for a long time, you will forget all attachments and concentration will come naturally. That is the art of zazen. Zazen is the Dharma gate of great rest and joy. (Tr. Dumoulin.)

Fukanzazengi exists in two recensions, 1227/33, and a revision (*rufobon*) which is the basis of the Eng. trs. of N. Waddell and Abe Masao (*Eastern Buddhist* (1973), 115–28), Yukō Yokoi and Daizen Victoria, *Master Dogen* (1976), and F. D. Cook, *How to Raise an Ox* (1978).

Zazengi (seated meditation): see TAO-HSIN.

Zeal (Gk., *zelos*, 'be hot, boil'). Enthusiasm which may become intemperate, and thus an ambiguous religious emotion. The *Septuagint used *zelos* to translate Heb., *qana*, 'to be dyed red', which expresses the visible change of appearance of those under strong emotion. In Jewish scripture, the zeal of God expresses his involvement in his chosen people (thus the promises to the new-born royal child in Isaiah 9. 1–6 are confirmed with the words, 'The zeal of the Lord of Hosts will perform this'), and this zeal may be expressed as anger or mercy. Conversely, people are full of zeal for God ('The zeal of thine house hath consumed me', Psalm 69. 5), but *zealots are not unambiguously good people. In the New Testament, the same ambiguity continues: Paul regarded himself as a zealot for the *traditions of Judaism when he tried to destroy the new movement which became Christianity (Galatians 1. 14), and *zelos* (or *zeloi* in the plural) are included in his list of vices in Galatians 5. 20 and 2 Corinthians 12. 21. Yet equally, he praises the Christians at Corinth for their zeal for the good of others (2 Corinthians 7. 7) and urges them to be zealous for the gifts of the Spirit (1 Corinthians 12. 31). By the time of *Aquinas, zeal is defined as an expression of love which acts for the good of its object (*Summa Theologica* I–II, qu. 28, art. 4), and it becomes described as the flame of love; but warnings continue to be given that zeal under this definition cannot act on behalf of the Christian faith in such a way that it assumes the harm (or damnation) of those who do not listen or respond.

Zealots. Jewish resistance fighters in the Jewish–Roman War, 66–73 CE. *Josephus described them as so-called 'as though they were zealous in the cause of virtue'. The movement stemmed from the activities of Judah the Galilean who 'incited his countrymen to revolt'. In the War against the Romans, one of the sons of Judah seized the fortress of Masada and took command of the Jewish forces in Jerusalem until his murder in 68. The majority of the Zealots died in the siege of Jerusalem; Masada fell in 73, and those who fled to Egypt were rounded up, tortured, and executed. There is considerable scholarly discussion as to the relationship between the Zealots and other groups—the Sicarii, the community of *Qumran, the Galileans under John of Gischala—but no firm conclusions have been drawn.

M. Hengel, *Die Zeloten* . . . (1961, 1976); D. M. Rhoads, *Israel in Revolution, 6–74 CE* . . . (1976).

Zeami Motokiyo (Japanese playwright and actor): see NŌ DRAMA.

Zechariah. Eleventh of the *Minor Prophets in the Hebrew scriptures and Christian Old Testament. The book is attributed to Zechariah, son of Berechiah, and three of the prophecies are dated between the second and fourth year of the reign of King Darius (520–518 BCE). Chs. 1–6 contain the accounts of eight visions concerned with the restoration of the City of *Jerusalem, and the 'two anointed ones that stand by the Lord of the whole earth' (i.e. Joshua the *high priest and *Zerubbabel the king). In chs. 7 and 8, the purpose of divine worship is discussed; it is not fasting but 'honest justice . . . judgment . . . mercy and compassion' which are stressed. The second section of the book (chs. 9–14) contain prophecies of the *redemption of *Israel, the victories of the Jews against their enemies, the punishment of the 'evil shepherds', God's protection of Jerusalem and its ultimate destiny as a *sanctuary, 'holy to the Lord'. Some scholars ascribe a different authorship to chs. 9–14. In the *aggadic tradition, Zechariah is identified with one of the three prophets who accompany the exiles in their return to Jerusalem. After their deaths, the *Holy Spirit was thought to have departed from Israel. The picture of a king riding humbly on an ass (9. 9) is recalled in the story of *Jesus' entry into Jerusalem (e.g. John 12. 14 f.).

Zekut(h) Abot(h) (merit of the fathers): see MERITS OF THE FATHERS.

Zelanti (Lat., *zelantes*, 'those who are eager'). Franciscans in the Franciscan Controversy of the 13th cent., who opposed any modification of the Rule as established by St *Francis in 1221 and revised by him in 1223. The Relaxati supported modification of the Rule. The term is also used of other strongly committed, and usually conservative, groups.

Zemban (Jap., 'Zen board'). Board used in long sessions of *zazen to prop up the chin in order not to fall forward if drowsiness sets in.

Zemirot (Heb., 'songs'). According to the *Sephardim, the verses and *psalms recited before the main part of the Jewish morning service. According to the *Ashkenazim, they are the hymns sung during and after the *Sabbath meals. Twenty-five of the better known ones are printed in many editions of the *Prayer Book.

N. Scherman (ed.), *Zemiroth: Sabbath Songs* (1981).

Zenana (Missionary Society): see ZANĀNA.

Zen arts: see ART.

Zen Buddhism (Jap., *zenna* or *zenno*, from reading Chin., *ch'an-na* or *ch'an*, a Chin. version of *dhyāna). A coalition of related ways for attaining realization, even beyond enlightenment, of the true nature underlying all appearance including one's own—and above all, that there is no duality within appearances, but only the one buddha-nature (*buddhatā, *busshō). Ch'an/Zen is summarized in the four lines attributed to *Bodhidharma, the key figure who, according to tradition, transmitted the *dharma from India to China: 'A special transmission outside the scriptures, | Not founded on words and letters; | By pointing directly to mind | It allows one to penetrate the nature of things to attain the buddha-nature.' These lines (first found in *Ts'u-t'ing shih-yüan*, Jap., *Sotei jion*, 1108), summarize important characteristics in Zen, especially its reliance on direct transmission from one already recognized as having experienced enlightenment rather than from one who demonstrates authority from mastery of texts or teaching (eventually formalized in lines of transmission, *hassu, especially through 'patriarchs', *soshigata). Tensions remain in the history of Zen, nevertheless, between those who regard *sūtra or text study as a preparatory path and those who 'tear up the sūtras'; and between those who think that enlightenment is a gradual process and those who think that it comes as a sudden blow.

Ch'an emerged as part of the *Mahāyāna development, though naturally it traces its lineage back to the *Buddha Śākyamuni. Bodhidharma is recognized as the key figure in the transition to China, though few historical details can be established for him or for the succeeding five patriarchs—a matter of total unimportance for Zen Buddhists, since truth belongs to the healing wisdom imparted, not in a decision about which if any details are historically 'true'. Conflict set in over the sixth patriarch, leading to the division into *Southern and Northern schools, with the difference of emphasis summarized in the saying, 'Suddenness of South, gradualness of North'. The North continued its line in China, but eventually died out, and the conflict had ended by the 8th cent. CE. The Southern school developed into many independent schools, often in relation to other forms of Chinese Buddhism. Tsung-mi lists seven schools (though he includes the Northern school as one), but of these, only two developed important and continuing lines, those established by *Ma-tsu Tao-i and by Shih-tou Hsi-ch'ien, in the third generation after *Hui-neng. Ma-tsu was dynamic and *kōan-based); Shih-tou was quieter and more reflective. From these two derive the 'Five Houses and Seven Schools' (*goke-shichishū), replicating these differences of emphasis: from Shih-tou, *Tsao-tung (Jap., *Sōtō), *Yün-men (*Ummon) and *Fa-yen (*Hogen); and from Ma-tsu, *Kuei-yang (Igyo) and *Lin-chi (*Rinzai); Lin-chi produced two further divisions (hence the 'seven schools'), Yang-chi (*Yōgī) and *Hüang-lung (Ōryu).

As Ch'an faded in China, the different schools and emphases flowed into Korea and into Japan, as indicated in the equivalent names above, but the two which have been of the greatest importance are *Rinzai and *Sōtō. Foundation figures for Rinzai were *Eisai and Enni *Ben'en; the dominant figure is that of *Hakuin who led the revival of the 18th cent. Sōtō adherents regard *Dōgen as the key figure. While he was indeed a towering master, he remains enigmatically elusive in the history of Zen. Zen means simply: realizing the truth that is already the case, not a goal which has yet to be constructed and found. In the words of Hakuin: 'Not knowing how near the Truth is, people seek it far away—what a disaster! They are like one who, in the middle of a lake, cries out in thirst imploringly.' The truth to be realized is that there is only the buddha-nature underlying all appearance; when one realizes that this also is what one is, all differentiation ceases and one rests in that nature. To know this intellectually is very different from realizing it as experienced truth; and Zen developed many ways of seeking and seeing that unity—hence the immense cultural consequences of Zen. See also ZAZEN; ART; and Index, Zen practice.

M. Collcutt, *Five Mountains: The Rinzai Zen Monastic Institution in Medieval Japan* (1981); H. Dumoulin, *Zen Buddhism: A History* (1988, 1990); B. Faure, *The Rhetoric of Immediacy: A Cultural Critique of Chan/Zen Buddhism* (1991); T. Hoover, *Zen Culture* (1977); P. Kapleau, *The Three Pillars of Zen* (1965); N. W. Ross, *The World of Zen: An East–West Anthology* (1962).

Zendō. Zen hall (also dōjō, 'way hall'). Large hall in Zen monasteries, in which *zazen is practised.

Zengyō (Jap.). 'Gradual enlightenment', the step-by-step approach to enlightenment associated with the northern school of Ch'an Buddhism (see SOUTHERN AND NORTHERN SCHOOLS)—as opposed to sudden enlightenment (*tongyō).

Zenjō. Jap. for *dhyāna; hence zenjō-bikuni, a nun; zenjo-mon, a monk.

Zenrin-Kushu (Collection of Sayings from the Zen Forest). An anthology of Chinese wisdom, from Ch'an, Confucian, and Taoist sources, compiled by Ijūshi, 1688.

Tr. (selections): S. Shigematsu, *A Zen Forest* (1981).

Zephaniah. *Prophet of the 7th cent. BCE. The Book of Zephaniah is the ninth of the *Minor Prophets, and the author is probably reacting to the abuses current in the days of King Manasseh (687–642 BCE). The book consists of a picture of the Day of Judgement, the *Day of the Lord, in which no one will be spared. *Jerusalem and the people of other nations are condemned and destruction predicted. The book ends on a note of hope (3. 9–20), and the prophet looks forward to the time when all people will call on the name of the Lord and will return to *Zion. The opening words of the Christian hymn, **Dies Irae*, are taken from the *Vulgate version of 1. 15 f.

Zera'im (Heb., 'Seeds'). One of the six orders of the *Mishnah. Apart from the first tractate, it deals with the agricultural laws pertaining to *Erez Israel.

Zerubbabel (6th/5th cent. BCE). Post-exilic Jewish leader. Zerubbabel worked with Joshua the *high priest as leader of the returned exiles from Babylon and as builder of the *Temple in *Jerusalem. Zerubbabel's activities are described in the books of *Ezra, *Nehemiah, *Haggai, and *Zechariah, but the exact chronology is confused. In the *aggadah, Zerubbabel is the grandson of King Jehoiachin who was chosen as one of God's special servants (*ARN* 43) and who served in the Great *Synagogue. According to the *midrash, Zerubbabel will explain the *Torah together with *Elijah in the world to come.

L. Ginzberg, *Legends of the Jews* (1947).

Zhen dong (*gzhan.stong*, 'Emptiness of Other'). At one time a heretical theory in Tibetan Buddhism that contributed to the downfall of the *Jonang school, but which was later resurrected to underpin the great eclectic *Rimé movement of the Tibetan Renaissance. The theory asserts that the two levels of truth—ultimate truth (*paramārtha satya*) and conventional truth (*saṃvṛti satya*)—are two distinct 'entities', in other words that ultimate truths (i.e. emptinesses) are empty of being the objects that are the basis of their imputation, and that objects (e.g. tables) are empty of being the emptiness that may be imputed on them. This involves the belief that a conventional truth (tables are just tables) is true from a conventional point of view, and that an ultimate truth (emptiness is empty of any phenomenal basis of imputation) is only true from a standpoint of meditative insight at which point all phenomena apparently cease. The *Geluk, who adopt the *rang dong theory and who condemned the Jonang for heresy, point out several errors, notably that the separation and independence of the two levels of truth amounts to substantialism by reifying the 'absolute'; that their understanding of an ultimate truth contradicts the Prajñāpāramitā (*Perfection of Wisdom) by separating emptiness from form; and that the absence of emptiness can never be true at any level.

Zikhronot (Heb., 'remembrances'). A *benediction in the *Musaf prayer of *Rosh ha-Shanah. The benediction remembers *Noah, the Israelite slaves in Egypt, the *covenant with the *patriarchs, and the *'Akeda. The reciting of Zikhronot is mentioned in the *Mishnah and may go back to the days of the *Temple.

Zikr (remembrance of God): see DHIKR.

Zimra (Jewish halakhist): see DAVID BEN SOLOMON.

Zimzum, also **tsimtsum** (Heb., 'contraction'). Jewish *kabbalistic doctrine. The kabbalists taught that, in order that *creation could take place, God had in some sense to make a space for it. See further, LURIA, ISAAC BEN SOLOMON.

Zinā' (Arab.). Sexual intercourse outside the permitted relationships (which, in Islam, include concubines as well as marriage). Zinā' is dealt with particularly in *Qur'ān, sūra 4. The punishment by *rajm appears in *ḥadīth, not in Qur'ān. See also ḤADD.

Zindiq (Pers., *zand*, 'free thinking'). A heretic, in Islamic law, whose teaching endangers the community. The penalty for public expression may be in this life death, and certainly in the next, damnation. Initially it appears to have referred to *dualists, e.g. the *Manichaeans.

Zinzendorf, Count (supporter of Moravians): see MORAVIAN BRETHREN.

Zion. A hill in the city of *Jerusalem. The stronghold of Zion was held by the Jebusites before it was captured by King *David and turned into his capital. The term Zion can refer to the city of Jerusalem (e.g. Isaiah 33. 14), to the whole of Judea (e.g. Isaiah 10–24), or just to the *Temple mount (e.g. Psalms 20–3). By the 1st cent. CE, Mount Zion included the Upper City which was surrounded by a wall. It is to Mount Zion that the *prophets (e.g. *Zephaniah) foretold that all people would turn, to learn about and call upon the name of the Lord.

Zion Christian Church. The largest independent church in S. Africa. It was founded by Enginasi Lekganyane (d. *c.*1948), a Pedi who had been influenced by a mission from J. A. Dowie's Christian Catholic Apostolic Church in Zion in Illinois; he separated from Eduard of Basutoland's Zion Apostolic Faith Mission in 1925 to form his own church in the Transvaal. It grew rapidly and now has an impressive holy city and headquarters, Zion City Moriah, near Pietersburg, where upwards of a million pilgrims from all over southern Africa are reported to assemble for the great *Easter festival. Healing is emphasized, through imposition of hands and water and other media that have been blessed. There is an emphasis on baptism and upon possession by the Spirit, with much singing and dancing in worship. The church has its own farms and shops, and co-operated with the government's separate development policy. Enginasi was succeeded briefly by one son and at his death by another, Eduard (1922–67), a progressive leader who in the 1960s attended the Dutch Reformed Church seminary at Turfloop near Zion City; his son, aged 13, became head in 1967, under a council.

Zionism. International, political, and ideological movement dedicated to restoring *Erez Israel to the Jewish people. The desire to return to the land of *Israel has been preserved in the *liturgy and folk consciousness of the Jews of the *diaspora since the time of the destruction of the Temple in *Jerusalem in 70 CE. Modern political Zionism was first conceived by Theodor *Herzl, and the movement was launched at the First Zionist Congress of 1897. Its stated aim was 'to establish a home for the Jewish people in Palestine secured under public law'. Herzl's vision drew on the long history of *messianic hope in the restoration of *Zion, and at the same time made an attempt to solve the problem of *anti-Semitism in the diaspora by meeting the desire for a homeland. Early Zionism was not supported wholeheartedly by the Jewish community. Many of the *Orthodox believed that the return to Zion would only be effected by divine intervention, and that it was wrong for human beings to anticipate divine providence. At the other extreme, members of the *Progressive movements were anxious to play down the ethnic and nationalistic aspirations of Judaism and were convinced of their successful future in the countries of the *diaspora. After the death of Herzl in 1904, Russian Zionists began to press for immediate colonization in Palestine, buying land, settling, and developing agricultural colonies. Others believed that Zionist aims could only be achieved by extensive diplomatic activity and they aimed to win the support of the Turkish and European Great Powers. Both approaches were adopted in the Conference of 1911. The Zionists succeeded in winning nominal British support of their aims in the *Balfour Declaration, but it was only after the full enormity of the Nazi *Holocaust was revealed that there was real international commitment to the idea of a Jewish homeland. After the State of Israel was established in 1948, the Zionist movement continued to raise money for Israeli projects and to encourage immigration. Today, Zionist activities are organized under the auspices of the World Zionist Organization which embraces all the various unions, federations, and associations. See Index, Zionism.

A. S. Halkin (ed.), *Zion in Jewish Literature* (1961); A. Hertzberg (ed.), The *Zionist Idea* (1960); W. Laquer, *A History of Zionism* (1972); H. M. Sacher, *A History of Israel* (1976).

Zionist Churches. A general term loosely used for the less orthodox, more *Pentecostal and more African *new religious movements in southern Africa, embracing several million Bantu and distinguished from the *Ethiopian churches. The term derives both from the Bible and from the mission from 1904 by J. A. Dowie's Christian Catholic Apostolic Church in Zion, in Illinois, which stressed divine healing and threefold-immersion *baptism. From American Pentecostal missionaries arriving in 1908 there was added the second baptism by the *Holy Spirit. Healing is associated with confession, repeated baptisms, purification rites, and *exorcisms, especially at 'Jordan' rivers, 'Bethesda' pools, and 'New Jerusalems' or holy villages established by chief-like founders. There is much singing, drumming, dancing, and symbolism, and many colourful uniforms and new festivals. The ethic is legalistic and *ascetic but often tolerant of *polygamy. Both the size of membership and the degree of Christian content vary considerably, but the more Christian movements resemble the *Aladura in W. Africa.

Zitzit (Heb., 'fringes'). Tassels attached by Jews to garments worn to fulfil the commandments of Numbers 15. 37–41 and Deuteronomy 22. 12. The *rabbis taught that wearing zitzit was a reminder to the Jew of his duty and identity. The fringes are tied in a particular way which, added to the numerical value of the word zitzit, adds up to the number 613, the number of the commandments. Very *Orthodox Jews wear a *tallit katan at all times to fulfil this *mitzvah; the less traditional only wear zitzit on the corners of their prayer shawls. As a positive time-bound commandment, *women do not have a duty to wear zitzit.

Ziyāra. Visit to a Muslim holy place or tomb, especially to *Muḥammad's tomb in *Madīna. The *Wahhābis allowed it (when they were ruling the area) even though they contested ziyāra in general as *bidʿa (innovation)—no doubt with an eye on the Shiʿa ziyāra, which is a ritualized visit to the tombs of *Imāms (*mashhad) regarded as martyrs (*shahīd), or of *pīrs, whose souls were often believed to remain close to the shrine, assisting those who come to them.

Zōbō (period in pure Land Buddhism): see SHŌZŌ-MATSU.

Zohar, Sefer ha- (Heb., 'Book of Splendour'). The central literary work of the *kabbalah. The *Zohar* is a collection of several books, many of which are supposedly the work of *Simeon b. Yoḥai (2nd cent. CE). It is a mystical commentary on the *Pentateuch and parts of the Hagiographia, and much of it is arranged according to the weekly portions of the *Torah. It first appeared in Spain and is thought to have been composed by *Moses b. Shem Tov de Leon who lived in the late 13th cent. It is partly written in Hebrew and partly in Aramaic Homiletic passages alternate with stories, legends, and short discourses and it was clearly influenced by earlier mystical works. The *Zohar* has been crucially important in the development of the kabbalah, and many commentaries have been written on it, the best known being *Ketem Paz* (1570) by Simeon Labi of Tripoli, *Or ha-Hammah* (publ. 1896) by Abraham b. Mordecai Azulai, the 18th-cent. *Mikdash Melekh* of Shalom Buzaglo, and *Elijah ben Solomon's *Yahel Or*.

Eng. trs. J. H. Sperling and M. Simon (1933), completed R. A. Rosenberg, *The Anatomy of God* (1973); I. Tishby (trs. D. Goldman), *The Wisdom of the Zohar* (1989).

Zoku Kōsōden (Buddhist biographies): see TAO-HSÜAN.

Zōmatsu (age of spurious dharma): see SAICHŌ.

Zoroaster. The name by which the ancient Iranian prophet Zarathustra has been known in the West. *Parsis often date him around 6,000 BCE, following Greek texts which misinterpret ancient Iranian sources. The significance for them is that he is the first of the world's religious prophets. There has been much W. scholarly debate over the dating. Until the 1980s the date most commonly given was the 6th cent. BCE (Gershevitch and *Zaehner), but more recently much earlier dates around 1200 BCE have been generally accepted (Boyce, Gnoli). The arguments centre partly on the identification of Zoroaster's patron, but more on the language, style, and (stone-age) imagery deployed in his teaching. There is a general acceptance that he lived in NE Iran. The broad setting of his religion was the Indo-Iranian tradition reflected in the *Ṛg Veda*, the language style of which seems roughly contemporaneous.

His teaching has been preserved in seventeen hymns, the *Gāthās, **Yasna* (hereafter *Ys.*) 28–34 and 43–53. Zoroaster was a practising priest (the only one of the great religious prophets known to have been such), and these hymns were meditations on the liturgy (*Yasna) cast into rather esoteric mantic poetry. They are, therefore, extremely difficult to translate and interpret, so that accounts of them differ considerably. The essential place to begin an account is with the prophet's conviction that he had seen God, the Wise Lord, *Ahura Mazda, in a vision. He believed that he personally had been set apart for his mission from the beginning, a conviction which resulted in a stress on personal responsibility in religion. There are, he taught, two opposing forces, the Bounteous Spirit of Mazda and the destructive power of *Angra Mainyu who created respectively life and non-life. Each person's eternal fate would be determined by the choice (s)he made between them (*Ys.* 30. 3): 'there are two primal Spirits, twins renowned to be in conflict. In thought and word, and act they are two: the better and the bad. And those who act well have chosen rightly between these two, not so the evil doers.' Zoroaster called upon his followers to worship the good Mazda, who he declared, in a series of rhetorical questions, is the creator of all things:

> The Father of Order . . .: Who established the course of the sun and stars? Through whom does the moon wax and wane? Who has upheld the earth from below, and the heavens from falling? Who (sustains) the waters and plants? Who harnessed swift steeds to wind and clouds? What craftsman created light and darkness? What craftsman created both sleep and activity? Through whom exist dawn, noon and eve. (*Ys.* 44. 3–6)

Elsewhere he speaks of Mazda as the creator of the physical body and of people's inner selves. Zoroaster's people were suffering from the violent raids of warrior nomads, and in the actions of the 'bloodthirsty wicked' he saw the expression of the cosmic forces of chaos and destruction, Angra Mainyu and his demonic forces, the *daevas (e.g. Fury and the Lie). The daevas and their counterparts the *ahuras* (*aśura) were part of the Indo-Iranian tradition, but the *ahuras* are identified with good and harmony in Zoroastrianism and the daevas with evil, the reversal of their roles in Hinduism. It seems likely that this reversal was part of Zoroaster's own teaching because of his equation of violent force with destructive evil. Central to Zoroaster's belief in Ahura Mazda are the *Amesha Spentas, a system of seven spirits which in later tradition at least were opposed to seven evil spirits. He therefore saw a cosmic divide between the forces of good and evil. The eternal consequences of the choice are elaborated in the Gāthās. Zoroaster accepted the traditional myth of individual judgement that is more fully elucidated in the later *Pahlavi texts. After death the soul is led by the *daena*, the conscience pictured as a maiden, to the Chinvat Bridge, or Bridge of Judgement. Those whose good thoughts, words, and deeds predominate cross over safely to a paradisal existence, an abode of song, but the wicked will fall from the bridge to be 'guests in the House of the Lie', a place of poor food, foul smells, of long torment, and woe (*Ys.* 31. 20; 49. 11; 44. 11; 45. 3). Because the Gāthās are but a fragment of Zoroaster's teaching, and difficult to translate, it is not possible to expound all his teaching—e.g. whether he believed that this post-mortem existence was eternal or that it was a prelude to a final resurrection and judgement as enunciated in the later tradition (*frasokereti) is not certain, though recent scholarship has tended to emphasize the reliability of the later texts as guides to the unknown parts of the prophet's teaching. He used the term which later referred to the expected saviour, Sōšyant, at least partly to refer to the work of himself and his followers, but also probably with a future sense as in the developed eschatology. Further, he refers to the fires of judgement at the final turning-point of existence (*Ys.* 43. 5 f.), again features associated with the second judgement in the later detailed expositions of the doctrine.

Zoroaster says that he was cast out by kinsfolk, rejected by many of his contemporaries, and refused hospitality when travelling. Clearly his teaching provoked opposition from the priests of his day, partly because his rejection of the daevas must have seemed to them a dangerous step. In later tradition a full account of his life is elaborated. It was said that he was the only child to laugh at birth, an appropriate reaction in a religion which emphasizes happiness. The evil forces sought to destroy the baby—e.g. through the work of evil priests, through a stampede of cattle, by wolves, and fire, but Ahura Mazda saved his emissary. In the course of his ministry the wicked priests had him imprisoned, but Zoroaster convinced the local king of the truth of his teaching by performing miracles to cure the ailments of the monarch's favoured horse. Thereafter the king and his court espoused the religion of the prophet. God therefore not only protected but visibly supported the work of his prophet, who in turn rejected all the seductions of evil to lead him from the path of Truth. According to tradition, he was slain (at the age of 77) by invaders while sacrificing at the altar. In modern Iranian Zoroastrian thought, the prophet is seen as the bearer of the great revelation, the inspiration or mouthpiece of the scriptural word. Among Orthodox Parsis, he is often seen as yet more than this, as a manifestation of the divine, almost as an *avatāra. He is the great role model for all Zoroastrians, the stalwart defender of the faith, the uncompromising enemy of evil, the supporter of the Good, whose vision of the divine all the followers of righteousness seek to share.

M. Boyce, *Zoroastrianism: Its Antiquity and Constant Vigour* (1979) and *Sources for the Study of Zoroastrianism* (1984); G. Gnoli, *Zoroaster's Time and Homeland* (1980); E. Herzfield, *Zoroaster and his World* (1947); A. V. W. Jackson, *Zoroaster, the Prophet of Ancient Iran* (1965).

Zoroastrianism. The religion of the followers of the prophet known in the West as *Zoroaster (Zarathustra to his followers). He is generally thought to have lived in NE Iran around the year 1200 BCE. His teaching was based on the Indo-Iranian tradition which he inherited and bears striking parallels to the teaching in the *Ṛg Veda*. He was convinced that he had been taught personally by God (*Ahura Mazda) in a series of visions, and the emphasis on personal responsibility is a hallmark of the religion throughout its history. His teaching grew in importance only slowly over the following centuries because it encountered opposition from the established religious authorities who believed that it undermined the foundations of their teaching. He called for the worship of the wholly good Ahura Mazda and rejected the *daevas (whom he described as forces of destruction) and the evil *Angra Mainyu. However, by the 7th cent. BCE, his teaching had spread across the Iran plateau, and when Cyrus the Great established the Persian Empire in the 6th cent., Zoroastrianism became the official state religion and so held sway from N. India to Greece and Egypt. The Persian Empire, ruled over by the Achaemenid dynasty, transformed the political world of the Ancient Near East. Within its borders, delegated authority was given to established local rulers, satraps, and an effective communications network (e.g., roads and a sort of postal system) facilitated trade; with the establishment of a strong legal system to ensure justice, there was a relatively stable and ordered society. The traditional religions of the various nations were encouraged: so, e.g., the Jews were encouraged to rebuild the temple destroyed by the Babylonians. In Deutero-Isaiah, Cyrus is hailed as the 'Anointed' (i.e, *messiah) of Yahweh (Isaiah 45. 1), acting under divine guidance, and following the obedient route of *Abraham. The evidence suggests that other nations also considered Persian rule beneficial, and there were few revolts. The main source of conflict was with the Greeks, who repelled the Persian invasion and, in the 4th cent., under Alexander, eventually conquered Iran. In the West, he is described as 'the great', but in Zoroastrian texts he is referred to as 'the accursed' because he destroyed the great royal and cultural centre of Persepolis and killed some of the priests, the *magi. For approximately 150 years the Hellenistic legacy of Alexander impressed itself on much of Persian culture, e.g. the architecture and coinage. But in the 2nd cent. BCE, native traditions began to reassert themselves under a new ruling power, the Parthians. They restored many of the old boundaries of the old Achaemenid Empire and ruled until the 3rd cent. CE. In this time they were the major force to stand against Rome. In the 200 years of frontier conflict between the two powers, the Parthians ruled over parts of Asia Minor and Syria, even capturing *Jerusalem (in 40 BCE, but Herod returned with Roman help and forced them out two years later). One consequence of this western expansion appears to have been that Jews and Christians were aware of, and influenced by, Zoroastrian teachings (especially the teaching on the end of the world, the *resurrection, *heaven and *hell, and aspects of the saviour imagery: see ESCHATOLOGY, BUNDAHISN; FRASOKERETI). Internally in Iran, the Parthians increased the number of fire temples (*Atas), began the process of collecting the sacred oral traditions to form a scriptural *canon, and fostered the epic traditions, all measures which eroded the *Hellenistic heritage.

In the 3rd cent. there was a revolt when the Sasanians from the SW of the country, Persia proper, overthrew the Parthian northerners. They legitimated their rebellion by presenting their rule as a reassertion of Zoroastrian power, publicity which has affected generations of W. scholars (e.g. R. C. *Zaehner's *Dawn and Twilight of Zoroastrianism*, 1961). The Sasanian era was perhaps the time of the greatest courtly splendour in Iran, with lavish royal patronage of great temples, with magnificent palaces decorated with mosaics, furnished with superb utensils, many of which have survived the ravages of history and enable scholars to reconstruct much of Sasanian magnificence. The monarchs threw their considerable power behind the official priesthood (magi), so Church and State were spoken of as 'brothers, born of one womb and never to be divided'. Once the authority of the chief priests had been declared, deviance from their teaching became not only *heresy, but treason. Whether that teaching was what historians consider 'orthodox' Zoroastrianism may be doubted. It seems rather to have been the 'heresy' of Zurvanism (*Zurvan), which not only contravened traditional Zoroastrian teaching on free will, but also questioned the essential goodness of the material world. The Sasanian period is the only era in Zoroastrian history where there is clear evidence of the oppression of other religions. Whether this was royal fervour or Zurvanite teaching is not known, but there were attempts to convert or suppress Jews and Christians (*Naujote).

The 1,200 years of Zoroastrian imperial history came to an end in the 7th cent. CE with the rise of Islam. The early battles were seen by the Iranians as local skirmishes resulting from Bedouin quests for booty. When the Muslim forces defeated the might of the Sasanian army at the battle of Nihavend in 642, it became clear that a permanent conquest was sought. The last Zoroastrian king, Yazdegird III, fled and was killed by one of his own people in 652. After the initial conquest, the imposition of Muslim rule on the lives of the people was a gradual affair. There were even benefits to some ordinary people. Islamic taxes were less than those imposed by magi and monarchs. The clarity of the new teaching and the evident success it enjoyed evidently appeared attractive to many. But as taxes increased, as Arabic was imposed as the national language, as Zoroastrians were increasingly oppressed and socially restricted, the future of the religion in its homeland came under increasing threat. There was some ambivalence over the position of Zoroastrianism as a religion of the book (*ahl al-kitāb), though in Islamic times the *Avesta had emerged as the holy text of the religion. Ever-increasing Muslim oppression forced the diminishing number of Zoroastrians to retreat from the big cities near trade routes to the desert cities of Yazd and Kerman and their neighbouring villages. In the 10th cent., a band of Zoroastrians left the homeland to seek a new land of religious freedom, and settled in India where they are known as the *Parsis, or the people from Pars (Persia).

The harshness of Islamic rule over Iranian Zoroastrians was punctuated by two extremely severe foreign invasions, the Seljuk Turks in the 11th cent., followed by the Mughals. Both conquerors were eventually converted to Islam, but for Zoroastrianism there was no such reprieve to compensate for the great slaughter which occurred. The Zoroastrians emerge into the light of history only occasionally over the succeeding centuries. Their courage, faithfulness, and determination were tested to the full under the Qajar dynasty (1796–1925; see AL-MAJLISĪ). They were rarely protected by the law, so they became prey to fanatics and ruffians; the *jizya tax increased into a crushing burden, travel was forbidden, they were humiliated, made to wear undyed cloth, forbidden to wear tight turbans or ride horses, made to dismount even from a donkey in the presence of a Muslim. The corresponding inducements to convert tempted some, but it is remarkable how many stayed faithful to their ancestral religion.

In 20th cent. Iran, the Zoroastrians experienced a revival of their fortunes. Due largely to the efforts of a Parsi, Manekji Limji Hataria, the jizya had been removed in 1882, and grinding poverty was eased. He and others laboured hard to make educational and medical provisions for the oppressed Zoroastrians, so that, at the start of the 20th cent., they had improved in learning, health, and wealth as a number of merchants began to flourish. In 1906, a parliament, the Majles, was established and a Zoroastrian was elected. In 1909, all minorities were given one representative, including the Zoroastrian representative, Kay Khosrow Shahrokh. When the Majles deposed the last Qajar monarch and enthroned the prime minister as Reza Shah Pahlavi, the physical circumstances of Zoroastrians improved considerably. They were generally seen as the true, the ancient, Iranians, and were recognized as reliable, industrious, and able. Parsis began to consider returning to the homeland as Zoroastrian voices became influential at court. Their position improved further under the second Pahlavi monarch who publicly proclaimed the pre-Islamic history and culture of his people. A Zoroastrian became a deputy prime minister and others achieved high positions in the armed forces and the professions. With the opportunities available in Tehran, Zoroastrians migrated in increasing numbers to the metropolis from their desert retreats. With the seductions of the modern world, a number left their tradition as well as their village behind, some converted to what they saw as the new world religion of the *Bahā'īs. Those who stayed in the religion often became westernized in their new urbanized setting. Ironically, therefore, the new opportunities brought their own threats to the religion.

When the Islamic Republic under Ayatollah *Khumayni assumed power in 1979, many Zoroastrians feared for their future, a few returned to their desert homes, more withdrew from any public profile, and a number migrated overseas—to Britain, Australia, Canada, and especially the USA—and joined the Parsi diaspora. Those who remained in the homeland have not suffered the persecution they feared, but their rights in law are not equal to those of Muslims; their opportunities in education and the professions are restricted. Always there is the fear of an outbreak of fanaticism. Yet, on official counts, numbers have increased. Whereas a 1960s census estimated that there were approximately 17,000 Zoroastrians, the Islamic authorities state that in the 1990s there are in excess of 90,000 Zoroastrians in Iran. Some outsiders are sceptical of this estimate, others explain it as the result of many people returning to Zoroastrianism during the 1970s, and later from the Bahā'īs. The future of the world's oldest prophetic religion in its homeland seems delicately poised as the third millennium approaches.

J. K. Amighi, *The Zoroastrians of Iran* (1990); M. Boyce, *Zoroastrians: Their Religious Beliefs and Practices* (1979), *Sources for the Study of Zoroastrianism* (1984), *A History of Zoroastrianism* (1979, 1982, 1991), and *A Persian Stronghold of Zoroastrianism* (1977); S. A. Nigosian, *The Zoroastrian Faith . . .* (1993).

Zucuto, Abraham ben Samuel (1452–1515). Historian and astronomer. Zucuto was the author of the astronomical work, *Ha-Hibbur ha-Gadol*, under the patronage of the bishop of Salamanca. After the expulsion of the Jews from Spain in 1492, he settled first in Portugal (where he advised Vasco da Gama) and then N. Africa. He also wrote *Sefer ha-Yuhasin*, a history of the *oral law based largely on original research, on which Moses b. Israel *Isserles subsequently wrote notes (publ. 1580).

F. Cantera Burgos, *Abraham Zucut* (1935).

Zugot (Heb., 'pairs'). The pairs of Jewish *sages who maintained the chain of *oral law. The zugot are seen as the link between the *prophets and the *tannaim (*Pe'ah* 2. 6). The earliest of the zugot were Yose b. Jo'ezer and Yose b. Johanan of the mid-2nd cent. BCE, and the last were *Hillel and *Shammai. Traditionally, the first-named of the zug was *nasi and the second av *bet din.

H. Mantel, *Studies in the History of the Sanhedrin* (1961).

Zuhd (Arab., *zahada*, 'abstain'). Abstinence in Muslim life, at first from sin and from all that separates from God; then (for those pursuing a *Sūfi path) from all that is created in order to cling only to the Creator. Although there is suspicion of *asceticism in Islam if it is taken to imply a rejection of the goodness of God's creation, moderation is commended: 'The poor man is not he whose hand is empty of possessions, but he whose life is empty of desires.'

Zunz, Leopold (Yom Tov Lippmann; 1794–1886). Jewish historian. Zunz was among the founders of the 'Science of Judaism'. Zunz became editor of *Zeitschrift für die Wissenschaft des Judentums* in 1823, the purpose of which was to redefine Judaism in accordance with the spirit of the times. His writings include a biography of *Rashi, a history of Jewish homiletics, a history of Jewish geographical literature, a history of the Jewish *liturgy, studies of the medieval *piyyutim, and various sermons and biblical studies. In his work, he presented Jewish themes in the context of human culture as a whole, and he demonstrated the development of Jewish thought and concepts through the ages: in this way, he believed that a perennial absolute could be discerned in the midst of cultural and historical change—'Particular virtues are a matter of fashion, but virtue is not.' He hoped that Jewish Studies would be recognized as an academic subject taught in secular universities. Although this aim was not realized in his lifetime, his work was continued after his death by the specially created Zunz Foundation (Zunzstiftung).

L. Wallach, *Liberty and Letters: The Thoughts of Leopold Zunz* (1959).

Zurvan. 'Time' in *Zoroastrianism, speculation on which subject appears to have given rise to a 'heresy' so powerful that it was dominant in Sasanian if not Achaemenid times. Essentially it appears to have been an intellectual interpretation of the doctrine rather than a formal cult, since there is no evidence of a separate priesthood or temples. Probably under Greek philosophical influence, Time was seen as the source and controller of all things, as the unity behind the polarity of the twin spirits of good and evil, *Ahura Mazda and *Angra Mainyu. If the idea of twins requires a father, then Zurvan was that father. But Time as the controller of all things led to a doctrine of predestination, fundamentally at variance with 'orthodox' teachings on free will (*Fravasi). One associated idea appears to have been that the world as we know it was under the control of Ahriman (see ANGRA MAINYU), and not simply a battleground where good and evil are in a state of mixture. The supremacy of Zurvan would appear to undermine the status of Ahura Mazda. Not only did Zurvanism have no clear cultic boundaries, it may not have had any doctrinal ones either, for there are Zurvanite tendencies in some otherwise 'orthodox' texts. It is, perhaps, best thought of as an intellectual trend among educated Iranians in imperial times, for Sasanian Iran has been shown to be a kingdom with a wide variety of religious trends.

S. Shaked, *Dualism in Transformation: Varieties of Religion in Sasanian Iran* (1994); R. C. Zaehner, *The Dawn and Twilight of Zoroastrianism* (1961) and *Zurvan: A Zoroastrian Dilemma* (1955).

Zushi (Jap.). A small shrine or sanctuary dedicated to the *Buddha or to a transmitter of *dharma.

Zutra, Mar. Three Jewish *exilarchs of the 5th and 6th cents. CE. Mar Zutra I (d. *c.*414), known as 'the pious', was famous for his compassion and exemplary character. Mar Zutra II (d. 520) defeated the Persians and set up an independent Jewish state,

513–20. His son, Mar Zutra III, was traditionally born on the day his father was executed. He left Babylon and eventually settled in *Erez Israel.

Zwingli, Ulrich (1484–1531). Swiss *Reformer. He was educated at Berne, Vienna, and Basle, where Thomas Wyttenbach inspired his commitment to biblical studies. After *ordination in 1526, he became pastor at Glaurus, where he devoted himself to the study of *Erasmus, biblical languages, *patristic theology, and the memorization of the *Pauline epistles. In 1516 he became chaplain of the Cloister at Einsiedeln where blatant abuses strengthened his desire for reform. He was appointed *priest at the Zurich 'Great Church' in 1518, gradually using his expositions to encourage reform. Zwingli defended his views in sixty-seven theses, on which he wrote *Auslegung und Gründe der Schlussreden*, i.e. his own commentary, and obtained the active support of the Zurich City Council, but a second disputation in 1523 led to a breach with two of his more radical colleagues, Conrad Grebel and Felix Manz, with Zwingli fearing that their 'Free Church' convictions would alienate the magistracy. Zwingli opposed their views about believers' *baptism, insisting on the baptism of all infants. At the same time, he encountered further theological difficulty over relationships with the *Lutherans, with the 1529 Colloquy of *Marburg failing to reconcile the *eucharistic views of German and Swiss Protestants. The Swiss Cantons fought over their divergent ecclesiastical loyalties, and the intensely patriotic Zwingli was killed at the battle of Cappel in 1531.

Zwingli placed great emphasis on the work of the *Holy Spirit. Thus although (as with *Luther) scripture has supreme authority, only the Spirit enables perception of its truth: prayer precedes perusal. Baptism he related to *covenant theology, and the *Last Supper he understood, not as initiating a sacrificial *mass, but as mediating the opportunity for faith to perceive the presence of Christ and to receive the benefits thereof: 'Those who have God's Spirit, who know that Christ is their salvation, who rely on the word, do not sin, because the only mortal sin is unbelief.'

G. W. Locher, *Zwingli's Thought* . . . (1981); G. R. Potter, *Zwingli* (1976); W. P. Stephens, *The Theology of Huldrych Zwingli* (1986); R. C. Walton, *Zwingli's Theocracy* (1967).

TOPIC INDEX

Note In this Index of general topics, the entries are to headwords of articles in the main text of the book. An entry followed by → means that the entry will be found in the main text under the headword given—e.g., Kashrut and Kosher appear in the index under Food; the reader is then directed to the article, Dietary laws, in the main text where they are discussed.

Where topics in the Index can provide further information to each other, cross-references are denoted by see/see also followed by small capitals—e.g. Mysticism see also SUFI BELIEFS.

In each topic, general entries, or those dealing with several religions, come first, followed (where applicable) by those related to particular religions.

The Index does not include accents, breathings, or italics.

Shinto (*cont.*): Magatsuhi-no-kami; Matsuri; Mikagura → Music; Mikoshi; Misogi; Mito; Motoori Norinaga; Musubi; New Sect Shinto → Sect Shinto; Nihongi; Niiname-sai; Ninigi; Norito; Okuninushi no Mikoto; Ritsu and ryo; Ryobu Shinto; Sect Shinto → Kyoha Shinto; Shimenawa; Shin kyoha Shinto → Sect Shinto; Shinbutsu-shugo; Shinsen; Shintai; Shinto; Shrine Shinto → Ise; Sect Shinto; Suiga Shinto; Tenrikyo; Torii; Ujigami; Ujiko → Ujigami; Watarai Nobuyoshi; Watarai Shinto → Ise; Watarai Nobuyoshi; Yamazaki Ansai; Yoshida family; Yoshida Shinto; Yuiitsu Shinto → Honji suijako; see also KOKUGAKU

Sin, offence, etc. Adam; Adharma; Atonement; Blasphemy; Christus Victor → Atonement; Confession; Dualism; Ethics; Excommunication; Expiation; Fall; Idolatry; Redemption; Sacrilege; Sin; Sodom and Gomorrah; Usury **Buddhist**: Abhabba-tthana; Anusaya; Asava; Dosa; Five deadly sins; Gogyaku-zai; Lobha; Mana; Moha; Nimitta; Nivaranas; Papa; Parajika-dhamma; Raga; Samyojanas; Tiracchana-katha; Upadana; Uposatha **Christian**: Absolution; Accidie; Ashes; Baptism; Black Mass; Deadly sins; Felix culpa; Immaculate conception; Imputation; Indulgence; Justification; Lapsi; Mortal sin; Original sin; Pardon; Penance; Predestination; Seven deadly sins; Venial sin **Hindu**: Adharmacarin → Adharma; Klesa; Krodha; Lobha; Mahapataka; Papa; Upapataka → Mahapataka **Jain**: Prayascitta **Jewish**: 'Al het; Azazel; Ba'al teshuvah; Bittul ha-Tamid; Bloodguilt; Book of Life; City of refuge; Day of Atonement; Days of Awe; Golden calf; Hillul ha-Shem → Kiddush ha-Shem; Hukkat ha-Goi; Idols → Iconography; Inclination; Kafir; Karet; Man; Moloch worship; Penitence; Rebellious son; Scapegoat; Teshuvah **Muslim**: Kufr → Kafir; Murtadd; Ridda; Shirk; Zina' **Sikh**: Five evil passions; Haumai; Kurahit; Manmukh; Patit; Tankhah **Taoist**: Chai; Chang Tao-Ling

Siva Abhiseka; Adinatha → Siddha; Appar; Ardanarisvara; Arunacala; Avatara; Basava; Bhairava; Bhavani; Bhubaneswar; Bindu; Brahma; Churning of the ocean; Damaru; Dance; Devi; Diksa; Durga; Durvasas; Duti puja; Elephanta; Ganga; Ghanta; Hara; Harappa; Hari-hara; Indus Valley; Jata; Jyotir-lingam; Kailasa; Kala; Kalaratri; Kali; Kama; Kapalika; Kashmir Saivism; Kaularnava Tantra; Kirtimukha; Lalla; Linga(m); Lingayats; Mahadeva; Mahakala; Mahendra; Mahesna; Mahesvara; Mohini; Naga; Nandi; Narmada; Nataraja; Nath; 'Nayanmar; Pancanana; Parasurama; Parvati; Pasupata; Pasupati; Rudra; Sabda; Sadhaka; Sahasrara; Saiva Siddantha; Saiva-agama; Saivism; Sakti; Samdhya; Sati; Siddha; Siva; Skanda; Tamilnadu; Tandava; Tantra; Trikasasana; Trilocana; Trimurti; Trisula; Uma; Urna; Vamacara; Vibhuti; Virabhadra; Visvanatha; Yamala

Slavery 'Abd; African-American religion; Afro-Brazilian cults; Bilal; Channing; Crowther; Deva-dasi; Exodus; Friends; Hamallism; Haroset; Jizya; Jubilee; Livingstone; Marriage (Islam); Philemon; Qurayza; Rabia; Ransom; Sabbath; Slavery; Southern Baptist Convention; Spiritual; Wilberforce

Societies see SECRET SOCIETIES

Soteriology Arminius; Atonement; Moksa; Naujote; Salvation; Sosyant → Frasokereti; Zoroaster; Teshuvah; Tetzel, J.; Trimarga; Universalism; Varnasramadharma; Videhamukti; Vidya; Vijnapti-matra; Vimokkha; Vimukti; Virgin birth; Weber, Max; Yoga

Soto Buddhism in Japan; Dogen; Eihei-ji; Genjo-koan; Hung-chih; Issinjo; Keizan; Menpeki; Ryokan Daigu; Soji-ji; Soto shu; Ts'ao-tung

Sound Ahata → Sabda; Anahata → Sabda; Anahata-sabda; Arabic; Aum → Om; Bija; Dadu Dayal; Dharana; Dharani; Dhikr; Fang Yen-kou; Ghanta; Koto-dama; Mandukya; Mantra; Nada → Sabda; Nipponzan Myohoji; Om; Pratyahara (2); Sabad; Sabda; Sat cakra bedha; Sphota; Vac; Vyahrti; see also MANTRA

Study of religion Anthropology of religion; Apollonian; Axial Age; Axis mundi; Biogenetic structuralism; Bricolage; Chthonian religion; Church-sect typology; Civil religion; Collective representations; Counterculture; Cult; Cults of affliction → Affliction, Cults of; Cultural relativity; Culture; Danielou, A.; Dionysiac; Dreams; Dream-time; Dualism; Dumezil, G.; Durkheim, E. → Festivals and fasts; Dying and rising gods; Ecstasy; Eliade, M.; Emic/etic; Enthusiasm; Enttraditionalisierung; Evans-Pritchard, E.; Evans-Wentz, W. Y.; Farquhar, J. N.; Florenz, K. A.; Folk religion; Frazer, J. G.; Freud, S.; Geertz, C.; Gemeinschaft → Ideal type; Gesellschaft → Ideal type; Great tradition; Heiler, F.; Henotheism; Herbert, E.; Hierophany; Holy; Homo religiosus → Eliade, M.; Horner, I. B.; Ibn Khaldun; Ideal type; Ideology; Invisible religion; James, W.; Jones, W.; Jung, C. G.; La Vallee-Poussin; Lamotte, E.; Levi-Strauss, C.; Magic; Maslow, A. H.; Muller, M.; Myth; Nanjo bunyo; Numinous; Nyantiloka; Olympian religion → Chthonian religion; Ontology; Orthopraxy; Otto, R.; Parapsychology; Patristics; Phenomenology; Philosophia perennis; Philosophy of religion; Protestant ethic → Weber; Psychodynamic theory; Psychology of religion; Rationalization → Weber; Religionsgeschichtliche Schule; Renan, E.; Retrogressive rituals; Reuchlin, J.; Rhys Davids; Rites of passage; Sacred and profane; Sapir–Whorf hypothesis → Cultural relativity; Schopenhauer, A.; Sects; Secularization; Shahrastani; Sociology of religion; Somatic exegesis → Cultural relativity; Stcherbatsky, T.; Suzuki, D. T.; Symbols; Syncretism; Tabu; Tambiah, S. J.; Totemism; Tradition; Trickster; Troeltsch, E.; Tubingen School; Tucci, G.; Turner, V.; Tylor, E. B.; van der Leeuw, G. → Phenomenology; Violence; Weber, Max → Theodicy; Wellhausen, J.; Zaehner, R. C.

Stupas Amaravati; Anuradhapura; Bharut; Borobudur; Caitya; Chorten; Dagaba; Gilgit; Goose Pagodas → Sian; Gorinsotoba; Kusinagara; Nalanda; Nipponzan Myohoji; Pagoda; Relics; Sanchi; Sarnath; Shwedagon; Sotoba; Stupa; Thread-cross; Toji

Sufi beliefs Abdal; Al-Insan al-Kamil → 'Abd al-Karim al-Jili; al-Insan al-Kamil; al-Niffari; Awtad → Abdal; Baraka; Barzakh; Bast; Dhikr; Dhu 'l-Nun; Fana'; Faqir; Ghaiba; Hadd; Hal; Kashf; Khidr; Qabd; Qutb; Sama'; Shath; Sober Sufism → al-Junaid; Sufis; Suluk; Tawhid; The Perfect Man → 'Abd al-Karim al-Jili; 'Urs; Wajd; Wali; Waqfa; Wird; Zuhd

Sufi orders 'Alawiy(y)a → Shadhiliy(y)a; Beshara; Darqawiy(y)a → Shadhiliy(y)a; Derwish; Hamallism; Hasafiyya → Hasan al-Banna; Kashmir Sufism → Sufis; Mawlawiy(y)a; Mevlevi → Mawlawiy(y)a; Mevlevis → Mawlawiy(y)a; Naqshbandiy(y)a; Ni'matullahi → Ni'mat Allah Wali; Nurbakhshiy(y)a; Qadiriy(y)a; Rishis → Sufis; Safavis → Safavids; Shadhiliy(y)a; Silsilah; Sufis; Tariqa; Tijaniya → Ahmad al-Tijaniya; Tijaniy(y)a; Yezidis

Sufis 'Abd al-Karim al-Jili; 'Abd al-Qadir al-Jilani/Jili; Abu Madyan; Ahl al-Suffa; Ahmad al-Badawi; Ahmad al-Tijani; Ahmad Sirhindi; al-Bistami; al-Busiri; al-Ghaz(z)ali; al-Hallaj; 'Ali Hujwiri; al-Junaid; al-Muhasibi; al-Niffari; al-Sanusi; al-Shadhili; al-Shibli; al-Tijani → Tijaniy(y)a; 'Attar; Chishti; Dhu 'l-Nun; Hasan al-Basri; Hujwiri, Ali → Sufis; Ibn (al-)'Arabi; Ibrahim b. Adham; Iqbal, M.; Jalal al-Din; Jami; Khirqa; Ma'ruf al-Kharki;

Theologians, philosophers (*cont.*): Nazzam; al-Razi, Fakhr al-Din; al-Tusi, Nasir; Averroes → Ibn Rushd; Avicenna → Ibn Sina; Ibn Rushd; Ibn Sina; Ibn Taimiyya; Sahl al-Tustari; Said Nursi; Wasil b. ʿAtaʾ

Theology Affirmative Way; Analogy; Anthropomorphism; Apophatic; Apotheosis; Biogenetic structuralism; Covenant; Death of God; Deus absconditus; Deus otiosus; Ethical monotheism; Feminist theology; Fideism; God; Grace; Holy Spirit; Immanence; Impassibility of God; Incarnation; I–Thou; Kataphatic theology → Affirmative Way; Moral argument; Occasionalism; Omnipotence; Ontological argument; Pantheism, panentheism; Paraclete; Physico-theological argument; Teleological argument; Theism; Theodicy; Theology; Throne of God; Ubiquity; Via eminentiae; Via negativa; Wrath of God → Wrathful deities **Christian**: Alexandria; Antioch; Barth, K.; Calvinism; Chalcedonian Definition → Chalcedon; Christology; Consubstantial; Feuerbach, L.; Filioque; Heilsgeschichte → Salvation history; Hypostasis; Justification; Liberation theology; Minjung → Liberation theology; Modalism; Monarchianism; Natural theology; Neo-Orthodoxy; Neo-Thomism; Ontologism → Ontology; Patripassianism; Paul; Political theology; Predestination; Process theology; Providence; Quinque viae; Salvation history; Scholasticism; Subordinationism; Thomism; Trinity **Hindu**: Avyakta; Brahman; Saiva Siddantha; Trimurti; Visistadvaita **Jewish**: Deuteronomic history; Sefirot; Shekinah **Muslim**: Allah; al-Maturidi; Badaʾ; Iman; Kalam; Kismet; Kursi; Muʿtazilites; Qadar; Tanzih; Tashbih; Taʿtil → Tasbih; Tawhid; Thanawiya; Wali **Sikh**: Nirgun

Tibetan religion Abhiseka; Adi Buddha; Amitayus; Atisa; Avalokitesvara; Bardo; Bardo Todrol → Tibetan Book of the Dead; Bhaisajyaguru; Bhavacakra; Body, speech, and mind; Bon; Breathing; Buddhist schools; Bu-ston; Chod; Chokyi Gyaltsen → Panchen Lama; Chorten; Dakini; Dalai Lama; Dorje; Drona; Drugpa Kunleg; Dzogchen; Emanations; Gampopa; Geluk; Gesar; Govinda; Great Perfection → Dzogchen; gShen; gzhan.stong → Zhen dong; Heruka; Iconography; Iconography (Tibetan); Jigme Lingpa → Klong-chen Rab-ʾbyams-pa; Jokhang; Jonang-pa; Kadam; Kagyu; Kailasa; Kalacakra; Kamalasila; Kanjur; Karma Kagyu; Karma-pa; kLong chen rab ʾbyams pa; Kumaraja → Klong-chen Rab-ʾbyams-pa; Kyabdro; Lama; Lamrim; Lhasa; Ma.gcig Lab.sgron; Mahamudra; Mandala; Manjusri; Mar-pa; Milam; Milarepa; Music; Naga (3); Naro chos drug; Na-ro-pa; Nyingma; Nyingmapa; Om mani padme hum; Padmasambhava; Panchen Lama; ʾPhags-pa Blo-gros-rgyal-mtshan; Prayer wheel; Rang dong; Red Hats; Rime; Ritroma; Sakya; Samye; Santarakshita; Santaraksita; Shambhala; Siddha tradition; Six Doctrines of Naropa; sman.bla; sPyan-ras-gzigs → Avalokitesvara; Tanjur; Tara; Terma; Thread-cross; Tibetan Book of the Dead; Tibetan religion; Tibetan wheel of life; Ti-lo-pa; Torma; Tsha-tsha; Tsong kha pa; Tulku; Vajra; Vajrayana; Visualization; Yab-yum; Yellow hats; Yidam; Zhen dong

Tirthankaras Adinatha; Adi-Purana; Arhat; Digambara; Ganadharas; Jina; Kevalin; Mahavira; Neminatha; Paramatman; Parsva; Pilgrimage; Rsabha; Tirtha; Tirthankara; Yaksa

Titles Svami **Buddhist**: Bhagava; Liu-tsu-ta-shih; Nyorai; Sakyamuni; Sammasambuddha; Sayadaw; Soshi; Tathagata; Thera; Zasu **Chinese**: Ho shang **Christian**: Aba Salama → Abuna; Abba; Abbe; Abbess; Abbot; Abuna; Amba; Apostle; Catholikos; Chorepiscopus; Curate; Ecumenical Patriarch; Exarch; Friar; Hegumenos; Metropolitan; Monsignor; Pontifex Maximus; Prebendary; Prelate; Primate; Rector; Rural dean **Hindu**: Babu; Bhagavan; Bhairava; Bhatta; Jagadguru; Ma; Mahendra; Sri **Jain**: Mahavira **Japanese**: Sensei **Jewish**: Chief rabbi; Exilarch; Gaon; Hakham; Maʿamad; Nagid; Nasi; Rebbe; Resh Kallah; Rishon le-Zion **Muslim**: Ayatollah; Faqih; Pasha; Saiyid; Shaikh al-Islam; Sharif; Shaykh **Sikh**: Baba; Bhai; Bibi; Sahib; Sardar **Taoist**: Celestial Master; Chang Tʾien Shih; Tʾien-shih **Tibetan**: Dalai Lama; Karma-pa; khen-po → Abbot; Kundun → Dalai Lama; Lama; mkhan-po → Abbot; Rinpoche **Zen**: Daishi; Daisho; Godo; Roshi

Torah Aaron; Aaron ben Jacob; Academies; Agudat Israel; Aliyah; Ark; Art (Jewish); Avot; Bible; Bimah; Birkat-ha-Torah; Breast-plate; Bridegroom; Caro; Chosen people; Codifications of law; Daʿat Torah; Din Torah; Elijah ben Solomon; Enoch; Ethics (Jewish); Golden Rule; Hagbaha, Gelilah; Hagbahah, gelilah; Hakhel; Halakah; Judaism; Kallah; Karaites; Kelal; Ket(h)er Torah; Maimonides; Mitzvah; Oral law; Pentateuch; Petihah; Pilgrimage (Judaism); Rebellious elder; Revelation; Scroll of the Law; Simhat Torah; Sinai; Six hundred and thirteen commandments; Sura; Synagogue; Tawrat; Torah; Torah ornaments

Torah reading see READING

Tradition see CUSTOMS

Translation Abraham bar Hiyya; al-Biruni; Amoghvajra; An Shih-kao; Aquila; Arabic; Aramaic; Aristeas, Letter of; Authorized Version; Bible; Boethius; Buddhabhadra; Bu-ston; Coverdale; Eknath; Fa-hsien; Fa-tsang; Hermeneutics; Hsuan-tsang; Hui-yuan; Ibn Hasdai; I-Ching; Jerome; Kagyu; Ke-yi; Kumarajiva; Marpa; Melanchthon; Nyantiloka; Onkelos; Padmasambhava; Pure Land; Quran; Rhys Davids; Sakya; Septuagint; Tao-te Ching; Targum; Tyndale

Upanisads Aitareya; Brahmasutra; Brhadaranyaka; Chandogya; Isa; Katha; Kausitaki; Kena; Mahanarayaniya; Mahavakya; Maitri; Mandukya; Mundaka; Prasna; Svetasvatara; Taittiriya; Upanisad

Vaisnava see VISNU

Vedanta Anubhava; Badarayana; Bhagavad-gita; Brahman; Brahma-sutra; Cit; Darsana; Drg-drsya-viveka; Karma; Mahasunya; Mithya; Nididhyasana; Nimbarka; Nirguna-Brahman; Prakrti; Ramanuja; Saccidananda; Sankara; Satkasampatti; Sri Harsa; Sri-Vaisnavism; Suddhadvaita; Upanisad; Uttara-mimamsa; Vaisnava; Vallabha; Vedanta; Vivekananda

Virtues **Buddhist**: Abhabba-tthana; Alobha; Anagamin **Christian**: Seven virtues **Hindu**: Abhaya-mudra; Abhaya-vacana; Ananda; Aparigraha; Asparsa

Visnu Abhaya-mudra; Acarya; Alvars; Ananta; Angkor; Aniruddha → Visnu; Avatara; Bhagavad-gita; Bhagavan; Bhagavata-purana; Brahma; Brahman; Buddha; Daityas; Dattatreya; Dhruva; Ganga; Garuda; Gaya; Govinda; Hara; Hari-hara; Hayagriva; Hiranyakasipu; Hiranyaksa; Jagannatha; Janardana; Kalki; Krsna; Kurma; Laksmi; Madhu; Mahendra; Matsya; Mayon; Mohini; Nara; Narasimha; Narayana; Nath; Padma-purana; Pancaratra; Parasurama; Prapatti; Rama; Ramanuja; Samkarsana; Sankaradeva; Sesa; Tamilnadu; Trimurti; Vaikuntha; Vaisnava; Vamana; Varaha; Vasudeva; Vasudeva (2); Visnu

Vows Abhiseka; Aparigraha; Hair; Oaths; Vows; Vrata **Buddhist**: Amida; Bhaisajyaguru; Bodhisattva vow; Homon; Hongan; Hui-yuan; Jikkai; Jujukai; Sila **Christian**: Baptism; Confirmation; Crusade; Francis Xavier; Habit (Christian); Jesuits; Nun; Opus Dei **Hindu**: Kapalika; Vratya; Yama (2) **Jain**: Ahimsa; Anuvrata; Brahmacarya; Diksa (Jain);

INDEX OF CHINESE HEADWORDS

WADE–GILES → PINYIN CONVERSION TABLE

A-lo-pen	A-luo-ben
An Shih-kao	An Shigao
Ch'an	Chan
Ch'ang	Chang
Ch'ang-an	Chang'an
Chang Chüeh	Zhang Jue
Chang Hsien	Zhang Xian
Chang Hsiu	Zhang Xiu
Chang Kuo-lao	Zhang Guolao
Chang Ling	Zhang Ling
Chang Lu	Zhang Lu
Chang Po-tuan	Zhang Boduan
Chang san-feng	Zhangsanfeng
Ch'ang-sha Ching-ts'en	Changsha Jingcen
Ch'ang-sheng Pu-ssu	Changsheng Busi
Chang Tao-ling	Zhang Daoling
Chang T'ien Shih	Zhang Tianshi
Ch'an-na	Channa
Ch'an-tsung	Chanzong
Chao-chou Ts'ung-shen	Zhaozhou Congshen
Ch'eng	Cheng
Ch'eng-chu	Chenzhu
Ch'eng Hao	Cheng Hao
Ch'eng-huang	Chenghuang
Ch'eng I	Cheng Yi
Cheng-i tao	Zhengyidao
Cheng-kuan	Zhengguan
Ch'eng-shih	Chengshi
Cheng-yi	Zhengyi
Ch'eng Yi	Cheng Yi
Chen jen	Zhenren
Ch'en T'uan	Chen Tuan
Chen-yen	Zhenyan
Ch'i	Qi
Chiang-I	Jiang Yi
Chiao	Jiao
Ch'ieh-lan	Qielan
Ch'ien ai	Qian ai
Chien-chen	Jianzhen
Ch'ien tzu wen	*Qian zi wen*
Chih	Zhi
Ch'i-hai	Qihai
Chih-che	Zhizhe
Chih-i	Zhiyi
Chih-kuan	Zhiguan
Ch'i-kung	Qigong
Chih Tao-lin	Zhi Daolin
Chih-tun	Zhidun
Ch'in	Qin
Ching	Jing
Ch'ing-ming	Qingming
Ch'ing-t'an	Qingtan
Ching-te Ch'üan-teng-lu	*Jingde Quangdenglu*
Ching-t'un	Jingtun
Chinju	Jingru
Chin-lien	Jinlian
Chin-tan	Jindan
Chou	Zhou
Chou Lien-ch'i	Zhou Lianqi
Chou Tun-(y)i	Zhou Dunyi
Chu	Zhu
Ch'üan-chen tao	Quanzhendao
Chuang chou	Zhuangzhou
Chuang-tzu	Zhuangzi
Chu Hsi	Zhu Xi
Chu-hung	Zhuhong
Ch'un Ch'iu	*Chun Qiu*
Chung-Kuo-Shih	Zhongguoshi
Chung-li Chuan	Zhonglizhuan
Chung-yang	Zhongyang
Chung Yüan	Zhong Yuan
Chung Yung	*Zhong Yong*
Chün tzu	Junzi
Fa	Fa
Fa-chia	Fajia
Fa-hsiang	Faxiang
Fa-hsien	Faxian
Fa-ju	Fazhu
Fa-jung	Farong
Fa-lang	Falang
Fang-chang	Fangzhang
Fang-chung shu	Fangzhongshu
Fang-shih	Fangshi
Fang Yen-kou	Fang Yangou
Fa-shun	Fashun
Fa-tsang	Fazang
Fa-yen Wen-i	Fayan Wenyi
Fei-sheng	Feisheng
Feng-kan	Fenggan
Feng-shui	Fengshui
Fen-yang Shan-chao	Fenyang Shanzhao
Fu-ch'i	Fuqi
Fu-lu (pai)	Fulu (bai)
Han Hsiang-tzu	Han Xiangzi
Han-shan	Hanshan

Lü-tsung	Lüzong
Lu tung-pin	Ludongbin
Ma-fa	Mafa
Man-ta-lao	Mandalao
Mao-shan	Maoshan
Mao Tzu-yuan	Mao Ziyuan
Ma-tsu	Mazu
Ma-tsu Tao-i	Mazu Daoyi
Meng Tzu	Mengzi
men-shen	Menshen
Mi-lo-fo	Miluofo
Ming Chi	Ming Ji
Ming-tao	Mingdao
Ming-ti	Mingdi
Mo-chao ch'an	Mozhao chan
Mo-chia	Mojia
Mo-kao Caves	Mogao Caves
Mo Ti	Modi
Mo Tzu	Mozi
Nan-hua chen-ching	*Nanhua zhenjing*
Nan-yang Hui-chung	Nanyang Huizhong
Nan-yuan Hui-yung	Nanyuan Huiyong
Nan-yüeh Huai-jang	Nanyue Huairang
Nei-ch'i	Neiqi
Nei-kuan	Neiguan
Nei-shih	Neishi
Nei-tan	Neidan
Nieh-pan	Nieban
Nien-fo	Nianfo
Nü-kua	Nügua
O-mei, Mount	Emei, Mount
O-mi-t'o	Emito, Mount
Pa-chiao Hui-ch'ing	Bajiao Huiqing
Pa-hsien	Baxian
Pai-Chang-Ch'ing-Kuei	*Baizhangqinggui*
Pai-chang Huai-hai	Baizhang Huaihai
Pai-lien-tsung	Bailianzong
Pai-ma-ssu	Baimasi
Pai-yün Kuan	Baiyunguan
Pa-kua	Bagua
P'ang-chu-shih	Pangzhushi
P'ang Yün	Pang Yun
P'an-ku	Pangu
Pa-tuan-chin	Baduanjin
P'ei Hsiu	Peixiu
P'eng Lai	Peng Lai
P'eng-tzu	Pengzi
Pi-ch'iu	Biqiu
Pi-ku	Bigu
Pi-yen-lu	*Biyanlu*
P'o	Po
P'u	Pu
P'u-hsien	Puxian
P'u-Hua	Puhua
Pu-k'ung Chin-kang	Bukong Jingang
P'u-sa	Pusa
P'u-t'i-ta-mo	Putidamo
P'u-t'o-shan	Puteshan
Ru-chia	Rujia
San-chiao	Sanjia
San-chieh-chiao	Sanjiejiao
San-ch'ing	Sanqing
San-hsing	Sanxing
San-i	Sanyi
San-pao	Sanbao
San-Shen	Sanshen
San-Sheng Hui-Jan	Sansheng Huiran
Shang-Ch'ing	Shangqing
Shang-Ch'ing	*Shangqing*
Shang-ti	Shangdi
Shang-tso-pu	Shangzuobu
Shan-tao	Shandao
Shao-lin-ssu	Shaolinsi
Shen	Shen
Sheng(-jen)	Sheng(-ren)
Shen-hsiang	Shenxiang
Shen-hsiu	Shenxiu
Shen-hui	Shenhui
Shih	Shi
Shih Chi	*Shiji*
Shih-chieh	Shijie
Shih Ching	*Shijing*
Shih-i	Shiyi
Shih-shu	Shishu
Shih-shuang Ch'u-yuan	Shishuang Chuyuan
Shou	Shou
Shou-i	Shouyi
Shou-lao	Shoulao
Shou-shan Sheng-nien	Shoushan Shengnian
Shu	Shu
Shu Ching	*Shujing*
Sian	Xi'an
Ssu-hsiang	Sixiang
Ssu-ma Ch'ien	Sima Qian
Ssu-ming	Siming
Ssu Shu	*Sishu*
Sun Wu-k'ung	Sun Wukong
Su-yüeh	Suyue
Ta-ch'eng	Dacheng
Ta-chu Hui-hai	Dachu Huihai
Ta Hsüeh	*Daxue*
Ta-hui Tsung-kao	Dahui Zonggao
T'ai-chi	Taiji
T'ai-chi-ch'üan	Taijiquan
T'ai-ch'ing	Taiqing
T'ai-chi-t'u	Taijitu
T'ai-hsi	Taixi
T'ai-hsü	Taixu
T'ai-i	Taiyi
T'ai-I Chin-hua Tsung-chih	*Taiyi Jinhua Zongzhi*
T'ai-i Tao	Taiyidao

Yüan-ch'i	Yuanqi
Yuan-chueh-ching	*Yuanzhuejing*
Yüan-shih t'ien-tsun	Yuanshi tianzun
Yüan-wu K'o-ch'in	Yuanwu Keqin
Yü Chi	Yu Ji
Yü-huang	Yuhuang
Yün-chi Ch'i-ch'ien	*Yunji Qiqian*
Yung-chia Hsüan-chüeh	Yongjia Xuanchue
Yun-kang	Yungang
Yün-men Wen-yen	Yunmen Wenyang
Yun-yen T'an-sheng	Yungan Tansheng

PINYIN→ WADE–GILES CONVERSION TABLE

A-luo-ben	A-lo-pen
An Shigao	An Shih-kao
Baduanjin	Pa-tuan-chin
Bagua	Pa-kua
Bailianzong	Pai-lien-tsung
Baimasi	Pai-ma-ssu
Baiyunguan	Pai-yün Kuan
Baizhang Huaihai	Pai-chang Huai-hai
Baizhangqinggui	*Pai-Chang-Ch'ing-Kuei*
Bajiao Huiqing	Pa-chiao Hui-ch'ing
Baxian	Pa-hsien
Bigu	Pi-ku
Biqiu	Pi-ch'iu
Biyanlu	*Pi-yen-lu*
Bukong Jingang	Pu-k'ung Chin-kang
Caishen	Ts'ai-shen
Caodong	Ts'ao-tung
Cao Guojiu	Ts'ao Kuo-chiu
Caoshan Benji	Ts'ao-shan Pen-chi
Chan	Ch'an
Chang	Ch'ang
Chang'an	Ch'ang-an
Changsha Jingcen	Ch'ang-sha Ching-ts'en
Changsheng Busi	Ch'ang-sheng Pu-ssu
Channa	Ch'an-na
Chanzong	Ch'an-tsung
Cheng	Ch'eng
Cheng Hao	Ch'eng Hao
Chenghuang	Ch'eng-huang
Chengshi	Ch'eng-shih
Cheng Yi	Ch'eng I
Cheng Yi	Ch'eng Yi
Chen Tuan	Ch'en T'uan
Chenzhu	Ch'eng-chu
Chun Qiu	*Ch'un Ch'iu*
Cunsi	Ts'un-ssu
Dacheng	Ta-ch'eng
Dachu Huihai	Ta-chu Hui-hai
Dahui Zonggao	Ta-hui Tsung-kao
Danxia Tianran	Tan-hsia T'ien-jan
Dao	Tao
Daoan	Tao-an
Daochuo	Tao-ch'o
Daodejing	*Tao-te Ching*
Daodetianzun	Tao-te t'ien-tsun
Dao Hongjing	T'ao Hung-ching
Daojia	Tao-chia
Daojiao	Tao-chiao
Daosheng	Tao-sheng
Daoshi	Tao-shih
Daoyi	Tao-i
Daoyin	Tao-yin
Daozang	Tao-tsang
Datongshu	*Ta T'ung Shu*
Daxue	*Ta Hsüeh*
Deshan Xuanjian	Te-shan Hsüan-chien
Di	Ti
Dicang	Ti-ts'ang
Dongshan Liangjie	Tung-shan Liang-chieh
Doushuai Congyue	Tou-shuai Ts'ung-yueh
Dunhuang	Tun-huang
Dunwu rudao yaomen-lun	*Tun-wu ju-tao yao-men lun*
Dushan	Tu-shun
Emei, Mount	O-mei, Mount
Emito, Mount	O-mi-t'o
Fa	Fa
Fajia	Fa-chia
Falang	Fa-lang
Fangshi	Fang-shih
Fang Yangou	Fang Yen-kou
Fangzhang	Fang-chang
Fangzhongshu	Fang-chung shu
Farong	Fa-jung
Fashun	Fa-shun
Faxian	Fa-hsien
Faxiang	Fa-hsiang
Fayan Wenyi	Fa-yen Wen-i
Fazang	Fa-tsang
Fazhu	Fa-ju
Feisheng	Fei-sheng
Fenggan	Feng-kan
Fengshui	Feng-shui
Fenyang Shanzhao	Fen-yang Shan-chao
Fulu (bai)	Fu-lu (pai)
Fuqi	Fu-ch'i
Ge Hong	Ko Hung
Geyi	Ko-yi
Gong'an	Kung-an
Gu, Ku	Ku, K'u
Gui	Kuei
Guifeng Zongmi	Kuei-feng Tsung-mi

Index of Chinese Headwords

Nieban	Nieh-pan
Nügua	Nü-kua
Pangu	P'an-ku
Pang Yun	P'ang Yün
Pangzhushi	P'ang-chu-shih
Peixiu	P'ei Hsiu
Peng Lai	P'eng Lai
Pengzi	P'eng-tzu
Po	P'o
Pu	P'u
Puhua	P'u-Hua
Pusa	P'u-sa
Puteshan	P'u-t'o-shan
Putidamo	P'u-t'i-ta-mo
Puxian	P'u-hsien
Qi	Ch'i
Qian ai	Ch'ien ai
Qian zi wen	*Ch'ien tzu wen*
Qielan	Ch'ieh-lan
Qigong	Ch'i-kung
Qihai	Ch'i-hai
Qin	Ch'in
Qingming	Ch'ing-ming
Qingtan	Ch'ing-t'an
Quanzhendao	Ch'üan-chen tao
Rujia	Ju-chia
Rujia	Ru-chia
Rujiao	Ju-chiao
Rulai	Ju-lai
Sanbao	San-pao
Sanjia	San-chiao
Sanjiejiao	San-chieh-chiao
Sanqing	San-ch'ing
Sanshen	San-Shen
Sansheng Huiran	San-Sheng Hui-Jan
Sanxing	San-hsing
Sanyi	San-i
Shandao	Shan-tao
Shangdi	Shang-ti
Shangqing	*Shang-Ch'ing*
Shangqing	Shang-Ch'ing
Shangzuobu	Shang-tso-pu
Shaolinsi	Shao-lin-ssu
Shen	Shen
Sheng(-ren)	Sheng(-jen)
Shenhui	Shen-hui
Shenxiang	Shen-hsiang
Shenxiu	Shen-hsiu
Shi	Shih
Shiji	*Shih-Chi*
Shijie	Shih-chieh
Shijing	*Shih Ching*
Shishu	Shih-shu
Shishuang Chuyuan	Shih-shuang Ch'u-yuan
Shiyi	*Shih-i*
Shou	Shou
Shoulao	Shou-lao
Shoushan Shengnian	Shou-shan Sheng-nien
Shouyi	Shou-i
Shu	Shu
Shujing	*Shu Ching*
Sima Qian	Ssu-ma Ch'ien
Siming	Ssu-ming
Sishu	*Ssu Shu*
Sixiang	Ssu-hsiang
Sun Wukong	Sun Wu-k'ung
Suyue	Su-yüeh
Taiji	T'ai-chi
Taijiquan	T'ai-chi-ch'üan
Taijitu	T'ai-chi-t'u
Taipingdao	T'ai-p'ing Tao
Taipingjing	*T'ai-p'ing Ching*
Taiqing	T'ai-ch'ing
Taishan	T'ai-shan
Taishang Daojun	T'ai-shang Tao-chün
Taishang Ganyingpian	*T'ai-shang kan-ying P'ien*
Taishi	T'ai shih
Taixi	T'ai-hsi
Taixu	T'ai-hsü
Taiyi	T'ai-i
Taiyidao	T'ai-i Tao
Taiyi Jinhua Zongzhi	*T'ai-i Chin-hua Tsung-chih*
Taiyue dadi	T'ai-yüeh ta-ti
Tanhuang	Tan-huang
Tanjing	*T'an-ching*
Tanluan	T'an-luan
Tantian	Tan-t'ien
Taoxin	Tao-hsin
Taoxuan	Tao-hsüan
Tian	T'ien
Tianchi	T'ien-chih
Tian Fang	T'ien Fang
Tiangu	T'ien-ku
Tianming	T'ien-ming
Tianshang Shengmu	T'ien-shang Sheng-mu
Tianshi	T'ien-shih
Tiantai	T'ien-t'ai
Tiantiaoshu	*T'ien-t'iao shu*
Tianwang	T'ien wang
Tiaoqi	T'iao-ch'i
Tong Zhongshu	T'ung Chung-shu
Tudi	T'u-ti
Tutanzhai	T'u-t'an chai
Waidan	Wai-tan
Waiqi	Wai-ch'i
Wang Anshi	Wang An-shih
Wangbi	Wang-pi
Wang Yangming	Wang Yang-ming
Wei	Wei
Wei Huazun	Wei Hua-tsun